CURRENT

BIOGRAPHY

WHO'S NEWS AND WHY

1 9 4 0

EDITED BY

Maxine Block

THE H. W. WILSON COMPANY

950 UNIVERSITY AVENUE . . NEW YORK, N. Y.

First Annual Cumulation—1940

Printed in the United States of America

Copyright 1940

by

The H. W. Wilson Company

Copyright © renewed 1968

by

The H. W. Wilson Company

REISSUED 1971

International Standard Book No. 0-8242-0477-8

Library of Congress Catalog Card No. (40-27432)

FOREWORD TO THE 1971 REISSUE

Responding to widespread demand from librarians and other researchers, The H. W. Wilson Company has brought back into print the six early volumes of Current Biography Yearbook, 1940-45. Although their style and format depart considerably from present editorial policy, the volumes constitute a rich source of information on persons of the World War II period. They provide contemporary viewpoints on major world figures and furnish valuable leads to further research into the lives of a host of authors, organization heads, war correspondents, and women military leaders. And their reference value is enhanced by photographs that are difficult or impossible to come by elsewhere. The Company is pleased to make these volumes once again available to serve the research and reference needs of the scholarly community.

CHARLES MORITZ

Preface

"Biography is by nature the most universally profitable, universally pleasant of all things: especially biography of distinguished individuals."—*Carlyle*

In the main the staff of CURRENT BIOGRAPHY is inclined to agree with the estimable Carlyle. Yet when a staff member assembles six biographical sketches of the same person from six newspapers, magazines and books, and finds that each differs radically from the others in dates and statements of facts, we begin to wonder. Then follows a period in which we try to arrive at the approximate truth. In many cases we have asked biographees to correct any errors and give us additional information. However, in no sense are these *official* biographies.

This volume is a cumulation of all the material in the monthly numbers of CURRENT BIOGRAPHY issued in 1940 (these can now be discarded). Additional sketches have been incorporated in this annual in place of a December monthly number. All names marked [Dec] in the complete index (Who's News and Why) at the end of the volume have not appeared in any previous issue. Each sketch and its accompanying list of references have been brought as far up to date as time and the printer's "deadline" have allowed. In writing of people who are making history today, each issue of a daily newspaper brings changes, so we have tried to incorporate into these sketches as much late material as possible.

The staff of CURRENT BIOGRAPHY includes the managing editor, E. Mary Trow, and the editorial assistants, Barbara Falkoff, Frances Jennings and Lillian Price, who, together with Ruth Lechlitner and Flora Kaiser, part-time writers, are responsible for most of the sketches in this annual volume. Herbert B. Grimsditch, London journalist who has written for other Wilson publications, also sent us sketches of many English statesmen, written between hasty trips to improvised shelters in bomb-torn London.

Efforts were made to obtain a photograph to accompany each biography, but this proved impossible to accomplish. We take this opportunity to thank all—individuals, organizations, publications—for their cooperation in furnishing photographs and information in response to our requests.

MAXINE BLOCK
Editor

Explanations

Authorities for forms of names are the Library of Congress and the Wilson Company bibliographical indexes. Exception is made to the authorized form when the shortened form of a name is better known: e.g., Monty Woolley instead of Edgar Montillion Woolley. If the full name is not given in the heading it will be found in the sketch itself.

After the name, pronunciation is given if the name is difficult, and then the date of birth as fully as possible. The date of death is given for those who have died. The occupation of the subject and the reasons for his news-worthiness follow. Next comes the sketch itself, followed by a list of references for further study. These include magazine and newspaper references (in one alphabet) and books. If the person is not living, references are made to obituaries in newspapers and magazines. Only books of an autobiographical or biographical nature are listed, including such well-known reference works as *Who's Who, Who's Who in America,* etc. The absence of a date following the title of an annual publication means that the volume used is the latest published.

The magazine articles listed under *References* are in abbreviated form (see list "Periodicals and Newspapers Consulted" for complete title). The form of entry is as follows: Ladies' H J 56:78-9 S '39 por. This means that an article supplementing our sketch will be found in Ladies' Home Journal, volume 56, pages 78-9, in the September 1939 number. The abbreviation *por* means that the article is accompanied by a portrait. In the case of newspapers, the name of the paper is followed by paging and date.

Contents

KEY TO ABBREVIATIONS

AAA	Agricultural Adjustment Administration	Dr.	Doctor	NBC	National Broadcasting System		
Abp	Archbishop	D. Sc.	Doctor of Science	nd	no date		
A. C. L. U.	American Civil Liberties Union	D. S. O.	Distinguished Service Order	NLRB	National Labor Relations Board		
A. D. C.	Aide-de-camp	ed	edited, edition, editor	N. M. U.	National Maritime Union		
A. E. F.	American Expeditionary Force	F	February	no	number		
A F of L	American Federation of Labor	FBI	Federal Bureau of Investigation	ns	new series		
Ag	August	FCC	Federal Communications Commission	NYA	National Youth Administration		
A M	Amplitude Modulation	FERA	Federal Emergency Relief Administration	O	October		
A. M. A.	American Medical Association			o.p.	out of print		
Ap	April	FHA	Federal Housing Administration	p	page		
A. P.	Associated Press	F M	Frequency Modulation	pam	pamphlet		
ASCAP	American Society of Composers, Authors and Publishers	Four A's	American Association of Advertising Agencies	P. E. N.	Poets, Playwrights, Editors, Essayists and Novelists (International Association)		
assn	association	F. P. A.	Franklin Pierce Adams	Ph. B.	Bachelor of Philosophy		
AYC	American Youth Congress	G. H. A.	Group Health Association	Ph. D.	Doctor of Philosophy		
B. A.	Bachelor of Arts	G. M.	General Motors	pl-s	plate, -s		
BBC	British Broadcasting Corporation	H. M.	His Majesty	por-s	portrait, -s		
B. D.	Bachelor of Divinity	il	illustration	P. R. M.	Party of the Mexican Revolution		
B. E. F.	British Expeditionary Force	I. L. A.	International Longshoremen's Association	pseud.	pseudonym		
B. L.	Bachelor of Letters	I. L. G. W. U.	International Ladies' Garment Workers' Union	PWA	Public Works Administration		
blvd	boulevard			R	Review		
bp	bishop	Inc	incorporated	R. A. F.	Royal Air Force		
B. S.	Bachelor of Science	INS	International News Service	RCA	Radio Corporation of America		
C. B. E.	Commander of (the Order of) the British Empire	I. R. A.	Irish Republican Army	RFC	Reconstruction Finance Corporation		
CBS	Columbia Broadcasting System	I. W. W.	Industrial Workers of the World	RKO	Radio Keith Orpheum		
CIO	Congress of Industrial Organizations	Ja	January	S	September		
		J. D.	Doctor of Jurisprudence	SEC	Security Exchange Commission		
C. M. G.	Companion of (the Order of) St. Michael and St. George	Je	June	ser	series		
cond	condensed	Jl	July	S. J. D.	Doctor Juristic Science		
C. P. A.	Certified Public Accountant	K. C.	King's Council	S. T. D.	Doctor of Sacred Theology		
CROM	Confederación Regional Obrera Mexicano (Mexican Regional Confederation of Workers)	Litt. D.	Doctor of Letters	sup	supplement		
		LL. B.	Bachelor of Laws	tab	tabulation		
		LL. D.	Doctor of Laws	TNEC	Temporary National Economic Committee		
		LL. M.	Master of Laws				
CTM	Confederación de Trabajadores Mexicanos (Confederation of Mexican Workers)	M. A.	Master of Arts	tr	translated, translation, translator		
		mag	magazine	T. U. C.	Trade Union Congress		
		M. D.	Doctor of Medicine				
		MGM	Metro-Goldwyn-Mayer	TVA	Tennessee Valley Authority		
D	December	M. Litt.	Master of Literature	UAW	United Automobile Workers		
DAR	Daughters of the American Revolution	M. P.	Member of Parliament	U. P.	United Press		
		Mr	March	U.S.S.R.	Union of Socialist Soviet Republics		
D. C. L.	Doctor of Civil Law	M. R. A.	Moral Rearmament	v	volume		
		M. S. or M. Sc.	Master of Science				
D. D.	Doctor of Divinity	My	May	V. M. I.	Virginia Military Institute		
D. Eng.	Doctor of Engineering	N	November	w	weekly		
D. Litt.	Doctor of Literature	N. A. M.	National Association of Manufacturers	WPA	Works Projects Administration		

KEY TO PRONUNCIATION

āle, chăotic, câre, ădd, ärm, sofá; ēve, ĕvent, ĕnd, makĕr; īce, ĭll; N=French nasal sound, as in boN; ōld, ŏbey, ôrb, ŏdd; fōōd, fŏŏt; out, oil; cūbe, ûnite, ûrn, ŭp, menü; kh=ch in German ich, ach; zh=z in azure; ″=secondary accent, ′=main accent

CURRENT BIOGRAPHY

1940

ABBOTT, GEORGE June 25, 1889- Playwright; theatrical producer
Address: b. 630 Fifth Ave, New York City

George Abbott, one of half a dozen of Broadway's best known producers, has achieved a reputation for "pulling rabbits out of shabby theatrical hats and turning them into ermine." His talents as a director, and frequently as co-author, have put over many a show which was no dramatic masterpiece.

As George Jean Nathan, the drama critic, said of Abbott: "His is the theatre of snappy curtain lines, wisecracking dialogue, mention of favorite brands of champagne, periodic, humorous excursions to the lavatory, sentimental relief in the shape of tender young lovers, and various analogous condiments, all staged as if the author had used a pepper shaker in lieu of an inkwell." But, according to Nathan, Abbott's ambition is to be a directorial Hamlet, "to produce more important plays than the trivial comedies and farces with which he has achieved big box office success." Abbott has few rivals in the field of rough and tumble popular entertainment, of fast-moving, side-splitting farce. Yet every time he has tried to establish himself as a producer of more exalted status he has had a flop on his hands.

"If Abbott," Nathan writes, "can't be the directorial Hamlet of his dreams, he may at least content himself in being a pretty satisfactory couple of other fellows from Ephesus and Syracuse." Nathan's allusion is to one of Abbott's hits, *The Boys from Syracuse,* a modern adaptation of Shakespeare's *Comedy of Errors,* with the songs and lyrics by Richard Rodgers (see sketch this issue) and Lorenz Hart. Rodgers and Hart had thought Shakespeare's classical plot of the twin brothers and their mistaken identities good enough for them, but Shakespeare wasn't good enough for George Abbott, who wrote the book for the musical comedy, *The Boys from Syracuse.* Abbott pitched out Shakespeare's dialogue because he liked his own better.

While some critics said that even Abbott's dialogue, Rodgers' and Hart's music instead of Shakespeare's poetry, and good comic actors failed to lighten the tedium of the tale or keep it from dragging, the play was a hit. It was not one of the outstanding Abbott successes, however, such as *Room Service, Boy Meets Girl, Three Men on a Horse* or *Brother Rat.*

GEORGE ABBOTT

As a producer, Abbott has not hesitated to use unknown material, and, as a matter of fact, has had his greatest successes on what Broadway characterizes as "hot hunches." *Room Service* was a "washed up" play property when authors John Murray and Allen Boretz brought it to Abbott. Sam Harris, the well-known producer, had tried the play out in Philadelphia with Metro-Goldwyn Mayer money, and it was a $23,000 flop. When the Harris option lapsed, Abbott looked at the script and suggested a few changes. It went on to wild acclaim on Broadway, and later Abbott sold it to RKO Radio for $255,000.

He undertook to produce *Brother Rat,* after it had been turned down by 31 managements, because it was a play about youngsters written by youngsters (John Monks Jr., and Fred F. Finklehoffe, Virginia Military Institute '32). The Abbott "touch" turned it into a Broadway hit and a $150,000 film property. Abbott's own *Three Men on a Horse* made an estimated profit of $650,000.

He has had flops, too. *Angel Island* and *Brown Sugar,* both playwriting efforts of Bernie (Mrs. Howard) Angus, flopped on Broadway in 1937. Of five productions Abbott had on Broadway during the 1939 to 1940 season, three were flops, closing soon

ABBOTT, GEORGE—*Continued*
after they opened. *Goodbye in the Night*
opened in March 1940 and quickly closed.

After *Too Many Girls* made a hit on
Broadway, Abbott went to Hollywood to
produce and direct it for RKO. It was
his first experience with the movies in which
he declared himself happy about the whole
thing, and he came back to New York
eager to get started on his first Broadway
productions of the fall of 1940 season: *The
White-Haired Boy* and *Pal Joey*.

It is true that producer Abbott has occasionally undertaken plays by established
authors—for instance Bella and Samuel
Spewack's *Boy Meets Girl,* which became a
smash-hit. But he prefers to pick them out
of a grab bag, or to help write them himself.

Abbott has co-authored many plays—
Broadway (with Philip Dunning); *Coquette*
(with Anna Preston Bridgers); *Three Men
on a Horse* (with J. C. Holm); *Four Walls*
(with Dana Burnet); *Love 'Em and Leave
'Em* (with J. V. A. Weaver); *The Fall Guy*
(with James Gleason) and others.

As for rules, superstitions or fetishes about
the theatre, Abbott says he has none. Too
many shows that have followed all the rules
and superstitions have flopped, he says. He
writes by the oral method—that is, he talks
to secretaries informally. Then he writes it
all out in longhand, and leaves it to the
secretaries to make what sense they can out
of it. There is usually enough sense to make
a play. And as a collaborator on sick manuscripts, Abbott performs miracles.

He started in the theatre as an actor in
1913. He was born in Forestville, New
York, June 25, 1889, son of George Burwell
and May (McLaury) Abbott, attended
Kearney Military Academy and Hamburg
High School, and received his B. A. from
the University of Rochester in 1911. He was
a student at Harvard the following year, and
the succeeding year an actor.

From 1919 on he wrote and directed plays
and films. He was director for Paramount
Pictures from 1927 to 1930. In 1933 he
became a partner of Abbott-Dunning, Incorporated, producers, and when the partnership was dissolved continued producing for
himself.

Abbott is an arch apostle of what he calls
"pace" in performance, but pace is not
necessarily speed, he says. "Tempo," he
asserts, "is variety." Actually many of his
productions which seem to move at break-
neck speed move slowly a large part of the
time. The effect, according to Abbott, is
achieved by contrast of character, of movement, of tone of voice, and not in making
actors speak and move in double quick time.

Abbott married Ednah Levis of Rochester,
New York in 1914. Mrs. Abbott died in
1930. He has one daughter, Judith Ann.

References

Fortune 17:72 F '38 por
Lit Digest 122:21 Ag 15 '36 por
Newsweek 10:30 N 1 '37 por

Theatre Arts 20:120-3 F '36
Time 30:30 N 1 '37; 32:36 S 26 '38
por
Who's Who in America
Who's Who in the Theatre

ABBOTT, ROBERT SENGSTACKE Nov
24, 1870—Feb 29, 1940 Negro publisher;
editor of *The Defender,* a weekly newspaper
devoted to the interests of the colored race

References

Who's Who in America
Who's Who in Colored America

Obituaries

N Y Herald Tribune p16 Mr 1 '40

ADAMIC, LOUIS (ă'dȧm-ĭk) Mar 23,
1899- Author; director of the Common
Council for American Unity
Address: R. F. D. 1, Milford, New Jersey

Louis Adamic is the man who heads the
Common Council for American Unity,
organized "to explore the complex racial
cultural situation" created by 38,000,000 non-
Anglo-Saxons and non-Protestants having
joined the older racial stocks in the United
States. Through the Council's quarterly,
Common Ground, which was given a grant
from the Carnegie Corporation and whose
first issue was published in the summer of 1940
under Mr. Adamic's editorship, the Council
will attempt to offer an "amalgam of belief
and unity" which can successfully hold together the varied temperaments, religions and
individualities of all Americans, new and old.

Something like the Council has been Mr.
Adamic's dream for a long time. He is
himself a new American, born in the little
village of Blato, Austria (now Yugoslavia)
in the Slovene province of Carniola on
March 23, 1899. The son of Anton and
Ana (Adamic) Adamic, he was brought up
in a family of seven brothers and sisters,
attended the Gymnasium of Ljubljana from
1910 to 1913. He didn't like it, didn't like
the career his parents expected him to
follow, thought much about America, but
might never have come here if he hadn't
read a book called *Do Not Go to America*
and hadn't been thrown out of school at
the age of 14. The ceremonious unveiling
of a statue of Franz Joseph had revealed a
monarch crowned with a very unbecoming
spitoon—Louis' contribution. Once out of
school, he kept right on going until he
reached the United States.

"Studious, idealistic, vaguely aspiring to
be a writer," the youthful immigrant dug
ditches, loaded freight, welded metals, wove
textiles, swept floors, waited on tables,
looked around in America's West—and
learned English as fast as he could. He
hadn't exactly expected to become a millionaire. Finally, when he knew enough English, he entered the University of California,
read all the books he could lay his hands
on. He was naturalized in 1918, entered

the United States Army during the World War, and after the War went right on discovering America—particularly from the point of view of its workers, its unskilled laborers, its immigrants. Someone once described him as "a tall young man with a look of eager curiosity."

Although Adamic had published numerous magazine articles, his first book wasn't published until 1931. It showed that he didn't like quite all he saw. Called *Dynamite*, it was a record of violence in the United States' labor movement from the Molly Maguires to the dynamiting of the Los Angeles *Times'* building. The year his book was published Adamic married Stella Sanders of New York. *Laughing in the Jungle* (the "jungle" was the United States, and the title might have been paraphrased "whistling in the dark") followed in 1932. That year Adamic also won a Guggenheim Fellowship by submitting the outline of a novel which he proposed to write during a visit to his native Carniola. What he actually wrote after his visit didn't turn out to be a novel, but it *was* a best seller. *Native's Return* (1934) was the first-person story of a young man who returns to his own country and finds that he cannot become a peasant again; it was Adamic's own story. Two sequels, *Grandsons* (1935) and *Cradle of Life* (1936), were also successful; his first novel, *The House in Antigua* (1937), was not so well received.

My America, published in 1938, received much critical acclaim. It has been described as "An Immigrant Author's Sixth Book in Search of a Character." A "mixture of memoir, social philosophy, anecdote and transient magazine article," its section headings reveal something of its contents: America in Action; New York; After the Native's Return; Ellis Island and Plymouth Rock; The Depression; The Workers; Random Portraits and Snapshots; The Long Road. Mr. Adamic has never subscribed to any particular political philosophy, but this, like his most casual writings, displays a rare personal honesty, a "complete integrity and a kind of cool passion for justice and democracy," and an almost mystical belief in "the American Process," which, in spite of countless failures and setbacks, he believes has been for 200 years working for "more and more social, economic and political liberty and equality."

After receiving a grant-in-aid from the Rockefeller Foundation in 1937, Louis Adamic worked for the Rockefeller and Carnegie Foundations in collecting the experiences of foreign-born and second-generation groups in America and trying to classify the attitudes toward them of native Americans of older stocks. *America and the Refugees,* a pamphlet, was published in 1939. Many of Adamic's magazine articles have dealt with the same problems—the feeling

LOUIS ADAMIC

of inferiority of millions of new Americans and its causes; the tragic situation faced by refugees from Fascist Europe who have entered the United States illegally. Adamic has also written sympathetically and from firsthand experience of the CIO, of sitdown strikes, of migratory workers in California, of labor in general, but perhaps it is the problems of the immigrant which he best understands and which most arouse his desire to help. The Council which he now heads might be said to have been conceived back in 1934, when he urged some sort of an organization which could give these millions a pride in their own cultural heritage and create a sympathetic understanding for them on the part of older Americans.

Mr. Adamic's newest book, *From Many Lands* (1940), has an identical purpose in mind. A collection of "illuminating and significant portrait-histories," packed with facts, it gives true records of the lives of certain immigrants—Meleski, Starkku, Steinberger, Evanich—each of whom came to America with a definite contribution to make to his adopted country and who had the good fortune to have it accepted. Said the New York *Times* reviewer: "In the heroic sweep of his material, the poetic thrust of the author's noble simplicity, the everyday heroisms and dauntless triumphs over disaster which are the stuff of which these lives are lived, Louis Adamic has given us such a saga as might be sung by heroes of old."

Adamic is a member of the Authors' League of America, the American Civil Liberties Union, the American Political

ADAMIC, LOUIS—*Continued*

Science Association and the Committee for Cultural Freedom.

References

Lit Digest 117:14 Ap 7 '34 por
N Y Sun p26 Je 14 '40
Newsweek 11:32 My 16 '38
Scholastic 24:7 Ap 7 '34 por
Wilson Lib Bul 9:8+ S '34 por; 9:182 D '34 por
[Adamic, L.] After Nineteen Years *In* Balch, M. ed. Modern Short Biographies and Autobiographies p116-47 1940
Adamic, L. Native's Return 1934
America's Young Men
McWilliams, C. Louis Adamic and Shadow-America 1935
Who's Who in America

ADAMS, THOMAS Sept 10, 1871—Mar 24, 1940 British architect and authority on town planning; widely known in the United States; director for the Regional Plan of New York (1923-30); professor at Harvard University and Massachusetts Institute of Technology

References

International Who's Who
Who's Who

Obituaries

N Y Herald Tribune p12 Mr 25 '40
N Y Times p15 Mr 25 '40 por

ADDINGTON, SARAH Apr 6, 1891—Nov 7, 1940 Author of children's books, among them *The Boy Who Lived in Pudding Lane, The Pied Piper of Pudding Lane, Pudding Lane People;* also contributed to magazines; wrote two novels, *Dance Team* (1931) and *Hound of Heaven* (1935); former newspaper writer; married Howard Carl Reid in 1917

References

Who's Who Among North American Authors
Who's Who in America

Obituaries

N Y Herald Tribune p18 N 8 '40
Pub W 138:2204 D 14 '40

ADDIS ABABA, PIETRO BADOGLIO, DUCA D' (äd'ĭs ä'bä-bä bä-dōl'yo) Sept 28, 1871- Ex-supreme chief of the general staff of the Italian Army

Address: Rome, via XX Settembre 8, Italy

Bulletin: Badoglio resigned on December 6.

In 1922, when Mussolini marched on Rome, it was Pietro Badoglio who begged for a battalion of Royal Carabinieri to "sweep away these Black Shirt upstarts." Had the King assented, he could have crushed the Fascist march. Four years after Mussolini seized power, legend says that the same man hustled up troops just in time to pre-

PIETRO BADOGLIO, DUCA D' ADDIS ABABA

vent an attempt on the Dictator's part to seize the throne of Victor Emmanuel. Staunch monarchist, "friend and favorite of the Italian aristocrats," said to rank high in the freemasons, Pietro Badoglio is still too useful a man to be retired to the obscurity that his Duce might find politically desirable for him. Whatever his personal views are today on the subject of Mussolini and the War, in his military rôle he has already won more victories for Italian Fascism than most Fascists, has been rewarded in the past with the titles of Marquis of Sabotino and Duke of Addis Ababa and in 1940 is supreme chief of the general staff of the belligerent Italian Army.

Badoglio comes from the province of Piedmont, whose people are "distinguished by unswerving perseverance." He was born of humble, peasant parents (Mario and Antoinette Badoglio) in Grazzano Montferrato in 1871. He attended a military school at Turin, in 1890 became a sub-lieutenant of artillery and later entered the War College and the Royal Army Corps. He has served in every Italian war since, his first experience being lieutenant of artillery in the East African campaign of 1895 to 1896, when the Abyssinian Emperor whipped Italy in Eritrea. At that time he helped save Adigrat, and was one of the survivors of Adowa. In the Libyan campaign of 1911 to 1912 he was credited with planning the victory of Zanzur which wrested Libya from Turkey. He was promoted to the rank of major.

The First World War found him, in 1915, a lieutenant colonel with the second army corps fighting the Austrians, and in 1916 he became colonel and chief of staff of the sixth army corps. Other promotions followed and the capture of Mount Sabotino from the Austrians which led to the victory at Gorizia earned him a generalship. Badoglio had just taken over the command of the second army when the Austrian surprise attack brought about the defeat of Caporetto. He helped General Armado Diaz and the Allied rescue staff reorganize the Italian defense forces, strengthened morale, himself prepared the defensive on the Piave, and the "final push" which he had planned at Vittorio Veneto in October 1918 resulted in complete victory over the Austrians.

That he can be firm is shown by his behavior as leader of the Italian Armistice Commission which negotiated with Austria in November of that year. At one point in the negotiations an Austrian officer began to protest at the terms. *"Basta!"* exclaimed Badoglio. "Under the circumstances we have nothing more to say!" He turned to his adjutant. "Please make a telephone call and see that the order for cessation of hostilities is withdrawn." The telephone call never had to be made.

Hailed as a national hero after the War, Badoglio was made chief of the general staff of the army, and later Senator for life. In 1921 he was visiting both Romania and the United States as envoy extraordinary. In 1922 came the march of the Black Shirts on Rome. The year 1924 found him Ambassador to Brazil; in 1925 he again served as chief of the general staff; in 1926 he acquired the title *Maresciallo d'Italia* (field-marshal); in 1928 he became Governor General of Libya; and finally in 1929 he was knighted as the *Marchese del Sabotino*. He governed Libya until 1933.

In the beginning Badoglio was supposed to have opposed the Abyssinian War, but when the elderly De Bono was leading the Italians to disaster in Ethiopia, he was, nevertheless, sent to replace De Bono in November 1935 as high commissioner for East Africa—thus making the Ethiopian conquest an affair of the regular army and shoving the responsibility for its success on to Badoglio's shoulders. He was equal to the task. In 1936, victorious, he was created Viceroy of Abyssinia and then relieved at his own request and made Duke of Addis Ababa. He is said to have "master-minded" Franco's victory in Spain, though he himself refused to campaign, saying proudly: "I have never been a chief of mercenaries." The lessons in mechanical warfare learned in Spain are undoubtedly proving useful to Badoglio in World War II, however.

Taciturn and modest, Badoglio's "square head and jaw and flattened nose often betray a pugnacious aspect. His deep-set eyes seldom smile. Yet . . . his manner is dashing, kindly, courtly. . . Despite his years, his back is straight as a ramrod, and few military shoulders are as nattily adorned." He is far from being the traditional Latin hothead. Seldom engaging in any large-scale operation until he has himself inspected things thoroughly and made careful plans, skeptical of reports he can't verify with his own eyes, he is as economical with lives as he is with material, and his men like him and have confidence in him. He used to have friendly arguments with General Gamelin (see sketch this issue) over the war of position versus the war of motion, but that was before September 1939. Not quite all his accomplishments are military. He seldom fails to win at *Boccia* (a kind of bowls played by Italian peasants), he is the author of a book, *War in Abyssinia* (1937) and he never overbids at bridge.

References

Collier's 97:12-13+ Ap 11 '36 il pors
Lit Digest 121:14-15 Ja 18 '36 il
Liv Age 350:317-20 Je '36
R of Rs 94:47 Ag '36 por
Time 35:26 Je 24 '40

Addis Ababa, P. B., Duca d'   War in Abyssinia 1937
Chi è?
Gunther, J. Inside Europe p261 1940
International Who's Who

ADDITON, HENRIETTA SILVIS May 14, 1887- Social worker
Address: Westfield State Farm, Bedford Hills, New York

On March 18, 1940 Miss Henrietta Additon assumed her duties as superintendent of Westfield State Farm, New York's only prison for women. She is the first woman superintendent of the prison section at Bedford Hills; the reformatory (just across the highway) which opened in 1901 has had only one woman superintendent, the late Dr. Katharine Bement Davis who later became Commissioner of Correction for New York City. The prison and the reformatory were united in 1933.

Miss Additon, succeeding the late Carl J. Kane, is responsible for the welfare of almost 600 delinquent women and girls in the farm's two branches. She must supervise the operation of the prison farms, the cannery, the laundry, a herd of cows and droves of pigs. She said she had never had any experience in cow and pig management, but expects to find out about it soon.

Henrietta Additon's ancestors came from Maine, but she was born in Utica, Illinois. Before many years her family moved to Flowery Branch, Georgia, where her father, Orville I. Additon, (Lucy [Benner] Additon was her mother) had a furniture business. She began her career as a schoolteacher there after she was graduated from Piedmont College in Demorest. Within a year she became an instructor in history in that Georgia college and in 1911 received an M. A. degree from the University of Pennsylvania in social studies.

Then Miss Additon became an agent for the Philadelphia Society for Organizing Charities and the following year probation

ADDITON, HENRIETTA—*Continued*
officer for the city's municipal courts. In three years she was put in charge of probation work in Philadelphia. During the World War she was director of the women's and girls' section of the War Department's Commission on Training Camp Activities.

After the War she was successively executive assistant to the United States Interdepartmental Social Hygiene Board; executive secretary and organizer of the Philadelphia Big Sister Association; in charge of the Girls' Service at the Sesquicentennial Exposition in 1926; consultant on protective measures of the American Social Hygiene Association.

In 1930 Miss Additon went to New York City to head the Crime Prevention Bureau, and when Edward P. Mulrooney became Police Commissioner he appointed her a deputy so that she might better carry on the bureau's work. As sixth deputy police commissioner she was put in charge of a newly organized Crime Commission Bureau. She resigned in September 1934 as a result of a disagreement with Mayor La Guardia (see sketch this issue), charging that the Mayor misunderstood and hindered the work of her bureau. Later the misunderstanding was patched up. The next year she was made a member of the State Crime Commission and was appointed to the State Commission of Correction in 1938.

Miss Additon became the director of the New York World's Fair Welfare Department in 1937 and in 1938 her duties were extended to include the supervision of housing. She and her assistants took care of 11,418 individuals during the first Fair season. They gave medical care to many who needed it; helped foreigners who couldn't speak English; supplied information on suitable living quarters; returned lost and runaway children, of whom there were more than 7,000, to their parents.

From her wealth of practical experience in crime prevention and juvenile delinquency Miss Additon has written articles for magazines and published two books: *City Planning for Girls* (1928), a study of the social machinery for case work with girls in Philadelphia, and *A Study of Brooklyn Girls* (1931). She has lectured extensively to social workers and to club groups on crime prevention, probation, penology and social work and has taught social economy at the Pennsylvania School of Social Service, Bryn Mawr, the New York School of Social Work and Hunter College.

Shouldering her new duties in her early 50's, Miss Additon is described as "a large woman with graying hair and brown eyes." She has a calm, competent, charming manner accompanied by a contagious smile. She had told herself that she would never accept a position in an institution, but the challenge of Westfield Farm and the possibilities of exerting an influence upon its inmates made her personal preferences give way to her sense of duty. As a social worker, "but with a sense of humor," she hopes to be able to help solve the problems, not of 600 inmates of the prison and reformatory, but of 600 individuals—"each with a separate background, and to help each individual herself so that upon release she can cope with the world."

References
> Am Mag 127:105 Je '39 por
> Ind Woman 19:139 My '40 por
> N Y Herald Tribune p1, 19 Mr 14 '40 por
> N Y Times VII p13, 20 Je 2 '40 por
> Scholastic 36:10 Ap 1 '40 por
> Survey 76:175 My '40 por
> American Women
> Who's Who in America

G. Maillard Kesslère

HENRIETTA ADDITON

ADLER, CYRUS Sept 13, 1863—Apr 7, 1940 Noted educator; president of Dropsie College in Philadelphia; president of the Jewish Theological Seminary of America, New York City

References
> Newsweek 12:26 S 19 '38 por
> Who's Who
> Who's Who in America
> Who's Who in American Jewry

Obituaries
> Bul Am Schools of Oriental Research p2, 3 Ap '40
> Christian Cent 57:523 Ap 17 '40

CYRUS ADLER

N Y Herald Tribune p12 Ap 8 '40
por
Newsweek 15:9 Ap 15 '40
Sch & Soc 51:474 Ap 13 '40

ADLER, HARRY CLAY Sept 8, 1865—
Mar 27, 1940 Executive of the Chattanooga
Times for 40 years; father of Julius Ochs
Adler, general manager of the New York
Times

References
Who's Who in American Jewry

Obituaries
N Y Herald Tribune p22 Mr 28 '40
N Y Sun p23 Mr 28 '40 por
N Y Times p23 Mr 28 '40 por
Time 35:58 Ap 8 '40

ADLER, MORTIMER JEROME Dec 28,
1902- Educator; author
Address: b. University of Chicago, Chicago,
Illinois; h. 20 E Cedar St, Chicago, Illinois

Attention in the educational field first
came to Mortimer J. Adler in 1930 when
President Hutchins of the University of
Chicago brought him there to be his right
hand man in instituting a "return to the
classics" theory of education. Then only 28
years old, Adler soon became known through
his publications as one of the most brilliant
thinkers in the United States. His *Art and
Prejudice* (1937) not only received the approbation of scholars, but came to wider
public notice because of its section on motion pictures as an art and the question of
their regulation by moral and political authorities. *How to Read a Book* (March 1940)
is Dr. Adler's first book for the man in the
street; one of the soundest in the "self-help"
category, it led the best-seller lists.

Most people can't read, Dr. Adler says,
and that's what's wrong with democracy.
After he had received his Ph. D. and began
teaching, he discovered that he himself
didn't know how to read, and set about
remedying the matter. Reading for amusement is ruled out in his discussion; by reading he means learning, or reading for understanding. In his first section of *How to Read
a Book* he says a book worth reading must
be read three times: for analysis, for interpretation and for evaluation. In the second
section of the book Dr. Adler lays down
rules for reading (as necessary, he says, as
for tennis or car-driving) such as spotting
clue-words and sentences, pivotal paragraphs and central ideas. His third section
is concerned with the connection between
reading and freedom. The whole process is
called active (as opposed to passive) reading, entailing "the most intense mental activity."

Reading in this way, Dr. Adler says he
can read at best 10 books a year. In an
appendix he lists books by 131 great authors
of all time, from Euclid to Thomas Mann.

The style of *How to Read a Book* is clear
and simple, informal and concrete enough
for the average level of "reader" intelligence.
The book has been highly praised by reviewers, one of whom claims it has taught
him, for the first time, how to read. It has
also been praised, but questioned in part, by
educators.

Mortimer J. Adler was born in New York
City December 28, 1902, son of Ignatz and
Clarissa (Manheim) Adler. In high school
he was editor of the De Witt Clinton High
School paper; but he never was graduated
because the principal objected to his trying
to run the school as well as the paper. He
left high school and became personal copy
boy to a newspaper editor. Soon he was
writing short editorials and taking extension
courses at Columbia University in the evening. When he was fifteen he read in John
Stuart Mill's autobiography that when Mill
was five years old he had read the *Dialogues
of Plato*. Adler hadn't even seen the *Dialogues
of Plato*, so he got a second-hand copy, read
it and decided to be a philosopher instead
of a journalist. On a scholarship he went
to Columbia, where he finished the four
year course in three years at the head of his
class. At that time one had to be able to
swim to get a degree; Adler couldn't learn
to swim. As he puts it, "no swimmee, no
A. B." It was not until after six years of
teaching that he became the recipient of a
Ph. D. in psychology (1929) from Columbia.

In 1926 Adler married Helen Boynton.
They live near the University of Chicago,
where Adler has taught since 1930, first
in the philosophy faculty, then in the law
faculty. With Dr. Hutchins (see sketch this
issue) he was co-teacher of the famous
course in philosophy of education. He
has also been an assistant director of the
People's Institute in New York. Since
1937 he has been a visiting lecturer at

MORTIMER ADLER

St. John's College, Annapolis. There, as at the University of Chicago, a return to the traditional basis of education has been established: close study of the classics of the Western World.

Known as one of America's foremost lecturers, Dr. Adler spoke during his 1940 tour on the themes of his recent books and on such topics as Progress in Progressive Education; The Social Influence of the Movies; Communism and Christianity; The Limitations of Science.

Besides *How to Read a Book* Dr. Adler is the author of *Dialectic* (1927); *Diagrammatics* in collaboration with Maude Phelps Hutchins (1932); *Crime, Law and Social Science* in collaboration with Professor Jerome Michael (1933); *What Man Has Made of Man* (1937) and *Art and Prudence* (1937).

The last-named book, ostensibly about the movies, is for the most part a formal, academic analysis of the views of Plato, Aristotle and St. Thomas Aquinas (of whom Adler is a disciple) on the relation of art to morals. Adler states that everything that can be said about films today was well said before films even existed. He calls "communication or social education" a function of art; as such, the cinema is a real successor to the arts as practiced by the ancients. He believes that the movies, like all other arts, should be judiciously regulated by moral and political authorities, the criteria to be applied not to production but to reception. Art stimulates the passions and sublimates them through "purgation." If "purgation" does not take place, social harm may result. Dr. Adler thinks most of the movie researches to date are doubtful as to method and inconclusive as to results.

Otherwise, he makes some extreme claims for the movies: "The arts, enriching the imagination and providing vicarious experience which can be directly appreciated, are almost indispensable in social education, both for children in schools and for the adult population. Of the arts, those of fiction serve best because of what they represent; their proper object of limitation is all of human life. Of the arts of fiction, the movies are at once the most popular and the most vivid representation of contemporary society. Their vividness, which is held to be responsible in part for the power they have over children, makes them exceptionally useful as an educational instrument."

How to Read a Book is another projection of Dr. Adler's theories on the meaning of a liberal education. He believes that a smaller proportion of Americans is literate now, in the real meaning of the term, than in the eighteenth century. As his reason for writing the book he says: "You know how many times people say, 'It's a good book, but it's 'way over my head.' That's all nonsense. Any person of intelligence has no right to say that any book is over his head. The technique of proper reading is intended to elevate one's head to those things that formerly were over one's head.

If one has no skill in reading he may even have difficulty in reading the funnies for pleasure. Once he has acquired skill he can find pleasure in reading Homer and Dante." Adler maintains that books should be lived with as friends: with this idea, he wanted to call his book *How to Become Friends with Books and Be Influenced by Them.* But the publishers didn't think much of that as a title.

The book itself was written during 16 days, a chapter a day. Each night Adler went to a movie, 16 in all. Apparently he reads more slowly than he writes: he cannot read more than two hours at a sitting, because he finds it quite fatiguing. His favorite relaxation, as may be gathered from his frequent references to the game in *How to Read a Book,* is tennis.

References

Commonweal 29:581-3 Mr 17 '39; 29:
680-3 Ap 14 '39; 30:548-51 O 13 '39;
31:504-7 Ap 5 '40; 32:119-22 My 31
'40
Nation 146:415-17 Ap 9 '38
N Y Herald Tribune p23 Mr 5 '40 por
N Y Herald Tribune Books p3 Mr
31 '40
N Y Sun p32 Mr 4 '40
N Y Times Book R p4 Mr 10 '40
N Y World-Telegram p20 Mr 21 '40
por
Sat R Lit 21:6 Mr 9 '40 por
Time 35:94-6 Mr 18 '40 por
America's Young Men
Who's Who in America (Addenda)
Who's Who in American Jewry

AITKEN, WILLIAM MAXWELL, 1ST BARON BEAVERBROOK *See* Beaverbrook, W. M. A., 1st Baron

ALDRICH, WINTHROP WILLIAMS
Nov 2, 1885- Banker
Address: b. 18 Pine St, New York City;
h. 15 E 78th St, New York City

Winthrop Aldrich, chairman of the board
of the Chase National Bank, organized the
Allied Relief Fund, one of the largest and
most important charities in the United
States for overseas relief during the Second
World War. Aldrich's contributions in
time and money to charitable and welfare work are notable, and it is not surprising that he should add the chairmanship of
the Allied Relief Fund to the dozen or more
directorships of welfare organizations he already heads. By October 1940 Mr. Aldrich
had helped Allied Relief raise about $1,600,000
in cash in addition to $800,000 worth of do-
nated supplies. Allied Relief was merged
with the British War Relief Society and Mr.
Aldrich carried on as president of this nationwide organization. Because of his "distinguished public service" Mr. Aldrich was
awarded the Goodrich Medal at the New York
World's Fair in October 1940.

Winthrop Aldrich is the son of Abby
Pierce Chapman Greene and the late
Senator Nelson W. Aldrich of Rhode Island, who was a power in the Republican
party and sponsor of the high tariff. Winthrop was born in Providence, Rhode Island, the tenth of eleven children. His
sister Abby married John D. Rockefeller
Jr., and his friendship with his brother-in-
law had much to do with starting Aldrich
in the banking business.

As a boy Aldrich attended the Hope
Street High School in his home town of
Providence, Rhode Island and then went to
Harvard. He was graduated from the Harvard Law School in 1910, tenth in his class,
then came to New York, where he got a job
with the firm of Byrne and Cutcheon. He
had a "ponderous thoroughness" and an intense desire to do a job by himself and soon
became a valuable man in corporate law
work for his firm. In 1916 he was made
a junior partner.

That same year he married Harriet Alexander, daughter of Charles B. Alexander,
a New York lawyer, a marriage which allied him to a social aristocracy as important
as the financial aristocracy of the Rockefellers. Aldrich was establishing himself as
an important member of society. He bought
a town house, built formal and informal
summer houses, traveled a good deal and
was active in charities and clubs. He and
Mrs. Aldrich have four daughters and one
son. About half his time is taken up with
welfare activities. Golf is a hobby but he
finds little time for it or for yachting.

He added to his knowledge of yachting
with a technical course in navigation at the
School of Navigation in New York City
and was commissioned a lieutenant in the
United States Naval Reserve. During the
First World War he was successively commander of patrol boats, navigating officer

of the *Niagara* and of the cruiser *New Orleans,* which operated as a convoy to transatlantic troop ships.

After the War his brother-in-law, John D.
Rockefeller Jr., suggested that Aldrich leave
his junior partnership at Byrne and
Cutcheon and enter the law firm of Murray, Prentice and Howland, for years chief
counsel of the Rockefeller interests. He
was chosen by his firm to represent the
old Equitable Trust Company, a Rockefeller
bank, and for eight years, from 1922 to 1930,
devoted almost all his time to the bank's
affairs.

He also handled successfully an outside
job for John D. Rockefeller Jr., the famous
proxy fight in which the Rockefellers were
successful in ousting Colonel Bob Stewart
from the chairmanship of the Standard Oil
Company of Indiana. Then, when the Equitable Trust Company merged with the Sea-
board National in 1929, Aldrich handled
the legal complexities of the merger. And
when Chellis A. Austin, the young president
of the new bank, died of heart failure three
months after he was installed in his new
office, Aldrich was called in to take over
Austin's duties temporarily, since he knew
more about the business than anyone else.
Aldrich had protested, "I'm not a banker,
I'm a lawyer," but a banker he became.

Three months later, when there was announced another merger of the Equitable
Trust Company, this time with the Chase
National Bank which Albert H. Wiggin had
built up in a series of mergers, Aldrich was
made president of the new Chase National
Bank. He was there primarily to see that
Equitable's interests were served in the
merger and was looked upon as a newcomer
who did not know much about banking.

Before the year was out, however, Aldrich
had learned a great many things about the
Chase National Bank. Under the direction
of Wiggin, then chairman of the board,
Chase Securities Corporation had been organized for underwriting investment loans
and selling securities. Under Wiggin's management the Bank and the Securities Corporation had poured large sums into specula-
tive loans which became increasingly sour
as the depression deepened during 1931 and
1932. Aldrich finally went to mat with
Wiggin on the issue. The important interests on the board of directors sided with
Aldrich, who won his insistent demands for
a conservative banking policy. Wiggin resigned on January 10, 1933 and Aldrich succeeded him as chairman of the governing
board.

Two months later Aldrich made his
famous depression banking statement during
the banking moratorium of March 1933, and
it has become one of the classics of Wall
Street. Aldrich called for a complete divorce
of commercial and investment banking.
Wall Street reverberated with anger.
Aldrich was accused of breaking Wall Street
tradition by not asking other bankers' advice
and not taking them into his confidence.

Pach Bros.

WINTHROP W. ALDRICH

But he made good his statement. In April he formally proposed to his directors the discontinuance of Chase-Harris-Forbes securities, an affiliate of the Chase National Bank. Congress enacted a law paralleling Aldrich's suggestion that affiliates selling securities be completely separated from commercial banks.

Only a month before his unconventional statement Aldrich had testified before the Senate Finance Committee. At that time, according to his own declaration, he knew nothing about Wiggin's personal speculations. In the fall of 1933, when Wiggin testified before the Senate Banking and Currency Committee that he personally had made $10,000,000 cash profits in open-market trading in Chase National Bank stock while Chase subsidiaries had lost money trading in pools, Aldrich jumped to his feet to protest that this was news to him. He declared he did not "approve of it and would not condone it while he was connected with the bank."

But there was general bitterness against the bank and its officers at this time and Aldrich's statement did him no good publicly. Some business and Wall Street observers turned a cold shoulder on Aldrich, first for his March 8, 1933 statement and now this, coming as it did on revelations of the bank's bad investments.

The bank came through with greater resources at the end of the year, however, and by 1936, despite the depression, was in better condition than it had ever been before. Aldrich's management has been entirely successful.

Aldrich has none of the smiling back-thumping cordiality expected by some of the banking fraternity. He enters his office "with stiff, cold strides" and goes to his desk by the nearest route. But of his moral rectitude and his intense loyalty to the ideas which have been bred into him there can be no doubt. They are not the kind of ideas "that would have encouraged reckless speculation or market rigging or fundamentally unsound practice of any kind."

Winthrop Aldrich is not a colorful figure. "A deliberate, precise, well-tailored gentleman," he cannot be catalogued or classified easily. His New England background has given him reserve and disinterest in personal publicity. To his staff he is friendly and approachable. Aside from his duties at the Chase National, his charities and his membership in more than two dozen clubs, yachting has been in the past his special pleasure. In the days when he had more time for it the New York Yacht Club was his favorite club. He climaxed a successful yachting career in 1930 by managing the New York Yacht Club Syndicate which built the cup defender *Enterprise*. He sailed as the navigator under Skipper Mike Vanderbilt when the *Enterprise* defeated the late Sir Thomas Lipton's *Shamrock V*.

References

Business Week p13-14 Ja 4 '33 por
Fortune 13:54-60+ Ja '36 il pors
Lit Digest 115:9 Mr 25 '33 por; 116:6 D 9 '33
Newsweek 10:28 O 25 '37 por
[Anonymous] Winthrop Williams Aldrich *In* Mirrors of Wall Street p115-29 1933
Smith, A. D. H. Winthrop W. Aldrich *In* Men Who Run America p95-102 1935
Who's Who in America
Who's Who in Commerce and Industry

ALEXANDER, ALBERT VICTOR May 1, 1885- First Lord of the British Admiralty; leader in the Cooperative movement
Address: 1 Victor St, S. W. 1, London, England

When Ramsay MacDonald included A. V. Alexander in his administration in 1929 as First Lord of the Admiralty, one press comment was: "At least he will be the first Cooperator and the first Baptist lay preacher to be the ruler of the King's Navy." There proved to be no need for misgivings. Alexander turned out to be a wise administrator then, and today, as Lord of the Admiralty again, he is again a wise administrator. Political observers now believe that in the twentieth century only one other First Lord has been a bigger man in the post—Winston Churchill (see sketch this issue).

Alexander is a Socialist. Not a campaigning, fighting, fiery Socialist, but one who believes in the cooperative movement as the cure for most social ills. Without conspicuous oratorical gifts or a wide, world view of political questions, he has nevertheless become a figure of importance in the progressive movement. He has figured in no "scenes," he has denounced nobody, he has emphasized not the abolition of Capitalism but the paramount virtues of Cooperation. And in doing this, as in acting as Lord of the Admiralty, his method has been one of quiet industry, of fact accumulation, of thorough knowledge.

Albert Victor Alexander was born in the pleasant seaside resort of Weston-super-Mare, the son of Albert Alexander, an artisan engineer. His boyhood was spent in the neighboring port of Bristol, where he went to public school. He left at 13 to become a junior clerk in the offices of the Bristol Education Committee. He was capable at his job, played football enthusiastically on weekends and began to read and study. Evenings he attended classes at the St. George Technical School in Bristol and generally, as the Victorians used to say, "improved himself."

When Alexander was 18 he left the Bristol Education Committee and went to work for the Somerset County Education Committee, with which he remained for 17 years, rising to be its chief clerk and serving as secretary to the Somerset branch of the National Association of Local Government Officers. Outside office hours he developed two absorbing interests. One was Cooperation, on which he made himself an expert. Eventually he became vice-president of the Weston-super-Mare Cooperative Society, after working on its management committee. The other was the Baptist religion. He became active in it locally, frequently preaching its doctrines.

With the coming of the First European War, Alexander joined the Artists' Rifles. After becoming a corporal he took a commission, served through the whole period of the War and rose to the rank of captain. After the War, in 1919, he acted as Education Officer for the Southwestern District.

It was in 1920 that Alexander secured his first national post in the Cooperative movement, as secretary to the Parliamentary Committee of the Cooperative Congress. When, in 1921, there was a proposal in Parliament to tax the undistributed dividends of the Cooperative societies, Alexander successfully led the opposition. He led it successfully again when the proposal was brought up in 1933.

In 1922 Alexander put up for Parliament in the Hillsborough division of Sheffield against a Cabinet Minister who had had the big majority of 7,000. Alexander won, by 3,318, and increased his majority in the 1924 election. During these two years in Parliament he acted as whip to the Cooperative Party. In 1924, when Labor formed its first government, he was appointed to the minor post of Parliamentary Secretary to the Board of Trade. Thrown out by a second election that same year, he was absent from Parliament until 1929 when, in Labor's second administration, he was made First Lord of the Admiralty and sworn a Privy Councilor.

Even though the First Lord is only the political chief who is advised on technical matters by Sea Lords, still there were a good many explosions in officers' messes when the appointment was announced. It wasn't long, however, before Alexander had won the respect of both officers and men by his grasp of essential detail and his obvious care for efficiency and the welfare of personnel. He improved the working conditions and quarters of the common sailor and at Dartmouth (the Naval College) saw to it that not only the wealthy public school boys but also secondary school boys should be eligible for entry.

His position on broad issues of policy was considered sane and sound. Like most progressives he is a pacifist by conviction, but still feels that the aims of peace would not be furthered by unilateral naval disarmament. He did what he could to make the Five-Power Naval Treaty of 1930 an effective instrument for peace; he went to Paris and, with the late Arthur Henderson, did his best to compose Franco-Italian differences. One of his aims was to abolish the submarine, but in this he failed.

When Labor suffered its crushing defeat in 1931, Alexander again lost his seat and returned to Cooperative work. In 1932 he was one of those who helped form a new National Cooperative Authority. In 1935 he was re-elected to Parliament and, even though he was in the Opposition when the present War broke out, the First Lord of that day, Winston Churchill, often consulted with him. When Churchill as Prime Minister formed his government in May 1940, he was quick to appoint A. V. Alexander head of the Admiralty.

Alexander is a man of medium height, clean-shaven, with a keen and intelligent face. In the House the general opinion of him is that "he is appreciated, but is not big, jolly or hearty enough to become popular." He is married to Esther Ellen, youngest daughter of the late George Chapple of Tiverton.

References

Picture Post p38-9 Je 1 '40
Author's and Writer's Who's Who
Cooperative Representatives in Parliament 1924
International Who's Who
Johnston, J. A. A Hundred Commoners 1931
Who's Who

ALLEN, GRACIE July 26, 1905- Radio and motion picture actress; member of team of Burns and Allen

Address: c/o National Broadcasting Company, Hollywood, California

Gracie Allen, whose full name is Grace Ethel Cecile Rosalie Allen, is the scatter-brained goof, the allegedly lightweight mental part of the team of Burns and Allen. In real life she is not so daffy. She and George Burns have been one of the major attractions of the networks since 1931.

As a guest on the *Information, Please* radio program in the summer of 1939, Gracie stacked up favorably with the most select experts, which is hardly in keeping with her professional dumbness on radio and screen. She played opposite James Cagney in a serious Irish playlet for a Screen Guild show, and did it very well. And one year the University of Southern California psychology students honored her by voting her Hollywood's most intelligent actress.

The actress' association with George Burns dates back to 1922, when she appeared for the first time with Burns at the Hill Street Theatre in Newark, New Jersey. Gracie had started her professional career in San Francisco, where she was born. Her father was a song and dance man, and when she was three and one half years old she joined his act. Later she attended a convent school in San Francisco, but at the age of thirteen or thereabouts joined three older sisters in vaudeville as a hoofer. Next she joined the Larry Reilly Company doing jigs and dances and playing Irish colleen parts. When the Reilly Company got to Hoboken, New Jersey, Gracie left over a question of billing. She thought she deserved billing other than the "and company." Reilly decided she didn't.

GRACIE ALLEN

Vaudeville jobs were scarce, so Gracie decided to take up stenography. She was taking a secretarial course in New York when she met George Burns, then teamed with Billy Lorraine in a song and dance act at Union Hill, New Jersey. One of Gracie's roommates was doing an act at the same theatre, and Gracie met George backstage one night.

The team of Burns and Lorraine was just on the verge of breaking up, and Burns (Nathan Birnbaum, born January 20, 1898, a Manhattan youth who had been doing variety turns since he was 12) asked Gracie to work with him. Gracie left stenography, and her career of professional giddiness began. At first Gracie asked the straight questions and Burns gave the quip answers, but it didn't work, so Burns reversed the routine. Gracie became the garrulous, dumb girl of the act and Burns claims that theirs was the first mixed act to coax laughs without funny clothes.

The Burns and Allen pay envelope for the first three days of their act at the Hill Street Theatre was $15. In 1940 they were reputed to be earning $9,000 a week for their radio act. But they put in hundreds of weeks of vaudeville before they got anywhere near that figure. They had steady work, however, and realized their ambition to play on the Orpheum Circuit touring the West Coast.

Back in New York they broke in a new act and celebrated the event by taking time off, while they were playing in Cleveland, to get married. This was in 1927. Burns quipped, "I owed Gracie $200 so we decided to take a gamble."

In New York they were seen by a Keith scout and the next day signed a five-year contract, the longest up to that time. Their salary is reported to have rocketed from $400 to $750 a week, and they took summers off to play in Europe. Their debut in radio was made in England in 1930, when the British Broadcasting Company asked them to do their act on the air.

Burns and Allen were playing at the Palace in New York on the same bill with Eddie Cantor in 1931 when they next appeared on the radio. Cantor, who at that time was broadcasting on a network program, asked Burns if he would allow Gracie to appear as a guest on his program. Gracie nearly stole the show from Cantor. The next day Burns and Allen had a radio offer. Since then they have remained in radio steadily, with little time off between changing sponsors.

Gracie's scatterbrained prattling and dumbness have made her a household by-word in the United States. Gracie popped in on countless programs in 1933 looking for her supposedly lost brother, and created such a sensation that her real brother George, a San Francisco accountant, had to go into hiding until the gag blew over. Her latest exploit on the Burns and Allen radio broadcast has given the act columns of publicity, for in 1940 Gracie entered the Presidential race as a candidate of the Surprise Party, and appeared unannounced on half a dozen network programs to air her politico-comic aims. "With what party are you affiliated?" she is asked. Gracie answers: "Same old party—George Burns." When it is pointed out that candidates always affiliate themselves with a party, Gracie says, "Well I may take a drink now and then, but I never get affiliated." Her political philosophy "is not one of overconfidence. I realize the President of today is merely the postage stamp of tomorrow," she says. Her *How to Become President*, prepared by the Gracie Allen Self-Delusion Institute, was published on June 19. The 1940 political campaign was not her first entrance into politics on the air. Once before, when Burns and Allen decided their program needed a little shot in the arm, Gracie ran for Governess of the State of Coma and created quite a sensation.

At home the comedienne is simple, unaffected, untheatrical. Her voice is mellow and entirely unlike that high-pitched thin voice she uses in her act. Of Irish descent, Gracie Allen is an attractive, petite brunette. Her hair is an auburn tone, her eyes hazel and her skin a creamy white. Most of the year she and her husband, George Burns, live in a 12-room Beverly Hills, California house with their two adopted children, Sandra Jean, born July 1934, and Ronald John, born July 1935.

The private lives of Burns and Allen have been without scandal or headlines, except for the trial of George Burns in 1939 on a charge of buying jewelry smuggled in by Albert Chaperau and avoiding paying the duty on it. Burns pleaded guilty and was fined $8,000.

Their radio act is an amiable bit of husband-and-wife teamwork. George knows that Gracie can get the laughs and has purposely selected the minor rôle for himself. While they employ script writers, George Burns himself often writes the jokes for Gracie Allen. He does not have the slightest jealousy of her popularity, but off the radio and screen, when they are at home, it is George who entertains the guests. Off the air George Burns is said to be one of the funniest men in the world, as well as a keen, matter-of-fact businessman who knows the show business.

Burns and Allen made their motion picture debut in short subjects while they were still in vaudeville. Later they appeared in feature pictures: *The Big Broadcast*, *We're Not Dressing*, *Love in Bloom*, *College Humor*, *Six of a Kind*, *The Big Broadcast of 1935*, *Soup to Nuts*, *Here Comes Cookie*, *The Big Broadcast of 1937*, *College Holiday*, *College Swing* and the *Gracie Allen Murder Case* (Gracie alone).

Apart from radio and screen work, Gracie has found time to indulge in a bit of painting in her own style of surrealism. In 1938 she gave an exhibit of her revolutionary surrealism in a Manhattan gallery. Some of the typical titles of pictures were *Gravity Gets a Body Scissors on Virtue as Night Falls Upside Down* and *Eyes Adrift as Sardines Wrench at Your Heartstrings*.

References

Arts & Dec 48:25-7+ Ag '38 il
Delin 129:64-5 Ag '36 il por
Ind Woman 19:198+ Jl '40 por
Liberty 17:45-6 Je 29 '40 por
N Y Herald Tribune X p14, 20 My 12 '40 por
Photoplay 52:27+ Ap '38
Time 32:21 D 26 '38; 35:36 Mr 18 '40 por
Variety 138:25, 31 My 8 '40
American Women
Variety Radio Directory

ALLEN, JOEL NOTT 1866—Mar 11, 1940 Artist

Joel Nott Allen, famous portrait painter, died at Port Jefferson, New York, March 11, 1940, at the age of 74. Born at Ballston Spa, New York, the son of the Rev. Edward B. and Margaret Copper (Nott) Allen, he attended the Mount Pleasant Military Academy in Ossining, New York, and studied art under Robert Blum and H. Siddons Mobray as well as at the Art Students League and the Metropolitan School. Mr. Allen's work is represented in permanent collections in the National Gallery, Washington, D. C.; the Gibbs Memorial Gallery, Charleston, South Carolina; the New York Chamber of Commerce, the Museum of Natural History and the Lotos Club, New York; and numerous private collections.

Obituaries

N Y Herald Tribune p22 Mr 12 '40
N Y Times p23 Mr 12 '40
N Y World-Telegram p30 Mr 12 '40

ALLYN, LEWIS B. 1874—May 7, 1940 Noted food chemist; head of the chemistry department of Westfield State Teachers College, Massachusetts from 1903 to 1915; writer on pure food standards

Obituaries

N Y Times p17 My 9 '40 por
Springf'd Republican p1, 2 My 8 '40

ALMAZAN, JUAN ANDREU (äl-mä-zän' huän an-drĕ-ōō') May 11, 1891- Defeated 1940 candidate for President of Mexico

December 1940 Bulletin: General Juan Andreu Almazán, officially defeated for the Presidency of Mexico in the elections of July 7, 1940, claimed that the Almazánistas had actually polled 90 per cent of the total votes and that he still had every intention of taking office on December 1. While he was seeking the support of American financiers and political leaders for his cause his fol-

Associated Press

JUAN A. ALMAZAN

lowers set up a rump Congress in Mexico City and were reported as using Texas as a base for operations in the north. Sporadic revolutionary attempts and guerilla warfare resulted in many deaths, and the hope of forestalling outright civil war which would give the United States a reason for intervention at this critical time was most likely the cause of increasingly conciliatory policies on the part of President Cárdenas' government and increasingly conservative statements on the part of President-elect Avila Camacho (see sketch this issue) as inauguration day drew nearer. In fact, Camacho has been accused of having appropriated Almazán's program in an attempt to win over his supporters. One of the most loyal of these was evidently the organ of the Spanish Fascist government, which in August 1940 described Almazán as "the future Mexican President, friend of Franco." In November 1940, however, prospects for a revolution seemed unlikely, especially after the United States government recognized Camacho's election. On November 27 Almazán, who had returned to Mexico, renounced his claim to the Presidency, although his followers continued to demonstrate.

From June 1940 issue:
On July 7, 1940, a new President will be elected in Mexico. If the United States press seems to be taking an abnormal amount of interest in the elections, it is because revolution is expected to be one of its by-products. On April 3, 1940 Cordell Hull (see sketch this issue) sent a note to the present government of President Cárdenas, calling attention to the strained relations now existing between the United States and Mex-

ico which have grown out of Mexico's 1938 expropriation of foreign oil and mining concessions and suggesting arbitration of the dispute. Since that time relations with Mexico have grown even more strained. On May 1, after organized demonstrations against "Yankee imperialism" in all of Mexico's 28 states, came the reply of the Mexican government refusing international arbitration for what it considered a domestic issue. A private and direct agreement was reached with the Sinclair oil interests, however, and the government indicated its willingness to negotiate with any other oil companies that care to do so. Of the remaining companies, it is Standard Oil that has the biggest stake in Mexico.

Up to this time the hope of United States oil interests has seemed to lie with conservative General Juan Andreu Almazán, who is opposing the Cárdenas party's candidate for President, General Manuel Avila Camacho, and who favors a policy of cooperation with the United States. The General claims to doubt the government's sincerity in promising a fair election, and has stated that he will hold a private election the day before or on the day of July 7; if votes in the two elections do not tally, he threatens force. "If the government attempts to thwart the will of the people by manipulating votes at the election of July, I shall know what course to follow." Two weeks before the election the Dies Committee (see sketch this issue) also proposes to hold an inquiry in Texas with regard to alleged efforts by Communists and Nazis to take over the Mexican government. This proposal, Mexican authorities charge, is designed purely to aid Almazán, whose clique would probably present testimony about such a conspiracy, and to give the United States an excuse for intervention. In the meanwhile there are rumors of heavy arms smuggling across the United States border and of a coming march against Mexico City or the establishment of an independent Rightist government in Northern Mexico by Almazán's followers. As a precaution the government will mass its troops to rally popular support and to overcome the opposition.

Forty-nine-year-old Juan Almazán has long taken an active interest in Mexican politics, although previously he was more concerned with bullets than ballots. He was born in 1891 in the mountains of Guerrero. His family were wealthy landowners, among the seven per cent which formed the aristocracy of Mexico at that time. When he quit his medical studies to join Francisco Madero's forces, which exiled dictator Díaz in the bloody Revolution of 1910, it may have been merely because of natural adventurousness, for it is certain that once in uniform he never showed any desire to return to medicine. In 1913, the year that Madero was forced out of office and murdered, Almazán was already commander of the garrison of Morelos. The reactionary

Huerta moved into power. Twenty-two-year-old Almazán did not revolt against tyranny for the second time, however, but served with Huerta. In fact "since Díaz' time," he says, pointedly, "I have never revolted against established government."

Almazán profited by the chaos of the middle '20s, revolt or no revolt, and became a "self-made general," leading 15,000 men. When Calles headed the government in 1924 it was Almazán who was chosen to command Monterrey, the country's most important army zone, and he held that same post under the three Calles-made Presidents who followed.

In 1928 Almazán was backtrailing Don Quixote in Spain—"on a well-fed and spirited Rosinante." In 1929 he distinguished himself by his quick suppression of a threatened revolt. In the meanwhile he was in a position to add to his private fortune. Privately he developed the resort property from Monterrey to Acapulco on the south Pacific coast. He became head of a construction company which landed one fat government contract after another and which in 1931 successfully took charge of one of the great engineering jobs of the world, the Pan-American highway. Often his soldiers were used in the work of construction; the Monterrey army post was entirely soldier-built, as was his summer home and resort center, constructed in 1933 on a mountain shelf 3,000 feet above Monterrey.

In late 1934 Cárdenas and the Party of the Mexican Revolution (P. R. M.) came into power, but Cárdenas was rather careful to leave Almazán alone. It was noted that in 1938 Almazán was not called upon to hunt down the rebellious Cedillo, and that there were practically no expropriations in Almazán's adopted state of Nuevo Leon. But Almazán was waiting for the psychological moment to make his appearance on the political scene. The young government was having its difficulties; six years was hardly long enough for the country to make a successful economic and financial adjustment to Cárdenas' sweeping reforms. The Constitution declared that the President may not succeed himself, and Cárdenas, loyal to its principles, refused to run again.

In 1939 General Manuel Avila Camacho, Secretary of National Defense and not known as a "strong man," was chosen as the candidate of the P. R. M., with the endorsement of Vicente Lombardo Toledano (see sketch this issue), Mexico's John L. Lewis. Although Mexico has never in all its history had a truly democratic election, Cárdenas promised that in the 1940 election the President would be elected by the people. The new law of Federal elections, the lack of political prisoners in the jails and the freedom of the press enjoyed by the opposition as well as by those sympathetic to the government seemed also to promise well.

In 1939, when Washington cut the price paid for Mexican silver and thus added the "next-to-last straw" to the country's financial worries, General Almazán, "big, erect, handsome in a leonine way," finally decided it was time to come down from his mountain shelf and offer to save the country.

Almazán is "supported by the Right and talks Left." He claims to have the backing of a large section of labor and of the P. R. M., but Northern Mexican industrialists are known to be solidly behind him, and some have claimed that he is backed by foreign oil interests. Vice-President Garner is one of his good friends outside his own country. His campaign is financed by "patriotism bonds, non-redeemable and suitable for framing," by his own personal fortune and by the fortunes of his friends.

Although calling himself "profoundly nationalistic," Almazán still opposes those forces which foster an anti-Yankee spirit in Mexico. "We can never have either the sympathy or cooperation of the American people to become a strong nation unless we establish bonds of true friendship with them. This must be based upon conscientious respect of our mutual rights," he has said.

To the Mexican people he promises peasant ownership of land instead of the present collectivist system. His speeches run like this: "Do you really own the land today? Or have you just traded the old landowner for a greater one in Mexico City?.. I will see that you own the land. You, Pablo, will have your 10 acres. You, Pedro, will have yours. You may cultivate it or you may sit and look at it. But when the workingman's crop comes in there will be no bookkeeping agent to rob him of it. That is what he fought for in 1910."

He claims that the present government and unions are overrun by corrupt politicians and racketeering labor leaders. "People of Mexico," he cries, "you overthrew your oppressors in 1910, but are being enslaved anew today by thousands of parasites and vultures who are reducing you to a deeper, more abject misery."

Of the reforms of the Cárdenas government he says: "This is a very fine dream. But are you eating?"

A Catholic himself, he has the support of a large number of Catholics because of his promise of freedom of education. His advocacy of woman suffrage has won him the backing of many Mexican women. Few observers at this time believe that his following is strong enough to assure his election against the Cárdenas candidate, however, even though Almazán has partially succeeded in splitting the ranks of union labor and of the Party of the Mexican Revolution.

An election campaign in Mexico has little in common with a fireside chat. Camacho posters are ripped down during the night and replaced with Almazán posters; the next night finds the Almazán posters torn down. Already there have been

ALMAZAN, JUAN—*Continued*

many pre-election killings, and at **one** time Almazán was given a bodyguard of 150 soldiers by Cárdenas.

Almazán maintains a costly home in Mexico City, but usually he spends most of his time in his "mountain aerie," 600 miles to the north. There he has a private zoo, where he can divert himself with all varieties of the country's wild animals. "I am a mountain man," he insists. "I do not feel right where things are flat."

References

Commonweal 30:390-3 Ag 18 '39
Cur Hist 51:37-9 Ap '40 (Same abr. Read Digest 36:87-90 Ap '40)
Life 9:19-23 Jl 1 '40 il pors
Liv Age 358:444-6 Jl '40
Nation 151:71-3 Jl 27 '40; 151:270-1 S 28 '40
New Repub 102:628-9 My 13 '40; 103: 109 Jl 27 '40
N Y World-Telegram p16 My 9 '40
Scholastic 36:9, 12 Ap 22 '40
Time 35:32 F 19 '40 por; 35:39-40 Ap 15 '40 por; 36:39-40 S 16 '40 por; 36: 34 S 30 '40

ALSBERG, CARL LUCAS Apr 2, 1877— Oct 31, 1940 Biochemist; worked in food biochemistry; chief of United States Bureau of Chemistry, 1912-21; second chemist to become government expert on pure food and drugs; director of Stanford University's Food Research Institute, 1921-37; dean of graduate studies at Stanford, 1927-33; director of Giannani Foundation of Agricultural Economics at University of California since 1937

References

Sci ns 54:244 S 16 '21

American Men of Science
Chemical Who's Who
Who's Who Among North American Authors
Who's Who in America
Who's Who in American Jewry

Obituaries

N Y Herald Tribune p12 N 2 '40 por
N Y Times p15 N 2 '40

ALTENBURG, ALEXANDER 1884—Mar 12, 1940 Artist

Well-known artist and member of the firm operating the Altenburg Piano Company of Elizabeth, New Jersey, Alexander Altenburg studied art in Europe and toward the end of his life spent most of his time painting there. He won favorable comment from American and European critics for his French landscapes. The French government purchased three of his paintings. A diploma of honor was awarded him at the Bordeaux International Exposition in 1927. His works hang in the Luxembourg Museum, the Salon d'Automne and the Jeu de Paume, all of Paris, the Brooklyn Museum and the 57 Fifth Avenue Gallery, New York.

Altenburg died after a long illness, at the age of 56, leaving a widow and three brothers.

Obituaries

N Y Herald Tribune p22 Mr 13 '40
N Y Times p23 Mr 13 '40

ALTER, GEORGE ELIAS May 8, 1868— Aug 18, 1940 Lawyer; former Attorney General of Pennsylvania (1920 to 1923); candidate for the Republican nomination as Governor of the state in 1923; began practice in 1893; served in House of Representatives of the state from 1908 to 1914; member of the commission on uniform laws **for** Pennsylvania

References

Who's Who in America
Who's Who in Law

Obituaries

N Y Herald Tribune p8 Ag 19 '40
N Y Times p17 Ag 19 '40

AMSTERDAM, BIRDIE Mar 25, 1902- Judge

Address: b. 51 Chambers St, New York City; h. 299 E 11th St, New York City

The first woman justice elected to the Municipal Court in New York County is 38-year-old Birdie Amsterdam. The attractive brunette judge was inducted into office January 3, 1940 by Presiding Justice Pelham St. George Bissell.

Judge Amsterdam's primary interest is social service. "To my mind, law is a social institution," she says. "A jurist should

BIRDIE AMSTERDAM

be socially minded, should be sympathetic, understanding, tolerant, patient and humane. Of all the institutions in our government, the courts are the bulwarks of Democracy. Theirs is the responsibility for safeguarding citizens against any invasion of their personal or civil liberties."

Born in New York City on March 25, 1902, Miss Amsterdam was one of six children in a family of Austrian Jewish immigrants. Today, two brothers are physicians, one a pharmacist; Miss Amsterdam's older sister was formerly a nurse, and her younger sister is shortly to be admitted to the Bar.

At the age of 12 Miss Amsterdam was graduated with honors from a grammar school in the heart of New York's crowded tenement district. To continue her schooling she worked in a candy store and at Mt. Sinai Hospital during the day and after high school attended evening classes in banking and economics at the College of the City of New York. Her law degree she obtained from New York University Law School.

In 1923 she opened her own office and practiced law for many years alone. Later she became associated with her brother-in-law and took an active role in politics. At one time she was a co-leader in Tammany Hall.

Miss Amsterdam's election to the Municipal Court is for a 10-year term during which her salary is $10,840 a year. But money is of minor importance to her; many of the clients in whom she has become most interested have been too poor to pay her anything for her legal aid.

This attitude Judge Amsterdam explains by saying: "At an early age I was taught to do justice, to love mercy and to walk humbly with my fellow man. This precept I have endeavored to practice at all times, and I hope to be given the strength of heart and mind to continue to dispense justice to the fullest measure of sympathy and mercy."

Judge Amsterdam's father, Joseph Amsterdam, is dead, but Mrs. Essie Amsterdam is living. "Any success I've had," says the justice, "I owe to those two people."

References
    Humanity Mr '40
    N Y Herald Tribune Ja 1 '40; p9 Ja 3
      '40 por; Ja 4 '40
    N Y Times II p4 N 5 '39 por; p19
      N 9 '39 por; p27 D 21 '39; Ja 4 '40;
      Ja 8 '40

ANDERSON, ABRAHAM ARCHIBALD
1847—Apr 27, 1940 Artist; philanthropist; ex-head of Yellowstone Forest Reserve; patron of aviation

References
    Who's Who in America 1932-33

Obituaries
    N Y Herald Tribune p32 Ap 28 '40 por
    N Y Times p37 Ap 28 '40 por

ANDERSON, GEORGE EVERETT Aug 20, 1869—Mar 17, 1940 Former United States Consul in the Far East, Europe and South America; specialist in the study of international trade and finance; writer on financial matters

References
    Who's Who in America

Obituaries
    N Y Herald Tribune p12 Mr 18 '40

ANDERSON, JOHN CRAWFORD Aug 5, 1863—Apr 27, 1940 Chief Justice of the Alabama Supreme Court for 26 years; held the Scottsboro boys were unfairly tried; became a judge in 1895

JOHN CRAWFORD ANDERSON

References
    Who's Who in America
    Who's Who in Law

Obituaries
    N Y Herald Tribune p32 Ap 28 '40 por
    N Y Times p36 Ap 28 '40

ANDERSON, MARIAN Feb 27, 1908- Negro contralto

Address: b. 30 Rockefeller Plaza, New York City; h. 762 S Martin St, Philadelphia, Pennsylvania

When Toscanini heard Marian Anderson sing he said: "A voice like hers come once in a century." The 75,000 people who came to hear her before the Lincoln Memorial on Easter 1939—the greatest crowd since Lindbergh's triumphal homecoming—and the thousands who buy tickets for her concerts months in advance are heartily in agreement.

This singer who, according to *Variety's* box office score, is topped in popularity only

MARIAN ANDERSON

by Nelson Eddy and Lily Pons, and whose concerts are now booked for two years in advance, was born of poor Negro parents in South Philadelphia in 1908. Her start was an early one. "Indeed," she says, "I have expressed myself through my voice as long as I have known myself." At six she joined the junior choir of the Union Baptist Church and at thirteen the senior choir as well. After her father died when she was 12, she helped support her family by singing at church concerts.

During her second year at the South Philadelphia High School for girls her remarkable voice gained the attention of John Thomas Butler, the distinguished Negro actor. He sent her to Mary S. Patterson, who offered to teach her without pay. Some months later the Philadelphia Choral Society gave her a benefit concert and sent her to work with a leading contralto and teacher, Agnes Reifsnyder, of Philadelphia. When she was 19 her high school principal, Dr. Lucy Wilson, helped her meet Giuseppe Boghetti, the famous teacher.

Boghetti remembers her first audition well. It came at the end of a long, hard day's teaching when he was weary of singing and singers, and there was a tall calm girl who sang *Deep River* in the twilight and made him cry.

In 1925 Boghetti entered Marian Anderson's name in a singing contest, the winner of which was to sing at the Lewisohn Stadium in New York accompanied by the New York Philharmonic Orchestra. She won against three hundred other singers and her concert was a triumph. An important manager placed her under contract. Nothing happened. Engagements were negligible. Everyone said: "A wonderful voice—it's too bad that she's a Negro." Marian Anderson spent a year being coached by Frank La Forge and left

the United States, discouraged by the barriers of racial discrimination.

Her first concert in Germany cost her $500. This was the last time Marian Anderson ever paid to perform. From then on success was swift. She sang before King Gustav in Stockholm and before King Christian in Copenhagen, and received one of his rare invitations from Sibelius, the great Finnish composer. When she came in to see him, Sibelius said to his butler: "We will have coffee." After she sang, he shouted: "Not coffee, *champagne!*" To her he dedicated his song, *Solitude*.

On December 30, 1935 Marian Anderson gave her first New York recital after her return from Europe, standing throughout on one foot, her other foot in a cast. In 1936 she was asked to give a solo at the White House. When President Roosevelt said to her: "Oh, hello, Miss Anderson, you look just like your pictures, don't you?" she had the only attack of stage fright of her life.

Despite her tremendous success, when her agent tried to book a concert at the D. A. R.'s Constitution Hall in Washington for Easter 1939, the D. A. R. told him that "all dates were taken." Immediate protests were made by famous musicians. Heifetz, scheduled to play in Constitution Hall, said he was "ashamed" to appear there, and Walter Damrosch, Deems Taylor (see sketch this issue) and others fought against this discrimination. Leading clergymen and statesmen protested, too. The fight was climaxed by Mrs. Roosevelt's (see sketch this issue) announcement in her syndicated column that she was resigning from the D. A. R. and by Secretary Harold Ickes' securing of the Lincoln Memorial Hall for her Easter concert. This concert was used as the subject of a mural design contest for the new Department of the Interior building, announced by the Federal Works Agency's Section of Fine Arts in October 1940.

Marian Anderson is now the most popular concert singer in America and possibly in the world. Critics can't praise her tone and expressiveness enough. They call it a "voice of many rewarding timbres, clear and silvery in the soft upper tones, full and warm in the lower register"; they rave "over its sheer loveliness." With its three octave range it is particularly amazing in songs like the *Erlkönig* or *Der Tod und das Mädchen*, in which she uses both her lower register and her soprano.

Her repertoire is varied—two hundred songs in nine languages, Purcell and spirituals. No program of hers is complete without spirituals. "They are my own music," she says, "but it is not for that reason that I love to sing them. I love the spirituals because they are truly spiritual in quality; they give forth an aura of faith, simplicity, humility and hope."

It's been a life devoted to music and to her people that Marian Anderson has led. She has never married. Her friends are few, Kosti Vehanen, her coach and accompanist, being her only close one. Her home is still in South Philadelphia across the street from the house in which she was born.

On July 2, 1939, Mrs. Roosevelt presented Marian Anderson with the Spingarn Medal, given annually to the American Negro who "shall have made the highest achievement during the preceding year or years in any honorable field of endeavor." When Mrs. Roosevelt presented it she told Marian Anderson: "Your achievement far transcends any race or creed."

References

Christian Cent 57:245-7 F 21 '40
Collier's 102:17+ D 3 '38 por
Etude 57:631-2+ O '39 por
N Y Times IV p2 Ap 2 '39 por; p30 Ap 5 '39; p15 Jl 3 '39
Newsweek 12:24-5 D 19 '38 por; 13: 33 Mr 6 '39
Read Digest 36:26-30 Mr '40
Time 33:23 Ap 17 '39; 33:38 Mr 6 '39 por
Stokes, A. P. Art and the Color Line pam 1940
Thompson, O. ed. International Cyclopedia of Music and Musicians 1939
Who's Who in America

ANDERSON, MARY Aug 27, 1872- Director of the Women's Bureau, United States Department of Labor

Address: h. 528 17th St, N W, Washington, D. C.

Mary Anderson, who has spent over twenty-one years as a bureau chief under five administrations, is today the dean among women in key appointive positions in the Federal government. Her job as head of the Women's Bureau of the Department of Labor has been to formulate standards and policies to improve working conditions for women, to increase their efficiency and to develop their opportunities for profitable employment. In doing this she has had to break down prejudices; she has had to build up understanding; she has had to inspire confidence among government officials, congressmen, employers, employees, labor unions, all kinds of women's organizations, economists and social agencies.

Miss Anderson was born in the small city of Lidköping in Sweden on August 27, 1872, the youngest of seven children. Her home was on a farm and Mary passed her days churning, carrying wood, helping with the housework, spinning and weaving. An older sister who had gone to America wrote back glowingly of life there, and when Mary was 16 she joined her. First she lived in Ludington, Michigan where her sister was working.

Mary couldn't speak a word of English **and** found herself working as a cook,

MARY ANDERSON

spending every free minute studying English. But this lasted only a year, for her sister married and moved to West Pullman, near Chicago, Illinois, taking Mary with her. Mary got a job in a garment factory and then in a shoe factory. For 18 years she earned her living by stitching shoes.

Mary didn't just do her job. She began to analyze the difficulties confronting the workers in that factory; she began to see that even though women had their own peculiar problems, it was only when all workers stood together on important issues that progress could be made. Much of her spare time was spent with her "local" of the International Boot and Shoe Workers' Union—after 10 hours of daily stitching in the factory she would dash off to union meetings, or to meetings of civic and educational groups in Chicago.

Because of "her innate ability and enthusiasm," eventually she was made president of Local 94, one of the oldest and best-known in the shoe industry. As president she traveled to other shoe centers, began to meet labor leaders in many industries and later became the only woman on the executive board of the International Boot and Shoe Workers' Union.

The American women's movement saw in her an invaluable aid toward furthering the progress of women wage earners, and she was asked to leave her shoe operator's machine to take a full-time position as organizer for the National Women's Trade Union League. Eight years of this work proved excellent experience. Mary Anderson learned to speak at a moment's notice; she gained knowledge of industrial, economic and legal matters, of sectional and national labor conditions, and particularly of the handicaps and hardships of women workers.

ANDERSON, MARY—*Continued*

When the United States entered the First World War Miss Anderson was drafted into service She explains how it all happened: "The suddenness of it took my breath. It was at the beginning of the World War when . . . I was busy helping a thousand women out on strike in Chicago. Mrs. Raymond Robins, then president of the League, announced to me at 9 o'clock one morning: 'You will have to take the noon train to Washington today.' She explained that I was to attend the meeting of the woman in industry section of the Council of National Defense. I protested that I didn't want to desert the girls, but Mrs. Robins insisted she would take my place. I never dreamed that what appeared to be just a brief interlude would end up in steady work in Washington."

Miss Anderson's first job was to supervise the laboring conditions of women munitions workers. One war job led to another and in July 1918 she was appointed assistant director of the Woman in Industry Service "to safeguard the interests of women during the War and to make their services most effective for the national good."

After the War she was appointed director of the Woman in Industry Service to succeed Mary van Kleeck, who resigned in August 1919, and when, in June 1920, Congress converted this agency into the permanent Women's Bureau, Miss Anderson was retained as director, the first "labor" woman to hold any responsible position in Washington. During the 20 years she has headed this bureau she has made intensive studies of conditions and problems among wage-earning women; she has been instrumental in formulating standards and policies for their safe and efficient employment; she has cooperated with many important organizations, assisting and advising in special projects pertaining to the welfare of women workers. It was she who was responsible for calling two important conferences on woman in industry in the United States, attended by representatives of all national organizations of women. When she attended the Seventeenth International Labor Conference at Geneva, Switzerland in June 1933 she was appointed chairman of the American delegation of official observers. In April 1937 President Roosevelt appointed her adviser to the United States Government Delegate to the Technical Tripartite Conference on the Textile Industry.

One of the busiest officials in Washington, gray-haired Miss Anderson is also one of the most approachable—ready to meet anyone who calls at the bureau. Women workers everywhere feel that Mary Anderson, the former factory worker, is still one of them, vitally concerned about their welfare. They know that her aim is "to safeguard the interests" of the millions of women in the United States who earn their living.

References

Survey G 25:93 F '36 por
American Women
Kirkland, W. M. and Kirkland, F.
    Mary Anderson, The Women's Bureau *In* Girls Who Became Leaders
    p59-66 1932
Who's Who in America
Who's Who in the Nation's Capital

ANDERSON, MARY [obit] *See* Navarro, M. de

ANGELL, JAMES ROWLAND (ān'jĕl) May 8, 1869- Educational counselor for the National Broadcasting Company

Address: b. 30 Rockefeller Plaza, New York City; h. 155 Blake Rd, Hamden, Connecticut

Dr. James Rowland Angell, who in June 1937 retired as president of Yale into the still very active position of its president-emeritus, actually merely changed "his base of educational endeavor from New Haven to New York, from a university to the air." Since that time he has been NBC's educational counselor, numbering the "students" under his guidance by the millions rather than the thousands.

Dr. Angell has spent by far the greater part of his life on university campuses. He is descended from nine generations of Rhode Islanders. His grandfather was president of Brown from 1868 to 1872, and his father, James Burrill Angell, was president of the University of Michigan for 38 years. His mother was Sarah Swope (Caswell) Angell. James Rowland himself was born in Burlington, Vermont on May 8, 1869—on the campus of the University of Vermont, where his father was president for a brief time. When he was 11 years old he spent a year with his parents in Peiping, where his father had been sent as Minister to China, but it wasn't long before he was back on a campus, and he ended up by attending the University of Michigan himself. He studied under John Dewey, played shortstop on the baseball team, won the university and state tennis championships, played clarinet in the university band, became a member of Phi Beta Kappa and Delta Kappa Epsilon, received his B. A. in 1890 and his M. A. a year later. It was also at Michigan that he fell in love with Marion Isabel Watrous of Des Moines, Iowa, whom he married in 1894.

Young Angell's great interest was psychology, and he next spent a year at Harvard studying under William James and Josiah Royce. He received his M. A. from Harvard in 1892, and then was one of the first to go to Germany to explore the field. In 1893 he was studying at the universities of Berlin and Halle, and he also traveled and studied at Vienna, Paris and Leipzig. Back in the United States the same year he secured a position as instructor in philosophy at the University of Minnesota, and then in 1894 he became assistant professor of psychology and director of the psychological laboratory at the University of Chicago. For 15 years he was engaged in psychological experimentation. In 1901 he became an associate professor, in 1905 professor and first head of Chicago's department of psychology. In 1908 appeared his *Psychology*, the first textbook after William James' to come into extensive use in schools and colleges. The same year Dr. Angell became senior dean, and, in 1911, dean of faculties at Chicago. *Chapters from Modern Psychology* (1911) and *Introduction to Psychology* (1913) followed his first textbook, and from 1912 to 1922 he was editor of *Psychological Monographs*, a series of research publications. He was fifteenth president of the America Psychological Association, and, with John Dewey, who was at Chicago at the same time, did much to shift the emphasis in modern psychology to the process of adaptation of the individual to his environment.

After serving in 1914 as an exchange professor at the Sorbonne and from 1918 to 1919 as acting president of the University of Chicago, Dr. Angell came to the Carnegie Corporation as its president in 1920. He was there only a year, however, before he was called to be Yale's first non-Yale president, shortly after a sweeping reorganization. He accepted the position.

Some Yale alumni were described as "stricken with grief and shame" at the very thought of a president who wasn't a Yale man himself. Their shame, at least, couldn't have lasted long. Although Dr. Angell never went so far as to acquire a nickname on the campus, and his second wife, the former Mrs. Katharine Cramer Woodman, whom he married in 1932 (his first wife died in 1931), is said to have outshone her husband as a New Haven character, his 16 years at Yale were great ones in the history of the University. He inaugurated the new College Plan; he doubled the amount spent annually for maintenance and instruction, rebuilt the campus almost completely; he trebled the value of the Yale plant, quadrupled the University's endowment; during his presidency the School of Nursing and the Institute of Human Relations were founded, and the Medical School, the Law School and the School of Fine Arts enjoyed a great renaissance.

Since all Yale faculty-men must retire at 68, in 1937 Dr. Angell celebrated his sixteenth and last commencement as president of the University, bestowing an honorary LL. D. on his friend Cordell Hull (see sketch this issue). Major Lenox R. Lohr, president of NBC, saw his opportunity, and approached Yale's president-emeritus, still "lively as a cricket despite what he called his 'obvious and offensive senility.'" Said Major Lohr, in effect: "Your father was a pioneer; you've been a pioneer; in our opinion here at NBC there is a still greater

William Haussler

JAMES ROWLAND ANGELL

pioneering opportunity in a new field that we believe has great possibilities for human good and public service." In 1937 NBC was planning to devote a much greater part of the networks' total broadcasting time to "educational programs," and Dr. Angell was offered the position of educational counselor, with a free hand "to devise and suggest methods," an executive office at Radio City and a reputed salary of $25,000 a year. After many conferences Dr. Angell accepted the post; he spent his first year studying foreign and American systems of broadcasting to determine just what the relationship between radio and education should be; and, following a survey abroad, he made the recommendations which at present pattern and guide NBC's expanding activities in the field of public service broadcasting.

Dr. Angell has always been concerned with the freedom of the university and has spoken against the teachers' oath bills which, he pointed out, certain university presidents must take, though Father Coughlin (see sketch this issue) does not. He has been almost equally disturbed at the cessation of the flow of small legacies caused by governmental taxation—according to *Time*, "who soaks the rich soaks him," and according to Dr. Angell himself, "the right to tax is the right to destroy." Nevertheless, as he said in 1936, "if our universities are fully to justify to the increasingly critical public their intellectual and moral freedom . . . they must . . . turn more of their attention toward those urgent and compelling problems upon whose solution depends the very existence of civilization itself." He finds the increasing study of the social sciences an encouraging symptom in this direction.

Dr. Angell is a member of numerous scientific societies, among them the psychology committee of the National Research Council,

ANGELL, JAMES—*Continued*

of which he was chairman from 1919 to 1920. He is vice-president of the National and International Committees for Mental Hygiene, since June 1939 has been national president of the English Speaking Union and is a director in the New York Life Insurance Company and the National Broadcasting Company. He holds honorary degrees from more than 20 universities and colleges, numerous decorations. Besides articles in scientific and popular journals, his recent works include *American Education* (1937) and *War Propaganda and the Radio,* a pamphlet published in 1940.

"A very successful social personality," he is a member of the Graduate Club of New Haven, the Yale Clubs of Boston and New York, The University Clubs of Boston and Chicago, New York's Century Club and the Cosmos Club of Washington, D. C. He has one daughter, now Mrs. William Rockefeller McAlpin, and his son, James Waterhouse Angell, is an "orthodox professor of economics at Columbia University."

The Order of the Past Participle, "that exclusive company of onetime college and university presidents who continue to function actively after retirement," also claims Dr. Angell as a member. He lives in Connecticut and commutes to Radio City, New York. His hobbies include sailing, golf and reading.

References

Sch & Soc 46:12-13 Jl 3 '37; 48:554 O 29 '38
Sci ns 81:358-9 Ap 12 '35
Time 27:41-4 Je 15 '36 por (cover); 30:52 Jl 5 '37 por
American Men of Science
Heidbreder, E. F. Functionalism and the University of Chicago *In* Seven Psychologies p201-33 1933
Leaders in Education 1932
Who's Who Among North American Authors
Who's Who in America

ANTONESCU, ION (än-tōn-ĕs-koō' ē-ōn') 1886-   Premier of Romania

Address: Bucharest, Romania

On September 5, 1940, only three days after his release from the prison where he had been interned for "prohibited political activity," General Ion Antonescu, known as the "Red Dog," was appointed Premier of Romania by hard-pressed King Carol II (see sketch this issue). Parliament and the constitution were dissolved and dictatorial powers acquired by the General. This did not appease his vociferous Iron Guard supporters, however, and after violent demonstrations on their part he was compelled the next day to demand the abdication of the King to whom he had sworn allegiance. Carol fled; his 18-year-old son Michael for the second time acquired a sceptre without much weight to it.

Among Antonescu's first acts as military dictator of Romania were to lift the press censorship, cancel the extraordinary police measures which had been in effect since King Carol's "one-party" rule, restore Maniu's National Peasants and Bratianu's National Liberals to their legal status and release Iron Guard prisoners. His intentions were obviously to establish a "broader national government with a strong army flavor, in which all political parties, as well as the Iron Guards, will be represented." He also issued "sweeping decrees aimed at those who became wealthy under 10 years of the rule of the deposed King," abolished Carol's Party of the Nation and the National Guard, and a great many arrests were made among those identified with the former government. Its anti-Semitic flavor was preserved, however, and even intensified, although Antonescu later announced that he "could not possibly accomplish miracles in one week," and that the Jewish population would suffer nothing if it did not "sabotage the régime either politically or economically." As for himself, he took over four cabinet posts—the Ministries of War, Armaments, the Navy and the Interior.

One of the major aims and also major difficulties of Antonescu's government was to appease Romanian resentment against Romania's losses to Hungary. Immediately after taking office the General dispatched messages to Hitler and to Mussolini assuring them both of Romania's devoted loyalty to the Axis powers and of her intentions to carry out the terms of the Vienna "arbitration" peaceably. In his alignment with Germany he had the support of the fascist Iron Guards, who even back in 1936 were calling for friendship with the Axis, but he also had some difficulty in reaching an agreement with them because of their extreme demands for power. Finally early in October 1940, shortly before Germany's occupation of Romania, the Premier appeared before an Iron Guard rally wearing the green shirt of the organization, and assumed supreme command. The Iron Guard murders which took place late in November, after Antonescu had officially aligned Romania with the Axis, seemed to show that he had lost authority over them, however.

Antonescu is officially a Nationalist, and although he has been tagged "pro-German" since his rise to power, he has been known as "pro-British" throughout most of his career. His present position might be ascribed more to tough-minded political realism than to natural sympathy with Nazi aims. He is something of a cosmopolitan. Born of an aristocratic family in Transylvania, then a part of Austria-Hungary, he was educated at military academies in France and married a Frenchwoman. During World War I he served in the Romanian Army (where the standing of graduates of French military academies was very high), finished with the rank of major and shortly after the Armistice was promoted to the rank of colonel.

ION ANTONESCU

During the latter half of the '20s he was a military attaché in Rome and London. Carol's 1930 *coup d'état* was partially arranged by a friend of Antonescu's, Major Precups (who in September 1940 was released by Antonescu after having been imprisoned for having later taken part in a plot against Carol's government), and Antonescu himself was at that time far from unfriendly toward the King. It was during Carol's rule that he became a general and was finally appointed chief of staff in 1937.

The summer of 1938 found him out of favor, however. Mr. M. W. Fodor, authority on Central Europe, tells us how it happened. Carol was giving a reception attended by Romanian society and prominent government officials, among them his chief of staff. Magda Lupescu (see sketch this issue) chose to appear on that occasion. Antonescu rudely refused to kiss her hand; he was "forced to go," demoted to the command of the third army corps. It was November 29, 1938 when he left the army, suspended because he had condemned Carol's suppression of the Iron Guard, and two days later there occurred the abortive revolt against Carol, most of the leaders of which were discovered and imprisoned. Antonescu was among them.

Freed not long afterward and given the post of Minister of War, Antonescu made himself one of the strongest critics of the policies of the various Romanian governments since the abolition of political parties. After the resignation of Tătărescu he is said to have appeared before the King and asked for a change in policies, but without success. In the early summer of 1940 he was forced to resign his cabinet post, and in July 1940 was once more arrested for opposing the cession of Bessarabia and Northern Bukovina to the U. S. S. R. (he

had always been known as anti-Soviet). His opposition to the surrender of territories increased his popularity with both the Iron Guard and Maniu's Peasant Party, however, and the greater part of both parties supported the replacement of Carol's royal dictatorship by his military dictatorship. One Romanian newspaper, at least, rejoiced:

"Here is General Antonescu, the man in whom the Romanian people have been putting their hope for a long time, the man who only three days ago was freed from the prison of Bistritza, where he was detained without justice and without judgment, the man who only now, in the eleventh hour and when the greatest part of our frontiers are lost, has been called to bring calm and consolation to a people embittered by a tyrannic form of government under which it has lived for ten years and during which time the youth of the Nationalist generation has been basely killed and from whom billions of *lei* belonging to the country have been stolen under the pretext of rearmaments."

General Antonescu has been described as "honest, serious, clever, well-informed." His photographs show him as bland, trim, square-jawed, with regular features and hair graying a little at the temples.

References

N Y Herald Tribune p4 S 5 '40; p1, 11 S 6 '40 por; p1, 4 S 7 '40; p4 S 9 '40
N Y Times p1, 6 S 5 '40 por; IV p4 S 8 '40; p10 S 11 '40; p5 S 13 '40
PM p4 S 5 '40

ARCO, GEORG WILHELM ALEXANDER HANS GRAF VON (är'kō) Aug 30, 1869—May 7, 1940 Radio engineer; quit career in German Army to become scientist; called "German Marconi"; considered expert on radio-electric subjects; telephone service overseas largely due to his studies

References

Wer ist's?

Obituaries

N Y Times p23 My 8 '40 por

ARMSTRONG, EDWIN HOWARD Dec 18, 1890- Inventor; electrical engineer

Address: h. 435 E 52nd St, New York City

The method of eliminating static in radio by means of wide band Frequency Modulation, announced in 1939 and perfected in 1940, will soon revolutionize radio broadcasting and reception. Since Frequency Modulation may supply also the keystone in television and facsimile broadcasting, it is likely to remake the whole face of mass communication in the next decade. F M broadcasts may start in January 1941 commercially, and in the autumn of 1940 Major, Armstrong gave a six-week series of lectures on this new art at the American Institute of Electrical Engineers.

ARMSTRONG, EDWIN—*Continued*

The story of this most important development in radio since its inception is largely the story of the work of one man, Edwin H. Armstrong, who modestly calls himself an electrical engineer, but who has to his credit three outstanding previous inventions in the radio field. He has been Professor of Electrical Engineering at Columbia University since 1936. In February 1940 he was one of 19 inventors and scientists awarded the American Pioneers' Plaque by the National Association of Manufacturers.

Edwin H. Armstrong was born in New York City December 18, 1890, the son of John and Emily L. (Smith) Armstrong. During his freshman year at Columbia University he commenced research with the vacuum tube. In his sophomore year, dissatisfied with Dr. Lee De Forest's explanation of how his tube worked, he set out to find an explanation for himself. His experiments led to the discovery that the vacuum tube was a generator of high frequency currents. Thus in 1912, at the age of 22, Armstrong invented the regenerative circuit for high frequency oscillations, revolutionizing radio transmission. The following year he filed for a patent on it; in 1914 De Forest filed an application for a patent embodying part of the same principle. A battle ensued that went on for some 18 years, with many costs, legal tangles and complexities. In 1924 the legal tide turned against Armstrong. In 1933 he again attempted to gain recognition of what he believed to be his priority to the invention, and won in the court of appeals, only to have the Supreme Court reverse judgment in favor of De Forest in 1934. But most radio engineers agree that the honor of the invention belongs to Armstrong.

After his graduation in 1913, Armstrong stayed on at Columbia as assistant in research to Michael I. Pupin. But at the outbreak of the War he went to France as a captain, later becoming a major in the United States Signal Corps in charge of aircraft and intelligence radio. Three months before the Armistice he perfected the superheterodyne circuit, which magnified the weakest signals on the shortest waves thousands of times. Major Armstrong returned to the United States with patents pending on this invention. Once again the question of invention priority came up, but was never passed upon. Armstrong went on with his work, however; and in 1920 he invented his superregenerative circuit, now in wide use in police and military radio, which has the distinction of earning more for him than any of his other inventions.

In 1929 Columbia University conferred upon him the honorary degree of Doctor of Science. He married Marion MacInnis December 1, 1923.

From the very start of his career Armstrong had been interested above everything else in the problem of conquering static.

Pupin had worked with him for a short time; but in 1924 he started out on his own to attack the problem. In 1925 he proved to his own satisfaction that radio waves and static had the same electrical characteristics. Discarding the dogmas already in the field, by 1928 he found himself on the right track. In 1933 he invited officials of the Radio Corporation of America to his Columbia laboratories to look at his system of special Frequency Modulation which eliminated static.

Frequency Modulation (F M for short) means changing the length of the radio wave. Frequency-modulated signals slip past such interference as lightning bolts or ice-box motors. Ordinary broadcasting uses Amplitude Modulation, obtained by changing the size of the swings of the signals. In F M all the swings of the waves are the same and modulation is obtained by varying the frequency. The wave-band is five times wider than that occupied by one A M station. If the receiving set is deaf to all amplitude changes, a system is constructed so insulated that static cannot crash in within the service area of the station.

At the 1935 demonstrations a sound reel recording was played, comparing the reception during a thunder storm of the old and new types of broadcasting—the latter showing a program free of static, though the station power was only one per cent that of the larger station. In demonstration also was the sending of a radio facsimile copy of the front page of a newspaper, static free. A musical program was transmitted at the same time. This was the first time in his experiments, Major Armstrong said, that music and the printed word were sent and received together.

The remarkable thing about F M is the brilliant clarity of reception secured. Faint musical passages come through perfectly, loud passages or sounds need not be tuned down. Homely, natural sounds are transmitted with fidelity—not by a sound-effects man, but by broadcasting the actual sounds themselves. A British journalist, after hearing the reception, told his readers at home that the reproduction was "ghastly" in its reality. He looked for gurgling water to run out of the loud speaker, and the scratching of a match seemed almost to burn his hand. In the pauses between numbers it was impossible to tell whether the station was on or off the air.

Armstrong set up his apparatus in the Empire State Building for further demonstrations, but RCA kept asking for more time before throwing its weight behind F M. Then Armstrong was asked to take his apparatus out to make way for television. He did so, but with no very friendly feeling toward RCA. Meanwhile he and his friend, Carman R. Runyon, who had an amateur radio station, worked together at the building of an F M transmitter. The results were so successful that in 1936 Armstrong applied to the Federal Communications Commission for a permit to erect a big F M station of his own.

Because television was seeking channels at the same time, the FCC held up Armstrong's permit, and it was not till 1937 that he constructed his own station, W2XMN, a 40 kilowatt station perched high atop the Palisades at Alpine, New Jersey. It has a 400-foot tower and three 100-foot cross-arms. If Armstrong had not used his own money to rush construction of this station, it might have been years before the public ever heard of F M. But W2XMN was heard clearly and steadily at distances of 100 miles. Armstrong gives credit for the development of the work necessary to two of his assistants, John Bose and James Day. Apparatus for the stations was designed in the Hartley Research Laboratories at Columbia University. The remainder of the equipment was constructed at Radio Engineers' Laboratory in Long Island City and the RCA Company of Camden, New Jersey.

Soon other F M stations were in operation. Among the first were Yonkers, New York; Hartford, Connecticut and Paxton, Massachusetts. The Yankee Network Incorporated, became interested, and set up an experimental station on Mount Asnebumskit, Massachusetts. This network is planning a high-powered station in New York City, and is moving toward a complete change over to the Armstrong F M system. In September 1940 there were 22 experimental stations licensed in the country, many applications for F M commercial stations pending.

The construction of F M receiving sets has been put on a commercial basis. Since July 1939 sets have been put on sale by the General Electric Company and the Stromberg-Carlson Company. Other companies are in process of preparing sets. The new sets, costing from $75 to $225, are constructed so that they will be able to receive both the old and the new kind of broadcasting.

An additional advantage of the F M system is that it will relieve the danger of air-wave monopoly, by making available a service on those ultra-high frequency channels that are comparatively unused at present. This promises to bring cheaper station operation and consequently more opportunity for local stations. Engineers envisage the possibility of replacing the wires used to transit programs between network stations with a system of low power, low cost F M radio relay transmitters.

A highly successful demonstration of F M capabilities was made in January 1940. The Major's co-experimenter, C. R. Runyon, sent out a program of music and speech over his F M station in Yonkers, New York. Armstrong's station W2XMN in New Jersey picked it up and relayed it to WIXOJ at Paxton, Massachusetts. From there the program was broadcast to

Bachrach

EDWIN HOWARD ARMSTRONG

an F M station at Mount Washington in New Hampshire, which reported reception absolutely clear. From here the signal was rebroadcast by a standard short wave station to a Yankee Network receiving outpost in Winchester, Massachusetts, sent by telephone wire to Boston, and thence back to Yonkers. This was an important demonstration because it pointed a way out of F M's major difficulty—limitation of range.

Frequency Modulation has a possible bearing upon television also. Since the range of a television broadcasting station is the horizon, this means that to achieve coverage television must have many more transmitters than radio. If television could be transmitted by F M, as Major Armstrong believes possible, an F M beam transmitter would handle as many frequencies as necessary in any given situation, over a completely static-free, undisturbed circuit, and could thus be substituted for the present co-axial-cable piping.

On the status of Major Armstrong's outstanding work, *Fortune* (October 1939) reports: "While the duty of the FCC in making short-wave-band allocations was clearly to get television on the air as quickly as possible (the British having already beat the United States by a couple of years), the Commission's failure to understand Frequency Modulation and to place the proper estimate on its technological importance is just as deplorable as the industry's failure to push it. Instead of encouraging substantial capital outlays, which the development of this invention would cause, the Commission has acted as a deterrent by relegating Major Armstrong to an experimental corner of the ultra-short-wave spectrum. What F M needs at the present time above all things is an allocation that

ARMSTRONG, EDWIN—*Continued*

will put it on a commercial status and will at the same time be large enough to permit it to operate to full advantage. Of the many ultra-short-wave bands that have been allocated but are not actually in use, one band six megacycles wide would accommodate thirty F M stations, and through duplication get F M off to a start all over the country. Relieved of the heavy duties of policing its present restrictive wave lengths, the FCC might thus open a new era of democracy in the air."

The last week in March 1940, the FCC had on its hands a bitter fight between Armstrong, and his advocates of static-less radio, and the television concerns. Armstrong was on hand to testify before the FCC and state the case for F M. He requested that F M be granted full commercial licenses, that its present maximum power of 1,000 watts be raised to 50,000, that a band of frequencies from 41 to 44 megacycles be allocated F M stations; that immediate permission for expansion of these allocations be made, since nearly 100 station applications from all over the country had recently come in. Since the 44 to 45 megacycle band is already television's number one channel, Armstrong's demand roused the RCA to battle all Armstrong claims. RCA and television received a set-back when the FCC withdrew its recently granted "limited commercial" status from all telecasters, fearful that the public might buy sets that would soon prove to be obsolete.

John Shepard III, of the Yankee Network, outlined a plan for a ten-year absorption by F M of present broadcasting methods, with a gradual change-over of transmitting and receiving equipment. Major Armstrong made some remarks of his own about television. "I am convinced," he said, "that the television people . . . will soon realize they can operate to better advantage in frequencies higher than those upon which they are now operating. . . If I hadn't been so busy showing the world how good F M is, I might have shown the television boys how to do it."

On May 20, 1940 a Federal Communications Commission ruling opened the air lanes to commercial stations using F M. The fact that any number of properly spaced F M stations can operate in the same air channel solves a headache for the FCC since it can now satisfy an almost unlimited number of license applicants. Major Armstrong believes that there isn't any reason now "why every city in the United States which can afford a radio station cannot have an F M station." And already radio manufacturers are predicting a great boom in radio, in which millions of dollars will be spent and thousands of persons employed in making, selling and installing F M equipment.

References

Christian Sci Mon p3 Mr 16 '40 il
Fortune 20:86-8+ O '39 por
N Y Herald Tribune p11 Mr 20 '40
  por; p7 Mr 29 '40; p20 My 21 '40
N Y Times X p12 Mr 17 '40; p46 Mr
  28 '40; X p12 O 20 '40
Newsweek 13:32-3 Ja 30 '39; 15:30
  Ja 15 '40; 15:30-1 Ap 1 '40 il por
Pop Sci 137:59 N '40 por
Sat Eve Post 213:18+ Jl 6 '40 il pors
Scholastic 36:10 Ap 15 '40 por
Sci ns 82:6 N 15 '35; 89:72 Ja 27 '39
Sci N L 35:355-6 Je 10 '39 por
Sci Am 154:3 Ja '36 por; 160:291 My
  '39
Time 34:47-8 Jl 31 '39 por; 35:36 Ap
  1 '40 por
Who's Who in America

ARNOLD, THURMAN WESLEY June 2, 1891- United States Assistant Attorney General in charge of the Antitrust Division

Address: b. Department of Justice, Washington, D. C.; Dover House, Jackson Hill, McLean, Virginia

Thurman Arnold, number one trust-buster of the nation, is a large, middle-aged man overflowing with human gusto, who "looks like a small-town storekeeper and talks like a native Rabelais." He has homesteaded in the foothills of the Rockies, run a sheep ranch, managed a thriving cattle-country law practice and taught at Yale. He has been Mayor of Laramie, Wyoming. In *The Folklore of Capitalism* (1937) and *The Symbols of Government* (1935) he has written satirical analyses of our legal, economic and political folk-ways, so witty and shrewd that some think the two books among the most significant of our time, but in *The Bottlenecks of Business* (1940) he stops kidding capitalism and asserts his faith in it—if the "economic toll bridges" which squeeze the American consumer can only be opened. It is possible to do it, he thinks, by applying the Sherman Antitrust Act.

Appointed United States Assistant Attorney General in charge of antitrust cases in March 1939, Arnold wasted no time in announcing a thorough-going drive against the trusts. His announcement created no small stir among the big cartels and trusts that had been hitherto left untouched by the very administration that was now determined to "thaw our frozen economic system" by attempting to give literal application to what had before been "beautiful generalities." Many scoffed at Arnold's ambition, maintaining that "in spite of more than 40 years on the books and decades of fulsome lip service from eminent thinkers, the antitrust laws have never been enforced before." Modern restraints of trade, chiefly consisting in competition-limited practices by groups of businessmen, flourished undisturbed on every hand. The laws, they asserted, "preserved the ideal but not the substance of free competition."

Arnold recognized the validity of their skepticism; he himself had said that instead

THURMAN ARNOLD

of restricting monopolies, "the actual result of the antitrust laws was to promote the growth of great industrial organizations by deflecting the attack on them into purely moral and ceremonial channels. . . In this way the antitrust laws became the greatest protection to uncontrolled business dictatorships." He maintained that "the nation cannot distribute goods because its prices are out of line with the power of the people to buy. . . The power to fix prices without public responsibility is the same as the power to tax without public responsibility. In the long run it cannot exist without governmental interference and regulation." Analyzing the situation further, he compared the affairs of the United States with those of Nazi Germany: "By January 1933 German business was so monopolistic that almost everyone in the country had to belong to a cartel or a trade association, or a chamber of commerce, or some other organization dedicated to preventing competition. The distribution system was too rigid. . . It needed a general to order the workers to work and the mills to produce. Hitler made himself that general. . . I predict that unless steps are taken to reverse the trend and restore free competition, our economic system will limp along on two cylinders for a good many decades." Arnold remained obdurate to all arguments that in trying to break the trusts he was going against a natural historical development. He knew what he was doing and he "meant business."

Arnold's drive grew out of the activities of the Temporary National Economic Committee. One of the principal purposes of the committee headed by Senator Joseph C. O'Mahoney was to look into the laws against monopoly and restraints of trade and see whether they ought to be changed. Arnold maintained that the laws didn't

need changes, but enforcement, and said he could enforce them if adequate money and personnel were available. He succeeded in obtaining funds and enlarged his department to include about 190 lawyers in contrast to the 18 in the department in 1932.

The field which touched most closely the problem of the bottled-up savings of the nation—a major problem considered by the TNEC—was the building industry. Arnold appeared before the TNEC and read what some of his colleagues regarded as a "declaration of independence" for the building industry in which he announced the first nationwide antitrust drive in the nation's history.

By May 1940, Arnold's antitrust drive in the building industry had resulted in 74 indictments in 11 cities, involving 985 defendants, both corporations and individuals. Of the 985 indicted, 680 were individuals, 200 of whom were union representatives; 214 were corporations, 58 were labor unions, 32 were trade and other associations, and one was a partnership.

Arnold's inclusion of labor unions in these attacks aroused severe criticism of the Roosevelt administration on the part of trade unions and their friends. Though Arnold explained that his drive was aimed only at unreasonable use of the union's strength, opponents contended that in setting up his own standards for determining which labor unions are "lawful" and which "unlawful" he was, in effect, subscribing to the view that the antitrust law was also meant to police labor. They held that since the courts and not Arnold ultimately decide these cases, and the judges of these courts act on their own idea of what constitutes "lawful" labor activities, he was again opening the door wide to the revised use of antitrust laws against labor.

When the leaders of the International Fur and Leather Workers' Union were indicted on a seven-year-old charge that "a conspiracy existed to restrain trade" and that the strike they held affected interstate trade, friends of labor fought the indictment on the grounds that "if the right to strike is recognized only on condition that interstate commerce will not be restrained, affected, or interfered with, it means in reality that the workers are deprived of their right to strike." And though Arnold claimed that he was interested in convicting only "bad" labor leaders, many replied that "there are numerous laws under which corrupt union officials can be charged with specific criminality." Arnold, however, maintains that: "The principle applicable to unions is the same as that applicable to other groups specially protected by law. Investors may combine into a corporation, farmers into a cooperative and labor into a union. The Antitrust Division has the duty to prevent the use of such legal rights of association in an illegal way for purposes far different from those contemplated in the statutes."

ARNOLD, THURMAN—*Continued*

The movie, milk and tobacco manufacturing industries were only a few of the other places where Arnold looked and found "restraint of trade," hurting the consumer. He stubbed his toes, though, when he tried to institute similar suits against certain oil companies. The National Defense Commission claimed, in the fall of 1940, that such suits would "complicate and delay" the national preparedness program. Arnold didn't think so, but any action against the oil companies was delayed while he thought about other things that slow up the national defense effort—monopolistic patent restraints, for instance, which he calls the "economic Fifth Column."

Thurman Arnold has been characterized by Attorney General Robert H. Jackson (see sketch this issue) as "a cross between Voltaire and a cowboy, with the cowboy predominating." His origin is decidedly picturesque. His family comes of old, solid Connecticut stock, with a village named for them. The placid homestead was first deserted by his grandfather, Franklin Arnold, who went to darkest Africa as a Congregationalist missionary. Laboring in the African vineyard, Franklin Arnold made friends with a young German Lutheran colleague, Pastor Ramsauer. One day Ramsauer sickened of yellow fever. His sister, Marie, warned by slow mail, sailed to nurse him. When Marie's packet reached the Gold Coast, Pastor Ramsauer had been dead for months. Franklin Arnold gave Marie his sympathy and friendship, fell in love with her and married her. Some time after that the Congregationalists transferred Franklin Arnold to Laramie, Wyoming— where, to Franklin's dismay, the large majority of Laramians turned out to be Presbyterians. But Franklin Arnold wrestled with his conscience, changed his faith— and is still remembered in Laramie as a devout man. His son, Constantine Peter, became an able lawyer and prosperous rancher. Constantine's son was Thurman, a gangling, precocious youth, growing up in a part of the West which was still wild and woolly. He was good enough at his books to go, at the age of 16, to Princeton, where he was elected to Phi Beta Kappa. Harvard Law School and a brief practice in Chicago were followed by three years of fighting in Mexico and in France. In the interval between the Mexican campaign and the World War, he married Frances Longan, a Missourian. After the War he returned to Laramie to settle down. There he went into politics and was elected Laramie's Mayor and later went to the state legislature. In 1927, being offered the deanship of the law school at West Virginia University, he came East. Three years later he took a law professorship at Yale.

At Yale he was "a professorial nine-days' wonder." His lectures, to which he insisted on bringing his dog, Duffy Arnold, became celebrated for their fascinating discursiveness. He frequently started on a set topic, wandered off into the mythical aspects of economics, progressed to the mores of politics, and so on until, lost at last, he brought himself up short with a genial: "Now what the hell am I supposed to be talking about?"

While still a professor at Yale he worked as special counsel to the AAA, trial examiner for the SEC, and finally, in March 1939, received his appointment as Assistant Attorney General in charge of antitrust cases.

Arnold has two sons, George and Thurman Jr., who are away at school and college most of the time. He and his wife live alone in a comfortable, unpretentious old house a little way out in the country, not far from Washington. His wife, a famous housewife, "feeds New and Old Dealers by turns and together, while her husband talks at, to, around and through them."

References

Business Week p13-14 My 28 '38; p14 Mr 25 '39; p18+ My 27 '39
Christian Sci Mon Mag p2, 12 My 11 '40 pors
Nation 149:596-7 D 2 '39
New Repub 99:177-8 Je 22 '38; 102: 494-6 Ap 11 '40
N Y Times IV p6 Ap 7 '40
Sat Eve Post 212:5-7+ Ag 12 '39 pors
Sat R Lit 21:3-4+ Mr 30 '40
Time 31:11 Ja 3 '38; 36:69-70+ S 9 '40 por
Vital Speeches 4:567-70 Jl 1 '38; 5:290 Mr 1 '39

America's Young Men 1936-37
Johnsen, J. E., comp. Trade Unions and the Anti-Trust Laws 1940
Who's Who in America
Who's Who in the Nation's Capital

ARONSON, LOUIS V. Dec 25, 1870— Nov 2, 1940 Inventor; creator of Ronson lighters and other inventions in metal art work; leader in development of non-phosphorous matches; president and founder of Art Metal Works; president of Industrial Office Building Company; vice-president and founder of Lincoln National Bank; leading Republican in Newark, New Jersey

References

Who's Who in American Jewry
Who's Who in Commerce and Industry

Obituaries

N Y Times p57 N 3 '40 por

ASHMUN, MARGARET ELIZA Died Mar 15, 1940 Author of children's books, including the *Isabel Carlton* series for girls

References

American Women
Who's Who in America

Obituaries

N Y Herald Tribune p14 Mr 18 '40

(Continued next page)

MARGARET ASHMUN

ASTOR, NANCY WITCHER, VISCOUNTESS
May 19, 1879- American-born member of the British Parliament

Address: h. 4 St James's Sq, London, S. W. 1, England

American-born Nancy Astor nearly all her life has been the subject of one kind of controversy or another. First woman member of the British House of Commons, temperance advocate, later reputedly the leader of the "Cliveden Set," in September 1940 she was the heroine of a ditty written by a British soldier in Egypt:

"And when the sandstorms blow,
    and get in body and in kit,
And you start to cough your lungs
    up and then begin to spit,
Just think of Lady Astor, who says
    you are not fit
To fight for King and Country and
    do your 'little bit'."

She was born Nancy Langhorne, the daughter of the late Chiswell Dabney Langhorne of Mirador, Greenwood, Virginia, and started life as a Southern belle, dancing all night, riding to hounds, noted for her vivacity, her wit, her charm—and her temper. Her sister Irene, who married Charles Dana Gibson, was equally celebrated. Nancy Langhorne was only eighteen when she married Robert Gould Shaw, and it was only six years later (in 1903) when she divorced him, taking their young son to England with her. There she met Waldorf Astor (who, incidentally, shares her birthday), and married him in 1906. He was then Conservative Member for Plymouth. Nancy helped him with his work in the constituency, and when he succeeded to the viscounty in 1918 and automatically passed to the House of Lords,

she decided to contest the division. Already a militant advocate of women's rights (in 1915 she had walked in a procession to ask Lloyd George to allow women to make munitions), she was the only woman elected in the "coupon" election of 1918, and since December 1, 1919 has been in the House without interruption as Conservative M. P. for the Sutton Division of Plymouth. Someone has accused her of starting "the evil tradition that the wife of a popular member has the natural reversion to her husband's seat."

It wasn't quite all roses, being the first woman to be seated in the House of Commons. There were a number of members determined to make her membership so uncomfortable that she wouldn't try to get it again. One story says that when a distinguished cabinet member finally congratulated her on her election she protested: "But I have been in the House six months and you have not taken the slightest notice of me." "No, I don't like women in Parliament," he answered, "and when you took your seat I endured the same kind of embarrassment as I would if a lady invaded my bathroom." But Lady Astor could be fully as rude as any male. "If I were as ugly as you," she quipped, "I should have no fear of any lady invading my bathroom."

The frequent frivolity of her remarks didn't help much, however, and when the House found that she was a "dry," a vigorous opponent of the brewers, it was material for a first-class battle—especially since the liquor question cut across all party lines. Nancy Astor was undismayed and sponsored a measure prohibiting the admission of people under 18 to licensed premises—a matter which all parties now consider non-controversial.

Lady Astor's talent for "incessant and irrelevant interruption," for picking quarrels with the "less responsible members of the Labor Party" on the slightest provocation, and for repartee which, "though always smart, would sometimes have been better left unsaid," continued to involve her in frequent scenes and to make her the object of such remarks as "Sit down!" "Shut up, Nancy!" "Go back to America." But Parliament eventually succumbed to her charm, and in the early '20s she was a picturesque symbol of woman's emancipation. Though without any sociological background to speak of, she showed herself particularly interested in exposing the evils of child labor in unregulated trades, in working for nursery schools, in the League of Nations, in anything affecting family life and the interests of women and children, and on one occasion she even had the courage to speak up strongly in favor of birth control. In 1922 she conquered the United States on a return visit. Even a writer for the *New Republic* who accused her of "always so infallibly hitting on the head only the largest and most accessible nails" couldn't help describing her as a

Pictures, Inc.

LADY ASTOR

"gay, friendly, girlish person, telling us all, with a gallant jerk of the head, things we already believe." In 1923 Lady Astor published *My Two Countries.*

It was at least two years before Munich that the term "Cliveden Set" came into being. Lady Astor's parties at Cliveden, her country mansion on the Thames, had long been famous for their vivacity, their comparative informality and the highly miscellaneous nature of their guests. One early observer gives a picture of the Socialist David Kirkwood, clad in a lounge suit, in animated converse with the Duke of Windsor, then Prince of Wales, robed in full evening glory. By the spring of 1936, however, Cliveden was famous because of rumors that it was a center of intrigue for a group with Hitlerian leanings. Described as Britain's "second Foreign Office," it was at Cliveden that British foreign policy was said to be decided by Sir Nevile Henderson, Lord Halifax, Sir Samuel Hoare, Sir John Simon (see sketches this issue) and other members of the appeasement clique.

The existence of any such group was finally denied by Lord Astor in the London *Times* (which is mainly controlled by his brother, Major the Hon. J. J. Astor) in a letter which pointed out that at seasons when momentous matters were reputed to have been discussed at Cliveden the house was actually closed and shuttered. Lady Astor herself denied the legend in an interview published in the *Saturday Evening Post,* and staunchly affirmed her belief in both peace and democracy. After Munich she unapologetically admitted backing Chamberlain in trying to get appeasement in Europe and described the Prime Minister as "a first-class administrator and a real

progressive social reformer." In March 1939, however, she urged him to protest against the invasion of Czechoslovakia.

Shortly before World War II broke out Lady Astor was urging United States women to cable the Women's World War Veterans to fight against war. When War was declared her sons went into service almost immediately and in October part of Cliveden was converted into a nursery for evacuated children. Lady Astor's main battles were once more in the House of Commons. She fought for a curb on champagne imports, against an allowance to unmarried women living with soldiers equal to that for soldiers' wives, for the rationing of supplies to brewers. In the summer of 1940 she was active in pressing governmental action on the child evacuation plan. It was an open letter she wrote to the editor of the London *Daily Mirror,* jeering at London's crack regiments for "sunbathing in Egypt" while their homeland was facing such grave danger, that inspired one hussar to verse in September.

Lady Astor has one son by her first husband, four sons and a daughter by Lord Astor. Her constituency is in the heart of industrial Plymouth, definitely working class and she has always pulled every string to help her constituents. She has also contributed liberally to *crèches* and to boys' clubs, and as a Member of Parliament has stood quite consistently for laws protecting the more defenseless members of society. Nevertheless, back in the '20s, the late George Lansbury, Labor Member of Parliament, called her the most ignorant woman in the House on social questions and stated that for so wealthy a woman to interfere in matters concerning the poor was "disgusting." Someone else said that "there is always about her democracy the sense of the great lady being kind to the poor." Perhaps it is because as the wife of a millionaire, Lady Astor has herself never acquired any sense of responsibility toward money and is not the type of person who spends long hours in libraries acquiring data even on those problems she is emotional and obstinate about. And although she has always stood for legislation involving reforms like shorter working hours for women, she is also inclined to work her own secretaries 18 hours a day. "For her a declaration of good will is equivalent to a realization of justice."

Still, "it must be nearly impossible to dislike Lady Astor." A Christian Scientist by faith, she has been called "the Pollyanna of the political world" and "the most honest of hypocrites." Her charm—"that damned charm"—has been extensively and unsuccessfully analyzed. Unaffected in manner, with blue-gray eyes and a crooked smile, an ever-changing face and a gift for comic mimicry, she has "the gift of speaking in headlines"—although her remarks don't seem so excruciatingly funny in cold print.

Those who have called her a Puritan have had reasons. Temperate in conviction as well as practice, Nancy Astor keeps a pitcher of barley water prominently displayed on the table at St. James's Square; she dresses simply in Parliament, usually wearing a sober black or blue suit with a white blouse, a string of pearls and a chaste, three-cornered hat; and there has never been anything remotely scandalous about her private life. When, long ago, the journalist Horatio Bottomley published a scurrilous article called *Lady Astor's Divorce,* it took little time before he was exposed for embezzling and sent to prison. Announced Lady Astor triumphantly: "The brewers paid Horatio Bottomley to try to take my moral character away. Well, I've still got my character, but Bottomley is in jail."

There are dozens of stories about her, a good many of them dealing with her shockingly informal attitude toward the great and the supposed great. To Lloyd George she announced one day: "Oh, you old ruffian, I cannot help liking you." Of the Prince of Wales: "I love that boy." She once had a three-hour interview with Gandhi and told him what she thought of Hinduism. She once interviewed Stalin and asked him when he was going to stop killing people. When he commented on the strangeness of a small island like England ruling a third of the world she explained: "Look at the map. It can't be might; it must be right. It's something in their thinking."

Someone once said: "There are four Nancy Astors—the charmer, the pope, the showman and—one whom few people know —the good little girl."

References
  Cur Hist 48:31-4 F '38 por
  Ladies' H J 52:5-7+ F '35 por
  Liv Age 338:416-19 Je 1 '30
  N Y World-Telegram p4 S 10 '40 por
  No Am R 227:385-91 Ap '29 por
  Sat Eve Post 211:5-6+ Mr 4 '39 pors
  Astor, N. W. My Two Countries 1923
  Bigger, R. V. My Miss Nancy pam 1924
  Gardiner, A. G. Lady Astor *In* Portraits and Portents p188-95 1926
  Hodgson, S. Lady Astor *In* Portraits and Reflections p139-45 1929
  Kircher, R. Women in Politics: Lady Astor *In* Englander p177-87 1928
  McGovern, J. T. Lady Astor *In* Diogenes Discovers Us p151-69 1933
  Who's Who
  Who's Who in America

ATALENA, pseud. *See* Jabotinsky, V. E.

ATHERTON, GERTRUDE Oct 30, 1857-
Author
Address: h. 2101 California St, San Francisco, California

One of the most popular American novelists, Gertrude Atherton has sustained the lively interest of feminine readers throughout her long career by basing her novels on problems of vital interest to women. Author of more than 45 books, her California novels in particular are said to present a complete social history of San Francisco, where she was born, grew up and still lives. One of the many interesting phases of Mrs. Atherton's life is her participation in the activities of Career Women, a San Francisco organization, at whose birthday dinner in June 1940 she presided. And careers for women play an important part in her new novel, *The House of Lee,* published in September 1940.

The Lees, like many other wealthy San Franciscans, are affected by the market crash of '29. Three generations of gentlewomen—the grandmother, Mrs. Edington; the daughter, Mrs. Lee; the granddaughter, Lucy—face the necessity of finding jobs (they consider relief a vast disgrace) to augment their income, which has been abruptly limited to $200 a month. Chang, their Chinese cook and butler, helps them keep up appearances by generously lending them his considerable savings. Grandmother, a strong-minded, rugged individualist of the old school, sallies forth and gets herself a fine position. Her more feminine-minded daughter earns money by teaching bridge to the new rich. Lucy, just out of college, determines on a career, but finds her intentions somewhat hampered by a suitor and the prospects of a good marriage. It is through Lucy that Mrs. Atherton expresses her irritation over Left ideologies: "The Pinkies and Lefties turn in their lips and bleat about the inevitable disappearance of 'class' every time one of us has to get out and work. . . When a big concern closes down and throws hundreds of men out of work, the sentimentalists sob over them but don't give a thought to the stockholders who may be wondering where their next meal is coming from. *We* don't count."

Gertrude Franklin Atherton was born October 30, 1857 on Rincon Hill in San Francisco. Her maternal grandfather (a grandnephew of Benjamin Franklin) was the editor of one of San Francisco's first newspapers and also a banker. Her mother, Gertrude Franklin, a Southern-bred girl who became a belle of the city, married Thomas Lodowick Horn, a Yankee businessman. After three years they were divorced. The only child, little Gertrude, was sent to be brought up on her grandfather's ranch near San Francisco. In her autobiography, *Adventures of a Novelist* (1932), Mrs. Atherton writes frankly of her childhood. She says: "I was the angel child in appearance, with golden curls and eyes of

ATHERTON, GERTRUDE—*Continued*

seraphic blue, but I must have been a little
fiend. It had amused my father to stand
me on the table when he was giving a
dinner party and encourage me to kick
the plates into the laps of the guests."
Thoroughly spoiled by the whole family,
Gertrude became a willful, egocentric "problem" child. No boarding school would
keep her and no nurse stayed long with
the family. Finally they got one who took
Gertrude in hand and "spanked with gusto."
The mother remarried, and Gertrude and
her new father disliked each other intensely
from the start. Mrs. Atherton thinks that
the abnormal conditions of her home life
"caused that dislocation of particles or
whatever it may be that produces fiction."

Her early schooling was irregular, but she
read a great deal. At 14 she first got the
idea of becoming an "authoress" and produced several stories, mostly unfinished.
When 17 she was sent to the Sayre Institute in Lexington, Kentucky, but when her
stepfather died she returned to San Francisco. There George Atherton (a former
admirer of her mother's) fell in love with
her and proposed, she writes, until she gave
in and married him. A son, George, was
born; a few years later a daughter, Muriel.
George died at the age of six. The children
were given over to the care of nurses (Mrs.
Atherton says she had no maternal instinct)
and, since her husband didn't care about
the things which interested her, she was
bored to death with her marriage.

Accordingly she wrote a novel, *The
Randolphs of Redwoods*, based on a local society scandal, which was published anonymously in *The Argonaut*. (In 1899 it was
republished in book form as *A Daughter
of The Vine*.) Although her husband
violently disapproved of her writing, she

continued with it. However, her second
effort, a historical novel, and her third were
rejected by publishers with painful regularity. Then, while en route to Chile, her
husband died on shipboard; his body,
"embalmed in a barrel of rum," was sent
home.

Gertrude Atherton definitely decided to
make writing her career, even though her
domineering mother-in-law, an eccentric
aristocrat of Spanish blood, didn't believe
women could be writers. "*Si* all were
known, you find the mens write those books
for them," she said. But Gertrude got her
way and went to live in New York; then
traveled in France and England. On a brief
return to America Mrs. Atherton explored
California with a view to writing about its
rich, historical past. From the wealth of material she discovered came *The Splendid Idle
Forties* (1902), Rezánov (1919) and other
California historical novels.

Her work was first recognized in England. It was not till the appearance of
The Conqueror (1902), a novel about Alexander Hamilton, that her reputation in
America was made. It became a best seller
and a critical success. But most of her
novels thereafter were written abroad.
Among the best of these was *Tower of
Ivory* (1910)—"my own favorite of all the
novels I have written," she says.

From 1916 to 1918 she was active in war
work and received three decorations from
the French government, including the
Légion d'Honneur. But between 1916 and
1923 she found time to write five more
novels, among them *The Living Present*
(1917) and *The Avalanche* (1919).

Then came her biggest best seller in the
field of fiction, *Black Oxen* (1923), in which
she told the story of Mary Ogden, a
woman of 58, who was reactivated by the
Steinach method and returned to her world
as Madame Zattiany, a new woman. It was
a story based on Mrs. Atherton's own experience. Following a period of mental
sterility she herself took the Steinach treatment under Dr. Harry Benjamin—a treatment consisting of X-ray stimulation of the
sex glands. *Black Oxen* was denounced
from the pulpit; but women from all over
the world who hoped to renew their youthful energies wrote to Mrs. Atherton inquiring about the Steinach treatment.

Mrs. Atherton wrote several more novels
—*Immortal Marriage* (1927); *Dido, Queen
of Hearts* (1929) are among the best known—
in rapid succession; then in 1932, when she
was 75, she took another Steinach rejuvena-
tion. At the age of 78 the energetic novelist,
when interviewed, said she had implicit
faith in the treatments. Her conversation
was brilliant, her hair still bright and blonde,
and, to enhance the youthful vigor, her
cheeks were rouged and her fingernails
carmined. A critic who has always admired
her work, Isabel Paterson, says: "Her
classic colonial profile [all her portraits are
taken in profile] might have been drawn

GERTRUDE ATHERTON

by Peale or Gilbert Stuart. Her eyes are very blue, her hair pale gold; she is of middle height and of that erect carriage one associates with an earlier generation which used straight-backed chairs as a matter of self-respect."

Mrs. Atherton says that among her likes and dislikes are: "Hate shams, toadies, sewing, bores, insincere and narrow-minded persons; like my friends, and with exceptions, keep them forever; like a certain amount of social gaiety when I am not working, meeting new people, going to strange places; above all like reading; also like the theatre and some movies; hate visiting; have a charming family and like being with them, but I prefer living alone."

She has received several honorary degrees and is a member of a number of nationally known clubs. Coincidental with the publication of her new novel, Mrs. Atherton, who heads the list of California's 13 most distinguished women, was fêted at a luncheon at the San Francisco Exposition.

Keystone

CLEMENT ATTLEE

References

N Y Herald Tribune p13 S 9 '40
N Y Herald Tribune Books p1 Ap 3 '32 por
N Y Times Book R p24 S 22 '40
Newsweek 6:40 D 14 '35
Wilson Lib Bul 5:428 Mr '31 por
American Women
Atherton, G. F. Adventures of a Novelist 1932
Cooper, F. T. Gertrude Atherton *In* Some American Story Tellers p245-64 1911
Hamilton, C. Gertrude Atherton *In* People Worth Talking About p87-95 1933
Hatcher, H. H. Post-War Reassertions *In* Creating the Modern American Novel p87-98 1935
Jackson, J. H. Gertrude Atherton pam 1940
Kunitz, S. J. ed. Living Authors 1937
Overton, G. M. Gertrude Atherton *In* Women Who Make Our Novels p2-7 1928
Who's Who
Who's Who in America

ATTLEE, CLEMENT RICHARD Jan 3, 1883- Lord Privy Seal; member of British Parliament

Address: Heywood, Stanmore, Middlesex, England

In the days before the Second World War began, England's Prime Minister Neville Chamberlain was faced, in many quarters, with a good deal of dissent and dissatisfaction. One of the most vocal dissenters was the Right Honorable Clement Attlee, leader of His Majesty's Opposition. To him the Munich settlement was a wrong one: "It is not a policy, it is only an attitude—an attitude of deference." Even after England united behind Chamberlain to fight the War, Mr. Attlee insisted that the Labor Party supported the War but did not support the present government. To the government he directed embarrassing questions on the feeding of the army, on the supplying of war material, on the conduct of the War itself.

On May 7, 1940 he went so far as to brand Chamberlain and his War Cabinet as "failures" in the most violent Parliamentary debate since the War began. Those in command, he said, "are men who have had an almost uninterrupted career of failure," and "the British people are not satisfied that the War is being waged with sufficient energy, industry or results." Shortly after, Chamberlain asked Attlee and Arthur Greenwood (see sketch this issue), also a leader of the Labor Party, to serve in a coalition cabinet, but they refused.

When the Chamberlain government fell on May 10, partly because of their refusal, Winston Churchill (see sketch this issue) immediately formed a coalition cabinet in which Attlee was made Lord Privy Seal and Greenwood Minister without Portfolio. Attlee took up his duties immediately and announced to the British public that it was his hope that Britain would be a socialistic country when the War was over, with cake for none until all had bread. In his new post Attlee is Churchill's parliamentary spokesman, "the No. 2 boss of England." He has published *War Comes to Britain* (1940) since coming into office.

Since 1935 Clement Attlee has led Britain's Labor Opposition in the House of Commons. Since the beginning of the century, he has been fighting for the cause of socialism. He has seen the Labor Party grow from thirty members to over eight million; he has seen it grow from five repre-

ATTLEE, CLEMENT—*Continued*

sentatives in Parliament to three hundred. And, as he says, "throughout these years I have never wavered in my faith in the cause of socialism."

At first sight Attlee seems to be one of the more academic of British Socialists. He was born on January 3, 1883, the son of a London solicitor, and was brought up in conservative British traditions. He went to Haileybury, a fairly expensive "Public School," and afterward to University College, Oxford, where he took an Honours degree in modern history. He left Oxford to study law but didn't stay at the Inner Temple long. He became interested in social work and went to live in East London, where he supported himself by taking jobs on the docks.

"The condition of the people in that area, as I saw them at close quarters," he says, "led me to study their causes and to reconsider the assumptions of the social class to which I belonged. I became an enthusiastic convert to socialism." In 1907 he joined the Fabian Society, socialist group of which George Bernard Shaw was a famous member, and the Independent Labor Party. In 1910 he became secretary at Toynbee Hall, a pioneer "social settlement" for university men desiring to live in an industrial area to study working-class conditions.

Major Attlee's next post was that of tutor and lecturer at the London School of Economics. He stayed there from 1913 until he entered politics in 1922. In between, however, he served in the War—in France, Gallipoli and Mesopotamia—and retired as a major with a few bad wounds. In between, too, he began to have his first taste of politics, as Mayor of Stepney, East London, (1919-21) and Alderman (1919-27).

In 1922 Mr. Attlee became parliamentary private secretary to the leader of the Opposition; in 1924 he was made under-secretary of state for war; in 1929 he was chancellor of the Duchy of Lancaster; in 1931 postmaster general; and in 1931 deputy leader of the Opposition. In November 1935 he became the Opposition's leader, the first to draw the official salary of £2,000 a year.

Mr. Attlee's rise in the world of politics has been attributed to his sincerity rather than to his eloquence. He is not one of Britain's best speakers. He has a high-pitched, rather staccato voice. "His experience at the Bar molded the character of his public speaking, forensic and unemotional; it certainly has not given him crusading fire." The *Manchester Guardian* says of him that, in general, "he does not coin a striking phrase, he has none of Mr. Churchill's power of self-dramatization about him, but he has profound integrity. He is wholly devoid of jealousy and pose. His convictions are profound and he fights for them with a tenacity that one has to meet in order to appreciate."

He has always believed in and worked for a League of Nations. He still says that his party is working for "a world cooperative Commonwealth of Nations in which every nation, while preserving its own distinctive civilization and organizing its life on the lines best suited to it, will combine with the others for the good of humanity." He has always believed in and worked for socialism. To him socialism is "the dominant issue of the twentieth century."

According to his beliefs, the "only motive which should guide the economic mechanism is the public need and the public well-being." He continuously stresses that his party is strongly opposed to all dictatorships, whether from the Left or the Right, and that it is devoted to the defense of democracy. In fact, the socialism that Attlee supports is far from a radical doctrine. It "owes more to the *Bible* than to *Das Kapital* or to *State and Revolution*. To Attlee socialism is another stage in the historical broadening of freedom in his country to be reached by entirely constitutional means." Communism is anathema to him. Nevertheless it was Attlee who introduced the bill in the House of Commons to establish a war-time dictatorship in England.

"Clem," as he is known to his friends and the gossip writers, is now 57 years old, "short and unimpressive in figure, with a benevolent air reminiscent of a safely berthed schoolmaster." In Stanmore, where he lives simply, he has a wife (the former Violet Helen Millar) and four children, a collection of pipes, a kit of carpenter's tools, a bag of golf clubs and a set of gardening implements.

References

Canad Forum 17:347 Ja '38
Christian Sci Mon p6 My 7 '40
Manchester Guardian p2 Ja 15 '40
New Repub 99:206 Je 28 '39
N Y Times p1 My 11 '40

Attlee, C. R. The Labour Party in Perspective 1937
Attlee, C. R. The Will and the Way to Socialism 1935
Johnston, J. A. A Hundred Commoners 1931
Socialist View of Peace *In* Geneva Institute of International Relations. Problems of Peace 9th ser p96-127 1934-36
Watchman, pseud. Right Honourable Gentleman 1939
Who's Who

AULAIRE, INGRI D' (dō'lĕr' ĕN-grē) Dec 27, 1904- and **AULAIRE, EDGAR PARIN D'** Sept 30, 1898- Authors; illustrators

Address: c/o Doubleday-Doran & Co, 14 W 49th St, New York City

The 1939 Caldecott Medal, named in honor of the famous English illustrator Randolph Caldecott and presented each year to the artist of the most distinguished picture book for children, was awarded to Ingri and Edgar Parin D'Aulaire for their *Abraham Lincoln*.

These author-illustrator collaborators are husband and wife. Ingri (Mortenson) D'Aulaire, the youngest daughter of a Norwegian government official, Per Mortenson, and Line (Sandsmark) Mortenson, was born in Norway in 1904. As a girl she was interested in painting and drawing and encouraged by Harriet Backer, a Norwegian painter, persuaded her family to let her study art in Munich. There she met Edgar, also an art student.

He was the son of a French portrait painter, Gino Parin D'Aulaire of Huguenot descent and an American mother, Ella D'Aulaire. He was born in Compoblenion, Ticino, Switzerland, September 30, 1898. As a child, under the influence of his artist father and of book collector friends, he made picture books with verses. Edgar fulfilled parental wishes by graduating from high school and studying architecture for one year. Then he gave up architecture and started a "pure study of nature" art training course at the Munich Academy.

Munich was in a state of siege in 1923. Ingri and Edgar, with many of the other students, fled to Paris. A year later they were married in Ingri's family's country place in Norway, but only after Edgar had earned the approval of the family by initiation into the Mortenson's annual 31 mile Christmas ski trip, although he had never been on skis before in his life.

The Aulaires established headquarters in Paris in a stable which had been turned into a studio. This became their base for six years. Edgar continued studying: "understanding of functioning of space, movement and expression" under Matisse; "principles of abstract composition" at Lhote's and "graphical arts" at Galani's. From their Paris base they traveled all over Europe and North Africa, Ingri doing portraits of children and Edgar studying frescoes in Florence and doing murals and illustrations in France and Norway. Two books illustrated by Edgar were published in Paris: Poe's *Aventures de Gorden Pym* with lithographs (1927) and a picture book with etchings, *Aventures Sentimentales* (1928). Fifteen titles with his illustrations were issued in Germany, including: Goethe's *Märchen* (1922), Poe's *Pfaals Mondreise* (1922) and *Blocksberg* (1925).

Pursuing their inclination to travel, the Aulaires came to America and liked it so well that they established their home here in 1929. Here they wrote and illustrated their first book for children, *The Magic Rug* (1931), based on their African travels. "We each had our different distinct way of expression," they say "and were as different as the countries we came from. When we paint we still manage to be ourselves." But when they began to make children's books they found that they might

Newspictures

INGRI and EDGAR D'AULAIRE

make a happy combination of Ingri's knowledge of children and Edgar's dramatic sense, so "we started to forget the You and I and became one unity with two heads, four hands and one handwriting when working on our children's books."

Working together, the Aulaires illustrated their books with lithographs in a technique derived from the old craftsmen. Each picture is sketched first on paper and then drawn with a lithograph crayon on a large stone block from which the lithograph is printed. This method enables them to use more colors and give a look of individuality and freshness to each picture. Edgar does the black or key drawing on the stone, and Ingri does the color work, drawing on a separate stone for each color, which means that for every color picture in *Abraham Lincoln* it was necessary to use five stones, for the pictures are in five colors.

For the writing of *Abraham Lincoln* the authors spent many months in discovering and getting the feel of Lincoln's land. With a car and tent they worked their way over the Lincoln trail. In spite of doubts, storms and hot weather they camped along the Ohio and Mississippi Rivers, high in the Kentucky hills, and in the broad Ohio valleys and recreated in their minds the country as Lincoln himself had known it. One reviewer wrote: "I think Lincoln himself might have enjoyed the humor of these designs: he had a liking for the grotesque, and the humor here is without malice and marked by evident affection."

The same procedure of careful research was used in writing *George Washington* (1936). The authors took a walking tour through the Virginia country which Washington had known as a boy. The figures of Lincoln and Washington were very real

AULAIRE, INGRI D' and **AULAIRE, EDGAR PARIN D'**—*Continued*

to Edgar: when he was a child his mother had told him many stories of her American childhood and of the adventures of her father, who owned a Southern plantation but had fought on the Northern side in the Civil War.

One of their most popular books, *Ola* (1932), the story of a small boy's wintertime activities in Norway and Lapland resulted from actual experiences in Ingri's homeland. It was followed by *Ola and Blakken* (1933), which described the adventures of Ola in the summertime on a farm with three girls and a cream-colored horse. *The Conquest of the Atlantic,* written the next year, recounted the story of travel across the Atlantic from Viking days to the present-day airplane flights. *The Lord's Prayer* was written in 1934. *Children of the Northern Lights* (1935), was the result of a journey by boat and sled into the north of Norway. Their latest book is *Animals Everywhere,* a first picture book for children published in the fall of 1940. Edgar has also illustrated a number of books which were published in America: Dhan Gopal Mukerji's *Rama* (1930), Dmitri Merejkowsi's *Leonardo da Vinci* (1931), John Matheson's *Needle in the Haystack* (1930), and H. H. Ewers' *Blood* (1930).

The Aulaires live in a studio apartment on lower Fifth Avenue in New York City, an apartment with Norwegian furniture and walls covered with pictures they have painted in many parts of the world. Recently the studio has become enlivened by "the presence of Per Ola Parin D'Aulaire, who might have stepped out of the pages of the *Ola* book itself, but who is a very real blue-eyed, blond-haired little boy growing up as his father did, surrounded by the smell of brushes, wet paint on canvas and richly glowing pictures."

References

> Horn Book 16:256-64 Jl '40 il por
> Library J 65:475-6 Je 1 '40 il por
> N Y Herald Tribune Books p6 Je 2 '40
> Pub W 137:2134 Je 1 '40 por
> Kunitz, S. J. and Haycraft, H. eds. Junior Book of Authors 1935
> Mahoney, B. E. and Whitney, E. comps. Contemporary Illustrators of Children's Books 1930

AUSTIN, WILLIAM LANE Jan 25, 1871-
Director of the United States Census

Address: b. Bureau of the Census, Washington, D. C.; h. 1412 Delafield Place, N W, Washington, D. C.

For the past 40 years William Lane Austin, with neat, housewifely precision, has been gathering statistics on business, manufacturing, mines, quarries, agriculture, crime, religion, death, income, housing. When he started in 1900 there were only 75,994,575 people living in the United States.

WILLIAM LANE AUSTIN

On the first day of April 1940, Mr. Austin started the sixteenth decennial census, in which he reckoned with a population of approximately 131,500,000. Actually the first figures released in November 1940 show the whole population of the United States as 131,409,881; with its territories and possessions, exclusive of the Philippine Islands, the population is 150,362,326.

Austin was born on "Hurricane Farm," Scott County, Mississippi, the son of Dr. Richmond Pearson and Sue D. (Lane) Austin. His family were of old plantation stock, some members of whom left England for America more than 200 years ago. For generations there have been Austins at "Hurricane Farm," most of whom became physicians and surgeons, surveying in the cool of the evening their cotton fields stretching "as far as you could see."

Young Austin received a degree from Harperville College in his home state in 1891; in 1897 and 1898 his Ph. B. and LL. B. from the University of Mississippi. In 1903 he married Eley D. Campbell of Forest, Mississippi.

In 1900 as the protégé of the late Senator John Sharp Williams he took a $900 clerkship in the Census Bureau in Washington. A statistician of brilliant attainments, he advanced from grade to grade in the Bureau, mostly in Republican administrations—he himself is a Mississippi Democrat—until in April 1933 he was made director of the Census. Austin's own specialized work has been in agricultural statistics: statistics on plantations, cotton, tobacco, irrigation, drainage and horticulture.

"Bland-browed, still placid of disposition after 40 years of brooding on government statistics," Austin, who generally wears a ruby stickpin and carries a 150-year-old watch, has run into many Congressional storms "over snooping census questions, and the present one does not worry him very much."

Austin remains cool over protestations such as the one delivered by Senator Charles W. Tobey of New Hampshire. "Ye gods!" said the excitable Senator, "Stalin and Hitler may play the game that way, but not in free America. Shame on our country for suggesting such a thing!" Even Mark Sullivan, ordinarily unruffled columnist, wrote that "the government curiosity about divorce, income, toilet facilities was an invasion of man's responsibility to God alone."

Austin knows that a census of the United States population every 10 years is mandatory. He knows that his department has been called "the greatest statistical organization in the world." The census took one month to complete and the results will be published during the next three years. With 135,000 workers in his department for the taking of the 1940 census he feels that the debate on the subject of how much the government is entitled to ask is purely political, since the census occurs during a presidential election year. He feels that possibly the Congressional hullabaloo might have been caused by the possibility that new census figures would result in a reapportionment of Representatives in some states.

People who are so indignant at the questions asked this year will find that the old-fashioned censuses were more impertinent than the 1940 cross-examination. In 1860, for instance, people had to report the value of all bonds, stocks, mortgages, notes, livestock, plate, jewels and furniture worth more than $100, and in 1850 the man at the door asked: "Are you deaf, dumb, blind, insane, idiotic, a pauper or a convict?"

In view of those questions Austin thinks we should not balk at what the census taker asks. For the first time the 1940 census will show employment status and the amount of wages earned in the past twelve months. Also for the first time the Census Bureau will be able to present us with a complete inventory of housing conditions. "We shall finally know," says Austin, "how precisely President Roosevelt was speaking when he said that 'one-third of the nation was ill-housed.'"

Austin feels that the employment questions "are designed merely to give complete and useful facts on unemployment, America's greatest problem." Endorsement was given the income questions by many influential business, farm and labor groups.

When the census director grows tired of statistics he has two hobbies—books (mainly history and biography), and flowers, which he grows in a well-planned garden.

References

Scholastic 36:10 Mr 18 '40 por
Time 35:12 Mr 11 '40 por
U S News 8:37 Mr 29 '40 por
Who's Who in America
Who's Who in the Nation's Capital

JOSEPH AVENOL

AVENOL, JOSEPH LOUIS ANNE (ă′ve-nŏl) 1879- Former secretary general of the League of Nations

On July 26, 1940 Dr. Joseph Avenol resigned as secretary general of the League of Nations, saying the "realities" of the present time made his office no longer necessary.

Dr. Joseph Avenol is the son of Ernest and Renée (de Hansy) Avenol. He was educated at Poitiers and the School of Political Science of the University of Paris (LL. D.). He began his career in 1905 as an official of the French treasury and later he was appointed Inspector General of Finance.

During and after the World War he represented France in inter-Allied financial relations in London (1916-23). Then he became the French representative at the League of Nations, later deputy secretary general, and in 1932 he was appointed secretary general. In addition to these duties he was a member of the League of Nations Inter-Governmental Refugee Advisory Committee. In Europe he is regarded as one of its leading financial experts. Bald-headed, wearing large horn-rimmed glasses, he has been described as "shy, reticent and incapable of indiscretion." Among his chief interests are medieval parchments and art treasures.

References

Illustration 185:341 Jl 1 '33 por
Lit Digest 118:14 S 29 '34 por
N Y Times p1 D 4 '39; p18 D 5 '39;
   p1 D 20 '39; p2 D 23 '39
International Who's Who
Who's Who

AYRES, LEONARD PORTER Sept 15, 1879- Economist

Address: War Department, Washington, D. C.; b. Cleveland Trust Co, Cleveland, Ohio

In October 1940 Leonard Ayres accepted the position of head statistician of the Assistant Secretary of War's office. This meant that he took leave from the vice-presidency of the Cleveland Trust Company and gave up his other business posts in order to spend his time "almost entirely on the progress of procurement under present contracts." Defense efforts up to that time he characterized as "decidedly leisurely."

"The country's No. 1 bachelor economist," Leonard Ayres' varied experience has made him an authoritative spokesman for the viewpoint of American capital. The son of Milan Church and Georgiana (Gall) Ayres, he was born on September 15, 1879 at Niantic, Connecticut. He was educated at Boston University, where he acquired his Ph. B. in 1902 with Phi Beta Kappa honors. He then accepted a teaching position in Puerto Rico, and by 1906 had become general superintendent of schools for Puerto Rico and chief of the Division of Statistics in that country. In 1908 he returned to the United States to become director of the departments of education and statistics at the Russell Sage Foundation, a position which he held until 1920. During that time he published many educational studies. He had also, among other distinctions, received his M. A. in 1909 and his Ph. D. the succeeding year from Boston University; had served in the World War as chief statistical officer of the United States Army, of the American Expeditionary Force and of the American Commission to Negotiate Peace. The government awarded him the Distinguished Service Medal.

In 1920 Colonel Ayres became vice-president of the Cleveland Trust Company and member of its executive committee, positions which he has now held for 20 years. In 1924 he served as economic adviser of the Dawes Commission. He is director of many railroads and of other corporations. Since 1932 he has been chairman of the Economic Policy Commission and of the Research Council of the American Bankers Association and he is a member of and has held offices in a great number of other associations, statistical, educational and economic.

Colonel Ayres has utilized his practical knowledge of finance and economics as the author of numerous published works. Until *The War with Germany* (1919), these had been mainly monographs on education, but in 1921 he began to speak for business, to concern himself with the problems of depressions and recovery, and as a statistician, economist and banker, he has been speaking for business in person and in print ever since. Perhaps best-known of his analyses is *Economics of Recovery* (1933), "a conservative analysis of the origins and

LEONARD P. AYRES

progress of the depression and of the measures that have been enacted in this country to meet it." *Turning Points in Business Cycles* (1939) is a technical study in economics pointing a moral which Colonel Ayres has been preaching in simpler form for a number of years: that recovery cannot be brought about by pump-priming in the form of stimulated spending for consumer's goods. The monthly *Business Bulletin* of the Cleveland Trust Company was also written by Colonel Ayres.

Both in his speeches and in his writings, Colonel Ayres has maintained a consistent position in favor of an "orthodox" rather than a "planned" recovery. He believes that governmental interference undermines the confidence in the prospects for future profits necessary to make business men take present risks—that "our troubles are political, not economic." For years he has been repeating, in one way or another, that "it is as futile for us to believe that we can spend ourselves rich as for us to suppose that a man can drink himself sober." In other words: "In the old days we did not know much about business cycles, but we did know that recovery would always come after awhile because nobody interfered with it. . . Business is optimistic by inclination, but now it has become pessimistic by information."

He also believes that "the really serious problem of this depression and of all American depressions, is that of putting back at work the producers of durable goods and keeping them profitably employed." But if the utilities were expanding "as they did in the last decade, their activities would largely solve the problem of the railroads, and the railroads and utilities together would largely solve our recovery problem."

As a prophet Colonel Ayres has a reputation that isn't quite undeserved. It is true that in December 1929 he didn't think a serious depression likely, and said so, in his annual business forecast before the Cleveland Chamber of Commerce; but in general his "batting average" has been about .850. It was also Colonel Ayres who in September 1918 predicted the First World War would end in the second week of November.

References
> Atlan 161:151-6 F '38
> N Y Herald Tribune p40 My 15 '40
> N Y Times IV p2 O 6 '40 por
> Newsweek 9:40 Je 26 '37 por
> Time 27:71 Ap 27 '36 por; 32:33 D 26 '38 por; 33:69 My 8 '39 por
> Vital Speeches 4:630-2 Ag 1 '38; 5: 185-7 Ja 1 '39
> Who's Who in America
> Who's Who in Commerce and Industry

AZANA, MANUEL Jan 10, 1880—Nov 4, 1940 President of Spanish Republic during Spanish Civil War; during monarchy, an obscure playwright and author, active plotter against the aristocracy; leading spirit of Republic of 1931; Premier under President Zamora; temporarily ousted in 1933; formed Left Republican Party; Popular Front landslide of 1936 brought him back as Premier; elected President in May 1936; after Franco's rebellion, played negligible part; fled to France in February 1939, declaring War was lost and refusing to continue struggle; rebuffed other Republican leaders who begged him to return to Madrid; resigned when France and Great Britain recognized Franco, writing "I gained nothing positive"

References
> Commonweal 24:145-7 Je 5 '36
> Cur Hist 47:46-52 D '37 il
> Eur Nouv 22:244 Mr 4 '39
> Harper 167:620-32 O '33
> Lit Digest 121:16 F 29 '36; 121:13-14 My 2 '36 il; 121:16-17 My 30 '36 por
> Liv Age 343:506-9 F '33
> Newsweek 5:11 Ja 5 '35
> Scholastic 25:19 O 27 '34 por
> Gunther, J. Spanish Civil War *In* Inside Europe p156-70 1936
> International Who's Who

Obituaries
> N Y Herald Tribune p26 N 5 '40 por
> N Y Times p25 N 5 '40 por

BACHRACH, ELISE WALD June 20, 1899—Mar 8, 1940 Artist

Although Elise Wald Bachrach did not seriously take up painting until a few years before her death, her oils, figures, still-lifes and landscapes have been widely exhibited throughout the country. She was born in New York City and attended Horace Mann School, later studying painting abroad. Mrs. Bachrach, whose home was in Great Neck, Long Island, maintained a studio in the artists' colony at Woodstock, New York, and also did some painting in the South.

References
> Who's Who in American Art

Obituaries
> N Y Times p49 Mr 10 '40

BACON, PEGGY May 2, 1895- Artist; author
Address: 131 E 15th St, New York City

Friends like to think that no other woman would describe herself with so devastating a sense of humor as Peggy Bacon shows in her book, *Off With Their Heads* (1934): "Pin head, parsimoniously covered with thin dark hair, on a short dumpy body. Small features, prominent nose, chipmunk teeth and no chin, conveying the sharp weak look of a little rodent. Absent-minded eyes with a half glimmer of observation. Prim, critical mouth and faint coloring. Personality lifeless, retiring, snippy, quietly egotistical. Lacks vigor and sparkle." One writer feels that Peggy had to put this description in her book "purely" in "self-defense—a weapon of words to ward off potential howls of protest from others described in the book."

Forty-five years ago Margaret Frances Bacon was born in Ridgefield, Connecticut, the daughter of two well-known artists—Charles Roswell and Elizabeth (Chase) Bacon. As a child her parents noted that she began to draw pictures even before she could talk. Always she has been interested in drawing faces, not as likenesses, but by distorting lines and adding emphasis, as sly caricatures. She received a diploma from the Kent Place School of Summit, New Jersey in 1913 and then attended the Art Students League and the School of Fine and Applied Arts of New York City, where she studied with such famous artists as Jonas Lie (see sketch this issue), John Sloan, George Bellows and George Bridgman. While a student at the Art Students League she met a promising artist, Alexander Brook, and they were married, May 4, 1920. This marriage was dissolved by divorce in July 1940. Their two children, Belinda and Alexander (called Sandy), have both shown aptitude for art studies.

Both Miss Bacon and Mr. Brook have taught at the Art Students League, and she has taught art (1933-35) at one of the most famous progressive schools in the country, the Fieldston Ethical Culture School. There she taught children drawing and composition.

For years she has been writing poems and making illustrations for the *New Yorker* and making illustrations for many other periodicals,

G. Maillard Kesslère

PEGGY BACON

has been writing and illustrating a number of books and holding shows of her paintings in New York art galleries. She works in dry-point, pen and ink, pastel, etching. Pastels, drawings and drypoints by Miss Bacon are owned by the Metropolitan Museum, the Brooklyn Museum, the Chicago Art Institute, the Whitney Museum of New York, the Los Angeles Museum, Carnegie Institute of Pittsburgh and the San Diego Fine Arts Gallery. Many private collectors eagerly seek her paintings and caricatures.

When asked how she managed all this and a full social life, she said: "I'm really an indolent person, I think. I'm sure I'm not systematic—I've never been able to schedule my time. No two days are alike because of family demands, and because I must visit editors and visit the people I'm drawing."

The witty but unmalicious verbal notes she writes to accompany her caricatures are almost as famous as the illustrations themselves. "There is no propaganda in Miss Bacon's work," says Thomas Craven, art critic, "no art for art's sake, no esthetic humbug; she has fastened upon personalities and has depicted graphically with expert craftsmanship, the various ways in which strength and weakness, character and conceit, shine out in the expression of the faces and the structure of the head. And more: to a rather astonishing talent for likenesses she has added her own sly, delving wit and the controlled vitality of her own personality."

Although Peggy Bacon has guillotined her former husband in *Off With Their Heads* thus: "A violent stare compounded of rage and gaiety, slightly berserk . . . an air of force and energy . . . mercurial, overbearing and intense," he with characteristic masculine

gallantry has written of her: "Her crowded plates are collections of humanized objects, viewed with the ruthless eye of an Olympian spitting contemptuously into the populous valley below. These satirical observations are also expressed in words, and the combination of these two mediums is the forerunner of a plate. The presence of the double appeal—the literary idea combined with the fine expression of a clear vision—is the cause, I believe, for the wide public which enjoys her work, in spite of the complete absence of any ingratiating traits therein."

References

Am Mag Art 27:137 Mr '34 por; 27: 529 O '34 por
Ind Woman 14:13+ Ja '35
Lit Digest 118:12 N 24 '34 por
New Repub 44:16-17 Ag 26 '25; 94: 363 Ap 27 '38
Scrib Mag 105:2 F '39 il por
Birchman, W. Peggy Bacon *In* Faces & Facts 1937
Mahony, B. E. and Whitney, E. comps. Contemporary Illustrators of Children's Books 1930
New Standard Encyclopedia of Art 1939
Who's Who in America

BADOGLIO, PIETRO *See* Addis Ababa, P. B., Duca d'

BAILEY, SIR ABE Nov 6, 1864—Aug 10, 1940 South African political leader; financier; sportsman and famous race horse owner; helped establish Union of South Africa; was in Transvaal gold rush in 1880's; made mining fortune estimated at 10 million pounds; friend of Cecil Rhodes; was active in the political struggle between Dutch settlers and English gold seekers; served in the Boer War; held seat in the Transvaal Legislative Assembly from 1910 to 1924; knighted in 1911; made baronet in 1919

References

International Who's Who
Who's Who

Obituaries

N Y Herald Tribune p30 Ag 11 '40 por
N Y Times p31 Ag 11 '40 por
Time 36:48 Ag 19 '40

BAILEY, GUY WINFRED May 7, 1876 —Oct 22, 1940 President of University of Vermont since 1920; former Vermont State Representative and Secretary of State

References

Leaders in Education 1932
Who's Who in America

Obituaries

N Y Herald Tribune p26 O 23 '40 por
N Y Times p23 O 23 '40 por

(Continued next page)

GUY WINFRED BAILEY

BAKER, ASA GEORGE Sept 27, 1866—
Sept 10, 1940 Publisher; chairman of the
board of directors and former president of
the G. & C. Merriam Company of Springfield, Massachusetts, publishers of the Webster dictionaries; member of many educational associations

References

Who's Who in America
Who's Who in Commerce and Industry

Obituaries

N Y Times p26 S 11 '40

**BAKER, RAY STANNARD [DAVID
GRAYSON, pseud.]** Apr 17, 1870- Au-
thor; historian
Address: Amherst, Massachusetts

The eight-volume biography of Woodrow
Wilson for which Ray Stannard Baker received the Pulitzer Award for 1939 represents a labor of fourteen years during which
Mr. Baker remained literally immured in
tons of paper, lost to the world.

The last letter Woodrow Wilson wrote
was addressed to him. On January 27,
1924, a week before the ex-President died,
he wrote to his friend asking him to write
the official biography. He said: "I would
rather have your intepretation than that
of anyone else I know." It has taken a
long time to get Mr. Baker's full interpretation, but in 1939 the world had the two
final volumes of the Wilson biography, and
on May 6, 1940 Ray Stannard Baker was
honored with the Pulitzer Prize of $1,000
for the best biography of the year.

Ray Stannard Baker (known to part of
his public as David Grayson) was born in
Lansing, Michigan April 17, 1870, the son of

Major Joseph Stannard and Alice (Potter)
Baker. As a child he attended a backwoods
school in northern Wisconsin, where he
began a habit of recording his rural experiences and observations in notebooks. He
took his B. S. degree at Michigan State
Agricultural School in 1889, studied law and
literature at the University of Michigan and
for a while played around with his father's
real estate business. By 1892, however, he
had decided he was a writer and nothing
else. From cub reporter on the old Chicago
Record he made himself sub-editor, then left
the paper in 1897 to be managing editor and
to write articles for *McClure's Syndicate,* having acquired the year before a wife (Jessie
I. Beal, the daughter of the noted botanist).
During all this time he was also a frequent
contributor to *Youth's Companion,* and his
first book, published in 1899, was titled
A Boy's Book of Inventions.

From 1899 to 1905 he was associate editor
of the famous muckraking *McClure's.* During this time his magazine articles on politics
and business were collected in book form
and published as *Our New Prosperity* (1900)
and *Seen in Germany* (1901), following a trip
to that country. Finally in 1906 he joined
in the purchase of the *American Magazine*
and became one of its editors along with
muckrakers William Allen White (see
sketch this issue), Ida Tarbell, Peter
Dunne, John Phillips and others. Baker
was associated with the magazine until
1915. His interest in sociology led him
to travel in many countries and in 1908
he published a collection of articles called
Following the Color Line, an exposition of
the Negro problem as he found it in his
travels. Another collection, *The Spiritual
Unrest,* followed in 1910, the year in which
his acquaintance with Woodrow Wilson
began.

In the meanwhile Ray Stannard Baker
was also publishing the contents of his
private notebooks in the *American Magazine*
under the name of David Grayson, and the
farmer-philosopher author of *Adventures in
Contentment* (published in book form in
1907) was enjoying a popularity of the best
selling variety which never came to Baker
under his own name. In 1910 came Grayson's *Adventures in Friendship,* in 1913 *The
Friendly Road,* in 1915 *Hempfield,* in 1917
Great Possessions. Some of these titles are
still selling.

The World War interrupted both Baker's
and Grayson's literary careers temporarily,
but brought Baker another. In 1918 he was
selected as special commissioner of the
State Department and sent on missions to
Great Britain, France and Italy. The following year he was appointed director of
the press bureau of the American Committee
to Negotiate Peace at Paris and in this
position was in constant and close association with Woodrow Wilson. A Republican
by tradition, he returned from Versailles one
of the President's most fervent admirers
and a crusader for the League of Nations,

Blackstone

RAY STANNARD BAKER

determined to educate the country to an understanding of the conditions under which the Versailles Treaty was made. *What Wilson Did at Paris* (1919) was written in three weeks; in 1922 came the three volumes of *Woodrow Wilson and World Settlement;* and these were followed by *The Public Papers of Woodrow Wilson* in six volumes, which Baker edited with William E. Dodd. It would seem that literary devotion could go no further. But on March 6, 1925 a truck rolled up to the Baker home containing fully five tons of documents, letters, state papers—Ray Stannard Baker was beginning the task which his friend had set him, not to be finished for fourteen years.

In 1927 the first two volumes of the *Life and Letters* appeared; in 1931 two more volumes. Then while working on volume five Baker fell seriously ill. He had made contracts for the syndicate rights to the biography, and in the midst of his illness these contracts were canceled, Wilson's news-value having somewhat depreciated, if his historical value had not. But still in poor health, and with his income from the biography averaging no more than $1,500 yearly, Baker continued. Farmer-philosopher David Grayson had been revived to support him in a financial way. In 1925 had appeared *Adventures in Understanding,* in 1931 *Adventures in Solitude,* in 1936 *The Countryman's Year.*

By 1935 the fifth book in the official biography was finished, in 1937 came the sixth, and last year, in time for World War II, the two final volumes were completed. Baker announced: "It appalls me when I think of it, and yet when I look back I have not the slightest regret. It was a grand experience! I thought I should be overjoyed at being a free man again, yet I confess that I have felt in the past few months more or less like a lost soul."

Baker, round-featured, with a clipped moustache and rimless glasses, looks more like a businessman than the outdoors person that he is. Since 1910 he has lived in Amherst, Massachusetts, in a house which he himself built beside a giant elm, looking over miles of farmland to the hills. There he will have more leisure now for his favorite recreations of gardening, bee-keeping and tramping. He has four children—two sons and two married daughters —and, at 70, an enviable capacity for enjoying living.

References

> Mentor 13:1-18 O '25 il pors
> N Y Herald Tribune p17 My 17 '40 por
> N Y Times p20 My 7 '40 por
> Rotarian 46:2 Mr '35 por
> Sat R Lit 22:13 My 11 '40 por (p5)
> Filler, L. McClure Idea *In* Crusaders for American Liberalism p80-9 1939
> Kunitz, S. J. ed. Authors Today and Yesterday 1933
> Who's Who in America

BALBO, ITALO (bäl'bō) June 6, 1896 —June 28, 1940 Italian Air Marshal and Governor-General of Libya; pioneer in Fascist Party who backed Mussolini's march on Rome in 1922; led mass air flight from Rome to the United States in 1933; killed in air battle over Tobruk, Libya during a British bombardment

References

> Nuova Antol 390:5-13 Mr 1 '37; 400: 3-13 N 1 '38

Wide World

ITALO BALBO

R Deux Mondes s8 32:134-48 Mr 1 '36
Chi è?
Gunther, J. Who Else in Italy? *In*
  Inside Europe p190-8 1936
International Who's Who
Who's Who

Obituaries
  N Y Herald Tribune p1, 8 Je 30 '40
    por; p3 Jl 1 '40
  N Y Times p1, 26 Je 30 '40 por;
    p18 Jl 1 '40
  Newsweek 16:31 Jl 8 '40 por
  Time 36:30+ Jl 8 '40 il por

BALDWIN, ROGER NASH Jan 21, 1884-
Director of the American Civil Liberties
Union
Address: b. 31 Union Sq, New York City;
h. Dell Brook Farm, Oakland, New Jersey

The American Civil Liberties Union has
been called "the organization which is doing
the most fruitful work to advance the so-
called Class War in America today," and
it has also been called "the staunchest defender of American democracy." Its own
statement of purpose is: "We stand on
the general principle that all matters of
public concern should be freely discussed
without interference."

It has been charged that the American
Civil Liberties Union defends only Communists and that its "occasional sideswipes
at non-radical cases are little more than
window dressing," but the Union itself
says its cases are not of his own choosing;
they are made for it by those who violate
civil liberties. For the same reason that it
defends Communists, it also defends Nazis
and members of the Ku Klux Klan. It defends,
not their doctrines, but their right to make
them known as guaranteed in the United
States Bill of Rights.

The Civil Liberties Union has come to
the defense of Sacco and Vanzetti, the
CIO, individual Communists, and it has
also said that Henry Ford has a right to distribute anti-union leaflets if he wishes.
When Mrs. Dilling, author of *The Red Network,* said the Union was financed by Moscow gold, the Union still offered to protest
for her to the Federal Communications
Commission when her speech was censored
by Station WOW. "The fact that the
A. C. L. U. fights for the rights of the
American Communists with its left hand
and for the rights of the Bund with its
right is why both parties have charged it
with inconsistency, incompatability, favoritism and certain crimes that can be stated
only in dirty words."

It was partly in answer to these charges
that the Civil Liberties Union in February
1940 excluded from membership on its governing committees or staff any person "who
is a member of any political organization
which supports totalitarian dictatorship in
any country, or who by his public declarations indicates his support of such a prin-

ROGER BALDWIN

ciple." Elizabeth Gurley Flynn, Communist
member of the Board of Directors, refused
to resign, and the board of directors announced her removal in May 1940.

One of the founders and the leader of the
American Civil Liberties Union, which since
1918 "has made itself the guardian of free
speech in this country," is Roger Baldwin.
To some, "the union is the irradiation of
his personality." Roger Baldwin has "a
family tree that can be traced back to an
acorn planted by William the Conqueror."
It was from his family that the Baldwin
apple obtained its name.

Roger Baldwin attended public schools in
Wellesley, Massachusetts and was graduated
from Harvard in 1904. In 1905 he received a
Master's degree in anthropology from Harvard. After Harvard he went to St. Louis,
where he taught sociology for three years
and was chief probation officer from 1917 to
1910. His book, *Juvenile Courts and Probation* (1912), written with Bernard Flexner, was the outcome of the years he spent
in social work in St. Louis. It was there
that Baldwin fought his first free speech
fight. The late Emma Goldman, anarchist,
came to town and was refused a place in
which to speak. Baldwin tried to get her
one, but she wasn't the least bit grateful to
him for his help.

When the First World War began, Baldwin
went to New York and joined forces with
other conscientious objectors in the American Union Against Militarism. After America entered, when it was no longer possible
to halt the War, the principal work of this
organization was snatching as many war
opponents as possible out of the jaws of
the Espionage Act. It became a work of
legal defense, not propaganda. From this
organization and the National Civil Liber-

BALDWIN, ROGER—*Continued*

ties Bureau the American Civil Liberties Union was born.

When Baldwin was drafted, he went to prison for a year rather than go to War. At his trial he said: "I know that as far as my principles are concerned, they seem to be utterly impracticable—mere moonshine. They are not the views that work in the world today. I fully realize that. But I fully realize that they are the views which are going to guide in the future."

After he came out of prison, Baldwin wandered all over the United States. He rode the rails, worked in a lead factory, in a brick yard, saw America. When he returned to New York it was to work for the newly formed American Civil Liberties Union and since 1920, as its director, he has been in the thick of every struggle for civil liberties in the United States and abroad. Many of these struggles have been famous. There was the Scopes "monkey" trial in Tennessee in 1925, in which the Union's lawyer, Arthur Garfield Hays, fought against the State's prohibition of the teaching of evolution. In 1938 and 1939 there was the fight against Mayor Hague's interference with civil liberties and the CIO organization in Jersey City which, after going to the United States Supreme Court, was won. Other struggles have been the small day-to-day ones to defend those whose rights have been infringed upon. From its office in New York the Union handles about 300 cases a year and at any given time has from 30 to 80 active cases on hand. With its branches all over the country, the Union is working on 75 to 100 cases a day.

Roger Baldwin is in the midst of all these cases, "a man of remarkable energy and executive ability." He himself tells us: "My public life for many years has combined a number of diverse activities, all relating to the maintenance of democracy and peace.

"While my jobs are mainly administrative, they require in this field continued public speaking, writing and teaching, in order to keep abreast of the manifold developments. A man engaged in so highly controversial a work must be clear in his own mind by taking a position on each major issue as it arises. The best recipe for that is teaching and public speaking. I have never confined myself to any one job, because it is so easy to fall into a routine which stifles growth. Most of the satisfaction in public work comes from fresh problems, new personalities and association with people on their best—their public—side.

"For recreation from a crowded routine I have made it for years almost a religion to escape to the country week-ends and for vacations. There I engage in all the juvenile sports in a rough wilderness retreat, where a canoe, a horse and a pair of skis will do full duty at the appropriate seasons." Very often Mr. Baldwin is accompanied into the country by his second wife, Evelyn Preston, whom he married in 1936, and by whom he has one child.

Peggy Bacon (see sketch this issue) describes him thus: "Dusty hair, a bit bedraggled. Turn-out clean but careless. Manner tumblingly hurried. Personality generous, self-disciplined, aristocratic, Galahadian, full of fervor and violent integrity, emotional, ethical, tirelessly seeking the Grail. A genuine article." Today, when the American Civil Liberties Union feels we may have even more "denials of civil liberties," than usual, Mr. Baldwin continues to seek "the Grail" of civil liberties for all the American people—unionists, Negroes, capitalists, aliens, Communists, Nazis.

References

Am Mercury 39:385-99 D '36
Christian Cent 57:237 F 21 '40
Forum 99:207-11 Ap '38; 100:312-16 D '38
Nation 151:326-8 O 12 '40
New Repub 81:209 Ja 2 '35 por
Scholastic 31:27S D 18 '37 por

Allen, D. ed. Galahad of Freedom: Roger Baldwin *In* Adventurous Americans p154-64 1932
American Civil Liberties Union The Bill of Rights—150 Years After 1939
Who's Who in America

BAMPTON, ROSE Nov 28, 1909- Singer
Address: 128 Central Park S, New York City

Rose Elizabeth Bampton had a very happy twenty-third birthday. Her debut at the Metropolitan on November 28, 1932 fell on that birthday, and like everything else in her charmed career it turned out an unquestioned success.

Her debut was in a contralto rôle— Laura in *La Gioconda*. But today Miss Bampton is singing soprano rôles. Back in the South Park High School in Buffalo, where Miss Bampton grew up, she began her singing career in a school Christmas pageant as a coloratura soprano. Later, while she was a student at the Curtis Institute of Music in Philadelphia, she was engaged for a concert in Buffalo, and was considerably excited over singing professionally in her home town. But she arrived in Buffalo with laryngitis, and no voice. The story is told that a doctor who came to look at her throat said: "You're a contralto?" "No," whispered Miss Bampton, "I'm a soprano." The medico is reported to have laughed. "So you think, my dear. You may as well know now that you are a contralto."

In Philadelphia once more, Rose told her teacher about the incident, and recalled that she had been having trouble with high notes. A renowned throat specialist was consulted. "You're a contralto," he agreed. "You have a remarkable range, but you're a contralto."

So Rose Bampton became a contralto, and made her debut at the Metropolitan as such. After three years of contralto rôles at the Metropolitan she wearied of the wicked and frustrated females she had to portray. She referred to herself in opera as "always a bridesmaid, never a bride." She was determined to sing soprano rôles, to become an operatic heroine. For, as she knew, after years of singing many of the lower-range artists develop new color and ability to produce the coveted higher notes. As Lauritz Melchior, present-day Metropolitan Opera tenor who sang baritone rôles for four years, explained to newsmen: "The voice is like a skyscraper. It must be built on a firm bedrock—then you can always build upward."

Rose Bampton did build her voice upward, and tried out her new soprano in Europe in the fall of 1936. She sang in Munich, Prague and Stockholm, but saved her United States soprano debut for the spring season. New York first heard her as a soprano in a Town Hall recital in March 1937, when she called upon her full range of two and a half octaves. Critics reported that "although her tones were rich and beautiful, Miss Bampton showed an overcautious interest in their production." However, they believed that when she became accustomed to her new power, she might be one of the most delightful lieder singers of the day. Their prophecy turned out true, for when she sang her first soprano rôle in *Il Trovatore* at the Metropolitan in May 1937, "audiences rejoiced that personable Miss Bampton was trustworthy in the high notes, could hit 'D' without difficulty, would now be able to sing soprano heroines instead of villainous contralto women."

Rose Bampton is the daughter of a Buffalo businessman, Samuel W. Bampton, an Englishman by birth. Her mother is an American whose family history dates back many generations in this country. Miss Bampton was born in Cleveland, and from there moved with her family to Massillon, Ohio, and later to Buffalo where she grew up. She led the life of a typical American child, the only girl in a family of three children. Although she studied piano from the age of six, it was not until she was in high school that she considered an operatic career seriously. She sang her first public solo in a high school Christmas pageant. A singing angel in the pageant had been taken ill, and the music director chose the tall, dark-haired, eager Rose Bampton to sing the part. "Chiefly," Miss Bampton says modestly, "because my name began with 'B,' and I sat in the first row." She was such a success that her teachers and parents encouraged her to take her voice seriously.

Her musical training began at the Curtis Institute of Music in Philadelphia. For four years she was the scholarship pupil

ROSE BAMPTON

of Horatio Connell, and during her fifth year at the Curtis Institute a pupil of Queena Mario.

In 1928 Miss Bampton began her operatic career with the Chautauqua Opera Association. She went next to the Philadelphia Grand Opera Company, with which she sang leading rôles through the Spring of 1932. She was something of a protégé of Leopold Stokowski, and the distinguished conductor engaged her for various appearances with the Philadelphia Orchestra. In April 1932 the stately brunette sang the part of the Wood Dove at the American première of Schönberg's *Gurre-Lieder,* both in Philadelphia and at the Metropolitan Opera House in New York, thus coming to the attention of the Manhattan critics. A month later she distinguished herself again at the Bethlehem Bach Festival and was encouraged by her teacher, Queena Mario, to apply for an audition at the Metropolitan Opera. After a second hearing Rose Bampton got the coveted Metropolitan contract, and made her debut, November 28, 1932 as Laura in *La Gioconda.*

Slender, brunette, with large expressive eyes, Miss Bampton is unpretentious, tremendously grateful for her voice. She is married to Wilfred Pelletier, one of the leading conductors of the Metropolitan.

Many American music lovers became acquainted with her through her regular programs on the National Broadcasting Company's network. She has sung throughout the length and breadth of the United States on concert engagements and with orchestras in Canada. She filled a London concert engagement in the home of Lady Astor (see sketch this issue) during the Jubilee celebration. She is scheduled to sing two

BAMPTON, ROSE—*Continued*
rôles in the 1940 to 1941 Metropolitan Opera
season.

References

Boston Transcript p6 Mr 1 '40
Musician 40:5 Mr '35 por; 45:52 Mr
'40 por
Newsweek 9:38 Mr 13 '37 por
Opera News 4:9-10 Ja 15 '40 pors
Time 29:48-50 My 17 '37 por
American Women
Pierre Key's Musical Who's Who

BANKHEAD, WILLIAM BROCKMAN
Apr 12, 1874—Sept 15, 1940   Late speaker
of the United States House of Representatives

December 1940 Bulletin: Speaker Bankhead died at 1:35 a. m. September 15,
1940 at the Naval Hospital in Washington. He had been in poor health for
the past several years. Representative
Sam Rayburn (see sketch this issue) of
Texas has been appointed Speaker of
the House.

From October issue:

William Brockman Bankhead and his
father before him have been representing
Alabama in Washington for an aggregate
of some threescore years. Sometimes called
the "best-loved man in Congress," still the
Alabama Congressman seems occasionally
to fall in the shadow of the rest of his family. Some people know him mainly as the
father of the glamorous actress Tallulah,
and of the equally glamorous Eugenia, who
has been married six times; others remember his Senator-brother, John Hollis Bankhead, who defeated Tom Heflin in 1930;
and then there is a sister who was mentioned as a gubernatorial prospect for 1938.

Wide World
WILLIAM B. BANKHEAD

But in the House of Representatives there
is little danger of Bankhead's being known
simply as "Tallulah's father." "Broad-shouldered, bald, completely untheatrical" but grave
and firm, it is Speaker Bankhead who "rises in
the House when 'the gentleman from
Palooka yields'—and no Republican hell-
devil can stop his bitter blast: 'May I
remind you, gentlemen?' And he steps forward with the grace of a leading man."

Long before the Civil War members of
the Bankhead family were prosperous
planters in Alabama, the name used for
towns, hotels, mines, roads, farmsteads.
William's father, "Cap'n John" Hollis Bankhead (he married Tallulah James Brockman), was both a prominent Alabama
Senator and Representative, and helped
sponsor the Bankhead Highways and War-
rior River development. The family was
always Methodist and anti-Ku Klux Klan.
William was born in Moscow, Lamar
County, Alabama on April 12, 1874 and was
educated at the University of Alabama,
where he played fullback on the University's
first football team, achieved Phi Beta
Kappa, took his B. A. in 1893 and his M. A.
three years later. In 1895 he received
an LL. B. from Georgetown University.
Throughout his college years he had nursed
dramatic aspirations (he had won the college medal for oratory, too), and after
finishing law school he almost ran away
from an apprenticeship in a Manhattan law
office to become a great actor. His Southern
accent actually brought him the offer of a
rôle in Boston, but when he received a letter
from his mother warning him of disaster
and disgrace he decided to stick to the law.

His next venture was as a struggling
lawyer in New York City again, where he
promptly joined both the Anawanda Club
and Tammany Hall. His first speech was
made in the Bowery from the tail gate of a
delivery wagon. He was soapboxing for
Robert Van Wyck for Mayor, and he
earnestly begged the New York populace to
"vote every star." Finally, finding the city
"too big a place for a country boy," he
went back to the South to be his brother's
law partner and in 1900 married Adalaide
Eugene Sledge of Memphis, Tennessee.
Entering politics in his own county, he was
from 1900 to 1901 Madison County representative in the State Legislature, then for
four years city attorney of Huntsville, and
from 1900 to 1914 served as Circuit Solicitor
of the fourteenth Judicial Circuit. In 1917 he
went to Washington as Democratic member
of the sixty-fifth Congress from the seventh
Alabama District, after having been defeated in the previous election. In 1915 he
married his present wife, the former
Florence McGuire, his first wife having died
and left him with two daughters, Eugenia
and Tallulah.

His father's advice before he entered the
House had been to "learn the rules." Bankhead followed this advice; he didn't make
himself particularly conspicuous in the
House, however. For a long time he was

merely an "amiable, well-liked but not particularly influential" Congressman with a vast knowledge of parliamentary procedure and well-disguised ambitions to become Speaker. On April 5, 1934 he was elected chairman of the House Rules Committee, but, when mentioned for the Speaker's office, temporarily abandoned his larger ambitions in favor of his friend Joseph Byrns from Tennessee. "You know I went fishing this summer with Joe Byrns down in the Gulf," Bankhead joked ruefully. "I now find I made a mistake in not throwing Joe overboard." But on January 2, 1935 Bankhead became majority leader in the House, and when on June 4, 1936 the House was shocked by the news of Byrns' sudden death, he himself was the natural choice for the office of Speaker.

As Speaker his duties are many and delicate: to "preserve order and decorum on the floor; to sign all acts, resolutions, writs, warrants and subpoenas ordered from the House; to use his vote to break deadlocks and to further the interests of his Party." Bankhead once summed up his own requirements for the office: "I should say that the most important is that the Speaker should be a parliamentarian. The second is that he should act impartially . . . and he should have a sense of humor."

These requirements and others that he didn't name have been filled by Speaker Bankhead more than adequately. He calls himself "a conciliator, not a combatant," and although he is generally known as one of the best speakers in Congress, with a resonant voice, an excellent vocabulary and an "unfailing sense of the dramatic," he can be counted on to get on his feet only when he really has something to say. Something of his unfailing calm and polished manner can be conveyed by two stories that people tell about him. Speaking for Al Smith in Alabama, back before his Speaker days, Ku Kluxers threw eggs at him. Brushing himself off, the Congressman turned to the chairman of the meetings. "Sir, I have been treated discourteously," he said—and continued his speech. At another time the early morning found the lower floor of his Washington house in flames. Roused from bed by his wife, Bankhead investigated and made his decision: "We had better return to our bedroom and await the firemen." When, after some time, the firemen arrived, they found the Congressman was as carefully dressed as always and he made his way down the ladder unescorted.

A consistent supporter of President Roosevelt even on his most unpopular proposals, it was Bankhead who on July 15, 1940 made the keynote address as temporary chairman of the Democratic National Convention. He himself also enjoyed a mild "boom" for the Vice-Presidency before former Secretary Wallace (see sketch this issue) carried the day. In spite of strenuous duties, his health is none too good: he suffers from occasional heart attacks and digestive disorders, so fishing is his only recreation. His hobby is collecting the gavels used by Speakers who preceded him: he now has six, and his is the smallest of them all.

References

    Christian Sci Mon Mag p2 N 25 '39 por
    Collier's 95:22+ Ja 5 '35 por
    Lit Digest 121:30 Ja 4 '36 por; 121:5 Je 13 '36 por
    Newsweek 7:9 Je 13 '36 por; 13:16 Ap 24 '39 por
    Scholastic 29:23 S 19 '36 por
    Time 30:12 N 29 '37 por (cover)
    Vital Speeches 6:613-16 Ag 1 '40
    Who's Who in America
    Who's Who in Government
    Who's Who in the Nation's Capital

Obituaries

    N Y Herald Tribune p12 S 16 '40
    N Y Times p18 S 17 '40 por
    Time 36:16-17 S 23 '40 por

BANNING, MARGARET CULKIN Mar 18, 1891- Author
Address: 617 Irving Pl, Duluth, Minnesota

Mrs. Banning has written, on the average, a book a year for the past 20 years and has contributed short stories and essays on phases of American life and activities to many magazines. In September 1940 her latest book, *Enough to Live On,* was published. A critic calls it "a readable and moderately entertaining book but not exactly escape fiction for most people."

She maintained that basically Americans are moral, that our modern law is based on the Ten Commandments. She was supported in her contention by Chester A. Kreider, a business man. Lewis Browne, author and university professor, disagreed with both of them. He called Americans the most "casual law breakers" and stated that we obey the law only because it is prudent to do so.

A native and resident of Minnesota, Margaret Culkin was born in the town of Buffalo. She is the daughter of William Edgar, an editorial writer on a Duluth newspaper, and Hannah Alice (Young) Culkin. Graduating from Vassar (1912) with Phi Beta Kappa honors, she became interested in philanthropic and social work. Later she received a certificate from the Chicago School of Civics and Philanthropy, and was a fellow in research at the Russell Sage Foundation the following year.

Margaret Culkin married Archibald Tanner Banning, a Duluth lawyer, in 1914. Two of their four children are living: Mary Margaret, the oldest, is taking post graduate work in physics at Johns Hopkins University, and her brother, Archibald Tanner Jr., is to complete his undergraduate work at Harvard in 1940.

MARGARET CULKIN BANNING

Six years after her marriage Mrs. Banning's first novel, *This Marrying*, was published by Harper's. Her stories appeal to many American women, for they deal with problems which always confront them. She describes her own contribution to literature: "The only possible reason why women should read anything I write might be because I might get a glimmer of truth once in a while and would pass it right along."

Out in Society (1940) is the story of what a girl gets into when she is in society, and what she gets out of it if she is out in it. Among her many novels are *The First Woman* (1935); *The Third Son* (1934); *The Iron Will* (1936); *Prelude to Love* (1929); *Mixed Marriage* (1930), *Too Young to Marry* (1938); and *Enough to Live On* (1940). Many short stories, articles and essays have appeared in magazines such as *Collier's, Delineator, American Magazine, Good Housekeeping, McCall's, Ladies' Home Journal, Saturday Evening Post, Pictorial Review, Atlantic Monthly* and *Harper's Magazine*. She has also published works in England.

Much comment was aroused and many reprints issued of *The Case for Chastity*, which Mrs. Banning wrote for the *Reader's Digest* (August 1937). This article was "based on extended research and interviews and on data supplied by doctors, psychologists and others who deal daily with difficulties arising from sex conduct."

Her productivity as a writer does not preclude other activities. She takes very seriously her duties as a citizen and as a mother. She is interested in her city, is a trustee of the Duluth Public Library Board and is interested in the Duluth Symphony Orchestra. In 1935 she was selected as the year's first citizen for the Duluth

Hall of Fame for her outstanding record in leadership in civic and welfare work—the first woman ever to have received this distinction.

She is interested also in houses, gardens, riding, current problems of women, war-relief work, Vassar College Alumnae and other clubs. She writes: "I belong to about 38 organizations and always intend to resign from 37."

Active in politics, Mrs. Banning is restless as a member of the Republican Party, yet unconvinced either that we can do without party government or that socialism would be practical. To become a Democrat instead of a Republican seems to her like turning over in bed. Much of her short-story material has developed out of the practical experiences of herself and other women in the political world.

An interesting speaker on either the radio or lecture platform, Mrs. Banning is chic, charming and unhurried. She has a flair for taking the impersonality out of hotel rooms—for always creating a homelike atmosphere about her. "As for writing," she says, "I do it everywhere. I write in the cottage and in the North and in the South. I wrote one of the *Letters to Susan* in Spain on the night before the Revolution and another in Paris that same year. I write on trains and on other people's typewriters. But in Duluth I have a bare room overlooking Lake Superior which is the best place in the world to be a professional writer, and when I can spend seven hours a day there for a few months I feel that I'm really on the job and earning my living."

References

Ind Woman 18:131 My '39 por
Sat R Lit 16:4 Je 12 '37 por
Writer 53:67-9 Mr '40
American Catholic Who's Who
American Women
Overton, G. M. Women Who Make Our Novels 1928
Who's Who Among North American Authors
Who's Who in America

BARBIROLLI, JOHN (bar-bĭ-rōl′lĭ) Dec 2, 1899- Orchestra conductor
Address: 113 W 57th St, New York City

John Barbirolli, "a musician of taste and fire and intensity, electric, vital, sensitive, dynamic, experienced," opened the ninety-ninth season of the New York Philharmonic-Symphony Orchestra in October 1940. Its permanent conductor since 1937, he has come a long way in popular opinion since he came as a young unknown to take Toscanini's place.

He had a reputation abroad, however, both as a conductor and as a cellist. But John Barbirolli started his musical career as neither; he had intended to be a violinist. Born in London, the son of Lorenzo Barbirolli, an Italian, and Louise (Ribeyrol) Barbirolli, a Frenchwoman, young John began to study music early. A boy whose father and grandfather had both played in the orchestra of La Scala in Milan had no trouble in getting encouragement from his family. It made them unhappy, though, to watch him play the violin: he kept striding up and down the room, always walking, never still. John's grandfather suddenly got an idea, and it wasn't long before John's practicing had been transferred from the violin to the cello and John was sitting in one place as he played.

By the time he was 11 he had received a scholarship to Trinity College of Music and had given his first public performance—the solo part of the Saint Saëns' Cello Concerto in A Minor. By the time he was 14 he had really started his professional career and, as he says, "it wasn't long before I had played everywhere except in the street—theatres, music halls, cinemas, in opera, orchestra and in chamber music. I went right through the mill. I think now it was the best possible thing that could have happened to me."

When he was 16 Barbirolli became a member of the Queen's Hall Orchestra in London, "and it was good schooling," he comments, "to work my way through such a large repertoire of orchestral works." He also played in the Beecham Opera Company at Drury Lane and got jobs once in a while in small theatre orchestras. He liked theatre jobs —"not much to do. . . All we did was to play the people to and from the bar in the intermissions. In the long waits between the act intervals I studied scores."

He kept studying scores because his real ambition was conducting, not cello playing ("bandmasters in parks were my heroes when I was young"). He got his first chance at conducting when he was in the army under a colonel who fiddled enthusiastically and formed a small orchestra The War over, Barbirolli returned to London feeling everything was a "mess." "Progress had been stopped for four years. Young men returned to their homes and had to start life all over again. So far as I was concerned," he adds, "I had my cello and I turned to that."

He became cellist of the International String Quartet in 1920 and stayed with this quartet until 1924. Then he began his first professional conducting. In 1925 he founded a chamber orchestra, the Barbirolli Chamber Orchestra, which was widely heard. After listening to a performance of it Fred Austin, of the British National Opera Company, offered him the position of conductor in his company. "In Newcastle, during my opening week," he says, "I conducted opera by Puccini, Verdi and Gounod—quite a job for a youngster with no previous opera experience."

This was in 1926. In 1927 Barbirolli became guest conductor of the London Symphony Orchestra and of the Royal Philharmonic Society concerts, and in that same year started his seven years' association with the International Opera Company at Covent Garden, London. From 1933 to 1936 he conducted the Scottish Orchestra and the Leeds Symphony, so successfully that "both organizations increased their audiences measurably and extended their seasons."

In 1936, after having conducted all of England's great orchestras and after having been a guest conductor in Russia and Finland, Barbirolli was invited to New York by the Philharmonic to have charge of the season's first 10 weeks. It was a hard job. Toscanini had just left and his memory was shining. But Barbirolli announced that he did not "intend to follow in the maestro's footsteps. . . I feel that music must go on. I am a simple person who is passionately in love with music. I wish to serve it."

When he first ascended the Philharmonic podium audiences were prepared to think him too young, too inexperienced for the leadership of that august body. But they watched him, "planting his feet widely, chin down," as he "swayed his shoulders delicately through the lyrical passages, hunched forward to demand a pianissimo, twitched his kinetic torso and wagged his flying tails to call for quickened tempi." And they listened to him. And they called him "a young conductor of high promise, venturesome, resourceful."

In that same year Barbirolli was appointed conductor of the New York Philharmonic for three years, the first permanent conductor of the Philharmonic since 1921. Music critics hailed the appointment as a "significant decision, marking a new era in the history of the Philharmonic Society," and pointed out how important it was to have a conductor of artistic integrity who could mould the orchestra into a "consistent personality and technical unity." The appointment was attributed also to the "amazing" attendance gains. In 1940 Barbirolli's engagement was extended until the season of 1942 to 1943.

At the end of the 1939 to 1940 season Samuel Chotzinoff (see sketch this issue) suggested that "a captious critic would perhaps say that the Philharmonic-Symphony, as a virtuoso body, continued this last season to show a certain deterioration." However, audiences continued and continue to be pleased. Much of this pleasure may be due to Barbirolli's ingenuity as a program maker. His tastes are catholic, he plays no favorites and he searches for novelties with "commendable zest." He himself says he has no favorites. "I love all music. Sometimes, as when I play Beethoven's Seventh Symphony, I think that is greatest. Again, perhaps when I am playing Brahms' Fourth Symphony, I think, 'What could be greater than this?' "

"A fiery, small man" who "dances about the podium, cutting the air with a great circular beat, stamping his foot, changing his baton from one hand to the other,"

JOHN BARBIROLLI

Barbirolli still insists that the more simple the baton technique the better, and that "with his eyes a conductor can convey many things for which the baton is impotent. A lift of the eyebrow, a look—nuances, subtleties." He is even more firmly convinced that the best technique is unimportant if the conductor himself is not a "born conductor." "No matter how much conductors study . . . their real progress begins only after the business of formal study has ended. . . A man either possesses the sum total of magnetism, communicativeness and perceptive ingenuity which make a master composer or he does not."

A conductor, even one with all these qualifications, is aided by being able to play "some if not all of the instruments he directs." And he "must be a good psychologist." Barbirolli feels that he knows how to handle an orchestra. He explains his first sessions with the Philharmonic thus: "All the men in the Philharmonic are A-1 musicians and I treated them so. I let them save all their nervous tension for the performances. The rehearsals were gay and carefree. . . I never worked them six hours a day as some conductors do." But he did, and he does often, rehearse one number hour after hour, insisting it be played as it was written. Then, "perhaps midway through the session, he will rap smartly with the baton, pass his fingers through his black hair and say: 'It is not good enough.' Then he may pause with a smile and add: 'It is not improper to become inspired in the cause of music.'" Barbirolli often, too, gets off gentle witticisms to his men like: "Gentlemen, that passage should sound like the night. You're playing it like the morning after."

"A short, slightly dark young man, somewhat Napoleonic in aspect, with a hint of Mediterranean intensity in his face," John Barbirolli is actually very British, except when he is on the platform. He was born in London's Bloomsbury, likes Bloomsbury and still maintains a four-room flat there. He likes Yorkshire ham, cricket matches and trim, English clothes. His wife, Evelyn Rothwell, is as British as he. They were married in July 1939, seven months after Barbirolli had received a divorce from Marjorie Parry, English opera singer, his first wife, whom he married in 1932. The present Mrs. Barbirolli was one of England's outstanding oboe players, soloist of the Scottish Orchestra of Glasgow, the Adolf Busch Ensemble and the Glyndebourne Festival Orchestra.

Since their marriage Mrs. Barbirolli has given up her career, though she did play with the Vancouver Orchestra in the summer of 1940 when Barbirolli was conducting it. She shares many but not all of his enthusiasms—he is a gourmet, an authority on liquors, and his idea of relaxation is to get all his shoes out of the closet and shine them brightly.

References

Etude 56:635-6 O '38 por
Lit Digest 123:24 Ja 16 '37
Musician 41:77+ Ap '36 por (p80)
N Y Herald Tribune N 1 '36
Time 27:42 Ap 20 '36 por; 28:50-1 N 16 '36 por
Shore, B. Eugene Goossens, John Barbirolli, Leslie Howard, Julius Harrison *In* Orchestra Speaks p83-92 1938
Thompson, O. ed. Cyclopedia of Music and Musicians 1939
Who's Who
Who's Who in America

BARCLAY, MCCLELLAND May 9, 1893- Illustrator

Address: 36 W 59th St, New York City

McClelland Barclay says he is "considered by some a versatile artist." This illustrator who created "The Fisher Body Girl" has also become known for his marine paintings, his portraits, his sculpture and his industrial designing. He has even taught art. In the summer of 1939 he started a school of his own on Long Island in which he tried to help young artists develop in a direction best suited to their particular talents. Before that he instructed many of the younger illustrators now appearing on the pages of America's magazines.

Good, sound art training is the basis for the success of this popular illustrator. He was born in St. Louis, Missouri, the son of Robert and Minnie G. (Hamilton) Barclay. It was in St. Louis that he received his first art lessons. His first known painting

McCLELLAND BARCLAY

was made when he was seven: he met Mark Twain and rushed home to do an oil portrait of him. After attending Central High School in St. Louis and studying at the St. Louis Museum of Fine Arts, Barclay moved with his family to Washington, D. C. There, from 1909 to 1912, he studied at the Corcoran School of Art. The next two years he spent at the Art Students League in New York. Five years later he returned to study and spent two years at the Chicago Art Institute. Barclay himself says that he has studied art as long as he can remember and expects to keep on studying.

McClelland Barclay's first illustrating job came in 1912, and from that date on his sleek, smooth, rounded, long-limbed young ladies and his firm-jawed young men have graced the pages of the *Saturday Evening Post, Good Housekeeping, Cosmopolitan* and other magazines. Innumerable advertisements for innumerable products have been enlivened and made attractive by his drawings, though "The Fisher Body Girl," a series of advertisements that ran for nine years, made the most money for Barclay and brought him the most fame.

Barclay married the model for "The Fisher Body Girl," Helene Coghill Haskin, in 1930. Many times he painted her picture in numerous poses and molded a portrait head of her. Later, when she became ambitious for a screen career, they were divorced, but they have continued to be friends.

Like most artists who draw beautiful women, Barclay is frequently called upon to judge beauty shows, or to give his opinions on the relative merits of American and foreign women, or to present his criteria of beauty. After many years of doing this he still believes "the modern American girl is the most beautiful any race or age has produced."

Barclay's ability to set things down clearly and attractively has nowhere been better illustrated than in the many posters he created during the last War. His recruiting poster was awarded first prize by the Conference Committee on National Preparedness; the Red Cross gave him another first prize for his *Fill the Breach*; his Marine Corps recruiting poster, *The Human Cross,* was awarded still another first prize.

McClelland Barclay likes to box and sometimes puts on the gloves with Arthur Donovan, noted referee and boxing coach at the New York Athletic Club. He is also a strong swimmer, plays a fast game of tennis, skis and rides horseback. He likes to rough it in the woods, too, or, even more, his great pleasure is to go to a lonely island off the coast of Maine, where he paints the waves. He doesn't smoke, he says, or "play cards, drink liquor or play golf."

References

Art Digest 13:28 My 1 '39
America's Young Men 1936-37
Birchman, W. McClelland Barclay
  In Faces & Facts 1937
Who's Who in America
Who's Who in American Art

BARLOW, HOWARD May 1, 1892- Symphony orchestra conductor
Address: b. Columbia Broadcasting System, 485 Madison Ave, New York City; h. 435 E 57th St, New York City

Howard Barlow, conductor of the Columbia Broadcasting System Symphony, was engaged as director of the Baltimore Symphony Orchestra for the 1940 to 1941 season. This did not affect his duties as conductor of the radio orchestra.

It seems quite natural that American music, just a stepchild to most symphony conductors, should find a staunch champion in Howard Barlow, a plain American from Plain City, Ohio, to which his family tree branched off from its New England beginnings. Barlow, the son of Earl W. and Nettie (Dunham) Barlow, made his debut at the age of six, in Urbana, Ohio, bravely singing a hymn at a Sunday School social. While his family hopefully anticipated the day when the youngster would enter his father's furniture manufacturing business, Howard heard a player-piano version of something from *Il Trovatore*, and immediately decided that he wanted to become a composer. So he studied the trumpet, piano, cello and drums. Of this period of musical devotion, he says: "Music was my greatest source of enjoyment, and as our town boasted neither music teachers nor music stores (except the place where dance records were sold), I was hard put to it to find the enjoyment I wanted. My only pieces were a book of Czerny exercises, Schumann's *Album for the Young* and a volume of baritone songs. I learned all of these on the piano, and then began all over

HOWARD BARLOW

again practicing them on the violin and the violincello. After that, I came to a stop."

Howard Barlow's family moved to Mt. Carmel, Illinois, then to Denver, where Howard became a pupil of a music teacher in the public schools, the late Wilberforce J. Whiteman, father of Paul Whiteman. Later he went to the University of Colorado, and Reed College in Oregon (B. A. in English literature), and then he received a scholarship to Columbia University in New York. While his family, a little less hopefully now but with admirable persistence, continued to suggest the furniture business, Barlow registered at a New York agency as an "American singer." Nothing came of that but he did get jobs conducting choral groups in New York City and surrounding places.

After the War, in which he served as a private and sergeant, he resumed his career, conducting several American music festivals, notably the MacDowell series at Peterboro, New Hampshire. In 1923 he formed an all-American orchestra of 75 musicians which did well for two seasons in New York, although bucking such strong opposition as the New York Philharmonic and the Damrosch Symphony. Barlow then obtained a job as music director at the Neighborhood Playhouse on Grand Street, where he arranged the music for its productions of The Dybbuk and Grand Street Follies. Under the name of Thomas Tilton he appeared as a singer.

On December 12, 1926 he was married to Miss Jeannette Thomas of Portland, Oregon. To the well-grounded musician the puny youngster called radio then made an appeal. On September 18, 1927 Howard Barlow stood before twenty-two musicians and "at precisely three o'clock" led them into Luigini's Ballet Egyptienne. With this hour of symphonic mu-

sic the Columbia network was inaugurated. In line with Barlow's oft-reiterated interest in American music, he conducted for the radio that evening selections from Deems Taylor's The King's Henchman (see sketch this issue).

"Because of its inherently democratic nature," says Barlow, "I believe that radio can be used to explore the vast field of native American music. The American performer and the American composer must be given a full, free chance to show what they can do in taking their places beside the foreign artists. So far, we have done this in only a limited way. We have progressed beyond the point where Americans were refused a chance in the arts and had to change their names—from Norton to Nordica!—to be heard at all. But there is still vast room for improvement. . . The one thing the American composer needs today is not a finishing year abroad, but a chance to be heard at home."

In 1937 he introduced six works by famous American composers who had been commissioned by the radio to write music specifically for broadcasting. Relatively unknown American composers have also had their works played. "None of them," he says of some 100 compositions out of 200 submitted to him, "was below the average of new, untried works anywhere in the world. We have an immense amount of creative talent, earnestness and vitality. . ."

Barlow is an expert program maker, memorizes everything and has been known to conduct for as long as a year and a half without repeating a major work. Muscular, with fine dark eyes and receding hairline, he is not the arty, musical type. He has made guest concert appearances with orchestras in Philadelphia, Duluth, Washington, D. C., and has conducted both Stadium concerts in New York City and Metropolitan Opera concerts.

Struggling small-town musicians anxious to know about "pull" for New York radio and musical work will be heartened by Barlow's: "When I arrived in New York myself, my only letter of introduction was to a cheese merchant."

References

Christian Sci Mon p7 F 28 '40 por
Etude 57:367+ Je '39 pors; 58:87 F '40
N Y Times p18 N 15 '39
Newsweek 12:19 Jl 4 '38 pors
Pierre Key's Musical Who's Who
Thompson, O. ed. International Cyclopedia of Music and Musicians 1939
Who's Who in America
Wier, A. E. ed. Macmillan Encyclopedia of Music and Musicians 1938

BARNEY, SAMUEL E. 1859—Feb 23, 1940 Civil engineer

Samuel E. Barney, professor emeritus of civil engineering at Yale University, died at his home after a heart attack. He was 81 years old. A native of New Haven, Connecticut, Mr. Barney was a descendant of the family which settled Salem and Taunton, Massachusetts. After being graduated from Yale in 1879, he became a consulting engineer for various municipalities and corporations and was an expert on the construction of breakwaters, watersheds and railroads. One of his important assignments was to make a valuation of the land taken for construction of the Ashokan Reservoir in the Catskill Mountains. He is survived by a widow, Mrs. Ida Bushness Barney, and two daughters.

Obituaries

N Y Herald Tribune p10 F 24 '40
N Y Times p13 F 24 '40

BARNOUW, ERIK (bar'now) June 23, 1908- Radio writer; instructor in radio writing and production at Columbia University

Address: 4414 Cayuga Ave, New York City

"Tall, dark, handsome Erik Barnouw, Holland-born, Princeton-built, author, dramatist, summer-stock trooper who might have become a matinee idol had he not chosen backstage radio writing" is in 1940 an instructor in radio writing and production at Columbia University. Monday and Tuesday nights he imparts to students facts about "commercials" and "continuities," about directing programs and "ad libbing" which he learned in the nine years he spent writing for Camels and General Foods, *True Story* and Barbasol, Orson Welles and *Liberty.*

Erik Barnouw has been teaching at Columbia since 1937 and in 1938 lectured on radio and drama at the Writers' Conference at the University of Colorado. In 1939 his *Handbook of Radio Writing* was published, a "thoroughgoing text on the tricks of the trade, with liberal examples quoted from radio worthies." According to the radio writer Norman Corwin (see sketch this issue) it "should be as much a part of every radio writer's equipment as a receiving set, a typewriter and a dictionary." The book starts with a general appraisal of the market and then proceeds to analyze the tools, technique, methods and devices of radio writing. It also gives "many interesting slants on radio both as a market and as a madhouse."

Erik Barnouw, his two brothers and his sister were all born in The Hague, Holland, where their father was a teacher in a Gymnasium and during the World War a foreign correspondent for *The Nation.* Erik went to elementary school in The Hague until the end of the War, when his father came to America to become one of the editors of the *Weekly Review* and later Queen Wilhelmina Professor at Columbia.

Then Erik attended Horace Mann School in New York City.

From Horace Mann, Erik Barnouw went to Princeton University in 1925. At Princeton he was editor of the Nassau *Literary Magazine* and collaborated with Joshua Logan on one of the Princeton Triangle Club musical plays. "It was called *Zuider Zee,*" he says, "and was about the boy who put his finger in the dyke, about whom I had never heard until I came to America." He also wrote, alone, a non-musical, three-act comedy satirizing Princeton, entitled *Open Collars,* successfully produced and later revived at Princeton and at a number of other colleges. Mr. Barnouw now says rather ruefully that "although I'd hoped to annoy the University with it, a little bit, the dean commended it and the Princeton University Press published it."

At college Barnouw made most of his spending money designing Christmas cards and bookplates for other Princetonians. One summer he spent tutoring a wealthy Scotch baronet on his estate in Scotland; another he spent being one of the founders and directors of the summer stock company at Falmouth, Massachusetts, first called the University Players. The group included Margaret Sullavan, Henry Fonda, Joshua Logan and Bretaigne Windust.

After he was graduated from Princeton in 1929 Barnouw spent some months as an actor in the Cukor-Kondolf Stock Company in Rochester, New York, but left this to join the writing staff of *Fortune.* Before the year was out he was in Europe traveling on a scholarship and studying under Max Reinhardt at his theatre seminar in Vienna.

Late in 1930 Erik Barnouw was back in the United States and in early 1931 he was working as an advertising writer for Erwin Wasey, Incorporated. For five years he

ERIK BARNOUW

BARNOUW, ERIK—*Continued*

stayed with the firm, moving up from writer to radio program director, directing programs for Camels, General Foods, Goodyear, Philco, Barbasol. In 1935 Barnouw became program director for another advertising agency, Arthur Kudner, directing programs for *True Story* and *Liberty*. He left to become a free-lance writer and, for a year, from 1936 to 1937, wrote the NBC serial, *The Honeymooners*. The best-known series he has done for radio is, probably, the *Pursuit of Happiness*. He has also contributed to the *Campbell Playhouse, Main Street* and the *Cavalcade of America*.

Mr. Barnouw says that the kind of scripts he prefers and specializes in are historical scripts and the adapting of classics. It is interesting to note that his *Handbook* gives as a sample script a radio version of *Macbeth*. Other Shakespearean plays have been arranged for school use and some of them have been published by *Scholastic* magazine.

In 1939 Erik Barnouw was married to Dorothy Beach, who comes from Fair Haven, Vermont and was a scholarship pupil of Madame Louise Homer.

References

> Time 34:57 N 6 '39 por
> Variety Radio Directory

BARR, FRANK STRINGFELLOW Jan 15, 1897- Educator

Address: St. John's College, Annapolis, Maryland

Stringfellow Barr is an educator who believes that a college education should be a liberal education, that it should prepare "men for the business of living—concerned that they meet not only their bills but other and subtler obligations which free men must meet." Only if American colleges scrap their text books, abolish the elective system and relinquish specialized education can they prevent the onset of another dark age.

These are the ideas on which the curriculum of St. John's College in Annapolis, Maryland is based. When Barr became president of this college in 1937 he and its board, made up of liberal educators and now headed by President Hutchins of the University of Chicago, decided to revive the traditional liberal arts college course. His and Hutchins' plan for a college education consisted of four years of reading and discussing the great books of the past.

To get a degree seniors must prove that they know the 120-odd classics of the world backwards and forwards; they must show competence in the liberal arts; they must have the ability to read at least two foreign languages; they must be proficient in mathematics and must have spent 300 hours in laboratory science. Their teachers are the great thinkers of the past. Dr. Barr asks

STRINGFELLOW BARR

interviewers: "Aren't you sorry for the students in all the other colleges who have nobody to teach them but oafs like me?" From the great thinkers of the past the students get all their knowledge, through reading, through working out the old principles in practical fashion, through seminar discussions of the classical works, through analyzing and criticizing terms and propositions, arguments and contradictions.

John Dewey is one of the critics of the St. John's system. He admits that this type of liberal education is the best possible —but only for those who can master it. It isn't the kind from which all students can benefit. Dr. Barr, however, points to his student body, many of whom come from small towns in Maryland and half of whom are working their way through school, and their evident absorption in their work. When others criticize the system on the grounds that it is impractical, Stringfellow Barr tells them that the student who has consorted with great minds can learn specialized subjects in a few months and probably more thoroughly than if he had studied them on the campus.

Stringfellow Barr was born in Suffolk, Virginia on January 15, 1897 and did much of his educational work in Virginia. He received his B. A. from the University of Virginia in 1916 and his M. A. in 1917. Because of his unusual record there, he was made a Rhodes Scholar (after a period driving an ambulance in the War), and spent the years from 1919 to 1921 at Oxford, from which he also got a B. A. and an M. A.

Dr. Barr continued with his studies after Oxford—at the University of Paris and at the University of Ghent. In 1924 he returned with his wife, Gladys Baldwin, whom he married in 1921, to Virginia to become assistant professor of modern European history. He stayed at the University of Virginia, as associate professor and professor, until 1936. At Virginia he was one of the university's most popular lecturers, famous, too, for his work in editing the *Virginia Quarterly Review,* probably "the South's most distinguished literary magazine."

While there he contributed, as he has continued to contribute, articles and book reviews to the country's important magazines and published his *Mazzini: Portrait of an Exile* (1935). In his writings he began to develop those ideas of modern, "liberal" education for which he is now well-known, ideas which formed and still form the basis for lectures all over the country.

In 1936 President Hutchins (see sketch this issue) of the University of Chicago drafted Dr. Barr to help him with a projected revival of the traditional liberal arts college course, but "red-haired, stocky" Professor Barr stayed there only a year and then left, with Scott Buchanan, to put President Hutchins' ideas into practice at St. John's. In May 1940 Dr. Barr inaugurated for CBS a weekly Sunday afternoon program, *Invitation to Learning,* on which Professor Barr and other educators discuss the great books read at the college.

References

Harper 179:64-75 Je '39
Life 8:61-7 F 5 '40 il por
Newsweek 10:40 S 20 '37 por
Progressive Educ 16:18-23 Ja '39
 (Same cond. Educ Digest 4:7-10
 F '39)
Sch & Soc 51:375 Mr 23 '40
Time 30:35-6 Jl 19 '37 por; 32:40-1
 O 24 '38 por; 36:58 O 21 '40
America's Young Men 1936-37
Who's Who in America

BARRERE, CAMILLE EUGENE PIERRE (bä-rär) Oct 1851—Oct 8, 1940 French diplomat; in 1880 French delegate on the international commission for the regulation of the Danube; Minister Plenipotentiary to Egypt and represented France in Stockholm, Munich, Bucharest before going to Rome in 1897, where he represented France for 32 years; is credited with winning over Italy from the Triple Alliance to the Triple Entente and inducing Italy to throw in her lot with the Allies in the First World War

Obituaries

N Y Times p25 O 10 '40

BARRETT, WILTON AGNEW Oct 26, 1885—Feb 18, 1940 Motion picture critic

Wilton Agnew Barrett, executive secretary of the National Board of Review of Motion Pictures since 1923, died at the age of 54 after a heart attack.

He was born in Philadelphia in 1885 and was graduated from the University of Pennsylvania in 1909. That year he joined

WILTON A. BARRETT

the staff of the National Board shortly after its organization by the People's Institute. Under his direction the Board began to review films. In time they were reviewing 98 per cent of all films produced. Credited with developing the Board's weekly bulletin method of classifying pictures for adult or children's consumption, he also started the monthly magazine which reviewed important films. Later he organized the committee on exceptional photoplays which annually selects the 10 best motion pictures.

Critics said that "his knowledge of motion pictures in all their ramifications was surpassed by few people in the United States either within or without the industry." He never worked in the industry and thus was able to maintain a detached attitude toward it.

Long an ardent foe of censorship, Barrett maintained that the Board was not a censorship organization, but merely a body to help the motion picture-goer select his film fare intelligently. The Board has consistently opposed all forms of state censorship and any proposal for national censorship. While Mr. Barrett believed strongly in decency in motion pictures, he maintained that the people themselves are the best judges of motion pictures. He wrote a book of poems, *Songs of the Journey,* and was a frequent contributor to poetry magazines and general periodicals.

References

International Motion Picture Almanac 1936-37

Obituaries

Nat Bd of R Mag 15:3 F '40
N Y Herald Tribune p14 F 19 '40
N Y World-Telegram p19 F 19 '40

Underwood & Underwood

EMILY DUNNING BARRINGER

BARRINGER, EMILY DUNNING Sept 27, 1876- Surgeon; gynecologist
Address: b. 114 E 54th St, New York City; h. New Canaan, Connecticut

Retiring as director of gynecology after 21 years at the Kingston Avenue Hospital, Brooklyn, New York, Dr. Emily Barringer was given an honorary dinner by her staff at the New York Academy of Medicine on March 2, 1940. On retirement, she becomes honorary consulting surgeon.

A pioneer in a profession which was virtually closed to women, Dr. Barringer was influential in opening the way for women physicians to obtain positions in the medical and surgical services of the New York City hospitals.

Dr. Barringer was born at Scarsdale, New York, September 27, 1876. After receiving a degree of B. S. from Cornell University in 1897, she entered the Cornell Medical School affiliated with Bellevue Hospital and was graduated with honors as the second in her class in 1901. She won first place in competition for a position at Mount Sinai Hospital, but the appointment was denied her because of her sex. She appealed to Mayor Seth Low, who ratified the appointment. She then took part in the competitive examination for Gouverneur Hospital (Bellevue and Allied Hospitals) and again won first place, and this was also denied her because of her sex. The following year brought the reform Mayor, Seth Low, and learning of the above, he said that if a woman physician won a place at the examination for Gouverneur Hospital, he would ratify it. Dr. Dunning again entered the competitive examination for Gouverneur Hospital, and this time won fourth place. True to his word, Mayor

Seth Low ratified the appointment, and Dr. Dunning became the first woman ambulance surgeon of New York City. As the city's only woman ambulance surgeon she attracted much attention and comment in the press of the day. She was known as "the beautiful girl on the Bowery run" during the year her route included the lower East Side.

In 1904 she married Benjamin Stockwell Barringer, also a surgeon. They have two children, Benjamin Lang and Emily Velona, and live in New Canaan, Connecticut.

Dr. Barringer is president of the Women's Medical Association of New York City, and has served for several years as chairman of the medical committee on minimum standards for delinquent girls of the National Committee on Prisons and Prison Labor. She is a fellow of the College of Surgeons and the New York Academy of Medicine. She has always been an active worker for the passage of progressive medical legislation. Her hobby is architecture; for recreation she likes skating and dancing.

References

N Y Herald Tribune p3 Mr 3 '40
N Y Times p37 Mr 3 '40
American Medical Directory
American Women

BARROW, JOSEPH LOUIS *See* Louis, J.

BARRY, PATRICK FRANK, BISHOP Nov 15, 1868—Aug 12, 1940 Bishop of the St. Augustine Diocese of the Roman Catholic Church; ordained in 1895 in Ireland; was pastor in Florida in various churches from 1895 to his death

BISHOP PATRICK BARRY

References
American Catholic Who's Who
Catholic Who's Who
Who's Who in America

Obituaries
N Y Herald Tribune p14 Ag 14 '40
por
N Y Sun p19 Ag 13 '40

BARTHE, RICHMOND (bär-tā) Jan 28, 1901- Sculptor
Address: 285 Eighth Ave, New York City

Richmond Barthé is a successful sculptor who has had only a couple of months of sculpture lessons in his life. His works can be seen at the Whitney Museum in New York and in museums all over the country, and he was awarded a Guggenheim Fellowship (April 1940) which gave him a year's real freedom for creative work.

Barthé is untaught because Jo Davidson advised him to be so. Born of mixed Creole, Negro and Indian stock in Bay, St. Louis, Mississippi, Barthé lived there until he was 23. As a youth, his talent was obvious, and a Catholic priest there, together with the novelist, Lyle Saxon, who lived next door to the home where Barthé worked as houseboy, encouraged him. Southern art schools would not admit him because he was a Negro, so he went to the Chicago Art Institute to study, earning his way by waiting on tables. It was towards the end of his stay at Chicago that he became interested in sculpture and came to New York for advice from Jo Davidson.

He stayed clear of sculpture lessons as Davidson suggested and within two years had taught himself enough to have a one-man show at the Chicago Women's City Club. This exhibition, his first, won him a Julius Rosenwald Fellowship. His first sculpture commission was to do a head of Toussaint l'Ouverture for the Lake County Children's Home at Gary, Indiana. In 1931 came his New York debut for which he received much critical praise. In 1932 he worked at the Art Students League for a couple of months. Shortly after he was invited by the Whitney Museum to exhibit there, and after that showing three of his sculptures were bought for the museum's permanent collection.

In 1934 Barthé took his first trip to Europe on a tour which, he says, "opened up a new world," and from which he obtained representation in private collections in Austria, Germany, Romania, France and England. In America, later, he was commissioned by the Treasury Department to do two eight and one-half by forty foot bas-relief panels for the Harlem River Housing Project Amphitheatre depicting a Negro dance group and the Exodus scene from *Green Pastures* and by the Federal Arts Project to create a military figure of heroic size for the dining hall at West Point. More recently he was commissioned to execute a memorial for James Weldon Johnson, Negro writer.

RICHMOND BARTHE

Most critics agree that it is not in his larger works—not even in those like the impressive and moving *Mother and Son* at the New York World's Fair, which shows a mother mourning over the body of her dead son, on whose neck is a rope mark—that he shows his full genius, but in his smaller figures. In them he meets Cellini's requirements that a sculpture should appear to advantage from many points of view. The *Blackberry Woman* at the Whitney Museum, for instance, is a statue "whose hard silhouette, legible from all around, is complemented by the beautiful view from above in which one gets the full value of the spreading feet and the low relief still life of leaves in the tops of the baskets." In these smaller figures Barthé has realized the racial genius for concentrating on an emotional state to the limit of the powers of the body. He has done this in *Benga* and *Wetta*, in the dignified but almost trance-like *African Boy Dancing*.

In these sculptures and in most of his others Barthé is a "physical" artist in the sense of his being immensely interested in the physical and spiritual life of the human body and very little concerned with mythological and literary ideas or the pursuit of fascinating processes and materials. Perhaps his best works are the simple, dignified studies of Negroes—his favorite among his own works is his first study in marble, a portrait head of his friend, Jimmy Daniels, a Negro singer. It's not Harlem Negro life which interests him, though he has presented it—in *Lindy Hop*, for instance —but the primitive and more simple aspects of his people's culture.

Barthé doesn't feel that he can show these aspects by artificial stylization—he prefers to simplify "naturally," keeping the spiritual and rhythmic qualities of his figures.

BARTHE, RICHMOND—*Continued*

His knowledge of anatomy is, as it has to be, strong. He learned it at the Art Institute of Chicago when he was studying drawing and he learned it as a student of dancing under Mary Radin of Martha Graham's group. Consequently he isn't so much at the mercy of models as most sculptors. "Indeed, models are at his mercy, for they are often obliged to do things which he is able to do and wants them to do."

In keeping with his desire to achieve simplicity, Barthé isn't much interested in materials for variety's sake. Although he has produced terra cottas and has one popular success in marble, most of his work has been meant for casting. Usually he models his figures in plasteline, a putty-like substance. He makes his own armature or skeleton out of lead wire and plumber's pipe and builds on this framework with plasteline bit by bit until the figure is finished. He then covers the finished plasteline model with green soap to form a protective covering, and finally casts it in plaster. From the plaster model, workmen in a foundry cast the final figure in bronze.

Barthé is known as a sculptor not only of figures but of portraits "which are much more than the traditional 'heads' which glut the galleries." Best known of his heads, perhaps, are those of Jimmy Daniels, of Maurice Evans (see sketch this issue) as Richard II and of John Gielgud as Hamlet.

Barthé is "a handsome representative of his race," a staunch Roman Catholic with none of the old plantation attitude about him but still with a feeling for the homely features of religion. He is anxious now to emphasize in sculpture the personal charm of Christ and His popularity during his human life. "Jesus was always being asked out to dinner," Barthé says. "People were crazy about Him."

References
Art Digest 13:20 Mr 1 '39 il
Art N 37:9 Mr 18 '39
Mag Art 32:232 Ap '39 il
N Y Herald Tribune p8 Ap 8 '40
Newsweek 14:38-9 Jl 24 '39 il por
Parnassus 12:10-17 Mr '40 il self por
America's Young Men
Brawley, B. G. New Temper in Painting and Sculpture *In* Negro Genius p317-30 1937
Who's Who in American Art

BARTOK, BELA (bär-tŭk′ bā′lȧ) Mar 25, 1881- Hungarian pianist; composer

Address: c/o Boosey & Hawkes Artists Bureau, Inc, 43 W 23rd St, New York City

Béla Bartók, Hungary's most outstanding modern composer is, according to critic Lawrence Gilman, "a tone-poet who is both an uncompromising modernist and the reviver of the ancient past . . . and is the most eminent of living Hungarian com-

BELA BARTOK

posers." He made his second appearance in the United States early in 1940 at the invitation of Mrs. Elizabeth Sprague Coolidge—to take part in the Coolidge Festival of Music. During that season Bartók performed with violinist Joseph Szigeti (see sketch this issue) in the Library of Congress, where they played his *Rhapsody* for violin and piano, and participated in a concert given in his honor by the League of Composers at the Museum of Modern Art in New York City. Besides his many solo appearances, Bartók also made several recordings of his works, and supervised the performance and publication of his latest composition, *Mikrokosmos,* 153 progressive piano pieces, a gigantic work that represents more than 10 years of labor.

In May 1940 Bartók returned to Budapest to organize Hungarian folk songs and returned to the United States in October to fulfill engagements as concert pianist and lecturer. His tour started on November 3 when he played his *Sonata* for two pianos and percussion at the concert of the New Friends of Music in New York, with his wife, Ditta Pasztory-Bartók, playing the second piano. From New York he started on his tour of the country to appear as soloist with orchestras in Cleveland, Pittsburgh, Montreal and in recitals and lectures at a score of universities, colleges and clubs.

Béla Bartók was born in Nagyszentmiklós, in the heart of "Alföld," the Hungarian Plain, on March 25, 1881. His father, the director of an agricultural school and an excellent pianist and cellist, died when Béla was only eight years old. His mother was forced to teach for a living and traveled all over Hungary with her family, teaching in small villages. Béla acquired through these travels a broad acquaintance with his native land that later proved of great value in his composing.

Music came naturally to Béla. By the time he was 10 he had already made a public appearance as pianist, and had composed several small piano pieces. In 1893, when his mother procured a post in Pressburg, Béla began his first systematic musical education—which, at that time, was almost exclusively German. He also wrote many compositions tinged with the influence of Brahms, none of which has been published. He studied piano under László Erkel and composition with Ernst Dohnányi. His spare time was spent in the many opera houses and concert halls of Pressburg, where he intensely absorbed all the different kinds of music. His final studies were taken at the Royal Hungarian Musical Academy at Budapest. While at the Academy he composed his first large works—a rhapsody for piano and orchestra and an orchestral suite—both extremely Hungarian in spirit.

Upon graduation from the Royal Academy in 1905, at the age of 24, Bartók collaborated with Zolton Kodály on a study of native folk music. This resulted in the discovery of an entire library of unknown Hungarian folk songs—some 13,000 of them, which in 1940 Bartók is organizing for publication. The Hungarian gypsy music of the type played by Emery Deutsch is termed by Bartók "semi-popular music." "This music," he says, "is non-peasant in origin. It is the music of an educated class. . There are hundreds of these melodies. Liszt used some of them, and Brahms, too. But they are not of folk origin, in spite of general belief. You might say they have the same function in Hungarian music as jazz and swing in the United States."

In 1907 Bartók was appointed professor of piano at the Royal Hungarian Musical Academy at Budapest, where he remained for five years. In 1913 he visited Biskra to investigate native Arabian folk music.

In the meanwhile he worked intensively on his own original music—which had a long and fierce struggle for recognition. At this time he turned toward Western European composers, particularly Debussy. This influence is in his newer compositions where, making no use of the musical literature of nineteenth century Hungary, he forms his own musical language based on the elements and spirit of Eastern European "primitive" folk music.

With the 1917 production of the ballet, *The Woodcut Prince,* at Budapest, Bartók finally received the recognition he deserved; "his unique vocabulary was beginning to become more and more decipherable." On March 1918 his *Second String Quartet* was performed for the first time. From that date onward he was recognized as the leading figure in Hungarian music.

The style of all of Bartók's compositions is greatly influenced by his enthusiasm for and prolific study of the folk music of Hungary. But there are certain distinct phases in his development of it. The first, comprising the *Funeral March,* the two *Rhapsodies* (for piano and orchestra and for solo piano) and the two orchestral *Suites,* is throughout dominated by a specifically national mode of thought, which is merely the outcome of the exploitation of certain melodic or rhythmic peculiarities of Hungarian folk music. "They belong to that movement which took rise towards the end of the last century and sought to base itself upon national sentiment and racial idioms."

As Bartók gained in individuality, the national element in his works decreased. Then followed an extraordinarily fertile period in which several piano pieces were composed, subjective investigations of the purely spiritual values of sound. "Looked at broadly," says Cecil Gray, "his whole artistic development is a progress from nationalism to complete individuality—or universality, if one prefers it."

In all his music—whether it is rich and elaborate or austere and restrained—Bartók shows a "definite logic and tonality in his harmony." "Every note of his music means something; it is there for a purpose and for a musical purpose." And whatever the method he uses, whatever the effect he works for, he is a "master of expression. His originality is the outcome of inclusiveness, not exclusiveness; Bartók is a fine stylist precisely because he has no style."

Bartók's fiftieth birthday was virtually uncelebrated in his native land, for Bartók had antagonized Hungary early in his career, when he simply and soberly declared Eastern Central Europe to be bound together by an inextricably intertwined folk lore. He said this when a lofty nationalistic purism was strongly prevalent throughout Hungary— definitely at the wrong time. Through Western Europe and the United States, however, his birthday was known and celebrated, for today Béla Bartók is one of the most popular of all contemporary European artists.

Bartók is enormously shy. He does not relish conversation even with his best friends; and he speaks with a soft and hardly audible voice. His preferences in modern music are few and far between—he reserves his greatest admiration for Stravinsky (see sketch this issue).

On November 25, 1940 Columbia University conferred án honorary degree on Béla Bartók. In awarding the degree Dr. Butler (see sketch this issue) called him: "A distinguished teacher and master performer of the piano; internationally recognized authority on the folk music of Hungary, Slovakia, Romania and Arabia; creator through his composition of a musical style universally acknowledged to be one of the great contributions to the twentieth century literature of music; a truly outstanding artist who has brought high distinction to the spiritual life of his country."

BARTOK, BELA—*Continued*

Bartók is a very hard worker—work, as a matter of fact, is his greatest diversion—and though he composes little, each of his compositions requires a colossal amount of revision and rewriting before he will permit it to be published. He spends much time, too, instrumenting various classical works by Bach, Mozart and Beethoven and writing books and numerous articles for musical journals dealing with the instruments, dialect and folk lore of his own land.

References

Musical Q 219:267-87 por; 19:260-6 Jl '33
N Y World-Telegram p8 My 25 '40
Newsweek 16:75-6 N 11 '40 il por
Time 33:37 Ja 23 '39 il; 35:54 Ap 29 '40 por
Blom, E. Béla Bartók as Quartet Writer *In* Stepchildren of Music p239-46 1926
Ewen, D. ed. Béla Bartók *In* Twentieth Century Composers 1937
Ewen, D. ed. Composers of Today 1936
Gray, C. Béla Bartók *In* Survey of Contemporary Music p194-209 1924
Haraszti, E. Béla Bartók, His Life and Works 1938
Rosenfeld, P. Bartók *In* Discoveries of a Music Critic p197-204 1936
Szentkirályi, J. ed. Béla Bartók pam 1940
Thompson, O. ed. International Cyclopedia of Music and Musicians 1939
Who's Who
Wier, A. E. ed. Macmillan Encyclopedia of Music and Musicians 1938

Donald H. Ross

WILLIAM C. BARTOL

BARTOL, WILLIAM CYRUS Nov 24, 1847—Oct 31, 1940 Emeritus professor of mathematics and astronomy at Bucknell University, known to thousands of alumni as Bucknell's "Grand Old Man"; professor at Bucknell in 1881, later was made head of departments of mathematics and astronomy and continued in that position until retirement in 1927; after retirement engaged in historical research for Bucknell's centennial in 1946, as university historian; author of college textbooks

References

Who's Who in America 1936-37
Who's Who in American Education

Obituaries

N Y Herald Tribune p18 N 1 '40 por
N Y Times p25 N 1 '40

BARTON, GEORGE Jan 22, 1866—Mar 16, 1940 Journalist; historian; writer of mystery novels

References

American Catholic Who's Who
Who's Who in America

Obituaries

N Y Times Mr 17 '40

BATES, ERNEST SUTHERLAND Oct 14, 1879—Dec 4, 1939 Author; editor; critic

On December 4, 1939, a few minutes after completing his new book, *American Faith,* a treatise on American religious beliefs, Dr. Bates died of a heart attack at his home, Edgehill Inn, Spuyten Duyvil, New York.

Born at Gambier, Ohio, son of Cyrus Stearns and Laverna (Sutherland) Bates, he was a graduate of the University School of Cleveland; received his B. A. and M. A. degrees from the University of Michigan (1902 and 1903); and in 1908 a Ph. D. from Columbia. His original intent was to enter the ministry but after studying philosophy he gave up the idea, although he continued a lifelong interest in the Bible. Probably his most important book, a best seller both here and in England, was *The Bible Designed To Be Read as Living Literature* (1936), which he edited, and in which he omitted lineages and repetitions and made radical changes from the arrangement of the King James version. His immense vitality, scholarship, range of interest and concentration can be shown by his literary output for the same year, 1936, in which he published *The Story of the Supreme Court; The Story of Congress* and *Hearst, Lord of San Simeon* (in collaboration with Oliver Carlson).

He was a tutor of English at Columbia University in 1907 and 1908 and for the next 17 years taught English at the University of Arizona and English and philosophy at the University of Oregon. Except for his Columbia doctor's thesis in 1908, Bates had never published a book and had con-

ERNEST SUTHERLAND BATES

Pub W 136:2259 D 23 '39
Sat R Lit 21:8 D 16 '39
Sch & Soc 50:756 D 9 '39
Time 34:59 D 18 '39
Wilson Lib Bul 14:358 Ja '40

BATES, GRANVILLE 1882—July 9, 1940
Noted stage and screen actor; spent 40 years
in profession; appeared on stage in *Rain;
Once in a Lifetime; Gentlemen of the Press;*
for films in *My Favorite Wife; Midnight;
Pursuit* and *Private Affairs;* mostly portrayed
business men and judges

Obituaries

N Y Herald Tribune p18 Jl 10 '40 por
N Y Sun p21 Jl 10 '40
Newsweek 16:6 Jl 22 '40

BATISTA Y ZALDIVAR, FULGENCIO
(bä-tēs'tä ē zäl-dē'vär fool-hĕn'sē-ō) 1901-
President of Cuba

Address: War Office, Havana, Cuba

Colonel Fulgencio Batista is "a swarthy,
chunky, middleweight edition of Jack Dempsey, with a velvet smile and an iron fist."
Time has called him "the most likeable of
Caribbean dictators." For seven years he
has been the real ruler of Cuba, while
Batista-made Presidents came and went. In
October 1940 the Colonel took a leave of absence from the army which he heads to fill
the Presidential office himself and announced
to the press: "the revolutionary cycle has
ended. I wish to be good and to be loved
by my people. I have no triumph. It is an
ideal that has triumphed—the ideal of the
revolution."

His career has been as fantastic as that
of most dictators. The son of a poor truck
gardener, he was born in the backwoods of
Oriente, a province at the extreme east of
Cuba. His grandfather was Chinese; he
himself is a racial blend of white, Negro,
Indian and Oriental. At nine he was in
school in an American missionary establishment in Oriente; at thirteen he was an
orphan slaving in the cane fields. He worked
as tailor's apprentice, grocery clerk, bar-
tender, railroad fireman, engineer, conductor; he studied to become a barber; during
the 1920 sugar boom he found himself administrator of an Oriente cane plantation.
Finally, at the age of 20, a civil service examination brought him into the army as a
stenographer.

That he was the best stenographer in the
Cuban Army there seems little doubt.
"Ingratiating, ever-smiling," he "had been
particularly well-known to the officers for his
energy, his accuracy, his dependability.
'Leave it to Batista!' had been a byword."
But even the best stenographer in the Cuban
Army couldn't have risen above the rank
of sergeant without the events of September
4, 1933.

A "clique of *politicos* and army chiefs"
(with more than a little indirect help from
Sumner Welles, then Ambassador to Cuba)

tributed chiefly to scholarly journals. Nevertheless, in 1925, he courageously resigned
his post at the University of Oregon in
protest against curtailment of academic
freedom, and came to New York to make
his living by his pen. From 1926 through
1929 he was literary editor of *The Dictionary
of American Biography* and from 1933 to
1936 he was an associate editor of *The Modern Monthly.* As a book reviewer for the
New York *Herald Tribune* since 1929 he had
become favorably known for his wide knowledge and sound judgment of social topics.

The man who wrote *Biography of the
Bible* and edited *The Four Gospels* would
not ordinarily be thought of as an authority
on the theories of Karl Marx, but Dr. Bates'
capacities easily encompassed both fields.
Much of his writings was based on the
research in which he was engaged for many
years and which he did not complete—
a gigantic, detailed history of the whole of
American culture.

Dr. Bates was married first, to Miss Florence Fisher of Bay City, Michigan, in 1902;
and after her death, to Miss Rosalind Boido
of Tucson, Arizona. After a divorce he
married Miss Gladys Graham at Astoria,
Oregon, in 1920. By his second marriage
he had a son, who now lives in Los Angeles.

In addition to the works listed above, he
was the author of *This Land of Liberty*
(1930); *Mary Baker Eddy—The Truth and
the Traditions* with J. V. Dittemore (1932);
and *American Hurly-Burly* with Alan Williams (1937).

References

Cur Hist 51:4 Ap '40
Who's Who in America 1938-39

Obituaries

N Y Times p27 D 5 '39 por
Newsweek 14:47 D 18 '39

Underwood & Underwood

FULGENCIO BATISTA

had finally succeeded in ousting the "butcher-dictator" Machado. Backed by Welles (see sketch this issue), Dr. Carlos Manuel de Cespedes was then made provisional President. Cuba, rejoicing at the overthrow of the hated dictator, nevertheless accepted Cespedes unenthusiastically. Anarchy and terrorism prevailed.

On September 4, 1933, twenty-four days after Cespedes had taken office, a group of six sergeants headed by Batista walked into officers' quarters and painlessly took over, while students and fellow conspirators, joined by military and police units, seized barracks, forts, ships about Havana. Incredibly, by the end of the day Batista was master—and without bloodshed. A military junta of five, selected to take over the government, chose as provisional President Dr. Grau San Martin, a liberal and a doctor, while Batista assumed the rank of colonel and chief of staff of the army and began to whip it into shape.

Ten days later President Grau established a virtual dictatorship until there could be a meeting of the Constituent Assembly. He announced a policy that sounded rather like "Cuba for the Cubans" to anxious United States citizens who owned four-fifths of the Cuban national wealth. Batista had to suppress revolts both from the Right and from the extreme Left. Dr. Grau began to concentrate on pro-labor, anti-banking decrees, soon acquired a "pink" label. The United States continued to refuse recognition to the new government, desperately in need of its credit. Things went on like this for months until Batista, convinced that the United States would withhold recognition until a President whose policies were agreeable to Washington was chosen, secured Dr. Grau's resignation on January 14, 1934. Not long afterward conservative President Mendieta

took office and the Cuban government was recognized.

In the meanwhile Batista was consolidating his own position, having settled down with his wife and children in the middle of the Columbia barracks on the edge of Havana. He "put shoes on the barefooted, amateur army of 9,000," set about increasing its man power to the largest in Cuba's history, drilling it into fitness and making himself popular with his men. Modern barracks were built for them; civilians did the potato-peeling; the sergeants became lieutenant colonels and took over pieces of the country for themselves.

Ruling military cliques seldom make themselves popular with the people, however. The Mendieta government went from arbitrary decree to more arbitrary decree. Unions were dissolved; strikes and threatened insurrections were brutally put down; the Cuban third degree was a commonplace; the press was censored; Batista made his own appointments to the universities; army officers, it is claimed, went in for embezzling and smuggling on a grand scale. And zigzag policies brought sugar prices down in a country where "sugar is the real dictator," resulting in widespread unemployment and near-bankruptcy for the government.

After two years of Mendieta, Sumner Welles persuaded Batista to hold a constitutional election for his successor. President Gomez was legally elected and duly installed in 1936, but the rule of machine gun and rifle abated very little. Seven months after Gomez took office he was impeached for "interfering" with Congress: Batista had wanted Congress to levy a nine-cent tax on each sack of sugar produced in Cuba to finance a program for the rural schools; the President had fought the measure. He was replaced by his Secretary of State Bru, a Batista man, who remained President of Cuba until 1940.

The Batista régime was not totally black, of course. As soon as he could Cuba's "man on horseback" went ahead with a program of building schools in remote rural districts, installing army sergeants as teachers, and thousands of children and adults began to learn to "read, write, delouse themselves, ply trades." Hospitals, particularly tuberculosis sanitoriums, and orphan asylums were built in great numbers. There were attempts—though by no means entirely successful—at cooperative agricultural projects, social security for workers and farmers, government control of the sugar industry. Nevertheless the anti-Batista forces were strengthening themselves, and in 1938 seventy per cent of the electorate stayed at home on voting day to boycott him. A change seemed imminent. Something had to be done.

Promptly Batista did another about-face. He ordered the Cuban *Falange* (an offshoot of Spanish Fascism) to dissolve itself. He legalized the Cuban Communist Party. He emerged a great "progressive" and "democrat," disavowing the more shady of his accomplices, apparently trying at the same time to gain the support of the Left and of certain parties of the Right. He made visits to President Roosevelt (in Washington, it is said, he was society's darling) and Mexico's Cárdenas, and was greeted with flattering demonstrations on his return. He preached against totalitarianism.

Finally, in December 1939, he quit his job, called for the election of a Constituent Assembly to draft a new Constitution, announced that he would become a candidate in the Presidential elections of February 1940 under the new rules. In voting for the delegates the Batista faction was left behind; it was opposition candidate Dr. Grau San Martin who headed the assembly, and while the Constitution was being drafted the elections were postponed three times. Nevertheless seven political parties threw their support to Batista, and on July 14, 1940 he was elected President of Cuba against his one rival. Even Dr. Grau had at one time withdrawn his candidacy and remained in the race only at Batista's request. Oddly enough, the Communist Party and the Socialist-Democratic coalition were among the groups which supported the once violently anti-Leftist Batista, while Dr. Grau had the support of the Cuban ABC, a group which nearly overthrew his liberal régime in 1933.

At the 1940 Havana conference Batista made a startling suggestion in regard to the disputed European possessions in the Western Hemisphere. "Why not give them independence?" he asked.

Batista and his wife, the former Elisa Govinez, have two children: a daughter, Mirta, and a son, Ruben Fulgencio (nicknamed "Papito"). Cuba's strong man is "a bantam in size, with a body of steel and a jaw of bronze, his crowning glory a glistening comb of coarse black hair, which he tosses about in eloquent gestures." He combines a sense of the dramatic with a sense of humor, talking very fast with a flowery vocabulary. By training he is more sportsman than economist or sociologist, but he is said to admire the American New Deal even more than American baseball. He is passionately fond of cockfighting, has a stable of his own.

Of him Carleton Beals once said: "One would have to travel to the East to find a similar combination of oily courtesy, intellectual keenness, insight into men, devious astuteness, ruthless purposefulness and extreme cruelty."

References

Collier's 99:12+ Je 19 '37 il por
Cur Hist 50:51 Ap '39; 51:15 Mr '40
Lit Digest 124:11 D 25 '37 por
Nation 141:152-4 Ag 7 '35; 147:658-60 D 17 '38
N Y Times p8 O 9 '40; p5 O 10 '40; p6 O 11 '40; IV p2 O 13 '40

Newsweek 8:10 D 26 '36 por; 12:13 Jl 4 '38 por; 12:15-16 N 21 '38 por
Sat Eve Post 211:8-9+ My 20 '39 il pors
Time 29:21-3 Ap 26 '37 por (cover); 32:17 N 14 '38 por; 34:30+ D 4 '39 por; 35:36 My 6 '40; 36:40 O 21 '40 por
International Who's Who
Strode, H. Pageant of Cuba 1934

BAUR, BERTHA Died Sept 18, 1940 President emeritus of the Cincinnati Conservatory of Music; served as president from 1912 to 1930; became director at death of her aunt, Miss Clara Baur, who founded the conservatory in 1867; institution is now part of the University of Cincinnati and has an average enrollment of 2,000 students a year

References

Etude 47:271 Ap '29 por

Pierre Key's Musical Who's Who
Thompson, O. ed. International Cyclopedia of Music and Musicians 1939
Who's Who in America 1928-29

Obituaries

N Y Times p23 S 19 '40

BEAVERBROOK, WILLIAM MAXWELL AITKEN, 1ST BARON May 25, 1879- British Minister of Aircraft Production; newspaper publisher
Address: h. Cherkley, Leatherhead, Surrey, England

When in May 1940 a reorganization of the British government gave Lord Beaverbrook, newspaper king of Shoe Lane and personal friend of Prime Minister Churchill (see sketch this issue), the office of Minister of Aircraft Production, he was surprised by his own popularity. Few commentators stated anything more unfriendly than the hope that "the Puckish-looking little peer and publisher will make the figures of bomber production rise as successfully as he has the circulation of the *Express*." Since few newspapers have come in for so much concentrated criticism as Lord Beaverbrook's three—the London *Daily Express* (largest in the world, published in three cities, circulation 2,500,000), the London *Sunday Express* and the *Evening Standard* (run largely by his subordinates)—this reception must have been something of a shock for the "146-pound Hearst of Britain."

It didn't upset him too much, though. With characteristic energy and genius for manipulation Lord Beaverbrook went to work. After a lightning survey of the status of aircraft production, his orders sent factory heads from all over the kingdom scrambling for interviews with him. He ordered Lord Nuffield ("the British Ford") to submit to a merger of his new aircraft works with the old-guard firm of Vickers-

Margaret Bourke-White

LORD BEAVERBROOK

Armstrong, Limited, purring: "The thanks
of the nation are due to Lord Nuffield."
He conferred with United States Ambassador Joseph Kennedy (see sketch this issue)
on speeding up shipments from the United
States, "and almost certainly Ambassador Kennedy and Minister Lord Beaverbrook clicked
with each other and with President Roosevelt."
Even though this tremendous job he has on his
hands is a completely new one, it seems unlikely that "the Beaver" has ever found anything too much for him.

In October 1940 Lord Beaverbrook was
officially made a member of the War Cabinet,
keeping his present position in charge of
aircraft production. By that time he had
actually doubled production, though by methods that "even his mildest critics" label
"slightly cracked."

His talents as a businessman can hardly
be overestimated. Born (quite without a
title) in Maple, Ontario, May 25, 1879, Max
Aitken was the son of a poor Presbyterian
minister, William Aitken, and Jean (Noble)
Aitken. He was selling newspapers when
he was six—perhaps a kind of prophecy
of his career. There wasn't much formal
schooling for him, but he didn't have to go
to school to decide that he wanted to be a
millionaire. It didn't take long, either.
After washing drugstore medicine bottles,
selling sewing machines, bonds, the young
man found his backer in an elderly Halifax
financier and became a promoter. He engineered mergers of banks, utilities, steel and
cement companies. His last merger of 13
cement companies into the Canada Cement
Company, Limited was "almost a dominion
scandal," but in 1907 he liquidated his holdings for $5,000,000 and went to London with
his bride of the year before, Gladys, daughter of Major General Charles Drury.

Here Max Aitken enlarged his ambitions.
According to his own statement, "if the chief
function of the American is to make money,
the chief function of the European is to
enter politics." To politics there are front
doors and back doors. Aitken tried both.
He sold Bonar Law some life insurance,
became his private secretary, eventually his
closest friend. He himself was elected to
Parliament in 1910 on the strength of
speeches for a high tariff, kept his seat for
six years on the same platform, but didn't
create enough of a stir there. Back doors
best suited his talents; he was a promotor;
he would be a power behind the throne. He
stood behind and "promoted" Bonar Law,
behind the scenes "shifted cabinet ministers
like puppets," made an alliance between
Lloyd George and Bonar Law, "merged"
the Lloyd George "Win the War" Cabinet
in 1917 and finally won a peerage for his
services. (He selected Beaverbrook, a
small town not far from his Canadian birthplace, as a name more distinguished than
"Maple.") In 1918 Lord Beaverbrook was
Minister of Information and Chancellor of
the Duchy of Lancaster.

Already he was in the newspaper business.
In spite of warnings, in 1917 he had bought
the "sick-dog" *Express* mainly to support
Bonar Law. The first year he lost $1,000,000,
the second year $300,000, the third year he
broke even; after that the paper began to
prosper. His first real challenge was from
Lord Northcliffe of the *Mail*, who began a
free insurance war with him; at one time
both were offering accident insurance policies
of 10,000 pounds to their subscribers. Then
there was the famous premium war of the
London newspapers, when bewildered readers found themselves offered everything from
free can openers to free radios. But in spite
of competition, "by giving London a cock-
neyed version of low-brow United States
journalism," Lord Beaverbrook found he
could do phenomenal things with his paper's
circulation. He even came to the United
States to study Hearst's methods, and he was
a good pupil.

The original purpose of the newspaper was
gone. In 1923 Bonar Law died of cancer of
the throat. He had resigned as Prime
Minister the year before, and his last words
for Max had been: "You're a curious fellow."
But Beaverbrook's paper could still be used
as a "crusading" organ, could make and
break other political figures. His political
views as a whole corresponded so closely
with those of press-tycoon No. 1, Lord
Rothermere, that a new word came into the
British vocabulary: "Beavermere." "Empire
Free Trade" was the cornerstone of Beavermere policy. This meant forming all the
peoples of the British Empire into a sort
of great customs union which would "devote
itself to repulsing foreign competition and
which would buy only the products of the
commonwealth that would thus be attained."
E. F. T. also implied isolationism: absolute
hostility to the League of Nations and all

the organizations which support it; no boundary guarantees, loans or alliances with any other country; no greater local autonomy for India and other colonial possessions. The Beavermere frontier was not the Rhine, but South Africa.

Although the papers of Lord Beaverbrook and Lord Rothermere professed to be Conservative, "in the past decade they have been politically consistent only in their inconsistency." In February 1930 after battling for a long time against Baldwin's free-trade candidates, Lord Beaverbrook and Lord Rothermere formed a United Empire Party whose program soon attained such popular support that the Conservatives were forced to adopt a milder version of Empire Free Trade, including nearly all its program but food taxes. Beaverbrook and Rothermere next offered to cease fighting Baldwin if they could have a controlling hand in choosing his next ministry, but the offer was rejected indignantly and the long feud between the newspaper barons and Baldwin was resumed. A writer much later summed up the feud by saying: "Did Beaverbrook get anything from it? Yes. He got an attack of asthma. He has it still. He is no longer a political force. He is a medical problem."

Besides using tactics designed to harass Baldwin and to mold the policies of the government, Beaverbrook and Rothermere sometimes threw their weight behind political parties other than the Conservative. Perhaps it was not as politically inconsistent as it seemed when the Express announced its support of new Prime Minister MacDonald, with only the warning: "If Mr. MacDonald and his colleagues attempt to force nationalization upon the industries and utilities of the country then the Daily Express will oppose them by every means in its power." But when in his crusade for Empire Free Trade Lord Rothermere waxed publicly enthusiastic about Sir Oswald Mosley (see sketch this issue) and his Blackshirts, Lord Beaverbrook refused to follow. His motto was: "Empire ever, Nazi-ism never." In matters of foreign policy, however, his newspapers were consistent propagandists of the belief that the British Empire had no quarrel with Fascism and that no crisis could lead to war. He criticized the Locarno agreement, besought England to keep out of the League, pleaded that Ethiopia be left to Mussolini's tender mercies, apologized for Franco in Spain. In 1938, during the Czechoslovakian crisis, the Daily Express staff drilled for a dash to the gasproof cellar beneath the "Black Glass House" in London, but Express headlines asserted confidently: THE DAILY EXPRESS DECLARES THAT BRITAIN WILL NOT BE INVOLVED IN A EUROPEAN WAR THIS YEAR, OR NEXT YEAR EITHER, while circulation reached an all-time peak. Both Rothermere and Beaverbrook gave their official approval to Munich, agreeing that the partition of Czechoslovakia might be the best means of preserving peace, and Chamberlain was praised by the Express as a "champ."

Only one dream involving alliance with a foreign power did Lord Beaverbrook ever permit himself, and that was the dream of an Anglo-American union which would rule the world. In 1936 he was the leading advocate of a military and naval alliance in the Pacific between the United States and Great Britain, perhaps forgetting that in 1932 he had been the most violent advocate of repudiating Britain's war debts to the United States.

Exactly how great an influence the newspaper magnate's opinions, as expressed in his papers and his books: Politicians and the War (1928); My Case for Empire (1930); Resources of the British Empire (1934), have had on recent British diplomacy it is impossible to say. But certainly his editorial policies have come in for a fair share of ridicule even from his own employees. One of them, Evelyn Waugh, in a novel, created the character of Lord Monomark of the Daily Excess, "a ludicrous egocentric who eats little but raw onions and oatmeal, is surrounded by slavish sycophants who toady to his ignorant misconceptions, abuses his distracted underlings and usually triumphs by some absurdly fortuitous accident." Another, the famous cartoonist, David Low, (see sketch this issue) for a long time has drawn cartoons for Beaverbrook's own Evening Standard which reduce his employer's pronouncements to absurdity. Colonel Blimp, "red-faced, walrus-mustached, paunchy Tory," is pictured as Lord Beaverbrook's typical subscriber, and has continually been caught in the middle of such statements as: "Gad, sir! Lord Beaverbrook is right! We must give up the League of Nations until it promises to have nothing to do with foreigners," or "Gad, sir! Lord Beaverbrook is right! The Tory Party must save the Empire if it has to strangle it in the attempt." Perhaps Lord Beaverbrook's most beguiling characteristic is his astonishing tolerance of such criticism. The impish publisher only chuckled when a poll of the Express staff on the question—"Do you approve of Express policies?"—returned an almost unanimous NO.

Even those who don't much like Lord Beaverbrook's ideas seem to be susceptible to his charm. John Gunther called him "one of the most provocative, original and lively public men in England." He knows all sorts of people—gamblers, taxicab drivers, aviators, steel workers, machinists. He knows people because he has a boundless curiosity and all his life has been asking questions and actually listening to the answers. Quite frankly a vulgarian, he's fond of slapping his trouser pockets and saying: "I have all the money any man can want!" while "conservative Britons shudder." Yet among those who find his company stimulating are such public figures as

BEAVERBROOK, WILLIAM—*Continued*
Air Secretary Sir Archibald Sinclair (see sketch this issue), United States Ambassador Joseph Kennedy, Prime Minister Winston Churchill and such intellectuals as Rebecca West and Noel Coward. In his home, palatial Stornoway House in London, a typical day for the restless little publisher used to be: up before 8 a. m.; listen to a typed summary of news; conferences; calls; bouts with two dictaphones; an hour's ride or walk; tea; a nap; dinner (with three or four uninvited guests who, if the conversation should grow dull, are likely to hear "Oh, God, I'm bored!"); later in the evening, a Bible reading. All this time Beaverbrook would be in almost continuous touch with his editors by telephone. "A bumptious, result-getting, self-made man," he owns a racing stable and the latest model in airships. Lady Beaverbrook, the former Gladys Drury of Halifax, Canada, died in 1927, leaving him a daughter, Jan (Mrs. Drago Montagu), and two sons: Max Jr., and Peter. Lord Beaverbrook has resigned from any active direction of the newspapers. His son, the Honorable Max Aitken, is now nominally the head ("though no doubt pa has his say"), and in 1940 was also a squadron leader in the British R. A. F.

References
> Am Mercury 38:433-7 Ag '36 (Same. Cong Digest 17:203-5 Ag '38; Same abr. Ref Shelf 12 no. 1:246-51 '38)
> Collier's 102:16+ Jl 2 '38 por
> Fortnightly 132:761-7 D '29
> Life 9:70-81 Ag 5 '40 il pors
> Liv Age 339:58-60 S '30; 342:85 Mr '32
> New Statesman & Nation 1:416 My 16 '31
> Read Digest 37:65-8 N '40
> Time 28:21-2 Jl 27 '36 il; 32:44-50 N 28 '38 por (cover); 35:36+ My 27 '40 por; 36:28+ S 16 '40 por (cover)
> Gardiner, A. G. Lord Beaverbrook *In* Portraits and Portents p47-56 1926
> Mackenzie, F. A. Beaverbrook 1933
> Middleton, E. C. Beaverbrook: the Statesman and the Man 1934
> Thompson, E. R. Lord Beaverbrook *In* Uncensored Celebrities p184-90 1919
> Who's Who
> Who's Who in Commerce and Industry

BEDFORD, HERBRAND ARTHUR RUSSELL, 11TH DUKE OF Feb 19, 1858 —Aug 27, 1940 One of the four wealthiest dukes in Great Britain; owner of many real estate districts in London; fortunes of family held by them since time of Henry VIII's rule; natural history expert; famed for large zoological collection; wife noted airwoman who took up flying at age of 62, set several long distance records and disappeared at sea while solo flying at 71; Duke was interested in science; gave large part of fortune to social causes

References
> Who's Who
Obituaries
> N Y Times p19 Ag 28 '40

BEEBE, LUCIUS Dec 9, 1902- Columnist; photographer of railway engines
Address: b. c/o New York Herald Tribune, 230 W 41st St, New York City; h. Wakefield, Massachusetts

Orchidaceous oracle of café society, Lucius Morris Beebe has been polishing up the glass of fashion and the mold of form in his famed column, *This New York,* since 1933. His elegantly archaic prose, with Boston inflections, informs over one and a half million readers of that glittering rivalry among the 500 "Chosen" to be seen at the right table at the right place. Many of his devotees may be amazed to learn that "Luscious Lucius" (Walter Winchell's term) is an authority on railroading. But his particular interest in steam engines is not the anomaly it might seem, since he regards them as symbols of the romantic, vanishing past. He has become a noted photographer of locomotives. His first book of annotated photos of the rail monsters in action, *High Iron,* appeared in 1938; his second, *Highliners,* was published in April 1940.

The 103 photos in *Highliners,* most of them of powerful old-timers, show why railway enthusiasts regard the streamlined electric locomotive with disdain. Beebe's own affections lie "close to the less pretentious roads of the Middle and Southwest and their often far from up-to-the-minute equipment." Some of the photos (not all are by Beebe) are excellent for their drama, others for their beauty of mechanical composition. In a foreword, Beebe says of his work: "Railroad photography in its most satisfactory form is conditioned by a technique that is neither known nor understood by photographers honored and successful in other specialized fields of endeavor. There are conventions governing train photography as rigid as the unities of the French classic drama and as exacting as the uses of diplomatic protocol." He writes of the difficulties of indicating motion, since modern speed cameras stop all action so completely it is difficult to tell whether the train is static or rolling at high speed.

Lucius Beebe is the descendant of a long line of Tory men of property. Junius Beebe, son of a wealthy dealer in leather, married Eleanor Merrick, whose father was a Harvard professor and close friend of Eastern *literati.* Lucius, their fourth child, was born at Wakefield, near Boston, Massachusetts, December 9, 1902. He spent his early years on the Beebe 140-acre farm, and encountered fist-fights at public school. The town blaster became his hero and friend, and Lucius was a leader in the rural sport of blowing up outhouses. This was the beginning of the Beebe legend of practical joking. Expelled from two private schools, he was sent to Roxbury, in Connecticut, and from thence went to Yale, the destiny of his most elect classmates.

Deciding to be a scholar and a dandy, he dressed from the start in cutaway and gold-headed cane. His rooms had Picasso drawings, a roulette wheel and a revolving bookcase-bar. His cultural pursuit resulted in a book of verse, *Falling Stars,* published while he was still a freshman. In his sophomore year an anti-prohibition outburst brought him to grief with the head of Yale's Divinity School, and he was dismissed. A year later he transferred to Harvard, for which President Angell (see sketch this issue) apologized to President Lowell. He attracted attention with new forms of practical joking, but managed to be graduated with the Class of '27, stayed at the Graduate School for a year to study poetry. He published a second volume of poems, a book about Villon, and for his Master's thesis wrote on Edwin Arlington Robinson and the Arthurian legend. He got the idea of printing and distributing as rare items several copies of a deleted passage from Robinson's *Lancelot.* Highly incensed at a bibliophile who informed Robinson of this, Beebe called on the traitor, who, in course of argument, suffered a fractured skull. Harvard, like Yale, washed its hands of the undaunted Lucius. "Nothing matters but the gallant gesture," he said.

After a literary session on the Boston *Transcript* he applied for a job on the New York *Herald Tribune* in 1929. His height, 6 feet 4 inches, and his weight, 180 pounds, so impressed City Editor Stanley Walker that he was hired as a reporter. After attending a fire in a morning coat, covering the wrong banquet and wasting his Boston erudition on petty thieves, he was transferred to the drama department. His portrayal of Hollywood as a den of iniquity caught the eye of the *Tribune's* syndicate manager, who felt that Beebe was just the man to exploit the Babylonic mire of New York society. Beebe's trial column, happily accepted in the hinterlands, was duly established as *This New York.* From the beginning it was a success, particularly among Manhattan's ineligibles. The column of the "sandwich man for the rich," as Kyle Crichton called Beebe, was taken up by many other papers, including one in an Alaskan fishing community.

Beebe has turned down fabulous offers from Hearst and Hollywood agents: money is no object to him, since he has a private income of some $20,000 annually. He is a bachelor and lives in a New York hotel suite. The apartment is decorated with innumerable photographs of Beebe; its closets hold the most publicized male wardrobe outside Hollywood. He owns about 40 suits at a time, has one dress coat lined with mink and collared with astrakan, sports valuable jewelry. But he leads a

N Y Herald Tribune

LUCIUS BEEBE

more circumspect life than his column suggests: gets up at 7:00, reaches the *Tribune* by 8:30, goes, after lunch, to the Turkish baths at the Biltmore and begins his social life at 6:00. This includes a theatre first night and a drop-in at El Morocco, where he picks up most of his column material. During the year he gives lectures to club ladies, spends vacations on the family farm. Though he has produced no more poetry (modern forms baffle him), in 1934 he wrote *Boston and the Boston Legend,* a 100,000 word study of his native city, which sold at $5 and aroused the ire of liberals by his flippant treatment of the Sacco-Vanzetti case.

His politics are strictly Republican, he has no patience with organized labor and is repelled by the American Newspaper Guild, which he calls "shabby, degraded and spurious." Some of his classmates have said he is intolerant and overbearing, but generous to his friends. Beebe claims he has not been respected enough and has been too often treated with derision. Once O. O. MacIntyre, upon meeting him, confused him with the scientist Beebe and asked if he had been catching any interesting fish. He likes to be known as a gourmet and to perpetuate such legends about himself as that of his nostalgic sleigh-race (he the lone racer) to the Central Park Casino. An incurable romantic, he has a genuine Bourbon hostility to change. "He would much rather be a bright leaf on the stream of a dying civilization than a fertile seed dropped in the soil of a new era."

References

Am Mercury 51:309-17 N '40
House & Gard 76:46-7+ O '39
Lit Digest 119:12 F 9 '35 il

BEEBE, LUCIUS—*Continued*

  New Yorker 13:24-9 N 20 '37; 13:25-9
  N 27 '37
  Read Digest 34:29-33 F '39
  Scrib Mag 102:84-8 O '37
  Time 32:39-40 O 31 '38 por

  America's Young Men
  Who's Who in America

BEER, THOMAS Nov 22, 1889—Apr 18,
1940 Author; most famous books *Stephen
Crane* (1923); *The Mauve Decade* (1926) and
Hanna (1929); contributed short stories to
magazines

  References

    Bookm 74:241-6 N '31
    Sat R Lit 10:689 My 12 '34 por
    Author's and Writer's Who's Who
    Baldwin, C. C. Thomas Beer *In* Men
      Who Make Our Novels p42-5 rev.
      ed. 1924
    Boyd, E. A. Thomas Beer *In* Por-
      traits p208-16 1924
    Kunitz, S. J. ed. Living Authors 1937
    Who's Who in America

  Obituaries

    N Y Herald Tribune p16 Ap 19 '40
      por
    N Y Times p21 Ap 19 '40 por
    Newsweek 15:6 Ap 29 '40
    Pub W 137:1664 Ap 27 '40
    Sat R Lit 22:3-4+ My 4 '40 por

THOMAS BEER

BEGG, ALEXANDER SWANSON May
23, 1881—Sept 26, 1940 Dean of the Boston
University School of Medicine since 1923;
formerly taught at Drake University from
1907 to 1913; taught at Harvard Medical
School from 1911 to 1921; during the World

ALEXANDER SWANSON BEGG

War served as a major and colonel while
commanding base hospitals in France

  References

    American Men of Science
    Leaders in Education 1932
    Who's Who in America
    Who's Who in American Medicine

  Obituaries

    N Y Times p23 S 27 '40

BEL GEDDES, NORMAN *See* Geddes,
N. B.

BENCHLEY, BELLE JENNINGS Aug
28, 1882- Director of Zoological Garden of
San Diego

Address: b. Zoological Garden, San Diego,
California; h. 5106 W Point Loma Blvd,
Ocean Beach, California

  San Diego's "Zoo Lady," the only woman
zoo director in the world, has written a
book about her experiences as "housekeeper,
chief dietitian and consulting physician as
well as homemaker" for her family of thousands in the Zoological Garden of San
Diego. *My Life in a Man-Made Jungle*
(1940) talks of animals not as though they
were humans, but as though they were individuals—amazingly complex and temperamental individuals, too. Their personal
likes and dislikes and eccentricities Mrs.
Benchley has learned not only to know but
to understand and respect during some 13
years of association with such friends as
Jiggs, the oranguatan (oranguatans are
"natural engineers"); Bum, "the affectionate
condor"; Empress, the teasing elephant;
Marie, the baby walrus who demanded her
milk by saying "Ma"; and, perhaps most
intimate friends of all, Mbongo and Ngagi,

the largest gorillas in captivity. Mrs. Benchley builds up and tears down a great many reputations—in fact, after learning that Hollywood's old horror-reliable, the gorilla, is not only affectionate and the one animal that will look straight into the human eye but also more fastidious than most people, the reader is ready to question almost everything he thinks he knows about animals.

Mrs. Benchley's book is warmly and simply written, and, besides dozens of fascinating anecdotes, contains a sizable chunk of information that will be completely new to anyone but another zoo director. Her duties aren't simple. A zoo director must work long hours, sometimes weeks without so much as a day off, years without a vacation. She must be prepared to meet "whatever the day brings forth," whether it is being nurse to a baby monkey or shipping "fifty dog or sand fleas" to a flea trainer. Mrs. Benchley tells in her book how she "brought back a sick Galápagos tortoise by feeding it raw alcohol mixed with castor oil, and putting it to bed close to the furnace; how the doctor operated on a stork that had swallowed but not digested a nail; how the beavers went all but crazy with furious damming activity when their pool was drained; and of Babe, the thousand-pound grizzly, who, in tropical San Diego, appeared to hibernate—and produced two fourteen-ounce babies." She tells how the modern zoo is built and arranged, how the specimens are acquired, how the animals are fed and cared for. She tells about curious relationships between animals and their human caretakers and about even more curious relationships between animal and animal —a bantam rooster which became the devoted admirer of a seal, a ring-necked dove which incubated, hatched and adopted a black bantam rooster, a Canadian goose which played Damon to a baby Patagonian seal's Pythias. There are a great number of excellent photographs.

Born near Larned, Kansas on August 28, 1882, the daughter of Fred Merrick and Ida Belle (Orrell) Jennings, Belle spent much of her childhood wandering over the rolling hills and rugged, rocky beaches of California's Point Loma with her younger sisters and brothers. She got acquainted in a friendly way with the rabbits, squirrels and birds that she saw; and she was taught to identify birds and shells and to classify flowers—otherwise, she says, nothing much in her youth showed that she was destined to spend much of her life in a zoo. In 1902 she was graduated from the San Diego Teachers College, and four years later married William L. Benchley.

It was in 1923 that she found herself a middle-aged woman with a son of high school age, Edward, to support. She had been divorced from her husband, and her only experience in earning a living had been as a teacher in Orange County, California. For short periods in 1923 and 1924

BELLE BENCHLEY

she was in charge of the Benchley Packing House in Fullerton, California and worked as cashier at the Hugh Miller Company, and then, in October 1925, a civil service examination brought her an appointment as bookkeeper in the Zoological Garden of San Diego.

It was more than a bookkeeper's job, though. There was a great deal of telephone-information work. People asked questions like: "How long is a hippo's tail?", asked her to prescribe for their sick canaries, inquired about the gestation period of an elephant, wanted her to identify snakes from only a vague description. She went to some trouble to answer their questions, and found she was learning a lot. The president of the Zoological Garden evidently found the same thing, for he first tested her out by getting things "in a hell of a mess" and going East to see what she would do with them, then, in July 1927, appointed her head of the Zoo staff: executive secretary of the Zoological Garden of San Diego.

For others with zoo-keeping ambitions Mrs. Benchley recommends a knowledge of the animal world gained from general study, "an insatiable curiosity," all organized so as to be usable automatically and patience for trying and trying again to solve the unexpected problems which inevitably come up. There must be no lapse in caution— it's foolish not to be afraid at the proper time. And there must be, above all, what can only be described as the "animal instinct," without which even knowledge and curiosity and patience aren't much good. That Mrs. Benchley had all these is very evident from her book.

As Mrs. Benchley became known to the animals as a friend whom they could trust and to the children of San Diego as the "Zoo Lady," she gradually found herself

BENCHLEY, BELLE—*Continued*

also something of a celebrity on the West Coast. Her speaking engagements increased —in 1939 she gave 150 half-hour talks; she spoke over the radio; appeared in news-reels; she contributed articles to *Nature Magazine, Westways, Parks* and *Recreation, Zoonooz* (the publication of the Zoological Society of San Diego); and became reconciled to seeing herself in print "in ungainly smocks such as no stout woman should ever wear and with my hair streaming in what one reporter said was 'no particular style.'"

Mrs. Benchley is still "a most domestic person," however. Famous for her dinners before she achieved more national fame, she is fond of collecting recipes for Christmas cakes and cookies from European countries, rolling pins, fancy cooky cutters in animal shapes. Another hobby of hers involves animals, too. From all over the world people have sent her wild animals in all sorts of materials, although her own collection is confined to early American glass picturing animals or in animal shapes. She used to collect American Indian blankets and baskets as well, but since she had to dispose of many of them when her home was broken up, only "a few real collectors' pieces" are left.

> *References*
>> American Women
>> Benchley, B. My Life in a Man-Made Jungle 1940

BENJAMIN, WILLIAM EVARTS Feb 19, 1859—Feb 24, 1940 Retired financier; noted manuscript collector

> *Obituaries*
>> N Y Herald Tribune p10 F 26 '40
>> Pub W 137:1315 Mr 30 '40

BENNETT, JAMES O'DONNELL May 1, 1870—Feb 27, 1940 Journalist

James O'Donnell Bennett, retired staff member of the Chicago *Tribune,* died of coronary thrombosis at the age of 69.

He was born in Jackson, Michigan, a son of Charles Henry and Mary (O'Donnell) Bennett. His uncle, James O'Donnell, a United States Representative from Michigan and editor of a paper, encouraged him in his desire to become a journalist. While a student at the University of Michigan, he made an outstanding record in drama and literature. After serving as press representative for a group of Shakespearean players he entered newspaper work in Chicago in 1892, and, with the exception of brief periods when he worked with Julia Marlowe, he remained a newspaper writer until his retirement from the *Tribune* on February 1, 1939.

One of his outstanding pieces of work was his report of the Eucharistic Congress in Chicago in 1926. Newspaper people

Chicago Tribune

JAMES O'DONNELL BENNETT

regarded his stories as masterpieces of reporting. Older citizens of Chicago remember him chiefly as a drama critic, although he wrote in every field. He served as reporter, critic, columnist and correspondent in the First World War during his 48-year career. He was the author of *Much Loved Books* (1927); *Private Joe Fifer* (1936); and compiler of *When Good Fellows Get Together* (1908).

> *References*
>> Who's Who in America

> *Obituaries*
>> N Y Herald Tribune p16 F 28 '40; p20 F 29 '40
>> N Y World-Telegram p31 Mr 1 '40
>> Time 35:64 Mr 11 '40
>> Wilson Lib Bul 14:546 Ap '40

BENSON, ALLAN LOUIS Nov 6, 1871— Aug 19, 1940 Author; Socialist Party candidate for President in 1916; only Socialist Presidential candidate other than Eugene V. Debs to receive more than 500,000 votes; argued against preparedness and American involvement in the First World War; former managing editor of the Detroit *Times;* leading writer on Socialism—his booklets on subject had immense sales—sometimes almost 2,000,000 copies each

> *References*
>> Cur Opinion 61:162-3 S '16 por
>> Lit Digest 52:807 Mr 25 '16 por
>> Outlook 112:865-9 Ap 12 '16
>> Who's Who in America

> *Obituaries*
>> N Y Herald Tribune p16 Ag 20 '40
>> N Y Times p19 Ag 20 '40

BENSON, EDWARD FREDERIC July 24, 1867—Feb 29, 1940 Author

E. F. Benson, prolific author of sprightly novels, numerous biographies, essays and poems, died February 29, 1940, at the age of 72. Benson was born at Wellington College, England, where his father, Edward White Benson, who later became Archbishop of Canterbury, was headmaster. He was one of six children. One of his brothers became the Very Reverend Monsignor Hugh Benson, a priest in the Catholic Archdiocese of Westminster, the author of several religious books, articles and pamphlets; he died in 1914. Another brother, Arthur Christopher, was master of Magdalene College, Cambridge, from 1915 until his death in 1925. He wrote numerous biographies and poems.

In *Our Family Affairs* (1921) E. F. Benson wrote of some of the events of his busy childhood. During his early years, all the members of the family were ornithologists, conchologists, geologists, poets and literary folk. An important influence of this early home life was a joint literary effort called the *Saturday Magazine,* to which every member of the family contributed when the children were home for holidays. The requirement of each was "at least four pages of prose or one page of verse" written on the father's sermon paper. Later E. F. Benson was to write of this enterprise: "This habit gave us all a certain ease in expressing ourselves if only because we expressed ourselves so freely." It was continued for years, even after the children were in college and were succeeding in more ambitious literary endeavors.

As a youth, E. F. Benson had a tutor, A. H. Beesley, whose knowledge of prose and of history later earned him a place as a historian. His more formal education young Benson received at Marlborough College and at King's College, Cambridge, where he was a Craven and Prendergast student. During his school years he edited *The Marlburian,* in which may be seen his imitations of Addison and Tennyson. During this period, too, he became interested in archeology. While he was at Cambridge, he discovered remains of Roman monuments embedded in the wall of the city of Chester, and William Gladstone showed him how to make blotting paper "squeezes," or casts, of the inscriptions.

After pursuing archeology for a while at King's College, Benson went to Athens in 1892 as an assistant in researches for the British Archeological Schools and remained there until 1895, at the same time writing novels. In the years 1895 to 1897 Benson spent his winters in Egypt doing work for the Hellenic Society, returning to Greece for the rest of the time. During these years he was writing steadily. After 1897 he gradually settled to writing as a career.

E. F. BENSON

In 1893, while he was in Athens, Benson's best-seller, *Dodo,* was published, as well as his *Six Common Things. Rubicon* appeared the following year. The manuscript of *Dodo* had been lying in a drawer for years, coming out now and again for revision. The novel created a mild sensation and, as P. W. Wilson said in the New York *Times* Book Review more than 40 years later, "the amusement was the more enjoyable because Dodos [modern girls of the period] had not been included up to that time within the ecclesiastical entourage of Primates at Lambeth Palace." The success of *Dodo* later proved something of a handicap to its author, for regardless of the great number of books he wrote meanwhile, years later he was frequently referred to as the author of *Dodo.*

From 1893 until 1936, with the exception of the years 1899 and 1909, Benson published at least one book every year. In some years there were as many as three. Altogether, he published 79 works. Creative ability, finished literary style and facility of writing were qualities of all his work. His was a keen wit that was never malicious, and a humor that was never forced. Of *As We Are: A Modern Revue* (1932) one critic wrote: "There is no room in which to dwell upon Mr. Benson's understanding, sympathetic and moving depiction of the War-generation."

Among his most successful novels were *Mammon and Co.* (1900); *The Princess Sophia* (1900); *The Relentless City* (1903); *The Challoners* (1904); *The Weaker Vessel* (1913); *Dodo Wonders* (1921); *Paying Guests* (1929) and several about the amazing Lucia Pillson, the first of which, *Queen Lucia,* appeared in 1920 and the last, *Trouble for Lucia,* the fall before his death.

BENSON, EDWARD F.—*Continued*

Benson also wrote a number of biographies and histories which were well received. In 1938 he published *Queen Victoria's Daughters* which Queen Victoria dominated, as she had in real life dominated the lives of her children. The New York *Times* said of it: "Mr. Benson . . . still writes with the urbane ease of a later Victorian novelist—a contemporary Anthony Hope, Stanley Weyman and the rest whose neatly worked-out romances, when we turn over the leaves, are as silks and satins still fragrant with crumpled roses that recall what can never be again. It is pleasant and cultured writing. These Victorians of the drawing room knew their language and, in the days before syncopation, were satisfied with a serene and melodious tempo." Although he wrote the book with obvious affection and respect, with his usual competence and sense of human values, the author was not prevented from indulging in "occasional irony of a suave and gentle sort." For this work, the Royal family turned over to Benson correspondence which had not been previously published.

His other biographical and historical works include *Sir Francis Drake* (1927); *The Life of Alcibiades* (1929); *Ferdinand Magellan* (1930); *As We Were* (1930); *Charlotte Brontë* (1932) which has been called "the first really fair biography of the Brontë family that has been written," *King Edward VII* (1933); *Queen Victoria* (1935); and *The Kaiser and English Relations* (1936).

Mr. Benson, who was made a member of the Order of the British Empire in recognition of his literary works, also served as Mayor of Rye from 1934 to 1937, and was an honorary fellow of Magdalene College, Cambridge.

References

Benson, E. F.   Final Edition   1940
Benson, E. F.   Our Family Affairs:
  1867-1896   1921
Kunitz, S. J. ed.   Living Authors
  1937
Who's Who

Obituaries

Manchester Guardian p12 Mr 1 '40
N Y Herald Tribune p16 Mr 1 '40
Pub W 137:1089 Mr 9 '40
Spec 164:334 Mr 8 '40
Time 35:64 Mr 11 '40
Wilson Lib Bul 14:546 Ap '40

BENSON, JOHN 1872-   President of the American Association of Advertising Agencies

Address: 420 Lexington Ave, New York City

The late Edward W. Bok, for 30 years editor of the *Ladies' Home Journal*, established a series of Annual Advertising Awards "to encourage merit and stimulate improvement in advertising." Administered by the Har-vard School of Business Administration from 1924 to 1930, the awards were discontinued early in the depression. In 1935 the magazine *Advertising and Selling* revived them and has continued to sponsor them.

The gold medal for distinguished services to advertising in 1939 was presented to John Benson, president of the American Association of Advertising Agencies, at the Annual Advertising Awards dinner in New York City on February 15, 1940. President Roosevelt sent Mr. Benson a letter of congratulation which said: "I am especially glad to know that this award is bestowed upon you for having made most constructive contributions to the betterment of advertising during the past years. Advertising which stresses truth and fairness to the public can be an immense aid in spreading distribution and in stimulating and maintaining production."

John Benson, the greater part of whose life has been devoted to the service of advertising, was born in Erie, Pennsylvania in 1872. He went to Erie Academy and also took lessons in English composition from a group of Harvard professors who called themselves the Hawkins Correspondence School of Cambridge, Massachusetts. His first job was learning the coal business as a miner in the pit of the Youghiogheny River Coal Company.

In 1906 he married Cora Handy of Chicago, and went, still on coal business, to Green Bay, Wisconsin. His top job was general sales agent of a small company. He was ambitious for more and tried to scribble business stories for the Sunday edition of the old Chicago *Tribune*. But there was no living in that. A friend advised him: "If you have a bent for writing, why not try ad-

JOHN BENSON

vertising? That would give you a better chance to eat."

Benson tried advertising for William D. McJunkin, a young Chicago agency head, who paid him $20 a week for a time and then offered him a partnership. After three years John Benson went into business for himself, attracted a few loyal clients and became senior partner of Benson, Gamble, Johnson and Read. It took him 23 years to get there, though. And they weren't easy years, even for a "studious and non-gregarious chap who was grizzling into middle age with four children."

He didn't get there in a flashy way, either. All he ever did in his agency, actually, was to hold the original loyal clients and attract a few more. Fancy writing wasn't in him. "He had, by early advertising standards, a hopeless penchant for the truth, and he not only told the truth but battled for it as a member of almost all the associations and committees which a serious advertising man could join."

In the first years of the First World War a group of successful advertising men felt that the five regional associations of advertising agencies in this country should unite for self-protection and for higher standards. The first meeting was held in Buffalo and the Four A's—the American Association of Advertising Agencies—was founded. In 1922 John Benson was elected president of the Four A's and in 1927 was asked to become permanent president on full time. John Benson—"quiet, informed, but self-effacing"—thought it over for a year and then accepted.

As president of the Four A's and as advertising man Mr. Benson prophetically said in 1930: "Advertising does not yet command sufficient confidence to become a buying guide. There is not enough information and helpful suggestion in it. Most advertising is too partisan. It tells too many half-truths. It does not look *through* the consumer's eyes." It is this creed that aids John Benson immensely in Washington where, through him, officials have learned the Four A's point of view: that legislation is right which (1) serves the public interest, and (2) restricts honest advertising as little as possible.

References
Adv & Selling 33:36-7 F 15 '40 por
N Y Herald Tribune p33 F 16 '40 por
Newsweek 15:61-2 F 26 '40 por
Who's Who in Advertising

BENTLEY, IRENE 1870—June 3, 1940 Musical comedy star; widow of Harry B. Smith, librettist for Victor Herbert; won fame on two continents; retired in 1910

References
Who's Who in America

Obituaries
N Y Herald Tribune p24 Je 4 '40 por
N Y Times p23 Je 4 '40
Variety 138:46 Je 5 '40

BENTON, THOMAS HART Apr 15, 1889- Artist
Address: h. 3616 Belleview Ave, Kansas City, Missouri

A novel and brilliant promotion scheme that has brought considerable attention to a group of American artists was devised by motion-picture producer Walter Wanger for his sea picture, *The Long Voyage Home* (1940). Nine famous painters were brought to Hollywood to do scenes and characters from the movie. The pictures, shown during August at the Associated American Artists' Gallery in New York, then toured the country through the museums.

Notable among the group, which included such names as Grant Wood, Luis Quintanilla and James Chapin (see sketches this issue), was the dynamic muralist, Thomas Hart Benton. As his subject from the movie Benton painted a crew on the London docks shaking their fists at the captain of a rival tramp steamer. Benton approved the Wanger scheme, saying it was "a sign of growing intelligence in Hollywood." He reported a fine time in the movie colony; but added that his main reason for being there was to study the locale for drawings he was doing for a limited edition of John Steinbeck's (see sketch this issue) *Grapes of Wrath*. He has already made a striking group of these drawings to illustrate the advertisements for the motion picture version of *Grapes of Wrath*.

A pioneering force in American art, Thomas Benton has been called by the art critic, Thomas Craven, "the most prominent, vigorous and virile of our painters." His famed Americana murals in New York, Chicago and his native Missouri have aroused much critical controversy, but a large American public has seen and liked them. Benton was born in Neosho, Missouri on April 15, 1889, the son of Maecenus E. and Elizabeth (Wise) Benton. He was named after his great-uncle, old Thomas Hart Benton, Missouri's first Senator. His father, Colonel Benton, was a lawyer with political aspirations, and as a boy Thomas accompanied him on his political tours. When his father was elected to Congress he went with him to Washington every autumn and returned in the spring. During the summers, however, young Tom had to take care of the farm: his father didn't want him to forget good old pioneer Missouri ways. His father had also decided that a Benton could be nothing but a lawyer. But his son perversely preferred the town bums and colored boys to Senators and judges, dime novels to studies. His love for drawing was totally incomprehensible to his father, but his mother encouraged him.

Ned Scott

THOMAS HART BENTON

Benton's first mural, he says, was painted at the age of six. It was a very long freight train in charcoal which ran up the stairway on the new cream-colored wall paper—the engine puffing heavy black smoke because of the steep grade. The storm of protest, rather than appreciation, which greeted this early effort was only a prophetic forecast, the artist wryly observes. During the Spanish-American War the young artist graduated to battleships—mostly the *Maine* being blown up. He also drew Indians, not like those found on the Indian territory nearby, but wilder ones.

At 17 he decided to be a professional artist and got a job drawing cartoons for the Joplin *American* at $14 a week. Then, feeling the need to get away from the small town and to associate with his own kind, he went to Chicago in 1907 to study at the Art Institute. There he couldn't stand making drawings of plaster casts and sneaked into the life classes. In Chicago they didn't think he was much of a genius either, so with his mother's backing he set out for Paris at the age of 19. Paris was ecstasy. But the conventional art schools repelled him just as they had in Chicago, and he set about painting by himself—thereafter "to flounder for 15 years without a compass in every direction." After three years he came back to New York, a great misfit with his pose of the typical Bohemian Paris artist. After a while he managed to pick up a few jobs, such as painting the portraits of the movie queens of the day for Rex Ingram. At that time his "serious" work was cubism and symbolism in the Paris manner. Taking up "synchronism," he exhibited a few pictures in the Forum show of 1916.

The War came, and Benton decided the safest place would be the navy. They first put him to loading coal boats in Virginia,

then he was transferred to the architectural service as a draftsman. This War experience marked the turning point in his art career: he came into contact with real things and with real American types. He began to express himself objectively and to break from the old pre-War art crowd influences. He also got married (in 1922)—to Rita Piacenza, an art student in the free art classes he taught at nights just after the War. She designed hats to help eke out their precarious income. Through a friend they were introduced to parties given by the higher strata of New York's underworld. Here Benton met and began to paint some of the types in his series of "American portraits."

Benton went on developing his interest in American subjects and learned much from the American artist Burchfield's way of painting native backgrounds. His first public success came in Philadelphia when his canvases attracted the attention of the collector, Albert Barnes. Summers he and his wife went to Martha's Vineyard, Massachusetts, where Benton painted the landscape and the old people of the countryside. Two children were born to them.

A return visit to Missouri in 1924 renewed his interest in Missouri types. He wanted to know a great deal more about America and started going places, traveling the back roads and byways throughout the country. Leisurely, often on foot, with a pack of drawing materials in his knapsack, he visited the towns and homes of common American people. He studied life in the Texas panhandle oil fields, on Mississippi towboats; he visited coal mines, steel mills, shipbuilding plants. He made trips on Ohio, Missouri and Mississippi river boats; and he lived among mountain people in the Ozarks and Tennessee. The account of this rich, first-hand contact with American lives, customs and folkways Benton has given in his delightfully written autobiography, *An Artist in America* (1937), illustrated with several drawings.

His interest in the vast panorama of America's present and past led him naturally to the field of mural painting. His first mural on a contemporary American theme was done for the New School for Social Research in New York City and met with severe criticism as well as praise. The preliminary studies of the mural were purchased by the Whitney Museum, and the values of his pictures went up. He then painted a mural for the Whitney Museum.

In 1933 he was commissioned to do the Indiana mural for the World's Fair at Chicago. This mural of Indiana history Benton felt represented his best work, and the folks at the Fair liked it too, even if some New York critics did not. Fellow Missourians wanted him to paint a similar mural for the home state, and in 1935 he was commissioned to do one for the state capitol at Jefferson City. Of this work he said, "I wanted plain Missouri people like the farmers to like my painting, and when my total design was not affected by their objections to some detail of fact I remedied the matter for them. I had all the evidence necessary to make me believe that my realistic conception of Missouri's social history and life was in line with the reputedly realistic psychology of the state's people." Representations of Frankie and Johnny, Kansas City's notorious Boss Pendergast and certain other realistic episodes and figures in Missouri's history drew pained and loud protests from local and neighboring stuffed shirts among editors, educators and politicians: "a great state is grossly libeled," they said. But the common folk refused to feel disgraced, and were proud of their state mural.

The critics themselves never agreed about Benton because, as Thomas Craven has pointed out, he falls into none of the ready categories of modern art. "To the conservatives he is a Red; to the radicals, he is a chauvinist. His art is too specifically real, too deeply impregnated with what I shall risk calling the collective American spirit, to touch the purists, methodists, and doctrinaires. . . He has the rawhide individualism, the cynical laugh, the rough humor, the talent for buffoonery, and something of the typical Westerner's sentimental slant on life." His designs in these murals were full of violent contrasts, with one unit rhythmically set against another to express the tense energy and raw power of America in development. Benton does not have a particular social alliance, painting without satire and with equal representation café society and striking workers, politicians and farm hands.

Although he helped found in New York the Associated American Artists, organized to stimulate wider interest in contemporary American art, Benton decided to go back home to live, and in 1936 the offer of a teaching job in the Kansas City Art Institute clinched his decision. His interest in American types and themes continued; but an exhibit of his later work held in New York in 1939 showed that his work was undergoing further change.

Among the 1939 paintings were symbolic nudes, still lifes and simple landscapes, all showing Benton's new and careful study of textures. The change began with his *Susanna and the Elders,* the manner being echoed in *Persephone,* in which subtlety is the keynote. Benton gives complete, sculptural life to each of the many forms represented in the paintings, which are done in highly-glossed oil tempera. Landscapes such as *Shallow Creek* and *Weighing Cotton* are studies in objective realism. Of these Howard Devree has written: "Benton appears to have come nearer maturely artistic stature in his easel paintings than in any earlier work. . . His color is more lively and clearer; his textural grasp sure and pleasing; his designs convincing; the strength of his draftsmanship makes itself felt; he is reassuringly painstaking of space and perspective." Since, however, Benton's art has changed constantly during the course of his career, most observers of his work believe that—considering his volatile nature and wide range of interests—he will continue experimenting, changing, developing— perhaps in other new directions.

References

Art Digest 13:10 Ap 15 '39 il; 14:16 F 15 '40 il
Mag Art 32:301-2 My '39 il
N Y World-Telegram p7 Jl 13 '40 por
Time 35:54 Je 10 '40 por
Benton, T. H. An Artist in America 1937
Craven, T. Benton *In* Modern Art p332-45 1934
Craven, T. Our Art Becomes American *In* Bower, W. ed. New Directions p303-20 1937
Craven, T. Thomas Hart Benton 1939
Who's Who in America
Who's Who in American Art

BERG, PATRICIA JANE Feb 13, 1918- Golfer

Address: h. 5001 Colfax Ave, South Minneapolis, Minnesota

Patty Berg turned professional in July 1940, ending one of the most amazing amateur careers in the history of women's golf. When she was 17 no one outside of Minneapolis, her home town, had ever heard of her; at 20 she had won every amateur golf title of importance.

At 22 she said goodbye to the ranks of the amateurs to sign up with a Chicago sporting goods company at a salary reported to be $7,500 a year. "That's $145 a week," as one newspaper writer commented at the time. "Quite a lot of money for a girl just 22 years old and taking her first job." Patty's duties on her $145-a-week job with the Wilson Sporting Goods Company are largely educational, with appearances at summer camps for girls and golf-coaching schools.

Miss Berg has realized almost painlessly the dream of thousands of girls to play golf and to be paid for it. She has always had a natural aptitude for sports. As a little girl she played quarterback on a boys' football team, played baseball, and was the despair of her mother, who couldn't keep tomboy Patty's clothes mended.

When Patty was 13 her father, Herman Berg, a Minneapolis grain broker and golf enthusiast, brought home to his young son a membership to a golf club. "Where is mine?" Patty teased. "Just because I'm a girl is no reason not to give me one." So Mr. Berg got his tomboy daughter four old clubs, supplied her with a golf club membership and made her promise to go out for practice every day. The Bergs probably thought golf might keep Patty from such pastimes as football and baseball.

Patty got her first golf clubs in 1932. "In the beginning my game was awful," she said. Nevertheless, Patty soon played pretty good

PATTY BERG

golf. Her father was her chief instructor.
A year after she got those first clubs she
qualified for the championship flight in a
Minneapolis tournament. By 1935 she had
won the Minnesota state championship, a
title she won again in 1936 and in 1938.

The young golfer first came into the national limelight in 1935 when she entered the
women's national, which that year happened
to be played on her home course, the Inter-
laken, in Minneapolis. Patty amazed the
galleries with her 200-yard-drive and her
earnestness. She beat five opponents in a
row and got to the finals, where she faced
the famous Glenna Collet Vare, who that
year had returned to the golf wars to win
her sixth national title. Mrs. Vare defeated
young Patty, but not before Patty had given
her a few anxious moments.

From then on Patty Berg was important
sports news. She furnished lively copy for
the sports writers, who predicted that it
would "only be a matter of time before the
17-year-old would prove herself the foremost
woman golfer in the United States." The
little girl who had only been playing golf
three years had "what it takes," they declared
—"the competitive spirit of a Bobby Jones
or a Gene Tunney" (see sketch this issue). One
sports writer called her a "Bobby Jones" in
skirts.

Patty has always been a favorite of the
galleries. She proved as great an attraction
for golf as Helen Wills Moody was for
tennis. Red-haired, blue-eyed, freckled-faced,
her nose shiny, her face devoid of makeup,
Patty is all business on the golf course.
About five feet one, sturdy and weighing
about 110 pounds, she is an appealing figure
on the links. For a long time she wore the
same old sweater and hat in tournaments because she said they brought her luck. She
usually wears slacks or a skirt and a sweater

for playing and has a blue beret perched on
the top of her head. Sometimes after a bad
shot the galleries can hear her mutter, "Patty,
you bum." She has a nice direct grin and,
despite her red hair, she has yet to show
temper on the links.

During a tournament Patty retires at
8:30 p. m., lining up all her clubs (thirteen
irons and five woods) against the wall of
her room. Her mother and father used to
follow their daughter's progress anxiously.
Mrs. Berg, who has been lame since girlhood, could not follow her daughter hole
by hole, but she watched her until she
was a mere speck in the distance. Mr.
Berg did follow, and when things went
badly for Patty he whittled away furiously
at a piece of wood.

In three years the hard-driving Patty
won 13 titles. After her performance in
the women's national of 1935 she did some
sensational playing on the Florida circuit
in the winter of 1936, winning the Punta
Gorda, Florida and the Miami-Biltmore,
Miami, Florida tournaments. The officers
of the United States Golf Association rewarded her with an invitation to accompany
the Curtis Cup Team to Scotland in May
1936 for the women's international matches
with Great Britain.

In 1937 Miss Berg came through to the
finals of the United States women's national again but was defeated by Estelle
Lawson Page. Patty was so jittery in the
finals she could hardly hold a club, and
sports writers laid her defeat to her youth
and lack of long experience. But the following year, in 1938, she again faced Mrs.
Page in the United States women's national finals and this time she dethroned
the champion. At 20 Patty Berg was the
national women's golf champion. It marked the best season of her career—her tenth
victory in 13 tournaments.

That year, in addition to the women's
national golf championship, she won the
women's Western championship, the Western derby championship, the trans-Missis-
sippi championship, the Minnesota state
championship and several winter Florida
tournaments. The Associated Press sports
writers selected her as the outstanding
woman athlete of 1938.

She well deserved the title, for little Miss
Berg was a natural athlete. A few years
previously she had taken up speed skating
and won the midget championship of Minnesota the first time she entered, placing
third in the nationals the next winter.
When she was attending high school in
Minneapolis she won a score of ribbons
for track victories.

That eventful year of 1938 Patty also
entered the University of Minnesota as a
freshman. Busy with her studies, she did
not play as much golf in 1939.

As a professional Miss Berg takes her
place with five other well-known women
golfers—Helen Hicks Harb, Mrs. Opal S.
Hill, Helen Dettweiler, Helen MacDonald
and Mildred (Babe) Didrikson. These six

make up the entire list of well-known women golf professionals.

When she was 19 years old Miss Berg solemnly told an interviewer that she would not marry—she was just going to play golf. It is a pretty good game at $7,500 a year.

References

Am Mag 122:85 S '36 por
Christian Sci Mon p11 Jl 3 '40 por
Collier's 97:26+ My 9 '36 por
Good H 104:44-5 My '37 pors
Lit Digest 121:40 Mr 7 '36 por
N Y Sun p27 Jl 10 '40
Newsweek 16:45 Jl 15 '40
Time 27:27 Mr 9 '36 por; 32:53 O 3 '38 por; 36:34 Jl 15 '40
American Women
Shehan, T. Patty Berg *In* Nason, J. and others Famous American Athletes of Today 7th ser. p3-33 1940
Who's Who in America

INGRID BERGMAN

BERGMAN, INGRID 1916- Motion picture actress

Address: c/o David O. Selznick Corp, Culver City, California

When Miss Bergman, Sweden's leading film star, came to Hollywood in the spring of 1939 to do the English version of a Swedish success, *Intermezzo,* no one paid any attention to her. Even in Hollywood, while she and Leslie Howard were making *Intermezzo: A Love Story,* she went about as she pleased with nary an autograph hound on her trail The film made an immediate sensation and people, entranced by her beauty and acting, announced a new star in the Hollywood firmament.

At 24, Miss Bergman had been an actress in Sweden for six years—two on the stage and four in the films. Before that she was a student for 11 years at the famous Stockholm Lyccum for Flickor. She is a bit tired of explaining that in Swedish *Flickor* means "girls" and has nothing to do with films. At school when she was 15 she took part in a play with such success that theatrical impresarios asked her to go on the stage. Then she spent a year at the Royal Dramatic Theatre School and was ready to play ingenues at the Oscar and Royal Theatres of her native city. After she made *Intermezzo* for the Svensk Filmindustri, she came to the notice of David O. Selznick.

When reporters met her in New York in January 1940 after her vacation in Sweden, they were amazed at her charm and the fresh beauty of her glowing Scandinavian coloring, which needs no makeup. She looks no more than 18 now. Taller than average (5 feet 8), she has light brown hair, deep blue eyes, an athletic figure, and a quality of deep serenity. Ordinarily a glamour star hides her marriage and parenthood, but Miss Bergman amazed hardened ship's reporters by appearing with her 15

months' old daughter, Pia, slung over her shoulder in a fur-lined "papoose bag."

"It would be wonderful," commented a reporter, "to have a picture of you with Pia peeping from the bag over your shoulder." "I'd love it, too," she replied, "for naturally I am very proud of her. But it is impossible. Strict orders from Selznick." Pia, whose odd name is a combination of the initials of the names of Ingrid and her husband, a doctor and professor at the Swedish Royal Academy of Medicine, is a smaller edition of her mother. Ingrid has been married three years and her husband was anxious to accompany her to Hollywood, but he is of military age and must remain in Sweden.

"I hope," says Miss Bergman, "that my next picture won't be made for a long time, so that I will have an opportunity to perfect my English. Of course I shall take lessons and I shall have a teacher right with me on the lot when I make the picture—I had one in *Intermezzo,* too—but the best way is to live in the country for a while." Her English seems delightful to listeners. She explained that she could always speak it a little, for in Sweden it is taught in the schools along with French and German.

In the spring of 1940 Ingrid Bergman opened in a revival of Molnar's *Liliom* on Broadway. The critic for *Theatre Arts* said: "She brings to the part of Julie a lovely, fresh innocence that has about it something of the peasant solidity, the strength of bone and fibre under its youthful charm which is an authentic contribution to the part. Her slight accent is no handicap to this very 'foreign' play, especially as she speaks with great clarity and has a pleasantly modulated voice." Other critics were equally kind in discussing her rôle.

BERGMAN, INGRID—*Continued*

She is a little frightened at becoming an American star. "In Stockholm I go everywhere alone. They recognize me, but no one pays any attention." One thing she is sure of: "If I become famous in Hollywood I will not forget my husband in Stockholm. My husband knows I would come back to him. He is a very clever man."

References

Collier's 106:13+ S 14 '40 por
N Y Herald Tribune VI p4 Ja 28 '40
N Y Post p11 Ja 17 '40 por
N Y Sun p22 Ja 16 '40
N Y Times X p5 Ja 21 '40 por
N Y World-Telegram p17 Ja 15 '40 por
Photoplay 54:14-16 Ja '40 por
Theatre Arts 24:315-16 My '40

BERLE, ADOLF AUGUSTUS JR. (bĕr'-lê) Jan 29, 1895- Assistant Secretary of State
Address: Department of State, Washington, D. C.

To be an official in the United States State Department these days demands the utmost in intelligence, understanding and energy. Adolf Augustus Berle Jr., "a ball of intellect and nervous energy," who has advised the Roosevelt government on taxation, on railroads, on banking; who has been City Chamberlain of New York and chairman of its Planning Commission; who had advised Secretary of State Hull (see sketch this issue) on trade treaties and conferred with foreign ministers, has the wide experience and dynamic vitality necessary in these ticklish times.

As Assistant Secretary of State he has called on both capital and labor to subordinate, during the European War, their respective desires for greater profits and higher wages in order to obtain the highest degree of national unity. This he considers essential for the freedom of the United States and even for the "ultimate salvation of civilization." As Assistant Secretary of State he has argued against "selfish isolationism" which is "neither possible, practical nor peaceful," and in its place urged a policy of "cooperative peace." We must stay out of the War, he insists, and yet remain "good neighbors." As Assistant Secretary of State he has been busy speaking and writing on President Roosevelt's foreign and domestic policy and he has been busy working out plans to deal economically with Latin America.

This is not the first time that Secretary Berle has appeared in a position close to the President. In 1932 he was one of the original "brain trust" that helped formulate Roosevelt's policies during his first years in office, its "cockiest member." Already known as a brilliant lawyer and a thorough analytical economist, it was he who advised President Roosevelt on bank and corporation affairs.

A. A. Berle is an infant prodigy who has made good. His father, Dr. Adolf Augustus Berle, a liberal minister and sociologist of Boston, had his own educational ideas, which he passed on to his son shortly after he left the cradle. At fourteen Adolf Jr. entered Harvard with high examination marks and short pants, and in 1913, only three years later, was graduated with honors. A year later he had his master's degree, and at 21 was the youngest man ever to graduate from the Harvard Law School.

Right out of law school he entered Louis Brandeis' law office. He stayed there for a year until he went to the War as a lieutenant in the infantry. He also saw service as an army intelligence officer, and his trips into the Caribbean added the sugar business, Latin American law and Caribbean politics and sociology to the subjects on which he was later recognized as an expert.

After the War Berle practiced law with the New York firm of Rounds, Hatch, Dillingham and Debevoise until 1923. In that year, at the age of 24, he went to the Peace Conference as an assistant to Frank Howard Lord, American High Commissioner to Poland, in the redrafting of the Eastern frontier of Germany. The solution finally incorporated in the draft treaty was absolutely unacceptable to him, and he resigned.

Back in New York he began active work in the Henry Street Settlement. He became interested in the welfare of Indians and defended their rights in several lawsuits. But the main line of his legal work gradually carried Berle into the accepted channels for a respectable and ambitious young corporation lawyer in New York City. He became an active Republican, relieved of financial cares by his marriage in 1927 to Beatrice Bend Bishop of New York. From 1925 to 1928 he lectured occasionally at the Harvard School of Business and in 1927 accepted a professorship in corporation law from Columbia University. He stayed at Columbia until he went to Washington, active as a teacher, as a lawyer and as an author of substantial and authoritative books on corporation finance.

In 1928 appeared his *Studies in the Law of Corporation Finance;* in 1930 his *Cases and Materials in the Law of Corporation Finance* (with Dr. Gardiner C. Means); and in 1932, also with Dr. Means, his most famous book, *The Modern Corporation and Private Property.* This now standard book is based on the most elaborate studies that have been made of the growth of American corporations, and its conclusion is that "the rise of the modern corporation has brought a concentration of economic power which can compete on equal terms with the modern state—economic power versus political power, each strong in its own field. The state seeks in some aspects to regulate the corporation, while the corporation, steadily becoming more powerful, makes every effort to avoid such regulation."

When Mr. Berle appeared before the Congressional Monopoly Investigation Committee in 1938 it was his books that inspired a good many of his suggestions. He cautioned the trust busters that bigness did not mean badness, and he criticized the technique of the New Deal for indulging in "shotgun imposition of regulation without adequate definition of standard." Yet, then and since, Berle has clung doggedly to the hope that bankers and business men will realize that restraint, higher standards of conduct and a sense of social responsibility are imperative if the capitalistic régime is to survive.

During the first Roosevelt campaign Berle did useful odd-jobs of economic analysis, sloganeering and drafting, but when Roosevelt was elected he refused office in the New Deal, preferring to be free to continue his teaching and practice. Yet as a "brain truster" he spent two or three days a week in Washington and during the one-hundred-day Congressional Session of 1932 to 1933 had a hand in varied pieces of legislation. He helped to write the Bankruptcy Act, the new Securities Act and the National Recovery Act. He was legal counsel to the Agricultural Adjustment Administration in obtaining sugar production and marketing agreements. Most important, he was special advisor to the Reconstruction Finance Corporation in charge of untangling the mess of railroad finances. As such he was primarily responsible for the system of Federal coordinators which Roosevelt adopted as his transitional railroad policy. As such, too, he infuriated Wall Street by his uncovering of one bit of skullduggery after another on the part of the railroads and banks.

In 1933 Berle was sent to Cuba as financial advisor to the United States Embassy there and arrived just as the second revolution broke out. From then on he became involved in New York City rather than Federal politics. From 1934, until the office was abolished by the new city charter in 1937, he served as City Chamberlain of New York under La Guardia (see sketch this issue), whose election he had supported long before the practical politicians and reformers could agree to pick the "Little Flower." Then he became chairman of the City Planning Commission, a member of the City Housing Authority, chairman of a committee to study the New York substitute teacher system.

In February 1938 he rejoined the Roosevelt Administration as Assistant Secretary of State. Under-Secretary of State Sumner Welles (see sketch this issue) is supposed to have been responsible for bringing this short and slender "financial and legal genius" back to Washington, for he worked closely with him at the Pan-American Conference at Buenos Aires. There was some opposition in Washington to the appointment, for Berle's "show of self-esteem had irritated many government officials with whom he came in contact." As one writer

A. A. BERLE JR.

put it: "Berle is an infant prodigy who has irritated everybody by continuing to be a prodigy after he has ceased to be an infant."

When Berle went to the State Department in February he retained his Columbia professorship because the new post "may not last more than a few months." In August of the same year he resigned, saying that his work on the pending British trade agreement was done and affirming to President Roosevelt his support of "your administration and you personally . . . against all your enemies, foreign and domestic."

In September of that same year President Roosevelt announced that Berle's resignation would not become effective on September 15th as originally was made public, but that Berle would continue in office for an indefinite period because of the international situation, though a leave would be granted him. In April 1939 that leave was cancelled. And with the world as it is today it looks as though it will be a long time before this "cocky little devil" of the sharp mind and the sharp pen will return again to the teaching of corporation law.

References

Am Mag 116:58 S '33 por
Fortune 17:162 Ap '38 por; 18:150 O '38 por
Newsweek 1:23-4 Ap 22 '33 por; 11:10 F 21 '38
Sat Eve Post 206:5 Ja 27 '34 por
Scholastic 32:13S F 26 '38 por
Scrib Mag 94:257-66 N '33 por
Survey G 24:469-73+ O '35; 25:596-7 N '36
Time 31:17 F 21 '38 por; 32:41 Ag 29 '38 por; 35:15 F 19 '40 por; 35:71 Je 24 '40

BERLE, ADOLF A. Jr.—*Continued*

Unofficial Observer [pseud.] Privy
Councillors *In* New Dealers p307-35
1934
Who's Who in America
Who's Who in Law
Who's Who in the Nation's Capital

BERRY, MARTHA MCCHESNEY Oct
7, 1866- Educator; social service worker
Address: Mount Berry, Georgia

The story of the Berry Schools, founded
by Martha Berry, is the story of a woman
who devoted her life to an ideal of service,
and who through her unselfish devotion to
that ideal opened the gates of opportunity
to thousands of poor Southern boys and
girls.

Martha Berry was brought up to a life
of ease and pleasure. The daughter of Captain Thomas and Frances (Rhea) Berry,
she was born on a plantation, several miles
from Rome, in northwest Georgia, in the
upland district on the edge of the higher
Appalachian belt. She and her sisters enjoyed the advantages of travel and a fashionable education. Martha Berry attended
a finishing school in Baltimore, and came
home to the huge white-pillared plantation
house to take her place in the society of
Georgia.

Almost at the door of the Berry plantation were the poor cabin homes of the
Georgia mountaineers, people of English
and Scotch ancestry, the sturdy, adventurous
type which formed the backbone of early
America. But as the hillside soils were
depleted, and as their contacts with the
rest of the world grew less frequent, the
later generations lived in poverty and ignorance. Even as a young girl Martha Berry
was aware of the little ragged mountain
children, growing up illiterate and unkempt.

One Sunday afternoon she gathered several of these neglected waifs in the old log
cabin on her father's plantation and told
them *Bible* stories. They came again the
next Sunday, and the next, and Martha
Berry soon had a real Sunday School class.
She rode out into the remote mountain sections where preachers never went, and
invited the mountain folks down for Sunday
services at the little log cabin. She became
known as the "Sunday Lady" of the mountains.

As she came in closer contact with the
mountaineers, she saw fine young boys and
girls growing up neglected, with no chance
for an education of even the most rudimentary sort, no chance to make anything of
themselves! Georgia, once the proudest
state in the union, had a deplorable record
in providing public education. For these
mountain boys and girls there seemed to
be little future.

And Martha Berry decided to do something about it. In the little log cabin across
the road from her home she opened a school
where all who liked might come and learn.
Thus in 1902 was laid the foundation for
the Berry Schools. Five boys were in Miss
Berry's first class. At the end of the first
week came wash day. But the boys were
mountain-reared. They refused to wash
their clothes, their bed or table linen. Washing was women's work.

Martha Berry, who had always had Negro
servants to wait on her, rolled up her sleeves
and stepped to the wash tub. "Very well,
boys," she said sweetly, "I'll wash your
clothes for you." Rather than see Miss
Berry do the wash, the boys capitulated.
Miss Berry had solved the first of many
problems which were to beset the Berry
Schools.

In 1940 when Martha Berry was selected
to receive the second annual humanitarian
award of the Variety Clubs of America, a
nation-wide showmen's organization, the
Berry Schools had 25,000 acres of land and
125 buildings, including an accredited college. Less than eight per cent of the students who were graduated from the schools
paid for tuition or board. The others
earned their way by working for the schools.

From the earliest days of the school the
students worked for their tuition. Mountain
pride had prevented them from taking
charity. Some boys brought a few chickens,
others a few yards of hand-woven cloth.
One boy came driving a team of oxen to
work for his year's tuition. Ways had to
be found to help the boys earn their own
way, and to make use of what they brought.
They made gardens, raised stock, planted
fruit trees.

The boys built the first school dormitory
of 10 rooms. Friends donated furniture
and dishes. Miss Berry bought cots. The
school grew and soon it was impossible
to accomodate all who came. The girls
wanted to come, too. Miss Berry had not
hesitated to sink her own small fortune into
the school, but still boys and girls had to
be turned away.

Determined to give an opportunity to as
many boys and girls as she could, Miss
Berry went to New York in an attempt to
raise funds. She had few influential friends,
only a list of people known to subscribe to
worthy causes. Her first check was from
R. Fulton Cutting, who gave her $500,
enough to send 10 boys to school for one
year. Since then other philanthropists, persuaded by Martha Berry's eloquence, have
given thousands, even millions, to the
schools.

For Miss Berry is as determined and as
undaunted by obstacles as she is kind and
charming. And she has devoted all her
energy and all her life to her mountain boys
and girls.

The result has been the Mount Berry
School for Boys, the Martha Berry School
for Girls, the Berry Model Practice School
and the Berry College—the latter established
in 1926. All are operated with a view to
fitting boys and girls for some definite work

in their community. The school is a self-sustaining city. A mill has been built, granite for the buildings has been dug from the hills, there are orchards, there are herds of cattle and goats, there is an automobile shop, a bakery.

The Berry Schools have an enrollment of 1,300 students from 11 Southern states, and about 5,000 applicants are turned away each year. Each student devotes two days, or 16 hours a week, to some form of labor in the operation of the schools. No city boys or girls, or those who can pay their way without working at the school, are admitted. The boys wear overalls, the girls chambray dresses and sunbonnets. In addition to the scholastic work there is practical training in farming, dairying, orcharding, truck gardening, landscaping, forest management, road construction, carpentry, blacksmithing, plumbing, cabinetmaking, brick manufacture, bricklaying, printing, laundry work, shoe repairing, automobile mechanics, general merchandizing, stenography, office work, cooking, sewing, millinery, nursing, cafeteria work, dental assisting, school teaching, music and the ministry.

Aside from the satisfaction she has enjoyed at seeing her missionary vision come true, Martha Berry has had honors heaped upon her by an admiring nation. The Georgia Legislature honored her as a "distinguished citizen" in 1924; she was awarded the Roosevelt Memorial Medal for services to the nation in 1925. She received the Pictorial Review Award of $5,000 for outstanding service in 1927; was voted one of the 12 greatest American women in a nationwide poll in 1931; received a gold medal from Town Hall of New York for accomplishment of lasting merit, 1931; was appointed the only woman member of the Board of Regents of the University System of Georgia, 1932; received the biennial medal of the Society of Colonial Dames for eminent patriotic service, 1933; and was received at the Court of St. James by the King and Queen of England in 1934.

These are only a few of the honors which "Mother" Berry has received. A doctor of pedagogy from the University of Georgia, 1920, honorary degrees have been bestowed on her by half a dozen universities and colleges.

But she has built herself a more lasting memorial—the gratitude of more than 10,000 boys and girls who go out in life with new vision and opportunities because of Martha Berry's work in founding and directing the Berry Schools.

A sign marked "The Gate of Opportunity" stands at the entrance of the schools. To it might fittingly be added another sign: "Opened by Martha McChesney Berry."

References

Christian Sci Mon A p15 F 19 '40 por
Good H 93:50-1+ Ag '31 por
Mentor 16:18-20 Ag '28 il por
Newsweek 15:37 Ap 22 '40 il por
R of Rs 71:593-7 Je '25 por

MARTHA BERRY

Sch & Soc 51:274 Mr 2 '40
Sch Arts 25:519-26 My 26 il
U S Dept of the Interior Educ Bul 9:49-53 1938
American Women
Bartlett, R. M. When Dreams Come True: Martha Berry *In* They Dared to Live p7-10 1937
Byers, T. Martha Berry 1932
Who's Who in America

BESTEIRO Y FERNANDEZ, JULIAN (bĕs-tī′rō) 1870—Sept 27, 1940 Socialist Speaker of the Spanish Cortes (1931-33); last Foreign Minister of the Spanish Republican government; stayed behind in Madrid to surrender the city to the Rebels; had been for many years professor of logic and dean of the faculty of philosophy at the University of Madrid; served as Spain's Minister to The Hague; died in Carmona Prison, where he was serving a 30-year sentence for "prolonging the war"

References

Eur Nouv 22:935 Ag 26 '39
Time 34:28 Jl 17 '39
International Who's Who

Obituaries

N Y Herald Tribune p12 S 28 '40 por
N Y Times p17 S 28 '40 por

BETHE, HANS ALBRECHT (bā′tĕ häns al′brĕht) July 2, 1906- Physicist
Address: 104 Northway Rd, Ithaca, New York

Professor Bethe was born in Strasbourg, Alsace-Lorraine. After studying at Kiel, Frankfort and Munich (Ph. D. 1928), he

HANS A. BETHE

taught at various German universities. Because his mother was Jewish he found it necessary to leave Germany in 1933 and go to England, where he taught and continued his researches in physics for a year. In 1935 he came to Cornell as assistant professor of theoretical physics and in 1937 was promoted to a full professorship. In 1940 and 1941 he is visiting professor of physics at Columbia University.

In 1939 Professor Bethe received the Morrison Prize of the New York Academy of Science for his researches in astrophysics concluding that "carbon must be the stuff that enables the sun to turn fragments of hydrogen atoms into sunshine." In January 1940 he made headlines again for confirmation for the first time of the theory that "the forces holding the nucleus of the atom together are transmitted by the recently found meson, the elementary particle." The meson had been first recorded two years before in cosmic radiation by two professors of the University of California, Anderson and Neddermeyer, and simultaneously by Street and Stevenson of Harvard, Dr. Bethe's findings were published in *Physical Review* in 1940.

"Modest, demure" Dr. Bethe is considered by American physicists a man with extraordinary mathematical equipment. He is the author of five major treatises and dozens of articles on nuclear physics. *American Men of Science* (1938) gives his interests as follows: "Theory of atomic collisions, metals, atomic nuclei, absorption spectra of crystals and atomic spectra, particularly those of hydrogen and helium, quantum electrodynamics and properties of very fast particles."

In the summer of 1939 Professor Bethe married Rose Ewald, daughter of a famous German theoretical physicist now exiled by the Nazis and living in Ireland. He likes "skiing, economics and riding on trains, but spends most of his time mulling over theoretical physics. His tools: a stack of reference books, a batch of paper, a slide rule, a fountain pen, a powerful brain."

References

N Y Times p27 D 15 '38; II p11 D 25 '38; p24 Ja 14 '40
Sci ns 91:sup8 Ja 19 '40
Sci N L 37:59 Ja 27 '40
Sci Am 161:18-19 Jl '39 por tabs
Time 33:69 F 27 '39 por; 35:42 Ja 29 '40 por; 35:67-8 My 6 '40

American Men of Science
Who's Who in America

BEVIN, ERNEST 1884- British trade union leader; present Minister of Labor

Address: b. Transport House, Smith Sq, London, S. W. 1, England

Soon after his appointment as Minister of Labor at the beginning of May 1940, Ernest Bevin said: "I hope the War Cabinet will not allow vested interests, profits or anything else to stand in the way of maximum production. If this is the policy of the government I will ask my people to work like hell to save the lives of our lads." This plain, forceful statement in the language of the people epitomizes the character of the man. From humble beginnings as a farm boy he has risen to his present great responsibilities (his latest is as a member of Churchill's War Cabinet) through proved merit as a trade union organizer and administrator. Trade unionism has been his life. He had never even been in Parliament until June 22, 1940 when he was reported to have been returned unopposed at a by-election in Central Wandsworth (London).

Bevin is a huge, ruddy-faced, bull-like man, with a voice to match. He has always been a fighter of redoubtable quality, and in the past has been the implacable political enemy of the present Prime Minister, Winston Churchill (see sketch this issue). Personally, however, they warmly respect each other, and Churchill has described Bevin as the ablest figure in British industry. His biggest single achievement so far has been the amalgamation of large numbers of separate unions into one huge body called the Transport and General Workers' Union, which numbers over half a million members. He has done valuable work on the Economic Committee of the Trades Union Congress (the co-ordinating body for all British trade unions) and in 1920, in a famous 11-hour speech, was instrumental in securing a minimum wage for the dockers. An enormous worker, forthright and unsubtle, he mistrusts the intellectual wing of the party. He is earnest, combative, sometimes dictatorial, and has high ideals, some of which he has seen come to realization.

Born in the country village of Winsford, Somersetshire, Bevin lost both his parents before he was eight and was brought up by a sister in Devonshire. But she was very poor, and in 1894, when he was only 10, she sent him to work on a farm, where he received his board and 12 cents a week. Very soon he left for the nearest large city, Bristol, where he became successively page boy at a restaurant, tram conductor, shop assistant and vanman. He was fired from tram conducting for making an excited speech at a Sweated Industries exhibition. As a truck driver his work lay at the Bristol docks; so when he came to join a union it was the Dockers' Union (Carters' Section).

He had frequent periods of unemployment, and from 1905 to 1909 was secretary of the West of England Unemployment Movement. The trade union pioneer, Ben Tillett, perceived that he had energy and merit and persuaded him easily enough to make union organization his career. In 1911 he became branch secretary of the Dockers' Union; then district secretary, national organizer and assistant general secretary. He saw that the weakness of the movement for collective bargaining lay in the multiplicity of unions covering similar trades and set to work to negotiate amalgamation. All these activities covered the period from 1911 to 1919.

In 1920 Bevin went up to London, and in February of that year delivered the famous 11-hour speech before the Transport Workers' Court of Inquiry which resulted in the dockers' receiving a standard minimum wage. By this speech Bevin first sprang into nationwide renown, and was dubbed "the dockers' K. C." (a King's Counsel being the highest grade of advocate in England).

Bevin had made an attempt at Parliament in 1918, contesting Central Bristol, but was heavily defeated by Sir Thomas Inskip. In 1919 he acted as one of fourteen mediators in a big railroad strike; in 1920 he became joint secretary of the Council of Action (a body envisaging political changes to be brought by industrial action); and in 1921 he did good work on a Tramway Inquiry.

The year 1922 brought the great triumph for which he had worked for many years, the merging of thirty-two unions into one big national organization, the Transport and General Workers' Union, with himself as general secretary. The fine headquarters building of the Union, Transport House in Westminster, London, now houses not only its own people but the Trades Union Congress itself. Its board room contains a bronze bust of Bevin by E. Whitney-Smith, presented in gratitude for the amalgamation and unveiled in 1930 by Ben Tillett.

Meanwhile Bevin's first two years in London had been filled with another major occupation. In 1920 Labor's newspaper, the Daily Herald, was a thin and poorly run sheet; and Bevin was one of those trade union leaders who believed that the movement's vital interests demanded an up-to-date and influential organ. He and his fellow unionists worked tirelessly to improve the Daily Herald. The turning point came in 1922 when the editorial direction was given over to H. Hamilton Fyfe (see sketch this issue), a journalist who had done distinguished service on the London Times and the Daily Mail. In four years he raised the circulation from 130,000 copies to 450,000. Bevin was co-opted to the directorial board; but from Fyfe's autobiography, My Seven Selves, it does not appear that he was very helpful on the editorial side. Fyfe resigned in 1926. The paper is now jointly run by the publishing house of Odhams and the Trades Union Congress and circulates well over a million copies. Thus another dream of Bevin's has come true.

In 1926 Bevin was on the general council of the Trades Union Congress and took an active part in the general strike. It was he who announced its beginning to the press. The same year saw him visiting the United States as member of a Government Industrial Mission of Inquiry. In 1929 he served on the Macmillan Committee on Finance and Industry and in 1931 again attempted Parliament, contesting Gateshead without success. He created some stir in 1933 with a well-thought-out scheme to deal with the crying problem of unemployment, his chief suggestions being the retirement of elderly workers on pension, the raising of the school-leaving age to 16, and the introduction of the 40-hour week.

Like most prominent Labor leaders in England, Bevin has often been assailed not only from the Right but from the extreme Left. In November 1933 there was heard an action by Bevin against the Communist organ, the Daily Worker, for alleged libel contained in an article accusing Bevin of betraying trade union interests. The decision was in his favor, and he was awarded the enormous sum of £7,000 (about $28,000) in damages.

Wm. Vandivert

ERNEST BEVIN

BEVIN, ERNEST—*Continued*

In September 1936 Bevin reached the highest position in the whole British Labor movement by his election as chairman of the General Council of the Trades Union Congress; and he had the unusual honor of being elected for a second term in 1937.

When Neville Chamberlain resigned office early in May 1940, Bevin was an obvious choice for high office, despite his lack of Parliamentary experience. It says much for Mr. Churchill's real desire to form the strongest possible government regardless of party lines that he should incorporate into his team this old adversary, whose views differ so radically from his own.

Bevin has begun well, but he has a colossal task in hand, not the least part of which is to adapt the ample reserves of available labor to the specific task of making munitions. He has wide compulsory powers for transference and so forth, but the British have noted with real satisfaction that so far he has not had to use them. Perhaps only a man with Bevin's record of service to labor could have ventured to ask the working man to work twelve hours a day for seven days a week.

References

Amalg Eng Union Mo J p39-41 Je '32
Collier's 106:15+ Ag 31 '40 por
Daily Express S 24 '36
Daily Herald S 24 '36
Life 9:107-16 N 11 '40 il
New Statesman & Nation 6:870 D 30 '33
Picture Post 7:18-9 Je 1 '40
Scholastic 37:10 S 23 '40 por
Fyfe, H. H. My Seven Selves 1936
Who's Who

BEVIS, HOWARD LANDIS Nov 19, 1885- President of Ohio State University
Address: Ohio State University, Columbus, Ohio

On February 1, 1940, Dr. Bevis left his position as professor of law and government at Harvard University and took over the presidency of Ohio State University. He succeeded George Washington Rightmire, president from 1926 to 1938, who has retired. Dr. Bevis was born on a farm at Bevis, Ohio, the son of Edgar and Cara (Corson) Bevis. He studied and later taught law at the University of Cincinnati, and first won fame as a Cincinnati political reformer. Urged by a classmate, Alma D. Murray (whom he married in 1914), he aided in the election of the first woman to Cincinnati's school board. While teaching law he took part in the practical work of organization politics—work which he considered a diversion from the serious duties of a professor. When he found that Cincinnati needed cleaning up he drafted a new city-manager charter.

HOWARD LANDIS BEVIS

Dr. Bevis was appointed Director of Finance for Ohio when former Governor George White took control of the state government in 1931. It was a difficult task, for funds of the state were dangerously low and revenues were falling. Bevis effected drastic economies by cutting Ohio's budget from $86,000,000 to $48,000,000. From 1933 to 1935 he sat as a Supreme Court judge, then was called upon to reorganize the state's finance department for Governor Davey. That task accomplished, he accepted a professorship at Harvard.

"Tall, ruddy, leathery Howard ('Stick') Bevis is a Methodist and a Democrat," and is well acquainted with the problems of administering the nation's fifth largest university. It has an enrollment of more than 13,000 students, and was founded in 1870 as a land-grant college with its main function to help farmers. Even now less than a fifth of its students enroll in the arts college.

Dr. Bevis is the author of *Cochran's Law Lexicon* (3rd ed.); *Ohio Law Quizzer;* and is co-author of *Private International Law in Ohio Jurisprudence*. He is also a frequent contributor to law periodicals.

References

N Y Herald Tribune p16 Ja 9 '40
N Y Sun p3 Ja 9 '40 por
Sch & Soc 51:47 Ja 13 '40
Time 35:74-5 Ja 22 '40 il
Who's Who in America

BINET-VALMER, JEAN (bē-nā′-väl-mẽr′) 1875—July 1940 French author; originated plan to bury an unknown soldier under the Arc de Triomphe in Paris; author of many novels, several of which dealt with the religious struggles of Switzerland in the sixteenth century; best-known work was *The Foreigners*

References

Europa v2

Obituaries

N Y Herald Tribune p14 Jl 24 '40

BINKLEY, ROBERT CEDRIC Dec 10, 1897—Apr 11, 1940. Head of the history department of Western Reserve University's Flora Stone Mather College; author

ROBERT C. BINKLEY

References

Who's Who in America

Obituaries

N Y Herald Tribune p18 Ap 12 '40
N Y Times p23 Ap 12 '40

BIRGE, RAYMOND THAYER Mar 13, 1887- Physicist

Address: b. University of California, Berkeley, California; h. 1639 La Vereda St, Berkeley, California

On February 29, 1940 Mr. Raymond T. Birge, University of California physicist, when presenting the Nobel Prize to Professor Ernest O. Laurence (see sketch this issue) announced the discovery of a radioactive form of carbon by Dr. S. Ruben and Dr. M. D. Kamen of the Radiation Laboratory of the University of California.

Since germs consume living tissues which contain carbon, and their excretions (which also contain carbon) are often the poisons that cause sickness, it should be possible to give animals the new electrified substance in food and then study how bacteria use it for their own ends. Other forms of radioactive carbon lose their electrical qualities rapidly, but the type discovered at the University of California has a relatively long life.

Dr. Birge has been chairman of the department of physics at the University of California since 1933. He was born in Brooklyn, March 13, 1887. He received B. A., M. A. and Ph. D. degrees at the University of Wisconsin. He was instructor in physics at Syracuse University, (1913-18), and at California has been professor of physics since 1920. In 1913 he married Irene A. Walsh of Redfield, South Dakota; their home is in Berkeley, California.

Dr. Birge has specialized in spectroscopy; band and line series relations in spectra; carbon and oxygen isotopes; probable values of general physical constants.

References

Newsweek 15:47 Mr 11 '40
Sci ns 91:323-9 Ap 5 '40

American Men of Science
Who's Who in America

BLACK, ALEXANDER Feb 7, 1859—May 8, 1940 Expert on photography; deviser of a method of accompanying lantern slides with narrative; called "father of the photoplay"; newspaper editor; artist; author

References

Who's Who in America

Obituaries

N Y Times p23 My 9 '40
Variety p32 My 15 '40

BLAKE, NICHOLAS, pseud. *See* Day-Lewis, C.

BLAKER, RICHARD Mar 4, 1893—Feb 19, 1940 Author

Richard Blaker, British novelist and screen writer, died at Santa Monica, California, after an illness of several weeks. He turned to fiction writing after receiving his master's degree at Oxford. His first novel, *Voice in the Wilderness*, was published in 1922. Among his popular books were *Medal Without Bar,* a war novel published in 1930; *Here Lies a Most Beautiful Lady* (1935); and *Love Went A-Riding* (1938). His last screen assignment was with Samuel Goldwyn on *MacIntosh.* He is survived by his widow, Mayo Blaker, and a daughter.

References

Sat R Lit 13:11 F 29 '36 por

Who's Who

Obituaries

Pub W 137:898 F 24 '40
Variety 131:141 F 28 '40

RICHARD BLAKER

BLANCH, ARNOLD June 4, 1896- American artist

Address: b. c/o Associated American Artists, 711 Fifth Ave, New York City; h. Woodstock, New York

"Temperamentally, he disagrees. He disagreed with millions of his countrymen in 1917. He disagreed with his father and became a painter, and, at one time or another, he has disagreed with most of his contemporaries on the subject of painting."

That is how a critic once characterized Arnold Blanch, 26 of whose most recent paintings were shown at the Associated American Artists' Galleries April 15 to May 4, 1940. They included both landscapes and portrait work—the products of eight months of travel through the West and the South —and other paintings stretching back over the last five years since his last exhibition. Of his landscapes the New York *Herald Tribune* said: "They reflect an honest search after truth, but that truth is curiously tinctured by a somewhat gloomy sentiment. It is in only one landscape, *Suwanee River,* that Mr. Blanch appears willing to strike a cheerfuller note." The New York *Post* speaks of the artist's blend of "romanticism", "tart realism" and "ironic humor," and finds the *Flower Makers* and *The People* strongest of his paintings. *Cue* particularly approves of *Sunday Landscape* and another landscape called *Swamp Folks,* but finds "*Suwanee River* and other artificially colored pictures . . . no more of the place than Al Jolson is Mammy's boy." *Time* considers him a remarkably unaffected painter who succeeds in presenting the United States scene without trimmings—"no gravy, no ketchup." It appears that the critics also disagree when it comes to Mr. Blanch.

He was born in the little town of Mantorville, Minnesota on June 4, 1896, the son of Louis and Bertha (Adler) Blanch. His mother painstakingly painted on china, his aunt conscientiously copied paintings and he began to draw as soon as he could hold a pencil. When the family moved to Minneapolis, Arnold attended the Minneapolis School of Fine Arts, and after four years of cast-copying and life classes won a fellowship for the Art Students League in New York. At that time such men as Robert Henri, John Sloan, George Bellows and Kenneth Hayes Miller were working and teaching there, and it was the latter who exerted a particular influence on the young student.

When War came the 21-year-old Blanch, then working as a commercial artist (he once designed advertisements for Pluto Water), was drafted into the American Expeditionary Force. He was unhappy about it until he managed to secure a year's educational leave in order to travel through Europe, visiting the museums, studying the old masters and painting in out-of-the-way places. Upon his return he did commercial work again for awhile, then around 1923 moved to the artists' colony at Woodstock with his wife, Lucille Blanch, another former student of the Minneapolis School of Fine Arts. There the young couple performed the almost unique feat of living by art alone, with occasional not-too-profitable ventures into running a cafeteria, looming rugs, hunting and fishing for their food. In 1926 two years later he again left the United States—this time to study in Italy; and upon Blanch gave his first one-man exhibition; his return in 1929 gave a second one-man show.

In 1930 he was offered a teaching position at California's School of Fine Arts in San Francisco and he promptly accepted, crossing the continent in his trusty old Ford. Although he had won prizes before, it was while in California that substantial recognition first began to come to him as an artist, for during this period of teaching the Metropolitan Museum, the Whitney Museum and the Palace of the Legion of Honor all purchased paintings of his.

In 1933 both Mr. and Mrs. Blanch were given Guggenheim Fellowships to travel abroad for a year, and for the third time Blanch painted in Europe, for the most part working near Renoir's home in Southern France.

In 1938 the painter was awarded the third Carnegie International Award of $500 for *The People,* shown in the recent exhibition. In the same year he was awarded the Carol H. Beck Medal for his *Portrait of a Man,* and his *Portrait of Doris Lee* has very recently been purchased by the University of Nebraska.

A great many of the paintings in the recent exhibition have as their source a summer spent teaching at the Colorado Springs Art Center in 1939. Although known as a

"Rehn member" of the Woodstock colony, a painter of many New England scenes, Blanch took advantage of his new geographical situation to make excursions to all parts of the West and the Southwest. In the winter he extended these excursions further South, and the result was a group of paintings ranging from the sharp mountain scenes of Colorado and the West to portraits of Negro preachers, Southern farmers and Suwanee River scenes. The year before, while an instructor at the Art Students League, he had completed murals for the post offices at Norwalk, Connecticut and Fredonia, New York.

As an artist, Arnold Blanch cannot be easily summed up. He has always been known as a painter of the "American scene," but his rejection of art for art's sake has never been so complete as in recent years. Most critics agree that his pictures have become more and more informed by philosophic statement, by his increasing interest in the world around him; one critic has said that even his earliest landscapes were characterized by more drama, more human comment than most, and that his simplest nudes and portraits were "more earthy, more aware of life as growth," than those of most of his contemporaries. In the past few years he has been generally known as a social painter, although *Time* describes his recent exhibit as "unburdened with 'social significance.'"

Blanch once stated his artistic credo thus: "A painter should not only create art, but use art in order to create." He felt that the fault of the public's indifference to art lay with painters, who "in their frantic endeavor for self-expression have lost the art of being understood," and he defended the "literary" element in his painting by saying: "I can go much further with a canvas now. The longer I work, the more possibilities open up. The canvas grows increasingly interesting as I paint on it, and when you just look around for a pleasant landscape or an attractive still-life to paint, that never happens." Whether or not this is his present theory, it explains a large part of his work.

Critics' estimates of his talent have varied; as is not unusual, some have praised his painting for the very qualities which others have found distinctly unpleasant. His New England scenes (such as *The Farmer, New England, Red House*) were briefly described by one critic as "drab and not very characterful landscapes," often "freighted with macabre symbolism." Another critic found in them "a nostalgia for the heroic past of our own country. His hunting and fishing take him back into this past—give him a sense of vigor and of solitude that are typical of it. And from these excursions come brooding, often lonely, pictures, imbued with a sense of tragedy." *The People*, the picture which won the coveted Carnegie Award in 1938, was described by one critic as "a mystifying and rather confused

Peter A. Juley & Son
ARNOLD BLANCH

statement of some sort of political ideology unredeemed by quality of painting" and brought forth the following unenthusiastic comment from another: "The artist appears to have a curious distaste for the people whose cause he pleads, and in this picture the figures resemble a group of actors waiting for the cue to vent the injustices of their fate. Meanwhile one can imagine that the artist, laying down his brush, is saying to himself virtuously: 'Thank God I'm not a lyric painter.'"

Conflicting with his apparent preoccupation with current social and economic problems is Blanch's love of rural, almost pioneer life. Though he has never worked in his native state (which, in turn, has never honored him by buying one of his pictures), "gray-thatched" Arnold Blanch still confesses a "chronic nostalgia for Minnesota." But he does not believe in regionalism in American art. "I shall never again believe," he said after his recent travels, "that an artist should settle in one place to paint. I have become conscious of the rich material all over the country, and I should like to go back again to Colorado, Arkansas, South Carolina, Georgia and so many other artistically exciting locales." He did get to Colorado in the summer of 1940 when he taught at the Colorado Springs Fine Arts Center.

References

Am Mag Art 27:548 O '34 il; 28:364-70 Je '35; 29:26 Ja '36 il

Art Digest 13:5 O 15 '38; 9:19 Mr 1 '35

Art N 37:9 O 15 '38 il

Cue 9:31 Ap 27 '40

London Studio 17 (Studio 117):3 Ja '39 il

BLANCH, ARNOLD—*Continued*

> Mag Art 30:312 My '37 il; 31:535 S '38 il; 31:662 N '38 il; 33:103 F '40 il
>
> N Y Herald Tribune p23 Ap 16 '40; VI p8 Ap 21 '40
>
> Time 35:39 Ap 29 '40 il
>
> Boswell, P. Jr. Modern American Painting 1939
>
> Who's Who in American Art

BLATCHLEY, WILLIS STANLEY Oct 6, 1859—May 28, 1940 Naturalist; state geologist of Indiana for 17 years; author of numerous textbooks

WILLIS S. BLATCHLEY

References

> Nature 19:135 Mr '32
>
> American Men of Science
>
> Who's Who Among North American Authors
>
> Who's Who in America

Obituaries

> N Y Herald Tribune p14 My 30 '40

BLAU, BELA 1896—Oct 21, 1940 Theatrical producer; former accountant and teacher of accountancy at the College of the City of New York; became member of business staff of Theatre Guild, for whom he introduced theatre cost system which other managements adopted; produced a number of plays, his most successful *Having Wonderful Time*, done in association with Marc Connelly; managed summer stock company in Harrison, Maine

Obituaries

> N Y Herald Tribune p24 O 22 '40 por
>
> N Y Times p23 O 22 '40 por

BLITZSTEIN, MARC (blits'stīne) Mar 2, 1905- Composer
Address: 496 Hudson St, New York City

In April 1940 Marc Blitzstein was awarded a Guggenheim Fellowship to help him continue his work in musical composition. An unorthodox composer whose experiments in new forms and tonalities once made him one of the more difficult moderns to listen to, with *The Cradle Will Rock* and *I've Got the Tune* he became one of America's popular musicians.

The Cradle Will Rock has been called "the American opera that many of us have waited for." On its opening night in December 1937 it looked as though we would have to wait for it a good while longer. Blitzstein had written it and Orson Welles had directed it for the Federal Theatre, but the Federal Theatre suddenly cut down on its activities and on opening night the crowd stood before the closed doors of the Maxine Elliott Theatre. They were told to wait, the cast came out and sang songs. Suddenly a little man in the crowd stepped up and offered to take everybody over to his theatre, the Venice, 20 blocks away. An upright piano was loaded on a truck and everybody went over to the Venice, where, without scenery, without orchestra, Blitzstein played the score of his opera and the rest of the company acted from seats in the audience. When the play was finally put on commercially much of this informality was kept.

The story of *The Cradle Will Rock* is the story of a capitalist who fights unionization. Mr. Mister controls Steeltown; he has a judge, a college president, a news editor and a doctor under his thumb and by bribery and intimidation has coerced them and other leading citizens to serve on a "Liberty Committee" to fight the union. The action centers in a night court. Here are a prostitute, a broken-down druggist and the "Liberty Committee" (brought by mistake). Here is painted a picture of the whole of Steeltown.

John Mason Brown called *The Cradle Will Rock* "the most exciting propagandist *tour de force* our stage has seen since Clifford Odets' *Waiting for Lefty* burst like a bombshell on this town." Its material is familiar enough, but its technique is original and striking, and it drives its point home with a vigor and cogency that cannot be denied. Realism and stylization, tragedy and farce, burlesque and passionate propaganda are mixed at will, "but to good effect." In fact the only critic who failed to be impressed by the force of this opera was George Jean Nathan, who said that *The Cradle Will Rock* "strikes me as being little more than the kind of thing Cole Porter (see sketch this issue) might have written if, God forbid, he had gone to Columbia instead of Yale."

It has been said that "Blitzstein's music has become alive since he embraced the people's cause; his best art has been propaganda art." Blitzstein himself firmly believes that we "must use art to fight Fas-

cism." He says he got these liberal ideas
"by seeing talented young people thrown
out into a world of topsy turvy values. . .
I soon saw that the artist, the writer, the
composer suffered. There seemed to be two
ways out for the sensitive artist: one to
live in a world bounded by G clefs and Bach
and the small talk of musicians—a world of
half-notes; the other I took. Feeling that
sharp, acute discontent I analyzed, dissected.
Finally I realized that this world I never
made needed change and as an artist I could
use my music as a weapon in that struggle."

Marc Blitzstein was born in Philadelphia,
where "there's a Blitzstein active in every
progressive movement," on March 2, 1905.
He went to grammar school there and
became a scholarship student at the University of Pennsylvania. But he flunked
gym and flunked out. "I didn't care," he
says, "that is, after a while. I had decided
on a musical career long before." He had
given concerts at five and composed at
seven, and at fifteen appeared as solo
pianist with the Philadelphia Orchestra.

Blitzstein attended the Curtis School of
Music, where he studied composition with
Rosario Scalero, and commuted to New
York to study piano with Alexander Siloti.
After he decided to become a serious
concert composer he went abroad, in 1926,
to study with Nadia Boulanger in Paris
and with Schönberg in Berlin. Schönberg
is said to have regarded him as "his most
talented United States pupil," and in turn
Blitzstein was influenced by Schönberg, as
well as by Stravinsky (see sketch this issue) and Hindemith.

Back in America he lectured for women's
clubs—"You know the sort of thing. West
86th Street to 1 University Place-dowa-
gers, debutantes and do-littlers. I was a
blender of musical pills." He lectured on
music at Columbia University, Vassar and,
later, at the New School for Social
Research. And he continued to compose.
He composed orchestral works—*Jig Saw*
(1927), a ballet; a *Romantic Piece* for
orchestra (1930); a piano concerto (1931).
He composed chamber music—a piano
sonata (1927), a string quartet, a serenade
for string quartet and *Percussion Music
for the Piano* (1929). He composed choral
works—*The Condemned*, (1933) a choral
opera, and the *Children's Cantata* (1935).

Many of these works have been performed at concerts of ultra-modern music
in New York, Paris and London and show
him "a vigorous and original voice in
modern American music." He himself does
not consider his music experimental; "for
materials I use what has been bequeathed
to our generation of composers by the
pioneers of the movement called 'modern
music.'"

Blitzstein's *Triple Sec* (1928), which was
a "little opera" given its première by the
Philadelphia Orchestra, was later incorporated into the *Garrick Gaieties* of 1930.
This was Blitzstein's first excursion into

Musical America

MARC BLITZSTEIN

the theatre. Another opera, *Parabola and
Circula*, followed in 1929. He continued
to do more in the same style. Then, as a
member of a composers' collective, he met
Hanns Eisler and Bertoldt Brecht, and it
was Brecht who gave him the idea for
The Cradle Will Rock.

Since *The Cradle Will Rock*, Blitzstein
has composed the music for the Mercury's
Julius Caesar, for Hemingway's movie, *The
Spanish Earth*, a sketch for *Pins and
Needles*. He is also the author of *I've
Got the Tune* (1937), a radio song-play
about a composer who wrote a tune but
couldn't think of any words for it. In the
play he travels around the world with his
secretary, "Beetzie, the shorthand speed
queen," in the hope that he will find someone who wants his tune. All the wrong
people get hold of it first—a decadent
German woman who runs a salon, a suicide,
a Fascist organization. But it finally finds
its rightful home when it is used by May
Day paraders. In 1939 Blitzstein composed
another opera, *No for an Answer,* based
on the chances of young aliens in the
modern world, which will probably be produced on Broadway in the 1940 to 1941
season. Since then he has been writing the
music and songs for the documentary film
Valley Town and composing the music for
Native Land, also a documentary film.

When he's not traveling, which he does
a good deal, Marc Blitzstein lives in New
York City, active as critic and lecturer
as well as composer and pianist. He has
no special method of composing, but works
whenever the mood seizes him. His great
interest these days is in operas such as
The Cradle Will Rock. But don't call them
operettas where he can hear you. He hates
the term. "To me it conjures up a world

BLITZSTEIN, MARC—*Continued*
of Viennese waltzes and Yum-Yums from
the *Mikado*."

References

Cur Hist 48:53 Ap '38
Daily Worker p5 D 7 '38
Mag Art 32:356-7+ Je '39 il
Musical Am 60:4 Ap 10 '40
Musical Courier 107:6 S 16 '33
Scrib Mag 103:70-1 Mr '38
Time 29:46+ Je 28 '37

Sobel, B. ed. Theatre Hand Book
1940
Thompson, O. ed. International Cyclopedia of Music and Musicians
1939
Who's Who in American Jewry
Wier, A. E. ed. Macmillan Encyclopedia of Music and Musicians
1938

BLOCH, CHARLES EDWARD (blŏkh)
Dec 22, 1861—Sept 2, 1940 Publisher of
Jewish periodicals and books; his publish-
ing house the oldest of its kind in the Eng-
lish-speaking world; active in Jewish affairs;
founder and former president of the Free
Synagogue of New York; founder of the
Jewish Institute of Religion

CHARLES EDWARD BLOCH

References

Pub W 131:37 Ja 2 '37
Who's Who in American Jewry

Obituaries

N Y Herald Tribune p20 S 3 '40
N Y Times p17 S 3 '40 por

BLOCK, RUDOLPH *See* Lessing, B.,
pseud.

KATHARINE BURR BLODGETT

BLODGETT, KATHARINE BURR Jan
10, 1898- Research physicist
Address: b. Research Laboratory, General
Electric Co, 1 River Rd, Schenectady, New
York; h. 18 N Church St, Schenectady, New
York

Dr. Blodgett has achieved outstanding
recognition as the discoverer of a long-
sought-for process for making glass invisible.
She was born at Schenectady in 1898, the
daughter of George Redington and Katharine
Buchanan (Burr) Blodgett. In 1917 she received a B. A. from Bryn Mawr and a year
later Chicago University gave her an M. S.
degree. Since 1918 she has been a research
physicist in the laboratories of the General
Electric Company in her home town. In 1924
she took a leave of absence and went to England for further study at the Cavendish Laboratories of Cambridge University. That year
she received her Ph. D. from Cambridge.

A plump, pleasant-faced woman with
sleeked-back dark hair, uptilted nose, horn-
rimmed glasses over a pair of merry eyes,
she received front page recognition in 1939
when she discovered a method of coating
glass which made it invisible. The coating is
colorless and exceedingly thin, in fact four
millionths of an inch. The day after her discovery was announced, two scientists using a
somewhat similar principle also announced their
formula for invisible glass.

As a basis for her "non-reflecting" glass,
Dr. Blodgett used scientific principles relating to the properties of thin films discovered
by a co-worker at General Electric's laboratory—Dr. Irving Langmuir (see sketch this
issue), Nobel Prize winner in chemistry.

"The process," said Dr. Blodgett, "is still
in a laboratory stage." With scientific caution, she does not admit that it can be offered
to the public yet. "However, we are hopeful

that we may soon do so," she says. When the new glass is placed on the market it will make it possible to see pictures framed under glass from all angles. Glare from reflected light has always been a problem of museums. Other uses are glass for automobile windshields, show cases, eye glasses and telescopes.

Dr. Blodgett is a petite person, just five feet tall. Resembling the unscientific members of her sex, she "loves gardening, is afraid of snakes, cooks well but won't if she can help it." She is a very modest person who admits that she is still puzzled by finding her name heading lists of outstanding women of 1939. In the book *Excursions in Science,* edited by Reynolds and Manning, (1939), she discusses in popular terms her work with Dr. Irving Langmuir in calculating the thickness of films that makes glass invisible, and explains the system of measuring gradations of color reflected on the films.

References

Ind Woman 18:36+ F '39; 19:29 Ja '40 por (p3)
N Y Times II p7 Je 12 '38; p19 D 27 '38; II p4 S 24 '39 por; p34 N 19 '39
N Y World-Telegram p22 F 16 '40
Time 33:33 Ja 9 '39 por
American Men of Science
American Women
[Blodgett, K. B.] Gauge That Measures Millionths of an Inch *In* Reynolds, N. B. and Manning, E. L., eds. Excursions in Science 1939

BLUM, LEON (blōom lâ-ō') Apr 9, 1872- Ex-Premier of France

In September 1940 Léon Blum was among those former French leaders uncomfortably quartered at the Château Chazeron not far from Riom, France, waiting to be tried there by the Vichy government. His Popular Front had been accused of "disrupting French home life, spreading sloth and dissatisfaction among French workers and generally running France by orders from the U. S. S. R.; he himself was indicted on October 19 for "betrayal of the duties of his charge." While he waited, before being taken to Riom in November 1940, the one-time Premier of France kept quietly to himself, "wearily stroked his straggling mustache, said little, did little"—probably thought much.

Léon Blum was born on April 9, 1872 at 151, Rue Saint-Denis, Paris. His father, Auguste Blum, an Alsatian Jew, was a fairly prosperous manufacturer of silks and ribbons; his mother, Marie Picart, was liberal-minded; his maternal grandmother, blind, but the owner of a bookstore, had "profound radical convictions" and used to hold political salons twice a week. Léon was the second of five boys, healthy and happy, his only handicap short-sightedness; his family expected him to become a brilliant

LEON BLUM

writer or an illustrious lawyer or both. From a little private school called the Pension Roux he went in 1881 to the Lycée Charlemagne, thence to the Lycée Henri IV, where he studied philosophy under Bergson, and in 1890 to the Ecole Normale Supérieure. Here he read philosophy for a year and failed two examinations, but after he transferred in 1891 to the law school at the Sorbonne he took his law degree in 1894 with highest possible honors. Not long afterward he passed the examination for *Conseil d'Etat* and became *auditeur* in that body. This meant that for 26 years his chief work was to aid the State in drafting legislation, in determining the bearing of new laws on those already in existence and in settling claims of individuals against the State. He was eventually to reach the top rank in civil service and become *maître de requêtes* (solicitor general).

Even before he was out of school Blum had begun to frequent the literary salons of Paris, becoming acquainted with well-known figures like Hérédia, Mallarmé, Valéry, Gide, Anatole France, becoming known himself as an intellectual and something of a dandy. His earliest passion was for the theatre, at which he was a frequent first-nighter, and in 1892 he began to contribute dramatic criticism to the snobbish *La Revue Blanche.* His anonymous *Nouvelles Conversations de Goethe avec Eckermann* was published there; after being introduced to horse racing at Longchamps he became so expert that he collaborated with Tristan Bernard in running its sporting page; next he was its literary editor until 1900; and he wrote for the review until it died in 1903.

After that it was dramatic criticism for *La Petite République, Le Matin* (for which he wrote until 1920) and, later, *Comoedia.* The young lawyer also contributed count-

BLUM, LEON—*Continued*

less articles on law, literature and life to other publications, but all so much on the *précieux* side that it is hard to believe he was already interested in anything so vulgar as politics. The librarian of the Ecole Normale had given him his first ideas of socialism; during the years of the Dreyfus controversy, from 1894 to 1899, Blum became an ardent Dreyfusard; and in 1899, three years after he had met and conceived a great admiration for the Socialist leader, Jean Jaurès, he joined the Socialist Party. From that time until the First World War Blum was an active Socialist, but still more an active journalist and man of letters. Both in 1902 and 1906 he refused when Jaurès urged him to stand for election to the Chamber, although when Jaurès founded *L'Humanité* as a Socialist daily early in the 1900's he became one of its chief contributors. His chief literary interest was still in the exclusive and the *précieux,* however. His book, *Du Mariage,* published in 1907, scandalized many by its advocacy of premarital experience for women. An excellent duelist, in 1912 he fought his last duel—with a dramatist whose work he had criticized. In 1914 he published one of his best critical works, *Stendhal et le Beylisme.*

The murder of Jaurès on July 13, 1914 not only robbed Blum of a close friend and beloved leader, but did much to drive him into active political life. When the Socialist, Marcel Sembat, took a portfolio in the "National Union" Cabinet and asked him to act as *chef de cabinet* he finally agreed. Sembat resigned in December 1916 and no Socialists served in the ensuing Clémenceau government, but the anonymous *Lettres sur la Réforme Gouvernmentale* which came out in *La Revue de Paris* at the end of 1918 gave Blum's ideas as to how the administration could be captured and run by Labor.

Early in 1919 Blum was made chairman of the Socialist Party executive board and elected to the Chamber from the first division of Paris. This meant giving up the *Conseil d'Etat* post; so Blum sat for the Bar examination, was admitted and soon had a lucrative practice, specializing in commercial and financial cases. He was able to live and entertain in comfort, but the stories about his being a millionaire and owning a magnificent collection of silverware have been discredited.

Blum's first speech in the Chamber profoundly impressed the deputies, and he was made Parliamentary Secretary to the Socialist Party. In 1921 he was a leader of the dissident group when the Socialist Party split at the national convention at Tours, the majority favoring affiliation with the Third International. *L'Humanité* thus became the Communist organ, but that same year Blum founded *Le Populaire* as the official organ of the Socialist Party. He gave the paper life and vigor and in time made it a powerful political force. Blum refused to think of collaborating as a member of a minority party in any government coalition, however. He opposed the governments of Millerand and Poincaré and the occupation of the Ruhr, was ejected from Parliament by Communist intervention in 1928 and remained outside for a year.

Returning in 1929 as deputy from Narbonne (an agricultural and mainly winegrowing constituency), Blum grew to be an increasingly prominent figure in the years when a Popular Front of Communists, Socialists and Radical-Socialists was created to combat the growing power of Hitler and the increasingly violent tactics of native Monarchist and Fascist organizations. On February 12, 1934 Blum and his onetime enemy, the Communist Marcel Cachin, spoke from the same platform at a big popular demonstration—and the Popular Front was in being at last. A gifted speaker, but obviously more at home in conference-room meetings than on the platform at huge mass meetings, to some Blum seemed a strange figure as its leader. On February 13, 1935 the scholarly intellectual nearly lost his life when he was attacked by a group of Fascists. Nevertheless the 1936 elections were an overwhelming victory for the Left, and on the evening of June 4 Blum became Premier of France's first Popular Front government.

He had waited a month before taking office, although the reactionary groups were desperate and rumors had been circulating that the Fascist leagues were about to stage a *coup.* In the meanwhile he had been making far-from-militant speeches asking for patience both from the "200 Families" and the Popular Front and had announced: "We want to collaborate with all the nations of the world, whatever their internal policy, in eliminating the causes of conflict which might someday lead to war. We reject war absolutely." Labor had been growing restive, showing its power by a wave of "stay-in" strikes. Blum took office on the crest of the wave, formed a Cabinet of Socialists and Radical-Socialists, and a week later most of the strikers were back at their machines. Promised social legislation was pushed forward with remarkable speed: the 40-hour week, vacations with pay, obligatory collective bargaining, the nationalization of the armament industry, the abolishment of the regency of the Bank of France, the dissolution of the armed Fascist leagues.

In spite of their enthusiasm for these measures the more Leftist elements soon began to question the foreign policy of Blum's government. Foreign Minister Delbos was observed making overtures to both Italy and Germany, saying that France had no intentions of doubting Hitler's promise to keep the peace; and there were still no conversations between the general staffs of France and the U. S. S. R. The cornerstone of Blum's policy seemed to be Franco-British amity. When in July 1936 Franco's insurrection began in Spain, Blum made a trip to London. After two days of conversations both he and Delbos decided to follow the British lead of observing strict neutrality, and Delbos proceeded to collect assurances from Italy and Germany that they would not interfere. Soviet proposals for aiding Spain were rejected, also advances on the part of the Turkish government. Blum declared a policy of "non-intervention," saying Britain would not support France if she should be drawn into war. Nevertheless the Right began to accuse his government of secretly sending arms and planes to the Loyalists, and on August 8 the embargo was made official. A cry of "Arms for Spain! Airplanes for Spain!" went up from the Left, and the Right was delighted, seeing the Socialist Party splitting wide open on the issue.

Big Business, always critical of the effect of Popular Front social legislation on the national economy, wasn't exactly inclined to help stabilize Blum's government. Attacks on the national currency resulted in the autumn of 1936 in devaluation and the Tripartite Monetary Agreement between France, Britain and the United States. As the conflict over Spain grew more serious, Blum and his government continued to claim that Italy and Germany were observing the non-intervention agreement and to paint vivid pictures of the war into which France might be drawn by changing her policy. A great many Socialists as well as Radical-Socialists were won over to this view, and as the dividing line between the different parties in the Popular Front grew more and more sharp over this issue, more legislative concessions had to be made to the Right.

In 1937 came the Paris Exhibition, designed to raise money, but the same year there was a new flight of capital from France. Though Blum had once said: "I would rather have a king than grant full powers!" he was forced to ask Parliament for decree powers in June 1937. On this issue he was defeated in the Senate, and although his Cabinet would not have had to resign, since a bill winning three times in the Chamber becomes law even though the Senate rejects it, Blum tendered his resignation. The one-year rule of his government was at an end. Two years later Blum said: "It was not the financial difficulties which conquered us; it was not even the adverse votes of the Senate—nothing would have overthrown us if we had not had the feeling that the working class was no longer responding to our advice."

During Blum's term in office appropriations for national defense had been highest in the peacetime history of France, but even at the time certain Rightist circles claimed that many of them were going for other purposes. In any case, the Vichy government accuses the Popular Front government of having squandered these funds by laws restricting production and thus leaving France totally unprepared for war.

In the succeeding Popular Front government Blum served under M. Chautemps as Vice-Premier. When on March 12, 1938 Hitler invaded Austria, Chautemps resigned and left his countless troubles to the Socialist leader. Blum wanted for the first time to form a Cabinet which would include both the extreme Left and the extreme Right, from Thorez to Marin, but the Right refused to collaborate. Again it was a group of Socialists and Radical-Socialists which he headed; again his was a policy of "non-intervention" in Spain; again he was defeated in the Senate. This time Blum was Premier only three weeks before resigning.

Although since that time Blum has held no Cabinet post, his political influence has been great. In September 1938 he was urging Roosevelt to act for peace in the Czechoslovakian crisis, but he could not approve of Munich, feeling more shame than relief at the shape that particular peace took. In January 1939 he quit law to devote all his time to politics and in March of that year he was opposing the bill to give Daladier (see sketch this issue) dictatorial powers. With the outbreak of World War II, however, his voice became remarkably similar to Daladier's. He was a strong supporter of the War; he defended the illegalization of the Communist Party; he scolded the British Laborites for their original opposition to pre-War conscription. In May 1940, attending the British Labor Party conference, he ridiculed the suggestion that the French government might impose a military tyranny on the nation and said the death penalty for the spreading of "seditious propaganda" was a "penalty for treason to the French people." After the fall of France it was reported that he had left the country, his last public appearance having been at the National Assembly at Vichy on July 12, where he voted against the Pétain (see sketch this issue) dictatorship; but on September 15, 1940 he joined France's two War Premiers in "administrative custody." During the interval he had been staying with friends in his electoral district near Narbonne, editing the newspaper, *République Sociale*, which attacked the Vichy government's suppression of the Masons and other secret societies.

Blum's "gray hair, long face with the spectacles and the wispy walrus mustache, his bent lean figure and the flailing motions with which his stringy arms accompanied and emphasized his words" for a long time have been a familiar sight to the French people and a delight to the caricaturist, as was his big black Latin Quarter hat. Though not quite so much ascetic as esthete, Blum is almost a teetotaler, smokes denicotinized cigarettes and isn't a really famous gourmet. In 1924 he said: "For 30 years I have done precisely the thing for which I was least fitted. What I really love is solitude and books." When Anthony Eden (see sketch this

BLUM, LEON—*Continued*

issue) saw Blum for the first time it was said that the conversation languished altogether until the two of them plunged into an enthusiastic discussion of Proust.

Blum doesn't have a great deal of physical stamina, has no shoulders, "only antennae," is noted for his high-pitched voice. It is said that his impeccable manners often made him seem distant and even cold, particularly before a working-class audience. After the Popular Front had been in control for a week an opponent consoled himself, saying: "After all, Léon *is* an aristocrat and a gentleman." Blum's tendency to compromise has been called both his strength and his weakness, and some have questioned his political realism. For instance, he received Dr. Schacht on the day Hitler doubled the length of military service in Germany and greeted him hopefully with: "You know that I am a Jew and that I do not agree with the anti-Semitic measures in Germany. And now we can talk things over!"

In 1896 Blum married Lise Bloch, whom he had known since childhood. A year after her death (December 1931) Blum married Thérèse Peyreyna, also Jewish, who died in January 1938. He has one son by his first marriage.

References

Atlan 160:431-9 O '37
Cur Hist 49:26+ N '38
Nation 144:719-20 Je 26 '37
N Y Herald Tribune p4 My 16 '40
Newsweek 16:29 S 23 '40
Time 29:17-18 Je 28 '37; 36:30-1 S 30
'40
Fraser, G. and Natanson, T. Léon
Blum, Man and Statesman 1938
Gunther, J. Daladier and Blum *In*
Inside Europe p145-65 1940
Qui Etes-Vous?
Simone, A. J'Accuse 1940
Stokes, R. L. Léon Blum 1937
Von Paassen, P. Men and Events *In*
Days of Our Years p162-209 1939
Who's Who
Who's Who in American Jewry

BLUMER, GEORGE ALDER May 25, 1857—Apr 25, 1940 Psychiatrist; formerly superintendent of hospitals in Utica, New York and Providence, Rhode Island; brought about reforms in care of insane; writer on psychiatry

References

American Medical Directory 1938
American Men of Science 1938
Who Who's in America

Obituaries

N Y Herald Tribune p18 Ap 26 '40
N Y Times p21 Ap 26 '40

A. T. Beals

FRANZ BOAS

BOAS, FRANZ (bō'ăz fränts) July 9, 1858- Anthropologist

Address: b. Department of Anthropology, Columbia University, New York City; h. Grantwood, Bergen County, New Jersey

It is to be expected that Franz Boas, "one of the world's most distinguished anthropologists," should be a firm and articulate foe of Nazi racial theories. In *The Mind of Primitive Man* (1911) he demonstrated conclusively that races and sub-races were mixed; that no language was superior to another or better capable of expressing ideas; that there was no such thing as a pure race or even a "superior" one. "If we were to select the most intelligent, imaginative, energetic and emotionally stable third of mankind, all races would be represented," he said.

In 1931 Dr. Boas went back to his native Germany to receive an honorary degree from Kiel University. From 1933 on he bitterly denounced the "race nonsense" preached by Hitler, Goebbels and Streicher, and sadly contemplated the decline of science in Nazi Germany. In retaliation for this his books were withdrawn from circulation in the library of Kiel University. According to first reports they were burnt. His only comment on the burning was: "If people want to be crazy what can you do about it?"

Dr. Boas believes firmly in the principles of democracy which are inherent in his anthropological theories, and during the past years has been one of the staunchest fighters for the freedom of science and thought. In 1938 he headed a committee of American scientists which issued a manifesto in December of that year, signed by 1,284 leaders in the field of science. This manifesto stated: "American scientists hold fast to their conviction that science is wholly independent of national boundaries and race and creeds, and can flourish only when there is peace and intellectual freedom. It is in this light that we publicly condemn the Fascist position toward science."

He has been a vigorous and articulate opponent of the Dies Committee (see sketch this issue), insisting that it is "fundamentally opposed to the spirit of our Constitution and to the democratic principles of free discussion." Since February 1939 he has been chairman and guiding force of the American Committee for Democracy and Intellectual Freedom, which works with educators and scientists on public issues. In April 1940 he received this year's Teachers Union Medal for outstanding services in the cause of education for democracy. He was one of the members of the Committee who signed a statement challenging Dr. Butler's (see sketch this issue) position on "academic freedom" in his speech to the Columbia faculty in October 1940. Dr. Boas explains his activities for democracy by saying: "My ideals have developed because I am what I am and have lived where I have lived; and it is my purpose to work for these ideals because I am by nature active and because the conditions of our culture that run counter to my ideals stimulate me to action." He urges that we "be ready to maintain our democratic ideals in these turbulent times," that we "shun war unless it is carried to our shores."

Professor Franz Boas was born in Minden, Westphalia, Germany on July 9, 1858. He tells us that "the background of my early thinking was a German home in which the ideals of the Revolution of 1848 were a living force; my father liberal but not active in public affairs, my mother idealistic but with a lively interest in public matters.

"An early, intense interest in nature and a burning desire to see everything that I heard about dominated my youth. I lived in the surrounding world without speculation, naively enjoying every new impression." From 1877 to 1881 Franz Boas attended the German Universities of Heidelberg, Bonn and Kiel and in 1881 received his Ph. D. from Kiel, with a thesis on *The Nature of the Color of Water.* "My university studies were a compromise," he tells us. "On account of my intense emotional interest in the phenomena of the world, I studied geography; on account of my intellectual interests, I studied mathematics and physics."

After graduation Boas wanted to go to Greenland on a ship which was to bring back a corps of meteorologists. Boas financed the trip with a newspaper contract for travel articles. During his stay in Baffin Land he became so deeply interested in the culture of the Eskimos that he stayed a year. "A year spent as an Eskimo among Eskimos had a profound influence on the development of my views . . . because it led me . . . towards the desire to understand what determines the behavior of human beings." When Boas had finished a book about the Eskimos, he was an anthropologist for life.

After a year in the University of Berlin he went to the United States to marry Marie A. E. Krackowizer, the daughter of a distinguished surgeon, an emigrant who had fled to America from Austria. For a while he was associate editor of *Science,* after which ne joined the faculty of Clark University and was in charge of anthropology at the Chicago World's Fair from 1892 to 1895. On expeditions to the northern Pacific coast he studied Indian art, music, religion. His *Tsimshian Mythology* is regarded by experts as a classic concordance of North American myths.

In 1899 Dr. Boas joined the faculty of Columbia University, where in his first years "he was something of a storm center. To his German-trained mind the idea of popularization was repugnant. He snorted savagely that some of the students whom his renown had attracted had no business to be anthropologists." Later he softened and even went so far as to write a few books for popular consumption, notably *Anthropology and Modern Life* (1928).

Dr. Boas taught at Columbia until 1937, when he became professor emeritus. During his years there he was president of the American Association for the Advancement of Science (1931) and an honorary member or fellow of all of the world's leading anthropological societies. During these years he published *The Growth of Children* (1904); *Changes in Form of Body of Descendants of Immigrants* (1911); the *Mind of Primitive Man* (1911); *Primitive Art* (1927) and *Anthropology and Modern Life* (1928).

Changes in the Form of Body of Descendants of Immigrants was written at the request of the United States Department of Immigration, which was interested in finding out just what changes, if any, had taken place among the immigrants' descendants. Dr. Boas piled up evidence to show that changes in appearance, in time of puberty, in motor habits do take place.

In his books, in his many writings, Franz Boas has invaded almost every branch of the science of anthropology—linguistics, primitive mentality, folklore, ethnology, growth and senility, the physical effects of environment. "He reminds his colleagues of the oldtime family doctor who did everything from delivering babies to pulling teeth."

Even after these many years in America, Dr. Boas still speaks with a German accent. "The entire department of anthropology calls him 'Papa Franz.' He has no hobbies except playing the piano, which he does very well, and his grandchildren, who go to him with personal problems and tough Latin passages."

References

Forum 103:156-7 Mr '40
Nation 147:201-4 Ag 27 '38
New Repub 98:300-3 Ap 19 '39
N Y Herald Tribune p14 Ap 21 '40
Time 27:37-42 My 11 '36; por (cover);
    32:36 D 19 '38 por

BOAS, FRANZ—*Continued*
   International Who's Who 1940
   Trattner, E. R. Boas: Theory of Man
      In Architects of Ideas p351-74 1938
   Who's Who in America
   Who's Who in American Jewry

BODANZKY, ARTUR (bō-dänz'kē) Dec 16, 1877—Nov 23, 1939 Metropolitan Opera conductor

G. Maillard Kesslère
ARTUR BODANSKY

References
   New Yorker 6:23-6 Mr 15 '30
   Opera News 4:13 Mr 1 '40 por
   Outlook 154:315 F 19 '30
   Pierre Key's Musical Who's Who
   Who's Who in America 1938-39

Obituaries
   Etude 58:144 F '40
   N Y Herald Tribune p1 N 24 '39
   N Y Times p1 N 24 '39 por; p16 N 25
      '39; p17 N 25 '39; IX p11 D 3 '39
   Newsweek 14:4 D 4 '39 por
   Time 34:47 D 4 '39 por

BOGGS, CHARLES REID Nov 22, 1883 —Apr 1, 1940 Chemist; one of the world's outstanding authorities on rubber chemistry; writer of technical papers; discoverer of various vulcanization accelerators; vice-president of the Simplex Wire and Cable Company of Cambridge, Massachusetts

References
   American Men of Science
   Chemical Who's Who

Obituaries
   Boston Transcript p9 Ap 1 '40
   N Y World-Telegram p30 Ap 2 '40

FRANCES PAYNE BOLTON

BOLTON, FRANCES PAYNE (bōl'ton) 1886- First United States Congresswoman from Ohio

Address: b. House of Representatives, Washington, D.C.; h. Lyndhurst, Cleveland, Ohio

When rich, socially prominent Mrs. Frances Payne Bingham Bolton was elected in February 1940 to fill the unexpired term of her husband, Chester Castle Bolton, United States Representative from Ohio, who died October 1939, she also inherited his title of "the richest man in Congress." Good looking, middle-aged, mother of three grown sons, Mrs. Bolton did not need to enter politics as a profession. She made just one public speech, and that a short one, for her Congressional campaign. After her victory she returned to the United States Treasury the $10,000 check which Congress had voted her as a widow of a member, with the comment that "to accept this under the circumstances would be excessive." It indeed would be pin money to the widow of Representative Bolton, old-guard Republican, son of the late Mark Hanna's business partner. Bolton had made a fortune in the steel business. His personal check for $125,000 had assured the city of Cleveland the 1936 Republican convention, his money had entertained political big-wigs at the convention.

Mrs. Bolton is supposed to be even richer than her husband. Daughter of a pioneer Cleveland banker and industrialist, granddaughter of Senator Henry B. Payne, she married Bolton in 1907. She took part in social, philanthropic and civic activities, but except for campaigning for her husband since 1932, her Congressional campaign was her first personal political venture.

Her philanthropies have reached from Miami, Florida, where she spends much of her time, to backwoods Kentucky, where she financed a log cabin nursery center. "She once took a flyer at improving the lot of chorus girls." In 1929 she gave $1,250,000 of the fortune left her by her father to endow a school of nursing at Western Reserve University. She lives at Lyndhurst, a suburb of Cleveland.

"Like her husband, whose 1938 campaign expenditures came to $120.94, Mrs. Bolton refused to spend any money to get elected. When, three years ago, a political boss blasted away at "royalists of the Republican party" and "pocketbook domination of its councils," Mrs. Bolton replied, "none of us has any rights except those we earn." Mrs. Bolton was elected to serve 10 months, the unexpired term of her husband. She will be the seventh woman member of Congress, and the first to be elected from Ohio, whose twenty-second district she represents.

References

Life 8:28 Mr 11 '40 por
N Y Herald Tribune p18 Mr 11 '40 por
N Y Post p6 F 28 '40 por
N Y Sun p14 F 29 '40
N Y Times IV p2 Mr 3 '40 por
Time 35:20 F 12 '40 por
Who's Who in America (Addenda)

BONCI, ALESSANDRO 1870—Aug 9, 1940 Italian lyric tenor; voice was once ranked by critics second only to that of Enrico Caruso; appeared at Metropolitan Opera House and Hammerstein's Manhattan Opera House; first sang here in 1906; his perfect technique won admiration in Europe and South America; was center of a celebrated controversy when Metropolitan Opera Company offered him a larger salary

Musical America

ALESSANDRO BONCI

and took him away from the Manhattan Opera Company; death occurred in Rome

References

De Bekker's Music and Musicians 1925
Who's Who in America

Obituaries

N Y Herald Tribune p30 Ag 11 '40 por
N Y Times p31 Ag 11 '40 por
Time 36:48 Ag 19 '40

BOOKER, EDNA LEE Newspaper reporter; author
Address: c/o Macmillan Co, 60 Fifth Ave, New York City

One of the first, and probably one of the youngest woman correspondents in China, Edna Lee Booker reports her activities and adventures over a period of 18 years in *News Is My Job*.

Miss Booker has been a newspaper reporter since she was 16. She was born in Danville, Virginia and taken to California as a little girl. She was sent back to a girls' school in Missouri, majored in journalism, and returned to Los Angeles to take a job as a reporter on the Los Angeles *Herald* for one year. She learned the "ropes" from "brilliant—temperamental" Adela Rogers St. John. For a few months she worked on the San Francisco *Call-Bulletin*, then attended a denominational school for two years.

She had two childhood ambitions: to be a reporter when she grew up and to go to China. The second was stimulated by listening to a distant relative of her mother's. Mrs. Carrie Chapman Catt (see sketch this issue), tell of her experiences trying to start a woman suffrage movement in China. Later Mrs. Catt was selected by *American Women,* for contributions to the Woman Suffrage and Peace Movements, as one of the 10 outstanding women of 1937.

In 1921 Miss Booker was able to realize both her ambitions. She went to China as a reporter on the *China Press*, leading American daily in Shanghai, and correspondent for the International News Service in the Far East. Her family permitted her to go only after she accepted an invitation to stay with friends during the year's assignment.

Learning the history and understanding the background of the city which she was "covering" necessitated the learning of its language. "Morning after morning," she writes, "I would study aloud as did the children in the old Chinese schools. I began to acquire a small vocabulary, and strutted each new expression; but after calling the duck we were having for dinner a 'tender shoe' I subsided."

From her first assignment, covering a parade the City God put on for the Hungry Ghosts in Shanghai, she soon graduated to more serious reporting. One of her most dangerous and difficult assignments was to

EDNA LEE BOOKER

interview the powerful war lords of China. Going far back into the war-torn interior (1922), she was successful in interviewing General Wu Pei-fu, the same General Wu who was unsuccessfully sought by the Japanese militarists in 1939 to head the puppet government at Peking.

She achieved the distinction of being granted the first interview ever given a woman correspondent by Marshal Chang Tso-lin, the Mukden Tiger, the audience having been arranged by Marshal Chang, who years later figured so prominently in the kidnapping of Generalissimo Chiang Kai-shek (see sketch this issue) at Sian-fu.

After the successful completion of this assignment she next interviewed Dr. Sun Yat-sen. He was in hiding on his gunboat following his dramatic midnight escape from Canton. She followed him down the Pearl River under shell fire, handling the boat herself when her boatman was wounded.

Early in her career Miss Booker married John Potter, American realtor from Pennsylvania. She then resigned from the *China Press*, continuing to report for the International News Service. From life "peaceful as a chapter out of David Grayson's *Adventures in Contentment* (see sketch this issue), six weeks after her marriage she went out on a story." The story was of a band of some thousand bandits who had derailed and wrecked the famous Blue Express train, the pride of China. Miss Lucy Aldrich of the Rockefeller family was among the kidnapped passengers. "For the first time I began to wonder about a newspaper career and marriage. I might be away two weeks, or two months, and I had been married six weeks! News was my job—but was it?"

Her subsequent career demonstrates that it was. She covered the Japanese earth-

quake; the flood disaster of the Yangtze Valley in which the Lindberghs (see sketch this issue) figured; the anti-foreign riots in 1925 and 1927; the Sino-Japanese War over Shanghai in 1932; the aerial bombardments of Canton and Hankow in 1938. She lived a life full of adventure and rich experience, traveling over 50,000 miles of Far Eastern hinterland during her 18 years of reporting. She has interviewed war lords, followed guerilla armies, covered bombings, earthquakes and floods, and come to know China and its people. She has spent summer months with her family in a village at the foot of the Great Wall of China; has visited a little known tribe in the mountains of Fukien; has penetrated far up the Yangtze Gorges into Szechuen and on southward into Yunnan.

News Is My Job ends on a serious note—a firsthand account of Japan's ruthless agression, vivid pictures of "Free China" and an appeal for action on behalf of the Chinese people. Her book has been variously reviewed. *Christian Century* says: "A well informed and eminently readable account of the fortunes and misfortunes of China from 1922 down to the middle of last year (1939), by a newspaper woman who resided in Shanghai through those years, and knows conditions and events with an expert and penetrating eye." The Boston *Transcript* writes: "The defects of the book are principally superficiality."

A personal friendship with Miss Soong Mei-ling, now Madame Chiang Kai-shek (see sketch this issue), began early in the reporter's career. She played tennis with Miss Soong, listened while she talked of her dreams of Democracy and Christianity for China; attended her wedding; kept in touch with her during the years when as Madame Chiang she was rising to fame as first lady of China. Recently Miss Booker made a hazardous trip into the far interior of Free China to talk with Madame Chiang, to bring directly from her a message to the women of America.

She was in Addis Ababa in Ethiopia at the outbreak of the Italian-Ethiopian War. With her husband and two children, Patty and John Jr., she has traveled twice around the world, spending considerable time in Germany, Italy, France and England.

In the fall and winter of 1940 Miss Booker lectured in the United States to women's clubs and college groups, describing her own experiences, talking on The Miracle of New China; America's Stake in the Far East Today; the New Woman of China; and Journalistic Careers for Women. A charming speaker, Miss Booker has not lost her Southern drawl after so many years abroad. She is blonde, with china-blue eyes and the placid appearance of a young matron of the "rocking-chair brigade."

Miss Booker is an active member of the American Advisory Committee in Shanghai, that group of representative American business men and missionaries who handle the disbursement of much of the money contributed by the Red Cross, Bowl of Rice, Famine Relief and Church groups for civilian relief in China.

References

N Y Herald Tribune Books p8 Mr 10 '40

N Y Times Book R p9 F 25 '40

N Y World-Telegram p27 F 13 '40

Booker, E. L. News Is My Job 1940

BOOTH, BALLINGTON July 28, 1859—Oct 5, 1940 Founder of the Volunteers of America which he organized in 1896; brother of Evangeline Booth, retired head of the Salvation Army and son of William Booth, founder of the organization; after rift with his father he parted from him and set up the Volunteers of America; previously he was commander of the Army forces in the United States and Australia

BALLINGTON BOOTH

References

Who's Who in America

Obituaries

N Y Herald Tribune p42 O 6 '40 por

N Y Times p49 O 6 '40 por

BORAH, WILLIAM EDGAR June 29, 1865—Jan 19, 1940 United States Senator

Dean of the Senate and member from Idaho for almost 33 years, William Edgar Borah died at his Washington home after a short illness which began with a cerebral hemorrhage. He was 74 years old.

When C. O. Johnson wrote *Borah of Idaho* in 1936, he filled more than 500 pages and even then was forced to confess that the biography was far from complete. "The shaggy, unpredictable doyen of the United States Senate lived long and lived hard. The story of his life is a long story, but never a dull one."

William Edgar Borah was born at Fairfield, Illinois, June 29, 1865, the son of William Nathan and Elizabeth (West) Borah. The Borahs, of mixed Irish and Bohemian ancestry, were an old American family, having come to this country in 1760, and with restless courage moved first to Pennsylvania, on to Kentucky, then across the Ohio River to Wayne County, Illinois. William was one of 10 children. His father, a prosperous, hard-working farmer, was a devout Presbyterian. Young Borah had the typical American school boy education of his time in a tiny place called Tom's Prairie. Then he attended the Southern Illinois Academy at Enfield, Illinois and the University of Kansas.

The late Senator's "first love was not statesmanship, politics, or even the law, but the theater. The crusty old Senator who never went out socially in Washington and never entertained, went frequently to the theater." His first ambition was to be an actor. At one time as a boy he ran away from his Illinois home and joined a rundown Shakespearean company in which he played Mark Antony. Growing tired of his slim food supply after three weeks, he returned home where he could be assured of three good farm meals a day.

While a student at the University of Kansas he "cut grass, waited on tables and did odd jobs" to finance himself through law school. In 1890, an accredited member of the Bar, he went to Lyons, Kansas and started to practice law. Day after day his office remained empty, and he gave the citizens one year to become clients. After that he closed up and, impelled by the inherited urge to "go West" decided to seek his fortune in Seattle. A chance acquaintance on the train suggested that he stop at the thriving Western metropolis of Boise, Idaho (population 2,500). There Borah saw a drunken lawyer trying a case and decided that if a drunken one could succeed, a sober lawyer ought to make a living. Borah during his whole lifetime never used coffee, tea or tobacco and was a total abstainer from liquor.

Boise was then a raw frontier town, and its horse stealing, cattle rustling, vice, gambling and gunplay gave the young lawyer plenty of practice. Later he became especially successful as a jury pleader (his Shakespearean training standing him in good stead), and he won fame for his participation in some sensational criminal trials as a State Prosecutor. One of these legal battles which Borah did not win but which brought him national fame was the case in which Clarence Darrow defended Will D. ("Big Bill") Haywood and others on charges of killing Governor Steunenberg during a strike of Idaho miners. Darrow described Borah then as "the ablest man" with whom he had ever contended.

WILLIAM E. BORAH

While busy with the law, Borah took time to play an active part in politics. He ran unsuccessfully for Representative as a "Bryanite Republican" in 1896. A year before he had married Miss Mamie McConnell, daughter of Governor McConnell. Borah had been McConnell's secretary. The Borahs had no children.

In 1903 the young lawyer ran for the United States Senate and lost because he would not consent to a "deal" with the legislative caucus. "Send me absolutely free, or not at all," he told them. Four years later he toured the state with the slogan "King Caucus must go." This time the party leaders could not stop his election—and the people of Idaho, so proud of the "Big Potato" of the Senate (as his colleagues called him), never considered sending anyone to Washington to take his place during a third of a century.

Many people thought that Borah was a struggling young attorney when he was first elected Senator, but in reality he was Idaho's most successful attorney with the state's largest lumber and mining companies as clients. He had amassed $100,000 before he went to Washington. At his death there was much surprise at announcements that he had left $207,000 in life insurance policies and government bonds. It had been thought that he was a poor man, so simply did he and Mrs. Borah live.

Young Borah was a terrible disappointment to the Old Guard Republicans, led by Senator Aldrich of Rhode Island. As a freshman Senator he already showed that strong streak of independence of thought which for a third of a century made him one of the imposing lights of the Senate and which was to carry the name of Borah to world-wide fame.

At once he became the champion of the underdog. Senator Aldrich told him that unless he stopped his advocacy of such laws as the eight-hour day and taxes to be paid on income, he would receive no patronage. "I don't want any," replied the amazing Borah. When Aldrich tried further to get Borah's Idaho constituents to make him "behave," he received the following letter from Idaho:

"I want you to understand clearly that in any case, I have no influence with Senator Borah, and if you discover anybody in Idaho who has, I would be grateful to you if you would send me his name."

Borah went to the Senate as a Progressive Republican, but during the years he got himself called conservative, reactionary, changeable, radical, bitter isolationist, fearless individualist, champion of the underdog. Nothing that stood in the way of his principles mattered to him—whether it was party politics or the interests of his own state. Once he remarked, "I will travel with the devil, if he is going in my direction."

A relentless fighter, Borah was co-leader of that "little band of willful men" who bitterly opposed Woodrow Wilson's foreign policy. He helped organize and led the fight against confirmation of the Versailles Treaty. Before the League of Nations Covenant had reached its final written form, Borah delivered the epic address which brought him world fame on November 19, 1919 and which dealt the death blow to the entrance of the United States into the League of Nations. From that moment he was looked upon as a leader "of isolationist sentiment in the Senate."

Borah, a student of Shakespeare and a practiced orator even in his school days, could disarm his most dramatic opponents by the force of his words. No customary Congressional bombastic oratory or excessive gesticulation marred the power of his words. The classic eloquence of his famous 1919 speech brought tears to the eyes of Senators, and Vice-President Thomas Marshall sent him a note: "Even a mummy on a pedestal could not remain silent after such a speech." It was declared by hearers the greatest ever delivered in that forum. Viscount Grey, then acting British Ambassador, said of Borah: "I have watched this debate most carefully and in all my experience I have never heard a debate on a higher plane than that conducted by Senator Borah."

Many opposing speakers heaped recrimination on President Wilson for his adherence to the League of Nations, but Senator Borah never let personal criticism enter his speeches. Shortly before Wilson died, he passed Borah while driving in Washington and said: "There is one irreconcilable whom I can respect."

Like every man in public life, Borah had his critics. Some felt that he voted on each occasion "as the spirit moved him" without a feeling for the inter-relation of the past and the future. Although he helped to bring about the Washington Disarmament Conference in 1921, they maintain that his inconsistency in defeating the League of Nations lost the very peace which the Disarmament Conference would have made possible.

Others criticized his changeableness, which was the source of many Senatorial discussions. Once when someone remarked that Borah's Ferry in Kentucky was named for Borah's ancestors, a Senator interrupted to remark that the name was "entirely appropriate, as our distinguished colleague has spent a lifetime going from one side to the other."

President Coolidge, on hearing that Borah had started out for a horseback ride (his favorite exercise in his younger days), remarked with his sparse Vermont humor: "I'm amazed that he can ride at all. I had always understood that a rider had to go in the same direction as his horse."

During his thirty-three years as a Senator Borah served under seven Presidents. Although all seven at times chafed under his objections, all respected his influence, his honesty and his force. In the eulogy delivered at his death, Senator Vandenberg (see sketch this issue) placed Borah "in the company of Clay, Webster and Blaine as a statesman who failed the Presidency, yet outshone successful rivals."

"I follow issues, not men," Borah frequently said—and that is primarily what cost him the Presidency. He had been a Presidential possibility as early as 1912. Several times he was offered the Vice-Presidency but declined it. He explained his failure to be nominated with: "I would rather be Borah than President."

In his long life as a Senator there was no important piece of legislation which could be called his own, although he influenced many members of Congress. He himself remarked that looking back over his years in the Senate, he was "proudest of doing what little I have been able to do to keep us out of Europe. I mean in terms of abiding by Washington's advice against entangling commitments. I do not mean isolation in economic matters of trade and so forth."

In addition to his strong isolationist policy, he campaigned for peace; for the release of political prisoners after the World War; was a leader in the dismissal of Harry M. Daugherty as attorney general during the Senate investigation of oil lands; urged restoration of normal relations with the Russian government; disagreed with President Hoover's farm relief policy.

He opposed some of the New Deal's emergency legislation; opposed President Roosevelt's proposal to reorganize the Supreme Court; shared in the unsuccessful fight against revision of the neutrality act in 1939. He felt deeply the present plight of Europe and insisted that we were in the war already except that we hadn't sent soldiers over. On his desk when he died was a planned protest against British interference with American mails. "I suppose they'll start howling again that I'm anti-British," he said. "I'm not anti-British, and I never have been. It's just that they do so many things to us that need to be called to the attention of the American people."

The late Senator spent most of his time in Washington and very little in Idaho. He referred to his wife as "Little Borah" and discussed all legislation with her beforehand. He was fond of meeting the press (who adored him) lying on an old couch in his office with an army blanket pulled up over him. Members of the press frequently said that when other Senators spoke they emptied the Senate chamber and filled the cloak rooms; when Borah spoke the chamber was filled and the cloak rooms emptied. He lived simply and ate little. His clothes, dark and loosely cut, were often unpressed and threadbare. One vanity he had—his small feet which were shod in expensive shoes, beautifully polished.

His death saddened Washington. Of him President Roosevelt said: "The Senate and the Nation are sadly bereft by the passing of Senator Borah. We shall miss him and mourn him, and long remember the superb courage which was his. He dared often to stand alone, and even at times to subordinate party interest when he presumably saw a divergence of party interest and the national interest.

"Fair-minded, firm in principle and shrewd in judgment, he sometimes gave and often received hard blows; but he had great personal charm and a courteous manner which had its source in a kind heart. He had thought deeply and studied patiently all the great social, political and economic questions which had so vitally concerned his countrymen during the long period of his public service.

"His utterances commanded the close attention of the Senate and of a far-flung audience whenever he spoke. A unique figure, his passing leaves a void in American public life."

In France it was recalled by the press that Borah had once said: "It is false to say I do not love France." In London, the Daily Mail observed that Senator Borah was "known to the average man in this country better than almost any other United States politician." Le Matin, French journal, said that once Borah declared that if he knew France "perhaps I would love her, but I wish to know and love only America." The German press praised Borah for "courage, decency and upright methods of combat which made him respected by friend and foe alike."

References

Christian Sci Mon Mag p5 S 9 '39 por
Collier's 97:12-13+ F 1 '36 por
Cur Hist 43:463-6 F '36; 51:6-7 O '39

BORAH, WILLIAM—*Continued*

N Y Times p3 Je 30 '38; VII p10 S 24 '39 por; p14 O 3 '39
N Y World-Telegram p22 Ja 19 '40
Newsweek 7:22 Ja 4 '36 por
Scholastic 28:16 My 16 '36 por
Green, H. ed. American Problems; a Selection of Speeches and Prophecies 1924
Johnson, C. Borah of Idaho 1936
Warren, C. Borah and La Follette and the Supreme Court of the United States 1923
Whaley-Eaton Service Wherefores of Borah 1926
Who's Who in America 1938-39
Who's Who in the Nation's Capital

Obituaries

Christian Cent 57:135-7 Ja 31 '40
Christian Sci Mon pl Ja 20 '40
Life 8:16 Ja 29 '40 por
Nation 150:87 Ja 27 '40
New Repub 102:131 Ja 29 '40
N Y Times p1 Ja 20 '40; p9 Ja 20 '40 pors
Newsweek 15:15-16 Ja 29 '40
Scholastic 36:3 F 5 '40 por
Time 35:18-19 Ja 29 '40 por

BOSCH, CARL Aug 27, 1874—Apr 26, 1940 Chemist; winner of the 1931 Nobel Prize for chemistry; discoverer of chemical substitutes credited with aiding Germany in First World War; chairman of German dye works

References

Sci Mo 34:278-83 Mr '32 por
International Who's Who
Wer ist's?
Who's Who

German Railroads
CARL BOSCH

Obituaries

N Y Herald Tribune p32 Ap 28 '40 por
N Y Times p36 Ap 28 '40 por

BOURKE-WHITE, MARGARET *See* White, M. B.

BOURNE, JONATHAN JR. (bŏŏrn) Feb 23, 1855—Sept 2, 1940 Republican Senator from Oregon from 1907 to 1913; first man elected to Senate under popular vote plan; author of the parcel post law; made a fortune in farming, mining and commercial enterprises

References

Ind 70:1411-12 Je 29 '11 por
McClure 37:507-11 S '11
Nation 103:460-1 N 16 '16
Who's Who in America

Obituaries

N Y Herald Tribune p20 S 3 '40 por
N Y Times p17 S 3 '40
Time 36:38 S 9 '40

BOWER, BERTHA MUZZY, pseud. Nov 15, 1871—July 23, 1940 Author of 57 Western novels of which the most famous were *Chip of the Flying U; Her Prairie Knight; Skyrider* and *Cow Country;* many made into films; signing herself B. M. Bower, she was often mistaken for a man; found her greatest reading public among adolescents

Keystone
B. M. BOWER

References

American Women
Who's Who Among North American Authors
Who's Who in America

Obituaries

N Y Herald Tribune p14 Jl 24 '40
N Y Times p21 Jl 24 '40
Newsweek 16:7 Ag 5 '40 por
Pub W 138:321 Ag 3 '40

BRADBURY, JAMES H. Oct 12, 1857—
Oct 12, 1940 Veteran comedian of stage
and screen; supported Edwin Booth, Dion
Boucicault and Edwin Arden; first great
hits in *Naughty Anthony* in 1900 and in
Eben Holden in 1901; two of best remembered performances in *Along Came Ruth* and
Shavings; last seen on Broadway in *Lady be
Good;* went to Hollywood in 1926, where he
appeared in *The Tide of Empire, The Woman
from Hell* and other motion pictures

References

Theatre 38:23 Ag '23 por
Who's Who in the Theatre 1936

Obituaries

N Y Herald Tribune p28 O 15 '40
N Y Times p23 O 15 '40

BRANDENBURG, WILLIAM A. Oct
10, 1869—Oct 29, 1940 President of Kansas
State Teachers College at Pittsburg and
the American Association of Teachers Colleges; taught in Oklahoma and was member
of the Oklahoma State Board of Education;
member Kansas State Board of Education
since 1920

Ferguson's Studio
WILLIAM A. BRANDENBURG

References

Who's Who in American Education

Obituaries

N Y Times p23 O 30 '40

BRANLY, EDOUARD Oct 23, 1844—Mar
24, 1940 French physicist; preceded Gug-
lielmo Marconi in experiments resulting in
the invention of the wireless telegraph and
radio

References

International Who's Who

Obituaries

N Y Herald Tribune p12 Mr 25 '40
por
N Y Times p15 Mr 25 '40 por
N Y World-Telegram p28 Mr 25 '40

**BRAUCHITSCH, HEINRICH ALFRED
HERMANN WALTHER VON** (brou'-
kĭch hīn'rĭk hĕr'män väl'tĕr fŏn) Oct 4, 1881-
Commander in chief of the German Army

Colonel general Walther von Brauchitsch
was little known to the man in the street
in Germany or to the world at large when
he was made Commander in chief of the
German Army in 1938. An American military expert remarked that a "military
mediocrity" had been selected for the post.
But after the lightning Polish campaign,
Von Brauchitsch was hailed as one of Germany's great military heroes.

In the cafés of Germany, men talk of Von
Brauchitsch as another Von Hindenburg, and
whisper that he would be the logical successor to Adolf Hitler, should anything
happen to the Führer. However, experts say
that he is in no way comparable to Von
Hindenburg as an officer. He is molded in
the same tradition of army caste, and is the
typical German officer, self-effacing, obedient,
and has the thoroughness and persistence
that has made the army the highest expression of German efficiency.

He has an impressive physical façade. Tall,
handsome, the grimness of his face is
punctuated by gray, intelligent eyes and
softened by a humorous mouth with a readiness to laugh.

His life has not been spectacular or brilliant. But he has succeeded in ingratiating
himself both with the old army class and
with the Nazis, and not even his divorce
from his middle-aged, wealthy wife, Elizabeth von Karstedt, and his marriage to the
younger and more attractive Charlotte
Schmidt, daughter of a Silesian judge, have
cost him anything in official regard. He has
two sons and a daughter.

Born in Berlin, a member of the old
Prussian feudal aristocracy (he traces his
forebears to 1259), Von Brauchitsch had
little choice of a career. As the fifth son
of a cavalry general, Bernhard von Brauchitsch, and Charlotte von Gordon von Brauchitsch, he was destined for the army. He
attended the Französische Gymnasium in Berlin, one of the best junior colleges in pre-War
Germany, and in 1900, at the age of 19, was
commissioned a lieutenant in the Royal Elizabeth Guard Grenadiers. But the Grenadiers
wore corsets and led a gay life, and Von
Brauchitsch got his father to transfer him to

Transatlantic

WALTHER VON BRAUCHITSCH

an artillery regiment. At the outbreak of the First World War in 1914, Von Brauchitsch had risen to the rank of captain. Throughout the World War he remained a general staff officer, and saw no fighting. Instead he was assigned to solving the logarithmic puzzles for staff officers on the Western Front. At the end of the War, like thousands of other officers, he was relegated to the reserve corps, his career apparently ended.

But General Hans von Seeckt, then reorganizing the Reichswehr to conform to the Versailles Treaty, got Von Brauchitsch an appointment as a major in Stettin. Three years later the young officer was in command of the artillery section of the Defense Ministry, and a key figure in Germany's miniature army. Next he became a lieutenant colonel, and served a term with a Prussian artillery regiment. His career, however, seemed to lie in office work, and after a succession of paper assignments he was appointed chief of military training further the Reich with the rank of colonel in 1930. He became a major general in 1931, and Reichswehr chief of artillery in March 1932. The next year, when Hitler came into power, Von Brauchitsch was given command of the East Prussian military area, one of the most important in Germany because of its vulnerability from both Poland and Russia. He was largely responsible for the construction of the new fortifications built there after 1933 to make East Prussia impregnable from the East.

Von Brauchitsch is not given to strutting, and has no interest in Hitler's Aryan gibberish. But he is an ambitious careerist. During the years he spent in an army swivel chair, he studied hard, mastering his own specialty, artillery, and then poring over the more theoretical aspects of warfare. And he became a strong believer of strong defense

as a prelude to any kind of warfare. But most important to his career was the fact that he had convinced himself that Hitler was a God-sent means to an end—the destruction of the Versailles Treaty, and the resurrection of the German Army. Like his Junker-class colleagues he was a diehard monarchist; but unlike most of his colleagues he was able to see in the Führer's avowed mission to regain for Germany her pre-War position, a reinstatement of the Reichswehr officer-class to its rightful place in the sun, and thus to give his sincere allegiance to the Nazi.

Marked as a man whom Hitler could trust, Von Brauchitsch's rise was rapid after the Nazis came into power. His chief of staff in East Prussia was General Walther von Reichenau, closest of all army officers to the Nazis, and the two men became good friends. In 1937 Von Brauchitsch became chief of the Leipzig Group Command, a key post that secured his future.

At this time Hitler was having trouble with his army leaders. Loyalties were split between the old army group opposing Hitler's impatience to begin his grabs of territory and the Nazi leaders in the army. When the purges came and General Werner von Fritsch, former Chancellor General Kurt von Schleicher, and General Field Marshal Werner von Blomberg lost their jobs, Von Brauchitsch played safe, and kept quiet. His good friend Von Reichenau recommended him to Hitler as the man to lead the army.

In February 1938 Von Brauchitsch took over the command of the army with the rank of colonel general, and became a member of the Secret Council created to advise Hitler on foreign policy.

Von Brauchitsch sold himself to Hitler and won the reputation of being the most skillful politician in the army and the most powerful military man among the politicians. He had one advantage over his colleagues in that he regarded the Führer as a gifted politician, and treated him as an equal and not as a parvenu as did many of the aristocratic officers. He became a confidant of the Führer, and won his friendship further by his approval of the Führer's first gamble in reoccupying the Rhineland in 1936. The reoccupation was against Von Brauchitsch's better judgment, but he believed the French and British would do nothing.

Von Brauchitsch also supported the Austrian seizure, although he is supposed to have told Adolf Hitler before the Anschluss, "Mein Führer, if you want to use the army to support a bluff by military pressure, you can depend on us. For more serious business we are not yet ready. Wait a few months— only a few months." A few days later he had taken over the command of the Austrian Army. Von Brauchitsch said the same thing before he marched into the Sudetenland, and also before he occupied Moravia and Bohemia. The army was not ready. But in August 1939 as motorized divisions began concentrating in Slovakia, Silesia and East

Prussia, Von Brauchitsch *was* ready and the campaign hung on him. Von Brauchitsch accomplished the job of taking Poland in 19 days, not counting the brave but futile hold-out by the citizens of Warsaw.

Von Brauchitsch's insistence on the completion of the fortifications in the West, when he took command of the army, had worked out as he had expected. Without its West Wall, where a major battle was in progress the middle of September 1939, Germany might have been overrun almost as fast as it overran Poland. But with the Western frontier fortified, Von Brauchitsch could plan his attack, and he chose the *Blitzkrieg*, the war of movement. He knew that to deliver a lightning blow Germany needed not only a superlative air force, but plenty of motorized strength, and he had concentrated on building up the armored motor divisions of the army. In 1937 Germany had only two such divisions. By September 1, 1939 she had six, each with an average strength of thirteen thousand men, besides a fleet of eight thousand tanks. It was this force that swept through Poland so swiftly, and took the rich Polish coal fields at the precise moment England blockaded Germany.

Von Brauchitsch not only deliberately prepared the conflict with Poland, but was one of the most important champions of a rapprochement between Germany and the Soviet. To him, the deeply-rooted Nazi feeling against Bolshevism did not count: only purely military points of view were possible and admissible as decisive. After 1919 it was the leading Reichswehr officers, among them Von Brauchitsch especially, who supported German tool deliveries to the Soviet in order that factories might be erected in Russian territory to make army equipment for Germany. A lot of hard work was needed, however, before he could succeed in bringing about far-reaching negotiations between Germany and Russia. When the Soviet ratified the pact in 1939, he knew that the campaign of Germany against Poland would be assured, and that the anticipated movement of the German Communists in the interior had been throttled.

The office of the highest military command in Germany today is an important one. Though Von Brauchitsch is an honest patriot, and an expert in military, political and economic affairs, it has long been known that his true leanings are in nowise toward National Socialism. He has shown himself to be a decisive alterer of Hitler's military policy; he also stands in opposition to Goering in his belief that the army must have precedence over the air force. It cannot be said definitely that he is playing a double game; but of all men in Germany it is he alone who in case of need could use his weapon, the command of the army, against the ruling régime, for general opinion holds that the Nazi dictatorship could be replaced in the future only by a military one.

References

Cur Hist 51:28-9 O '39 por; 51:29 F '40 por
Life 8:58 Ap 1 '40 por
Liv Age 357:448-51 Ja '40
N Y Sun p20 F 15 '40
Scholastic 35:20S N 6 '39 por
Time 34:25-6 S 25 '39 il por

Dutch, O. Hitler's Twelve Apostles p164-73 1940

BRECKENRIDGE, LESTER PAIGE May 17, 1858—Aug 22, 1940 Professor emeritus of mechanical engineering of Sheffield Scientific School at Yale University; inventor; consulting engineer; was professor at Yale from 1909 to 1923; invented an automatic recording machine and smoke-prevention appliances for soft coal; served on a United States survey for power machinery

LESTER PAIGE BRECKENRIDGE

References

Cassier 37:747-8 Ap '10 por (p654)
American Men of Science
Who's Who in America
Who's Who in Engineering

Obituaries

N Y Herald Tribune p8 Ag 24 '40
N Y Times p13 Ag 24 '40

BRIDGES, ALFRED BRYANT RENTON *See* Bridges, H.

BRIDGES, HARRY July 28, 1900- Labor leader

In the autumn of 1940 Harry Bridges is once more being "investigated." Perhaps so much governmental curiosity has never before been directed against a single person, but then perhaps Harry Bridges "isn't a

HARRY BRIDGES

single person but a shrewd, tenacious, resourceful organization reaching into many fields of business and industry." Though in January he was officially cleared of Communist connections, in May 1940 the House of Representatives singled him out for deportation by passing a special bill that didn't mention any crime. The Senate Immigration Committee and Attorney General Jackson (see sketch this issue) found its constitutionality dubious, but authorized a special squad of FBI agents to investigate his "general status and activities in San Francisco, Seattle, Portland and Los Angeles" in order to determine once more "whether he ever was or is a member of the Communist Party." Under the Smith Act, passed since Bridges' first trial, an alien can be deported for having been affiliated with the party.

There is no doubt at all that Harry Bridges is an alien. He was born in Melbourne, Australia on July 28, 1900, christened Alfred Bryant Renton Bridges, but soon nicknamed Harry. His father, Alfred E. Bridges, a fairly prosperous real estate man and "a regular British Tory," began teaching him the real estate business when he was barely in his teens by sending him out to collect rents from poor families. He didn't enjoy it. His mother, Julia (Dorgan) Bridges, whose family had migrated from Ireland to Australia, reared him in the Catholic faith. That didn't stay by him long, either. Nor did he like the job he found when he left St. Brennan's Parochial School at 16: clerking in a retail stationery store. He went away to sea as soon as he could, was in two shipwrecks off the Australian coast, and finally in 1920 shipped on a barkentine bound for San Francisco. He was already pretty militant. Two of his uncles had been actively interested in the

Labor Party, he himself belonged to the sailors' union and had taken part in strikes, he had read Jack London and books on labor, economics and sociology and he had been having a good look at the world for three years. When the skipper of his ship tried to make the men work on a religious holiday young Bridges led the men in objecting, and when they docked at San Francisco he paid his head tax and quit. (He was later legally admitted to the United States.)

Then followed two years on American vessels. Bridges sailed around South America, Central America, Mexico, New Orleans, acquired the nickname "Limo," in 1921 was arrested for picketing in a New Orleans maritime strike, did a "trick" with the Coast & Geodetic Survey, was quartermaster on a government ship chasing rumrunners—then in 1922 decided to settle down in San Francisco as a longshoreman.

It wasn't long—in 1924—before he and some other men tried to organize a branch of the International Longshoremen's Association. It collapsed, however, when somebody embezzled the union's funds, and it wasn't until 1933 that an attempt to get the majority of longshoremen into a noncompany union was successful. Harry Bridges was on the payroll as organizer and not very important until a strike for recognition of their union, wages of more than $10.45 a week, a 30-hour week, a coastwide agreement and union control of hiring halls was called on May 9, 1934 after the owners refused to negotiate. Soon the other marine unions and the teamsters joined them and shipping stopped. The newly-formed Joint Maritime Commission of which Bridges was chairman was pledged to hold out for a coastwide agreement, and the men won virtually all their demands when on July 31 the government's National Longshoremen's Board handed down an arbitration, but only after the strike had expanded into a general strike that the press called a "revolution."

Harry Bridges was by this time "the bogey man of the Pacific." He was "privately and publicly damned as a Communist, an alien agitator, a ruthless doctrinaire, an unscrupulous wrecker with a lust for power." But the longshoremen elected him president of the San Francisco I. L. A. local, with a weekly salary of $40. Bridges neither affirmed nor denied that he was a Communist, but freely admitted his willingness to accept Communist assistance and advice.

Next, "before the shipping industry knew what was going on," Bridges had formed the Maritime Federation of the Pacific, which in 1935 seven marine and water front unions voted to set up. In 1936 Bridges was elected president of the West Coast district of the I. L. A., his salary raised to $75.

By September 1936 the 1934 award to the marine unions had lapsed, and while the unions demanded further gains the employers refused to renew their contracts unless concessions were made. On October 30, 1936 a strike was called for all unions affiliated with the Maritime Federation. All Pacific shipping stopped like clockwork, rather than gradually, as in 1934. It was the most costly seamen's strike in the nation's history, and dragged on until February 1937, when the unions won. The West Coast I. L. A. then began to organize the warehousemen of the Pacific Coast as their affiliate, and unionization of lumber-workers, industrial workers and even the Newspaper Guild was speeded up. Harry Bridges began to sing the praises of the CIO; by June 1937 the longshoremen and warehousemen as well as many other West Coast unions had joined forces with John L. Lewis. In July 1937 Bridges was appointed West Coast regional director of the CIO. That same year the National Maritime Union was formed, with jurisdiction over most of the seamen in the Eastern and Gulf ports.

"Anti-Bridges agitation from such powerful groups as the Associated Farmers, the Waterfront Employers' Association, the Southern Californians, Incorporated, and scores of business and civic organizations aided by most urban newspapers and virtually all the rural press" was, logically enough, stronger than ever. "Deport the alien agitator!" was their cry and that of the American Legion and Dies (see sketch this issue) Committee, and in February 1938 Bridges asked the Department of Justice to determine his status once and for all. Under pressure from other groups Miss Frances Perkins (see sketch this issue), Secretary of Labor, finally issued a warrant for his deportation on the ground that he was a Communist. The hearing was postponed pending the Supreme Court's decision on a similar case and the warrant not reissued until June 1939, when for 10 weeks Professor James M. Landis of the Harvard Law School sat on Bridges' case as a special examiner, hearing conflicting testimony as to his beliefs and connections.

During the entire trial Bridges denied membership in the Communist Party, although he said he considered Communists good unionists and would work with them. He denied that the welfare of the workers was identical with the welfare of their employers . . . admitted believing that the United States should be so far socialized as to liquidate big companies and substitute public ownership of their properties, but also thought it could eventually be done "under the Constitution we've got now" and affirmed his faith in democracy, which "we [in the unions] practice every day." He also said that he had long wanted to become an American citizen. His first papers, filed twice, had lapsed both times because of technicalities.

Professor Landis' final verdict, rendered in January 1940, was: "That Bridges' aims are energetically radical may be admitted, but the proof fails to establish that the methods he seeks to employ to realize them are

other than those that the framework of democratic and constitutional government permits." Organized labor, most particularly the CIO, greeted the verdict as a great victory.

It was not a final victory, however. The costly ship clerks' strike had been Bridges' first water-front defeat, and many West Coast employers claimed he hadn't been able to get anything for his men since 1936. They warned the East that he was therefore on the move, inspecting Eastern opportunities in the warehouse field. Having made one New York raid on Local 65 of the United Retail and Wholesale Employees' Association, by the summer of 1940 Bridges was asking the CIO for jurisdiction over all warehouse workers, thus arousing the URWEA's belligerency. And in the meanwhile Congress had been acting. Representative Allen of Louisiana had denounced Landis' report as a "whitewash," and introduced a bill into the House that would deport Bridges to Australia. Dies and others contended that Bridges had once cried, "To hell with the President of the United States!" and advocated the sinking of American warships; it was also claimed that "the warehouse union linked with water-front workers could even interfere seriously with military operations anywhere in the nation," and it was true that Bridges had once shown a certain amount of power by ordering union members not to load scrap iron into the hold of an Italian freighter during the Ethiopian War. Representative Vito Marcantonio of New York, who led a futile fight against the bill, read a long letter from Bridges himself in which he pointed out that as CIO director he had investigated Nazi and Fascist activities in aircraft and munitions plants on the coast and turned the names of suspects over to the Department of Justice and the Department of Labor.

When the Allen bill was passed in the House 330 to 42, a large part of even the conservative press condemned it and Attorney General Jackson stated his "emphatic disapproval" of "the first deportation in which the alien was not even accused either of unlawful entry or of unlawful conduct while here." Finally, on August 15, 1940 the Senate Immigration Committee blocked the bill, approving instead a measure to investigate Bridges' "subversive" connections.

"Dark, razor-faced, with the quick, lithe movements of a fencer," when in action Harry Bridges nervously struts back and forth on the platform with "a sort of sailor's walk," speaking in a "soft, low, emphatic voice" that used to have a pronounced Australian accent but has now lost most of it. Under pressure he is unfailingly cool. Away from his duties he "would rather hang around a beer parlor on Skid Row than argue over the coffee dregs in some intellectual's study." He lives in a modest apartment, drives a Ford, dresses unpretentiously, stops at sailors' hotels and eats sailors'

BRIDGES, HARRY—*Continued*

food and is a strong believer in rank-and-file control of unions. "Labor unions cannot sell out their followers when all decisions are subject to referendums," he says. He is "incorruptible by cash, favors or flattery."

His daughter, Patricia, (he married Agnes A. Brown in 1924) is his devoted admirer. And although it is reported that Harry Bridges' influence in the Pacific Northwest has been waning in recent months and that in November of 1940 he was at odds with John L. Lewis over certain West Coast jurisdictional issues, it is said any critics among his men are likely to be answered with: "What are you guys kickin' about? Harry's gotcha better pay and conditions, ain't he?" But a great many other people in the United States think of him as "a composite of Stalin and Boris Karloff."

References

Cur Hist 50:9 Ag '39
Fortune 16:123-8+ S '37 il pors
Forum 101:195-9 Ap '39 por
Nation 142:576-80 My 6 '36 il; 143:
    753 D 26 '36; 148:192-3 F 18 '39;
    150:638 My 25 '40; 150:743 Je 22
    '40; 150:771 Je 29 '40; 151:420 N 2
    '40
New Repub 94:72 F 23 '38; 99:289 Jl
    19 '39; 100:128-9 S 6 '39; 101:6 N 8
    '39; 102:36 Ja 8 '40; 102:841 Je 24
    '40
Newsweek 14:11-12 Jl 24 '39 il por;
    15:15 Ja 8 '40; 16:50+ Jl 1 '40
Sat Eve Post 210:25+ My 14 '38
Time 30:12-14 Jl 19 '37 pors; 32:12 S
    26 '38 por; 34:13 Jl 24 '39 il por;
    34:15-16 Ag 14 '39 por
Minton, B. and Stuart, J. Harry
    Bridges: Voice of the Rank and File
    In Men Who Lead Labor p172-202
    1937
Ward, E. E. Harry Bridges on Trial
    pam 1940
Who's Who in Australia

BRISTOW, GWEN (brĭs'tō) Sept 16, 1903- Author

Address: h. 726 N Rodeo Dr, Beverly Hills, California

Miss Bristow sends us the following biographical sketch: "According to the archives, the ancestor who bequeathed me my surname left England in 1647 and came to live in Virginia. One of his progeny married a Miss Tazewell, and they moved to South Carolina, the colony where the family that was destined to produce my mother was already planting rice not far from the town of Charleston. The Bristows knew nothing about them, however, and did not discover their existence for more than two hundred years, because the Bristows were planting cotton in the up-country—that is, the hill region north of the Santee River—and the up-country and the low-country were a long way apart in those days.

"My mother's forebears were Scotch, German, English and French. My predecessors on both sides were very devout. As a young man my father [Louis Judsen Bristow] was a newspaper correspondent, and while serving in the army during the Spanish-American War he combined military duties with covering the war for the Charleston *News and Courier*. After the War he entered a theological seminary and was ordained a minister. He and my mother [Caroline Cornelia (Winkler) Bristow] were introduced when he happened to visit her home town and she asked a mutual friend to make her acquainted with the reporter-soldier whose newspaper articles she had read with so much enjoyment. They were married a year later and went to live in Marion, a village near the coast, north of Charleston. It was there that I (their first child) was born September 16, 1903.

"So many people ask writers when they first decided they were going to be writers that I might as well say immediately that I cannot answer because I don't remember. It simply never occurred to me that I was going to be anything else. From the time when I first discovered the use of a pencil I have never been able to see a pile of white paper without wanting to scribble on it.

"My first appearance in print occurred when I was 12. Our school had won first place in the competitions of County Field Day, and I wrote a piece about it which was published on the weekly School Page of *The State*, Columbia, South Carolina, and it had my name printed at the end. The morning the article appeared I spent a quarter, which was all the money I had, buying copies of the paper. I do not remember what became of them.

"During the next few years my effusions were printed only in the school paper, but when I was graduated from high school I covered myself with what I believed to be deathless glory by writing a play in two acts that was presented by the graduating class. Believing the theatre to be my destiny, I wrote several other plays while I was in college, which, when they were presented, made me so pleased with myself that I was probably hard to live with. By this time, however, I had discovered the joys of writing for profit; for I had gone into the essay business. I would write anything assigned by any teacher to anybody, with a price range of from twenty-five cents to three dollars, depending partly on length and partly on whether the purchaser insisted upon getting a good grade for the essay or would be satisfied with a passing mark. The emoluments of this undertaking kept me happily provided with pickles, chocolate bars and eventually a typewriter.

"That college, by the way, deserves a book all to itself. Founded in 1837 as the Judson Female Institute—named for Ann Hasseltine Judson, an early foreign missionary—it has been a landmark in Alabama ever since. Released from that famous institution [B. A. 1924], I went as fast as I could where I had wanted to go all the time, the Pulitzer School of Journalism at Columbia University in New York. I had a wonderful year. As clergymen rarely get great financial rewards in this world and there were younger children in our family to be educated, I had precious little money, but that was in the joyous days before the depression and it was easy to earn more. I was nursemaid to rich women's children, typed theses for graduate students, wrote rags-to-riches biographies of successful businessmen and sold them to trade journals and was secretary to a Central European baroness who had come to this country after the War.

"From the School of Journalism I went to work on the New Orleans *Times-Picayune* [1925]. As a newspaper reporter I had the time of my life. I covered holdups, murders, meetings of the Rotary Club, football games and investigations of Huey Long; sat around waiting for juries to make up their minds, nearly got shot during a jailbreak and roasted alive on a burning oil tanker, interviewed celebrities, criminals and political candidates, wrote Sunday feature articles about romantic spots, went out on still-smashing expeditions with the Prohibition raiders, rode the elephant in the circus, covered a Mississippi River flood, and was married [January 14, 1929].

"My husband, Bruce Manning, was a New York newspaperman who after an illness had been advised by his doctor to look for a job in a milder climate. He was a reporter on a rival newspaper, the *Item*. One of the biggest compliments either of us ever received was that nobody on either paper suggested that our being husband and wife might interfere with our doing our best to beat each other on exclusive stories. It didn't; on the contrary it made us grimmer professional rivals than ever, and our eagerness to outwit each other was responsible for some of the best stories we ever dug up for our respective papers.

"Meanwhile we were both doing a lot of private scribbling between assignments. It was not easy to write at home, for the tranquility of our apartment was persistently broken by the man next door, who had the loudest and most raucous radio I have ever heard, which he played from nine o'clock every morning until eleven o'clock every night. Requests, threats, even appeals to the police had no effect on the mechanical screams that poured from his window, and we could not find another comfortable apartment at a price we could afford to pay. Bruce and I got some spiritual relief by devising various schemes to murder that man without being caught up with. One evening at dinner, with the radio blaring next door, we made up an exceptionally diabolical plan of murder. While we were polishing it up the idea struck us that this particular plot against our neighbor could be written, and might be sold, and might

GWEN BRISTOW

bring enough money to enable us to move.

"The book was called *The Invisible Host* [1930]. It was made into a play by Owen Davis called *The Ninth Guest*, and later made into a moving picture under the latter title.

"With a book, and a play, and a movie, Bruce and I immediately got very grand and of course very silly. We quit the papers, took a house on the Mississippi Gulf Coast, and settled down to what we thought was the literary life, which meant having a lot of house parties and writing more detective stories. We did write three more books of murder, which we both blush to remember, and might have spent our lives on that beautiful beach had not the depression— which we had heard of, but ignored— suddenly swooped upon us and sent us scurrying for shelter. I ran back to New Orleans and the *Times-Picayune*. The managing editor smiled wisely and told me I could go back to my old desk. Bruce began writing radio scripts about a gangster named Angelface.

"While I continued to cover the events of the day for the paper I wrote another novel, which nobody would publish. Bruce was occupying his spare time writing stories for the screen, one of which was finally sold to a Hollywood studio. We jubilantly quit work again and departed in grandeur, this time to Connecticut, where Bruce went on writing screen originals and radio scripts and I wrote another novel. This made four novels, not counting the detective stories we had written in collaboration. Nobody would publish that one either.

"Then all of a sudden Bruce was given a chance to come to Hollywood and do a real screenplay. When we arrived here I had grimly determined not to write any more novels. I had written four, and no publisher would have anything to do with

BRISTOW, GWEN—*Continued*

any of them, and when I looked at the manuscripts I had to confess in all honesty that they deserved no better. As I had really worked hard on them, it seemed obvious that I had been mistaking desire for ability. I had written good newspaper stuff and collaborated with Bruce on detective stories, but I had concluded that I might as well own up to it that a serious novel was beyond me. There was no reason why I should go on writing anyway. Here I was in the fabulous town of Hollywood, and my husband's salary, though small by Hollywood standards, was sufficient to support me in idleness. So I sat down in the well-known sunshine and decided to be idle.

"Then, as the vacant weeks dragged along, I discovered that I was the victim of a certain mental aberration. There is a Latin phrase for it: *cacoethes scribendi*. It means that you are impelled to write, and neither outer circumstances nor inner determination to the contrary can stop you.

"There was no provision for a study in our apartment, because I had announced decisively that I was done with writing, and my husband did his at the studio. So, almost stealthily, as if I might be caught at a shameful occupation, I set up a card-table in the corner of the bedroom, bought some yellow paper at the dimery and began to write Novel Number Five. There was no reason for writing it except that I was unhappy not writing it.

"It was the summer of 1934 when I came to Hollywood; by the next summer I was half way done with a novel of Louisiana in colonial days. My plan was, if somebody would be so kind as to publish this one, to write three novels, each complete in itself but the series forming a record of several typical families who might have lived in Louisiana from the time of the Colonial settlements until the twentieth century. The first of the series, *Deep Summer*, was finished in the spring of 1936 and sent off with prayers and jitters.

"After several weeks during which I soothed my impatience by beginning the second novel of the series, pretending to be confident that *Deep Summer* would be published, which I certainly wasn't—I received a blessed letter. It said that the Thomas Y. Crowell Company would take *Deep Summer* on condition that they could wait a year to bring it out, as their current list was complete. Waiting a year to see my book in print didn't matter to me at all. I got a taxi and went to the Brown Derby on Vine Street for lunch. I do not remember what I ate. I do remember looking around at the celebrated people having lunch at nearby tables and thinking, 'You are merely movie stars, but I have written a book.' I went home and spent the afternoon writing furiously on my next novel, which was to be called *The Handsome Road*.

"When *Deep Summer* was published [1937] Louisiana State University invited me down to make a lecture tour. I scampered all over the state in a car driven by Annette Duchein of the university's graduate school, whose job was not only to drive and to make the introductory talk, but to stand around with a watch so she could drag me away from one town in time to reach the next, for the university had given me a schedule that demanded not only split-second efficiency but the constitution of an ox. In short, I lectured in twenty-one towns in nine days. I did it again the next year when *The Handsome Road* was published [1938], only this time it was thirty-six towns in fourteen days. It sounds horrible, but I'm afraid I must own that I enjoyed it. Just before my third book, *This Side of Glory*, was published, I went on another lecture tour, this one in the Middle West; it occupied the months of February and March, and I nearly froze to death. I don't think I ever really appreciated the California climate before.

"*This Side of Glory* was published in the spring of 1940. The first part of it was written in a hotel room in New York, on stationery that the bellboys kept bringing up with wondering remarks on the extent of my correspondence, and the book was finally finished in my home in Beverly Hills. We live in Beverly Hills now, for when it became apparent that we would be denizens of the moving picture colony for some time we bought a house here. There were two unnecessary luxuries I had dreamed of all my life—not delights I thought I would ever experience but just sweet wistful yearnings to indulge at moonrise. One was a swimming pool and the other was a private study with a really big desk, an even bigger sofa and plenty of windows. Now at last I have both. The swimming pool sounds much more glamorous than it looks, for it is not one of the blue-tile-with-dolphins-spouting-spray affairs pictured in the fan magazines, but we can swim in it, which is quite good enough for us.

"My husband works at Universal Studio, where for several years past he has been turning out scripts, mostly for Deanna Durbin. The first Durbin script he worked on was *One Hundred Men and a Girl*, the most recent to be produced was *First Love*.

"A lot of people ask us how we manage with two writers in the same family. It's really very simple. He never sees anything I write until it is printed and I never see anything he writes until the picture is on the screen. So, as that leaves us nothing to argue about, we can spend our leisure time outdoors playing games, which is what we both like to do anyway."

References

N Y Post p10 Ap 17 '40 por
Pub W 137:1155-8 Mr 16 '40 il por
American Women
Who's Who Among North American Authors

BRONSHTEIN, LEV DAVIDOVICH *See* Trotsky, L.

BROOKES, GEORGE S., REV. Congregational minister

"Within the shadow of my thirtieth birthday I sat alone with bowed head in a corner of the Pennsylvania Railroad station wondering which way to take in this country of opportunity. A battered trunk and a battered courage were my sad companions. Will tomorrow be like yesterday? Is America really for everybody or for the few? Where shall I sleep tonight? These were the questions I asked myself."

And these are the questions Reverend Brookes answers in *Thank You, America!* (1940), his tribute to his adopted country. "After the flip criticism of hasty visitors, who often reveal unflattering truth with holy glee, it is a welcome change to hear the grateful praise of one who, though not blind to faults, sees America as still the land of opportunity," writes one reviewer.

George S Brookes, the son of a bricklayer's laborer, was born in a mining town conspicuous for its unattractive appearance, in the Black Country of the English Midlands. His pious and poor parents took him out of school at the age of 13 to start working in a nut and bolt factory; then, on the advice (for a shilling) of a phrenologist, they apprenticed George to a printer. At the end of seven years he progressed from printer's devil to compositor, but had no steady job. In the meantime he had married the same girl "he used to play hopscotch and make mud pies with" and they had three children. Tales of travelers returned from "the land of promise" across the ocean inspired him to go to America. Having no funds or relatives "worth a shilling," he penned, printed and published a booklet, *Silent Memories* (1912), of which sympathetic friends bought copies enough to pay his passage.

A social worker advised the newcomer to go to Philadelphia because New York was so congested that authorities were offering free transportation to all immigrants who were willing to move on as far as that. After days of seeking employment and living in the railroad station, which he described as "clean, cheap and comfortable," he went to work on the Homestead, Pennsylvania *Messenger*. In spite of his "greenness" he made real progress and by December of his first year had become foreman of his shop.

Because of his thorough knowledge of the *Bible* Mr. Brookes was asked to become pastor of a small Welsh Congregational Church at a weekly salary of $15. With the two salaries ($18 from the newspaper) he was able to send for his family in 11 months. But his most thrilling adventures were in getting an education. An older friend suggested that if he had more schooling he might look forward to a ministerial career. He was astonished at the idea of a

Bachrach

GEORGE S. BROOKES

grown man going to school, but he was assured that such a thing might happen quite easily in America, and so it did.

By special supplication Mr. Brookes was permitted to study and take an examination in a few months for a course of reading that usually required three years. The examination resulted in his ordination in the Western Pennsylvania Association of Congregational Churches and Ministers and was followed by a full time pastorate at Sharon. He gave up newspaper work.

It wasn't long before he received a call to the village church at Seal Harbor, Maine with the chance to study at Bangor University. The community spirit in the summer colony was strong, and when John D. Rockefeller Jr., William Adams Brown and others drew up a plan for a community church, it was, and continued to be, successful. Other members of the summer congregation included Henry Van Dyke, Harry Emerson Fosdick (see sketch this issue), Francis G. Peabody and Fritz Kreisler.

In 1918 Reverend Brookes was graduated from Bangor Theological Seminary, presenting as his thesis *Where Christianity and the War Meet.* It was based on the principle that religion and war should fight together for the defense of right against wrong, the weak against the strong. He writes: "It would take more than a shoestring of courage to deliver that thesis now." He learned by teaching. He taught school in addition to his ministerial duties, increased the interest in the community and established a library in the school from the proceeds of entertainments. As an instructor he managed to keep just a little ahead of his students. Reverend Brookes moved to the First Congregational Church of Ellsworth, Maine and was graduated from the University of Maine in 1925, receiving a

BROOKES, GEORGE S.—*Continued*

B. A. from the University of Orono and B. D. from Bangor Seminary at the same time.

When he became naturalized in 1919 he queried: "Why 37 out of every 100 Englishmen enjoying all the advantages of American life have not become citizens is an enigma to me. Here is everything we need to make life happy—a real home among all nationalities; the help of a friendly education; an asylum of freedom, tolerance, equality; a marvelous chance to develop self-respect, independence and enterprise. What more could we ask?"

While pastor at Rockville, Connecticut, Reverend Brookes studied over a period of 10 years at Hartford Seminary and in exchange for a decade of research received a Ph. D. His research resulted in his writing *Friend Anthony Benezet* (1937), a biography of an eighteenth century American Quaker, a teacher and philanthropist notable as one of the earliest crusaders against slavery. It was dedicated to "America, whose institutions of learning I increasingly enjoy and appreciate." His later book closes with: "You bestowed upon me your choicest gift —all the rights and privileges of citizenship in the best country of the world. So thank you, America!"

> *References*
>> Christian Cent 57:454 Ap 3 '40
>> N Y Times Book R p24 Mr 31 '40
>> Brookes, G. S. Thank You America! 1940

BROUN, HEYWOOD (broōn) Dec 7, 1888 —Dec 18, 1939 Newspaper columnist; president of the American Newspaper Guild; probably the best-loved figure in American journalism; born in Brooklyn, New York; attended Harvard; worked on New York *Morning Telegraph, Tribune, World, Telegram, World-Telegram*; his column, *It Seems to Me*, ran in last three papers for 18 years, most of the time crusading for some liberal cause; a prodigious writer, responsible for some 21,000,000 words; made innumerable speeches; once ran for Congress; founded the American Newspaper Guild, became its president in 1934, its "presiding saint"; went from Socialism to Communism in his sympathies, but was converted to Catholicism after second marriage in 1935; ran Broun's *Nutmeg*, a Connecticut weekly; one of his best-known books was *The Boy Grew Older* (1922)

> *References*
>> Cath World 149:494-5 Jl '39
>> Cur Hist 50:55+ My '39
>> Lit Digest 118:12 N 10 '34
>> Nation 146:580-3 My 21 '38
>> N Y Times p4 F 7 '38; p2 Ag 23 '38; p9 N 16 '38
>> New Yorker 3:18-22 O 1 '27
>> Time 33:64-6 My 22 '39 por
>> Wilson Lib Bul 11:238 D '36 por

HEYWOOD BROUN

> American Catholic Who's Who
> Bruce, B. and others Heywood Broun pam 1940
> Newspaper Guild of New York Heywood Broun as He Seemed to Us 1940
> Who's Who in America 1938-39
> Who's Who in Journalism

> *Obituaries*
>> Christian Cent 57:5 Ja 3 '40
>> Commonweal 31:215 D 29 '39
>> Liv Age 357:545+ F '40
>> Nation 149:698 D 23 '39
>> N Y Times p23 D 19 '39 por; p23 D 21 '39; p13 D 23 '39
>> Newsweek 14:25 D 25 '39 por
>> Pub W 136:2332 D 30 '39
>> Time 34:35 D 25 '39 por; 35:33 Ja 1 '40
>> Wilson Lib Bul 14:358 Ja '40

BROWN, A. TEN EYCK 1878—June 8, 1940 Architect; designer of many important buildings throughout the South

> *Obituaries*
>> N Y Herald Tribune p18 Je 10 '40
>> N Y Times p17 Je 10 '40

BROWN, FRANCIS SHUNK June 9, 1858—May 6, 1940 Noted lawyer; former attorney general of Pennsylvania; member of Bar for 60 years; headed Girard $89,000,000 trusts

> *References*
>> Who's Who in America
>> Who's Who in Government
>> Who's Who in Law

> *Obituaries*
>> N Y Times p25 My 7 '40 por

BROWN, JOHN FRANKLIN 1866—Feb 15, 1940 Educator; author; editor of secondary school publications for the Macmillan Company

H. R. Ware Co.

JOHN FRANKLIN BROWN

References

Who's Who in America 1932-33
Who's Who in American Education

Obituaries

N Y Herald Tribune p18 F 16 '40
N Y Sun p23 F 16 '40
Sch & Soc 51:240 F 24 '40

BROWNSON, JOSEPHINE Catechist; awarded Laetare Medal for 1939 in recognition of outstanding work in Catholic education

Address: 1440 Seyburn Ave, Detroit, Michigan

In 1883 Notre Dame University established the custom of awarding the Laetare Medal each year to an outstanding member of the Catholic laity. Miss Brownson is the eleventh woman to receive the medal, the first since 1934. It is the first time since the inauguration of the award that a descendant of a former medalist has received the honor. Her father, the late Major Henry F. Brownson, well known journalist, received the award in 1892.

In 1906 Miss Brownson established the Catholic Instruction League in Detroit to give religious instruction to Catholic children attending public schools. When Miss Brownson received the Laetare Medal there were some 400 teachers and 13,000 students under her supervision. Formerly an instructor of mathematics in a Detroit school, she resigned her position to devote her time to religious instruction.

In announcing the award, the Rev. John F. O'Hara, president of the University of Notre Dame, made the following statement: "While this year's Laetare Medal is awarded in tribute to the pioneering spirit and the long faithful devotion of Miss Brownson to the cause of religious instruction, it contains at the same time a recognition of a very important section of Pope Pius XI's program of Catholic Action. Miss Brownson was one of the first Catholics in any country to organize on an extensive scale the catechetical instruction ordered by Pope Pius X in his encyclical *Acerbo Nimis* published in 1905."

Miss Brownson was the recipient of a Papal decoration, *Pro Ecclesia et Pontifice,* in 1933, conferred on her in recognition of her contribution to the cause of Catholic Action by the late Pope Pius XI in 1933. The literary traditions of her family, begun by Orestes A. Brownson, her grandfather, the celebrated "father of American philosophy," and convert to the Catholic Church, are carried on by Miss Brownson. She is the author of *Catholic Bible Stories from the Old and New Testament* (1919); *Living Forever* (1928), a text in religion for high school students; *Stopping the Leak* (1928); and the Learn of Me series of eight books for the first eight grades in religion: *Come Unto Me* (1938); *Feed My Lambs* (1938); *Come and See* (1939); *Keep My Commandments* (1939); *Thou Art Peter* (1938); *Living Water* (1939); *I Am the Vine* (1939); and *To the Heart of the Child* (1934).

Among others who have received the Laetare Medal in former years are: Dr. Albert Zahm, occupant of the Guggenheim chair of aeronautics in the Congressional Library; Honorable Alfred E. Smith; John McCormack, Irish tenor; Richard Reid, Southern editor and writer; and Dr. Irvin

JOSEPHINE BROWNSON

BROWNSON, JOSEPHINE—*Continued*
Abeill of Louisville, Kentucky, president of
the American Medical Association.

References

America 60:602 Ap 1 '39
Cath School Journal 59:15A My '39
Cath World 136:746 Mr '33; 149:237
My '39
American Catholic Who's Who

BRYAN, JULIEN HEQUEMBOURG
(bri'an) May 23, 1899- Photographer
Address: Bronxville, New York

One of the most widely printed photographs to come from European war zones
was that of a little Polish girl kneeling in a
field beside the blood-stained body of her older
sister. Julien Bryan took this photograph—
along with many others—in Poland during the
days of the German invasion in September
1939. Well-known as a photographer and lecturer, a man who has been in all parts of the
globe to take pictures of people, Julien Bryan
had been in Bucharest, and planned a bit of
quiet picture-taking in Warsaw en route to
America. He was taking a bath in his
Warsaw hotel on September 4, 1939 when
the German bombing of Poland began and
he learned that the American Ambassador,
and all correspondents and press photographers had left the city. It was a photographer's dream come true—and in spite of
the great danger, Bryan stayed on: "I had
the siege of Warsaw all to myself."

The story of this siege of Warsaw has
been told by Julien Bryan in a documentary
film, *Siege,* and in a book published in April
1940 by the same name with a foreword by
Maurice Hindus. The first part of the
book is a dramatic narrative of Bryan's
personal experience; the second part is a
group of 48 full-page photographs. His are
the only uncensored pictures of the Polish
invasion. Well-written, factual, vivid—
Bryan catches with an artist's eye the small,
significant detail—the text is an account of
a city and its people under fire for three
fearful weeks. The courageous Mayor of
Warsaw gave Bryan all possible assistance,
for the Poles were anxious that the outside
world should have a photographic record
of what was happening to them at the hands
of the Nazis. Bryan was encamped most of
the time, with several refugees, in the
cellar of the American Embassy. Bombings
and shellings were less feared by day when
planes could be seen, than at night, when
one could only listen and wait. Soon finding, as the Poles did, that fear could be best
overcome by activity, Bryan worked hard.
"I was much happier when busy in the open,
and toward the end was excited but not
terrified as I filmed bombers power-diving
a few hundred yards away." The Poles,
he says further, took the whole siege
patiently, bravely, asking only one question:
why do not England and France help us?

Bryan took pictures of a bombed hospital, women and children killed in a shelled
apartment house, a cellar in a maternity
hospital, coffins unearthed in cemeteries,
breadlines, peasants killed by machine guns
in the fields, dead horses in the streets.
There is quiet humor as well as pathos in
some: a peasant woman with her cow in
the city streets, selling milk from house to
house; a family in the midst of its salvaged
household goods carrying on in the open
the small, everyday routine of washing,
cooking, sleeping. Several of the pictures,
apart from the story, are actually of more
propaganda than artistic value. Among
those notable as definite contributions to
photographic art (and considering the extreme difficulties under which they were
taken, it is remarkable there are so many)
are: a child refugee with her dog in her
arms, the strikingly strong face of an old
woman who had saved two spoons and a
pair of scissors, another shawled woman
holding a loaf of bread, a patient's unfinished meal on a hospital bedside table, the
faces of four Polish women who have
looked upon death.

Bryan and other foreigners in Warsaw
were evacuated September 21, courteously
aided and given safe passage out by the
Germans. Before he sailed home from
Stockholm, he tells of going, in Germany,
to see a moving picture of the taking of
Poland: throughout its showing, he says,
there was not one sound of applause.

Julien Bryan was born in Titusville,
Pennsylvania, May 23, 1899. On his tenth
birthday someone gave him a camera, and
his life career was settled for him then and
there. He took pictures all during his high
school days in Titusville; a camera went to
Princeton with him. But in 1917 he left
college to serve at the front with the
French ambulance service. He had no idea
that the war pictures he took then, and
the lecturing for the government he did at
the age of 18, were to begin his career as a
documentary photographer and popular lecturer. He went back to Princeton after the
War; while he was still an undergraduate
his *Ambulance 464*, describing and illustrating his experiences in the War, was published. He was so eager to study other
nationalities that between his junior and
senior year he shoveled coal on a liner to
get to Europe, made pastry on another boat
to pay his way home.

After he was graduated, Bryan, following
family tradition, became interested in the
ministry and spent three years at the Union
Theological Seminary and Columbia University. But he soon found that a career
within four walls was too limited for him,
and around 1920 began the travels with a
camera that have been his adventure and
his living. During a 20-year period he
has visited and photographed scenes and
people in the Orient, Mexico, Siberia, Soviet
Russia, every part of Europe. No little
part of his success taking pictures in

JULIEN BRYAN

strange corners of the world is due to the fact that he genuinely likes people. He says: "I have never yet encountered, in years of exploring foreign countries with a camera, a national group or people who were inherently hostile to all outsiders." A good many primitive groups looked upon him with suspicion at first: their confidence had to be won slowly, and care taken that their *mores* and their hospitality were never violated. He had amusing experiences and friendly treatment among such peoples as the Tungus, who look like Eskimos and cultivate reindeer. When he showed them a picture of Santa Claus and his reindeer flying over housetops, they said: "Artist no good. He's drawn the reindeer all wrong—and besides, even our children know that reindeer can't fly!"

It was in 1930 that he first went to Russia, with a party led by Maurice Hindus, and took films which were shown on his return to the United States in several theatres. Burton Holmes became interested and invited Bryan to tour with him in the spring of 1933 on a joint program, "Russia as it was—Russia as it is today." Since then he has gone back again and again to Russia; in the summer of 1939 he was in Holland, Belgium and Switzerland. His films have been featured by the *March of Time* program, and his many lecture tours have been enthusiastically received not only because of his photographs but because of their educational value.

Bryan himself is a big, friendly person with a broad smile, an inquiring nose and a high forehead with receding hair. As the photographs reproduced in *Siege* indicate, he takes considerable pains with his work. He says that he does not "shoot" scenes at random, taking pictures of just pretty or unusual things. "Instead I map out and

film, in a methodical, analytical way, a logical series of scenes that tell the true story of the life of the people there." In his pictures and lectures he has tried, he says further, to give Americans a truer understanding of how other nations live and work and play, in an effort to counteract those unjust prejudices we are apt to harbor against people in other lands. "I have learned one thing from my travels; that whatever the dictators and the militarists of the world may desire, the vast majority of all populations, the common people like ourselves, want peace and are bitterly opposed to war."

Julien Bryan is married, and lives with his family on Perry Street in New York City. His wife teaches dancing at Sarah Lawrence College, and he has a young son, born in 1939. Bryan has never yet toured America to photograph it, but during the summer of 1940 he hopes to go on a camera tour of South America. He says he feels that the United States will last a few more years, and wants to do the other countries first.

References
Greenwich Villager p12 My 16 '40
Pop Mech 73:328-32+; 552-7+ Mr-Ap '40 il pors
Read Digest 36:27-32 Ap '40
Scholastic 34:23E My 13 '39 por
Bryan, J. H. Siege 1940

BRYCE, ELIZABETH MARION, VISCOUNTESS 1853—Dec 29, 1939 Widow of Viscount Bryce; promoter of Anglo-American friendship

Viscountess Bryce, widow of the famous Liberal statesman and British Ambassador to the United States (1907-19), died in London at the age of 86. Daughter of Thomas Ashton, she was married to Lord Bryce in 1889 and continued an active public career after his death in 1922. He was the author of *The American Commonwealth,* internationally known analysis of political and social life in America. Lady Bryce had been president of a committee of the English Speaking Union; long a powerful supporter of better understanding among English-speaking peoples; and a worker for rights and welfare of women in England.

References
Who's Who

Obituaries
N Y Herald Tribune D. 29 '39 por

BRYSON, LYMAN July 12, 1888- Educator
Address: b. Columbia University Teachers College, 525 W 120th St, New York City; h. 400 W 118th St, New York City

During 1939 and 1940 Professor Lyman Lloyd Bryson of Columbia University has acted as dinner host and conductor of the Columbia Broadcasting System's informal forum, *The People's Platform.* This is just one of the programs he has charted as chairman of the

LYMAN BRYSON

CBS Adult Education Board, which is attempting to present adult education in new and stimulating forms.

Each evening that the program is presented Professor Bryson has four guests discuss a topic with which they are familiar or on which they are experts. Before they go on the air he gets them talking easily over dinner, served in the studio, and then the microphone picks up their informal, unrehearsed conversation. It is he who gets the shy ones to voice their opinions and keeps the orators from making rehearsed speeches—who, in fact, keeps the program moving vigorously.

Educational work, in one form or another, has been Lyman Bryson's interest for many years. He was born in Valentine, Nebraska on the edge of an Indian reservation, the son of a pioneer druggist, George E. Bryson, and Nancy Melissa (Hayes) Bryson. His boyhood was spent in the cattle country and in Omaha and his first job was that of reporter on the Omaha *Bee*. After he received his B. A. from the University of Michigan in 1910 he spent several years in Omaha and Detroit as a reporter. He then went back to the University with his wife, Hope Mersereau, whom he had married in 1912, to teach in its rhetoric and journalism departments and to get his M. A. in 1915.

When the War came Lyman Bryson went East and worked for the army several months, then for the American Red Cross at National Headquarters. In 1919 the Red Cross sent him abroad. There he was put in charge of the Junior Red Cross program and later made aide for the commissioner for Europe. Then, for the International Red Cross, he was director of the Junior Division until he became director of publications. He says: "I was constantly on

the move in Europe and later in Asia investigating social conditions in the interest of international philanthropy."

From 1925 to 1932 Professor Bryson was an extension lecturer at the University of California and during his last three years in California acted as executive director of the California Association for Adult Education. In 1934 he was visiting professor of education at Teachers College, Columbia University and from 1935 on professor there. While at Columbia Professor Bryson started the "readability laboratory," the aim of which is to develop new versions of books on economics, sociology, politics, political economy, rewritten in simple, vigorous style.

Professor Bryson believed that a true picture of the readers of America "would count out about 15,000,000 adults who cannot read well enough to understand anything that has a serious meaning." Because he felt the need of a "common language" for difficult works, he asked the American Association for Adult Education for funds to develop writers for the mass of people. With about 20 writers he set to work. It wasn't easy, for, as Professor Bryson pointed out, "it is not a mere matter of using shorter words, shorter sentences, shorter paragraphs. It reaches deeper than that. It is a matter of developing a style so distinctive that as yet it isn't on the market."

Most of Professor Bryson's educational ideas and theories are presented in his textbook, *Adult Education* (1936). Here are given the historical background, the philosophical and theoretical bases and the practical workings of the adult education movement in America. It has been called "the ideal introduction to adult education," and commended for its simplicity and directness.

Professor Bryson is, perhaps, best known for his work in the development of public discussion. At California University, as Forum Leader for the Des Moines, Iowa Adult Education Project (1932-34), as lecturer on social and educational topics at Town Hall, New York, at the Chautauqua Institution at Chautauqua, New York and before many clubs and forums all over the country, his aim was always to stimulate discussion in his audiences. And he was one of the first college teachers to develop courses in discussion methods. Undoubtedly he has had a good deal to do with the spread of the forum movement in the United States.

In what he calls "more frivolous moments", "ruddy, shake-haired" Professor Bryson has written a number of short stories, a prize-winning one-act play *(The Grasshopper)* and poetry. "My volume of verse," he says, "is a very scarce collector's item—or it would be if anyone wanted to collect it." Away from teaching, Professor Bryson is, he insists, "a very fancy billiard player and an enthusiastic but very bad tennis player." He collects nothing but books, likes comedies but never goes to a serious film and prefers, in the order named, French and Chinese cooking.

References
> Library J 61:455 Je 1 '36
> Lit Digest 121:33 F 22 '36
> Who's Who in America
> Who's Who in New York

BUCHAN, JOHN, 1ST BARON TWEEDSMUIR (bŭk'an) Aug 26, 1875— Feb 11, 1940 Governor General of Canada; author

Lord Tweedsmuir, born John Buchan, Governor General of Canada since 1935 and author of some 60 books, died less than a week after suffering a brain concussion resulting from a fall. He was 64 years old. Just before his death, he had completed and sent to his publishers (Houghton Mifflin) the final chapters of his autobiography, which was published in 1940 under the title *Pilgrim's Way: An Essay in Recollection,* as well as a manuscript of a completed novel, entitled *The Mountain Meadow,* which is expected to come out in the spring of 1941.

John Buchan was born in Peeblesshire, Scotland, the son of the Rev. John and Helen Buchan. With the aid of scholarships he managed to work his way through Glasgow University and then Brasenose College, Oxford. Considered one of the finest scholars of his time, young Buchan was a "small, thin, retiring and studious lad who found satisfaction in debate and became president of the Oxford Union."

After two years in South Africa, as private secretary to Lord Milner, he returned to England, joined the publishing firm of Thomas Nelson and became a director of Reuter's News Agency. During the World War he was a member of the Headquarters' Staff of the British Army in France, and was later promoted to director of information in the War Office. From 1927 to 1935 he represented the Scottish Universities in Parliament. As a speaker then he was polished and eloquent, one of the few who maintained "the grand manner." Once his oratorical delivery was interrupted by a heckler's shout of "let us pray," but as time went on he lightened a natural solemnity and became a popular speaker.

Shortly after his appointment as Governor General of Canada he became the first Baron Tweedsmuir, choosing the title from Tweedsmuir in Peeblesshire, where his family had lived for generations. As Governor General he arranged the visit of the King and Queen of England in 1939 and also delivered an historic speech in September of that year when Canada declared war on Germany.

All through the years from college on, Buchan continued to write as a journalist, novelist, biographer and historian. Once in

Karsh

JOHN BUCHAN, 1st BARON TWEEDSMUIR

an interview in Canada he said: "I've written too many books; they weigh upon my conscience." He worked at top speed and turned out a book a year for many years. Some of his books were frankly thrillers, but even these showed his sound training as a classical scholar. Probably his finest stories were the trilogy of secret service work in the World War—*The Thirty-Nine Steps* (made into a prize winning movie); *Greenmantle* and *Mr. Standfast.* These brought him fame in the United States. In non-fiction, he was the author of *Augustus; Oliver Cromwell; A History of the Great War* (four volumes); his juvenile books included *A Book of Escapes and Hurried Journeys* and *Prester John.*

References
> Atlan 165:620-9 My '40; 165:798-807 Je '40; 166:67-75 Jl '40
> Lit Digest 119:11 Ap 6 '35 por
> N Y Sun p1 F 8 '40
> Newsweek 5:15 Ap 6 '35 por; 6:28-9 N 9 '35
> Pub W 131:1586 Ap 10 '37
> Queen's Q 43:353-63 N '36
> Sat R Lit 17:5 O 30 '37 por (p1)
> Wilson Lib Bul 3:422 Ja '29 por
> Kunitz, S. J. ed. Living Authors 1937
> Kunitz, S. J. and Haycraft, H. eds. Junior Book of Authors 1935
> Who's Who

Obituaries
> Christian Sci Mon Mag p3 F 16 '40
> Manchester Guardian p3 F 12 '40 por
> N Y Herald Tribune p1 F 12 '40; p18 F 13 '40
> Sat R Lit 21:8 F 17 '40
> Time 35:27-28 F 19 '40

BUCHANAN, THOMAS DRYSDALE
bū-kăn'n)   Mar 9, 1876—Mar 21, 1940
Physician; outstanding specialist in the field
of anesthesia; held many hospital posts

References

American Medical Directory
American Men of Science
Who's Who in America

Obituaries

N Y Herald Tribune p18 Mr 22 '40
N Y Times p19 Mr 22 '40 por

**BUCHMAN, FRANK NATHAN DAN-
IEL, REV.** (book'man) June 4, 1878- Clergy-
man; founder of the Oxford Group religious
movement
Address: 61 Gramercy Park N, New York
City

To assert that a bespectacled, obscure ex-
Lutheran minister and Y. M. C. A. secretary, driven from the campus of Princeton
University, should have a leading place in
determining British foreign policies may
sound fantastic, but it is true. During the
Munich discussions and the successive international crises of the summer of 1939
Dr. Buchman was busily engaged on the
Continent and in England in presenting his
religious principles of peace in our time
and appeasement to English statesmen. In
Great Britain endorsers of the principles of
Dr. Buchman's Moral Rearmament increased by the thousands. Moral Rearmament means "to keep the peace and make
it permanent; to make the wealth and work
of the world available to all and for the
exploitation of none; and with peace and
prosperity as our servants and not our masters, to build a new world, create a new
culture, bring in the Golden Age."

Moral Rearmament's grandiose but seemingly impractical pronouncements have been
endorsed by the leaders of Great Britain in
a pamphlet (1939) of which 500,000 copies
have been sold. In that same year Britons
opened 5,000,000 milk bottles with MRA
on their tops; 10,000 billboards were donated
to Dr. Buchman to advertise MRA for a
month; half a million letters were marked
MRA.

The proverb—a prophet is without honor
in his own country—might have been written for Dr. Buchman, who, although an
American, has never aroused enthusiasm in
the United States comparable to that which
he enjoys in Europe. He was born of solid
Swiss-Dutch stock in the small town of
Pennsburg, Pennsylvania, son of Frank and
Sarah A. (Greenawalt) Buchman. His
father, a local hotel owner of German-
Lutheran religious belief, claimed descent
from a clergyman who was the successor of
Zwingli in the chair of theology at Zurich.

In 1899 young Buchman was graduated
from Muhlenberg College (awarded a D. D.
there in 1926) and then went on to study
for the ministry at Mount Airy Lutheran

Theological Seminary. Students there at
the time speak of him as "a fair but not
exceptional student" who was ordained in
1902.

"In his early environment," said the late
Ernest Sutherland Bates (see sketch this
issue), "he found the two religious traditions
that have raised him to greatness. The
Lutheran Church, which never broke away
completely from its Catholic origin, retained
auricular confession as a means of spiritual
growth. . . According to Quaker belief, it
was possible for every man to obtain
spiritual guidance from God by consulting
the Light Within. Through combining
these two essentially antagonistic principles,
as no one with a logical mind could have
done, and vulgarizing both of them in subjection to salesmanship needs, Dr. Buchman
was at last able to cross-breed the exotic
flower of 'Buchmanism.' "

After his ordination Dr. Buchman's rise
in the ministry was slow. For a while he
served as pastor at Overbrook, Pennsylvania. Then he founded the first Lutheran
settlement house for poor boys at Philadelphia in 1907. The "awakening" to which
he traces the origin of the Oxford Group
occurred in 1908 when he had gone to
England after an angry quarrel with the
trustees of the organization. One afternoon, low in spirit, he stopped at a wayside
church where he heard a woman preacher.
"It produced in me a vibrant feeling," he
said, "as though a strong current of life
had poured into me, and afterwards a dazed
sense of a great spiritual shaking up."

From that moment he was a "called" man
with an unshakeable mission. He discovered within himself a new power—he
could "change the life" of a friend. In 1909
he returned to the United States and became Y. M. C. A. secretary at the Pennsylvania State College. There he evolved the
principles of his "life-changing" religion,
which he called *A First Century Christian
Fellowship*. He found much sin on the
campus and began to convert or, as he
called it, "change" students. As time went
on he "perfected himself in the great art of
extracting confessions from adolescents."

By 1915 he was seeking new pastures
and became a missionary, beginning the
travels which have taken him around the
globe "as casually as other men drive
around the block." He went to Japan,
India, Korea under Y. M. C. A. auspices,
then worked in France during the War
looking after German prisoners. At the
close of the War he gave his first house
party in a summer resort in Kuling, China.
A wealthy Chinese diplomat converted to
the new evangelist invited 80 people to his
country estate. Buchman succeeded in
"changing" several guests who confessed
their sins and promised to be led by God
in the future. Generous sums of money for
further "life-changing" were made available
to Dr. Buchman. From the first he developed his ability to extract money from
converts painlessly. He found that "money

Portrait by M. David

FRANK BUCHMAN

rolls in with freedom and timeliness that are considered truly providential." In later years, when he was asked why he and his workers always traveled in luxurious liners and stayed at swank hotels, he answered: "Why not? Isn't God a millionaire?"

Buchman came back to the United States to introduce his new form of evangelism to the great universities—Yale, Harvard and Princeton. The last named furnished him with intensive work against sin. In house parties there he revealed the principles of "sharing" and "guidance" to enthusiastic students. "Sharing" was the old Catholic-Lutheran principle of private confession transmogrified by having the confessions made in the presence of the whole group. Then a "quiet time" came when "guidance" was given from above during a period called "listening-in to God."

Naturally students' confessions were mostly trivial in nature or a matter of sex experience. The erotic nature of the meetings came to the attention of the president of Princeton and he promptly banished Dr. Buchman from the grounds. Although suffering a severe setback, Dr. Buchman did not give up, but moved his field of operation to Oxford University, England, a place which "for an American aiming at a crusade, ranked high among unlikely places." Armed only with "his own quasi-messianic sense of mission and a letter of introduction," his success was spectacular. Although the authorities rebelled, Dr. Buchman changed the name of his movement to the Oxford Group and became "soul surgeon" to most of the British aristocracy. The Oxford Group sped along a sex-tinged confession path mainly among the moneyed class. In 1924 the Reverend Buchman came to the United States to find results rather disappointing, for "only a few sheepish

sheep were gathered into the fold." But in subsequent trips his success increased and thousands all over the country flocked to hear him speak.

In England once again, Dr. Buchman, smarting under the criticism of vulgarity in the sex confessions of callow college students, dropped such confession almost completely from his movement. He also began a more general campaign for working-class people in the movement when it was criticized for appealing only to persons of wealth and social position. The list of his supporters contained an imposing array of those highly placed in government, religious and professional life. Buchman and his workers traveled in the best society, put up at the best hotels and with a seemingly never-ceasing flow of money went from nation to nation expounding the principles of "sharing" and "life-changing" before enthusiastic crowds which many times numbered 25,000. A limerick went the rounds:

"There was a young man from Peoria
Whose sinning grew gorier and gorier
By confession and prayer,
And some savoir-faire
He now lives at the Waldorf-Astoria."

Dr. Buchman does not look like the traditional evangelist "who always has a strong personality, gifted of tongue and capable of moving vast crowds to emotional fervor." He believes that religion should not be solemn but hilarious, filled with jokes and laughter. His "mien of scrupulously shampooed and almost medical cleanliness so characteristic of the hygienic American" is accompanied by "the ingratiating and beamingly confident manner of a well-trained salesman for one of the better class business firms. He claims to be on intimate terms with his employer. 'I know that He is a personal God,' he has said. 'Look what He has done for me.'" The "soul surgeon" is a bachelor. A receiver of divine messages for his every action, he has been asked why he didn't marry: "Just because I have never been guided to marry."

About 75 books have been written on the subject of the Oxford Group, Moral Rearmament and Dr. Buchman. Rose Macaulay used the movement in a satiric manner in *Going Abroad*. Rachel Crothers wrote *Susan and God,* in which Gertrude Lawrence (see sketch this issue) in 1935 and for some time on scored a hit as a silly rich woman whose life was transformed by a religion which might well be Buchmanism. In 1940 Joan Crawford and Fredric March appeared in a highly successful film made from the play.

Great numbers of people all over the world confess that after "quiet times" and "testifying" to their sinful pasts in public they experience a miraculous change in their lives. Employers such as Louis B. Mayer, movie magnate, George Eastman, Kodak manufacturer; and labor leaders such as David Dubinsky, head of the International Ladies Garment Workers, and Dan J. Tobin,

BUCHMAN, FRANK—*Continued*

head of the International Brotherhood of Teamsters, speak of the wonderful results to capital and labor. Both in England and the United States the movement is credited with settling strikes. William Rowell, executive of the Trades Union Congress of Great Britain and a leading Buchmanite, declared that "labor and capital should lie down together in one of Dr. Buchman's 'quiet times.'" He hoped that the labor leader would abandon his union demands and the employer "agree to stop trying to triple his profits."

Applied to international relations in the shocking year of 1940 Buchman's plan of sitting down quietly waiting for "God's dictation" does not appear to have notable success. It would be quite difficult, even for Dr. Buchman, with his spectacular success in appeasement in Europe's former international crises, to induce Hitler, Mussolini, Pétain (see sketch this issue) and Churchill (see sketch this issue) to solve their difficulties in a "quiet time."

References

Friday 1:21-2 My 31 '40 il pors
New Yorker 8:22-5 Ap 23 '32
Time 35:59 Je 17 '40

Landau, R. Man Whose God Was a Millionaire: Dr. Frank Buchman *In* God Is My Adventure p172-200 1936
Murray, R. H. Oxford Group Movement *In* Group Movements Throughout the Ages p285-372 1936
Who's Who
Who's Who in America

BUDD, RALPH Aug 20, 1879- Railroad president; member of the National Defense Commission

Address: b. War Department, Washington, D.C.; h. 936 Lake Shore Drive, Chicago, Illinois

Ralph Budd, president of the Chicago, Burlington and Quincy Railroad, was appointed on May 29, 1940 by President Roosevelt to the National Defense Commission, to direct transportation. It will be Mr. Budd's job to see to it that no railroad congestion develops such as happened in the First World War, to see that goods move promptly. With a lifetime of railroading experience behind him, Ralph Budd is one of those Commission members with "expert knowledge of the fields to which they are assigned and the backing of the industries in which they are leaders."

Since 1932 Mr. Budd has headed the Chicago, Burlington and Quincy Railroad. Half his time he spends out on the road, either traveling between business engagements, seeing people who live along the line, inspecting jobs and tracks (often in a small auto rail car), or just getting the feel of the trains and sounding out rider opinion. He says, "I'm much happier outside," but he also likes to spend time compiling statistics on his railroad's operations and handling the finances of the Burlington, the budget of which is a staggering sum.

During the years he has been with the Burlington, Mr. Budd's most spectacular achievement has been the development of streamlined Diesel-engined trains. His railroad, which has a large number of comparatively short branch lines over the section west of Chicago, needed an economical way of providing service. Heavy steam trains were too costly to operate. First Budd tried out gasoline-motored one and two car trains, but the "puddle jumpers," as they were called, were not popular. Budd experimented on various kinds of trains and finally evolved the streamlined, Diesel-motored, stainless-steel Zephyr trains, created, he insists, not "to startle the public into riding in something new and different," but by a need "for economy consistent with public fancy and demand."

All his adult life Ralph Budd has been working for and with railroads. He was born on August 20, 1879 in Waterloo, Iowa, in the heart of the fertile farm county his railroad now serves. He was brought up in Iowa and went to school in Iowa—to Highland Park College at Des Moines, from which he was graduated with a degree in civil engineering in 1899.

Budd started his railroad work in the engineering department of the Chicago Great Western Railway and by 1902 had acquired a wife—Georgiana Marshall, whom he married in 1901—and the position of assistant engineer. From 1902 to 1906 he was successively roadmaster, general superintendent of construction and divisional engineer with the Rock Island Railroad. It was at this point that he began to do more interesting and important things. In 1906 he went to Panama where he served for three years as chief engineer of the Panama Railroad. During those three years the old railroad was rehabilitated and the new Panama Railway laid out and nearly completed. "That job," says Budd now, "was an engineer's paradise."

Back in the United States in 1909, he became chief engineer with the Oregon Trunk Railway, the Spokane, Portland and Seattle Railway and the Spokane and Inland Empire Railroad. Then came what Mr. Budd considers the most important phase of his life—the 19 years he spent with the Great Northern Railway. He started in 1913 as assistant to the president and chief engineer, and in 1919 became president, a position he held until 1932. It was here, working under James J. Hill, famed pioneer builder of the Great Northern, that he got much of his knowledge, skill and experience. It was here, too, that his engineering skill found a new outlet.

The Great Northern, winding over the mountains of the Northwest between Chicago and the Pacific, had more than $150,-000,000 in property improvement put into it during Budd's term as head and paid divi-

RALPH BUDD

dends steadily. The many improvements, feats of engineering skill, include the eight mile Cascade Tunnel, the longest railroad tunnel on the American continent, built at a cost of about $25,000,000. Working on this and on the general maintenance of the railroad, 10 to 16 hours of work a day were usual for Mr. Budd. Often after inspection trips over the Great Northern, after a day which left his associates gasping and fagged, Budd could be found at midnight poring over statistics, maps and data.

It was Mr. Budd's experiences on this road which attracted the Soviet government, when in 1930 its representatives came here to look for some good American railroad man to advise them about building and operating railroads in Russia. The Great Northern, they saw, traversed just about the same sort of country as the Siberian line in Russia and they saw in Budd just the man they wanted. Budd went to Russia—his first vacation in years, and a busman's vacation at that—and spent three months riding around Russia on its railroads. His report recommended among other things, that the Russians proceed with their program, using heavier and larger cars and heavier ties and rails instead of the standard light capacity equipment commonly in use in Europe.

In 1932 Budd began to manage the affairs of the Burlington Railroad, which is owned by the Great Northern and the Northern Pacific. During the years in which he has been its head he has come to believe that a loyal and efficient personnel is the greatest asset a railroad can have. An employer and capitalist, he still makes no table-pounding attacks on radicals and regimentalists and bureaucratic spendthrifts, though he has, of course, disapproved on occasion of some New Deal policies.

Budd is a "quiet, unassuming, kindly, thoughtful" sort of man who in his own office, it is reported, was once mistaken for a filing clerk. Tall and spare in appearance, he is pleasant to meet, and despite his lack of "good fellowship" traits makes friends easily. He has none of the ordinary businessman's hobbies. He doesn't play golf or visit luncheon clubs, and he hates to waste time in table talk, but likes to attend baseball games and rides horseback whenever the opportunity affords. His hobbies are maps and history reading. He has a large collection of maps and is always on the lookout for more. He likes to study, particularly, the historical background of that part of the United States running from St. Paul to the Pacific Northwest. His knowledge of it is extraordinary and his associates used to say that if all the printed histories of the early Northwest were destroyed, Ralph Budd could probably replace the most important ones from memory.

References

Business Week p39-40 Mr 12 '30 por; p15-16 Je 15 '40
Christian Sci Mon Mag p3+ N 24 '37 il por
N Y Sun p16 My 29 '40; p1 My 30 '40
N Y Times p1, 15 My 29 '40
Who's Who in America
Who's Who in Commerce and Industry
Who's Who in Railroading

BULGAKOV, MICHAEL AFANASIEVICH (bool-ga'kŏf a'fä-nä'sĕ-ĕ-vich) 1891 —Mar 10, 1940 Novelist; playwright

The death of Michael Bulgakov, a member of the right wing of contemporary Russian literature, at the age of 49, was reported March 10, 1940. Bulgakov's most famous play was *Days of the Turbins*, which depicts sympathetically a White Russian family. This play was first produced at the Moscow Art Theatre in 1927, but two seasons later was removed because of censorship. The production of several other dramas by the playwright was also forbidden, and it was said that as a result Bulgakov went directly to Josef Stalin, through whose intervention Bulgakov became an official at the First Arts Theatre in Moscow, and the much discussed play was revived in 1933.

Following this experience, Bulgakov presented in his play *Molière* the predicament of the playwright under censorship. His other writings include *Zoe's Lodging, The Scarlet Island, The Deviliad, The Flight* and, in collaboration with Vassily Sachnovsky, a dramatization of Nikolai Gogol's *Dead Souls*.

References

International Who's Who

Obituaries

N Y Herald Tribune p12 Mr 11 '40
Variety 138:47 Mr 13 '40
Wilson Lib Bul 14:548 Ap '40

BULLITT, WILLIAM CHRISTIAN Jan
25, 1891- Former United States Ambassador to France

December 1940 · Bulletin: William C.
Bullitt came back to the United States
in July 1940 to make his personal report
on the fall of France to the President.
His first comment absolved the Vichy
government, headed by his friend Pétain
(see sketch this issue), from the charge
of Fascism and favored continued diplomatic relations. Not long afterward
Joseph Alsop and Robert Kintner revealed that the American Ambassador
had stayed in Paris after French authorities had fled in order to instruct
the Germans in their occupation of the
city, in the face of threatened revolt by
the French Communists. Next, in his
August speech in Philadelphia's Independence Hall (published as a 29-page
pamphlet under the title, *Report to the
American People*), Bullitt emphasized the
lesson of appeasement and stated that
only Great Britain and her navy stood
between the United States and the
Nazi peril. This, "Bullitt's personal
declaration of war on the Reich"—presumably delivered with the approval of
the Administration—brought on Bullitt's
head the wrath of isolationists in
Congress. Thereafter he was kept busy
denying his supposed promises to
France of war aid by the United States.
In a speech in October he quoted from
a letter from Daladier (see sketch this
issue) to show that he had made our
intention to stay out of war clear to the
French government. Nevertheless he
still sees aid to Great Britain—and
China—as our first task. In November
1940 he resigned his Ambassadorship.

From July issue:

In 1914, from the balcony of his aunt's
home, William Bullitt saw the air raid on
Paris, the first in history. Now a quarter of
a century later, he has once more seen the
skies of France dark with German planes,
has witnessed the occupation of Paris by
German troops, has heard the tragic order
to surrender—this time from the American
Embassy in Paris, where he has represented
the United States as Ambassador to France
since 1936. Days after the occupation came
word from Paris that none of the Embassy
staff had been injured.

Our Ambassador to France is credited
with a "behind-the-scenes" influence on
America's foreign policy which far out-
weighs that of the ordinary career diplomat.
Since the outbreak of the Second World
War he has been in almost constant communication with the White House, supplementing long and informal letters and reports with several trans-Atlantic telephone
conversations with the President each week.
His letters are not always seen even by
Secretary of State Hull (see sketch this

issue), and there are those who fear his
influence and speak of him as the "Colonel
House of the Administration." Even prior
to the War examples of his influence were
apparent. In the Czechoslovakian crisis,
after President Roosevelt had sent a note
to Hitler pleading for a peaceful solution
and Berlin had rejected the plan, the
President wanted to write another note. The
State Department objected on the ground
that American public opinion would not
permit such intervention in foreign affairs.
It was Bullitt whom Roosevelt turned to for
advice, and it was Bullitt who not only
urged the President to send the second note,
but offered to take the blame if the public
was outraged. Again, after the war started,
Bullitt overruled protests of army and navy
officials by arranging for a French Air Mission to buy United States built airplanes before the United States had access to them—
a fact which was later uncovered accidentally
through an airplane crash in California.

His presence at the White House or with
the President at Warm Springs, Georgia, has
always been regarded in diplomatic circles as
"a prelude to possible administrative changes
in the Department of State, shifts of Ambassadors and Ministers in the field to other
posts, or a sharpening of diplomatic policy
toward Central Europe or the Far East at
times when aggressive actions of dictator
states were causing apprehension." No
poker-faced, tight-lipped diplomat, Bullitt is
allegedly "the soul of indiscretion," yet by
background and education he is certainly
well-equipped to be one of President Roosevelt's most trusted informants and advisers
on European affairs.

A co-worker once said of William Christian Bullitt: "He rose from the rich." He
was born January 25, 1891 into a wealthy
and distinguished Philadelphia family which
traced kinship with George Washington,
Patrick Henry, Pocahontas and with many
aristocratic Virginia families. His grandfather, William Christian Bullitt, had come
to Philadelphia from Louisville to assist in
liquidating a bank, and had decided to remain in the legal center of the country. The
Bullitts had been following the profession
of law for 300 years; William Christian
Bullitt's father was a lawyer; he was himself destined for the law. After an active
career at Yale, where he distinguished himself as a student of political science, editor
of the *Yale News*, member of Phi Beta Kappa,
and where he raised his voice in protest
against snobbery, he entered the Harvard
Law School. The elder Bullitt's death interrupted his legal schooling, however, and the
future ambassador sailed with his mother for
a trip to Europe.

They were caught in Russia when the
First World War broke out. Young Bullitt
saw opposing armies marching off to war,
each with the conviction that they were
fighting for righteousness, each with the
idea that their cause was blessed. It gave
him an earnest desire to end wars, to get

behind the scenes and learn just what started them. He decided upon a career as newspaper correspondent, but when he returned to the United States the best he could find was a job on the Philadelphia *Public Ledger* as police reporter at $10 a week. He took it and in his spare time wrote editorials on the European situation. Encouraged to write more about foreign affairs, in one tremendous leap Bullitt found himself promoted to the position of associate editor.

In 1916 Bullitt married Ernesta Drinker, a Philadelphia girl of great beauty and of fine social background. They spent their honeymoon, in Germany, Austria and Belgium, where they traveled as guests of the German High Command, and Bullitt continued to write articles for the *Ledger* on what he saw. On their return he was put in charge of the Washington Bureau of the paper, and there formed a friendship with Colonel House, President Wilson's right-hand man. In return for information on economic and civic affairs in Europe, House gave the young newspaperman many exclusive beats.

When the United States entered the War Bullitt was put in charge of the State Department Bureau of Central European Information. Here he served until the end of the War, analyzing European speeches and trends, supplying material for the President's papers. Bullitt made an idol of Wilson; he thought of him as the one man who could outlaw war. And he was pleased when he himself was selected to be a member of President Wilson's Peace Mission when it sailed in 1918.

Wilson, in turn, thought highly of young Bullitt and relied on his judgment of European conditions. Thus when the question of Soviet Russia came up in peace discussions Wilson and Lloyd George sent Bullitt, then 27 years old, on a secret mission to find out if Soviet Russia was permanent and stable enough for recognition. After interviews with Soviet officials, he came back with a proposed peace treaty given him by the Russians and his own recommendation that the Allies recognize the Soviet. He made the mistake, however, of reporting to Lloyd George first. Bullitt now believes that to be the reason Wilson cut him, suppressed his report and let the Soviet go unrecognized.

Disillusioned over the neglect of his Soviet report, Bullitt became even more disillusioned when he read the draft of the Versailles Treaty which Colonel House gave him. He told House, "This isn't a treaty of peace; I see at least 11 wars in it." He ended matters by resigning as a member of the Peace Commission, writing to Wilson: "I am sorry you did not fight our fight to the finish and that you had so little faith in the millions who like myself had faith in you."

Bullitt made his letter of resignation public and sailed for home still in a quandary about whether to expose all the horse-

WILLIAM C. BULLITT

trading on the peace terms he had witnessed behind closed doors. This was soon solved for him when he was called before the Senate Committee on Foreign Relations. His testimony covered 139 pages, and gave the opponents of the League of Nations the ammunition they wanted. Soon afterward President Wilson collapsed, and with him American participation in the League. As for Bullitt, he found himself roundly denounced by Wilson partisans for his "disloyalty," and cut politically dead by the party chieftains. His diplomatic career was apparently over.

For 12 years Bullitt lived in retirement from public life. He lived first in New York, then in Ashfield, Massachusetts, where he built a country home. In 1921 he spent a year as managing editor of the Famous Players-Lasky Corporation. In 1923 Mrs. Bullitt obtained a divorce, and shortly afterward Bullitt married Louise Bryant Reed, widow of John Reed, American Communist. The two traveled about Europe, Bullitt examining private papers, diaries, unpublished memoirs and other revealing documents of the World War period. He also wrote a novel, *It's Not Done*, published in 1926, and in the same year obtained a divorce from the second Mrs. Bullitt. He was given custody of their daughter.

Bullitt was finally recalled from his political oblivion when President Roosevelt entered the White House. Bullitt was thoroughly sympathetic with the Roosevelt policies, had long desired to re-enter the diplomatic service, and had known Roosevelt since the time when the two men occupied adjoining offices in the State, War and Navy Building during the First World War. Even before Roosevelt entered the White House, Bullitt had made

BULLITT, WILLIAM—Continued

a hurried trip throughout Europe on a mission for the President-elect. It was Raymond Moley, however, who suggested that he be appointed assistant to Secretary Hull. Moley saw Bullitt as "pleasant, keen-minded, idealistic and widely informed"; but he thought he also detected in him a "deep and somewhat disturbing strain of romanticism." Foreign affairs, according to Moley, were to Bullitt's imaginative mind "full of lights and shadows, plots and counterplots, villains and a few heroes—a state of mind that seemed to me dangerous, if not constantly subjected to the quieting influence of some controlling authority." Bullitt's position as special assistant to the Secretary of State seemed like such a job. In that capacity he served as executive officer for the American delegation at the London Economic Conference and worked over many of President Roosevelt's speeches, but he was not to be long in the State Department. The United States at last recognized Soviet Russia and, naturally enough, it was Bullitt who became its first United States Ambassador, going to his post in Moscow in November 1933.

Bullitt had gone to his post with rejoicing; at last his bargaining for Russia had borne fruit. But again he was to find disillusionment. His rôle in Moscow turned out to be "neither mute nor glorious." "He began by loving his Russians well and not wisely and ended by disliking them neither wisely nor well. The Russians trusted him in neither stage and told him nothing. He lost all of his temper and most of his friends." In 1936, when Bullitt was transferred to France, he welcomed the change with relief. Again those close to him admitted his mistakes, but promised that he had reformed, "that from now on he will be teachable and tactful." Said one commentator: "Bullitt is one of the President's risks. And ours also."

In France Bullitt was tremendously popular. His family connections and his many previous visits to the country gave him a wide circle of friends, and he was on intimate terms with high French officials. From France he carried on a one-man campaign against Nazi aggression, continuing to maintain that the United States must give moral support to the European democracies. After Munich he was temporarily summoned home for consultations with Roosevelt together with Ambassadors Kennedy and Phillips (see sketches this issue), and among them it was agreed that it was time to do "something practical" to stop Germany, Italy and Japan and to assist England and France—time to revise the Neutrality Act. When in January 1939 Bullitt rushed back from a Florida vacation to communicate his secrets of state to a closed session of the House and Senate Military Affairs Committees, he did not succeed in sufficiently alarming them, however.

In the spring of 1940, after the War had been going on for some months, the Germans published a *White Book* which purportedly was compiled from confidential papers of the Polish Ministry of Foreign Affairs containing pre-War conversations with Ambassadors Bullitt and Kennedy, as reported by the Polish Ambassador in Washington to his chief in Warsaw. One of the main German contentions was apparently that Bullitt and Kennedy, "by their indiscreet indications of the probability of American assistance to Poland and the Allies, had strengthened Polish and Allied resistance to the German claims and in effect caused a war which would not otherwise have taken place." Bullitt is supposed to have informed the Polish Ambassador that "America is ready to place its entire resources in the way of finances and raw materials at their (the Allies') disposal," to have stated that we would "undoubtedly" participate in a war to force the capitulation of Germany, though "only after England and France had stirred themselves," and to have claimed that the United States was already (in November 1938) "in a psychosis similar to that existing before America's declaration of war on Germany in 1917." His reported opinion on the reason for the United States' willingness to participate was that President Roosevelt "wanted to distract the attention of the American public from difficult and complicated domestic problems, especially between capital and labor." Bullitt is also supposed to have made disparaging remarks about Russia and Italy and to have tried to encourage a conflict between Russia and Germany.

Upon publication of the German *White Book* isolationist Senator Reynolds (see sketch this issue) made a Congressional move to question Bullitt on these alleged conversations. But Bullitt's denial of them was accepted by the Executive Department without question, and most of those who found the authenticity of the *White Book* not unlikely still found nothing more dangerous in the remarks attributed to Bullitt than in many other expressions of American opinion not spoken in any official capacity. No action was therefore taken which would delay the Ambassador's sailing for Paris, and on April 6, 1940 he once more left the United States.

The second Mrs. Bullitt having died in 1936, Bullitt has been particularly close to his motherless daughter, who visits him during vacations from school in Virginia. Blue-eyed, bald, pink-skinned, an active sportsman, the Ambassador looks like a twin of his younger brother, Orville, a Philadelphia banker. But Orville is a conservative Democrat, and Ambassador Bullitt can hardly be called a conservative. The story goes that Felix Frankfurter asked him many years ago: "Well, Bill, have you learned to keep your shirt on yet?" "Absolutely," replied Bullitt. "It's nailed down this time." But Bullitt has been a dissenter most of his life, and it's not probable that he has changed very much, nor that he intends to.

References

Fortune 20:50 D '39
Ladies' H J 57:12 Jl '40
Lit Digest 122:10-11 S 5 '36 por
New Yorker 14:30-3 D 10 '38; 14:22-7 D 17 '38
Newsweek 13:11-13 Ap 24 '39 il por; 8:9 S 5 '36 por
Sat Eve Post 211:5-6+ Mr 11 '39 il por; 18-19+ Mr 18 '39 il por
Time 28:12 S 7 '36; 33:20 Mr 6 '39 por; 35:15 Ap 8 '40
Earle, H. P. Blackout 1939
Flanner, J. An American in Paris 1940
Flanner, J. Mr. Ambassador In Balch, M. ed. Modern Short Biographies and Autobiographies p338-58 1940
International Who's Who
Moley, R. After Seven Years 1939
Who's Who
Who's Who in America

BUNAU-VARILLA, PHILIPPE (bü-nō' và-rē-yà' fēl-lēp') July 25, 1859—May 18, 1940 French engineer; soldier; chief engineer of the French Panama Company which planned the Isthmus cut in 1885; sold the project to the United States while Panama Minister; designed Paris' subway system

References

Outlook 122:333 Je 25 '19; 98:653 Jl 22 '11 por
Qui Etes-Vous?

Obituaries

N Y Times p15 My 18 '40
N Y World-Telegram p29 My 18 '40
Newsweek 15:8 My 27 '40 por

CHARLES K. BURDICK

BURDICK, CHARLES KELLOGG Feb 7, 1883—June 22, 1940 Professor of law and former dean of the Cornell Law School; chairman of the New York State Law Revision Commission; member of the New York State Commission to Investigate the Administration of Justice from 1931 to 1939; was professor of law at Tulane University and the University of Missouri before joining the faculty of Cornell in 1914; author of articles and books on various law problems

References

Who's Who in America
Who's Who in American Education
Who's Who in the East

Obituaries

N Y Herald Tribune p26 Je 23 '40 por
N Y Times p31 Je 23 '40 por

BURKE, EDWARD RAYMOND Nov 28, 1880- United States Senator from Nebraska

Address: b. First National Bank Bldg, Omaha, Nebraska; h. 4907 Davenport St, Omaha

As one of the authors and proponents of the Burke-Wadsworth conscription bill (passed September 16, 1940) the name of Senator Edward R. Burke has been much in the news. In April 1940 he was defeated in the Nebraska Democratic primaries. On July 18 he bolted the Democratic ticket, predicting an organized Willkie (see sketch this issue) drive by anti-third-term Democrats. Nebraska's Democratic National Committeeman Quigley announced that he was "glad to hand him over to Willkie"; that "Burke is finally getting into the political party he has been supporting for the last six years." Said the President: "Senator Burke did not bolt the Party, the Party bolted Burke."

Edward Raymond Burke was born in Running Water, South Dakota on November 28, 1880, the son of Patrick Dorsey and Mary (Nolan) Burke. After attending the public schools he went on to Beloit College in Wisconsin, where his senior year found him star left tackle and captain of the football team. He acquired his B. A. in 1906 and then continued his education at Harvard Law School. The year 1911 brought him an LL. B., a wife (Henrietta Flinn of De Kalb, Illinois) and admission to the Nebraska Bar. He has been in practice in Omaha ever since, except for two years during the World War when he served as second lieutenant in the Air Service (1917-19).

In 1932 he was a "successful, but largely unknown, corporation lawyer." The only public office he had held had been the presidency of Omaha's school board (1927-31), although he had also been president of Omaha's Bar Association from 1926 to 1927 and a member of the general council of the American Bar Association from 1928 to 1932. Nevertheless, with the backing

EDWARD R. BURKE

of Arthur Mullen, Roosevelt floor-leader at the Chicago convention, Roosevelt's triumph carried him to Washington in 1933 as a member of the 73rd Congress from the 2nd Nebraska District. He merely sat and listened during the Hundred Days Congress, after which his speeches began to attract attention. By 1934 Roosevelt and Farley were both plumping for him in the Senatorial race, Roosevelt mentioning Burke's definition of the New Deal—which Mullen called the best ever written—in one of his own speeches: "The New Deal is an old deal— as old as the earliest aspirations of humanity for liberty and justice and good life . . . "

He was elected Senator from Nebraska for the term beginning January 3, 1935, after having defeated Nebraska's Governor, a brother of William Jennings Bryan, for the Democratic nomination—thus "smashing the 40-year reign of the Bryans."

Although known at the time of his election as "a New Dealer through and through," once in the Senate Burke became increasingly critical of the New Deal. He voted for the World Court, for the President's veto of the soldiers' bonus and for the $4,800,000 Work Relief Bill, but found other New Deal measures less agreeable. He voted against the tax bills of 1935 and of 1936, in which year he resigned as Democratic National Committeeman for Nebraska; he fought the Guffey Coal Act, the Utility Holding Company Act; and as a member of the Senate Committee on the Judiciary he was one of the leaders in the fight against Roosevelt's plan to enlarge the Supreme Court, warning against the centralization of authority in Washington which, if continued, he said, meant "one-man rule." The Wagner Labor Relations Act he found "fatally defective" from its inception and he is still fighting to amend it; the National

Labor Relations Board is to him Public Enemy No. 1. Only the Administration's foreign policy went uncriticized. Shortly after World War II opened he spoke for the repeal of the arms embargo as "a step toward peace," and he has long advocated compulsory military training.

A third term for President Roosevelt Senator Burke found "an attempt at self-perpetuation in the office of the Presidency." He had supported Vice-President Garner, whose close friend he is, earlier in the race, and after Roosevelt's nomination threw his support to Wendell Willkie. He later headed a Senate Judiciary Subcommittee which considered two Constitutional amendments: (1) limiting the tenure of the President to one six-year term and (2) outlawing re-election to a third term.

Thin-lipped, thin-haired, conservatively dressed, Senator Burke is no longer a football star, but his compact build shows that he still keeps fit by golfing and bowling (and taking on political opponents). He is a Congregationalist. There are two Burke daughters, Beatrice and Barbara.

References

Business Week p15 My 7 '38 por
Christian Sci Mon Mag p1-2+ Mr 25 '39
Cong Digest 18:243-4 O '39
Lit Digest 118:5 Ag 25 '34 por; 118:7 N 17 '34 por; 122:15 D 19 '36; 123:5 F 27 '37 por
New Repub 91:72-3 My 26 '37
N Y Times p1, 8 Jl 20 '40; p1+ Jl 24 '40; p1+, p13 Jl 25 '40; p1, 10 Jl 26 '40; pl, 13 Ag 1 '40
Newsweek 4:12 Ag 25 '34 por
Time 29:15 Mr 15 '37 por
Who's Who in America
Who's Who in the Nation's Capital

BURLEIGH, GEORGE WILLIAM (bûr'lē) Apr 18, 1870—Mar 15, 1940 Lawyer; soldier; leader in New York civic affairs

References

Who's Who in America
Who's Who in Law 1937
Who's Who in New York 1938

Obituaries

N Y Herald Tribune p10 Mr 16 '40
N Y Sun p29 Mr 15 '40
N Y Times p15 Mr 16 '40 por
N Y World-Telegram p46 Mr 15 '40

BURLIUK, DAVID (bûrl-yook) 1892- Artist

Address: 321 E 10th St, New York City

The work of a distinguished Russian painter, who has lived in the United States since 1922 and who has contributed to many exhibitions in this country was shown in a one-man exhibition of oils and water colors at the Boyer Galleries, New York City, from March 25 through April 13, 1940. David Burliuk belongs to no one country (though he has lived in many), but to international culture. The richness and variety of his work owe much to the fact that he has had the opportunity to participate in three historic periods of art development in three different countries.

Burliuk was born at Kharkov in the Ukraine in 1882, and at the early age of seven or eight began to paint. In 1902 he was called to military service; a year later he studied in Odessa, then in Paris under the landscape and historical painter, Fernand Cormon. He soon came under the influence of Van Gogh, and started painting in the modern manner. In 1907 he exhibited with modern French and Russian painters in Moscow. He helped found the Bubnovy Valyet (the Jack of Diamonds) group of Russian painters.

Young Burliuk became in 1911 one of the daring band of German painters called *Der Blaue Reiter,* a modern art movement launched by Kandinsky and Marc. They made Munich famous with their colors and credo of expressionism in the days before the War. Before the Russian Revolution he became one of the leaders of the Russian revolutionary painters. In Russia today Burliuk is remembered not only as a painter, but as a poet and teacher of Mayakovsky, whose heroic poems were acclaimed by Russian youth during the days of the consolidation of Bolshevik power. After painting in the Urals (1918-20), he lived for two years in Japan.

In 1922, at the close of the epoch of futurism in the U. S. S. R., Burliuk came to America. Though he quickly absorbed the American scene and the fascination of industrial life, he never lost his love for two things: the old feudal Russian village life with its roots deep in the soil; and the tumultuous days that brought social revolution to Russia in 1917. Though Burliuk saw the destruction of that ancient pre-industrial village life, he affirmed the revolution as good and necessary. While in the United States, he continued, however, to paint from memory pictures containing the symbols of the village, his landscapes marked with the slow rich movement of the seasons. Of this aspect of his work, Charmion von Weigand has written:

"Burliuk knows and understands the age-old drama of the soil and of man's labor with it. He paints dreams of it, like clouds hovering over summer fields. He revives in memory the primitive collective of the village, where people banded together against the terrors of nature and war, organically bound to the soil and strong as Anteus from contact with the earth." She states further that, at the same time, "Burliuk has no fear of the future, but knows a robust acceptance of life and a tender sensuousness towards its smallest and most insignificant objects. There are no shadows in his canvases; no ghosts in his universe. The future is a part of the past. Creation and destruction are both

DAVID BURLIUK

necessary parts of a process; there is no beginning and no end to life; only being and becoming. There is nothing lost in destruction, merely a changing of the original elements into new forms."

In 1923 Burliuk was represented by 44 canvases in the Russian art exhibition at the Brooklyn Museum, and contributed to exhibitions in Philadelphia and Pittsburgh. He exhibited at the Whitney Museum of American Art, New York, in 1932. Between 1933 and 1939 several one-man shows of his work were held in San Francisco, Philadelphia and Portland, Oregon; exhibitions in 1939 and 1940 in the San Francisco Museum of Art, the Tacoma Art Association Gallery, the Duncan Phillips Memorial Gallery, Washington, D. C. and the Boyer Galleries, New York.

Paintings exhibited at the last-named, in 1939, included *Lover of Books,* showing a victim of too much reading gone mad with the printed page; *Halibut Point, Massachusetts,* a staccato of brush drawings held together by simplified black line drawings; a portrait, *Mrs. Burliuk,* executed in Burliuk's new departure—complete relief in brilliant tones applied directly from the tube; and several floral pieces of magnificently executed details, set off by irridescent blue and violet backgrounds.

His work is permanently represented in the Whitney Museum of American Art, the Phillips Memorial Gallery, the Solomon R. Guggenheim Foundation and the Société Anonyme-Museum of Modern Art and numerous private collections here and abroad.

Burliuk's painting, even his earliest, has always been cyclonic. He has been successively influenced by the broken style of the Impressionists, by the Byzantine ikon and the Japanese print. Concerning his own theory of art, Burliuk wrote:

BURLIUK, DAVID—*Continued*

"A painting is the result of a movement. To be dead is to be immobile in the meadows of eternity. Drawings or paintings are seismographic recordings. They express psychological cataclysms; eruptions of emotions, different passions, because only souls of academicians are mournful and sleepy as swamps. Then again, real life and real creations are symbolically so near to the revolving convulsions of tigers ... this man-eating jumper is the highest note on the claviary key-board, representing greatest energy, vitality. To create means to jump; a creator is a jumper—to beat and to bite everybody who prefers the tranquility of a cemetery."

Powerful land paintings of Ukranian peasants and horses, overloaded with explosive color and thick impasto, are representative of Burliuk's greatest work. It seems that the longer and farther he is removed from his native land and from the primitive life of his childhood, the more dynamic grow his solid, retrospective memories of the Russian steppe. He has often suffered the appellations "wild" and "fantastic" for the eccentric and original strength of his work.

The 1940 exhibition at the Boyer Galleries contained 22 oil paintings and 12 water colors. Critics maintained that it represented the painter at the full powers of his maturity. Four of the pictures are outstanding in size of conception as well as of dimension. *Coming Home from the Steppe* is characteristic of his work that recalls scenes from the past: the figures in the painting are seen as though foreshortened through the telescopic lens of his memory. *Tea Party* solves a problem of faces under artificial light (an oil lamp). It represents the interior of a Russian peasant's home, with a big stove in the corner. A man is telling a tale to a group around the tea table, one of whom is amazed, one ready to disagree and one sitting quietly. *Watering Horse by Moonlight* is another study of figures in artificial light. *Shore of Hospitality* is a Pacific Ocean memory of a tropical island, showing female nudes with parasols waiting for company from a sail ship anchored nearby. The majority of the paintings and water colors, however, are views in and around New York, indicating how successfully Burliuk has adapted the American scene.

References

    Art N 37:13 Ap 22 '39
    Color and Rhyme 12:7-8, 14-15 Ja-F '40
    Who's Who in American Art

BURNS, GEORGE   *See* Allen, G.

BURNS, JAMES ALOYSIUS, FATHER Feb 13, 1867—Sept 9, 1940 Former president of the University of Notre Dame (1919-22); assistant superior general of the Congregation of the Holy Cross; considered one of the leading Catholic educators in America; author of books on the Catholic school system

FATHER JAMES A. BURNS

References

    Cath School J 31:275 Ag '31 por
    American Catholic Who's Who
    Leaders in Education 1932
    Who's Who in America

Obituaries

    N Y Herald Tribune p24 S 10 '40
    N Y Times p23 S 10 '40

BURTON, CHARLES EMERSON, REV. Mar 19, 1869—Aug 27, 1940 General secretary of the National Council of Congregational Churches from 1921 to 1931 and of the General Council of Congregational and Christian Churches from 1931 until 1938; since then secretary emeritus; ordained in 1898; author of religious books and editor of the annual *Year Book of the Congregational and Christian Churches* from 1922 to 1938; served as pastor in various churches

References

    Who's Who in America
    Who's Who in New York

Obituaries

    N Y Herald Tribune p22 Ag 28 '40 por
    N Y Times p19 Ag 28 '40

BURTON, LEWIS WILLIAM, BISHOP
Nov 9, 1852—Oct 17, 1940 Retired Bishop
of the Episcopal Diocese of Lexington,
Kentucky; rector of All Saints' Church and
Saint Mark's Church in Cleveland, Ohio
until 1884, when he became rector of St.
John's Church in Richmond, Virginia; in
1893 became rector of St. Andrew's Church in
Lexington, a post held for three years, when
he was consecrated Bishop of Lexington, the
first to hold that position

References

> Who's Who
> Who's Who in America

Obituaries

> N Y Times p21 O 18 '40

BURTON, RICHARD Mar 14, 1861—
Apr 8, 1940 Writer; poet; critic; professor
of English at Rollins College since 1933;
chairman of the fiction-award for the
Pulitzer Prize from 1924 to 1929

Pinchot

RICHARD BURTON

References

> Wilson Lib Bul 4:52 O '29 por
> Rittenhouse, J. B. Richard Burton *In*
>   Younger American Poets p248-68
>   1904
> Who's Who in America

Obituaries

> N Y Herald Tribune p22 Ap 9 '40
> N Y Times p23 Ap 9 '40
> Sch & Soc 51:477 Ap 13 '40

BUSH, VANNEVAR (văn-ē-var) Mar 11,
1890- Scientist
Address: b. Carnegie Institution of Washington, Washington, D. C.

Dr. Vannevar Bush, "a small, keen-eyed,
fast-thinking, tireless, eloquent Yankee,"
who became president of the Carnegie Institution of Washington in 1939, taking over
the highest administrative position in one of
the world's largest scientific foundations,
was appointed in June 1940 to head the
President's National Defense Research Committee.

When Andrew Carnegie set up the Institution in 1902 he presented it with a
total endowment of $22,000,000 which has
since grown to $34,000,000. Today its
budget runs about $1,500,000 a year; its ex-
peditions study magnetism in Peru, anthropology in Java; research bodies delve into
the mysteries of plant biology, embryology,
genetics, terrestrial magnetism, nutrition;
Mount Wilson Laboratory and a division of
historical research are under its wing. And
Dr. Bush, famed scientist in his own right,
administers and guides all the vast workings of the Institution.

The son of the Rev. Richard Perry Bush
and Emma Linwood (Paine) Bush, and
grandson of a whaling sea captain, Vannevar Bush was born in Everett, Massachusetts on March 11, 1890. He went to
school near home and then to Tufts College, from which he received his B. S. and
M. S. degrees in 1913. He got a position
right after college with the test department of the General Electric Company, but
left after a year to work with the inspection
department of the United States Navy. In
the academic year of 1914 to 1915 he was
back at Tufts, teaching mathematics. The
following year he was promoted to assistant professor of electrical engineering.
On September 5, 1916 he married Phoebe
Davis of Chelsea, Massachusetts, and they
have two children, Richard Davis and John
Hathaway.

During the War he served the government by doing research on submarine detection devices and after the War was over
returned both to private industry and to
teaching. He was with the American
Radio and Research Corporation from 1917
to 1922 as consulting engineer and at the
same time was associate professor of electrical power transmission at the Massachusetts Institute of Technology, from
which he had received his Doctor of Engineering degree in 1916. In 1923 he was
appointed full professor and in 1932 vice-
president and dean of engineering.

As professor of electrical power transmission, Dr. Bush made a comprehensive
study of the undergraduate curriculum in
electrical engineering in order to develop
the most efficient methods of teaching in
this field. At M. I. T., too, Dr. Bush built
the famous differential analyzer, a mathematical robot which solves complex differential equations in a short time. It was
in recognition of his work with mathematical analyzing instruments that he was
awarded the Levy Medal of the Franklin
Institute in 1928 and the Lamme Medal

Harris & Ewing

VANNEVAR BUSH

of the American Institute of Electrical Engineers in 1935.

When Dr. Bush was made head of the Carnegie Institution, President Karl T. Compton of M. I. T. said: "Dr. Bush is so eminently qualified for his new position and the post is of such great influence and opportunity in the field of science and human welfare that his colleagues at Technology are unanimous in their approval of his selection." Dr. Compton went on to point out the "good judgment and analytical power" Dr. Bush had shown in his administrative work as vice-president of M. I. T.

Dr. Bush, whose "rustic grin and cracker barrel drawl about engineering conceal an unorthodox scientific mind of whiplash speed," is, besides, president of the Carnegie Institution and head of President Roosevelt's new research defense committee, chairman of the National Advisory Committee for Aeronautics and of the National Academy of Science's division of engineering. He is also member or fellow of most of this country's scientific societies. His interests, outside of science, include raising turkeys on his farm in New Hampshire and playing the flute.

References

Aviation 39:76 Jl '40 por
Newsweek 15:58 Je 24 '40 por
Sci N L 33:397 Je 18 '38
Sci Mo 47:188-90 Ag '38 por
Time 35:44 Ja 1 '40 por
American Men of Science
Blue Book of American Aviation
Who's Who in America
Who's Who in Engineering

BUTLER, NICHOLAS MURRAY Apr 2, 1862- President of Columbia University

Address: b. Columbia University, New York City; h. 60 Morningside Dr, New York City

A speech made by Dr. Nicholas Murray Butler to the assembled faculties of Columbia University on October 3, 1940 made the issue of academic freedom and its meaning once more a subject of heated debate. Dr. Butler defined the present war as between "beasts and human beings," and suggested that faculty members should resign if their convictions brought them into open conflict with the "university's freedom to go its way toward its lofty aim." Academic freedom, he said, was only for "accomplished scholars," having no meaning for students, and in any case should be subordinate to "university freedom."

Although Dr. Butler's plea for wholehearted university cooperation with the government in its national defense program brought him little but praise, a number of people began to wonder audibly if his conception of academic freedom was or was not similar to that of the totalitarian states. John Dewey, H. G. Wells, John Haynes Holmes, Charles Beard, a group of prominent Columbia professors, the American Student Union, the editors of the *Columbia Spectator* and the executive council of the New York College Teachers Union were among those who announced themselves either very much opposed or very much puzzled. Others said that Dr. Butler could not be construed as advocating limitation of freedom of discussion in the classroom—only outside—and some came out staunchly in support of his attitude, among them Dean Virginia Gildersleeve (see sketch this issue) of Barnard College. She challenged Dr. Butler's critics to point to any other college that has enjoyed more academic freedom than has Barnard College under Dr. Butler's presidency, and said that while she agreed with him, her interpretations of his meaning were not theirs. "My interpretations," she said, "are based on many years of association with him. I have always found him enlightened, progressive, open-minded and dedicated to the protection of academic freedom."

On October 10 two letters from Dr. Butler clarifying his speech were made public. He expressed surprise that it had been "misinterpreted," and asserted that "academic freedom is and has long been so firmly established at Columbia that no one should have the least fear that our university opinion would permit its abandonment or qualification." Students were entitled to "student freedom," faculty members were "certainly at full liberty to think and to talk as they please upon any subject which interests them, whether it be popular or unpopular."

However its president's words have been interpreted, not everyone is agreed that there have been invasions of academic liberty at Columbia in the past. It is true that many incidents have been so labeled. In 1911 a professor was dismissed after he had been threatened with a breach of promise suit; a professor who protested was also dismissed. In 1916 a professor was dropped after referring to Plattsburg in a derogatory way; the next year another was discharged after his pacifism had been attacked by the press as "treason" and "sedition"; still another was dropped after activities in the People's Council for Peace. Three weeks later Dr. Charles A. Beard resigned, saying the "status of a professor at Columbia was lower than that of a hired laborer." His economic interpretation of the Constitution had caused Columbia's trustees to catechize him as to his own 100 per cent Americanism.

As recently as 1932 the editor of the *Columbia Spectator* was expelled after charging that the dining halls were mismanaged and the football administration commercial, and that same year a meeting hall for students wishing to discuss the problems of chain gang labor was refused. In 1933 a member of the department of economics active in Communist groups was dropped; not long afterward an anti-Fascist member of the Italian department was transferred to the French department; and in 1936 an American Student Union leader was expelled after having taken part in a demonstration against Columbia's sending of an official representative to Nazi Germany's Heidelberg anniversary celebration.

But it was the former Dean Kirchwey who said: "There are only two classes perfectly free to say what they think—tramps and Columbia University professors," and Alva Johnston maintained in 1930 that under Dr. Butler's rule "Columbia has become a hotbed of liberalisms, including those varieties which he personally abhors." The President himself has stated that "no member of Columbia University is ever questioned as to either his political or religious beliefs," that genuine cases of the invasion of academic freedom are "non-existent and wholly imaginary." "It is a misnomer," he once said, "to apply the high and splendid term 'academic freedom' to exhibitions of bad taste and bad manners"; actually dismissals have taken place only because of "conduct or failure in satisfactory academic performance."

Nicknamed "Nicholas Miraculous" by Theodore Roosevelt, Dr. Butler is said to be "the only university president who has made an impression on this generation." H. G. Wells once called him "the champion international visitor and retriever of foreign orders and degrees"; he is "the most comprehensively decorated individual extant," the "semiofficial boss of American letters"; "no international pie is free from his ambitious finger"; and if he also thinks of himself as "Minister of Education" for the United States, it is with some reason. Once he signed a series of articles—most suitably—by the pen name "Cosmos."

He was born in Elizabeth, New Jersey on April 2, 1862, the son of Henry Leny and Mary Jones (Murray) Butler. According to Dr. Butler "at least three of the grandparental strains were exceptional by reason of their intellectual character, their religious ardor and their influence upon their fellow men." When young Nicholas was a few days old his grandmother carried him up to the cupola of the house with an American flag, a $10 gold piece and a *Bible*, and there "dedicated his life to patriotism, wealth and piety."

In 1864 the Butler family moved to Paterson, New Jersey, and in its public schools Nicholas was lucky enough to be educated at a time when, he tells us, "the present-day notion that an infant must be permitted and encouraged to explore the universe for himself as if everything were at its beginning and there had been no human experience whatever, had, fortunately, not yet raised its preposterous head." He was a prodigy. He finished high school at 13 and in 1878 became a freshman at Columbia College, then an unpretentious institution whose five buildings centered around Madison Avenue and 49th Street.

After playing cricket, editing the *Acta Columbiana* and the junior yearbook, young Butler was graduated in 1882 with $1,000 already in the bank—he had earned his way ever since his freshman year by teaching and by journalistic work. His career was already chosen. Although he had at first planned to become a lawyer, Columbia's president had persuaded him that the almost unexplored field of educational theory —"pedagogics"—was his field. Butler, with the Fellowship in Letters, took his M. A. in 1883 and his Ph. D. a year later, still finding time to do more journalistic work and to take on a couple of political ap-

White Studio

NICHOLAS MURRAY BUTLER

BUTLER, NICHOLAS MURRAY—*Cont.*

pointments (his father was important in New Jersey politics). By the time he was 22 he was studying education in Berlin and Paris and already "talking with the wise and dining with the rich." Letters of introduction enabled him to collect conversations with everyone from Pope Leo XIII to Bismarck and Gladstone. As someone once said: "From his earliest youth he was a lion-hunter, and to this day appears to have associated with nothing but lions." In maintaining his associations he has since crossed the Atlantic more than fivescore times.

Butler returned from Europe in 1885 to become a mere tutor in Columbia's philosophy department. But he was obviously slated for big things. His first accomplishment was winning support for his idea that education was a subject worthy of study and overcoming the opposition of the board of trustees to his proposals for establishing a course in "pedagogics." In 1889 New York College for the Training of Teachers was established (renamed Teachers College in 1892). Butler had no sooner been promoted from an instructorship to an adjunct professorship of philosophy when he was offered a job as Stanford University's first president. It was the first of many such offers which he was to have the privilege of refusing. Soon afterward he found himself dean of Columbia's philosophy department.

In 1891 Butler founded the *Educational Review,* which he edited for 30 years; he started the *Great Educators Series* and the *Teachers Professional Library*; and it was he who was chiefly responsible for the formation of the National Education Council and the College Entrance Examination Board. He also began working at putting his own plan for the reorganization of Columbia into operation. In 1899 Columbia's summer school was founded. And five years after Nicholas Murray Butler was inaugurated president of Columbia College (on April 19, 1902, at the age of 40), the college had actually been turned into a university. Under his guidance—and talents for collecting endowments—it was to grow to be one of the largest universities in the world, with 68 buildings and more than 30,000 students.

A "lifelong active participant in the work of political organization and political education," Dr. Butler has been a delegate at 14 consecutive national Republican conventions—all of them before 1936, when he found himself thoroughly disillusioned. He has known all the Presidents from Hayes on, seven of them "more or less intimately." He was particularly familiar with Theodore Roosevelt, but in 1912 turned against him when he proposed judicial recall and himself campaigned against him as Vice-Presidential candidate on Taft's ticket. Although the Vice-Presidential nomination was the only one which Dr. Butler ever accepted,

in 1926 he claimed that he had had the "offer of every nomination worth having at home and abroad." Among the offers have been: New Jersey legislator; United States Representative, Senator, Commissioner of Education, Ambassador to London or Berlin, Secretary of State; Mayor of New York City; Governor of New York. In 1920, however, Dr. Butler's only aspiration toward political office was unfulfilled when he campaigned for the Republican nomination for President of the United States under the slogan "Pick Nick for President and Pic-Nic in November."

Dr. Butler has been on more or less intimate terms with "almost every man of light and learning who has lived in the world during the past half century." His correspondence is "a grain elevator of international confidences." Besides an extensive acquaintance with men of science and letters he has known every British Prime Minister except two since Gladstone; he was holding conversations with Lenin in 1908, though certainly never afterward; he knew and admired Kaiser Wilhelm II, Dr. Stresemann, Von Hindenburg; he has debated the merits of Fascism with Mussolini in a friendly way; he was extremely close to Briand; he is a warm friend of Kerensky. Of all the countries which he knows he has a particularly friendly feeling for the British Commonwealth, which, he said in 1926, "now carries its beneficent rule into every continent and every clime." Once, it is said, he himself steered England through a House of Lords crisis.

One of Dr. Butler's favorite phrases is "the international mind." He has it. During the Spanish-American War he had announced that the United States entered it "in the most unselfish spirit and from the loftiest motives." In 1910, however, he persuaded Andrew Carnegie to establish the Carnegie Endowment for International Peace, to the presidency of which he was re-elected in May 1940. In 1913 he was praising the German Kaiser as a great pacifist, in 1914 opposing preparedness, but shortly grew so enthusiastic about the First World War that he was calling La Follette a "traitor" and becoming impatient with Wilson's dilatoriness in entering it. By the fall of 1918 he was demanding universal military training.

Dr. Butler never approved of either Wilson's manners or theories, and in 1920 he endorsed Harding's stand toward Wilson's League of Nations, but he afterward found the United States' failure to participate in the League a "tragedy." In 1921 he was embarrassed at being called America's Unofficial Ambassador while visiting Europe in the interests of post-War reconstruction. Throughout the '20s and early '30s he worked for disarmament; he almost singlehandedly sold the 1928 Pact of Paris (the "Kellogg Pact") first to Briand and then to the world; in 1931 he shared the Nobel Peace Prize with Jane Addams; in

1932 he was fairly sure that our last war had been fought. Yet he could never have been accurately described as a pacifist. He has spoken continually about "uprooting the causes of war," but has also said that there is a point at which the rule of force may be needed. To him that point was not in September 1938, when, he thought, a World War between the "Despotisms and Democracies" could have "but one end . . . the destruction of our civilization," but in 1940 some have accused him of declaring war before the United States has made it official.

To Dr. Butler's way of thinking "the true liberal is a conservative." He is also unalterably opposed to government "interference" with the individual, in whatever form it may appear. Upton Sinclair has called him the "intellectual leader of the American plutocracy," but Dr. Butler has indirectly called Upton Sinclair far worse names. As early as 1912 he described socialism as "a sort of glorified lynching," and he hasn't changed his mind much. In 1915 he thought youth should be protected from professors who propagandized for socialism—and woman suffrage, too. In 1917 he warned against the menace of the "academic Bolsheviki." He fought the income tax, the excess profits tax of 1920, condemned high inheritance taxes, found laws ending child labor as dangerous as the Eighteenth Amendment to American liberties, and met the depression by urging the wealthy to devote part of their fortunes "to public service through public benefaction," like the Rockefeller, Carnegie and Harkness families. The charge of "non-distribution of wealth" was "sheer invention." New Deal tax measures were a "steal-the-wealth" program. Most unions were led by racketeers who forced the workingman to do what he didn't want to do—strike and pay dues. Advocates of the closed shop were "Fascist-minded." Administration boards and commissions were a dangerous form of bureaucracy. Government restriction of the laborer's hours of work invaded his freedom and also helped breed the false doctrine that such things as classes and a class struggle existed. If the latter did exist it was "a revolt of the unfit, due to an inferiority complex," and anyway it didn't. The economic interpretation of history was "important," but very much "subordinate."

Nevertheless there have been many who have thought of Dr. Butler as a liberal. He "made the wet cause respectable" and consistently fought the Eighteenth Amendment, which offended his "intelligence," his "moral sense" and his "political principles." Back in the '80s he campaigned for higher education for women (although he thought an "educated proletariat" dangerous) and he has always wanted women admitted to the Columbia law school. He has also spoken disapprovingly of the greed of munitions makers. Professor E. R. A. Seligman once commended his "unfailing ability to take the broad rather than the narrow view of the case."

In 1887 Dr. Butler married Susanna Edwards Schuyler, who died in 1903. His second wife is the former Kate La Montagne, whom he married in 1907. There is one daughter, Sara Schuyler Lawrence. A "stout figure, garbed in impeccable business suits," complete with derby, cane and "cold-weather spats," there is little of the absent-minded professor or dreamy scholar about Dr. Butler. In spite of the pressure of his many activities he seems always "calm and composed and cheerful" and is noted for "a grand and nearly imperturbable complacency." His schedule is fairly regular. At 11:30 a. m. he is in the habit of mounting the steps to the library at Columbia; he takes a private elevator and works for two hours. In the afternoon there are meetings—"he probably belongs to more committees and boards than any other American." Then back to his palatial home on Morningside Drive, called "The Social Register House" by Columbia students because of the calibre of its guests; a two-hour nap; a shower; and, usually, out for dinner.

According to the Columbia charter its president must be an Episcopalian, and Dr. Butler was confirmed in the Protestant Episcopal Church in 1897. His wife is a Catholic. Dr. Butler has been "increasingly vocal" in praise of religion and the church, and once even suggested that the public schools be closed one afternoon each week for the purpose of religious instruction. He has edited any number of publications, especially on the subject of education, and is the author of an almost terrifying number of books. In 1940 *Why War?* and the second volume of his autobiography, *Across the Busy Years*, were published. Besides these, his personal correspondence is collected in a dozen unpublished volumes, and somewhere he keeps 40 huge scrapbooks devoted to articles and clippings about himself. His public addresses have been called "those interminable miasmas of guff" by Dorothy Dunbar Bromley, but Alva Johnston finds that they display the respective strengths and weaknesses of a "pundit since infancy," and are distinguished by "robust energy, sagacity, imagination, and, occasionally, a certain rugged grace."

The Paris *Figaro* once summed up Dr. Butler, if it is possible to sum up a public institution so easily: "A gentleman of distinguished exterior."

References

Am Mercury 34:286-98 Mr '35

Nation 135:343-4 O 19 '32; 139:550-2+ N 14 '34; 140:617-18 My 29 '35

New Yorker 6:28-32 N 8 '30; 6:33-4+ N 15 '30

Newsweek 8:41-2 O 17 '36 (Same abr. Read Digest 29:90 D '36)

Sat R Lit 20:7 S 30 '39 por

Time 34:55-6 S 25 '39 por

Butler, N. M. Across the Busy Years v1-2 1939-40

BUTLER, NICHOLAS MURRAY—_Cont._

Johnston, A. "Cosmos": Dr Nicholas
Murray Butler _In_ New Yorker
(periodical) Profiles from the New
Yorker p219-38 1938
Leaders in Education 1932
Who's Who
Who's Who Among North American
Authors
Who's Who in America
Woolf, S. J. Nicholas Murray Butler
_In_ Drawn from Life p97-105 1932

BUTLER, SMEDLEY DARLINGTON
July 30, 1881—June 21, 1940 Retired major
general of the United States Marine Corps;
fought in every Marine Corps campaign
from the Spanish-American War to the
World War; won many medals for his
bravery; in 1924 left the Marines to clean
up vice in Philadelphia as director of public
safety but returned to service within a year;
almost court-martialed in 1930 for calling
Mussolini a "hit-and-run driver"; retired in
1931, he became a lecturer for complete
isolation coupled with strong defenses;
wrote a book called _War Is a Racket_ (1935)

SMEDLEY BUTLER

References
Butler, S. D. Old Gimlet Eye 1933
Who's Who in America
Obituaries
N Y Herald Tribune p12 Je 22 '40
pors
N Y Times p15 Je 22 '40
Newsweek 16:47 Jl 1 '40 por
Time 36:55 Jl 1 '40

CAHILL, MICHAEL HARRISON (cā'-
hǐl) Nov 19, 1874—Mar 26, 1940 Retired
president of the Missouri, Kansas and Texas
Railroad

References
Who's Who in America 1934-35

Obituaries
N Y Herald Tribune p22 Mr 27 '40
por
N Y Times p21 Mr 27 '40 por

CAIRNS, HUNTINGTON (kârnz) Sept 1,
1904- Lawyer; author
Address: b. United States Treasury Department, Washington, D. C.; h. 2219 California
St, N W, Washington, D. C.

Huntington Cairns, author, lawyer and
member of CBS's _Invitation to Learning_
program along with Mark Van Doren and
Allen Tate (see sketches this issue), is the
assistant general counsel of the United States
Treasury Department. He is, besides, official
guardian of American morals against all possible contamination by imported works of art
and literature from foreign countries.

All books or objects of art of which our
customs officials are suspicious are temporarily detained at the port of entry and
sent to Mr. Cairns for his approval. If he
decides that the confiscated object is immoral and not redeemed by esthetic
standards it is burned in the presence of
witnesses; but if he gives it his approval
it is returned to its importer. This is all in
accordance with the statute which governs
these materials. None of Mr. Cairns' rulings on such books—which extend over a
period of six years—has been reversed by
the courts. Passing upon material of this
kind, however, is only a minor part of his
work in the Treasury.

Mr. Cairns was born in Baltimore, Maryland, the son of James Duncanson and
Helen Huntington (Heath) Cairns. Before
he was 10 years old he began to collect
his library, which today covers the walls,
from floor to ceiling, of three large rooms.
He claims that he needs 25,000 books and
won't be happy until he has them. His art
collection is still small, but choice, and
is securely protected under individual glass
covers.

He attended the Washington County
Maryland High School from 1918 to 1920
and then transferred to Baltimore City
College, and was graduated in 1922. He
received his LL. B. in 1925 from the University of Maryland School of Law. He
was admitted to the Maryland Bar that same
year and in 1926 became an associate in
the law firm of Piper, Carey and Hall.
Four years later he was married to Florence
Faison Butler of Washington, D. C., and
three years after that, in 1933, he became
a partner in the law firm. After he had
been a special legal adviser to the United
States Treasury Department and a lecturer
on taxation at the law school of the
University of Maryland, Mr. Cairns became

HUNTINGTON CAIRNS

assistant general counsel to the Treasury in 1937.

It was in the '20s that Mr. Cairns began to review books for the Norfolk *Virginian-Pilot*. For nine years he reviewed books weekly for the Baltimore *Evening Sun* and since he came to Washington in 1937 he has been a regular contributor to the Washington *Post*.

Mr. Cairns' first book, *Law and the Social Sciences*, was published simultaneously in London and New York in 1935. His second book, *Tax Laws of Maryland*, appeared in 1937 and he has continued to edit revised editions of the work biennially. Because of his work in taxation, he is a member of the Maryland Tax Revision Commission appointed by the Governor to modernize the Maryland tax laws. His third book, *The Theory of Legal Science*, will be published in January 1941 by the University of North Carolina Press. Mr. Cairns is also a contributor to the Columbia, Yale, Harvard and other law reviews and has published articles in the *Atlantic Monthly*, in the *Annals of the American Academy of Political and Social Science*, and in the *Philosophy of Science Journal*. He has contributed numerous biographies to the *Dictionary of American Biography* and is represented in eight symposia and anthologies, two of them in the Modern Library.

Mr. Cairns abhors all kinds of sports and any kind of physical exertion, but he is an ardent chess player and an enthusiastic devotee of the Chinese military game of Go, which is the oldest board game of which there is any record. It is a more complicated and more subtle game than chess and is said to have been invented by a Chinese emperor to teach his son to think. Mr. Cairns is vice-president of the American Go Association and Go players

from far places call on him in his library in Washington for a quiet game, which they play sitting cross-legged on the floor.

When Mr. Cairns was graduated from law school he was awarded the first prize for his thesis on the law of charitable trusts. In 1935 he was awarded the Civic Medallion for the most significant contribution to the progress of Baltimore in that year.

References

Lit Digest 118:12 N 10 '34 por
Pub W 126:1569 O 27 '34

America's Young Men
Who's Who in America
Who's Who in Law

CALDWELL, ERSKINE Dec 17, 1903-
Author
Address: Point O' Woods Rd, Darien, Connecticut

Jackpot, published in August 1940, is "a full-dress parade" of Erskine Caldwell as a short-story writer. In it are all the stories contained in four earlier volumes together with nine new ones, each narrative prefixed by the author's own comment. In it are "gusty tales of sub-human folk of the type set forth in *Tobacco Road*"; in it are tragic episodes of the black and white life of the South.

It is this black and white life of the South which forms the theme of his latest novel, *Trouble in July* (March 1940). Its story is the story of a lynching; of Sonny Clark, 18-year-old Negro accused of raping a white sharecropper's daughter of Sheriff Jeff McCurtain who finds himself in a tough spot, of the farmers who are out to "get" Sonny. What happens when the whites take things into their own hands, when Sheriff McCurtain tries to avoid all the trouble by going fishing, when the sharecropper's daughter reveals that she has been lying—winds into a story termed "one of the most dramatic and intensely human Caldwell has ever created." There are critics, however, Clifton Fadiman among them, who believe that this book, good as it is, shows that Caldwell "is beginning to repeat himself."

Erskine Preston Caldwell was born in the village of White Oak, Coweta County, Georgia. His father, the Reverend Ira Sylvester Caldwell, is a Presbyterian minister in Georgia (Caroline Preston Bell is his mother) who continuously moved from town to town, carrying his family along with him. This was no doubt largely responsible for the younger Caldwell's wanderlust. The fact, too, that Southern ministers are about the poorest paid in the profession contributed to Caldwell's early reliance upon himself.

He left home at the tender age of 14. For two years he roamed about, taking in his stride the deep South, Mexico and Central America. Upon his return, he managed

Margaret Bourke-White

ERSKINE CALDWELL

to complete his high school education (actually, he spent but one year in public school and one year in high school).

While attending the University of Virginia in 1925 (on a $25-a-month allowance from home), Caldwell was married to Helen Lannigan of Charlottesville, Virginia—and at the same time decided to write for a living. Until then he had knocked about, working in a cottonseed oil mill, picking cotton, driving cabs in Tennessee, playing professional football in Pennsylvania, reporting for an Atlanta newspaper—all in order to go to college. But he quit school to write. He moved to Maine and wrote for seven years before any of his work was published.

Caldwell first received fame with the publication, in 1932, of the now almost legendary *Tobacco Road*. First written as a novel, it was soon after dramatized by Jack Kirkland and produced on Broadway the following year. In *Tobacco Road* Caldwell delved into "Cracker depravity" and revealed its source in the decadent agricultural system of the South. Although greeted on the Great White Way with roars of laughter and interpreted as a comedy, the play was not meant to be funny. It is reported that every time Caldwell went into the theatre the laughter "sent him wandering the streets in tight-lipped rage." In 1940, seven years after it opened, *Tobacco Road* is still on Broadway, having broken all records for long run performances.

The attacks on *Tobacco Road* came mostly from Southern critics, who quite naturally resented so vivid a portrayal of their home territory. One reviewer in defending the book said: "Erskine Caldwell digs around in Southern muck, flings the muck into the literary sky. . . With no

pretense of being a prophet or reformer. . . The characters in *Tobacco Road* are an integral part of what someone has called that 'miserable panorama of unpainted shacks, rain-gullied fields, straggling fences, rattletrap Fords, dirt, poverty, disease, drudgery and monotony that stretches for a thousand miles across the cotton belt.' "

God's Little Acre (1933) was followed in 1935 by *Journeyman,* a story "concerned with the adventures of a fabulous traveling preacher who descends upon a remote Georgia community to drink whisky, seduce its women, arouse it to orgy in a revival meeting and then disappear one morning in an automobile acquired by the aid of a beneficent Providence working through the instrumentality of a crap game." The play version of *Journeyman* was scathingly denounced by Broadway reviewers—it was attacked as being lewd, filthy, immoral and along with the books *Tobacco Road* and *God's Little Acre* was banned from many public libraries and was brought before the courts as immoral.

When such charges are leveled against his work, Caldwell doesn't fight back. All he says is simply: "I try to hold up a mirror to nature in the South and to my own nature, to human nature. I don't say that lynching is evil or that cruelty is bad. But by showing people as they are, cruel, and by showing their victims, by showing people oppressed to hopelessness and impoverished to hopelessness—perhaps in that way I'll have some effect on many lives."

In 1936, together with Margaret Bourke-White (see sketch this issue), whom he married in 1939 after obtaining a divorce from his first wife, he wrote *You Have Seen Their Faces.* This was one of the first books of the reportorial-photographic school. Traveling through the heart of the deep South, Caldwell and Margaret Bourke-White took pictures of the people and the land, and re-created what they had heard and seen into a "tremendously vital and gripping document." Caldwell here not only points out the problem, but he also brings forth his approach to a possible solution of it. He proposes that a Federal commission be created to study the problem—then to seek the solution in order to plan for immediate action.

The immediate public reception of *You Have Seen Their Faces* encouraged Caldwell and Miss Bourke-White to do another book along similar lines. In 1938, just before the Munich crisis, they again made a trip, this time through what once was Czechoslovakia, and wrote *North of the Danube.* The book is full of the drama which filled the air in those early autumn days of 1938.

Besides these novels, a documentary study of regional America called *Some American People* (1935), and numerous articles for magazines and newspapers, Caldwell has published four books of short stories— *American Earth* (1931); *We Are the Living* (1933); *Kneel to the Rising Sun* (1935); *Southways* (1938); and *Jackpot* (1940).

Erskine Caldwell is a tall, quiet man with an unobtrusive sense of humor. He enjoys being alone, and in order to do this lives in the country where he is sure he won't have to be bothered by the social graces. He seldom reads novels; prefers timely magazines and newspapers. He has read widely and variously, and in his youth soaked up a lot of history and economics which he now finds extremely valuable in understanding and interpreting current social and economic problems.

Caldwell's three children by his first marriage live with their mother in Maine. His eldest son, aged 14, whom he fondly calls "Pixie," earns his own money by raising rabbits and vegetables—Caldwell wants his children to develop initiative and self-reliance with which to meet their future problems.

References

Am Mercury 49:493-8 Ap '40
Christian Cent 55:204-6 F 16 '38
Darien R p1-2 S 5 '40 por
Nation 146:190 F 12 '38
N Y World-Telegram p21 F 23 '40
Sat R Lit 19:10 F 18 '39 por
Wilson Lib Bul 7:600 Je '33
Kunitz, S. J. ed. Authors Today and Yesterday 1933
Van Doren, C. C. Revisions *In* American Novel, 1789-1939 p349-66 1940
Who's Who Among North American Authors
Who's Who in America

CALDWELL, MRS. ERSKINE *See* White, M. B.

CALDWELL, TAYLOR Sept 7, 1900-
Author

Address: h. 703 W Ferry St, Buffalo, New York

Janet Taylor Caldwell (she does not use her first name) was born in Manchester, England, on September 7, 1900. Both her father, Arthur Francis Caldwell, a commercial artist who died nine years ago, and her mother, Anna (Marks) Caldwell, who now lives in Buffalo, were born in Glasgow. She comes from a long line of Scotch Presbyterian teachers, artists, landed gentry, shipbuilders, publishers and distillers. At a very early age he was sent to a private school in the little suburb of Reddish, where she readily acquired a strong dislike for the snobbishness of the decayed-gentlewoman teacher.

Her father had a strange antipathy for almost everyone but Scotsmen, Presbyterians and Caldwells, and because in England his profession was full of Germans he brought his family to America in 1907—where, though he little suspected it, conditions were virtually the same. It was during that crossing that Taylor Caldwell got her "first lesson in undemocracy": she found herself in a kind of second-class quarantine, snubbed by the first-

TAYLOR CALDWELL

class youngsters and forbidden to play with the third-class children. She remembers the porpoises, however, with a good deal of pleasure, as well as the icebergs, porridge with treacle, ice cream and the first electric fans she had ever seen. On a soggy day in March they entered New York harbor, and during a violent argument with the customs inspectors got a wholly unpleasant impression of the "bloody Yankees."

At the age of nine she began to write and illustrate books. The first appears to have been a tale of a lurid seduction in the days of Nero—with copious realistically anatomical drawings. She wrote at least 10 huge books a year, by hand, at the kitchen window and succeeded in working up a thoroughgoing contempt for children. "Father frequently disappeared furnaceward with armfuls," she says, "for I lost interest in the books when they were done." She also turned out a lot of poetry about this time, pages and pages that never mentioned love but were ridden with mysticism, religion and Life. She was quite sure that she had a Message. (When she sometimes catches herself believing that even now, she becomes very severe with herself.) And before she reached her teens she had also written some music and executed some fair portraits and sculpture. She came to the conclusion that she would get nowhere if she scattered her energies, and so threw everything but writing overboard.

Her father disapproved of higher education for women, so she set out at the age of 15 to earn some money; and after a long siege at Buffalo University evening sessions she received her B. A. in 1931.

By her first marriage, to William Fairfax Coombes in 1918, she had a daughter, Mary Margaret; and by her second, to Marcus Reback in 1931, another daughter, Judith

CALDWELL, TAYLOR—*Continued*

Ann. Her husband, a gifted linguist, was in the Intelligence Service during the World War, afterward became adviser to President Hoover, and is now a government official.

Taylor Caldwell has been writing madly ever since her early juvenile enterprises, and conservatively estimates that she has destroyed two or three forests. But nothing reached publication until *Dynasty of Death,* in September 1938. It was a huge, somewhat theatrically contrived novel about the intrigues of the Barbours and Bouchards, munition-makers. Reviews of this best seller were mixed, indeed, but the author had the pleasure of seeing several far-from-naïve critics take it for the work of a somewhat seasoned literary gentleman. A motion picture version of the book is planned for release in 1941.

In early 1940 she published a further projection of the armaments theme, *The Eagles Gather,* a later glance at the war-fomenting activities of a dynasty established in her earlier novel. *The Earth Is the Lord's* was published in the fall of 1940—a novel about the life and times of Genghis Khan.

Taylor Caldwell laments the fact that she is always trying to "get somewhere," which, says she, is the curse of the British. She is a passionate believer in trade unions but confesses to being skeptical of the intelligence of the masses. The professions and politics, she insists, are already overstocked with women, and she has a mean opinion of the average female wit and intelligence: education for women has become too universal —it makes them go about "'clear-eyed' and gallant, and inquisitive and snobbish and generally imbecilic." She was brought up in a violently conservative British home, with "books, arguments, boiled beef and cabbage"; has been called a conservative and a Fascist, but considers herself as probably "just a Democrat."

References

Newsweek 12:33-4 O 3 '38 por
Pub W 134:1442 O 15 '38
Sat R Lit 21:5 Ja 6 '40 por

CALLOW, JOHN MICHAEL July 7, 1867—July 27, 1940 Metallurgist and mining engineer; holder of 18 patents; inventor of the settling tank and traveling screen; retired in 1933 from the presidency of the General Engineering Company; in 1925 received the James Douglas Gold Medal from the American Institute of Mining and Metallurgical Engineers in recognition of distinguished achievement in non-ferrous metallurgy

References

Who's Who in America 1934-35

Obituaries

N Y Times p27 Jl 28 '40

CAMAC, CHARLES NICOLL BANCKER (kĕ-măk') Aug 6, 1868—Sept 27, 1940 Physician; educator; authority on clinical medicine; taught clinical medicine at Columbia University from 1910 to 1938; was a member of the faculty at Cornell University Medical College, 1909 to 1910, and at Polyclinic Hospital and Medical School in New York City, 1934 to 1936; was an assistant to Sir William Osler, whose writings he later compiled; was himself the author of many medical texts and articles in medical journals

References

American Medical Directory
American Men of Science
Who's Who in America
Who's Who in American Medicine

Obituaries

N Y Herald Tribune p36 S 29 '40
N Y Times p43 S 29 '40

CAMACHO, MANUEL AVILA (kä-mä' chō mä-nuĕl ä'vĭl-à) Apr 24, 1897- President of Mexico

Until General Camacho was inaugurated President of Mexico on December 1, it was impossible to say how much was settled in the Mexican Presidential election of July 7, 1940, for both candidates claimed their own elections. On July 16 the Mexican ministry advised all Mexican diplomats that General Camacho, the government candidate, had been chosen by an overwhelming vote of the people, and the Mexican Congress on September 23 officially announced a 16 to 1 majority for him. General Almazán (see sketch this issue), his outstanding rival, complained of fraud and the use of force to prevent the Almazánistas from voting, however (there had been bloodshed on both sides throughout the campaign), and repeatedly announced he would himself take the oath of office on December 1. Having left the country not long after the elections, he was reported biding his time and attempting to gain more support abroad while waiting for the signal to set up his own government. Whether this would be a signal for revolution no one knew, but Almazán's hopes were considerably dashed in November 1940 when President Roosevelt appointed Vice-President-Elect Wallace as his representative to Camacho's inauguration. And on November 27 Almazán officially renounced his claim to the Presidency.

According to a New York *Times* correspondent General Camacho is "a big man as Mexicans go, with heavy shoulders and thick neck. His hair and bushy eyebrows are black, as are also his eyes, and he has a small, thin-lipped mouth set in an elongated, rather plump face. He gives the impression of being fundamentally earnest and serious-minded; his occasional smiles are engaging and he possesses considerable charm of manner and ability to make friends." One of his brothers is Governor of a native state, another brother Mayor of Puebla. He is a three-goal polo player whose team won third in the 1936 Olympics, and owns a string of ponies which has traveled as far as Long Island; he is also said to be more student and thinker than man of action. He looks no more like a people's President than his rival.

Born in Teziutlán in the State of Puebla on April 24, 1897, Camacho started life as the son of an obscure farmer: Manuel Avila Castilla. His mother was Euprosia Camacho de Avila. Young Manuel was trained to be a bookkeeper, but after completing his course in accounting rode away in 1914 to join the forces revolting against Huerta. The revolt was successful, and for the next 15 years Camacho continued to "guess right on every upheaval." In 1923 he was fighting beside Cárdenas and Calles with United States' aid against rebellion. In 1924 he was specially cited for his defense of Moralia. But his main talents were as an arbitrator; he won so many battles with his tongue alone that the Mexicans sometimes jokingly call him "The Unknown Soldier" or "The Virgin Sword." In the Cristero rebellion of 1927 he is remembered for having walked unarmed into a saloon to meet the chief of the enemy forces and for having walked out an hour later with the rebel's promise to lay down his arms. In Michoacan in 1929 he talked 12 enemy generals into surrender.

He had begun army life as a second lieutenant; he rose to the rank of captain, major, colonel, brigadier general. Under President Rodriguez he served as chief of staff of the Ministry of War and the Navy, and the reforms he instituted at that time brought him an appointment as Secretary of National Defense in the Cabinet of President Cárdenas. In that office he advocated the purchase of United States airplanes, equipped the Mexican Army with tanks, trucks and anti-aircraft guns, and in 1938 achieved the highest rank in the army—division general —by his suppression of the bandit Cedillo.

Devoted to his wife, polo, history, biography and social studies, General Camacho became known as "a mild, pleasant moderate who hates excesses or extremes in any form," also as a loyal Cárdenas man. When he resigned from the Cabinet early in 1939 to campaign for nomination for President by the PRM (Party of the Mexican Revolution, the government party which has won the elections in Mexico since 1910), it was with the blessing of some of the more conservative elements in Mexico. Soon, however, his candidacy was also endorsed by Lombardo Toledano (see sketch this issue), radical head of the CTM (Confederation of Mexican Workers, a powerful and militant labor organization 1,000,000 strong), who believed that he would carry on the progressive program of President Cárdenas. The endorsement of the National Farm Confederation and of other labor and agricultural organizations followed, as well as that of

MANUEL CAMACHO

Cárdenas and his junta, and on November 3, 1939 Camacho won the nomination of the government party.

His most dangerous rival was General Almazán, who, backed by the great part of both Mexican and foreign business, American and British oil interests and those who were persuaded that the country was being run by a "corrupt labor bureaucracy" shot through by agents of the Comintern, promised to wipe out much of Cárdenas' program and pledged himself to cooperation with the United States. According to the correspondent of the *Christian Science Monitor* many of the men backing Almazán were ardent supporters of General Franco during the Spanish Civil War. His promises to give the land outright to the peasants and to revive the now-forbidden Catholic Church schools brought him some adherents from the people, however; the press and the middle classes were largely won to his side; and the loyalty of the Mexican Army generals is even now doubtless divided between the two camps.

Camacho's speeches, however, began to grow somewhat more conservative as the campaign went on. He pledged himself to "consolidate but not experiment," also favored transferring the title of land to the peasants who till it, the slackening of restrictions on the Church, the encouragement and protection of foreign capital if it does not hinder the welfare of the Mexican people. And, he announced: "Under present world conditions, we must find very close cooperation with Washington." Nevertheless, although his personal liking for the radical Lombardo Toledano is not at all certain, he never went so far as to break with the CTM. The greater part of labor continued to support him, and when, after his election, Congress met in August to ratify credentials of newly-elected Senators and

CAMACHO, MANUEL AVILA—*Continued*
Deputies, strong contingents of Camacho's peasant supporters were on hand to prevent a possible military *coup* by the opposition.

Both Camacho and Almazán are generals, both wealthy; they do not look unlike; their programs do not even sound as dissimilar as they might. And since his election Camacho has advanced a program that differs less and less from Almazán's. He has professed himself a good Catholic and promised to dedicate as much care to the spiritual as to the economic needs of the Mexican people. What is more, he has denied that he is a Socialist, has stated that neither Lombardo Toledano nor the Communists would have any part in his government and has said that he intends to defend American interests in Mexico. As a result, a number of Almazánistas have come over to his side and, revolution or no revolution, may stay there. On the other hand, many progressives have expressed the fear that the social gains of the past years will come to an abrupt halt under his conservative leadership.

References
> Christian Sci Mon p1, 6 Jl 8 '40
> Liv Age 356:447-9 Jl '39
> Look 4:24-7 Jl 2 '40 il
> New Repub 103:441-2 S 30 '40
> N Y Times IV p6 Jl 7 '40 por; p12, p20 Jl 9 '40; p7 Ag 2 '40; p6 Ag 12 '40; p10 Ag 14 '40; p8 S 13 '40; p9 S 20 '40
> Newsweek 15:12 Ap 29 '40
> Time 35:40+ Je 10 '40; 36:24-7 Jl 15 '40 il por

CAMPBELL, MRS. PATRICK Feb 9, 1865—Apr 9, 1940 English actress; estab-

Museum of the City of New York
MRS. PATRICK CAMPBELL

lished as star by performance of *Second Mrs. Tanqueray*

References
> Baring, M. Mrs. Patrick Campbell *In* Punch and Judy and Other Essays p65-85; Pélléas and Mélisande p325-6 1924
> Who's Who in America 1916-17
> Who's Who in the Theatre
> Winter, W. Mrs. Patrick Campbell in Several Plays *In* Wallet of Time 2:338-67 1913

Obituaries
> Manchester Guardian p3 Ap 11 '40 por
> N Y Herald Tribune p24 Ap 11 '40 por
> N Y Times p25 Ap 11 '40 por
> Newsweek 15:6 Ap 22 '40 por
> Time 35:53 Ap 22 '40
> Variety 138:55 Ap 17 '40

CANAVAN, JOSEPH J. Sept 6, 1887—Oct 10, 1940 Chairman of the New York State Parole Board and authority on parole; started career as newspaperman on the New York *Sun* and later on the *World*; induced to enter parole work by Governor Lehman of New York; because of his success in New York was made chairman of nationwide Committee of Standards and Procedures for Parole Selection and Release

Obituaries
> N Y Times p21 O 11 '40 por

CANBY, AL H. 1856—Oct 15, 1940 Retired theatrical manager and former actor and newspaperman; acted in, managed and produced a number of hits, including *The Prince of Pilsen* and *The Circus Girl*; associated in the management of Mrs. Patrick Campbell and for five seasons was manager of Alla Nazimova; before retirement in 1930 was associated with David Belasco and John Golden

Obituaries
> N Y Herald Tribune p26 O 16 '40
> N Y Times p23 O 16 '40

CANTON, ALLEN A. Sept 27, 1889—Mar 20, 1940 Electrical engineer; inventor of electrical, mechanical, naval and aeronautical devices

Obituaries
> N Y Herald Tribune p18 Mr 22 '40

CANTU, GIUSEPPE (kän-too') May 24, 1873—Oct 24, 1940 Italian commissioner general to New York World's Fair; served as officer aboard warship in Italo-Turkish War of 1911 to 1912 and saw service on five vessels during First World War; made rear admiral in 1925 and named director general of general personnel and

GIUSEPPE CANTU

military services of Navy Department; promoted to full admiral in 1935 and made president of Council of Royal Italian Navy; retired from active service in 1936

Obituaries

N Y Herald Tribune p10 O 26 '40 por
N Y Times p15 O 26 '40 por

CAREWE, EDWIN Mar 5, 1883—Jan 22, 1940 Director of silent films; real name Jay Fox

EDWIN CAREWE

Obituaries

N Y Herald Tribune p18 Ja 23 '40 por
Newsweek 15:2 F 5 '40
Time 35:57 Ja 29 '40
Variety 137:4 Ja 24 '40

CARMODY, JOHN MICHAEL Administrator of the Federal Works Agency

Address: b. Federal Works Agency, Washington, D. C.; h. 2101 Connecticut Ave, N W, Washington, D. C.

When President Roosevelt advised Congress on April 25, 1939 that "I find it necessary and desirable to group and consolidate under a Federal Works Agency those agencies of the Federal government dealing with public works," he transferred five agencies to the new agency. On June 23 he nominated John Michael Carmody to be administrator of the Federal Works Agency. Mr. Carmody was quickly confirmed by the Senate and assumed the duties of his new post on July 1.

The new Federal Works Agency combines under one administrator those agencies of the Federal government dealing with public works and administering Federal grants or loans to state and local governments for the purposes of construction. Their main functions are: 1. The *Work Projects Administration*, which provides work for needy persons on useful public projects; 2. The *Public Works Administration*, which finances, through loans and grants, public works having an estimated total cost of approximately four billion dollars; 3. The *United States Housing Authority*, which has as its major purpose the administering of loans and grants-in-aid to local public housing authorities for construction of low-cost housing; 4. The *Public Roads Administration*, which manages the Federal roads program in cooperation with state and local governments; 5. The *Public Building Administration*, which handles the allocation of space to Federal agencies and the construction of Federal buildings.

For six years before his appointment as administrator Mr. Carmody had served in various government administrative posts and prior to that had spent more than 20 years of equally varied responsibilities in the private industrial field.

Mr. Carmody was born in Towanda, Pennsylvania, the son of Michael John and Catherine (Collins) Carmody. In 1899 he was graduated from the Elmira (New York) Free Academy and the following year was graduated from the Elmira Business College. Subsequent education included work at Lewis Institute in Chicago in 1908 and at Columbia University in 1926.

Mr. Carmody began work in 1900 as a clerk and bookkeeper, and worked with various structural steel manufacturing concerns until 1914. In that year he left the steel field to become production and merchandising manager in the garment industry, which he did not leave until 1923. In

JOHN MICHAEL CARMODY

It was the combined FWA agencies which presented a series of displays at the New York World's Fair (1940). Here the dramatic story of these agencies was graphically presented through exhibits, through photomurals (one of which was the largest at the Fair), through actual demonstrations of spinning, weaving, serum making, highway research, model making and other nationwide projects which furnish useful employment. Here also was told the story of America's new schools, its pack horse libraries, its new hospitals and clinics, its public housing projects. In the theatre such famous movies as *The Plough That Broke the Plains* and *The River* (see sketch this issue under Pare Lorentz) were shown, as well as Technicolor movies and puppet plays.

Mr. Carmody was married in 1913 to Margaret Cross. They have one daughter, Catherine Cross Carmody.

References
    Am City 54:5 Ag '39
    Who's Who in America

1922, however, he identified himself with his third major industrial field when he made a special study of labor relations in the bituminous coal industry for the United States Coal Commission.

In 1923 Mr. Carmody joined the coal industry as vice-president in charge of industrial relations for the Davis Coal and Coke Company, and was vice-president and general manager of its merchandising subsidiaries from 1923 to 1926. In 1927 he became editor of *Coal Age* and of *Factory and Industrial Management* for the McGraw-Hill Publishing Company of New York and remained with McGraw-Hill until he came into the Federal government service in 1933. In 1931 he made a survey of industrial developments in Russia for the McGraw-Hill Company.

Mr. Carmody came to the Federal government as mediator for the Wagner Labor Board which was set up in connection with the NRA. Shortly thereafter he became chairman of the Bituminous Coal Labor Board. From November 1933 to September 1935 he served as chief engineer for the Civil Works Administration and the Federal Emergency Relief Administration, which initiated the Federal work relief program during the depths of the depression, and he was also a member of the National Mediation Board. He served on the National Labor Relations Board and in 1937 was appointed administrator for the Rural Electrification Administration. He relinquished this post to become Federal Works administrator.

When Carmody took over his new position he stated that he did not intend to have a large over-all staff in the Federal Works Agency but preferred a small coordinating unit, "working through the existing machinery of the FWA agencies."

CAROL II Oct 16, 1893- Former King of Romania

December 1940 Bulletin: In November 1940 Carol was merely another one of Europe's former crowned heads—and in more unfortunate circumstances than some. Under house arrest in Spain with his companion-in-exile, Magda Lupescu, he was begging President Roosevelt to exert his diplomatic influence in his behalf. Events had moved fast. After a large strip of Southern Dobruja had been surrendered to Bulgaria and more than half of Transylvania to Hungary, largely through the intervention of the Axis powers, and after German armored divisions had begun moving into Romania, civil war there had been forestalled only by Carol's surrender of supreme authority to Iron Guard sympathizer General Ion Antonescu (see sketch this issue). A day later, on September 6, Carol was forced to abdicate in favor of his son, and early the next morning he was nearly assassinated by the Iron Guard as his train sped toward the Yugoslav frontier, Magda Lupescu on board. The famous couple and their retinue reached Spain on their way to Portugal, where they had permission to stay, but after intervention on the part of Antonescu's government they were placed under house arrest by the Spanish authorities. It was asked that Lupescu be brought back to Romania for trial. As for Carol, one of the main accusations against him was that he had squandered public funds. Although his financial holdings in Romania itself were frozen by order of Antonescu's government, it was well-known that the greater part of his wealth (and it is considerable) had already been transferred to other countries.

From August issue:

In July 1940 two planes at the palace airfield in Bucharest stand ready for the instant flight of King Carol from Romania "in case of emergency." There is no longer room in Europe for a man who would be both a king and a dictator. The fate of Carol II is now under the control of two powers: Nazi Germany and Soviet Russia. Since September 1939 the hot kettle of the Balkans has sizzled at high pressure; trying to hold down the lid, Carol has been anything but happy. The fall of France in June 1940 forced him precipitously into the Nazi totalitarian camp: this meant the release of his old enemies, the Iron Guardists. Within a week came Russia's long-predicted taking of Bessarabia from Romania which Carol, minus the intervention of his Axis partners, was helpless to prevent. Broken in spirit, sleepless, forgetting to shave, endlessly smoking cigarettes, Carol paces the floor of his suite, nervously considering abdication in favor of the 18-year-old Crown Prince Michael.

The "playboy of the Balkans," who became head of a country whose riches are greatly coveted, was born in 1893, son of the late King Ferdinand and Queen Marie, born Princess of Great Britain and Ireland, Duchess of Saxony. Like a modern Prince Hal, Carol grew up a roistering escapader who later turned out to be a serious ruler. His father, having romantically eloped with a commoner and renounced his throne, had been persuaded to marry Queen Victoria's 17-year-old granddaughter. Marie soon took the reins in her own hands, intrigued with the house of Bratianu, and brought Romania to the Allied side in the World War. At Versailles she succeeded in doubling Romania's territory at the expense of Russia and Hungary. She married off her daughters advantageously, but she couldn't do anything with Carol, who was developing a mind of his own. A match with the daughter of Czar Nicholas failed to come off. The young prince defiantly left his regiment during the War, married the daughter of a Romanian officer, and renounced his rights to the throne. The marriage was annulled, the girl paid off, and Carol sent on a trip. When he got back his family forced him to marry Helen, sister of the present King of Greece, in March 1921. A son, Mihai (Michael), was born in October 1922.

But Carol had no intention of remaining a faithful husband—even in public. Soon favored among his mistresses was the divorced half-Jewish wife of an army lieutenant, titian-haired Magda Lupescu (see sketch this issue). In 1925 Carol ran away with "Bibi," as he always called her, penned a letter renouncing the throne from the same hotel as his father had before him. Little Mihai was declared successor.

CAROL II

But the Bratianu court was not holding its own. The opposition planned to bring Carol back in June 1930—on condition that Magda was dropped. Carol, however, brought Magda with him to Bucharest. Helen departed. Sentiment, particularly anti-Semitic, was strong against "that witch Magda." She was accused of being responsible for every evil in the country, and was particularly hated by the Fascist Iron Guard, which also sought to draw Carol away from his ties with the Balkan Entente, France and Czechoslovakia (through them with Britain) and to hitch Romania to Hitler's chariot. They assassinated one Premier, Duca, and Carol took sporadic measures of reprisal against them, but in 1937, temporarily appeased them with his appointment of violently anti-Semitic Premier Goga. Finally, in February 1938, agitation was so extreme that Carol assumed dictatorial power, formed a one-party state and discreetly retired Magda to a country villa, where her hobby was raising white turkeys. Calinescu was made Premier.

Things went on like that for awhile. Britain and France, who owned part of Romania's oil wells, competed against the German trade agreement. Intrigue was rife in brilliant Bucharest, "Paris of the East," swarming with resplendent officers and smartly-dressed women—many of them spies. The stock market soared, business and building boomed, the King's palace at Cotresceni got two new wings.

The wily Carol, later in 1939, visited England; he also dropped in on Hitler. He signed a new trade treaty with Germany, but when he got home shot or put into concentration camps most of the pro-Nazi Iron Guardists, whose leader, Codreanu, had been murdered by the government the year before. In September 1939 they retaliated

CAROL II—*Continued*

by assassinating Calinescu and attempting a *coup* in Bucharest.

When war began in September, Carol at once formally declared Romania's neutrality. And, while Italy and Turkey bickered over the subject of a Balkan federation, King Carol sat tight. After Russia took Finland, however, he saw the writing on the wall and rushed defense fortifications in Bessarabia. Feeling assured of the backing of England and France, he dared Stalin to cross the border. "Romania will fight as one living wall if we are invaded," he said. "Bessarabia will always remain Romanian." But the Soviet calmly started maneuvers off the Bulgarian coast, and Moscow signed a trade treaty with Bulgaria. Italy and Hungary began conferences.

To continue a vast war, Germany was highly in need of Romania's oil and grain. In March 1940 Hitler offered King Carol a pledge of "security" in return for a virtual monopoly on Romania's produce. Carol was most indignant at the suggestion that he also give amnesty to the imprisoned Iron Guard. But on April 25 he was forced to do this. With the pressure of Italy's entrance into the War, he was also forced to confer with Iron Guardist leaders on forming a dictatorship favoring the Axis powers. Although pro-Ally, his Premier Tătărescu remained in office. But on June 21, as soon as France fell, Carol had to cast his lot ostensibly with Germany. He formed a new "Party of the Nation," in which the anti-Semitic Iron Guard played a big part. Over the radio he ordered the people to reverse their entire mental attitude and asked the younger generation "to work also in this beehive of the national resurrection." His new "friend," Iron Guard leader Horia Sima, said: "The King's new party will enable us to face the future."

The "future" was just around the corner. Russian planes made flights over Bessarabia —border clashes were reported. The Axis powers failed to promise aid to Carol, and on June 28 the Red Army's motorized units marched into Bessarabia. On the heels of the Soviet ultimatum Hungary sent a time limit communication to Carol's government on its claims in Transylvania, and moved up troops. Italy and Germany did exert restraining pressure on Hungary. But Carol's new government pleased neither Berlin nor the Iron Guard extremists, who held Carol responsible for the loss of Bessarabia. There was much uncertainty about the position of Carol himself who, in Hitler's opinion, jumped too late on the band wagon and who, for all they knew, was still privately intriguing with Britain. Privately irked that the Russian grab of Bessarabia brought the Soviet Union within reach of Romania's oil fields, the Nazis felt that a strong government in Romania was imperative. On July 4 Tătărescu was replaced by Prime Minister Ion Gigurtu, and Horia Sima became Minister of Culture, with other Iron Guardists given key posts. Within four days the Iron Guardists

tendered their resignations, prompted by the realization that cessions of territory to Hungary and Bulgaria are probably inevitable: Sima himself comes from Transylvania. Carol tried to reinstate the Iron Guardists, and meantime entertained the young Soviet ambassador and gave him assurances of Romania's desire to be friendly.

King Carol's present difficult position is to please the Nazis and at the same time not to displease Russia. And always around him are his old enemies the Iron Guardists, who have not forgotten that he once put them in a concentration camp. King Carol looks nervously out the window toward the waiting plane—but it is not definitely reported what country will welcome him when "the emergency" comes.

References

Christian Sci Mon p5 Je 11 '40
Nation 150:769-70 Je 29 '40
N Y Herald Tribune p4 Je 22 '40; p2 Jl 2 '40; p1 Jl 4 '40; p1, 6 Jl 5 '40
N Y Times p1, 4 Je 22 '40; p23 Je 23 '40; p14 Je 28 '40; p12 Jl 9 '40; p4 S 7 '40 por
Newsweek 16:31 Jl 15 '40; 16:26-8 S 16 '40 il por
PM p4 Je 27 '40 por; p4 Je 28 '40
Time 34:25-8 N 13 '39 il por; 35:24-5 Ja 15 '40 por; 36:25-6 Jl 1 '40; 36:23 Jl 29 '40; 36:34+ S 16 '40 il por

Bercovici, K. That Royal Lover 1931
Bolitho, H. Roumania Under King Carol 1940
Carr, A. Alexander, Metaxas, Carol: Ferment in the Balkans *In* Juggernaut p129-45 1939
Gay, G. King Carol of Rumania pam 1940
Gunther, J. Lupescu Comedy *In* Inside Europe p339-53 1936
Hoven, H. von der King Carol of Romania 1940
International Who's Who

CARPENTER, SIR HENRY CORT HAROLD Feb 6, 1875—Sept 14, 1940 Noted English metallurgist; was professor of metallurgy at Victoria University, Manchester from 1906 to 1913; at his death was professor at the Royal School of Mines, London; had received many outstanding honors in the United States, Japan and Europe; was awarded the Carnegie Gold Medal of the Iron and Steel Institute in 1905 and other awards during the next 30 years; had written widely for iron and steel journals; knighted in 1929

References

Nature 140:675 O 16 '37
Who's Who
Who's Who in Commerce and Industry

Obituaries

N Y Herald Tribune p14 S 16 '40
N Y Times p19 S 16 '40

CARPENTER, LEWIS VAN Dec 23, 1895—May 10, 1940 Engineer; professor of sanitary engineering at New York University; one of the nation's authorities in that field; author of many technical books

LEWIS VAN CARPENTER

References

Who's Who in Engineering
Who's Who in New York

Obituaries

N Y Herald Tribune p42 My 12 '40 por

N Y Times p49 My 12 '40 por

CARREL, ALEXIS (kä'rĕl ä-lĕk'sĭs) June 28, 1873- Scientist

Address: Rockefeller Institute, 66th St and York Ave, New York City

Dr. Alexis Carrel was born at Sainte-Foy-lès-Lyon, France, June 28, 1873, the son of a silk merchant. He took his M. D. at the University of Lyon in 1900. While a medical student, he acquired surgical dexterity not only by extended anatomical studies and dissection, but by carpentry and sewing. For instance, he trained himself to take stitches with a very fine needle and very fine thread in ordinary paper so that the stitches did not show on either side of the paper. The line of research he wished to pursue after graduation was so far off the beaten track that none of the professors at Lyon was interested. He thought of going into cattle raising and went to Canada in 1904. Once there he was set back on the track of science again and went to work in the Hull Physiological Laboratory in Chicago. His professional reputation was established by his discovery of a new way of sewing together the ends of an artery, and by his success in removing a dog's thyroid

and putting it back upside down for thyroid functioning. It was Simon Flexner who asked Carrel to come to his newly-organized Rockefeller Institute for Medical Research in New York in 1906. He was made a member in 1912.

Dr. Carrel married Anne de la Motte, handsome widow of the Marquis de la Mairie, in 1913. Having long wanted to be a soldier, he rushed into the French Army at the outbreak of the War, won the Légion d'Honneur, and soon became a major. Mrs. Carrel served as a head nurse of the French Red Cross and directed a mobile surgical ambulance at the front. With chemist Henry D. Dakin, Carrel perfected the famed Carrel-Dakin antiseptic solution for the treatment of infected wounds. Following his honorable discharge from the French Army Medical Corps in 1919, he returned to the Rockefeller Institute, where he developed new techniques for the cultivation of tissues and, in later years, for the cultivation of organs outside of the animal body.

Dr. Carrel won the Nobel Prize in 1912 for success in suturing blood vessels and the transplantation of organs. He won the Nordhoff-Jung Cancer Prize in 1931; the Newman Foundation Award at the University of Illinois in 1937. It was January 1912, at the Rockefeller Institute, when Dr. Carrel began the cultivation in the juice of chick embryos of a few fragments of embryonic chick heart. From the sub-cultures obtained from these fragments was derived the strain of connective tissue, or fibroblasts, which has grown actively ever since. It is now under cultivation in a private laboratory. It was recently rumored that this heart was dead, but as New York's *World-Telegram* headlined it: Cancel that obituary on the chicken heart. The report, it seems, was exaggerated.

In 1935 the name of Carrel whirled up to fresh fame because Charles Lindbergh, aviator and bio-mechanic, designed for him a perfusion pump, or artificial heart, with which to pump life into organs *in vitro* such as the heart, kidneys and ovaries, and such glands as the thyroid. The new technique of tissue culture perfected by Carrel leaves classical anatomical dissection far behind; and it was to make known the use of Lindbergh's perfusion pump that Carrel and Lindbergh published in collaboration in 1938 their *Culture of Organs*.

The function of this germ-proof pump is not only to keep separate vital organs alive in fluid, but, by changing the contents of the fluids, to make them develop abnormalities which may be readily studied. Carrel hopes that in the future organs removed from the body, during operations or soon after death, may be revived in the pump and made to function again; and that larger human organs such as the pancreas can be made to manufacture substances *in vitro* now supplied to patients only by animals. Also, diseased organs might be transferred to the pump for treatment, cured, then replanted in the patient. The cultivation of organs in the

ALEXIS CARREL

pump would allow the discovery of the nature of the specific chemicals demanded by these organs for growth and normal function. It would then be possible to feed such chemicals to the body instead of supplying the hormone by injection, such as is done in the case of diabetes. Thus, after 123 years, through the perfusion pump for keeping alive organs isolated from the body, the conception of the physiologist Le Gallois has been realized.

The pump, like the human body, is a "closed system"—its orifices protected by cotton-wool filter bulbs and cement sealed so that no air gets into the pump after it is connected to the rest of the apparatus. The temperature of the pump is maintained at the level of the organism by keeping it in an incubator. A "rhythmic pulse" is supplied by a pressure of gas driven forward at regular intervals by compressed air escaping through a rotating valve.

Dr. Carrel retired from the Rockefeller Institute in June 1939, with the title of Member Emeritus. Shortly thereafter he went to France, and in September 1939 was given a special mission by the French government. In May 1940 he returned to New York, where he is pursuing extensive studies on man and environment and where he designed a mobile hospital for war work.

Dr. Carrel is a stocky, trim, broad-faced, broad-browed and pink-complexioned Frenchman, with piercing but kindly eyes. Of him Lindbergh has said: "Dr. Carrel has one of the most brilliant, penetrating and versatile minds I have ever met. His every action is filled with character and the record of his life could not fail to interest anyone who cares about human personality."

Dr. Carrel is also the author of *Man, the Unknown*, published in 1935. Into this book he put the essence of his experiences, philoso-

phy and intuition as a doctor and as a man. Its theme is that science has itemized most of the facts of mankind but never added them up to the total of man's potentialities. Dr. Carrel proposes a High Council to rule the world for its own good, at a "thinking center" where political leaders would come for advice. The council members would dedicate their lives to the economic, psychological, physiological and other phenomena manifested by the nations and their individuals. "An institute of this sort," says Dr. Carrel, "would acquire enough knowledge to prevent the organic and mental deterioration of civilized nations." He also maintains that high councilors would correct errors concerning democratic equality. Individuals, he thinks, are not equal: the feeble-minded and the man of genius should not be equal before the law. The stupid and unintelligent have no right to a higher education, nor to the same voting power as intelligent beings. Unless certain changes are made, Dr. Carrel says, "men cannot follow civilization along its present course because they are degenerating."

References

Lit Digest 124 (Digest 1):35 S 11 '37 il
N Y Herald Tribune p6 Jl 28 '40
Newsweek 15:43 Ja 29 '40
Sat Eve Post 211:5-7+ Jl 23 '38 il pors
Sci ns 81:621-3 Je 21 '35; 83:516-17 My 29 '36
Sci N L 33:413 Je 25 '38
Sci Am 154:235 My '36 por
Time 26:41-2 Jl 1 '35 por; 26:40-3 S 16 '35 por (cover); 31:40+ Je 13 '38 il por (cover); 34:37 N 20 '39 por
American Catholic Who's Who
American Men of Science
Beard, A. E. S. Great Medical Investigator: Dr. Alexis Carrel *In* Our Foreign-Born Citizens p107-17 1939
Carrel, A. Man, the Unknown 1935
Kaempffert, W. B. Carrel *In* Science Today and Tomorrow p181-93 1939
Law, F. H. Alexis Carrel: Surgeon *In* Modern Great Americans p63-76 1926
Ratcliff, J. D. Life's Beginning *In* Modern Miracle Men p196-210 1939
Who's Who
Who's Who in America

CARSON, JOHN RENSHAW June 28, 1887—Oct 31, 1940 Mathematician and electrical engineer; as member of the engineering department of the American Telephone and Telegraph Company installed the first carrier current system; joined Bell Telephone Laboratories in 1934; received the Liebmann Memorial Prize from the Institute of Radio Engineers in 1924; in 1935 was awarded Doctor of Science degree from the Brooklyn Polytechnic Institute and in 1939 won the Elliott Cres-

Blackstone

JOHN RENSHAW CARSON

son Medal from the Franklin Institute; author of scientific books and articles

References

American Men of Science
Who's Who in America

Obituaries

N Y Herald Tribune p18 N 1 '40
por
N Y Times p25 N 1 '40

CARTON DE WIART, ADRIAN (wē′är) 1880- Major General in command of British forces in Norway

In April 1940 when the battle front of the War between Germany and the Allies had shifted to Norway, Major General Adrian Carton de Wiart, in command of the British forces in central Norway, came in for a good deal of attention. This 60-year-old veteran, minus one eye and one arm, wears the decorations of three wars, surmounted by the—Victoria Cross, England's highest award for valor.

General Carton de Wiart, who was born in 1880 in Brussels, received his education at Balliol College, Oxford. In 1899 he enlisted as a private in the Imperial Yoemanry for the Boer War. He later won a commission and was promoted to captain in the Fourth Dragoon Guards in 1910. In the World War he first saw service in South Africa with the Somaliland camel corps, where he was twice wounded and lost an eye. He was mentioned in dispatches and awarded the Distinguished Service Order.

From 1915 to 1918 General Carton de Wiart served in France, where he was lieutenant colonel and, before the War ended,

commander of a Gloucestershire regiment. He was wounded nine times and lost his left hand at Zonnebeke. One of his most legendary exploits was at La Boiselle, where he rallied three battalions which had lost their commanding officers. The wavering British line began to reform and advance, when Carton de Wiart strolled casually toward the German trenches. Inspired by his nonchalance, the battalions drove forward. Carton de Wiart received the Victoria Cross for this exploit.

In 1923, when he was attached to the British mission to Poland, Carton de Wiart participated in the final battles between Russian and Polish troops outside Warsaw. In that year he retired from the army.

For years General Carton de Wiart lived quietly in Poland on a 300,000-acre estate lent him by the family of Prince Radziwill. The estate was only eight miles from the old Russian border and once was part of the shooting grounds of Czar Nicholas. The General's wife is the Countess Frederica, daughter of Prince Fugger Babenhausen and Nora, Princess Hohenlohe.

General Carton de Wiart left his retirement in September 1939 to become a member of the British military mission to Poland.

A six-footer, Carton de Wiart wears a patch over his lost eye and his armless sleeve is fastened at his side. "He is no D'Artagnan type, but rather a typical old-style British fighting man with a handsome, heavy, gray mustache." In the clubland of Pall Mall and St. James's Street, where oldtime British fighting men assemble after dinner to recall war exploits, no veteran is more surrounded with legend and fame than General Adrian Carton de Wiart.

ADRIAN CARTON DE WIART

CARTON DE WIART, ADRIAN—*Cont.*

References

N Y Herald Tribune p2 Ap 22 '40
N Y Times p5 Ap 22 '40
Scholastic 36:10 My 13 '40 por
Time 35:19 Ap 29 '40 por
Who's Who 1940

CARVER, GEORGE WASHINGTON

1864-   Agricultural chemist; director of the Research and Experiment Station, Tuskegee Institute, Alabama

Address: Tuskegee Institute, Alabama

One of the three recipients of the Roosevelt Medal in 1939 was George Washington Carver, who was given the award for "distinguished service in the field of science," the citation reading "to a scientist humbly seeking the guidance of God and a liberator to men of the white race as well as the black." For his "brilliant achievements" he was awarded in June 1940 a bronze plaque by the International Federation of Architects, Engineers, Chemists and Technicians, a CIO affiliate. These are only two of the many honors that have come to Carver during his more than forty years as a scientist. Born a slave toward the end of the Civil War, near Diamond Grove, Missouri, today he is internationally known as an agricultural chemist, holds B. S., M. S. and Ph. D. degrees and is a fellow in the Royal Society of Arts of London.

Carver's contributions to the field of agricultural chemistry have gained for him such names as the "Wizard of Tuskegee," the "Negro Burbank", "Goober Wizard", "Columbus of the Soil," and have greatly expanded the agricultural economy of the entire South. Salad oil; an oil remedy for infantile paralysis, dyes of 19 different shades from peanuts; stains and face powder from clays; flour and shoe blacking from sweet potatoes; paving blocks from cotton; dyes from dandelions, tomato vines and trees—these are among the "brilliant achievements" that have made Carver known throughout the world.

But all of this was almost lost to the world, for when the future scientist was a slave baby only a few weeks old he and his mother Mary (his father was Moses Carver) were stolen by night raiders from the plantation of their German-born master, whose name was Carver. The master sent a messenger in pursuit, who ransomed the child with a race horse valued at $300. Ill with whooping cough, which almost proved fatal, he remained sickly and frail throughout childhood.

As the child, whom the Carvers called "George Washington," grew older he helped Mrs. Carver with household tasks. She encouraged him to study and gave him a blue-backed speller, from which he got his earliest education. Later she gave him a *Bible*, large portions of which he committed to memory.

Though the Carvers were interested in George's getting an education, they could not afford to help him. So at the age of ten he left their home and found a school eight miles away which he attended two years, supporting himself by doing odd jobs. When he learned all that this school had to teach him he moved on to Minneapolis, Kansas, where he completed high school. He then began to earn money for college, doing fine laundry work, knitting, tatting, embroidery and odd jobs. For three years he attended Simpson College, earning his tuition by working in the college laundry. After he was graduated he entered Iowa State College of Agricultural and Mechanical Arts. At the end of five years he held two degrees from Iowa State College—a Bachelor of Science degree and a Master of Science degree.

He was invited to remain at Iowa State College as a member of the staff in charge of the work on systematic botany, the bacteriological laboratories and the greenhouses. It was there that two years later (1898) Booker T. Washington discovered him and asked him to join the staff of Tuskegee Institute, Alabama, where he has been since.

One of Carver's first interests after he arrived in the South was the study of crop rotation. After experimentation he suggested peanuts, pecans and sweet potatoes, as satisfactory money crops in place of cotton. How he drove around the countryside showing the farmers what they could raise was dramatically portrayed in a recent movie, *The Story of Dr. Carver* (a Pete Smith short released in June 1938). He was not always listened to, but he kept on until he had convinced the Alabama farmers that they could grow something besides cotton. Today the peanut, which in 1898 had scarcely any commercial value, ranks next to cotton as a money crop in Alabama, and in the whole South there are more than a million and a half acres of peanuts in cultivation bringing more than $60,000,000 a year in income.

When the Alabama farmers took his advice about growing peanuts, Carver began to find ways of using this once unimportant plant. He has found almost 300 ways. In 1921, when Congress was considering the Hawley-Smoot tariff bill, the Southern farmers asked for a tariff on peanuts. Carver was among those called before the Ways and Means Committee for advice. When he had talked his allotted 10 minutes he was prepared to stop; but other men clamored for him to go on. They listened, fascinated, for an hour and three-quarters, during which time Carver enumerated 145 products which he had made from the peanut, as well as 100 from the sweet potato and 60 from the pecan—milk, condiments, axle grease, plastics, ink, flour, insulating board, coffee, starch, mock coconut, preserved ginger, library paste and many more—both edible and non-edible.

From the red clay soil of Alabama Dr. Carver has extracted valuable pigments— blue, purple and red; he is said to have rediscovered a secret of lasting colors that was known to the ancient Egyptians. From cottonstalks he has made starch, gums, dextrins; from the palmetto root, veneers; from palmetto and green wood shavings, a synthetic marble; from cornstalk fiber, rope.

Though Dr. Carver spends most of his time in his laboratory, his fame has spread far beyond Tuskegee and far beyond the United States. Thomas Edison once offered him $50,000 a year for five years to do research for him, but he refused. A synthetic marble company of Mississippi asked him to join its firm, at any figure he named; when he declined, the company moved to Tuskegee, where they could have the benefit of his advice—advice that is given free. In 1928 the Crown Prince of Sweden spent several weeks with him to obtain information about using agricultural waste substances for industrial raw materials. The Duke of Windsor, when he visited the United States as Prince of Wales, spent several hours in Dr. Carver's laboratory, fascinated.

Whatever service Dr. Carver can give he gives freely. He has sought no patent on the peanut oil that has proved effective in many paralysis cases, and it is available at any drugstore for 65 cents a gallon. His peanut oil therapy he has turned over to the medical profession. When peanut growers sent him a check for eradicating a disease of the plant he returned it.

Recognition of Dr. Carver's services has been given in other ways: in 1916 he was made a fellow in the Royal Society of Arts of London, an honor conferred upon few Americans; in 1923 he received the Spingarn Medal for the most distinguished contribution by a Negro to science; in 1935 he was appointed collaborator in the Bureau of Plant Industry, United States Department of Agriculture. During a series of anniversary celebrations held at Tuskegee Institute between November 1936 and April 1937, called the "Carver Fortieth Anniversary," one of the highlights was the presentation to the Institute of a life-size bronze bust of the great scientist done by the distinguished Atlanta sculptor, Steffen Thomas, and paid for by Carver's admirers of both races, mostly by dollar subscriptions.

The George Washington Carver Foundation, to perpetuate research in agricultural chemistry, was established at Tuskegee in February 1940 through the donation by Dr. Carver of $30,000, his life savings, much depleted by a bank failure. The Foundation will study problems of soil fertility, new uses for the native plants and creation of useful products from otherwise wasted material. It will include a unit, already established, for the study of infantile paralysis; and it will house the Carver Museum, where are found hundreds of products discovered by the scientist and about a

GEORGE WASHINGTON CARVER

hundred of his paintings, one, *The Rose*, promised to the Luxembourg Galleries upon his death.

A documentary film made on location by the Bryant Production Company, with Dr. Carver taking the lead, was released in April 1940. It was designed to show not only the story of Carver but also something of the history of the Negro in America.

Dr. Carver explains the amount of work he is able to do by saying: "I have made it a rule to get up every morning at four. I go into the woods and there I gather specimens and study the great lessons that Nature is eager to teach us. Alone in the woods each morning I best hear and understand God's plan for me."

References

Am Mag 114:24-5+ O '32 il por (Same abr. Read Digest 30:5-9 F '37)
Commonweal 31:441 Mr 15 '40
Liberty 15:19-21 Ja 8 '38 por
Lit Digest 123:20-1 Je 12 '37 por
N Y Times p16 Mr 31 '39; p22 O 10 '39; p7 O 28 '39; IV p2 F 18 '40 por; p20 F 27 '40; p17 Je 3 '40
Newsweek 10:20 S 6 '37; 15:42-4 F 26 '40 il por
Time 29:54 Je 14 '37 por; 31:41 My 16 '38 por
American Men of Science
Borth, C. First and Greatest Chemurgist *In* Pioneers of Plenty p226-40 1939
Bullock, R. W. George Washington Carver *In* In Spite of Handicaps p45-51 1927
Hunter, J. Saint, Seer and Scientist pam 1939
Merritt, R. H. From Captivity to Fame 1929

CARVER, GEORGE WASHINGTON—
Continued

>Ovington, M. W. George Washington Carver *In* Portraits in Color p169-80 1927
>Who's Who in America
>Who's Who in Colored America

CASEY, EDWARD PEARCE June 18, 1864—Jan 2, 1940 Architect

After 50 years spent as a leading architect, Edward Pearce Casey died in New York at the age of 75. He was born in Portland, Maine, the son of General Thomas Lincoln and Emma (Weir) Casey, the grandson of Major General Silas Casey. After graduation from Columbia University School of Mines, in 1886, he studied for three years at L'Ecole des Beaux Arts, Paris.

In the New York City Hall architects' competition of 1893 in which 134 architects competed, he was one of the six equal prize winners. In 1900 he was a co-winner of the first prize for the design of the memorial bridge over the Potomac River at Washington, and he won first prize in 1902, again in competition, for the design of the Grant Monument, Washington. Plans for the Library of Congress were altered by Mr. Casey, who was in charge of plans for the building from 1892 to 1897. Among his other Washington designs were Memorial Continental Hall, the Commodore Barry Monument, New York State monuments for the Civil War battlefield at Antietam, Maryland and Gettysburg, Pennsylvania and the American College at Beirut, Syria. He was married in New York City to Lilian Berry, June 20, 1929.

References

>Who's Who in America 1938-39
>Who's Who in New York

Obituaries

>N Y Times p21 Ja 3 '40

CASEY, RICHARD GARDINER Aug 29, 1890- First Australian Minister to the United States, appointed January 1940

Address: Australian Legation, Woodland Dr, Washington, D. C.

With the appointment of the Right Honorable Richard Gardiner Casey as the first Minister to the United States from Australia, New Zealand is the only member of the British Commonwealth of Nations left without representation in the United States. The outbreak of the Second European War in 1939 has made Australia, heretofore represented in Washington only by the British Ambassador, anxious to establish direct diplomatic contacts with this country which also has active interests in the Pacific.

Richard Gardiner Casey, handsome, lean-faced and mustached, born in Brisbane, Australia, famed throughout his country as an airplane pilot, was Minister of Supply and Development during the year 1939. He was educated at the University of Melbourne and at Cambridge and saw active service during the First World War, being mentioned in dispatches from France and Gallipoli and receiving the D. S. O. and the M. C. Since 1931 he has been a member of the House of Representatives from Corio. He was married in 1926 and has a son Conn and daughter Jane.

The President of the United States in turn nominated an American Minister to Canberra, capital of Australia. He is Clarence E. Gauss, veteran American Consul General at Shanghai.

References

>N Y Herald Tribune D 26 '39 por; p17 F 22 '40 por
>N Y Sun p6 Ja 8 '40 por; p11 Mr 30 '40 por
>N Y Times p1 D 25 '39 por
>Time 35:14 Mr 4 '40 por
>Who's Who
>Who's Who in Australia

CATT, CARRIE CHAPMAN Jan 9, 1859- Women's leader

Address: 120 Paine Ave, New Rochelle, New York

In November 1940 women leaders from all over the country met in New York City to celebrate the Woman's Centennial Congress in honor of twenty years of woman suffrage and to celebrate the hundredth anniversary of the beginning of the suffrage movement. They charted a course for women to follow for the century to come, for their leader, Mrs. Carrie Chapman Catt, believes that it takes "a hundred years to change the public's mind on an important question." She called the meeting and prepared a *Declaration of Intentions* similar to the *Declaration of Sentiments* which set the pace for the first woman's rights convention a hundred years ago.

Mrs. Catt began to champion her sex and struck her first blow for it back in the Sixties, when she was six and in the first grade in school. In Ripon, Wisconsin it was, when every boy laughed at one of her classmates losing her hoop skirt. Carrie "firmly, deliberately and with righteous conviction" marched up to the most boisterous and slapped him in the face. When she was seven her parents, Lucius and Maria (Clinton) Lane, moved to Iowa and brought her up on a farm near Charles City. There she struck her second blow. Her brother Charles chased her with a snake. She was afraid of snakes, but she caught one and chased her brother. Although he was three years her senior, he recognized a grim purpose in her blue eyes and ran. At the age of 13 her purpose gained a point when she realized that her father could vote, that her mother could not; that her mother could hold no property in her own name and that if she worked could not collect her earnings.

Robert Ingersoll was her favorite author in high school.

After teaching for a year she went to the Iowa State College at Ames. When her savings from her $20-a-month teaching job proved insufficient to pay her way through three years at college, she supplemented them with dish washing at nine cents an hour and library work at ten cents an hour. She made a further step in her fight for the rights for women in college when she secured physical education instruction for girls after noticing that the boys were given free military training.

After receiving a B. S. in 1880 she showed her independence by entering a lawyer's office to read law. But apparently the citizens did not object too strenuously, because the next year they made her principal of the Mason City High School and two years later appointed her the first woman superintendent of schools.

In 1884 Carrie Lane married Leo Chapman, editor and owner of the Mason City *Republican*. In the first year of her married life she independently organized a small group of friends to canvass Mason City with petitions for the passage of a bill in the State Legislature for municipal suffrage for the women of Iowa. The appearance of this petition from a town where there was no suffrage club led the state suffrage association to invite her as a delegate to their state convention.

Two years after their marriage, Mr. Chapman sold his newspaper and went to San Francisco. There he became ill and died of typhoid before his wife could reach him. His widow became a newspaper reporter, but stayed in San Francisco only long enough to learn that women, especially pretty women, had a hard time competing with men in the business world, and to meet some of the pioneers in the woman suffrage movement—Susan B. Anthony, Julia Ward Howe, Lucy Stone.

Mrs. Chapman returned to Iowa in 1887 with the twofold purpose of earning a living and beginning to work to "change people's minds about woman's function in society." She started out as an organizer for the Iowa Woman Suffrage Association and in 12 years rose to a position of national leadership. From 1900 to 1904 she was president of the National American Woman Suffrage Association. In 1909, known as "the brains of the woman suffrage movement," she organized the suffrage forces on the lines of political parties, without belonging to any party.

Her work was not interrupted by her marriage to George William Catt, a civil engineer, in Seattle, Washington in 1890. She was able to return to South Dakota to campaign, and there made the first outdoor speech ever made by a woman for suffrage. Arriving in a small town with another worker and finding that no meeting place had been arranged, they hired a democrat wagon and drove to the center of the town,

CARRIE CHAPMAN CATT

alternately ringing a dinner bell and introducing each other to attract a public. Mrs. Catt spoke so eloquently that the words of Secretary George (Chairman of the Senatorial Committee on Woman Suffrage) were most apt: "There isn't a man in Christiandom that can answer that woman's arguments, but I'd rather see my wife in her coffin than going to vote."

Mrs. Catt retired from the presidency of the National American Woman Suffrage Association in 1904 due to her own failing health and the illness, followed by death, of her husband. She returned to a home she had established in New York. In 1915 she directed the state suffrage campaign and was drafted again as president of the organization to lead the drive for the passage of the Nineteenth Amendment. The first legislative victory had been made in Wyoming in 1869, the next in Colorado in 1893. The three years from 1917 to 1920 were "the climactic ones of her work." She conducted the drive on Congress to submit the Amendment, then the drive on the state legislatures to ratify it—living on trains, in hotels, in conferences. She was able to carry on the struggle with a million dollars which Mrs. Frank Leslie bequeathed to the cause. Mrs. Catt campaigned through nearly all the states in the Union, and in 1920 Tennessee was the thirty-sixth state to ratify the Amendment and make it a part of the Federal Constitution. The inner story of the suffrage movement with an analysis of its opposition—*Woman Suffrage and Politics*—was published in collaboration with Nettie R. Shuler in 1923. A chapter, *Wyoming: the First Surrender*, from this volume, was adapted for publication in *Victory*; *How Women Won It*, issued in the fall of 1940.

In 1919 Mrs. Catt founded the National League of Women Voters to help women

CATT, CARRIE CHAPMAN—*Continued*

vote intelligently, and she has been honorary president of the organization since then. An International Woman Suffrage Alliance was organized at her instigation in 1904. She was president of that organization until 1923, and since then honorary chairman. She made tours of Europe, went around the world to bring women of the oriental races into the Alliance, helped sponsor the first suffrage conference of Pan-American women in Baltimore in 1922 and finished her suffrage labors with a tour of South America in 1923. The Turkish government issued a postage stamp bearing her portrait in honor of the founding of the Alliance in 1935. In 1930 she won the $5,000 *Pictorial Review* Award for outstanding achievement and was selected as one of the 10 outstanding women of 1937 by *American Women*. Mrs. Catt also won an award for bringing about better understanding between Christians and Jews in 1933. Other awards include a medal from the National Institute of Social Science, in May 1940, and honorary LL.D.'s from the University of Wyoming, Iowa State College and Smith College.

When the suffrage battle was won Mrs. Catt plunged into another—the cause of peace. First she was a member of the woman's committee of the Council of National Defense. Then she founded and was chairman (1925-32, honorary chairman since) of the National Committee on the Cause and Cure of War; in 1925 she called a Washington conference; in 1935 she published an essay *Because If We Do Not Destroy War Now, War Will Destroy Us* in the collection *Why Wars Must Cease*. She is still fighting for peace. The theme of the meeting of women celebrating the Woman's Centennial Congress at the New York World's Fair August 26, 1940 was that "all women must be alert in defense of democracy and to save this country from war."

Mrs. Catt has many hobbies. She loves her garden. Flowers bloom their earliest and brightest for her. She is a thorough housekeeper and knows how to prepare delicious food. She specializes in jellies and pickles, made the old-fashioned way. There is nothing in her home that reflects the real Mrs. Catt so much as her library, and her desire to share it with useful results. In 1937 she gave her Peace library to Iowa State College and in 1939 presented her Feminist library to the Library of Congress, where it is now placed in the room with Benjamin Franklin's Library.

A friend writes: "Throughout the years of Mrs. Catt's advancement of rights for women she has revealed the mind of a statesman. Her statesmanship has been the fundamental kind—broad vision, a scholarly background, an enormous sense of fair play, unswerving honesty, patient tolerance, a love for her fellow men, ready tact and the genius to appeal to an opponent's intelligence rather than to his prejudice. These are the qualities that have made Mrs. Catt the greatest leader of women of her time."

References

 Christian Sci Mon Mag p8-9 Ag 24 '40
 Good H 93:34-5+ O '31 por
 Scholastic 34:20 F 4 '39 por
 World Tomorrow 13:358-61 S '30 por
 Allen, D. ed. Changing the Mind of a Nation, Carrie Chapman Catt *In* Adventurous Americans p165-78 1932
 American Women
 Kirkland, W. M. and Kirkland, F. Carrie Chapman Catt, Crusader *In* Girls Who Became Leaders p76-87 1932
 National American Woman Suffrage Association. Victory, How Women Won It; A Centennial Symposium 1840-1940 1940
 Who's Who in America

CATURANI, MICHELE GAETANO (kä-tur-a′ne me′kel′ gä-ä-tä′nō) Nov 11, 1873—Feb 24, 1940 Physician; expert on gynecology; founder of the Parkway Hospital in Manhattan

MICHELE GAETANO CATURANI

References

 American Medical Directory

Obituaries

 N Y Times p58 F 25 '40

CAVERO, SALVADOR 1851—Feb 19, 1940 First Vice-President of the Peruvian Republic

Obituaries

 N Y World-Telegram p26 F 20 '40

CHADDOCK, ROBERT EMMET Apr 16, 1879—Oct 21, 1940 Statistician and professor at Columbia University where he taught since 1911; since 1925 member of the American Statistical Association's Advisory Committee to the United States Director of the Census; also improved the government's statistical methods as a member, from 1933 to 1936, of the Committee on Government Statistics and Information Services; was founder of the Cities Census Committee, which developed a system for enumeration and tabulation in New York which other cities adopted; author of books on statistics

References

Who's Who in America

Obituaries

N Y Herald Tribune p42 O 22 '40 por

N Y Times p25 O 22 '40 por

CHADWICK, HELENE Nov 25, 1897— Sept 4, 1940 Star of silent films; started career in 1916; co-starred in many silent films; became a featured player when sound came in and thereafter obtained only bit parts

Photoplay-Movie Mirror
HELENE CHADWICK

References

Motion Picture Classic 11:22-3-+ Ja '21 pors
Motion Picture Mag 21:24-5+ Jl '21
Photoplay 22:36-7 Ag '22 pors

Obituaries

N Y Herald Tribune p18 S 6 '40 por
Variety 140:46 S 11 '40

CHAMBERLAIN, JOHN RENSSELAER Oct 28, 1903- Author; critic

Address: Cheshire, Connecticut

As a book reviewer and critic on the New York *Times* and other publications, more recently as an editor of *Fortune,* John Chamberlain became known, in spite of his youth, for his mature consideration of social and economic matters. Published in March 1940, his second book, *The American Stakes,* commanded the respect of critics for its calm evaluation of the current political and economic scene in the United States. Chamberlain belongs to that generation under 40 which did not get "lost," but which has become the product of an "enlightened disillusionment." In some respects he might be called its liberal spokesman.

Chamberlain preceded the present volume with *Farewell to Reform,* published in 1932. It was a presentation of the rise and course of liberal thought in America, in politics and in literature, during the last 30 years. In it he considered the muckrakers, the progressivism of the Roosevelt and Wilson eras, and the theories of planned economy as proposed by such men as Chase, Soule and Beard. Chamberlain's conclusion was that reform methods had failed to advance the welfare of democracy. He says that if he were writing it again, he would come to some different conclusions. He no longer sees history as a lesson in the failure of reform. How he does see it, today, he attempts to tell us in *The American Stakes.*

Economic factors are the prime determinants in history and in our world, John Chamberlain believes. In a democracy political rights have no reality except as a function of economic rights. We should not overthrow, but modify, the capitalist system in order to obtain these rights—and it is in the interest of capitalists to take part in this process of modification. In 1932 Chamberlain had only scorn for such a "planned capitalism," saying that the situation could make one "either a cynic or a revolutionist." In 1940 he leans toward social democracy, or political pluralism, in which he adopts the "gradualist" approach to reform. He tends to reverse his previous sympathy for Marxism by saying that "no clear cut victory of any class over any other class is immediately at hand." All that he finds left to admire in the Soviet Union is the New Economic Policy. He analyzes the products of New Deal reformism, and indicates that they point the way toward participation in the benefits of a "limited racket" government. Mayor La Guardia (see sketch this issue) appeals more to him than does President Roosevelt.

Other topics discussed by Mr. Chamberlain are consumers' cooperatives, monopolies, foreign trade, and isolationism. He would have us produce and consume cooperatively at home, stay out of Europe's War, and extend our economic aid when a unified Europe was willing to lower trade barriers everywhere. He does not attempt to answer all the questions he brings up,

JOHN CHAMBERLAIN

preferring to look forward to their answers through possible gradual change and accomplishment.

John Chamberlain was born in New Haven, Connecticut October 28, 1903, the son of Robert Rensselaer and Emily (Davis) Chamberlain. He attended the Loomis Institute at Windsor, Connecticut; and then, as a matter of geographical convenience, went to Yale. There he was a good, but not brilliant student, having done little serious reading. He wrote a little poetry, was on the board of the *Yale Literary Magazine*, ran a column à la F. P. A. in the *Daily News*, and was chairman of the *Yale Record*. He specialized in history; but his roommate, William Troy (now also a critic) drew his attention to contemporary literature.

After receiving a Bachelor of Philosophy degree at Yale in 1925, he got a job, which lasted four months, with the Thomas F. Logan Advertising Agency. Then he became a reporter on the New York *Times* from 1926 to 1928. He preferred covering Washington, since his interests tended more and more toward national politics and economics. He got a good practical grounding in the contemporary American scene that was to serve him well when he became a reviewer of books on socio-economic problems. He became assistant editor of the New York *Times* Book Review in 1928; and in 1932 published his *Farewell to Reform*. He wrote no other books until *The American Stakes*, but subsequently became a contributor to symposia such as *The Critique of Humanism* (1932); *Challenge to the New Deal* (1934); and *After the Genteel Tradition* (1937).

He served for a few months in 1933 as an associate editor of the *Saturday Review of Literature*; and in that year became daily book columnist for the New York *Times*. His work as a daily book reviewer—and a good one—for three years, moved his friend Clifton Fadiman to admiration. Mr. Fadiman said of it: "His stuff has been analytic, more like monthly periodical journalism than like the hurried product of the daily grind. How did he do it? For one thing, he has that peculiarly journalistic gift of being able to write—and write well—under pressure. And he writes quickly, straight on to the typewriter, without much revision, 1,200 words in an hour and a half (which makes him a good typist too.)" Fadiman says further that Chamberlain has a phenomenal memory for facts. But he had to give up book reviewing because he felt that his "universe of ideas became fragmented."

He was book editor of *Scribner's Magazine* in 1936, and the same year became an editor of *Fortune*. The latter job he likes because of the opportunity it offers for various contacts and associations. "One month they will be with business men," he says, "the next month with New Dealers, the month after that with specialists in foreign exchange, and the month following—who knows? It all depends on the type of assignment." He has been a lecturer at the Columbia School of Journalism and the New School for Social Research; and at present does book reviewing for *Harper's Magazine*.

He married Margaret Sterling of New Haven, Connecticut, April 16, 1926. They live in Cheshire, Connecticut.

John Chamberlain, as his friend Clifton Fadiman describes him, looks even younger than he is. "He owns a shy, deprecating smile (complete with dimple) and a tentative manner of speaking, both tending to obscure the fact that his mind has a sharpness and an unbluffability quite remote from that of the conventional college graduate. He is the kind that will never try to out-argue anyone, but on the other hand will rarely permit himself to be fooled."

Of the books he has read which have radically impressed him, Chamberlain names *This Side of Paradise*, by F. Scott Fitzgerald, Randolph Bourne's *Untimely Papers* and the works of Thorstein Veblen and William Graham Sumner. He thinks Edmund Wilson and Van Wyck Brooks the best living American critics, and prefers Archibald MacLeish (see sketch this issue) to any other contemporary American poet. Among reviewers he admires Malcolm Cowley and Robert Cantwell. He believes that Heywood Broun was the best all-around journalist in America.

Chamberlain thinks that his generation, compared with its predecessor, knows more but has less personality. It tends to think more about the world than of itself. This objectivity marks the difference between men of Hemingway's War generation and those who were too young for the War. Fadiman believes that in Chamberlain's case it is not only a matter of seriousness of temperament, but of genuine modesty. "He is the only literary man I know who blushes when you praise him."

But it is the opinion of many that Chamberlain's ability tops his modesty. Good things are expected of him, beyond his present accomplishment, because he keeps an open, skeptical mind, is willing to admit errors in judgment and to change his opinions and tries to be an objective observer, even though he describes himself as "a free-lance radical who refuses to be bound."

References

Nation 150:395 Mr 23 '40
N Y Herald Tribune Books p6 Mr 24 '40
N Y Times Book R p2 Mr 17 '40
N Y World-Telegram p31 Mr 15 '40
Pub W 129:219 Ja 18 '36; 134:2086 D 17 '38 por
Sat R Lit 13:10-11 Mr 7 '36 il por; 21:5, 25+ Ap 6 '40 por
Time 35:72 Ap 1 '40 por
America's Young Men
Who's Who in America

NEVILLE CHAMBERLAIN

CHAMBERLAIN, NEVILLE Mar 18, 1869—Nov 9, 1940 Ex-Prime Minister of Great Britain; Conservative; son of Joseph Chamberlain; christened Arthur Neville Chamberlain; half-brother of Sir Austen Chamberlain; before First World War a manufacturer in Birmingham, interested in town planning, housing, municipal banking; Lord Mayor of Birmingham one year; entered House of Commons, 1918; Postmaster General, 1922; Paymaster General, 1923; appointed to Health Ministry, 1923, 1924, 1931; as Chancellor of Exchequer, 1923 to 1924, 1931 to 1937, carried through tariff reform and greatest loan conversion in history; head of Conservative Party; became Prime Minister in 1937; adopted policy of negotiation with authoritarian states, reversing policy of collective security; Anthony Eden (see sketch this issue) resigned as his Foreign Minister in February 1938; his efforts for "peace in our time" culminated in trip to Munich in September 1938 and consequent partition of Czechoslovakia; his umbrella became symbol of appeasement; after Hitler's occupation of Czechoslovakia in March 1939 pledged aid to Poland against aggression, mistakenly believing this would make it necessary for Hitler to consult with him before marching; brokenhearted, declared war on Germany, September 3, 1939; took Winston Churchill (see sketch this issue) and Anthony Eden, his old opponents, into Cabinet; forced to resign on May 10, 1940, after Norwegian debacle and statement that Hitler had "missed the bus"; his complete elimination demanded by Liberals and Labor, but made Lord President of the Council; repeatedly denied favoring peace negotiations with Germany; finally resigned from all connections with the government on October 3, 1940 because of ill health

References

Business Week p54 My 22 '37 por
Canad Forum 18:230-1 N '38
Christian Cent 57:1269 O 16 '40
Collier's 100:18 O 16 '37
Cur Hist 50:48 My '39
Gt Brit & East 52:409 Ap 13 '39; 54:36 Ja 18 '40; 54:53 Ja 25 '40 por
Liv Age 351:224-7 N '36; 352:417-19 Jl '37, 355:134-6 O '38
Spec 158:789 Ap 30 '37; 164:440 Mr 29 '40; 164:680+ My 17 '40
Audax, pseud. Neville Chamberlain *In* Men in Our Time p24-56 1940
Begbie, H. Mr. Neville Chamberlain *In* Windows of Westminster p65-82 1924
Hodgson, S. Man Who Made the Peace: Neville Chamberlain 1938
Shaw, D. K. Prime Minister Neville Chamberlain 1939
Soward, F. H. Neville Chamberlain and the British "Diplomatic Revolution" *In* Moulders of National Destinies p187-98 1940
Walker-Smith, D. Neville Chamberlain: Man of Peace 1940
Who's Who

Obituaries

N Y Herald Tribune p1+ N 10 '40; p1, 8 N 11 '40 pors
N Y Times p1, 4 N 11 '40 pors
Time 36:34+ N 18 '40 il por

CHAMBERLAIN, PAUL MELLEN Feb 28, 1865—May 27, 1940 Mechanical engineer; internationally known horologist; possessed some 1,500 watches and clocks, comprising one of the world's largest collections of ancient and modern historic timepieces

CHAMBERLAIN, PAUL—*Continued*

References

American Men of Science
Who's Who in America

Obituaries

N Y Herald Tribune p18 My 29 '40
por
N Y Times p23 My 29 '40 por

CHANG SHAN-TZE (shäng shan-tsä) 1878—Oct 20, 1940 Chinese artist noted especially for his pictures of tigers; had colorful career ranging from major general to revolutionary, from artist to diplomat; since the hostilities with Japan traveled through Europe and the United States for the Chinese Government Relief Mission to raise funds

References

Asia 39:696-7 D '39
Time 34:30 Jl 24 '39 por

Obituaries

N Y Herald Tribune p14 O 21 '40 por
N Y Times p19 O 21 '40 por

CHAPIN, JAMES (chä-pǐn) July 9, 1887- Artist

Address: b. 182 W 4th St, New York City; h. R. F. D..1, Annandale, New Jersey

A retrospective exhibition of James Chapin's paintings selected from work done between 1924 and 1940, and held at the Associated American Artists' Galleries in New York City in March 1940, attracted considerable public interest and critical attention. Fellow artists such as Grant Wood (see sketch this issue) put him in the front rank of American painters. The New York

JAMES CHAPIN

Times art critic says that this show "establishes his position as second to none in our contemporary roster. It contains some of the finest paintings of our time."

James Chapin was born in West Orange, New Jersey in 1887, the son of James A. and Delia S. (Ryder) Chapin. He left school at the age of 16 and worked as a bank runner in New York while studying at Cooper Union at night. Later he entered the Art Students League and went abroad to study at the Royal Academy of Art at Antwerp, Belgium, where he received the first award and gold medal for drawing. On his return to New York after two years, he earned a meager living as illustrator of books such as his friend Robert Frost's *North of Boston* and of magazines.

In 1924 he left New York to go back to live in the farm lands of lower New Jersey. There he turned from post-impressionism to the painting of the American scene. He rented a log cabin near Newton, for $4 a month, from a primitive farm family named Marvin. The Marvins don't know it, but portraits of them, as symbols of Americana, now hang in the Duncan Phillips Memorial Gallery in Washington, D. C., in the John Herron Art Museum in Indianapolis, in the Pennsylvania Academy of Fine Arts and in the Art Institute of Chicago. Four of these Marvin family portraits are among the high spots in the 1940 exhibit. One of the series received the Temple Gold Medal for the best painting by an American at the Pennsylvania Academy of Fine Arts in 1928.

In addition to the Marvins, the 56 oils in the show depict almost all phases of the American scene. There are other portraits, including those of Robert Frost and Katharine Hepburn. There are the rolling New Jersey farm lands, first memorably painted by George Inness. *Bank of a Stream* (1924) still shows an affinity for the impressionism of Cézanne; but *Planting Potatoes* has the very smell of the soil in it; and *Barn in Snow* (1931) is essentially a near-abstract design. Critics say that his *Grindstone* is a "felicitous example of his successful merging of penetrating characterization achieved through a realistic approach, with rhythmic, plastically animated composition."

The exhibition contains also the painting, *Pork Chops*, a scene of butcher and customer in a city meat-market; a fine *Old Man in a Railway Coach;* a young High Bridge, New Jersey, *Ball Player;* and an Ethel Waters *Blues Concert* in Carnegie Hall—a concert which the artist attended in 1939 with his 20-year-old son, a swing enthusiast. His work in the late '30s is represented by *Railroad Workers, Lime Kilns* and *Quarry* and *Strawstacks in Utah*.

Chapin's works are owned in the permanent collections of several art institutes and colleges and by private collectors and he was one of the artists commissioned to do a painting for Walter Wanger's *The Long Voyage Home*. He maintains a Greenwich Village studio in New York, but for the past eight years has rented a modest farm near

High Bridge, New Jersey. He lives there with his second wife, Louise Vermont, whom he married in 1925. The shy, grizzled painter teaches one day a week at the Pennsylvania Academy of Fine Arts in Philadelphia, explaining that he used to be a seven-day-a-week artist but is now a six-day painter. "Art," he says, "is just about my whole life."

References

Mag Art 33:190 Mr '40 il (p173)
N Y Times X p9 Mr 3 '40
N Y World-Telegram p6 Mr 2 '40 il
Newsweek 15:38 Mr 11 '40 il
Time 35:57 Mr 11 '40 il
Who's Who in American Art

CHAPLIN, CHARLIE Apr 16, 1889-
Comedian; moving picture actor and producer

Address: Charles Chaplin Studio, 1416 La Brea Ave, Los Angeles, California

Few pictures in the history of filmdom have been awaited as eagerly as Charlie Chaplin's *The Great Dictator*, in which he plays a double rôle: that of the lovable little tramp with a soup-strainer mustache and baggy pants, who, as the late Will Rogers had said, is better known in Zululand than Greta Garbo is in Arkansas; and the ranting, roaring Führer with an identical mustache and a mania of grandeur. His "satire on monomaniacs" was in preparation for two years; little information was given out about it, and the work going on at the Charles Chaplin Studio was veiled in secrecy. When *Life* tried to print some of the pictures before Chaplin deemed it suitable, that publication was threatened with a suit and had to withdraw the pictures. There were vague stories of threatening letters from representatives of "interested powers," of sabotage —according to Chaplin himself, these rumors were mostly exaggerations. But they served to build up an atmosphere of anticipation that culminated in mobbing the theatres in which the picture was finally shown.

The reviews ran the gamut from unqualified praise to regrets that Chaplin left the realm of pure comedy to descend to propaganda. Everybody loved the part where Charlie, as the little barber, shaved a startled customer to the tune of Brahms' *Hungarian Dance*; or his dance as Führer Hynkel with the balloon on which the world is painted—a delicate and barbed piece of satire. Most repeated was the objection to the impassioned speech with which Chaplin, stepping completely out of character, ends his picture. One critic wrote: "This is not a great Chaplin picture. . . No time for comedy. Yes, time for Chaplin comedy. No time ever for Chaplin to preach . . . no matter how deeply he may feel what he wrote and says." Perhaps the most searching comment was: "He wants to be more than the great clown. He wants to play Hamlet and be a political thinker and cry out in the wilderness. He's the boss, so he

G. Maillard Kesslere
CHARLIE CHAPLIN

does." Chaplin himself said simply: "I had to do it. . . All my life I've hated oppression and stupidity and now I have a chance to do something about it when it needs doing worst."

Every big picture produced by Chaplin in the last decade was reputedly his last one, and the next one was invariably hailed as a comeback. The fact is Chaplin simply produces pictures at his leisure; he is one of the millionaires in the industry (he had something like $6,000,000 before he started making *The Great Dictator*, into which he put $2,000,000 and he can afford to take his time, all the more so since he is the producer and the chief actor; being, besides, a rabid perfectionist, he does take his time. He keeps his staff on a payroll during all the idle months, "storing up energy," so that they are ready to start at a minute's notice.

Charlie Chaplin was born in a poor district of London—oddly enough, four days before Adolf Hitler was born. His father, Charles Chaplin, was a vocalist on the variety stage, his mother, whose stage name was Lily Harley (her real name was Hannah—the name of the girl in *The Great Dictator*), was a singer. Charlie's boyhood was an unhappy one and affected his later character considerably. His parents had separated and he and his brother Sydney, also a well-known comedian in his time, lived with their mother. His mother had a profound influence on his life. Chaplin was always proud of the strain of gypsy blood that came from his mother's side and that, he claims, was responsible for his ability as an actor. She had a gift for story-telling and mimicry that used to delight him when he was a child.

The Chaplins lived in abject poverty— Charlie's mother died in the poorhouse and

CHAPLIN, CHARLIE—*Continued*

the boys had to work for a living when barely out of school. When Charlie was 14 he took a job with a printing press establishment. But he had a tremendous passion for the stage and he and his brother Sydney used to hang around backstage looking for a chance to show their talents. Their parents' connections made it easy for them. In 1899 he was touring music halls as one of the dancing team called the *Lancashire Lads*. His first significant debut in the theatre was in 1905 as page boy Billy in *Painful Predicament of Sherlock Holmes*, with William Gillette.

Later he joined Fred Karno's company in music hall sketches. Little by little he built up his originally small part (he had been pinch-hitting for his brother Sydney, who at that time was the better known of the two) until he became the mainstay of the act, which broke up when he left it. The troupe came to the United States in 1910. Chaplin was a success here. People came away remembering the wistful little man who leaned against the proscenium and commented on the antics of the other actors in eloquent dumb show. He was hired to make films for the Keystone Company under Mack Sennett. There he was paid $150 a week and produced pictures the way a Roman candle throws off sparks. During the time he worked for Sennett he made 50 films. His first picture was called *Tillie's Punctured Romance*, with the late Marie Dressler. It was when he was shooting the second picture that he evolved his present immortal costume. He cut down his comical walrus mustache to an even more comical little brush. The rest of the costume with the jaunty cane and derby was based on the attire of the shabby but genteel little London clerks. Chaplin has used the same costume since, keeping the huge cracked boots in ether between productions.

The pace was terrific. One of the things that contributes to the present leisurely pace of Charlie's pictures is the memory of the Sennett days when he shot pictures "off the cuff" at the rate of one a week. In 1915 he changed over to the Essanay Company and then to Mutual Film Corporation. By that time he was beginning to be very well-known: the two studios were fighting for his services. His threat to resign threw the Mutual producers into panic and got him a million-a-year contract which enabled him in 1918 to set up his own studios. Chaplin was the first to become a millionaire in pictures. In 1920, together with Mary Pickford, the late Douglas Fairbanks (see sketch this issue), and D. W. Griffith, he founded the United Artists Corporation of which he is still a major stockholder.

Meanwhile the world was deluged with Chaplin pictures: small chronicles of lamentable adventures of the little tramp who is constantly sideswiped by life and who every time comes up slightly dazed but jaunty and goes on his duck-footed way twirling the indomitable cane. He was a lovable mass of crazy contradictions: utterly ragged, he cultivated princely airs; an arrant coward, he was driven to unbelievable lengths by gallantry and a wish to impress his love; and small and pitiful as he was, he yet managed to protect those even smaller than he. He combined a gamin's mischief with a sense of genuine tragedy, and as often as not your heart broke while you were laughing at his predicaments.

At first he produced only two-reelers, including the inevitable chase by mustachioed Sennett cops and pie-throwing. Later, when he got on his own, he began also to produce six-reelers. In 1918 he made *Shoulder Arms*, a satire on militarism. Then followed *The Kid* (1920), with Jackie Coogan, whom Chaplin discovered, and *The Pilgrim* (1922). In 1925 came *The Gold Rush*. Most of Chaplin's big pictures are based on some real event: *Gold Rush* was suggested by the Brenner Expedition tragedy. It will long be remembered for the marvelous scene in which starving Chaplin, for want of anything better, cooks his boots, eats shoelaces as if they were spaghetti and with consummate grace picks nails out and sucks them with relish. As independent producer Chaplin made *The Woman of Paris* (1920), the only picture in which he himself does not appear. In spite of baleful predictions it turned out to be an artistic success. After *The Gold Rush* the pace of his productions fell off. The next film was *The Circus* in 1928; it did not come up to the level of his other pictures, reputedly for personal reasons: the shooting of *The Circus* coincided with the breaking-up of his marriage to Lita Grey, his second wife (the first was Mildred Harris, also an actress), and the prolonged suit about the custody of his two children.

Meanwhile the talkies had come in without Chaplin's paying any attention to them at all. He could say what he wanted to without uttering a word and he was understood the world over. His *City Lights* (1932) began with what amounted to a "Bronx cheer" directed at the talkies: a speaker addressing a crowd in confused, indistinct, blurry utterance that was characteristic of the talkies when they first began. In *Modern Times* (1936) he broke into sound with his wordless little song—a sort of Katzenjammer French—that delighted the audience hugely. In *The Great Dictator*, he speaks—in the fervent gibberish that is a travesty on Hitler's speeches ("Demokratien shtoonk! Libertad shtoonk! Frei Sprecken shtoonk!") and in the gentle, diffident voice of the little barber with its somewhat British accent.

Chaplin has been living in Hollywood since he was 24 and has become one of its legends. There are all kinds of picturesque rumors about him—about the strange influence he has exercised on the characters and lives of all who came in contact with him. All his leading ladies were supposed to have failed in pictures—Mildred Harris, Lita Grey, Virginia Davis. That jinx has been broken by his present wife, Paulette Goddard, who has played with him in *Modern Times* and *The Great Dictator* and is a well-known actress in her own right. But "Hollywood is full of workers who carry on after they have left him bearing the stamp he gave them—Menjou is a celebrated instance." Many of the people who work with him have been with him since the beginning of his career—Al Reeves, whom he took on from the old Fred Karno act, Henry Bergman, and Rollie Totheroh, who has not missed shooting a Chaplin picture in those 25 years. His brother Sydney is now his manager.

Chaplin is a small man with baby-pink complexion, a pompadour of gray hair and dark, tragic eyes. Someone said: "No one who sees the eyes of Chaplin can feel like laughing." His hands and feet are tiny. He is a superb gymnast—is a good enough tennis player to give Fred Perry a good game, is an agile acrobat, is a fine swimmer and an excellent dancer, with a sound ballet training. His little dances are a delightful and important part of his pictures. He is also a good musician, excelling particularly in pipe organ and, besides directing his pictures, writes most of the music.

His temperament is volatile; he has moods of dark depression and of extreme elation when he convulses his companions by his marvelous mimicry. He is a mass of contradictions: he is one of the best businessmen in Hollywood, in spite of that unworldly look. All his pictures have made money, yet he hates to have anything to do with money, does not like to pay checks (this has given him his reputation of a penny pincher), preferring to have everything charged. He used to have a mania about being poor. Long after he had become well-known and had made a lot of money, he was living in a modest room at a club. His brother Sydney had to bully him into getting a car and a house, after which he got more or less into the swing of spending money. He went through a period when he sought acquaintance with celebrities: was visited by Harold Laski, Aldous Huxley, John Steinbeck (see sketch this issue) and others. Yet he has always remained somewhat of a hermit, shunning Hollywood's social functions. He likes low comedy and burlesque shows and goes down to Los Angeles' toughest quarters to see them. Without any formal schooling, he has a sort of instinct about things that saves him from making blunders. "He knows what he knows in his bones." He is a merciless disciplinarian when on the job, yet hates any sort of routine. He is considered a radical in Hollywood; yet when Upton Sinclair was running for office he refused to support him, in spite of having approved of his EPIC plan.

His popularity has remained unimpaired. He is loved as Charlot in France, as Carlitos in Spain, as Carlino in Italy (perhaps not so much now after his lampoon of Mussolini). His pictures are shown on Africa's Gold Coast and in Timbuctoo and the natives love them. He is an idol with the Japanese, who yearly celebrate his birthday with a parade. His latest picture, though, is for purely domestic consumption.

References

Atlan 164:176-85 Ag '39 (Same abr. Read Digest 35:34-7 S '39)
Christian Cent 57:816-17 Je 26 '40
Christian Sci Mon Mag p7+ S 7 '40
Collier's 105:20+ Mr 16 '40 il por
Ladies' H J 57:18+ Jl '40 il pors
N Y Times VII p8-9+ S 8 '40
New Yorker 1:9-10 My 23 '25
Bowman, W. D. Charlie Chaplin 1931
Burdett, O. Art of Mr. Chaplin *In* Critical Essays p148-55 1925
Frank, W. D. Charles Chaplin *In* In the American Jungle p61-73 1937
Harris, F. Charlie Chaplin *In* Contemporary Portraits 4th ser. p56-76 1923
Hughes, F. Charles Chaplin *In* Famous Stars of Filmdom (Men) p91-111 1932
Nathan, G. J. Chaplin Buncombe *In* Passing Judgments p210-14 1935
Seldes, G. V. "I Am Here To-day": Charlie Chaplin *In* Seven Lively Arts p41-53, 361-6 1924
Von Ulm, G. Charlie Chaplin, King of Tragedy 1940
Who's Who
Who's Who in America
Who's Who in the Theatre
Woollcott, A. Mr. Chaplin *In* Enchanted Aisles p53-8 1924

CHAPPEDELAINE, LOUIS DE (shăp-dĕ-lĕn lū-ē) 1876—Dec 9, 1939 French statesman

Obituaries

N Y Times D 9 '39

CHASE, CHARLEY Oct 20, 1893—June 20, 1940 Screen comedian; started in Mack Sennett's old *Keystone Kop* series; later remained under contract for 17 years to Hal Roach, writing and producing comedies as well as acting in them; featured in many "shorts" of the lighter or slapstick variety

References

International Motion Picture Almanac

Obituaries

N Y Sun p19 Je 21 '40
N Y Times p21 Je 21 '40

(Continued next page)

CHARLEY CHASE

CHASE, EDNA WOOLMAN   Mar 14, 1877- Editor in chief of *Vogue*

Address: b. 420 Lexington Ave, New York City; h. 333 E 68th St, New York City

In August 1940 an event of great significance took place in the world of fashion —one presaging great changes. At about this time every year Edna Woolman Chase, the editor in chief of *Vogue,* broadcasts news of the French collections from Paris to the American audiences. This year, however, she addressed them over NBC in New York and her subject was American collections and fashion trends. The blackout of Paris has turned the eyes of the world to New York, which is taking this opportunity to make a bid for becoming the world fashion center—with the approval of no less a personage than Mayor La Guardia (see sketch this issue), who has been promoting this trend with his usual energy.

Mrs. Chase, as one of the high priestesses of fashion, holds in her hands the sartorial destiny of New York. For many thousands of women she is the final authority in all matters of fashion. Her pronouncements in that field are held in respect not only in New York but in Paris and London, where independent editions of *Vogue* are published under her guidance. She holds high hopes for the progress of American design and has no qualms about the future, when the American designers will have emerged from the tutelage of the French *haute couture* and blossomed out on their own. "Many American designers," she says, "learned and were inspired through the authority of Paris. Yet many others who never went to Paris have designed very wearable, much-sold models." As one who has been responsible to a great degree

for the fostering of French design in the United States, she is anxious to keep here some of its better features: for example, the cooperation between designers and fabric makers which has made the French *ateliers* famous for the high quality of their products.

Edna Woolman Chase was born in Asbury Park, New Jersey, the daughter of Franklyn and Laura (Woolman) Alloway. On her mother's side she is a descendant of a Quaker divine, John Woolman. Her Quaker ancestry, however, does not seem to get in the way of her rather worldly profession—on the contrary, she claims that it has endowed her with a sense of proportion which she finds invaluable. She passed through the usual gamut of private schools and tutors that is the lot of well-to-do young ladies. Then, when she was 22 years old, she joined the staff of *Vogue,* at that time a small weekly written "by society for society."

Mrs. Chase's 35 years of successful publishing are closely connected with the fortunes of *Vogue*: she has never been associated with any other publication. Her excellent business sense and unerring good taste have contributed to a large extent to transforming what was originally an amateur society chitchat sheet into the enormously successful fashion magazine. When Condé Nast acquired *Vogue* in 1909 he was so impressed by what he described as "her steel-trap mind . . . combined with all the intuitive qualities of a woman," that he made her managing editor. That he has shown superlative judgment in this is borne out by the fact that under Mrs. Chase's stewardship *Vogue's* revenue is far in advance of the other Condé Nast publications. In 1914 Mrs. Chase became *Vogue's* editor in chief, and later Paris and London editions also came under her control. She has continued in this position until now at a salary reputedly between $50,000 and $75,000.

Mrs. Chase has left a significant mark on the fashion publishing world. She has been an assiduous importer of new things from abroad—particularly from France, thereby meriting the gratitude of the French Republic in the guise of the tiny red ribbon of the Légion d'Honneur bestowed upon her in 1935. Under her, *Vogue* has kept abreast of the newest trends in decorative arts— in photography, decoration and illustration as well as designing. She was the first to introduce the application of modern art into the fields of illustration and advertising, by contracting shortly after the War for the services of modern artists like Lepape, Martin, Marty, Brissaud, Guy Arnoux and Benito. This was a dish that at first was strange to the palates of the American public. Now, of course, the application of the canons of modern art is general throughout the publishing and advertising world.

The appearance of Mrs. Chase is extremely deceptive. Far from being an

Baker

EDNA WOOLMAN CHASE

aggressive executive type, she is a tiny and very feminine person, with a fluffy aureole of snow-white hair and lively brown eyes. In fact she is something of a pocket edition of her actress-daughter, Ilka Chase, her only child by a first marriage (to Francis Drake Chase). Ilka has taken a page from her mother's book and, besides being a successful actress, has been getting considerable attention as a fashion and gossip commentator on the radio.

Mrs. Chase can best be described as an ardent perfectionist. She ascribes her success as editor to the fact that she is extremely hard to please. "My waste basket is my strongest ally," she says. "I discarded what was bad, also anything that was merely 'good enough.' . . Many a photograph, many a fashion was brought to me that could have been published without the public seeing anything wrong. . . But over a period of time such a policy would have had its deadly effect." She possesses "the ruthlessness of an expert taste and the courage to insist upon it"—in no uncertain terms, either. Characteristic was her address to the Shoe Guild in 1939, the year when the heel-less shoe campaign got into full swing. She said: "Gentlemen, I want to plead with you to stop this promotion of the open-toed, open-backed shoe for street wear. . . Today you see millions of women all over America slop-slopping along the streets with not only their toes out, but their heels out too. . . All this makes me very sad."

People who work for Mrs. Chase find her exacting and difficult to please. She herself dresses beautifully—usually in simply cut clothes, but always with a feminine touch of a soft jabot or a rich pin. She expects the same unerring good taste in clothes

from her staff. College-girl job seekers distress her: the fine minds inside their heads are too often entirely eclipsed by the "unspeakable hats on top of them." She also feels uncompromisingly that "sex is definitely out as a business asset."

In private life Mrs. Chase is the wife of Richard Newton. She herself has planned their country home at Oyster Bay, Long Island, a charming, long, low house with the poetic name of "Four Winds," surrounded by apple trees and facing a small lake. She likes to work in the garden and play golf.

References

N Y Herald Tribune p19 Ag 20 '40 por; p16 Ag 28 '40
N Y Times p28 S 27 '40
Newsweek 6:25-6 Ag 24 '35 por
Time 35:51 My 22 '39 por

American Women
Who's Who in America

CHASE, MARY ELLEN Feb 24, 1887-
Educator; author
Address: b. Smith College, Northampton, Massachusetts; h. 16 Paradise Rd, Northampton, Massachusetts

Mary Ellen Chase is known in literary circles as the author of some good novels with a Maine background; but her life work has been in education, and she prefers to think of herself as a pedagog. She loves to write, but loves even more to teach. In 1940 a professor at Smith College, she looks back on 30 years of teaching experience; it is of this she writes in her latest book, *A Goodly Fellowship,* published in December 1939.

A modest but salty chronicle, it is full of delightful reminiscence and comment, keen and witty, a continuation, autobiographically, of the story of that Maine childhood which Miss Chase wrote of in *A Goodly Heritage* (1932). She begins with the teaching she herself received, particularly at home from her parents. At her father's request she began teaching in a Maine district school before she finished college. If you had anything in you, he said, teaching in a country school would bring it out. Her first real job was with the Hillside Home School in Wisconsin, a fine school that would probably be called "progressive" today. Following work at a fashionable girls' school in Chicago, and a brief period of study in Germany, she returned to teach in Montana—and also to write.

Miss Chase concludes with her happy experiences at Smith College, and pays a warm tribute to William Allen Neilson, until recently its president. Two things she objects to in the educational field: courses in education and its theories, not supported by experience; and the general quality of teaching found in graduate schools. Miss Chase writes also of some of her experiences as an itinerant lecturer.

MARY ELLEN CHASE

Mary Ellen Chase was born in Blue Hill, Maine, February 24, 1887. Her parents were Edward Everett and Edith (Lord) Chase. She has written much about her New England childhood in the two books mentioned above. She started in early trying to depict the scene and its people. But her first short story, published when she was 21, wasn't about Maine at all—it was a football story sold to the *American Boy* for $17. Miss Chase sold more stories to help pay her way through college. She also taught school— and has written fervently and most amusingly of that first country-school job in the village of South Brookfield, Maine. In such a small backwoods village a teacher was an object of high suspicion, and had a great deal to live down if she came from college. And during this spring term there were several big boys of 16 and over who might otherwise have been at sea. Miss Chase had only one defense: her father had presented her, as a parting gift, with a stout razor strop. She stormed up and down the aisles madly flourishing this, though her knees were quaking; but she had no trouble with discipline after that.

She took degrees at the Universities of Maine and Minnesota, and taught in Western boarding schools until 1918. She was instructor and professor of English at Minnesota from 1918 to 1926; and since 1926 has been a professor of English literature at Smith College. There she devotes three days a week to teaching (nineteenth century prose writers being her specialty); the rest of her time she spends writing and filling her lecture engagements. She has spent many of her summers in England, exploring small country villages and towns in the Southern part of the country. Her humorous essays on English weather, trees, manners,

food, railway travel, etc., have appeared in a collection, *This England* (1936).

Besides textbooks and the above-mentioned works, Miss Chase has written numerous short stories, two adventure tales for girls and novels. Of these latter the best known are *Mary Peters* (1934), a story of a girl who passed her childhood on board her father's sailing ship, her later youth in a Maine village—a novel striking for the vigor and beauty of its prose; *Silas Crockett* (1935), a story of four generations of a New England seafaring family that is also a rounded history of Maine culture; and *Dawn in Lyonesse,* a retelling of the Tristram legend.

An artist as a writer, Miss Chase regards good teaching also as a fine art. Her students throng eagerly into her classroom, not only because of her enthusiasm for and thorough knowledge of English literature, but because she genuinely likes and understands young people. She approves the consuming interest of the younger generation in matters of national and international importance. She admires their capacity for ignoring the barriers of age and position, their honesty and their abhorrence of fraud and sentimentality.

References

Am Assn Univ Women J 33:74-9 Ja '40
Boston Transcript p1 Jl 7 '34
Col Engl 1:291-9 Ja '40; Same. Engl J 29:1-9 Ja '40
Ladies' H J 56:21 D '39
Scholastic 30:4 Ap 17 '37 por; 36:17, 18+ F 26 '40 por
Wilson Lib Bul 8:322 F '34 por
American Women
Chase, M. E. A Goodly Fellowship 1939
Chase, M. E. A Goodly Heritage 1932
Who's Who Among North American Authors
Who's Who in America

CHASE, STUART Mar 8, 1888- Author; economist

Address: h. Georgetown, Connecticut

For many years the tragedy of waste— waste in man power, natural resources, money—and what to do about it, has been the lively concern of economist Stuart Chase. To the lay reader his books on our economic and industrial system, compared to others on the subject, are made refreshingly understandable by the use of simple terminology and concrete illustration. But Mr. Chase felt that he and many other writers failed in communicating their exact ideas and meanings to readers because of a slack or meaningless use of words, particularly abstract words, leading to false or diverse concepts. Accordingly, Mr. Chase examined word-waste in *The Tyranny of Words* (1938), taking up the science of semantics. A few serious students of semantics pooh-poohed Mr. Chase's theories. But other critics found useful his attempt to clear away the confused use of abstractions in popular writing and oratory; and Sinclair Lewis called it the most important book published in 1938.

In *Idle Men, Idle Money* (August 1940) Stuart Chase confronts again the old problem, the tyranny of waste, with some initial acid remarks—via semantics—on the loose use of the terms "government" and "business." Waste of money is not so great an evil as waste of man power, Mr. Chase says. But how shall we keep prosperous on butter rather than guns? He points out that since the German Blitzkrieg our unbalanced national budget has ceased to be a moral issue. Our money is built on debt. The way in which income is divided among various groups, however, lies at the root of our difficulties.

Mr. Chase denounces over-saving, and is all for a system of taxation which encourages rapid spending. He approves the kind of government spending that has built, for instance, the Grand Coulee Dam. From the testimony given by industrial heads he further notes that today the money for plant and equipment upkeep comes from the firms' own "depreciation" funds: hence the investment banker is going out of business. Following an amusing divagation in a chapter called "Design for 1960" Mr. Chase sets before our current President six practical proposals for a solution of the idle money-idle men situation:

(1) Set up a permanent PWA for housing, dams, soil conservation, schools, highways, etc. (2) Put the Federal budget on a business basis, meaning the separation of capital expenditures from running expenses. (3) Amend the social security law to give every citizen unemployed after 65 a monthly old-age pension. (4) Increase personal income and inheritance taxes and corporate income taxes. (5) Provide a flexible WPA program for the remaining unemployed. (6) Create a new bank for long-term capital loans.

He ends his book with the statement that unless we are to go against a massive world trend, we must put men first and money second.

The Yankee-minded economist who denounces waste, and likewise over-saving, has nine generations of New Englanders behind him. He was born in Somersworth, New Hampshire, March 8, 1888, son of Harvey Stuart and Aaronette (Rowe) Chase. He attended the Massachusetts Institute of Technology for two years, then specialized in economics and statistics at Harvard, receiving his B. S. *cum laude* in 1910. Stuart Chase wanted to be an architect but instead practiced public accounting in his father's office until 1917. He disliked it but was good at it. His first wife was Margaret Hatfield, whom he married on July 5, 1914. They spent their honeymoon representing themselves as an out-of-work couple and became acquainted at firsthand with the un-

STUART CHASE

employment problem. They published their experiences on job-finding, factory conditions, etc., in a book, *A Honeymoon Experiment* (1916). Two children, Robert and Sonia Hatfield, were born of the marriage.

During the War Mr. Chase was in charge of the control of packers' profits under the Food Administration Department. After the War he was with the Federal Trade Commission investigating the meat industry; later he took charge of the accounting features of a milk investigation. In 1921 he joined the Technical Alliance in New York and became interested in the problem of waste from the wider engineering viewpoint. He has been with the Labor Bureau, Incorporated, since 1922 and has made studies for various labor and cooperative organizations on costs and on the general problem of waste in competitively organized society. He was one of the founders of Consumers' Research.

In 1924 Stuart Chase won *Life's* contest prize for his recipe for bigger and better wars; and a little later the Boni & Liveright prize of $500 for the best review of Gillette's *The People's Corporation*. His first important work in his own field was *The Tragedy of Waste*, published in 1925. The book was praised by forward-looking economists for its sound suggestions for the prevention of waste of man power and of natural resources; but *Your Money's Worth* (1927) written in collaboration with F. J. Schlink, had a more popular appeal. A book of facts for the consumer about buying and selling, it discussed the real value of things bought compared with their cost.

Mexico; A Study of Two Americas (1931) compared the civilization of the two Americas, one based on handicraft, the other on the machine, and deplored the Yankee invasion of Mexico to destroy its vigorous

CHASE, STUART—*Continued*

craft culture. Mr. Chase's second wife, Marian Tyler, whom he married in 1930 after a divorce, collaborated with him on the book, learning Spanish in order to help him with the research. *A New Deal* (1932) described the growth of our economic and industrial systems and proposed ways to revise the economic structure without breaking entirely with the past. The title furnished the Democratic Party with its 1933 political slogan. *Rich Land, Poor Land* (1936) was a survey of waste in natural resources and of what the government was trying to do in the way of reclamation. He and Marian Tyler collaborated further in *The New Western Front* (1939), a brief, popular exposition of reasons why the United States should keep out of European and Far Eastern conflicts.

Mr. Chase doesn't like cities and prefers to do most of his work in the country. The Chase home in Connecticut is a rebuilt barn furnished with Mexican rugs and handicraft, and has a workroom where Mr. Chase tries his hand at furniture-making. He also likes to swim, play tennis, take hikes and chop wood to get into good writing condition. Before writing a book he does a tremendous amount of research, jotting down notes on cards. He writes rapidly in longhand and is a bad speller. Energetically interested in a good many things besides economics, Mr. Chase knows what he likes and doesn't like. "I like good conversation, white wine, Mexican Indians, high mountains, Fire Island, mighty bridges, pine forests, clean-cut thinking, Russian folk songs, Charlie Chaplin (see sketch this issue). . . I do not like billboards, hot dogs, high-pressure selling, radios, chambers of commerce, the stock exchange or Radio City." He is an avowed sun worshiper, spending as much time in the sun all year round as possible, and wishes the American public would learn to "go native." His own skin is nearly as brown as a Mexican's and he has a lean, lithe body and an inquisitive snub nose to go with it. "His hair is a sandy kind of gray that doesn't add anything to his years or his dignity. . . He is friendly, intelligent, alert, unpretentious and eager."

References

New Repub 97:331-3 Ja 25 '39
N Y Herald Tribune Books p3 Ag 25 '40 por
Newsweek 11:32 Ja 24 '38 por
Sat R Lit 17:21 Ja 22 '38 por (p5)
Wilson Lib Bul 6:336 Ja '32
Kunitz, S. J. ed. Authors Today and Yesterday 1933
Who's Who
Who's Who in America

CHASE, WILLIAM SHEAFE, REV. Jan 11, 1858—July 16, 1940 Clergyman; retired minister of Christ Protestant Episcopal Church, Brooklyn who served there for 28 years; nationally known reformer for past 40 years; in pulpit, public forum and legislative hall fought liquor, jazz, birth control, movies, drinking and betting

Pach Bros.

REV. WILLIAM CHASE

References
Who's Who in America
Obituaries
Christian Cent 57:958 Jl 31 '40
N Y Herald Tribune p18 Jl 17 '40 por
N Y Times p21 Jl 17 '40 por

CHERNE, LEO M. (chŭrn) 1912- Editor; executive of the Research Institute of America; author

Address: b. 292 Madison Ave, New York City; h. 910 Grand Concourse, The Bronx, New York City

It can be stated without fear of exaggeration that Leo M. Cherne, "America's Outstanding Civilian Authority on M-Day," and the answer to a baffled businessman's prayer, is one of America's most brilliant young men. Still in his 20's, he is called upon to interpret the New Deal regulations to business, to testify before the Senate as to the advisability of such projects as Senator Vandenberg's (see sketch this issue) proposal on incentive tax and profit sharing (December 7, 1939), and to lecture before the United States War College. His latest emergence into the public eye was Simon & Schuster's publication of his *M-Day and What It Means to You*, a concise and dispassionate analysis of America in wartime. This is a lavish pamphlet written in the question and answer method beloved by Simon & Schuster, a popular adaptation of material previously used in *Adjusting Your Business to War* (1939).

Cherne's career presents a satisfying spectacle of a Bronx boy making good. He was born somewhere near Willis Avenue in 1912, a son of a Romanian composer, Max Cherne, and his wife Dora (Ballin) Cherne, who owned a printing and stationery store. He went to public school and was pretty good in chorus practice, having a fine voice of which he is still rather proud. At the age of 12 he joined the chorus of the Metropolitan Opera Company. He sang there for four years and got enough money to enable him to go to New York University. While going to college he did some journalistic work on the side: for the *Daily Mirror* and "a short-lived competitor" of The Bronx *Home News.* In 1931 he entered the New York Law School and was graduated from it in 1934. He was admitted to the Bar in 1936, after working for a year with the law firm of Blau, Perlman and Polakoff. Then he got a job with a publishing house called Whitgard Services by answering an advertisement in the New York *Law Journal.*

He was put to work editing a loose-leaf volume called *The Payroll Tax-Saving Service* which provided information on social security legislation. It immediately became clear that the young lawyer had found his berth. His colleagues, Edward Whittlesey and Carl Hovgard, regarded him as the "editorial brains of the business." It was his suggestion to turn the rather cumbersome compilation of the material into a publication giving specific information on concrete cases. The result was the *Social Security Coordinator.* At about that time Cherne acquired an interest in the business, Whittlesey having sold out his share. Whitgard Services eventually became the Research Institute.

The first *Coordinator* proved a success and Cherne put out another—*Federal Tax Coordinator*—and began work on his *Business and Legislative Report* in 1936. It came out in 1937, a rich-looking volume designed to appeal to the esthetic sensibilities of businessmen and abounding in political and economic chitchat. Among the books put out by the Institute were: *Guide to Tax Economy* (1937); *Adjusting Your Business to the New Legislation* (1939); and *Chart of Illegal Business Practices,* a pamphlet put out in the beginning of 1940.

The Research Institute, of which Leo Cherne is executive secretary, is a boon to harassed businessmen swamped in the flood of New Deal legislation, much of which is conflicting. The *Business and Legislative Reports* which Cherne edits is a fortnightly newsletter and its value lies in the extensive information which it supplies to its clients and in its uncompromising objectivity. The latter policy is pursued at the risk of offending the clients who often don't like some of Cherne's predictions.

But so far the policy of telling the clients what is so rather than what they wish to hear has been a profitable one. It has enabled the *Reports* to keep a fairly high score on accurate predictions: thus they have been uniformly successful in predicting

LEO M. CHERNE

Supreme Court decisions. It is the fairly prompt fulfillment of their prophecies that keeps them going. Cherne claims that if the CIO-General Motors settlement which he had predicted had been delayed for a few more weeks, the newsletter would have been ruined. As it is, the firm will probably make something like $1,000,000 this year. Admittedly Cherne does not publish everything that comes his way, and Ferdinand Lundberg has pointed out that, for example, like other big "constructive and pro-business" newsletters in the United States, his *Reports* "are reticent about the activities of business lobbies and the corporation lawyers in Washington." At any rate they say more than is approved in higher government circles and have on occasion drawn oblique reproof from the Administration.

Cherne's first book on M-Day was written with the same ruthless objectivity and cold-blooded disregard for his reader's feelings. In March 1939 he went to Washington to find out more about it, and, after six weeks of research with full cooperation of the War Department, wrote *Adjusting Your Business to War,* a straightforward, unemotional account of what will happen to business on the M-Day, "that day without date when the United States goes to war." The book created considerable sensation in Washington, was used as a basis for a neutrality discussion in the Senate. The *Annals of the American Academy of Political and Social Science* in a scathing review called it "a blueprint for Fascism" which neglects to tell how "this Leviathan, once established, could ever be immobilized." On the other hand the Springfield *Republican* said of his *M-Day: What It Means to You* (1940), which was a popularized rehash of the first book: "Cherne has really written what, in another

CHERNE, LEO M.—*Continued*

time, might be regarded as anti-war propaganda." Cherne is neither for nor against M-Day. His job is to prepare his clients against its coming by giving information about it. He used the material he collected for another loose-leaf book called *War Coordinator.*

Now Cherne has added to his reputation as a student of government interference that of an expert on M-Day. He has been writing articles and giving lectures about it. His presentation of the subject—written or spoken—is lucid and orderly. The theme of his presentation is that: "Control by priorities will be the keystone of any control over industries exercised by the government in a war period. . . It will then become necessary to divert labor, capital and raw materials from industrial operations of a character non-essential to the purposes of the war to activities which are essential." Another element which he emphasizes is fixed prices.

Cherne may be found in his rather ornate office in the Research Institute Building. Against its impressive Gothic background he "looks like Ronald Colman in Technicolor." He is dark, slender and very handsome, a high-powered young executive with a dashing presence. In 1936 he married Julia Lopez, a girl whom he knew from his high school days, and is now the proud father of a daughter called Gail Stephanie, whose birth he hailed in a newsletter parody jocosely entitled *Labor and Procreation Report.*

His favorite hobby besides M-Day is music. He does some amateur composing on the side and enjoys singing his compositions, upon request, to whatever friends visit his palatial penthouse on the Grand Concourse (his roots are still in The Bronx). His wife accompanies him on the piano. A song of his entitled *I'll Never Forget* will be published in the fall.

> *References*
>
> Cong Digest 18:11-13 Ja '39
> Harper 180:469-73 Ap '40; 181:113-24 Jl '40
> New Yorker 16:23-8+ O 5 '40
> Vital Speeches 6:680-3 S 1 '40

CHESSER, ELIZABETH SLOAN 1878— Feb 16, 1940 Outstanding English physician; lecturer; author

> *References*
>
> Who's Who 1940
>
> *Obituaries*
>
> Manchester Guardian p10 F 17 '40 por

CHIANG KAI-SHEK (chĭ-äng' kĭ-shĕk) Oct 31, 1888- Chinese military and political leader

Address: c/o The Generalissimo's Headquarters, Chungking, China

CHIANG KAI-SHEK

Slim, poker-faced Generalissimo Chiang Kai-shek controls the destinies of China today more absolutely perhaps than any other living dictator controls his country. For Chiang is the symbol of Chinese unity and resistance against Japan. What war lords have been unable to do in thousands of years of Japanese history, Chiang Kai-shek has done. He has united China from a mass of provinces into a nation, fighting to the last ditch to stem the Japanese invasion.

The question as to what manner of man is Chiang Kai-shek, and how did he reach his position, is not easily answered. Chiang Kai-shek is full of contradictions, full of riddles. Even to the Chinese the self-contained, ruthless Generalissimo is not well-known. Unlike other strong men such as Mussolini, Hitler or Stalin, he shuns speech-making and publicity. He is first of all a soldier, hard-headed and practical. Statesmanship and diplomacy are to him merely the by-products of his successful soldiering.

Chiang Kai-shek's father, a wine merchant in Chikow, Chekiang Province, died when the future Generalissimo was nine years old. Soon afterward young Chiang Kai-shek was sent to relatives in Fenghu, where he was to go to school and to be apprenticed to a trade. But Chiang ran away and joined the provincial army. Since at that time the culture-loving Chinese considered soldiering the lowest form of occupation, his relatives prophesied that Chiang would come to no good. Chiang, however, surprised his relatives by taking first place in tests for entrance to the newly established military school at Paoting, the West Point of China, and went north to learn soldiering in scientific fashion.

In the meantime, according to Chinese tradition, he had been married off to a Miss Mao of Fenghu, a young lady whom he had never seen until the wedding. He was said to be about 15 at the time of his marriage, and was already the father of a son, Ching-kuo, when he went off to school at Paoting.

His mother, with whom his bride and child lived, approved of young Chiang's education. After a year at Paoting he was sent to the Military College at Tokio and it was his mother who sent him his living expenses and took care of his wife and child.

Chiang Kai-shek remained in Japan for four years. Japan in those days was the center of liberal and radical movements, and revolutionary Chinese were plotting with the Japanese for establishment of republican principles. Dr. Sun Yat-sen, future founder of the Chinese Republic, was an active figure in the organization of Chinese youth in the schools and colleges of Japan. Chiang heard Dr. Sun Yat-sen, became imbued with his revolutionary doctrines, returned to China and joined Dr. Sun Yat-sen's fight for the overthrow of the monarchy. He commanded a regiment in the first revolution.

In the next few years Chiang Kai-shek's fortunes rose and fell with the success and failure of the Nationalist cause. At one period he was a poverty-stricken clerk in Shanghai, at another a successful young officer. But he was still unknown to the great Dr. Sun Yat-sen, leader of the Nationalist movement. Chiang, with characteristic ambition and industry, succeeded in finding himself a patron, however, a wealthy revolutionist-financier who became interested in him.

Caught short in the stock market after a fling at business, Chiang was sent south by his patron with a letter of introduction to Dr Sun Yat-sen. It meant the beginning of a close association with the Nationalist leader and a permanent identification with the revolutionary Nationalist cause.

Dr. Sun had formed an entente with the Russian Communists, and Chiang Kai-shek was sent to study Soviet military methods and political institutions. When Chiang returned a year later he organized the Whampoa Military Academy, later to become the nucleus of Nationalist China's Army. Chiang realized that if the Nationalist cause was to be successful, it must have a trained patriotic army to fight the ever-recurring revolts against Dr. Sun's newly established government in Canton. He became principal of the Academy, which attracted a high type of Chinese youth with revolutionary ideals, and under his training these youths won the day for the Nationalists when Dr. Sun's Canton government stood close to defeat. Dr. Sun looked upon Chiang with new approval, and Chiang became commander in chief of the Koumintang (Nationalist) Army.

When Dr. Sun Yat-sen died in 1925, Wang Ching-wei and Hu Han-min were regarded as his rightful heirs, destined to carry on his political ideals and philosophy. Chiang had also been close to Dr. Sun Yat-sen, but he was a soldier rather than a politician. It took a hard headed, practical soldier to command the loyalty of the Koumintang after Dr. Sun Yat-sen's death, however, and Chiang's political influence increased with his military victories against the feudal war lords whom the Koumintang had set out to conquer.

His sympathies at this time were turning to the side of the Chinese against the Russian Communists. But he did not yet break with the Communists. He used them on his march north. Michael Borodin, Russian Communist organizer, went ahead of the army, organizing workers, stirring up revolt and creating converts to the Koumintang flag. And Chiang and his army followed, using bribery or bullets, as the situation demanded, to conquer the feudal war lords.

From Canton to Hankow, Chiang marched victoriously: Southern China was uniting under one banner. But Borodin's work had been too thorough. The peasants demanded more than lip service: they wanted abolition of excessive taxes, dispossession of the gentry. Chiang was alarmed. Even if he had at one time been a believer in the revolutionist ideology he was not going to have a social revolt interfere with his military plans for a united China. At any rate, he made an about-face. He turned to the Shanghai bankers for aid. They were to support Chiang and his establishment of new governments at Nanking and Shanghai and Chiang in turn was to rout the Communists. There followed a wholesale murder of Reds, as Chiang began his long attempt to bleed the Koumintang Army white.

A tremendous howl went up within his own party. In the split that followed Chiang Kai-shek resigned. But he had followed the old maxim: "never resign until you are indispensable." The Nationalist leaders decided a united China was worth all differences of opinion and recalled him. He resumed his post January 4, 1928, and on February 1 the National Executive Committee elected him chairman of the National Military Council. He was back stronger than ever.

In the few weeks while still plain Mr. Chiang, the Generalissimo took care of a matter of the heart. He married Soong Mei-ling (see sketch this issue under Chiang Mei-ling), daughter of a wealthy merchant and banker, an American-educated Chinese girl, who was to become China's most beloved first lady. The marriage took place in December 1927, after Chiang won another victory by overcoming the objections of his wife's family to his suit. He declared his first wife had been divorced by him, although there appeared to be some question as to the validity of the divorce.

CHIANG KAI-SHEK—*Continued*

Chiang's new wife was to have a tremendous influence on him. She interpreted the Western world to him, made him conscious of the social changes China needed and influenced him to become converted to Christianity. Intelligent and energetic Mei-ling could be entrusted, too, with political offices that could be trusted to no one else.

The first few years after his marriage Chiang Kai-shek was busy with civil wars in China, as he attempted to wipe out the Reds. After the Japanese invasion and the Manchurian incident his troubles increased. The Chinese, particularly the Communist element, were crying for war against Japan rather than his own people. Chiang thought his army was not yet ready. He continued a policy of appeasement.

The climax came when Chiang Kai-shek was kidnapped at Sian December 1936 by the forces of young Marshal Chang Hsueh-liang, his ally. The young Marshal's soldiers were calling for action against Japan and declared they were uniting with the Reds to fight Nippon. For two weeks Chiang's fate hung in the balance. Hsueh-liang finally freed Chiang, however, and offered himself as a prisoner to be punished. The whole incident was shrouded in mystery; writers give various explanations of it. All that is certain is that after the kidnapping Chiang stopped his war on the Reds and began fighting the Japanese.

Chiang has fought his war with Japan with a united China, Reds and all. It has been a fight of guerilla warfare and retreat for Chiang, but entrenched in the mountain fastness of Chungking, he is still confident of ultimate victory, still leads the Chinese people in a war to the death "still buoyant, dynamic and more optimistic than ever before." The "scorched earth" he has left behind to the enemy. He is still China's "strong man" and more than ever China's destiny depends on his success or failure.

Chiang has been called a dictator. He denies this, declaring that after a period of tutelage the people will have a voice in the government. His ambition to see a united, independent China is certainly unquestioned. He is utterly patriotic, ready to die for China. He has been called cruel and ruthless, and yet he has been generous, too. Chiang is in truth a Chinese enigma—an enigma that stands for the China of today and one that only future historians can solve.

References

Asia 39:405-6 Jl '39; 40:258-61 My '40; 40:646-8 D '40
Collier's 99:17+ Ap 10 '37 por
Cur Hist 50:40-3 Ap '39 por
Int Concil 359:138-9; 163-70 Ap '40
Liv Age 353:422 5 Ja '38
Sat Eve Post 210:5-7+ Mr 19 '38 il pors

Time 31:12-16 Ja 3 '38; 33:29-32 Je 26 '39 il pors; 34:21 Jl 17 '39 por; 35:31-2 Ap 22 '40
Berkov, R. Strong Man of China 1938
Chiang, K. and M. New Life Movement 1937
Chiang, M. General Chiang Kai-shek 1937
Crain, M. Rulers of the World 1940
Ekins, H. R. and Wright, T. China Fights for Her Life 1938
Gunther, J. Generalissimo Chiang Kai-shek *In* Balch, M. ed. Modern Short Biographies and Autobiographies p441-51 1940
Hedin, S. Chiang Kai-shek 1940
International Who's Who
Mathews, B. J. Wings Over China (Generalissimo and Madame Chiang Kai-shek) pam 1940
Mowrer, E. A. The Dragon Wakes 1939
Parker, W. Peace Terms to Chiang Kai-shek *In* Benjamin, R. S. ed. Inside Story p10-27 1940
Soward, F. H. Marshal [Chiang] Kai-shek and the Freedom of China *In* Moulders of National Destinies p229-39 1940
Who's Who in China 1936

CHIANG KAI-SHEK, MME. *See* Chiang Mei-ling

CHIANG MEI-LING [MME. CHIANG KAI-SHEK] (chi-äng′ kī-shĕk′) 1898-
Director of the New Life Movement in China

Address: c/o The Generalissimo's Headquarters, Chungking, China

Madame Chiang Kai-shek has been called variously "the brains of China", "Madame Dictator" and "the first lady of China." The Chinese-born, American-educated wife of Generalissimo Chiang Kai-shek (see sketch this issue) has certainly had her hand in the destinies of her country since she married the commander in chief of the Chinese Armies, December 1, 1927.

Much of what she has known and learned about China during the years of its war with Japan is told in her book, *This Is Our China*, published in May 1940. It is a book that is "eloquent and stingingly outspoken"—no book to read "if you are planning to write an essay on Japanese culture." In it are travel sketches, stories, tales of old dynasties; in it is expressed her firm belief that China must fight on.

After having studied at Wellesley College from 1914 to 1917 the petite sweet-faced Miss Soong returned to her native land, and there in 1922 met the Generalissimo, at that time one of the most trusted disciples of her brother-in-law, Sun Yat-sen, founder of the Chinese Republic. Chiang Kai-shek was several years Mei-ling's senior, and a direct contrast to her in every way. He was cold, silent, practical, ruthless. Mei-ling was vivacious, sensitive. Chiang Kai-shek had never been in any foreign countries except Japan and Russia and was thoroughly Chinese in thought and background. Mei-ling had been educated in America and was, as she once told an intimate friend, "Chinese only in looks." Nevertheless the two fell in love.

But the rich and powerful Soong family objected to the romance of its youngest daughter, Mei-ling, with the hard, ambitious young general. In the first place the Soongs were all Christians, and Chiang, as a Buddhist, was not only not a Christian, but not even a monogamist. He had been married before, and it was rumored that he had had concubines.

Mei-ling's family was rather remarkable. Her father had come to the United States in 1880, a poor hammock peddler from the Hainan Island, off the coast of South China. At the Fifth Street Methodist Episcopal Church of Wilmington, North Carolina, he became a Christian; at baptism he added the name Charles Jones to his family name of Soong, in honor of the man who was his religious sponsor, the captain of the ship in which he came to the United States.

Charles Jones Soong was an ambitious youth. An American became interested in him and sent him to school. Charles Jones completed his education, got an English theological certificate and returned to China to become a teacher and a Southern Methodist Episcopal missionary. He subsequently married a Miss Ni, member of a cultured Chinese family and a pillar of the church in Shanghai, and with her help founded the Chinese Y. M. C. A.

The shrewd Charles Jones also saw his opportunity in the demand for *Bibles* that the missionaries were creating in China. He printed Chinese *Bibles*, invested his earnings at the exorbitant Chinese interest rates, and became a merchant prince. All his children were American educated. The eldest daughter married H. H. Kung, a merchant banker and a lineal descendant of Confucius; the second daughter married Dr. Sun Yat-sen. His sons were China's richest bankers; T. V. Soong became an international figure.

Charles Jones Soong did not live to see the marriage of his youngest daughter, Mei-ling, but at the Soong summer home in Japan in 1927 General Chiang Kai-shek finally won Mother Soong's consent to the marriage. Madame Soong at first said that he could marry Mei-ling only on the condition that he became a Christian. Chiang replied that he could not swallow Christianity like a pill, for it was a philosophy that must be absorbed. He promised to study it, however. This pleased Mother Soong, and the marriage was solemnized with a Christian ceremony in Shanghai.

Proof of the influence of Mei-ling on her husband is the fact that he became a Christian three years after their marriage, and was baptized at the home of his mother-in-

MME. CHIANG KAI-SHEK

law by the Chinese pastor of the All-American Church.

Whether Madame Chiang Kai-shek is the real ruler of China and the dictator of Chiang Kai-shek's policies is open to debate. Yet even though Chiang Kai-shek is not a man who needed a woman's prodding, undoubtedly his wife has had a hand in shaping his policies. When Chiang inherited the mantle of Sun Yat-sen and became China's leader, he was more the ambitious war lord than the inheritor of the ideology of Sun Yat-sen. He might have remained a hard-headed, ruthless, though patriotic war lord, had it not been for Mei-ling.

Under Mei-ling's influence his war lord ambitions were curbed and redirected. Mei-ling, educated in the ideals of Christianity and democracy, brought some of those ideas back to China with her. China's New Life Movement, for instance, which is such an important factor in the social awakening of China, is Madame Chiang Kai-shek's idea. Although she gives her husband credit for it, the New Life Movement, according to American correspondents in China, originated in the minds of some Christian missionaries who thought the great masses of Chinese peasants were getting little out of the revolution. They approached Madame Chiang Kai-shek, who in turn approached her husband. Thus the New Life Movement, based on four old Chinese virtues—courtesy, service, honesty and honor—was born, with Madame Chiang Kai-shek its director and one of its most ardent propagandists.

The New Life Movement, although it was given a Chinese background, might have been lifted from the American credo: "Don't spit; safety first; good roads; watch your step; keep to the right; fresh air and sun-

CHIANG MEI-LING—*Continued*

shine; swat the fly; brush your teeth; stop, look and listen; better babies; clean up and paint up." Sewer systems have been built; people have been taught to boil and wash vegetables. The Chinese masses are slowly being made conscious of sanitation, of solving social problems and of the necessity for overcoming their centuries of superstition and lethargy.

Madame Chiang Kai-shek has had a tremendous influence in arousing sympathy for her country in its fight against Japan. She has written many articles for American magazines, attempting to show that China's cause is the cause of the democracies of the world and interpreting her country to Americans. In 1940 she published two books—*China in Peace and War* and *This Is Our China*—which again stated her country's cause, and incidentally aroused more admiration for the indefatigable Mei-ling.

Help from American women in the form of shipments of dressings and first-aid kits for China has been sent through Madame Chiang Kai-shek's influence. She herself is an ardent war worker, and her efforts have made many Chinese society women, who, despite the New Life Movement, still regard a coolie as just a coolie and unworthy of notice, take part in war work. Madame Chiang Kai-shek does not ask Chinese women to do what she herself will not do. She has dressed soldiers' wounds, has done sewing and active relief work.

War orphans and women in industry are her two chief concerns. In her relief work she travels from village to village, and her sound judgment and energy have resulted in accomplishments which high Chinese officials have not been able to effect. She has influenced factory owners to move factories out of war zones; obtained hand looms for refugees so they can weave simple cotton stuff to circumvent the Japanese blockade; and has been everywhere to arouse Chinese women to their new tasks.

But no matter how hard she works, and no matter how hot or sticky the weather, Madame Chiang Kai-shek is always immaculately groomed, always the picture of elegance in her simply cut Chinese clothes. She has charm, graciousness and beauty.

In addition to her position as director-general of the New Life Movement, Madame Chiang Kai-shek has served in an official capacity as secretary general of the Chinese Commission on Aeronautical Affairs. In 1936 the Generalissimo appointed his wife to the post in order to effect a radical reorganization. Chinese politics were so shot through with graft that Chiang, faced with buying airplanes quickly and cheaply, could trust no one but his wife to dicker with foreign salesmen and get the best bargains for China.

Madame Chiang Kai-shek also played an important rôle in getting the release of her husband when he was kidnapped in the Sian mutiny in his party in 1936. It was Madame Chiang Kai-shek who kept her husband's followers from firing on Sian and thus perhaps endangering his life and throwing China into a civil war, and it was she who courageously went into the Sian camp to complete negotiations for his release.

War worker, patriot, founder of the Association of Chinese Women to Support the National Defense, director of the New Life Movement, it can be truthfully said that Madame Chiang Kai-shek converted her husband's desire for a united China from a mere political task to a crusade.

In their book, *China Fights for Her Life* (1938), H. R. Ekins and Theon Wright say of Madame Chiang Kai-shek: "It is quite true that if Chiang dies, the rule will pass into the slim hands of Mei-ling. She has not only been the supreme influence of his life since 1927, but she has obviated the need for understudies.

"More men probably would stand ready to act on the word of Madame Chiang than on the word of the Generalissimo. She has fewer enemies. Her husband has been ruthless, and held his subordinates by fear of his wrath and power; Madame Chiang has held them through admiration and almost nationalized love for this sweet-faced woman."

References

Asia 39:405-6 Jl '39
Collier's 99:17+ Ap 10 '37 il por
Forum 93:354-60 Je '35 por; 91:131-4 Mr '34 por
Ind Woman 16:35-6+ F '37 por; 18: 54 F '39 il por (cover)
Lit Digest 122:15-16 Ag '29 '36 por
Liv Age 353:422-5 Ja '38
Time 31:12-16 Ja 3 '38 por; 28:12-15 D 28 '36 por
Bartlett, R. M. First Woman of the Orient *In* They Did Something About It p94-111 1939
Chiang, M. General Chiang Kai-shek 1937
Ekins, H. R. and Wright, T. China Fights for Her Life 1938
Gunther, J. Generalissimo Chiang Kai-shek *In* Balch, M. ed. Modern Short Biographies and Autobiographies p441-51 1940
International Who's Who
Mathews, B. J. Wings Over China (Generalissimo and Madame Chiang Kai-shek) pam 1940
Mowrer, E. A. The Dragon Wakes 1939
Who's Who in China

CHOTZINOFF, SAMUEL (shŏts'ĭ-nŏf)
July 4, 1889- Music critic; pianist
Address: b. c/o New York Post, 75 West St, New York City; h. 29 W. 85th St, New York City

Samuel Chotzinoff's life is like a Horatio Alger yarn in its triumphant struggle against poverty and adversity. Born in

Russia, he came to New York City with his parents at the age of six, and lived in what is now chic Sutton Place but was then a shabby, overcrowded haven for poverty-stricken immigrants. When his father died, the responsibility of supporting the family fell on young Samuel's shoulders. He was the family breadwinner at the age of 13.

"We went in strongly for culture," Chotzinoff recalls, "because it was cheaper than any other form of entertainment." Chotzinoff learned to play the piano largely through his own methods, and soon was teaching others in his neighborhood for 25 cents a lesson. It took a great deal of courage and hard work to get through high school. College seemed almost impossible, but a sympathetic friend helped him, and possibly influenced the entire course of his life.

"He was a dentist," Chotzinoff recounts, "and therefore, in my estimation, an extremely wealthy man." The dentist paid a year's tuition in advance for his son and daughter, to whom Chotzinoff was then teaching music, and the ambitious young musician was able to pay his tuition at Columbia University.

Chotzinoff kept at his music, and three years later when Efrem Zimbalist, the famous violinist, offered him the post of accompanist, he left Columbia. After several tours with Zimbalist, he played for Alma Gluck, Jascha Heifetz and many others.

In 1925 Chotzinoff made his debut as a newspaper music critic. Deems Taylor (see sketch this issue), becoming known as a composer, resigned his post as critic of the New York *World* and Chotzinoff asked for and got the job. He remained on the paper until its demise in 1930. He went to the New York *Post* as music critic in 1934.

To thousands of music lovers Chotzinoff became known chiefly through his rôle of commentator for the National Broadcasting Company's Saturday night broadcasts of Arturo Toscanini's symphony programs. It was Chotzinoff whom David Sarnoff (see sketch this issue), president of the Radio Corporation of America, sent to Milan, Italy, early in 1937, to broach the subject of radio broadcasts to the great Toscanini.

When Toscanini accepted the radio proposition which his friend, Chotzinoff, had been commissioned to present, National Broadcasting officials began considering the whole problem of serious music in radio. They reasoned that it would be a good idea to have someone with a double background of active musician and critic to supervise NBC music presentations in order to make sure that the musical art offered was of the highest type obtainable. Chotzinoff was sounded out on the idea, and became NBC's director of serious music.

SAMUEL CHOTZINOFF

To his job at NBC Chotzinoff adds the duties of music critic on the *Post*, with a full quota of concerts to be covered each week; he commutes to Philadelphia one day a week to teach a course in music criticism at the Curtis Institute of Music; directs activities at the Chatham Square Music School; contributes articles on music to various magazines and lectures occasionally.

Chotzinoff in 1939 was an important figure in a promotion stunt which his paper, the New York *Post*, arranged and which other papers have copied, so successful has the venture been. The *Post* arranged to have the Victor Recording Studio make a special series of recordings by important symphony orchestras playing anonymously and to sell music albums at cost to its readers. Chotzinoff chose the music and acted as key man in the scheme because he was close to Sarnoff, RCA's president. The Washington *Star*, taking over the scheme, formed a national music appreciation committee, and began distributing the symphonic records at $1.39 a set. The idea has spread nationally.

Dark, velvet-eyed, stoop-shouldered, sensitive, Chotzinoff is familiarly known as "Chotzi." He was married in 1925 to Pauline Heifetz, sister of the violinist. They have two children, Blair and Anne.

References

Fortune 17:62-8+ Ja '38 por

Time 34:26 Jl 3 '39 por

Thompson, O. ed. International Cyclopedia of Music and Musicians 1939

Variety Radio Directory

Who's Who in America

Who's Who in American Jewry

CHRISTIE, AGATHA Author

Address: h. 58 Sheffield Terrace, London, W. 8, England; Ashfield, Torquay, England

Known for years to every detective and mystery story fan in England and America, Agatha Mary Clarissa Christie tops the good and growing list of feminine crime-careerists in the "whodunit" field. Next to the immortal Sherlock, Mrs. Christie's eccentric, rapier-keen little Hercule Poirot has attained the widest international reputation among fictional detectives.

The queen of sleuth-puzzlers does not depend solely, however, upon Poirot's Gallic talents: she has used other detectives, both professional and amateur. But with or without Hercule, no mystery addict would miss a Christie thriller. Possibly no rival in the whole detective-story camp has been able to turn out so many books with as consistently high a degree of merit as Agatha Christie has done for the past two decades. Since 1921, when her first was published, she has produced nearly 35 full-length novels and a considerable number of short stories as well. Her novels make the best-seller lists; her work has often been serialized in popular magazines before publication in book form. *And Then There Were None* (1940) appeared serially in 1939; *The Patriotic Murders*, which ran serially (August-September 1940) in *Collier's*, will appear in book form (February 1941) in this country.

The countryside of Devon, England has been the setting for a good many of Agatha Christie's stories. She was born there at Torquay. Her father, Frederick Alvah Miller of New York City, died while she was a child and she was educated at home by her mother. "An intelligent woman of great charm and character," the mother encouraged her highly imaginative daughter to write poems and stories. "As a youngster, it never occurred to me to be a writer," Mrs. Christie has said. "I was an atrocious speller and had a terrible mortification, when at school in Paris later, of having 42 faults in my *dictée*. No other girl had more than five, so I felt completely humiliated!" It was when she had a bad cold and couldn't go outdoors that her mother told her to write a story. The first one didn't come easily, but later she wrote others. "For some years I enjoyed myself very much writing stories of unrelieved gloom where most of the characters died. Also a good deal of poetry and a novel with an impossible number of characters in it."

Her great interest, however, was music; and when she was 16 she went to Paris to study piano and singing. But she did not take it up professionally because she was too nervous to play in public and her voice was not big enough for opera, which she cared about most. She went with her mother to Cairo for a winter and there wrote her first novel. She showed it to Eden Phillpotts, their friend and neighbor in Torquay;

AGATHA CHRISTIE

it was his encouragement that made her decide to go on writing.

A few months after the outbreak of the War in 1914 she married Colonel Archibald Christie of the Royal Flying Corps. They had one daughter, Rosalind, born in 1919. While her husband was in France, Mrs. Christie worked in a Red Cross hospital in Torquay and had little time for writing. She did, however, plan a detective story. It was at the challenge of her sister, who said almost no detective story was written in which one didn't know right away who had committed the crime, that she wrote *The Mysterious Affair at Styles*. It was rejected by several publishers before it finally came out in 1921.

In 1928 she received a decree of divorce from her husband and spent the next few years traveling, mostly in the East, while her daughter was at school. She visited Ur in 1930, where she met Max Mallowan, an archeologist then assisting Sir Leonard Woolley with archeological excavations there. In September of that year she and Mr. Mallowan were married. Since then she has spent part of each year in Syria or Iraq, helping with the photography on her husband's expeditions. She likes the desert and finds it a good place to write. An archeological expedition is the background for her mystery, *Murder in Mesopotamia* (1936).

Like most mystery story writers, Mrs. Christie lives quietly, avoiding publicity. She has, indeed, been called the Greta Garbo among them: she won't be interviewed, and even her publishers know little about her. But in 1927, briefly, she herself was headline news. Her car was found deserted in the Sussex downs. Mrs. Christie had disappeared: posses were sent in search, airplanes flying over the downs could find no trace of her. Then the police received a clue letter—the handwriting said to be strangely like Mrs. Christie's own. Eleven days later she was found at a Harrogate hotel registered under the name of the woman her husband later married. Specialists said she was suffering from amnesia; others were skeptical as to this. Nevertheless the whole affair enormously increased the sale of Christie books.

Most of Agatha Christie's mysteries have been written in the Conan Doyle tradition, in which the egotistic, mustached, passionately neat little Belgian Poirot uses his brain cells—and his intuition—and gets results as surely as the thorough, scientifically analytical Mr. Holmes. For its deviation from pattern, and for the skill of its "trick" ending, her best-known novel is *The Murder of Roger Ackroyd* (1926). Many other detective story writers have questioned the legitimacy of the device she uses in it; but others—among them Dorothy Sayers—have rushed to her defense. The story undoubtedly stands among the classics in the modern detective field. Among her numerous books may be named *The Murder on the Links* (1923); *The Big Four* (1927); *Mystery of the Blue Train* (1928); *Partners in Crime* (1929); *The Murder at the Vicarage* (1930); *Peril at End House* (1932); *Thirteen at Dinner* (1933); *Death in the Air* (1935); *Dead Man's Mirror* (1937); *Murder for Christmas* (1939); *Murder Is Easy* (1940); and *Sad Cypress* (1940).

And Then There Were None (1940) represents Mrs. Christie at her slickest, rule-breaking best. It is a hair-raising thriller full of murders, past and present. Eight guests and two servants gather in a luxurious mansion on Indian Island off the coast of Devon: the hosts are missing. The guests suddenly find themselves doomed to die for crimes which they are alleged to have committed. As a warning of what is to come, a copy of the nursery rhyme, "Ten little, nine little, eight little Indian boys," etc., hangs in each bedroom. A terrific storm isolates these guests on the island, and one by one they depart from the land of the living. There is no Hercule Poirot present in this book, to stay the hand of the killer.

Agatha Christie says that the three severest critics of her books are her sister, her young daughter—whose judgments are very severe—and her archeological husband, whose comments are usually different from everyone else's. "As for my tastes, I enjoy my food, hate the taste of any kind of alcohol, have tried and tried to like smoking but can't manage it. I adore flowers, am crazy about the sea, love the theatre, but am bored to death by the talkies, and am very stupid at following them, loathe wireless and all loud noises, dislike living in cities. I do a lot of traveling, mostly in the Near East and have a great love of the desert."

References

Delin 130:29 F '37 il por
Sat Eve Post 209:100 O 31 '36 por;
   209:108 N 7 '36

Sat R Lit 19:13 Ja 7 '39 por
Time 31:67 F 28 '38 por
Author's and Writer's Who's Who
Kunitz, S. J. ed. Authors Today and Yesterday 1933
Thomson, H. D. Masters of Mystery 1931
Who's Who

CHRYSLER, WALTER PERCY Apr 2, 1875—Aug 18, 1940 Auto manufacturer and president of the Chrysler Corporation which he founded; at the age of 17 began his career as a 5-cent-an-hour locomotive wiper at a roundhouse; rose from job to job until in 1911 was manager for the American Locomotive Company in Pittsburgh; studied motor car construction; General Motors offered him a job as works manager for Buick cars; later became executive vice-president of General Motors; in 1920 undertook the revitalization of the Willys-Overland and Maxwell companies; in 1924 brought out the Chrysler car; sold $5,000,000 worth of them in first year; four years later his corporation was considered one of the "big three" auto manufacturers and made, besides the Chrysler, the Plymouth, Dodge and De Soto cars; in 1935 left the presidency of the company but retained his chairmanship of the board and remained the corporation's chief executive; organized, financed and built the Chrysler Building in New York City, second in size to the Empire State Building

References

Fortune 12:30-7+ Ag '35 il pors
Newsweek 1:22-3 Ap 29 '33 por; 6:19
   Ag 3 '35 por; 9:7-9 Ap 3 '37
Pop Sci 137:76-7 Ag '40

Blank-Stoller

WALTER P. CHRYSLER

CHRYSLER, WALTER PERCY—*Cont.*

Sat Eve Post 209:5-7+ Je 19; 16-17+
Je 26; 210:20-1+ Jl 3; 20-1+ Jl
10; 20-1+ Jl 17; 20-1+ Jl 31; 20-1+
Ag 7; 20-1+ Ag 14 '37 pors
Scholastic 30:24 Ap 24 '37
Time 29:14-15 Ap 5 '37 por
Foster, O. D. Walter P. Chrysler *In*
Forbes, B. C. Automotive Giants of
America p30-43 1926
Walter Percy Chrysler *In* Mirrors
of Wall Street p197-212 1933
White, T. M. Walter Percy Chrysler
In Famous Leaders of Industry 3d
ser. p17-27 1931
Who's Who in America
Who's Who in Commerce and Indus-
try
Woolf, S. J. Walter P. Chrysler *In*
Drawn from Life p339-46 1932

Obituaries

N Y Times p1+ Ag 19 '40 por
Newsweek 16:36 Ag 26 '40 por
Time 36:56 Ag 26 '40

CHURCHILL, BERTON 1877—Oct 10,
1940 Stage and screen character actor; attained first real success in theatre in 1925
in *Alias the Deacon* and appeared in many
Broadway productions; began film career
in 1929 and acted in hundreds of rôles,
most often cast as a bluff, hearty businessman or a small-town "leading citizen";
active in Actors Equity Association and
served as a vice-president and a member of
the executive council

References

Am Mag 102:36-7+ N '26 por

Obituaries

N Y Herald Tribune p22 O 11 '40 por

BERTON CHURCHILL

N Y Times p21 O 11 '40 por
Newsweek 16:6 O 21 '40

**CHURCHILL, WINSTON LEONARD
SPENCER** Nov 30, 1874- Prime Minister
of Great Britain; author

Address: b. 10 Downing St, S. W. 1, London,
England; h. Chartwell, Westerham, Kent,
England

There are several schools of thought in
Great Britain about Britain's Prime Minister, and not even his own party is united
in its estimate of his abilities. Among
Right-wingers there are some who think
him one of the cleverest men of his age;
"brilliant" is the adjective they most commonly use. Others of the same group think
him much too clever and mistrust him, not
because they doubt his integrity, but because they belong to that British upper-
class stratum which, as a matter of principle, looks askance at high intelligence.

Left-wingers in general dislike him, because to them he typifies an old England
of "the squire and his relations," a class-
conscious, possessive, grind-the-faces-of-the-
poor England which they want to see transformed. In all groups there are large
numbers who consistently bring up three
dreadful words—Antwerp, Gallipoli and the
Murman Coast—words which in their time
meant blood, bereavement, muddle, horror
and disgrace. Churchill was responsible for
all three of these fearful misadventures in
the last War. That is enough for some
people.

Winston Churchill is a vivid, colorful personality, who may be detested, perhaps, but
never ignored. "He is impulsive, impatient,
quick-tempered, hasty at times in making
up his mind, intemperate in putting and
defending his conclusions." Nevertheless
he stands out among English public men
as a man of "character, of initiative, of independence and of tenacity."

Churchill's blood is very blue English
and very red American. According to Philip
Guedalla some key to Winston Churchill's
life can be found in his combination of
English and American traits. He is the
eldest son of Lord Randolph Churchill, third
son of the seventh Duke of Marlborough and
descendant of the original Duke, the victor
of Blenheim. His mother was an American,
the former Jennie Jerome of New York. Her
father, Leonard Jerome, cleaned up $6,000,-
000 in the panic of 1857, led a dashing
existence and had Jerome Park and Jerome
Avenue in The Bronx, New York named
after him. It was in 1867, when he took
his wife and their three daughters to Paris,
that his daughter Jennie met and married
Lord Randolph Churchill, even though his
father, the Duke of Marlborough, was
"slightly shocked" at the thought of a transatlantic marriage.

Churchill went to school at Harrow, one
of the two most famous English "public
schools," noted for the number of statesmen

it has turned out. From there he went to Sandhurst (the British West Point) and afterward served as an officer in several campaigns. He was with the Spanish forces in Cuba, the Malakand Field Force, the Tirah Expeditionary Force and the Nile Expeditionary Force. During the South African War he went out as war correspondent for the *Morning Post*. He contrived to get himself captured by the Boers (or rather by an individual Boer, who was none other than Louis Botha), and owed his life to the fact that he had lost his revolver. Later he escaped under the very noses of the sentries and scrambled aboard a train, eventually rejoining the British.

In 1900 Churchill began his Parliamentary career as a Conservative member. A reproach that is often brought against him is that he has changed about from party to party according to which happened to be in power at the moment. The year 1906 brought the big landslide to Liberalism, and surely enough Churchill appeared that year as a Liberal, being returned for North-West Manchester. His first job, beginning that same year, was that of Under-Secretary for the Colonies, and he held it for two years. In 1908 he was married to Clementine Hozier (their son Randolph was elected to Parliament in October 1940), after having been beaten in a by-election at North-West Manchester on promotion to the presidency of the Board of Trade. He was returned for Dundee (for which he continued to sit until 1922) and passed from the Colonial Office to the post of president of the Board of Trade, which he held until 1910. In that year and the next he acted as Home Secretary.

In 1911 Churchill became First Lord of the Admiralty. He is now generally recognized to have been a success there, and to deserve much of the credit for the Fleet's preparedness in August 1914. The disasters of Antwerp and Gallipoli at the time did his reputation no good, however. In 1915 he first sank to the minor office of Chancellor of the Duchy of Lancaster, and then went out to France as an officer. He had yet another narrow escape from death while there, moving from one dugout to another just a few moments before the first one was utterly obliterated by a shell.

In 1917 Churchill made a political comeback as Minister of Munitions, and between 1919 and 1921 was Secretary for War and Air. It was in 1919 that he conceived the extraordinary idea of sending an expeditionary force to northern Russia to assist the anti-Bolshevik projects of Wrangel and Denikin. There was no mandate from the British public for this, and the expedition came back with its tail between its legs; but this much can be said: the men who went out were volunteers. Churchill next went to the Colonial office again in 1921, but in the following year he lost his seat in Parliament. During the next couple of years he made several attempts to re-enter

WINSTON CHURCHILL

the House at by-elections, but his stock was very low and no constituency would have him. In 1924 he was returned for Epping, a country district northeast of London, and has sat for this division ever since. He was returned as an Independent, but voted with the Conservatives and was made Chancellor of the Exchequer. This office ended with the advent of the Labor Government in 1929.

According to John Gunther, for years Churchill seemed to stand on the wrong side of great social issues. He had been against the suffragists, against a liberal constitution for India, against "every shade and aspect of even the very mild brand of socialism advocated by the British Labor Party", "against the working classes"; and "during the General Strike, when he edited the official government newspaper," he had "behaved like a schoolboy." But this did not mean that he was in good standing with the Tories.

In recent years Churchill has always been in the background, but not very far back in it; and there has invariably been a strong body of opinion that favored the use of his talents in the government of the country. He was kept out of office by his lack of party orthodoxy on several important points. He disagreed with the official Conservative policy on India, for example; he was strongly against Mr. Neville Chamberlain's policy of "appeasement," and as a result he has been classed by Herr Hitler with Anthony Eden and Duff Cooper (see sketches this issue), as a "warmonger."

But the strong body of opinion prevailed. To the great satisfaction of most of England, Chamberlain appointed Churchill First Lord of the Admiralty seven hours after the War broke out in September 1939. There was satisfaction, too, when in April 1940 he was

CHURCHILL, WINSTON—*Continued*

made Chairman of the Armed Services Committee, which meant, actually, head of all the war forces as well as head of the admiralty. In May 1940 he became Prime Minister, and his appointment brought hope to many. To them his vigor, toughness and forcefulness were in sharp contrast to the apparent ineptness of his predecessor. Sir Archibald Sinclair (see sketch this issue), leader of the Liberal Opposition, stated in the House that six months of Winston Churchill before the War would have been six nails in Hitler's coffin. In October 1940 he was unanimously elected leader of the Conservative Party.

When Churchill describes the strength of the R. A. F. or the fighting spirit of the British people, his bold speeches also distinguish him from Chamberlain. "He has brought back the arrogance and splendor of Elizabethan language. Like Shakespeare Churchill detests the enemies of England and says so in words that carry across the seven seas." The English people love his snarling, scornful pronunciation of invective upon the "nahzies," and they find encouragement in such phrases as "In the end we'll break their hearts."

At the times when Churchill has not been in politics, he has been very prolific as an author and journalist. One of the highest paid journalists in England, it is said that he can command as much as $500 for a thousand-word newspaper article. His historical and biographical works are marked by a brilliant power of exposition, a masterly handling of sources, a breathlessly interesting narrative and an elegant and polished style. His large book, *The World Crisis* (1923-29), is one of the most important works produced by the last War, and his recent *Marlborough* (1933-38) is acknowledged to be one of the best biographies of modern times. In fact, a commentator on *Marlborough* stated that, if Churchill hadn't made politics his career he might have been one of the most popular writers of his generation. His latest book is *Blood, Sweat and Tears* (November 1940).

Some years ago Churchill learned the craft of bricklaying, and whenever there is a building job at Chartwell Manor, his country home in Kent, he goes right out with his trowel. His other spare time hobby is painting, at which he spends a good deal of time and in which he is reputed to have acquired a good deal of skill. Some of his closest personal friends are artists like Sir William Nicholson and connoisseurs like Sir Edward Marsh.

In his appearance there is little which suggests the man's latent power. He is elderly, stodgy, fat, with a countenance that has been called both "puckish" and "cherubic." His figure, his black bow tie and the long cigar perpetually clenched between his teeth make him a pleasure to caricature. To much of England he looks and acts the perfect personification of "John Bull." Actions like his entrance into the Admiralty seem typical. He, with other officials, received a pass to admit him, but, an eternal enemy of red tape, he tore it up the first day, explaining to the doorman: "My face is my fortune." Another story tells of him walking in the slums of the Midlands. "Fancy," he said, "living in one of these streets—never seeing anything beautiful—never eating anything savory— *never saying anything clever!*"

References

Christian Sci Mon Mag p2 Mr 9 '40 por

Manchester Guardian p6 Ja 29 '40; p3 F 28 '40

New Repub 102:787-8 Je 10 '40

N Y Times VII p3+ Ap 14 '40 por; VII p4+ My 19 '40 por; p1, 4 My 20 '40; VII p7 S 8 '40 por; p7 O 10 '40

New Yorker 16:14 Je 22 '40

Read Digest 36:33-6 F '40; 37:152-92 Jl '40

R Deux Mondes s8 35:343-57 S 15 '36

Time 34:20 N 20 '39 por; 35:25 Ja 29 '40 por; 35:38, 40 My 27 '40; 35:88 Je 10 '40; 36:22-4 S 30 '40 por

Audax, pseud. Winston Churchill *In* Men in Our Time p57-82 1940

Begbie, H. Mr. Winston Churchill *In* Mirrors of Downing Street p97-108 1923

Broad, C. L. Winston Churchill, Man of War pam 1940

Buchan, W. Winston Churchill pam 1939

Churchill, W. L. S. My Early Life 1934

Dawson, R. M. Winston Churchill at the Admiralty 1940

Germains, V. W. Tragedy of Winston Churchill 1931

Gunther, J. The Incomparable Winston *In* Inside Europe p321-33 1940

International Who's Who

Kircher, R. Winston Churchill *In* Engländer p117-30 1928

Kraus, R. Winston Churchill 1940

Phelan, J. L. Churchill Can Unite Ireland

Roberts, C. E. B. Winston Churchill 1936

Watchman, pseud. Right Honourable Gentlemen 1939

Who's Who

Woolf, S. J. Winston Spencer Churchill *In* Drawn from Life p132-40 1932

CIANO, GALEAZZO, CONTE (chä'nō gä'lâ-ät'tsō) Mar 18, 1903- Italian Foreign Minister

When Italy joined Germany in the present war her Foreign Minister, Count Galeazzo Ciano, was in command of a bomber squadron. The man who together with Mussolini did his best to bring about the

Rome-Berlin axis, fought for that axis, undoubtedly with all the "reckless bravery" he demonstrated in the Ethiopian War. Now that the War is progressing from county to country, from battlefield to battlefield, Count Ciano has been found successfully conferring with Spain, urging Romania to yield to the Axis' demands, pushing Italy's demands upon Greece. He has been in conference with Hitler and Von Ribbentrop over the whole Balkan situation.

Mussolini is proud of his Foreign Minister and son-in-law—proud of him as a fighter and as a diplomat; and because of his success in carrying out Il Duce's commands, Ciano is the man whom "Mussolini has chosen to succeed himself as dictator of the Italian Empire." Although from time to time Mussolini snorts: "My successor has yet to be born," and although he probably believes that MUSSOLINI can have no successor, he has groomed the husband of his favorite daughter Edda with great care for the post.

Ciano has responded. Ideologically and practically he has followed Mussolini's lead closely. What Mussolini thinks, so does Ciano. He lives the motto: "Mussolini is always right." He even tries to look like Mussolini. "Daily he acquires more of the jaw-thrusting mannerisms of his father-in-law"; he stares with the same frown; he holds his arms akimbo in the same way.

Ciano was a Fascist zealot before he was out of his teens. He was born in 1903 in Livorno, which the English call Leghorn. He was the son of S. E. Constanzo Ciano, an Admiral who in the last War defeated the Austrians on the Adriatic and the seamen's unions on the Tyrrhenian waterfront, and was rewarded with a longtime post of Minister of Communications. In Fascism's early days Father Ciano was the first Italian of national prominence to join the struggling editor, Benito Mussolini, and to become a Fascist. Mussolini made him a count.

After Galeazzo Ciano took his law degree at the University of Rome, he became a theatre and book reviewer on *Nuovo Paese*, the first Fascist newspaper in Rome. He also wrote two plays on which all comment has now been forbidden. In 1925, three years after the March on Rome, Ciano took examinations for the diplomatic service, "which he barely passed," and immediately was appointed to routine duty in South America. From South America he went to Peiping as diplomatic representative.

During this time Admiral Ciano discovered that Mussolini was about to solve the "Roman Question" by making a treaty with Pope Pius XI. He had his son released from China just in time to squeeze him into the Italian Embassy to the Holy See as First Secretary. Ciano did a good job there and was soon on the upgrade. His marriage to Mussolini's daughter Edda in 1930 didn't hurt his career either. According to some sources the marriage was the result of a "passionate courtship";

CONTE CIANO

according to others it was arranged by old Count Constanzo Ciano.

It is impossible to consider Ciano's career without considering his wife Edda. "Of all the yes-men around the Duce," they say in Rome, "Edda is the only one who sometimes says no." She has her father's jaw, and she has her father's ability and intelligence. There's a rumor that she isn't the daughter of the present Mrs. Mussolini but is really the result of a *grande passion* between Benito and a Russian woman socialist, in the days when Mussolini was a powerless, ranting radical.

"Gaunt, pale-faced." chicly-dressed, Edda is supposed to be "the only intimate of a man now lonely in his greatness," loved and admired by her father for her wit, her spunk, her daring, for her successful intriguing and string-pulling. Since the Fascist State rules that woman's place is in the home and that woman has no place in politics, Edda has had to play her rôle in the recent realignments of Europe through her husband, Ciano, but there is little doubt in many minds that it is her political perspicacity that guides him. Nor is there doubt that it is her great ambition for Ciano to become Dictator of Italy—an ambition which her father seems willing to satisfy—in the future.

Soon after Edda and Ciano were married, they sailed for Shanghai, where Edda's first son (they now have three children) was born. Edda nicknamed him Fabrizio, which means "Little Chink," and still calls him that. As Italian Consul General in Shanghai, Ciano became president of the League of Nations Commission which enquired into Japan's bombardment of Shanghai. Soon he was promoted to Minister to China, and as such was sent to the London Economic Conference, at which he secured an adjust-

CIANO, GALEAZZO—*Continued*

ment of Italy's Boxer Rebellion indemnity claims on China.

Back in Rome in 1933 the Cianos proceeded to cut a great social swath. Their parties were famous. Handsome and swarthy and neat, Count Ciano wore, and still wears, good clothes that fit him well. And he began the practice he still maintains of working late, seeing Mussolini for high pressure contact on world affairs and then joining his friends at Rome's best club or best hotel for recreation. Then and recently, when young ladies ask political questions, he whispers to them what is in the afternoon papers—"only it is a secret strictly between you and me," he tells them.

In 1934 Ciano became head of the government's press office, and in June 1935 was made Minister for Press and Propaganda. As such he never could seem to understand why the foreign correspondents didn't write with the same pro-Fascist zeal which came so naturally to him when he was a reporter. When Italy invaded Ethiopia, Ciano, as an aviator, dropped the first bombs and was the first Italian to alight in Addis Ababa. An indifferent pilot, but recklessly brave, he returned to Rome after the War, a conquering hero.

In June 1936, when he was 33, Ciano became Italy's Foreign Minister, the youngest foreign minister of any great power. As Foreign Minister, his trips to Berlin, Vienna, Budapest and Albania confirmed his rôle of vice-Duce and successor. No one else except Mussolini ever was given so much headline space or had his picture so frequently on the front page. He worked out agreements with Germany, strengthened Italy's position in Central Europe and signed a Mediterranean pact with British Ambassador Sir Eric Drummond. When the Anglo-Italian agreement was signed in April 1938 cries of "Ciano, Ciano," took precedence for the first time over the more usual ones of "Duce, Duce."

As Foreign Minister, Ciano has had his greatest success—if such it can be called now—with Germany. When he first went there as Minister in November 1936, he was rapturously greeted. There were parades, he laid wreaths on the graves of dead storm troopers, pink-cheeked Hitler youths saluted him and pink-cheeked Hitler maidens offered him posies. And it was Ciano who signed the Axis treaty from which came German-Italian cooperation in Spain, Italian support for Germany in the Czechoslovakian crisis, German support for Italy's invasion of Albania, the military alliance signed in the spring of 1939, and finally, Italy's entrance into the European War on Germany's side in June 1940.

There were some who once considered Ciano a playboy because of the parties he attended, because of his habit of speeding in his roaring car over Italy, because he used to take the ambassadors of other coun-

tries out of their swallow-tails and put them into swimming trunks. They are now probably wishing it were true.

References

Am Mercury 51.30-3 S '40
Collier's 100:19-20 O 30 '37 pors
New Repub 94:385-6 My 4 '38
N Y Sun p1 Je 11 '40
Newsweek 11:19 Ja 24 '38 por
R Deux Mondes s8 43:183-93 Ja 1 '38
Sat Eve Post 212:25+ D 23 '39
Time 28:15-16 N 2 '36 il por; 34:18-20 Jl 24 '39 il pors
Chi è?
Gunther, J. Who Else In Italy? *In* Inside Europe p255-67 1940
International Motion Picture Almanac 1937-38 (under Di Cortellazzo, H. E.)
Who's Who

CLAPPER, RAYMOND   May 30, 1892-
Newspaper correspondent

Address: b. 1013 13th St, N W, Washington, D. C.

Raymond Clapper was born in 1892 in LaCygne, Kansas, the son of John William and Julia (Crow) Clapper. After being graduated from high school in Kansas City, Kansas, he enrolled at the University of Kansas in 1913 and married Olive Ewing the same year. They have two children, Janet and Peter. After three years of college Clapper left and worked for a few months as a reporter on the Kansas City *Star*, then joined the United Press and saw the country—reporting in Chicago, Milwaukee, St. Paul, New York and Washington.

From 1923 to 1928 he was chief political writer for the Washington Bureau of the United Press; special writer on the Washington *Post* for the next year; and since 1936 he has been political commentator for the Scripps-Howard newspapers and the United Feature Syndicate.

From his well-written daily syndicated column many thousands of readers over the country obtain their opinions about what is going on in Washington. Henry Ford once described Clapper in these words: "Mr. Clapper knows this nation. He has constantly traveled its length and breadth, observing its trends, studying its methods, familiarizing himself with the wide variety of mind and motive which marks its citizens and reporting these with the efficiency and high impartiality which characterize our best journalism." *Time* calls him "one of the ablest of United States political commentators." He once was "rated a New Deal sympathizer" even though "his particular passion was Republican progressivism," but about the time of the Supreme Court reorganization bill he became somewhat less sympathetic, and in 1940 he supported Wendell Willkie (see sketch this issue) for President. Before the German invasion of the Low

RAYMOND CLAPPER

G. Maillard Kesslère

MARGUERITE CLARK

Wolf Hopper; appeared in Victor Herbert's *Babes in Toyland;* in 1915 went to Hollywood, where she was a beloved figure and a box-office hit in such films as *Snow White, Mrs. Wiggs of the Cabbage Patch* and *Wildflower;* retired at the height of her fame in 1920, saying: "I knew enough to go home when the party was over."

Countries he was highly suspicious of Roosevelt's foreign policies, and even afterward grew to advocate a "kind of limited imperialism" for the United States rather than direct intervention.

In 1933 Clapper wrote *Racketeering in Washington,* which he describes as "being an account from authoritative records of the grafting in small and great things by our Senators and members of the House of Representatives and executives in public departments who line their private pockets, living in the lap of luxury at the expense of the taxpayer, and indulging in nepotism, junketing, padded expense accounts and many wastes and extravagances at the very time that millions of our citizens are out of work." From this it can be seen that Mr. Clapper looks at the Washington scene with the slightly-jaundiced, irreverent eye of a newspaperman who sets very few lawmakers up on pedestals. And Quincy Howe (see sketch this issue) says that he differs from his Washington colleagues in that "he does not believe that God has summoned him personally to save the American people."

References
Time 35:18 Mr 18 '40 por
America's Young Men
Clapper, R.   Racketeering in Washington 1933
Howe, Q.   The News and How to Understand It p63-4   1940
Who's Who in America

CLARK, MARGUERITE   Feb 22, 1887—Sept 25, 1940   Former star of the stage and early silent movies; died of pneumonia in New York City; co-starred at 15 with De

References
Am Mag 84:42+ D '17 pors
Motion Picture Classic 5:45+ O '17 pors; 9:18-19 O '19 pors; 12:44-5+ Jl '21 pors
Motion Picture Mag 13:103-6+ F '17 pors; 14:79-80 Ag '17 por; 15:60-3+ Jl '18 il pors
Photoplay 17:28-9 Ja '20 il pors
Who's Who in America 1928-29

Obituaries
N Y Herald Tribune p18 S 26 '40
N Y Times p23 S 26 '40
Newsweek 16:6 O 7 '40 por
Time 36:57 O 7 '40

CLIVE, EDWARD E. (clīve)   1884—June 6, 1940   British stage and screen star; noted for his portrayal of butler parts; on Boston stage for 14 years: appeared in 1,159 legitimate plays before going into motion pictures

References
International   Motion   Picture   Almanac

Obituaries
N Y Herald Tribune p18 Je 7 '40 por
N Y Times p23 Je 7 '40 por

COCHRAN, CHARLES BLAKE (kŏk' răn) Sept 25, 1872- British impresario
Address: 49 Old Bond St, W. 1, London, England

CHARLES B. COCHRAN

When in September 1940 the British Broadcasting Corporation gave C. B. Cochran a *Cochran Hour* every Saturday evening from eight to nine, a good many Britishers thought: "And high time, too." More than once it has been suggested that Cochran would be an ideal choice for director general of British broadcasting. Certainly, if entertainment is considered the major function of radio, it would be hard to think of anyone with qualifications for that position as impressive as his.

In the last 40 years Cochran has produced some of the most spectacular and successful shows the British stage has ever seen. And his activities have by no means been limited to the stage. Any kind of entertainment that might be popular and profitable has appealed to him—he was chiefly responsible for the craze for roller skating just before the last War; he has organized circuses and rodeos; he has acted as manager to Suzanne Lenglen; he has promoted big boxing and wrestling matches; his "young ladies" (as the chorus is always known) are always famous for their beauty and charm; and he has made and lost several fortunes.

Though Cochran's name and origins are Irish, he was born in the English village of Lindfield in Sussex, the son of James Elphinstone and Matilda (Walton) Cochran. He was one of a family of 10 children. The first play he ever saw was the pantomime, *Sinbad the Sailor*, with Arthur Roberts as the chief comedian. Immediately young Cochran decided that he, too, would be a comedian. Of course he had to go to school first. From his first school, at Eastbourne, he was expelled because of disorderly behavior. His second was Brighton Grammar School, where he shared a study with the later famous Aubrey Beardsley.

Cochran left school when he was 16 and went into a surveyor's office. But he still wanted to get on the stage, and kept trying. In August 1890 he succeeded. He was supposed to sing comic songs, but the whole venture, as he says in his book *Secrets of a Showman* (1925), "was a complete failure. My turn finished with the first song and the manager refused to pay me."

The end of that same year he arrived in the United States as a steerage passenger and for two years beat up and down the country with touring companies, making little money and scoring no success at all. One small-town critic in Pennsylvania wrote of him: "A more ridiculous chump has never been seen on the local stage." Richard Mansfield, whom he met in America, quite agreed that Cochran was no actor, but he liked him, thought he had business sense and made him his secretary. The two men quarreled in 1895 and Cochran went to New York, where he set up an academy of acting with E. J. Henly. That same year he put on Ibsen's *John Gabriel Borkman,* his first try at production. Two years later he returned to London.

Cochran's acquaintance with the Beardsley family procured him introductions to prominent people in the *Yellow Book* group such as Sir William Rothenstein, Sir Max Beerbohm and Ernest Dowson, but his ambitions never turned to literature. Despite poverty and failure, Cochran was determined on the theatre for his career. In Paris he saw a performance of *Cyrano de Bergerac.* Immediately he cabled Mansfield and, their quarrel settled, Mansfield put on the play in New York with Cochran once more his secretary. The play was a tremendous success; people lined up hours in advance to get seats; there were fights among them and one man was shot, another stabbed.

Back in England again, Cochran set up in business as a theatrical agent and in time represented most of the world's famous players—Eleanora Duse, Houdini, Elisabeth Bergner, Mistinguett. The light play he put on in 1902, *Sporting Simpson,* failed, but that failure was more than compensated for by the success of his management of the famous wrestler, Georges Hackenschmidt, with whom he arranged a bout with Madrali, known as "the Terrible Turk." He then started a "Fun City" with sideshows, and before the First World War put on his biggest project, *The Miracle*, which was produced on Christmas Eve, 1911 with a chorus of 500, an orchestra of 200 and in the Madonna's part the celebrated beauty, Lady Diana Manners. Cochran ran a big circus in 1912 and in June 1914 turned his attention to boxing.

During the First World War the public craved light entertainment and Cochran had his chance to introduce the French idea of the *revue*. His first one, *Odds and Ends*, ran for 500 performances and was followed by Irving Berlin's *Watch Your Step* and many others. Then, after "going serious" with the two Brieux plays, *Damaged Goods* and *The Three Daughters*, in 1917 Cochran produced *The Better 'Ole*, a comedy which at first looked like a flop but in the end ran to 817 performances. The next year Cochran had another enormous success with *As You Were*.

In 1919 Cochran took over the Garrick and Aldwych Theatres and promoted many important boxing matches at the Holborn Stadium, including Billy Wells versus Joe Beckett and Joe Beckett versus Georges Carpentier. But his career was halted by illness and a long period of recuperation in Spain. When Cochran returned to London he brought a band of Russian entertainers known as *Chauve-Souris*, run by Nikita Balieff. Then he did a season for Lucien Guitry, staged a return for the 63-year-old Duse and proceeded to burn his fingers financially over a rodeo which he put on at Wembley. An accident the first night and a good deal of journalistic censure persuaded the British public that the animals were being cruelly treated, and the rodeo fell flat. It was in that same year (1924) that everything seemed to go flat and Cochran was forced into bankruptcy.

He emerged from it with a Pirandello season in 1925. In 1927 he acted as manager for the singer Chaliapin; in 1929 he produced Sean O'Casey's *The Silver Tassie*; and in 1931 he shared Noel Coward's great success in *Cavalcade*. Before then and afterwards Noel Coward wrote much for him, and the collaboration was fruitful for both. In 1932 Cochran's second book, *I Had Almost Forgotten*, was published.

To follow through all the productions of Cochran, who at one time has had as many as seven plays running simultaneously, would be to present a history of the lighter stage in England during his time. In Cochran's history there have been ups and downs but the general impression is one of sheer business ability, plus a grand sense of scale, a feeling for the spectacular and a great deal of real taste. A genial, friendly man, Cochran is well-liked by his employees and all who do business with him. He is married to Evelyn Alice Dade and has no children.

References

Bridges, T. C. and Tiltman, H. H. Charles Cochran *In* Kings of Commerce p33-46 1928
Cleugh, J. Charles B. Cochran 1938
Cochran, C. B. I Had Almost Forgotten 1932
Cochran, C. B. Secrets of a Showman 1930
Who's Who
Who's Who in Commerce and Industry
Who's Who in the Theatre

COCHRAN, JACQUELINE (kŏk'răn)
Aviatrix; cosmetician
Address: b. 630 Fifth Ave, New York City; h. Stamford, Connecticut

Jacqueline Cochran has been piling up aviation honors steadily since 1937 and now holds 17 official national, international and cross-country records. She added the two latest records to her list in April 1940 when she won a new national speed record for 100 kilometers with an official mark of 292.6 miles an hour, and set a new speed mark for the 2,000 kilometer distance by flying 331 miles an hour.

To win she had to fly these distances faster than any man or woman alive. In endurance, in stamina, in flying ability she is the match of male aviators and she has wrested many aviation trophies from men. She won the Bendix Transcontinental Race, crack event of the National Air Races, in 1938 over nine male contestants.

But she is extremely feminine in one respect—she won't tell her age. To interviewers she talks frankly of everything else but her personal life. She is voluble on the subject of flying, on her cosmetic business, on everything but dates and ages. Except for the date of her marriage to Floyd B. Odlum on May 10, 1936, biographical sketches of her are vague as to dates.

Jacqueline Cochran's life sounds like a story book. "That's why I don't like to talk about it," she says. "People think I'm plagiarizing on the story books." Born in Pensacola, Florida, she was orphaned at four and reared by a family in Columbus, Georgia. She started helping to earn her way when she was 11 years old by making $1.50 a week and her room and board running errands for a beauty parlor. She made herself so useful that at 13 she was doing the work of a full-fledged operator. From that time on she has stood on her own feet. She had a beauty shop of her own at 19.

JACQUELINE COCHRAN

She was working in a beauty salon on Fifth Avenue in New York when she became seriously interested in flying. "I loved flying," she says, "but I thought of it primarily as a sport." She soon realized, however, that it was rather an expensive sport and looked about for some way to combine it with business. She conceived the idea of approaching several cosmetic companies, which had urged her to go on the road to sell their products, with a plan for using an airplane. By using a plane, the bright young beauty operator reasoned, she could cover more territory, sell more cosmetics and get added publicity.

Being a woman of determination, Jacqueline Cochran put her plan into action. In August 1932 she presented herself at Roosevelt Field, Long Island and announced, "I'm starting on a six weeks' vacation and I want to spend it learning to fly. Do you think I can learn enough in those six weeks to get my pilot's license?" She learned enough in two and one-half weeks to pass the Department of Commerce examination.

Although she now had a license to fly, she realized how little she actually knew about it and decided to make herself a competent pilot. She took her savings and went to California for a year's intensive training. There Lieutenant Theodore C. Marshall gave her the equivalent of the regular navy course of instruction in groundwork and flying. By the end of that time she had obtained a limited commercial license in San Diego, California, and later a transport license.

Miss Cochran was then a full-fledged pilot. She also took a course in blind flying from Wesley Smith, rated the best in his field. She was the first woman to conquer the problems of blind flying.

Miss Cochran's first important competition was the London to Melbourne Air Race in 1934, which she entered under the sponsorship of Mabel Walker Willebrandt, former assistant attorney general of the United States. She and Wesley Smith took off on the race to Australia with 19 other planes. Their original plane had been damaged in transit and they were using a much smaller plane than they had planned. In Bucharest they were forced down and decided not to continue.

This was the beginning of three years of flying mishaps for Jacqueline Cochran. She was forced out by trouble of one kind or another and failed to place in her next four races. In 1935 she entered the Bendix Transcontinental Race and was forced down at Kingman, Arizona. She explained she was tired and decided to quit before anything happened. The next year, while preparing for another event, her plane caught fire near Indianapolis when she was 12,000 feet up. She brought the plane down in one piece.

Miss Cochran did not make excuses for her failures to place, but men pilots said she was flying planes of experimental design and construction.

The year 1937 marked the beginning of a long string of aviation successes for her. She came in third in the Bendix Transcontinental Air Race that year, placing first in the women's division. The same year she set a new world's record for women over a three kilometer course at Detroit, flying a Seversky pursuit plane an average of 293 miles an hour, 17 miles an hour faster than the former record.

Other records followed in rapid succession. She set a new non-stop record from New York to Miami, covering the distance in four hours and twelve minutes; she set national women's speed records for 100 and 1,000 kilometers.

In 1938 she put herself at the top of the nation's list of aviators when she came in first in the Bendix Air Derby in competition with nine men fliers. The course from Los Angeles to Cleveland was flown in particularly bad weather. Pilots who landed complained bitterly of the "dirty weather." Miss Cochran emerged after her time-clocked trip of eight hours, ten minutes and thirty-one seconds, casually, with no weather complaint. She merely said, "Yes, it was bad weather," in answer to questions. She had been smoking an oxygen pipe all the way across the country, and all she wanted was a cigarette and to talk to her husband when she landed.

After 15 minutes at the field she took off again for Bendix, New Jersey to become the holder of a new transcontinental record for women. She made the cross-country trip in 10 hours and 12 minutes. That evening she flew back to Cleveland in a transport plane for the air race ball. The day's work had netted her $12,500—$9,000 for the Bendix race; $2,500 for being the first woman to finish and $1,000 more for continuing to Bendix, New Jersey.

The first lady of the air lanes has received the highest aviation awards given to her sex. She received the Harmon Trophy four years in succession as the outstanding woman flier of 1937, 1938, 1939 and 1940. She was selected by *American Women* as one of the ten outstanding women of 1938. She received the William E. Mitchell Award for achievement in aeronautics, was cited along with Howard Hughes by the International League of Aviators for accomplishment in aviation in the United States. Mayor La Guardia (see sketch this issue) in May 1940 presented her with the William J. McGough Memorial Trophy in behalf of the American Legion Post 501.

Miss Cochran's apartment overlooking the East River in New York is full of mementos of her successful aviation career. But she does not confine her activities to flying. She has several beauty salons and a cosmetic business which she directs. She has a ranch in Indio, California. And she and her husband have a home in Stamford, Connecticut.

Fair-haired, attractive and affable, Miss Cochran is a young woman who does a man's job of flying without looking the least bit masculine. Oddly enough she doesn't think women should pilot transport planes. "It's too big a strain," she says, "and too monotonous day after day." Women, she believes, would make excellent instructors in radio and blind flying, and would be good radio operators because they are patient.

References

N Y Times VII p8 S 25 '38; II p5 My 12 '40 por

Newsweek 12:39 S 12 '38 por

American Women

Blue Book of American Aviation

COLE, JESSIE DUNCAN SAVAGE 1858—Oct 27, 1940 Portrait and landscape painter; works exhibited at Society of American Artists, National Academy of Design and many other galleries; assisted John La Farge in stained glass work and murals and executed murals for Harvard University and several famous American churches and homes

Obituaries

N Y Herald Tribune p10 O 28 '40

N Y Times p17 O 28 '40

COLEMAN, GEORGIA 1912—Sept 14, 1940 Once acclaimed as the world's greatest diver; winner of the Olympic championship in 1932; won second place in the Olympics of 1928 when she was 16 years old; took many important diving titles in the succeeding years until 1937, when she was stricken with an attack of infantile paralysis; made a remarkable recovery and learned to swim all over again

References

Am Mag 115:35 My '33

Obituaries

N Y Herald Tribune p42 S 15 '40 por

Newsweek 16:59 S 23 '40 por

COLLINS, EDDIE Jan 30, 1884—Sept 1, 1940 Screen comedian; was inspiration for the dwarf character Dopey in the Disney motion picture, *Snow White and the Seven Dwarfs*; played the rôle of Jiggs in the original stage production of *Bringing Up Father*; played in burlesque before becoming featured comedian in films; appeared in such films as *Young Mr. Lincoln, Drums Along the Mohawk* and *The Blue Bird*; passed the bar examination in Indiana but never practiced law

EDDIE COLLINS

References

International Motion Picture Almanac

Obituaries

N Y Herald Tribune p22 S 4 '40 por

N Y Times p23 S 4 '40 por

COLLINS, EDWARD DAY Dec 17, 1869 —Jan 1, 1940 Former acting president of Middlebury College

Dr. Collins, who died at the age of 71, was the adopted son of I. D. R. and Mary E. (Tenney) Collins. He received his B. A. and his Ph. D. from Yale (1896 and 1899) and taught history at Yale. From 1905 to 1909 he was principal of the State Normal School at Johnson, Vermont; then he became professor of pedagogy at Middlebury College. He has been Middlebury's acting president, provost and controller. He was known chiefly for the creation and administration of the summer session language

COLLINS, EDWARD DAY—*Continued*
schools at the college. After retirement in 1925 he directed the Ecole Champlain, a French camp for girls, in Ferrisburg, Vermont. Surviving are his wife, Mrs. Ruth Mary (Colby) Collins, a son and two daughters.

EDWARD DAY COLLINS

References
Who's Who in America
Obituaries
N Y Herald Tribune Ja 2 '40

COLLINS, GEORGE LEWIS Feb 19, 1874—June 16, 1940 Retired medical direc-

U. S. P. H. S.
GEORGE LEWIS COLLINS

tor in the United States Public Health Service; specialized in eye, ear, nose and throat surgery; worked to eradicate trachoma in the Southern states

References
Who's Who in American Medicine
Who's Who in the East

Obituaries
N Y Herald Tribune p18 Je 18 '40
N Y Times p23 Je 18 '40

COLLINS, LORIN CONE Aug 1, 1848 —Oct 18, 1940 Judge and lawyer; member of Illinois House of Representatives from 1879 to 1884 and Speaker in 1883; circuit judge from 1884 to 1893, when he resigned to practice law in firm of which Clarence Darrow was member; appointed Associate Justice of the Supreme Court of the Canal Zone in 1905 and served a six-year term, after which he practiced law in New Mexico; returned to Chicago in 1922 and practiced in special cases

References
Collins, L. C. Autobiography 1934
Who's Who in America 1938-39
Who's Who in Law
Obituaries
N Y Times p50 O 20 '40

COLQUITT, OSCAR BRANCH (col' quit) Dec 16, 1861—Mar 8, 1940 Governor of Texas 1911 to 1915; member United States Board of Mediation 1929

References
Who's Who in America
Obituaries
N Y Herald Tribune p10 Mr 9 '40
N Y Times p15 Mr 9 '40

COMPANYS, LUIS 1873—Reported dead Oct 1940 Former president of Catalonian Spain; leader of Catalan *Esquerra*; journalist; lawyer of Syndicalists; prominent for 25 years in Republican and Catalan Independence movement; became President of Catalonia in 1936; in 1940 discovered in Nantes, France by the German Gestapo; reported executed in Spain on orders from Franco

References
Lit Digest 121:16 Mr 7 '36 por
Time 29:26 My 17 '37 por
International Who's Who

Obituaries
N Y Herald Tribune O 17 '40
N Y Times O 18 '40

COMPTON, ARTHUR HOLLY Sept 10, 1892- Physicist
On May 15, 1940 Dr. Arthur H. Compton received the Franklin Medal awarded to

workers in physical science or technology whose efforts have done most "to advance the knowledge of physical science or its application." This is just one of the many awards Dr. Compton has received. The American Academy of Arts and Sciences gave him the Rumford Gold Medal in 1927; he received the Nobel Prize in physics in that same year; the Radiological Society, the Italian Academy of Sciences and learned societies all over the world have honored him.

Dr. Compton's main work, like that of Robert Millikan (see sketch this issue), has been to discover the secret of cosmic rays. He started this work in 1931 and since then has roamed the world climbing mountains, descending to the sea, tracking the Arctic wastes and the equator, seeking knowledge of the invisible, powerful rain of cosmic radiation that pours upon the earth from space. In 1932, with funds from the Carnegie Corporation of New York, he organized an elaborate world-wide cooperative enterprise for the collection of cosmic ray data. The earth was divided into several regions for this enterprise, and eight associated expeditions within eight zones of cosmic ray research, equipped with a new electroscope that Compton had invented, made findings and reported them to him.

When his conclusions were made public at a meeting of the American Association for the Advancement of Science in 1932, it was found that his conclusions and Millikan's differed. Compton said cosmic rays were mostly electric particles while Millikan held that they were mostly photons (electrically inert bundles of radiation). It wasn't until January 1936 that Compton presented a résumé of his researches which was considered a victory for his conclusions.

Compton's most recent feat in his prolonged attempt to wrest the secret of the cosmic ray from nature was a high altitude flight to photograph the ray. In a big air liner flying above 29,000 feet, Dr. Compton and his assistants took 400 pictures under what were described as "ideal conditions," and Compton believes that these photographs will "materially assist" in unlocking the mystery of cosmic rays and their importance to man.

It was for his work on X rays that Dr. Compton received the Nobel Prize. With an apparatus "so sensitive it measured one ten-millionth of the energy of a mosquito climbing an inch of screen," he brought forth the "Compton Effect," which showed that X rays, through radiation, act like solid particles when scattered by reflection from atoms.

Arthur Compton was born at Wooster, Ohio on September 10, 1892, into a family whose every member has made his mark. His father, Elias Compton, is a Ph. D. and a D. D., a Presbyterian clergyman and long-time professor of philosophy and psychology at the College of Wooster. His mother, Otelia (Augspurger) Compton, received an

Acme

ARTHUR HOLLY COMPTON

LL. D in 1932 from Western College at Oxford, Ohio "for outstanding achievement as a wife and mother." Arthur's oldest brother Karl has been president of the Massachusetts Institute of Technology since 1930 and is also a famous physicist; his sister, Mary (Compton) Rice, is the wife of the president of a missionary college in India and heads her own missionary school; his brother Wilson is a lawyer, manager of the National Lumber Manufacturers' Association, economics adviser to the Department of Commerce and a professor of economics at George Washington University. All three Compton sons were graduated with Phi Beta Kappa keys from Wooster College, all received Ph. D.'s from Princeton and all are listed in Who's Who in America. Mrs. Compton says she trained her children "on the Bible and common sense."

Arthur Compton showed a scientific bent early, and his family encouraged him. There was the time when eight-year-old Arthur showed his mother an essay he had written. "Here is what I think about this elephant question," he declared. "I have gone through a lot of books. They all say that African elephants have three toes and Indian elephants five toes. I believe this wrong. I say African elephants have five toes and Indian elephants have three toes and this," he concluded, pushing the papers in front of her, "is why I think so." Mrs. Compton looked gravely at the essay and congratulated Arthur on having gone into the matter so thoroughly. Thirty years later she asked him whether he remembered it. "Yes," he replied grinning, "and mother, if you had laughed at me then it would have finished my urge for research."

COMPTON, ARTHUR HOLLY—*Cont.*

In his teens Arthur built a glider that actually flew, published articles on aeronautics, made an astronomical clock for a telescope and took pictures of Halley's Comet. He went to Wooster College in 1909, and while there invented a patented gyroscopic device for airplane control. By then he had decided that he was going to become a mechanical engineer, but Karl, five years older, steered him away from engineering by interesting him in advanced mathematics and physics.

In 1916 Arthur Compton received his Ph. D. in physics from Princeton University, *summa cum laude,* and right after graduation married Betty Charity McCloskey of New Waterford, Ohio. With his wife he went to the University of Minnesota to teach physics, but after only a year there left to enter industry. For two years he worked in the Pittsburgh laboratory of the Westinghouse Electric Company, where he was engaged in the development of electric light lamps. Then he said to his wife: "Betty, I'm going back to university work."

He got a research fellowship in the Cavendish Laboratory at Cambridge under Thomson and Rutherford, and it was this year's research which led him to make fundamental discoveries in the field of light. He returned to America in 1920 to become professor and eventually head of the physics department at Washington University, St. Louis. Since 1923 Dr. Compton has been a professor at the University of Chicago. For the past years he has been teaching one class a day, at 8:00 a. m., after which he works in his office, "which has a black steel desk, cream walls, tan curtains, gray rug, a cosmic-ray counter clicking away in a corner; or in the laboratories just outside where he has $50,000 worth of equipment for his own researches."

Dr. Compton is a leading spokesman for those who see no conflict between religion and science. In 1935 he expounded his views in *Freedom of Men,* in which he showed how the newer discoveries of atomic physics lend support to the ancient basic ideas of religion. For years he taught Sunday School at the Hyde Park Community Baptist Church of which, though a Presbyterian, he was deacon, and in 1937 he was elected general chairman of the Laymen's Missionary Movement; in 1938 he was made co-chairman of the Conference of Jews and Christians. To Compton "science can have no quarrel with a religion which postulates a God to whom men are as his children." To him "science is the glimpse of God's purpose in nature, and the very existence of the amazing world of the atom and radiation points to a purposeful creation, to the idea that there is a God and an intelligent purpose back of everything."

With his wife and two sons Dr. Compton lives in Chicago in a big brick house filled with souvenirs from all over the world. He doesn't know the taste of hard liquor and almost never smokes. "A tall, rugged man with deep-set eyes and a heavy chin," he plays a fast game of tennis, swims powerfully and strokes a canoe manfully. Several times a month he puts in an evening of mandolin-playing with three friends. When his graduate students have finished an examination, he likes to take them out to dinner and the theatre.

References

Fortune 16:145 D '37 por
Lit Digest 120:15 N 9 '35 il por
Newsweek 3:32 Ja 6 '34 por; 12:23 D 12 '38; 15:4 Ap 29 '40
Sci Mo 51:185-9 Ag '40 il
Time 27:28+ Ja 13 '36 pors; 32:20 Jl 11 '38 por; 34:37 N 20 '39 por
American Men of Science
America's Young Men
Hylander, C. J. Arthur H. Compton *In* American Scientists p160-3 1935
Jaffe, B. Radiation *In* Outposts of Science p369-416 1935
Who's Who in America

CONLEY, WILLIAM GUSTAVUS Jan 8, 1866—Oct 21, 1940 Former Republican Governor of West Virginia; taught in public schools before admitted to Bar; attorney general of West Virginia from 1908 to 1913; from 1924 to 1929 was vice-chairman of the State Board of Education and served as Governor from 1929 to 1933; member of many law associations

Obituaries

N Y Herald Tribune p24 O 22 '40 por
N Y Times p23 O 22 '40

CONNOLLY, WALTER Apr 8, 1887— May 28, 1940 Stage and screen actor;

WALTER CONNOLLY

joined films in 1932; generally regarded by critics as a character actor of the first rank; toured with Sothern and Marlowe from 1911 to 1914

References

Lit Digest 119:19+ Mr 23 '35 por
American Catholic Who's Who
International Motion Picture Almanac
Who's Who in the Theatre

Obituaries

N Y Herald Tribune p18 My 29 '40 por
N Y Times p23 My 29 '40 por
Newsweek 15:6 Je 10 '40 por

CONVERSE, FREDERICK SHEPHERD
Jan 5, 1871—June 8, 1940 Composer; former dean of the New England Conservatory of Music and former professor of music at Harvard University; composer of *The Pipe of Desire,* the first American opera ever presented at the Metropolitan Opera House in New York; composed five symphonies, several tone poems, a cantata, several operas, chamber music for various combinations of instruments, songs and piano pieces

Musical America
FREDERICK SHEPHERD CONVERSE

References

Etude 56:2 Ja '38 por
Ewen, D. ed. Composers of Today 1936
International Who's Who
Scholes, P. A. Oxford Companion to Music 1938
Thompson, O. ed. International Cyclopedia of Music and Musicians 1939

Who's Who in America

Obituaries

Musical Am 60:16+ Je '40 por
N Y Times p44 Je 9 '40

COOK, FREDERICK ALBERT 1865— Aug 5, 1940 Explorer in both the Arctic and Antarctic; laid claim to discovery of the North Pole, later disputed by Peary and many scientists; given a sensational welcome in the United States; claim caused a nationwide controversy; practiced medicine; accompanied Amundsen and Peary; sought credit for climbing Mount McKinley which was later discredited; government convicted him in an oil stock scheme; spent 7 years in prison; granted a pardon by President Roosevelt

Wide World
FREDERICK A. COOK

References

Read Digest 35:79-83 Ag '39
Time 27:8+ Ap 13 '36; 34:34+ D 4 '39 por
Greene, L. comp. Peary and Doctor Cook *In* America Goes to Press p343-5 1936

Obituaries

N Y Herald Tribune p15 Ag 5 '40 pors
N Y Times p19 Ag 6 '40 por
Time 36:62 Ag 12 '40

COOLIDGE, DANE Mar 24, 1873—Aug 8, 1940 Author; internationally known naturalist; expert on Indian and cowboy lore; third cousin of Calvin Coolidge; was author of about 40 novels of Western life, praised for their authenticity; many of his novels were used in motion pictures

(Continued next page)

DANE COOLIDGE

References

> Who's Who Among North American
> Authors
> Who's Who in America

Obituaries

> N Y Herald Tribune p8 Ag 9 '40
> N Y Times p15 Ag 9 '40 por
> Pub W 138:477 Ag 17 '40
> Time 36:48 Ag 19 '40

COOPER, ALFRED DUFF Feb 22, 1890-
British statesman; Minister of Information
Address: 90 Gower St, London, S. W. 1, Eng-
land

When, on a day of glorious May weather
in 1940, the British public heard that German mechanized units had forced their way
between the French and British Armies to
Boulogne and Abbeville, there was not a
man or woman in the country who underestimated the gravity of the news; not one
but felt that war had come to his very
doorstep.

That evening there came a calm, cultivated but not complacent voice on the
radio, making no attempt to gloss over
the danger, but quoting the familiar *Henry
V* lines about St. Crispin's day, deprecating
not only panic itself but the very thought
of panic. This was not Mr. Churchill (see
sketch this issue), with his "blood and toil
and sweat and tears." This voice was like
a steadying hand on the shoulder; no one
who heard it could have failed to be
heartened by it. It was the voice of Alfred
Duff Cooper, on May 12, 1940 appointed
to the Ministry of Information. Most of
the listeners knew that the speaker was
himself a soldier of the last War, with a
very gallant record. And many of them

must have felt that here was the man who
had all along mistrusted Hitler—and had
been proved right.

Alfred Duff Cooper is the complete temperamental Tory, not necessarily because
he is the nephew of one duke and married
to the daughter of another, but because he
sees in Toryism an ideal, a system tending
to the preservation of old and tried things
that he esteems worthy of survival. The
whole of his career (except his incursions
into the columns of a popular evening
paper) has been on strictly upper-class
lines—Eton, Oxford, the Foreign Office,
the Brigade of Guards, the War Office, the
Admiralty. It would have been strange
indeed if a man with such antecedents
should have political views other than those
he possesses.

At one time the very strength and purity
of his convictions almost brought his political career to an end, for Cooper's attitude
over the Munich settlement and his consistent opposition to any suggestion of
"appeasement" caused him to be bracketed
by Hitler with Mr. Churchill and Mr. Eden
(see sketch this issue) as one of the principal "warmongers."

Born in 1890, he is the only son of the
late Sir Alfred Cooper, Fellow of the Royal
College of Surgeons, and Lady Agnes Duff,
sister of the first Duke of Fife. He went
to Eton, and thence to New College, Oxford, where he took honors in modern
history. He then passed into the Foreign
Office, but at the outbreak of the last War
he transferred to the Grenadier Guards,
served with great distinction in France for
four years and returned with the Distinguished Service Order Award. In 1919
he married Lady Diana Manners, daughter
of the eighth Duke of Rutland, a celebrated
beauty and an actress of some distinction,
who had played, among other parts, that
of the Madonna in *The Miracle* in the
United States.

In 1924 Cooper entered Parliament as one
of the two Members for Oldham, Lancashire.
His maiden speech showed assurance and
high competence, and he began to be noticed as a "back-bencher." In 1928 Mr.
Baldwin made him financial secretary to
the War Office; but this did not last long,
for in the following year occurred Labor's
first big set of gains, and it was hardly to
be expected that a Tory should be able to
hold an industrial constituency like Oldham.

Cooper's name was put down as prospective candidate for Winchester, but he was
soon to return to the House for a safe
London constituency after an election notable for its acrimony. At this time Lords
Beaverbrook (see sketch this issue) and
Rothermere, who between them control
most of the popular Conservative Press,
were attacking Mr. Baldwin; and when a
by-election occurred in the division of St.
George's, Westminster, Lord Beaverbrook
decided to run an unofficial Conservative
candidate, a certain Sir Ernest Petter.

Baldwin picked on Cooper as official party candidate, and the brickbats began to fly.

Cooper exchanged slang for slang, accused Beaverbrook of not having "the guts of a louse," and eventually topped the poll with a majority of nearly 6,000. This was in 1931; and in the general election of the same year he was returned unopposed. He returned to his financial secretaryship at the War Office, and since the Secretary of State (Lord Hailsham) was in the Lords it fell to him to present the army estimates to Parliament three times. This he did with astonishing aplomb and grasp of minute detail and without consulting any notes.

During the session of 1934 to 1935 Cooper was financial secretary to the Treasury; and in the 1935 election he won his seat by a huge majority against a Labor candidate. From 1935 to 1937 he held his first Ministerial post as Secretary of State for War. Signor Mussolini's Abyssinian adventure was on at the time, and Cooper neither minced words about it nor about the lowering dangers of the European situation in general. He was often denounced as a panic-monger by those who hoped against hope to find some *modus vivendi* with the dictators.

Mr. Chamberlain transferred Cooper to the Admiralty, where he served as First Lord for about 18 months, until the Munich settlement of September 1938 caused his resignation. He placed no faith whatever in any promises from Hitler and felt that the peace then bought at great cost to Czechoslovakia could be no more than a brief respite. His "personal explanation" to the House was telling and dignified, and it was obvious that it pained him to be a prophet of doom at a time of general rejoicing.

It is a curious example of time's revenges that Cooper should then become the weekly political oracle of the London *Evening Standard,* which is the chief evening organ of the Beaverbrook Press (though his lordship's son, Max Aitken, is now in control). Cooper's weekly articles maintained his intransigent attitude toward the dictatorships and keenly emphasized the need for rapid rearmament and preparedness for the test of war.

It was hardly to be expected that Mr. Chamberlain should invite his collaboration; but he was taken into the Ministry of Mr. Churchill early in May to control Information. This Ministry has been severely criticized since the War began, and with good reason, for the paucity and slowness of its news releases and its comparative feebleness in counteracting German propaganda abroad. "It has been seriously supposed in some neutral countries, for instance, that there is a food shortage in Great Britain, whereas the truth is that there is plenty of everything, even of the three or four commodities that are rationed." Cooper's task is to scotch these falsehoods, to put the Allied case plainly and forcibly,

Acme

ALFRED DUFF COOPER

and to see that British journalists get every scrap of news (other than news likely to help the enemy) quickly and easily: It was felt that as a journalist himself and as the brilliant biographer of *Talleyrand* (1932) and *Earl Haig* (1935-36) he should be able to talk to writing men in their own language; while as a former serving officer and Services Minister he should have a precise appreciation of what information it is unsafe to make public.

He started out with a series of pungent radio addresses which were enthusiastically received. It wasn't long, however, before to some he seemed to have slipped up when he organized a "Silent Column" to suppress defeatist talk and hired canvasers to conduct house-to-house interviews asking Britons how they felt about the War. Immediately these interviewers became "Cooper's Snoopers," and there was strong criticism in Parliament of both schemes. Cooper was forced to abandon them and has been concentrating on getting out stories on the War, on British resistance, on British power.

Cooper's record shows that he has always been a fighter and never a man prepared to trim his sails according to the prevailing wind. He speaks with assurance (a shade too much at times), and his style is combative and forthright. Agree with him or not, at least there is no doubt about where he stands. He was in the United States early in 1940 and returned to England in March after lecturing in 60 of the larger American cities.

References
Illustration 194:385-6 Jl 25 '36
Nat R 111:665-75 N '38
Newsweek 16:22 S 2 '40
Picture Post 7:16-7 Je 1 '40
Sat R Lit 141:183-4 F 13 '26

COOPER, ALFRED DUFF—*Continued*

Strand Mag Jl '40
Time 35:29 My 6 '40 por

Audax, pseud. Duff Cooper *In* Men in Our Time p158-80 1940
Cooper, A. D. Second World War 1939
Nichols, B. Are They the Same at Home? *In* Oxford—London—Hollywood 1931
Watchman, pseud. Right Honourable Gentlemen 1939
Who's Who

COOPER, COURTNEY RYLEY Oct 31, 1886—Sept 29, 1940 Author; former circus publicity agent and newspaperman; committed suicide in New York City; at 16 ran away from home to become a clown in a circus; later worked on the Kansas City *Star,* New York *World* and Chicago *Tribune;* became press agent for Sells-Floto Circus, and later with Ringling Brothers and Barnum & Bailey; began contributing to magazines in 1912; wrote some 500 stories and articles on circus and animal life; also wrote novels on crime and scenarios of many motion pictures

Woods

COURTNEY RYLEY COOPER

References

Read Digest 37:31-4 Jl '40

Overton, G. M. Coming!—Courtney Ryley Cooper—Coming! *In* Cargoes for Crusoes p290-303 1924
Who's Who in America

Obituaries

N Y Times p36 S 30 '40 por
Time 36:57 O 7 '40

COPLAND, AARON (cōp'land) Nov 14, 1900- Composer
Address: c/o Whittlesey House, 330 W 42nd St, New York City

Aaron Copland, once considered one of the least understandable of American musicians, is now writing music for the people. His *Billy the Kid* and *The Second Hurricane,* his scores for *The City, Of Mice and Men, Our Town* and other motion pictures have made him almost universally recognized as "probably the most generously gifted composer among living Americans." They have made his name known to many.

All his life Aaron Copland has been striving to make his own works and those of his contemporaries familiar to the general public. The Copland-Sessions Concerts, which functioned from 1928 to 1931, presented largely unheard music to the public; festivals of American music were organized by Copland at Yaddo in Saratoga Springs, New York; in 1935 an educational campaign for modern American music was started, at which the works of the five most important younger composers—Roy Harris, Virgil Thomson (see sketches this issue), Roger Sessions, Walter Piston and Aaron Copland—were presented; and in May 1940 Copland was elected the first head of the American Composers' Alliance, which aims to encourage the performance of serious American compositions and to provide means for obtaining just compensation to the composer for performances. As a writer of articles for magazines and the author of *What to Listen for in Music* (1939), as a lecturer at Harvard and the New School for Social Research, New York City, he has been "a tremendous force in bringing further recognition and a maturer understanding to the new music of modern composers everywhere." But it is only now, when he is consciously striving for simplicity, that Aaron Copland has achieved for his own works the broad audience he has come to believe modern composers should have.

Aaron Copland was born in Brooklyn on November 14, 1900 "on a street which can only be described as drab." He was the youngest son of Sarah (Mittenthal) Copland and Harris Morris Copland, a Brooklyn storekeeper who thought his name was Kaplan until an immigration official wrote it to suit his own ears. "No one had ever connected music with my family," says Copland. "The idea was entirely original with me. And unfortunately the idea occurred to me seriously only at 13 or thereabouts—which is rather late for a musician to get started."

The idea of being a composer, he says, "seems gradually to have dawned on me some time around 1916 when I was about 15 years old." Before then Aaron had taken the usual piano lessons and had tried to learn harmony from a correspondence course. When he found that these methods wouldn't work, he began harmony lessons in the fall of 1917 with Rubin Goldmark. By the spring of 1918 he had been graduated from high school and was able to devote all his energies to music.

Rubin Goldmark was a conservative teacher and it wasn't from him, certainly, that Copland learned about modern music. He says that he just "happened upon it in the natural course of my musical explorations." Goldmark disapproved strenuously, and the climax came when Copland brought him a piano composition of his own called *The Cat and the Mouse.*

Copland was becoming a bit discouraged, when he read in a musical journal of a summer school in the Palace at Fontainebleau. He was the first American student enrolled. In 1921 he went there and was taught by Paul Vidal, who "turned out to be a French version of Rubin Goldmark except that he was harder to understand." Then, after he had got over the mental hurdle of being taught by a woman, he began to study with Nadia Boulanger. For three years he stayed in Paris. "It was a fortunate time to be studying music in France," he says. "Paris was an international proving ground for all the newest tendencies in music. . . It was a rarely stimulating atmosphere in which to carry on one's studies." During these years he composed several *Motets* for unaccompanied voices, a *Passacaglia* for piano, a song for soprano with flute and clarinet accompaniment, a *Rondino* for string quartet and a one-act ballet called *Grohg,* his first essay in the orchestral field.

With these pieces under his arm Copland returned to America in June 1924, without the slightest idea of how composers managed to get their compositions performed or published and without the slightest idea of how he was going to earn his living. The first thing he did in America was to write a symphony for organ and orchestra which Nadia Boulanger had asked him to furnish for her coming performances with the New York Symphony and the Boston Symphony. He wrote it while he was pianist for a hotel trio in Milford, Pennsylvania.

The first American performance of Copland's works was in November 1924 by the League of Composers. In the following January, Damrosch, with Boulanger as soloist, presented the symphony for organ and orchestra. After the performance Dr. Damrosch turned and addressed the audience: "If a young man at the age of twenty-three can write a symphony like that, in five years he will be ready to commit murder." Koussevitzky (see sketch this issue), however, liked the symphony and encouraged Copland.

The young composer's main concern was still how to earn a living. He opened a piano studio in New York, but not one pupil came. Then, in 1925 and 1926, his problem was settled by the grant of two Guggenheim Fellowships. He was free to write. He wanted to write in the American idiom. *Music for the Theatre*—"music of such sparkle, intoxicating freshness and contagious vigor that it clearly proved the fact that a new, significant

AARON COPLAND

voice had now been added to the choir of American composers"—was his first piece in the new idiom. It was followed by a concerto for piano and orchestra which "represents the jazz period in its most dazzling aspect—dissonant, unleashed primitivism—but handled with an unexpected mastery of material for a young composer of 26." For these compositions critics everywhere praised Copland. He had brought a new dignity to jazz and had proved emphatically that jazz has a definite place as a serious musical expression.

In 1929 RCA Victor offered $25,000 for a symphonic work. Copland started one, but wasn't able to finish it in time and submitted, instead, three movements from his old ballet, *Grohg.* The prize was divided among a number of contestants, and Copland won $5,000. The *Symphonic Ode* which he had started for the contest was later finished and performed as one of the works celebrating the fiftieth anniversary of the Boston Symphony.

The *Ode* marks the end of a period. The works which follow are "no longer so grand or so fulsome." The *Piano Variations* (1930), the *Short Symphony* (1933), the *Statements* for orchestra (1935) are, according to Copland, "more spare in sonority, more lean in texture. They are difficult to perform and difficult for an audience to comprehend."

It was after this group of compositions that Copland began to feel the importance of being understood, of reaching a wider audience. He became dissatisfied with the relations between the music-loving public and the living composer. "It seemed to me," he said, "that we composers were in danger of working in a vacuum. Moreover, an entirely new public for music had grown up around the radio and the phonograph. It made no sense to ignore them and to continue writing as though they did not exist.

COPLAND, AARON—*Continued*

I felt that it was worth the effort to see if I couldn't say what I had to say in the simplest possible terms." In his recent works he does— in the lively *El Salon Mexico* and *Music for Radio,* written on commission from the Columbia Broadcasting Company; *Billy the Kid,* a "close-knit, percussive, incisive" piece of music based on cowboy songs; *The Second Hurricane,* "a clean-cut, refreshingly unhackneyed, in instances magnificently sonorous little score"; and the music for many motion pictures, including that for *Of Mice and Men* and for *Our Town,* which was given its première before the film was opened to the public.

Copland is still a young man, "tall, energetic, large-nosed, engagingly toothy," full of an electrical energy that seems to course through his body, making his gestures nervous and abrupt.

References

Christian Sci Mon Mag p8-9 Mr 17 '37 por
Mag Art 32:522-3+ S '39 por (p498)
Musical Q 25:372-6 Jl '39
New Repub 91:48 My 19 '37
N Y Sun p28 Je 10 '40
N Y Times p23 My 24 '40; IX p3 Je 23 '40
Newsweek 6:41 N 2 '35 por
Time 33:60 Je 5 '39 por
Chandler, T. W. Aaron Copland *In* Cowell, H. ed. American Composers of American Music p49-56 1933
Ewen, D. ed. Composers of Today 1936
Rosenfeld, P. Copland *In* Discoveries of a Music Critic p332-7 1936
Saleski, G. Famous Musicians of a Wandering Race 1927
Thompson, O. ed. International Cyclopedia of Music and Musicians 1939
Who's Who in American Jewry

CORCORAN, THOMAS GARDINER (cor'co-ràn) Dec 29, 1900- Special counsel to Reconstruction Finance Corporation

Address: b. 827 Lafayette Bldg, Washington, D. C.; h. 1610 K St, N W, Washington, D. C.

Ordinarily Washington lawyers meet the President through an arranged conference —Thomas Gardiner Corcoran met him by singing to him in 1933 at an informal White House party. The President applauded Corcoran's sentimental Irish ballads, sea chanteys and mountain laments, then enthusiastically asked for more. Thus he met Corcoran, whom he was later to dub "Tommy the Cork," the man whose brilliant legal talents were the basis for many intricate and weighty New Deal legislative measures. Corcoran, the genial silver-tongued Irishman, clothed always in anonymity, consequently became the favorite subject for dinner conversation in the Nation's capital during the ensuing years.

On March 4, 1940, the 39-year-old drafter of New Deal legislation, an avowed bachelor, set the famous town to talking again when he married his secretary, Margaret Dowd. For seven years the pretty redheaded "Peggy" had served him well, causing him to remark again and again: "God bless her, she's a wonder," because she always matched his grinding pace of work.

Together with his working partner, Benjamin V. Cohen, Corcoran has been called by government officials the "little hot dog"; the "Gold Dust Twin" (taken from the advertising slogan, "Let the Gold Dust Twins do your work"). A catalytic agent and a political opportunist, he has been warmly commended and bitterly reviled by various Washington political figures.

Corcoran is labeled "little hot dog" because he was one of former Professor Felix Frankfurter's most brilliant students at Harvard. He has come a long way with the New Deal. Born in Pawtucket, Rhode Island, of a conservative family, young Corcoran amazed his schoolteachers with his mental gifts. At Brown University he carried off prize after prize in debate and English composition and became the intellectual star of the Class of 1921 when he received his B. A. In 1922 he was awarded his M. A. During the summer vacations he worked to help pay his tuition.

Enrolled at Harvard Law School, he came under the influence of Professor Frankfurter, who, since the Administration of Woodrow Wilson, has been supplying brilliant young lawyers to Washington. Corcoran topped his class and after receiving his LL. B. and S. J. D. degrees (1925-26) he was awarded the highest honor possible for a Harvard Law School graduate—a year's job as secretary to the late Supreme Court Justice Oliver Wendell Holmes. He used to read the classics aloud to the beloved Holmes. Dante and Montaigne were the young scholar's favorite writers. Latin and Greek texts presented no difficulties to him. The young man became a walking *Bartlett's Quotations.* From those golden days, he carried away a store of literary sparklers with which he has sprinkled the "ghosted" parts of the speeches of President Roosevelt. For instance, for the first time in history, Dante has broken into an American Presidential acceptance speech.

In 1927 Corcoran joined the law firm of Cotton & Franklin, in New York City. Eugene Mayer, then chairman of the RFC, in 1932 asked Professor Frankfurter to recommend a good lawyer. Remembering the marvelous mental agility of young Corcoran, Frankfurter sent him. So Corcoran went to Washington, really working under the Hoover administration, although many people think that Roosevelt brought him to the capital. While a member of the Cotton & Franklin legal firm Corcoran fought mightily for the big corporation heads who were clients; for the RFC he went to work energetically against them. This experience on both sides of the fence helped him in drafting legislation for the New Deal.

One cannot speak of the work of Corcoran without mentioning that of his partner, Benjamin V. Cohen. They lived together for years in Washington and frequently work together for 20 hours at a stretch. Cohen does most of the actual bill-drafting while Corcoran goes out to persuade politicians to the President's way of thinking. Called "thinkers of almost legendary existence whose skill at totalitarian induction makes neophytes of the former Regimenters," Corcoran and Cohen are responsible for the Securities Tax of 1933; the Securities Exchange Act of 1934 (called the act that "outsmarted Wall Street"); and the Public Utility Holding Company Act of 1935. In addition they worked on the judiciary reorganization plan; the wages and hours legislation; the TVA; the Electric Farm and Home Authority and the extended RFC.

Besides helping the President with his speeches (they do what they call the "technical information"), they advise Congressmen privately and publicly. They testify before Congressional committees. They report to the President the results of patient investigation in Washington bureaus (their latest report resulted in the shift of alien control from the Department of Labor to the Department of Justice). This investigation is made by the numerous brilliant young lawyers whom Corcoran has brought to Washington. When officials speak of the Corcoran Gallery they do not mean the famous Washington art gallery but the numerous, strategically placed staff of Corcoran.

"Tommy the Cork" likes to boast of two tricks in his method of drawing up proposed bills. He likes to make them complicated so that the average lawyer will fail to spot some of the far-reaching implications. Moreover, he words bills more strongly than he desires, so that any chopping down on the part of Congress will not destroy the intentions he wanted realized. Called the "greatest legislative drafting team in American history," Cohen and Corcoran make their bills models of legal brilliance.

The early days of the New Deal found the statesmen of Capitol Hill rudely jolted by Corcoran's energy and ingenuity in carrying out the President's ideas. It was not without good reason that he came to be known as the foremost legislative architect of the New Deal. When he slipped into the White House, usually through a side door, the President would say: "Tommy, here's a 400-page report. Will you make a digest of it?" or "Tommy, there's a row in a House committee over a bill. Will you find out what it's all about?"

And "Tommy the Cork" would be seen whisking through the Capitol corridors, busily conferring with Senators and Congressmen, arguing, pleading, cajoling and

THOMAS CORCORAN

threatening in order to line up support behind New Deal measures.

He is a glutton for work—keeping a 10 a. m. to midnight schedule. Once or twice a week he has managed to dine out, but more often he spends the evening and sometimes the night working. His marriage may change it—but in the past he always surrounded himself with bachelors because he said they never objected to the irregular hours and tremendous amount of office work.

Corcoran has been assistant to the Secretary of the Treasury in 1933, and special assistant to the attorney general of the United States from 1932 to 1935. He retired from the RFC—"temporarily at least"—in September 1940 to campaign for Roosevelt without accusation of violating the Hatch Act, which he is supposed to have written. He has learned how to handle politicians and he can be gentle or rough about it. Mentally and physically, he is tough. With his own two hands he built a cabin on Mt. Washington. He goes there week ends to chop wood and cook for his guests. Music is his great passion—as a boy he hoped to be a concert pianist. He can play the Gilbert and Sullivan operettas from end to end with scarcely a glance at the notes. He has an encyclopedic knowledge of Irish ballads and old American folk tunes.

"Stocky but buoyant, with the shoulders of a halfback, Corcoran presents a picture of affability on all occasions. His black wavy hair is streaked with gray." His amazing mental qualities and charm combined with "an almost unparalleled industry" have made him a favorite of the President's. Eventually he wants to establish the law firm of Corcoran and Cohen in New York City. Thus far, he has stayed in the political background, letting President Roosevelt

CORCORAN, THOMAS—*Continued*
take all the credit for the New Deal measures he drew up.

References

Am Mag 124:22-3+ Ag '37 por
Am Mercury 43:38-45 Ja '38
Collier's 102:14+ S 10 '38
Life 8:105 Mr 18 '40 por
Lit Digest 120:38 Jl 27 '35 por; 123: 7-8 My 22 '37 por; 124 (Digest 1): 24-5 S 11 '37
Newsweek 6:24-5 Jl 13 '35 por; 15:14 Ap 1 '40; 16:13 O 14 '40
Sat Eve Post 210:5-7+ Jl 31 '37; 211:8-9+ N 12 '38
Time 32:22-4 S 12 '38 por (cover); 36: 10 Ag 5 '40
America's Young Men
Who's Who in America

CORDIER, CONSTANT (kor'dē-ā') May 31, 1880—Feb 24, 1940 Soldier and diplomat who helped organize the American Expeditionary Force

Obituaries

N Y Times p39 F 25 '40

COREY, PAUL July 8, 1903- Author
Address: b. c/o Bobbs-Merrill Co, 468 4th Ave, New York City; h. Cold Spring, New York

"Move over, big boys, to make room for Iowa's Paul Corey." So reads the heading of the review of Mr. Corey's new novel, *The Road Returns* (October 1940) in the Des Moines *Register*. The reviewer continues: "That name is going to mean something in American literature and we might as well get used to saying it." Iowa is proud of its statesmen, artists and writers. And its pride in Iowa-born and Iowa-raised Paul Corey is justified by the opinion of nationally known critics. Of *Three Miles Square* (1939), the first in a series of three novels on the Iowa scene, Lewis Mumford (see sketch this issue) wrote: "One of the best novels of agricultural America that anyone has produced in our generation. . . I recommend it to all those who wish to read more intimately the living face of America." Louis Bromfield found it "full of truth and understanding and beautifully done," and Iowa's Grant Wood (see sketch this issue), an artist also concerned with interpreting Midwestern life, found in *Three Miles Square* "realism of the best sort."

Its economic and social background an Iowa farm community in the years just before the World War, *Three Miles Square* begins the story of the Mantz family when, on the father's death in 1910, the mother is left with four children and the responsibility of a farm at a time when agricultural problems are acute. Supported by the energy and courage of her eldest boy, 14-year-old Andrew, she decides to keep the farm. The foreground of the novel is built upon the intensely human drama of the struggles, fortunes and misfortunes of the Mantz family, collectively and individually, their personal conflict forming one pattern set against the larger pattern of the whole neighborhood, pictured with a remarkable "clarity and perfection of detail."

The Road Returns, starting with America's entrance into the World War, tells about those years of feverish prosperity for Iowa farmers, when the land boom made some greedy for increased acreage, others sell out for enough to retire on in California or in nearby towns. The draft takes young Andrew Mantz, blasting his hopes of becoming an architect after he got the farm on its feet; the Widow Mantz sells the home place and moves to Elm, the county seat town. She figures that now the second son, who has hated the farm, will have his chance to be a mechanic, and her youngest son Otto will go to high school and college. But Mrs. Mantz soon discovers that her seeming security was only a dream: the War market falls; Andrew, home from France, marries and can't get a job; Wolmar, also married, and facing bankruptcy, bleeds his mother of what little she has banked to start his own garage; the married daughter with her children descends on them; Otto's hopes of a college education seem shattered. The farmer to whom the home place has been sold defaults on his payments, and the only thing left for the Mantzes is to take the farm back: the road returns. Interwoven with all this are the experiences of their farm neighbors and their new neighbors in town. "Mr. Corey tells a full, rich story, sweeping in its scope, and leaves the possible implications to the reader. *The Road Returns* is an honest and admirable novel which deals with living people juxtaposed against a community. . . It recreates superbly an era of the first importance," comments Edith Walton in the New York *Times* Book Review.

Paul Corey was born July 8, 1903 on a farm in Shelby County, Iowa, son of Edwin Olney and Margaret Morgan (Brown) Corey, the youngest in a family of five boys and two girls. His paternal grandfather was a Mexican War veteran and an adventurer in the gold rush of '49 who did not, however, find gold. He was a descendant of Giles Corey, famed as the only man to be tortured to death for witchcraft in this country: stout-minded Giles met death by having planks laid across his chest and stones heaped upon them. When young Paul was not yet two his father died, and the struggles of his mother to keep her family together on the farm were similar to those he told concerning the Mantz family in *Three Miles Square*. When she moved to Atlantic, Iowa in 1918 Paul went to high school there. In 1921 he entered the University of Iowa, where he worked his way chiefly as geology librarian. During the summer of 1923 he also worked in a California redwood lumber mill. His mother lived to see her youngest son get a college education and died in the year of his graduation, 1925.

Leaving for Chicago in the summer of 1925, Corey worked first in Krock's bookstore there, then on *The Economist*, a trade paper. Having already written a novel and several short stories (which came back regularly with rejection slips), like many other Midwestern young people with literary ambitions, he came to New York. He wrote nights and held jobs variously with the Retail Credit Company, the Brooklyn Directory of the New York Telephone Company and the *Encyclopaedia Britannica*.

In February 1928 he married Ruth Lechlitner, poet, and poetry critic for the New York *Herald Tribune* Books. Before she came to New York from Michigan they had met at the University of Iowa while she was working on the *Midland*, a national literary magazine edited by John T. Frederick. The Coreys combined their savings to go to Europe for a honeymoon in the fall of 1928; they spent several months traveling and writing in France, Spain and England. On their return to New York they took office jobs again; but long hours of work all day and trying to write at night seemed to them a futile and hopeless struggle. They decided to get away from the city and bought a few acres of land in the Highlands of the Hudson near Cold Spring. In the spring of 1931 they left their jobs and went to the country to live.

William Seabrook (see sketch this issue) in an article, *Pioneer Spirit, '39 (Reader's Digest* September 1939), writes of this venture: "They lived for a while in a one-room shack, clearing, planting, starting baby chicks. Mrs. Corey said, 'The first night was bad. We had a cot, two chairs and a box for washstand and table. We wished we hadn't come. But soon it got to be fun.'" They had no money to have a house built, so Corey, though he had never studied carpentry, decided to build his own. After all, his grandfather and his father before him had built their own houses. "Stones were our main crop," the Corey's said, "so why not put them into walls for a house?" Having terraced a rocky hillside into level beds, as they had seen the French farmers do, they raised their own vegetables.

"By winter Corey had built a small cottage. He spent about $500 on the materials and built it so well that after they had lived in it for a few years he sold it at a profit. Meanwhile he had started a bigger stone house on his hilltop, and they slept in one partly-finished room. While they were building the new house they had done well with their chickens. . . Their garden yielded vegetables. They were still writing and selling. In those years it cost them 'nearly $300 to live.' They are prospering now; on less than $1,000 a year cash income they live in absolute independence." They both spend their mornings writing; in the afternoons they work on the house, or in the garden or with the chickens. Corey keeps

PAUL COREY

seeing places to add on a new room or two to the house, and his wife is alarmed: she is afraid that after this house is finished he may want to start all over again on another one.

Paul Corey is very blond, with hair that is beginning, he says, a forehead "pincer-movement," blue-eyed, and hard-muscled from having mixed, according to his estimation, "a hundred thousand pounds of sand and cement" to say nothing of handling "a thousand tons of stone" at his housebuilding. He likes good food, railway engines and cats; his special dislike is the one billboard visible on the Post Road across the fields from the Corey front yard. He is busy at work on his third Iowa novel, tentatively called *County Seat Town*, to be published in 1941, and has also planned one on lumber-milling. The manuscript of his first novel, *Three Miles Square*, has been presented to the University of Iowa, where, according to Wilbur Schramm, professor of English, it will form the nucleus of Iowa's projected collection of original manuscripts to be kept in the rare book room of the University library.

References

Des Moines Register Ja 14 '40 por; O 13 '40
N Y Herald Tribune Books p2 O 1 '39 por; p2 N 10 '40 por
N Y Times Book R p7 S 24 '39 por; p6 O 20 '40 por
Read Digest 35:42-6 S '39
Sat R Lit 20:6 S 23 '39 por

CORTELYOU, GEORGE BRUCE (kôr' têl-yōō) July 26, 1862—Oct 23, 1940 First Secretary of the Department of Commerce and Labor and Postmaster General and Secretary of the Treasury under Presi-

GEORGE BRUCE CORTELYOU

dent Theodore Roosevelt; was assistant secretary to President McKinley and later to Theodore Roosevelt; from 1909 to 1935 was president of the Consolidated Gas Company; president of the Edison Electric Institute and vice-president of the Chamber of Commerce of the State of New York (1924-28)

References

Shumway, H. I. George Bruce Cortelyou, Secretary to Presidents and Cabinet Officials *In* Famous Leaders of Industry p75-88 1936
Who's Who in America

Obituaries

N Y Times p25 O 24 '40 por

CORWIN, NORMAN May 3, 1910- Radio dramatist
Address: c/o Columbia Broadcasting System, 485 Madison Ave, New York City

Six-foot tall, brown-eyed Norman Lewis Corwin (he does not use his middle name) is an important figure in the radio world. He has written radio dramas—the best-known is probably *They Fly Through the Air with the Greatest of Ease*—he has directed dramas and produced them. Though he says "worrying" is one of his hobbies, people who should know think it a pretty silly one for a man of his achievements and abilities.

He was born in Boston, Massachusetts on May 3, 1910, the third son of Samuel H. and Rose (Ober) Corwin, and spent his childhood in Boston. He attended the East Boston High School for two years, then switched to the Winthrop (Massachusetts) High School when his family moved to Winthrop. He was an undistinguished stu-

dent, Mr. Corwin remembers, barely scraping through mathematics and flunking Latin in his first year, but he was always near or at the top in English and literary studies, and he led the class in chemistry. Mathematics and foreign languages mystified him.

He decided before being graduated from high school that he wanted to be a newspaperman. He canvassed, by letter, 80 daily newspapers in Massachusetts. Through the letters he obtained a job on the Greenfield *Daily Recorder*, the editor John W. Haigis, who later became state treasurer and ran unsuccessfully for Governor.

Corwin fibbed his age, which was 17, and was accepted as 24. In a month he became sports editor of the paper, and continued for about three years to combine sports writing with feature work, court reporting and film reviewing. His picture-review column was entitled *Seeing Things in the Dark,* and got him in trouble with theatre managers. They finally banned him from their theatres.

At 19 he joined the staff of the famed Springfield *Republican,* having been recommended for the job by his eldest brother, Emil, who was leaving that paper to join the Providence *Journal.* Before Norman left the *Recorder,* however, he recommended another brother, Alfred, as a successor to himself. As a result, for about a year all three brothers were editing on different New England newspapers.

For seven years, during the depression, Norman worked on the Springfield *Republican.* He was regarded as the best "color" writer on the staff, and sometimes got good assignments on that account, but never in all that time did he get a by-line—that was against the policy of the paper. Finally in 1932 the *Republican* entered an agreement with radio stations WBZ-WBZA, operating in Springfield and Boston, to furnish a nightly news commentary of 15 minutes. At that time such newspaper-radio relationships were rare, and the leased news wires for radio were unheard of. But because Corwin's voice was "baritonish" and he read well, he got the job, name credit on the air and eventually a sizable following in New England.

In 1931 Corwin got a leave of absence and took the few hundred dollars he had been saving for five years and went to Europe. He had nothing but bad luck in his travels —got colitis in Italy, broke his portable typewriter and glasses, sprayed fountain pen ink over his only suit, etc. After three months of this he returned to the *Republican.*

In 1935 he became radio editor of the paper, and worked hard trying to create a new kind of service to listeners. His reforms in program listing were permanently adopted by the paper and are still carried on. Then his brother Emil again recommended him for a job. It was that of radio director for Twentieth Century-Fox Films in New York, and the chief responsibility was writing a weekly script which film-fare commentators around the country could read readily to their listeners. It plugged Fox products in a nice way. For such services the *Film Daily* cited him editorially.

While working for Fox, Corwin yearned for the exhibitionism of broadcasting personally—something which had begun years ago with newscasts and continued with a couple of unnoticed sustaining programs over WBZ and WMAS—one called *Rhymes and Cadences,* the other *Norman Corwin's Journal.* (The latter was notable for the fact that the total mail for a period of twenty weeks was three letters.)

Corwin at length wrote a letter to Elliott Sanger, program chief of New York's "quality" independent station, WQXR. The letter outlined an idea for making poetry—the forgotten art—palatable to the ear. Sanger took a chance, and for 40 weeks Corwin did a broadcast every Wednesday night, discussing and "saying" verse, and later experimenting with dramatizations.

Luckily for him one of the best broadcasts of his *Poetic License* series on WQXR was favorably reviewed by the trade magazine *Variety* and led indirectly to a guest appearance on NBC's then-popular variety program, *The Magic Key of RCA.* W. B. Lewis, vice-president in charge of the Columbia Broadcasting System, heard of Corwin's work at WQXR and, liking it, engaged him in April 1938 as a director-performer. Corwin was to fit into a new educational program, his function being to make general literature as easy to swallow as he was apparently making poetry. But before Columbia's educational advisory committee could agree on the shape of such a program he was set to work directing shows. It was another lucky break, because he then turned his entire efforts to the absorption of new techniques and the acquisition of a new type of creative effort: production. The experience was invaluable. For six months he directed *Americans at Work* and *Living History,* working closely with Gilbert Seldes on both programs.

For months at CBS Corwin declined to have his name go out on the air in connection with the programs he directed: he didn't feel he was good enough to be credited. He attempted one *Workshop* script, a satire, but tore it up halfway through. Late in 1938 he conceived the idea for *Words Without Music,* asked Mr. Lewis for an audition budget, and proceeded to make a record of a show which incorporated his new ideas on augmentation and orchestration. The performance was hailed by executives and by the CBS writing chief, Max Wylie (see sketch this issue). Wylie pushed hard for a series based on the audition, and it was finally arranged. Corwin then entered upon a very active period. For 25 weeks he wrote, adapted, cast and produced *Words Without Music,* doing all his own research and sometimes composing music for it. After nearly six months of this he came close

NORMAN CORWIN

to physical collapse, and CBS packed him off on a vacation.

Corwin's first general recognition came from *The Plot to Overthrow Christmas,* an original rhymed fantasy, done on Christmas Day 1938, and it was followed a few weeks later in the *Words Without Music* series by a verse drama entitled *They Fly Through the Air with the Greatest of Ease.* This, based on the Fascist conception of the beauty of war, and having to do with the bombing of a Spanish city by a lone Italian bomber, drew a number of blessings from unexpected quarters, and later that year was awarded first prize by the Institute of Education by Radio (Ohio State University) as the best dramatic program of the year. Other highlights in *Words Without Music* (which got top award as the 1938 series "best demonstrating the cultural, artistic and social uses of radio") were his adaptations of Carl Sandburg's (see sketch this issue) *The People, Yes,* Whitman's *Leaves of Grass* and Masters' *Spoon River Anthology.*

At the request of Douglas Coulter of the CBS executive staff Corwin later wrote a dramatic essay called *Seems Radio is Here to Stay.* This made quite a stir within the industry, and was privately published by CBS for distribution among agencies, clients and the press. Another Coulter suggestion was that Corwin write a radio play based on Lucille Fletcher Herrmann's story, *My Client Curley.* It made a hit and had to be repeated within a month.

In October 1939 Corwin was asked to direct *The Pursuit of Happiness,* and this led to his first extensive contact with people of stage and screen. Not long after the program was started, composer Earl Robinson, whom Corwin had never met, approached him to discuss ideas he (Robinson) had for an opera based on *The People, Yes.* Robinson casually

CORWIN, NORMAN—*Continued*

mentioned his *Ballad of Uncle Sam,* which a year back had died, struggling, in a Federal Theatre revue named *Sing for Your Supper.* The basic idea seemed to Corwin unworthy of early death, and he asked Robinson to play it for him. Corwin immediately interested CBS executives, and all three in turn got Paul Robeson interested. Then Corwin shortened the score, changed the name to *Ballad for Americans,* brought together Robinson and Robeson, and directed its first performance on *The Pursuit of Happiness,* November 5, 1939. It created a national sensation and was repeated on the Christmas broadcast a few weeks later. The broadcast marked the start of Earl Robinson as a widely recognized American composer, and also gave wide prominence to the librettist of the *Ballad,* John LaTouche (see sketch this issue).

The Pursuit of Happiness tried hard to keep a high standard, though it sometimes ran into terrible streaks of bad luck—stars were forced to drop out at the last minute or suffered untimely illnesses. But before the program went off the air for lack of a sponsor it had presented the first performance of Bernard Schoenfeld's great *Johnny Appleseed,* the première of Maxwell Anderson's and Kurt Weill's *Magna Charta,* and Corwin's own adaptations of writings by John Steinbeck (see sketch this issue), Thomas Wolfe and Stephen Vincent Benét. In the latter two he directed Charles Laughton and Elsa Lanchester, and began an association which continued later in Hollywood. He afterward wrote *To Tim at Twenty* expressly for the Laughtons.

Soon after the termination of *Pursuit of Happiness* Corwin was offered a long-term writer-producer-director contract by RKO Pictures, but turned this down in favor of a one-picture writing commitment, which he fulfilled in the summer of 1940.

During the summer of 1939 he lectured at the University of Colorado. Previously he had lectured at Columbia University, New York University and Amherst College.

References

Newsweek Jl 31 '39
Scholastic Ap 8 '40
Time N 20 '39; Ap 15 '40
Variety Jl 26 '39

COTTON, JOSEPH BELL Jan 6, 1865— Aug 5, 1940 Attorney; specialist in railroad and mining law; member of Minnesota House of Representatives in 1893; practiced law for 52 years; descendant of John Cotton, Puritan divine, and of the noted colonial New England Cotton Mather family

References

Who's Who in America
Who's Who in Law

Obituaries

N Y Times p19 Ag 7 '40

COUGHLIN, CHARLES EDWARD, FATHER (kŏg'ln) Oct 25, 1891- Priest of the Shrine of the Little Flower

Address: h. Woodward & Twelve Mile Rd, Royal Oak, Michigan

> December 1940 Bulletin: On September 20, 1940 Father Coughlin announced that he had abandoned his plan for a new series of weekly radio talks, scheduled to open on October 20. According to Father Coughlin, "men powerful in the field of radio and other activities" had "forced the decision upon me."

From September issue:

The famous "radio priest," Father Charles E. Coughlin of the Shrine of the Little Flower, owns a 47-station network, once headed a political organization, the National Union for Social Justice, publishes the magazine *Social Justice,* now heads the Social Justice Poor Society, Incorporated. Recently his popularity has declined because of his violent anti-Roosevelt and anti-Semitic stand. But in June and July 1940, he became headline news again on two counts. The July 1 issue of *Social Justice* came out with Father Coughlin's candidates for President and Vice-President: Wendell Willkie (see sketch this issue) and Charles A. Lindbergh. He has since said (after Willkie repudiated his support) that he "could not in good conscience support either candidate." His political announcement closely followed his statement on June 24 on the acquittal of 17 members of the Christian Front, an anti-Semitic, pro-Fascist organization with which he was connected: "The Christian Front movement will emerge more vigorous and potent than ever." When the Christian Fronters were first charged with conspiracy to overthrow the government with force of arms the radio priest disavowed knowing them, called them "fakers." But evidence that *Social Justice* had long encouraged the Christian Front included a speech by Father Coughlin in July 1939 in which he counseled them to follow the "peaceful way" until "there is left no other but . . . the Franco way." In face of such evidence Father Coughlin reversed his position: "I take my stand beside the Christian Fronters. . . My place is by their side."

Commonweal, a Catholic publication, accused the radio priest of being directly responsible for the plight of the arrested men. So many complaints against Father Coughlin came in to the Dies Committee that Representative Voorhis of the committee urged an investigation of his activities. But such an investigation on the part of Martin Dies (see sketch this issue) has not yet been forthcoming.

The priest of a small parish at Royal Oak, Michigan, whose radio expenses are, according to his own estimate, some $10,000 a week, and whose assets are said to have reached nearly half a million in 1938, once wrote in the foreword of a book on his work: "If I threw away and denounced my faith, I would surround myself with the most adroit highjackers, learn every trick of the highest banking and stock manipulations, avail myself of the laws under which to hide my own crimes, create a smoke screen to throw into the eyes of men and—believe me—I would become the world's champion crook. If I didn't believe in religion and in a happy beyond I would get everything for myself I could lay my hands on in the world."

Father Coughlin was born of pure Irish stock in Hamilton, Ontario, Canada on October 25, 1891, the son of Thomas J. and Amelia (Mahoney) Coughlin. His father was a stoker on the Great Lakes who later became sexton in a Catholic Cathedral; his mother was a seamstress. From the parochial schools young Coughlin entered St. Michael's College, Toronto. After his graduation he considered politics as a career, but was persuaded to enter the Church. He was incardinated at the Diocese of Detroit in 1923 and sent to be pastor of the Shrine of the Little Flower, Royal Oak, Michigan in 1926. For four years he broadcasted sermons and talks to children over WJR of the Detroit *Free Press* without gaining recognition. But in 1930, when he injected economics and politics into his sermons and got results, Father Coughlin organized the Radio League of the Little Flower and branched out.

His "rhetorical, florid tirades," larded by the philosophy of the encyclicals of Pope Pius XI and Leo XIII, brought him letters by the thousand, many with contributions. He rented time on a 16-station Columbia hookup. He devoted a series of talks to Communism in which he charged that Russia was fomenting revolution in America. He attacked prohibition. When he talked on the "menace of Hoover" his mail brought him nearly a million congratulatory letters. When the Detroit banks closed in 1933 Father Coughlin became a spokesman for the New Deal: at the White House he conferred with Raymond Moley, he employed his own brain trust and hired priests to take care of his parish work. But his income in 1934 fell to a low figure, and by the end of 1935 he was anti-New Deal—as was big industry and finance. With his anti-Roosevelt stand, money began to flow back into his coffers—enough to help him launch his National Union for Social Justice.

Meanwhile complaints against the radio priest caused the Columbia network to ease him out, and he created his own network. The National Union for Social Justice campaigned in 1936 for William Lempke. During the campaign Father Coughlin was forced by the Pope to apologize for calling President Roosevelt "a liar," which apology he later retracted in a speech. His "lobby" (he did not call it a political party) had headquarters at the Shrine of the Little Flower, exempt from taxation because it is church property. According to statistics gathered by John L. Spivak in his investigation of Father Coughlin's ventures, the

Bachrach

FATHER COUGHLIN

Union for Social Justice was formed on money borrowed from his parish funds, from the Radio League of the Little Flower—which, according to sworn statement, is a non-political organization to raise funds for the Shrine—and from the magazine, *Social Justice.*

"I am neither Republican, Democrat nor Socialist," he has declared. "I glory in the fact that I am a simple Catholic priest endeavoring to inject Christianity into the fabric of an economic system woven upon the loom of greed." His party lifted certain planks from the Farmer-Labor platform, but there was no word in its policy of democratic government or the right of free speech.

Lempke defeated, Father Coughlin gave up active political campaigning and continued his extracurricular activities through his Social Justice, Incorporated. *Social Justice* magazine is not an organ of the church but a privately owned publication. It became this when Archbishop Mooney of Detroit tried to censure its pronouncements. In 1937 the Social Justice Publishing Company asked tax exemption because it was owned by a "non-profit-making corporation named the Radio League of the Little Flower." The sole stockholder of Social Justice, Incorporated is Father Coughlin, and his board of directors consists of himself and two secretaries. The directors of the Radio League of the Little Flower are the same. The president of Aircasters, Incorporated, an agency handling Father Coughlin's radio time, is also general manager of *Social Justice.* The Social Justice Poor Society, which, as a charitable organization is not required to publish any statements, is actually (according to *Look,* April 4, 1940) a holding company for the cor-

COUGHLIN, CHARLES EDWARD
Continued

poration Social Justice, Incorporated, organized for profit.

Social Justice is the mouthpiece for Father Coughlin's anti-Communist and anti-Semitic campaigns. John McCarten (*American Mercury*, June 1939) says that much of the material used in Father Coughlin's anti-Semitic campaign has been culled directly from *World Service,* a Nazi propaganda organ. He attacks the Jews for having introduced "Communist international banking," and lists Bernard Baruch and Eddie Cantor as America's two most dangerous Jews. He once told his listeners that there are three kinds of communism today: "the industrial communism of Russia, the military communism of Japan and the financial communism of Wall Street." When several radio stations refused to allow him the air for his 1938 anti-Semitic campaign, among those quick to defend him were Wilhelm Kunze, press-agent of the German American Bund, Edward Smythe, one of the organizers of the Christian Front, and Allen Zoll, arrested for trying to extort money from station WMCA in return for calling off a Christian Front picket line he had thrown around the station. Zoll was bailed out by Seward Collins, editor of the *American Review.*

With regard to the Detroit priest's stand on labor, Raymond Gram Swing (in his book, *Forerunners of American Fascism*) says that Father Coughlin "believes in government-organized unions such as Germany and Russia have. . . . He denounces at the same time capitalism and communism. After reading and hearing many of his speeches I am struck with their technical similarity to those of Hitler." Father Coughlin refused to employ union labor in building his shrine. According to R. J. Thomas, president of the United Auto Workers, Father Coughlin, who had always lashed out against the CIO, in 1937 helped Henry Ford to split union ranks by offering his support to Homer Martin, then head of the UAW, to start a "new union" at the Ford Motor Company—provided Martin left the CIO.

In 1935 the Detroit *Free Press* brought to light that, while the flexible Father was denouncing Wall Street, he was at the same time using the services of a Wall Street broker to handle his 500 shares of Kelsey Hayes stock. He orated vociferously against the silver market, but when the government published the list of all holders of silver the largest in Michigan proved to be the secretary of Father Coughlin's own organization. It is believed that the Detroit priest "tipped the scales against the World Court" when, backed by William Randolph Hearst, he fought with Huey Long against it.

The Catholic Church authorities say that Father Coughlin is given "permission to speak—not approval." He speaks as an American citizen, not for the Church. If he says anything "that affects our moral doctrine, it's the duty of the Church to take it up. If it is politics, economics and social conditions, then it does not come within the scope of the Church."

He is the author of three books—*Christ or the Red Serpent* (1930); *By the Sweat of Thy Brow* (1931); and *The New Deal in Money* (1933).

His own Church, the Shrine of the Little Flower, has become the mecca of many tourists. It is an architectural miscellany with a cruciform tower 150 feet high that has frequently been compared to a silo, and its builder irreverently called "silo Charlie." Powerful lights play upon it at night. On the corner of the property is the Shrine Super-Service Station and hot dog stand. Outside and inside the Shrine itself all kinds of souvenirs are for sale.

Father Coughlin's business offices (he has a staff of more than 100 clerks and stenographers) are in the Shrine tower. He is, according to Mr. Swing's (see sketch this issue) description, a likeable enough person. "Once a caller reaches him—and he can make himself as inaccessible as a bank president—he finds him quite the human being. He is quick, intelligent, friendly, unpretentious in his dealings, leaps up and paces the floor, talks in a flood of language. He smokes cigarettes endlessly. He dots his conversation with manly sounding 'damns' and 'hells.' Furthermore he is sincere, if sincerity means the aim of his enterprise is not to line his own pockets. But ambition preys on his soul."

What form that ambition may take remains debatable. Because of his Church ties, Father Coughlin can look to no future as an independent political leader, and he has cut off all chance for advancement in the Church itself. It is said that his *Social Justice* has been operating on a large deficit for some years, yet at the same time he has been adding to his radio stations even though his broadcasts cost some $500,000 a year. The question has been raised by more than one observer as to who is meeting the radio priest's deficits. His recent acknowledged connections with the pro-Fascist Christian Front has added to the suspicions of many concerning Father Coughlin's trend and influence. A. B. Magil in the *New Republic* (June 24, 1936) has said: "The American Hitler may have died with Huey Long, but the Paul Joseph Goebbels of Royal Oak believes his successor will come."

References

Am Mercury 35:293-300 Jl '35; 47:129-41 Je '39
Commonweal 31:114-16 N 24 '39
Look 4:19-21 Ap 9 '40 il pors
New Masses 33:3-12 N 21 '39 por; 33:3-9 D 12 '39; 33:10-17 D 19 '39; 33:11-15 D 26 '39; 33:4-7 Ja 2 '40
New Repub 87:196-8 Je 24 '36; 87:226 Jl 1 '36
N Y Times p12 Je 26 40; p21 S 21 '40
Time 35:19 Ja 29 '40
American Catholic Who's Who

Kernan, W. C. Ghost of Royal Oak
 1940
Magil, A. B. Truth About Father
 Coughlin 1935
Mugglebee, R. Father Coughlin, the
 Radio Priest, of the Shrine of the
 Little Flower 1935
Riley, W. B. Philosophies of Father
 Coughlin 1935
Spivak, J. L. Shrine of the Silver
 Dollar 1940
Swing, R. G. Father Coughlin *In*
 Forerunners of American Fascism
 p34-61 1935
Unofficial Observer [pseud.] Micro-
 phone Messiah (Father Coughlin)
 In American Messiahs p33-54 1935
Who's Who in America

COULTER, CALVIN BREWSTER (kōl'-
ter) Jan 3, 1888—May 11, 1940 Pathologist; noted bacteriologist; professor of Long
Island College of Medicine; chief bacteriologist of Kings County Hospital, New
York City

References

American Medical Directory
American Men of Science

Obituaries

N Y Herald Tribune p16 My 11 '40
N Y Times p19 My 11 '40

COVARRUBIAS,   MIGUEL   (kō-vär-
rōō've̅-äs) 1902- Artist
Address: c/o Museum of Modern Art, 11 W
53rd St, New York City

Miguel Covarrubias is going to use the
Guggenheim Fellowship which he was
awarded in April 1940 to prepare a book
on the culture of the Isthmus of Tehuantepec. A Mexican himself and long a student
of the types, customs and cultures of the
world's people, he is extraordinarily well-
equipped for the job.

Covarrubias is best known, perhaps, for
his caricatures, but his *Island of Bali* (1937)
established him as an ethnologist and anthropologist, as well as a superb reporter
and artist. He and his wife, Rose, went to
Bali for the first time in 1932 and brought
back pictures that "reflect the beauty that
belongs to the women of this enchanted
island, showing them in characteristic poses
and parades." They went back in 1936,
and *Island of Bali* was the fruit of their
two long stays there. It deals with the
art and culture, the background and everyday life of the Balinese as seen through
the sympathetic and understanding eyes of
an artist. *The Nation* says that the book
"is a sound piece of scientific work, a real
contribution to knowledge, and will probably be the standard English work on
Balinese culture for years to come." It is
also a lively book and a handsome one, pro-
fusely illustrated by Covarrubias' drawings
and his wife's photographs.

Steichen

MIGUEL COVARRUBIAS

In his six mural maps of the cultural
and economic contribution of the peoples
of the Pacific areas for the interior of Pacific House at the San Francisco World's
Fair (1939-40), Covarrubias again shows his
firm grasp on ethnology, sociology and eco
nomic geography. The freshness and beauty
of these maps are equalled by their value
as visual educators. For them he consulted
thousands of sources, and with researchers
at the University of California studied flora
and fauna, racial stocks, costumes, specific
products and industries.

When Miguel Covarrubias arrived in New
York in 1923 with a limited scholarship from
the Mexican government, he was without
friends, influence or means. But in his first
four years in New York he published two
books, illustrated a third, did scenery and
costumes for Shaw's *Androcles and the
Lion,* designed three ballets, drew hundreds
of caricatures, published a remarkable suite
of Negro drawings, contributed regularly to
Vanity Fair (sometimes as many as eight
drawings in a single issue), made weekly
sketches for the *New Yorker,* and went once
to France and twice to Mexico.

Covarrubias was born in Mexico City in
1902. As a child he used to draw and make
caricatures, but he received no formal art
education (or any other kind of education,
for that matter). He never finished what
he called his "sentence at preparatory
school," and he never was in an atelier in
Paris or an academy in New York or London. What he learned he learned through
personal observation, through constant hard
work.

Covarrubias' first New York exhibition
was held at the Whitney Club shortly after
he arrived there. It was a tremendous
success, and he suddenly found himself "in

COVARRUBIAS, MIGUEL—*Continued*

the position of one of the most indulged youths of that great city." *Vanity Fair* asked him to contribute, and he continued as a contributor until the magazine was suspended in 1936. His first book, *The Prince of Wales, and Other Famous Americans* (1925), with caricatures of the great and the spectacular, "definitely opened the doors of fame to him."

As a caricaturist "he has caught Harold Lloyd in his shark-like laugh and Chaplin in the convulsive contraction of a mouth that no longer knows how to laugh. The comical part of a caricature lies in the contrast between the changing mobility of a person and a paradoxical impression of the same person fixed in a movement that condemns it to perpetual immobility." In a sharp line or a shadowed curve, in the placing of an eyebrow or the drawing of a series of criss-cross lines the essence of the person drawn—whether it is Greta Garbo or John D. Rockefeller—is caught and transmitted. And yet, as Diego Rivera says: "In Covarrubias' art there is no malice; a humor that is young and clear; a precise and well-defined plasticity."

In his painting of types and aspects of Negro, Mexican, American and European life, Covarrubias has gone further than caricature. These are plastic interpretations achieved through his own original modes of expression and personal technique. In 1925 Covarrubias became known as the discoverer of the Negroes in Harlem, and his *Negro Drawings* (1927) made him the first artist in America to bestow on the Negro anything like the attention Gauguin gave to the South Sea natives. In these drawings of blues singers, sheiks along Lenox Avenue, "higher-yaller" flappers, revivalist preachers, are humor, truth, aliveness and "a feeling of actuality." After looking at them the London *Times* said: "As an artist Mr. Covarrubias deserves all that his introducers say about him—even if their references to Giotto, El Greco, Picasso are unnecessary. He has an extraordinary control of plastic form, his colour is rich and haunting, and, above all, his work is full of vitality."

Covarrubias has done lithographs and oil paintings. He has illustrated many books; he has painted scenery; he has written about the popular Mexican theatre; he has published a book on life in Bali; in May 1940 he selected material for the modern painting section of the New York Museum of Modern Art's "Twenty Centuries of Mexican Art" show. And now he is going to work on his book on Tehuantepec. If his previous work is any indication, again we will have a book which will be "as superb a piece of reporting, of anthropological and artistic understanding as you will find in a dozen campusfuls of pompously scientific works."

References

Fortune 17:56-7 My '38 19:60-4 My '39 il
N Y Herald Tribune p25 My 15 '40
Time 33:24 Mr 6 '39 por; 35:68 Ap 15 '40
Mérida, C. Miguel Covarrubias *In* Modern Mexican Artists p35-6 1937
New York City. Museum of Modern Art Twenty Centuries of Mexican Art p185 1940
Velázquez Chávez, A. Miguel Covarrubias *In* Contemporary Mexican Artists p69-70 1937
Who's Who in America

CRAMER, STUART WARREN (krā'mer) Mar 31, 1868—July 2, 1940 Textile industry leader who planned or equipped one-third of the South's cotton mills; holder of 60 patents in industry, chemistry and physics; former leader of the Republican Party in North Carolina; Naval authority; father of Mrs. James Rowland Angell, wife of the president emeritus of Yale University

References

Who's Who in America
Who's Who in Commerce and Industry

Obituaries

N Y Herald Tribune p8 Jl 4 '40 por
N Y Times p15 Jl 4 '40 por

CRAVATH, PAUL DRENNAN (kra-văth') July 14, 1861—July 1, 1940 Lawyer; famous for his defense and reorganization of corporations; in 1931 elected president of the board of directors of the Metropolitan Opera Company; at his death, president of

Musical America

PAUL CRAVATH

the Metropolitan Opera Association, Incorporated

References

New Yorker 7:21-5 Ja 2 '32
International Who's Who
Who's Who
Who's Who in America
Who's Who in Law
Who's Who in the East

Obituaries

N Y Herald Tribune p20 Jl 2 '40 por
N Y Times p20, 21 Jl 2 '40 por
Newsweek 16:6 Jl 15 '40 por
Time 36:55 Jl 8 '40

CRAWFORD, MORRIS BARKER Sept 26, 1852—Oct 9, 1940 Professor emeritus of physics at Wesleyan University and member of the Wesleyan faculty for 44 years until his retirement in 1921; believed to be the first person to take an X-ray picture of a broken bone for the purpose of reducing a fracture

MORRIS B. CRAWFORD

References

American Men of Science
Leaders in Education 1932
Who's Who in America 1928-29

Obituaries

N Y Herald Tribune p20 O 10 '40

CRAWFORD, PHYLLIS Feb 8, 1899-
Author
Address: h. 57 Charles St, New York City

Rated one of the best writers of books for children in their early teens, Phyllis Crawford, who in 1938 won the Julia Ellsworth Ford Foundation Award for *Hello,* *the Boat!,* recently published (October 1940) *Walking on Gold.* The characters in this new book for boys and girls are from Arkansas, where Miss Crawford was born and grew up. It is the story of a company of fortune-seekers, the Arkansas Travelers, who followed the trail in the spring of 1849 to the California gold mines. In particular it is the story of this exciting trek as experienced by a red-headed boy, Peckerwood.

The account of this journey by covered wagon across rough pioneer country and wide deserts full of the hazards of wild life and Indians is one that any boy (or girl, for that matter) should follow with the most lively interest.

The narrative moves swiftly; at the same time the details are exceptionally vivid and realistic. The characters are real people with genuine Arkansas folk speech. Particularly good is Miss Crawford's handling of Indians. They are not stereotyped bloodcurdling redskins, but have humanly varying characteristics, as tribes and as individuals. It is expected that *Walking on Gold* will top the appeal which *Hello, the Boat!* had for young readers. The latter, a story of riverboating on the Ohio, was called "that rare thing, a pioneer story which is original and unhackneyed both in setting and plot."

Phyllis Crawford was born February 8, 1899 in Little Rock, Arkansas, daughter of Thomas Dwight and Elizabeth Daviess (Williams) Crawford. "As a little girl," she says, "I was so terribly shy that I would walk down the opposite side of the street rather than pass the home of someone I knew, so I didn't have many friends." She played games with her brother John and their boy cousin, who were always doing Wild West plays in which they condescendingly created minor female parts for Phyllis to act. She didn't become interested in reading until she was about eight, when she found a copy of a particularly lush romance for adults, *Lady Betty Across the Water.* Only one thing in the book puzzled her: the "cocktails" the people were always having; she had never heard of a cocktail. But from then on she avidly read everything she could find. She hated *Elsie Dinsmore,* but her great passion was *Little Women,* which she read over and over.

She went through the Little Rock High School in three years, because her brother had done so, and was class artist and class poet. Although at 10 her modest ambition was "to be the world's greatest violinist, or the greatest artist, or the greatest writer," she now settled upon writing." I decided it was a good means of communication when the cat got your tongue and there wasn't a safe place for your hands and feet," she says, "and the equipment was both cheap and handy." She went to Randolph Macon Woman's College, where she edited the monthly literary magazine staff and helped establish a writing club called the Quill Drivers. After her graduation in 1920 she taught English for a year at Fairfax Hall in Virginia, a girls' school, but didn't like having to chaperone the girls. Then she decided to

CRAWFORD, PHYLLIS—*Continued*
be a librarian and went to the University
of Illinois Library School, where she received her B. L. S. degree.

In 1924 she was employed by the H. W.
Wilson Company in New York as editorial
assistant on the *Standard Catalog.* She was
co-editor of the *Song Index* published in
1926. In 1928 she married Cyril Kay Scott,
artist and novelist, and went to Santa Fe,
New Mexico to live. After her divorce in
1931 she returned to work again at the
Wilson Company, editing the *Vertical File
Service* catalog as well as the current supple-
ments to the *Children's Catalog* and *Song
Index.* Her first two books were published
in 1930: *Elsie Dinsmore on the Loose,* a satire
for grownups, under the pseudonym Josie
Turner; and *The Blot: Little City Cat,* for
children, under her own name. She left the
Wilson Company in 1935 to work on the
Index of American Design of the Federal Arts
Project. She resigned in 1937. Deciding to
devote her time wholly to writing, she went
to work on *Hello, the Boat!* which won, the
following year, the $3,000 Ford Foundation
Prize.

Miss Crawford is small, charming, dark-
haired, with an engaging twinkle in alert,
wide-set hazel eyes. She talks as well as
she writes and is interested in any number of
things, "especially cats—and more cats."
She is also fond of antiques, American
primitives in particular. She lives in New
York City and is at work on a new book
for young people, *The Secret Brother,*
announced for 1941 publication.

References
Pub W 133:2359 Je 18 '38 por
Sat R Lit 18:10 Jl 30 '38 por
American Women

PHYLLIS CRAWFORD

CRAWSHAW, WILLIAM HENRY Nov
6, 1861—July 2, 1940 Former dean and
acting president of Colgate University;
joined Colgate faculty as English instructor
and later became professor; dean of the
undergraduate college from 1897 to 1930;
acting president in 1897, 1907 and 1908 and
president pro tem from 1908 to 1909; famous
as Shakespearean scholar

WILLIAM H. CRAWSHAW

References
Crawshaw, W. H. My Colgate Years
1937
Who's Who in America
Who's Who in New York
Who's Who in the East
Obituaries
N Y Times p17 Jl 3 '40 por
Newsweek 16:6 Jl 15 '40 por

CRIPPS, SIR STAFFORD Apr 24, 1889
British Ambassador to Soviet Russia

On June 12, 1940, Sir Richard Stafford
Cripps (he does not use Richard), Britain's
newly-appointed Ambassador to Russia, arrived
in Moscow on the same plane with the new
French Ambassador Erik Labonne. The
appointment of a Left-wing member of
the British Labor Party as Ambassador to
the Soviet at this time marked a new phase
in British diplomatic policy, especially since
former Ambassador Sir William Seeds had
been "on leave" from Moscow since January, and since Cripps was expelled from
the executive council of his party early in
1939 for advocating a united front of British
Laborites, Liberals and Communists against
the Chamberlain National Government.

Member of Parliament since 1931, Sir
Stafford Cripps is known professionally as a
brilliant radical lawyer, privately as "Red
Squire" of the Cotswolds, politically as the

enfant terrible of the British Labor Party. The youngest son of Sir Charles Alfred Parmoor (Lord President of the Council in the last Labor government) and Theresa (Potter) Cripps and nephew of the Webbs, he was born April 24, 1889. He was educated at Winchester and at University College, London, and in 1913 set himself up as barrister-at-law in Middle Temple. In 1914 he was with the Red Cross in France, in 1915 he was assistant superintendent of His Majesty's factory at Queen's Ferry, Cheshire, and after the War Cripps began to make his reputation as the greatest authority on company law in Great Britain, one whose fees as a King's Counsel have been estimated at $150,000 a year.

In 1930 he entered politics as Solicitor-General in Ramsay MacDonald's second Labor government (a regime that has since been labeled "anti-democratic, anti-Socialist and therefore pro-war"), was knighted, and with the formation of a National Government in 1931 went into opposition. Since the by-election of 1931 he has been Labor Member of Parliament for Bristol East, and during the past decade has created a great stir in the British political arena. Founder and chairman of the Socialist League within the parliamentary Labor Party, "one of the half-dozen figures in the movement with a national appeal," often called the party's best mouthpiece, he has made himself feared almost as much by the conservative British trade unions as by the Tories, has found himself described as "inconsistent", "indiscreet", "a dangerous character," a "heretic," and also as England's most courageous fighter against entrenched privilege.

Sir Stafford Cripps once told a political audience that as a lawyer he met the people of the ruling classes. "They pay me fabulous and fantastic sums to get them out of their difficulties," he said. "I have no hesitation in saying that the working class of this country are more capable of ruling than they are." This was his sincere belief. And he was a Socialist who, mindful of the history of MacDonald's government, had become convinced "that half-measures and compromises, timidly concurred in by a labor government on taking office, doom that government to sterility and ultimate defeat."

According to Sir Stafford the policies of Chamberlain's National Government showed Great Britain's rapid and dangerous trend toward Fascism, the first definite and conscious step having been the Trade Disputes Act of 1927. The 1931 elections themselves had been "essentially Fascist in nature": the "forces of capitalism had such a triumph at the polls that there was no need for any formal personal dictatorship." "The worker is being, and has been, disciplined not viciously and ruthlessly as in Germany and Italy, but gently and firmly as one would expect from a country-gentleman-Fascism in Britain. Colored shirts are not necessary and are embarrassingly obvious; a special

SIR STAFFORD CRIPPS

constable is much cheaper and attracts less attention."

In 1934 he had become a member of the national executive council of the Labor Party. "But because he argued that the new tasks which confront democracy call for a new technique and a swifter procedure, it suited the Tory and Liberal press to pretend that he was advocating some species of dictatorship. It called on the Labor Party to clear its good name by repudiating him." Always known for his "brutal frankness," during one speech listing the opposition which a government intent on a rapid socialization of the country must face, Sir Stafford mentioned Buckingham Palace, thereby committing another blasphemy which neither the press nor his stunned audience soon forgot.

In 1935 he fell out with his party over a question of foreign policy, finally resigned from the executive council, and was not re-elected until 1937. By then he was gathering wide support among the intellectuals of his party in his campaign against Fascism both abroad and in his own country. Within the Labor Party there were divisions on many issues. Sir Stafford's main quarrel with accepted policy was Labor's support of rearmament by the Chamberlain government; he insisted that "if Fascism chose to gamble on war, only a Labor government would wage that war for working-class ends." What is more, while Sir Walter Citrine and the trade unions seemed willing to make terms with Winston Churchill (see sketch this issue) in return for a firm policy toward Germany, Sir Stafford Cripps and the Socialist League signed an agreement for joint action with the Communists and the Independent Labor Party on the main issues of the day, continued to talk "Marxism with an English accent," to fight for a united

CRIPPS, SIR STAFFORD—*Continued*

front, for an alliance with Russia, for a really Socialist national policy. Already there had been talk of expelling him and his followers. Said Harold Laski, one of the four members of the executive council then known as Left-wingers: "Comfortable trade union officials, liberals who have joined the party without ever changing their views, pushing middle-class intellectuals who want to be in the Cabinet as quickly as possible, these may demand Sir Stafford's head on a charger. But the day they get it will mark the end of the hope of most of us that this generation may still see in England a great forward move toward socialism."

On January 13, 1939 Sir Stafford presented a memorandum to the executive council, asked for a special meeting to consider certain proposals. Their substance was that unless Chamberlain and his National Government could be defeated in the next election "British democracy was threatened with destruction by both internal and external enemies." Acting alone, the Labor Party was not powerful enough to elect its own candidates, and could only divide and weaken the power of the groups opposed to the Tory government. He therefore proposed that the Labor, Liberal and Communist Parties should for the term of a single Parliament agree to concerted action on a previously agreed-upon program of social progress at home and opposition to Fascism abroad.

After discussion, the memorandum was defeated. The next day, however, leading members of the Party and its constituent organizations received the same memorandum in the mail, and a request for support. This being considered a grave breach of discipline, Sir Stafford was shortly afterward requested to withdraw his memorandum; he refused, was expelled from the executive council. This did not stop the controversy, however. The London *Daily Express* announced that by the expulsion the Socialist Party was "blowing its brains out." Sir Stafford continued to ask support for his program, to form Petition Committees; everyone connected with the Labor Party was taking sides; the efforts of four of Sir Stafford's allies ended in their own expulsion. After a speech before the Southport Congress in which he found himself blackballed, Sir Stafford asked for reinstatement, at last promised "to abide by the decisions of the conference on a Popular Front," but was refused.

After World War II began Sir Stafford Cripps was still contending that a British alliance with Russia would have prevented the conflict. Late in April 1940 he arrived in London. He had just made a leisurely tour of the world, including visits to Japan, India, the Philippines and the United States as well as a flight from Chungking to Moscow and back, during which he had presumably talked to Molotov (see sketch this

issue). In the United States he had expressed it as his opinion that the German-Soviet pact could be broken if the Western countries, including the United States, were to resume economic relations with Russia, and it is supposed that he went to Chamberlain with whatever information he had gathered on this score. It was not until Winston Churchill replaced Chamberlain, however, that Sir Stafford was listened to. First sent to Moscow as the head of a small British trade mission, he was given en route the rank of Ambassador when Great Britain was informed that Russia would be unable to accept a special envoy to discuss trade matters which could be dealt with by Ambassador Seeds or anyone appointed to replace him. Before reaching Moscow on June 12 Sir Stafford had made stops in Athens, Sofia and Bucharest in order to study the Balkan situation, and after his interview with Premier Molotov on June 14 it was said that concrete discussions on the possibility of a commercial agreement between Russia and Great Britain were to be started immediately. In October 1940 Sir Stafford was still sufficiently optimistic about a Soviet-British agreement to send for his wife and two of their daughters, although to most observers there seemed to be few tangible reasons for optimism, and British Left-wingers were claiming he was being used as a "front" for the policies of Lord Halifax (see sketch this issue), who had always been anti-Soviet.

Sir Stafford Cripps is "a thin, grave man who drinks no spirits, eats no meat," young-looking, "meticulously dressed, with a serious, scholarly face." In 1911 he married Isobel, second daughter of the late Commander Harold Swithinbank, and the couple have three daughters and a son who has already been a Parliamentary candidate. Sir Stafford has fathered two books as well as legal works; *Why This Socialism?* (1934) and *The Struggle for Peace* (1936). He recently remarked to a fellow-diplomat: "Of all the various occupations I thought I might follow, that of Ambassador never was among them. When any one here addresses me as 'Your Excellency' I involuntarily glance over my shoulder to see whether some excellency is standing behind me."

References

Canad Forum 19:112-14 Jl '39
Christian Cent 51:108-9 Ja 24 '34
Nation 144:92-3 Ja 23 '37; 148:724-6 Je 24 '39
New Statesman & Nation 17:171-2, 207, 247, 283-4, 324-5, 358-9 F 4-Mr 11 '39
N Y Times p6 My 28 '40; p4 My 30 '40; p11 Je 5 '40 por; p8 Je 8 '40 por; p25 Je 16 '40; p35 O 20 '40
PM p7 Jl 22 '40 por
Time 33:24 Je 12 '39 por; 35:35-6 Je 10 '40 por; 36:17 Ag 12 '40
World Tomorrow 17:80-1 F 15 '34; 17: 167 Mr 29 '34

Gunther, J. Left and Right in England *In* Inside Europe p256-66 1936
International Who's Who
Who's Who

CROMPTON, ROOKES EVELYN BELL

May 31, 1845—Feb 15, 1940 Pioneer English electric lighting engineer; installed first electric lights in Buckingham Palace and Windsor Castle; twice president of the Institute of Electrical Engineers

Wide World

ROOKES CROMPTON

References
   Who's Who

Obituaries
   N Y Herald Tribune p18 F 16 '40
   Newsweek 15:6 F 26 '40 por

CROMWELL, JAMES H. R.

1897- Ex-United States Minister to Canada, 1940; candidate for United States Senator from New Jersey

Address: Somerville, New Jersey

Long known as an amateur in sports, social philosophy, economics and politics, James Henry Roberts Cromwell became a professional diplomat upon his appointment at the age of 43 as United States Minister to Canada by President Franklin D. Roosevelt early in January 1940. On April 19, 1940 he formally announced his candidacy for the Democratic nomination for United States Senator from New Jersey in a statement in which he described himself as a "liberal" and on May 23 he resigned his Ministerial post to devote himself to his campaign. He received the nomination, Mayor Hague calling him the "ideal" candidate, but was defeated after a campaign in which his opponents called him "Mayor Hague's

puppet" and he insisted that he wore "no man's collar." In November 1940 his rival's campaign expenditures were being investigated.

Mr. Cromwell was born in New York City, the son of Oliver Eaton and Eva (Roberts) Cromwell. When he was 15 years old, his mother, after the death of Oliver E. Cromwell, married the late Edward T. Stotesbury, senior partner of J. P. Morgan & Company and head of the Philadelphia banking house of Drexel & Company, for whom his stepson had great affection and admiration. Young James grew up in Philadelphia. Mrs. Stotesbury is known as a leader in society and as dowager queen of the Palm Beach winter colony.

James H. R. Cromwell attended Central High School in Philadelphia as well as private schools (Fay and Lawrenceville) and the University of Pennsylvania. He left the university during the World War to enlist in the Navy. Later he transferred to the Marines, where he attained the rank of captain.

On June 17, 1920 he married Delphine Dodge, daughter of automobile manufacturer Horace E. Dodge. They had one child, Christine. This marriage ended January 1928 in an "amicable separation" followed by a Reno divorce later the same year. On February 13, 1935 Mr. Cromwell was front-page news because of his marriage to 22-year-old Doris Duke (daughter of tobacco magnate James Buchanan Duke), who is known as "the richest girl in the world." She is said to be the heiress to a fortune of between $30,000,000 and $53,000,000. In 1936 the Senate Committee on Campaign Expenditures reported that she had contributed $50,000 to the Democratic campaign that year. After the 1940 Senatorial campaign she separated from her husband, however.

The Cromwells lived on a 2,500-acre estate at Somerville, New Jersey and also maintained a home in Palm Beach and estates in Newport, Rhode Island, North Carolina, Antibes and a $1,000,000 "guest-proof" mansion in Honolulu which was designed, at Mrs. Cromwell's request, without spare bedrooms. In Ottawa they occupied the spacious Ministerial residence in Rockcliffe, overlooking the Ottawa River.

"Jimmy" Cromwell is an accomplished amateur sportsman, with special skill in golf, tennis, horsemanship, swimming, boat-racing. As an amateur boxer, he stood up for three rounds in a bout at Palm Beach with Tommy Loughran, then light-heavyweight champion of the world. For years he was a playboy. His parties were famous, and he once said: "For a long time in my life I thought the world was just a nice big pie, and I cut myself a slice."

But Cromwell, who is now said to scorn the "idle rich" and who on his arrival in Canada urged newspapermen to "forget all this richest girl in the world stuff," settled down to a serious study of economics after the collapse of the Florida land boom in

JAMES CROMWELL

the middle 1920's and the stock market crash of 1929. He had returned from the War to be introduced to the mysteries of banking as a clerk in the house of Drexel & Company. He then turned to the automobile financing business and later was vice-president of the Peerless Motor Company of Cleveland, and a partner in the New York advertising firm of H. R. Doughty and Associates. He is said to have been personally responsible for the sale of Dodge Brothers Company, after the death of his father-in-law, for the prodigious sum of $160,000,000. In 1925 Cromwell became president of the British-American Improvement Company of West Palm Beach. With Stotesbury and Dodge backing, he and his associates (among them the former King of Greece and the Countess of Lauderdale) created the town of Floranada, midway between Palm Beach and Miami, which was to be the center of the "American Riviera." The collapse of the land boom ruined the enterprise.

Cromwell was bitter over the law suits which followed this unfortunate venture. He turned with enthusiasm to economics, politics, social criticism, statistics, theories of constitutional law and lecturing. As a youth he was orthodox in his economic beliefs, and once he resigned from a Wharton School course because an instructor made disparaging remarks about a utility company of which Mr. Stotesbury was chairman, citing it as an example of "predatory plutocracy."

Nearly 20 years later, however, Cromwell went in somewhat the same direction. Although he still maintained reservations on behalf of his stepfather, in *The Voice of Young America,* published in February 1933, a month before the first inauguration of President Roosevelt and while the author

was still vice-president of the Peerless Motor Company, Cromwell severely lectured the parasitic rich and called for government ownership of transportation and public utilities. He also advocated that the issuance of any additional tax-exempt securities be prohibited; that United States tariffs be gradually reduced; that a blanket moratorium be declared on all international debts; that the government of Soviet Russia be recognized by this country. Although the book pointed out that men who have built their own fortunes by satisfying a need should not be confused "with those multimillionaires who have gained their wealth through the unconscionable exploitation of public monopolies or through the acquisition of special privileges by which they have obtained an unfair advantage over competitors," the author emphasized that his position was that of a capitalist who wanted capitalism to continue but felt that without considerable changes in the structure of our government, capitalism could not continue in this country.

Later Cromwell became one of the founders of the Sound Money League in which he was associated with the Rev. Charles E. Coughlin (see sketch this issue), radio priest, and for which he wrote booklets called *What Is Sound Money?* (1934) and *The Lion's Share* (1935). He so frequently conferred with Father Coughlin regarding the banking situation in November 1934 that the report arose that he had provided the Priest with inside information on bankers. Cromwell denied this, however, and said that the conferences were devoted to interpreting the attitude of bankers toward reforms sought by the Sound Money League and to impress on Father Coughlin that the system was at fault, not the bankers. The league pleaded with young men to unite for the reform of society within the framework of capitalism. With H. E. Czerwonky, Cromwell wrote *In Defense of Capitalism,* which was published in 1937. Written for business men, this work is "an explanation of the functioning of our capitalistic system of today and specific measures which would correct its defects."

Before his appointment to the "comfortable, socially pleasant, politically important" post of Minister to Canada, James H. R. Cromwell had no previous diplomatic experience, though he has long been interested in public affairs and has been a personal friend of President Roosevelt. Although he has been especially friendly toward some of the President's policies, particularly those dealing with foreign affairs, he cannot be termed a New Dealer in the full sense of the word. Some political commentators considered his appointment largely a political move to pave the way for him to run for election to the Senate, and events have proved them right. "Some said," according to *Time,* "it was because an election was coming, as well as drafts on the Democratic war chest; some said the moves were like a shot in pocket pool, in which the eight ball smacked the six, the six hit the three and James Cromwell dropped into the corner pocket." The Canadian post is considered one of the most important in the diplomatic service because of the economic relations of the two countries as well as their proximity. Mr. Cromwell's appointment to it was very popular in Canada where, headed by Prime Minister Mackenzie King (see sketch this issue) one of the largest crowds Canada ever turned out to greet an arriving American Minister met him and his wife on their arrival at Ottawa, with the thermometer at 15° below zero, on January 22, 1940.

The new Minister's popularity in Canada was considerably increased by his address, on March 19, 1940 at a joint luncheon of the Canadian and Empire clubs of Toronto, in which he praised Anglo-French war aims, blasted Germany and attacked American isolationists. His speech, however, raised a storm of protest in the United States where Senators and House members, believing his statements entirely outside the authority of an official representative of the United States government and likely to involve the nation in the War, demanded his recall. Cromwell settled the problem himself by his resignation, but didn't change his mind. During his Senatorial campaign he ardently defended conscription and all aid to Britain (France now being out of the picture) short of war.

James Cromwell is an enthusiastic person who enjoys life. Friends come easily and he is good company, ready to start anything or to talk business. His increased serious activities have not caused him to withdraw from society, though he has, of course, lessened his play hours. According to Elsa Maxwell, "he is never in doubt about anything and he feels he could cure the ills of this republic if given half a chance." According to others, some of his beliefs have borne a strong resemblance to those of Sir Oswald Mosley (see sketch this issue), British Fascist leader. Strong, tall, slender, he moves and speaks quickly. He has sandy, curly hair and a warm smile. Arthur Krock has written in the New York *Times*: "Mr. Cromwell is an engaging young man of wealthy antecedents and connections who deserves credit for having tried to amount to something in his own right."

References

Christian Cent 57:436 Ap 3 '40

Ladies' H J 55:22 D '38 pors

Life 8:24 F 5 '40 il pors; 8:28 Ap 1 '40 por

N Y Times p17 F 17 '33; p23 F 14 '35 por; p1 Ja 5 '40; p20 Ja 10 '40; p1, 6 Mr 20 '40; p9 Mr 21 '40; p26 Mr 24 '40; p9 Ap 20 '40; p11 My 24 '40; p26 Je 4 '40

Newsweek 15:14-15 Ap 1 '40

Sat Eve Post 212:9-11+ Mr 23 '40 il pors

Scholastic 36:10 F 5 '40; 36:2 Ap 1 '40

Time 35:12 Ja 15 '40; 35:15 Ap 1 '40 por

Who's Who in America (Addenda)

CROSS, MILTON JOHN Apr 16, 1897-
Radio announcer of NBC

Address: b. 30 Rockefeller Plaza, New York City; 60½ Riverside Drive, New York City

"The house lights are being dimmed. In a moment the great gold curtain will go up. . ." To ten million people who have sat enraptured before their radios listening, the "cultured, genuflecting" voice of Milton J. Cross, announcer for the Metropolitan Opera broadcasts, is more widely known than that of any other American with the possible exceptions of President Roosevelt and Charlie McCarthy.

In 1940, with 19 years of radio experience behind him, Cross is the second oldest radio announcer in point of service. Born in New York City, he lived as a boy in the tough Hell's Kitchen section and dreamed of a career in music. So "music-struck" was he that on vacation he fought for the privilege of personally delivering butter to Louise Homer, merely to gaze at the great singer. He even paid to carry a spear in a Metropolitan Opera production. After the regulation high school graduation he registered at the Institute of Musical Art under the direction of Dr. Frank Damrosch and received a diploma entitling him to become a music supervisor at a public school. But he never applied for such a position for while he was a student he became interested in radio. "Today," he says, "I look back with amazement to my own start in radio. As a profession it was practically non-existent. It held no attractions for an ambitious young man. I sang tenor and had engagements as second tenor in several excellent church choirs."

One evening in 1921 he met an electrically-minded young man who had picked up broadcasts from the Westinghouse studios (WJZ) outside of Newark. Cross was fascinated and rushed to compose a letter asking if they needed a singer. They did, and without pay on September 15 he sang in a partitioned-off corner of the women's rest room. He was asked if he would like to become a second announcer. "The offer was made," explains Cross, "due to the fact that I was familiar with foreign names and musical terms and had a natural respect for good diction. My first inclination was to refuse, with thanks. My future interest, I felt, lay in the field of music." He was naturally hesitant "about accepting any closer connection with this interesting but distressingly noncommercial enterprise." He did accept, however, with a small salary which did not cover his tuition at the music school, supplementing these slim earnings by singing in a Presbyterian Church (his own faith), Jewish Synagogues and Catholic Churches. Soon he was earning $40 a

MILTON CROSS

week for singing, announcing, impersonating, "enthusing" over household supplies, operating the Ampico player piano, reading the Sunday funnies and reciting Uncle Wiggily.

Cross concentrated upon his work as an announcer after WJZ joined the National Broadcasting Company. Nowadays his resonant "bass-viol" tones soothe the hearer into a reverent mood. In 1929 his superb diction won for him a gold medal from the American Academy of Arts and Letters. People have wondered where he learned his pronunciation of foreign words. No easy achievement, Cross has spent a year in study of Italian at the Institute of Musical Art, studied French with teachers at NBC, and had four years of German study in high school. In 1939, anxious to improve his diction further, he joined a course at Columbia University.

Although Cross has not had an experience so painful as that of the St. Louis announcer who was told to fill in pauses with "plugs" for his sponsor's product during a papal broadcast and said: "The next words you will hear will be those of Pope Pius XI,"—a pause—then, the plug: "Ajax is the beer for me"—Cross' tongue double-crossed him on an *A & P Gypsies* hour when, after a great burst of introductory music, he announced: "The A & G Pypsies !"

Ordinarily his diction is fine, however—rolling r's with Italian, and beautiful Wagnerian *ich's* and *ach's*. "The announcer's job," says Cross, "is most highly specialized. The best way for a young man with a good voice and good ideas to prepare to enter the radio field is first to perfect his diction, his acquaintance with foreign names—musical names and terms, geographical names, proper names, political terms—and to increase his ability to *ad lib*

or fill in extra minutes of time with spontaneous comments of his own."

Ad libbing brings up to Cross' mind the most wretched experience of his life. This occurred in Chicago, where NBC some years ago was broadcasting a single act of Verdi's *Trovatore*. It was subscribers' night at the Chicago Civic Opera Company. Just as Cross was ready to announce the rising of the curtain, word was brought that Samuel Insull would read an annual report which was not to go over the air. Cross had no script for the emergency, only a brief account of the action of *Trovatore*. First, he told the story of the plot. Then, in other words, he retold it. Then he described how the scenery would probably look. From there he went to other scenery he had seen for the opera. Then he recounted the cast. . . He reviewed other casts that came to his mind. . . He slowly recounted the whole of Verdi's life. "Mr. Insull is still speaking," whispered an aide. Cross started on the history of opera—the history of the Chicago Civic Opera—the auditorium in which the opera was housed—launched into an exciting description of the underground passage between the auditorium and a hotel. Mercifully someone handed him a list of the railroad cars to be used by the opera company on tour.

With passionate earnestness he went on: "Rosa Raisa will travel in car 244, Tito Schipa in car 241, etc." After 35 minutes of horror Mr. Insull stopped and the orchestra started. Insull came to him and said: "I know you will be grateful to me for leaving out the last 15 minutes of my speech."

Since Christmas Day 1931, when Milton Cross announced *Hänsel and Gretel,* he has never missed a Metropolitan Opera broadcast. Millions of listeners have enriched their knowledge of opera through his painstaking descriptions of the plot, costumes, scenery. He sits in at rehearsals on new or rarely played operas. When no opera is going on he announces station identification every 15 minutes. · For these services he receives about $80 a week. This is a very small salary, and even with additional commercial announcing he does not average the salary of announcers whose voices are more adaptable to commercial products. For the half-hour *Information, Please,* he receives $100 a week. Here he is at home, his voice suitable to accompany that of Clifton Fadiman, master of ceremonies and reputed to have one of the finest radio voices on the air. Other programs Cross announces are the *Radio City Music Hall,* the *Town Hall* program, a children's Sunday morning hour and a program for the Sherwin Williams Company called *Metropolitan Opera Auditions.* This last, with *Information, Please,* are the only two commercial programs for which separate salaries are paid.

Cross is a portly man, six-feet-two, with wavy hair, horn-rimmed glasses and a double chin. "I really love exercise," he says, "but I just don't have much time for it." Horseback riding is his favorite sport, although he likes swimming and handball, too. He was married to Lillian Ellegood, who is now dead, and has one daughter, Lillian G. Cross.

One would imagine that after all these years *ad libbing* would hold no terrors for him. Yet he admits that the moment before the conductor raises his baton, when the concluding remarks must be timed to the split second, is his zero hour.

References

    Christian Sci Mon Mag p9 N 25 '39
      por
    Etude 55:367-8 Je '37 pors
    Opera News 4:11-14 Ja 1 '40 por
    PM p55 Ag 18 '40 por
    Time 34:60 D 18 '39 il por
    Variety 137:40 Ja 31 '40

    Variety Radio Directory
    Who's Who in America

CROWLEY, JOHN J., FATHER Dec 9, 1891—Mar 17, 1940 Priest known as "the Padre of Death Valley"; pastorate covered 10,000 square miles

Obituaries

    N Y Herald Tribune p14 Mr 18 '40
    N Y Times p19 Mr 18 '40 por

CULBERTSON, ELY July 22, 1893- Bridge authority

Address: 16A E 62nd St, New York City

The man who founded an empire on a pack of cards, who made 10 million American homes contract-dizzy, who revolutionized life with the Forcing Two-Bid—this is the fabulous celebrity, the publicized world-renowned bridge authority, Ely Culbertson. According to his own reckoning, Culbertson's annual income amounts to half a million dollars. It accrues from various sources: his best-selling books on bridge, (*The Contract Bridge Blue Book* 1930; *Contract Bridge for Auction Players* 1932; *The Gold Book* 1936, etc.) on which he is said to receive the largest royalties in the publishing business; syndicate of his bridge column in some 200 daily newspapers; film shorts based on bridge problems; radio shorts; magazine articles on problems of bidding and playing; commercial endorsements; lectures, conventions, and teachers' fees; technical advice to bridge concerns; of many bridge gadgets, including score pads and playing cards.

But the Bridge Master, the celebrity whom the public sees, is actually only one of seven Ely Culbertsons, he tells us in his long autobiography, *The Strange Lives of One Man,* published in April 1940. Early in the book he names the other Elys, or "control-facets" of his personality: the epicurean, the idealist, the child, the philosopher, the family man, the businessman. The last-named, latest to develop, created the celebrity; the family

man seems to have been the most dubiously successful of the Ely personalities.

Only the last part of the book is the story of the bridge expert's career, already fairly well known to bridge enthusiasts. But the public will doubtless be amazed to learn of the strange dual heritage, the unorthodox growing up, the uncommonly interesting and diverse trend of events and adventures that made up the early life of Ely Culbertson.

His father's people were American, his mother's Russian. She was the daughter of a Cossack ataman or chief. His paternal grandfather, of Scotch descent, lived in Pennsylvania. News of the discovery of oil in the Caucasus brought his father, Almon, to the home of the Rogoznys. From the time that Almon drank, heroically, two great horns of Russian liquor as a challenge of strength, he determined to find out all he could about Cossack life. He learned to speak Russian, began to woo Xenia Rogozny and eloped with her. Their first-born was Eugene, who was later to become a soldier, then a monk. Two daughters died in childhood. Illya (Ely) was born July 22, 1893 at Poyana de Verbilao, Romania; his family had moved there on hearing of the discovery of new oil fields in the region. Another brother, Sasha, was born two years later; he was to become a famous violinist.

His family having returned to the Caucasus, Ely played with the Cossack village boys until he was six, when his father moved to America. A short stay brought his father to the conclusion that he was no longer at home in America, so they returned to settle definitely in Russia. A home was built—an American-styled house—at Grozny, near the oil fields. New oil fields were discovered, and the father gradually became rich.

Ely was sent to the Gymnasium at Vladikavkaz in 1904: he and his brother Eugene, as "Amerikantzi," were the school's oddities. Ely didn't get along very well with his schoolmates, and in many ways his life was made miserable until success in sports helped him win a place for himself. At 15 he developed strong religious interests, resolved to retire to a monastery and become "the greatest saint on earth," just as later he hoped to become the "greatest bridge player on earth." Sex awakening came to him as the temptation of the Devil; he suffered a severe nervous illness, and finally gained a saner viewpoint on the healthy advice of his doctor. He decided to be a rebel, and to sow a few wild oats; a brawl over women landed him in jail. Then his violinist-brother Sasha entered the Rostov Conservatory, so Ely transferred to the Gymnasium there. He began to read voraciously, admiring especially the works of Tolstoy, Dostoievsky and Edgar Allan Poe. He resolved to be a writer. His first story was about a man who was sane in all respects but one: he believed his *derrière* was not flesh and bone, but composed of fine, precious crystal.

ELY CULBERTSON

The story was not accepted for publication; later, for a schoolboy trick, Ely was expelled from the Gymnasium.

In common with many wealthy youths, Ely felt that his life was that of a wastrel, and he became interested in the problems of the peasants and workers. He took part in a socialist demonstration that was brutally broken up by the Cossacks. When he fell in love with Nadya, a beautiful student-revolutionist, he joined the party. In a riot Nadya was killed by the Black Hundred; seeking to avenge her death, Ely was arrested, and in prison met a number of Russian revolutionists. His mother's influence, however, secured his release.

Culbertson's father persuaded him to go on with his education, and sent him to America to go to Yale. But he soon left Yale to spend his time around the Bowery in New York. He went to Canada and worked as a timekeeper at a labor camp during the building of the Grand Trunk Pacific. He lost his job when he tried to organize the men. He hoboed around for awhile, then went to Mexico, where he didn't have much luck trying to "join the revolution." An abortive adventure in Spain preceded a decision to study in Paris and Geneva. It was in Geneva that he first learned to play auction bridge. Known as Geneva's "worst player," he resolved to be soon the world's best. He also adopted the young daughter of a French prostitute.

The Russian Revolution of 1917 wiped out the fortunes of Culbertson's parents. He came with his father and brother Sasha to America, all of them broke. Ely's father had always wanted him to give up card playing, which he abhorred. Destitute, however, he consented to Ely's earning money for them in the only way he knew. Through a friend, young Culbertson gained access to the Knickerbocker Whist Club; and, using a system which he announced as his own, found his winnings increasing. He began a scientific diagnosis and classification of his errors and successes.

At the club, the queen of the inner circle was Josephine Murphy Dillon, an attractive young widow with a reputation as America's greatest woman bridge player. Culbertson credited her with having a man's mind—and charm as well. He soon converted her to his System, but it took him much longer to win her heart. Finally, on June 11, 1923, they were married. For awhile bad luck and severe illness pursued the Culbertsons, then the tide turned. He began teaching his Culbertson System, and they resolved to become the best bridge players in the country, organizing tournaments and challenging experts. Two children were born to them: Joyce Nadya and Bruce Ely (nicknamed Jump Bid).

Culbertson went on with his plan to build himself up as a great public figure via contract bridge. This personality was to be "tough, cocky, comically conceited, not unwitty, perhaps kind, and certainly eccentric." To his Adam, Mrs. Culbertson was to be the publicity Eve. Unable to get backers for his promotion plans, he went ahead, on his own, shaping an organization from which issued his magazine, *The Bridge World*. The editor-owner had to play his hardest in clubs in order to make enough to meet his first payrolls. In order to raise money to arrange a bridge match between England and America, he inaugurated a beautiful scheme of taking orders for a special autographed edition of his forthcoming *Contract Bridge Blue Book,* which was completed in two frantic weeks. They went abroad to meet the British team, and they won the match. A cablegram from New York said that the *Blue Book* was an enormous success, going into several editions. (A later *Summary,* prepared entirely by Mrs. Culbertson, sold even better).

Thus, early in 1931, the Culbertsons returned triumphantly to America, rich and famous. They went to revisit Russia during the summer, but Culbertson, super-salesman, failed to get anywhere when he approached the Russian Card Trust on the promotion of contract: the Bolsheviks were all for outlawing playing cards, since their kings and queens represented "the remnants of a feudalistic régime."

Back again in America, the Culbertson expansion went on. But the 12 other bridge authorities in the country united in a war against him. Culbertson's reply was a challenge to a match: he and his wife against the opposition's team of Lenz and Jacoby. It was played off during December 1931. The story of the match was given considerable space on the front pages of newspapers; there were breathless telegraphic dispatches on the playing and winning of each hand. During Christmas, Theodor Lightner replaced Mrs. Culbertson in the tournament; the arena was shifted to the

Waldorf-Astoria to accomodate the mobs. At last, after 33 days, the Culbertson team won its final bid, and the match.

The Culbertsons became world-famous. Ely established elaborate headquarters at Rockefeller Plaza for a tremendous organization promoting such super-activities as the annual World Bridge Olympic, in which thousands of people take part, each contestant paying a dollar fee. A bridge network supported by 4,000 licensed Two-Demand instructors was set up. An enterprise to manufacture Kim (chemical plastic) playing cards sent him deeply into debt; but after some months of hair-raising and nerve-straining holding out for higher bids from buyers, he sold it at a tremendous profit. With the money he built a magnificent house on East Sixty-Second Street, New York, and moved his Crockford's Club, a most exclusive bridge-playing organization, into the adjoining building.

By 1937 Ely, the Business Manager, felt that he had everything, materially, that one could desire. But, as an industrial and social robot, he wasn't happy. He became nervous and depressed, even indifferently lost a bridge match. He began to quarrel with Jo, and this kept up. Finally they decided to get a divorce, but to continue their public life in bridge, sharing its profits. And they decided to keep the same house, he living on one floor, she on another, and both meeting in the apartment of the children, which was "neutral territory."

Culbertson's chief interest, besides bridge, is psychology and its application. He proudly admits to psychological methods in selling bridge. It is said that the Bridge Master has an impressive and theatrical personality. He is "tall and lean, sandy-haired, with piercing gray eyes, a lofty forehead and slightly vulpine teeth. In manner he is fastidious, surrounding himself with all kinds of continental fripperies, and expending a tidy fortune upon his personal tastes. He maintains a suite in New York and a million-dollar estate in Ridgefield, Connecticut. He has a pretty flair for caviar, goose liver and vintage wines. He is the sort of man who always mixes his own salad dressing at the table. . . He speaks six languages, all of them with a crisp and crackling Russian accent which is not displeasing. In brief, he has adopted the Grand Manner."

Culbertson hopes to do something besides bridge, to continue with his writing. In addition to a projected work on "mass psychology," he is now working on a play, and has a mystery novel on the fire.

References
> Am Mag 114:36-7+ D '32
> Am Mercury 38:69-77 My '36 (Same abr. Read Digest 28:71-4 Je '36); 51:434-41 D '40
> Christian Cent 49:16-17 Ja 6 '32
> New Yorker 16:16-17 Ap 27 '40
> Newsweek 15:37 Ap 8 '40 por
> Pub W 137:1398-9 Ap 6 '40

> Sat Eve Post 205:12-13+ Jl 16 '32
> Sat R Lit 21:10 Ap 20 '40 por
> Culbertson, E. Strange Lives of One Man 1940
> Who's Who in America

CULLEN, GLENN ERNEST Apr 1, 1890 —Apr 11, 1940 Authority in the field of child medicine research; professor of biochemistry in the Graduate School of the University of Cincinnati; professor of research pediatrics at College of Medicine. University of Cincinnati

GLENN E. CULLEN

References
> American Men of Science
> Who's Who in America

Obituaries
> N Y Herald Tribune p18 Ap 12 '40

CULVER, ESSAE MARTHA President of the American Library Association
Address: State Library Commission, Baton Rouge, Louisiana

Complete and adequate library service for all the people in the United States and Canada was the keynote of President Essae Martha Culver's address to the members of the American Library Association meeting at the Taft Auditorium in Cincinnati, May 31, 1940. After she received the four-leaf clovers, horseshoes and rabbit's-foot from retiring President Ralph Munn, President Culver outlined a four-point program for the 15,000 members of the association in her *Call to Action.*

President Culver has fought hard and worked long for the extension of library service to the many millions of people who are not served by libraries. Born in Emporia,

ESSAE M. CULVER

Kansas, the daughter of Joseph Franklin and Mary (Murphy) Culver, Miss Culver attended college in Claremont, California and received a Bachelor of Letters degree from Pomona College in 1905. After working as assistant librarian in the Pomona College Library she determined to supplement her practical experience with library school training and went to the New York State Library School in Albany, New York in 1907 and 1908. Then she returned to the West coast, going to the Salem (Oregon) Public Library, where she was librarian from 1909 to 1914.

Miss Culver entered county library service in the romantic days when "a librarian on horseback with a pack mule and Indian guide might go over steep trails, through unfrequented country, taking with her mental food to the remotest dwellers" and where counties are larger than many states. She was successively librarian of Glenn, Butte and Merced Counties in California from 1914 to 1925. Her county library administration was interrupted from 1921 to 1923 when she served as a library visitor for the California State Library. In the county service she experienced "the joy of work which comes from the satisfaction of being able to meet the great need of the rural people."

Going to Louisiana as executive secretary to the State Library Commission (1925), Miss Culver again had an opportunity to develop her interest and experience in an all-embracing library service. There she conducted the first state-supported regional library experiment. In this experiment, made up of three political units—five libraries and 11,600 books served a population of 32,000 white persons, 11,916 of whom became library borrowers. In less than a year the circulation approximated 220,000. Books were distributed through 24 branch libraries and 37 bookmobile stops at a total cost of $25,000. So great was the success of the experiment— started to see if the whole state of Louisiana could be served through rural libraries—that an appropriation of $100,000 was granted in 1938 for future demonstrations.

Miss Culver has written many articles for library periodicals describing her crusade for the extension of library service. She has taught (summer sessions 1935, 1936, 1938) classes in extension work at the School of Library Service at Columbia University. She has been active in library groups: League of Library Commissions (president 1931 to 1933), Southwestern Library Association (president 1936 to 1938) and the American Library Association (second vice-president and member of the executive board 1936 to 1938, first vice-president and president elect 1939 to 1940); active in professional groups: Louisiana Federation of Women's Clubs, Louisiana Business and Professional Women; active in social groups: The Orleans, Petit Salon.

A calm, self-possessed person, Miss Culver has dark eyes and smooth brown hair. She speaks with a sense of humor, but never loses sight of her belief that "talkers are not doers" and that deeds and not words will provide an opportunity for librarians "to work together toward the goal of freedom and opportunity to read for all the people."

References

A. L. A. Bul 33:262 Ap '39
Library J 65:528 Je 15 '40 por
American Women
Who's Who in America
Who's Who in Library Service

CURIE, EVE (kü'rē') Dec 6, 1904- French writer; lecturer
Address: c/o W. Colston Leigh, Inc, 521 Fifth Ave, New York City

Eve Curie came to New York on her first visit in 1921. She was a young girl of 16, and her own fledgling charm was eclipsed by the fame of her scientist mother, Marie Curie. Marie Curie had come to the United States to receive as a gift from the women of America a $250,000 gram of radium—the precious radium she had discovered, but was too poor to buy. It was a triumphal tour, climaxed by an impressive ceremony at the White House at which President Harding made the presentation. Madame Curie was accompanied by her two daughters, Irène and Eve, and when the work-worn, exhausted scientist could not attend all the receptions and dinners which an adoring public wished to shower on her, the two girls substituted for her—but they were merely "Madame Curie's daughters," not yet famous in their own right.

But when Eve Curie made her second visit to the United States to lecture early in 1940, she was already well-known to Americans. Her biography of her mother, translated into English by Vincent Sheean, was a popular best seller, and acclaimed by critics as a great human document. Her third trip was made in the fall of 1940 after she had fled from France.

Tall, slender, with deep blue eyes, fair skin and dark hair, Eve Curie looked like something that had stepped out of a French fashion magazine. She had beauty, brains, charm, and she won the hearts of her audiences. American journalists waxed lyrical describing her chic and her wit. She was described as "the woman who has everything."

If Eve Curie "has everything," she has developed her own talents in a field foreign to that in which she had been brought up. Her parents, Marie and Pierre Curie, were absorbed in their scientific researches. They had scarcely any interest outside of science. Eve Curie's sister, Irène, was to follow in her mother's footsteps, and become completely absorbed in scientific research. For Irène, like her mother, has received the Nobel Prize in collaboration with her husband, Frederic Joliot (see sketch Irène Joliot-Curie this issue).

But Eve showed no interest in science. She must have amazed her puritanical, unworldly mother. She loved fine clothes, loved fun and had the French flair for life. Born in Paris, she was graduated from the Sévigné College as Bachelor of Science, and later as Bachelor of Philosophy, in both cases with honors. She became interested in music and devoted several years to the study of the piano.

Her debut as a concert pianist was made in Paris in 1925. She followed it with many concerts in Paris, in the French provinces and in Belgium. Not wishing to trade on her family name, she began writing music criticism under a pen name and won some renown as a critic, acting for several years as the music critic of the weekly journal *Candide*. She wrote regularly for the Parisian journals and periodicals, mainly on music, the theatre and motion pictures. In 1932 she translated and adapted for the French theatre the American play, *Spread Eagle*, by George S. Brooks and Walter B. Lister. It was produced at the Théâtre du Gymnase under the title *145 Wall Street*, and had a long run.

When United States publishers approached her with the idea of writing a biography of her mother, Mlle. Curie was willing to undertake the job, but was terrified by the task. She kept putting it off and had to be badgered constantly to finish it. The biography, *Madame Curie*, is a heart-warming, poignantly-moving tribute to her mother. Although it is written with a daughter's sentimentality and is tinged with hero-worship, it gives a picture of the Curies as none but one intimately acquainted with them could give. The modest, retiring Curies had hidden themselves from the public. The story of the little Polish girl, Marie Sklodowska, who became Marie Curie, and who overcame sickness and poverty to give the great gift of radium to the world, needed

EVE CURIE

to be told. Although Eve Curie's book met with reviews ranging from lukewarm to rave pieces, no reviewer could altogether overlook it as a human document of a noble character. One reviewer wrote: "It is difficult to characterize this exquisite story of Madame Curie's life without using superlatives which seem out of place in describing an account of a life so simple and at the same time so sublime, and which is reproduced in lines equally simple, accurate and appropriate. The writer has put her soul into a work which only she could have done." Another wrote: "It would be easy to point out faults in this book, considered only as a biography. . . But to stress such limitations would be churlish. This is a great book because its subject is a great subject." Still another said of the book on Marie Curie: "Her daughter's presentation has obvious defects. She is richer in sentiment than in science, and her style is exuberantly adjectival. But when all has been said, there emerges from the book a charming and impressive picture of one who might be termed a Saint of Science."

Madame Curie was the December 1937 choice of the Literary Guild; it was chosen by the American Library Association as "the best non-fiction book of the year." And it won for Eve Curie the Clement Cleveland Medal awarded annually by the New York Cancer Committee to one who has achieved distinction in the fight against cancer. It was also the prelude for the lecture tour of the United States which brought Eve Curie to the attention of Americans as a unique figure in her own right.

When the time came for her first United States lecture tour, Mlle. Curie was working 10 hours a day in the Paris Giraudoux Office of Censorship and Propaganda as direc-

CURIE, EVE—*Continued*

tor of women's activities. But she took time to lecture in cities all over the United States on the cause of France during her tour, beginning in January and ending in April, 1940. And somehow she managed to get together a Schiaparelli (see sketch this issue) wardrobe about which fashion reporters wrote columns and which gave both Schiaparelli and Mlle. Curie added reams of publicity, just as it had been designed to do. One fashion reporter wrote of Mlle. Curie: "In any place in the world a beautiful young woman who makes an entrance in a Schiaparelli original is allowed to rest on her laurels a bit. She may even titter and make very little sense, and people are inclined to be lenient, but when beauty arrayed by Schiaparelli can discuss music, painting, skiing, writing and international affairs in any language you choose, the plot thickens."

After France fell, Mlle. Curie fled to England and thence to the United States, where in the fall of 1940 she continued to lecture on the War and the importance of British victory. Her sympathies are with the "free French" forces of General De Gaulle (see sketch this issue).

Louis Bromfield, one of her writer friends, had written of her: "When I think of her, she is somehow associated with the freshness and beauty and soft glittering quality of snow. . . She is like Diana. . . I realize that what I have written may sound rhapsodical, yet I only feel that my effort has been inadequate. She is a woman—in the common, vivid speech of our times—who has everything." This appeared in the conservative New York *Herald Tribune*.

Between Eve Curie, chic, worldly, and her mother, so different in her tastes, there existed a close companionship. During her childhood, Eve had been brought up by governesses, generally Polish, and her mother's early background in Poland was vivid and real to her. In her biography of her mother, Eve Curie wrote in a foreword: "My mother was 37 years old when I was born. When I was big enough to know her, she was already an aging woman who had reached the summit of renown. And yet it is the 'celebrated scientist' who is strangest to me—probably because the idea that she was a 'celebrated scientist' did not occupy the mind of Marie Curie. It seems to me rather, that I have always lived near the poor student, haunted by dreams, who was Marie Sklodowska long before I came into the world."

Eve Curie lived with her mother after her sister's marriage and made many trips with her in France, and to Italy, Belgium, Switzerland and Spain. Marie Curie was a fine sportswoman, and she taught her children to like sports. Eve Curie swims particularly well, skis and skates.

It was Eve who was with her mother in her final illness, who nursed her and who accompanied her to the sanatorium in Savoy and was with her until the end, July 4, 1934.

References

Atlan 165:603-13 My '40
Christian Sci Mon p2 Ja 19 '40
Ind Woman 18:129 My '39
N Y Herald Tribune p5 Ja 18 '40; p10 Ja 26 '40 pors
N Y Times p8 Ja 19 '40; p13 Ja 20 '40; II p6 Ja 21 '40 por
Time 34:30 D 11 '39 por; 35:25-9 F 12 '40 por (cover)
Curie, E. Madame Curie 1937

DALADIER, EDOUARD (dä-läd-yā' ä'dwär) June 18, 1884- French statesman

Five men who ruled the destinies of France have in 1940 been formally indicted by the Supreme Court at Riom in the "war blame" investigation. Among them was Edouard Daladier, who had fled to Casablanca on June 20, when France's fate became apparent. He was brought back to the Château Chazeron to await his trial, and then transferred to Riom in November 1940. The charges were that as Premier he declared war without consulting Parliament and as Minister of War for many years failed to equip the army with necessary material.

Since 1919 Edouard Daladier has been a figure in French politics. He has held posts in twelve Cabinets, has three times been Premier of France. He has been granted powers greater than those accorded to any French Premier before him, and much of the responsibility for France's present situation lies on his shoulders.

Edouard Daladier comes of peasant, artisan stock. He was born in 1884 in the village of Carpentras, the department of Vaucluse, in Southern France—a rugged, mountainous country. His father was a baker. His two grandfathers were bakers. His sister worked in a bakery all through her childhood; his brother still carries on the family tradition. His own entrance into politics was something of an accident, for it was while attending the Lycée Duparc at Lyon that he first met the man who was to direct his first political footsteps, Edouard Herriot, then a teacher. Herriot took an unusual interest in his young pupil, made him his protégé. In 1909 Daladier himself was teaching history, first at the University of Nîmes, then at Grenoble, Marseille, Lyon, and finally at the Lycée Condorcet, Paris. While still teaching at Grenoble he was elected Mayor of Carpentras, and at Lyon he again came under the influence of Herriot, leader of the Radical-Socialist Party.

But it was 1914. For four years Edouard Daladier was in the trenches—as common soldier, as sergeant, as captain. He received the Légion d'Honneur, the Croix de Guerre and three citations for bravery. In 1919 he returned to teaching at the Lycée Condorcet, but this time for only two weeks. Herriot persuaded him to run for Parliament as Radical-Socialist deputy for Vaucluse, and he was elected. For 21 years he was to be returned to Parliament as deputy for that department.

Daladier did not immediately distinguish himself as a parliamentarian. He was not a lawyer, he was a teacher. And for a long time he remained in the shadow of Herriot. It was true that during the years 1921 to 1924 he was condemning the French occupation of the German Ruhr, advocating friendship with the post-War Weimar Republic, and speaking vaguely of the economic reorganization of Europe, but it was mainly by his knowledge of army affairs that he made himself recognized. He had traveled some in the Soviet Union, in Great Britain and in Germany, always with an eye to things military, and by 1923 he was acknowledged as his party's best spokesman on army matters.

In 1924, at the age of 40, Daladier held his first Cabinet post, as Minister for the Colonies under Herriot. That same year he married Mlle. Laffont. She was the daughter of a country doctor, and during the War had been his "Marianne"—the unknown girl whose letters he received while in the trenches.

By 1927 Daladier had become leader of the Left-wing Radical-Socialists (neither radical, Socialist, nor very far Left), and in 1928 he was elected president of his party. Herriot's protégé had stepped permanently out from under that somewhat massive wing.

During the next three years Daladier held the post of Minister of Public Works in three Cabinets, the post of Minister of War in another, and early in 1933 he became Premier of France for the first time—on the day after Hitler became Chancellor of Germany. In the Cabinet which he formed the Right was pleased to find no Socialists represented, and it was also in this Cabinet that Georges Bonnet received his first job of major rank in the French government—that of Daladier's Minister of Finance. Daladier himself took the post of Minister of War, and the French generals found him "suitable and compliant." At this time his hope was to reach some kind of an understanding with Germany, and it was during his term in office that the Four Power Pact between France, Great Britain, Italy and Germany was signed, in June 1933. Four months later he was out of power.

Upon the resignation of Chautemps, January 27, 1934, Daladier again became Premier—for 11 hectic days. Encouraged by the Rightists and Fascists, riots in protest against the Stavisky scandal of Chautemps' administration were breaking out all over Paris. Daladier's transfer of Police Chief Jean Chiappe to another post was hardly a satisfactory answer. On February 6 an angry mob of 30,000 demonstrators was moving over the bridge across the Seine on its way to storm the Chamber of Deputies. Daladier ordered out his Garde Mobile. Suddenly, unbelieving cries were heard from the crowd: "They are shooting, they are really shooting!" In the resulting rout at least seventeen were killed,

EDOUARD DALADIER

hundreds wounded. Daladier, fearing a "Fascist coup," had ordered his Guards to fire, and they had done their job efficiently.

Forced to resign the next day, branded a murderer by the Rightists, nicknamed "Le Fusilleur," it seemed that Daladier's public career must be over. But the Rightists were losing ground; the movement toward the Popular Front was gaining momentum in France. For 18 months Daladier remained in comparative retirement—then, on July 14, 1935, Bastille Day, the leader of the Radical-Socialists made a spectacular public appearance. With Léon Blum (see sketch this issue), the Socialist leader, and Maurice Thorez, the leader of the Communists in France, he marched in the Popular Front demonstration. In the shadow of the Bastille he gave the clenched-fist Communist salute, swore fidelity to the Popular Front. In the elections of the next year it was the Front Populaire which won heavily, and when Blum became Premier on June 15, 1936, Daladier was appointed his Minister of War.

Some of the statements from speeches made by Daladier during this period are interesting in view of his sharp swing to the right two years later. He had joined the Popular Front because "I represent the *petite bourgeoisie* and I declare that the middle class and the working class are natural allies." "France is now in the hands of a financial oligarchy, from whom power must be wrested and given back to the people." "It is our aim to reconcile the spirits which stormed the Bastille and defended Verdun." "What is to be desired is a blend of nationalism and democracy."

Under Blum's Popular Front government the power of the financial oligarchy of France's 200 families and of the Bank of France was reduced, aviation nationalized, the railways coordinated; the 40-hour week

DALADIER, EDOUARD—*Continued*

and other social legislation long fought for by Labor was introduced; but France's very shaky financial condition did not improve. Wobbling from Left to Right on its political legs and finding that neither would support it, Blum's Cabinet fell at last. On April 4, 1938, the day Hitler was holding a plebiscite in Austria, Edouard Daladier for the third time "took over."

Almost immediately he performed a swing to the Right which would provoke the admiration of any acrobat. In the interests of armament production, one of his first announcements was that it was time to abolish the 40-hour week. Although, while Blum was Premier he had complained that he was prevented from helping Republican Spain, now he himself sealed the Spanish border, and with it, some say, the fate of Spain. In the interests of national unity against the growing threat of war, he soon asked Parliament for full powers, and was three times granted temporary power to rule by decree. His Foreign Minister was Georges Bonnet, whose notoriously pro-German policy paved the pathway to Munich. After Munich, when Daladier was given new plenary powers and his Cabinet reshuffled, his new Minister of Finance, Paul Reynaud (see sketch this issue), instituted drastic financial and economic legislation that brought about the famous November strikes.

In May 1939, Daladier did not bother to go through the formality of tendering his resignation after the Presidential election; the work of the Chamber itself was by this time almost entirely limited to discussion of the new electoral system. People who mumbled of dictators could be answered with his comment: "Am I no longer a Republican because I insist on respect for Republican law and order?" And it was also true that the sentiment of a great number of French people, as well as of the army, was behind Daladier; although he had followed Chamberlain's policy as far as Munich, under his régime presumably France was at last seriously preparing for war.

When the War came in September it brought with it a further curtailment of parliamentary government: strict censorship, further harsh decrees. The 1940 general elections were postponed until 1942. Communist deputies in the Chamber were arrested, the party suppressed. The War itself developed into a "Sitzkrieg." But, although Daladier proclaimed that he was growing tired of "this sleepy war," Bonnet remained in his Cabinet, though finally transferred to the Ministry of Justice. At that time Daladier added the portfolio of Foreign Minister to his own. With the development of the Russo-Finnish War he sent arms and ammunition to the Finns, wished to declare war on Russia and to override the objections of the Scandinavian countries. Parliament was growing even more restive. When the Russo-Finnish peace was made the growing discontent with the French government

came to a head. Criticisms had been made of Daladier's Cabinet; it was assumed that a new Cabinet would be formed before the meeting of the Chamber of Deputies on March 19.

On that afternoon Daladier appeared in the Chamber with his old Cabinet. In the stormy secret session that followed a vote of confidence in his government's effective prosecution of the War was introduced; the vote was 239 affirmative, 1 negative, 300 abstaining. Among the abstainers were Rightists and a number of Radical-Socialists as well as 155 Socialists. Since in France it is an unwritten rule that one does not vote against a government in time of war, Daladier took this as a "moral defeat," refused to form a new Cabinet, on March 20 offered his resignation. On March 21 Paul Reynaud accepted the office of Premier, and Daladier was appointed to the post of Minister of National Defense which he had held all during the time of his own Premiership. On May 19, with the German forces threatening Amiens, Reynaud took over the Defense Ministry, and Daladier was appointed to the post of Minister of Foreign Affairs. He was not removed from the Cabinet until June 5.

Edouard Daladier is described by John Gunther as "short and stocky, with big shoulders and heavy hands. His eyes are a bright blue, below uncombed eyebrows that dart upward. The forehead is broad, the hair sparse. He smiles almost continually when he talks: a quick, perceptive smile, punctuated by short bursts of rather hard laughter. His conversation is quick and to the point. He likes badinage, but doesn't waste much time on it. He can lose his temper easily."

He is not a sociable man. Since his wife's death in 1932 he has lived with his sister and his two sons, students in a Paris school, in an unpretentious apartment on the Rue Anatole de la Joige. Seldom seen at fashionable receptions, he liked walking, riding, swimming, reading. Before the dignities which came to him in the past few years he would often be seen on his bicycle, earnestly pedaling away from the Chamber of Deputies.

He seems to have little regard for money, and has never been mixed up in any financial scandal. He does enjoy good food, and in quantities; he is a heavy drinker and smoker. His great interests are the history of the Middle Ages and the Renaissance and military affairs, and his one book, published in 1939, was titled *In Defense of France*.

Daladier has been called a "strong man" of France. Critics, however, have pointed to his vacillation at times of crisis and to his domination by Georges Bonnet and by the Marquise de Crussols, with whom he became very friendly shortly after the death of his wife and at whose salon he is supposed to have made his peace with Big Business. Essentially he is a stubborn rather than a strong man, his strength "lavished on parliamentary jousts and ministerial tilts" and vanishing "in the face of momentous historic events." Many have been impressed by his frankness and genuineness—John Gunther admired his ability to speak "the language of the average Frenchman," found in his taciturnity and natural suspiciousness a proof of his closeness to the peasant; others, for the same reasons, have called him "mediocre", "a machine politician *par excellence.*" Daladier has described himself as "the last Jacobin." It was probably an overestimation.

References

Am Mercury 50:477-83 Ag '40
Christian Sci Mon Mag p1-2 Jl 8 '39 il por
Collier's 106:11+ S 7 '40 il por
Cur Hist 51:19-21 Ja '40 (Same abr. Read Digest 36:13-18 Ja '40)
Good H 109:30+ O '39 il
Liberty 17:22-4 N 2 '40 por
Liv Age 354:136-9 Ap '38
New Repub 99:327-8 Jl 26 '39
Sat Eve Post 213:16-17+ S 21 '40 il por
Time 28:24 Jl 27 '36 por; 31:25 Ap 18 '38 por; 35:22 F 19 '40; 35:20-1 Ap 1 '40

Crain, M. Rulers of the World 1940
Gunther, J. Daladier and Blum *In* Inside Europe p145-65 1940
Lapaquellerie, Y. Profile *In* Daladier, E. In Defense of France p3-38 1939
Leeds, S. B. These Rule France 1940
Ray, O. Life of Edouard Daladier pam 1940
Romains, J. Seven Mysteries of Europe 1940
Simone, A. J'Accuse 1940
Who's Who

DALI, SALVADOR (dä'lē săl-vä-dor') Mar 11, 1904- Surrealist painter
Address: c/o Julien Levy Gallery, 15 E 57th St, New York City

When Salvador Dali's very real surrealist rage caused him to crash through a swank Fifth Avenue shop's plate-glass window 'way back in 1939, he was arrested, but an official suspended his sentence with the announcement: "These are some of the privileges that an artist with temperament seems to enjoy." In July 1940 it was reported that the Master of the Limp Watches had been arrested in Spain on charges of opposing Franco's Fascist régime; he had made irreverent noises during a demonstration of Falangist youth. He has now fled back to the United States, claiming to be "a reformed and much more conservative man." He plans to paint surrealist Biblical pictures in Virginia, to have an exhibition in the near future and to publish an autobiography.

Although this can't quite classify as a publicity stunt Dali does have a genius for landing in the newspapers. Perhaps this is why he is the only surrealist that the public knows much about. Born in Figueiras near Barcelona in 1904, the son of a notary who wanted another notary in the family, young Salvador refused him that satisfaction and at 14 began to attend the Academy of Fine Arts in Madrid. There he puzzled his teachers both by his facility at copying the works of the masters with a touch of quite personal satire and his love of what has since become known as "doodling."

Nobody then had discovered the immense Freudian and artistic significance of the simple "doodle," and Dali was finally expelled for insubordination. By the time he arrived in Paris in 1927, however, surrealism was the talk of the cafés. With already well-developed neuroses, he took to it with no effort at all. When he first exhibited his subconscious in the form of small canvases, he sold every picture, and in his enthusiasm went on to write surrealist poems and to help produce the first two surrealist films: *Le Chien Andalou* (with emphasis on pianos filled with the carcasses of dead donkeys) and *L'Age d'Or.*

By 1934 art dealer Julien Levy decided the United States was ready to receive Dali's message. Both the artist and his exhibition here created an immediate sensation, particularly the picture containing the well-known drooping timepieces, *The Persistence of Memory* (now owned by the Museum of Modern Art). He had recently married Gala Eluard, former muse of all Parisian surrealists, and newspapermen all over the land were made happy by such statements as: "I used to balance two broiled chops on my wife's shoulders, and then by observing the movement of tiny shadows produced by the accident of the meat on the flesh of the woman I love while the sun was setting, I was finally able to attain images sufficiently lucid and appetizing for exhibition in New York." Promptly taken up by New York socialites, a Dali Ball, in which the artist himself wore on his chest a glass case containing a brassiere, put the subconscious of the Social Register into costume, décor and history.

Perhaps Dali's vogue in the United States reached its peak, however, after the surrealist exhibition at the Museum of Modern Art in December 1936. The previous summer he had made his impression on London during a lecture in which he appeared wearing a deep-sea diving suit with a jeweled dagger at its belt, carrying a billiard cue and leading a pair of Russian wolfhounds. Nearly suffocated before his helmet could be unscrewed, he had explained: "I just wanted to show that I was plunging deeply into the human mind." At another lecture in Barcelona during the Spanish War he balanced on top of his head a loaf of bread whose significance is still unexplained In America, all New York came to the Museum, looked, scratched its collective head and went out discussing such titles as *Three Young Surrealist Women Holding in Their Arms the*

SALVADOR DALI

Skins of an Orchestra or *Suburbs of the Paranoiac-Critical Afternoon (on the Outskirts of European History).* Magazine covers and department store windows began to take on a familiar nightmarish look.

The Dali vogue has had remarkable persistence, too. It was in March 1939, two years after the exhibition, that the famous Bonwit Teller department store episode took place in which changes made in a display Dali created for them caused such indignation in the artist's breast that an attempt to destroy the fur-lined bathtub in their window caused him to smash the plate glass and topple into the street. It was at the New York World's Fair in 1939 that the Dali-created *Dream of Venus,* a "reconstruction of a very Freudian subconscious in the medium that Broadway calls a 'girl show'" startled the public. And meanwhile there have been Dali ballets—notably one about a red-wigged Tristan's love for Isolde, music by Wagner and Cole Porter (see sketch this issue); more Dali lectures; Dali articles on surrealism; even a Dali attempt at a scenario for Harpo Marx, whose portrait he painted in Hollywood along with Mae West's. (The artist is among those who classify the Marx Brothers' pictures as surrealism applied to films.)

A little proud of the very remunerative persecution complex which supposedly inspires his canvases, Dali says: "The only difference between me and a madman is that I am not a madman. I am able to distinguish between the dream and the real world." Although he claims to paint "for the masses, for the great common man, for the people," he finds it perfectly natural for the public not to understand his pictures. "I do not understand them at first myself. Then I begin to grasp the symbols, though there are often some symbols which I can never explain." Most people find his titles any-

thing but explanatory of the symbols, however, and ask questions. The mystery of *Debris of an Automobile Giving Birth to a Blind Horse Biting a Telephone* he once cleared up by explaining the telephone as representing "the blackened bones of my father passing between the male and female figures in Millet's *Angelus.*" (The telephone appears and reappears in his pictures, as do other symbols said to represent "the horrors that have beset him from infancy to the present," among them nearly all "man-made devices.")

Dali says his two greatest influences have been Leonardo and Vermeer—"the former by his spirituality, the latter by his objectivity," and defines painting as "photography, by hand and in colors, of concrete irrationality and the world of the imagination in general." Not long ago he announced that the period of surrealist dream-documentation was about over, the period of "paranoiac painting" just beginning. For a long time he has defined surrealist painting itself as the interpretation of paranoiac dreams, however, and often employs on his canvases such devices as the paranoiac multiple image.

As for what people think of him—there's nothing really unanimous about it. Some say he's crazy, wasting a very real talent on nonsense. Some find him merely an amusing opportunist. Most will admit that his miniaturist style shows "extraordinary technical facility as a draughtsman" and a remarkable feeling for color, even though they may find his paintings more interesting for their illustrational qualities than for their experiments in form, which are few. Fellow surrealists, perhaps resentful at being neglected, admit he can paint, but find his soul "commercial." And then there is Edward Alden Jewell of the New York *Times,* who rhapsodized: "So far as ideology goes, all this is quite beyond debate. It is beyond life and death. It is beyond everything."

Slight, dark, restless, with "a clipped cinemactor's mustache" and the "eyes of a crystal gazer," Dali doesn't look much like an artist except, perhaps, when he wears his favorite knitted Catalan liberty cap. He probably knows more English than he claims to, speaks fluent French in a soft voice with a pronounced Spanish accent, and names Freud as his favorite reading matter. He has no particular work habits. Sometimes he paints eighteen hours a day, sometimes goes weeks without touching a brush; some of his pictures are finished in two weeks, others not for months.

Opinion is divided as to whether he amuses himself mightily with the public or takes himself with almost unprecedented seriousness. It is possible that he does both. Certainly he takes very seriously the right of an artist to create as he pleases. When in August 1939 the World's Fair authorities forbade him to put fishes' heads instead of fishes' tails on his Dream of Venus beauties the mermaids remained conventional in that one respect, but he issued an indignant manifesto which ended: "Artists and poets of America! .. Loose the blinding lightning of your anger and the avenging thunder of your paranoiac inspiration!"

They have not, as yet.

References

> Art Digest 9:16 Ja 1 '35; 11:7 Ja 1 '37 il; 11:17 Mr 1 '37; 12:7 F 15 '38; 13:12 My 1 '39; 13:12 Jl '39; 13:9 Ag '39
> Arts & Dec 42:46 Mr '35 il
> Cur Hist 50:48-9 Ap '39 il
> Mag Art 30:60-1 Ja '37
> New Repub 81:360 F 6 '35
> New Yorker 15:22-7 Jl 1 '39
> Parnassus 8:15 D '36 il
> Time 28:31 Jl 13 '36 por; 28:62 D 14 '36 por (cover); 33:31 Mr 27 '39 il; 33:43 Ap 3 '39 il
> Bulliet, C. J. Salvador Dali *In* Significant Moderns and Their Pictures p129-30 1936
> New Standard Encyclopedia of Art 1939

DAMON, LINDSAY TODD (dã'mŏn) Nov 8, 1871—May 6, 1940 Chairman of the English department of Brown University for the last 10 years; supervising editor of Scott Foresman & Company; writer

Bachrach

LINDSAY TODD DAMON

References

> Who's Who Among North American Authors
> Who's Who in America 1938-39
> Who's Who in American Education

Obituaries

> N Y Times p25 My 7 '40

DANIELS, ARTHUR HILL Oct 19, 1865—Apr 2, 1940 Former acting president of the University of Illinois; professor of philosophy

ARTHUR HILL DANIELS

References

> Who's Who in America
> Who's Who in American Education

Obituaries

> N Y Times p23 Ap 3 '40
> Sch & Soc 51:476 Ap 13 '40

DANNAY, FREDERIC *See* Queen, E., pseud.

DAUGHERTY, JAMES HENRY June 1, 1889- Artist; illustrator

Address: c/o Viking Press, Inc, 13 E 48th St, New York City

Writer and illustrator of *Daniel Boone*, a children's life of the famous frontiersman, James Daugherty received the 1939 John Newbery Medal. He is the first man in 10 years to win the award. Mr. Daugherty has illustrated many other books for children, and is also a muralist of note. Since he made the drawings for Stewart Edward White's biography of Boone in 1928, he has been particularly interested in this pioneer whose image is "ever young in the heart and bright dream of America marching on." The lusty, muscularly rhythmic crayon drawings in terra cotta, green and black blend ideally with Mr. Daugherty's text to express physical fortitude, frontier energy and savage action. He writes of Boone's growing up, his expeditions into Kentucky, constant combat with the Indians and adventures with the British; of Boone's love of the wilderness that kept him ever-moving Westward in spite of the honors his countrymen thrust upon him.

Among other books illustrated by Mr. Daugherty are Sandburg's (see sketch this issue) *Abraham Lincoln Grows Up*, Irving's

JAMES DAUGHERTY

Knickerbocker History of New York, Three Comedies by Shakespeare and Benét's *John Brown's Body.* A reviewer of children's books has said of his work in illustration: "Mr. Daugherty's pictures stand out as the richest imaginative contribution to the reading and study of American history which has been made in my time."

James Daugherty was born in Asheville, North Carolina, June 1, 1889. His earliest recollections are of a farm in southern Indiana and a little Ohio town in the corn belt, of neighbors quiet, hospitable, book-loving. Often he listened to his grandfather tell stories of Daniel Boone; his Virginia-born mother told tales of the old South. When he was nine his family moved to Washington, D. C. where his father was employed as an agricultural statistician. His father, a university-educated man, liked to read out loud to the children from Shakespeare, Thackeray, Keats, Poe and Dickens. While the readings were going on young Jimmie would make illustrations of the stories. These drawings admitted him to the Corcoran Art School. His teacher there would conclude his instruction with: "Be like the Irishman at Donnybrook Fair: when you see a head, hit it."

After a year at the Philadelphia Art Academy, the young artist at 17 went abroad with his father. England, France and Italy, filled with art treasures, were ultra-romantic places to him in those pre-War days. In London he studied under Frank Brangwyn, and in London he first read Walt Whitman. This vision of America brought him back home to take a studio in Brooklyn Heights. "Then came the Armory show and Modern Art, now so mellow; and me going cubist with a new wife and baby to support; weary soliciting of magazine editors for illustration; and drudging at advertising drawing—a waste of precious years too well-known to many American artists." During the War Daugherty had a job camouflaging ships; then he got the opportunity to paint murals in Loew's moving picture palaces.

Studio life, with many newly-formed friendships and serious work, went on. The artist and his family then decided to move to the quiet of the country and took a cabin in Connecticut. About this time May Massee, children's book editor then with Doubleday, Page and Company, became interested in his work and assigned him to illustrate White's *Daniel Boone.* He has illustrated some 50 books since then, and his work has appeared in such magazines as the *New Yorker, Forum* and *Golden Book.*

In 1935, under the Federal Arts Project, Daugherty began a number of murals for the Stamford, Connecticut High School, and in six months completed the undertaking. The school, which has 2,500 pupils, lent itself to the project, faculty and students posing as models for the more than 200 figures used. Of the four main panels of this mural on democracy, one is devoted to historical New England, a second to the music of America, a third to the varied activities of the school, and a fourth pictures the complexities of the world outside the school. "Done in subdued blues and terra cotta, swirling with life and small boys, their style resembles that of a somewhat superficial Curry, a gentle Hogarth."

James Daugherty has become one of the best-known illustrators of books for young people. His wife, Sonia V. Daugherty, is an author; and his son Charles is a graduate of the Yale School of Fine Arts. A friend describes "Jimmie" Daugherty in these words: "Tall, muscular, straggling, possessed of arms and legs that defy all dancing school theories of grace but that never appear awkward, alive with a vitality and a rhythm that color and shade his personality, he might have stepped from any one of the number of books he has illustrated."

References

Horn Book 16:231-46 Jl '40 il por
Library J 65:473-4 Je 1 '40 il por
N Y Times p21 My 29 '40 por
Pub W 116:2073-6 O 26 '29 il; 137:
    2135-6 Je 1 '40 por
Survey G 24:227-9 My '35
Time 30:46 Jl 26 '37 il
Bolton, T. James Daugherty *In* American Book Illustrators p46-8 1938
Kunitz, S. J. and Haycraft, H. eds. Junior Book of Authors 1935
Mahoney, B. E. and Whitney, E. comps. Contemporary Illustrators of Children's Books 1930
Who's Who in America
Who's Who in American Art

D'AULAIRE, INGRI and D'AULAIRE, EDGAR PARIN *See* Aulaire, I. d' and Aulaire, E. P. d'

DAVIDOVITCH, LJUBA 1863—Feb 19, 1940 Twice Premier of Yugoslavia; last of pre-World War Serbian statesmen who participated in the creation of Yugoslavia

Obituaries

N Y Times p21 F 20 '40
N Y World-Telegram p19 F 19 '40

DAVIES, WILLIAM HENRY Apr 20, 1871—Sept 26, 1940 Noted Welsh "tramp" poet; spent many years roaming in America with hobos; at 34 completed his first book of poems and published it at his own expense with money earned as a peddler; book attracted the attention of George Bernard Shaw and started Davies on a long career as a writer during which he turned out some 50 books including his very popular *Autobiography of a Super-Tramp* (1917)

References

Cath World 149:671-9 S '39
Fortnightly 153 (ns 147):80-6 Ja '40
Scholastic 25:9 O 27 '34 por
Adcock, A. St. J. William Henry Davies *In* Gods of Modern Grub Street p63-9 1923
Cunliffe, J. W. Masefield and the New Georgian Poets *In* English Literature in the Twentieth Century p292-334 1933
Davies, W. H. Autobiography of a Super-Tramp 1917
Davies, W. H. Later Days 1926
Kernahan, C. W. H. Davies *In* Five More Famous Living Poets p17-48 1928
Kunitz, S. J. ed. Living Authors 1937
Maynard, T. W. H. Davies: A Case of Dual Personality *In* Our Best Poets p107-15 1922
Moult, T. W. H. Davies 1934
Sitwell, E. William H. Davies *In* Aspects of Modern Poetry p90-8 1934
Williams, C. W. S. William Henry Davies *In* Poetry At Present p70-81 1930

Obituaries

N Y Times p23 S 27 '40

DAVIS, CHESTER CHARLES Nov 17, 1887- Governor of Federal Reserve System; member of President Roosevelt's National Defense Commission

Address: b. Federal Reserve Bldg, Washington, D. C.; h. 5217 Reno Rd, N W, Washington, D. C.

Chester Davis was appointed in May 1940 by President Roosevelt as the member of the new National Defense Commission with the responsibility for agricultural problems. Because he has spent his entire adult life

thinking about farmers, the country agrees with General Hugh Johnson that his appointment was "by all odds the very best selection that could have been made."

Born on a farm in Iowa, the son of a tenant farmer, "Chet" Davis rode "lead horse" to a binder almost before he was old enough to toddle and sweated in wheat field and corn patch all through boyhood. He and his five sisters and brothers worked hard to help their father meet the payments on the land, to win the never ceasing struggle against droughts, pests and mortgages. Schooling was secondary, and what education he had then came in winter, in the farm's slack season, at a little country schoolhouse.

Davis enrolled in Grinnell College, Iowa in the fall of 1906, working at whatever he could get to do to pay expenses, including tuition. The middle of his senior year he dropped out for a year, which he spent running two weekly newspapers in South Dakota, returning to be graduated in 1911. After college he decided to push on to the Pacific Coast, but when he stopped off in Bozeman, Montana he met Helen Smith, whom he married in 1913. He also met Joseph Dixon, a fighting progressive. He stayed in Montana.

In 1917 Davis was offered the editorship of the Montana *Farmer* and in the four years he edited the paper made it "a force not only in agriculture but in the battle for good government, tilting bravely against the rule of the copper companies." In 1921, because of his good work there, he was made commissioner of agriculture and labor for the state of Montana when his friend Dixon became Governor.

After four years as commissioner, the copper kings "booted out the 'reformers.'" By this time, however, Davis knew clearly that farm relief was his life work. He went to Illinois and became associated with George Peek, at that time the foremost apostle of the agrarians. His job was to be director of grain marketing for the Illinois Agricultural Association, and his principal duty was lobbying. Davis was "a lobbyist without money for hotel suites, lordly dinners and Havanas, making up for the lack by demoniac energy."

In his early years he had been nominally a Republican but voted for Cox-Roosevelt in 1920, La Follette-Wheeler in 1924. In 1928 he was associated with George Peek in the management of the agricultural campaign for Alfred E. Smith, and four years later campaigned actively for Roosevelt. When Roosevelt was elected Davis was one of those who helped formulate the Agricultural Adjustment Act, and became director of its production division under Administrator George Peek. When Peek left in December 1933 Davis became administrator.

The manner in which Davis handled the drought which came shortly after the AAA started "explains the high regard in which he is held by the present Administration from the President down." And the manner in which he evolved plans for soil conserva-

CHESTER CHARLES DAVIS

tion and helped carry them through won the endorsement of the farmers in referendums conducted in 1934 and 1935. To Davis the AAA was never a fascinating experiment in social revolution or a place to try out theories. His job there was to him a "very definite assignment to bring about a better balance between farm production and market requirements." "The Agricultural Adjustment Act," Davis said, "enables farmers for the first time in the troubled history of agriculture to furnish goods to the world on the same basis as that enjoyed by other industries."

As head of the AAA Davis was successful. Farm income rose from a little over four billions in 1932 to six billions in 1934. As "head and driving force" he launched vast production programs for wheat, cotton, tobacco, sugar, rice, corn, hogs, and helped negotiate innumerable marketing agreements affecting producers of milk and speciality crops. And during all the convulsions that rocked the Department of Agriculture in those years "he kept all his old friendships." Very seldom was he known to get angry. Once, he did, however. He read an advertisement which appeared in a Joplin, Missouri newspaper: "Dandy way to make money; buy this 13 acres for hog-raising. Sign up with the government not to raise, say, 500 hogs. It will pay you $1,000." Davis is supposed to have hit the ceiling. "Preposterous," said he. "I shall begin an investigation."

Soon after the AAA was declared unconstitutional Davis began to evolve the Soil Conservation Act as a substitute. But "overwork to the brink of collapse" caused President Roosevelt to send him to Europe in "honorable exile." His job in Europe was "to size up in a realistic way just what are the prospects for American farmers to sell more of their goods." He returned in May 1936 after a six-weeks tour to report: "There is not the slightest hope we can regain for some important commodities the great markets [in Europe] we once enjoyed."

In June 1936 Davis was appointed a governor of the Federal Reserve Board. The unoccupied seat had been earmarked for a farmers' spokesman, and Davis was obviously the best man for it, although he was no banker. When he got the appointment he thought he was "sailing from a storm-tossed sea into a comparatively smooth and protected harbor," but the recession of 1937 dispelled any such ideas. As Federal Reserve Board member he has been mainly concerned with farmers' problems and has dealt with them with the understanding born of long years of experience. In 1939 he was awarded the American Farm Bureau Federation's Medal for Distinguished Service to Agriculture.

Mr. Davis, "slight, gray, silent," has always distinguished himself from other Washington leaders. "Where others in Washington stalk headlines with almost Indian cunning, Mr. Davis is so retiring that newspapermen have to hunt him with mole traps." The real reason for this is that he loves his work and always has: "farming is his passion and farming his infatuation."

References

Collier's 96:28+ O 5 '35 por
Lit Digest 120:38 Ag 10 '35 por
N Y Times pl, 15 My 29 '40
Newsweek 6:8 Ag 3 '35; 6:9 N 2 '35; 7:16 Mr 21 '36
Time 27:16 Je 1 '36; 27:63 Je 15 '36; 30:45 Jl 5 '37 por; 35:19 Je 10 '40
Who's Who in America
Who's Who in Commerce and Industry
Who's Who in the Nation's Capital

DAVIS, ELMER Jan 13, 1890- Radio commentator; author
Address: h. 423 W 120th St, New York City

The reputation of a thorough student of history and politics, a story writer and a novelist who has won popular acclaim stands behind Elmer Holmes Davis, Indiana-born, well-traveled, shrewd and tolerant news analyst. His life interests follow the two traditional Hoosier industries, politics and literature; in his most recent career as radio commentator he achieves a synthesis of both. He was engaged by the Columbia Broadcasting Company August 23, 1939, just as the big war news was breaking, when its ace commentator, H. V. Kaltenborn (see sketch this issue), was in Europe. For some time his essays on a number of things had been appearing in *Harper's, Forum, Saturday Review of Literature* and other periodicals. In March 1940 about a dozen of these were collected in one volume, *Not to Mention the War*.

Elmer Holmes Davis was born January 13, 1890 in Aurora, Indiana, the son of a banker, Elam H., and Louise (Severin) Davis. He took his B. A. at Franklin College in 1910, his M. A. was awarded a year after he left, for courses taken while in residence. In 1910 he won a Rhodes Scholarship to Oxford, where he was elected president of the American Club. While studying at Oxford he began cultivating an interest in foreign affairs and politics, and spent his summers traveling abroad. It was in Paris that he met Florence MacMillan of Mt. Vernon, New York. They were married February 5, 1917 and have two children: Robert Lloyd and Caroline Ann. They live at Mystic, Connecticut in the summer, during the winter in New York City.

His first job was teaching at the Franklin, Indiana High School from 1909 to 1910. Then for a year he was on the editorial staff of *Adventure*. As a boy he had been printer's devil on the Aurora *Bulletin*. Ten years later, 1914, he became a cub reporter on the New York *Times,* rising in another ten years to become feature man on American politics, expert correspondent and editorial writer. He acquired a reputation by creating, during the 1920 Democratic Convention in San Francisco, a character named Godfrey Gloom from Amity, Indiana. Godfrey (Davis) was sent for 16 years to conventions, until Davis finally killed him off, and Arthur Krock of the *Times* solemnly wrote his obituary.

Apart from his newspaper career, Elmer Davis found time to do considerable writing, both fiction and non-fiction. His *History of the New York Times* appeared in 1921. In 1923 he published his first novel, *Times Have Changed,* a fantastic fiction spoof. Among the novels which followed were: *The Keys of the City* (1925), an Indiana-locale, Main-Street type of tale; *Friends of Mr. Sweeney* (1925), an excellent newspaper novel; *Strange Woman* (1927), the story of the wife of a college president and *Giant Killer* (1928), an historical novel based on the life of David. Two collections of his short stories have been published: *Morals for Moderns* (1930) and *Love Among the Ruins* (1935).

Davis has won in a short time nationwide repute as an analyst. He felt no little trepidation, he says, at the time he was called to take Kaltenborn's place: it was like being asked to pinch-hit for Joe DiMaggio. But his discourses are clear, calm, well-reasoned, justly tempered; he speaks with a straight-from-the-shoulder manner, a down-home twang. His scholarly background and his broad, liberal viewpoint (although one writer says that "today he would barely qualify as a liberal"), no less than his skeptical mind, enable him to plow through propaganda and rumor in an effort to find the real truth in a report. Even in times of war crises Davis keeps his calm, unhurried manner, sorting conflicting reports, carefully checking all information. When asked recently, however, if he still had "mike

ELMER DAVIS

fright," he said: "I haven't yet lost the fear that some day I will go insane at the mike and begin spouting treason, blasphemy and (worse) libel." But so far his manner has been so quiet and casual that he has been called "a master of understatement."

It is likely that Elmer Davis prefers to be known as a scholar and observer, rather than a public figure or celebrity, since he avoids anything in the way of "showing-off." He dresses inconspicuously in quiet gray tweeds, and always wears a black bow tie. He is tall, well-proportioned, energetic; he has strong features, gray hair and thick, black brows above keen brown eyes. It would not be hard to single him out in a crowd as a man of action and distinguished accomplishments.

A great deal may be learned about the real Elmer Davis from his book of essays, *Not to Mention the War*. Having to talk about the War every day, he found considerable pleasure and release in writing these non-War sketches, and published them with the hope that people may like to read about things not immediately connected with these troubled times. But he discovered that he was unable to avoid the War or Hitler, or other current topics even when writing of quite different matters—about Thucydides, cats, music, the world of 1913 or bridge.

He likes nothing better than to see today in terms of history; he is something of an authority on the decline and fall of the Roman Empire, as his essay, *The Logic of History,* shows. As a student of the classics, he believes that reading Thucydides, for example, will help us understand the times we live in better than all the works by moderns. His knowledge of history and politics breaks out in shrewdly drawn parallels when he writes on such matters, for instance, as cats

DAVIS, ELMER—*Continued*

and music. He is very fond of cats, "the most dignified and independent of living creatures." He has been intimately associated with some 15; at present he owns a silver Persian, but he likes alley cats, too. His essay *On Being Kept by a Cat* is one of the most amusing and brilliant in the collection, whether one likes cats or not. Writing of them, he remains the shrewd social commentator. He observes that independence is most conspicuous in alley cats, who are practitioners of rugged individualism. "This ought to make the alley cat the favorite animal of the conservative rich; yet I suspect that if you took a census of these gentry you would find that most of them prefer the docile dog; their definition of individualism is usually 'individualism for me.'"

In opera he has a decided preference for Wagner's *Ring* cycle. He draws a pithy parallel between the tale of Siegfried and a modern event, recalling that when the sword Siegfried forged was brandished in the air, Wotan's umbrella fell to pieces. The cycle is not yet finished. "All we can be sure of, so far, is that Hitler makes a better Siegfried than Siegfried himself; he knows what to do with the ring."

In *On the Eve: Reminiscences of 1913,* Davis says that this was the year in which, as a person, he sat up, began to take notice. He feels nostalgic about that period, which seems to him now the peak of a Golden Age, an age of innocence and security. He remarks in another essay that it has twice been his fortune to be reported missing in a catastrophe, probably dead. The second time was during the hurricane of 1938. When he returned afterward to New York, he felt he saw a look not unmixed with resentment on friends' faces. The next time he is reported dead he is not going to deny the rumor.

His style is both pungent and friendly; he is blunt, candid, witty—a person of broad sympathies and tolerance. Critics are generally delighted with his well-balanced prose, rich with allusion, classical or otherwise, and find he has the indispensable light touch.

It may be no paradox, in this day of paradox, that an analyst of contemporary politics and events should claim Horace and Catullus (read in the original) as his favorite poets and list the *Bible* as the greatest book ever written, without a runner-up. And it is comforting to hear from a student of history:

"With an irrational optimism befitting an alumnus of the absurd age in which I came to the surface, I still believe that higher peaks of human felicity may be ahead; that our race, if it keeps on trying, might make quite a habitable place of the planet on which it resides."

References

Harper 177:382-90 S '38 (Same abr. Read Digest 33:89-92 O '38); 178: 536-42 Ap '39; 179:579-88 N '39
New Repub 98:35-7 F 15 '39
N Y Times Book R p2 Ap 14 '40
Pub W 137:781-2 F 17 '40 (Same Sat R Lit 21:8 Mr 2 '40); 138:1965-6 N 23 '40 por
Time 34:50 D 25 '39; 35:55 Ja 22 '40 por
Davis, E. Not to Mention the War 1940
Howe, Q. The News and How to Understand It 1940
Ringel, F. J. America as Americans See It p206-14 1932
Who's Who in America

DAVIS, HERBERT JOHN May 24, 1893- College president

Address: Smith College, Northampton, Massachusetts

Old-world and New-world Northamptons were linked when Herbert John Davis, 46-year-old chairman of Cornell's English Department, assumed the presidency of Smith College on October 17, 1940. He succeeded Dr. William Allen Neilson, who had retired early in 1939. Mrs. Dwight W. Morrow was acting president in the interim.

Herbert John Davis was born May 24, 1893, in the heart of England in the town of Northampton, about 30 miles from the Shakespeare country. His father (Carter Davis) was a boot manufacturer, and his mother (Martha Ann Sheldon Davis) descended from a family which for many generations had been farmers in the Midlands. He went to the Council School until he was twelve, and then, after the death of his father, by hard-won scholarships got six years at the Northampton Grammar School.

All the while he was bent on taking orders in the Anglican Church. He stood examinations, "won an exhibition" for St. John's College, Oxford, and received his degree in 1914 at the outbreak of the First World War. Defective vision kept him from the first volunteer ranks, but after a year at Wells Theological College in Somerset he went to France, took charge of a social center and then in 1916 joined the colors as a gunner in the ranks. A year later he was made lieutenant and saw active fighting in the Battle of Arras. He was assigned to the Army of Occupation, following the Armistice, and served there until September 1919.

The War destroyed the pattern of his life, and when he was mustered out his earlier eagerness to take orders for the Church was gone. He returned to Oxford and received his M. A. degree. For the next two-and-a-half years he was a lecturer in English literature at the University of Leeds. In 1922 he accepted a call from University College, Toronto and remained there 16 years except for one year when he was guest professor at the University of Cologne (1924-25): he was

HERBERT DAVIS

References
N Y Times p2 D 3 '39
Newsweek 14:34 O 30 '39
Sch & Soc 50:57 O 28 '39
Time 34:40 O 30 '39

associate professor until 1935, when he became full professor of English in University College and was elected chairman of the English Department. In the summer of 1937 he was Frederick Ives Carpenter visiting professor at the University of Chicago. In September 1938 he went to Cornell to succeed Professor William C. De Vane—made Dean of Yale—as head of the English Department, and in 1939 was appointed Goldwin Smith professor of English literature.

Davis first married Gertrud Lucas, daughter of Landrat Lucas, a high official of the Rhineland, Germany; she died in 1928. In 1930 he married Gladys Wookey of Toronto. They have two girls, Elizabeth Ann and Jane Sheldon.

As head of the English Department at Cornell, Davis built up his staff, secured greater appropriations for assistants and for books for collateral reading and reference. Here, as well as at Toronto, Davis encountered women students in large numbers, and he can, therefore, approach Smith girls, 2,000-strong, without any vestige of fear. His accent is pleasantly British, but he has, nevertheless, a thorough mastery of the American idiom.

He hopes—perhaps not too optimistically—that his administrative duties at Smith will not prevent him from continuing his edition of Swift, of which five volumes are already completed. He has contributed scholarly articles and reviews to various English, Canadian and American journals and has made studies both of contemporary and seventeenth and eighteenth century English literature.

Davis is tall, thin, and fair-haired, with regular features and a friendly mouth. He plays as hard as he works, and he has a well-established reputation as an all-weather golfer in the British tradition.

DAVIS, NORMAN H. Aug 9, 1878-
Chairman of the American Red Cross
Address: b. American Red Cross, Washington D. C.; h. 804 Prince St, Alexandria, Virginia

Norman Hezekiah Davis (he uses only the initial of his middle name) was born in Bedford County, Tennessee in 1878, the son of Maclin H. and Christina Lee (Shoffner) Davis. He attended Vanderbilt and Stanford Universities. Just out of college he ran away to Cuba, where he had a successful business career, becoming head of a trust company at 27. In 1917 he entered public life and has since held many important positions at home and in the capitals of Europe.

During the First World War he visited England, France and Spain as a special adviser on financial affairs. He was chairman of the American Delegation to the Disarmament Conference at Geneva; chairman of the American Delegation to the Naval Conference at London, 1935 and 1936; chief delegate of the United States to the Nine Power Conference at Brussels in 1937. While serving under three Presidential Administrations he has been a spokesman abroad for the United States. As chairman of the financial section of the Supreme Economic Council of the Allies he did notable work. When the War was over he served as Assistant Secretary of the Treasury in President Wilson's Cabinet and later as Under-Secretary of State. With the ending of the Wilson Administration, Mr. Davis returned to private life until 1927, when he was chosen as one of the

Blank-Stoller

NORMAN H. DAVIS

DAVIS, NORMAN H.—*Continued*

American delegates to the International Economic Conference at Geneva. For several years he acted as President Roosevelt's "roving ambassador."

President Roosevelt appointed him chairman of the Red Cross in April 1938. A tireless worker for world peace, he accepted the appointment with the hope that he could continue his peace efforts. "Short, white-haired" Norman Davis feels that the Red Cross faces an ever-increasing burden in helping non-combatants as well as soldiers. "Something must be done," he says, "to restore civilization to a sanity which will at least stop the killing of the helpless and innocent by warring forces!" In November 1940 he was reappointed to his position for a term expiring December 11, 1941.

References

Am Mag 120:54 Jl '35 por
Commonweal 30:468-70 S 15 '39
Layman's Mag 2:10-11 Mr '40
New Outlook 163:37 My '34
N Y Times p14 My 17 '38 por; p18
   Je 9 '38 por; p9 N 11 '39 por; p6
   N 18 '39 por; IV p6 Ap 26 '40 por
Newsweek 1:4 My 20 '33 por; 3:15 Je
   9 '34 por
Scholastic 30:24 Ap 24 '37 por
Survey G 29:215 Ap '40
Time 31:11 Ap 25 '38 por; 32-13 Jl 4
   '38 por
U S News p45 Ja 5 '40 por
Who's Who in America

DAVIS, STUART   Dec 7, 1894- Artist
Address: 43 Seventh Ave, New York City

In the 1920's Stuart Davis produced his first *Eggbeater. Eggbeater No. 4* was bought in February 1940 by the Phillips Memorial Gallery in Washington, D. C. None of the four looks like an eggbeater, of course, and none is intended to. Davis' purpose, he says, was to recreate the idea of eggbeater into "a real order in three dimensions."

"Unfaltering in his allegiance to the abstract," Stuart Davis' pictures have been inspired by other mechanical devices. Some of these he calls simply *Composition* and gives a serial number. He did a series called *Gas Pumps*—these, he found, lent themselves particularly well to abstract treatment. To those who find abstract art a little hard to follow, Davis is quick to explain his method and ideas: "A picture," he says, "must tell a story. This story can have pictorial existence only through the artist's concept of form. There are an infinite number of form concepts available. My own is very simple and is based on the assumption that space is continuous and that matter is discontinuous."

Since Davis' works are in some of the most conspicuous places in this country and admired here, his meaning and purpose must be clear. The men's lounge in Rockefeller Center, New York City, is hung with a 12 by 18-foot abstract mural called *Men Without Women*. This mural collects a group of typical masculine articles—pipes, playing cards, sports equipment—and arranges them in the way Davis has made his own.

At the Communications Building at the New York World's Fair Davis had an enormous mural symbolizing the development of communication. In it he put "a big spiral, meaning the universe, a seashell suggesting the origins of sound. Then you see man rising out of chaos, sign language, writing by letter, the first printing press, the first telephone instrument, semaphore, a human ear, a carrier pigeon, radio towers, light signals, the United States mail and a lot of other things."

New York City's broadcasting station, WNYC, has a mural with a saxophone, radio antennae, an operator's panel, a graph of radio frequencies in it. "The forms," Davis explains, "aren't directly reflective of the things they come from, but rather of their colors, shapes, directions—dissociated from their actual environment."

Davis' abstractions of Paris and of America have been collected by many art lovers, and many museums have Davis' pictures in their permanent collections. These include the Museum of Modern Art and the Whitney Museum in New York, the Newark Museum, the Los Angeles Museum and the Milwaukee Art Institute.

This "most daring and powerful of the Left-wing American moderns" was born in Philadelphia on December 7, 1894, the son of Edward Davis, who was art director of the Philadelphia *Press* in the 1890's. The workers on that paper in Edward Davis' department included John Sloan, George Luks, William Glackens and Everett Shinn. It was easy for Stuart Davis to decide to become an artist.

Most of his art education he got at the Henri School of Art in New York, which he attended from 1910 to 1913. At nineteen he was precociously represented with six water colors in the celebrated Armory Show, "that cataclysm in the course of American art." During the War he continued with his art—drawing maps in the Army Intelligence Department, and with the War over found himself "hard at work" moving toward the abstractionist painting he now does. To him the purpose of "naturalism"—aping nature in paint—no longer existed. The camera did it better. "An abstract painting, on the other hand, became an analogy, a synthesis of the subject in terms the artist chose. The abstract artist was free from the commonplace and took his post in the real where 'pure esthetic experience' reigns and 'enjoyment of line, color and form' is sufficient end in itself."

Davis went to Europe for the first time in 1928 and painted abstractions of Paris, "remarkably evocative of the city and its typical aspects and done with great charm and humor." He discovered that the work

STUART DAVIS

being done in America "was comparable in every way with the best of the work over there by contemporary artists." Since that trip Davis has been working in America, much of the time in Gloucester, Massachusetts, where marine shapes appeal to him.

One of the most articulate of modern artists, Stuart Davis has consistently allied himself with the Left-wing artist groups. In his youth he was a frequent contributor to the radical magazines, the *Masses* and *Spawn*. In 1934 he helped organize the artists' union and urged other artists to join. "The artist does not join the union merely to get a job," he said. "He joins it to fight for his right to economic stability on a decent level and to develop as an artist through development as a social human being." Again and again he has insisted that "the artist participates in the world crisis." In 1936 Davis was a leader of the American Artists' Congress, formed with the main purpose of opposing Nazi racial ideas in the field of culture, but he resigned from the organization in April 1940 because he felt that the "present active membership" of the group was incompetent to carry out the aims of the organization.

References

Am Mag Art 28:476-8+ Ag '35
Art N 30:10 Mr 12 '32
Nation 149:112 Jl 22 '39
N Y Sun Ap 28 '34
N Y World-Telegram p13 F 21 '40
    pors
Who's Who in America
Who's Who in American Art

DAVIS, WILLIAM ELLSWORTH Dec 30, 1896- Medical missionary to the Belgian Congo
Address: c/o Reynal and Hitchcock, Inc, 386 Fourth Ave, New York City

Four ordinarily unemotional scientists— Arthur H. Compton, Kirtley F. Mather, Harlan T. Stetson and Edward L. Thorndike—writing in the *Scientific Book Club Review,* call Dr. William E. Davis' book, *Ten Years in the Congo* (March 1940), "a truly remarkable book that gives a rather detailed and inclusive picture of that part of the Congo where he and his wife lived, taught, and practiced for ten years." They call Dr. Davis "a true man of science" and recommend his book. It was selected as the April 1940 book by the Scientific Book Club.

Dr. Davis, while thoroughly sympathetic with evangelizing missionaries and their teaching, devotes only one chapter of his book to the church work in the Congo. The greater part of his work has to do with jungle life, travel, diseases, social customs and a record of the changes that have come over the Belgian Congo in recent years. He holds that the natives have gained immeasurably by their contact with civilization and disagrees sharply in this respect with the French writer, André Gide. Some idea of the immense amount of medical assistance Dr. Davis gave the natives can be approximated by the information that in his last year at his medical station he treated 65,000 patients at his hospital dispensary and performed 536 major operations under the most primitive and intolerable conditions.

Dr. Davis tells us that he was born in Morton, Oregon on December 30, 1896, the son of Nona Austin and Maud Mary Davis, a very devout Christian couple. His early life was a period of wandering, with a year's interlude in Mexico and farm life near Lynchburg, Virginia from 1912 to 1917. He attended Lynchburg College, and Whitman College at Walla Walla, Washington, receiving a degree in 1920. His college course was broken up by a year in War service as a pilot in Boston and Miami. Out of college, he worked as a science teacher and athletic coach at Pasco, Washington.

All this time he thought of various careers which would fulfill his love of travel and explains how he finally decided to become a medical missionary. "I had been the janitor of our Church [Christian Disciples'] during my senior year at college," he says, "and I had met a man in the preacher's study one day who had suggested the possibility of missionary work. He had pictured it in such a way as to make it seem an interesting and worthwhile line of endeavor."

In order to fit himself for missionary work he enrolled at the College of Missions, and Butler University at Indianapolis. In 1922 he began the study of medicine and en-

WILLIAM E. DAVIS

tered Northwestern University. Meanwhile he had met and fallen in love with a young missionary, Martha Newell Trimble, whose station was in Africa. "The years in the medical school," says Dr. Davis, "were long years, not without many bitter thoughts upon the circumstances that separated me from Africa and from my fiancée. They were hard to endure but they eventually came to an end and we were married in the Summer of 1927, after her return to America on a furlough from Africa."

"I've traveled considerably," he says, "all over the United States, most of Europe [University of London School of Tropical Medicine, 1927 to 1928; University of Grenoble, Grenoble, France, 1931 to 1932] and a good part of Canada; into Mexico as far as Vera Cruz and right smartly in Africa. I've done a bit of this and that—farming, harvest fields, lumber woods, construction gangs, mule skinning, cowpunching, taxi driving, flying, schoolteaching, bookselling (I didn't sell many books), fruit picking, doing night guard duty for the railroad during a strike, preaching for a Chicago church, doing a couple of turns as a singing evangelist, male nursing, etc. I rang the college bell at Lynchburg, delivered papers, swept and mopped out a ladies' dress shop, janitored a church, washed dishes, etc., while at Whitman College."

With that wealth of experience behind him Dr. Davis and his wife went to Wema in the Belgian Congo in 1928—he as medical missionary and she as a missionary teacher. "If I expected much of it," he says of Africa, "I have never been disappointed. The reality of the Congo has surpassed any dream I ever had. My 10 years in the jungle have been for me a tremendous experience that I would not exchange for any other."

To Dr. Davis one of the amazing things about the Congo is the coming of the machine age. He says: "The discovery of practically all the other considerable sections of the world took place before the arrival of the machine age, but the Congolese are being confronted with a mass of modern developments which are still amazing to us and must be positively overwhelming to them. I know of no other people who have been called upon to make so great and so sudden a shift in ideas and culture. The untutored savage, who has never before seen so much as a wheelbarrow, is put to work on complicated machinery. He comes naked out of the jungle and goes to work in a garage. With no place to go for escape, the forest dwellers are caught and impaled upon the sudden prong of Western iron and steel."

The Davis' two sons were born in Africa, William E. Jr., in 1929 and Thomas Austin, in 1934. The older was the first white child to be born in all the region around Wema, and the natives had quite a time deciding on a name for him, Dr. Davis recalls.

In 1938 the family returned to the United States, and Dr. Davis spent a year studying at Columbia University Post Graduate Hospital in New York City. Then he and his family settled in North Middletown, Kentucky, which has a population of 500. He hopes, he says, to spend the rest of his life there. With true Chamber of Commerce sentiment he says: "I think that the Blue Grass section of Kentucky is the best place in the world to live and my ambition is to have a small farm near North Middletown and vegetate."

References

Davis, W. E. Ten Years in the Congo 1940

S. J. Woolf

RUFUS CUTLER DAWES

DAWES, RUFUS CUTLER July 30, 1867—Jan 8, 1940 Financier; president of Chicago's Century of Progress Exposition; brother of the former Vice-President of the United States

References

Who's Who in America 1938-39

Obituaries

N Y Herald Tribune p14 Ja 9 '40
N Y Sun p1 Ja 8 '40
Newsweek 15:41 Ja 22 '40

DAY-LEWIS, CECIL [NICHOLAS BLAKE, pseud.] Apr 27, 1904- Author

Address: Brimclose, Musbury, Axminster, Devon, England

An able spokesman for that group of Left-wing poets who emerged from Oxford during the first post-War decade is Cecil Day-Lewis, and with the publication of his second novel, *Starting Point* (1938), he remains (despite the nature of his literary vehicle) essentially a poet.

C. Day-Lewis was born in Ballintogher, Ireland in 1904. At the age of three he was taken to England to live, and when he was only six he made a conscious attempt to write. He was sent to Sherborne School and then entered Wadham College, Oxford, where he was a co-editor of *Oxford Poetry, 1927*. For eight years he held successively three positions as schoolmaster, and then withdrew in 1935 in order to apply himself entirely to the art of writing and to Left-wing political activities. In 1928 he married Constance Mary King; they have two children and make their home at Brimclose in Devon.

Day-Lewis is, obviously, identified with a group-poetry and with a group-ideology which holds that "a revolution in literature is now taking place" but that "a revolution in society is incomparably more important, and without it the other would be futile and meaningless. . . Evolution is the dance, revolutions are the steps." But, he continues, it does not follow that any kind of lyric proselytizing is good poetry.

Long accustomed to domestic ease and rural pleasures, he might well have decided to go to court for poetry in the decadent though still acceptable Victorian tradition. But the genuineness and strength of his belief that society was not merely temporarily indisposed but acutely diseased brought him, like Anthony in the closing pages of *Starting Point*, to a conviction that unless intelligent young men would pool their conscious energies there would be no rebuilding of a new social order. This was the "point from which it was impossible to turn back." At least as early as 1933

Day-Lewis had expressed this same belief in somewhat similar phraseology. In his *Letter to a Young Revolutionary*, published in Michael Roberts' *New Country* (1933), he said: "The certainty of new life must be your starting point."

Day-Lewis' work suffers at times from a lack of imaginative intensity; his most gaping weaknesses are, perhaps, an occasional undergraduate exuberance, "Look West, Wystan, lone flyer, birdman, my bully boy" —or a rather obvious derivation, such as "Spoon out the waters of comfort in kilogrammes" from T. S. Eliot's "I have measured out my life in coffee spoons." Although not a technical innovator, he has made skillful use of internal rhymes and feminine endings.

An earlier novel by Day-Lewis was *The Friendly Tree* (1937), a delicate and lyric story of youthful love. He has published six detective stories under the pseudonym of "Nicholas Blake": *Question of Proof* (1935); *Thou Shell of Death* (1936); *There's Trouble Brewing* (1937); *The Beast Must Die* (1938); *The Smiler with the Knife* (1939); and *Summer Camp Mystery,* also known as *Malice in Wonderland* (1940). He has also written some tales for children. Fundamentally, however, he remains a poet.

It is his belief that only poetry and the fairy tale (or parable) will survive: the first, "partly through metaphor but chiefly through rhythm, can penetrate into strata of man's mind that nothing else can touch," and the second because it is "primitive . . . universal . . . can slip past the defences of our intellect and talk to the deep unconscious levels within us. Cinderella, the Tin Soldier, the Prodigal Son can go places where there is no admittance for Herr Goebbels or the Board of Education."

CECIL DAY-LEWIS

DAY-LEWIS, CECIL—*Continued*

References

Time 32:55 Jl 25 '38 por

Who's Who (under Lewis, Cecil Day)

DEASY, LUERE B. (dēz'ĭ) Feb 8, 1859— Mar 13, 1940 Former Chief Justice of Maine

References

Who's Who in America
Who's Who in Government
Who's Who in Law

Obituaries

Boston Transcript p11 Mr 13 '40

DE CHAPPEDELAINE, LOUIS *See* Chappedelaine, L. de

DEFAUW, DESIRE (dē-fō) Sept 5, 1885- Belgian violinist and conductor; guest leader of the NBC Symphony Orchestra in 1939 and 1940

Address: c/o National Broadcasting Company, 30 Rockefeller Plaza, New York City

The first of the distinguished guest conductors occupying the podium, relinquished until March 1940 by Arturo Toscanini, is the Belgian violinist and conductor, Désiré Defauw, who has had a dashing musical career on the Continent and who is credited with sufficient wit to "tell a good story with a Cockney accent." On December 9, 1940 he again took over Toscanini's baton as guest conductor of the NBC Symphony.

Désiré Defauw was born in Ghent on September 5, 1885, the youngest of five children. At the age of eight he entered the Ghent Conservatory, with a strong plea to study violin, because, as he himself declared, "I already know the piano." He was a student of Johan Smit. Six years later a visiting impresario heard the lad in recital and offered his parents 35,000 francs for the privilege of taking the youthful virtuoso to America. The proposal was refused: the child was not yet ready for a public career. At 15, however, he became concertmaster of the Concerts d'Hiver in Ghent, and toured as a violinist with great success until the outbreak of the World War in 1914.

Defauw's musical energy was by no means stifled, however, by the War. From 1914 to 1918, with Lionel Tertis, violist, Charles Woodhouse, pianist, and E. Doehard, cellist, Defauw formed the Belgian Quartet and toured England. Ernest La Prade, now NBC's director of musical research, provided a second violin for quintets and also played viola in Tertis' absence.

After the Armistice Defauw conducted the concerts at the Théâtre de la Monnaie in Brussels until his appointment, in 1925, as Director of Concerts in the Royal Conservatory in Brussels. In addition to his conservatory duties Defauw holds the post of musical director of Belgium's Institut National de Radiodiffusion, conducting an 84-piece symphony orchestra formed expressly for radio broadcasting. He is, moreover, president of the Belgium Section of the International Society for Contemporary Music.

References

Newsweek 14:44 D 18 '39 por
Time 34:55 D 18 '39

Thompson, O. ed. International Cyclopedia of Music and Musicians 1939
Wier, A. E. ed. Macmillan Encyclopedia of Music and Musicians 1938

DE GAULLE, CHARLES (dĕ-gōl shȧrl) Nov 22, 1890- Head of Provisional French National Committee in London

Once a general of France and at the end of 1940 an exile dismissed from the army and condemned to death by his country, Charles André Joseph Marie de Gaulle, leader of the French forces that will not surrender, is a "gallant and romantic figure." Under him French soldiers, sailors and airmen in Europe and in the colonies are banded together to fight against Germany to the end, determined not to acquiesce in the Pétain (see sketch this issue) capitulation. Daily they raid enemy air objectives with the British; daily they work for the defense of Britain against the enemy; daily they strive to unite all "free Frenchmen."

De Gaulle, who was once a great admirer of Pétain, appealed to the French people immediately after the Compiègne armistice was declared. To them he broadcasted: "This capitulation was signed before all means of resistance had been exhausted. . . There is no longer on the soil of France an independent government capable of upholding the interests of France and the

DESIRE DEFAUW

French overseas." He set up his Provisional Committee in London and began organizing his forces and started his daily broadcasts to the French people, in which he urged them not to work in the factories, not to make war against Great Britain, not to become Germans.

In these activities he had been supported by the British government, but it wasn't until August 7, 1940 that a formal agreement was signed. By its terms the volunteer Frenchmen pledged themselves to fight to the end against Germany but never to take up arms against France. By its terms General De Gaulle's forces, even though they retain their French character, will be under nominal British command. The British government also has agreed to finance De Gaulle's efforts to gather together as many men as possible and to grant pensions to the dependents of those men in the service who are killed or injured.

Tall, melancholy, handsome, this man whom Winston Churchill (see sketch this issue) calls "the leader of all free Frenchmen" has long had a reputation as a brilliant army officer, even though promotions have not been swift. He was born in Lille, France on November 22, 1890. In 1911 he was graduated from the military school of Saint-Cyr near the head of his class and immediately became a sub-lieutenant in the 33rd infantry regiment. It was here that he had his first contact with Pétain, then commander of the regiment.

As soon as the First World War was declared De Gaulle was sent to the front and was wounded at Dinant. In September 1915 he was promoted to the rank of captain, took part in the Verdun operations and received three citations for his military valor. The next year he was taken prisoner and spent two years and eight months in a prison camp.

In 1924 De Gaulle was admitted to l'Ecole Supérieure de Guerre and after passing a brilliant examination was placed on the staff of the Army of the Rhine, assistant to Marshal Pétain. Three years later he was placed in command of the 19th infantry battalion and sent to Beirut. After his return to France some years later he was appointed to the secretariat of the Conseil Supérieur de la Défense Nationale where, until 1937, he held a number of important positions. In that year he was made a colonel, after a period at the Centre des Hautes Etudes Militaires.

During these years in the army De Gaulle consistently pleaded for a highly mechanized French Army. As long ago as 1928 he described France's inevitable doom if tanks were not built in a hurry, and foreshadowed the range and mobility of the tanks of the future. In 1935 he urged the Chamber of Deputies to authorize the mechanization of at least 10 army divisions. His articles and books, especially *Vers l'Armée de Métier* (1934), *Le Fil de l'Epee* (1932) and *La France et Son Armée* (1938), were discussed to

CHARLES DE GAULLE

some extent, but the leaders of the French Army and of the French Republic paid too little attention to what he urged; only the Germans took over some of his best tank ideas.

Still, De Gaulle's varied experience and training and grasp of military matters were finally recognized, and 15 days after the War started he was made a brigadier general and later promoted by Pétain to major general. On June 6, 1940 Premier Reynaud (see sketch this issue) made De Gaulle his special assistant in charge of war department matters in his Cabinet. Shortly after, De Gaulle was sent to England, ostensibly to confer on military matters for France. He remained in England, still conferring on military matters—but they were different matters and for a different France.

On August 2, 1940 De Gaulle was condemned to death in absentia by a French military tribunal. His reply to the sentence was that it was made by "a court largely under the influence and possibly even under the direct orders of the common enemy. The enemy will one day be driven from the soil of France. On that day I will submit myself willingly to the judgment of the people."

He continued to rally the "free French" forces and in September approached Dakar in Sénégal with six troop transports. Eight times he tried to land and eight times he was repulsed. After three days of attack De Gaulle called off the expedition, "not wanting to be a party to a fight between Frenchmen." Immediately relations between the French government of Vichy and Britain became even more strained than they had been; French airmen bombed Gibraltar in reprisal and a court was set up to try all De Gaulle partisans. Resentment in Britain was widespread, even though De

DE GAULLE, CHARLES—*Continued*

Gaulle himself assumed full responsibility for the abortive attack.

Yet De Gaulle's headquarters in London maintained that "the moral prestige of General De Gaulle and his troops remains intact. The magnificent efforts of free French forces will not be relaxed merely because of the failure of Dakar." A number of French colonies had already declared their support for him. On September 3, Tahiti had gone over to his side; the New Hebrides and New Caledonia followed later in the same month; all French Equatorial Africa was reported to be with him. And on October 10 General De Gaulle landed in Duala, capital of the Cameroons to carry on the struggle. Meanwhile groups were formed in the United States and other countries "to act in close cooperation with the free French forces."

According to *De Gaulle and the Coming Invasion of Germany* by James Marlow, a pamphlet published in October 1940, De Gaulle believes that a land invasion will be necessary, for the German Army must be destroyed. When the Germans are "war-weary and slack," he says, he hopes to attack them "with tanks and guns, thousands of airplanes, tens of thousands of airplanes."

References

> Collier's 106:11+ Ag 10 '40 por
> Cur Hist & Forum 52:50-1 S '40
> **Le Temps** Je 1 '40
> Liv Age 359:35-8 S '40 por
> N Y Times; p1 Ag 3 '40; p11 Ag 8 '40; p6 S 4 '40; p5 S 23 '40; p4 S 25 '40; p8 S 27 '40; p2 O 7 '40; p5 O 11 '40
> Newsweek 16:35 S 9 '40; 16:24-5 O 7
> Scholastic 37:10 S 23 '40 por
> **Time** 36:25 Jl 1 '40 por
> Marlow, J. De Gaulle and the Coming Invasion of Germany 1940

DE GUISE, JEAN PIERRE CLEMENT MARIE, DUC *See* Guise, J. P. C. M., Duc de

DELL, ROBERT EDWARD 1865—July 20, 1940 British author; correspondent at Berlin, Paris and Geneva for the Manchester *Guardian* for 30 years; contributor to *The Nation*; lectured in New York; was working on his autobiography at the time of his death; edited two art magazines in England; wrote *Socialism and Personal Liberty*; *Germany Unmasked* and *The Rise and Fall of the League of Nations*

References

> International Who's Who

Obituaries

> Nation 151:65 Jl 27 '40
> N Y Herald Tribune p24 Jl 21 '40 por
> N Y Times p29 Jl 21 '40 por

Maurice Goldberg

ROBERT EDWARD DELL

DENNY, GEORGE VERNON JR. Aug 20, 1899- Director of the radio program, *America's Town Meeting of the Air*; president of The Town Hall, Incorporated

Address: b. The Town Hall, 123 W 43rd St, New York City

George Vernon Denny Jr., is the man who brought the town meeting back to America. His town meeting covers the entire United States, for it is broadcast by the Blue Network of the National Broadcasting Company over stations from coast to coast. When the town crier rings his bell and calls "Town Meetin' Tonight," millions of radio listeners tune in as eagerly to hear questions of national interest discussed as if they were actually attending a town meeting.

A chance remark about a neighbor gave Denny the idea for *America's Town Meeting of the Air*. The neighbor had refused consistently to listen to President Roosevelt's fireside chats. Denny, who was at that time associate director of Town Hall of New York, passionately believed that the Town Hall's work of presenting all sides of political questions was one of the great educational services of the country. And he was shocked by his neighbor's refusal to listen to anyone whose political views differed from his own.

If people shut their minds to all discussion, the great American principle of free speech and free discussion, in a word, the democratic form of government, was endangered, Denny reasoned. The intimacy of early American communal life with its town meetings for discussion of public affairs was gone. In a complex, industrial civilization a man might shut himself up and read only the newspapers he approved, listen only to friends who believed as he did, close his mind to all opposite thought. Denny pondered on how he could recapture the democratic way of thinking and of solving problems.

The result was *America's Town Meeting of the Air*. The meetings began with a series of six experimental programs, starting May 30, 1935 and ending July 4. After the first broadcast at which four speakers—Lawrence Dennis, A. J. Muste, Norman Thomas and Raymond Moley—discussed: "Which Way America—fascism, communism, socialism or democracy?" 3,000 letters poured into the offices of Town Hall and NBC stations. The response was a surprise because the program had received little publicity, and Americans supposedly were politically indifferent.

The letters were enthusiastic. They showed that Americans were stirred by this new *America's Town Meeting of the Air* with its free discussion of public questions. Apparently the program filled a vital need.

However, the success of *America's Town Meeting of the Air* is due, to a large extent, to Denny's fine sense of showmanship and drama. Denny started life as a teacher of play production and as an actor, and he knew how to give the town meeting discussions a dramatic touch. They were not just dry debates. It was fun to go to a town meeting as the crier sang out, "Town Meetin' Tonight, Town Meetin' Tonight." And Denny as moderator kept the town meeting moving at a quick, dramatic pace.

The moderator of *America's Town Meeting of the Air* was born in Washington, North Carolina, a town of 7,000, on August 29, 1899, the son of George Vernon and Carrie Ricks (Cobb) Denny. He attended the University of North Carolina and received his B. S. in commerce in 1922. During his sophomore year a new college professor, Frederick H. Koch, came to the University to start a department of dramatic arts and formed the now famous student acting troupe, the Carolina Playmakers. Denny joined the Playmakers and became company manager at $50 a month. He served as instructor in dramatic production at the University from 1924 to 1926.

A leading lady in the Playmakers' first productions was Mary Traill Yellott, who came to the University of North Carolina from Bel Air, Maryland. Denny was cast in the rôle of her lover and he has never stepped out of it. They were married in June 1924. They have three children, Mildred Nelson, George Vernon 3rd and Mary Virginia.

Denny came to New York as an actor in 1926 and did rather well, except that most of the plays he was in closed. So the young actor got himself a job as manager of a lecture bureau. Indirectly this led to his next job with Columbia University, which was then looking for a man with lecture-bureau experience to manage the extension work of its Institute of Arts and Sciences. Here the League for Political Education heard of him.

GEORGE V. DENNY JR.

The League for Political Education had since the 1890's presented distinguished orators of various political creeds and opinions from its platform. Denny became the assistant of Robert Erskine Ely, director of the League, in 1928. In 1937, when Ely retired, he turned his job over to Denny. Denny changed the name of the organization to Town Hall, Incorporated as soon as he came into power.

Denny has followed the spirit and tradition of the League for Political Education, which built the Town Hall of New York in 1920. As president of Town Hall, Incorporated since 1937, he has kept alive its many lectures, discussion groups and short courses. But he has broadened its influence immeasurably as one of the "yeasty" influences in American democracy with his *America's Town Meeting of the Air*.

Denny is convinced that a small but enlightened bloc of independent voters controls the balance of political power, and it is this bloc he hopes to reach and influence to action. It is this bloc that he says must stop the drift toward dictatorships.

But if Denny's job is primarily that of educator, his *Town Meeting of the Air* is so well sugar-coated with showmanship that it does not show. His radio program brings in more than 60,000 letters each season. After five seasons on the air it is still going strong. In 1939 eighty-three stations broadcast the program twenty-six times without pay, and the National Broadcasting Company contracted for its continuance three years in advance.

America's Town Meeting of the Air is good theatre. It has conflict, differing opinions voiced about affairs that concern us all. It avoids the old-fashioned debate technique. The individual who rises in the meeting to ask a question is part of the program. Denny

DENNY, GEORGE VERNON, Jr.—*Cont.*

has often made the heckler good entertainment. Nobody knows when something exciting is going to happen at *Town Meeting,* and 10,000,000 listeners who tune in Thursday nights feel the dramatic import of stern controversial issues being thrashed out.

The radio audience had some rare treats—the night Mrs. Eugene Meyer went to mat with Mrs. Roosevelt (see sketch this issue) over the New Deal; the night the late Heywood Broun and Julian Mason almost came to blows on the Town Hall platform; the night Ickes and Gannett spoke their minds about the freedom of the press. Wendell Willkie, Dorothy Thompson, Frank Knox, Frances Perkins, Burton K. Wheeler, Carl Sandburg (see sketches this issue), John Gunther, Jan Masaryk, Pearl Buck are some of the persons who have appeared on the program.

But no matter how important the speakers are, Denny is a stern ringmaster. His blue eyes snap behind silver-rimmed glasses, his high forehead is brilliant under the Town Hall stage lights, and no one is allowed to run past his time. In the same stern fashion he deals with those who rise to ask questions. Personalities are barred; issues alone must be considered. And as an added dramatic touch groups in distant places have shot in their questions by radio to New York's *Town Meeting.*

As a result of *America's Town Meeting of the Air,* town meeting listening-discussion groups have sprung up all over the United States. Town Hall has set up an advisory service which supplies hundreds of these groups in all states with complete background materials in advance of each program. From Kobe, Japan, to Alaska and the Argentine, listeners have written of their enjoyment of the program.

> *References*
>> Christian Sci Mon Mag p3 N 16 '38 il por
>> Cur Hist 51:32 Ja '40 por; 51:33-5+ F '40 il por (p41)
>> Liberty 16:41-5 D 9 '39 il
>> America's Young Men
>> Overstreet, H. A. and Overstreet, B. W. The Story of America's Town Meeting of the Air pam nd (reprinted from Town Meeting Comes to Town (1938)
>> Who's Who in America

DERMOT, JESSIE *See* Elliott, M.

DES GRAZ, SIR CHARLES LOUIS
Mar 2, 1860—Oct 24, 1940 Member of British diplomatic corps; entered service in 1884 and served as secretary in Constantinople, Teheran and Athens; councilor of Embassy in Rome in 1905; later Minister to Peru and Ecuador; Minister to Serbia through the First World War; retired in 1920; knighted in 1915

> *References*
>> Who's Who
> *Obituaries*
>> N Y Times p21 O 25 '40

DE VALERA, EAMON (dĕ vȧ-lā′rȧ ā′mûn)
Oct 14, 1882-　Prime Minister of Eire
Address: Bellevue, Cross Ave, Blackrock County, Dublin, Eire

In the Second World War Ireland, like Europe's other neutral countries, is in a ticklish spot. Southern Ireland fears that Hitler may try to use it as a springboard for an attack on Britain or that he may land troops in Northern Ireland, which is belligerent territory. It fears, too, that there is danger that Britain may send in troops to forestall the Germans. It is doing all in its power to maintain the strictest neutrality.

At the beginning of the War Prime Minister Eamon De Valera announced that Ireland was neutral and would stay so. Yet precautions were immediately taken: Ireland's army was brought to war strength; an air raid precaution service was instituted; censorship was clamped down. As De Valera put it, "There is but one danger over this country . . . and there is but one safeguard—to be prepared to defend the liberties we won against anyone who might try to invade them."

For his actions De Valera has been called both pro- and anti-British. The extremists of the Irish Republican Army, determined by any means to bring the six northern counties which are now a part of England under the flag of Eire (the Irish Free State), think he is playing the British game. The British, angrily contrasting Eire's neutrality with the enthusiasm of New Zealand or Canada, balked by De Valera in their desire to have a British armed force strengthen Irish preparations against possible German invasion and in their effort to lease naval bases, aware of the fact that Eire's neutrality makes it possible for a German Minister to be alarmingly close to England, feel that De Valera is far from doing his bit. Others say he would give in to Britain's demands if it were not for his people's passionate desire for neutrality and suspicion of British ambitions.

On the other hand, a great many believe De Valera's only wish is for a peaceful, united Ireland, free of Great Britain. With "rigid self-control, fanatic faith in his duty to Ireland, extreme seriousness of mind, complete unworldliness, stubbornness and humanity" he has spent almost all his life fighting for this goal.

This Prime Minister of Ireland, who says his ambition is the unity and self-determination of all Irish people, actually is only half Irish and is of American birth. Eamon De Valera was born Edward De Valera in New York City; his father, Vivian De Valera, was a Spanish immigrant; his mother, Catherine (Coll) De Valera, was an Irishwoman recently arrived from Limerick. When Edward was two years old his father died and he was sent to Ireland to live in his grandmother's home near Bruree in County Limerick. His mother, who stayed in America, remarried.

In Ireland, Edward, whose name was changed to the Gaelic equivalent, Eamon, lived on a farm and went to the local school. Because of his skill in mathematics he won a scholarship to the Christian Brothers' School near Cork and from there went to Blackrock College near Dublin. At school he read everything, was a star runner and rugby player and a brilliant mathematician. His B. A. degree he got from the National University of Ireland.

After leaving the University, De Valera learned Gaelic. His wife, Jane Flannagan (S. Ni Fhlannagain), whom he married in 1910, was a teacher at the University. Then he got himself a job teaching mathematics, a "tall, long-nosed, serious fellow, dressed in rough homespun and wearing a queer sort of deerstalker cap." It wasn't long before his career as a nationalist and a revolutionary began. Like most Irishmen he resented Britain's domination over Ireland.

On Easter Monday, 1916 a few thousand determined Irish decided that "Britain's extremity is Ireland's opportunity," and rebellion against England's rule was started. As a commandant in the Republican Army the young, gawky professor of mathematics led out fifty partly-armed men to hold two miles of strategic railway line and canal in Dublin. When British troops approached he admonished his men: "You have but one life to live and but one death to die. See that you do both like men." The rebellion was crushed and all its leaders, except De Valera, sentenced to death and shot. Because he was an American citizen De Valera was given penal servitude for life and sent to Dartmoor Prison.

De Valera stayed in prison only a year, for in the general amnesty of 1917 he was freed, to become an Irish hero, his portrait in thousands of Irish homes. Immediately he was elected president of the Sinn Fein ("ourselves") Party and made Sinn Fein Member of Parliament for Clare, though he never took his seat since he refused to take the necessary British oath of allegiance. In 1918 he was back in jail again. After that year's general elections the newly-elected M. P.'s had met at Dublin as the Dáil Eireann (Assembly of Ireland), and at the very same time the British had "discovered" a pro-German plot and carted off to England hundreds of prominent Sinn Feiners among them De Valera.

He escaped from Lincoln Prison (where he mastered Einstein's theory) by having a key made (it is a most romantic story) and went to Manchester, where he hid in the house of a priest. From there he made his way to Liverpool and thence to Ireland, once disguised as a seaman, once hidden in sacks of potatoes. Eventually he

EAMON DE VALERA

went to America disguised as a stoker. His arrival here was stirring—the police were still scouring Ireland and England for him. De Valera spoke all over the United States and raised money for the Irish cause.

Back in Ireland in 1920, De Valera was elected President of the Dáil Eireann, which was made up of the Sinn Fein deputies from Southern Ireland who had refused to take an oath to the King and had proclaimed their independence. Civil War began, in which the Black and Tans and Irish Nationalists slaughtered each other until July 1921, when a truce was declared. Five months later the Irish Treaty was signed, which gave Ireland dominion status but separated the Free State from Ulster. De Valera had been arguing about this treaty with Lloyd George for a long time—Lloyd George said: "Negotiating with that Irishman is like trying to scoop up mercury with a fork"—but when it was finally negotiated and signed by his men, he denounced it. The Dáil Eireann, however, approved it and there was Civil War again. When it began De Valera was arrested while making a speech. Released 10 months later, after the War had stopped, he climbed the same platform and quietly began: "As I was saying when I was interrupted. . . "

Until 1926 De Valera held out in his demand for an all-Ireland Republic. Then he suddenly proposed that his party of Sinn Feiners enter the Dáil if they would not have to swear allegiance to the King. When his proposal was rejected he left the Party, formed his own Fianna Fail (Soldiers of Destiny), and later took the oath and entered the Dáil himself. Many called him "traitor" (some still do), and it took him six years to fully recover his political influence. Forty-three of his men came into the Dáil in 1928; in the next election there were fifty-seven; in 1932 De Valera's

DE VALERA, EAMON—*Continued*

Party had won a majority by a coalition with the Labor Party and De Valera was the Dáil's President, a position he held until 1937.

In that year De Valera drew up a new constitution for the Irish Free State which was adopted in April, and in 1938 the Irish Free State, having adopted the name of Eire, separated itself from the British Commonwealth, with Douglas Hyde as its first President and De Valera as Prime Minister. As the Constitution put it, Eire "is a sovereign, independent, democratic state" which may choose to associate itself with Great Britain in international affairs but may at any time revoke that association by act of the Irish Parliament. The payment of land purchase annuities was suspended, British ships were forced out, the British Governor was scared away from his vice-regal lodge in Dublin, and Ireland found itself involved in economic warfare with England.

Out of this warfare, under De Valera's "adroit manipulation," came a considerable degree of self-sufficiency for Ireland, aided rather than hampered by a trade treaty with England concluded in 1938. But despite this independence De Valera says he will not be satisfied until Northern Ireland is part of Eire and all Ireland is entirely free of Great Britain. This must come, however, through peaceful means and not by I. R A. terrorism (since the War started he has jailed some terrorists without trial and told the rest that they may expect no quarter). There have been two hangings.

There is a minority in Eire which believes that by his actions De Valera has made "the union of Ulster and the Free State even more remote"; which describes him as a "vain, egotistical schemer whose real study is Machiavelli rather than mathematics, whose policies are crippling the country, whose life has been a curse to Ireland." Many others say that "the government is no longer aiming at a republic," perhaps because if the thousands of middle-class young men and women who emigrate to parts of the British Empire were forced to find work at home they would challenge the tremendous influence of the clergy in Ireland. And De Valera is deeply religious. According to a writer in *The Nation,* "he lives in a veritable dictator's paradise, a paradise *sans* purges, *sans* martyrs, thanks to the British Empire, which takes to its bosom the more refractory of his fellow-citizens." But most of Eire apparently believes that this deeply religious, this fanatically Irish Irishman has been the deliverer of his country.

All his followers call him "Dev." To them a free Ireland is typified in his spare, rugged frame clothed almost always in rusty black, in his homely face with its long nose and deep lines to the mouth. They listen with wild Irish enthusiasm to his speeches, often plodding and overelaborated. (Someone once said about them: "De Valera is marching on Dublin at the head of 20,000 words.") They support his policies. In return De Valera gives Ireland all he has to give. His life is simple and frugal—he, his wife and six children live in a small house, and his salary is only £1,500. His hobbies are walking, chess and mathematics but he gives them little time, for each day is a grueling one and he has never taken a holiday. He once told an interviewer, "It's not a question of what I want, but what the people of Ireland want."

References

Am Mag 126:35+ S '38 por
Atlan 162:374-81 S '38
Cath World 148:304-8 D '38
Christian Sci Mon p5 My 27 '40; p1, 6 Ag 12 '40 por; p18 S 7 '40
Commonweal 27:455-7 F 18 '38
Harper 173:311-17 Ag '36
Nation 149:442 O 21 '39; 150:335-7 Mr 9 '40
Time 35:30+ Mr 25 '40 il pors
Crain, M. Rulers of the World 1940
Gunther, J. De Valera *In* Inside Europe p366-76 1940
Gwynn, D. R. De Valera 1933
O'Faoláin, S. Life Story of Eamon De Valera 1933
Pechell, G. M. De Valera 1938
Ryan, D. Unique Dictator 1936
Soward, F. H. Eamon De Valera and the Making of Eire *In* Moulders of National Destinies p209-18 1940
Stuart, F. President De Valera *In* Men of Turmoil p201-11 1935
Who's Who

DEWEY, THOMAS EDMUND Mar 24, 1902- District Attorney of New York County

Address: b. 137 Centre St, New York City; h. 1148 Fifth Ave, New York City

In 1940 one of the leading contenders for the Republican Presidential nomination was Thomas E. Dewey. The young District Attorney, whose name has been as familiar to Americans during the past few years as that of Clark Gable, Henry Ford, Charles A. Lindbergh, Joe Louis (see sketch this issue) or Joe DiMaggio, was born in Owosso, Michigan, March 24, 1902, the son of George Martin and Annie (Thomas) Dewey. His father, who died in 1927, was for many years Republican county chairman, postmaster of Owosso and publisher of the Owosso *Times*. The Dewey who was hero of Manila Bay was his grandfather's third cousin. Nobody could possibly find anything scandalous in his boyhood, or anything particularly remarkable, either. He was a Boy Scout, sang in a choir, organized a magazine agency and won a bicycle for his services to the *Saturday Evening Post,* made a record for never being late or absent at the local public schools that he attended, occasionally won' debating contests—but no one could have predicted his spectacular career from these facts. Even when he went to the University of Michigan in 1919 he made no teams, was never nominated for the presidency of his class, didn't head the debating society, but instead specialized in winning singing contests. In 1923 he acquired a B. A. and a scholarship for a brief period at a Chicago music school. He continued his singing lessons at another branch of the school in New York. At the same time he began to attend Columbia Law School, however, and hired his voice out to church choirs and synagogues in order to help pay expenses. It took him only two years to finish Columbia's three-year law course. In 1925 he must have at last decided that an LL. B. was more useful than a beautiful baritone, for that year Thomas Dewey entered legal practice in the firm of Larkin Rathbone & Perry, where he was to stay a year before associating himself with McNamara & Seymour.

It was after this that things began to happen. In the first place, the summer of 1925 was the time when Thomas Dewey first grew his famous mustache, during a bicycle tour of France. Frances Hutt approved of it. Since Frances Hutt was to become Frances Dewey in 1928, after a romance that had begun at music school several years before, her opinion must have carried some weight. Dewey kept the mustache. Evidently his clients approved of it, too, for by 1931, when he left McNamara & Seymour for a position as chief assistant to George Medalie, newly-appointed United States Attorney for the Southern District of New York, he was making $8,000 a year in private practice.

Dewey was chief assistant to Medalie for two years and nine months. Toward the end of this period he was beginning the trial of his first big racketeer, Waxey Gordon, later sentenced to the Federal penitentiary for 10 years as a tax dodger. Two days after the trial had begun Medalie resigned, and for five weeks his assistant was United States Attorney. He worked for himself for the next 18 months until, in July 1935, the New York Grand Jury asked Governor Lehman to appoint somebody to investigate racketeering and vice in New York. Medalie suggested Dewey for the position, and after four other prospects had refused the job, he was offered the office of Special Prosecutor. He accepted, called on the public to come forward with information on racketeering.

In 1936 he began his spectacular assault on the prostitution industry in which Lucky Luciano was crowned "King of Vice" and was convicted with eight others accused of "shaking down" prostitutes. This conviction was said to have cost $110,000 of the people's money, but the testimony of the ladies concerned brought Dewey so much publicity that later, more prosaic investigations of rackets in the poultry, trucking, restaurant and baking businesses became "a sort of front-page Arabian Nights series about New York, with the same hero for each installment."

In 1937 New York's anti-Tammany faction, headed by Fiorello La Guardia (see sketch this issue), picked Dewey to run on its ticket as candidate for District Attorney.

Underwood & Underwood

THOMAS DEWEY

He accepted the nomination, and after a campaign conducted with his own inimitable "cops-and-robbers technique" (Dewey's "private and public conversation always emphasized the menace of the underworld, omnipresent, almost omnipotent, crouched for a leap"), on December 31, 1937 Thomas Dewey became New York City's District Attorney by a margin of more than 100,000 votes. It was an office not held by a Republican in nearly two generations, and victory meant he had come a long way from the early days when he began his political career by ringing doorbells, canvassing for votes for the Republicans, and getting himself elected chairman of the board of directors of the Young Republican Club. The New York World-Telegram announced: "Hoodlums Start Out As Dewey Starts In."

During Dewey's term as District Attorney the crimes and consequent punishments of such figures as Richard Whitney, Jimmy Hines, Fritz Kuhn and Lepke were brought to the attention of newspaper readers all over the country. Not so well publicized was his creation of the Volunteer Defenders, a panel of the best legal talent which handles a certain number of cases every year without fee. When, during the end of his first year in office, Dewey ran against Lehman for Governor of New York, the people of that state showed what they thought of him by giving him so many votes that a switch of 35,000 would have meant his election. And after his defeat he added to his record the prosecution and conviction of such varied public menaces as Judge Manton, Fritz Kuhn, subway employees responsible for the theft of a fortune in nickels, ambulance-chasing lawyers and landlords whose tenants

DEWEY, THOMAS—*Continued*

burned to death in tenements which violated the New York fire laws.

In the fall of 1939 a petition was circulated among leading Republicans beginning: "Convinced that he possesses above all other leaders in the country today the ability, temperament and training which the next President of the United States must have, we have decided to cooperate in the movement to elect Thomas E. Dewey President in 1940." Public sentiment seemed to be trending in the same direction, for by January 1940 the Gallup polls revealed 60 per cent in favor of his candidacy. On December 1, 1939 Thomas Dewey formally announced he would accept the Republican nomination if it were offered.

During the heaviest cross-country campaign ever undertaken by a candidate for the Presidential nomination, Dewey drew enthusiastic bouquets from voters all over the country and also made himself the "top-flight clay pigeon of the political sharpshooters." It was charged by his opponents that he was too young and inexperienced for the Presidential office (Ickes announced: "The District Attorney of New York has finally thrown his diaper into the ring"); he was accused of "bullying hostile witnesses and coddling favorable ones, demanding exorbitant bail, wire-tapping, condoning the use of perjured testimony"; he was called "pompous and conceited"; he was supposed to be "groomed by the moneyed crowd"; and Samuel Grafton (see sketch this issue) said of his social philosophy that "if a young man is as cold as this at 37, he will reach absolute zero by 50." His supporters, in turn, pointed out that some of the experienced people then in office hadn't "polished off the nation's rough spots" too satisfactorily, that he was "the only one of the leading candidates of proved executive ability," that he had proved by his acts that he would not tolerate financial crookedness and that he had sympathy for the poor; that "he came from good, typical American people . . . was taught family life . . . and believes that men and women when they get married, get married for keeps and raise a family." His honesty, morals and good health were never questioned by anyone.

Although the Republican nomination finally went to Wendell Willkie (see sketch this issue), Dewey and Robert Taft (see sketch this issue) ran a fairly close race at the Philadelphia Convention. Afterward, the District Attorney campaigned for Willkie, eloquently condemning the New Deal on the grounds of inefficient rearmament, open war on American business, defeatism, bureaucracy, extravagance, corruption. His book, *The Case Against the New Deal*, was published shortly before the 1940 election.

Even aside from his amazing record as a District Attorney, Thomas Dewey has many political assets. As an orator he "lacks Franklin Roosevelt's charm but he can deliver the smokiest platitude in such a way that it sounds like a bit of brand-new evidence just mined by a special investigator." He is personally attractive—something over five-feet-eight, with piercing brown eyes which he rotates furiously to "punctuate and emphasize his speech"; "at climactic moments he can pop them, almost audibly." (Photographs seldom show him in the act of popping, though: his favorite study is "to appear close-mouthed, intent, looking into the future.")

The District Attorney lives with his two small sons and his attractive wife, a former prima donna in George White's *Scandals*, in an eight-room apartment in Manhattan, and spends his summers with them on a 300-acre farm near Pawling, New York. Though the Deweys represent the "younger married set," they live rather sedately, are not yet in the Social Register, have few even minor vices. Mr. Dewey, an Episcopalian and a Mason, smokes a pack of cigarettes a day, didn't drink at all during Prohibition and never has more than two highballs at a sitting now, plays penny-ante poker with a nickel limit. He hates speed, hates night clubs, likes sleep, the opera, Sunday concerts, singing duets with his wife, and wishes he could attend church more than once a month. Perhaps the cruelest thing ever said about him, even during the heat of the campaign, was one Democratic hostess' epigram: "You have to know Mr. Dewey very well in order to dislike him."

References

Am Mercury 50:135-47 Je '40
Collier's 105:14-15+ Je 8 '40 il por
Cur Hist 51:35-9+ Ja '40 por
Life 8:19-21 Mr 4 '40 il pors; 8:28-9
    Ap 15 '40 il pors; 8:84-6+ Ap 22 '40
    il pors
Nation 150:282 F 24 '40; 150:356-60
    Mr 16 '40; 150:551 Ap 27 '40
New Yorker 16:24-8+ My 25 '40 il
Survey G 29:286+ My '40
Time 35:15-17 F 26 '40 pors; 35:18-19
    Ap 15 '40

America's Young Men
Hughes, R. Attorney for the People
    1940
Powell, H. Ninety Times Guilty 1939
Who's Who in America
Who's Who in Government
Who's Who in Law

DE WIART, ADRIAN CARTON *See* Carton de Wiart, A.

DIES, MARTIN Nov 6, 1901- Congressman; chairman of the House Committee Investigating un-American Activities

Address: b. House of Representatives, Washington, D. C.; h. Orange, Texas

The House Committee Investigating Un-American Activities has received more publicity since its creation in May 1938 than any other current governmental committee. It has been called "the correct mechanism for defending democracy" and a "disgrace" to this country. It has aroused violent denunciations and has enjoyed "unprecedented popular support."

Much of the argument has centered about its chairman, Martin Dies of Texas, who has been raised by the committee to the position of a national figure, his picture in the newspapers almost every day, his name in headlines, his methods the subject of adulation or attack from Roosevelt down. For his activities as committee head Martin Dies has been called a "Fascist," a "dangerous demagogue," an "enlightened politician," the "one-man Gestapo of Texas," and a "warder-off of ruin."

Martin Dies has spent most of his short life in politics. He was born in Colorado, Texas, the son of Martin and Olive (Cline) Dies. His father was a member of Congress for 10 years and under Woodrow Wilson achieved minor fame for his opposition to the War. With his father Martin spent many of his high school years in Washington and "by the time he had long pants he had soaked up more practical political lore than most men ever possess."

He studied at Wesley College (Greenville) and at the University of Texas, and received his LL. B. from the National University in Washington, D. C. At the age of 19 he was admitted to the Bar and spent nearly two years in law practice in Marshall, Texas. While he was practicing there he married Myrtle Adams in 1920. On January 1, 1922, he moved to Orange, Texas, where he became senior partner of the law firm of Dies, Stephenson and Dies.

When Martin Dies was first elected to Congress in 1931 he was under 30, the baby of the 1931 to 1933 session. When the New Deal began in 1933 Dies was strongly with it, an advocate of monetary inflation and a critic of a conservative Supreme Court. He was chiefly noticed, however, because he was thought to be a protégé of Vice-President Garner. In some quarters his elevation to the powerful House Rules Committee was "attributed to Mr. Garner's benevolence," though others claimed he "campaigned" for the position, as any good politician would.

This position on the Rules Committee was an important one for Dies mainly because it left him free from service on other committees. He seemed, then, to have "infinite leisure. He would sprawl his six-foot length on the tufted leather couches of the House cloak rooms and deliver himself of roughly-phrased, often very comical observations on his colleagues." About this time the Demagogues Club was founded, the members of which were pledged never to vote for a tax bill or against an appropriations bill. It has been called an "unofficial organization of House members addicted to flamboyant speeches saturated with hokum." Its first president and the

leader of this not quite pro-New Deal organization was Martin Dies.

Early in the New Deal Dies had said that the way to cure unemployment was to deport the six million aliens he estimated were in this country. In February 1937 he was one of those who fought against Supreme Court reorganization, and was one of the first to attack the sit-down strikers in the General Motors strike. It has been whispered "that he did so with Mr. Garner's backing." Overnight he gained prestige and became one of the recognized anti-Roosevelt Democrats in the House. Later in the same session he was a leader in the fight against the Wages and Hours Bill.

From 1936 on, Martin Dies had kept trying to get Congress to instigate investigations of one sort or another. In fact, he suggested seven investigations in three years—on the Administration's restriction of the freedom of the press and radio, on the problem of aliens, on Ickes' charge that 60 families control the United States, etc. "From the first," says a newspaper commentator, "he made no secret of the fact that he was looking for a safe political horse on which to ride to headlines and glory."

He got his chance in 1938 when Representative Dickstein of New York—worried by Fritz Kuhn and the Nazi Bund camps—supported him, and the Committee to Investigate Un-American Activities was set up, with Dies as chairman and with an appropriation of $25,000. Dies wasn't discouraged by the small sum which, under ordinary conditions, should have allowed him to investigate for about one month. He went ahead without any staff, without counsel and with volunteer help.

The first hearing of the Dies Committee was held in the latter part of July 1938. In his opening statement Dies said: "We shall be fair and impartial at all times and treat every witness with fairness and courtesy. The Committee will not permit any 'character assassination' or any 'smearing' of innocent people." There had been similar hearings before. In 1932 Hamilton Fish had investigated Communist activities, roused some stir and had then been forgotten; in 1934 Representatives McCormack and Dickstein had investigated Nazi and other propaganda and had also been forgotten. But as soon as the Dies hearings began they created excitement and controversy. The first investigations of the Nazis were quiet enough, but when John Frey of the American Federation of Labor accused the Communists of a number of things, there was a stir. Hundreds of people objected and hundreds of people wrote and wired to Dies asking to appear as witnesses and offering to pay their own fares.

Dies next aimed at Hollywood and discovered that a number of Hollywood figures had aided Communism by sending greetings to the Leftist French newspaper Ce Soir. Among them was Shirley Temple. Ickes got mad. "They've gone into Hollywood,"

Joseph Stonehill

MARTIN DIES

he said, "and there discovered a great Red plot. They have found dangerous radicals there, led by little Shirley Temple. Imagine the great committee raiding her nursery and seizing her dolls as evidence." There were others, however, who felt just as vehemently that Dies was doing a great service to the United States.

Just before the November 1938 elections there was testimony before the Dies Committee that Frank Murphy (see sketch this issue), then running for Governor of Michigan, was a "Communist or Communist dupe." At a press conference President Roosevelt denounced the committee and its methods, saying: "The Dies Committee made no effort to get at the truth, either by calling for facts to support mere personal opinion or by allowing facts or personal opinion on the other side."

The Department of Labor, the WPA Federal Theatre and Writers' Project, the National Labor Relations Board and the Wages and Hours Board, the American League for Peace and Democracy and the Workers' Alliance were some of the groups that came under surveillance by the Dies Committee and were accused of having Communists or "Communist dupes" among their members. It was said that if Mr. Dies "once puts his mind to it he can find Reds anywhere along the political spectrum." It was also argued that "all who tried to undermine confidence in the existing social system, promoted the idea that it is a governmental duty to support the people, advocated regimentation of industry, agriculture and labor, were equally subjects of inquiry along with Communists." On the other side it was stated that "Congressman Dies and his committee are doing a splendid thing in bringing to the attention of our

people the activities of Communists and all un-American organizations."

Dies' first year's investigation drew much blood from radical and liberal opinion and was, as he himself admitted, "slipshod." Yet its first report that the Communist and Nazi parties were branches of the Soviet and German governments, respectively, and that the Communists held key positions in federal agencies and projects and in the CIO "so caught the imagination of the American public that in January 1939, Dies had no trouble in getting the life of the committee extended with a fourfold appropriation."

The Committee was continued in rather different form. Representatives Voorhis and Casey, both strong New Dealers, were substituted for other committee members, several former FBI agents were employed, Rhea Whitley, with the FBI for 10 years, was taken on as counsel, and J. B. Mathews, a "former Communist fellow traveler," was hired as investigator.

Dies and his Committee got still more publicity when they investigated the American Youth Congress and the consumer groups. During the investigation of the Youth Congress and the American student Union, in the fall of 1939, Mrs. Roosevelt (see sketch this issue) appeared with those about to testify, sat through the proceedings with them and invited them to lunch at the White House. When the Dies Committee came out in December 1939 with the assertion that the Milk Consumers' Protective Committee, the League of Women Shoppers, Consumers' Union, the Consumers' National Federation and other consumer groups were Communist "transmission belts," there was a good deal of hue and cry. Mrs. Roosevelt protested strongly in her syndicated column, while a group of Westchester housewives strongly supported Mr. Dies' contention, put out as the findings of himself and Mr. J. B. Mathews. Hue and cry was stirred up, too, when the mailing lists of the Washington members of the American League for Peace and Democracy were seized. President Roosevelt called this a "sordid procedure."

The full report of the activities of the Dies Committee was made public on January 2, 1940. Boiled down from 7,000 pages of testimony from 205 witnesses, "it was a document that no radical could have expected from the Dies Committee." Its material was evenly divided between Communists and Fascists, and in its 15,000 well-chosen words there was nothing to justify the fuss which preceded it.

It begins: "Every modern democratic nation is confronted by two pressing problems. The first is the preservation of the Constitutional liberties which their people have gained through the years of struggle; the second is the problem of adjusting their economic life to the difficulties of the machine age." It says further that the main problem in combating groups trying to undermine democracy is to avoid action "which would undermine the fundamental structure of Constitutional liberty itself."

According to a number of commentators, the report is as calm as it is because an initial, original report by Mr. Dies alone was turned down by Voorhis, Casey and Dempsey, the New Deal members of the Committee. They threatened to issue a minority report, if the original report was submitted, which would have made a new Congressional appropriation difficult to obtain.

Before and after the report was submitted there had been a good deal of pressure on Congress both to continue and to end the Dies Committee. Large groups of churchmen, the National Association for the Advancement of Colored People and other groups asked that it be ended, while the New York State Chamber of Commerce and other groups asked that its life be assured for another period. One side put it that "if civil liberties are to be preserved in this country," the Dies Committee must be discontinued; the other, that "if we are to preserve America, if the America of the future is to protect our boys and girls as we have been protected, then this Committee should be authorized to proceed further." On January 23, 1940, the House voted to continue the Committee for one year with an appropriation of $75,000.

Some of Dies' most publicized acts in 1940 were an investigation of Fifth Column activities along the Mexican border which, the *New Republic* charged, was actually designed to aid Almazán (see sketch this issue); the revelation that Communists had obtained information on a Federal Writers' Project which would enable them to paralyze the City of New York (the local WPA Administrator calmed fears with the statement that none of the information was confidential, anyway); the clearing of 20 movie celebrities of the charge of Communism. He consistently urged that Communist, Nazi and Fascist groups be outlawed, and in August asked for another appropriation to continue his inquiry.

The main controversy about Martin Dies and his Committee has raged, not so much about the information which is being gathered and given out, as about the method by which it is being obtained. According to one critic, "the vital distinction between investigation and persecution has escaped Mr. Dies." Wendell Willkie (see sketch this issue) denounced him "for undermining democratic procedure." Others have criticized him for concentrating on Communists almost to the exclusion of the Nazis, and for his total lack of concern with native Fascist movements such as those led by Father Coughlin (see sketch this issue) and Gerald Winrod.

It has been said in extenuation, however, that "Dies' perpetually scandalized method of listening to everybody, hauling in back-fence radical gossip, old shoes, scandals,

guesses and wild charges was perhaps the best method of building up the picture of the elusive world of United States Communism," and Stanley High says, "Mr. Dies may not be quite the finest bloom of the hothouse of Texas politics, but he certainly is a handy man with a flit gun." Mr. Dies says in defense of his own methods: "America is a free country and I would defend with my life the rights of its citizens, but when they take the oath of allegiance and then seek to undermine our government, I say what amendment in our Constitution protects these spies and agents of foreign governments?"

The findings of Martin Dies' Committee to Investigate un-American Activities were summed up in his book, *The Trojan Horse of America*, published in October 1940. According to one critic, it is "a restrained, informative primer about United States Communists and Fascists, what they are, how they work." His book "should be serviceable to those who do their own thinking and should curl the hair of others." Other critics, however, find fault with the fact that Dies devotes 324 pages to the Communists and only 42 to the Nazis and Fascists, and object to false inferences, which, if taken too seriously by the public, "together with his haunting suspicion of all aliens," will result in "an epidemic of witch-hunting and lynching which will crack our national unity instead of cementing it." In November 1940 the Dies Committee published a *White Paper* concerned with Nazi activities in the United States, raided offices in many cities, and promised further revelations. At the same time Dies criticized the work of the FBI as ineffectual compared to his own.

Away from his committee Martin Dies is a "practical politician of the New South." He talks in a "homespun folksy way" which is not affected. There have been rumors that his hunt to free America from un-American activities may be in some way linked with the Presidential election of 1944. But when he is asked about what he is going to do or where he intends to go in politics, Dies replies: "Not interested." He professes rather to prefer playing pool at home in the evenings with his three young sons and doing a little bird-shooting down in East Texas every summer and fall to "running around the country on any political campaign."

References

Am Mag 129:22-3+ My '40 il pors
Atlan 165:232-7 F '40
Christian Sci Mon Mag p3 Ja 20 '40
Cong Digest 18:267-70 N '39
Cur Hist 51:29-30 D '39 por; 51:8
    Ja '40
Nation 149:512 N 11 '39; 149:641 D 9
    '39; 149:669-70 D 16 '39
New Repub 101:185-9 D 6 '39; 102:
    10-13 Ja 1 '40; 102-137-9 Ja 29 '40;
    102:532 Ap 22 '40; 102:592 My 6
    '40; 103:337 S 9 '40

DIES, MARTIN—*Continued*

Propaganda Analysis 3:no4 Ja 15 '40
Time 34:15-17 O 23 '39; 35:13-14 Ja
15 '40

America's Young Men
Michie, A. A. and Rhylick, F. What
So Proudly They Wave *In* Dixie
Demagogues p45-67 1939
Who's Who in America
Who's Who in the Nation's Capital

DIETERICH, WILLIAM H. Mar 31,
1876—Oct 12, 1940 United States Senator
from Illinois from 1933 to 1939; practiced
law in Rushville, Illinois; from 1913 to 1917
was special inheritance tax attorney for the
State and from 1917 to 1921 a State Representative; in Congress from 1931 to 1933 as
Representative

References

Who's Who in America
Who's Who in Law
Who's Who in the Nation's Capital

Obituaries

N Y Times p48 O 13 '40

DIETZ, DAVID (dēts) Oct 6, 1897-
Science editor, Scripps-Howard newspapers
Address: b. Cleveland Press Building,
Cleveland, Ohio; h. 2891 Winthrop Rd,
Shaker Heights, Ohio

Lecturer in general science at Cleveland
College of Western Reserve University and
science editor of the Scripps-Howard newspapers, blond, mustached David Dietz was
the recipient of the B. F. Goodrich Award
for Distinguished Public Service in the field
of science in August 1940. Acknowledging
the award in the Goodrich Arena at the

DAVID DIETZ

New York World's Fair, he regretted that
"while American science has been working
for the good of humanity, the dictators of
Europe have plotted and launched a war
which threatens to destroy all those things
in life which Americans hold dear." He
pointed out the development by Dr. Waldo
L. Semon (see sketch this issue) of *Ameripol*,
a synthetic rubber, for the Goodrich Rubber
Company, as an illustration of the way in which
the nation is being freed from dependence on
foreign sources of supply for essential materials
not already produced here.

David Henry Dietz was born in Cleveland, Ohio on October 6, 1897, the son of
Henry William and Hannah (Levy) Dietz.
His interest in science began as a boy, for
his father was an enthusiastic amateur
astronomer and young David was looking
at the pictures in astronomy books before
he was old enough to read. His interest
continued to grow, and at Central High
School, Cleveland, he was elected president
of the Faraday Club, the school's scientific
society, and achieved a grade of 99 for the
year in his physics class. He began to combine these talents with journalism when he
became Central High School correspondent for
the Cleveland *Plain Dealer* in 1913 and again
when he entered Western Reserve University in 1915, earning his way by working
for the Cleveland *Press*. The first scientific
article which he wrote was in 1915, an interview with Professor Dayton C. Miller, and
he has been writing about science for the
Cleveland *Press* ever since.

Leaving school to enlist in the army in
October 1918, a few days after his marriage
to Dorothy B. Cohen, David Dietz received
his honorable discharge barely two months
later. His B. A. from Western Reserve he
acquired in 1919 and subsequently he carried
on graduate studies at both Western Reserve University and the Case School of
Applied Science. Since 1921 he has been
science editor of the Scripps-Howard
newspapers and in that capacity has attended important scientific meetings and
visited important scientific institutions in all
parts of the United States and in Europe.
He was a charter member and first president of the National Association of Science
Writers, and in 1926 was appointed lecturer
in general science at Cleveland College of
Western Reserve University.

His book, *The Story of Science*, in 1940
in its fourth edition, was published in 1931.
"With the gifts of a born popularizer," Mr.
Dietz dealt with the leading achievements
of astronomy, geology, physics, chemistry
and biology so successfully that Harry Elmer Barnes decided "there is no longer any
reason why a man who owns a radio cannot be mentally nearer its mysteries than
he is to the stone hatchet." A second book,
Medical Magic, came out in 1937. (Its British
title is *Builders of Health*.)

In 1933 Mr. Dietz added to his professional duties that of science correspondent
for the United Press Association. Journal-

istic distinctions followed. In 1937 he was awarded the Pulitzer Prize in Journalism, in 1938 the New Orleans Trophy of Zeta Beta Tau.

Mr. Dietz shares a love of music with his wife and three children—Doris Jean, Patricia Ann and David Henry II. He himself has played the violin since he was five. Other hobbies are collecting books on the history of science and golf. He is a fellow of the Royal Astronomical Society and the Société Astronomique de France. The City and Professional Clubs in Cleveland and the National Press Club in Washington also claim him as a member. He is a member of the Board of Trustees of the Shaker Heights Public Library.

References

N Y World-Telegram p9 Ag 26 '40
American Men of Science
Who's Who in America
Who's Who in American Jewry

DILLARD, JAMES HARDY (dĭl'ard) Oct 24, 1856—Aug 2, 1940 Educator; rector of the College of William and Mary since 1917; received the Theodore Roosevelt Medal for 1937 for his work in furthering understanding between the white and Negro races; career as an educator extended over a period of 60 years; head of the Jeanes Foundation which provided for the training of Negro school teachers

References

Sch & Soc 45:712 My 22 '37
Brawley, B. G. Doctor Dillard of the Jeanes Fund 1930
Who's Who in America
Who's Who in American Education

JAMES HARDY DILLARD

Obituaries

N Y Herald Tribune p8 Ag 3 '40 por
N Y Times p15 Ag 3 '40

DISNEY, WALT Dec 5, 1901- Producer of animated cartoons

Address: 2719 Hyperion Ave, Hollywood, California

Walt Disney made his reputation on a mouse—a pathetic little fellow who wormed his way into the hearts of millions of people all over the world by making them laugh. The mouse was called Mickey Mouse, and it was Walt Disney's first important animated cartoon creation.

Since the birth of Mickey Mouse in 1928, many other characters have appeared in the Mickey Mouse series—Donald Duck, Minnie Mouse, Goofy and Pluto, and Walt Disney has made motion picture history with his feature-length animated cartoons, *Snow White and the Seven Dwarfs* and *Pinocchio*. But Mickey Mouse and his friends continue to be the favored short subjects of the Walt Disney studios.

Stories of Mickey Mouse's origin differ. One says that the original Mickey was a little fellow who lived in a wastebasket where Disney worked drawing sketches for a farm journal in Kansas City. The mouse got so tame he ran across the cleat along the top of Disney's drawing board, and the young artist formed quite an attachment for him. He named him Mortimer, then Mickey. Another version is that Walt Disney, returning to Hollywood after he had broken with the distributor of his first animated cartoons, thought up Mickey Mouse during a sleepless night in an upper berth.

Whatever the genesis of Mickey Mouse there is no doubt about his popularity. In Japan, in Russia, in Africa, in Alaska, in every country in the world, Mickey Mouse is beloved by both children and adults. Learned theses have been written on the reason for Mickey Mouse's tremendous popularity. Religious magazines have carried articles on Walt Disney's animated cartoons; artistic criticism have been written on the subject of Mickey Mouse; and the Phi Beta Kappa magazine in July 1939 in an article called "But Is It Art?" mentioned Walt Disney's Mickey Mouse in the same breath with some of history's greatest creations in art.

But Walt Disney himself doesn't bother much about art. The word "art" is never mentioned in his studios. The genius of the animated cartoon field is a slim, unassuming young man (the office boys call him by his first name) who works very hard, tries to make good pictures and lets the savants figure out just what it is that gives his animals and fairy creatures that lovable, emotionally-appealing quality. Nevertheless, his work has won him numerous awards in the motion picture industry and has even

DISNEY, WALT—*Continued*

earned him honorary degrees from Yale University, Harvard University and the University of Southern California.

Walter Elias Disney had little formal instruction in art. A brief period at the Chicago Art Academy and at an art school in Kansas City, each at different stages, constituted his entire instruction. The son of a contractor, he was born December 5, 1901 in Chicago, and spent his boyhood on a farm near Marceline, Missouri and in Kansas City. His family made the move to Marceline when Walt was quite young, and the boy got acquainted with the animals on the farm and took to drawing them along the margins of his schoolbooks, flipping the pages so rapidly the figures seemed to move.

When he was 10 or 11 years old he did his first commercial art work for the town barber shop. The barber gave him a free haircut for a weekly sketch which was displayed on the barber shop wall. Apparently Disney was always an energetic person. After school in Kansas City he delivered newspapers, and during his high school career he worked as a news vendor on trains. At 16 he was in Chicago taking a night course in cartooning at the Academy of Fine Arts.

When the First World War broke out Disney was too young to join the army, but he managed to get overseas as a driver of a Red Cross ambulance. He returned to Kansas City after the War and got a job with an advertising firm sketching illustrations for farm journals. At the same time he was making cartoon slides for a film company in his private studio over his father's garage. He called the cartoons *Laugh-O-Grams,* and had some success with them, as he did with other free-lance cartoons during this period.

Animated cartoons interested the commercial artist, and with a group of local cartoonists Disney spent six months making a series of short features. But the venture failed and Disney decided to try Hollywood. He arrived in Hollywood in 1923 with a print of the cartoon, *Alice in Cartoonland,* and $40. His brother Roy was already in Hollywood, had a steady job and $250 in the bank. The two got a loan of $500 from an uncle and set up a studio in a garage.

After three dismal months Disney succeeded in getting a producer and distributor for his cartoon. The distributor was M. J. Winkler of New York, for whom Disney worked for four years doing a series of cartoons in which Oswald the Rabbit was the central character. Then, when Winkler would not step up the costs of production and expand as Disney wished, Disney left, abandoning the rights to Oswald.

It was then that the necessity of creating a new character presented itself, and Mickey Mouse was born. The first two Mickey Mouse adventures, *Plane Crazy* and *Gallopin' Gaucho,* were disappointing and were both shelved. The third, *Steamboat Willie,* the first to employ sound, made its debut in New York in October 1928 and was an instant success.

With the launching of Mickey Mouse, Disney was on his way to fame. He and his brother were besieged by offers from producers and distributors. However, he and his brother Roy and their wives have retained full interest in Walt Disney, Incorporated, although they have had various arrangements with picture companies for the financing and distribution of the films. Walt has charge of all production and Roy supervises the finances.

After Mickey Mouse was established in popularity, Disney launched another series of cartoons called *Silly ·Symphonies,* each picture based on a musical theme and confined to the realm of the unreal.

Even before he made any feature-length cartoons, Disney had won a reputation for himself as a producer of short subjects. Another producer of animated cartoons said of him, "We're businessmen. Walt Disney is an artist. With us, the idea with shorts is to hit 'em and run. Disney is more of a Rembrandt." The Academy of Motion Picture Arts and Sciences also thought so and gave Disney the accolade of its approval by giving *Trees and Flowers,* the first animated cartoon ever to be made in Technicolor, its award in 1932, when short subjects were first included for recognition by the Academy. *Three Little Pigs,* which sent the whole country chanting *Who's Afraid of the Big Bad Wolf,* was the shorts prize winner in 1933; *The Tortoise and the Hare,* 1934 prize winner; *Three Orphan Kittens* and *The Country Cousin* were the Academy's choices in 1935 and 1936.

The feature-length cartoon was invented of necessity. The double-feature programs were crowding the short subjects completely off the theatre's program, and Disney felt he must change his product to meet the demands of the day. He decided to make a feature-length animated cartoon.

When news leaked out that the Disney studios were planning to produce *Snow White and the Seven Dwarfs* as a full-length feature, Hollywood thought Walt Disney mad. How could a picture without a name, without a star, a mere fairy tale hold audience interest for seven reels, they asked. Although Disney had every honor bestowed on him by the picture industry, he did not have much money. Short subjects did not earn much, and what profits the Disneys did have were always reinvested in their studio. The venture was referred to as Disney's folly. Made on borrowed bank money, it had to gross $2,500,000 to become a Disney asset.

Snow White and the Seven Dwarfs took three years to make. Some 2,000,000 drawings and sketches had been made, and approximately 250,000 of them photographed. Production costs amounted to $1,600,000. The film was released December 1937 with considerable ballyhoo and some misgiving.

But no one was prepared for the sensational success *Snow White and the Seven Dwarfs* turned out to be. It broke all established records by showing an intake of $8,000,000 shortly after it was released, and the complete total was estimated at $10,000,000. It was sound-tracked in eight languages and in every place it was shown it left audiences enthralled. The seven dwarfs made their appealing little *Heigh, ho, heigh, ho, it's off to work we go,* practically an international melody. The dwarfs Dopey, Grumpy, Doc, Sneezy, Bashful, Happy and Sleepy caught on commercially in all manner of objects.

Critics began showering serious praise on Disney. The film was called "a combination of Hollywood, the Grimm Brothers and the sad, searching fantasy of universal childhood . . . an authentic masterpiece to be shown in theatres and beloved by new generations long after the current crop of Hollywood stars, writers and directors are sleeping where no Prince's kiss can wake them." Disney was said to have proved that "the pen is mightier than the personality of the greatest star." Then Disney marched on to new fame. *Pinocchio,* his second feature-length animated cartoon, released Christmas 1939, found an eager audience and praise quite as handsome.

It is only a little more than a decade since Disney started his small studio in a Hollywood garage. In 1940 he moved into a new plant at Burbank, California, consisting of about 20 buildings on a 51-acre tract. The studio is a little city in itself and employs more than 1,000 men and women.

It is years since Disney has drawn any of the cartoons for his pictures, but he still supervises every detail of their production, and he is not easily satisfied. He is in on each story conference, still finds time to be the voice of Mickey Mouse, works until six or seven o'clock each night, and in busy times works round the clock. Hollywood hot spots see him seldom. He and his wife (he was married in 1925 to Lillian Bounds of Lewiston, Idaho, one of the first girl assistants who helped him in the Hollywood garage studio) have a charming home with a large garden, and live a quiet, domestic life. They have three small daughters.

Disney still has no formula for making successful pictures. "I've never made pictures for a child audience alone," he says. Pressed for an answer as to why he does the kind of work he does, he says, "We just try to make a good picture." However, the routine of making an animated cartoon is set. First there is a story conference to decide on continuity and action; next come a musical score and rough timing with the sketches showing continuity from beginning to end; then come the animators' drawings.

The artists who are senior animators sketch out the important points of action of the figures, and assistants follow through with the intermediate steps. When an an-

WALT DISNEY

imator and his assistants complete a scene a test camera photographs the sketches, which Disney then approves before they go to the inking and painting department. It is a highly technical and complex process to draw in background and scenery, to synchronize action and sound and to make a complete, living picture.

The latest Disney production is a highly ambitious film, *Fantasia,* combining classical music by the Philadelphia Orchestra conducted by Leopold Stokowski, and cartoon. It was released in November 1940, and was recorded by an entirely new method requiring special projection equipment. Deems Taylor (see sketch this issue) acted as narrator for the film.

Critics decided that Disney had again done something revolutionary—and, on the whole, successfully. Otis Ferguson announced: "The screen itself when the music is playing is the only excuse I have ever seen for having eyes and ears at the same time." *Time* thought "critics may deplore Disney's lapses of taste, but he trips, Mickey-like, into an art form that immortals from Eschylus to Richard Wagner have always dreamed of."

Bambi, Felix Salten's story of a deer, is another new Disney feature in production. He also plans a combination cartoon and acting film in which an actor playing Mark Twain will appear with cartoons of his characters, and *The Reluctant Dragon* with Robert Benchley.

Walt Disney, Incorporated has joined the ranks of Big Business; Disney stock is listed in 1940 with the Securities and Exchange Commission. The SEC statement showed that Disney received the company's highest salary in 1939—$108,298. But Mickey Mouse is still an old stand-by of the studio, and Walt Disney, Incorporated will go right on

DISNEY, WALT—*Continued*

producing *Mickey Mouse* and *Silly Symphony* shorts, according to present plans. Says Disney: "We don't even let the word 'art' be used around the studio. If anyone begins to get arty, we knock them down."

References

Atlan 166:689-701 D '40
Bet Homes & Gard 18:13-15+ Ja '40 il pors
Christian Sci Mon p3 Mr 8 '40 il por
N Y Times VII p6-7+ N 3 '40
New Yorker 7:23-7 D 19 '31
Pop Mech 73:17-24+ Ja '40 il por
Read Digest 32:25-6 Je '38
Scholastic 36:10 Ap 8 '40 il
Theatre Arts 25:55-61 Ja '41 il(cover)
Time 30:19-21 D 27 '37 il por; 36:52-5 N 18 '40 ils
America's Young Men
Charlot, J. Disney Disquisition *In* Art from the Mayans to Disney p263-80 1939
Ferguson, O. C. Extra Added Attractions *In* Bower, W. ed. New Directions p273-6 1937
Who's Who in America
Who's Who in Commerce and Industry

DITMARS, RAYMOND LEE (dĭt'märs) June 20, 1876- Curator of the New York Zoological Park

Address: b. Zoological Park, The Bronx, New York City; h. 855 Post Rd, Scarsdale, New York

Raymond Ditmars' exploits with animals usually are of the dignified kind that fill scientific papers or make amusing lecture material. But once when he was 15 years old and a student at the Barnard Military Academy in New York they called for police interference. Young Ditmars used to spend his Saturdays and Sundays collecting garter snakes in the park and along the Hudson River and by saving his lunch money he managed to buy a four-foot water snake to add to his collection. Wishing to give his pet a little air and breathing space, he made a barricade for the snake on the fire escape of his home. The neighbors took one look at the formidable looking reptile and called the police, and Ditmars' water snake, never very popular with his family, had to go.

His snake banned, young Ditmars got his parents' consent for a collection of frogs. But alas, a fine collection of horseflies he had gathered to feed his pets escaped into the Ditmars home, and the frogs also had to go. So Ditmars started a collection of insects, gathering moths and such creatures. Mounted and dead these insects could do no harm, he reasoned.

This hobby led to his first job. One day the boy took his collection to the New York Museum of Natural History to check the name of a moth. The neatly-arranged specimens showed a knowledge of classification and an aptitude for mounting. The curator offered him a job mounting specimens.

The Ditmars family did not think too highly of this offer, although Raymond was excited about it. The boy was preparing for West Point and was to take his entrance examinations that fall, and his parents looked with disfavor on his bug hunting. But Raymond persuaded his parents to allow him to take the job. It was the beginning of a five-year association with the Museum of Natural History in the department of entomology, where Ditmars became an assistant curator. During these years he made his first insect-hunting expedition to Florida and acquired a scientific interest in snakes that has lasted until the present and has made him an outstanding authority on reptiles.

Ditmars, however, was looking for more lively work than mounting and classifying dead things at the museum, and during his spare time studied shorthand with the intention of becoming a Congressional reporter. With characteristic thoroughness he learned to write shorthand with both right and left hands.

In the meantime he got a position on the New York *Times* as a reporter, doing court work for the most part. One afternoon the city editor said to Ditmars, "Go up to the Bronx and see what this new highbrow Zoological Society means by saying it's going to have the largest zoo in the world." The surveyors were still staking out the land, and the zoo collection at that time consisted of a bear cub, a wolf pup and a snapping turtle.

Ditmars found Dr. William T. Hornaday, director of the Zoological Society, and the two had a very satisfying interview. Dr. Hornaday found the young reporter's interest and knowledge of reptiles and insects astonishing. "You don't want to work on a newspaper. You want to come out here and help us build up this park," he told Ditmars.

Ditmars did just that. He joined the New York Zoological Park staff that year, 1899, and was put in charge of reptiles. Since 1910 he has been curator of reptiles and mammals.

Ditmars' position has been spiked with adventure, and he has filled a dozen volumes —*Forest of Adventure* (1933); *Book of Zoögraphy* (1934); *Confessions of a Scientist* (1934); *Reptiles of the World* (1934); *Strange Animals I Have Known* (1934); (with Bridges, William) *Snake-hunters' Holiday* (1935); *Book of Prehistoric Animals* (1935); *Reptiles of North America* (1936); *Book of Living Reptiles* (1937); *Making of a Scientist* (1937); *Snakes of the World* (1937); (with Bridges, William) *Wild Animal World* (1937)—with materials drawn from his expeditions and his experiences with animals. Tall, lean and military in bearing, Ditmars is grave and calm in manner, although perceptive and quick. His hands are sensitive and quick,

RAYMOND LEE DITMARS

and his manual dexterity is an outstanding feature of his work. He has handled as many as two hundred snakes in two hours with never an accident from their poisonous venom.

He was one of the pioneers in research work which, through the perfection of serums against snake bites, has saved hundreds of thousands of lives. When Dr. Albert Calmetee of the Pasteur Institute at Paris, France had completed early experiments toward producing a serum to neutralize bites of poisonous serpents, he wanted information on American types of snakes.

Ditmars undertook experiments with his reptiles and developed an ingenious method for extracting venom. He worked for a time with Dr. Hideyo Noguchi, the brilliant Japanese scientist.

In addition to animals Ditmars has one hobby—meteorology. He likes to observe hurricanes and enjoys spending vacations in the Caribbean looking for a nice one. One room in his home has been fitted up as a complete weather station. Ditmars lives in a comfortable house in Scarsdale, New York with his wife, who also likes animals and who, with their two daughters, has often accompanied him on expeditions. In the back yard of their home is a "pill box" in which is stored more than 500,000 feet of motion picture film that Ditmars has made of strange animals. Some of the film has been shown in all parts of the world.

Ditmars was born in Newark, New Jersey and came to New York as a boy. His father, a fur merchant, discouraged his career as a curator and laughed at Raymond's interest in bugs and animals. But Ditmars stuck with it with the same persistence with which he stole snakes into his home as a boy. He has helped make the New York Zoological Park

the best known in the country and he has grown with it.

References

Am Mag 114:24-5+ Ag '32 il por
New Yorker 4:24-7 Jl 14 '28
Pop Sci 137:76-7 Jl '40
American Men of Science
Ditmars, R. L. Confessions of a Scientist 1934
Ditmars, R. L. Making of a Scientist 1937
Gillis, A. and Ketchum, R. Raymond Lee Ditmars: Animal Lover *In* Our America p151-67 1936
Kunitz, S. J. and Haycraft, H. eds. Junior Book of Authors 1935
Who's Who in America

DIX, DOROTHY, pseud. of **ELIZABETH MERIWETHER GILMER** Nov 18, 1870- Newspaper columnist

Address: h. 6334 Prytania St, New Orleans, Louisiana

Almost every American newspaper reader knows the name of Dorothy Dix and her advice to the lovelorn. Not everyone knows that she is in private life Mrs. Elizabeth Meriwether Gilmer, white-haired, vivacious little old lady who lives quietly in her New Orleans home and who is reputed to earn between $70,000 and $80,000 a year from her syndicated writings.

Mrs. Gilmer started her career as a $5-a-week woman's page writer on the New Orleans *Picayune* in 1896. Her weekly sermonette, written for women readers under the title of *Sunday Salad,* was a success from the first. She disregarded that period's vogue for high-sounding phrases and flowery writing and wrote instead in everyday colloquial style. On occasion she dared to point out that parents were not always infallible, that domestic troubles might be the woman's fault—revolutionary writings for a newspaper columnist in those days.

Her own marriage had been a tragic one. Born in Woodstock, Tennessee November 18, 1870, the daughter of impoverished Southern gentry, she spent a tomboyish girlhood riding her father's horses, climbing trees and getting little formal schooling. "We were sent to school to 'Miss Alice's' or 'Miss Jenny's,'" Mrs. Gilmer recounts, "not because they were either trained or qualified to teach, but because their fathers had been either colonels under Beauregard or had been killed at Shiloh, and somebody had to help the poor souls along. And so I could climb like a squirrel and ride like a jockey long before I knew a great deal about the three R's." At the Clarksville Grammar School Mrs. Gilmer did distinguish herself by her essay writing. However, there was no thought then or later of any professional writing.

At 18, she writes in a brief autobiographical sketch, "I tucked up my hair and got married, as was the tribal custom among my people." Her husband was George O.

DOROTHY DIX

Gilmer, a debonair gallant in his late 20's and a brother of Mrs. Gilmer's step-mother. One gathers that it was because young Elizabeth was flattered by the attention of an older man that she followed the "tribal custom." Soon after the marriage, it developed that Gilmer had fallen victim to an incurable mental disease. For 35 years the disease ran its slow course until Gilmer died in a madhouse.

If Mrs. Gilmer needed to develop courage and character in order to become the nation's chief confidante, the early years of her marriage provided it. She tried to make a home, to keep up appearances in front of pitying friends. She had no way of earning money and had, in fact, been brought up in an atmosphere that looked upon self-support in a woman as somehow shameful. After a year or two she suffered a nervous collapse.

She went to recuperate at a little resort on the Mississippi coast and during the long leisure hours took to scribbling stories. One, a fictionized version of how an old family servant had saved the Meriwether family silver during the Civil War by hiding it in a tomb, she showed to a friend, Mrs. E. J. Nicholson, owner of the New Orleans *Picayune*. Mrs. Nicolson bought the story outright for $3 and offered Mrs. Gilmer a job on the *Picayune*.

The *Picayune* during this era used an alliterative style, and so Mrs. Gilmer chose the name of Dorothy Dix—Dorothy because she liked it, and Dix in honor of the old family slave Dick, who had saved the Meriwether family silver. Her column, *Sunday Salad*, caught the public fancy at once and the title was changed to *Dorothy Dix Talks*, a heading it still bears.

Meanwhile Mrs. Gilmer was learning the technique of news writing and news gather-

ing. She became a full-fledged reporter and right-hand man to the aging editor Major Nathaniel Burbank. Her salary was increased from the original $5 a week to $15 and then to $20.

At this time William Randolph Hearst had come out of the West, and his talent scouts were looking for big names and unusual features. Mrs. Gilmer was offered a place in the Hearst organization at a flattering figure. But she refused because she felt a debt of gratitude to Major Burbank, who had taught her all she knew of newspaper work and who, she felt, needed her. Shortly afterward, when Major Burbank died, she accepted the Hearst offer and came to New York.

She went to work for the New York *Journal* in 1901. The *Dorothy Dix Talks* appeared in the *Journal* three times a week, and they elicited hundreds of daily responses. The shrewd Hearst editors realized that something about Dorothy Dix invited confidences, and they made the fullest use of that quality. Dorothy Dix was to become one of the greatest sob sisters of her time.

One day a sensational murder, the killing of an 18-months-old child by its stepmother, occurred in New Jersey. The newspapers could get no information from officials or relatives. "I know one person who can get somebody down there to talk," the *Journal* city editor said, "Dorothy Dix." She was given a roll of bills, told to go to New Jersey and to get the story. It was Mrs. Gilmer's first murder story. By a stroke of luck she found a former beau of the arrested woman. The erstwhile beau drove Mrs. Gilmer around, helped her find sources of gossip, and proposed matrimony.

As a sob sister Mrs. Gilmer was a decided success. She was so good that for the next 15 years she covered sensational murder trials, vice investigations and heart-interest features. In addition she wrote her column. "I was dreadfully tired of murder stories," Mrs. Gilmer said. "They didn't do anyone a bit of good, and I did feel that my *Dorothy Dix Talks* were of help to people who needed help. Time and time again I received letters telling me how someone had taken my advice, and that it had solved his or her problem."

When in 1917 the Wheeler Syndicate offered Mrs. Gilmer a contract which allowed her to devote herself exclusively to the *Dorothy Dix Talks*, she accepted. Three days a week she wrote the sermonettes and on the other three days she published actual letters and the answers.

In 1923 the *Dorothy Dix Talks* were taken over by the Ledger Syndicate, which has published them ever since. They appear in 273 papers and her publishers estimate that Dorothy Dix has 60,000,000 readers in the United States, England, Australia, New Zealand, South America, China, Mexico, Hawaii, the Philippine Islands, Puerto Rico and Canada. In 1939 Dorothy Dix received 100,000 letters. Each letter that is signed and bears a real return address is answered, either through publication or an individually mailed reply. Routine inquiries are turned over to Mrs. Gilmer's secretary.

Replies to inquiries not under routine classification are dictated by Mrs. Gilmer, who also dictates her *Dorothy Dix Talks.* A methodical worker, Mrs. Gilmer keeps a supply of three-months talks in a safety deposit box in a bank to be used in case of her illness or incapacity. She has traveled to every corner of the globe and has always kept ahead of her schedule. She has never been late with her copy in 45 years of newspaper work.

Nearing 70, she works daily from 9 to 12 in her pleasant, seven-room apartment in New Orleans, goes for a drive through Audubon Park every afternoon, engages in a pleasant social life, although she attends few parties. Childless, she is devoted to the family of her brother, Charles E. Meriwether, a New Orleans businessman.

She has a maternal feeling for her woebegone public with its yearnings for advice on domestic problems, puppy love, on its heartaches and heartthrobs, on everything from clandestine romance to advice on methods for removing superfluous hair. Mrs. Gilmer has taken their problems seriously and has tried to give them sincere, honest advice.

When, in the early days of her career, people advised her to get a divorce, she said: "I never once thought of divorce. I could not say to others 'Be strong' if I did not myself have strength to endure." Twice she has published books of her advice, her latest being *How to Win and Hold a Husband,* published in 1939. Although her advice is strait-laced, she has kept pace with the times and with changing morals and social standards. Plump, full of vitality, she knows the problems of succeeding generations and answers them with hard-headed realism.

Her books include: *Dorothy Dix, Her Book* (1926); *Mirandy Exhorts* (1922); *My Trip Around the World* (1924).

References

Life 8:104-7 Ap 22 '40 il pors
Lit Digest 118:10 Jl 21 '34; 123:31 Ap 17 '37
Sat Eve Post 210:16-17+ Jl 10 '37 il pors
Time 34:66 Ag 14 '39 por
American Women
Who's Who Among North American Authors
Who's Who in America

DODD, WILLIAM EDWARD Oct 21, 1869—Feb 9, 1940 Historian; author; United States Ambassador to Germany (1933-38)

Dr. William E. Dodd left a quiet life as professor of history at the University of Chicago in 1933 for the political maelstrom of an Ambassadorship to Germany. He

WILLIAM E. DODD

knew the old Germany from his youth as a student at the University of Leipzig and he had high hopes of fostering better German-American relations.

His first few months in Germany were encouraging. The then President Von Hindenburg received him cordially, and the two men exchanged speeches stressing German-American desire for friendship and cooperation. The German people and the new Ambassador liked each other. But as Nazi storm troopers started assaults on Americans for not giving the Nazi salute (twenty such cases were reported in Dr. Dodd's first six months in Germany), and Germany's moratorium on debt payments was announced, his hopes faded.

Dr. Dodd became one of the most bitter critics of the Nazi régime. He finally resigned late in 1937 and returned to the United States in January 1938, issuing a statement which said that he had found representing America in Berlin "a hopeless task."

He declared: "In a vast region where religious freedom is denied, where intellectual initiative and discovery are not allowed, and where race hatreds are cultivated, what can a representative of the United States do?"

The Hitler régime in Germany had filled Dr. Dodd with bitterness, and had in a measure made his relations with Washington strained. His departure from Berlin was unattended by the customary amenities accorded diplomats. Hitler gave him no farewell audience, and the German Foreign Minister omitted the dinner usually given to departing diplomats.

Back in the United States Dr. Dodd resumed work on his history of the Old South, which his diplomatic work had interrupted. But the last two years of his life were

DODD, WILLIAM E.—*Continued*

plagued with trouble. Relieved of his diplomatic status, he continued his attacks on Nazi Germany in outspoken terms before audiences in Canada and Eastern United States. This, coupled with his work on his book, led to a partial physical breakdown. His wife, the former Martha Johns of Wake County, North Carolina, died in May 1938. In December of the same year his automobile struck and seriously injured a Negro child near Hanover Court House, Virginia. Dr. Dodd was indicted as a hit-run driver, pleaded guilty and was fined $250 and costs. It was brought out that he had paid to the child's parents medical and hospital bills totaling $1,100.

Dr. Dodd was born at Clayton, North Carolina, on October 21, 1869. He was graduated from Virginia Polytechnic Institute with a Bachelor of Science degree in 1895 and received a Master of Science degree in 1897. He then went to Germany for three years and won his Doctor of Philosophy degree at the University of Leipzig in 1900. He returned to this country to become professor of history at Randolph-Macon College, and went to the University of Chicago in 1908. Dr. Dodd received honorary Doctor of Laws degrees from Emory University, the University of Alabama, the University of North Carolina and the University of Cincinnati. He was president of the American Historical Association in 1934 and was a member of the Mississippi Valley Historical Association, the Social Science Research Council, the Quadrangle and Chicago Literary Clubs in Chicago and the Cosmos Club in Washington.

Dr. Dodd was the author of a number of important historical works and is especially well-known for those dealing with the Old South. In 1924 and 1926, with Ray Stannard Baker (see sketch this issue), he edited *The Public Papers of Woodrow Wilson.* In 1920 he wrote *Woodrow Wilson and His Work.* Among his other important books are *Life of Jefferson Davis* (1907); *Statesmen of the Old South* (1911); *Lincoln or Lee* (1928). He was also editor and joint author of *The Riverside History of the United States* (1911).

Dr. Dodd died February 9, 1940 of pneumonia at his home at Round Hill, Virginia. He is survived by a son, William E. Jr., and a daughter, Mrs. Alfred Stern.

References

Nation 136:681 Je 21 '33
Pub W 133:941 F 19 '38

Kraus, M. Frontier and Sectional Historians *In* History of American History p492-545 1937
Who's Who in America 1938-39

Obituaries
Am Hist R 45:756-7 Ap '40
Nation 15:268 F 24 '40
N Y Herald Tribune p8 F 10 '40
N Y Times p15 F 10 '40 por
Newsweek 15:8 F 19 '40
Sch & Soc 51:210 F 17 '40

DOHERTY, HENRY LATHAM May 15, 1870—Dec 26, 1939 Public utilities operator; engineer

"A shrewd and aggressive iconoclast with an uncanny knack of knowing which way the wind was blowing while his competitors still were holding their moistened fingers in the air," is the summing up one critic gave to Henry Latham Doherty, who started his amazing career as a newsboy at 10; became in succession a gas company employee at 20; engineer of many companies at 27; millionaire at 35; and a multi-millionaire at 40. Reputedly worth $200,000,000 in 1929, he was still a multi-millionaire at his death in Philadelphia at the age of 69 after spending much of his last 12 years in bed.

He was born in Columbus, Ohio, the son of Frank and Anna (McElvain) Doherty, of English, Scotch and Irish ancestry. His father had been an inventor and engineer, but family reverses made it necessary for him to follow the well-trod path to riches—selling newspapers at 10 and leaving school at 12. "My preliminary education was largely obtained from the study of catalogs and handbooks," he explained. Thereafter he rose rapidly in the Columbus (Ohio) Gas Company until he attained the position of chief engineer in 1896 and subsequently became engineer or manager of public utility companies in more than 30 cities. At 35, an expert in public utility operation in the West, he came to New York, grew a beard to impress Wall Streeters with his age, and tried to borrow money. The beard didn't work and he had to borrow from Europe. In 1905 he organized Henry L. Doherty and Company and in 1910 Cities Service Company, which was a "super de luxe" holding concern for more than 190 public utility and petroleum properties combining assets of more than a billion dollars.

HENRY L. DOHERTY

A recognized leader in industrial America in gas, electricity and petroleum, his associates called him a human "dynamo of energy with business conferences as likely to be at 2 a. m. as at 2 p. m." When one group left Mr. Doherty's home at midnight, others were waiting to confer with him. When the collapse of Florida real estate sent droves of operators scurrying from that state, Doherty stepped in, bought up 11,000 once valuable properties (Miami Beach's Roney Plaza, Palm Beach's Biltmore, etc.) for the proverbial song. He thereupon started an enthusiastic campaign for Florida's return to prosperity and soon in those lean depression years found his holdings worth $25,000,000.

Suddenly in 1926 arthritis put a stop to his manifold activities. He recovered, but for the last three years of his life remained at a hospital under constant treatment, conducting his businesses from his bed. The devoted nursing in 1928 by the 40-year-old widow of Percy Frank Eames, International Harvester official, led him to renounce his lifelong bachelorhood at the age of 58. He was reputed to have spent $250,000 on the Washington debut of his stepdaughter in the heart of depression days. In 1931 he bought a half-interest in the Kansas City *Journal-Post,* after his handling of his vast utility empire had been the subject of bitter attack by the powerful Kansas City *Star.* He announced openly that he wanted to present his side of the case, naïvely unaware that one-sided paid advertisements were one thing, while biased front-page domination of a newspaper was a vastly different matter.

He was a man of simple tastes, without car or yacht long after these were supposedly necessary appendages to the rôle of financier. In his vast penthouse atop one of his skyscrapers commanding a view of New York harbor he was troubled with mosquitoes, so he started a campaign for their extermination. Also he thought the Statue of Liberty would enhance his view if it were lit up, so he started a campaign to get flood-lighting for it. His apartment was full of ingenious devices, the principal one being a bed, powered by motor, which slid along a track so that he could sleep in any room desired without getting out of bed—an invention which might well be put into general use.

References

N Y Times p8 F 17 '38; p31 Mr 23 '38 por; p8 My 31 '38
Newsweek 1:23-4 My 6 '33; 2:22 Ag 5 '33
Outlook 158:484 Ag 19 '31
Who's Who in America 1938-39

Obituaries

N Y Herald Tribune p1, 18 D 27 '39 por
N Y Sun p17 Ja 11 '40
Newsweek 15:5 Ja 8 '40 por
Time 35:52 Ja 8 '40

ARNOLD DOLMETSCH

DOLMETSCH, ARNOLD Feb 25, 1858— Feb 29, 1940 French musician; gave concerts of old music on the instrument for which it was written; lectured at Harvard

References

Christian Sci Mon Mag p4-5 N 11 '36 il pors
Etude 57:712+ N '39 il pors
Mag Art 32:599 O '39
Time 31:48-50 Mr 7 '38 por
Pierre Key's Musical Who's Who
Who's Who

Obituaries

Musical Am 60:32 Mr 10 '40 por
N Y Herald Tribune p16 Mr 1 '40
Spec 164:328-9 Mr 8 '40
Variety 137:54 Mr 6 '40

DORIOT, JACQUES 1888- Leader of the French Popular Party

"Hulking, bull-voiced" Jacques Doriot, leader of the French Popular Party, is the man whose name is most often mentioned when changes are rumored in the Vichy government of France. In the autumn of 1940 Doriot and Pierre Laval (see sketch this issue) were said to meet often in Vichy, and it was hinted that M. Doriot is "the 'trump' that M. Laval is holding back for use if trouble breaks out and a strong, popular man is needed, particularly in Paris and the suburbs." Doriot has headquarters in Marseille, and his propaganda work has been particularly active in the provinces, in the French Army and among the demobilized soldiers.

Doriot was born in 1888 in St. Denis, a suburb of Paris, which has always been his home. His father was a blacksmith, and he himself began his career as a me-

Pictures Inc.

JACQUES DORIOT

chanic and metalworker. At first a member of the Communist youth organization, he eventually became the most important member of the French Communist Party, a member of the Central Committee. For 16 years "Red" St. Denis elected him its Mayor, and his St. Denis organization was the pride of the Communist Party in France, approximately one-fourth of its entire French membership being drawn from his constituency. He was also an influential member of the Paris Municipal Council, being suspended only once, when in 1927 he returned from an agitatorial tour of the Far East and was arrested and imprisoned for "subversive activities."

But although a brilliant orator and expert organizer, Doriot was not too willing to obey orders from the Communist International or Central Committee. In 1933, according to Ludwig Lore, he began calling publicly for an alliance with the Socialists to oppose Fascism—before the Party advocated such a step. He was therefore removed from his strategic post in the Central Committee and Maurice Thorez put in his place. Nevertheless, in 1934 another attempt at a united anti-Fascist front came from Doriot. The Comintern invited him to Moscow; he refused and was expelled. Almost immediately the official movement toward a Popular Front began. Enraged at such treatment, it seems that Doriot went from Trotskyism to the most extreme anti-Communist position possible, and by mid-July 1936 was ready to launch his own political party, which he called the *Parti Populaire Français*. Its following drawn mostly from the middle classes from the respectable suburbs of Paris, with a sprinkling of workers, war veterans and "bearded academicians wearing the Légion d'Hon-

neur," it stood for opposition to the Popular Front on every issue: for Franco, for Mussolini, for Japan, for an "understanding" with Hitler. Furious at the Comintern and the French Communist Party, Doriot had for a long time been shouting its innermost secrets from the housetops and demanding a parliamentary investigation of financial relations between the U. S. S. R. and the Communist Party of France. Now the tenuous Franco-Russian military pact was to his movement "what the Versailles Treaty was to Hitler." He accused the Popular Front of trying to drive Europe into war, and in an interview which he gave to a Hitler organ in October 1936 he revealed as the three cornerstones of his Party's policy: (1) Destruction of the Communist Party of France; (2) Repudiation of the Franco-Russian alliance; (3) An alliance between Germany and France.

He was getting support, too: at first from a *Croix de Feu* group that had broken with De La Rocque, soon from other groups. While Premier, Pierre Laval ordered the Paris police not to interfere with his fight against Communists. "Jules Romains lent his name and the prestige of his *Juilletiste* movement." Hennessey, the cognac distiller, "supplied funds and a special blessing." A reporter of *L'Illustration* saw him as "preaching the crusade of union to all good Frenchmen." Many of the Rightist papers lauded him. The insurance interests were said to be supporting him financially, as was Goebbel's propaganda bureau (the latter fact was always denied). Well versed in "social lingo," Doriot also won over a great many of his St. Denis constituents, and consistently outpolled the Communists in that suburb.

His fame even reached to Great Britain, where the *English Review* for June 1937 hailed him as an "outstanding figure in French politics today"—the "first great popular orator the Right has possessed for many a long year"—"the Joseph Chamberlain of his country." His speeches were proclaimed "masterpieces of reasoned argument," and it was said that "as Mayor of St. Denis he has transformed that suburb of Paris from a byword for squalor into a model municipality, and alone among French politicians he is really interested in social problems." But then the *English Review* was confident that there was "nothing of the Fascist about him."

By May 1937 Doriot was financially able to launch a daily newspaper; his party had formerly been publishing nothing more ambitious than a weekly, *L'Emancipation Nationale*. It became known that he had obtained control of *La Liberté,* a daily long held by the Rightist André Tardieu. Almost at once Blum's (see sketch this issue) government removed Doriot from his office as Mayor of St. Denis by edict of the Ministry of the Interior, charging that the deficits of his party's whirlwind financial campaign had been covered by ordering the payment of fictitious bills for coal and other supplies out of the St. Denis Treasury.

Doriot asserted: "The accusations against me are fantastic... It is fundamentally a political battle. I have never refused battle and I am going to fight." In protest, he resigned as municipal councilor in June, and so did other councilors belonging to his party. When at the elections of June 20, the Popular Front won an overwhelming victory, Doriot also resigned as deputy in order to "consecrate himself" to the battle against Communism. Wherever he spoke there were threats of general strikes, propaganda posters appeared on walls, workers gathered around the meeting halls to blockade demonstrations and engaged in battle with his "private army of declassed proletarian mercenaries"; but his movement grew.

That same year (1937) an interview with Doriot made Ludwig Lore conclude that "his denunciation of Communism and—just a little less violently—of Socialism, his condemnation of 'international bankers and alien financiers' would have done credit to our own Father Coughlin [see sketch this issue], who also emphatically denies Fascist or anti-Semitic aims." To Doriot "an awakened nationalism is the answer!"—as it had been in Germany, as it had been in Italy. Today he advocates a National Socialist form of government for France.

Doriot is described as more than six feet tall and as weighing around 250 pounds. "To an American he looked like one of our own *Bible*-yodelers come out of the South, stocky, inexhaustible, with a massive head and a comical touch of horn-rimmed glasses concealing a myopic stare," yet friendly, intelligent, direct, a pleasing personality."

References

Cur Hist 46:60-2 Ap '37 por
Engl R 64:717 Je '37
Eur Nouv 19:680 Jl 4 '36; 19:1140-1 N 14 '36; 21:899-902 Ag 20 '38
Illustration 194:372 Jl 18 '36 por; 197:283 Je 26 '37 por
Liv Age 351:132-5 O '36
Nation 143:299-300 S 12 '36; 145:369-72 O 9 '37
Time 29:21 Je 7 '37 por

DORNAY, LOUIS 1876—Aug 12, 1940 Operatic and concert tenor; singing teacher; developed a repertoire of principal tenor rôles in leading Italian, French and German operas; appeared at the Royal Dutch Opera at The Hague, in Covent Garden, London, in Berlin and in New York in various opera houses

Obituaries

N Y Times p19 Ag 13 '40

DORPFELD, WILHELM Dec 26, 1853—Apr 26, 1940 German archeologist; aided Heinrich Schliemann in search for Harbor of Troy; one of the best-known figures in Greek archeology; first to study the construction of ancient Greek theatres

References

Europa v2

Obituaries

N Y Times p15 Ap 27 '40

DOS PASSOS, JOHN (dŏs păs′us) Jan 14, 1896- Author; winner of 1940 Guggenheim Fellowship

Address: Provincetown, Massachusetts

As one of the creators of a fresh and original technique in novel writing, and as a champion of the underdog, John Dos Passos has already left an indelible imprint on American letters. Some critics have gone so far as to say that his trilogy, *U. S. A.* (1937), is the nearest thing we have to "the Great American Novel" and the first successful attempt to depict America as a whole in fiction. Others, while they find the technical versatility and imagistic brilliance of the trilogy interesting, think the novels lacking in warmth and convincing characterization. However, there is no doubt that *U. S. A.*, which includes *The 42nd Parallel, Nineteen Nineteen* and *The Big Money,* places Dos Passos definitely in the foreground of interpreters of the American scene.

That this is so is borne out more fully by the fact that the John Simon Guggenheim Memorial Foundation in 1940 awarded John Dos Passos a fellowship for the second time, in order that he might complete a series of essays on the basis of present American conceptions of freedom of thought, which he began in 1939.

John Roderigo Dos Passos made his first serious mark as a writer with his *Three Soldiers*, his second novel, published in 1921, which was an outgrowth of his experiences in the World War. But the book that established his reputation as a writer was *Manhattan Transfer*, published in 1925. A kaleidoscopic panorama of 25 years of New York City life on all levels of society, it is still considered one of the best attempts to catch in fiction the elusive quality of New York. It has been called the "Rhapsody in Blue of contemporary American fiction." Sinclair Lewis described the book as presenting "the panorama, the sense, the smell, the soul of New York," and predicted that it might be "the foundation of a whole new school of novel writing." It was indeed the foundation of a new school of novel writing for Dos Passos and for a host of his imitators.

The ordinary reader is apt to find some of Dos Passos' writing difficult, for he has used James Joycean stream-of-consciousness devices, and Cummings-isms, particularly in the section of his trilogy called *The Camera Eye.* But these parts contain some of his finest writing. Dos Passos' work has been acclaimed and denounced largely on the score of its manner—the rapidity of his narrative, the coined words and run-together phrases. He regards the ¯novel

JOHN DOS PASSOS

as something more than "the mere chronicle of private lives."

As a chronicler of the American scene, John Dos Passos has an appropriate background. He was born in Chicago, January 14, 1896, a true product of the various racial strains in the melting pot of America. His grandfather had been a Portugese immigrant, a shoemaker in Philadelphia. His father, who went to the Civil War as a drummer boy, was, as Dos Passos describes him, a "self-made literate" and a corporation lawyer by the time young John Roderigo was born. His mother came of old Maryland and Virginia stock and bore her son at the age of 48.

As a boy John Roderigo moved all over the world with his parents, living in Mexico and in England (where he went to a private school for a while), Belgium, Washington, D. C., and on a Westmoreland County farm in Tidewater, Virginia. He was graduated from the Choate School and in 1916 received his B. A. *cum laude* from Harvard University: After his graduation from Harvard he went to Spain to study architecture, but was sidetracked by the War. In 1917 he was a volunteer in the ambulance service of the Allies, and when America entered the War he served in the United States ambulance service and finally in the United States Medical Corps.

After the War he wandered about Spain, Mexico and the Near East as a newspaper correspondent and magazine free-lance writer. During his adolescent years Gibbon's *Decline and Fall of the Roman Empire* was his *Bible,* and it was from this and not, as is generally supposed, from Karl Marx that Dos Passos got his taste for history in great perspectives. The world has been his province since an early age. But from each of his journeys he has returned to

confront America as a novelist, after putting down in travel books the sensory impressions of a dozen countries.

John Dos Passos' first book came out of his experiences as an ambulance driver. It was *One Man's Initiation,* published in England in 1917, a highly subjective record of Dos Passos' days with the French ambulance service, "as plotless as a diary," and callow and inexpert in its writing. *Three Soldiers,* which followed in 1921, was a much better book and is generally regarded as one of the more powerful and effective fictional indictments of war.

In 1923 another Dos Passos novel, *Streets of Night,* appeared. It was arty and pretentious and read like a typical first novel. But in 1925 Dos Passos published *Manhattan Transfer,* a book which was an obvious turning point in his career as a novelist. It marked the beginning of the Dos Passos style, and was a sort of trial balloon of his later innovations in the technique of the novel. It was both an "art novel" and one of the most successful attempts to paint a collective portrait of New York City.

Dos Passos did not publish another novel until five years later when *The 42nd Parallel* came out. In the interim he had experimented with play writing and another travel book. His travel books, *Rosinante to the Road Again* (1922); *Orient Express* (1927); *In All Countries* (1934); show even more than his novels Dos Passos' broadening sympathies and interest in "the little man."

Dos Passos was developing an ever deepening social consciousness. First he had a sympathy for the Soviet Union; the civil war in Spain enlisted his interest; the Kentucky miners found a champion in him; during the Sacco-Vanzetti demonstration he was arrested in the picket line in front of the Boston State House. In Russia Dos Passos was immensely popular as a "proletarian" novelist. But he has said farewell to Europe as far as its power politics are concerned. Even while the Communists were hailing him as a literary fellow traveler because of his sympathy for the underdog, he was saying to those who called him Red, "I'm merely an old-fashioned believer in liberty, equality, fraternity." Later his attitude became definitely anti-Communistic.

His novels from *Manhattan Transfer* on have been infused with a hatred of "the iron combination of men accustomed to run things." Disillusioned about Europe, he clings to a hope of a just social order in America. In 1939 he wrote: "I think there is enough real democracy in the mixed American tradition to enable us, with courage and luck, to weather the social transformations that are going on without losing our liberties or the humane outlook that is the medium in which civilizations grow."

Dos Passos' sympathies for the Spanish refugees from the Franco government led him to work for their relief. When the Ecuador government in the spring of 1940 signed a contract with the New World

Settlement Fund of New York to establish in Ecuador Spanish refugees then in France, John Dos Passos was named the recognized representative of the fund in the contract providing for the establishment of farm colonies.

Personally Dos Passos is anything but the picture of a cynical, disillusioned, ultra-sophisticated writer that one might expect from his novels. Scrupulously polite, given to deprecatory gestures, he is youthfully enthusiastic. He is shy and will not speak in public or over the radio, hates literary affectations and shop talk. Year after year he has mixed expeditions to strange places with periods of quiet living on Cape Cod, where he writes mornings and swims and sails in the afternoons.

His wife, Katharine (Smith) Dos Passos, formerly of St. Louis, whom he married after the War, writes for women's magazines. Dos Passos spends his leisure dabbling with sketching and painting, and in 1937 had an exhibit of 30 of his sketches in a New York gallery. Baldish, extremely nearsighted, he is a kindly, pleasant-looking man not at all arty or sophisticated in appearance.

The Dos Passos trilogy, *U. S. A.*, follows 20 or 30 characters in various strata of American life through 30 years of history. Intermingled with their stories are impressionistic biographical sketches of various historical figures of the period: Eugene Debs, Burbank, William (Big Bill) Haywood, William Jennings Bryan, Carnegie, Edison and other idols of the time. There are fragmentary "newsreel" sections or excerpts from newspaper headlines and popular songs, and *The Camera Eye* paragraphs, which are poetic, subjective records of the author's point of view. Although the devices of the biographies, the camera eye and newsreel were artificial, they enabled Dos Passos to take in a whole era and a whole country, to depict all the facets of American life in its industrial, economic and social aspects. He shows the "little man" the goat of the industrial system.

Dos Passos' latest novel, published in 1939, *Adventures of a Young Man*, was considered by most critics slight in comparison with the books in the *U. S. A.* trilogy. It is a satire on the American radical movement as it has become under the sway of the Communists. In addition to his five important novels, *Adventures of a Young Man* (1939); *Manhattan Transfer* (1925); *The 42nd Parallel* (1930); *Nineteen Nineteen* (1932); and *The Big Money* (1936), Dos Passos has published several plays—*The Garbage Man* (1926); *Airways, Inc.* (1929) and *Fortune Heights,* which were combined in one volume, *Three Plays* (1934); *Journey Between Wars* (1938), made up of excerpts from three of his books; a book of verse, *A Pushcart at the Curb* (1922).

References

Lit Digest 123:26-7 F 6 '37 il
Nation 150:15-18 Ja 6 '40 por
N Y Times p2 My 8 '40

No Am R 244 no2:349-67 [D] '37
Sat R Lit 20:3-4+ Je 3 '39 il pors
America's Young Men 1936-37
Beach, J. W. Abstract Composition: Dos Passos *In* Twentieth Century Novel: Studies in Technique p501-11 1932
Cowley, M. Dos Passos: Poet Against the World *In* Cowley, M. ed. After the Genteel Tradition p168-85 1937
Edgar, P. Four American Writers: Anderson, Hemingway, Dos Passos, Faulkner *In* Art of the Novel, from 1700 to the Present Time p338-51 1933
Hartwick, H. The Anarchist *In* Foreground of American Fiction p282-93 1934
Hatcher, H. H. Critical Spirit *In* Creating the Modern American Novel p127-39 1935
Kunitz, S. J. ed. Living Authors 1937
Loggins, V. Revolution *In* I Hear America p249-81 1937
McCole, C. J. John Dos Passos and the Modern Distemper *In* Lucifer at Large p175-200 1937
Van Doren, C. C. New Realisms *In* American Novel, 1789-1939 p334-48 1940
Who's Who in America

DOVER, ELMER Apr 14, 1873—Oct 3, 1940 Former Assistant Secretary of the United States Treasury (1921-22); began his political career as secretary to Senator Mark Hanna in 1897; served the Republican Party for many years, was friend of six United States Presidents; last public office was as clerk of the Federal Court for the Western District of Washington

References

Who's Who in America 1936-37

Obituaries

N Y Herald Tribune p18 O 4 '40

DOWDING, SIR HUGH CASWELL TREMENHEERE Apr 24, 1882- Former chief marshal of the British Royal Air Force

December 1940 Bulletin: Air Chief Marshal Sir Hugh Dowding will be sent to the United States on "special duty" by Lord Beaverbrook, Minister of Aircraft Production (see sketch this issue), it was announced in November 1940. He will be replaced by Air Vice-Marshal Sir William Sholto Douglas.

From November issue:

The British Royal Air Force has for many weeks taken heavy toll of the *Luftwaffe* in the intensive German raids that come every day, sometimes as often as six times a day. Much of the success of British defenses can be attributed to Air Chief Marshal Sir Hugh Dowding. He is the man who convinced the British Air Council

SIR HUGH DOWDING

that eight synchronized machine guns should be placed on the British fighter plane; he is the man who is responsible for the decision to place the cockpit on the Hurricane behind the engine, where the pilot would have maximum protection, and on his own initiative worked with a firm of glass manufacturers for a year until they developed a pilot's windshield that would shed machine bullets; and he is the man who has built up and now controls the whole British system of defense against air raids—fighters, antiaircraft guns, the observer corps and the balloon barrages.

"A thin, inscrutable figure in blue," he sits at headquarters directing his fighter pilots by radio. By a vast complicated telephone system he knows the position of every bomber over the country and directs the defense to meet every maneuver of the raiders. His junior officers idolize him, and when comments are made on British effectiveness in the air they all say: " 'Stuffy' did it."

The service calls him "Stuffy" mainly because of his reserved manner and his "university don" appearance. Dowding is an officer of the intellectual type whose interest in aviation goes back to 1913. A Scotsman, he was born at Moffat, Dumfriesshire and was educated at Winchester College and the Royal Military Academy, Woolwich. On August 18, 1900 he was gazetted to the Royal Artillery and for some 13 years pursued the ordinary humdrum career of a subaltern, serving in India and the Colonies.

In 1913 he was made a captain and in the same year took a flying course at the Central Flying School, Upavon, Wiltshire. When the First World War began he was attached to the Number 6 Squadron of the Royal Flying Corps and flew in it to Bruges

on October 7, 1914—only to find the action lost when he arrived. For about a month he was stationed at St. Omer and on November 18 was appointed general staff officer, third grade.

In March 1915 Dowding was put in charge of the Number 9 (Wireless) Squadron and was sent to England, where he was prominent in organizing the first home wireless school of the Royal Flying Corps—this was only the first of the many times in which he played a useful part in the development of radio communication. By July he was back at St. Omer commanding the Number 16 Squadron, which did some only moderately successful reconnaissance and photography prior to the Battle of Loos. Through intensive work and experiment in the next six months this arm's efficiency was increased so that it was more successful at the Somme Battle which began in July 1916. Throughout the Somme offensive Dowding, now a wing commander, led the ninth wing until he was succeeded in December by Sir Cyril Newall (see sketch this issue).

Dowding spent the rest of the War period in England. During 1917 he was at Salisbury commanding the Southern Training Brigade and in 1917, when the Royal Air Force was established, he was attached to the headquarters of the northeastern area of England with the temporary rank of brigadier general. In 1916 he had been mentioned in dispatches and in January 1919 was made a Companion of the Order of St. Michael and of St. George.

The War over, Dowding had to choose between the Army and the Royal Air Force. Without hesitation he chose the R. A. F., even though it meant reversion to the rank of group captain. It was only a little over two years, however, before he became an air commodore and later chief staff officer of the inland area. In September 1924 he went out to Iraq as chief staff officer to Air Vice-Marshal Sir John Higgins, there helping to organize raids against Akhwan tribesmen. In 1926 he was back in England again as director of training at the Air Ministry and in 1929 was made an air vice-marshal.

In September 1929 Dowding went to Palestine and Transjordania for three months as temporary air officer in command, and at the end of the same year he was brought to England to take over the fighter command. In September 1930 he was appointed a member of the Air Council for Supply and Research; in January 1933 an air marshal's baton followed; and in June of the same year he was knighted.

When in June 1936 the R. A. F. was arranged in three big commands, Bomber, Fighter and Coastal, Dowding was put in charge of Fighters. He has worked ever since that time in raising that group to its present state of efficiency. It was in January 1937 that he became an air chief marshal and principal air A. D. C. to the King, and in July of that year he was awarded the additional knighthood, Grand Cross of the Victorian Order—his previous knighthood was Knight Commander of the Bath.

In September 1940 he was promoted a stage in the Order of the Bath, to Knight Grand Cross.

Dowding is a quiet man, noted for his "unsmiling wit, his stubborn Scottish temper and his quick decision in battle." He is a widower with one daughter and a son who is now a pilot.

References

Listener 22:964 N 16 '39
N Y Times p9 S 29 '40; VII p5+ D 15 '40 il pors
News R 9:15 My 30 '40
Pollard, A. O. Leaders of the Royal Air Force 1940
Who's Who

DROSSAERTS, ARTHUR JEROME, ARCHBISHOP (drŏs'sĕrts) Sept 11, 1862—Sept 8, 1940 Roman Catholic Archbishop of San Antonio; came to this country from Holland just after his ordination in 1889; served in various churches; celebrated his golden anniversary as a priest in 1939; was made a Count by the Pope in recognition of his work for the church against the Mexican government

References

Central-Blatt 32:276 D '39
Extension 25:35 O '30
National Catholic Welfare Conference (Bulletin) R 12:24 S '30
American Catholic Who's Who
Who's Who in America

Obituaries

N Y Times p15 S 9 '40 por

DROUET, BESSIE CLARKE (drōō'ā) 1879—Aug 27, 1940 Internationally known author of psychic works; known as painter and sculptor; wrote *Station Astral* and many other books on psychic methods; was friend of the late Sir Arthur Conan Doyle and the late Sir Oliver Lodge; was co-founder of the American Students' Foundation, Incorporated, in 1934, and its president

References

Who's Who in American Art

Obituaries

N Y Times p19 Ag 29 '40

DU BOIS, WILLIAM EDWARD BURGHARDT (dü'bwä') Feb 23, 1868- Editor; author; Negro leader
Address: Atlanta University, Atlanta, Georgia

For 55 years Dr. W. E. B. Du Bois has been fighting for the Negro. He has fought to give him his place in American history; he has fought to give him his place in American life today. His has been mainly the battle of the pen. In the periodical, the *Crisis,* in articles in many magazines, in books, he has told of discrimination against his race and has preached to his race courageous independence.

In preaching independence he was a pioneer. Booker T. Washington, Negro leader, had urged upon his race "dependence, and through compromise an emergence into an economic, social and cultural stability never quite equal to the white man's." Du Bois urged instead "a fight to obtain without compromise such rights and privileges as belonged to members of the civilization of which he was a part."

Dr. Du Bois was born in Great Barrington, Massachusetts on February 23, 1868. He received his B. A. from Fisk University in Tennessee in 1888 and the same degree from Harvard in 1890. From Harvard he also received his M. A. in 1891 and in 1895, after a period of study at the University of Berlin, he acquired his Ph. D. His thesis was the *Suppression of the African Slave Trade,* still the standard work on this subject.

Right after he left Harvard Dr. Du Bois married Nina Gomer of Cedar Rapids (they have one daughter), and taught for a short while at Wilberforce University. For some time he was an assistant at the University of Pennsylvania, during which period he worked on *The Philadelphia Negro* (1899). It was the research for this book which gave him that intimate knowledge of the practical problems with which the Negro masses had to contend.

Already, in 1896, he had accepted the professorship of history and economics at the old Atlanta University, and there he remained until 1910. At Atlanta he was the moving spirit of the Atlanta Conference which assembled each year during commencement week, and through his annual

W. E. B. DU BOIS

DU BOIS, WILLIAM—*Continued*

editing of the *Studies of Negro Problems* became known as one of the leading sociologists of the day. He contributed to the *Atlantic Monthly, World's Work* and other magazines.

Disillusion had begun for Du Bois early and it continued at Wilberforce. In Atlanta, however, he was reborn. He learned to play as well as work and he formed some of his strongest friendships. In *Souls of Black Folk* (1903) there was cynicism, bitterness, but a great sympathy. In it he stated that "the problem of the twentieth century is the problem of the color line," and he who had been the critic of his people now became their defender: "I saw the race-hatred of the whites as I had never dreamed of it before—naked and unashamed! The faint discrimination of my hopes and desires paled into nothing before this great, red monster of cruel oppression. . . I emerged into full manhood, with the ruins of some ideals about me, but with others planted above the stars . . . determined, even unto stubborness, to fight the good fight."

In 1905 twenty-nine Negro men launched the Niagara Movement, whose aims included the abolition of all distinctions based on race or color, the recognition of the principle of human brotherhood as a practical present creed and the recognition of the best training as the monopoly of no class or race. Du Bois wrote most of its manifestoes and was a leader of the movement, but, because it lacked coherence, the life of the organization was short.

Nevertheless it had paved the way for a larger and stronger organization. In 1909 some persons of both white and colored races in New York determined upon a new effort for the full freedom of the Negro. The result was the National Association for the Advancement of Colored People. Dr. Du Bois was called from Atlanta in 1910 to be director of publicity and research and he began to edit the *Crisis,* the organ of the Association. For 24 years he remained in this work, wielding a tremendous influence on Negro thought and letters through his articles and editorials.

In 1919 Dr. Du Bois organized the Pan-African Congress, which had its first meeting in Paris, and in 1920 he was awarded the Spingarn Medal, given yearly to the Negro who reflects most credit on the race in any field of honorable endeavor. In 1932 he went to the new Atlanta University to devote his time mainly to historical research.

During these years Dr. Du Bois wrote many books, historical and imaginative. *Souls of Black Folk* (1903) was the first product of combined feeling and thinking. "It is in this book that he grows to fullness as a writer, fusing into a style that is beautifully lucid the emotional power that later made his *Crisis* editorials unsurpassed by any writing of their kind." In 1909 appeared his biography, *John Brown.* In 1911 *The Quest of the Silver Fleece,* his first novel, was published. This was not so much a novel as fact fictionized, endeavoring to impress the mind by a reasonable exposition of facts about the economic status of the Southern Negro. In 1920 came *Darkwater,* a collection of essays, editorials, sketches and six poems, many of which had appeared in the *Atlantic Monthly* and the *Independent* and most of which had been published in *Crisis.*

Dr. Du Bois' second novel, *Dark Princess* (1928), has been called a "strange compound of revolutionary doctrine and futilistic philosophy, refuting, it seems, Dr. Du Bois' own text of aggressive independence." In 1935 appeared *Black Reconstruction,* which has been called "remarkable" and "an important and enlightening book," and which fills the gaps white historians have left in the history of the South in the years between 1860 and 1880. In 1939 he wrote *Black Folk: Then and Now.* In the fall of 1940 he published *Dusk of Dawn,* "the autobiography of a concept of race," and also a picture of a "dark man of genius, with a tough mind and a tender skin, in a white world." This year, too, he launched a new *Review of Race and Culture.*

References

Sat R Lit 13:4 Ja 18 '36 por

Allen, D. ed. Wings for God's Chillun: Burghardt Du Bois *In* Adventurous Americans p192-202 1932

Brawley, B. G. Protest and Vindication *In* Negro Genius p190-230 1937

Brawley, B. G. W. E. Burghardt Du Bois *In* Negro Builders and Heroes p185-90 1937

Bullock, R. W. William Edward Burghardt Du Bois *In* In Spite of Handicaps p67-72 1927

Du Bois, W. Dusk of Dawn 1940

Kunitz, S. J. ed. Authors Today and Yesterday 1933

Ovington, M. W. W. E. Burghardt Du Bois *In* Portraits in Color p78-91 1933

Redding, J. S. To Make a Poet Black p49-92 1939

Who's Who in America

Who's Who in Colored America

DUFF COOPER, ALFRED *See* Cooper, A. D.

DUFFY, EDMUND Mar 1, 1899- Winner of 1939 Pulitzer Award of $500 for best editorial cartoon

Address: b. The Sun, Baltimore, Maryland; h. 901 Cathedral St, Baltimore, Maryland

Being on the list of Pulitzer winners has become habitual with Edmund Duffy, political cartoonist for the Baltimore *Sun* since 1924. In 1931 he won the award for his cartoon showing a Russian Communist

EDMUND DUFFY

pulling a cross from a mosque. In 1934 he repeated the feat, with *California Points with Pride*—a drawing of two San José lynch victims hanging from a gallows. On May 6, 1940 he received this recognition (and $500 cash) for the third time. *The Outstretched Hand*, published October 7, 1939, shows Hitler with outstretched right hand, dripping in blood, labeled "the peace offer"; in his left hand torn papers marked "broken promises, treaty and no more territorial demands"; crouched before him a group of people marked "minorities"; in the background, smoking ruins. Only one Pulitzer winner can rival Duffy's record, and that is Rollin Kirby, the Scripps-Howard political cartoonist, who also has received three awards.

Edmund Duffy, the son of Anna (Hughes) and John Joseph Duffy, a Jersey City policeman, was born in that city on March 1, 1899, but "as soon as possible crossed over to New York." He began his education in the ordinary way, but wound up by discarding algebra for drawing and at 15 found himself a student at the Art Students League. There he stayed for five years, under such instructors as George Bridgman, John Sloan and Boardman Robinson.

When Duffy was graduated in 1919 his "first job of any consequence was a page of the Armistice celebration printed in the Sunday magazine section of the New York *Tribune*," although he also contributed drawings to the New York *Herald* Sunday magazine and sports sections, to the New York *Evening Post's* Saturday magazine and sports' pages, and illustrated stories for *Scribner's* and *Century*. In 1920, with a hard-earned $150, the 22-year-old artist boarded a Liverpool-bound ship and arrived in England by steerage with $90 left. A job on the London

Daily News was both a stroke of luck and a financial necessity, and when Duffy grew tired of poverty in London he was free to try the Parisian variety. He moved over the Channel to "study art, investigate Montmartre night life, and sip vermouth at the Café du Dôme," at the same time contributing drawings to the New York *Herald's* Sunday section by long distance. Finally in 1922 he returned to the United States, "lugged his lanky frame into the Brooklyn *Eagle* offices," and proceeded to waver with his drawings between their offices and those of the short-lived New York *Leader* until he was offered a job on the Baltimore *Sun* on Labor Day 1924.

Duffy immediately took the job, and with the assistance of his artist-wife, Anne Rector, whom he married on November 26 of that same year, and his daughter, Sara Anne, has managed to remain in one spot ever since, physically speaking. He boasts that he never exercises, and complains that "aside from a slight weakness for horse-racing, which I developed after coming to Maryland, I have no hobbies." He contributes cartoons to *The Nation* and to the *Saturday Evening Post* and sometimes writes for the Sunday papers—for the most part book reviews. But chiefly—and most important—he is active on his own paper in a Pulitzer sort of way.

References

Lit Digest 116:11 O 21 '33 por
N Y Herald Tribune p17 My 7 '40 por
N Y Times p20 My 7 '40 il por
Newsweek 5:37 Ap 6 '35 il
America's Young Men
Who's Who in America
Who's Who in American Art

DU FOURNET, LOUIS RENE MARIE CHARLES DARTIGE (dü'fŏŏr'nā') 1856 —Feb 18, 1940 French vice-admiral who commanded the Allied Fleet in the Mediterranean during part of the World War

Obituaries

N Y Times p21 F 20 '40
N Y World-Telegram p19 F 19 '40

DUGAN, RAYMOND SMITH May 30, 1878—Aug 31, 1940 Professor of astronomy at Princeton University; faculty member for 35 years; special field of study was that of eclipsing variable stars, commonly known as double stars; was credited with having the most accurate photometric observing eyes in the world; writer on astronomy; made millions of measurements of stars

References

Sci N L 31:174 Mr 13 '37
American Men of Science
Who's Who in America

Orren Jack Turner

RAYMOND SMITH DUGAN

Obituaries

N Y Herald Tribune p18 S 1 '40 por
N Y Times p21 S 1 '40 por

DU MAURIER, DAPHNE (dü-môr'yä)
May 13, 1907- Author

Address: b. c/o Curtis Brown, Ltd, London,
England; h. Bodin-nick-by-Fowey, Cornwall,
England

Described as blonde, blue-eyed, athletic,
and "pretty enough for a screen test in anybody's studio," Daphne du Maurier is in her
early 30's a noted English novelist, the
author of five novels and two biographies.
Her novel *Rebecca,* published in 1938, was a
best seller, as was her *Jamaica Inn* in 1936.

She first came to the attention of American readers with her witty and frankly indiscreet story of her family, *The Du Mauriers* (1937) and the biography of her
famous actor-father, *Gerald* (1936). In these
were recorded the doings of the remarkable
tribe which for well over a century has
produced famous actors, dramatists and
novelists.

The story of her family tree, which
Daphne du Maurier presents like some absorbing novel in *The Du Mauriers,* began at
the turn of the eighteenth century with
Mary Anne Clarke, an actress who was the
toast of London and mistress of the Duke
of York. When the lovely but scandalous
Mrs. Clarke's connection with the Duke
became too public, she went to France.
There in Tours her daughter Ellen married
a young inventor named Louis Mathurin du
Maurier, son of a schoolmaster.

They had two sons, George and Eugène,
and a daughter, Isabel. George du Maurier
became famous as a caricaturist and novelist, the author of *Trilby* and *Peter Ibbetson.*
George du Maurier's two sons carried on

the family tradition. Major Guy, although
a soldier by profession, was the author of
An Englishman's Home, and Sir Gerald du
Maurier, Daphne's father, was the famous
British actor.

It was not strange, therefore, when David
O. Selznick came to produce the motion
picture of Daphne du Maurier's novel,
Rebecca, that he was amazed at the small number of changes necessary to transform the
book into a photoplay. Daphne du Maurier
was a true daughter of the theatre, and
her book fell naturally into the dramatic
medium. Not only her father but her
mother had been on the stage. Her sister
and half-sister were actresses; her uncle was
a dramatist.

Daphne du Maurier was born in London
May 13, 1907, the second daughter of Gerald
du Maurier. Her famous grandfather,
George du Maurier, died 11 years before,
and Miss du Maurier says that one of her
greatest sorrows is that she never knew
him. As a child, she was said to have
borne an extraordinary resemblance to his
drawings of *Trilby.*

Educated privately in England and
France, Miss du Maurier began writing at
the age of 19. Her poems and short stories
appeared in the *Bystander* and the *Sunday
Review.* She wrote her first novel, *The
Loving Spirit,* when she was 22. When the
book was published in 1931 it received enthusiastic praise from Rebecca West and
other well-known critics. There followed,
however, two more novels, *I'll Never be
Young Again* in 1932, and *The Progress of
Julia* in 1933, before Miss du Maurier wrote
her first major success, *Jamaica Inn,* an exciting story of smugglers and wreckers on
the Cornish coast more than a 100 years
ago. Séan O'Faoláin described it as a tale
Robert Louis Stevenson would not have
been ashamed to have written.

Miss du Maurier was married in 1932 to
Major Frederick A. M. Browning of the
Grenadier Guards. They have two daughters, Tess and Flavia. Since her marriage,
Miss du Maurier has written her books at
whatever place her husband happened to
be stationed. For a while they divided their
time between a small cottage in Hampstead
and their place at Fowey, Cornwall, the
little seaport where Miss du Maurier wrote
her first novel. Much of *The Du Mauriers*
was written in Alexandria, Egypt, where
Major Browning was stationed temporarily.
Rebecca was started in Alexandria in September 1937, and finished in England during April 1938.

Miss du Maurier follows a workmanlike
schedule in her writing. She does it just
like going to an office, she declares. "I
usually work from about ten to one o'clock,
have an hour for lunch, and then get at it
again from two to four. That way I can
finish a novel in about three months.

"It is a strange and rather puzzling
thing," she observes, "that the profession
of writing should cause more interest and
curiosity in the mind of the layman than

any other craft on earth." She cannot
understand why the artist, be he writer,
actor, composer or painter, "should be considered as though he were a species apart,
a rare being, dreamy and temperamental,
who lives in another world, working when
he chooses and when the spirit moves him.
"How nice," she says, "it would be to
lock the door every morning and simply
turn on the tap.
"As for me, I may determine to write a
gay, light romance. But I go for a walk
on a moor and see a twisted tree and a pile
of granite stones beside a deep, dark pool,
and *Jamaica Inn* is born.
"I find a lot of old letters in a forgotten
drawer belonging to my grandfather and
his father before him, and I must know
why they wept and why they suffered, and
what strange memories enfolded these Du
Mauriers of 60 and a 100 years ago."

Miss du Maurier's husband once told her
she would never be a great writer until
she wrote a happy story about happy people.
Sometimes, Miss du Maurier says, she believes that he is right. But she can't do
anything about it.

During the Second World War, Daphne
du Maurier turned from novelist to war
worker. She told an interviewer early in
1940, when she was in Kent where her husband was stationed, that she had an idea
for a new book, but had little time or will
to write it because it was to be about peace.
And the post-War, which she intends to put
in her next novel, "won't be real peace, but
chaos," she said.

One reason Miss du Maurier put off the
novel is that work on a committee looking
after 250 Grenadier Guardsmen's families,
learning to be of use in case of air raids,
and other War work took a great deal of
time. And although her two children were
staying with her mother-in-law she still had
too many interruptions to do much writing.

Although her novels have had great success in America, Miss du Maurier has never
visited the country, and is a little timid
about going there. "They're frightfully
hospitable there, aren't they?" she asked an
interviewer. "Lots of cocktail parties, I
understand. I really don't like so much
social life." She likes looking for birds and
studying them. She likes walking because
it's something she can do while she looks
for birds and identifies them by their songs.

Before the War broke out, she and her
husband had dreams of buying a boat, going
to the United States to get it, and cruising
around in Southern waters for a while.
Miss du Maurier says she is not a good
sailor, but likes it.

Despite her attractiveness, the author is
no artificial glamour girl. She is modest
and unassuming. The village in Kent where
she was living during the early days of the
Second World War knew her simply as
Mrs. Browning.

When the movie version of *Rebecca* was
being made she was hoping for the best.
She didn't like what the movies had done

DAPHNE DU MAURIER

to *Jamaica Inn,* which starred Charles
Laughton.

"I came to London and went to see
Jamaica Inn all by myself," she said. "I
bought a seat in the three and sixes (the
cheaper section) and nearly wept. About all
that was left was the title."

Miss du Maurier has been most fortunate
at the hands of the critics. *Rebecca,* the
melodramatic story of the young, sensitive
second wife haunted by events that re-
volved around her predecessor, received unqualified praise. The New York *Times*
wrote: "Almost in a class by herself, Daphne
du Maurier's special forte becomes increasingly established: the ability to tell a good
story and people it with a twinkling reality."

The *Christian Science Monitor* said of it:
"Many a better novelist would give his eyes
to be able to tell a story as Miss du Maurier
does, to make it move at such a pace and
to go with such mastery from surprise to
surprise."

Despite its obvious and unashamed melodramatic quality, the craftsmanship in *Rebecca* won admiration from critics, several
of whom compared it to a Charlotte Brontë
story, and predicted it would be a best-
seller. It has fulfilled that prediction.

The American Booksellers' Association, in
announcing its national book awards at a
luncheon in New York on February 1939,
chose *Rebecca* as the booksellers' favorite
novel.

In November 1940 a slim Christmas book,
Happy Christmas, was published. Reviewers
liked that, too.

Miss du Maurier was as fortunate with
her other books. The *Saturday Review of
Literature* described *The Du Mauriers* as
"so readable one cannot put it down. It

DU MAURIER, DAPHNE—*Continued*
is a fitting sequel to that most beguiling
story of *Gerald*."

References

Newsweek 12:29 S 26 '38 por
Sat R Lit 15:7 Ap 24 '37 por
Springf'd Republican p12 F 21 '40
Wilson Lib Bul 11:14 S '36 por
Author's & Writer's Who's Who
Du Maurier, D. The Du Mauriers
  1937
Du Maurier, D. Gerald 1936
Who's Who

DU PONT, PIERRE SAMUEL   Jan 15,
1870- Industrialist
Address: b. Wilmington, Delaware

Although at present only a director and
member of the finance committee of E. I. du
Pont de Nemours & Company, Pierre
Samuel du Pont is one of the best-known
members of "the family which has built
up the most spectacular industrial dynasty
in history," with an empire of more than
70 factories. The Du Ponts have been
named by the Securities and Exchange Commission as one of the three American
families who exert most influence on the
economic and political life of the United
States through their hold on industry; in
Delaware their "ducal estates line both
banks of the Brandywine above the ruins
of the old powder mill and stretch across
the state line into Pennsylvania"; "no other
family so completely dominates a state as
they do" through their journalistic, banking
and political connections.

Pierre Samuel du Pont is the great-grand-
son and namesake of a refugee from the
French Revolution, who in 1802 with his
second son set up as a powder maker on the
banks of the Brandywine. Pierre's father,
Lammot, was a partner in the powder company, but never became the head of it; his
mother, Mary Belin, was of an old French
family. He himself was born in Wilmington,
Delaware on January 15, 1870, and 14 years
later Lammot du Pont's death in an explosion left him to father his younger
brothers and sisters. His brothers Lammot
and Irénée still call him "Dad."

After preparing at the Penn Charter School
in Philadelphia, Pierre went on to the Massachusetts Institute of Technology, where he
emerged in 1890 with a B. S. in chemistry
and a position as chemist with the family
company, helping to develop a smokeless
powder. For two years he was assistant
superintendent of the Brandywine Black
Powder Mills; for seven years superintendent
of Carney's Point Works. But his rise
didn't seem to him sufficiently rapid, so in
March 1899 he went to Lorain, Ohio to
liquidate the real-estate holdings of a certain
Johnson Company and, with the $50,000
which his father had left him, to become
president of the company. In Lorain, too,
he acquired the stenographic services of a

shrewd young man called John Jacob
Raskob.

In 1902 Coleman du Pont brought Pierre
back into the family company, together
with Alfred du Pont, and the three cousins
organized the corporation of E. I. du Pont
de Nemours & Company, which purchased
and took possession of the properties previously owned and operated by a corporation
of the same name. Pierre was first elected
treasurer of this new corporation, afterward
became successively vice-president and member of its executive and finance committees.
As his assistant, Raskob came with him.

Originally more than 50 per cent of the
corporation's stock was held by the triumvirate of cousins, Coleman owning the most,
but after a consolidation in 1903 they ceased
to be controlling stockholders. In 1915 a
group headed by Pierre bought Coleman's
stock for their "family investment trust"
(the Du Pont Securities Company, now the
Christiana Securities Company). When Alfred fought the sale as a breach of trust he
was ousted from the corporation by its
directors. On March 6, 1915 Pierre became
president of E. I. du Pont de Nemours &
Company, and it is the three brothers
(Pierre, Lammot, Irénée) who have held
control ever since.

In October 1915 Pierre married his cousin,
Alice Belin, although there had been so many
earlier marriages between Du Pont cousins
that a family dictum had already been laid
down against the practice.

Du Pont sales during the World War
meant unprecedented profits—are said to
have represented 276 years of "normal" business. After the Allies agreed to pay $1 a
pound for powder, contracts were let so
rapidly that, as one executive wrote later,
"we were forced to start a new plant nearly
every day." It was during the War, too,
that Pierre bought the Wilmington *Journal*—
it is claimed for the purpose of fighting
Alfred, who had bought the Morning *News*.
Pierre afterward acquired the *News* from
Alfred and finished the job by adding the
Every Evening to the family holding company, combining it with the *Journal*.

During all this time Pierre du Pont had
been assisted by Raskob's very able advice.
It was Raskob who brought first Pierre and
then the Du Pont Company into General
Motors, and after the War, two years after
buying the first shares in the company, 49
Du Pont millions were used to buy absolute
control. On May 1, 1919, when Alfred's
litigation against Pierre was definitely settled
in Pierre's favor, Pierre became board chairman of both Du Pont and General Motors,
passing the presidency of Du Pont on to
Irénée, while Raskob became vice-president
of Du Pont and finance committee chairman
of General Motors.

There followed a period of tremendous
expansion. The seizure of German patents
by the United States government in 1917 had
opened the way for large-scale entry into
the dyestuffs industry. And the Du Pont
Company after the War had a surplus on

hand large enough to acquire a vast "chemical empire." A large number of industries were also acquired by exchange of stock, and by 1935 the scope of Du Pont enterprises was to include, besides explosives and sporting and military powders, the making of rayon, paints, lacquers, varnishes, pigments, plastics, cellophane, ammonia, acids, chemicals, Duco, Fabrikoid, Ethyl gas, shatterproof glass, motors and airplanes (the "Lindbergh line"). According to Raskob, in 1934 the Du Ponts controlled "a larger share of industry, through common stock holdings, than any other group in the United States."

In the meanwhile there had been ventures into politics. It was in 1925 that Pierre was appointed tax commissioner for Delaware for his first term, serving until 1938. Then, although a Republican in state politics, in 1928 he supported Al Smith for the White House and Roosevelt for Governor of New York—both anti-prohibitionists, as was Pierre. The Association Against the Prohibition Amendment also received his strong financial support, and in 1933 he was given the job of Delaware's single liquor commissioner, a non-political appointment which he held until 1938, and a part in writing the state's liquor control law. In 1932 he supported Roosevelt for President; in 1934 he was appointed to the National Labor Board which mediated labor disputes under the NRA.

But he was not to support the Administration long. In 1934 a Senate munitions investigation committee headed by Senator Gerald P. Nye charged that the Du Pont Company during the World War had not only made huge profits from munitions but had "defrauded the government on war contracts on a gigantic scale." Although the company was exonerated, that same year marked the founding of the anti-Administration Liberty League, sponsored with others by Pierre du Pont. Mr. Du Pont states that his "change of position was entirely due to the failure of the Administration to carry out any of the pledges of the platform which adherents had been promised without qualification." Then about the time that the Liberty League was getting into high gear, the government, through the Bureau of Internal Revenue, pounced again: Du Pont and Raskob were charged with having evaded $1,824,112 in taxes through a 1929 transaction involving cross sales. To this Pierre du Pont replied that the prosecution was merely "part of a scheme to injure me and to force a compromise of claims in a manner amounting to extortion," and in 1936 he and Raskob were prime movers in the Liberty League campaign to get Roosevelt out of the White House.

On May 20, 1940, at the age of 70, Pierre du Pont retired as chairman of E. I. Du Pont de Nemours & Company, though retaining his membership on the board of directors and the finance committee. Perhaps he was "ready to retire to his enormous hothouses at Longwood Gardens, where he plucks

Hazel Ives

PIERRE SAMUEL DU PONT

orchids and figs, to sit in the evening on his broad plaza and watch his $500,000 fountain swish and spurt in beams of many-colored lights" or listen to his powerful $250,000 organ, built especially for his wife, who is growing deaf. But his 1,000-acre estate, Longwood, is not his only hobby. Education and philanthropy are others. A former member of the State Board of Education (1919-21), long a member of the Corporation of the Massachusetts Institute of Technology, he has contributed millions both to the building of Delaware schools and to M. I. T. He has also contributed $750,000 to roads, has built a hospital in Pennsylvania in memory of his favorite chauffeur and lends his financial support to the Metropolitan Opera Association.

Pierre and his wife are childless, and Longwood is said to be rather lonely except on the days when the great gardens are thrown open to the public, especially since the young nieces for whom Pierre used to give elaborate dances in the conservatory have grown up. Perhaps that is why he takes a great personal interest in the younger men who work for him and won't let his chauffeurs wear livery because he likes to dine with them away from Wilmington. He has few close friends outside the family, but is uniquely generous with his friends, keeping cars and chauffeurs in both New York and Paris especially for their convenience. They usually occupy his box at the Metropolitan, too. He is the most insured man in America: in 1932 he carried policies amounting to $7,000,000. An article in *Fortune* described him as "inclined to heaviness around the waist and jowls. His head is large and bald; his nose is large, thick and heavy, topped by spectacles or pince-nez; his eyes are small and mild. Like most of the Du Ponts he wears collars that are too high and slightly

DU PONT, PIERRE SAMUEL—*Cont.*

oversize." He also wears the rosette of an Officier de la Légion d'Honneur.

References

Business Week p13 F 10 '34 por; p31 S 15 '34

Fortune 10:72-3 N '34 por; 16:85 D '37; 22:56-60+ Jl '40

Lit Digest 118:6 S 22 '34 il; 121:40 Ja 25 '36 por; 121:41 F 15 '36

New Repub 80:212 O 3 '34; 85:338-9 Ja 29 '36

Newsweek 7:27 Ja 18 '36; 7:13 F 1 '36 por; 9:38-9 My 22 '37 por

Time 29:16 My 17 '37 por; 34:69 D 4 '39 por; 35:70-1 Je 3 '40

World's Work 60:62-3 F '31

Lundberg, F. America's 60 Families 1937

Myers, G. History of the Great American Fortunes 1910

Smith, A. D. H. The Du Ponts *In* Men Who Run America p64-72 1936

Who's Who in America

Who's Who in Commerce and Industry

Winkler, J. K. Du Pont Dynasty 1935

DUROCHER, LEO (dü-rō-shā') July 27, 1906-   Baseball player; manager of the Brooklyn Dodgers

Address: b. Brooklyn Dodgers, Ebbets Field, Brooklyn, New York; h. Lindell Towers, St. Louis, Missouri

In 1940 the Brooklyn Dodgers made a serious bid for the championship of the National League. According to most sports writers and fans much credit for their amazing successes should go to Leo Ernest Durocher who has been managing them for

LEO DUROCHER

not quite two years and who has signed a contract to manage them in 1941. "Leo, the Lip," who has been "the talkingest, most talked about and most talked against shortstop in baseball," has finally won support for himself from his team and from the fans. It has taken a good many hard years, but "baseball's ugly duckling" has become baseball's swan.

Durocher has been playing baseball for as long as he can remember. Born in West Springfield, Massachusetts of French parents, he attended the local parochial school and high school in Springfield. In high school he played a fast game of basketball, a powerful game of football and baseball that was already distinguished. After being graduated he went to work for the Wyco Electric Company, learning to make motorcycle batteries and playing shortstop for the factory's baseball team. His playing was noticed by Yankee scouts and in 1925 he got a contract with the Yankee's Hartford, Connecticut farm team.

The Yankees sent him to Atlanta in 1926, where he played 154 games as shortstop, and then to St. Paul in 1927. In 1928 they brought him up to their home team. From the first day he showed up with the Yankees, Durocher was "the cockiest player in the training field." "His voice was loud, but his wardrobe was louder" and his vocabulary was something "worthy of the typewriter of Ring Lardner." He played in the 1928 World Series and stayed with the Yankees until 1929. That was the year that Yankee Manager Miller Huggins, with whom Durocher was a favorite, died. Leo was left without a friend on his team, with a reputation for being wild and untamable, with a good many debts. His fielding, somehow, seemed less steady and less spectacular, and his batting, which was never very good, seemed less so. So the Yankees, without regrets, "palmed him off" to the Cincinnati Reds.

During the seasons of 1930, 1931 and 1932 Durocher alternated second base and shortstop for the Reds. In 1930 they finished seventh; in the next two years eighth. After three seasons with them Durocher, in 1933, was traded to the St. Louis Cardinals and became a star. That 1934 World Series was a memorable one. When it was over the Cardinals had beaten Detroit in seven games, and Durocher was recognized as the best fielding shortstop in baseball and as a hitter as well, for his average for the series was .259. In 1935 he was made team captain of the Cardinals and in 1936 was selected for the National League All-Star Team.

It was while he was with the Cardinals that Durocher made his second, successful marriage. His first marriage, to Ruby Hartley in Cincinnati in 1930, ended in divorce in 1933. They had one child, Barbara. In September 1934 Durocher married Mrs. Grace Dozier of St. Louis and she became "the rudder that was finally to steer his course in a straight line." On the day after their marriage "she sat down and made out countless checks to clear up all his remaining obligations." At home in St. Louis, where Mrs. Durocher is owner of a large dress manufacturing concern, the Durochers live at the Lindell Towers.

After four years as "keyman" with the Cardinals, Durocher was traded to the Brooklyn Dodgers in exchange for four players. The fans thought the officials were out of their mind. By this time Durocher was along in years as baseball players go and besides had a reputation for fighting. It was true that he had "never booted a grounder or muffed a throw in a World Series," but he had an attitude of "noisy bravado" about his hitting and was always involved in rows.

In 1938 Durocher was made captain of the Dodgers and in that same year he asked Larry MacPhail for the job of manager. To the surprise of a good many people, he got it. When he took over the Dodgers they had been a bad seventh. They went out West in 1939 and received six straight beatings. Then Durocher proceeded to "give them hell" together and individually and swore to send them all back to the "sticks" unless they played real ball. Within two weeks after that they were in third place. And when the season was over Durocher had been given the Sporting News Award for being the outstanding manager of the year.

The Dodgers' success in 1939 was more than matched in 1940, when they came right to the top of their league as one of the main contenders for the pennant. When Durocher was asked how he had done it he said: "All you have to do is get a lot of good ballplayers together, make them hustle all the time and the percentage is bound to be with you."

> References
>> Collier's 104:14+ Ag 5 '39 por
>> Sat Eve Post 212:14-5+ Ag 19 '39 il pors
>> Who's Who in Commerce and Industry
>> Who's Who in Major League Base Ball

DUSSER DE BARENNE, JOANNES GREGORIUS (du̅-sā′ de bär-ĕn′) June 6, 1885—June 9, 1940 Physiologist and neurologist; won renown by recent discoveries about the brain; former teacher of physiology at the Universities of Amsterdam and Utrecht; Sterling professor of physiology at Yale University since 1930; member of the editorial board of the *American Journal of Physiology* and co-editor of the *Journal of Physiology*; author of several books on neurology

> References
>> American Men of Science
>> Who's Who in America

JOANNÉS DUSSER DE BARENNE

> *Obituaries*
>> N Y Herald Tribune p18 Je 10 '40 por
>> N Y Times p17 Je 10 '40

EDEN, ANTHONY June 12, 1897- Appointed British Foreign Minister, December 1940; former British Secretary of State for War
Address: 17 Fitzhardinge St, W. 1, London, England

Anthony Eden, who has spent the whole of his public life in a strenuous and single-hearted effort for peace, is in 1940 England's Secretary of State for War. The man who told Neville Chamberlain: "I do not believe we can make progress in European appeasement," who urged a "firm spirit" against the dictator nations and resigned from the office of Foreign Secretary rather than go along with Chamberlain's policies is now organizing the British Army.

Robert Anthony Eden (he never uses the Robert) was born at Windlestone Hall in Durham, the son of Sir William Eden, a man who added to the usual preoccupations of a country gentleman a nice talent as a water colorist. In 1906, he was sent to Sandroyd Preparatory School in Surrey and from there, in 1911, went to Eton where he "worked industriously and behaved quietly, seldom making himself conspicuous either by prowess or by misdeed." In 1915 he obtained a commission as second lieutenant in the 21st battalion of the King's Royal Rifle Corps. He spent two years on the French front, won the Military Cross and rose to be captain and brigade major.

In 1919 Eden entered Christ Church, Oxford, where he specialized in Oriental languages so successfully that he was once able to amaze the Aga Khan by making an entire speech in Persian and the Arabian

ANTHONY EDEN

envoy by quoting fluently in Arabic from the *Koran*. He was graduated with first-class honors in 1922 and immediately contested a Durham seat for Parliament with the ringing declaration: "I am a Conservative, always have been a Conservative and expect to die a Conservative." Despite, or perhaps because of this declaration, he was unsuccessful. In 1923, however, he was returned for Warwick and Leamington. In that same year he married Beatrice Helen Beckett, daughter of the Honorable Sir Gervase Beckett, an influential banker who owned the Yorkshire *Post*. They have two sons, Nicholas and Simon.

After his marriage Eden settled down in London, dividing his time for the next three years among the House of Commons, where he spoke "prosaically" on subjects of which he had special knowledge, journalism and travel. In 1925 he traveled around the world and published a book on his experiences which dealt mostly with the scenic beauties he had seen.

It was inevitable that Eden's rise in politics should be rapid: good family, impeccable clothes, conventional good looks, private means, good war record, education at Eton and Oxford, a handsome wife and two sturdy boys, and—what other "young-men-about-politics" lacked—tact, skill, patience and the ability to work hard. By 1925 Eden had become Parliamentary Private Secretary to Commander Locker-Lampson and in 1926 he was under the late Sir Austen Chamberlain. His was a post which offered unrivaled opportunities for studying the work of the Foreign Office from within and for knowing, at first hand, everything going on in the world. In it Eden "fetched and carried, unobtrusive and industrious," remembered as a "somewhat frail fellow with a marked stoop and the tired eyes of

a student rather than the arresting gaze of a leader."

His first government post came in 1931 when he was made Under-Secretary for Foreign Affairs, and in 1934 a special post was created for him, when he was made first Lord Privy Seal and later minister without portfolio for League of Nations Affairs. In 1934 he was a leading figure in the negotiations and plebiscite for the return of the Saar to Germany. With the Foreign Secretary, Sir John Simon (see sketch this issue), he traveled to Berlin, Moscow and Warsaw to discuss an Eastern mutual assistance pact and by himself went to Rome, where Mussolini is supposed to have spluttered words to the effect: "The nerve of the British government to send, as their representative in dealing with me, a little boy!"

Because of his efforts for the League of Nations he became to the British public a sort of "Knight in Shining Armour" and "the natural idol of that mass of British public opinion which was firmly convinced that world disarmament could and would be achieved." When Simon was replaced by Sir Samuel Hoare (see sketch this issue) Eden worked under him, but it wasn't long before he was in active opposition to Hoare's compromise policies and after the Hoare-Laval (see Laval sketch this issue) proposals for ending the Ethiopian war were made, came out squarely against him.

When, in October 1935, public opinion drove Hoare out of office, Eden became Foreign Secretary, the youngest Britain had had in almost a century. Strenuously he advocated sanctions against Italy. He later engineered the non-intervention treaty in Spain, however, and although it was flouted by the other signatory powers he insisted on maintaining the Spanish embargo. Yet all this time it was clear that a clash between him and Chamberlain was inevitable. Eden hated appeasement, according to some commentators not because of democratic indignation but because of "an old fashioned diplomat's contempt for botched negotiations and for truckling to gangsters."

Their differences came to a head over Mussolini's demand that the British come to Rome to talk peace "now or never." Eden could not agree with the proposed plans for closing the London-Rome breach. "I cannot recommend to Parliament a policy with which I am not in agreement," he said and resigned on February 20, 1938, "to the delight of Rome, Berlin and Tokyo" and to the dismay of many of the British. Crowds thronged the streets of London, shouting, "Chamberlain must go! Hitler and Mussolini must not dictate to Britain! Eden must stay!" But Eden did not stay and two days later Winston Churchill (see sketch this issue) sadly commented that Eden was "the one fresh figure of first magnitude arising out of the generation which was ravaged by the War."

It was felt then that Eden might break with the Conservative Party, and observers were even more certain right after Munich that a break was inevitable. But Eden, instead of leading dissident Conservatives, asked for "unity" in the Party, and shortly after left for America to express unofficially "the British view." In the United States he was received with "friendliness and enthusiasm which no foreign statesman has had since the days of the Allied War missions."

He returned to government work in 1939 when Chamberlain made him Secretary of State for Dominion Affairs shortly after the outbreak of the Second World War. In that same year his book, *Foreign Affairs*, was published. It is a "collection of his speeches on foreign affairs from his maiden speech on air defence, in 1924, to his speech in New York in December 1938." When Winston Churchill took office he promoted Eden to the position of Secretary of State for War. In November 1940 Eden returned from an inspection of British forces in the Mediterranean with an optimistic pronunciamento: "The future is safe." In December he received his new appointment.

Eden has always seemed to many a "glamour" politician, not only because of his high-minded opposition to appeasement but because of his appearance. A model of sartorial elegence, his trousers faultlessly creased and his shoes flawlessly polished, he moves with a sort of angular grace, tall, slightly stooped, his dark hair just beginning to be flecked with gray. But he is more than good looking and well-bred. Anthony Eden is "a man of great knowledge and intelligence . . . animated by intense seriousness of purpose."

References

Atlan 157:526-32 My '36
Collier's 97:25+ My 9 '36 pors
Cur Hist 50:1-4 Ag '39
Foreign Affairs 16:691-703 Jl '38
Ladies' H J 56:29+ Mr '39 il pors
Time 31:22-3 F 28 '38 por; 32:9-10 D 19 '38 por

Audax, pseud. Anthony Eden *In* Men in Our Time p121-43 1940
Gunther, J. Men of Whitehall *In* Inside Europe p334-54 1940
International Who's Who
Johnson, A. C. Anthony Eden 1939
Raskay, L. Anthony Eden 1939
Slocombe, G. E. Abyssinian Crisis *In* Mirror to Geneva p282-304 1938
Soward, F. H. Anthony Eden, British Spokesman for the "Lost Generation" *In* Moulders of National Destinies p199-208 1940
Watchman, pseud. Right Honourable Gentlemen 1939
Who's Who

EDEY, BIRDSALL OTIS June 25, 1872— Mar 17, 1940 National commander of the Girl Scouts and former president of the

Mrs. W. Burdell Stage

BIRDSALL OTIS EDEY

organization (1930-35); pioneer in the women's suffrage movement

Obituaries

N Y Herald Tribune p12 Mr 18 '40
N Y Times p17 Mr 18 '40 por

EDISON, CHARLES Aug 3, 1890- Democratic Governor-elect of New Jersey; former Secretary of the Navy

Address: b. West Orange, New Jersey; h. Llewellyn Park, West Orange, New Jersey

Charles Edison was elected Governor of New Jersey in November 1940. However, his formal announcement of his candidacy for Governor of New Jersey on the Democratic ticket, made on March 30, 1940, took political leaders and business executives by surprise. It was only in January of the same year that he had been appointed Secretary of the Navy. At a time when naval defense is one of the main concerns of this country, his resignation from the cabinet aroused a good deal of speculation.

Former Ambassador Walter E. Edge of New Jersey attacked the move strongly. He said that the naval post was the most important office in this country outside of the Presidency and asserted that if the Secretary "was an ideally equipped man for the post, as he must have been, or surely the President would not have appointed him, then, in these days, with the War brought almost to our very door, he should remain Secretary of the Navy. That would be his duty as a patriotic citizen."

Edison himself said that he had discussed his move with President Roosevelt and "he is entirely in sympathy with what I am doing." To some, the reason for the President's support and Edison's candidacy was that

CHARLES EDISON

Roosevelt was anxious to bolster his chances of getting New Jersey's electoral vote for a third term. To others, Edison left because, as they thought, the President was *not* running for a third term and Cabinet changes in November would deprive him of his post as Navy Secretary. There were still others who questioned Edison's efficiency as Secretary of the Navy.

Those who detracted from Edison's forcefulness and efficiency in his Navy Post pointed out that although Edison had been assistant head of the Navy since 1936, that although 1939 was a year of great preparedness, Roosevelt got along with the ailing, aging Swanson as head of the Navy for many months, and then with no Secretary of the Navy, after Swanson died in July 1939, until December 1939. Edison's supporters pointed to his record, and to the complete sympathy between his naval views and President Roosevelt's.

When soft-spoken Charles Edison was made Assistant Secretary of the Navy in November 1936 he stated: "My own personal belief is that we should have a very strong, very fine navy for defense. . . I don't see any sense in being weak in defense. No one respects you if you are." His main job has been that of building ships. It is true that he didn't "know the front of a ship from the back," but he did know business and manufacturing; he was a strong supporter of the New Deal; and he was not in awe of gold braid.

When Edison became Secretary of the Navy at the beginning of 1940, his creed was a Navy "so invincible" that it could at all times bring the enemy to "our terms as quickly as possible while keeping him at a safe distance from our shores." The most ambitious naval program in the history of this country was already under way. Two billion dollars were to be spent to increase our combatant strength from 272 to 372 ships. Edison urged this spending and more. He argued against those who felt that air power was more important than sea: "So far as the United States is concerned battleships were, are and will be for many years the backbone of our first line of national defense. Trust your fleet."

As Secretary of the Navy Edison worked hard, and admirals were often disturbed by calls for Saturday afternoon or all-day Sunday conferences. In only one case was there any conflict between him and the government. Shortly after he took office he proposed that direct contracts instead of competitive bidding be used for naval construction, for with bidding the result was an "unstandard ship" and "huge wastage through differences in plans and duplications." Immediately the House Naval Affairs Committee put him on the carpet for suggesting that Congress empower the President to make United States manufacturers take Navy orders on Navy terms. There was discussion, argument and disturbance. Edison apologized: "I was taken completely by surprise by all the commotion. I ask the country not to jump to the conclusion that I am so intrigued with the idea of national defense that I would sell democracy short to get it."

On June 24 Edison quit his post, 30 days after the New Jersey primary, because "during these trying times there must not be the slightest suspicion that decisions of a Secretary of the Navy are influenced by political expediency." Roosevelt gave him his blessing and wished him success.

This was the first time that Edison aspired to elective office, although he has been in politics since 1932. And his power to get votes in New Jersey, "the state where I was born, the state where I have lived for most of my life and the state that I love," has been proved. Mayor Hague of Jersey City gave him "100 per cent support," even though Edison was not an ideal candidate so far as his own political interests were concerned.

The new Governor of New Jersey, who likes to collect books, who is "happiest when perched at his piano dashing off impromptu tunes and boisterous jingles," has cleancut features and prematurely gray hair that remind many people of his father, Thomas Alva Edison, the inventor. He has his father's deafness, too, and his father's prodigious capacity for work, but not his father's creative genius.

He was born in Llewellyn Park, in West Orange, New Jersey on August 3, 1890, the eldest son of Edison's second marriage to Mina Miller. Gifted with none of Thomas Edison's inventiveness and "blessed with an appreciation for the trivia of living," young Charles Edison spread his share of wild oats around Llewellyn Park. It wasn't until he had labored through the Massachusetts Institute of Technology (he came out in 1913) and settled down in the business end of the loosely joined Edison Industries that Charles got along well with his father. He gradually took over the management from him and reorganized the business. Here he attacked the business problems of the many Edison enterprises as energetically as his father attacked the technical ones. Frequently he could be found in his gray-walled office in West Orange for 17 hours at a stretch.

In March 1918 Edison was married to Carolyn Hawkins of Cambridge, Massachusetts, who loved the job of naming ships which was frequently hers when her husband was Secretary of the Navy, but who "just turns green" on water. She does accompany him occasionally on the fishing trips of which he is so fond, however Once she caught a 104-pound tarpon, but it was so big she couldn't bear to think she had killed it and it made her cry. The Edisons, who have no children, have a large stone house in Llewellyn Park, a private residential section in West Orange.

Charles Edison's first acquaintance with the Navy was during the last War, when Thomas A. Edison served as President of the Naval Consulting Board under Assistant Secretary of the Navy Franklin D. Roosevelt. It was then, too, that he first came to know Roosevelt, of whom he has always been a firm supporter and close friend. Since 1932 he has been in politics, the only Democrat in a Republican family. He supported Roosevelt strongly for the Presidency and after the election "few businessmen gave their support to the New Deal earlier or more enthusiastically than Charles Edison."

The New Deal was only a month old when Edison plastered the walls of the plant in West Orange with messages urging his 3,500 employees to "get going" behind the President: "Buy something—buy anything —anywhere. Paint your kitchen. Send a telegram. Get a car. Pay a bill. Rent a flat. Fix your roof. Get a haircut. Get married." He handed each employee $5 and told him to spur on recovery by buying something he wouldn't have bought otherwise. When the New Deal was being criticized by other business men, Edison voiced his belief in Roosevelt. "I believe in the new experiments going on. It takes courage to try new things and it takes courage to stop them if they are not successful."

Edison became an important cog in New Jersey New Deal politics. He was successively a member of the State Recovery Board, of the Regional Labor Board, NRA Compliance Director, State Director of the National Emergency Council and a member of the National Industrial Recovery Board. When the Federal Housing Act was being drafted, Edison was a consultant and later was made regional director of the Federal Housing Administration.

He has, it has been said, consistently refused the position of head of the FHA.

In 1940 for the first time, he ran successfully for elective office with the support and blessing of the Roosevelt Administration he has served since 1933. In announcing his candidacy he said: "I have been deeply impressed by the sincerity of those who think I might be of some help to New Jersey... Candidly I should like to be of service to New Jersey." Now he has his chance. Among other things, he wants to revise the New Jersey constitution and election laws, giving the Governor "a veto that would stick" and a longer term, giving every bill a public hearing before it becomes law, making it easier to pass amendments.

References

China W R 91:101 D 16 '36 por
Cur Hist 51:32 Mr '40 por
N Y Herald Tribune p4 Ja 3 '40; p1 Ja 23 '40; p21 Ja 28 '40; p16 F 5 '40 por; p18 Mr 21 '40 por; II p10 Mr 24 '40; p1 Ap 3 '40
N Y Times VII p9, 16 Ja 14 '40 il pors; p11 Ja 28 '40; p1, 19 Mr 21 '40; p19 Je 5 '40
Newsweek 8:18 N 28 '36 por; 15:13-4 Ja 8 '40 por
Time 28:12 N 30 '36 por; 33:12-14 F 20 '39 por (cover) map; 34:10 S 18 '39 por (cover); 35:19 Ja 8 '40; 35:17 Ja 22 '40 por; 35:73 My 20 '40
Who's Who in America
Who's Who in Commerce and Industry
Who's Who in the Nation's Capital

EGLOFF, GUSTAV (ĕg'lŭf) Nov 10, 1886- Chemist

Address: 310 S Michigan Ave, Chicago, Illinois

Dr. Gustav Egloff, one of the world's greatest experts in the field of petroleum and hydrocarbon chemistry, was awarded the gold achievement medal of the American Institute of Chemists in May 1940 for his "prodigious contributions" to this field.

For 25 years Dr. Egloff has been conducting research into oil and oil products; he has written almost 400 articles relating to the oil industry; and he holds more than 250 patents for the processing of petroleum, shale oil, coal and hydrocarbon derivatives. Perhaps his greatest contribution to crude oil refining is the multiple coil cracking process "which increases the yield of high octane gasoline from crude oil." This process "is now used in every refinery of any size in the world," makes it possible to operate high speed planes and motor cars of today "with 40 per cent increased efficiency."

In 1939 Dr. Egloff created quite a stir by his announcement that he had devised a new way to make synthetic rubber from butane gas. Butane, used for heating, welding and motor fuel, is present in natural gas and is a by-product of oil refining and so

Associated Press

GUSTAV EGLOFF

is extremely plentiful and cheap. The rubber made from it, Dr. Egloff stated, "is not only more wear resistant in tires, hose and shoes than natural rubber but has in addition other valuable properties in that it is resistant to acids and alkalies and to heat." After almost a year's further work on this synthetic rubber Dr. Egloff told the Institute of Chemists, when they presented him with their medal, that the potential supply of synthetic rubber from United States oil wells was 200,000,000,000 pounds or nearly 200 times more than the quantity of natural rubber used in this country in 1939.

Dr. Egloff was born in New York City on November 10, 1886 and was graduated from Cornell University in 1912. From Cornell he went to Columbia, which gave him a master's degree in 1913 and a Ph. D. in 1916 after two years as a Barnard Fellow.

While working for his Ph. D., Dr. Egloff spent one year with the United States Bureau of Mines and as soon as he received his degree started to work for the Aetna Chemical Company as engineer and chief chemist. He stayed there only one year and then went to the Universal Oil Products Company of Chicago. He is still with the same company, director of its research.

While with the Universal Oil Products Company Dr. Egloff has lectured at many of the great colleges of the United States. He has been official delegate to numerous technical conferences in many countries and in 1937 he was elected vice-president of the World Petroleum Congress. He has been honored by many lands for his work.

References

Nat Petr N 29:16 Je 23 '37
N Y Herald Tribune p28 My 19 '40
    por

Newsweek 14:46 Jl 17 '39 por; 15:6
    My 27 '40
Time 34:35 Jl 17 '39 por
American Men of Science
Who's Who in America

EILSHEMIUS, LOUIS MICHEL (ĕl-shēm'ĭ-ŭs mĭ-shĕl') Feb 4, 1864- Artist
Address: 118 E 57th St, New York City

"For 20 years Manhattan's most persistent exhibition-goer was a little old gentleman with a beard, a beady eye and baggy trousers. Standing before a painting, preferably a high-priced one, he would mutter: 'Pffft! Such crude pigments! My, such a stencil technique—brr—let me get away!' He stopped other gallery-goers to tell them he was the world's greatest artist, passed out handbills describing himself as 'Mesmerist-Prophet and Mystic, Humorist Galore, Ex All Round Athletic Sportsman (to 1889), Scientist Supreme: all ologies, Ex Fancy Amateur Dancer...'

"He wrote crank letters to the newspapers. His letterhead: 'Mahatma Dr. Louis M. Eilshemius, M. A. etc., Mightiest Mind and Wonder of the Worlds, Supreme Parnassian and Grand Transcendent Eagle of Art.' His paintings, on the rare occasions when he could get them shown, brought horse laughs from critics and public alike."

Recently, Louis Eilshemius has been hailed as "the greatest living master," but this time by somebody else. In October 1939 three Manhattan galleries were simultaneously showing his pictures while other Eilshemius exhibitions were touring the country. A biography of him, *And He Sat Among the Ashes* (October 1939), had just been published and was stirring up a good deal of enthusiasm and attention. At the age of 76, more than a half century after his first paintings were shown, Eilshemius won recognition.

The story of Louis Eilshemius is the story of a gifted man who was his own worst enemy: a man whose career got off to a bad start because of "an almost incredible blindness in the art world of the nineties," and who, as his failures continued year after year, resorted to "frenzied publicizing of his own talents and, finally, to pathological self-glorification."

His was a happy childhood. He was born on February 4, 1864 in Arlington, New Jersey, in a spacious manor bought by his father who had come to this country from Dutch Friesland. With his many sisters and brothers, Louis spent much of his childhood traveling abroad and studying in foreign schools. In 1881 he received his diploma from the Dresden, Germany, Realschule.

At 17 Eilshemius already knew that art was his proper calling. But his father thought differently and got him a job as bookkeeper in a wholesale glove house. That didn't work, and as another compromise between what he wanted and what Louis wanted, his father suggested that he go to the State College of Agriculture at

Cornell University. Louis wasn't unhappy there, for he continued with his drawing and began to write poetry, "neither better nor worse than the run of its kind."

However, he made up his mind that he wasn't going back for his senior year, and he proceeded to study art at the Art Students League and with Robert Minor. With the grudging blessing of his father but with his father's hard cash, Eilshemius set out for Paris in the fall of 1886. Shortly after he had begun studying there he submitted a painting, *Evening, Milford, Pennsylvania,* to the American National Academy of Design and it was accepted. In 1888 two more of his paintings were accepted by the Academy. Neither of them sold, but it seemed like a promising start.

Although none of his pictures was ever accepted by the Academy again, Eilshemius kept on working. In 1892, made rich by a legacy left him by his father who died in that year, he went to Algeria, stopping off at Spain on the way back. His canvases up to that time had been painted more or less under Minor's influence, but now they began to show the influence of Impressionism while still being distinguished by a "new, personal idiom." Always there was diversity in them, for "Eilshemius had a healthy scorn of repetition."

Eilshemius traveled again—to Europe, to Samoa, and continued his painting. He started writing poetry, too, with rather more facility than inspiration. One critic said, then, of his poetry: "We have searched these volumes faithfully for one line of poetry and if there is such a thing in either of them it has been most artfully concealed." He himself advertised his verse by calling himself "most original—most prolific—most versatile—unique, towering with all the giants of past ages above the workaday world."

In 1909 Eilshemius started a magazine, *The Art Reformer,* a 10-cent pocket monthly, mostly devoted to praising himself. A reporter came up to interview him about it after Eilshemius wrote a letter to his editor saying: "I am perhaps the greatest inventor of the age. . . I am the Da Vinci of modern times." The magazine died very shortly.

In 1914 Eilshemius gave an exhibition of his own works to which nobody came and in which nothing was sold. In 1917 he sent his paintings in to the Society of Independent Artists, and Marcel Duchamp (*Nude Descending a Staircase*) declared that Eilshemius' *Supplication* was one of the two really important paintings in the entire exhibition. From then on Duchamp took an interest in him, tried to get him to meet people and tried to interest people in his work.

When Eilshemius was 57, in 1921, he found himself poor. The rent for his studio was increased, and he had sold no pictures. He "put aside his brushes and paint for good and all." During this period and

LOUIS EILSHEMIUS

later, he spent much of his time writing letters to the New York *Sun,* on art, on the subject of premonition, on Walt Whitman, on bananas, on himself.

In 1920, through the efforts of Duchamp and Katherine Dreier, Eilshemius was given a one-man show by the Société Anonyme. The efforts of these people and of Henry McBride, art critic of the New York *Sun,* finally brought results when in 1926 the Valentine Gallery gave him a one-man show of 31 paintings. The criticism was almost completely adverse, with one critic going so far as to say that the pictures "ranged from something terrible, up through pathetic, to almost good." It was six years before the Valentine Galleries would exhibit his works again.

When the Valentine Galleries did show him again, in 1932, he received a good deal of praise and became something of a fashion. In this year the Whitney Museum showed his *Delaware Water Gap Village* which was bought later by the Metropolitan Museum of Art. In 1934, Eilshemius finally broke into a history. In *Art in America,* edited by Alfred H. Barr Jr., and Holger Cahill, the latter wrote: "Naïve and visionary and romantic in style, Eilshemius has a note of unexpectedness and fantasy which is very delightful. Altogether he is one of the most extraordinary 'singulars' in contemporary American art." From then on frequent Eilshemius exhibitions were held in New York. In April 1940 he was given his first one-man Boston show.

There has always been and probably always will be a good deal of controversy on the importance and effectiveness of Eilshemius' work. It is so varied—there are gentle, uncontroversial water colors; there are fanciful landscapes and romantic ones; there are wild nudes and tender ones. The

EILSHEMIUS, LOUIS—*Continued*

general consensus of opinion seems to be, however, that "there are reminders of Ryder, the Barbizon School and the Impressionists, but, by no means dominated by any one influence, a victorious and very definite Eilshemius emerges." The future will probably judge that "neither the greatest nor the least of his contemporaries, he ranks high among them."

Although dealers have snapped up for a song his lush romantic landscapes, his pictures of Samoa, his moonlit fantasies, his clear sun-lit American scenes, his strange nude nymphs bathing in improbable streams, and have sold them at high prices, Eilshemius until recently was in want. Even now he still lives with his brother Henry in his old brownstone house on East 57th Street in New York. His chair exactly faces the door of his room. "From it he can see down the dark hall of the house to the stairs that bring people to him. Callers come now. They never used to. They come to him, he does not go to them. They climb those stairs, approach along the dark hall, walk through his door and stand before him. They are coming to him. To Eilshemius. A light suddenly smolders in the old anguished eyes."

References

> Art News 37:12 Je 3 '39
> Boston Transcript V p7 Ap 13 '40 il
> Mag Art 32:694-7+ D '39
> N Y World-Telegram p13 F 20 '40 por
> New Yorker 11:24-28 S 14 '35
> Newsweek 14:40+ O 23 '39
> Time 34:58 O 23 '39
> Barr, A. H. Jr., and Cahill, H. Art in America 1939
> Charlot, J. Louis M. Eilshemius *In* Art from the Mayans to Disney p161-7 1939
> Schack, W. And He Sat Among the Ashes 1939
> Who's Who in America
> Who's Who in American Art

EISEN, GUSTAV (ī'zen) Aug 2, 1847—Oct 29, 1940 Archeologist, biologist and author; soon after he came to the United States from Sweden in 1873 did research that led to the growth of California fig industry; succeeded in having the government establish Sequoia Park; made studies of earthworms which attracted attention of Charles Darwin; later his interests turned more and more to archeology; gained fame for researches on the Chalice of Antioch; published many monographs and books on archeology, antique glass, biology, figs and raisins.

References

> American Men of Science
> Who's Who in America

Obituaries

> N Y Herald Tribune p22 O 30 '40 por
> N Y Times p23 O 30 '40 por

ELIOT, GEORGE FIELDING June 22, 1894- Author; lecturer; radio war commentator

Address: b. Columbia Broadcasting System, 485 Madison Ave, New York City; h. 19 E 88th St, New York City

If England has its famed military expert, Captain B. H. Liddell Hart (see sketch this issue), America's equivalent must surely be Major George Fielding Eliot. He was born in Brooklyn, the son of Philip Park and Rena (King) Eliot, but when he was eight his family emigrated to Melbourne, Australia. When the World War broke out, young Eliot had just been graduated from Trinity College, University of Melbourne. He immediately joined the Australian Imperial Force (infantry), where his school cadet corps training won him a second lieutenant's commission. Later he was promoted through the ranks to acting major. He saw four years of fighting in the Dardanelles, Egypt, the Western front, the Battles of 1st Somme, Arras, Passchendaele, Amiens, Hindenburg Line.

After the War Eliot came back to the United States, and here earned his major's title during eight years' service as a reserve officer with the Military Intelligence Reserve (1922-30).

In Kansas City, Eliot became an accountant, a field he had studied before the War. This occupation he must have found less than exciting after his war experiences, and when he picked up a pulp magazine called *War Stories*, he decided he could certainly write as well as its authors. He thereupon typed out an account of one war experience and received $100 for it. Several years later he dropped accounting to concentrate on writing and lecturing. In 1928 he came to New York, and began occasional serious military writing for *The Infantry Journal* and the *United States Naval Institute Proceedings.*

When one of these articles was read with much interest by a captain on a United States battleship at Norfolk, Virginia, Eliot was invited to visit him. On the steamer he met Sara Elaine Hodges, whom he married December 23, 1933. After collaborating, in 1937, with Major R. Ernest Dupuy on his first book, *If War Comes,* Major Eliot's reputation was increased and his skill as a lecturer put him in the higher brackets of authors booked by the important lecture bureaus.

"This book should be required reading for every American," commented Dorothy Thompson (see sketch this issue) of his second book, *The Ramparts We Watch* (1938). It is a serious analysis of "the problems of American national defense" written for the layman in non-technical language by a soldier who is in no sense a jingoist. The critics received it enthusiastically.

GEORGE FIELDING ELIOT

Major Eliot makes a plea for a large navy and for a small but mobile army. Attack by air he considers not a grave danger for us.

So long as our Star-Spangled Banner waves Eliot will have titles for his books, for his recently published one is called *Bombs Bursting in Air* (1939). In it, he regards air power as one of the three revolutionary changes throughout the world's history of warfare—the other two being military discipline and gunpowder. "The true measure of air power," he says, "as a means of waging war lies as yet hidden behind the veil of the future." The book fills a distinct need at the present when jittery Americans, hysterical over the menace of airplanes in war, are asking the War Department for anti-aircraft protection even in towns as far inland as Tucson, Arizona.

On May 17, 1940 Eliot's publishers rushed his latest work—*Strategy Map of Europe*—off the press. Designed by Richard E. Harrison, well-known map artist of *Fortune,* it is valuable for its new picture of Europe's many war fronts.

Major Eliot is an extremely busy man these days. He is military and naval correspondent for the New York *Herald Tribune,* with semi-weekly articles syndicated in 40 newspapers. He broadcasts a war commentary nightly for the Columbia Broadcasting System. He is a regular contributor to *Life*; his articles have also appeared in *Harper's, Foreign Affairs, New Republic, Current History, American Mercury, Saturday Evening Post, Fortune* and other magazines.

He is a member of the United States Infantry Association, Army Ordnance Association, Military Intelligence Reserve Society, the United States Naval Institute, American Military History Foundation, Foreign Policy Association and Institute of Pacific Relations, and is a fellow of the American Geographical Society.

References

New Yorker 15:14 Ja 20 '40
Scrib Mag 105:3 F '39
Time 32:67 N 28 '38 por
Who's Who in America

ELLERMAN, FERDINAND May 13, 1869—Mar 20, 1940 Nationally known astronomer; pioneer in modern solar photography; member of the staff of the Mount Wilson Observatory for 33 years

References

American Men of Science
Who's Who in America

Obituaries

N Y Herald Tribune p24 Mr 21 '40
N Y Times p25 Mr 21 '40

ELLIOT, KATHLEEN MORROW Feb 14, 1897—Mar 3, 1940 Author

Kathleen Morrow Elliot, poet and author of books for children, died in New York City, March 3, 1940. Surviving are her husband, Arthur H. Elliot; a son, Arthur, Jr.; and a daughter, Patricia.

Mrs. Elliot was born in Illinois in 1897, the daughter of the Reverend and Mrs. Winfield Morrow. She was graduated from Wooster College at the age of 19, and three years later married Arthur H. Elliot, an executive of the Standard-Vacuum Oil Company, stationed in the Dutch East Indies. Most of their married life has been spent in the Far East, first in the Straits Settlements, later in Java. During her years in the Orient Mrs. Elliot became noted as

KATHLEEN MORROW ELLIOT

ELLIOT, KATHLEEN MORROW—*Cont.*
a hostess, entertaining almost every important visitor to Java. When her children were old enough to go to schools in the United States, she began to write.

Her poems have appeared in a number of contemporary poetry magazines. Her three books for children, *Riema* (1937); *Soomoon* (1938); and *Jo-Yo's Idea* (1939), all treat of the East India scene and its people, and have received high critical praise.

References
> N Y Herald Tribune p22 Mr 6 '40
> American Women

Obituaries
> Pub W 137:1165 Mr 16 '40

ELLIOTT, HARRIET WISEMAN July 10, 1884- Educator; member of the National Defense Commission
Address: b. Federal Reserve Bldg, Washington, D. C.; h. 316 McIver St, Greensboro, North Carolina

Miss Harriet Elliott, only woman member of President Roosevelt's National Defense Commission, was appointed in May 1940 to represent the "consumers" of this country. She has promised American housewives that food prices will be watched against undue rising and that standards of living will be protected. "Hungry people, ill people are a liability in a defense program," she said. "The President is thinking in terms of a unified nation, of a people mentally and physically prepared to meet the responsibilities which the impact of the world crisis forces upon us." She has warned, however, that at present many millions of Americans are living below the "safety line."

Miss Elliott's job is a big one, but she is optimistic about its success. "We are in a better position today—1940—than we were in 1917. We start with a relatively stable cost of living standard. We start with some unused manpower and surplus commodities—with unusual plant facilities in some fields. We have a better national attitude to assist. All of this combines to make, for the moment, a less critical situation, if we use our available information and ingenuity in an intelligent way."

Without doubt, "agreeable round-faced" Harriet Elliott is well equipped for the task of seeing that prices stay down and living standards up. In 1940 she was elected president of the Social Service Conference, a group significant for its broad interest in all social questions. During the period of the Emergency Relief Administration, she was appointed a member of the State Advisory Commission of the ERA by the Governor of North Carolina. For many years she has been a professor of political science at the University of North Carolina.

HARRIET WISEMAN ELLIOTT

Born in Carbondale, Illinois, Miss Elliott, the daughter of Allan Curtis and Elizabeth Ann (White) Elliott, received her B. A. from Hanover College in 1910 and her M. A. from Columbia University in 1913. Right out of Columbia, she went to the University of North Carolina to teach political science. Her great interest then was woman suffrage, and she organized the first woman's suffrage group in North Carolina. Then, as now, she believed that women should have "responsible freedom."

This is the phrase that guides her now and has been the symbol of her relationship with the students at Woman's College, University of North Carolina, where, since 1935, she has been dean of women as well as professor of political science. When Miss Elliott went there it was a small normal school. Now it is one of the largest colleges in the country. During those 27 years Miss Elliott has built up not only her own political science department, but the whole social régime on the campus. She emphasizes that a broad educational policy means more than training girls in the skills; it means an appreciation of human relationships and of beauty.

As a political science teacher the classes she has taught have always been active discussion groups, with students encouraged to provoke questions at all times. An able speaker, Miss Elliott is constantly in demand by groups not only of women, but of men, for her "searching opinion" of the affairs of the day. In 1935 she toured the country, speaking from coast to coast, as director of an educational program for the women's division of the National Democratic Committee.

Miss Elliott has been associated with the government before her present position. In 1936 she was a member of the Woman's Advisory Committee of the Democratic National Convention. To the White House Conference on

"Children in a Democracy" in 1940 she gave her wholehearted support. And now this dynamic dean of women is glad to serve her country because she is a feminist who believes that "for the first time in history women today are equally important with men, not only in a crisis but in all the affairs of the nation," and because she is a woman who knows that "this is a time when we must have unity in every phase of national life." Although she insists that her major interest is still in education, Miss Elliott says that "when the President says I am needed, I shall be glad to go."

References

Business Week p22+ S 7 '40 por; p25 O 19 '40
Christian Sci Mon Mag p7 O 19 '40 il pors
N Y Herald Tribune p29 Je 9 '40; p19 O 23 '40; XI p8+ O 27 '40 por
N Y Times p1, 15 My 29 '40; p8 Je 9 '40; VII p10+ Jl 21 '40 por; p33 Ag 30 '40
N Y World-Telegram p21 Je 4 '40 por
Scholastic 37:14 O 7 '40 por
Time 36:67-8 N 4 '40 por
American Women

ELLIOTT, MAXINE Feb 5, 1873—Mar 5, 1940 Actress

Long before the term "glamour girl" was coined, Maxine Elliott was the personification of that term. She was one of the most beautiful women the American stage has ever known. And while she was a competent actress, it was her beauty and personal charm that sent reviewers home to write of her in glowing adjectives and superlatives, and audiences to exclaim about her grace.

Daughter of a New England sea captain and brought up in a middle-class household, she was to charm two continents with her personal magnetism, to win fame and fortune and to become the friend of crowned heads. She was born in Rockland, Maine, February 5, 1873, and began life as Jessie Dermot, daughter of Thomas Dermot, a sea captain, and Adelaide (Hall) Dermot. As a young girl she made several trips on her father's sailing vessel and took a long voyage to South America and Spain. She studied at the Notre Dame Academy at Roxbury, Massachusetts, and, becoming interested in school theatricals, decided on a stage career.

At 16 she came to New York to study under Dion Boucicault. He suggested that she change her name to one that would be more striking for stage purposes, and thus "Maxine Elliott" was born. She made her first public stage appearance in 1890 in a minor part, that of Felicia Umfraville, in *The Middleman*, at the American debut of E. S. Willard, a noted English actor. For three years she played small parts in Willard's company, winning a few more important rôles occasionally, and then went

Culver

MAXINE ELLIOTT

to play supporting rôles for the late Rose Coghlan in *Diplomacy, A Woman of No Importance* and *Forget-Me-Not*.

Despite her industry and beauty, she served a five-year apprenticeship before she became at all well-known. It was in 1895, when Augustin Daly engaged her as one of the many who supported his star, Ada C. Rehan, that she began bowling over reviewers and stirring up controversy over whether it was her beauty or her acting ability that attracted attention. An anonymous reviewer describing her in her appearance with Ada Rehan in *A House of Cards* in 1896 said: "A wondrously beautiful woman who can act." The next year, when she appeared in *An American Citizen*, another reviewer was willing to grant her loveliness but to question her skill. "Maxine Elliott," he wrote, "contrary to recent testimony, is no more an actress than before, although her undoubted beauty is quite sufficient again to make one overlook other shortcomings."

However, whatever her acting ability at the time, Daly's strenuous demands on his players was an excellent training school for the future star. Three or four days after a new play was produced, its successor was put into rehearsal, and Maxine Elliott got plenty of experience. She went to London with Daly's company, playing Shakespearean rôles, and gained considerable success. In 1897 she left the Daly entourage and spent a summer in Tim Frawley's stock company in San Francisco in the Columbia Theatre, where later the star's dressing room was to be called the "Maxine Elliott Room."

Early in her stage career the young actress had married George A. McDermott, New York lawyer and marshal to Mayor William

ELLIOTT, MAXINE—*Continued*

R. Grace. She divorced him in 1896, and two years later, on February 20, 1898, married the late Nat C. Goodwin, whom she had met on one of her tours and with whom she was co-starring at the time of her marriage.

For several years she and her husband toured together, appearing in such hits as *Nathan Hale*, *A Gilded Fool* and *The Cowboy and the Lady*, and playing not only in the United States but in England and Australia as well.

When their stage partnership began Nat Goodwin was a veteran of the stage and one of the most popular comedians in the United States. Miss Elliott was comparatively little known. But she soon began stealing the show. When Goodwin presented *The Merchant of Venice* she won further acclaim; she was recognized as a player in her own right, and this was reflected in her contract for $200 a week salary and half the profits over $20,000.

Finally on September 28, 1903 she saw herself billed alone when Clyde Fitch's *Her Own Way* opened. Charles B. Dillingham had elevated her to stardom, and it marked her ultimate professional triumph over her husband. The reviews of *Her Own Way* sounded as if the reviewers had all collaborated. For almost every reviewer, impressed by her beauty and her performance, began his account of the show with the obvious: "Maxine Elliott had *Her Own Way* at the Garrick Theatre last night." Ethel Barrymore, seeing her for the first time, said: "She's positively beautiful. She's the Venus de Milo with arms."

Maxine Elliott was to have "her own way" as a star and a woman for the next 10 glittering years. She had already made successful appearances in London in *When We Were Twenty-One*, and in 1905 she took *Her Own Way* to London. The play was a marked success there, and so was Miss Elliott. She won the praise of King Edward VII, who asked that she be presented to him, and thereafter remained one of her warm admirers.

Mr. Goodwin had in the meantime passed out of her life, obtaining a divorce from her in Reno, Nevada, in 1908. Miss Elliott never married again.

When she returned to the United States she opened her own theatre. The Maxine Elliott, as the first woman manager and owner in New York. She opened in *The Chaperon* on December 30, 1908. From then on she began devoting more time to her theatrical enterprises and less to acting. She spent a great deal of time traveling abroad, scouting for plays she thought Americans would like. In 1911 she returned to England, bought a large estate, Hartsbourne Manor at Bushey, set up residence for herself and the family of her sister Gertrude, wife of Sir Johnston Forbes-Robertson, and embarked on a brilliant career in British society. The Duchess of Sutherland, Lord Rosebury and Lord Curzon were among her close friends. She received international social notice when she was invited to Belvoir Castle, the ancestral seat of the Duke of Rutland, who was said to be so bored by society that for days at a time he would not exchange a dozen words with acquaintances in his clubs.

Her appearance in *Joseph and His Brethren* with Sir Herbert Beerbohm at His Majesty's Theatre in London in 1913 was a sensational success, but it marked the end of her theatrical career, except for desultory appearances between 1918 and 1920.

The War really ended the most glamorous period of her life. She threw herself into war work, and except for professional nurses was said to have been the first woman permitted at the front. She had her automobile transformed into an ambulance, and enlisted as a Red Cross nurse. She outfitted a fleet of barges to carry relief supplies to civilians along the canals of Belgium, devoting her entire income to this project. She scrubbed decks, cooked, did not spare herself. As a reward she received the Belgian Order of the Crown, and also decorations from the French and British governments.

Miss Elliott returned to the United States in 1917 and tried the silent motion pictures for a brief engagement, toured with William Faversham in *Lord and Lady Algy* in 1918 and 1919, and in 1920 appeared for the last time on the American stage as Cordelia in *Trimmed in Scarlet*, at her own theatre.

She refused to return to the theatre later, saying she "wished to grow middle-aged gracefully." In an interview in the United States in 1937 she was quoted as saying: "I never did like playing—never did really. All I care about are my friends and peace." This was looked upon as explaining in a sense the fact that, although she was one of the most important figures of the American theatre, she was never acclaimed as one of its greatest actresses.

After 1925 she spent most of her time on the Riviera. Her estate near Cannes, Villa de l'Horizon, was a show place, and European royalty and the elite of the social world gathered there. She was one of the most popular hostesses on the Riviera. At one dinner party in 1938 her guests were the Duke and Duchess of Windsor, Winston Churchill (see sketch this issue) and David Lloyd George. The Duke of Windsor, the former Edward VIII, leased the Villa de l'Horizon in 1936 when he was planning his first holiday away from England following his accession to the throne. There was a sentimental link between Maxine Elliott and the Duke of Windsor, whose grandfather, Edward VII, had been the actress' friend.

Maxine Elliott won wealth as well as international popularity. Many had worshiped her from afar, like the late Robinson Locke, editor and publisher of The Toledo *Blade,* who compiled a three-volume scrapbook of her career which was bequeathed to the New York Public Library. It is one of the fullest available sources of the biography of the dark-haired statuesque beauty.

As in the case of many beautiful women who start out with glamour as their only asset, there was gossip about Maxine Elliott, and people speculated on whether her wealth was the result of her own earning and investments or whether she profited by market tips from men friends who were "in the know" in Wall Street. Despite whispers Maxine Elliott went calmly about her business untouched by scandal, was deeply affectionate to her family and took good care of them. It was through Maxine's efforts that her sister Gertrude began her stage career in Goodwin's troupe.

She was known as a shrewd business woman and died a wealthy woman. She had owned two valuable residences in New York, and the Villa de l'Horizon was built at a cost of $350,000. Its rear wall was soundproof and its swimming pool was hewn from solid rock. She had in addition a valuable estate in Bushey and was reported to have given her niece, a namesake and a daughter of Sir Johnston Forbes-Robertson, $500,000 as a wedding present in 1924.

One of her hobbies was dressmaking, probably a hangover from the early days of her career when she made her own dresses. She insisted on sewing for the Forbes-Robertson children, who adored their Aunt Maxine. And, strange to say, in her later years she sought comfort more than beauty. While other women dieted Maxine Elliott ate what she liked and weighed over 200 pounds on her last visit to the United States. "I love a quiet life," Maxine Elliott said, but to the end she was a lavish hostess.

She died at her villa near Cannes after a half-year's illness of heart disease.

References

Who's Who in America 1924-25
Who's Who in the Theatre

Obituaries

Manchester Guardian p8 Mr 7 '40
N Y Times p15 Mr 9 '40
Newsweek 15:8 Mr 18 '40 por
Time 35:65 Mr 18 '40
Variety 138:44 Mr 13 '40

ELLIOTT, WILLIAM THOMPSON, REV. Nov 15, 1880—June 20, 1940 Canon of Westminster since 1938; lecturer in theology at Durham University; past president of Rotary for Great Britain and Ireland

WILLIAM THOMPSON ELLIOTT

References

Who's Who

Obituaries

N Y Times p21 Je 21 '40

ELSON, ARTHUR Nov 18, 1873—Feb 23, 1940 Music critic; author

Arthur Elson was born in Boston in 1873. He attended Harvard University from 1892 to 1895 and received a B. S. degree from Massachusetts Institute of Technology in 1897. He was a frequent contributor to newspapers and magazines. Among his books are: *A Critical History of Opera* (1901); *Orchestral Instruments and Their Use* (1902); *Modern Composers of Europe* (1904); and *The Book of Musical Knowledge* (1915). He was unmarried and is survived by his mother.

References

Who's Who Among North American Authors
Who's Who in America

Obituaries

N Y Herald Tribune p33 F 25 '40
N Y Times p39 F 25 '40

ENTERS, ANGNA (anj-nä) April 28, 1907- Mime; painter; author

Address: b. c/o Newhouse Galleries, 15 E 57th St, New York City; h. 113 W 57th St, New York City

"The art of Angna Enters defies analysis," says one critic. "She isn't a monologist because she never says a word on the stage. She isn't exactly a dancer. She can't with accuracy be classified as an actress because she hasn't been in a play for a long time.

ANGNA ENTERS

She doesn't sing either." Angna Enters, who always packs in crowds to her performances, remains the great "What is it?" of the theatre.

This doesn't bother the audiences at all. The people who really worry are the critics who get very learned and technical after they have seen one of her performances. After listening to some of their highbrow dissertations, Angna Enters retorts: "Esthetics of the dance! I leave those to my colleagues. I plan my compositions to be interesting. I'd like to have the audience think of my performance as just a good show."

In *First Person Plural* (1937) Angna Enters describes the trend of her own life and recounts the background and evolution of the figures which compose her repertory. She wrote it partly to give some facts about herself and her compositions, partly because the Civil War in Spain, of which she was a witness, caused her "to realize that art alone, like bread, is not enough for life" and made her want to speak not as an artist but "as a person about persons."

When Angna Enters achieved success in 1927 rumors about her dark past began to circulate. There were reports that she was an Italian aristocrat who had fled from vast Italian estates because of thwarted love. Or some older woman would remark at a matinée: "My dear! My dear! They say she is a former nun! Fancy." Actually there is no mystery. Though she was born in New York, "today, with beer, Angna Enters is one of the things Milwaukee is proud of."

She says she would like to begin *First Person Plural* with a little anecdote about how she began to dance and mime (she pronounces it "meem") at the age of two,

but can offer only a prize which she won when she was four for coloring a newspaper drawing. As a child she studied ballet "for no special reason . . . just to be accomplished," but these studies stopped almost as immediately as her formal education, for Angna Enters' childhood was "harried by poverty."

Her study of painting was limited "to an intermittent elementary school course, some work (chiefly swimming) during an adolescent summer month in a camp, and one unfinished evening semester at the New York Art Students League." The evening course was unfinished "because what I earned by day at commercial lettering in an advertising concern wasn't enough to pay for the course. I had augmented my earnings as a 'free lance,' getting assignments from other advertising offices during my lunch hour, but these additional jobs could be done only after my nightly attendance at the Art Students League. That obliged me to work half the night."

In the intervening time, between job and night course, Angna Enters began working in the studio of Michio Itow, the Japanese dancer. She toured with him, portraying a Japanese dancing girl. In 1924 and 1925 she played a small part in *The Lady Cristalinda*, in which she was a Japanese girl.

She kept on with her painting and it was painting that drew Miss Enters to "mime," as it was her "miming" that brought fresh vision to her painting. "Working directly with myself as a medium instead of with a brush on canvas might solve a lack of approach—just as now the study of painting seems to help me in the study of form in movement." But times were hard and in 1925 she was up against it. She spent time with her art, she did lettering for printers and advertising agencies.

Late in that year she decided to give a recital of her miming. She borrowed $25 for the theatre and the money to print handbills. She mailed the handbills to names picked at random from the telephone book. At her performance on February 26, 1926, to everyone's surprise, there was a fairly good attendance. She cleared expenses and short, vivid sketches. Sometimes she gave another recital, this time together with a singer and a violinist because she didn't have enough numbers to fill up a whole evening. She continued to borrow money and put on shows until suddenly in 1927 she was successful.

Today Angna Enters is a complete one-woman theatre. Quite by herself, without scenery and without dialogue, she gives short, vivid sketches. Sometimes she dances, sometimes she remains quite motionless in a chair or at a table and conveys her characterization by movements of her hands or the expression on her face. The characters she has imagined are realistically commonplace—like the girl practicing the piano; or they are rich and strange—a sultry, majestic Spanish girl of the sixteenth century dancing the slow pavana; or they are humorous—a young woman reversing the strip tease act; or they are socially significant—*Spain Says Salud.*

The dances are built up bit by bit from odds and ends scribbled in black-bound notebooks. These volumes, the size of a high school student's composition book, contain water colors, pencil sketches and disconnected paragraphs. Out of these workbooks come ideas for costumes as well, for Miss Enters does all the cutting and fitting of her stage garments.

Miss Enters has won a reputation for herself, too, as a painter. From 1933 on she has had seven successive New York exhibitions, two of them in conjunction with two Guggenheim Fellowships awarded in 1934 and 1935 and she has had a number of exhibitions in many cities of this country and Europe. One of her paintings, *Spain Says Salud* was bought by the Metropolitan Museum of Art in 1940. Of her art work one critic said: "Taken either as spadework for her miming or as independent creations, her paintings and drawings of archaic Greek and Oriental forms, Spanish bullfighters, imagined figures from history are fresh, economical, expert." She has also written the play, *Love Possessed Juana* (1939), which deals with the inquisition in Spain and has stage settings and music by the author.

No matter what she is doing, Angna Enters works very hard, from 12 to 14 hours a day in her studio, on costumes, on musical arrangements, on details of her tours and on painting. Her tours are mostly one-night stands, the most tiring for an artist, and there was a time when Miss Enters suffered a breakdown because she was trying to do too much. She is a "chic, puckish young woman with bright black eyes and thick black bangs."

References

Am Mag 113:74 F '32
Arts & Dec 44:37 F '36 por
Collier's 98:11+ Ag 1 '36; 99:34 Ap 24 '37 il
Cue p6-7+ D 12 '36
N Y Sun p8 Ja 19 '40 por
Newsweek 8:39 D 26 '36 por
Sat R Lit 17:5+ D 18 '37
Time 31:24+ Ja 3 '38 por
American Women
Enters, A. First Person Plural 1938
Rosenfeld, P. Dance of Angna Enters *In* By Way of Art p209-16 1928
Untermyer, L. From Another World 1939
Who's Who in American Art

ERLANGER, MITCHELL LOUIS (âr'läng-er)   Feb 15, 1857—Aug 30, 1940 Former Justice of the Supreme Court of New York (1907-27); after retirement was appointed for life as official referee of the Supreme Court; brother of noted theatrical producer, Abraham Lincoln Erlanger, who was once the owner of more theatrical properties than any other producer in the world; upon death of brother took over management of theatrical properties

References

Who's Who in America 1930-31
Who's Who in American Jewry

Obituaries

N Y Herald Tribune p10 Ag 31 '40 por
N Y Times p13 Ag 31 '40 por

ERNST, MORRIS LEOPOLD   Aug 23, 1888-   Lawyer
Address: b. 285 Madison Ave, New York City; h. 46 W 11th St, New York City

When Franklin D. Roosevelt was Governor of New York State he called Morris Ernst to Albany and asked him to become a member of the State Banking Board. Ernst accepted. "And now, Morris," said the Governor, "I'd like to ask for one favor. Don't try to free Tom Mooney tomorrow."

Morris Ernst is a lawyer who has helped organize movements to save the Scottsboro boys and who fought Mayor Hague of Jersey City for the CIO when the Mayor expelled or locked up CIO organizers for giving out leaflets. He is also an authority on literary censorship, libel, radio legislation, taxation and finance. He is the attorney for the National Jewelers' Board of Trade, for the Society of American Composers, for the Sauerkraut Workers' Union, for the American Civil Liberties Union, for the Authors' League, the Dramatists' Guild and the Macaroni Workers' Union.

It is probably as a censorship lawyer, however, that he is best-known. For years he has waged an almost continuous fight against Federal, state, local, private and ecclesiastical censorship bodies. In 1927 he gained the right of general sale for Dr. Marie Stopes' *Married Love.* Radclyffe Hall's *The Well of Loneliness*, Schnitzler's *Casanova's Homecoming* and James Joyce's *Ulysses* were put on sale through his court fights. And it is largely due to his own efforts that Morris Ernst was able to say in March 1940: "Now no book published by a regular publisher or reviewed by a regular critic, no book published honestly and without surreption is in any danger of suppression."

When Morris Ernst argues a censorship case, he doesn't use any courtroom tricks. Once in a while, as in the case of *Ulysses*, he uses the sort of argument which states that, since *Ulysses* is the essence of frankness it is also the essence of purity. But mostly he relies on making a public issue of the case. He himself says: "As a good many of my professional associates know, I am not a good office lawyer. We have boys in our office who know more law than I do. As an outside man, however, occasionally I do pretty well."

MORRIS ERNST

When Morris Ernst does his regular routine of business and commercial law for his firm (Greenbaum, Wolff and Ernst) he makes a good deal of money. His cases and his clients are important ones; he has bested such opposing counsels as John W. Davis and the late Samuel Untermyer (see sketch this issue) before the Supreme Court, and has acted as counsel for Maurice Evans (see sketch this issue), Edna Ferber and others. He has to make a good deal of money to be able to take those long layoffs in which he indulges in non-revenue or low-revenue producing pursuits—defending unions, fighting for civil liberties, acting as a member of the State Banking Board.

Ernst does not and never has belonged to the American Bar Association, though he is an active member of the less conservative Lawyers' Guild. He refused to join the American Bar Association because it won't admit Negroes. When the association asked him to become a member, he wrote back asking whether colored attorneys were eligible for membership. In return he received an apology, which he still treasures, which said that the invitation was sent under the assumption that Ernst was white.

Much of the law in which he has been involved and much of what he believes is incorporated in the books and articles which Ernst has written. With Pare Lorentz (see sketch this issue) he wrote *Censored* (1930); with Alexander Lindey he wrote *Hold Your Tongue!* (1932) and *The Censor Marches On* (1939). He also wrote *America's Primer* (1931), which chartered a new order of things and presented several of the fundamentals of the New Deal, and the *Ultimate Power* (1937), a study of the Supreme Court, voted one of the 10 best non-fiction books of 1937 by a jury of distinguished critics. His latest book, published in June 1940, is *Too Big*,

a study of Big Business in this country— coal, steel, insurance, banks, movies—in which Ernst concludes that the "pursuit of size as a symbol of success is ruinous to our society. . . We are developing a race of clerks devoid of initiative, stripped of individuality and barren of imagination."

Ernst started law as a shirt manufacturer. He was born in Uniontown, Alabama, the son of a country general storekeeper, S. Carl Ernst, and Sarah (Bernheim) Ernst. When he was about two, his family moved to New York, where his father made a comfortable living from real estate. Ernst finished Horace Mann High School at 16 and then went to Williams College, from which he was graduated in 1909. After college he started in the shirt business in Brooklyn, making what he called "the world's ugliest shirts"—"nifty numbers" at $3.75 to $4.50 a dozen.

While manufacturing shirts he went to the New York Law School at night. After about a year or so he quit the shirt business and went to work selling furniture in Ludwig Baumann's Brooklyn store, where he rose to be manager. But he got his law degree in 1912 and in 1915 left the store to form the law partnership of Greenbaum, Wolff and Ernst. In his first year of practice Ernst made about one-sixth of what he made in the furniture store, and was probably overpaid at that, he says. "Very quickly I realized the inadequacy of my part-time preparation. I started out to make up for it by exhibitionism and have never recovered."

Very soon after he started practicing law, Ernst was included in a group formed for the discussion of a free employment service, to be run by New York State. Ernst got the job of drafting a bill which the Legislature later adopted. Within a few years newspapers were referring to him as a "labor expert," and as such he was made a member of the United States Shipping Board during the War.

After the War Ernst became involved in a fight for the truck farmers around New York, alleging that the public markets were graft- and racketeer-ridden, and for years he was involved in a number of labor cases. In 1934 he was appointed Mayor La Guardia's (see sketch this issue) personal representative to try to settle the taxi drivers' strike, and he brought about a settlement. He was the champion of the Newspaper Guild and won its biggest case in the Supreme Court. Besides labor, he has particularly championed the causes of the book trade, achieving lower postal rates, fighting censorship, arguing for fair trade practices.

"A small man, broad-shouldered and vital looking, with a keen apperceptive face and an easy manner which can change in a minute to something that just misses being too aggressive," Ernst spends four months of the year at Nantucket, building furniture, garages and houses, and sailing in his boat, *The Episode*. In New York City his cocktail parties are distinguished for the diversity of guests. At any one you might find labor leaders and Morgan partners; fan dancers and leading authors all together. Winter, spring and fall weekends are spent with his wife and three children on their farm in New Jersey. In 1924 he married Margaret Samuels, a teacher in the City and Country School and author of several books on etymology. (His first wife, Susan Leerburger, died in 1922.)

Ernst himself is a general contributor to a number of magazines, and a chronic contributor to *The Nation*. Once, and only once, he wrote a love story, which *Cosmopolitan* bought for $500, "unaware," says Ernst, "that I would have given $500 to be able to say it had been accepted."

References

Lit Digest 117:14 Ap 7 '34 por
N Y Herald Tribune p23 Mr 13 '40
Pub W 130:2305 D 12 '36 por; 137: 1735 My 4 '40
Sat R Lit 21:3-4+ Ja 6 '40
Scrib Mag 101:78+ Ap '37; 104:7-11+ Jl '38 il por
Who's Who in America
Who's Who in American Jewry
Who's Who in Law

ESTIGARRIBIA, JOSE FELIX (ĕs'te-gär-rē'byä hō-sā' fä'lĕks) Feb 21, 1888— Sept 7, 1940 Dictator of Paraguay; killed in airplane crash

From June issue:

Conquering hero of the Chaco War, diplomat, president and dictator is the path that General José Félix Estigarribia's life has followed. The outbreak of hostilities between Paraguay and Bolivia over the Chaco region in 1932 found Estigarribia in command of the first division of infantry in the Chaco and well prepared to take command of the field. When he returned to Asunción in 1935 at the head of his victorious armies, he was hailed as a conquering hero. To honor him the Paraguayan Congress created the rank of general of the army, equivalent to that of marshal, and he was also granted a life pension of 1,000 gold pesos a month. And it seemed only natural that a grateful people further reward a national hero with the post of Minister to the United States, and later elect him President of Paraguay.

José Félix Estigarribia was born in Caraguatay, Paraguay, February 21, 1888, the son of well-to-do parents, Mateo and Casilda (Insaurraldo) de Estigarribia. When he was a child his parents moved to Asunción, and young José Félix received his education there, attending the military college. In the army he was assigned to the infantry. A year later, in 1911, he supplemented his military studies by attending the military college in Chile for two years. On his return to Paraguay he rose rapidly in army rank. In 1923 he was appointed principal of the Military School of Asunción with the

JOSE FELIX ESTIGARRIBIA

rank of major. In 1924 he was sent to L'Ecole Supérieure de Guerre in Paris, France, for a three-year military course. Once more back in Paraguay in 1927, he was promoted to the rank of lieutenant colonel, and appointed deputy chief of staff. Early in 1931 he was named inspector general of the army and in that capacity went to the Chaco to organize the first division of infantry.

When hostilities broke out he was commissioned to organize the defense of the Chaco. He covered himself with glory. After a hard-won victory at Fort Boqueron in 1932 he was advanced to the rank of colonel. His victories in the "green hell" won for him successively the titles of chief of the first army corps, then of a sector of the Chaco, next, of all the Chaco forces, and, finally, of all campaign forces, with the rank of general of division.

There was only one setback in the career of Paraguay's war-hero President. When Colonel Rafael Franco, another Chaco hero, seized the Presidency in a revolution that upset the administration of President Ayala, Estigarribia and Ayala were exiled for a brief period in 1937.

But in 1938 Estigarribia's star was again in the ascent. In March of that year he was appointed Minister to the United States and also represented his country on the governing board of the Pan-American Union. While he was Minister to the United States Estigarribia tried his hand at making peace between Paraguay and Bolivia. A truce had been arranged in 1935, but the efforts of the United States, Argentina, Brazil, Chile, Uruguay and Peru to settle the conflict seemed to be doomed to failure. As late as June 1938 armed incidents were increasing between Bolivian and Paraguayan troops. The tide was

ESTIGARRIBIA, JOSE—*Continued*

turned by Estigarribia. Leaving his post in Washington, Estigarribia conferred with neutral delegates and his own countrymen. As a result of his work common sense prevailed, and in July 1938 Paraguay and Bolivia signed a treaty ending their bloody war in the Chaco swamps. Paraguay got most of the Chaco, but Bolivia got a free port on the Paraguay River.

Estigarribia's election as President in 1939 was unopposed. Estigarribia was not even on the scene; he was in Washington, serving as Minister.

The Paraguayan President is a small, military-mannered man, a bit taciturn. He is 5 feet 6 inches tall, weighs between 130 and 140 pounds and is a man of direct action. He wasted little time after his election in setting himself up as a dictator. In a radio address made February 18, 1940, following a decree he had issued, Estigarribia told the people of Paraguay that the nation faced anarchy and that as soon as orderly government was restored he would call an election of a national assembly to draft a new constitution. The old document, in force since 1870, was out of date, Estigarribia declared. Paraguay, he insisted, must proclaim a new democracy which must be a social as well as an economic one. In setting himself up as a dictator, President Estigarribia put to a public test the popularity he won as a war hero. The new Constitution was signed on July 10, 1940.

Both as Minister and President, Estigarribia has worked for Paraguay's economic advancement through financial and trade agreements with the United States. He wrote to Secretary of State Cordell Hull (see sketch this issue) of the United States just prior to leaving to take up his duties as President of Paraguay: "The peaceful and successful settlement of the boundary dispute between Paraguay and Bolivia which was agreed upon by the two parties with the assistance of six mediatory nations at the Chaco Peace Conference leaves my country free to devote itself to the constructive task of developing its natural resources. Paraguay knows from bitter experience what sacrifices and what diversion of energies from economic and social progress are imposed by war. It turns from the sword to the plowshare with deep satisfaction, and as a result of the freely-expressed choice of the Paraguayan people. I realize, as do my fellow citizens, the magnitude of the task which faces us, but we are determined to succeed and to obtain those benefits of modern civilization which will mean happiness and prosperity to the country."

References

Bul Pan Am Union 72:405 Jl '38 por; 73:469-72 Ag '39 pors
Christian Sci Mon p18 Mr 9 '40; p2 Mr 14 '40; p5 Jl 23 '40
N Y Herald Tribune p2 F 19 '40
Scholastic 33:10 S 17 '38 por
International Who's Who
Who's Who in Latin America

Obituaries

N Y Herald Tribune p1 S 8 '40 por
N Y Times p28 S 8 '40 por
Newsweek 16:8 S 16 '40

EVANS, MAURICE June 3, 1901- Actor; manager

Address: St. James Theatre, New York City

In 1935, when Maurice Evans, without any preliminary fanfare, sailed quietly from London to play Romeo with Katharine Cornell, nobody could possibly have prophesied that within the brief space of five years he would climb to a position of commanding importance in the American theatre. Yet Mr. Evans has done this, single-handed. He has become known to Times Square and to Texas, to Boston and to Ohio. "If his career should close tomorrow," says one theatre expert, "Maurice Evans would have earned a chapter for himself in any subsequent history of the American theatre."

Maurice Evans has been acting almost since he can remember. He was born on June 3, 1901, the son of a Justice of the Peace in Dorset, England. His father, who was "something of a local light," used to dramatize for amateur performances the novels of another local light, Thomas Hardy. Maurice made his debut as a shepherd lad in *Far From the Madding Crowd* when he was seven. Later he held the post of musical director for another of these performances. This meant that he played the pianola between acts.

He attended the Grocer's Company School and spent much of his time appearing as a boy singer and amateur actor. During the War, he says, he "would go around to the war hospitals and torture the poor wounded soldiers" with his singing. After his voice broke he continued his musical career as assistant cashier at Chappell's music publishing house, Bond Street, London. Mr. Evans says that he wasn't much good at Chappell's because he was very bad at figures. While pretending in the daytime to be a cashier he appeared regularly with an amateur company every night. "It was down in a slum, but I went there every evening and played everything." It was while he was playing Saint Francis of Assisi in an amateur offering that he got his first chance. The owner of the Cambridge Festival Theatre saw him and liked him and insisted that he give up commercial life and act professionally at Cambridge. His first professional appearance was on November 26, 1926 as Orestes in *The Orestia* of Aeschylus. He stayed in Cambridge for one season, acting everything from Greek tragedy to Sweeney Todd, the "Demon Barber of Fleet Street," in which, because of a defective trap slide, he suffered a case of near concussion.

Maurice Evans' first London appearance was on August 25, 1927 in *The One-Eyed Herring,* in which he portrayed a policeman who arrived at an opportune moment with the authority of the law and three lines of dialogue. He had a lot of jobs after that, none very good, until what he calls "his first burst on the London public" came in John Van Druten's *Diversion.* He was a success in a number of plays and a tremendous success as Second Lieutenant Raleigh in *Journey's End* (January 1929).

After *Journey's End,* Maurice Evans was one of London's leading actors. In 1929 he also went into pictures and was seen in *White Cargo, By-Pass to Happiness, Wedding Rehearsal* and others. But while he was making a name for himself in the London theatre and in the films, he established and carried on the "Nine to Six Cleaners" in Bloomsbury, one of the first cleaning and dyeing places in London where customers could get service within a day. "He was deluged with dirty clothes in the daytime and applause at night and was pleased with both."

"Probably the most important move in his life" came when Dame May Whitty, with whom he was playing in *The Voysey Inheritance,* persuaded him to join the "Old Vic" company, for the same reason that Charles Laughton and John Gielgud had joined it—to study the classics. In the one year that he was there, from 1934 to 1935, he played Octavius Caesar in *Antony and Cleopatra;* Benedick in *Much Ado About Nothing;* Petruchio in the *Taming of the Shrew;* Iago in *Othello;* Richard II; and Hamlet, as well as rôles in three or four Shaw plays and the title rôle of a Greek drama.

At a party in London one night he was introduced to a man named Guthrie McClintic. McClintic had been searching for a Romeo from Broadway to Hollywood and back and thence to London, where he saw Maurice Evans in *Hamlet.* Immediately upon introduction, McClintic asked Evans: "How would you like to go to the United States and play Romeo with Mrs. McClintic?" Evans dodged the answer and rushed a friend off to a corner to ask him: "Who is this Mrs. McClintic?" When he found out that it was Katharine Cornell, he said he'd be delighted.

He acted Romeo with Katharine Cornell on tour throughout the fall of 1935 and made his first New York appearance in it on December 23, 1935. He was a success, even though he confesses that he really doesn't care much for Romeo. "He is disagreeable, really," Evans insists. "He falls in and out of love at the beginning of the play in very fickle fashion; he is directly responsible for the killing of his friend, Mercutio; he sobs like a child in the Friar's cell; he leaves the newly-wedded Juliet to face the consequences alone; in fact, he was not even

MAURICE EVANS

permitted to propose to her—she herself did the proposing."

While Evans was playing Romeo with Katharine Cornell, she wrote Shaw (who always likes to be consulted) asking who should play the Dauphin in his *St. Joan,* which she was planning to put on next. Shaw wired back: "If you can find Maurice Evans, engage him." She did. That Maurice could play the Dauphin, "a richly satiric portrait," right after Romeo is proof of his astonishing versatility. According to one critic, he conveys much of the differences between characters through a flexible voice of variable range and quality. For Romeo it is "rich, full and steady," for the Dauphin it rises into falsetto and has a sharp edge. According to some critics, it is "his best assct."

As Napoleon in *St. Helena* in 1937, Evans gave proof of "how remarkable is his talent." But *St. Helena* was a failure. Because this play, Evans' first solo effort in America, had failed and because there was a lot of Shakespeare on the stage that year, first-night audiences looked forward with a good deal of doubt to Evans' production of *King Richard II* in February 1937. "But if the first curtain had risen on more doubt than certainty, the final curtain brought unanimous yells of enthusiasm that proclaimed one of the most startling triumphs in years."

It is said that *Richard II* had been made possible by a still anonymous Evans fan who handed him a check for $25,000 at the Gotham bar one afternoon.

In November 1937 Maurice Evans appeared as Falstaff in *Henry IV, Part I.* "In Evans' shrewd and comprehending hands Falstaff lurched over the footlights not only for the last, true ounce of his classic self, but with an amiable clarity and beaming self-criticism that many hams who

EVANS, MAURICE—*Continued*

previously have battened on him have denied him."

"In the entire history of the English-speaking stage since 1600," says Clayton Hamilton, "I can find no record of any other actor who having achieved success as Falstaff, was also willing to attempt the part of Hamlet." Maurice Evans not only attempted the part of Hamlet; he attempted it in an uncut version in October 1938. Of this version, which started at 5:30 in the afternoon, most critics are agreed that the spectators "receive not only a heightened and intensified emotional impression of the play but a sense of its logical structure and motivation which none of the condensed versions has achieved."

The critics are not agreed, however, on Evans' interpretation of the melancholy Prince of Denmark. Evans himself said: "I wanted to produce a *Hamlet* which was a play and not a study of dyspepsia." John Mason Brown thinks he succeeded splendidly: "Unlike most recent Hamlets, Mr. Evans' is not a neurotic princeling with a pale visage who strikes despairing poses under spotlights. He is the first entirely masculine Hamlet of our time." But by others, Evans' Hamlet is called a work of "bold showmanship rather than profound interpretation": it is said to "shed no light on Hamlet himself, to add no cubit to his stature." *Time* says Evans makes Hamlet into "more of a Great Dane than a melancholy one."

In October 1940 Mr. Evans and Helen Hayes opened in Boston in *Twelfth Night*, preparatory to bringing it to New York. He was commended for having found "something that seems to be new for the part in a slight cockney accent" although "he has skillfully followed the tradition, with richly varied means, to emphasize the humorous connotations of the dilemma."

Maurice Evans, who lectured on Shakespeare during the fall of 1940 for the British War Relief Fund, has enjoyed producing and acting in the United States—"it's more alive," he says. And he has been commended by George Jean Nathan for his attitude towards America. "He's giving the American theater the doggone best that's in him; he shows frankly that he is doggone tickled to death that the American theatre likes him; and we gladly give him back what he doggone well deserves."

When you meet Maurice Evans minus the blond wig of Richard or the pot-belly of Falstaff, "you discover a young man who might easily be a rather firmly-set businessman with a flair for wearing a brown and white checkered jacket with dark trousers. His black-brown hair is close-cut and he has a neat set of features, including a good forehead and chin which balance nicely. He loves to sail his boat, he likes to swim, to play golf and to eat heavy meals before performing. And he loves his dog Hamish. Hamish hates mice and the last time Evans called London to talk to his family—he's

unmarried—they held Hamish up to the telephone. Evans made a noise like a mouse with a file and Hamish said "woof."

In everything he does, Evans is clipped and briskly efficient. "When he found out he was really going to produce *Richard II*, he put a telephone call through to London to Margaret Webster (see sketch this issue) to arrange her coming over to direct it. . . As he snapped out one item after the other—when, and on what boat she was to sail, what the designer was to do, and a dozen and one other things—Miss Webster could only cling to the phone in silent prayer that she'd remember each crackling detail. Abruptly he stopped. 'We've half a minute left,' he said crisply. 'How's the King?'"

References

Collier's 100:55-6 O 23 '37 por
New Repub 96:361-2 N 2 '38
N Y Herald Tribune VI p5 Mr 24 '40
N Y World-Telegram p8 Ap 13 '40
Newsweek 13:30 F 13 '39 por
Theatre Arts 24:86-8 F '40
Time 32:53+ O 24 '38 por; 35:53-4 Ap 22 '40 por

Brown, J. M. Maurice Evans as Richard II *In* Two on the Aisle p24-8 1938
Who's Who in America
Who's Who in the Theatre

EVES, REGINALD GRENVILLE 1876-
English portrait painter
Address: 149 Adelaide Rd, London, N. W. 3, England

After fighting had been going on for two years in the First World War the British decided to appoint a number of official artists to record scenes on the various battle fronts and at sea. Sir Muirhead Bone was the first and the greatest of these, but there were a number of other fine painters similarly occupied, and their works are now to be seen in the Imperial War Museum, London. This time the official artists were appointed a few weeks after war had begun. The best-known among them is Reginald Eves, and since he is a portrait painter his chief task will probably be to put on canvas the features of generals, admirals and statesmen. That he is an excellent choice is proved by his existing portraits of Earl Jellicoe, Earl Beatty, Sir Charles Townshend and other military figures.

Though Eves is a full-fledged member of the Royal Academy he is not like the popular conception of an Academician either in his appearance or in his painting. Typical of the man is his conversation with a reporter who called to ask him how his portrait of Sir Giles Scott was painted. "How did I paint him?" Eves replied. "Well, I took a brush and I took some paint and I took a canvas, and he came half a dozen times and I painted him." Said the reporter, "That's not what I meant; I mean, in what clothes did you paint him?" Eves thought.

"I can't remember . . . wait a moment; let me think. Yes, I remember; he was wearing a medal!"

Nor is he much interested in money. When acting as visiting teacher at an art school (which he does from time to time) he is quite capable of dashing off a fine drawing to illustrate some point and leaving it, endowed with obvious commercial value, as a gift to the student concerned. He is said to be "no businessman," and leaves financial matters in the hands of a brother who carefully watches the painter's best interests.

As for his work, it is "academic" only in the sense that it is correctly drawn and does not go in for distortion. His strong, breezy handling of paint, his keen, penetrative sense of character and his mastery of color combine to make him a portraitist second only to Augustus John. And over and above this better-known work are his water colors, big drawings comparable in size to those of the late George Ennis, but not otherwise similar; for where Ennis handled his brush with a Sargent-like largeness and dash, Eves almost dissolves his subject in color and light, producing ethereal poems which place him among the first half-dozen water-colorists of England.

He was born in London, the son of the late W. H. Eves, Justice of the Peace, and began to draw and paint as soon as he could write. He was using water colors at the age of 10 and started on oils soon afterward. He attended University College School, Hampstead, London, but left in 1891 at the comparatively early age of 16, after winning an award called the Trevellyan Goodall Scholarship which would maintain him through a course at the Slade School (the art department of University College, London).

While at college Eves won another award, the Slade Scholarship, and so was able to complete his course, winning his diploma in 1894. His parents—like most parents of would-be artists, when there is no family fortune in the offing—objected to his taking up painting as a career; but his father went so far as to grant him a small allowance, and on this he lived for five years on a farm at Holwick, in Yorkshire, concentrating on painting animals and landscapes.

It was the Royal Academy that began Eves' real career by accepting a picture called *Waiting* in 1899 and hanging it "on the line" (that is, at eye-level)—an unusual honor for a newcomer. This made him decide to try his fortunes in London, and when he set up a studio there in Fitzroy Street, where many of the younger and poorer artists gather, he was lucky enough to pick up three portrait jobs almost at once. He painted with energy and en-

thusiasm, studied the works of the past at the National Gallery and at the British Museum, and in 1900 moved out to the more prosperous artistic quarter of St. John's Wood, two miles north of the Marble Arch. In 1902 he exhibited at the academy a portrait of Miss Bertha Sybil Papillon, his fiancée. Two portrait commissions at $500 each the same year made him feel more financially secure, and in 1903 he married. The couple now have one son.

Since that time Eves' career as a portrait painter has shown steady progress. He has exhibited regularly at the Royal Academy, of which he was made Associate in 1933 and full Academician in 1939. The Paris Salon has also honored him, granting him a silver medal in 1924 for *Sir Charles Townshend* and a gold medal in 1926 for *Sir Acton Blake*. He is a member of the Royal Society of Portrait Painters and the Royal Institute of Oil Painters, and in 1933 was elected an honorary member of the Royal Institute of Painters in Water Colors. His list of distinguished sitters is extensive. Royal patrons have included the ex-Queen of Spain, Princess Beatrice and Lord Leopold Mountbatten; politics have brought him Earl Baldwin; from legal circles he has painted the famous judge Lord Darling; from the services Lord Jellicoe and Lord Beatty; from literature Thomas Hardy and Max Beerbohm; from the stage Lady Diana Manners and Leslie Howard. He is represented in the Tate Gallery, the National Portrait Gallery, the Luxembourg, and the National Gallery of Australia.

Eves lives in Hampstead, London, a suburb which is the residence of many other British writers, actors and artists.

References

Artist D '33
Royal Inst Brit Arch J s3 43:14-15 N 9 '35 il
Who's Who
Who's Who in Art

EYDE, SAMUEL (ā'dē') Oct 29, 1866— June 21, 1940 Norwegian chemist; founder of the Norwegian chemical industry; noted for his extraction of nitrogen from air; Norwegian Minister to Warsaw from 1920 to 1923; one of the first industrialists to establish modern housing for industrial workers

Obituaries

N Y Herald Tribune p12 Je 22 '40
N Y Times p15 Je 22 '40

FAIRBANKS, DOUGLAS May 23, 1883 —Dec 12, 1939 Film actor

Douglas Fairbanks was the son of H. Charles Ulman, a New York lawyer and Shakespearean scholar who went West to

DOUGLAS FAIRBANKS

Museum of the City of New York

WILLIAM FAVERSHAM

look after mining interests. Shortly after Douglas' birth, in Denver, Colorado, his mother was divorced and resumed the use of the name of her first husband, John Fairbanks. Young Fairbanks attended the Colorado School of Mines, spent five months as a special student at Harvard, and then struck out for the stage, working up from Richmond, Virginia, to Broadway. After a dull stretch in a Wall Street office and a little tramping as a hardware salesman he landed some rôles on Broadway again, and came eventually into his fabulous career on the screen.

Fairbanks was thrice married: in 1907 to Beth Sully, an actress, the mother of Douglas Fairbanks Jr.; two years after his divorce from her, to Mary Pickford (1920); and a year after his second divorce (1935), to Lady Ashley, Sylvia Hawkes of stage fame.

References
Am Mag 84:33 Je '17; 94:36 Ag '22
Everybody's Mag 35:729 D '16
Sunset 61:38 O '28
Who's Who in America 1938-39

Obituaries
N Y Herald Tribune p18 D 13 '39
N Y Times p26, 30 D 13 '39; p17 D 16 '39; IX p7 D 17 '39
Newsweek 14:25 D 25 '39 por
Time 34:30 D 25 '39; 35:52 Mr 11 '40
Variety D 13 '39

FAVERSHAM, WILLIAM (făv'ẽr-shăm)
Feb 12, 1868—Apr 7, 1940 Actor; matinee idol; popular for 20 years; famed for rôle in *The Squaw Man*

References
Who's Who in the Theatre

Obituaries
N Y Herald Tribune p11 Ap 8 '40 por
Variety 138:43 Ap 10 '40

FEDOROVA, NINA (fĕd-or-ō'vä nē'na or fyo'dō-rō-vä) Mar 7, 1895- Author
Address: h. 1848 Moss St, Eugene, Oregon

One of the novels to attract special interest in the fall of 1940 was *The Family* by Nina Fedorova, which won the *Atlantic Monthly* prize of $10,000 for its surprised author. An extremely successful first novel, it has drawn consistently favorable reviews from the critics, one of whom commented that "*The Family* is written in the tradition of the great Russian novelists; it may, indeed, be rated as the best Russian novel that has emerged in the last two decades. Neither Tolstoi nor Dostoievski would be loath to give a smile of brotherhood to Nina Fedorova. . . Out of a welter of suffering, imprisonment, exile, poverty and incredible hardship, she has fashioned a simple tale of essential goodness and compassion."

Not all the critics are ready to agree that Nina Fedorova is ready to receive the mantle of greatness right off the shoulders of Tolstoi and Dostoievski. Lewis Gannett of the New York *Herald Tribune* sees her rather as a compound of Chekhov, Pearl Buck and Alice Hegan Rice, while Charles Poore of the New York *Times* called the book halfway between *Grand Hotel* and *Mrs. Wiggs of the Cabbage Patch*. There seems to be no doubt, however, that Nina Fedorova has written an entertaining and excellent book, a story of human sorrow but alive with both humor and gaiety.

Nina Fedorova's book deals with the story of a White Russian family, eking out its existence among thousands of other refugees by running a boarding house in the British Concession of Tientsin. The family consists of "a granny, a mother, a daughter and two nephews," and their story is closely interwoven with the fantastic tales of all the transients who make a brief stay at the shabby boarding house. Yet somehow this pageantry of the defeated—including an Englishwoman of means regrettably addicted to the bottle, a Russian scientist once internationally known, a Bessarabian fortune teller—is not a gloomy spectacle. On the contrary, the whole book is permeated by a sort of innocent merriment and joy of living; tragedy and heartbreak alternate with sudden disconcerting flashes of humor, so that the book becomes a "sunlit parable of this world in which almost everyone is in some sense a refugee." And "The Family" is what gives the sense of reality to the crumbling and illogical world in which we live.

The novel has a distinct ring of authenticity—the incidental characters, the customs, the local color of the war-torn Tientsin (the story takes place in 1937) are sketched with confidence and deftness that betoken personal knowledge rather than research. Until 1938 Nina Fedorova (in private life Mrs. Antonina Riasanovsky) had lived in Harbin as one of the ever-present colony of the White Russian refugees. She claims that her life has been rather ordinary —but her attitude in that respect is reminiscent of the characters in her novel, with their capacity for taking in their stride the unusual and disturbing things that happen to them.

The daughter of Fedor Dimitrievitch Podgorinov, she was born in Poltava, a small South Russian town of historical importance: Peter the Great had routed the Swedes there. Her life, until the Revolution, pursued the smooth, even tenor of the pre-revolutionary middle-class existence. She went to the local Gymnasia—high school. Afterward she attended the University of Petrograd—now Leningrad—for three and one-half years, studying philology and history. The great storm that was the Revolution swept her, together with many other people of her station in life, eastward and over the Russian border. She migrated across Siberia into Manchuria and settled in Harbin.

In Harbin Nina Fedorova taught literature, history, psychology and logic in a high school and at the same time attended courses at the Y. M. C. A. college. In 1923 she married a Russian exile, Valentine A. Riasanovsky, a brilliant professor of law. The Japanese invasion of Manchuria drove the Riasanovskys out of Harbin and to Tientsin, where the author of *The Family* helped to balance the family budget by writing for the English-language papers.

The War, however, pursued them to Tientsin, and in 1938 they decided to come to

NINA FEDOROVA

the United States and settle in Eugene, Oregon. The selection of the town seems to have been based on a typically Russian feeling for family. While poring over maps and travel books in search of a place to settle, Nina Fedorova's eye was arrested by the name of her present residence because her sister's name is Eugenia. An omen! Accordingly, to Eugene the Riasanovskys went. They have since lived there with their two sons, Nicholas and Alexander, and are now in the process of becoming American citizens.

The author bears a marked resemblance to some of the nicer characters in her book; her face, with its typically Russian high cheekbones, is intelligent, sensitive and humorous. Until June, when her first novel, submitted at the last minute, won the *Atlantic Monthly* prize for 1940, she had been living the simple and modest life of a small-town housewife with her husband and their two young sons, one of whom is studying at the University of Oregon. For months before she won the prize, her happiness was darkly clouded by the illness of her husband—"I spent three months with him actually living in the hospital," she says, "while the boys imitated Robinson Crusoe at home." Now, she writes, he is "firmly on the way to a complete recovery." And her prize money has helped pay the bills, as it has paid for a new house, called, in honor of its source, "Atlantic Laurels." Nina Fedorova admits to being a little old-fashioned: she does not smoke or drink or even dance, she confessed on her arrival in Boston to collect the prize from her publishers, The Atlantic Monthly Press and Little, Brown & Company. "I like classic literature and music. I do not follow fashion closely."

FEDOROVA, NINA—*Continued*

Nina Fedorova says about her life: "A considerable part of it has been spent in moving from place to place (Europe, Asia, America), and a great amount of my energy in different kinds of short-lived activities connected with the needs of the moment and the place... Now I am developing a taste for peace and solitude."

She has no time for many hobbies. If she had she would like to collect old porcelain teacups. Also, "if given another life," she would devote it to astronomy. Her great passions are reading and symphonic music. She would like to spend the rest of her life "living in a very small town, seeing mountains from my windows, studying Italian and reading Dante and Petrarch in the original." Eugene, Oregon seems to have been made to order for her and her family.

References

Boston Transcript p3 S 21 '40
N Y Herald Tribune Books p1 S 22 '40 por
N Y Times Book R p4 S 22 '40
Pub W 138:33 Jl 6 '40 por
Sat R Lit 22:15 Jl 6 '40

FENIMORE-COOPER, SUSAN DE LANCEY 1857—Feb 25, 1940 Head of girls' school; last surviving grandchild of James Fenimore Cooper

Obituaries

N Y World-Telegram p10 F 26 '40

FERRIS, HARRY BURR May 21, 1865—Oct 12, 1940 Professor of anatomy at Yale School of Medicine; after graduation from the Yale School of Medicine became instructor there in 1891 and rose quickly to full professor and chairman of the department of anatomy in 1895; professor emeritus since 1933; author of several scientific books

References

American Men of Science
Who's Who in America
Who's Who in American Education

Obituaries

N Y Herald Tribune p38 O 13 '40 por
N Y Times p49 O 13 '40 por

FEW, WILLIAM PRESTON Dec 29, 1867—Oct 16, 1940 President of Duke University; taught English at Trinity College, Durham, North Carolina from 1896 to 1910, when he became president of the college; was instrumental in influencing the late James B. Duke to establish a trust fund for the creation of Duke University, which now includes Trinity College; served as president of Duke from 1924 until his death; well-known as a Shakespearean scholar

Morton-Van Dyke

WILLIAM PRESTON FEW

References

Leaders in Education 1932
Who's Who in America

Obituaries

N Y Herald Tribune p28 O 17 '40 por
N Y Times p25 O 17 '40 por

FINCH, FLORA 1869—Jan 4, 1940 Pioneer film comedienne

Obituaries

Newsweek 15:49 Ja 15 '40 por
Time 35:60 Ja 15 '40 por
Variety 138:54 Ja 10 '40

FINKELSTEIN, LOUIS, RABBI June 14, 1895- Professor and president of the Jewish Theological Seminary of America

Address: b. 3080 Broadway, New York City; h. 612 W 112th St, New York City

In September 1940 an "august collection of Nobel Prize scientists, college professors and clergymen of all faiths" met in a Conference on Science, Philosophy and Religion, called to find unifying principles strong enough to meet the challenge of totalitarianism. Dr. Louis Finkelstein, president of the Jewish Theological Seminary and one of the founding members of the Conference, opened its first meeting and answered the humanist arguments of Dr. Albert Einstein. He pointed out that "a natural scientist has a great responsibility when speaking in the field of philosophy and religion; he should realize that he must speak with as much reserve in these fields as he habitually does in his own field of natural science." With differences of this sort cropping up time and again, the participants admitted that their search for unity was a hard one, but they intended to try for it again in 1941 and 1942.

At this conference tall, lean, bearded Dr. Finkelstein, chosen chairman of the executive committee, was a prominent figure. He has been a prominent figure in intellectual and religious life for many years. Since 1920 he has taught at the Jewish Theological Seminary of America; from 1934 to 1937 he was assistant to the Seminary's president, in 1937 its provost, and he is, today, its president. The Jewish Theological Seminary, established in 1902 "for the perpetuation of the tenets of the Jewish religion, the cultivation of Hebrew literature, the pursuit of Biblical and archeological research, the advancement of Jewish scholarship, the establishment of a library and the formal education and training of Jewish rabbis and teachers," ordains rabbis and confers academic degrees. It also conducts the Institute of Interdenominational Studies "to enable ministers of all faiths to study under the guidance of eminent theologians of the various denominations." In the session of 1940 to 1941 Dr. Finkelstein is giving a course, together with Professor Robert L. Calhoun of Yale University, entitled "Two Ancient Philosophers and the Problems of the Present Day."

At the Seminary Rabbi Finkelstein is both president and Solomon Schechter professor of theology: his duties are both executive and professorial. An outstanding Jewish scholar, literature, philosophy and theology have been his interests all his life. He was born in Cincinnati, Ohio, the son of Rabbi Simon and Hannah (Brager) Finkelstein. He received his B. A. from the College of the City of New York in 1915 and his Ph. D. from Columbia University in 1918.

After studying at the Jewish Theological Seminary in New York for a year he became the Rabbi of the Congregational Kehilath Israel in New York City, a position he held until 1931. Meanwhile, in 1920, he had become a member of the Seminary's faculty and in 1921 received the Abraham Berliner Award for research in Jewish history. Two years later he was awarded the *Hattarat Horash,* the highest form of rabbinical ordination, by the seminary. His books began to appear: in 1924 *Jewish Self-Government in the Middle Ages;* in 1929 *The Pharisees, Their Origin and Their Philosophy;* in 1938 *The Pharisees: the Sociological Background of Their Faith.*

By 1931, when he left his rabbinical post to teach full time at the Jewish Seminary, Dr. Finkelstein was acknowledged to be one of the greatest living Jewish scholars. After teaching Talmud and lecturing in theology, in that year he became Solomon Schechter professor of theology. Others of his books were published—perhaps the one best-known to laymen is *Akiba—Scholar, Saint and Martyr* (1936)—and articles by him appeared in the *Journal of Biblical Literature,* the *Harvard Theological Review,* the *Jewish*

RABBI LOUIS FINKELSTEIN

Quarterly Review and other publications, both American and foreign.

Dr. Finkelstein is known as a leader in Jewish rabbinical life as well as a scholar. From 1928 to 1930 he was president of the Rabbinical Assembly of America. In 1932 he became a member of the executive committee of the United Synagogues of America, a position he held for seven years; from 1932 to 1934 he was on the Hillel Foundation Commission; and in 1940 he is a delegate to the Synagogue Council of America, a member of the executive committee of the American Jewish Joint Distribution Committee and of the publication committee of the Jewish Publication Society of America, honorary vice-president of the United Palestine Appeal and a member of the executive committee of the American Jewish Committee.

Dr. Finkelstein is well-known outside Jewish circles. In 1937 he lectured at Johns Hopkins University; in 1939 at Oberlin College; and in 1940 was Carew lecturer at the Hartford Theological Seminary Foundation.

Dr. Finkelstein was married in 1922 to Carmel Bentwich. They have three children, Hadassah Nita, Ezra Michael and Faith.

References

Newsweek 16:53-4 S 23 '40

Who's Who in America

Who's Who in American Jewry

FINLEY, JOHN HUSTON Oct 19, 1863 —Mar 7, 1940 Editor; educator; philanthropist

Dr. John H. Finley, editor emeritus of the New York *Times,* former president of the College of the City of New York and

FINLEY, JOHN—*Continued*
former New York State Commissioner of
Education, died March 7, 1940. He was 76
years old. Throughout his long career Dr.
Finley held many journalistic and professorial positions, was also active in civic
and philanthropic work and was the author
of several books. His recent positions and
offices held include: vice-president of the
National Institute of Arts and Letters and
the National Institute of Social Sciences;
president of the American Social Science
Association, the National Dante Committee,
the National Recreation Association, the
National Child Welfare Association and the
New York Adult Education Council; director of the Hall of Fame of New York
University; national chairman of the Phi
Beta Kappa campaign for intellectual freedom; and vice-chairman of the Near East
Relief. He served a number of years as
trustee of the New York Public Library,
and in 1939 was made honorary member of
the American Library Association.

Like several other educators, Dr. Finley
rose from farm boy to college president.
But his record is unusual in that he did not
content himself with a college presidency,
but continued his work in various fields,
taking an active part in human affairs at
an age when most men have long since
retired. When he became editor in chief
of the New York *Times* at the age of
73, he came to his office daily at nine and
put in his full quota of editorial and
routine work.

John Huston Finley was born on a farm
near Grand Ridge, Illinois, on October 19,
1863, of solid Scotch ancestry, the son of
James Gibson Finley and Lydia Margaret
(McCombs) Finley. He passed his boyhood on the farm, where he plowed, hoed
and split rails. In his spare time he learned
the printer's trade. He paid his tuition at
Knox College by running a job-printing
office and reading proof for one of his professors. He was graduated in 1887 and for
two years was a student at Johns Hopkins
University, taking courses in politics, economics and history to prepare himself for
work in the field of journalism. He assisted
in the editing of economics publications while
there, working with Dr. Richard T. Ely.

In 1892 he returned to Illinois and became
president of Knox College, his alma mater.
He was then 28 and the youngest college
president in the country. After serving as
president for seven years, he returned to
the East to be editor of *Harper's Weekly*.
He planned and helped found *World's Work*,
intending to stay with the publication; but
in 1900 was offered the newly established
chair of politics at Princeton. His methods
of teaching there made the science of politics
a living thing to his students.

After three years, Dr. Finley was asked
to take over the presidency of the College
of the City of New York. For 10 years
he maintained high standards of scholarship and efficiency at the college: under

his direction the institution grew, and educational plans were forwarded. In 1913 he
resigned to become Commissioner of Education of the State of New York, emphasizing the value of physical training during
his régime. He studied his job thoroughly,
often walking throughout the State incognito,
visiting the country schools to learn at
firsthand what educational conditions were
like.

When the United States entered the
First World War Dr. Finley happened to be
in France on a special mission to the schools
of that country. He offered his services to
General Pershing and carried out his war
work as head of the Red Cross Commission
to Palestine and the Near East in 1918 and
1919. It was work to his liking, for he could
take long walks in the Holy Land, the
country that had always fascinated him.

In 1921 Dr. Finley was appointed to the
position of associate editor on the New York
Times; in 1937, after the death of his predecessor, Rollo Ogden, he became editor in
chief. But several months later he was
stricken with a severe illness which took
heavy toll of his health, and on November 16,
1938 Dr. Finley took the title of editor
emeritus, heartily approving the appointment
of Charles Merz as his successor in charge
of the editorial page of the *Times*. Among
his other manifold activities Dr. Finley was
Harvard exchange lecturer at the Sorbonne,
Paris, in 1910 and 1911, in which connection
he wrote two books on the French and
French education; he was lecturer on the
Watson Foundation, University of Edinburgh, 1929 and on the Earl Foundation,
Pacific School of Religion, 1931.

In 1935 he went to Scotland, representing
the six American Carnegie trusts at the
Andrew Carnegie centenary observances.
He has received various honors in America,
including a bronze bust from City College,
New York, on his seventieth birthday; and
he has been the recipient of innumerable
decorations from foreign countries, including
the Légion d'Honneur of France and Commander of the Order of the White Rose
of Finland. He has been a director of the
English Speaking Union since 1923, and of
the Russell Sage Foundations of Knox and
Berea Colleges.

Surviving Dr. Finley are his wife, the
former Martha Ford Boyden, of Sheffield,
Illinois, whom he married in 1892; two
sons, Dr. John H. Finley Jr., of Cambridge,
Massachusetts, associate professor of the
classics at Harvard, and Robert L. Finley,
of New York City; and a daughter, Mrs.
William H. Kiser Jr., of Atlanta, Georgia.

Besides his journalistic and academic interests, Dr. Finley was a noted pedestrian.
He considered walking not only a matter
of health, but a mental benefit. "As a
farm boy in Illinois," he said in a recent
interview, "I remember leaving my plow,
going to the house and changing into my
suit of black, walking eight miles to take
an examination in solid geometry which I

had studied by myself, passing it and walking eight miles home again. A good walk clears the mind, stimulates thinking. I walk to the *Times* office each morning. At least once each year I walk around Manhattan, 32 miles. I have walked 70 miles in a day in the White Mountains. Several times I have walked from New York to Princeton. Even on an ocean crossing I will walk 100 miles. Gramercy Park circuit is just equal to the deck circuit on the *Aquitania*."

While Commissioner of Education for New York he had a medal made: the figure of a walking boy and the motto, "à la Sainte Terre." This was designed to be awarded to Boy Scouts and others who have become faithful walkers, and to cripples who have overcome handicaps and learned to walk. Once, on visiting a home for incorrigible boys about 30 miles from his office in Albany, he promised a medal to the first boy who would walk to his office. One day six of them arrived, and Dr. Finley walked the 30 miles back to the school to deliver the six medals in person.

Several years ago he made a tour on foot along forgotten bypaths in the Great Lakes and Mississippi River country and in Eastern Canada. While in France and in Scotland he also went for long tramps over the countryside, getting acquainted with the scene and the people. Bridges fascinated him. There was not a bridge built within the New York region during his long residence in this city which he did not cross afoot soon after its opening. He used a pedometer to clock off the miles he walked from home to office; and constantly he carried with him a *Baedeker,* by which method he transferred the distance he walked in New York to some imagined point or town of interest. Such imaginary "journeys" took him to many parts of the world he had never visited.

Dr. Finley was for many years interested in the Boy Scouts; at his death he was a member of the Scouts' National Executive Board. Daniel Carter Beard, National Scout Commissioner, was among the many who expressed deep sorrow at the news of his death. "Dr. Finley was my idea of a real pedestrian," he said. "He was as thrilled by the sights in a walk through a congested district as by the beautiful scenic effects afforded in the open country. Several years ago I became enthralled as I listened to Dr. Finley recount his experiences of a day's hike around the edge of Manhattan Island. . . He described at least 30 persons he saw on that trip.

"When I asked him if he saw nothing but people, he told me he also was delighted to find potato patches, small gardens of cabbages, lettuce and other vegetables tucked away in the most unexpected places near the shoreline. He appeared pleased when I told him that while everybody considered him a good editor I knew he was a good reporter, as he had proved it from his account of that trip."

JOHN HUSTON FINLEY

In spite of his many interests, and the demands made on his time by various organizations which engaged him to speak and preside at dinners, Dr. Finley found time also to write a number of books. Among these were *The American Executive and Executive Methods* (1908), in collaboration with J. F. Sanderson; *French Schools in War Time* (1917); *A Pilgrim in Palestine* (1918); and *The Debt Eternal* (1923). He was also one of the editors of Nelson's *Encyclopedia* and greatly interested in the *Dictionary of American Biography*. Three days before his death he had finished reading proof on another book, *The Coming of the Scot,* which was published late in March 1940. It is a study of the part the Scottish people had in the development of America.

Dr. Finley's close friends knew him as a man of kindliness and affection, filled with deep appreciation of his fellow men and to whom nothing was ever too much trouble. He was a constant visitor to friends and acquaintances who were sick, though he himself had never known a sick day till his serious illness in 1938. His travels abroad and at home made him a citizen of the world, giving him a deep understanding of all human problems.

Of him, Dr. Nicholas Murray Butler (see sketch this issue) has said: "Dr. Finley was an American of the highest type. His learning was always at the service of some good cause and his religious faith gave richness and elevation to his character. His human sympathies made him as much beloved as he was admired. His influences upon our people will be permanent."

References

J Adult Ed 11:229-34 Je '39
Library J 64:555 Jl '39
Lit Digest 123:30 My '37 por

FINLEY, JOHN—*Continued*

Nat Educ Assn J 28:sup 11 Ja '39
Newsweek 9:27 My 1 '37 por
Recreation 30:252+ Ag '36; 33:562 Ja '40 por
Time 29:47-8 My 3 '37 por
Wilson Lib Bul 14:68 S '39
Who's Who in America

Obituaries

N Y Herald Tribune p22 Mr 8 '40; p10 Mr 9 '40; p40 Mr 10 '40
N Y Times p16, 17 Mr 8 '40 por; p16 Mr 9 '40; p22, IV p9 Mr 10 '40
Time 35:82 Mr 18 '40
Variety 138:44 Mr 13 '40

FINN, WILLIAM JOSEPH, FATHER
Sept 7, 1881- Founder of Paulist Choir
Address: b. 411 W 59th St, New York City

Father William Joseph Finn is the organizer of one of the world's best-known corps of singers, the Paulist Choir of the Church of St. Paul the Apostle, Manhattan. The choir has traveled throughout the United States and in Europe; it has appeared on national radio programs and in the leading concert halls of the country and it was one of the attractions of the New York World's Fair. Yet its programs have been for the most part the sacred music of the sixteenth century. Father Finn has made modern lay audiences like the heavy musical fare of the medieval church. He has resurrected the sacred music of the sixteenth century and made it a living thing.

Father Finn has had much to do with bringing boys' choirs back into prominence. The rebirth of the boys' choirs began in 1903 when members of the American Catholic clergy were shocked by the Pope's encyclical letter deploring the lax custom of employing women sopranos and urging the churches to return to orthodoxy and to have only men and boy singers.

Soon after this, as one writer puts it, "the ear-splitting noises of the boy choirs were all but driving the worshippers from church." It was in this crisis that Father Finn was summoned to take charge of a Paulist Choir in Chicago, in a district so tough that priests were often accompanied by policemen on their parish visits.

Before he came to Chicago, Father Finn was undecided between a musical education and a religious education. He was born in Boston, September 7, 1881, son of James Anthony Finn, a physician, and Margaret (Hussey) Finn. There were musicians in the family, including one or two professionals, and amateurs on both sides, and his father was also musically inclined. Father Finn's preoccupation with ecclesiastical music began when he was 14 and his mother dragged him to a Tenebrae service at the Boston Cathedral. For the first time the music of the medieval church burst upon his consciousness, to become his greatest interest.

The future Paulist priest prepared for college at the Boston Latin School, the oldest boys' high school in the country, and studied organ at the same time. At 16 he was the organist at the Carmelite Monastery in Boston. He attended St. Charles College near Baltimore for two years and then began his theological studies at the Catholic University in Washington in 1900. Then, leaving his theological studies incomplete, he went back to Boston for more musical study.

He went in 1904 to Chicago to take charge of the Paulist Choristers at St. Mary's Church. He was ordained in 1906, and for 11 years afterward not only directed the choir but acted as curate of the parish.

One of Father Finn's practical aptitudes is for managing choirboys. No one is better at reducing mischievous barbarians of about 12 or 14 to order and to music. Father Finn himself cannot sing a note! Two boyhood operations on his larynx flattened his voice forever. But he took the street urchins from his tough Chicago parish and turned them into angelic boy sopranos by reviving the medieval "Spanish tenor" or "counter tenor technique of singing the boys through the adolescent change of voice." This means that soprano boys whose voices are about to mature are trained to perform the alto parts in the choir. As the Chicago Paulist Choir began attracting attention, boys with fine voices volunteered their services, and Father Finn had a wider field from which to choose his choir.

The first great triumph for the Paulist Choristers and Father Finn came in 1912 when the choir toured Europe and won an international contest in Paris in competition with 96 choirs. The choir so delighted Pope Pius X in a private concert that the Pontiff gave Father Finn the title of Magister Cantorum (Master of Singers). Father Finn was also honored by the French Academy.

In 1918, when the Paulist Choristers already had an international reputation, Father Finn was transferred to New York and became associated with the Church of St. Paul the Apostle. Here in 1919 he started a choir school which flourished as a regular boarding school, with grammar school and college preparatory courses. By having a place to board the boys, Father Finn found he could have his pick of voices from all over the United States. It was impossible to keep up with the expense of the school, however. What the choristers took in from concerts did little more than meet the expenses of the unit. Today the choristers are recruited from the New York metropolitan area, although Father Finn still hopes some day to have a choir school.

The Paulist Choristers have become known to a great many people through their regular appearance on the *Catholic Hour*, broadcast by the National Broadcasting Company over a network of 40 stations. Those who are accustomed to the cold formality of choral performances are amazed at what Father Finn has accomplished with the Paulist Choristers. The ecclesiastical restraint of the medieval music is permeated with warmth, sincerity and an ethereal quality. Father Finn's interpretations of heavy musical fare such as the *Requiem* of Brahms, the Mozart *Requiem* and the *St. Matthew Passion* music of Bach have been astonishingly popular.

Despite his classical tastes in music Father Finn has a flair for showmanship. The Paulist Choristers have been a huge attraction to radio audiences of all creeds. The Paulist Father gets letters from people in all walks of life and of all religions telling him what a deep emotional experience the music of the Paulist Choristers has given them.

The Paulist Choristers have sung their way around the United States, Canada and Europe. They have given innumerable benefit performances for charitable and civic undertakings. In 1918 they took a six months' tour of the United States to raise money for the rebuilding of the Rheims Cathedral. During the First World War the choristers gave more than 300 concerts for War relief measures. They have appeared with symphony orchestras, on commercial radio programs, in an annual concert at the Metropolitan Opera House and at the World's Fair.

They have received the unstinted praise of metropolitan music critics, and have received various radio awards. But the choir members, about 60 boys and 35 men, remain anonymous. Father Finn strives for and achieves this perfect anonymity of the individual voices called for in orthodox church music. Normally, the soloist just happens. He may be discovered singing at rehearsals or in some other uncompetitive way. His station is no more exalted than that of the other youngsters from nine years to fifteen years old who work hard at rehearsals.

In addition to their regular NBC Sunday evening performances on the *Catholic Hour,* the choristers sing regularly for Sunday high mass and the church festivals of Christmas and Easter. At the minimum they have three rehearsals a week; at the maximum they may be required every day of the week, as benefit performances or special occasions pile up. They are on probation for six months, and the only pay they get is 50 cents for supper money on Sunday night. The choristers are not fanatically sectarian. When they sang before Pope Pius the head solo boy was a Protestant, and there is always a sprinkling of non-Catholic boys.

Father Finn follows the routine of the monastic order of St. Paul, of which he is a member. He rises for mass at 6 a. m., then attends a chapel service before lunch, another before supper and then night prayers. But he not only finds time to keep the

William Haussler

FATHER FINN

choristers up to the high standard they have attained but to write books and compose appealing melodies that are always a hit with audiences when the choristers sing them on secular occasions.

He is America's foremost authority on choral music. He is the author of the *Epitome of Choral Technique,* published in 1934, and *The Art of the Choral Conductor,* 1938. In 1939 he conducted a short course in choral music for 75 choirmasters, organists and music teachers, Catholic and non-Catholic, from all over the country. He is also the composer of a large number of Christmas carols and other choral music.

About 25 years ago Father Finn began going abroad a few months at a time to study and listen to the music of the old masters. He studied the hints left by the great medieval conductors and also modern choir technique, but has taken little from his research. His music has been a matter of intrinsic intuition. It has been living music instead of dead, scholarly research. Father Finn has one complaint against operatic and orchestral music. The instruments it relies upon, he says, are mechanical, while his instrument is the human voice in massed chorus.

A big burly man with white hair, Father Finn has an Irish twinkle in his eye that shows he likes a wisecrack. He lives in the rectory and observes the vows of poverty of his order. He has a sister who is a nun in Newfoundland, another sister married to a curator of a Vienna museum, and two more sisters and a brother who live in New York.

References

Commonweal 29:712-13 Ap 21 '39
Eccl R 101:370-1 O '39

FINN, WILLIAM JOSEPH—*Continued*

New Yorker 6:26-8 D 20 '30 por
Newsweek 14:30 Jl 17 '39 il por
American Catholic Who's Who
Who's Who in America

FISCHER, ISRAEL FREDERICK Aug
17, 1858—Mar 16, 1940 Former chief judge
of the United States Customs Court in New
York City; first associate and then presiding judge for 33 years

ISRAEL F. FISCHER

References

Who's Who in America 1936-37
Who's Who in American Jewry
Who's Who in Government

Obituaries

N Y Times p48 Mr 17 '40

FISCHER, LOUIS Feb 29, 1896- Author;
European correspondent

Address: c/o W. Colston Leigh, Inc, 521 Fifth
Ave, New York City

Russia's conquests in the Baltic and her
invasion of Finland will probably be one of
the most stupendous boomerangs of modern
times according to Louis Fischer, special
European correspondent and noted author,
who, with his family, in early 1940 returned to
the United States to deliver a series of lectures.

Mr. Fischer, the son of David and Shifrah
(Kantzapolsky) Fischer, was born in Philadelphia. He attended the Philadelphia School
of Pedagogy from 1914 to 1916, then taught
in the public schools for the next two years.

When he was 25 Mr. Fischer became a
contributor to the New York *Post* from
Berlin. The following year *The Nation*
sent him to Russia as its special European
correspondent. There he met and married

Bertha Mark of Libau, Latvia. Their two
sons, George and Victor, were born in Russia and their current stay in the United
States is their first visit to their own country. Like their father, both boys speak
Russian and German, as well as English.
Mr. Fischer also speaks French and understands Spanish.

In addition to having been the regular
European correspondent for *The Nation* for
18 years, Mr. Fischer contributes articles
to the Baltimore *Sun, New Republic, Current
History, New Statesman and Nation,* the Paris
L'Europe Nouvelle and the Prague *Tagebüch.*

He has written many books. His first,
published in 1926, *Oil Imperialism,* describes
the international struggle for the vast petroleum concessions in Russia. It was variously reviewed as "well-documented" and "a
shrill-voiced and furious indictment of all
capitalistic nations." The *Soviet in World
Affairs* which followed in 1930 is "a standard
reference for all students of Russian activities." This work might have been written
"either by a journalist with scholarly leanings or a scholar with journalistic leanings,"
said one commentator.

Why Recognize Russia? (1931) presented
arguments for and against the recognition of
the Soviet government by the United States.
Machines and Men in Russia (1932), illustrated with photographs by Margaret Bourke-
White (see sketch this issue), an account of the life, industry and future plans
of Soviet Russia, "filled with a great deal of
shrewd observation and common sense," is
"a fine, honest, informing book," and "not
wholly impartial."

In the introduction to his *Soviet Journey*
(1935) Mr. Fischer says: "I want to try to
make the reader see, hear, feel and smell
Russia. I want him to travel with me on
trains and boats, go with me into homes
and factories, probe with me the private
thoughts and private life of various kinds
of Soviet citizens. I would like to make
Russia concrete and real to the person who
has never seen it or whose knowledge is
incomplete. I will stress the permanent
fundamentals which enable one to watch
future developments."

A reviewer in the *Christian Science Monitor*
wrote: "It is nothing short of an acrobatic
feat to remain as poised as Louis Fischer
in the vast arena of Red Russia, to see so
much and to see so clearly, to probe depths,
to indicate shallowness, to discern the human
and the barbaric."

Today Mr. Fischer believes that not only
has Russia made herself more vulnerable to
attack by the great nations of the West,
now and in the future, through her seizures
of Baltic lands, but that through her aggression she has lost an opportunity for the
moral leadership of the world. He also believes that her invasion of Finland has alienated the sympathy of the working class
throughout the world.

There is "no difference in principle between the British tenure of Gibraltar and

Bachrach

LOUIS FISCHER

Russian occupation of the Estonian Islands of the Gulf of Finland," he says. But, by the break with her traditional policy against all imperialism, Russia has lost her right to champion the cause of the proletariat the world over. The cause of world labor is not identical with that of Russian territory.

Although Mr. Fischer's headquarters have been in Moscow for the past 18 years, he has made frequent and long visits into Germany, into what were Austria and Czechoslovakia, into France and Italy. He also covered the Ethiopian conquest.

Mr. Fischer was in France when War broke out in September 1939 and a little later went to London to watch developments in the various diplomatic maneuvers which followed. He interviewed all the Allied governments' heads and was in constant touch with many behind-the-scene leaders both in France and England. He was certain "that the Allies neither want nor expect active military participation by the United States. The chief problem of this War is materials and all they are asking for at present is goods sold for immediate cash and carried in their own ships."

On the lecture platform "he has a pleasing presence and a strong personality. His voice is deep and resonant and he likes nothing better than answering questions."

In addition to the books on Russia Mr. Fischer wrote *The War in Spain* (1937) and *Why Spain Fights On* (London, 1937).

References

Who's Who in America
Who's Who in American Jewry

FISHBEIN, MORRIS July 22, 1889- Physician; editor

Address: b. 535 N Dearborn St, Chicago, Illinois; h. 5543 Blackstone Ave, Chicago, Illinois

Americans pay $3,210,000,000 annually for doctors' bills and for many persons the financial burden is too great. Some of them don't get care and some of them don't pay their bills. One way of bringing medical services to persons who can't budget for sickness, and of improving, at the same time, the incomes of physicians—in 1929 one out of every four doctors was earning less than $2,300 a year—is the medical cooperative.

With the medical cooperative doctors are hired for fixed salaries which are paid out of health-insurance "premiums." In addition to their prepaid doctors' care, the members receive free physical examinations and other medical benefits. In November 1937 such a cooperative was formed in Washington, D. C.—the Group Health Association—and in less than a year it had nearly 2,500 members.

Around the Group Health Association of Washington has raged one of the major storms of modern medicine. Organized medicine, under the banner of the American Medical Association and led by Dr. Morris Fishbein, immediately opposed the plan. The A. M. A. stated that "physicians who sell their services to an organization like the G. H. A. for resale to patients are certain to lose professional status." The Medical Society of Washington, D. C. (a branch of the A. M. A.) threatened the doctors who worked for the group plan with loss of membership in the A. M. A. and in August 1938 expelled one. It also applied pressure upon the Washington hospitals to exclude Group doctors.

In July 1938 the United States Department of Justice indicted the A. M. A., the local society and 21 physicians under the Sherman Anti-Trust Act on charges of restraining trade. In August 1939 the indictment was dismissed in a District Federal Court on the ground that the term "trade" didn't include the medical profession. In March 1940 the Circuit Court of Appeals reversed this decision and said that the A. M. A.'s interference with doctors who worked for the Group was a violation of the Sherman Antitrust Act. Medical Association members were up in arms over this decision. And no one was more wrought up than Dr. Morris Fishbein, editor of the A. M. A.'s *Journal* and of *Hygeia*.

For many years Dr. Fishbein has been a strong and voluble opponent of "socialized medicine" in any form. When the American Medical Association's Committee on the Costs of Medical Care drew up a set of principles for medical care in 1937, beginning with the proposition that "the health of the people is a direct concern of the government," Dr. Fishbein was one of the leading A. M. A. members who "rejected it with enthusiastic unanimity" and

MORRIS FISHBEIN

was in the forefront of the movement which led to the ousting of the Committee.

For many years Dr. Fishbein has been contributing articles and editorials to medical and popular magazines, pointing out the evils which he believes inherent in any system of dispensing medical care other than that by which the average American doctor practices. He has stated firmly that George Washington's dictum, "he who would surrender liberty for security is likely to lose both," is directly applicable to those who would support socialized medicine. He has called compulsory socialized medicine "another insidious step towards the breakdown of democracy." He has insisted that socialized medicine isn't possible "until that' time comes when human beings have been standardized."

His arguments against any form of group health insurance or governmental aid in medical care can be summed up, from his writings, as follows: He feels, first of all, that it is not preventive insurance, but merely aids people after they have become sick. Second, he feels that it "breaks down that initiative and ambition which are the marks of a young country going ahead," for the young doctor who steps into a regular job "begins a mechanized routine type of service that is harmful not only to his patients but to his own character and advancement." Third, he feels that it "brings into the picture of medical practice business methods and commercialization which are fatal to medical science." Fourth, he believes that with any governmental system, such as now prevails in most European countries, we would get "incompetent political control." Fifth, it seems to him that a real epidemic would send any insurance scheme into bankruptcy.

Dr. Fishbein's solution to the problem of the people in this country who cannot afford medical care is the exercise of a little common-sense economy by the average man and the support of hospitals from the motive "which makes the care of the sick a high moral objective."

Dr. Fishbein has received a good deal of support for his views among American Medical Association members, and he has also aroused a good deal of opposition, both from doctors and laymen. To many people his view seems rather old-fashioned in light of the social security and unemployment programs this government has instituted, in light of the various hospitalization plans to which many Americans subscribe, in light of the widespread practice of socialized medicine in England, Scandanavia and most of the countries of Europe. In fact, *Fortune* Magazine said that Dr. Fishbein "hasn't displayed much flexibility when faced with new medical and political realities. He has, in a word, failed to develop in social consciousness as fast as the needs of the day require."

Dr. Fishbein is, without doubt, the most prolific and articulate of the leaders of the American Medical Association. He writes 15,000 words a week, reads 3,000 manuscripts submitted annually, and daily goes over 30 to 40 medical magazines. Three times a day on the average he is asked to make a speech and every three days, on the average, he does. He is the author of fifteen books and the editor of five more. He contributes to lay periodicals—from *Plumbing and Heating* to the *Saturday Evening Post*—and syndicates a daily column in 200 newspapers.

Dr. Fishbein has written articles not only about socialized medicine, but about obstetrical care, muscles, colds, hay fever, social diseases, harmonious hormones, poliomyelitis, medical quacks, influenza and the truth about candy. His books include *Medical Follies* (1925); *Your Weight and How to Control It* (1927); *Fads and Quackery in Healing* (1932); *Frontiers of Medicine* (1933); *Syphilis* (1937); *Do You Want to Become a Doctor?* (1939); and the *Modern Home Medical Adviser* (1935) of which he was editor.

Actually, Dr. Fishbein has never practiced medicine on his own. He was born in St. Louis, Missouri on July 22, 1889, the son of Benjamin and Fanny (Glück) Fishbein, and was brought up in Indianapolis and educated in Chicago. Since childhood he has spoken with a Hoosier twang, as does his wife Anna. He received his B. S. from the University of Chicago in 1910 and his M. D. from Rush Medical College in 1912. After receiving his degree he spent one year as a fellow in pathology at Rush Medical College and then had one year's service in the Durand Hospital of the McCormick Institute for Infectious Diseases, which was the extent of his personal contact with patients.

Morris Fishbein was first spotted as a bright young man by Dr. Ludvig Hektoen, who in 1913 proposed him for the post of assistant to the late Dr. George H. Simmons, editor of the *Journal* of the A. M. A. In 1924 Dr. Simmons retired and Dr. Fishbein became editor of the *Journal* and of *Hygeia*.

As editor of the A. M. A.'s publications and chairman of several A. M. A. councils, "Dr. Fishbein," according to *Fortune*, "has been a promoter. He has promoted the A. M. A. from a mild academic body into a powerful trade association." He has done this by his writings, and by his speeches given all over the country. When he talks he is "easy, charming and as poised as a master of ceremonies. His addresses are interspersed with jokes and he is constantly being reminded of the one about the etcetera." In 1931 he started a speech to the A. M. A. House of Delegates: "Unaccustomed as I am to public speaking," and the delegates rolled in the aisles.

His wife Anna (Mantel) Fishbein, whom he married in 1914, goes with him on all his trips around the country and on the road acts as his personal secretary and purchasing agent (ties, shirts, socks). Since he is subjected to a good many libel suits, he turns over his entire income ($30,000 to $40,000 a year) to her as a precaution. They have three children, Barbara, Marjorie and Justin.

Some of Dr. Fishbein's colleagues who have shown their appreciation of his work by electing him to the American Association for the Advancement of Science, to the American Public Health Association, to a Fellowship in the American Medical Association, still feel that his speeches and his lectures and even some of his writings aren't quite in keeping with the dignity of the profession, and his outside activities have been criticized before the A. M. A. House of Delegates. Since one of the main ethical tenets of the A. M. A. is the prohibition of self-advertising, some doctors believe that he does put himself in an ambiguous position "by inspiring murder-sized headlines wherever he goes."

"Dr. Fishbein," according to one commentator, "is precisely the sort of person that people who take Dale Carnegie courses would like to be. He is the great winner, the great influencer." His associates keep saying that he would make a "good advertising man." Most laymen and doctors agree that that is what he already is. He intends to stay that in the medical field. He has turned down a number of attractive bids from business—the largest one $50,000 a year from the Great Atlantic and Pacific chain of grocery stores—and intends to keep turning them down.

References

Fortune 18:152+ N '38 por (p89)
N Y Times p25 Ap 23 '40
Newsweek 4:24 D 8 '34; 14:33 Ag 7 '39
Outlook 152:221 Je 5 '29; 154:21 Ja 1 '30
Rotarian 47:13+ N '35 por (p64); 55: 15+ S '39 por (p64)
Scholastic 36:2 Mr 18 '40
Time 29:28+ Je 21 '37 por (cover)

American Men of Science
Bealle, M. A. Medical Mussolini 1938
Who's Who in America
Who's Who in American Medicine
Who's Who in American Jewry

FISHER, JOHN STUCHELL May 25, 1867—June 25, 1940 Governor of Pennsylvania from 1927 to 1930; backed William S. Vare's right to a Senate seat; lawyer who made exhaustive study of the State's banking laws and when Governor reorganized Pennsylvania's fiscal system; supervised the largest state building program in the history of Pennsylvania

References

Who's Who in America
Who's Who in Commerce and Industry
Who's Who in Government

Obituaries

N Y Herald Tribune p22 Je 26 '40 por
N Y Times p23 Je 26 '40 por
Newsweek 16:55 Jl 8 '40 por

FISHER, STERLING May 24, 1899- Director of Education and Radio Talks of Columbia Broadcasting System
Address: b. 485 Madison Ave, New York City; h. Wilson Park, Tarrytown, New York

Since the summer of 1936 Mr. Fisher has officiated as director of the CBS presentation, *American School of the Air*, also of *The School of the Air of the Americas*, which he founded; as director of religious broadcasts, including Columbia's *Church of the Air*, and editor of *Talks*, a quarterly magazine, and of the CBS *Student Guide*, a monthly publication.

Extension of the *American School of the Air* to the other countries of the Western hemisphere was started in the fall of 1940, and at present 15 countries other than the United States are participating in this radio educational project. According to Secretary of State Hull (see sketch this issue): "It would be difficult to devise a form of international cooperation which holds more promise for the deepening and broadening of understanding between the peoples of the American republics." In the United States these radio programs are used in 210,000 classrooms by about 8,000,000 pupils.

Sterling Wesley Fisher (he does not use his middle name) spent his boyhood in San Antonio, where he was born, and San Marcos, Texas. His primary and secondary education was received in the Coronal Institute, of which his father, for whom he was named, was president. His mother was Sue (Harper) Fisher. He studied for two years at Southern Methodist University, Dallas, and one year at the University of Texas, receiving his B.A. in 1919.

STERLING FISHER

From 1919 to 1921 Mr. Fisher taught in the Middle School, Himeji, Japan, and also at the University of Western Japan (Kwansei Gakuin) in Kobe.

He then returned to the United States, and from 1921 to 1922 took courses at the School of Journalism at Columbia University and also at Teachers College. He next devoted his time to teaching English at the Georgia School of Technology, and followed that experience with further study at the Graduate School of the University of California in Berkeley, where in 1924 he received his M. A.

Then followed a further stay in the Orient, and from 1924 to 1929 he was professor of English language and literature at the University of Western Japan in Kobe.

After his long sojourn in Japan, Mr. Fisher came back to his native country and joined the editorial staff of the Springfield (Massachusetts) *Republican,* remaining in that post until November 1929. His next journalistic venture was on the New York editorial staff of the Associated Press. From August 1930 until 1937 Mr. Fisher served as a writer on the New York *Times* and also as the Far Eastern authority on that newspaper. In October 1935 he was sent as the representative of the publisher of the New York *Times* to the inauguration of the Commonwealth of the Philippines. He remained in the Far East to report Japanese activities in northern China, Manchuria and Korea for the *Times.* Soon after his return to this country he was assigned by the *Times* to write articles on the Yosemite Conference of the Institute of Pacific Relations.

It was in April 1937 that he joined the staff of the Columbia Broadcasting System and in the fall he was sent on President Roosevelt's Pacific and Northwestern tour to arrange special broadcasts. Mr. Fisher was subsequently instrumental in organizing the CBS Adult Board of Education (in 1938), whose chairman was and is Professor Lyman Bryson (see sketch this issue). He was further responsible for the arrangement of the working agreement between the *American School of the Air* and the National Education Association, an organization comprising 983,000 members, and likewise won the favor of the Pan American Union for the *School of the Air of the Americas.* He attended the Second Conference of American Secretaries of State in Cuba in July 1940, when he inaugurated the new radio *Escuela de Las Americas* as an official part of the agenda of the Conference, finally completing arrangements for holding in February 1941 the first International Conference of the *School of the Air of the Americas.*

Although Mr. Fisher has devoted a great deal of time to study and teaching, he has had his share of exciting experiences, particularly when he was in China for the New York *Times.* He was successful in obtaining for his newspaper a copy of the map of the hitherto unknown double-track B. A. M. strategic railroad in Siberia. Being thoroughly familiar with the Japanese language enabled him to get this exclusive information and the ink sketch. During this period he was instructed by cable to go from Shanghai to Tientsin, a distance of about 1,000 miles. When his plane was over the Tientsin landing field, the pilot and others observed on grounded planes below the red ball insignia of Japan. When Mr. Fisher's flying machine landed it was soon afterward visited by Japanese army officers, who had their eyes out for cameras. Although Mr. Fisher had a camera, the fact that he spoke Japanese so well won the favor of the Japanese officers and caused them to abandon their aggressive search of the Chinese-American plane.

Mr. Fisher is an honorary life member of the American Museum of Natural History, a member of the Philosophical Society of Texas, of the Sigma Delta Chi, an honorary journalistic fraternity; also a member of Pi Kappa Alpha; of the executive committee of the Federal Radio Education Commission, and of the advisory committee of the Chicago Radio Council.

Mr. Fisher, who was married in 1923 to Jean Alice Callahan, has two sons. His hobbies are tennis and reading, especially reading history and biography. He is a contributor to the New York *Times* Magazine, *Current History* and other magazines and is the editor of many radio booklets, including *Americans at Work* and the CBS *Student Guide.*

References

Cur Hist 51:40-2 Ap '40 por
Who's Who in America
Who's Who in American Education

Who's Who in Radio
Who's Who in Transportation and
Communication

FITZMAURICE, GEORGE Feb 13, 1885—
June 13, 1940 Motion picture director;
wrote and supervised *The Perils of Pauline*;
later directed such stars as Greta Garbo,
Jean Harlow, Cary Grant, Ronald Colman

References

> Boyd, E. A. Later Playwrights *In*
> Contemporary Drama of Ireland
> p142-69 1917
> International Motion Picture Al-
> manac

Obituaries

> N Y Times p21 Je 14 '40
> N Y World-Telegram p31 Je 14 '40
> Newsweek 15:8 Je 24 '40
> Time 35:47 Je 24 '40

FLAGG, JAMES MONTGOMERY June
18, 1877- Artist

Address: 340 W 57th St, New York City

James Montgomery Flagg, whose posters
covered the land during the First World
War, is again drawing patriotic messages.
Famous for his beautiful young women and
strong-jawed young men in magazines and
in advertisements, Mr. Flagg is able also to
produce encouraging posters for national
defense.

"At an age when many limners have put
away their drawing boards, he is doing
more work than ever before and with a
zip." He has always worked incredibly
fast and is still able to turn out about 250
pictures a year, less three months' vacation.
These pictures are frankly commercial ones
—done for the "slick" magazines to illustrate stories and for large companies to
promote their products—for Mr. Flagg has
no pretensions toward being an "artist."
He says the difference between the artist
and the illustrator is that the latter knows
how to draw, eats three square meals a day
and can pay for them.

In the years that he has illustrated stories
and articles, Mr. Flagg has, inevitably, become an authority on women—"physically
attractive women are the most plentiful
thing produced in America," he says. His
idea of a beautiful woman is that she should
be "tall, with wide shoulders, a face as sym-
metrical as a Greek vase, thick, wavy hair,
either dark or light, thick, long lashes,
straight, short nose tipped up a bit at the
end, a wide, rippling, full-lipped mouth, even
white teeth, eyes so full of feminine allure
that your heart skips a beat when you gaze
into them." But physical beauty, according
to this authority, isn't enough. To be really
beautiful a woman must have "certain fundamental qualities of spirit—serenity, kindness, courage, humor and passion."

Flagg's first drawings weren't of women,
however. They began when he was two.

Hāl Phyfe

JAMES MONTGOMERY FLAGG

He was born in Pelham Manor, New York,
the son of Elisha and Anna Elida (Coburn)
Flagg. His first published drawing appeared in *St. Nicholas* when he was 10. By
the time he was 14 he was a regular illustrator for the magazine. He was, of course,
going to school, too—to New York City's
public schools and Dr. Chapin's private
school. After he began drawing for *Judge*
and the old *Life* in 1892 he studied at the
Art Students League and later at Her-
komer's Art School in England and under
Victor Marec in Paris.

For a while Flagg painted portraits—in
Paris, St. Louis and New York. These
were exhibited in the Paris Salon in 1900
and at the National Academy of Design
and the New York Water Color Club. It
was about the beginning of the century, too,
that Flagg became famous for his adventures of "Vervy Nat, a bibulous ne'er-do-
well and imposter who was living by his
wits in Paris." His first book, *Yankee Girls
Abroad*, appeared in 1900. This was followed
by other funny or satiric books—*Tomfoolery*
(1904); *If—A Guide to Bad Manners* (1905);
Why They Married (1906); *All in the Same
Boat* (1908); *City People* (1909) and others.
One of his more successful books was *The
Well-Knowns as Seen by James Montgomery
Flagg* (1914), a collection of caricatures.

When the United States entered the First
World War Mr. Flagg was appointed New
York State military artist for the duration
of the War and was kept busy designing
posters to stir up enthusiasm for recruiting
and for liberty loans. After that commissions for illustrations began coming in, and
still do, for some of the most important
products in this country. Besides illustrating and writing, Flagg also wrote a series
of motion pictures, *Girls You Know,* and
satirical comedies for famous players.

FLAGG, JAMES MONTGOMERY—*Cont.*

Flagg's first marriage, to Nellie McCormick of St. Louis, took place in 1899. The first Mrs. Flagg died in 1923 and in 1924 Mr. Flagg was remarried—to Dorothy Wadman. They have one daughter, Faith.

When Flagg works he wears tortoise-shell glasses. He twirls his big black eyebrows as he talks. "His mind has the speed of a roulette wheel and his tastes are fastidious. He is openly hostile to ignorant people."

References

Good H 102:86 Ap '36 por
Read Digest 30:11-13 Ap '37

Birchman, W. James Montgomery Flagg *In* Faces & Facts 1937
Flagg, J. M. Boulevards All the Way—Maybe 1925
Who's Who in America
Who's Who in American Art

FLEMING, ARTHUR HENRY Apr 3, 1856—Aug 11, 1940 Philanthropist; lumber manufacturer; gave $5,000,000 for founding of the California Institute of Technology; became known internationally when he gave 100,000 francs to the French government for the establishment of a pavilion and park in Compiègne forest as a shrine for the railway car in which the Armistice was signed after the First World War; was made a member of the French Légion d'Honneur

ARTHUR HENRY FLEMING

References

Who's Who in America
Who's Who in Commerce and Industry

Obituaries

N Y Herald Tribune p8 Ag 12 '40 por
N Y Times p15 Ag 12 '40 por
Time 36:48 Ag 19 '40

FLEMING, JOHN ADAM Jan 28, 1877-
Geophysicist; magnetician

Address: b. 5241 Broad Branch Rd, N W, Washington, D. C.; h. 8 Drummond Ave, Chevy Chase, Maryland

On Easter Day 1940 radio communication with Europe was cut off and the teletype in America "talked like a jabberwock." "Sun spots," was the immediate opinion of the learned and the layman, and according to John Adam Fleming, director of the department of terrestial magnetism of the Carnegie Institute of Washington, sun spots it was.

He confirmed the theory that the upset was caused by a new rash of sun spots and cyclonic disturbance among them. The heavyside surface deflected their electrical charges North and South to the poles, scrambling air traffic, although it is this same barrier which routes our communications in an orderly way around the earth, keeping us talking to ourselves instead of to other planets, "which is perhaps just as well, considering our present contribution to the music of the spheres."

Dr. Fleming has been observing the actions of the spheres and of this earth for more than 40 years. He was born in Cincinnati, Ohio on January 28, 1877, the son of Americus V. and Catherine B. (Ritzmann) Fleming. He went to school in Cincinnati and received his B. S. degree from the University of Cincinnati in 1899, from which he later was awarded an honorary degree. Right after graduation he started to work for the United States Coast and Geodetic Survey, first as an aide, then as assistant and finally as magnetic observer.

While he was working for the government, Dr. Fleming married Henrietta C. B. Ratjen of Lawrenceberg, Indiana, who died in 1912, leaving one daughter, Margaret Catherine. In 1913 he was married again, to Carolyn Ratjen, also of Lawrenceberg, Indiana.

In 1904 Dr. Fleming began work with the Carnegie Institute in Washington and has stayed there, holding the following positions: magnetician, chief of the observatory division, chief of the magnetic survey division, assistant director and finally director in 1935. He has held a number of other important positions in his field: trustee of Woods Hole Oceanographic Institution since 1930; president of the Association of Terrestial Magnetism and Electricity of the International Union of Geodesy and Physics, 1930 to 1939; member of the executive council of the International Council of Scientific Unions since 1937.

Many honors have been given Dr. Fleming for his work in terrestial magnetism. He is a fellow of the American Association for the Advancement of Science and of the American Physical Society; he is a member of the National Academy of Sciences and an honorary member of the State Russian Geographical Society. There are many published works to Dr. Fleming's credit and he is a frequent contributor of articles and reviews to magazines and journals.

A young disciple of Dr. Fleming's once summed up Dr. Fleming's importance in the field of terrestial magnetism and the scope of that field. It was just after an expedition had emerged from a year in the Arctic ice. When the disciple was asked to tell something about the scientific gains of the expedition, he said: "We will have to leave that to Dr. Fleming. Polar discoveries boil down mostly to terrestial magnetism, and if Dr. Fleming could spend 20 or 30 years at the Pole, we might learn something."

References

N Y Sun p22 Mr 26 '40
Sci Mo 46:583 Je '38 por
American Men of Science
Law, F. H. Maxwell, Hertz, and Fleming: Leaders in Radio Communication *In* Civilization Builders p220-1 1939
Who's Who in America
Who's Who in the Nation's Capital

FLEMING, PHILIP BRACKEN Oct 15, 1887- Administrator of Wages and Hours Division of the United States Department of Labor

Address: b. Department of Labor Bldg, Washington, D. C.

Colonel Philip Fleming, serving as administrator of the Wages and Hours Division since October of 1939, was officially appointed to the position—and salary—on the 19th of February 1940 by the passage of a special amendment to the Defense Deficiency Bill.

Born in Burlington, Iowa, the son of John J. and Mary (Bracken) Fleming, he was educated at the University of Wisconsin and the United States Military Academy. He has had a long military experience, starting as a West Point Cadet in 1907 and being promoted through the ranks to colonel in January 1940. He temporarily held the rank of colonel during the First World War.

Colonel Fleming, quiet, grizzled and unmilitary in appearance, has earned the confidence of President Roosevelt and the title of "trouble-shooter" for the New Deal Administration. "Both as executive officer and deputy administrator of the Public Works Administration he was largely responsible for early organization of that undertaking. He started building on the Passamaquoddy project and was later picked to straighten out the snarl in the Resettlement Administration after Rex Tugwell retired from the Brain Trust."

His latest task has been to unwind the tangles of the Wages and Hours Division in the second year of its existence. In following Administrator Elmer F. Andrews, Colonel Fleming stepped into what was literally a hot spot. The Wages and Hours Administration, subject to much scrutiny from its be-

PHILIP B. FLEMING

ginning, had been recently criticized for slowness in establishing minimum wages for workers in other than the textile industries. There had also been opposition from the South to the ruling that there should be no distinction between wages paid workers in the textile industry in the North and South, and President Roosevelt finally upheld the Southern viewpoint.

"It is taken for granted," said *Survey Graphic* at the time of this appointment, "in informed Washington circles that his connection with the Wage-Hour Division is temporary—an assignment of a year, or even less. He is brought in, not as a liberal spokesman, or an expert in Labor legislation, but as an ace administrator."

When former Administrator Andrews resigned, Fleming's appointment could not be made because of a Federal law of 1870 which forbids army officers on active duty to hold civilian office. A "dummy administrator," former administration-chief of the Division, Harold Duane Jacobs, "whitemaned, competent publicity man ... a onetime Scripps-Howard editor who is capable of going to work in a green sports coat with orange stripes, pea-green vest, blue tie, gray shirt and gray flannels," was appointed.

Fleming discharged his duties while in fact he was only an assistant to this "phantom boss," until the passing of the Adams amendment to the Defense Deficiency Bill made it possible for the chief to administer—officially.

Colonel Fleming, recent army district engineer in St. Paul (as reported by *Business Week*), "doesn't relish his new job, but it's a good bet that neither employers nor unions will push him around." His appointment was coolly received by both Capital and Labor. Labor resented the power of an

FLEMING, PHILIP BRACKEN—*Cont.*

army officer, and business anticipated that the new chief might enforce the law too rigidly. Now that Colonel Fleming has been in office a year, Labor, while sensible of his opposition to reduction of wage and hour benefits because of national defense, still feels that under him "effectiveness of a number of standards has been greatly weakened and their application to several large groups of wage earners completely surrendered." Business believes that he should grant employers more concessions. Both parties, however, do concede that he has been an able and efficient administrator.

One of his first official acts (March 18, 1940) was the approval of upward minimum-wage adjustments affecting about 24,500 of the 83,000 employees in the knitted underwear and knitted outerwear industries. He approved a minimum-wage recommendation of 33½ cents an hour, made by the knitted underwear and commercial knitting committee, and a minimum-wage recommendation of 35 cents an hour, made by the knitted outerwear committee. This is above the minimum of 32½ which went into effect on October 24, 1939 for the textile and hosiery industries. Since then other industry committees have been set up and have made their recommendations for minimum wages.

In October 1940 he issued a new ruling exempting certain classifications of administrative and professional employees from the provisions of the Wages and Hours Act.

On December 5, 1914 Fleming married Dorothy Carson; he has two children, Carson and Joselyn, both in college. He has retained an interest in his place of birth, continuing to hold the position of president of the William Carson Company in his native city.

References

Boston Transcript p10 Ap 18 '40
Business Week p7 O 21 '39 por; p32
  Mr 30 '40 por
Nation 151:381 O 26 '40
N Y Times p38 Ap 11 '40; p1, 11
  O 14 '40; p22 O 16 '40; IV p10 O 20
  '40
Newsweek 14:48 O 30 '39 por
Scholastic 36:5-6+ My 13 '40
Survey G 28:730 D '39 por
Time 34:12 O 30 '39 por
Who's Who in America
Who's Who in the Nation's Capital
  1934-35

FLY, JAMES LAWRENCE Feb 22, 1898-
Chairman of Federal Communications Commission

Address: New Post Office Bldg, Washington, D. C.

The recent television controversies between the government and private corporations reached new pro and con peaks during April 1940. Bearing the brunt of these controversies, as chief protagonist for the government, is Chairman James Lawrence Fly of the Federal Communications Commission, versus David Sarnoff (see sketch this issue), president of Radio Corporation of America. Lawyer "Jim" Fly is a tall, rangy, level-headed Texan who has made his name with the New Deal TVA's general counsel since 1937, winning its two major cases in the Supreme Court. President Roosevelt appointed him Chairman of the FCC in August 1939 to succeed Frank R. McNinch, who resigned because of illness. Since Fly had previously won the respect of utilitarians for his tact and moderation, many observers hoped that he might bring some degree of house-cleaning order into the turbulent FCC. In September 1940 President Roosevelt made him head of a National Defense Communications Board to coordinate the nation's telephone, telegraph, radio and cable facilities.

He was born February 22, 1898 in Seagoville, Dallas County, Texas, son of Joseph Lawrence and Jane (Ard) Fly. After his graduation from the Dallas High School in 1916 he entered the United States Naval Academy, from which he was graduated in 1920. He saw service as a midshipman during the War; for three years after his graduation he was commanding officer aboard the *U. S. S. Idaho* and the *U. S. S. Baltimore*. In 1923 he retired from the Navy, and in that year also married Mildred Marvin Jones. They have two children: James Lawrence and Sara Virginia. He is a member of the Protestant Church.

Deciding on law as a profession, Fly entered the Harvard Law School, where he received his LL. B. degree in 1926. He entered private law practice and was associated with the firm of White and Case of New York City. He then engaged in antitrust work as special assistant to the United States Attorney General, 1929 to 1934. Then he became general solicitor and head of the legal department of the Tennessee Valley Authority, and served in this capacity until 1937, when he became general counsel of the TVA. In 1939 President Roosevelt nominated him as the new Communications Commission chairman.

The current television problem began in 1938, when the major television receiver manufacturers, chief among them RCA, had formulated, through the Radio Manufacturers' Association, a group of television transmission standards and recommended their adoption by the FCC. But other companies objected to the Manufacturers' Association's standards. It is essential, however, that specifications be fixed: in television, unlike radio, receiving and sending must correspond technically. If the transmitter is improved, the receiver must likewise be adjusted or improved, or it becomes useless. The principal concern of the FCC has always been that no one company, such as RCA, shall control transmission, and that owners of television sets may be able to pick up telecasts on any radio bands with any type of set. President Roosevelt, for instance, remarked that he wanted to be able to use his own television set to see either a town hall meeting or a prize fight, although there was "little essential difference between them." Despite fears and difficulties, the commission, however, had made an order allowing semi-commercial television broadcasting, scheduled to begin September 1, 1940. At the same time Fly warned against any attempts to "freeze" the standards of television transmission, and emphasized that it must remain on an experimental basis.

On Easter morning 1940 the radio industry was shocked to read that the commission had rescinded the September 1st order. A definite reason was given: RCA had suddenly begun a concentrated commercial advertising campaign, offering sharply reduced prices for their receivers. This activity was not in line with the commission's policy. And, at about the same time, the backers of Frequency Modulation for radio, led by Major Edwin Armstrong (see sketch this issue), appeared before the FCC demanding one-fifth of television's ether surface.

Private business and Republican newspapers were quick to attack what they called the FCC's "arbitrary restriction of a new and promising industry" and "government interference in business." Chairman Fly was forced to answer the bombardment on two national networks. His argument was that, if RCA's transmission methods should be superseded by technological developments, its sets would be useless to purchasers. Ironically, he broadcast this over NBC's red network, owned by RCA, at a cost to them of $10,000.

On April 11 the case came up for debate before the Senate Interstate Commerce Committee, of which Senator Burton K. Wheeler (see sketch this issue) is chairman. The Committee was asked to ascertain whether the FCC had exceeded its authority, interfered with private enterprise. At the same time a bill was introduced into the Senate to curb the FCC. In his defense, Chairman Fly urged flexibility in both television receiving sets and transmitters so the public could view all systems and make its choice. David Sarnoff said RCA had no intention of "freezing" standards, and that RCA receivers could be adapted to any new type of transmission at a cost of about $40 a set. Senator Wheeler said he hoped RCA would build a receiver capable of taking all transmissions, and that the industry would stop fighting within itself and get together. Morton Davis of RCA said that if the FCC specified what standards were to be, the RCA was prepared to build receivers on which the public could receive programs from FCC licensed transmitters.

Apparently the FCC did not decide immediately to fix standards, but indications in late April 1940 were that it would accept the industry's assurances at face value: a license was granted to Allen B. DuMont

JAMES LAWRENCE FLY

for a Class 2 "public programme service" television station to be located in New York City. This station will operate alternately on the several proposed types of transmission, and the public can compare results by adjusting flexible receivers.

References

Business Week p22+ Ap 20 '40 por
Christian Sci Mon p16 Ap 11 '40
Collier's 104:54 Ag 5 '39
Nation 150:447-9 Ap 6 '40
N Y Herald Tribune p22 Ap 11 '40
N Y Times p14 Ap 12 '40; p9 Ap 13 '40; p20 S 25 '40 por
Time 34:32 Ag 7 '39 por; 35:81 Ap 15 '40 por
America's Young Men
Who's Who in America
Who's Who in the Nation's Capital

FLYNN, EDWARD J. Sept 22, 1891- Chairman of the Democratic National Committee

Address: b. 60 E 42nd St, New York City; h. 2728 Henry Hudson Parkway, New York City

Edward J. Flynn accepted the position of Chairman of the Democratic Party in August 1940 as "an honor, a privilege and a duty most welcome." Most political observers agreed that he took on a hard job, for he had the third term issue to contend with; he had to fight against the unpopularity in some quarters of Wallace's (see sketch this issue) nomination as Vice-President; he had to conciliate the many important Democrats who were alienated by the "purge" of 1938; he had to line up strongly the city machines; and he had to consistently yet tactfully remind the public of the billions in bounties dispensed by the administration

EDWARD J. FLYNN

in the last years. That he did his job well is evidenced by the Roosevelt and Democratic successes in the November 1940 elections.

When, at the insistence of President Roosevelt, Ed Flynn took the job, he said he didn't hope "to equal the record of my predecessor and friend, Jim Farley, but—I will do my best." Comparisons between the two men were, of course, inevitable. The New York *Times* said that Mr. Flynn "can hardly match Mr. Farley in energy"; others pointed out that although Flynn knows the "big wig" Democrats, still he is a stranger "to thousands of local party hacks whom Jim Farley calls by their first names." Personally, it was felt, Flynn lacks a certain warmth and ease with people which Farley exercises to perfection.

Nobody doubted, however, that Flynn has much of Farley's political astuteness and that he is a first class campaigner. For 18 years he has been Democratic leader of The Bronx—Wendell Willkie (see sketch this issue) calls him "Boss Flynn of The Bronx"—and in these 18 years he has made The Bronx "proportionately the strongest Democratic borough in New York City."

This six-foot-two handsome Irishman, the son of Henry Timothy and Sarah (Mallon) Flynn, was born, brought up and educated in The Bronx. He went to public schools there and then to Fordham University, from which he got his law degree in 1909. He was only 18 then and had to wait three years before he could go before the Bar. After he was admitted he opened law offices in The Bronx, and his firm of Goldwater and Flynn is still prospering.

Flynn first stepped into real politics in 1917, when he was elected to the New York State Assembly. He spent three terms there and then, in 1921, was elected sheriff of

Bronx County. It was only a year later that he was made Democratic leader of The Bronx, much to the dismay of Tammany. "He didn't even speak the language and probably didn't understand it. Him with his fancy talk and expensive suits. How could that kind of a guy be boss of a borough?" But Tammany leader Charles Murphy knew him to be one of his "brightest young men" and a clean young fellow— which was what the Democrats needed then.

Since then Flynn has bossed The Bronx successfully. He has come unsmeared through every municipal scandal, including the Seabury affair, and he has "been careful to keep his coattails clean in connection with the courts." The only accusation of this sort against him was made by Dewey, (see sketch this issue) when he was running for Governor of New York State in 1938. He charged that Flynn had appointed Arthur (Dutch Schultz) Flegenheimer, an ex-convict and trigger man for Legs Diamond, as special deputy sheriff in The Bronx. Flynn easily convinced the public that Dewey had "deliberately distorted" the facts and that Flynn had appointed Flegenheimer before he was known as Schultz and had revoked the appointment when he was found in Diamond's company.

In his borough of well over a million, Flynn is said to know personally thousands of voters, and to have built a closely knit, highly efficient machine which repeatedly turns in huge Democratic majorities. Of course, any organizer who builds up a well-oiled machine comes in for both praise and criticism, but probably the most general impression even among his opponents is that Flynn is a "practical politician, perhaps no better but certainly no worse than political bosses everywhere."

During these years, from the pre-convention campaign of 1924 on, Flynn has always been a staunch friend and supporter of Roosevelt. Mr. and Mrs. Flynn (Flynn was married in 1927 to Helen Margaret Jones, and they have two sons and a daughter) are frequent Roosevelt guests, and have been hosts to the President and Mrs. Roosevelt at their Lake Mahopac summer home, where Ed Flynn has many acres under cultivation and 56 cows. When Roosevelt became Governor of New York, Flynn became his Secretary of State, and it has been said that Roosevelt "constantly sought and followed his advice." Flynn was an early supporter of Roosevelt for the Presidency and worked with Farley to bring about his nomination in 1932. Since then he has taken the course desired by the President in all Democratic Party clashes in New York. And he has often been heard to say, "I'm for anything Roosevelt is for. I'm for whatever he wants."

When Lehman took Roosevelt's place as Governor, Flynn continued as Secretary of State until 1939, when ill health caused him to resign, but he was always regarded as a Roosevelt man. In New York City politics he allied himself with Alfred E. Smith in the fight to get rid of Mayor John Hylan when Jimmy Walker's campaign was considered a reform effort. When Walker got in he appointed Flynn City Chamberlain. But it was over Walker that Flynn broke with Tammany when Walker wanted to run for Mayor after having resigned under charges.

The next year, in 1933, he waited until late in a heated Mayoralty campaign and then bolted the Tammany candidate, John P. O'Brien, to support Joseph V. McKee as a Recovery Party nominee. Because of the split he made in Tammany's ranks, La Guardia (see sketch this issue) was elected. As a result, there wasn't much enthusiasm at Tammany Hall when Flynn's appointment to head the Democratic Party was made known in August 1940. Most of the statements had about the same warmth as that of Tammany Leader Christopher D. Sullivan, who said: "Ed is a well-known man. I have known him for 30 years. He has a lot of practical experience in politics."

Since 1939 Mr. Flynn has been the United States Commissioner General for the New York World's Fair. On August 17, 1940 he took over his Democratic Party duties from James Farley, after a series of conferences with him and the President, with forces "trained to victory" and intentions of running the campaign as "thoroughly as though the results were doubtful." After election he announced that he would keep the job, maintaining a New York office and commuting when necessary, but that he would not take on the duties of Postmaster General.

Edward J. Flynn is "trimly built, iron-gray and dresses splendidly"; in fact he is known as the best-dressed politician in New York. He has read widely, is informed about economics, plays a fair game of golf and collects Pennell etchings. He loves to argue and when not arguing can "carry on a lively conversation on almost any subject." His friends say, "Ed is just like a successful uptown businessman whose business happens to be politics."

References

Collier's 106:14+ O 12 '40 il por
Cur Hist & Forum 52:14-15 S '40
Look 4:14-15 N 5 '40 pors
Nation 151:106-7 Ag 10 '40
N Y Herald Tribune p1, 14 Ag 2 '40 por
N Y Times p1, 5 Ag 2 '40 por; p14 Ag 3 '40; IV p3 Ag 4 '40; p13 Ag 6 '40; VII p7+ S 15 '40 por
PM p2 Ag 1 '40; p7 pors, p12 Ag 2 '40; p18 S 8 '40
Sat Eve Post 213:27+ O 5 '40 por
Time 36:13 Ag 12 '40 por
American Catholic Who's Who
America's Young Men 1936-37
Who's Who in Law

FOLKS, HOMER Feb 18, 1867- Secretary of State Charities Aid Association of New York

Address: b. 105 E 22nd St, New York City; h. 428 Hawthorne Ave, Yonkers, New York

Education, public health, child care—these have been the chief preoccupations of white-haired, distinguished-looking Homer Folks, who on October 27 was presented with the Roosevelt Distinguished Medal for 1940, almost since the day when he stepped up to receive his diploma from a small Michigan college in 1889. He was born in Hanover, Michigan on February 18, 1867, the son of James and Esther (Woodliff) Folks. He was 22 when he received his B. A. from Albion, went on to take another B. A. from Harvard, and immediately stepped into a position as superintendent of the Children's Aid Society of Pennsylvania. A year later, in 1891, he married M. Maud Beard of Albion, Michigan, and it was 1893 when he became secretary of the State Charities Aid Association. This is the position which he has held ever since, with the exception of a two-year interval from 1902 to 1904, when he was Commissioner of Public Charities of New York City, and during his service abroad with the American Red Cross.

His duties as chief executive officer of the Association only begin to describe the extent of Mr. Folks' activities, however. There is hardly a field of social service in which he has not been a pioneer. In his unceasing fight for child care, he organized the first agency in New York for aiding homeless mothers to care for their children (1894). In 1902 he published a book, *The Care of Destitute, Neglected and Delinquent Children.* In 1909 he was first vice-chairman of the White House Conference on Dependent Children. In 1935 he became vice-chairman

Vandamm

HOMER FOLKS

FOLKS, HOMER—*Continued*

of the National Child Labor Committee, of which he is now chairman; in 1936 chairman of the Governor's Commission on Illegitimacy, in 1940 chairman of the report committee of the White House Conference on Children in a Democracy, and in February 1940 he was appointed by Frances Perkins (see sketch this issue) to select a group to carry out the recommendations of the Conference over a 10-year period.

A pioneer in the battle against tuberculosis, Homer Folks attended the first international tuberculosis meeting in Washington in 1909 and later went to Albany to try to get help from the State in building much-needed hospitals and dispensaries. He was told that the taxpayers wouldn't stand for it. The counties took over the work, however, and in 1930 the State itself built three tuberculosis hospitals for counties which couldn't afford their own. One was named after Homer Folks, who in 1912 was the first layman to be elected president of the National Association for the Study and Prevention of Tuberculosis and at present is a member of both the National and the New York Tuberculosis Associations. The fact that from 1907 to 1939 the State's death rate from that disease was reduced 75 per cent must have made the taxpayers more amenable.

One of the by-products of the tuberculosis campaign in New York was the establishment of the Special Public Health Commission in 1913, of which Mr. Folks was appointed secretary. A new public health law (through which the State Public Health Council was established) was enacted through this Commission's efforts, and when in 1930 another Special Public Health Commission was appointed Mr. Folks was again one of its members.

Mr. Folks has very definite ideas about the matter of public health. He is not a proponent of socialized clinical medicine, believing the rôle of a public health authority should be a preventive one, though by no means limited to indigents. But so far, he thinks, we have only scratched the surface. Since 1913 he has been vice-chairman of the New York State Public Health Council, and he is a member of the board of the National Committee for Mental Hygiene, of the technical committee of the New York City Health Department, and chairman of the governing board of the East Harlem Nursing and Health Demonstration. Most recently, Governor Lehman appointed him to head a Committee to make a complete survey of the State's mental hygiene services.

Homer Folks' responsibilities have by no means been limited to this country. In 1900 he was a special agent of the United States Commission to the Paris Exposition, and he has also been a special agent to the military government of Cuba. During the First World War he organized and directed the department of civil affairs of the American Red Cross in France, after the Armistice served as chief of the American Red Cross Survey Mission to Italy, Greece, Serbia, Belgium and France, and in 1921 was adviser to the American Red Cross in Europe. A book, *The Human Costs of the War,* was published in 1920.

In Mr. Folks' opinion this is an era in which wealth will be redistributed by raising the social, educational and health levels of all the people, and taxpayers might as well resign themselves to the fact. At the time when he became secretary of the State Charities Aid Association, he said, "There was just as much yelling about high taxes then as there is now, but it wasn't organized. Today it is organized, therefore it carries more weight." Nevertheless, what made the taxpayers indignant in those days is today taken as a matter of course: for instance, State hospitals rather than almshouses for the care of the insane.

In 1934 Mr. Folks said, in an article entitled *Making Relief Respectable*: "I see no reason for thinking that we shall ever wholly outgrow the need for a public relief system. . . My plea, therefore, is to accept it, not as a necessary evil, not as a makeshift, not as something demoralizing and unsocial. . ." From 1935 to 1936 he himself was a member of the Governor's Commission on Unemployment Relief. In the days before the institution of Federal relief he was commissioner of public charities in the City of New York (1902-3), president of the National Conference on Charities and Correction (1911), and in 1923 a member of the National Conference on Social Work. At present he is chairman of the executive committee of the Welfare Council of New York City.

Mr. and Mrs. Folks have two daughters, Gertrude Homera and Evelyn Esther. Mr. Folks is a Republican and a member of the University, Harvard and National Arts Clubs. His fraternity is Alpha Tau Omega. He holds honorary LL. D.'s from both his own Albion College and from Ohio Wesleyan, and in November 1940 Albion presented him with a Phi Beta Kappa key.

References

N Y Herald Tribune p25 O 17 '40 por
N Y Post p11 F 20 '40 por
Who's Who in America

FORBES, GUILLAUME, ARCHBISHOP Aug 10, 1865—May 22, 1940 Roman Catholic archbishop of Ottawa, Canada since 1928; served 52 years in the Church

References

Who's Who in Canada

Obituaries

N Y Herald Tribune p20 My 23 '40
N Y Times p23 My 23 '40

FOSDICK, HARRY EMERSON, REV.
May 24, 1878- Pastor of the Riverside Church, New York City

Address: b. 490 Riverside Drive, New York City; h. 606 W 122nd St, New York City

"Fuzzy-haired, magnetic" Harry Emerson Fosdick has been known for the past decade as a "sectless theological liberal" and probably the most influential clergyman in the United States. He is the pastor of the Riverside Church in New York City, built especially for him by his good friend John D. Rockefeller Jr. (Raymond Fosdick, his brother, is president of the Rockefeller Foundation.) In August 1940 he spoke against the "hysterical haste" with which the nation is being rushed into military conscription. "Conscription of wealth, conscription of industry, conscription of factories, conscription of labor, conscription of educators—why is not that democratic also if conscription of life is?" he asked.

For three centuries Dr. Fosdick's ancestors have been Puritans. Born in Buffalo, New York on May 24, 1878, he is the son of the late Frank Sheldon Fosdick, for 25 years principal of a Buffalo high school, and of Amy I. (Weaver) Fosdick. He attended Colgate University with no intentions of becoming a minister. Known as "Fuzzy" there because of his "flocculent, dark hair," he was prominent in the debating society, editor of the college paper, cheerleader. It was at college that he learned about a man named Darwin. Writing to his father about his discovery, he was amazed to get this letter: "Dear Harry: I believed in evolution before you were born." When he returned to school for his junior year he announced: "I'm throwing over my old idea of the universe! I'm building another—and leaving God out." He did build another in the next two years, but he couldn't quite manage to leave God out. By the time he was graduated in 1900, a member of Phi Beta Kappa, he had decided to attend Union Theological Seminary in New York City, even though not quite sure that his ideas weren't too "radical" for any church to risk him as its preacher.

Harry Emerson Fosdick was ordained for the Baptist ministry in 1903, and in August 1904 married Florence Allen Whitney of Worcester, Massachusetts. (They have two daughters, Elinor Whitney and Dorothy.) He received his B. D. from Union Theological Seminary in 1904 and the same year became pastor of the First (Baptist) Church at Montclair, New Jersey. In 1908 he acquired his M. A. from Columbia University, published his first book, *The Second Mile,* and began teaching homiletics at the Seminary.

He was very popular with his Montclair parishioners, but didn't impress them as particularly "radical." He led a campaign against the town's saloons, but in general his ministry was quiet. A new building was erected for the church, and the membership was trebled. Once he joined four

REV. HARRY EMERSON FOSDICK

other ministers in a gymnasium class, and the New York papers published a picture with the heading: "Five Muscular Christians." For the most part, he tried to be that. In 1915 he left Montclair to become a professor of practical theology at the Seminary, and the same year published his second book, *The Meaning of Prayer.* He also preached in colleges and universities, lectured in England and spoke to the British and American troops at the front in France and Flanders during World War I.

The aftermath of the War brought changes in religious feeling as well as in everything else. Dr. Fosdick felt that the unity that had sometimes manifested itself even among Catholics, Jews and Protestants during the grimmest days of the War made the time ripe for an experiment in interdenominationalism. In New York City two other churches were merged into the First Presbyterian Church, and Dr. Fosdick, a Baptist, was called in as minister. It was to be "a house of prayer for all people."

Dr. Fosdick preached the right of science to its place in the modern world, the right of scholars to trace the origins of the books of the Bible, the validity of faith which doesn't rest on any miraculous element, the duty of the Church to be something more than a defender of the social *status quo.* Presbyterian Fundamentalists shook their heads and some businessmen didn't approve, but the storm didn't really break until after the famous sermon delivered on May 21, 1922: "Shall the Fundamentalists Win?" In the uproar that followed, the general assembly of Presbyterian Churches finally asked Dr. Fosdick politely to take the Presbyterian vows or resign. He did the latter, severing relations on March 1, 1925. "I wouldn't live in a

FOSDICK, HARRY EMERSON, REV.—
Continued

generation like this and be anything but a heretic," was his opinion. And in May 1925 he was called to the Park Avenue Baptist Church, John D. Rockefeller Jr., agreeing to build him a $4,000,000 temple on Riverside Drive at .122nd Street to accommodate the overflow of worshipers.

The heresy charges served to make Dr. Fosdick's name better known than ever and, as he said, really put a "sounding-board" in back of his opinions. There were many other ministers of unpublicized unorthodoxy preaching to unshocked congregations, but it was Harry Emerson Fosdick who became the spokesman for "modernists" all over the United States. As the radio became more and more common his following grew enormously, even among those who didn't read his books, which sold over a million copies during the 1920's.

Some agnostics claimed Fosdick's attempt to reconcile religion with the modern world was not so much a battle with the Fundamentalists as with the material universe. They said he asked such questions as "Is God unnecessary?" and was forced to return always to the fact that he knew Christ's existence because he had "experienced direct contact with him," that he believed only because he believed. Also his "original intellectual contributions" were not numerous. But most liberals praised him as much for his views as for his courage, seeing the future of the Church as dependent on ministers of similar ideals. Fosdick himself was as confident that modernist theology would triumph over materialism as over Fundamentalism. "Each age of unbelief is followed by an age of belief; after Epicurus came Christ; after Descartes came Kant; after Spencer and Nietzche someone must come. It is now near the time."

In 1927 Dr. Fosdick's professional manner was described by an interviewer as resembling that of "the famous specialist of nervous diseases where the illness is largely imaginary, needing only confidence for its cure." Actually "specialist of nervous diseases" was not so far off the mark. Dr. Fosdick had revived and streamlined the "confessional," and with a knowledge of the rudiments of psychiatric procedure was attempting scientifically to diagnose the spiritual ailments of those who came to him for help. He ended by working with seven or eight specialists in nervous diseases. An energetic and tremendously alert little man, with a humor and self-confidence that never failed, Dr. Fosdick kept a regular schedule, taught a series of classes in the modern use of the *Bible* at the Seminary, spent long hours preparing his Sunday sermons, continued to publish books which continued to be read all over the world. Some of them are: *The Hope of the World* (1933); *The Secret of Vic-*

torious Living (1934); *The Power to See It Through* (1935); *Successful Christian Living* (1937); *A Guide to Understanding the Bible* (1938).

Although Dr. Fosdick's receptiveness to scientific theory has never grown less, his inherent mysticism has been deepening over a period of years. In 1935 he claimed that "the Church must go beyond modernism," astonishing those who still thought of him as modernism's most popular exponent. He also challenged the conception that it is religion's business to adjust man to his environment, especially if it is an environment that should be changed. Since the First World War he has been preaching vigorously against "putting Christ in uniform." An anti-war sermon which he delivered in June 1939—*Dare We Break the Vicious Circle of Fighting Evil with Evil?*— was later printed in pamphlet form by John D. Rockefeller Jr., and 50,000 copies distributed.

Dr. Fosdick is a firm believer in democracy, and defines it as "the conviction that there are extraordinary possibilities in ordinary people and that if we throw wide the doors of opportunity so that all boys and girls can bring out the best that is in them, we will get amazing results from unlikely sources."

References

Christian Cent 52:1480-2 N 20 '35; 52:1549-52 D 4 '35; 56:1539-42 D 13 '39
N Y Times p2 Ag 8 '40
New Yorker 3:18-20 Je 18 '27
Outlook 153:208-10 O 9 '29 por
Read Digest 30:79-81 My '37; 32:73-5 F '38 (Abr. from Vital Speeches 3: 567-9 Jl 1 '37)
R of Rs 95:54-5 My '37
Time 26:32 O 14 '35 por; 34:45 Jl 3 '39
World's Work 58:56-8 Jl '29 il por
Burns, P. G. Fosdick and the Fundamentalists pam nd
Jones, E. D. Harry Emerson Fosdick *In* American Preachers of Today p27-35 1933
Lotz, P. H. ed. Vocations and Professions 1940
Rusterholtz, W. P. Harry Emerson Fosdick: Emerson Again *In* American Heretics and Saints p273-89 1938
Shepherd, W. G. Harry Emerson Fosdick *In* Great Preachers as Seen by a Journalist p29-38 1924
Who's Who in America

FOURNET, LOUIS RENE MARIE CHARLES DARTIGE DU *See* Du Fournet, L. R. M. C. D.

FOWLER, ALFRED 1868—June 24, 1940
Astronomer; authority on solar spectra; member of five British eclipse expeditions; ex-head of Royal Astronomical Society; winner of many awards

References
    Who's Who
Obituaries
    N Y Herald Tribune p22 Je 26 '40
    N Y Times p23 Je 25 '40

FOWLER-BILLINGS, KATHARINE

June 12, 1902- Geologist; author; explorer

Address: c/o W. W. Norton & Company, Inc, 70 Fifth Ave, New York City

Because Katharine Fowler-Billings (then Fowler-Lunn), herself a geologist, was forbidden by the British Foreign Office to accompany her geologist husband to the Gold Coast, West Africa and was not to be "downed so easily," she set out independently for Sierra Leone (West Africa), a region that remained almost unscratched from a scientist's point of view. She went very specifically *not* to write a book, but in the course of a few years *The Gold Missus* was inevitable.

Katharine Fowler was born June 12, 1902, the daughter of William Plumer and Susan Farnham (Smith) Fowler. She had a typically Bostonian Puritanical upbringing; survived the regimen of a select girls' school; sternly refused to "come out" socially; and because she had never set foot out of New England settled upon Bryn Mawr as an acceptable college. Here she took courses in geology —hay-fever retreats in the White Mountains had endeared her to this—and biology. During her sophomore year her aunt took her to Europe: "Persuading Auntie that she needed a rest . . . I scaled the Jungfrau, the Breithorn and the Eiger. The trip up the Eiger was unfortunately visible through the telescope at our hotel in Mürren. The strain of knowing our movements for 13 hours, when we encountered difficult going and had to cut steps in the ice all the way up and down the Eiger's cone, was too much for Auntie. We took the next train to London. . . "

She pursued graduate studies at the University of Wisconsin (M. A. 1926) and here got her first geological field-work. She hitch-hiked through the Black Hills and beyond, and found that in order to get into some of the Montana mines she had to be smuggled along as a boy. At Columbia University she continued her studies, and wrote her Ph. D. thesis (1930) on the Laramie Mountains, Wyoming.

In the summer of 1929 she went to the International Geological Congress held in South Africa; did some exploring along the Congo tributaries; and on a clammy day in December of that year was married in a London registry office to James W. Lunn, also a geologist. It was the red tape surrounding his transfer by the British Foreign Office that drove her into feministic desperation—and the depths of West Africa.

After a divorce she was married, in April 1938, to Marland P. Billings, Harvard professor of geology. Since, she has been periodically engaged in the mapping of the Mount Washington (New Hampshire) quadrangle. Until recently she was instructor of geology at Wellesley; her son, George Bartlett Billings, was born in the summer of 1939.

References
    Fowler-Billings, K. Gold Missus; a
    Woman Prospector in Sierra Leone
    1938

FOX, JOHN MCDILL

Jan 3, 1891—Apr 18, 1940 Former dean of the Catholic University Law School (1930-35); trial examiner in charge of hearings for the Food and Drug Administration of the United States Department of Agriculture

References
    American Catholic Who's Who
    Who's Who in America

Obituaries
    N Y Times p17 Ap 20 '40

FRANK, GLENN

Oct 1, 1887—Sept 15, 1940 Noted liberal; editor; university president; author; political adviser; was killed in an automobile accident (together with his son) on the election eve of his first campaign for public office; in 1925 resigned as editor in chief of *Century Magazine;* became the famous "boy president" of the University of Wisconsin; ousted in 1937 by Governor La Follette after they differed over policies of administration; became chairman of a group which drafted plan for the Republican Party in 1940; long known as a bitter foe of the New Deal; was campaigning for Senator of Wisconsin at the time of his death

S. J. Woolf

GLENN FRANK
(Continued next page)

FRANK, GLENN—*Continued*

References

Am Mercury 31:149-59 F '34
Christian Sci Mon Mag p3+ My 4 '40
il pors
New Outlook 164:30 S '34
Newsweek 2:24-5 Ag 5 '33 por; 10:23
Jl 24 '37
Time 30:41 Jl 26 '37 por
Leaders in Education 1932
Who's Who in America
Who's Who in Journalism

Obituaries

Christian Cent 57:1184 S 25 '40
N Y Herald Tribune p1, 14 S 16 '40
por
N Y Times p1, 19 S 16 '40 por
Newsweek 16:59 S 23 '40 por
Sch & Soc 52:231 S 21 '40
Time 36:45 S 23 '40

FRANK, WALDO DAVID Aug 25, 1889-
Author
Address: c/o Doubleday, Doran, 14 W 49th
St, New York City

Waldo Frank's recent program for the
world's future, *Chart for Rough Water:
Our Rôle in a New World* (1940), brought
him once more into the public eye as the
defender and advocate of "the rebirth of
our lost humanism." His concern is with
"the new world which reaches further back
in time than the World War of 1914 and
extends into a future far beyond Hitler."
It is also, in the last chapter, with the problems presented to America by the present conflict in Europe. The concrete proposal
Frank makes for a solution to the "rough
water" in which the United States finds itself in 1940 is that "we make ourselves
non-belligerent allies of the Allies" who are
fighting to preserve "The Great Tradition."
The merit of Mr. Frank's book, according to Max Lerner, author and professor, is
that "it dares deal greatly with a great
theme. Its complexity lies in the multiple
rôle Mr. Frank essays of being at once religious prophet, moral exhorter, fashioner of
new myths, social analyst, historian of ideas,
political polemicist."

The most consistent criticism leveled at
the book is that it has been "miscalled *Chart
for Rough Water.*" One critic complained
that "there is nothing in it of the simple accuracy the word chart implies... It is confused, contradictory and tormentingly dull...
Its confusion and dullness are compounded
of a number of ingredients—Mr. Frank
wants everybody to get religion but doesn't
say so right out."

After the First World War, Frank, like
many other writers, veered sharply to the
Left. He was forced slowly but surely into
the arms of radicalism, though "he did not
surrender without a protracted inner
struggle." He accepted the doctrine of the
class struggle and the ends proposed by

Marxism—"the establishment of collective
society," but never in orthodox Marxist
form.

By the time 1936 came around Frank had
written a novel, *The Death and Birth of David
Markand* (1934), dealing with the workers
of the mining region in Kentucky, and had
gone so far as to say that "only the swift
maturity of a mass party of revolutionary
Communism, manned by Labor and by the
enlightened guards of petty bourgeoisie and
intelligentsia, can destroy American Fascism
by destroying the Capitalist system before it
has time to enter the last period of par-
oxysm, euphoria and catalepsy." *The Bride-
groom Cometh* (1939), a sequel to *David
Markand,* developed the same theme. However, Frank, though a sympathizer, was no
Communist, and at the time of the Trotsky
trials had definitely broken with the Communists. After the outbreak of World War
II Waldo Frank believed that "with every
ounce of our economy, of our political prestige, we should make ourselves non-belligerent allies of the Allies." It was because
he felt this belief was not shared clearly
enough by the *New Republic* that he resigned from that magazine in May 1940.
This resignation, like that of Lewis Mumford's (see sketch this issue) created a stir,
for Waldo Frank had been a consistent contributor to the magazine and long a member
of its staff.

Waldo Frank made his first protests
against this "godless" world on August 25,
1889 in Long Branch, New Jersey. He was
the son of Julius J. and Helen (Rosenberg)
Frank. Young Frank was a precocious lad;
by the time he was five years of age he had
written a play, and at the age of sixteen had
a novel accepted by a publisher. He attended Yale University, receiving both his
B. A. and M. A. degrees there, and in 1911
was elected to Phi Beta Kappa. While in
his senior year he ran a column as drama
critic on the New Haven *Courier-Journal.*

After graduation he did some writing for
the New York *Times* and the New York
Post and in 1913 left the United States for a
year in Europe. Back in New York in 1914,
he lived in an East Side block similar to
the one in *City Block* (1922) and free-
lanced as a writer. In 1916 he founded the
short-lived *Seven Arts* magazine with James
Oppenheim.

In 1917 Frank objected to the War for
political reasons, and to elaborate his beliefs
wrote an essay, *Our America* (1919). During that period he was a correspondent for
La Nouvelle Revue Française and *Europe,* two
Parisian publications, was a contributing editor
of the *New Republic* and *Masses* and lectured
on modern art and literature at the New
School for Social Research, New York City.

Frank married Margaret Naumburg in
1916. Miss Naumburg, well-known as the
founder of the Walden School, was a leader
in the application of psychoanalysis to education. They had one son, Thomas. Later
they were divorced, and Frank married

WALDO FRANK

Alma Magoon in 1927. They have two children, Michal and Deborah.

Frank has received more recognition from foreign lands than from his own country. He has an honorary degree from the Universidad Nacional de San Marcos, Lima, Peru, and most of his life has lectured abroad. "Handsome, dark, intense," he makes his strongest appeal mainly to the French and Spanish (his book on Spain, *Virgin Spain* [1926] is accepted as a classic by the Hispanic peoples), though he has a good-sized following in the United States. Included among his numerous works are the novels, *Rahab* (1922); *City Block* (1922); and *Holiday* (1923), which first made his reputation abroad. There are also biographical sketches, a play, *New Year's Eve* (1929), many articles, translations and a number of books which he has edited.

References

Nation 148:433-4+ Ap 15 '39
New Repub 89:8-10 N 4 '36; 102:568-73 Ap 29 '40; 102:603-8 My 6 '40
New Statesman & Nation 16:410-11 S 17 '38
N Y Times Book R p4 Je 23 '40 por
Sat R Lit 22:3-4+ My 25 '40 por; 22:12-13 Je 15 '40
So Atlan Q 35:13-26 Ja '36
Baldwin, C. C. Waldo Frank *In* Men Who Make Our Novels p174-79 1924
Beach, J. W. Expressionism: Woolf, Frank *In* Twentieth Century Novel p485-500 1932
Frank, W. Waldo Frank *In* Schreiber, G. ed. Portraits and Self-Portraits p41-45 1936
Kunitz, S. J. ed. Living Authors 1937

Michaud, R. Reinforcements: Willa Cather, Zona Gale, Floyd Dell, Joseph Hergesheimer, Waldo Frank *In* American Novel To-day p238-56 1928
Millett, F. B. Contemporary American Authors 1940
Munson, G. B. Waldo Frank 1923
Rosenfeld, P. Waldo Frank *In* Men Seen p89-109 1925
Who's Who in America
Who's Who in American Jewry

FRATELLINI, PAUL   Died Nov 1940
Most famous clown in the world; solemn one of *Les Trois Fratellinis*, three brothers beloved by all of France; played for audiences in nearly every country, appearing before Americans many times

References

Seldes, G. V. Further Note on the Fratellini *In* Seven Lively Arts p380-82 1924
Seldes, G. V. True and Inimitable Kings of Laughter *In* Seven Lively Arts p297-305 1924

Obituaries

N Y Herald Tribune p22 N 7 '40; p18 N 8 '40

FRAZER, SPAULDING   Oct 7, 1881—Mar 7, 1940 Dean of the law school of Newark University; nationally known attorney; represented the Congress of Industrial Organizations in its successful action to restrain Mayor Frank Hague from interfering with civil liberties

SPAULDING FRAZER
(Continued next page)

FRAZER, SPAULDING—*Continued*

Obituaries

Boston Transcript p9 Mr 8 '40
N Y Herald Tribune p22 Mr 8 '40
por
N Y Times p21 Mr 8 '40

FRAZIER, EDWARD FRANKLIN Sept
24, 1894- Professor of sociology; author
Address: Howard University, Washington,
D. C.

Professor E. Franklin Frazier, Negro
educator, of Howard University, has been
twice honored in 1940. In April he was
awarded a Guggenheim Fellowship for a
year in Brazil and the West Indies to make
a comparative study of the Negro family
there. In May he received the John Anisfield Award, presented each year for "a
sound and significant book published in the
previous 12 months on the subject of racial
relations in the contemporary world."

The book for which Dr. Frazier received
the Anisfield Award is *The Negro Family
in the United States* (July 1939), a history
of the Negro family group from the days
of slavery to the present. Although the
main study of the book is never obscured,
it incidentally throws much light on such
specific subjects as Negro education, the
Negro in business and industry, Negro
housing and similar problems. "Few studies," according to competent reviewers,
"have done as much to illuminate the obscure processes of social change as this
thorough-going treatment." Most significant, perhaps, is its revelation of wide variations in the standards of different social
classes among the colored population and
of the still wider variations in the behavior of different individuals. The substantial, authenticated material is often given
added point by the very successful organization of the whole and the engaging
manner in which it is presented.

Long before the publication of *The Negro
Family in the United States* Dr. Frazier was
recognized as an authority on Negro problems. His first sociological writing on the
Negro, *Durham: Capital of the Black Middle Class*, appeared in the *New Negro* in
1925. In 1932 the University of Chicago
Press published his *The Negro Family in
Chicago;* his study of *Traditions and Patterns of Negro Family Life* came out in
1934. Numerous magazines, including
academic ones such as the *American Journal
of Sociology* and the *American Sociological
Review,* and popular ones like *Forum, Current History* and *The Nation,* have published his articles. His *Negro Youth at the
Crossways,* prepared for the American Youth
Commission, was published in 1940.

Dr. Frazier's writings are based on firsthand study and firsthand knowledge. Frequently he has directed research projects,
and in 1935 and 1936 headed an economic
and social survey of Harlem for Mayor

EDWARD FRANKLIN FRAZIER

La Guardia's (see sketch this issue) New
York Commission on Conditions in Harlem.
From this came his study, *Negro Harlem*;
from his surveys in Chicago had come his
book on the Negro family in Chicago; and
from his personal study of Brazil and the
West Indies will undoubtedly come a well-
documented, analytical survey of the Negro
family.

Edward Franklin Frazier was born in
Eastern Shore, Maryland on September 24,
1894, the son of James Edward and Mary
(Clark) Frazier and received his schooling
in Baltimore. From high school he went to
Howard University, from which he was graduated *cum laude* in 1916. Right out of college
he got a job—teaching mathematics at Tuskegee Institute in Alabama—but he stayed there
only a year and then went to St. Paul's Normal
and Industrial School in Lawrenceville, Virginia. A year later he was teaching mathematics again—at the Baltimore High School.

In 1919, however, Dr. Frazier took a leave
of absence from teaching to get his master's
degree in sociology from Clark University
(1920). He did so well there that the New
York School of Social Work gave him a
year's research fellowship, after which he
went to Denmark as a fellow of the American-Scandinavian Foundation. In Denmark
Dr. Frazier studied "folk" high schools.

Back in the United States in 1922 he married Ellen Brown and became an instructor
in sociology at Morehouse College in Atlanta, Georgia. He stayed there until 1924,
when he became director of the Atlanta
School of Social Work. Then he went to
Fisk University, first as a special lecturer
in the department of sociology and then as
research professor in the same department.
From 1934 to the present he has been professor and head of the department of sociology at Howard University in Washing-

ton, D. C. During his years of teaching Dr. Frazier found time to earn his Ph. D. from the University of Chicago in 1931.

Full-faced, energetic Professor Frazier has made his classes at Howard University significant not only to his students but to Negroes and white people everywhere. His influence as a sociologist is far-reaching, and the two awards he received in 1940 are but further recognition for a man who has already made himself and his work a force in this country.

References

    N Y Herald Tribune p8 Ap 8 '40
    Sat R Lit 22:8 My 11 '40
    Who's Who in Colored America
    Who's Who in the Nation's Capital

FREEDLANDER, ARTHUR R. 1875— June 24, 1940 Portrait painter and art teacher; chairman of the New York Chapter of the American Artists' Professional League; former head of art school in Vineyard Haven and later director of the Martha's Vineyard School of Art; frequent exhibitor in shows of the National Academy of Design

References

    Art Digest 10:40 Jl '36 il
    Who's Who in American Art
    Who's Who in American Jewry

Obituaries

    N Y Herald Tribune p22 Je 26 '40
    N Y Times p23 Je 26 '40

FREYBERG, BERNARD CYRIL (frī'-bĕrg) Mar 21, 1889- Commander in chief of the New Zealand Expeditionary Force

Address: 7 Clarendon Pl, W. 2, London, England

General Freyberg, who in 1940 has charge of the New Zealand troops in the Near East, was one of the most picturesque figures to emerge from the First World War. His feats of valor in that War read suspiciously like fiction. Not only does he hold the Victoria Cross, but he won the Distinguished Service Order no less than three times, the first episode which gained him this distinction being one of the most amazing in the whole history of warfare. He has also gone rapidly up the ladder of army promotion: at the age of 28 he became a temporary brigadier general and at 45 a regular major general of peacetime status, after a uniquely short army service of only 18 years.

Though he was born in London, Bernard Cyril Freyberg went out to New Zealand as a child and was brought up there as a colonial, even learning the Maori language. He was educated at Wellington College, New Zealand, and at the Staff College, Camberley, England. As a youth he was a notable oarsman and boxer and won many trophies at swimming. There are journalistic stories about the years just prior to the First World War which should be treated skeptically. It is reported that Freyberg served against Victoriano Huerta in the Mexican Civil War of 1913; that in 1914 he was a dentist in New Zealand; that he sold his swimming cups to raise the fare to England; that when he reached London he buttonholed Winston Churchill (see sketch this issue), demanded a commission and received one. But a circular letter to the English press sent out by Freyberg to correct misstatements contains no allusion to these episodes. It states clearly that he was trained at the Staff College, Camberley, and joined the New Zealand forces in 1911, which would seem to rule out Mexico, dentistry and the improbable-sounding Churchill story.

Leaving conjecture for fact, it is certain that Freyberg was commissioned to the royal naval division in 1914, that he served with it in the abortive Antwerp expedition (where he received his first wound) and that in 1915 he went out to the Dardanelles as a lieutenant commander in the Hood battalion. It was then that the exploit described above as one of the most amazing in the history of warfare occurred. On the evening of April 24 a number of warships were maneuvering off Gallipoli. That night the destroyer *Kennet* staged a feint landing, and it was planned that the following night a platoon of the Hood battalion should be thrown ashore to light flares as a further feint. Freyberg, however, suggested that this would mean useless casualties; but that, being a strong swimmer, he might be rowed to within a mile of the shore, where he could swim off and light the flares. This was agreed to, and on the night planned for the feint Freyberg, naked, and with his body dark-stained, lowered himself into the water and set off, towing a waterproof bag containing oil flares, calcium lights, a knife and a revolver. He swam for an hour and a quarter in bitterly cold water, landed, lit his first flare, swam some 300 yards, lit his second flare, and crawled up the slope to some trenches, which he discovered to be dummies. He then lit a third flare on the beach, and set off once more into the bay, in pitch darkness. It was not until 3 a. m. that he was picked up. By means of this astounding feat the Turks were kept guessing for many hours about a part of the coast that was not really menaced, while the real landing was taking place much further south. For this Freyberg was awarded the D. S. O.

Freyberg served right through the Gallipoli campaign and then went, still with the royal naval division, to France. He was commissioned to the army on May 19, 1916. In November 1916 he won his Victoria Cross by leading the attack on Beaucourt (not Beaumont Hamel, as sometimes stated). Though he was wounded four times during the day, he pressed on to the

FREYBERG, BERNARD CYRIL—*Cont.*
capture of the village and five hundred German troops by savage hand-to-hand fighting. He was weak with loss of blood, but refused to be carried back to a dressing station until the position had been thoroughly consolidated.

Freyberg rose steadily. in rank and in June 1917 was promoted to a brigadier generalship. He won two bars to his D. S. O.—that is, he earned the distinction twice again. The first bar came from another piece of Freybergian dash and daring. The only way of investigating the position on his brigade's left flank was by a road running through No Man's Land. Freyberg got hold of a bicycle, pedaled down the road under heavy fire, reorganized the position and pedaled back again. Altogether he was wounded nine times in the War and mentioned in dispatches five times. In 1919 he was made Companion of the Order of St. Michael and St. George.

Peacetime soldiering inevitably entailed a slipping back in rank, but Freyberg was gazetted to the aristocratic Grenadier Guards. He was granted leave in April 1921 for a world tour to recuperate from his wounds and in 1922 married the Honorable Mrs. Barbara McLaren, widow of the Honorable Francis McLaren, an M. P. who had been killed in an air crash in 1917. His best man at the wedding was the late Sir James Barrie, a great friend of his.

In October 1922 Freyberg stood for Parliament as an Independent, with Liberal leanings, at South Cardiff, Wales, but was not elected. His military career continued with distinction, and he preserved all his fondness for strenuous outdoor pursuits. At one time he is reported to have made a practice of walking in from Windsor, where he was stationed, to London, 22 miles away. The yarn even credits him with walking back again in the afternoon! At all events, on August 5, 1925, at the age of 36, he set out to swim the English Channel. He was 16 hours and 44 minutes in the water, but was taken out only 500 yards from Dover, defeated by an old War wound.

On February 4, 1929 Freyberg obtained his lieutenant colonelcy in command of the first battalion, the Manchester regiment. He rose to full colonelcy in 1931, when he became assistant quartermaster general of the Southern command. In 1933 and 1934 he was a general staff officer, first grade, at the War Office, reaching the rank of major general in the latter year. Then on October 16, 1937 he went on retired pay, and in April 1938 was adopted prospective National and Conservative candidate for the parliamentary division of Spelthorne, Middlesex. When in September 1939 the New Zealand Expeditionary Force was formed, Freyberg was placed in charge of it and in February 1940 went out to Egypt.

Freyberg has one son who was 16 years old and at Eton College when World War II broke out. He ran away from school to join the army, was sent back again because of his age and had to content himself with Sundays spent doing War work in factories with other Eton boys.

References
> Birmingham Post F 13 '40
> Daily Mail F 13 '40
> Life 8:13 Mr 11 '40 por
> London Evening Standard Jl 9 '40
> Manchester Guardian F 13 '40
> News Chronicle F 13 '40
> Scotsman F 13 '40
> Who's Who

FULLER, CLARA CORNELIA 1852—Nov 8, 1940 Principal of Ossining School for Girls for 44 years until school closed in 1932; it became known as "Miss Fuller's School"; active member of Daughters of the American Revolution

Obituaries
> NY Herald Tribune p10 N 9 '40

FULLER, GEORGE WASHINGTON Nov 17, 1876—Oct 24, 1940 Historian and librarian; ordained a Unitarian minister in 1902 and after holding two pastorates in California from 1903 to 1906 became a field agent for the American Unitarian Association in Idaho and Montana; pastor First Church of Spokane, Washington from 1907 to 1911, when he became librarian of the Spokane Public Library, a post he held until retirement in 1936; his *History of the Pacific Northwest* (1931) is used as a textbook in college history departments

References
> Leaders in Education 1932
> Who's Who in America

GEORGE WASHINGTON FULLER

Who's Who in American Education
Who's Who in Library Service

Obituaries

N Y Herald Tribune p10 O 26 '40

FUNK, WALTHER (foōnk) Aug 18,
1890- German Minister of Economics;
president of the Reichsbank

Address: Deutsche Reichsbank, Berlin C 111,
Germany

Dr. Walther Immanuel Funk is the man
who succeeded Dr. Schacht, in title at least,
as ruler of the entire German national economy: the creation of money, the direction of
trade and economic policy. He would like also,
to be called "Minister of World Economics,"
and in the summer of 1940 was kept busy
issuing dire warnings to the United States—
denouncing free trade, denouncing the
United States' cartel scheme, declaring
barter the only salvation for world commerce, threatening to peg all European currencies to the Reichsmark (the "work
dollar"). His tone makes it difficult to believe that actually he is a friendly, fat little
man, "the gentlest of the Nazis," who lets
others put most of his theories in his mouth
and who is respected as a great political
economist mainly by his musician friends.

He was born of an aristocratic Königs-
berg family, the son of Walther and Sophie
(Urbschat) Funk, in Trakehnen in East
Prussia. After attending high school at
Intersburg and the Universities at Berlin
and Leipzig, acquiring his doctorate, he
became a reporter on a small provincial
paper. He changed jobs frequently, and
1916 found the 26-year-old journalist in
Berlin on the editorial staff of the Berlin
Börsen-Zeitung, a stock exchange paper.
There his job was to express the desires of
the Pan-Germans, the heavy industries, the
coal barons, the East Prussian military caste,
the large agriculturists. Throughout and
after the First World War, Dr Funk fought
socialism, fought inflation, published propaganda for I. G. Farben, Krupp and Thyssen
(see sketch this issue) for a suitable remuneration. Finally, marriage in 1920 to Luise
Schmidt-Sieben, the daughter of a wealthy
manufacturer, brought him into circles
where he occasionally acquired inside information that gave him a reputation for
understanding finance. By 1926 he was
chief editor of the paper.

On political currency questions it is said
that his friends Helfferich and Schacht used
Dr. Funk for a mouthpiece, and he preached
the obnoxiousness of foreign credits, the
pre-eminence of the home market, the importance of a national trade policy and increased production—theories of two men
who were at that time liberals, but whose
views were perfectly agreeable to Hitler.
At that period, however, Dr. Funk showed
no trace of anti-Semitism, moving respectfully, even obsequiously, among Jewish industrialist and banking acquaintances. The

WALTHER FUNK

head of the economic department of the
Nazi Party was also one of his friends, urged
him to join, but industry's hesitation in supporting the movement kept him cautiously
away.

In the end it was Dr. Funk who linked
the industrialists and their capital to the
National Socialist Party by introducing
Krupp, Thyssen and others to the Nazi
leaders. The result was the first election
success of 1928. And when some sort of
scandal lost him his newspaper position in
1930 he no longer hesitated to join the economic department of the Party—according
to the *New Republic* it was simply that "he
had lost a job and needed a new one." His
duties were to continue obtaining financial
support, to supervise money matters, to
keep the Party apparatus and propaganda
running smoothly. It was true that under
his guidance the National Socialists were
enormously in debt by the time of the 1932
election defeat, but when Hitler became
chancellor a month later the entire money
resources of the state became available to
them.

In 1933 Dr. Funk was appointed chief of
the Reich Press Bureau, and when Dr.
Goebbels expressed a desire to handle the
affairs of the press himself Funk became his
state secretary. But his positions as chairman of the Berlin Philharmonic Orchestra,
the Radio Corporation and the Filmkredit-
bank he found not only more remunerative
but also more soul-satisfying: his home was
a center for highbrow soirées at which he
would himself perform at the piano whenever
permitted, and he had always found the company of musicians, film stars and artists
highly agreeable. Perhaps he thought of
himself as a thwarted artist: back in his
Börsen-Zeitung days he had once paraphrased Goethe by writing under a para-

FUNK, WALTHER—*Continued*

graph of his own to be published in a press almanac: ."Only he who knows what the stock market is, knows what I suffer."

Dr. Funk had remained on good terms with Dr. Schacht (he had a talent for remaining on good terms with people who had not only turned Nazi) but had been given the Ministry of Economics and the presidency of the Reichsbank. Though acknowledged as the financial wizard of the Reich, he was independent, and when finally he thought he foresaw economic disaster as the result of obeying orders from above, he refused to be responsible. In 1938, therefore, he was forced to resign the Ministry of Economics, and the pliable Dr. Funk took his place, with his main task to justify the new Nazi trade agreements. Though Dr. Schacht cooperated with him for a while as president of the Reichsbank, a conflict with the Nazi leaders soon arose. Schacht refused unlimited expansion of credit on the basis of note issues, and Dr. Funk inherited the second office, too. Doing what he was told to do with "neither theoretical nor practical scruples," economic considerations were increasingly subordinated to military ones as German currency began to lose practically all connection with world markets.

Doubtless there was time free to play the piano, however, for in practice the management of the bank was turned over to a Berlin banker, the Ministry of Trade to Funk's secretary, and after Funk had made a rather disastrous Balkan tour in October 1938 the former chief of the Foreign Exchange Office was called on for similar duties arising in the future.

In December 1938 Dr. Funk acquired an additional title—Commissar for Increasing Production, at the head of the shipbuilding, motor, machine and most other industries— but in January 1940 even his nominal powers were reduced when a General Economic Council was devised which pared down his staff and his jurisdiction, transferred final authority to Goering.

A plumpish, thick-necked little man, not quite bald, Dr. Funk is known more for his happy-go-lucky opportunism than for his energy. He manages to get along. Besides, he has other assets: "he knows the best years for wine from the Rhine to Bordeaux" and is said to be the funniest after-dinner speaker in Berlin. There was humor even in his appeal to the German people to save not "real" wealth, but marks and pfennigs: "Some people are hoarding even bathtubs, although they can neither eat them, wear them around their necks, nor pay taxes with them."

It takes an artist to put humor into German taxes.

References

Business Week p55 D 4 '37 por
Liv Age 353:513-14 F '38
New Repub 98:12-13 F 8 '39 tab
N Y Times p2 Ag 12 '40

Newsweek 13:17 Ja 2 '39 por; 13:22 Ja 30 '39 por
Time 32:23 O 17 '38 por; 35:24 Ja 15 '40 por; 36:59 Ag 5 '40 por
Dutch, O. pseud. Dr. Walther Funk, the "Thwarted Artist" *In* Hitler's 12 Apostles p174-85 1940
International Who's Who
Pernot, M. German Trade Policy pam 1938
Wer ist's?
Who's Who in Commerce and Industry

FYFE, H. HAMILTON Sept 28, 1869-
Journalist
Address: The Cliff, Roedean, Brighton, England

Hamilton Fyfe is one of the ten most famous journalists in Europe. There is nothing he doesn't know about news gathering and presentation, about scoops and the workaday life of a pressman. He has been an editor, he has contributed to many of the world's journals, written over 20 books and several plays. But though he might easily have made a fortune, in 1940 he is writing mainly for *Reynolds News*, the organ of the British Cooperative Movement. After the last War he decided that he had so great a care for his conscience and political ideals that he would never again write anything for the Conservative press except non-political matter such as book reviews. He has kept that determination.

Henry Hamilton Fyfe (he uses only the H of the Henry) was born in London, the eldest son of the late James Hamilton Fyfe, a barrister and journalist who for some years was Parliamentary correspondent of the London *Times*. When Hamilton was only 10 his father died, but Hamilton's mother was able to send him to Fettes in Scotland. It was unusual for an English boy to attend a Scottish public school, but Mrs. Fyfe had heard Fettes described as the "Scottish Eton" and, since she couldn't afford the real Eton, sent him there.

At 17 Fyfe started to work for the London *Times*, first at odd jobs and later at reporting and sub-editing. Since his mornings were free he spent them studying and writing free-lance articles. Eventually he became editorial secretary to the London *Times'* editor, George Earle Buckle, and through this position was able to meet people prominent in the political, literary and art worlds. He also wrote reviews, dramatic criticisms and occasional leading articles.

In 1902 Fyfe committed the first of many actions which his friends considered rash or unworldly. The Licensed Victuallers' Association, the trade organization of the saloon-keepers, asked him to take over the editorial chair of their daily newspaper, the *Morning Advertiser*. Fyfe, well set as editorial secretary on the most dignified daily newspaper in the world, immediately threw up his job to run a journal which only saloonkeepers buy—he saw scope for initiative.

The late Lord Northcliffe, who missed nothing, saw the great improvements Fyfe was making in the victuallers' journal and in 1903 took him on to the *Daily Mirror,* then just starting to make its fortune as the first London all-picture daily. Fyfe stayed with the *Daily Mirror* four years and invented for it the very short leader and other devices to appeal to the public to which the *Daily Mirror* caters. In 1907, still under Northcliffe, Fyfe moved over to the *Daily Mail,* for which he acted as special writer, covering such notable stories as the Blériot cross-Channel flight.

By this time Northcliffe had gained control of the London *Times* and in 1913 sent Fyfe to cover the Carranza revolution in Mexico. The next year found Fyfe reporting the Ulster ferment over Irish home rule and, when the First World War broke out in August, Fyfe went immediately to France. His account in the London *Times* of the retreat from Mons was spectacular and his other reports were journalistic feats. In 1915 Fyfe was sent to Russia and Romania (he was there during the German attack); then back to Russia, from which he gave the British public its first account of the strange career and tragic death of Rasputin. In 1917 he reported from Spain and Portugal, then from Italy, and finally was sent to the United States as honorary attaché to the British War Mission. In 1918 he was in London preparing propaganda to be distributed among the German Army and civilians.

The year 1919 marked a turning point in Fyfe's ideas and career. He refused a knighthood and also refused to do anything but neutral reviewing for the *Daily Mail,* for this was a strongly Tory paper while his own views were going more and more toward the Left. He got a chance to work for a paper with which he was more in sympathy in 1922 when he was asked to become editor of the *Daily Herald,* Labor's first real attempt at a national daily. When Fyfe took over it was a poorly published sheet with a circulation of only 130,000. Fyfe made it into a real newspaper and within four years had brought its circulation up to 450,000.

Nevertheless, he wasn't entirely happy there. He had a number of disagreements with Ernest Bevin (see sketch this issue) and other trade union leaders on matters of procedure. Still, during the General Strike of 1926 he ran a successful emergency edition called the *British Gazette.* That same year he resigned. For a while he did some work on the *Daily Chronicle* until it was merged with the *Daily News.* He also ran for Labor candidate at Sevenoaks, Kent in 1929 and at Yeovil, Somerset in 1931. Both times he was defeated.

In 1907 Fyfe married Eleanor Kelly, daughter of the late William Kelly, an official at the War Office. Mrs. Fyfe accompanied him on many of his journeys in search of news. Today he lives at Roedean, near Brighton. His books include *Northcliffe, an Intimate Biography* (1930); *The British Liberal Party* (1928); *Pinero's Plays and Players* (1930); *Life of T. P. O'Connor* (1934); and an autobiography called *My Seven Selves* (1935). He has also written several plays, including a wordless drama called *The Pool,* which was successfully produced in London in 1912.

References

    Author's and Writer's Who's Who
    Fyfe, H. H. My Seven Selves 1935
    Who's Who

GALLI, ROSINA (gäl'lē) 1896—Apr 30, 1940 Former première danseuse and ballet mistress of the Metropolitan Opera Company, New York City

Musical America

ROSINA GALLI

References

    Forum 62:11-21 Jl '19
    Sat Eve Post 205:11 D 3 '32 por

Obituaries

    N Y Herald Tribune p22 My 1 '40 por
    N Y Sun p23 Ap 30 '40
    N Y Times p24 My 1 '40 por
    Newsweek 15:8 My 13 '40

GALLUP, GEORGE HORACE (gäl'lup) Nov 18, 1901- Public opinion statistician
Address: The Great Rd, Princeton, New Jersey

Founder and director of the American Institute of Public Opinion, Dr. George Gallup, streamlined tabulator of the democratic viewpoint, has in the past few years

GEORGE HORACE GALLUP

become America's foremost soothsayer. Unlike most oracles, he is generally right. The election year of 1940 has been a busy one for him and one, he feels, which has definitely established scientific sampling polls. Observers agreed with him that he hadn't "got out on a limb" as other polls have done at election time, but they felt, too, that he had hedged considerably in predicting the returns. There is no doubt that he underestimated the Roosevelt vote, though he has scientific reasons to explain this.

The Institute of Public Opinion is at present equipped to measure within three per cent of accuracy the views of the electorate on current social and political questions. For this reason the Gallup polls, appearing three times a week (with two Sunday surveys) in more than a hundred newspapers throughout the country, are read eagerly by many groups and interests. The Institute maintains a research office at Princeton, New Jersey, which sends out thousands of ballots every week. There are also a predetermined number of personal interviews by nearly 300 staff reporters stationed across the United States. Six categories, or "controls," of population-types are used to reflect opinion from all social strata. Dr. Gallup in 1940 has in operation four independent checking systems for the results of the surveys. In June 1940 a book on the Institute's methods and results, by Dr. Gallup and Saul Forbes Rae, called *The Pulse of Democracy*, was published.

The man who thus keeps his finger on the collective pulse of America was born in Jefferson, Iowa, November 18, 1901. His father was a speculator in ranch and farm lands, something of an eccentric, who spent a lot of time trying to develop a new sys-

tem of logic. He was also a staunch advocate of "dry" farming; Dr. Gallup says that he contributed to the formation of the Dust Bowl. Land values fell, and financial reverses came to the family while young Gallup was attending the University of Iowa. On his own, he organized a towel service in the swimming-pool locker room; and when a junior became editor of the college daily. He raised the paper to professional status by covering local news, obtaining a national wire service and a substantial amount of advertising. This made such an impression on university authorities that after his graduation they asked Gallup to be an instructor in journalism. The story is told that his first survey was of the campus to select the prettiest girl. The girl who won was Ophelia Smith Miller of Washington, Iowa, whom Gallup married December 27, 1925.

For the thesis of his Ph. D. in journalism, Gallup told how he had developed and tested a method of measuring reactions of newspaper readers to certain features by questioning a small selected number of them. This was the germ of the Gallup Institute method. While teaching journalism at Drake University, and at Northwestern in Evanston, Illinois, he continued to make his surveys of newspaper readers, financed by the Des Moines *Register and Tribune*. His work came to the attention of Young & Rubicam, a New York advertising agency, who hired him in 1932, and for whom he has been piling up statistics since, estimating the number of people who listen to their clients' radio programs or read their advertisments in the magazines.

In 1935 Gallup set about organizing the American Institute of Public Opinion. His first test question was to get the reaction of the average man on New Deal spending. But the first real test of the Institute was the Presidential election of 1936. The business of predicting the election became almost a contest between Gallup's new Institute and the traditional *Literary Digest* poll. The *Digest* poll was made up of names culled from subscription lists; automobile registration; and the telephone directory. Gallup, who had sold his service to papers on a money-back guarantee, got paler and paler as November came. His figures kept showing up for Roosevelt, whereas the *Digest* figures calmly proclaimed Landon. Abusive blasts against him he filed in a "Dirty Editorials" file. He worked himself into a state, knowing that if wrong this once, his Institute was ruined. But it is history now that Gallup's poll predicted the election results better than those of anyone else; and though he had to spend five months resting up after election, the Institute was saved.

Granting their accuracy, and despite their values, there have been objections to the Gallup polls on the grounds that they are a bad political influence. Dr. Gallup once answered that objection by pointing out, among other factors, the continued existence of the Republican Party. And undoubtedly people like being questioned on a Gallup poll. When an Arkansas tenant farmer was recently asked his opinion on a third term for Roosevelt, he was amazed and pleased. "You're asking *me*? Does my opinion count? Nobody ever asked me for it before."

Dr. Gallup also started in 1936 the British Institute of Public Opinion, which uses the methods of the American Institute. He is the author of *A New Technique for Measuring Reader Interest.*

In private life Dr. Gallup, who has been called the most discussed man in the advertising world, is a pretty typical and model American. His own reactions and opinions check almost exactly with the majority of those received on his polls. One writer has described his appearance as that of "a grown-up, dog-eared edition of a 4-H Club boy. His heavily muscled shoulders, draped in tailored tweeds selected by his wife, are the best features of his solid torso. His face is round and amiable and photographs badly, mainly because of an insolent, tip-tilt nose. His black hair is thinning but his eyebrows remain nicely bushy." Dr. Gallup's childhood friends all call him "Ted." He likes to sprawl at his desk; he has professorial fits of forgetfulness; and his own filing system consists of putting everything into a heap and pulling one piece out at random.

Dr. Gallup, his wife and three children, George, Jr., Alec and Julia, live in a pleasant early-American farmhouse near Princeton. Here Dr. Gallup has some 300 acres, where he raises a purebred herd of Aberdeen Angus cattle. He says his prime motive in life is to make his family comfortable. His chief aversions are flummery and red tape; an occasional beer, horseback riding and heroic novels his favorite relaxations.

References

Am Mag 128:88 Ag '39 por; 130:31+ N '40 por
Cur Hist 51:23-6+ F '40 por
Forum 103:92-5 F '40
New Yorker 16:20-4 Mr 2 '40
Newsweek 14:30-1 O 30 '39 il por
Read Digest 33:55-6 D '38
Sat Eve Post 211:8-9+ Ja 21 '39 il por
Scholastic 35:29-30 O 2 '39 por
Scrib Mag 100:36-9+ N '36
America's Young Men
Who's Who in America

GAMELIN, MARIE GUSTAVE *See* Gamelin, M. G.

GAMELIN, MAURICE GUSTAVE (găm'lăN) Sept 20, 1872- Former commander in chief of the Allied Armies and former chief of the French national defense

General Maurice Gustave Gamelin, former "Generalissimo of the Allied Armies of Air, Sea and Earth," was in the autumn of 1940 under arrest, on trial at Riom for his acts that "led to the passage from the state of peace to a state of war . . . and thereafter aggravated the consequences of the situation thus created." General Gamelin, who for a time was reported to have been executed, to have committed suicide "following a definite invitation of the French High Command," to have fled France, had previously been interned along with others of France's former leaders at the Château Chazeron, busy preparing his defense brief.

Even though he may now be accused by the Vichy government of sacrificing ill-equipped troops to cover his own blunder, of depending on a Maginot Line that was no defense—accused by others of lack of action and the tactical blunder of moving the French Army into Belgium, still it is certain that "no commander in chief in the First World War came to his task as Gamelin did last September, because none had, like Gamelin, gone through another World War." And it also seems certain that few commanders so enjoyed the entire confidence and respect of their men. In the last War Gamelin displayed an amazing talent for being right rather than rash, and for disentangling himself from engagements with minimum losses. Soldiers appreciate that particular brand of economy. And French people had often been heard to say: "He will bring us victory and peace, but not by talking about it."

Maurice Gustave Gamelin was born just across from the War Ministry in Paris on September 20, 1872. His father was a former controller general of the French Army; his uncle had been the last Governor of Strasbourg before the city was lost to the Germans; on his father's side he was descended from at least five generals, and many of the ancestors of his mother, a distinguished painter, had been officers in the French Army. But as a boy a literary career was predicted for him. He consequently attended the Collège Stanislas, "a strict and scholarly Catholic school with considerable social standing and a military flavor," and disciplined his mind by memorizing 10 lines of prose at night and reading a book of philosophy a week. Upon graduation in 1891 he succumbed to the military tradition by attending St. Cyr, French training school for army officers, but he never recovered from the habit of philosophy.

At St. Cyr young Gamelin had overawed his classmates by being second in his entrance examinations, by graduating first in a class of 449, and most of all by his physical endurance in being the only one among them never to fall asleep during evening lectures. He now began his career in the infantry, spending three years with an Algerian regiment in Africa, where a different kind of physical endurance was necessary. In 1895 he was promoted to the rank of lieutenant, and soon afterwards was seconded to the Army's cartographical service, where he spent three years because "he liked to paint landscapes in water color, survey and map."

MAURICE GAMELIN

By 1898 Gamelin was back in Paris at l'
Ecole de Guerre for French officers, where
Foch was one of the instructors. There he
studied "topography and a species of military metaphysics then in vogue," but was
saved from too extreme a military mysticism by Foch's critical attitude: "Remember, the solution now counts only 25 percent, the application of the solution in war
later on 75." He finished in 1901 with
a record marked, "very good," and was
promptly posted to the staff of Corps XV
with the rank of captain. In 1904 he was
given a company of chasseurs.

From 1906 to 1911 Gamelin was on
Joffre's staff as confidential officer. It was
an amazing combination, and one that was
to become famous. Joffre having "all the
practical experience and Gamelin all the
theory it was then possible for officers of
the French Army to acquire," together they
formed very nearly "an intellectual entity."
When in 1911 General Micheler was relieved
of his command in the midst of the "perennial war scare," Joffre became commander
in chief of the French Army, and Gamelin
head of his small group of advisers, with
the title "Chef de Cabinet." There was an
interval of staff work in 1913, but in 1914,
when war broke out, Gamelin was officer
and chief of staff at general headquarters,
still Joffre's "ears and eyes, hearing of
everything that happened in the Army and
knowing, before anybody except Joffre,
what the Army was going to do next."

Joffre called him "one of my red blood
corpuscles." In September of 1914 it was
Gamelin who worked out the strategic
move which stopped the German advance
on Paris and saved the Allied cause at the
famous Battle of the Marne. The story
goes that Gamelin, detecting a weakness in
the German position, presented Joffre with
his arguments for an early attack. "I agree.
Write the order," Joffre said. Replied
Gamelin, pulling it out of his pocket: "Here
it is, my General"

"Very much all there," one British general
was reported to have characterized the calm
little tactician—and it seems he was, in
more than one sense. In 1916, when things
looked darkest, he asked for an active post,
and was given command of a brigade of
chasseurs, with the rank of colonel. He was
in Alsace; in the Somme; he was twice
mentioned in army orders; and at the end
of the year he was promoted to the rank
of brigadier general. He was then recalled
to serve again on Joffre's staff, and when
Joffre was superseded he was shifted to the
post of chief of staff to General Micheler,
commanding the group of Armies of Reserve.
Then from May 1917 to the end of the
War he commanded the Ninth Division
which made such a brilliant record in some
of the last offensives of the War.

After the War Gamelin was away from
the home army until 1925 on an assignment
as head of the Military Mission to Brazil,
counteracting German influences in that
country, and reorganizing the Brazilian
Army on the French pattern. In 1925 he
was sent to Syria as commander of the
French forces in Levant to suppress a rising
of the Djebel Druse and to relieve the
besieged outpost of Soneida. There he displayed "an almost irritating complacency
and deliberateness, working out his plan of
campaign and accumulating men and material." In one report local authorities announced sarcastically: "Gamelin now has
more men than the entire population of the
Druses, men, women and children included.
When he gets some more reinforcements he
may perhaps attack."

Gamelin, however, continued to do things
in his own studied way, and Soneida was reoccupied with almost no losses on the part
of the French, Damascus beseiged and the resistance of the tribesmen finally completely
broken down, although it must be said that
he showed little interest in inflicting minimum losses on the enemy.

In 1928 he returned to France and was
given command of Corps XX at Nancy
(Foch's command in 1914). Two years later
he was made chief quartermaster of the
Paris general staff, and in 1931 he became
chief of the general staff of the French
Army. At that time he believed war between France and Germany inevitable, but
believed it would be a "war of movement"
rather than a war of numbers. The actual
war was only four years closer when he succeeded Weygand (see sketch this issue) as
head of the army, and, as such, also inspector general and vice-president of the Higher
Council of War, responsible for the drafting
and execution of all plans and for the organization, equipment and training of the
army.

The "Gamelin Plan" for the anticipated
coming war was known as one to knock

Italy out as quickly as possible by an attack through the Alps. But there must be plans for fighting any combination anywhere—as Gamelin put it: "Like a timetable.. Trains in all directions." He extended the conscript period from a year to eighteen months to two years, supposedly speeded up the mechanization of the army, extended the Maginot Line of fortifications from the Rhine to the English Channel, originated the defense system of Belgium, on the Italian side created a system of defense considered so perfect that there would never be the slightest fear of attack by Mussolini at France's "back door."

At the same time he was a sincere advocate of collective security and favored the Russian alliance. In 1936 he urged Léon Blum (see sketch this issue) to pitch in with the Loyalists in Spain. When the Germans reoccupied the Rhineland in the same year he went to the government to say he could chase them out if given permission. At the time of the Munich crisis he begged Daladier (see sketch this issue) to support Czechoslovakia and went to London to tell British statesmen that his army was ready to fight. Finally, when all failed, his trips to London during the numerous crises that followed Munich had much to do with the forging of close plans for the cooperation of British and French forces.

On January 23, 1939 Gamelin became chief of the general staff of the National Defense, and it was understood that France would be entitled to the nomination of commander in chief for the Allied land forces when war broke out, since France had the largest army. On September 1, 1939 Gamelin became almost automatically Generalissimo of the Allied Armies, which were later to include those of Belgium and Holland as well as France and England.

Criticized for lack of action during the first few months of the War. Gamelin explained the situation thus: "The last War developed a stage of stagnation after the fall of 1914. This one begins with stagnation. The other then developed a stage of attrition, with the Allies trying to kill two Germans for every Allied casualty. This has been a war of accumulation, with us building two planes for every one the Germans can build. The object is the same—to reach a definite superiority." It was generally agreed that Gamelin was waiting for the Germans to attack or for the Allied strength to be so great that an attack on the Allied side would overwhelm them, although Reynaud (see sketch this issue) said: "Time is not necessarily on our side. She is a neutral who will rally to force."

On May 10, 1940 Gamelin's order of the day to the allied troops read:

"The attack which we have forseen since last October was launched this morning.

"Germany has begun to fight to the death against us.

"The orders are for France and her Allies: Courage, energy, confidence."

As for the growing danger of Italy entering the arena on the side of the Axis powers, his reported comment was sardonic: "If Italy should remain neutral, I need five divisions to watch her. If she goes over to Hitler, I should need some ten divisions to beat her. But if Italy should join the Allies, I should need fifteen divisions to help her." This was his last order.

This little general "with gray hair, a small gray mustache, a small, neat dignity" was both a disciple of Bergson and a world authority on Napoleon's movements.

Past the ordinary retirement age, but looking extremely young for his years, Maurice Gamelin was first married not many years ago, on his fifty-fifth birthday. "Madame la Générale" is "as neutral-toned as her husband, a kindly, unpretentious woman who dislikes publicity" and who is on the directorates of at least a dozen war charities. A note received by a needy woman from General Gamelin in the fall of 1939 tells something about both the extent of his wife's activities and his own sensitiveness. "I am sorry," it began, "that my wife is too busy to answer your request..."

Gamelin hated publicity even more than his wife, and perhaps that's why his face often looked so grim in newspaper photographs. Actually it was a rather kindly face, that of "a sceptical but indulgent Dutch uncle in a Frans Hals painting." ("One must not command, but persuade," he often said.) He had a quiet voice, and a "curious detachment of manner which those who are not admitted to his friendship consider cold and aloof," but he was not unsociable: he didn't mind the luncheons and dinners he had to attend, he had friends on every general staff except the German, he enjoyed going out evenings to hear opera and ancient music. His Paris apartment near the Bois de Boulogne, where his wife continued to stay, and where he actually was, tending its rose garden in the days when rumors of his death and disappearance flew fast, was strictly in keeping with his modest income. In more normal times it was his habit to get up at 7 a.m. and to work straight on through until evening, only stopping sometime in the afternoon to take his big police dog out for a brisk walk. He was a "methodical but also an imaginative worker with a special passion for maps," treated his staff with "benevolent formality" and was always willing to learn from subordinates. In religion he was a Catholic, "a believer but not a strict observer," and politics he left alone. The politicians should leave the army alone, too, he thought. Occasionally he rode, and he had had so much experience walking all over France that he kept his feet and legs comfortable even when he was in full regalia, with at least 20 ribbons obligatory. Mountain skiing used to be his favorite sport, but there's been little of that for a long time, and he hasn't touched a paint box in years.

GAMELIN, MAURICE—*Continued*

References

Cur Hist 51:29 O '39
Harper 180:34-40 D '39
Illustration 220:86-7 My 21 '38 pors
Liv Age 353:144-6 O '37; 358:49-51
    Mr '40; 358:228 My '40
N Y Times VII p7˙F 4 '40 por
New Yorker 16:24-7 My 11 '40; 16:
    22-6 My 18 '40
Read Digest 36:83-6 Mr '40
Sat Eve Post 213:12-13+ S 28 '40 il
    por
Scholastic 34:24S My 6 '39 por; 35:
    20S N 6 '39
Time 33:22 Ap 24 '39 por; 34:20-3
    Ag 14 '39 pors; 35:35 Je 10 '40; 36:
    25 Ag 12 '40; 36:31 S 30 '40
Finn, A. Gamelin: the Man Nobody
    Knows *In* Benjamin, R. S. ed.
    Inside Story p117-27 1940
International Who's Who
Ray, O. General Gamelin pam 1939
Romains, J. Seven Mysteries of Eu-
    rope 1940

GANFIELD, WILLIAM ARTHUR Sept 3, 1873—Oct 18, 1940 Retired president of Carroll College at Waukesha, Wisconsin; ordained in the Presbyterian ministry and served as pastor at Green Bay, Wisconsin; president of Centre College, Danville, Kentucky 1915 to 1921 when he went to Carroll College; member of Republican National Advisory Committee

References

Leaders in Education 1932
Who's Who in America

Obituaries

N Y Herald Tribune p12 O 19 '40
N Y Times p17 O 19 '40

GARLAND, HAMLIN Sept 14, 1860—Mar 4, 1940 Author

Hamlin Garland was one of the great literary pioneers. His pioneering was not in literary style, for his prose was as direct and honest and as unaffected as the country about which he wrote. But he was one of the first "dirt farmer novelists"—the first American to write successfully about the West, and "to sell what he had written to sophisticated publishers and readers in Boston."

At the time of his death of a cerebral hemorrhage at the age of 79 in Hollywood, California, he was called the "dean of American letters." It was a title he richly deserved. He had worked hard for it, enduring poverty and privation, floundering grimly in a world of letters new to him, yet always refusing to compromise artistic standards, or to write anything he considered cheap or untrue.

Hamlin Garland had come to Boston in the 1880's, a lean, gawky boy with hands calloused by the plow, and eyes used to the limitless distances of the western prairies. He was born in West Salem, Wisconsin, September 14, 1860, and spent his entire boyhood in the West and Midwest. His father was Richard H. Garland, a native of Maine; his mother, Isabelle (McClintock) Garland, of New England and Scottish ancestry. The couple had trekked westward in the immigration wave of the '50s. Richard Garland had enlisted in the Union Army in the third year of the Civil War, and one of Hamlin Garland's first childhood recollections was of his father's return from the War, a memory he incorporated in *The Return of the Private,* an ironic short story.

In 1869 the Garlands and their children moved to Minnesota, and then to Iowa, building a homestead in Mitchell County, in northern Iowa. Here at 10 young Hamlin was following a plow, turning two acres a day in a 10-hour stretch, after first getting up to do the chores.

The Garlands moved to Osage, the county seat in 1876, and Hamlin entered the Cedar Valley Seminary. Here farm chores were forgotten for a while, and new vistas to literature, oratory and debate were opened. Young Garland was graduated from the Cedar Valley Seminary in 1881, and his first work outside of the farm was a year of school teaching in Illinois. In the interim there had been, too, another move for the Garland family, this time to Ordway, South Dakota, after a plague of grasshoppers and chinch bugs had descended on the Iowa homestead. There was also a tramping tour on which Hamlin and his brother Franklin went about the country, digging ditches, shingling roofs and doing odd jobs for board and lodging. The two boys went to Chicago, Niagara Falls, Boston and New York. But Hamlin was terrified of the cities, and at 23, after a winter of school teaching, he staked out a claim in McPherson County, South Dakota. It looked as if "his literary ambitions might be plowed under," but two withering summers and three blizzards ended his farm career.

He went East again. His life at this period is graphically described by Joseph E. Chamberlain of the Boston *Transcript.* Chamberlain writes: "He lived in bleak little attic rooms, breakfasted on eight cents, dined on fifteen, and supped on ten; wore his prairie-born coat to a frazzle, and was shrunken thin by low fare; but his head was up and his manner, though grave, was confident.

"He would not equivocate or compromise or deny anything that he really believed in. When he was earning $8 a week, and sent a part of that to support his father and mother, whose crops on their claim in Dakota had for two years running been entirely eaten by grasshoppers and chinch bugs, he refused to write anything for a newspaper that he was not willing to sign with his own name, or to write romantic love stories for a magazine. 'We have had enough of those lies,' he said, and went off and dined on a dime."

Mr. Garland's interest in oratory led to an opportunity to deliver a lecture, and subsequently to his appointment as an instructor of English and American literature in the Boston School of Oratory. He also wrote occasionally for the *Transcript,* but his first literary contribution of consequence was a story on corn husking which he sold to *Harper's Magazine* for $25. Boston was beginning to discover the slender 27-year-old farm boy-author.

In 1890 he sold a story to *Century* for $500 and in 1891 published his first book, *Main Traveled Roads,* a collection of his best short stories, now considered a classic. The following year he published his first novel, *A Spoil of Office.*

Meanwhile he had met Boston's literary celebrities, William Dean Howells, who before Hamlin Garland had the title of "dean of American letters," and others, and had formed many lifelong friendships.

But the cities did not make a lasting impression on his writing, although they made him articulate. His most famous books are realistic pictures of the Midwest he knew so well. Among the best remembered is the trilogy, *A Son of the Middle Border, A Daughter of the Middle Border,* which won the Pulitzer Prize in 1921, and *Trailmakers of the Middle Border,* all three of which were largely autobiographical and recorded the efforts of the Garland and McClintock families to transform the raw prairie land into livable homesteads.

As his writing and lectures found a steady market, Hamlin Garland traveled. He lived in New York for a time. Then he went to Chicago for the Columbian Exposition in 1893. He took his parents on a trip to California and persuaded them to return to New Salem, Wisconsin, where he bought a comfortable home for them. There was also an interlude in 1898 when he and a former classmate went to the Yukon in Alaska.

Returning from Alaska, he married Zulime Taft, sister of Lorado Taft, the Chicago sculptor, in November 1899. Mr. Garland lived in Chicago until 1916, then returned to New York, where he remained until 1930. That year he established a home in California.

He made one excursion into the political arena, when he made a speaking tour of the West for the Farmers' Alliance and the People's Party, to expound Henry George's philosophy of the single tax in the nineties.

The country boy who had learned to read from *McGuffey's Reader* on an Iowa homestead, lectured on literary style and won honorary literary awards. He was elected to the American Academy of Arts and Letters in 1918, later becoming its president. He won the Pulitzer Prize in 1921. And in 1931 he was awarded the Roosevelt

HAMLIN GARLAND

Memorial Association Medal "for distinguished service as a social historian." Hailed as one of the first realists in a period dominated by the traditions of a Victorian Europe, he disliked the term "realist." His stark, realistic and sometimes grim picture of pioneer life he preferred to describe as that of a "veritist," a word he coined to express his attitude towards his writing.

He was ever an interested observer of life. When he moved to Hollywood and became a neighbor of Cecil B. De. Mille, the motion picture director, he became interested in the doings of the motion picture colony.

At the time of his death Mr. Garland was completing the final chapters of a book, *The Fortunate Exile,* describing his 10 years in California, and had instructed his family that he wanted it published only after his death.

He had two daughters, Mrs. Constance Harper and Mrs. Mindret Lord, both of whom took part indirectly in his writing, the former by illustrating several of her father's books, and the latter by making his works better known by her readings before audiences.

In addition to the *Middle Border* trilogy, which made for him a lasting place in American literature, Mr. Garland was the author of *A Spoil of Office, Jason Edwards, A Little Norsk, A Member of the Third House, Crumbling Idols, Wayside Courtships, Prairie Songs, The Spirit of Sweetwater, The Eagle's Heart, Her Mountain Lover, The Captain of the Gray Horse Troop, Hesper, Light of the Star, The Tyranny of the Dark, Money Magic, Boy Life on the Prairie, The Shadow World, Cavanagh Forest Ranger, Victor Olnee's Discipline, Other Main Traveled Roads, The Forester's Daughter, The Trail of the Gold-Seekers* and a biography of Ulysses

GARLAND, HAMLIN—*Continued*
S. Grant. In 1936 he published *Forty Years of Psychic Research*, a summary of his interest in the subject.

References

Bookm 70:138-52, 246-57, 392-406, 514-28, 625-38; 71:44-57, 196-208, 302-13, 423-34 O '29-Jl.'30
Wilson Lib Bul 3:466 F '29 por
Garland, H. A Daughter of the Middle Border 1921
Garland, H. A Son of the Middle Border 1917
Garland, H. Trailmakers of the Middle Border 1926
International Mark Twain Society Hamlin Garland Memorial pam 1940
Kunitz, S. J. ed. Living Authors 1937
Who's Who in America

Obituaries

N Y Herald Tribune p22 Mr 5 '40 por; p24 Mr 6 '40
N Y Sun p19 Mr 5 '40
Pub W 137:1089 Mr 9 '40
Scholastic 36:27 Mr 18 '40 por
Time 35:64 Mr 11 '40
Times [London] Lit Sup p138 Mr 16 '40

GARVEY, MARCUS 1880—June 10, 1940
West Indian Negro who once set himself up as "Emperor of the Kingdom of Africa" in New York's Harlem and appeared before the League of Nations as representative of "the black peoples of the world"; leader of the "Back to Africa" movement; formed the Black Star Steamship Line to transport Negroes to their homeland; con-

MARCUS GARVEY

victed of mail fraud in 1923 and subsequently deported

References

Ovington, M. W. Marcus Garvey *In* Portraits in Color p18-30 1927

Obituaries

N Y Herald Tribune p22 Je 12 '40 por
N Y Times p25 Je 12 '40
Newsweek 15:8 Je 24 '40 por

GATES, WILLIAM 1874—Apr 24, 1940
Former professor at Johns Hopkins University; devoted 30 years to archeological work; outstanding authority on Mayan history, language and culture; author of numerous books

Obituaries

N Y Herald Tribune p20 Ap 25 '40 por
N Y Times p23 Ap 25 '40 por

GATTI-CASAZZA, GIULIO (gät'tê-kä-sät'sä jōōl'yô) Feb 3, 1869—Sept 2, 1940
Former impresario of the Metropolitan Opera in New York for 27 years; died in

Musical America
GIULIO GATTI-CASAZZA

Italy a few months after the death of his wife, Rosina Galli, former ballet mistress of the Metropolitan; prominent in opera and music for over 40 years; produced 15 American operas in 27 years; discovered Caruso; brought Chaliapin, Flagstad, Toscanini and many others to New York; retired from the Metropolitan in 1935

References

Am Mercury 35:33-40 My '35
Commonweal 22:20 My 3 '35

Lit Digest 118:26 N 17 '34 il por
Musician 39:3 N '34
Nation 140:495 My 1 '35
New Yorker 1:9-10 F 21 '25
Sat Eve Post 206:5-7+ O 28; 20-1+
N 11; 26+ N 25; 18-19+ D 9; 26-
7+ D 23 '33
Thompson, O. ed. International Cy-
clopedia of Music and Musicians
1939
Who's Who in America 1934-35
Wier, A. E. ed. Macmillan Encyclo-
pedia of Music and Musicians 1938

Obituaries
N Y Herald Tribune p1, 17 S 3 '40
pors
N Y Times p1+ S 3 '40 por
Newsweek 16:8 S 16 '40
Time 36:38 S 9 '40

GAULLE, CHARLES DE *See* De Gaulle,
C.

**GAUTHIER, JOSEPH ALEXANDRE
GEORGE, ARCHBISHOP** (gō′tyā) Oct
9, 1871—Aug 31, 1940 Roman Catholic
Archbishop of Montreal since 1939; Coad-
jutor Archbishop for 16 years; ordained as
priest in 1894; noted as foe of sit-down
strikes; staged a mass wedding for 105
couples as protest against divorce; ex-rector
of the University of Montreal

References
Catholic Who's Who
Who's Who

Obituaries
Cath World 152:107 O '40
N Y Herald Tribune p18 S 1 '40 por
N Y Times p28 S 1 '40 por

GAYDA, VIRGINIO (gī′dà) Aug 12, 1885-
Italian editor
Address: h. Paläzzo Sciarra, Rome

The latest blasts of Virginio Gayda, editor
of *Il Giornale d'Italia* and spokesman for Mussolini, have been directed against the United
States. "By participating with too much
indiscretion in European affairs and in the
solution of problems that are entirely European in their origin and significance," he said,
"the United States is automatically giving
to the European powers the right to retaliate
today or at any future time in American
history and on American territory." His
latest activity has been the formation, with
Otto Dietrich, German press chief, of a
new international society of journalists "to
fight against falsehood, which is the favorite
tactic of the enemy."

The most quoted Italian of all is Gayda,
to many outside of Italy, Fascist No. 3.
Daily, in anywhere from two to four columns spread across the front page of *Il
Giornale d'Italia,* he announces, explains and
defends Mussolini's foreign policy. On
Sundays his comments appear in *La Voce*

Pix

VIRGINIO GAYDA

d'Italia; his reviews appear weekly in serious
magazines; books and special articles appear
constantly under his name. The most prolific journalist in Italy and probably in the
world, Gayda's weekly output has been estimated at 50,000 or 60,000 words.

Gayda's style is more conspicuous for
its tones of "wounded innocence, anger and
threats" than for its clearness. As quoted
in the foreign press his messages are clear
and striking enough, but they have usually
been taken from the mass of verbiage which
surrounds them when printed in Rome.
They are not, as is sometimes supposed,
directly dictated by Mussolini, and as a
matter of fact Gayda seldom submits his
copy for approval to Mussolini or Ciano
(see sketch July issue). What happens is
that "Mussolini or Ciano strikes a note on
the Fascist political piano and Dr. Gayda
writes the theme song." But he is careful
to get it right. Almost every statement is
bolstered with columns of figures, facts and
quotations, and almost daily Gayda calls at
the Chigi Palace of the Foreign Ministry
to confirm his own impressions.

Virginio Gayda, the son of Stefano and
Clotilde (Stratta) Gayda, was born in Rome
of Piedmontese stock and was originally cut
out to be a political economist, but after
being graduated from the School of Political
Economy of the University of Turin he
plunged into newspaper work. His first
job, which he got in 1908, was as reporter
on *La Stampa,* a Turin newspaper. As reporter he was sent to the Balkan Peninsula
and Turkey and finally to Austria, where
he stayed for over five years. When the First
World War broke out he was in Rome, together
with the principal Italian politicians exiled
from Austria, directing the Italian policy
toward intervention on the side of the
Entente Powers.

GAYDA, VIRGINIO—*Continued*

In 1915 Gayda was sent to Russia as a special envoy of the Milan *Corriere della Sera* and later became special envoy of the Rome *Il Messaggero*. When Italy went into the War he became an attaché in the Italian embassy at St. Petersburg, entrusted with arranging exchanges of Austrian prisoners for Italians captured by the Austrians. In May 1917 Gayda left Russia, and in the next eight years occasionally carried out a few minor diplomatic tasks in Sweden and England.

In 1921 Gayda became editor of *Il Messaggero*. Little is known about how he came to be a front rank Fascist, for Gayda makes light of whatever part he played in the Fascist revolution. It is known, however, that as editor of *Il Messaggero* he was one of the first to give Mussolini's movement his complete support. His position as editor of *Il Giornale d'Italia* was secured for him in 1926 when Count Ciano was Minister of Press and Propaganda and was looking for a mouthpiece for the Foreign Office. Without official status or title in the Fascist Party, Gayda has become one of its leaders.

A "small, mild little man with twinkling blue-grey eyes behind shell-rimmed spectacles," with "a wispy brownish mustache stained by ceaseless cigarette smoking," Gayda certainly looks little like the foreigner's idea of a powerful Fascist leader. He is a notoriously poor conversationalist who prefers to let off steam on his typewriter, hammering with his two index fingers at an amazing rate of speed. His home is a modest villa in Rome, every room packed from floor to ceiling with books. When Gayda leaves Rome he goes mountain climbing or looks after his kennel, which specializes in Pekinese.

References

Cur Hist 50:47 Je '39
Liv Age 356:543-5 Ag '39
N Y Sun p1 Je 6 '40; p3 Je 8 '40; p26 O 15 '40
Scholastic 31:28S D 11 '37 por; 37:13 O 14 '40
Chi è?
Who's Who

GEDDES, NORMAN BEL　Apr 27, 1893-
Theatrical producer; stage and industrial designer; author
Address: b. 50 Rockefeller Plaza, New York City

Those who know anything about Norman Bel Geddes know that nearly all his life the famous designer has been trying to create a world of tomorrow—today. For the New York World's Fair of 1939 and 1940 he designed the General Motors' *Futurama,* but the exhibit by itself is a toy. This pioneer of the streamline is not content merely to make predictions; what really interests him is seeing that his own predictions come true. And, since he has shown himself to be an amazingly persistent person, it seems probable that some of them will.

He was born in Adrian, Michigan, April 27, 1893, the son of a Scottish father and a German mother, Clifton Terry and Lulu (Yingling) Geddes. He was a poor boy. His schooling was irregular—public schools in Michigan, Ohio, Pennsylvania, Illinois, Indiana—and he was finally expelled from the ninth grade for drawing a caricature of the principal on the blackboard. At 13 he was working, and for several years it was at anything he could get to help him keep his head above water. Reports are that he had early experience as a vaudeville magician ("which may have taught him the showmanship of producing effects"), that he spent three months at the Cleveland School of Art and seven weeks at the Chicago Art Institute, working as a bus boy in exchange for his meals and as a super for the Chicago Opera Company, and that his earliest recognition came as a portrait painter. The young artist then found a a job with some company which started him at $3 a week. He stayed there until he was promoted to a $125-a-week position, commissions extra, and that same year sold his first play, a drama of American Indian life. Whether or not it was a good play is not stated, but from then on it was the stage that occupied all his spare time and enthusiasm.

It was to be the stage for some time. In 1916 Geddes had married Helen Belle Schneider of Toledo, Ohio; in 1917 he threw up his safe job and was off to Los Angeles to stage his own and five other plays for the Los Angeles Little Theatre. That same year there was a brief excursion into Hollywood, where he wrote and directed *Nathan Hale* for Universal. It took him just six weeks to learn that he didn't like directing movies, and being a man of action, he quit. Sitting on a Los Angeles park bench one hot summer afternoon in 1918, he was counting his diminishing worldly possessions (at this point a wife, a daughter and $5.83) when a newspaper headline caught his attention. "Millionaires Should Help Young Artists," it said flatly. This interesting statement led to an interview with Otto Kahn, the banker patron of opera and the stage. After paying for a two-page telegram asking Mr. Kahn to lend him enough money for two weeks in New York while he looked for a job as stage director, Geddes had four cents left over. Twenty-four hours later he received $400 by cable, the following Saturday he arrived in Mr. Kahn's office with a soapbox full of sketches for novel theatrical sets, and within a week he was stage designer for the Metropolitan Opera. What he did with the four cents is unknown.

From then on, Norman Bel Geddes was to do a job of artistic pioneering. His was not a talent for ornamentation and pictorial effects, but a unique sense of clean, functional form that inevitably made him much more than a stage designer. Because he believed that every detail of the stage should be "the organic outgrowth of the action of the play," he must be director as well as designer, for he maintains that "the art of design and the art of direction are inextricably part of one scenic pattern." True scenery to him consisted of "three-dimensional plastic space, lighting and clothes"—not of extraneous pictures. The audience "was not to be conscious of any scenery or background other than the mood in which the characters of this particular play should move."

During his career in the theatre he was in charge of more than 200 productions, among them *Pélléas et Mélisande;* Max Reinhardt's *The Miracle* and *The Eternal Road; Jeanne d'Arc* (with Eva Le Gallienne); Sidney Kingsley's *Dead End; Hamlet.* Of his famous set for *Dead End* (produced in 1935), Stark Young said:

"By force of emphasis it becomes more convincing than actuality. And, though few persons there might know it, the gasps and applause of the audience when this setting is first revealed, are not so much that the scene is so like any actual scene as that so many actual scenes appear to be swept up into and expressed in this scene. It could not be any actual place, but any actual place could be it."

But for Geddes it was not enough to revolutionize the artistic concept of the stage. His philosophy (for it was as much a philosophy as it was good art and showmanship) could be carried over into more than one field. In 1927 he became an industrial as well as stage designer, and in 1935 he entered into partnership with George Howe, the well-known architect, in order to "provide domestic and commercial building owners with a broad survey of mechanical and architectural trends for their consideration and use." He created radio cabinets, furniture, refrigerators, office, restaurant and airplane interiors, a medal to commemorate the silver anniversary of General Motors (now a part of the permanent exhibit at the New York Metropolitan Museum), gas stoves, window displays, automobile tires, gasoline service stations. He was largely responsible for popularizing streamlining in America. He designed the first combined focus and flood lamp for stage lighting, the first streamlined ocean liner, the first ocean-going streamlined yacht. He was architect for the Ukrainian State Theatre of the U. S. R., for the factory and administration buildings of the Toledo Scale Company, for the Theatre Guild Theatre in New York (with Howard Crane).

In the meanwhile, he expounded his ideas in print as well as in practice, contributing to the theatrical section of the *Encyclopedia Britannica,* to various magazines, and publishing two books (*A Project for a Theatrical Presentation of the Divine Comedy of Dante Alighieri,* 1923; *Horizons,* 1932). His paintings, models and drawings were exhibited in New York, Chicago, Amsterdam, Milan, London. Norman Bel Geddes' name **became known internationally.**

Leon de Vos

NORMAN BEL GEDDES

Finally in 1938 the unprecedented happened: Big Business "backed an artist on a gigantic scale." General Motors engaged Geddes to design its entire World's Fair exhibit, and when the Fair opened in 1939 "the adventurous quality of this artist's dream" drew greater crowds than any other exhibit on the grounds.

Superlatives were tossed around freely in describing the architecture of the vast exhibition building, *Highways and Horizons.* "It is not classic. It is not diluted Gothic. It is not Colonial. It is not American Factory. It is not familiar and conventional. It has not been done before. It is original, different, striking, adventurous. It is pure form, in eye-surprising movements, angles, and dimensions. . ." The building was totally without ornamentation, only the various necessary signs being sculptured. The architectural forms used on the exterior were "a translation of the streamline forms used in the design of automobiles, trains, and other transportation units, interpreting not so much the automotive, but the artistic characteristics." And, true to Geddes' theories of function, the whole design and casting of the General Motors' building was to orient it on its plot after a careful study of the actual traffic flow past it.

Perhaps most talked-about of all the exhibits within was the *Futurama,* Geddes' miniature model of the world of 1960 in action. And certainly the most astonishing feature of that world is its traffic system. Far from the cities, cars move in segregated traffic lanes at different speeds, automatically directed from control towers. This is no whimsical idea of Geddes, however; he has actually brought it to Washington, and a book, *Magic Motorways,* published in 1940, expounds the same idea. He is very serious about his plan for roads and traffic control.

GEDDES, NORMAN BEL—*Continued*

and violent in his condemnation of "haphazard planning and resulting congestion implicit in a traffic system that has grown up helter skelter from carriage paths and Conestoga wagon ways." He says, very sensibly: "The roads we have today should be designed in terms of. the automobile." In the last 20 years $30,000,000,000 has been spent in road building, and he believes that the same amount could be utilized in a planned program for the next 20 years that would make his world of 1960 a reality. Nevertheless the Federal Bureau of Public Roads has so far been inclined to poohpooh his suggestions as impractical, and economicly-minded Rexford Tugwell points out that a nation fitted out with his magic motorways "could not tolerate the slums of Brooklyn or of the Mississippi Delta, the miseries of California ditch-banks, or of Pennsylvania coal towns." "Nor," he adds, "the particular professions of General Motors. Either this book is nonsense, or most of solemn industrial America is; how shall we choose?"

Housing officials are keeping a less skeptical eye on Geddes, however. In January 1940 it was announced that he was at work developing a pre-fabricated house for low-income families. Although at that time the material was not decided, the house was to contain a living-dining room, two bedrooms, kitchen and bath; there was to be a system of air circulation and overhead, indirect lighting; it was to be set up in a day; and the estimated cost (exclusive of land) was to be $2,350. His backer is Theodore Backer, brother of the owner of the New York *Post*. His latest activity is in a still different field—the redesigning of the Ringling Brothers Circus in Florida.

Geddes, who has two daughters, Joan and Barbara, by his first wife, was married a second time in 1933 to Frances Resor Waite of New York. He lives in New York City, and has his offices in Rockefeller Center. Members of his design staff say that the "massive blond" artist is a hard man to work for. He approaches no problem without a fantastic amount of preliminary research, and he is a hound for detail. But it is also true when the facts are all assembled he calls the entire staff into a conference where free speech isn't merely a catch phrase. He is a stimulating driver, and experimental even in his recreations: naval and military strategy and tactics and motion picture photography.

Geddes' philosophy of design which has done so much to change at least the expression of part of the face of the modern world has been summed up in a paragraph:

"For every given set of conditions there is an ideal form which does not need to be ornamented or decorated to make it beautiful. The preamble to finding the successful solution is to master first all the facts which may properly condition that solution. This done, the designer must pursue his research

for the right form with every bit of ability and honesty he possesses. The acceptance of traditional things which have been outdated is evidence of mental laziness. Think things out fundamentally. Then express them—in the same terms."

References

Arch Rec 78:47 Jl '35 por; 84:125-8 Jl '38
Arts & Dec 43:29 D '35 por; 50:35 Je '39 por
Forum 102:191 O '39 il
New Repub 85:21 N 13 '35; 92:211-12 S 29 '37
New Yorker 16:82 Ap 27 '40
Newsweek 5:18 Je 8 '35 por
Read Digest 35:9 Ag '39
Sat R Lit 21:3-4 Ap 13 '40
Theatre Arts 20:776-83 O '36 il; 24: 872-81 O '40 il
Vital Speeches 6:117-18 D 1 '39
Brown, J. M. House That Geddes Built *In* Two on the Aisle p260-2 1938
Brown, J. M. Raymond Massey's Dane *In* Two on the Aisle p55-8 1938
Brown, J. M. Norman Bel Geddes *In* Upstage p162-7 1930
Who's Who in America
Who's Who in American Art

GEHRIG, LOU (gĕr'ĭg) June 19, 1903- Former baseball star; parole commissioner *Address:* b. 139 Center St, New York City; h. 5204 Delafield Ave, New York City

After 15 years of outstanding performance, Henry Louis Gehrig, the idolized "Iron Horse" of the baseball world, was retired from the New York Yankees in 1939 at the age of 36. An account of his life and exploits is being prepared by sportswriter Richards Vidmer.

Born of sturdy German stock in a congested neighborhood of upper Manhattan, Henry Louis Gehrig was one of a sickly family of four children. Three perished during the struggle of his parents to rear a family in their constricted home, but from a sickly tot "Lou" grew into a robust youngster, one with the strength and stamina of four ordinary boys. He went in early for all sports—baseball, football, basketball, skating and swimming.

He began to play ball with the students of the Sigma Nu fraternity house at Columbia University, where his mother was cook and his father man-of-all-work. "Heinie," as the boys called him, was "then big for his age and had reached the period when the change from short to long trousers was imminent, but still wore short ones whose tightness exaggerated the size of his fat, round legs."

He attended the New York High School of Commerce, where he starred in all sports activities under Coach Harry Kane. In the 1920 inter-city championship game, played with Lane Tech at Wrigley Field, Chicago, the schoolboy slugger of the New York team amazed the fans by hammering a homer over the right-field fence. He duplicated this feat twice when he paid a return visit to the same field in the World Series of 1932.

Lou just missed being a member of the rival New York team, the Giants. He was invited to the Polo Grounds in the spring of 1921 for a trial by former manager John J. McGraw. The Giants arranged for him to go to Hartford, where he played a few games under the name of "Lewis." Then he was rescued by Columbia's graduate manager of athletics, the former fraternity house manager. McGraw has since placed Gehrig on first base in his All-Star Team of All-Time.

Aided by the sacrifices of his parents, Lou entered Columbia University in 1921, remaining until his junior year. He had not been ready at first to take the entrance examinations, but six rather painful months in the extension school got him by. He continued to get by for two years, and meanwhile played on the football team in 1922 and was alternate pitcher and first baseman for the baseball team in 1923.

One spring afternoon, in a college game, he hit the longest homer that any Columbia, perhaps any undergraduate, player had ever made—more than 400 feet. Reports of this hit brought some scouts from professional teams to see him. Much to the concern of his parents, who wanted no "bummer" for a son, Lou gave up college to sign with the Yankees. He was farmed out to Hartford, Connecticut in 1923 and 1924 and was assigned to first base on the Yankee team in June 1925.

Known as the "Iron-Horse," Lou Gehrig established one of the most remarkable careers in the history of baseball. Over a period of 14 years, while compiling a lifetime batting average of .341, he played 2,130 consecutive major-league games besides seven World Series and hundreds of exhibition games. Some of his batting records surpass even those of Babe Ruth's. Gehrig has led the league four times in runs scored, four times in total bases, five times in home runs.

"Buster," as his teammates called him, was one of the best-liked players in the game. For his honesty, courage and modesty the "sparkplug" of the Yankees received the Best Player Award of the major-league four times. He was a strong defensive first baseman, one of the greatest hitters of all time, and has averaged more runs driven in per season than any other contemporary player. Even the old-timers, diehards though they are, call him the greatest first baseman of all time. In December 1939 the Baseball Writers Association of America waived the rule that a candidate must be out of play for at least a year and unanimously voted Lou Gehrig into Baseball's Hall of Fame at Cooperstown, New York.

George Burke

LOU GEHRIG

When asked if he was going to be married shy Lou told reporters "my mother makes a home comfortable enough for me." But finally, six years after meeting Eleanor Twitchell (who owned and operated an apartment house in Chicago), comments and questions of friends rushed him into marriage. His wife was worried about her ability to cook, particularly to prepare "pickled eels," about which there were many Gehrig legends. She wrote: "I had never pickled an eel in all my life. I wouldn't know how to begin. It was terrible. Our happiness might be smashed by eels. Lou's batting average might slump. At the first opportunity I broached the subject. 'Lou,' I said wistfully, 'are you so very fond of eels?'

" 'Why, I never ate an eel in all my life,' he replied. 'I like to catch 'em.' "

Dimple-cheeked, piano-legged Lou Gehrig, standing six feet one inch tall and weighing 205 pounds, allowed neither injuries nor sickness to snap his streak of consecutive games. A strong wrestler with huge hands and bulging, bony wrists, he kept healthy by taking care of himself. Off-season he used to play 54 holes of golf every day until he found it cramped his batting swing. Now he walks or goes fishing for the sporty marlin. He plays bridge well, but can take it or leave it alone. He goes hatless most of the time, leaving his dark curly hair uncovered, and even on the coldest days tries to slip out of the house without an overcoat. Usually his wife catches him and makes him wear one.

In the spring of 1939, when he had succeeded in getting only four hits and driving only one run in the first eight games of the season, Lou Gehrig voluntarily benched himself. Examination proved that a rare

GEHRIG, LOU—*Continued*

form of paralysis, "amyotrophic lateral sclerosis," now called "Lou Gehrig's disease" even by his physicians, had ended his baseball career.

But he was still able to walk and to live a normal life if he avoided overexertion. When Mayor La Guardia (see sketch this issue) called him in and suggested the position of Parole Commissioner for New York City, Lou modestly urged his lack of training and asked for three months to think it over. He took home stacks of books and reports on crime, prisons and psychology, and spent the summer in hard study and visits to jails.

Meanwhile he had a dozen offers of soft jobs with fancy salaries—in night clubs, hotels, commercial testimonials and Hollywood, merely for the use of his name and prestige. "But Lou believes in working for what he gets." Though at the peak of his baseball career he earned $36,000 for one season's work, he was born poor and knows what it is to struggle. He took the city job at a salary of $5,700 a year—no more than he received by vote of his teammates for sitting on the bench in the World Series.

On January 2, 1940 Henry Louis Gehrig became a parole commissioner. "This is the luckiest thing that ever happened to me," he said, speaking of his appointment. And *Scholastic* thinks "it is the luckiest thing that ever happened to the youngsters of New York to have men like Gehrig— honest, conscientious, human and public spirited—going to bat for youth."

References

Am Mag 116:57 S '33 por
Collier's 95:20+ My 25 '35 il; 95:14+ Je 1 '35 por
Cur Hist 50:42-3 Je '39
New Yorker 5:22-5 Ag 10 '29
Newsweek 14:22-4 Jl 3 '39 pors
Scholastic 35:5 O 30 '39
Time 34:24 Jl 3 '39
Atkinson, L. and Lake, A. Henry Louis ("Lou") Gehrig: "Larruping Lou"—Manufacturer of Home-Runs *In* Famous American Athletes of Today 3d ser p83-103 1932
Busch, N. Little Heinie (Lou Gehrig) *In* Twenty-One Americans p321-32 1930
Carlson, S. W. Lou Gehrig: Baseball's Iron Man 1940
Who's Who in Major League Baseball
Who's Who in New York

GEORGE, ALBERT BAILEY Oct 23, 1873—Mar 23, 1940 Outstanding leader of the Negro race; only Negro ever elected a judge in Chicago

References

Who's Who in Government

Obituaries

N Y Times p30 Mr 24 '40

GERAUD, ANDRE [PERTINAX, pseud.] (zhā-rō') Oct 18, 1882- French journalist

When the Armistice of Compiègne was signed André Géraud, known the world over as Pertinax, was among the first of the French journalists to flee France. In July 1940 he arrived in the United States from Montreal and in the winter of 1940 to 1941 he is going to publish a book explaining how and why France fell.

Pertinax escaped from France because he faced a jail sentence if caught: his escape has cost him his money and property, which have been confiscated by the Pétain (see sketch this issue) government. This famous French correspondent, whose "political dispatches sparkle like champagne at a diplomat's table," who has been called "France's most distinguished writer" and "Europe's mouthpiece," has been forced to leave his native country because of his strong anti-German stand and his firm belief in a French-English alliance.

For more than a decade, at first almost alone among French observers, he has insisted that a reborn Germany would bring Europe to a new crisis. His articles have been dominated by his fear and hatred of pan-Germanism; he has fearlessly campaigned against the timidity of French statesmen in their policy toward the Reich.

During these years, and particularly in the past few years, he has advocated a French-English alliance. "France and Britain," he said, "only if joined to each other in the closest bonds, can hope to uphold their traditional civilization." And as late as June 1940 he stated that an "Anglo-French union is an instrument from which we expect not only victory but the reconstruction of Europe." Called an "Anglophile" by many, Pertinax has, however, opposed the Chamberlain group in England and has insisted firmly that his politics are not this or that, but "France."

Charles Joseph André Géraud was born in St. Louis de Montferrand on October 18, 1882. He attended the Lycée of Bordeaux and took the highest degree in history in the university there. Soon out of school, in 1908, he became the London correspondent of the *Echo de Paris* and his writings began to appear in English papers as well, in the *Daily Telegraph* and the *Pall Mall Gazette*. He knows English thoroughly; the English articles were written in English and continue to be.

Géraud served as interpreter during the greater part of the First World War. In 1917 he became foreign editor of the *Echo de Paris* and first used the name of Pertinax. From then on articles on foreign policy, on world politics came almost daily from his pen, published in his own paper, in Eng-

ANDRE GERAUD

lish papers, in many American papers. The Manchester *Guardian* spoke of him as the man "who usually says today what the French Foreign Office denies tomorrow but confirms the day after." When in 1938 the *Echo de Paris*, a Rightist and Catholic paper, merged with *Le Jour*, an even more Rightist paper, Géraud resigned and devoted his full time to the editorship of a weekly, *L'Europe Nouvelle*, while continuing his pieces for foreign newspapers and journals. In 1929 his book, *Le Partage de Rome*, on the reconciliation of Italy and the Vatican appeared and created quite a stir. In 1931 he accompanied Laval (see sketch this issue) to the United States to see Hoover; in July 1934 he came with Barthou to London.

During these years Pertinax's comments on foreign affairs gave a good many people the impression that he had just left the French foreign ministry. Pertinax denied this and explained his methods simply: "My good friends telephone me; the others I telephone."

Stocky, with an impressive monocle and mustache, Pertinax is always beautifully dressed, usually in a gray suit, a gray homburg and gray gloves. He is, his friends say, "essentially a homebody," and in fact complained in 1939, when the European crisis was at its height, that the effect on him had been "to destroy my home life and ruin my exercise." "I am," he says, "a lover of dogs, good food, fine French wines and sports."

References

Foreign Affairs 18:601-13 Jl '40
Time 31:30 Ap 11 '38 por
Who's Who

GESELL, ARNOLD (gĕ-zĕl') June 21, 1880- Psychologist
Address: h. 185 Edwards St, New Haven, Connecticut

Dr. Arnold Lucius Gesell believes that "the first five years of life are the most consequential in the formation of the human individual." "Coming first," he says, "they inevitably influence all the years that follow": in them are laid down the social and individual behavior patterns which later manifest themselves in the adult. It is to the study of these patterns that Dr. Gesell has devoted most of his life, and the Yale Child Development Clinic under him has become the nation's foremost laboratory for the study of infant behavior.

Dr. Gesell was born in Alma, Wisconsin, the son of Gerhard and Christine (Giesen) Gesell, on June 21, 1880. He went to grade school in Wisconsin and later to the State Normal School at Stevens Point, Wisconsin. From there he went to the University of Wisconsin, from which he was graduated in 1903 with a Bachelor of Philosophy degree. Immediately after graduation Arnold Gesell went East to attend Clark University, from which, three years later, he received his Ph. D. in psychology.

His first position was teaching psychology in the Los Angeles State Normal School. He stayed there for three years, until 1911, when he became assistant professor of education at Yale. It was during his first year at Yale that he established the Yale Psycho-Clinic (now the Child Development Clinic) at the Yale School of Medicine. Four years later he was made professor of child hygiene at the Yale Graduate School.

Before he received his professorship Dr. Gesell had received his M. D. While working with children he decided that medical training would be a tremendous, in fact, indispensable help, so he took medical studies at Yale, which awarded him the degree in 1915.

Dr. Gesell's first interest at Yale was in the study of backward children, but the course of his interest soon changed. While dealing with abnormal children it seemed to him that the age at which abnormality might be discovered and diagnosed could be pushed farther back, even to babyhood. He became a pioneer in studying the mental growth of babies—from the time they were born until the time they went to school. As he studied the "preschool" abnormal child it became clear to him that unless more was known about the mind of the normal infant and child, it wasn't possible to deal adequately with the abnormal. By 1919 his original interest in the mentality of abnormal school children had been changed into an interest in the mental development of the normal infant.

Since tools and techniques were lacking Dr. Gesell had to work out a system of observing and measuring infant behavior. His

ARNOLD GESELL

chief work has been to show that the mental growth of the child reveals itself "in consistent and characteristic behavior patterns, governed by laws of growth similar to those which control the development of his body." Thus he works with children not in terms of psychology alone, but in terms of physiology and medicine as well.

Dr. Gesell's main instrument in the Child Development Clinic and in the "Guidance Nursery" which was added to it in 1926 is the motion picture camera. This to him is a scientific instrument by means of which infant behavior patterns can be charted, for it captures behavior in its totality; "it crystallizes any given moment of behavior in its visible entirety"; and it records the developmental cycle. As the infants and children play, eat, wash, dress, sleep, they are under observation. By means of an ingenious screen device they are watched without knowing it and pictures are made on every phase of child activity. Dr. Gesell considers his collection of pictures as perhaps the most important achievement of the clinic.

From Dr. Gesell's long years of work with infants and children have come many books. Some of them are: *The Preschool Child from the Standpoint of Public Hygiene and Education* (1923) ; *Mental Growth of the Preschool Child* (1925) ; *An Atlas of Infant Behavior: A Systematic Delineation of the Forms and Early Growth of Human Behavior Patterns,* illustrated by 3,200 action photographs (with collaborators) (1934) ; *Feeding Behavior of Infants* (1937) ; *Biographies of Child Development* (with collaborators) (1939) ; *The First Five Years of Life* (with collaborators) (1940). He has also prepared a volume on *Developmental Diagnosis* designed for medical students and practitioners. In his books and in his many articles Dr. Gesell writes with

a style that is "thorough, very scientific and more than a little difficult. Colleagues have been known to smile over the doctor's preference for long words compounded in the Teutonic manner where a simpler term would do as well."

Besides being head of the Yale Clinic, Dr. Gesell is attending pediatrician at the New Haven Hospital, has been school psychologist for the Connecticut Board of Education, a member of the Connecticut Commission on Child Welfare and member or director of innumerable scientific societies, conferences and associations.

Now, in 1940, Dr. Gesell is "handsome, distinguished with that variety of white hair known as 'leonine.'" Mrs. Gesell, the former Beatrice Chandler of Los Angeles, whom he married in 1909, was a supervisor of primary education in the Los Angeles Normal School. Her interests, like Dr. Gesell's, lie in the field of child psychology and education. In fact, Dr. Gesell's first book, *The Normal Child and Primary Education* (1912) was written in collaboration with Mrs. Gesell. It has been rumored, too, that the Gesells used to try out their theories on their own two children, Gerhard Alden and Katherine Gesell Walden.

References

New Outlook 165:34-5 F '35
N Y Herald Tribune p4+ Jl 21 '25
American Men of Science
Murchison, C. ed. Psychological Register 1929
Who's Who in America
Who's Who in American Education

GIBBS, GEORGE Apr 19, 1861—May 20, 1940 Engineer; safety expert; world authority on railroad engineering and electrification; designed first all-steel car

References

American Men of Science
Who's Who in America
Who's Who in Engineering
Who's Who in Railroading

Obituaries

N Y Herald Tribune p22 My 21 '40
N Y Times p23 My 21 '40 por

GIBSON, ERNEST WILLARD Dec 29, 1871—June 20, 1940 United States Senator; elected to House of Representatives in 1923; appointed Senator from Vermont in 1933; Republican member of Naval Affairs Committee; served as colonel in the First World War; was head of Vermont State Senate, 1908.

References

Who's Who in America
Who's Who in Law
Who's Who in the Nation's Capital

Obituaries

N Y Sun p21 Je 20 '40 por
N Y Times p21 Je 21 '40 por

GIDEONSE, HARRY DAVID (gĭd'ē-ŭns) May 17, 1901- Economist; president of Brooklyn College

Address: b. Brooklyn College, Brooklyn, New York

Brooklyn is only one of New York City's five boroughs, but it could be a metropolis in its own right. Its population (2,792,000) is bigger than that of any other American city except Chicago. But it wasn't until 1930 that Brooklynites had a free municipal college of their own. In that year the New York Board of Higher Education began giving Brooklyn boys and girls higher schooling in offices and lofts in the downtown business section. In 1937 the college shifted to a more scholarly atmosphere: a $7,100,000 campus and five buildings in residential Flatbush.

In 1940, with 13,700 students and a faculty of more than 500, Brooklyn College is the largest college of its kind in the United States. Its arts and sciences enrollments outnumber those of Barnard, Columbia, Williams, Amherst, Colgate, Smith, Vassar, Mount Holyoke and Princeton combined.

Since October 1939 the job of handling this vast enterprise has been in the hands of "a brilliant young economist," Harry David Gideonse. Dr. Gideonse, who has taught in four colleges and who has made his ideas on higher education widely known, has already busied himself in stimulating the academic and "other than intellectual" activities of his college. In 1940 and 1941, as professor of economics, he is also teaching a course on "Freedom and Order."

Harry Gideonse, the son of Martin Cornelius and Johanna Jacoba Helena Magdalena (de Lange) Gideonse, was born in Rotterdam, The Netherlands, on May 17, 1901 and was brought to the United States when he was three. He did his undergraduate work at Columbia University—he received his B. S. in 1923—and did graduate work there, too (M. A. 1924). Right after he received his M. A. he became a lecturer in economics at Barnard College and Columbia College and stayed there until 1926, when he went to Switzerland to become director of international students' work in Geneva. In 1928 he received the Diplomé des Hautes Etudes Internationales from the University of Geneva. In Switzerland he met Edmee Koch, and they were married on June 17, 1926. In 1928 Dr. Gideonse returned to the United States to become assistant professor of economics at Rutgers University.

Dr. Gideonse "settled down" as associate professor at the University of Chicago in 1930 and all was quiet until the war between him and President Hutchins (see sketch this issue) of the University of Chicago got under way. It started with President Hutchins' book, *The Higher Learning in America* (1936) in which Hutchins proposed that United States universities try to restore order to a

HARRY D. GIDEONSE

confused world by teaching people the truths uttered by the great philosophers of the past.

Gideonse replied with *The Higher Learning in a Democracy* (1937). What Dr. Hutchins proposed, said he, was "intellectual dictatorship," and pointed out that due to its faculty, not its president, the University of Chicago was stressing "the understanding and enrichment of twentieth-century human life in all its phases." After his book was published Harry Gideonse continued to teach at the university. "Tall, lanky," he used to "stride about the campus with his big German shepherd dog, Bob, at his heels," sometimes taking the dog to class.

While his controversy with President Hutchins brought him his chief fame, in eight years at Chicago he acquired a reputation as a crack economist—he published *America in a World Economy* (1934) and *The Commodity Dollar* (1936)—and became "the most popular speaker on the University's radio *Round Table.*" Nevertheless his rank still remained that of associate professor and his salary stayed at $5,500. Three times his colleagues recommended that he be appointed to a full professorship. Three times President Hutchins ignored the recommendation.

In June 1938 Harry Gideonse quit the University of Chicago to take "a comfortable job as professor" at Barnard College, Columbia University. On leaving he said: "There has been no personal quarrel between President Hutchins and me. . . Dr. Hutchins and I have simply not seen eye to eye on educational policy. . . I expect to find a more congenial atmosphere at Columbia."

Dr. Gideonse taught economics at Columbia until he was offered the $17,500 post at Brooklyn College. He mulled the offer over for two months before deciding to

GIDEONSE, HARRY DAVID—*Continued*
accept what he called Brooklyn's "challenge."

The Dies Committee (see sketch this issue) has pictured Brooklyn College's 7,700 men and 6,000 women as "dominated by Reds." But Gideonse has had no trouble in that quarter. There is the more or less apocryphal story of the group of young Communists who came to him shortly after he took office to get permission to sell the *Daily Worker* on the campus. Certainly you may sell it, he said, if you'll also let me allow *Social Justice* to be sold. On the issue of academic liberty he agrees with Dr. Butler (see sketch this issue).

President Gideonse has, however, come into conflict with his student body a couple of times since he took office. At two meetings in March 1940 he warned the undergraduates that "splinter" groups such as the American Student Union were in control of extracurricular activities at the college, and told them that he wanted "truly representative activities on the campus." In June he ordered the Student Union disbanded and found his home picketed as a result. There was also a student strike after a teacher was suspended.

In fact, President Gideonse, who considers the Brooklyn student body "less rah-rah and more grown-up than most collegians," has had, in the first months of his occupancy, a little difficulty in getting his educational ideas across to the entire student body. To him the college is a trifle too intellectual. He thinks Brooklyn could easily build up the best band in the country and a crack football team.

Dr. Gideonse is something of a pessimist. As early as June 1940 he predicted a possible thirty years' war and announced that "the sooner we get over this oratorical rubbish about preserving the social gains of the last ten years the better. . . The only question asked today of any proposal must be 'Does it contribute to total productivity?'" How Brooklyn College answers this question he has not said, but at his installation "the tall good-looking president" told the delegates from 250 other colleges that: "No college can live by training mind alone. . . Talent must be shifted from sheer cultivation of the intellectual virtues to education for the *whole man,* for men as "knowers and doers and appreciators.'" He begged the students to remember Brooklyn College's size: "If we go slow—and if we seem somewhat impersonal—keep the arithemtic in mind."

References

Assn Am Col Bul 25:493-504 D '39
Fortune 18:110 Ag '38 por
N Y Herald Tribune p7 Ja 23 '40
  por; p8 Je 15 '40; p3 Ag 2 '40
N Y Times p21 Mr 22 '40; p17 S 23
  '40
Newsweek 14:34 O 30 '39 por
Sch & Soc 50:557 O 28 '39
Time 31:26 Je 13 '38 por

America's Young Men
Who's Who in America

GILBRETH, LILLIAN EVELYN May 24, 1878- Engineer
Address: h. 68 Eagle Rock Way, Montclair, New Jersey

The rambling Gilbreth house at Montclair, New Jersey is run with factory-like efficiency and precision. Despite the procession of 12 children and grandchildren who wander in and out, and the confusion that might be expected to develop from a large family, there is not a step of waste motion. The house is divided like a factory into work centers, work surfaces, work motions. Work is done by charts and a follow-up system.

That is because "Mother" Gilbreth is an efficiency engineer and specializes in the elimination of fatigue and waste motion in industry and the home. "Mother" Gilbreth is really Dr. Gilbreth and has almost as many major degrees as she has children. She is a Bachelor of Letters, a Master of Literature, Doctor of Philosophy, Doctor of Science, Master of Engineering, Doctor of Engineering and a Doctor of Laws, holding her degrees from the University of California, Brown University, Rutgers College, the University of Michigan and Russell Sage College.

Dr. Gilbreth is the widow of Frank Bunker Gilbreth, efficiency engineer, with whom she pioneered in the study of the relationship between the machine and the human beings who run it. She was born in Oakland, California May 24, 1878, the daughter of William and Annie (Delger) Moller, and was graduated from the University of California in 1900. She intended to follow a career in psychology and to become a dean of women. Instead she married Frank Bunker Gilbreth October 19, 1904 and devoted her energies to making a "best marriage."

The Gilbreths had twelve children, six boys and six girls, and both parents were tremendously interested in their home, sharing alike in its responsibilities. Frank Gilbreth was the kind of an industrial engineer "who discovers with interest that motion and energy can be saved by lathering the two sides of the face at once with two shaving brushes." It was natural therefore, that the Gilbreth marriage should develop into a partnership in the designing of model nurseries, model kitchens and the reduction of office and factory routine to a state of efficiency. With so much to do, the Gilbreths had to find an efficient way of doing it. Their efficiency work became almost a ritual.

When Frank Gilbreth died in 1925, his wife sailed for a scheduled European conference two days after his burial, reading his papers before the convention and taking his place on committees. She explained her fortitude with the remark: "I am only adhering to my husband's principles—the elimination of waste motion." After his death, she devoted herself almost exclusively to those principles, becoming a bona fide engineer in her own right. Her motion-saving devices can be found in a number of American plants.

Lecturer, author and teacher, she has done a man's job in woman's sphere—the home. She has put thousands of United States kitchens on an efficiency basis. Once, at a National Organization of Better Homes in America, she stopped 4,000 busy housewives so that she could measure the distance from their elbows to the floor to get information on the proper height for stove and sink. Dr. Gilbreth is president of Gilbreth, Incorporated, consulting engineers in management; has been professor of management at Purdue University since 1935; and is a lecturer at Bryn Mawr College.

As combination of successful career woman and mother, Dr. Gilbreth is perhaps unexcelled. Honors which have been bestowed on her have taken into consideration her domestic background as mother of 12 children. A citation read to her at a dinner given for her in New York, when the Engineering Woman's Club honored her in 1940 by making her an honorary life member, is an example. It read: "For your scientific achievements in the field of industrial psychology, for your pioneer work in applying these principles to the practical problems of the efficiency of human labor, for your intelligent womanhood, and for the esteem in which you are held by your fellow members."

Dr. Gilbreth's writings, too, reflect her double interest in efficiency and the home. She has written articles ranging from *This Grandmother Job* to *Reducing Federal Expenditures* and *Efficiency of Women Workers*. She is the author of *Psychology of Management* (1912); *The Home-Maker and Her Job* (1927); and *Living With Our Children* (1928). She is coauthor with her husband of *Time Study* (1920); *Fatigue Study* (1919); *Applied Motion Study* (1917); and *Motion Study for the Handicapped* (1919).

Engineers and efficiency experts have honored her for her outstanding work. She is an honorary member of the American Management Association, of the Society for the Advancement of Management, of the Society of Industrial Engineers. She was also chosen by *American Women* as one of the 10 outstanding women of 1936. In addition to being a member of various engineering societies and professional organizations, she has found time to serve on the President's Emergency Committee for Unemployment and the President's Organization for Unemployment Relief. She was a member of the New Jersey State Board of Regents from 1929 to 1933.

She is fond of music and reading and her favorite recreation is walking.

References

Am Mag 119:37 Mr '35 por
Fortune 12:82 S '35 por
N Y Herald Tribune p17 Mr 27 '40
Parents' Mag 5:26 O '30

LILLIAN EVELYN GILBRETH

American Women
Who's Who in America
Who's Who in Engineering

GILDER, ROBERT FLETCHER Oct 6, 1856—Mar 8, 1940 Newspaperman; archeologist; discoverer of the Nebraska "Loess man," oldest human remains found in America; landscape painter

References

Who's Who in America

Obituaries

N Y Herald Tribune p10 Mr 9 '40
N Y Times p15 Mr 9 '40

GILDERSLEEVE, VIRGINIA CROCHERON Oct 3, 1877- Dean of Barnard College, Columbia University

Address: h. 3007 Broadway, New York City

Doctor of Philosophy, Doctor of Literature, Doctor of Laws, recipient of many honorary degrees and medals, Dean Gildersleeve was described in an article in *Literary Digest* as having "enough caps and gowns to fill an ordinary New York apartment closet." She is undoubtedly one of the foremost women in American education.

She was born in New York City in 1877, the daughter of a Supreme Court Justice, Henry Alger, and Virginia (Crocheron) Gildersleeve. A vital, dark-eyed, dark-haired figure, she is tall and erect and has the poise and dignity becoming to her position. Dean of a women's college for almost 30 years, she has little good to say about coeducational institutions. Once at a convention of the American Association of University Women in 1937 she advised women to steer clear of coeducational institutions and their "lordly Male complex" and denounced

Pach Bros.

VIRGINIA C. GILDERSLEEVE

male professors and presidents of women's colleges as "softies" whose decisions "are more often swayed by emotion than women's." Although she has a strong interest in the youthful worries of her charges, she has never yielded to the desire to be called "The Dear Dean" and to pry into their private affairs. She calls students by their last names and herself prefers to be a stern "older sister," rather than a "mother" to her girls.

"Everyone knows that the Dean is a good executive, a magnificent speaker, a wise woman, an intellectual," Alice Duer Miller has written of her, "but not everyone knows she can lose her temper over examples of stupidity and spite, and that, therefore, her tact and calm are the more to be admired, since they are achieved and not wholly innate."

Dean Gildersleeve is inclined to deprecate her own accomplishments. She once said to an interviewer: "I never had to try for anything in my life. My father sent me to college and after that everything fell into my lap." However, she has a passion for perfection. As a student she was dissatisfied unless she received an "A" rating on every paper. In 1899 she was awarded her first degree, B. A., from the college where she is now dean, and received her M. A. from Columbia University. Before being appointed dean, she was instructor in English at Barnard College.

Archeology is her greatest hobby. Her idea of a perfect life is one spent among the ruins of some ancient castle. On summer vacations she used to look for old stones on the traces of early Roman roads near the cottage of a friend who lives in Sussex, England, and always hoped some day to find a Carthaginian penny. She plays deck tennis for relaxation. Occasionally she smokes a cigarette and enjoys a glass of claret with her meals. She is fond of dogs, and of books on polar exploration. The "Deanery," her home in the college, is a comfortable apartment with the living room filled with many soft chairs and lamps, and lined with books.

Although she is a gifted scholar in English and Latin literature, Dean Gildersleeve also takes an active interest in current national and international affairs. She served twice as president of the International Federation of University Women, from 1924 to 1926, and again from 1936 to 1939. In politics she is a vigorous Independent Democrat and internationally she is urging American aid for the Allies. She belongs to the school of current opinion which finds American youth too "soft."

References
> Assn Am Col Bul 25:258-67 My '39
> Lit Digest 121:35 F 29 '36 por
> Newsweek 7:46 F 22 '36 por; 9:34 Mr 27 '37
> American Women
> Who's Who Among North American Authors
> Who's Who in America

GILMER, ELIZABETH MERIWETHER
See Dix, D., pseud.

GILMORE, MELVIN RANDOLPH Mar 11, 1868—July 25, 1940 Ethnologist; curator of ethnology at the University of Michigan; authority on American Indian lore; wrote extensively on Indian folklore and tribal customs; conducted expeditions into the Southwest; formerly held post at the Museum of the American Indian in New York City

References
> American Men of Science
> Who's Who in America

Obituaries
> N Y Sun p15 Jl 27 '40
> N Y Times p13 Jl 27 '40

GILMOUR, JOHN May 27, 1876—Mar 30, 1940 British Minister of Shipping since October 1939; member of Parliament for 22 years; served as Home Secretary and Minister of Agriculture

References
> Who's Who

Obituaries
> N Y Herald Tribune p32 Mr 31 '40 por
> N Y Times p45 Mr 31 '40 por
> Newsweek 15:8 Ap 8 '40 por

GLENN, MARY WILCOX Dec 14, 1869—
Nov 4, 1940 Leader in local, international,
national social welfare and charity organizations, among them American Red Cross,
International Migration Service, Association
of Volunteers, Mobilization for Human
Needs; had been president of National Conference on Charities and Corrections, National Council of Church Mission for Help,
Family Welfare Association of America,
American Association for Organizing Family
Social Work; married John M. Glenn, also
a social worker, in 1902

References

American Women

Obituaries

N Y Herald Tribune p26 N 5 '40 por
N Y Times p25 N 5 '40 por

GOLDENWEISER, ALEXANDER A.
gōld-ĕn-wī'zer) Jan 29, 1880—July 6, 1940
Anthropologist; sociologist; author of several well-known college texts on anthropology; widely known as lecturer and professor; taught at Columbia University,
Reed College, University of Wisconsin,
Leland Stanford University and others

References

Who's Who in America
Who's Who in American Jewry

Obituaries

N Y Herald Tribune p14 Jl 23 '40

GOLDMAN, EMMA June 27, 1869—May
14, 1940 Anarchist; internationally known
figure; deported from the United States;
disillusioned by Lenin and Trotsky; her
autobiography *Living My Life* (1931) is
regarded as one of the important books of
its kind

EMMA GOLDMAN

References

Nation 138:320 Mr 21 '34
Goldman, E. Anarchism and Other
Essays 1910
Goldman, E. Living My Life 1931
Goldman, E. My Further Disillusion-
ment in Russia 1924

Obituaries

N Y Herald Tribune p20 My 14 '40
por; p28 My 15 '40
N Y Times p23 My 14 '40 por

GOLDMARK, PETER CARL Dec 2,
1906- Engineer; inventor of color television
Address: b. Columbia Broadcasting System,
485 Madison Ave, New York City; h. 129
E 69th St, New York City

Color television is now an established development. On August 29, 1940, in the Columbia Broadcasting System's laboratories, Dr.
Peter C. Goldmark, Columbia's chief television
engineer, demonstrated his new method of
full-color television to James L. Fly (see
sketch this issue), chairman of the Federal
Communications Commission. The new development is said to be the most important
contribution to television in the last 15 years.
The Columbia Broadcasting System expects
to have color television ready for commercial
use by January 1, 1941.

Dr. Goldmark's method produces a rapid
alternation of three colors, red, green and
blue, along rapidly moving rows of three
hundred and forty-three dotted lines (one
hundred lines less than required in black
and white pictures), shifting with such speed
from row to row that the eye is given the
illusion of a single full-color picture. The
color itself is produced by a rotating filter
placed before the camera. The method
requires only one camera at the pickup
point, one transmitter and a single wave
band for transmission instead of three colors
and three bands. It is estimated that the
cost will not be substantially more than for
black and white images.

A further demonstration was given September 3rd for the press. As reported by
PM (September 5, 1940): "The program of
color selected for the demonstration made
all major stops along the spectrum. 'Small
multi-colored object,' the first subtitle announced, and the picture flashed was of a
variegated bowl of flowers and a girl's
hands. 'Intense color,' the next one said,
and a brilliant zinnia appeared against a
Maxfield Parrish sky. Then there were
other gay samples: nodding black-eyed
Susans; red sails in a sunset; a group of
textiles. There was a startlingly beautiful
brunette girl in a red scarf; and a peach-
bloom blonde in a beach robe applying lipstick ('Red on Pink').

"For a motion test, to show that color
television does not run, the blonde girl
slipped out of her beach robe and chased
a bounding red, white and blue beach ball
into the surf. To cap everything, just like

PETER GOLDMARK

a minstrel show, the last scene was the American flag, waving in the breeze in tele-genic, dry-cleaned splendor." The marked contrast between images in black and white and the same scenes in color was revealed by having a standard screen alongside a television receiver equipped for color. The texture of velvet and other fabrics, indistinguishable in black and white, was immediately discernible in color.

The brilliant young inventor of color television, Peter C. Goldmark, was born in Budapest, Hungary, December 2, 1906, the son of Alexander and Emmy Goldmark. His heritage of scientific skill is attributed to a grand uncle, Joseph Goldmark, who served in the Hungarian Parliament in 1848. He won fame as a chemist through the discovery of red phosphorus, a nonpoisonous substance used in match manufacture; and, after arriving in this country, for the invention of percussion caps which were first used in the rifles of the Northern Army during the Civil War.

Peter Goldmark was educated at the Universities of Berlin and Vienna, received his doctorate in physics from the latter institution. While still a student there he read a thesis on "A New Method for Determining the Velocity of Ions" before the Academy of Science in Vienna. Following graduation he was employed by Pye Radio, Limited, in Cambridge, England, assuming control of its television activities. He remained with the British company until 1933.

In 1936 Dr. Goldmark, having come to this country as a consulting engineer, joined the Columbia Broadcasting System's television research department. Later, as CBS's chief television engineer, he supervised installation of the television transmitter atop the Chrysler Building. He has also had several patents issued on his various inven-

tions. These include the CBS type of film scanner, which he completed in 1938, and the scientific reverberation device, which was first demonstrated shortly thereafter. Dr. Goldmark discovered that synthetic reverberation could be made equally useful in sound broadcasting and recording. Based on the electro-optical principle, it adds reverberation to a "dead" studio.

Dr. Goldmark is proud of the American citizenship which he acquired a few years before his marriage in 1940 to Frances Trainer of New York City. Her ancestors settled in New England early in the seventeenth century.

He is fond of outdoor sports, preferring tennis, swimming and skiing. His favorite indoor pastime, besides television, is music. He is an accomplished pianist and cellist, for music is another family heritage. His grandfather's brother is the late Carl Goldmark, distinguished Viennese composer of opera, orchestral and chamber works. Dr. Peter Goldmark himself performed at concerts in Vienna and played in university recitals while employed in the Pye television plant in England.

References

Business Week p20 S 7 '40
N Y Times p18 S 5 '40 por
Newsweek 16:59-60 S 9 '40
PM p13 Ag 30 '40 por; p13 S 5 '40
Variety Radio Directory

GOLDSMITH, LESTER MORRIS July 1, 1893- Engineer
Address: b. 260 S Broad St, Philadelphia, Pennsylvania; h. 1012 W Upsal St, Germantown, Pennsylvania

Chief engineer of the Atlantic Refining Company, Philadelphia, Pennsylvania, Lester M. Goldsmith was awarded the Melville Medal at the annual meeting of the American Society of Mechanical Engineers at Philadelphia, December 6, 1939.

Mr. Goldsmith was born July 1, 1893 at Pottsville, Pennsylvania, son of George Jay and Sara R. Goldsmith. He attended the Philadelphia public schools, the Northeast Manual High School and Drexel Institute. He married Florence Frankel June 26, 1921. They have three children: George Jay, Richard Lester and John Charles.

In 1914 he held his first position as research engineer for the Perpetual Fuse Company, Philadelphia. He became inspector of the Gas Engineering Department of Public Works, City of Philadelphia, in 1915. Since 1916 he has held, in order, the following positions with the Atlantic Refining Company of Philadelphia: mechanical draftsman, research engineer, engineer of tests and superintendent of the Mechanical Laboratory, technical assistant to the President, consulting engineer, manager Engineering and Construction Department, chief engineer.

Since 1929 Mr. Goldsmith has been vice-president and director of the Atlantic Pipe

Line Company; from 1931 to date a director of the Atlantic Oil Shipping Company and chief engineer for the Atlantic Pipe Line Company, the Keystone Pipe Line Company and the Buffalo Pipe Line Corporation.

Mr. Goldsmith is the author of the following papers relating to various processes and instruments in engineering: *New Process for Gas Purification, Pitot Tube Testing Methods, Measurements with Knife Edge Orifices, Diesel-Electric Drive for Tow Boats* (presented personally before the Institution of Engineers, Greenock, Scotland), *Diesel-Electric Drive for Tankers, Diesel-Electric Drive for Pipe Lines, Diesel-Electric Power Plants, Earth Resistivity Measurement, Smith Rotary Type Displacement Meter for Tank Truck Service* and *The High-Pressure, High-Temperature Turbine Electric Steam Ship J. W. Van Dyke.*

He is a member of the American Institute of Electrical Engineers, the American Petroleum Institute, the American Society of Mechanical Engineers, the American Welding Society, the Society of Automotive Engineers and the Society of Naval Architects and Marine Engineers, all located in New York City; of the American Society of Naval Engineers of Washington and of the Engineers Club of Philadelphia.

Mr. Goldsmith has obtained eight United States patents and is awaiting action on four more, relating to oil refining, oil heating, ship, motor truck, centrifugal pump and oil engine design. Several of these patents have been granted by Canada and Great Britain.

His home is in Germantown, Philadelphia, Pennsylvania. Although his chief interests have always been those of the professional engineer, he has several hobbies, among them amateur photography (both still and motion pictures), boating and fishing.

References

Who's Who in American Jewry
Whos' Who in Engineering

GOLER, GEORGE WASHINGTON Aug 24, 1864—Sept 18, 1940 Physician; pioneer in child health and hygiene; known for having established the first municipal milk station and first prenatal clinic in the country; director of the Rochester Board of Health from 1896 to 1932; was the author of many papers on hygiene and sanitary science

References

American Medical Directory 1938
Who's Who in America
Who's Who in American Medicine 1925

Obituaries

N Y Times p23 S 19 '40

GOMA Y TOMAS, ISIDORO, CARDINAL (gō'mä ē tō'mä) Aug 19, 1869—Aug 22, 1940 Archbishop of Toledo; Primate of Spain since 1933; noted supporter of the Church during the Spanish Civil War; celebrated Mass on ruins of the Alcazar after siege was lifted; was ardent supporter of Generalissimo Francisco Franco's forces and organized world-wide relief work in behalf of the Insurgents; appointed Cardinal by Pope Pius XI in 1935; had been priest for 45 years

References

Tablet 175:350 Ap 13 '40
Time 35:35 Ja 15 '40 por
International Who's Who

Obituaries

N Y Times p15 Ag 23 '40
Newsweek 16:55 S 2 '40

GOODRICH, JAMES PUTNAM Feb 18, 1864—Aug 15, 1940 Republican Governor of Indiana from 1917 to 1921; active figure in national politics for more than 40 years; made four visits to Soviet Russia as emissary of President Harding and as agent for the American Relief Administration; noted as arch foe of radicalism; was "favorite son" of Indiana's Republicans for Presidential nomination in 1920

References

Who's Who in America
Who's Who in Government

Obituaries

N Y Herald Tribune p10 Ag 16 '40
N Y Times p15 Ag 17 '40

GORDON, JOHN SLOAN 1868—Oct 12, 1940 Artist; leader of the Canadian impressionist movement in art and associate of the Royal Canadian Academy of Art; art master at the Hamilton Technical School; painted the Congressional Library ceiling

Obituaries

N Y Herald Tribune p12 O 14 '40

GORMAN, HERBERT SHERMAN Jan 1, 1893- Author

Address: Wappingers Falls, New York

Called the best and most complete study of the author of *Ulysses* yet written, Herbert Gorman's biography, *James Joyce,* was published early in February 1940. Mr. Gorman is well known as a writer of several excellent historical novels: *The Place Called Dagon* (1927); *Jonathan Bishop* (1933); *The Mountain and the Plain* (1936); and for critical studies of literary figures and biographies: *The Incredible Marquis, Alexandre Dumas* (1929); *The Scottish Queen, Mary Stuart* (1932). In 1924 he wrote a short analysis: *James Joyce —His First Forty Years.* The present book, on which Gorman has spent 10 years gathering material, covers Joyce's complete career to date.

It is a careful, well-documented biography, written with skill and clarity, interesting because of its intimate portrait of Joyce himself, with whom Gorman spent a great

HERBERT GORMAN

deal of time. Noteworthy chapters in the book include Joyce's revolt in youth against his religious education and Dublin as a center of culture and "Nationalism"; a destitute period in Paris when the young writer all but starved; his marriage and journeys from one European city to another to find teaching jobs; his years of struggle with publishers to get his work published, and published as he wrote it—particularly the struggle for esthetic freedom versus censorship that involved the publication of *Ulysses*. A good many of Joyce's letters are printed in the book, and it contains several hitherto unpublished poems, including the satiric *Gas From a Burner* and *The Holy Office*.

Herbert Gorman was born in Springfield, Massachusetts, January 1, 1893. A writer of commendable Irish wit and frankness, he sends us the following biographical details about himself:

"Father: Thomas, born in Ireland, 1842, died 1924. A hard-riding, hard-drinking, improvident cuss with a fiery temper. Fought in the Civil War. A great horseman, noted in Western Massachusetts as a racing driver in the days of sulky racing. Always broke. Gave me a Gawd-forsaken, poverty-stricken childhood. Mother: Mary Longway, born 1860, still living. Daughter of Louis Longway and Lucinda Griswold. Small, dark, talkative, an inveterate bookworm.

"Education: Public schools and high school, Springfield. But most of it came from the public library. I used to read about 15 hours a day for months on end. How could a penniless boy get 'eddycated' any other way? Jobs: Was assistant to a cobbler, pasted up newspapers in a newspaper mailing room, worked in a rubber-stamp factory where I nearly lost my finger, spent a year in a bank (Springfield National) as the worst bank clerk ever born, labored for a lumber company where had first love affair with a stenographer. She turned me down cold. Spent about a year and half (circa 1912) trying to be an actor. Was frightfully stage-struck. Played in stock, in vaudeville and with Robert B. Mantell. I simply stank.

"About 1914 started reviewing books for Springfield *Republican*. Had written oceans of poetry, some of it placed in small newspapers and fly-by-night magazines. About 1915 became reporter for Springfield *Union*. Later assistant literary editor, then motion picture editor. In 1916 was called to New York to work for the Liberty Loan Publicity Bureau, Second Federal Reserve.

"Travels: After end of war went to Europe every chance I could get. Returns home became farther and farther between. (Whatever that means—sounds like Gertrude Stein trying to write like Colonel Stoopnagle.) Lived for a number of years in France. All my furniture is still stored in Paris, and I hope to return there as soon as this crewel crewel war is finished. Lived also for a year or more in London. Spent some time in Mexico. Also Switzerland. Also Scotland. Also Ireland—ooh, pardon me, Eire.

"Am a member of P. E. N. Was once member of the Players but dropped membership. Or rather, they dropped me for nonpayment of dues. . . Was close friends with Edwin Arlington Robinson, Vachel Lindsay, Elinor Wylie, Ford Madox Ford, Padraic Colum, James Joyce, etc.

"No religious affiliation but lean toward Roman Catholicism. No political affiliation. Am anti-Communist and anti-Nazi. Lean rather toward the Right. As bad as it is it isn't so bad as the Left. Do NOT believe in the equality of people but DO believe in justice for all. Desire the utmost freedom—every man and woman in the world to be able to say anything he or she desires to say at any time and in any place. But *not* by persuasion or conspiracy to limit the freedom of others.

"Love (outside literature) music—NOT swing; painting (very pro-Picasso, Modigliani, Vlaminck and Utrillo); sculpture, football and boxing (to watch); dancing (do only a one-way fox-trot); and flirtation. Love my liquor and love it strong, but can drink beer all night.

"Passion for hot spicy foods, curries, Chinese dishes, etc. Two secret passions: 1) to be a chef; 2) to meet Myrna Loy."

Herbert Gorman was married to Jean Wright of Cleveland in 1921; the marriage was dissolved in 1932. Jean Wright is now Mrs. Carl Van Doren. In 1932 Gorman married Claire O. Crawford (Schneider) of New York. They have one daughter, Patricia Anne d'Auray, born on Shakespeare's birthday, 1933. The Gormans are living at present in the country near New York City. He is working at a novel on

General Boulanger, tentatively called *Brave General*.

References

N Y Herald Tribune p19 F 15 '40
N Y Post p15 F 15 '40
N Y Sun p23 F 14 '40
N Y Times p1, 19 F 18 '40
Newsweek 15:35-6 F 19 '40
Sat R Lit 14:1 Ag 15 '36 por
Who's Who Among North American Authors
Who's Who in America

GORT, JOHN STANDISH SURTEES PRENDERGAST VEREKER, 6TH VISCOUNT
July 1886- British inspector general to the Forces for Training

Address: 98 Mount St, W. 1, London, England

VISCOUNT GORT

When General Lord Gort was appointed chief of the imperial general staff in 1937 over the heads of 32 generals, veteran General Sir Ian Hamilton said: "Thank God, we have got a proper soldier. Now we shall not be shot sitting." The confidence of England in General Gort is still high, not only in spite of Dunkirk, but even because of Dunkirk. That this military disaster did not degenerate into something even worse was due to the qualities of the troops, the work of the navy and in no small measure to the leadership of Britain's "miracle man," Lord Gort, then commander in chief of the B. E. F. in France. As the Birmingham *Post* put it, "Lord Gort has shown himself to be not only a great fighting soldier, but a brilliantly skillful general. Generalship of the highest order has extricated the B. E. F. from a position from which, a few days ago, there seemed no way out."

Lord Gort is the complete practical soldier and has won more medals actually on the field than any other officer in the last 30 years. Field Marshal the Earl of Cavan said of him: "A man with those medals has no right to be alive. By all the laws of averages he should have been killed half a dozen times." It is generally agreed that the authorities have been wise to confide the training of the British Army to a man who has wide experience and personal knowledge of the conditions under which this War is being fought.

John Vereker (he succeeded to his Irish viscounty in 1902) is the son of the fifth Viscount Gort and is descended on his father's side from John Vereker, a Royalist leader in Cromwellian days. His mother (who died in 1933) was the daughter and co-heiress of R. S. Surtees of Hamsterley Hall, County Durham, author of the famous "Jorrocks" hunting books. Gort was brought up partly in County Durham, where he learned to ride, and partly at East Cowes, on the Isle of Wight, where he acquired a great love of yachting. At 14 he went to Harrow, passing from there in 1904 to the Royal Military College, Sandhurst, from which he was gazetted on August 16, 1905 as a second lieutenant in the Grenadier Guards. He was known to his intimates then as "Fat Boy" (the nickname "Tiger" is merely an invention of newspaper men) and led the normal life of a young officer with little incident until his promotion to captain on August 5, 1914.

From then on action piled itself up with a vengeance. Gort alternated staff appointments with periods spent in the thick of the fighting in France. He won the Military Cross in June 1915; in September 1917 he was awarded the Distinguished Service Order; and during 1918 he won it twice more (gaining two bars to the medal). In September of that same year he was given that rare distinction, the Victoria Cross. This was gained for performing "a suicide job" near Flesquières on the Canal du Nord. Gort was ordered to lead his men across the canal under heavy fire and on marshy ground. Though wounded early in the action, he carried on, crossed open ground and boarded a tank, from which he proceeded to direct enfilading fire at the enemy. He was again wounded, but when the men began to wither under heavy punishment he directed operations from a stretcher and so heartened the troops that they rallied and took their objective.

At the end of the War Gort had been acting lieutenant colonel for 18 months. In January 1919 he was appointed to the general staff in London. The next year, however, he took the first post-War course at the Staff College, at Camberley, "to learn something about this business of soldiering." With theoretical studies in strategy and tactics added to his practical experience Gort was appointed to the instructional staff of the College in January 1921.

GORT, VISCOUNT—*Continued*

Four years later Gort was made a colonel and spent the year of 1926 as chief instructor at the Senior Officers' School. On January 24, 1927 he was appointed general staff officer to the Shanghai and North China Defence Force. While in China he had a narrow escape from death when he rescued some nuns from Chinese bandits and was saved only by the intervention of a French Jesuit named Jacquinot who was known in the neighborhood.

Gort returned from China in November 1927 to take charge of the Eastern Command in England. He was appointed to be commanding officer of the Grenadier Guards on January 1, 1930; in November 1932 he sailed for India, with the rank of brigadier, as director of military training. March 1936 found him commandant of the Staff College; in September 1937 he became military secretary to Leslie Hore-Belisha, then Secretary of State for War. That same year he rose to the rank of general and reached the eminent position of chief of the imperial general staff.

An even greater honor was his when he was made commander in chief of the British Expeditionary Force immediately after the Second World War started. Visitors to his headquarters in France were all impressed by the plainness and severity of its furnishings and by the extreme informality of its routine. André Maurois, looking for some place to put his cigarette butt, was astonished to be told, "Chuck it on the floor." After his visit, Maurois wrote of Gort: "I admired the precision of his information and the clarity of his mind. Much good sense. Gaiety. And always the astonishing vitality, coming out in his laugh, his movements, the rapidity of his words."

Gort is strong and stocky, five feet nine inches tall. "Red faced in the best British officer tradition," he has a wide face, a bald head with sandy hair at the sides, a close-clipped mustache and pale blue eyes. He is physically very tough and stays that way by daily cold baths, by walking when others taxi, by hunting and yachting and by flying—he was the first military commander in Europe to pilot his own plane. He is free from the frosty superciliousness of the typical Guards officer and is a frank and forthright talker. There are times when he gets stirred up by people, but once his views have been forcibly expressed, he forgets all about it and resumes his usual friendly attitude.

In January 1940 Gort was given the Grand Cross of the Legion of Honor and, after the Dunkirk evacuation, the Grand Cross of the Order of the Bath. In 1911 he married Corinne, the daughter of George Medlicott Vereker, and in 1925 he divorced her. He has a daughter and a son and heir, Charles Standish Vereker. In 1938 he married Yvonne Frances, the daughter of Geoffrey and Lady Aline Barnett, Sopwell, St. Albans.

References

Cur Hist 51:29 O '39 por
Time 30:21 D 13 '37 por
Karslake, Sir H. Leaders of the Army 1940
Laverton, R. H. Life Story of General Viscount Gort pam 1939
Tuohy, F. Twelve Lances for Liberty 1939
Who's Who

GOUDGE, ELIZABETH (gōōzh) Apr 24, 1900- Author

Address: b. c/o Coward-McCann, Inc, 2 W 45th St, New York City; h. Providence Cottage, Westerland, Paignton, South Devon, England

Elizabeth Goudge is the author of novels that are light without being lightweight, stories about "really nice people" that, for most readers, seem to stay on the right side of sentimentality. Those who require more reassurance about the world than can be found in most current problem-novels and who appreciate a magically evocative prose style when they find it are apparently numerous enough to make her name appear on best-seller lists with unfailing regularity.

Best known for her ability to conjure up a romantically beautiful yesterday, her first novel dealing with contemporary characters is *The Bird in the Tree* (1940). The setting, however, is the eighteenth century home of the Eliots, Damerosehay, "tucked away between the marshes and the sea on a forgotten stretch of the Hampshire coast," and much of the action leads back into the past. It is most of all the story of a family's love for Damerosehay and what it symbolizes. Bought by widowed Lucilla Eliot years before in order that one might "come to it weary and sickened and go away made new," its peace is threatened by her grandson's love for his uncle's divorced wife. *The Bird in the Tree* is that old-fashioned thing, a story with an inescapable moral, and the moral is an old-fashioned one, too: something to do with renunciation. A few critics were afraid Miss Goudge was preaching, wondered if there might not be a little too much "sweetness and light," but most of them found her faith in living as refreshing as her unique understanding of children, her humor, her fantasy and a kind of "lyrical joyousness" found more often in poetry than in prose.

Most of her life Miss Goudge herself has been living in and falling in love with old houses, usually within sight and sound of one cathedral or another. Both are as important in her books as any of the human characters. She was born in 1900 in Wells, Somersetshire, England, where her father, Henry Leighton Goudge, was vice-principal, later principal, of the Theological College. Her mother, Ida de Beauchamp Collonette, was an invalid with a marvelous gift for storytelling; she herself was "a watery child," on the plumpish side, who climbed mulberry trees, wrote a monthly magazine with a neighboring family of little boys, and every other summer visited her Norman-French grandparents in the Channel Islands (later to become the setting for *Island Magic*). When she was 11 her father was made canon of Ely Cathedral in Cambridgeshire, "another small and beautiful cathedral city"; at 14 she went to a boarding school from whose high garden the lovely tower of Christchurch Priory could be seen, and stayed there quite happily all during the War, though "a dunce at everything except English composition and the court curtsey."

Once through with school it was considered necessary to learn to make a living, and after Elizabeth had been discouraged from the idea of becoming a nurse she turned to writing children's stories. The magazines wouldn't buy them, though, and the one volume of fairy stories that was published didn't sell. During this period she earned all of 15 shillings and ended by turning to art as possibly more lucrative. For two years she attended the Art School of Reading University, where she not only "fell devastingly in love" but "conceived a passionate attachment for William Morris and all the pre-Raphaelites." Upon returning home, she turned her house into a studio and proceeded to find students of design and applied art among the good ladies of Ely.

Moving to Oxford in 1923 when her father was appointed Regius Professor of Divinity there, she lived in still another old house in Tom Quod, Christ Church. Life in a big university town she found at first "most alarming" for a naturally shy person—it was necessary to return calls, go to dinner parties—but soon it was more stimulating than alarming, and she found herself wanting to write again. In her odd moments (she was still teaching art) she began to work on plays and continued even after London managers showed themselves unimpressed. Finally in 1932 a play she had written about the Brontës achieved a London performance and good reviews, and though no publisher wanted to bring out her plays one suggested that she write a novel.

She did. It was *Island Magic* (1936) published in England in 1935 after having been revised and rejected twice. There followed *City of Bells* (1936); *Pedlar's Pack and Other Stories* (1937); *Towers in the Mist* (1938); *The Middle Window* (1935); *Sister of the Angels* (1939); and in 1940, *The Bird in the Tree*. In October 1940 appeared her first story for the children about whom she writes so understandingly: *Smoky House*, a story of smugglers, free traders and a "spy who bewitches the countryside with marvelous music" in the West Country of England of a century ago.

In 1939 a volume of three of Miss Goudge's plays was published in England. It is possible that she is prouder of that than of all her other accomplishments, for, she tells us: "Plays, just because they are so difficult and I never have any success with them, are still my first love."

ELIZABETH GOUDGE

References

Christian Sci Mon Mag p11 Je 8 '40 por
Scholastic 34:29 Mr 4 '39 por
Goudge, E. Elizabeth Goudge; an Autobiographical Sketch pam nd

GRAFTON, SAMUEL   Sept 7, 1907-
Newspaper columnist

Address: b. c/o New York Post, 75 West St, New York City

Samuel Grafton, columnist for the New York *Post*, Philadelphia *Record* and other newspapers, is one of those individuals ("rare" to everyone but a student of statistics) actually born in New York City. He received a B. A. from the University of Pennsylvania in 1929 and married Edith (Kingstone) Grafton June 28, 1931. They have one daughter, Abigail Alice, born in 1940.

When asked to tell us something of himself, he replied: "I have no hobbies that make any sense whatever. I read as much in American history as my time allows. Wrote for comic magazines while at college, and for the *North American Review* and the *New Republic* while a junior. Became an editorial writer immediately on graduation, thanks to a sudden impulse which hit J. David Stern, publisher of the Philadelphia *Record*. That was 11 years ago; Mr. Stern still publishes my column."

Mr. Grafton's column is called *I'd Rather Be Right*. The title derives from the saying: I'd rather be right than President. Although Mr. Grafton has a great fan mail from well-wishers, occasionally he receives letters de-

SAMUEL GRAFTON

manding "Who asked you to be President, anyway?"

During the heat of the 1940 Presidential campaign, Sidney Skolsky called Mr. Grafton "the best political columnist now writing in the United States." Grafton's columns have been reprinted by newspapers which do not syndicate his column.

In November 1940 Grafton's book *All Out!*; *How Democracy Will Defend America* was published. Wythe Williams said the book "should be read by every living American. In no other book have I read a more succinct picture of the present world situation."

GRANT, ETHEL WATTS MUMFORD *See* Mumford, E. W.

GRANT, ROBERT Jan 24, 1852—May 19, 1940 Ex-judge; member of commission that approved Sacco-Vanzetti verdict; author of 30 books; Harvard overseer for 25 years

References
> Grant, R. Fourscore; an Autobiography 1934
> Who's Who Among North American Authors
> Who's Who in America
> Who's Who in Law

Obituaries
> N Y Times p17 My 20 '40 por
> N Y World-Telegram p26 My 20 '40
> Pub W 137:2279 Jc 15 '40

GRAVES, FREDERICK ROGERS, BISHOP Oct 24, 1858—May 17, 1940 Retired missionary bishop in charge of the Protestant Episcopal Church's work in Shanghai; wrote books in Chinese; aided in founding a national church in China

References
> Who's Who
> Who's Who in America

Obituaries
> N Y Herald Tribune p12 My 18 '40
> N Y Times p15 My 18 '40 por

GRAVES, WILLIAM SIDNEY Mar 27, 1865—Feb 27, 1940 Major general of United States Army; commanded the American Expeditionary Force in Siberia from 1918 to 1920; author of *America's Siberian Adventure*, containing rather sensational revelations as to America's rôle at the time

WILLIAM S. GRAVES

References
> Who's Who in America
> Who's Who in the Regular Army

Obituaries
> N Y Herald Tribune p16 F 28 '40 por
> N Y Sun p10 F 27 '40
> N Y World-Telegram p19 F 27 '40
> Newsweek 15:9 Mr 11 '40

GRAYSON, DAVID, pseud. *See* Baker, R. S.

GREEN, JULIAN Sept 6, 1900- Author
Address: b. c/o Harper & Bros, 49 E 33rd St, New York City

Julian Green, American novelist who has lived in France almost all his life, has been in the United States since the summer of 1940, working on a new novel to be published in March 1941. Its tentative title is *Then Shall the Dust Return*. The book which precedes it is *Personal Record, 1928-1939* (1939), an introspective journal which tells of Green's

JULIAN GREEN

References

Bookm 70:180-2 O '29 por; 75:349-53
  Ag '32 por
Forum 103:IV F '40
N Y Herald Tribune Books p7 N 12
  '39
N Y Times p9 D 3 '39
Sat R Lit 14:7 S 5 '36 por
Time 34:88 N 13 '39 por
Wilson Lib Bul 3:518 Mr '29 por
Green, J. Personal Record, 1928-39
  1939
Kunitz, S. J. ed. Living Authors 1937
Who's Who in America

work and life, of his friendships with Gide, Dali (see sketch this issue), Gertrude Stein, Cocteau and Malraux.

This book, like all his others except the one he is now working on, was written in French, for though Julian Green's parents were Americans of Scotch-Irish ancestry, he was born in Paris and brought up as a typical young Frenchman. During the First World War he saw active service near Verdun and on the Italian Front. One year after the Armistice he saw America for the first time. He enrolled in the University of Virginia and for two years studied English and American literature, Latin and Greek, teaching French in his spare time. It was while he was in Virginia that he first appeared in print—with a long story called *The Apprentice Psychiatrist* published in the college magazine.

Back in France, Green republished this story in French and began to study art and music, uncertain of what his career should be. It wasn't long, however, before he was writing again: essays on English literary figures, on religion, on art. In 1926 came his first novel, *Mont Cinère,* translated as *Avarice House* (1927). This was a success, and his next novel, *Adrienne Mésurat,* translated as *The Closed Garden* (1928), was awarded the Femina-Bookman Prize for the best French work suitable for English translation. His next, *Léviathan,* translated as *The Dark Journey,* was the Harper prize novel in 1929.

In all these novels and in his short stories Julian Green writes in a "dark manner." His work is sombre, psychologically penetrating, neurotic. But André Maurois feels that his work will eventually become lighter, more tranquil, and perhaps his first novel in English, written in America, will reveal this newer trend.

GREENE, FRANK RUSSELL Apr 16, 1856—Jan 20, 1940 Artist; member of the National Academy

Obituaries

N Y Herald Tribune p28 Ja 21 '40
N Y Times p15 Ja 13 '40; p34 Ja 21
  '40

GREENWOOD, ARTHUR 1881- British Labor Party leader; Minister without Portfolio in the Churchill Cabinet

Address: Transport House, Smith Sq, S. W. 1, London, England

The Socialist movement in England has drawn its most valuable recruits from two very different kinds of people. To it have come manual workers who have progressed by sheer ability—men like Lord Snell who began life as a farm boy or Ernest Bevin (see sketch this issue), ex-tram conductor. To it have come, too, many intellectuals —Dr. Alexander D. Lindsay, Master of Balliol College (a position soundly entrenched in the English social and intellectual system), has Labor views. It is to this second group that Arthur Greenwood, long a leader in the British Labor Party and now a Minister in the Cabinet, belongs. Though his origins are fairly modest, he has never worked with his hands.

Arthur Greenwood is a native of Yorkshire, a section celebrated for the dour, dogged, unsentimental type of mind it produces. He attended the ordinary state elementary and secondary schools in his native city of Leeds and then went on to University College, Leeds, then a part of the old Victoria University. His career there was brilliant. He won frequent prizes in the history and theory of education and in economic research and was graduated with a B. S. degree. Immediately after college he started to teach. From various elementary and secondary schools in different parts of Yorkshire he progressed to a lectureship in economics at his old University and then to the headship of the department of economics at Huddersfield Technical College.

Greenwood's labor views declared themselves early, and for some time he helped run a labor monthly at Leeds. Even more important was the part he played in working-class education. With Dr. Albert

ARTHUR GREENWOOD

Mansbridge, J. J. Mallon and R. H. Tawney he was one of the moving spirits in the establishment of the Workers' Educational Association, which now controls a great network of classes all over the country. He was chairman of its Yorkshire district and later became vice-president of its central organization.

Just before the First World War Greenwood left Yorkshire for London to become general secretary of the Council for the Study of International Relations. Mr. Lloyd George (with his genius for finding able lieutenants off the conventional lines) appointed him secretary to the Reconstruction Committee in 1917 and in the same year made him one of the secretaries at the Ministry of Reconstruction. He served there effectively until after the Armistice and also worked on the Committees on Profiteering and on Trusts.

In 1920 Greenwood came to the parting of the ways. A safe, prosperous, useful career in the Civil Service was his for the asking. He decided to work for Labor instead. He joined the general headquarters of the Labor Party as secretary of advisory committees and within 12 months had become head of the Labor Research and Information Department for which the Labor Party and the Trades Union Congress are jointly responsible. He also founded the University Labor Federation and served as its president until January 1940, when he resigned after an anti-War resolution had been passed.

Greenwood's first attempt at Parliament was in 1918 at Southport, Lancashire, a smart seaside resort largely populated by retired cotton merchants. It was a hopeless constituency for Labor, and of course he failed miserably. In 1922, however, he was returned for Nelson and Colne (Lancashire industrial districts), and during the short Labor government of 1924 acted as Parliamentary Secretary to the Ministry of Health. When Labor came back in 1929 he was made Minister of Health, a post which gave scope for social reforms near his heart: reforms in housing, slum clearance, public health and widows' pensions. He was sworn a privy councilor in 1929 and in the following year was made honorary Freeman of the City of Leeds and awarded an honorary LL. D. by the University of Leeds.

The general election of 1931, conducted as it was in an atmosphere of financial panic, cleared out most of the Labor Ministers, Greenwood among them; but he returned to Parliament at a by-election a year later, winning Wakefield, Yorkshire, by a narrow majority. He now found himself one of a greatly diminished Labor group constantly at loggerheads with an enormous Conservative majority. He pitched into the "National Government" on every possible occasion, particularly for its weakness in the face of the growing menace from the dictator countries. The strength of his views on this issue caused him to be classified by Hitler with Churchill, Eden and Duff Cooper (see sketches this issue) as a "warmonger." Greenwood is no "warmonger"; he has emphasized the folly and wickedness of war time and again—but he still has never wavered in his belief that England must stand up to the dictators.

Because of his ability, his beliefs and his position in the Labor Party (he was acting leader of the Party during Attlee's [see sketch this issue] illness in 1939), Winston Churchill was quick to take Greenwood into a coalition Cabinet as Minister without Portfolio: At The Labor Party Congress held shortly after the appointment was made, shouting Labor hecklers accused him and Attlee of "treachery to Labor" because they had joined the government. "Such accusations are a foul lie," Greenwood roared back. "It would have been treachery if we had seen other countries go under the harrow and refused to do our share."

It's only on rare occasions that Greenwood roars. Tall and spare in build, he is usually quiet and dignified in manner and looks what he is—a scholar. From time to time he has written books on social and educational matters and is credited with having devised and inspired some of the most effective literature the Labor movement has produced in the last 20 years. Yet in this literature Greenwood is less interested in scholarly theory than in the practical business of organization and government. He has an encyclopedic grasp of detail, together with the gift of quickly clearing away the non-essentials in an argument and leaving the important issues clearly defined. His appetite for work is colossal, and he can turn quickly from departmental duties to a rousing platform speech and then back again to the very different kind of speech that "goes down" at Westminster. Energetic, highly intelligent and socially conscious, he is an important part of the coalition which faces the gigantic task of preserving England.

References
> Picture Post 7:14-15 Je 1 '40
> Time 35:38 My 27 '40
> Who's Who

GRENFELL, SIR WILFRED THOMASON Feb 28, 1865—Oct 9, 1940 Founder of the world-renowned Labrador Medical Mission; started as surgeon for poor fishermen in Labrador and set out to colonize and improve conditions there; from 1892 to 1935 remained in Labrador building hospitals, schools, cooperative stores, orphanages; wrote many books, mainly on life in Labrador; knighted in 1927; received honors from a score of colleges and universities in the United States and England

SIR WILFRED GRENFELL

References
> Christian Cent 57:1300 O 23 '40
> Mis R 59:197-200 Ap '36
> R of Rs 96:25-6+ Jl '37
> Time 36:64-6 O 21 '40 por
>
> American Medical Directory 1938
> Bridges, T. C. and Tiltman, H. H. Grenfell of Labrador *In* Heroes of Modern Adventure ⌐132-42 1927
> Grenfell, W. T. Adrift on an Ice-Pan 1929
> Grenfell, W. T. Labrador Doctor: Autobiography 1929
> Hall, A. G. Dr. Wilfred Grenfell nd
> Hayes, E. H. Forty Years on the Labrador 1930
> Mathews, B. J. Wilfred Grenfell, the Master-Mariner 1923

Parkman, M. R. Deep-Sea Doctor: Wilfred Grenfell *In* Heroes of Today p51-77 1917
Tiltman, Mrs. M. H. Putting Labrador on the Map: the Story of Sir Wilfred Grenfell's Great Work *In* God's Adventurers p124-43 1933
Waldo, F. L. Grenfell 1924
Waldo, F. L. With Grenfell on the Labrador 1920
Wallace, D. Story of Grenfell of the Labrador 1922
Who's Who in America

Obituaries
> N Y Herald Tribune p20 O 10 '40 por
> N Y Times pl, 25 O 10 '40 por
> Newsweek 16:6 O 21 '40 por

GRISWOLD, AUGUSTUS H. Sept 29, 1879—Feb 24, 1940 Senior vice-president and director of the International Telephone and Telegraph Company; spent last 12 years developing properties of the company throughout the world

References
> Who's Who in America 1938-39
> Who's Who in Commerce and Industry

Obituaries
> N Y Herald Tribune p32 F 25 '40 por
> N Y Times p39 F 25 '40 por

GROFE, FERDE (grō-fā) Mar 27, 1892- Composer; conductor
Address: b. c/o National Broadcasting Company, 30 Rockefeller Plaza, New York City; h. 195 Norma Rd, Teaneck, New Jersey

Ferde Grofé (he was christened Ferdinand but has since shortened it and discarded the von in his name) is a "bland-spoken" composer who believes that there is a real place for symphonic jazz in American music. "I am not foolish enough to try to place myself in a class, for example, with Ravel and Sibelius, whom I admire immensely," he says, "but I am going on to try to describe America in music."

Grofé's America is bounded by Manhattan (his *Tabloid Suite),* by New Orleans *(Mardi Gras),* by Hollywood *(Hollywood Suite).* It includes the scenic wonders portrayed in the *Grand Canyon Suite* and the clanging industry of *Symphony in Steel.* With an inimitable flair for melodic inventions and a tremendous skill in orchestration, Ferde Grofé has translated into musical terms much of the face of America.

He has always written music: "It was the first thing my mother taught me before I knew how to write English." Grofé was born in New York City near Battery Park and moved to Los Angeles when he was very young. His mother, Elsa Johanna (Bierlich) von Grofé, a graduate of the Leipzig Conservatory and a cellist of "eminent ability," taught him the rudiments of theory and harmony. His father, Emil von Grofé was a

FERDE GROFE

singer with a light opera company, and his grandfather, Bernhardt Bierlich, premier cellist in the Los Angeles Symphony Orchestra, and his uncle, Julius Bierlich, concert master of the same orchestra, coached him in chamber music.

Ferde Grofé started studying piano and violin when he was five. When he was 14 he ran away from home. He worked as a bookbinder, in an iron foundry, as a truck driver, as a theatre usher. He kept on with his music, too, and eventually earned his keep pounding the piano in California mining town dance halls until his family got him a job as violist in the Los Angeles Symphony Orchestra in 1909. In that year came his first published composition—*The Elks' Grand Reunion March*—a notable feature of the Elks' convention.

For 10 years Grofé remained with the Los Angeles Symphony, learning from his grandfather to play the brass instruments as well as the violin and viola. But he wasn't making much money. Dance halls and ballrooms began to supply him with the major part of his income. It was in 1919 while he was leading an orchestra at a dance hall named the Portola Louvre that he met Paul Whiteman. Whiteman had happened by chance to walk in. Before he left he had engaged Grofé for his orchestra as pianist and arranger. To the disgust of Grofé's grandfather, who looked upon anything that savored of dance music as "shoo-fly" music, Grofé went to San Francisco. He stayed with Paul Whiteman for 12 years.

It was Grofé who added melodic shimmer to such Whiteman numbers as the *Song of India* and *Chansonette*. It was Grofé whose early arrangement of Whiteman's rendition of *Whispering* sold more than a million and one-half records. It was Grofé who was "the power behind King Whiteman's throne" and

as such "dressed up many a sleazy Tin Pan Alley Cinderella and made it the belle of the ball." And it was Grofé who brought both George Gershwin and himself fame by his scoring, in 1924, of the *Rhapsody in Blue*, "a mere sketch until he got hold of it."

It was in this same year that Grofé retired from active playing in Whiteman's orchestra and devoted himself mainly to arranging, as well as to making piano roll records for the Ampico Company and phonograph records. What with all the arranging business he got, Grofé was so busy writing other people's music that he had little chance to write any of his own. But from time to time he did turn out an orchestral piece in conservative jazz style, "more notable for expert workmanship than for sizzling licks or hipwrenching tunes." His first serious effort at composing resulted in a tone poem called *Broadway at Night* (1924), which received little attention. The following year came the famous *Mississippi Suite* with the well-known "Mardi Gras" and "Huckleberry Finn" movements. *Metropolis,* a fantasy of New York, followed in 1927, and *Three Shades of Blue,* "a delightfully imaginative number in the modern style," was written in 1928. Then followed a series of smaller piano pieces, and finally in 1931 came the *Grand Canyon Suite,* hailed by musicians and critics as "one of the finest pieces of American music ever produced."

After the success of this suite, Grofé did much less arranging and more composing. He wrote more suites. In 1935 his first ballet was produced in the Hollywood Bowl and in 1938 his second, *Café Society,* "added a persuasive point in his lifelong argument for 'symphonic' jazz."

In January 1937 Grofé made his debut as a conductor in Carnegie Hall, New York City, playing a program of his own music. The jazzy, tuneful, descriptive music made good listening and was often good for a laugh. In his *Symphony in Steel* Grofé employed a siren and pneumatic drills; in *Hollywood* there were the banging and scraping of carpenters and electricians, the ennui of "stand-ins," the barking of a director and a "precision routine" in which the percussion section drummed on its shoes with rhythmic ingenuity to suggest a dance routine. "There's so much noise I can't hear," one member of the audience complained that night.

Grofé has led and continues to lead prominent orchestras, in concerts and broadcasts. He has taught orchestration at the Juilliard School in New York City. His compositions are widely heard. In fact, so strong is his influence with rhythms and harmonies that people are beginning to talk of the "Ferde Grofé School."

There is publicity value in descriptive, alive, fresh music like Grofé's and leading industrialists long ago recognized the advantages of a tie up with him. The American Rolling Mills Company put him on its regular payroll while he composed the *Symphony in Steel* and the Ford Motor Company supported him while he created the suite, *Wheels.* During 1939 and 1940 he has been presenting the New World Ensemble as a main feature of the Ford Exhibit at the New York World's Fair. This ensemble, composed of four novachords and a Hammond organ, sounds like a full-size orchestra and reproduces the tone of every instrument used in the average symphony. With it Grofé presents some of his own works and many masterful arrangements of favorite pieces, old and new.

On May 11, 1929 Grofé married Ruth Harriet MacGloan; they have two children—Ferdinand Rudolf Jr., and Anne Carlin.

References

Etude 56:425-6+ Jl '38 por; 58:293+ My '40 il
Musician 44:47 Mr '39 por; 44:86+ My 39 por (p89); 44:173 O '39 por; 45:49 Mr '40 por
New Yorker 16:74 My 25 '40
Newsweek 9:25 Ja 30 '37
Scrib Mag 90:594 600 D '31
Time 29:38 F 1 '37 por; 32:42 N 28 '38
Thompson, O. ed. International Cyclopedia of Music and Musicians
Wier, A. E. ed. Macmillan Encyclopedia of Music and Musicians 1938

GROPPER, WILLIAM (grŏp'per) Dec 3, 1897- Artist; cartoonist

Address: h. Mt Airy Rd, Croton-on-Hudson, New York

For several years William "Bill" Gropper's trenchant cartoons of social protest and satire have been known to the American public. Only recently has Gropper been recognized also as a skilled and effective painter. In New York City during February 1940, "Twenty Years of Bill Gropper" was celebrated with a rally in Mecca Temple; a Gropper monograph of 36 reproductions, with text by his fellow-artist Joe Jones (see sketch this issue); and an important show of his recent paintings at the A. C. A. Gallery. Among these new paintings on exhibit, in oil and water color, are several typically class-conscious canvases: *The Shoemaker,* bare footed, mending other people's shoes; *Brenda in a Tantrum,* satirizing the 1939 Glamour Girl; *The Kibitzer,* a youth absorbed in a poker player's royal flush; and *Art Patrons,* two socialite gallery-goers viewing a picture with disapproving hauteur. At present his paintings are represented in the permanent collections of the Metropolitan Museum of Art, the Museum of Modern Art, the Phillips Memorial Gallery in Washington, the Hartford, Connecticut Museum and elsewhere.

Gropper was born in New York City, on the lower East Side, December 3, 1897, son of Harry and Jenny (Nidel) Gropper. On his way to school he would carry to a sweatshop the bundles of sewing his mother did at home. His first job was in a clothing store at $5 a week. Later he attended the National Academy of Design (1913-14), and the New York School of Fine and Applied Art (1915-18). He has been awarded several prizes for illustration, and in 1937 won a Guggenheim Fellowship.

Though he wanted to paint, Gropper, like Daumier, had to earn his living by drawing cartoons. His first job as a cartoonist was with the New York *Herald Tribune* (1920). One day he was assigned to caricature an I. W. W. rally. But Gropper was so moved to sympathy that he became a convert to Left-wing activity. So, in his own phrase, he "fired the *Tribune,*" and became successively a Labor organizer, oiler on a freighter, itinerant sign painter and illustrator. He still draws cartoons, willingly and without pay, for the *New Masses* and the *Sunday Worker;* and for the *Freiheit,* Yiddish Communist paper, getting paid only when the *Freiheit* can afford it. He makes his living free-lancing for capitalist and conservative publications such as *Fortune* and *Vogue.* And he has been commissioned as a mural painter for hotels and public buildings. Notable among his murals are those for the post office at Freeport, New York; his Cuban scenes for the Schenley Products Company, New York; and the mural in the new Department of the Interior Building in Washington, D. C. Gropper never embarrasses his conservative employers by making paintings of social comment for them. "To paint a mural that doesn't fit the place would be like painting swastikas in a synagogue," he says. "My only interest, when I haven't got a free hand, is to do as good a job as possible."

William Gropper has been described as "a short, thick man with dreamy gray eyes and an air of subdued but uninhibited amusement." He paints as he draws, usually from memory or from imagination, in fast, bold

WILLIAM GROPPER

GROPPER, WILLIAM—*Continued*

strokes, with bright reds, yellows, blues, slashes of white.

Gropper is a member of the Society of Mural Painters and The American Group. Three books of his illustrations have been published: *The Golden Land* (political cartoons), (1927); *Fifty-Six Drawings of U. S. S. R.* (1928); *Alay-Oop* (story in pictures), (1930). He is considered America's ranking satirist, not only in his forte, black and white, but also in oil. In August 1935 he created quite a stir when the Emperor of Japan demanded an apology from the United States State Department for Gropper's caricature of him. His artistic derivations are Brueghel, Rouault and George Grosz. Among his better known paintings are *Waiting,* a cow dying of thirst, on whom buzzards have already lit; *Burning Wheat,* an echo of the now defunct AAA program; *Klansman,* the modern equivalent of the rider of death; *Survivors,* a full lifeboat on the sea, suggested by the Vestris disaster; and *Burlesque,* a footlight Venus type. A recent exhibit, dedicated to "the defenders of Spanish Democracy," included water colors and oils inspired by the news from Spain. In these, Gropper expressed the helplessness of refugees, the terror of people during air raids, the senseless destruction of human beings.

In 1924 Gropper married bacteriologist Sophie Frankle of Youngstown, Ohio. Soon after their marriage they spent a year in Russia, where Gropper worked on *Pravda,* official organ of the Communist Party. They have two sons, Gene and Lee. They live at Croton-on-Hudson, New York, where they built their own nine-room stone house.

The sharp, dramatic form of his paintings, their discipline of clean line and comment, owe much to Gropper's training as a cartoonist. There are actually two worlds represented in his painting. One, a kind of life that calls for social comment and protest, usually takes the form of a grim portrayal of poverty, cruelty or violence. In these drawings the background of sky, clouds, hills or trees reflects the mood of the painting, and the lives of the figures appearing in it. In *Southern Landscape,* for instance, the gnarled branch of a pine tree is extended like clutching bony hands across the lowering sky. At the base of the picture, startlingly white against a dark rock, lies a half-naked, prostrate figure, with two dark vigilante forms nearby. Even his paintings without figures can express social meaning. In *Still Life* Gropper paints a cheap vase holding faded flowers, with a solitary undernourished herring on a white plate.

Another world is reflected in his paintings with bright, robust activity and portraiture. In singular contrast to his water color *Sweatshop* is the physical exuberance of two woodcutters in *Landscape;* the pathos of his American slum children to the plump, glowing health of *Little Girl—U. S. S. R.* Then there is the gay, colorful landscape of *Grape Gatherers,* with figures in pleasant, zestful occupation. In such landscapes there is no flat, somber gray: the skies are clear and blue, the buildings stand out in sharp, vivid colors.

Discussing the quality of his social comment work, through which he has achieved his real distinction, Ernest Brace writes: "William Gropper's painting is unequivocally effective. Whether he paints the agile mouth of a Senator or the thin, tight lips of a judge, prisoners being marched off to execution or the prostrate victims of an air raid, the briefest glance tells the story. . . Gropper's purpose seems as inseparable from his painting as the pigment. And even when his protest against injustice is loudest and most vehement, it never becomes shrill or raucous with personal animosity. . . He is concerned not with an individual, but with the forces that have conditioned him."

References

Am Mag Art 29:188-9 Mr '36 il
Art Digest 11:9 Ap 15 '37
Forum 103:288 My '40 il
Mag Art 30:464, 467-71, 514 Ag '37 il pl; 33:174 Mr '40 il
Time 31:41 Mr 21 '38; 35:41 F 19 '40 il; 35:41 F 19 '40 il

Boswell, P. Jr. Modern American Painting 1939
Who's Who in America
Who's Who in American Jewry

GRUENBERG, SIDONIE MATSNER (grü'en-burg sē-dō'nē' măts'ner) June 10, 1881- Educator

Address: b. 221 W 57th St, New York City; h. 418 Central Park West, New York City

Parents' Magazine's annual award for the outstanding book for parents published during 1939 was given to Mrs. Sidonie Matsner Gruenberg for *We, the Parents,* a book written to give parents constructive help in understanding and working toward a solution of basic problems of childhood and family life. In 1930 the same magazine awarded her the medal for Distinguished Service in Parental Education.

Born near Vienna, Austria, Sidonie Matzner (the spelling now changed to Matsner) attended the Hohere Tochterschüle in Hamburg, Germany. When she was 14 years old her parents, Idore and Augusta Olivia (Bassechés) Matzner came to New York City. Soon after, her father died. Her mother, descended from a wealthy cultured family and having led a sheltered life, was faced with the problem of making a living for herself and five children. She engaged in rubber importing, a most unusual business occupation for a woman.

Sidonie was graduated from the Ethical Culture School (1897), later took special training in the normal department and then did graduate study at Columbia University. In 1903 she married Benjamin Charles Gruenberg, who was born in Bessarabia,

Russia, and came to the United States when a child.

They have four children: Herbert M., a physician; Richard M., a businessman; Hilda Sidney. a writer; and Ernest M., a medical student. From her study and from her experiences in bringing up her own children, as well as two grandchildren, and helping to meet the problems of other parents, Mrs. Gruenberg is well qualified to advise on all problems of childhood.

One of Mrs. Gruenberg's biggest jobs is directing the activities of the Child Study Association of America. She has been with that organization since 1906, has been its director since 1921. She was Chairman of the sub-Committee of the White House Conference on Child Health and Protection (1930); a member of the President's Conference on Home Building and Home Ownership (1931); and of the 1940 White House Conference on Children in a Democracy. In addition she is a member of the advisory council or board of almost 20 organizations, ranging from the Advisory Board of the Junior Literary Guild to the Council of 100 of the American Association for Adult Education. Most recently she was appointed a member of the Executive Committee of the Progressive Education Association.

A member of the lecture staff at Columbia University Teachers College, 1928 to 1936, and at New York University since 1936, Mrs. Gruenberg also lectures before women's clubs, parents' and teachers' organizations and social workers—her audiences varying from 19 to 9,000. She contributes articles on child training, children's literature, family relationships and educational problems to magazines and has written a number of books.

Her first book, *Your Child Today and Tomorrow* (1913), is a book for parents, dealing with some of the problems of child training. The author's objective is expressed in the introduction: "It has been my chief aim to show that a proper understanding of and sympathy with the various stages through which the child normally passes will do much towards making not only the child happier, but the task of the parents pleasanter."

Sons and Daughters (1916), which followed, has to do with the training of older children—boys and girls of adolescent age. A critic has written: "The author's attitude is wise and sane; her methods unite what is best of the old and new ideals in child training. She points out that many of the supposed innovations in bringing up children are only efforts to restore to them what they have lost in the advance of industrial civilization."

Modestly, Mrs. Gruenberg says that she does everything with her author-educator husband and admiringly states that his record of achievement in *Who's Who in America* is longer than hers. They coauthored *Parents, Children and Money* (1933), which is an elaboration of the simple pedagogical dogma

G. Maillard Kesslère

SIDONIE GRUENBERG

that children learn to do by doing. And so, using the "allowance," no matter how small, as the best instrument by which education can be carried on, they discuss the various phases of that training in the home and the ways in which the allowance can be used to make the child feel his responsibility, develop his intelligence and train his understanding of his relations with other members of the family.

Our Children (1936), coedited with Dorothy Canfield Fisher, is a volume made up of 27 articles on the care and training of children, written for parents by specialists in medicine, psychology, physiology and education.

Parents' Questions (1936) answers questions brought to the Child Study Association by inquiring parents.

Mrs. Gruenberg, a striking-looking woman, has brown eyes and is very dark—a "Spanish" type. Her secretary describes her as having a "marked outgoing personality." Without a trace of accent, she has a low-pitched voice and speaks beautifully. Good health, says Mrs. Gruenberg, and the cooperation of her family and staff are the primary essentials which enable her to participate in so many activities which all converge about the problems of parenthood and children. While gardening and travel are her hobbies, her real hobby, as well as her work, is child study.

References

New Outlook 165:37 F '35
N Y Herald Tribune p22 Mr 20 '40
N Y World-Telegram p28 Mr 29 '40
Parents' Mag 15:126 Ap '40 il; 15:104 My '40 por
American Women
Who's Who in America
Who's Who in American Jewry

GRUPPE, CHARLES PAUL (groop'ĕ) Sept 3, 1860—Sept 30, 1940 Noted landscape painter who won acclaim in the United States and Europe; born in Canada and came to this country at the age of six; works on exhibition in many museums of the country; works once adorned the collection of former Kaiser Wilhelm of Germany and the Queen Mother of Holland; awarded gold medals in Rouen, Paris and Philadelphia

References

Who's Who in America
Who's Who in American Art

Obituaries

N Y Herald Tribune p22 O 1 '40
N Y Sun p21 O 1 '40

GUILLAUMAT, MARIE LOUIS ADOLPHE (gĕ-yō-mà) Jan 4, 1863—May 18, 1940 French general; War Minister under Briand; commanded Allied Force at Salonika in 1917 to 1918; commanded Army of Occupation; reported Reich rearming in 1927

References

Dictionnaire National des Contemporains 1936
International Who's Who
Qui Etes-Vous?

Obituaries

N Y Herald Tribune p32 My 19 '40
N Y Times p43 My 19 '40 por

GUISE, JEAN PIERRE CLEMENT MARIE, DUC DE (gēz) Sept 24, 1874 —Aug 25, 1940 Pretender to the vanished French throne; spent 14 years in exile in Sicily, Brussels and Spanish Morocco; has issued many manifestoes from his exile; asked for dictatorship in his country under a monarchy which he would head; in 1940 it was said he would succeed Pétain (see sketch this issue) as chief of France and re-establish the monarchy

References

International Who's Who

Obituaries

N Y Herald Tribune p14 Ag 27 '40 por
N Y Times p21 Ag 27 '40 por
Time 36:47 S 2 '40

GUNTER, JULIUS CALDEEN Oct 31, 1858—Oct 26, 1940 Democratic Governor of Colorado from 1917 to 1919; member of Colorado Bar for nearly 60 years and served on bench for many years; former president of Colorado State Bar Association

References

Who's Who in America
Who's Who in Law

Obituaries

N Y Times p44 O 27 '40

GUTHRIE, CHARLES ELLSWORTH, REV. (gŭth'rĭ) May 26, 1867—July 26, 1940 Clergyman; nationally prominent in the Methodist Church for many years; former general secretary of the Epworth League; served as pastor in Methodist congregations in Baltimore, Washington and Wilkes-Barre

References

Who's Who in America

Obituaries

N Y Herald Tribune p8 Jl 27 '40
N Y Times p13 Jl 27 '40

GUTHRIE, WILLIAM BUCK Sept 6, 1869—Nov 6, 1940 Professor emeritus of government at City College, New York; formerly chairman of government department; authority on constitutional government; retired in February 1940; known as "Big Bill" Guthrie because of girth and height; several times named most popular instructor at City College, where he had taught since 1903; writings include *Socialism Before the French Revolution* and *The Housing Problem in Germany*; coauthor of *American Government*; working on three law books at time of death

References

Who's Who in America

Obituaries

N Y Herald Tribune p22 N 7 '40 por
N Y Times p25 N 7 '40 por

HAAKON VII, KING OF NORWAY (häk'kŭn) Aug 3, 1872- King of Norway

After they fled from the Norwegian port of Molde, only 28 miles from the German-occupied Aandalsnes, the King of Norway, his family and most of the members of his government reached London on June 10, 1940. In April 1940 had come the announcement from Berlin that neither King Haakon nor the old Norwegian government would have any authority in the occupied territories because they had placed themselves on the side of the Allies.

Interviewed two days after his flight from the Norwegian capital of Oslo on April 9, 1940, the King was reported as saying: "Since I left Oslo Tuesday I have not taken off my shoes and have hardly slept. All civilization seems to have come to an end. I cannot understand how such terrible things can happen. I can no longer be sure of anything.

". . . My people can evacuate to Sweden I will have to stay in my country as long as there remains a single inch of Norwegian soil."

This fugitive monarch who has presided over conservative, liberal, radical, peasant and labor governments in Norway for 34 years is, strangely enough, not even Norwegian-born. He was born Prince Charles of Denmark (Christian Frederick Charles George Waldemar Axel) on August 3, 1872, the second son of Crown Prince Frederick (later Frederick VIII). At thirteen he was known in Denmark as "the sailor Prince" because for nine months he served in the royal navy as midshipman, the lowest post in the service. In 1896 he married Princess Maud, the daughter of Edward VII of England, and on July 2, 1903 a son, Alexander, was born.

At this time Norway was still annexed to Sweden, having been ceded in 1814 after the dissolution of a four-century union with Denmark. Although Sweden was dominant, Norway had retained her own Constitution and the right to local self-government. When Norway finally separated from Sweden in 1905, its Republican Party was not in a majority, however. Norway wanted a king. And Edward VII of England was prompt to suggest his son-in-law for monarch after Oscar II of Sweden had refused to select one of his own sons. On November 18, 1905, Prince Charles was elected King of Norway by popular referendum (not a strange procedure for a monarchy so democratic that all hereditary titles were abolished by its Constitution of 1814); the same month Charles first set foot in Norway, carrying his young son in his arms; and early the following year he was crowned King Haakon of Norway in the cathedral at Trondheim. Princess Maud became Queen Maud, and Prince Alexander became Crown Prince Olaf. In 1938 the nation mourned the death of Queen Maud.

Although the Norwegian government's power is divided between royal authority and the elected representatives of the Storting (Parliament), with the King presiding over the state council, actually his is "a purely decorative office, closely resembling that of the President of the Republic of France, just as far removed from active participation in the running of the state and just as much of a pompous misnomer." According to the Constitution he has a greater latitude of initiative than the King of England, but his veto rights are limited and he has no power to dissolve Parliament. Fortunately King Haakon, unlike his grandfather, Christian IX, was liberal-minded and easy-going, and he quickly made himself popular with both Parliament and the people. His knowledge of foreign affairs won respect for his statesmanship as well. The first year of his reign found Sweden's attitude toward Norway rather threatening, but in 1907 an Integrity Treaty was signed by which the strategic powers—including Great Britain, France and Russia—guaranteed Norwegian independence. After that treaty King Haakon's reign was one of close cooperation with the other Scandinavian powers—and, until now, of peace for Norway.

When the First World War broke out in 1914, a Scandinavian conference was quickly called in which the monarchs of the "Oslo Nations" affirmed their neutrality

Norwegian

HAAKON VII

and their determination to preserve it. It was the first of many such conferences, always for the same purpose—in 1917; in 1918; "Scandinavia Day" in October 1936, in celebration of a "common front of democracy and tolerance"; in 1938; in September 1939; again in October 1939. Journalists who noted that at the 1917 conference Sweden's King Gustav kissed King Haakon on only one cheek while honoring both cheeks of his brother Christian X of Denmark also noted that the brothers were treated alike at the October 1939 conference, and saw it as a symbol of Scandinavia's strengthened ties. Crown Prince Olaf's marriage to Martha, niece of the Swedish King, had also taken place in the interim.

In Oslo Norway's King drove around the streets unescorted in a modest car, granted audiences to whoever asked, was known for his sea yarns, his habits of strolling down to the waterfront and of talking informally to everyone from fishermen to clerks. The royal family had an estate at Skangum, a summer home at Bygdöy; in winter there were winter sports, in the hunting season there was riding to hounds; King Haakon, "erect, slender and well over six feet in height," was at least as fond of outdoor sports as of diplomacy, and it was not unpleasant to be a King in a country where even the people were so democratic that they didn't bother to stare at the spectacle of a royal family acting quite normally.

The governments over which King Haakon presided went through many changes, however, as did the national economy. In 1935 the Liberals fell from power when they refused to levy higher taxes for the relief of the unemployed. The Agrarians, normally rather conservative in their views, threw their weight behind the Labor Party of Norway, and in 1936, seventy members of

HAAKON VII—*Continued*

the Labor Party were among the Storting's one hundred and fifty representatives. With the avowed aim of gaining the cooperation of the middle classes by a program of not-too-radical social legislation, Labor still succeeded in winning the serious antagonism of the Conservative Party and of Norwegian business interests by such measures as a 30 per cent income tax, 10 per cent sales and corporation taxes, and a 25 per cent tax on all interests on bank deposits.

Norway had joined the League of Nations in 1920; nevertheless the Scandinavian policy had always been as much isolationist as against large-scale military preparation. The Scandinavian conference of July 1938 had proclaimed sanctions non-obligatory; the neutrality of the Oslo nations continued to be rigidly guarded after war broke out and, in spite of pressure from the Allies, during the war in Finland.

Not long after the Finnish peace, Great Britain, with the announced intention of saving the Scandinavian countries from the results of their isolationist policies, mined Norwegian waters. On April 8, 1940, between midnight and noon of the next day, the Norwegian capital, principal seaports and principal coastal defenses were seized by the Germans in a naval coup which startled the world and which, it is claimed, had been planned weeks in advance. Fully equipped Nazi troops leaped from German transport planes; innocent merchant vessels turned out to be Nazi convoys; Nazi ships landed other troops in the Fjord, meeting with almost no immediate resistance because, reported the journalist Leland Stowe (see sketch this issue) some days later, Norwegian war ships had been ordered by Nazi-sympathizing commanders not to resist, and mines had been electrically disconnected. Three thousand singing, parading Nazis held Oslo for 48 hours, its 300,000 population stunned, until German transports carrying more than 20,000 troops arrived on April 11. Communications and radio stations were seized, censorship established. Quisling (see sketch this issue), Nazi sympathizer, former Minister in the King's council, was temporarily proclaimed Premier.

In the meanwhile King Haakon, Crown Prince Olaf, and most of the Storting and Council had fled to Hamar, where the Storting voted to refuse to capitulate and ordered mobilization. Pursued there by the Germans, they fled to Elverum, where farmers and local guards beat off the Nazis, fighting behind barricades of overturned cars. A *White Book* released by the fugitive government reveals that German attempts to negotiate with Haakon for the formation of a friendly government were at one time on the verge of success, but when Hitler redoubled his demands he was met with a proclamation of war, further orders for mobilization and the formal declaration of alliance with Britain and France. Next Ger-

man planes leveled Elverum to the ground, but Haakon and his government were already in Nybergsund. There planes bombed their hotel; the party, escaping in automobiles, was bombed four times as it took shelter in the woods. Harried from village to village, but refusing to recognize the Nazi-controlled interim government headed by Christiansen, the attitude of Haakon's government stiffened the resistance of the Norwegians. Nine days after the invasion British troops landed to help them, but they were defeated.

Since then the tired 68-year-old monarch who said, not without reason: ". . . I can no longer be sure of anything," has rejected a plea to abdicate, presented him by members of the German dominated Parliament in July 1940. He told the Presidential Board of the Storting that he would conform to the wishes of the Norwegian people if they really wanted him to abdicate, but insisted he would never bow to the wishes of the German Army of Occupation. Two months later the Norwegian Parliament declared that Haakon VII was no longer able to function and named a regent in his place. However, it decided to postpone until after the War the final question of whether he will be allowed to return to his country.

References

Christian Sci Mon Mag p18 F 24 '37
Life 8:26 My 13 '40
Lit Digest 122:14 O 31 '36
N Y Herald Tribune p10 S 12 '40
N Y Times p1-2 Ap 15 '40; p5 Ap 25 '40; p1, 10 Jl 9 '40
Newsweek 8:12 O 24 '36 por; 15:17-21 Ap 22 '40 por
Sat Eve Post 204:6 Ap 23 '32 por
Scholastic 35:8 O 30 '39 por
Time 35:23-4 Ap 22 '40; 35:19 Ap 29 '40
Travel 72:6-12 Mr '39
Arneson, B. A. The Democratic Monarchies of Scandinavia 1939
International Who's Who
Olson, A. L. Scandinavia—the Background for Neutrality 1940
Rothery, A. Norway, Changing and Changeless 1939

HADDON, ALFRED CORT May 24, 1855 —Apr 20, 1940 English anthropologist; ethnologist; Fellow of Christ College, Cambridge; lectured extensively in the United States

References

International Who's Who
Who's Who
Who's Who in Commerce and Industry

Obituaries

N Y Herald Tribune p12 Ap 22 '40
N Y Times p17 Ap 22 '40 por

HADFIELD, SIR ROBERT ABBOTT
Nov 29, 1858—Sept 30, 1940 World-famous
English metallurgist; inventor of manganese
and silicon steel and many other alloy steels;
knighted in 1908 and created a baronet in
1917; received many honors in the United
States and Europe including the Carnegie
Bessemer Gold Medal of the Iron and Steel
Institute; was considered the world's greatest authority on the production of steel;
was engaged in war armament for the British Navy at the time of his death

References
    Author's & Writer's Who's Who
    Bridges, T. C. and Tiltman, H. H. Sir
        Robert A. Hadfield and His Story
        In Kings of Commerce p90-8 1928
    Who's Who
    Who's Who in Commerce and In-
        dustry
Obituaries
    N Y Times p23 O 2 '40

HAGGARD, WILLIAM DAVID Sept 28,
1872—Jan 28, 1940 Surgeon; president of
the American Medical Association in 1925;
president of the American College of Surgeons in 1933; professor of gynecology and
clinical surgery in Nashville, Tennessee

References
    American Medical Directory
    Who's Who in America 1938-39
Obituaries
    N Y Herald Tribune p8 Ja 29 '40 por
    Sch & Soc 51:145 F 3 '40
    Time 35:48 F 5 '40

HAINISCH, MICHAEL (hī'nĭsh) Aug
15, 1858—Feb 29, 1940 German economist
and author; first President of the Republic
of Austria 1920 to 1928

MICHAEL HAINISCH

References
    International Who's Who
    Wer ist wer
    Who's Who in Central and East-
        Europe
Obituaries
    N Y Herald Tribune p16 Mr 1 '40
        por
    N Y World-Telegram p30 F 29 '40

HALDANE, JOHN BURDON SANDER-
SON (hôl'dān) Nov 5, 1892- Biologist;
author
Address: University College, Gower Street,
W. C. 1, London, England

Professor of biometry at London University since 1937, "bald, burly, tweedy, shaggy"
J. B. S. Haldane is one of the best-known
living popularizers of science. His most
recent book is *Science and Everyday Life*
(1940), a collection of 70 brief articles in
which he has tried to give not only a few
facts not yet found in textbooks and "which
a student leaving a university with an honors
degree would not be expected to know,"
but also "to bring these facts into relation
with everyday life." Without the use of
a technical vocabulary or the assumption
of any previous technical knowledge on his
reader's part, he talks about marriage and
earthquakes, weather and superstition, the
laws of probability and "the economics of
cancer." Non-Marxist reviewers find his
analogies between science and society the
least valuable part of the book, but agree
that the eminent biologist has once more
"accomplished his purpose of writing an
understandable book of real scientific
worth."

John Burdon Sanderson Haldane was
born on November 5, 1892, the son of J. S.
Haldane, an experimentally-minded scientist.
He was also the nephew of the Viscount
Haldane who became Lord Chancellor.
Since his parents both came from Scotland
he was brought up to think of himself as
a Scot, and it was in an "atmosphere of
intellectual curiosity and freedom" that he
grew up. After attending an Oxford Preparatory School and Eton he took his M. A.
at New College, Oxford just in time
to go off to the First World War. He was
with the Black Watch in France and in Mesopotamia, was wounded twice, became a captain
in 1915. It seems unlikely that the War
left any serious scars on him, for he once
commented (perhaps frivolously) that at the
time he quite enjoyed shooting Germans.

From 1919 to 1922 Haldane was a Fellow
of New College, and then became a reader
in biochemistry at Cambridge University.
After he was involved as correspondent in a
London divorce action in 1925 Cambridge
put him before a disciplinary body. A year
later he married Charlotte Franken, a writer.
From 1930 to 1932 he was also Fullerian
professor of physiology at the Royal Institution, but it was not until 1933 that he

J. B. S. HALDANE

left Cambridge to become professor of genetics at London University. Since 1937 he has held a life tenure of that University's chair of biometry.

Besides publishing numerous scientific papers on such subjects as human chemical physiology, genetics and natural selection, Haldane began early in the '20s to make a reputation for himself as a popularizer of science. He was never in any sense a "pure" scientist, however: speculation on the philosophic implications and practical possibilities of modern knowledge made every book an adventure to him as much as to his readers. Some of them were *Possible Worlds* (1928); *Animal Biology,* with J. S. Huxley (1927); *Science and Ethics* (1928); *Facts and Faith* (1934); *Heredity and Politics* (1938).

With no desire to shut himself up in the laboratory or classroom away from the problems of the ordinary citizen, Haldane became increasingly concerned with just those problems. In 1935 he was urging that England make herself less vulnerable to attack by storing away a great quantity of food, providing her people with gas masks and building underground shelters that would be both bomb- and gas-proof. In 1936 he spent six weeks in Madrid during the Christmas siege of the city by Franco's forces. Already known as an authority on poison gas, in 1938 he published a little book called *Air Raid Precautions* which sold for 6d and didn't reassure anybody very much about the horrors of modern warfare. "I hate having to write this book," he began, without mincing words. "Air raids are not only wrong, they are loathsome and disgusting. If you had ever seen a child smashed by a bomb into something like a mixture of dirty rags and cat's meat you would realize this fact as intensely as I do." He wanted England

to adopt a two-year program of digging 1,100 miles of brick-lined tunnels at a depth of 60 feet to house the entire metropolitan population—the work to be done by 100,000 unemployed miners.

Since 1914, Haldane once expressed it, he had been living in an "heroic age." His knowledge of Fascism made him doubtful of "surviving into another epoch of peace and quiet," and for a long time he had been convinced that "our civilization will either break up or go forward to a 'new form." But although he had frequently quoted Marx, Lenin and, particularly, Engels in his writings, it was not until 1938 that he became an avowed Marxist. *The Marxist Philosophy and the Sciences* (1938) deals with mathematical, physical, biological and sociological problems from the Marxist viewpoint, and so do many of his 27 essays, lectures and broadcasts collected into *Adventures of a Biologist* (1940). Of the last book, however, Clifton Fadiman says that it is mainly "straight popularization of a high order, succinct, dryly humorous, clear."

Science and politics were not the only subjects of Haldane's literary ventures. He also wrote a book of nonsense stories for children called *My Friend, Mr. Leakey* (1938). Mr. Leakey is a magician, so that the book is full of delightful but quite unscientific miracles, but there are any number of facts tucked in with the fantasy.

Since the outbreak of World War II Haldane has continued both to work for better defenses for England and to contribute articles to the London *Daily Worker.* Although University College in London was evacuated in September 1939, he refused to go and has since then "made some discoveries." He has also "been doing work of a somewhat dangerous character designed to save the lives of certain members of the British forces."

Since 1928 Haldane has been a corresponding member of the Société de Biologie; from 1932 to 1936 he was president of the Genetical Society; and in 1937 he was made Chevalier of the Légion d'Honneur for his scientific services to France. He has a reputation for "epigrammatic discourse" which makes him a delight to reporters. Typical remarks: "I have never yet met a healthy person who worried very much about his health, or a really good person who worried about his own soul"; "Luxury is the mother of all human kindness."

In an essay titled, *What I Require from Life,* Haldane gives a fairly good idea of his philosophy. His requirements are work that is hard but interesting; a decent wage for it; more freedom, particularly more freedom of speech; health; friendship, in a society of equals; adventure (as distinguished from "thrills"). He would also like to see every other man and woman at work, controlling their conditions of work, healthy, with "class and sex subjection" at an end. To him this means socialism.

He also makes certain requirements of death. Socrates' death, he believes, couldn't have been better. He died for his convictions, having completed all the work he could reasonably have hoped to do, and his last words were joking words. If Haldane can fulfill even two of these conditions he doesn't think he would deserve anybody's pity.

References
Lit Digest 114:20 O 1 '32 por
Newsweek 15:24 Ja 22 '40 por
Sci N L 38:139 Ag 31 '40
Time 32:18 O 3 '38 por; 33:46-7 Mr 13 '39 por
Wilson Lib Bul 3:619 My '29 por
Belgion, M. Men Like Ants *In* Essays of the Year, 1933-34 p366-78 1934
Bridges, T. C. and Tiltman, H. H. Experimenter Who Is His Own Rabbit *In* Master Minds of Modern Science p104-16 1931
Who's Who

HALE, ARTHUR, REV. 1861—Feb 29, 1940 Clergyman; philanthropist; chairman of the United States Coal Exporters Association; chaplain of the United States Senate for many years; last of the four children of Dr. Edward Everett Hale, author of *The Man Without a Country*

Obituaries
N Y Herald Tribune p8 Mr 2 '40; p36 Mr 3 '40
N Y Times p12 Mr 2 '40

HALIFAX, EDWARD FREDERICK LINDLEY WOOD, 3RD VISCOUNT Apr 16, 1881- Former British Foreign Secretary; Ambassador to the United States

Address: 88 Eaton Sq, London, S. W. 1, England

December 1940 Bulletin: On December 23, 1940 the appointment of Lord Halifax as British Ambassador to the United States was announced. Anthony Eden succeeds him as Foreign Secretary.

From September issue:

The change of name caused by the grant of or succession to a British peerage causes a great deal of confusion, for it is difficult to realize that three names can belong to one person. In the case of Lord Halifax it might almost be said that each of his names is associated with a different phase of personality. Plain Mr. Edward Wood was an ordinary gentleman until he was nearly 30, and thereafter a not-very-striking member of Parliament and Minister; Lord Irwin was a reformist Viceroy of India who prepared the way for the Round Table Conference; Lord Halifax, succeeding to his viscounty at 53, became a Foreign Secretary who was considered by some the most influential behind-the-scenes member of Chamberlain's National Government, at one time pointed out as probable successor to the Premiership. In all three

Times—Wide World

VISCOUNT HALIFAX

phases he has left his mark, for good or ill, on the policy and destiny of his country. And this same Edward Wood once said he would rather be master of foxhounds than Prime Minister.

Gentleman, sportsman, scholar and devout churchman, Lord Halifax has sometimes been called the "saintliest" character in British public life. He is "a tall, big-boned man with a high forehead, clear, slightly myopic eyes, a firm chin, a sensitive mouth"—unassuming, friendly, quiet-spoken, with a natural dignity and a charm that caused one gentleman to complain: "You know, one trouble with the fellow is that everyone who comes at all into close contact with Halifax becomes enamored of him." Unquestionably he represents the highest type of British aristocrat and since March 1939 he has more than earned the enmity of the Nazis. Yet in the summer of 1940 H. G. Wells was pressing for the removal of Halifax from Churchill's (see sketch this issue) Cabinet along with other men connected with the policy of appeasement, while the *New Statesman and Nation* stated the earnest hope that such an action would facilitate "democratic counterrevolu-ion" against Hitlerism throughout the continent. In October 1940 when Churchill reorganized his Cabinet his retention of Halifax was even more severely criticized by the Liberal and Labor Press. The *News Chronicle* stated that he was "inextricably involved in the policy of appeasement, signs of which still linger too ominously. . . Until he has gone, distrust of British intentions abroad cannot finally be removed." And again H. G. Wells, now visiting the United States, was quoted as saying: "The man I want to see go is Halifax, the quintessence of what all English-speaking men should be afraid of. I have a feeling, being

HALIFAX, VISCOUNT—Continued

a British citizen, that I have never been so misrepresented as by my present Foreign Minister." Lord Halifax's integrity has seldom been impugned; yet earlier in his career Harold Laski predicted: "We shall pay in the end a heavy price for his high character and the moral beauty of his inner life."

In the meantime Lord Halifax was finding refuge from air raids in London's famous Hotel Dorchester, where he and Lady Halifax had rented eight rooms which included a chapel for the Foreign Minister.

Wood grew up on a spacious estate at Garrowby, Yorkshire, where he was riding almost before he could walk, in spite of the disability of a withered left arm. His father, the second viscount of Halifax (who married Lady Agnes Elizabeth Courtenay), lived to the hale old age of 92, leading an active life to the last. He was not only a pious high churchman like his son, working all his life for the reunion of the Anglican and Roman communions, but an enthusiastic collector of ghost-lore. Edward went from Eton to Oxford, where he was an undergraduate of Christ Church, took a first class in history, proceeding M. A., and was elected a Fellow of All Souls. A biography of the churchman, John Keble, was published during his student days.

Right through his 20's he led the life of a country gentleman and showed no special interest in politics; but in January 1910—when even country gentlemen were feeling seriously upset by the Liberals' far-reaching measures of social legislation—he was persuaded to put up for Parliament, and was elected for the Yorkshire constituency of Ripon in the Conservative interest. The year before he had married Lady Dorothy Evelyn Augusta Onslow, daughter of the fourth Earl of Onslow. (They now have one daughter and three sons, his heir being the Hon. Charles Ingram Courtenay Wood).

Wood made no special mark as a backbencher in the House of Commons, but he got on friendly terms with two other more or less obscure politicians, Stanley Baldwin and George (later Lord) Lloyd. The latter was a fellow Etonian, and from his talks with Wood about the destiny of the Conservative Party there emerged a book called *The Great Opportunity*, which they wrote in collaboration. With the coming of the First World War, Wood went to France with the Yorkshire Dragoons, was twice mentioned in dispatches, ended as colonel of his regiment. At the "khaki election" of 1918 he retained his seat, and at the War's end was one of 200 Conservative M. P.'s who signed a demand for harsher terms with Germany, though he fought Lloyd George's ruthless Irish policy. In 1921 he was made Parliamentary Under-Secretary for the Colonies, serving until 1922. Then, when the Conservative Party repudiated the Lloyd George Coalition and Stanley Baldwin rose from nonentity to the Premiership, his friend Wood was remembered and from October 1922 to January 1924 served in his Cabinet as president of the Board of Education; in October 1924, after a brief Labor interlude, he became Minister of Agriculture and served until November 1925.

In 1925 Wood was raised to the peerage in his own right as Baron Irwin of Kirby Underdale before becoming Viceroy of India. (His grandfather, incidentally, had been Secretary of State for India). It was Good Friday in the year 1926 when Lord Irwin arrived in the country in which he was to act as the King's representative for five years, and he immediately impressed the religious-minded natives by refusing to disembark on a holy day. During his term as Governor he showed himself willing to work on a long-term basis for some measure of self-government, brought matters so far forward that the Round Table Conference could be held and succeeded in winning and holding Gandhi's respect and admiration in spite of the fact that at one time during his rule as many as 37,000 Indian Nationalists languished in British prisons. Gandhi called him "a man I can trust to tell me what he thinks", "the Christian Viceroy", "one of the noblest of Englishmen"; Indians referred to him as "that thin tall Christian"· British Conservatives found him somewhat over-anxious to compromise with the Nationalists; and British Left-wingers went so far as to admit "he made British imperialism look less stark and ugly than it was under Lord Reading or Lord Willingdon."

Back from India in 1931, the next year Lord Irwin at long last became Joint Master of the Middleton Hunt, an office which he was forced to give up six years later. The same year he published *Indian Problems;* from 1932 to 1935 he served again as president of the Board of Education; in 1933 he became chancellor of the University of Oxford; and in 1934 he succeeded his father as Lord Halifax. He was Secretary for War in 1935, Lord Privy Seal from 1935 to 1937, Leader of the House of Lords from 1935 to 1938, Lord President of the Council from May 1937 to 1938. His duties as master of foxhounds being almost more demanding than those of his public offices, outwardly it looked as if he was "on the shelf" politically. Those in the know recognized his influence, however. While Anthony Eden (see sketch this issue) was Foreign Secretary, Halifax was accustomed to pinch-hit for him in his diplomatic absences, was given the tag "pro-German" by some circles, and in November 1937 gained Eden's enmity when sent on a visit of "exploration" to Germany. He talked to Nazi chieftains, was impressed with the Nazi International Hunting Exhibition, and, according to Duff Cooper (see sketch this issue), came back with a report which said in essence "that they were very queer fellows, but that he could see no harm in them and he was glad to say that Hitler had promised him never to interfere with Austria or Czechoslovakia." In March 1938 he succeeded Eden as Foreign Secretary, as a man actually representing Chamberlain's point of view and yet possessing the sympathy and respect of both friends and foes of appeasement. (Even Churchill calls him "a gentleman, a fox hunter, a friend.")

It is reported that when Halifax received word of the Nazi conquest of Austria on March 12, 1938 he buried his face in his hands and murmured "Horrible, horrible!"—although on March 10 he had "prolonged discussions" with Ribbentrop. Munich to him was "at best the lesser of two frightful evils." Nevertheless until Hitler's seizure of Czechoslovakia on March 1939 he continued to hope that it was possible to remain on good terms with the dictators. Without questioning his sincerity, those who found his views unrealistic called him an "instrument of the country-house aristocracy" which felt that war must be avoided at all costs, described him as "a mystic who could hardly explain his intellectual processes even to himself. He dislikes the clear-cut principle and the downright mind." But five days after the German troops entered Prague he made a speech in the House of Lords finally admitting the necessity for collective security, followed by guarantees of Poland, Romania, Greece and Turkey and the introduction of conscription.

During the earlier stages of World War II it was one of Halifax's rôles to defend the way in which the War was conducted by the Chamberlain National Government, to condemn "amateur strategists," to preach against the danger of "large-scale adventures." Under Churchill's leadership he has become an eloquently religious spokesman for British determination to continue the struggle. When on July 22, 1940 he answered Hitler's bid for "peace," the keynote of his uncompromising reply was: "This is a crusade of Christianity." His closing of the Burma Road (later reopened) brought criticism on his head once more, however.

The tall, reedy, saintly country gentleman with a sense of public duty now finds himself in the anomalous position of one who is scornfully dubbed "Chaplain of the British Empire" and "Britannia's funeral orator" by his country's enemies, yet asked by many of the Britons to withdraw to a position where he "can do no further harm." It could not have happened to a simple master of foxhounds.

References

Am Mercury 49:161-3 F '40
Atlan 164:610-20 N '39; 165:737-43 Je '40
Contemp 157:312-19 Mr '40
Liv Age 354:139-41 Ap '38
N Y Herald Tribune p2 Jl 23 '40; p3 O 5 '40
N Y Times p6 Ap 11 '40; p5 My 9 '40; p1, 3 Jl 24 '40
19th Cent 119:592-603 My '36
Strand Mag 90:148-55 Je '38
Time 30:18-19 N 29 '37 por; 35:21-2 Ja 15 '40 il por (cover); 36:21 Ag 12 '40

Audax, pseud.   Lord Halifax   *In* Men in Our Time p83-100 1940
Gunther, J.   Inside Europe 1940
International Who's Who
Who's Who

HALL, JAMES   Oct 22, 1900—June 7, 1940
Ex-film actor; once starred with Bebe Daniels; appeared on Broadway in plays; appeared in the film, *Hell's Angels,* with Jean Harlow

JAMES HALL

References

International Motion Picture Almanac 1936-37

Obituaries

N Y Herald Tribune p12 Je 8 '40 por
N Y Times p15 Je 8 '40

HAMBRO, CARL JOACHIM   (hăm' brō) Jan 5, 1885- Former president of the Storting (Norwegian Parliament)
Address: c/o Appleton-Century Co, Inc, 35 W 32nd St, New York City

Carl Hambro, president of the Norwegian Parliament for 14 years and chairman of the Norwegian Foreign Affairs Committee, is spending the winter of 1940 and 1941 lecturing and writing in the United States. *I Saw It Happen in Norway,* his story of the invasion of Norway, was published in September 1940, "the first authoritative historical account of the Norwegian phase of the War" and is an "excellent book for those who do not want to see 'it' happen here."

On March 15, 1940 Carl Hambro arrived in Stockholm "on a trip for information." It was generally accepted that he was there to discuss the idea of a defensive military alli-

Harris & Ewing

CARL J. HAMBRO

ance of Sweden, Finland and Norway. He remained in Stockholm, but his mission had changed. He was there "to complete a speaking engagement," and because the government considered his trip opportune. Overnight what he sought to prevent had happened, and his country had become the unwilling Northern front for the Second World War.

On April 28, 1940 Carl Hambro announced, in reply to the charge of the Reich Foreign Minister in Berlin, that Norway "aided and abetted" plans for an Allied Scandinavian front so that Germany could be destroyed: "We now have irrefutable proof that Germany prepared detailed plans for the invasion of Norway months before it actually occurred. We would have been in a better position today if the British really had troops ready to land and even more so if the Allied intelligence service, which knew of the German preparations, had warned us previously."

Hambro stated that it was also undeniable that the Germans had a detailed plan for the occupation of Denmark, where they have established a Nazi régime, and for an invasion of Sweden, to come later.

This 55-year-old statesman, once described as "short, rotund and merry-eyed," has been known as a spokesman of peace rather than of war during the greater part of his career. He was born in Bergen, Norway on January 5, 1885, and studied at Oslo University. After having worked on the large Oslo morning newspaper, the *Morgenbladet,* while still a student, he took his final examination in 1907 and that same year found a position as teacher in the Oslo Commercial High School. In 1910 he married; in 1913 he became chief editor of the *Morgenbladet,* a position which he held until

1921; and in 1919 he was elected a representative to the Storting from the Conservative Party.

In 1920 Norway joined the League of Nations, and Hambro became known as one of the most active supporters of disarmament. He was fond of saying that peace can be just as interesting and just as "dangerous" as war. In 1926, the year he was elected President of the Storting, he was also appointed Norwegian delegate to the League, and became active on many committees of the League of Nations as well as being associated with many non-political organizations such as the New Theatre in Oslo, the Norwegian Students Association, the Norwegian-American League. He was honored with the Grand Cross of the Royal Order of St. Olaf, the highest Norwegian decoration. In December 1939 he was elected president of the League Assembly at Geneva, called especially to consider Finland's pleas for help against Soviet agression.

Hambro is something of a literary figure in his own country—the author of many studies on immigration, on the League, on political and economic questions; the Norwegian translator of such authors as Kipling, Victor Hugo, Dickens, Sinclair Lewis; and, until recent events, one of the literary critics of the *Morgenbladet,* the newspaper which he edited for such a long time.

As a speaker he is familiar to lecture audiences in the United States where he has filled many speaking engagements. In 1935 it was the Oxford Movement rather than the Germans which had swept through Norway and Denmark like wildfire; as a convert to Buchmanism, Hambro "testified" in the Metropolitan Opera House in New York City that the Oxford Group had "changed his life," and told the bankers, lawyers and business men of the Bankers' Club that Europe never would settle its problems until the statesmen themselves ceased their hypocrisy and met on an equal basis of honesty and unselfishness in accordance with the fundamentals of Christian ethics.

He has been denounced by the Germans as a Jew and a relative of the London founders of Hambro's Bank.

Johan Hambro, 24, studying journalism and history as a guest student at Columbia University in New York City, is one of his four sons. His comment on the invasion of Norway was:

". . . We have believed too much in disarmament."

References

Lit Digest 120:16 N 30 '35 por
N Y Herald Tribune p3 Mr 16 '40; p15 Ap 10 '40
N Y Times p2 Ap 12 '40
International Who's Who
Norwegian Who's Who

HAMILTON, GEORGE LIVINGSTON
July 24, 1874—Sept 25, 1940 Professor of
romance languages at Cornell University
since 1911; specialist in folklore; had taught
previously at the University of Michigan,
Trinity College and the University of Cincinnati; author of a commentary on Chaucer's *Troilus and Criseyde* and many monographs on romance languages

GEORGE L. HAMILTON

References
  Who's Who in America

Obituaries
  N Y Herald Tribune p18 S 26 '40
  N Y Times p23 S 26 '40

HAMLIN, CLARENCE CLARK Jan 7,
1868—Oct 29, 1940 Publisher of the Colorado Springs *Gazette* and *Telegraph*; one
of the West's best known attorneys, who
represented many large interests in his corporation practice; Republican national committeeman for Colorado for many years

References
  Who's Who in America
  Who's Who in Law

Obituaries
  N Y Times p23 O 31 '40 por

HAMMOND, AUBREY LINDSAY Sept
18, 1893—Mar 19, 1940 British artist; stage
designer; pioneer in the development of the
modern technique of camouflage

References
  Who's Who

Obituaries
  N Y Herald Tribune p28 Mr 20 '40
  N Y Times p27 Mr 20 '40

HANSON, OLE Jan 6, 1874—July 6, 1940
Ex-Mayor of Seattle; lawyer; head of real
estate developments in California; earned
national fame in 1919 as the "Fighting
Mayor" when he broke Seattle's general
strike which involved 65,000 workers by the
use of United States Army troops

References
  Who's Who in America

Obituaries
  N Y Times p17 Jl 8 '40 por
  Newsweek 16:6 Jl 15 '40

HARADA, TASUKU, REV. Nov 10, 1863
—Feb 22, 1940 Professor emeritus of Doshia-
sha University, Kyoto, and of University of
Hawaii, Honolulu; clergyman; lecturer and
author of books on the Christian movement
in Japan

References
  Who's Who

Obituaries
  N Y Times p15 F 23 '40

HARDEN, ARTHUR 1865—June 17, 1940
Biochemist most widely known for his re-
search in fermentation; winner of Nobel
Prize in 1929; joint editor of the *Biochemical
Journal;* emeritus professor of biochemistry
at London University; knighted in 1936

References
  International Who's Who
  Who's Who

Obituaries
  N Y Herald Tribune p18 Je 18 '40 por
  N Y Times p23 Je 18 '40

HARDY, ASHLEY KINGSLEY Apr 6,
1871—July 29, 1940 Educator; senior member of faculty of Dartmouth; taught Old

ASHLEY K. HARDY

HARDY, ASHLEY KINGSLEY—*Cont.*
English and German; member of faculty for 43 years; trustee of the Dartmouth Savings Bank; president of the Howe Library

References
Who's Who in America

Obituaries
N Y Herald Tribune p16 Jl 30 '40

HARINGTON, SIR CHARLES May 31, 1872—Oct 22, 1940 British general; chief of staff of the Second Army in the World War, where his tactics won the memorable attack on Messines in 1918; commander in chief of the British Army in the Black Sea region in 1920 and commander in chief of the Allied Forces in Constantinople from 1921 to 1923; later in India; was Governor of Gibraltar from 1933 to 1938, when he retired

References
International Who's Who
Who's Who

Obituaries
N Y Times p25 O 24 '40 por

HARKNESS, EDWARD STEPHEN Jan 22, 1874—Jan 29, 1940 Financier; philanthropist

Edward Stephen Harkness died at his home in New York City at the age of 66. He had been ill two weeks with intestinal grippe and complications. Few persons in the whole United States have given as much as he has to medical, educational and civic institutions. Although he gave away millions, he was known as "a self-effacing man who shunned the public" and had never made a public speech or granted a newspaper interview. He was born in Cleveland, Ohio, the son of Stephen V. and Anna M. (Richardson) Harkness. He received a B. A. from Yale in 1897 and an M. A. in 1925. The University at St. Andrews, Scotland conferred an LL. D. in 1926, as did Columbia University in 1928. He married Mary Stillman of Brooklyn, New York on November 15, 1904.

Harkness inherited his father's and mother's estates, (Standard Oil Company), valued at more than $60,000,000, and his brother, Charles W. Harkness, a director of the Standard Oil Company, left him $36,000,000.

No complete list of his benefactions has ever been known, but estimates are that he gave away more than $100,000,000 to institutions in this country and abroad for hospitals, medical research and education. Among them are Harvard, where he established house systems of education following those of Oxford University; Yale University; Columbia University, which received medical funds and a library; Phillips Exeter Academy and other preparatory schools. He aided, in addition, various English and Irish

Press Portrait Bureau
EDWARD S. HARKNESS

institutions. He was director of the New York Central Lines and the Southern Pacific Railroad Company.

References
Time 27:48-9 Je 22 '36 por
Who's Who in America 1938-39

Obituaries
N Y Herald Tribune p1+ Ja 30 '40 por; p14 Ja 31 '40
Time 35:48 F 5 '40

HARLAN, OTIS 1865—Jan 20, 1940 Retired stage and motion picture actor; made his debut in *The Hole in the Ground* in 1887;

OTIS HARLAN

appeared with such stars as Weber and Fields, Elsie Janis and Anna Held; started in movies in 1920 and appeared in *Show Boat, Diamond Jim*; was the voice of Happy in Walt Disney's *Snow White*

References

Who's Who in America 1934-35

Obituaries

N Y Times p35 Ja 21 '40
Newsweek 15:2 Ja 29 '40 por
Variety 137:47 Ja 24 '40

HARPER, ALEXANDER JAMES 1877—Sept 23, 1940 Architect; practiced his profession for 34 years; worked on the design of the General Post Office in New York City, the Cleveland railroad terminal, the Gimbel Brothers building in Philadelphia, the Aetna Life Insurance Company building in Hartford, Connecticut and the library at Columbia University, New York City

Obituaries

N Y Herald Tribune p18 S 24 '40

HARRIMAN, FLORENCE JAFFRAY HURST July 21, 1870- United States Minister to Norway
Address: h. "Uplands," Foxhall Rd, Washington, D. C.

"Daisy" Harriman first distinguished herself diplomatically in the First World War because she was said to have out-talked the German Minister to Norway at a "ratio of about 700 to 1." It was in connection with the United States freighter, *City of Flint,* which had been seized by a German prize crew, searching for contraband material, in the opening days of the Second World War during October 1939. Contrary to international law, the German crew had sought to anchor in Norway's neutral waters. When the vessel arrived at Bergen, Norway, in November, the German naval convoy claimed that an emergency had made the call at a neutral port necessary. Without delay, dynamic Mrs. Harriman made straight for the port. The German Minister to Norway came racing after her, claiming jurisdiction over the vessel. The two Ministers fought it out, with the victory on Mrs. Harriman's side. *The City of Flint* sailed for the United States; an impasse over neutral ships was averted; and Nazi spokesmen hinted ominously of an "acute situation between Oslo and Berlin."

This diplomatic job was a long way from "Daisy" Harriman's girlhood and her social triumphs in Washington. For Madame Minister Harriman had started adult life as a debutante who had nothing more serious than teas and dances to think of. She was born in New York City of well-to-do parents, Francis William Jones and Caroline Elise (Jaffray) Hurst, attended a fashionable finishing school, spent her summers in Newport and at 19 married J. Borden Harriman, a New York banker. As a young matron, she lived in Westchester County, traveled, spent a winter in Egypt and devoted herself to social affairs. She helped organize New York's exclusive Colony Club in 1904 and remained its president from its organization until 1916.

Her abilities as an organizer were put to a wider social purpose in 1906 when she was appointed manager of the New York State Reformatory for Women at Bedford, a post she held for 12 years.

Her first taste of politics came in 1912 when she took an active part in the Wilson campaign. She worked hard, and President Wilson rewarded her by appointing her to the Federal Industrial Relations Commission. The only woman on the Commission, she served on it from 1913 to 1916.

J. Borden Harriman died in 1914, and Mrs. Harriman moved to Washington and settled down to a career there. During the War she became chairman of the Committee on Women in Industry of the Council of National Defense and helped organize the Red Cross Women's Motor Corps, going to France in 1918 to take charge of 500 drivers. She also helped found the Women's National Democratic Club, whose leading spirit she has been for many years.

But Washington knew her chiefly as one of its foremost and most envied hostesses. Her Sunday night salons were sometimes referred to as "Mrs. Harriman's teacup chancellery." In her home, the "Uplands," on the outskirts of Washington, on a Sunday evening one could find judges, Senators, political bigwigs. She did not draw party lines and delighted in throwing conservatives and liberals together. Her Sunday night salons found radical newspaper columnists such as the late Heywood Broun side by side with conservatives such as Justice Roberts, George Creel and David Lawrence. Her book, *From Pinafores to Politics* (1923), is a sparkling account of the events for which she was fortunate enough to have a "box seat in the America of her time."

The depression swept most of the Harriman fortune away, but Mrs. Harriman still entertained lavishly. She eked out her income by renting her luxurious home at times to well-to-do paying guests, once to Otto Kahn during the Pecora investigations, another time to James A. Moffett, while he was Federal Housing Administrator. She even tried her hand at interior decoration for her friends.

The 12 long years of Republican régime dimmed "Daisy" Harriman's political star. An opportunity for a political comeback came in 1932, when as Democratic National Committeewoman for the District of Columbia she was one of the District's delegates to the Democratic National Convention in Chicago, but she made the mistake of supporting Newton D. Baker instead of Roosevelt. However, she was soon back in the Roosevelt graces. It was said that

HARRIMAN, FLORENCE—*Continued*

the battle was waged in the "Uplands" where members of New Deal aristocracy were favored guests. At any rate Mrs. Harriman was the official hostess at the Democratic National Convention in Philadelphia in 1936 and one of Roosevelt's most ardent supporters. (She supported him strongly again in 1940.)

President Roosevelt rewarded her with the post of Envoy Extraordinary and Minister Plenipotentiary of the United States to Norway. Norway took five weeks to confirm the appointment, although it usually takes about 24 hours for an appointment to be confirmed. It may have been that Norway was uneasy about a woman minister. But in June 1937 she became the second woman to be appointed by the United States as a minister to a foreign country.

The Norwegians and Mrs. Harriman liked each other. Mrs. Harriman's physical prowess was interesting to them. Although she is almost 70, Madame Minister's posture is as fine, her back as straight, as any young cadet's. Perhaps it is the result of her early Spartan training. Her father, a Union officer in the Civil War, had an army sergeant drill his three young daughters, three times a week. Mrs. Harriman learned to swim in the Hudson River when she was four and in the summer she used to swim every afternoon in one of Norway's picturesque fiords; in the winter she skied, a sport she quickly picked up from the Norwegians. "I found it easy," she told friends in the United States. "It's mostly a matter of balance, and I had that from riding horseback all my life."

"Daisy" Harriman is an imposing figure. Tall, her gray hair neatly bobbed, her eyes a deep blue, she is partial to blue for daytime wear, and severe black gowns for evening. She has a straightforward, almost brusque charm that made her as popular in Norway as she was in Washington.

When Mrs. Harriman went to Norway, her main concern was to see the signing of a reciprocal trade treaty between the United States and Norway. But the Norwegians, who pride themselves on their self-sufficiency, were not in a bargaining mood. Mrs. Harriman, nevertheless, found her time well filled. She spent mornings answering mail, making reports. Her luncheon hours were almost always taken up with visiting American tourists. Genuinely interested in social reform, she tried to sell Americans on Norway and its cooperative and social advancement. In the evenings she had to attend innumerable state functions and there hobnob with *le grande monde* of Norway.

With the coming of the War to Norway all that was changed. Mrs. Harriman found herself in the thick of the fray, the first to inform the United States State Department of the outbreak of hostilities. She remained as close to King Haakon (see sketch this issue) and his court as she could until air raid after air raid made her decide to make

for Sweden, where she could get better communication facilities.

In May 1940 she was actively working to get American women in Norway out of that country into Sweden and appeared in vigorous health, despite her 70 years. It was not until September that she returned to the United States.

Her experiences as United States Minister to Norway, culminating in the German invasion are told by Mrs. Harriman in a book to be published by Lippincott in the spring of 1941. It will be called *Mission to the North*.

References

Christian Sci Mon Mag p3 Jl 6 '38 por
Ind Woman 16:130-1 My '37 por; 19: 128b My '40 por
Life 8:32 My 13 '40; 30:31+ S 9 '40 pors
Liv Age 357:444-8 Ja '40 por
N Y Herald Tribune p23 Ap 10 '40 por; p1 Ap 13 '40 por
N Y Sun p14 Ap 9 '40
Sat Eve Post 212:24+ Je 22 '40 il pors
Time 29:21 Ap 12 '37 por
American Women
Harriman, F. J. From Pinafores to Politics 1923
Who's Who in America

HARRINGTON, FRANCIS CLARK Sept 10, 1887—Sept 30, 1940 National Work Projects Administrator; member of the United States Army Engineers from 1909 to 1935; assisted in the construction of the Panama Canal; chosen in 1935 by President Roosevelt to become Assistant Administrator of the Works Progress Administration; in 1938, when Harry Hopkins left to become

FRANCIS C. HARRINGTON

Secretary of Commerce, was advanced to top position; since July 1, 1939, when the Work Projects Administration replaced the Works Progress Administration, he had been commissioner

References

Time 33:8 Ja 2 '39 por
Who's Who in America
Who's Who in the Nation's Capital

Obituaries

N Y Herald Tribune p22 O 1 '40 por
N Y Times p23 O 1 '40 por
Time 36:57 O 7 '40

HARRIS, ROY   Feb 12, 1898-   Composer
Address: h. 160 Cabrini Blvd, New York City

As late as 1925 Roy Harris was earning his living as a truck driver. Today he is one American composer who has found a ready market for his works. Frequently his music is broadcast over national hookups; much of it is recorded; and the great orchestras of this country rush to include a new Harris composition on their programs. His recent *Folk-Song Symphony* was written on a commission from the National Committee of Music Appreciation and his *Challenge, 1940* came at the request of Artur Rodzinski (see sketch this issue) for a composition for a Philharmonic Lewisohn Stadium concert.

Harris' popularity may be due, in part, to the strikingly American character of his writing. His pieces seem to "taste and breathe the vast American soil"; in them is an energy that seems especially American, "muscular, spare, adventuresome." This nativeness is a basic quality of the music in *Symphony, 1933,* for instance, or the *Third Symphony* which Koussevitzky (see sketch this issue) called "as completely outside European experience as the prairie morning itself." It is both intrinsically and extrinsically identified with works like *When Johnny Comes Marching Home,* based on a familiar American tune, or *A Song of Occupations* or *Challenge, 1940,* the words of which are the preamble to the Constitution of the United States.

Harris himself says: "If we create an indigenous music worthy of our people, it will make its way swiftly and unfalteringly. . . Whether it be a little more or less 'dissonant' or 'original' is of small import—but it must have the pulsing life stuff in it—creative urge and necessity of continuity. It cannot be a scholarly mosaic of all the materials and forms of the last 200 European years."

Harris' is not modernistic music. It is classical music in the sense that his works embody organically developed musical ideas. But in his conservatism Harris does not imitate older styles. Rather he creates through great labor a self-built style which "is original because he originated it himself, but which is not always new." Many of his rhythms are delightfully novel and vigorous. Many of his "plaintive, originally

G. Maillard Kesslère

ROY HARRIS

modulated bitter-sweet melodies" are equally distinctive. In fact, many critics agree that Harris' "melodic gift is his most striking characteristic."

Often Harris' technical equipment is questioned because he started composing so late, and it is true that there is a certain awkwardness in his early works both in handling his material and in writing for instruments. Gradually, however, "this awkwardness becomes part and parcel of his style, taking on a charm of its own." Yet it has been pointed out frequently that Harris' work is still "unequal." His slow movements, especially, with a tendency toward soft sentiment, seem out of style with the rest of his work.

Harris has listened to his own music critically, aware of its unevenness or its occasional patchiness, and ultimately rejected the inferior among his works. He has "put compositions ruthlessly back on to the stocks when they needed reworking and cut away whole movements and substituted better, and furiously labored at the improvement of his style and form." This "spare, gangling Oklahoman" is in "deadly earnest with a devoted sincerity to musical ideals and with boundless enthusiasm as to his own possibilities."

Roy Harris was born in an Oklahoma log cabin, the son of a farmer and of a waitress who had been brought to the United States from England when a baby. At five he was taken to California, where he lived the life of a farmer. His mother taught him to play the piano and he had a few lessons on it and on the clarinet. Then his father bought a phonograph and some records. "We played them nearly every evening, even in the late summer evenings after a long day's work," he says.

HARRIS, ROY—*Continued*

At public school Roy played piano in occasional concerts, but decided to give up music and go in for athletics. "I grew to normal masculine stature, learned to dance, to neglect my studies and to be at ease in the presence of my schoolmates. All this was probably necessary." Then came the War, and when it was over Harris spent two years at the University of California. But "I could find nothing definite to get hold of," he says.

Then he discovered that music was what he wanted. His job was that of a truck driver, delivering 3,000 pounds of butter and 300 dozen eggs around Los Angeles, but four years of truck-driving were for him "years crowded with enthusiasms. Each new harmony, each new melody each composer discovered was a milestone for me." He began to write "unbelievable commonplaces of harmony like a schoolboy's first exercises, melodic fragments of no distinction, rhythm all half-note blocks in four-four meters." But Harris pointed them out "with the firm conviction that they were potential masterpieces."

"Then one week, in desperation," he says, "I wrote a work for orchestra." He took it to Arthur Farwell, his friend and teacher, and it was performed in a festival at Rochester by Dr. Howard Hanson and repeated in a New York Lewisohn Stadium concert and at the Hollywood Bowl. This *Andante*, Harris knew, "was poor, heavy-footed, fumbling. It conveyed none of the racy, taut springiness which I felt as I wrote it. But at last something seemed to be expected of me. People said I was a 'fresh talent' but needed 'technique.'"

In 1927, as a result of this *Andante*, Harris was awarded a Guggenheim Fellowship and went to Paris to study with Nadia Boulanger. For a time he began to pick up sophisticated "tricks" but he kept his drive and "a bit of ungainliness which he has never quite outgrown." After two years he returned to America, where he was, at first, unhappy. "Nobody really cared whether I wrote good music or not. Good American citizens resented one of their own making a lifework out of music unless it netted money." During this period he suffered a fractured spine and spent six months in a plaster cast—a "blessing," actually, because it forced Harris to read and to write music without depending on the piano.

Soon Harris won a creative fellowship from the City of Pasadena. His performances began to receive encouraging reviews; Elizabeth Sprague Coolidge sponsored his chamber music when the Pro Arte quartet decided that it was "virile United States music well worth playing widely."

Harris is a fairly prolific composer, lavish in his ideas and in his development of them. Best known among his works, perhaps, are the *Symphony*, 1933, which Koussevitzky called the first tragic American symphony; *A Song for Occupations*, a vigorous setting for *a cappella* choir of Whitman's words; *When Johnny Comes Marching Home*, an "American Overture" commissioned and recorded in 1934 by RCA Victor Company, "rough-hewn, sinewy and directly outspoken"; the *Third Symphony*, which Koussevitzky gave a première almost immediately and which then was broadcasted by Toscanini and came to be the "most talked about American composition in a decade." Harris' chamber music, like his orchestral works, is consistently outstanding for its elevated manner, "sublime for all its ruggedness."

Harris, who in 1938 was head of the composition department of the Westminster Choir School in Princeton, New Jersey and in 1940 is teaching and composing in New York, still looks and sounds his Western origin. "He is rather spare in build, and his voice has the barest suggestion of both lisp and twang. He has fair hair and eyes of bluish gray; his eyes can light up with humor or restrained sarcasm and he has the gift of listening." In his personality he has "a plain, driving force, undampable conviction, ruggedness," much of which is reflected in his music.

In the fall of 1940 *Singing Through the Ages: Melodic and Harmonic Songs* was published. It was edited by Harris and Jacob Evanson.

References

Am Mercury 34:490 Ap '35
Christian Sci Mon Mag p8-9 Mr 17
    '37 por
Mag Art 32:638-9+ N '39
Musical Q 25:376-9 Jl '39
Musician 40:19 O '35 por (p1)
N Y Times p27 Je 26 '40
Newsweek 15:44+ My 6 '40 por
Time 26:36-7 N 11 '35 por; 35:45
    Ap 8 '40 por; 36:46-7 Jl 8 '40
Cowell, H. Roy Harris *In* Cowell,
    H. ed. American Composers on
    American Music p64-9 1933
Ewen, D. Roy Harris *In* Twentieth
    Century Composers p247-56 1937
Pierre Key's Musical Who's Who
Rosenfeld, P. Harris *In* Discoveries
    of a Music Critic p324-32 1936
Thompson, O. ed. International Cy-
    clopedia of Music and Musicians
    1939
Wier, A. E. ed. Macmillan Ency-
    clopedia of Music and Musicians
    1938

HART, BASIL HENRY LIDDELL- *See* Liddell Hart, B. H.

HART, LORENZ *See* Rodgers, R. and Hart, L.

HART, MOSS Oct 24, 1904- Playwright; librettist

Address: b. 1501 Broadway, New York City

In the fall of 1940 George Kaufman and Moss Hart presented Broadway with their seventh collaborated production, *George Washington Slept Here*, while their sixth, *The Man Who Came to Dinner*, was still playing to crowded houses.

Since Kaufman and Hart have built up the most smoothly integrated collaborating team in Broadway history, it is difficult to tell what particular gifts Moss Hart brings to their work. His feeling for satire combines readily with the more experienced Kaufman's sense of humor in situation and careful attention to the fine points of production. They satirized Hollywood (*Once in a Lifetime*, 1930) before either of them had ever been to the movie coast; they satirized New Deal politics (*I'd Rather be Right*, 1937), though neither had ever played the political game in Washington. But they were near-celebrities themselves when, as theatre-goers know, they satirized celebrity-worship in *The Man Who Came to Dinner* (1939), and their satirization of the woes of a New York family in a Bucks County, Pennsylvania farmhouse is close to their own experiences.

With critics and public agreed that *The Man Who Came to Dinner*, the story of a touring Great Man who breaks a hip and stays for weeks with a much enduring Midwest family, is one of the best and funniest of the Kaufman-Hart plays, Warner Brothers of Hollywood have negotiated with the playwrights for its screen production in 1941. *George Washington Slept Here*, however, was a disappointment to the critics (one called it: *George Kaufman Slipped Here*) who found that, despite tremendously amusing sequences, the story of the making over of a dilapidated Colonial farm house just wasn't enough for three acts.

Prototype of the bright-young-man who makes good on Broadway—from obscurity to riches in a decade—Moss Hart likes to say he was born on the wrong end of Fifth Avenue, New York, the son of Barnett and Lillian (Solomon) Hart. The place was 107th Street, the time October 24, 1904. The theatre began for him when he was seven years old and his Aunt Kate took him on a trip clear downtown to Manhattan to see a play called *Life* by Owen Davis, presented at the Manhattan Opera House. The boy at once knew that this world behind the footlights was the world he would live for. He made playwriting his objective while still in high school; he took up the study of the short story at Columbia University, but never got far with it. His parents were poor, so to help support them he went to work in cloaks and suits. His first contact with the theatrical world came when at 17 he became secretary to August Pitou, theatrical manager. His small salary was turned over to his family, but he did get passes to all the theatres. At 19 he wrote his first play, *The Hold Up Man*

Vandamm

MOSS HART

(or, *The Beloved Bandit*) and persuaded Pitou to produce it. The play actually ran for five weeks in Chicago, but Pitou lost so much money on it that he and his young secretary soon parted company.

Moss Hart next became a Little Theatre director. Then he got better paying jobs as entertainment director in large summer camps for adults. He found that one of the world's toughest jobs is keeping city folks sufficiently entertained when they are confronted with a few weeks of Nature. He stole most of the plays he produced for them on drama nights—and he played the lead in all of them. One season when it rained during 15 days the entertainment director had to devise a bit of palm reading, fortune telling, bridge tournaments and tap dancing on the side.

After one such harrowing summer Moss Hart announced to his family that he was going to write a play, that he must live away from New York in order to have peace and quiet to do it. Accordingly he and his family fled from The Bronx into the wilds of Brooklyn. There *Once in a Lifetime* was written. The young playwright hopefully took it to Jed Harris, who turned it down. It was Sam Harris who suggested that he might get George S. Kaufman to collaborate with him on its rewriting and production. Hart had long looked upon Kaufman, who was 15 years his senior, as a god, and could scarcely believe his good fortune when Kaufman liked the play and would work with him. But he now calls his first job working with Kaufman the "Days of Terror," since the daily schedule meant working from 10 a. m. "until exhausted" or starving, since Kaufman seldom ate anything while working. They might spend two hours shaping a sentence, or a whole day discussing an

HART, MOSS—*Continued*

exit. A Kaufman-Hart play is never completely written; it is gone over, cut, rewritten time and time again before, during, and even after rehearsals.

Further opportunity came to Moss Hart, while he was still comparatively unknown, to collaborate with another brilliant theatrical personage: Irving Berlin. Hart was librettist for two successful reviews, Berlin writing the scores; *Face the Music* (1932) and *As Thousands Cheer* (1933). In 1935 he wrote, with Cole Porter, (see sketch this issue), *Jubilee*. This lightly satirized a social situation similar to one then developing at the Court of St. James; but in Hart's story the Royal Family is ordered to a gloomy castle as the result of a Communistic threat perpetrated by a mischievous prince. The family escapes from the castle and goes on a bust of its own devising, incognito.

But since his initial success Hart's best work has been done in the plays that are Kaufman-Hart combines. *You Can't Take It With You* (1936) won the Pulitzer Award for drama that year. This, an outstanding motion picture success after its long run on Broadway, was a farce-comedy of the clowning Sycamore family: Grandfather Vanderhof who gave up business because he wanted to relax, his daughter Penelope who wrote plays because someone left a typewriter by mistake at the house, her husband who manufactured fireworks in the cellar. Only the youngest granddaughter is conventional enough to be an efficient secretary—and marry the boss' son. In 1937 came *I'd Rather Be Right*, the New Deal satire in which George M. Cohan as President Roosevelt helped roll up a tremendous box office score. *The Fabulous Invalid* (1938) was a cavalcade of the New York stage since 1900, showing the long struggle of a theatre and a producer-manager: everything is going to kill the theatre—but it always survives. *The American Way* (1939) was the type story of the immigrant, a German carpenter, who comes to this country to find freedom and work, raises a family, makes a fortune, loses a son in the War, is impoverished by the financial crash, and dies a martyr to freedom.

The Glamor Boy of New York first nights, whose meteoric rise has behind it some intensively hard work, is described as "a tall, pleasant looking man with lots of dark hair, a full face, eyebrows like inverted V's, and a rushing enthusiasm." He is unmarried, and fond mamas with marriageable daughters yearn over him. But sweet young things usually bore him; he prefers wise and witty and more experienced companions like Beatrice Lillie and Fanny Brice. He says that his home life is "a glamorous mixture of New York, Hollywood, insomnia, nervous indigestion and a childlike passion for the theatre." He likes dogs, has a dark room for amateur photography and always plenty of space for parties, since he has a phobia about eating alone.

His home in New York is a beautiful remodeled Victorian brownstone filled with Victorian furniture, much of which he picked up at auctions. In Bucks County, Pennsylvania he has a farmhouse in the center of a theatrical and art colony.

Moss Hart's idea of solid luxury is a gold monogram—several of them—on everything from belt buckles to bottle-stoppers. He is a spendthrift on haberdashery and gadgets; he spends not only on himself, but generously on his family and friends: lavish jewels, furs, silks. When he had his first success with *Once in a Lifetime* he established his family in an elegant hotel apartment refitted by the best interior decorators. He spent his royalties as fast as he got them, a procedure he still follows; fortunately there are usually more coming in.

In spite of the aura of success that surrounds Moss Hart, those who know him best believe that much more than a love of glitter is bred in his bones. His good friend but not-yet collaborator, Edna Ferber, writes of him: "Iron is stronger than gold, and he has plenty of that hardy metal in him. As his social sense wanes, he will write more and more out of his own emotional and intellectual findings. The theatre is an integral part of him. He sees people and events with an eye which is at once dramatic, technical and human—the craftsman's eye. There's not the slightest danger that he will one day be hopelessly snarled up in all those monograms, neckties, dressing-gowns and engraved dinner invitations."

Moss Hart has finished, on his own, a play tentatively called *Lady in the Dark*, in which Gertrude Lawrence (see sketch this issue) will star. *George Washington Slept Here*, a new Kaufman-Hart play, opened in New York in the fall of 1940.

References

House B 82:44 Ap 1 '40 por
Lit Digest 118:10 Ap 11 '34 por
Nation 149:474-5 O 28 '39
New Repub 70:97 Mr 9 '32
Stage 11:22 O '33; 14:58-61 N '36; 14:41-3 D '36 por; 15:36-8 Ap '38 il por
Theatre Arts 21:96-7 F '37 il (p92); 22:862-4 D '38 il (850); 23:162-4 Mr '39 il (p158); 23:788-98 N '39
Time 34:65+ N 20 '39 pors

Brown. J. M. Gridiron Club and I'd Rather Be Right *In* Two on the Aisle p286-9 1938
Mantle, B. Contemporary American Playwrights p8-13, p15-20 1938
Who's Who in America
Who's Who in American Jewry
Who's Who in the Theatre

HAWES, ELIZABETH Dec 16, 1903- Designer; writer
Address: b. c/o PM, 27 Sixth Ave, Brooklyn, New York; h. 217 E 48th St, New York City

Elizabeth Hawes has been referred to as "Fashion Is Spinach" Hawes, which indicates the popularity of her debunking book by that title. Whether or not she has indeed come to the conclusion that "fashion is spinach" as far as she personally is concerned and has decided to forsake it for journalism, remains to be seen. Apparently she is engaged in both careers at present.

She closed her very exclusive dressmaking establishment in January 1940 with the announcement that she planned to open a "small laboratory" where she would make clothes and accessories for a very limited number of women with the hope eventually of applying the designs to mass production. Shortly after the announcement the shop was supplanted by Hawes Customers, Incorporated, run by Miss Hawes' former employees, and for which the former owner occasionally did some designing.

The announcement was almost coincidental with her acceptance of the post of editor of the "News for Living Department" of New York's new tabloid, *PM*, which made its appearance in May 1940. The "News for Living Department" took the place of the conventional woman's pages in newspapers, and, according to *PM* editors, was to help its readers eat better, dress better and have more fun for less money. It was, in effect, a new kind of woman's department, which gave a digest of advertisements, shopped for unadvertised bargains in clothes, listed 20 best buys in food each day, and searched for new trends in cosmetics, apartments, schools and entertainment. This department was discontinued in the fall of 1940, but Miss Hawes continues to write Sunday pieces for *PM*.

It was a far cry from Hawes, Incorporated, exclusive *couturière*, but yet entirely in keeping with the aims Elizabeth Hawes expressed in her best seller, *Fashion Is Spinach*, in 1938. For Elizabeth Hawes is definitely of the opinion that the American woman is not getting her money's worth in her clothes because she is the victim of that "deformed thief," fashion. And fashion, according to Miss Hawes, is something entirely different from style. Style, she says, is functional, while fashion is the whim of designers and manufacturers. A dress that is in good style may be worn for three years, she declares.

Giving women advice and information about clothes is certainly in Elizabeth Hawes' sphere. She began making clothes as a child in Ridgewood, New Jersey, where she was born the daughter of John and Henrietta (Houston) Hawes. She was sewing her own clothes by the time she was nine or ten years old, and at twelve she was making clothes for children of her mother's friends.

She wanted to go to art school, but somehow, after her graduation from the Ridgewood High School, found herself in Vassar, chiefly because her mother had been a student there and her older sister was attending the college. At the end of her sophomore year, however, she did attend an art school for a three months' summer term, the Parsons School of Fine and Applied Arts, in New York. The following

Mary Morris

ELIZABETH HAWES

summer, in 1924, still determined to become a designer and convinced that no art school could teach her, she went to work as an unpaid apprentice at Bergdorf Goodman, exclusive specialty shop, in New York.

For this privilege, obtained through a friend who bought her clothes at Bergdorf Goodman, she worked from 8:30 a. m. each morning, and it was 7:30 at night before she got to her suburban home. "I was so tired I cried every night when I got home," she writes in *Fashion Is Spinach*. "I learned how expensive clothes were made-to-order." But the experience apparently did not discourage her. During her senior year at Vassar she supplemented her meager allowance by designing clothes for a shop near the campus.

She was determined to go to work in Paris to learn the fashion business at first-hand. Soon after she was graduated in the summer of 1925 she set out for Paris with a Vassar classmate. There was no parental objection to overcome, and Elizabeth Hawes started off on her quest of a career armed with a letter to the Paris office of Bonwit Teller (New York exclusive specialty shop), and two fashion reporting jobs—one a $10-a-month job for her local newspaper and the other a $15-a-month job for a Wilkes-Barre, Pennsylvania department store.

From July 1925 to August 1928, when she returned to America permanently, Paris and the fashionable resorts of Europe were Elizabeth Hawes' stamping ground. Her first job was with a Paris copy house at the munificent salary of $20 a month. The copy house was a bootleg establishment which copied the models of the famous French designers for its special customers. Miss Hawes assisted with this bootlegging and for a while found her work a pleasure,

HAWES, ELIZABETH—*Continued*

since she was learning to recognize the styles of the important French designers.

After three seasons she quit to make sketches for American buyers and manufacturers in Paris. This work consisted of accompanying buyers to the important fashion openings and sketching surreptitiously those dresses they wanted to copy, but did not wish to buy. She made some comparatively quick money in this way, and it left her free between buying seasons. Her next experience was as correspondent for an American fashion syndicate; she also was Paris correspondent for the *New Yorker* and for short periods a Paris stylist for Macy's and for the Lord & Taylor specialty shop in New York. She quit it all, however, to take a job with the French designer, Nicole Groult, for $20 a month so that she could do designing.

But, after a season with Groult, the young *couturière* decided that French designing was not for her. She was out of sympathy with the life of the French leisure class. She wanted to design clothes for American women, to make clothes that suited the lives they led. "No use trying to design clothes in Paris for a group of people whose lives were nothing to me," she said.

She returned to America in September 1928 with no job, only with an idea that she wanted to design American fashions, a thing almost unheard of then, since the tradition of copying French models was still very strong. By chance she heard of Rosemary Harden, a debutante of the year before, who wanted to do something besides go to parties. Rosemary's father set the girls up in a dress business.

The firm of Hawes-Harden opened on East 56th Street on December 16, 1928, Elizabeth Hawes' twenty-fifth birthday. Launched with considerable publicity, the shop did $60,000 worth of business the first year, but lost $10,000, which Mr. Harden obligingly paid. Hawes-Harden was having more of a success making beautiful clothes than making money. In 1930, when Rosemary Harden was married, the Hardens gave Miss Hawes their share of the business for $1.

Although Miss Hawes now had a business of her own, it was not easy going. The depression was just around the corner, and it looked rather dark for the shop for a time. But the ever-energetic Miss Hawes was full of ideas. Probably one of her most unusual stunts was the exhibition of her American fashions in Paris, July 4, 1931. It was the first time the world's style center had known invasion from overseas, and it won Miss Hawes considerable publicity.

Until this time, Miss Hawes' designing had been done exclusively for the woman who could afford to buy made-to-order clothes. But in 1933 she hired herself out to a Seventh Avenue (the manufacturing row of New York) dress manufacturer to design ready-made clothes. Hawes' moderately priced designs were blazoned forth in advertisements and promotion pieces. Miss Hawes also designed gloves and bags for the retail market.

Color combinations that the retail trade thought startling and designs they declared very novel were merely duplications of things done in her made-to-order business several years before, Miss Hawes says. She made enough out of her first year's work with a dress manufacturer to pay for newer, larger quarters for her own business. Hawes, Incorporated, opened in its new quarters on East 67th Street in 1933. Soon afterward Miss Hawes left Seventh Avenue because she said she found Hawes' fashions being made in inferior materials and badly put together.

Elizabeth Hawes has dubbed herself an "American" *couturière*, and has built her success on that. She is, in fact, one of the pioneer American women's clothes designers of note. Her *Fashion Is Spinach* was thought by some to bear the faint tinge of press-agentry. A discussion of the ins and outs of fashion from the autobiographical standpoint, the book was called destructive by trade papers. Nevertheless it made the ranks of the best sellers. If it did press-agent Elizabeth Hawes, it was honest and entertaining.

Miss Hawes' *Men Can Take It*, published in 1939, was an indignant attack on the uncomfortable clothing men wear. The designer advocated functional clothing without stiff collars, heavy belts and stiffly buttoned coats, and predicted that colored slack suits would be the common business attire of the future. It was not her first attempt to do something about men's clothes. She had held a men's fashion show with clothes designed by her and previously had written articles on the subject.

The energetic Miss Hawes has tried her hand at fiction, also, and has had several short stories with a dress-designing background published. After *Fashion Is Spinach* was published she says she made more money from writing than from dress designing. Incidentally, writing, talking and bicycling are, she declares, her chief hobbies.

Miss Hawes has been married twice. Her first husband, whom she married December 12, 1930, was Ralph Jester. After a divorce, she was married to Joseph W. Losey, July 1937. They have one son, Gavrik, born in 1938.

References

Am Mag 115:40 My '33 por
N Y Post p4 F 24 '40
Newsweek 11:29 Mr 28 '38 por; 15:54
    F 19 '40 por
American Women
Hawes, E. Fashion Is Spinach 1938
Who's Who in New York

HAYNES, ROY ASA Aug 31, 1881—
Oct 20, 1940 Federal Prohibition Commissioner under Presidents Harding and Coolidge; editor of Hillsboro, Ohio *Dispatch* for many years; during prohibition service wrote *Prohibition Inside Out* (1923); active in business after retirement as prohibition commissioner in 1927

References
> Who's Who in America

Obituaries
> N Y Times p17 O 21 '40

HEAD, SIR HENRY Aug 4, 1861—Oct 9, 1940 British neurologist; made some of the most important contributions to knowledge of nervous disorders; former editor of *Brain*, a medical publication, and author of works on neurology; member of Royal College of Surgeons and Royal College of Physicians, Fellow of the Royal Society; author of a volume of poetry; knighted in 1927

References
> International Who's Who
> Who's Who

Obituaries
> N Y Herald Tribune p20 O 10 '40
> por
> N Y Times p25 O 10 '40
> Time 36:66 O 21 '40

HEATH, S. BURTON Dec 20, 1898-
Journalist
Address: b. c/o New York World-Telegram, 125 Barclay St, New York City

"An anonymous postcard made a muckraker out of me," said S. Burton Heath of the New York *World-Telegram*, whose exposé of the illegal extra-judicial activities of former Judge Martin T. Manton of the United States Supreme Court of Appeals won for him the 1939 Pulitzer Award for best reportorial work.

Mr. Heath is a muckraker of the modern variety, and that means that when he gets through playing around with records and facts and figures something has to happen besides a series of articles in an evening newspaper. In this case Judge Manton resigned, was tried, convicted and sentenced to prison. Because of Heath's other muckraking activities, he tells us, "two judges have left the bench by resignation under fire; three of the largest insurance companies stand condemned in the public conscience; cheap equitable insurance is available to more than 12,000,000 in New York State; the taxpayers of New York were saved more than $3,000,000 on a few foul, sewage-swept acres of unused ocean bottom."

Although Heath, the son of Horace Burton and Ida Victoria (Marine) Heath, was born on December 20, 1898 in Lynn, Massachusetts, he really hails from Vermont, where his parents still live. He attended the Bradford, Ver-

S. BURTON HEATH

mont High School and while a sophomore there, worked as hand compositor on the Bradford *Opinion*, the town's weekly newspaper. It is possible there wasn't much going on in Bradford that really required muckraking at the time. In 1917, a year after young Heath was graduated, he became editor-manager of the weekly Groton (Vermont) *Times*; in 1917 he enlisted in the Vermont National Guard, later was sent to France and returned to the *Times* with two citations for war-time service and two wound stripes. In 1919 he bought the newspaper. Shortly afterward he was forced to retire from the newspaper business because of poor health, but retirement was only temporary. Heath began to study at the University of Vermont and there he worked on the Burlington *Free Press*; when he was graduated in 1926 there was another newspaper job waiting for him with the New Haven Bureau of the Associated Press; in 1928 he came to the New York *Telegram*. He has been with the *Telegram* and the *World-Telegram* ever since, aside from a two-year interval (1930-32) during which he served as secretary of the St. Lawrence Power Development Commission.

It was not until 1933 that Heath began muckraking, though, and then his career was begun almost by accident. The anonymous postcard that Heath spoke of was one suggesting he investigate the judgments against one of the 48 justices in New York City's "poor man's court." He did, and the uncovering of the facts had such immediate and practical results that Heath used the same method to become the "unofficial scourge of Tammany Hall." His articles exposing Tammany's corruption provided considerable ammunition for the Fusion forces in driving Tammany from the City Hall that year, and until 1936 he

HEATH, S. BURTON—*Continued*

continued to specialize on municipal affairs. Later investigations included one on industrial insurance which was followed (April 1938) by the passage by the State Legislature of the Savings Bank Insurance Act, which allows savings banks to handle small insurance policies of the poorer citizens.

The first article on Judge Manton's activities appeared on January 27, 1939, but it was the result of patient research on Heath's part since the summer of 1938, with time out only to cover Dewey's (see sketch this issue) campaign for Governorship. "Research" to the modern muckraker means burrowing in ledgers, court files, tax reports. According to Heath it means having the "combined qualities of analytical accountant, mathematician, chess master, crossword-puzzler and jigsaw addict. It needs also a smattering, at least, of curbstone law." It was suspected that Judge Manton had been sitting on cases which involved persons from whom he had received financial benefits; simultaneously the New York County Grand Jury was investigating him. But it was up to Heath to provide the leads and work them up to prove that Manton was unfit to sit on the bench. His first article describing the control held over various corporations by Judge Manton brought about the Judge's resignation within three days. Shortly afterward Manton was indicted and on June 3, 1939 he was convicted, fined $10,000 and sentenced to two years in prison.

The process of muckraking, modern style is, Heath says, "one of calm analysis of cold records: the collection and tabulation of facts and figures, their meticulous sifting and evaluation, and eventually their organization into a syllogism in which both premises are indisputable and the conclusion is inescapable." Those are big words, but they seem to have brought results.

In the fall of 1940 Burton Heath's book, *Yankee Reporter* tells how his kind of reporting is done. In it he tells of following clues through court records, statistics and personal interviews; in it he gives sidelights on various personalities he has met; in it he tells of his own life in Vermont, New Haven and New York. This, says Harry Hansen in the New York *World-Telegram* is a book "that was crying to be written."

Mr. Heath is a sharp-faced Vermonter, "mild and courteous," with a wife (he married Emily Dodge in 1923) and one daughter, Nancy, five years old. He is very fond of French fried potatoes and doesn't like fruit or vegetables. His first name unfortunately cannot be divulged for the sake of any record; he has been trying to keep it secret for 20 years.

References

Am Mercury 46:421-8 Ap '39
N Y Herald Tribune p17 My 7 '40 por
N Y Times p20 My 7 '40 por
N Y World-Telegram p5 My 7 '40
Heath, B. S. Yankee Reporter 1940

HEDIN, SVEN ANDERS (hĕ-dēn' sfĕn än'dürs) Feb 19, 1865- Explorer; author

Address: c/o E. P. Dutton & Co, 300 Fourth Ave, New York City

For more than 50 years Sven Hedin, "the Marco Polo of our day," has been wandering through the unmapped regions of the world. "His yak-dung fires have burned in innumerable Himalayan passes; he has run the risk of death from cold, hunger, wolves, thieves; over and over again, from one remote and desolate spot he has gone through storm and flood, through Himalayan cold and the unspeakable dirt of Tibetan villages, to reach another equally remote and desolate spot merely for the satisfaction of drawing a new line on the map of the world." About 20 published volumes of which *The Wandering Lake* (April 1940) is the latest, tell the story of his adventures and discoveries.

Hedin has always been an explorer. In *My Life as an Explorer* (1935) he tells us: "At the early age of 12 my goal was fairly clear. My closest friends were Fenimore Cooper and Jules Verne, Livingstone and Stanley . . . particularly the long line of heroes and martyrs of Arctic exploration." When Nordenskjöld returned to Stockholm in 1878 (the city where Hedin was born in 1865), after a trip of incredible hardships through the Arctic, Sven Hedin was one of the crowd that cheered him. "All my life I shall remember that day," he says. "It decided my career."

Hedin then delved into everything about Arctic expeditions he could find. He read, he studied maps and during the northern winters he rolled in the snow and slept by open windows "to harden myself." But he never became an Arctic explorer. In 1885, while he was at the University of Stockholm, he was offered a job as a tutor in Baku on the Caspian. He went, "and for the rest of my life I was to be held by the enchanting power that emanates from the largest continent in the world."

From Baku, Sven Hedin went to Persia (1890) where he had the first of the many thrilling and amusing adventures that were to color his travels. Before he left Stockholm he had been asked by a professor at the university to bring back the crania of some Persian fire worshippers. He found three fine skulls. The customs official examined his luggage, and asked, "What's in that bag?" pointing to the one with the heads. "Human heads," Hedin replied. "Take a look." The official did, and sent Hedin through fast, perfectly certain that a foul triple murder had been committed.

In 1889 Hedin returned home. One of his professors called him to the attention of Baron von Richthofen, the famous Asiatic authority, and Hedin visited Richthofen in Berlin and studied Asiatic geography with him. Then he returned to the East. *A Conquest of Tibet* (1934) tells some of his earlier adventures, his unsuccessful effort to reach Lhasa in disguise frustrated in a very gentle and polite fashion by Tibetan officials, his adventures and observations in a Tibetan monastery, his friendship with the Panchen Lama, his discovery of the sources of the Indus. Here and there in the book one sees mention of the Lop-nor, the mysterious wandering lake in Central China that flits through many of his books like a *Fata morgana* and finally forms the theme of his latest one.

From the turn of the century on, Sven Hedin continued to travel and explore Asia's deserts, Mongolia, India, Arabia, Tibet, Mesopotamia. The result of almost each expedition is a book, both scientific and exciting. *Overland to India* (1910); *Jerusalem* (1918); *Jehol, City of Emperors* (1932) are only a few of them. In *Across the Gobi Desert* (1931) we see Hedin as the executive, the head of a great Swedish and Chinese scientific expedition, directing its affairs from Peiping, the base in the Gobi Desert, the United States and back in the Gobi again. The affairs of that expedition, which employed a staff of 13 scientific specialists, run through his next book, too, *Riddles of the Gobi Desert* (1933). But here Hedin is no executive at a desk, recording contacts with lords and bureaucrats. He travels by auto, dugout and camel, on foot and by horse through the heart of the Gobi Desert.

In between his trips of exploration, Sven Hedin would return home. He would get the pictures he had taken into shape for publication and go over the drawings he had made. He always relied more on drawings, for as he said: "A landscape which I've painted I never forget." In Stockholm his father and his sister Alma would help him copy his manuscripts. But he never stayed with them long. Soon he would think of "the slow, measured step of camels and the sound of copper bells."

One summer evening in 1933 Sven Hedin was guest at the German Embassy in Peiping, where some officials of the then existing Chinese government were also present. One of these officials asked Hedin if he had any suggestion about how the Chinese government could retain control of Sinkiang, a Chinese dependency stretching from Mongolia to Tibet. Hedin said: "Yes. Motorize the Silk Road." The Chinese government didn't know what the Silk Road was. Hedin had to tell them it was the caravan route traveled by Marco Polo in the days when China exchanged her silk and spices for European goods. The Chinese government asked Hedin to make a map of the Silk Road so they could motorize it. Hedin knew there were about 5,000,000 maps already in existence, but he accepted. He had been over the route a dozen times, on camel, elephant, horse and coolie back,

SVEN HEDIN

but he liked the thought of going over it in a well-equipped Ford motor truck.

It wasn't so simple. China was disorganized during the years of 1933 and 1934. *The Flight of Big Horse* (1936) is the first of the three books which deal with this expedition. It is the story of the Hedin expedition as its adventures were intertwined with those of Ma Chung Yin, "Big Horse," a swash-buckling, 23-year-old general with the ambitions of a Tamerlane. Asiatic politics and gunplay and prison, victory and disaster make up a story of exciting Chinese adventure. *The Silk Road* (1938) continues the story of the perilous expedition that succeeded in laying out the famous road over which the present Chinese government is now consolidating China.

In the last book of the trilogy, *The Wandering Lake* (1940), Hedin covers a special province of that last expedition. This lake, Lop-nor, has been wandering in and out of Hedin's writings for the last 50 years. Now, at last, he examines it in detail, fixes its present geographical position and outlines and settles the arguments of the cartographers.

For his work in discovery Sven Hedin has received great homage from his countrymen and from other nations. He has been given a seat in the Swedish Academy, he has been knighted, he has received doctorates from Oxford and Cambridge, from the University of Berlin and from the University of Heidelberg. He has been awarded the Grand Gold Medal of the City of Paris and the Gold Medal of the Japanese Geographical Society.

Sven Hedin is 75 years old now, but this amazing and romantic figure is still going— "his energy and drive, his powers of production, his powers of observation, his flair for adventure undiminished for being now housed in a body that is no longer as sturdy and

HEDIN, SVEN—*Continued*

efficient as it once was." His latest book, published in November 1940, is on Chiang Kai-shek (see sketch this issue).

Hedin is in the news today not only as an explorer and author but as a diplomat. He has figured in politics from time to time before. Once he was diplomat from Sweden to the Shah of Persia, and before the First World War took an active part in "bringing about dissension between Sweden and Russia." To him has been attributed part of the responsibility for the "Peasants' March" to the Royal Palace in Stockholm, just before hostilities began, which resulted in "the triumph of those who sympathized with Prussia and her system of the government of the many by the privileged few."

Swedish Sven Hedin has always been on Germany's side. During the World War he strongly supported Germany and was the author of pamphlets urging Sweden to arm itself against the Allies. In 1937 he wrote *Germany and World Peace,* from Germany's point of view, and he has been called by the Berliner *Tageblatt* "a true friend of Germany." On his 75th birthday, on February 18, 1940, Hitler presented him with "the grand cross of the distinguished service of the German eagle."

Now that Germany is again at war, the explorer Sven Hedin is once again prominent in his less familiar rôle as statesman. On March 5, 1940 there was a report that in an interview with Hitler he had offered to mediate the Russian-Finnish War. According to *Time,* Sweden "picked him as her salesman." In April 1940 Hedin urged the American people not to side against Germany, not to take part in the War, not to supply the Allies with any materials.

In May 1940, when the War had advanced to Scandinavia, a good many people were curious about his position and feelings toward Germany. The New York *Times* book critic, before reviewing *The Wandering Lake,* told about the decoration Hitler gave Hedin only a few weeks before and asked: "I wonder if he has the ribbon in his button-hole now?"

References

Bücherei 7:65-72 Mr '40
Forum 103:217-18 Ap '40
Liv Age 346:49-51 Mr '34; 348:107-10 Ap '35
Nation 139:130 Ag 1 '34
N Y Times p23 Ap 10 '40
Newsweek 12:36 D 12 '38
Time 35:19 Mr 18 '40
Haslund-Christensen, H. Men and Gods in Mongolia (Zayagan) 1935
Hedin, S. A. My Life as an Explorer 1925
Hedin, S. A. To the Forbidden Land; Discoveries and Adventures in Tibet 1934

Key, C. E. Through the Wastes of Asia and Tibet *In* The Story of Twentieth-Century Exploration p36-83 1938
Montell, G. Sven Hedin's Archaeological Collections from Khotan 1938
Wer ist's?
Who's Who

HEIDENSTAM, VERNER VON July 6, 1859—May 20, 1940 Swedish writer (full name Karl Gustaf Verner von Heidenstam) who won the Nobel Prize in literature in 1916; was an intense nationalist; known for descriptions of travels and epics of homeland

VERNER VON HEIDENSTAM

References

Am Scand R 27:138-41 Je '39
Gustafon, A. Six Scandinavian Novelists 1940
International Who's Who
Kunitz, S. J. ed. Authors Today and Yesterday 1933
Marble, Mrs. A. R. Heidenstam of Sweden *In* Nobel Prize Winners in Literature p189-97 1901-31
Who's Who

Obituaries

N Y Herald Tribune p22 My 21 '40 por
N Y Times p23 My 21 '40
Pub W 137:2224 Je 8 '40

HEMING, ARTHUR HENRY HOWARD Jan 17, 1870—Oct 30, 1940 Artist, noted for his paintings of Canada's North and woodlands; color blind until age of 60, Heming sketched in only three tones, black, white and yellow; when he was able to see color painted in vivid shades with such

Richard Jack

A. H. H. HEMING

success that the Fine Arts Society of London invited him to give a one-man exhibition; particularly liked to show early historical figures against a background of wild life; wrote and illustrated a number of animal stories, among them *Spirit Lake* and *The Living Forest*

References

    International Who's Who
    Who's Who in America 1922-23
    Who's Who in American Art

Obituaries

    N Y Herald Tribune p22 O 31 '40
    por
    N Y Times p23 O 31 '40

HENDERSON, LEON May 26, 1895- Economist; member of the National Defense Commission

Address: b. Federal Reserve Bldg, Washington, D. C.; h. Millville, New Jersey

The career of Leon Henderson ever since he came to Washington in 1934 has aroused more controversy than that of any other member of the President's National Defense Commission. Henderson, who describes himself as a broker in economic ideas, and who looks like a Sunday-supplement caricature of a radical," is the terror and despair of those who oppose New Deal economic policies, for it is he who is supposed to be, and is, largely responsible for much of the economic activity that comes out of Washington.

It was Henderson who was one of the first and sternest evangelists of the consumer-purchasing power theory, today the New Deal's avowed economic policy. It was Henderson who shouted for relief expenditures. It was Henderson who was foremost in urging an attack on business

monopoly. It is Henderson who "has put his mark on the present Administration more firmly than anyone save Mr. Roosevelt." "A baffling mixture of personal humility and moral arrogance, his impact on Washington was not unlike that of the New England hurricane, except that the Henderson hurricane, after descending on Washington, has never passed."

Nevertheless, although every other appointment that Leon Henderson has received has stirred up hornets' nests, there has been surprisingly little uproar about his new job to watch over raw materials and price stabilization for the Defense Commission. Hugh Johnson, perhaps, sums this up best. "I brought Leon Henderson into this government from obscurity to an important post," he says. "I believe that he is too biased and pinkly partisan for his job in the SEC and with the monopoly committee but he will be, I think, ideal for this job."

There is no doubt that Henderson, who has already impressed business leaders with the need for holding prices down, is working as hard at this job as he has worked at everything he has ever done. He was born in Millville, New Jersey and went to school there. Then, "as the result of reading too many success stories," he decided that all he needed for riches was a college education. His father had just plunged all but 56 cents of his life-savings into the purchase of a farm, so Leon got a job long enough to earn enough money to take him to the University of Pennsylvania, from which he switched to Swarthmore College.

At Swarthmore Henderson had at least 14 sources of income. He was a newspaper reporter, referee, factory worker, salesman. He waited on table, worked on a farm, took care of children evenings and acted as secretary for Dr. Louis N. Robinson, who was later a member of President Hoover's Crime Commission. After two years of Swarthmore the War came along. Henderson served in the ordnance department starting as a private and finishing as a captain. He returned to college after the War and was graduated in 1920.

Then came a whirl at the Chautauqua business and a few years of teaching college—at the Wharton School of the University of Pennsylvania and at Carnegie Tech, where he got himself into characteristic hot water by taking his class to hear the Socialist Eugene V. Debs talk. In 1923 he began work in Pennsylvania, in charge of personnel and the classification of state employees. Then he organized the retirement system; later he became director of accounts and deputy secretary of the Commonwealth. With a new Administration Henderson's jobs in Pennsylvania—he held five simultaneously under Pinchot—were divided into $28,000 worth of titles. His pay had been $5,000 a year.

In 1925 Henderson married Myrlie Hamm (they have three children) and started to work for the Russell Sage Foun-

LEON HENDERSON

dation in New York City, where he stayed for eight years. Here he was director of the department of remedial loans and it was his job to run down loan sharks. Largely through the efforts of his department, laws against loan sharks were enacted or improved in some thirty states during the eight years he was there.

Henderson got his start in the government when he attended a consumers' conference in 1934, staged by the NRA. There he roused General Hugh Johnson's admiration by the epithets he hurled against Johnson's régime as head of the NRA. Johnson immediately appointed him as temporary assistant "to be purely critical," and within two months Henderson was made head of the NRA division of research and planning. As such he made reports on various industries, including one in which "every sore toe in the automobile industry was carefully trod upon."

Henderson was a member of the National Industry Recovery Board in 1935 when the Supreme Court knocked the blue eagle off its perch. He got a job then as economic advisor to the Senate committee on manufacturers but left it to become economic adviser to the Democratic National Campaign Committee at the request of President Roosevelt. His job as economist for the Democratic Committee was certainly the most peaceful position Henderson ever had. It was while he was turning out data for campaign use that he saw coming the slump that anti-New Dealers labeled the "Roosevelt Recession" a year later. "No blushing violet," he made as much noise as possible about it, and while other economists shilly-shallied over the need for "more facts," Henderson was proved right.

In 1936 Henderson showed his "phenomenal vigor and his facility for digesting great gobs of statistics, transforming them into entrancing, apparently profound diagnoses of national ills." He wrote a treatise entitled *Boom or Bust* when he was a consulting economist of the WPA, a job which he kept until 1938, when he became executive secretary of the newly created Temporary National Economic Committee.

Before the TNEC investigation, for which he was considered largely responsible, Henderson said: "We are in a strategic point in our economy. If we go on as we are, we are in for stagnation and decline. We do not stop. We either go forward or back." He believed that the investigation had to find a way to increase the earning-consuming quotient of the nation's low-pay masses. Through Henderson's "swift and durable head" passed all the data presented to the committee—tables of statistics, price charts, graphs. As executive secretary and then as committee member he was, it has been said, the "guiding genius" of the committee, even though his appointment, according to Raymond Moley, "sent chills down the spine of the business community."

In May 1939 there was even more fuss about a Henderson appointment. He was appointed a member of the Securities and Exchange Commission to fill the vacancy left when William O. Douglas was appointed to the Supreme Court, and his appointment "aroused more criticism and resentment than the naming of any other member to that agency in the five years of its existence." Because he had little technical knowledge of finance, because of his opposition to "big business," because of his truculent temper, Wall Street tried to head off his appointment, couldn't and was more or less calmed by the appointment of Jerome Frank as the SEC's chairman. As member of the TNEC and as SEC member, Henderson has repeatedly affirmed and reaffirmed his hatred of monopoly and his sincere belief in competition. It is as deep, he says, "as a declaration of faith."

Raymond Moley calls Leon Henderson "the Falstaff of New Deal economists," and there seems some superficial justification for the epithet. Truculent, harried, Henderson whirls around Washington "in clothes almost sensationally unkempt." In summer when you call he may receive you with his 200 and more pounds clad only in shorts and then proceed to argue either classical or radical economies long and well, fishing thousands of statistics from the depths of his mind as he goes along.

Shortish, dark, with immense shoulders and chest, Henderson has a temper inconsistent with Falstaffian jollity. On one 10-day trip to New York he had fights with two taxicab drivers and one truck driver. Then he went to a football game and tossed a drunk over a parapet into the arms of three policemen, who tossed *him* in jail. Once at Swarthmore, in a huff at the coach who told him to retire from the basketball court, he took off his clothes and marched out naked, and once as an economics instructor, when a football hero he had flunked got nasty, Henderson threw him down the steps. Though he calls himself "the best damned no-trump player in the United States," he has been known to put his fist through the card table when his bridge luck is against him. He can get just as truculent when he is championing the consumer, swinging statistics about to show the influence of rigid prices on the cost of living.

References

Business Week p7 F 16 '35 por; p18 S 10 '38 por; p13 D 3 '38 por; p15 S 14 '40 por
Collier's 103:13+ Ja 7 '39 por
Lit Digest 117:38 Ap 7 '34 por
New Repub 99:3 My 10 '39
N Y Times pl, 15 My 29 '40
Newsweek 13:43 My 8 '39; 16:64 O 7 '40
Sat Eve Post 212:11 Mr 30 '40 por
Scholastic 34:24S My 6 '39 por
Time 32:13 D 12 '38 por; 33:20 My 1 '39 por
America's Young Men
Who's Who in America
Who's Who in the Nation's Capital

HENDERSON, SIR NEVILE MEYRICK June 10, 1882- Diplomat

Address: Lyncroft, Oxford, near Sevenoaks, Kent, England

The Second World War was declared on Sunday, September 3, 1939. On Monday morning, September 4, The Right Honorable Sir Nevile Henderson left Berlin and shortly after 8 p. m. on Thursday, September 7 reached Victoria Station. "It had taken us three days and eight hours to get from Berlin to London," Sir Nevile says in *Failure of a Mission.* "My mission to Berlin had terminated and the failure was complete."

Sir Nevile Henderson began this mission in 1937. As British Ambassador to Germany he went there determined "to do my utmost to see the good side of the Nazi régime as well as the bad and to explain as objectively as I could its aspirations and viewpoint to His Majesty's Government," and determined "to labor for an honourable peace." He says: "I was, above all, convinced that the peace of Europe depended upon the realization of an understanding between Britain and Germany."

In a *Blue Book* published in England at the end of September 1939, in a *White Paper* given out at the end of October, and in his autobiographical *Failure of a Mission,* published in March and April 1940 in *Life* Magazine in condensed form, and in book form in April 1940, Sir Nevile Henderson has told the story of his attempt, and his failure, to avert the calamity of European war. *Failure of a Mission* was selected as the May 1940 Book-of-the-Month Club choice.

In the documents which Sir Nevile sent as his reports to Lord Halifax, British Foreign Secretary, he contrived to bring to the Stationery Office publications the "quality of the best seller." The 75,000 first printing of the British *Blue Book* sold like hot cakes in London, for in it he had "turned in a world scoop, a still warm drop of the very blood of history," a terrifying picture of how war is born, some penetrating glimpses of Goering, Von Ribbentrop, Von Weizsäcker and, above all, a never-to-be-forgotten firsthand sketch of Hitler.

The *White Paper,* written as Sir Nevile's final report to Lord Halifax (see sketch this issue) and released at the end of October 1939, is a 12,000-word intensive study of Hitler, the Nazis and the German nation. "Perceptive, witty and compassionate as a Jane Austen novel or a Lytton Strachey biography, it steers hard away from the old 1914 concept of the Germans as Huns or their ruler as the Beast of Berlin." Instead it describes them as understandable dupes and Hitler as a powerful but pitiable man.

Failure of a Mission is a story of world drama told within a few months of its happening by one of its principal actors. Looking back over the three years of his mission Sir Nevile sees them as Greek tragedy moving inexorably toward disaster in spite of anything that can be done to avert it.

The year 1937 is, to him, the background of the drama. It was a time of preparation for Germany, of increasing military might and impatience to march on toward the glowing destiny of the Third Reich which Hitler had proclaimed. Throughout this section of the book are given descriptions of Sir Nevile's meetings with Hitler, Goering, Hess, Von Ribbentrop, Himmler and the other Nazi leaders.

The years 1938 and 1939 are treated by Henderson as the tragedy proper, divided into four acts: Austria, Czechoslovakia, the occupation of Prague and Poland. Sir Neville was alert in those tragic days when Schuschnigg played out his desperate game in Austria. He waited tensely while the fate of Czechoslovakia trembled in the balance between May 21 and 28, 1938, and in September went to join Chamberlain on his visits to Berchtesgaden and Godesberg. Henderson was witness to Munich. There were the desperate months when he tried to save Poland until, after the last hopeless appeals and ultimatums, France and England were brought into the War.

H. V. Kaltenborn (see sketch this issue) says of *Failure of a Mission*: "This is the first source book on the Second World War. It will remain one of the most important." John Gunther states: "It is not an indiscreet book— no one of the type of Nevile Henderson could ever be more than mildly indiscreet—but there are sidelights on the Nazi leaders of the utmost value. I read these pages with complete fascination. They are indispensable to the student of contemporary world tragedy." *Failure of a Mission* is both an important historical record and a very human story, the story of a man who failed disastrously but who tried with "every resource of heart and mind compatible with honor

HENDERSON, SIR NEVILE—*Continued*
to keep the lamps from going out all over Europe once again."

Sir Nevile Henderson, knighted in 1932, was appointed to his post as Ambassador to Germany after a long and varied career in the British diplomatic service. He was born on June 10, 1882, at Sedgwick Park, Horsham, Sussex, England. His father, Robert Henderson, who died in 1895, was for a long time a director of the Bank of England. His mother, Emma Hargreaves, was a sister of Reginald Hargreaves, who married the original of *Alice in Wonderland,* Alice Liddell. Sir Nevile's grandfather, also Robert Henderson, was a Scot who had gone South about 100 years before and had made a fortune in England.

Sir Nevile was educated at Eton, 1895 to 1900, and then went abroad to study languages before going into the diplomatic service. He entered the British Foreign Office in May 1905 and was sent to St. Petersburg as an attaché in December of that year. The 1905 Revolution came while he was in St. Petersburg and he watched the occupation of Bosnia and Herzeviinia and the beginning of the Balkan crisis which led to the First World War. It was during this first appointment that he nearly brought his budding career to an end by all but strangling his chief, the British Ambassador, Sir Arthur Nicolson, whom he mistook for a burglar.

Sir Nevile was in Japan from 1909 to 1912 and marked the occupation of Korea and Japan's first advance into the mainland of Asia. He was in Rome in 1914 at the outbreak of War and in Serbia during her fight against Austria in 1914 and 1915. From 1915 through the peace conference he was in Paris. Four times, during the course of the War, he tried to resign from the Foreign Office to join the army, but was refused every time.

After the War, Henderson continued to be in the thick of things and went to Constantinople in 1921. Mustapha Kemel and Turkey were a main spot of interest in those years. When Sir Horace Rumbold left, Sir Nevile remained in charge as acting high commissioner in Constantinople from 1922 to 1924. In 1924 he returned to England, but was sent out on 24 hours' notice with the rank of Minister to reinforce Lord Allenby's staff in Cairo.

1928 and 1929 found Sir Nevile in Paris with the rank of Minister (second in command at the Embassy), and it was during this period that the Kellogg Pact was signed. At the end of 1929, Sir Nevile was sent to Belgrade, again as Minister, but this time in sole charge. This was his first absolutely independent diplomatic appointment, although he had been acting high commissioner at Constantinople and Cairo. In Belgrade diplomatic relations were complicated by the invariably bad relations between Italy and Yugoslavia, the internal dispute with Croatia, the dictatorship of King Alexander and his murder at Marseille in 1934.

Sir Nevile's next post was in Argentina. He remained in Buenos Aires from November 1935 to March 1937 during which period the Anglo-Argentine Trade Agreement was concluded. In March 1937 he set out for Germany and his mission that failed.

Sir Nevile Henderson is unmarried. He is good at and likes golf, fishing and polo, but his favorite sport is hunting. His ability to shoot a stag through the heart with one bullet did much to win him Goering's favor, an important asset during those troubled years in Germany.

References

Atlan 165:791-7 Je '40
Scholastic 36:10 Ap 8 '40 por
Time 34:26 O 2 '39; 34:29-30 O 30 '39
Henderson, N. Failure of a Mission 1940
International Who's Who
Who's Who

HENIE, SONJA (hĕn'ē)　Apr 8, 1913-
Champion ice skater; motion picture actress
Address: b. Twentieth Century-Fox Film Corp, Beverly Hills, California

No other feminine sports figure in the world is the drawing card that Sonja Henie is. And no other feminine athlete to date has made as much money as Sonja Henie has made from her skating. It got her into the movies and together with her ice shows has netted her more than a million dollars—some say two million.

Sonja Henie has turned an athletic performance into an art. She performs the standard ice skating figure executions, but she puts beauty, sex appeal and theatre into them. Typical of how Sonja revolutionized amateur figure skating is her performance in Oslo, Norway in 1927 when she won her first world's figure championship for women. Six women skaters had appeared before her in the contest. All were quietly and modestly dressed, all cut their figures accurately and exhibited excellent technique. Polite applause greeted their efforts. Then the judges announced, "Fröken Sonja Henie," and a small figure in a dazzling white silk and ermine costume with very abbreviated skirt skated out, spread what there was of her skirt in a curtsey, and gave the judges a big smile. Sonja skated with her dimpled smile working full force; she dramatized every figure, like a ballet dancer, with a tilt of the head and a swing of the free leg. She brought something new and exciting to skating and she soon had a host of imitators.

Miss Henie won the world championship figure skating contests for 10 consecutive years, an unequaled record. She also won the seven European championship contests she entered and the Olympic championships in 1928, 1932 and 1936. And when she terminated her amateur career in March 1936 it was only to begin a new and fabulously successful professional career.

Two great worries of Sonja Henie's life were first that she might kill or maim herself in her dangerous profession and second her friends' concern over her unmarried state. She corrected the latter on July 4, 1940 by marrying Daniel Reid Topping, New York sportsman, in Chicago, after a romance which had been making the headlines for several months, but which Sonja denied had any significance.

As for the danger in her skating, Sonja says that despite all precautions, she has taken falls which she believes would have killed a less experienced skater. To keep the ice clear of objects that might send her spinning upside down while she is traveling at 35 miles an hour, her troupe is forbidden to wear hairpins, and the electrical superstructure over the rink is scrupulously vacuumed. The shapely Henie legs are insured against accident for the largest sum Lloyds of London would underwrite, $5,000 a week.

The "queen of the ice," as she had been called, first put on skates when she was eight years old. Her father, Wilhelm Henie, an Oslo fur merchant and once a champion amateur bicycle rider, got them for her for Christmas of that year, and her brother Leif gave her her first lesson. By the following year the chubby little blond Sonja had practiced so diligently that she won Oslo's junior competition. Five years later, when she was only 14, she won the Norwegian championship. Much of what happened in those years and later is told in her autobiography, *Wings on My Feet* (October 1940).

That year, 1924, was an Olympic year, and Sonja went to Chamonix to try out in the games. The little Norwegian champion placed third and was so disappointed she withdrew from competition and began practicing seven hours a day. Sonja could not brook serious rivals and with characteristic determination she set out not to have any. Because Norway had no indoor rinks and had good ice only for several months, Sonja followed the ice and Papa Henie financed lessons with teachers in Germany, England, Switzerland and Austria. To develop her sense of rhythm Sonja studied ballet under Madame Karsavina in London. There was nothing too hard or too trying for Sonja to do so that she might excel in her career. Her mother traveled with her and was her constant companion even after she turned professional.

In 1926 Miss Henie entered the world's championship matches at Stockholm and placed second. There followed another year of training, and in 1927 she came in first. In the ensuing 10 years her reign as amateur queen of the ice was undisputed. Kings, princes, queens, official dignitaries were her devoted fans. Norway's King Haakon (see sketch June issue) telegraphed her before each public performance. In Nor-

SONJA HENIE

way huge crowds met her at trains, docks. She was a national idol such as Norway had not worshiped since Ibsen.

But Sonja still had one ambition—to become a movie actress—and with the advice of an American friend and promoter she planned to go out of amateur athletics in a blaze of glory in the 1936 Olympics and then go to Hollywood. But despite a sensationally successful barnstorming tour through the United States, Sonja found no Hollywood producers knocking at her door. So far as Hollywood knew, Miss Henie was just another woman athlete. So Sonja gave a skating exhibition in Hollywood and showed them.

Twentieth Century-Fox offered her stardom, and in 1937 the "Pavlova of the Ice" made her debut in pictures. From the first, her pictures were a tremendous success. *One in a Million* played to packed houses; *Second Fiddle* was equally successful. The five-year contract for two pictures a year at an average of about $125,000 a picture was proving a good investment. In the *Motion Picture Herald's* exhibitors' poll in 1939 Miss Henie was placed as Hollywood's third ranking box office attraction, following only Shirley Temple and Clark Gable. Critics were less enthusiastic concerning her acting ability. Her motion picture success also increased her drawing ability in her ice exhibitions. Henie ice revues sold tickets with a top of $4.40, and the shows she put on, as extravagantly staged and costumed as any musical comedy, were often sellouts in advance. Her latest show is *It Happens on Ice*, which opened in October 1940. With sets by Norman Bel Geddes (see sketch this issue), humor by Joe Cook and ice skating by "young women who not only are beautiful but also have that special air of radiant health which for

HENIE, SONJA—*Continued*

some reason seems to attack all disciples of this difficult art," still, because Miss Henie is only a producer and not a performer, the attendance hasn't matched that of her other shows.

Miss Henie is shrewd in her business dealings, knows what she wants. Once a roly-poly, the little skater, five-feet-two, now weighs 110 pounds; takes two massages a day, one in the afternoon, the other before retiring; diets carefully; never smokes. Even on vacations, strenuous exercise is a daily routine for her; if not skating, then swimming, expert skiing or tennis (she once ranked second on Norway's list of most skillful women tennis players.)

After almost 20 years of skating Miss Henie is still at the apex of her career—a record few professional athletes can equal.

References

Am Mag 124:32-3+ N '37 pors
N Y Times p15 Jl 5 '40
New Yorker 16:38 O 19 '40
Newsweek 15:38 Ja 29 '40 pors
Time 34:51-4 Jl 17 '39 il pors
Henie, S. Wings on My Feet 1940
International Motion Picture Almanac

HENRY-HAYE, GASTON (hĕn'rē-hā or än'rē-ī) 1889- French Ambassador to the United States

Address: b. 1601 V St, N W, Washington, D. C.

Gaston Henry-Haye arrived in the United States in September 1940 to take up his new duties as Ambassador from the Vichy government. He stepped out of the plane to be greeted by pickets bearing the legends, "Heil Haye"; "Haye, Made in Germany." "Gee whiz," said the Ambassador. Then he hastened to add: "I am pro-French. I have no brown shirt, just white ones," and he affirmed that any charges that he opposed French armaments and made friends with the Nazis are "unfounded and stupid."

Those who accuse the new Ambassador of pro-German sympathies point out his "curious association" with the German Ambassador to Vichy, Herr Abetz, alleged to be the underground pre-War organizer of the Fifth Column in France. They quote his desire for a new "dynamic" state; his urging of the Chamber of Deputies and the Senate to do business with Hitler and Mussolini and not offend them; his opposition to "frantic and hysterical" rearmament. In answer to them M. Henry-Haye reminds the American public that he opposed the evacuation of the Rhineland and voted for the construction of the Maginot Line. As he explains the situation: "I was one of the political men who favored some kind of *modus vivendi* between the French and German nations. I knew we were not prepared

for a war against Germany. Unfortunately, history has shown that I was right."

Robert Murphy, Chargé d'Affaires of the American Embassy in Vichy, strongly supports M. Henry-Haye. He is, he says, "a courageous man, a patriotic Frenchman and the best man for the position. . . Any thought of him being Nazi or pro-German is the bunk." At least fourteen prominent American writers disagree with him, however, for on October 26 a joint statement was issued suggesting that we "beware of the men of Vichy who now spread the seeds of totalitarianism in America" and describing Henry-Haye and others as "pathetic wooden mannikins mouthing the words of the Nazi ventriloquists." Actually, the consensus of opinion seems to be that the new Ambassador is a Rightist who loves France and who presumably will serve the best interests of the Vichy régime.

It is going to need someone who is as "genial, astute and successful a politician" as Henry-Haye to do this. First of all there is the problem of our attitude toward the Pétain (see sketch this issue) régime, complicated by the relation of the United States toward the French colonial empire. One ticklish situation in this relationship has already arisen—the Pétain government is reported as intending to bolster the fortifications on Martinique Island, a plan which Roosevelt far from approves. Others will certainly arise and there may be cases in which our government's interests will be better served by recognizing the forces of "free Frenchmen" under De Gaulle (see sketch this issue).

There is a feeling in some quarters that the appointment of M. Henry-Haye, rumored to have been made through the intervention of our Ambassador to France, William C. Bullitt (see sketch this issue), removes the danger of President Roosevelt's withdrawing recognition from the Pétain government. Actually, however, in receiving the new Ambassador, the President made no reference to the Vichy government and said only that he was "pleased to hear that France in its travail bears still in its heart the ideals for which it took up arms." It should be remembered, too, that an acceptance of change in ambassadors of governments with which we have maintained diplomatic relations doesn't imply either recognition or non-recognition but merely a continuation of the *status quo*.

Another problem which M. Henry-Haye faces is that of the French credits now frozen in this country. Partly in answer to the fears of those who hesitate to release them, he told the members of the French Chamber of Commerce of the United States that he was surprised by the feeling in America that the Vichy government was a mere puppet of the Germans. "France is not dead," said M. Henry-Haye. "You will see very shortly that the spirit of all true Frenchmen still is alive."

It was the same sort of reply that he gave to those who picketed New York's swank Fefe's Monte Carlo, where he was a guest of the Friends of France, Incorporated. He looked at the signs of the members of the Committee to Defend America by Aiding the Allies ("Give all aid to Britain"; "Down with Henry-Haye, emissary of the Vichy government") and said: "If I understand their purpose they are picketing against food that should reach France through the blockade. If that is their purpose I feel sorry for them, but I want to assure them that no food sent from here to France will fall into German hands." One of M. Henry-Haye's main jobs, undoubtedly, is to get supplies of food and medicine to "my suffering country."

There is no question that the new Ambassador is well fitted for his complicated task—he knows America well and he is an eloquent writer and speaker, whether in French or in fluent English. This gray-haired, partly bald, ruddy-complexioned Frenchman was born at Chatou, a small town on the Seine near Paris. His family was not rich and when his father died he had to work. He decided to go to the United States and in 1906 arrived here to work as a bellboy in a large New York hotel and eventually to work with the American Worthing Pumps. Several times he crossed the continent, on foot, by car and train, by bicycle. Once he was arrested as a tramp, it is reported.

When the First World War broke out Henry-Haye returned to France to fight, and rose from a non-commissioned officer to captain. He saw heavy fighting in Champagne, on the Somme and at Verdun; was wounded; was cited five times for bravery and awarded the Légion d'Honneur and the Croix de Guerre. In 1917, when the United States entered the War, he was sent to America to instruct recruits and did a good job of it. He liked it, too. "My Sammies and I were the best pals in the world," he says. "I taught them soldiering and they taught me their *joie de vivre*, their great American optimism which has been a big help to me in life ever since."

After a year in the United States M. Henry-Haye returned to France but was back in this country in 1919 on a money-raising campaign for France and as the representative of coal consumers who were trying to buy coal. He put his son Pierre in school here and went all over the country, writing and lecturing, extolling France as the savior of democracy and pleading for money for her rehabilitation. His mission was considered a "brilliant success."

From 1921 to 1928 M. Henry-Haye was in business (industrial research) in Paris and at the same time active in war veterans' activities. Unknown in politics, he suddenly decided to run for Deputy from Versailles. He appeared from nowhere without any political tag, backing or connection with any party and announced: "I am a Repub-

GASTON HENRY-HAYE

lican Democrat but I am going to attack parliamentary customs and morals and the routine of bureaucracy which are the bane of my country." He was elected. In 1932 he was re-elected and in 1935 he was sent to the Senate, representing the department of Seine-et-Oise as an *Indépendant de Gauche*.

In the Senate M. Henry-Haye was a key figure in the Senatorial Commission on Foreign Affairs, known for his "purely pragmatic politics" and his gift for oratory; for his urging of a "dynamic" policy and his belief that direct negotiations with Hitler and Mussolini would avert war. In 1935 he was elected Mayor of the City of Versailles. Several times in his career M. Henry-Haye was offered ministerial portfolios. Each time he refused. "I prefer to be first in my village," he said, "rather than a cipher among the ephemeral and interchangeable excellencies who run our country so badly."

As Mayor of Versailles M. Henry-Haye did a good deal of city planning and also erected a monument in honor of French-American friendship and the A. E. F. When the Blitzkrieg struck he saved Versailles from being burned and pillaged—he had things so well in hand that "scarcely a teacup was cracked"—and later fed and provided for the 10,000 inhabitants who refused to abandon their homes.

During the Blitzkrieg and afterward M. Henry-Haye repeatedly told the world that in the hearts of Frenchmen was "a force which no power can crush." It was with this thought and the statement that "the ideal for the defense of which my countrymen courageously took up arms again only 20 years after the most bloody of victories, still remains alive in the heart of French men" that M. Henry-Haye presented his credentials from the Vichy government of

HENRY-HAYE, GASTON—*Continued*
Marshal Pétain to President Roosevelt and
the American people.

References
> Christian Sci Mon p4 N 16 '40 por
> N Y Herald Tribune p3 Jl 31 '40 por;
> p6 S 7 '40 por; p3 S 14 '40; p5 S
> 28 '40
> N Y Times p6 Jl 31 '40; p18 Ag 11 '40;
> p2 S 7 '40 por; p4 S 14 '40 por; p12
> S 29 '40; p8 O 2 '40
> PM p9 S 6 '40; p9 S 8 '40; p7 S 17 '40;
> p8 O 27 '40 por; p7 O 28 '40; p7 N 1
> '40

HERING, HERMANN S. (hā'rĭng) Aug
24, 1864—May 15, 1940 Christian Science lecturer; formerly first reader and president of
the Mother Church in Boston; became interested in Christian Science in 1893; worked with
Mrs. Mary Baker Eddy

References
> Who's Who in America

Obituaries
> N Y Herald Tribune p23 My 16 '40

HERRICK, FRANCIS HOBART Nov 19,
1858—Sept 11, 1940 Professor emeritus of
biology at Western Reserve University;
widely known for his study of the American
eagle; spent years in study of the bird, even
erecting a tent on a platform in a tree to
observe eagles day and night; author of
many books on American wild life

FRANCIS H. HERRICK

References
> American Men of Science
> Leaders in Education 1932
> Who's Who in America

Obituaries
> N Y Herald Tribune p20 S 13 '40

HERTZ, EMANUEL Sept 2, 1870—May
23, 1940 Attorney; outstanding authority on
Abraham Lincoln; wrote 70 books on Lincoln;
collector of thousands of rare items relating to
the President; presented Lincoln documents to
the Library of Congress

EMANUEL HERTZ

References
> Who's Who in America
> Who's Who in American Jewry

Obituaries
> N Y Herald Tribune p18 My 24 '40
> por
> N Y Times p19 My 24 '40
> Newsweek 15:2 Je 3 '40
> Pub W 137:2145 Je 1 '40

HEYWARD, DU BOSE Aug 31, 1885—
June 16, 1940 Novelist of Negro life; poet;
wrote *Porgy* and *Mamba's Daughters;*
George Gershwin did the music for *Porgy
and Bess* made from his novel

References
> Sat R Lit 20:14 Ag 19 '39 por
>
> Allen, H. Du Bose Heyward pam nd
> Clark, E. Du Bose Heyward *In* In-
> nocence Abroad p235-50 1931
> Hatcher, H. H. Exploiting the Negro
> *In* Creating the Modern American
> Novel p140-51 1935
> Kunitz, S. J. ed. Living Authors 1937
> Who's Who
> Who's Who in America

DU BOSE HEYWARD

Obituaries

N Y Herald Tribune p14 Je 17 '40 por
N Y Times p15 Je 17 '40 por

HILL, EDWIN C. Apr 23, 1884- Columnist; radio commentator

Address: b. 515 Madison Ave, New York City

Edwin Conger Hill (he uses only the initial of his middle name) had a long career as a star reporter before he became a columnist and a radio commentator. Even as far back as his public school days in his home town of Aurora, Indiana his ambition was to become a newspaperman. The son of Harvey Boone and Mary (Conger) Hill, he was born April 23, 1884. Upon his graduation from Indiana University in 1901 he began his newspaper career as a cub reporter on the old Indianapolis *Sentinel*. Later he moved on to the *Press* and the *Journal* of the same city and then on to Fort Wayne and Cincinnati.

He had already covered important assignments, such as the funeral of President Benjamin Harrison and an interview with James Whitcomb Riley, when he came to New York and a position on the New York *Sun* in 1904. He began by writing on space rates for the *Sun*, a precarious business at best. Just at that time the empty Proctor Theatre was slighly damaged by fire. Hill's story of the small fire and what might have happened won him his first recognition on the paper: it was such an excellent account that it was put on the front page. It was the first of a long series of poignant human-interest stories written by Hill, and within a few months the Hoosier boy was one of New York's crack reporters, covering the most important stories of the time.

Hill remained on the New York *Sun* until 1923. He met the great and the near great. He traveled with President Theodore Roosevelt; went to Europe, South America and Central America on assignments. He attended state and national conventions; he wrote about murders, about wrecks and inconsequential human-interest stories; he covered the sinking of the *Titanic*. He was, in a word, one of New York's star reporters.

Edwin C. Hill was one of the best-dressed newspapermen in New York. When he began interviewing important personages he decided that he would dress to impress visitors. He was one of the first to sport a cane in Park Row. Tall, courtly in manner, he made an impressive appearance.

By 1923 Hill felt he had exhausted the possibilities of newspaper work. He had a fling at the movies, working for Fox Film Corporation as newsreel director, scenario editor and supervisor in Hollywood.

But his movie career was comparatively short-lived. In 1927 he appeared at the *Sun* office. "A real newspaperman will never be content with any other job," he said, and went back to the old grind as a feature writer. Later he went to the King Features Syndicate, and his column, *The Human Side of the News*, was syndicated and appears in many newspapers throughout the country.

Hill has a deep, rich voice that was a "natural" for radio, bringing to it dramatic and graphic pictures of news stories. He made his first appearance in radio in 1931. In 1932 he had a contract to broadcast *The Human Side of the News* five times a week. The popularity of these broadcasts spread, and in addition he was called upon to conduct special radio programs to give his impressions of great news events. The

EDWIN C. HILL

HILL, EDWIN C.—*Continued*

Radio Editors of America in 1933 and 1934 elected him leading news commentator. Although news commentators since that time have increased and there is hardly a station that does not have several newscasts a day, Hill's program has remained steadily on the networks.

Hill divides his time between writing his syndicated column, broadcasting and other writing. He has published a novel, *The Iron Horse* (1925), based on the conquest of the West by the railroad builders; *The American Scene* (1933), which reviewed events of the year 1932; and *The Human Side of the News* (1934). Despite his activity he finds time for recreation. He likes horseback riding and golf and is an ardent fly fisherman.

He was married in 1922 to Miss Jane Gail of New York City.

References

Hill, E. C. Human Side of the News 1934
Variety Radio Directory
Who's Who in America

HILL, HOWARD COPELAND Dec 20, 1878—June 25, 1940 Professor of social sciences at the University of Chicago; author of 50 textbooks on social science, literature and economics

References

Who's Who in America
Who's Who in American Education

Obituaries

N Y Herald Tribune p22 Je 26 '40
Pub W 138:38 Jl 6 '40

HILLMAN, SIDNEY Mar 23, 1887- Labor leader; member of the National Defense Commission

Address: b. Federal Reserve Bldg, Room 2055, Washington, D. C.; h. 237 E 20th St, New York City

In May 1940 President Roosevelt appointed a National Defense Commission to energize American industry for mass production of the weapons our armed forces need. On the board, with Knudsen of General Motors (see sketch this issue) and Stettinius of United States Steel (see sketch this issue), is Sidney S. Hillman, president of the Amalgamated Clothing Workers of America, CIO.

Sidney Hillman has been placed in charge of non-military personnel for the new program. To the A F of L this has been a blow. Matthew Woll, vice-president of the A F of L, attacked the appointment sharply; to him Hillman of the clothing industry is not competent "to deal with employment problems affecting workers in the metal trades, aviation, steel, munitions and other industries vitally and directly concerned with national defense." To other A F of L leaders it seems unfair that both the A F of L and the CIO haven't been given representation. Part of the CIO, too, isn't completely satisfied with the appointment because of differences of opinion between him and John L. Lewis which had been going on for some time before the November 1940 CIO convention, at which the friction seems to have been smoothed over, particularly by the election of Philip Murray (see sketch this issue) to the presidency of the CIO.

To much of the country at large, however, Sidney Hillman is a good man for the job, one of the main hopes for labor's teamwork in working for industrial preparedness. For almost 30 years he has been in the labor movement. For 25 years he has been president of the Amalgamated Clothing Workers, "one of the most potent and importantly pioneering unions in the country." For almost five years he has been a leader of the CIO. And in all these years he has urged labor to be "industry conscious." "We cannot ask from industry more than it can soundly afford to give," says Hillman. On the National Defense Commission Hillman has charted a plan for voluntary youth training in technical defense jobs; he has formed his Labor Advisory Committee to avoid labor disputes; and he has aroused a good deal of controversy over his statement that government contracts should be withheld from firms which violate the National Labor Relations Act. For these activities he has been assailed. When the training plan for youth was announced Representative Cox of Georgia exclaimed: "God alone can save this Republic if our youth are put under a man like Sidney Hillman." When his announcement on government contracts, supported by Attorney General Jackson (see sketch this issue) was announced, there was a tremendous furor over the possible disruption to national defense, as a result of which both he and Jackson backed down. This, in turn, resulted in criticism from labor, which has continued to protest that his division has not been reviewing defense contracts to see that they comply with labor rules. And there has also been a good deal of criticism of his continuing to receive his salary of $12,500 a year from the Amalgamated Clothing Workers while working for the government. His answer to that was that, unlike Knudsen and Stettinius, he could not afford to forego his salary and live on $1 a year.

Sidney Hillman was born in Zagare, Russia, the son of a small merchant. As a boy he studied for the rabbinate because almost all men in his family were rabbis. But he wasn't satisfied with this. He broke with his family over orthodoxy and at 15 went to a larger city, Kovno. Here he worked in a chemical laboratory for a living and at night studied the economists. What they said came to mean for him the demand for shorter hours of work. He paraded with the students for a 10-hour day. The police attacked the parade and threw scores into jail, Hillman among them. For eight months he was in jail. After he got out he fled to England, where a prosperous uncle received him cordially. But he stayed there only seven months.

In 1907 he came to America—to Chicago. For two years he was a clerk and then went to Hart, Schaffner and Marx to learn the trade of a cutter of men's garments. For a while he worked without pay; then he made $6 a week. Three years later he was still there making $11 a week for 54 hours' work.

Conditions generally were terrible in the clothing industry. Children of 12 worked in the shops or at "home work." There was night work, speed up, low pay, long hours. In some places there were no toilets or drinking water so employees wouldn't have to take any time off from their work.

On September 22, 1910 five girls struck against Hart, Schaffner and Marx. They were joined by 6,000 other employees. Within three weeks 45,000 other men's garment workers in Chicago were on strike. For the first 10 weeks Hillman was a picket. Then he was chosen one of a committee to combat the influence of William Haywood, who was trying to lead the strikers into the IWW camp. Eventually Hillman was leading the strike. The Hart, Schaffner and Marx employees won theirs and got an agreement, the main point of which was the setting-up of an arbitration committee. The rest of the clothing employees, however, had to call off their strike.

Hillman's skill in the strike brought him a call in 1914 to do for the women's garment industry what the Hart, Schaffner and Marx agreement was doing for the men's clothing industry. He became chief clerk of the Cloakmakers' Union in New York and was doing fine when his own union called him back to lead a fight against the United Garment Workers to which it belonged. The members were dissatisfied with their "autocratic" leadership, with the failure of the leadership to recognize their problems. When dissenting delegates were barred from the national convention they held a convention of their own and asked the A F of L to recognize them rather than the other group. Hillman they nominated for president, warning him of the dangers to him in accepting this job in an "upstart" union. He gave up his job in New York and stayed. "When I came to America," he said, "I looked for a nine-dollar job and I was worth all of six. Well, the tailors made me. They can have me."

He led the revolt and in December 1914 the Amalgamated Clothing Workers of America was formed with Hillman as president. "From then on the careers of the Amalgamated and of Hillman have been practically inseparable." Born of rebellion against autocratic rule, the Amalgamated has stressed democracy in its constitution and actions. All these years it has followed Hillman, who believes in the democratic proc-

esses and who understands the problems of the rank and file. The members, so sure of his knowledge of their problems, have even been known to cheer his recommendation that they accept a 15 per cent wage cut.

Within time the clothing workers of New York, Chicago, Rochester, Cincinnati, Montreal, Toronto and many other large cities were completely unionized, though according to Benjamin Stolberg under "lower standards than any other needle-trades union," since Hillman's aim has usually been "to gain union recognition, to collect dues directly from the employers and make as little fuss as possible about union standards." In 1937 Hillman signed a contract with the manufacturers of the men's garment industry on a national basis. Ninety-five per cent of the industry was covered and $30,000,000 in wages and increases was won for the workers.

Through the union's efforts production techniques which have increased output and saved overhead have been introduced. The manufacturers' needs have always been considered and the Amalgamated has gone so far as to lend money to firms which needed it. Before negotiations are even started a survey of the employer's business is made, and unless he can really afford raises they are not asked for.

Under Hillman's leadership the Amalgamated has established two banks, has inaugurated low-cost housing for its members, has given its members unemployment insurance. Under Hillman the Amalgamated originated the idea of an "impartial chairman" for disputes, which has been of great service to labor and industry generally. Under Hillman a union of a few thousand workers has grown to one of a quarter of a million.

Hillman has been an important figure in the labor movement as a whole, not only in his own union. The government recognized this even before his appointment to the National Defense Commission. In 1933 he was a member of the Labor Advisory Board of the NRA and used his position to bring about quickly the 36-hour week in the garment trades; in 1935 he was a member of the National Industrial Recovery Board. He has been a member of the National Advisory Board of the National Youth Administration, and in 1938 was a member of the Textile Committee of the Fair Labor Standards Board.

Hillman, too, was "Lewis' right-hand man in building up the CIO" though commentators are now prophesying a split between the forces led by the two men. In 1933 Hillman's union had finally joined the A F of L, but in 1935 it left to join the CIO. In the CIO, of which he was made first vice-president in 1937, Hillman has helped in the organization of steel, has arbitrated the factional struggle in the automobile industry and, most significant, has been in charge of the CIO's efforts to organize the textile field.

HILLMAN, SIDNEY—*Continued*

The textile field at the time he went into it was a mess: "it would take a Moses or a Mussolini to bring order out of its chaos." But within 10 months Hillman had increased the membership of the Textile Workers Organizing Committee from 30,000 to 450,000 workers and had signed contracts affecting half a million workers—all without violence or bad blood.

Although Hillman has worked to increase the strength and power of the CIO, still he is a firm believer in the necessity of A F of L-CIO unity in the labor movement today. He was a member of the committee that met in March 1939 to discuss peace, and he and his union have strongly advocated it. At the convention of May 1940 he went so far as to say that Lewis' position on peace was "a mistake" and that "labor and the nation stand to gain so much from a unified labor movement that no effort should be spared to achieve it."

There has, of course, been criticism of Sidney Hillman from both labor and capital. Labor has often assailed what it feels to be his collaborative tactics; capital has been aware of the fact that his is, on the whole, a socialist union and that he has a good deal of power in the American labor movement. Yet on the whole because he is a "conservative in the labor movement who stresses social responsibility," both employers and employees have consistently respected him. Even the caricaturists have not "gone to town" on him. That is probably, however, because there is little about him to caricature. "Except when on the platform his person and personality affect you like a quietly uttered understatement just before you recognize it as such. Then you notice the alert look in the brown eyes that make his glasses seem only an aid to an already keen vision." When on the platform his chin takes on a bulldog thrust, his voice rasps and rings, his consonants become hard and sharp and it is easy to see that his English, though correct, is acquired.

Sidney Hillman was married in 1916 to Bessie Abramowitz, one of the five girls who led the original Hart, Schaffner and Marx strike. She, too, is active in the Amalgamated Union. With their two children the Hillmans live in New York.

References

Atlan 162:47-56 Jl '38 (Same abr. Read Digest 35:104-7 Jl '39)
Business Week p33 Ag 20 '38; p28 D 24 '38 por; p37 Ja 14 '39 por; p20+ My .6 '39; p31 Je 8 '40 por; p15 O 12 '40
Canad Forum 20:50-2 My '40 por
N Y Times p41 My 17 '40; p25 My 23 '40; pl, 15 My 29 '40; p12 My 30 '40; p22 Je 11 '40; p13 Jl 6 '40; p10 O 2 '40; pl, 9 O 19 '40
Newsweek 1:19 Ap 29 '33; 11:34 My 23 '38 por; 15:55+ Je 24 '40
Sat Eve Post 213:12+ O 19 '40 il pors
Survey G 26:338-9 Je '37 por
Time 31:13 Je 20 '38 por; 33:16 Mr 13 '39 por; 34:17 O 23 '39 por; 36:15-17 D 2 '40 pors
Allen, D. ed. Labor Can Lead: Sidney Hillman *In* Adventurous Americans p233-47 1932
Soule, G. H. Sidney Hillman, Labor Statesman 1939
Who's Who in America
Who's Who in American Jewry

HILLYER, ROBERT SILLIMAN (hĭl'yēr) June 3, 1895- Poet; professor of English literature

Address: b. Harvard University, Cambridge, Massachusetts; h. Venily, Pomfret, Connecticut

A new book of verse, *Pattern of a Day,* (August 1940) is the nineteenth published volume by Robert S. Hillyer, winner of the Pulitzer Prize for poetry in 1934 and professor of English at Harvard University since 1919. In 1937 Professor Hillyer succeeded Charles Townsend Copeland to the distinguished post of Boylston professor of rhetoric and oratory at the University.

A poet who writes with excellent technique in the sound tradition of English and American verse, Robert Hillyer was born June 3, 1895 in East Orange, New Jersey, son of James Rankin and Lillian Stanley (Smith) Hillyer. His preparatory education was at Kent School, Connecticut, and he took his B. A. degree at Harvard in 1917. From 1917 to 1919 he was an ambulance driver and lieutenant with the American Expeditionary Force. In 1919 he became an English instructor at Harvard, and from 1920 to 1921 studied in Copenhagen as a fellow of the American-Scandinavian Foundation. Following two years on the faculty of Trinity College in Connecticut he returned to Harvard as associate professor in 1928 and there continued his teaching of English literature. He was married in 1926 to Dorothy Hancock Tilton of Haverhill, Massachusetts. They have one son, Stanley Hancock Hillyer, and make their home in the country near Pomfret, Connecticut.

Robert Hillyer's first book, *Sonnets and Other Lyrics,* was published when he was 22. His next two collections of verse came out in 1920: *The Five Books of Youth* and *Alchemy: A Symphonic Poem.* The latter, based upon symphonic movements, revealed the skilled understanding of and love for music that has influenced much of his writing and underlies the subtlety of his rhythm and lyric tone. In 1923 he compiled an anthology called *The Coming Forth of Day* from the Egyptian *Book of the Dead.* His next book of poems, *The Hills Give Promise,* contained lyrics and sonnets on the emotions of romantic love. Two further collections preceded *The Seventh Hill* (1928), the volume which won for him his first real recognition. The poems were commended by Louis Untermeyer and other critics for their variety of subject

Johan Durup

ROBERT S. HILLYER

and thought and for the maturity and mastery of their technical composition. Mr. Hillyer received, however, wider notice in England because his work, though written in America, was not local in treatment but had a closer identity with the Georgian tradition. It was highly praised by English writers, including Arthur Machen and Middleton Murry.

A single excursion from poetry was Mr. Hillyer's novel, *Riverhead* (1932). Combining realism and symbolism, it told the story of a young man's canoe trip up the Connecticut River and back. Hillyer's *Collected Verse*, for which he was awarded a Pulitzer Prize, appeared in 1933. No other work of importance followed till 1937, when *A Letter to Robert Frost and Others* was published. These were for the most part tributes to personal friends that were at the same time criticisms of contemporary thought and letters. Of them Mr. Untermeyer said: "Superficially like Pope, the epistles are actually Horatian in spirit; underneath the clinched couplets a living philosophy declares itself."

Pattern of a Day, Robert Hillyer's most recent volume, contains several nature lyrics with a New England background, characteristic of the poet at his best, and a few satirical character sketches. It concludes with *In Time of Mistrust,* a Phi Beta Kappa poem read at the College of William and Mary and published separately in 1939.

Several critics of poetry admire Mr. Hillyer's technical accomplishments, but deplore the fact that he is in no way concerned with the temper and events of our time. Alfred Kreymborg has said of him: "One admires the self discipline of the poet, but cannot help hoping that a gust will shatter the lamp and drive the poet outdoors." Mr. Hillyer prefers not to come

outdoors. Of contemporary poets he most admires Robert Bridges, "incomparably the greatest poet of modern times." He says further: "Most of the poets who are petulant about the wasteland of these years have been happily sheltered from the confusions they deplore." In *Unregimented,* a poem in *Pattern of a Day,* he says that he abhors poets who espouse a cause, and thinks of himself as

"Freed of all obligation to enlist
On any side, triumphant Quietist."

References

Forum 95:320, sup9 My '36
N Y Herald Tribune My 14 '37
Poetry 51:267-70 F '38
Kreymborg, A. Our Singing Strength p588-9 1929
Kunitz, S. J. ed. Authors Today and Yesterday 1933
Untermeyer, L. ed. Modern American Poetry p545+ 1936
Who's Who in America

HITZ, RALPH   Mar 1, 1891—Jan 12, 1940
Hotel executive

Ralph Hitz, perhaps America's best-known hotel host, died after a heart attack in New York on January 12, 1940, at the age of 48. He was born in Vienna and came to the United States in 1906. From a three-dollar-a-week job scrubbing floors, washing dishes and peeling potatoes, he worked his way up to the presidency of the $22,000,000 Hotel New Yorker and a chain of seven other hotels. His motto was, "Give 'em value and you get volume." He is credited with having introduced many novel ideas in hotel service which carried his hotels through the depression days.

RALPH HITZ
(Continued next page)

HITZ, RALPH—*Continued*

References

Fortune 15:139-44+ My '37 il por
Who's Who in America 1938-39

Obituaries

N Y Herald Tribune p10 Ja 13 '40 por
N Y Times p231 Ja 16 '40
Newsweek 15:41 Ja 22 '40
Script 23:22 Ja 27 '40
Time 35:75 Ja 22 '40

**HOARE, SIR SAMUEL JOHN GUR-
NEY, 2ND BART** (hōr) Feb 24, 1880-
British Ambassador to Spain

Address: 25 Cadogan Sq, London, S. W. 1,
England

Sir Samuel Hoare, England's Ambassador
to Spain, has one of the most delicate tasks
in the British Empire. In view of Franco's
obligations to Italy, now at war with England, his efforts to "promote friendly relations" between Spain and Great Britain
will need consummate diplomatic finesse.
When Sir Samuel arrived in Spain in May
1940 students immediately demonstrated
against British possession of Gibraltar and
since then Spain's cries for the fortress have
been growing ever louder.

That Sir Samuel Hoare, who was given
no place in Winston Churchill's (see sketch
this issue) War coalition, should be given
this important post is most probably due
to his well-known reputation as an "appeaser," which would make him unsuitable
for Cabinet rank in a fighting government,
yet acceptable to Spain. It should be remembered, too, that Sir Samuel opposed the
sanctions against Italy at the time of the
Ethiopian War and fathered the Hoare-
Laval plan for the partition of Ethiopia.

SIR SAMUEL HOARE

Samuel John Gurney Hoare comes of old
Quaker banking stock. The Hoares are the
oldest banking family in London; the Gur-
neys (one of whom was Samuel's great-
grandmother) are an old banking family of
Norwich. The baronetcy was created in
1899 and the first baronet married Katharine
Louisa Hart Davis. Their son, Samuel, was
educated at Harrow and at New College, Oxford, where he stood out both as a scholar
and as an athlete. He took a "double first"
in classics and a "first class" in history and
represented his University in skating and
tennis. He married Lady Maud Lygon,
daughter of the Earl of Beauchamp.

In 1905 Hoare became assistant private
secretary to the Honorable A. Lyttleton, the
Colonial Secretary, and in the following year
had an unsuccessful shot at Parliament by
standing for Ipswich. He turned to municipal
politics after his defeat and served on the
London County Council, where his special
interest was education and his special desire
to see smaller classes and higher salaries
for teachers.

In 1910 the Conservative Party accepted
Hoare as candidate for Chelsea, a London
constituency which includes a good many
impecunious artists as well as a good many
arrived ones and which has always been a
safe Tory seat. Hoare won it easily enough
and has represented it ever since. He attended to his duties at Westminster until
the War when he joined the Norfolk Yeo-
manry as an officer. When winter came,
however, he contracted rheumatic fever and
was invalided out of the service.

While he was convalescing, Hoare decided
to learn Russian and after six months' tutoring and study could speak and write it.
The British Military Intelligence then sent
him to Russia, where he remained until the
beginning of the Kerensky régime. He was
the first Englishman to hear of the death
of Rasputin and certain persons even went
so far as to suggest he was responsible for
his murder! Because he knew Italian as
well as Russian, Hoare then went to Italy.

After the War Hoare was appointed
deputy high commissioner of the League of
Nations for the care of Russian refugees.
A year later, in 1922, Bonar Law made him
Air Minister and he held that office, except
for the brief spell of Labor rule in 1924,
until 1929. When he became Air Minister
he learned to fly, and at a time when the
Air Ministry was something of a Cinderella,
did much to forward its work.

When the second Labor government was
routed in 1929, Hoare was one of those
Conservatives who were actively engaged
in the formation of the "National Government." Mr. MacDonald included him in
his Cabinet as Secretary of State for India.
It became Hoare's task to pilot the India
Bill through the Commons—a huge and
complicated measure that ran to 400 clauses,
all of which Hoare had to know and defend
against criticism. He was opposed line by
line and clause by clause by one of the
House's most formidable debaters, Win-

ston Churchill. It was a terrific fight and John Gunther estimates that Hoare answered 15,000 questions, made 600 speeches and read 25,000 pages of reports.

When Baldwin transferred Hoare to Foreign Affairs in 1935 Sir Samuel was utterly weary with the struggle. The Abyssinian War broke out in October of that year. Hoare, who had opposed sanctions, stopped off in Paris on his way to a holiday in Switzerland and had interviews with Laval (see sketch this issue). When their joint proposals were disclosed there was immediate and widespread indignation. Members of Parliament received scores of letters from their constituents protesting against any attempt to give, Italy a large slice of Abyssinia. The London *Times* trained its heavy guns on the Foreign Secretary, and when he cut short his holiday and faced the House he found nothing but hostility. There was nothing to do but to resign.

The general feeling against Hoare was so strong that it was supposed that his political career was finished. Yet he was brought back to office again in June 1936 as first Lord of the Admiralty. In May 1937 Mr. Chamberlain made him Home Secretary and he gained a good deal of approval by bringing in a Criminal Justice Bill designed to lighten some of the more drastic penalties prescribed by law.

Sir Samuel had moved right up the ladder which leads to the Premiership, for the Home Secretaryship is the position next to the top. And yet, either because of the Hoare-Laval proposals and his general reputation of being an appeaser or because it was felt he could serve his country best in his present Ambassador's job, he found no place in Winston Churchill's coalition.

The English admire and respect Hoare for his intellectual standing, for his Oxford record, his linguistic ability, his wide literary culture, the mastery of detail evident in his management of the India Bill. But few like him, for he is a man of emotional half tones, "not one who mixes with the throng or feels at home in a crowd." In personality and in his speeches he is all cold precision and his thin voice and lack of fire have contributed toward making him "perhaps the dullest speaker in the House of Commons."

In addition to his baronetcy, to which he succeeded in 1915, Sir Samuel is a Knight of the Order of the Star of India and of the Order of the British Empire and holds honorary doctorates from the Universities of Oxford, Cambridge and Reading. At the age of 60 he is president of the Lawn Tennis Association and is still a devotee of ice skating. Alfred Duff Cooper (see sketch this issue) tells of the time Hoare invited his friends to see an exhibition of his ice-skating skill. "Slim and dapper, perfectly dressed for the occasion, he whirled around like a ballet dancer before the eyes of his astonished colleagues, seeming anxious to prove to them that there was no feat of balancing he could not perform."

References
Am Mercury 49:164-6 F '40
Liv Age 348:507-11 Ag '35
N Y Times p8 My 27 '40; p27 Je 9 '40
R Deux Mondes s8 31:231-40 Ja 1 '36
Audax, pseud. Sir Samuel Hoare *In* Men in Our Time p199-217 1940
Gunther, J. Men of Whitehall *In* Inside Europe p237-55 1936
Hoare, S. J. G. Flying Visit to the Middle East 1926
Hoare, S. J. G. India by Air 1927
International Who's Who
Nicholson, A. P. The Real Men in Public Life 1928
Watchman, pseud. Right Honourable Gentlemen 1939
Who's Who

HOBSON, JOHN ATKINSON July 6, 1858—Apr 1, 1940 English economist; author; professor

References
Hobson, J. A. Confessions of an Economic Heretic 1938
International Who's Who
Who's Who

Obituaries
N Y Herald Tribune p18 Ap 2 '40
N Y Times p25 Ap 2 '40

HOELLERING, FRANZ (hŭl'ĕr-ing) July 9, 1896- Author
Address: Box 52, Stamford, Connecticut

The Defenders (1940) is a first novel by a distinguished Austrian journalist which John Chamberlain (see sketch this issue) calls "history in the three dimensions of space and the one dimension of time" and Edmund Wilson "a steadying contribution to the creative critical consciousness of our world." Nearly 500 pages long, the novel takes as its canvas nothing less than the entire society of Vienna—Vienna of February 1934, when democracy was being slowly strangled but could still stir a little. Without theorizing or propagandizing but "through the nerve ends of a score of vital protagonists," the author, Franz Hoellering, shows how it came about that the Vienna of the country-house aristocracy, of the university and coffeehouse intellectuals, of the Socialist workers and Social Democrat bureaucracy could become finally lost to the home-grown Fascists: the Italian-controlled Heimwehr who broke the ground for Hitler by their assault on the Socialist working classes. He does it in such a way that one has "the illusion of living in Vienna with letters of introduction."

It is a broad canvas; it was a complex and disunited society. There are the escapists who in the end failed to escape; the café

FRANZ HOELLERING

society of self-centered artists and writers; Baron Weisner, the cultivated and skeptical remnant of the last War who understands what is happening but still hopes to retire from his diplomatic post to "an honorable private life"; Franz Steiger, famous scientist and director of the Technological Institute, whose science knows no politics, who says: "Leave the present to those who have ruined it... There is never a time when all is lost." There are the Socialists, never sure of when to take a stand against the government: Councilor Birkmeier, grown complacent with years of Social Democratic rule; his son Joseph, a half-hysterical radical; Hippmann, weary party leader, preaching "passive tolerance" and "calmness and unity" in the face of attack. There are the Nazis and the incipient Nazis ("we must win the next war"). And there are, finally, the workers, the Left-wing conspirators of the Defense Corps who do at least meet force with force, too late, and who go down fighting.

Weaving the many threads together is the love story of Maria Steiger, 19-year-old daughter of Professor Steiger whom Baron Weisner plans to take with him into retirement but who instead chooses the real, challenging and dangerous world of Karl Merk.

This is history, but it does what history cannot do: "it lives, it moves." It is a book that belongs to its characters and its time, the author seeming to stand aside and with almost conscious self-restraint avoiding both heroics and the kind of mysticism common to novels of similar scope, only directing its intricate architecture. He speaks with no one voice, but Lewis Gannett interprets him as saying "that the men of honor must, in this primitively dangerous

age, also learn to live—and to act—dangerously."

Whether for all its integrity this is merely the novel of a particular situation is for the reader to decide. Clifton Fadiman finds that it is not "written on a level of universality," while Leane Zugsmith accuses every character of having "a French counterpart, even an American counterpart," and Lewis Gannett says: "It is Vienna; it is all Europe; it is frighteningly like America."

Of the author himself Gannett says: "He has had a romantic, a terrifying, and an inspiring life." Born in Baden bei Wien, Austria on July 9, 1896, the son of Georg and Maria Magdelana (Zahradnik) Hoellering, Hoellering grew up in a typically Viennese atmosphere in which politics, music and the theatre played leading rôles. His mother was a German from Czechoslovakia, his father a German from the Sudetenland who moved closer to Vienna, organized a musicians' union, became a candidate of the Deutschnationale Partei for a seat in the Austrian Parliament, later founded the Wiener Tonkünstler Orchestra and became general manager of the Friends of Music in Vienna. Franz played the violin from the time he was five; read intensively; published a volume of poetry in his teens. In those years a friend with a common interest in the theatre was Elisabeth Bergner.

Hoellering had attended public schools and the Realschule in Vienna; he was 18 and a student at the University of Vienna when War broke out. Volunteering, he served on the Russian, Italian, Serbian and Romanian fronts, won every possible medal. In 1916 a copy of the Kaiser's tricky peace offer fell into his hands. In sudden disgust he returned his medals and regimental insignia to his commanding officer, announced his opposition to the War. He was not court-martialed as he had expected, however, but sent to posts at the front where he should logically have been shot. Not caring much, he survived both bullets and brandy for breakfast; was shell-shocked in 1918, sent home, returned to the front; miraculously continued to survive.

When peace came unpeacefully in 1918 he plunged into the revolutionary student movement in Vienna, where he encountered Elisabeth Bergner again. But after taking his doctorate of law and economy at the University of Vienna in 1921 (he had been studying another officer's law books for a year while at the front), he found he had lost taste for both revolution and law. He turned to the theatre. By 1926 he found himself in Berlin writing the movie script of an Ibsen play, after having edited a theatre magazine, and directed German theatres in Brno and Teplitz-Schönau. Then he became a reporter, and it was as a reporter that he conceived the idea of founding a literary magazine about sports. The magazine, *Arena,* was a success principally "because none of us knew anything about sports, so we understood our readers," and his next venture, the A. I. Z., "sort of a working-class *Life*," attained a 350,000 circulation within a year.

That same year Hoellering went to Russia to see the tenth anniversary celebration of the Revolution. He came back to Germany to resign from his paper and take a non-political job as head of the dramatic department of the Ullstein group of publications. He published a novelette, *Fanny, the Story of a Maid,* a series of short stories, a study in criminology. But there was no escaping politics. While Hitler's star was in the ascendancy Hoellering became editor in chief of Ullstein's *B. Z. am Mittag,* a popular democratic newspaper, and made it militantly anti-Hitler. The public liked it; the owners were frightened; the Social Democrats attacked him for "overestimating" Hitler; and when, on December 12, 1931 he published Hitler's secret instructions to henchmen to form an aviation service, the sensation and scandal that it created caused Bruening's Cabinet to protest to the publishers. Hoellering refused to submit to "house censorship," was dropped from the staff. This compromise, which Von Ossietzky called "the most scandalous capitulation to National Socialism on record," did the publishers little good. Fourteen months later the House of Ullstein was taken over by the Nazis.

In 1932 Hoellering was in America working as a correspondent, but he returned to Germany at the beginning of 1933 with a book about the United States which was later torn up by the storm troopers. When Hitler became Chancellor, Hoellering was editor of the Leftist daily, *12 Uhr Blatt,* and the weekly *Montag Morgen.* On February 26 he wrote: "Unless something happens, the Chancellor cannot win the election." Something did happen—the Reichstag fire. There was a censor, but *all* of the contradictory reports of the fire sent out by the Nazis that night appeared the next day in Hoellering's paper under the sub-head "Official Reports of the Prussian Government News Service." The paper was suspended.

Hoellering fled, taking the train first to Dresden, then to Czechoslovakia, where he proceeded to found a German newspaper in Prague for anti-Nazis in exile. In 1934 he came to America and in 1937 married Marta Troyanova, a well-known Czech actress who is also the Czechoslovakian translator of Theodore Dreiser. The next year Hoellering came to *The Nation* as movie critic, a position which he still holds.

But he had watched democracy dying in Europe and had asked too many questions not to try to answer some of them. The result was *The Defenders.* It was set in Austria before the *Anschluss,* begun in New York, written in German on a typewriter lent by Hendrik van Loon, finished early in 1939, translated by Ludwig Lewisohn, published in the United States in August 1940.

Dr. Hoellering is particularly concerned with the problems of democratic authors whose books can no longer be published in Nazi-occupied territory, and he urges the establishment of a foundation for the publication of uncensored works in German, French, Czech, Polish, Dutch, etc. He does what he can to aid refugee authors both in the United States and abroad. Aside from that he divides his time between writing and tending his Stamford, Connecticut garden—both occupations which "involve a great deal of weeding." He is working now on a second novel whose scene will be laid in Europe and America from 1880 to the present.

References

Pub W 138:546-7 Ag 24 '40 por

Gannett, L. Franz Hoellering and His Novel "The Defenders" pam 1940

HOFFMAN, MALVINA June 15, 1887- Sculptress

Address: 157 E 35th St, New York City

"HAVE PROPOSITION TO MAKE DO YOU CARE TO CONSIDER IT? RACIAL TYPES TO BE MODELED WHILE TRAVELING ROUND THE WORLD." As a result of this telegram from the Chicago Field Museum, sculptress Malvina Hoffman undertook a "head-hunting" expedition in 1930 which lasted five years and took her to the farthest corners of the earth. From 3,000 artists Malvina Cornell Hoffman (she does not use her middle name) was singled out to receive this, the largest sculptural commission ever given a woman, and possibly the largest ever completed by one sculptor anywhere. In the Hall of Man at the Field Museum are 101 life-size bronze statues, standing as an enduring monument to her perseverance, energy and creative genius.

"She has modeled the pygmies of Africa, enticing them from the jungles with cakes of chocolate and with beads; she has used cannibals for models; she has done an East Indian woman while her suspicious husband sat with a knife across his knees; her sitters have varied from lovely Balinese temple dancers to warriors and hunters."

The sculptress' childhood was spent on Forty-third Street in New York City, where she was born June 15, 1887, the daughter of Richard and Fidelia (Lamson) Hoffman. In those days Lillian Russell lived there, too, and the continuous stream of visitors to the actress' house provided the child with a "panorama of excitement."

Of her youth, Miss Hoffman says: "Born and brought up as I was in the lurid atmosphere of Broadway and Forty-third Street, I was nevertheless one of a household which conserved the traditional habits of Puritanical forefathers and conventional groups of numberless relatives."

Miss Hoffman studied painting for six years, but she turned to sculpture because she felt the need of three-dimensional form

G. Maillard Kesslère

MALVINA HOFFMAN

to make some adequate portrait of her father. Richard Hoffman was the English infant prodigy who, at the age of 15, had come to America to accompany Jenny Lind on her first concert tour under the management of P. T. Barnum. The marriage of Malvina's mother to the piano teacher was for many years regarded as a disgrace by the Lamson family.

Malvina's father was her idol. When she had completed the portrait of him the old man examined her work carefully. "My child," he said, "I'm afraid you're going to be an artist. It's a long hard road and you have to travel most of the time entirely alone. I am 78 years old and can leave you very little of this world's earthly goods, but if I can leave you my ideals, perhaps they will be worth more to you than anything else. Above all, you must *be* an artist; after that you may create art."

When she was only eight Malvina encountered "suicidal despair" for the first time and the experience made a profound impression on her youthful mind. As she watched a snow storm from her mother's bedroom window she saw a beautiful woman climb on to the window ledge opposite, discard her filmy gown and plunge 30 feet into a snow bank, narrowly missing the postman as she fell. The revelation of "naked young physical beauty" thrilled her unforgettably and probably awakened within her the first urge to translate her feelings into reality.

At the age of 16 Malvina modeled her first figure, a woman in the grip of despair, which expressed to her youthful mind all that she knew of grief. "It seemed to give me a certain sense of peace and satisfaction to feel that I had collected and concentrated my many conflicts and unshed tears into this concrete image," Miss Hoff-

man remembers. "Perhaps the artist does regain a sort of equilibrium from the transference of his emotions into his art."

After her father's death in 1910, Malvina and her mother sailed for Paris, armed with two marble busts, $1,000 and a letter of introduction from Mrs. John Simpson of New York to Rodin, the famous French sculptor. After five attempts to see the artist, the 23-year-old girl finally gained entrance to his studio and succeeded in interesting him in the marble heads she had carved of her father and Samuel Bonarios Grimson, a friend of the family, whom she married on June 6, 1924.

On this first visit to Rodin's studio Miss Hoffman was locked in and left to explore every inch of the room while Rodin went out with some friends. When he returned he found her sketching small plaster hands, so completely absorbed that she had let the fire go out.

It was during these early days in Paris that Miss Hoffman became aware of the importance of understanding the craft as well as the art of sculpture. She became convinced that she must know her profession from the very beginning in order to attempt competition with men in the field. Accordingly she devoted hours to learning the technicalities of sculpture at the foundries where her work was reproduced.

International acclaim was first accorded Miss Hoffman in 1915 when she completed *Pavlowa Gavotte* and *Bacchanale Russe*. These two pieces of sculpture were the only work she took with her to New York when, following a mental and physical collapse, her doctor ordered her to leave Paris and take an absolute rest.

During the next few years Miss Hoffman divided her time among three continents. In Yugoslavia she directed work in the child-feeding centers which Herbert Hoover had organized following the World War. In 1926 she yielded to her restlessness and left New York again to find "the island of the Lotus Eaters" off the coast of Africa. Her African experiences proved invaluable to her when the proposal came from the Field Museum three years later.

On most of these trips Sam Grimson accompanied his wife, taking moving pictures of her subjects. In the interval between Africa and the world tour, however, Miss Hoffman spent a winter in Rome studying alone and some time in Yugoslavia working under Ivan Meštrović (see sketch this issue), the famous sculptor whom she numbers among her most intimate friends.

The exciting years between 1930 and 1935 are described in her book, *Heads and Tales*, an autobiography, (1936) which she sat down and wrote while the "Hall of Man collection was becoming one of the most popular exhibitions in the world." From the standpoint of anthropology as well as that of art, this group of 101 statues is considered perfect. Miss Hoffman's attention to detail distinguishes all her work and she has received the highest awards for it all over the world.

In 1939 Miss Hoffman wrote *Sculpture Inside and Out,* which is a combination of autobiography and technical information. Of this book it has been said: "With a generous inclusive enthusiasm and a broad, sympathetic attitude towards many radically different styles, Miss Hoffman writes on a wide variety of topics, all more or less related to sculpture, hoping that what she has said 'might be of use to serious students and of interest to the general public.'"

As a rule the sculptor prefers to let her work do her talking. "For better or for worse," she says, "it expresses my thoughts, my ideals, in brief, my way of meeting life and people who are so rich a part of life."

Her *International Dance Fountain* was considered one of the outstanding pieces of sculpture at the New York World's Fair. It consists of seven dancers of different nationalities modeled in high relief on a cylindrical form and was selected by the committee to remain as one of six pieces to decorate the Flushing Meadows Park after the close of the Fair.

Permanent exhibitions of Miss Hoffman's work are to be found in museums in many large cities throughout Europe and the United States. The most extensive collection is, of course, in Chicago, but many pieces are to be found in the Museum of Natural History and the Metropolitan Museum of Art in New York City and the Brooklyn Institute of Arts and Sciences.

While her own work "derives from the great tradition," she is never intolerant toward experiment or development from the classic mood. "Is it not exciting to be alive in an age of experiment and pioneering?" she writes. "We should all feel the urge to turn over the fresh earth and constantly plant new seeds of thought and action. Nothing is more deadly than the apathy of indifference or self-satisfaction."

In appearance, Miss Hoffman is tall, slim and gray-haired. She is a member of eight art societies and an honorary member of three others. In 1937 the degree of Doctor of Literature was conferred upon her by Mount Holyoke College, and that of Doctor of Fine Arts by the University of Rochester.

Her critics believe that Miss Hoffman is unconsciously describing herself when she says of the giants of art: "They seem to spring from the center of the earth, naked souls, living apart from the world's riches and distractions, and by some unexplained miracle living in close contact with elemental forces which endow them with super-energy and wisdom."

References

Am Mag 117:45 Je '34 por
Asia 33:423-33+ Jl '33 pors
Ind Woman 18:97 Ap '39 por
Lit Digest 117:13 Ja 6 '34 por
Newsweek 8:31 O 3 '36 il
Parnassus 11:41 N '39
Time 28:44+ O 5 '36 por

American Women
Hoffman, M. Heads and Tales 1936
Hoffman, M. Sculpture Inside Out 1939
Kirkland, W. M. and Kirkland, F. Malvina Hoffman, Sculptor of Types *In* Girls Who Became Artists p110-15 1934
Who's Who in America

HOHENLOHE-WALDENBURG, STEFANIE RICHTER, PRINCESS (hō'ĕn-lō'ĕ-wäl'dĕn-boorg') 1896- European political figure

December 1940 Bulletin: The request of Princess Hohenlohe for a renewal of her temporary visitor's permit has been denied and unless she leaves the United States by December 21, 1940 deportation proceedings will be started, the United States Department of Justice announced. She was with Captain Fritz Weidemann, German Consul at San Francisco. The Princess' presence was regarded as "inimical" to this country's best interests because of her close association with Nazis.

Her long imposing name reduced to "Steffi" or "Toffi" by her friends, the Princess is also known to the tabloids as "the mystery woman of Europe" and has been described as "a very, very shrewd and a very, very dangerous woman." The mystery surrounding her is so fantastic that one candid reporter described her thus: "A stumpy, determined middle-aged woman . . . with mouse-brown hair" and another says she is "small, plump, with red gold hair, sleeked up-style."

Still surrounded by clouds of mystery after losing her bizarre law suit against Lord Rothermere (1939), Princess Steffi,

Acme

STEFANIE HOHENLOHE-WALDENBURG

HOHENLOHE-WALDENBURG, STEFANIE—*Continued*

her son and her mother, Baroness Szepessy, came to New York from London, December 22, 1939. The Princess is reputed to have been born into a middle-class Jewish family named Richter in Vienna in 1896. Her father was an attorney. To this, Steffi, onetime close friend of Adolf Hitler, impatiently said: "They say my father was in prison, that I am a Jewess named Richter and that I was arrested in France as a spy. I won't dignify those statements by confirming or denying them."

The sensational suit which she filed against the Nazi-admiring Lord Rothermere who controls the London *Daily Mail, Evening News* and *Sunday Dispatch* besides numerous provincial papers, was to force him to pay her $20,000 yearly for the rest of her life. She affirmed that he paid her some $185,000 (he says it was over $250,000) for her services as "foreign political representative." She declared that Lord Rothermere in 1927 "had decided to work for the restoration of the Hohenzollern and Hapsburg dynasties. He wanted to be a modern Warwick-the-King-Maker and work on the European rather than the English field."

It is said that in 1931 she arranged a $400,000,000 loan through the pro-German British publisher to Hitler. Her career as a leading "intrigante" started long after her marriage. On May 12, 1914 she married Prince Friedrich Franz Hohenlohe-Waldenburg-Schillingsfürst. The Almanach de Gotha listed the marriage as "not in conformity with the princely house of Hohenlohe." Six years later, after their son was born, they were divorced. In Germany she became a powerful personality in the intrigues of the country when she met Captain Fritz Weidemann, Hitler's aide-de-camp, now in 1940 German Consul in San Francisco. Through him she met Goebbels and it was decided that though she was a non-Ayran, she could be useful to the cause. She was given the title "Honorary Ayran" and was hostess during Viscount Runciman's mission to Prague, where, surrounded by Germans and Sudetens, she explained the Nazi viewpoint to Runciman. She is credited with arranging meetings which helped to bring about the Munich Pact.

During the trial in London it was brought out that when in 1933 she was reported in the French press as expelled from France because she was a Nazi spy, Lord Rothermere told her not to sue French papers, as he would defend her. Steffi's closeness to Hitler was brought out by a letter from German Consul General Weidemann, who wrote: "There is no doubt in my mind that he [Hitler] will grant to her any help he can in her fight to re-establish her personal honor and financial status."

The Princess says she has come to New York to write her memoirs, for which she is asking a very high price. Her agent is Curtis Brown. In her book she expects to recount her friendships with Hitler, Lord Rothermere and Fritz Weidemann. She thinks it will take a year to write, for she has never written any books before. Asked how her writing was coming along she replied airily, "I expect to start in a few weeks." It is believed that she is here because she is no longer useful to Hitler after the publicity attending her trial, unwelcome in England and not allowed to enter Italy, which she tried. While here she is the subject of close scrutiny by both the New York Police Alien Squad and the Federal Bureau of Investigation.

Refusing to discuss international politics with reporters, she said: "If you like to write something about me you might say I am known for my loyalty to my friends, my love of music and my taste in dress. I have also won two beauty contests, one in England and another in Austria." Her taste in dress is attested by a reporter who wrote: "She wore a silver fox turban with a provocative pink rose perched on it, a silver fox finger-length coat, a black silk jersey (Alix model) and black kid Perugia sandals with sky-blue platform soles. Gorgeous diamond ear-clips were fastened on her small and pretty ears and a scintillating diamond clip lightened her dark dress."

References

> Liv Age 356:43-6 Mr '39
> N Y Post p1 Ja 12 '40 por
> N Y Times p25 N 16 '39; p5 D 8 '39
> N Y World-Telegram p3 Ja 12 '40 por
> Time 34:24+ N 20 '39 por

HOLLANDER, JACOB HARRY July 23, 1871—July 9, 1940 Educator; professor of political economy at Johns Hopkins University for past 15 years; former treasurer and financial director of Puerto Rico; noted for many years as an economic expert; advised several Presidents on financial procedure

References

> Who's Who in America
> Who's Who in American Jewry

Obituaries

> N Y Herald Tribune p18 Jl 10 '40 por
> N Y Times p19 Jl 10 '40
> Sch & Soc 52:41 Jl 20 '40

HONEYWELL, HARRY E. Sept 19, 1871—Feb 10, 1940 Noted American balloonist and Spanish-American War veteran who won the national balloon races three times and took second place in seven other competitions

Obituaries

> N Y Herald Tribune p40 F 11 '40 por
> N Y Times p48 F 11 '40

HOOPER, FRANKLIN HENRY Jan 28, 1862—Aug 14, 1940 Editor emeritus of the *Encyclopedia Britannica;* supervised five editions of the *Encyclopedia;* retired in 1928

FRANKLIN H. HOOPER

after 39 years, the longest service of any American editor of the work; supervised the selection of the 3,700 experts on various subjects who wrote for each edition

References

Who's Who in America

Obituaries

N Y Herald Tribune p17 Ag 15 '40 por
N Y Times p19 Ag 15 '40 por
Pub W 138:554 Ag 24 '40 por
Time 36:56 Ag 26 '40

HOOTON, EARNEST ALBERT Nov 20, 1887- Anthropologist

Address: b. Harvard University, Cambridge, Massachusetts; h. 13 Buckingham St, Cambridge, Massachusetts

Dr. Hooton, noted anthropologist, sends us the following sketch of himself:

"I was born on November 20, 1887, at Clemansville, Wisconsin, a tiny farming town about four miles from Oshkosh. My father, William Hooton, was at the time Methodist minister in that town, in which his uncle, also named William Hooton, was one of the most prosperous members of the farming community. My father was born in Rampton, Nottinghamshire, England, the son of a Methodist circuit rider. He emigrated to Toronto, Canada about 1878 and worked for a while in his half-brother's jewelry store. He then attended for some short while the theological school of McGill University, and, for one year, was a missionary on the Manitoulin Island in Lake Huron. In Toronto he met Margaret Newton, a young schoolteacher of Scottish descent. After their marriage they moved to

Wisconsin, where my father continued in the ministry for some 50 years.

"Father was a sentimentalist and a bookworm. His sermons were full of fine writing and stuffed with quotations from the poets. His knowledge of literature was vast. Otherwise he was a gentle, easygoing daydreamer, whom everyone liked. He was totally dominated by my mother except on occasion when his English obstinacy was aroused and he became quite unmanageable. Mother was a woman of great intellectual ability, a brilliant student, very practical and unswerving in her industry and devotion to her family and to her duties as a pastor's wife. She was by upbringing a Scotch Presbyterian and she loathed sentiment and verbosity. She was the most direct and forcible female speaker I have ever heard. She and my father were devoted to each other and she managed him in every activity except the writing and delivering of sermons. She also managed all of her children. I was brought up under a matriarchate and since I have married I have continued in another.

"I had two elder sisters, one quite gifted at the piano and the organ, the other sensitive, delicate and scholarly. Methodist ministers had to move every three or five years, so that we lived in many towns in eastern Wisconsin. Mother and father had two obsessions—religion and education. We possibly received too much of each. I started in the public kindergarten at the age of five and at the age of six put on spectacles for short-sightedness. This malady grew faster than I did and is still growing, although I am beginning to shrink. I think that I was objectionably precocious. Nearly every winter I contracted bronchitis or some respiratory ailment and was forced to stay out of school. Mother would then teach me at home and when I went back to school I would skip a grade. I was not small for my age, but I was always in classes with children two or three years older than I. I had to compensate for my physical inadequacy by the use of a sharp tongue and a certain facility in invective.

"Thus I entered the high school at Manitowoc at the age of 11—a pallid, spectacled child among bearded stalwarts of 18 or 19 years who chewed tobacco and spat the juice out of the windows. Of course some were younger and chewed gum. Wisconsin had a fine population of Germans, Scandinavians, Czechs, Poles, with a sprinkling of English, Scotch, Welsh and Old American stock. My friends were of all of these descents and some others. It was a splendid, small town life, geographically, temporally and socially, intermediate between that of Tom Sawyer and that of Penrod Schofield. Neither the sacred nor the profane was neglected. In the summer I cut lawns or worked in pea-canning factories; in the winter I was assistant janitor in the high school and head janitor in the church. I earned $10 a month in the winter and was unbe-

Bachrach

EARNEST A. HOOTON

lievably rich. I bought a cornet and a gold-filled watch and also became an amateur photographer. Thus at a tender age I became a social nuisance.

"One sister was a year ahead of me in school and the other two years. We were all sent to Lawrence College, Appleton, Wisconsin, a small Methodist school [B. A. 1907]. We all specialized in Latin because my mother considered that subject to be the foundation and superstructure of a real education. I also specialized in college journalism, including amateur cartooning and scurrilous verse—both bad. In my senior year I went to Madison, Wisconsin to take the examinations for the Rhodes Scholarships. These examinations were in Greek, Latin and mathematics. After becoming eligible for a scholarship at Oxford I did not immediately present myself as a candidate, but spent three years at the University of Wisconsin doing graduate work in the classics [M. A. 1908 and Ph. D. 1911]. During this time I was supported by scholarships and teaching fellowships. The most terrifying experience I had was teaching freshman Latin prose to a class of 40 coeds. This resulted in my permanent intimidation as regards the weaker sex. Otherwise I learned something about Roman religion, archeology and the textual emendation of Greek and Latin manuscripts. I also discovered in the library a book called *Anthropology and the Classics* and decided that I would have a little flyer in anthropology when I went to Oxford.

"In 1910 I entered University College, Oxford as Rhodes Scholar from Wisconsin. I was the only American in the college. The master welcomed me by saying that they had had one American before and had not liked him. He hoped that they would like me better. I think he was disappointed.

I attended one session of Gilbert Murray's seminar on Sophocles which convinced me that I was not going to be a Greek scholar. So I went over to R. R. Marett, reader in social anthropology, at Exeter College. Anthropology was a hardly respectable subject; so Marett received me with enthusiasm and open arms. I found myself let in for all sorts of subjects, including anatomy and physical anthropology. I had always scorned the sciences with all of the superciliousness of the pure Classicist. Thus I entered upon the study of bones and cadavers with revulsion, but quickly acquired a possibly morbid fondness for these carnal relicts. In fact I found that I liked skeletons better than declensions and considered apes more interesting than philosophers. In my second year at Oxford I became demonstrator in physical anthropology—which was an euphemism for laboratory assistant. I took the diploma in anthropology (with distinction) and finished up my thesis for the Ph. D. in classics at the University of Wisconsin. In my last year I took a research degree at Oxford—the B. L. Meanwhile I spent some time in going about England pronouncing professional judgment upon bones dug up in excavations—such as the remains of a saint disinterred at Carnavon, Wales and a group of skeletons brought to light in an early Anglo-Saxon cemetery at East Shefford, Berks. In the winter vacations I hung about Paris and other European capitals; in the summer I returned to the United States.

"On my way back to Oxford for my third year I became acquainted with a young lady from Chicago, Mary Beidler Camp, who, being graduated from Smith College, was going to Berlin for the ostensible purpose of studying at the university there. I spent my vacations that year pursuing this girl about Europe and ultimately succeeded in getting her to agree to marry me. This seems to have been the brightest thing I ever have done.

"At the end of my last year at Oxford [1913] I was fortunate enough to secure a position as instructor in anthropology at Harvard, the junior member of a three-man department. In the next summer vacation I returned to England to dig Bronze Age barrows in Wiltshire and was caught there when the War broke out, but got back in time for the opening of the university. At the end of the next academic year (1915) I married, and my wife and I set out for the Canary Islands, where I planned to dig caves in the interest of the newly founded Harvard African Studies. However, the Spanish government stopped my excavating, so that I spent most of the time in measuring skulls in the museum at Teneriffe. The results of these studies were eventually published in a large tome called *The Ancient Inhabitants of the Canary Islands* (1925). In the meantime there had been added to my duties as instructor in anthropology the post of curator of somatology in the Peabody Museum of Harvard University. This job involved the care of the numerous skulls and skeletons of the museum collection. It was a congenial task.

"In the summer of 1916 I attended the Second Business Men's Military Training Camp at Plattsburg, at the end of which I was honorably discharged as too blind for active duty. My subsequent efforts to get into the army were frustrated and I was obliged to remain at Harvard and teach during the War. After the Armistice I did some mapping of Africa for the Colonel House Peace Commission of experts, but I have no reason for suspecting that my maps were ever used. I spent the summer of 1919 at Camp Grant in Illinois, where I was in charge of measuring some 8,500 soldiers at demobilization. The summer of 1920 was spent in the excavating of Indian skeletons at the ruined pueblo of Pecos, New Mexico. The archeological project was being conducted for Philipps Academy, Andover, Massachusetts, under Dr. A. V. Kidder, and I had engaged to study the skeletal specimens which were to be deposited in the Peabody Museum of Harvard University. More than 1,000 skeletons were recovered—the largest collection from any site in the New World. My report, *The Indians of Pecos Pueblo*, was published by the Yale Press in 1931.

"The years between 1920 and 1925 were filled with hard work and the vicissitudes incidental to the acquisition and retention of three offspring. My wife and I went abroad one summer. I finished my studies of skeletal collections and began to promote research in race mixture in several parts of the world, the field work done mainly by young anthropologists sent out from Harvard.

"In 1926 I began an anthropological study of criminals in Massachusetts which was extended to cover 10 states and included the measurement and observation of some 17,000 criminals and check samples of civilians. It involved an enormous amount of reduction of statistical data and raising money for fieldworkers and clerical and statistical helpers. This is the biggest and toughest job I have ever undertaken or ever will. Publications up to the present include *Crime and the Man* (1939), a semipopular (but actually very unpopular) preview, and *The American Criminal*, of which volume I is called *The Native White Criminal of Native Parentage* (1939)—a vast statistical and technical work. Two other volumes are projected. In this work the biological inferiority of criminals and the insane was demonstrated, to the satisfaction, at least, of the author. During the period 1918 to 1933 I also edited the *Harvard African Studies* of which some 10 large volumes were published. These years were active in Harvard anthropological expeditions to Africa, which I organized but

did not attend. These years were also most fruitful in studies of race mixture carried on by my students in various parts of the world. In 1929 I accompanied Professor A. M. Tozzer on a brief archeological reconnaissance in Panama.

"In 1930 I took up golf and wrote a non-technical book on human evolution called *Up From the Ape*, which was published the next year. I wrote the book, which I hoped would be popular, in order to gain a respite from ponderous scientific writing which no one read. I took up golf because I was bullied into it by my wife and my friends. *Up From the Ape* is still making a modest amount of money for me, but not enough to pay for my golf. I have played the latter game assiduously for the past decade, displaying an ineptitude which is nothing short of phenomenal. There can be no doubt that I am a golf moron. I have no other hobby, although I do read a great many detective stories and other volatile literature—literally as a soporific.

"In 1932 I organized the Harvard Anthropological Survey of Ireland which carried on field work in archeology, social anthropology and physical anthropology for more than five years. All of the actual work in Ireland was carried on by my junior colleagues. I am at present engaged upon the writing of the report on the physical survey of 10,000 adult Irish males.

"My present and future interest in applied physical anthropology has to do with the relation of the human constitution to pathology—mental and physical—and to social behavior. Such studies require the cooperative investigation of anthropologists, physicians, psychologists and sociologists. Most of my public speaking has been devoted during past years to an attempt to awaken in the educated and more or less intelligent public the realization that biological deterioration is at the bottom of our sociological and political troubles and that we must do something to check human degeneration. The medical profession must be aroused to play its proper and leading rôle in our biological redemption. I have pointed out its shortcomings in this duty. I have also attacked the social redemptionists who lay all of the evils of mankind to institutions and environment.

"My recent more or less popular books have dealt with these problems and have consisted mostly of public lectures on the various phases of the subject which I have given. These books are: *Apes, Men, and Morons* (1937); *Twilight of Man* (1939); and *Why Men Behave Like Apes, and Vice Versa* (1940).

"I regard my principal function as that of a university teacher and a trainer of professional workers in physical anthropology and I have taught unintermittently at Harvard for 27 years without any sabbatical or leave of absence. My pleasantest duty and

HOOTON, EARNEST—*Continued*

most prized privilege is lecturing to Harvard students."

References

Life 9:95 N 15 '37 por; 7:60 Ag 7 '39 por
N Y Sun p10 Jl 29 '40
Sat R Lit 16:26 O 16 '37
Time 30:68 N 8 '37 por; 34:50 O 2 '39 il
Wilson Lib Bul 14:712 Je '40 por

American Men of Science
Leaders in Education 1932
Who's Who in America

HOOVER, J. EDGAR Jan 1, 1895- Director, Federal Bureau of Investigation, United States Department of Justice since 1924

Address: b. United States Department of Justice Bldg, Washington, D. C.; h. 413 Seward Sq, S E, Washington, D. C.

In October 1940, J. Edgar Hoover, asked to issue a report on efforts to combat Fifth Columnists, reassured the American public:

"The nation is safer from spies and saboteurs than ever before. There has been a negligible amount of sabotage in the second World War in contrast to a similar period in the first World War.

"This situation exists largely because law enforcement throughout every municipality, county, state and the nation is far better prepared to deal with these matters than at any time in the past."

Although many times as many complaints have been pouring into the offices of the Federal Bureau of Investigation as during any year in the past, the FBI chief feels it is well equipped to cope with its tremendous responsibilities, and warns against vigilante hysteria.

Director of the Federal Bureau of Investigation since 1924, and connected with the Bureau since 1919, John Edgar Hoover has succeeded in acquiring in that time a great number of fervent admirers (including Walter Winchell, the late Courtney Ryley Cooper, Shirley Temple and thousands of G-man worshipping kids) and a great number of as fervent enemies. Like Martin Dies (see sketch this issue), he seems to be more a "national issue" than a man—at least in the spring of 1940, when criticism of his bureau was at its height.

He was born January 1, 1895 in "a pleasant frame house" in "an unpretentious section" of Washington, D. C., the son of Dickerson and Annie (Scheitlin) Hoover. He grew up in the Capital. At Central High School his nickname was "Speed," and although he weighed only 110 pounds and was the smallest boy in his cadet company, he became captain of the cadets by the time he was a senior. It is said that what he lacked in size he made up in loudness of voice when it came to drilling his company. Besides that, he sang in the choir at the Church of the Reformation, and from all available evidence was something of a model boy. " 'Speed,' " said a friend of his much later, "chastised us with his morality." He was graduated in 1913, valedictorian of his class and a young man determined to go places.

He did. He worked as messenger in the Congressional Library and studied law evenings at George Washington University. By 1916 he had his Bachelor of Laws degree from George Washington, and the following year he received his Master of Laws, was admitted to the Bar, and for a short time was a practicing lawyer. He had some experience in war-time counter-espionage; then in 1919, after the War, he was appointed special assistant to Attorney General Palmer. As such he was director of the newly-created General Intelligence Division, known as the anti-radical" division.

In 1921 Hoover was appointed assistant director of the FBI, and three years later became its director. It is an office which he has since held under every Administration.

His anti-radical activities were not yet over. But it was not such activities, but his dramatic campaign against organized crime that first made "compact, wiry-haired" J. Edgar Hoover's name familiar to every schoolboy, moviegoer and reader of comic strips. When he became director of the Federal Bureau of Investigation it was a "sloppy, demoralized agency." From such a beginning, *Time* said in 1935, Hoover built "one of the finest, most efficient law enforcement agencies the world has ever known." He began to replace untrained men with members of the Bar or experienced accountants. New departments of training were instituted, new scientific methods of criminal detection studied and a central bureau for fingerprints set up. The appropriations asked of Congress for the Bureau were also continually increased, and the authority of the Bureau tremendously extended. In the first few years his agents were without authority even to carry arms or to make arrests. Armaments and automobiles were provided for them in 1934 (Hoover's men are now trained to use tear gas, machine guns and arms), and in that same year they also acquired the authority to investigate nearly all sorts of Federal violations, including "racketeering."

In the early '30s it was Hoover's blasts against "public enemies," the dramatic capture or death at the hands of G-men of such criminals as Baby Face Nelson, John Dillinger and Pretty Boy Floyd, the solution of a large number of kidnapping cases and the extensive publicity given to the part the FBI played in all these cases which served to spotlight his Bureau and its accomplishments, although a relatively small percentage of the cases handled by his Bureau are of this spectacular variety. Some thought Hoover carried self-advertising a little too far: his face appeared on everything from advertisements to comic strips, and he seemed to be an indefatigable speaker and writer of magazine articles. Hoover and his supporters justified what publicity they did not disown, however. They said that the taxpayers were entitled to know exactly how their money was being spent, and that it is healthy for public morality when a G-man can be given more glamor than a gangster.

There was more serious criticism. It was claimed that many of the FBI gangster raids were not legal in all their aspects; agents of the Secret Service and of the Post Office Inspectors' Service made frequent complaints that "in scores of cases . . . their men have built up the evidence and located the criminal only to have the FBI step in for the kill and credit"; G-men were accused of needless shooting; it was said that Hoover's "head-line-stalking" delayed the solution of many cases, and that there was little cooperation between Federal and local law enforcement agencies; Hoover's attacks on what he called "the abuses of the parole system" were called assaults on prison reform. What is more, the *New Republic* asserted that his "crime statistics and his claims for great returns for the millions he spends have been assailed by reputable criminologists as unreliable."

None of these charges were ever verified, however, and Hoover remained philosophic. He pointed to the Department of Justice's record of convictions—in one year, 94 per cent of all it brought to court—and to the great number of kidnappings solved. On the radio in his office was a framed sentiment entitled *The Penalty of Leadership* which no doubt reflected his own attitude: "In every field of human endeavor, he that is first must perpetually live in the white light of publicity. . . When a man's work becomes a standard for the whole world, it also becomes a target for the shafts of the envious few." Congress appropriated with increasing generosity, in 1936 the Boys' Club of America presented him with their Distinguished Service Medal, and J. Edgar Hoover continued to make speeches. In 1939 five thousand addresses were made by the Director of the FBI and his agents.

With the outbreak of the European War in September 1939, J. Edgar Hoover again organized his General Intelligence Division and with 1919 enthusiasm started to compile an up-to-date index of those he considered engaged in subversive activities. He soon showed himself capable of action as well as definition. On January 14, 1940, about the time he was asking Congress for a 33 per cent increase in his annual appropriation (four times as much as a decade earlier), he released the story to the newspapers that 18 alleged members of the Christian Front had been arrested for a conspiracy to overthrow the government. Before any jury trial had taken place Hoover was pointing out to reporters that "it took only 23 men to overthrow Russia," was having "Rogue's Gallery" photographs of the men made and turned over to a weekly. But the fact that meanwhile the accused had spent weeks in jail, unindicted and unconvicted, caused Congressman Martin Kennedy to call this "an occurrence which we would very loudly

Paul Frehm

J. EDGAR HOOVER

protest if it were permitted in a foreign country."

Next sensational move of the FBI was early in the morning of February 6, 1940, when in Detroit 10 men and a woman were awakened from sleep, handcuffed, chained, stripped, searched and marched off to prison. It turned out that they had been indicted three days before under an 1818 statute for soliciting volunteers for the Spanish Loyalist Army. In prison they were admittedly held incommunicado and refused the right of consulting an attorney until 15 minutes before they were arraigned, and, according to a prompt letter of protest from Senator Norris, "subjected to third-degree methods from the time they were arrested until three o'clock in the afternoon."

Attorney General Jackson (see sketch this issue) quashed the Detroit indictments under pressure of public indignation, but Senator Norris, supported by Senator Wheeler (see sketch this issue), continued to demand an investigation of Hoover and his Department of Justice. When Jackson gave both a clean bill there followed a second protest, and Jackson finally ordered a departmental, though not an independent, investigation. Its report Norris also termed a "whitewash"; nor was he appeased by the new Neutrality Division set up about the same time, since the White House said it would not curb Hoover's powers.

In the meantime a campaign of protest against the FBI on these and other counts had long been raging in the liberal (and part of the not-so-liberal) press. Hoover was its target. He was criticized for wintering in Florida; his habit of frequenting night clubs, often in the company of Walter Winchell, caused Vito Marcantonio to label him a "Stork Club detective"; and when Hoover himself revealed that his operators had been tapping

HOOVER, J. EDGAR—*Continued*

wires, a practice which had been made a felony in 1934, the storm had broken in all earnest. It was demanded of Jackson that he take action against Hoover other than his order barring wire-tapping by FBI agents in the future. Westbrook Pegler (see sketch this issue), who had previously called Hoover "a night-club fly-cop" and "a publicity hound pandering to gent's-room journalism," raised the ante, saying: "He would be a great attraction as a keyhole columnist and logroller, and he should be worth something at current rates, with 15 minutes of hysterics on the air composed of unimportant and unconfirmed innuendoes about people too big and too contemptuous to talk back." The FBI was frequently referred to as the "American Gestapo." Of Hoover's much-discussed card file *The Nation* suggested: "If it really is a list of persons dangerous to our form of government, it ought to include a card for 'Hoover, J. Edgar.'"

Hoover and his supporters, of course, were not remaining idle either. Headlines in the New York *Journal-American* and in other Hearst papers announced: "Reds 'smear' FBI." In speeches Hoover gave his opinion that criticism of his methods came directly or indirectly from un-American groups. Hugh S. Johnson (see sketch this issue) wrote: "This attack on such a man and his work is nothing less than obscene. . . Sucker commentators and sucker politicians who have allowed themselves to be duped into support of this sabotage are unwittingly doing great harm. . . If the reward for such victories over crime and corruption—such improvements in police methods everywhere—is a political smearing out from public life, then why should any cop be capable, be brave, efficient or honest?"

By November 1940 most of this tempest had died down, but Attorney General Jackson was taking up the cudgels in defending the efficiency of the FBI against attacks by Martin Dies.

The subject of this storm of controversy is a thick-set man in his 40's with "the constitution of a locomotive"—which is fortunate. His "hard, black eyes look down a nose that widens considerably as it turns south." He doesn't look like a man who would have a cheerful idea of human nature, and he hasn't; very recently he made a speech in which he estimated that "our army of criminals numbers into the millions." A bachelor, he is very careful of his reputation, and the only girl he has ever been photographed kissing is Shirley Temple, although he once received something like 500 proposals upon publication of an interview stating his requirements for his ideal girl. They ended: "She must remain upon the pedestal upon which I have placed her."

Hoover approves of sports because they "teach a man to take defeat and dig in all the harder." He is fond of the electric horse in the Department of Justice gym, plays tennis and jujitsu, and says he likes nothing better than a wrestling or boxing match or a baseball game. His favorite dishes are green-turtle soup and hamburgers, his hobby collecting Chinese antiques at auctions (his study is filled with them), his favorite reading (according to one newspaper sketch) Edgar Guest and a few poems of Robert W. Service. If he doesn't find time for reading many books, that doesn't mean he doesn't enjoy words, though. Anything with five syllables is said to have particular appeal for him, and he is a man to whom fishing has become a "piscatorial diversion."

He is an unremitting foe of corruption in politics—"Old Man Politics" can be blamed for much of the crime in our national life today, he believes.

References

Liberty 17:7-10 Mr 16 '40 por; 17:37-40 Mr 23 '40 por
Nation 144:232-4 F 27 '37; 144:262-4 Mr 6 '37; 150:323 Mr 9 '40; 150:380 Mr 23 '40
New Repub 102:330-2; 102:345 Mr 11 '40; 102:364-5 Mr 18 '40; 102:393-4 Mr 25 '40; 102:429 Ap 1 '40
New Yorker 13:20-5 S 25 '37; 13:21-6 O 2 '37; 13:22-7 O 9 '37
Newsweek 6:34 Jl 20 '35; 12:29 Ag 22 '38
Read Digest 31:42-5 D '37
Scholastic 33:13S Ja 14 '39 por; 35:21 Ja 22 '40 por; 35:18 Mr 11 '40
Time 26:10-12 Ag 5 '35 il por (cover);
America's Young Men 1936-37
Who's Who in America
Who's Who in the Nation's Capital

HOPKINS, LOUIS BERTRAM Aug 11, 1881—Aug 10, 1940 President of Wabash College, Crawfordsville, Indiana since 1926; had long business career before becoming an educator; was personnel director for

LOUIS B. HOPKINS

Northwestern University (1922-26); originated the Wabash plan which called for a well-balanced, highly co-ordinated system of education which overstressed no part of college life

References

Who's Who in America

Obituaries

N Y Herald Tribune p30 Ag 11 '40
N Y Times p30 Ag 11 '40

HORLICK, WILLIAM JR. Dec 12, 1875 —Apr 1, 1940 Son of the founder of the multi-million-dollar Horlick malted milk fortune; philanthropist; aided, explorers

References

Who's Who in America 1938-39

Obituaries

N Y Herald Tribune p18 Ap 2 '40 por
N Y Times p26 Ap 2 '40

HORNER, HENRY Nov 30, 1878—Oct 6, 1940 Governor of Illinois; only native Chicagoan ever elected to the state's highest office; only Democratic Governor of Illinois elected to a second term since 1870; had been ill for two years; before entering politics had been judge for 18 years and protégé of the late Anton J. Cermak; gathered one of the world's greatest Lincoln libraries, a collection of more than 6,000 volumes and many manuscripts and letters; gave this collection to the Illinois State Historical Library

Herbert Georg

HENRY HORNER

References

Fortune 14:52 Ag '36 por
Time 35:17 Mr 18 '40 por

Who's Who in America
Who's Who in American Jewry
Who's Who in Government
Who's Who in Law

Obituaries

N Y Times p1, 17 O 7 '40 por

HORTHY DE NAGYBANYA, NICHOLAS (hô'tĭ) 1868- Regent of Hungary
Address: Budapest I, Királyi Vár, Hungary

There are few commentators on foreign, and especially Balkan, affairs who do not point out that Nicholas Horthy wears an admiral's uniform in a country that has no navy and is head of a kingdom which has no king. On the question of his attitude toward social and economic ideas they disagree, but they are unanimous in considering him, "loyal to his country and ever watchful of its needs."

Admiral Horthy has lasted longer than any other post-War ruler—"the most solid figure in the Continental flux," Anne O'Hare McCormick (see sketch this issue) calls him—and despite the movements and machinations of Europe's other rulers, it looks as though he will last a good while longer. During the past two years, however, Hungary has been an important pawn in Hitler's plans for Europe, because of its strategic position in the Danube Valley and because of its wheat and bauxite. So far Horthy has made out well. In 1938, just after the Munich settlement, his country was given Ruthenia, "a nibble of Czechoslovakia." In September 1940 a second Hitler award took half of Transylvania from Romania and gave it to Hungary, which had had it before the First World War. Awards like these cause their recipients to step warily, but Admiral Horthy, "the only head of a foreign country for whom Führer Hitler has deep respect," knows the advantages to Germany of having Hungary between it and Russia and believes firmly that this award is to the best advantage of his country. He may believe that it is also to Hungary's advantage to be part of the Berlin-Rome-Tokyo axis, which it joined in November 1940. Or he may know that it was definitely to Hungary's disadvantage not to join when asked.

Regent Horthy, who is 72 but looks less than 60, has been the dictator of Hungary for 20 years. Born in Kenderes, Hungary, the fourth son of Stephen de Horthy, a member of the House of Magnates, and of Paulette (de Halassy) Horthy, he is the descendant of a family of landed gentry which can trace its ancestry back to the thirteenth century. His father was a Protestant who took his five sons to the Protestant church in the village; his mother, a Catholic, took her daughters to Mass.

Young Nicholas attended the Reformist College at Debreczen for a while, but he had always been fascinated by the sea and ships and at a very early age entered the Imperial Naval Academy at Fiume with the necessary endorsement of the Emperor. In

NICHOLAS HORTHY DE NAGYBANYA

1886 he entered the Austro-Hungarian Navy and in 1900 was made a lieutenant. For many years he cruised around the world, at one time in a sailing frigate which provided the escort for an Austro-Hungarian scientific expedition into the South Seas. Tall, slender, with a long mustache and a collection of beautiful uniforms, he was a prominent and attractive figure and, in 1901, married Magdalene Purgly, the pick of all the eligible young ladies, "one of those beautiful Hungarian girls who seem to have stepped out of fairy tales." (They have two sons and one daughter.)

After having been stationed in various places, in 1908 Horthy was put in command of the *Taurus* at Constantinople, and proceeded, with his wife, to plunge into the whirl of diplomatic life there. When the Revolution of Young Turks occurred in 1908 his reports on it won him favorable attention. The next year Emperor Franz Josef made him his aide-de-camp, a job he was able to keep for a number of terms. Vital and even excitable, Horthy still knew when to hold his tongue and when to speak.

He rose rapidly in the Navy and just before the First World War was made a captain. When the War began Captain Horthy commanded the battleship *Hapsburg* for 10 months and then the cruiser *Novara*. In 1915 he was engaged in the attack of the Austro-Hungarian fleet on the Italian Adriatic coast and that same year sank the transports bound for the relief of Montenegro in the port of San Giovanni di Medua. When the Allies bottled up the Austro-Hungarian fleet in the Adriatic in 1917, it was Horthy who induced his superiors to undertake the Austrian Navy's only bold expedition of the War. As leader of the cruiser squadron he broke through the Allied blockade in the Straits of Otranto. Overtaken by superior forces, wounded in the leg, he was still able to outmaneuver the enemy and returned to port safely. For this exploit he won a decoration, became a national hero overnight and was, the next year, promoted by Emperor Charles I to the position of rear admiral in command of the fleet, over the heads of older officers. In that same year he was made vice-admiral. But then the Austro-Hungarian monarchy collapsed and Admiral Horthy had to turn over its Navy to the newly formed South Slav government.

Emperor Charles I went into exile and Nicholas Horthy became "a national hero on half pension." Then came the Communist revolution under Béla Kun, and when the counter-revolutionists needed a man "with name, luck and love of adventure" to lead their forces, they chose Horthy to create Hungary's national army. He became Minister of War, the Communists were crushed and the White Terror set in. Concentration camps, the first in post-War Europe, were set up, the Jews were persecuted, thousands of people were killed. And, according to John Gunther, when the members of a British delegation investigating the atrocities complained to Horthy that the officers responsible had not been punished, he replied indignantly: "Why, they are my best men!"

After the Civil War strong authority was needed to build the country. On March 1, 1920 the National Assembly at Budapest elected Horthy Regent Governor of Hungary with the title of "Serene Excellency" and the privilege of keeping the position as long as he lived. Since then there have been one or two abortive *putsches* by ex-Emperor Charles, who mistakenly believed, when he came back in 1921, that Regent Horthy was just keeping the throne warm for him. But the job of Regent has been firmly Horthy's.

Since 1920 Admiral Horthy's power has been immense under Hungarian law. "He can dismiss premiers, as he has done repeatedly, and be sure that Parliament will always ratify his action." His veto is so strong that it is almost impossible for Parliament to override it. He issues decrees, appoints judges and other officials and determines the foreign policy of his country. Considered reactionary and even feudal in his social and economic ideas, he is, nevertheless, immensely popular among Hungary's people, to them "a loyal and courageous patriot."

"Straight as a sentry, his thick black hair hardly touched with gray," Admiral Horthy still holds a hunter's rifle firmly, his step is springy and "he wears his cap at a young officer's rakish angle." He has remained aflame with vitality. According to John Gunther: "At one moment, he may burst a collar discussing Hungarian revisionism; at the next, pick up a paper knife and go through the gestures of murder to illustrate a point; at the next, mention with tears in his eyes how good a human being old Franz Josef was."

From the time he was made Regent, Horthy has lived in the royal palace on the Danube, but behind the imposing façade of marble corridors and miles of stairways, the Admiral works in a "small, rather shabby room." He and Madame Horthy, famous for the Winter Relief Fund she organized and supervises, spend as much time as they can in their pleasant country house at Kenderes, where Nicholas Horthy indulges his hobbies of painting and playing the piano.

References

Am Mercury 50:176-83 Je '40
Cur Hist 49:55-6 Ja '39
Lit Digest 102:62-4 S 14 '29 por
N Y Times p14 S 9 '40
Newsweek 12:15 Ag 29 '38 por

Forbes, R. Admiral Horthy, Regent of Hungary *In* These Men I Knew p97-106 1940
Gunther, J. Hungary and Dr. Habsburg *In* Inside Europe p418-27 1940
International Who's Who
Marcosson, I. F. Some Central European Personalities *In* Turbulent Years p370-95 1938
Who's Who
Who's Who in Central and East Europe

HOSHINO, NAOKI (hō-shē′nō nä-ō′kē)
1888- Minister in the Cabinet of Prince Fumimaro Konoye

Address: General Affairs Board, Hsinking, Manchukuo

When Prince Fumimaro Konoye (see sketch this issue) formed his Cabinet, one of the first men he summoned was Naoki Hoshino, chief administrator of the Manchukuo State council and known abroad as "Manchukuo's dictator." In the Cabinet Hoshino is minister without portfolio and also president of the Cabinet's planning board, the government's most important administrative organ, where concrete measures for enforcing national policies are drafted.

Hoshino's previous career well qualifies him for his new job. It was he who originated Manchukuo's state-controlled economy, and, because Konoye's plans for Japan include the government's intensification of state-controlled industries, he picked him out. Since 1932 Hoshino has been in Manchukuo. He went there as a vice-minister in the finance department and in 1936 became chief administrator. It was Hoshino who announced Manchukuo's five-year development plan and who gave the Japanese financial world something to talk about again when, shortly after the outbreak of the Sino-Japanese hostilities in 1937, he succeeded in effecting Manchukuo's adoption of a revised expansion program with an increased appropriation.

Hoshino was born in Tokyo and was graduated from the Law College of Tokyo Imperial University in 1917. He immediately went into Japan's finance ministry and became chief of the indirect taxation section and later chief of the state property section. But though his experience was received in the finance ministry, he is not of the orthodox, conservative career-man type. He isn't afraid of undertaking bold enterprises, as his plans for Manchukuo show.

When Hoshino arrived in Tokyo to become a member of Konoye's Cabinet he provided the newspaper reporters with good copy. He came by plane with only one suit, and that a soiled one. He also wore large, thick, shell-rimmed spectacles which accentuated his short stature of five feet two inches. His hair, thin but long, was disheveled. He startled the Japanese, too, when they found out that he had no home of his own in Tokyo and had to stay at a friend's place. He had gone to Manchukuo in 1932 with the intention of living there all his life and had given up all his Tokyo property and connections.

Hoshino, who is married and the father of two sons and one daughter, is said to be a man without a hobby. His only diversion is reading—mainly foreign books and periodicals. Unlike many men in Japanese public life he is easily approachable. Shortly after his appointment he amazed a reporter who was seeing him for the first time by greeting him like an old friend.

References

N Y Times p19 Jl 21 '40; p3 Jl 22 '40; p5 Ag 5 '40
Japan Manchoukuo Year Book 1937
Who's Who in Japan

HOUSTON, DAVID FRANKLIN (hūs′-tŭn) Feb 17, 1866—Sept 2, 1940 Former Secretary of Agriculture (1913-1920) and for-

DAVID F. HOUSTON

HOUSTON, DAVID FRANKLIN—*Cont.*
mer Secretary of the Treasury (1920-1921);
as Secretary of Agriculture helped organize
the Federal Reserve Bank system; board
chairman of the Mutual Life Insurance Company of New York; vice-president of the
Bell Telephone Securities Company; served
as president of the Agricultural and Mechanical College of Texas; president of the
University of Texas; chancellor of Washington University in St. Louis

References

> Leaders in Education 1932
> Who's Who in America
> Who's Who in Commerce and Indus
> try

Obituaries

> N Y Herald Tribune p20 S 3 '40 por
> N Y Times p17 S 3 '40 por
> Newsweek 16:8 S 16 '40

HOWARD, BART B. May 13, 1871-
Winner of 1939 Pulitzer Award for distinguished editorial writing
Address: b. St. Louis Post-Dispatch, St.
Louis, Missouri

Bart Howard of the St. Louis *Post-Dispatch* is a man who is fond of saying:
"There are three great documents that
everybody needs to know: the Sermon on
the Mount, the Magna Carta and the Bill
of Rights. In them are distilled all the
religion, all the politics, all the rules for
good living that any man needs." For
more than half a century he has also had
the habit of memorizing an outstanding
passage from his favorite authors each day,
among them Homer, Cicero, Aeschylus,
Seneca, Gibbon and Macaulay. And he has
been a newspaper man for nearly 50 years.
That may give some idea of the kind of
editorials that won for him the 1939 Pulitzer
Prize for distinguished editorial writing
during the year, "the test of excellence
being clearness of style, moral purpose,
sound reasoning and power to influence public opinion in what the author conceives to
be the right direction."

Bart Howard is a New Englander, born
in North Brookfield, Massachusetts on May
13, 1871. He went to Phillips' Exeter
Academy and thence to Williams College,
where his talents as a second baseman outshone even his scholastic ability. He was
so good that when he left college he went
into professional baseball and in the depression of the mid-nineties was earning from
$175 to $200 a month, a salary which enabled him to "afford the luxury of going
to work as a cub reporter at $6 a week"
on the Schenectady (New York) *Gazette*.

After Howard was graduated from cub
reporting there was a brief period in South
America; then he went to Joplin, Missouri
to become editor of both the *News-Herald*
and the *Globe* and to discover Ann Picher,
whom he married. (They have one daughter, Virginia.) While there he was "men

tor" for at least a couple of younger newspaper men who since haven't done badly
by the profession: Ben Reese, present managing editor of the *Post-Dispatch,* and Wesley Winans Stout, editor of the *Saturday
Evening Post.*

Next Bart Howard went to Ohio as managing editor of the Columbia *Sun* until it
suspended publication two years later. Then
the St. Louis *Republic* took him on as feature
writer, sports expert, conductor of the
"Whatyamacallem" column of local fame.
After that and after three years' experience
as editorial writer with the *Daily Oklahoma*
of Oklahoma City, he joined the St. Louis
Post-Dispatch staff on May 6, 1919 (having
worked for the paper briefly in 1910), and
there he has been for the past 21 years.

Bart Howard's editorials are known not
only for a respect for words that is unusual
in the breezy journalism of today, but for
the "deep and abiding convictions" that they
evidence. He can be indignant—against
Fascism, or corruption in business or government, or any flaunting of the human
rights which he believes in so sincerely. He
can be sonorous, too, much in the style of
his favorite Macaulay. He can call Germany, epigrammatically, "a Colossus in
growing pains," or he can use the "latest
bit of slang fresh from Tin-Pan Alley." But
there is a dignity and earnestness to all his
writing that makes a Bart Howard editorial
immediately recognizable.

He hasn't lost his fondness for baseball—
or, for that matter, for anything else, whether
it is flowers or good food, or simply the
day's work. But he likes to recall the good
old days in St. Louis (he calls it "the Golden
Age") when his favorite beer was still being
served by Tony Faust and when "the automobile had not yet banished the democracy
of the street car."

References

> St Louis Post-Dispatch p1C My 7 '40
> por

HOWARD, ROY WILSON Jan 1, 1883-
Newspaper publisher
Address: b. 230 Park Ave, New York City

Roy Howard is a newspaper man who not
only writes and publishes news but makes it.
He made it when he got a "knock-out" interview with Lloyd George in 1916; when
he gave out news of the false armistice in
1918; when he got a private interview with
Emperor Hirohito of Japan in 1933; when
he had an exclusive session with Stalin in
1936; and when President Roosevelt, in
August 1940, pointed him out as the "one
exception" who had refused to help in the
defense program.

Roosevelt wanted Roy Howard to go to
South America to sound out opinion among
political leaders and publishers and report on Fifth Column activities. But Howard pointed out that he hadn't been in South
America for any length of time for almost 20

years, knew no Spanish or Portuguese and was totally unfamiliar with Latin America. This, said he, was why he had refused, and "it would be erroneous to believe that my personal affairs played any part in my decision. No personal considerations have ever or ever will interfere with my rendering to you or anyone in your position, any public service for which I am qualified."

But though energetic Roy Howard states his willingness to render "public service" to Roosevelt, he and the Scripps-Howard newspapers under him, especially the New York *World-Telegram*, did their best to see that whatever service Roy Howard eventually gave would be given under Wendell Willkie (see sketch this issue). At the Republican Convention in June, Howard "buzzed around Philadelphia in a green sports coat, green striped flannels, green bow tie, green shirt, green pocket handkerchief" and then took Willkie away for a week end on the Howard yacht. Immediately his papers began "thunderously thumping" for the Republican nominee.

There was a time, however, when Roy Howard was enthusiastically for Roosevelt—"we have a leader," he rejoiced in 1933. A few years later the Scripps-Howard papers were delivering stinging attacks on the New Deal, partly in editorials, partly through their columnists, Raymond Clapper and Westbrook Pegler (see sketches this issue). Howard himself, in 1935, wrote Roosevelt: "There can be no recovery until the fears of the businessman have been allayed through the granting of a breathing spell to industry." His papers opposed spending, the tax program, the "dictatorial" Supreme Court reorganization plan, "politics in WPA," the Wagner Act. Nevertheless, even though 61 of 75 editorials written in a four-month period were anti-New Deal, as late as 1939 Roy Howard refused to admit that his papers had changed and rebuked the New York *Daily News* for suggesting he had turned sour on the New Deal program.

There are a good many commentators who feel that along with Roy Howard's swing away from the New Deal has come a general swing to the Right; that the Scripps-Howard newspapers, once liberal, have become more and more conservative. In foreign policy, in the autumn of 1940 Roy Howard was busy plugging the maintenance of good relations between the United States and Japan.

Roy Howard, now head of the Scripps-Howard chain which includes 24 newspapers; the United Press; the NEA, the world's largest newspaper feature syndicate; minor radio feature and photographic adjuncts; and millions of dollars worth of property, still "views himself as a thirty-eight-dollars-a-week reporter, in their daily, pitching hay with the rest of the hands." This is partly due to the fact that he is today actual working editor of the New York *World-Telegram*; mainly to the fact

ROY W. HOWARD

that Roy Howard started as a reporter and worked up from one.

His first job was in Indianapolis, where his family moved when he was quite young. Howard was born in the little town of Gano, Hamilton County, Ohio. His father, William A. Howard, was a brakeman on the railroad who earned about $60 a month. Roy had to work. He got himself two newspaper routes in Indianapolis and, at the Manual Training High School earned his lunches by working behind the school cafeteria counter and his pocket money by acting as high school correspondent of the Indianapolis *News* at space rates. He was graduated in 1902.

When he got out of school the *News* offered him a full-time job at $8 a week. He took it. It was shortly after that that his father died and Roy had to support his family on what he could make. His present-day "tightness" is supposed to be due to that hard period of his life—"even today, when his income runs to half-a-million a year, he is a string-saver, a waste-paper folder. He will walk around the block to dodge a hat-check tip" and for many years he was "notorious for paying smaller salaries than any newspaper owner in the country."

From the *News* Howard went to the Indianapolis *Star* as sports editor at $20 a week. While there he went to Chicago to look for another job and was told by the editor who interviewed him not to come back until he "wouldn't look funny in long pants." He got another job, in St. Louis, on the *Post-Dispatch*, and from there went to the Cincinnati *Post* as news editor. The trouble with this last job was that Howard preferred to find and tell news, rather than edit it; so he went to New York in 1906 as correspondent for the Scripps-McRae League.

HOWARD, ROY WILSON—*Continued*

When Edward Wyllis Scripps, founder of the chain, first met Howard he is reported to have said: "That young man will never get indigestion from licking my boots." In the same year that he was hired Howard became New York manager of the new Scripps Publishers Press Association and the next year found him New York manager of the United Press when it took over the Publishers Press Association. Working 15 hours a day, Howard filed news, assigned reporters, organized bureaus, sold the service and set up a compact European news service. He also bought stock in the U. P., economizing to pay for it by living modestly with his mother, Elizabeth (Wilson) Howard, until he was married in 1909 in London to Margaret Rohe, pioneer newspaper correspondent and magazine writer. In 1912 Howard became president and general manager of the United Press. Under him it expanded from 21 bureaus serving 267 clients to 104 serving more than 1,350. There is no doubt that he was "in great measure responsible" for the U. P.'s success.

When the First World War broke out Howard went to Europe, "where he shuttled with tireless energy between trenches and foreign offices, running down news less energetic correspondents somehow missed." Because of his activities then and later a veteran newspaper man once described him as "three jumps ahead of the news—three jumps ahead of himself."

In 1921 E. W. Scripps told Howard he was going to be made a chairman of the board and business director of the Newspaper Enterprise Association and all the Scripps-McRae newspapers, as well as chairman of the board of the United Press Association, in partnership with Scripps' son Robert. Howard is supposed to have "put up a big kick." He didn't want to be a business manager; he wanted to be an editor. He took the job, however, and was able to get his chance in 1925, when he took over the editorial direction of all these enterprises in association with Robert Scripps. By this time the chain was no longer the Scripps-McRae newspapers: it was the Scripps-Howard chain.

In 1931 Howard engineered the merger of the New York *World* with the *Telegram* and proceeded to take a greater interest in that paper than in any other. In 1936 Howard resigned the chairmanship of the board of the Scripps-Howard enterprises "to associate himself more closely with Robert P. Scripps, the controlling stockholder, in purely editorial activities, especially those pertaining to national and international relationships." As he put it more informally, "I have never been one of those birds who could sit back and say, 'All right, boys, go

get them.' I have to say, 'All right, boys, let's go get 'em.'" After Robert Scripps, who had actually never taken much part in the work (he always wanted to be a poet) died in 1938, Howard, chairman of the executive committee, was in full editorial control.

Free from the cares of management, Howard continued traveling and reporting, "self-assured, light-heartedly truculent, uninhibited, peripatetic, striving to shrink the earth in the service of his solid mistress, the news, and her unstable sister, opinion." His five-foot-five slim figure continued to be seen all over the world, talking to crowned heads and head waiters—"gregarious, a first-rate story teller, an excellent mixer, he never forgets people worth while." And they seldom forget him, despite or maybe because of his "gift for spontaneous insult equaled by few men" and his "special Hoosier proficiency in the use of epithet and profanity," delivered in a "high, arid, twanging voice."

Howard is easy to remember, too, because of his taste in clothes. Whether he is game hunting or news hunting, he "favors checks. His shirts run through the spectrum and are often yellow, green or one of the gaudier shades of purple. He carries walking sticks, his folded pince-nez invariably swings across his waistcoat and to see him stride through a city room on one of his best days is to see an army with banners."

References

Lit Digest 121:38-9 Mr 14 '36 por; 121: 35-6 Je 27 '36 por
Nation 143:158 Ag 8 '36; 146:548 My 14 '38; 148:553-6 My 13 '39; 148: 580-4 My 20 '39
New Repub 95:322-5 Jl 27 '38
Sat Eve Post 210:5-7+ Mr 12 '38 pors
Time 27:29-30+ Je 29 '36 por; 36:12 S 2 '40 por

Who's Who in America
Who's Who in Commerce and Industry
Who's Who in Journalism

HOWE, FREDERIC CLEMSON

Nov 21, 1867—Aug 3, 1940 Lawyer; economist; special assistant to Henry A. Wallace (see sketch this issue), Secretary of Agriculture; former consumers' counsel of AAA; leader in civic reforms; appointed special expert on the Mediterranean question at Paris Peace Conference by President Wilson; perennial champion of liberal causes and reform movements; United States Commissioner of Immigration at the Port of New York (1914-19)

References

Howe, F. C. Confessions of a Reformer 1925
Who's Who in America
Who's Who in Law

FREDERIC C. HOWE

Obituaries

N Y Herald Tribune p28 Ag 4 '40 por

N Y Times p33 Ag 4 '40 por

HOWE, QUINCY Aug 17, 1900- Author; editor; radio commentator

Address: b. Simon & Schuster, Inc, 1230 Sixth Ave, New York City; h. 108 E 82nd St, New York City

What Quincy Howe probably considers his most telling achievement in a distinguished career as author, editor and radio commentator is the fact that he once riled the imperturbable British. In fact, the British Lion has always been his *bête noire,* and his avocation has long been pulling the said royal beast's tail. This pastime attained results when his book, *England Expects Every American to Do His Duty,* provoked a storm of indignation in England in 1937.

Quincy Howe is a caustic-tongued, canny Yankee—by heritage as well as by inclination. He is the son of Boston's famed librarian and biographer, Mark Antony De Wolfe Howe, (who won the Pulitzer Prize of 1924 for *Barrett Wendell and His Letters*). On his father's side he descends from James Howe, who emigrated from England in 1637. Through his mother, Fanny Huntington Quincy, he descends from Josiah Quincy, the president of Harvard. Quincy Howe was born in Boston, and his wife, Mary L. Post, whom he married in 1932, also comes from Boston.

Young Howe attended St. George's School in Newport, Rhode Island and later went to Harvard. In 1918 he served in the United States marine unit of Harvard's Students' Army Training Corps. After he

was graduated, *magna cum laude,* in 1921 he spent a year abroad traveling in Europe and studying at Christ's College, Cambridge. His English critics explain his Anglophobia by hinting slyly that he did not enjoy his stay in Cambridge. Mr. Howe claims he did and that the British are a decaying race anyhow.

From 1922 to 1929 he worked with the Atlantic Monthly Company in Boston, where he was one of the editors of *Living Age,* a monthly devoted to translating and reprinting articles from the foreign press. In 1928 the magazine was sold to Archibald Watson of New York and after six months, during which he was assistant to the editor of the *Atlantic Monthly,* Mr. Howe followed it there as editor in chief. While editing *Living Age* he published a startling exposé of the arms traffic. This material formed the basis of the sensational article, *Arms and the Men,* which later appeared in *Fortune* and led to the Nye Senate investigation.

His first book, *World Diary: 1929-1934,* came out in the fall of 1934. A summary of his extensive knowledge of the foreign and domestic scene, it elicited a great deal of favorable comment. "Mr. Howe's volume . . . is one of the clearest and most consistent interpretations of events during the depression period that I have encountered anywhere. It is moreover an interpretation which no one can afford to ignore," wrote one critic.

A year later Quincy Howe became editor in chief of Simon & Schuster. Under him that firm has brought out three books "expressing respectively suspicion of the motives, amusement at the manners and rage at the methods of the massive muddling empire of George VI." The first was Howe's own *England Expects Every American to do His Duty* (1937); the others were Margaret Halsey's *With Malice Toward Some* (1938) and Robert Briffault's *Decline and Fall of the British Empire* (1938). He, too, was responsible for selecting that best seller of 1936, Dorothea Brande's *Wake Up and Live.*

But it was his own book, published in 1937, that produced a minor furore. His thesis was explicit in the title. Quincy Howe wrote a sardonic analysis of the ceaseless flood of British propaganda inundating the United States via such influential institutions as the English Speaking Union, the New York *Times* and Nicholas Murray Butler (see sketch this issue). He claimed that "ever since the unpleasantness of 1776 the American Dominion has been making the world safe for the British Empire." His forthright denunciation of the Anglophile policy of our State Department placed him in the ranks of eminent isolationists with a concretely outlined program of self-sufficiency.

The British reaction to his book was satisfying in the extreme. It provoked a debate on the floor of the House of Commons and a special meeting in London of the English Speaking Union, attended by Lady Astor, Lord Lothian (see sketches this issue)

QUINCY HOWE

and other eminent Englishmen. The British reviews ran the gamut from a Podsnap-like sneer to an outraged howl. There even came a reaction from H. G. Wells, who contributed a nasty little parable on "Dame Quincy Howe," who smugly watched other people's houses being burned until her own caught fire. Quincy Howe was matched at a press luncheon debate with Sir Wilmott Lewis, who accused him of seeing an Englishman under every bed. Howe replied to Sir Wilmott's rather superior speech by saying in effect that his honored opponent is the best illustration of how persuasive and dead wrong an Englishman can be at the same time.

Howe was one of the crop of commentators on world affairs that was brought forth by the Czechoslovakian crisis in 1938. He analyzed the news for the Mutual Broadcasting System. Since August 1939 he has been commenting three times a week on WQXR. Devoid of breathless sensationalism, his comments, delivered in a somewhat flat Bostonian monotone, have been amazingly canny and original. The impressive mixture of thorough knowledge and clarity in his broadcasts, plus an ingratiating homespun humorous quality, has made him a popular commentator.

In the spring of 1939 he wrote his third book, *Blood is Cheaper Than Water,* in which he described the attributes of what he called "the peace and war parties" of the United States and the state of mind of the average American who, "if he cannot entirely share the idealism of the peace party, finds the realism of the war party even less to his taste." No longer a total isolationist, Quincy Howe is himself the embodiment of the small group of people, who, unable to prevent the chaos into which the world is being plunged, nevertheless prefer to go

through it with their eyes wide open. That same year he also wrote an introduction to and edited David Low's *Cartoon History of Our Times* (see sketch this issue). In the fall of 1940 his latest book, *The News and How to Understand It, in Spite of the Newspapers, in Spite of the Magazines and in Spite of the Radio,* inspired by his own editing and radio experiences was published.

Quincy Howe is a slight, pleasant-spoken New Englander with a keen, expressive face. Vital and restless, he produces an impression of constant alertness, of always being on the go. Characterized by Clifton Fadiman (whom he succeeded at Simon & Schuster as editor in chief) as "one of the most brilliant editors working in New York today," he is without doubt also one of the busiest. Besides "editing other people's books," he keeps busy on his own. In 1940 and 1941 he will also be effectively occupied by a lecture tour throughout the country, speaking on subjects of topical interest. He has not much time for hobbies, smokes incessantly and will discourse fluently on any subject with a cigarette hanging precariously from the corner of his mouth. He likes to play tennis, sail and walk but gets time only for walking. He has two children—a son, Quincy Jr., and a daughter Mabel Davis. His sister, Helen Huntington Howe, is a well-known monologuist.

References

> Newsweek 10:36 Ag 21 '37 por
> Time 32:69 D 5 '38 por; 36:75-6 N 25 '40
>
> America's Young Men
> Who's Who in America

HUCKEL, OLIVER, REV. Jan 11, 1864— Feb 3, 1940 Lecturer; author of 30 volumes; held pastorate in Greenwich, Connecticut (1917-35)

References

> Who's Who in America 1938-39

Obituaries

> N Y Herald Tribune p34 F 4 '40
> N Y Times p40 F 4 '40

HUGHES, EDWARD EVERETT Mar 14, 1862—Jan 19, 1940 Retired head of the Franklin Steel Company; founder of the Rail Steel Bar Association

Obituaries

> N Y Sun p17 Ja 20 '40
> N Y Times p15 Ja 20 '40

HUGHES, LANGSTON Feb 1, 1902- Poet; novelist

Address: h. Hollow Hills Farm, Monterey, California

Of the young Negro writers in America, James Langston Hughes is credited with having best expressed, particularly in his poetry, the real consciousness and feeling

of his race. The Negro people themselves—
dock hands, porters, domestic workers and
factory workers, streetwalkers—are given
voice in poems that employ primitive or
folk forms and racial rhythms such as the
"Blues" and the "Shout." Mr. Hughes has
further written of a typical Negro family in
a novel; of the race problem in a play,
Mulatto; and of the relations of white people
and colored in various short stories. But
the life of a talented Negro in social, literary
and artistic circles during the last two
decades is likewise a subject of special interest and significance; and that is the subject of Langston Hughes' autobiography,
The Big Sea, published in August 1940.

The Big Sea is a tolerant, candid, but unpretentious chronicle, richly underlaid with
race experience, of a Negro boy's growing
up, of his adventures in travel and in literature. Since little beyond the most meager
facts concerning the publication of his
books has been written about Langston
Hughes, *The Big Sea* is an authentically
valuable biographical source as well as a
vital human and social document. Early in
his autobiography the author tells us that
he is a "brown" Negro of mixed blood: on
his father's side both male great-grand-
parents were white; on his mother's, French
and Indian blood contributed to his heritage.
His ancestors were intelligent, freedom-lov-
ing people; one of them was a follower of
John Brown and was killed in the raid on
Harpers Ferry. Young Langston was born
in Joplin, Missouri on February 1, 1902,
son of James Nathaniel and Carrie Mercer
(Langston) Hughes. But he grew up
mostly in Lawrence, Kansas. His father
and mother were separated: his father was
in Mexico, where his one ambition was to
make big money and forget his race; his
mother was forced to travel about in search
of jobs. His grandmother brought him up.
At her death he went to live with "Auntie"
Reed, very kind, and very religious. At 13
he attended a revival at Auntie Reed's
church, hoping to "see Jesus" and get converted. All the children were soon saved
but Langston, who felt so embarrassed at
being the last one in his seat that he thought
he'd better get up and say he was saved.
But it was a bitter disappointment: he
hadn't seen Jesus.

The boy worked at odd jobs after school,
and went to see all the road shows he
could. Though he had never written a
poem, when he was graduated from grammar school he was elected class poet; that,
he says, is how he began to write poetry.
His mother remarried when he entered
high school and his family moved to Cleveland. There he went to Central High School
and wrote poems for the school magazine.
He read much of Carl Sandburg (see sketch
this issue), whom he greatly admired, and
began to write poems like his. "I wrote
about love, about the steel mills where my
stepfather worked, the slums where we
lived, and the brown girls from the South."

LANGSTON HUGHES

He was also on the track team and in his
senior year edited the year book. His best
friend was a Polish boy, but he had lots
of Jewish friends, too. He worked during
vacations; at night he read. The world of
books became the real world to him. He
began sending poems to magazines, but they
all came back.

The summer of 1919 he spent in Mexico
with his father, who associated with money-
making whites and hated both poverty-
stricken Negroes and peons. He intensely
disliked his father and went back to Cleveland, but returned later on his father's
promise to give him a college education.
At this time he wrote *The Negro Speaks of
Rivers*, a poem which, published in the *Crisis*,
first won him attention. He finally persuaded his father to let him go to Columbia
University instead of to an engineering
school, and went to New York City. But
he didn't like the bigness and loneliness of
Columbia, couldn't study, and quit at the
end of the first year.

At 20 he moved to Harlem and began life
on his own. Leaving the world of books
to see the real world, his first big adventure came when he signed up on a ship
going to Africa. He returned with a wealth
of experience but with a pet monkey as his
only material asset. Another sea-faring
venture landed him at last in Paris, penniless
but enchanted by all that Paris offered a
romantic young man. He became assistant
cook at the Grand Duc Café, where many
famous Americans dined. After learning a
good deal about Parisian night life he spent
some time beachcombing in Italy and dipping into Spain before coming back to New
York. Broke, he joined his mother in Washington, worked in a laundry, and because he
was unhappy (he always wrote when unhappy, he says) composed a number of

HUGHES, LANGSTON—*Continued*

Negro blues and spirituals. While working as a bus boy in a hotel he met Vachel Lindsay, who was enthusiastic about his poems and made him known to the literary world of the '20s. With *The Weary Blues* he won first prize in a poetry contest held by *Opportunity* magazine.

Langston Hughes now found himself riding into fame on the new Negro vogue in New York—the vogue that saw the rise of Paul Robeson, Countee Cullen, Florence Mills, Josephine Baker, Roland Hayes—that took white people in droves to Harlem and the Cotton Club. Many white writers and philanthropists became interested in Negro culture: the "new Negro" was being created. Elegant banquets and parties, at which Negro artists were feted, were given by the intelligentsia. Chief among these party-givers was Carl Van Vechten, through whose influence Langston Hughes' first book of poems, *The Weary Blues*, was published in 1926, a book highly praised by critics for its force, passion, directness and sensitive perception. A second volume, *Fine Clothes to the Jew* (1927), was almost as well received by the white press, but generally condemned by Negro critics such as Benjamin Brawley, who missed its satire and felt that it was "holding up our imperfections to public gaze."

Aware of the need of completing his education, Langston Hughes then became a student at Lincoln University in Pennsylvania, where he also began to write what he hoped would be a novel of typical Negro family life in Kansas. At this time he was receiving substantial financial aid from a wealthy New York patroness interested in his work. He felt deep gratitude and respect for his benefactress (whom he does not name). But when he wrote a satirical poem on the opening of the new Waldorf Hotel when thousands were hungry and homeless, she did not like it. Because of things she later said his violent anger resulted in a period of physical illness. About this time he realized that the "Negro renaissance" could not last and he determined to finish his novel and strike out on his own as a writer. *Not Without Laughter* (1930), narrating the life of the colored boy, Sandy, was commended as a good piece of work because it kept sanely to a middle course between the sentimental and the sensational in stories of Negro life. In 1931 this novel received the Harmon Prize of $400 and a gold medal.

Langston Hughes' own story of his life in *The Big Sea* ends with the waning of the Negro vogue in 1930 and the publication of his novel. Because of his interest in the common folk from which he came and his sympathy for all persecuted peoples, he soon became active in workers' movements and his writing began to take on a new degree of social consciousness. This was to be noted in the poems in *Scottsboro Limited* (1932) and a collection of stories showing the relations between white and colored told from the Negro viewpoint, *Ways of White Folks* (1934). *The Dream Keeper,* a number of poems for children, was published in 1932. In 1933 he was in Russia assisting in preparing a scenario on Negro life for a motion picture to be made in Moscow. He was selected by Dr. Charles Austin Beard in 1934 as one of America's 25 most interesting personages with a socially-conscious attitude. He was awarded a Guggenheim Fellowship in creative writing in 1935; and in that year his play, *Mulatto,* opened on Broadway. It was not well received; critics thought that Hughes, an excellent poet, should not be encouraged as a dramatist.

Meanwhile he continued his travels and observations, both in this country and abroad; and his sympathies for the Loyalist cause in Spain took him to that country during the Spanish Civil War in 1936 as Madrid correspondent for the Baltimore *Afro-American.* Since the publication of *The Big Sea* he has been living in Chicago and California and plans for the fall of 1940 a travel and lecture tour in the United States.

References

Nation 146:123-4 Ja 29 '38
New Repub 103:600 O 28 '40
N Y Times Book R p5 Ag 25 '40 por
Brawley, B. G. New Realists *In* Negro Genius p231-68 1937
Hughes, L. The Big Sea 1940
Kunitz, S. J. ed. Living Authors 1937
Ovington, M. W. Langston Hughes *In* Portraits in Color p194-204 1933
Redding, J. S. Emergence of the New Negro *In* To Make a Poet Black p93-125 1939
Who's Who in Colored America

HULL, CORDELL   Oct 2, 1871- Secretary of State

Address: b. Department of State, Washington, D. C.

"Cord wasn't set enough to be a schoolteacher, wasn't rough enough to be a lumberman, wasn't sociable enough to be a doctor and couldn't holler loud enough to be a preacher. But Cord was a right thorough thinker." That's what the father of the present United States Secretary of State said about him, and later others considered Cordell Hull "thorough thinker" enough to emerge as Democratic possibility for the Presidency of the United States in 1940.

It is true that Hull may not be the most popular man in the country in the spectacular sense of the word, but somebody once called him "the least unpopular," and sometimes that's safer. In all Hull's years in a New Deal Cabinet he has managed to keep out of (and what's more, keep quiet about) domestic policies so completely that many conservatives consider him "a 'sound' man who happens to find himself in the Cabinet of a wild-man President," yet lib-

erals can't point to very much in his record
that's unprogressive. Two Republican
former Secretaries of State, Stimson (see
sketch this issue) and Charles Evans
Hughes, were among his staunch supporters.

Hull himself has never asked any "monument in life except a deep nick in a tariff
wall." It has taken him most of his life
to make that nick, and if today we have
"unconditional most-favored nation reciprocal trade agreements" with 22 nations, with
which we have been doing 60 per cent of
our foreign business, it is largely due to
the persistence of this gaunt, white-haired,
drawling Tennessean.

Cordell Hull wasn't born 'an internationalist. He was born and grew up in a community so backwoodsy that in 1937 there was
one telephone in the whole countryside. The
exact spot was on Star Point, in a log cabin
among the haze-hung mountains of northern
Tennessee, and the date October 2, 1871.
His shrewd, tough, "ornery-dressin'" father,
still remembered as "Uncle Billy" and celebrated as Pickett County's great man, was
married to a girl with Cherokee blood in
her veins: "tall, dark, sweet-eyed" Elizabeth
Riley. Of their five sons Cord was the favorite: "always just like a grown man from
the time he could walk," studious, quiet, but
the most expert log-rafter and the best
speaker and debater in the family. Billy Hull
had become a timberman with $1,000 earned
from moonshining, and as a timberman he
prospered. The Hull boys and the neighbors' children consequently went to a one-
room school that Billy had built himself,
and when Cord was 15 he went away to college, though not a very big one: Mont
vale in Celina, Tennessee, where half the
faculty was Joe McMillin, professor of surveying, geometry, anatomy and Greek. During the off months Cord worked in his
father's lumber business, and besides, attended every political meeting he could.
This was the part of the South where every
Yankee was a "damyankee," an old-fashioned community where politicians still
gathered at the country schoolhouse for
their campaign oratory. Long before he
was of voting age Cord was therefore not
only an ardent Democrat but had even
given a campaign speech (for Benton Mc-
Millin, Joe McMillin's brother, and a candidate for re-election to Congress), and
had driven the Governor of the state
around from town to town in a rented
horse and buggy just in order to listen
to the man's speeches over and over again.
His family and neighbors didn't have to
be particularly astute to predict a political
career for him, even if they didn't know
quite how far he would go.

In 1889 Cord attended the National Normal University at Lebanon, Ohio; the following year he spent 10 months at the
Cumberland University Law School; and in
1891 he was admitted to the Tennessee Bar.
The young lawyer wasn't yet 20. He prac-

Bachrach

CORDELL HULL

ticed law for a year or two in Celina (probably he didn't get a chance to practice
much), and then got himself elected to the
State Legislature. Already under the influence of Benton McMillin, fighter for free
trade and author of an early income tax
bill which had been defeated, Hull began to
study taxation problems. When the Spanish-
American War came, however, the youthful
politician's more adventurous instincts suddenly asserted themselves and he left statistics to recruit a company of mountaineers
and to join the Fourth Tennessee Regiment.
Although the Fourth Tennessee arrived in
Cuba too late to fight, Cordell Hull acquired
more than local fame there for his poker-
playing and a "command of language which
was the envy of all the sergeants in Cuba."

In 1903 Hull was appointed judge of the
Fifth Tennessee Circuit, with headquarters
in Carthage, Tennessee, although his rivals
had tried to keep him off the bench by picturing him as a "wild-eyed young poker-
playing lawyer." Far from not taking his
duties seriously, though, Hull turned out
to be "so tough on the sinful that crime lost
much of its allure and nearly all of its
profits," and he once fined his own "pappy"
five dollars for sitting in court with his hat
on. This period of his life must have been
a very happy one for some reason, for Hull
would still rather be called "Jedge" than
anything else. But he was a politician at
heart, not contented for very long in a
small-town courtroom, and in 1907, after a
campaign in which he "wore out three
horses, busted three wheels and two sets
of springs on his buggy and stunned the
mountaineers with tax talk," Hull went to
Congress from the Fourth Tennessee District. He had been elected by the skin of
his teeth and 17 votes.

HULL, CORDELL—*Continued*

In Congress Hull quickly became identified with his tariff and taxation program: low tariffs and the provision of revenues by direct taxation of wealth. He was something of a fanatic; it is said that he still prefers a "seven-page pamphlet on tariff statistics to a seven-course dinner." For 18 years he served on the Ways and Means Committee. In 1913 he authored the first Federal Income Tax Bill, in 1916 the Revised Act, and in the same year was author of the Federal and State Inheritance Tax Law. In the House he was leader of Wilson's economic program, and by 1919 he was calling for world economic conferences to level trade barriers "h'ar—thar—and ev'ry-whar." The Harding landslide put him temporarily out of the office the following year, but he was soon back in the House with his Jeffersonian free-trader's recipes for economic health and in 1931 he brought them to the Senate.

In 1933, five hours after Roosevelt's inauguration, it was Cordell Hull who was sworn in as his Secretary of State. Immediately there was speculation about the appointment, especially since Roosevelt's views didn't precisely agree with those of the 62-year-old Senator's, and since this unassuming gentleman from Tennessee "with one string to his bow" seemed a little drab in contrast to the youthful and aggressive brilliance of the Brain Trusters. In fact it was generally accepted that Roosevelt's was a purely political move, "part of the involved maneuvering to bind the dry, *Bible*-totin' Democratic fundamentalists of the South" to the New Dealers, and when powerful Raymond Moley was appointed Assistant Secretary of State people began to be a little sorry for "the Hon. Mr. Milquetoast at the State Department rookery who 'didn't know what it was all about'" Newspaper reporters nicknamed Cordell Hull who at first avoided his press conferences as much as possible "Old H'ar-Thar-and-Ev'ry-whar." When in June 1933 he headed the American delegation to the London Economic Conference, which ended in failure, a Britisher impressed with the ascendancy of Moley over Hull began to chant: "Moley, Moley, Moley, Lord God almighty."

It seemed that a lot of people were mistaken in their estimate of the tall Tennessean, however. He was quiet and he didn't have the manners of the conventional diplomat, but he knew his own mind and he knew how to make people like him. At the Pan-American Conference at Montevideo that same year his easy informality and genuine friendliness did more to wean the South American delegates away from their suspicion of the policies of the United States than any reassuring speeches on the part of his predecessors. Calling on them individually early in the morning (*too* early, maybe), the Secretary of State announced himself to the other delegates simply as "Hull from the United States," chatted a while, and left with some pronouncement like: "Just give me a ring if you want to take anythin' up with me, and I'll be right ovah." It was at this conference that a Good Neighbor policy was really formulated, Hull supporting a pact which declared in part: "No state has the right to intervene in the internal or external affairs of another," and it was Hull who laid the groundwork for the abrogation of the Platt Amendment in Cuba.

What is more, it began to become evident that when someone tangled with Hull it was not Hull who got the worst of it. Moley was soon out of the State Department entirely; more and more Cordell Hull gained the President's ear and confidence. On June 12, 1934 the Trade Agreements Act was passed, designed specifically for the reconquest of Latin-American markets and for the re-establishment of United States predominance there, and providing that the President should have authority to raise or lower existing tariff rates by as much as 50 per cent for those nations willing to make reciprocal concessions. This was a great triumph for Hull's views on international trade.

The Secretary of State has been criticized for concentrating on trade treaties and leaving many important problems of foreign policy to others. Some say this is because "the real State Department is in the White House," and that "like a good first officer, Mr. Hull has obeyed orders." Others say that actually "his influence on American foreign policy in this critical period has been very real." In general it has been Wilsonian and internationalist, although the isolationist temper of the country has not made it possible for him to have given as much encouragement to the League of Nations as he might have wished, and although he shares the responsibility for the Spanish policy by his note to Senator Pittman opposing any action on the arms embargo. In 1940 his views follow President Roosevelt's very closely. He advocates the strongest possible national rearmament, a police force for the Western hemisphere, all aid short of war to the Allies. From July 1940 on, in the face of Japanese declarations for an Asiatic Monroe Doctrine, he reaffirmed the United States' Far Eastern policy of maintaining the *status quo* and condemned the Japanese moves in Indo-China. Cordell Hull played a prominent part in the Pan-American Conference in Havana in the summer of 1940, which he feels has made the Americas ready to meet unitedly any threat from abroad, and which resulted in the so-called Act of Havana, providing for a Pan-American trusteeship of any European possession in the Western hemisphere felt to be in danger of a change in its present status.

For a long time Hull's reciprocal trade agreements remained as important as ever in his speeches, however, in spite of spectacular international and domestic events.

To the public Cordell Hull skillfully refuses to commit himself on any issues which can be avoided, and at press conferences his favorite cliché is a vague: "We are looking into all phases of the situation." His views on domestic issues are therefore practically unknown; he says "I 'tend to mah int'national affairs." But on the whole he is regarded as "in the New Deal but not of it." It is known that he is a sincere prohibitionist, it is reported that "what he said privately about the New Deal amiability toward sitdown strikes couldn't be printed on asbestos," and "toward the entire New Deal school of economics his thoughts reputedly parallel Mr. Garner's." For instance, he regards the NLRB as unfair to all sides—the employer, the worker and the public; the SEC, he believes, needs simplification and conservative administration.

Six feet one, with thick white hair and bright dark eyes, "as lean as a fence rail," Hull is said to possess the shy charm of one "who is uneasy in the world in which he moves." There is something broodingly Lincolnesque in his "look of frontier Weltschmerz"—he looks at you as if "he is ready to forgive and forget the shenanigans you have no intentions of pulling." Many people find the "finest expression of Mr. Hull's character" in his long, sensitive, almost poetic hands, which he uses freely. He speaks "two languages"—English and the Tennessee mountain lingo. His voice is high and rasping, his plates give him a slight lisp which interfere with his "r's," he is "inept at phrase-making and so devoid of literary sense that the men who compose his speeches sometimes nearly weep over the interpolations he chooses to make in them." Nevertheless even those who don't find him effective on the speaker's dais are impressed by his absolute sincerity and lack of affectation.

In 1917 he married Rose Frances Whitney of Staunton, Virginia. Mr. and Mrs. Hull are childless, and live in a seven-room hotel apartment in Washington. They live quietly and simply, without benefit of many social affairs except those which Mr. Hull's official position requires him to attend, and the Secretary's main recreations are reading or an occasional game of croquet. Almost the only indication that he isn't entirely self-effacing is the wall of his office, which is covered with framed news pictures telling the story of his official life.

References

Am Mercury 49:391-9 Ap '40 (Same abr. Read Digest 36:114-17 Je '40)
Collier's 105:13-14+ My 4 '40 por
Cur Hist 51:24-7 My '40 pors
Life 8:79-85 Mr 18 '40 il por
Nation 141:71-4 Jl 17 '35; 146:576 My 21 '38; 146:607-10 My 28 '38; 150: 729-31 Je 15 '40; 151:107-9 Ag 10 '40; 151:291-2 O 5 '40
New Repub 95:92-4 Je 1 '38; 102:720-3 My 27 '40
Newsweek 13:48 Je 26 '39; 15:14, 52 Ja 22 '40 pors; 15:16, 17 Ap 8 '40; 16:21-2 O 14 '40 por
Sat Eve Post 210:8-9+ Ja 15 '38; 212: 21 Jl 15 '39 por
Time 34:19 Jl 17 '39 por; 35:14-17 Ja 8 '40 pors (cover, p14, 15) 35:20 Ap 15 '40; 36:11 Ag 12 '40
Babson, R. W. "Moley's Friend" (Cordell Hull) *In* Washington and the Revolutionists p138-55 1934
Unofficial Observer [pseud.] Sops to Cerberus *In* New Dealers p270-306 1934
Who's Who in America
Who's Who in the Nation's Capital

HULL, HELEN R. Author; teacher

Address: b. Columbia University, New York City; h. 878 West End Ave, New York City

During the first months she began writing fiction, Helen Rose Hull says she papered one whole wall of her house with rejection slips. But she kept right on writing, and gradually the "acceptance wall," distressingly bare for a long time, began filling up. She began her professional work with short stories that have appeared in most first-class American magazines, and in several English ones. Her first novel, *Quest,* was published in 1922, but it was 10 long years before she achieved recognition on a large scale. In 1932 *Heat Lightning* was the choice of the Book-of-the-Month Club, and it introduced her to thousands of new readers.

The 10 years between were punctuated by a number of happy literary events in her life. There was the Guggenheim Fellowship for creative writing which she received in 1931, and which gave her time for travel and study. And there were several new novels: *Labyrinth* (1923); *The Surry Family* (1925); *Islanders* (1927); and *The Asking Price* (1930).

Miss Hull combines a career of writing and teaching. Born in Albion, Michigan, of a teaching family, it was natural for her to gravitate toward teaching. She attended Michigan State College, spent one summer at the University of Michigan, and took her degree of Bachelor of Philosophy at the University of Chicago in 1912. From 1912 to 1915 she was instructor in English at Wellesley College. She has been teaching at Columbia University since 1916—as an instructor in the extension division until 1919; instructor in English from 1919 to 1923; an assistant professor until 1939, and an associate professor, giving courses in writing, since. In connection with her school work, she interviews hundreds of people, helping them with practical advice to find their ambitions and abilities. Cock Robin, a wire-haired terrier, who, according to his mistress, believes only in "art for art's sake," is her most appreciative au-

HELEN HULL

dience, a listener-in on all her courses and companion in all her adventures.

Miss Hull does most of her writing at her summer place, "Bayberry Farm," in the Blue Hill region of Maine. After a few years of renting the farmhouse, Miss Hull bought it and renovated it, for she likes the country with modern conveniences. "Bayberry Farm" is a sort of modern, rural Eden, judging from others' descriptions of it. The house stands in 15 acres of pasture and woodland, sloping down to the ocean. "There is a flower garden, a vegetable garden and an iris-bordered path leading to the door. At the foot of the lane is Blue Hill Bay, whose fine waters tempt motor boats or sailboats."

The minute college is out, Miss Hull is on her way to "Bayberry Farm." Here she dons slacks or a linen suit, and gives herself over to the simple life. There is a small building on the farm which Miss Hull calls the workhouse. When she is doing a book she conceals herself there mornings, with Cock Robin to guard the door. In the afternoons she gardens, walks, swims or sails. "She does not care for golf or politics, refuses to acknowledge the existence of bridge. She likes to cook, and could compete with any writing-chef in soufflé-making or birthday cake architecture. She shuns publicity and book reviews."

According to her own description of her writing methods, Miss Hull apparently follows the rewrite system. She says she can never make merely marginal corrections or erasures in her first draft. She reads her previous day's output, and always finds that the last page or two are inferior to the rest. She rewrites this portion.

She has the artist's absorption in and impatience to complete her work once the initial business of planning her story is completed. "The necessary interruptions of sleeping, eating, being pleasant to friends, taking the dog for walks and attending to other tasks are brambles and fences and thick brush on what the book would prefer to be: one swift cross-country run." When the book is finished, she is free again—that is, until "that distant day when at the horizon [she] sees a cloud, no bigger than a man's hand, which means that the strange urge to write another book is rising."

Miss Hull's latest novel, *Through the House Door* (1940), is a character study of a woman suddenly thrown on her own resources when her husband becomes blind. Although one reviewer complained that it "smacks too much of the woman's magazine public, the critic of the Boston *Transcript* called it "her best book so far." This was preceded by *Frost Flower,* published in 1939, a study of everyday life in an American suburban family. Drama enters the story through the mother's past, threatening to break up the peaceful family life. The New York *Times* said of it: "This novel gives Miss Hull added stature as a creative artist. Her writing is delicate and sensitive, her characters distinct and real as individuals." Other reviewers received it warmly, although some were not as enthusiastic. Phyllis Bentley wrote in the *Saturday Review of Literature*: "This portrait of a modern housewife, 1939 vintage, though not perhaps very subtle, is accurate, detailed and entertaining. The rest of the characters are lightly, but adequately sketched."

In a vignette of Helen Hull and her work, Olga Owens wrote: "I believe that Helen Hull's unique quality is her ability to put into lucid words the elusive ideas that have always fallen just short of crystallization in one's own mind. We are spared the effort of articulating these deeply sensed thoughts, but we come upon them in her prose with a delighted familiarity. Her style is simple and direct. It is extremely difficult to believe that Miss Hull has not enjoyed several brands of husbands, and has not been the mother of assorted sons and daughters."

Miss Hull's *Experiment*, published January 1940, is a collection of four stories, all of which appeared previously in magazines. A reviewer says of it: "This is a collection of four short novels, or four long short stories, however the reader prefers to think of them. The title of the book has a twofold significance. It is the name of the last and best story in the group. It also undoubtedly refers in the author's mind to the experiment she is making in a length halfway between the short story and the novel. . . *Experiment* presents four readable, well-constructed tales."

Miss Hull's novels include, in addition to *Quest* (1922); *Labyrinth* (1923); *The Surry Family* (1925); *Islanders* (1927); *The Asking Price* (1930); *Heat Lightning* (1932); *Frost Flower* (1939); and *Through the House Door* (1940); the following: *Hardy Perennial*

(1933); *Morning Shows the Day* (1934); *Uncommon People* (1936); *Candle Indoors* (1936); *Snow in Summer* (1938), published with other writers' contributions under the title of *The Flying Yorkshireman*; and *Through the House Door* (1940).

References

Wilson Lib Bul 5:114 O '30 por

American Women

Overton, G. M. Helen R. Hull *In* Women Who Make Our Novels p178-9 1928

Owens, O. Helen Hull and Her Work nd

Who's Who Among North American Authors

Who's Who in America

HUTCHINS, ROBERT MAYNARD Jan 17, 1899- Educator; president of the University of Chicago

Address: b. University of Chicago, Chicago, Illinois; h. 1146 E 59th St, Chicago, Illinois

In 1929, when Robert Maynard Hutchins became the president of the University of Chicago at the age of 30, he was immediately dubbed the "Boy President," a sort of infant prodigy of the educational world. Today he is a veteran among college presidents—only eight universities out of thirty-three have kept their presidents as long as Chicago has kept Dr. Hutchins—but he is still considered the "most dangerous man in American education," watched by his fellow pedagogues with an admiration not unmixed with apprehension.

For the "terrible young man" is a breaker of shibboleths, an iconoclast, and, to boot, not afraid to express himself. He cares nothing for time-honored traditions of university life. The social contacts a boy can make in the University of Chicago may be negligible; the football team is terrible. But the president is not dismayed: he feels that the function of the university is not "social or athletic," that primarily students must "come to college to learn to think. . . To do that the old disciplines are needed—grammar, logic and mathematics—but don't let that scare you, for these are only the arts of reading, writing and reckoning." As a result, some of the letters Dr. Hutchins has been getting sound like the famous letter an indignant Princetonian wrote to Woodrow Wilson: "You are turning my dear old college into an educational institution." But in the meanwhile the University of Chicago is on the same level of achievement as Harvard and Yale—Hutchins himself claims that "compared with the University of Chicago, Yale is a boys' finishing school"—and the students attending it are doing some serious studying and thinking.

Tall, handsome Dr. Hutchins, who in appearance "compares favorably with a Greek god" and who has proved himself to be an accomplished administrator and a crack money raiser, has education in his blood and won't leave this field for any

ROBERT MAYNARD HUTCHINS

inducements. And there have been many of them: Hearst had offered him a job; President Roosevelt wanted him in the NRA; he was offered the presidency of the New York Stock Exchange and was mentioned as a possibility during the last three Supreme Court vacancies; and the Sinclair Lewises once nominated him for President of the United States. But Dr. Hutchins only wants to be able to teach and to get his educational reforms accepted.

He has been staying out of politics except for that one time in 1932 when he came out for President Roosevelt. Later he threatened to vote Socialist unless either of the two major parties better defined its issues. His latest public statement had to do with the draft. He did not favor exemption from the draft "for college and university students as such," claiming that it would result in young men regarding enrollment in a college as a method of avoiding conscription.

Hutchins comes from a family of educators. He is the son of William James and Anna Laura (Murch) Hutchins. His father, a Presbyterian minister, was the president of Berea College, Kentucky and was succeeded in that post by Robert's brother Francis, known for his activities in Yale-in-China. Robert was born in Brooklyn, New York on January 17, 1899. Later on the family moved to Oberlin, Ohio, where the father taught homiletics. In 1915 he went to Oberlin College and after two years transferred to Yale. He worked his way through Yale by organizing a cooperative tutoring bureau. In his college days he gained a considerable reputation as captain of the Yale debate club. In 1917 he went abroad with an ambulance corps and a year later was fighting with the Italian Army. He came back to Yale after the War and was graduated in 1921, celebrating his gradu-

HUTCHINS, ROBERT MAYNARD

ation by marrying Maude Phelps McVeigh, a charming and gifted young sculptress.

Robert Hutchins spent the next year teaching English and history at a Lake Placid school. Then he came to Yale to study law and started teaching it as soon as he was graduated from the law school (1925). In two years he was the dean of the Yale Law School, which under him became one of the outstanding law schools of the country. In 1929 he became the president of the University of Chicago, probably the most dynamic and colorful personage in American education.

The first reform Dr. Hutchins inaugurated was his famed Chicago Plan, which was passed by the overawed faculty in 12 minutes. It achieved a great measure of liberalization by offering to treat students as adults desiring to learn rather than truant children who must be herded to classes. He eliminated required class attendance and the course credits system, substituting for them general examinations whenever the student was ready for them. This was an attempt to adapt the educational process to the student and to alter the previous student psychology. It was a good thing for the teacher as well as for the student, keeping the former mentally alert and preventing him from falling into a rut.

President Hutchins' other ideas did not meet with as prompt and enthusiastic a reception as the Chicago Plan. His curriculum, made up on the basis of his rather revolutionary ideas, was thrice rejected. And today he feels that even in his own university he is facing an unhappy spectacle of "wrong things being taught the right way." The bad aspects of the American educational system are vocationalism and specialism. "An American university," he states acidly, "will teach anything which will attract philanthropy or student fees." Hutchins is not concerned with making the student a "whole, well-rounded personality"— the Dewey concept of education. For him, higher education is primarily intellectual. He merely wishes to teach the student how to think so that he may himself discover the truth. To him that comes even before natural sciences. Education must cultivate certain permanent values, such as intellectual honesty, love of truth, ability to think clearly, moral qualities. This can be done by bringing the student's mind in contact with those of the greatest thinkers of mankind, rather than "putting them through little fake experiences." One of Hutchins' contributions was a course in which his students read and discussed the great classics—ancient and modern—from Homer to Freud, instead of predigested prepared pills in the form of textbooks. In 1939 Columbia University made a similar course compulsory for freshmen.

Dr. Hutchins is for the Jeffersonian principles of differentiation and selection, which means that "a pupil should attend an institution suited to his needs." He would combine the last two years of high school and the first two years of college to create so-called junior colleges which would provide the students with general education. Many of them would need to go no further: their careers would be better furthered in technical and vocational schools. The rest would be sent on to the universities. In that way a B. A. degree would mean something more than a "sheepskin to clothe intellectual nakedness." He places more emphasis on the study of metaphysics and classics (he himself is on the board of St. John's College in Annapolis where the study of classics forms the heart of the curriculum) than on natural sciences—although he does not underestimate the latter. He has consistently opposed the waste and duplication of facilities in universities. Less advertisement and commercialism would be necessary if universities got together on expensive research projects, fostered the German idea of migration of students when convenient and pooled their resources together in other ways. His ideas were expressed in his book, *Higher Learning in America*, which came out in 1936 and was a veritable *Gone With the Wind* among books on education.

The ideas of President Hutchins, and the didactic way in which he states them, have brought a storm of controversy upon him. Many see something ominously medieval in his preference for Thomas Aquinas and Aristotle and insist that metaphysics is simply a technical word for superstition. Many critics, the most violent being Dean Clark of the Yale Law School, have taken issue with his absolutism and suggested that his ideas spring from the same philosophy that forms the basis of Fascism. President Hutchins is not dismayed by these attacks. In the first place he can take care of his opponents singlehanded, being a brilliant polemicist; in the second place, even his enemies cannot deny his record as a liberal from the time he defended Sacco and Vanzetti. Even Clark has said that his defense of freedom of thought and expression are "noble additions to our priceless heritage of human liberty."

Under him the faculty has known the true meaning of "university freedom." In 1935 when Hearst and the financial community of Chicago charged the university with "sedition," raising a "red scare," Hutchins replied stirringly: "Socrates was accused of corrupting the youth. Some people would like to visit upon the educators of America the fate which Socrates suffered. . . Athens missed Socrates when he was gone. . . Those who have made these charges are either ignorant, malicious, deluded or misinformed." In 1933, as regional chairman of the first National Labor Board, he decided in favor of a striking bus drivers' union and was dubbed a Communist. His reputation for integrity was advanced when he resigned from the board of the New York Exchange, where he was serving as a "representative of the public interest," because the Exchange refused to investigate the "ethics of Whitney's confidants in Wall Street."

Yet in spite of his complete integrity and independence, often caustically expressed— he once told a fractious donor of $25,000 that "donors of less than $50,000 are not allowed to open their heads"—Hutchins is a crack money-raiser and has brought into the Chicago University coffers contributions trailing only slightly behind those to Yale and Harvard. His is the rare capacity of getting the money without toadying, and from the most unexpected quarters: such was a contribution of $550,000 from Walgreen, who had started the "sedition" investigation in 1935. Things like that keep the trustees from firing him, in spite of their wailings about his "Rooseveltian finance." His was practically the only university that did not cut the professors' salaries during the lean years, although administrative salaries were cut. He does not believe in economizing on education.

Dr. Hutchins has the physique of a Yale oarsman in spite of a marked disinclination for exercise: he ascribes his excellent health to the fact that whenever the impulse to exercise comes over him he lies down until it passes over. He is not on too familiar terms with either the students or the faculty. Mortimer J. Adler (see sketch this issue), whom he brought to Chicago from Columbia to teach his "great books" course, is a good friend of his and he numbers Felix Frankfurter, William Douglas of the United States Treasury and Alexander Woollcott among his friends. But he is rarely seen on the campus and never fraternizes with anyone on it: for one thing he is too busy to entertain the faculty; besides, he refuses to capitalize on his well-known charm. His manner toward the students is that of friendly disdain. He intimidates them in the classroom by his didactic coldness and by pouncing on them whenever they say something vague or mediocre. Nevertheless they worship him from a distance and much of the talk in the halls centers on Hutchins' latest activities.

Although gifted with all characteristics that a demagogue would welcome, he scorns to bring them into play. Thornton Wilder says that his epitaph should be, "Here lies a University President who has never used the word 'Ideal.'" He prefers to appeal to intellect rather than to emotions. He is witty and a brilliant conversationalist. His chief fear is to come to a board meeting and find all the trustees agreeing with him—that would mean that he is getting old and settling down. He hates the publicity which is brought upon him by his position and reputation. When his daughter was born (he has two, Frances Ratcliffe and Joanna Blessing) he remarked acidly to the reporters who cornered him: "Gentlemen, believe it or not, this is not a publicity stunt."

References

Am Mercury 45:482-4 D '38 (Same cond. Read Digest 33:61-3 D '38
Commonweal 32:112-14 My 31 '40
Harper 178:344-55 Mr '39; 178:543-52 Ap '39
Ladies' H J 55:22-3+ S '38 por
Sat Eve Post 212:8-9+ N 11 '39
Time 33:56 Je 12 '39 por
Vital Speeches 5:586-8 Jl 15 '39 (Same abr. Forum 103:15-17 Ja '40); 6: 546+ Jl 1 '40
America's Young Men
Gideonse, H. D. Higher Learning in a Democracy 1937
Leaders in Education 1932
Who's Who Among North American Authors
Who's Who in America

HUTCHINSON, RAY CORYTON Jan 23, 1907- Author

Address: c/o Farrar & Rinehart, Inc, 232 Madison Ave, New York City

"This," R. C. Hutchinson said a year ago, "is a day for journalists. The novelists can't keep up with the stream; the breadth and depth and fullness and lovely proportions of the art—as the masters have revealed it—cannot show themselves in this uproar." And yet, out of this uproar Mr. Hutchinson, now on active military service with the British Army, has managed to produce a novel which "will be long remembered by anyone who reads it, a novel certain to add substantially to his already secure reputation," a novel which William Lyon Phelps calls the best he has read this year.

The Fire and the Wood was written at a time when it has become "increasingly hard to concentrate for several hours a day on the fortunes of two people." But it is in Mr. Hutchinson's concentration on the two main characters of his book, against a background of Nazi Germany, that its power and moving quality lie. The story is that of Dr. Josef Zeppichmann, a young bacteriologist fanatically interested in discovering a cure for tuberculosis. Unable to find facilities for his research at the hospital where he works, he fits up a laboratory in his rooming house and begins to treat Minna, the housemaid there, for the disease. His formula is one he has so far tried out only on rats. The treatments go on; Zeppichmann (he is a Jew) loses his job; and Minna becomes, instead of a human guinea pig, someone he loves.

Zeppichmann is interned in a concentration camp and Minna in a sanitarium. Half cured, she procures Zeppichmann's escape and the two of them flee on a canal boat across the border into safety. According to most reviewers, it is in this last half of the book that Mr. Hutchinson falls down; its first part is real, its characterization meaningful.

S. J. Woolf

RAY CORYTON HUTCHINSON

What faults belong to the whole are faults of "unevenness," of "too much invention."

These are the faults which have been pointed out in all of Mr. Hutchinson's novels since 1932; yet the virtues of *The Fire and the Wood* are persistent enough throughout all his work to inspire some reviewers to calling him "a great novelist"; and even the more cautious ones do not hesitate to prophesy that he will be "one of the most interesting of England's post-Second World War novelists."

R. C. Hutchinson's first published novel was *Thou Hast a Devil* (1930). He himself says: "I have read many first novels, but not, on my oath, anything quite so excruciatingly naïve as this one. I then wrote what I thought was a pot-boiler. So far from boiling the pot it was (rightly) refused by nearly every publisher in London. My third book, *The Answering Glory* (1932), was better, I think."

The notable quality of *The Answering Glory* is its "ability to depict character," one reviewer wrote when it came out. It is the story of Miss Thompson, a missionary in Africa who is carried unwillingly back to England. There she dies, but the inspiration of her example sends another woman out to take her place. It is a warm and moving story "with plenty of stamina in it," but its material, somehow, "has not been thoroughly melted down."

Two years later, in 1934, appeared *The Unforgotten Prisoner*, a story of the Germany of post-War disintegration which, when published in England, was a Book Society choice and caused "tremendous furore." "Uneven", "too long," in plan "too haphazard," it was yet felt to be "an indictment of war as poignant as any tale of horror at the front." Its successor was

One Light Burning (1935), a tale of a don who ran away from women until he was past 40 and then began to run after one whom he had taken to idealizing with a kind of old-fashioned sentimentality. Some said it had "a silly plot," and some found it confusing; others felt that it was an "extraordinarily compelling story with deep spiritual overtones."

This novel was followed by *Shining Scabbard* (1936), in which Mr. Hutchinson presents Colonel Séverin, whose main aim in life is to have the stain of a courtmartial removed from his name; the Eurasian wife of his son Pierre and their two children. It is in the relationship to one another of the Séverin family that the essential interest of the book lies, a relationship, some critics feel, "that will leave no reader unmoved."

Testament, a novel of the Russian Revolution, was published in 1938, won the London *Sunday Times'* gold medal for fiction and was translated into five languages. Phyllis Bentley called it "undoubtedly the outstanding English novel of 1938," and its author was called "the most mature and the most accomplished of the English novelists." And yet there were those who felt about *Testament*, as about Mr. Hutchinson's other books, that he "invents too copiously and writes too easily," that he is "a man of many words."

"I wrote stories as far back as I can remember," Mr. Hutchinson says. He was born in Middlesex, the son of Harry Hutchinson, and was brought up in what he calls "an exceedingly comfortable home in a London suburb." At 13 he went to boarding school (Monkton Combe), where he wrote his first novel, a "thriller" of 20,000 words, and where he was miserable with homesickness. From there young Hutchinson went to Oriel College, Oxford, "where I wasted my time." While there he joined the cavalry section of the O. T. C., but found that his "temperament was incompatible with that of the horse." He gave this up and went into the air squadron, where he learned how to take up an airplane and bring it down without smashing it.

A great deal of Mr. Hutchinson's last year at school was spent "nervously shadowing" an undergraduate. This, he says, "was the one sensible thing I did at Oxford and we became betrothed almost immediately after I had sat for my final "schools." They (the girl's name was Margaret Jones) were married in 1929 and now have four ("rather pleasant, I think") children—girl-boy-girl-boy.

After college Mr. Hutchinson went into the firm of J. and J. Colman, Limited, manufacturers of mustard and "a lot of other things." First he was in the foreign dissection department and then in the advertising department, where he was chief assistant to the manager for almost six years. "But I never found the business of selling things such an outsize thrill as some people do," he says, and in 1935 he quit to give his full time to writing.

By this time he had already had five books published after a more or less unsuccessful attempt at writing short stories, and a little acting at Norwich. These had all been written in the evenings after a full day's work: *Shining Scabbard* was the first book to which he was able to devote all his time.

When he sends a manuscript in to his printers Mr. Hutchinson invariably accompanies it with a letter that reads something like this: "I have at last finished the book. Here it is. Someday I hope I shall write a really good one." There are Englishmen, and Americans, too, who believe that R. C. Hutchinson has already written "a really good one," and that what will come eventually from his pen is "a really great one."

References

Sat R Lit 19:4 Ja 28 '39
Wilson Lib Bul 13:584 My '39 por
Davenport, B. R. C. Hutchinson: An
    Appreciation pam 1940
Who's Who

HUTTON, MAURICE 1856—Apr 5, 1940 Retired professor and principal emeritus of University College, University of Toronto; served on the college staff from 1880 to 1928; author

MAURICE HUTTON

References

International Who's Who
Who's Who
Who's Who in Canada

Obituaries

N Y Post p22 Ap 6 '40
N Y Times p17 Ap 6 '40

IGLESIAS, SANTIAGO (ē-glĕ'se-äs) Feb 22, 1872—Dec 5, 1939 Resident commissioner representing Puerto Rico in Congress

Harwood Hull

SANTIAGO IGLESIAS

References

Time 28:12 N 8 '36 por
American Catholic Who's Who
Who's Who in America 1938-39

INGERSOLL, RALPH MCALLISTER (ĭn'gēr-sŏl) Dec 8, 1900- Editor; publisher
Address: b. 27 Sixth Ave, Brooklyn, New York; h. Shadow Rock Farm, Lakeville, Connecticut

Ralph McAllister Ingersoll became front page news when he brought to life a new kind of metropolitan newspaper—*PM*, which made its debut in New York City June 18, 1940 without a line of advertising, a neat 32-page edition, smaller and squarer than the regular tabloids. It solved the question of revenue by charging five cents for a paper. To keep its readers informed of bargains, sales and announcements of new merchandise it presented a digest of retail advertising as news. The paper was a departure from the conventional newspaper in other respects also; it was a new kind of tabloid in its treatment and writing of news and in its technical make-up.

If *PM* is a success Ingersoll will make a permanent name for himself in the journalistic hall of fame. Since 1895 only three big dailies have been born in Manhattan, and all of them were tabloids financed by rich men who could afford to spend millions on them. One, Bernarr MacFadden's *Evening Graphic*, died in infancy. The other two, Joseph Medill Patterson's *Daily News* and William Randolph Hearst's

RALPH McALLISTER INGERSOLL

Daily Mirror, survive and prosper. Ingersoll had no such private resources as Hearst's or Patterson's upon which to draw. He started out backed by $1,500,000, invested by a group of stockholders in lots of about $100,000.

Ingersoll is a comparatively young man to be the father of a new kind of journalistic effort. Thirty-nine years old when *PM* was born, he already had had a long career as an editor. He had been managing editor of the *New Yorker,* managing editor of *Fortune,* vice-president and general manager of Time, Incorporated, and publisher of *Time.*

Born in New Haven, Connecticut, December 8, 1900, son of an important consulting engineer, Colin Macrae Ingersoll, and Theresa (McAllister) Ingersoll, he was graduated from Yale University's Sheffield Scientific School in 1921 to follow in his father's footsteps as an engineer. He continued his education at Columbia University the following year, then got a job as a mining engineer with a California gold mine, working underground as a miner. After several months he got another job with a copper mining company in Bisbee, Arizona, and went underground again to work as a miner. In 1923 he became a division engineer for a mining company in Mexico.

The end of the year brought a complete change of work for the young mining engineer. He had written a book, *In and Under Mexico* (1924), and largely on the strength of that had obtained a job as a reporter on the New York *American.* He stayed with the *American* until the end of 1924, and then did free-lance writing in New York and abroad. This led to reporting for the *New Yorker.* In 1925 when he was 25 years old he became managing editor

of the *New Yorker,* and remained in that position for five years.

His next move was to the associate editorship of *Fortune,* published by Henry R. Luce, a fellow alumnus of Yale and the Hotchkiss School. Thence he moved to the managing editorship of *Fortune,* serving in that capacity from 1930 to 1935, when he became vice-president and general manager of Time, Incorporated. This involved publishing of the Time enterprises—*Time, Fortune, Life* and the *Architectural Forum,* and the sponsoring of the radio and cinema productions of *March of Time.* In 1937 Ingersoll was appointed publisher of *Time,* remaining in that position until he resigned to begin *PM,* the new paper.

Tall, bald, shambling, Ingersoll was regarded as one of the possible heirs to the mantle of Henry R. Luce while he was on *Time.* He had a reputation on *Time* for being the magazine's No. 1 hypochondriac, and his desk was littered with pills and unguents. He wrote copious memoranda about filing systems and other trivia. His salary in 1938 was reported as $30,000, income from stock, $40,000.

Ingersoll is something of a socialite. *Who's Who in America* lists Ralph Ingersoll as a member of the Yale, Union, Racquet, Tennis and Cloud Clubs. He was married in 1926 to Miss Elizabeth Carden of New York.

Back in 1933 Ingersoll got an idea that he wanted to start a radically different newspaper. He was then publisher of *Time.* But the project was entirely Ingersoll's and *Time* had no desire to go into the newspaper business. Rumor that Henry Luce's money was tied up in the new project was denied. So Ingersoll went ahead on his own. He figured that without advertising, a paper selling for five cents would break even with a daily circulation of about 200,000, and that a newspaper such as he planned could get that many subscribers without disturbing the circulations of other New York newspapers. To succeed as a commercial venture, it has been estimated, such a paper would need a steady circulation of about 300,000.

Editor Ingersoll set up a small office under the name of Publications Research, Incorporated to figure costs and make plans. In the meantime he was busy turning out dummies and planning the editorial policy and content of the proposed paper with a staff of well-known writers, laboring without pay. By April 1939 things had progressed to the point where Ingersoll was ready to resign his job with *Time*—with six months' pay.

Then began the problem of raising money for the project. Ingersoll went about delivering forceful sales talks and writing dynamic prospectuses. By August 1939 he had found three "angels" to back him. But just then Hitler marched into Poland, the stock market soared upward, and two of the backers decided their money was better invested in the stock market. One, Mrs. Marion Rosenwald Stern, daughter of the founder of Sears, Roebuck & Company, remained.

Ingersoll started finding new backers, this time trying the idea of selling stock in lots of about $100,000. It took four months of wining, dining, talking and persuading before he finally raised the $1,500,000.

The list of stockholders of *PM* read like Dun and Bradstreet's top rating. It included Marshall Field III, John Hay (Jock) Whitney, Lawyer Garrard Bigelow Winston, Lessing Julius Rosenwald, M. Lincoln Schuster, George Huntington Hartford II, Philip Knight Wrigley, Producer Dwight Deere Wiman and Columnist Dorothy Thompson (see sketch this issue).

The paper was financed on terms of non-intervention by stockholders, however. The legal guarantee of management control is a five year employment contract between the 20 directors representing the preferred stock, and Ralph Ingersoll. The contract is accompanied by $500,000 worth of insurance on Ingersoll's life as investment protection, and gives Ingersoll "complete, absolute and exclusive power to formulate the editorial, advertising, circulation, production and promotion policies."

At the end of three months, marked with many changes and considerable experimentation, it became apparent that *PM* had run through the $1,500,000 cash which its original 18 stockholders had put up to found it. Most of the money had gone into the tremendous build-up which preceded the launching of its first issue and into the equipment. But Ingersoll had chosen his backers well. In October 1940 one of them, Marshall Field III, one of the richest men in the United States, became the paper's sole angel, forming a new corporation, and paying back the original stockholders 20 cents on the dollar. He also added $500,000 more to the depleted coffers of *PM*. The editorial policies will remain unchanged, Ingersoll retaining full control as publisher. Ingersoll himself has been writing editorials, some of which, particularly an attack on Lindbergh and an appraisal of the conscription bill, had aroused considerable comment and praise. The only changes envisaged would be enlargement of the paper with a view to greater news coverage. Ingersoll reportedly was not discouraged by the reorganization, confident that the circulation was going up. As a matter of fact, he took time off to go to London "in search of a scoop," according to some sources, and returned to write a series of feature stories.

In a prospectus sent out to subscribers, Ingersoll, prior to the publication of *PM,* said the editorial purpose of the newspaper would be to tell as much of the truth as it could find out. More specifically he wrote: "We are against people who push other people around, just for the fun of pushing, whether they flourish in this country or abroad. We are against fraud and deceit and greed and cruelty and we will seek to expose their practitioners. We are for people who are kindly and courageous and honest. We respect intelligence, sound accomplishment, open-mindedness, religious tolerance. We do not believe all mankind's problems are now being solved successfully by any existing social order, certainly not our own, and we propose to crusade for those who seek constructively to improve the way men live together. We are Americans and we prefer democracy to any other principle of government."

Technically *PM* has a number of innovations. Each story is complete on its page. There are no "continued on page-." It uses both photographs and artists' drawings to illustrate news stories. Its various departments—foreign, national, New York, labor, business, opinion, the press, theatre, movies, radio, living, food and advertising digest—and the page number on which they appear on the issue are listed on the front page. In addition, the radio news programs of each day are listed on the front page. Thus one column of the front page is given over to a table of contents and the day's news by radio, and the remaining three columns to a news story or picture. The tabloid technique of telling a story in pictures is employed often, but is not a rule. Some others use no picture illustrations at all. The statement that *PM* imitates no other newspaper is apparently true.

The paper is now housed in a three-story brick and stucco factory in downtown Brooklyn, which will gradually be transformed into modern, permanent editorial offices. The name *PM* was an accident. A typographer had slapped *Newspaper* across the masthead of a dummy copy and Ingersoll thought the name *Newspaper* good enough for temporary purposes. Prospectuses and correspondence referred to the prospective daily as simply *Newspaper*. Then a gossip columnist, mistaking a gag credited to playwright Lillian Hellman as the truth, called the paper *PM* in his column. So many outsiders began using the name that Ingersoll decided to leave it at that. The name inspired a popular song called *6 PM*, which so pleased Ingersoll that he has been paying a supplementary royalty to its authors.

References

Business Week p38-40 Mr 23 '40
Nation 150:700-3 Je 8 '40
New Yorker 12:20-5 N 28 '36 (Same cond. Scholastic 33:9-10+ N 19 '38); 16:13-14 My 18 '40
Time 35:38 Ja 22 '40 por
America's Young Men
Who's Who in America

INGERSOLL, RAYMOND VAIL (ing'-ger-sŏl) Apr 3, 1875—Feb 24, 1940 Borough President of Brooklyn, New York

References

International Who's Who
Who's Who in America 1938-39
Who's Who in Law

RAYMOND V. INGERSOLL

Obituaries

N Y Herald Tribune p1 F 25 '40 por; p14 F 26 '40
N Y Times p1 F 25 '40

IRONSIDE, SIR EDMUND May 6, 1880- Former chief of the British Imperial General Staff; now commander in chief of the home forces

Sir William Edmund Ironside stands six feet four and weighs 258 pounds, which is why his troops nicknamed him "Tiny." When "Tiny" Ironside, "attired in yellow corduroy trousers and sport coat, took over his duties as chief of staff at the War Office in September 1939, his massive frame, his brindle bulldogs, his long cigars, his battery of pipes and his very name furnished British journalism with copy and color. Great Britain had found not only the man to direct her troops but also a rugged symbol of her war efforts."

Sir Edmund has always been a soldier. He was born on May 6, 1880, the son of Surgeon Major William Ironside, a Scot in the British Army (Royal Horse Artillery) Medical Service at Ironside, Aberdeenshire, Scotland. In 1899 young Edmund started his military career with the Royal Artillery and started what has come to be the Ironside legend. His name is mentioned in dispatches of the Boer War in which he is "supposed to have seized a Boer in his arms and crushed him to death." Later, as a wagon driver, he joined German troops in a campaign against rebellious natives in German South Africa, his duties those of a spy. After a couple of narrow "squeaks," he completed his job, and "disappeared into the routine existence of a British army officer."

Then came the World War. Ironside was the first British officer to land in France, and he proceeded to get himself promoted from gunner captain to brigadier general in 1916, after winning a Distinguished Service Order. A major general at 38, he was given one of the hardest assignments possible. He was sent as commander in chief of the Allied forces to the North Russian port of Archangel in 1918 to forestall a German thrust to the Arctic. The Germans didn't advance, and Ironside found himself opposed by Bolshevik propaganda instead of the Kaiser's soldiers. The morale of the varied Allied forces was far from high, and Ironside, haranguing in many languages, "performed prodigies in maintaining discipline and inspiring his listless troops with a spirit of cohesion." His superiors summed him up after Archangel. They called him "that rare combination, a good staff officer and theoretical soldier who has been successful as a practical combat officer." For his Arctic services Ironside received a knighthood in 1919.

Ironside's next post was also one of lost hopes. He took over the command of the Ismid force at Constantinople and dealt with Turks, Greeks, Bolsheviks and the intrigues on the Golden Horn. Again he accomplished a feat of extrication, maneuvering against the Turkish troops of Kemal Pasha. It was at this time that he wryly told a friend, "I seem to have become a specialist in retreats."

He appeared as retreat specialist again in 1920 in North Persia, where another Allied scheme for crushing the Bolsheviks hadn't worked out. He supervised the withdrawal of the North Persian force from the Caucasus region of Russia and later from Mesopotamia. An airplane accident in

SIR EDMUND IRONSIDE

which both his thighs were broken closed Sir Edmund's Near Eastern chapter.

In 1922 he took over the command of the Staff College at Camberley, four years later was commander of troops in India, and three years after that, in 1929, was appointed to the lieutenancy of the Tower of London. "This honor, conferred usually upon decorative gentlemen in their dotage, seemed to mark the end of his military career."

However, in 1936, a full general at 56, he advanced to the command of the Middle Eastern forces, one of the key posts of Britain's Imperial defenses. Then he returned to assume command of England's eastern area, and when in 1938 he took over the governor generalship of Gibraltar it certainly did not mean demotion. At Gibraltar, Ironside overhauled defenses and added a new item to the Ironside legend. "There was a catchy image in the association of two names, of man and rock: Ironside and Gibraltar."

When Hore-Belisha in the War Ministry started housecleaning Britain's military set-up, Sir Edmund was chosen over 50 officers of senior rank as inspector general of the Overseas forces. When War was declared in September 1939, he was made chief of the Imperial General Staff, the highest military job in England. On May 26 he relinquished that office to become commander in chief of the home forces and was succeeded by Sir John Greer Dill.

A few weeks after the declaration of War, Ironside became a familiar figure to the English public, impressed by his physique, intrigued by reports of his success as a linguist and his brilliant conversation. The spotlight was turned on his family, too. In 1915 he had taken a week's leave between two offensives to marry Mariot Isobel Chayne. They have one daughter and one son. When their fifteen-year-old son, Edmund Jr., visited French headquarters upon General Gamelin's (see sketch this issue) invitation, there was a good deal of anger in the House of Commons at the idea of such a privilege having been extended to a minor and a civilian. Young Edmund, upon his return from his visit to the army, assured reporters that he still wished to join the navy.

"Ironside spends his rare moments of leisure at a small cottage in Hingham, Norfolk. Here the General's horses are kept. In years gone by, Ironside has greatly enjoyed riding to hounds. While he never has excelled at sports, he loves fox hunting and fine jumping horses. In the hunting field the massive General on a still more massive hunter cuts an impressive figure. But his disrespectful fellow huntsmen were wont to cry, 'Here comes the tank,' when Sir Edmund hove into view."

References

Cur Hist 51:21-3+ Ap '40 il por (cover)
For Affairs 18:671-9 Jl '40
Manchester Guardian p13 Ap 6 '40
N Y Herald Tribune p1 Ap 6 '40 por
Newsweek 14:17 Jl 31 '39 por
Scholastic 35:20S N 6 '39 por
Eastwood, J. General Edmund Ironside pam 1939
International Who's Who
Who's Who

JABOTINSKY, VLADIMIR EVGEN-EVICH [ATALENA, pseud.] (jă-bō-tĭn'-skē vlăd'ĭ-mēr ev-gĕn'evĭch) Oct 18, 1880 —Aug 3, 1940 Zionist leader; author; soldier; world leader of New Zionist Organization since 1935; worked on plan for mass emigration of Jews to Palestine from Eastern and Central Europe; incurred wrath of Great Britain for his demands of an independent Palestine for Jews, free from British mandate; not allowed to enter Palestine during past 10 years; last book *Jewish War Front* was published in the fall of 1940

VLADIMIR JABOTINSKY

References

Christian Cent 55:1204 O 5 '38
New Statesman & Nation 11:45 Ja 11 '36
International Who's Who
Who's Who in American Jewry

Obituaries

N Y Herald Tribune p10 Ag 5 '40 por
N Y Times p13 Ag 5 '40 por
Sat R Lit 22:8 Ag 17 '40

JACKSON, CHEVALIER Nov 4, 1865-
Physician; surgeon
Address: Temple University Hospital, Philadelphia, Pennsylvania

The House of Delegates of the American Medical Association voted to Dr. Chevalier Jackson the Distinguished Service Award of the A. M. A. "for achievement in the art and science of medicine" in June 1940.

CHEVALIER JACKSON

Dr. Jackson is famous for his work in the development of methods for seeing into the esophagus, larynx and stomach and for his skill in removing foreign bodies from the throat and lungs. Nails, safety pins, hair pins, buttons, jackstones, coins and even false teeth have all been successfully retrieved by him. There was a time when 98 per cent of those who inspirated foreign bodies died, but Dr. Jackson's successful use of the bronchoscope has now made it possible to remove safety pins or false teeth through the mouth without the slightest risk or harm to the patient.

Dr. Jackson is known, too, for his campaign to have poisons, especially lye, labeled as poisons. For years he tried to interest people and the government in the need for this; for years he lobbied in Congress and finally, in 1927, saw his aim fulfilled.

The life of Chevalier Jackson, told in his autobiography (1938) has been a hard yet singularly happy one—a life simple in its devotion to medicine. He was born in Pittsburgh on November 4, 1865, but his family, shortly after his birth, moved to Greentree Township in Pennsylvania. As a boy, he says, "I had no intimate friends and few companions," and his school life at the Greentree Township Public School was an unhappy one. Undersized and frail, inter-

ested in his studies, he felt keenly the difference between the miners' sons there and himself, and the miners' sons felt it, too. "Jeering, taunting and physical abuse" were a regular feature of recess periods.

When "Chev" was still in his teens, his family suffered sharp financial reverses. They opened a summer hotel which never was much of a success, and "Chev" worked there summers. He always knew he wanted to be a doctor, even though he was fully aware of the hardships it would mean, and finally he entered the Western University of Pennsylvania, now the University of Pittsburgh, to take his pre-medical course. He commuted from home, earning whatever he could by painting china and glass.

In 1884 Jackson entered Jefferson Medical College in Philadelphia with exactly 63 cents a day to meet all his expenses, outside of tuition, for the year. He cooked his own meals, lived in a dollar-a-week room, spent his summers selling medical textbooks and fishing for cod. In 1886, after two years of privation and hard work, he was graduated.

Jackson knew he was interested particularly in the throat, even though doctors were, at that time, discouraged from specializing, and he scraped up enough money to go to Europe and study laryngology. Most of the money came from an old guest at his parents' hotel who told Jackson to get the best information so that he could treat his chronic laryngeal ailment. The time abroad was profitably spent, and when he returned Jackson opened an office in Pittsburgh, specializing in diseases of the throat.

Most of his time was spent with the poor, and Jackson was poor himself. He invented the esophagoscope and then became interested in bronchoscopy. But his constitution, always frail, went back on him—"most of my life," he says, "has been a battle against impaired health." In 1911 he was stricken with tuberculosis. He kept working, resting 12 hours out of every 24. In 1913 he had a very bad attack and was forced to go to bed. Somehow he enjoyed that attack. His wife, Alice White, whom he had married in 1899, took good care of him, and he was able to write the book he long had wanted to write —*Peroral Endoscopy and Laryngeal Surgery* (1914). The book was well received and has come to be regarded as marking a new era, that of direct inspection. All his other books—*Bronchoscopy, Esophagoscopy and Gastroscopy* (1934) ; *Foreign Body in Air and Food Passages* (1934) ; *Diseases of the Air and Food Passages of Foreign-Body Origin* (1936) ; and *The Nose, Throat and Ear and Their Diseases* (1929) which he edited and to which he contributed—have been welcomed by doctors everywhere.

By the time of publication of his first book, Dr. Jackson was famous. He was on the staff of 14 Pittsburgh hospitals, he was a medical professor at Western Pennsylvania Medical College and he had built up an international reputation. But he still was poor— "I could never mentally interpret achievement in terms of dollars."

In 1916 Dr. Jackson pulled up his stakes and moved to Philadelphia to establish a bronchoscopic clinic. Here he suffered another attack of tuberculosis, but recovered shortly and soon found himself in more comfortable circumstances than he had ever enjoyed—mostly because he hired a financial secretary to take care of all his money matters. In Philadelphia medals began to come thick and fast, and he was simultaneously on the faculties of all five medical colleges of Philadelphia, a most unheard-of thing.

Dr. Jackson is now considered the dean of laryngologists. His method of removing foreign bodies from the lungs by the insertion of tubes through the mouth and his techniques of laryngeal surgery have been universally adopted. Though an old man now, Dr. Jackson still devotes all his time to his work, still enthusiastic and agile.

His renowned clinic on the second floor of Temple University Hospital annually handles about 5,000 cases, and "a Ford-plant assembly line works no more smoothly." Dr. Jackson operates on Mondays and Thursdays, with his son and co-author, Dr. Chevalier L. Jackson, and two staff men assisting. There is always a fifth present—a fortunate doctor who has won the privilege of working with the master for a three months' period.

Now, as during all his life, he has very little social life, not because of an unsociable nature, he says "but simply that I felt I could not spare the time from the completion of a life's work." He eats sparingly, avoids meats and never drinks or smokes. He says he has always been grateful for "the clear eye and steady hand that only total abstinence from alcohol and tobacco could give."

Dr. Jackson is and always has been a reserved man, happy to be alone with his work and the painting he does for diversion. One of his colleagues once said: "Dr. Jackson is generous to a fault, eager to help anybody out of difficulty at almost any sacrifice. We have long been working together. He has done many kind things for me during the past 10 years, yet I feel I do not know him any better now than the day I first met him."

Dr. Jackson has devoted himself to his work with almost the devotion of an anchorite. And the dominating passions of his life have been his faith in human nature, his "love of truth, of little children, animals, nature and his great desire to relieve human suffering."

References
Collier's 98:71 N 7 '36
Etude 57:5-6 Ja '39 por
Lit Digest 121:45 Ap 18 '36 por
N Y Times p27 Je 11 '40 por
Newsweek 8:22 Jl 4 '36 il por
Rotarian 52:41 F '38
Time 27:43 Je 1 '36 por
American Medical Directory
American Men of Science
Directory of Medical Specialists 1939
Jackson, C. The Life of Chevalier Jackson 1938
Who's Who in America

JACKSON, ROBERT HOUGHWOUT (how'ŭt) Feb 13, 1892- Attorney General of the United States

Address: b. Department of Justice, Washington, D. C.; h. Lakewood Rd., Jamestown, N. J.

The appointment of Robert H. Jackson, January 4, 1940, as Attorney General of the United States, was no surprise to anyone who had followed his notable career. Most people recognized his position as "favorite son" of President Franklin D. Roosevelt, who thinks Jackson will some day be a great liberal President of the United States.

The son of William Eldred and Angelina (Houghwout) Jackson, Robert was born on the family farm at Spring Creek, Pennsylvania, February 13, 1892. When he was a boy, his father, a horse breeder, moved the family to Jamestown, New York, because Western New York was better suited to horses. A precocious youngster, by the time "Bob" reached his middle teens he had absorbed the learning of the Jamestown and Frewsburg, New York high schools and was sent off to Albany to study law at the Albany Law School. He never went to college, but he spent many summers studying at the home seat of learning, Chautauqua Institute, and received from it their B. A. degree.

When he was 21 "Bob" Jackson was admitted to the New York Bar and hung out his lawyer's shingle in Jamestown, the largest town of the district, where he still maintains his residence. On April 24, 1916 he married Irene Gerhardt of Albany. They have two children—William Eldred (born in 1919) and Mary Margaret (born in 1921).

Jackson never received a law degree—with the exception of an honorary LL. D. awarded him in 1938 by National University. After he left Albany Law School he obtained practical law experience through a practice of tremendous range. Every type of case came his way in those early years, and labor unions and large corporations alike were his clients.

As his practice grew, Jackson became increasingly identified with the business life of Jamestown. "Repeatedly," writes Marquis W. Childs in *Forum*, "he found himself on the side of the local enterprise, the native industry, that was fighting for independence, resisting the encroachments of monopoly control. For years he fought the battles of the Jamestown Telephone Corporation, which is still an independent company." After the crash of 1929, he directed the consolidation of the three banks in Jamestown, and was made a director of the new Bank of Jamestown. Jackson has served as vice-president and general counsel of the Jamestown Street Railway Company

ROBERT H. JACKSON

and of the Jamestown, Westfield and North-western Railroad, as well as of the James-town corporation counsel.

Jackson has never been elected to public office. He first entered the government in 1934 as general counsel of the Bureau of Internal Revenue. There he earned a reputation as "the most zealous tax collector Uncle Sam ever had." After exploring the infinite ramifications of the Mellon empire, he brought a tax claim totaling, with penalties and interest, more than three million dollars. The hearing before the Board of Tax Appeals ran for eight weeks in Pittsburgh and in Washington. The tax liability was finally reduced to about $750,000, but in a dissenting opinion the minority paid high tribute to the case Jackson had built up. Before this decision was handed down Jackson had been sent to the Securities and Exchange Commission to take charge of the government's Electric Bond & Share case to test the holding-company law of 1935.

Jackson's appointment, in 1936, as Assistant Attorney General in charge of the anti-trust division was a natural result of his recent excursions into the ways of Big Business. He hates entrenched wealth as much as he despises political corruption. Before he went to the Department of Justice he had definite ideas about antitrust procedure. As soon as he was in charge of the division he began to put those ideas into effect, basing his policy on the interest of the public in the prosecution of monopoly. He started the drive against monopoly in 1937 with the suit against Mellon's Aluminum Company of America. He later instituted the cases against the big oil companies and against the motor finance firms. It was largely on his suggestion that a formal, extensive investigation of monopoly was started.

In 1937, partly to build him up for the Presidency, for which the Governorship of New York is the best stepping stone, and partly because he had become a political force to be reckoned with, some of Jackson's friends persuaded him to run for Governor of New York. Jackson, to be sure, remained skeptical of the move, as well he might, for neither Postmaster General James A. Farley, who dominated the Democratic Party machinery in his State, nor other political bosses would support Jackson.

So Jackson went back to Washington. Appointed Solicitor General of the United States (chief of the government's legal staff) in 1938, he has argued more Supreme Court cases involving constitutional law than Daniel Webster. During the term ending in June 1939 he argued 24 cases, of which he lost only three. Despite contrary economic views, even the older members of the Supreme Court pay high tribute to Jackson's ability, and Chief Justice Hughes has called him "the ablest Solicitor General." A few weeks before his forty-eighth birthday, Jackson was appointed Attorney General.

Jackson has subscribed to the ideals and objectives of the New Deal since long before the New Deal was heard of. He has fought for them unspectacularly but brilliantly. He has sacrificed nothing for position but has consistently promoted the cause of men who were particularly suited for certain key positions, or whose appointments would best further the purposes of the New Deal. One Washington columnist has written of him: "Many contemporary Washington figures seem to have been eroded by the passage of time. But Jackson's stature has not been impaired."

Marquis W. Childs has written of Robert Jackson: "He will stay in Washington as long as he feels he is useful. At 48 he has an incurable belief in the processes of democracy. Those who have watched him in Washington believe that ... his star inevitably will rise in the future."

Since his appointment Robert Jackson has been the busiest—and some say the most harassed—man in Washington. In June 1940 the whole alien problem was dumped in his lap when the Bureau of Immigration and Naturalization was transferred to his department. He proposed and took charge of alien registration and had to fight the alien discrimination tendency that followed. He had to carry on the investigation of Fifth Column activities, while at the same time trying to counteract the vicious effects of the Fifth Column scare and defend the Bill of Rights. He instigated anti-trust action against oil-companies and faced the Supreme Court on the regulation of the bituminous industry. He recently clarified the Hatch "clean politics" Act, rapping both parties on the fingers.

Two of his rulings created considerable stir: The first was his opinion of September 4, 1940 when he upheld President

Roosevelt's action in sending over-age destroyers to Great Britain. In October he created an uproar by holding that companies judged by the National Labor Relations Board to be guilty of unfair labor practices should be barred from further government contracts. "The findings of the NLRB," he wrote in answer to a question from Sidney Hillman (see sketch this issue) "are binding and conclusive upon other agencies of the executive branch of the government unless and until these findings are reversed by a court of competent jurisdiction." Since this ruling affected important firms like Ford and Bethlehem, it was greeted with objections from many quarters. Cries of rage subsided, however, when he explained that this opinion had no bearing on the awarding of defense contracts which need not be withheld because of labor policies of contractors. This was resented by many labor leaders as a backing down on the part of the Administration.

In 1940 Jackson's new book, *The Struggle for Judicial Supremacy*, was published.

The Attorney General is moderate in all things but his capacity for work. He does not smoke and seldom takes a drink. "There is about him a quality of buoyant health and well-being." A thoroughly unaffected person, he likes simplicity. He is probably the only Cabinet member who drives his own car. As Solicitor General he was given a suite of two rooms: a huge and imposing room and a small one meant to be a study. Jackson chose to work in the study and put his secretary in the spacious office.

An outdoor man, Jackson is fond of sports—especially of fishing, shooting and horseback riding. He is a good softball pitcher and a fine campfire cook. He and his gay and charming wife are accomplished figure skaters, and enjoy dancing together as well. Jackson's chief hobby is raising horses, which was his father's business. All the Jacksons look forward to summer vacations on their farm in Jamestown, and to long hours of riding, roughing it and camping. Jackson keeps a small power boat, the "Alibi," on Lake Chautauqua. "The best thing about it," he says, "is that it has no telephone."

References

Business Week p24 F 10 '40 por
Forum 103:148-54 Mr '40
Look 4:10-13 Mr 12 '40 il pors
New Repub 102:455-6 Ap 8 '40
N Y Herald Tribune p1 Ja 5 '40 por; II p2 Ap 7 '40 por
N Y Times p1, 11 Ja 5 '40; p7 Ap 15 '40
No Am R 248 no2:334-44 D '39
Time 33:16-17 Je 12 '39 por; 35:11-12 Ja 15 '40; 16:76 O 4 '40
Who's Who in America
Who's Who in Law
Who's Who in the Nation's Capital

JACOBS, JOE 1896—Apr 25, 1940 Boxing manager; helped Schmeling to world title; managed Tony Galento

References

Collier's 104:16+ Jl 1 '39 por

Obituaries

N Y Herald Tribune p20 Ap 25 '40
N Y Times p24 Ap 25 '40 por
Newsweek 15:41-2 My 6 '40 por
Time 35:50 My 6 '40

JACOBS, PHILIP PETER 1879—June 12, 1940 Director of personnel training and publications of the National Tuberculosis Association; honored by the Danish government in 1924 for his work in the control of tuberculosis; author of three books on tuberculosis and contributor to medical publications

PHILIP P. JACOBS

Obituaries

N Y Times p23 Je 13 '40
N Y World-Telegram p35 Je 13 '40

JAMES, ARTHUR HORACE July 14, 1883- Governor of Pennsylvania

Address: Harrisburg, Pennsylvania

One of the "dark horse" candidates for the Republican Presidential nomination in 1940 was Governor Arthur H. James of Pennsylvania, who in 1938, following the administration of New Deal Governor Earle, restored to Pennsylvania the long reign of conservative Republican control. His campaign theme was economy. He pledged himself to operate the commonwealth upon a principle of thrift and husbandry. "We are going to take relief out

Bachrach

ARTHUR JAMES

of politics," he said. "We are going to humanize relief."

A coal mine boss' son who became a corporation lawyer, stocky, redheaded Arthur James was born in the heart of the anthracite region in Plymouth, Pennsylvania, July 14, 1883. He was the eldest son of James D. and Rachel (Edwards) James, Welsh immigrants. Governor James likes to recall that he was not born to riches and luxury, but went down into the mines during his boyhood. This was during summer school vacations. He started as breaker boy (slate picker) but rapidly rose as a nipper, brakeman and bratticeman. Once he drove mules ahead of loaded coal cars through the colliery gangways. At night after doing his homework he read slowly and distinctly from two *Bibles,* Welsh and English, to his father, who was studying shorthand. To this early practice he attributes his public speaking ability.

Ambitious to become a lawyer, Arthur James entered the Dickinson School of Law at Carlisle, Pennsylvania, youngest member of his class. He was active in sports and a member of the basketball team. In 1904 he received his LL. B. He was admitted to the Bar of Cumberland County, and later opened his own office in Plymouth. His first years were lean, but he steadily established himself until he was able to open another office in Wilkes-Barre. In 1912 he married a young school teacher, Ada Morris. Twins were born to them in 1915, the girl, Dorothy, surviving. A second son, born four years later, died in 1939. The death of Mrs. James occurred in 1935.

Arthur James entered politics in 1919 when elected district attorney of Luzerne County. During the War he administered the selective service laws and became known as a good law enforcer. He became the State's

Lieutenant-Governor in 1926: as presiding officer of the Senate he was characterized by "a grasp of intricate legislative complexities." In 1932 he was elected judge of the Pennsylvania Supreme Court, thus keeping intact his record of never having been defeated for office.

In 1937, with a Democratic Administration in control, James decided he would lead staunch Republicans to victory. He conducted a big campaign, trekking all over the state and making as many as 25 speeches a day. He assured the people he was a poor boy up from the mines, a man who shared their lot. "Thirty years ago when I left that coal mine in Plymouth I left my heart with the people in it." He was elected by a strong majority.

To keep his economy pledges, Governor James first repealed outright or amended the enactments of "fat cat" Earle's administration, abandoning most of Earle's projects. His opponents complain that he repealed the labor and workmen's compensation laws, authorized sheriff sale of tax-delinquent property, gave industry the right to work women till midnight, postponed state subsidies to schools and health institutions, and that he further financed the deficit by cutting the relief appropriations in half at a time when there was a simultaneous cut in WPA rolls. The amendment of the state's "little Wagner Act" provisions to protect employers as well as employees kept several industrial concerns in the state, however, and the outbreak of the War in 1939 resulted also in increased production in the steel plants. These "new" industries were to give those on relief jobs—the "Give-a-job" plan.

Accordingly a series of advertisements under the signature of James appeared in the *Saturday Evening Post* and *Nation's Business* saying: "Production is up, employment rising, industry expanding . . . figures show stimulation of employment by industry to the extent of 400,000 new jobs." His political adherents claimed that he had also saved the State millions of dollars by abolishing 2,000 useless and unnecessary government positions and that he had put relief on a business basis. Nevertheless writers in the *New Republic* and other papers who toured the state found a large number of "ghost" mining and steel towns, others with almost all families on relief, a four-day strike in May 1940 of 4,500 miners near Pittsburgh in protest against indiscriminate firing of miners.

Governor James is fond of all sports, particularly duck-hunting, fishing, rowing, swimming. He is frequently heard singing as he takes his morning walk. He is a member of the Board of Trustees of the Methodist Church, first president of the Plymouth Kiwanis Club and a member of Plymouth Fire Company Number One. He has been given numerous honorary degrees. His love of hiking is as typically a part of him as reading the *Bible,* for from both practices he obtains comfort and inspiration. His favorite Biblical quotation is found in Psalms: "I will lift up mine eyes unto the hills, whence cometh my help."

References

Friday 1:6 My 10 '40; 1:11 My 17 '40; 1:12-15 My 24 '40
New Repub 102:599-601 My 6 '40 por
Newsweek 11:8 My 30 '38; 15:52 Mr 11 '40
Time 32:14 N 21 '38; 35:20 Ap 15 '40
Who's Who in America
Who's Who in Law

JENKINS, MACGREGOR Apr 14, 1869—Mar 6, 1940 Author; former publisher of the Atlantic Monthly Company

References

Who's Who in America

Obituaries

Boston Transcript II p11 Mr 6 '40
Pub W 137:1232-3 Mr 23 '40
Springf'd Republican p3 Mr 7 '40

JENKS, LEON E. Oct 20, 1876—Mar 9, 1940 Research chemist for the General Chemical Company of New York; professor of chemistry

References

American Men of Science

Obituaries

N Y Herald Tribune p40 Mr 10 '40
N Y Times p48 Mr 10 '40

JOHNSON, ARTHUR NEWHALL Nov 11, 1870—July 11, 1940 Dean emeritus of the University of Maryland College of Engineering; called "father" of Maryland's hard-surface road system; recognized as pioneer in highway construction; received the Bartlee Award for outstanding contribution to highway progress in 1933

References

Who's Who in America
Who's Who in Engineering

Obituaries

N Y Times p15 Jl 12 '40

JOHNSON, CLIFTON Jan 25, 1865—Jan 22, 1940 Author; illustrator; editor

References

Who's Who in America 1938-39

Obituaries

Pub W 137:719 F 10 '40

JOHNSON, HAROLD OGDEN *See* Olsen, J. S.

JOHNSON, HUGH SAMUEL Aug 5, 1882- Newspaper columnist
Address: b. 1626 K St, N W, Washington, D. C.; h. Okmulgee, Oklahoma

Hugh Johnson Says is a column that reaches a large part of the American public every day. What Hugh Johnson says is usually sulphurous, bumptious, opinionated —seldom pulling any punches. "Hell hath no fury like General Johnson's scorn." For a long time Johnson has been one of the most outspoken Democratic critics of the New Deal and even claimed credit for having unwittingly launched the Willkie boom by his statement that if Willkie (see sketch this issue) were nominated he would make a powerful candidate and, if elected, a great President. The Presidential campaign found him warning us that Roosevelt's reelection would mean "the last of democracy as we have known it" and offering to eat his own column if Gallup's (see sketch this issue) poll had predicted the results correctly. Although General Johnson favors a strong national defense and was an ardent advocate of conscription, he believes the President is leading the United States into war, and this idea makes him use his most original adjectives and nouns. Among other things, President Roosevelt is "the real appeaser." And, Johnson asks, "what are we doing and risking in Asia?"

Former cavalry officer, writer of boys' books, businessman, NRA and WPA administrator, the General is one of the most colorful characters in public life and one of newspaperdom's greatest masters of invective. He was born August 5, 1882 in Fort Scott, Kansas, the son of Samuel and Elizabeth (Mead) Johnson. There he "ate, slept, and learned to spell to the discordant accompaniment of bugle calls, whinnying cavalry horses, and bawling top sergeants." The children in the neighborhood remember him at the age of four for his cry: "Everybody in the world is a rink-stink but Hughie Johnson and he's all right!" At 15, after his family moved to the Oklahoma Territory, he tried to run away to join the Rough Riders, was caught on the station platform by his father, dissuaded only by the promise of West Point. Upon finishing Oklahoma Northwestern Teachers College in 1901 he got the promised appointment and was graduated from the military academy two years later, the youngest in his class, with a reputation as "one of the most talented hazers" who ever attended the school and a memory of two years' membership in the Salt Creek Club, whose motto was: "Never bone today what you can bugle tomorrow." He was commissioned a second lieutenant of cavalry and the following year married Helen Kilbourne. (They now have one son, Captain Kilbourne Johnson.)

There followed years of routine military service in Texas, San Francisco and the Philippines, during which he acquired the nickname "Tuffy," published *Williams of West Point* (1908) and *Williams on Service* (1910), "two boys' books chockfull of chivalry, courage and last-minute touchdowns," wrote numerous short stories and ended by being sent by the army to the University of Cali-

JOHNSON, HUGH SAMUEL—*Continued*
fornia. There he finished in two years a
three-year course which gave him both B. A.
(1915) and Doctor of Jurisprudence (1916)
degrees. After California he was a member
of the Pershing Punitive Expedition which
dashed over the Mexican border after Villa,
but in October 1916 was transferred to the
office of the judge advocate in Washington.

Johnson tells with pride in his book, *The
Blue Eagle from Egg to Earth* (1935), how,
months before the United States declared
war on Germany, he originated the majority of the provisions of the Selective
Service Act; how, illegally and without
authority, he had 30,000,000 registration
forms printed before the act was passed;
how he wrote Wilson's proclamation ("It
is in no sense a conscription of the unwilling; it is rather a selection from a
nation which has volunteered in mass");
how he "sold" conscription to the American people.

His talents next brought him to the War
Industries Board as representative of the
Army general staff, where he helped a
group of men headed by Bernard Baruch
regiment industry, and then to the head
of the Purchase, Storage and Traffic Division of the general staff, in effect for the
last four months of the War. By 1918 he
had acquired the title of brigadier general,
commanding the 15th Infantry Brigade,
but wasn't allowed to go to France.

When Johnson resigned from the service in February 1919 he could have had
his pick of several hundred good jobs in
private industry. He chose to become
general counsel (later vice-president) of
the Moline Plow Company, in association
with George N. Peek. The farm slump
soon forced liquidation, and although in
1925 the business was reorganized with a
new company, by 1927 Johnson had become
associated with Bernard Baruch as industrial and economic adviser. Since Baruch
had achieved the unofficial position of adviser to United States' Presidents, Roosevelt's frequent consultations with both
Baruch and Johnson soon after his nomination came about naturally. And it was
natural enough, too, that Johnson should
receive the position of administrator for
Roosevelt's newborn NRA on June 16,
1933, with the job of selling industry the
idea of "fair-trade-practice codes reminiscent of those of war-time."

"When Johnson first struck Washington he gave the most exciting press conferences within the memory of the oldest
inhabitant," according to the late Heywood Broun. Looking rather like Captain
Flagg in *What Price Glory,* "gruff and
tough," his pet phrases "you guys", "cut out
that guff", "bunk", "hooey", "chiselers," tireless, rabid in his devotion to his job, the fiery
general dramatized the New Deal as no one
else could. He turned out to be a better
evangelist than administrator, however—or
that seems to be the consensus of opinion.

Business winced at his tirades and constant
threats to "crack down"; labor complained
more and more that his eloquence in defense of its rights stacked up with few
of his actions; economists attacked his
theories; others found him inconsistent,
unable to stick to a decision. Although
Roosevelt's faith in him never wavered, in
1934 Johnson resigned, still friendly to the
Administration and the New Deal.

In March 1935 came his courageous blast
against Father Coughlin (see sketch this issue)
and the late Huey Long while speaking at a
dinner given him by *Redbook,* which was publishing his autobiography. United features
promptly signed him up to do his present
"fighting" daily column. Shortly afterward he
accepted the position of Works Progress Administrator, although in his column he had
called the new relief program "a new, if more
ambitious kind of leaf-raking" which looked
like "$4,000,000 worth of boondoggling" to
him. "Anyone who congratulates me on
this job is crazy!" he announced when he
took it; and he held it only until October
1935. The summer of the next year found
him working as labor counsel for RCA
during a strike in which, liberals claim, the
RCA management employed "every union-
busting dodge in the book." In 1937 Bromo
Quinine ("for colds and simple headaches")
signed him up for four broadcasts a week.

For some time Johnson's column had
been enthusiastic neither about President
Roosevelt's advisers nor various features
of the New Deal which followed his beloved
NRA; he had never been a "yes-man";
but he did not definitely turn against Roosevelt himself until the spring of 1937 brought
demands for the enlargement of the Supreme Court. Then his editorial warnings
of the Administration's threats to democracy
grew more alarming daily, while he was
already painting equally alarming pictures
of a Fascist invasion of the American
continent and plumping for the heaviest
possible national rearmament. In 1940 he
was violent against the third term "draft."

Johnson isn't quite the brusque "Man
of Action" that he sometimes pretends. He
is an Anglican Catholic. At his Cedarhurst,
Long Island home he likes nothing better
than tending his roses and his collection
of rare plants, raising wire-haired terriers,
reading political science and economics.
He has read almost everything and can
produce an "unexpected, apt quotation from
the Scripture" for any occasion. (Recently
he brought clerical wrath down on his head
by using Holy Writ for a pro-conscription
broadside.) He is something of a hero-
worshipper: Ludendorff, Newton D. Baker
and Bernard Baruch are among the idols
to whom he remains faithful; and Roosevelt used to be in the same gallery.

His charm is almost as famous as his
energy; few even of Johnson's political
enemies find it possible to dislike him personally. His wisecracks are "rapid and
sizzling." He has a "childlike trick of
abruptly holding little muttered conversa-

tions with himself" which is utterly disarming. And the effect of his smile, a "combination of shyness and hard-boiledness," is "as surprising as though an army tank suddenly paused, reached out a lily-fingered hand and handed you a posy."

References

Am Mag 116:20-1+ S '33 por
Harper 169:585-96 O '34
Nation 139:4 Jl 4 '34; 144:314 Mr 20 '37; 144:447 Ap 17 '37; 146:297-300 Mr 12 '38; 148:718-19 Je 24 '39; 151:113 Ag 10 '40
New Repub 79:304 Ag 1 '34; 80:129 30 S 12 '34; 82:212 Ap 3 '35; 93: 252 Ja 5 '38
New Yorker 10:21-5 Ag 18 '34; 10: 23-28 Ag 25 '34; 10:22-8 S 1 '34
Newsweek 1:23 My 27 '33; 1:3 Je 24 '33 por (cover); 3:15 Je 23 '34 por; 4:27 Jl 21 '34 por; 4:34 Ag 25 '34 por; 5:30 Ap 27 '35 pors; 5:5-7 Mr 16 '35 por
Sat Eve Post 212:9+ Je 22 '40; 213: 18-19+ N 2 '40
Time 26:12 Jl 8 '35 por; 28:56-8 S 28 '36 por; 30:32+ O 4 '37 por; 36: 53-4 Jl 8 '40 por; 36:42 Ag 12 '40
Howe, Q. The News and How to Understand It p55-6, 77-9 1940
Johnson, H. S. Blue Eagle from Egg to Earth 1935
Unofficial Observer [pseud.] Industrial Ogpu *In* New Dealers p28-73 1934
Unofficial Observer [pseud.] Rally-Round-the-Flag Boys (Hugh Johnson) *In* American Messiahs p212-38 1935
Who's Who in America
Who's Who in the Nation's Capital

Thomas D. McAvoy

NELSON TRUSLER JOHNSON

JOHNSON, NELSON TRUSLER Apr 3, 1887- United States Ambassador to China

Address: c/o Department of State, Washington, D. C.

During the first two months of 1940 the State Department of Washington felt anxiety concerning the life of our Ambassador to China, because of announcement by Japanese Army spokesmen that the Chinese were planning his assassination as a means of embarrassing the Japanese in their international relations. But in March 1940 Ambassador Johnson was back in Chungking after his three-months' tour of Japanese-occupied cities, well and unharmed.

A career diplomat, Nelson Trusler Johnson was born in Washington, D. C. in 1887 and studied at the Sidwell's Friends School and at George Washington University. Languages were his best subjects at college, and he disclosed other linguistic abilities by mixing with the Southwestern Indians and learning their dialects. When a professor suggested a language appointment in the foreign service, Johnson took the examination, passed it easily and

was sent to China. There for the past 30 years he has represented the United States in various capacities, except for short intervals in Washington.

During his early years in China he was shifted around so much that he developed a restlessness which still clings to him. In 1923 he was appointed chief of the Far Eastern Division of the State Department in Washington, in 1927 he was made Assistant Secretary of State, and two years later Minister to China. In 1935 he became Ambassador, with a salary increase from $10,000 to $17,000 per year. In China, a country to which he quickly became devoted, Johnson easily became adept at reading and speaking Chinese and has been of great service in making friends for the United States. He is a typical American who is able to translate his homey, honest viewpoint to the Chinese, who have great faith in him. His attitude has always been a cautious one in regard to Japanese aggression in China. In general he has followed the course advised by the State Department—"self-denial and restraint"; no provoking of Japan in regard to our interests in China; "sitting tight on the *status quo*." Johnson has been through hair-raising times in China—civil war, the Manchuria invasion, the Shanghai battles of 1932—and has found comfort in his favorite books, which he carries in his pockets—the *Analects of Confucius* in one and *Alice in Wonderland* in the other.

At 43, and regarded as a life-long bachelor, he married a school teacher from Cody, Wyoming, who was in Peking on a round-the-world tour. They have two children, Nelson Beck and Betty Jane. His wife and children stay in Peking while he transacts business at Chungking, where he may at any time be awakened in the middle of the

JOHNSON, NELSON—*Continued*

night by an air raid alarm and be forced to seek shelter in a dugout until the danger is over.

Described as "a regular Old King Cole," Johnson is "plump as a pillow. He has thinning pale-gold hair, with lashes and brows to match, a face all shades of pink, from salmon to sunset, big enough nose, strong chin, mouth with a chronic smile. In ricksha, cutaway, or gas mask he looks more like a tire salesman than an Ambassador."

References

Lit Digest 119:38 Je 22 '35 por
New Outlook 163:39 My '34
N Y Post p2 F 3 '40 por
N Y Times IV p2 F 18 '40
N Y World-Telegram p1-2 Ja 25 '40
Newsweek 10:10 D 27 '37 por
Scholastic 31:20S O 2 '37 por
Time 34:17-19 D 11 '39 il por
Who's Who in America

JOHNSON, OSA Mar 14, 1894- Author; explorer

Address: J. B. Lippincott Company, 250 Park Ave, New York City

Unsettled world conditions cannot stop Osa Johnson, widow of Martin Elmer Johnson, from returning to the jungles of East Africa, to the little compound which she calls home. She could never bear staying here in civilization for long, she says. "There is tropical fever, yes. But in the jungles there are no diseases comparable in number and deadliness with those of civilization. There are savage animals. I have been stalked by man-eating tigers. I have walked head on into ambushed lions. But always I was superior. I was the intelligent and stronger one, armed with a weapon. . . The dangers of the jungle are trivial compared with the dangers of civilization. Nature made the one, man the other. I have implicit trust in Nature's goodness."

For 27 years she had worked at her husband's side in Africa, Borneo, Australia and the South Sea Islands. Resting under an equatorial sun, drenched by tropical rain or freezing in the bitter cold of high mountains by water holes, they waited with camera or notebook until nearly all the wild beasts came to be captured with the lens.

Chanute, Kansas was the birthplace of Osa Helen Leighty, daughter of William Sherman and Ruby Isabel Leighty. At the age of seven Osa asked her father for 10 cents, an unprecedented amount for a brakeman father to give a child of seven—a sum that would buy a pound of steak or a gallon of gasoline. It was to have six pictures of her three-year-old brother taken by an itinerant student photographer. The photographer, Martin Johnson, on his first adventure and 11 years her senior, was the man she married when she was 16. In the meantime he had worked in his father's jewelry store in In-

OSA JOHNSON

dependence, Kansas; with only $4.25, traveled to Europe on a bet; and accompanied Jack London on the voyage of the "Snark."

Discouraging months of haphazard trooping, with Martin lecturing and showing the cannibal pictures taken on the "Snark's" trip, accompanied by Osa singing and dancing, marked the early days of their marriage. Finally they got an Orpheum booking which enabled them to save enough to plan an expedition to the South Seas. They were captured by Malekula cannibals and released by the intervention of a British gun boat. Several years later (1914), they returned to the same island, and with movies of their previous visit made friends with the islanders—completed a camera record to establish the existence of cannibalism among savage tribes. This was the first of 15 motion picture features, some produced under their own name, Martin Johnson Pictures, Incorporated.

They returned home periodically to show the records of their trips and lecture about their adventures, but never stayed for long. In 1917 they went to explore North Borneo around the upper reaches of the Kinabatangan River, to photograph wild animal life and the savage Murat and Tengarrah tribes.

In 1921 they made their first expedition to Africa and were so enchanted with the abundance of wild life that they have made repeated return trips, producing their historic feature films, *Simba, Congorilla* and *Baboona*. They discovered Lake Paradise, a crater lake on the Northern frontier, and there spent four years filming the vanishing wild life for the American Museum of Natural History, New York.

In 1932 the couple adopted airplanes and in two Sikorsky amphibians, "The Spirit of Africa" (painted to resemble a giraffe) and "Osa's Ark" (so named because Mrs. Johnson was always rescuing wounded animals), flew 60,000 miles over all parts of the African continent.

Following an airplane crash which claimed the life of her husband in California in 1937, Osa Johnson dedicated her life to carrying on their scientific and film work, and returned in that year to Africa to make the largest motion picture expedition ever undertaken, resulting in the motion picture *Stanley and Livingstone.*

She collaborated with her husband in writing *Cannibal Land* (1922); *Camera Trails in Africa* (1924); *Lion* (1929); *Congorilla* (1931); and *Over African Jungles* (1935). Independently she has written a number of children's books—*Jungle Babies* (1930); *Jungle Pete* (1932); and *Osa Johnson's Jungle Friends* (1939)—and many stories for children which have been published in magazines. *I Married Adventure* is the Book-of-the-Month Club selection for June 1940, and a motion picture of the same title has been released. Both deal with the 27 years' adventure Osa and Martin Johnson faced in dangerous jungles in all corners of the world.

Mrs. Johnson is listed in *American Women* as an explorer, motion picture producer, author and lecturer. As a lecturer of five-feet-two, weighing 112 pounds, she is "chicly dressed, with a pert little hat perched over one eye, has lovely eyes and tiny feet, and the African sun doesn't seem to have damaged her complexion."

She has also achieved note as a designer of animal toys, animals resembling as nearly as possible those she has had as jungle pets. These toys are sponsored by the National Wild Life Federation, as a means of interesting young children in wild life conservation.

Fond of clothes, she has been acclaimed as one of the 12 best-dressed women in America, and says: "I'm a woman in the jungle. At the end of the day I get into royal blue satin tuxedo pajamas which have zippers on the sides and buttons of lipstick red." She and Irene Castle were the first in this country to have permanent waves She was described by one interviewer as "having the face and form of a movie star, the heart of a home-loving woman, and the courage of a lion."

References

Christian Sci Mon p9 F 16 '40 il pors; p11 Mr 23 '40 por
N Y Times VII p10+ Ap 21 '40
Springf'd Republican p4 D F 18 '40 pors
American Women
Johnson, O. H. I Married Adventure 1940

JOLIOT-CURIE, IRENE Sept 12, 1897- (zhol-yŏ' kü-rē ē-rĕn') Scientist; winner with her husband, Frederic Joliot, of the Nobel Prize in chemistry, 1935; also Barnard Gold Medal for Meritorious Service to Science, 1940

One cannot tell the story of Irène Joliot-Curie without telling of her parents, for she is the daughter of Pierre and Marie Curie, famous discoverers of radium. She was born while they were searching for radium, and practically grew up in the laboratory. She was only a little girl when her parents won the Nobel Prize of 1903 jointly for their work in discovering radium. Her father was killed in an accident in 1906, and Marie Curie continued the scientific work alone, winning in 1911 the second family Nobel Prize, this time for isolating radium.

Irène Curie became her mother's assistant, working with her at the Radium Institute of the University of Paris. There she met Frederic Joliot, eager young scientist and one of her mother's assistants. Marie Curie lived to see her daughter Irène marry young Joliot in 1926, lived to see her begin the same kind of scientific partnership which she and Pierre Curie had enjoyed. Her old age was gladdened by being able to watch the two young people develop into fine, able scientists.

Marie Curie did not live to see her daughter and son-in-law duplicate the honor she and Pierre had, the joint winning of a Nobel Prize. The Nobel Prize in chemistry awarded jointly to Frederic and Irène Joliot-Curie in 1935 was the third in the Curie family. The Joliot-Curie's won it for discovering that radioactivity can be produced artificially, a pioneer work of the atom smashers. The cash award amounted to about $41,000.

The Joliot-Curie pair were honored again in 1940 when they won the Barnard Gold Medal for Meritorious Service to Science. The prize, established by the will of Dr.

IRENE JOLIOT-CURIE

JOLIOT-CURIE, IRENE—*Continued*

Frederick A. P. Barnard, former president of Columbia University, is awarded every five years for outstanding discoveries "in physical or astronomical science, or such novel application of science to purposes beneficial to the human race." They have also been co-recipients of the Henri Wilde Prize and the Marquet Prize of the Académie des Sciences.

In many respects Irène Joliot-Curie is like her famous mother. The elder of the two Curie children, she not only inherited her mother's love of science, but her mother's lack of interest in clothes or the usual feminine vanities and fripperies.

Eve Curie (see sketch this issue), the younger sister, who took to music and writing and had no interest in science, never failed to be amazed at Irène's personality. Writing a sketch of the famous Irène in a Parisian weekly, she tells how even as a child her elder sister's conduct seemed to her entirely incomprehensible. "It used to dismay me," she says, "to see Irène Curie get a box of bonbons, put it away in her small yellow pine cupboard, always in such meticulous order, take it out once to eat a single bonbon, and finally forget all about the existence of this treasure, which I should have devoured in a few hours. I have seen her accumulate in her savings bank, franc by franc, sums which seemed enormous to me but which she never spent—simply because she never wanted anything."

Eve Curie tells of her sister's punctuality, her perfect record in doing homework, neatly and well. "This young person, so unsociable, so slow-moving and hard to approach, lacked the dash of the brilliant pupils," Eve says of Irène. "She had something better; knowledge once acquired was fixed firmly in her well-ordered mind. The examination periods for the bachelor's and master's degrees, which had made even our mother in her time feverish and nervous, were for Irène Curie just like any other days. She went quietly to the Sorbonne, came back certain of being accepted, and then waited without much emotion for the results, of which she was sure in advance."

Thus Irène Joliot-Curie acquired her B. A. and M. A. degrees, and quietly, with no hesitation, began her life's work of scientific research. In 1921 she published her first essay on physics. Fourteen years later when she was 38 she received the Nobel Chemistry Prize with her husband.

During the First World War Irène Curie served as a nurse, and her unruffled calm and constant good humor proved a boon to wounded soldiers, just as it did later to the laboratory students whose experiments she supervised at the Radium Institute in Paris. "I have never succeeded in making Irène angry," Eve Curie writes, "nor have I ever heard her say anything nasty, and to my knowledge she has never told a lie in her life." But on the other hand Madame Joliot-Curie will not do anything that bores her, such as seeing importunate people, taking interest in clothing or showing interest at public receptions.

She likes sports, and even when she has been working hardest has found time to ski, to canoe, swim and climb mountains. She hates city life, and has a house both in surburban Paris and in Brittany so that she can work all year round in a healthy atmosphere and lead a simple family life.

When she and her husband were married they agreed that the family name should be Joliot-Curie, and thus the name Curie has been perpetuated in their 12-year-old daughter and 7-year-old son. The name is also perpetuated in the "curie," the unit by which radioactivity of elements is measured. Madame Joliot-Curie signs her scientific papers Irène Curie, however.

Marriage made Irène Joliot-Curie more human, more tractable, Eve Curie says in an article translated from the French in *Living Age*. "I have seen her adapting herself little by little to family life, transforming herself into a housewife, growing deeply attached to the two children she has brought into the world. The impassive physicist now gets excited about social questions, even about political doctrines."

But tall, slim, bushy-haired, grave Madame Joliot-Curie has not allowed public questions or anything else to interfere with her scientific research. She was undersecretary for scientific research in the Blum Cabinet from June to September 1936, but resigned to continue her 10 or 12-hour day in the laboratory. Even the Nazi occupation of France could not keep her long from working: although the Germans requisitioned her equipment after the fall of France, in November 1940 they put it once more at her disposal. Nor has her pretty, fashionable sister, Eve, succeeded in making her more style-conscious. "All my efforts to get her to take care of her fine hair and to make up her face, with its firm and beautiful features, like a primitive portrait, have been in vain," writes Eve.

Madame Curie is a scientist first, a woman afterward. And she is carrying on from where her mother left off.

References

Delin 130:10 Ja '37 por
Lit Digest 118:32 Jl 14 '34
Liv Age 351:40-2 S '36
N Y Times p19 Mr 18 '40
Newsweek 6:25 N 23 '35 por
R of Rs 94:54+ O '36
Sci Mo 42:86-8 Ja '36 por
Time 26:52 N 25 '35
International Who's Who

JOLSON, AL   May 26, 1886- Comedian; singer

Address: c/o The Lambs, 130 W 44th St, New York City

The Jolson legend started on another chapter when the famous blackface comedian and mammy singer came back to Broadway after a year's absence in a sprightly comedy called *Hold On to Your Hats*. The 1940 Jolson is streamlined. He has discarded the burnt cork and has, by some miraculous means, cured himself of his trick of falling to his knees whenever his songs touch on the sacred subject of his "mma-a-a-mmy," —a time-honored practice that, he himself claims, has "given him that knee-sprung look." The critics greeted him with cries of joy. Besides being tops in entertainment, the production has turned out to be a nostalgia-fest. At the première Jolson sang *April Showers, Swanee, Sonny-Boy, Mammy*, of course—all the old favorites that had wrung the hearts of audiences many years ago and caused strong men to "totter out to send a night letter to their mothers."

"Jolson is a great, great man," wrote one critic. "He is one of the greatest dominators in the theatre. Every once in a while he leaves the stage to change his suit and snatch a drag at a gasper, but to his fans those brief absences are what might be called 'stage waits.'" All of the critics paid tribute to his inexhaustible ebullience: "His voice is a good 80 per cent of what it was 20 years ago, his vitality apparently 90 per cent... At the première he made many men over 40 cry as he sang [the old favorites from his stage career]. It was a nostalgic success and Mr. Jolson was very happy." Another critic says: "No doubt Jolson really does represent a phenomenon of cultural history. He has a style which he to some extent invented and which proved to be exactly what a large public wanted— a style which combined a persistent form of sentiment with a new sort of frenzied rhythm. Nor does he seem to have lost his knack, for when he lets himself go there is no great difference between the Jolson of today and the Jolson of the remote '20s."

The Jolson legend began with its hero fleeing his father's home for the doubtful and vagrant life of a minstrel. His father was a respectable Rabbi. The Yoelsons (Al Jolson's original name was Asa Yoelson and he had come from Russia with his parents when he was about seven years old) lived in Washington, D. C., and young Jolson's earliest ambition was to be a cantor. That ambition faded early in life, to be succeeded by a burning desire to be an actor. The boy began to run away from home, singing in cafés and saloons, following circuses. He tried at the age of 15 to join a Spanish American War regiment. From all of these ventures he was sent home or to one of his many relatives, penniless, often sick, but never discouraged. Once his father, in despair, sent him to a house of refuge.

His first appearance in the legitimate theatre was in 1899 in Israel Zangwill's *Children of the Ghetto*, in which he played in a mob scene. After that he traveled around with vaudeville and minstrel shows and passed through a long apprenticeship as an "end man" with Lew Dockstader's Min-

AL JOLSON

strels. He discovered "mammy," and America discovered him in 1909 in San Francisco, when he had to pinch-hit for one of the stars and sang his first mammy-song in blackface. After the last anguished invocation had shaken the rafters Jolson was a made man. Growing constantly more popular, he finally was engaged to play in the productions of the Winter Garden Theatre. His first show—a great success—was *La Belle Paree*, in 1911.

In the 14 years Jolson spent on the stage before Hollywood called him he was featured in a whole series of productions loosely known as Winter Garden Shows, in which he mostly appeared as "Gus," a stock character played in blackface. The productions were: *Vera Violetta* (1911); *The Whirl of Society* (1912); *Honeymoon Express* (1913); *Dancing Around* (1914); *Robinson Crusoe Jr.* (1916); *Sinbad* (1918-20)—all of them lavish Shubert extravaganzas. In 1921 he played in *Bombo* in a theatre that was named after him and in 1925 appeared triumphantly in *Big Boy*.

The impact of the Jolson personality on the American audience was terrific. Dynamic, vital, witty, he created a style of his own and precipitated a flock of imitators. His style of singing was emotional and tear-jerking—he depended on smashing abandon to put a song across, used such tricks as falling on his knees, talking off the second verse of a song. He has been called the greatest master of hokum in show business. Gilbert Seldes wrote of him: "No one else . . . so holds an audience in the hollow of the hand. . . I have heard Jolson in a second-rate show before an audience, listless or hostile, sing [an] outdated and forgotten song and . . . saw also the tremendous leap in vitality and happiness which took possession of the audience as he sang it."

JOLSON, AL—*Continued*

In 1927 Jolson started on his movie career by making *The Jazz Singer*, the first talking picture, for Warner Brothers. Based on his own story, it was a smashing success. He followed up with others, most of them glorifying his personality—a mush-mouthed mammy-singer with a voice and heart of gold. At about that time, too, he discovered the possibilities of father love and wrung people's hearts with his *Sonny-Boy,* which he made popular in *The Singing Fool.* He came back to Broadway in 1931 in a somewhat more sophisticated rôle in *Wonderbar.* That was his swan song. He left the theatre for the movies and the radio. Among the pictures that he made were: *Say It With Songs* (1929); *Big Boy* (1930); *Hallelujah I'm a Bum* (1933); *Wonderbar* (1935); *Go Into Your Dance* (1935); *The Singing Kid* (1936) and *The Rose of Washington Square* (1939). His influence in the motion picture industry as producer of *The Jazz Singer* remained considerable. He had a lot to say about the stories and plays bought by Warner Brothers. As new and more streamlined stars dawned on the horizon his popularity fell off and his pictures grew few and far between. He concentrated on the radio. He began his radio programs in 1932, varying his singing routine with "serious stuff." Later he shifted to weekly broadcasts from Hollywood over WABC of the Columbia Network, with Parkyakakus and Martha Raye. His style was usually running monologue interspersed with songs.

Throughout his career in the theatre as well as in the films he managed to keep America interested in him as one of its most fascinating personalities, even dabbling in its political destiny as he campaigned songfully for Harding, Coolidge and Roosevelt. A confirmed and joyous extrovert, he has made headlines with his domestic affairs. He was married three times: to Henrietta Keller in 1906, in 1922 to Alma Osborne, known on the stage as Ethel Delmar, and to Ruby Keeler in 1928. The nation was constantly posted as to his marital bliss or vicissitudes, suffered when his marriages broke up, watched breathlessly his courting. In 1935 he and Ruby Keeler (an ex-Follies girl and a well-known motion picture star in her own right) adopted a son, to whom Jolson has made many affectionate references on the radio. In 1939 he and Miss Keeler were divorced. That however, did not prevent her from staying temporarily in the Chicago production of *Hold On to Your Hats.*

In 1933 the country rocked when he knocked Walter Winchell out at a prize fight. Jolson's fistic victory over the gray-haired columnist who had been his friend was perhaps as much due to the not too serious lessons in boxing given to him by his friends Dempsey and Max Baer as to his opponent's being out of condition. The ensuing publicity caused him to remark philosophically that: "You have to sock a columnist before you're really famous." Winchell's favorable comment about *Hold On to Your Hats* probably terminated the enmity.

Jolson's most characteristic trait is his inexhaustible vitality. He is a brown, lean man with a rolling eye and an irresistibly droll smile. He is an unashamed sentimentalist: used to have a youngster near the microphone when singing *Sonny-Boy,* and has been known to shed tears at a particularly enthusiastic reception. He likes to confide in his audience: to tell them how much money he sank in the show, what a wonderful girl Ruby is, something about his baby boy back in California. He is an inveterate gambler. He has been known to lose a fortune on a horse and is one of Broadway's heaviest stock plungers: likes the feel of ticker tape on his fingers. The only card game he is fond of is hearts.

Although he has never studied voice, for a time he nurtured operatic ambitions and he is interested in song writing. He has long wanted to direct a motion picture. He likes to sail, fish and play golf, has a farm in San Fernando Valley, California, where he raises walnuts and oranges, and in 1935 was elected the Mayor of Encino, a small town near his farm. His life has been full and exciting in all its aspects—theatrical as well as domestic. It can be best summed up by something else that Gilbert Seldes had written about him: "Whatever he does he does at the highest possible pressure."

References

Commonweal 11:715 Ap 23 '30
Life 9:60-2 Jl 29 '40 il pors
Nation 151:281-2 S 28 '40
N Y Herald Tribune VI p2 S 8 '40 por (p1)
N Y Times IX p1, 2 Jl 21 '40; IX p3 O 20 '40
Theatre Arts 15:366-9 My '31 por
Seldes, G V. Daemonic in the American Theatre *In* Seven Lively Arts p191-200 1924
Who's Who in America
Who's Who in American Jewry
Who's Who in the Theatre

JONES, E. STANLEY, REV. Jan 3, 1884- Missionary

Address: Clifton Springs Sanatorium, Clifton Springs, New York

Destined to become one of the greatest Christian missionaries, Dr. Eli Stanley Jones (he uses only the initial of his first name) was, at the age of 17, an untamed youth with little knowledge of or interest in religion. He and a group of boys went to church one day to hear an English minister because they had heard he pronounced English queerly. Young Jones was deeply moved by the sermon and joined the church. Other matters took up his time, however, and it was two years before he heard another sermon that made him think seriously of religion.

Through the Rev. Bateman, young Jones was induced to study at Asbury College, Wilmore, Kentucky, from which he was graduated in 1906. It was while he was still in college that he felt the call to go abroad as a missionary. There was some conflict within him, for his mother was opposed to his going, and others believed that he should do evangelistic work at home. Nevertheless, in 1907, at the age of 23, he went to India as a missionary of the Methodist Episcopal Church.

The work was heavy for an inexperienced missionary. During the next eight years he was pastor of the English Church at Lucknow, superintendent of the Lucknow District, and principal of the Sitapur Boarding School. His work at this time was largely with the low castes. But as Dr. Jones writes in his book, *The Christ of the Indian Road* (1925), he "was strangely drawn to work among the educated high castes, the intelligentsia."

After work, Dr. Jones often played tennis at an Indian clubhouse with the high-caste Hindus and Mohammedans. One evening a Hindu official asked him why he had gone only to the low-caste Hindus to tell of Christ. Dr. Jones answered that he didn't think the higher castes were interested. The official answered: "It is a mistake. We want you, if you will come in the right way."

Thus began Dr. Jones' work among the high castes, the educated and student groups in India. That he has found the "right way" is evident from the esteem in which the Indians hold him. They call him "Rishi" (a saint). Yet Dr. Jones had not started his work without misgivings and questioning of his own abilities. In an interview he once told of the tense, nervous struggle of those early days in India, of the public debates he held, arguing the superiority of Christianity with Buddhists, Moslems, Hindus.

Dr. Jones asked Gandhi what should be done to naturalize Christianity in India. Gandhi, Dr. Jones declared, told him that the Christian missionaries should live more like Jesus Christ, that they should practice their Christian religion without adulterating it or toning it down and that they should study the non-Christian faiths more sympathetically in order that they might have a more sympathetic approach to the people.

These points, Dr. Jones declared, he decided to put into practice because they went to the heart of things. He did put them into practice. In 1926 he spent several months in the school of the Indian Christian poet, Dr. Rabindranath Tagore, studying India's culture and religion. Dr. Tagore and Mahatma Gandhi are among his intimate personal friends, as was the late Charles F. Andrews, missionary and biographer of Gandhi. Dr. Jones also counts among his friends scores of other Indian leaders.

While Dr. Jones is officially a missionary of the Methodist Church, serving among the

REV. E. STANLEY JONES

high castes, his fame as a preacher, lecturer and author has spread far beyond India. He has been heard by hundreds of thousands of persons in Japan, Korea, Burma, China, the Philippines and Malaya. South Americans, a few years ago, thronged a series of meetings which he held in their principal cities, and his following in the United States and Canada is probably unequalled by any other living religious leader.

A few years ago, when he conducted the annual Lenten services of the Greater New York Federation of Churches, his addresses were broadcast across America by a chain of radio stations. In the autumn of 1938 he toured America as chief speaker in a University Christian Mission of the Federal Council of Churches, and brought his dynamic, intensely personal messages to young people in a dozen universities.

The department of evangelism of the Federal Council of Churches gave more Americans an opportunity to hear him in the summer of 1940 at two Christian Ashrams (Indian for retreats) held at Westminster Lodge, Saugatuck, Michigan and at Blue Ridge, North Carolina. Dr. Jones spoke at both retreats daily.

Dr. Jones' books, too, have enjoyed a tremendous popularity. His first, and one of his most popular and best known, *The Christ of the Indian Road,* he wrote in a month between speaking engagements when he was on furlough in America in 1925. He pounded it out in haste, for he was anxious to get back to his work in India. He was writing the book at the urging of a church executive who wanted a record of Dr. Jones' missionary impressions. He left the manuscript and thought no more of it until a printed copy reached him in the interior late in the year.

JONES, E. STANLEY, REV.—*Continued*

By that time the book was fast becoming a best seller. An honestly written, straightforward account of his evangelistic experiences in India, it is a story of a religion in practice, of Christian precepts freed from prejudice and self-interest. It so impressed certain political leaders in England that they asked their party's members in Parliament to read it as a help towards understanding India.

The Christ of the Indian Road sold 600,000 copies, an unusually high number for a religious book. It was translated into 12 foreign languages, several Indian vernaculars and into Braille. It made Dr. Jones an international figure.

On the heels of the success of the book came Dr. Jones' election as a bishop of the Methodist Episcopal Church in 1928, an office from which he resigned at once (24 hours after his election) because he wished to continue his work in India. Twice later he refused to be elected a bishop, preferring to devote his entire time to his missionary work.

The Christ of the Indian Road was followed by eight other books, written at intervals of about every two years. All have had wide audiences and have been translated into many languages. Dr. Jones has also been a prolific contributor to religious publications.

Dr. Jones has decried the rivalry between various denominations and the petty quarrels over ritual. He believes that all divisive labels of Christianity should be dropped and that the denominations should become members of a Church of Christ in America.

Dr. Jones was born in Clarksville, Maryland, January 3, 1884 and was educated at the City College of Baltimore and at Asbury College. He received his M. A. degree in 1912 from Asbury College, his D. D. from Duke University and S. T. D. from Syracuse University. He was married in 1911 to Mabel Lossing. They have one daughter, Eunice, born in 1914.

References

> Am Mag 108:48-9 Jl '29 por
> Christian Cent 52:787-9 Je 12 '35
> Lit Digest 115:15 Ap 1 '33 por; 120: 17 O 26 '35 por
> Missionary R of the World 52:603-5 Ag '29
> Newsweek 16:46 S 2 '40 il pors
> Time 32:47 D 12 '38
> Jones, E. S. The Christ of the Indian Road 1925
> Lotz, P. H. ed. Vocations and Professions 1940
> Who's Who in America

JONES, GROVER 1893—Sept 24, 1940
Veteran screen writer; career in Hollywood began in 1913; one of the industry's best-known writers; had worked for nearly every studio in Hollywood; wrote many articles and short stories for *Saturday Evening Post*

and *Collier's*; wrote scenario for *Lives of a Bengal Lancer, The Plainsman, If I Had a Million, Abe Lincoln of Illinois* and *The Virginian*; won the Academy of Arts and Sciences Award in 1932; had written or collaborated on more than 400 films

References

> Collier's 96:26+ S 21 '35; 98:24+ D 5 '36 por
>
> International Motion Picture Almanac

Obituaries

> N Y Herald Tribune p24 S 25 '40
> N Y Times p27 S 25 '40
> Time 36:63-4 O 7 '40 por
> Variety 140:12 S 25 '40

JONES, JACK *See* Jones J. J.

JONES, JESSE HOLMAN Apr 5, 1874-
United States Secretary of Commerce; Federal Loan Administrator

Address: b. Department of Commerce, Washington, D. C.; Federal Loan Agency Bldg, 811 Vermont Ave, N W, Washington, D. C.; h. Shoreham Hotel, Washington, D. C.

> December 1940 Bulletin: In the fall of 1940, Jesse Jones, acting in his capacity of Federal Loan Administrator, has signed an agreement to lend Brazil $20,000,000 to set up her own steel industry and has been negotiating the question of further loans to China in exchange for essential defense products needed by the United States.

From October issue:

There were no dissenting voices when President Roosevelt announced his choice for Secretary of Commerce to succeed Harry Hopkins. His selection of Jesse Holman Jones meant, everyone felt, that he had offered that office "to a man who by training and experience is fit to hold it." A successful businessman and for the past eight years a successful government administrator, Mr. Jones is considered by both Republicans and Democrats, by New Dealers and anti-New Dealers "a splendid demonstration that government in business can be competent."

His job since July 1939 has been that of Federal Loan Administrator, in charge not only of the Reconstruction Finance Corporation and its affiliates which he formerly headed, but of the Federal Housing Administration, Electric Home and Farm Authority, Export-Import Bank of Washington, the Home Owners' Loan Corporation and the Federal Home Loan Bank system. President Roosevelt asked Congress to permit Jesse Jones to continue as Federal Loan Administrator while he is Secretary of Commerce, and most commentators agree that with the two offices he will be better able to coordinate the work of the Federal agencies in the Western Hemisphere.

Jesse Jones, who has loaned millions of the government's dollars to thousands of its citizens, knows personally "what it feels like for a businessman to lay a million dollars on the line." He has been a successful businessman since his teens. His father, William Hasque Jones (his mother was Anne Holman), was a tobacco planter in Robertson County, Tennessee, where Jesse was born, and Jesse worked for and with him almost from the time he was old enough to go out into the fields alone. His schooling was intermittent but his practical experience was large. There was the time when he wanted a horse, but got a small pig instead. Jesse didn't complain. He fed that pig until it was big enough to swap for a calf and he brought that calf up until he was able to get a horse in trade for it. He raised tobacco for himself on a plot near the house where "the turkeys and the chickens would pick off the worms for me" and made money on it.

When Jesse was 20 his father died, and Jesse went to Dallas, Texas, where an uncle had a lumber business. Within a year he was manager of the company in Dallas and by 1898 he was general manager of its main office in Houston. It was in Dallas that Jesse Jones began seriously to borrow money, make a profit on it, invest his profit and make more. He started by borrowing $500 from the local bank. "I didn't have any use for it," said Jones, "but I knew I'd need money some day soon, if I was ever to get a start." He put the money away in a drawer and later paid it back. He did the same with larger sums, always repaying them promptly. Then he found he needed $10,000 to buy up some timberland and was able to get it. Within five years he had disposed of this land for a profit of fifty thousand dollars.

In Houston Jesse Jones branched out from the lumber business, and he is considered mainly responsible for the city's growth after the panic of 1907. He built skyscrapers, office buildings, stores, a hotel, a theatre, and then spread out to Fort Worth and Dallas. He organized and became chairman of the Texas Trust Company and was active in most of the banking and real estate operations of Houston.

During the First World War Jones spent 18 months in France as director general of the department of military relief of the American Red Cross and took charge of the building of canteens and recreation halls in all the American Army camps. In 1919 he was sent back to Europe to help organize the League of Red Cross Societies of the World.

When the War was over Jesse Jones was married to Mary Gibbs of Mexia, Texas, and went back to his old jobs of putting up buildings and organizing banks. The field of his operations this time was New York City, where he put up one apartment house on Park Avenue and one on Fifth Avenue, built an apartment hotel, a theatre

JESSE JONES

and a professional building. Then he went back to Houston, bought the Houston *Chronicle* and started to become active in politics. From 1924 to 1928 he was director of finance for the Democratic National Committee, and in 1928 chairman of the advisory finance committee. In that year he was personally responsible for getting the Democratic convention to Houston.

It was a Republican, however, who first brought him to Washington. In 1932, when the Reconstruction Finance Corporation was organized, President Hoover asked Garner, then Democratic leader in the House, for a list of Democrats from which he could select a director. Garner handed in one name, that of Jesse H. Jones. In 1933, when Roosevelt was President, Jones became chairman of the RFC, which was given more scope and power. The RFC became "easily the public's favorite New Deal Agency and he perhaps Washington's favorite administrator."

The RFC with its 32 branches lends money to all sorts and sizes of borrowers. Chairman Jones' main questions to prospective borrowers when the cases came to his office were: "Will the loan add to employment?" "Have you exhausted all private loan sources?" "Is too much money being spent on high executive salaries and dividends?" And, "Will the loan be repaid?" Jones always believed that "the greatest disservice you can do a man is to lend him money he can't repay." His job, he said, was not to give away money but to *lend* it—"on the best terms possible both to the government and the borrower." And in the years that Jesse Jones headed the RFC it not only helped thousands of people but made money as well, since it was able to get money from the Treasury at one per cent less than it charged borrowers.

JONES, JESSE—*Continued*

In July 1939 Jesse Jones resigned as chairman and member of the board of directors of the Reconstruction Finance Corporation to become Federal Loan Administrator and in August 1940 he was offered the Cabinet post of Secretary of Commerce. During these years he has remained on excellent terms with Republicans and Democrats, considered by many a "Democrat rather than a starry-eyed New Dealer." During these years his large, six-feet-two frame, his blue eyes, white hair and dimpled cheeks have become familiar to all of Washington. And his reputation for being a hard and successful worker has grown. At 6:30 each morning he gets up and starts reading office papers before breakfast. Twelve and fourteen hours later he is often still working, and working well. President Roosevelt once said "Jesse Jones was the only man in Washington who could say yes or no intelligently 24 hours a day."

References

Collier's 97:42+ F 15 '36 por
Fortune 21:44-51+ il pors; 21:140+ My '40
N Y Herald Tribune p18 Ag 27 '40
N Y Times p34 Ag 25 '40 por; VII p8+ O 6 '40 por
Newsweek 16:17 S 23 '40
Read Digest 35:82-6 D '39
Sat Eve Post 213:9-11+ N 30 '40 il pors; 213:29+ D 7 '40 por
Scholastic 37:10 S 23 '40 por
Time 29:12 Ja 25 '37 por
Shumway, H. I. Jesse Holman Jone , Builder and Banker *In* Famous Leaders of Industry 4th ser. p207-20 1936
Unofficial Observer [pseud.] Mad Money *In* New Dealers p104-41 1934
Who's Who in America
Who's Who in Commerce and Industry
Who's Who in the Nation's Capital

JONES, JOE Apr 7, 1909- Artist
Address: c/o A. C. A. Gallery, 52 W 8th St, New York City

Joe Jones, the former member of the St. Louis House Painters' Union whose first Manhattan exhibit in 1935 brought him immediate fame as one of the most gifted among American painters of social protest, in November 1940 had his fifth New York one-man show at the A. C. A. Gallery. *Cue* announced: "The champion of the underdog finds things not a whit better than when he first joined the strikers."

Born "on the faintly respectable edge" of a St. Louis slum on April 7, 1909, Joe Jones' early life led him to a "desperate kind of hooligan rebellion." His father was a house painter, and in his teens he began slapping paint around, too, meanwhile acquiring a great ambition and a "colossal ego" without doing much about it. Finally he drifted into a job in a shoe store. The manager made a hobby of painting—on canvas rather than walls—and at 18 Joe was induced to try it. From then on there was no stopping him. Entirely self-taught, picking up his knowledge "from looking, listening and reading, in about that order of importance," his talent didn't long go unrecognized in St. Louis. In 1931 he won the Baldwin portrait prize, in 1932 both the Spaeth Prize for modern painting, and the Healy Prize for lithograph work. His canvases were big, bold, often violent, always honest—he wanted to paint "things that will knock holes in the walls." When he was 23 he became a Communist; he called the Diego Rivera of that period a "bourgeois reactionary." There were patrons who suggested that he might find Mexico both more paintable, and more palatable than St. Louis, but Joe wanted to paint St. Louis as he saw it—and he did. In 1933 he was awarded a prize of $100 for the best work of art in the St. Louis Artists' Guild show of that year. There wasn't much disagreement; as one critic said: "In a St. Louis show with hundreds of pictures . . . suddenly there was Joe Jones."

But exhibiting in St. Louis and in upper Manhattan's exclusive galleries are two different things. Joe Jones found that out when he came to New York and spent most of the spring of 1935 lugging one of his canvases and a portfolio of photographs from one art dealer to another before getting a showing at the A. C. A. Gallery in May. Then his depictions of evicted women, striking workers, lynchings with hooded Ku Klux figures, all painted while living on a Missouri houseboat propped "on the ruined levee," created a sensation among the New York critics. They greeted him as a genius, compared him not only with Gropper (see sketch this issue) but with Goya. Archibald MacLeish (see sketch this issue) spoke of him as having "digested a lot of the good ideas of a lot of good people" and as having "more scope, more vitality, more fecundity and more promise as well as more mastery than most artists a decade his senior."

After going to Arkansas that summer to paint a mural for Commonwealth College (in "grays, blues and fiery reds," it included sharecroppers, coal miners, Negro lynching victims, a dust storm, a farmer plowing his cotton under), Joe Jones spent the rest of the summer in the wheat fields near St. Louis, painting the grain and its threshers. He wanted "to understand the farmers and present them on their own feet." The artistic results of that summer were exhibited in New York at the swank uptown Walker Galleries in January 1936, eleven wheat-field pictures forming the main part of the show. Of the eleven, *Threshing No. 1* was most discussed, critics varying in their opinions of this new phase of his work but for the most part finding it as distinctly his own as before. They spoke particularly of his "blazing, clear skies," his dramatic color sense, though one critic found his landscapes less interesting than his other work: "It is when he paints the human figure singly or in groups that his work takes on organic vibrancy and warmth of human understanding." One of his wheat-field pictures was purchased for the Metropolitan Museum of Art.

In spite of his success, however, some of Jones' friends told him his work was getting too "slick." In atonement he went home and painted a Negro prostitute. "That's us," he told his New York representative. "We all prostitute ourselves."

The next year found the artist of social revolt among the recipients of a Guggenheim Memorial Fellowship, a paradox which inspired one art journal to head an article: "It Can Happen Here." His third Manhattan exhibition displayed an even greater "militancy" than the others, for the most part depicting the disasters of Fascism. Henry McBride was alarmed: "Carried too far, it's danger; it is death." Edward Jewell of the New York *Times* disposed of him in short order by describing *Without Mother*, perhaps the most typical of his canvases, as "a piece of sentimental posturing. . . Joe Jones seems still one of those characters in search of an author . . . lacking the clear, pure flame of a unique artistic purpose." But Klein of the New York *Post* called the new exhibit "a great forward step in technical realization," and Emily Genauer of the *World-Telegram* placed *Without Mother* "the tops." Of Jones himself she said: "His work is emphatically social again. But from it he has sloughed whatever characteristics it had in common with message-bearing political posters. Today his pictures have a much more profound human content. There is in them cosmic perspective, passionate insight."

By the autumn of 1939, when new work by Joe Jones appeared once more in New York's A. C. A. Gallery, something had happened. Some of his paintings still dealt with harvesters and railroad workers, but in general "violent social protest played a minor rôle." *Nude with White Cloth, Three Trees* and *Road to Verplanck* were pleasant pictures pleasantly mentioned by critics, but created little stir. Nor did his 1940 show, although again concerned with the social scene. It was sometimes agreed that the artist, now only 31, had, perhaps, been "over-rated" or recognized too early. In any case there was still plenty of time for him to find himself.

Jones once insisted that "art must please and instruct the plain brain." Following his own advice, the best of his work has won praise for its "superb color, sound technique and unquestionable honesty," its "strong and simple compositional unity." His color sense leads him to "dramatic, nacreous whites tinged with faint pearl-like pinks, bronze browns, rich greens and blues, permeated with smoky shadow." Technically he has mastered his art; whether he will develop into the important American painter that his first work seemed to foretell is for the future to decide.

References

Art Digest 12:22-3 N 15 '37; 14:12 D 1 '39
Fortune 12:68-9 D '35 il
Mag Art 28:486-8 Ag 8 '35 il; 29:188-9 Mr '36; 32:717+ D '39 il
Newsweek 6:21 Ag 31 '35 il por; 7:28 F 1 '36
Time 27:46 F 3 '36 il por
Cheney, M. C. The Painters Discover America *In* Modern Art in America p132-3 1939
Who's Who in American Art

JONES, JOHN JOSEPH Dec 8, 1873- British trade unionist and Labor Party politician

Address: 9 Wanlip Rd, Plaistow, E. 13, London, England

When "Jack" (as he is invariably known) Jones retired from Parliament in February 1940 because of poor health, the British legislature was robbed of one of its most picturesque and unconventional figures. The very first time Jones opened his mouth in the House he was instantly called to order because, instead of using the usual formula of "Mr. Speaker, Sir. . ." he began his speech with "Gentlemen. . ." That one was only a slip, but in a stormy 21 years of Parliamentary life Jones was frequently in conflict with authority: called to order, escorted out, even carried out. From a back seat under the Gallery he would fire interjections, and was quite capable, when aroused, of shouting "Liar."

Jones' constituency was Silvertown, and *Punch* once alluded to him as "the honorable Member for Silver-Tongue." Shortly after he was elected the London *Sunday Chronicle* said of him: "The man who has been thrown up to the top by the maelstrom of the new Parliament seems to be Mr. Jack Jones, the burly Labor member for Silvertown. . . He has proved that there is solid stuff in him. True, he is unconventional, really and unconsciously unconventional. His statement that the house he occupies in Silvertown is so cramped that he has to open the windows to swing his braces when he puts his trousers on was made in all sincerity, and his look of amazement when the House laughed immoderately was really funny. . . He is called frequently and he always has something to say that is worth listening to."

Jones can hardly be described as a statesman and was never awarded office; on the other hand, he is by no means a clown. He went into Parliament, as he went into the trade union movement, with the simple idea of ameliorating the condition of the workingman. Once there it did not occur to him to adapt his style to the august halls. "I simply spoke in the Parliament of 1919 in my natural manner," he wrote in his autobiography. "I could not invent a

JONES, JOHN JOSEPH—*Continued*

false 'Parliamentary' style even if I would, and I certainly would not. So you see complete naturalness became quaint in an assembly where the sense of tradition, the sense of importance and sometimes the sense of false pride and pomposity undoubtedly affect like a plague many of its members."

Born at Nenagh, Tipperary, Ireland, Jack was the son of laboring parents, John and Margaret Jones. He was sent to the Christian Brothers' School at Nenagh village, but stayed there only until 1884. In that year his father died and his mother went across to Liverpool, England, as so many poor Irish do when they are looking for work, since it is the nearest port. Jack began his working life as an errand boy to a Liverpool draper at $1 a week. In 1889 he became a page in a hotel, but soon grew too big for this and went to work at the Liverpool docks at 10 cents an hour.

It was there that he joined his first trade union. Soon, though, he left the docks for the engine sheds of the old Lancashire and Yorkshire Railway at Horwich, Lancashire and after 15 months there was fired for attempting to form a union. He joined the Social Democratic Federation and in 1897 was sent to prison for persisting in speaking at Nelson, Lancashire, in defiance of a police order. It was in that year that he met Arthur Hayday, a trade unionist working in West Ham, London, who persuaded Jack that he could do useful work in the metropolis.

The move was made, and Jones found himself in West Ham, a grim, swarming industrial region of East London, abutting on part of the dockland. He immediately started a very active life there as a trade union organizer and municipal politician. He served on the Board of Guardians (the body charged with the maintaining of the poor laws), was elected to the town council and rose to be Mayor of the borough.

Jones' first attempt at Parliament was made in 1906 for the tin-mining division of Camborne, Cornwall. He was howled down and polled only a miserable 108 votes. He tried again in 1910, this time for Poplar (the London division including the West Ham district and made famous by the stories of Thomas Burke), and again failed. Eventually he reached Parliament at the end of 1918 as Labor member for Silvertown (a West Ham division). From that time on he was regularly returned for Silvertown at every election; and even in 1935, the peak of the National Government's popularity, he came back with a majority of 13,901. During these years in Parliament Jones occupied a position with the National Union of General Workers, from which he retired, under the age limit, in December 1938.

Unsophisticated and unruly though he proved to be, in Parliament Jones was soon seen to be capable of contributing valuable elements to debate. Never a well-informed,

expert Parliamentary hand like Herbert Morrison or Clement Attlee (see sketches this issue), his speeches were, nevertheless, well constructed and full of shrewdness, force and sincerity. He never allowed himself to forget that he was a poor man from a slum representing thousands just like himself and often turned debate from academic lines to urgent practical consideration. A celebrated remark of his was: "I do not want to rise from the ranks but with the ranks."

One of his main interests as an M. P. was in housing reform, and Jones lived to see gigantic improvements in housing. He has also always been a defender of the workingman's right to drink his pint of beer and often spoke vigorously against the restrictions which, imposed during the War of 1914 to 1918, were partially continued into the peace. Many of the causes he worked for and the experiences he went through in Parliament are described in *My Lively Life* (1928), a discursive autobiography which presents a very good picture of Parliamentary life and one or two ill-founded political prophecies—for instance he pointed out Oswald Mosley, Fascist leader, (see sketch this issue) as a coming. man in the Labor Party.

Jones is a large, roundheaded, ruddy man who cares less than nothing for sartorial niceties and .never troubles about a crease in his trousers. He has often poked fun at Labor members who wear Court dress when in office. "Boiled shirts and knee breeches look best to me in pictures," he wrote, "or on old Court officials. The poor chaps look quite pleased with themselves dressed up like ninepenny rabbits, and why shouldn't they? If it pleases them and does no harm to anybody else, let them get on with it. For myself, I like a comfortable old suit and a low collar."

References

Johnston, J. A Hundred Commoners 1931
Jones, J. My Lively Life 1928
Who's Who

JONES, SAM HOUSTON 1897- Governor of Louisiana

Address: b. State Capitol, Baton Rouge, Louisiana; h. Lake Charles, Louisiana

Elected Democratic candidate for Governor of Louisiana in a run-off primary election in early 1940, Sam Houston Jones broke the 12-year reign of the Huey Long machine in that State. He was overwhelmingly elected in the formal election of April 16 against the first Republican candidate in many years, W. W. Tuttle. Celebrating the defeat of Governor Earl Long, during whose régime several Long henchmen were indicted, huge victory parades were held in Baton Rouge. The Long defeat was decisive: only 37 of the 100 members returned were Long adherents.

On May 15 a record-breaking crowd gathered to see him inaugurated and to participate in a giant barbecue. Immediately afterward the new Governor launched a terrific clean-up. He swept through the state bureaus and departments chucking out dead timber and began, with the assistance of legislative consultants, to draft bills to repeal the dictatorial laws enacted by the Long machine. He made it clear that while the effects of the Long machine rule cannot be immediately wiped out, he is determined to rebuild the state government. At the first sign of interference, he says, he stands ready to appeal directly to the people who had elected him.

Sam Houston Jones' career has been one of quiet but steady advancement; and—in contrast to Huey Long's—it has been entirely unspectacular. He was born in 1898 in a two-room farmhouse near Merryville, Louisiana, close to the Texas line, one of a large family. His parents had settled there when Sam Houston was a living hero. Later they moved to De Ridder, and there young Sam first went to school. He wanted to go to the State University to study law, but the family had no money. He got work at a neighboring sawmill, earned enough to enter the University and worked his way through.

When the United States entered the First World War, young Jones joined the infantry. After the Armistice he read law for himself, in 1922 was admitted to the Bar and hung out his shingle in De Ridder. After a term as city judge there he moved to Lake Charles, where an oil boom had started. For nine years he was assistant parish prosecutor. Always active in the American Legion, known for his speeches at conventions, he was made State commander of the Legion in 1930 and 1931, and afterward served as national committeeman.

At the time Huey Long was launching his share-the-wealth plan, Sam Jones returned to private law practice. In 1934, the same year, he married his former boyhood sweetheart, Louise (Gambrell) Boyer. They have two children, Carolyn and Robert; and he is the stepfather of two boys, Jimmy and Billy Boyer.

The gigantic Huey Long machine was careening from scandal to scandal, and settling-up time had come. Disclosures were followed by a Federal investigation. The State was in bad financial shape when Sam Houston Jones, prosperous and respected lawyer, was put on the ballot with other candidates to run against Earl Long in the Democratic primaries. During his campaign he never missed an engagement. He has the voice of an excellent orator and makes a good platform appearance. In the courtroom, however, he is quiet, methodical, positive. On the stump in the country he knows how to talk to people in homely vernacular. And he has the knack of turning in his own behalf the weapons chosen by his

SAM H. JONES

enemies. Longsters had called him "High-Hat, Sweet Smellin' Sambo." At his inauguration he gibed, "I take off my high hat," and perfume hawkers sold "Sam Jones sweet smellin' perfume."

Mr. Jones sees his job in Louisiana as one of the biggest since Reconstruction. He hopes to put forward a complete house-cleaning program to get rid of the practices developed during the 12 years that Huey Long and his heirs ruled the State. On the day of his formal election, four Constitutional amendments proposed and indorsed by incumbent Governor Earl Long were swept to defeat. The vote was interpreted as an overwhelming indorsement of Jones' program. Among his campaign pledges were promises of $3 automobile license plates, better farm-to-market roads, regular auditing of books of State departments, increase of old-age pensions, continuation of free lunches for needy children, no rattle of arms at or between elections, repeal of the one per cent State sales tax. "We are again a democracy," he says. "Louisiana has been given back to the people and the people will rule."

References

Christian Sci Mon p2 Mr 18 '40 por
Christian Sci Mon Mag p3+ Ap 27 '40 il por
Cur Hist 51:50 Ap '40
Newsweek 15:36 My 27 '40
N Y Herald Tribune p15 F 22 '40 por; p10+ S 15 '40 il por
N Y Times VII p7, 18 Mr 3 '40 por; p10+ S 15 '40 il por
Scholastic 36:23 Mr 4 '40 por
Time 35:15-16 Mr 4 '40 por; 35:22 My 27 '40

Who's Who in America

JOSEPHSON, WALTER S. 1889—Mar 7, 1940 Founder of the dry ice industry

Obituaries

N Y Herald Tribune p12 Mr 11 '40
N Y Times p48 Mr 10 '40

KAI-SHEK, CHIANG *See* Chiang Kai-shek

KALTENBORN, HANS VON (käl'tĕn-born") July 9, 1878- NBC news commentator

Address: b. National Broadcasting Co, 30 Rockefeller Plaza, New York City; h. 9 Garden Pl, Brooklyn, New York

H. V. Kaltenborn, the "suave Voice of Doom" familiar to so many radio listeners, terminated his long association with the Columbia Broadcasting System in the spring of 1940, and also canceled a projected trip to Europe. His version of what's-happening-this-minute-and-why can now be heard over NBC.

Kaltenborn's crisp voice has reported the day-to-day events of so many wars—those that didn't quite happen and those that did—that his wife once expressed her amazement at the people who really believed Orson Welles' broadcast of the invasion from Mars. "Why, how ridiculous!" she said. "Anybody should have known it wasn't a real war. If it had been, the broadcaster would have been Hans." In Europe the radio is sometimes known as war's "Third Front" (the other two supposedly being military and economic), and it is here that Kaltenborn has taken up his position. "I get no joy out of war," he said a few months ago. "I would rather discuss a fireman's ball than spend one word combatting the propaganda of the 'Third Front.' But," he added, "while knowledge makes for peace, and the truth can set men free, I hope to remain at my post." Quincy Howe (see sketch this issue) announces, however, that he has now "become indistinguishable from those Americans who can think of American problems only in terms of defending the British Empire."

H. V. Kaltenborn (the V is for "von," which he dropped during the World War) is "technically a baron," since the Kaltenborns have been nobility since 1352. His father was Baron Rudolph von Kaltenborn, a Hessian Guards officer who came to America in protest against absorption of Hesse by Prussia, and who married an American schoolteacher, Betty Wessels, and settled in Milwaukee. Hans was born there on July 9, 1878, but spent most of his childhood in Merrill, Wisconsin. After only a year in high school he ran away to work in a lumber camp, then for five years worked for his father in the building-material business at $3 a week, at the same time doing odd jobs for the local newspaper. When he was 19 the Spanish-American War came along and he went as first sergeant in the 4th Wisconsin Volunteer Infantry. He never got any closer to the war than an Alabama camp, but he started his newspaper career by covering it for the Milwaukee newspapers, writing his accounts in both English and German.

He came back to be city editor of the Merrill *Advocate* for a year, but found himself bothered with wanderlust. It was the year 1900 when he picked out a freight train bound for New York, hopped it and from New York made his way casually to Europe on a cattle boat. For two years he was a traveling salesman in France, selling stereoscopes to pay his way. Then in 1902 he came back to the United States, this time found a job on the Brooklyn *Eagle* as a reporter, stayed with the *Eagle* until he decided there was something to formal education after all. In 1905 he entered Harvard at the age of 27 as a special student, having prepared for the entrance examinations by himself (he didn't pass his entrance examination in algebra until two weeks before being elected to Phi Beta Kappa). There he debated, studied speech, won prizes in oratory and acquired the accent which, superimposed on his original Midwestern, has caused so many listeners to wonder about his birthplace. From 1907 to 1908 he was secretary to the Harvard-Berlin Professional Exchange in Berlin, a year later he took his B. A. degree from Harvard *cum laude* and sailed away to the West Indies on the *Nourmahal* as Vincent Astor's tutor. In Berlin in 1910 he married the beautiful young Baroness Olga von Nordenflycht. Then once again back to the *Eagle* and the impecunious life of a newspaperman.

Kaltenborn was with the *Eagle* for 20 years. During that time he was consecutively drama editor, assistant managing editor and associate editor, but most of his experience was as editorial writer and commentator. That experience prepared him to lecture on current events for the paper, and this speaking experience, in turn, meant that when radio came he was prepared to speak over the air. In 1922 he became radio's first news analyst. Because he was used to talking to living audiences he was at first troubled with "mike fever"—to this day he makes gestures and changes his expression as if his ether-audience were really visible—but he had a great advantage in being able to speak extemporaneously from nothing more than a few jotted notes. Thus he began building up a solid, if not a sensational reputation with the radio public. He continued spending most of his summers increasing his already wide knowledge of foreign affairs by travel and study abroad, usually accompanied by his wife. From 1926 to 1927 he was in Russia and in the Far East as a correspondent; from 1929 to 1934 he was a member of the

Russian-American Chamber of Commerce delegation in Russia. Finally in 1930 he left the *Eagle* to become news analyst for the Columbia Broadcasting System, and he was with Columbia during one of the most troubled decades in history.

During the past 10 years Kaltenborn has been lecturer on current history for various universities and study groups, and since 1932 has reported the Republican and Democratic Conventions, the London Economic Conference, the League of Nations sessions and every major crisis.

The Spanish War he covered under highly unusual circumstances. At the front during its early days, Kaltenborn was the first to bring the sounds of an actual battle to a radio audience. It was on a point in a sharp bend of a river where French territory extended right into the battle line that he found a farmhouse with a telephone line, arranged for a radio connection through the wire, and took up his position in the shelter of a haystack with a coil of cable under his arm. After nine hours, and after mending the cable when an exploding shell broke it, he succeeded in establishing radio connections with the outside world. At last America heard the familiar dignified diction, the famous Kaltenborn-clipped consonants, only this time punctuated by the rattle of machine gun fire. A description of Kaltenborn under fire is rather typical of the man: he was "a solid, substantial figure in a well-cut business suit and pince-nez, Phi Beta Kappa key dangling across his ample vest front; but as a slight concession to the adventurous nature of his trip he wore a steel helmet over his thinning hair."

During the days of the Czechoslovakian crisis which terminated in Munich, Kaltenborn slept on a couch in the studio, subsisted mainly on onion soup prepared and brought to him by his wife ("a crisis is a fine opportunity to lose weight," he says). Between sorting out the constant bombardment of fresh dispatches, talking by radiophone to European capitals, listening to speeches of European statesmen and to short-wave broadcasts in French and German he managed to give 85 broadcasts in 18 days. This almost superhuman feat brought him 50,000 letters and telegrams, telephone calls from Herbert Hoover and Alfred Landon, and all sorts of cups, medals, scrolls and special citations.

During the summer of 1938 the Kaltenborns stayed home for the first time in many years: they wanted to enjoy their infant granddaughter and their new country place at Stony Brook, New York. The summer of 1939 brought no such opportunity, however. Kaltenborn spent three weeks in Europe on a flying trip, mostly interviewing key men on the ominous political situation, and when war came in September it was a war that he had predicted. Until the spring of 1940, when he became news analyst for the National Broadcasting Company, he reported the Second World War for Columbia.

H. V. KALTENBORN

This "tall, ruddy-faced, white-haired" man is the only radio commentator to go on the air without a script. From his newspaper experience he knows how to avoid libel and giving offense. His training and background have enabled him to read a news bulletin at a glance and explain it without a pause, and for this purpose it is also enormously helpful to have had personal contacts such as his with men like Hitler, Chamberlain, Mussolini. He talks rapidly, but so distinctly that listeners seldom complain that they can't understand him, and he says that short sentences, simple language and frequent repetition are very important in making oneself clear to a radio audience. In his opinion it is the news analyst's job to present all sides of a question, not to take sides—to "calm emotions, not to incite them"; and he believes it is proof of his impartiality that he has been accused of being pro-German, pro-Roosevelt, pro-Japanese, pro-Communist, and pro-British—one as often as another. One woman wrote criticizing his "Oxford accent": "Your sentiments may be pro-British, but please keep your voice neutral." In all his years of broadcasting he has never allowed himself to be interrupted by commercial announcements.

Kaltenborn tries to read all the books on foreign affairs as they come out, and every day there are bulletins of various associations, newsletters, newspapers and domestic and foreign magazines of such varying types as *The Japanese American* and *The Soviet World Today* waiting for him to look over, as well as innumerable letters and telegrams from listeners or personal correspondents either begging for more information on some point or volunteering some information of their own. He makes his job more difficult by insisting on fulfilling lecture engagements besides. He is his own manager, travels by

KALTENBORN, H. V.—*Continued*

plane, speaks without fees when it is for a cause which particularly appeals to him, and prides himself on never delivering the same lecture twice. Somehow he has found time to write and publish three books: *We Look at the World* (1930) ; *Kaltenborn Edits the News* (1937) ; and *I Broadcast the Crisis* (1938). He also finds time for an occasional trip to the Harvard Club for a "good sweat, swim and massage." And somehow he manages to keep right on bumping into adventures. One of his exploits was to be mistaken for a robber while on a lecture tour and arrested when he got off a plane in a strange city. It took so much time to persuade anyone that he really was H. V. Kaltenborn that he almost missed his broadcast that time.

Mr. and Mrs. Kaltenborn live in Brooklyn, New York and have two children, Ánais and Rolf. Mr. Kaltenborn is also listed as winner of first place in a newspaper poll for "most popular radio commentator" conducted by the *Motion Picture Daily* and the Scripps-Howard press in 1939.

> *References*
> Cur Hist 51:35-9 O '39 por
> New Yorker 16:4 Ap 27 '40 por
> Read Digest 34:52-4 F '39
> Scholastic 34:23-4E+ F 4 '39 il pors;
>   35:34-5+ N 6 '39 por
> Howe, Q. The News and How to
>   Understand It 1940
> Variety Radio Directory
> Who's Who Among North American Authors
> Who's Who in America

KANDER, LIZZIE BLACK   1858—July 25, 1940 Author; social worker; wrote the

LIZZIE BLACK KANDER

famous *Settlement Cook Book* which went into 23 editions and has been translated into many foreign languages; used $75,000 royalties from the book to organize the Milwaukee Jewish Center; has been called the Jane Addams of Milwaukee

> *References*
> Who's Who Among North American Authors 1931-32
>
> *Obituaries*
> N Y Times p17 Jl 26 '40
> Pub W 138:321 Ag 3 '40

KAUP, FELIX F., FATHER (koup) June 8, 1879—Mar 18, 1940 Vicar-general of the Roman Catholic Diocese and rector of the Sacred Heart Cathedral of Richmond, Virginia

> *Obituaries*
> N Y Times p25 Mr 19 '40

KEENAN, WALTER FRANCIS JR. 1884 —Mar 18, 1940 Mechanical engineer; director and vice-president of the Foster-Wheeler

WALTER F. KEENAN JR

Corporation; supervised the design and installation of boilers in several vessels of the United States Navy

> *Obituaries*
> N Y Herald Tribune p20 Mr 19 '40

KEITEL, WILHELM (kï'těl) Sept 22, 1882- Chief of the Supreme Command of the Armed Forces of Germany; member of the Cabinet for Defense of the Reich

Address: Ministry of War, Berlin, Germany

It was Colonel General Wilhelm Keitel, Hitler's chief of staff, who read the long document which spelled France's ruin on that historic day in June 1940 when Hitler and members of his Cabinet met representatives of the French government in a railway car in Compiègne forest to dictate to them the terms of the German peace.

The fact that Keitel read the peace terms indicated his high position in the German Reich. Colonel General Keitel was Germany's spokesman on all military and naval matters and had been since February 4, 1938. That was the date on which Hitler reorganized the army with a Napoleonic gesture, firing Von Blomberg, Minister of War, and Von Fritsch, commander in chief of the army, on grounds of "ill health," and himself assumed personal and direct command of all of Germany's armed forces.

Under the new order of things there was no position of Minister of War. Hitler, like the Kaiser, was the all-high chief. His authority was exercised through a "Supreme Command of the Armed Forces headed by General Wilhelm Keitel." Thus Keitel became technically Von Blomberg's successor, but without the latter's authority. He took over the War Ministry and in accordance with Chancellor Hitler's decree was, during times of peace, to have "charge of national defense in all fields." The new German armed hierarchy was now first Hitler, then General Keitel, as a kind of administration officer in charge of liaison to the three fighting services—Marshal Goering for the air, Admiral Raeder for the navy and Von Brauchitsch (see sketch this issue) for the army.

Later Keitel also became a Cabinet Minister. On August 31, 1939, on the heels of mobilization in Poland, Hitler organized his government on a war basis, appointing a "Cabinet Council of Defense of the Reich." Keitel, as chief of the Supreme Command of the Armed Forces, was, of course, a member of the new Cabinet.

Keitel's appointment, like Von Brauchitsch's position as commander in chief of the army, was not looked upon in Germany as a political appointment. General Keitel was a good soldier and not a politician. Born September 22, 1882 in Helmscherode, he was descended from an old family of German army officers. He started his officer's career with the artillery in 1901 and rose slowly through the ranks by seniority. In 1902 he was made a second lieutenant. It was 1910 before he became a first lieutenant.

During the First World War he was a captain, spending most of his time on the general staff in the Ministry of War. After the War he served successively in the field artillery and the general staff and was instructor of the Reichswehr Cavalry School from 1920 to 1922. In 1923 he was promoted to the rank of major and served in the Reichswehr (Army) Ministry from 1925 to 1927; he was made lieutenant colonel in 1929; colonel in 1931; and major general in 1934, commanding the 4th Infan-

WILHELM KEITEL

try Division with headquarters at Bremen. From 1935 to 1938, when he became chief of the Supreme Command of the Armed Forces, he was chief of the administration department in the War Ministry.

General Keitel apparently has stood well in the graces of his Führer since he became his chief of staff. In a personal letter written to Keitel in November 1938 Chancellor Hitler expressed his congratulations to his chief of staff for "his valuable cooperation." General Keitel was also promoted to the rank of colonel general at this time.

The General has accompanied the Führer on many of his most important missions. He was with Chancellor Hitler on the latter's visit to Rome in May 1938; was present during the visit of Prime Minister Chamberlain in Berchtesgaden, September 1938; and was also present at the Munich Conference of September 1938.

What influence, if any, he has on Chancellor Hitler is not known. French military writers, however, generally credited Keitel with a strategic victory over Admiral Erich Raeder by persuading Hitler to concentrate air forces on the Western Front instead of diverting a large proportion of them to a coordinate attack rôle with the German Navy. Hitler is said to have wavered, but finally concurred in the idea of concentrating Germany's air forces on the Western Front. The result and the smashing of the Maginot Line is history.

Again Keitel was said to have had a voice in arguing against the German air offensive in Britain in the summer of 1940. According to an English newspaper which attributed its information to the "most neutral sources," a serious difference of opinion among Adolf Hitler's advisers delayed the airplane invasion of Great Britain. It was said that Marshal Goering, Propaganda Minister Goebbels and

KEITEL, WILHELM—*Continued*

Colonel General Keitel were insisting that the invasion must not be launched because the risks were too great, while Foreign Minister Von Ribbentrop and Heinrich Himmler, chief of the Gestapo, were pressing for the invasion.

In October 1940 Keitel took over the Axis African command, succeeding Italian Marshal Rodolfo Graziana, shortly after the Brenner Pass conference between Hitler and Mussolini.

Colonel General Keitel was married April 18, 1909. He has three sons and two daughters. He is described as "hard, unsmiling and always mysterious."

References

N Y Post Jl 25 '40
N Y Sun p26 O 5 '40
N Y Times p1, 3 F 5 '40; p1 O 10 '40
Newsweek 16:13 Jl 1 '40 por

Europa v2
Wer ist's?

KELBERINE, ALEXANDER 1904—Jan 30, 1940 Russian concert pianist

Musical America

ALEXANDER KELBERINE

Obituaries

N Y Herald Tribune p1 Ja 31 '40 por
N Y World-Telegram p9 Ja 31 '40 por

KELLY, FLORENCE FINCH May 27, 1858—Dec 17, 1939 American newspaper woman; author

References

Kelly, F. F. Flowing Stream; The Story of Fifty-Six Years in American Newspaper Life 1939

Who's Who in America 1938-39

Obituaries

Pub W 136:2259 D 23 '39

KENNEDY, JOSEPH PATRICK Sept 6, 1888- Former United States Ambassador to Great Britain

Address: h. 294 Pondfield Rd, Bronxville, New York

Fortune described Joseph Kennedy's career as picaresque even before he was appointed United States Ambassador to Great Britain: "The legends of Joe Kennedy make him at once the hero of a Frank Merriwell captain-of-the-nine adventure, a Horatio Alger success story, an E. Phillips Oppenheim tale of intrigue, and a John Dos Passos [see sketch this issue] disillusioning report on the search for the big money." And it is true that he has had an assortment of experiences any one of which might last another man a lifetime. Joseph Kennedy has never been able to decide whether he is an athlete or a banker, a Wall Street wolf or the investor's guardian, a businessman or a statesman. The only stable and permanent classification he falls into is that of a father.

It was on East Boston's Meridian Street that he was born, on September 6, 1888, the son of Patrick J. and Mary (Hickey) Kennedy. His father was sort of a "soft-spoken, benign-appearing" political boss, with a coal business and part-interest in a couple of saloons besides, so that the Kennedys were moderately well-off. Just the same Joe peddled papers, sold candy on an excursion steamer, took tickets on a sight-seeing boat, and went to Parochial school until the seventh grade. Then he attended the Boston Latin School, where he made records for himself in basketball and football and won the Mayor's cup for his batting; on to Harvard in 1908, to major in economics, make the basketball team, Hasty Pudding, Institute of 1770, Dicky and D. U.; and out into the world in 1912, with a B. A. degree and the experience of $5,000 already earned by running a sight-seeing bus to Lexington during three summers.

Joseph had decided he would have a million by the time he was 35, but temporarily contented himself with a bank examiner's job at $125 a month, traveling around eastern Massachusetts. (His father was a director of the Columbia Trust Company.) After only 18 months on this comparatively humble job he managed to borrow enough money to buy a great part of the stock of the Columbia Trust around the time First Ward National Bank seemed about to take it over; and in 1914 he was elected president of the bank. He was only 25, the youngest bank president in the United States. He was making a good start toward that million.

On October 7, 1914 Joe Kennedy married the daughter of the Mayor who had presented him with the cup for batting six years before: her name was Rose Fitzgerald. The young couple moved to Roxbury, and his father-in-law made Kennedy the director for the city of the Collateral Loan Company, a job that turned out to be troublesome enough to keep anyone else out of politics for more than 20 years. In 1917 Kennedy quit banking for a while and became assistant general manager of the Fore River (Massachusetts) plant of the Bethlehem Shipbuilding Corporation. He spent 20 months building ships for Bethlehem Steel and Assistant Secretary of the Navy Franklin Delano Roosevelt, got himself on the board of trustees of the Massachusetts Electric Company, and finally in 1919 joined the Boston branch of the Hayden-Stone Company, investment bankers, as their manager. (He had met Mr. Stone while trying to interest him in ordering ships.) Until 1924 Kennedy moved in the "intense, secretive circles of operators in the wildest stock market in history, with routine plots and pools, inside information and wild guesses"—and he learned market operations thoroughly. "Anyone can lose his shirt in Wall Street if he has sufficient capital and inside information," he summed up his experiences.

It wasn't quite an accurate description, though. In 1919 Kennedy had bought control of a New England chain of 31 small movie houses and taken a brief flier in production. Then in 1926 he sold part of his little theatre chain, bought control of the Film Booking Offices of America, and started making about one picture a week—mainly Westerns and melodramas. It was a highly profitable venture. In 1928 he became special adviser on the board of Pathe, in 1929 chairman; he bought a controlling interest in Keith, Albee, Orpheum Theatres Corporation and for five months served as chairman of their board; finally a general reshuffling of stocks and the formation of Radio-Keith-Orpheum left him holding a fortune in RKO. He retained only the chairmanship of Pathe, and left that position in 1930, but when he quit the movies he had something like $5,000,000. He was also 32 pounds underweight and had to go to the hospital before he could "clarify his social views."

He emerged looking for "a leader who will lead," and decided it was Franklin D. Roosevelt. It is reported that he gave $15,000 to the 1932 Democratic campaign fund, lent $50,000 more, and is supposed to have contributed another $100,000 indirectly. In 1932 he traveled with the Roosevelt campaign train and all kinds of rumors went around about him; it was said he was the man who had brought Hearst into the Roosevelt camp, and it was known that he was friendly with Cardinal Pacelli and Father Coughlin (see sketch this issue). After Roosevelt's election he didn't get a Cabinet position, however, although he is supposed to have wanted the job of Secretary of the Treasury, and 1933 found

JOSEPH P. KENNEDY

him back on Wall Street cleaning up in a pool in stock of the Libbey-Owens-Ford Glass Company.

In 1934 a good many people were startled when his appointment as the head of the Securities Exchange Commission was announced. Putting a speculator in charge of a commission formed to protect the investor caused most liberals to break into a cold sweat and decide that Wall Street had captured the New Deal. John T. Flynn described Kennedy as an "antisocial gambler, a blundering wrecker of corporations, a tool of other capitalists, and a conscienceless market manipulator to boot." But when Kennedy resigned in September 1935 after 431 strenuous days it was not only the praise of the conservative press that was ringing in his ears, but the same John T. Flynn was calling him the "most useful member of the Commission."

Back to private life, Kennedy worked for a short time as an independent corporate consultant reorganizing RCA, making a report on Paramount Pictures and reorganizing the Hearst properties. He also published a campaign volume, *I'm for Roosevelt* (1936), in which he claimed that the New Deal was doing away with the necessity for more drastic changes in the American way of life. Then in 1937 he was asked to be chairman of the newly-formed Maritime Commission, set up to create an American merchant marine and to administer the United States Merchant Marine Act. He was in charge for 75 days, performed a remarkable job of settling ship operators' claims against the government, worked out a scheme for subsidizing shipping companies to the tune of $25,000,000 a year, which caused some to tag him a lobbyist for the shipowners, and got himself called a "union-wrecker" by the N. M. U. because of his advocacy of legislation to

KENNEDY, JOSEPH PATRICK—*Cont.*

outlaw strikes and to make arbitration of labor disputes compulsory. His own opinions of the Merchant Marine Act and of Frances Perkins (see sketch this issue) grew less and less printable, and when in December 1937 he was appointed the United States' (first Irish and first Catholic) Ambassador to Great Britain it was probably a happy day. But Kennedy waved farewell with a plaintive: "I am simply a babe thrown into a foreign country to do the best I can."

In England Kennedy was hailed as "Jolly Joe Kennedy" and "The U. S. A.'s Nine-Child Envoy" (Joseph P., John F., Rosemary, Kathleen, Eunice, Patricia, Robert, Jeanne, Edward). The new Ambassador made a hole in one at golf the first Sunday, said he was fond of Rugby, rode horseback in Rotten Row, put his feet on his desk during his first press conference ("You can't expect me to develop into a statesman overnight"), told Queen Elizabeth she was "a cute trick," didn't wear knee breeches when he presented his credentials to the King but found it "no fun to go to one of those parties and be the only man in long pants," and ended up by making himself very popular. Perhaps that is why he was called the most pro-British Ambassador the United States has ever had. A great friend of Chamberlain's, it was said that he worked closely with the appeasers. In October 1938 a Trafalgar Day speech he made caused the New York *Post* to comment: "If this precious specimen of diplomatic expediency had been written in the British Foreign Office it could not have served better to bolster the propaganda of Prime Minister Chamberlain." By this time Kennedy was saying openly that he didn't approve of all of the New Deal, and President Roosevelt was hearing reports that he had assured British conservatives that there would be a "safe" man in the White House after 1940.

But it was not long after Munich when Kennedy changed his tune and began issuing frantic warnings that 1939 would be a year of war. In September 1939, two hours before it was delivered, he read Chamberlain's speech declaring war. "It's the end of the world," he said. In those early days of September the American Embassy was working day and night, and the cable wires to Washington were equally busy. Ambassador Kennedy moved to a country house outside London after his family left for the United States, but drove into the city each morning.

In November he was holding conferences in Paris with Ambassador Bullitt (see sketch this issue); early in 1940 he was in Washington conferring with Bullitt and Secretary Hull (see sketch this issue). As usual, rumors flew busily about. It was reported that he was trying to enlist Roosevelt's support for an Italo-Vatican peace move; it was reported that he was going to resign. Kennedy made it known that he

had no intentions of resigning, at least. "I cannot forget that I now occupy a post which at this particular time involves matters so precious to the American people that no private considerations should permit my energies or interests to be diverted," he said. In February he returned to London, and the next month was occupied in visiting Gibraltar, Rome and Paris with Under-Secretary Sumner Welles (see sketch this issue), denying German press reports that he had criticized the Allies, keeping silent on the revelations of the German White Book as to his statements on the United States' War policy (already denied by Roosevelt and Hull). June found him working for the evacuation of British children and cabling pleas to Roosevelt for aid to the Allies. He was said to have warned the United States previously of the probability of German successes. In August he narrowly escaped death when a German bomb fell within 300 yards of his country house.

In October 1940 Joseph Kennedy arrived in the United States, and when asked whether he was planning to hand in his resignation, refused to comment, as Hull refused to comment. He immediately proceeded to spike rumors of a rift between him and Roosevelt by making a radio speech strongly advocating his re-election. Not long after election an "off the record" interview printed in the Boston *Globe* created quite a sensation. Kennedy was quoted as having said the presence of Labor leaders in the British Cabinet was merely a sign that "national socialism" was growing out of the British war effort; that "democracy is finished" in England. Late in November 1940 he announced his resignation, saying that as a private citizen he wanted to help the President keep the United States out of war.

Kennedy has said: "I never liked what I had to do until I did it; then it became my career." Red-faced, with receding sandy hair and spectacled blue eyes that usually have an affable glint in them, he has been summed up as "athletic, unperplexed, easily pleased, hot-tempered, independent, impatient and restless as they come." He is "a back-slapper, a good cusser, almost a teetotaler." He likes exercise, plays golf in the 80's, swims, rides, plays tennis, enjoys good food, detective stories, warm climates, long battles, speech-making, talking pictures, music. He used to play the piano himself and has an excellent collection of records, of which Beethoven's *Fifth* is his favorite. He gave up smoking in 1937 and now is a great candy-eater and gum-chewer.

It is quite obvious that he is a family man. His family is as attractive as it is large, consisting of pretty, youthful-looking Mrs. Kennedy, five daughters and four sons. John got his LL. D. at Harvard; the subject of his thesis was non-intervention in the Spanish Civil War. *Why England Slept* (1940) in his contribution to a much-debated problem. Joseph Jr. worked for a time in the Paris office of Ambassador Bullitt. Another member of the family that shouldn't be forgotten is Edward Moore, "nurse, comforter, friend, stooge, package-bearer, adviser," who used to be the secretary of Mrs. Kennedy's father and who is now Joe Kennedy's personal aide.

References

Am Mag 105:32-3 My '28 por
Collier's 96:14 Jl 27 '35 por; 103:11+ Ap 8 '39 il por
Fortune 16:56-9+ S '37 il pors
Ladies' H J 56:23+ F '39 il pors
Nation 146:234 F 26 '38; 147:555 N 26 '38; 151:593-4 D 14 '40
New Repub 79:264-5 Jl 18 '34 tab; 84:244 O 9 '35; 103:78 N 25 '40
No Am R no2:267-76 [D] '38
Time 31:17 F 28 '38; 32:17 O 31 '38 por; 34:13-14 S 18 '39 pors; 36:19 N 4 '40 por; 36:16 N 18 '40
American Catholic Who's Who
Who's Who in America

CHARLES FRANKLIN KETTERING

KETTERING, CHARLES FRANKLIN

(kĕt-ēr-ing)   Aug 29, 1876-   Engineer; manufacturer

Address: b. Winters Bank Bldg, Dayton, Ohio

"Most people think of research as one of two kinds," Charles Franklin Kettering once told a group of businessmen, "either high-brow or nuts." He believes it's neither. "Research is an organized method of finding out what you are going to do when you can't keep on doing what you are doing now."

Kettering, who is now vice-president of General Motors Corporation in charge of its Research Laboratories Division, has gone along on this premise ever since the day when, a "loose-jointed, raw-boned six-foot-three country boy just turned twenty-seven," he got off the train at Dayton, Ohio and walked over to the offices of the National Cash Register Company to ask for a job. He was asked to develop a motor to run cash registers. He made one.

Since then he has made or had a hand in making Delco-lighting, which provided cheap lighting for farms; Duco paint, which reduced the time needed to paint cars from seventeen days to about three hours; the Diesel engine; the hypertherm, which treats diseases by artificially induced heat; the crankcase ventilator; Ethyl gasoline; the self-starting motor; Frigidaires; and a gadget for opening bedroom windows without getting out of bed.

This "monkey wrench scientist" was born on an Ohio farm near Loudonville on August 26, 1876, the son of Jacob and Martha (Hunter) Kettering. He went to the small district school near his home and to high school, earning extra money by working on country telephone lines. After high school Kettering got a job as a country school teacher, but left it a year later to go to Ohio State University.

It took Kettering six years to get through Ohio State, mostly because of an eye ailment which kept him out of school for two years and made it necessary for him to have somebody read to him. In 1904, at the age of 27, he was graduated, threw his diploma into the wastebasket, and went after the National Cash Register Company job. The next year he married Olive Williams and was on his way in the career that was to make him head of the Dayton Engineering Laboratories Company, with Edward Andrew Deeds; president of the General Motors Research Corporations; president of C. F. Kettering, Incorporated, and vice-president of the General Motors Corporation.

There were three men who had contributed to Kettering's understanding of science and research. They all taught him that "formulas should always follow facts and not facts formulas." His country schoolteacher, John Rowe, used to teach square root by whittling out blocks of wood; he did the facts first and then developed the formula. His friend, Neil McLaughlin, taught him that most things in this world are related, and a carriage maker named Sweet in the town where he was teaching school taught him the joy of invention and discovery.

For the past 36 years Charles Kettering has been a researcher. Not the ivory tower kind, but the sort of researcher who firmly believes that he "needs the practice of experience and commercialism." His fellow engineers gave him the Washington Award in 1936 for "accomplishments which pre-eminently promote the happiness, comfort and well-being of humanity."

Humanity's happiness and well-being are promoted by labor-saving devices, Kettering knows, but he knows, too, that it is the

KETTERING, CHARLES F.—*Continued*

labor-creating inventions which can do even more to increase the well-being of great numbers of people. Kettering regards the creation of jobs as a "primary responsibility," and for an example points out that because of researches on Diesel engines the General Motors Electro-Motive plant near Chicago, where his only son Eugene is an engineer, has created work enough to employ 2,000 men.

In these past 36 years Kettering has become less and less interested in the research that turns out annual improvements in Chevrolets or Frigidaires. The most important research job in the world right now, he thinks, is "to find out why grass is green." To discover the answer he set up a thorough study of photosynthesis at Antioch College which costs him about $30,000 a year. He is interested, too, in the practical research which means basic changes in the things around us. He insists: "Time and change are tied together so eternally that we cannot separate them."

This research is mostly carried on now in the special 11-story building in Detroit that houses the General Motors Research Division. Forty per cent of the work here is consultative engineering at the request of the manufacturing divisions; about forty more per cent is advanced engineering, to discover the upper limits of Diesel performance, for instance; about twenty per cent is "pure science," to discover the nature of combustion, perhaps, or of friction. But the whole is "900 per cent Charles Franklin Kettering."

They know him in the laboratory as "Boss Ket." Engineers in rival factories say that you have to be a yes-man to work for "Ket." That's not strictly true, since he does love to argue and insists on a certain amount of it. "But you can't help noticing how the department heads fall unconsciously into his ways of speech and constantly quote him. It's doubtful if even the strongest-minded engineer could work for him without showing it. Sometimes, when in a vein of iconoclastic preaching, the Boss reminds you of an old-womanish Abe Lincoln. At others, when he is tinkering with a stroboscope or drawing graphs on his big office pad, he looks like a young and impish Ichabod Crane."

At 63 he is as loping and active as he was when he first walked into the National Cash Register Company. His eyes still glisten and peer from behind thick lenses just as they did when he was an Ohio farm boy fighting for an education against blindness and poverty. "What makes them gleam now is a prodigious intellectual curiosity." But "Ket" is not satisfied merely to solve problems; he must moralize on his methods.

All around his office are aphorisms: "A man must have a certain amount of intelligent ignorance to get anywhere." "Nothing is so conducive to thought as the sheriff." "Any problem thoroughly understood is fairly simple."

For Kettering economic problems are not exceptions to these rules. "We have too many men out of work, too much idle capital, and too many raw materials," he states firmly. "So, obviously, we have too few projects." In April 1940 he told the Temporary National Economic Committee that more new machines and more projects were the answer to the ills of our economic system.

He tries to remedy this situation by his General Motors' research, the chief purpose of which, he claims, is to supply new industrial projects to society. Thousands of projects go into the G. M. Laboratory and it's often impossible to tell how or in what form they will come out. "The only sure thing is that General Motors' research will sooner or later produce something, and the probability is that it will make General Motors some money, fill a new human want and put some men to work."

References

> Am Mag 109:11-13 Ja '30 por; 124:
> 14-15+ D '37 por
> Christian Sci Mon p1 Ap 9 '40
> Fortune 19:44-52+ Mr '39 il por
> Pop Mech 58:586-7+ O '32 il por
> Sat Eve Post 213:32 Jl 6 '40
> Sci Mo 43:181-4 Ag '36 por
> Time 26:70 D 16 '35 por
> U S News 8:13 Ap 26 '40 por
> American Men of Science
> Bartlett, R. M. "World Isn't Finished" *In* They Did Something About It p1-17 1939
> Who's Who in America
> Who's Who in Commerce and Industry
> Who's Who in Engineering

KEY, BEN WITT June 11, 1883—June 5, 1940 Noted eye surgeon; one of the first surgeons to transplant human cornea; was known internationally as surgeon, diagnostician, research worker and contributor to journals of ophthalmology

References

> American Medical Directory
> Directory of Medical Specialists 1939
> Who's Who in New York
> Who's Who in the East

Obituaries

> N Y Herald Tribune p26 Je 6 '40 por

KIERAN, JOHN (kĭ-rŭn) Aug 2, 1892—Sports columnist of the New York *Times*; member of the *Information, Please* radio program

Address: c/o New York Times, 229 W 43rd St, New York City

The popularity of the question and answer program on the radio shows that Americans still hanker for the parlor games of three generations ago. Evidently Americans yearn for self-improvement—for culture in easy, painless capsule form. Europeans smile at our naïveté, yet there is something refreshing in the thought of millions of people sitting in their comfortable living rooms waiting for the clarion call of *Information, Please:* "Wake up, America! Time to stump the experts!"

One "walking encyclopedia" who has answered many hundreds of questions correctly on the *Information, Please* program over a period of almost three years is John Francis Kieran (he does not use his middle name). He was born, as he puts it, "of poor but Irish parents" in New York City in 1892. His father, a native-born New Yorker, now deceased, was James Michael Kieran, scholar and teacher of the classics, a man of deeply analytical and factual turn of mind who was president of Hunter College in New York City. His mother, Kate (Donahue) Kieran, was a public school teacher before her marriage. "She wrote poetry," says Kieran, "but showed no other signs of mental derangement." Completely opposite in temperament to her husband, she was a romantic who loved music and books. When winter came it was her habit to settle herself in an upstairs sitting room with piles of books close at hand and have all her meals brought up by the maid. She read during practically all her waking hours and could, naturally enough, quote poetry by the yard. Kieran says: "Mother quoted the classics on the slightest provocation." An accomplished musician as well as a student of literature, Mrs. Kieran instilled a love of music in all her children.

As a child John Francis was something of a prodigy. He was tremendously interested in music but showed no disposition toward a musical career. By the time he was 10 he knew most of the music and something about the lives of the great composers. At the same time he read avidly whenever he could get away from his schooling. He maintains that a poor boy can get a lot of pleasure from library books at no cost. But to assume that Kieran and his numerous brothers and sisters led a completely bookish life is incorrect. They were Irish and fond of every kind of boisterous fun and sport. "At high school and college," says Kieran, "I played many games but none too well. Was on the varsity baseball team and fancy diver on the swimming team. Later I won a newspaper golf championship. Now I play tennis and chop wood for regular exercise."

When he was graduated, *cum laude,* from Fordham University in 1912 his father remarked that if he had been a less distinguished shortstop he would probably have been a more distinguished student. For a year after graduation he taught a country school in Dutchess County, New York. He had only six pupils, received $10 a week and ran a poultry business on the side. Both these occupations left him with leisure time, which he spent reading twice, two thick volumes of Blackstone from cover to cover and making voluminous notebooks filled with

JOHN KIERAN

his own comments. The inquiring mind of his father and the love of books and poetry of his mother definitely showed up in the young man. He played no favorites—every kind of book was his constant companion.

He noticed birds in his walks and began to study them. Now he can identify the plumage and the call of nearly every bird in Eastern America. From birds his interest went to flowers and insects. For Kieran to become interested meant to read everything on the subject he could find. As one study led to another he began building up his tremendous memory.

A year of schoolteaching seemed enough for Kieran and in the fall of 1913 he got a job as timekeeper for a sewer construction project. The workers were Italian and Kieran promptly learned the language—not only the words but the gestures and fiery Italian enthusiasm that went with them. This job was an hour by subway from his home. He made the trip six days a week with a French book and a dictionary instead of a newspaper. During 12 hours a week for 12 months Kieran taught himself French— "you can learn a lot of French in that time," he says—and he did.

All this time he wanted to become a journalist. He kept sending in pieces to the New York *Times.* In 1915 he joined the staff of the paper in the capacity, he says, "of added starter in the sports department." At the *Times* he admired from afar the chief of the telephone operators, Alma Boldtmann. Eyewitnesses report that at the time he was very bashful and "too small for his clothes." "I thought he was the new office boy," she recalls. The World War snatched him away from her, however, and he went overseas with the 11th Engineers. Kieran's tunic was undoubtedly the most unshapely in the whole A. E. F.

KIERAN, JOHN—*Continued*

It was stuffed at various times with volumes of Dickens, Thackeray, Shakespeare, Keats and George Borrow.

"I did no harm," Kieran recalls, "to anybody on either side in the War; collected no wounds but was scared to death many times. After the War I returned to newspaper work. After a short term with the New York *Herald Tribune* and Hearst I returned to the home team January 1, 1927 to start the first daily signed column ever published in the New York *Times*. It's still going on. So am I." Meanwhile in 1919 Kieran had married Alma Böldtmann. They went to live in Fieldston, a suburb on the edge of New York City, and have lived there ever since. They have three children—a girl, and two boys who are students at Yale.

Kieran says that his luckiest break in the pursuit of culture was his assignment to go on the road with New York baseball teams. "Nobody on a ball team," he explains, "gets up early and I had almost every morning to myself." Thus he discovered the "culture potential" of every large city in the country—where the libraries were; the parks; the museums; the art exhibitions.

During the years Kieran's curiously dual nature expanded—a scholar and student discussing in true "sports argot" southpaw pitchers, shortstops and winners on the race track, while finding time to dip into the Latin text carried in his pocket. In addition to his sports writings—he has been called one of the world's really great authorities on sport—he found time to rent from the city of New York the concession for the rowboats of the three lakes in Central Park. He did well with them until the profitable venture was put to an end by some trouble with a man named Peter Pappas. One of the Kieran children's earliest recollections is a family chant which went, "PE-ter PAP-pas did PAP-py out of PARK."

Kieran, called the "know-it-all" of *Information, Please,* is essentially a very modest man. That modesty conceals a streak of pugnacity, however. As a boy he was called the "fightingest" Irish. During the War he was given the title "The Battling Supply Sergeant" for taking care of a bullying noncom; once he was formally presented by his fellow sports writers with a plaque—"To John F. Kieran, The New World's Champion" for putting into his place an offensive sports writer.

In 1939 Kieran was asked to address a very swank preparatory school. The professor who introduced him said that it was not customary for the school to invite sports writers. Kieran's Irish flared up. Then the professor went on to say that Kieran was no ordinary sports writer. That maddened Kieran as a reflection on his profession. Finally the learned professor wound up with a "salvo of Latin" in order to put the squirming guest in his place.

"But the Lord," says Kieran, "delivered him into my hands." Kieran arose. "I am sure," he said, "that you will forgive me for correcting one conjugation and one case in your quotation." He corrected them. Then he proceeded to deliver a 30-minute extemporaneous speech, every word of which was in Latin.

The radio program *Information, Please* did not "make" Kieran. He was recognized as a journalistic phenomenon long before. Brooks Atkinson, dramatic critic of the New York *Times* and one of its top intellectuals, once introduced Kieran to his wife, Oriana. Kieran immediately replied with the verse from Tennyson's ballad:

"My heart is wasted with my woe,
    Oriana
There is no rest for me below,
    Oriana"

"That," said Atkinson, "is the first time that any one ever recognized the literary ancestry of my wife's name."

Once, when William Lyon Phelps was asked to write his estimate of the New York *Times*, he startled the editors by passing over its outstanding qualities and writing of Kieran's column—"it is generally conceded that nothing like that column—'Sports of the Times'—was ever seen before among sports pages. Kieran knows the things about sports that every sports writer is expected to know and a good many things that are not required."

The man who carried Thoreau's *Walden* and Carlyle's *French Revolution* through the War, and whose coat pocket houses a book as part of his wardrobe, was a natural for *Information, Please.* The story goes that Dan Golenpaul, who first started the program, met Kieran at the Dutch Treat Club luncheon in New York and was astonished by Kieran's "knowledge of Greek philosophers, obscure composers, classic poetry and other erudite subjects." Since May 1938 Kieran has continued to astonish his listeners.

He denies that his memory is out of the ordinary. "I remember what I'm interested in," he says. "Everybody does. I just happen to be interested in a lot of things—most of them, luckily, the kind that don't cost much." He uses no memory tricks and has but two mottos: "Improve each shining hour" and "Whenever a new book comes out, I reread two old ones."

Since the program started he has answered extemporaneously more than a thousand questions on subjects ranging from "ornithology to mythology, from sports to dead languages, from Shakespeare to ceramics." With him appear F. P. Adams, Oscar Levant (see sketch this issue), and Clifton Fadiman, who acts as master of ceremonies. A successful series of motion picture shorts made without rehearsal has carried the fame of this "omniscient pack" to every corner of the country, and a new *Information, Please* book published in November 1940 records their radio errors and triumphs for posterity.

Kieran receives about $500 a week for the radio hour. This in addition to his *Times* salary amounts to a substantial income, but the family lives simply, almost frugally. They have a summer cottage on an island near the city. With the family away for the summer, Kieran prepares his own breakfast and spends the week in town. Mrs. Kieran told him to be careful not to put wet clothes in the hamper as they might mildew. When she returned to see how he was getting along she found 17 shirts hanging from chairs, light fixtures and furniture in his bedroom. "But I made my bed every morning," he reminded her.

"Neither Kieran nor his brow was built to wear the laurel wreath that the public has bestowed upon him," remarks a critic. "In person he is small, rosy and bashful. His hair is gray; his face and his cumbersome ears authentically Irish; his body slightly bent at the middle. He quotes the classics softly and well. But the accent is unmistakably New York." That accent has given people cause for reflection. It is so definitely what one writer called "Tenth Avenoo": unaffected and candidly no scholarly accent.

Some people feel that Kieran's memory is almost never at a loss when it comes to poetry. One of the most amusing stories concerning him is the time Clifton Fadiman asked him to give the second verse of three famous poems sent in by a Yale undergraduate—one John F. Kieran Jr. Kieran answered two parts correctly but was stumped on the third—stammered and gave up—then called upon a Kieranized Shakespearean line for the last word. "How sharper than a thankless tooth it is," he said, "to have a serpent child."

References

> Christian Sci Mon Mag p4 D 21 '38 il por
> Ladies' H J 57:20+ Mr '40 pors
> Liberty 17:57 Mr 16 '40
> Scholastic 35:21-2E+ S 25 '39 por (Reprinted from Editor & Publisher My 13 '39; same cond. Read Digest 34:103-6 Je '39)
> Time 33:36 Ja 9 '39 por
> Variety Radio Directory
> Who's Who in America

KIMBALL, WILBUR R. 1863—July 29, 1940 Aircraft inventor; engineer; builder of first helicopter in the United States in 1908; associated in his youth with Alexander Graham Bell and Thomas A. Edison; holder of many patents in aeronautics; builder of early electric streetcars; his early work in the development of aircraft using rotary wings instead of the fixed wings of ordinary airplanes received much attention in late years from army engineers

Obituaries

> N Y Herald Tribune p12 Jl 31 '40
> N Y Times p17 Jl 31 '40 por

KING, WILLIAM LYON MACKENZIE
Dec 17, 1874- Prime Minister of Canada
Address: Laurier House, Ottawa, Ontario, Canada

For the duration of the War parliamentary government in Canada was virtually abandoned. The election of March 26, 1940 was such an overwhelming victory for the Liberal government that there were left in Parliament only a few men capable of criticizing its work. The man who was granted almost dictatorial powers at that time was Prime Minister Mackenzie King, who for years has guided Canada's policy down the middle of the road, and the rapid march of events since his election has brought to the country a great deal of unprecedented legislation designed to galvanize Canada's war machine into action. Although the Opposition at first showed symptoms of wishing to displace him, the session of Parliament that ended in August 1940, not to reconvene until November, brought him tributes from the leaders of all parties. If he serves his full term of five years he will have been Canada's Prime Minister for 19 years. To Canadians his is a familiar figure: "small, black-coated . . . with inches of starched shirt cuff, the single wisp of hair sprawling over the forehead, the bouncing little stride, the battered red dispatch case under his arm"—familiar, and perhaps reassuringly undictatorial in appearance.

It was a bold and shrewd move on King's part that turned possible political embarrassment into victory, back in the first months of 1940. Shortly after Canada declared war on Germany, Mitchell Hepburn, provincial Premier of Ontario and dissident Liberal, persuaded the Liberal members of the Ontario Parliament to pass a vote of censure on the Prime Minister for lax conduct of Canadian war activities. Dr. Robert J. Manion, leader of the Conservative minority in Parliament, took up the cry, charging that King's conduct of the War had been "half-hearted, incompetent and neglectful." To the sessional opening of Parliament on January 18, 1940 Opposition leaders came all primed to insist upon their Parliamentary right to facts and figures, which, they believed, would expose unfair campaign censorship and patronage in awarding war contracts, previously hidden under a cloud of "dictatorial secrecy." They were surprised; after walking "like a trained actor through all the preliminary ceremonies," the Prime Minister, without a word of warning, dissolved Parliament four hours after it assembled, called for a "direct and unquestioned mandate from the people." Dr. Manion, after protesting that King wished to gag the House, after calling "Dictatorship! Why should we fight for democracy in Europe and lose it at home?" was met with the quiet retort: "Democracy doesn't

WILLIAM LYON MACKENZIE KING

mean that I am answerable to the leaders of the Opposition—but to the people."

The people answered two months later by giving the Liberals more seats in Parliament than ever before, by re-electing all the government ministers, and by defeating Manion in his own home town. It is supposed that Manion's program seemed more than a little vague, particularly without the hoped-for "facts and figures," and that King's promises to fight the War with vigor, to spread war sacrifices as evenly as possible over all sections of the people, and not to draft men for war service seemed more dependable than those of a comparatively unknown Opposition.

Mackenzie King was born in Kitchener, Ontario, Canada, December 17, 1874, the son of Isabel Grace and John King, a law lecturer at Toronto. His maternal grandfather, William Lyon Mackenzie, was a "Scottish journalist and politician who played some part in obtaining parliamentary government for Canada in early colonial days" and who gave him his name. Young King's first and last interests have always been economics and political science. Of a scholarly turn of mind, he took B. A., LL. B. and M. A. degrees from the University of Toronto, went on to Harvard to add another M. A. and a Ph. D. to the long string of letters after his name, became a protégé of Harvard's President Eliot, won a fellowship in political science and a traveling fellowship which enabled him to study European social and economic conditions, and finally polished off his education at the University of Chicago. Here for a while he did social work under Jane Addams at Hull House. When he returned to Canada he had more than adequate background for making his bow in sober Canadian politics, and in 1900 he entered the Canadian civil service as Deputy

Minister of Labour, became editor of the *Labour Gazette*. At this time he was beginning to acquire the reputation of a radical, a reputation perhaps not entirely deserved even then, for during the eight years in which he served almost continuously as Deputy Minister his main claim to such description was the authorship of the Industrial Disputes Investigation Act of 1907, limiting Capital and Labor in the rights to strikes and lockouts.

In 1909 Sir Wilfred Laurier, the late Liberal leader, cast his eye about for a brilliant young Minister of Labor and found 35-year-old Mackenzie King. King served for two years under Prime Minister Laurier, and though defeated in the election of 1911 when the Conservatives came into power, he remained Laurier's faithful lieutenant until the older man's death in 1919. From 1912 to 1914 he was president of the General Reform Association of Toronto; during the War he was not at the front, but engaged in industrial relations investigations under the sponsorship of the Rockefeller Foundation in the United States, where he worked out a plan of employer-employee representation that was put into practice by the Colorado Fuel and Iron Company, the Bethlehem Steel Company and other great industrial concerns; finally in 1919, at the death of Sir Wilfred, he was chosen by the Liberal National Convention as their new leader. Although at the end of the War he had published a book titled *Industry and Humanity* (1918), whose main thesis was that "autocratic government in industry must be superseded by a system in which all the parties to industry are represented," when the Liberals returned to power and King became Prime Minister in 1921 his government "steadily avoided responsibility for labor questions" on the plea that they fell within the jurisdiction of the provinces. This Liberal government held office until the debacle of 1930, with only a brief period out of office in 1926; 1930 to 1935 were years "in the wilderness"; then in 1935 Mackenzie King once more became Canada's Prime Minister, President of the Privy Council, Secretary of State for External Affairs.

Traditionally the Canadian Liberal Party, polling most of the rural and French vote, stands for provincial rights, low tariffs, curtailment of central orders-in-council, equality of farmer-labor interest with those of urban industrialists. But under the pressure of economic necessity most of these policies have been slowly reversed, until the Liberals have been accused of having become, if anything, more conservative than the Conservatives. During King's premiership there has been little pampering of Labor. Although his Conservative predecessor had inaugurated various "New Deal" measures—unemployment insurance, laws for the regulation of hours and conditions in industry—the new Prime Minister, a firm believer in individual enterprise, who opposed much of the economic program of his friend across the border, had these Canadian laws referred to the Courts. They were declared *ultra vires*. Of low tariffs and free trade he remained a strong advocate, however, and he welcomed the opportunity to negotiate the Canadian-American trade treaty in 1935.

In matters of foreign policy King's outlook is said to be "essentially North American and nationalistic." For many years he was an isolationist. From 1928 to 1936 he served as a member of the League of Nations' Council and vice-president of the assembly, but he disapproved of the military sanctions of the League of Nations' Covenant, talked of making the League over as a body of conciliation only and at one time repudiated a Canadian representative who wanted to impose oil sanctions against Italy during the Ethiopian conquest. Still, although he played "a large part in shaping the cause of the Imperial Conference of 1926, which registered the emancipation of the Dominion from the control of Downing Street," he believed in maintaining close relations with both the United States and Great Britain. Before the present War some Canadians were even suspicious of the degree of cooperation between Canadian and English military authorities, and it is said that the Opposition had little reason to criticize the Prime Minister for neglect of war preparations, for it is now coming to light that significant preparations of that kind were made in 1938 and early 1939. When England declared war on Germany, Canada was the first of the colonies to follow suit.

In June 1940, with a warning that "Germans may be crossing the oceans now in a fleet they have seized to conquer new lands," the Prime Minister introduced in the House of Commons a measure to conscript all men between 18 and 45 for military service within the country. Under other legislative measures in the interest of national defense wealth can be conscripted, Canadian taxation has become the heaviest in the country's history, and for the first time unemployment insurance has been introduced. August 1940 marked the creation of a Permanent Joint Defense Board for Canada and the United States— one of the Prime Minister's "fondest dreams."

His function, as Mackenzie King sees it, is to "ascertain all the conflicting views of his party, weld them into the best compromise possible," and at this he is said to be past master. Because in Parliament he is a "cautious, cool, ponderous speaker" who, you feel, "has never uttered a sentence here without visualizing it in his mind on the printed pages of Hansard," most observers characterize him as without much color or human appeal, but one reported: "On the stump he looks tired and smart, something like J. Ramsay MacDonald on the downhill trail; a veteran performer, capable of twisting the interruption of a

heckler into an outburst of applause, and playing on the emotions of any audience as Fritz Kreisler does with a violin." The care of government he does not take lightly; in the recent campaign he "likened himself, with an ingratiating smile, to Abraham Lincoln and William E. Gladstone, with such an air of depreciating aplomb that the observer knows he thinks of himself in terms of historic statesmanship, and is wearing himself out no longer merely for office, but for rank in world history."

Mackenzie King has never married and has few intimate friends. "Bachelor-like, he has lavished his affection on an Irish terrier by the name of Pat, now 17 years of age, wobbling on his pins and too gloomy to permit his picture to be taken." Society as a whole bores him; he has been dubbed "the Hermit of Kingsmere," after the beautiful country home where he spends so much of his time. In the winter he lives in Laurier House, an old-fashioned stone house in Ottawa which Sir Wilfred left to the Liberal Party, and here a light can almost always be seen burning in the Prime Minister's top-floor study. "Politics and government are his life and he has no other interests." He is, perhaps, "the scholar, the dreamer, dragged from his books, his bric-a-brac, his papers and his dog, by the accident of politics and the drive of his own ambition"; he is, surely, the most powerful and one of the ablest men in Canada.

References

Business Week p51 My 4 '40
Canad Mag 82:17 Ag '34
Cur Hist 46:28-35 Jl '37 por; 51:15 Mr '40
Life 8:16 F 5 '40 por
Newsweek 14:16 O 23 '39 por; 15:25 F 5 '40; 15:27-8 Ap 8 '40 por
Scholastic 36:10 Mr 18 '40; 36:3 Ap 8 '40 por
Spec 164:433 Mr 29 '40
Time 35:25 F 5 '40 por; 35:24 Ap 8 '40 por; 36:26-8 S 2 '40
Locke, G. H.   William Lyon Mackenzie King *In* Builders of the Canadian Commonwealth p285-6 1923
Vining, C. Mr. King *In* Bigwigs p83-5 1935
Who's Who
Who's Who in Canada

KIPLING, CAROLINE STARR BALESTIER Dec 31, 1865—Dec 19, 1939 Rochester-born widow of Rudyard Kipling

Obituaries

Newsweek 15:40 Ja 1 '40 por
Time 35:41 Ja 1 '40

KLEE, PAUL 1879—June 30, 1940 Swiss-born artist, generally identified with contemporary school of German modernists; works are in numerous European and Ameri-

KLEE, PAUL—*Continued*
can galleries and museums but banned by Nazis

References

Art Digest 9:13 Mr 15 '35 il; 10:19 N 1 '35
Beaux Arts p6 Jl 15 '38
Parnassus 9:8-11 N '37; 7-9+ D '37
Time 31:39 Ap 11 '38 il
Bulliett, C. J. Paul Klee *In* Significant Moderns and Their Pictures p172-4 1936
International Who's Who

Obituaries

N Y Times p17 Jl 3 '40

KNICKERBOCKER, HUBERT RENFRO Jan 31, 1898- Journalist

Address: c/o International News Service, 235 E 45th St, New York City

H. R. Knickerbocker (he uses only the initials of his name) is an "astringent redheaded Texan" who has been reporting the world since 1923. Wherever big events happen, wherever history is being made, he has a ringside seat. From Munich, from Moscow, from Vienna, Jerusalem, Prague, Ethiopia, South America, Spain and China he has cabled out his sensational stories, his beats so varied, his material so important that even a hardened newspaperman like Alexander Woollcott was moved to write: "Not since I first met Richard Harding Davis five and twenty years ago have I myself encountered any journalist whose panache so completely fitted in with my slightly romantic notions about the profession."

With his "pleasant but unmistakable drawl," H. R. Knickerbocker, in March

H. R. KNICKERBOCKER

1940, began lecturing all over the United States about his experiences and the conclusions he drew from them. He assured audiences that if Hitler wins the present War the United States will not be much better off than was Czechoslovakia in 1938; he urged this country to throw its whole weight behind the Allies, not with troops, but with arms, money, air force and the navy. And when listeners objected to his strong interventionist stand he asked them: "Why all this talk about not being emotional? What did God give us emotions for? To protect us from fear, of course..."

After revisiting the battlefields of Europe Mr. Knickerbocker came back to the United States in October 1940 persuaded that "we should go into war today—as soon as possible," and ready for another four-months lecture tour.

The son of Hubert Delancey Knickerbocker, an itinerant Methodist preacher, and Julia Catherine (Opdenweyer) Knickerbocker, Hubert Renfro was born in Yoakum, Texas and got his college degree at Southwestern University in Texas in 1917. For a while he drove a milk wagon in Austin, Texas, but sold his route to study psychiatry in New York. When, in 1919, he arrived at Columbia University "all he could afford was a course in journalism," so he took that instead. Before that he had spent a few months in the army as a telegraph operator on the Mexican border.

After a year at Columbia, Knickerbocker got a job on the Newark (New Jersey) *Morning Ledger* and was conspicuous mainly for his success in conducting a vice crusade. From there he spent a short time on the New York *Evening Post* and another short time on the New York *Sun*. In 1922 he was head of the department of journalism at Southern Methodist University.

Knickerbocker hadn't really given up his idea of becoming a psychiatrist, however, and in 1923 he went to Germany to study. He enrolled at the University of Munich and to pay his way took a job as occasional correspondent for the United Press. He was in Munich when Hitler gathered together his followers for his first unsuccessful *putsch*. After a year Knickerbocker left Munich for Berlin, where he enrolled in the university and where he became assistant Berlin correspondent for the New York *Evening Post* and the Philadelphia *Public Ledger*. In 1925 he got his first job with Hearst's International News Service and spent two years in Moscow.

In 1928 Knickerbocker was back in Berlin, covering news both for INS and the Philadelphia *Public Ledger*. He got his *Ledger* position by introducing Sinclair Lewis to Dorothy Thompson (see sketch this issue). When Lewis married her he stepped right into what had been her job. Up to the time Hitler came to power "Knickerbocker's income and prestige topped that of any other foreign correspondent." In the winter of 1931 to 1932 he created a sensation by touring Germany, by writing 90,000 words in 48 days and never missing a cable filing. "After only a minimum of editing" came his book based on these stories, *The German Crisis* (1932). Before its publication he had already (in 1930) been awarded a Pulitzer Prize for a series of 24 articles on *The Red Trade Menace*.

When the Nazis came to power they quickly marked him as an observer out of sympathy with Nazi views; the market for his books and lectures fell; gradually he was edged out of Germany. Hearst immediately gave him an assignment as roving reporter. For Hearst he covered the Abyssinian War; he was with Franco's Army in the Spanish Civil War, the first reporter to reach it after the outbreak of hostilities; in 1937 he covered the Sino-Japanese War; he did a series of articles on Palestine; he saw German troops march into Austria and then into Czechoslovakia. After one month on the Allied Front, covering the Second World War, he took a leave of absence, flew back to the United States and started giving lectures on Europe and the part the United States should, according to his views, play in the international scene.

During these years he published *The Red Menace* (1931); *Fighting the Red Trade Menace* (1931); *The German Crisis* (1932); *Will War Come in Europe?* (1934); *Siege of the Alcazar* (1937). Nearly all reviewers found these books extremely readable, vivid and exciting as reporting, although many complained of Knickerbocker's over-simplification, inconclusiveness or hastiness in the rôle of interpreter of the international scene. The New York *Times* called his *Seige of the Alcazar* neither an "enlightening" nor "even a reliably informative book." As a newspaperman, however, readers and fellow correspondents alike agree that this slight, bespectacled reporter with a "shock of wavy flame-red hair (balding on top)" has a "capacity for sensing copy which will be weighty with significance when it appears across the water in the American press." Quick at sifting the facts, "quick at detecting the relevant from the irrelevant, writing directly in cablese," he is usually, too, the first to get out his story. Nevertheless, H. R. Knickerbocker has always been less interested in spot news than in trends. His has been the long-range view of politics. Four years before the Anschluss he predicted in a dispatch that Germany wanted and would get Austria. "Adolf Hitler," he wrote, "was born in Braunau on the Inn. He will never rest until his Austrian homeland has become a part of his, the third Reich."

References

New Outlook 162:28 D '33
Time 26:41 O 14 '35 por; 36:35 Ag 26 '40; 36:75 O 14 '40 por
America's Young Men
Author's and Writer's Who's Who
Davis, F. My Shadow in the Sun 1940

Howe, Q. The News and How to Understand It 1940
Who's Who in America

KNOPF, SIGARD ADOLPHUS (knŭpf') Nov 27, 1857—July 15, 1940 Physician; world authority on tuberculosis; pioneer in combatting the disease; for 40 years led fight against "white plague"; prolific author in field; book on tuberculosis was translated into 30 languages; professor at Post-Graduate Medical School, New York City for 12 years

SIGARD ADOLPHUS KNOPF

References

American Men of Science
Who's Who in America

Obituaries

N Y Herald Tribune p14 Jl 16 '40 por
N Y Times p17 Jl 16 '40

KNOX, FRANK Jan 1, 1874- Secretary of the Navy

Address: b. Navy Department, Washington, D. C.; h. 1320 Sheridan Rd, Lake Forest, Illinois

On the eve of the formal opening of the 1940 GOP National Convention in Philadelphia came the news that President Roosevelt had invited former Secretary of State Henry Stimson (see sketch this issue) and newspaper publisher Colonel Frank Knox to enter his Cabinet as Secretary of War and Secretary of the Navy respectively, and that the two Republicans had accepted. Since a coalition Cabinet had never been formed by any United States President since George Washington, Messrs. Stimson and Knox soon became officially ex-Republicans, and political observers all over the world began

FRANK KNOX

to emit sounds of pleasure or displeasure as they examined the implications of the appointments. The two men have often been called "interventionists." Whether the nomination of Knox for the post of Secretary of the Navy made the Democratic Party a "war party" or simply showed abandonment of partisanship in a time of national emergency was a matter for the Naval Affairs Committee and the Senate to fight out before finally confirming his appointment on July 10, 1940.

William Franklin Knox (known as Frank) has little in common with his President but his middle name and a foreign policy. He was born in Boston on New Year's Day 1874, the son of an oyster-market man, William Edwin Knox, and of Sarah (Barnard) Knox. Four years after he was born his family moved to Nova Scotia to enter upon an unsuccessful lobster-market project. Then they moved back to Boston, broke, and from there to Grand Rapids, Michigan, where his father opened a small grocery store. Frank was seven then. The grocery business prospered not much more than his father's other ventures. At 11 Frank was attending the Jefferson Street School, writing prize English themes, and getting up at 3 a. m. to deliver newspapers. After high school he went West and hustled around as a salesman until the panic of '93 lost him his job. Then he attended Alma College, "a rather aggressively Christian (Presbyterian) college in Michigan," and managed to earn enough money to continue his education there by coaching gymnasium classes, painting signs on barns and spading up gardens for faculty wives. It was 1898 when he took his B. A. and left football, Latin and Greek to enlist in the Army and to become one of Theodore Roosevelt's Rough Riders.

Theodore Roosevelt became Frank Knox's lifelong hero. For the next 10 years he was to be a "Roosevelt man at a distance," but at 24 he began his own political and newspaper career by helping to put over Senator William Alden Smith's campaign and by being rewarded with a job on the Senator's Grand Rapids newspaper, the *Telegram-Herald*. Arthur H. Vandenberg (see sketch this issue), present Senator from Michigan, went to work as a cub reporter on the same newspaper on the same day.

It was on a cub reporter's salary that Knox married his college sweetheart, Annie Reid, in December 1898, but he had advanced from city editor to circulation manager before he left the Grand Rapids paper in 1901 to engage in his first publishing venture. His wife had succeeded in saving $500 from his pay envelope, and he borrowed another $1,000 in order to buy a half-interest in Sault Sainte Marie's weekly *News*.

As a country editor Knox was a belligerent crusader against vice, gambling and corruption, and he still likes to tell stories about his experiences in the colorful little town of "Soo." Lumberjacks and sailors were being robbed in "protected" saloons; Knox was out to clean up the town, and at one time was so zealous as to knock out a saloon-keeper. For a while things were pretty uncomfortable, but he continued fighting not only the saloons but the "interests"; managed the campaign for the Michigan Governor who first imposed heavy taxation on the Michigan Central Railroad and introduced the first workman's compensation law; was given the chairmanship of the Republican Central Committee in 1910 and finally branched out into national politics.

In 1911 it was Knox who was Theodore Roosevelt's pre-convention Midwest campaign manager, and it was Knox more than anyone else who dragged him into the unfortunate 1912 campaign on the Progressive ticket. That same year, after selling his expanded publishing properties in Sault Sainte Marie for $50,000, Knox moved to New Hampshire to become half-owner of the Manchester *Union* and *Leader,* papers which are still running smoothly under his partner's guidance. His "business life," someone said, has been a pattern of settling in strange towns and making good."

Knox's crusading instinct was as strong as ever, but soon the crusades were of a different nature. Long before the United States' entrance into the First World War his New Hampshire papers were raging at President Wilson for being "too proud to fight." When war was finally declared the 43-year-old publisher enlisted in the Army as a private, went overseas with the 78th Division, and by the time of the Armistice had become a major of field artillery. Grown more conservative in his views (or perhaps it was the times that had changed), in 1920 he was floor manager for General Wood, another defeated Rough Rider, at the Chicago Republican Convention; in 1922 he was successfully fighting the imposition of a state income tax in his state; and in 1924 he himself sought the Republican nomination for Governor of New Hampshire but was defeated. By 1927 he was quite ready to retire, but Hearst offered him approximately $1,000 a week, put him in complete charge of his Boston *American* and *Advertiser,* and early in 1928 made him general manager of all the Hearst newspapers at a salary three times as large.

Knox was with Hearst only five years, but during those five years he earned half a million dollars. By 1931 he was ready to retire again, actually resigned from his position—and then heard that the Chicago *Daily News* was up for sale. The *Daily News* in Chicago was more than a newspaper—it was an institution. Frank Knox couldn't resist bidding for a controlling interest.

One of Knox's first announcements as publisher was that he would "never Hearstify" the *News.* Through its columns he fought the corrupt Len Small Republican régime; from time to time with "steaming" front-page editorials, written over his own name, he came out for such issues as academic freedom; and it is rumored that one of his best reporters nearly lost his job for asking him how he wanted him to write a certain story. But when the New Deal came along he found himself labeled reactionary by those who liked neither his "Communist-alarmist" attacks on the régime of President Franklin D. Roosevelt nor his attitude toward labor.

Knox's first anti-New Deal editorial, in August 1933, when Roosevelt placed a blanket code on industry, lost him 5,000 readers; but the editorials continued, and in 1934 he went on a trip to Russia, Italy, Austria and Germany for fresh anti-New Deal ammunition. He found it. A pamphlet later in the year denouncing the European dictatorships caused many Republicans to see him as a party hope, and after he had gone around from city to city making speeches to raise money for the Republican chest, rumors began going around that he was a candidate for the Republican Presidential nomination. It was Roosevelt he was attacking rather than the Democrats: the President's aides were "fanatics," the President himself a "shadow boxer," the suggested Republican slogan "Fewer and better Roosevelts!"

He himself believed firmly in economic *laissez-faire,* in the competitive system. He condemned the AAA, the Social Security Act, the Wagner law, wanted to pay veterans' bonuses from the billions appropriated for relief, suggested that pensions be administered by the states rather than by the government.

It was only after having received the Republican nomination for Vice-President and having been defeated in the 1936 elections that Colonel Knox began to find any of Roosevelt's policies to his liking. Knox was opposed to all world courts and leagues of nations, "axiomatically a nationalist." In December 1937 he publicly supported President Roosevelt for perhaps the first time in his stand against "peace at any price" in the *Panay* incident with Japan. Even before World War II began he was pointing out the threat of the importation of Nazism from Europe to South America, the need for achieving superiority over any enemy on the high seas (he had always been a "big Navy" man), throwing out "dark hints about a future United States extending from the North Pole to the Equator." He suggested getting the British and French West Indian Islands in payment for debts, making a special trade agreement with Brazil. At that time, however, he argued against involvement in European quarrels and asserted that "it will never be possible to make a decisive attack on us by air."

Shortly after the War began, however, he was advocating all possible help to the Allies short of an expeditionary force, and when Germany invaded Holland in May 1940 he published a two-column editorial on the first page of his newspaper calling for uncompromising rearmament and unflinching defense of the entire Western Hemisphere. A few days later he was authorized to organize civilian groups to cooperate with the government in training 10,000 pilots at volunteer "air Plattsburgs"; shortly afterwards it was reported that Knox was being considered for a secretaryship in a coalition cabinet; but it was not until June 1940 that Roosevelt's nomination for successor to the post of Navy Secretary Charles Edison (see sketch this issue) was announced.

In August the Colonel left his paper for the duration of his services as Secretary of the Navy. In October he professed himself well pleased with the progress of the two-ocean Navy building program, and stated that the United States now had the "most powerful fleet afloat."

Stocky, smooth-shaven, with a "large, pleasant face and rather reddish hair," Colonel Knox, "like the late Dean Briggs of Harvard, acts like an editor, swears like a trooper. The look of energy and shrewdness is just what you would expect, the heartiness, the manner of the successful business man, the brisk gestures, even the pipe." It is said that those who work for him call him "a swell guy." He has a home on Chicago's North Shore, and he's an honorary member of Chicago's swank Commercial Club, a member of Room 100 of the Chicago Club, the Old Elm and the Union League, but home still means a great red brick colonial house on the outskirts of Manchester, New Hampshire, "maple-shaded and enclosed by an old stone fence." Here publicity-shunning Mrs. Knox lives most of the time with her sister, ready to welcome the Colonel home every month or so. In Manchester he goes to Rotary meet-

KNOX, FRANK—*Continued*
ings, rides horseback, plays "mediocre golf."

References

Atlan 164:75-80 Jl '39
Fortune 12:109-12+ N '35 pors
Lit Digest 121:7 Mr 7 '36 por; 122:4-5 Ag 8 '36 por
Nation 142:219-20 F 19 '36; 142:248-9 F 26 '36; 142:351 Mr 18 '36; 142:843 Je 27 '36
Newsweek 6:22-3 Ag 24 '35 por
Time 26:13-15 O 14 '35 por
U S News 9:22-3 Jl 12 '40
Vital Speeches 4:243-7 F 1 '38; 6: 418-22 My 1 '40
Beasley, N. Frank Knox, American 1936
Shumway, H. I. Colonel Frank Knox, Veteran of Wars, Campaigns, Newspapers *In* Famous Leaders of Industry 4th ser. p235-52 1936
Who's Who in America
Who's Who in Commerce and Industry

KNUDSEN, WILLIAM S. (nŭd′sĕn) Mar 25, 1879- Member of the National Defense Commission

Address: b. War Department, Washington, D. C.; h. 1501 Balmoral Drive, Detroit, Michigan

Famed industrial expert appointed by President Roosevelt to the National Defense Commission is William Signius Knudsen (he uses only the initial of his middle name), president of General Motors Corporation. Mr. Knudsen was given a leave of absence from the corporation to enable him to devote his time to the Commission. He stated in an interview his belief that America could turn out sufficient munitions for national defense and General Motors could, if need be, match Henry Ford's offer to produce 1,000 airplanes a day. On June 3, 1940 Secretary Morgenthau (see sketch this issue) turned over to Knudsen the direction of mobilizing machine tools for the defense program. It was expected that the work which Secretary Morgenthau had been doing in the aircraft and aeronautical engine fields would also go to Mr. Knudsen.

Since that time, the other six members of the National Defense Commission have faded a little into the background, for the chief problem of the Commission is production, and it is production that Mr. Knudsen is in charge of. The President of the United States has final say, but Knudsen can advise, suggest, request—and he has personally supervised the placing of all contracts. He got the President to agree to the bill permitting manufacturers to amortize the cost of defense plants within five years, argued for the removal of restrictions that the House put in the excess profits tax bill, and fought Attorney General Jackson's (see sketch this issue) ruling

concerning the awarding of contracts to violators of the labor laws. "Certainly," he said, "the Defense Commission has no authority and does not want to undertake the job of enforcing the labor laws." If by October 1940 contracts amounting to $8,253,000,000 had been cleared, with only $4,000,000,000 remaining to be awarded, it was chiefly due to Mr. Knudsen. Since September all his connections with the General Motors Corporation have been severed.

The man who headed the huge General Motors plants, and who earned one of the 10 biggest incomes in the country, was born in Copenhagen, Denmark March 25, 1879 and came to America at the age of 20, when he could speak scarcely a word of English. In Copenhagen his father was a customs inspector, and young Knudsen had a good education, excelling in mathematics. He wanted to go to sea, but his father apprenticed him instead in a bicycle factory. There he startled the townspeople by building and riding the first tandem ever seen in Copenhagen.

On arriving in America he got a job in the shipyards in New York, learned "American" from the children in the streets, and also how to use his fists. After a session repairing boilers in an Erie Railroad roundhouse, he became stockroom keeper, and in 1902 superintendent, of the John R. Keim Mills, a Buffalo bicycle factory. This company began producing automobile parts for Henry Ford, and Ford took it over in 1911. Knudsen began his career with Ford as an installer of assembly plants all over the country. He wanted to go to college, but with a substantial salary increase he was married instead, in 1911, to Clara Elizabeth Euler, a Buffalo girl. The Knudsens have four children: Elna, Clara, Martha and Semon. It was in 1914 that Knudsen became an American citizen, and thereafter giving up his name—Signius Wilhelm Poul —became plain "Bill" Knudsen.

During the War years he became Ford's production manager and right-hand man; but in the depression years that followed differences arose between them, and he resigned. General Motors immediately annexed him; and at the age of 40 Knudsen became vice-president and manager of Chevrolet. His job was to build a Chevrolet to outsell Ford's Model-T. He did this so successfully that in 1927 Ford shut down his plant and changed his philosophy of motorcar making. In 1933 Knudsen became executive vice-president of General Motors, with five lines of automobiles to manage. He put each division so rapidly on its feet that in 1937 he was appointed President of General Motors, with Alfred P. Sloan (see sketch this issue) moving to the post of Chairman of the Board.

It was in 1937 that Homer Martin, heading the United Automobile Workers, called sitdown strikes that closed 14 General Motors plants. Governor Murphy of Michigan (see sketch this issue), as mediator, tried to bring Knudsen and Martin together. But Knudsen wanted the withdrawal of the strikers, whom he denounced as "lawless trespassers." He felt himself under obligation both to his workers and to General Motors' stockholders. President Roosevelt sat tight and refused to intervene or take sides in the strike. Governor Murphy hoped there would be no violence, but when trouble arose between strikers and non-strikers at the Chevrolet plant and 19 were injured, the National Guardsmen were mobilized. The long strike was finally settled by an agreement in which neither General Motors nor the CIO could be considered victor, and for the settlement of which Governor Murphy was given credit. Knudsen emerged, however, with an epitaph on strikes: "Let us have peace and make automobiles." A report of the La Follette Civil Liberties Committee charges General Motors with employing a great number of labor spies during Knudsen's management. Knudsen has also been charged with having produced the "speed-up" system, but refutes the charge, saying that the only thing that produces good work is accuracy. He objects to the CIO because he believes in craft unionization. Having learned, since the General Motors strike, to think of industry as a whole instead of in terms of a few plants, he says he looks forward to the time when unions will be as responsible as management is today, and collective bargaining will be a matter of course.

Hard-working, forthright, genial, thoroughly democratic, Knudsen has always held the respect and affection of the men working for him. He is large: six-feet-three inches, with a boxer's slope-shouldered frame; some time ago he gave up boxing, but he still likes to swim. His strong, well-shaped hands compel attention. "In repose, their half-curled stiffness testifies eloquently to a past of manual labor. They seem to demand a spanner or marlinespike. That they could grasp a marlinespike competently you know when you learn that the sea sang in his boyhood dreams, that his home is adorned with marine paintings and that he warms inwardly when anything nautical is mirrored in his sea-blue eyes." These same hands are nimble performers on the accordion and the xylophone. Knudsen loves music and he likes dancing parties too, with plenty of young people—his "kits." Since coming to Washington, where his home overlooks scenic Rock Creek Park, he flies back to Detroit nearly every week end to see those same "kits."

He always wears a hat at his desk. "I think better in a hat," he explains. His voice is soft and quiet (but he can shout like John L. Lewis when he wants to) and he uses words simply and effectively. He doesn't like women secretaries since one burst into tears once at the language he used in conference. He depends on the one-page reports of a small staff of assistants to show him the curve of progress in national defense production, and he doesn't interfere with their work.

In spite of his still broad accent, Knudsen is a good extemporaneous speaker. He has

WILLIAM S. KNUDSEN

gone back to Europe every two years or so on business but he much prefers traveling in America, visiting the small towns where "they show you something they're going to build." But he has a staunch loyalty for his native land (several of his good friends in America are Danes like himself) and for all Scandinavia. He has been knighted by Denmark's King Christian, but this embarrasses him because his daughters like to tease him about it. In 1938, when he returned from a visit to Germany, the New York *Times* reported him as saying that the transformed Reich was "the miracle of the twentieth century." He has changed his mind since then, however.

Knudsen has great respect for book learning and, although he never had a formal education, he reads much. His library is said to contain one of the world's finest Spinoza collections. From his experience as a workman and a boss, however, his advice to the young man today is to get some kind of work to do with his hands—to learn how to create with practical skill, whether he adopts mechanics or a desk profession as a career.

References

Am Mag 127:20-1+ Je '39 por (Same abr. Read Digest 35:70-2 D '39)
Christian Sci Mon p1, 13 F 10 '40 por; p10 Ag 10 '40
Forum 101:159-62 Mr '39 por
Lit Digest 123:38 My 15 '37 por
Newsweek 11:36-7 My 16 '38 por (cover); 16:29 Ag 26 '40 por
Sat Eve Post 209:5-7+ Ap 17 '37 il pors
Time 29:17-19 Ja 18 '37 por (cover); 30:66-7 N 8 '37 por; 35:76-7 My 6 '40
U S News 9:14 O 18 '40

KNUDSEN, WILLIAM S.—*Continued*
Who's Who in America
Who's Who in Commerce and Industry

KOHLER, WALTER JODOK Mar 3, 1875—Apr 21, 1940 Republican Governor of Wisconsin (1929-30); prominent manufacturer; built model village for employees; aviation enthusiast

WALTER JODOK KOHLER

References
Business Week p13 Ag 18 '34
N Y Times p2 Je 28 '38
R of Rs 91:30 My '35
Sat Eve Post 205:21+ N 12 '32
Who's Who in America
Who's Who in Commerce and Industry
Who's Who in Government

Obituaries
N Y Herald Tribune p12 Ap 22 '40 por
N Y Times p17 Ap 22 '40 por
Newsweek 15:60-1 Ap 29 '40 por

KONOYE, FUMIMARO, PRINCE (kō-nō-ĕ fū-mĭ-mä-rō) Oct 1891- Premier of Japan
Address: Tokyo, 26 Nagatacho Nichome, Kojimachiku

In July 1940 Prince Fumimaro Konoye became Premier of Japan. Immediately it was felt that the way had been opened up for a totalitarian régime and the Chungking press went so far as to say that Konoye was merely a puppet set up by the army to mask the reality of a totalitarian state. When he formed his cabinet it was called "the most totalitarian minded and antiliberal in Japa-

nese history," and his new political party, it was indicated, would be organized on Fascist lines. All other political parties were dissolved.

However, there were some commentators who believed that Konoye intended to try his hand "at something that will combine Fascism with Democracy," and as Hugh Byas in the New York *Times* put it: "The ideal party or political structure that Prince Konoye is trying to find is one that will allow the Japanese to be governed with their own cooperation. . . It will be a government in which the people can respectfully express their wishes." In any case, it seemed clear that Konoye was trying to keep his government free of the Axis powers, for in his first speech he declared for the "establishment of a new order in East Asia" to be achieved "by our own power."

In September the announcement of the Rome-Berlin-Tokyo Axis took the world by surprise, but was speedily followed by the United States' embargo on scrap iron to Japan, and Britain's reopening of the Burma Road in October. Threats of Japanese reprisals—even of war—did not have their expected effect.

Now "the most popular statesman in Japan," Prince Konoye has a difficult political job ahead of him. First, he must bring about a favorable settlement in China as quickly as possible. Second, he must unite the dissident and disorganized old political parties of Japan into what he calls "a strong national and political structure." He must, too, some observers feel, meet the problem of disciplining the army which in three years has "developed practically unbreakable habits of willfullness." And all this while faced with an increasingly tough-minded United States and Britain and a Russia that had always been unfriendly. The "new order in East Asia" seemed likely to encounter more obstacles than had been looked for.

Konoye, who at one time was "a melancholy Marxist," who later was called a liberal because he sent his son, nicknamed "Butch," to Princeton, and is now labeled a Fascist, comes from a family of the highest rank and prestige. One of his ancestors was an important enough empire builder to have his face on ten-yen notes today. His father, Prince Atsumaro Konoye, was "a great man," an intimate and protégé of Prince Kimmochi Saionji, last of the Genro (Elder Statesmen). Although Prince Atsumaro died when he was only 42 he contributed much to the development of parliamentary government as president of the House of Peers and performed valuable services in guiding diplomatic policy during the Sino-Japanese and the Russo-Japanese Wars.

Eight days after Prince Fumimaro Konoye was born his mother died, and he was only thirteen when his father died. Prince Konoye still remembers incidents with creditors and debtors, how friends grew fewer as his money grew less. All this, he says, "bred in my susceptible mind a hatred of injustice. I was a gloomy youth throughout my student days, with an inclination to read extremist literature from Western Europe." In 1914 Konoye went to Kyoto Imperial University and was graduated with a law degree in 1917.

It was clear during his student days that Prince Saionji was grooming him for an important rôle in state affairs and after Prince Konoye left the University he went into the home ministry. He still continued to read Marx and other Western authors and went so far as to consider renouncing his titles and going to live in the United States. But Prince Saionji was able to persuade him to be his secretary at the Paris Peace Conference.

Shortly before leaving for Paris, Konoye published a dissertation setting forth what he considered the principles governing the peace and happiness of mankind. In it he stressed the importance of greater justice among individuals and equalities of rights and opportunities among nations. The Conference was a disappointment to him.

Back in Japan, Konoye devoted himself to repairing the family fortunes. Notable friends and a successful marriage helped, and today he is a man of independent means. He entered the House of Peers and identified himself with one of its political clubs, the Kenkyu-kai. Soon he became a power, credited with a large part of the responsibility for Japan's adoption of universal manhood suffrage. In fact, in the many years he was a member and president (1933 on) of the House of Peers, it has been said that "not a single important national issue has failed to receive his thoughtful consideration or to feel his influence before settlement."

In 1934, when amiable Japanese-American relations had been disrupted as a result of the "Manchurian incident," Konoye was sent to the United States on a good-will tour "to make a few official friends unofficially." He came bringing dolls with him as good-will emblems; he met many leading Americans and made many friends.

In 1936 Konoye was offered the Premiership for the first time and refused it. He said he couldn't accept because of ill health. This was the first important appearance of Konoye's famous "ill health" on the political scene. Whenever, in his first Premiership, which began in 1937, Konoye was conscious of bickering and strife and loud criticism he would go home to his villa, lock the door and announce that he was "sick." When he came back wan and pale the difficulty would usually be over. When the army rammed through its embarrassing National Mobilization Law, Konoye had a bad "cold." When the China Incident broke out he was taken with a "heat stroke." It has been figured that he has spent one-half of his political days in bed. Some suggest that the basis of his ill health

Japanese American News Photos

PRINCE FUMIMARO KONOYE

can be found in the deprivation and exhaustion Konoye suffered in the great earthquake and fire of 1923, when he was searching for his family. But others stoutly maintain that he uses his frail health "as a sort of storm cellar into which he retires whenever he see a political twister coming."

When Konoye became Premier in 1937 it was as the head of a "New Party." Immediately after he was appointed he sat down and rang up the prospective ministers of what was soon tagged "The Telephone Cabinet," and described as "the broadest, the most nearly 'national' in Japan's history." His job, as Konoye put it, is "to heal strife and eliminate friction." That meant that he had to "conciliate the powerful army (ruler of every Tokyo cabinet since the Manchurian War), recognize the disgruntled civilian parties and win the sympathy of the electorate."

There were observers at that time who felt that in his marshaling of all parliamentary groups Konoye had set up the initial state of a totalitarian government. They felt, too, that he was using his liberal reputation to hold the nation behind the army's policy. But it was over a quarrel with the army that Konoye resigned. Unwilling to sanction the army's demand for limiting industrial profits, in the winter of 1938 he gave up his position. When he was made Premier again, in 1940, after the army forced the resignation of Premier Yonai (see sketch this issue) he was acting as president of the Privy Council.

"Very dark, very sad, very tall—morose, indolent and possessor of perhaps the only gangling figure in all the Empire," Prince Konoye is said to be a "bundle of nerves." He's so fussy about hygiene that he sprinkles alcohol on an apple before eating it and dips the raw fish Japanese eat in

KONOYE, FUMIMARO—*Continued*

boiling water before touching it. He also suffers from insomnia. His main interests are talking and reading, but he does like to watch wrestling matches and occasionally plays a couple of holes of golf with his son, Fumitake, who, known as "Butch," won himself a reputation at Princeton as a golfer and was voted "most likely to succeed." He has three other children—one son, and two daughters, both of whom married into the nobility.

References

Asia 37:544-5 Ag '37 pors; 37:678-80 O '37 il (p665)
Christian Sci Mon p4 Jl 17 '40 il
Collier's 102:11+ O 1 '38 por
Cur Hist & Forum 51:40-3 Ag '40
Liv Age 352:425-8 Jl '37
N Y Times p6 Je 25 '40; p9 Jl 19 '40; p6 Jl 20 '40; p9 Jl 23 '40; p9 Jl 24 '40
Newsweek 9:12 Je 12 '37 por; 16:31-2 Jl 29 '40; 16:30 S 9 '40; 16:28-30 O 14 '40 por
Time 29:22 Je 14 '37 por; 35:23 Ja 8 '40 por; 36:29-30+ Jl 22 '40 pors; 36:22 Jl 29 '40 por; 36:30 S 9 '40; 36:40 O 14 '40 por
International Who's Who
Who's Who in Japan

KOUSSEVITZKY, SERGE (kōō″sủ-vǐt′- skê sĕr′gā) July 26, 1874- Conductor of the Boston Symphony Orchestra

Address: b. Symphony Hall, Boston, Massachusetts; h. 88 Druce St, Brookline, Massachusetts

The Boston Symphony Orchestra, "unquestionably the finest in the world," started its sixtieth season in 1940. For 26 of these seasons Serge Koussevitzky has been its conductor; to Back Bay, Boston, "an idol, firmly pedestaled"; to musicians, the "number one full-time conductor in the United States."

A consistent champion of modern music, Dr. Koussevitzky has in these years brought to the American public Sibelius, Honegger, Gruenberg, Walton (see sketch this issue), Kodály and other contemporaries. "Over a similar period no conductor in America has produced so many valid new works, both domestic and foreign," for Koussevitzky firmly believes that "we cannot refuse a careful performance and a fair hearing to the composers who are working in our own time."

It is Koussevitzky, too, who is responsible for the Berkshire Music Center, for the Symphonic Festivals held at Tanglewood every summer since 1934 and the Berkshire Music School, begun in 1940. The Symphonic Festivals started in a tent; eventually a shed was built and in it the Boston Symphony presented and will continue to present works of the classic masters and the significant moderns. When Tanglewood, the 150-acre estate of Mrs. Gorham

Brooks and her aunt Miss Sara Aspinwall at Lenox, Massachusetts, was presented to the Orchestra as a permanent home, and a donation given by the Rockefeller Foundation, Dr. Koussevitzky was able to see the "realization of my long cherished dream" of an American music center.

At this music center Dr. Koussevitzky hopes to bring together "the greatest writers, the greatest musicians, the greatest painters to work with one another in creating a new . . . form growing out of our life." Already the music school is well under way. "We have a junior orchestra and orchestra classes for higher studies. We have conducting and opera classes. We have drama classes and composition classes. We have some of the best composers and lecturers," among them Aaron Copland (see sketch this issue), Paul Hindemith, Herbert Graf, Roy Harris (see sketch this issue), Olin Downes. Dr. Koussevitzky is willing to be modest in his promises for this American music center, "but by no means modest in our aspirations."

Serge Koussevitzky, "a pince-nezed Russian who strongly resembles a diplomat of the Napoleonic era," conducts the Boston Symphony Orchestra, whether at Tanglewood, Boston, Philadelphia or any other place, with energy, nervous intensity and fire. As a conductor he has an "instinct for building dramatic effects, for color, for correct phrasing, for expressive dynamics"; he has an "unusual ability to cull sonorities of great richness from the brasses and a wonderfully singing tone from the strings." Neat, precise, faultlessly tailored, his gestures are graceful, his beat straightforward, and, merely glancing at the score he always keeps on the stand, he presents performances that are almost consistently brilliant.

They are brilliant because Koussevitzky himself at his best "is a singularly inspired and inspiring conductor"; they are brilliant because his orchestra of faultless players has been drilled to the point where he can receive, "almost as a reflex action," any response he seeks. At rehearsals, dressed in "baggy rough trousers, a soft white shirt and an old gray sleeveless sweater," Dr. Koussevitzky "shouts, sings, gesticulates, lunges and paddles with his baton, grins froglike at pleasant sounds, scolds frantically in heavily battered English." No slip is allowed to pass; no interruption is permitted—if asked a question Dr. Koussevitzky has been known to say, "Do not spik. If you spik I go home." He shouts to his men in French, Russian, English. "No!" he shouts to the violins. "No! It's *Da Da Dadada DA*," he sings, stressing the rhythm. And always he tells the orchestra, "Sing, always sing your phrases. There is no music without singing."

Sergei Alexandrovich (as he was christened) Koussevitzky, who has been called a "haughty, gray-haired, tyrannical aristocrat," was born in the small Russian town of Iver, the son of poor but musical parents.

His father, Alexander Koussevitzky, gave lessons on the violin; his mother, Anne (Barabeitchik) Koussevitzky, who died shortly after Serge was born, was a pianist. Serge took piano lessons and learned to play other instruments, but always wanted to be a conductor. He used to make believe he was one. He would line up empty chairs and put an open score on a music stand. Next, "entering the parlor stiffly, he would majestically bow to the empty seats and then, rapping his stick sharply on his stand, would give the imaginary orchestra the signal to begin. Suddenly he would begin to gesture wildly and would sing the different parts of the orchestral score at the top of his voice." Later he conducted a band of real musicians who played at performances of the strolling actors of Vyshnü Volochok and toured with them.

By the time he was 14 Koussevitzky had exhausted the musical possibilities of his home town and with three rubles in his pocket and a bundle of clothes on his back he set out to Moscow to seek his musical fortune. When he reached the Philharmonic Conservatory of Moscow he found that the only scholarships open were for horn, trombone and double bass. He decided on the double bass and when he was graduated in 1894 was able to get a position playing it in the Moscow Imperial Theatre Orchestra. From 1896 to 1905 he gave solo performances on the double bass in Russia and in Europe's great cities, playing the ungainly instrument as though it were a cello. Today he is the "greatest living double bass virtuoso."

Dr. Koussevitzky first saw his wife, Nathalie Oushkoff, when he was giving a double bass concert and she was sitting in the audience. It was two years, however, before they met and two years more before they were married in 1905. After their marriage they settled in Berlin, where Serge had studied under Artur Nikisch and where, in 1906, he made his debut as a conductor with the Berlin Philharmonic Orchestra. Later in that same season he conducted in London, Paris and Vienna.

It was in 1907 that Koussevitzky got his own orchestra, a wedding present from his wife's father, one of Russia's wealthiest merchants. With his orchestra Koussevitzky introduced composers rarely heard; he made symphonic music familiar to Russians and brought leading European conductors, composers and soloists to Russia. One of his innovations was a series of popular Sunday concerts at which young conductors led and young soloists had a chance to perform. His greatest, however, was the series of tours in Russia which he led in 1910, 1912 and 1914. Down the Volga for 2,300 miles in a chartered steamer Koussevitzky and his orchestra stormed Russia, bringing music to people who had never had it.

Koussevitzky and his wife founded the Russian publishing firm which printed and distributed those new Russian works he had

Bachrach

SERGE KOUSSEVITZKY

introduced. Probably it was these years of Russian success that account for Oscar Levant's (see sketch this issue) famous dictum on the conductor: "He is unparalleled in the performance of Russian music, whether it is by Moussorgsky, Rimsky-Korsakoff, Strauss, Wagner or Aaron Copland."

When the Russian Revolution arrived Koussevitzky's orchestra and publishing house were liquidated, but he was made director of the Russian State Orchestra. He held this post until 1920, when, discouraged by performances in mittens in freezing Soviet halls and by his belief that there was "no chance there for artistic endeavor," he left for Paris, abandoning almost all his money and personal property. For the next four years he conducted in Paris, England, Italy, Spain, Portugal, and his *Concerts Koussevitzky* which he founded in Paris in 1921 became an important feature of French musical life.

In 1924 he was invited to become conductor of the Boston Symphony Orchestra. This orchestra, founded in 1881, had fallen upon hard days. After a brilliant period under Karl Muck (see sketch this issue), who was interned during the War, it had deteriorated under the leadership of Henri Rabaud and Pierre Monteux. Its ablest musicians had been lured away and, with the failure of a general strike to establish a union in the orchestra (it is today the only important non-union symphony orchestra in the country), more than 20 of the best players, including the concertmaster, had resigned. Within one season under Koussevitzky the orchestra changed—older players were pensioned; those who couldn't meet his standards were dismissed; the country was sifted for the best orchestral material.

KOUSSEVITZKY, SERGE—*Continued*

Immediately painstaking rehearsals were started and when the concerts came they came with real musicianship, lighted by Koussevitzky's "flair for showmanship" and his gift for program building. "One of the most brilliant program makers before the public," Koussevitzky gave Boston programs "electric in their experimentalism" yet well balanced in their combination of classical, romantic and modern music. And Boston, which at first found him "somewhat exaggerated and theatrical," soon admitted that he had an "uncannily transparent tone" and a repertoire more varied than that of any other conductor in the United States. It did hear a mediocre performance occasionally; mostly it heard inspired ones.

Today the Boston Symphony Orchestra is great and its conductor adored by Boston. But this slender, rather short man with iron-gray hair and rugged features and his "pleasant, portly Russian wife" give Boston and its social life little attention. All Dr. Koussevitzky's days are "regularly and carefully apportioned, with so much time allowed for rehearsing, so much for walking, so much for studying his scores." He studies new ones by reading them through and playing sharp dissonances on the piano. "Then the work begins," he says, "the work which is required before the music can be brought to life by performance. I study, study, study . . . then finally I arrive at a point where I feel that I realize what the composer wished to say."

He does this studying in "a large, sunny room, neat and simple and bare," in a large rented house in the "quiet, substantial, somewhat stuffy Boston suburb of Brookline." The room contains countless musical scores, a grand piano, a chest of drawers, two easy chairs and one stiff little armchair in front of Koussevitzky's worktable. "On the table is a music stand, two or three volumes of music, two stop watches and a Russian *Bible*."

In private life Dr. Koussevitzky is "an affable, courtly, talkative, rather posey Russian . . . of the old school. . . Temperamentally a romantic, he loves to brood over the oniony ideas of such dank German philosophers as Schopenhauer and Nietzsche." But his manner is far from gloomy —"as enthusiastic as champagne"—and his conversation, "always accompanied by violent gesticulation, is loaded with rhetorical *ahs* and wreathy superlatives." Nevertheless, this attractive, pleasant Koussevitzky is a tyrant on the podium and many legends have graced his reign over the Boston Symphony. Perhaps the best-known one tells of a musician who played four sour notes. "You're fired," Koussevitzky shouted. "Ged out. Ged out." On his way out the musician passed the room where Koussevitzky was sitting hunched over a score. "Nuts to you, Koussevitzky," he bellowed. Koussevitzky haughtily turned his head. "It's too late to abologize," he snapped.

References

Atlan 158:748-57 D '36
Christian Sci Mon Mag p7, 12 Jl 6 '40 pors
Harper 179:589-91 N '39
Life 8:42-6 F 26 '40 il pors
N Y Times IX p5 Jl 7 '40
Newsweek 16:33 Jl 22 '40
Time 32:28+ O 10 '38 por (cover); 36:38 Ag 12 '40
Ewen, D. Koussevitzky *In* Man with the Baton p227-40 1936
Kaufman, Mrs. H. L. and Hansl, Mrs. E. E. Vom B. Sergei Koussevitzky *In* Artists in Music of Today p63 1933
Lourié, A. Sergei Koussevitzky and His Epoch 1931
Saleski, G. Famous Musicians of a Wandering Race 1927
Shore, B. Sergei Koussevitsky *In* Orchestra Speaks p101-8 1938
Thompson, O. ed. International Cyclopedia of Music and Musicians 1939
Who's Who in America
Who's Who in American Jewry

KRUEGER, MAYNARD C. (krü′ger) Jan 16, 1906- Educator; economist

Address: b. University of Chicago, Chicago, Illinois; h. 6630 University Ave, Chicago, Illinois

Thirty-four-year-old Professor Maynard C. Krueger was the Socialist Party candidate for Vice-President in the 1940 Presidential electio . The son of Fred C. and Nelle C. (Hoev ing) Krueger, he was born in Clark Count , Missouri and reared on a farm. Before he was 17 he was teaching a one-room rural school, with a year of university work already behind him. He was graduated from the University of Missouri in 1926, became an instructor in the department of history and received an M. A. degree the following year. In 1927 he was one of six Americans to receive scholarships to the Geneva School of International Studies. He has studied at various times at the University of Paris, University of Berlin and the Universities of Pennsylvania and Chicago.

Most of Professor Krueger's time from 1925 through 1928 was spent in Western and Central Europe, and he has returned there twice since then, although he has been unable to get a German visa since early 1933. It was the failure of a study of diplomatic records of the summer of 1914 to throw any very useful light on the causes of the First World War which led him to the study of economics and its relation to war, and which "today leaves him skeptical about the ability of diplomacy to rectify or alleviate international situations which are basically economic."

During the ascendancy of the League of Nations, Professor Krueger served one term as tutor in the Geneva School of International Studies. He then taught international relations and history at Albion College, Michigan during the school year 1927 to 1928. After four years on the faculty of the Wharton School of Finance and Commerce of the University of Pennsylvania he went (1932) to the University of Chicago, as assistant professor of economics.

At the University of Chicago he married Elsie C. Gasperik. They have two daughters, Karen and Linda.

Professor Krueger's hobby is politics. As a student he took an active part in "campus politics." Motivated by a "fine ethical spirit which frequently puts him at odds with the dominant trends of the day," he has been an active member of the Socialist Party. He served as chairman of the Party in 1934 and previously was chairman of local groups in Pennsylvania and Illinois. He was associate editor of their *Campaign Handbook* (1932). As official delegate in 1933 to the Socialist and Labor International Congress he presented a majority report criticizing the NRA because "it did not give labor adequate representation in the control of industry." He was the keynote speaker at the St. Louis National Convention (1940). He was vice-president of the American Federation of Teachers for three terms and is an active member of the League for Industrial Democracy and the American Civil Liberties Union.

As a lecturer "his wit and humor are made to serve the purpose of enlightenment rather than unprincipled ridicule." He has participated in the University of Chicago *Round Table Broadcasts* over NBC. A round table in which he took part at the time of the Munich crisis was immediately translated by NBC and rebroadcast to Germany by directional shortwave with the approval of the American State Department, but without that of the German State Department.

In addition to writing magazine articles, Professor Krueger is the editor of *Issues of the Day*, a Socialist Party pamphlet service. He contributed to the *National Industrial Recovery Act* (1933), one of the series, and wrote *Inflation: Who Wins and Who Loses?* (1934). He is also the author of *Deflation and Capital Levy* (1933) and coauthor of *Economics Question Book*.

Professor Krueger believes that while we can operate our automobiles and telephones quite successfully without knowing how they really work, we cannot operate an economic and political system without knowing how it really works; that is, we cannot if we want it to be operated by the people instead of a dictator. He believes, too, that objectivity in the analysis of pressing problems is not synonymous with sitting on the fence, and that the most controversial of subjects can be discussed in such a manner as to achieve truly educational results.

Brooks

MAYNARD C. KRUEGER

References

N Y Times p4 F 22 '31; p5 Ag 24 '33; p1, 3 Ap 7 '40 por
Newsweek 16:28-9 O 14 '40 por
America's Young Men

LAGERLOF, SELMA (lä'gur-luf" sel'mä) Nov 20, 1858—Mar 16, 1940 Novelist

Selma Ottiliana Lovisa Lagerlöf, the grand old lady of Swedish letters, died at the age of 81 at her family home, Marbacka, in Sunne, in the province of Värmland, Sweden. Her books were translated into 30 languages; she won the highest literary honors. She was the first woman to win the Nobel Prize for literature, and the first woman to become a member of the Swedish Academy.

The fourth child of Lieutenant and Mrs. Erik Gustaf Lagerlöf, Swedish gentlefolk of the landowner class, she was one of a large family of brothers and sisters. She had a sickly childhood and, instead of romping around the Sunne farmlands with her brothers and sisters, spent her time reading. At 15 she had read and reread every book in the house, and she had started writing her own poetry.

Miss Lagerlöf went to Stockholm at the age of 22 to study for a teaching career. In 1882, after a year at Sjoberg's Lyceum for Girls, she entered the Royal Women's Superior Training College, where she completed her education. Three years later she became a teacher at a girls' school at Landskrona in Skåne in southern Sweden, and remained there from 1885 to 1895.

But while she was teaching she continued studying and writing. In 1890 she began work on *Gösta Berling*. When a Swedish magazine offered a money prize for the best 100-page novelette she submitted the

SELMA LAGERLOF

first five chapters of her work, and won the contest. When the completed novel was published later, it was widely acclaimed for its imaginative power and its treatment of Värmland legendary material.

Miss Lagerlöf continued teaching until after the publication of her second book, *Invisible Links*, in 1894. Through financial aid extended by King Oscar of Sweden and his son, Prince Eugen, and by the Swedish Academy, she was able to give up teaching in 1895 and to devote her entire time to writing. She made a trip to Italy that year, and the result was her third novel, *The Miracles of Antichrist* (1897). There followed *Jerusalem* (1901)—after a trip to the Orient—and two volumes of short stories, *From a Swedish Homestead* (1899) and *The Adventures of Nils* (1906-07), the latter written at the request of Swedish school authorities for a book for primary school children.

In 1904 Selma Lagerlöf received the gold medal of the Swedish Academy. Three years later she was honored with the degree of Doctor of Philosophy at the Linnaeus Jubilee of Upsala University, the first of several honorary degrees. She was awarded the Nobel Prize for literature in 1909. It was said that the prize had been withheld from her for three years because members of the Swedish Academy feared they might be accused of favoring their own countrywoman. But literary critics throughout the world were now clamoring for recognition for Selma Lagerlöf, and the Swedish Academy bowed to popular judgment. Miss Lagerlöf was herself made a member of the exclusive Swedish Academy in 1914.

A modest, unassuming woman, Miss Lagerlöf cared little for the doings of modern society, though she was hospitable to a fault and loved to see people about her. Velma Swanston Howard, Miss Lagerlöf's chief English translator, described her as "a woman of medium height, with a fine, fair face, splendid head, superbly set on neck and shoulders. . . Her sense of humor was keen. There was a twinkle in her eye, a twist about the mouth and a certain sly humor that preceded her speech, while her chuckle was inimitable."

The famous novelist spent her summers at Mårbacka Manor, the place of her birth. Winters she often spent at Falun, Delarne, where *Jerusalem* was written. Her family had lost Mårbacka at the death of her father. Selma Lagerlöf determined to buy it back and eventually did so with the profits from her novels. She lived there alone after the death of her mother in 1916.

Mårbacka Manor, to which hundreds of visitors made pilgrimages each year to see the scene of *Gösta Berling*, was modernized by Miss Lagerlöf, but its old dignity and simplicity remained. She cultivated 140 acres of land and looked after 53 tenants during her years there.

Dr. Lagerlöf's first novel, *Gösta Berling*, one of her masterpieces, was written several times unsuccessfully before it achieved its final form. The author started to write it in verse, then rewrote it in realistic prose, and then rewrote it again in the romantic style which distinguished all her later writings. A Stockholm author, who recognized her talent, aided and encouraged her with the novel, it is said.

In Sweden Dr. Lagerlöf was appreciated largely because of her skill in putting into vivid prose the background of contemporary Swedish life. Abroad it was the manner of her writing rather than the substance which won fame for her. Her writing of the Northern sagas had a rich Homeric sweep. Hugo Alfén, the Swedish composer, once said of her: "Reading her books is like sitting in the dusk of a Spanish cathedral. You do not know whether what you saw or felt was a dream or reality. You certainly were on holy ground." Folklore, magic, superstitions, customs, the farm, the countryside, the family and childhood associates—all furnished material for her novels, and all of them she colored with her gift of understanding, intuition and sympathy.

An editorial written on her work after her death described her as having the "true storyteller's art of making the unreal seem as plausible as the real."

On her seventieth birthday Miss Lagerlöf was honored with the Order of St. Olaf, first class; the Danish Distinguished Service Medal and the diploma of the French Legion of Honor.

During her last years, she wrote almost exclusively of her childhood, writing, as Lewis Gannett in the New York *Herald Tribune* said, "miraculously like a child." She published *Memories of My Childhood* (1930 to 1932) and *The Diary of Selma Lagerlöf* (1937).

In the early days of the Third Reich, Nazi publications sang her praises as the "Nordic poetess," but when she began helping German intellectual refugees they changed their minds.

Although her death was caused by peritonitis, it was said that her grave anxiety over the future of Sweden and Scandinavia in warring Europe contributed to her illness. A firm believer in peace, she was shocked by the Second World War and later by Russia's invasion of Finland. She cherished the hope that the United States might lead the world to peace, and her only visit to the United States was in 1924 as a delegate to the Women's Congress in Washington. Only two months before she died she gave her gold Nobel Medal to the Swedish national collection for Finland.

In addition to the saga of *Gösta Berling*, her most famous novel, she also wrote *Invisible Links* (1895); *The Adventures of Nils* (1906-07), published in the United States as *The Wonderful Adventures of Nils* and *The Further Adventures of Nils*; *The Miracles of Antichrist* (1897); *From a Swedish Homestead* (1899); *Queens of Kungahälla* (1899); *Jerusalem* (1901); *Herr Arne's Hoard* (1904); *The Girl from the Marsh Croft* (1908); *The Emperor of Portugallia* (1914); *The Outcast* (1918); *Mårbacka, the Tale of a Manor* (1922); *Memories of My Childhood* (1934); *Harvest* (1933); and *The Diary of Selma Lagerlöf* (1937). Other books were published in the United States under the titles of *Christ Legends*; *Liliecrona's Home*; and *Treasure*. Three short novels, *The General's Ring* (1925); *Charlotte Löwensköld* (1925); and *Anna Svärd* (1928) have been published in English separately, and in a single volume entitled *The Ring of the Löwenskölds*.

References

Liv Age 343:368-9 D '32
Scholastic 30:13 F 20 '37 por
Berendsohn, W. A. Selma Lagerlöf 1932
Björkman, E. A. Story of Selma Lagerlöf *In* Voices of To-morrow p139-53 1913
Cooper, A. P. Selma Lagerlöf *In* Authors and Others p81-97 1927
Gustafson, A. Six Scandinavian Novelists 1940
Kirkland, W. M. and Kirkland, F. Selma Lagerlöf, Who Listened and Remembered *In* Girls Who Became Writers p13-25 1933
Kunitz, S. J. ed. Living Authors 1937
Lagerlöf, S. The Diary of Selma Lagerlöf 1937
Lagerlöf, S. Memories of My Childhood 1934
Marble, Mrs. A. R. Selma Lagerlöf— Swedish Realist and Idealist *In* Nobel Prize Winners in Literature, 1901-31 p104-23 1932
Who's Who

Obituaries

N Y Herald Tribune p38 Mr 17 '40 por

N Y Times p49 Mr 17 '40 por
Newsweek 15:8 Mr 25 '40 por
Pub W 137:1232 Mr 23 '40
Theatre Arts 24:227 Ap '40 por
Time 35:71 Mr 25 '40

LA GUARDIA, FIORELLO HENRY
(là gwär'dyà fē-ô-rĕl'ō) Dec 11, 1882- Mayor of New York City

Address: b. City Hall, New York City; h. 1274 Fifth Ave, New York City

Fiorello La Guardia, New York City's "short, swart, tousled" Mayor, already has on his hands the second or third toughest political job in the United States, but he has found time to do a lot of traveling around the country and even to take on new duties. Since 1936 he has been president of the Conference of Mayors. In August 1940 he was appointed head of the joint board to coordinate American and Canadian defense measures. "The problem," he commented, "is whether or not strategic points in the Western Hemisphere shall be taken for offensive action by a potential enemy or used as points of defense for the Western Hemisphere."

This political dynamo with the Italian name of "Little Flower" is not only generally agreed to be the best Mayor New York City has ever had, but is actually a New Yorker by birth. His father was Achilles La Guardia, composer, conductor and cornettist, who came to this country with his wife, the former Irene Coen Luzatti, a "Sephardic Jewess from Venice," to be accompanist to the famous singer Patti. He stayed to become army bandmaster at various frontier posts, and his family went with him: first to Fort Sully, South Dakota, then to the Whipple Barracks near Prescott, Arizona. It was in Prescott, where the La Guardias lived until the Spanish-American War, that young Fiorello attended high school, learned to make spaghetti sauce in his mother's kitchen, to play the cornet, to love Italian opera. Then he spent a short time as unsalaried correspondent for the St. Louis *Dispatch*. In 1898 his father died after eating putrefied meat—army rations—and not long afterwards his mother took him to Budapest. He was only 19 when he got a job in the consulate there; a few months later he was transferred to Trieste as an interpreter; next (in 1904) he went to Fiume as United States Consular agent.

Finally in 1906 La Guardia resigned from the consular service, returned to the New York he had left two decades before, and a year later, while studying law in the evening school of New York University, found himself an interpreter's job at Ellis Island. His assorted experiences there and abroad gave him a speaking knowledge of Italian, German, Croatian, French, Spanish and Yiddish. In 1910 he acquired his LL. B., was admitted to the bar, changed his middle name from "Enrico" to "Henry" and hung

FIORELLO H. LA GUARDIA

out his shingle. His first real clients were garmentworkers during the strikes of 1912 and 1913.

Living in Greenwich Village, Tammany's home base, stubborn young La Guardia became a Progressive Republican. In 1914 he got himself on the Republican ticket for Congress (nobody knew him, but it didn't matter—Tammany always won), and after strenuous campaigning astonished the Republicans by snaring 14,000 votes that usually belonged to Tammany. As a reward he was appointed Deputy Attorney General of New York in 1915, but he decided he would actually win that Congressional seat. He continued to make friends in the district, offered free legal advice to its pushcart peddlers, icemen and shopkeepers, mobilized the letter carriers and garmentworkers to campaign for him, and in the election morning of 1916 pulled flophouse voters out of bed before Tammany was awake. He won by 257 votes, and was the first Republican ever to go to Washington from his district. The Republicans weren't too pleased with him, however, since the first thing he did when he got there was to join House liberals in battling for liberalization of House rules. They even threatened a recount. He laughed.

When the First World War came Congressman La Guardia voted for entrance into the War and for the draft, and then decided to go to War himself and resigned his seat. Only five-feet-two, he was turned down at Plattsburg but found himself a flying instructor and ended up as captain of the American aviators in Italy, the "flying Congressman." He returned with all conceivable decorations and honors, the rank of major, a wife (he had met Thea Almerigotti in Trieste and married her in 1919), and when he campaigned for Congress once more even Tam-

many wasn't opposing him. Again he failed to make himself popular in Washington, though: in 1919 the War hero was opposing military and naval appropriations, fighting A. Mitchell Palmer's espionage acts, speaking against post-War loans to the Allies. One of the few things the rest of Congress agreed with him about was woman suffrage.

In 1919 La Guardia ran for the presidency of New York City's Board of Aldermen, and won. He proceeded to fight graft and corruption, make an alliance with the Mayor against Tammany, accomplish very little, irritate almost everybody (they called his tactics "Blackguardia," and at one meeting someone suggested: "Hit that little wop over the head with the gavel")—but the experience in municipal government must have been valuable. There was also a big scrap over New York's famous five-cent fare, and the Republicans, who had promised to nominate him for Mayor in 1921, decided he was too radical.

In 1921 blow after blow followed in quick succession. La Guardia was defeated in the primaries; he had a serious operation; his new home was rifled by burglars; his year-old daughter died of spinal meningitis; his wife succumbed to tuberculosis. He was apparently a broken man. But by the next year he had not only recovered his combative instincts but had blackmailed the Republicans into nominating him for Congress from East Harlem by threatening to run as an independent against their candidate for Governor. Delivering some of his campaign speeches in Yiddish, he won, and was to be re-elected for five terms from his predominantly Italian-Jewish district.

In Congress there followed 10 years of "apparently fruitless opposition" to almost everything: the Drys, judicial corruption, Congressional "pork," letting Henry Ford have Muscle Shoals. "In Congress in 1924 I was taken off all my committees," he said later, "but I didn't whine about it. I told Nick Longworth that if he wouldn't let me attend his caucuses I wouldn't let him attend mine, and I'd hold mine in a telephone booth."

In 1924 the Single-taxers, Farmer-Laborites, Socialists, Liberals and Progressives fused interests and voted for him. In 1925 he made history in the House by pulling a lamb chop from his pocket, then a steak, then a $3 roast. "What workman's family can afford to pay $3 for a roast of this size? What are we coming to?" During the height of the "dry era" he manufactured beer at a drugstore counter in the Capital, defied police to arrest him. Senators Wagner, Wheeler (see sketch this issue), Norris and La Follette liked him and he worked with them. He got an anti-injunction bill passed that abolished the "yellow-dog" labor contract; fought for a shortened working day, old-age pensions, national unemployment insurance, employers' liability laws; wanted Andrew Mellon impeached and tried to keep him from reducing income taxes. With the 1929 crash he sailed into Insull and Richard Whitney, and anticipated most of the find-

ings of the Seabury investigations while running for Mayor of New York against the
debonair Jimmy Walker, who called him a
"Red." And when La Guardia was one of
the Congressional casualties in the Democratic victory of 1932, Samuel Seabury and
A. A. Berle Jr., (see sketch this issue)
managed to put him across with the reformers' Committee of Fourteen as the nominee
for Mayor on the 1933 Fusion ticket. On
January 1, 1934 he became New York City's
ninty-ninth Mayor.

At one of the last big Fusion rallies
La Guardia had warned: "You've nominated
me but don't expect any patronage if I'm
elected!" He kept his promise, appointing
to important posts staunch Democrats and
"foreigners" from other states if he found
them best suited to the jobs, and getting
almost twice as many highly paid positions covered by Civil Service rules as was
the case under Tammany. He got a new
charter for the city, tried to put New York
on a pay-as-you-go basis, and, having found
the $41,000,000 budget out of balance, suc-
ceeded in balancing it by raising half in
taxes and saving the remainder. Though he
increased total expenditures, his own salary
was cut from $25,000 to $22,500, and the
city began to get its money's worth in new
parks, highways, hospital facilities, low-cost
housing developments, sewage-disposal
plants, school seats, transit improvements—
even an airport at North Beach. When the
sales tax which he had previously fought
against was introduced, said the Mayor:
"It is wholly wrong except for one thing—
it raised the money we need." Labor didn't
like it much, but it liked other things. For
the first time the union label appeared on
city printing, and a clause was written into
the municipal franchise requiring bus operators to bargain collectively with their employees. And in spite of the disapproval of
"silk-stocking" Republicans, complaints that
the explosive little Mayor insisted on doing
everything himself and in his own way, and
occasional feuds with the press, in 1935
La Guardia was re-elected with the support
of the American Labor Party.

During his next term in office La Guardia
was frequently criticized from both Left and
Right. In 1937 I. F. Stone wrote in the
New Republic: "He is a friend of labor, but
he took New York's taxi drivers for a ride.
He has been better than Tammany on
relief, but he assailed the leader of an unemployed demonstration as a 'yellow dog.'
He makes strong speeches on power, but he
sabotaged the fight for a municipal power
plant in New York City. . . He is a leader
of democratic forces, but a dictator by
nature. . . He is loud in denouncing the
Interests but cautious in dealing with them.
Wall Street knows that he is more bark
than bite; a tub-thumper rather than a
radical." At about the same time a writer
for the American Mercury was complaining
that he was a rabble-rouser, that he had
failed to curb the strike tactics of labor
groups, that "he does not intend to use the
forces of law and order to protect property
owners and taxpayers," while Republicans
continued to accuse him of being more pro-
New Deal than most Democrats. Nevertheless, in the 1937 campaign he was supported
by the "Republicans, the independent pro-
Republican Democrats, the American Labor
Party, the Socialists and the Communists"—
from the New York Herald Tribune to the
Daily Worker, from Park Avenue to the Popular Front. Even most of those who criticized
him announced their firm intentions of
voting for him, and there was hardly a
dissenting voice to Oswald Garrison Villard's (see sketch this issue) opinion
that "never have we had in the City Hall
anyone more certainly or completely honest, more rigidly set against all graft, all
favoritism." As returns were coming in
from the November election that year an
eight-year-old tugged at the Mayor's coattails: "It's a landscape!" was the news.
"La Guardia by $500,000!"

During his third term La Guardia's increasing preoccupation with foreign affairs
has been noted. Although he had never
before expressed any opinion of Mussolini,
he had already shown his healthy disregard
for Nazi feelings by publicly suggesting
Hitler for a "chamber of horrors" at the
coming World's Fair, by illegally refusing
to renew a license for a German masseur
back in 1935, by giving a Nazi delegation
an escort of Jewish police. He was known
as a pacifist, however. As a member of the
House Military Affairs Committee he had
battled against compulsory military training in
colleges, in 1937 told a delegation of American Legionnaires they should parade to the
steady rhythm of "mind your own business,
mind your own business!" As late as 1939
he told an annual parley of the A F of L
that it was the workers who suffered in a
war, that we were well out of the European
mess, and that he would prefer to have
voted against American entrance into the
First World War. But early in World War
II he made a speech in Boston in favor of
lifting the embargo, later showed himself
anxious to send arms to the Finns. In June
1940 he told an international audience that
Hitler and Mussolini were in the same boat
and that to American noses "the bilge
stank," asked for an anti-Nazi plank in the
Republican platform; in July he suggested a
united military organization of the United
States, Canada and Latin-America to defend
the Western Hemisphere, pleaded for compulsory military training as "the only means
of keeping us out of war."

La Guardia has also been much talked
about for national public office and before
the party nominating conventions was often
mentioned for a Senatorial post, for the
Vice-Presidency or even the Presidency, if
Roosevelt did not run. He was said to
have stated that this term would be his
last as Mayor, but in August 1940 friends
gave assurances that if Willkie (see sketch
this issue) were elected, La Guardia would
again run for Mayor of New York City.

LA GUARDIA, FIORELLO H.—*Cont.*

while if Roosevelt served a third term he would become Secretary of War. In September 1940 La Guardia pledged his support to Roosevelt in the Presidential campaign.

At the same time labor thinks it has detected a growing conservatism in La Guardia's administration, accuses him of having made his peace with both Tammany and the bankers in order to further an ambition for higher office.

Even when he is receiving an honorary degree from some university (as he did from Yale in June 1940), Mayor La Guardia is no guardian of municipal dignity. "In structure and temperament he is a queer combination of a bull and a baby—of the dominating male and the worried little boy." He looks a little like Napoleon, likes to shout and pound, swears with enthusiasm and originality—but when he sits down his feet dangle a foot from the floor, he can turn his temper off as fast as he turns it on, and his voice is inclined to get shrill. The voters find these traits endearing.

Though he likes to rage against the "politicians," it is said that La Guardia is no purist himself when it comes to electioneering, that he knows all the tricks of preconvention tactics and has even shown himself willing to endorse such "reactionaries" as George Harvey or Bruce Barton if it is expedient in a particular campaign. In such matters as the source of campaign funds no one could be more the purist, however. He has also been called "a demagogue" and, more tactfully, "a virtuoso in exploiting his temperament" for the benefit of the public, but—as he once told a bunch of actors—"What the hell—how else are you going to get people excited about a sewer?" So, whether he is leading a vice raid or a band, pulling the lever of a steam shovel on a big construction job or climbing a ladder at a fire, there is always drama. The horseplay that goes on at City Hall itself "frequently reminds one of life in a prep-school dormitory": once the Mayor turned off the heat in a room where negotiators were sitting wrangling over a coal strike; once he proved the efficiency of his police force by turning in a riot call in front of the Stock Exchange.

In 1929 he married Marie Fisher, who used to be his secretary in Washington, and they have adopted two children. Home life is happily quiet, after the strenuous days. Both Mayor and Mrs. La Guardia are fond of music, particularly Haydn, and the Mayor once asked: "Would you ruin my enjoyment of music by talking politics?"

References

Atlan 161:55-63 Ja '38
Christian Sci Mon Mag p6 N 4 '39 por
Collier's 103:16-17+ Mr 11 '39 il pors
New Repub 92:376 N 3 '37
New Yorker 5:26-9 Ag 31 '29

Time 30:14 Ag 2 '37 por (cover); 36: 11 S 2 '40 por
Yale R ns 29 no 1:11-27 [S] '39
Allen, W. H. Why Tammanies Revive: La Guardias Mis-guard pam nd
Carter, J. F. La Guardia 1937
Kern, P. J. Fiorello H. La Guardia *In* Salter, J. T. ed. American Politician p3-46 1938
Limpus, L. M. and Leyson, B. W. This Man La Guardia 1938
Tucker, R. T. and Barkley, F. R. La Guardia: A Roistering Rebel *In* Sons of the Wild Jackass p368-98 1932
Unofficial Observer [pseud.] Disquiet on the Eastern Front (Rush Holt, Curley, La Guardia) *In* American Messiahs p193-211 1935
Who's Who in America

LAIDLAW, SIR PATRICK PLAYFAIR
Sept 26, 1881—Mar 20, 1940 British physician and scientist; discovered the cause of and developed a serum to combat distemper in dogs; identified for the first time the germ which causes influenza; deputy director of the National Institute for Medical Research in Great Britain; knighted in 1935

References

Who's Who

Obituaries

N Y Herald Tribune p8 Mr 23 '40
N Y Times p26 Mr 23 '40
Newsweek 15:7 Ap 1 '40

LAMOND, FELIX (lä-mon) 1863—Mar 16, 1940 Director of the department of musical composition of the American Academy in Rome since its foundation in 1921; organist and chorus master at Trinity Chapel, New York City

Obituaries

Musical Am 60:42 Mr 25 '40
N Y Times p51 Mr 17 '40

LAMONT, THOMAS WILLIAM (lä-mŏnt') Sept 30, 1870- Banker
Address: b. 23 Wall St, New York City; h. 107 E 70th St, New York City

Of Thomas W. Lamont, Ferdinand Lundberg said, "He has exercised more power for 20 years in the Western Hemisphere, has put into effect more final decisions from which there has been no appeal, than any other person. Lamont, in short, has been the First Consul *de facto* in the visible Directory of post-War high finance and politics, a man consulted by presidents, prime ministers, governors of central banks, the directing intelligence behind the Dawes and Young Plans." Of him it has also been said: "Few can be more charming, more considerate or more generous. Few have led cleaner lives; he is the soul of respectability. Banker that he is, he is not a covetous or grasping man; his fortune is by no means great."

Executive committee chairman of J. P. Morgan & Company; executive committee chairman of the Guaranty Trust Company until June 1940; on the board of banks controlling industrial empires; director in the United States Steel Corporation, the A., T. & S. F. Railway Company, Lamont, Corliss & Company, the International Agricultural Corporation and numerous other enterprises, Thomas Lamont is second in prestige not even to J. P. Morgan, whose best publicist he is. "Mr. Morgan speaks to Mr. Lamont and Mr. Lamont speaks to the people." For many years a director of the Crowell Publishing Company, Mr. Lamont's literary and journalistic ties are almost as important as his business connections. He maintains correspondence with writers and editors all over the world; has often entertained H. G. Wells, André Maurois, John Masefield and other literary notables; is an intimate friend of Henry Seidel Canby of the *Saturday Review of Literature*, Ellery Sedgwick, formerly editor of the *Atlantic Monthly*, and Walter Lippmann (see sketch this issue), who went with him on a trip to the Near East in 1931; numbers among publisher-friends Henry Luce of *Time*, Arthur Sulzberger of the New York *Times*, Mrs. Ogden Reid of the New York *Herald Tribune*; once even made a pilgrimage to the California ranch of William Randolph Hearst. Newspapermen who cover Wall Street have instructions to see him regularly, and when newspaper references are made to the "consensus among bankers" or "prominent banking opinion" it is often taken for granted that the reference is to Lamont.

Articles under Lamont's name, mainly on finance and international affairs, have appeared in leading magazines, more often in past years than recently. Nearly every word written about J. P. Morgan passes through his hands or those of his staff of readers, after its publication, if not before. He is quick to detect errors in fact or criticisms which he considers fallacious and to attempt to have them corrected or retracted.

Mr. Lamont has a great interest in education. In January 1936 he made a gift of $500,000 to Harvard University, of which he had been an overseer from 1912 to 1925, suggesting that it might be used for a professorship of political economy. He has also given large sums to Phillips-Exeter Academy.

A lifelong Republican and in the past, at least, one of the most reliable sources of Republican campaign funds, Lamont was "a mentor of Woodrow Wilson in Wilson's second administration as well as of President Hoover throughout his fateful single term in the White House," and in 1940 his name has been linked with Wendell Willkie's (see sketch this issue). Surely Lund-

THOMAS WILLIAM LAMONT

berg's description of him as "Protean" is apt: he is "a diplomat, an editor, a writer, a publisher, a politician, a statesman."

He was born in Claverack, New York on September 30, 1870. His father, Thomas Lamont, was a Methodist minister who had once been a teacher of Greek. His mother was Caroline Deuel (Jayne) Lamont. He grew up in a parsonage where cards, dancing or even walks "outside the yard" on Sundays were considered sinful, but managed to make up for the uneventfulness of parsonage life by extensive reading—for the most part novels and romances. He attended Phillips-Exeter Academy, New Hampshire; was graduated in 1888 and then worked his way through Harvard, acquiring his B. A. in 1892. From 1893 to 1894 he was a financial reporter on the old New York *Tribune* which later merged with the *Herald,* and in October 1895 he married Florence Haskell Corliss of Englewood, New Jersey. From 1903 to 1905 he served as secretary and treasurer of the Bankers Trust Company, from 1905 to 1909 as vice-president, from 1909 to 1911 as vice-president of the First National Bank. It was 1911 when he accepted a partnership in J. P. Morgan & Company, bankers.

A large part of the criticism which has been directed at the House of Morgan has been for its rôle in selling to the Allies and floating their bond issues early in the First World War, when the United States was still ostensibly neutral. Disclosures of the Nye Committee investigation were intended to show that subsequent pressure exerted by the House of Morgan helped to bring about the United States' declaration of war. Mr. Lamont, however, has always emphatically denied not only propaganda and attempts to influence Washington, but even that there could have been any motivation for such

LAMONT, THOMAS WILLIAM—*Cont.*

pressure. He states that although his firm's sympathies were naturally heart and soul with the Allies, several Morgan partners actually favored keeping out of the conflict until Wilson recommended United States' entry, and he has often publicly wished that "someone would run down the sources of the idea that businessmen are inclined to war."

In 1918 Lamont acquired the New York *Evening Post* from Oswald Garrison Villard (see sketch this issue) and terminated "Villard's critical attitude toward Wilson." He sold the paper in 1922 at a reputed loss of $2,000,000. In 1919 he served as representative of the United States Treasury on the American Commission to Negotiate Peace at Paris. According to William Boyce Thompson, he "wrote the financial part for Wilson's League of Nations and was more relied upon abroad in financial matters than was Bernard Baruch."

Although the rest of the Morgan camp was split on the issue, Lamont became and remained an ardent supporter of Wilson's League of Nations, led the *Post's* pro-League newspaper campaign and in 1920 backed Cox because of his pro-League stand.

In 1922 he gave up the *Post* and soon afterwards privately financed Henry Seidel Canby in founding the *Saturday Review of Literature*. In 1929 he became one of two alternate delegates on the Committee of Experts on German Reparations at Paris, headed by Owen D. Young. And although President Coolidge insisted that the American government had no connection with the project, the resulting Young Plan was later found acceptable here.

Thomas Lamont was said to have been one of President Hoover's two principal advisers, the other having been the late Dwight Morrow. When Lamont was not in Washington the telephone wire between the White House and 23 Wall Street was rumored "in almost constant use." For a long time Lamont had favored the moratorium on war debts which Hoover finally declared in 1931; he had conferred with Hoover just before Hoover announced the extension of time limits on New York bank credits to Germany, on the theory that there was no danger of German collapse; he shared with Hoover the persistent idea that the depression should be allowed to "take its course."

With Roosevelt in the White House another Lamont thesis still found friends outside: that New Deal spending was paving the road to ruin. On the other hand, he favored Hull's (see sketch this issue) trade agreements, and was even more cheerful than the Administration on the question of World War II. In 1936, returning from one of his frequent trips to Europe, he signed a reassuring statement for the press: "I do hope and trust and believe that Europe will keep the peace," he said.

With the actual coming of World War II Lamont almost immediately affirmed his belief that the United States should avoid armed conflict, speaking before the Academy of Political Science at the Hotel Astor in November 1939. This he proposed we do by encouraging the Allies to buy defense supplies here, by a vigorous defense program of our own and by making the United States so strong economically and financially that it could cooperate toward "lasting peace." Writing somewhat later, he saw the ideal solution of the War as an economic United States of Europe—though naturally "the Allies must win." In April 1940 he again urged that the United States remain aloof from the European War, although his participation in the founding of the Committee to Defend America by Aiding the Allies created a little suspicion that he was not quite on the isolationist side.

Mr. Lamont is not only hurt but puzzled by those who are "given to spinning fantastic 'spider webs' of capitalist ownership," often pointing out how small J. P. Morgan's actual holdings are in various corporations. The House of Morgan frequently bears the brunt of public criticism while its clients profit from its operations, and Mr. Lamont is sensitive about it. It is also true that he himself is not an extremely wealthy man.

One of his sons, Thomas S. Lamont, is also a Morgan partner; another is Corliss Lamont, formerly instructor in philosophy at Columbia University, well-known Leftist author and one-time national chairman of the Friends of the Soviet Union. Mr. Lamont himself is a member of the Harvard, University, Union League, Metropolitan, City, Century, New York Yacht, Down Town, Links and Englewood Country Clubs.

References

Nation 125:671 D 14 '27; 141:527 N 6 '35; 141:612-13 N 27 '35
Sat R Lit 11:161+ O 6 '34; 15:5-8 D 5 '36; 20:3-4+ Jl 29 '39
Time 27:22 Ja 6 '36 por; 28:16 Ag 31 '36; 31:63 My 9 '38 por
Vital Speeches 4:251-3 F 1 '38; 6:108-10 D 1 '39
[Anonymous] Thomas William Lamont *In* Mirrors of Wall Street p99-112 1933
Lundberg, F. America's 60 Families 1937
Smith, A. D. H. Men Who Run America 1935
Who's Who in America
Who's Who in Commerce and Industry

LANGMUIR, IRVING Jan 31, 1881-
Chemist

Address: h. 1176 Stratford Rd, Schenectady, New York

Dr. Langmuir has been described as a scientist who "chose a trail into the infinitely little as his way of satisfying the great curiosity, and out of that highly specialized pursuit has come new light on familiar mysteries, a new understanding of fundamental phenomena, a whole new branch of science. New industries, new products, new conveniences, as well as new ideas, emerged from his findings—yet he had no practical end in view when he entered upon the search."

He was born in Brooklyn, New York, one of four sons of Charles and Sadie (Comings) Langmuir. The father was a self-made businessman who started as a clerk at 14 and accumulated a tidy fortune by the time he was 35. However, he lost it, and his middle years were filled with financial struggles. As a result the four Langmuir boys early developed a serious attitude toward life. The boys were taught to record systematically everything that went on in their lives in minutely-kept diaries—an inherited habit which both their parents carried to an extreme.

Young Irving early showed an overwhelming curiosity about everything in his daily life and particularly about chemistry. Once, when he was six, walking with his brother Arthur (a student of chemistry), he was asked to smell a bottle of gas, and inhaled so much that he almost strangled to death. It gave him no inhibitions about science—at nine he made a childish workshop and at twelve had a laboratory of his own in which to conduct his experiments. The father's business made it necessary for the family to live in Europe and Irving "hated" the rigorously disciplined French school and, in his own words, "did poorly at it." But always his tremendous interest in chemistry stayed with him, and his happiest hours were in scientific discussion and experimentation with his brothers.

On his thirteenth birthday his mother wrote to a friend: "Irving's brain is working like an engine all the time, and it is wonderful to hear him talk with Herbert [his brother] on scientific subjects. Herbert says he fairly has to shun electricity, for the child gets beside himself with enthusiasm, and shows such intelligence on the subject that it fairly scares him."

After attending Pratt Institute, Langmuir went to Columbia University where he received a degree in 1903 and then went abroad for further study at the University of Göttingen, Germany, where he obtained his doctorate. Then he returned to the United States to spend three unhappy years teaching at Stevens Institute of Technology, where the piles of papers to be graded and the elementary chemistry to be taught to ofttimes uninterested students proved unsatisfying.

In the summer vacation of 1909, instead of his usual mountain climbing, he decided to work in the laboratory of the General Electric Company at Schenectady, New York. Fascinated by the freedom for research, the equipment, the uncommercial atmosphere, he never returned to the class-

IRVING LANGMUIR

room. It was a turning point in his life—one which led to the heights of scientific achievement. Since 1932 he has been associate director of the laboratory. Years of tireless experimenting and amazing results achieved have given him his reputation as "one of the outstanding figures in the world of science."

His investigations, in many fields, have been the result of an insatiable curiosity. In 1932 his work in the field of molecular films won for him the coveted Nobel Prize in chemistry—the first industrial chemist in the United States to be so honored.

Earlier, at the Schenectady laboratory, his extensive studies of "hot filaments in gases produced important improvements in incandescent lighting." This discovery—the result of Langmuir's curiosity about "what goes on in a lamp"—became the basis of a huge industry. It superseded the use of the vacuum incandescent lamp and the arc. "United States sales alone in 1939 of [Langmuir's] type of lamp were in excess of $58,000,000, and it has been estimated that the use of these lamps saves the public about $1,000,000 a night."

Another great industry was built on Dr. Langmuir's work on "the behavior of electrons in vacuum," which formed "the foundation for our present knowledge of vacuum tubes and their application to radio." A third important industry resulted from Dr. Langmuir's work in the atomic hydrogen welding torch, which is used in industry in welding metals which require quick melting and high temperatures.

Dr. Langmuir's most recent work has been in invisible films. These findings were the basis for the discovery of "invisible glass"—a process for coating glass which made headline news in 1939 and brought fame to Langmuir's coworker, Dr. Kathar-

LANGMUIR, IRVING—*Continued*

ine Blodgett (see sketch this issue). During the First World War Langmuir worked on submarine detection devices. More than 60 patents have resulted from his studies, about half being in the field of radio engineering, and the latest is for an "image reproducer" designed to make dim X-ray fluoroscopic images intensely brilliant so they may be photographed by an ordinary camera.

Maintaining that the task of the scientist does not need expensive and elaborate apparatus to achieve important results, Dr. Langmuir says: "Dr. Katharine Blodgett and I have been using a simple method, which does not require expensive or complicated apparatus, to measure the sizes of molecules that are only one ten-millionth of an inch in diameter." This feeling for simplicity characterizes Langmuir. The man to whom *Who's Who in America* devotes a third of a page for the recording of the honors and decorations which United States and foreign scientific bodies, universities and honorary scientific fraternities have bestowed upon him leads a quiet life in Schenectady with his wife and their two children. He has lots of hobbies, among them aviation. Close contact with the experiments of Colonel Charles Lindbergh has deepened his interest in aviation. He also enjoys winter sports and mountain climbing, and Lake George, nearby, affords fine motorboating.

References

> N Y World-Telegram F 26 '40 por
> Sci Am 157:131 S '37 por; 160:41 Ja '39
> American Men of Science
> Chemical Who's Who
> Gray, G. W. Chemist on Vacation *In* Advancing Front of Science p168-93 1937
> Hylander, C. J. Irving Langmuir *In* American Scientists p131-8 1935
> Jaffe, B. Langmuir *In* Crucibles p313-18 1930
> Kendall, J. Some Young American Chemists *In* Young Chemists and Great Discoveries p225-67 1939
> Who's Who in America

LANSBURY, GEORGE Feb 21, 1859—May 7, 1940 Churchman; lecturer; editor; called "Britain's No. 1 pacifist"; Labor Party leader; Privy Councilor

References

> Christian Cent 52:1339-41 O 23 '35
> Sat R Lit 149:253-4 Mr 1 '30; 155:67 Ja 21 '33
> Spec 155:499 O 4 '35
> Who's Who

Obituaries

> Christian Cent 57:660 My 22 '40; 57:711 My 29 '40

N Y Times p23 My 8 '40 por
Springf'd Republican p1, 2 My 8 '40 por

LATOUCHE, JOHN TREVILLE (la'-tōōsh') 1917- Playwright

Address: c/o National Broadcasting Co, 30 Rockefeller Plaza, New York City

John Latouche, coauthor with Earl Robinson of *Ballad for Americans*, is a "short, dark and dynamic" Virginia poet who has written what has been hailed as the "long-awaited great American epic."

Described as "Whitmanesque in scope," *Ballad for Americans* was heard by American radio audiences for the first time early in November 1939, when Paul Robeson, Negro baritone, sang it over CBS on the Sunday afternoon *Pursuit of Happiness* program. The results were startling. The demonstration in the studio continued for 20 minutes after the program went off the air. CBS switchboards in New York, Chicago and Hollywood were deluged with calls. On December 31 Robeson repeated the ballad on the same program; enthusiasts in the Southwest sent chain letters to friends urging them to listen in.

Since then the song, published by the Robbins Music Corporation, has been bought by nearly every high school and college in America. Clubs and civic organizations are learning it, and to get the Victor album of four sides recorded by Mr. Robeson "you enroll your child before birth." Lawrence Tibbett sang it over the air a few months after its introduction. In fact, so great was the response to the song that Metro-Goldwyn-Mayer purchased it for a Judy Garland-Mickey Rooney musical at the reputed sum of $6,000. Early in 1940 the song was booked for three performances by Robeson and his chorus with the Philadelphia Orchestra in the fall; was scheduled to be sung at the Philharmonic Stadium concerts in New York during the summer and was chosen by the Republican Party to open its national convention. The Westminster Choir included it in its repertory.

On the strength, many believe, of the wide success of the ballad, 29-year-old Earl Robinson, who wrote the music, has been given a $2,000 Guggenheim Fellowship; he plans to write a full-length ballad-operetta based on Carl Sandburg's (see sketch this issue) *The People, Yes*.

Ballad for Americans was originally a long poem Latouche had written about human rights. "It comes out of my own country," says Latouche, "out of my home state, and out of the South, out of the young people of the South—out of a younger generation that does not accept a defeatist philosophy."

While working in *Sing for Your Supper*, Latouche, at the instigation of Harold Hecht, adapted the poem into a ballad for the stage. It was presented as *Ballad for*

Uncle Sam in the finale of *Sing for Your Supper,* but failed to make an impression. Latouche saw the possibilities of projecting a musical background for it. At the same time Earl Robinson had also entertained the idea of a ballad with a musical background; he had even written the music and was looking for a lyric writer. The two met during a production of *Sing for Your Supper,* and *Ballad for Americans* was born.

The ballad, which is a chant with antiphonal choral responses and occasional spoken lines, is written in the vernacular and presents the soloist as a composite American type of all races, creeds and activities. It traces the development of the United States from the Revolution through our Western Expansion and Civil War to the Machine Era. The soloist is an epic figure who embodies the hopes, the fears and the spirit of all the people. In each of the four eras the ballad covers, he re-affirms, half spoken, half sung, his belief in America. In the final passage, the soloist expresses his conviction that liberty will continue to be the keystone of American democracy.

Latouche calls the song a "pamphlet for democracy" and is dismayed at some public comment that it is a George M. Cohan flag-waver. "That," Latouche denies stoutly, "is the farthest thing from my intentions. Americans should be proud of their traditions, but never smug about them."

Although he looks French (he is dark-complexioned and has light blue eyes) and his name is French, Latouche is actually of Irish descent. The explanation is that at the time of the Edict of Nantes many Frenchmen came to Ireland and settled there; later many came to America. Among those was his great-grandfather, who became a wealthy landowner in Virginia, where, a few generations later, John Treville Latouche was born, the son of the late Burford Latouche and of Mrs. E. E. Tupper Latouche.

Latouche, beginning to write at the age of six, composed poems, drew pictures and wrote plays which he put on as one-man shows, directing and acting in them himself. At the age of 14, while attending the Richmond Academy of Arts and Sciences, he submitted a fanciful story in a short-story contest and won the grand prize. James Branch Cabell, who was one of the judges, became interested in the young prize winner. He suggested that Latouche leave the South, where he was unhappy—he was revolted by the harsh treatment of the Negro there—and continue studying and writing in the North. So the following year the 15-year-old prize winner, armed with a scholarship left his home and came to New York to attend the Riverdale Preparatory School on the Hudson. At school Latouche was so active and gave the authorities so much trouble that they debated whether to graduate him and rid themselves

of him that way, or to fail him and punish him by keeping him in school. However, on the strength of a grade of 100 on an English college entrance examination, Latouche was graduated into Columbia.

At college he majored in modern French literature, and in his freshman year made himself prominent by being the first freshman to win the Columbia Award for both poetry (*Legend of a Great City*) and for prose. In his sophomore year he again won the Columbia Poetry Award (*The Sea Gull*) and split the prose award with Leonard Robinson. The following year he wrote the book, lyrics and some of the music for the college varsity show, *Flair Flair from Paris,* from which he later sold some of the songs to the American Music Hall. The show, a parody on current theatre forms, took many characters out of Proust and Rabelais, and aroused a storm of controversy. Many critics were shocked with its boldness; others, among them Lucius Beebe (see sketch this issue), defended it as one of the best out of Columbia and gave it laudatory write-ups. As a result of all the comment aroused by the show, Columbia University, for the first time in its history, was moved to set up a board of censorship for its future musicals.

His success with the Columbia production drew Latouche into the theatre, where he received encouragement and assistance from Ira Gershwin and song-writer Vernon Duke. Soon afterwards he met Erika Mann (see sketch this issue), whose play, *The Pepper Mill,* he adapted into English. Once when the leading man, Kurt Bois, was unable to perform Latouche stepped in and played the rôle himself.

Green Mansions, a summer resort where Harold Rome was director of entertainment, attracted him next. He wrote satirical sketches and lyrics, two of which he sold to *Pins and Needles.* Later he wrote for the WPA production, *Sing for Your Supper.*

In New York City Latouche lived in an old Greenwich Village house built over a creek where the rebels in the Revolutionary War used to hide out from the British. Engaged in working on experimental radio forms for NBC and as a writer for its Saturday night *Listeners' Playhouse,* he believes that "Homer's lute was a weak instrument compared to the microphone, which is yet to be touched by an audience of millions." Besides his radio work, Latouche is writing a novel, *Crosstown,* which will deal with life in a great metropolis; a Negro show called *Little Joe* with Vernon Duke; and is also working on an adaptation of Shakespeare's *Much Ado About Nothing* with George Abbott (see sketch this issue). With Vernon Duke he wrote the music for the successful Negro musical, *Cabin in the Sky.* Secretly engaged for two years, Latouche married on October 30, 1940 Theodora Griffis, socialite daughter of Stanton Griffis, motion picture executive of New York City.

LATOUCHE, JOHN TREVILLE—*Cont.*

References

Collier's 106:80+ O 19 '40 il por
N Y Herald Tribune X p17 Jl 7 '40
  por
N Y World-Telegram p19 Ap 19 '40
New Yorker 16:10 Je 29 '40
Newsweek 15:40 Mr 25 '40 por; 16:45
  Ag 5 '40

LAVAL, PIERRE (lä"väl') June 28, 1883- Former Foreign Minister of Vichy Government in France
Address: h. Châteldon, L'Allier, France

December 1940 Bulletin: On December 14, 1940 Laval was removed from his post.

In France the same politicians have the habit of turning up over and over again, not always in the same party. Pierre Laval, after numerous prominent appearances in Cabinets of every shade of political opinion, has since 1936 been simply Senator and Mayor of Aubervilliers. In 1940 the "new" France found him again at the fore, this time as Vice-Premier and eventual successor to Marshal Pétain (see sketch this issue) as Chief of the French State, and, since the shake up in Pétain's Cabinet, the only politician in the government. On October 28, 1940 he became Foreign Minister for the Vichy Government.

"A chubby, olive-skinned little man with wiry hair, a pouting lower lip and a tinny toy trumpet voice," French wits have often pointed out the fact that L-A-V-A-L spells the same thing from Left to Right as from Right to Left as an indication of its owner's character. All things to all men, Pierre Laval has been on thee-and-thou terms with more people than anyone in France, numbering men of every party among his friends, being careful to remain on speaking terms even with his enemies and trusting no one completely. His slipperiness is almost as famous as his reticence, and he used to be called the Calvin Coolidge of France.

He was born June 28, 1883 in Châteldon, in the Auvergne, whose thrifty, close-mouthed people are sometimes known as the Scotsmen of France. Actually there is a heritage of Moorish blood. His father was village butcher, unsuccessful innkeeper, and also ran the mountain mail coach. As a boy Pierre used to drive it—reins in one hand, Greek grammar in the other—and, gaining the interest of a passenger-priest by such studious habits, won a scholarship to St. Etienne. Then he taught in the village school for two years and went on to the Universities of Lyon and Paris, earning his way as school crammer and taking degrees first in natural science, then in law. He was a brilliant student, though with little interest in abstractions or the arts. Even then he was, above all things, practical.

In 1907 he was admitted to the Bar in Paris (nominally he is still a barrister at the Paris Court of Appeals), and as a labor lawyer proceeded to win his first case—that of defending an anarchist. He was never a particularly good pleader, however: his talents were mainly for "inside" jobs on corporate work. And for politics. He was at first an ardent Socialist, and in 1914 was elected both Socialist deputy for the Seine and Mayor of "Red" Aubervilliers. During the First World War he made a reputation for himself in the Chamber as a "dangerous" antimilitarist, refused to volunteer in the army, escaped all but rudimentary military service on the grounds of varicose veins, but, they say, at the same time made a small fortune in munitions supplies. It is also reported that he had the privilege of refusing an offer to become Clemenceau's Under-Secretary of State.

In 1919 he lost his deputy's seat and was also beaten when he ran for Mayor on the Socialist slate. Shortly afterward, following a split in the Tours Socialist Party when he voted for affiliation with the Third International, he is said to have taken membership in both the Socialist and Communist Parties—just to be safe!—and in 1923, running again for Mayor of Aubervilliers as an Independent Socialist, he was elected. (Since then he has been perpetually Mayor of the industrial suburb, whose inhabitants think of him affectionately as "Pierrot.") The following year he was re-elected to Parliament as well.

In 1925 he began his long Cabinet career, first as Minister of Public Works in the Left coalition headed by Painlevé, then as Briand's Under-Secretary of State and Minister of Foreign Affairs. In 1926 those who voted for him voted for him as an Independent, and he was elected Senator for the Department of the Seine. In the same year he was Minister of Justice in several Briand Cabinets, but the crash of the Left coalition, when Poincaré came into power, made him realize that it would be wise to cultivate the Right as well. This he did, in the person of Tardieu, and in 1930 Tardieu appointed him Minister of Labor. It was at that time that Laval forced through the unpopular Social Insurance Law.

Still flirting with both Briand and Tardieu when the latter was overthrown in January 1931, Laval became Prime Minister and Minister of Foreign Affairs at the insistence of Briand, but by making Tardieu his Minister of Agriculture sacrificed Left support. During this term he upset precedents by making trips both to Berlin and to the United States, where he spoke for the non-payment of French war debts and is supposed to have rebuked President Hoover for declaring a moratorium without consulting France. By February 1932 he was out of office, having angered both the people and the Bank of France; but he reappeared in the Doumergue Cabinet as

Minister of Colonies in February 1934, as Minister of Foreign Affairs in October 1934, and served in Flandin's Cabinet in the same office. Then, according to John Gunther, after the Banque had permitted the financial crisis of June 1935 in order to beat Flandin, Laval took over both as Minister of Foreign Affairs and as Prime Minister, with the right to legislate by decree until November 1935; having learned his lesson, he obeyed the Banque in a "merciless policy of deflation" which manifested itself in the De Wendel-Laval Decree Laws of July and August 1935. (Laval had for a long time been the munitions king's intimate law counsel.)

In the meanwhile, with Laval's talents for "saving both faces," foreign relations had been growing amazingly complicated. In the spring of 1935 he had negotiated the Franco-Russian pact of mutual assistance, which those who favored a system of alliances against Germany had long been demanding, but kept deferring its ratification; he had permitted military conscription in Germany, too. He had tried to remain friendly at once with Great Britain and with Italy, making a visit to Mussolini in January in which Il Duce agreed to frustrate German ambitions in Austria, the Danube and the Balkan countries in return for a slice of French territory in Africa. He had smoothed Italian-Jugoslavian tension; he had helped Hitler by seeing to it that France had nothing to do wih policing the Saar Plebiscite; he had obtained Italian-British support for the French attitude toward Germany's rearmament, forming the "Stresa Front."

His juggling seemed to be going remarkably well, however, until Italy declared war on Ethiopia and it developed that Mussolini considered he had been given a free hand in Abyssinia by Laval; until the British accused him of failure to uphold the League by taking his stand against sanctions; until, finally, there was revealed the Hoare-Laval (see Hoare sketch this issue) agreement by which France and Britain were to make peace between Italy and Ethiopia at Ethiopia's expense. Both advocates of collective security and Anglophiles, including Reynaud (see sketch this issue), worked up a popular storm against the Prime Minister; the Left also complained of his hesitancy in ordering dissolved the French Fascist leagues; while most of the Right considered itself irrevocably committed to French-Italian solidarity, and its press campaigned as violently against Britain as against collective security. Though both British and Italian relations were now strained, Laval remained in power until January 1936, even his opponents showing no great desire for taking over the reins of government before that time.

After the tragic sequels to the Ethiopian debâcle Laval explained his diplomacy of that period as aimed toward gaining both Italian support for preventing the Germans

Pictures, Inc.

PIERRE LAVAL

from taking Austria and British support for preventing Nazi fortification of the Rhineland. When he later opposed war at the time of Munich, he said it was in order to stall for time really to prepare against Hitler.

At the outbreak of World War II Laval is reported to have refused a seat in the Daladier government, keeping up relations through Alfred Mallet, former managing editor of the *Petit Journal*. In March 1940 United States newspapers named him as at the forefront of those pressing Daladier (see sketch this issue) to "find a battlefield and make war," but Michel Gorel, a former writer for the Paris *Midi,* claims that three days after the Russian-Finnish peace Laval told Daladier: "You have uselessly irritated Russia by promising support to Finland, but you could not prevent the Finnish defeat. You drove Italy into Germany's arms. The French Army is demoralized, the blockade is a myth and the British Empire will be slow to get under way. We must make peace." According to the same writer, in return for the Ministry of Foreign Affairs Laval promised mediation by his intimate friend Mussolini, with whom he had remained in close contact throughout the winter, and who offered "a white peace to offset the Red danger." Daladier, however, is supposed to have hesitated and have been finally ousted "because of a plot against him by Paul Reynaud and Léon Blum" (see sketch this issue). Daladier himself claims that before the Armistice Laval and other Rightists induced him and his companions to go to North Africa to prepare a new seat of government there, merely in order to get them out of the way. These are all, however, unconfirmed rumors.

What is known is that when Laval became Vice-Premier in France's new authori-

LAVAL, PIERRE—*Continued*

tarian régime of July 1940 he stated that France is through being "a humanitarian crusader for other nations" and will devote her efforts purely toward "national reconstruction within the framework of a European bloc of nations." Reynaud, Blum, Daladier were to be tried for responsibility for the War, all Popular Front personages eliminated from power. Since then his own position has continued to be strengthened despite, or perhaps because of, his continued parleys with German officials and Hitler himself. He is known to favor a National Socialist form of government for France.

Laval is married, but his wife does not appear often in public life. They have one daughter, José, who is the wife of Count René de Chambrun, now in the United States. Laval owns a villa in Paris, a château in Châteldon, two or three country estates. He adores animals, and when Premier, used to interrupt state conferences to telephone to one of his farms and ask about the welfare of his cows and pigs. He has "homely manners," bad teeth, dresses carelessly, wears a perpetual washable white tie, has a phobia against railway sleepers, appreciates food, smokes around 80 cigarettes a day, plays around with his own provincial newspapers (*Le Moniteur* among them) but has never written a book, speaks badly, is said to be totally without vanity or temper. He is a devout Catholic. He has "grown rich without explanation"— perhaps by munition supplies during the First World War, real estate profits and speculation on the currency exchange with advance political information as a guide. He may have other information. Reports are that astrology, in the person of M. Maurice Privat, has played no small part in his conduct of foreign and other affairs!

References
Collier's 96:22+ Ag 17 '35 por
Cur Hist 43:532-5 F '36; 43:645-7 Mr '36; 51:14 Ag '40
Illustration 202:448 Ap 15 '39 por
Life 9:43-5 Jl 22 '40 pors; 9:74-5 S 23 '40 il pors
Lit Digest 120:39 N 2 '35 por; 120:12 D 14 '35
New Statesman & Nation 8:817-18 D 8 '34; 10:365-6 S 21 '35; 10:625-6 N 2 '35; 11:105-6 Ja 25 '36
N Y Times p30 Je 30 '40; p4 Jl 11 '40; p10 Jl 16 '40; p4 Ag 12 '40 por; p5 O 24 '40
Sat Eve Post 213:18-19+ N 23 '40 il
Time 26:22-4 Ag 19 '35; 27:18-19 Ja 6 '36; 27:25-6 Ja 27 '36; 36:26 D 23 '40

Gunther, J. More About Frenchmen *In* Inside Europe p182-99 1940
Romains, J. Seven Mysteries of Europe 1940
Simone, A. J'Accuse 1940
Slocombe, G. E. Abyssinian Crisis *In* Mirror to Geneva p282-304 1938
Who's Who

LAWRENCE, CHARLES EDWARD Dec 24, 1870—Mar 15, 1940 British author; playwright; joint editor of the *Quarterly Review*

References
Who's Who

Obituaries
N Y Sun p30 Mr 15 '40
N Y Times p15 Mr 16 '40
N Y World-Telegram p4 Mr 16 '40

LAWRENCE, ERNEST ORLANDO Aug 8, 1901- Nobel Prize winner in science, 1939; professor of physics

Address: b. Radiation Laboratory, University of California, Berkeley, California; h. 111 Tamalpais Rd, Berkeley, California

Dr. Lawrence was born at Canton, South Dakota, the son of Carl Gustavus and Gunda (Jacobson) Lawrence. His father is an educator, now teaching at Northern State Teachers' College, Aberdeen, South Dakota. Young Lawrence studied at St. Olaf College, Northfield, Minnesota, received a B. A. from the University of South Dakota in 1922; did graduate work at the University of Minnesota and the University of Chicago; received his Ph. D. from Yale in 1925. He received honorary Doctor of Science degrees from the University of South Dakota in 1936, Stevens Institute of Technology, Yale University and Princeton University, and an LL. D. from the University of Michigan.

He married Margaret Kimberly Blumer and has three children, a boy and two girls. He has taught physics at Yale and in 1940 is director of the Radiation Laboratory at the University of California.

Dr. Lawrence, a jovial good-looking young man, joins 12 other United States scientists as recipients of the highest honor a scientist can receive—the Nobel Prize. It was awarded to him for the invention of the cyclotron, a "Rube Goldberg contraption of steel, copper and aluminum weighing 220 tons and used to study one of the tiniest units of the physical world, the nucleus of the atom." About 10 years ago he invented the first one which weighed a mere 60 tons. In 1940 he hopes to work on a 4,900-ton cyclotron, for in April the Rockefeller Foundation promised him $1,150,000 to build it and to "smash atoms as atoms have never been smashed before." In his special Radiation Laboratory on the campus of the University of California, Dr. Lawrence and his coworkers "have already created scores of artificially radioactive substances, including common salt, and have even created a few atoms of gold." What the 4,900-ton machine will uncover in "the inner heart of matter" no one knows, but no physicist doubts that it will "unlock many a treasure house of secrets."

All over the world in scientific laboratories there are other cyclotrons which are being used to study the world's supply of

ERNEST ORLANDO LAWRENCE

energy, locked inside the nucleus. Many physicists who studied under Dr. Lawrence are now working independently. With his brother, John Hundale Lawrence, the Nobel Prize winner is considering cyclotron treatments for cancer.

Other awards made to Professor Lawrence include: Elliott Cresson Medal of the Franklin Institute (1937); Research Corporation Prize and plaque (1937); Comstock Prize of the National Academy of Sciences (1937); Hughes Medal of the Royal Society (1937); William K. Dunn award of the American Legion (1940); and the William Du Bois Duddell Memorial Medal of the London Physical Society, one of the highest awards of English science (December 1940).

References

Life 8:42-3+ F 5 '40 il por
N Y Times p6 N 8 '39; p25 N 10 '39 por; p14 N 11 '39
Newsweek 14:50 N 20 '39 por
Sci ns 86:7 Jl 2 '37; 86:405-7 N 5 '37 (Excerpt Sci Mo 45:571-2 D '37 por); 86:578 D 24 '37
Sci N L 36:323 N 18 '39 por; 36:394-6 D 16 '39 il
Sci Am 162:259 My '40 por; 163:68-71 Ag '40 (Same abr. Read Digest 37: 121-4 Ag '40)
Time 30:37-8+ N 1 '37 il por (cover); 32:41 N 28 '38 por; 34:36 N 20 '39 por; 35:48 Ap 22 '40 il
American Men of Science
Who's Who in America

LAWRENCE, GERTRUDE July 4, 1901-
Actress
Address: 17 W 54th St, New York City

Gertrude Lawrence, who has been called the "undisputed queen of the light comedy stage," has led a storybook life with all the standard plots, including the ancient from rags to riches one. After a hard life, fortune and fame are hers. Fame has come, as it should come for actresses, in the form of Standing Room Only signs outside the theatres in which she is playing; it has come, too, in the form of awards and medals. The latest added to her already large collection are the gold medallion awarded by the New York Academy in February 1940 "for the best performance of the year" and the annual award of the Comedia Matinee Club, also "for the most outstanding theatrical performance of the year."

This famous British star—actually she's half Danish and half Irish—was born in London on July 4, 1901 and named Gertrud Alexandra Dagma Lawrence Klasen. She made her first public appearance at the age of two when her father, an interlocutor in a minstrel show, put her in a chair in the lobby and told her to smile. Her smile helped sell the programs. Her parents were divorced soon after and Gertrude went to live with her mother, a very minor actress. When her mother had a bit in a play there was meat to eat; when she didn't there was only very thin soup.

At nine Gertrude was dancing in a pantomime in London and later was one of fifty girls playing in *The Miracle*. Noel Coward was one of the fifty boys who played in it, and he acted, too, in *Hannele* in which they both appeared in 1913. He remembers her then as "a vivacious child with ringlets to whom I took an instant fancy. She wore a black satin coat and a black velvet military hat with a peak, her face was far from pretty but tremendously alive. She gave me an orange and told me a few mildly dirty stories, and I loved her from then onwards."

Gertrude studied dancing under Madame Espinosa, and elocution and acting at the Italia Conti Dancing Academy, first as a pupil and then as a student teacher. Whenever she had a spare shilling she went to the theatre. She began to get small parts. "I went on the stage to make money," she says now, to those who speak with awe of the glamor of the theatre. "I had to earn a living and that seemed the most attractive way to do it."

It wasn't a very attractive way at first. For seven years she played in the English provinces: "I danced and sang and acted and did everything but sell tickets." There was the time when she was playing in Shrewsbury and the manager skipped, leaving the company flat without money to pay hotel bills. The landlady told Gertrude she could stay on until something turned up if she'd lend a hand in the bar. She was glad to do it. She stayed as barmaid until the next acting company reached town and wanted a girl to sing before they began their play, *The Rosary*. Someone said: "There's a pretty nifty bar-

GERTRUDE LAWRENCE

maid down at the Red Lion. She's had stage experience. Why not get her?" "So they got me," she says, "and I put on a nun's habit and sang *My Rosary* before each performance and then scampered back to the bar."

Eventually Gertrude Lawrence got to London as dancer and understudy in a revue called *Some* and got her real start as a chorus girl in one of the earlier *Charlot's Revues*. Charlot signed a three-year contract with her for £3 a week for the first year and £6 a week for the next two. In return for this Miss Lawrence was to dance and sing and understudy a couple of parts. She understudied Beatrice Lillie's rôle and Miss Lillie was kind enough to break her leg by falling from a horse. Miss Lawrence took over Bea Lillie's routine—successfully. But in the next revue she was back in the chorus again—until Miss Lillie decided to get married and leave the show. Gertrude got her part for keeps at £6 a week and rave notices with it.

In 1924 Gertrude Lawrence came to New York for the first time. She was already married (the marriage was later dissolved) to Francis Gordon-Howley, by whom she had one daughter, Pamela, now living in New York City. She came to New York with Beatrice Lillie to do *Charlot's Revue* of 1924. Singing a number called *Limehouse Blues* Gertie Lawrence was a hit. She was even more of a one when, dressed in a dazzling white dress, she sang insinuating patter.

In the annual *Charlot's Revues* Gertrude Lawrence always "danced with magical lightness and her voice was true and clear; the personification of style and sophistication, she could still convulse an audience with a bit of cockney horseplay or bring tears to its eyes with a sentimental ballad—the ideal musical comedy star," her admirers said.

After five years of musical comedy in London and New York, Gertrude Lawrence got her first "straight" part—in the Viennese comedy, *Candlelight*. "I hadn't much experience in playing a legitimate part," she says, "but I'd played in a lot of sketches, some dramatic, some comic. An actress is like a piece of blotting paper. You don't consciously learn the technique of acting, you absorb it." According to a couple of critics, in *Candlelight* Gertrude Lawrence "was as charming and as decorative as ever, but she turned on all the comic stops at once and overplayed consistently."

Overplaying is a fault of which Miss Lawrence has occasionally been accused. Noel Coward used to try to cure her of it and to a large extent succeeded. She knows all about her tendency. "Now and then," she frankly admits, "I find myself reverting to the old habit of overplaying a part or emphasizing and banging home points that should be underlined. But now, thank goodness, I know when I'm doing so and I have a horrible thought of what Noel would say were he out front."

Gertrude Lawrence has been associated with Noel Coward a lot, of course, since the time they first met in *Hannele*. He's written plays for her; he's acted, sung and danced with her. *Private Lives* (1930), which he wrote for her, is the play that made her the acknowledged queen of the light comedy stage, for her portrayal of Amanda Prynne was "a brilliant, sustained and restrained piece of high comedy acting." Her "sureness of touch and fluency of expression" were astonishing in another of Coward's plays, *Tonight at 8:30,* presented in New York in the winter of 1936 to 1937. *Tonight at 8:30* was a series of nine short plays, three of which were given at each performance. In the cycle Miss Lawrence had to play comedy, high and low, tragedy, melodrama or revue—do everything but balance a rubber ball on her nose—all in an evening.

When Miss Lawrence toured in this country in 1935 with John Golden's production of *Susan and God* the play broke attendance records in practically every city where it appeared. Critics were unanimous in heaping on Miss Lawrence for her "dazzling performance" the sort of praise previously reserved for Helen Hayes and Katharine Cornell.

Miss Lawrence's latest appearance is in *Skylark* "which fortunately has Gertrude Lawrence to give it wings." When the play opened in October 1939 the critics agreed that this comedy owed a good deal more to her bright, particular sparkle than to its own merits, and some went as far as to say that it was merely "an inadequate vehicle for her vivid talents and ingratiating personal charm."

After her marriage on July 4, 1940 to Richard S. Aldrich, theatrical producer whom she met on Cape Cod when *Skylark* was being tried out, Miss Lawrence went on tour with *Skylark*. In the spring of 1941 she is going to appear in *Lady in the Dark* by Moss Hart (see sketch this issue), where her rôle will be that of a woman who is being psychoanalyzed.

Those who know Miss Lawrence away from the stage insist that she is just as charming as when she is in a play especially designed to show off her talents. Her voice has the same throaty resonance; her manner is just as pleasing. Off stage and on she is lovely to look at, "tall, somewhat angular, yet lithe and graceful," with a "winning smile, eyes that sparkle and a nose that can crinkle delightfully."

References

Am Theatre Mag 1:56-7 Mr '40 por
Collier's 105:11+ F 10 '40 por
Forum 100:238-9 N '38
Lit Digest 123:22 My 15 '37 por
N Y Herald Tribune p17 F 16 '40 por; p7 Jl 4 '40 pors
N Y Times p17 Jl 4 '40 por
Theatre Arts 23:714-16 O '39 por (p696)
Time 34:36 O 23 '39 por
International Motion Picture Almanac
Sobel, B. ed. Theatre Handbook 1940
Who's Who
Who's Who in the Theatre

LAWRENCE, MARJORIE 1908- Soprano
Address: c/o Metropolitan Opera Company, Broadway and 39th St, New York City

There is little doubt that the most startling event of the 1936 Metropolitan Opera season was the dashing exit of Brünnhilde on horseback in the last scene of the *Götterdämmerung*. For years buxom prima donnas had led ancient nags across the stage by the bridle or left them in charge of a stable groom. But on the evening of January 12, 1936, Marjorie Lawrence charged boldly on her horse in the direction of the funeral pyre.

Such a feat, however, is to be expected of a soprano, the daughter of William and Elizabeth (Smith) Lawrence, who was born and brought up in Australia and spent much of her youth rounding up cattle and sheep. This was in Dean's Marsh, a country village of some 140 people in the heart of the bush country. There were four Lawrence boys and two girls, all of whom attended the little village school from which Marjorie used to escape by the window when she'd been kept after school for misbehaving. "I was an impossible child," she now says of herself. "I wanted to be a boy like my brothers. I simply never did what I was told, and my relatives and neighbors wondered what would happen to me when I grew up."

Marjorie's first music lessons came from the Reverend A. J. Peerce, Dean's Marsh's Church of England parson, who had already taught her most of the world's great reli-

Musical America

MARJORIE LAWRENCE

gious music by the time she was 18 and beginning to realize that she wanted to sing more than anything else in the world.

Her father was against Marjorie's having a career, and so one day she and her brother Cyril, now her manager, stole away to Melbourne. For two years she studied with Ivor Boustead while supporting herself by working as a seamstress. In 1929 she won an operatic contest sponsored by the Melbourne *Sun* which sent her to Paris for study under Madame Cecile Gilly. After three years of hard study learning rôles and vocal technique, she made her debut in Monte Carlo as Elisabeth in *Tannhäuser,* and shortly after made her Paris debut as Elsa in *Lohengrin.* Marjorie Lawrence's Metropolitan debut was on December 18, 1935 as Brünnhilde in *Die Walküre.*

From the time of her first debut Marjorie Lawrence has been recognized as "one of the truest Wagnerian interpreters, alike for the stirring magnificence of her Brünnhilde and the tender simplicity of her Sieglinde, the stately loveliness of her Elsa and the compelling malevolence of her Ortrud."

Marjorie Lawrence, actually, isn't much like *Tannhäuser's* saintly Elisabeth or stalwart Brünnhilde, with her "saucy blond head" and "pert little nose." Nor is she like the general idea of operatic artists. There was the night she strode into the smoker of a midnight train armed to the teeth in full battle regalia, brandishing Brünnhilde's shield and spear while strong men ran for the door. Or the time the Metropolitan mouse that hid in her ermine wrap picked the center of the Astor Hotel lobby to jump out. She herself insists on being Marjorie Lawrence. "For heaven's sake, don't let me catch you calling me a prima donna or a diva," she'll tell you. "And I'm not Madame Lawrence, or any-

LAWRENCE, MARJORIE—*Continued*

thing like that. I'm just Marjorie. I don't have a favorite recipe for kugelhupf or spaghetti. I hate cities and crowded rooms and stuffy people and I just can't wait until I get out in the fresh air with a good horse or my bike. How I love a bike!"

In Paris, which she still considers her home city and where she maintains a "wonderful, crazy" studio in Montmartre, she has established an unique place for herself, and can be counted on to put some new sensation into almost any opera season—"whether because Brünnhilde rides again, or because all seven of Salome's veils come off on schedule in a dance outdaring even Mary Garden's, or merely because Marjorie Lawrence is singing."

References
    Christian Sci Mon Mag p14 Je 22 '40
      pors
    Etude 56:593-4 S '38 pors
    Metropolitan Opera Program p6-7+
      F 14 '40 por
    N Y Post p11 F 2 '40 por; p4 Mr
      23 '40 por
    Thompson, O. ed. International Cyclopedia of Music and Musicians 1939

LAYCOCK, CRAVEN Sept 30, 1866—Apr 4, 1940 Dean emeritus of Dartmouth College; associated with the college for 42 years; served as lawyer before joining faculty; his statue on the campus was an "exam" charm for students before tests

CRAVEN LAYCOCK

References
    Who's Who in America
    Who's Who in American Education

Obituaries
    N Y Herald Tribune p16 Ap 5 '40
    N Y Times p21 Ap 5 '40
    Sch & Soc 51:477 Ap 13 '40

LEE, JOHN CLARENCE, REV. Oct 15, 1856—Sept 16, 1940 Author; clergyman; university president; was the fifth president of St. Lawrence University (1896-99); was for the next 19 years pastor of the Universalist Church of the Restoration in Philadelphia; author of many religious and philosophic books

References
    Who's Who in America

Obituaries
    N Y Times p23 S 17 '40
    Sch & Soc 52:231 S 21 '40

LEE, MANFRED B. See Queen, E., pseud.

LEHRBAS, LLOYD (lĕr'bäs) Oct 15, 1898- Associated Press' "roving correspondent"

Address: c/o The Associated Press, 50 Rockefeller Plaza, New York City

Lloyd Lehrbas, who was given honorable mention for his foreign dispatches in the 1939 Pulitzer Awards, has crowded an improbable amount of experience into his life. Born in Montpelier, Idaho, on October 15, 1898, he attended school there and at Boise, spent a year as a student at the University of Idaho and as local correspondent for the Salt Lake *Tribune,* then enrolled in the school of journalism of the University of Wisconsin. After two years at the university his roving began, and he has been on the move ever since.

First it was the World War. Young Lehrbas quit school to enlist in the air service, and although the Armistice came before he got to France, he didn't go back to Wisconsin, but found a job as reporter on the San Francisco *Chronicle.* He wasn't there long; he had an itching foot that got him onto an army transport in a bellboy's uniform, and eventually brought him to Siberia, China, Japan, the Philippines. Back in the United States, he tried Chicago, and joined the staff of the Chicago *American;* he returned to the Philippines, and worked nine months as night editor of the Manila *Bulletin;* he was with the Shanghai *Evening Star,* on a Hearst paper in New York City, two years with a Washington newspaper, editor of Fox Movietone News in New York, a freelance reporter in the Orient and in Europe. Finally, on December 4, 1933, he joined the state department of the Associated Press in Washington, D. C., expressing his desire to become their "roving correspondent."

It was evident that he already had a good many qualifications for the job. In December 1935 A. P. sent him to London to cover the Naval Conference. In January 1936

Associated Press

LLOYD LEHRBAS

he was back in Washington, covering the Republican and Democratic conventions. In November of the same year he was in Buenos Aires with Cordell Hull (see sketch this issue), and at last, early in 1937, he set sail for Shanghai with the roving commission.

From then on Lloyd Lehrbas kept bumping into history, maybe because he kept following it around. He was in the thick of the Chinese-Japanese War. He was in Warsaw at the time of the German air-raids on Poland, and from his apartment, telephone in one hand, gas-mask in the other, he dictated the story of the first air-raid on Warsaw to a fellow correspondent in Budapest who had telephoned to find out if "anything was doing." When it became necessary to leave, he started for the border town of Lwow in an ancient German automobile, while "bombs fell in front of us and bombs fell behind us." Continuing to Bucharest, he arrived just before the assassination of Rumanian Premier Calinescu, and managed to score a world beat for the Associated Press by getting the story out before the censor clamped down.

Lehrbas returned to the United States late in 1939 and spent a short time as correspondent for the A. P. in Washington, but in May 1940 he was on his way back to Europe again.

Firm-jawed, with high cheekbones, Lehrbas belongs to the rugged type of newspapermen who make legends and who somewhat justify Hollywood's romantic versions of the press. Fellow newspapermen say there has not appeared such a combination of ace reporter and colorful character since the late Webb Miller.

References

St Louis Post-Dispatch p1C My 7 '40 por

LEIGH, DOUGLAS (lē) May 24, 1907-
Advertising executive
Address: b. 630 Fifth Ave, New York City

Times Square in New York has been called the Louvre of advertising spectacles. From the Square to Columbus Circle, about 200,000 electric bulbs and 25 miles of neon tubing blazon forth the glories of innumerable products. What used to be the largest sign of them all, the Wrigley Gum aquarium scene opposite the Hotel Astor, was put up by the General Outdoor Advertising Company. Most of the next largest signs and those which seem to fascinate most gapers were put up by a former General Outdoor Advertising employee, Douglas Leigh. And in October 1940 his "mazda-piece" was opened —the largest animated cartoon ad in the world.

When Douglas Leigh arrived in New York in 1929 he had $8.25 in his pocket. Today, his firm, Douglas Leigh, Incorporated, has physical assets of half a million dollars, mostly in erected signs, and holds contracts of an aggregate face value of more than a million.

He was born on May 24, 1907 in Anniston, Alabama, the son of an executive of a local manufacturing concern. At 10 he was earning $2 a week selling magazines for an Anniston drugstore. At 13 he entered high school in Greenville, North Carolina and for four years was advertising manager of the year book. In his spare time he ran a magazine agency and during his senior year made as much as $150 a month. Summertimes he visited an uncle and aunt in Atlanta and worked up a magazine route there.

In 1927 Leigh entered the University of Florida, where he was none too good in his studies. But he made money there. In his freshman year he bought the advertising rights to the year book for $2,000 credit. Advertising had never run over $1,500, so this looked like a good price to the editors. Leigh sold more than $7,000 worth of advertising that year.

Next year the editors wouldn't sell him space, but he had other ideas. Through program concessions, through selling buckles, raincoats and stickers with the college seal he made $5,000 and, with the profits from his two years in college, quit. "When he was asked whether he had worked his way through college, he replied: 'Well, in a way. It's really a business and I went there to make money.'"

Leigh worked for a sign company in Birmingham, Alabama, then in Atlanta, where he led all the salesmen and got several increases. But the increases didn't come fast enough to suit him, so he resigned. Right after the stock market crash he landed in New York, broke—he always had a talent

DOUGLAS LEIGH

for dissipating money and had been helping a brother in medical school.

In New York he got a job with the General Outdoor Advertising Company at $50 a week. As the depression got worse he received salary cuts, though he did good work selling billboard space and bulletins in Brooklyn. When his bosses wanted to cut him to $30 a week, he begged to be allowed to sell Broadway spectaculars (signs with more than 200 feet of neon tubing or the equivalent in electric light bulbs). He was told that one needed social prestige for that job. He quit.

He had $50 and a second-hand Ford and the day after he quit he came down with the mumps. When he really got started was on the day President Roosevelt closed the banks in March 1933. "After breakfasting at the Automat where he always ate, Leigh bought a 50-cent Japanese camera and a roll of film and took a subway up to Fordham Road in The Bronx, a neighborhood he had scouted before. He walked along Fordham Road until he came to a likely sign spot on the roof of a building. He talked the owner of the building into giving him an option on the space, on credit, and took snapshots of it. An unemployed artist friend enlarged the shots, on credit, and painted in a sign, singing the praises of the St. Moritz Hotel. Armed with his composographs, Leigh dropped in on the business manager of the tony hostelry on Central Park South and sold him the space."

Leigh peddled his Ford to get some of the money necessary to put up the sign and got from the hotel a two-room suite for a year, rent free plus $50 a month. He made his office in the bedroom and used hotel stationery with a rubber stamp of his name on top. Then he proceeded to ex-

plore Times Square with his camera, got the help of his artist friend again and took his pictures around to dozens of firms. Finally the A & P signed a contract and Leigh put up his first spectacular, the central figure of which was a large cup which gave off white clouds like a cup of steaming-hot coffee.

Since then he has erected the Kool cigarette advertisement with the penguin that blinks 3,600 times a minute, the Ballantine beer sign that has clowns tossing quoits on a peg, the huge Schenley advertisement over Columbus Circle, the Gillette razor spectacular with a clock and Westminster chimes, the Trommers sign with the German beer pixies and the Four Roses whisky spectacular, the highest sign on Broadway. "His Coca-Cola sign on Columbus Circle giving weather forecasts is a masterpiece of imagination, sold to the Coca-Cola people on the strength of their own slogan, 'Thirst knows no season.'" Once he put up a Coca-Cola sign in Bryant Park and a woman tenant used to hang her wash in front of it every Monday. She said she had been hanging it in the same place for 20 years and didn't intend to change. Leigh has been mailing her $2 a week with the understanding that she send her laundry out to be done.

The most talked of of all Leigh's signs are his two animated cartoon comics, advertising Old Gold cigarettes and Wilson's whisky. In 1936 he obtained the American rights to the animated cartoon patent, an invention of Kurt Rosenberg, an Austrian. The cartoon is made on film and is projected onto the bank of photo-electric cells. The cells are activated and the current transmitted to mercury tubes, where it is magnified and passed onto the corresponding outside bulbs on the sign itself. When Leigh sold the sign to the P. Lorillard Company, he inserted a clause in the contract promising that the spectacular would attract more attention than any other in New York, and permitting the company to cancel its $4,000 a month contract if he failed to deliver. He doesn't have much to worry about. The sign "draws the biggest standee crowd along the Rialto."

Leigh gets the ideas for the comic strips himself, as he gets all the other ideas he develops and sells. A couple of years ago he excited a reporter into doing a long article when he prophesied he was going to rent the Empire State Building's mooring mast from Al Smith and develop it into an electrically lighted 100-foot cigarette which would give off smoke and be visible 100 miles away. When pressed, Leigh will admit he knows it's a pretty far-fetched idea.

Physically Leigh is slight and "looks like an actor who will always be cast in juvenile rôles." "His manner is mousy"; he speaks softly and answers everyone with a "Yes, Sir," or "No, Sir," even the tobacconist who sells him cigarettes. He's scared to death of high places and won't live in an apartment above the third floor.

If by some chance he has to take a hotel room above the third floor he loops one end of a sheet around his ankle and the other end to the bedpost before retiring. He hates banks and won't borrow from them, maybe because he found it hard to borrow when he first started; maybe because the man he admires above all, Henry Ford, doesn't like banks either. There's a story that when Leigh was taking a course at Columbia University, a professor referred to Ford slightingly. Leigh stood up, walked out and never came back.

In 1936 Leigh met Patricia de Brun, the pretty daughter of a New York manufacturer, and shortly after asked her to marry him. Her family objected because she was only 18. Leigh and Miss de Brun eloped, by Long Island Sound ferryboat, and were married in Stamford, Connecticut. Now "his wife need never worry about being supported; he has a little notebook in which 11 pages are filled with substitute ways of making money in case anything ever happens to his spectaculars."

References

Christian Sci Mon Mag p6 S 22 '37 por
Friday 1:21 N 8 '40 pors
N Y World-Telegram p25 Ap 24 '40 por
Sat Eve Post 211:20-1+ Ap 15 '39 il por
Time 32:42+ Jl 18 '38 por
America's Young Men
Streyckmans, F. B. Today's Young Men p9-10 1940
Who's Who in Commerce and Industry

LEINSDORF, ERICH (līnes'dorf ĕr'ĭk) Feb 4, 1912- Chief conductor, Metropolitan Opera Company

Address: c/o Metropolitan Opera Co, Broadway and 39th St, New York City

Chief conductor of the largest opera house in the world is an enviable title, but as a job it is one of the toughest. As one critic has said, it requires a man who is "showman, diplomat, handshaker, politician, executive, psychologist"—and, not purely incidentally, musician. Being chief conductor of the largest opera house in the world at the age of 27 is just plain unprecedented, and perhaps that's why Erich Leinsdorf has been one of the most publicized and most argued-about young men of the year. Having now survived his strenuous first season in that position, it seems likely that the Metropolitan Opera Company will go on permitting him indefinitely to live down his age while wielding its baton.

Erich Leinsdorf began his career early. Born in Vienna in 1912, he was taking piano lessons under Paul Emerich by the time he was seven, studying to be a concert pianist. When he was 13 he began also to

Musical America

ERICH LEINSDORF

study the cello, musical theory and composition. By the time he was 18 he knew where his ambitions really lay: in interpretation. And four years later he was already beginning to achieve them.

He was engaged for the 1934 Salzburg Festival as an assistant conductor to Bruno Walter when it was found that they needed someone familiar with the Italian language for the opera *Don Giovanni*. After the opera was produced successfully Leinsdorf was asked to stay for other work.

Back in Vienna the next spring he was asked to play the piano rehearsals of Kodály's *Psalmus Hungaricus* conducted by Toscanini because no pianist was available who knew the score well enough to work with the great conductor. At the concert he was pianist for the Kodály work and for Beethoven's *Ninth Symphony*. In May 1935, he worked again under Walter at the Florence Festival, and at the Salzburg Festival that same year he was general assistant to both Walter and Toscanini, preparing both singers and chorus. In the fall and winter of 1936 he had several operatic and symphonic engagements at Bologna, Trieste and San Remo, and in 1937 he once more assisted at the Florence and Salzburg Festivals, making himself known as Toscanini's right-hand man.

At about this time the general manager of the Metropolitan Opera of New York City, "gray-haired, wiry" Edward Johnson, was looking for an assistant conductor of German opera for his over-worked chief conductor, Artur Bodanzky. At the recommendation of Toscanini, young Leinsdorf was engaged for the 1937 to 1938 season, sight unseen. He had never publicly conducted an opera, and his duties were supposed to consist largely of piano rehearsals with the singers.

LEINSDORF, ERICH—*Continued*

The young conductor's debut was for a performance of *Die Walküre* on January 21, 1938. His appearance was something of a triumph. Said the late Lawrence Gilman, music critic of the New York *Herald Tribune*, of the audience that night: "They saw an astonishingly boyish figure, short, small of build, graceful, with one or two of the familiar gestures of his great master (Toscanini). . . Though he wiped his brow occasionally with his handkerchief . . . he soon made it evident that he was entirely at home."

The same critic spoke of his "remarkable musical memory," his "clear and intelligible" beat, his "musical feeling, taste and authority." He noted in conclusion that Leinsdorf was "a very welcome acquaintance, an artist whom one must admire and, better yet, respect."

That same season Erich Leinsdorf conducted 10 performances, earning admiration by taking over the performance of *Parsifal* at Easter on 12 hours' notice after Bodanzky became suddenly ill. For his second season, ending in the spring of 1939, thirty-six performances of operas by Wagner and Richard Strauss were turned over to him. At the end of the season he conducted four performances of the NBC and one of the Montreal Symphony Orchestras, and spent the fall season with the San Francisco Opera Company conducting *Pélléas et Mélisande.*

In the next season Leinsdorf expected to conduct only twenty-five to thirty performances of four or five operas. Three weeks before opening night he returned to find his chief again in ill health. In those three weeks the young man prepared and rehearsed nine German operas—and six days before the opening curtain on Thanksgiving came Artur Bodanzky's catastrophic death. Leinsdorf was suddenly forced to assume all that veteran conductor's assignments in addition to his own; and this meant all performances of 13 works, many of which he had never before conducted in public. During his first Metropolitan season Leinsdorf had conducted *Die Walküre, Parsifal,* Richard Strauss' *Elektra;* on tour that same season he had added *Lohengrin* and *Tannhäuser;* in his next season with Metropolitan he had also conducted *Siegfried* and *Das Rheingold.* But in one season *Die Meistersinger, Tristan und Isolde, Götterdämmerung, Orfeo ed Eurydice, Der Rosenkavalier* and *Pélléas et Mélisande* had to be added to his repertoire.

It would have been a tremendous assignment for a conductor of many years' experience. The reaction of many of the critics might be summed up in the words of one: "One might reasonably ask if this is not excessive. It might not be if the incredible had happened and Mr. Leinsdorf proved himself at a step a young Toscanini. But that is not the case, and was not expected to be." Mr. Leinsdorf's great precocity and talent were universally acknowl-

edged, but as the season wore on there was criticism that his inexperience made him rather unheedful of the needs of singers—reluctant to give cues, given to playing in different tempi and to varying his interpretations from performance to performance.

Late in January 1940, some of this criticism on the part of members of his company was pounced upon by the press. Lauritz Melchior was quoted on January 25 as having acknowledged Leinsdorf as a "genius" but as stating flatly that he was "not yet ready to be senior conductor of the finest department of the greatest opera house in the world." Kirsten Flagstad was reported to have hinted that she would not continue with the Metropolitan that season if Leinsdorf continued as conductor. "Since Mr. Leinsdorf is inexperienced in playing Wagner," she was quoted, "he watches the music. I see his arms moving, but I can't tell where the music is."

General Manager Edward Johnson, however, was firm in defense of his "young Toscanini." He spoke darkly of certain "old boats in the company . . . who, because they have exalted egos since they have no competition for their rôles, would like to be dictators of the Metropolitan." Of Mr. Leinsdorf he said: "He will be so acclaimed in a few years that they won't want to remember that they opposed him." Leinsdorf himself maintained a dignified silence.

It was a poor time for a musical feud— the time of the campaign to raise a million dollars to pay for the purchase of the opera house from the Metropolitan Opera and Real Estate Company. And it was true that box-office receipts were even larger in the 1939 season than 1938, indicative of the approval of Leinsdorf by a large section of the public. On the evening of January 25, 1940 at the performance of *Götterdämmerung,* Melchior and Leinsdorf appeared together and at the second act it was Leinsdorf who was given an ovation by the audience. One critic said of his conducting that evening: "It was clearly an exhibition of youth, if not of emotional depth, subtlety and finesse." On the evening of January 29 the feud was officially ended by a handclasp at the performance of the *Die Walküre,* amid further ovations by the audience. And in February, Flagstad appeared on schedule.

By the end of the regular 1939 to 1940 season Erich Leinsdorf had given a total of 55 performances. Music critics of Boston were uniformly kind during the Boston tour. W. S. Smith said of Leinsdorf: "He was last year and the year before [1938-39] a young man working for his place next to the older colleague—now, young as he is, he is the master of whom we expect confidently mastery." The consensus of critical opinion was that he had acquitted himself remarkably well in "one of the most grueling schedules a Metropolitan Opera conductor ever faced." Mr. Leinsdorf, however, claimed that he was not at all tired, that he had even put on weight. "Why all this talk about too much work?" he asked. "I am glad I had the opportunity to work so much. It doesn't exhaust me—on the contrary, it's stimulating, and I'm in better condition right now than I was at the beginning of the season. Why, in Vienna, where I got my training, we had a ten months' opera season, with nightly performances, and there were only three conductors. Each of them had more work than I undertook at the Metropolitan this year."

Whether the exercise of his profession is or is not ideal to keep one in physical trim, it is the only exercise Erich Leinsdorf gets during the winter seasons, and his short, chunky figure is that of an athlete, topped by broad shoulders. During the summer months he plays a little tennis, but, he says, "poorer than second-rate."

In this country less than three years, the young Viennese is becoming rapidly Americanized. His English has scarcely a trace of accent; he already has his first citizenship papers; he is at least a conservative supporter of swing music and he is an enthusiastic believer in operas in English with American casts. In August 1939, he married Anne Frohnknecht. The young couple have set up housekeeping in a rambling, old-fashioned five-room apartment just off Central Park West, and Erich spends most of his time there when he is not working. He doesn't like parties, and claims one cocktail gathering tires him more than conducting *Götterdämmerung*.

He has definite—and mildly revolutionary—ideas as to what he would like to do with the Metropolitan of the future, although no real plans are possible. It should be put on a permanent, year-round basis, he thinks; conductorial training should be offered to at least one or two especially talented young American musicians; he would like to give a representative cycle of German operas there—something besides Wagner; and there should be a "summer training camp for younger singers." "For five decades the Metropolitan has been buying readymade singers. Now, I think, it is our duty to grow our own," Erich Leinsdorf says, firmly.

References

Boston Transcript III p6 Ja 27 '40
Christian Sci Mon p3 Ja 30 '40
Cue p23 D 16 '39 por
Lit Digest 125:22 F 19 '38
Musician 44:107 Je '39 por
N Y Herald Tribune p1 Ja 25 '40; p1 Ja 26 '40; p7 Ja 29 '40
New Yorker 14:12 N 26 '38
Newsweek 11:22 Ja 31 '38; 15:36-7 F 5 '40 por
Time 35:56 F 5 '40 por

Streyckmans, F. B. Today's Young Men p99-100 1940

Thompson, O. ed. International Cyclopedia of Music and Musicians 1939
Wier, A. E. ed. Macmillan Encyclopedia of Music and Musicians 1938

LENROOT, KATHARINE FREDRICA

Mar 8, 1891- Chief of the Children's Bureau

Address: b. Children's Bureau, United States Department of Labor, Washington, D. C.; h. The Kennedy-Warren, Washington, D. C.

In 1911 a blond-haired girl who was still a Junior at the University of Wisconsin appeared before the legislature in Madison to speak for a minimum-wage law. Armed with statistics, she sought legal protection for the workers of the state. Today that same woman, Katharine Lenroot, as chief of the Children's Bureau of the Department of Labor, is interpreting those provisions in the Fair Labor Standards (Wages and Hours) Act which apply to children.

The law forbids, as a general rule, the employment of children under 16. However, it confers upon the chief of the bureau authority to permit youngsters of 14 and 15 to work in an occupation which will not interfere with their health or education. It likewise gives the head of the bureau the right to decide which occupations are so dangerous that boys and girls under 18 may not be employed in them. Miss Lenroot's decisions are not only important for the welfare of the children involved but have an economic effect upon the industries in which children have been employed.

Born in Superior, Wisconsin, Miss Lenroot has been interested in progressive welfare movements and social problems since she was a little girl. She accompanied her father, Judge Irvine Luther Lenroot, Republican member of the House of Representatives and of the Senate, to Washington for a year and observed the workings of the government. Her mother was Clara Pamelia Clough of Superior.

Miss Lenroot was graduated from the Superior State Normal School in 1909 and then studied under Dr. John R. Commons, sociologist and labor legislation authority at the University of Wisconsin. She received her B. A. in 1912 and an honorary LL. D. in 1938.

In 1913 Miss Lenroot was appointed, as a result of a state civil service examination and not through the influence of her father, woman deputy of the Industrial Commission of Wisconsin. It paid $1,200 a year. She made cost-of-living investigations in Milwaukee, preparatory to the development of plans for administrating the newly enacted minimum-wage law for which she had fought while a student. She resigned in December 1914 to accept a position as special agent in the newly created United States Children's Bureau for which she had qualified again through civil service examination.

Blackstone

KATHARINE F. LENROOT

In the summer of 1915 she attended the New York School of Social Work, then was assigned to the Social Service Division of the Children's Bureau. She served as assistant director until June 1921, making studies concerning provision for dependent children and methods of juvenile court administration.

In 1921 Miss Lenroot was appointed director of the Editorial Division, a position which she administered until November 1922, when she was promoted to the rank of assistant chief. After 20 years of tracking the footsteps of Grace Abbott, second chief of the Children's Bureau, she grew big enough to step into Miss Abbott's shoes. She was appointed by President Roosevelt in 1934. Of the appointment the *Journal of Home Economics* wrote: "She has a thorough understanding of the aims and needs [of the bureau] and of its relation to other organizations and workers, governmental and private, who are concerned with similar social welfare problems. That she has the confidence of social workers is shown by the fact that they have made her president of the National Conference of Social Work (1935)."

Five years after the Bureau was created, Miss Lathrop, the first chief, proposed a public program for maternity and infancy. The program suggested was based on Federal and State cooperation. Three years later it was put into effect. Between 1921 and 1929 a beginning was made in direct Federal cooperation with the State and in Federal aid for mothers and babies. Now we have the Social Security Act and the Fair Labor Standards Act.

From its inception the Bureau has served as a clearing house for information. It gathers all possible data on child health not only in this country but throughout the world. And the Bureau does not stop at investigating and reporting. It also plays a part in the administration of the maternal and child welfare provisions of the Social Security Act, and, under the direction of a physician, it works in cooperation with the states in allotting financial assistance for study and services for improving the health of mothers and children, for the medical care of crippled children, for the public health nursing units and for assisting communities in regular child welfare activities.

Miss Lenroot is "probably the most valiant fighter" in the battle for the Child Labor Amendment, proposing that Congress shall have the power to limit, regulate and prohibit the labor of persons under 18 years of age. The bill passed the House and Senate in 1924 and since has been ratified by 28 of the 36 states necessary to make it a law.

In 1937 and 1938 she served as a member of the Advisory Committee on Education appointed by the President to review Federal relations to State and local conduct of education, was research secretary of the Delinquency Committee of Child Health and Protection and in 1940 was executive secretary of the White House Conference on Children in Democracy. Miss Lenroot lapped up a Spanish grammar in order more ably to represent her department at three Pan-American Child Congresses. She was chairman of the United States delegations to the Cuba (1927) and Peru (1930) meetings.

Miss Lenroot is a member of the board of directors of the American Public Welfare Association and a fellow of the Child Hygiene Section of the American Public Health Association. She is also a member of the Technical Advisory Committee on a National Relief Policy of the National Resources Planning Board and of the Council of the International American Institute for the Protection of Childhood (which has headquarters in Montevideo, Uruguay), and she represents the United States on the Advisory Committee on Social Questions of the League of Nations.

In addition to supervising the many publications of the Children's Bureau, Miss Lenroot contributes to many magazines articles on child care in this country and South America.

There is an air of the school teacher about her, likewise a suggestion of the social worker, but she possesses one trait which distinguishes her from the serious-minded with whom she works. She has a sense of humor which even serious subjects cannot down. She smiles often as she talks, her laugh is infectious, her voice low and musical. Her wide-set blue eyes and her round face—that still dimples—betray her Scandinavian ancestry. Streaks of white show in her wavy golden hair, which she wears parted on one side. She is a comfortable-looking person, kindly, almost matronly.

Although dealing with dry statistics for years had made an impression upon her, she "has not lost her sense of the ills which afflict the children of the world." "The progress of the bureau, its tradition of concern for the whole child," she says, "is in her bloodstream."

References

Am Mag 119:61 Ap '35 por
Good H 102:39 Ja '36 por
J Home Econ 27:101-2 F '35
Lit Digest 118:10 D 15 '34 por
N Y Times VI p6 Ap 18 '37 por;
   VIII p11 Ja 16 '38 por; VII p10
   Ja 15 '39 por
Parents' Mag 10:36 Ja '35 por; 15:34
   N '40 por
Scholastic 25:22 Ja 5 '33 por
American Women
Who's Who in America
Who's Who in the Nation's Capital

LESSING, BRUNO, pseud. of RUDOLPH BLOCK Dec 6, 1870—Apr 29, 1940 Newspaper columnist; inaugurated his widely syndicated column—"Vagabondia" in 1928; famous for his collection of 1,400 walking sticks

References

Who's Who in America
Who's Who in American Jewry

Obituaries

N Y Times p21 Ap 30 '40 por
N Y World-Telegram p24 Ap 29 '40

LEVANT, OSCAR Dec 27, 1906- Pianist; composer; conductor; radio wit
Address: h. St. Hubert Hotel, New York City

Thousands of people would never recognize the name Oscar Levant if it hadn't been for a hot summer day in 1938. Nobody was in town and the producer of the New York radio program, *Information, Please,* needed a fourth performer. He remembered an amusing and musically inclined young man named Levant and he invited him to join. So, quite by accident, radio listeners became acquainted with the uncanny musical knowledge of a young man who has been a legend to his friends. S. N. Behrman, the dramatist, feelingly observes that if Levant "did not exist," he "could not be imagined."

Oscar Levant was born in Pittsburgh, the son of Max and Annie Levant. His father is dead but his mother is living. A brother and an uncle are also musicians, so it was natural that the boy when he had to leave high school at fifteen to earn his living should choose music for a profession. He came to New York in 1922 determined to take the metropolis by storm, but cannily decided to use the piano as a means of earning a living. While he was playing for young ladies' ballet classes he studied piano with

Eric Schaal

OSCAR LEVANT

the noted Sigismund Stojowski and even once performed for Paderewski. Later he developed a more popular technique and learned to play anything "from the accompaniment to a violin cadenza at a ladies' luncheon to hot jazz tunes in hideaways" off Broadway. In 1928 he became an actor in *Burlesque,* in which he played the piano in a speakeasy scene. When the play was made into a motion picture, Oscar went along to Hollywood. There for a time he says he was "Twentieth Century-Fox's private WPA." In reality, though, he became an assistant to a producer of Westerns, a composer of film and popular music and a student of the ultra-modern composer, Arnold Schönberg.

Oscar has been called a musical dilettante, but his works refute that accusation. "In the space of a year and a half," notes Sidney Carroll, "he composed two string quartets, a piano concerto, a nocturne for symphony orchestra, music for two films, some smaller piano pieces, and a handful of popular songs. Such production is not the mark of a poseur. And when he feels like it, Levant can compose popular ditties with the best of them. . . Even among musicians, Levant is considered an important musician." He has been soloist with symphony orchestras in many cities; composer of musical comedies for Fred Stone; radio concert artist; and music composer and conductor for *The American Way* in 1939.

He also became an actor in 1940 when he played a part modeled after Oscar Levant in a picture called *Rhythm on the River,* which starred Bing Crosby and Mary Martin.

"Oscar is not on the handsome side," comments a critic, "but his physiognomy may explain the source of a great deal of his glibness. 'When I first meet somebody,' Oscar says, 'I have to destroy that

LEVANT, OSCAR—*Continued*

first impression.' He is medium tall, husky and dark. He has black hair, large eyes and a large mouth. He is known for his carelessness of dress. Lately he has been straightening his tie and he often combs his hair."

His living habits merit attention and in some respects may explain his character. After a round of New York night spots which begins regularly at Lindy's, Broadway restaurant patronized by music and theatre crowds, and includes the Stork Club, rendezvous of café society, Oscar retires regularly at 5 a. m. He does not drink, and relies on his own acidulous comments for stimulation. In order to get to sleep at that queer bedtime he resorts to sleeping tablets. Arising next midafternoon, he is so befogged by the tablets that he starts his incessant chain cigarette smoking and coffee drinking. It is said that rarely does a day go by that doesn't see Oscar imbibe from 20 to 30 cups. Trying to go to sleep again after that intake, he must resort to sleeping tablets. This routine, explains Oscar, is a regular one, for he likes to lead a regular life.

In spite of so bizarre a routine he manages to work intensively. He can practice a piano concerto while dictating letters and listening to a radio broadcast of a big league baseball game. Baseball, by the way, is his passion. He hoped as a boy to play professionally. Country life, sunshine and cozy apartment living he dislikes intensely. He lives in a hotel, the St. Hubert, on 57th Street, New York. On December 1, 1939, at Fredericksburg, Virginia, he married June Gale, Hollywood cinema actress and in October 1940 a daughter was born to them. Previously he was divorced in 1933 from Barbara Smith, musical comedy actress.

The numerous listeners to *Information, Please* are frequently amazed when he identifies a symphony after hearing a few bars, or unravels a tangled phrase of music and places it as part of a Broadway musical. In his book, *A Smattering of Ignorance,* published by Doubleday, Doran (1940), Levant hastens to dispel illusions about his fabulous musical knowledge. He speaks of "a widespread misconception" that he is "infallible in musical knowledge." That misconception, he adds, "flourishes exclusively among people largely ignorant of music. Most persons professionally engaged in music, who have been reared in a musical atmosphere, would qualify as well to answer the average questions that are asked. The questions, generally speaking, are taxing only to a layman's knowledge of music, not a musician's." Such acutely self-deprecatory words are open to question.

Levant is a strange mixture of impudence and artistic integrity. His book, filled with malicious anecdotes, some new, some bearded, while amazingly readable, is a bit of a disappointment. His is the type of brilliant wit which is wonderful around a dinner table but somehow, like a freshly baked cake exposed to a rush of air, seems to fall a bit when encased in the confines of a book. While it is a first attempt and should not be too harshly criticized, the style, instead of being colloquial, is stiff, awkwardly formal and inclined to a strange use of language.

His friends claim that once the name of Levant is mentioned, it becomes necessary to discuss him for hours. S. N. Behrman speaks of "his hard-bitten integrity which, if it does not spare his friends, does not spare himself either." Once when he parked himself, a "penthouse beachcomber," on the Gershwins for a visit which went on indefinitely, he made some distasteful remark which caused Mrs. Ira Gershwin to say: "Get out of this house." Levant, in the midst of buttoning his jacket, stopped, sat down and said, "I'm not going." "Why not?" she asked. "Because I have no place to go," replied Levant and, comfortably sitting down, he stayed another two years.

At one time in New York he received a wire from Harpo Marx in Hollywood asking him to come and promising to pay half his fare. "Fine," wired Levant, "I'll go to Kansas City." He went, however, and as a joke refused to say a word to his host for four months while eating breakfast, lunch and dinner with him.

The number of enemies his book will make for him leads one critic to call him a "Broadway James McNeill Whistler." Of Stokowski Levant says: "I would like to have been present, if I could have my choice of all moments in musical history, when Stokowski suddenly became conscious of his beautiful hands. *That* must have been a moment." Of Serge Koussevitzky (see sketch this issue): "He is unparalleled in the performance of Russian music, whether it is by Moussorgsky, Rimsky-Korsakoff, Strauss, Wagner or Aaron Copland." Of Toscanini: "Many orchestral players consider him cruel, inflexible and even petty. He would have done more for American music had he played none at all."

Levant is passionately in earnest when he speaks of music. He gives American music and American composers their due. His good friend George Gershwin was treasured as an artist.

What makes Oscar mad is that the public wants everything from him but the accomplishment which he cares about the most. "Yeah," he roared at his editor, "movies, radio, Broadway, popular songs—and now books! You guys want me to do everything but my own racket. Do you know what I am?" he wailed. "I'm a concert pianist and nobody'll believe me!"

References

Esquire 13:36+ Ja '40
Etude 58:316+ My '40 por
Harper 179:527-35 O '39; 179:589-91 N '39
Life 8:55-7 F 5 '40 il por
N Y Times VI p12 Ja 21 '40

New Yorker 15:61-62 Ja 13 '40
Pub W 137:883-5 F 24 '40 por
Time 35:36 Ja 15 '40 por
Thompson, O. ed. International Cyclo-
pedia of Music and Musicians 1939
Variety Radio Directory
Who's Who in America
Wier, A. E. ed. Macmillan Encyclo-
pedia of Music and Musicians 1938

**LEVENE, PHOEBUS AARON THEO-
DORE**   Feb 25, 1869—Sept 6, 1940 Internationally noted biochemist; member of
the Rockefeller Institute for Medical Research from 1905 to 1939; authority on
foods, nutrition, vitamins and enzymes;
contributed nearly 500 original papers to
the literature of science; received the Willard Gibbs Medal of the American Chemical
Society in 1931 and its William H. Nichols
Medal in 1938

PHOEBUS A. T. LEVENE

References

Sci ns 86:464 N 19 '37

American Men of Science
Chemical Who's Who
Who's Who in America
Who's Who in American Jewry

Obituaries

N Y Herald Tribune p10 S 7 '40 por
N Y Times p15 S 7 '40

LEVIN, MEYER   (lĕ-vĭn' mī-yer)   Oct 8,
1905-   Author

Address: b. c/o Viking Press, Inc, 18 E 48th
St, New York City; h. 264 S Vendome St,
Los Angeles, California

Free-lance writer, reporter, editor, actor,
theatrical producer, worker with marionettes

—these are careers in the background of
Meyer Levin, outstanding among the
younger American novelists. Most of his
novels, particularly the later ones, deal with
some strong aspect of the social scene;
their setting is Chicago, where Mr. Levin
was born and grew up.

Meyer Levin's latest novel, *Citizens*
(March 1940), is a story based on the Memorial Day picketing during the 1937 steel
strikes in Chicago, when 10 men were killed.
Because it combines factual historical record
with the human details of real lives, and
because it tries to analyze the underlying
causes of industrial conflict in our social
structure, *Citizens* is an unusually well-
rounded and effective work.

Much of the material of *Citizens* is taken
from the report of the La Follette Civil
Liberties Committee. Evidently Mr. Levin,
who knows Chicago well, was an eyewitness,
too, of the scenes he describes so vividly in
Citizens. An article written for *The Nation*
(June 12, 1937) called *Slaughter in Chicago,*
is a graphic, firsthand account of Memorial
Day 1937, outside the Republic Company
steel plant of Chicago.

Meyer Levin, the son of Joseph Levin, was
born in Chicago October 8, 1905. In 1921 he
entered the University of Chicago; during
his freshman year he edited the *Chicago High
School News*, and during his last two years
there he worked on the Chicago *Daily News*
under the late Henry Justin Smith. He was
graduated from the University in 1924, in the
same class as John Günther; Vincent Sheean
had been graduated a year or two before.
Levin went to Europe for about a year. His
next few years in the United States were "a
jumble of trying to earn money so I could
have time to write, working for the *News*
again, working as a press agent, writing a
column, going to Palestine and working
with the pioneers, stopping to write a
book. . ." He became a special writer for
the Jewish Telegraphic Agency in 1931;
from 1933 to 1939 he was successively
reader and editorial assistant on *Esquire,
Coronet* and *Ken* magazines.

Levin married Mabel Schamp Foy on
February 19, 1935. They have one child,
Eli Jonathan.

Though he wrote two short novels preceding it, the novel *Yehuda* (1931) first made
Meyer Levin known. Written from firsthand experience, it was a story dealing with
life in an agricultural commune in Palestine—the first novel of modern Palestinian
life to appear in English. In 1932 appeared
The Golden Mountain, a book of Chassidic
legends centering around the wonder-working Rabbi Israel Baal Shem Tov (Master
of the Name) and his followers. This volume opened the way for several studies of
this sect. *New Bridge* (1933) was a vivid
story of an evicted family, and *The Old Bunch*
(1937) a deftly drawn social study of a
group of Chicago Jewish boys and girls
who leave high school and start on their
various careers.

MEYER LEVIN

Besides his writing, Mr. Levin has always been interested in photography, the theatre, and marionette theatre production. He taught marionette production at the New School for Social Research, New York City, from 1931 to 1932. He presented *The Hairy Ape, The Crock of Gold, From Morn to Midnight*, and other plays with marionettes. He writes: "Although the author of several novels and numerous short stories, often find myself better known for my work with marionettes, which extended over several years, even after I had begun to publish novels; and also for my work as *The Candid Cameraman*, a motion picture criticism department in *Esquire*."

Levin has also been strongly interested in the acting side of the theatre, and appeared behind the footlights on Broadway in *If I Were You* and *Counsellor-at-Law*. Though his acting career was ended by acute appendicitis, he became director of the summer experimental theatre in Brookfield Center, Connecticut in 1932.

References

Nation 144:670-1 Je 12 '37
N Y Herald Tribune Books p4 Mr 24 '40
N Y Times Book R p2 Mr 31 '40
New Yorker 16:73 Mr 30 '40
Read Digest 29:101-2 D '36
Sat R Lit 15:1 Mr 13 '37 por
Scholastic 32:4 Ap 23 '38 por
Who's Who in American Jewry

LEWIS, ALBERT BUELL June 21, 1867 —Oct 10, 1940 Anthropologist; former teacher of anthropology at the Universities of Chicago and Nebraska; in 1908 became assistant curator of Melanesian ethnology for the Field Museum in Chicago and in

1937 curator; went on expeditions to Fiji, New Caledonia, the Admiralty Islands and elsewhere

References

American Men of Science
Who's Who in America

ALBERT BUELL LEWIS

Obituaries

N Y Times p21 O 11 '40

LEWIS, CECIL DAY- *See* Day-Lewis, C.

LEWIS, FRANCIS PARK May 19, 1855 —Sept 10, 1940 Internationally known oculist; president of the New York State School for the Blind at Batavia; founder and vice-president of the National Society for the Prevention of Blindness; promoted international use of silver salt solution to save eyes of babies; received the Leslie Dana Medal in 1928 for "outstanding achievement in the prevention of blindness and the conservation of vision"; in 1929 founded the International Association for the Prevention of Blindness

References

Directory of Medical Specialists 1939
Who's Who in America

Obituaries

N Y Herald Tribune p26 S 11 '40 por
N Y Times p25 S 11 '40 por

LEWIS, MARY Jan 28, 1897- Fashion director of the 1940 New York World's Fair

Address: b. 647 Fifth Ave, New York City

Success stories on the career of Mary Lewis usually have stressed two facts—that she has a Dresden doll-like, blonde prettiness and that income tax lists of 1937 and 1938 gave her salary for those years respectively at $56,527 and $54,622. Apparently it made a strong impression on interviewers that a self-made woman, who started working at $9 a week and became one of the best-known and highest paid women in retail merchandising and advertising, had not lost any feminine attractiveness on the way.

Mary Lewis does things quietly and efficiently and without a blatant executive air. In the spring of 1940 when she was preparing to open her own shop and at the same time to take over the duties of fashion director of the New York World's Fair, probably two of the most important steps in her business career, she went about her work with unruffled efficiency. She said, "I get to the office at 9, work until 6 and then forget about it at night."

Miss Lewis has had long training at getting jobs done. She was born in Louisville, Kentucky, the daughter of Henry and Mary (Hicks) Lewis. She came to New York at the age of 13 with her widowed mother. Mrs. Lewis was employed as a stenographer in a bank and later as a lawyer's secretary, and little Mary had to begin working at an early age. After her graduation from the Wadleigh High School she got a job in an interior decorator's shop—without pay. She decided to seek her fortune at Macy's and wrote a letter asking for a job. She got one at $9 a week, first in the basement upholstery department and later designing "occasional" furniture. This was in 1917.

She was promoted to $18 a week and a job writing copy in the advertising department, where she worked with an old school acquaintance, Estelle Hamburger, who had been instrumental in getting her into the department. Miss Lewis made a hit with the first advertisement she wrote for Macy's by slugging a miscellaneous lot of merchandise for which she could find no other heading: "Made in America." In 1918 "Made in America" was a popular thing to say.

Women's Wear Daily, Bible of the retail trade, had hailed the "Made in America" advertisement as a stroke of Macy genius, and Mary Lewis' upward climb began. The First World War found her working far into the night as enlistments depleted the staff. Her salary rose to $35 a week and then in one step to $45. But declaring the $10 raise an undervaluation, she left in a huff and in October 1919 got a job at Best and Company, Fifth Avenue women's wear shop, as a copywriter at $65 a week.

By 1930 she had risen to the position of vice-president at Best's. Her fashion innovations became as well-known as her promotional exploits. Ideas that have been credited to Miss Lewis include the shirtwaist dress, the dirndl, the denim suit, the fireman shirt, the Dutch girl dress and

G. Maillard Kesslère

MARY LEWIS

the resurrection of cotton as a fashionable dress fabric. One of her better known promotional stunts was the two girls who looked like twins but were unrelated and who went about to fashionable resorts wearing Best's clothes and incidentally popularizing Best's styles.

Miss Lewis remained with Best and Company for 19 years. She left in April 1938, and six months afterward joined Saks Fifth Avenue as vice-president in charge of promotion. She resigned from Saks in December of 1939 and a few months later had opened her own shop.

In addition to running her retail shop she is fashion consultant to several large stores throughout the country, among them Sears, Roebuck and Company. Clothes she sells in her second floor Fifth Avenue shop may also be sold through a syndicate arrangement throughout the country. The year she became her own boss Miss Lewis also stepped into the limelight as the director of the Fashion Building at the New York World's Fair. As an added attraction in its second year the Fair was beginning a series of novel fashion shows offering the first coordinated display of fashion interest —from basic materials to the finished product. These shows were a huge success and gave the Fair columns of publicity.

Although her entire career has been identified with fashion Miss Lewis calls herself not a designer but an "editor" of clothes. She says she merely tells manufacturers what she wants and how she wants it made. She prefers the fundamentally classic styles, although many of her novel fashions have swept the country. And, unlike many successful fashion executives, she believes a woman is not smart in ratio to what she pays for her clothes but that good taste is possible at any price.

LEWIS, MARY—*Continued*

Career-woman Mary Lewis' personal life has received little publicity. She was married from 1920 to 1937 to Arthur Finley, a commercial artist. Discussing the question of a career versus marriage with an interviewer, Miss Lewis was quoted as saying (and this was after the breakup of her own marriage) that she would "chuck the whole business of a career to be a wife."

Despite her topflight position as a business executive Miss Lewis apparently does not take herself too seriously. *Life* magazine in July 1940, in an illustrated story of her career, showed her taking exercises in shorts (she has an hour's daily workout in a Fifth Avenue salon), showed her barefooted in a housecoat, and photographed her in a gay mood at her Cold Spring, New York home where she spends week ends with her mother and stepfather.

References

Fortune 18:130 N '38 por
Life 9:43-5 Jl 22 '40 il pors
Mlle 11:123 My '40 por
N Y Post p9 F 7 '40 por; p16 Mr 30 '40 por
N Y Sun p11 Ag 12 '40 por
N Y Times p9 F 6 '40; p23 F 7 '40
American Women
Hamburger, E. It's a Woman's Business 1939

LEY, ROBERT (li) Feb 15, 1890- Head of the German Labor Front

Address: Berlin W 57, Potsdamerstr. 75, Germany

Dr. Robert Ley, head of the German Labor Front, has become more and more "the spokesman of German doctrine, the utterer of slogans, the salesman of ideas." He it is who delivers the stirring pronouncements on the War. War, itself, says he, is "a blessing of God, the eternal fount from which new generations of men are born"; it is "the expression of the highest and best in manhood." And this War against Britain is intended to bring Europe and the whole world "to their senses."

Now when Germany wants to bring its people to a full appreciation of this War Ley sings out about the War. Before, when the party wanted discipline, he ranted against nicotine, alcohol and debauchery (even though he himself has been known to indulge too generously on "Strength through Joy" outings). When Germany needed man power he lectured the Many Children League on the "natural, healthy" phenomenon of illegitimacy. When vilification of Britain was in order he branded the enemy "a rich parvenue wishing to play world policeman" and insisted that "a German laborer is worth more than an English lord."

In his ability to incite and to entertain Ley has "combined the talents of Billy Sunday and Billy Rose" (see sketch this issue). It was he who staged the vast Nürnberg Party rallies each year, and he who created in November 1933 the "Strength Through Joy" organization which "mass-produced recreation, playgrounds, loyalty—all convertible for war uses." Apart from Hitler himself, "Ley probably has more influence on the morale of the masses in Germany than any other one person."

This leader of the Nazi Party was born in Niederbreitenbach, Germany, the son of Ludwig Ley, a farmer. From an early age he was interested in chemistry and studied the chemistry of foodstuffs at the Universities of Jena, Bonn and Münster, from which he received his Ph. D. From school he went right into the First World War as a pilot and almost lost his leg from a severe wound; from 1917 to 1920 he was a prisoner of war in France. Back in Germany he became a chemist in the dye industry and stayed in a factory in Leverkusen until 1928.

Ley entered the Nazi Party early—in 1924, after reading an account of Hitler's trial after the abortive Munich *Putsch*. Himself a fanatical anti-Semite and Nationalist who had already been building an independent organization along Hitler's lines, he was appointed to a leading position almost immediately. Up and down his native Rhineland he went, haranguing all who would listen. In 1925 he was made head of the party district for the Rhineland. He founded, wrote, proofread and edited two newspapers, one of which has been described as "the wildest, maddest anti-Semitic publication which ever made use of the German language." But he believed that National Socialist ideas could be put over even better "by the fist and the beer mug" than by intellectual weapons, and innumerable times was imprisoned for his violent acts.

Both the frays in which he took part and his unbridled attacks against Jewish businessmen and financiers brought him special distinction in the Nazi movement, however, and in 1928 he became a National Socialist deputy. In April 1931 he was transferred to party headquarters at Munich, made leader of the chaotic organization there, and proceeded to compile the first service rules for the political organization of the party—perhaps his greatest contribution to National Socialism. The next year, after the resignation of Strasser, he was made head of the whole party organization—a position which he still holds. In March 1933 Ley became a member of the Prussian State Council and on May 5, 1933, Hitler further rewarded his unswerving loyalty with the job of liquidating the free trade unions and a position as head of the Labor Front.

"Brutally and ruthlessly," as Hitler had told him to, Ley occupied union premises, seized their property and arrested their leaders All union members, except Jews, were told that they were automatically

ROBERT LEY

members of his Labor Front; the only other choice was starvation or a concentration camp. A month later, when Ley entered the great hall in Geneva to take part in a session of the International Labor Conference, a fierce cry went up: "Jailer of the German Workers!" It marked the end of participation in the work of the International Labor Office both for Ley and for Germany.

Under his governing hand, however, the Labor Front grew until it now includes 95 per cent of all gainfully employed persons in Germany, a total of between 25,000,000 and 30,000,000 human beings. What is more, "it was Dr. Ley who supported with all his energies the plans of Hitler, Goering and Schacht for combatting unemployment by introducing general conscription in Germany, and switching German industry completely over to armaments."

Abroad, and perhaps even in Germany, Ley's reputation is none too good. He has been in the police courts several times, once for wrecking a beer hall in Cologne and once for assault. He is considered the greatest toper in the party, said to have been in insane asylums off and on. He is married, and his home is a luxurious villa in Berlin that once belonged to a Rhineland industrialist, but it is said that in the evening he finds a tavern more to his liking.

References

N Y Herald Tribune p8 My 15 '40 por
N Y Times p3 Mr 28 '40
Sat Eve Post 123:14-15+ Jl 27 '40 pors
Time 35:17-18 Ja 1 '40 por
Dutch, O., pseud. Dr. Robert Ley, the Jailer of the German Working Classes *In* Hitler's 12 Apostles p123-38 1940

Gunther, J. Two Radicals *In* Inside Europe p77-8 1940
International Who's Who
Wer ist's?

LICHTENBERGER, ANDRE (lĭkh'tn-bĕrkh'er) 1870—Mar 25, 1940 French writer on social problems and books for children; known in the United States for the book *Mon Petit Trott;* received French Academy Award in 1900; served as aide to the Military Governor of Paris during the First World War

References

International Who's Who

Obituaries

N Y Times p21 Mr 26 '40
N Y World-Telegram p30 Mr 26 '40

LIDDELL HART, BASIL HENRY (lĭd'el) Oct 31, 1895- Author

Written before the outbreak of War in September 1939, the defensive theory expounded in Captain Liddell Hart's latest book, *The Defence of Britain*, was "among the many things which died on the morning of May 10, 1940." Until then Captain Liddel Hart's authority as a military strategist, and his known influence upon recent British policy, gave weight to his analysis of strategy and his ideas concerning the future rôle of Britain's army. The first part of the book presented his basic theory: that since Britain could not attack others save by the process of economic strangulation, she must be made secure through defense. Thus land participation must be limited, with sea and air effort stressed. The analyst further discussed England's "forward positions"— France, the Low Countries, and Switzerland. A final section of the book was devoted to the reorganization of the British Army. Captain Liddell Hart believed that if England made the most of a defensive position, Germany would be defeated in the present struggle just as in 1918.

Allied practice in the first months of the War followed his theory closely, and as late as March 1940 Captain Liddell Hart had not changed his mind about the inadvisability of a spring offensive by the Allies, nor about the dangers to Germany if she attempted such an offensive. But with the Nazi invasion of the Low Countries Britain began to wonder if actually the best defense was not offense.

Still, there seems to be a good deal of justice in Liddell Hart's claim that the policy of a waiting war would have worked if it had been consistently practiced as he expounded it. It wasn't.

Basil Henry Liddell Hart was born October 5, 1895. He was sent to St. Paul's in London, and as a small boy had a more-than-average fondness for tales about military and naval heroes. "Waterloo" and

Pictures, Inc.

BASIL LIDDELL HART

"Wellington" were so strangely but mystically fused in his own imagination that the broad expanse of rails at Waterloo became the battlesite itself and he could see Wellington riding up and down his line.

The World War cut into his university days at Corpus Christi College, Cambridge. He was twice wounded during a long service (1914-18); was placed on half-pay status in 1924; and retired in 1927. In those years of fighting he saw not only real but "artificial" history in the process of manufacture: too often the "record" was all-hallowed, the actualities negligible. He recalls how Field-Marshal Haig once contended that the poor physique of his prisoners was proof of the excellence of his offensive, and then immediately phoned advance instructions that all able-bodied prisoners be removed from the corps cages before his arrival with the Prime Minister.

By 1926 Liddell Hart had established a real reputation as a military strategist and on request made official visits to the training centers of the French, and later the Italian, Armies. From 1925 to 1935 he was Military Correspondent of the London *Daily Telegraph;* more recently he was with the London *Times,* but a nervous breakdown forced his retirement to the West of England after a disagreement with the *Times* on questions of policy. Since then he has been writing for a number of English journals.

With *A Greater Than Napoleon: Scipio Africanus* (1926), the only English forerunner of which was an 1817 book by a country clergyman, he made a serious plunge into military biography. He was particularly interested in illuminating Scipio's remarkable understanding of the interplay of economic, military and political forces. In the two years following came *Great Captains Unveiled*

and *Reputations—Ten Years After.* The second of these was a combination of personal estimate and official military record. A year after *The Real War* (later expanded into *A History of the World War*) came a full-length profile of *Foch—The Man of Orleans.* T. E. Lawrence, his much admired friend, said of it: "You demolish him thoroughly as a soldier; as a politician he needed no other evidence than his own to discredit him. But as a human being he came out well and honorably in what you wrote."

As early as October 1929 Liddell Hart had been approached with the task of placing the Arab Revolt, and T. E. Lawrence's part in it, in proper historical perspective. The book finally emerged as *T. E. Lawrence—In Arabia and After.* Lawrence himself once credited Liddell Hart with being "one of the few Englishmen who can see the allusions and quotations, the conscious analogies, in all I say and do, militarily."

In May 1937, at the suggestion of Sir Thomas Inskip, Minister for the Co-ordination of Defence, Captain Liddell Hart began the preparation of a paper on the reorganization of the Army, recommending four anti-aircraft divisions of the existing scale and a doubling of the number of guns. Not until the German invasion of Austria the following March did it find any favor with the general staff. At the risk of becoming a "private nuisance" in the eyes of Mr. Hore-Belisha, he suggested a number of advantageous changes in official jurisdictions. By midsummer 1939 an amazing number of his reforms had been achieved, and all of them were embodied in his national and imperial approaches to *The Defence of Britain.*

Captain Liddell Hart was married, in 1918, to Jessie Stone, by whom he had one son, Adrian John.

His literary domain extends, obviously, well beyond field strategies, and he has actively supported the Association of Writers for Intellectual Liberty. His achievements as both historian and authority on the art of warfare did much to break down a part of T. E. Lawrence's pessimistic observation that because the creative mind is seldom allowed a hand in the actual building of a military structure the evolution of military science still remains no more than a "swing of the pendulum."

References

New Repub 102:714 My 27 '40
Sat R Lit 20:5 O 14 '39 por
Time 35:30 Mr 18 '40
Who's Who

LIE, JONAS (lē yō-nas) Apr 29, 1880—Jan 10, 1940 American artist; former president of the National Academy

Jonas Lie, well-known artist and pioneer in the revolt against conservative policies of the National Academy, died on January 10, 1940, in New York, at the age of 59. Mr Lie, who came to this country when he was

JONAS LIE

13, was born in Moss, Norway, the son of
Sverre and Helen Augusta (Steele) Lie.
His mother was an American and had lived
in Connecticut before she went to Norway,
and his father was a native of Norway.

Soon after the family moved to this
country, the father died and young Lie went
to work as a designer in a cotton factory to
support his mother and sisters. He submitted a painting to the National Academy,
then called the National Academy of Design,
and it was accepted. During the years he
achieved fame as a painter of landscapes
and marine scenes. His work has been
bought by the great museums of the world.
He was married twice, first to Charlotte
E. Nissen, and after a divorce in 1916, to
Inga Sontum, a Norwegian dancer. She died
in 1925 and one daughter, Sonja, survives.

In 1919 Lie led a small group of "moderns," including George Bellows, Paul Manship (see sketch this issue) and Joseph Pennell, in revolt against the conservative leadership of the National Academy, and succeeded
in deleting Design from its name and modernizing its principles. From 1934 to 1939
he was president of the Academy. In his
later years radical painters called him a reactionary, and he became the center of many
bitter disputes.

References

Art Digest 8:14 Ap 1 '34; 13:7 Jl '39;
    14:13 O 15 '39
Arts & Dec 43:27 O '35 por; 49:8-9+
    D '38 pors
Boswell, P. Jr. Modern American
    Painting 1939
New Standard Encyclopedia of Art
    1939
Who's Who in America 1938-39

Obituaries

N Y Herald Tribune p18 Ja 11 '40;
    Ja 13 '40; p30 Ja 14 '40
N Y Times p17l Ja 12 '40; p43l Ja 14
    '40
Newsweek 15:41 Ja 22 '40
Time 35:75 Ja 22 '40

LILLARD, GEORGE W. (lĭl-ard) 1884—
Oct 24, 1940 Founder of the Hartford College of Law (1921) which was joined with
the Hartford College of Insurance in 1939;
former member of the Department of Justice and headed staff of FBI agents in Connecticut during the First World War; in life
claims department of Travelers Insurance
Company from 1919 to 1935, when he left to
devote full time to the law college

Obituaries

N Y Times p21 O 25 '40

LIN YU-T'ANG Oct 10, 1895- (lĭn yü'-
täng') Author; philosopher
Address: b. c/o Reynal & Hitchcock, Inc, 386
Fourth Ave, New York City; h. 2393 Castilian
Dr, Los Angeles, California

In October 1940 Dr. Lin Yutang (his
books use this spelling instead of the Library of Congress form above) returned to
the United States from a trip to China insisting that "China can never be conquered
by the Japanese—even if China gets none
of the help to which she is entitled from
the democracies." What Dr. Lin says
carried weight, since for many years this
brilliant young Chinese philosopher has
lectured and written in the United States.
Among his best known books are My Country and My People (1936); The Importance of
Living (1937); Moment in Peking (1939); and
With Love and Irony (1940), his latest. This
collection of 50 essays, sketches and satires
has been praised for "the sparkling, thrust-
ing quality of his thought." The subjects
of his lectures and books are varied: the
importance of living—and loafing, China
and the War, Chinese national traits, and
curious American customs.

Lin Yutang was born in Changchow,
Fukien Province, China. His father was a
pastor in the American Reformed Church
Mission, a "second-generation Christian"
who loved his parishioners. In his childhood he had been a peddler of sweetmeats,
a bamboo-shoot seller, and a seller of rice at
the prisons. Lin was early associated with
peasant life and became interested in the
welfare of the masses. As a young boy he
was fascinated by machinery, had done some
inventing, and still believes he is going to
invent the best Chinese typewriter. He
was educated at mission schools and went
to St. John's College in Shanghai. He
thought for a time of taking up the ministry
but, unable to accept the doctrine of the
virgin birth and other precepts, gave it up
to become what he calls "happily a pagan."

LIN YU-T'ANG

After being graduated, Lin became a teacher of English at Tsinghua, the American Boxer Indemnity College. He married a girl who was also born in a mission family. To her he pays the highest of tributes, adding that he has always been devoted to her because she allows him to smoke in bed. With characteristic Chinese modesty, however, he does not tell us the year of their marriage. He and his wife came together to America, where he studied at Harvard for a year (1919-20). Afterward they went to Jena and Leipzig. He received an M. A. from Harvard, a Ph. D. from Leipzig, his subject being philology.

On his return to China, Dr. Lin Yutang was appointed a professor in Peking National University, 1923 to 1926. He was counted among the radical professors, and took part in many student demonstrations, where he learned to fight with bricks and poles. When his name was put on the blacklist he had to spend months in hiding. The rebellion was then stirring China, and he joined the new Wuhan government as secretary in the Ministry of Foreign Affairs. He liked revolutions, but not all revolutionaries; and he threw over politics after four months because he said he realized he was "a herbivorous, rather than a carnivorous animal, vastly better at minding my own business than that of others." Seeing through the farce of the revolution, he says he "graduated into an author, partly by inclination, and partly by necessity."

The Lins have three daughters, Adet, 16, Anor, 13, and Meimei, 9, who in 1939 wrote a book called Our Family, which threatened to rival their father's in charm and popularity. It contained shrewd and witty comments on the Lin family, and the children's impressions of the United States, Europe and China.

In My Country and My People (1936), a book giving a lively picture of what the Chinese are like today, Lin speaks of China's debt to Western civilization and discusses the country's needs and future rôle. He loves China, but he criticizes her more frankly and honestly than do any other Chinese. His History of the Press and Public Opinion in China (1937) is a monograph on the fight for freedom of the press in modern China.

The Importance of Living (1937), a Chinese philosophy for Western readers, has been described by its author as "a personal guide to enjoyment." In a style pleasingly simple yet urbane and ironic, Dr. Lin presents the philosophy of generations of Chinese sages, pointing out their wisdom for modern use. It is full of the salt and tang of daily living. A reviewer writing in the Atlantic Monthly said of it: "When a book by an Oriental has the style of a sophisticated contribution to the New Yorker, we are put at once on our guard. If this author has become so completely one of us, we ask, can he have anything to say for himself? But if the reader suspects this book he soon changes his impression. Dr. Lin has learned to talk our language as we might wish to talk it ourselves, but he has not changed his spiritual home. His insight is too subtle to be merely clever. In the midst of his colloquial banter he preaches a gospel that applies to all men, and behind his sense for the apt American word is the artist's awareness of the universal."

Lin Yutang's first novel is Moment in Peking (1939). This long chronicle of life in China begins with the Boxer Rebellion and takes us down to the epic flight of China's millions to the interior in 1938. Its story is the story of three wealthy upper middle-class Chinese families, and in it Lin Yutang has achieved "the quintessence of Chinese life." The technique, even, is Chinese rather than Western, and according to almost every critic demands slow, leisurely reading.

Clifton Fadiman says: "The book is a remarkable panorama; you must sit back in your seat and allow it to flow past your eyes. Its charm and significance inhere not in any detail or any particular episode but in the movement itself, the flow of time, the incessant flux of gesture, people, habits, architecture, interiors, relationships — all somehow loosely uniting to give one a sense of a life at once alien and beautifully familiar."

In an essay, Faith of a Cynic, published in The Nation May 6, 1939, Dr. Lin has some pertinent things to say about contemporary religion. "Stated in the simplest terms, science is but a sense of curiosity about life, religion is a sense of reverence for life, literature is a sense of wonder at life, art is a taste for life, philosophy is an attitude toward life based on a greater or lesser, but always limited, comprehension of the Universe so far as we know it."

The greatest enemy of old religions, he says, is the 200-inch telescope. And he repudiates the ideal of the perfect man for the reasonable man. We are living in a barbaric and cynical time: "International morality has never sunk so low." He is of the opinion that the only kind of religious belief left for the modern man is a kind of mysticism that consists of reverence and respect for the moral order of the universe and the effort to live in harmony with it. Dr. Lin likes to discuss democracy and fascism from the Chinese viewpoint. He believes in the ultimate triumph of democracy because dictatorship is inhuman, and "anything inhuman cannot last. To be human is the great thing in life; and to be allowed to live human, individual lives is the primary longing of every human being." The Chinese ideal is that "he governs best who governs least."

Lin Yutang likes to combine idealism and cynicism, whimsy and common sense. He loves contradictions, such as seeing safety-parade busses kill pedestrians. Once he went a long way to a temple in Western Hills near Peiping to see a eunuch's sons. He is interested in everything from atoms to pretty girls, from literature to electric dry shavers, from music to all kinds of scientific gadgets. He models clay, and for his pastime drips colored wax portraits and landscapes on glass from candles. He doesn't like the sea, possibly because he can swim only "about three yards," but adores mountains.

He doesn't go in much for sports, except walking, or lying on the ground in Central Park when the police aren't watching. "I have an abhorrence of physical effort and have never sat on a fence, nor have I turned a somersault, physical, spiritual or political." He doesn't play Mahjong, but he does like poker. As a matter of fact his favorite recreation is reading. He reads everything: politics, fiction, religion, science; Greek, Chinese or contemporary English and European writers. He likes to read the papers for scientific and medical news, but is contemptuous of statistics, and thinks all academic jargon is a way of hiding lack of understanding. He can not stand Kant; but he loves Heine and Stephen Leacock and Heywood Broun.

Socially, he has no desire to impress people. He hates a tuxedo because he says it makes him look exactly like a Chinese waiter; and he avoids having his picture published because he says he doesn't want to spoil the reader's illusion of him as a bearded grand old wise man from the East. Among the things which would make him happy he lists a nice comfortable not-very-tidy room of his own, a pair of old shoes, freedom to wear as little as he cares to, old trees in the neighborhood, a good cook, good library, good cigars, some bamboos in front of his study window. And he wants good friends, "friends who are as familiar as life itself, to whom I need not be polite, and who will tell me all their troubles, matrimonial or otherwise, who can quote Aristophanes and crack dirty jokes, friends who are spiritually rich and can talk dirt and philosophy with the same candor."

Pearl Buck, who well understands China and the Chinese, writes of Lin Yutang: "He is Chinese to the core, far more Chinese than most of his Western educated contemporaries. He is a great patriot and lover of his country and has done more than any other person to make China intelligible but likeable. But he is more than a Chinese. Any one can talk with him with complete frankness and intellectual honesty, for his is an honest intelligence. He is afraid of nothing and of no one. . . He is sophisticated and keen and knows himself. He enjoys success but he laughs at it and at himself a little, being at heart too large for petty vanity. He takes the truth without flinching and has an unshakable integrity of judgment beneath the brilliance of his talk. To a crowd which he feels is responsive he will deliver an entertainment of wit and laughter and hard hits. But if he doesn't like the crowd, he disappears into a slight, stiff, masked figure, academic and remote—and knows what he is doing and doesn't care."

References

Asia 36:743-5 N '36; 38:334-7 Je '38
40:123-5 Mr '40
Forum 97:83-8 F '37; 98:195-9 O '37
Harper 175:143-50 Jl '37
Mag Art 31:70-6+ F '38
Newsweek 10:31 D 6 '37 por
Scholastic 32:21-23E Mr 19 '38
Time 36:28 S 2 '40 por
Wilson Lib Bul 11:298 Ja '37 por
Buck, P. Lin, Yu-t'ang pam 1937
International Who's Who
Who's Who in China

LINDBERGH, ANNE SPENCER MORROW 1907- Author; aviator

Address: h. Englewood, New Jersey

When Anne Morrow was a shy English major at Smith College, contributing short stories and poems to the college paper, she wrote one poem that began:

"Everything today has been
Heavy and brown
Bring me a Unicorn
To ride about town."

It ended:

"And I will kneel each morning
To polish bright his hoofs
That they may gleam each moon-night
We ride over roofs."

There are few roofs in any country in the world that Anne Morrow has not ridden over since she became Anne Lindbergh; and her life has been both more adventurous and more tragic than if she had literally achieved her wish.

LINDBERGH, ANNE—*Continued*

She was born in Englewood, New Jersey in 1907, the daughter of the late Dwight Whitney Morrow, Morgan partner, Senator and at one time Ambassador to Mexico; and of Elizabeth Reeve (Cutler) Morrow, poet, and in 1940 acting president of Smith College and active with the Committee to Defend America by Aiding the Allies. Anne was graduated from the fashionable Miss Chapin's School in New York City and in 1923 attended Smith College, where she didn't take much part in social events but was known as "a shy girl of unusual charm and great literary ability," remembered for her "unaffected manner" and "lovely disposition."

She was graduated in 1927 with special honors, being awarded the Mary Augusta Jordan Prize for the most original piece of work and the Elizabeth Johnson Prize for the best essay on "Women of Dr. Johnson's Time." When in 1929 her engagement to America's most eligible bachelor was announced after Colonel Charles A. Lindbergh's good will flight to Mexico, where he visited the Morrow family in Mexico City, a dispatch from Northampton called her "an argument . . . for old-fashioned femininity." She was described as "a brunette, slender and graceful . . . a studious, diffident girl, said by her friends to be interested in modern literary and artistic movements, but at the same time domestic." It was surely the most publicized romance of the '20s, for the nation immediately began to consider "Anne" its property as much as "Lindy." But rumors that the engagement was a case of mistaken identity and that the famous flyer had really preferred her "more beautiful" sister could not have added to Anne Morrow's comfort in finding herself living in a spotlight.

Nevertheless on May 27, 1929 Anne and "Lindy" succeeded in getting themselves married in a ceremony at which the press was notoriously absent and in which even the guests didn't know in advance for what they were assembled. The honeymoon, too, was private until a photographer learned they were at sea and began circling around them in a motorboat. The attraction of the lost Mayan cities, whose cliff dwellings the young couple explored that same year, seems quite understandable.

Her husband had been teaching her to fly, but it was not until 1930 that Anne Lindbergh made her first solo flight. (She got her private pilot's license in 1931.) It was also in 1930 that "we three" made a transcontinental record, Anne acting as co-pilot and navigator. It was in June of that year that Charles Augustus Jr., was born.

The following year came the Lindberghs' flight across the Pacific to act as "ambassadors of American good will in the Orient." *North to the Orient*, published in 1935, tells Anne's story of this voyage from New York to Japan and China. Her friendship with the Chinese people made at this time lent earnestness to her radio plea for funds for Chinese flood relief in February 1932

In Shanghai in October 1931 the Lindberghs had been informed of Senator Morrow's death. A few months later, in March 1932, nearly every newspaper in the world carried large, black, shocked headlines telling of the kidnaping of Charles Augustus Lindbergh Jr. The discovery of the child's body in May, near the Lindberghs' New Jersey estate, did not end the glare of sympathetic but undesirable publicity, for the case was still unsolved. And when in August a second son, Jon Morrow, was born, threats against his life began to come. False arrests, false clues, false hopes about the solution of the first son's death were innumerable. There were constant rumors that the Lindberghs were about to take up residence abroad, though these were always denied.

In June 1933 the Lindberghs gave their estate as a welfare project for children, and shortly afterward made a five-months, 40,000-mile flight over five continents to survey transatlantic air routes, returning to the United States in December. For her work as co-pilot and radio operator Mrs. Lindbergh received the Cross of Honor of the United States Flag Association, in 1934 was the first woman to be presented with the Hubbard Gold Medal of the National Geographic Society, and in December 1935 was to be listed by Carrie Chapman Catt (see sketch October issue) as one of ten leading American women. *Listen! the Wind*, published in 1938, is her account of 10 days during this trip—in Santiago, an island off the African coast; in Bathurst, a British town on the African seacoast; and over the Atlantic, flying from Africa to South America.

In 1934 the government's cancellation of air-mail contracts caused the Colonel to protest to Washington, and during the investigations that followed he was called upon to testify more than once. In September of the same year a German carpenter was arrested as a suspect in the kidnapping of Charles Augustus Jr., and all through 1935 the Hauptmann case—trial, conviction, sentence, appeals—dragged on, giving the tabloids a holiday which reached ghoulish proportions. It was necessary for the Lindberghs to appear and testify many times.

Finally, however, the Lindberghs set sail for England with their three-year-old son, in December 1935, not planning to return to the United States. By this time there were few who were anything but sympathetic with their desire for privacy and protection for their child which America could not give them—including, paradoxically enough, the press itself. There was no visit to the United States again until 1937, and during the interval the Lindberghs took up residence in Kent, England, though making flying visits to France, Germany, Denmark, Ireland, Italy. During their first visit to Berlin in July 1936 the Colonel visited German flying fields for a week and made a speech on the horrors of aerial warfare which was much applauded in America as well as in Germany. In May 1937 another son, Land Morrow, was born, but the Lindberghs refused to stay put. October found them receiving an ovation at the Munich Air Congress and being entertained by Goering.

In December 1937, when the Lindberghs left their children in England and unexpectedly revisited the United States, they were once more beset with crank telephone calls and letters, threats, photographers. Upon their return to Europe in March 1938 they proceeded to find a refuge on the Island of Illiec, near Port-Blanc, France, within rowing distance of the island laboratory of Dr. Alexis Carrel (see sketch this issue), with whom Lindbergh invented the mechanical glass heart. They were also reported as frequent visitors to Lady Astor's (see sketch this issue) Cliveden estate. In August 1938 they visited Russia for the second time (Anne had written very pleasantly of her first visit in 1933); the Colonel attended a Soviet air circus, later saw certain officials in Czechoslovakia, visited Paris, saw Lady Astor in England—and soon the press was full of rumors. It was reported that he had described German air power as so strong and Soviet air power so weak that the authors of Munich were able to use his information as a justification for the partition of Czechoslovakia.

Lindbergh was widely attacked, particularly by the Soviet press, which claimed he had orders from British reactionaries to make just such a report. On the other hand there were denials that he had seen enough of Russian air strength to have given any report at all. He himself refused to comment. When in October 1938 he accepted German hospitality for the third time, however, and was presented at a banquet with the Service Cross of the Order of the German Eagle, suspicions seemed more reasonable. In November the Lindberghs were reported as thanking Goering for his hospitality and planning residence in Berlin. In December Harold Ickes criticized the Colonel publicly, his name was removed from the TWA air-line slogan, and in a small, upstate New York town even Anne Lindbergh's best-selling Listen! the Wind was banned. The Lindberghs did not return to Berlin, however, but rented a Paris apartment.

In April 1939 Anne and the two small Lindberghs arrived in the United States to stay for a while at the Morrow home in Maine before going on to Englewood, New Jersey. The Colonel was already in this country as special adviser to the Army on aircraft production. After making a quick survey of American aviation plants he submitted a report to the President and returned to private life in September. That

ANNE MORROW LINDBERGH

same month, after the outbreak of World War II, he gave a radio address pleading for United States' isolation. In October he denounced Canada's entry into the War and advocated the sale of only "defensive" weapons to belligerents in a speech whose tone brought renewed accusations that his sympathies were with the totalitarian powers—that he was, at best, advocating "appeasement."

Other radio addresses by Colonel Lindbergh since that time have not allayed that suspicion among a large part of the American public. On October 3, 1940 was published The Wave of the Future, Anne Lindbergh's third book—just a day after her first daughter was born. This book Lewis Gannett finds "a subtler, less dogmatic, more persuasive statement of the philosophy expressed by her father-in-law, the pacifist Representative Lindbergh, in the early years of the last War, which has been echoed, mingled with dubious overtones, in the younger Lindbergh's speeches." Mrs. Lindbergh, like her husband, calls for "reform at home rather than crusade abroad," but unlike him asserts that "if we do not better our civilization, our way of life, and our democracy, there will be no use to 'save' them by fighting; they will crumble away under the very feet of our armies." It is, she says, a confession of faith, though James Thurber (see sketch this issue) finds her faith utterly mystifying.

All of Anne Lindbergh's books have brought her a reputation as "a two-career woman, a flier and a writer, and both with honors." Lewis Gannett said of her first book, North to the Orient (1935), that it "has a rare and delicate intimacy and a winning girlish charm, and it reveals Mrs. Lindbergh as far more than a wife and a daughter. The girl can write." Reviewing

LINDBERGH, ANNE—*Continued*
Listen! the Wind, which in February 1939 won the American Booksellers Association Award, Amy Loveman said that Mrs. Lindbergh "has the seeing eye and the singing heart." Clifton Fadiman finds that "Mrs. Lindbergh's books, quite apart from their value as aeronautical history, are small works of art." In them she shows herself serious, sensitive, fond of daydreaming, fond of philosophic speculation on such matters as time and space, but also capable of remarkable impersonality and detachment. She observes and describes small things with an eye that is scientific as well as poetic.

The late Amelia Earhart once described her: "She is small of stature, and has a charming dignity when surrounded by people. . . Her dress is simple, like her direct manners. . . About her mouth a smile always seems to lurk." A head of Mrs. Lindbergh, done by the sculptor Charles Despiau, created a sensation in Paris. It was regarded as the symbol of "a mother's martyrdom in a disturbed era."

> *References*
> Lit Digest 100:38-46 Mr 9 '29 por; 105:39-40 Ap 12 '30 il por; 105:11 My 3 '30 il; 121:28 Ja 11 '36 por
> Mag Art 33:481 Ag '40 il
> Nation 142:35 Ja 8 '36
> New Repub 59:145-7 Je 26 '29
> Newsweek 2:16 D 16 '33 por (cover)
> Read Digest 36:1-8 Ja '40; 37:1-12 N '40
>
> American Women
> Lindbergh, A. S. M. North to the Orient 1935
> Who's Who in America

LINDLEY, ERNEST HIRAM Oct 2, 1869—Aug 21, 1940 Chancellor of the University of Kansas from 1920 to 1939; in 1924 removed from position by Governor Jonathan M. Davis on demands of the Ku Klux Klan; dismissal aroused widespread protests and brought about Dr. Lindley's reinstatement; began to teach philosophy at the University of Indiana in 1893; in 1917 was named president of the University of Idaho

> *References*
> Sch & Soc 49:59 Ja 14 '39
> Who's Who in America
> Who's Who in American Education
>
> *Obituaries*
> N Y Herald Tribune p16 Ag 22 '40 por
> N Y Times p19 Ag 22 '40 por
> Newsweek 16:55 S 2 '40 por

LIPPINCOTT, JOSHUA BERTRAM (lĭp'ĭn-kŏt) Aug 24, 1857—Jan 19, 1940 Dean of American publishers; board chairman of J. B. Lippincott Company

J. BERTRAM LIPPINCOTT

> *References*
> Pub W 128:624 Ag 31 '35 por
> Who's Who in America 1938-39
>
> *Obituaries*
> N Y World-Telegram p36 Ja 19 '40
> Newsweek 15:2 Ja 29 '40 por
> Pub W p37:410 Ja 27 '40

LIPPMANN, WALTER Sept 23, 1889- Author; editor
Address: c/o New York Herald Tribune, 230 W 41st St, New York City

To a good many of the 8,000,000 who read his syndicated column, *Today and Tomorrow,* Walter Lippmann is truly "the Man with the Flashlight Mind, the Great Elucidator," as the New York *Herald Tribune* called him. "Master of a lucid style"— cynics call it "the best prose on the market" —his comments on America and the world are simple, straightforward and forceful.

Most of the argument between his loyal followers and loud critics seems to center about the question of Walter Lippmann's "liberalism." Many who know his past feel that he has "sold out," that he is now using "the vocabulary of liberalism to support the doctrine of the mortgage note holders." They point to the "pleasant old ladies on Park Avenue who like to think themselves as a shade to the left of William McKinley" and who have adopted his column "as part of the morning ritual with their warm tub and their orange juice." They say that "Lippmann has moved steadily to the right and his prestige and prosperity have increased concomitantly."

But there are others, and their number is legion, who still believe that Walter Lippmann is "one of the most prominent and influential liberals of our generation," a man whose greatest wish is to bring a "good society" to the world. There are still others who find in him one of the most successful and powerful supporters of the cause of capitalism and who read him for that reason.

There is no doubt that Mr. Lippmann has come a long way since his student days when, together with John Reed, he organized the Harvard Socialist Club. He was born in New York on September 23, 1889, the only child of a successful Jewish manufacturer, Jacob and Daisy (Baum) Lippmann. After winters at private schools and summers in Europe he entered Harvard University in 1906. In only three years he was graduated with honors.

It was while he was at Harvard that Walter Lippmann first became socially conscious. There was a bad fire in a poor section of Boston, and when the students were called out to help, Lippmann saw misery for the first time in his life. It was a shock. It was then that the Harvard Socialist Club was formed. It was at Harvard, too, that a scathing criticism in the college paper of a book which said the poor were pretty well-off brought him to the attention of William James, whose friend and disciple he became.

After graduation Lippmann spent a year at Harvard as assistant to George Santayana, professor of philosophy. In 1910, when his year was about over, Lincoln Steffens, reporter of the "muckraking era," asked the Harvard professors: "Who among the new graduates has the ablest mind which can express itself in writing?" The unanimous choice was Walter Lippmann. He became Steffens' assistant in investigating corruption in big business and politics. Of Lippmann at 21 Steffens wrote: "Keen, quiet, industrious, he understood the meaning of all he learned; and he asked the men that he met for more than I asked him for. . . He searched them; I know it because he searched me, too, for my ideas and theories."

Steffens' articles were intended for *Everybody's Magazine,* and when his work with Steffens was through Lippmann went to the magazine as sub-editor. He didn't like it much, since his job consisted mainly of reading stories and editing jokes, so he left after a few months to become secretary to the Socialist Mayor, George R. Lunn, of Schenectady, New York, helping him clean up a very crooked city.

In the summer of 1912 Lippmann quit his job and went to a cabin in the Maine woods to write *A Preface to Politics* (1913), the first of his 17 books on politics, morals, economics, personalities and social life. Theodore Roosevelt wrote an enthusiastic review of it, from which a warm friendship developed. Through Roosevelt, Lippmann became associated with Herbert Croly and the *New Republic* and continued as one of its editors until 1921. During the early years of Wilson's Presidency the *New Re-*

WALTER LIPPMANN

public "was the almost official White House organ," and Lippmann was a frequent visitor to Washington.

In June 1917 Lippmann was called to Washington to be special secretary to Newton D. Baker, Secretary of War, to handle the relations between the War Department and organized labor in building cantonments. In September of that year Wilson made him a member of Colonel House's committee to help in preparing maps and data for the peace conference. A year later he was commissioned a captain of military intelligence and sent to France. When the War ended he was a member of the American Commission to Negotiate Peace, but he disagreed with its policies and resigned.

In 1921 Lippmann joined the editorial staff of the New York *World*; two years later he was in charge of the editorial page; eight years later he was editor. During those years he wrote brilliant editorials on the Harding scandals, the Scopes trial, the Dawes Plan, the defects of the Hoover Administration. His editorship "made and kept the *World's* editorial page the brightest lighthouse in United States journalism."

Hard times sent the *World* out of existence in 1931 and in that same year Walter Lippmann was hired by the New York *Herald Tribune* "to provide in its ample pages a little corner of mild Left-wing philosophy to offset its own conservative columns." He was told he could write whatever he pleased—all the paper wanted was four articles a week on whatever appealed to him in the news of the day. He is still with the *Herald Tribune,* his column syndicated in over 170 papers.

In 1932 Lippmann was for Roosevelt and in 1933 he supported the NRA. He began to oppose Roosevelt's banking acts, the stock exchange and securities act. How-

LIPPMANN, WALTER—*Continued*

ever, later he was against the Utility Holding Company Act and the Neutrality Act. After two years of the New Deal he said "the courts will do an historic service . . . if they liquidate a major part of the central regulation to which the New Deal has committed itself." And in 1936 he announced that he would vote for Landon. In 1940, however, he did not go along with the *Herald Tribune's* support of Wendell Willkie (see sketch this issue). Whatever his political position in 1940, it is clear that "Big Business has always respected Mr. Lippmann's utterances. He has those rare qualities of investigation and judgment, as Thomas W. Lamont (see sketch this issue) once said." By then "liberals" were sadly saying: "Mr. Lippmann's brand of liberalism is the intellectual garment of capitalist power; it is the liberalism of the . . . professors and editors and lawyers who want at the same time to preserve the *status quo* and their self respect"; they were regretful, for "with his active mind, his great talent, his industry and his brilliant style," he "might have been a rain that would have helped freshen the streams of American thought."

Walter Lippmann does his writing mornings. He starts at 8:30 and usually finishes from 700 to 1,200 words in about two hours, writing furiously and illegibly in longhand on white paper. His afternoons and evenings are given over to a rather full social life, in which he "is more apt to be on intimate terms with Morgan partners than with union leaders." Husky and powerful, Lippmann rides, fishes, plays golf ("fairly"), tennis ("better") or referees a polo game. He and his second wife, Helen Byrne Armstrong, whom he married in 1938 (he was first married to Faye Albertson in 1917), have three houses—in Manhattan, Florida and Long Island.

References

Am Mag 114:16+ S '32 por
Commonweal 30:348-50 Ag 4 '39; 31: 296-8 Ja 26 '40
Nation 137:7-10 Jl 5 '33; 137:36-8 Jl 12 '33; 137:67-70 Jl 19 '33; 137:126-31 Ag 2 '33; 145:589-90 N 27 '37; 146:464-7 Ap 23 '38; 150:654 My 25 '40
New Repub 88:180-1; 88:183-4 S 23 '36
Time 30:45-8 S 27 '37 pors
Wilson Lib Bul 4:94 N '29
Howe, Q. The News and How to Understand It 1940
Kunitz, S. J. ed. Living Authors 1937
Who's Who in America
Who's Who in American Jewry
Who's Who in Journalism

LITTLE, WILLIAM LAWSON JR. June 23, 1910- Golf champion

Address: c/o A. G. Spalding & Bros, 105 Nassau St, New York City

Lawson Little is the winner of the 1940 United States open golf championship. The sixth player to win both the American amateur and open championships and the first to win both the British and American amateur titles in succeeding years, Little started his golf career in 1917. His father, Colonel William Lawson Little, an officer in the medical corps, and his mother, Evelyn Baldwin (Ryall) Little made golf their avocation, though neither was a championship player.

The Little family was transferred to many army posts in remote corners of the world. William Lawson was born at Fort Adams, Newport, Rhode Island, and was a baseball fan up to the age of seven. One day Dr. Little, when stationed at Old Point Comfort, Virginia, broke a golf club on one of his morning rounds. Junior displayed an interest in the broken shaft and inherited it. He spent hours swinging the club as he had seen his father swing it.

During the war years of 1918 and 1919 the elder Little was shifted to El Paso, then to San Antonio as district surgeon. Here Lawson Jr., practiced and caddied occasionally for his father. From Texas they were transferred to Manila. There Junior shot his first round of nine holes with his mother when his father was unable to play one day, and turned in a score card of 53. In China, at the Tientsin post, the family encountered the macabre local links' rule: "ball may be lifted without penalty from open graves." The course there bisected a Manchu cemetery which followed the custom of leaving coffins on the ground so that the departed ones might sink gradually into the soil, a process that required from 15 to 20 years.

After they returned to the United States the Littles moved from post to post along the Pacific Coast. Now known in the golf world as a powerful hitter whose sturdy frame rifles a ball 300 yards on occasion, it is remarked that Little might not be the powerhouse he is were it not for the competition supplied him by a boy several years his senior when his father was stationed at Vancouver Barracks, Washington. Then 12 years old, Lawson used to play with George Van Way, now Lieutenant Van Way of the United States Army. Being older, Van Way could naturally drive farther than Little and seized every opportunity to twit the younger player. As a result Lawson kept pressing all the time to equal George, hitting every ball just as far as he could. For three years he waited to outdrive the older boy. Finally he did. This experience has now become a part of his teaching, and he advises all young boys to put all their strength into their shots. "When they become good enough to enter tournaments," he says, "they can cut down their power for greater accuracy—and still get distance."

Mel Smith, the professional, and Dr. Oscar F. Willing, a former United States Walker Team Cup member at the Waverly

Club, Oregon, became interested in Lawson and taught him a great deal. He entered his first real tournament test in that state and won a place in the select circle of Oregon golfers with a 163, two strokes better than his father. He was defeated, however, in the first round, but went on to win the first flight.

In California, when the Little family was transferred to The Persidio, Lawson Jr. was coached by Larry Brazil and reached the fourth round of the San Francisco junior championship tourney. He won the North California amateur championship that same year, 1928.

In 1929 Lawson gained his first national reputation by defeating Johnny Goodman, the "man who defeated Bobby Jones" in the United States open championship at Pebble Beach, when he was only 19. The following year he entered Stanford University and disappointed football devotees who saw great possibilities in the young giant with the wide shoulders. Lawson turned his back on the chance to shine on the football field and became the constant companion of Eddie Twiggs, golf coach, to whom he gives great credit for developing his short game. But his record with the Stanford golf team was not outstanding "perhaps because he had his eyes focused upon championships." He never became an intercollegiate star and was seldom rated higher than third best golfer at the University. Although he won the Pacific Coast interchampionships in 1931 and 1933, he found it difficult to mix studies and golf, and his play in 1931 and 1932 was "so dismal that the boy wonder of Pebble Beach became just another flash-in-the-pan in newspaper stories."

But he believed in himself from the very beginning and in his ability to win against any and all opponents. He trained sedulously. He ran three miles very early in the morning, had a light breakfast and then played from 27 to 36 holes. He came back in 1933 to the semifinals at Kenwood in Cincinnati. This qualified him for the American Walker Cup team in England. He returned from Prestwick, Scotland with the 1934 British amateur championship cup and then proceeded to the Brookline Country Club in Massachusetts to win the American crown.

Lawson Little repeated the two records the following year. To accomplish this he won 31 consecutive matches, most of them over the 18-hole route. In all 31 he only once had to play off a tie. At Cleveland he played 156 holes 19 under par, went through the whole tournament without taking more than five strokes on any hole. The double victory in both amateur championships was regarded as fine a performance as has ever been known in golf, and while it was not as brilliant an achievement as was Bobby Jones' when he won all four tournaments in 1930, it ranks a close second. Sports editors regarded Little as the outstanding athlete of 1935, and, in spite of some lack of public popularity and an "egotistic, ruthless reputa-

LAWSON LITTLE

tion," voted him the James E. Sullivan Memorial Award.

A sports writer says: "It is debatable whether Little's most potent weapon on the links is his cool and methodical brain or his unusually powerful physique. To his unusual strength this champion adds an enviable tournament temperament. From the first hole of the first match he sets about winning in a businesslike way, and the vicissitudes of the ancient game have little effect on his control. His admirers say that his coolness in a crisis is his most admirable trait. He is never discouraged and never plays a hurried or sloppy shot. He has the power of concentration of a wild animal trainer."

In 1936 Lawson Little turned professional, won the Canadian open championship (with 271, the lowest recorded score) and married Miss Dorothy Hurd, the daughter of Mrs. Robert Maxon of Chicago. The round-faced, snub-nosed, curly-haired player has built up a reputation of affability, particularly while touring the country giving instruction and demonstration for a company manufacturing golf equipment. He is now serving as director of golf at Bretton Woods, New Hampshire and won the 1940 United States Open by defeating Gene Sarazen at Cleveland.

References

Christian Sci Mon Mag p15 Je 29 '40
Lit Digest 118:38-9 S 8 '34; 120:32-3
   Ag 31 '35 por
Time 26:49 S 23 '35 por
America's Young Men
Atkinson, L. William Lawson Little Jr: the Greatest Athlete of 1935 *In* Atkinson, L. and others Famous American Athletes of Today 5th ser. p217-50 1937

LLEWELLYN, RICHARD, pseud.
(loo-ĕl'lĭn) Author

Address: c/o Macmillan Co, 60 Fifth Ave, New York City

Richard Llewellyn's *How Green Was My Valley* (1940), the first novel of an unknown Welsh writer, is a best seller in both England and America. This story of life in a Welsh mining community before South Wales had become a "depressed area" is told by Huw Morgan, the last of his family, just before he leaves the valley forever.

The novel is made up of Huw's rememberings. He remembers the valley before industrialism came to it, before the slag heaps had risen to blacken its green. "Happy we were then for we had a good house, and good food, and good work." They were a fine family, the Morgans, in the little house on the hill—father, mother, five sons besides young Huw and three daughters. Hard working they were, and their lives were simple and primitive.

A time came, however, when wages were cut and a new order of things began. Huw's father, Gwilym Morgan, who was a leader in the valley, put his trust in reasonable argument; but argument failed, and the men struck tentatively, doubtfully, without organization. They won the strike, but their wages were lower than before. That was only the beginning. Other strikes and increasing bitterness were ahead. Davy and Owen, Huw's brothers, fought hard to build the union, but they were struggling against forces that bore them down with the years. The closing of a single pit left 400 men idle. Times grew blacker as the slag rose. Strangers appeared in the valley and found hearers, and to men like Huw Morgan it was sad to know that the brave ideas "and the brave ones of early days had all been forgotten in a craziness of thought that made more of the notions of foreigners than the principles of Our Fathers." The alien notions prevailed and at last there was war in the valley. But that came after the Morgan sons had been scattered abroad and Gwilym himself didn't live to see much of it.

How Green Was My Valley has been acclaimed by critics for the characterization, the emotional intensity, the poetry in the story of the Morgans. "In one book the author has done more than all his predecessors to show the English what Wales really is, giving us with tingling vivacity, quenchless spiritual force, the prose epic of a nation." It has been called "vivid", "eloquent", "poetical," and though slight charges of over-poetical writing and sentimentality have been brought against it, the consensus of critical opinion is that *How Green Was My Valley* is a "beautiful story" "well performed."

Of himself Richard Llewellyn tells us: "I have two birth dates and the honour of choice between two birthplaces, one the largest, and the other the smallest city in

RICHARD LLEWELLYN

the world: London, and St. David's in Pembrokeshire. My school days were spent in St. David's, Cardiff and London. At 16 I was sent to Italy to learn hotel management, starting in the kitchen. In Venice I studied painting and sculpture in my spare time, and worked with an Italian film unit, learning the rudiments of the cinema.

"I should describe the years up to 19 as turbulent. Realizing a need for discipline, I joined the ranks of H. M. Regular Army and served both at home and abroad. Returning in 1931, jobless, I turned to the cinema and entered the studios as extra player in order to study the methods of men then in charge of production. In an interval I became a reporter on a penny film paper, and it was during this period that I started writing for pleasure."

Mr. Lewellyn returned to the cinema to become assistant director, scenarist, production manager, and finally director. Then a slump in the industry turned him to playwriting and his *Poison Pen,* a psychological mystery play, was successfully produced in London.

How Green Was My Valley was begun in St. David's from a draft written in India and was rewritten in Cardiff and again "in St. James's Park, London, during a period of unemployment." After another period of work in Wales, Mr. Llewellyn returned to London, where a friend introduced him to the publisher who accepted the manuscript of the novel he 'had been working on for so long. "That was the happiest day of my life," he says.

Altogether he has written five novels and destroyed them, and three plays, "one of which was produced, one is now in production, and one was written purely for pleasure." In 1940 he was a captain in the Welsh Guards, defending England.

References
> Christian Sci Mon Mag p11 F 24 '40 por
> N Y Times Book R p3, 19 F 11 '40
> Sat R Lit 21:5 F 10 '40 por

LLEWELLYN LLOYD, RICHARD DAVID VIVIAN *See* Llewellyn, R., pseud.

LOCKE, CHARLES EDWARD, BISHOP Sept 9, 1858—Mar 3, 1940 Bishop and retired Methodist Church leader; conducted funeral of President McKinley on September 15, 1901; author of many religious books

BISHOP LOCKE

References
> Who's Who in America

Obituaries
> N Y Herald Tribune p22 Mr 5 '40 por

LOCKRIDGE, RICHARD Sept 26, 1898- Drama critic; author
Address: b. c/o New York Sun, 280 Broadway, New York City; h. 74 Washington Pl, New York City

As drama critic for the New York *Sun* Richard Lockridge's judgment is independent and, according to fellow critics, "his perceptions are excellent and his observations are generally sound." As the creator of the *Mr. and Mrs. North* whose saga frequently appears in the *New Yorker* and whose adventures have been the subject of two books, *Mr. and Mrs. North* (1936) and *The Norths Meet Murder* (1940), written in collaboration with his wife, he has shown himself an author of humor and understanding. The new Frances and Richard Lockridge mystery novel, *Murder Out of Town,* will be published in January 1941.

When Mr. and Mrs. North first appeared in book form, reviewers defied readers to "suppress" their "mirth in a staid chuckle." They pointed out the sense they got of having read "an unobtrusive but far from negligible contribution to current Americana" and hoped that this delectable couple would appear sometime, not only in short sketches, but in a novel. Four years later they got their wish when fluttery-minded Mrs. North and her sometimes troubled husband met murder in New York City. A "good crime puzzle," the book had the added charm of "excellent characterization" and infectious humor of writing.

Mr. Lockridge's first book, *Darling of Misfortune: Edwin Booth* (1932) combined his interests as dramatic critic and author. In this biography of the great American tragedian he shows that Booth frequently had to act in life as tragic a part as any on the stage. An arresting book, with much important detail collated from all kinds of sources, critics were almost unanimous in its praise.

Richard Orson (he does not use the middle name) Lockridge has had a lot of jobs in his life, but since his first position on the Kansas City *Kansan* his main interest has been newspaper work. He was born in St. Joseph, Missouri, the son of Ralph David and Mary Olive (Notson) Lockridge. His public school education was capped by two years at the Kansas City Junior College, from 1916 to 1918, when he left to enlist in the Navy. He never really got to see the War—his job was to scrape paint off warships in the Brooklyn Navy Yard.

When the War ended, Lockridge began working for the United States Census Bureau and at the same time started to study journalism at the night school of George Washington University. Tired of this, he went back home and spent one semester of 1920 at the University of Missouri, after which he got himself a job in a wholesale grocery company. That didn't last long either, and Lockridge drifted from one kind of work to another in the South—part of the time he worked as roustabout with a carnival. Then he returned to Kansas City, Missouri and spent a couple of months in the Post Office as printer and registry clerk.

It was in 1921 that Richard Lockridge was hired as a reporter by the Kansas City *Kansan.* He stayed there a year until he went back to Missouri to the Kansas City *Journal.* While on this paper he met Frances Davis, a reporter on the Kansas City *Post,* and they were married on March 4, 1922. They both decided it would be a good idea for them to go to New York to try free-lance newspaper work, but homesickness overcame them and within a few months they were back in Kansas City, this time Mr. Lockridge getting a job on the Kansas City *Star.*

Before the year was up, however, they decided to try New York again, and this time they stayed. Richard Lockridge got a

RICHARD LOCKRIDGE

job on the New York *Sun* as a reporter. From 1923 to 1928 he covered general assignments, did rewrite work and reported many of the important trials, including the Hall-Mills, Ruth Snyder and Judd Grey and Browning cases. He also managed to get assigned to second-string reviews.

In 1928 his keen interest in the theatre bore fruit and he succeeded Gilbert Gabriel as the *Sun's* drama critic, a position he continues to hold. In his reviews Richard Lockridge is without doubt the most accurate reporter in New York City, if not always the most exciting. According to *Variety's* box-office poll of dramatic critics, his score was the highest in the season of 1939 to 1940. Of seventy-three plays reviewed he was right in his estimate of sixty-five and wrong about only eight—which makes for the high average of accuracy of eighty-nine per cent.

His reviews are written in his apartment in Washington Place and picked up by *Sun* messengers around 1 a. m. Between theatre seasons Lockridge continues his old trade of City Room rewrite and manages to spend a good deal of time at his country house at Brewster, New York.

References

Morehouse, W. Forty-five Minutes Past Eight 1939
Who's Who in America

LODGE, SIR OLIVER JOSEPH June 12, 1851—Aug 22, 1940 Eminent English scientist; inventor; spiritualist; although outstanding in the realm of pure science, won world-wide acclaim for his belief in communication with the dead; first expounded this view in 1908; professor of physics at University College, Liverpool (1881-1900);

president of Birmingham University (1900-19); invented the rudiments of the radio loud speaker; mastered the principles of wireless telegraphy before Marconi; wrote a great number of books on science and spiritualism; knighted by King Edward VII in 1902

References

Fortnightly 142:273-84 S '34
Pub W 128:1015 S 21 '35
Bridges, H. J. Sir Oliver Lodge and the Evidence for Immortality *In* Criticisms of Life p121-46 1915
Bridges, T. C. and Tiltman, H. H. Solving the Riddles of Space *In* Master Minds of Science p129-38 1931
Keith, Sir A. Sir Oliver Lodge *In* Men of Turmoil p307-16 1935
Lodge, Sir O. J. Letters—Psychical, Religious, Scientific and Personal 1932
Lodge, Sir O. J. Past Years 1932
Wallace, A. Religious Faith of Great Scientists *In* Religious Faith of Great Men p139-73 1934
Who's Who

SIR OLIVER LODGE

Obituaries

Christian Cent 57:1068-9 S 4 '40
N Y Herald Tribune p10 Ag 23 '40 por
N Y Times p15 Ag 23 '40 por
Newsweek 16:55 S 2 '40 por
Time 36:47 S 2 '40

LOEB, FRITZ (lōb) 1895—June 19, 1940 Major General of the German Army; instrumental in building Germany's air force; Goering's "key man in the four-year-plan"

Obituaries
N Y Herald Tribune p6 Je 26 '40
Newsweek 16:31 Jl 3 '40

LOFTUS, CISSIE Oct 22, 1876- Actress
Address: h. Halifax Apartments, 6376 Yucca
Ave, Hollywood, California

Marie Cecilia Loftus set all London talking about her impersonations in 1893 and
after five decades of legitimate, vaudeville
and motion picture acting still has people
talking about her impersonations. Her voice
has echoed with startling accuracy hundreds
of well-known personalities, from the
throaty singing of Florence Reed to the
East Side accents of Fanny Brice. She may
impersonate John or Ethel Barrymore;
be George M. Cohan at his Yankee-
Doodliest or Sarah Bernhardt at her
stateliest; successfully imitate Gertrude Lawrence (see sketch this issue) or Beatrice
Lillie. She has also given impersonations of
Lynn Fontanne, Pauline Lord, Norma
Shearer, Libby Holman, Robert Morley
and others.

Cissie probably inherited her gift of
mimicry from her mother, Marie Loftus, a
Scottish music hall singer who delighted
the patrons of Harry Miner's in the Bowery
with such ditties as *I'm So Shy.* Ben Brown,
her father, was a member of the trio of
Brown, Newland and LeClerce which
played the music halls the world over in
one minstrel skit, *Black Justice,* and nothing
else, for 45 years.

When her mother went on a tour of the
United States, Cissie (born in Glasgow,
Scotland), then six, was left in a school in
Cambridge, Massachusetts. Her education
was continued in the Convent of the Holy
Child, Blackpool, England. During the
holidays she attended the theatre with her
mother and, watching the performers from
the wings, thought she could do better
than an impersonator who failed to change
her voice with each characterization.

Cissie made her first appearance at 16
on the stage of the Alhambra in Belfast
singing the ballad, *Molly Darling,* and at
17 was at the Oxford Music Hall in London, achieving instantaneous popularity by
her "simplicity, reserve, cool sweet inexperience" and a complete absence of make-up.
Her vocal abilities were discovered by Sir
Arthur Sullivan, who took her to Blanche
Marchesi for a tryout. Cissie was surprised to learn that she had an unusual
voice fit for grand opera, but "her mother
thought that it was very nice of them to say
such things, but the music hall was her
world, and she had lived it all her life, and
she didn't know any other."

During Cissie's early career Scotti and
Caruso were among the guests at a
party in New York. They were playing and
singing. Finally young Cissie was called
upon, and said she would imitate Caruso.
The accompanist, expecting a burlesque,

Elmer Fryer

CISSIE LOFTUS

asked her what key she would sing in.
She said in Caruso's own, and proceeded
to sing the song Caruso had just sung.
When she finished the tenor rushed up
to her and nearly poked his finger through
her breastbone, shouting "*Madonna Mia*!
It is my voice, and it is in you."

During her first year in London (1893)
Cissie had the regular part of Haidee in
Don Juan at the Gaiety. In 1894 she married Justin Huntly McCarthy, son of Justin
McCarthy, the leader of the Irish Party in
the House of Commons. After her honeymoon she joined the company of Augustin
Daly and played with Ada Rehan. After
leaving Daly's company she appeared in
vaudeville at Koster and Bails in 1895, doing
her sensational imitations. A collection of
30 poems, *First Verses,* of which 100 copies
were privately printed and inscribed to
"Justin," was the pride of her husband, who
at the time was the dramatic critic on the *Pall-
mall Gazette.*

In April of 1895 she was playing in *The
Highwayman* at the Lyceum. She returned
to the music halls of London in 1897, giving imitations, then appeared with Martin
Harvey in *The Children of the King* and
came back to America in 1900 to make her
debut in comic opera as Bettina in *The
Mascot.* Later she joined Madame Modjeska's company as Leonie in *The Ladies,
Battle,* Viola in *Twelfth Night,* Hero in *Much
Ado About Nothing;* then worked under
Daniel Frohman at Daly's Theatre, appearing
as Elsie in *The Man of Forty,* Lucy in *Lady
Huntworth's Experiment,* Lady Mildred Yester
in *The Shades of Night.* At the turn of
the century she was E. H. Sothern's leading
lady in *If I Were King,* a play written by
her first husband just as they were being
divorced.

LOFTUS, CISSIE—*Continued*

From 1902 on Cissie alternated between England and America, between vaudeville and the theatre. Among other rôles she played Marguerite in *Faust* with Sir Henry Irving and Nora in *The Doll's House.* Her son, by a second marriage to Dr. A. H. Waterman of Chicago, she named Peter for her favorite rôle in *Peter Pan. Peter Pan's* author, James M. Barrie, was godfather to the child. While playing in *The Lancers* in 1908 she sustained an accident in rehearsal and underwent a serious operation. In 1911 her voice failed and after that she made only occasional appearances at the Coliseum and other variety houses in her imitations of popular actors and actresses.

She returned to the United States in 1923 to make a comeback, and 14 days later her voice was gone again. In reduced circumstances and with her son to support, Cissie Loftus went into the *Ziegfeld Follies.* Gradually she re-established herself, first by giving private concerts, of which there were 24 the first year, then by stage parts. Since that time she has appeared in many plays: as Mrs. Rimplegar in *Three-Cornered Moon;* as Aunt Chloe in *Uncle Tom's Cabin;* in *Tonight at 8:30;* as Frau Lucher in *Reunion in Vienna* and in many others.

When she inaugurated her Sunday night shows in 1938, *An Evening With Cissie Loftus,* "a white-haired veteran of many battles with life and art, she stopped a Broadway show with her witty caricatures of stage stars. Her audience cried for more and more." After touring the country with her *Impressions and Impersonations* she went to Hollywood and appeared in such motion pictures as *East Lynne, The Old Maid* and *It's a Date.* She intends to continue her recitals and is also doing radio broadcasts.

References

> Harper's Bazaar 72:52-3+ Je '38
> Lit Digest 116:9 S 16 '33 por
> N Y Daily News p46 Ap 29 '38 por
> Sobel, B. ed. Theatre Handbook 1940
> Who's Who
> Who's Who in the Theatre

LOGAN, WALTER 1877—Mar 11, 1940

Violinist; composer; conductor and music director of Station WTAM, Cleveland; friend of Victor Herbert

Obituaries

> N Y Herald Tribune p22 Mr 12 '40
> N Y Times p23 Mr 12 '40

LOMBARDO TOLEDANO, VICENTE

(lōm-bär'thō tō'lä-thä'nō vē-sěn'tä) July 16, 1894- Mexican labor leader

Address: Villa Rosa María, San Angel, Mexico City, Mexico

December 1940 Bulletin: In 1940 Vicente Lombardo Toledano's term as head of the Confederation of Mexican Workers comes to an end, since re-election is spe-cifically forbidden by the Constitution of the CTM. His successor is expected to be Fidel Velásquez. (Rumors that he has been removed from his position by President Cárdenas are false.) He remains president of the Federation of Latin American Workers.

From August issue:

As secretary-general of the CTM Vicente Lombardo Toledano, frequently called the "John L. Lewis of Mexico," has a particularly hard job in an election year. The labor movement in Mexico is closely identified with politics and Lombardo Toledano has spent much time keeping his organization solid under "the pulls and strains of the complicated Mexican political patterns." It is to avoid this that he is trying now through his Workers' University, his daily newspaper, *El Popular,* through political activities and through the building up of a workers' militia, to create an independent labor movement which will remain strong whether the President of Mexico is pro- or anti-labor.

"Vivacious, magnetic, confident and relentless in forcing his reasoning to its conclusions, Lombardo Toledano is now the greatest influence in Mexican labor circles" —the "undisputed dictator of Mexican labor" some call him. It is he who heads the million members of the CTM and it is he who is president of the Federation of Latin American Workers, formed in 1938.

Lombardo Toledano's union was founded in February 1936 when a number of labor groups united under him and other labor leaders in opposition to the CROM (*Confederación Regional Obrera Mexicano*) which, according to some of its members, was a "tool of North American imperialism," backward, conservative, merely a governmental agency. Lombardo Toledano had belonged to the CROM and had even been one of its secretaries but he resigned his membership in 1932.

The CTM has been called "the most important labor organ ever formed in Mexico, both in the number of its constituent elements and in its program and the tactics that it has employed." It is made of national industrial syndicates and local federations of syndicates in all the economically important regions of the country and is both vertical and horizontal corresponding to the needs of Mexican economic life. Under Lombardo Toledano the CTM has made many contracts, has succeeded in extending the operation of the labor laws and has raised the minimum wage in every state in Mexico. Its syndicates participate in the operation of many Mexican industries. They manage the national railways, have a share in the management of the oil industry, manage municipal services and control many mills.

In making these gains the CTM has had the "emphatic support" of President Cárdenas and it has been rumored that Cárdenas frequently calls on Lombardo

Toledano for advice. In fact, rumor goes so far as to credit the labor leader with having played a large part in the determination of the expropriation of the oil properties.

Because the program of the CTM extends to the consideration of national problems; because the ambition of Mexican labor is the socialization of all national wealth; because it is an active, new union, the CTM has occasionally been called Communistic, and Lombardo Toledano has even been called "the archpriest of Mexican Communism." Toledano denies his Communism, though he avows his Marxism. Diego Rivera, however, holds that "Lombardo Toledano has closely intertwined his fate with that of the Soviet oligarchy in the Kremlin," and Cedillo once said: "Toledano—one day he is a Nationalist, the next day a Communist. He fools no one though." Others have insisted just as strongly that Lombardo Toledano is not a member of the Communist Party "and not entirely trusted by Communist leaders." It should be pointed out, too, that although Lombardo Toledano went to Moscow in 1938, in that same year he announced the solidarity of the Federation of Latin-American Workers not with the Third (Communist) International but with the Second (Socialist) International, "to which most labor leaders outside Russia belong."

A lawyer and author, "almost the only intellectual ever to secure a following among the Mexican workers," (his enemies call him "a labor leader who has never labored") Lombardo Toledano is well-born and well-educated. He was born in Teziutlán in the State of Puebla on July 16, 1894, of part Indian heritage. At the time of his birth his father and grandfather were on the way to becoming well-to-do operators of a copper mine development which his grandfather had founded when he emigrated from Italy in 1850. Young Vicente was educated in the French Commercial School and the National Preparatory School of Mexico City and in 1919 received his licentiate in law from the National University of Mexico. In 1920 he received his M. A. and in 1933 his Ph. D. During these years he became an attorney-at-law.

In 1917 he became secretary of and professor in the Mexican Popular University and from 1918 to 1933 was professor of law and philosophy in the National University of Mexico. In 1920 he first entered politics as secretary of the Government of the Federal District and in 1923 became Governor of the State of Puebla; in 1924 member of the municipal council of Mexico City; in 1926 and 1928 federal Deputy to the Legislature. During these years his philosophy had undergone a change, mainly inspired by a trip to Europe: "I was at close range when Fascism marched into Italy," he said. "I

was witnessing the dubious successes of social democracy in Germany, and for the first time I became aware of Karl Marx."

Because of his radical views, which increased during the years, he was expelled from the National University of Mexico in 1933. Immediately he founded his own university, devoted almost exclusively to workers and to peasants. This, late in 1935, emerged as the Universidad Obrera with Lombardo Toledano as rector. During these years he had been active in the CROM, later among the workers in general and finally in the founding and development of the CTM.

It was Lombardo Toledano who in 1938 was cofounder and first president of the Latin American Federation of Workers. At their first convention he said: "The principal task of the Latin-American working class consists in winning full economic and political autonomy for Latin-American nations... Fascism is opposed to the objectives of the proletariat and must be combatted in all its forms." "We will," he said, "fight today and tomorrow to drive Fascism from the face of the earth."

"Slight of build, quick in action and in intellectual reflex, Lombardo Toledano is a good example of what the world thinks of as Latin characteristics." In fact he has been said to resemble "the conventional idea of a Latin-American screen star rather than the popular conception of a great labor leader." Dressed in clothes with a distinctly Bond Street cut, his fiery orations are quoted, praised, reviled constantly "in the press, on the lecture platform and at the coffee-clotch forum." With the elections and their outcome a vital concern for him and his union, he affirmed and reaffirmed that "our big job now is to consolidate the gains that we have made in the last six years under President Cárdenas. Our job is to build an independent economy, free of domestic feudalism or Yankee and British imperialism." This distrust of the United States and Great Britain, reflected in his paper, caused frequent accusations of pro-German sympathies until, under pressure, he changed his line and declared: "There was never truer friendship between North American and Latin-American peoples."

References

Am Scholar 6 no4:471-80 [O] '37
Ann Am Acad 208:48-54 Mr '40
Business Week p48 Mr 12 '38 por
Christian Sci Mon p4 Jl 9 '40
Commonweal 24:173-4 Je 12 '36; 28:389 Ag 5 '38; 29:94-6 N 18 '38
Newsweek 12:36 Ag 22 '38 por
PM p5 N 7 '40
Time 32:22 S 19 '38 por; 35:37 Je 24 '40; 36:30 O 7 '40 por
International Who's Who
Senior, C. Mexico in Transition pam 1939
Who's Who in Latin America

LONGMAN, SIR HUBERT HARRY Nov 29, 1856—Mar 18, 1940 Retired British publisher; partner in Longmans, Green and Company; created a baronet in 1909; member of the Longmans firm for 53 years

SIR HUBERT LONGMAN

References

Who's Who

Obituaries

N Y Herald Tribune p14 Mr 18 '40

LORAM, CHARLES TEMPLEMAN (lōr'ŭm) May 10, 1879—July 8, 1940 International authority on race relations; Sterling professor of education at Yale University since 1931; expert on racial problems of the South African native and the American Negro; spent most of his life in South Africa as an educator

References

Sch Life 21:209-10 Ap '36

Who's Who in America

Obituaries

N Y Times p19 Jl 10 '40 por
N Y World-Telegram p30 Jl 9 '40
Sch & Soc 52:41 Jl 20 '40

LORENTZ, PARE (lo-rentz' pār) Dec 11, 1905- Motion picture director; author; critic

Address: h. Sneeden's Landing on the Hudson, New York

In 1934 Pare Lorentz, who until then had been no closer to the motion picture industry than a critic's seat in the audience, was called to Washington to vivify the government's output of documentary films. March 6, 1940 was the première of his third major production, *The Fight For Life.*

A 68-minute film visualizing unforgettably the unending battle in the United States against disease and death during pregnancy and childbirth, *The Fight For Life* is based on the chapters on maternal welfare in Paul de Kruif's book of the same name. The death of a patient in a modern, well-equipped, abundantly staffed urban maternity hospital inspires a young doctor to affiliate with the renowned De Lees Maternity Center in Chicago. In the heart of the slum area the doctor learns the exacting routine of the Center's prenatal examinations, accompanies senior doctors and nurses to squalid, airless tenements, and finally, as a full-fledged doctor, saves the life of a woman who is having a hemorrhage.

Mothers in the waiting rooms of the Maternity Center, undernourished children playing dangerously in the streets—the people of the tenements themselves are the real actors of this film. Of the professional actors two actually studied at the Center to qualify as clinicians, and the others were taught to act as though they were not acting, as though they belonged to the clinic. For the delivery shots one mother was filmed for four hours, then went home and had her baby.

The New York Maternity Center says that because of its stark realism, this is a "dangerous film, one that should not be shown to young people throughout this nation. Pare Lorentz depicts the abnormalities of childbearing in such realistic terms that the movie-goer is overwhelmed, dazed, frightened. Never once does he intimate that the maternal death rate is steadily coming down; that 996 out of 1,000 mothers come through safely; or that the coming of a baby is the biggest, happiest time in the life of a young couple. There is hardly a smile in the whole picture. Everything is stark, sombre."

Movie critics, however, differ. The New York *Times*: "It's as dramatic as life itself. The drama has been solidly built on human experience, on the tissue of life, on the beat of the human heart itself. . . We wish there were some form of Pulitzer Award for the kind of cinema journalism Mr. Lorentz has been doing"; the New York *Herald Tribune*: "A stirring and eloquent drama, as well as a document of profound significance. It is strong and even terrifying drama at times, but it never resorts to sensationalism. Here is a memorable tribute to the medical profession, accented by challenging social overtones. . . It is a film like no other you have ever seen. It is one you are not likely to forget soon"; and *Cue*: "Powerful, excellently produced dramatization . . unusual, accurately detailed, carefully prepared."

Pare Lorentz was born in Clarksburg, Virginia in 1905. He attended the West Virginia Wesleyan College and then the University of West Virginia, where he edited the humorous magazine, *Moonshine*. At 19, in his junior year, he left school and went to New York City. His first job was editing the General Electric Company's house organ; his second, reviewing motion pictures for *Judge*, lasted 10 years. From 1930 to 1932 he was movie critic for the New York *Evening Journal* and the year following for *Vanity Fair* as well.

Lorentz achieved a national reputation as a serious student and critic of the movies, though he was frequently referred to as a "director's critic." His beginnings in motion picture criticism coincided with the closing years of the silent film, then in its richest development as pictorial expression. His later work as writer and director of motion pictures has been said by a number of commentators to reveal certain techniques reflecting his close observation of the silent screen in its finest period.

From 1934 to 1936 he wrote a movie column for King Features Syndicate, and covered movies for *Town and Country*. He also wrote a nationally-syndicated political column, *Washington Sideshow*, commenting on people and events in the fast changing scene of national affairs. This job was short-lived. In an early column Lorentz praised Henry A. Wallace (see sketch this issue), then Secretary of Agriculture, and also praised the New Deal's farm program. He was fired by wire from San Simeon.

He has never been limited to one activity at a time. He has written miscellaneous work, articles and short stories for a number of publications, including *McCall's*, *Fortune*, *Harper's*, *Scribner's*, *Forum* and *Story Magazine*. One of his articles, *A Young Man Goes to Work*, was reprinted from *Scribner's* (February 1931) as part of a college textbook.

In collaboration with Morris Ernst (see sketch this issue) he wrote *Censorship: The Private Lives of the Movies* (1930), which argues for a more adult and intelligent acceptance of realism on the screen. *The Roosevelt Year* (1933) is a dramatization in still photographs and text of the significant events of the first year of Roosevelt's Presidency. It was written only after Lorentz had vainly tried to persuade "some people down in Wall Street to put up the money for a skillfully edited compilation of newsreel material in narrative form."

In June 1935 he was called to Washington to be consultant on motion pictures. A number of government officials, dissatisfied with dull two-reel films on such subjects as the manufacture of paving bricks, hog-breeding and the love life of the honey bee, asked Lorentz to propose a movie program which could present with dramatic forcefulness of a quality comparable with Hollywood's technical resources some of the problems of American agriculture.

The consultation resulted in Lorentz's heading a new film unit which released in 1936 *The Plow That Broke the Plains*. This is the story of how and why the great favorite central plains of the United States

PARE LORENTZ

became a desert. Here, as in the succeeding films, Lorentz stuck to a stubborn realism, stating the immediate problem simply but so eloquently that the far greater social problem was implicit in the statement.

With three cameramen and a skeleton shooting script, they took thousands of feet of film of the dust bowl area and its people. Back in the cutting room a triple process of creating took place. While Virgil Thomson (see sketch this issue), at the piano, worked out a musical score for the picture, Thomas Chalmers, the narrator, rehearsed the lines into a moving story of the ruin of a great section of this continent by carelessness, selfishness and the lack of a planned far-sighted program of soil conservation.

Hollywood, which had refused all cooperation in making the film, refused, when it was finished, to distribute it through any of the regular booking channels. Lorentz took the can of film under his arm and went from town to town, arranging private showings for the critics, saying: "If you like it, please say this picture can't be shown in your town." Universal critical acclaim and public demand opened many independent theatres to it, and it has been shown to hundreds of schools, clubs and other organizations.

The Plow That Broke The Plains, produced under the sponsorship of the Resettlement Administration under Rexford Tugwell, cost a little less than $20,000. In spite of this relatively low figure, governmental red tape had complicated the financial aspects of production, and Lorentz, who was paid a salary a little lower than that of his cameramen, often had to meet some immediate expenses from his own pocket. He went to Tugwell's office when the picture was finished, stated his grievances and resigned. As he walked out he pointed to a

LORENTZ, PARE—Continued

map on the wall. "There," he said, "you guys are missing the biggest story in the world—the Mississippi River." Tugwell called him back, raised his salary, gave him a $50,000 appropriation, and work began immediately on *The River*.

With a camera team Lorentz traveled 26,000 miles up and down the River, taking 80,000 feet of film. Again his "actors" were just the people who lived along the banks of the Mississippi. Paring the film down to the required 3,000-foot length took six months, working 18 hours a day. The narrative was written after the film was cut and the music set. James Joyce said of it: "This is the most beautiful prose I have heard in 10 years." Mr. Lorentz himself, in the printed text of *The River* (1938) states: "It was intended as functional text to accompany Mr. Virgil Thomson's score, and to fit the tempo of the sequences of the picture." This time the picture was distributed by Paramount, shown in more than 5,000 theatres in the United States, and televised in England by the British Broadcasting System. It was voted the best short dramatic picture of the year in a pool of movie operators. It took first prize (the Nobel Prize of the Movies) over 70 other "documentaries" at the International Cinematographic Exposition in Venice in 1938. Each of his pictures has been rated as "exceptional" by the Exceptional Photoplays Committee of the National Board of Review.

All the films are an exceptional integration of sound and music, words as soliloquy or narration, and pictures. Lorentz obtained the services of outstanding men in their various fields. For his first two pictures Virgil Thomson, the young American composer, wrote the music. For *The Fight For Life* Louis Gruenberg did the score. In each case Alexander Smallens conducted the orchestra, using at various times musicians from the New York Philharmonic, the Los Angeles Philharmonic and the Metropolitan Opera.

Mr. Lorentz wrote the original outline for *The City* (1939), a documentary film on city planning, financed by the Carnegie Corporation of New York and sponsored by the American Institute of Planners.

In 1938 the *Columbia Workshop* program broadcast a short play by Lorentz, *Ecce Homo*, a radio version of a preliminary sketch for the latest documentary picture the government film unit has been working on. The theme is unemployment and the script was voted the best dramatic presentation of the year. In July 1938 the government named him head of the United States Film Service, whose function is to coordinate and supervise all government films.

In March 1940 the Labor-Federal Security Appropriation Bill, including an item of $106,400 to continue the United States Film Service, came before Congress. Previously the funds had been supplied by the WPA and PWA. The House Appropriations Committee found no existing law that would authorize the appropriation; the Senate voted down the bill and the United States Film Service flickered out of existence. Its films are being stored, leased or returned. In May the staff was working without pay. Just what will happen to *Ecce Homo*, the film on unemployment, has not been determined. Mr. Lorentz has not announced any future plans.

Pare Lorentz describes himself as "a reporter and a dramatist." He lives in a large pre-Revolutionary house at Sneeden's Landing on the Hudson with his wife Sally (Bates), a former actress, and their two children, Pare Jr., and Tillie. He is dark-haired, brown-eyed, strong-jawed. He has an abundance of energy, imagination and ideas. His manner is dramatic; he dresses dashingly; he likes direct and quick action. Hollywood has tried to lure him with tempting offers. In the past he has said no; in the future he may change his mind.

References

Am Mag 125:109 My '38 il por
Collier's 106:22+ Ag 3 '40 por
Life 8:98-101 Mr 18 '40
Look 4:34-7 Mr 12 '40
Nat Bd of R Mag 15:11-13 Mr '40 il
Read Digest 37:73-6 Ag '40
Scrib Mag 105:7-11+ Ja '39 por
Time 35:15 My 6 '40

LOTHIAN, PHILIP HENRY KERR, 11TH MARQUIS OF (lō'thē-àn) Apr 18, 1882—Dec 12, 1940 Late British Ambassador to the United States

> December 1940 Bulletin: Lord Lothian died suddenly at 2 a. m. on December 12, 1940 at the British Embassy, of uremic poisoning.

Shortly before the outbreak of World War II Lord Lothian (he is actually the possessor of several other titles) was appointed British Ambassador to the United States. Although it was his first diplomatic post, the choice was by no means a careless one. As a veteran of 15 trips to this country, as a visitor to 45 out of our 48 states, as secretary of the Rhodes Trust that sent 32 United States students to Oxford every year, Lord Lothian was well qualified to become tactful chief spokesman for British interests in the United States. Since that time he has further proved his qualifications by becoming one of this country's most popular speakers at commencement exercises, dinners, at World's Fair celebrations. On October 15, 1940 he left the United States for his first visit to London since the War began and returned in November to tell the United States that England may soon be in need of credits to purchase materials here.

The Right Honorable Philip Henry Kerr was born on April 18, 1882, son of the late Major General Lord Ralph Kerr of the "crabbed Kerrs," devout Roman Catholics whose ancestral land titles go back to King Harold, and of Lady Anne (Howard) Kerr. He is proud of being Scotch and insists on being referred to as a Scotsman. After attending the Roman Catholic Oratory School at Birmingham and New College, Oxford University, he went to South Africa in 1904 as a member of the Railway Committee of South Africa Railways. From 1905 to 1908 he was assistant secretary of the Inter-Colonial Council of the Transvaal and Orange River Colonies, working under Colonial Administrator Lord Milner, who was pushing reconstruction and attempting to reconcile the Boers. In 1907 he also took on the duties of secretary of the Transvaal Indigency Commission. As a member of "Milner's Kindergarten," which also included the late John Buchan (see sketch this issue) and John Dawson, editor-to-be of the London *Times*, he helped in the beginnings of the formation of the Union of South Africa. It is said that he was influenced by Milner's philosophy of Empire —that it must be democratized, liberalized —and particularly so after studying the *Life of Alexander Hamilton* and *The Federalist*.

From 1908 to 1909 Philip Kerr was editor of *The State,* a magazine published in South Africa advocating union of the South African colonies; then, back in England, from 1910 to 1916 he edited *The Round Table,* "a scholarly journal of political philosophy." A member of the Liberal Party, in the midst of the First World War in 1916 he became secretary to Prime Minister Lloyd George. He made two secret trips to Switzerland in an attempt to convince the Austrians that further fighting was hopeless and after peace came he went with Lloyd George to Versailles, helping to draft the Treaty. He did not resign as Lloyd George's secretary until 1922, when he was recognized with the Cross of the Companion of Honor.

For the next three years Philip Kerr devoted his time to travel and to journalism —he has been a director of the United Newspapers, Limited (1921-22), political director of the *Daily Chronicle* and a frequent contributor to the London *Times* and the *Observer;* in 1925 he became secretary of the Rhodes Trust, an office which he held until his appointment to the Ambassadorship in 1939; and in the First National government in 1931 he became chancellor of the Duchy of Lancaster. The year before, upon the death of his cousin, he had succeeded to the title of 11th Marquis of Lothian, becoming also Earl of Ancram, Earl of Lothian, Viscount of Brien, Baron Kerr of Newbattle, Baron Jedburgh, Baron Kerr of Kersheugh and heir to 28,000 acres and three country houses. These included Monteviot in Roxburghshire, Newbattle Abbey in Midlothian, which he donated to Scottish universities as an adult education center, and his present chief seat, Blickling Hall, a great English castle complete with a ghost—Henry VIII's second wife, Anne Boleyn, who carries her head tucked inconveniently underneath her arm.

International

LORD LOTHIAN

In 1931 Lord Lothian became under-Secretary of State for India and chairman of the Indian Franchise Committee, with the task of laying a franchise foundation for a system of responsible government in India. He attended the Round-Table Conferences on the Indian Constitution, visited Delhi (where he was greeted with the sign "Lothian, go back"), lived in a mud hut next to Gandhi's and conceived a great admiration for the Indian leader, whom he has called "the only man of whom one can honestly say that he is both a politician and a saint." In 1932, when the Liberals split over trade policy, he resigned from the Cabinet. He himself had always favored closer United States-British trade relations.

Throughout the '20s and '30s Lord Lothian wrote much on international affairs. A believer in private enterprise, free trade and "social reform," he laid the responsibility for wars and "technological unemployment"—in fact, all the world's major evils—on "international anarchy." Back in 1933 he predicted a new World War if the state of anarchy continued. The solution as he saw it did not lie in giving teeth to the League of Nations and enforcing collective security, but in disarmament, and, while Hitler was growing strong, he suggested giving him non-strategic colonial areas in return for armament limitation. He himself made several trips to Germany, where he met Hitler and other leading Nazis; in 1935, after a visit to the Führer, he announced, "I believe he is sincere."

In 1936 Lord Lothian was already advocating a federation of nations in which the national State surrenders some part of its sovereignty to a common authority representing the whole—sort of a "Union Now" plan. (When Clarence Streit's [see sketch

LOTHIAN, LORD—*Continued*

this issue] book appeared he likened its importance to Adam Smith's *Wealth of Nations*.) He was also advocating Anglo-American cooperation in matters of sea policy, and an Anglo-American treaty of guarantee to France. Other alliances he found undesirable, however: "The alliance system is the murder-trap of the nations."

As a close friend of Lady Astor's (see sketch this issue) he was damned as a member of the Cliveden Set, but, like most of its alleged members, denied its existence. He was, however, a member of the Anglo-German Fellowship. In 1937 he was saying frankly that war was inevitable unless some adjustment was made with Hitler. He also thought France and England would lose the first few years of such a war unless United States aid came swiftly. Still, "I have always understood that it is a first principle of National Socialism to respect the political and economic independence of other races and peoples so long as they respect the independence of the Germans." Just before the *Anschluss* in 1937 he was being reassuring about Hitler's intentions toward Austria; in April 1938 he was said to have been instrumental in forcing Anthony Eden's (see sketch this issue) resignation from the British Cabinet, though he always denied it; it is rumored that he was the chief author of Munich. In 1939, however, he read or reread *Mein Kampf* and called for general conscription in England. Before war finally broke out he was one of those most anxious for the United States to amend her Neutrality Act.

When he was appointed Ambassador to the United States in August 1939, Lord Lothian immediately made himself popular with the American press by holding a press conference right after his first visit to the White House; by posing cheerfully for photographers with a black cat which strolled across his path; by showing an approachability and friendly informality attributed to few of his predecessors. He broadened the circle of Embassy guests, made contacts with New Dealers, was so often at the State Department that a few even criticized his visits as overfrequent. At first he declined hundreds of speaking engagements, though this did not prevent the late Senator Borah and Senator Reynolds (see sketches this issue) from attacking him as a British propagandist.

Lord Lothian's tact was invincible. As early as 1938 he had suggested that Britain make a payment on her War debt, and he still found it a good idea. He predicted that the United States would be the strongest power of the twentieth century; he named Abe Lincoln as his political saint; he admitted that the United States had won the First World War; he was grateful for the American Revolution as having shown Britain how to run her Empire better; Southern fried chicken was his "favorite dish"; his secret ambition was to be a Western orange rancher; he even could flatter the American language by using such colloquialisms as "socking them in the nose!"

But he had another more serious job to do aside from making himself generally liked. In June 1940 Lord Lothian delivered commencement addresses at Columbia and at Yale after having been presented with honorary degrees by both universities. His speech at the Yale alumni luncheon which followed the latter address summarizes his attitude toward America's stake in the War as he had expressed it many times before and since: "The outcome of this grim struggle will affect you almost as much as it will affect us. For if Hitler gets our fleet, or destroys it, the whole foundation on which the security of both our countries has rested for 120 years will have disappeared. . . I am not concerned today to attempt to tell you what you should do in this grave matter. That is your business. But I am concerned that if and when the crisis arises you should not be able to turn on me and say, 'Why did you not warn us about these facts?'" He is responsible for the expression: "Britain is the United States' Maginot Line." He is convinced that in World War II Britain stands at "Armageddon and the battle for the Lord," and he considers the First World War "a successful war of liberation." As for Hitler, "what force alone constructs has neither permanence nor life." In July 1940 he believed that if Britain could hold out for two years the United States would be ready to enter the struggle; in August his country had won the "Battle of Britain"; in September he was begging for "more of everything—and quickly." In November King George VI conferred a knighthood of the Order of the Thistle on Lord Lothian in appreciation of his work.

Lord Lothian's three sisters live with their bachelor brother in Washington, and on the Embassy staff are more than a hundred people, including an expert on international law and four personal secretaries. As for Lothian himself, he is as famous for the great quantities of orange juice he consumes as for anything else. He is a Christian Scientist and hasn't touched alcohol in 25 years, but broadmindedly serves excellent wines to his guests. He spends an hour or two a day in religious reading, is a "good golfer" (he once tried for the amateur golf title in England), can pilot a plane and likes to drive his own car at terrific speed. His main social talent, he says, is the ability to tell the make of any car in the world merely by a quick glance at it as it goes by.

In appearance, "minus his spectacles, with his broad forehead and high-arched Roman nose, Lord Lothian looks like a Roman of some intermediate period a few centuries before Rome's sliding fall. That appearance is strengthened by the mildly indulgent character of his bulky frame—a respectable paunch, the lazy slope of his broad shoulders. His family motto is the indulgent apposite *Sero sed serio*—'Late, but in earnest.'"

References

Christian Sci Mon Mag p1-2 Jl 28 '37; p7+ My 6 '39
Collier's 105:18+ My 25 '40 por
N Y Post p12 Mr 2 '40 por
Scholastic 34:8 My 13 '39 por
Time 34:15 S 11 '39 por; 36:53 Jl 1 '40 por; 36:16-18 Jl 8 '40 por (cover)
Lothian, P. H. K. Lord Lothian vs Lord Lothian 1940
Who's Who

Obituaries

N Y Herald Tribune p1, 22 D 13 '40 pors
N Y Times p1, 27 D 13 '40 por

JOE LOUIS

LOUIS, JOE May 13, 1914- World's heavyweight champion
Address: b. 550 E 61st St, Chicago, Illinois

Nobody wants to fight the "Brown Bomber." Eleven times Joe Louis (he doesn't use his surname Barrow) has successfully defended his heavyweight crown— a feat never approached by any other world champion titleholder—and at 26 remains the two-fisted terror of the ring. Fight-promoter Mike Jacobs, who owes his fame and fortune to the million-dollar gate drawer, is worried: the customers won't turn out unless some challenger can be found good enough to stand up under Joe's diabolical fists. When Max Baer, after downing Tony Galento (July 2, 1940) refused a bout with Louis, the desperate Jacobs decreed that the champion would defend his title but he couldn't say when or with what fighter. Fight fans think that Joe ought to fight the winner of the Bob Pastor-Billy Conn battle which was won by Conn on September 6, 1940. But that doesn't mean that Joe will meet real opposition, say these fans. He has already whipped Pastor twice; and Conn, a light heavyweight, isn't seasoned enough to face the devastating dead-pan of the champion.

The big Negro boy, whose phenomenal rise in three years of professional boxing made him the youngest champion ever to wear the world's pugilistic crown, was born May 13, 1914 near Lafayette, Alabama. His family lived in a one-room shanty set in the cotton fields. His father, Munn Barrow, a sharecropper, died when Joe was four; and his mother, Lilly Reese, took in washing to support her large brood of growing children. When Joe was seven she married Patrick Brooks, who transported his new family to Detroit, where he hoped to find work. But jobs were scarce, and Joe and his brothers sold papers, shined shoes and ran errands to get enough to eat. Then Joe got a real job as assistant to an ice-wagon

driver: toting heavy ice, he says, helped early to develop his big shoulder muscles. At 16 he became a sparring partner in a makeshift gymnasium. There he learned to punch. But in his first local boxing bout he was floored six times in three rounds. His next three fights he won with knockouts and became popular in Detroit sporting circles. At a tournament in Boston, however, he was thoroughly beaten by Max Marek, ex-football star; and later outpointed by Bob Evans. For a while after that he held a steady job in the Ford auto plant. He continued his boxing, though, and in April 1934, as an amateur, won the National A. A. U. light-heavyweight title in St. Louis.

Three months later he decided to become a professional boxer, taking the name Joseph Louis. It was Jack Blackburn, a Negro trainer, who saw the possibilities in the young fighter, taught him how to punch, and from that time has been the fighting brains behind Joe's natural gift for superb body coordination. After he won his first eight professional victories he became known as the "Brown Bomber of Detroit." Knocking out Stanley Poreda and Lee Ramage brought him national attention. Mike Jacobs, then an obscure Bronx promoter, took on Louis after James Johnston of Madison Square Garden had turned him down. When Joe became world champion, it was Jacobs who replaced Johnston as professional czar of American boxing.

After winning 22 professional bouts, Louis was signed in 1935 to fight Primo Carnera. His defeat of Carnera entitled him to the big battle with Max Baer, another former titleholder, whom he took in four rounds. When he next knocked out Charley Retzloff in the first round, he became known as a killer who terrified all comers. Then came

LOUIS, JOE—*Continued*

a setback. In June 1936 he was matched with Max Schmeling—and the bets were ten to one on Louis. But in the twelfth round Schmeling blasted Louis with the first knockout he had taken since 1933. Matched with Jack Sharkey in a comeback bout, he won, and later downed Eddie Simms in 20 seconds after the opening bell. Bobby Pastor, who had studied how to keep out of Louis's reach, lasted 10 rounds with him.

Then Louis fought the titleholder, James J. Braddock, June 22, 1937. The "Brown Bomber" became the world's new champion when he knocked the great Irishman out in the eighth round of the battle. He had made the top in three years; he had also saved his earnings and was known as one of the richest boxers in history. He was matched in his first title-defense bout with the British heavyweight Tommy Farr, who went the 15-round limit with him. But Louis was declared winner on points. In a return battle with Max Schmeling, June 22, 1938, Louis found sweet revenge by knocking out the German in the first round. No one expected "two-ton" Tony Galento to last long with Joe in July, 1939—and at the end of the fourth round Tony, terrifically battered, went down. A far different opponent for Joe was the wily South American, Arturo Godoy, whom he fought in February 1940 to a 15-round decision, baffled throughout by the peculiar crouching, unorthodox boxing technique Godoy used. A return bout with Godoy in June drew a very small gate, however. This time Louis was ready for Godoy, and punched the South American into submission in eight rounds. "Toughest man I ever fought," said the laconic Louis. It was the eleventh successful defense of his crown.

Lacking the fighting character, temperament, vivid personality and intelligence of men like Dempsey or Tunney (see sketch this issue), Joe Louis owes his success to a magnificent physique and two equally fine fists—a natural fighting machine developed by a skilled trainer. Blackburn early taught him to use his hands, to get his body behind every punch. He is a "place" puncher—one of the best in boxing history. He is a flat-footed boxer who in training has been forced to step to drawn diagrams on the ring floor. Psychologically, his outstanding quality as a fighter is his murderous, dead-pan calm—a face that never betrays the cold, precisely calculated moves of the quick, muscled body. "Sometimes I get mad inside," Joe admits, "but I don't let nobody know about it." Actually most of the time he is bored by fighting and does it because he doesn't know how to do anything else.

Unlike Tunney, Joe Louis does not read Shakespeare. He refuses to read any books at all. But he does like the comic strips (his favorite is *Superman*) and movies, if they are about gangsters. He dislikes the theatre, politics, formal society, but thoroughly enjoys hot jazz, chiefly records by Jimmy Lunceford. When he plays a record he dances around the room with a phantom partner, grinning from ear to ear. He sleeps 12 to 14 hours a day. When not in training he drinks four quarts of milk daily and eats enormous in-between-meal snacks; in training, prodigious breakfasts and dinners, the latter topped off with a quart of ice cream. He has invested most of the $1,500,000 he made in six years by knocking out white men at the rate of three-a-year, and owns two apartment houses, two homes for himself and family, a restaurant, a farm with prize cattle and hogs, a big black Buick (state license number KO) and 30 suits of clothes costing $100 each. Swanky models in checks and plaids, with green predominating, are his favorites.

In 1935, two hours before his fight with Max Baer, he married Marva Trotter, a pretty young Chicago stenographer. Their marriage has been a bit less than idyllic chiefly because they dislike each other's friends: Marva is socially ambitious, has an expensive apartment and many furs and jewels, and enjoys formal gatherings, which bore Louis. His best friends are mostly his childhood playmates who, being poor, are a serious drain on his income; Marva calls them parasites. Joe's utter lack of snobbishness has endeared him to most people who know him. Asked his impressions when he once shook hands with Roosevelt he said, "I didn't think nuthin' of it." He is well liked even by his opponents in the ring and he is the idol of every Negro home in the United States. In Harlem hundreds of Negro children, cats and dogs are named after him.

The brains behind Louis, in addition to Jack Blackburn, are John Roxborough and Julian Black, also Negroes from the Midwest, who manage his business affairs, teach him manners and keep him out of trouble. They may have had something to do with his much publicized support of the Republican nominee in the Presidential campaign of 1940. They have taught him to speak politely of and to complement defeated opponents, and to keep away from strange females. Since they once discovered him driving his car at 90 miles an hour, he has been forbidden to drive and to pilot a plane. His mother has always been a big influence in his life; he bought her a fine home and often visits her. Because he likes animals and loves to ride horseback, he goes often to his 447-acre farm in Utica, Michigan. He has ideas of turning the place into a colored dude ranch, tourist camp and picnic grove. Most of all he'd like to retire there. "I been terrible lucky," Louis says, "and I don't want nuthin' to change."

References

　　Collier's 95:16+ Je 22 '35 pors
　　Cur Hist 51:49-50 Mr '40
　　Liberty 17:25-6 Je 22 '40 por; 17:41
　　　D 7 '40 por
　　Life 8:48-50+ Je 17 '40 il pors

Look 4:46-8 Jl 22 '40 pors; 4:48-9
Ag 27 '40 pors
New Repub 99:277 Jl 12 '39
PM p30 Je 21 '40; p28 Jl 28 '40
Sat Eve Post 208:14+ Je 20 '36 il por
Atkinson, L. Joe Louis: the Brown
Bomber In Kaese, H. and others
Famous American Athletes of To-
day 6th ser. p133-66 1938
Mitchell, J. Joe Louis Never Smiles
In Walter, E. A. ed. Essay An-
nual, 1936 p115-20 1938
Ray, O. Joe Louis, the Brown
Bomber pam 1939
Van Deusen, J. G. Brown Bomber
1940
Van Every, E. Joe Louis 1936
Who's Who in Colored America

LOUISE CAROLINE ALBERTA, DUCHESS OF ARGYLL, PRINCESS (ar"gīl') Mar 18, 1849—Dec 3, 1939 English sculptress; daughter of Queen Victoria; widow of Marquess of Lorne, who was the eldest son of the eighth Duke of Argyll

References
Who's Who

Obituaries
Newsweek 14:8 D 11 '39

LOW, DAVID Apr 7, 1891- Cartoonist
Address: 3 Rodborough Rd, N. W. 11, London, England

"In one way war makes a cartoonist's work simple," says David Low, "because there is only one subject." In other ways it makes it harder. "Cartoonists have to be students and when they have to work ahead they also have to be prophets and to be a prophet these days is no joke." When Low does a cartoon for a foreign newspaper one month in advance he knows that "if Hitler doesn't do what I think he is going to do, I shall have to eat that cartoon. I may say that I have taken long chances on that fellow and haven't had to eat one yet. Perhaps it's because we're both artists."

To David Low the Second World War has meant harder work under more difficult circumstances. He feels strongly that "the defence of the decencies of life is part of a cartoonist's business and deflating the flocks of humbugs, hypocrites and incompetents that seem always to grow and flourish like the green bay tree in time of war." It has meant, too, working in black-out days without light; "my studio is all glass on one side but the light is dimmed by sheets of transparent paper stuck on to prevent my becoming a human pincushion if I happen to be there when a bomb drops in." Of course, there has been a lighter side to the War, too, for a cartoonist. Low likes to see and reproduce "everybody walking around with their little gas mask boxes on their shoulders, people with luminous

paint metals on their hats in the black-out, sedate suburbanites hopping out of bed and banging into holes in the ground at the sound of the siren's song."

Even before the War began David Low had "worthily earned the enmity of Hitler, Mussolini and their accomplices." It's been said that when Halifax (see sketch this issue) visited Berlin in 1937 to discuss vital matters with Hitler, the first half hour of his interview consisted of a violent harangue by the Führer on the subject of Low's cartoons. There have been pointed caricatures of Hitler by Low and a prize one of Hermann Goering dressed as a fat and sluttish Rhine maiden. Mussolini, Daladier (see sketch this issue), Franco, Stalin—none of Europe's leaders has escaped him.

Nor have his own countrymen fared any better. There is a famous cartoon in which Neville Chamberlain kneels at Mussolini's feet to wash his hands in the Mediterranean; there is the picture of a confused Chamberlain, standing in front of an ambulance with a stretcher addressing a group of well-fed wolves with a bone (Czechoslovakia) before them: "Excuse me, but did you hear a piercing scream?" Low gives Stanley Baldwin a look of porcine stupidity; he shows Halifax as "the horsefaced Englishman come to life." And he has created Colonel Blimp.

Colonel Blimp is a fat and pompous old gentleman with a walrus mustache who objects to change in anything, detests the working classes of all countries, sees "Red" influences upon all but himself and "makes even Neville Chamberlain look like a tool of Moscow."

Low's gift for caricature has been called the "greatest we have known in our time," and it is true that his pen has probably deflated more self-important leaders and stuffed-shirt statesmen than any in the business. Even though his material very often runs counter to the Tory opinions of Lord Beaverbrook (see sketch this issue), owner of the *Evening Standard* for which Low now works, still they are published, for "Low is not only more admired than any cartoonist in England, he is also more eagerly followed, by hundreds of thousands of people, than any political commentator."

Low works hard at his cartoons, every day. He starts at 8 a. m. by digesting the daily papers. Then breakfast is a political meeting, with the cartoonist, his wife and his two daughters thrashing out the news. After breakfast Low retires to his studio, where, "with much pacing and squirming and pipe smoking," he struggles to express a complex idea in a few vivid lines and a brief, usually wry, caption.

David Low, the son of David Brown and Jane Caroline (Flanagan) Low, was born in Dunedin, New Zealand. He got his start as a political cartoonist in 1902. He was 11 years old and drew a cartoon for the *Spectator* in his native town of Christchurch in New Zealand. It represented the local authorities

LOW, DAVID—*Continued*

as lunatics because of their reluctance to remove certain trees that obstructed traffic. David's mother wanted him to become a bishop and some people "scarred by his corrosive brush" have reason to regret that he didn't follow her advice.

Instead, after attending the Boys' High School in Christchurch, he did free-lance work. When he was 19 he went to Australia, where he got a job on the Sydney *Bulletin* and continued to do free-lance work as well. In 1919 David Low went to England. There he was political cartoonist for the London *Star* until 1927, when Lord Beaverbrook hired him for his *Evening Standard*. In 1920 he married Madeline Grieve Kenning.

During his years on the *Star* and the *Evening Standard* Low's cartoons have been seen in many journals and collections of them have been published in book form. In 1939 *A Cartoon History of Our Times* was published in this country with an introduction and text by Quincy Howe (see sketch this issue). In it Low traces the history of our times through cartoons on six main subjects—disarmament, collective security, the Far East, Spain, the Axis, and the British Empire. In it he shows brilliantly both his gift for caricature and his critical intelligence.

Low often draws portraits of himself, which show him a rather puckish-looking man with a slightly Shakespearean beard. He says that he grew the beard "just to pass the time. When I got home the youngsters wouldn't let me cut it off. I hate it but I'm a martyr to family life." Besides his distinguished beard Low also wears a large black hat and likes to smoke down cigars until they threaten to set his whiskers on fire.

In 1937 he visited America with his wife and children. Prudence and Rachael had looked forward all the way over to visiting Coney Island and eating corn on the cob. "But now that we've come all the way from England," said Low sadly, "they tell us it isn't the season." He did make one discovery, though. "Coming up from South America I discovered hot cakes and syrup. I propose to have them every morning the rest of my life."

References

Lit Digest 122:31-2 N 21 '36 il
Liv Age 351:324-6 D '36; 357:408-9 Ja '40
New Repub 100:80-1 Ag 23 '39
N Y Times p12 Mr 25 '38; VII p4, 5 F 18 '40 il, self por
Sat R Lit 20:5 Jl 22 '39
Scholastic 32:15S Mr 26 '38 por
Time 34:21-2 Jl 3 '39; 34:46 N 6 '39 por
Birchman, W. David Low *In* Faces & Facts 1937
Cape, J. Best of Low 1930
Hodgson, S. Mr. Low *In* Portraits and Reflections p85-90 1929

Low, D. and Howe, Q. A Cartoon History of Our Times 1939
Who's Who

LUHAN, MABEL DODGE (lo͞o′hän) Feb 26, 1879- Author
Address: Taos, New Mexico

One of the most discussed of American women writers, probably America's leading hostess to authors, stage and screen personalities, musicians, psychologists, sociologists—in fact every type of American celebrity—returned to New York in the winter of 1939 after a quarter of a century spent on her pueblo of adobe houses in Taos, New Mexico. She re-opened her literary salon at One Fifth Avenue, fashionable Greenwich Village hotel.

When Mrs. Luhan, then Mrs. Dodge, returned from Europe in 1912, she moved to General Sickles' house at 23 Fifth Avenue and for the next four years held court over the nearest approach to a Paris salon to be found in America. Such long dead "isms" as cubist painting, the I. W. W., anarchy, women's rights and birth control were freely discussed by such personalities as John Reed, Leo and Gertrude Stein, Hutchins Hapgood, Robert Edmond Jones, Walter Lippmann (see sketch this issue), Isadora Duncan, Lincoln Steffens, Amy Lowell and "Big Bill" Haywood. This period of her life is set forth with astonishing candor in volume three of her memoirs, *Movers and Shakers.*

These many years later her son, John Evans, a novelist in his own right, convinced her that New York needed a salon once more. She hoped to capture the bloom of the old ones, but found New York changed, although among the speakers for her "at homes" every other **Friday** night were Roger Baldwin, Mor-

MABEL DODGE LUHAN

ris Ernst (see sketches this issue), Thornton Wilder, Dr. A. A. Brill and John Collier.

She remained in New York only until March 1940, when she rejoined her fourth husband, a full-blooded Pueblo Indian, Tony Luhan, in New Mexico. At the present time she is doing no writing but plans further revelations in the future.

Among her books are four volumes of *Intimate Memoirs,* of which the first is *Background;* second, *European Experiences;* third, *Movers and Shakers;* and fourth, *Edge of Taos Desert. Winter in Taos* has been written of as follows: "Perhaps no book about the Southwest would have more to say than this one does to an outsider who hopes that he may some day live there." For an understanding of the enigma of both D. H. Lawrence and Mabel Dodge Luhan, her book, *Lorenzo in Taos,* is recommended reading. Mabel has recently been described as a "spry . . . brown-eyed grandmother with long graying bangs, horn-rimmed glasses, a thirst for new experiences."

References

> N Y World-Telegram p19 F 21 '40; p15 Mr 5 '40
> New Yorker 15:14+ F 3 '40
> Sat R Lit 19:12-14 N 26 '38 por
> Time 35:80 Ja 22 '40 por
>
> Kunitz, S. J. ed. Authors Today and Yesterday 1933
> Who's Who in America

LUNDEEN, ERNEST (lŭn-dēn') Aug 4, 1878—Aug 31, 1940 United States Senator from Minnesota killed in airplane crash; called one of the country's most outspoken opponents of war; in 1917 was one of 50 Representatives who voted against the declaration of war on Germany; in 1940 was

Harris & Ewing

ERNEST LUNDEEN

in the public eye as an isolationist opponent of the draft; elected to House of Representatives in 1916, 1932 and 1934 as a Farmer-Laborite; elected Senator in 1936

References

> Christian Sci Mon Mag p5 D 16 '36
> Who's Who in America
> Who's Who in the Nation's Capital

Obituaries

> N Y Herald Tribune p1, 18 S 1 '40 por
> N Y Times p6 S 1 '40 por

LUNN, KATHARINE FOWLER   *See* Fowler-Billings, K.

LUPESCU, MAGDA   (loo-pes'koo) 1904- Exiled Romanian favorite

Called "the Cleopatra of the Near East" and King Carol II's (see sketch this issue) "uncrowned queen," Magda Lupescu has since the early '20s been "a king's favorite in the grand line of Du Barry and De Pompadour," perhaps both the best-hated person in Romania and one of the most influential women in history. In September 1940 she and King Carol were reported about to take up residence in Portugal after fleeing from Romania, the King's abdication in favor of his son Michael having been forced by General Ion Antonescu (see sketch this issue). With the former Minister of the Palace, Ernst Urdareanu, the couple were staying in Seville, Spain when, late in October, both Lupescu and Urdareanu were arrested. Accused of complicity in the assassination of Iron Guard leader Codreanu in November 1938, their extradition had been requested by the Romanian authorities. Meanwhile, back in Bucharest, Lupescu's home was being inspected by the public at 10 cents a head, and it was reported that its furnishings were to be auctioned off for the benefit of the families of slain Iron Guardists. It seemed that for Lupescu and King Carol there was to be no second idyll.

Officially Lupescu was born in Jassy in 1904; actually she is probably well into her forties. So much about her is rumor and legend that it is difficult to separate fact from fiction. The one thing about her that is surely more than legend is the famous flaming hair that might have been painted by Titian.

It has been said that her father was a Jew named Wolff (keeper of an apothecary shop, innkeeper, junk dealer or moneylender) who had been baptized and had changed his name to the Romanian equivalent—Lupescu. It has also been said that Magda took the name Lupescu only after becoming Carol's mistress. Everyone seems to agree that her mother was a Viennese Catholic, an "Aryan"; but Magda herself has been variously described as born and brought up in both the Roman Catholic and the Romanian-Greek Orthodox Church.

European

MAGDA LUPESCU

John Gunther says that she did not even know of her Jewish blood until she was grown and already infected with anti-Semitism, and that the discovery resulted in a great deal of conflict in her own mind.

Magda was educated in a convent and afterward married an army officer named Timpeano. One story, highly improbable, says that even before her marriage she had done a little glimpsing of King Carol from afar and was already dreaming of greater things. Another story says that she eloped with a colonel not long after her marriage, repented, returned to her husband and bore him two children, both of whom died. She may or may not have been a stenographer at one time.

It was in either 1921 or 1923 that Lupescu first met King Carol officially—whether in the "glass-domed Officers' Casino at Bucharest" or in Sinaia, the summer capital of Romania, seems unimportant. The heir apparent to the Romanian throne was married to Princess Helen of Greece (a previous marriage to Zizi Lambrino, a commoner, had been annulled). He promptly fell in love with Magda, she with him. She quietly divorced her husband; he not so quietly alienated his royal wife, his royal parents and a large part of Romania's aristocracy by his scandalous attentions to the beautiful Jewess.

It has been often said, however, that Carol's love affair, one among many in the youth of "the bad boy of the Balkans," was not so much the cause as the excuse for his banishment from Romania in December 1925. Premier Bratianu was his political enemy, according to this version of the event. After attending a royal funeral, King Carol met Lupescu in Milan, where he received a message from his parents which had been inspired by the wily Prime Minister. It

told him to return immediately to Bucharest without Lupescu or forfeit the succession. Angry, he sent a refusal; Bratianu wangled the council into accepting his "abdication"; and five years of exile followed. Upon the death of King Ferdinand, Carol's young son Michael ascended to the throne, and Princess Helen divorced Carol in 1928. In the meanwhile King Carol and "Bibi," as he called Lupescu, were living happily in a garden-enclosed stone villa in the Parisian suburb of Neuilly.

In June 1930 came King Carol's famous musical-comedy *coup d'état.* With the support of Premier Maniu and his Peasant Party the royal exile flew back to Bucharest in a plane chartered by Elsie De Wolfe, American actress, and, meeting no resistance and not much surprise except in the foreign press, proclaimed himself King. The chief political casualty was his mother, Chief Regent Marie, whom the Peasant Party was very glad to get out of the way. Supposedly King Carol was to renounce Lupescu, become reconciled with his former wife. But things did not work out quite like that. In spite of all Prime Minister Maniu could do, rumor soon had Lupescu back in the country, and fact soon had the long-suffering Helen packing up and leaving.

Madame Lupescu was living quietly in a red brick villa at No. 2 Alea Vulpache, in the residential outskirts of Budapest—a villa with a large garden and chicken coops whose pedigreed inhabitants she cared for herself. In the garden of the palace grounds, though situated on the main street of Bucharest, was a smaller cottage, and sometimes she stayed there, too. More often she was in Sinaia with King Carol. She was notoriously discreet, seen by no more than a handful of people, never mentioned by the press, always claiming to be utterly disinterested in politics. But there were those who claimed that in reality she was head of the palace *camarilla,* had her own secret service, chose the people who filled the big jobs, decided what could and could not be done by Romania's Prime Ministers—that she was, in fact, more Romania's ruler than Carol himself and that her influence was ruining the country. Maniu, her enemy, was supposed to have lost his position as Prime Minister on her account, and he and his Peasant Party remained her enemies. The Fascist-minded, violently anti-Semitic Iron Guardists were also sworn to drive her out of the country, although at one time she had supported and worked with them.

Early in 1934 her *camarilla* was broken up after the assassination of Prime Minister Duca by the Iron Guardists, Titulescu having demanded its abolishment as the price of his entering the government. A new *camarilla* speedily took its place. Next the Iron Guard put Madame Lupescu at the top of its list for assassination, No. 2 on the list being Titulescu himself; and in May 1934 more than 100 prominent men were arrested, involved in a fantastic plot for her kidnapping and murder. The following month Maniu threatened a peasant revolt (which didn't materialize) against "sinister Jewish influence at the palace," and in September 1934 he proclaimed: "As long as Madame Lupescu remains in Romania, nobody will be able to accomplish anything good. Through her meddling in politics, thirteen Governments and four elections have followed on each other's heels. Madame Lupescu is responsible for almost every evil in this country."

Whether or not Lupescu went into hiding during this period, with King Carol dodging out of town incognito in a battered old car when he wanted to see her, it seems very unlikely that she became the "stricken, pale creature with a haunted look" that some correspondents wrote piteously about. It was true that anti-Semitism in Romania was steadily growing, and she was its chief target. She received threatening letters; there were demonstrations at restaurants when she appeared; students shouted insults at her garden gate; peasants whispered: "A red-headed witch lives in the palace and lives off gold plates. We cannot even find straw for our hungry children." But in 1938 she told a British correspondent firmly that she had no intentions of ever leaving Romania.

Early in September 1940 it was rumored that King Carol had finally yielded to pressure and agreed to her expulsion from the country, preparatory to placing dictatorial powers in the hands of General Antonescu, Iron Guardist sympathizer who is supposed to have resigned as chief of the general staff as the result of Madame Lupescu's influence. With the abdication and flight of King Carol himself a few days later the famous couple were united once again, at least temporarily.

King Carol once said of Lupescu: "The truth about my little friend is that she is the other half of my being, the other half of my brain. The story that I renounced my claim to the throne because of her is a lie. I was compelled to leave Romania for purely political motives, because I was the enemy of graft and bribery.

"She stood by me as nobody else did. Her sympathy and understanding was a thing I was entirely unable to do without." It was reported, however, that Carol showed himself markedly indifferent to his companion in exile in Spain, hardly speaking to her.

Madame Lupescu's devotion to King Carol has never been questioned. Neither frivolous nor avaricious, she has persuaded King Carol to save his money (she herself is reported to own considerable interests in Bucharest banks, in newspapers, and in a foreign motor car company), has never given him any illegitimate children, has always been "the soul of discretion." Growing a little fat these days, sometimes she has been described as neither beautiful nor striking. But a correspondent in 1938 could still write of her as "tall and of remarkable beauty," with "large green eyes, a small

straight nose, delicately bowed mouth, full lips and a Greek profile." She speaks fluent French and German and a little English and has been both credited with and denied remarkable intelligence. Among the few qualities which no one has denied her are the great personal charm and commanding personality that have more than once swayed the destiny of a Balkan kingdom.

References

Collier's 107:10+ Ja 4 '41
Lit Digest 121:12 Je 13 '36 por
Liv Age 354:48-9 Mr '38
N Y Sun p10 S 5 '40
N Y World-Telegram p1 S 5 '40 por; p4 S 6 '40
Newsweek 6:13 S 21 '35
World's Work 59:69 Ag '30

Gunther, J. Carol, Lupescu, and Rumania *In* Inside Europe p438-443 1940

LUQUIENS, FREDERICK BLISS (lü-kyăN′) Dec 10, 1875—Apr 18, 1940 Chairman of the department of Spanish and Italian at Yale and since 1935 Street professor of modern languages; authority on Spanish-American literature; author

FREDERICK BLISS LUQUIENS

References

Who's Who in America

Obituaries

N Y World-Telegram p34 Ap 18 '40

LYNDON, EDWARD 1879—Nov 6, 1940 Electrical engineer; inventor of prism reflector used in New York subway turnstiles to magnify coins dropped in turnstile slots; for a time associated with Simon Lake in early submarine work; helped develop

LYNDON, EDWARD—*Continued*
searchlight mirrors for Army Engineer Corps during the First World War; after War became president of company manufacturing searchlight mirrors, technical lenses and prisms

Obituaries

N Y Herald Tribune p22 N 7 '40
N Y Times p25 N 7 '40

MACARTNEY, WILLIAM NAPIER Feb 25, 1862—June 15, 1940 Physician; practiced medicine for many years in up-state New York, covering 14,000 miles a year on his calls; author of *Fifty Years a Country Doctor* (1938)

References

Who's Who in New York

Obituaries

N Y Herald Tribune p32 Je 16 '40
N Y Times p38 Je 16 '40 por

MCCARL, JOHN RAYMOND Nov 27, 1879—Aug 2, 1940 Lawyer; Controller General of the United States (1921-36); served under four Presidents; was called "watch dog of the treasury" for his violent disagreements with government officials over spending United States funds; wielded unlimited power during his 15 years in office

References

Collier's 96:28 S 21 '35 por
Lit Digest 122:6 Jl 11 '36 por
Newsweek 8:10-11 Jl 11 '36 por
Sat Eve Post 207:22 Je 15 '35; 209: 22 Ag 8 '36
Who's Who in America
Who's Who in Law
Who's Who in the Nation's Capital

Obituaries

N Y Times p15 Ag 3 '40 por

MCCORMICK, ANNE O'HARE Foreign correspondent; member of the New York *Times* editorial board
Address: b. New York Times, 229 W 43rd St, New York City; h. 326 Cherry Dr, Dayton, Ohio

Anne O'Hare McCormick must surely be one of America's most modest women. She does not appear in the current *Who's Who in America* or in the numerous women's biographical publications, nor does her own paper, the New York *Times,* know much of her personal life. When she received the citation of "Woman of 1939" from prominent women's organizations in the country, such as the American Women's Association, the New York Career Tours Committee (a composite of many American women's organizations) and the National Federation of Press Women, she said with characteristic modesty:

"I think the emphasis was on the year rather than on the person. A newspaper woman who specializes in international affairs is chosen for this award rather than a more distinguished representative of some other career, because in 1939 the interest of the world is focused on news. I have been moving around among thunderous events, and I have stolen some of the thunder."

Anne Elizabeth O'Hare was born in Wakefield, Yorkshire, England in the '80s, the daughter of Teresa Beatrice O'Hare, poet. She was educated at private schools in this country and abroad and has a B. A. degree from St. Mary's Academy near Columbus, Ohio. The University of Dayton awarded her an honorary LL. D., as did Smith College in 1939 and Elmira College a year earlier.

She became associate editor of the *Catholic Universe Bulletin* before she began work for the New York *Times.* As the wife of Francis J. McCormick, an importer of Dayton, Ohio, she acquired the background for her journalistic career when she accompanied him on many trips abroad.

In 1921 she timidly suggested to the New York *Times* that she would like to become a free-lance contributor and send back articles from Europe if this would not conflict with regular foreign correspondents. The *Times* gave her permission. From Italy she sent back stories on the rise of Fascism and Mussolini. At that time she was perhaps the first reporter to see that a young Milanese newspaper editor, lantern-jawed, hungry and insignificant, would attain world importance. She became friendly with him and obtained dozens of stories.

Since that time she has interviewed De Valera, Blum (see sketches this issue), Hitler, Stalin, Venizelos, Dollfuss, Stresemann, Schuschnigg and most of the important national leaders in the United States. She has covered national conventions in the United States, has made campaign surveys all over the country and has been "on the spot" for most of the post-War revolutions in the proteanlike capitals of Europe.

In 1939, during five "hair-raising" months, she traveled in 13 countries to study conditions and to obtain firsthand information. While she generally saw the leaders, it was her plan to rove over the country, chatting with farmers, small shopkeepers, mechanics—the people who could give her a cross section of the life of a country.

A tumultuous climax to her journeying was the day in early March 1939 in Huszt, Carpatho-Ukraine, where in a period of 27 hours she lived under three flags. That day Huszt, a town whose location would probably stump the most famous student of geography, made world-wide headlines. Anne O'Hare McCormick saw history in the making that day as a newly-born republic perished before it could draw breath. Hour after hour she cabled home what she was seeing. And it made a story of international significance. In the first two months of 1939, studying the date lines of Mrs. McCormick's stories is enough to make one dizzy. "Although some dates have been omitted, her schedule was approximately this: January 1, Cairo; January 6, Jerusalem; January 13, Rome; February 3, Budapest; February 10, Belgrade; February 12, Vienna; February 17, Berlin."

Now in her 50's, "energetic, sparkling, short, red-haired" Anne McCormick, "dressed not smartly but with taste and a sense of style," has managed to be in places where things were happening.

Practically every European chancellery has been invaded by the New York *Times* reporter. She is greeted by her colleagues with, "You're here again! What's going to happen now?" This question might well have been put to her on the day she was in Rome when Chamberlain came to see Mussolini—on the day she visited Parliament in London when Chamberlain, apprehensive over Germany's ominous attitude toward Poland, abruptly cast aside the "policy of appeasement."

"Crises were popping all over Europe at the time," explains the matter-of-fact Mrs. McCormick, "so it isn't strange that I bumped into a few." Her tramping over Europe has given her "greater knowledge of post-War Europe than almost any other woman possesses."

When asked about her rules for interviewing figures of state, she says that she never takes notes, as it might distract them. She treats important figures as human beings and does not expect information on their political views. If they have important statements they are not given to reporters, but rather are held for public speeches. The interview is valuable only for the opportunity to study personality.

Before she went to see Mussolini she read (in her halting Italian) the then new *Law of Corporations,* a thick and imposing legal volume. Mussolini asked her what interested her most in Italy and she replied: "The new law for the corporate state." When she admitted that she had read it, *Il Duce* smiled, extended his hand, rose and said: "My congratulations; you and I are the only ones who have!" Naturally there was no difficulty in seeing him after that.

Any woman has a difficult time becoming an outstanding journalist—for it is commonly supposed to be a "man's world." To become outstanding on the New York *Times* is even more difficult because that paper has "remained a man's preserve." In 1936 Anne McCormick attained a new high in feminine achievement by being made a member of the then eight-man board of the editorial writing staff, sitting in conference with the board which "decides the policy of America's most influential paper."

Mrs. McCormick has written *Hammer and the Scythe: Communist Russia Enters the Second Decade* (1928). It received excellent

ANNE O'HARE MCCORMICK

reviews. Dorothy Thompson (see sketch this issue) said of it: "Mrs. McCormick has an eager eye, a delightful talent for noting significant details, and an active intelligence which plays upon all that she sees."

In 1937 Anne McCormick won the Pulitzer Prize for European correspondence. She was the first woman to be awarded a major Pulitzer Prize in journalism. All these honors have left her still a very modest woman. Sometimes she appears on the lecture platform and on the radio. After journalism, her hobby is art. When she lived in Ohio years ago she was one of the directors of the Dayton Art Museum, a post she still holds, although Dayton has not seen this globe-trotter in some years. In New York she lives quietly at a hotel. Certainly a quiet place should appeal to a woman who remembers a tea one afternoon in Palestine with the District Commissioner of Jerusalem—a tranquil, beautifully served tea in the best British tradition. Afterward the official walked with her through the delightful garden to the road where her taxi was waiting. They stood on a low stone wall chatting, and then she took her leave. Twenty minutes later the wall was blown to bits by a time bomb set the previous night and ominously ticking away the minutes under her feet as she made her leisurely adieux.

References

Cur Hist 50:27+ Jl '39
Ind Woman 18:192b Jl '39 por
J Crim Law 30:964 Mr '40
N Y Times My 4 '37; p21 F 25 '40
Newsweek 7:33 Je 20 '36 por
Think 5:16 D '39

American Catholic Who's Who

MACCORMICK, AUSTIN H. Apr 20, 1893- Penologist

Address: b. Osborne Association, 114 E 30th St, New York City; h. 9 Gracie Sq, New York City

On January 15, 1940 Austin Harbutt Mac-Cormick resigned from the position of commissioner of correction for the city of New York to become executive director of the Osborne Association, Incorporated, a privately supported organization whose aim is to promote more effective methods of dealing with adult criminals and juvenile delinquents.

He knows prisons and prisoners at first-hand and through long experience. In his last year at college he became interested in the work of Thomas Mott Osborne, advanced penologist, and wrote a commencement address on modern penology. Immediately after graduation he had himself locked up in the Maine State Penitentiary at Thomaston, booked as a forger. MacCormick picked half a dozen lifers, most of them in for murder, as his particular cronies and cultivated them assiduously. They were the aristocrats of the prison and had the most to offer an earnest young investigator. He stayed in prison a week, seeing everything there was to see, and when he came out described the prison as "a disgrace to the state" and declared that conditions were "worse than barbarous."

Again he served a voluntary prison sentence, this time with Thomas Mott Osborne, as a deserter. They were investigating the naval prison at Portsmouth, New Hampshire under the direction of the Secretary of the Navy. Shortly after they had made their report to Washington, the United States went into the War and MacCormick joined the Navy. After a commission as ensign he was assigned as executive officer to Osborne, then commander of the prison. From July 1917 until May 1921 they worked to make it the ideal expression of their theories, an institution without walls, one in which the inmates shared in the prison government.

Just before going to Portsmouth, Mac-Cormick had married Gertrude Albion, daughter of a Universalist minister in Portland, Maine. He and his wife lived with Commander Osborne during the reformers' terms of duty there. "On and off duty, Osborne dominated their lives, talking about his theories, reading poetry to them, playing the piano to them. MacCormick regarded Osborne as his spiritual father, and considers himself today to be Osborne's spiritual heir and successor."

In collaboration with Paul W. Garrett, as field representatives of the Osborne Association, MacCormick visited all the prisons and reformatories in the United States except three, in 1927 and 1928. The two investigators reported their findings in the 1929 edition of *The Handbook of American Prisons and Reformatories.* The *Handbook*

includes complete descriptions and critical comments on all the institutions visited by the authors.

Going to the United States Bureau of Prisons as assistant director (1929), he assisted Sanford Bates in the introduction and initiation of programs of probation, parole, social service and education, including libraries, in all the Federal prisons. He made an outstanding contribution to penology, and during the period of his service the Federal prisons became models for all state prisons and reformatories.

The Education of Adult Prisoners, which MacCormick published in 1931, is a book that ought to be under every warden's pillow. In 1927 and 1928 he made a study of educational and library work in American prisons and reformatories. He found the educational work in the penal institutions to be so limited that he soon realized that the principal task was not to describe what was being done, but to formulate a workable program demonstrating what could be done with adequate financial support and competent personnel. There are chapters on the aim and philosophy of education for prisoners, the teaching of illiterates, vocational education, the library as an agency of education, health education, class rooms, shops and equipment, etc.

From the United States Reformatory at Chillicothe, Ohio, where he was on temporary duty reorganizing the institution, Mayor La Guardia (see sketch this issue) called Mr. MacCormick, then acting superintendent, to head the New York City Department of Correction in January 1934. Welfare Island, the city penitentiary, was notorious for gambling, vice, political control and narcotic smuggling. One observer described it as a "country club gangsters," ruffians who led lives of incredible luxury and power, usurping the hospital quarters from which they had driven the really infirm, regaling themselves with costly food and drink, waited upon by obsequious prisoners and prison officials.

On the day that the Commissioner "raided" the institution, less than a month after his appointment, the institution tension ran high. The prisoners had been locked in their cells, improper privileges were suspended and a search was being made for drugs, weapons and other contraband. Nerves were on edge.

Commissioner MacCormick, a small wiry man, "almost frail looking" according to the New York *Sun,* but "a bundle of nervous energy," moved about briskly, and his "cold nerve and complete mastery of the situation was demonstrated when 800 prisoners filed into the mess hall for the evening meal. After a turbulent day in which he had experienced at least one narrow escape from injury, the Commissioner astounded his associates by walking into the big mess hall alone, unprotected.

"The men were seated at their tables. A big, husky guard turned pale at the gills when he saw the little Commissioner.

There was an ominous silence. Slowly, with measured tread, Commissioner MacCormick continued down the long hall, unmindful of the angry glances of the prisoners.

"Then two convicts broke into a slow grin. They recognized and appreciated such nerve. Their grins eased the situation. Others followed suit, and soon all the prisoners were smiling. 'Hey, Commissioner, how do you like us now?' one of the prisoners called. This brought laughter. The Commissioner smiled and continued his inspection."

In 1937 the outdated prison at Welfare Island was closed and the population moved up the East River to a new and modern institution at Ricker's Island. There was developed a model city institution, the largest in the world, with an intake of 25,000 men annually—an institution well-run, up-to-date, free from political and boss control.

During Commissioner MacCormick's administration a number of improvements in the New York City prison set up were inaugurated: segregation of prisoners, system of classification, a well-rounded medical program and a complete educational service, including a library of 10,000 volumes with a trained librarian in charge. From its former scandalous condition the Department of Correction was raised to a high standard of efficiency and integrity.

In 1935 Commissioner MacCormick was a member of the faculty at Columbia University, lecturing on criminology. In 1938, Georgia, the state famous for its chain gangs, called him to aid in working out a new penal system. He has recently been invited by four different states to help on widely differing penal problems.

Mr. MacCormick is an indefatigable lecturer, delivers innumerable addresses to prison conventions and other conferences, advocating the use of socialized and educational techniques in the rehabilitation of prisoners. He has spoken to many organizations, clubs and colleges and contributed articles on prison education, medical service, libraries, discipline, food problems and on various phases of delinquency and crime to periodicals and journals. In 1939 he was president of the American Prison Association, and is either an officer or director of many other organizations.

Mr. MacCormick, a blue-eyed, dark-haired, dapper, young-looking man, was born in Georgetown, Ontario, Canada, April 20, 1893. He was brought to the United States by his parents, the Reverend Donald (Scotch Presbyterian Minister) and Jean (Green) MacCormick in that same year. After he had been graduated from Bowdoin College, Brunswick, Maine (1915), he was an English instructor at that institution (1916-17) and alumni secretary (1921-28). The college awarded him an honorary Doctor of Science degree in 1934. He received his Master of Arts degree from Columbia Uni-

AUSTIN H. MACCORMICK

versity in 1916 and the Honorary Doctor of Laws was conferred by St. Lawrence University, Canton, New York, in 1937. In 1928 he was assistant for one year to the president of Bennington College, Vermont, in charge of fund-raising in New York City.

Mr. MacCormick has two children, Joan, 18, and James A., 16. On January 6, 1936, after having been divorced by his first wife during the previous year, he was married a second time—to Mrs. Patricia Welling of New York City.

He takes his work—and himself—very seriously, and yet has a reputation as a humorous after-dinner speaker. His conviviality serves somewhat to disguise his real, evangelistic self, as does also his dead-pan expression, which enables him to see everything while appearing not to see anything.

He places great confidence in prisoners, and has cultivated the ability to talk with them on an equal footing without letting them lose sight of the fact that he is not one of them. He is said to have talked with more prisoners than any other man in the country. Many of them look him up when they get out, and he does what he can to help them. He keeps his wardrobe thinned down to bare essentials, most of the time, by giving away suits and other clothing to ex-convicts who come to see him.

Many disillusioning experiences have not soured his faith in the ultimate success of rehabilitating prisoners: of making them over, to some extent at least, substituting decent for twisted viewpoints and ambitions by means of healthy activity, vocational training, education, work, reading, the careful segregation of the mentally and physically abnormal who need specific treatment, and case work with the families of prisoners.

MACCORMICK, AUSTIN—*Continued*

References

Bul Osborne Assn News 11:1-3 F '40 por
Lit Digest 117:5-6 F 3 '34 por
N Y Herald Tribune X p6, 17 S 2 '34 por
N Y Times p15 Ja 12 '40 por
New Yorker 10:26-29 My 26 '34 por
Who's Who in America
Who's Who in Government

MCCORMICK, WILLIAM PATRICK GLYN, REV. June 14, 1877—Oct 16, 1940

Vicar of St. Martin-in-the-Fields, London, and a chaplain of the British King since 1928; went to Transvaal in Boer War as chaplain and remained in South Africa as Vicar; was chaplain in France during First World War; became vicar of Croydon in 1919 and an honorary canon of Canterbury in 1923; relinquished both offices in 1927 to become vicar of St. Martin-in-the-Fields; sermons and addresses frequently broadcasted

References

Who's Who

Obituaries

N Y Herald Tribune p28 O 17 '40
N Y Times p25 O 17 '40 por

MACCRACKEN, HENRY NOBLE Nov 19, 1880- Educator

Address: President's House, Vassar College, Poughkeepsie, New York

For over 25 years Henry Noble Mac-Cracken has been the president of Vassar College. For over 25 years he has spread his doctrines of liberalism throughout the school he heads. To him any sort of ivory tower attitude is out of place on the campus: "the modern college must lead in defining moral and social objectives."

This college president who has done much in his life to further the causes of democracy believes that "it is the moral obligation of a college in a democracy to teach democracy." Since this can best be done through living, "the college becomes a laboratory for democracy, through conference, through discussion, through voicing its ideals and through organizing all activity in committees democratically formed."

Both the students and faculty have, in these many years, responded to Dr. Mac-Cracken's ideas and ideals. Today Vassar is one of the leading liberal women's colleges in the United States. Today it is equipped to teach its students all those subjects which make for successful living in a democracy.

Students and faculty alike have responded, too, to the quiet charm of Dr. MacCracken's personality. It has been said that one of his most striking characteristics is "his capacity for understanding exactly how an undergraduate feels." He is with these undergraduates a good deal. He likes to browse around the campus with them; he takes parts in their plays; he joins the faculty in baseball games against the students. After dinner in one of the campus houses he often reads poetry aloud; he goes with the Student Association on picnics and there cooks steaks and sings amusing songs in several languages. Dr. MacCracken is a rather shy man, but "despite his shyness there is a great deal of warm friendliness in his manner."

Dr. MacCracken's progressive ideas about women's education and his beliefs in equal opportunity for women, as well as his many publications, have made him one of America's outstanding educators. Yet he had no intention of becoming an educator at all, despite his family background. His father, Henry Mitchell MacCracken, was for many years Chancellor of New York University; his elder brother, John Henry MacCracken, was at one time president of Lafayette College.

Henry Noble MacCracken was born in Toledo, Ohio, the son of Henry Mitchell and Catherine (Hubbard) MacCracken, and almost from the time he could read "always wanted to be an explorer." When he was eight he won as a prize a copy of Nansen's book on the first crossing of Greenland, and his desire for travel and adventure was sharply stimulated. To prepare himself he studied many languages.

In 1900 Dr. MacCracken received his B. A. and a Phi Beta Kappa key from New York University and tried to get himself some sort of an exploring job, or a position with a scientific expedition. He was unsuccessful and as a sort of compromise went to the American College at Beirut in Syria to teach English. He stayed there for three years and while there wrote his first book, *First Year English* (1903). In 1903 he was offered the position of dean, but his health had been weakened by a bad bout of typhoid and his father came to take him home to regain his strength.

By the time he returned to America Dr. MacCracken had discovered that he loved teaching and that this, rather than travel, was going to be his life work. He went back to New York University to get his Master's Degree and then went on to Harvard, where he got both his M. A. (1905) and his Ph. D. (1907). He has since been awarded an LL. D. by Smith College and by Brown University.

Right after Dr. MacCracken got his Ph. D. he was married to Marjorie Dodd of New York and spent the first year of his married life as a John Harvard Fellow. Then, in 1907, he became an instructor in English at the Sheffield Scientific School of Yale University, staying there as instructor and assistant professor through 1913. During these years there appeared his second textbook, *English Composition in Theory and Practice* (1909), written in collaboration with others; he was author or

HENRY NOBLE MACCRACKEN

part author of *An Introduction to Shakespeare* (1910), *Minor Poems of Lydgate, Part I* (1912), and *The College Chaucer* (1913); and he edited *The Serpent of Division* (1911).

From 1913 until 1915, the year in which Dr. MacCracken went to Vassar, he taught English at Smith College. Here and since he has continued to publish books—in 1927 appeared *Ten Plays of Shakespeare* and *John the Common Weal;* in 1934 Part II of the *Minor Poems of Lydgate*. Always his main fields have been Chaucer and Shakespeare, though his interests have been as wide as literature and the world.

When, at the age of 35, Dr. MacCracken went to Vassar, the first question he was asked was: "Where do you stand on the issue of suffrage?" He answered calmly that he had no doubts that women should vote. In the same calm way he has continued to take the lead in the liberalization of women's education and in progressive teaching, changing the curriculum and the methods of presenting it whenever necessary.

Today Dr. MacCracken looks more like the head of a bank or a prosperous businessman than a scholar and college president. "He is tall and somewhat heavily built," and his manner is quiet and emphatic. "In conversation he talks freely with a smile in his eyes; often, but not always, in rather involved phrases. His writing, by contrast, is simple and direct."

References

Christian Sci Mon Mag p3+ Je 1 '40 il por
N Y Times VII p8+ S 24 '39 il por
Who's Who in America
Who's Who in American Education

MCCULLERS, CARSON Feb 19, 1917-
Author

Address: c/o Houghton Mifflin Co, 432 Fourth Ave, New York City

The most highly praised and widely discussed work in fiction to be published during the summer of 1940 was *The Heart Is a Lonely Hunter*, a first novel by a 23-year-old Southern girl. Critics in general agree that Carson McCullers, considering her youth, has written a remarkable story. Since it goes well beyond the "promising" stage of competent first novels, her future output will be watched with unusual interest.

Written with symbolic and realistic variations on the theme of human loneliness, *The Heart Is a Lonely Hunter* concerns a group of people in a small Southern mill town. The realism, natural and convincing, centers around Mick Kelly, tomboy girl in a down-at-heels family of several children. The girl's awkward, intense adolescence, her driving dream of being a musician and her healthy physical growing-up are handled with a tough-minded yet tender touch. The symbolism hangs upon the mystical deaf-mute, John Singer, whose Christ-like, apparent serenity invites the secret soul-confidence of the story's other characters. He is more of a focal-point than a personality; but his strange, maternal-like affection for another deaf-mute, the fat, greedy, mentally dull Greek, Antonapoulos, is strongly reminiscent of the relationship between Steinbeck's (see sketch this issue) George and Lennie in *Of Mice and Men*. Other characters in the book have come obliquely out of Faulkner or Caldwell (see sketch this issue).

The theme is the plot: the hungry search of these people for an escape from individual loneliness, for self-expression and for identification with what each most idealizes in human living. The author claims for her novel a larger intention: "The book is a parable in modern form, and the fundamental idea is ironic. Indeed it is a story of Fascism, but it must be understood that the word is used here in its very broadest terms and that it deals with the spiritual rather than the political side of that phenomenon." Very few readers will get any idea from the story that it is about a struggle between Fascist and anti-Fascist forces in the human soul. As Clifton Fadiman says in his review of the book: "On this level, it's a failure; Miss McCullers simply hasn't got what such a myth takes. On the simpler level, it's a story with an extraordinary obsessive quality, eerie and nightmarish, yet believable."

The author's style supports her realism, but is not adequate to the purposive symbolism. The book, she says, is a parable; and indeed the opening sentence is parable-styled: "In the town there were two mutes and they were always together." Beyond this, however, the writing is alien to that of the parable or myth. Nor does the narrative follow the direct narrative form the

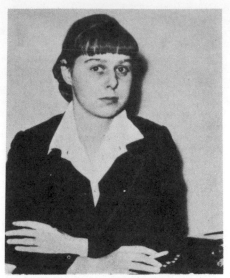

CARSON MCCULLERS

parable demands. But as a whole *The Heart Is a Lonely Hunter* has a cool power and violence rare in so young a writer's work; it shows a precociously exact command of significant incident; and its characters as a group are much superior to the symbolic theme the author wishes upon them.

Carson McCullers was born in Columbus, Georgia on February 17, 1917, the daughter of Lamar and Marguerite (Waters) Smith. Her father's ancestors were French Huguenots who came to this country to escape persecution; her mother's people were from Scotland. "I have been writing since I was 16 years old," she says. "After finishing high school very early I loafed for almost two years before getting off to New York and to school again. I began to write at about this time. For several years before then my main interest had been in music and my ambition was to be a concert pianist. My first effort at writing was a play. At that phase my idol was Eugene O'Neill and this first masterpiece was thick with incest, lunacy and murder. The first scene was laid in a graveyard and the last was a catafalque. I tried to put it on in the family sitting room, but only my mother and my eleven-year-old sister would cooperate. My father, who was startled and rather dubiously proud, bought me a typewriter. After that I dashed off a few more plays, a novel, and some rather queer poetry that nobody could make out, including the author.

"When I was 17 I went to New York with the idea of going to classes at Columbia and at the Juilliard Institute. But on the second day I lost all my tuition money on a subway. I was hired and fired from various part-time jobs and went to school at night. But the city and the snow (I had never seen snow before) so over-

whelmed me that I did no studying at all. In the spring I spent a great deal of time hanging around the piers and making fine schemes for voyages. The year after that *Story* bought two of my short stories and I settled down to work in earnest."

She married Reeves McCullers in the fall of 1937, and before returning to New York she and her husband lived for two years in North Carolina. There Mrs. McCullers worked on *The Heart Is a Lonely Hunter* and for recreation took long walks in the woods or played the piano and listened to phonograph records. She and Mr. McCullers are now living in New York City in an apartment lined with books that reveal her tastes: Dostoievsky, Marcel Proust, James Joyce, Thomas Mann, Thorstein Veblen among them. She is much interested in the refugee problem, and feels deeply about the refugee children. "Although we have awfully little money," she says, "we talk about adopting a refugee child from France. We feel we should give one a home, if only for a few years, until the parents get a fresh start. Or perhaps one whose parents are lost." It is reported that Carson McCullers' new book on which she is hard at work will be about the refugees. During the summer of 1940 she was awarded a fellowship at the Bread Loaf Writers' Conference, Middlebury, Vermont. In August she sold a novelette to *Harper's Bazaar—Reflections in a Golden Eye*. After running serially it will be published in January 1941.

Carson McCullers has been told that she looks like a cross between Garbo and Slim Summerville, and she doesn't seem to mind.

References

N Y Herald Tribune Books p11 Je 23 '40
N Y Times Book R p6 Je 16 '40
N Y World-Telegram p12 Jl 1 '40
New Yorker 16:77-8 Je 8 '40
Sat R Lit 22:6 Je 8 '40

MCCUNE, CHARLES ANDREW Oct 17, 1879—Oct 13, 1940 Research engineer; helped develop non-destructive method of testing metals for flaws; developed arc-welding electrodes and cylinders for safe storage and transportation of acetylene; author of many papers and several books on metallurgy and welding; since 1932 associated with Magnaflux Corporation

References

Who's Who in Engineering

Obituaries

N Y Herald Tribune p12 O 14 '40
N Y Times p19 O 14 '40

MCDANIEL, HATTIE June 10, 1898- Motion picture actress
h. 2177 W 31st St, Los Angeles, California

In March 1940 Hattie McDaniel was given an award by the Academy of Motion Picture Arts and Sciences for her performance as Mammy in *Gone With the Wind,* the first Negro ever to win an "Oscar." She had wanted the part badly and when it came her turn to be tested she just "opened her heart and let the tears flow out." There were no more Mammy tests after that, for Selznick put her under contract at once.

Her latest rôle, in *Maryland,* confirms the fact that the Hattie McDaniel who once took in washing is in the movies to stay. She was the thirteenth child of a Baptist minister, Henry McDaniel and his wife, Susan (Holbert) McDaniel, born in Wichita, Kansas on June 10, 1898. While she was still a baby her parents moved to Denver, Colorado and she was graduated from the public school there and spent two years at the East Denver High School. It was in Denver that fame first came to her, when she was 17 and sang over the radio with Professor George Morrison's Orchestra. At 18 she won a gold medal from the Women's Christian Temperance Union for reciting *Convict Joe.*

Immediately she plunged into her stage career, playing the entire South for the Shrine and Elks Circuits. Then she got on the Pantages Circuit and headlined it in 1924 and 1925. They began to call her "the colored Sophie Tucker" and the "female Bert Williams." She was writing her own act, too. When bookings were slow she would get herself a job in somebody's kitchen until things picked up.

Things looked worst the time she arrived in Milwaukee, without money and with no prospects for a job. All she could get was a place as maid in the ladies' room of Sam Pick's Suburban Inn. But one night, after all the entertainers had left, the manager called for volunteer talent from the help. Hattie sailed right out of the ladies' room and launched into *St. Louis Blues.* She got herself a job starring in the floor show and stayed there for two years until she decided to try the movies.

In 1931 Hattie McDaniel arrived in Hollywood and began the rounds of the studios. She managed to get a few extra and atmosphere rôles, but not enough to keep going on, and in between she took in washing. But she didn't stop making the rounds of the casting offices. Finally she landed fairly good parts, the cooking and laundry jobs grew fewer and fewer and Hattie was seen on the screen more and more.

She appeared in *Judge Priest, The Little Colonel* and *Showboat,* in which she sang *I Still Suits Me* with Paul Robeson and another number with Irene Dunne. Work kept coming. *Saratoga, The Mad Miss Manton, Nothing Sacred* are only a few of the movies she was seen in. Meanwhile she got the rôle of Hi-Hat Hattie in a popular radio show and that of "Mammy" on the radio *Show Boat* coast-to-coast program.

Round-faced Hattie McDaniel has been married twice. Her first husband died and she was divorced from her second. Now,

HATTIE MCDANIEL

with her niece, she keeps house in Los Angeles.

References

Photoplay 54:80 Je '40 por (p71)
International Motion Picture Almanac

MACDONALD, SIR GEORGE 1862—Aug 11, 1940 English authority on ancient coins; one of foremost classical scholars in England; expert on Roman Britain; medalist of the American Numismatic Society in 1926; appointed permanent secretary of the Scottish Education Department from 1922 to 1928; knighted in 1927

References

Who's Who

Obituaries

N Y Times p15 Ag 11 '40

MCGUIRE, WILLIAM ANTHONY July 9, 1887—Sept 16, 1940 Playwright; scenarist; greatest success as a playwright came in the 1920's with *Six Cylinder Love* and *Twelve Miles Out*; until 1926 was associated with Florenz Ziegfeld; wrote many of that producer's revues, including *Kid Boots; The Three Musketeers; Smiles* and *The Follies* of 1922 and 1923; became one of the highest paid scenarists in Hollywood; wrote *The Kid From Spain; Roman Scandals; The Great Ziegfeld; Rosalie; Girl of the Golden West* and *Lillian Russell*

References

Burns, M. Contemporary American Playwrights p305-18 1938
International Motion Picture Almanac
Who's Who in America
Who's Who in the Theatre

MCGUIRE, WILLIAM ANTHONY—
Continued

Obituaries

N Y Times p23 S 17 '40 por
Newsweek 16:59 S 23 '40
Time 36:51 S 30 '40

MACKENZIE, CLINTON 1871—Mar 9, 1940 Industrial architect associated with group which planned model industrial city of Kingsport, Tennessee; yachting enthusiast

Obituaries

N Y Herald Tribune p12 Mr 11 '40
N Y Sun p19 Mr 11 '40

MCKENZIE, RODERICK DUNCAN Feb 3, 1885—May 6, 1940 Chairman of the department of sociology at the University of Michigan since 1930; served on President Hoover's Research Commission on Urban Problems in 1929

RODERICK DUNCAN MCKENZIE

References

Leaders in Education 1932
Who's Who in America

Obituaries

N Y Times p25 My 7 '40

MACLEAN, MALCOLM SHAW Jan 4, 1893- Educator

Address: Hampton Institute, Hampton, Virginia

The election of Dr. Malcolm Shaw MacLean as the sixth president (all have been white) of Hampton Institute, Negro educational institution, was announced May 7, 1940. Hampton Institute was founded in 1867 by the American Missionary Asso-

ciation which, being concerned with the fate of freed slaves, purchased a Civil War hospital in Virginia and with three teachers and fifteen students, started what was destined to become an outstanding college for Negroes. Today, with an endowment of $10,000,000, Hampton Institute occupies 74 acres, has 139 buildings and an enrollment of 987 Negro students. It offers vocational courses in farming, business, teaching, homemaking and trades.

The new president, the son of Lester and Mary Dewey (Shaw) MacLean, was born in Denver, Colorado. He attended East Denver High School, then went to Hamilton College (1912-14) and received his B. A. from the University of Michigan in 1916. Immediately after graduation he married Marion Hastings Brown. Later he did graduate work, earning his Ph. D. from the University of Minnesota in 1929 and taking courses at Northwestern and Michigan Universities. But, writes Dr. MacLean: "A very large portion of my education has come from experience outside of the classroom as sheep herder, soda jerker, office boy, delivery boy, newsboy, librarian, tutor, sewer cleaner, gardener, carpenter and newspaper man."

Dr. MacLean's rise to fame in the field of education began as an English instructor at Northwestern University. After three years there he taught at the University of Minnesota for one year. Following an interval of newspaper work (editor Laguna, California *Beach Life,* 1920 to 1921, and successively copy reader, financial editor, night editor of the Minneapolis *Tribune* from 1921 to 1924) he returned to the University of Minnesota, staying for five years as student counselor and instructor. Then he became professor and later assistant director of the Milwaukee Center of the University of Wisconsin Extension Division.

In 1932 Dr. MacLean was appointed director of the University of Minnesota's General College, an experimental school for "misfit college students" once dubbed "Moron Hill" and "Capsule College" because it concentrated upon those students who were unable to meet the entrance requirements for other departments of the University and trained them in practical vocational fields. Under MacLean "The University of Tomorrow" has become one of the leading experimental colleges in the country.

In order to determine the effect of a college education Dr. MacLean made a survey, reaching the conclusion that: "It is appalling to discover that there are few, if any, observable differences, in other respects than earning power alone, between the graduates and non-graduates. . . They are culturally much alike: they listen to the same radio programs, read the same magazines, go to the same movies, feel much the same about their jobs and their families and their health, carry on the same, and for the most part, spectator types of recreations, and almost uniformly find democratic par-

ticipation in social and civic affairs dull as
dishwater and comparatively unimportant."

From Dr. MacLean's work have come
many publications. In 1930 he compiled
Men and Books with E. K. Holmes, a
collection of essays from various types of
minds, on men and books as additional testimony to the use of reading. *Scholars,
Workers and Gentlemen* (1938), an Alexander Inglis Memorial lecture delivered at
Harvard, is a diagnosis of our educational
ills which proposes cures and is "well conceived, rigorously and clearly presented"
and "merits careful attention." Besides
articles on college and adult education in
periodicals, he has edited the *American
General Education* series, including *Students
and Occupations* (1937), *What About Survey
Courses?* (1937) and *Income and Consumption*
(1936 and 1937); and contributed to *Effective General College Curriculum* (1937), *The
Rôle of the Library in Adult Education*
(1937), *Write What You Mean* (1938), and
other books.

Dr. MacLean is chairman of the National
Committee on General Education; a member of the National Committee on Intellectual Freedom and Democracy; a member of
the advisory board of the Institute of Propaganda Analysis; a member of the National
Council of Parent Education, a member of
its executive board (1936-40), vice-president
(1938-39); Fellow of the American Academy
of Political and Social Science.

Handsome, silver-haired Dr. MacLean is
"sharp-eyed, square-jawed and dynamic."
He writes us: "My hobbies are: first, fishing
(my General College staff at Minnesota has
just presented me with a magnificent deep-
sea rod and reel to insure my recreation at
Hampton Institute); second, gardening,
with a particular passion for flowers in the
blue ranges; photography, with a special
bent toward what have come to be known
as documentary pictures, particularly of
human beings, supplemented by Koda-
chrome shots at great magnification of
minute subjects (I have, for example, a
shot of a mosquito on a house screen which,
when projected, makes him six feet long in
the body with a nine-foot wing spread and
a business proboscis that looks like a canoe
paddle); laying rock wall and doing stone
masonry; and finally, reading vast quantities of detective novels. The only trouble
with this hobby business is that I don't
get time enough to do it. My chief business outside of education—particularly experimental education to try to make education make sense—is my home and family
life with my three children and Mrs. Mac-
Lean. The eldest son is married to a lovely
girl, has a small apartment in St. Paul, and is
entering his sophomore year in medicine
on his way to psychiatry. The second son
is already a master photographer and is
looking forward to getting his Ph. D in
education, with training to enable him to be
an interpreter to students of all the arts.
My daughter, Mary Katharine, a sophomore at Stephens College, is putting in

Cheyne

MALCOLM SHAW MACLEAN

four or five hours a day at the piano. In
consequence of all this, and particularly
because he who experiments in education
must work from dawn until dark and after
six days a week, spend the seventh getting
ready to work six more, there are not
nearly enough hours in a twenty-four-hour
day for all that I should like to do."

References

N Y Herald Tribune p10 My 8 '40
    por
Newsweek 14:41-2 S 18 '39; 15:38 My
    13 '40 por
Time 34:38 S 18 '39 por; 35:46+ My
    13 '40 por
Who's Who in America

MACLEISH, ARCHIBALD (màk-lēsh')
May 7, 1892- Poet; head of the Library of
Congress

Address: b. Library of Congress, Washington, D. C.; h. Farmington, Connecticut

Sometimes a writer or public figure who
tries to keep his humanitarian outlook free
of intellectual bias or partisanship becomes,
ironically, the storm center of that partisan
controversy he decries. This has happened
more than once in the career of Archibald
MacLeish. A poet who believes in public
speech by poets, the head of the Library of
Congress who believes that a library must
in all ways serve the public, MacLeish found
himself once again the subject of public
attack following his address May 23, 1940
before the Adult Education Association.

This was a speech condemning the pacifist
attitude of the younger generation in
America, its lack of belief in the "final
things for which democracy will fight," its
apparent lack of conviction that "Fascism

ARCHIBALD MACLEISH

is evil and that a free society of men is good and is worth fighting for." The responsibility for this attitude MacLeish placed upon the writers of his own generation who knew the last War: books like Dos Passos' (see sketch this issue) *Three Soldiers,* Hemingway's *Farewell to Arms,* Aldington's *Death of a Hero.* These words against war, he said, were written by honest men with great skill, but they have borne "bitter and dangerous fruits." MacLeish, who himself felt as these writers did and wrote as they were writing, now feels that what they wrote "was disastrous as education for a generation which would be obliged to face the threat of Fascism in its adult years."

By many people this latest attitude of MacLeish is regarded as a startling about-face for the author of *The Fall of the City* (1937) and, particularly, *Public Speech* (1936); for the chairman of the 1937 Congress of the League of American Writers, a Left-wing organization; and for the active speaker in defense of Loyalist Spain. Most writers and critics agree that his attacks upon such books about the last War are unjustified. They feel that the widespread general skepticism among youth is not the result of reading Hemingway and Dos Passos (many of them never have done so) but derives from the same causes that produced the books in the first place; youth is by no means convinced that this time it would be fighting for a "free society." Ernest Hemingway replied to the attack by saying: "If the Germans have learned how to fight a war and the Allies have not learned, MacLeish can hardly put the blame on our books." Edmund Wilson represents a further viewpoint. At this moment of excitement, he said, it does not create reassurance to hear the Librarian of Congress

talking about "dangerous" books, saying that "certain kinds of writers should be discouraged from giving expression to certain kinds of ideas." And the League of American Writers has issued a protest stating that MacLeish's address, "however it was intended, does suggest censorship and censorship is an instrument of Fascism. Coming at this critical moment, it gives aid and comfort to those reactionary forces which sought to block Mr. MacLeish's appointment as Librarian of Congress."

MacLeish's speech was a continuation of an attack previously launched from another angle in a speech before the American Philosophical Society on April 19, 1940, printed in an article, *The Irresponsibles* (*The Nation,* May 18, 1940), censuring scholars and writers for their blindness, their failure to recognize the peril that is Fascism. This was later published in book form. Hitherto divided, scholars and writers must unite in one profession to "defend the disciplines of thought." Critics of MacLeish have replied that it is not the words of writers which have caused a revolution, or a Hitler; that the real failure of liberals and intellectuals has been their inability to unite on common ground in defense of the ideals of democracy: while they argue and disagree, a united Fascism conquers. The present quarreling and dispute over MacLeish's statements might be taken as a case in point.

MacLeish pursued the theme of the militant writer in the keynote speech made during October 1940 at the tenth annual New York *Herald Tribune* Forum. The rise of Fascism has made necessary the mobilization of all resources, material and spiritual, for the defense of democracy—it is a mobilization of which American writers and artists are a part. But their function is to defend themselves not by interrupting their lives but by fulfilling them through creating for the future.

When President Roosevelt, in 1939, decided to appoint Archibald MacLeish, whom he termed "a scholar and a gentleman," Librarian of Congress, MacLeish became the target of considerable controversy. The House rafters rang with opposition: he was known as a fellow-traveler of the Communist Party, had spoken on the same platform with Communists, had defended Loyalist Spain. To the attack leaped the American Library Association, headed by Milton J. Ferguson: the most important library in the world needed for its head an experienced library administrator, not a mere poet. But scholars and writers in general, and some librarians, applauded the appointment. Dr. Herbert Putnam, MacLeish's predecessor, warmly listed his qualifications: "There is first the Scot in him—shrewd, austere, exacting, but humorous. There is the poet in him—whose stuff is not made of mere dreams but of realities. . . There is the humanist, keenly sympathetic to all that calls for social sympathy. The lawyer—trained to analysis through determination of exact issues. The soldier—pledged to duty under discipline. The athlete—pledged to fair play. And finally there's the orator—capable of vivid and forceful speech."

Archibald MacLeish is not the man to take an important job on sinecure terms. He believes the burden of education has fallen upon libraries, and he has a dream of the library as a vast, popular, people's information service. Practically, his plans included the listing of some 1,800,000 unrecorded volumes in the main catalog of the Library of Congress; the creating of 50 new positions in the processing division; the getting of books at the copyright office at the time they go to reviewers; seeing about raising the disgracefully low salaries of library workers—under $2000 a year—a reflection of the general salary level of librarians throughout the country. As head of the Library of Congress, MacLeish has thus far proved himself a man of energy, insight and real executive ability. But lovers of poetry—many critics consider him the most significant poet of our time—hope that he may also continue the work that he has temporarily been forced to put aside.

Archibald MacLeish was born May 7, 1892 in a wooden chateau overlooking the waters of Lake Michigan at Glencoe, Illinois, son of Andrew and Martha (Hillard) MacLeish. His father was a Scot born in Glasgow, one of Chicago's early settlers and a successful merchant; his mother was a Connecticut woman who taught at Vassar College. A normal, democratic American boy, "Archie" MacLeish hated the fashionable Connecticut preparatory school to which he was sent. At Yale he led an active undergraduate life. He was on the football and swimming teams (he was a water polo player and diver and still performs creditably on the springboard); he was editor of the Literary Magazine and made Phi Beta Kappa. He says he went to the Harvard Law School to avoid having to go to work: he led his class there, but never liked law. At Harvard, however, he won the lasting friendship and admiration of Felix Frankfurter. He married Ada Hitchcock of Farmington, Connecticut in 1916 while still in Law School.

During the War MacLeish was with the field artillery in France, later rose to the rank of captain at Camp Mead. He writes that in the War he won no distinction "but the fact that my brother, Kenneth, had been a great flier and had been killed." After the War he taught for a year at Harvard, then successfully practiced law for three years in Boston. But MacLeish never wanted to be a lawyer; he wanted to write poetry. So in 1923—the year he says his "real life" began—the MacLeishes went with their two children to live in France, in or near Paris. They also cruised for a time on the Mediterranean and spent one spring in Persia. MacLeish was greatly influenced, technically, by French poetry:

Laforgue, Rimbaud, Valéry. His earliest writing showed also the influences of Eliot and Pound. Between 1924 and 1928 he had published four books of verse. After his return to America he went, in 1929, to Mexico to gather background material for his long narrative poem, Conquistador, following by pack mule the entire route of Cortez to the Valley of Mexico. It was Conquistador that won for him, in 1932, a Pulitzer Prize.

In order to support himself and his family, MacLeish variously taught, lectured and took on jobs in journalism. In 1930 he began writing for Fortune. A writer-editor of Fortune has no easy task; but his associates on that magazine were amazed at MacLeish's energy and capacity for organizing his work. "He would come to the office in the morning at nine, get through a prodigious amount of mail, tell his researchers just what he wanted and where to get it and then write graceful, forceful prose until five in the afternoon." He wrote almost all of the Japanese issue of Fortune in two months' time; and every article save one collected in the book, Background of War, was written by him. From 1938 to 1939, prior to his appointment as Librarian of Congress, MacLeish was curator of the Nieman Collection of Contemporary Journalism at Harvard.

The head of the Library of Congress may find recorded in its catalogs some 15 books of his own verse. Critics of contemporary American poetry have been interested in tracing MacLeish's development from the personal or private in subject, romantically colored and highly imitative early work through a transition period in which he developed a more objective, historical outlook, to the later powerful lyrics and verse-plays with a keenly developed, critical social viewpoint. The Happy Marriage (1924), a sonnet sequence on marital love, in the romantic tradition, was followed by The Pot of Earth (1925), showing the marked influence of Eliot's Wasteland. Streets in the Moon (1926) was unimportant except for the notable long poem, Einstein; but in New Found Land (1930) MacLeish had perfected his own technique, best illustrated in the lyric, You, Andrew Marvell. This book brought him critical acclaim, and Conquistador (which he personally now likes least of his books) a much wider audience. It describes the conquest of Mexico as narrated by Bernal Diaz, an old fighter under Cortez, an epic of greed full of dramatic and colorful imagery. MacLeish's shift to the realism of social protest came in 1933 with the publication of Frescoes for Mr. Rockefeller's City, satiric poems on past corruption in American life and various aspects of the contemporary scene. MacLeish's humanitarian conscience was in evidence here; yet because the evidences of health in America that he saw and his ideals for it were apart from organized partisan movement, Michael Gold and other Communist critics bitterly attacked the

MACLEISH, ARCHIBALD—*Continued*
book. But MacLeish kept on the way that seemed right to him. He felt that he had something to say, but needed a larger medium than the lyric for saying it. Accordingly he wrote *Panic* (1935), a play in verse on the bank crisis, in which the rôle of the proletariat versus capitalism was shown. Produced three times, it received on its third night, from an audience of poorly paid clerks, laborers and unemployed, such an ovation that MacLeish said, much moved, "Now I have found my audience." He was convinced from then on that a poet must face the real world, that he cannot shut out public matters and concentrate on personal matters, that the significant poet is one who employs a "public speech." In his book, *Public Speech,* he projected his image of mankind:

"The brotherhood is not by the blood certainly:
But neither are men brothers by speech
—by saying so:
Men are brothers by life lived and are hurt for it."

Because he felt that the radio could be, for the poet, a means of reaching a great audience, MacLeish wrote *The Fall of the City,* first performed by the *Columbia Workshop* in 1937. This play against the coming of Fascism was followed in 1938 by *Air Raid,* less effective as poetry, but more strongly anti-war. *Land of the Free* (1938) was another experiment in media: the America of strikes, dust bowls, depressions, sharecroppers, told through a series of fine photographs with an accompanying verse-commentary. *America Was Promises* (1939), his most recent poem, is another "public speech," a call to Americans for action before the "others" (Fascists) take over. Leaner in effect, weaker as good verse than his previous writing, the poem at the same time forecast MacLeish's attitude as expressed in his speech before the American Association for Adult Education, condemning the pacifist stand.

John Chamberlain (see sketch this issue) has said that MacLeish may seem to have wavered between various Leftist ideologies, but he has never deviated from democratic and humanistic values. Independent, courageous, he is not easily influenced; as a man of great personal charm and conviction, he often influences others. His manner is quiet, forthright, wholly without pose or affectation. His voice, his quick, boyish grin, his crisp hair that shows little gray make him look much too young to have grown-up sons; his wife, Ada, blonde and vivacious, looks even younger. The MacLeishes like people and have varied friends and interests; but they like to spend as much time as possible on their farm near Conway, Massachusetts.

References

Am Mercury 51:369-74 N '40
Atlan 165:786-90 Je '40

Christian Sci Mon Mag p6+ Mr 23 '40 il pors
Commonweal 27:602-3 Mr 25 '38
Library J 64:864+ N 1 '39
Nation 148:689 Je 17 '39; 150:618-23 My 18 '40; 150:678 Je 1 '40
New Repub 99:171 Je 21 '39; 102:789-90 Je 10 '40
No Am R 243:330-43 Je '37
Pub W 137:2125 Je 1 '40
Sat R Lit 20:10-11 Je 24 '39 por
Time 33:18 Je 19 '39 por
Wilson Lib Bul 14:560-1 Ap '40
Kunitz, S. J. ed. Living Authors 1937
Loggins, V. Intellectualism and Experiment *In* I Hear America p307-30 1937
MacLeish, A. Archibald MacLeish *In* Schreiber, G. ed. Portraits and Self-Portraits p67-70 1936
Who's Who in America
Zabel, M. D. Cinema of Hamlet *In* Zabel, M. D. ed. Literary Opinion in America p415-26 1937

MCNARY, CHARLES LINZA (màc-nā'rē lǐn'zà) June 12, 1874- Senator; 1940 Republican Vice-Presidential candidate
Address: b. United States Senate, Washington, D. C.; h. Salem, Oregon

When Senator Charles Linza McNary, "best lubricator and trouble shooter in the Senate," was nominated by the Republican National Convention as Wendell Willkie's (see sketch this issue) running mate, he accepted the nomination philosophically: "I am grateful for the confidence reposed in me by the convention," he said, "but I wish they had imposed the chore on someone else. However, I am a good soldier and will do the best I can."

"Geographical considerations apparently played a major part in the decision of party leaders to pick me," he explained further. The tall, slender Senator from Oregon, representative of the West and farming interests, did, to the Republicans and much of the country, present a perfect complement to Mr. Willkie, representative of the East and business interests. Willkie is a public utilities man—not much of a recommendation in the West; McNary is against public utilities. Willkie is strongly for reciprocal trade treaties, McNary is against them; Willkie is weak in practical political experience, McNary, who has been in the Senate 23 years, is "serpent wise in politics."

Although there may have been occasional doubt whether the combination of Willkie and McNary was a correct one, there was complete unanimity on McNary's qualifications for the Vice-Presidency. In 1936 McNary was frequently mentioned as a Republican Presidential candidate and the late Senator James Couzens of Michigan offered to put up $100,000 to start a campaign for him. But McNary scotched that idea. On the back of a Senate restaurant menu he scribbled a

message one day and sent it across to
Couzens:

"The presidential bee is a deadly bug
I've seen it work on others.
Oh Lord protect me from its hug
And let it sting my brothers."

McNary was mentioned for the Presidency
and nominated to the Vice-Presidency because of his enormous popularity—a press
gallery poll once chose him as the most
popular Senator—because of his liberalism,
because of his pro-farmer activities, because
of his political wisdom.

In his campaign speeches, McNary credited the Roosevelt Administration with "certain social gains" but attacked it for its
defeatism, "stop-gap" farm legislation. He
conceded defeat on the election night before his running mate did and promised to
give "Mr. Roosevelt and his associates a
worthy and vigilant opposition."

As minority leader of the Senate since
1932, Senator McNary has been called "the
best political catalyst in the Republican
ranks." In these years he has often strayed
from the conservative fold, but he hasn't incurred the dislike of conservative Republicans. In early New Deal days his job was
a hard one, for his party was divided and
the voters back home wanted no party politics and little opposition to the President's
program.

McNary tried to dissuade Republican headquarters from launching broadside attacks on
the Roosevelt program and refused to participate in the 1934 Republican campaign because
he considered it too anti-Administration in
tone. From 1933 to 1935 he voted with
the New Deal nine times and against it
seven. He voted for the Wagner Act, the
National Recovery Act, bills for additional
funds for TVA, old-age pensions, additions
to the appropriations for the Department of
Agriculture. His only speech in the Senate
in Roosevelt's first term was a 15-minute
defense of the Social Security Bill, in which
"he exhibited willingness to go further than
Roosevelt had gone."

However, Senator McNary is a long way
from going along with Roosevelt and at times
has attacked his proposals strongly. It was
he who moulded the Senate minority into a
potent opposition and his strategy that
handed the New Deal its most crushing Congressional defeat when the Supreme Court
Reform Plan was introduced. Instead of
rushing in to attack it, McNary withdrew to
a secluded spot and imposed silence on his
fellow Republicans—a tough job. "Let the
boys across the aisle do the talking," he
would say, "smiling dreamily as he shot his
cuffs." The boys across the aisle did, and it
was the Democrats who took the headlines
in the Supreme Court debates and finally
defeated the plan.

In 1938 McNary urged drastic revision of
the Federal farm labor and social security
statutes. He pleaded for government economy and the return of relief administration

CHARLES L. MCNARY

to the states. In 1939 he took a leading part
in the fight for cuts in the President's relief
fund request. Always he has opposed revision
of the Neutrality Law and has been firmly
against Roosevelt's reciprocal trade treaty
policies. In 1940 he went so far as to say
that the New Deal had forced on the people
"a temporary depression as a permanent way
of life."

When the New Deal is working for the
farmer, however, McNary is right along
with it, for he is one of the staunchest supporters of agrarian interests in the Senate.
Among the farmers he is said to have "a
more genuine backing than any other member of his party." He first appeared as the
hope of agrarian organizations in 1926 when
he sponsored the McNary-Haugen Farm
Bill which would have permitted the government to sign contracts with grain growers to sell abroad at lower prices than in
the home markets and to receive recom-
pense through an equalization fee paid out
of a tax bill. This, the most radical measure to pass a conservative Congress, was
twice vetoed by Calvin Coolidge.

McNary's belief that "substantial support
must be given to the farmer," is only one
plank in a program he advocated in 1938
for the Republican Party. He advocated,
first of all, that it be "progressive," continuing many New Deal policies. He advocated more economy and decentralization
in the handling of relief; clearer definition
of the laws against monopoly; simpler forms
of taxation; and a "conduct of international
relations that will maintain American rights
with a minimum of risk of embroilment in
foreign wars."

Even though there are a few Republicans
who don't go along with McNary in his
ideas and proposals, he is still the most
effective minority leader the Republican

MCNARY, CHARLES L.—*Continued*

Party has seen for many years in the Senate. "Mild and pleasant in manner, invariably cheerful and rarely losing his temper," he is no drill sergeant who maintains discipline by whipcracking methods. His cloakroom negotiations are always skillful —so skillful that he is often called into consultation by factions of the Democrats. After all these years he has many firm friendships which include "blown-in-the-bottle old line Republicans, rampant progressives, New Dealers and unreconstructed and bellicose Southern Democrats."

McNary, the "best-liked man in the Senate and its ablest parliamentarian," has been a Senator since 1917. He was born on June 12, 1874 on a farm near Salem, Oregon which his grandfather, an emigrant from Tennessee had tilled. When he was four his mother died and his father a few years later. His eldest sister Nina was left to rear a family of nine children.

After high school in Oregon, McNary entered Leland Stanford University in 1896, but left after only two years, in 1898, the year he was admitted to the Oregon Bar. He went into the law office of his brother, the late John H. McNary, and stayed there until 1913 when he was appointed a justice of the Supreme Court of Oregon to fill an unexpired term. In 1915 he stood for election to the Court but lost out by one vote. When his friends urged a recount, he said: "To the hell with it."

The next two years McNary acted as chairman of the Republican State Central Committee and in 1917 was appointed to the Senate to fill a vacancy. In 1918 he was elected to a full term and has been reelected every six years since then. In Oregon he has become a "political tradition," a man who was able to carry his state in 1936 when Roosevelt won the electoral college votes.

When sandy-haired, impeccably-dressed Charles McNary first came to the Senate in 1917 a curious reporter asked him what he was interested in. "Nuts," said the Senator. He meant filberts. He has twenty acres of them on his farm five miles north of Salem, Oregon, as well as extensive orchards of walnut, cherry and pear trees. Whenever he can get away from Washington Senator McNary hurries with his wife, the former Cornelia Morton, whom he married in 1923 (his first wife died many years ago) and his adopted daughter, Charlotte, to his farm, famous as a bird sanctuary, a laboratory for horticultural experiments and the home of the largest prune grown, the Imperial, which Senator McNary developed himself.

References

Christian Sci Mon Mag p1, 2 Ap 27 '38 por

Lit Digest 117:9 F 10 '39 por; 118:12 S 29 '34 por; 121:36 Ja 11 '36 por; 125: 9 Ja 22 '38 pors
N Y Herald Tribune p1, 3 Je 29 '40; p7 Jl 4 '40
N Y Times p1, 3, 4 Je 29 '40; p1 Jl 1 '40
Newsweek 3:19 Ja 20 '34 por; 15:9 My 6 '40
R of Rs 89:31 F '34 por
Scholastic 28:23 F 1 '36 por
Time 30:11 Ag 23 '37 por; 34:11 Jl 31 '39 por; 35:20 Ap 15 '40
Who's Who in America
Who's Who in Law
Who's Who in the Nation's Capital

MACNEIL, NEIL Feb 6, 1891- Newspaperman

Address: b. New York Times, 229 W 43rd St, New York City

Neil MacNeil has found time to write a book on journalism despite the fact that he is in the hurly burly of active newspaper work. As assistant managing editor of the New York *Times,* MacNeil has put the paper to press five nights a week for ten years. He knows the business of putting out a newspaper from A to Z; he knows the problems of the reporter, the editor, the mechanical departments and the business office.

And he has explained them all in a remarkably clear and interesting book, *Without Fear or Favor,* published March 1940. To the layman the book performs a real service in taking him behind the scenes of a business that may seem complex and puzzling to him. To the student of journalism it should prove a valuable, informative handbook. For MacNeil knows whereof he speaks, and speaks honestly.

News background and news problems have been a life-time study to this "tall lantern-jawed Scot who looks like a football coach." He has a vast reading background of history, economics, sociology, government. He has studied news-gathering problems at firsthand on visits to most of the news centers of the world. Born in Boston, Massachusetts, February 6, 1891, he was graduated in 1912 from St. Francis Xavier University, Nova Scotia. Before coming to the *Times* in March 1918 he had already served as city editor for two Montreal newspapers (*Gazette* and *Daily Mail*), as well as serving during the World War in the trade test division of the personnel department of the United States Army. Since the fall of 1914 he has thus had a major rôle in the coverage of every important story, and he continued this while becoming, successively, assistant telegraph editor, head of the city copy desk, foreign editor, night city editor and in 1930, assistant managing editor of one of the world's most important newspapers.

In all these 28 years of experience, handling hundreds of thousands of stories, MacNeil is proud to be able to say that there has never been a libel action on any story written, edited or directed by him.

N. Y. Times

NEIL MACNEIL

MacNeil is proof of the fact that the modern successful newspaper man is not the whisky-guzzling, swearing "tough-guy" portrayed in popular movies and plays. As the author remarks in his book: "The city staff of the metropolitan newspaper is a smooth, fast-functioning machine, one of the most competent of this age of efficiency. The reporter and his city editor are quiet, capable and educated gentlemen."

The city staff of tomorrow's metropolitan newspaper will be an even more efficient machine, by the way, if a prediction made in MacNeil's book comes true. He forecasts two newspapers for every home, one carrying local news exclusively, the other a worldwide newspaper edited at one central office and transmitted by sound photo to key cities throughout the country for simultaneous distribution.

In addition to his regular newspaper work and occasional free-lance writing, MacNeil sandwiches in time somehow for his hobbies of walking, golf and travel. He is also a former governor of the New York Athletic Club, former president of the Clan MacNeil Association of America and a member of the Dutch Treat Club.

In 1920 he married Elizabeth Quinn. They live in Forest Hills, Long Island, and have three children Mary Rose, Nancy and Neil, Jr.

References

N Y Herald Tribune Books p10 Ap 7 '40

N Y Times Book R p4 Ap 7 '40

Newsweek 15:42 Ap 1 '40

American Catholic Who's Who

MCNUTT, PAUL VORIES July 18, 1891–
Administrator Federal Security Agency
Address: b. Federal Security Agency, Washington, D. C.; h. 3025 N. Meridian St, Indianapolis, Indiana

In 1925, when Paul McNutt was dean of the Law School of the University of Indiana, his cronies at card games frequently heard him say: "It would be kind of nice to be President of the United States, wouldn't it?" In 1940 the dream came close to reality as his backers got busy rounding up votes for the Presidential convention. McNutt's candidacy however hinged entirely on Roosevelt's decision about the third term, and in the middle of the convention he dropped out as a possible candidate with a plea for the nomination and election of President Roosevelt.

"Tall, tan, terrific" Paul McNutt, known as a democratic glamour boy, was born in a simple frame cottage at Franklin, Indiana, the son of John Crittenden and Ruth (Neely) McNutt, third-generation Indiana residents of Scotch-Irish descent. He was a delicate, only child whose mother liked to dress him in Lord Fauntleroy suits which promptly made him the target for the town's rougher boys. In high school at Martinsville, Indiana, he was president of his class, pitcher on the base ball team, organizer of a dramatic club and founder of a school publication. Entering Indiana University in 1909, he continued to exercise his amazing ability to achieve leadership by becoming editor of the campus paper, class president etc. It is interesting to note that his rival for campus leadership was a radical student named Wendell Willkie (see sketch this issue). As a student McNutt was conservative and "something of a snob."

After he received his B. A. in 1913 his family obtained a loan on their home in order to send him to Harvard to study law. IIis father, at 76, is still a lawyer at Martinsville and is a former state judge. For a few months after Paul received his degree from Harvard in 1916 he practiced law at home, but his keen eye was searching the horizon for more exalted work. In the summer of 1917 he enlisted in the army and emerged with the rank of major, although he saw no overseas service. He married Kathleen Timolat of San Antonio and they have one daughter, Louise, a student at Indiana University.

After the War McNutt became a professor at Indiana University in the law department, and was made dean of the law school at the age of 34—youngest dean in the history of the law school. While dean, McNutt showed an interest in the local American Legion Post of which he was a charter member. With his ability to organize and assume leadership, he won the post commandership, later the state command, and finally the national command (1928-29), although many of the delegates wanted a commander with overseas experience.

PAUL V. MCNUTT

As commander he became known in every state and especially in Indiana. Although a Democrat in a strongly Republican state, his American Legion experience pointed the way for the Governorship and in 1933 he was elected. As Governor he instituted progressive legislation and "plucked the state from a bad economic and civil crisis." He was appointed United States Commissioner to the Philippine Islands in February 1937, and left that post in 1939 to become Federal Security Administrator in Washington.

On December 3, 1940 he was designated by the President as "coordinator of all health, medical, welfare, nutrition, recreation and other related fields of activity affecting the national defense." The new duties will not affect his status as Federal Security Administrator.

Jack Alexander in an article in the magazine *Life* describes him thus: "He is conscious of his bodily grandeur—his six-feet-two of height, his 195 lbs., his pale blue eyes and umbrageous black brows—and has got more out of a head of platinum hair than any other American, barring possibly the late Jean Harlow. . . He smokes menthol cigarets, reads detective mysteries, drinks moderately, plays poker and shoots golf in the 90's. During a campaign he sleeps four or five hours a night and dozes sitting upright in an automobile speeding 75 m. p. h. from one engagement to another."

References

Am Mag 129:26-7+ Ja '40 por
Am Mercury 41:430-7 Ag '37; 49:30-6 Ja '40
Christian Sci Mon Mag p7+ Ap 20 '40

Collier's 92:10-11+ N 18 '33; 104:13+ Jl 22 '39 por; 105:14+ Ja 20 '40 por
Cur Hist 50:7 Ag '39; 50:32 S '39 por
Ladies' H J 56:58 D '39 por (p23)
Life 8:64-73 Ja 29 '40 il pors
Nation 147:86-8 Jl 23 '38; 150:415-8 Mr 30 '40
Time 29:10 Mr 1 '37 por; 34:15-17 Jl 10 '39 il pors; 34:18 N 27 '39 por
Who's Who in America 1938-39
Zink, H. Paul V. McNutt *In* Salter, J. T. ed. American Politician p62-76 1938

MACROSSIE, ALLAN, REV. 1861—Mar 2, 1940 Methodist Church leader; organizer and director of the Methodist ministerial training courses in 1921

Obituaries

N Y Herald Tribune p36 Mr 3 '40

MALTZ, ALBERT (mältz) Oct 28, 1908- Author; playwright

Address: c/o Little, Brown & Co, 34 Beacon St, Boston, Massachusetts

The discipline of literary economy which the theatre imposes on the playwright has, presumably—and certainly this is true of the writings of Albert Maltz—a carry-over effect in the execution of a good short-story. Maltz is concerned with that one-third of a nation that is ill-fed, ill-clothed and ill-housed, and he proceeds with what Michael Gold calls the emotion of identity—"no mere slummer's pity . . . but a fraternalism that becomes an identification and a philosophy. . . These are his people, and what happens to them also happens to him. . ."

Albert Maltz was born on October 28, 1908, in Brooklyn, New York. His parents had come to America as immigrant children: his father, Bernard Maltz—who began as a grocer boy and became a contractor and builder—from Lithuania; his mother, Lenz (Sherry) Maltz, from Poland. He attended public schools and then entered Columbia, where he majored in philosophy, was elected to Phi Beta Kappa and was graduated in 1930. He studied playwriting (1930-32) at Yale under George Pierce Baker. And in October 1931 he and George Sklar, neither of whom had been able to ignore the social effect of the Tammany machine, were set upon turning out a play which would arouse intelligent indignation.

Their *Merry-Go-Round*, with a good cast, opened on the following April 22, at the Provincetown Theatre in Greenwich Village. Soon outgrowing Macdougal Street, it was scheduled to open at the Avon on May 3. But the Commissioner of Licenses had informed the Police Commissioner that the Avon had no license (nor did 100 of the 166 theatres in the city). A week elapsed before four city department heads com-

Talbot

ALBERT MALTZ

pleted inspection—and approval—of the building.

Merry-Go-Round was an indictment—implicit but sharp—of city government in New York; and the revelations of the Seabury Investigation which was taking place at the same time only strengthened its innuendoes. The play ran until mid-June; screen rights (*Afraid to Talk*) were bought by Universal.

The Theatre Union took *Peace on Earth,* a Maltz and Sklar anti-war collaboration, for its first production (1934); and in 1935 staged *Black Pit,* the tale of a young West Virginia coal miner who is forced by exterior circumstances to become a stool pigeon and is eventually trapped. For concentration of motif and clarity of projection it was decidedly good theatre. The best of Maltz's three one-act plays, *Private Hicks,* won first prize in the New Theatre League Contest in 1935 (see *Best Plays of the Social Theatre,* 1939).

Meanwhile he was writing short stories, seven of which were later collected in 1938 under the title, *The Way Things Are. Man on a Road (New Masses,* January 8, 1935), said to have been reprinted in more labor journals than any other piece of American fiction, loomed into the forefront at the time of the silicosis investigations by Congress (January 1936), because of its startling resemblance to the testimony of the tunnel-diggers from Gauley Bridge, West Virginia; and *Season for Celebration,* a novelette laid in a Bowery flophouse on New Year's Eve, was included in *The Flying Yorkshire-man,* a Book-of-the-Month Club choice for May 1938.

The Happiest Man on Earth, a study of unemployment's most corrosive effects on the morale of young men, brought Maltz first prize in the 1938 O. Henry Memorial

Awards. It moves with the same nervousness that underlies the central character's quiet but reckless eagerness to regain a few comforts for his family.

His first novel, *The Underground Stream,* was published June 26, 1940. It is a story about a Communist automobile worker in Detroit. "It might, with a few minor changes, have been about an early Christian martyr," according to Lewis Gannett.

Maltz married Margaret Larkin of New Mexico in 1937, and they live with their son Peter in New York City. He is an instructor of playwriting at the Writing Center, School of Adult Education, New York University, and is a member of the Council of the Author's League. He has taught at summer writers' conferences at Boulder, Colorado.

References

New Repub 83:302-4 Jl 24 '35
Scholastic 32:12 Mr 5 '38

MAMLOK, HANS J. 1875—Nov 11, 1940 Leading pioneer of modern dentistry in Germany; head of Dental School of University of Berlin until he came to United States in 1937; his works standard textbooks in many countries for more than a decade; longtime editor of Germany's leading dental periodical; research resulted in many technical improvements, notably "Mamlok fixation" for tightening loose teeth, treatment for arresting pyorrhea; treated many famous international figures; Friedrich Wolf's anti-Nazi play, *Professor Mamlock,* supposedly based partially on his life; soon after its production in Switzerland life in Germany became too uncomfortable or him to stay there

Obituaries

N Y Herald Tribune p20 N 12 '40 por
N Y Times p23 N 12 '40 por

MANDEL, GEORGES (măn-dĕl) June 5, 1885- Former French Minister of the Interior

First on the list of civil trials at Riom in 1940 was the name of Georges Mandel, former French Minister of the Interior noted for his "deadly" efficiency. M. Mandel was charged with treason—plotting with Great Britain "against the security of France"—and with general guilt in having brought France into World War II. A further indictment accused him of "corruption in speculating in the value of the franc." Since the Riom prosecution would have very much enjoyed making an outstanding example of him, it must have been somewhat embarrassing for Pétain (see sketch this issue) that his enemy had already been acquitted of the treason charge before a military court at Meknes, Morocco, where he fled after the Armistice in an attempt to rally the Colonial Army in North Africa to continue the fight against Germany as Britain's ally. Rumors that M. Mandel had

Wide World

GEORGES MANDEL

sent bulging *dossiers* abroad with which he could "blow the lid off" the French situation could not have made the Vichy government more comfortable, either.

The man whom Clemenceau once called "not conspicuous, but very serviceable," was born in France on June 5, 1885. His name was originally Jeraboam Rothschild. The first anyone seems to have heard of him was when he appeared in the offices of Clemenceau's *Aurore* in 1904, "rather pale, with wide-awake, searching eyes, the nose of a gourmet or a hunter, and a thin, scornful mouth," and asked for a job on the newspaper. "You are an ugly rat," the Tiger is supposed to have said. "So I can see in that mirror," replied the stranger, pointing to the glass opposite Clemenceau. The latter, with his instinct for making use of other men's talents, eventually recognized in Mandel a "bloodhound, a conscientious agent, a Jack-of-all-trades," and hired him. He ended up by nicknaming him "mon ami Pierrot," telling him he would never learn how to write, but not to mind, just to remember: "A subject, a verb, a direct object. When you have to use an indirect object let me know."

For after all, if the "solemn, peremptory" Mandel couldn't write, there were other things he could do. Reporting on the Moroccan situation, for instance, he could collaborate with the more literary M. Albert, dictating to him "with the look of a chief mourner." (Clemenceau had told Albert jokingly: "Mandel, who would know everything if he knew how to write, will give you the ideas.") But it was really true that Mandel was as remarkable for his erudition as for his devotion to the Tiger. And although when Clemenceau became Minister he didn't make his protégé a member of the

Cabinet, Mandel served in Sarraut's Cabinet later, and after Sarraut's resignation his association with Clemenceau became permanent. The Tiger treated him roughly, made jokes about him, but never deserted him; Mandel in turn spent much of his time amusing himself sadistically by reading the most critical portions of Clemenceau's "press" aloud to his chief, but was unswervingly loyal.

During the First World War, when Clemenceau was made Premier, Mandel became his *chef de cabinet* (1917-20), and his power was almost unlimited. Leaving Clemenceau's mind free for matters more military and international, he virtually took charge of France's domestic policy during the War as well as preparing her post-War domestic policy of unity against Bolshevism—the elections of 1919 were his work—and, although dozens of deputies pleaded with the Tiger to get rid of him, the requests were always refused. Mandel also served as Clemenceau's private secretary with unusual powers, had his own secretary, a luxuriously appointed house.

In December 1919 Mandel was elected deputy and general counselor from the Gironde. He also ran for Mayor of Souillac, but when, in January 1920, Clemenceau was defeated for the Presidency, he renounced any career outside of Parliament. It had been generally (and often hopefully) hinted that Mandel would vanish when Clemenceau did, but instead he became "a sort of invisible Richelieu, an *éminence grise* behind the scenes," during the early '20s leader of the *Bloc National* and a bitter enemy of the Socialists and those Radical Socialists who had withdrawn from it.

He kept making enemies both Left and Right, however, by his manner—in public "peremptory, harsh and aggressive"—by his sharp and skillful tongue, his love of recrimination, his refusal ever to yield a point to an opponent, his infallible memory for everything others would prefer to forget. He in turn was as scornful of popularity as he was of criticism, made his way by will power, a quick intelligence notable for its clarity and logic, an unfailing instinct for making himself useful to great men and a love of complications for their own sake that sometimes passed for expert diplomacy and sometimes for complete lack of principles.

In 1924 Mandel was defeated for deputy and not re-elected until 1932, but this did not lessen his power. A word to the left, a word to the right, intervention from the Tribune of the Chamber, and Briand was overthrown through his influence; in 1930 he was reported to be "the man behind Tardieu" and was surely "the most hated and most slandered person in France."

In 1932, when he was re-elected, he became president of the Independent Group in the Chamber, also president of the Commission of Universal Suffrage—an office which he had held before in 1929. By 1934 it was being said of him: "It is certain that in this period of Fascism he remains one of the most amazing Parliamentary figures. He loves Parliament in so far as he despises it and feels able to dominate it. But he loves it sincerely." And almost in the same breath he was still being called such names as a "jungle beast without heart or nerves," a "magnificent sadist."

Up to November 1934 he had steadily refused any formal office. When Flandin became Premier, however, he accepted the position of Minister of Posts and Telegraphs, and in the Bouisson and Laval (see sketch this issue) Cabinets of June 1935 and in Sarraut's of January 1936 he continued to hold this office. He could have the wires of both his political friends and enemies tapped indiscriminately, and there seems to have been little doubt that he did. Even Flandin, it was said, couldn't outwit Mandel's listeners; and although Mandel's information on the "secret life of the Third Republic" must already have been encyclopedic, it became even more formidable. No one has accused him of being inefficient, however. He went in for reform—removed the personnel of his department from labor union politics, took commercial advertising out of broadcasting, improved radio programs, encouraged progress in television, initiated a highly efficient information and messenger service for the benefit of telephone subscribers.

About this time, as Mandel himself put it, the Franco-Soviet Pact was creating alarm among many Nationalists because they feared it might encourage the French Communist Party. "Their hostility, which was shrewdly stimulated by foreign propaganda, grew more intense when the French Communists took steps to weld the Popular Front." As an Independent Republican in the Chamber, a former member of the commission investigating the Stavisky affair, Mandel had a certain prestige with the Rightists. He persuaded many of their most influential members that any attempt to introduce Fascism by a *putsch* would bring on civil war, with the masses in an anti-Fascist mood. In April 1938, when he became Minister of Colonies in Daladier's (see sketch this issue) Cabinet, he insisted that no commitments be made in London contrary to the Franco-Czech and Franco-Soviet Pacts. He had never been accused of any tendencies toward German appeasement, even though his sympathies during most of his career might have been said to be with the Right and at times he had even been suspected of authoritarian leanings; and as a Nationalist deputy he had exposed the secret rearming of Nazi Germany. Now he was counted by Hitler among the more notorious "Franco-Russes," assailed by certain factions on the Right as "a sinister devil in the pay of the Jews, seeking to erect a Jewish-dominated France on the ruins of the Fatherland."

As Minister of Colonies, Mandel created colonial armies in preparation for the conflict which he foresaw; united them under the first colonial chief of general staff; fortified French Indo-China with anti-aircraft guns, coastal batteries, improved harbors; initiated public works there; expanded the light industries and the production of coal, tin, rubber, iron and rice. He thought that Daladier was for a policy of resistance and was intending to get rid of Bonnet. But before Munich, in protest against French policy, he resigned from Daladier's Cabinet. Soon after Munich, Italy, with her eyes on the Suez Canal, was holding anti-French demonstrations. The Suez Canal Company adopted "an intransigent position." Announced Mandel, sardonically: "Now we can feel safe. The Suez Canal Company is going to save the honor of France—with dividends as usual, of course!"

Reinstated as Minister of the Interior in March 1940, after Reynaud (see sketch this issue) succeeded Daladier as Premier, Mandel worked for the fullest possible collaboration between France and England. He said: "France—the France of Richelieu, of Danton and of Clemenceau—has never failed in a test of will." In May he ousted many officials for the safety of the French State. When France seemed on the verge of defeat he was one of those who advocated the merged Franco-British State proposed by Churchill (see sketch this issue), and was one of the strongest opponents of Pétain's armistice decision—perhaps because he knew more about the potential military strength of the French Colonial Empire than any other statesman. During the first 24 hours of Pétain's rule he was arrested while sitting with a general and a lady in a Bordeaux café. He was charged with hoarding arms to overthrow the Pétain government. Although released a few hours later with apologies, he refused to shake hands with Pétain. Shortly afterward he escaped to Morocco on the steamer *Massilia*, and it was in Meknes, Morocco, that he was acquitted of the charge of treason. It was necessary to bring him back to Riom for the second trial, and in France the news of his previous acquittal was suppressed until October 1940. The more recent charges of "corruption" were possibly based on the rumor that "Rothschild's fortune and Mandel's wiles were pooled for their joint benefit." Mandel has no great fortune, however.

Georges Mandel is described as a "pale, slender man" with "a sharp profile, dangling arms and a generally well-groomed appearance." At the Château Chazeron he was described as complaining about the cold, about his teeth. Confinement is not good for his disposition.

References

Cur Hist 44:109 Ap '36
Illustration 206:42 My 11 '40 por
Life 9:68 Ag 26 '40 por

MANDEL, GEORGES—*Continued*

Liv Age 338:23-5 Mr 1 '30; 346:51-4 Mr '34
N Y Times p2 Ag 16 '40; p7 O 4 '40
Newsweek 16:27 O 14 '40
Time 36:35-6 Ag 19 '40
Gunther, J. More About Frenchmen *In* Inside Europe p195 1940
International Who's Who
Katzin, W. tr. Monsieur Georges Mandel *In* As They Are p81-90 1923
Qui Etes-Vous?
Simone, A. J'Accuse 1940

MANLY, JOHN MATTHEWS Sept 2, 1865—Apr 2, 1940 Chairman of the English department at the University of Chicago from 1898 until 1933; wrote several textbooks on literature; known chiefly as a Chaucerian scholar

JOHN MATTHEWS MANLY

References
Leaders in Education 1932
Who's Who in America

Obituaries
N Y Herald Tribune p18 Ap 4 '40

MANN, ERIKA (män) Nov 9, 1905-
Author; lecturer
Address: h. c/o Farrar & Rinehart, Inc, 232 Madison Ave, New York City

Of all the political refugees from Hitler's Germany perhaps one of the most vocal and articulate is Erika Mann. From lecture platforms and in writing she has exhorted against the barbarism of the Nazi dictatorship and painted graphically the state to which the Hitler régime has reduced the Germans.

The daughter of Thomas Mann, the famous novelist (Erika and her brother Klaus are sometimes called "the Mann brats"), Miss Mann was, like her father, expatriated for her frank criticism of the Hitler régime. After the fall of 1936 she made the United States her home and traveled the length and breadth of the land delivering lectures. In the summer of 1940 she was in besieged London, doing journalistic work, helping with the evacuation of refugees, and broadcasting to the German people through the BBC. She came back to the United States in October 1940.

Erika Mann's early ambition was to be an actress, and she was, in fact, on the stage until the advent of Hitler turned her mind toward politics and made her a crusader for freedom. She was born in Munich, November 9, 1905, the eldest of the six children of Thomas Mann and Katja (Pringsheim) Mann. Despite the poverty of the First World War years (she tells of going barefooted from spring to fall because there were no shoes) Erika had an idyllic childhood. She and her five brothers and sisters spent the summers at their Tolz house and winters in Munich. There were amateur theatricals with the children of Bruno Walter, who was the Mann's neighbor in Munich, and never-to-be-forgotten hours when their father read them stories and they heard the manuscript of *The Magic Mountain* and the *Joseph* novels as they were being written.

Erika remained in Munich until she finished school. First she attended the backward Bavarian high schools from which she and her brother Klaus (see sketch this issue) had to be transferred because their relations with anti-Republican schoolmates and teachers became so strained. Next she attended a progressive type of school near Heidelberg. But all through her school days she took no interest in politics. As Miss Mann told an interviewer in America: "I was of the mistaken opinion that politics was the business of the politicians and that people should mind their own business. A lot of us thought so; that's why Hitler came to power."

When she left school she went to Berlin to study for the stage under Max Reinhardt. After a year in Berlin she went to Bremen and later to Hamburg. On the stage in Hamburg she met a young Left-Wing actor, Gustaf Gründgens, whom she married. When Hitler began gaining power Gründgens turned about face and became a Nazi, and later was elevated to the managership of the Berliner Staatstheater. Although she was no Jewess, Miss Mann divorced him and returned home to Munich. She acted at the Staatstheater there.

Even while she was still on the stage Miss Mann's restless energy manifested itself in outside activities. She traveled around Europe in an automobile-driving contest, driving 1,000 kilometers (621 miles)

a day, completing the trip in 10 days and telephoning reports to the newspapers from all stopping places. She won first prize for Ford in the competition and got the car as a keepsake.

She was already writing little articles and stories at this time. *Rundherum* (1929) was a book which she and her brother Klaus had written recording their around-the-world journey. She wanted to act in plays she had written herself, and *The Pepper Mill* was an outgrowth of this.

The Pepper Mill, a political-literary revue which Miss Mann had founded and produced, had just opened in Munich when Hitler became Chancellor of the Reich. *The Pepper Mill* lampooned the Nazis, but nevertheless it was still playing to capacity audiences when the Reichstag was burned, and it stopped only when Hitler's regent, Von Epp, appeared in Munich and the Nazi flag was hoisted on public buildings. Erika had to flee.

The elder Manns were in Switzerland on a holiday, and the Mann children telephoned them advising them to stay a while longer because "the weather in Munich was unpleasant." The next day they left to join their parents. That was March 12, 1933, and except for one secret night Erika Mann has not set foot in Germany again.

She went back once secretly to rescue the manuscript of her father's novel, *Joseph and His Brothers,* which had been left behind when Thomas Mann thought he was merely going off for a few weeks' holiday. The Mann house was being watched and the Nazis had forbidden the transfer of any of the Mann possessions. But Erika, wearing peasant costume and dark glasses for disguise, stole into the house, spent a few hours inside in total darkness and stole out again with the manuscript under her arm. The manuscript was with the tools under the seat of her car when she crossed the German border.

After she left Germany Miss Mann took *The Pepper Mill* through Holland, Switzerland, Austria, Czechoslovakia, Belgium and Luxembourg. It had 1,043 performances before it was banned after German government protests and an organized gas bomb riot in Zurich. The theatrical venture cost her her citizenship, but she was already English through her marriage in 1935 to W. H. Auden, the British poet, who, like herself, was an ardent anti-Fascist.

When Miss Mann came to America in 1936 it was her second trip to this country. The first time she came in the winter of 1927-1928 she took the United States more or less for granted. When she came with her family in 1936 it was after their voluntary exile from their own country, and she saw the United States anew as an example of the democratic way of living.

Miss Mann has appeared on the lecture platform jointly with her father, who occupies a chair at Princeton University, and with her brother Klaus, and by herself.

ERIKA MANN

Tall, dark, with closely-cropped hair, she is a vital figure. Her charm, and her tact in handling questions endear her to audiences. If she has turned from acting to writing and lecturing, she has nevertheless brought something of the appeal of the stage to the lecture platform with her eager, intelligent and tremendously alive personality.

Although she had had her start as a writer in Europe and had just published a juvenile adventure story, *Stoffel Fliegt übers Meer* (1932), before she left Munich, her most effective writing has been done since she came to America and turned crusader for the cause of democracy.

Her *School for Barbarians,* published in October 1938, reported scathingly what was happening under Hitler to Germany's children and Germany's once fine educational system. The book was thoroughly documented and contained a preface by her father. When it was published she was in Prague ready to fight with the Czechs against Adolf Hitler's forces. By winter she was back in the United States again, telling her story from the lecture platform.

Her next book, published in 1939 with her brother Klaus as coauthor, *Escape to Life,* gave a picture of German emigration, not only that of the Manns, but of others who represented German culture in the pre-Hitler days.

Erika and Klaus Mann jointly published another book, *The Other Germany,* in January 1940, which was something of an apology for the German neglect of politics which the Manns declared made Hitler possible. But the Germany of Hitler, the authors declare, is not the real Germany. There is "The Other Germany," fighting and sabotaging under cover.

MANN, ERIKA—*Continued*

Miss Mann followed this with a book of her own published in the spring of 1940, *The Lights Go Down,* which tells in true-story form what happened to various German citizens under the Hitler dictatorship. As examples she uses a priest, a doctor, a mother, a sailor, a newspaperman, a storm-trooper, a tradesman and an industrialist, and shows sympathetically how their private lives are affected by the privations imposed on them by the Hitler government.

References

Atlan 163:441-51 Ap '39
Time 32:45-6 O 10 '38 por
Wilson Lib Bul 13:728 Je '39 por
Mann, E. and Mann, K. Escape to Life 1939
Mann, E. and Mann, K. The Other Germany 1940

MANN, KLAUS (män) Nov 18, 1906-
Author; lecturer
Address: b. c/o Modern Age Books, Inc, 432 Fourth Ave, New York City; h. Bedford Hotel, 118 E 40th St, New York City

Although Klaus Mann has been writing since he was 17 years old and has published about 25 books, he is still referred to as Thomas Mann's son. He once told an interviewer that "the hyper-criticism with which people usually approach the son of a great writer rather hinders than helps him."

Klaus Mann, like the rest of his family, is an exile from Nazi Germany. But even before Hitler he lived abroad more than he lived in Munich, his birthplace, or in Berlin. From his earliest youth on, young Mann had Left-wing leanings. "Since I was 19 I have never ceased to protest—though with

Stein

KLAUS MANN

too weak a voice and with inadequate arguments—against reaction, imperialism, militarism, against nationalism and exploitation," he has said. "Most likely the Nazis would have killed me if they could have [reached] me. I left the Reich on March 12, 1933 and have never set foot in it since."

Young Mann wrote for newspapers and was a dramatic critic for a Berlin paper before his first novel, *The Devout Dance,* appeared when he was scarcely more than 20. Before his voluntary exile he had published about twenty books in German, including seven novels, several volumes of essays, and short stories. He also wrote a play, *Anja and Esther* (1925), in which he acted with his sister Erika (see sketch this issue) and which had a long run in Hamburg. They went on tour together with his second play, *Four in Revue.*

When the Nazis deprived him of his citizenship Mann became a citizen of the Czechoslovakian Republic in the days before it fell under Nazi domination. He has also lived in France, Switzerland and Holland. From 1933 to 1935 he edited a literary monthly, *Die Sammlung,* in Amsterdam, Holland and tried to use it as a medium for continuing fine German literary traditions and for fighting Fascism. He was forced to suspend publication, however, when his father, still in Germany, was threatened by the Nazis.

In 1936 he came to the United States and has been lecturing and writing in this country ever since. He has contributed to various American periodicals, including the *Atlantic Monthly, The Nation,* the *New Republic, Survey Graphic, Common Sense* and the *Saturday Review of Literature.* He has lectured by himself and also with his sister Erika Mann, warning against Fascism and dictatorships.

His first book published in English was *The Fifth Child,* in 1927, shortly before his first visit to the United States. There followed a novel, *Alexander* (1929), based on the life of Alexander the Great. *Journey into Freedom* (1936) was his first book published in exile.

There followed *Symphonie Pathétique* in 1935, a novel based on the life of Tschaikowsky, and the two books in coauthorship with his sister Erika, *Escape to Life* (1939) and *The Other Germany* (1940), both of which received excellent reviews.

Klaus Mann is unmarried. He was once engaged to Pamela Wedekind, who is now a member of the Berlin Staatstheater and married to Carl Sternheim.

References

Survey G 28:478-81 Ag '39
International Who's Who
Mann, E. and Mann, K. Escape to Life 1939
Mann, E. and Mann, K. The Other Germany 1940

MANNERHEIM, CARL GUSTAF EMIL, BARON VON   June 4, 1867-   Finnish statesman; military leader

Baron von Mannerheim, who, more than any other man, was responsible for the effectiveness of Finland's stand against Russia, has been called "ruthless", "a leader of truly heroic mold", "an individualist." Actually he is all of these.

Mannerheim was born in 1867 on his family's estate at Louhisaari, the third of eight children. The first Mannerheim of record was a Swedish merchant named Marheim who died in 1667. His grandson picked up a title and his son moved to Finland. The next Mannerheim was a judge and entomologist and the next one, Carl's father, started out as a spoiled intellectual rebel and ended up as a tycoon with a rich wife. In Carl himself was "a little of the tycoon, a little of the scientist, a great deal of the rebel."

The favorite story about Mannerheim's childhood, told by his family to point up his later success, is about a winter's day when he was eight years old. As he rushed across the city street leading his schoolmates in a snowball battle, he was run down by a sledge which passed over his body. The driver, horrified, stopped and asked the little boy who he was. As young Carl struggled to his feet he replied with as much pride as haste allowed, "I am general of the third grade," and rushed off to continue the attack.

At the age of 14 Carl was sent to the Hamina Cadet School and shortly after to the Nikolaev Cavalry School in St. Petersburg, from which he left with the rank of second lieutenant. Two years later he wangled a transfer to the Czar's Chevalier Guard. With no money or family connections, unable to speak the Russian language, his rise was amazing. It was his "striking looks, his unique horsemanship, and his instant grasp of military tactics which sent him upward like a rocket in the court of decadent Czardom."

After his marriage to Anastasia, daughter of Major General Nikolai Arapov of the Czar's suite, advancement was even more rapid. Although Anastasia bore him two daughters, this marriage never was a success, partly due to her bad health, partly to the excessive demands made upon him by court and military life. In 1903 they separated and she took the children to the South of France, to live there the rest of her life.

In 1893 Mannerheim became a first lieutenant, in 1899 a second captain, in 1901 a captain of cavalry. In 1904, when the Russo-Japanese War broke out, he clamored for front-line service. He arrived just in time to have his prize steed shot from under him at Mukden, in one of the most disastrous routs of the War. Mannerheim spent the rest of the campaign covering retreats and returned to Russia a colonel, with three decorations.

BARON VON MANNERHEIM

His fame as a horseman and reputation for military judgment were so great that he was picked to head an expedition through Asia to Peking to gauge the effect of Russia's lost war on the nations and tribes and to pick up military data for possible future use. The Mannerheim party traveled 8,750 miles on horseback during two years. For the army Mannerheim brought back topographic maps and a detailed analysis of all the military factors encountered. On his own account he had extended the expedition to the scope of a scientific expedition as well.

In 1913 he rose to be commander of the Czar's Uhlan bodyguard, and when the War broke out he was a major general. His reputation as a tactician was born soon after the War started. When the division of which his brigade was a part was attacked by strong Austro-German forces, his general, Delsal, ordered him to cover the right flank. Major General Mannerheim retired to the left, guarded the only road of retreat and saved the division. He received the order of St. George for that, and a special citation for insubordination.

After the March Revolution in Russia (1917), Mannerheim was in a ticklish spot. According to some accounts "suffering from a broken ankle," and according to others "conveniently developing a sprained foot," he left the front. Since the independence of Red Finland had just been declared, Mannerheim started for home. There are many stories of how he got there. One version states that he wore his dress uniform and commandeered a train, another that he awed the Russian privates with his commanding presence so that they let him pass through to a train unmolested, another that he disguised himself as a porter.

MANNERHEIM, CARL—*Continued*

When he reached Helsinki he found the city, and Finland, in turmoil. There had been rioting since March, with a Red Guard supporting the Social Democrat Party which had just lost its majority in the Diet, and a White Guard in the process of organization. The White members of the Diet named Mannerheim "commander in chief." Mannerheim outfitted his army in discarded Russian uniforms, rushed a garrison to get arms and the war was on.

Meanwhile Germany's General Von der Goltz had landed in Finland with 12,000 Germans. They took Hanko for the Whites, moved on to Helsinki, took Viipuri, and the Reds fled into Russia. On May 16, 1918, Mannerheim rode into Helsinki in triumph.

There are many conflicting versions of the White Terror that followed the Civil War, but nobody denies that Reds were executed by the thousands. The Soviet press claims 30,000 were executed, the *Encyclopedia Britannica* says 15,000, the Finnish government puts the figure at 2,000 executions, 10,000 dead of the flu. Whatever the figure, the Finnish Workers' Republic was ended.

Shortly after this Mannerheim resigned: according to one version it was because he insisted on emptying the huge prison camps and putting the nation back to work, while Germany was more interested in keeping the Reds broken and behind bars than in the restoration of Finnish strength; according to another, because Mannerheim wanted to move on Petrograd with the British Murmansk expedition while his pro-German government vetoed any cooperation with England. In fact, through the Finns' invitation, the Kaiser soon proposed his brother-in-law for King of Finland, and the Diet elected him.

The end of the War found Finland in an unhappy position, starving and with a German King. The only man who could get Finland out of it was Mannerheim. He did. He gained diplomatic recognition from London and Paris, and food ships were on their way even before his return from abroad. It was his cousin, Jacob de Julin, who negotiated the necessary loan from the United States.

Mannerheim was made Regent of Finland in 1918 and remained Regent for six months, after which he ran for President. He was defeated. The people were tired of war and soldiers, tired of his insistence on vengeance against the Reds, and they elected Professor K. J. Ståhlberg President by 143 votes to 50 on a platform of amnesty for the Reds.

Mannerheim's first act as a private citizen was to found the Mannerheim Institute for the Care of Children, which he made within a year one of the strongest stabilizing influences in war-racked Finland. His most consistent work as a private citizen was to bring his country into a state of preparedness for war. He wrote four textbooks on defensive tactics, he organized the Civic Guard 100,000 strong as a permanent reserve force, he urged the government into increasing its military appropriations each year. He picked out promising young officers in the army and had them sent to France and Germany to study military science.

In 1931 Mannerheim was made president of the Council of Defense and two years later became Finland's only field marshal. It has been said that he threatened to have nothing further to do with defense unless the government established conscription. It did. It was under Mannerheim's guidance that the now famous *Mannerheim Line* was built.

Before that fortification gave way, Baron Mannerheim declared: "We shall fight to the last old man and the last child. We shall burn our forests and houses, destroy our cities and industries, and what we yield will be cursed by the scourge of God." In 1940 the Finnish people are looking to him as their leader to bring reconstruction again, as he did in 1918.

In 1940 Baron Mannerheim is still fit for the task. He stands well over six feet. He still rides early every morning and there is no trace of gray in his jet-black hair. The Finns feel that he is equal to the task of reconstruction. To them he is still the "Liberator of Finland."

References

Christian Sci Mon p4 Mr 18 '40
Christian Sci Mon Mag p3 D 30 '39 il por
Cur Hist 51:48 F '40
Liberty 17:7-11 Ap 20 '40; 17:23-8 Ap 27 '40; 17:25-8 My 4 '40; 17:42-4 My 11 '40
N Y Herald Tribune X p4, 29 F 25 '40; p2 Mr 14 '40; p3 Mr 18 '40
N Y Times p5 Mr 18 '40
Time 35:29+ F 5 '40 il por; 35:26 Mr 25 '40
Borenius, T. Field-Marshal Mannerheim 1940
Forbes, R Tribute to Field-Marshal Mannerheim *In* These Men I Knew p273-82 1940
International Who's Who

MANNING, WILLIAM THOMAS, BISHOP May 12, 1866- Protestant Episcopal bishop

Address: Bishop's House, Cathedral Heights, New York City

As long ago as 1930 Bishop William T. Manning of the Protestant Episcopal Diocese of New York criticized Bertrand Russell (see sketch this issue) in a sermon delivered at the Church Club of New York. On Easter Sunday, March 12, 1940, without mentioning Russell's name, he appealed to his congregation "to make an open issue" with college and university heads and others who were supporting the appointment of

Lord Russell as professor and head of the department of philosophy of the College of the City of New York.

Bishop Manning supplemented his remarks with two letters to the New York *Times*. The first, on March 1, charged that Bertrand Russell was a propagandist against religion and morality, and a defender of adultery. The second, on March 12, gave additional quotations from Russell's writings to substantiate these charges.

Bishop Manning's protests started a vigorous campaign against Professor Russell's appointment. The Board of Higher Education of New York refused to reconsider their decision, by a vote of 11 to 7. An injunction was secured, however, and on March 30th the appointment was revoked in a 17-page decision by Justice McGeehan of the Supreme Court. Professor Russell was declared unfit for the position because (1) "of his immoral and salacious attitude toward sex"; (2) he is not legally qualified, since he is not a citizen of this country; and (3) the New York State Constitution was violated because Mr. Russell was not subjected to competitive examination. Recently Bishop Manning took a stand on other secular matters by coming out for selective service and for aid to the British.

Bishop Manning, the son of John and Matilda Manning, was born in Northampton, England. He was 16 years old when his parents came to the United States and settled in Southern California. They sent him to the Sewanee, Tennessee Seminary to be trained for the ministry. He received the degrees of Bachelor of Divinity (1893) and Doctor of Divinity (1906) from the University of the South; Doctor of Divinity from the University of Nashville (1901) and Princeton (1919); Doctor of Sacred Theology, Columbia University (1905) and Hobart (1908); Doctor of Laws from King's College, Nova Scotia (1919) and New York (1922).

The Bishop's experience and progress in the ministry are almost as varied as the number of degrees conferred upon him. He was deacon (1899), priest (1891), and rector (1892) of the Protestant Episcopal Church of Redlands, California; professor of dogmatic theology at the University of the South (1893-95); rector of the Lansdowne, Pennsylvania Christ Church (1896-98); rector at Nashville (1903-08); vicar of St. Agnes' Chapel, New York (1903-08); assistant rector (1904-08) and rector (1908-21) of Trinity Parish, New York. On May 11, 1921 he was consecrated bishop.

On America's entrance into the First World War, Bishop Manning served as a volunteer chaplain in 1917 and 1918 at Camp Upton. In 1919 he received the Chevalier Légion d'Honneur from France and the Office Order of the Crown, Belgium.

While a young clergyman he married (1895) Miss Florence Van Antwerp, daughter of a well-to-do Cincinnati family. Their two children are Frances and Eliza-

Pach Bros.

BISHOP MANNING

beth. The latter, for awhile proprietress of a fashionable tourist agency in New York, is now the wife of Griffith Baily Coale of New York City.

Bishop Manning is constantly in the news. His sermons range from Pacifism to World Conditions. His office, says the *New Yorker*, "is one of the most august berths in the United States and one of the most difficult. Low-Churchmen rail at the Bishop for wearing a hat of High-Church block; the orthodox grumble at his failure to purge the diocese of scoffers in reversed collars. . . He is too high, too low, too broad, too middle, too arrogant, too meek, too adamant, too supple. He is courteous, approachable, genial, sympathetic; it is only under the compulsion of what he conceives to be sacred duty that he becomes the reproving, rebuking, admonishing, denouncing, pontificating prelate."

Uncompromising, Bishop Manning has never pursued ambition at the expense of principle. In 1915, as rector of Trinity Church, he took an unpopular stand in one of the church disagreements of the time and temporarily disbarred himself from advancement. Three years later he engaged in an odd crusade against textbook publishers. During the steel strike (1918) he recommended that churchmen interfere as little as possible "with definite political and economic issues as to which few representatives of the church are qualified to speak wisely." In the Bishop Manning-Judge Lindsey "brawl" he denounced Judge Lindsey's teachings, saying they were "immoral and destructive, foul and wicked; and his *Companionate Marriage* was one of the most filthy, insidious and cleverly written pieces of propaganda ever published in behalf of lewdness, promiscuity, adultery and unrestrained sexual gratification."

MANNING, BISHOP—*Continued*

Bishop Manning "will go down in history as one of the great cathedral builders," says the *North American Review*. He has been effective in raising funds for the Cathedral of St. John the Divine, started by Bishop Potter, a cathedral edifice a tenth of a mile in length, to soar to a height of 460 feet, and to be the longest and highest (exterior) cathedral in the world and in area the largest Gothic and the second largest cathedral in the world. The *Review* continues: "By his wise administration and his keen sense of justice he had already endeared himself to the great majority of his clergy and flock. And he enjoyed the confidence of the community as a whole. . . In his personal relationships he is definite and direct, but always sympathetic. There is nothing of good-natured heartiness or backslapping geniality about him. He is kindly and courteous, and surprisingly ascetic for a man so delicately attuned and responsive to the reality of the world about him."

References

Christian Cent 57:1069 S 4 '40
New Yorker 7:24-36 F 28 '31
No Am R 229:345-50 Mr '30
Outlook 156:604 D 17 '30 por

Johnston, A. First Churchman: the Rt. Rev. William T. Manning *In* New Yorker (periodical). Profiles from the New Yorker p154-64 1938
Who's Who in America

MANSHIP, PAUL Dec 25, 1885- Sculptor
Address: 319 E 72nd St, New York City

Among the works that had aroused the most comment at the now defunct New York World's Fair are three groups by Paul Manship. His *Moods of Time* and *Time and the Fates of Man* on Constitution Mall and his *Celestial Sphere* in the Court of States held sight-seers spellbound with admiration or curiosity. And when these visitors would stop in New York to see Rockefeller Center, Manship's *Prometheus* Fountain in the lower plaza was the first of the many imposing sights they saw.

Paul Manship, who has been called "the most hopeful figure in American sculpture," is represented by works in many of the world's famous places. The New York Metropolitan Museum of Art, the Washington, D. C. Post Office, the New York Zoological Park, the American Academy in Rome, the Musée de Luxembourg in Paris, are only a few of the important spots where Manship's work can be seen. "Possessed of seven-league boots," Manship has produced "a galaxy of contemporary masterpieces sufficient for seven sculptural lives."

Most of these masterpieces are varied. Manship is a medalist of rare power and precision. He has done bronzes, "small and exquisite, admirable *objets d'art*." He has done gigantic memorial gates, 36 feet high and 42 wide. He has done portrait busts and terra-cotta flower boxes, a *Centaur and Driad* and a portrait of his daughter *Pauline*. But versatile as his production is, most critics agree that Paul Manship belongs in "the true line of descent from Greek archaic art." He has been called a "true academic," with "academic" defined as "having qualities which are derived from a study of accepted or approved styles and methods."

According to one commentator, Manship, "without a halt even at Paris, jumped straight from Minnesota to Rome and then with all possible speed to Greece." He was born in St. Paul, Minnesota on Christmas Day 1885, the son of Charles Henry and Maryetta (Friend) Manship. Unlike a good many so-called "American" artists, he is native to the core. His ancestors arrived before the Revolution; his father fought in the Confederate Army.

Manship started early to be interested in art, but intended to become a painter or commercial artist. With this thought in mind he became a student at the Art Institute of St. Paul, Minnesota, but found out rather soon that his interests didn't lie in painting. He decided on sculpture and began to study under Solon Borglum. Soon he left Borglum to enter the Pennsylvania Academy of Fine Arts in Philadelphia, where he worked under Charles Grafly and Isadore Konti.

In 1909 he won the much-coveted award of a fellowship at the American Academy in Rome. There he "learned no more and no less than he required." In Rome and in Greece his gleanings and assimilation of the works of bygone ages and his original development of their antique essence became part and parcel of his sculptural development. He would make his own the message portrayed in some bit of modeled ornament from Pompeii or Herculaneum or he would avidly seize upon the stylized figures from the best of the painted Greek vases.

When Manship returned to New York after three years in Rome, he had already hit his stride. An exhibition of his bronzes, the result of his Rome activities, scored an instant success and induced Herbert Adams, president of the National Sculpture Society, to write to La Farge, then secretary of the American Academy in Rome: "It seems to me that here is a man, who, if given a chance to work out his natural bent may do American art an incalculable good. . . It is not impossible that this man alone may be worth to American art all the effort the American Academy in Rome has cost!"

A list of the honors and awards Paul Manship has received is evidence that Mr. Adams' prophecy has been fulfilled. In 1913 Manship received the Helen Barnet Prize, National Academy of Design; in 1914 the George D. Widener Gold Medal, Pennsylvania Academy; in 1915 the Gold Medal, San Francisco Exposition; in 1921 the Gold Medal of the American Institute of Architects. He has received numerous other medals and awards, was made a member of the French Legion of Honor in 1929, was the first American whose works were exhibited at the Tate Gallery in London in 1935.

Critics are agreed on the originality of his conceptions and of his combinations. In *Girl Dancer and Gazelles* he uses a feminine form from East Indian art, but he clothes her in archaic Greek drapery and conceives the whole in the Hellenic mode. His *Air* is a compilation from a dozen different styles, and his *Centaur and Driad* is archaic in part while the effect of the whole isn't archaic Greek at all.

Critics do not agree, however, on the essential meaning behind what he has done. "All that manner, style and taste—added to superlative craftsmanship—can do may be enjoyed in Manship's work," says one, "but there is no meaning inside of it, the pieces are all outsides." "An exhibition of his work creates a curious indifference in the beholder, like a plethora of jewels." On the other hand it has been said that from his study of the work of sculptors of other ages Manship has "formed a powerful and intensely personal style which never diverges one inch from the standards set up by his predecessors."

Critics have argued, too, about his individual works. It's perfectly true that his "creations have been the topic of more discussion than those of any other sculptor of recent times." According to one critic, the reason for this lies in the fact that he is a "curiously unequal" artist, some of whose exhibits (*Nude Reclining,* for instance) are about as bad as sculpture can be, while others are superb. Other critics disagree about individual works. Manship's bust of Rockefeller has been called "faithful without brutality, simple without extremity of formalism, true to life as well as to character," and it has also been questioned: "The nicety of handling rather belittles the power of our famous plutocrat. Where is all the fabled ruthlessness?" The Rockefeller Center *Prometheus* Fountain has probably come in for more criticism than any other piece he has done. Probably one of the kindest things any adverse critic said was: "You'd think the bringer of fire would have sense enough to stay away from the water."

The public, however, has, by its purchasing of Manship's work and by its viewing of it, shown its approval or at least interest in it. Henry McBride of the New York *Sun* wrote after he saw an exhibition of the sculptor's works: "The cultured people of this generation almost instantly recognized Mr. Manship to be their sculptor. They get from him what they would get in surgery from the best surgeon of the day, in engineering from the best engineer, and so on. . . The American people did not wait for European approbation before adopting Mr. Manship. They joined forces with him

PAUL MANSHIP

the moment he swam into their ken. It was a case of instinct, and instinct is always swifter and more unerring than intellect."

Paul Manship is "a short, unassuming, serious-looking man" who "might be mistaken for a broker or a prosperous operator in real estate." He lives a quiet life wholly devoted to sculpture and his family: wife (he married Isabel McIlwaine), three girls and a boy.

References

Carnegie Mag 11:110-3 S '37
New Yorker 4:21-3 S 1 '28
Newsweek 5:35 Je 22 '35
Canfield, M. C. Paul Manship *In* Grotesques and Other Reflections p79-85 1927
Casson, S. Paul Manship *In* XXth Century Sculptors p41-54 1930
New Standard Encyclopedia of Art 1939
Who's Who in America
Who's Who in American Art
Who's Who in Art

MARBLE, ALICE Sept 28, 1913- Tennis player

Address: c/o Radio Station WNEW, 501 Madison Ave, New York City; h. 457 Arden Blvd, Los Angeles, California

On November 12, 1940 Alice Marble, holder of the women's amateur tennis crowns of the United States and England, announced her decision to join the professional ranks. She will tour 50 United States cities, and for her first year is guaranteed $25,000 and a cut of the gate. In the fall of 1940 Alice Marble had won the women's national singles tennis championship for the fourth time. "The greatest of all

Harold Stein

ALICE MARBLE

women players," Miss Marble has been winning championships since 1930.

Alice Marble started to play tennis when she was 15, after her family decided she was spending too much time on baseball. This was in San Francisco. She was born in Plumas County, California, the daughter of Harry Briggs Marble, a cattle rancher, and Jessie (Wood) Marble. It was while she was attending the Polytechnic High School of San Francisco—she was graduated in 1931—that Miss Marble first began to realize that tennis wasn't a sissy's game.

When her masculine type of game first began to be noticed, Eleanor Tennant, former national ranking player, took her under her wing. It wasn't long before Alice became Miss Tennant's secretary and most promising pupil, and it was only two years later, when she was seventeen, that Alice Marble won the California junior tennis championship. From that time on her career has been one of successes on the courts. In 1931 she won the national girls' doubles championship at Philadelphia and narrowly missed winning the singles.

The next year she won the California women's championship and rose to No. 7 in national ranking, and one year later, in 1933, she had forged ahead to No. 3 behind Helen Wills and Helen Jacobs. In 1934 Alice Marble had her first setback. She and five other girls went to Paris to play international team matches. At the beginning of the first match she swayed, turned halfway and crumpled on the court in a heap. The doctor diagnosed sunstroke and Alice was rushed off to the hospital in an ambulance. Two weeks later she was sent back to the United States on a stretcher, warned by the doctors that she should never play tennis again.

Two years later she won the national women's singles from Helen Jacobs. A doctor had diagnosed her trouble as secondary anemia and had proceeded to cure it. From then on tennis meant triumphs for Alice Marble, in the United States and at Wimbledon, England. Among other championships, she won the national singles and the national doubles in 1938 and 1939; the Wimbledon mixed doubles in 1937 and 1938; the Eastern grass court feminine championship in 1938.

After she had won the 1938 singles Alice Marble capitalized on her pleasant contralto voice and made her debut as a professional supper club singer at the Sert Room of the Waldorf Astoria Hotel in New York. Since then she has also sung over the radio, designed tennis clothes, endorsed advertisements, lectured at women's colleges and clubs. In 1940 she got herself a new job as staff sports announcer for New York's radio station WNEW and began her career with programs devoted largely to predictions of college football games. She says cheerfully: "You know football isn't as difficult a game to play as tennis."

In all these activities Miss Tennant, "one of the shrewdest managers in the business," has been Miss Marble's constant coach, friend and adviser. It was she who had much to do with shaping Alice's game—with developing her twisting service, her powerful forehand and backhand drives—with developing, too, Alice's mental attitude. Today Miss Marble's greatest assets for her smashing play are her assurance and her ability to withstand the strain of tournament competition.

This lithe, blonde Californian who has been called a "glamour girl" as well as "a natural athlete," has not only been voted the outstanding woman athlete in this country by an Associated Press Poll in 1939, but was also selected by *American Women* as one of the 10 most outstanding women of 1938.

References

Good H 105:38-9 S '37 pors
Newsweek 16:58 O 21 '40 por
Time 36:63 N 25 '40 il por
American Women
Fenno, J. B. Tennis Career of Alice Marble *In* Nason, J. and others. Famous American Athletes of Today 7th ser. p305-338 1940
Who's Who in America

MARGOLIOUTH, DAVID SAMUEL Oct 17, 1858—Mar 23, 1940 Arabic authority; author of many works on Arabic literature; professor of Arabic at Oxford University; educator for 59 years

References

Who's Who

Obituaries

N Y Times p30 Mr 24 '40
Sch & Soc 51:409 Mr 30 '40

MARIUS, EMILIE ALEXANDER (mä' rĭ-us) 1853—Mar 27, 1940 Concert singer and teacher of voice; first American woman to be elected to the French Academy

Obituaries

N Y Times p23 Mr 28 '40
Variety 138:54 Apr 3 '40

MARKHAM, EDWIN Apr 23, 1852—Mar 7, 1940 Poet; lecturer

Famed for his poem, *The Man with the Hoe,* Edwin Markham, called by many "the Dean of American Poetry," died at his home in Staten Island, New York City, March 7, 1940. He would have been 88 years old on April 23rd.

Edwin Markham was born in a log cabin in Oregon City, Oregon, April 23, 1852. His parents, excited by Frémont's vision of the great Northwest, had sold out their establishment in Michigan and trekked with an ox team westward, eventually opening a store in Oregon City. When Edwin was about five years old his mother, still filled with the pioneer spirit, left her husband to tend his cattle range, and with her children went to California. She bought a wheat and sheep ranch in a valley near Sacramento, later went in for cattle. Young Markham learned to sow and plow wheat, and to care for the cattle.

Up to his fifteenth year he had had little more than a year of schooling and was eager for more. In the autumn of that year a new teacher came to the school which young Edwin was attending. He became interested in the boy and listened to his descriptions of the things he had observed while herding cattle. He decided there was a real vein of poetry in the boy and told him about the great poets, quoting from their work. There were no books of poetry in that whole region. Young Markham plowed rough farm land, at a dollar an acre, so that he could buy the poetry of Tennyson, Thomas Moore and Bryant, and a dictionary. The discovery of Byron opened a new world to him, and under his inspiration he began to write.

The young poet wanted to go to the San Jose Normal School, but his mother wanted him to become a prosperous farmer. So, packing his few possessions, he rode northward on horseback in search of adventure and learning. After he had been gone for some months, his mother discovered his whereabouts and decided to help him get to college. Then one day, while digging for soaproot, he found a bag full of gold pieces, presumably buried long before by some miner. His schooling was assured, and in 1872 he had his diploma, ready to teach.

Clara E. Sipprell

EDWIN MARKHAM

Markham's first position was in a remote California mountain settlement, where he helped build the rough schoolhouse. In 1880 his first poem to appear in print, in a California magazine, was *The Gulf of Night.* Years passed while he moved from one place to another, teaching and writing poems. At the age of 34 he came across Fourier's *Social Science.* This, together with his own experience of years of hard work, made him determined to write an epic of labor.

In 1897 Markham married Anna Catherine Murphy, who died in 1938; their one son, Virgil, survives his father.

When Markham was 47, head of the Teachers Training School in Oakland, he went to see Millet's famous painting, *The Man with the Hoe,* then on exhibition in San Francisco. "For an hour I sat enthralled in front of it, and when I left I was like one under a strange enchantment. It was as though this awe-inspiring shape, full of terror and mournful grandeur, had risen before me from Dante's dark abyss; yet at the same moment I was filled with exaltation as though the heavens had opened and given me a message for mankind." Immediately after, Markham wrote *The Man with the Hoe* (1899), the poem for which he became famous. First printed in the San Francisco *Examiner,* it was reprinted in many other papers throughout the country, editorials were written about it and its subject, lecturers took it up. Publishers besought Markham to bring out a book of his verse. The poem was translated into several languages, and also adopted by labor groups.

Markham claims to have been equally inspired on the occasion of composing his *Lincoln, Man of the People.* It was written to be read at a banquet given to celebrate

MARKHAM, EDWIN—*Continued*

the first Lincoln's birthday anniversary of the twentieth century.

With the success of these two poems, Markham's financial future seemed assured. From 1900 to 1905 he made some $10,000 a year writing; the sales of *The Man with the Hoe* mounted continuously. But through a number of unfortunate financial investments Markham lost his money. In 1912, at the age of 60, he had little left. He began lecturing and giving readings to support himself, which was a handicap to his output. But he found time each year to work on his ten-volume anthology, *The Book of Poetry,* consisting of thousands of notes and pages of selections from the poets of all time.

His first book of poems, *The Man with the Hoe,* was published in 1899. Shortly after came a series of articles on the problem of child labor, called *The Hoe Man in the Making.* Among his other books are: *Lincoln and Other Poems* (1901); *California the Wonderful* (1915); *Gates of Paradise* (1920); *Ballad of the Gallows Bird* (1926); and *Eighty Poems at Eighty* (1932).

Markham was inclined to attribute his success to good fortune rather than genius. But he had his own theories of what poetry should be. Of the test of greatness in a poet, he said: "Sublimity is the test. Very few poets have it—Homer, Aeschylus, Dante, Shakespeare—that's about all. Americans, on the whole, are too much taken up with material concerns to make poets. They are too much devoted to the dollar hunt, and yet there is a great future for American poetry." On another occasion he said further: "A true poet is both born and made. One can acquire by study and observation much that is needful for this career; yet, unless he has been endowed from on high with an intangible lyric spirit at birth, he will never write great poetry."

Edwin Markham came to settle in the East when he was an old man, first living in Brooklyn, New York, then on Staten Island in a little house overlooking the Lower Bay. His later work was not accorded the wide attention of his earlier poetry, but several literary honors were given him. Since 1928 he has won a number of contest prizes; and in 1936 the Academy of American Poets announced that it had made a "special prefatory" award of $5000 to him for his poetry. In his later years he was given special honors on his birthdays. In 1930 his birthday was proclaimed a holiday on Staten Island, and hundreds of school children took part in a pageant in his honor.

On the day of his eightieth birthday, when his *Eighty Songs at Eighty* was published, he spoke on his work to a large audience at Carnegie Hall: the proceeds of the evening were used to send him and his wife on their first trip abroad. On February 12, 1940 the Staten Island Chamber of Commerce presented on the radio the voice of Markham reciting *Lincoln, Man of the Peo-*ple. In addition, it presented nine of his poems about Lincoln, which he wrote in 1925, read over the air by his son Virgil.

Critical estimate of Edwin Markham's work have been many and varied. Benjamin de Casseres said of him: "Edwin Markham is the *Blessed Damozel* of American poetry... He is really Mrs. Grundy riding Pegasus, the veritable Pegasus, for Edwin Markham is a real poet, sometimes a great poet, but always a poet. He has proved that Demos and Prometheus are not enemies."

On the publication of his *Eighty Songs at Eighty,* William Rose Benét wrote: "Markham has retained unusual vigor both in his personality and in his writing. He has always been a dogmatic poet, but with a great liberality of spirit and an accomplished knowledge of versification. He has never surpassed his *Hoe* and *Lincoln* poems. They were the work he was primarily born to do."

References

Am Mag 106:26-7 S '28 por
Am Mercury 9:398-9 D '26
Christian Cent 50:723 My 31 '33
Lit Digest 118:24 D 22 '34 por
Newsweek 9:23 F 22 '37 por
Overland ns 88:337 N '30
Sat R Lit 8:685 Ap 23 '32
Time 35:45 F 19 '40 por
Fitch, G. H. Markham, the Poet of the American People *In* Great Spiritual Writers of America p136-45 1916
Hind, C. L. Edwin Markham *In* Authors and I p195-200 1921
Kunitz, S. J. ed. Authors Today and Yesterday 1933
Power, M. J. Edwin Markham *In* Poets at Prayer p83-93 1938
Who's Who in America

Obituaries

N Y Herald Tribune p23 Mr 8 '40; p10 Mr 9 '40; p41 Mr 10 '40; p12 Mr 11 '40
N Y Times p21 Mr 8 '40; p15 Mr 9 '40
Pub W 137:1165 Mr 16 '40
Scholastic 36:25 Mr 25 '40
Time 35:82 Mr 18 '40
Variety 138:44 Mr 13 '40

MARQUIS, FREDERICK JAMES, 1ST BARON WOOLTON *See* Woolton, F. J. M., 1st Baron

MARSHALL, GEORGE CATLETT Dec 31, 1880- Chief of staff of the United States Army

Address: b. War Department, Washington, D. C.

General George Catlett Marshall is one of the people most likely to be glimpsed if you do much wandering around the corridors of the United States Capitol, for in these days the chief of staff is much in demand. President Roosevelt may be calling on him to ask about the progress of rearmament; the Defense Advisory Council may be wanting his advice on production schedules; or the Congressional Appropriations and Military Affairs Committees may be asking that he do a little explaining about the army's expenditures.

General Marshall, the sixth chief of staff who isn't a graduate of West Point, was promoted to his present top-ranking army position over the heads of twenty major generals and fourteen brigadier generals who were his seniors in rank because the President decided that here was the man most capable of peacetime planning for what the army will do and how it will do it. (In time of war the field commander of the armies will probably top him in rank.) Marshall's is the desk across which flow all the army's plans for national defense, and it's up to his office, under Secretary of War Stimson (see sketch this issue), to develop and execute them. Naturally this doesn't mean that national defense is a one-man job. On the contrary, there are five divisions of national defense experts under the general—the army's War Plans, Personnel, Military Intelligence, Operations and Training and Supply Departments—but it is Marshall who must coordinate their work in such a way that the result is a "steady, dependable and rapid increase in military power." With the formation of the new War Department General Headquarters, Marshall now holds a post combining functions usually held by two officials: chief of staff of the army and field force commander.

George Catlett Marshall was born on December 31, 1880 in Uniontown, Pennsylvania, the son of Laura (Bradford) and George Catlett Marshall, a great-grandnephew of Chief Justice Marshall. There wasn't any great military tradition in his family aside from his father's service with the home guard of the Union Army when he was 16, but George's older brother attended Virginia Military Institute and George followed in his footsteps after trying in vain to wangle a West Point appointment. He entered V. M. I. in 1897, "a clumsy, unpromising recruit, ill-looked upon by the exacting faculty of the ancient institute," and was graduated in 1901 with the highest military rank in the cadet corps in addition to the honor of having been an all-Southern football tackle. He was promptly commissioned a second lieutenant of infantry.

Early the following year young Marshall married Elizabeth Carter Coles of Lexington, Virginia, and shortly afterward was assigned to the thirtieth infantry in the Philippines, where he remained only until 1903. In the course of his career he was to change his address more than 20 times— from the Philippines to Oklahoma, Kansas, Massachusetts, Arkansas, Texas, California, New York, France, China, Georgia, South Carolina, Illinois, Washington, and finally

GEORGE C. MARSHALL

Washington, D. C. But to an army man "home is where you hang your hat." In 1907 Marshall was an honorary graduate of the United States Infantry-Cavalry School; the following year he finished the course in military theory for officers given at the newly-established Army Staff College at Fort Leavenworth, Kansas; from 1908 to 1910 he was an instructor there; and by 1913 he was back in the Philippines again, this time as a lieutenant of infantry.

It was in the Philippines that Marshall first showed something of his genius for organization. Manila's defenses were being tested, and he was merely assisting the adjutant of the "defending" forces in routine duties when the chief of staff was suddenly taken ill. Someone remembered Marshall's training and sent for him. Asked the commander: "Lieutenant, do you know how to draw up a field order?" "Yes, I think I do," Marshall replied. "Well, go ahead and draw one up," he was instructed. He did. Having learned the positions of the "defending" and "attacking" troops, calmly and without hesitation he dictated orders which disposed of the men, brought up supplies and started an immediate counter-attack in such a way that the departmental commander afterwards described his as the best plan for Manila's defense that he had ever seen. "Keep your eyes on George Marshall," he said, "he is the greatest military genius of America since Stonewall Jackson."

When the United States entered the First World War in 1917 Marshall went from the Philippines to France as a captain on the general staff of the first division, and in a year was promoted to the rank of colonel. He participated in the battles of Cantigny, Aisne-Marne and St. Mihiel. Then, in September 1918, he found himself chief of

MARSHALL, GEORGE C.—*Continued*

operations of a section of the first army at the time when a large part of the American force had to be transferred from St. Mihiel for the Meuse-Argonne offensive. It took him only about two weeks to arrange and manage the transfer, to organize the supplies and lay out the attack positions, and it is greatly to his credit that the offensive was "smashingly successful." One British newspaper called his one of the finest pieces of work of the World War.

Later Marshall was promoted to be chief of staff of the eighth army corps with the rank of brigadier, but when he returned from France in 1919 as aide to General John Pershing he reverted to his pre-War rank of captain.

After the War the president of a large corporation is said to have remarked: "A man with an organizational brain like his would be worth $20,000 a year. I'd like to see him and make him an offer." When the remark was repeated to Marshall he replied: "I am a soldier. My country trained me as a soldier. There is not much advancement ahead. I'll stick to the service."

Until 1924 Marshall served as Pershing's aide, but rose slowly in the military hierarchy, not achieving the rank of brigadier again until 1936. From 1924 to 1927 he saw service in China; in 1927 he was an instructor in the Army War College at Washington; from 1927 to 1932 he was assistant commandant of the Infantry School at Fort Benning; in 1933 commander of the eighth infantry; from 1933 to 1936 senior instructor to the Illinois National Guard; from 1936 to 1938 commanding general of the fifth brigade. His first wife had died in 1927, and in October 1930 he married Katherine Boyce Tupper Brown of Baltimore, Maryland, who had three children by a previous marriage: Molly Pender, Clifton Stevenson and Allen Tupper.

From July to October 1938 Marshall was chief of the War Plans Division of the general staff, and then in October General Craig brought him to Washington, D. C., to be deputy chief of staff. In May of the following year, as chief of a military mission to Brazil, he made trips to inspect strategic areas such as the Natal District of Brazil, and to exchange views with ranking military men of other American nations. Finally on July 1, 1939, after General Craig's retirement as chief of staff, Marshall moved into his big, gray-paneled War Department office to be acting chief of staff, with the rank of major general. It was not until he took over the post of chief of staff, on September 1, 1939, that Marshall acquired the rank of general.

When General Marshall took office he brought about a minor revolution. It had been years since army men had had experience vaguely resembling actual wartime duty. Marshall changed that. In the winter of 1939 seventy thousand men were put in the field for mass maneuvers, and mimic warfare was waged through the South. At the same time he was pessimistic about the state of military preparation of the United States, in his "dry, impersonal voice" telling reporters who attended his weekly press conferences: "We are not ready for war. We are not even ready for defense." He complained of the smallness of military appropriations in the years since the First World War and urged that a sizable army be maintained even in peacetime.

By the summer of 1940 Marshall was even more urgent. On June 4 he predicted trouble in South America "within the next month or so." A week later he was telling the graduating class of V. M. I. that the next few days would probably be "the most fateful in history." In testimony before the Senate Appropriations Subcommittee General Marshall stated that "we cannot at present expand beyond a force of 1,200,000 without destroying our present organizations." This he considered a reasonable minimum to discourage anyone from attacking the Northern Hemisphere or the Caribbean area, but did not find it adequate for complete hemisphere defense, which, he claimed on August 20, might require between 3,000,000 and 4,000,000 men. Nevertheless on conscription his viewpoint was: "No one can say with certainty, the way things are going abroad, that we won't need the additional man power without delay. Time is the dominant power, and time is fleeting." On several occasions he described the situation facing the United States within the next six months as "critical."

The chief of staff is described as a "rangy, lean six-footer in negligently neat mufti, a field soldier with reflective blue eyes, a short, pugnacious nose, broad, humorous mouth, a stubborn upper lip." He never appears hurried, but is actually "streamlined and speedy"; he is a strict disciplinarian, yet, some say, the best storyteller in the army. Something of an athlete and even more of a perfectionist, he plays tennis, rides, dances, gave up golf only because he didn't have time to play it "as well as he should," tries to get some hard exercise every day even though there is little time now for anything but work. His reading consists mostly of military science and history. On duty, he and his wife live at the chief of staff's big house at Fort Myers, but they also have a summer home on Fire Island, New York, where the General likes to go surf fishing. An Episcopalian and a member of Kappa Alpha fraternity, he possesses the United States Distinguished Service and Victory Medals and decorations from the French, Montenegran, Italian, Panamanian and Brazilian governments.

General Marshall once commented during the First World War that "the principles of war are unchanging." He still thinks so. While some of his predecessors believed that success in warfare depended upon such factors as individual heroism or great man power, his faith is in organizational perfection plus the infantryman, who collectively wins a war." To him "the German success was in the coordination of all branches, thorough training, skill, and in the remarkable way the staff was able to keep in touch with all the new and old arms of battle to insure teamwork." He doesn't say a democracy isn't capable of as great organizational perfection, but does deplore the democratic habit of telling military secrets in peacetime. "We're playing poker with everyone looking at our hand," he says.

References

Cur Hist 50:9 Jl '39
Look 4:54-5 O 8 '40
N Y Herald Tribune p1+ D 29 '39 por; p29 Je 13 '40; p3+ Ag 11 '40; p1+ Ag 21 '40 por
N Y Times p18 Jl 14 '40; p1+ Ag 21 '40; p2 Ag 25 '40
New Yorker 16:26-35 O 26 '40
Newsweek 14:19 D 11 '39; 15:39 Je 17 '40
Sat Eve Post 212:25+ Jl 15 '39 por
Time 36:30-3+ Jl 29 '40 por (cover); 36:19 Ag 26 '40
Who's Who in America

MARTIN, EDGAR STANLEY JR. Mar 8, 1873—Aug 9, 1940 National director of publications of the Boy Scouts of America; with group since inception in 1910; cited by Theodore Roosevelt and Woodrow Wilson for Red Cross work; formerly an educator in Tully, New York and Racine, Wisconsin

Underwood & Underwood
EDGAR STANLEY MARTIN JR.

References

Who's Who in America

Obituaries

N Y Times p13 Ag 10 '40 por

MARTIN, JOSEPH WILLIAM JR. Nov 3, 1884- Chairman of the Republican National Committee; Republican leader of the House of Representatives

Address: b. House of Representatives, Washington, D. C.; h. 54 Grove St, North Attleboro, Massachusetts

When Wendell Willkie (see sketch this issue) chose Representative Joseph Martin to head the Republican National Committee in July 1940, he picked a man who "walks on sure political feet," a man who knows how to set up political organizations and "get out" the vote. As leader of the Republicans in the House of Representatives, Joe Martin is thoroughly familiar with the nation's problems, district by district; no backslapper, he still knows the first names of the men who make the local organizations tick, and he knows how to set them in motion.

Since 1912 Joseph Martin has been active in Republican politics; since 1924 he has been a member of Congress. The "stocky, bright-eyed, black-browed," Scotch-Irish Representative from Massachusetts was born in North Attleboro, Massachusetts, the son of Joseph William and Catherine (Katon) Martin. His father was a blacksmith and Joe the eldest son in a family of eight children. That meant he had to go to work early, and when he was only six he was peddling newspapers. Later he worked in jewelry shops and as night telephone operator in the North Attleboro exchange.

In high school Joe distinguished himself as a baseball player—in his senior year he was captain of the team—and known as an all-round athlete. When he was offered a scholarship to Dartmouth, he declined and went to work instead. Many years later he sent his two youngest brothers through Dartmouth. Joe's first job was as reporter on the North Attleboro *Evening Leader;* his second as reporter on the North Attleboro *Sun.*

After he had worked as a newspaper reporter for five years, Joe found he had one thousand dollars saved up. He persuaded several local citizens to go in with him to buy the North Attleboro *Evening Chronicle,* and in 1908, at the age of 24, Joseph Martin was the youngest newspaper publisher in the country. The paper prospered, its daily circulation rose from 800 to 2,800, and before many years Martin bought up the shares of the other partners and became majority stockholder. He still publishes the *Chronicle,* now edited by his brother Charles.

In 1912, "with a sudden passion for politics," Joseph Martin got himself elected to the Massachusetts House of Representatives and stayed there until 1914, when he was elected to the State Senate. While in the legislature he served as secretary of the Joint Rules Committee under Senator Calvin Coolidge and also acted as chairman of the Republican Legislative Campaign Committee.

Greystone

JOSEPH W. MARTIN JR.

Martin retired from politics in 1917, intending to devote himself to business, but in 1920 he was a Republican Presidential elector and in 1922 he was drafted by Massachusetts Republican leaders to consolidate and harmonize party factions. He was made executive secretary of the Republican State Committee and in that same year directed the campaign that saved Henry Cabot Lodge's Senate seat. In 1924 he ran his own campaign and went to Congress in 1925 by a plurality of 9,600.

For many years after his election Martin was "only a rear-row private in the ranks of the army of smug Republican leaders who marched invincibly through the '20s." His first assignment was to the Committee on Foreign Affairs, his next, in 1929, to the House Rules Committee. In 1933 he was assistant to the Republican floor leader and in 1936 he began to emerge from the ranks of Representatives. In that year he was Landon's floor leader at the Republican Convention and later his Eastern campaign manager. Two years later Martin, who had always been liked for his warmth and directness and respected for his political acumen, began to be known as a good "political mechanic." As chairman of the Republican Congressional Campaign, "shrewdly and tirelessly he combed the field for able new candidates, concentrated his funds and fire in districts where the Republicans had at least a fighting chance to win, swung around the country and chatted with candidates by long-distance telephone about the problems of their campaigns." It was his skill that helped get 80 new Republicans elected to the House.

In 1939 Martin was made minority leader in the House, his job to direct his party group's machinery of committees and con-

ferences, to decide its floor strategy, to unify it in shaping and agreeing on party policy. Immediately he proceeded to whip a "frazzled minority into a tough opposition." He enlarged the Republican steering committee; he initiated regional Republican conferences to discuss legislation and general policy; he set up committees to study special pieces of legislation. So informed, disciplined and effective a body of legislators did he form that in cooperation with varying groups of Democrats they were able to pass the arms embargo, revise the WPA, put through the Hatch Bill, start an investigation into the National Labor Relations Board and bury the President's spend-lend plans. Martin has gone along with some of the New Deal's reform measures, but on the whole he has been "quite vehemently against it." As he puts it: "What we were seeking was not Utopia, but a sane revival of old-fashioned Americanism."

As a boss, however, Martin is "probably the most democratic floor leader either party has possessed in long years." He urges every Republican Congressman, even the greenest, to air his views and take part in discussion and decision. "The boys like it," he says. "It gives them a feeling of pride and responsibility. They get enthusiastic." Picked as the ablest Representative by a Washington correspondents' poll, there's no doubt that he "plays the rough and tumble game of politics hard, but nobody has ever accused him of playing it unfairly or dishonestly and he is known as the man without a single Congressional enemy."

Representative Martin is of medium height, dark-haired, smooth-faced, "a bit on the homely side" and scarcely a dandy. When the Congressional reception committee went to meet the King and Queen of England, it was a state occasion. Joe Martin made the concession of wearing morning clothes, but wore a derby on his head. And all his clothes are "comfortable, rather than costly or well valeted."

Joe Martin's home is still in North Attleboro, where he lives with his invalid mother, a widowed sister and a brother. He has never married. Between sessions of Congress he drops into his newspaper office every day to talk with cronies and callers, and spends most afternoons riding around his district to find out what his constituents are thinking about. "If you met him walking down the street in North Attleboro," according to a Life correspondent, "you could hardly mistake him for anything but what, at base, he is: a plain, sober, hardworking, successful, popular, businessman-politician of a type to be met on almost any Main Street."

In Washington he has a two-room apartment in the Hay-Adams House. He doesn't drink, smoke, golf or dance and his only real passions outside of politics are attending games of the Washington American League baseball team, reading history and biography, especially political biography, and walking in the rain.

References

Christian Sci Mon Mag ·p5 Ap 1 '39
il por
Collier's 106:12+ N 2 '40 por
Cur Hist & Forum 52:14 S '40
Life 8:48-54 Ja 1 '40 pors
N Y Herald Tribune II p2 Mr 17
'40; p1 Jl 9 '40
N Y Times VII p7+ S 15 '40 por
Newsweek 14:44 Ag 21 '39
Time 31:12-14 Ap 11 '38 por (cover);
36:15-17 S 9 '40 pors
American Catholic Who's Who
Who's Who in America
Who's Who in the Nation's Capital

MARTLAND, HARRISON STANFORD
Sept 10, 1883- Physician

Address: b. City Hospital, Newark, New Jersey; h. 180 Clinton Ave, Newark, New Jersey

The medical life and training of one "of the most colorful personalities" who has reached a high place among medical investigators and leaders of the country has been a comparatively simple one. Dr. Harrison Stanford Martland, the son of Dr. William Henry and Ida (Carlyle) Martland, was born in Newark, New Jersey. After receiving a B. A. from Western Maryland College in 1901 he says that, because his father had been a doctor and because there was nothing else to do, he, too, decided to become a doctor.

He attended the College of Physicians and Surgeons in New York City and after graduation in 1905 interned for 18 months at New York City Hospital on Welfare Island. Then he spent a period of two years in pathology and bacteriology at the Russell Sage Laboratory. In 1908 he returned to his place of birth to be the pathologist at the Newark City Hospital, and except for a period of service during the First World War has held that position ever since.

Dr. Martland entered the army in 1917 as a member of the Bellevue Hospital Unit. His services were so distinguished "that he was made a colonel in the reserve corps in 1919, and the Rockefeller Foundation desired him for the directorship of the Institute of Hygiene to be established for the government of Mexico." But it was too hot even to consider going to Mexico and when the War was over he resumed his post at the Newark City Hospital.

Dr. Martland's pathological museum at City Hospital, which was built up mostly through his own efforts, has come to be known as one of the best in the country. In the museum he does all his work himself, including the making of his own drawings and illustrations. In his laboratory, whose atmosphere is more like that of a university than a city hospital, he demonstrates an ability to explain things clearly. He is described as an "outstanding teacher, not given to formal methods—informally he is always teaching—in his laboratory, with exhibits, etc." He spends most of his time in the laboratory. It is the best place to find him, especially late at night. Here he is an unceasing worker, making "no difference between weekdays and Sundays."

Until 1916 Dr. Martland worked and studied: he soaked up information at firsthand, both in his laboratory and at the postmortem table, and expanded his interests to include morbid anatomy, pathological histology, forensic medicine, bacteriology and clinical law. Then in 1916 he began to write for publication. Since then he has written more than 50 medical papers. Original works include *Punch Drunk* (1928), a medical analysis of that "goofy, cuckoo slug-mouth condition" in prize fighters, and *Dr. Watson and Mr. Sherlock Holmes* (1939), a history of medical techniques in detective fiction.

As chief medical examiner of Essex County (appointed 1925) Dr. Martland has been able to develop his interest in criminology. His most famous court appearances and research came in the case of the investigation of radium poisoning of five women workers in watch factories. He proved that the luminous paint which these women used in painting the dials caused their deaths—and possibly the deaths of many other workers. He also published a series of articles showing the results of occupational poisoning in manufactures of luminous watch dials, with a general review of the hazard caused by ingestion of luminous paint, with especial reference to the New Jersey cases.

Dr. Martland was appointed assistant professor and shortly afterward, in 1935, made professor of forensic medicine at New York University College of Medicine. In the same year, at the age of 52, he received an honor that usually does not come during a doctor's lifetime: The Essex County Anatomical and Pathological Society established the Harrison Stanford Martland Lectures.

Besides his extensive court work, numerous papers and appearances at medical meetings and crime conferences, Dr. Martland finds time to participate in gratis duties at the New York Academy of Medicine. There he directs the scientific exhibits of the Graduate Fortnights.

Dr. Martland is heavy but distinguished looking, with hazel eyes and black hair that has a bit of gray in it. He generally works in his shirt sleeves, sans tie, and characteristic photographs show him smoking a cigarette while performing an autopsy. Besides criminology, he is interested in Chinese checkers, string quartets and photography. His wife, Myra C. (Ferdon)

MARTLAND, HARRISON—*Continued*
Martland, looks after her shy "absent-minded" husband and their two children.

References

> Bul New York Academy of Medicine 12:317-20 My '36
> American Medical Directory
> American Physicians and Surgeons 1931

MARVIN, DWIGHT EDWARDS, REV.
Feb 22, 1851—Feb 28, 1940   Former pastor of Flatbush Presbyterian Church, Brooklyn, New York; one of the most prolific writers in the Presbyterian clergy

References

> Who's Who in America

Obituaries

> N Y Herald Tribune p20 F 29 '40

MARVIN, HARRY   1863—Jan 12, 1940
Pioneer film and radio inventor

Obituaries

> N Y Herald Tribune p10 Ja 13 '40
> N Y Times p15 Ja 13 '40

MARY JOSEPH BUTLER, MOTHER
1861—Apr 23, 1940   Superior general of the Religious of the Sacred Heart of Mary; founder of the Marymount Colleges in the United States and Europe

References

> Religious Orders of Women in the United States 1930

Obituaries

> N Y Herald Tribune p20 Ap 25 '40
> N Y Times p15 Ap 27 '40

MASSINE, LEONIDE   1896-   (măs-sēn′ lä-ō-nēd)   Choreographer; dancer
Address: c/o Hurok Musical Bureau, 30 Rockefeller Plaza, New York City

The Russian Ballet is no longer a foreign institution. Theatres in New York and points West, North and South are packed to the rafters when the *Ballet Russe de Monte Carlo* comes to town. Even its financial backing is now American. In the "dancing talent, creative gifts and executive ability" of Léonide Fedorovitch Massine "American millionaires have invested a small fortune." And Léonide Massine rides around America in a trailer.

Former ballet master at Roxy's, student in the Imperial Theatre in Moscow, creator of some of the most popular modern choregraphy, Massine is now the *Ballet Russe's* artistic director, choreographer, ballet master and principal dancer.

Massine, whose genius has been universally acclaimed, was born in 1896 in Moscow, the son of a musician and an opera singer. He gave his first performance at the Imperial Theatre School there at the age of 12. When Léonide was 17 Diaghilev, the famous ballet impresario, saw him carrying a ham on a tray across a stage during a performance of *Don Quixote*. He liked him. He liked his elegant carriage and his "deep burning eyes in a face already touched with melancholy, like a Tolstoy hero."

Diaghilev took Massine back to Paris with him. He placed him under the tutelage of Cecchetti and taught him music, painting, sculpture. Within a few months, in 1914, Massine made his Paris debut in *La Légende de Joseph* and in 1915, when he was just 18, was entrusted with the choreography of a ballet, *Le Soleil de Nuit*. His first important work was *Les Femmes de Bonne Humeur,* "a sparkling dance comedy" based on a play by Goldoni and danced to the music of Scarlatti. In 1917 Massine collaborated with Jean Cocteau, Erik Satie and Pablo Picasso in the concoction of a curious hodgepodge called *Parade,* a cubist ballet given at a time when cubism was the last word in art.

An early work of Massine which still remains immensely popular is *Le Chapeau Tricorne (The Three-Cornered Hat),* produced in 1919 to music by De Falla and décor by Picasso. This is a ballet which Massine dances "with an electrifying intensity which grips an audience and holds it spellbound, and then sweeps it into hysterical enthusiasm." *La Boutique Fantasque,* Stravinsky's *Pulcinella, Chant du Rossignol* and *Sacré de Printemps* are others of his works composed during the years of his association with Diaghilev.

Early in 1921 Massine left Diaghilev. He felt he was grown-up and needed freedom. With a company of his own he toured South America and other countries and didn't return to Paris until 1924. In that year he created the very popular *Beau Danube* and rejoined Diaghilev to stay with him intermittently as choreographer until Diaghilev's death in 1929. From the day when Diaghilev first saw the 17-year-old Massine until the day he died, his admiration for Massine never dimmed. "He has that keen intelligence," he used to say, "that understands things before one says them."

For three years, from 1927 through 1929, Massine was premier danseur and ballet master at Roxy's in New York. Diaghilev almost had a stroke when he heard Massine had taken the job and, as an English critic put it, "slaving in such an environment . . . must have been distinctly irritating to one of his tastes." But there are others who feel that at Roxy's Massine learned a number of things Diaghilev never heard of. "He learned the art of American showmanship and he learned to work fast. He also learned how money is made in American show business."

Early in 1932 Colonel Wassily de Basil and M. René Blum formed a ballet company at Monte Carlo with George Balanchine as ballet master. Léonide Massine was invited as guest choreographer to stage *Jeux d'En-*

fants to the music of Bizet, and the next year succeeded Balanchine as principal choreographer of the De Basil Company. At this time he began his first experiments in symphonic ballet, the form in which he has made his most important contributions to the dance. *Les Présages,* based on Tschaikowsky's *Fifth Symphony,* was his first symphonic ballet and this paved the way for *Choreartium,* which received its first performance in London on October 24, 1933. Many musicians had protested when Massine proposed to dance Tschaikowsky's *Fifth Symphony;* when he dared to lay hands upon Brahms and "desecrate" the *Fourth Symphony* itself they declared it was blasphemy. Hector Berlioz' *Symphonie Fantastique* was his third symphonic ballet, and his transcription of Beethoven's *Seventh Symphony,* in 1938, his fourth.

During the years of his association with the De Basil *Ballet Russe* Massine devoted his best energies to his experiments in the symphonic ballet, but he also created several other works of varying interest. *Union Pacific,* given in 1934, was the first ballet on an American theme to be presented by a Russian company. The scenario, written by Archibald MacLeish (see sketch this issue), told of the completion of the first transcontinental railway. His attempts to use American themes have, however, not been too successful. His *New Yorker,* to the music of George Gershwin, produced in 1940, was, according to a critic, "cursed with bad choreography, poor dancing and feeble music."

In 1937 Massine and De Basil parted company, and their separation was taken into an English law court, with Massine maintaining that he had exclusive rights to all the ballets for which he had designed the choreography. The Honorable Mr. Justice Luxmoore held that property rights can be claimed in the dance steps of a ballet and granted exclusive right in some of his ballets to Massine, while allowing De Basil to have an option on those created while Massine was in his employ.

Just about this time Julius Fleischmann, of the yeast Fleischmanns, and some other American businessmen were looking around for an artistic venture in which to invest. They chose Léonide Massine and created an organization called Universal Art, Incorporated, which has already put vast sums into new ballet productions and plans to continue to do so as long as Massine continues to create them. They know him to be "the completely unrivaled stylist of our time, the greatest force in ballet today."

When the *Ballet Russe de Monte Carlo* is in New York you can find Massine in the twilight backstage of the theatre, "a slight man, fortyish, his black hair thinning, with enormous deep-set eyes in the thin face of an athlete trained fine." In worn costume trousers and an old sweater he is

Maurice Seymour

LEONIDE MASSINE

doing leg stretches and knee bends. "Slick, wire-taut muscles slip under his wet shirt."

An hour later he is on the stage in a dashing hussar's uniform, leaping and stamping and swinging a ballerina to his shoulder in a spirited Strauss waltz. And after that he can be found soothing a temperamental ballerina or a sulking male dancer, or severely dressing down an imperfect performer. "On the stage he is a panther; in rehearsal he is a roaring lion."

Massine now keeps records of his ballets on moving picture film and uses the film to settle disputes and to refresh his memory. He consults them even for his own solos. "At 44, which is considered an age for slippers and easy chair among dancers, he is still unrivaled in rôles ranging from the cancan and the cakewalk to St. Francis of Assisi. Electric, vibrant, smooth as a cat, he flashes through his solos leaving an incandescent trail of excitement."

References

Christian Sci Mon Mag p4 O 5 '38 il pors
Collier's 105:17+ F 17 '40 por
Newsweek 10:27-8 N 1 '37 por
Time 30:26-8 Ag 30 '37 il
Beaumont, C. W. Léonide Massine *In* Complete Book of Ballets p685-757 1938
Haskell, A. L. Dancing Around the World 1938
Lifar, S. Ballet, Traditional to Modern 1938
Liven, P. A. The Birth of Ballets-Russes 1936
Moore, L. Léonide Massine *In* Artists of the Dance p216-24 1938
Propert, W. A. Russian Ballet in Western Europe, 1900-1920 p84-93 1921

MASSINE, LEONIDE—*Continued*

Stokes, A. Russian Ballets 1936
Who's Who
Who's Who in the Theatre

MAURIER, DAPHNE DU *See* Du Maurier, D.

MAX, ADOLPHE Dec 31, 1869—Nov 6, 1939 Burgomaster of Brussels, Belgium

Burgomaster Max, last of the great Belgian war figures, who had refused a Baronetcy and declined a Premiership ("I would rather be Burgomaster than Premier"), died in Brussels, November 6, 1939, of pneumonia.

Max entered Brussels University at sixteen, got his law degree four years later, wrote copiously for the press, became one of the heads of the Liberal Party, and in 1909 was made Burgomaster of Brussels. The dramatic episodes surrounding his resistance to German troops during the World War have become a part of military legend. He was arrested in September 1914 for his "irreconcilable attitude" and was not released until the month of the Armistice.

"Our Max" was slight of build, had brown hair and a short-pointed beard. Laurels of various kinds were conferred upon him, among which was the Grande Croix de la Légion d'Honneur, an award usually reserved for heads of states.

References

International Who's Who

Obituaries

Commonweal 31:87 N 17 '39
N Y Herald Tribune p22 N 7 '39
N Y Times p25 N 7 '39 por; p2 N 9 '39; p23 N 10 '39
Time 34:44 N 13 '39

MAY, HENRY JOHN 1867—Nov 19, 1939 Secretary for 26 years of the International Co-operative Alliance, an organization with 70,000,000 members in 38 countries

References

International Who's Who

Obituaries

N Y Times p21 N 30 '39

MAYNOR, DOROTHY Sept 3, 1910- Negro soprano

Address: c/o Columbia Concerts Corp, 113 W 57th St, New York City

There is a decidedly Horatio Alger or Aladdin's Lamp cast to the story of Dorothy Maynor, newly-discovered Negro soprano who made her debut in New York on November 19, 1939.

Dorothy Maynor was born in Norfolk, Virginia, the daughter of the Rev. J. Mainor (the spelling was changed for professional reasons), who was a Methodist minister. Her only early musical training was singing in the choir of her father's church. At 14 she entered Hampton Institute, there received her first formal voice instruction,

and in 1929 toured Europe with the Institute's famous choir. Shortly afterward she entered the Westminster Choir School of Princeton, New Jersey, intending to become a teacher of voice. On the advice of friends she came to New York in 1936, studying first with Wilfred Klamroth and then with John Alan Haughton, her present instructor.

In August 1939 she went to the Berkshire Music Festival near Stockbridge, Massachusetts, with only a thin hope of getting an audition with Koussevitzky (see sketch this issue). She had it, and on the day following she sang everything from Negro spirituals to Wagner at Koussevitzky's private picnic, to which members of the orchestra and hand-picked critics had been invited.

She returned to New York, where she lived in an upper West-side apartment, and began practicing for her debut recital. Her success was almost unqualified. In February 1940, by unanimous vote, she was selected as the winner for 1940 of the Town Hall Endowment Series Award. The award is made each season to the artist under 30 years of age whom the New York music critics and the Town Hall music committee consider to have given the outstanding performance of the year at Town Hall. Her recital in October 1940 showed, according to Olin Downes, "an impressive advance. The glorious voice has now filled out and come under finer control."

Miss Maynor is four feet ten inches, warm-smiling, buxom, and disturbingly modest about her own accomplishments. And it was Koussevitzky who called her voice a "musical revelation."

With the aid of her patroness (Miss Mary Hayden of Boston) she is "now in the bank-account class." She has appeared with four symphony orchestras, New York Philhar-

De Bellis

DOROTHY MAYNOR

monic, Boston, Philadelphia and Chicago. She has engagements in twenty-seven states and is making two cross-country tours durin the 1940 to 1941 season.

References

> Ind Woman 19:4 Ja '40 por
> Liberty 17:55-7 N 30 '40 por
> Musical Am 60:33 Mr 25 '40
> N Y Times X p7 N 19 '39 por; p15 N 20 '39; IX p8 F 25 '40
> Newsweek 14:26-7 Ag 21 '39 por; 14: 25 N 27 '39
> Springf'd Repub p1+ Mr 15 '40
> Time 34:45 Ag 21 '39 por; 34:58 N 27 '39
> Who's Who in America (Addenda)

MAYO, KATHERINE 1867—Oct 9, 1940 Author; best-known work *Mother India* (1927), for which she was burned in effigy and denounced in lecture halls half around the world; helped bring about creation of New York State Police in 1917; is supposed to have wielded a strong influence in keeping the Filipinos from achieving independence; author of many crusading books and articles; was working on a book dealing with the international traffic in narcotics at the time of her death

K. S. Woermer

KATHERINE MAYO

References

> American Women
> Author's and Writer's Who's Who
> Who's Who Among North American Authors
> Who's Who in America

Obituaries

> N Y Herald Tribune p20 O 10 '40 por
> N Y Times p25 O 10 '40 por
> Newsweek 16:6 O 21 '40
> Pub W 138:1602 O 19 '40

MEAD, MARGARET Dec 16, 1901- Anthropologist

Address: b. American Museum of Natural History, New York City; h. 43 W 93rd St, New York City

Margaret Mead has found that to be an anthropologist involves "not only scientific research but the practice of rough, tropical medicine, care of children, organization and maintenance of camps in the bush, cultivation of rapport with primitive peoples and many varieties of writing necessary to record the results." Since 1925 Dr. Mead has been roaming over much of the world and studying its peoples. New Guinea, the Admiralty Islands, Bali, Samoa are some of the places she has visited and studied.

From her travels and studies have come books and articles. Her first two, *Coming of Age in Samoa* and *An Inquiry into the Question of Cultural Stability in Polynesia*, were published in 1928; in 1930 came *Growing Up in New Guinea*; in 1932 *The Changing Culture of an Indian Tribe;* in 1935 *Sex and Temperament in Three Primitive Societies*. Miss Mead's latest book, *From the South Seas* (1939), is a reprint of three of her earlier books and warmly recommended by the critics to "anybody with an inquiring mind and a philosophical interest in the human race."

Margaret Mead was born in Philadelphia, Pennsylvania, the daughter of Professor Edward Sherwood Mead of the University of Pennsylvania and Emily (Fogg) Mead. During childhood she wanted to be a portrait painter; in college she majored in English. Her first year of college, from 1919 to 1920, she spent at De Pauw University; her next three at Barnard College, from which she was graduated with a Phi Beta Kappa key in 1923. From Barnard she went to Columbia and received her M. A. in psychology in 1924.

The year after she received her Master's Degree Dr. Mead received a National Research Council Fellowship and was able to spend six months studying adolescents in Samoa. A later fellowship for one year (1928-29) from the Social Science Research Council enabled her to continue her studies. Much of her work in the years after Columbia (she received a Ph. D. from the University in 1929) was concentrated on children and on studies in sex. In New Guinea, for instance, Dr. Mead studied three tribes "to discover to what degree temperamental differences between the sexes were innate and to what degree they were culturally determined." And from her studies she has drawn scientific conclusions on many phases of cultural life all over the world— her latest conclusion is that warfare is "an

MARGARET MEAD

invention like any other of the inventions in terms of which we order our lives, such as writing, marriage, cooking our food instead of eating it raw, trial by jury or burial of the dead, and so on."

From 1928 to 1933 Dr. Mead's New Guinea studies were made in collaboration with Dr. Leo. F. Fortune. During this period Dr. Mead studied four New Guinea tribes, living in native villages, participating in the community life and speaking the native languages. In 1936 Dr. Mead was married to Gregory Bateson, English anthropologist of St. John's College, Cambridge, England, and they have one daughter, Mary Catherine, born in December 1939. Her last expedition, in collaboration with Mr. Bateson, was to Bali and New Guinea from 1936 to 1939.

Since 1926 Dr. Mead has been an assistant curator of ethnology of the American Museum of Natural History in New York and in 1940 was appointed a visiting lecturer in child study at Vassar College. Her latest trip was to Bali and to New Guinea—she went there in 1936 and returned in 1939. For her contributions to anthropology, in discoveries, in books and articles, in her teaching and museum work, she received in June 1940 the annual National Achievement Award of Chi Omega Sorority.

Youthful-looking, small, dark-haired Miss Mead has discovered in these years of work that anthropology is a completely satisfying study. "The study of human culture," she says, "is a context within which every aspect of human life legitimately falls and necessitates no rift between work and play, professional and amateur activities."

References

Scholastic 30:11 My 15 '37 por
Wilson Lib Bul 5:306 Ja '31 por

American Men of Science
Who's Who in America

MEARNS, HUGHES (mûrns hūz) Sept 28, 1875- University professor; author
Address: b. School of Education, New York University, New York City; h. 531 W 124th St, New York City

Besides being a teacher and author of wide reputation, Professor Mearns is known for the authorship of a nonsense quatrain which was sweeping the country as a "hit parade" popular favorite in early 1940. He was born in Philadelphia, Pennsylvania, the son of William Hughes and Lelia Cora (Evans) Mearns. He studied at the School of Pedagogy, Philadelphia, and in 1902 received a B. A. from Harvard. For the next five years he studied at the University of Pennsylvania Graduate School. Even with all this pedagogical training, Mearns had no idea of becoming a professor.

He wanted to write, for the stage preferably, but he needed money to live on, so he accepted a teaching job in Philadelphia which paid $1,000 a year. In 1904 he had married Mabel Fagley of Philadelphia. They have one daughter, Emma. Professor Mearns had always been extremely fond of children. He determined at the Philadelphia school to try experimenting with the creative processes of children. He would gather the children around him on the lawn, and, as he says, "began by quietly exploring outside of school classes the creative possibilities of children from three to eight years old." He "came upon a hidden individual spirit of surprising keenness and of stubborn honesty." He typed notes of their conversations; he learned how to make them forget an adult was around; never asked them questions and never showed surprise no matter what they did or said. His method was good, for he found children had amazingly acute observation, were completely selfish and merciless to each other. While some parents think children speak too freely, Professor Mearns has the opposite idea—he feels that children's individualities, the source of their creative efforts—are smothered because parents and teachers try to mold them into prissy little ladies and gentlemen.

From 1905 to 1920 Mearns was a professor at the Philadelphia School of Pedagogy. The Rockefeller Foundation became tremendously interested in the kind of creative work he was doing and they asked him to start a five-year experiment at the Lincoln School, Teachers College, Columbia University. In 1925 during intervals away from his young charges, he "dashed off" his widely acclaimed book, *Creative Youth,* which established him as one of the leading progressive educators of the country and won him a post at New York University.

Since 1926 Professor Mearns has been Chairman of the Department of Creative Education at New York University. He dislikes scholarly formality, says: "Imagine calling another man 'Professor' with nobody else around!" His classes are conducted without the solemnity common to many university classes in education. He teaches no less than 1,000 students, mostly adults, each term by a method he calls "education by exposure." At first he found it an almost unsurmountable difficulty to get people to be themselves, but he has convinced himself and them that "every man has the machinery for a full, honest and individual life within him if he will but throw off the shackles of artificiality. He tells them of a clubwoman at a meeting who astonished her hearers by saying candidly: "I never liked Wordsworth, and now, for the first time in my life, I'm going to say so." Then he reminds them of Robert Benchley's review of the play, *Strange Interlude*, by the idolized Eugene O'Neill. No one at the time had the effrontery to utter a word against that figure of perfection. Benchley, however, complained of the play's length, then quickly, in parentheses, wrote: "All right, Jove, strike me dead!"

"There has always been a danger in placing the artist in a special class," says Professor Mearns. "It turns us all into foolish worshipers instead of independent fellow craftsmen; we are then too easily satisfied with the American picture of a few highly-paid professional performers before a nation of mutes. Admitting the excellence of the experts, we do not need to be dumb before them. We have our own excellences."

In 1929 he wrote *Creative Power*, in which he tells how, "in his free school, he encouraged the creative activity of apparently ordinary children." He includes many illustrations of the poetry and prose which the experiments brought forth in children. In 1940 he published *Creative Adult*, which explains the work done in his classes in strengthening the native cultural gifts of adults. Professor Mearns feels that many adults cannot truly be happy because they are fettered by mediocrity, and too ready to conform to "the mores and the folkways of the masses."

In 1938 in the Wrightstone Survey of 200 years of educational reform in America and Europe, Professor Mearns is named among the 10 "most notable contributors," in a list which includes Adler, Parker, Hall, Cattell, Thorndike, Terman and Dewey.

Professor Mearns, a "tweedy, loquacious educator, boyish, despite his 64 years, and unbowed by his ponderous scholastic title" does not feel that he has suffered any loss in prestige by being known as the author of *The Little Man Who Wasn't There*. The quatrain has been set to music by two Broadway songwriters, Harold Adamson and Bernard Hanighen, and was known as the number one rhythm song, tagged as a "hit parade" tune on the radio. In 1910 Professor Mearns composed it as part of a play, *The Psyco-ed*, which he wrote for a group of theatrical

HUGHES MEARNS

amateurs calling themselves *Plays and Players*. The quatrain goes:

"As I was walking up the stair
I met a man who wasn't there.
He wasn't there again today.
I wish, I wish he'd stay away."

In the drama in which the ditty appeared, a psychology student sang it to a ponderous professor who analyzed it at great length. Professor Mearns, without a trace of bitterness, tells people that the authorship of the ditty has been ascribed to "nearly every modern writer except George Bernard Shaw, whose mind would presumably never run in such channels." Even his students have from time to time brought the ditty to him as their own—"a plagiarism he always condones." Far from being proud of it, Professor Mearns waited until 1921 to have it printed, and then it appeared in F. P. A.'s *Conning Tower*.

When the song writers wrote the song they assumed the verse was anonymous and in the public domain. However, the music company found out that Professor Mearns was the author, and they offered to pay the startled educator one cent per copy for sheet music plus one third of the royalties on recordings. So far the song has sold 35,000 copies in sheet music and 165,000 in recordings.

Mearns is also the author of many light novels, the first, *Richard, Richard,* written in 1916. They sell well in England. One, *The Vinegar Tree,* is popular, he says, among 16-year-old girls. He confesses that he has also written innumerable one-act plays, all of which he has destroyed.

References

N Y Times VI p3 Ja 31 '40
N Y World-Telegram p15 Ja 15 '40
    por

MEARNS, HUGHES—*Continued*

New Yorker 15:15 S 30 '39
Newsweek 15:43-4 Ja 15 '40 por
Scholastic 30:5-6 Ap 17 '37 por
Who's Who in America

MELLOR, WALTER Apr 25, 1880—Jan
11, 1940 American architect and designer
of the Chapel at Bony, France and the
American Battle Monument at Ypres

Obituaries

N Y Sun p23 Ja 12 '40
N Y Times p17 Ja 12 '40
N Y World-Telegram p36 Ja 12 '40

**MENDENHALL, HARLAN GEORGE,
REV.** Apr 12, 1851—May 15, 1940 Clergy-
man; former moderator of Presbyterian
Synod of New York and president of the
Presbyterian Ministers Association; pastor
emeritus of the Chelsea Presbyterian
Church, New York City

References

Who's Who in America

Obituaries

N Y Herald Tribune p22 My 16 '40
N Y Times p23 My 16 '40 por

MEREDITH, BURGESS Nov 16, 1907-
Actor

Burgess Meredith knocked around in a
surprising number of odd jobs before he
decided to become an actor. A year of
working his way through Amherst College,
washing dishes, tending furnaces, having no
money for recreation or social life, left him
with debts and no taste for a higher education. He didn't even have enough money
to leave Amherst at the end of the year.
But he heard of an annual declamation
contest, hastily memorized the last scene of
Cyrano de Bergerac, shouted it at the
judges and won the $50 prize. Then he
departed from Amherst to make his mark
in the world. This was in 1928.

There followed about a year and a half
during which Meredith went from job to
job with rather lightning rapidity as he
was fired, or just moved on. He turned
up during the Christmas rush at a New
York department store selling neckties;
found himself behind a complaint desk in
a Fifth Avenue shop; sold or rather tried
to sell vacuum cleaners from door to door;
sold roofing, toilet articles—all very unsuccessfully, throughout various cities. For
two months he was a runner in Wall Street.
He lived with other impecunious young
men, a week here, two weeks there, always
from hand to mouth. Once he lived for a
week on free samples of breakfast food.

Meredith ended this "commercial" career
with a voyage—definitely not of the de
luxe kind. He shipped as a seaman on a
tramp steamer, and made one trip unevent-
fully. The food was regular, so he made a

second trip, but got himself into trouble.
He overstayed his shore leave in a South
American port, and made the voyage back
in the ship's brig under arrest. The story
goes that he relieved the tedium of the
voyage by reciting out loud everything he
could remember. He was so pleased with
his voice that he decided to become an
actor.

His desire to go on the stage was not
without precedent in his family. Although
he did not know it at the time, his mother
had been in stock. Going through an old
scrapbook of his mother's after her death,
he found she had not only been on the stage,
but had received rather good notices in her
short career. The daughter of a Methodist
revivalist, she had run away from home, and
spent 10 months in stock before she was
brought back home by the pleas of her irate
preacher-father.

He had an uncle in vaudeville, and a
brother in a jazz band for a short time, but
otherwise young Meredith had no encouragement to follow a stage career.

Meredith was born November 16, 1907, the
son of Dr. William George and Ida
(Burgess) Meredith, in a suburb in Cleveland where his father was a doctor. As a
boy he sang solos in the Methodist Church,
and at the age of 11, over 75 competitors,
won a scholarship in vocal training at the
Paulist Choir School in New York. The
Methodist tradition was too strong in his
family to allow his entrance into a Catholic
choir school, so instead he was sent to New
York to enter the choir of the Cathedral of
St. John the Divine.

In 1923 when he was no longer a plaus-
ible soprano he was sent to the Hoosac
Preparatory School at Hoosick Falls, New
York. There he distinguished himself by
editing the school paper and by leaving it in
the red financially. At the Christmas Yule
Log Festival he always played the jester.
He also won the David Brook Anglo-
American Prize essay cup for his essay,
"The Benefit to Christian Civilization From
a Complete Understanding and Friendly Re-
lationship between the United States of
America and the British Empire."

His father was obliged to retire in 1926
and there was no further money for Meredith's education. With the help of a scholarship and aid from an uncle he entered Amherst College in 1926. He came too late
to get any work, however, and left after a
few weeks to return the following year.

At Amherst between tending furnaces,
washing dishes and trying to get an education, Meredith didn't find life very satisfactory. He tried out for the dramatic club
and won, but his scholarship, according to
the dean, was such that he was ineligible for
extra-curricular activities. Determined to act,
he went to Northampton, Massachusetts to
play Sir Toby Belch in *Twelfth Night* for
the Smith Dramatic Club, and was nearly
dismissed when the Dean heard about it.

When Meredith decided to embark on a dramatic career, he was not discouraged by the fact that young men seem to have a pretty hard time getting on the stage unless "they have been on the stage betore." He wangled a letter of introduction to Eva Le Gallienne from a kindly man in the theatre. On the strength of the letter which praised his qualifications without saying exactly what they were, Meredith, in December 1929, became an apprentice without pay in Miss Le Gallienne's Civic Repertory Company. He lived with his married sister in East Orange, New Jersey and awaited developments in his stage career.

The ambitious young student finally got one line to say—the part of the servant to Juliet's nurse in *Romeo and Juliet*. From that he progressed to bit parts and by spring was making $20 a week. For the next two years he alternated between summer stock and Miss Le Gallienne's company. When in the fall of 1931 Miss Le Gallienne left the stage for a year Meredith had no rôles except for a short appearance in *People on the Hill*.

It was at this stage in his career that a clerk in some casting office summed up Oliver Burgess Meredith's (he has dropped the Oliver) qualifications on his application card thus: "young, homely, large head, blond." Nevertheless Meredith had already attracted some attention in the summer theatres. In the summer of 1930 a White Plains reporter, seeing him as Marchbanks in George Bernard Shaw's *Candida*, wrote with frantic enthusiasm: "A young man of remarkable genius walked out on the stage last night and began creating a Marchbanks that became one of the most beautiful and poetic things seen in the theatre anywhere and at any time."

During the "no rôle" period Meredith and a roommate tried to organize an acting company, operating on a profit-sharing basis, but failed. Meredith went back to stock in 1932, and between performances married Mrs. Helen Berrien Derby, ticket-taker for the company, on the stage of the summer theatre at Cape May, New Jersey. They were divorced in September 1935 just when Meredith began his part in his great success, *Winterset*.

Meredith went back to the Civic Repertory Theatre in the fall of 1932 when Miss Le Gallienne reopened it, and played in a variety of small parts. At one period he even had three animal parts in *Alice in Wonderland*. He left in the middle of his career in the animal parts for his first Broadway play, *The Three Penny Opera*. It lasted one week.

Meredith made his first impression on Broadway in the spring of 1933 when he played the part of Red Barry in *Little Ol' Boy*, the Albert Bein play of reform school life. The play brought him a rather stupefying (after the

BURGESS MEREDITH

$30 a week in the Civic Repertory Theatre) three-figure-a-week salary, and was a huge critical success. One critic wrote of Meredith that his performance "was as near perfection as could be imagined" and that what he achieved "was worth a hundred performances up and down town." The play, however, lasted only nine days.

Although Meredith had flops after that, he was never without rôles again for any length of time. He next appeared on Broadway in *She Loves Me Not*, a prodigious success which won for him acclaim as an actor of robust comedy parts. His success in *She Loves Me Not* under Howard Lindsay's direction brought him to the attention of radio and gave him the part of Red Davis, a typical American boy in a program sponsored by a chewing gum company, for 40 weeks at $350 a week.

His greatest success came while he was working under the direction of Guthrie McClintic. McClintic drew out in Meredith those qualities which led the actor to be dubbed by a press agent "The Hamlet of 1940." McClintic directed him first in a small rôle in Miss Cornell's revival of *The Barrets of Wimpole Street*, then again with Miss Cornell in *Flowers of the Forest*, where Meredith, according to critics, "came near walking away with the production."

It was under McClintic's direction, too, that Meredith appeared in *Winterset*, the Maxwell Anderson play that won the Critics' Award, and the following year in another Anderson play, another Critics' Award prize play, *High Tor*.

Meredith's success in *Winterset* somehow guaranteed him stature and importance in the theatre. He took a house at Sneden's Landing on the Hudson. It was while he was living

MEREDITH, BURGESS—*Continued*

there that he met Margaret Perry, a young divorcee who also had a home there. They were married January 10, 1936, and although the marriage seemed a happy one at first, they were divorced July 20, 1938.

Meredith also played in the movies the part of Mio in *Winterset*, which he had interpreted so beautifully on the stage. His eight-year movie contract calls for a picture a year at a time to be chosen by him, and started with $1,500 a week to be raised so that he will make $3,500 a week when the last picture under the contract is made. In addition to *Winterset* Meredith's movies include *Of Mice and Men, Spring Madness, There Goes the Groom* and *Idiot's Delight*.

His most recent plays were *Star Wagon* and the revival of Molnar's *Liliom* in which he played in 1940. At 32 his place in the theatre is assured. His acting has been described as brilliant, impressive, heartbreaking, sinewy and sensitive.

Meredith has not become brash with praise. "I am sure I never would have had any success if I had not been lucky enough to play under excellent direction both in New York and summer stock," he says. "Directors, I don't mind saying, made me. The actor's opportunity to learn his craft lies in the chance to work under a good director."

About five-feet-seven inches tall, Meredith has a pointed face that might "reasonably belong to a jockey," and ginger-colored hair. His friends call him "Buzz" or "Bugs," and the name seems to suit him and his offhand, crumpled clothes.

He has served as vice-president and president of the Actor's Equity. On March 18, 1939 Amherst, which he left so disillusioned in 1928, honored him at the dedication of the new Kirby Memorial Theatre at the college by presenting him with an honorary Master of Arts degree.

References

Am Mag 124:32-3+ Ag '37 por
Collier's 99:24+ Ap 10 '37 por
New Yorker 13:26-30+ Ap 3 '37
Sat R Lit 20:9 O 7 '39
Scholastic 31:22E Ja 22 '38 por
Theatre Arts 20:51-2 Ja '36
America's Young Men
Eustis, M. Burgess Meredith *In* Players at Work 1937
International Motion Picture Almanac
Sobel, B. ed. Theatre Handbook 1940
Who's Who in America
Who's Who in the Theatre

MERRILL, JOHN DOUGLAS 1865—Jan 9, 1940 Editor of *The Harvard Alumni Bulletin* for 37 years; political reporter for the Boston *Globe* for 50 years

JOHN D. MERRILL

References
Who's Who in America 1938-39

Obituaries
N Y Herald Tribune p18 Ja 10 '40

MESSERSCHMITT, WILLY 1898- Aircraft designer; manufacturer

Hanson Baldwin of the New York *Times* wrote in December 1939: "At present Germany is probably stepping up her airplane production faster than Britain, France and the United States combined." The man who is mainly responsible for the growth of the Nazi plane industry and for the lethal speed of Nazi pursuit planes is Willy Messerschmitt.

Willy Messerschmitt is a "sharp-nosed, sandy-haired citizen of the placid medieval town of Augsburg, Germany." He was born in 1898 in Germany and was educated at the Munich Technical High School. He started flying when he was 15 and designed his first plane in 1916. In 1923 he founded the firm of Messerschmitt; while its director, he was also chief engineer, specializing in speed, for the Bayerische Flugzeugwerke, until it amalgamated with the Messerschmitt works in 1938. He was made chairman of the German Institute for Research in Aviation in 1936, was awarded the gold medal of the Association of German Engineers in 1937 and the Lilienthal Prize for Research in Aviation in the same year. In 1937, too, he became a member of Germany's Council of War.

Willy Messerschmitt, member of Hitler's Council of War and inventor of his pursuit planes, was reported in December 1939 to be missing. One rumor had it that he had fled to the Netherlands; another that he "hadn't been out of Germany since the War

Newsphotos

WILLY MESSERSCHMITT

started." There still is some question in the minds of foreign correspondents as to his present whereabouts.

There is also a good deal of question in the minds of airplane experts as to the exact efficacy of the Messerschmitt planes. In April 1939 one of the Messerschmitts set up an absolute record of 469 miles per hour, with the ship "undoubtedly stripped and 'souped up' for the test." In combat with United States Curtis fighters which hit a top speed of about 330 miles per hour, "Messerschmitts," with their long, flat, square-tipped wings, have been proved "lacking in maneuverability and rate of climb," however.

It is possible that the lessons that Germany is learning in warfare now are being incorporated in new designs, for experts agree that so far as airplanes are concerned, "new types, new maneuvers, new designs will determine balance-of-power in the air rather than sheer quantitative production." It is to improve the designs of German airplanes, so vital in the War, that Willy Messerschmitt comes in, "if he hasn't gone out."

References

Time 34:23 D 4 '39

International Who's Who

MESTROVIC, IVAN (mesh'trô-vĭch) Aug 15, 1883-   Sculptor

Address: Mletacka ul. 8, Zagreb, Yugoslavia

Ivan Meštrović whose fifty-seventh birthday came on August 15, 1940, has been internationally renowned as a sculptor since 1911, when one of his large-scale conceptions dominated the Serbian Pavilion at the International Exhibition in Rome. Represented at the Brooklyn Museum, the Art Institute of Chicago, the galleries of Detroit and San Diego and the museums of Vienna, Budapest, Paris and Rome as well as by the Canadian War Memorial, he has had the honor of exhibitions at great public galleries like the Victoria and Albert Museum, the Tate Gallery in London and the Musée du Jeu de Paume in Paris.

Art critic André Michel once described Meštrović as "the only Serbian artist having a European reputation," and as long ago as 1915 Sir Michael Sadler, British scholar and connoisseur, began a movement to raise a fund for the national purchase of one of his pieces. As one French commentator wrote: "He is great because he pursues a higher reality showing through appearances and makes of every work at once an affirmation of the present, an appeal to the future and an aspiration towards the divine."

Meštrović was born at Vrpolje, Slavonis, the son of a small builder whose home was at Otavitze, on the Dalmatian plateau overlooking the Adriatic Sea. The family was very poor, and the village primitive and entirely devoted to agriculture. Ivan tended sheep in the mountains, was 15 before he saw anything of the life of a town and 16 before he walked on the streets of a great capital city. His education he got from his father, who taught him to read and write and encouraged him when he started to carve bits of wood and stone. Some of these carvings aroused comment in a local paper, and as a result some neighboring monks commissioned him to make a devotional carving, offering him a *florin* for the job. Meštrović held out for three and got his price.

When he was 15 a retired officer, Captain Grubišić, started a collection at Drniš to cover his higher training. Ivan's father sent him to Spalato for a year's apprenticeship to a master mason, after which Captain Grubišić was able to finance him for an attack on the wider world of Vienna. In 1902 he arrived there, poor, raw and bewildered. He found humble lodgings with a Czech family and went round to various schools and teachers, trying in vain to get taken on as a pupil. One pompous art master greeted his efforts with: "We want no Balkan prodigies here."

Finally he got his lessons, first from O. König and then from E. von Hellmer. At the same time his general education was continued by an official of the department of fine arts. When Meštrović had been in Vienna a year, with Hellmer's help he was able to enter the Kunstakademie and win a stipend for his lessons there in open competition.

After Vienna Meštrović's first important move was to set up a studio in Paris in 1907. He had already participated in the Vienna Secession Exhibitions and held one-man shows at Belgrade in 1904 and Zagreb in 1905. Now, in Paris, he was able to meet sculptors like Rodin, Bourdelle and Maillol,

Clara E. Sipprell

IVAN MESTROVIC

who taught him much without in any way changing the proud nationalistic spirit which had already shown itself in his work. Various visits to Italy likewise failed to turn him from his personal style. From 1907 to 1908 he was working on a huge scheme for a temple at Kossovo, its theme medieval Serbia in the grip of Islam. The temple was never built, but the model, exhibited in Rome at the International Art Exhibition of 1911, created a profound impression.

From 1911 to 1914 the sculptor lived in Rome, where he studied the sculpture of Michelangelo and the style of the archaic Greeks. From there he went to England, where prominent critics praised his work, where exhibitions were held, where Meštrović was commissioned to execute portrait busts of such important people as Sir Thomas Beecham and Lady Cunard. Part of the period of the First World War Meštrović spent at Geneva and at Cannes. And as stone became more and more scarce, he turned increasingly to wood sculpture, in which he became a master.

When the War was over Meštrović went back to his native country (now the principal constituent of an enlarged Yugoslavia) and in 1922 was given the post of rector of the School of Fine Arts at Zagreb, a post which he still holds. Many commissions and honors came to him and continue to come to him.

Meštrović is both a carver and a modeler. He works in wood, stone and bronze and in addition to his sculpture practices painting, engraving and lithography. He has tackled practically every kind of sculpture—from portrait busts to huge architectural schemes. But no matter what he does he impresses on it the mark of a virile intelligence and a far-reaching imagination. During the years

he has varied his style a good deal, sometimes, as in *Virgin and Child*, showing Byzantine feeling, sometimes being at once dramatic and realistic, as in *The Indian*, and sometimes showing a vein of tenderness, as in *The Artist's Mother*.

Most commentators divide his work into three classes. There are the "heroic" sculptures, designed to illustrate Yugoslavian history or legend, or created under the violent stimulus of the wars in which Serbia had been continuously engaged from 1912 to 1918; there are his studies in form "in which his strong originality in composition is pre-eminent particularly in female figures"; finally there are his "exquisite and rhythmic reliefs carved in wood or in a similar technique in stone, with two simple planes of relief." His *Bishop Nin*, *Widows* and *Maiden of Kossovo* all illustrate the first and earlier style; *Girl with a Guitar* shows the second; *Christ and the Woman of Samaria* is an example of the third.

Meštrović is married. He is a member of the Roman Catholic Church, and has executed a number of devotional works. He is short, stocky and dark, with piercing eyes and what has been described as "an attitude of restrained friendliness." He is not given to writing or speaking much about his art, but a significant phrase occurs in a short monograph which he wrote on Michelangelo. "The artist must have a profound and slowly ripening conviction," he wrote, "and no work of art can live without some remote religious conception."

References

Connoisseur 96:241-2 O '35

Ali, A. Y. Meštrović and Serbian Sculpture 1916

Casson, S. New Movement in Sculpture *In* Some Modern Sculptors p59-87 1928

New Standard Encyclopedia of Art 1939

Who's Who

METAXAS, JOHN (mĕt-äks-äs') Apr 12, 1871- Dictator of Greece

Address: 150, Od Patissiou, Athens, Greece

One small European country after another has been drawn into the orbit of the current War. In October 1940 Greece became another battleground. Accused by Italy of maltreating Albanian minorities and of murdering an Albanian "patriot" and faced with an ultimatum demanding virtual surrender of Greek independence, Greece and John Metaxas, her dictator had been compelled to go to war against Italy, whose armies attacked as soon as the ultimatum expired. Metaxas' firm stand has helped to increase his popularity among his subjects.

Greece and her harbors are important strategic points in World War II. Today they serve as shelters for British convoys and keep open for Britain communications in the East Mediterranean. In Italian hands these harbors could serve as valuable bases against Egypt and the Levant.

Ideologically and economically the sympathies of John Metaxas, dictator of Greece who is officially Greece's Premier and Minister of War, Marine, Air and Education, had been previously on the side of the Axis. For many years Germany has been the greatest consumer of Greek agricultural products and minerals, and the Nazi influence has been strong in radio, consumers' goods, railroad supplies and armaments. Metaxas himself, who attended military school in Germany and supported Germany in the First World War, is considered by some Germanophile and is also supposed to have understudied Mussolini and to have set up his own state "on strictly Fascist lines."

When Metaxas came to power on August 4, 1936 as the result of a *coup*, he immediately proceeded to reorganize Greece according to the examples set him by Hitler and Mussolini. In September of that year the secret police arrested more than 4,000 Liberals, Communists and Republicans and herded them into penal colonies. Arrests and deportations continued; and Metaxas went so far as to exile a young barber for "excessive and dangerous politeness, provocative of Communism."

Books were burned, the universities were purged, castor oil treatments were frequent, censorship was "clamped down." Editors were sometimes given even the headlines to use on the government propaganda articles they printed. Metaxas explained this to the British press when there was criticism: "England," said he, "can afford the luxury of a free press. Greece cannot afford to offend her neighbors." And he explained to the newspaper editors how they must follow him like soldiers in battle, "never consulting the general, nor criticizing him, nor exchanging opinions with him, but always having confidence in him."

Reforms, however, were established. A minimum wage was set up, an eight-hour day was declared, some of the debts of small landowners were canceled, workers were given medical care and vacations. Metaxas was and still is proud of these reforms and the support he thinks they have brought him. "I have raised the burden of debt from the small landowner. I have increased wages. I have trebled the minimum wage. Is it likely that my work is not appreciated? My government is directed toward bettering the lot of the poor. I feel that they are with me."

Many observers think that Metaxas deceives himself and that "a vast majority of the population is opposed" to his dictatorship. Actually, rising prices have offset any rise in wages; the minimum-wage laws are generally ignored; the medical care is almost non-existent; complainers are sent to prison; the eight-hour day is ignored "by most factories." But though "a dictator without popular support until the outbreak of the war between his country and Italy,

Associated Press

JOHN METAXAS

Metaxas has continued in power for four years because he has been supported by the army and by the King.

John Metaxas was born in Cephalonia, the son of Panaghi and Helene (Trigoni) Metaxas, and is the descendant of a long line of military and governmental officials. Almost from birth he was intended for the army. He went to the Military School of Greece and in 1890 was made an officer. His first battle came in 1897 when he fought against the Turks. Always impressed by German military methods, he then went to the Kaiser's Military Academy at Potsdam in 1899 and stayed there for four years. The German professors, impressed by his brilliance, used to call him "Little Moltke" after the hero of the Franco-Prussian War.

From 1903 to 1912 Metaxas served in the Greek Army and in 1912 was active in the war against the Turks and Bulgars as assistant chief of staff. In 1915 he became chief of staff and military adviser to the former pro-German King Constantine of Greece. It was partly on Metaxas' advice that Constantine supported Germany in the War. But Constantine abdicated, Greece joined the Allies and Metaxas was dismissed from the army and exiled to Corsica in 1917.

In 1921 Metaxas was back in Greece and a supporter of King George II. The Republic was established in 1924 and in 1926 Metaxas was made Minister of Communications in the coalition government. He continued active though not prominent in politics until 1934, when he started a Fascist-Monarchist party of his own which was severely defeated at the polls. In 1935, when George II was restored to the throne, he was made Vice-Premier and War Minister though his party had only six seats in Parliament. In April 1936 he was made Premier.

METAXAS, JOHN—*Continued*

At the time when King George returned, the country had been in great confusion, its treasury empty, its political parties constantly feuding, its people discontented. The King tried to restore order but wasn't too successful. In August, on the eve of a general strike, in order to combat "political divisions and the menace of Communism," Metaxas staged a *coup d'état* and declared himself dictator. Demoralized by years of parliamentary squabbles, the Republican and Monarchist parties accepted his proposal that he rule until some agreement was reached, and plump, bespectacled, shabbily-dressed Metaxas declared: "I shall become a sort of modern monk. I shall renounce everything in the world and shall live only for Greece." After four years, he is still dictator in his own country but surrounded by the dictators of larger nations: the Fascist country he has built up is now threatened by the Fascist countries he admired and copied.

References

Canad Forum 19:78-9 Je '39
Cur Hist & Forum 52:10 N 26 '40
Fortnightly 148 (ns 142) :722-9 D '37
Lit Digest 121:14 Ap 25 '36 por; 122: 13 Ag 15 '36 il; 122:17-18 N 14 '36 por
Liv Age 353:52-5 S '37
Nation 145:197-8 Ag 21 '37 (Same abr. Lit Digest 124 (Digest 1) :27 S 11 '37)
Newsweek 16:31-2 N 18 '40
Time 36:20 O 28 '40; 36:24-7 N 4 '40
Carr, A. Alexander, Metaxas, Carol: Ferment in the Balkans *In* Juggernaut p129-45 1939
International Who's Who
Who's Who in Central and East-Europe

GEORGE JULIAN MEYERS

MEYERS, GEORGE JULIAN Apr 10, 1881—Dec 7, 1939 Rear Admiral in the United States Navy who spent 20 years of active duty at sea

References

Who's Who in America 1938-39

Obituaries

N Y Times p25 D 8 '39

MICHELIN, EDOUARD (mĕsh-lăn) 1856—Aug 25, 1940 French tire manufacturer; inventor of the rubber tires which bear his name; his company was one of the world's largest rubber firms; created a tourist guide organization which placed milestones on French roads; established a standard road map service covering nearly all of Europe

Obituaries

N Y Herald Tribune p8 Ag 26 '40

MICHELSON, CHARLES (mĭ'kĕl-son) Apr 18, 1869- Director of publicity for the Democratic National Committee

Address: b. National Press Bldg, Washington, D. C.; h. The Westchester, Washington, D. C.

Charles Michelson, who has been handling Democratic publicity since 1929, is "the greatest silent orator in America." Those Democratic speeches in an election year which seem to come from Senators, Cabinet members, Governors or local spellbinders usually find the source of their eloquence in the typewriter of Charley Michelson—"puppet master to a troupe of Democratic politicians," is what the Republicans call him. Some politicians will take a speech from him and not even bother to read it until they get to the microphone; others will bring their own ideas into headquarters to get them "polished, perfumed and packaged."

As public relations and publicity man for the Democrats, Charley Michelson has more to do than to write speeches. He has to process the news, explaining away or minimizing unfavorable events and playing up the favorable ones. Much of this he does in his weekly column sent out free to the newspapers of the country. It is called *Dispelling the Fog* and is devoted to proving that the "Republican elephant is no more than a mouse with a snout." He also has to confer almost daily with party leaders, plan policies and advise on strategy, and he works very closely with Roosevelt and Flynn (see sketch this issue). When Roosevelt holds his press conferences, "Charley sits off to one side, looking gloomy, dreamy and abstracted, but missing no phrase or intonation. One day when the reporters filed in the President said there was no news 'except that Charley Michelson needs a haircut.' Charley stirred from his abstraction. '*Somebody's* got to economize around here.'"

Charley Michelson was born in the little silver mining camp of Virginia City, Nevada in 1869, the son of Samuel and Rosalie

Michelson, who had migrated there a few months before he was born. His is a distinguished family. His sister Miriam was the author of *In the Bishop's Carriage*, a very popular novel of 35 years ago; his brother A. A. Michelson became a famous physicist, won the Nobel Prize and conducted experiments in the speed of light on which the Einstein theory was largely based.

But Charley had a prejudice against scholarship and because his family insisted on educating him, ran away from home at 13 and went to Arizona where he became a sheepherder, a miner and a driver of 40-ox teams. His brother-in-law, owner of the Virginia City *Chronicle*, liked the letters Charley wrote home and offered him a job as a reporter. He accepted, and when he got a chance at a $7 a week job with the San Francisco *Post* he knew he was going to be a journalist. He started as a reporter by chasing horse-drawn fire engines and Barbary Coast desperadoes.

He reached fame with the Hearst papers. The New York *Journal* sent him in 1896— the year he was married to Lillian Sterrett— to Cuba where the Spanish-American War was brewing. The Spaniards threw him into jail in Morro Castle for a while, but let him out in time to cover the War. After the War, Michelson stayed with Hearst as managing editor and editorial writer until 1913 when he began writing scenarios for Essanay. In 1917 he was put in charge of the Washington Bureau of the New York *World*. Here his "crackling reportorial style and ungloved handling of men and events put him in the forefront of the correspondents." There was one time when he approached Coolidge at a reception and said: "I don't think you know me, Mr. President. I'm Michelson of the *World*." "I know you," the President replied. "Wish you were a Republican."

In 1928 Charles Michelson was put in charge of publicity for the Democratic Party. John J. Raskob, manager and "angel" of the Democratic Party, was smarting from the 1928 defeat. "I have never been connected with an enterprise that was a failure," said he, "and I'm not going to this time." As a first step he hired Charley at the unheard of sum of $20,800 a year (since raised to $25,000) and gave him an entirely free hand. He hired him because he was a "crackerjack reporter, a shrewd and witty commentator and an old student of politics and politicians."

Michelson had hardly started when the stock market crash and the depression came along. "Charley joyfully proceeded to hang that depression right around President Hoover's neck." "Hundred-tongued Charley" put attacks into the mouths of Democratic bigwig Senators or Governors whose names would carry the headlines. Republicans became able to identify his speeches. If a Senator made a dull one, it was probably his own. If the Hoover Administration was "picking splinters out of its skin for a week afterwards, it was a Michelson speech." The Republicans cried out against his job as "one

CHARLES MICHELSON

of the most infamous incidents in American political history," but Charley's "Smear Hoover Campaign" went right ahead.

From the moment he was hired, ignoring the publicity man's usual system of "canned handouts" which reporters throw in wastebaskets, "his high powered press agentry laid the groundwork for the Democratic landslide which put Franklin D. Roosevelt in the White House." But after the 1932 elections Michelson insisted: "We performed no miracles. The table was spread and there was nothing to do but eat the meal."

This "gray haired, round-shouldered, pleasantly homely little man" whom everybody calls Charley found one of his main jobs in 1932 was to act as sharpshooter against Raskob, Al Smith and the others who had originally hired him when they became leaders of the anti-Roosevelt Liberty League. It wasn't long before the country had a picture of them as a lot of silk-hatted old plutocrats warring on the common people; it wasn't long before Charley had looked up all Al Smith's old speeches and found a good many contradictions and one amazing phrase—"put the Constitution on the shelf"; and it wasn't long before Michelson had succeeded in converting the enmity of the Liberty League into a Roosevelt asset.

As press agent for the Roosevelt Administration, Charley really shone. He delivered blows and he parried them. He expertly smothered bad publicity with good— for instance, right after it was announced that the air mail was going back to civilians, a defeat for Roosevelt, he told the country that Mellon and others were to be investigated on income tax charges. He was tremendously useful in advising the Administration on what to ignore, with prophetic

MICHELSON, CHARLES—*Continued*

powers to estimate the developments which look big and menacing today but are forgotten by next week if left alone.

In 1933 Michelson was sent into the Treasury Department. There he "insisted that the Treasury's intricately worded statements be reduced to language which he could understand; then he gave them to the press." From the Treasury he switched to the CCC which was just being organized, but within a short time was sent to another "hot spot in the New Deal's press relations" —the London Economic Conference. He had been credited "with getting the American delegation on through its severe ordeal with far less loss of prestige than might have been the case without his ministrations."

After the Economic Conference there was a little trouble with the NRA, so Michelson was appointed its Director of Public Relations. He was behind all its publicity and behind its eventual smooth running. "The wise Ulysses," wrote General Hugh Johnson (see sketch this issue) later, "who kept my erring feet on the path when he could reach me was Charley Michelson. As long as I was where Charley could edit my speeches or manage NRA publicity, I never made any very bad blunders."

By 1936 the Republicans began to regard the little man with gray hair, clothes and complexion with a "kind of superstitious dread." They had felt the burn and sting of his phrases. They saw him as a Machiavelli behind all the Democratic successes. "If *we* only had a Michelson," moaned the Republican leaders. They hired Franklyn Waltman to do for them what Charley had done for the Democrats. Charley greeted him nicely in his column. He pointed out that Waltman had once been a Democrat but said he was no doubt "true to the code of the honest soldier of fortune who fights his best under the flag of whatever cause engages him."

In 1937 Charley stirred up quite a rumpus in both his own party and in the Republican when he accepted a post as publicity director of the Crosley Radio Corporation along with his Democratic job. His own party thought it unwise because party strife was still echoing over the Supreme Court plan's defeat, and the New York *World-Telegram* solemnly warned: "The New Deal can't afford this. . . It is not illegal but it is certainly improper."

An insatiable worker, Charley paid no attention and kept right on writing speeches and press releases, conferring with Democratic leaders. To the casual eye, however, he always seems to work very little. "He seems to spend a large part of every day in the back room of the press club playing dominoes or chess with his old newspaper cronies." But some say he "can think out a whole speech while pondering over a chess move." And when he does write he turns out fast and polished copy.

Now over 70, Charley Michelson is "stooped and frail and looks as if the wind would blow him away." But he conceals an unexpected spryness and goes around the golf course in the 90's. He likes hunting and fishing, too, and once said, his "small countenance seamed, lined and puckered into an expression of boredom and gloom" with only the eyes showing the sharp wit beneath, that he would like to be appointed minister to some small state where there would be nothing to do but to go fishing.

References
> Am Mag 129:26-7+ Ap '40 por
> Lit Digest 117:28 My 26 '34 por
> New Outlook 164:26-7 Jl '34
> Newsweek 2:16-17 Ag 26 '33 por;
>   10:16-17 Ag 7 '37 por
> Sat Eve Post 208:5-7+ My 30 '36
> Time 29:14 My 24 '37 por; 30:14 Ag
>   9 '37 por
>
> Who's Who in America
> Who's Who in American Jewry
> Who's Who in the Nation's Capital

MILLAR, ALEXANDER COPELAND, REV. May 17, 1861—Nov 9, 1940 Editor of Arkansas *Methodist* for 26 years; former president of Hendrix College, Conway, Arkansas; ardent dry; became head of Arkansas Anti-Saloon League in 1923; leader in "good roads movement" of Arkansas; leader in opposition to modification of State divorce laws; active in other legislative matters

References
> Who's Who Among North American Authors
> Who's Who in America

Obituaries
> N Y Herald Tribune p46 N 10 '40 por
> N Y Times p57 N 10 '40

MILLER, MAX Feb 9, 1901- Author; journalist

Address: h. La Jolla, California

When Max Miller, in 1936, found himself "sitting in a Hollywood studio with five new pencils, three different colored stacks of paper and a well-oiled typewriter, wondering what to do about a girl and boy in the United States Coast Guard," he knew he had met the fate that comes to well-known authors whose auto needs a new top or whose roof needs creosoting. But his stay there, described wittily and bitterly in *For the Sake of Shadows* (1936), was short.

He had been many places before then and his 10 books tell a good deal about them. He was born in 1901 in Traverse City, Michigan, but, as he says, "this makes no difference, as the earliest place I can remember is Everett, Washington." In time his family moved to "Montana to take up a homestead 18 miles Northeast of Conrad," and his life there is described in his third book, *The Beginning of a Mortal* (1933).

Max Miller's first newspaper job was in Everett, Washington, where he worked on the old *Tribune* to get through grade and high school. He left because "the War seemed an easier career, so, though under-age and under-weight, the Navy let me in after I filled up on lemonade before standing on the examining scales." After the War he attended the University of Washington for the "customary four years" and from there went to Australia, the Solomon Islands and New Guinea, paying his way by doing newspaper copy.

I Cover the Waterfront (1932) was Max Miller's first book and, perhaps, his best known one. He says that it is "merely my own story of trying to reconcile myself to failure somehow, for every time I attempt to put my neck up my ears are slapped back," but the critics found these sketches of life along the San Diego waterfront "tragic, touching and strange," and the public read them widely.

The philosophical cast to *I Cover the Waterfront* is the mainstay of a good many of Max Miller's books. *He Went Away for a While* (1933), which contains the quiet thoughts of days by the sea, *The Second House From the Corner* (1934), which gives sketches of his own life and the life around him, and *The Man on the Barge* (1935) are all the results of his thoughtful consideration and thoughtful reporting of what he has seen, felt or known.

In *The Great Trek,* published in 1935, Max Miller first appears as a travel reporter. This account of the five-year drive of a reindeer herd through the icy wastes of Alaska to northern Canada and his later *Fog and Men on Bering Sea* (1936) have the sort of vivid realism that caused one critic to say of *Fog and Men*: "It makes one see and hear and smell the coast of Alaska and the Bering Sea." This book is Max Miller's account of his own adventures, of adventures past and present, true and legendary, along the northern coastline.

Mexico Around Me (1937), like *Fog and Men,* is no conventional guide to a country. It tells about the "Land of No Tourists" in the extreme southern part of Mexico and about Mexico City and without being a tourist's book, "sums up Mexico complete-ly." Even those who call it "self conscious" and "occasionally tedious" agree that it is one of the best travel books on Mexico.

In all these travel books is evident Max Miller's strong love for this continent. As he puts it, "I dislike every American who puts on an European swish to sniff: "Pffff! and *what* is a desert?""

MAX MILLER

A Stranger Came to Port, which appeared in 1938, was Max Miller's first novel, the story of a tired business man who suddenly disappears from his family and his business and lives for a year alone on a houseboat, his only friends fishermen and beachcomb-ers. This book is a mixture of story telling, reporting and moralizing, whose best parts, all agree, are the descriptions of tuna fishing. *Harbor of the Sun* published in October 1940 is a "rather easy-going his-tory of San Diego, oldest port on our West Coast."

Max Miller is now living in La Jolla, California. He has traveled widely; he has tried the Orient, the Arctic, Australia, Alaska and Mexico—and there has come to him finally the idea of staying home.

References

America's Young Men

Miller, M. The Beginning of a Mortal 1933

Miller, M. I Cover the Waterfront 1932

Who's Who in America

MILLER, WEBB Feb 10, 1892—May 7, 1940 Newspaper correspondent; general European manager of the United Press; covered Mexico, the First World War, Paris, Italy, India, the Near East, the Spanish Civil War and Munich; author of *I Found No Peace*

References

Newsweek 8:57-8 N 14 '36 por
Time 28:58-60 N 23 '36 por

Miller, W. I Found No Peace 1936

Acme

WEBB MILLER

Obituaries

N Y Times p9 My 9 '40 por
Newsweek 15:54 My 20 '40
Pub W 137:1916 My 18 '40
Time 35:61 My 20 '40 por

MILLER, WILLIAM LASH Sept 10,
1866—Sept 1, 1940 Outstanding Canadian
authority on chemical thermodynamics; head
of the University of Toronto chemistry department from 1921 to 1937; member of the
staff for 48 years until retirement; one of
seven leading physical chemists asked to
give lectures at the opening of the Sterling

WILLIAM LASH MILLER

Laboratory at Yale University; associate
editor of *The Journal of Physical Chemistry*
from 1910 to 1926

References

American Men of Science
Who's Who

Obituaries

N Y Times p15 S 2 '40

MILLES, CARL (mĭl'ĭs) June 23, 1875-
Sculptor
Address: Cranbrook Academy of Art, Bloom-
field Hills, Michigan

Carl Milles has been hailed as the greatest
fountain sculptor in the world. His latest
masterpiece, however, attracted public attention not only because of its beauty but
because it was the center of an art controversy in a city famous for its art squabbles.
The fountain in question was his *Wedding
of the Rivers,* erected on Aloe Plaza in St.
Louis as a memorial to Louis P. Aloe,
merchant and alderman. The 19 heroic
nudes which depict the meeting of the male
Mississippi with his coy bride Missouri, attended by a troup of playful naiads and
tritons, were viewed askance by the Board
of Aldermen, as a "convocation of Nordic
Monsters" and a "wedding in a nudist colony." The statues were duly unveiled,
however, and Milles in his dedication speech
archly urged "boys and girls in the pool" to
"behave well . . . enjoy life but remember
that at every sunrise you have to be here."

Carl Milles was born on June 23, 1875 at
Lagga, Sweden, the eldest son of Lieutenant Emil (or Mille) Anderson and his wife
Walborg (Tissel) Anderson. Carl's father
was a picturesque figure, a veteran of the
Franco-Prussian War, so well-known and
liked in the vicinity that his first name was
gradually adopted as a surname instead of
Anderson for his children, who were generally known as "Mille's children." Carl was
a delicate and rebellious child with a great
love for the countryside. He missed it
sorely when he was sent to the Jacob
School in Stockholm at the age of 10. He
developed a passionate love for ships and
wharves to compensate for his lost fields
and forests and when he was 14 unsuccessfully tried to run away to sea.

Since it was obvious by that time that
the boy hated going to school, his father
decided to apprentice him to a cabinetmaker
as a disciplinary measure and also because
he had shown unusual manual skill since
early years. Young Carl did not neglect his
wood carving. He attended evening classes
in the Technical School, won a scholarship
in the more advanced grade, where he received instruction in carving and orna-
mental modeling. At that time, too, he decided that he was going to be a sculptor like
the famous Johan Börjeson whose workshop was across the street and whom the
youngster worshiped. In 1897 he was
awarded the Swedish Arts and Crafts So-

ciety Pride of 200 *kroner*. With this modest prize he set off to Chile, where he hoped to make a living teaching Swedish gymnastics in a school run by a friend.

Milles never did get to Chile. He stopped off at Paris and was so enchanted with it that he decided to stay and follow his ambition to become a sculptor, whatever the cost. The next few years he led the traditional existence of a starving genius. He did a few odd jobs here and there: worked for a coffinmaker who allowed him to sleep in the shop in his own handiwork, was a waiter in restaurants and clubs, worked for a firm of Italian ornament makers. Yet he somehow found time to attend a few classes at the Academy Colarossi and to take a thorough course in life drawing and in anatomy. He also found time to visit the *Jardin des Plantes* to study plant forms and make sketches of animals. By 1900 he was beginning to be known: his marble *Hylas* got honorable mention at the *Salon des Artistes Français* and his study of an adolescent girl received a silver medal at the Paris World Exposition. That year, too, he first met the great sculptor Rodin, who conceived a great liking for the talented young Swede and for whom he worked for a while as an assistant in his studio at Meudon. His poverty was somewhat alleviated by orders of small bronzes by the firms of A. Collin and Blot.

Recognition came when he was awarded fourth place for the Sten Sture monument in Upsala. The award was later changed to first place on demand of the student body. Because of disagreements and lack of funds the completion of the monument was postponed until 1925, but young Milles' reputation in Sweden was made. During the next two years he made a series of notable animal groups and rounded off his stay in Paris with sculptural designs for the new Dramatic Theatre in Stockholm. Then, tiring of Paris with its exclusively impressionist preoccupations, he went to Munich in 1904, where he married Olga Granner, a young Austrian artist. Soon after his marriage, years of strain and overwork took their toll. Milles was ill for several years and it was only in 1908 that he was able to come back to his native land and settle down near Stockholm. He began at that time to build his famous villa near Lidingö, which was to house his rapidly accumulating works and to become known throughout Sweden for its exceptional charm as well as its embodiment of his art theories. In 1914 his achievements were recognized by a special exhibition of his works at Malmö.

In 1917 such a radical change had taken place in Milles' concepts that he actually felt it necessary to destroy the major part of his earlier work. He suddenly threw off the shackles of academism that had bound his earlier work to some extent, and his work of the period that followed is marked by individualism and unconventionality. His highest tribute to impressionism had been

his monument to Schéele, erected in the city of Köping. The following years brought works so different that many critics objected. The first was a gigantic figure of Gustavus Vasa, rich and solid, made of polychrome wood—a medium that Milles used again in his wood relief in the Time and Life Building, Radio City, New York.

During the next decade he began and completed eight monumental projects, in addition to many minor works. Among the former are his Halmstad *Europa,* a ruggedly rhythmic work, his marvelous *Rudbeckius* monument, a massive gothic figure with a chubby sprite perched humorously on its shoulder, the *Folkunga* fountain, with the sardonic figure of the legendary King, Folke Filbyter, on a horse. Perhaps the most remarkable thing about Milles' work aside from his versatility is his sense of site, of placing. This is particularly visible in his fountains, in which water becomes an essential part of the sculptural concept and lends a dynamic quality to the sculptured form. The works of his later period are remarkable, too, for their exuberance and rugged humor. Milles uses the Greek myth freely but imparts to it a vivid Gothic quality. Such is the sly, sharp face of the god Poseidon over his dripping classic body; a homely pungent quality is added to the whole fountain by the treatment of the eels he holds in his rugged hands. Or observe the original treatment of the young Diana, a sleek stripling who tiptoes through the forest teeming with lurking beasts.

In 1920 Milles became professor of modeling in the Royal Academy of Art in Stockholm—a position in which he found himself increasingly at odds with the academic world around him because of his new stylistic development. However, in spite of criticism of his later work, he was gaining an ever-increasing recognition in Sweden and abroad. In 1923 his new works were given a prominent place in the Tercentenary Exhibition at Gothenburg. In 1926 his works were exhibited at the Tate Gallery in London—a signal honor and his first showing outside of Sweden.

In 1929 came his first visit to the United States in order to design a fountain on the same theme as his *Diana* fountain in the court of the Swedish Match Company Building in Stockholm. Thereafter he agreed to spend at least a part of every year teaching in the Cranbrook Academy of Art and in 1931 he left his lovely villa at Lidingö and took up permanent residence at Cranbrook, where he now teaches and which is the source of all of his latest designs. His first years in the United States were occupied with the completion of his fine *Orpheus* fountain (1936), commission for which was given to him in 1926 and which was set up in Stockholm. Other works were the whimsical *Jonah* fountain and the *Peace Monument* in St. Paul, Minnesota, a great opalescent monument in white onyx, on the Indian theme of the Great

MILLES, CARL—*Continued*

Spirit. In 1939 Milles was given a prize at the Golden Gate Exposition. Two of his statues, the monumental and savage *Astronomer* and the highly stylized *Pony Express,* were shown at the New York World's Fair. Among other recent works wrought at his Cranbrook studio are his *Monument to Genius,* a tragic and powerful winged figure reminiscent of his demonic *Orpheus,* plucking at a vast harp, and his *Nature and Man,* wood reliefs for the Time and Life Building.

Carl Milles is a handsome man, of typically Swedish appearance, blond, apple-cheeked and stocky, with a wide, smiling face and a soft voice. He has a tremendous capacity for work, as the long roster of his sculptured figures indicates, and is content to live up to the motto on the gates of his Lidingö home: "Let me work while the sun endures." He likes gardening, is fond of flowers and animals, and has made many interesting and vital studies of animal life, replete with exuberance. His views on art can be summed up in his own words: "Nothing," he said once, "is ugly save stupidity." And on another occasion: "Art is not decorating nor is it literature. It is the ultimate desire of the eye."

References

Apollo 20:31-4 Jl '40 il
Artwork winter '40
Life 8:110-12 Je 10 '40 il por
Mag Art 31:422-4 Jl '38 il; 31:599 O '38
Newsweek 15:31-2 My 6 '40
Parnassus 6:7-9 Ja '34 il
Studio 90:3-9 Jl '25
Time 31:31 Je 6 '38 il

Baeckström, A. F. E. Carl Milles, the Swedish Sculptor 1935
Casson, S. Carl Milles *In* Twentieth Century Sculptors p25-40 1930
International Who's Who
Rogers, M. R. Carl Milles: An Interpretation of his Work 1940
Verneuil, M. P. Carl Milles 1929
Who's Who
Who's Who in American Art

MILLIKAN, ROBERT ANDREWS (mĭl'ĭ-kàn) Mar 22, 1868- Scientist

Address: b. California Institute of Technology, Pasadena, California

Chance made a physicist of Dr. Robert A. Millikan. One of the world's greatest scientists might have been a teacher of Greek or mathematics if a vacancy had not occurred in the science department of Oberlin College during his junior year. Young Millikan was working his way through college, and was majoring in Greek and mathematics when he was asked to teach a class in elementary physics.

He knew little about physics, but he boned up on it, and managed to keep one jump ahead of his class. He made such a good record as president of his class, member of Phi Beta Kappa and teacher that when he was graduated from Oberlin College he was given a job as instructor of physics at $600 a year.

Thus started his interest in science. With characteristic thoroughness and industry, Millikan set about making himself proficient in the profession into which chance had thrust him. He continued his studies at Oberlin College and two years later was awarded a fellowship at Columbia University for graduate work. Here he came under the influence of Michael Pupin, eminent scientist, who encouraged him to go on with his studies.

After taking his Ph. D. in 1895 at Columbia University, Dr. Millikan studied in Berlin and Göttingen. Soon after his return to America he took a teaching position at the University of Chicago, where he became assistant to Dr. A. A. Michelson, the world-renowned scientist who perfected an instrument for astronomical measurements. Dr. Millikan remained at the University of Chicago for 25 years, doing the research which led to the measurement of the electron there. He left in 1921 to become director of the Norman Bridge Laboratories at the California Institute of Technology and chairman of the executive council of the Institute, positions he still holds.

For almost 20 years Dr. Millikan has worked on the mysteries of the cosmic rays. He has carted balloons through the Andes and the Rockies, has had airplanes take electroscopes up at various heights to learn something of those mysterious cosmic rays which seem to be constantly bombarding the earth. Dr. Millikan was the first to name them "cosmic" rays.

Even now, in his 70's, he still is on the field for every detail of his research on cosmic rays, besides carrying out his strenuous duties as head of the California Institute of Technology, writing and teaching. In the summer of 1939 when he might have been taking a long vacation he and two young assistants went to Tasmania to send up balloons carrying electroscopes which would measure minute amounts of electricity emanating from cosmic rays. In June, 1940 he has disclosed in his annual report "a promising" new attack by science upon cancer.

In the field of practical science, Millikan was one of the group which developed the three-electrode telephone relay and speech amplifier which now underlies much of the science of communications as well as of talking pictures. He worked for six exhausting and patient years on the experiment of measuring the electron, one of the fundamental physical and chemical constants.

His capacity for work is amazing. An interviewer wrote of him: "Apart from his inherent ability, Millikan's greatest strength, it seems to me, lies in his habits of work, apparently so easy and effortless, yet withal so steady, devouring and persistent." During one of the stages of his cosmic rays experiments, when army planes were carrying electroscopes to various heights in a 72-hour continuous test, Millikan and his assistant would check the electroscopes every hour, day and night. Between times, Dr. Millikan would lie down on a cot and take a nap. At the end, when the other workers were near the breaking point, he seemed as fresh as when the ordeal started. He will get up several times in the middle of the night to check experiments and then quickly go back to sleep. After dinner or an evening out, he goes back to the laboratory for several hours' work. "This tireless quality is due partly to his powers of relaxation."

Dr. Millikan learned habits of industry and thoroughness at an early age. The son of a Congregational minister, the Reverend Silas Franklin and Mary Jane (Andrews) Millikan, he was born in Morrison, Illinois in 1868, and when he was seven years old moved with his family to Maquoketa, Iowa. The Rev. Millikan believed in hard work and education. Young Millikan and his brothers raised chickens, tended cows, mowed lawns. It may be partly because of his early training and the years in which Millikan supported himself through school that he is now probably one of the best salesmen among scientists. He has been to sell the value of scientific research in universities to millionaires and to raise the budget for the California Institute of Technology.

Dr. Millikan's early religious background, too, colored his life. He has maintained that there is no real conflict between religion and science. "New discoveries in science are to him but further indications of the wonders of God's creation." But his religion has nothing in common with the Fundamentalists, the dogmatists of religion. His is a broad and liberal faith based upon the Golden Rule and the Sermon on the Mount.

The mature thinker, he believes, finds that science does not disturb the inner spirit of a man's religious faith. He quotes Einstein's statement: "It is enough for me to contemplate the mystery of conscious life perpetuating itself through all eternity, to reflect upon the marvelous structure of the universe, which we dimly perceive, and to try humbly to comprehend even an infinitesimal part of the intelligence manifested in nature." "I myself," Millikan says, "need no better definition of God than that."

Dr. Millikan is a small, sturdy man with white hair, blue eyes and a sunburned complexion. He looks younger than his years and more like a business man than a scientist. Despite all his work, he has time for a devoted and comfortable family life. He tries to get in golf once a week, and he and Mrs. Millikan lead a fairly busy social life. They also take an active interest in church work. They have three sons.

ROBERT ANDREWS MILLIKAN

For his scientific work, 22 colleges and universities have given Dr. Millikan honorary degrees. Various societies and organizations have given him prizes and gold medals. He holds 15 medals, including the 1923 Nobel Prize in physics. He has written more than a dozen books on scientific subjects, among them *Elements of Physics* (1917); *Science and Life* (1923); *Evolution of Science and Religion* (1927); *Science and the New Civilization* (1930); *Cosmic Rays* (1939), and numerous papers and lectures in scientific periodicals, all in a field which he entered by chance.

He explains it thus: "If chance thrusts you into work apart from your inclination or training, you need not necessarily be a misfit. It really doesn't matter a whole lot what line of work you happen to fall into so long as you follow through to the limit, with the individual abilities God gave you."

References

Am Mag 120:34-5+ D '35 por
Cur Hist 34:702-3 Ag '31
New Repub 80:311-12 O 24 '34
Newsweek 4:42 O 13 '34; 14:36 D 25 '39 por
Time 34:60 Ag 28 '39
American Men of Science
Hylander, C. J. Robert A. Millikan *In* American Scientists p139-45 1935
Jaffe, B. Matter *In* Outposts of Science p317-68 1935
Jaffe, B. Radiation *In* Outposts of Science p369-416 1935
Lotz, P. H. ed. Vocations and Professions 1940
Wallace, A. Religious Faith of Great Scientists *In* Religious Faith of Great Men p139-73 1934
Who's Who in America

MILLIS, HARRY ALVIN May 14, 1873-
Chairman of National Labor Relations Board
Address: b. National Labor Relations Board,
Washington, D. C.; h. 5729 Kenwood Ave,
Chicago, Illinois

It seems that in Chicago whenever A F of
L or CIO members or their employers had
a dispute that needs settling the man they
were most likely to pick out to settle it was
"tall, burly, square-jawed, deaconesque"
Harry Alvin Millis, who, since 1916, had
been professor of economics at the University of Chicago. In October 1940 he
took a position as permanent referee between the General Motors management and
the CIO's United Automobile Workers, but
had been General Motors' man for only
six weeks beore he was called to head the
National Labor Relations Board, succeeding
J. Warren Madden. He will serve for a
five-year term ending August 27, 1945.

Little criticism of Dr. Millis' appointment
was heard even from the most conservative
employers. He is known as a "confirmed,
but minimum" liberal—neither pro-labor
nor pro-employer—and as a friend of William M. Leiserson, leading Right-wing member
of the National Labor Relations Board,
though himself a member of no faction. Primarily an arbitrator, Dr. Millis belongs to
the school of thought which believes there
are few labor problems which cannot be
solved if employer and employee can be
brought together. And "racketeering by
union leaders usually appears in conjunction
with racketeering by employers," he says.
One of his first pronouncements after his
appointment was that although he believed
in the 40-hour work week, it would be
lengthened if necessary in the interests of
national defense. He did not see any such
necessity in the near future, however, while
there are still millions unemployed.

Millis was born in Paoli, Indiana on May
14, 1873, the son of John and Maria
(Bruner) Millis. He took his B. A. at
Indiana University in 1895, dividing his time
between baseball and more serious matters,
took his M. A. a year later, and by 1899 had
his Ph. D. from the University of Chicago.
His first teaching job was at the University
of Arkansas in 1902, where he was professor
of economics and sociology. The year before he had married Alice M. Schoff of Cincinnati, Ohio. (There are now three children:
Savilla, John S. and Charlotte Melissa.)

The young couple next made their home
in California, for in 1903 Millis was offered
a position as assistant professor of economics at Stanford University. He was an
associate professor before he left in 1912
to become professor and head of the department of economics at the University of
Kansas, and when in 1916 he joined the staff
of the University of Chicago as professor
of economics he apparently decided to
settle down. He remained at Chicago until
1940, and in 1928 was made chairman of his
department.

While in California Dr. Millis had worked
as director of investigations in the Rocky
Mountain and Pacific states for the United
States Immigration Commission for two
years (1908-1910), and after coming to
Chicago served as director of investigations
for the Illinois State Health Insurance Commission from 1918 to 1919. Material for
The Japanese Problem in the United States
(1915) and *Sickness and Insurance* (1926)
was doubtlessly collected during these
periods. Then from 1919 to 1923 he served
as chairman of the trade board and later
chairman of the board of arbitration for
the men's clothing industry, bodies which
keep the peace between Chicago clothing
manufacturers and the Amalgamated Clothing
Workers of America; at that time he formed
a friendship with Sidney Hillman (see sketch
this issue). Since 1923 he has been a member of the arbitration panel maintained by
the American Newspaper Publishers' Association and the International Printing
Pressmen's Union; he settled a great many
railroad labor disputes; and from 1934 to
1935 he was a member of the old NRA National Labor Relations Board. He is also
an active member of the American Economics
Association, of which he was president in 1934,
of the American Association for Agricultural
Legislation and of the National Tax Association; and in 1938 he was on a three-man Emergency Board which presented a report to President Roosevelt against a cut in rail wages.
His study, *Labor Economics,* written with R.
E. Montgomery, two volumes of which
were published in 1938, speaks with considerably more than academic experience.

Though he likes golf, Dr. Millis seldom
gets time to play it; and though he has been
planning a vacation with his wife for some
time, that probably won't materialize either.
But Dr. Millis is in the habit of working a
seven-day, 84-hour week (most of the time
with his pipe in his mouth), and is no doubt
resigned to no play. He looks on the
NLRB appointment as in the nature of a
"draft."

Dr. Millis' popularity as a labor arbitrator
was probably a little disconcerting at times.
He couldn't ever be sure exactly what all
his obligations were. It wasn't until June 1940
that he learned that he had been appointed
in May to arbitrate charges arising from
the settlement at Chicago between the
Hearst papers and the Newspaper Guild,
and would automatically be called upon
to settle an argument if either the A F of L
or the CIO thought it was being discriminated
against. He was usually good-natured about
things, though. There is a story that he
got a call one day from a total stranger.
"Come on down and arbitrate," said the
voice. "We're in a deadlock with our
employer, and so it's up to you."

"What have I to do with it?"
"You're our arbitrator."
"Who says I am?"

HARRY ALVIN MILLIS

"Why, it says so right in the agreement that was signed 10 years ago and renewed every year since then. It's printed right here in the book, Rule No. 6. How soon can you get here?"

"Oh, hell," Millis grumbled. "If it's printed in Rule No. 6, I guess it's up to me. The arbitration hearings will open next Tuesday at 10 a. m."

It is reported that Dr. Millis is the man who was offered the vacancy on the National Labor Relations Board which has existed ever since Chairman Madden's term expired.

References

Business Week p36-8 S 28 '40 por; p42 O 19 '40; p32-3 N 29 '40 il
N Y Times VII p12+ N 24 '40 il por
Newsweek 16:39-40 N 25 '40 por
PM p19 N 10 '40 por
Leaders in Education 1932
Who's Who in America

MINARD, GEORGE CANN Aug 28, 1879 —July 3, 1940 Professor in the New York University School of Education since 1925; authority on delinquent children; educational adviser of the Children's Village at Dobbs Ferry, New York; head of a survey on the care of delinquent children in the Southern States; president of the National Conference of Juvenile Agencies in 1939

Obituaries

N Y Herald Tribune p8 Jl 4 '40
N Y Times p15 Jl 4 '40

MIRO, JOAN (mĭ-rŏ′ jhō-än′) Apr 20, 1893- Spanish artist
Address: c/o Valentine Gallery of Modern Art, Inc, 16 E 57th St, New York City

It is difficult to believe that there is no way of deciding when a painter is a surrealist painter and when he is not. Some of the critics, including those who viewed his five paintings in the Spanish show at the Valentine Galleries in New York City April 1 to 27, 1940, say Joán Miró used to be a surrealist but can no longer be given that name; some call him a "nonconforming surrealist," a neo-surrealist, or make up an interesting new ism for him; such as "plastic lyricism." Some years ago Miró informed his public: "It is very difficult for me to talk about my own painting, because it is always conceived in a state of hallucination created by a shock either objective or subjective, for which I am utterly irresponsible." This certainly didn't help the controversy very much.

Probably less well-known to the general public in this country than Salvador Dali (see sketch this issue), their names are often linked together—not so much because of their similarity as because of their different approaches to what is generally agreed to be the same problem: the expression of the subconscious on canvas. Dali's dream-language contains objects that are familiar enough, only his grammar is startling. In contrast, Miró's is a "pictographic language of the subconscious," a kind of shorthand in which objects in the familiar world are seldom referred to at all except by subtle suggestion. In any comparison Dali usually comes out a bit battered by the critics, one of whom called him "a sort of ten-cent store version of Miró." Another said: "If Dali is the Courbet of the dream-world, then Miró is its El Greco, or better its Picasso." Miró himself thinks Dali's work over-representational, literary, while Dali calls Miró, simply, "a failure."

Whether it is necessary to define Miró's work in order to enjoy it seems doubtful. Even in his most abstract fantasies audiences seldom fail to appreciate Miró's gaiety of patterning, his imaginative use of color, his unfailing sense of design—above all, the indescribably witty something that is conveyed by his assemblages of little forms resembling nothing exactly and to the obvious-minded suggesting nothing so much as sunbursts, stars, fish, insects, microbes. Critics, of course, find deep significance in these same symbols. One French critic says, pictorially: "Here is where the comma falls in love with the period " A Freudian states that Miró's "expression of the subconscious in symbolical terms" is closely related to prehistoric rock drawings, and shows a flight to the caveman, pure and simple. Another more poetic critic speaks of his "romantic, poetic disposition which probes the apparent, the 'real' for the 'unreal,' the infinite mysteries which lie hauntingly beneath the seen, as beneath the ocean or the canopy of the sky." Still another critic sums up his artistic credo in a sentence: "All painting to Miró is lines, **areas, and interceptions."** Henry McBride

Balthus

JOAN MIRO AND DAUGHTER
DOLORES

of the New York *Sun* was particularly impressed with his sincerity and assured his readers that Miró was "as honest as death."

Although he is now in middle-age (he was born in Barcelona, Spain, on April 20, 1893), Joán Miró achieved recognition when much younger. At 14 he was attending art school in Barcelona. He was temporarily forced to leave school and take a job as clerk in a store, but by the time he was 18 he was again studying art—this time under Gali, who taught a sense of form by having his pupils draw objects which they knew only by touch, and model in clay. By 1918 Miró was ready to exhibit in Barcelona, and when his first show was successful he began looking for a wider horizon. For the young artist there was only one—Paris. The next year he found himself in Montparnasse, not much more financially secure than any of its struggling geniuses, but distinguishing himself from the rank and file by "his tidy, carefully brushed clothes and well-groomed hair and nails"—and by a talent which was easily recognized.

Miró's painting was at this time more or less naturalistic, even imitative. The influence of the academics was strong as well as the later influences of Van Gogh, Matisse, Picasso. But when he exhibited for the first time in Paris in 1921 he found other artists already willing to acknowledge him as a genius. Picasso bought a self-portrait. Picabia, Léger, Matisse and Braque were kind to him. And not least important among others who helped him was André Breton, the poet, editor of *La Révolution Surréaliste*, the literary organ of the surrealist movement.

As Breton says, this was a time when "painting was forced to beat a retreat and to retrench itself behind the necessity of expressing internal perception visually." The surrealist movement courted such painters as Picabia, Picasso, Chirico, Max Ernst and Paul Klee, and many artists whose work was afterward to develop along more independent lines were at this time flirting with automatic painting, the exploration of the subconscious and of the night world of dreams and insanity.

In 1922 Miró painted what some critics still regard as his masterpiece, *The Farm*. A daydream of his ancestral farm in Tarragona, it had taken him nine months to paint, and was an odd mixture of the old and the new—for details were realistic, the pattern of the whole was at least partially cubistic, and yet the barns of the picture were laid open as if X-rayed. It was acclaimed as a surrealist *chef d'oeuvre*, and when in 1924 the surrealist school felt itself well-enough organized and defined to publish its manifesto, Miró was hailed as the painter who best conformed to its specifications, with Max Ernst, possessor of "the most magnificently haunted brain of them all," as his chief rival.

But any painter of integrity has a horror of repetition. One critic has said that "the painting of Joán Miró manifests a progression, or series of progressions, from that of the poet-painter to that of the painter-poet."

Thus, although Miró's earliest work was largely "literary," a matter of images described in paint, imitative of actual objects, his canvases gradually became less and less crowded, more simplified, his color and color contrasts increasingly intensified, until by 1927 he was painting almost complete abstractions. In 1926 came *Dog Barking at the Moon,* which is much more representational than many of his works of the same period (its fantastic forms are easily identified as dog, moon, ladder, though as simplified as a nursery rhyme), but which nevertheless illustrates the trend of his development. Herbert Read has described his more typical work of the period as "a single sensitive line exploring a field of pure color."

By 1928 Miró had gone so far in this one direction—he was beginning to be accused of sterility, of painting by formula—that some revitalizing influence was required. He found it in a temporary return to observation—not observation for the sake of photography, but for the suggestions implicit in the forms of natural objects. A visit to Holland in 1928 and the influence of Vermeer were the sources of *The Potato,* a painting which reveals Miró's "subconscious reactions to the suggestions which spring from the vegetative outgrowths of the potato." At about the same time Miró began to re-experiment with color. He had been known for his fresh, clear colors, sparingly used—pastel combinations, primary colors, large divisions of blacks and whites and earth tones; his colors were often more angry, more violent now. His objects became generally larger, more recognizable, though never really representational.

His was a "spiral" development rather than a reversal, however, for this second phase of observation also reached a more abstract conclusion, and again Miró began to simplify, to search for a shorthand which could express symbolically what he had to say without becoming a "mere calligraphic scribble."

Still best-known, perhaps, for the whimsically mystic mood of such pieces as *Dog Barking at the Moon* and *Mrs. Mills in 1740 Costume* (the latter shown in the recent New York show), Joán Miró is able, "by adroit turns of composition and tone, to conjure up an emotional sequence ranging from laughter to horror." In 1937 one critic commented on his *Still-life with an Old Shoe*: "For morbid, gangrenous coloring and generally stomach-turning qualities in purely abstract form . . . (this picture) takes all prizes for the (1937-38) season." Perhaps it is not unreasonable to suppose that events in Spain made Miró unwilling or unable to express anything less "morbid" and "gangrenous"; if so, his ability to produce such revulsion in the spectator by purely abstract form seems as much a proof of the communicativeness of his symbols as his ability to amuse.

Like his countrymen, Pablo Picasso and Juan Gris, whose canvases appeared in the Spanish show along with his, Joán Miró has lived the larger part of his artistic life in Paris, with frequent visits to his farm in Spain. In his cramped studio in Paris it is probable that he continues to paint, concerned with more important issues than varied reports as to exactly what he is painting. In the early '20s he married a native of Mallorca and is the father of a daughter, Dolores.

References

Art Digest 8:13 Ja 15 '34; 12:21 My 1 '38 il; 13:18-19 Ap 15 '39 il
Art N 35:11+ D 5 '36 il; 36:13 Ap 30 '38; 37:14 Ap 15 '39 il; 38:10 N 4 '39; 38:27+ Ap 6 '40
Beaux Arts p4 Je 23 '39; p7 Je 4 '37 il; p4 Ja 7 '38
Cahiers Art 10 no5-6:115-16 '35 il; 14 no 1-4:73 '39; 15 no3-4:37-47 '40 il
Mag Art 32:315 My '39
New Repub 81:360 F 6 '35
Parnassus 8:13-15 O '36 il
Bulliet, C. J. Joán Miró *In* Significant Moderns and Their Pictures p107-10 1936
New Standard Encyclopedia of Art 1939

MIX, TOM Jan 6, 1880—Oct 12, 1940 Cowboy and hero of Western film thrillers killed in auto accident in Arizona; fought in Spanish-American War and Boxer Re-

TOM MIX AND DAUGHTER
THOMASINA

bellion; served as sheriff in Kansas and Oklahoma and then as Texas Ranger; in 1906 joined Miller Brothers' "101" Ranch, a Wild West show, and three years later the Sells-Floto Circus; identified with motion pictures since 1910 and millions of fans idolized him and his horse "Tony"; dropped out for a while when "talkies" came in but returned to screen in *Destry Rides Again*, *My Pal*, *The King* and other movies; since 1933 with Tom Mix's Circus and Wild West Show

References

Ladies' H J 44:14-15, 234-5 Mr '27 il pors
Motion Pict 43:48-9, 90, 98 Mr '32 il pors
Motion Pict Classic 9:56-7, 86 O '19 pors; 28:55, 86 F '29 il pors
Motion Pict Mag 17:66-7, 110 F '19 pors; 22:57, 112 O '21 il pors; 32:21, 101 N '26 por
Movie Classic 3:24-5, 78 S '32 il pors
Photoplay 27:46-8, 114 F '25 pors; 30:34-5, 135 S '26 pors; 31:42-3, 114 Ja '27 pors; 33:38-9, 110 Ja '28 il por
Christeson, H. M. and Christeson, F. M. Tony and His Pals 1934
Who's Who in America

Obituaries

N Y Herald Tribune p1, 25 O 13 '40 por
N Y Times p1, 48 O 13 '40 por
Newsweek 16:6 O 21 '40 por
Time 36:63 O 21 '40
Variety 140:4+ O 16 '40

MODJESKI, RALPH (mŏ-jes'kē) Jan 27, 1861—June 26, 1940 Engineer; son of the late Helena Modjeska, famous tragedienne;

MODJESKI, RALPH—*Continued*
chief engineer of the Thebes Bridge at Thebes, Illinois, the McKinley Bridge at St. Louis, Missouri, the Quebec Bridge over the St. Lawrence River, the Manhattan Bridge over the East River in New York, the Mid-Hudson Bridge at Poughkeepsie, New York and many others; recipient of many honors for engineering

References

> W Soc E J 36:69-79 Ap '31 il por
> American Men of Science
> Who's Who in America

Obituaries

> N Y Herald Tribune p18 Je 28 '40 por
> N Y Times p19 Je 28 '40 por
> Variety 139:46 Jl 3 '40

MOLOTOV, VIACHESLAV MIKHAILOVICH (mŏl′o-tŏf ·vyä-che-slav′ me-khī′lo-vich) 1890- Russian Premier; Foreign Commissar

Address: The Kremlin, Moscow, U. S. S. R.

Viacheslav Molotov, Russia's Premier and Foreign Commissar, has played an important part in Europe's intrigues during 1940. It was he who in the first months of the year was his country's spokesman for the Finland-Soviet warfare and he who, in November, created world-wide speculation by his visit to Berlin.

Officially the conferences which took place were described as aimed at developing a long-range program of Soviet-Nazi co-operation. What actually transpired is, in December 1940, still a mystery. Probably Turkey, the chief obstacle to a Nazi *Drang nach Osten,* was a main topic; the Balkan states were at least talked over; the Sino-

VIACHESLAV MOLOTOV

Japanese situation may have been considered. In any case, Britain took a gloomy view of the meetings. "The fact that the visit comes so soon after the American elections is not encouraging," said the London *Daily Mail* which also pointed out that a new phase of the War seemed to be starting.

The trip to Berlin was the first journey outside of Russia of Russia's Foreign Minister and Premier who was born Viacheslav Mikhailovich Skriabin, the son of a low salaried clerk. He was educated at the St. Petersburg Polytechnic School and was an early worker for Communism. He took the name of Molotov when he took the oath of loyalty in 1906.

For the past 19 years he has been Premier of Russia. In May 1930 Foreign Commissar Maxim Litvinov, suddenly pleading ill-health, resigned, and since then Molotov has filled the position of Foreign Commissar in addition to his duties as Premier. Some European circles profess to believe that Litvinov's resignation was not because of ill-health but because Stalin did not agree with Litvinov, an "experienced diplomat who did his own thinking." These critics maintain that Stalin wanted a "yes man" and chose Molotov, his immediate assistant, and "one of his most trusted aides."

Since the Russian Revolution a number of prominent Soviet men have disappeared, been executed or exiled. Molotov has been one of the few who remained in a trusted position. Lenin called him the "best filing clerk in the Soviet Union."

Molotov has held a number of government posts, among them President of the Council, Secretary of the Communist Party of the Ukraine and since 1921 Secretary for the whole U. S. S. R.

In 1935 he aided in drafting reforms in the Constitution. Although he has not had the foreign experience of his predecessor, he has for many years helped in establishing the foreign policy of the Soviet, and as President of the Council he was for a time Litvinov's superior.

Now middle-aged, there is a strong supposition in Europe that some day he might succeed Stalin. A writer describes him as "broad-shouldered, bushy-mustached, pince-nezed" . . . resembling "the late Theodore Roosevelt." The pince-nez, his clothes and manner give him a certain elegance, rather English, which distinguishes him from his colleagues. In 1936 his wife visited the United States. Favorably impressed, she influenced him in our favor although since then he has not tried to maintain the best relations between this country and his. In August 1940 he said to the Russian Parliament: "I will not dwell on our relations with the United States ,of America if only for the reason that there is nothing good that can be said about them." Most of the statements on the United States and foreign affairs in general have been made by Molotov.

Molotov stutters badly. It is said that in 1937 when he addressed the highest legislative body in Russia, the Soviet Congress, he "made three great efforts before his speech impediment would permit him to utter the most important cry in Russia: 'Long Live Comrade Ssss. . . Long Live Comrade Sttt. . . Long Live Comrade Stalin !' "

During his busy days he has found time to write a number of books in Russian including *The Party's Policy in the Villages; Elections to the Soviets* and *On the Lessons of Trotskyism.* Translations in English have been made of *Second Five-Year Plan* (1936) ; *Soviet Prosperity* (1935) and *Tasks of the Second Five-Year Plan* (1934).

References

Christian Sci Mon p5 Mr 30 '40
Liv Age 356:449-51 Jl '39 (Same cond. Cur Hist 50:39 Jl '39 por)
N Y Sun p1 Mr 23 '40; p1 Mr 29 '40
N Y Times p8 N 1 '39 por; VII pl N 26 '39 pors; p29 D 7 '39; IV p4 D 31 '39
Scholastic 34:18S My 20 '39 por
Time 34:23 N 13 '39 por; 36:19-20+ Jl 15 '40 por (cover); 36:30-2 N 18 '40
Gay, G. Molotov, Author of the Soviet-Nazi Pact   pam 1940
International Who's Who

MONTESSORI, MARIA (môn'těs-sō-rě) Aug 31, 1870-   Educator

On August 31, 1940 Dr. Maria Montessori, the great Italian educator now interned in India as an enemy alien, celebrated her seventieth birthday. Since 1909 Dr. Montessori's name has been a household word and though the effectiveness of her educational method has occasionally been challenged, no history of modern education would be complete without some account of it.

The central ideas of the Montessori method are that children are best educated by allowing them to find things out for themselves; that training of the sensory faculties by handwork is of prime importance; that the teacher or parent should not impose his own personality on the child; that rewards, marks and punishments should be abolished; and that discipline should be entirely free and self-imposed. This tripartite method (The Doctrines of Freedom, Auto-Education, Sense Training) has been used all over the world—in America Douglas Fairbanks Jr., and the grandchildren of Alexander Graham Bell are products of it.

Maria Montessori, the first Italian woman to be awarded the degree of Doctor of Medicine, was born at Chiaravalle, Ancona, Italy, the only daughter of Chevalier Alessandro Montessori and Renilde Stoppani. She attended the University of Rome, where she studied both medicine and literature.

MARIA MONTESSORI

After taking her M. D. degree she became an instructor in the psychiatric clinic of the University, her main field the training of mentally defective children. From the cretins and morons in the clinic she learned that if a child has something to touch or twist with his hands, his brain will function responsively. In 1898 she gave a lecture on the sensory training of defectives at the Turin Educational Congress. This was heard by the Minister of Education, who was so impressed by her arguments that he appointed her in that same year directress of the Scuola Ortofrenica, an institution devoted to the care and education of retarded children.

Dr. Montessori might have had a much easier life as a university instructor, but this appointment was a chance to try out those theories in which she firmly believed. She proceeded to enter several eight-year-old defectives for the State examinations in reading and writing and achieved what has been called "the first Montessori miracle." The defectives not only passed, but passed higher than the "normal" children.

In 1900 Dr. Montessori left the Scuola Ortofrenica and went back to the University of Rome to take courses in philosophy and experimental psychology. She also spent much time visiting the principal European schools, making extensive notes on how (in her opinion) they were failing to secure the best educational results. Her idea was that complete equipment in medicine, psychiatry, psychology and practical pedagogy was necessary for a new educational method.

Early in 1907 Maria Montessori got her big chance. The filthy and overcrowded Roman slum region of San Lorenzo was taken over by the Instituto di Beni Stabili. The entire population was rehoused and to

MONTESSORI, MARIA—*Continued*
each block of houses was added a *Casa dei Bambini,* or children's house, which took in all children between three and seven while their parents were out at work. Dr. Montessóri was put in charge of one of these houses and proceeded to apply to these poor but normal children the methods she had successfully used with defectives. She gave these children objects to handle, encouraged them to express themselves, never hurried them or punished or rewarded them. The results were excellent.

Dr. Montessori's experiments aroused interest and comment and in 1908 the Humanitarian Society of Milan decided to follow her method. In 1909 Dr. Montessori published her *Metodo della Pedagogia Scientifica,* which was hailed by educators as a highly important document and which, with many of her later works, was ultimately translated into most of the principal languages of the world.

For two years more Dr. Montessori headed her *Casa dei Bambini* and then spent her time mainly in writing and in wide organizing activities connected with the spreading of her principles all over the world. In 1911 many of the Swiss state schools for infants introduced her method and in 1913 she gave a theoretical and practical course in Rome, which brought together students of 17 different nationalities. The serious press of France, Great Britain and the United States hotly canvassed the merits and demerits of the Method—it was and is a highly controversial subject—and books on it began to appear, the first important one *From Locke to Montessori,* published in 1914 by Dr. William Boyd.

With the First European War Dr. Montessori's propaganda and experimentation were slowed down, but even in that troubled period neutral Spain established a research institute in Barcelona in 1917. After the War, in 1919, Dr. Montessori gave the first of many training courses in London and a British Montessori Society was founded; a few years later schools for teachers were established in Rome and in London. In 1922 Dr. Montessori was made a Government Inspector of Schools in Italy, but after the Mussolini régime was established she became "so impatient with government indoctrination" that she soon left for anarchist Catalonia with her adopted son Mario (the Dottoressa is unmarried), for she had heard there was no government there at all.

Since 1931 annual congresses have been held and Dr. Montessori, now "a dumpy old lady," has continued to travel pretty well all over the civilized world, lecturing on her method and organizing new centers. She has continued to write—*The Secret of Childhood* (1939) is her latest book—and has continued to receive honorary degrees and membership in scientific academies in many countries.

There are some educators who feel that the Montessori Method has passed its heyday and is now overshadowed by the system of Froebel and the Dalton plan. There are educators, too, who feel that it lays too much stress on manual training, to the neglect of the intellect and imagination. But it was and is an experiment of great importance which, directly or indirectly, has had a vital and salutary effect on educational practice all over the world, even in quarters where the teaching profession has by no means been prepared to swallow it whole.

References
> Time 30:41 Ag 16 '37 por; 34:30 Jl 31 '39 por
>
> Chi è?
>
> Fisher, D. C. Montessori Mother 1912
>
> Fynne, R. J. Montessori and Her Inspirers 1924
>
> Who's Who

MOORE, RAYMOND 1897—Mar 8, 1940 Pioneer in the summer theatre field; founder of the Cape Playhouse and Cinema at Dennis, Massachusetts

Obituaries
> Boston Transcript II p1 Mr 9 '40
> N Y Herald Tribune p40 Mr 10 '40
> N Y Sun p13 Mr 9 '40
> N Y World-Telegram p1 Mr 9 '40

MOORE, T. ALBERT, REV. June 29, 1860—Mar 31, 1940 Leader of the United Church of Canada; one of the most widely known preachers in the Dominion; general council secretary of the United Church (1925-34)

References
> International Who's Who
> Who's Who in Canada

Obituaries
> N Y Times p19 Ap 1 '40

MOORLAND, JESSE EDWARD, REV. 1863—Apr 30, 1940 Negro clergyman; member of the International Committee of the Young Men's Christian Association (colored) from 1898 to 1924; trustee of Howard University; member of the American Negro Academy

REV. JESSE E. MOORLAND

References

Who's Who in Colored America

Obituaries

N Y Herald Tribune p18 My 2 '40

MORA, FRANCIS LUIS July 27, 1874—
June 5, 1940 Artist; one of the most outstanding muralists, etchers and illustrators in
the United States; paintings appear in museums
of United States and Canada; his portrait of
Warren G. Harding hangs in the White
House

References

Art Digest 8:11 D 15 '33 il
Who's Who in America
Who's Who in American Art

Obituaries

N Y Herald Tribune p26 Je 6 '40
N Y Times p25 Je 6 '40
Time 35:64 Je 17 '40

MOREHOUSE, WARD Nov 24, 1897-
Newspaper columnist; playwright; motion
picture scenarist

Address: c/o The Dial Press, Inc, 432 Fourth
Ave, New York City

Ward Morehouse does not look like a
glamour boy, being about five-feet-six, on the
plump side, chestnut-haired and devoted to
horn-rimmed glasses. But to the prosaic
"leg" and "rewrite" reporter he is a glamour
boy of journalism because he has been for
almost two decades an outstanding Samuel
Pepys of the nighttime doings of Fifty-
second Street and Broadway in New York,
Sunset and Vine Streets in Hollywood, and
the West End and Piccadilly Circus in
London.

The theatre is one of the earliest memories
of Mr. Morehouse, who was born in Savannah, Georgia, and began to write plays practically as soon as he could hold a pencil.
Instead of a long apprenticeship and desk
drawers filled with unproduced manuscripts,
his two dozen plays were early discovered by
amateur and semi-professional groups of his
state. Student life at Georgia College,
Dahlonega, Georgia, had no lure for the
stage-struck boy, and at 17 he joined an
itinerant professional Shakespearean reader
for a tour of Southern towns and hamlets.
At Roanoke, Ward amiably parted company
with his partner and got a job on the
Savannah *Press* as reporter and sports writer
at $9 a week. Then he went to the Atlanta
Journal in 1918. Atlanta, he says, "was a
good theatre town; it had always been a
good news town right on through Sherman's
time to the Leo Frank case and the furor
over the Ku Klux."

He married the best Latin scholar in the
history of her college, a Georgia girl, niece
of the jurist who presided over the trial of
Leo Frank. His thoughts turned to New
York just as had those of other distinguished reporters on the *Journal* before him—
Grantland Rice, Ward Greene, Don Marquis,
Keats Speed, Laurence Stallings, Bill Farns-
worth and Harold Ross.

When he had sold three short stories
and "run his savings up to $750" he came
to New York, found a job on the *Tribune*
as rewrite man and later as assistant night
city editor, then went into the theatrical
department, writing stage news and second
string reviews. At this time he refuted the
legend of the lazy, slow, shuffling man of
the South by undertaking the herculean task
of two daily full-time jobs! As he tells it,
he had a friend on the *Tribune* called "Fitzgerald, the Man Who Never Sleeps," a copy-

WARD MOREHOUSE

MOREHOUSE, WARD—*Continued*

writer rated "as one of the best" who worked a full day shift on the Brooklyn *Times* and an eight-hour shift on the *Tribune*. He persuaded Morehouse to do likewise. The job in Brooklyn was kept by Morehouse off and on for five years. "In those days I used to have endless vitality," he explains.

In 1926 he was fired from the *Tribune,* which was undergoing a series of volcanic eruptions. He joined the New York *Sun,* and is still there conducting his nationally famous *Broadway After Dark.* Anyone reading his columns can see that the term "glamour boy" is applicable to a newspaperman who has as intimate friends such personalities as Helen Hayes, Lunt and Fontanne, Jed Harris, Tallulah Bankhead, the late Percy Hammond, Edna Ferber, Maxwell Anderson, the late Jeanne Eagels, Katharine Hepburn, Peggy Wood, Darryl Zanuck. In theatrical and newspaper circles, both national and international, he knows nearly everyone worth knowing.

After a divorce from his first wife some fifteen years ago he married Jean Dalrymple, theatrical agent. They were divorced three years ago. He has written his column in many parts of the world—in remote hamlets in the United States, in European capitals, Egypt and the Near East. When asked in 1931 if he would like to undertake the dangerous flight around the entire South American continent, he replied that he was ready as soon as he could pack a bag. In France in 1930 he had a widely-quoted interview with Eugene O'Neill. He is the author of the Broadway success, *Gentlemen of the Press,* which might have been a smash hit if it hadn't unfortunately been produced at the same time as *The Front Page.* He also wrote *Miss Quis,* and is coauthor of *Forsaking All Others. Gentlemen of the Press* and five other scripts he wrote have been made into motion pictures. His book, *Forty-Five Minutes Past Eight,* published by Dial Press in late 1939, has been called "a list of names; a gay, gleeful, slightly bewildering and just a little too vociferous roll call of celebrities." "A history of his world and its people seen through a wine glass lightly, during the roaring '20s and staggering '30s," says another critic.

In the fall of 1940 he has completed a new play, *U. S. 90,* which is under option to Guthrie McClintic.

References

> Morehouse, W. Forty-Five Minutes Past Eight 1939
> Who's Who in Journalism

MORGENTHAU, HENRY JR. May 11, 1891- United States Secretary of the Treasury

Address: b. Treasury Dept, Washington, D. C.; h. Hopewell Junction, New York

Building up our national defenses is an expensive proposition, and the man who must find the money has one of the hardest jobs in the administration. Henry Morgenthau Jr., Secretary of the Treasury, has, during the summer and fall of 1940, drafted a program together with spokesmen of industry for increasing plane production; obtained from the British the American rights for the manufacture of Rolls Royce airplane engines; asked the machine tool builders "How can you give us for national defense what we want when we want it?"; presented a new tax bill which institutes for five years a supertax, boosts income and excise levies 10 per cent and lowers exemptions to $2,000 for married and $800 for single persons.

Without doubt Henry Morgenthau is one of the hardest-working men in the administration, but there are widely differing views as to his actual effectiveness. One commentator called him "probably the best organizer and administrator in the New Deal," and there is a consistent body of opinion which believes that it is he who "has done more than any other Cabinet member or high official to keep the administration's financial feet close to the ground." On the other hand, it has been said that "personally he does little." Henry Morgenthau "is no more Secretary of the Treasury than Max Baer. His duties are to see that the work is done and that the will of the Leader is carried out. Henry is nothing more than a glorified foreman," said one critic.

The opinion that much of the country holds, however, is probably that "in no sense has he been a brilliant Treasury head, but neither has he been a flop." Secretary Morgenthau has done a better-than-average job of managing his department and he has carried out the financial policies of the administration efficiently. Under him the Stabilization Fund, a wholly new instrument, has been developed into a permanent part of the Treasury's equipment. It is he who "superintended the transfer from Wall Street to Washington of the financial capital of the United States," he who helped stabilize the silver market here and in 1936 the franc abroad. Under Morgenthau an "almost unbroken record of financing successes and lower Federal interest rates" has been established.

It is true, on the other hand, that under Morgenthau the national debt of the United States has increased—because of a number of circumstances—and that the government has become involved in a policy of gold buying to which objections have been raised. "Inherently a conservative," it is probable that Henry Morgenthau may not always have acted as he himself would choose, but he has defended the administration's policies with vigor, which may be more ammunition for those who believe he is the willing instrument of the President.

Their real ammunition, though, comes when Mr. Morgenthau steps out from his office to face the public. At press conferences he "fidgets, squirms and gives the

impression of being extremely pained."
His "shy taciturnity"—President Roosevelt
playfully calls him "Henry the Morgue"—
makes him uncertain in public speeches and
"it is a happy day for the hyenas on Capitol
Hill when they can call the young secretary
to the witness stand to challenge his monetary policies." Observers say that recently
his manner has become more comfortable.

Before Henry Morgenthau was appointed
Secretary of the Treasury, there was little
in his career which seemed to have fitted
him for the position and its duties. He was
born in New York City on May 11, 1891,
the son of Josephine (Sykes) and Henry
Morgenthau, our Ambassador to Turkey
under Wilson. Morgenthau Sr. was a
lawyer who made most of his money in
real estate: "his real estate dealings were
so widespread that eventually nearly every
piece of property in The Bronx passed
through his fingers at one time or another." He also invested heavily in the
Underwood Typewriter Company.

Henry Jr.'s youth was uneventful. He
went to private school not far from home
and then to Exeter, where he stayed three
years. He left when he was 16 and spent
the next two years "vegetating." In 1909
he entered Cornell University to study
architecture as training for the taking over
of his father's real estate business, but he
didn't like it and didn't stay. He got a job
as timekeeper on a construction job and
kept it for about six months; then he became a machinist in the Underwood Typewriter Company.

While there Henry got typhoid and went
to Texas. He was then 18. When he came
back he knew he wanted to be a farmer,
but Henry Sr., had other ideas for him.
For a while he worked in his father's office
and later in a banking house, but then
went back to Cornell to study farming.
He didn't take a degree, but left in 1913
to engage in practical farming. His father
bought him 1,400 acres of rich land back
of Fishkill Hooks, near the Hudson, in
New York State, which he converted into a
farm, the chief product of which is apples.
Henry still makes a profit on the farm
and has made one every year even during
the depression. In 1916 he married Elinor
Fatman of New York, "the charming and
intelligent woman whose wisdom and
knowledge of the world are still great props
to him."

Morgenthau's farm is about 15 miles from
the Roosevelt estate. Morgenthau met
Roosevelt shortly after he started to cultivate it; their social acquaintance developed into close friendship and eventually
into political association. During the First
World War Roosevelt gave Morgenthau
a position in the Navy Department after
Henry's faulty eyesight disqualified him for
active service. When Roosevelt was
nominated for the Vice-Presidency in 1920
Morgenthau was in charge of the notifica-
tion ceremony.

HENRY MORGENTHAU JR.

In 1922 Morgenthau bought the *American
Agriculturist,* a farm journal, and "immediately breathed life into the paper, removing
the more highly scientific articles and replacing them with homely hints for good
pies and sewing circles." The magazine
prospered and its circulation grew. He
kept it until 1933.

When Roosevelt campaigned for Governor of New York State in 1928 Morgenthau was business manager of Roosevelt's
campaign tour. When Roosevelt got in
he appointed Morgenthau to organize an
Agricultural Advisory Commission. Morgenthau got together important farm leaders and experts and for four years served
as chairman of the commission which
drafted a broad program for farm relief in
New York State. In Roosevelt's second
term as Governor, Morgenthau was made
Commissioner of Conservation and played
an important part in the $2,300,000,000 state
reforestation program.

During his 1932 campaign for President,
Roosevelt used Morgenthau to maintain
contact with the farm organizations
throughout the country. Morgenthau
wanted to be made Secretary of Agriculture
when Roosevelt was elected. Instead he
was made Chairman of the Farm Board
and given the job of consolidating the government's nine agricultural credit agencies
into the Farm Credit Administration and
of applying the $2,300,000 farm mortgage
relief program.

As governor of the Farm Credit Administration, Morgenthau was frequently called
on to give advice and execute commissions
entirely outside of the duties of his position.
He played an active part in the early trade
negotiations with Russia and assisted in
developing the administration's gold purchase policy. Morgenthau didn't stick to

MORGENTHAU, HENRY JR.—*Continued*
his Washington desk, but traveled from the
Atlantic to the Pacific explaining in simple
language the New Deal in agriculture. No
orator, the farmers and businessmen
seemed to understand his simple language
and the "result of his trips was a better
comprehension of the President's plans."

In 1933 Morgenthau was made acting
Secretary of the Treasury and on New
Year's Day 1934 he was made Secretary, an
appointment which was the "culmination of
years of devotion to and adoration of his New
York neighbor." When he took over the Cabinet position there was reason to believe that
it would prove to be "a brief and probably
an unfortunate appointment." Nothing in
his record, except a brief excursion into
gold purchasing policies, had prepared him
for the duties of this office and so far as
anyone knew he had never shown any particular aptitude in the field of finance.

His start was inauspicious. He immediately ordered that all publicity should
pass through the hands of his personal publicity assistant, Herbert Gaston, and that
no one should discuss official business with
outsiders unless Gaston gave permission.
"This is not a censorship," he said, "but
I'm used to running my own shop. I want
to know what's going on in it and what
is going out from it." His motive was
unimpeachable—to stop leaks to Wall
Street and elsewhere—but his approach was
clumsy, and "groans and hisses" greeted
the order, with vague mutterings about
freedom of the press. The policy was
continued, however; and since press conferences have been held twice a week
"correspondents volunteered that they have
been obtaining more information than they
had before."

His next order also aroused ridicule.
He ordered the Treasury guards to stand
at attention, to dress neatly and to speak
courteously. Then the tall and serious
Secretary proceeded to organize his department efficiently. Bureau heads were called
in and ordered to pay no attention to
political influences from either party.
Weekly conferences were set up, in which
each bureau chief had to read a report of
the week's work in his bureau. The Internal Revenue Bureau was prodded to
collect some $800,000,000 in income tax
deficiencies. Morgenthau had a review
prepared of each large tax case pending
and passed on it himself and put an end—
for the time being at least—to the custom
of settling these cases in court at a big loss
to the government. The whole office began
to run, and continued to run, like clockwork. Anyone with an appointment seldom has to wait longer than 30 seconds,
and when his time is exhausted Morgenthau stands up and out the visitor goes.

Morgenthau's work is his whole life. He
plays no golf and accepts none but official
invitations. His main pleasures are taking
care of his farm, riding and playing tennis

there and going on picnics with his wife
and three children. He presents a neat
figure, his pince-nez worn with an intellectual air. His voice is low and rather nervous, he "occasionally stutters and is always
forgetting names." He is devoted to President Roosevelt, whom he calls "the Boss,"
and says that the two men who have influenced him most are "Dad" and "the
Boss."

References

Am Mercury 34:12-21 Ja '35
Business Week p27+ Je 15 '40
Lit Digest 115:6 Ap 8 '33 por; 117:9
Ja 13 '34 por; 117:7+ F 17 '34 por
Nation 141:182-4 Ag 14 '35; 144:638-9
Je 5 '37
N Y Times p9 My 20 '40; p15 My 28
'40
Newsweek 1:4 Je 24 '33 por; 15:60
My 13 '40 por
Sat Eve Post 211:8-9+ Ap 1 '39 por;
211:16-17+ Ap 8 '39; por; 211:25+
Ap 15 '39
Time 34:13 N 20 '39 por
America's Young Men 1936-37
Unofficial Observer [pseud.] Mad
Money *In* New Dealers p104-41 1934
Who's Who in America
Who's Who in American Jewry
Who's Who in Commerce and Indus-
try
Who's Who in the Nation's Capital

MORRISON, HERBERT STANLEY Jan
3, 1888- Home Secretary and Minister for
Home Security; leader of the London Labor
Party
Address: 55 Archery Rd, Eltham, S. E. 9,
London, England

An ex-errand boy and ex-telephone oper-
ator who became Leader of the London
County Council, ruling the social service of
a community of some eight million people,
Privy Councillor and architect of the modern
British system of traffic regulation—that is
Herbert Morrison, the erstwhile Minister of
Supply, who has been given in October
1940 the vital task of commanding the
London front line as Minister for Home
Security. In his first statement he rejected
the idea of deep raid shelters, but hinted
that London's entire subway system might
be taken over for that purpose.

A forceful, logical speaker who can elu-
cidate the fine points of a complicated measure, lightening his discourse from time to
time with a Cockney wisecrack, Morrison
has long been one of the outstanding personalities in the British Labor movement. He
is known in the United States, too, for he
traveled widely in this country in 1936 and
1937, and in the spring of 1938 was invited
by the American Labor Party to give his
advice on its reorganization on national lines.

He was born at Brixton, a London suburb, the son of Henry Morrison, a policeman, and an ex-housemaid; and within three

days after his birth suffered an eye injury which has always necessitated his wearing glasses. No special signs of cleverness appeared at his primary school (which he left at 14); and indeed it took long years of self-education to release his potentialities. He was first a shop boy, running errands, then an assistant in a shop, and then a telephone operator at a brewery. But while other youths of his age and class were reading novelettes and trying to find the winner of the "three-thirty," Morrison was turning his mind to the apparently arid, but highly important, subject of municipal organization.

He became especially interested in the ideas of Sidney and Beatrice Webb, joined the Social Democratic Federation, and began to contribute articles to the Labor press (then small and uninfluential). He next joined the Independent Labor Party, which thirty years ago was regarded as the fighting force of the movement, but which has now shriveled to a little group of three men. He progressed from the chairmanship of his local branch to become secretary for South London, and then chairman of the divisional council covering London and all the southern counties.

In 1913 Morrison got his first chance of paid work in the Labor movement (though the pay was nothing much). A paper called the *Daily Citizen* was founded, and he was taken on its circulation staff. In 1915 he was receiving $5 a week as part-time secretary of the newly formed London Labor Party; in 1919 he was promoted to full-time secretary; from 1920 to 1921 he was Mayor of the London borough of Hackney and was one of the London Labor Mayors who pursued Mr. Lloyd George up to Gairloch in the wilds of Scotland to ask what he proposed to do about unemployment. In 1922 he was elected to the London County Council, the authority responsible for the local government of the huge district of Greater London, comprising twice the population of Switzerland. A year later he was elected to Parliament as member for South Hackney, but his stay there was brief, for he failed to hold his seat in the 1924 election.

Five years passed before Morrison appeared again in Parliament, but they were years of intensive and able work in the background which had a great part in increasing his party's influence in the country and the municipalities. He became chairman of the National Labor Party in 1928, presided over its annual conference in 1929 and in the same year was re-elected to Parliament for his old constituency.

Labor was now entering on its second period of administration, as the largest party at the polls, though it held office only by sufferance of the Liberals. Morrison was awarded the post of Minister of Transport, and at once set in motion two measures of the greatest importance. The first of these was the Road Traffic Act. Road casualties and congestion had long been a problem, and there were many anomalous conditions. The

HERBERT STANLEY MORRISON

Act made third-party insurance compulsory, forbade the over-working of long-distance lorry-drivers, raised the speed limit from 20 to 30 miles per hour and introduced a whole series of safety regulations comprised in a "highway code."

The second enactment was the London Passenger Transport Act, which coordinated a number of separate bus and subway undertakings and placed them under one authority run as a public utility company responsible to Parliament. Morrison went out of Parliament again in the Labor debacle of 1931, before the Act had gone through all its stages, so that when it eventually became a law some of its provisions had been altered.

Morrison was again returned to Parliament for South Hackney, London, in 1935, and has remained there ever since. He has been an unsparing critic of the Chamberlain administration on grounds of both home and foreign policy. His municipal work has continued with unabated vigor, and it is in the sphere of local government that he has made his most solid reputation. When a London Air Raid Precautions Committee was set up he became its chairman, and it was his organizing genius that was mainly responsible for the smooth working of the evacuation scheme at the beginning of this War, when some 750,000 school children were sent out into the country without mishap of any sort.

When Mr. Chamberlain resigned in May 1940, in favor of Mr. Churchill (see sketch this issue) and the obstacle to Labor's collaboration in the government was removed, it was almost inevitable that Morrison should be offered a portfolio. As Minister of Supply he had applied to a severe national task his characteristic qualities of drive, organization and imagination.

MORRISON, HERBERT—*Continued*

Morrison is a clear, logical, persuasive speaker, but no emotional ranter. Work rather than words has been his way of furthering social amelioration. It has been Morrison, for example, more than any other, who has pushed on the important project of preserving a Green Belt around London; and he has done notable service in the demolition of slums and the reconstitution of obsolete schools.

He is a constitutionalist, and as such anathema to the small but vociferous Communist Party, which constantly attacks him. He is quite capable, however, of giving as good as he gets in any kind of debate. He is a stickler for party discipline and is no friend to Liberal or Tory converts who refuse to adapt themselves full-bloodedly to the Socialist program.

Morrison is no "boiled shirt Socialist," but remains in habits and demeanor a simple working man. He pays little attention to clothes; he is no social climber; and he takes his holiday with his wife (he married Margaret Kent in 1919) and daughter, at some watering-place under the auspices of the Workers' Travel Association. Despite his commanding personality he is not a grim, apocalyptic figure like the late Lord Snowden, but is friendly, charming and humorous in his dealings. He has been a prolific journalist for many years (when not in office) and has written *Socialisation and Transport* (1933) and *How Greater London is Governed* (1935). He is a "hot tip" for the Premiership some day, if ever Labor comes back.

References

Christian Sci Mon Mag p4+ Mr 23 '38 pors
Harper 170:498-9 Mr '35
Lit Digest 123:12 Mr 20 '37
Liv Age 349:342-4 D '35
New Repub 99:206-7 Je 28 '39
Newsweek 9:18 Mr 13 '37
Time 35:84 My 27 '40

Gunther, J. Left and Right in England *In* Inside Europe p256-66 1936
International Who's Who
Watchman, pseud. Right Honourable Gentlemen 1939
Who's Who

MORROW, HONORE WILLSIE 1880—Apr 12, 1940 American historical novelist; perhaps best known for her Lincoln trilogy: *Forever Free* (1927); *With Malice Toward None* (1928); and *The Last Full Measure* (1930)

References

American Women
Kunitz, S. J. ed. Living Authors 1937
Overton, G. M. Honoré Willsie Morrow *In* Women Who Make Our Novels p216-8 1928

HONORE WILLSIE MORROW

Obituaries

N Y Herald Tribune p10 Ap 13 '40 por
Newsweek 15:8 Ap 22 '40 por
Pub W 137:1594 Ap 20 '40

MORSE, JOHN LOVETT Apr 21, 1865—Apr 3, 1940 Physician; twice head of the American Pediatric Society; one of the nation's leading authorities on children's diseases; author of numerous medical texts

References

American Men of Science
Who's Who in America
Who's Who in American Medicine

Obituaries

Boston Transcript p10 Ap 3 '40
N Y Sun p23 Ap 4 '40
N Y Times p23 Ap 4 '40

MORTON, HENRY HOLDICH 1861—May 3, 1940 Physician; widely known authority on venereal diseases; wrote textbook on subject which was revised for six editions; helped systematize methods used by United States Army in combating the diseases

References

American Medical Directory
Directory of Medical Specialists 1939
Who's Who in America

Obituaries

N Y Herald Tribune p40 My 5 '40

MORTON, JAMES MADISON JR. Aug 24, 1869—June 26, 1940 Judge of the Federal District Court for 27 years; judge of the Circuit Court of Appeals for the First District from 1931 until his retirement in 1939; gained

attention for ruling that double prosecution for the same offense was legal; after the War barred citizenship to evaders of military service

References

Who's Who in America
Who's Who in Government
Who's Who in Law

Obituaries

N Y Herald Tribune p20 Je 27 '40
N Y Times p23 Je 27 '40 por

MOSCOVITCH, MAURICE Nov 23, 1871 —June 18, 1940 Character actor; made theatre debut in 1885 in Odessa, Russia; toured in Europe, United States, South America, Africa and Australia; played first English rôle when he was 47 years old; in motion pictures since 1936, appearing in *Susannah of the Mounties, Everything Happens at Night* and *The Great Dictator,* among other pictures

References

Who's Who in American Jewry
Who's Who in the Theatre

Obituaries

N Y Herald Tribune p22 Je 19 '40 por
N Y Times p23 Je 19 '40 por

MOSES, ROBERT Dec 18, 1888- New York City park commissioner

Address: b. State Office Bldg, New York City; h. 25 East End Ave, New York City

"The park that flanks the Hudson is
A veritable bed of roses
It fills my heart with pride that this
Is Gotham. Glory be to Moses."

This is the song that Margaret Fishback sings, and most New Yorkers pay spontaneous tribute to their energetic, La Guardia-appointed park commissioner, Robert Moses. Thanks to him New York City's parks and parkways, products of a genius for planning with an eye to beauty plus utility, rank with skyscrapers as things visitors simply must see. Thanks to him numerous beaches within the metropolitan area have been built and rebuilt, Jones Beach in particular made a show place to challenge the Riviera. And it was Mr. Moses who chose the site and cleared and filled in Flushing Meadow for the New York World's Fair. The park commissioner was not exactly interested in the Fair. What he foresaw on this site was the conversion of the exposition grounds into a fine, modern recreation development.

The National Institute of Arts and Letters will present the recently created Order of Merit to Park Commissioner Robert Moses on January 18, 1941.

The man who has made public service his career was born in New Haven, Connecticut, December 18, 1888, son of Emanuel and Bella (Cohen) Moses. His parents were of Spanish-Jewish descent, but not orthodox;

Blank—Stoller
ROBERT MOSES

his father was the proprietor of a prosperous department store. The boy was sent to the Mohegan Lake Preparatory School at Peekskill, New York, where he remained an unhappy cadet until graduation. He entered Yale, where he won a victory over Walter Camp in the matter of pooling athletic funds so the profits in football would take up the deficits in other sports. He was graduated in 1909, a member of the Senior Council and with Phi Beta Kappa honors. Going on to Oxford to continue his studies in jurisprudence, he became captain of the swimming and water-polo teams and was the first American to be president of the Oxford Union, a debating society. On his return to this country he went to Columbia to get his Doctor's degree (1914), his thesis being *The Civil Service of Great Britain.*

His first job was with the Bureau of Municipal Research, studying city governments. In New York, while assisting John Mitchell's Fusion régime in budget-making, he met Mary Louise Sims of Dodgeville, Wisconsin, then secretary of the Bureau. They were married August 15, 1915 and spent their honeymoon mountain-climbing near Lake Placid. They have two daughters, Barbara and Jane.

In 1919 Governor Smith appointed Moses secretary of his non-partisan State Reconstruction Committee to study and revamp outmoded state government machinery. Moses' reports and recommendations are regarded as classics in state papers. His association with Governor Smith was an auspicious one: Smith admired him to the point of awe, and it is said that Moses wrote most of the Governor's speeches and fathered his social policies. In 1924 he became chairman of the State Council of Parks and began his parkway system along Lake Ontario and the Niagara Frontier program.

MOSES, ROBERT—*Continued*

For four years he was a member of the State Fine Arts Commission. When Franklin D. Roosevelt became Governor of the state in 1928 he and Moses clashed from the start: Roosevelt forced Moses from his position as Secretary of State. But he did approve in 1929 his investigation of the collapse of the City Trust Company; Moses' report on banking abuses has been described by Walter Lippmann (see sketch this issue) as the best government report of its kind ever written.

Robert Moses continued his work on the development of State parks and in 1933 hoped to be New York's Fusion nominee for Mayor. He threw his support, however, to Fiorello La Guardia (see sketch this issue), who, when elected, let Moses name his choice of city jobs. Moses promptly chose to be Commissioner of Parks. Of all his numerous offices (he has a comfortable private income and salary is not essential), it is the only position for which he receives a salary—$13,000 a year. Without pay, he is chairman and chief executive officer of the Triborough Bridge Authority, chairman of the State Commission of Parks, head of the Henry Hudson Parkway Authority, chairman of the Jones Beach State Parkway Authority, chairman of the State Emergency Public Works Commission, Civil Works Administrator for Long Island Parks.

Under La Guardia, Moses wasted no time before undertaking the much-needed reorganization of the City Parks Department. His first step was to eliminate the five Borough commissioners and their pensioners so that he might be sole boss and coordinate park enterprises. He brought his own staff of engineers and experts, and soon had some 70,000 PWA workers employed. By 1937 he had increased the number of playgrounds from 119 to 362—the number since raised to 420—all newly equipped. Swimming pools, tennis courts and golf clubs for adults were built. Central Park itself got a fine new zoo, a big restaurant, a new children's playground. Decorative and play areas were constructed along such new highways as the Henry Hudson Parkway. Fort Tryon Park at the north end of Washington Heights, accessible by subway, is sixty acres of wooded slopes providing a lovely framework for the famed "Cloisters" of the Metropolitan Museum.

For the establishment and extension of several new parkways, along with the parks themselves, Commissioner Moses spent in five years some three hundred million dollars, two-thirds of which came from Federal funds for work relief. He built Grand Central Parkway and extended the Bronx Parkway up the Hudson River. Connecticut's admirable new Merritt Parkway is an extension of Moses' own Hutchinson River Parkway through Westchester County. Around the southeastern rim of Long Island he has been building the Circumferential Parkway. One arm sweeps eastward to connect with the parkway lead-ing off The Bronx-Whitestone Bridge. Another arm reaches around the tip of Brooklyn to come within swimming distance of lower Manhattan and Brooklyn, the whole project—33 miles of parkway and 69 bridges—to cost $28,000,000. He and Manhattan Borough President Stanley Isaacs share supervision of the park and drive under construction along the East River. As a member of the Triborough Bridge Authority Moses supervised the construction of this great traffic-facilitating enterprise, which has a capacity of as many as 80,000 cars daily. Though its cost was $61,000,000, it has since been refinanced by a private bond issue at a profit to the Federal government. At its inception, however, the New Deal tried to oust Moses from his Triborough post, but finally backed down.

Moses' proudest achievement is his Long Island park project, a model of planning which he began some 15 years ago. He viewed the whole of Long Island as a possible gigantic city playground: the entrenched aristocracy, however, considered it their private property. With them the undaunted commissioner began a real battle: he sliced through red tape, begged, bought and condemned land. It took five years to build the admirable Jones Beach: with thirty-eight million cubic yards of sand artificial dunes were built, on which the WPA workers even planted sand grass. Everything was made immaculately shipshape, from the sailor-garbed attendants to the old ships' funnels used for refuse. Its 78 acres of parking space take care of the thousands of people who proudly drive there for Sunday outings.

Robert Moses' one departure from park building was essayed in 1934 when he ran as a candidate for Governor of New York. Fortunately for the future of the City's parks and highways, candidate Moses was soundly defeated, free to go back to his 1,800 planned projects for the city, all of which have, to date, been started or finished.

The man whose works have made him a municipal Aladdin has been called a human firecracker, "a persistent hell-raiser who combines intelligence with the temper of a wounded lion." It has also been said that Moses would cross Fifth Avenue on a tight wire if he were sure of a row on the other corner. He has vast vitality and enthusiasm; his ruthless, high-pressure methods of getting things done have won him the admiration of many. His "arrogance and intolerance of contradiction" have made enemies: the editor of the Babylon, Long Island paper, who doesn't like him, calls him Lord Moses or Mussolini. La Guardia, who respects fighters, has nevertheless often clashed with his commissioner, though admitting the soundness of his projects. Every once in a while Moses gets a note from the Mayor saying, "Dear Bob: You're right—" adding plaintively, "you always are."

Moses, who usually gets in his punches first, "talks forcefully, sometimes eloquently, and as often as not in barnyard idiom." He is "firm-jawed, with a large, straight, executive nose; he has a generous mouth, his strong white teeth affording a striking contrast to smooth olive-hued skin, sombre eyes and heavy black eyebrows. . . His large strong hands, with tapering fingers, suggest a sculptor." It is said that his one financial problem is to remember to carry enough change to pay cab fares, and that the only person he can't get tough with is Tammie, the family Scottie.

A planner for the future whose public spending is thoroughly New Dealish, Moses is something of a political paradox. He is an old-guard Republican who has worked best with Al Smith and La Guardia—the latter anything but a devout Republican. He has kept politics out of his own enterprises, however: his Long Island park supervision is run on a strict non-partisan basis. In spite of his political fiasco in 1934, many who know Robert Moses believe that when he finally steps out of public service he will go into politics. He likes a fight, win or lose, as much as he likes to get things done.

References

> Am Mag 126:144-5+ Jl '38
> Atlan 163:225-34 F '39
> Cur Hist 50:26-8+ S '39
> Fortune 17:70-9+ Je '38 il por
> Harper 176:26-37 D '37
> New Yorker 10:26-9 Mr 10 '34
> Sat Eve Post 212:12-13+ F 24 '40
> Time 32:17 O 17 '38 por
>
> MacKaye, M. Public Servant: Robert Moses *In* New Yorker (periodical). Profiles from the New Yorker p287-96 1938
> Who's Who in America
> Who's Who in American Jewry
> Who's Who in Government

MOSLEY, SIR OSWALD ERNALD

Nov 16, 1896- Former Member of Parliament; leader of the British Union of Fascists

On May 23, 1940 Sir Oswald Mosley, leader of the British Union of Fascists, was arrested. Mosley and his followers formerly had been allowed to agitate against the government in favor of peace with the enemy without molestation, and, in fact, the police frequently arrested hecklers who tried to break up their meetings. But with the Germans just across the Channel, all this changed. The British government cracked down on all suspected enemies within its gates, and Mosley was taken into custody.

The British government has reason to suspect him, for Mosley's creed derives much from Hitler's and Mussolini's. It is strongly anti-Semitic, strongly in favor of the corporate state—"a mixture of Italian castor-oil economics with a still more concentrated dose of German politics." Even the salute of his group is "Mussolini via Hitler." And Mosley has or had a group of militant, devoted, well-disciplined followers whose numbers at one time were estimated as high as 500,000.

Ever since the British Union of Fascists (known also as the British Union) was formed in 1932, Mosley has argued for its truly British character. He used to assure his audiences that his Blackshirts would never resort to force, that Fascism meant peace, not war, that he would never tamper with the monarchy (he closed his meetings with *God Save the King*) and that a corporate, self-contained England with a legislature composed of experts, instead of the present House of Commons, was the solution to a stronger, more powerful England and a more prosperous people. Yet the phrases he used had a familiar sound; the black shirts of his followers and the fasces they used as a symbol were certainly not original with him; the tune of the Union's marching song was the tune of the Nazi *Horst Wessel;* the tactics of provocation when Mosley and his army descended into the heart of London's Jewish and anti-Fascist East End were the usual tactics.

Mosley himself comes from impeccable British ancestry, the sixth baronet of a title created in 1781. His schooling was impeccably British. He was educated at Winchester and at the Royal Military College, Sandhurst. During the First World War he fought as a cavalry officer and as an aviator.

Right after the War, in 1918, when he was only 22, Mosley entered Parliament as the conservative member for Harrow. Since then he has been an "ex" almost everything—an ex-conservative, an ex-independent, an ex-Socialist and an ex-leader of his own New Party. "A lone wolf, it has been said that on a fox hunt he would side with the fox." With every quality for political leadership "except judgment," his impatience has carried him from party to party, from rôle to rôle.

When he entered Parliament, he was immediately conspicuous. He was rich, he could speak, he was one of the best fencers in England, he belonged to the aristocracy and he married (1920) Lady Cynthia Curzon, daughter of the former Viceroy of India. In the Conservative Party he was singled out as of Cabinet caliber. But in 1923 he left the Conservative Party to become an Independent. As an Independent he impressed the country with his ability to win an election solely on the basis of his energy and platform ability.

In 1924 Mosley switched again—this time to the Labor Party, but was defeated in the elections by 77 votes. For two years he was out of the House, but he stayed in the public eye. He made speeches on the general strike, on India, on Anglo-Chinese relations. He traveled to other countries, including the United States. In 1926 he was returned to Parliament as member for Smethwick, Birmingham and held this seat in 1929 when he went into the Ministry as Chancellor for the Duchy of Lancaster. In

SIR OSWALD MOSLEY

the Labor Party, Mosley was a protégé of Ramsay MacDonald and even as late as 1931 he was told he was certain to be the next Labor Prime Minister if he would merely work and wait. But he wouldn't. In February 1931 he founded his own party, the New Party.

The New Party had among its adherents such Socialists as John Strachey and Oliver Baldwin, and its platform stressed the need for economic planning, for housing reform, for unemployment relief. Its weekly paper, *Action*, was edited by Harold Nicolson. Yet, on October 1, 1932, after a pilgrimage to Rome, Mosley organized the British Union of Fascists.

In all these years of changing politics Mosley's wife, Lady Cynthia Curzon, was by his side. With Sir Oswald she was active in labor politics and as a Socialist member of Parliament was close to Ramsay MacDonald. Together they enjoyed politics eleven months a year and then spent one month on the French Riviera. It was partly his wife's money that helped finance the British Union of Fascists in its hard, early years—her mother was the daughter of the multimillionaire Chicagoan, Levi Z. Leiter. She used to say: "I was one of the lucky ones. I could have had a good time and just enjoyed myself in life, for it happened that under this system I would never have had to work. But I could not get it out of my head that there were millions of mothers who would have their babies and then face years and years of gray dreariness." In 1933 she died, leaving three children. Mosley moved into a two-room flat, declaring: "I hate the junk of modern civilization with which bourgeois people litter their lives and rooms." But in 1937 he married Mrs. Diana Guinness Mitford, third daughter of the second Baron Redes-

dale and sister of Hitler's former friend, the notorious Unity Mitford-Freeman.

The start of the British Union of Fascists in 1932 was inauspicious, and at the beginning the adventure seemed doomed. Mosley dickered for help from Hitler and Mussolini, but got none. His street meetings were booed, minor street fights were a nightly occurrence and Mosley and his wife were often close to physical mauling. His book, *Greater Britain* (1932), was practically ignored.

Then, on January 15, 1934 Lord Rothermere, newspaper owner, announced his conversion to Fascism. He hailed Mosley and his movement as the only alternative to the menace of Socialism and the impending dictatorship of "hooligans and riff-raff." He urged young men earnestly to join and save England from the "hidden hand of Bolshevism." For three months Lord Rothermere's press supported and publicized the British Union of Fascists.

The Blackshirts began to attract attention. Mosley capitalized on economic discontent, on the proved impotence of the Labor Party, on the plight of the middle class. "Next to Winston Churchill (see sketch this issue), the finest orator in England," Mosley's speeches drew crowds. They were pure propaganda, dogmatic and bombastic, but they were fire. He could wheedle and coax and woo large audiences as few men can. To each meeting he gave an atmosphere of drama, a sense that great things were about to happen.

Blackshirt headquarters sprang up all over, and in 1934 there were over 200 official centers in Great Britain. The members were given instruction in boxing, jujitsu and fencing. An air training school was run for them and there were special summer training camps. The Fascist center in London housed treasury, research, publicity and legal departments, all the principal officers and a defense force. Fifteen to twenty headquarter propagandists were always on tour.

On June 7, 1934 a Fascist mass meeting turned into a wild riot. Uniformed Blackshirts "mercilessly" beat and kicked listeners for breaking into Mosley's speech and over 50 people needed medical attention. There was a debate on this in the House of Commons, but little came of it. The legions continued to parade through Jewish districts carrying anti-Semitic banners. And Mosley worked like an ox to achieve his ambition of a Fascist Britain. He never took a vacation; his social life was almost non-existent. He said, then, that he disliked cards, detested "irrelevant conversation," loathed dinner parties and social fawning and hated "entrenched old age whether it is sitting on a parlor sofa or in a Parliament seat." He kept himself in crackerjack condition to give the 200 or more speeches a year he made. He ate sparingly, drank nothing except a little beer and relaxed occasionally with some tennis or swimming or championship fencing.

In the winter of 1937 there was one especially violent sally on London's East End. After this "Bloody Sunday" laws were finally passed forbidding the wearing of political uniforms and placing Mosley's marches and provocations under scrutiny by the police. Mosley continued to wear his uniform, trying to goad the government into arresting him, but instead police squads were sent to protect him. Then he changed it. Dressed completely in black suit, tie, shirt, socks—in the words of John Gunther "like a skating champion"—solidly built and rather handsome, with a short, black moustache and intense, dark eyes, he used to create a striking picture as he carried on his work in the years before the second World War.

But the British Union of Fascists never again reached the flowering of 1934. In 1939 it still drummed up crowds at its meetings, but was given very silent treatment by the press and orthodox politics. Typical of its own reactions was the meeting addressed by Sir Kingsley Wood, Air Minister (see sketch this issue), in 1939. A group of the Union tried to stop the meeting and there was much rioting. Then Sir Kingsley Wood stepped forward, started *God Save the King*. The Fascists stood at attention and joined in the anthem until the police came and threw them out.

With Mosley and eight of his lieutenants in custody; with Britain making a concerted drive on all suspected enemies of the state, on all who would interefere with the most successful conduct of the present War, the outlook for the British Union of Fascists is not a cheerful one. Admirers of Hitler and Mussolini are not exactly *personae gratae* in England these days, and the chances of Mosley's being the first dictator in the English-speaking world look exceedingly slim.

References

> Christian Cent 50:741 Je 7 '33
> Collier's 94:10-11+ S 1 '34 il pors
> Cur Hist 39:542-7 F '34
> Harper 169:492-501 S '34
> Lit Digest 124 (Digest 1):13-15+ Jl 24 '37 il por
> Liv Age 346:46-8 Mr '34; 346:441-5 Jl '34
> N Y Times pl, 4 My 24 '40
> Newsweek 13:22-3 F 13 '39 por
> International Who's Who
> Strange, M. [pseud.] Who Tells Me True 1940
> Who's Who

MOTON, ROBERT RUSSA (mō'tn) Aug 26, 1867—May 31, 1940 Negro educator; succeeded Booker T. Washington as president of Tuskegee Institute in Alabama; earned recognition as one of the most famous Negro educators in America; ex-chairman of education to Haiti

References

> So Workm 63:335-6 D '34; 64:71-2 Mr '35 il; 67:151-2 My '38
> Brawley, B. G. Leaders in Education *In* Negro Builders and Heroes p211-25 1937

ROBERT R. MOTON

> Bullock, R. W. Robert Russa Moton *In* In Spite of Handicaps p15-21 1927
> Leaders in Education 1932
> Ovington, M. W. Robert Russa Moton *In* Portraits in Color p64-77 1927
> Who's Who Among North American Authors
> Who's Who in America
> Who's Who in American Education
> Who's Who in Colored America

Obituaries

> N Y Herald Tribune p34 Je 2 '40 por
> N Y Times p15 Je 1 '40
> Sch & Soc 51:730 Je 8 '40
> Time 35:88 Je 10 '40

MOTTA, GIUSEPPE (mŏt-tä' jōō-sĕp'pē) 1871—Jan 23. 1940 President of Switzerland for five terms

References

> International Who's Who

Obituaries

> N Y Herald Tribune p18 Ja 23 '40 por
> N Y Sun p19 Ja 23 '40
> Newsweek 15:2 F 5 '40
> Time 35:57 Ja 29 '40

MOWRER, LILIAN THOMSON Journalist; lecturer

Address: c/o Wm. Morrow & Co, 386 Fourth Ave, New York City

"We met in a railway carriage, without benefit of introduction." This is how Lilian T. Mowrer begins *Journalist's Wife* (1937), the story of the 20-odd full and hectic years she spent with Edgar Ansel Mowrer, correspondent for the Chicago *Daily*

LILIAN THOMSON MOWRER

News, Pulitzer Prize winner and author of *Germany Puts the Clock Back*.

It was in 1911 and she was on her way from London to Liverpool after years of study in Paris to become a speech specialist. A young man sat down beside her. "You interest me very much," he said. "May I talk to you?" Before the train reached Liverpool she and Edgar Ansel Mowrer were fast friends.

Five years passed before they were married, in February 1916. From their wedding day, when they were detained by the secret service in spy-ridden France, every period of the Mowrers' life "has been touched by the thrilling uncertainty of human history in the making." Rome, Edgar's first assignment, seemed remote from the War, but Mrs. Mowrer was in Venice when the city was bombed. With the Armistice she was nursing her husband, delirious (in three languages) from the effects of influenza. She observed the Supreme Council of the Allies at San Remo and witnessed the Fascist march on Rome. She lived in Italy until the "last hopes of a wholehearted Italian cooperation in international reconstruction and reorganization grew dim" and it became increasingly difficult to circumvent the censor.

With Diana Jane, their daughter, who had been born in May 1923, the Mowrers set out in March 1924 to "cover" Germany. In Germany, Lilian Mowrer, whose greatest interest since her student days had always been the theatre, decided it was absurd "to live in a country with the best theatre in the world and not have money enough to go as often as I like." She sought and found a job as German dramatic critic on the old London *Referee* and for years acted as critic for the important plays throughout the country.

Lilian Mowrer was interested in Germany's theatre, but she was even more vitally interested in Germany itself. She saw the Germany of the tolerant Weimar Republic fade into the despotism of Adolf Hitler's régime. She was a witness of the "brutality" and "terror" of the days that followed the Nazi rise to power. Edgar Mowrer's book, *Germany Puts the Clock Back*, published in December 1932, annoyed the Nazis. The German government went to his paper with a "mixture of argument and veiled threats." In August 1933 his chief wired him to leave Germany immediately, and the American Embassy was informed by the German government that it "simply couldn't guarantee his safety." The Mowrers left for Paris.

In Paris, in 1934, Lilian Mowrer heard men on the boulevards shout themselves hoarse against someone called Stavisky. She saw the growth of the Front Populaire and its defense of French democracy. In November 1936 she went to Russia, where her husband was covering the adoption of the new Soviet Constitution, and left it "a little baffled by that strange phenomenon."

Lilian Mowrer, who "can be as much at home in Tirana or Vienna as in her native London or her husband's Chicago," has won a reputation as writer, dramatic critic and lecturer. She lectures about Hitler's War, the European Theatre and about her own experiences. And the summation of this last is: "It has been a wonderful life so far. For a journalist these days knows no tranquility. And we wives sit around in strange countries, waiting till the assignment is finished and our men come home. The suitcases are hardly unpacked but they must be dragged out again; the welcome has not died on our lips and we must whisper goodbye. Then the old excitement flares, there is the rush to get everything ready; always improvising and adapting, always working against time—(can I possibly get the laundry back?)—but we don't have a dull life."

References

New Yorker 16:36+ Jl 20 '40
Sat R Lit 17:21 N 13 '37 por (pl)
American Women
Mowrer, L. Journalist's Wife 1937

MUCK, KARL　Oct 22, 1859—Mar 4, 1940
Symphony orchestra conductor

Dr. Karl Muck's meticulous, copperplate-like reading of Wagnerian scores, and his striking resemblance to the great composer (especially in profile) combined to make him one of the most effective interpreters of Wagnerian music both in America and in Europe. He was the favorite conductor of Wagner's widow, Cosima, and conducted the Wagner Bayreuth Festivals for 30 years

He was not a brilliantly popular conductor in the sense that he could sweep an audience off its feet emotionally. But to the musically-elect and initiated, his impeccable taste, his strict adherence to score gave him the reputation of one of the greatest interpreters of classical music.

This precise, distinguished musical genius became a central figure in the anti-German hysteria that swept America during the World War. Dr. Muck had conducted the Boston Symphony Orchestra in 1906 and 1907 on the invitation of its founder and director, the late Major Henry L. Higginson. His exact genius suited Boston, and he became permanent conductor of the Boston Symphony in 1912.

The tide of war-time hysterical patriotism found its first mark in Dr. Muck in the fall of 1917 when a patriotic group had requested that *The Star-Spangled Banner* be played at an appearance of the Boston Symphony Orchestra in Providence, Rhode Island. For some reason the anthem was not played. Dr. Muck afterwards explained that a symphony orchestra was not a military band, and that *The Star-Spangled Banner* was not a suitable vehicle for it. Major Higginson exonerated the German conductor, declaring that the request had been received too late, and that Dr. Muck had heard of the plan only as the orchestra was entraining for Providence, and that there had been no time for rehearsal. Subsequently *The Star-Spangled Banner* was played by the Boston Symphony at concerts in the East. But it was too late. Dr. Muck's lack of tact had brought down a thunder of extravagant denunciation. He was called "an alien menace," and "pro-German." The affair finally resulted in his resignation from the orchestra, and his internment as an enemy alien on March 26, 1918 at Fort Oglethorpe, Georgia. Major Higginson, who had supported Dr. Muck throughout the entire name-calling frenzy, promptly resigned from the orchestra. Without its chief patron, and its conductor, the Boston Symphony fell on lean days, and almost passed out of existence. It was not to regain its prominence as one of the world's great orchestras until 1924, when Serge Koussevitzky (see sketch this issue) took over the baton.

Back in Germany after the War, Dr. Muck conducted in various cities until 1922 when he became conductor of the Hamburg Philharmonic concerts, which he raised to a high artistic standard. Many rich offers were made to bring him back to the United States, but no power on earth could drag him back, so embittered and hurt was he at his treatment during the War. Reports that he was at odds with Hitler arose from his resignation from the Hamburg Orchestra in 1933. However, Dr. Muck declared that he had resigned as conductor because of the Hamburg Senate's decision to merge the Symphony Orchestra with Hamburg's Municipal Theatre. This was borne out by the fact that Dr. Muck was decorated on his last birthday by Hitler himself with the Order of the German Eagle, highest honor for culture in Germany.

KARL MUCK

The famous conductor's last public appearance as a national music figure was during the Leipzig observance of the fiftieth anniversary of Richard Wagner's death in February 1933. He had promised Cosima Wagner he would always help her son, Siegfried Wagner, with the Bayreuth Festivals, and he kept his word, conducting the festivals almost uninterruptedly from 1901 to 1930 when Siegfried Wagner died. He had shared the conductor's podium with Arturo Toscanini from 1927 to 1930. And in 1933, although he was very ill, he returned to conduct once more.

The last years of his life were spent at the home of Baroness von Scholley in Stuttgart where he died. The Baroness was the daughter of a former German Consul General in New York, who had been one of Dr. Muck's oldest friends and his former prison mate at Fort Oglethorpe. His was a lonely, ailing old age. His wife had died in 1921. Their only child, a son, died in 1881. Partially paralyzed from nicotine poisoning, said to be the result of his consumption of about 100 cigarettes daily over a long period of years, Dr. Muck immersed himself in Oriental philosophy and rarely left the house the last three years of his life.

He had lived through three phases of German life—the pre-War monarchical days when he won fame; the Weimar Republic in which he sought refuge after his humiliating experience in America during the War; and the totalitarian world of Adolf Hitler's Germany. He was born October 22, 1859 in Darmstadt, the son of a councilor of the government of Bavaria, which was then not part of the German Empire. A musical prodigy, he made his first public appearance when he gave a piano solo at a chamber music recital at the age of 11 years. He

MUCK, KARL—*Continued*

also played the violin with a local symphony orchestra as a boy. At 16 he entered Heidelberg University, one of its youngest pupils. A year later, he entered the University of Leipzig. While there he studied music at Leipzig's famous conservatory and made his solo debut as a pianist in Leipzig at the age of 20, the same year he took his degree of Doctor of Philosophy.

In 1880 he became choirmaster of the municipal opera in Zurich. Later he conducted opera in Zurich, Salzburg, Brünn and Graz. He became conductor of the Deutsches Landestheater in Prague, where he attained nation-wide fame, ranking with Hans Richter and Felix Weingartner as Germany's finest conductor. He toured Europe with the Prague orchestra, playing before Kaiser Wilhelm in Berlin, the Russian Court at St. Petersburg and the wealthy burghers at Hamburg. He conducted the Wagner *Ring* performances at St. Petersburg and Moscow in 1889, succeeding Seidl as conductor of the traveling Wagner theatre.

Still further musical honors were bestowed on him in 1892 when he became conductor of the Berlin Royal Opera, and conducted the symphony concerts of the Royal Orchestra under the patronage of the Kaiser. In 1899 he conducted the Wagner performances at Covent Garden in London and toured widely as a guest conductor. He was offered the Metropolitan Opera House podium at a reputed $27,000 a year, but for some reason refused. In 1901 began his long association with the Bayreuth Festivals, where he always conducted *Parsifal*. From 1903 to 1906 he alternated with Mottl as conductor of the Vienna Philharmonic Orchestra. He was the general music director of the Berlin Royal Opera when he was given leave in 1906 and 1907 to conduct the Boston Symphony, which he joined permanently in 1912. From May 14 to 26, 1915, he conducted the orchestra in 13 concerts of music of all nations at the Panama-Pacific International Exposition in San Francisco. He kept the already great Boston Symphony at its high level, winning over New York critics as well as Boston. Dr. Muck steered clear of strange or inner meanings in scores, preferring to think "that a dotted eighth note was a dotted eighth note without any secret significance," and insisted on the quiet, precise interpretations that made him so beloved by those who knew music well.

References

Ewen, D. Karl Muck—An American Tragedy *In* Man with the Baton p143-59 1936
Thompson, O. ed. International Cyclopedia of Music and Musicians 1939

Obituaries

Musical Am 60:5+ Mr 10 '40
N Y Herald Tribune p22 Mr 5 '40 por; II p11 Mr 17 '40

N Y Times XI p7, 8 Mr 10 '40
Time 35:64 Mr 11 '40
Variety 137:54 Mr 6 '40

MUMFORD, ETHEL WATTS Died May 2, 1940 Playwright; poet; novelist; writer of numerous novelettes, short stories, magazine articles; one of short story judges of O. Henry Memorial Award for five years

References

American Women
Who's Who Among North American Authors
Who's Who in America 1936-37

Obituaries

N Y Times p21 My 3 '40

MUMFORD, LEWIS Oct 19, 1895- Author

Address: Amenia, New York

Lewis Mumford, social philosopher and architectural authority, first sounded his summons to action in 1938 when in *A Call to Arms,* published in the *New Republic,* he advocated a policy of militancy by the United States to safeguard this country against the "imminent onslaught of Fascism." He followed this, in 1939, with a demand that *Men Must Act,* in which he denounced the Chamberlains and Daladiers whose policies of appeasement "we must regard with extreme skepticism, not to say hostility," and proposed that America engage in a policy of non-intercourse with the Fascist states, while beginning to "build up our own defenses." In September 1940 he published his *Faith for Living,* "a call to imperative action."

In *Faith for Living* Lewis Mumford warns us that the present victories of the Fascist powers so threaten our civilization that, unless we devise and translate into action a faith for living, all of us will revert to barbarism. Addressed to the liberal intellectuals, the conservatives and the militant radicals of this country, the book proposes a program with three main points: restoration of the family; re-establishment of ties with the soil; the development of personality. Calling it both "a moving sermon" and a "piercing shriek," critics have disagreed heartily on its merits, on its message, on its meaning for our times. And Mumford has been called, because of this book, a "warmonger" and "a prophet in the land."

This is certainly not the first time that Lewis Mumford has stirred up a row among the intellectuals and the liberals. Early in June 1940 he upset them when he resigned from his 13-year-old post as a contributing editor of the *New Republic,* disgusted with the magazine's slowness in rallying to the cause of all possible aid to the Allies. Two months before, in an article called *The Corruption of Liberalism,* printed in the *New Republic,* he had soundly spanked the liberals for "their unwillingness to defend civilization" when "confronted with the imminent threat of a world-wide upsurgence of barbarism," and it was clear that the rift was inevitable. He created another stir that same spring when he resigned as vice-chairman of the American Artists' Congress because it refused to condemn the Soviet Union's policy toward Finland.

Sturdy, sun-tanned, brown-eyed Lewis Mumford was born on October 19, 1895, the son of Lewis and Elvina (Baron) Mumford, into a home of extreme poverty. He spent his boyhood experimenting with the wireless and in his early teens wrote articles on radio telegraphy for electrical magazines. He attended Stuyvesant Technical High School in New York in order to become an electrical engineer. There he came into contact with various socioeconomic schools of thought, and occasional hints of such new ideas in science as relativity and the electronic theory of matter. He also attended Columbia University, the City College of New York and New York University.

The most important influence of his young life came to him, in 1915, in a book written by Patrick Geddes, a Scottish biologist who had trained under Thomas A. Huxley. Geddes had turned to sociology and to the study of Edinburgh and other cities. Mumford followed suit by becoming a student of New York City. Within the next few years he covered the city systematically on foot, studied architecture, learned to tell the approximate date a tenement was built from a glance at the fire escape or the cornice. Mumford maintained a long correspondence with Geddes until 1932, when the scientist died.

"Dislike of mathematics and a youthful love affair caused him to decide to be a writer," and in 1919 he began contributing reviews to the Dial, of which he became associate editor. In 1920 he was acting editor of a British publication, the Sociological Review.

From the late '20s on Mumford was able to combine his knowledge of New York City and its architecture with his desire to be a writer in the column called The Sky Line, which has been a frequent feature in the New Yorker and has been called "the most perceptive, severe and expert column of architectural criticism in the United States." Mumford notes in it the erection of New York's new apartment houses, office buildings, bridges and tunnels. He also wrote articles for the New Republic, the Freeman, the American Mercury, Harper's Magazine and for architectural journals. He collaborated with Paul Rosenfeld, Alfred Kreymborg and Van Wyck Brooks on The American Caravan (1927-36), a volume published annually in which they attempted to give a broad perspective of contemporary American writing.

Helen Post

LEWIS MUMFORD

Education has always been one of Mumford's greatest interests. For a short period he taught at the New School for Social Research in New York, and from 1931 to 1935 he was professor of art at Dartmouth College. From 1935 to 1937 he was a member of the Board of Higher Education of New York City, and is today a member of the Commission on Teacher Education, of the American Council on Education, and a member of the Commission on Resources and Education of the National Educational Association and the Progressive Education Association.

In 1939 Lewis Mumford wrote the narrative for The City, a documentary film shown at the City Planning Exhibit of the New York World's Fair. To him the city is not only a form of life, but is, through its layout and architecture, a form of art, "potentially the form of forms."

Mumford was married to Sophia Wittenberg in 1921; they have two children, Alison and Geddes. Among Mumford's most important works are: The Story of Utopias (1922); Sticks and Stones (1924), a study of American architecture and civilization; The Golden Day (1926), a study of American experience and culture; Herman Melville (1929), "an exhaustive criticism of the great imaginative American writer"; The Brown Decades (1931), a study of the arts in America from 1865 through 1895; Technics and Civilization (1934); Culture of Cities (1938); Men Must Act (1939).

References
Atlan 166:274-6 S '40
Commonweal 32:50 My 10 '40
New Repub 94:337 Ap 20 '38; 102: 568-73 Ap 29 '40; 102:827-8 Je 17 '40; 103:357 S 9 '40

MUMFORD, LEWIS—*Continued*

N Y Times p19 Ap 15 '40
Time 31:40-3 Ap 18 '38 il por (cover); 36:65 S 2 '40
Yale R ns 25:23-5 S 19 '35
Kunitz, S. J. ed. Living Authors 1937
Mumford, L. Lewis Mumford *In* Schreiber, G. ed. Portraits and Self-Portraits p117-20 1936
Mumford, L. Men Must Act 1939
Who's Who in America

MUNCH, EDVARD (mōōnk) Dec 12, 1863- Artist

Address: Ekely, Norway

At Ekely, near Oslo, a grand old painter, Edvard Munch, is spending the last days of what should be an honored old age. It is to be hoped that the German occupants of his country pay him due respect, for his work, though international in repute, belongs especially to the Germanic school and was in its day a vital influence on the modern Expressionist Movement. In the words of Herbert Read, he "occupies in modern Germany a position comparable to Cézanne's in French painting. He saved German art from a slavish following of the Post-Impressionist School and returned to a form of expression more consonant with the Nordic genius." He has done big stage settings and murals and is a lithographer of note. Some of his lithographs have a power that is almost terrifying. It may not be fanciful to see in his productions an affinity with the stark drama of his compatriot, Henrik Ibsen, and to detect in it also the pervasive loneliness and grandeur of his native landscape.

Edvard Munch was born at Løten, Norway, son of the physician Christian and his wife, Laura (Bjordal) Munch. His family had already produced a genius before him —A. P. Munch, an eminent Norwegian historian. Edvard was possessed of a true artistic temperament from his youth: he was a delicate, nervous boy. His parents intended him to be an engineer, but his artistic capacities had become apparent so early that in 1882 he was sent to the School of Arts and Crafts at Oslo. There he studied under Hans Heyerdahl and Christian Krogh, the greatest representatives of the Impressionist Movement in Norway. He paid a brief visit to Paris in 1885, staying long enough to become a devotee of Velásquez. It was, however, a sojourn in the Norwegian summer resort of Aasgaarstrand that had started him on his characteristic landscape style. He became known for his landscape studies of the Arctic summer nights.

The following year, which he himself regards as a decisive one in his life, he won a state scholarship which enabled him to study in Paris; he stayed in Léon Bonnat's life class for four months, saw the great French paintings of the century at the *Exposition Universelle*, and made friends with prominent painters like Claude Monet, Camille Pissarro and Denis Seurat, being especially interested by the *pointilliste* technique of the last. Canvases like *Rue de Rivoli* (1891) and *Gaming Room at Monte Carlo* (1892) show that he did not remain insensible to Impressionism, though the influence was not abiding.

Munch followed his Parisian stay by a period in Berlin from 1892 to 1895, though he continued to spend his summers at his favorite Aasgaarstrand. During that time he exhibited by invitation at the Association of Berlin Artists, precipitating a scandal of proportions by the daring of his subjects. The show had to be closed and the Association itself split into two warring sections. After that he exhibited in other cities with similar sensational results. During that period he also painted a number of portraits including *Strindberg* and *Ibsen*, and began to produce the wild, tormented, highly subjective lithographs like *The Cry*, *Melancholy* and *Death Room*, which remain his best-known works.

The next few years were spent in extensive travel. Restlessness has always been a characteristic of Munch's personal life. He traveled from Berlin to Lübeck and Thüringen, from Paris to Italy, Paris and Berlin being his main headquarters. In Lübeck he stayed with Dr. Max Linde, a collector, who had written a book about him (1902) and commissioned him to paint portraits of his four children. Count Harry Kessler, considered one of Europe's notable collectors, commissioned a portrait in 1906. In the same year Munch designed settings for Ibsen's *Ghosts* at Reinhardt's Deutsches Theater and in 1907 finished his big *Frieze of Life*, which was never placed in a building but broken up in 1912 and distributed among the Kronprinzenpalais, Berlin, the Lübeck Museum, and the Rode Collection, Oslo.

During that time Munch became the center of a group of German painters who called themselves *die Brücke* (the Bridge) and acknowledged Munch as their source of inspiration. From this group "originated that much wider movement in modern German art known as Expressionism"—not to be confused with the French variety. It remained a most active influence in German art until it incurred the disapproval of Herr Hitler on his accession to power. At about that time, too, Munch's style of painting became marked by Neo-Impressionistic traits —intercrossing lines of pure color. On the whole, however, one may say that Munch has sacrificed tone to line. Huneker wrote of him: "He distorts, deforms, and with his strong fluid line modulates his material as he wills, but he never propounds puzzles in form, as do the rest of the experimentalists."

In the autumn of 1908 Munch became seriously ill. During his long stay in a sanatorium at Copenhagen he made many

Soibelman Syndicate

EDVARD MUNCH

Huneker, J. G.   Kubin, Munch, and
  Gauguin: Masters of Hallucination
  In Ivory Apes and Peacocks p222-
  39 1915
Linde, M.   Edvard Munch 1902
Read, H.   Art Now 1933

MUNDY, TALBOT CHETWYND Apr
23, 1879—Aug 5, 1940 Author; started to
write in 1909 after adventurous life in
India, British East Africa, Near East,
Egypt and Arabia; produced 28 novels,
innumerable short stories, radio scripts and
several motion picture scenarios; his tales
of intrigue and fictional adventures generally
included sudden death, slow torture and fighting men

TALBOT MUNDY

portraits of doctors and nurses and did a
series of animal lithographs. In 1912 he
decided to abandon town life for a while
and settled at Kragerö, where he painted
a fine set of murals for the aula of Oslo
University and executed many landscapes.
His animated studies of galloping horses
belong to that period. He moved to Moss
in 1913 and spent his summers at Hvitsten,
a seaside village on a fiord. His paintings
of that period deal with rural subjects. In
1918, apparently tired of being too far removed from city circles, he took a house at
Sköien, a suburb of Oslo. An important
commission came to him in 1922—for murals
in the Freia chocolate factory at Oslo.

During the last 30 years there have been
several important exhibitions of Munch's
work. Zurich showed him in 1922, Manheim
in 1926, and in 1927 there was a great show
of 244 works at the Kronprinzenpalais,
Berlin. He was first shown in an extensive
London exhibition as late as 1936. His
works have been bought by public collections chiefly in Nordic cities—Basel, Berlin,
Bergen, Bremen, Stockholm, Copenhagen,
etc.—although they can be seen also in
Moscow, Prague and Tokyo. In the United
States he is represented in Detroit.

Munch has been living quietly at Ekely
for some time now. A series of self-portraits done at various phases of his life
show him changing from an extraordinarily
handsome stripling to a majestic old Viking.
He is indeed Norway's "grand old man."

References

Fortnightly 96:336-46 Ag '11
Kunst 69:sup5 Ja '34 por
London Studio 13 (Studio 113):42-3
  Ja '37 il
Parnassus 9:21-4 Mr '37 il
Times [London] p14 O 22 '36

References

Author's and Writer's Who's Who
Who's Who in America

Obituaries

N Y Herald Tribune p10 Ag 6 '40
  por
N Y Times p20 Ag 6 '40
Sat R Lit 22:8 Ag 17 '40

MURPHY, FRANK Apr 13, 1893- United
States Supreme Court Justice
Address: Department of Justice, Washington,
D. C.

President Roosevelt's latest appointment
to the Supreme Court, his good friend and
ardent New-Deal supporter Frank Murphy,
took the oath of office February 5, 1940.
The naming of Murphy clinched a five-man
liberal majority control over the nine-man
tribunal: it is assumed that the new Justice,
according to behavior in his career to date,

FRANK MURPHY

will be watchful of the rights of minorities and legislate against all forms of racketeering, and at the same time can be counted upon to do his own thinking. In April 1940 he was the one to write the Supreme Court decisions invalidating antipicket laws. But since his appointment, observers have deduced that Frank Murphy cares not too much for his Court position, and liked much better his man-of-action job as Attorney General.

One of the most dynamic figures in contemporary political life, Frank Murphy has combined in his career the characteristics of a Blitzkrieg Galahad and a mailed-fist aesthete. Tall, lean, red-headed, with shaggy eyebrows that rival those of John L. Lewis and John N. Garner, he was born of Irish-American parents—John F. and Mary (Brennan) Murphy—at Harbor Beach, Michigan, April 13, 1893. As a boy his work in a local starch factory gave him a lasting hatred for "industrial slavery," conditioned him for his defense of the underprivileged. His mother was his idol. She gave him a *Bible* when he was graduated from the eighth grade which he carries with him wherever he goes, and on which he has taken more than one oath of office. She also got him to promise, at the age of 12, never to drink alcohol in any form. He never has. Neither does he use tobacco, and it has been said he is a vegetarian. His mother also taught him to love all races and peoples alike—and that teaching he also strictly followed.

Murphy worked his way through the University of Michigan Law School. It is said he rounded up backsliding Catholic students and got them to attend Mass; but his best friend at Ann Arbor was a Jew, and he wouldn't join a fraternity because this friend was barred from it. After his graduation he became a law clerk at $5 a week in Detroit,

teaching night school on the side. When the First World War started he enlisted in the army, was sent to France, promoted to the rank of captain there and sent with the army of occupation to Germany. At the close of the War he studied law in London and at the University of Dublin. Back in Detroit he became assistant United States Attorney and for three years never lost a case.

In 1924 he became Judge Murphy in Detroit, handling criminal cases. His political career really began when Senator Couzens backed him to run for Mayor of Detroit in 1930, and he was elected. Fortunately he was one of the early supporters of Franklin Roosevelt at the Chicago convention; like the elephant, Roosevelt never forgot. He appointed Murphy to the Philippines as Governor General in 1932. The up-and-coming Murphy did this job well, and on his return became in 1936 Michigan's Governor. Here he ran into a career crisis. At the very time of his inauguration the General Motors employees were holding the largest and most dangerous sitdown strike in the State's history. General Motors obtained a court order to compel the strikers to quit the company's plants. This order Murphy refused to enforce because he feared it might cause bloodshed. In a talk with union men he did, however, threaten to use troops. The strike was settled the next week, and Murphy for his stand won the adulation of liberals. But he lost the support of Michigan politicians (and of a good many workers also) and suffered a defeat in the 1938 election. It is now said by some that Murphy received his orders on handling the strike situation from Roosevelt. But he still blames his defeat in re-election on the work of the Dies (see sketch this issue) Committee, which accused him of being a Communist in cahoots with the CIO. Since this was an affront to his staunch Catholicism, Murphy remains bitter about it.

The setback, however, was a stepup: it was Roosevelt's turn to come to the aid of Murphy. Of four posts offered him, he chose that of Attorney General, which Homer Cummings was quitting. Just the thing for a born crusading spirit, the position suited Murphy exactly. Many opposed the appointment on account of his "strike condoning," but apparently the Democrats needed someone to offset the works and growing popularity of Republican racket-buster Thomas Dewey (see sketch this issue). Murphy went immediately into gang-smashing action. He forbade his subordinates to make press statements regarding this action, which cut off J. Edgar Hoover (see sketch this issue) from an adoring public. But Murphy soon began making airplane raids around the country, crashing down on local political racketeering—and Hoover was with him, very much in the picture again. The ruthless war was on; and among those brought down during Murphy's crusade were Kansas City's Boss Pendergast. Later he indicted Philadelphia's Moe Annenberg for income tax evasion, prosecuted Federal Judge Martin Manton for "selling justice" in Manhattan, proceeded against Louis (Lepke) Buchalter and other lesser big shots. All in all, Murphy's idealism manifested itself in a fairly thorough cleanup. One of his last acts as Attorney General was to have 16 alleged Communists and fellow-travelers indicted in Detroit for having recruited volunteers for Loyalist Spain. Liberals throughout the country protested. It was Murphy's successor, Robert Jackson (see sketch this issue), who ordered dismissal of the indictments. But Earl Browder, general secretary of the Communist Party, was found guilty of a passport fraud, and scores of indictments were made against union labor leaders.

Not in 15 years had the Department of Justice been so active as under Murphy. It is small wonder, observers feel, that Murphy does not relish the comparatively cloistered atmosphere of the Supreme Court Bench. But for all his delight in racket-smashing, Murphy's manner is quiet, his speech soft, unctuous. His deliberate, soft "purr" at first irritated the hard-boiled Washington newspapermen, who called him "Holy Joe, the Airedale Angora." But because of their newsiness and calm courtesy, Murphy's press conferences soon became second in popularity in Washington to the President's. His sister, Mrs. Margaret Teahan, is still kept busy denying that she ever said, "he looks more like Jesus every day."

Although his pious upbringing and his asceticism are well publicized (too well, his best friends think), men who meet Murphy for the first time are said to be astonished: that a man could actually be so good seems incredible, almost unhealthy. It is a goodness bolstered by an earnest lack of humor. He says solemnly that he seldom reads novels because "no novel could be so exciting as my life." But he likes to dance, he is the fashion plate of the Administration, and can be most charming to women, although he is still unmarried.

Thomas Corcoran (see sketch this issue) says Murphy is the modern counterpart of the fighting abbots of the Middle Ages. Frank Murphy's own motto is: "Speak softly and hit hard." What he dislikes most is to have political phrase-mongers call him "New Deal Glamour Boy No. 1." Of his own aspirations he recently said: "I should like to belong to that small company of public servants and others who are content to do some of the homely and modest tasks of perfecting integrity in government and making government more efficient and orderly."

References

> Commonweal 29:312 Ja 13 '39; 31:275 Ja 19 '40

Liberty 17:25-7 Mr 2 '40 por
Lit Digest 1:7 Ag 14 '37
New Repub 99:279 Jl 12 '39
Newsweek 15:60 Ja 15 '40
Read Digest 35:77-9 S '39
Scholastic 35:9 Ja 15 '40 por (p10)
Time 33:13 Ja 9 '39 por; 33:9 Ja 23 '39 por; 34:14-17 Ag 28 '39 pors; 35:14 F 26 '40 por
American Catholic Who's Who
Who's Who in America
Who's Who in Law

MURPHY, FREDERICK E. Dec 5, 1872 —Feb 14, 1940 Publisher of the *Tribune* newspapers of Minneapolis; a director of the Associated Press

References

> R of Rs 93:45-6 F '36
> American Catholic Who's Who
> Who's Who in America 1938-39

Obituaries

> N Y Herald Tribune p18 F 15 '40 por
> N Y Sun p21 F 14 '40 por
> N Y World-Telegram p36 F 14 '40

MURRAY, AUGUSTUS TABER Oct 29, 1866—Mar 8, 1940 Professor of classical

Boye

AUGUSTUS T. MURRAY

literature at Stanford University; translator of Greek; author of many textbooks and articles

References

> Who's Who in America

(Continued next page)

MURRAY, AUGUSTUS TABER—*Cont.*

Obituaries

N Y Herald Tribune p40 Mr 10 '40
  por
N Y Times p48 Mr 10 '40 por

MYERS, JEROME   Mar 20, 1867—June 19,
1940 American artist, one of the first to
interpret on canvas New York street scenes;
received many awards from the National
Academy; one of the initiators of historic
New York Armory Show in 1913; on his
seventy-third birthday published his autobiography, *Artist in Manhattan*

References

Art Digest 14:31 Mr 15 '40
Myers, J. Artist in Manhattan 1940
Who's Who in America
Who's Who in American Art

Obituaries

N Y Herald Tribune p20 Je 20 '40 por
N Y Times p23 Je 20 '40 por
Pub W 138:38 Jl 6 '40

MYSORE, MAHARAJA OF   *See* Wadiyar, S. K.

NAVARRO, MARY DE   July 28, 1859—
May 29, 1940 Actress; widow of Antonio
Fernando de Navarro; was one of the
most widely known actresses of her day;
retired in 1890 at the height of her career

References

Arts & Dec 22:24-5 Mr '25 il; 46:
  12-15 Mr '37 il por
House B 63:281-5 Mr '28 il
Ladies' H J 40:15 N '23
Lit Digest 60:24-5 Ja 11 '19 (Cond.
  from Scrib Mag 65:1-13 Ja '19)
Pict R 25:22 Je '24
Sat Eve Post 199:38 F 26 '27 por;
  194:15 Mr 11 '22
Scrib Mag 65:1-13 Ja '19
Sobel, B. ed. Theatre Handbook 1940
Who's Who in America
Who's Who in the Theatre

Obituaries

N Y Herald Tribune p14 My 30 '40
N Y Times p17 My 30 '40 pors
Time 35:88 Je 10 '40

NEAL, HERBERT VINCENT   Apr 3,
1869—Feb 21, 1940 Biologist; former dean
of Tufts College Graduate School; authority
on the nervous system; author of several
books on anatomy

HERBERT V. NEAL

References

American Men of Science
Who's Who in America

Obituaries

Boston Transcript p7 F 23 '40

NEUMANN, HEINRICH   (noi'män, hïn'-
rikh) June 16, 1864—Nov 6, 1939 Austrian
ear, nose and throat specialist

References

N Y Times p4 Mr 15 '38; p7 Jl 8 '38
International Who's Who

Obituaries

N Y Herald Tribune p22 N 7 '39
N Y Times p28 N 7 '39
Time 34:79 N 20 '39

**NEWALL, SIR CYRIL LOUIS NOR-
TON** Feb 15, 1886- Newly-appointed Gov-
ernor General of New Zealand; Marshal of
R. A. F.

December 1940 Bulletin: In February 1941
Sir Cyril Newall will take up his post as
Governor General of New Zealand. He
will relinquish the position of chief of
the air staff of Great Britain to Sir
Charles F. A. Portal. He will be promoted to Marshall of the R. A. F.

From August issue:

With the British left to face alone the
full fury of the totalitarian states it seems
safe to say that no head in this world bears
a more terrible weight of responsibility than
that of Sir Cyril Newall. For the moment
the British Army must take a secondary
position in the defensive system while the
brunt of the work must be borne by the
Navy and by the Royal Air Force. And

the Air Force must not only repel bombers and carry on with the protection of shipping, but repeatedly attack military objectives in German territory. Luckily for Britain, the head that has to bear this load is a cool one, well supplied with brains of proven quality.

Newall is little-known to the British general public. There are almost no "personality stories" about him, except that he is an enthusiastic gardener, for he shuns publicity and is reputedly difficult to approach. His record, however, shows him to be not only a bold and resourceful officer but a far-sighted administrator who has devoted the whole of his adult life to the adaptation of flying to warfare.

Born at Mussoorie, United Provinces, India, he is the son of the late Lieutenant Colonel William Potter Newall, of the Indian Artillery. As with most English boys born in India, he was sent home for his education, going to Bedford School and to the Royal Military College, Sandhurst. In the summer of 1905 he was gazetted to the Royal Warwickshire Regiment as second lieutenant and returned to India for service. Some three years later he had his first experience under fire, in a minor frontier brush with the Zakka Khels tribesmen. In September 1909 he was raised to lieutenant and transferred to the 2nd Gurkha Rifles.

Toward the end of 1910 the British and Colonial Aeroplane Company arranged a flying demonstration in India. The young subaltern saw immense possibilities for the use of airplanes in war; and when he went home on leave the following summer spent almost his whole furlough learning to fly. Having no means but his pay, he had to raise the funds for his instruction from his lawyer. In those days of canvas "box-kites" and 50-horsepower engines, to fly at all was a great adventure, and there were heavy casualties among learners; but without mishap Newall duly qualified from the Bristol School of Aviation and received Royal Aero Club certificate No. 144.

Returning to India at the end of 1911, Newall could think and talk of nothing but aviation. "Flying had gone to his head like champagne," said a brother officer. He badgered his superiors persistently until at last they sent him back to Upavon, Wiltshire in 1913 to take a special course in flying instruction. On the completion of this he went back once more to India, won promotion to the rank of captain, and transferred to the Sirmoor Rifles.

When the War broke out in 1914, Newall at once took ship for England to serve in the newly-formed Royal Flying Corps. He was appointed a flight commander and carried out the organization of a squadron from very puny resources in men and material. During 1915 he rose quickly to be squadron commander and wing commander and by September 6th of that year had the No. 12 Squadron in France ready for the Battle of Loos.

SIR CYRIL NEWALL

In January 1916 Newall won his first decoration for an act of great gallantry. At St. Omer a warehouse containing some 2,000 bombs caught fire while the door was locked. With the help of three others Newall first poured water through a hole made by the flames; and then, when the key was obtained, went inside and succeeded in putting out the fire, even though incendiary bombs were furiously burning and many of the wooden cases were charred to a cinder. Since military decorations may be awarded only for action in the face of the enemy Newall was awarded the Albert Medal of the First Class.

Newall did little or no actual flying in France. His skill in organization and in training was far too valuable for that risk to be taken; but he spent much of the War period at the front. In February 1916 he was sent back to England to help Brigadier General Salmond with a scheme for the better training of pilots. At the end of the year he was in France again in command of the Ninth Wing; and early in 1917 he organized some of the earliest successful low-flying attacks on infantry.

The frequent raids on London had by this time determined the British High Command to institute reprisals against German industrial targets. The 41st (Bombing) Wing was formed for that purpose, with Newall in charge. From October 1917 to June 1918 it carried out 57 raids on such towns as Karlsruhe, Mannheim, Cologne, Mainz, Stuttgart, Coblenz, Thionville and Saarbrücken. Whether it was this or the improvement of antiaircraft measures that caused the Germans to abandon air attacks on English open towns is not clear, but they were abandoned from May 1918 to the end of the War.

NEWALL, SIR CYRIL—*Continued*

At the end of 1917 Newall became a brigade commander with the temporary rank of brigadier general and as commanding officer of the Eighth Brigade did splendid work under Sir Hugh Trenchard. His War honors comprised three mentions in dispatches, the C. M. G., the military C. B. E., the Belgian Croix de Guerre and the rank of officer in the French Légion d'Honneur, the Italian Order of the Crown and the Belgian Order of Leopold.

Although on August 1, 1919 Newall reverted to rank of wing commander on taking up a permanent commission in the Royal Air Force, he became a group captain a week later and was made deputy director of personnel at the Air Ministry. This post gave good scope for his already well-tried ability in the organization of large-scale training schemes, and he had much to do with the establishment of the R. A. F. Cadet College at Cranwell in 1920, the Staff College at Andover in 1922 and the Halton School of Technical Training for Boys, which insures that all air mechanics shall become highly trained craftsmen sure of ready absorption into industry when their period of service is over. From June 1923 until the end of 1924 Newall acted as Air A. D. C. to the King, after which he was promoted to air commodore and placed in charge of the Special Reserve and the Auxiliary Air Force —the latter a body of "week-end" airmen, some of whom have already rendered distinguished service in the present War.

For the first two months of 1926 Newall was on special duty with the League of Nations Disarmament Committee and shortly afterward became director of Operations and Intelligence and deputy chief of the air staff at the Air Ministry. At the beginning of 1930 he was raised to the rank of Air Vice-Marshal and co-opted as an additional member of the Air Council. There followed a period of eight months in command of the Wessex bombing area, which allowed of the fullest study of home defense problems, and some three years in charge of the Middle East command.

Recent years have seen the rapid continuance of Newall's steady rise in rank and responsibility. In January 1935 he was appointed again to the Air Council, as Air Member for Supply and Organization. By July he was Air Marshal; by April 1937 he was Air Chief Marshal, and in September of that year he became Chief of the Air Staff. He has thus had about four years before the outbreak of war in which to work out a complete system of defense for the British Isles. The balloon barrages and the blackout (on the rigorous observance of which he has insisted, in spite of the appalling automobile casualties which have ensued) are parts, and essential parts, of this defensive system; so are the escorts for convoys and the "security patrols" in the neighborhood of Norderney and Sylt.

Newall also believes in vigorous attack as a concomitant of defense and day after day there comes news of night attacks by the R. A. F. on enemy oil storage tanks and railroad yards with disastrous effects. Newall's cultivation of individuality rather than uniformity in his officers seems to have led to their fighting with brains as well as with bombs and machine guns.

Newall has a real and close link with the United States in that he married Olive Tennyson Foster, daughter of Mrs. Francis Stores Eaton, of Boston, Massachusetts. They have a boy and two girls. Newall is of medium height and build, ruddy of complexion, gray-haired. It is recorded that when Sir Kingsley Wood (see sketch this issue) was Air Minister, Newall once flashed a torch from the Ministry steps to guide him as he left his car in the blackout. Sir Cyril just escaped a reprimand from an air raid warden!

The "Sir" came about in June 1935, when Newall was created a Knight Commander of the Order of the Bath. He has since gone up a step in the Order, to Knight Grand Commander.

References

Listener N 16 '39
Liv Age 357:247-51 N '39
Manchester Guardian S 11 '39
Observer O 29 '39
Scholastic 35:20S N 6 '39 por
Time 33:23 Ap 24 '39 por
Pollard, A. O. Royal Air Force p9-45 1939
Tuohy, F. Twelve Lances for Liberty p185-202 1940
Who's Who

NEWTON, ALFRED EDWARD Aug 26, 1863—Sept 29, 1940 Noted bibliophile; essayist; world's leading authority on Dr. Samuel Johnson; had library of 10,000 volumes; owned manuscript of Hardy's *Far From the Madding Crowd* and Lamb's *Dream Children*; books were his avocation; vocation was the electrical manufacturing field in which he worked for 36 years; wrote many articles and books including *The Amenities of Book Collecting and Kindred Affinities*, which sold 30,000 copies; in 1935 and 1936 was the Rosenbach lecture fellow in bibliography at the University of Pennsylvania

References

Pub W 138:1497 O 12 '40
Scholastic 25:6 D 15 '34 por
Elkins, W. M. Eddie Newton's Ride pam 1934
Kunitz, S. J. ed. Living Authors 1937
Sargent, G. H. Busted Bibliophile and His Books 1928
Sargent, G. H. Writings of A. Edward Newton 1927
Who's Who in America

A. EDWARD NEWTON

Obituaries

N Y Times p17 S 30 '40 por
N Y World-Telegram p24 S 30 '40
Pub W 138:1414-97 O 12 '40

NICOLSON, MARJORIE HOPE Feb 18, 1894- Educator

Address: Columbia University, New York City

For a woman who believes that it is "easily possible to be a scholar and a gentleman, but it is hard to be a scholar and a lady," Marjorie Hope Nicolson has done rather well along both lines. She has been nominated president of the United Chapters of Phi Beta Kappa, and is the first woman to head the distinguished honorary scholastic fraternity since it was founded at William and Mary College in 1776. The first of the Greek letter societies, Phi Beta Kappa was originally social and secret, but evolved into the nation's No. 1 honorary society, choosing its members on the basis of scholastic merit.

Since nomination is equivalent to election, in September 1940 Dean Nicholson became the head of the 132 chapters of Phi Beta Kappa, and leader of the army of 86,000 members who wear the gold keys of academic wisdom. She heads a group that includes such notables as Franklin D. Roosevelt, Henry L. Stimson (see sketch this issue), Bruce Barton, John D. Rockefeller Jr., Charles Evans Hughes and Pearl Buck, and is composed of about one-third women and two-thirds men.

In an interview following her nomination as president of Phi Beta Kappa, Dean Nicolson explained that women's failure to find high places in music, mathematics, philosophy and religion boiled down to the fact that it was hard for them to be both

scholars and ladies—"they have no wives to look after social contacts and to perform the drudgery for them."

And, opined Miss Nicolson, an absent-minded professor may be picturesque, but a lady with unkempt hair and undarned stockings is definitely not picturesque. But darning stockings takes time from more important work.

If Dean Nicolson has had to put in the usual allotment of time on the equivalent of darning stockings, she has nevertheless found time to attain a full measure of scholastic honors. She holds honorary degrees from colleges, has written and edited half a dozen books, and has contributed to philosophical and literary periodicals in addition to her teaching.

Yet she is in no sense a blue stocking. At 45 she has a full, winsome face, blue eyes and dark auburn hair, and a youthful spirit undulled by 26 years of teaching. She likes to read detective stories and "sweet love tales" for relaxation, and her conversation ranges from "Galileo to Gulliver, from Milton to the movies." Her speech before 2,000 best brains of the country at the second annual dinner of the United Chapters of Phi Beta Kappa in New York, when she appeared as the body's presidential nominee, was witty and non-academic.

Her contention that "too little attention to duty makes some men playboys, all work and no play make Jill a dull girl" has kept her from falling into the dull Jill class. She agrees, however, that women do not carry their learning lightly.

The daughter of Charles Butler and Lissie Hope (Morris) Nicolson, she was born in Yonkers, New York, February 18, 1894, and received her early education in Halifax. She attended the University of Michigan, received her B. A. degree there in 1914, and started her teaching career the same year at Sagiversity during this period. In 1926 she taught in the Detroit public schools, and took her master's degree at the University of Michigan. She took her Ph. D. at Yale University in 1920.

After receiving her doctor's degree at Yale, she went to the University of Minnesota as instructor of English, later becoming assistant professor. She left in 1923 to become assistant professor at Goucher College and remained there until 1926, taking graduate work at Johns Hopkins University during this period. In 1926 she won a Guggenheim Fellowship, and spent a year in Europe, browsing in libraries and discovering old letters and pictures. On her return to this country Miss Nicolson was appointed associate professor of English at Smith College, and in 1929 was appointed professor and dean.

Dean Nicolson holds an honorary degree of Doctor of Letters from Mt. Holyoke College awarded in 1933, and another Litt. D. from the University of Michigan, awarded in 1937. She has served as a member of the committee on awards of the

MARJORIE HOPE NICOLSON

John Simon Guggenheim Foundation from 1930 to 1935 and again from 1936 to 1937; as vice-president of the Modern Language Association of America in 1937 and 1938; and as senator and vice-president of the Phi Beta Kappa.

Her elevation to the presidency of Phi Beta Kappa is not her first trail blazing for women. She was the first woman to win the John Addison Porter Prize awarded by Yale University for original work. She received that award in 1930, and, in 1938 one of her pupils was the second woman ever to receive it.

Dean Nicolson was also the first woman to hold the office of vice-president of the Modern Language Association of America. The organization which gives recognition for distinguished scholarship in English and modern languages has never had a woman president.

She will also be the first woman to hold a full professorship on Columbia University's graduate faculty when she takes up her duties there in February 1941. Her appointment as professor of English was announced by Nicholas Murray Butler (see sketch this issue) in May 1940.

In addition to her teaching and research she has had another occupation, a sideline she engaged in during the early days of her career. It was newspaper work. She grew up in a newspaper family. Her father was editor in chief of the Detroit *Free Press* during the First World War, and later Washington correspondent for the paper. Dean Nicolson got her first newspaper experience writing dramatic reviews for the Detroit *Free Press*. Later she worked with her father in his Washington Bureau, once, during the Harding Administration, running the entire office when her father was ill for three months.

But newspaper work was merely a sideline. Teaching and research have always remained her first loves. She considers it fun to go to the library and "work like a dog." Her particular field of research has been in English literature, primarily the 17th century, and the influence of science on literature.

Her books include: *The Art of Description* (1926); *Conway Letters* (1930); *The Microscope and English Imagination* (1935); and *World in the Moon* (1937). She has edited *Selections from Shelley and Keats* (1923) and *Selections from Tennyson* (1923). In addition she has contributed to various scientific and philosophical periodicals, and to the *Atlantic Monthly* and the *Yale Review*.

References

N Y Times VII p8+ Mr 17 '40 por; p21 My 8 '40
Newsweek 15:35 Mr 4 '40 por
Sch & Soc 51:639 My 18 '40
Springf'd Republican p2E F 18 '40

American Women
Who's Who in America

NIJINSKY, WASLAW (nē-jĭn'skĭ väs'läf) Feb 28, 1890- Dancer
Address: c/o Emilia Markus, Budapest, Hungary

A mild, shy, bald-headed man whose reputation "as the supreme male dancer" once jammed theatres was in the summer of 1940 at the home of his mother-in-law in Budapest waiting for permission to come to the United States to continue his treatments for dementia praecox. Nearly 20 years ago Vaslav (as his first name is usually translated) Nijinsky was pronounced incurably insane and has spent most of the years since in a Swiss sanatorium. Two years ago insulin shock treatments brought marked improvement and enabled Nijinsky to leave the sanatorium and live a more normal existence in Adelboden, Switzerland. Dr. Manfred Sakel, who administered the insulin, is now in New York City, and the Nijinskys wish to follow him for further treatment.

Madame Nijinsky has sold the motion picture and play rights to *Nijinsky* (her account of their lives, published in 1934) to pay the cost of the trip; the United States Labor Department has indicated that Mr. Nijinsky would not be barred because of insanity; a former associate, Mr. Anatole Bourman, now conducting a dancing school in Hartford, Connecticut, has offered the invalid a home and has offered to finance medical treatment here. But on May 9, 1940 the American Consulate at Zurich refused a six months' visitor's visa because the spread of the war might prevent Nijinsky's return to Europe. The Washington authorities were reported on July 28 to be reviewing the case, but a visa was finally refused.

Vaslav Fomitch Nijinsky was born at Kiev, South Russia on the 28th of February,

1890. The date is agreed upon, but not the profession of his parents. Madame Nijinsky has described his parents as of Polish origin: his mother Eleanora (Bereda) Nijinsky was a former student of the Imperial School of Ballet in Warsaw and danced up to within an hour of the birth of Vaslav, her second son. His father, Thomas Nijinsky, was a "first-rate exponent of classical ballet and also an excellent character dancer. His grandparents were dancers before them."

Others report that the parents were connected with the circus and that an uncle still works in "some circus show or other." The exponents of the latter belief explain Nijinsky's extraordinary physical gifts by this circus lineage: "the generations of acrobats back of him. His lightness which was beyond all technique, his renowned elevation ... his natural and inherent physical gifts were due to and sprang from the circus."

A delicate child, "awkward, temperamentally backward and slow thinking," Vaslav was admitted to the Imperial School in St. Petersburg when he was nine. His first teacher, Nicholas Legat, had noticed the extraordinary development of the muscles of his legs and his ability to jump. At the school Nijinsky literally leaped into fame. In his leap he didn't seem to jump, but to rise effortlessly, describe a long parabola of flight and finally descend slowly and lightly to the ground. He is said to have twice done 10 *entrechats,* not on the stage, but in his classroom. Few living dancers can do eight, and when more than four are done they are rarely cleanly performed.

In 1907 Nijinsky made his debut in Mozart's *Don Juan* at the Maryinsky Theatre, St. Petersburg. Still a pupil, he "eclipsed other members of the ballet, including his teachers." At his graduation performance in May 1908 he danced a *pas de deux* with Ludmilla Schoolar in a ballet arranged by Fokine, and after graduating became a partner of Mathilda Kchessinskaia, sometimes dancing as the soloist, although he was only a member of the *corps de ballet.*

During his first season with the Imperial Ballet he met Serge Diaghilev, and their acquaintance continued over a long period of both enmity and friendship. Two years later Nijinsky was dismissed from the ballet for wearing an improper costume in the presence of the Dowager Empress. Responsibility for this accident has been attributed to Diaghilev, who, it is said, "wished to assume full control of Nijinsky's career." Whether or not the incident was planned it had that result, and was the cause of the establishment of the Diaghilev Ballet and of bringing Nijinsky to the Western world.

The Diaghilev Ballet opened in Paris in 1911. One of Nijinsky's principal rôles was in *Le Spectre de la Rose,* in which he "not only was as light as a rose petal itself, but brought to it something of the gentleness of a moonlit night," and it created quite a stir. A favorite

Wide World

WASLAW NIJINSKY

portrayal of Nijinsky's was that of *Petrouchka,* a tragic puppet with the soul of a man, which revealed as much acting as dancing ability. Nijinsky's first composition as a choreographer, to Debussy's *L'Après-Midi d'un Faune,* was an immediate success and was followed by *Jeux* and Stravinsky's (see sketch this issue) *Le Sacre du Printemps.*

Nijinsky lived for his work. "In the theatre he was untiring; never ceasing to work; practicing, practicing, on the stage, in the rehearsal room, wherever he could find space." Off the stage he presented a colorless figure: "pale face, high cheekbones, small and slightly Mongol eyes, with thin hair nondescript in color—taciturn, glum and a little bewildered." As soon as he approached the stage he became the character he was to portray and his concentration upon his rôle was so intense that he seemed to walk in a dream.

In the summer of 1913 the Diaghilev Ballet sailed for a tour of South America, leaving its director in Europe. It was the first time Nijinsky had been separated from Diaghilev since the beginning of their association. The director had exercised a "tremendous influence over the dancer and protected him from all the unpleasantness of life; he had sincerely tried to educate him and to develop the cultural side of his existence; but he had also monopolized him to an abnormal degree." Once free of the immediate presence of Diaghilev, Nijinsky proceeded to do the one thing which destroyed their friendship and all hope of future collaboration between them. On September 10, 1913, in Buenos Aires, he married Romola de Pulszky. She was the daughter of Emilia Markus, a famous Hungarian actress, and had studied and joined the ballet for the express purpose of following Nijinsky, with whom she was infatu-

NIJINSKY, WASLAW—*Continued*

ated. (Their daughter, Kyra, born in 1914, has achieved some distinction as a dancer.)

Diaghilev was exceedingly displeased and dismissed Nijinsky by cable. When he returned to Europe Nijinsky organized a small troupe and secured an engagement at the Palace Theatre in London. But he had small talent for business affairs, and in spite of a weekly salary of $5,000 was forced to close in two weeks.

Internment in an Austrian prison camp at the beginning of the First World War prevented him from joining the first American tour of the Diaghilev Ballet after he and Diaghilev had settled their quarrel. "Under prison surveillance he fretted himself ill because he could not dance; planned ballets, worked on an intricate system of dance notation, to help him keep his balance." In 1916, largely through the efforts of Diaghilev, he was released and came to America. He made his American debut at the Metropolitan Opera House.

During his tour of North and South America the persecution complex which had clouded his actions became intensified by financial worries. Nijinsky made his last appearance on the stage in Montevideo at a benefit performance of *Les Sylphides*. Returned to Europe and making his home at St. Moritz, Nijinsky was planning a new system of dance notation when his illness became acute and it was necessary to place him in a sanatorium. An exhibition of his drawings, paintings, water colors and pastels done while in the institution was presented by the London Group Theatre in 1937 to raise funds for the Nijinsky Foundation.

References

N Y Herald Tribune p15 Ap 23 '40 por; p2 Jl 28 '40
N Y Sun p5 May 9 '40

Beaumont, C. W. Vaslav Nijinsky *In* Complete Book of Ballets p648-55 1938
Bourman, A. and Lyman, D. Tragedy of Nijinsky 1936
Deakin, I. Vaslav Fomitch Nijinsky *In* Ballet Profile p41-52 1936
Haskell, A. L. Diaghileff 1935
Liven, P. A. Nijinsky *In* The Birth of Ballets-Russes p315-26 1936
Moore, L. Vaslav Nijinsky *In* Artists of the Dance p193-202 1938
Nijinsky, R. Nijinsky 1934

NIPKOW, PAUL GOTTLIEB (nĭp′kō)

Aug 22, 1850—Aug 24, 1940 German television pioneer whose "Nipkow Disk" invented in 1884 was indispensable in the production of television until a few years ago when it was superseded by other devices; in 1934 received public recognition when made honorary president of the German Television Society; died in Berlin, Germany

PAUL G. NIPKOW

References
Wer ist's?

Obituaries
N Y Herald Tribune p30 Ag 25 '40
N Y Times p35 Ag 25 '40

NIXON, LEWIS

Apr 7, 1861—Sept 23, 1940 Naval designer; outstanding figure in the designing of scores of warships, among them the *Oregon, Indiana* and *Massachusetts*; before the First World War was asked by the former Czar of Russia to design the ships in the Russian Navy; for a brief period at the turn of the century was the leader of Tammany Hall in New York City, succeeding Richard Crocker; was head of the Nixon Nitration Company and the Raritan Sand Company of New Jersey

References
Who's Who in America
Who's Who in Commerce and Industry

Obituaries
N Y Herald Tribune p18 S 24 '40 por
N Y Times p23 S 24 '40

NORDMANN, CHARLES

1881—Nov 14, 1940 Astronomer; authority on star photometry; scientific writer for French publications; amused United States in 1923 by claiming minds of New York City dwellers suffered from excessive exposure to electric waves; among scientific posts, director of Paris Observatory

References
Tout Paris 1939

Obituaries
N Y Herald Tribune p16 N 15 '40

NORMAN, MONTAGU Sept 6, 1871-
Governor of the Bank of England

Address: b. 37 Grace-Church St, London, England; h. Thorpe Lodge, Campden Hill, W. 8, Kensington, England

No one could look and act less like the conventional idea of a great financier and banker than Montagu Norman, Governor of the Bank of England since 1920. There's nothing about him of the large, clean-shaven, heavy-jowled, portly, brusque and tough figure occupied only with money that the movies have made recognizable to most Americans. Instead, he is like nothing so much as a Velásquez portrait, with his thin, sensitive hands, his high forehead, his keen, slightly ironical eyes and his well-trimmed, pointed, white beard. Nor does Mr. Norman drive up to his bank in a long black limousine. As often as not he uses the subway. What is more, he is an art connoisseur whose home is on Campden Hill, Kensington, where many of England's famous artists live, and whose close friend is Augustus John, the portrait painter.

His manner is one of distinguished courtesy, not only when he deals with individuals but when he is carrying out matters of large policy. The late Lord Snowden, a Socialist, had a high opinion of him. "I never hear uninformed remarks about the callousness of international finance," he said, "but I think of the injustice done through ignorance to the high and unselfish motives of the Governor of the Bank. No man with great responsibilities ever tried more faithfully to discharge them with the single aim of promoting national and international well-being. It took but a short acquaintance with Mr. Norman to know that his external appearance was the bodily expression of one of the kindliest natures and most sympathetic hearts it has been my privilege to know."

At the same time, however, because of his position which has given him a hand in almost every major European financial crisis of the past two decades and because of his passion for privacy, a large body of legend has grown up around Montagu Norman. A quip once current in banking circles said that Mr. Norman enters his office unseen, "disguised as a Bank of England note." Everyone does not share Lord Snowden's unreserved admiration. Hugh Dalton, Under-Secretary for Foreign Affairs in the second Labor government, once complained that Norman pursued a foreign policy of his own based on the premise that "unless Germany is economically strong and prosperous, it is impossible to balance the one-sided political strength of France on the Continent." Harold Laski thinks that England has been conquered not once, but twice, by the "Normans," and chafes under the yoke.

The Bank of England, which he heads, is a private body which belongs to the owners of stock, its management in the hands of a governor, a deputy governor

MONTAGU NORMAN

and a court of directors. Although it is not controlled by the British government, it is banker to the government; it is the center for the issue of bank notes, it handles the daily operations of the government, manages its stocks and bonds, issues new government loans and advises the government on problems in which public policy is related to business and finance.

For his tremendously important position Montagu Collet Norman is fitted by background and experience. He was born at Moor Place, Much Hadham in Hertfordshire, the eldest son of the late F. H. Norman, a partner in the banking house of Martin's, a powerful and independent concern. His grandfather, George Warde Norman, had been a director of Brown, Shipley and Company, and of the Bank of England, and his grandmother had been a Miss Stone, daughter of a partner in Stone and Martin, bankers. Montagu was sent to Eton College and from there went to King's College, Cambridge. He stayed only a year and left without a degree, though he has since been given an honorary one.

Out of the university, Norman joined the firm of Brown, Shipley and Company and spent some time in America with their associated house, Brown Brothers (now Brown Brothers, Harrison and Company) of New York and Philadelphia. In 1900 he was made a director of the firm. He took a leave of absence that same year to fight in the Boer War, in which he was mentioned in dispatches and won the Distinguished Service Order and the Queen's Medal with four clasps.

There is an informal understanding that a director of Brown, Shipley should be on the board of the Bank of England, and Norman was elected to it in 1907. Eight years later he left the private banking

NORMAN, MONTAGU—*Continued*

house to become deputy governor of the Bank of England, serving under Lord Cunliffe. When Cunliffe died in 1920 Norman was elected to the governorship. Before his election it was customary to elect a new governor every two years, but Montagu Norman has remained in office for twenty years, his last unopposed reappointment being in April 1940.

Soon after the First World War Mr. Norman put England back on the gold standard and has argued strongly for it. Since England left the gold standard in 1931 (it is reported that he fainted when it did), his activities have done much to prevent inflation. Although there is disagreement about the measures which have been taken under his régime, there is no difference of opinion as to his intelligence and banking knowledge. In 1930 Mr. Norman became a director of the Bank for International Settlements.

Montagu Norman remained a bachelor until quite late in life. In 1933 he married Priscilla, daughter of the late Major Robert Reyntiens of the Belgian Artillery and Lady Alice Josephine, daughter of the seventh Earl of Abingdon.

References

Eur Nouv 21:830 Ag 6 '38
Liv Age 356:225-8 My '39
N Y Times p37 Ap 3 '40 por
Strand Mag 96:628-36 Ap '39 pors
Einzig, P. Mr. Montagu Norman's Policy *In* Bankers, Statesmen and Economists p35-46 1935
Einzig, P. Montagu Norman 1932
Gunther, J. Men of Whitehall *In* Inside Europe p334-54 1940
Hargrave, J. Professor Skinner, Alias Montagu Norman 1939
Kircher, R. McKenna to Banbury *In* Engländer p257-67 1928
Who's Who
Who's Who in Commerce and Industry

NORRIS, HENRY HUTCHINSON Apr 26, 1873—Apr 14, 1940 Electric transit engineer; personnel manager for the Boston Elevated Railroad; former head of the electrical engineering department at Cornell University

References

American Men of Science
Who's Who in America
Who's Who in Engineering

Obituaries

N Y Herald Tribune p12 Ap 15 '40

NORRIS, JAMES FLACK Jan 20, 1871— Aug 3, 1940 Professor of organic chemistry at Massachusetts Institute of Technology; director of its organic research laboratory; internationally known in his field; **former**

president of the American Chemical Society; was an expert during the First World War on poison gas and chemical research in England; elected an honorary member of the Royal Institute in London in 1925; author of many books and papers on chemistry

JAMES FLACK NORRIS

References

American Men of Science
Chemical Who's Who
Who's Who in America

Obituaries

N Y Herald Tribune p10 Ag 5 '40 por
N Y Times p13 Ag 5 '40 por

NORTHRUP, EDWIN FITCH Feb 23, 1866—Apr 29, 1940 Electro-thermic engineer; holder of 104 patents on high-temperature measurement; professor of physics at Princeton from 1910 to 1919; officer and adviser of Ajax Electro-Thermic Corporation for 20 years

References

American Men of Science
Who's Who in America
Who's Who in Engineering

Obituaries

N Y Herald Tribune p18 My 2 '40
N Y Times p24 My 2 '40

NOVOTNA, JARMILA (nō-vät'nä jarmě'lä) Opera singer

Address: c/o The Metropolitan Opera Co, Broadway and 39th St, New York City

A beautiful young Czech singer, as Violetta in *La Traviata,* received an ovation at New York's Metropolitan Opera House

February 7, 1940. Critics acclaimed her the greatest Violetta in 20 years. In addition to her beauty and the excellence of her voice, the young soprano also set a new standard for acting at the Metropolitan.

Born in Prague, the daughter of a banker, Jarmila Novotna studied music privately for a few years, since she was too young to study at the Conservatory in Prague. At 17 she made her debut in *La Traviata*. In her first year at the National Opera House of her native Prague, her repertory included the heroine rôles of *Eugene Onegin, The Magic Flute, The Barber of Seville* and *La Bohème,* all sung in Czech, although she later sang some of these rôles in both Italian and German.

Among her first successes was the title rôle of *The Bartered Bride,* a leading favorite in Bohemia and in Vienna, where during one season she sang Marie to the Hans of Richard Tauber. It is this part which Edward Johnson of the Metropolitan assigned to her for the 1939 to 1940 season's revival in German. She has also sung *The Bartered Bride* in a European film version, although she never saw the finished product of her work. In the film the hero was transformed from a farmer's son to a postilion, riding from town to town; otherwise Smetana's opera was treated with respect.

The young soprano soon extended her career beyond her native country. Franz Schalk advised her to continue her education in Milan, where she worked with Tenaglia. Her Italian debut was as Gilda in *Rigoletto,* singing opposite Lauri Volpi, in Verona. She was later introduced to Neapolitan audiences, and sang Antonia in a performance of *Tales of Hoffmann* at the Florence May Festival.

Madame Novotna received most of her acting experience under the direction of Max Reinhardt, and became known in Europe as an actress and film star as well as an opera singer. She has often been a guest artist at the State Opera in Berlin, where she sang in *Die Fledermaus* under Reinhardt's direction. Toscanini was impressed with her singing at Salzburg in 1937. She calls "the most beautiful time of my life" a performance of *The Magic Flute* there, in which she sang Pamina under his direction. "He made everything clear, like a picture," she says, "and in spite of what people say, he was not at all strict." At another Salzburg performance came an opportunity to sing Eurydice opposite Thorborg's Orfeo, under Bruno Walter.

Having been chosen by Toscanini to sing the heroine of *La Traviata* at a special season planned for the World's Fair in the spring of 1939, Jarmila Novotna came to this country. But the contract failed to materialize. Her disappointment, however, was offset by her activities in various opera rôles in the autumn. In San Francisco she made an excellent impression in the title rôle of *Madame Butterfly.* She was assigned to several famous rôles during the

JARMILA NOVOTNA

1939 to 1940 Metropolitan season, and has also fulfilled radio engagements.

In private life she is the wife of Baron George Daubek and the mother of two children. While in New York City, she keeps house in a duplex apartment on Park Avenue. When not busy in other countries with her art, she has in previous years found rest and relaxation in the garden of her 6,500-acre baronial estate at Liten, outside of Prague. Here she and her husband, when he was able to take time from his industrial and agricultural interests, had profited from the seclusion of their country place. There was swimming in summer, excellent shooting and freedom for the amusements of the children.

References

Arts & Dec 52:16-17 My '40 il por
Boston Transcript III p6 Mr 2 '40
Life 8:86-7 Mr 4 '40 pors
Metropolitan Opera Program p18 Ja 4 '40
N Y Times p7 Mr 3 '40
Opera News 4:7-10 O 30 '39 il pors
Time 35:60 F 19 '40 por

OBERTEUFFER, GEORGE (ō-ber-tŏf'-er) 1878—May 13, 1940 Artist; member of the National Academy; instructor of painting; represented in the permanent collections of the Brooklyn Museum, the National Gallery of New South Wales, Duncan Phillips Gallery in Washington, D. C., the Milwaukee Art Institute and the museums of Columbus, Ohio and Grand Rapids, Michigan

References

Who's Who in American Art

Obituaries

Boston Transcript p7 My 14 '40

OBOLER, ARCH (ō'bôl-ĕr) Dec 1909-
Radio dramatist
Address: b. c/o Leland Hayward, Inc, 9200
Wilshire Blvd, Beverly Hills, California

From 1938 on Arch Oboler has been
writing and producing a weekly half-hour
program series of dramas for NBC. In
the spring of 1938 he came from NBC's
Chicago studio to New York with the recorded script of his play, *The Ugliest Man
in the World,* and so impressed was NBC's
production manager that *Arch Oboler's
Plays* were launched. The dramas may be
comedy, realism, fantasy, satire or tragedy,
but are marked always by their originality
and skilled direction. Oboler is credited
with having developed the monologue and
the stream-of-consciousness story for radio
use. One of his plays, *Alter Ego,* starring
Bette Davis, was chosen as the best original
air drama of 1938.

Arch Oboler, the son of Leo and Clara
Oboler, grew up in Chicago; and his boyhood ambition was to be a naturalist. So
the bedroom of his home became a zoo of
turtles, frogs, tortoises, salamanders, snakes,
scorpions and other members of the animal
kingdom. The zoo gave him the idea for
a story which he wrote, and sold, at the
age of 10. He was fascinated by the world
of science in high school; and he enrolled
at the University of Chicago for its course
in electrical engineering. He always liked
to write, however, and he wrote a lot. While
still a student he submitted to NBC a fantasy called *Futuristic.* It was so striking
a work that they bought it and used it as a
salute program in ceremonies attending the
opening of Radio City in New York.

That was in 1934. Since then Arch Oboler has written 400-odd original dramas.
In 1935 he turned out playlets for the
Grand Hotel program, and began writing
sketches for such personalities as Don
Ameche, Henry Fonda, Joan Crawford,
Walter Huston and Edward G. Robinson,
who were glad to appear on his program
even at the minimum union rate, $21.
In 1936 he began to write for *Lights Out,*
an after-midnight spooky horror series of
dramas. Unable to top his own horrific
thrillers, he quit after two years; but learned
a great deal about radio technique while
producing the flesh-creepers. During this
period he married Eleanor Helfand, a University of Chicago student. For their honeymoon they went on a tour of all the haunted
houses in New England.

Oboler made a hit in 1936 with *Rich Kid,*
starring Freddie Bartholomew on the Rudy
Vallee Hour. Vallee repeated the sketch
three times, adopted the author as his protégé, and has since presented many Oboler
plays. A high point of achievement for
Oboler in his *Plays* weekly series was a full
hour special broadcast in 1939 of a dramatization (*The Lonely Heart*) with the Russian actress Alla Nazimova as star, and
the use of the NBC symphony orchestra.

Ernest A. Bachrach

ARCH OBOLER

It was the story of the strange relationship between Tschaikowsky and his patron,
Nadejda von Meck.

In October 1940 Arch Oboler's first commercially sponsored series of half-hour
plays began—Oxydol's *Everyman's Theatre,*
which can be heard every Friday evening.
Mr. Oboler also has a three-and-one-half-
year contract as author-director in Hollywood (he was responsible for the script of
Escape), and a collection of his scripts,
Fourteen Radio Plays, was published late in
1940 by Random House. *Ivory Tower,* a collection of three radio plays, limited to a
thousand signed copies, appeared in November 1940. He is kept busy.

Dark-haired, energetic, half-pint size
Arch Oboler likes to wear polo shirts and
unpressed bags in correct Radio City. As
a hangover of his early scientific interests,
he once kept a horned toad in his studio,
but it died of overindulgence. He has a
pet rabbit named Flopsie at home—an old
brownstone house with a fine library.
In California Frank Lloyd Wright is building him another, far less conventional
house, which will hang over the side of a
mountain and have a brook trickling right
through its living-room. Arch likes to wear
old clothes and prowl around odd parts of
New York City in search of plot material.
He uses a dictaphone in getting his plots
into shape; and it is said he names characters after friends, enemies or the heroes
and heroines of books. He puts on ear-
phones and directs his production (standing
on a table where he can be seen) from the
studio itself rather than the control room.
He says he has dreamed some of his plays,
and that he gets inspiration for others by
listening to the music of great composers.

References
   Christian Sci Mon Mag p5+ Ag 31
      '40 il pors
   Newsweek 14:38 S 4 '39 por
   PM p13 N 15 '40 por
   Script 23:26 Mr 9 '40
   Time 34:30 S 4 '39 por
   Variety Radio Directory

O'GORMAN, PATRICK F., FATHER
July 11, 1867—Mar 15, 1940 Prefect of
studies at Georgetown Preparatory School;
member of the Society of Jesus for 55
years

Obituaries
   N Y Herald Tribune p10 Mr 16 '40
   N Y World-Telegram p4 Mr 16 '40

OLSEN, JOHN SIGVARD Nov 6, 1892-
and **JOHNSON, HAROLD OGDEN** Mar
5, 1895- Actors
Address: Winter Garden Theatre, 1634 Broadway, New York City

OLSEN AND JOHNSON

Since 1914, when they first met, Olsen
and Johnson have been getting laughs. All
they want to do is to make people laugh.
"Here are two comics," says Ole, "who
don't want to play Hamlet." "That's a
lie," Johnson says, "I'd love to play Hamlet. Think of the fun we could have with
you as the Dane and me as the ghost."

"It's belly laughs" that Olsen and Johnson want, and it's "belly laughs" that they
have been getting. Their *Hellzapoppin,* in
the two editions New York has seen so
far, has been one of Broadway's biggest
hits. The "strictly screwball doings" of
this revue include a woman who wanders
up and down the aisles yelling for Oscar,
a man who keeps coming in to deliver a
plant, which before the curtain goes down,
has grown into a full-sized tree, people
trying to sell tickets to other shows, and
volley after volley of shots ringing out
offstage and on. The critics didn't like it—
they thought it "vulgar", "rowdy and confused." Only Walter Winchell found it
"wildly hilarious" and plugged it. But it
didn't make much difference what the
critics said or thought. The first night had
three solid hours of laughs and every night
since the first one has been a box-office
success. It will be filmed in 1941, and a
third edition will also appear on Broadway
in the fall of 1941

"Vaudeville has been dead for a decade,"
said one commentator, but Olsen and Johnson "have never known enough to lie
down." It's vaudeville which they present
in *Hellzapoppin* and it's been vaudeville which
they have been presenting profitably for the
last 25 years. Olsen, called Ole, has always
been the straight man, preparing the way
for the laughs his stooges get. Johnson,
called Chic, takes it away. He's the fatter
one, with "a wide, lardy, fat-man's face
with bulging eyes that resemble poached
eggs with pale blue yolks."

From almost the beginning of their
career Olsen and Johnson have been sure-
fire between Cleveland and California. They
both started out to be musicians: when Ole
was a boy in Peru, Indiana he intended to
be a violinist; Chic, who comes from
Chicago, was sure he was going to be a
pianist. When they met Ole had been
graduated from Northwestern University
(1912) and was playing the violin with the
"College Four," singing with illustrated
slides and offering a little ventriloquism to
fill in now and then. Chic was advertising
himself as the greatest ragtime pianist in
the Midwest and was doing an act in small-
time vaudeville. He says "Olsen was a
funny looking guy with big yellow shoes."
Ole says, "Chic didn't even have shoes
when I met him."

Within a few weeks Olsen and Johnson
were a team. Chic played and Ole sang.
They got jobs in beer halls and finally
worked up to Mike Fritzel's *Frolics.* From
there they went to vaudeville. They first
really caught on at the Majestic in Milwaukee. The two actors before them sang a
song called *Rolling Stones.* Once, during a
dull matinee, Olsen and Johnson came out
and rolled two stones across the stage as
they started to sing. The audience howled
and from then on things were different.
Olsen and Johnson would sing a comic
song dead-pan and clown a serious one;
they would do silly, unexpected things,
always aiming for the "belly laugh."

They got on the Pantages circuit, where
they were considered "vaudeville at its
best," and stayed there for five years. By
then they had four stooges working in the
audience and using all the props they could
get, from elephants to doves, from airplanes to toy autos. From Pantages they
went to the Orpheum circuit, "the Big

OLSEN, JOHN and JOHNSON, HAROLD—*Continued*

League" of vaudeville, and were making about $2,500 a week. They were the originators of the "after piece" idea in which all acts on the bill would get together for a general jamboree at the finale.

The first revue of their own was *Monkey Business,* presented in Los Angeles in 1926. It was in that year that they went to Australia for a ten weeks' booking and returned after two years. They toured all over the United States and Europe and were always top-notch successes. That is, until talking pictures came in and vaudeville died. When trouble came they left the circuit, organized a show of about 40 people and toured the country with it. The show lasted about 70 minutes and was played as a unit.

It wasn't in one of their own shows, however, that they first appeared on Broadway away from vaudeville. They appeared at the end of the Broadway run of *Take a Chance,* and were told by the critics that they were "as broad as some of their scenes seem long." But audiences laughed, and they went on the road with *Take a Chance* after the show closed in New York. In 1936 they were introduced to a radio audience by Rudy Vallee and presented *Comedy News* over WABC. Their jokes, some commentators felt, were hackneyed and laughed at too much by Olsen and Johnson themselves. They got in the movies, too, and were seen in *Fifty Million Frenchmen, O Sailor Behave* and *Gold Dust Gertie.*

Then they went back to their road shows, among them one called *Hellzapoppin,* named after a festival (spelled with one *l*) they had clowned for in Buckeye, Arizona. Lee Shubert went to Philadelphia to see it and suggested that it be enlarged and brought to his 46th Street Theatre in New York. While this was happening Johnson was fishing in Canada. He got a wire from Olsen by Indian runner which said: "Phone me right away." He walked to the nearest phone, which was 16 miles away. "Lee Shubert wants us to do eight shows a week," yelled Olsen. "If it's eight, take it," said Johnson, brought up on the "five-a-day." With sets from old musicals and secondhand costumes *Hellzapoppin* opened in September 1938. It was soon shifted over to the Winter Garden to accommodate the crowds and has stayed there.

Off the stage, except for playing occasional practical jokes like rounding up a lot of seedy bums to bring to a party when asked to bring their friends in the show, both Olsen and Johnson are serious men. They save their money and are well off. Olsen has a home at Brentwood, California and another at Malverne, Long Island; Johnson has a house at Santa Monica, California and a farm at Libertyville, Illinois, which he uses mostly for hunting and fishing. Both men are devoted to their families. Mrs. Johnson is the woman in *Hellzapoppin* who pursues "Oscar" up and down;

her daughter June is an actress in Hollywood. Olsen has three children and one of them holds cakes of ice and lets off pistols in the show. He went to Ohio State University and the University of Southern California, in order, his father says, "to wind up as a shot offstage."

References

> Collier's 102:16-17+ D 10 '38 il
> New Yorker 14:20-5 Ja 28 '39
> International Motion Picture Almanac

O'NEIL, GEORGE 1898—May 24, 1940 Hollywood scenarist; playwright and author; wrote Keats biography; did screen versions of *Magnificent Obsession* and *High, Wide and Handsome*

References

> Mantle, B. Contemporary American Playwrights 1938

Obituaries

> N Y Herald Tribune p12 My 25 '40
> N Y Times p17 My 25 '40

OROZCO, JOSE CLEMENTE (ō-rōs'kō hō-sā' klĕ-mĕn'tĕ) Nov 23, 1883- Artist
Address: Av. Alvaro Obregon 290, Mexico City, Mexico

In July 1940 José Clemente Orozco completed his mural, *A Dive Bomber and Tank,* for the Museum of Modern Art in New York City as part of its "Twenty Centuries of Mexican Art" Exhibition. During the painting of the fresco visitors were allowed to watch its progress, and there was a good deal of speculation, particularly since, as Orozco says, the six detachable panels on which it is painted can be shown right side up or upside down with any two or three shown together in any order.

According to most critics *A Dive Bomber and Tank* isn't intended to be a realistic picture of a dive bomber, but was painted to convey primarily a sense of the power of a machine monster of modern war. Orozco himself insists that there is no political significance at all in the selection of the subject. He wished merely to paint an aspect of modern life. "That is what modern art is, the actual feeling of life around us or the mood of whatever is just happening."

In his "slashing, dynamic mural style" Orozco has never been interested in recording facts but "in communicating his emotional reaction to them." On the walls of Mexican and American buildings he hasn't painted merely external clashes—the violence and bloodshed of the Revolution—but "the spiritual clashes of a race he loves and understands."

This painter, who with Diego Rivera has gone "a long way towards rescuing the mural from the degraded existence it has led since the Renaissance," is represented in the United States by murals at Pomona

College, Claremont, California; at the New School for Social Research and the Museum of Modern Art in New York City and at Dartmouth College, Hanover, New Hampshire. In Mexico many important public buildings have been decorated by him. Orozco has done much other work, but he prefers murals. To him they are the most disinterested form of painting; they are all for the people.

Orozco was born in Zapotlán, Jalisco in 1883, the son of Ireneo and Rosa Flores Orozco. He was graduated from the National School of Agriculture in Mexico City in 1900 and later studied mathematics at the National University of Mexico and architectural drawing at the Academy of Fine Arts. Eager to be an architect, it wasn't until 1909, when he was 26, that Orozco got around to art. Before then he had worked for a time as an architect's draughtsman.

When he started painting, Orozco was intolerant even then of the pretty, sunlit school of painting. He "expressed his contempt by painting prostitutes and used dark, lurid colors. To this day he has never painted landscape." In 1913 he painted a canvas in the former Museum of San Juan de Ulua in which he depicted the retreat of the Spanish Army in 1882. About the same time he published in several magazines some caricatures "which strike the eye at once with their originality, vigor and ferocity." He was beginning to be known and his first exhibition in Mexico City in 1915 was a success. He continued to paint, traveling around Mexico and to California where he spent two years.

In 1922 Orozco joined the Painters' Syndicate and was appointed to decorate the National Preparatory School. In 1923 he married Margarita Valladares of Mexico City. They have three children—Clemente, Alfredo and Eugenia. A little later he received a commission to decorate the Industrial School of Orizaba. In 1927 he went to the United States where, in spite of the Revolutionary politics that colored his works, he was welcomed. Several exhibitions of his work were held and he received a commission for the murals at Pomona College.

In 1932 Orozco made his first trip to Europe, but nothing he saw there nor anything he saw in the United States "has had any effect on his work." It remained and it remains completely indigenous. Orozco "still lives in the sun and shadow of his native land: the types and symbols, the physiognomies of his people, remain, as in his Mexican pictures, unaltered and unalterable." It was this fact that caused most of the stir when Orozco began to decorate the Baker Library at Dartmouth in 1932.

The subject of the murals was the rise of civilization in America, portrayed largely through themes from ancient Mexican culture. Not only were the frescoes called "hideous" and "grisly" but it was asserted

Paul Hansen

JOSE CLEMENTE OROZCO

that such frescoes, themes and such an artist did not belong to the New England tradition. In reply came the even firmer assertion that the "spiritual vitality of genuine New England is better embodied in Orozco's murals than in any amount of local history tamely recorded by local artists," and a Dartmouth professor added that Orozco's work "has many of the qualities that we like to associate with the college. It is forthright, unmannered and contemporary. It is democratic and deeply concerned with social values." After the shouting died down perhaps the most pertinent comment was that of E. M. Benson: "I relish the sweet irony of events which made it possible for a college originally founded for the purpose of converting the heathen Indian to be converted, in turn, by one."

In April 1934 an exhibition of the greater part of Orozco's work was held in the civic auditorium of La Porte, Indiana which "definitely established him as one of the greatest painters in America." Right after it Orozco returned to Mexico City, where he decorated one of the wings of the great hall in the Palace of Fine Arts. Here he developed the theme of war in a way that led Antonio Castro Lean, then head of the Mexican Department of Fine Arts, to declare: "If there are other Mexican painters who have succeeded in portraying with art and vigor the revolutionary ideas of present Mexico, it is unquestionable that no one has expressed as Orozco the eternal, tragical and human aspect of our civil and social struggles." In 1936 Orozco decorated the University at Guadalajara and after doing other commissions for the Mexican government was commissioned in the spring of 1940 by President Cárdenas to take charge of the decoration of the new

OROZCO, JOSE CLEMENTE—*Cont.*
building under construction for the Mexican Supreme Court.

"A slight, gentle, bespectacled man with about 20 teeth, Orozco . . . has no left hand, no hearing in his left ear and very poor eyesight. His disabilities have always been supposed to have been the result of a chemistry laboratory explosion in his teens, but Orozco says: "I was just playing in the street with some powder. It was just an ordinary explosion." Orozco has been having a fine time in New York doing his latest murals. He says: "The whole life is very amusing," and is corroborated by John Abbott, vice-president of the Modern Museum. According to Mr. Abbott, "Orozco has a great grasp of night life from Harlem to the Battery. He talks knowingly of floor shows all over town."

References

Am Mag Art 26:440+ O '33 il por
Art Digest 8:5-6 S '34; 10:13 Mr 1
  '36 il; 14:26 Jl '40
Bul Museum Modern Art Ag '40
Mag Art 33:434 Jl '40
New Repub 80:231-5 O 10 '34
N Y Times p13 Jl 4 '40
New Yorker 16:13 Jl 6 '40
Charlot, J. Jose Clemente Orozco
  In Art From the Mayans to Disney
  p100-08 1939
Craven, T. Mexicans (Diego Rivera
  and José Clemente Orozco) *In*
  Modern Art p346-64 1934
Flaccus, K. ed. Orozco at Dartmouth 1933
Mérida, C. J. Clemente Orozco *In*
  Modern Mexican Artists p137-8 1937
New York City. Museum of Modern
  Art. Twenty Centuries of Mexican
  Art p188 1940
Pach, W. Mexico: José Clemente
  Orozco, Diego Rivera *In* Queer
  Thing, Painting p281-94 1938
Twenty Centuries of Mexican Art
  p188 1940
Velázquez Chavez, A. José Clemente
  Orozco *In* Contemporary Mexican
  Artists p167-8 1937
Who's Who in Latin America

OSBORNE, OLIVER THOMAS Nov 14,
1862—Nov 11, 1940 Member of Yale Medical School faculty 1911 to 1925; professor emeritus since 1925; did pioneer work in tuberculosis; a chairman of Gaylord Farm Tuberculosis Sanatorium from 1933 to 1940

References

Lit Digest 115:22 F 25 '33 por
American Men of Science
American Medical Directory
Who's Who in America
Who's Who in American Medicine

Obituaries

N Y Times p23 N 12 '40

OWENS, ROBERT BOWIE 1870—Nov 1, 1940 Electrical engineer; inventor; molecular physicist; discoverer of Alpha ray and of electromagnetic system for guiding ships and airplanes through fogs; secretary of Franklin Institute, 1910 to 1924; chief signal officer at London headquarters of A. E. F. during First World War

References

Who's Who in America 1932-33
Who's Who in Engineering 1925

Obituaries

N Y Herald Tribune p40 N 3 '40
N Y Times p56 N 3 '40

PADDON, HARRY LOCKE 1880—Dec 24, 1939 Physician associated with Sir Wilfred Grenfell in his work in Labrador

Obituaries

N Y Herald Tribune D 26 '39

PAGE, MARIE DANFORTH 1870—Mar 3, 1940 Artist

Marie Danforth Page, who had won numerous honors and prizes for her portraits, died March 3, 1940 in Boston, where she was born 70 years before. Mrs. Page, who was the daughter of John Nourse and Hannah Marie (Rhodes) Danforth, studied at the Gannett Institute and at the School of the Museum of Fine Arts. She received an honorary M. A. from Tufts College in 1933. In June 1896 she married Calvin Gates Page, Boston physician, and they were the parents of two daughters.

Mrs. Page was awarded a bronze medal at the Panama Exposition in 1915, the Richard S. Greenough Memorial Prize of the Newport Art Association in 1919, a medal at the Sesquicentennial Exposition in Philadelphia and numerous prizes of the National Academy of Design, to which she was elected in 1927. Mrs. Page, who was an Episcopalian, was a member of the Connecticut Academy of Fine Arts, the Guild of Boston Artists, the Grand Central Galleries.

References

American Women
Who's Who in America 1938-39
Who's Who in American Art

Obituaries

Boston Transcript p4 Mr 4 '40
N Y Herald Tribune p22 Mr 5 '40

PALEY, WILLIAM SAMUEL (pā'lĭ)
Sept 28, 1901- President of the Columbia Broadcasting System
Address: b. 485 Madison Ave, New York City; h. 29 Beekman Pl, New York City

When radio network officials began fretting over the Federal Communications Commission's unfavorable monopoly investigation report on networks made in 1940, William S. Paley, president of the Columbia

Broadcasting System, was the first to voice his objections to the report. In a letter to affiliate stations he described it as error-laden and biased. And as chief of CBS Paley's opinion bears more than a little weight.

Paley is both the oldest and youngest chief of a huge radio network—the oldest because he has been president of CBS since September 25, 1928, and youngest in point of age. He took office as president three days before his twenty-seventh birthday.

Paley is an example of a rich young man who has made good. Born in Chicago on September 28, 1901, the son of Goldie (Drell) and Samuel Paley, he attended Western Military Academy at Alton, Illinois and went to the University of Chicago for one year before he had his first fling at business. His father and his uncle, Jacob Paley, had a cigar factory in Chicago. When they had labor troubles they decided to open a branch in Philadelphia, and Samuel Paley went there, taking his son with him.

Young Paley had already spent two vacation periods working around tobacco in Havana in preparation for entering his father's business and he was apparently just gaining more experience that summer in Philadelphia. But when the elder Paley was called back to Chicago by his father's death young William took over. Just then the Philadelphia workers decided to walk out on strike. William had the whole thing settled and the factory running before his father returned.

He went back to school, however, in the fall, this time to the University of Pennsylvania, from which he was graduated in 1922. After graduation he entered the cigar business in earnest and soon was made vice-president in charge of advertising and production.

The story is that while he was abroad in the summer of 1927 his father and uncle negotiated a $50,000 advertising contract for their Congress Cigar Company without consulting their young vice-president. The contract called for 13 weeks of radio broadcasting over the newly-formed Columbia Broadcasting System. The elder Paley is supposed to have called the signing of the contract "the biggest mistake I ever made."

When young Paley got back from Europe the Congress Cigar Company's La Palina cigars were on the air and sales were jumping. Paley found his attention fixed on radio and became tremendously interested in it. The Columbia System was then owned by Jerome Louchheim of Philadelphia, a friend of the Paleys. Louchheim's major interests were elsewhere and he found the broadcasting business more than he cared to handle. The upshot of it was that young Paley, with nothing more substantial as a guide than his own faith in the future of radio, bought Louchheim's holdings.

Paley was brilliant and anxious to show he was more than a young man with a lot of money to play with. When he took

WILLIAM S. PALEY

office as president of CBS on September 25, 1928 the system had 19 stations in the Northeastern part of the United States. By January 8, 1929 Paley had completed negotiations for 22 more stations. Today Columbia has 121 stations in the United States, Canada, Hawaii and Porto Rico on its network.

The young president of CBS stuck to his desk nine or ten hours a day, called up with suggestions and orders at all hours of the night, and made a name for himself with some of the policies he initiated. In the mushroom radio field of those days and under Paley's aggressive leadership, Columbia grew "like a dream." Rival motion picture interests went after Paley with offers to buy the network, and Paramount-Publix Corporation offered $1,500,000. Paley refused to sell. Nine months later, on June 15, 1929, he sold Paramount-Publix a half interest for $5,000,000. Within three years he bought back the half interest for $5,200,-000.

Back in the early days of his presidency irreverent young employees called Paley "Pale Billy" (purely a trick of transposition, for Paley is anything but pale). Six feet tall, heavy-set, handsome and usually well-tanned, Paley is capable of the greatest excitement over either business or fun. He likes to deal with men of his own age and has surrounded himself with a group of sprightly young executives. Paley moves fast and bothers little with details.

He rushes at both business and hobbies with zest. He has run through water-color painting, oil painting, motorboating and photography in quick succession. In business his impetuosity is deceptive because "it breaks down into shrewd caution whenever necessary." He chooses his words with astute grace when anything important is at

PALEY, WILLIAM S.—*Continued*
stake, but usually prefers the extravagance
of mixed metaphors.

Under Paley's direction Columbia has
pioneered in many radio ventures. One of
Paley's chief concerns is news, and even in
the early days of newscasting CBS sacrificed paid advertising programs to put on
the air events of international significance.
Technical problems of transmission have
been overcome. Columbia has covered the
abdication of King Edward VIII, the
Austrian *Anchluss,* the Czech crisis, the
dismemberment of Czechoslovakia. Columbia, too, organized its own news-gathering
service, the Columbia News Service, when
the radio stations began to have trouble
with newspapers over the broadcasting of
news. Many newspapers refused to run
listings of radio programs, but before the
newspaper-radio feud gathered much momentum, Paley, together with officials of
NBC, made their peace with the newspapers.
Paley had to give up his news service, and an
arrangement was made in 1933 whereby the
networks had use of newspaper wire services.

Another CBS venture close to Paley's
heart was the *American School of the Air,*
which, through daily programs with the
cooperation of the United States Department of the Interior, made radio education
available to school children. It was started
in 1930. On October 7, 1940 the *School of
the Air* was extended as an educational
project for the entire Western Hemisphere,
serving an audience of school children
estimated to number more than 15,000,000.

An outstanding scientific achievement in
the art of visual broadcasting was demonstrated in September 1940 when Columbia
introduced its color television.

Paley's musical interests (he was a promising pianist as a child and gave a concert at
11) were instrumental in bringing to Columbia the great symphony orchestras, and at
one time four nationally-known orchestras
were heard on CBS stations each week.
President Paley takes credit for bringing
important operatic programs to CBS and
for discovering Kate Smith (see sketch this
issue), Morton Downey and Bing Crosby.
He is proud also of the dramatic program,
Columbia Workshop, and the station's spot-
news coverage. It was Paley who in 1935
started a program which broke radio's
political neutrality and a radio tradition. It
was *America's Hour,* which editorialized on
current conditions by dramatized programs
of the kindly-employer-and-faithful-worker
combination and denounced radicals who
preached discontent.

It was the first time a great network had
thus editorialized. A CBS spokesman said:
"Mr. Paley felt it was our responsibility
to take people who can't see further than
their noses and make them realize they have
in America something to be proud of."

Despite his achievements, Paley is inclined
to be self-effacing. Once after he had made a
speech before the Academy of Political Science he swore he wouldn't make a speech
again. And at least once he suffered a bad
case of microphone fright. It was in April
1938 when he put his annual stockholders'
report on the air in direct competition with
Kay Kyser's dance orchestra on the NBC
network. He read quickly and nervously:
"The broadcasting industry should unite on
a definite program of service, of progress
and of protection... The newly organized
National Association of Broadcasters . . .
may well be the instrument."

One reason for Paley's perturbation was
the fact that the Federal Communications
Commission had just begun an investigation
of radio and had appointed a committee to
look into charges of monopoly. The National Association of Broadcasters, organized the previous week, was a self-regu-
lating, self-censoring body.

Paley, in addition to the presidency of the
Columbia Broadcasting System and the posi-
tion of chairman of the boards of several
broadcasting stations, is a director of the
Museum of Modern Art, a director of the
New York World's Fair, the Pan-American
Airways Corporation and the Philharmonic
Society. He is a member of the Lotos, the
Sands Point, Turf and Field, and Rocke-
feller Luncheon Clubs.

He was married in 1932 to Miss Dorothy
Hart Hearst of Los Angeles, California.
They have one son, Jeffrey, and one daugh-
ter, Hilary.

References

Newsweek 2:18 D 23 '33 por; **6:28**
   Jl 27 '35 por
Time 31:64 Ap 18 '38 por
World's Work 61:37+ Mr '32 por
America's Young Men
Shumway, H. I. William Samuel
   Paley, a Youthful Builder of a
   Great Radio Network *In* Famous
   Leaders of Industry 4th ser. p265-
   75 1936
Variety Radio Directory
Who's Who in America
Who's Who in American Jewry
Who's Who in Broadcasting
Who's Who in Commerce and In-
   dustry

PALMER, ALBERT DEFOREST July
26, 1869—Jan 13, 1940 Former chairman of
the department of physics, Brown University

References

Who's Who in America 1938-39

Obituaries

N Y Herald Tribune p30 Ja 14 '40

PAPE, WILLIAM JAMIESON Dec 1, 1873- Publisher of the Waterbury (Connecticut) *Republican and American*

Address: b. 61 Leavenworth St, Waterbury, Connecticut

As the result of a campaign in the Waterbury (Connecticut) *Republican and American,* Mayor Frank Hayes of that city and 19 colleagues were convicted in August 1939 of the operation of an eight-year conspiracy which plundered the municipal treasury of more than $3,500,000. The public service rendered by the newspaper has been recognized by the 1939 Pulitzer Gold Medal given to the paper, whose editor is E. Robert Stevenson (see sketch this issue). As publisher of the Waterbury paper, William J. Pape has also been honored.

He was born in Liverpool, England on December 1, 1873, the son of Robert and Martha (Burnett) Pape. At the age of 14 he came to the United States and became a naturalized citizen eight years later. The Pape family lived in Passaic, New Jersey, and young William had his first newspaper experience there. After he was graduated from the Passaic High School in 1890 he became a cub reporter on the Passaic *Daily News,* and sped straight up the newspaper ladder, from city editor in 1892 to business manager in 1895 to editor in 1897. In 1898 he married Julia E. F. Bolton of Passaic. He remained editor for four years, and then bought his own newspaper, the Waterbury *Republican,* in 1901, consolidating it with the Waterbury *American* 21 years later.

William Pape demonstrated his "ability as an organizer and his bulldog tenacity" by turning the *Republican,* "the weakest of run-down newspapers" when he bought it, into one of the most substantial newspaper properties in New England and a powerful organ of public opinion. He has always fought courageously against machine politics, and has been out of its good graces for a long time. In 1913 he began a persistent fight to divorce the utility companies from Connecticut politics with an attack on J. Henry Roraback, railroad lobbyist and successful candidate for chairman of the Republican State Central Committee. Mr. Pape's argument was that "a man cannot simultaneously serve a favor-seeking corporation and the voters of a major party," and over a period of time a good many Connecticut editors came around to his way of thinking. In 1930, seventeen years later, with Mr. Roraback political dictator of Connecticut and president of the Connecticut Light and Power Company, Mr. Pape himself sought the Republican nomination for State comptroller, though unsuccessfully.

Mr. Pape is prominent in newspaper circles. He is a member of the New England Daily Newspaper Association and was its president, 1926 to 1927. He has been a director of the Associated Press since 1937. A Republican and an Episcopalian, he belongs to the Rotary Club as well as other clubs, and has a strong interest in the little theatre movement. He was with the Yale School of Drama (1925-27), organized the Waterbury Little Theatre in 1929, and was president of the local theatre group in 1932.

Mr. and Mrs. Pape have four grown children: three sons and one daughter.

References

Nation 131:263-5 S 10 '30
St Louis Post-Dispatch p1C My 7 '40
por

Who's Who in America
Who's Who in Commerce and Industry
Who's Who in Journalism

PARRAN, THOMAS Sept 28, 1892- Surgeon General of the United States

Address: b. Bureau of the Public Health Service, Washington, D. C.; h. 3734 Oliver St N W, Washington, D. C.

Public health preparedness, according to Dr. Thomas Parran, Surgeon General of the United States, must become a vital part of the national defense program. "The rearmament program envisioned by the President," he said, "means vast concentration of workers in communities, many of which as yet are not prepared with needed sanitary safeguards to insure against disease spread." Also, he pointed out, "history shows that war breeds epidemics. We must guard against the spread of epidemics from the war-torn areas to this hemisphere."

National defense and the War abroad are merely two more reasons why we must defend and preserve the health of this nation. To Dr. Parran public health should always and must always be one of the main concerns of the government and its people. For years he has urged funds for public health and bitterly contrasted the millions of dollars spent on the control of hog cholera, the boll weevil, the tick and the fruit fly with the beggarly thousands contributed by the Federal government for the promotion of health work among human beings.

Dr. Parran, "dark, dynamic and a good deal of a zealot," has been "the nation's family doctor" since 1936. Tuberculosis, syphilis, cancer and other diseases; research into mental diseases and drug addiction; into the causes and prevention of disease; the supplying of adequate hospital and medical facilities for the country; the spreading of information about germs and disease into millions of homes—these are only some of the concerns of the United States Public Health Service under Dr. Parran.

It was Dr. Parran who was the man behind the crusade in 1936 to take the prudery out of the war against social diseases, and it was and is Dr. Parran who, with his staff, is working with "high and burning purpose" to tackle syphilis scientifically and wipe it out of this country. When the campaign against syphilis began Parran stated that "if all conditions due to syphilis were

Bachrach

THOMAS PARRAN

reported as such, it would be found the leading cause of deaths in the United States. It is responsible for 10 per cent of all insanity, 18 per cent of all diseases of the heart and blood vessels, for many of the still births and deaths of babies in the first weeks of life. Syphilis has always seemed to me the mad dog of the communicable diseases and needs swift action to control it."

Before the campaign, the subject was taboo. There could be no reference to it on the screen; the Columbia Broadcasting Company wouldn't permit the word "syphilis" to go out over the air from its stations; newspapers, when they printed the word, which was seldom, printed it usually in the smallest possible type in the most inconspicuous place. Now, due to Dr. Parran's crusade, there has even been a motion picture on the subject—*Dr. Ehrlich's Magic Bullet;* radios are freer; and the newspapers no longer consider the topic taboo. Due to Dr. Parran's crusade, major universities have been persuaded to open classes for physicians unfamiliar with the latest methods of treating social diseases.

In the same way Dr. Parran has attacked the problem of cancer research and education. After the National Cancer Institute Act was passed in August 1937 the government's buying of radium, training of doctors and education of the public was under his jurisdiction. In the same way he has campaigned for more hospital facilities. In 1939 and 1940 his staff conducted a painstaking county by county survey of hospital facilities in the 48 states. A plan was evolved under the Wagner health bill for little one-story hospitals, each planned to house 100 beds and to cost about $150,000 apiece, including X-ray equipment, surgical

instruments, laboratory machinery—everything but bed linen.

On any matter of public health Dr. Parran shows the same direct enthusiasm that was his when he once milked a cow on a city street to boost milk consumption. Almost all his working life has been spent in public health service. Dr. Parran was born in St. Leonard, Maryland, son of Benjamin and Mary (Latimer) Parran, in a glazed brick house which a Parran had built in 1655. He went to St. John's College, Maryland and was graduated in 1911. In 1915 he received both his M. A. and his M. D.— his M. A. from the University of Maryland and his doctor's degree from Georgetown University.

Dr. Parran entered the health service of the United States in 1918 and never left it. In that year he was married to Angela Bentley Vandoran and in that year he began working at Muscle Shoals. There, where government men were working to build a dam, 10,000 men were sick with influenza. They were dying in improvised barracks that looked like emergency hospitals in a battle zone. Parran was in charge, and to his frantic wires for supplies no answers came. He had no sheets, bandages, medicine. When he went to the railroad yard to see if anything had arrived he found a trainload of army supplies destined for a camp. He thought of court-martial and of his influenza sufferers and stole the supplies. Instead of being court-martialed he was promoted.

In 1919 he became the executive officer of the medical division of the War Risk Insurance Bureau and after that director of the Tri-State Sanitary District. From 1921 to 1923 he was director of the rural sanitation division for the Missouri Board of Health and from 1923 to 1925 director of county health for the Illinois State Department of Public Health. In 1926 he got his first job working directly against the venereal diseases he fights so vigorously as Surgeon General—as chief of the division of venereal diseases in the United States Health Service. He stayed there until 1930, when he was made commissioner of the New York State Department of Health.

The year Governor Roosevelt called him to that position he, a widower with four sons, married Buda Carroll Keller. They all took a big white farmhouse in the hills at Castleton, New York overlooking the Hudson, 10 miles south of Albany. There he could ride, train setters, split firewood, bake waffles and on Sundays go decorously with his whole family to Mass in the Roman Catholic Church in the village. Dr. Parran hated to leave it when President Roosevelt appointed him Surgeon General in April 1936, at a salary of $9,800 a year (he had been getting $12,000 in Albany).

Middle-aged doctors "were generally opposed to Dr. Parran's appointment," for Dr. Parran believes strongly in "socialized medicine, with free drugs and hospital service to every inhabitant of the United States who cannot afford them." As far as the practice of doctors is concerned, he would permit the private system to continue, would have private practitioners dispense the free drugs and assign patients to the free hospitals. With this plan, thousands of the 170,000 doctors in this country would have to take jobs with city, state or federal medical agencies. But because the opposition to Parran and his view was "politically unfocused," it fizzled out and the Senate quietly confirmed his appointment.

Dr. Parran is a member or fellow of most of the medical societies and has been honored time and time again for his excellent work. In December 1939 he was awarded the Sedgwick Memorial Medal "for distinguished service in public health."

References

Am Mag 124:94 S '37 por
Collier's 98:52+ S 19 '36
Lit Digest 122:18-19 O 31 '36 por
N Y Times p21 My 17 '40; p20 Jl 24 '40
Time 27:50-2 Ap 6 '36 por; 28:60-4 O 26 '36 por (cover) 35:34 F 12 '40 por
American Catholic Who's Who
American Men of Science
America's Young Men 1936-37
De Kruif, P. H. Ghastly Luxury *In* Fight for Life p253-330 1938
Ratcliff, J. D. U. S. P. H. S. *In* Modern Miracle Men p179-95 1939
Who's Who in America
Who's Who in the Nation's Capital

PARSONS, LOUELLA Aug 6, 1893- Motion picture columnist

Address: 619 N Maple Dr, Beverly Hills, California

Every day in more than 400 newspapers in this country, France, England, Canada, China, Egypt and India appears Louella Parsons' column devoted to news of motion pictures and motion picture stars. From it fans all over the world can find out who is going to marry whom, what 20th Century-Fox's latest acquisition wore at the Brown Derby on Wednesday, what MGM's latest production plans are and how air conditioning is going to be used when filming desert scenes.

Louella Oettinger Parsons, who has been in Hollywood for 15 years, gets her information from the producers and stars themselves—it has been said that stars who don't keep her informed of their private lives find themselves let in for "petty sideswipes." She gets it, too, from her two paid assistants and hundreds of "volunteer scouts and spies." Despite the variety of her sources or maybe because of it, Miss Parsons' information is called by critics "consistently inaccurate." The picture, *The President Vanishes*, for instance, appeared in her column first as *The Vanishing American* and later as *The President Disappears.*

G. Maillard Kesslère

LOUELLA PARSONS

The first literary effort of Miss Parsons on record was a high school essay entitled, *When is Rebellion Justified?* She wrote it in Freeport, Illinois, where she was born on August 6, 1893, the daughter of Joshua and Helen Ida (Wilcox) Oettinger, third generation German-Irish stock. While still in high school Louella branched out into newspaper work. She became the dramatic editor and assistant to the city editor on the Dixon, Illinois *Morning Star,* for $5 a week.

In 1910, when she was 17, Louella married John Parsons, whose business was real estate, and went with him to Burlington, Iowa. When he died four years later, leaving her with her three-year-old daughter Harriet, Louella packed, went to Chicago and landed a job on the *Tribune* at $9 a week. While she was still a reporter, in 1912, Louella made her first movie contact. She sold a script called *Chains* to the old Essanay Company for $25. After this was made into a one-reeler starring Francis X. Bushman, Louella was hired at $18 a week as story editor.

The response was merely mild when Miss Parsons started a movie column in the Chicago *Record-Herald* in 1914, and when Hearst took over the paper in 1918 she found herself out of a job. Undaunted, she and her daughter went to New York, where she became movie critic on the old *Morning Telegraph.* It wasn't long, particularly after she had praised Marion Davies in a review, before Hearst was trying to get her back. After a good deal of bargaining back and forth she got a three-year contract at $250 a week. Louella Parsons had been shrewd, but Hearst had been shrewder: the contract stipulated that she had to turn over one-third of all she made on the side to Hearst, while he could syndicate her material without paying her anything extra.

PARSONS, LOUELLA—*Continued*

However, it all seemed at an end in 1925. Miss Parsons had a bad case of tuberculosis and was told that she had about six months to live. She decided to spend these last months in California. At the end of them she was flourishing and a short time later, at Hearst's suggestion, was writing her column there. Her salary was raised to $350 a week and in 1929 to $500. Today she is getting $600 a week for her column. In Hollywood, in 1931, she was married to Dr. Harry Martin, who has worked as technical medical adviser for the films, and has become a member of the civil service commission and chairman of the State Boxing Commission. Louella, in private and in public, calls him "docky-wocky."

Miss Parsons, who has achieved part of her fame on the radio, first appeared before the microphone in 1928 and interviewed movie stars. When this didn't work out she explained that some of the "guests" couldn't even speak English "and I don't mean the foreign importations." Five years later she tried again, again unsuccessfully, but in 1934 she came through with her *Hollywood Hotel* program. During the years she put it on for Campbell's soup, Campbell's Crosley rating jumped from 39th to 10th place and "something like $2,000,000 worth of moving picture talent" appeared gratis in her company. All the guests received was a case of soup. On return engagements they were allowed to specify the kind of soup they preferred.

On the *Hollywood Hotel* program current pictures were dramatized and Miss Parsons, "the first lady of Hollywood," selected and sponsored them. A picture presented on her program usually came through at the box office. As a result Louella found herself wined, dined and loaded with gifts. When there was a problem, "producers would say 'Give Lolly a ring and see what she thinks about it.'" Louella even crashed the movies when *Hollywood Hotel* was made into a film in 1938.

All this radio success ended when the Radio Guild, in the summer of 1938, set out to stop all free talent broadcasts and Louella's main drawing card was gone. The program went on without her, and she went back to her column, her features, her outside writing.

Three secretaries help her. They arrive at 10:30 and immediately the three telephones start ringing and never stop. Miss Parsons' material goes by teletype direct from Hollywood to the Los Angeles *Examiner* and from there is dispatched to New York for distribution. She's always in a hurry, "being about 20 minutes late mentally from the time she rises until the time she reaches her bed again."

In the autumn of 1940 Louella was traveling all over the country pretending the stage of various theatres was her office at the Los Angeles *Examiner* and shaking a couple of rhumba rattles besides. The audiences loved her.

Known as a lavish party thrower and generous giver of gifts, Miss Parsons admits she has "312" friends. At premières, parties, night clubs and the race track she is a familiar figure. "Plump and breathless, she has dark hair, hazel eyes and an expression of blank bewilderment that no longer fools anybody."

References

Sat Eve Post 212:8-9+ Jl 15 '39 il
pors
Time 31:38 Ja 24 '38 por
American Women

PASSOS, JOHN DOS   *See* Dos Passos, J.

PASTERNACK, JOSEF ALEXANDER

July 1, 1881—Apr 29, 1940   Orchestra conductor; attracted Toscanini's attention when viola player and Toscanini helped him become conductor; conductor for several seasons of the Metropolitan Opera Company, of the Philadelphia Philharmonic Orchestra, of the Boston "Pops" Orchestra; conductor of radio programs since 1928

References

Thompson, O. ed.   International Cyclopedia of Music and Musicians 1939
Who's Who in American Jewry
Wier, A. E. ed. Macmillan Encyclopedia of Music and Musicians 1938

G. Maillard Kesslère

JOSEF A. PASTERNACK

Obituaries

N Y Herald Tribune p18 Ap 30 '40
por
N Y Times p21 Ap 30 '40
Variety 138:26 My 1 '40

PATRI, ANGELO (păt-rē′) Nov 1877-
Educator

Address: b. P. S. 45, 2502 Lorillard Pl, The
Bronx, New York City; h. 601 E 170th St,
New York City

For almost 40 years Angelo Patri has
been a teacher and principal in New York
City's public schools, and as a teacher, as a
writer, as the author of a syndicated column,
Our Children, he has made, according to
Dorothy Canfield Fisher, "one of the finest
contributions to civilized life in our nation."
Since 1913 Angelo Patri has been principal
of Public School No. 45 in The Bronx, New
York, a pioneering school in liberal education. In this school little emphasis is placed
on book learning; here pupils are encouraged to develop whatever talents they
have. Open to them are many shops and
studies in which they can model in clay,
paint, draw, write, work in wood or metal,
sew, weave, play in an orchestra, plant
fruit or vegetables, and every child is able
to develop his creative powers while he
studies the fundamentals of reading, writing
and arithmetic. That this unusual school
exists at all is in large part due to the
persevering leadership of its principal.

Angelo Patri was born in Italy and came
to this country in the '80s with an almost
uneducated father and mother. Until he
was 12 life here was very much like that
in Italy. His family lived in close-knit
clannishness with other Italians in Little
Italy in New York City, and it wasn't until
he went to school that little Angelo began
to realize that he was living in America.
A "pale, delicate, Italian boy," he found
school hard at first, but eventually became
acclimated. From New York's public
schools he went to the City College of New
York, from which he was graduated in 1897.
Patri was 20 when he left City College.
At 21 he found himself a teacher in the New
York public schools, bewildered and ill-
prepared. Most difficult was the problem of
discipline, for his superiors insisted on the
most rigid standards of behavior. Difficult,
too, was the system of teaching "methods,"
which meant that a prescribed program had
to be followed in what Patri felt to be
nothing but a "deadly mechanical grind."
He became discouraged and decided to
study pedagogical principles and methods
further. In his first year at Columbia
University he discovered nothing new. In
his second he discovered John Dewey's
Ethical Principles, in which it was stated that
conduct was "the real test of learning. The
teacher must watch and guide, he could not
force." Fortified with this knowledge and a
Master's degree which he received in 1904,
Patri went back into New York's public
schools.
In his first school after Columbia, Patri's
supervisors objected to his use of Dewey's
principles. Patri changed schools and found
a principal whose motto was "serve the
children." Everything was all right then.
In 1908 he became principal of P. S. No. 4

G. Maillard Kesslère
ANGELO PATRI

and five years later of P. S. No. 45. One
of the first things Dr. Patri did when
he became principal was to build up a relationship between the school and the children's parents. He started after-school
activities for the pupils and got their parents
interested in what was happening to the
point where a Parents' Association was
formed. He began holding assemblies
where folk tales were acted out, where there
was dancing and singing. Most important,
he began to take a special interest in children who were above or below the normal
level of accomplishment.

Children who failed were examined carefully to find out the cause of the trouble—
their eyesight and hearing were tested; their
teeth and tonsils examined; their home life
looked into; their interests discovered.
There was the boy who came to P. S. 45
after seven years of failure. "I can't learn
anything," he said doggedly. "My father
says I'm no good. I gotta low I. Q. The
quicker you put me out of here the better."
Yet after a year that boy had done a wood
carving that made both the principal and
the boy's father proud. Children brighter
than usual, too, were given special attention,
placed in special classes, given special work
and liberty of action.

Out of Dr. Patri's school have come many
people famous today as sculptors, etchers,
doctors, lawyers, writers. John Garfield, the
actor; Joy Davidman, the poet and novelist;
John Amore, winner of the Prix de Rome in
sculpture; William Hassler, the scientist, are
only a few of the graduates of whom P. S.
45 and Angelo Patri are proud.

In this large, plain school, whose walls
are decorated by pupils' work, whose books
have been rebound by pupils, it has always been emphasized that the teacher

PATRI, ANGELO—*Continued*

must continually ask the child, that the teacher must know the child, that "the school must stop doing things for the people and get the people to doing for themselves by putting the work before them in such a way that they will be able to do it."

Many of the principles by which Angelo Patri guides his school have been presented to a wider public than the pupils of P. S. 45 through his syndicated column and through his books. His column, *Our Children*, has, Dorothy Canfield Fisher says, "uplifted family life in countless American homes." Years ago President Eliot of Harvard said: "Whatever else Patri does, he must never stop those irreplaceable talks to teachers and parents in the newspapers." Many parents feel exactly the same. Together with his wife, Dorothy C. Patri, whom he married in 1910, Dr. Patri is a consulting educator, concerned with the problems of children.

Dr. Patri's first book for parents and teachers, *A School Master of the Great City*, was published in 1917. *The School That Everybody Wants* and *Child Training* followed in 1922. In 1925 came *School and Home*; in 1926 *Problems of Childhood* and *What Have You Got to Give?*; in 1930 *The Questioning Child*; in 1940 *Parents' Daily Counselor*. There were, too, books for children, including a translation of *The Adventures of Pinocchio* (1937), *Pinocchio in Africa* (1911) and *Pinocchio in America* (1928); *White Patch* (1911); and *Spirit of America* (1924).

References

Collier's 70:7-8 S 16 '22 pors
Read Digest 36:101-5 Je '40
Beard, A. E. S. Italian Immigrant Who Influenced Public School Education: Angelo Patri *In* Our Foreign-born Citizens p266-74 1939
Leaders in Education 1932
Who's Who in America
Who's Who in New York

PATRICK, MARY MILLS Mar 10, 1850—Feb 25, 1940 Founder and president emeritus of the Istanbul College for Women at Istanbul, Turkey

References

American Women
Who's Who
Who's Who in America 1938-39

Obituaries

N Y Herald Tribune p22 F 27 '40 por
N Y World-Telegram p19 F 27 '40
Sch & Soc 51:274 Mr 2 '40
Springf'd Republican p9 F 27 '40
Time 35:57 Mr 4 '40

PATTERSON, ELEANOR MEDILL Nov 7, 1884- Editor; publisher

Address: b. Times-Herald, Washington, D. C.; h. 15 Dupont Circle, Washington, D. C.

A red-haired woman editor who dictates newspaper policies by whims and changes her mind between editions sounds like something out of a scenario writer's imagination. Employees of the Washington, D. C. *Times-Herald* know these things can happen in real life, though, for their editor and publisher, Eleanor Patterson, probably outdoes all fictional editors, male or female, in unexpected and sensational moves.

Eleanor Patterson is the only woman editor-publisher of a large metropolitan daily in the United States. Wealthy, society-bred, she does not try to follow any conventional pattern in her work. Flanked by her three French poodles, which have the run of the office, she may sweep into the office in riding habit or in evening clothes. So much firing and rehiring has this mercurial lady editor done that she had seven news editors in the first decade of her editorship.

But even her enemies—and she can make bitter enemies—acknowledge that she is a good newspaper woman. She took over Hearst's moribund morning newspaper in Washington, the *Herald*, with a circulation of 60,000, and in several years had raised it to the 115,000 mark, with the Sunday edition at 225,000. Later she took over the Hearst evening paper, the *Times*, and now runs both combined in the *Times-Herald*, with morning and evening editions.

When she bought the papers in 1939 veterans of the newspaper business wondered if she could make them pay in the competitive and hard-to-get advertising revenue field of Washington. They wondered, too, if the newspapers were not just another whim of Eleanor Patterson's that she might decide to change at any moment. But in 1940 she told an interviewer the papers were beginning to pay. Deficits were being cut, and "dashes of black ink were appearing on the ledgers."

Whether "Cissy" Patterson, as her friends know her, continues to run the papers or not, she will have given Washington gossip-lovers some exciting moments. The *Interesting, But Not True* box which appeared on the *Herald's* front page soon after Mrs. Patterson took over its editorship in 1930 is now Washington newspaper history. The report was that Mrs. Patterson's cousin, Ruth Hanna McCormick, was to run for the Senate and that Alice Roosevelt Longworth would campaign for her. Mrs. Patterson denied the report in a brief item signed by her and headed *Interesting, But Not True*. She wrote: "Mrs. McCormick takes no advice political or otherwise from Mrs. Longworth. Mrs. Longworth gives no interviews to the press. Mrs. Longworth cannot utter in public. Her assistance, therefore, will resolve itself, as usual, into posing for photographs."

Washington loved this sort of thing, a revival of a girlhood feud between Alice Roosevelt and Mrs. Patterson, just as it loved Mrs. Patterson's other sharp forays. The *Herald's* circulation boomed.

"Cissy" Patterson comes by her interest in newspapers naturally. Her grandfather, Joseph Medill, moved from Cleveland to found the Chicago *Tribune,* and laid the basis of a distinguished family with it. One of Medill's two daughters, Elinor, married Robert Wilson Patterson, a Chicago reporter who rose to a high position on the *Tribune,* succeeding his father-in-law as editor. The Pattersons had two children, Joseph Medill and "Cissy." Joseph Medill Patterson became founder and publisher of the New York *Daily News,* and Cissy, always an admirer of her brother and her father, was also bitten by the newspaper bug. Her mother's sister had married Robert S. McCormick and their son, Colonel R. McCormick, became the publisher of the Chicago *Tribune.* Another son was the late United States Senator, Medill McCormick.

"Cissy" was born in Chicago, November 7, 1884, and her mother planned a brilliant social career for her. After Miss Hersey's finishing school in Boston there were debuts in Chicago and Washington, where the family maintained a huge, pretentious house in Dupont Circle. Eleanor married when she was 19. Her husband was Count Joseph Gizycki, a handsome, dashing young Polish cavalry officer whom she had met abroad and who had pursued her from continent to continent.

The marriage was unhappy from the beginning. The Count's castle was heavily mortgaged, and apparently he regarded his wife as another chattel. Cissy stuck it out for three years and then in 1907 left with her baby daughter. The Count followed her to England, abducted the child, hid her in a convent in Austria, and there ensued some of the most sensational stories of the decade. American newspapers railed at "foreign fortune hunters," letters passed from President Taft to the Czar of Russia, and wire-pulling at the Russian court by the McCormick family went on at top speed as the search for the baby continued. Finally the Countess recovered her child and arrived in New York in 1908, heartbroken. It still was not the end of the marriage. "Cissy" was unable to get a divorce until 1917, and the Count, it was said, "came out of the affair about half a million dollars richer."

Mrs. Patterson married again, a month after her daughter Felicia's marriage in 1925. Her second husband was Elmer Schlesinger, New York lawyer and United States Shipping Board counsel. In 1929 he died suddenly on a golf course of a heart attack, and "Cissy" found herself alone again. She had been drifting aimlessly for almost 20 years. She was well known in New York and Washington society, had

S. J. Woolf

ELEANOR MEDILL PATTERSON

spent years on a ranch in Wyoming, hunting and riding, and had done some writing. She had published two novels under the name of Eleanor M. Gizycka—*Glass Houses* in 1926 and *Fall Flight* in 1928, the first having thinly-disguised Washington personages as its characters.

But she had a hankering for the newspaper business. In 1930 she persuaded William Randolph Hearst, an old friend, into letting her try her hand at editing his Washington *Herald.* That same year she thrust aside the names of Countess Gizycka and Mrs. Schlesinger and had her name legally changed to Mrs. Eleanor Patterson.

William Randolph Hearst probably thought the publicity of Mrs. Patterson's name would be worth her $10,000-a-year salary. But she went into the work with all her tremendous energy, put all her wit and emotion into it. She was not too proud to go out on stories herself. When unemployment was running high in Washington, Mrs. Patterson disguised herself as "Maude Martin," a penniless woman in search of food, shelter and a job, and spent three nights in Salvation Army headquarters and days in employment agencies, later writing the story of her experiences.

She walked into Al Capone's guarded mansion and got a story from the bootlegger. She started a campaign to get hot lunches for children. And she was quick to recognize the importance of society news in Washington, printing pages of it while other papers were using columns. She tackled the business end, too, getting after the shopkeepers with whom she traded for ads and using her imposing residence to give parties for prospective advertisers who might be flattered by invitations from the social Mrs. Patterson.

PATTERSON, ELEANOR—*Continued*

By 1937 she was so absorbed in her newspaper career that she leased the *Herald* from Hearst and also his evening paper, the *Times*. When Hearst's competitor in the morning field, Eugene Meyer, publisher of the *Post*, began dickering for the *Herald*, Mrs. Patterson bought it together with the *Times*. Mrs. Patterson's feuds with Meyer over circulation and talent have made another picturesque chapter in her newspaper career. After Mr. Meyer won a court battle for the use of the comic strip, *The Gumps*, Mrs. Patterson sent him a pound of raw meat, neatly wrapped, with the implied message that he could have "his pound of flesh."

Mrs. Patterson says she plans to carry on, "make the paper soundly profitable and then divide up some of the shares with the employees." The red-haired lady newspaper publisher needn't worry about not having enough left for herself. Her holdings in the New York *Daily News* and Chicago *Tribune* will keep her comfortably even if she should decide to give up her *Times-Herald* or at least part of it.

References

Am Mag 130:28-9+ Ag '40 il pors
Newsweek 10:35 Ag 14 '37 por; 13:29 F 6 '39
Sat Eve Post 211:22-3+ My 6 '39 pors
Time 30:21 Ag 2 '37 por; 35:36 Mr '40 por
Allen, R. S. and Pearson, D. Washington Merry-Go-Round p12-14 1931
American Women
Who's Who in America
Who's Who in Commerce and Industry

PAUL, ELLIOT Feb 13, 1891- Author

Address: Hotel Lafayette, 9th St and University Pl, New York City; Pumpkin Hill Farm, Brookfield, Connecticut

When Elliot Harold Paul published a highly successful mystery novel in 1939, *The Mysterious Mickey Finn*, many people wanted to know if this was the man who also wrote that best-selling novel, *The Life and Death of a Spanish Town* (1937). He is the same Elliot Paul; and in 1940, as successor to his first mystery venture, appeared a second, *Hugger Mugger in the Louvre*. Like *The Mysterious Mickey Finn*, subtitled "Murder at the Café du Dôme," the scene of the new story is Montparnasse in Paris during the expatriate heyday. Mr. Paul knows well the Paris of these years through his journalistic work there, and his editorship with Eugene Jolas of *transition* brought him in contact with the literary and art movements of the time. In addition to its hilarious and breath-taking merits, *The Mysterious Mickey Finn* notably involved a millionaire art collector, several French artists and American celebrities, the sleuth being talented young Homer Evans. Its lack of traditional formula, its clever satire on art and on the general antics of expatriates were further distinguishing features. In the book, *Hugger Mugger in the Louvre,* Homer Evans is again on hand, as are also some of his friends of the Mickey Finn events. The story begins with the theft from the Louvre of a valuable Watteau, companion piece to one not stolen. An art museum as a crime scene has unique possibilities, not excluding mummy cases; and a copy of Joyce's *Ulysses* adds sophistication to the local color. While *Hugger Mugger in the Louvre* has a smaller quota of corpses than its predecessor, a taxidermist, a sharp-shooting gal from Montana, an American bottle-and-jar satrap and a Marchioness function as living thrill-producers.

Mayhem in B-Flat, described by the *Saturday Review of Literature* as a "sizzling concoction of murder, merriment and madness, which, this time, gets slightly out of control —if you care to notice it," also appeared in 1940. So did *Fracas in the Foothills,* the fourth in the series of Homer Evans which brings many of the familiar characters to the badlands of Montana. *The Death of Lord Haw-Haw* (1940), written under the pseudonym of Brett Rutledge, is another mystery in which an English-speaking Nazi radio spieler located in Manhattan" is "scotched by a Yankee-born French intelligence department ace." This one wasn't so favorably received by reviewers, however: the New York *Times* reviewer reported that "the total effect of the book is something like reading a mystery story while listening to the War news over the radio."

Elliot Harold Paul, the son of Howard Henry and Lucy Greenleaf (Doucette) Paul, was born in Malden, Massachusetts, in 1891. After being graduated from high school, he left comfortable New England for the American Northwest to join his brother Charles, a hydraulic engineer, on irrigation work in Idaho and Wyoming. After long days at surveying and timekeeping, he returned to Boston and took up newspaper work, until he went to France during the War with the 317th Field Signal Battalion of the A. E. F., serving as private and sergeant, He covered the French and Belgian occupation in the Ruhr, and as a newspaper correspondent traveled extensively in European countries. His journalistic affiliations have been with The Associated Press and the Paris editions of the Chicago *Tribune* and New York *Herald*.

Elliott Paul's published works include three early impressionistic novels—*Indelible* (1922); *Imperturbe* (1924); and *Impromptu* (1923)—and in the past few years, *Low Run Tide* (1929); *Lava Rock* (1929); *The Amazon* (1930); *The Governor of Massachusetts* (1930); *Concert Pitch* (1938); and the Book-of-the-Month Club selection, *The Life and Death of a Spanish Town*. With Jay Allen he also wrote in 1939 *All the Brave*.

Until Paul and his second wife (he married Flora Thompson Brown April 15, 1935) and her small son were rescued by a German destroyer, *Die Falke,* in September of

1936, he spent five years in the little town of Santa Eulalia, on the Island of Ibiza, in the Balearic group bordered by Spain and Africa and Sardinia. Here he became part of the village life, settling down to tranquil days among the islanders—fishermen, storekeepers, café owners, mechanics, farmers, priests and military officers—they who in days to come were to divide their last *pesetas* and red wine and beans and gay spirit with him. He loved them all—their docile beasts, the shadows of trees making Picasso-violet shadows on their white houses. . . "I was proud of Eulalia, and of the Spanish Republic, and of so many good men and lovely girls for whom vistas were opening."

The simple village folk took him to their hearts and called him "Xumeu" (Bartholomew), affectionate name for friends and friendly strangers. With Pep Torres, farmer and town wag, Paul organized an orchestra which was much in demand for weekly dances and feast days, and especially for weddings and rural pig-slaughters. Pep exercised his colorful tenor voice and was responsible for violin and trumpet accompaniment, while Paul played the accordion and an antiquated piano lent by the proprietors of the local theatre. Others played the lute, Spanish mandolin, guitar, castanets, tambourine, chimbumba and triangle. Besides Spanish favorites, Paul arranged American dance tunes—*Tammany, Harvest Moon* and *It Ain't Goin' to Rain No More*, which were always encored again and again and earned the players glasses of cognac. Later, during menacing revolutionary days, Pep and Paul kept up their spirits by collecting Ibicenco music and preserving it in various forms on paper. Apart from his activities in the musical life of the village Paul also organized a daily class in English for the young girls and boys.

In *The Life and Death of a Spanish Town* he captures the spirit of the happy island people as they were before the merciless invasion of civil warfare. His friends were shot, 400 of them herded together and mowed down by Italian and Rebel machine guns and most of the hospitable houses crushed by alien bombs.

Now Santa Eulalia is a dead village and Paul is left with memories of the tranquil, enchanted days . . . "whenever I think of the slopes and woods and acres under cultivation, the shapes of my favorite trees and the smell of rosemary and laurel, the gait of the peasant girls and the greetings of the peasant men, I cannot forget the produce. Perhaps that was most beautiful of all. I am in the stores of Santa Eulalia, or the market place in Ibiza, Valencia, Palma, Barcelona, Alicante, Madrid. I shall not say Ninevah because I was never there. As a child I regretted lost cities, but what need have we of such reminders now?"

Leaving the tragedy of a dead Spanish village, Elliot Paul in his next novel returned to the American scene. *The Stars and Stripes Forever*, published early in 1939, is a

Libsohn-Ehrenberg
ELLIOT PAUL

swiftly paced strike novel laid in a Connecticut manufacturing town and based on documentary material. Showing the class division of forces over the issue of the right to organize and bargain collectively, it contains the typical strike ingredients: picketing, labor spies, committees, arrests, finks, lockouts, state troopers. But in Paul's book the situation has a new slant because the story is told by the factory owner's brother-in-law, who sympathizes with the strikers and works with them. The novel also excellently portrays the effect of strike warfare on the town itself, combatants and non-combatants alike. Critics in general, however, are of the opinion that Paul wrote less convincingly of the life and death of an American town than he did of the life and death of a Spanish town.

Since 1925 Elliot Paul has lived most of the time in Europe, and his literary career has been that of an expatriate who has written much about Americans, but with less success than about Spanish characters. His recent mystery stories have a foreign setting, and a mixture of foreign and transplanted American types. Though Paul lately made a return trip to Paris, he is at present making his home in the United States.

References

Newsweek 10:27 Ag 14 '37 por
Sat R Lit 17:3-4 N 6 '37
Time 35:48 Mr 4 '40 por
Who's Who in America

PEABODY, ENDICOTT, REV. May 30, 1857- Former headmaster of Groton School
Address: Groton, Massachusetts

After 55 years as headmaster of Groton School, which he founded (with Sherrard

S. J. Woolf

REV. ENDICOTT PEABODY

Billings and William A. Gardner) in 1884, the Reverend Endicott Peabody retired in June 1940, in his 83rd year. The school which he founded "for manly Christian development" is considered exemplary among American secondary institutions. Many of its 1,400 graduates, including President Roosevelt and his sons, are famous; and probably to all of them Dr. Peabody is looked upon with respect and awe as "the greatest natural force in the United States, with the possible exception of Niagara Falls and the Mississippi River." Dr. Peabody was succeeded by the Rev. John Crocker.

Endicott Peabody was born in Salem, Massachusetts, May 30, 1857, the son of Endicott and Marianne (Lee) Peabody. He was sent to England to be educated and was graduated from Cheltenham College, England, in 1876. He received from Cambridge an LL. B. (1880) and an LL. M. (1884). His father at that time was a partner in the British branch of the House of Morgan. On returning to the United States, Dr. Peabody studied theology, taking a Bachelor of Divinity degree at the Episcopal Theological Seminary, Cambridge, Massachusetts. Since 1885 he has been a priest of the Protestant Episcopal Church.

He was 27 years old when he and his friends built the first school building, Brooks House, in the little town of Groton, 45 miles from Boston. A year later (1885) he married Fannie Peabody of Danvers, Massachusetts. They have six children: Malcolm Endicott, Helen (Mrs. R. M. Sedgwick), Rose (Mrs. W. B. Parsons Jr.), Elizabeth Rogers, Margery, Dorothy (Mrs. F. T. Davison).

For his excellent work in education, Dr. Peabody has received honorary degrees from Harvard and Yale Universities. In 1935 he was given an honorary L. H. D.

by the University of the State of New York. At the dinner on that occasion, President William M. Lewis of Lafayette College praised Groton above other secondary schools. Groton boys use excellent English, their manners are flawless, and their record as public servants is unique among graduates of swank schools.

From the beginning Groton has been a school for the upper class. Among its first pupils were Higginsons, Whitneys, Harrimans, Rogers, Morgans. Theodore Roosevelt sent his three sons there. Groton is an "inbred" school: out of a student body fixed at 180 boys, 94 are sons of alumni. Ten boys are given scholarships each year by competitive examination. Among its famed alumni are, besides Franklin D. Roosevelt, Joseph Clark Grew, Bronson Cutting, Robert McCormick, Payne Whitney, George Whitney, Ellery Sedgwick, Arthur Train, Sumner Welles (see sketch this issue), E. Roland Harriman, Dean Acheson, Junius S. and Henry S. Morgan, Oliver La Farge.

Groton is modeled much on the English public school system. The boys dress for dinner, aid in the choice of a senior prefect and play "fives," a game which originated at Eton. To outsiders Groton is snobbish; within, its discipline is democratic and somewhat Spartan. Endicott Peabody, who was a great oarsman at Cambridge, believes in rigorous exercise and encourages the rougher team sports, as well as tennis and golf.

One Grotonian, George Biddle, in an autobiographical essay (*Harper's*, August 1939), *As I Remember Groton School*, speaks with high praise of Dr. Peabody, "the Rector," as the boys called him. Though Groton had a distinctly English ring, he made several innovations that included breaking down the wall that had separated boys and masters, the introduction of the honor system, and a modification of the English fag and hazing traditions. The Groton code, Mr. Biddle says, was snobbish rather than military: precise and socially conservative, it exacted, first of all, obedience. It seems that the Rector had a way of winning the liking and respect of each boy individually. One of the boys once said of him: "You know he would be an awful bully if he weren't such a terrible Christian." His "look" is famous; of it, there has come down through the years the story of a first-former's comment: "Did you see the way the rector looked at that cat? And the cat—why, the cat just kept on going."

Mr. Biddle says of him: "Dr. Peabody is not a scholar himself. He is a great administrator and a warm Christian. I should define his Christianity as an unshaken faith in his particular God and a fervent wish to keep physically fit, sexually clean, morally honest, and—in every sense of the word —a gentleman. I fancy he dislikes a dirty collar as much as a dirty word, and is shocked by an East Side accent as well as by outspoken Atheism."

Franklin D. Roosevelt, class of 1900, has always been an admirer of Dr. Peabody. He has said: "As long as I live, his influence will mean more to me than that of any other person next to my father and mother." And Mr. Biddle tells the story of how, at a Union Club dinner (where Roosevelt had been roundly condemned) the Rector loyally defended his former pupil as "a gallant and courageous gentleman."

Dr. Peabody, though retiring at the age of 83, is tall, fit, pink-cheeked, with twinkling blue eyes and a quick wit. As every boy and master knows, he still misses nothing. His favorite sports are bicycling and horseback riding, and he hopes to devote much of his time henceforth to these. Handsome Mrs. Peabody often rides with him.

References

Harper 179:292-300 Ag '39
Lit Digest 119:18 Ja 19 '35 por
N Y Times VII p13, 26 My 12 '40 por
Newsweek 16:34 Jl 1 '40 il por
Sat Eve Post 213:16-17+ S 14 '40 il pors
Time 26:26+ O 28 '35 por; 35:11 Mr 11 '40 por

Who's Who in America
Who's Who in American Education

PEATTIE, DONALD CULROSS (pē-tē) June 21, 1898- Botanist

Address: 224 Buena Vista Rd, Montecito, Santa Barbara, California

A botanist with a poet's inspiration, a naturalist with a philosopher's insight, Donald Culross Peattie has won high critical acclaim for his several books on plant life and nature. His *Flowering Earth* (1939), called the best horticultural book of the year, was awarded a silver medal on June 11, 1940 by the Commonwealth Club of California.

Flowering Earth demonstrates Mr. Peattie's equal love for the world of flowers and the world of words: a fine lyric touch distinguishes a prose style pervaded by a continuous sense of beauty. A story of the miracle of plant life written for lay readers, it has been said of *Flowering Earth* that it does for the plant world what Alexis Carrel (see sketch this issue) has done for medical research. The book is not burdened with chemical formulas and it has no formal botanical glossary; but it is a complete, vital story of chlorophyll and of protoplasm, of algae and seaweeds, conifers and cycads. Mr. Peattie describes in terms of human behavior what plants have done; he gives a convincing sense of nature's oneness in Illinois, in California and in the South as he has seen and felt it.

Donald Culross Peattie was born June 21, 1898 in Chicago, Illinois. His father was Robert Burns Peattie, journalist and wit; his mother, Elia (Wilkinson) Peattie, a

Ward Wicart

DONALD CULROSS PEATTIE

novelist, essayist and for many years literary critic on the Chicago *Tribune*. Young Peattie was graduated from the Chicago University High School in 1916 and was a student at the University of Chicago from 1916 to 1918. He received his B. A. *cum laude* from Harvard in 1922, where he specialized in the natural sciences. In that year he also won the Witter Bynner Poetry Prize.

Between 1918 and 1919 he was a publisher's reader for the George H. Doran Company; but immediately after being graduated from college took a position in the Department of Agriculture as botanist in the office of foreign seed and plant introduction under Dr. Fairchild. From 1922 to 1923 he worked with J. Arthur Harris in Miami, Florida on frost resistance in tropical plants.

Peattie married the novelist, Louise Redfield on May 23, 1923. They have three children: Malcolm Redfield, Mark Robert and Noel Roderick. Mrs. Peattie collaborated with her husband in the writing of two of his earlier books.

After the publication of his first book, *Cargoes and Harvests* (1926), Peattie left the Department of Agriculture to freelance in his own field and began a nature column in the Washington *Star* which ran for 10 years. In 1928 he took his family to the south of France, where at Vence and Menton they made their home for five years. During these years he published three books of fiction. In 1930 he wrote *Vence, the Story of a Provençal Town.* The Peatties returned to America in 1933.

Many critics have reacted ecstatically to all of Donald Culross Peattie's writing. But their highest praise has been showered upon *An Almanac for Moderns* (1935). This has been described as "an essay in biology in

PEATTIE, DONALD—*Continued*

365 parts, the day by day revelation of a sensitive and incorruptible mind." It consists of short, beautifully written reflections on and interpretations of the various manifestations of nature. Of it Mark Van Doren (see sketch this issue) has written: "Not merely is it the best book of its kind that I have read in years: it is one of the best books I ever read. I suspect it of being a classic." As the book of the year most likely to become a classic, *An Almanac for Moderns* was awarded the Gold Medal of the Limited Editions Club in 1935.

The same year Peattie's *Singing in the Wilderness,* a delicately written, somewhat over-sentimentalized memoir of Audubon and his wife, was published. In 1936 came *Green Laurels,* biographical sketches of the lives and achievements of the great naturalists. Mr. Peattie is further distinguished for his *Book of Hours* (1937), 24 essays after the manner of those in *An Almanac for Moderns*; *A Prairie Grove* (1938), the story of a small section of Illinois prairie from the days of its formation to modern times; *A Gathering of Birds* (1939), an ornithological anthology; and *Audubon's America* (1940), for which he wrote the introduction and biographical notes. His column *The Nature of Things* appears each month in *Bird Lore.*

To enable him to continue his work in nature study Mr. Peattie was awarded a Guggenheim Fellowship for 1936 to 1938. He is at present preoccupied with Western nature and history and for the past year or two has lived in Santa Barbara, California.

References

N Y Times VII p14-15+ Je 2 '40
Scholastic 36:22 My 13 '40 por
Wilson Lib Bul 10:362 F '36

America's Young Men
Who's Who Among North American Authors
Who's Who in America

PEGLER, WESTBROOK (pĕg'lĕr) Aug 2, 1894- Newspaper columnist
Address: b. Scripps-Howard Newspapers, 230 Park Ave, New York City; h. New Canaan, Connecticut

James Westbrook Pegler (he dropped the James early in his career) has been in hot water so many times as both newspaper reporter and columnist that he must, by this time, have developed the skin of a rhinoceros. The man who has made dissention a philosophy and the word *agin* his battle cry is read daily by 6,500,000 people in 114 newspapers throughout the United States. The fact that his yearly income is estimated at $60,000 shows that Americans still cling to pioneer journalism—rich in salty abuse, personalities and a strong conviction that in every controversy both sides are wrong.

Pegler was born into a newspaper family in Minneapolis, Minnesota, in 1894. His father, Arthur James Pegler, came from England as a young man, thrilled by tales of American cowboys, and his mother, Frances (Nicholson) Pegler, was born in Minneapolis. Pegler Sr., became a star reporter in Minneapolis, Chicago and New York. Now in his 70's, he was actively at work for the New York *Daily Mirror* until a few years ago. In 1913 Pegler Sr. and Charles Washburn wrote the classic tear-jerker melodrama, *Little Lost Sister,* taken from some sensational articles Pegler wrote on Chicago vice rings. In 1940 it was playing in New York City to hilarious crowds under the title, *She Gave Him All She Had.*

At five young Westbrook began to show that inquisitive instinct which makes a good reporter. He wanted to know how it feels to ride in a patrol wagon! So when his father took him and his brother for a Sunday morning stroll downtown, he disappeared, rushed to the police station, told the chief he was lost, and while his father was frantically searching the town, had a triumphant ride home in the patrol wagon.

Pegler attended the Horace Greeley School and the Lane Technical High School in Chicago, but his heart was set on entering the newspaper business as soon as possible. At home he lived in an atmosphere of newspaper shop talk. When he couldn't get his father to let him "run copy" to the newspaper, he induced a newspaper photographer to let him carry his camera. One time this involved photographing the disinterred skeletons on a "murder farm" in Indiana. It had no lasting deleterious effect on Pegler, who in 1910, "a raw kid, as freckled as a guinea egg," got $10 a week at the United Press in Chicago telephoning short accounts of newspaper stories to small dailies. "Bud," as he was called, began to think he was pretty good and asked for more money. "I won't give it to you," said the bureau manager, "but I'll give you some advice. If you ever want to be a newspaperman, you'll have to go back to school." So Pegler went to Loyola Academy for two years.

Pegler met "Tad" Dorgan, the cartoonist, and showed him some cartoons he had laboriously sketched. "Isn't there anything else you can do?" commented "Tad" after a glance at them. During a two weeks' job with the International News Service in 1912 Pegler first met the late Arthur Brisbane, whom he later used as subject for one of his most devastating parodies. Brisbane was a very important person. "Here, boy," he said, holding up several sheets of copy, "run these down to the wire." Pegler didn't know who he was but he did know that he himself was no messenger. "Run it down yourself," he replied.

The United Press re-employed him and started him up the newspaper ladder, first with the Des Moines *News*; next gave him a fancy title (Southwestern manager for the United Press) and sent him to St. Louis. Then they sent him to Texas, where as manager of the bureau he did such good work that in 1916 they asked the 22-year-old reporter to join the staff in London as a foreign correspondent.

Pegler maintains that he was one of the lowest-paid war correspondents with the American Expeditionary Force. Very soon he was in hot water with the officer in charge of British Operations. The United Press was asked to keep the brash young Pegler out of conferences because he embarrassed the general by asking too many questions. As soon as the United States entered the First World War, Pegler lost no time in getting "in bad" with Admiral Sims and then with General Pershing. Although he was perfectly right in wanting the answers to questions, he was about to be shipped home, a failure. Evidently desiring some peace and quiet after his one-man war against generals, Pegler joined the Navy, in Liverpool, in the spring of 1918. At the end of the War he returned to the United States and went into sports-writing for the United Press, candidly admitting that he noticed "that the big salaries on newspapers usually were paid to the sports men." Floyd Gibbons had told him to stop signing himself J. W. Pegler because "a Pullman-car name like 'Westbrook' will help sell your stuff."

Pegler noticed that many sports men wrote in the "poetic, romantic school." Seeing few writers in the tough, rowdy-phrase school, he decided he'd have a better chance with less competition and lined up with them. He wrote slowly, carefully, and chose funny or fantastic sports happenings. Soon he was a star writer who by "tireless arguments" had "pushed up his salary to a fabulous $125 a week." As a "rather self-conscious happy-go-lucky reporter" Pegler served as a model for *Young Man of Manhattan*, by Katharine Brush.

In 1925 Pegler made a very important change. The Chicago *Tribune* hired him at $250 a week to write a daily sports story for syndication around the country. When there weren't any sports happenings of interest to write about, Pegler tried his hand on other topics. Thus by accident he changed from a sports writer to a commentator on national affairs. In 1933 he was asked to write a syndicated column for the New York *World-Telegram* and other papers. He was nervous about this promotion "to the ranks of the think men." He didn't want to make a fool of himself and he was modest concerning his own talents. He wrote: "I am not very well acquainted among the gold-standard crowd, the NRA crowd, the Governor-do-your-duty crowd, and the whither-are-we-drifting writers, but new around here. And I have a feeling just from the looks of them that there will be days over here in the Sacred Heritage of Liberty Department when I will pine for good old Primo and the Ol' Bambino."

Right at the start, with Pegler-prediliction-for-hot-water, he plunged in, writing the famous column which seemed to justify a lynching in California although it was aimed against self-righteousness. That got him into grave trouble with the intelligentsia, whom he labels "doubledome Babbitts." Dipping his scalpel in gall instead of ink,

WESTBROOK PEGLER

he has outraged at one time or another practically everyone who reads his daily column. When he went abroad and sent back a series of scathing attacks on Mussolini and Hitler (whom he called racketeers at a time when other writers were hesitating about them) the intellectuals liked him. In more recent years they have been calling him a reactionary, Fascist, Tory and Red baiter, detest him because he constantly attacks the CIO and other labor unions, Communism and Roosevelt, whom he labels "mamma's boy."

Pegler has made a fetish of irritation. He assumes that both sides are generally wrong. Identifying himself with the "common man," he asks embarrassing questions. Fascism rouses him to fury, as do crooked politics, spoiled rich people, James Farley, Harold Ickes, the Newspaper Guild, Eleanor Roosevelt (see sketch this issue) and the income tax. In the matter of income tax he has been carrying on a personal war with the tax collector. His agitation against tax exemptions of state salaries has brought about a "corrective act in the New York legislature." He has attacked Huey Long, Florida gambling and Upton Sinclair. He is the only man forbidden (in advance) to attend Walter Winchell's funeral. He is numbered by Quincy Howe (see sketch this issue) among those columnists who are "perhaps more conservative than the high-brows, more set against change because they have traveled farther to reach the positions they enjoy today." Pegler can find nothing good in unions, and delights in rummaging around for evidence that will back him in his contention that they are all either Red or rackets. Singlehanded in 1940 he unearthed damaging evidence against William Bioff, head of Hollywood movie unions, which resulted in Bioff's recall to Chicago to serve an old prison sentence.

PEGLER, WESTBROOK—*Continued*

It was Pegler who revealed the information in April 1940 which led to the indictment of George Scalise, resigned head of the Building Service Employees International Union, A F of L. Scalise said: "I've been Peglerized."

An amusing controversy was one in which Pegler critized Beniamino Buffano's model of the colossal statue of St. Francis of Assisi proposed for San Francisco. Pegler wagered that he could make a better statue. He promptly went to the studio of a friendly sculptor and concocted "an elf toting a gingerbread homunculus in one hand and a sheaf of carrots in the other while a fascinated mouse looks on." Pegler explained its odd look by saying: "My figure included a cornucopia, but two grapes and a pineapple were lost in the casting." The contest seems to have ended in a draw with the $200 wagered going to charity.

Reading Pegler day by day one finds him very uneven. He is sometimes funny—such as the time he waggishly repeated one sentence 50 times to make up his entire column: "I must not mix champagne, whiskey and gin." At other times he shows that he is way out of his depth, discussing questions which he will not or cannot think through. But no matter what he says, he says it always well and sometimes magnificently. These sentences, brisk, easily read, seem to be dashed off. Actually it takes him hours of slow toil to polish each phrase. He writes in the country, at his home in New Canaan, Connecticut, and hates New York City. About three or four times a year he tours the country to find out what is going on and what he should be *agin*.

His irritated, scornful, suspicious columns seem to be written by someone who is always "on the point of biffing somebody on the jaw." Actually this is a complete fiction. He is friendly and approachable, "Peg" to most people and "Buddy" to a few. "His sandy hair is graying over the temples," writes Milton Mackaye in *Scribner's*. "A gangling kid as a reporter, he has begun to put on a little weight at the middle. He is just under six feet tall, has a sulky Mick mouth (his mother was Irish), a crooked smile and skeptical, angry eyes."

Pegler's marriage is a "storybook romance." At a murder case in 1920 he met Julia Harpman, a reporter on the New York *Daily News*. Their marriage was postponed for two years because Miss Harpman spent more than a year in a hospital as the result of a broken back received in an automobile accident.

Pegler has published two books of reprints of his columns. The first was *'T Aint Right* (1936) and the second, *The Dissenting Opinions of Mister Westbrook Pegler* (1938). One critic said: "If one article incites you to want to kill the writer, calm yourself and read another, you may want to telegraph him congratulations."

Certainly Pegler does not mean everything he says. He even dissents from his profession by writing: "Of all the fantastic fogshapes that have risen off the swamp of confusion since the big war, the most futile and, at the same time, the most pretentious, is the deep-thinking, hair-trigger columnist or commentator who knows all the answers just offhand and can settle great affairs with absolute finality three days or even six days a week."

References

Life 8:34 My 6 '40 pors
Nation 146:273-6 Mr 5 '38
Newsweek 12:22-3 Ag 29 '38 il por
Sat Eve Post 213:10-11+ S 14 '40 pors
Sat R Lit 16:10-11 Je 26 '37 pors
Scholastic 32:20E Mr 26 '38 por
Scrib Mag 104:7-9+ O '38 por
Time 32:22 O 10 '38 por; 36:13 S 2 '40 por
American Catholic Who's Who
Howe, Q. The News and How to Understand It p51-3 1940
Who's Who in America

PENARANDA, ENRIQUE (pän'à-rän'dà ĕn-rēk') Nov 17, 1892- President of Bolivia

Address: La Paz, Bolivia, South America

General Enrique Peñaranda is a war hero who became President of his country. Commander in chief of the Bolivian Army during the latter part of his country's six-year bloody Chaco War with Paraguay, General Peñaranda was the army's choice for President.

His election was hailed as Bolivia's first return to constitutional government since 1931. It was the first time since March 1931 that the Bolivian government had changed hands without a coup. Bolivians went to the polls in 1940 in orderly, democratic fashion, although only 100,000 of the country's 3,500,000 population (most of them Indians) voted.

While Bolivians had an opportunity to vote for a President for the first time in eight years, they did not have much choice. Two other candidates had been invalidated because they had not fought in the Chaco War, and in the interest of harmony it was said that General Peñaranda would be the sole candidate for President. Five parties presented candidates for Senators and Deputies, however, and a coalition government was promised.

Nevertheless Peñaranda's election was not without some faint repercussions. Two weeks after his election a plot to capture the President-elect and to assassinate Provisional President Carlos Quintanilla was uncovered and nipped in the bud by the army chief of staff. The revolting soldiers marching on the palace were halted without a gunshot, and Peñaranda took over the reins of government peacefully on April 15, 1940.

The popular General Peñaranda had been offered the Presidency twice before and had refused for personal reasons. He has no easy job with Bolivia's complicated economic and political problems. His predecessor, Provisional President Carlos Quintanilla, had taken over after the suicide of Germán Busch, who had set himself up as a dictator in July 1937 after the revolution and had suspended part of the constitution. When Busch was found dead several weeks later, Quintanilla took charge and by restoring the constitution promised an end to the long régime of force and revolution since the military revolt during the Chaco War.

President Peñarando is a dark, fun-loving man. He is an almost pure-blooded Indian. Born November 17, 1892 in the Province of Larecaja, Department of La Paz, son of Teodocio and María Castillo de Peñaranda, he received his early education in the schools of La Paz. He entered the Military College in 1907, graduating in 1910 with the rank of second lieutenant

He rose steadily in the army. He was promoted to lieutenant in 1913; captain in 1917; major in 1921; lieutenant colonel in 1925. In 1932, three months after the start of the war with Paraguay, he became a colonel. The insignia of brigadier general he received on the field of battle in December 1933 and the same month was appointed commander in chief of the Bolivian Army in the field, a post which he held until after the termination of the Chaco War.

After the signing of the Peace Protocol of Buenos Aires, Peñaranda was promoted to the rank of division general "for his example and constancy in defending the country, for his skill in leading troops and for his influence in maintaining the morale of the soldier high and steady."

Bolivians were hopeful that in Peñaranda's four-year tenure as President their country would see the beginning of a new era through the solving of its economic, political and social problems. When he took office, General Peñaranda himself talked enthusiastically about the return of democracy, while welcoming and guaranteeing foreign capital invested in Bolivia to improve communications and to build hydroelectric plants.

But although he continued to speak enthusiastically of democracy after taking office, by September 1940, according to the *Christian Science Monitor's* correspondent, Peñaranda's emphasis on a "healthy nationalism" had made the quality of his enthusiasm suspect in certain circles. By Peñaranda's order the Leftist Congress was dissolved; a former Presidential candidate, the Rector of Oruro University, and many others who participated in the Congress were thrown into prison; and an amnesty law for political prisoners was vetoed by the President. His Minister of Agriculture, Alcides Argueda, openly favored a dictatorship.

Wide World

ENRIQUE PENARANDA

Oddly enough, while Bolivia was electing as President its war hero, General Peñaranda, its neighbor, Paraguay, was beginning its first year under the Presidency of Chaco War hero, the late José Felix Estigarribia (see sketch this issue).

References

Bolivia 7:5 Mr-Apr '40 por (p4)
Bul Pan Am Union 74:576 Ag '40 por
Christian Sci Mon p2 Ap 15 '40 por; p2 S 6 '40
N Y Times p37 Mr 10 '40; p6 Mr 27 '40 por; p11 Ap 16 '40
Scholastic 36:4 Mr 25 '40
Time 35:36 Ap 29 '40 por

PERKINS, FRANCES Apr 10, 1882-
United States Secretary of Labor
Address: Department of Labor, Washington, D. C.

Frances Perkins, the only woman member of the United States Cabinet, hates references to her sex. "Being a woman," she says, "has only bothered me in climbing trees." It has bothered others, however, and in the fall of 1940 opinions were sharply expressed by Wendell Willkie, Robert Moses (see sketches this issue) and others that the Secretaryship of Labor was a man's job. "The attitude of both labor and employer toward Miss Perkins," said Mr. Moses, "is a good deal like that of habitués of a water-front saloon toward a visiting lady slummer—grim, polite and unimpressed."

It is true that labor has been "lukewarm in her support" and that industry has considered her "one of the least important members of our government." Yet there are

FRANCES PERKINS

few persons in either camp who are not aware of her "strength of character, her devotion to the truth," of the fact that she is "a forward-looking person in touch with all reform movements, sympathetic to social control and social responsibility."

Frances Perkins came to the Department of Labor from the social work field and her broad *a's*, her neat tricorne hats, her New England background combine to set her aside from the rather more tough and businesslike Secretaries of Labor who preceded her. She was born in Boston, Massachusetts and brought up in Worcester. Her father, Frederick W. Perkins, was a classical scholar and businessman who founded the firm of Perkins and Butler, twine manufacturers, in Worcester. Both he and her mother, Susan (Wight) Perkins, were, like their New England forebears, "conservative and puritanical." They were, besides, Republican.

"Fanny" went to Worcester Classical High School, where she was a good but not outstanding student. Album pictures "indicate that she was pretty and she was, by her own account, articulate." When she was 16 she entered Mount Holyoke College, where she majored in biology and chemistry. She was also a fair campus politician, chairman of the Y. W. C. A. committee and elected permanent president of her class of 1902.

Although she was offered a job as an analytical chemist after graduation, Frances Perkins remained in Worcester for the next two years doing social work for the Episcopal Church, since her family didn't believe that women should work outside of the home. They did, however, permit her to take a position teaching chemistry in a girls' school near Chicago. Once there, it was inevitable that she should drift toward Hull House. For six months she lived there, trudging around to inspect tenements and sweatshops, becoming friends with the social workers there. Then Miss Perkins decided she needed more training in the social sciences. She entered the University of Pennsylvania and while she was studying economics and sociology acted as executive secretary of the Philadelphia Research and Protective Association, which combined placement with social case work. Because of her work, Columbia University offered her a fellowship and she received her Master's degree from the University in 1910.

Very shortly afterward she became executive secretary of the New York Consumers' League, which investigated industrial conditions and fought for protective legislation, especially for women and children. It was in 1911 that Frances Perkins witnessed the Triangle Shirtwaist Company fire in which 146 girls died. She never forgot it and for the next six years devoted much of her time to safety legislation. She conducted an investigation into cellar bakeries of New York City, as a result of which regulations were enforced, and in 1912 she became executive secretary of the New York Committee on Safety, a position she held until 1917. During this time, from 1912 to 1913, she was director of investigations for the New York State Factory Commission. Because of this position she traveled all over the state investigating, and frequently went to Albany. She had gone to Albany before —to help put over legislation for a 54-hour week for women workers—and had become acquainted with the politicians there—Al Smith, Robert F. Wagner, Franklin D. Roosevelt and Big Tim Sullivan, Tammany leader who helped teach her politics. He liked her. "You can look right at a man and know he is lying and never show it," he once commented. It was during this time, too, in 1913, that she was married to Paul Caldwell Wilson, a financial statistician who became secretary and financial adviser to John Purroy Mitchell, reform Mayor of New York City.

In 1919, after she had served for two years as executive director of the New York Council of Organization for War Service, she was made a member of the New York State Industrial Commission by Al Smith, and as commissioner continued writing, speaking and working for industrial and labor legislation. It was she who was largely responsible for the 54-hour week for women being changed to 48, for monthly statements on employment trends, for the standardization of state industrial legislation. In 1921 she became director of the Council on Immigrant Education, in 1922 a member of the New York State Industrial Board and in 1926 its chairman. In 1929 Roosevelt, when he became Governor, made her Industrial Commissioner of New York State. And when Roosevelt became President of the United States in March 1933 one of his first acts was to appoint her Secretary of Labor.

Immediately there was opposition. William Green, president of the American Federation of Labor, railed: "Labor will never be reconciled to her appointment"; the politicians objected to a woman in her position; business felt her to be rather too pink a liberal, with too little experience with Big Business to understand its problems. Only liberal magazines like *The Nation* came out with statements in praise of her suitability, her "diversity of interest within the broad field of labor and industrial relations and superlative personal achievement." Miss Perkins herself remained unperturbed and busy, too busy to buy an inaugural costume. What her daughter Suzanne and a friend bought for her, however, "was precisely as ordered: Rock of Gibraltar, rather, with a dash of style and a discreet touch of feminine appeal."

Her goal as Secretary of Labor, she said in 1933, was to get more pay, more comfort and more security for the ordinary worker. Her first act was to disband a group of undercover men hired by her predecessor, Doak, "to investigate violations of the alien-labor law, Bolshevism, moral turpitude, grand duchesses, foreign movie actors who overstay their leaves and similar menaces." She then proceeded to put in a system of fact finding about unemployment and unemployment statistics. Under Miss Perkins the Children's Bureau and the Women's Bureau have run smoothly and the Department of Labor Standards, the Bureau of Labor Statistics have all grown and functioned perfectly.

Still, Miss Perkins played only a small part in the growth of other labor agencies and services. The NRA was not put into the Department of Labor; neither was the National Labor Relations Board. The Wages and Hours Board and that for the Walsh-Healy act, though in her department, were made semi-autonomous. Partly because she was unable to build up her department and partly because so many activities were carried on over her head, by 1935 *The Nation*, which had so warmly welcomed her appointment, felt that she was "one of the least important members of our government"; others felt that "she herself has played no important rôle in the labor movement" in a period when labor problems have been to the fore, that her "department remains just a bureau, the Secretary just an office holder."

Most commented upon was her ineffectiveness as a conciliator and what Benjamin Stolberg calls her "ineptitude with the tougher variety of politicians both in the labor movement and in Congress, with the more hard-boiled industrialists and newspapermen." She started out bravely when, shortly after she took office, she stated the case for organization in the steel industry and then toured the steel towns, defying the company police who tried to keep her from speaking. Yet a few years later Big Steel was settled without a strike and she accomplished nothing in the Little Steel strike, which was lost. During the automobile strike of 1934 she was on the sidelines; during that of 1937 she created headlines by telling reporters that Sloan (see sketch this issue) of General Motors "ran out on me." By then reports were current that Edward McGrady, the assistant secretary, who had brought about a number of settlements in coal and automobile strikes, would take her place.

Labor seemed somewhat to resent her "welfare worker outlook" and remarks such as: "Sometimes violence comes from one side and sometimes from the other"— delivered when she was asked for a comment on a current situation. They, too, like the rest of the country, were conscious of her failure to bring about peace between the CIO and the A F of L—as one commentator put it, "All she did was to flutter solicitously between the two camps and to play down the difficulties in terms of her wish fulfillment." And at the same time it was felt by capital, as the New York *Sun* expressed it on June 4, 1940, that "by her opposition to repair of the Wagner Labor Act and by her support of other jug-handled legislation the Secretary herself . . . has strengthened the subversive elements in the American Labor movement."

Much of the work of the Immigration and Naturalization Service (transferred in 1940 from her department to the Department of Justice) was criticized, and criticism reached a head in February 1940, when a resolution was offered in the House instructing the Judiciary Committee to inquire whether she should be impeached for her failure to deport Harry Bridges (see sketch this issue). It was defeated and hearings were held on the deportation charges.

In November 1940 there were rumors, notably in the New York *Times*, that she had resigned as Secretary of Labor but would be connected with the Administration in some capacity. Miss Perkins denied this.

There are many people in Washington who find Miss Perkins in public life "earnest, rather humorless, briskly official," who tend to resent her sharp way of speaking up. Newspapermen, particularly, ever since they first tried to get "feature" stories from her and were told: "We New Englanders keep to ourselves," have seldom felt her to be a sympathetic personality. They have commented on her habit of talking "as though she had swallowed a press release, no asides, off-record confidences or personal comments." There are others, however, who feel that she has a "great deal of real charm. She is surprisingly feminine. She has large brown eyes, vivacious and intelligent; her hands are beautiful and she uses them expressively." That her clothes are not "surprisingly feminine," all agree. Her hats are almost always tricornes and her street clothes have been said to "look as though they had been designed by the Bureau of Standards."

PERKINS, FRANCES—Continued

Although Miss Perkins' private life is strictly her own, with very little known about it except that she has a house in New England and often spends week ends in New York with her daughter Suzanne, "who was never in the least interested in her mother's reforms and is married to David Meredith Hare, a New York socialite," everybody in Washington knows that Frances Perkins is one of the hardest workers in public life. She is in the office from nine in the morning until dinner and she works there until midnight at least twice a week. When she first came to Washington the chauffeur assigned to drive her official car resigned after a few weeks. He was tired, he said.

References

Am Mercury 32:398-407 Ag '34; 42: 416-26 D '37

Collier's 94:16+ Jl 28 '34 por

Good H 106:28-9+ Mr '38 por

Nation 136:192 F 22 '33; 136:253 Mr 8 '33; 140:353-5 Mr 27 '35; 142:303 Mr 11 '36

N Y Times p1, 20 N 25 '40 por

New Yorker 9:16-19 S 2 '33; 9:20-4 S 9 '33

Sat Eve Post 206:29+ S 16 '33 por; 213:9-11+ Jl 27 '40 il pors

American Women

Babson, R. W. "That Woman!" (Frances Perkins) *In* Washington and the Revolutionists p81-118   1934

Gillis, A. and Ketchum, R. Frances Perkins: Friend of Labor *In* Our America p281-98   1936

Kirkland, W. M. and Kirkland, F. Frances Perkins, the Girl Who Never Forgot *In* Girls Who Became Leaders p44-50   1932

Unofficial Observer [pseud.] Utopia on Tap *In* New Dealers p172-202 1934

Who's Who in America

Who's Who in the Nation's Capital

PERLA, DAVID July 13, 1900—June 14, 1940 Pathologist; immunologist

December 1940 Bulletin: Dr. David Perla died June 14, 1940 of a heart attack in his laboratory at Montifiore Hospital, New York City. He was 40 years old.

From June issue:

The discovery of a method for the prevention and treatment of surgical shock (prostration or collapse that may occur during or after a severe major operation) was announced by Dr. David Perla, young scientist and physician of Montefiore Hospital in the Bronx, New York. Experimentation on, development and results of the new technique were made public in a report by Dr. Perla in the Proceedings of the Society of Experimental Biology and Medicine, March 1940.

Observers believe that the discovery is equal in importance to Crawford Long's use of ether and Banting's discovery of insulin. Success already in 30 cases indicates that the procedure may blaze a new trail in the field of surgical care. It should save many lives not only in the operating room but also in the emergency operating ward and particularly in the hospitals on European battlefields.

The publication of Dr. Perla's paper followed 12 years of research in the field of natural resistance, and nearly two years of carefully controlled experiments with rats and mice.

The new antishock treatment consists of injections of the vital hormone (desoxycorticosterone acetate) secreted by the adrenal gland, in combination with the administration of solutions of common table salt.

Since the development of general anesthesia nearly a century ago, surgeons have long been aware of the dangers of shock that frequently follows an operation, regardless of the physician's skill. It consists of a sudden drop in blood pressure, and the withdrawal of blood from the brain and extremities to stagnate in the large vessels of the abdomen. The condition is known outside the operating room also. It may follow a fall, a bad burn, a limb injury; or it may be brought on by a severe emotional shock.

For a number of years scientists in medicine had been aware of the similarity between the signs and symptoms of "adrenal insufficiency" and those of secondary surgical shock. It was suggested that failure of the adrenal cortex, following an operation, was responsible for the shock. It was known also that the suprarenal cortex plays an important part in the mechanism of natural resistance to intoxications, poisons and bacterial infections. Dr. Perla attacked the problem with a view to finding out whether the patient's resistance could not be built up prior to the operation by supplementing or assisting the function of the adrenal gland.

He began his experiments at the Montefiore laboratories by using the cortical hormone derived from the adrenal glands of cattle, segregated two years before and since used only in the treatment of Addison's disease, and a saline solution which previously had proved effective in building shock-resistance. He divided a number of rats into four groups. He left the first group untreated, administered saline solutions to the second, cortical extract to the third, and both saline and cortin to the fourth group. Then all the rats received lethal doses of histamine, a chemical that lowers blood pressure by dilating the small blood vessels—a condition thus similar to the shock-condition following operations. Of the first group of untreated rats only 40 per cent survived; of those treated with saline, 55 per cent survived; of the cortin-treated, 75 per cent; and of those with both saline and cortin, 100 per cent survived. Similar experiments, with similar results, were made with mice. It was discovered that the resistance of animals could be built up to a point where they could withstand much greater doses of poison.

On the basis of these experimentations a plan for the prevention of surgical shock was carried out in preparing a series of patients for surgical procedure. These were suffering from major chronic diseases, such as tuberculosis and cancer, but were poor surgical risks because of their debilitated condition. From the fifth to the second day before operation they were given specified amounts of the desoxycorticosterone acetate intramuscularly, and the saline solution intravenously.

"In all instances," Dr. Perla reports, "the patients were strikingly benefited. There was no objective evidence of shock. The blood pressure was maintained or elevated. The temperature in general returned to normal within 24 to 48 hours. Post-operative exhaustion and toxemia were definitely lessened. Complications did not occur. And operative recovery appeared, to the surgeons concerned, to be more rapid than in their preceding surgical experience in our hospital."

However, since many of the gravest operations must be performed after accidents, or wounds received in battle, when there is no opportunity to build up such a resistance to shock, studies were made to determine the use of the preventive medicines after the operation. To simulate this situation rats and mice were given doses of killing poison first, and then divided into four groups. As in the previous experiments, one group was untreated, another given saline only, a third only the cortin, and a fourth both saline and cortin. And, just as the prophylactic treatments were successful in preparing the system for approaching shock, so the therapeutic treatments acted to neutralize the killing poison. Dr. Perla points out, however, that the prophylactic effect of the cortical hormone and saline was much greater than its therapeutic value.

Since the amazing success of the preoperative treatment at Montefiore Hospital, the method is being used in two other large hospitals in the Metropolitan area, where a wider experience can be established. Working with Dr. Perla on the development of the method were Drs. David G. Friman, Marta Sandberg and Sidney S. Greenberg.

Dr. Perla holds the rank of associate pathologist and immunologist at Montefiore Hospital and is instructor in medicine at Columbia University. He was born in New York City in 1900, the son of Jozue Perla and Fannie (Herzruecken) Perla. He received the degrees of B. S. and M. D. at Columbia University, the latter in 1923. His internship was at Montefiore Hospital (1923-

Newspictures

DAVID PERLA

24); he was assistant superintendent at Bedford Sanatorium (1924-25); research fellow at Henry Phipps Institute, Pennsylvania (1925-26); and studied in Berlin and Freiburg from 1926 to 1927. He became associate pathologist and bacteriologist at Montefiore Hospital in 1927. He is the author of many articles in scientific periodicals, and in collaboration with his wife, Dr. Jessie Marmorston, of works on the physiology of natural resistance. He is the father of three daughters. His hobby is portrait painting—when he finds time for it.

References

N Y Herald Tribune p21 Mr 12 '40
N Y Times p25 Mr 12 '40
N Y World-Telegram p1, 6 Mr 11 '40 por
Sci ns 89:132-3 F 10 '39
Time 35:158 Mr 25 '40

American Medical Directory
American Men of Science
Who's Who in American Jewry

Obituaries

N Y Herald Tribune p32 Je 16 '40
N Y Times p15 Je 15 '40

PERTINAX, pseud. *See* Géraud, A.

PETAIN, HENRI PHILIPPE (pā'täN' äN'rē') Apr 24, 1856- Marshal of France
Address: Vichy, L'Allier, France

Hero of the Battle of Verdun, Premier of defeated France (June 16, 1940) at the fall of the Reynaud (see sketch this issue) fight-to-the-end Cabinet, aged Marshal Henri Philippe Pétain became, on July 8, 1940, head of a "completely totalitarian system of government for France."

MARSHAL PETAIN

Thought to be in actuality the figurehead of a régime whose real dictator is Vice-Premier Pierre Laval (see sketch this issue), the 84-year-old Pétain is seen by many observers to be re-enacting the rôle of Hindenburg in Germany after the First World War.

Little was known about Marshal Pétain before his achievement at Verdun elevated him to chief of staff in 1917 and made him one of the most revered figures in France. His was the famous rallying cry, *"Ils ne passeront pas"* (They shall not pass)—a cry made familiar in more recent years as the watchword of the Loyalists in Spain, while its progenitor was, ironically, supporting Franco.

Pétain's life before Verdun was that of an obscure organizer of the French Army. He was born in 1856, educated at the St. Cyr School, early destined for a military career. An officer since 1878, he became in 1900 a battalion commander and for a year thereafter was a professor in a military school. He became a colonel in 1911 and brigadier general in 1914, when he attracted attention for a courageous charge at the head of his troops with a riding crop in one hand and a revolver in the other. In 1914 he received command of the 33rd Army Corps. In 1917 he became commander in chief of the French armies on the Western Front.

The first few years after the War Pétain spent in temporary retirement on his Riviera farm, where he cultivated prize roses. In 1920 he married Madame Hardon. He was recalled to service in 1925 to command the army sent against the Riffs in Morocco. In 1929 he succeeded Foch among the immortals in the French Academy. He served as vice-president of the Supreme War Council, and in 1934 became War Minister of the "sacred union" Doumergue Cabinet after the

Stavisky scandals. During these years Pétain made only one voyage outside his country—that was in 1931 when he came to the United States. He was met at the Battery by General Pershing and was given a triumphal parade to City Hall, where he was welcomed to this country. Of his visit he said that "it surpassed everything of which I ever dreamed." After Franco's victory in Spain, Pétain, who had once taught Franco military tactics and who had always admired him, became Ambassador to Spain. He was recalled from this post to assume the Premiership of France when the Reynaud government fell.

To observers of the less-publicized aspects of Pétain's career, it was no surprise that his first official act as Premier was to tell the nation it must ask Hitler for peace. During a crashing thunderstorm he spoke in a broadcast from Bordeaux. In his aged, cracking voice the one-time hero of Verdun announced that the Maginot Line had broken, that the German columns were plunging southward. "I have applied to our opponent," he said, "to ask him if he is ready to sign with us and, as between soldiers after the fight, and in honor, put an end to hostilities." Franco was asked, at Pétain's request, to be peace-mediator; and those leaders in France who had always been for surrender to the dictators were given Cabinet posts. Weygand (see sketch this issue) was named Minister of National Defense (it was recalled that his sympathies had always been Rightist); Chautemps, who had paved the way for the Daladier (see sketch this issue) régime, was named Vice-Premier; and Jean Ybarnegaray, vice-president of the Croix de Feu, French Fascist organization, was also awarded a Cabinet position. In spite of the strictest censorship, the people of France soon came to believe that France had been undermined as much by treachery as by incompetence and a strictly military defeat.

Some critics maintain that feeling in France became widespread against this pro-Fascist government. Pétain had many years before been suspected of being a patron of the Croix de Feu. Documentary evidence later revealed that Pétain's name, along with Laval's, was among those in the Fascist scandal of the "Hooded Men" during the Premiership of Chautemps. The aim of this organization was to replace the Republic with a totalitarian dictatorship; and at that time Pétain was asked if he were willing "in case of national emergency" to "head a strong government." When the "emergency" finally arrived in May 1940 two other factors made Pétain the favored and logical choice of the pro-Fascists: from the start he had exerted pressure on France to recognize Franco's government; at the same time he was a remembered military hero to all French citizens—an excellent patriot. He was paternally fitted to chastise the people of France after their defeat; his further broadcast to them has been interpreted in some quarters as a deliberate attempt to develop defeatism among them. "France had too few allies, too few children, too few arms and too few men," he said. "Since the World War victory, the spirit of sacrifice has been absent from France. We have sought more than we have given."

When the British expressed indignant criticism of France's separate peace, Pétain led the French reply and accusation, declaring · that Churchill (see sketch this issue) was not the best judge of French interests, that he was trying to divide France "at a moment when the country suffers," and that Britain failed to send sufficient aid to stop the German attack. Pétain accepted, with the terms of the armistice, the fact that "our airplanes and our fleet are coming under the control of Germany and Italy." "Nevertheless," he said, "the government remains free and our honor is safe." There was no explanation from the Pétain government as to why it refused to follow the example of Norway and the Netherlands—move to England, and continue the War from there. British editors, such as Vernon Bartlett, M. P., declared that France's famed "200 families" and their spokesmen—Laval, Flandin and Bonnet—had willingly sacrificed France to preserve their own interests. Even before an armistice was asked they had worried less about the German advance than the possibility of "social" troubles in France.

The Pétain government had said that the French fleet would be turned over to German control. The British, however, had other ideas about this. When, on July 3 at Oran, British battleships opened fire on French ships, the Pétain government directed French warships thereafter to stop all British merchant ships on the high seas and ordered French vessels at Alexandria to fight their way home. At the same time the government was busy drafting a new constitution eliminating "'unwieldly democratic procedure," under which Parliament's only task would be to aid the government.

Five days later, July 8, a complete totalitarian system was announced, based on that of the Franco dictatorship in Spain. President Lebrun's resignation was asked; Pétain would be nominal head of the new régime, with Laval key man. The government in reality would be dominated by a triumvirate consisting of General Weygand, Pierre Laval and Adrien Marquet, former Labor Minister. Pétain, "tremendously impressed" by Franco's reconstruction methods in Spain, asked that they be followed in France's reconstruction. He gave additional leaders in the Croix de Feu powerful positions. The Vatican, through its official organ, approved Pétain as head of the reconstruction of France, saying that he was "an inspiration to the youth of France."

As the foundation of the new constitution, the new slogan for France—replacing "Liberty, Equality and Fraternity"—was to be: "Labor, Family, Fatherland."

On July 11 a national plebiscite was placed before the people, after which 80 negative votes from Parliament were cast on the Pétain plan. September found a new Cabinet set up, with M. Laval the only parliamentarian left · in it, found France's "new order" more clearly defined. Anti-Semitism was already one of its features. In October strikes and lockouts were banned; prices, foreign commerce and exchange were controlled; France went off the gold standard; the Entente Cordiale with Great Britain was entirely repudiated, and a policy of "true nationalism" and collaboration with Germany announced. After a meeting between Pétain and Hitler later in October it was feared that this policy of collaboration might even include joining the Axis in warring upon Great Britain as well as allowing Nazi use of the French Navy. This was denied, but the meeting was followed a few days later by the suppression of all colonial general councils and local assemblies in fear of a general movement toward De Gaulle (see sketch this issue), the placing of the textile industry under totalitarian control, and a speech in which Pétain announced that France will work in collaboration with Germany "to maintain French unity . . . within the new European order." "This policy," said M. Pétain, "is mine. The Ministers are responsible only to me. It is I alone history will judge."

That he will remain alone seems unlikely.

References

Cur Hist & Forum 51:11 Ag '40

Nation 150:769 Je 29 '40

N Y Herald Tribune p2 My 19 '40 por; pl Jl 5 '40; pl, 2 Jl 9 '40

N Y Times p4 Je 17 '40 por; p6 O 31 '40

Newsweek 16:28-9 Je 29 '40; 16:11 Jl 1 '40; 16:29 Ag 5 '40; 16:29-30+ N 11 '40 por

Time 35:34 My 27 '40; 36:25 Jl 1 '40; 36:26 Ag 26 '40; 36:31 S 30 '40; 36:33-4 O 21 '40 por

Johnston, C. H. L. Henri P. Pétain: Defender of Verdun *In* Famous Generals of the Great War p171-9 1919

Liddell Hart, B. H. Pétain: Military Economist *In* Reputations Ten Years After p209-30 1928

Simonds, F. H. Pétain, Soldier of Verdun *In* They Won the War p42-58 1931

Who's Who

PETRILLO, JAMES CAESAR (pĕ-trĭl-lō) Mar 16, 1892- Labor leader

Address: b. American Federation of Musicians, 175 W Washington St, Chicago, Illinois; 1450 Broadway, New York City

James Caesar Petrillo is a tough labor boss who is supposed to ride in a bullet-proof car and keep a pistol in his desk drawer; he "murders the King's English, forces the nation's leading symphony orchestra off the air and hasn't earned his living as a player in over a generation." He has been called the "Mussolini of music," a "pettifogging parasite . . . who machinated his way into control of the American Federation of Music." He is also a labor leader who "for more than 20 years has been boosting the wages and increasing the employment of musicians," in the face of canned music in theatres, dance halls and over the radio. Because of Petrillo "the musician in the theatre pit who used to receive $12 a week now gets $99," and he gets union help when he is sick and his widow gets benefits when he dies.

Petrillo, who stays at the Waldorf-Astoria when he is in New York and in an apartment building he owns when he is in Chicago, was born on Chicago's tough West Side. His father had come there from Italy and had a job as a sewer digger for the city. Young Jim went to the Dante Elementary School and in nine years was able to get through the fourth grade. "They bounced me around," he complains. "One year I would be in the fourth grade and next year in the third. They drove me nuts. After nine years I gave it up."

He got jobs while at school and after, peddling newspapers, running an elevator, selling popcorn. He also made his way as a musician. He had started to play the

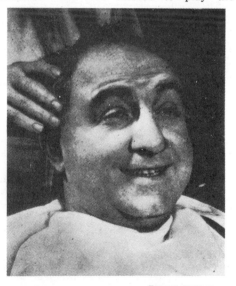

Bernard Hoffman
JAMES CAESAR PETRILLO

trumpet when he was eight and soon was a member of the *Daily News* band, in which he played for many years "without audible improvement." Then he organized his own orchestra which played for beer gardens, Italian dances, Jewish weddings and band wagons. He was the trumpeter—"loud but lousy" is his own description—until by popular request he switched to the drums. On the side he ran a cigar stand for a time and was at one time partner in a saloon. Finally he entered union politics.

Petrillo says he got started on his union career because "I liked punching holes in the other guy's arguments." His first affiliation was with the American Musicians' Union, a Chicago independent. At twenty-two he was its president and stayed at its head for three years. Then he was beaten in the elections in 1917 and quit the A. M. U. to join its rival, the American Federation of Musicians. The first speech he made in the Chicago local of the Federation got him boos. Still, in 1919 he became its vice-president and in 1922 its president, at $100 a week.

He immediately began fighting for Chicago's musicians. When radio began taking jobs away from musicians he stepped in. "Right away I found I had a fight on my hands." Petrillo won that fight: "Instead of seven days, the radio musicians worked six days, then five days for seven days' pay." He was a pioneer with the "standby" system, by which outside union men playing for radio stations must either join the union local or pay a musician to stand by and do nothing. He even arranged it so that the men who turn records when recorded music is broadcast are union musicians, paid union rates.

Petrillo got into a big fight in 1927 when the Chicago theatres disputed his powers. Two thousand musicians went out on strike. But in four days the strike was over and theatre musicians were all unionized. In 1931 Petrillo told the managers of all Chicago's hotels there would be no music on New Year's Eve unless they signed with the union. They signed. In 1936 he forbade Chicago musicians to make recordings for use in broadcasting; in 1938 a contract was signed which gave the American Federation of Musicians control over the output of canned music in 589 radio stations. Petrillo saw to it that no high school band played where a union band might; when a giant panda was to be welcomed by a troop of Chinese Boy Scout buglers, he demanded that eight union men be hired as well—and they were; he convinced the politicians that political sound trucks should resound with live music, not recordings. And he became active in Chicago politics, a "pal" of Mayor Kelly.

In 1933 Petrillo had himself appointed to Chicago's Park Board. He asked the Board: "If I prove the people want concerts will you appropriate for them?" The Board let him try, and in 1935 Petrillo organized free, open-air concerts in Grant Park, with his union footing the whole bill. The next year the Board paid for the concerts, and since 1935 some 15,000,000 persons have jammed Grant Park to hear them, and many union musicians have had jobs.

The threats to Petrillo's power in Chicago were negligible. In 1933, it is true, there were rumors of his having been kidnapped, and an injunction was issued to restrain him from using union funds, since, it was alleged, he had paid his ransom from members' dues. But Petrillo had the union books audited, bought $4,700 worth of newspaper advertising to tell the world his case, and all came out well for him. When the CIO started, John L. Lewis approached 2,500 members of the Chicago independent American Musicians' Union with the offer of a CIO charter. Petrillo immediately informed the independent musicians that the usual initiation fee of $100 would be waived (the rate to them was $4) and within a week had them rounded up into his union. This activity may have been the inspiration for Petrillo's active dislike of the CIO leader and his order in 1939 that references to Lewis be censored out of the *Man Who Came to Dinner* and George White's *Scandals*. Every newspaper in the country assailed him, and Petrillo had to backtrack: "I sure went the wrong way on that one," he said. "I was the most surprised man you ever saw when I read I was attacking the foundations of democracy. I certainly didn't want anybody to call me that kind of a guy—against free speech."

Petrillo's members in Chicago in 1934 sent him and his wife on a two months' tour of Europe—Petrillo came back saying: "They didn't have anything over there we wanted." In 1938 his members presented him with a $25,000 summer home at Fontana, Wisconsin. Petrillo isn't surprised by these gifts. "I don't abuse the power I have. I'm on the square with our members, so they give me things." In June 1940 his local members, who pay him a salary of $26,000 a year, helped elect him to the national presidency of the American Federation of Musicians. And Petrillo told them: "My services have never been for sale—only to the musicians I represent. . . I made you and you made me."

Petrillo has been a member of the A. F. M.'s national executive board since 1931. He had tried to get on it in 1927—"I got beaten very bad"—in 1930, and finally made it in 1931. When he wanted to become national president he helped vote the incumbent a $20,000-a-year pension, and took office on June 24, 1940 at a salary of $20,000 from the national office and $26,000 from Chicago, whose head he remains. Five days later he barred sustaining name bands from NBC and CBS in an effort to force two stations to pay minimum wages to a certain number of local musicians whether they were needed or not. This was settled by a compromise. Then Petrillo forbade RCA Victor to allow the Boston Symphony, the only non-union symphony orchestra, to make any more recordings. (It is because of Petrillo that the Boston Symphony hasn't broadcasted in more than a year.) "They're through," Petrillo announced. "We've taken them off the radio and off the records."

The real storm Petrillo stirred up, however, came in August 1940, when he informed the instrumentalists of the American Guild of Musical Artists (Heifetz, Horowitz, Zimbalist, Iturbi, etc.) that they had to join the American Federation of Musicians by Labor Day or be barred from radio and recording. "They're musicians and they belong to me," he declared. "Since when is there any difference between Heifetz playing a fiddle and the fiddler in a tavern? They're both musicians."

Immediately Lawrence Tibbett, president of the American Guild of Musical Artists and later of the American Federation of Radio Artists (September 1940), sought an injunction to prevent Petrillo's "blitzkrieg," which reflects "the personal ambition of one man to make himself the dictator of culture and entertainment in America." Tibbett pointed out Petrillo's control over his union—his power to fine up to $5,000, to call a strike at will, to set aside any except a financial provision of the union's constitution. Petrillo pointed out, in answer, that he personally had never called a strike and that the executive board, not he, had power to impose fines, and sadly shrugged: "Everybody calls me the tsar, the chieftain and this and that. What can I do?" Justice Steuer on November 19, 1940 refused to grant the temporary injunction to Tibbett who is continuing to fight Petrillo, nevertheless.

The controversy between Petrillo and Tibbett was heightened by the contrast between the two men personally. The cultured elegance of Lawrence Tibbett seemed so remote from "horny handed" Petrillo, who "except on formal occasions has never been known to use an adjective when he could use profanity; who frequently becomes grammatically involved"; whose face is fleshy, jaw hard. Petrillo is "stumpy, five feet five inches," with a paunch that is hidden by good tailoring ("I spend a lot of dough for clothes"). In summer he weighs 175 pounds, in winter 165, with the difference explained by his bottomless capacity for beer in hot weather.

Petrillo was married in 1916 to Marie Frullate, a girl from his old West Side neighborhood in Chicago. One of their children died of an infection from a football injury; the two others are Leroy, who is now helping to build the Chicago subway, and 16-year-old Marie. "She's beautiful!" says her father. Neither has musical ambitions.

References

Am Mag 130:30-1+ O '40 pors
Am Mercury 51:281-7 N '40 (Same abr. Read Digest 37:31-5 N '40)
Musical Am 60:3-4 S '40 por

PETRILLO, JAMES CAESAR—*Continued*

N Y Times IX p5 S 1 '40; p23 N 20
'40
Newsweek 16:57 Jl 15 '40; 16:57-8 S 9
'40
PM p42 S 8 '40
Sat Eve Post 213:12-13+ O 12 '40
pors
Time 29:24 Ja 4 '37 por (Same abr.
R of Rs 95:75 F '37); 35:60 Je 24
'40; 36:32 Jl 15 '40 por; 36:45 S 2
'40

PEYNADO, JACINTO B. (pä-näd'ō hä-
thin'to) Feb 15, 1878—Mar 7, 1940 President of the Dominican Republic

References

Bul Pan Am Union 72:504 S '38 por
International Who's Who

Obituaries

N Y Herald Tribune p22 Mr 8 '40;
p10 Mr 9 '40
N Y Times p21 Mr 8 '40; p15 Mr 9
'40

PHILLIPS, ALBERT 1875—Feb 24, 1940
Veteran stage and radio actor who played
General Ulysses S. Grant in Drinkwater's
Abraham Lincoln, and Stephen Douglas in
Sherwood's *Abe Lincoln in Illinois*

Obituaries

N Y Herald Tribune p10 F 26 '40
N Y Sun p19 F 26 '40
N Y World-Telegram p26 F 26 '40
Variety 137:47 F 28 '40

PHILLIPS, WILLIAM　May 30, 1878-
United States Ambassador to Italy

Address: h. 17 Commonwealth Ave, Boston,
Massachusetts

December 1940 Bulletin: William Phillips
resigned as Ambassador to Italy during
a leave of absence in the United States
in the summer of 1940. He has been convalescing from an illness. On December 18 Secretary of State Hull announced that Ambassador Phillips
would return to his post in Rome. It
is supposed that Italian war reverses
make the move necessary.

From July issue:

When in 1936 William Phillips was appointed United States Ambassador to Italy,
one commentator announced: "Mr. Phillips
has now gone to the Embassy in Rome,
where his skill in saying nothing will serve
him and his country well." Mr. Phillips'
"skill in saying nothing" has been serving
him and his country well for many years,
in all corners of the globe: London, China,
The Netherlands, Belgium, Canada, Washington. He is "everything that Henry James
could have hoped for in a United States
diplomat. Complete assurance behind
which there is an appealing shyness; capa-

city for being entirely graceful under any
circumstances and in any language; ability
to say yes or no with such distinction as
to leave one in doubt as to whether the sun
sets in the East or West; warm and friendly courtesy which could not possibly fail
under any exasperation; proud lineage and
acceptance by the best families—all these
are William Phillips'."

The first Phillips arrived in New England around 1630 and proceeded to found
Phillips Andover and Phillips Exeter Academies. Another Phillips was the first Mayor
of Boston. The Phillips family fortune was
made conventionally in shipping and real
estate and preserved in the best New England tradition. Probably when William
Phillips was born in Beverly, Massachusetts
on May 30, 1878, the son of John Charles
and Anna (Tucker) Phillips, it would therefore have surprised no one to learn that he
was to become one of the "bulwarks of
conservatism within the State Department."

William attended Milton Academy, in
1900 received his B. A. from Harvard, where
he was three years ahead of Franklin Roosevelt, spent two and a half years at Harvard
Law School and in 1903 entered the diplomatic service as private secretary to the
venerable Joseph H. Choate, United States
Ambassador to the Court of St. James. The
"sauve and elegant" young man soon attracted attention, and in 1905 he found himself second secretary at the American legation at Peking. But Peking was very far
away. In 1907 he resigned, gave up his
seniority, and started all over again in the
Gilbert-and-Sullivan-sounding position of
assistant to the third Assistant Secretary of
State on Far Eastern Affairs. His salary
was no more than an office boy's, but like
most of those who follow his career he had
independent means. The next year he was
himself third Assistant Secretary of State,
and the year after that he returned to London as first Secretary of the Embassy.

In 1910 Phillips married Caroline Astor
Drayton of New York, whose family, fortune, tact and charm would have been an
asset to any rising diplomat. In 1912, at
the age of 34, he retired on a leave of absence from London to become regent of the
College and secretary of the Corporation at
Harvard. But in 1914, when war broke out,
he accepted from Woodrow Wilson the
position of third Assistant Secretary of State
which he had held before, and he remained
in that position until he was appointed Assistant Secretary of State in 1917. During
1914 and 1915 it was to the Phillips' home
in Washington that Colonel House was accustomed to go to discuss the American
government's attitude toward the War.

In 1920 Phillips was in Europe as Minister to the Netherlands and Luxemburg,
in 1922 back in Washington as Under-Secretary of State, in 1924 in Belgium as Ambassador, and in 1927 he became the United
States' first Minister to Canada. Canada
was a convenient post because the Phillips

children could go to school in the United States, but the United States Minister and Mrs. Phillips unfortunately never found a house large enough to suit them! In 1929 he resigned and retired once more to Beverly, where he headed the Massachusetts drive of Herbert Hoover's private Committee on Unemployment until President Roosevelt called him back to the State Department in 1933. "That Republican Phillips was so honored by two Democrats (Wilson and Roosevelt) was proof both of his ability and his studied disdain of politics."

Once more Under-Secretary of State, Phillips' job was to supervise the acts of 800 members of Secretary Hull's (see sketch this issue) State Department and of 3,500 United States representatives scattered all over the globe, as well as to confer with the foreign representatives in Washington. Yet, although he would perhaps have been more at home under an old deal than a new, not once did a diplomatic break, a muddled situation or "so much as a misplaced comma" develop to haunt him. He remained "tight-lipped, adroit, correct in all formal punctilio from boutonnières to syntax, never caught offside in any close diplomatic huddle." For a time it was also his duty to make all diplomatic appointments in the State Department, but here he showed such an "overpowering preference for Social Registerites and career boys" at the expense of ambitious campaign contributors, and he developed such a personal horror of politics that all political comers were finally bundled off to another office.

In 1935 Phillips was a United States delegate to the London Naval Conference. In June 1936, after the resignation of Breckinridge Long, he sailed for Italy to take up his duties on August 4 as Ambassador to that country, to "keep watch in Rome on Europe's fever chart."

Someone once said of Phillips: "He has had the happy knack of always associating himself with the right men. His ladder to success has been Joseph H. Choate, Theodore Roosevelt, Elihu Root, Charles E. Hughes and Franklin D. Roosevelt, but he has climbed of his own ability, initiative and personality."

In spite of a good sense of humor, Ambassador Phillips is "so cautious and deliberate in his choice of words that he supplies his small world with few *bons mots*." But many years ago he supplied the perfect diplomat's answer to an interviewer's question: "There are jarring notes only when there are jarring personalities." Veteran Phillips is justly famed for his avoidance of jarring notes. Tall, lean, faultlessly tailored, complete with Harvard accent, shapely head, "sleek parting of the hair at the top of his high forehead," long nose and "aristocratically petulant mouth," he is "of the polished and professional type, cool to all but their closest friends"—surely "the career man's perfect picture of a diplomat."

Ambassador and Mrs. Phillips have three sons—William, Drayton and Christopher; two daughters—Beatrice and Anne; maintain homes in both North Beverly and in Boston. In Rome their home is a "great Italian Renaissance villa, with stucco walls, marble trimmings and gleaming classic statues galore on the roof and terrace."

References

> Business Week p18 N 30 '35 por
> Harper 174:227 F '37
> New Outlook 163:34 My '34
> N Y Sun p13 F 27 '40
> Newsweek 15:22 My 13 '40
> Time 26:18-19 D 9 '35 por (cover);
>   28:13 Jl 13 '36 por
> U S News 8:41 My 17 '40 por
> Moley, R. After Seven Years 1939
> Who's Who in America
> Who's Who in the Nation's Capital

PICK, BEHRENDT Dec 21, 1861—May 3, 1940 German numismatist; taught at University of Jena for 36 years; author; widely known as archeologist; visited the United States

References

> Wer ist's?

Obituaries

> N Y Times p17 My 30 '40

PIERCE, PALMER EDDY Oct 23, 1865—Jan 17, 1940 Brigadier General of the United States Army; former executive of the Standard Oil Company of New Jersey

References

> Who's Who in America 1920-21

Obituaries

> N Y Herald Tribune p18 Ja 18 '40 por
> N Y Times p23 Ja 18 '40 por

PINKERTON, KATHRENE SUTHERLAND June 9, 1887- Author

Address: c/o Brandt and Brandt, 101 Park Ave, New York City

Kathrene Pinkerton's story, *Wilderness Wife*, published early in 1939, of how she and her husband, who was ill, spent five arduous years in the Canadian North Woods aroused much popular interest as a modern pioneer venture. Mrs. Pinkerton was born June 9, 1887, in Minneapolis, Minnesota. After graduation from the University of Wisconsin she worked for the Russell Sage housing investigation, and then as field secretary for the Wisconsin anti-tuberculosis association.

In 1911 she married Robert E. Pinkerton, a writer, and for a time collaborated with him on short stories and novels. Soon after their marriage she and her husband—he on doctor's orders, she a city-bred girl with no experience of outdoor life—went to the Ontario wilderness. They had a capital of

KATHRENE SUTHERLAND PINKERTON

$80, and hoped to earn money by writing. It is the adventure of those years that Mrs. Pinkerton describes in *Wilderness Wife*. The stories at first didn't sell; while her husband served as a hunter's guide, she learned to cook and to manage a dog team, undertook trapping and fur trading, and even had a baby. Later writing success came, and they left their wilderness life.

"On our return to the States," Mrs. Pinkerton writes us, "we motored Westward, before there were surfaced highways. Lived in the high Rockies, on the desert, in the Sierra Nevada mountains and on the Pacific Coast. Because of our work, we could live where we wished, and it was our custom to settle in a place we liked, work for six months, move on. In 1924 we bought a small boat and cruised the British Columbia coast for three months. Liked it so well we bought a larger boat and lived on it almost continuously for the next six years, cruising the entire British Columbia coast and all of Southeastern Alaska. Once we did not sleep ashore for 522 nights."

They have traveled extensively since then, and in 1940 are staying in California. Their possessions, however, have been reduced for car traveling, and at any moment the Pinkertons can be foot-loose again.

Besides *Wilderness Wife,* Mrs. Pinkerton is the author of *Woodcraft for Women* (1915); *Penitentiary Post* with Robert Pinkerton (1920); *The Long Traverse* with Robert Pinkerton (1920); *Three's a Crew* and *Adventure North* (1940). She and her husband are coauthors of some six million words of magazine fiction.

PIRIE, JOHN TAYLOR (pĭr'ē) Sept 11, 1871—Feb 25, 1940 Chicago civic and financial leader; board chairman of Carson, Pirie, Scott & Company, Chicago department store

References

Who's Who in America 1938-39

Obituaries

N Y Herald Tribune p10 F 26 '40 por

PITTMAN, KEY Sept 19, 1872—Nov 10, 1940 United States Senator from Nevada; chairman of Senate Committee on Foreign Relations; president *pro tempore* of Senate; stockholder and officer in mining and industrial enterprises when elected to Senate in 1911; became known as "silver Senator" because he wanted silver pegged at high mark; backed President Wilson on ratification of peace treaty and League of Nations; became chairman of Foreign Relations Committee in 1933; fathered London Economic Conference's eight-power silver agreement of 1933; advocated sanctions against Italy during Ethiopian War, early embargo on all war supplies for Japan; led fight for passage of original Neutrality Act; wrote revisionary cash-and-carry statute passed in 1939; for Pan-American solidarity

References

Am Mercury 50:306-13 Jl '40
Cur Hist 51:6 N '39 por
Who's Who in America
Who's Who in Government
Who's who in the Nation's Capital

Obituaries

N Y Herald Tribune p12 N 11 '40 por
N Y Times p1+ N 11 '40; p12 N 11 '40 por

POLLAIN, RENE Nov 6, 1882—Nov 1940 Former conductor of New Jersey Symphony Orchestra; first viola player of New York Philharmonic Symphony Orchestra until 1935, when pensioned because of ill health; came to United States from France in 1918; became American citizen; sailed for France in summer of 1939, expecting to return to conduct 1939 to 1940 season of New Jersey Symphony Orchestra

Obituaries

N Y Times p23 N 13 '40 por

POORE, HENRY RANKIN Mar 21, 1859—Aug 15, 1940 American artist and author; widely known for his portrayals of animals and of hunting scenes; represented by paintings in museums of Europe, South America and the United States; author of many books on art; won many art prizes, including the $2,000 prize of the American Art Association

References

Who's Who in America
Who's Who in American Art

Obituaries

N Y Herald Tribune p10 Ag 16 '40
por
N Y Times p15 Ag 16 '40 por
Newsweek 16:51 Ag 26 '40 por

PORTER, COLE June 9, 1892-   Composer

Address: c/o Richard J. Madden 515 Madison Ave, New York City

That a boy from a farm in Peru, Indiana should become one of the best-known composers of sophisticated musical comedies with an international flavor is something of an anachronism. And perhaps Cole Porter, the boy in question, knows it because he has worked so hard at being a playboy.

Born in 1892, the son of Samuel Fenwick and Kate (Cole) Porter, on his parents' 700-acre farm near Peru, Indiana, Cole Porter began playing the violin and piano at the age of six. He didn't play much with other boys, he didn't do much of anything but practice and go to school because his parents thought he had talent. For fun he visited the winter quarters of the Hagenbeck and Wallace circus nearby, and became proficient at circus acrobatics practiced at home. But even before he left the confines of Peru, he composed a piece, *The Bobolink Waltz,* inspired by the song of the bobolink, and sent it off to a Chicago publisher. Although he was informed the song would be published, he never saw a check or the manuscript.

The Porter family was well off financially, Cole's grandfather having established the family fortunes when he started for forty-niner gold and ended up by buying Virginia timberland on which coal was found. Cole was sent to the East Worcester School for Boys, then Yale, where he distinguished himself by writing the famous football songs, *Bingo* and *Bulldog Yale,* and where his ballad *Miss Antoinette Birby* who "lived down in Derby" and whose adventures in that fountain of knowledge—Yale College—became undergraduate legend.

After he was graduated from Yale, he went to Harvard Law School for one semester, but quickly changed to the Harvard Music School, which he attended for two years. Later he supplemented this musical education by studying under Vincent d'Indy, the French composer, at the Schola Cantorum in Paris.

Armed with a Yale degree, a Harvard musical education, entree into the best cocktail parties, and the reputation for playing amusing songs, Porter might have begun his playboy career right then and there. Instead he elected to work. He wrote a musical comedy, *See America First,* in 1915, which turned out to be a dismal failure. It was his first important flop, and Porter was deep in melancholy.

Nelson

COLE PORTER

At this point an acquaintance suggested that the young composer would improve his compositions if he had the inspiration of more play life, saw something of the world and had more stimulating experiences than one circle of friends and one environment could give him. Porter disregarded this advice and set to work doggedly again. Then, when he seemed unable to create music, he joined the French Foreign Legion in desperation. He would see life, he would live dangerously, bravely, perhaps be killed. Instead, with the French Foreign Legion, Porter learned to be a playboy. The Legionnaire worked hard and played hard. Porter marched with a portable piano which looked like a zither slung across his back along with his pack, and when the regiment rested, he struck up the strings and played the men's favorite songs. He found himself composing tunes, creating in the abandon of play.

When the American troops began to arrive in France, Porter was transferred to a French artillery school to learn how to teach French gunnery methods to his fellow countrymen. He was far back of the fighting lines, and on leave had gay times in Paris. His sky-blue uniform, his Croix de Guerre (the French government had decorated him not for bravery but for good comradeship and personality) and his champagne parties are still remembered by Parisians.

During this period he married in Paris Mrs. Lee Thomas, daughter of William P. Lee of Louisville, Kentucky and former wife of Edward R. Thomas, well-to-do socialite. Porter now entered society and became a playboy in earnest.

He also began writing more music and did the scores and lyrics for two successes, *Kitchy Koo* and *Greenwich Village Follies. An Old*

PORTER, COLE—*Continued*

Fashioned Garden from *Kitchy Koo* was a huge success, and a few tunes from *Greenwich Village Follies* caught on. But Porter was still just one of the Tin Pan Alley troop, and not among the ranks of important composers.

Porter, however, did not lead the kind of life of other young men in Tin Pan Alley. He was Park Avenue at its most frivolous. He flitted from one party to another, from one yacht trip to another. He was at the opening of society's season in Paris; gave enormous parties at the Lido, Venice; held a salon at his home in the Faubourg St. Germain; week-ended in Morocco; was off on a world cruise. Producers shied away from him. They were afraid to put their shows into the hands of such a playboy.

Cole Porter's career came to a standstill. From 1923 to 1927 he could not get into a theatrical producer's office. He continued composing, however, for fun and for a circle of appreciative friends. He sang and played at Elsa Maxwell's and Noel Coward's parties. He amused the élite. The then Prince of Wales—Edward—liked his music. People described it as smart, but not commercial. Since Broadway had turned him down, Porter decided to chuck the works, retire to Venice and take up painting.

He tried to think he didn't want anything more to do with producers and acted the part of a bored young man, but when he saw Ray Goetz, the famous theatrical producer, on a beach at Venice, he confesses that his heart leaped. He knew he hadn't been playing for the fun of it. Goetz needed a composer to write scores for a musical comedy to be called *Paris*, which was to star Irene Bordoni. He wanted an American who could write songs with a Parisian flavor, and he didn't think any of the hard-working New York composers could do it.

So Cole Porter got the job, and went to work—or rather to play. For he worked hardest when he played hardest. He turned out not only *Paris* with its popular *Let's Do It Again,* but also *Fifty Million Frenchmen, Wake Up and Dream* and *The New Yorkers.* In 1932 there followed *The Gay Divorcee,* with its never-to-be-forgotten *Night and Day,* which swept the country, and in 1934 the tremendous hit, *Anything Goes,* which sent the whole country humming *You're the Top,* a song that was parodied so much that Porter had to take steps to forbid any but the original words from being broadcast on the radio. *Anything Goes* served to push Porter up to the top rung of the ladder of fame. Debutantes, stenographers, the man in the street were singing *You're the Top.*

Porter had written the score and lyrics for *Anything Goes* while drifting lazily down the Rhine River sheathed in a richly colored bathing suit. The music had been written for a musical comedy based upon an explosion on a ship at sea. But just before the show went to rehearsal the American excursion boat, *Morro Castle,* burned, and a comedy about an explosion seemed in execrable taste. The book had to be re-written quickly, with the boat afloat, and Porter began again to play and to compose. Only two songs, *You're the Top* and *Blue Bird,* were retained from his original score.

Cole Porter's *Du Barry Was a Lady,* which opened in New York in December 1939, was the first show in four years to charge $7.70 on opening night, with tickets being "scalped" at $50 and $75 a pair. The Cole Porter music and lyrics, and the personalities of Bert Lahr and Ethel Merman (later replaced) in the star parts were considered golden guarantee. The musical comedy had several good songs, among them *Friendship* and *Katie Went to Haiti,* but it was not Porter's best. It was still running strong in the winter of 1940, however, with seats still at a premium. *Panama Hattie,* his latest, opened with Ethel Merman in the title rôle in the fall of 1940 and has been enormously successful.

A working schedule for Porter means three or four parties a night, a wink of sleep between sunup and 10 a. m., and then a stretch of work from 11 a. m. to 5 p. m., when he starts the gay night life again. He does his best work lying on his back, looking up at the ceiling; he has his most successful inspirations while he is hard at work playing. He doesn't need a piano, paper and pencil to compose his lyrics. He thinks everything through, and then sets it down in a few minutes or dictates it to his secretary. His songs generally start with a title. Then he composes the melody, writes the last line of the chorus lyric, and works backward to the verse.

Porter has been called the heir apparent to the throne of Jerome Kern as the nation's top ballader. He followed *Anything Goes* with *Jubilee* in 1935. A song in *Jubilee* which scarcely raised a fuss was made into a dance arrangement by Artie Shaw in 1938. It became one of Porter's greatest hits, *Begin the Beguine.*

In 1938 he fractured both legs when he was thrown from a horse on the bridle path at Long Island's swank Piping Rock Club. In spite of the handicap of crutches he continued his visits to night clubs. While he was in bed he wrote part of the music and lyrics to *Leave It to Me.*

Porter is small, slender and slick-haired, cast in the image of Broadway. He moves, however, in a society of wealth and culture. A round-faced man, with saucer-like, gentle brown eyes, he has roaring enthusiasms. "I don't know why they say I'm bored," he told an interviewer. "I'm the most enthusiastic person in the world. I like everything as long as it's different. I like to go back to Peru, Indiana. I like hunting, swimming, parties, food, drink, composing. I like cats and voyages. You know I couldn't be bored or I couldn't compose. I am spending my life escaping boredom, not because I am bored, but because I don't want to be. I'm a hard-working boy from Indiana and I'm engaged in the business of entertaining myself, which enables me to entertain, as much as I can, the world." But one of these days, Porter says he is going to rest—"gardening, you know . . . in my back yard in Paris. I'm going to take a long rest from play and hoe and dig."

Mr. Porter's works include the scores of *See America First*, produced in 1916; *Kitchy Koo* (1919); *Greenwich Village Follies* (1924); *Paris* (1928); *Wake Up and Dream* (1929); *Fifty Million Frenchmen* (1929); *The New Yorkers* (1930); *Gay Divorcee* (1932); *Nymph Errant* (1933); *Anything Goes* (1934); *Jubilee* (1935); *Red Hot and Blue* (1936); part of the lyrics and music to *You Never Know* (1938); *Leave It to Me* (1938); *Du Barry Was a Lady* (1939); *Panama Hattie* (1940). He has also contributed numbers to other shows and written scores for several movies.

References

    Am Mag 119:62-3+ Ap '35 por
    Life 3:108 N 8 '37
    New Yorker 16:24-34 N 23 '40 por
    Scholastic 32:20E Ap 30 '38 por; 26:
      23 Mr 16 '35 por
    Stage 12:35 D '34; 15:43-6 Ag '38
    Theatre World 24:107 S '35
    Time 34:45 D 18 '39; 36:65-7 O 28 '40
      pors
    Vanity Fair 35:47 F '31
    Sobel, B. ed. Theatre Handbook 1940
    Who's Who in America
    Who's Who in the Theatre

PORTER, KATHERINE ANNE May 15, 1894- Author

Address: 1050 Government St, Baton Rouge, Louisiana

Rated by most critics as the outstanding stylist among living American writers, Katherine Anne Porter received on April 3, 1940, the gold medal of the Society for the Libraries of New York University for her book, *Pale Horse, Pale Rider,* published in 1939.

Few writers in the United States have been praised as highly as Katherine Anne Porter for publishing so little. *Flowering Judas,* published with other stories in a volume of that title in 1930, was one of her first published stories and the one that made her reputation. In 1935 the volume was reissued with two short and two longer stories added. Miss Porter continued to write after the publication of *Flowering Judas,* but only a few stories a year appeared and it wasn't until 1939 that her second book, *Pale Horse, Pale Rider,* was published. The reason for her unusual renown among connoisseurs of good prose, despite the smallness of her output, lies in the sheer excellence of all she writes; she commands in her work the most essential and exacting attributes of what constitutes good, as distinguished from esoteric or experimental, style.

G. Maillard Kesslère

KATHERINE ANNE PORTER

Katherine Anne Porter was born at Indian Creek, near San Antonio, Texas, May 15, 1894, daughter of Harrison Boone and Mary Alice (Jones) Porter. She is a descendant of Daniel Boone; and one of her ancestors, Colonel Andrew Porter of Montgomery County, Pennsylvania, was a colonel on Washington's staff. She is quite proud of him: "It seems that he went where he was needed and did the best he could. There is nothing in the record to suggest that he was a careerist or politician." Other ancestors were educators. Miss Porter was brought up in Texas and Louisana and educated at small Southern schools for girls. She says she was "precocious, nervous, rebellious, unteachable." Writing stories, from a very early age, was her real life, her one interest: "This has been the intact line of my life which directs my actions, determines my point of view, profoundly affects my character and personality, my social beliefs and economic status and the kind of friendships I form."

During all those early years she came in contact with no other writers, an isolation which probably saved her from direct influences and membership or alliance with special groups. She worked as a newspaper reporter in Dallas, and then in Denver, until she became seriously ill with influenza. After recovering she began to travel, in the United States, in Mexico, and abroad, doing reviewing, articles and hack writing of all kinds to support herself. "I have very little time sense," she says, "and almost no sense of distance. I have no sense of direction and have seen a great deal of the world by getting completely lost and simply taking in the scenery as I roamed about getting my bearings. . . I have a personal and instant interest in every human being that comes within ten feet of me, and I have never

PORTER, KATHERINE—*Continued*

seen any two alike, but I discover the most marvelous differences. It is the same with furred animals. I love best remembered landscapes two or three countries away."

She lived and worked for some time in Mexico, and arranged the first exhibition of Mexican popular arts sent to the United States. Mexico was the background for some of her first published stories. Her stories began to appear in *Century, transition,* the *New Masses, Scribner's* and *Hound and Horn.* When the collection, *Flowering Judas,* appeared in 1930, it received unanimous critical acclaim. Typical of the reaction to these six stories was Louise Bogan's estimate: "It is to Miss Porter's high credit that, having fixed upon the exceptional background and event, she has not yielded, in her treatment of them, to queerness and forced originality of form. . . She rejects the exclamatory tricks that wind up style to a spurious intensity, and trusts, for the most part, to straightforward writing, to patience in detail and to a thorough imaginative grasp of cause and character. . . Miss Porter should demand much work of her talent. There is nothing quite like it, and very little that approaches its strength in contemporary writing."

In 1931 Miss Porter was awarded a Guggenheim Fellowship and went abroad to travel and to write. While abroad she met Goering, Goebbels and Hitler, whom she considered "detestable and dangerous." In Paris in 1933 she married Eugene Pressly. Miss Porter continued her writing in the United States on her return a few years later. She was a Book-of-the-Month Club Fellow for 1937. She has lectured at the Olivet Writers' Summer Conferences since 1937. During the past few years she has become associated with that group of Southern writers centering at Louisiana State University, whose leader is Robert Penn Warren, editor of the *Southern Review.* In 1938 she divorced her first husband and married Albert Russel Erskine Jr., assistant editor of the Louisiana State University Press and business manager of the *Southern Review.*

Pale Horse, Pale Rider (1939) contains three novelettes. One, *Noon Wine,* is a psychological tale of murder on a small farm in Southern Texas: a tragedy presented not sensationally, but with vividness and conviction. The other two stories are related. In *Old Mortality* we are shown, through the eyes of two little girls, particularly freckle-nosed Miranda, the romantic, captivating person of Aunt Amy, a Southern belle, and the disintegration of her family. In the title story Miranda appears again: it is 1918, she is in love with a soldier, Adam, both get influenza, and Adam dies. It is a bitter, heartbreaking tale of young love and the horror of war. Miss Porter calls it the best story she has ever written. Of this book Paul Rosenfeld writes: "Katherine Anne Porter moves

in the illustrious company headed by Hawthorne, Flaubert and Henry James. Beautifully modeled, petal-like sentences abound in the three novelettes. But unlike those of other conscious stylists, Kay Boyle for example, they never seem to stud the prose and pirouette in the direction of imaginary footlights. They move unobtrusively and precisely. So, too, do the narratives, without breaks and with inflexible steadiness and suppleness, easily, almost with sprightliness."

In spite of her reputation as a stylist, Miss Porter does not try to be one; she actually does not want to write for connoisseurs. She is enjoyed by a relatively small number of readers because she writes sensitively and subtly, with a non-vulgar, non-slick quality. It is probable that she would gain more readers if her style were tougher in fiber, more robust: "vulgar" in the broad, human sense.

For concentration, she likes privacy when writing; but she also likes people and guests, so an isolated life is seldom hers. First, she says, she goes through a long period of thinking out the story. Once she starts writing (the beginning usually comes hard) she writes practically at white heat. Each of the three novelettes in *Pale Horse, Pale Rider* was written in less than a week. She uses a kind of typewritten shorthand, writing "as long as I am allowed by God, guess, and awkwardness." She makes revisions in the first draft, retypes it, makes a few more corrections, and that's all.

Miss Porter is quiet, charming, likes to cook and sew, reads medieval documents and modern poetry. She and her husband live on a tree-shaded street in Baton Rouge. For some years she has been working off and on at a biography of Cotton Mather; and for the past few years on a full-length novel, which she expects to have ready for the publisher soon. She refers to it as the *Promised Land,* although her publishers have advised her to think of a more original title. Its setting is on shipboard, and there are over 40 main characters. Though some critics doubt whether Miss Porter's style and method would be successful on so large a canvas, it must be remembered that, with Katherine Anne Porter, writing isn't a career—"it's a way of life."

References

Nation 150:473-5 Ap 13 '40
N Y Herald Tribune p9 Ap 6 '40
N Y Times Book R p20 Ap 14 '40
Pub W 118:1747 O 11 '30 por; 133:
   2382 Je 18 '38
Sat R Lit 19:7 Ap 1 '39 por
Scholastic 28:5 Mr 7 '36 por
Sewanee R 48:206-16 Ap '40
Time 33:75 Ap 10 '39 por
American Women
Kunitz, S. J. ed. Authors Today and
   Yesterday 1933
Who's Who in America

PORTINARI, CANDIDO   (pôr-tē-nä′rē căn-dē′dō) 1903- Artist

Address: c/o Museum of Modern Art, New York City

In the fall of 1940 there were three American exhibitions of the work of the Brazilian artist, Cândido Portinari. In August and September the Detroit Institute of Arts presented a showing of his paintings, and his work was represented at a Latin-American Exhibition at the Riverside Museum in New York; in October and November he was given a one-man show at New York's Museum of Modern Art. And his art will be permanently before the public in a volume of reproductions which the University of Chicago Press will bring out in 1941.

From these exhibitions a definite impression of the artist emerges. His is an art that is "remarkably varied in technique, in style and in theme." There are portraits with "a Renaissance straightforwardness and force of simple modeling and linear clarity"; there are female groups magnificent in their monumental qualities—*Women Planting*, for instance. From the architecturally impressive *Sao Joao Festival*, his paintings vary through a "looser technique of flowing surfaces" in his genre subjects and in his "picturesque and flamboyant studies of girls embracing, conversing and couples strolling," to designs like *Carcass* or *Burial* or *Scarecrow* that are fantastic, macabre, eerie, surrealist.

Portinari paints Brazil, mainly—"the red water carafe, the gaily decorated round-topped box which contains whatever the poor Brazilian considers precious . . . the stiff little flag on the mast outside of the village church, the inevitable kerosene can which the women use to carry water on their heads." He has shown the native workers of Brazil without romanticism, without exoticism, as real people who work, play, love, marry and die. *Burial in the Hills*, "a quiet story about life and death—as natural as the hills and the horizon," is typical.

Particularly he has painted the Negroes who make up 30 per cent of Brazil's population. In *Morro*, for instance, which was bought in 1939 by the Museum of Modern Art, he shows a hill in a poor Negro quarter and shows it with sympathy and dignity, untouched by propaganda. Portinari has painted, too, the Indians of South America —one critic insists that he "is at his best when he paints the Indians." In these pictures occasionally there is a tendency toward exaggeration and even distortion for dramatic effect and in these pictures there is little conventional beauty—"Portinari paints ugly things," some critics complain.

Nearly all of Portinari's work, no matter what the style or subject, is distinguished by fresh color. He likes "violent yellows, rich red-browns, green-blacks and electric blues," particularly blues. He himself says, "People are all colors in Brazil, especially

CANDIDO PORTINARI

blue." His work is, distinguished, too, except in evanescent fancies like *Scarecrow*, by studious and effective draughtsmanship.

Portinari's "peculiarly powerful style and vigorous mannerisms are especially adapted to monumental productions," most critics agree, and though he only recently turned to the fresco medium there is no doubt that some of his most successful work has been done in this field. In 1939 he completed a monumental series on the regional occupations of Brazil for the new Building of Education and Health in Rio de Janeiro, and in that same year painted three murals for the Brazilian pavilion at the New York World's Fair. In his frescoes, Portinari's "figures are large and dramatic, his backgrounds highly patterned and his palette rich in cool tones and singing darks. Like the Mexicans he cubes his forms and distorts his shapes to add to their effect of power, but he is an excellent draughtsman, capable of being rigidly naturalistic . . . as in a woman's head, *Retrata de nimha mae*, or decoratively abstract and whimsical as in *Figura e boizinho.*"

Cândido Portinari has painted since he was eight. He was born in the state of Sao Paulo in Brazil, the second of the 12 children of coffee workers who had immigrated there from Italy. His schooling was brief and irregular, for he had to help in the fields. It was in one of his short periods at school that Portinari broke his leg playing soccer and was left with a permanent limp. He says now that he is glad he did break it because it left him with more time for painting and none for soccer.

At school and at work Portinari scribbled drawings on paper, fences, walls. The first important one, he remembers, was of an apple on a table in a framework representing another "similar to the one on the table but,

PORTINARI, CANDIDO—*Continued*

naturally, larger." A few years later some itinerant painters came to the little town of Brodowski, where he and his family lived, to decorate the local church. Cândido was allowed to hang around and watch; soon he was given permission to mix the paint; finally, he was allowed to paint stars on the ceiling. That was when he determined to become an artist.

When he was about 15 his family had saved enough money to send him to Rio de Janeiro with three shirts and one pair of pants wrapped in a flour bag. In Rio, Portinari got lodgings in the bathroom of a boarding house and had to be out at five in the morning when the boarders would want to bathe. He enrolled at the art school, got himself a job with a photographer drawing enlargements of photographs and for many years continued to study and live skimpily on whatever he could make from portraits.

In his early 20's Portinari began to receive a few medals and prizes and a few more portrait commissions. Finally, in 1928, he won the *Prix de Voyage* which enabled him to go to Europe. In Europe he visited galleries, talked with people, read and did almost no painting at all. It was in Paris, Portinari says, that "I really commenced to see my native village. I have found that I can paint nothing at first sight. I must wait and let imagination work." He returned to Rio with only one small canvas, scandalizing the art world which was used to seeing painters return from a *Prix de Voyage* with truckloads of art.

He came back broke and with a Uruguayan wife, Maria, whom he had met in Paris. His first job was to convince a graduating class of 40 architects that he would do their portraits cheaper than a photographer would; his next to do them. In 1932 things began to pick up. The painter Foujita visited Rio and became interested in Portinari's work. Through him Portinari got to know the people in the diplomatic and foreign colony and was asked to paint their portraits. He became something of a fashionable portrait painter.

Portinari first came to the attention of Americans in 1935 when his *Coffee* won a second honorable mention in the Carnegie International Exposition. The next year he got his first adequate money-making position—on the faculty of the University of the Federal District in Rio—and stayed there until the spring of 1939, when the University closed. It was in Rio that Portinari got his first fresco commission and in Rio that the first comprehensive exhibition of his work was held in 1939.

With his work exciting attention in the United States in 1940 and with the opening of the Museum of Modern Art's exhibition, Portinari, his wife and their one and one-half year old son, Joao Cândido, came to the United States for the first time. Portinari, who has been going to American movies every day for many years, found Manhattan disappointingly mild. He was impressed, though, by a "What do you call it? A cafeteria? It was beautiful. And the fruit of the United States so polished and well kept just as though it had been waxed."

Interviewers found Portinari a sandy-haired, five-foot-five, slightly plump young man, with a lively and often satirical sense of humor. But most of them were hampered in their search for feature material by the fact that he speaks only Portuguese and a smattering of French. What many of them did discover was that several months before his baby's birth he began setting aside some of his choicest paintings for the baby's art collection, which is already impressive, and that he still has a small house near his family in Brodowski, where he is "still the simple son of the Italian coffee pickers."

References

Arts & Dec 52:15+ N '40 il
Bul Pan Am Union 73:503-6 S '39 il
N Y Herald Tribune VI p5 Ag 11 '40 il; p16 S 18 '40 il por; VI p8 O 13 '40 il
N Y Times p17 Ag 6 '40; p29 O 9 '40; X p9 O 13 '40
New Yorker 16:16 O 19 '40
Newsweek 16:48 O 21 '40 il por
Time 36:37 Ag 12 '40 il
New York City. Museum of Modern Art. Portinari of Brazil pam 1940

POST, WILLIAM STONE May 10, 1866 —July 8, 1940 Architect; designed a number of well-known buildings—among them the New York Stock Exchange (in collaboration with his father); the buildings for City College, New York; the Wisconsin State Capitol and a great many Statler hotels in various cities

References

Who's Who in America

Obituaries

N Y Times p21 Jl 9 '40

POTTER, ALFRED CLAGHORN Apr 4, 1867—Nov 1, 1940 Librarian emeritus of Harvard College; associate at Huntington Library, San Marino, California; directed buying of books for Harvard collection for nearly half a century until retired in 1936

References

Leaders in Education 1932
Who's Who in America
Who's Who in American Education
Who's Who in Library Service

Obituaries

N Y Herald Tribune p12 N 2 '40
N Y Times p15 N 2 '40

POWYS, LLEWELYN pŏ'ĭs hlōō-ĕl'ĭn)
Aug 13, 1884—Dec 2, 1939 English author

"I want to live to a great old age. . ."—
such was the hope of Llewelyn Powys, who
came of a family rich in literary tradition
and who died December 2, 1939 at Davos
Platz, Switzerland, at the age of 55.

The author of *Black Laughter, The Verdict of Bridlegoose*, and *The Pathetic Fallacy*
had suffered for 30 years from tuberculosis. He was born at Dorchester, Dorset,
England, the son of a clergyman. From the
Sherborne School he went to Corpus Christi
College, Cambridge, and in 1908 visited
America on a lecture tour. Discovering his
disease in 1909, he sought relief in Switzerland and finally in British East Africa,
where he raised stock from 1914 to 1919.
Returning to England, he left shortly again
for America and earned a sketchy living
as a journalist in New York until 1924. In
that year he took his American wife, Alyse
Gregory, managing editor of the *Dial*, back
to England. After a journey to Palestine
in 1928 and to the West Indies in 1930 he
took final refuge in Switzerland.

LLEWELYN POWYS

References
Sat R Lit 18:13 My 28 '38 por
Kunitz, S. J. ed. Living Authors 1937
Who's Who
Who's Who in America 1936-37

Obituaries
N Y Herald Tribune p26 D 5 '39
N Y Times p28 D 5 '39
Pub W 136:2259 D 23 '39
Sat R Lit 21:8 D 16 '39
Time 34:59 D 18 '39
Wilson Lib Bul 14:356 Ja '40

PRALL, DAVID WIGHT (präl) Oct 5,
1886—Oct 21, 1940 Professor of philosophy
at Harvard University; taught philosophy
at Cornell University, the University of
Texas and Amherst College before joining
the faculty of Harvard University in 1920;
from 1921 to 1930 was at the University
of California and then returned to Harvard,
where in 1938 and 1939 he was acting head
of the philosophy department; author of
Aesthetic Judgment (1929) and *Aesthetic Analysis* (1936)

References
Who's Who in America

Obituaries
N Y Herald Tribune p24 O 22 '40
N Y Times p23 O 22 '40

PRELLWITZ, HENRY (prĕl'vĭts) Nov 13,
1865—Mar 13, 1940 Artist; treasurer of
the National Academy of Design since 1928;
winner of many art prizes

References
Who's Who in America
Who's Who in American Art

Obituaries
N Y Herald Tribune p24 Mr 14 '40
N Y Post p21 Mr 14 '40
N Y World-Telegram p42 Mr 14 '40

PRENTIS, HENNING WEBB JR. July
11, 1884- President of the National Association of Manufacturers

Address: b. Armstrong Cork Co, Lancaster,
Pennsylvania; h. 151 School Lane, Lancaster, Pennsylvania

In 1940, after a long period of leadership
in its councils, Henning W. Prentis Jr., was

Acme

HENNING WEBB PRENTIS JR.

PRENTIS, HENNING WEBB JR.—*Cont.*

elected president of the National Association of Manufacturers in recognition of "his leadership in American industry." Both a scholar and a businessman, he was born in St. Louis, Missouri, the son of Henning Webb and Mary Norton (McNutt) Prentis, educated in the public schools of that state and received his B. A. degree from the University of Missouri in 1903. Later, in 1907, he received an M. A. in economics at the University of Cincinnati. For two years he was secretary to the president of the University of Missouri, then served in the same capacity at the University of Cincinnati.

In March 1907 Mr. Prentis left academic life and became assistant to the manager of the insulation division of the Armstrong Cork Company. He has been connected with that organization ever since. He rose from position to position within the company until he assumed the presidency in 1934, with direct charge over 11,000 employees in the United States and abroad. In 1909 he married Ida Bernice Cole of Portsmouth, Ohio.

In addition to serving as director and vice-president of the N. A. M. he was head of a committee which made a two-year survey of the "best" practices followed by outstanding firms of the nation. These were put together in a manual entitled *Constructive Industrial Practices.* His interest in education brought him a position as head of a committee on educational cooperation—a group formed "at the request of distinguished educators to give advice on educational problems too broad in scope to be solved by schoolmen alone." In August 1939, together with 50 educators and industrialists, he took part in a Congress on Education for Democracy at Columbia University. There he asserted that "our founding fathers created a republic as distinguished from a democracy, between which there is indeed a wide gulf. The solution of our problems does not lie in more and more democracy."

Mr. Prentis finds himself frequently in the news these days. He spoke before 2,000 business leaders in May 1940, telling them that "no profit in war" was the policy of the N. A. M. "The association and business as a whole," he declared, "approve an adequate national defense, but oppose any idea of participation in war." "Mobilization for Understanding of Private Enterprise" is the association's platform as a counter-offensive for what Prentis calls "creeping collectivism." In September 1940 he announced that the N. A. M., its industrial council and 243 affiliated organizations are conducting their own survey of defense potentialities of the nation's plants, as one of four major points in an N. A. M. program of industrial cooperation with the preparedness program.

Critics have said that Mr. Prentis "detests the NLRB. He loathes the CIO and doesn't care much for unions in general. Doubtful about the ability of people to govern themselves, Mr. Prentis has warned against the 'pitfalls of democracy.'" Armstrong Cork makes about half of the linoleum sold in the United States. In June 1940 the employees held and won an NLRB election. "Democracy at work is well illustrated by the National Labor Relations Act," declared Mr. Prentis. "Under its provisions 50 per cent of the employees of any concern are empowered to speak for all—thus disregarding certain rights of the minority."

Governing a huge body of employees, writing on industry and education, making speeches and participating in leadership of the N. A. M. and many other organizations take most of Mr. Prentis' time. On his farm, where he goes for relaxation from his many activities, Mr. Prentis raises horses, cattle and chickens. A few years ago he took up water-color painting and has since made many landscapes of the farm. Throughout his business life he has retained his deep interest in the educational field. He is a member of Phi Beta Kappa, holds two honorary Doctor of Law degrees —one from Hampden-Sydney College and one from Grove City College.

References

Christian Sci Mon p13 My 18 '40 por
N Y Herald Tribune p35 S 19 '40 por
Newsweek 14:62 D 11 '39 por
PM p22 Je 23 '40
Who's Who in America
Who's Who in Commerce and Industry

PRENTISS, HENRIETTA 1880—May 14, 1940 Former head of the department of speech and dramatics at Hunter College,

Bachrach

HENRIETTA PRENTISS

New York City; one of the foremost authorities in the country on speech; faculty member for 31 years

Obituaries
N Y Herald Tribune p26 My 15 '40

PRITCHARD, STUART Mar 31, 1882—Aug 4, 1940 Physician; tuberculosis authority; president and general director of W. K. Kellogg Foundation at Battle Creek, Michigan; sent as delegate to outstanding conventions on pulmonary diseases and tuberculosis at The Hague in 1932 and at Rome in 1928; president of the National Tuberculosis Association in 1933 and 1934; prolific writer on public health

W. R. French

STUART PRITCHARD

References
Who's Who in America

Obituaries
N Y Times p13 Ag 5 '40

PROCOPE, HJALMAR JOHAN (prō'cō'-pä' hăl'mar' yō-hän) Aug 8, 1889- Finnish Ambassador to the United States; economist

Address: b. 2416 Tracy Pl, N W, Washington, D. C.

"The peace is hard, but Finland is not defeated... Her needs are great and urgent. The assistance of the American people in meeting these needs is of vital importance to us." These words were spoken by Hjalmar J. Procopé, Finnish Minister to the United States, when Finland signed a peace treaty with Russia on March 13, 1940. The future fate of Finland may be uncertain, but Procopé, whose task has been an arduous one during the past few months,

expects to keep on working for Finland. His immediate concern centers around the continuance of fund collecting by American organizations for the relief of Finland: in October 1940 Procopé reported that unless aid is forthcoming, thousands of Finns evacuated from Russian-occupied territory will face "famine and cold" this winter. A weighty problem is what to do with the $20,000,000 which the Administration had planned to lend Finland through the Export-Import Bank. According to Loan Administrator Jesse Jones (see sketch this issue), it is still available for rehabilitation work.

Hard-working, intensely patriotic Hjalmar Procopé, busiest and handsomest foreign diplomat in Washington, was born in Helsinki in 1889, the oldest son of a prosperous Helsinki lawyer. He was graduated from the University of Helsinki in 1914, and began practicing law a year later. When Finnish freedom came with the Russian Revolution's elimination of the Czarist hold on Finland, Procopé was a judge. During those unsettled and exciting years, Procopé twice stood before a Bolshevik firing squad, and twice by incredible circumstances escaped. The new Finnish government was finally established and regconized young Procopé's abilities. He was a brilliant lawyer, a linguist who spoke English, French, German, Swedish and Norwegian.

In 1918 he entered the foreign service, after being a member of the Helsinki Municipal Council for a year. He became a member of Parliament. In 1920, when he was 31, he was named Minister of Commerce and Industry. He visited England and laid the foundation for a thriving commerce between the two nations. He was appointed Minister of Foreign Affairs in 1924, which position he held through six Cabinets. He was Minister to Poland from 1926 to 1927. He became Finnish Representative to the League of Nations Council, and for six years was active in the work of the League. His work at Geneva educated him in the pressing problems of the world: disarmament, ethnic minorities, the arbitration of international disputes. Procopé believed in the League, up to 1928, as a stronghold of Finnish independence; after that he saw that it would be vain for his government to put any trust in the League. Finland launched a strong military program for defense and began to look to the development of a firm friendship with the United States.

From 1931 to 1938 Procopé was managing director of the Finnish Paper Mill Association, largest exporter of European paper to all quarters of the world, and especially to the United States. There were few American newspaper publishers whom Procopé did not know when he arrived here officially in 1939. He first visited the United States, however, in 1925, as Finland's delegate to the Inter-Parliamentary Union meeting in Washington. At that time he traveled extensively throughout the United States, get-

Blackstone

HJALMAR J. PROCOPE

ting acquainted with journalists, labor leaders and businessmen. He learned all that he could about America to help his country model its ways after the best that he found in the United States. His second visit was in 1937 to strengthen trade relations between the two countries.

Because of his experience at Geneva, because of his knowledge of the United States, and because of the growing gravity of Finland's position in the international situation, in November 1938 the Finnish government chose Procopé for the Washington post. Illness, however, delayed his arrival for five months. When he arrived at the Finnish Legation in March 1939, duties were light: three persons took care of all the business. But since the "Peace of Munich" Procopé and other Finnish leaders were expecting the worst. Risto Solanko, in 1940 Procopé's first secretary, made an economic survey of Finnish resources and the war uses to which they could be put; Colonel Per Zilliacus studied modern warfare in Europe's military colleges. It was Procopé's job to pave the way for the United States to assist Finland in every way "short of war." When hostilities finally broke out between Russia and Finland, it came as no surprise to the Finnish Minister. But after that day the number of men and women working at the Finnish Legation grew from three to thirty, the Legation had its own switchboard going 24 hours a day.

Intelligent and friendly, his erect, tall figure and sure stride well-known in Washington, Procopé had no personal difficulty in enlisting sympathy for his country—a sympathy already predisposed because of the publicity attending Finland's payments of its "war debt." Procopé knew that the raising of money was all-important. This meant hours of hard work daily: he seldom went

to bed till 2:30 a. m., and was up again at 7. He went out to dinner every night, with people who could offer the best avenues of information or help.

Procopé sought first a loan in Wall Street, but soon donations from the American people rained in upon his busy Legation—from $1,000 a day in December 1939 to $6,000 in February and March of 1940. Many stories are told about individual donations during the fund-raising drive. A well-dressed woman from Virginia walked into the Minister's office and took a bracelet from her wrist. "This is for Finland," she said. It was worth $2,500. When Procopé entered a Washington shop to get his fountain pen repaired, the shop-owner promptly donated the 25-cent fee to Finland's treasury. A taxi-driver put a quarter with a note under the Legation's door: "This is all I can spare. Good luck." An American Legion Post in Missouri donated a mule for the Finnish artillery.

The two organizations most active in money-raising, and with which Procopé closely cooperated, were Herbert Hoover's Finnish Relief Fund and General John O'Ryan's Fighting Funds for Finland. These made collections running into the millions. Since all loans were specified to be used for non-military purposes, the Finns were greatly disappointed that they failed to get an American governmental loan to buy munitions. Procopé was restrained in his comment, but there were times when he felt he had failed in his mission. He once remarked that Paavo Nurmi, the Finnish athlete, was the best envoy Finland ever sent to the United States. But throughout the campaign Procopé's personal popularity grew. At the Gridiron Club banquet in Washington in December 1939, he received one of the most rousing ovations ever accorded a guest. He is in demand socially as a superior conversationalist with an amazing range of knowledge, and a capacity for listening as well. He has many requests to make speeches, and often complies. He once spoke over the telephone from Washington to 250 Finnish-American students at Suomi College in Northern Michigan. There were tears in his eyes, and the voice coming over the amplifiers in the college auditorium had a catch in it: it was oratory as moving as any the students had ever heard, burning with deep feeling for a homeland in distress. At its finish Procopé slumped in his chair; and at the college was a deep silence, then a great burst of cheering which he never heard.

At 50, Procopé looks little more than 40, and his step is still jaunty, though his hair is graying from past months of arduous work and worry over the fate of his country. On March 30, 1940 he was married to Miss Margaret Shaw of Sutton-on-the-Forest, York, England, at the historic Virginia home of B. Walton Moore, counselor of the United States State Department. The couple had met two years ago in London. She is the daughter of Mrs. Adela Shaw and a niece of the Dowager Countess of Lindsay. Procopé's previous marriage ended in a divorce in 1939, Legation attachés said. He has one son, 23 years old, in Finland.

References

N Y Herald Tribune X p7, 23 Mr 24 '40 por
N Y Times p28 Mr 31 '40
Newsweek 15:16 Mr 25 '40; 15:6 Ap 8 '40
Scholastic 31:28S O 30 '37 por; 36:10 Mr 25 '40 por
Springf'd Republican p22 Mr 31 '40
International Who's Who
Who's Who in Commerce and Industry

PUSEY, WILLIAM ALLEN (pū'zĭ) Dec 1, 1865—Aug 29, 1940 Outstanding Chicago dermatologist; educator; author; president of the American Medical Association in 1924; during fifty-one years of medical practice was honored by five foreign countries; early leader in the fight against syphilis; campaigned for sane birth control in 1925; wrote many technical books

References

American Men of Science
Directory of Medical Specialists 1939
Who's Who in America

Obituaries

N Y Herald Tribune p10 Ag 31 '40
N Y Times p13 Ag 31 '40

PUTNAM, JAMES WILLIAM Jan 18, 1865—Jan 23, 1940 Former president of Butler University, Indiana

JAMES W. PUTNAM

References

Who's Who in America 1938-39

Obituaries

Christian Cent 57:257 F 21 '40
N Y Herald Tribune p18 Ja 24 '40
N Y Sun p23 Ja 24 '40

QUEEN, ELLERY, pseud. of **FREDERIC DANNAY** Jan 11, 1905- and **MANFRED B. LEE** Oct 20, 1905- Author of murder mysteries

Address: c/o F. A. Stokes & Company, 445 Fourth Ave, New York City

Detectives spring up in the most unexpected places! Ellery Queen, whose murder mysteries were dramatized over the Columbia network, started his career over a luncheon table 11 years ago. Frederic Dannay, art director of an advertising agency, and Manfred B. Lee, movie publicity man, sat at lunch one day and toyed with the idea of collaborating on a mystery story for a magazine contest. The conversation bore fruit in a manuscript, *The Roman Hat Mystery* (1929). It won hands down but the magazine folded before the authors received payment.

The book publishing house of Frederick A. Stokes took over the manuscript rights, however, and Ellery was off in a cloud of startling deductions. Three years later (after the publication of *The French Powder Mystery* in 1930 and *The Dutch Shoe Mystery* in 1931) the writers were able to quit their jobs and concentrate all their time on their fiction detective, who was by then a best seller.

Since then they have produced fourteen Ellery Queen books, four Barnaby Ross novels, two collections of detective short stories and a mystery-story anthology. Most of these have sold 5,000 copies, and some have gone into popular editions and sold as high as 50,000.

No one wondered about Ellery's identity until Columbia University's School of Journalism in 1932 invited the detective to lecture on mystery writing. They flipped a coin; Lee lost, and Ellery Queen went to Morningside Heights wearing a mask. He spent a good part of that year masked, sitting on tables in department stores autographing books.

Dannay and Lee are cousins, were born the same year in Brooklyn, New York, and have been friends all their lives. Lee attended New York University, where he had his own orchestra. He still plays the violin. They look as much alike as oboe players; they are both of medium height and stocky build. Although they are still under 40, baldness is threatening to push their foreheads up over their heads to their back collar buttons. This made it duck soup for Ellery Queen when he donned a black mask for a lecture or other public appearance, for either could put on the mask and defy Barnaby Ross (author of *The Tragedy of X*, 1932, and

MANFRED LEE [ELLERY QUEEN]

other Drury Lane mysteries), their mystery story colleague, to tell them apart.

Barnaby Ross (Lee) appeared on the platform with Ellery Queen (Dannay) in most of his lectures. Audiences from coast to coast have been thrilled by the contests of wits between these two ratiocinative wizards. Queen would outline a plot; Ross would toss in a complication; and on they would battle, seeking to stymie each other's mental processes, only to arrive finally at a mutually triumphant conclusion that would leave the customers limp. Even the lecture agent didn't know they were collaborators. He thought he had sent out two competing authors to do battle.

Ellery Queen even wore a mask on the stage when he appeared after the first night as coauthor of the play, *Danger— Men Working* which he wrote with Raymond Moore. Their publisher, Frederick Stokes, is supposed to have revealed their identity when he gave a cocktail party to celebrate the publication of *The Devil to Pay* (1938). According to another story Paramount gave the secret away when Ellery Queen went to Hollywood.

"There's enough material in Hollywood for a thousand books," they reported on their return.

"Don't let anyone tell you that fantastic stories of Hollywood are exaggerated

"They don't tell the half of it. Our first assignment was to do a racing story

"Neither of us had ever seen a horse race and we haven't yet

"But we found a man who knew racing from the ground up, lived with him for three days and nights and wrote the picture

"Which delighted the producer."

Both Dannay and Lee have families; Dannay has two sons and Lee two daughters.

For some years both lived in Mt. Vernon, but Mr. Dannay moved to Great Neck some time ago, and Lee to New York. They put in about 12 hours of work a day, doing much of their writing at their homes and meeting to consolidate their material at their hideout, a tiny office near Fifth Avenue unknown even to their wives.

Gum-shoeing Ellery Queen has been in the movies, on the stage, on the lecture platform and last year on the radio as both actor and author. Splitting the detective's name between them, Dannay as Ellery and Lee as Queen, the two writers collaborated on the *Author! Author!* program in which literary riddles and radio charades were aired on Monday nights on the Mutual Broadcasting System. Various other writers served as guests, and S. J. Perelman as wisecracking master of ceremonies.

For the latest radio venture Ellery Queen wrote a $350-a-week mystery drama, a murder play in which he matched wits not only with the murderer, but with a board of invited guests who were given all clues and then challenged to fit the pieces together. The radio audience meanwhile was given a chance to outguess the murderer, detective and group of experts. For a conclusion the rest of the murder drama was then played off, showing listeners and guests just where they blundered in their deductions.

The authors were somewhat reluctant to make a radio character out of Ellery Queen. However, George Zachary, the radio producer who conceived the idea for the show would not let him escape. He had read through 200-odd stories before finding Ellery Queen, and didn't believe he would find another if he read 200 more.

A sort of intellectual Siamese twinship binds them together. Whenever they get

FREDERIC DANNAY [ELLERY QUEEN]

together to cook up a mystery thriller they toss their brains into the same pot. Their minds blend so easily and naturally that a third person, talking to them, gets the slightly uneasy impression that he is conversing with one man. Never prompting each other by as much as a glance (in one hour-long interview neither ever once addressed the other), one would begin a sentence, in the middle of which the other would hook on a subjunctive clause, with the first reappearing in the caboose of the train of their thought.

"Almost everywhere we went as Ellery Queen and Barnaby Ross we were asked to work on some local mystery

"But we remembered Van Dine's experience when he undertook to solve a murder mystery out in Jersey

"He worked long and hard at it and was getting nowhere

"When along came a flatfoot who didn't know the difference between analytical deduction and postular acne

"And solved it in two hours."

A chart which Ellery Queen worked out for judging detective stories gave Van Dine's *Green Murder Case* a 79 per cent rating; Agatha Christie's (see sketch this issue) *Murder of Roger Ackroyd* the same and Barnaby Ross' *Tragedy of X* 89 per cent. When asked, "How come?" Ellery Queen answered:

"Oh, we felt we ought to give Ross a break

"Because we didn't want to let a pal down."

References

N Y Times p19 N 15 '40
N Y World-Telegram p30 F 21 '38
New Yorker 16:26-7 Mr 16 '40
Newsweek 13:26 Je 26 '39 il pors
Pub W 130:1512 O 10 '36; 133:1026
    F 26 '38
Time 34:55 O 23 '39
Starrett, V. Books Alive p303-4 1940
Thomson, H. D. Masters of Mystery
    1931
Who's Who in America

QUINN, DANIEL JOSEPH, FATHER
May 12, 1864—Mar 9, 1940 President of Fordham University (1906-11); teacher; priest; parish worker

References

American Catholic Who's Who 1934-35
Who's Who in America 1920-21

Wide World

FATHER QUINN

Obituaries

N Y Herald Tribune p41 Mr 10 '40
N Y Times p51 Mr 10 '40 por
Sch & Soc 51:342 Mr 16 '40

QUINTANILLA, LUIS (kĭn-tä-nē'yä)
1900- Artist
Address: c/o University of Kansas City, Kansas City, Missouri

Luis Quintanilla, for years "one of Spain's most dreaded satirists and an active revolutionary in his personal life," is now teaching at the University of Kansas City. Appointed in the fall of 1940 to start the first university school of fresco painting in the United States, he will have 40 or 50 pupils who will help him paint on wet plaster a real fresco, in the Liberal Arts Building auditorium, "possibly of Don Quixote in a modern setting."

Quintanilla, who is known to America through his exhibitions, through his book, *All the Brave* (1939), through his picture painted for Walter Wanger's movie, *The Long Voyage Home*, is a Spaniard of Basque descent, a nephew of the Bishop of Burgos. He was brought up by his religious and conservative family in a wealthy home at Santander and sent to study at the Jesuit University at Deusto. At 14 he ran away from home to become a sailor in the Spanish Navy. At 20 he was in Paris, studying art and sharing a leaky studio with the late Juan Gris, cubist painter. He learned to paint, he says, "by talking about it all the time."

It wasn't until 1927 that Quintanilla became known in Spain. Then a traveling fellowship was arranged for him which allowed him to study frescoes in Italy.

QUINTANILLA, LUIS—*Continued*

When he returned the director of Madrid's Modern Art Museum began to collect his works and hold exhibitions of them. It wasn't long before he was recognized as "one of the finest artists of the people since Goya," and before his brilliantly colored frescoes were to be seen in Cologne, Germany, Hendaye, France, and Madrid, Spain.

During these years Quintanilla was becoming an active Socialist. Before the first "bloodless revolution" he gave over his apartment in Madrid as a hiding place for arms and, on the night of Alfonso's abdication in 1931, ran up the Republican flag with his own hand before the abdication was definite and then led the Republican forces to the palace. Three years later, when the government had swung to the Right under Lerroux, he offered his home as a refuge for four of his party's committeemen. Government officials raided the place, arrested Quintanilla and the committeemen, charging them with storing arms, and put them into jail. Quintanilla was sentenced to 16 years' imprisonment.

Ernest Hemingway, Quintanilla's friend, received a cable: "Luis hoosegowed," and while the artist was behind bars arranged for the first American showing of his work in December 1934. These were etchings, though Quintanilla had done painting, too, and they were etchings without revolutionary significance. Satirical and humorous Spanish street scenes dominated the show— a picture of a fat and cheerful Madrid dandy having his shoes shined in a park, for instance. Hemingway pointed out that Quintanilla "does not take money and rant and rave to save his soul. He has painted great frescoes in the Casa del Pueblo and the Cuidad Universitario in Madrid and there are no symbols of capitalism or any symbols in them. Always there are people, as there are people in the etchings."

Quintanilla was soon let out of jail and spent the years until the outbreak of the Spanish Civil War in 1936 completing the murals in 11 panels for the Memorial to Pablo Iglesias, Socialist leader who died in 1925 in University City. That done, he made himself a hero by joining the Republican forces and leading the attack which took the Montana barracks in Madrid. Four months after the War had begun Premier Negrin sent Quintanilla out of danger on a diplomatic mission to France. In 1937 he was back at the front, this time to draw, at the government's command, a series of picturizations of the War.

By this time almost all of Quintanilla's important paintings had been destroyed and the Iglesias memorial was just rubble. When Hemingway inquired about his work Quintanilla quietly answered: "It's all gone. . . Let's not talk about it. When a man loses his life's work, everything that he has done in all his working life, it is much better not to talk about it."

The war drawings, however, were saved, and it was these which were exhibited in the United States in March 1938 at New York's Museum of Modern Art. These drawings of war's effect on the streets of Madrid, on the villagers of Andalusia, on prisoners and wounded men were marked by an "absence of overstatement and bitterness which makes them unique among war pictures." These drawings, "at once so delicate and so strong, so ruthlessly real and so instinct with compassion," were done with a fine quill pen in a uniformly unexcited style. War in them was shown not in terms of melodrama, "but rather in its relation to the humble folks who . . . had no word in bringing it about."

During the Spanish Civil War Quintanilla left Spain to paint frescoes for what was to be the Spanish building at the New York World's Fair. But the War ended and there was no Spanish building. Soon, forbidden to return to Spain, he brought all his drawings to the United States, took out his first citizenship papers and rented a small studio in New York City. As he put it in a letter to Hemingway: "I arrived here sad and demoralized. I didn't know whether I should commit suicide or get married, which is to prolong life: I married—[an American girl whom he had met in Madrid]. I didn't know whether to take to alcohol or to work, and I worked. Little by little I took from my palette the bitter memories of Spain and by dint of brush strokes I came to feel myself an individual again and to love colors as old friends who for a long time have been forgotten."

In America Quintanilla worked at top speed and in November 1939 an exhibition of his paintings was held at the Associated American Artists Gallery. Nearly thirty paintings and five large frescoes, *Love Peace and Hate War*, originally commissioned for the Fair, were shown. These frescoes, according to Edward Alden Jewell, have "lightness, gaiety and decorative charm" and are "delightfully painted; for the most part, admirably composed." Other critics pointed out the "pleasing freshness in point of view," the "dignity and emotional appeal," the "able draftsmanship" of these panels, but seemed to agree with Mr. Jewell that Quintanilla "is decidedly at his best in the drawings and etchings."

The canvases in the show were mostly on American subjects: *A Daughter of Revolution in White and One in Red*, *Abandoned Poets of Fourteenth Street*. In addition, the sole painting left after Quintanilla's Madrid studio was bombed, *Brunete War Landscape*, and many of his war drawings and etchings were shown.

It was in 1939, too, that Quintanilla's book, *All the Brave*, was published—drawings by Quintanilla with a preface by Ernest Hemingway and text comment by Jay Allen and Elliott Paul (see sketch this issue). Unanimously the critics pointed out the deep feeling and great technical skill of these drawings—"savage, ironic, tender, infinitely delicate." Frequently they compared Quintanilla to Goya and frequently they commented on the book's meaning—"This is what happened to Spain. This is totalitarian war and its triumph."

Quintanilla is thin and dynamic, with bright black eyes and a roguish sense of humor. He works furiously and when he is not at work loves long conversations, gay French songs and a good game of pelota.

References

    Art Digest 9:18 D 1 '34 il; 12:23 Ap 1 '38; 12:16 My 15 '38; 14:11 N 15 '39 il

    Art N 36:14+ Ap 2 '38

    Nation 146:395 Ap 2 '38; 149:567 N 25 '39

    Newsweek 4:30 D 1 '34; 14:46 N 20 '39

    Parnassus 11:16-19 N '39 il

    Time 31:26 Mr 28 '38 por; 35:54 Je 10 '40; 36:53 S 23 '40

    Who's Who in American Art

VIDKUN QUISLING

QUISLING, VIDKUN (kvis'ling) July 18, 1887- Norwegian officer and diplomat; head of the State Council

Address: Oslo, Norway

Presumably Major Vidkun Quisling's political ambitions were at last fulfilled on September 25, 1940, when he was proclaimed the sole political leader of Norway, entrusted with the task of imposing Germany's "new order" on his country. The subjugation of Norway has with these measures fallen into the usual Nazi pattern after a period of unwonted indulgence. The cold-eyed, thin-lipped Major has become the exponent of the Führer principle: his party, the *Nasjonal Samling*—National Union—is the only one permitted in Norway; even the existence of such groups as the Temperance League, women's associations and religious auxiliary organizations is endangered on the ground that it is doubtful that they can adequately serve the interests of Major Quisling's new order.

Major Quisling's career until September 1940 has been one rife with disappointments. Even his moment of triumph, when Germany invaded Norway and he became a puppet premier, was short-lived. True, he seemed to be on the way to achieving immortality in a rather unexpected way, via the joyous exploitation of his name by the British:

"Major Quisling," wrote the London *Times* scathingly, soon after Norway was invaded, "has added a new word to the English language. . . To writers the word Quisling is a gift from the gods. If they had been ordered to invent a new word for traitor . . . they could hardly have hit upon a more brilliant combination of letters. Actually it contrives to suggest something at once slippery and tortuous. Visually it has the supreme merit of beginning with a 'Q,' which . . . has long seemed to the British mind to be a crooked, uncertain and slightly disreputable letter, suggestive of the questionable, the querulous, the quavering of quaking quagmires and quivering quicksands, of quibbles and quarrels, of queasiness, quackery, qualms and quilp. . . Major Quisling is to be congratulated. He has performed the rarish feat of turning a proper name into a common one." Ever since then the discomfited Major has had to listen to his name being declined in several languages (Quisling—I quisle, you quisle, he or she quisles).

Major Quisling's early years held no promise of his later unexpected contribution to the English language. His was a typical career of a brilliant young officer and diplomat. He was born in Fyresdal, Norway, in 1887, the son of Jon Lauritz and Anna Caroline (Bang) Quisling. From early youth he was trained for a military career. After completing his education in 1905 he was admitted into the army as an officer and his military advancement went on concurrently with his diplomatic career. He passed the War College examination in 1911, became an assistant of the general staff in 1916, got his commission as captain in 1917 and in 1931 was a major in the field artillery.

His diplomatic service unfolded mostly in Eastern Europe. He was sent to Petrograd as a military attaché from 1918 to 1919. In 1919 he was with the Norwegian legation in Helsinki. He served, too, in many international commissions of the League of Nations. From 1922 to 1923 he represented Norway on the International Russian Relief Committee in the Ukraine and in 1923 was a representative of the League's High Commissioner for Refugees

QUISLING, VIDKUN—*Continued*

in the Balkan States. From 1924 to 1926 he was secretary and delegate to the Armenian Commission of the League. On several occasions he was closely associated with Fridjof Nansen's relief expeditions. Reputedly the great explorer had been very fond of his capable young colleague, whose competence and efficiency he greatly valued. It has been said that young Quisling owed his rapid advancement and eventual participation in the government to Nansen's attachment to him.

From 1927 to 1929, while serving in Moscow on the Norwegian legation staff, he was given charge of the British legation during the time when Russian and British diplomatic relations were temporarily severed. As a reward he was named an honorary commander of the Order of the British Empire on November 22, 1929, in recognition of the services rendered to the British government in Russia. His name was struck off the rolls of the Order in June 1940, in recognition of the services rendered to the German government in Norway.

The height of Quisling's career—in independent Norway, that is—was reached in 1931, when he became the Minister of Defense in Karlstad's Cabinet. By that time he had made a considerable name for himself as an expert on Russian affairs. He had written a few books in that field, among them *Russia and Ourselves* (1931) and *Politica Occidentale Orientale*. He spoke Russian as fluently as if it were his native tongue. He was married to a Russian woman —Maria Vasilievna Pasek, a native of Kharkov, whom he married in 1923 when he served on a relief committee in the Ukraine. All this however, did not prevent him from being a rabid anti-Communist. His suspicions of Russian influence in the Scandinavian Peninsula caused him to accuse all the Norwegian labor leaders of being in Russia's pay and planning revolution— charges which he failed to prove. Nevertheless, he resigned from the Farmer Party in 1932 and began to build up his own party.

His reactionary attitude did not make for harmonious relationship with his colleagues in the Cabinet—there was no place for a conservative among the progressive Norwegian laborites. Quisling had made many enemies. There were rumors of complaints, of an investigation committee set up, and it has been hinted that only the collective resignation of the Cabinet prevented Quisling's expulsion from his post. However that might be, he went to the voters in 1933 at the head of the party he founded— the *Nasjonal Samling*—on a platform calling for the suppression of "revolutionary" parties and the "freeing" of labor from union domination.

His party, with its marked Fascist tendencies, was not a success—the trend in Norway was precisely toward the "revolutionary" parties that Quisling deplored. The National Union polled only 28,000 of the 1,240,000 votes cast in the 1933 elections. Nor did it grow in strength; its 1933 vote was halved at the 1936 elections; it never succeeded in electing even one member to the Storting and was in a state of virtual dissolution by the end of 1939.

Although without honor in his own country, the head of the *Nasjonal Samling* was successful in attracting the attention of Hitler, who was even then preparing his scheme for world domination and was not overlooking any bets. In spite of his minute following and signal lack of success at the polls Quisling had extremely valuable connections in the army and the navy and his party was reputedly nourished by big industrialists. Quisling began to get very friendly with Alfred Rosenberg, the "philosopher" of National Socialism, and to appear at various Nazi gatherings abroad. In July 1937 a conference of Nazi emissaries took place in the German legation in Riga to discuss General Haushofer's favorite theory of Nazi domination of the Baltic. Quisling represented the Norwegian Nazis and assisted Rosenberg, who was chairman of the meeting. At that time reputedly he got Hitler's promise of Premiership in Norway.

Major Quisling was in Berlin on the night of Friday, April 5, 1940, presumably putting the last touches on the German campaign in Norway. Three days later the German warships successfully ran the gauntlet of Norse forts and naval units along the Olso Fjord and were able to overrun Norway with the connivance of Major Quisling's military friends and sympathizers. Quisling's army connections, not to mention the information he had to offer as a former Minister of Defense, proved invaluable to the Nazis.

While the Germans were trying to lay their hands on the elusive King Haakon (see sketch this issue) long enough to obtain his abdication Major Quisling proclaimed himself Premier, apparently by the simple expedient of announcing it over the air. His government was not recognized even by the Germans themselves, who were mostly concerned with coming to terms with Haakon. According to the Norwegian *White Paper* this attempt failed with Haakon's categorical refusal to recognize Quisling as governmental chief. So a week after his *coup* the disappointed Major resigned and was succeeded by Ingolf Elser Christensen, the 68-year-old Governor of Oslo Province. He himself was put in charge of Norwegian demobilization in the German-occupied areas and later went to Berlin.

He came back from Germany on August 20 in order to make another bid for Premiership and to build up a following. The German authorities were divided in their feelings toward him: although he was backed by Dr. Alfred Rosenberg he had failed to win the favor of Josef Terboven, the Reich Commissioner to Norway. Also he found it difficult to find prominent Norwegians who were willing to participate in the projected Cabinet. With his arrival, besides, the stubborn though mute opposition of the Norwegians crystallized into violent action. Because of the German uncertainty about him, the Norwegian press and public opinion were comparatively free to criticize him. On August 26 the *Arbeiderbladet* went so far as to publish a resolution adopted by a meeting of the Association of Young Workers, who denounced the possibility of the Quisling government as "a humiliation to the Norwegian people."

Up till then the Germans counted on the Storting's producing its own puppet government. The latter having proved disobliging in that respect, the German patience broke. The editor of *Arbeiderbladet* was arrested for exposing "an exponent of National Socialism . . . to degrading judgments." Quisling was proclaimed Norway's sole political leader, heading a State Council of 13 German-controlled commissioners. Josef Terboven, the Reich's Commissioner to Norway, also announced the end of Norway's monarchy and parliament and stated that the only "avenue by which the Norwegians can regain a large measure of freedom and independence is the *Nasjonal Samling*." It is possible that the riots that followed this decree expressed the lack of reassurance that the Norwegians felt upon learning that their sole hope of freedom lay in the man whose name has, among many people, come to stand for "traitor." In November the publication of a massive edition of *Quisling Has Said*, sort of a Norwegian *Mein Kampf*, could not have added to their hope.

References

Christian Sci Mon Mag p3 My 11 '40
Eur Nour 23:514 My 11 '40
Life 8:98 My 6 '40 por
Liv Age 358:446-8 Jl '40 por; 359:104-5 O '40
N Y Post p2 Ap 23 '40
N Y Times p6 S 5 '40; p16 O 7 '40
Newsweek 15:19 Ap 22 '40
Time 35:23-4 Ap 22 '40 por; 36:28-9 O 7 '40 por; 36:23 O 28 '40 por
Hambro, C. J. I Saw It Happen in Norway 1940
International Who's Who

RAGON, HEARTSILL Mar 20, 1885—Sept 15, 1940 Judge of the United States District Court, Western Arkansas District since 1933; member of the Arkansas House of Representatives from 1911 to 1913; district prosecuting attorney from 1916 to 1920; member of the Sixty-eighth to the Seventy-second Congresses, from 1923 to 1933; regarded as an expert on tax questions before the House

HEARTSILL RAGON

References

Who's Who in America
Who's Who in Government
Who's Who in Law

Obituaries

N Y Sun p19 S 16 '40

RANDOLPH, ASA PHILIP Apr 15, 1889-Negro labor leader
Address: b. 217 W 125th St, New York City

There are many labor leaders today who believe that the success of the labor movement in this country depends upon its ability to include Negro workers. A. Philip Randolph, president of the Brotherhood of Sleeping Car Porters, has fought most of his life to bring Negroes into the organized labor movement and to end discrimination, in industry and in labor, against his people. He has been praised as "Negro labor's champion" and branded "the most dangerous Negro in America."

Because of his strong support of the trade union movement and his feeling that it is through the trade union movement that Negroes can make gains, Randolph's resignation from the presidency of the National Negro Congress on April 28, 1940, because of his opposition to its working with the CIO's Labor's Non-Partisan League, came as a surprise to many people. He said that any agreement with the League would "split the mass action of this Congress" and added that he would be just as opposed to tying up with the A F of L.

Randolph's attitude against accepting John L. Lewis' invitation to work with Labor's Non-Partisan League, even when the Negro Congress as a whole accepted it, can be attributed to his dislike in taking what

ASA PHILIP RANDOLPH

seemed possibly a first step toward participation in a third party movement if the Democratic and Republican Presidential nominees and platforms were not satisfactory.

Mr. Randolph resigned, too, because he was opposed to accepting money from the Communist Party and unions affiliated with the CIO. He stated firmly that he believed the Congress "should be dependent on resources supplied by the Negro people alone. The ground for my belief is that history shows that where you get your money you also get your ideas and control."

A. Philip Randolph, son of a poor Negro clergyman in the African Methodist Church, was born on April 15, 1889 at Crescent City, Florida. As a child he spent most of his time earning enough to keep the family going, as clerk in a grocery store, selling newspapers, picking up odd jobs. When he grew older and stronger he got work as a section hand on a railroad, digging and shoveling dirt, loading flat cars with sand, laying crossties and rails.

When he had completed his high school course at the Cookman Institute in Jacksonville, Philip traveled North. He took courses, mostly in political science and economics, at the College of the City of New York. He had a succession of varied jobs— as a waiter on the Fall River Line, as an elevator operator, as porter for the Consolidated Edison Company of New York.

Randolph married in 1915. Two years later he and Chandler Owen launched *The Messenger*, a monthly magazine with the subtitle: "The only radical Negro magazine in America." Because of the militant stand against the World War which Randolph adopted he was arrested in Cleveland in June 1918 by the Department of Justice, but released after a few days in the city jail.

Randolph began to contribute to other publications; he became an instructor in the Rand School of Social Science in New York. In 1921 he ran as the Socialist candidate for New York Secretary of State, and at other times for the Assembly and Congress. Until 1925, even though he had organized a union of elevator operators in New York City in 1917 and participated in organizational campaigns among motion picture operators and garment trade workers, he still considered himself a writer and editor rather than a labor organizer.

In August of that year he and a small group of men met in a Harlem recreation hall to outline a campaign to organize sleeping car porters. Randolph was elected president and general organizer of the union, which as yet existed only on paper. Shortly afterward the masthead of *The Messenger* changed to read "The official organ of the Brotherhood of Sleeping Car Porters."

By 1928 the Brotherhood, with over half the porters and maids organized, was ready to threaten strike if the Pullman Company refused to negotiate, but the strike was canceled.

The case between the Brotherhood and the Pullman Company dragged on for many years. It came before the Board of Mediation, before the Interstate Commerce Commission, before a Federal Court. In 1934, when the Railway Labor Act was amended, porters were brought within the scope of the law. Membership jumped, and when an election was held in 1935 the vote was 6,000 for the union to 1,400 against it. In August 1937 A. Philip Randolph was finally able to announce the signing of a contract with the Pullman Company giving the employees $2,000,000 in pay increases and guaranteeing them shorter hours with pay for overtime. At the biennial convention of the BSCP in September 1940 approval was given to negotiations with the Pullman Company in which a reduction from 240 to 210 monthly average working hours for porters would be asked. "Porters were looked upon as clowns," Randolph says. "Now they must be taken seriously."

Beyond its immediate tasks, Randolph has always looked upon the Brotherhood of Sleeping Car Porters as an example to other Negro workers, helping to draw them into the union movement. He feels that if Negroes are organized "the barriers against race and color will be broken down and eventually destroyed." As the head of the only all-Negro union with an international charter from the A F of L, which officially condemns race discrimination but 20 of whose unions draw the color line, Randolph challenged the delegates at the A F of L National Convention in November to really tackle the problem. He wasn't answered.

Randolph is still a Socialist, though not an "orthodox Marxian." In his spare time he is writing two books—one a social history, the other autobiographical.

References

N Y Times p17 Ap 29 '40; p14 S 15
'40
Newsweek 16:42 S 30 '40
PM p10 S 19 '40
Time 30:10 S 20 '37 por
Minton, B. and Stuart, J. A. Philip
Randolph: Negro Labor's Cham-
pion *In* Men Who Lead Labor
p143-71 1937
Who's Who in Colored America

RAUTENBERG, ROBERT (rou'tĕn-bērg)
1858—Feb 21, 1940 Sculptor

Robert Rautenberg, sculptor, widely
known early member of the single-tax
colony at Arden, near Wilmington, Delaware and the subject of several short sto-

ROBERT RAUTENBERG

ries by Victor Thaddeus, died at his home
in Arden at the age of 82. He left a widow,
Mrs. Louisa Rautenberg, a son and a
daughter. Mr. Rautenberg was born in Silesia, Germany, and as a youth studied wood
and stone carving in Berlin, Paris, Vienna
and Rome. He specialized in ecclesiastical
work, and some of his statues were placed
in leading churches in Vienna, Paris and
Berlin. In Berlin he became a close friend
of the philosopher Albert Dulc. Soon after
he came to this country in 1887, Mr. Rautenberg became an American citizen. He
worked with St. Gaudens, Charles Grafley
and other well-known sculptors. His best
known work is the statuary and figure work
for the main staircase of the Library of
Congress. The marble statue of *The Blessed Virgin* in the Roman Catholic Cathedral

of SS. Peter and Paul in Philadelphia has
also won the praise of critics.

Obituaries

N Y Times p23 F 22 '40

RAYBURN, SAM Jan 6, 1882- Speaker
of the United States House of Representatives
Address: b. United States House of Representatives, Washington, D. C.; h. Bonham,
Texas

On September 15, 1940 the House of Representatives mourned the death of its Speaker,
William Bankhead (see sketch this issue). On
September 16 Sam Rayburn, Democratic majority leader of the House, was elected
Speaker. It is the second time that he has
succeeded to an office held by Bankhead. In
1935 the two men were rival candidates for
the Speaker's office, increased annual salary and
shiny limousine, but the late Joe Byrns carried
them all away; in 1937 Bankhead was elevated
from his post of majority leader to the
Speakership, and Rayburn succeeded him as
majority leader.

The dark-eyed, "bald, stocky, rugged farmer-
lawyer from the red clay country of Texas"
(full name Samuel Taliaferro Rayburn)
was born in Roane County, Tennessee, on January 6, 1882, the son of W. M. and Martha
(Waller) Rayburn. His parents moved to
Texas, where they were not too well off, but
stories say that as a boy he used to tell visitors
at the family homestead that he was going to
college, that he would become the Speaker
of the Texas Legislature and that he would
end up in Congress. He did all of those
things. Sent to East Texas College with his
father's blessing and $25, he took his B. S.
degree there, then studied law at the University of Texas and began his practice at
Bonham, Texas, where "his neglected law
shingle still swings in the wind." He was
elected to the Texas House of Representatives,
where he served for six years and spent
the last two as Speaker of the House; then
in 1913 he went to Congress as Democratic
Representative from the fourth Texas district. He has been there ever since.

Rayburn is seldom known to make
speeches and usually gives no more than
five minutes to remarks on pending legislation, but as one of Vice-President Garner's
trusted lieutenants he has nevertheless been
a power in the House for years, maneuvering its Democratic majority behind the
scenes. One writer pictures him at the
back of the chamber, "standing by the
hour with his arms on the rail behind the
rearmost row of seats, quietly keeping an
eye on what is happening, conferring in
whispers with colleagues." "Unspectacular,
undemonstrative," even "unimpressive," still
when he does speak he is capable of a
"don't-give-up-the-bill doggedness" that has
put through many pieces of legislation
simply by outfighting and outarguing his
opponents. He is well liked, however.
Everyone calls him "Sam," and new mem-

S. J. Woolf

SAM RAYBURN

bers are impressed when Sam greets them by their own carefully memorized first names. He has served on only one committee. Having been born in a "hamlet on a branch-line railroad," he made railroads his hobby and became an expert on transportation problems and chairman of the Interstate Commerce Committee.

It was Rayburn who in 1932 managed Garner's bid for the Democratic Presidential nomination, Garner who in 1935 pushed him forward for the job of Speaker; but in spite of the close friendship between the two men Rayburn has never wavered in loyalty to Roosevelt. If the President was a New Dealer, he himself was a New Dealer, and he won Roosevelt's gratitude for his fight for the Wheeler-Rayburn Utilities Bill (see sketch of Wheeler this issue) and the Securities Exchange Act of 1934. Elected Democratic majority leader in 1937, Rayburn mourned Roosevelt's defeat over the Reorganization Bill, asking: "Is it possible . . . that this is a leaderless land?" And in June 1938 he eulogized the work of the outgoing Congress in typical New Deal terms. "The record of the last Congress," he said, "is one of which any four-year administration could be justly proud. The array of accomplishments of this Congress is impressive indeed. I do believe that the Congress has done its part well. It now remains to be seen whether others will do their part. We must all realize that all classes and all sections are interdependent. We must stand or fall together. No large sector of our people can be poor and the other part remain long rich. Each of us is responsible not only to our group but to the whole of our population."

Again in 1940 Sam Rayburn offered his support to Vice-President Garner for the 1940 Presidential nomination, calling him an "outstanding Texan and liberal Democrat," but after President Roosevelt's renomination he made a speech at Williamsport, Maryland in which he characterized the President as the greatest humanitarian to occupy the White House for 50 years, and promised him his full support. Sam Rayburn is, above everything else, a "party man."

The new Speaker is a bachelor and lives in a two-room apartment in Washington. He isn't fond of the social side of Washington life but he is fond of jokes that date back to the Civil War, friends who date back nearly as far, and occasional literary excursions into pedigrees and battles. If he shows "only a slight bulge in the midriff" at his age perhaps it's because he also likes trotting around a golf course on a Sunday morning and taking long walks. Often he walks halfway to and from his apartment and the Capitol and takes a taxi the rest of the way. Every day he smokes a pack or two of cigarettes. His favorite hero is Robert E. Lee, and there are three pictures of the great Southerner on his office walls.

As for vacations, they are a different matter. His sister, whom he calls "Miss Lou" (she calls him "Mr. Sam"), has been keeping house for him and his farmer-brother Tom in a pleasant, white, two-story house two miles west of Bonham ever since their parents died. There are 150 acres of farmland, hackberry trees, and it is natural for friends and relatives to gather in the Rayburns' back yard on hot summer afternoons. At home Sam Rayburn can wear old clothes, tend a herd of blooded Jersey cows, work right out in the fields with the farmhands—and put politics out of his mind.

References

Collier's 95:22+ Ja 5 '35
N Y Sun p29 F 16 '40; p1 O 9 '40
N Y Times p29 Ap 11 '40; p10 S 16 '40
Newsweek 8:20 D 26 '36; 16:20 S 23 '40 por
Scholastic 37:14 O 7 '40 por
Time 28:15 D 14 '36; 31:16 Ap 18 '38; 36:15 S 30 '40 por
U S News 9:33 S 27 '40 por
Vital Speeches 4:592-5 Jl 15 '38

Who's Who in America
Who's Who in the Nation's Capital

REAVIS, SMITH FREEMAN Nov 11, 1893—Feb 24, 1940 Editor and writer for 20 years for the Associated Press; his interview in 1927 with the French Foreign Minister Aristide Briand credited with laying the groundwork for the Kellogg-Briand Treaty to outlaw war

Obituaries

N Y Herald Tribune p32 F 25 '40
N Y Times p38 F 25 '40
Newsweek 15:4 Mr 4 '40
Time 35:57 Mr 4 '40
Variety 139:44 F 28 '40

REED, EDWARD BLISS Aug 19, 1872—
Feb 16, 1940 Poet; author of books on
English poetry; professor of English at
Yale; director of education of the Com-
monwealth Fund of New York

References
Who's Who in America 1938-39

Obituaries
N Y Herald Tribune p8 F 17 '40; p22
Mr 13 '40
N Y Sun p23 F 16 '40

REED, HERBERT CALHOUN Oct 16,
1873—July 25, 1940 Chemist; noted internationally as an analytical and consulting chemist to the leather industry and
allied trades; former state Senator in Connecticut in 1909; president of the Reed-Blair
Laboratories; original founder of the
American Leather Chemists Association

Obituaries
N Y Herald Tribune p10 Jl 26 '40
N Y Times p17 Jl 26 '40

REED, JOHN HOWARD 1860—Mar 12,
1940 Dentist; founder and director of the
old New York Dental School which merged
with the Columbia University School of
Dental and Oral Surgery

J. HOWARD REED

Obituaries
N Y Herald Tribune p22 Mr 13 '40
por
N Y Times p23 Mr 13 '40

**REISNER, CHRISTIAN FICHTHORNE,
REV.** (rēs'nẽr) June 3, 1872—July 17, 1940
Founder and pastor of the Broadway
Temple Methodist Church, New York City;
nationally famous for his advertising and
publicity schemes to further religion; estimated at one time that he had converted
10,000 persons, which he credited chiefly
to his widespread use of newspapers, handbills, electric signs and other advertising
media; wrote many religious and inspirational books

References
Am Mercury 18:79-87 S '29
Shepherd, W. G. Christian F. Reisner
In Great Preachers as Seen by a
Journalist p101-13 1924
Who's Who in America

REV. CHRISTIAN F. REISNER

Obituaries
Christian Cent 57:958 Jl 31 '40
N Y Herald Tribune p18 Jl 18 '40 por
N Y Times p19 Jl 18 '40 por
Newsweek 16:4 Jl 29 '40
Sch & Soc 52:41 Jl 20 '40
Time 36:35 Jl 29 '40

**REITH, JOHN CHARLES WALSHAM,
1ST BARON** (rēth) 1889- Head of the
British Ministry of Works and Buildings

In the British Cabinet reshuffle of October 1940 Baron Reith was moved from
his position of Minister of Transport to
the head of a newly created Ministry of
Works and Buildings, made necessary by
the damage which German aerial bombs
have done to houses and other structures.

For many years Sir John has been
prominent in Britain but "there is little
evidence that anyone has ever liked him."
The general impression that emerges from
the many articles on his career and work
is that of a hard, ruthless and highly
efficient administrator, ruling entirely by

Acme

BARON REITH

fear. Of his efficiency—much needed in his new Cabinet job—there is no doubt. It is he who made the British Broadcasting Corporation what it is today and he is also largely responsible for the organization of Imperial Airways.

R. S. Lambert, former editor of *The Listener,* in his book, *Ariel and All His Quality* (1940), has much to say of his 10 years' association with Reith. "For a long while," he writes, "I was handicapped by the sense of fear which he inspired; and for many years, whenever I received a summons to his room, I had to go apart for a minute in order to control my heart beats and allow the mist which rose up in my brain to clear away." Lambert reports, too, that Reith had three seats in his office for visitors—a hard one for nobodies, an armchair for senior subordinates and a luxurious sofa for high dignitaries or people he wished to placate. "He would work himself into a fuss about titles, orders of precedence and correct modes of address. . . He liked being 'sirred' and was once heard to explain the infrequency of his tours round the offices on the ground that his entry would embarrass the staff by causing them to stand up in the midst of their work."

Other associates have reported similar facts: Vernon Bartlett, M. P. and *News Chronicle* journalist, for instance, who records that on Reith's desk at the BBC there was perpetually kept a certificate from his boyhood Sunday School, stating that he had never missed attendance. And the *Frankfurter Zeitung* doesn't sound too prejudiced when it says: "There are numerous anecdotes about Reith, illustrating the hatred of this Scottish minister's son for tobacco, alcohol, jazz music on Sunday and worldliness in any form, his temperament of

an Aberdonian, his arrogance, his thirst for personal revenge." It goes on to quote the remark of an American Quakeress to him in 1917: "Vengeance is mine, saith the Lord," to which Reith is reported to have answered: "Certainly vengeance belongs to the Lord, but it lies with me to be an instrument of that vengeance."

Some people have explained Reith by saying he never got over the fact that he was unable to complete his education at Oxford or Cambridge. He is the fifth son and seventh child of the Reverend George Reith, D. D., a Presbyterian minister of Aberdeen, Scotland, and Adah Mary (Weston) Reith, an Englishwoman. John Reith went to Glasgow Academy and then to Gresham's School, Holt, one of the minor English public schools. He was then trained as an engineer at the Royal Technical College, Glasgow, from which he received the degree of M. S. and became a member of the Institution of Civil Engineers. After five years' apprenticeship in Glasgow, Reith began his first job, with the London engineering firm of S. Pearson and Son, Limited.

When the First World War broke out Reith took a commission in the Royal Engineers, served in France and rose to the rank of major before being invalided out in 1916. When he had recovered from his wounds he spent more than a year in the United States contracting for munitions. Then, in 1918, he went to the department of the Civil Engineer in Chief at the Admiralty and spent the year of 1919 liquidating ordnance and engineering contracts for the Ministry of Munitions. In 1920 he returned to civilian engineering as general manager for William Beardmore and Company. This was his last engineering position.

In 1922 Reith answered an advertisement and was selected out of 55 applicants to be the first general manager of the British Broadcasting Company. Its title was soon changed to Corporation and in one year Reith became its managing director. From 1927 to 1938 he had supreme power over the BBC as director general. Under his control the technological side of broadcasting was rapidly developed; a wide variety of programs was arranged; and the government's policy of running the radio in absolute freedom from advertising and without political bias was faithfully carried out.

Although under Reith considerable imagination was shown in the broadcasting of unexpected and out-of-the-way programs and the talks on various specialized subjects reached a high level, there were complaints. The newspapers used to howl that Reith was making BBC programs the dullest on all the world's air waves and there was persistent criticism about Sunday broadcasts in particular. But Sir John was unmoved: "So long as I am the director general," he said, "there will be no change in the character of Sunday programs. . . The BBC has never attempted to give the public what it wants. It gives the public what it ought to have."

There was criticism on the internal administration of the BBC, too. Reith tended to surround himself with yes-men and freeze out really original subordinates. He appointed a number of military and naval officers to key positions, though they lacked any obvious qualifications and according to the London *Evening Standard* of February 26, 1937: "No candidate for any one of the more important posts was appointed without first of all being examined by Sir John, who always attached great importance to the answer made to the question: 'What games do you play?'" Any aberration from the most conventional moral standards meant instant dismissal and to be involved in a divorce case was the end of working for BBC.

In 1938 Reith resigned from the BBC, a year after the world had heard him announce the abdication of King Edward VIII, to become chairman of Imperial Airways. Before he took over, Imperial Airways had a reputation for bumbling along and it was the job of this "dour, ascetic Aberdonian" to reorganize it efficiently. Immediately he began the top-to-bottom installation of the "rigid quarter-deck punctilio" he had commanded at BBC.

In February 1940 Sir John Reith was appointed Minister of Information, in supreme charge of censoring the British press and getting publicity for the British cause. As Minister a Parliamentary seat had to be found for him, so the member for Southampton stood down in his favor, and in the same month Sir John was returned unopposed. There was not a little criticism of his carrying out of this post and in Winston Churchill's (see sketch this issue) reconstructed government of May 1940 he was transferred from Information to the position of Minister of Transport and then to the position he now holds in the Ministry of Works and Buildings.

Reith stands six-foot-six and is described as having "blazing blue eyes, an impressive dome and a fearsome scar across his left cheek, result of a war wound." He lives in the pleasant Chiltern village of Beaconsfield, convenient to London. He was knighted in 1927 and made a baron in October 1940 in recognition of his services.

In 1921 he married Muriel Katharine, younger daughter of the late John Lynch Odhams of Southwick, Sussex, and they have one son and one daughter.

References

Gt Brit & East 54:21 Ja 11 '40 por
Nature 145:61 Ja 13 '40
N Y Herald Tribune p4 O 4 '40
N Y Times p4 Ja 7 '40
News R Ap 25 '40
Time 31:31 Je 27 '38 por; 25:20 Ja 15 '40 por

Allighan, G. Sir John Reith 1938
Gunther, J. Men of Whitehall *In* Inside Europe p334-54 1940
Lambert, R. S. Ariel and All His Quality 1940
Who's Who
Who's Who in Commerce and Industry

REVUELTAS, SILVESTRO (rā-vōō-ĕl'-täs) Dec 31, 1899—Oct 4, 1940 Mexican composer; toured United States as concert violinist before he was 20 and in 1919 played first violin in Chicago Symphony Orchestra; began composing in 1934 while assistant conductor of the Mexican Symphony; his compositions include many works for motion pictures and dance orchestras; appointed a director of National Conservatory of Music in Mexico in 1937

References

Thompson, O. ed. Cyclopedia of Music and Musicians 1939

Obituaries

Musical Am 60:36 N 10 '40 por
N Y Herald Tribune p24 O 22 '40

REYNAUD, PAUL (rā'nō' pōl) Oct 15, 1878- French statesman

Indicted at Riom on October 19, 1940 by the Vichy government on charges of "embezzlement of public funds," wiry little Paul Reynaud, former Premier of France, was said to be devoting the greater part of his day to physical culture—boxing, skipping rope—while awaiting trial.

Born in 1878 in the French Alpine village of Barcelonette, Paul Reynaud has been described as "a tough little mountaineer with a hard head for business." His grandfather, a French soldier who fought in Mexico under Maximilian and who did not leave that country until he had founded the family's substantial dry goods business there, seems to have possessed that same hard head. Reynaud's father, a Conseiller General, and his uncles, all Deputies or Senators, may have influenced his choice of careers. His family moved to Paris when Paul was a child, and upon graduation from the Lycee Louis le Grand he promptly decided to study law at the Sorbonne.

Reynaud did not begin law practice immediately after graduation, however; instead, he set out on the first of those voyages which have since won him the distinction of "Most Traveled French Statesman." His trip was around the world, and he traveled slowly, by branch railway, horse, canoe—making careful observations as he went. When he returned to Paris to set up practice as a corporation lawyer he employed these same faculties of observation in listening to the pleas of the famous lawyers in the Palace of Justice. Results of either the observation or his assorted other talents were so successful that he later became general secretary of the Paris

PAUL REYNAUD

Bar Association and husband of the daughter (Jeanne) of one of its presidents, Henri Robert.

He returned to Paris to enter post-War politics and to join the overruled minority who believed it was to France's interest to prevent a complete economic breakdown in Germany. In 1924 he was defeated as Deputy to Parliament from his own Basses-Alpes district; in 1928 he was elected to the same office, this time representing the sixth Paris district, which centers around the Stock Exchange. He has represented this same Parisian constituency for 12 years.

Specialist in many fields, in the next few years Reynaud served in a number of Cabinets: in 1930, as Minister of Finance under Tardieu; in 1931, as Minister for the Colonies under Laval; in 1932, as Minister of Justice under Tardieu. He was already regarded as a heretic in circles of orthodox financial theory because early in the depression he advocated the devaluation of the franc; he now embarked upon a career of dissent with other official policies. In 1934 he was one of a delegation of voters who went to the President's palace to beg him to dismiss the Daladier (see sketch this issue) government. In March 1935, influenced by De Gaulle (see sketch this issue) he introduced a bill to form 11 mechanized divisions in the French Army, but it was turned down by Daladier. In 1936 he was fighting Laval's (see sketch this issue) pro-Italian policy in Ethiopia. Though no friend of Communism nor of the People's Front, he favored the Franco-Russian pact and the policy of "collective security," and fought appeasement. In 1938, as Minister of Justice under Daladier, he was one of the deputies who are said to have offered their resignations after Chamberlain's visit to Berchtesgaden. At about the same time Flandin's pro-Munich attitude caused Reynaud to break with the Alliance Démocratique, with which he had formerly been allied. He has not since officially allied himself with any political faction, although he calls himself a moderate conservative.

At one time Reynaud summed up his "lone wolf" political position thus: "I have always had the 11 governments which rule France against me: the Bank of France, the Institute, the great industrial and financial trusts, the Veterans, the bondholders, etc.—in short, the whole of official France."

Time has summed it up otherwise. The next stage in Reynaud's career, probably, best justifies that publication's description of him as a man who "built a career on his belief that France is primarily a nation of small shopkeepers," that "two-thirds of the French people are *not* the Masses." On November 1, 1938, Reynaud became Minister of Finance as the result of a Cabinet reshuffle. On November 12 his decrees were announced. Based on a policy of increased production and lowered consumption for the purpose of building the military power of France as rapidly as possible, in many quarters of the nation they were not greeted with joy. Under Reynaud's predecessors the public debt had swelled enormously, the franc had fallen to less than half its normal value, and gold was pouring out of the Bank of France. Reynaud frankly proclaimed a "policy of sacrifice," of "facing the facts and getting to work." Ruthlessly he slashed expenses, increased taxes. Prices, profits, wages, exchange—all were controlled. The franc was to be further devaluated. Armaments took the place of public works, subway and bus fares were raised, pensions reduced, 40,000 railroad workers fired. On November 30 the people retaliated with a general strike, which was broken.

In April of 1939 further decree laws were announced. By the beginning of the War the five-day week had totally disappeared ("the week with two Sundays," Reynaud scornfully called it), Blum's (see sketch this issue) 40-hour week had been lengthened to 45—in munitions plants to 60—hours, and prices of such commodities as tobacco, wine and coffee had jumped tremendously. Women were mobilized for labor. Civilian France, at least, was being made painfully aware that a war was going on.

By December 1939, France's Minister of Finance was able to make an impressive report: a return to the treasury of 14 billion francs in exported capital, 10 billion francs in gold. And in the same month, on December 25, 1939, Reynaud and Sir John Simon (see sketch this issue) signed the equally impressive agreement binding France and England in a financial and economic union. By this agreement the respective strengths of the two currencies were linked and the material resources of the two empires pooled, to be shared proportionately in the prosecution of the War. The clause prolonging this partnership until six months after the peace, Reynaud believed, "could be the point of departure for that long-awaited reorganization of Europe."

On March 21, 1940 Paul Reynaud became France's new Premier, after a vote of confidence in Daladier's prosecution of the War failed to give him an affirmative majority.

The capacity for rapid and aggressive action that had marked Reynaud's career in the past was not lost in his acceptance of the Premiership. His Cabinet was formed in 24 hours, and immediately succeeded in antagonizing Marin's extreme Rightist group and others by its inclusion of five Socialists. His first statement of policy to the Chamber was made in four minutes flat. Its keynote was: "My government has but a single aim—to conquer. To win is to save all. To succumb is to lose all."

Reynaud's initial appearance found the Chamber unenthusiastic and its vote of confidence gave him a precarious majority. But in one month the opposition had temporarily "melted away." In spite of the fact that Reynaud's censorship and other restrictive measures were even harsher than those of Daladier's régime, on April 19, in the midst of the War in Norway, the Chamber gave him a unanimous vote of confidence after an all-day debate on his War measures. He fought against the withdrawal of British troops from Norway; he tried to put pressure on Belgium to abandon her neutrality; he wanted to dispense with the slow-moving Gamelin (see sketch this issue), although he did not immediately. His own policy was one of vigorous prosecution of the War. But, as Pertinax (see sketch this issue) points out, he surrounded himself with men of a different, a semi-totalitarian temper. The Countess Hélène de Portes, whose intimate friend he had been for a great many years, and who was rumored to be a lobbyist for several Big Business interests, was also a member of the influential clique which met nightly in his apartment.

On May 19 Weygand (see sketch this issue) succeeded Gamelin as commander of the French forces, and Pétain (see sketch this issue) became vice-president of Council and supreme technical adviser to Reynaud's Cabinet. Louis Marin, Rightist leader, and Jean Ybarnegaray, parliamentary chief of what had been the Croix de Feu, were also taken into the Cabinet in May. Daladier was not ousted until June 5, and it was not until June that De Gaulle became chief assistant at the War Ministry. The stage was getting set for the fall of France. It was only under pressure that on June 12 Reynaud asked Churchill to release France from her promise not to make a separate armistice; after Paris fell Reynaud appealed from Bordeaux to the United States for "clouds of airplanes"; when Britain proposed union to France, Reynaud himself voted for the British proposals, voted against any armistice, spoke of continuing the War from the Colonies. But most of the men he had put into office were against him, and when he was voted down he "meekly gave way," resigned, let Pétain take over, and, according to Pertinax, was actually ready to go to the United States to serve as Ambassador from Pétain's government. He even telegraphed to Churchill (see sketch this issue), begging him to be satisfied with the arrangements made about the French fleet. "Reynaud has betrayed me three times," Churchill said, and didn't answer.

Later in June, Devaux and Leca, two of Reynaud's closest advisers, were said to have been caught in Spain on their way to the United States with 50,000,000 francs in their bags (in banknotes, gold, jewels belonging to the Countess de Portes). Reynaud was not appointed Ambassador to the United States. And on June 28 news was received of the automobile crash on the French Riviera in which the Countess de Portes was killed, Reynaud injured. His friend dead, his career ruined, France in the hands of his enemies, even his honor not quite intact, he went from the hospital to imprisonment in the Chateau Châzeron, the boxing gloves and the skipping rope.

Small, agile, Reynaud is said to appear much younger than his 60-odd years. The American press often describes him as "dapper," and apparently the adjective is apt. In 1932, at a Hoover rally in Madison Square Garden, the crowd took the top-hatted Frenchman for Jimmy Walker, and called out to him, railingly: "What are you doing here, Jimmy?" His political soubriquet is "the cat." "With his somewhat Asiatic features and pinched eyes," says Antonina Vallentin, more poetically, "Paul Reynaud resembles in moments of tranquility a Chinese god carved in ivory. But his face is seldom tranquil—nor is it ever completely mobile. His glance alone is serious, vivacious, agitated."

Reynaud's favorite sport was a strenuous one: bicycling—and his hobby of maps was made more active than most. He has set foot in every continent at least three times, and is particularly familiar with the English language and institutions. He has published four books: *Waldeck-Rousseau; Les Trois Glorieuses; Jeunesse, Quelle France Veux-Tu?; Le Problème Militaire Français* (the latter inspired by the theories of De Gaulle).

References

Christian Sci Mon Mag p5 F 17 '40 pors

Liberty 17:14-15 N 9 '40 por; 17:10-14 N 23 '40 ils; 17:50-54 D 7 '40 il

Liv Age 354:318-20 Je '38; 354:327-30 Je '38

Nation 150:407-8 Mr 30 '40

New Repub 102:423 Ap 1 '40

REYNAUD, PAUL—*Continued*

Newsweek 12:21 N 14 '38 por; 15:18-
19 Ap 1 '40 por; 15:20 Ap 29 '40;
15:27 My 13 '40; 15:20 Je 17 '40

Time 27:19 Ja 6 '36 por; 32:26 N 14
'38 por; 34:19 Ag 21 '39 por; 35:20-1
Ap 1 '40 por; 35:30-2 Je 17 '40 por
(cover)

Yale R ns 24:66-82 S '34

International Who's Who
Simone, A. J'Accuse 1940

REYNOLDS, JAMES A. 1887—Apr 6,
1940 Electrical engineer; professor of
engineering at Tufts College for 22 years;

JAMES A. REYNOLDS

former Somerville, Massachusetts health
board chairman

Obituaries

N Y Times p45 Ap 7 '40

REYNOLDS, ROBERT RICE June 18,
1884- Senator from North Carolina
Address: b. Senate Office Building, Washington, D. C.; h. Asheville, North Carolina

"No. 1 Senatorial alien-baiter is North
Carolina's Robert Rice Reynolds, an ex-football star who scrimmages against the Menace
of Internationalism 24 hours a day," according to the *American Mercury.* For a long
time the "sandy-haired, ruby-cheeked Tarheel" has been arguing that "the time has
come for changing the tradition that the
United States is an asylum for the oppressed
of the world," has been insisting that "the
millions of foreigners who are about to
begin the rape of this country" should be
deported or interned in concentration
camps—or, at least, fingerprinted. Only

lately has his voice been even feebly echoed
in Congressional legislation, however.

Born in Asheville, Buncombe County,
North Carolina, on June 18, 1884, the son
of William Taswell and Mamie (Spears)
Reynolds, nothing much stood in the way
of a political career for Bob Reynolds. His
father was court clerk, his Uncle Henry
chief of police, his Uncle Dan sheriff, his
Uncle Gus tax collector. He, however, left
home at the age of 12, being somewhat independent minded, and proceeded to become
barker for a carnival and a few other things
before he even thought about attending the
University of North Carolina in 1902 and
taking his law degree there in 1906. At
the University he had also displayed his
versatility by captaining the varsity track
team and playing end and halfback on the
football team, and it is little wonder that
when he decided to set up law practice he
selected an ingenious way of getting himself a little advertising. Virtually unknown,
he campaigned for prosecuting attorney in
1910 (it cost only $50 to get on the ballot),
and went into the mountains astride a de-
crepit mare with his saddlebags stuffed
with sticks of candy. These he passed out
to children; they were inscribed, "Tell your
daddy to vote for Bob Reynolds." To the
voters he announced frankly that he was
out for the job and the money—and was
more surprised than anyone else when he
won the election. Another Reynolds was
in local politics. It was, perhaps, destiny.

His political luck deserted him temporarily, though. In 1912 he overturned a
normally Republican district to be elected
solicitor by a large majority, but shortly
afterward he resigned this post and ran
unsuccessfully for the national House of
Representatives. Then came World War
I. By that time he was a widower with
two children, Frances Jackson and Robert
Rice, his wife, Frances Jackson, whom he
married in 1909, having died. In 1914 he
married Mary Bland and sometime during
the War he resigned the captain's commission which he had held in the National
Guard.

In the next years he was, among other
things, to become proprietor of an ice skating rink, to make a million dollars, mainly
in real estate, to lose his fortune in land
deals and bank failures and to return to
North Carolina politics. In 1924 he was
campaigning for the job of Lieutenant Governor of the state. It was another unusual
campaign. Equipped with a North Carolina
Year Book and a voters' list, he mailed
some 175,000 postcards to his "God-fearin'
'tater-raisin', baby-havin' constituents," and
returned to North Carolina just before the
primaries. He lost. Nothing daunted, he
entered the 1926 Senatorial campaign,
amassed 90,000 votes, though not the office,
and then went blithely to work in preparation for the 1932 primaries. There were
graduation exercises to be attended in one-
room schoolhouses, mountaineers to be
championed before the Bar without fees

until Bob Reynolds was recognized everywhere as "Little Father of the Poor." And when campaign time came around Reynolds, without machine affiliations or fame, with only a two-year-old Ford and $20, stumped the State for six months. He had meanwhile divorced his wife and was married again in 1930—this time to Eva Brady, an ex-Follies girl, who died in 1934.

His opponent for the 1932 Senatorial nomination, Cameron Morrison, had been in Congress for such a long time that his constituents were used to marking their ballots for him almost automatically. But when Reynolds announced that the Senator ate "caviah, which is nothin' but fish aigs," and asked, "Do y'all want a fish-aig Senator?" they began to wonder. Reynolds' car rattled and he chewed wads of cut plug in public. He raised the banner against the Interests, Wall Street and the International Bankers; he blamed Hoover, the Reconstruction Finance Corporation, the moratorium and the Eighteenth Amendment for the wheat and cotton that was rotting while children froze and famished; he called the American Legion "the greatest body of heroes that ever lived in this or any other civilization." And he was elected by 100,000 votes.

In the Senate people weren't sure what to expect of Reynolds, and were rather relieved at first, deciding he didn't have to be taken seriously. Reynolds had known the late Huey Long "when the Louisiana 'Kingfish' was a patent-medicine peddler," and he became his friend at a time when other Senators were ostracizing him. Everyone liked Reynolds. Gregarious and convivial, it is said that he modeled his own manners and style of oratory after the Kingfish's, and was soon known as the Senate clown, the "Tarheel Toreador," filling the record with "turgid pages on his favorite subjects—himself, his travels, his slickness," garnering publicity, being photographed kissing Jean Harlow, endorsing Lucky Strikes—though never forgetting his North Carolina voters. During one housing debate he announced: "If $700,000,000 of the people's money is to be expended, I want North Carolina, God bless her, to have her part—although she does not need it particularly." In general he supported New Deal social legislation. And although he began crusading against "the alien" after a 1935 call at the San Simeon estate of William Randolph Hearst, it merely seemed like "a safe and effective issue in a State that had the highest percentage of native white population in the country." In May 1938 the Senate pages voted him their favorite Senator.

Not until after Reynolds' trip to Germany after his re-election in 1938 on a pledge to support the New Deal, did the Senator apparently decide to try really seriously to save the country from impending "rape" by "millions of foreigners." Upon his return he announced that "unquestionably the Germans have made a tremendous, a phe-nomenal progress and have done a great deal for their people," and admitted "in all fairness" that he had been deeply impressed by the Nazi setup. By winter the *Washington Merry-Go-Round* was calling him the "Tarheel Führer," accusing him of "acclaiming Hitler as a great man." Reynolds rose to defend himself. "Those who would picture him as anything other than the protector of the nation from 'isms,' all kinds of 'isms,' Hitler's and Mussolini's included" were being grossly libelous. But in the Senate he continued to make such statements as: "France and England are through. Democracy is finished in Europe. Hitler and Mussolini have a date with destiny. It's foolish to oppose them, so why not play ball with them?" Later he was found arguing for Franco's cause in Spain, defending Hitler's seizure of Czechoslovakia as an innocent outburst of "frontier spirit."

He also quit the New Deal camp. It is said that he wanted to get on the Foreign Relations Committee, and that South Carolina's Jimmy Byrnes fixed it and thus lured Reynolds' vote to a group bent on cutting relief deficiency funds when there was a crucial one-vote margin—in January 1939.

On January 31, 1939 Reynolds announced the creation of the Vindicators, a "mass movement of Americans" to "discuss Americanism." The Vindicators were a chain of patriotic societies without dues, contributions or salaries. The official organ, *The Vindicator,* cost $1 a year, a sum which also paid for the organizational work and three official emblems: a "banner" for every unit of fifty members (coiled rattler on a yellow background with the legend "Don't tread on me"); a red, white and blue button for each member's lapel; a red, white and blue feather for each member's hat. Mottoes were "America for the Americans; America first; Crush the enemies of America." Objectives were to keep us out of the War which, Reynolds warned, British and French propaganda was seeking to draw us into; register and fingerprint all aliens; stop all immigration for the next 10 years; banish all foreign "isms," most particularly Communism; deport all alien criminals and undesirables, whose number was, he was sure, legion.

Although appeals were made for supporters "regardless of race, creed or politics," he advanced "scientific" proof that "the Jewish people do not become integral parts of American life, except after generations and under pressure," and Jews were actually barred from membership. Excerpts from *Social Justice* have also penetrated Reynolds' Senate speeches, and his friendship with George Deatherage, leader of the Fascist, anti-Semitic Knights of the White Camellia has been held to show the real nature of his "Americanism." Reynolds has been called "chief Nazi spokesman in the United States"; it has been pointed out that "the decorations in his Washington office . . . are very graphic about Communism, say nothing about Nazism," and some

REYNOLDS, ROBERT RICE—*Continued*
have asserted that "German correspondents
and diplomats faithfully report to Berlin all
his anti-alien tirades." Many others have
taken him less seriously, however, saying
that he merely imitates Dies (see sketch
this issue) and "his success at rabble-rous-
ing," that he is still merely playing at publicity (like the time he kissed Jean Harlow) or at politics ("I play politics all day—
every day").

Recently Reynolds has not been completely consistent. He spoke against conscription, saying, among other things, that
"the squirrel hunters of North Carolina and
Kentucky can keep Hitler or anyone else
off until the Marines arrive and the situation is well in hand," but voted for the bill
itself. He shows every symptom of sticking
by his anti-alien guns, however, and was
an ardent supporter of the Smith Amendment and the Allen bill to deport Harry
Bridges (see sketch this issue).

The Senator has a reputation for having
said that he visited "Hungria" on his latest
trip to Europe, and that he thought Hitler
had "done wrong to take the Sudan," but
he also has a reputation for being the best
actor in the Senate (as a matter of fact,
he has been a professional), and his ignorance is probably artful. Actually he is the
most widely traveled man in Congress, having been around the world "six or eight
times" and chatted earnestly with half the
statesmen in Europe. He has even written
two travel books, *Wanderlust* (1913) and
Gypsy Trails. When Italy seized Albania
he was the first to observe that it had been
sold to Italy by King Zog I a decade before.

He holds other records, too. "Florid, fleshy,
and fresh," he is seen oftener than any other
member in the Senate gymnasium; he gets
more mail, telephone calls and visitors than
any of his colleagues; and he is the prime
dandy of the Senate, posing in double-breasted
suits and violent cravats except in campaigning, when he wears old clothes and
drawls "No'th Ca'lina." Someone called him
"the Duce of the Senate haranguers" and
pointed out unflatteringly that "the fact that
a Reynolds can happen at all is a signal example of the chances we must accept for the
sake of a democracy." But those who vote
for him are devoted to him and call him "Our
Bob."

References

Am Mercury 27:140-7 O '32; 48:304-11
N '39
Business Week p7 Ap 13 '40 por
Collier's 101:36+ My 21 '38 por
Lit Digest 119:12 Ja 26 '35 por; 120:3
S 14 '35
Newsweek 13:15-16 My 1 '39 por
Time 26:35 S 16 '35 por; 27:13 Je 1
'36 por; 28:38 Ag 10 '36 por; 33:16
F 13 '39 por
U S News 8:15 My 31 '40
Vital Speeches 4:363-5 Ap 1 '38

Michie, A. A. and Ryhlick, F. Tarheel
Fuehrer *In* Dixie Demagogues p221-
41 1939
Who's Who in America
Who's Who in Law
Who's Who in the Nation's Capital

RIASANOVSKY, ANTONINA *See* Fedorova, N.

RICHARD, LOUIS 1869—July 12, 1940
Sculptor; designed and executed work for
public buildings in this country and in
Canada; sculpture used for the Dominion
Parliament Buildings at Ottawa, Canada,
the New York Public Library, the Grand
Central Terminal Building in New York
and as ornaments for the entrance to the
United States Military Academy; executed
commissions for many of the best-known
mansions in New York and in Newport,
Rhode Island, among them the homes of
Henry C. Frick, William K. Vanderbilt,
Henry Spiers and Charles M. Schwab

Obituaries

N Y Times p13 Jl 13 '40
N Y World-Telegram p24 Jl 13 '40

RICHARDSON, NORVAL Oct 8, 1877—
Oct 22, 1940 Author and former United
States diplomat; was chargé d'affaires in
Copenhagen for short period, after which
he went to Rome as second secretary of the
American legation; later sent to Chile, Lisbon and Tokyo; resigned from diplomatic
corps in 1924; author of 15 books, many of
them dealing with his diplomatic experiences

References

Richardson, N. My Diplomatic Edu-
cation 1923
Who's Who in America
Who's Who Among North American
Authors

Obituaries

N Y Herald Tribune p26 O 23 '40
por
N Y Times p23 O 23 '40

**RICHMOND, CHARLES ALEXANDER,
REV.** Jan 7, 1862—July 12, 1940 Former
president of Union College, Schenectady, New
York (1909-29); noted as author, lecturer and
administrator; former Presbyterian minister; was pastor of the Madison Avenue
Presbyterian Church, Albany, New York
for 15 years

References

Who's Who in America
Who's Who in American Education

Obituaries

N Y Herald Tribune p8 Jl 13 '40
N Y Times p13 Jl 13 '40

RICKENBACKER, EDWARD Oct 8, 1890- President and general manager of Eastern Air Lines, Incorporated

Address: Eastern Air Lines Building, 10 Rockefeller Plaza, New York City

Edward Vernon (generally known as Eddie) Rickenbacker, aviation hero of the First World War, stepped out of his well-established rôle of businessman in 1940 to talk and write publicly again on aviation. In magazine articles and in speeches he urged that the United States build up its national defense with more planes and train more pilots. As one of the most glamorous of the United States' War heroes and as an important figure in the aviation industry, Rickenbacker's opinion can be expected to have weight with the public.

Eddie Rickenbacker's life follows one of the most beloved American patterns—the poor orphan whose exploits on the automobile race track and in the air led him on to prosperity and success in business. He was born in Columbus, Ohio, the son of William and Elizabeth Rickenbacker. As a boy, Eddie, according to his own description of himself, was a "tough little kid with an uncontrollable temper," the leader of his gang. His father died when he was twelve, and Eddie, the third of seven children, made up his mind to do something to help his mother.

The day after his father's funeral, instead of going to school, he started off in the direction of the Columbus factories. At the glass works he said he was 14 and got a job for $3.50 a week. He worked a twelve-hour night stretch, walked four miles to work to save carfare and turned every cent he made over to his mother.

He was always interested in motors and in mechanical things, so he enrolled in a correspondence school for a course in engineering and drafting. In order to be near engines he got a job with the Frayer-Miller Cooled Car Company in Columbus. An aggressive youngster, he went from the engineering phase of automobile manufacture to the sales division.

When the future war ace was 20, automobile racing caught his fancy and from 1910 to 1917 he was the daredevil of the American automobile race tracks. He won championships at national and international meets. When the United States declared war in 1917 Rickenbacker was preparing a racing team for the English Sunbeam Motor Company. He dropped his plans and a month later enlisted in the army.

His efforts to get government sanction to enlist all the automobile racing men into one squadron of fighting pilots did not meet with success, so he went to France as a chauffeur assigned to drive General Pershing's car. But flying still fired his imagination and he asked to be transferred to the Air Service. On August 25, 1917 he was sent to Tours, France, for preliminary training in flying. Subsequently he was transferred to Issoudan Training Field as

Wide World

EDDIE RICKENBACKER

chief engineering officer with rank of lieutenant.

But he still was not in the thick of fighting and to a daredevil like Rickenbacker this was not satisfactory. Requests to be transferred to the front were met with the answer that he could not be spared at Issoudan Field. He finally had to get himself sent to the hospital for two weeks to show that he was not indispensable and to get his way about going to the front.

His career as an American War ace began when he was transferred to active duty with the 94th Aero Pursuit Squadron, first American air unit to participate actively on the Western Front. In September 1918 he became the commander of the squadron which became known as the "Hat-in-the-Ring Squadron" and world-famous. The squadron was credited with 69 victories, the largest number of any American unit. Rickenbacker headed the list by bringing down 26 planes himself. Miraculously, he was uninjured.

At the end of the War he retired with the rank of major and a reputation as one of the most glamorous of America's War heroes. He was honored with the Croix de Guerre with four palms and the Légion d'Honneur from the French government and with the Distinguished Service Cross with nine palms and the Congressional Medal of Honor from the United States.

Rickenbacker returned to the automobile industry after the War, organizing and becoming vice-president of the Rickenbacker Motor Car Company. When the company was dissolved he joined the Cadillac Motor Car Company as assistant sales manager in charge of the La Salle division. After a year in that position he was transferred by General Motors Corporation to the Fokker Aircraft Corporation of America

RICKENBACKER, EDWARD—*Continued*
as vice-president and director of sales, with headquarters in New York City.

From 1932 to 1933 Rickenbacker was with the Aviation Corporation as vice-president of its American Airways, Incorporated. Then he became associated with North American Aviation, Incorporated, as vice-president, and on January 1, 1935 he became general manager of Eastern Air Lines, Incorporated.

As a director of North American Aviation and manager of its Eastern Air Lines, Rickenbacker ran Eastern almost like a one-man line. When the Air Mail Act of 1934 was passed forbidding one company to manufacture airplanes and also to have air mail contracts, North American Aviation found itself in an embarrassing position. North American built only military planes, so it got away for a time with its ownership of Eastern Air Lines and its air mail contracts. But when the government began looking askance North American decided to sell Eastern Air Lines. It was excellent property, having been the only major air line to show a sizable profit of $270,000 in 1937.

Rickenbacker's pleasant position as boss of Eastern Air Lines was threatened by Transcontinental's and Western Air Lines' bid to buy Eastern. Rickenbacker got Wall Street banking firms' backing and they offered $3,500,000 for Eastern Air Lines, outbidding the Transcontinental and Western. Air Lines. Rickenbacker remained not only general manager in complete control of operations but was made president of Eastern Air Lines when the deal was consummated in 1938.

Rickenbacker has been married to the former Mrs. Adelaide F. Durant since September 16, 1922. They have two sons.

References

Aero Digest 32:78 My '38 por (p64)
Business Week p17 Mr 12 '38 por
Look 4:8-9 Ag 27 '40 il por
Pop Mech 74:321-4 S '40 il
St Nicholas 63:20 N '35 por
Time 31:60+ Mr 14 '38
Blue Book of American Aviation
Rickenbacker, E. V. Fighting the Flying Circus 1919
Who's Who in America
Who's Who in Commerce and Industry

RICKETTS, LOUIS DAVIDSON Dec 19, 1859—Mar 5, 1940 Mining engineer; copper company executive; awarded James Douglas Medal of the American Institute of Mining and Metallurgical Engineers February 1940; author of technical papers

References

Who's Who in America 1938-39
Who's Who in Engineering

Obituaries

N Y Herald Tribune p22 Mr 6 '40
por
N Y Sun p9 F 15 '40

RIESMAN, DAVID Mar 25, 1867—June 3, 1940 Physician; educator; professor of clinical medicine at University of Pennsylvania for 28 years; wrote scientific works; practiced for 40 years in Philadelphia; lecturer on astronomy; known as expert on Italian Renaissance and archeology

DAVID RIESMAN

References

American Medical Directory
American Men of Science
Directory of Medical Specialists 1939
Who's Who in America
Who's Who in American Jewry
Who's Who in American Education

Obituaries

N Y Herald Tribune p24 Je 4 '40
N Y Times p23 Je 4 '40 por

RIGGS, AUSTEN FOX Dec 12, 1876—Mar 5, 1940 Specialist in neuropsychiatry; founded Austen Riggs Foundation, Incorporated for the free treatment of psychoneurotic patients without means; professor; author of books and medical papers

References

American Medical Directory
Who's Who in America 1938-39

Obituaries

N Y Herald Tribune p22 Mr 6 '40
N Y Sun p23 Mr 6 '40
Springf'd Republican p20 Mr 8 '40

RIPLEY, JOSEPH Jan 3, 1854—Sept 28, 1940 Engineer; assistant chief engineer in the construction of the Panama Canal; former advisory engineer to the New York State Department of Public Works; career was devoted chiefly to the construction of public projects, mostly in Michigan and New York State; for nine years was adviser on New York State canals

References

Who's Who in America
Who's Who in Engineering 1925

Obituaries

N Y Herald Tribune p36 S 29 '40

ROBB, HUNTER 1863—May 15, 1940 Gynecologist; author of many papers on surgical technique and diseases of women; first surgeon to use rubber gloves while operating and one of first to use foot pedals for water faucets; collaborator with the late Dr. Harvey Cushing on *The Life of Sir William Osler*

References

American Medical Directory
Who's Who in America

Obituaries

N Y Herald Tribune p22 My 16 '40
N Y Times p23 My 16 '40

ROBERTS, FLORENCE Mar 16, 1861—June 6, 1940 Stage and film actress; played "Granny Jones" in *The Jones Family* series of motion pictures; began on stage when 19 years old; received film start with Mack Sennett; should not be confused with another actress by the same name who died in Los Angeles in 1927 after spending seven years in films

References

N Y Dram N 60:1 O 10 '14
Theatre 6:152-3 Je '06
International Motion Picture Almanac

Obituaries

N Y Times p23 Je 7 '40 por

RODGERS, RICHARD June 28, 1902- **and HART, LORENZ** May 2, 1895- Composers of musical comedy
Address: b. c/o Music Corp of America, 745 Fifth Ave, New York City

When a team like Gilbert and Sullivan or Rodgers and Hart appears on the scene, the first question laymen ask is: "Which do you write first, the music or the words?" Dick Rodgers, of Rodgers and Hart, says there's no answer to the question. "My favorite blight and partner, Mr. Lorenz Hart, often hands me a completed lyric to be set to music. More often I have a tune ready for him to work on. Sometimes we sit in a room and hate each other until we get a title; then I throw Larry out

of the house and fool around until I get a satisfactory melody, inspired entirely by the title and not by nostalgia for Venice in the spring."

It was by this method, at least, that in 1940 the Rodgers & Hart-John O'Hara musical comedy, *Pal Joey*, got its lyrics and tunes written.

Since they first met in 1919, when Hart was 23 and just out of Columbia and Rodgers was 16 and just going in, they have never done a stick of work apart. "It was love at first sight," they say. And it has stayed that way. Between them they have turned out well over a thousand songs, many of them hits, including *Thou Swell, The Lady is a Tramp, Ten Cents a Dance, With a Song in My Heart*. Between them they have been responsible for at least one and sometimes two musical comedy successes on Broadway nearly every year.

Almost all his life Richard Rodgers has been writing music. "For the sake of color," he says, "I should have been a singing waiter at Nigger Mike's. Unfortunately I was a doctor's son and very well fed as a kid." He was born on June 28, 1902 in New York City. His mother was a "merry, musical woman who liked to sing and play the piano." She would sing songs from the *Merry Widow* and *Mlle. Modiste*, and when Richard was four he was able, by ear, to pick out the melodies on the piano. His family encouraged him, as he grew older, to write music.

Dick Rodgers turned out his first song, *My Auto Show Girl*, when he was 14, and proceeded to become precociously active in the amateur-show business. He wrote the music and some of the lyrics for the shows put on by the Akron Club, a social organization to which his elder brother, now a Park Avenue obstetrician, belonged, and for various other benefit performances around town. Between shows he tried to peddle mimeographed copies of his songs to music publishers, most of whom listened to a couple of numbers without emotion and then, rising, said: "Thank you very much." "This, a courteous phrase, always courteously spoken in the show business, is generally a death verdict, but it had a violent and healthy effect upon Rodgers."

He entered Columbia University in the fall of 1919 determined to write the music for the Varsity Show the next spring. The show was called *Fly With Me*, and he was the first freshman ever to compose the score of a Columbia Varsity Show. After this achievement he was acclaimed a prodigy by the Columbia faculty and the New York press to such an extent that he never went back to Columbia—partly because he feared an anti-climax, partly because, through *Fly With Me*, he had met Lorenz Hart.

Rodgers tells about their first meeting. "A friend of mine, Phil Leavitt, told me he would like to introduce me to a fellow called Hart. It appeared that this Hart

RODGERS AND HART

knew something about lyric writing but had no composer. I knew something about composing but had no lyricist. We ought to get together. On a Sunday afternoon I was taken to Larry's house. Well, we sat around and talked theatre and song-writing. I played some tunes for him about which he was highly agreeable, and he told me his ideas about lyric writing. . . Neither of us mentioned it, but we evidently knew we'd work together, and I left Hart's house having acquired in one afternoon a career, a partner, a best friend and a source of permanent irritation."

Lorenz Hart grew up on West 119th Street in New York City, the son of a promoter, Max M. Hart, and Frieda (Isenberg) Hart. In spite of the fact that his father generally promoted the wrong thing, the Hart household was a lively and genial one. At Columbia University he became locally famous as a versifier, and though he left in 1918, he was called back to write the lyrics for the Varsity Show for which Rodgers did the music.

Rodgers' and Hart's first professional collaboration was on a song called *Any Old Place With You* which was interpolated in a Lew Fields' comedy, *A Lonely Romeo.* But in spite of the first small flurry of success on Broadway the early nineteen-twenties were mainly a long and futile period of hanging around Broadway. Finally Rodgers went to the Institute of Musical Art to study under Frank Damrosch and at the end of the year was chosen, as one of the Institute's most promising students, to write the music for its annual show.

When Rodgers left the Institute he found once more that there was nothing for him on Broadway. With Larry Hart he put on some 20 amateur shows in the next year

or two for girls' schools, churches and synagogues. He was just on the point of going into the children's underwear business when Benjamin Kaye, a lawyer, told him the Theatre Guild needed some new tapestries and wanted to put on a small amateur show Sunday nights to pay for them. Dick refused to write the music for the show. "No more amateur shows for me."

After Kaye had explained the advantages of meeting "Terry" Helburn and working with Guild Theatre understudies, Rodgers gave in, but, he said: "I'll have to have Larry Hart write the lyrics." Hart had been translating plays and musical comedies into English for the Shuberts and had, with the money from his translations, gone into the producing business with two fairly spectacular failures: one a play starring Vera Gordon, and another chiefly notable because there were only two people in the cast.

The Garrick Gaieties, their musical comedy for the Guild, opened on a Sunday night in May 1925 "to the hosannas of public and critics, and soon became a riot with nightly performances and two matinees a week." It played 214 performances on Broadway. One night in 1939 "when Dick Rodgers and Larry Hart attended one of the Theatre Guild's stately first nights, Larry nudged Dick and murmured, 'See those tapestries? *We're* responsible for them.' 'Hell,' said Rodgers, 'they're responsible for *us!*' "

Since then Rodgers and Hart have worked on almost 30 shows together. Most of them —*The Girl Friend, A Connecticut Yankee, Dearest Enemy, On Your Toes, I'd Rather Be Right, Babes in Arms,* for instance—have been hits. In May 1940, they had two musicals running simultaneously—*Too Many Girls* and *Higher and Higher,* both full of "youth and freshness." There have been one or two flops—*Betsy* and *Chee-Chee* are examples—but their batting average is unusually high. As one critic put it: "Their services to musical comedy can be exaggerated, but hardly their success."

Rodgers and Hart have made a lot of money. When they collaborate with one or more authors on a show, their combined royalty is six per cent of the gross box-office receipts. They get about $20,000 a year apiece from royalties on the performance of their songs and their income from the sale of sheet music and records runs high. They make money in Hollywood, too, though Rodgers prefers Broadway. In Hollywood his usual experience was to hand in a score, and, when the picture was produced, find the score either missing or massacred. Once Rodgers and Hart worked for 15 months at MGM and turned out only five songs. Said Rodgers: "In New York we often write five songs in one week. In three weeks we did the entire score of *I'd Rather Be Right.*" He remembers well the time when "Rodgers and Hart" were credited in the sheet music made for the movie *Mississippi* with the song *Swanee River*.

In composing his songs Rodgers is more methodical in his work and calmer in his attitude than Hart, the lyric writer. He starts about 11 in the morning and if the collaborators have agreed to work that day in Rodgers' apartment he puts in a series of telephone calls to Hart, beginning around 10 o'clock. After the two have met and roughly completed the score, they separate until the show is ready to go into rehearsal, and their collaboration then becomes for each man "a matter of grim and solitary labor." Hart dashes off to Atlantic City while Rodgers puts on a torn brown sweater buttoned up the front and shuts himself in his study to write the music. He insists that tunes never come to him in the middle of the night. "No tunes have ever come to me anywhere. I've had to go to them." he says.

"To begin with, I write scores and not isolated song numbers; therefore the particular song in question must bear a family resemblance to the other musical material in the piece." Rodgers and Hart have been trying for many years to write musical comedy that will be as well constructed as straight drama, but it has been hard to convince authors and producers that any sentence implying the presence of the moon or a feeling of frustration isn't sufficient cue for a boy and girl to walk into a spotlight and sing about love. In *On Your Toes* they felt they had come close to a reasonable combination of plot and song, but it wasn't until *Babes in Arms* that they were able to turn out a show in which every number was a "plot" number including the hit song, *The Lady is a Tramp*.

"A song is words and music and nobody ever fused words and music more effectively than Rodgers and Hart." When Rodgers' melodic line expresses gaiety, sadness, humor, Hart's lyrical line invariably complements and fulfills it. Rodgers, who believes that, aside from Jerome Kern, nobody has influenced him musically, is "not only master of a tonal palette filled with surprise and delight, but is constantly searching for new forms across the known boundaries of his medium. The dream music for *Peggy Ann* and 12 years later the music for *I Married an Angel;* the *Slaughter on Tenth Avenue* ballet music for *On Your Toes;* the march of the clowns in *Jumbo* are imaginative and charming beyond the accepted standards of musical comedy music."

Rodgers and Hart are as different at a first-night as they are in appearance and in their personal life. As Dick tells it: "Larry is more fortunate than I am on these occasions since he is able to work off the nervous tension by walking up and down in back of the audience, cursing softly if a joke fails to get a laugh and rubbing his hands vehemently if a song goes over well. I seem compelled to take it sitting down.

I cringe in the last row where I can run to the nearest exit in case of mis-fire."

Rodgers is "poised, immaculate and humorous. He is under five feet seven inches in height but seems tall in comparison with the exact five feet of his partner, a small tumultuous man, rumpled and amiable behind a large cigar which he takes out of his mouth only in order to make excited gestures with it." Nothing about Rodgers worries Hart except his own conviction that Rodgers encourages the orchestra to play too loudly: "So you want to drown out my lyrics?" he wails. Rodgers regards him peacefully and inquires: "Do you want the audience to go out whistling the lyrics?"

All this bickering is affectionate, the kind that can go on for 20-odd years between two friends, even though their lives are different. Rodgers married Dorothy Feiner in 1930 and "now lives rather formally with his wife, two daughters and three servants in a pleasant duplex apartment on East 77th Street. Larry is a bachelor and his home life is a happy pandemonium shared by his mother, his brother Teddy, the actor, and Black Mary, the general maid who has been with the Harts for some 20 years."

"Mr. and Mrs. Rodgers, gay, attractive, sociable, are frequently seen with friends at first nights, in restaurants, and at parties. Larry likes parties, too, but the thought of a white tie dissolves him and he prefers to give parties at home, always loudly and almost tearfully proclaiming any soirée of his a failure if even one guest has departed sober."

Dick was once asked: "Don't you and Hart ever fight?" He replied: "And how! Though I must explain that the fighting is all on a theoretical basis. It is difficult to prove this, but in over 20 years of coping with each other, we have never had a disagreement over policy or credit or money or, for that matter, any of the things that cause partners to part."

References

Cue 9:35 Ap 13 '40
N Y Times X p3 My 5 '40
New Yorker 14:29-33 My 28 '38; 14:23-7 Je 4 '38 il
Theatre Arts 23:741-6 O '39
Time 32:35-9 S 26 '38 pors
America's Young Men 1936-37
Who's Who in the Theatre

RODRIGUEZ, NICOLAS 1897—Aug 10, 1940 Mexican Fascist leader of Gold Shirts, anti-Communistic and anti-Semitic organization begun in 1934; exiled as enemy by President Cárdenas in 1936; spent exile in the United States; received permission to return to Juarez to die; in 1938 boasted that he had 800,000 men on border ready to march against Mexican government; received title of General from Francisco

RODRIGUEZ, NICOLAS—*Continued*
Villa; active as a rebel since 1920; many clashes with United States government

Obituaries

N Y Herald Tribune p8 Ag 10 '40 por
N Y Times p15 Ag 12 '40 por

RODZINSKI, ARTUR (rud-jĕn'skē) Jan 2, 1894- Conductor
Address: 11001 Euclid Ave, Cleveland, Ohio

The 1940 season of the New York Philharmonic Orchestra at Lewisohn Stadium in New York was opened with an all Brahms concert, conducted by Artur Rodzinski. The Lewisohn concerts, frequently attended by as many as 20,000 people, offer the best music and the best conductors to New York City at prices from 25 cents up.

Mr. Rodzinski, who has conducted at Salzburg and Warsaw, in Budapest, Vienna and Paris, who is the permanent conductor of the Cleveland Symphony Orchestra, is at home at the Lewisohn concerts. For many years he has been pleading for the democratization of music. For many years he has insisted that music should belong to all who want to hear it. However, concerts like the Lewisohn ones are only a step in the right direction, for these concerts are not free, they are supported by millionaire philanthropists and they are local. Rodzinski's idea is that great orchestras and opera should be turned over to the people. The owner of every radio, he suggests, should be taxed $1 a year and with this money a Department of Art under the Secretary of the Interior could be set up. The people do want music. This way they could get it.

Artur Rodzinski, "in the front rank of the younger generation of symphonic leaders of today," was born at Spalato on the Dalma-

Musical America
ARTUR RODZINSKI

tian coast of the Adriatic, where his Polish father had been sent temporarily on a military assignment. His father wanted him to be a lawyer and sent him to the University of Vienna, from which he received a Doctor of Laws degree. While he was at Vienna he studied as much or more music than law. He watched rehearsals, he attended every performance, spent every spare minute going over scores and was able to get his Doctor of Music degree very shortly after his law one.

Rodzinski's musical career began at Lwow, Poland with modest choral direction but he soon had a chance to try conducting at the Lwow Opera. His "sparkling" performance of *Ernani, Carmen* and other operas brought him to the attention of Warsaw and after one trial there he was given a contract. It was a hard job. Day and night he had to keep ahead of the orchestra by studying and memorizing scores he had scarcely seen before.

For five successful years Rodzinski conducted opera and the Warsaw Philharmonic Orchestra until one day in 1924 a "tall blond man" appeared in his dressing room after a performance of *Die Meistersinger* and asked him: "How would you like to go to America?" The quiet, young conductor of 30 decided he'd like it very much and the next year went with Stokowski to Philadelphia.

Rodzinski spent four years in Philadelphia as assistant conductor of the Philadelphia Orchestra of which Stokowski was conductor, as director of the orchestral and operatic departments of the Curtis Institute of Music, as principal conductor of the Philadelphia Grand Opera Company. During these four years he appeared with the New York Symphony, the Detroit Symphony and the Rochester Philharmonic as guest conductor.

The next four years Rodzinski spent as conductor of the Los Angeles Philharmonic, appreciated there for his "untiring efforts and consummate musicianship," as the scroll given him on his departure attests. He left, it has been said, because of the Philharmonic's money difficulties, which led the directors to think that maybe a change of conductors might be a drawing card. They engaged Otto Klemperer, and Rodzinski went to Cleveland in 1933 to become the second conductor that city's orchestra had ever had.

Today, in its seventh season under Rodzinski "the Cleveland Orchestra stands at the height of its virtuosity, rich in tonal beauty, balance and unity, a splendid fulfillment of a conductor's lofty aims." Besides building up the audience for regular symphony series, Rodzinski added opera to his schedules and made his Wagnerian performances famous. He worked to make this orchestra serve the whole community, through educational work and so-called "popular" performances. Educational work in music, based on close cooperation with the public schools, began in the orchestra's first season and has become a model plan adopted in many parts of this and other countries.

His programs with the Cleveland Orchestra, both in Cleveland and on tour, are widely popular, for Rodzinski has emphasized the classics and at the same time welcomed new creative effort. He has conducted a good deal of American and foreign modern music; he was the first in America to perform Shostakovitch's *Lady Macbeth from Mzensk.* "First time in Cleveland" is a familiar marking on his programs.

In August 1936 Rodzinski made his debut at the Salzburg Festival—the first permanent conductor of a United States Orchestra to lead there. After one performance Toscanini stepped to the podium and led the cheering. Then he turned to the president of the Festival and said: "Next year you won't need me—you have him," with a nod at the 43-year-old Cleveland conductor.

Since Salzburg Rodzinski has conducted in most of the capitals of Europe and in 1937 was guest conductor of the New York Philharmonic. As such he brought from the orchestra "some of the best balanced music of the year." There, in defiance of popular custom, he appeared with score and baton. To him, conducting from memory is "the craziest thing in the world"; the men fear the conductor will forget and the batonist inevitably finds himself "conducting cues, not music."

When NBC asked Toscanini to conduct a series of concerts in 1938, Toscanini specified, among other things, that Artur Rodzinski select and train the new orchestra. Rodzinski succeeded in persuading fine concert artists to join and coaxed others away from their positions in other orchestras. He was especially proud of the strings. "There are no second violins," he says. "They are all firsts." Rodzinski has conducted this orchestra himself in nation-wide broadcasts.

Rodzinski has often been called a "conductor's conductor," one of the highest tributes in the world of music. In him are all the qualities essential for a great orchestra leader—"profound musical knowledge, masterful baton technique and a high capacity for the projection of emotional intensity." His beat is flexible and his phrasing ingenious. Some musicians feel that occasionally he exaggerates certain passages beyond necessity—the second movement of Sibelius' *Second Symphony,* for instance, which he takes more slowly than any other conductor alive. Most are aware only of the meaning and musicianship he gets out of whatever he is conducting.

Severely formal on the podium, Rodzinski is an affable and humorous personality in moments of leisure. He spends most of them with his second wife, the grandniece of Wieniawski, the famous Polish violist-composer (he was divorced from his first wife), at their estate at Stockbridge, Massachusetts, where they raise white goats. Rodzinski sells the milk not only in the Berkshires but in New York and other Eastern cities.

His son Witold also makes his home in the United States.

Dr. Rodzinski started raising goats after he discovered that goats' milk was a cure for his tortured stomach. Today on his 200-acre farm he has about 70 goats and 40 acres which he personally plowed, harrowed and seeded to raise alfalfa for feed. There are a large pasteurization plant, milking rooms, exercise grounds, and Dr. Rodzinski is interested in all the latest scientific discoveries in the goat world. There is trade talk right now about dairy radios to sooth or stimulate at milking hour with music, but Dr. Rodzinski is skeptical about that. "I have music enough," he says.

References

Christian Sci Mon p2 F 7 '40 por; p6 Jl 20 '40; p10 Ag 3 '40
Musician 39:4 My '34 por; 39:12 O '34 por; 39:6 D '34
N Y World-Telegram p9 Jl 5 '40
Newsweek 9:35 Mr 6 '37; 9:28 Ap 3 '37 por
Scholastic 32:8 F 5 '38 por
Springf'd Repub E p6 Mr 3 '40
Time 27:42 Ap 20 '36 por; 29:52 Mr 8 '37
Armsby, Mrs. L. W. Tristan of the Orchestra *In* Musicians Talk p169-74 1935
Thompson, O. ed. International Cyclopedia of Music and Musicians 1939
Who's Who in America
Wier, A. E. ed. Macmillan Encyclopedia of Music and Musicians 1938

ROGERS, NORMAN MCLEOD July 25, 1894—June 10, 1940 Defense Minister of Canada; succeeded Ian Mackenzie as Minister in 1939; had been Labor Minister since 1935

References

International Who's Who
Who's Who
Who's Who in Canada

Obituaries

N Y Herald Tribune p11 Je 11 '40 por
N Y Times p9 Je 11 '40 por

ROMANO, EMANUEL (rō-män'o) Sept 23, 1904- Artist

Address: 39-72 44th St, Long Island City, New York

In October 1940 Emanuel Romano's one-man show at the Marie Sterner Galleries, New York City, received critical acclaim. The drawings, in silverpoint, graffito and other original techniques show "an unusual talent for draftsmanship." One critic said: "Romano injects into his drawings an old master quality that is yet fresh and contemporary." Another said: "The solid mastery of draftsmanship that pervades all his

EMANUEL ROMANO

work is never obscured by the rich play of fantasy which makes him one of the most imaginative and interesting artists of his generation."

Visitors to both 1940 World's Fairs—San Francisco and New York City—found on view murals executed by Emanuel Romano for the Metropolitan Life Insurance Company. Mr. Romano wrote us that "the New York mural is 75 feet long and 11 feet high. Unfolding like a scroll, it is the story of insurance and at the same time the story of American family life today, designed to leave a lasting impression of family activities." The mural, which took a year to paint, shows a vivid contrast between city and country life and between youth and age. Variations in color, texture and shape have been employed to express that contrast. The scale is monumental and the whole has great decorative quality.

Emanuel Romano was born in Rome September 23, 1904, of Jewish ancestry, the son of Enrico Glicenstein, internationally famous sculptor and etcher who has exhibited with Rodin and twice was awarded the *Prix de Rome.* Not wishing to trade on his father's fame, the youthful Emanuel adopted the name Romano. The boy and his sister, Beatrice, grew up in an artist's environment. She is a worker in gold, silver and leather; their mother is a ceramist and sculptor. Always their homes, in widely scattered places, have been a beehive of artistic activity, as each member has pursued his own speciality. Romano admits that as a child he was ever in search of new forms for expressing himself in color and line. He has lived in Venice, Florence, Naples, Geneva, Paris and on the Riviera. Although he has studied at the University of Geneva, he had no formal art educa-

tion—only his father's strict artistic discipline and his own personal studies of the Old Masters throughout the museums of Europe. "The artist," says a critic, "has never lost contact with his early teachers. He sees the relationship between the expressionists and primitivists and abstract painters of today and the imagery of the past."

John Erskine, writing of Romano's one-man show in 1931 in New York, notes this resemblance in the artist's work to the Old Masters, particularly Michelangelo, "partly," he says, "because the proportions even in a small drawing are heroic, partly because the posture of the body stimulates an intellectual emotion, and at times suggests abstract ideas."

After achieving some note in Europe, where his pictures are owned by colleges and private collectors in Italy, Switzerland and France, Romano came to the United States in 1928. He spends his time in his studios in New York City and Boston. In 1931 he held his first one-man show in New York. The art critic of the New York *Times* noted the zeal which Romano showed in his paintings and drawings, a zeal which had nothing to do with the subject matter: "On the contrary, in these pictures farmers are leaning on their scythes; the family sits around the table, eating and drinking and cutting lovely hunks of bread; the mother nurses her baby; the workman chuckles over his newspaper. The line of the drawings is delicate; the color, that of faded fresco. But the delicacy is never precious and there is nothing weak about the sensitiveness."

In shows of his work held since 1931 Romano's pictures encompass a surprising range of material. Working in water color, gouache, oil, pen, crayon and silverpoint, he has painted landscapes and still-lifes, but his principal interests are people and animals. He has always shown a great love of the circus, and much of his work is dotted with acrobats, harlequins and punchinellos. Here the vivid color, strong light, fantastic costumes "lend themselves to bold patterns and pronounced dramatic moods."

In 1937 he designed and executed a two-panel mural called *Circus* which covers 500 square feet and is placed in the New York City Home for Dependents on Welfare Island. One panel depicts a ring master, a circus horse, trapeze performers and several clowns; the other shows a strong man balancing a girl, while other performers and monkeys delight a painted audience. Brilliant in strong greens, yellows and reds, it was designed by the artist to compensate the inmates of the home for the melancholy aspects of their present lives.

Romano believes that every artist is a propagandist for something—that art for art's sake is meaningless. Years ago before it became the fashion for artists to paint "social protest subjects," he painted many

canvases portraying the working man—
frequently shown struggling under heavy
burdens. "While many contemporary painters are literal and journalistic in their pictorial descriptions of workers and the
unemployed," says one critic, "Romano, accustomed to the theme, maintains his artistic
balance. His social depictions have consequently greater artistic validity. They are
well-knit in design, strong in pictorial elements of form, texture, color."

An exacting worker, Romano is constantly aware of the emotional values of
color. Using ancient formulas, which he
hunted for in Italy, he mixes his "pigments
himself, prepares the grounds, experiments
with all sorts of combinations and textured
effects." His draftsmanship is sure in
whatever styles he essays—moods of subtle
delicacy forming strong contrasts with other
pictures of bold, smashing color and
brusque execution. "In general," says John
Erskine, "Romano draws like a sculptor,
with an eye for three dimensions rather
than for the receding planes which painters
look for."

Of average size, fair-skinned, with receding hair line and melancholy deep-set black
eyes, Romano, in common with all his
family, has strong social consciousness. He
is a tremendous worker who never finds
enough hours in the day to do all he wants
and who never is satisfied with his work.

References

Art Digest 5:15 Ap 1 '31
Art N 29:12 Mr 28 '31; 38:12 O 21
    '39
Chicago Tribune O 20 '32
N Y Herald Tribune S 15 '37
N Y Times Mr 28 '31; S 15 '37
Theatre Arts 15:1027 D '31
Who's Who in American Jewry

ROOSEVELT, ELEANOR Oct 11, 1884-
Journalist; educator; wife of the President
of the United States
Address: h. Hyde Park, Dutchess County,
New York; The White House, Washing-
ton, D. C.

That the First Lady, Anna Eleanor
Roosevelt, should have a third term is the
unanimous opinion of her many admirers—
and these include a considerable number
who were against a third term for her husband. When Franklin D. Roosevelt became President in 1932, the public life and
many activities of Mrs. Roosevelt brought
a storm of criticism; now there are few
to challenge the often-made statement that
she is the greatest President's wife since
Dolly Madison. A Gallup (see sketch this
issue) poll in January 1939, showed that 68
per cent of the American people approved of
Mrs. Roosevelt (her husband received a smaller
popularity poll)—and this percentage included
a large number of Republicans. More young
people than older people are for her; and
she is more popular with the low income

ELEANOR ROOSEVELT

than with the high income group. Women
in small homes on Main Street throughout
the country—especially those who read her
column, *My Day*—like her informal, folksy,
neighborly manner. The opinion of the
small shopkeeper, the factory worker, the
taxi driver is apt to be: "She's a democrat,
Joe—a little 'd' democrat."

Even were she not the wife of a President,
Eleanor Roosevelt would be a distinguished
woman in her own right. She has made a
career for herself in the social service field,
including her work in the Women's Trade
Union League; in 1927 she became a teacher
on the staff of the Todhunter School; she
has traveled extensively and lectured on
topics that interest women; she is the author of six books, not including the published collection of her newspaper columns,
My Days (1938). Two are for children; one
is an autobiography, *This Is My Story*
(1939); the others collections of essays: *It's
Up to the Women* (1938); *This Troubled
World* (1938); and the recently published
(September 1940) *The Moral Basis of Democracy*. A new biography, *Eleanor Roosevelt*, by Ruby Black, appeared on Mrs. Roosevelt's birthday, October 11.

The Moral Basis of Democracy is based on
Mrs. Roosevelt's conviction that democracy
and religion ("Love thy neighbor as thy-
self") may together produce a way of life
able to withstand any totalitarian assault.
She discusses the great historic documents
of democracy, including our own Declaration of Independence based on the ideas
of Tom Paine. We have, however, "allowed
a situation to arise where many people are
debased by poverty or the accident of race
in our own country, and therefore have no
stake in democracy, while others appeal
to the old rule of the sacredness of property
rights to retain in the hands of a limited

ROOSEVELT, ELEANOR—*Continued*

number the fruits of the labor of the many." In Mrs. Roosevelt's basically sound though undistinguished writing there are some contradictions. She states emphatically that democracy means "individual liberty." Yet the first thing she lists among what we must sacrifice in order to retain democracy is the "privilege of thinking and working for ourselves alone," that we must "submit our ideas to the test of what the majority wishes." She does not tell us how what the "majority wishes" shall be decided in these days of crisis; nor, how, if individual liberty (democracy) must be temporarily sacrificed in time of crisis, it will be gotten back again when and if that crisis is passed.

Although Eleanor Roosevelt received in April 1940 *The Nation's* first annual award for distinguished service "in the cause of American social progress," she has been under fire in connection with her sponsorship of the American Youth Congress and her membership in the American Newspaper Guild. The former, charged the Dies (see sketch this issue) Committee, was Communist dominated; the latter, Westbrook Pegler (see sketch this issue) charged, was also run by Communists: hence Mrs. Roosevelt should resign. Once several years ago Louis Howe, the President's personal adviser, grumbled to the First Lady: "If you aren't called a Communist before the President leaves the White House we'll all be lucky." Mrs. Roosevelt has always been vitally interested in young people. Her favorite government agency is the National Youth Administration, and she feels that the problems of youth today represent our greatest social concern. Accordingly she continued her friendship with the Youth Congress leaders and took notes at all the hearings before the Dies Committee. Said she: "If they are accused of Nazi or Communist domination that is no reason for turning our backs. It is unfair unless you find out the facts and help them." As answer to Pegler's Newspaper Guild charge, she refused to resign, but said she meant hereafter to take an active part in Guild affairs "so long as I am a newspaper writer." At a stormy meeting on September 25, 1940 she listened quietly, taking notes, while her husband's policies were severely castigated, and voted with the minority pro-Roosevelt group.

Anna Eleanor Roosevelt was born in New York City October 11, 1884, daughter of Elliot and Anna (Hall) Roosevelt. She has described her family background and her childhood years with frank charm in her autobiography, *This Is My Story* (1939), familiar to many readers. She was the shy, unattractive, awkward daughter of a beautiful mother; it was her father whom she adored: he called her "little Nell" and took her traveling with him. There were two younger brothers. The mother died in 1892; the father two years later. She went to live with her grandmother and, since she had no playmates, read voraciously. When she

was about 15 she spent her holidays at her Uncle Theodore's at Oyster Bay. There were parties; and shy, gangling Eleanor suffered the fate of a wall flower. "I was a poor dancer, different from all the other girls. . . I still remember my gratitude at one of these parties to my cousin Franklin when he came and asked me to dance with him!"

After private schooling in England and vacation-traveling abroad, Eleanor "came out," and began to see more of cousin Franklin. Their engagement was announced when she was 19; they were married March 17, 1905. Because Uncle Theodore came to the wedding, the guests were so interested in the presence of the President that the newlyweds were totally neglected. After a honeymoon summer abroad they returned to America. In 1906 Anna Eleanor, the first baby, was born; and the following year, James. Servants brought up the babies; Mrs. Roosevelt writes that she wishes now she had learned to care for them herself. A second son, Franklin, died in 1909; in 1910 Elliott was born. Two more sons, Franklin Jr., and John, completed the family.

When Franklin Roosevelt entered politics they moved to Albany, where Mrs. Roosevelt attended her first political convention (1912). The next move was to Washington: Roosevelt was appointed Secretary of the Navy by President Wilson. The War came, and Mrs. Roosevelt was active working in the Navy Hospital; after the War she and her husband again went abroad together. It was during the summer of 1921, while they were at Campobello, that he became stricken with infantile paralysis. Long months of hospitals, then convalescence, kept the Roosevelts from public life. When Roosevelt recovered, and was subsequently elected to the Governorship of New York, Mrs. Roosevelt again continued her growing interest in social and political matters. She gives full credit to the League of Women Voters for having grounded her in citizenship and government; and in 1928 she helped originate the nation-wide web of active units of Democratic women.

When the Roosevelts entered the White House in 1932, she was fully prepared for an amazingly active public career. It is said that during the last seven years she has traveled some 280,000 miles, written a million words, earned and given away over half a million dollars, shaken as many hands, delivered several hundred lectures and radio speeches, attended to her colossal mail (150,000 letters in 1939) and in-between times knitted garments for her nine grandchildren.

Her innumerable trips all over the United States, lecturing, or just seeing how people live, have made her the butt of many a joke and cartoon. But on these trips she chats with anyone she meets on plane, bus or train; she goes to see engineering and housing projects and talks with workers; she visits with women in small towns. She is the moving spirit behind Arthurdale, a pioneer project for West Virginia coal miners. She went to see the Okies in the *Grapes of Wrath* country and was appalled by conditions: "At one place I saw a water pipe line next to a privy." A migrant's wife said, "She's nice—just as homey as we are." Because of all this, some observers believe that Mrs. Roosevelt has done more to popularize the Roosevelt Administration than any other person or factor.

Her column, *My Day,* started in 1935, now reaches some 4,500,000 readers. Purposefully chatty, naive, full of trivialities and platitudes, it seems to tell all—but by no means does so. During the past year it has been given over to more political comment than previously. Mrs. Roosevelt, however, refuses to believe that what she writes or does is responsible to the electorate, since "I have never been elected to any office." But Quincy Howe (see sketch this issue) points out: "The one thing a reader of her column might bear in mind is that Mrs. Roosevelt sometimes releases trial balloons for her husband, and when she writes about politics she almost always expresses a point of view that has the blessing of the White House." And it is known she confers with the President and reports to him on what she has heard and seen. "But I would never presume to make recommendations," she says.

Desperate appeals for help come to Mrs. Roosevelt from all over the country, and she often uses her own capital in setting up people in small businesses. She has been particularly interested in the Negro people; memorable is her sharp action on the move to exclude Marian Anderson, the singer (see sketch this issue), from Constitution Hall in Washington; and she once gave a White House party for delinquent Negro girls. She is an admirer of the work of Richard Wright, Negro novelist (see sketch this issue). She is always cordial to the many visitors who make demands on her time; usually equal to all situations. However, the story is told that when one day a pompous Southern lady called at the White House, Mrs. Roosevelt's dog bit her on the ankle. To her colored maid Mrs. Roosevelt exclaimed: "Mamie, that settles it: from now on we have iodine kept in this room."

She is still shy; she is not a good speaker, especially over the radio; only in the last few years has she learned to dress well. But her energy, warmth and naturalness win every group. Newspaper women have the greatest affection for her. She likes best to meet people at informal picnics at her Hyde Park cottage, Val-Kill. Usually she cooks the hot dogs and hamburgers herself. Her hot dog picnic for the visiting King and Queen of England in 1939 made history. Interested in the activities of her children, she visits them when she can,

writes to them often: they never write to each other, and this distresses her.

At the suggestion of a future political career for herself, Mrs. Roosevelt says, "Nothing under heaven could ever persuade me to run for any public office!" Whether or not she became First Lady for a third term, her newspaper contract was sure to go on. It is also reported that Bryn Mawr College is looking for a new President and that they want Anna Eleanor Roosevelt. When she does become an ex-First Lady, Mrs. Roosevelt will doubtless be able to set another precedent.

References

Cur Hist 51:47-8 Mr '40 por
Fortune 21:774 My '40
Harper 180:129-39 Ja '40
Life 8:70-6+ F 5 '40 il pors
Look 4:12+ O 8 '40 pors
N Y Times VII p3+ Ja 21 '40 il pors;
    p11 Mr 8 '40; p18 My 2 '40 por;
    p10 S 18 '40
N Y World-Telegram p1 Mr 21 '40;
    p3 Je 12 '40; p3 Jl 19 '40
Sch & Soc 51:543 Ap 27 '40
Time 35:17 Ap 15 '40

American Women
Black, R. Eleanor Roosevelt 1940
Howe, Q. The News and How to
    Understand It 1940
Roosevelt, A. E. My Days 1938
Roosevelt, A. E. This Is My Story
    1937
Unofficial Observer [pseud.] Praetorian Guard *In* New Dealers p203-
    33 1934
Who's Who in America

ROOT, OREN JR. June 13, 1911- Lawyer
Address: b. 15 Broad St, New York City; h. 455 E 57th St, New York City

Oren Root Jr. is the "affable effervescent young man of 28" whose whirlwind campaign to make Wendell Willkie (see sketch this issue) the Republican candidate for President achieved startling and stupendous success. It all started one morning when Mr. Root read Willkie's article in *Fortune* magazine called *We, the People.* He was impressed. That same afternoon he went to hear Willkie speak at Town Hall in New York; that same night he got busy.

In the winter of 1939 he drafted declarations and had 800 petitions for Willkie for President printed at his own expense. All the next week end he spent sending them to the younger alumni of Harvard, Yale and Princeton. At the same time one of Root's friends began an advertising campaign in the New York *Herald Tribune.* In the public notices column he inserted: "Wendell Willkie for President! Help Oren Root Jr. organize the people's demand for Willkie. Send Root a contribution to 15 Broad Street, New York."

The response to the petitions was greater than even Root had dreamed, and when the newspapers started printing stories about his

OREN ROOT JR.

one-man campaign, the three switchboards of the law firm where Root worked became so choked that none of the partners could get a line. "There was nothing to do but move out," Root said. He set up makeshift political headquarters in the apartment where he lives with his mother. This didn't work either, and soon a regular office was set up with a staff of six paid workers and about fifteen volunteers.

Root hadn't even met Willkie while all this was going on. After the campaign was swinging on, Willkie invited him up. He was dubious about the whole business. "Still he liked me," Root says, "and said I could go ahead. But he wouldn't lift a finger to help me."

Without Willkie's help Root managed to collect petitions from every state and territory of the United States, managed to win over to the Willkie side large numbers of the Republican Party and was one of those who can be given much of the credit for the landslide at the Republican Convention which made Willkie the Republican candidate for President.

Root was able to do this mainly because of his own firm and great faith in Willkie. One of his campaigning letters went so far as to state that "If we elect him President we will see the dawn of a New World." When he was asked to explain what he meant, he admitted: "Gosh, I have no idea," and said it had been dashed off in a white heat right after his first meeting with Willkie when he had been so affected by his "colossal charm" that he had just let himself go. Since then he has insisted with equal conviction that "each person who is for Willkie is for him heart and soul. There is a quality and a strength in this support for Willkie, especially among the inde-pendent voters, in which may lie the seeds of victory for the Republican Party in November."

Blue-eyed, six-foot Oren Root is the grandnephew of the late Elihu Root and the son of Oren Root, who worked himself up to be head of the Hudson and Manhattan Railway. He is also the grandson of another Oren Root, a professor of mathematics at Hamilton College known to generations of students as "Square Root," and the son of Oren and Aida (de Acosta) Root. Young Root was graduated from Princeton in 1933 and received his law degree from the University of Virginia in 1936.

After graduation he went into the law firm of Davis, Polk, Wardwell, Gardiner and Reed in New York and until the spring of 1940 was kept busy handling the legal affairs of some of the charitable organizations represented by his firm, drawing wills and occasionally appearing in court. He had, however, already sallied forth into politics as a member of the New York County Republican Committee, a campaigner for Mayor La Guardia in 1937 and for Thomas Dewey (see sketches this issue) for Governor in 1938. After the Convention he became head of the Associated Willkie Clubs of America, and after the election he urged that the clubs become a permanent organization "dedicated to the preservation of free government in America." "We the People" was his suggested title.

References

Life 9:78 S 30 '40 por
N Y Sun p14 Ap 20 '40; p3 Je 8 '40 por
N Y Times p7 Jl 18 '40
N Y World-Telegram p4 Je 8 '40 por
New Yorker 16:10-11 Je 8 '40
Newsweek 15:30 My 13 '40

ROSE, BILLY Sept 6, 1899- Theatrical producer

Address: b. Hotel Paramount, New York City; h. 33 Beekman Pl, New York City

The trouble with showmen, Billy Rose thinks, is that there are too many geniuses and not enough showmen among them. As for me, this "mighty midget" says, "I sell ballyhoo, not genius." Selling it, he has achieved "such fame as has not been achieved in the show business since Phineas Barnum brought the original Jumbo to this country and put a sign over the exit of his museum saying: 'This way to the Egress.'"

A tiny man who bounces when he walks, the entire success of Billy Rose, son of David and Fannie Rosenberg (he has had his real name, William Samuel Rosenberg, legally changed to Billy Rose) is founded on an immense enthusiasm fed by an abnormal desire for fame. This desire has been part of his life since he went to Public School 44 in The Bronx, New York and was merely intensified when he became Fanny Brice's husband and heard himself called "Mr. Brice." Billy's father was "a salesman who would have difficulty selling a famished dog a bone." Billy wanted to be someone.

He started being someone in P. S. 44 by becoming a sprinter, "learning to jump the gun without detection." "A steal of two yards enabled him to win the gold medal for eighty-five pound sprinters in an interscholastic meet in Madison Square Garden in 1914." When a medal for English was offered in a city-wide competition Billy studied hard and won it. It was as a shorthand speed demon, however, that Billy won his first national fame. Every contest he entered he won and pretty soon was round-shouldered from hanging medals on his shallow chest "so his mother could exhibit them proudly to her horde of relatives."

Soon the inventor and head of the Gregg system of shorthand heard of Billy. Those were the days of the great battle of Gregg versus Pitman, and Mr. Gregg decided to use Billy as an example of the superiority of his pothooks. He trained him. Three men dictated to Billy in relays at increasing rates of speed. When the dictators broke under the strain, a special phonograph was constructed which fired 350 words a minute at Billy. Drilled and trained for the shorthand contest of the world, Billy broke his index finger the day before. But he won anyway by shoving his pen through a potato and holding the potato in his fist. At 18 he was the shorthand king of the world!

Billy demonstrated his speed at the Steel Pier in Atlantic City by taking dictation from all comers in all languages and at all speeds and reading it back, and he went on tour for Mr. Gregg. During the War he organized the stenographic bureau for Bernard M. Baruch's War Industries Board and recorded all of Mr. Baruch's confidential work.

In 1920 Billy decided to give up shorthand and leave New York. His parents were sure he was crazy—wasn't he making about $300 a week? But Billy went West. By the time he got to San Antonio he was broke. Fortunately for him the Republican Party of Texas was having a state convention and when the convention broke up in a row, with the Negro delegates seceding and holding their own convention, Rose took a word by word account of their meeting. He got all the speeches in full, mimeographed them and sold copies at 25 cents a page. He started back home with almost $1,000.

Legend has it that on his way back from San Antonio Billy Rose met a girl, distantly related to the Shuberts, who informed him how much money Irving Berlin made as a song writer. Billy decided to be a song writer. He learned how in the New York Public Library. Patiently he read most of the song hits published in the twentieth century. He indexed them for phrases, rhymes and sounds and discovered that the only important line in a song was the first line of the chorus, but that sounds were very im-

White

BILLY ROSE

portant. The best sound, he found, was "oo."

His first song was *Barney Google*. He took it around to where the song writers hung out and just declared he was a song writer. The song was a success. Other hits followed *You Tell Her I Stutter, Follow the Swallow, Mmmmm, Would you Like to Take a Walk?, Don't Bring Lulu,* etc.—until as a song writer Billy Rose had a top ASCAP rating.

Billy became bored with song writing. He needed more scope for his talents. So he went into the night club business. He took a shabby little place, called it "The Back-Stage Club," announced that it was a hangout for people of the stage and was soon doing a flourishing trade—about $4,000 profit a week. Ambition soared and Billy opened the "Fifth Avenue Club," across the street from the residence of John D. Rockefeller Jr. The cover charge was $5 and the trade was smart society and gangster. When he found out the club was too near St. Patrick's Cathedral to sell liquor, he breathed a sigh of relief and sold it for $15,000. He had never liked it there. His haughty headwaiter wouldn't let him on the floor, because he felt that Billy lowered the tone of the place.

Fanny Brice and Billy Rose met when she was in the *Follies*. She liked the lines, "In the middle of a moment you and I forgot what 'No' meant" from *In the Middle of the Night,* and asked to meet the author. Her face fell when Rose was introduced. "You're disappointed," he said, "because I'm not a tall Spaniard with eyes like live coals." There was a long courtship, in the course of which Fanny showed her love by referring to Billy as "that pasty-faced dope," and they were married on February 8, 1930, Billy's first try at marriage and Fanny's third.

ROSE, BILLY—*Continued*

Rose couldn't bear to be swallowed up by his wife's reputation. He went to Hollywood, hoping for fame greater than hers. For six months he wrote for MGM at a salary of $1,000 a week and never had a line accepted. By this time, what with the depression and the radio, the song business wasn't so good and Billy wasn't making money at it. He decided to produce a musical comedy.

Its name was *Sweet and Low* and it was a flop. Undaunted, Billy Rose turned it into a tabloid review, called it *Crazy Quilt* and toured the country with it. It became "one of the most profitable theatrical enterprises of recent years." Billy had learned how to ballyhoo. Operating through chambers of commerce, boards of trade and grangers' organizations he impressed the citizens for 100 miles on each side of his itinerary of the glory which Billy Rose was conferring on their section by having *Crazy Quilt* visit it. He stirred up their civic pride by asking them to remember the Alamo and the Maine and not to sell America short, by turning out in hordes for *Crazy Quilt*. He roused their enthusiasm by calling it "Three Shows in One," a "Theatrical Colossus," by describing the chorus as "Notable Nymphs", "Statuesque Odalisques" and "Dashing Demoiselles." When the tour was over, Billy Rose knew that he was Barnum's spiritual heir. He slipped only once—when he got sidetracked in 1932 into producing *The Great Magoo*, a straight drama and a quick failure.

He got a new idea—a combination of theatre and restaurant. But before he started he scientifically studied all earlier attempts at the same thing and decided that they had been too expensive and formal. His own, the Casino de Paree, was a success—"tony but with an undercurrent of 'honky tonk.'" Then he hired a theatre around the corner and called it Billy Rose's Music Hall. Billy Rose was practically the only person who made money from the night club business in the late '30s. His Casa Mañana and Diamond Horse Shoe also herded in the customers.

But he wasn't satisfied. Finally he got an idea that was really colossal. "Kid, I found out the other day," he said, "that a circus sometimes makes as much as $50,000 in a one-night stand. I said to myself, that's the racket for me." Rose hired the Hippodrome in New York, bought the biggest elephant in the world, got Rodgers and Hart (see sketch this issue) to write the words and music, Ben Hecht and Charles MacArthur to write the play and Jimmy Durante to star in it. *Jumbo* was a year in production and postponed five times until its first performance in 1935. It was Billy Rose's idea of a circus, which meant that it started out with countless myriads of dream women—"the tour of the big tent should be a migration of maddening madonnas." Which

meant, too, that instead of 50 or so unrelated acts, as Barnum did it, *Jumbo* was a more or less unified drama, with Paul Whiteman and a zoo thrown in for good measure.

If the ballyhooing before *Jumbo*—which included an elephant parade in Wall Street—was noticeable, it was mild compared with that for the Fort Worth Centennial celebration in Texas. Billy Rose brought newspapermen from New York in airplanes; he covered every barn and fence in 48 states with propaganda. It was a mad and monster entertainment, and Billy Rose rode easily through all Fort Worth's hurly burly, incessantly smoking through an 18-inch cigarette holder made from an albatross quill, and phoning Fanny Brice in New York. Fanny was proud—"a Jewish Noel Coward," she called him.

Billy Rose put on other shows. His *Aquacade* at the 1939 and 1940 New York World's Fair was "one of the most amazing success stories" in the anthology of show business. "To many of the civic patriots who conceived the Fair, a Rose girl show had no place in their vision of the World of Tomorrow. How Rose thawed their attitude so thoroughly that he eventually got the Fair's choicest ready-built concession for a figure 10 per cent under that of the highest bidder is a Broadway legend." The *Aquacade*, a slick, streamlined revue in a swimming pool 300 feet long with a cast of about 300—Billy says 500—was the most spectacular feature of the Fair's amusement section.

Billy married its leading lady, Eleanor Holm, in the fall of 1939 after he got a divorce from Fanny Brice. Eleanor thinks him "the most fascinating man I've ever met." She and the "mad Mahout" have just taken a five-story house in New York, "a setting lavish as Billy's productions." Billy has four offices, but works in his bedroom, dressed in pajamas. He hates to get dressed and even Eleanor hasn't been able to do anything about it.

Billy has money—the furnishings of his house are supposed to have cost about $200,000—and he has the fame he's always fought for. He has the money because he is one of the shrewdest economists in the entertainment world who hires a C. P. A. to watch him and everyone of his lieutenants relentlessly. He has fame because of his press agent, Dick Maney, and because he is Billy Rose, and this fame is guaranteed by a never-ceasing flow of "colossal" ideas. His latest concerns a Sky Show—sort of an Aquacade of the air, and he is also reported working on a giant Broadway sports palace.

References

Am Mag 122:90 Jl '36 por: 123:48-9+ Ja '37 por
Collier's 96:22+ Jl 20 '35 por
Fortune 20:118-21+ Jl '39 il por
Life 8:112-14+ My 13 '40 il pors

New Yorker 11:22-9 Ap 27 '35
Newsweek 7:20 Je 27 '36
Sat Eve Post 213:16-17+ D 21 '40 il
pors
Time 26:39-41+ O 28 '35 il por; 34:
31-3 Ag 21 '39 il por
Variety 139:39 Jl 3 '30
Sobel, B. ed. Theatre Handbook 1940
Who's Who in American Jewry

ROSETT, JOSHUA 1875—Apr 4, 1940
Professor of neuro-anatomy at the College
of Physicians and Surgeons, Columbia University; author of many books dealing with
the mechanics of the brain

Blackstone

JOSHUA ROSETT

References
American Men of Medicine
American Men of Science
Who's Who in American Jewry

Obituaries
N Y Herald Tribune p16 Ap 5 '40
N Y Times p21 Ap 5 '40

ROSS, BARNABY, pseud. *See* Queen, E.,
pseud.

ROSS, SIR EDWARD DENISON June
6, 1871—Sept 20, 1940 Director of the British Information Bureau for the Near East;
one of the most accomplished linguists of
his generation; could read 49 languages and
speak coherently in 30 of them, specializing
in Oriental tongues; authority on Indo-
Iranian culture; author of a score of books;
came to the United States in 1931 to deliver
a series of lectures at Princeton and Northwestern Universities

References
Nature 140:185 Jl 31 '37
Near East 44:602 My 16 '35
Who's Who

Obituaries
N Y Herald Tribune p12 S 21 '40 por
N Y Times p19 S 21 '40 por

ROSS, NELLIE TAYLOE Director
United States Mint
Address: b. Treasury Bldg, Washington,
D. C.; h. 2126 Connecticut Ave, Washington,
D. C.

Mrs. Nellie Tayloe Ross, first woman
Director of the United States Mint, supervises the manufacture of all coins and is
responsible for the safekeeping of the government's vast gold and silver stocks,
amounting to 20 billion dollars. She directs
the activities of eight mint institutions
throughout the country as well as the
Bureau of the Mint in Washington, D. C.

When Mrs. Ross was appointed Director
of the Mint in 1933, activities were at a
low ebb owing to the depression, and personnel had been reduced to a skeleton.
Coincidental with the enactment of new
monetary laws, a load of work was laid
upon the Mint under which the skeleton
force staggered. Gold from all over the
world began flowing into the Mints, soon
to be followed by great deposits of silver.
With the upswing of business that began
in 1934 a demand for coin also began, which
has continued until the present. All records for coinage were broken in October
and November 1939; so heavy have been the
coinage requirements since, that frequently
the Mints have operated 24 hours a day, including Saturdays and Sundays.

Such drastic and sudden increase in the
activities of the Mint service necessitated
expansion of facilities of man power, machinery, vault space and working space.
The skeleton force of 1933 has trebled, and
equipment has been expanded in proportion,
new machinery installed, new vaults provided or old vaults modernized in every
field institution. Three new Mints have
been constructed. A guard force formerly
composed of "broken-down" employees has
been supplanted by one of stalwart men,
trained in the use of arms.

Mrs. Ross was appointed by President
Roosevelt to head the Treasury Assay Committee, which in February 1940 tested the
coins minted during the past year. In
this annual event two out of every 10,000
coins are weighed; each must assay 900
parts silver to 100 parts copper.

Mrs. Ross, the first woman director of
the Mint, is the first woman to have her
likeness on one of the mint medals. One
side shows a profile of Mrs. Ross and on
the reverse is an idealized figure seated
before a balance, weighing coins. On the
medal also may be seen a copy of the

NELLIE TAYLOE ROSS

Treasury seal, a coining press, bars of gold and stacks of coin.

Her name appears also on the cornerstone of the United States Bullion Depository (for gold) at Fort Knox, Kentucky; the United States Bullion Depository (for silver) at West Point, New York; and the new Mint building at San Francisco. These three impressive structures, as well as the addition to the Mint building at Denver, have been built since 1933.

Mrs. Ross is of medium height, has brown hair with a little gray in it now, and very large, expressive blue eyes. She claims the woman's prerogative of not making her age public. Although she is called "a daughter of the old South," she is a native of St. Joseph, Missouri. Her father, James Wynne Tayloe, was descended from the distinguished Tayloe family. One of its members erected the celebrated Octagon House in Washington, and later the equally famous Cameron House which served as the home of President Madison after the White House had been destroyed by the British during the War of 1812. Her mother, Elizabeth Blair Green Tayloe, was descended from Samuel Ball Green, whose mother, Patty Ball, was a cousin of the mother of George Washington.

She was educated in public and private schools and under private teachers. In 1902 she went to Wyoming as the youthful bride of William Bradford Ross, a young Tennessee attorney, who had chosen Cheyenne as his home. They had four children, one of whom died in infancy.

In 1922 Mr. Ross was elected Governor of Wyoming. In the middle of his term he died, and Mrs. Ross was elected to fill out his unexpired time, January 1925 to January 1927. Thus, although she and "Ma" Ferguson of Texas were elected on the same date, Mrs. Ross has the distinction of being the first woman Governor of any state because her inauguration preceeded that of Mrs. Ferguson by two weeks. She ran for a second term, but was defeated in a close election. Some commented that "she had been too cautious in action."

Mrs. Ross was state representative; then vice-chairman of the Democratic National Convention. She seconded the nomination of Al Smith at the Houston Convention of 1928. For the four following years she was in charge of activities of Democratic women, with an office in Washington, and she directed the 1932 Roosevelt campaign among women.

In addition to supervising the activities of the Mint institutions and the home she maintains for herself in one of the spacious, older apartment buildings in Washington, she acquired a farm in Maryland a couple of years ago, and devotes as much attention as possible to developing it. Tobacco is the principal crop raised at La Trappe, as the historical old place is called. Mrs. Ross spends her week ends as well as her summer vacations at the farm.

In her youth Mrs. Ross was very proud of the prizes she took with her embroidery and was quite famed in her community for her needlework. Today, she has little leisure to devote to a hobby, although she has a great interest in antiques. "I always hesitate," writes her secretary, "to say this for publication, because immediately after it appears in print we are deluged with letters and calls from people who want to sell her one of their *heirlooms.*"

Those who know her believe that while her success in a public career is based partly on political opportunity, "her fine intellect, lovely personality and most of all her capacity for hard, grueling, sustained work" have contributed to that success.

Mrs. Ross contributes articles on political subjects to women's magazines and is in demand as an interesting and entertaining speaker, "impressing her hearers with her earnestness and sincerity." She had never made a formal public address of any kind when she first addressed the State Legislature as Governor. Then her only training for such an event had been that which she had received as president of the Women's Club in Cheyenne.

Emily Newell Blair reported (1939): "Few women have known more women or been beloved by so many. And why not? I saw her recently speaking before almost a thousand women. . . Her plea for lasting peace was as valiant, earnest and intelligent as she herself was winsome and winning. Women recognize in her a woman who, when called on, can meet any and every situation with distinction, yet remain always feminine."

References

Business Week p24 F 24 '40 por
Cong Digest 9:245-6 O '30
Good H 102:39 Ja '36 por

Ind Woman 17:276 S '38 por
Newsweek 1:18 My 6 '33
American Women
Who's Who in America
Who's Who in the Nation's Capital

ROWELL, CHESTER H. Nov 1, 1867-
Editor
Address: b. San Francisco Chronicle, San
Francisco, California; h. 149 Tamalpais
Road, Berkeley, California

Chester Harvey Rowell, called "one of the
leading newspaper editors of his generation"
and a Pacific Coast leader in the Committee
to Defend America by Aiding the Allies,
was one of the three Americans presented
on October 27 with the Roosevelt Distinguished Service Medal for 1940.

Mr. Rowell was born in Bloomington,
Illinois on November 1, 1867, the son of
Jonathan Harvey and Maria Sanford
(Woods) Rowell. He received his Ph. B.
from the University of Michigan in 1888,
a year after his marriage to Myrtle Marie
Lingle of Webb City, Missouri, and did graduate work not only at Michigan but at the
Universities of Halle, Berlin, Paris and Rome.
He then taught at academies in Kansas, Wisconsin and California, for a year (1897-98)
was an instructor in German at the University
of Illinois, and in 1898 became editor and
publisher of the Fresno *Republican*. He was
to remain its editor for 22 years, at the
same time taking active part in politics.
From 1889 to 1891 he had been a clerk on
the committee on elections in the United
States House of Representatives, and in
1901 he published his *Digest of Contested
Election Cases in the House of Representatives of the United States, Fifty-sixth Congress*. Among other activities he was a
member of the Republican State Committee
from 1906 to 1911; in 1910 chairman of the
Republican State Convention; he was a
delegate to both Republican and Progressive National Conventions (from 1912 to
1916 he was a member of the Progressive
National Committee); and he organized
and served as president of the Lincoln-
Roosevelt Republican League from 1907 to
1911.

After 1923, having ceased to be editor
and publisher of the Fresno *Republican* in
1920 and at the same time having given
up the position as president and general
manager of the Fresno Republican Publishing Company which he had held since
1912, Mr. Rowell began to devote much of
his time to foreign travel, lecturing and
newspaper syndicate writing. To mention
only a few of his actitivies, in 1924 he was
a delegate to the International Congress of
Penal Law at Brussels, in 1925, 1927, 1929,
1931 and 1936 a member of the Institute of
Pacific Relations Conferences, in 1939 a
delegate to the International Labor Conference at Geneva.

Since 1926 he has been a member of the
National Crime Commission, and since 1927

president of the California League of Nations Association. From 1927 to 1934 he
lectured on political science at the University of California and at Stanford, and he
also did extensive lecturing elsewhere on
educational, civic and political subjects. His
interest in social problems brought him to
the presidency of the California Conference
on Social Work (1928-29); in 1928, 1929
and 1931 he was a member of the Presidential Emergency Boards on railroad
strikes; since 1935 he has been a member
of the American Youth Commission; and
he is a member of the Social Research
Council of the Pacific Coast.

This does not mean that Mr. Rowell has
ceased to be either a newspaper editor or
an active worker in the Republican Party.
In 1932 he became editor of the San Francisco *Chronicle*, his present newspaper. An
active supporter of Hoover even before his
nomination in 1928, in that year Mr. Rowell
was a delegate to the Republican National
Convention. In 1936 he was again a delegate, and argued for "a positive program
for the Republican Party," for, he thought,
"the governmental and economic institutions
of America are menaced with literal revolution, which must be stopped now or never."
In the years 1938 and 1939 Mr. Rowell was
a member of the National Republican Program Committee.

In many of his articles, published in magazines and newspapers all over the country,
the editor of the San Francisco *Chronicle* has
expressed concern for the freedom of the
press as well as for the freedom of business from excessive governmental influence.
Speaking of pressure from advertisers and
other unofficial sources, he inquires: "What
profiteth it a nation that its press be free of
the law, if it makes merchandise of its own
soul?"

Mr. Rowell has one son, Jonathan Harvey
Rowell, and two married daughters, Mrs. J.
A. Givens and Mrs. W. D. Laughlin. He
and Mrs. Rowell live in an attractive home
in Berkeley, California.

References

N Y Herald Tribune p25 O 17 '40
Who's Who in America

RUMPLER, EDMUND 1872—Sept 9, 1940
Internationally noted German airplane construction engineer; a "non-Aryan" who became one of Germany's "forgotten men"
upon the rise of Hitler; gained fame in the
First World War with his scouting planes
which climbed to a height of 8,000 meters;
after the Treaty of Versailles turned to
automobiles and invented the first streamlined German car; published many technical
books and articles; in 1927 designed a huge
plane for transatlantic flights

References

International Who's Who
Wer ist's?

RUMPLER, EDMUND—*Continued*

Obituaries

N Y Herald Tribune p24 S 10 '40 por

N Y Times p23 S 10 '40 por

RUSHMORE, DAVID BARKER Aug 21, 1873—May 5, 1940 Electrical engineer; official of the General Electric Company; organized American participation in the World Power Conference, 1924; member of Boy Scout Council

References

Factory and Ind Management 80:69 Jl '30 por

American Men of Science

Who's Who in America

Who's Who in Commerce and Industry

Who's Who in Engineering

Obituaries

N Y Sun p21 My 6 '40

N Y Times p25 My 7 '40 por

RUSSELL, BERTRAND ARTHUR WILLIAM, 3RD EARL May 18, 1872- Philosopher; educator; author

Address: Barnes Foundation, Merion, Pennsylvania

It was a housewife, Mrs. Jean Kay, (with a daughter of 18) who instituted the legal action which led to the voiding on March 30, 1940 of the appointment of Lord Russell to the philosophy faculty of the City College of New York. "I was glad," she cried, "that right and decency have triumphed." A reporter visiting her home found by cross examination that Mrs. Kay "was fond of reading philosophy ... Elbert Hubbard and Emerson."

The affidavit protesting the appointment alleged that Mr. Russell was "lecherous, salacious, libidinous, venereous, erotomaniac, aphroditous, atheistic, irreverent, narrow-minded, bigoted and untruthful"; that the doctrines which he calls philosophy were "just cheap, tawdry, worn-out, patched-up fetishes, devised for the purpose of misleading the people."

Justice John E. McGeehan, in a 17-page decision, ruled that the appointment should be revoked on three counts: Lord Russell was not subjected to competitive examination, a violation of the Constitution of the State of New York; he was not a citizen, a violation of the State Education Law; and the appointment would be a violation of "the public health, safety and morals of the people."

Many individuals, organizations and church groups rejoiced in the decision, including the Rt. Rev. William T. Manning (see sketch this issue), Bishop of the Episcopal Diocese of New York, who had asked in the pulpit: "What is to be said of colleges and universities which hold up before our youth as a reputable teacher of philosophy, and as an example of light and leading, a man who is a recognized propagandist against both religion and morality, and who specifically defends adultery?" and continued the attack in print.

Acting President Nelson Prentiss Mead of City College replied: "Mr. Russell has been invited ... to teach courses in mathematics and logic ... and not to discourse on his personal, ethical and moral views." The Committee on Cultural Freedom stated: "When the history of intellectual bigotry is written the denial of Bertrand Russell's right to teach will take its place on the record along with the persecution of Socrates and Galileo, whose critical tradition and belief in free inquiry Bertrand Russell carries into the world today."

Mr. Russell was supported by educators such as Franz Boas, Robert M. Hutchins, Marjorie Hope Nicolson (see sketches this issue) John Dewey; by groups such as officers of nine book publishing houses, The American Committee for Democracy and Intellectual Freedom, the American Federation of Teachers; by 330 administrators and 1,880 students of the City College of New York.

His opponents were led by the Hearst press and individual clergymen; by groups such as the Knights of Columbus, the Greater New York Federation of Churches, the National Catholic Alumni Federation, the National Society of New England Women, the New York County Board of the Ancient Order of Hibernians and the New York Post Office Holy Name Society.

The American Civil Liberties Union, Russell's counsel, indicated that Russell was willing to come to New York whenever necessary to answer charges of immorality. They intended to institute charges of breach of contract. But—Mayor La Guardia (see sketch this issue) in the meanwhile eliminated the $8,000 appropriation for the position from the city budget. As a result of the uproar the New ' York State Legislature authorized a $30,000 appropriation to investigate state wide education expenses and the activities of the Board of Higher Education.

Russell, who was silent during the entire controversy, wrote: "I am not as interested in sex as Bishop Manning, who is greatly concerned with it. Sex is only a small part of what I have written. Bishop Manning and his supporters have noticed only this part. They don't notice that almost all of my writing has been on other subjects. . . Precisely the same accusations were brought against Socrates—atheism and corrupting the young."

Even though La Guardia warned that the fight would be futile, Russell's case was to be argued again in the Appellate Division and in the Court of Appeals at Albany in the fall of 1940. In October, however, it was announced that Russell had signed a five-year contract to deliver one lecture a week at the Barnes Foundation, Merion, Pennsylvania, beginning January 1, 1941. In the meanwhile he was delivering the

William James Foundation lectures in philosophy at Harvard. The Board of Higher Education therefore decided "to take no further steps in reference" to the dispute.

A United States resident since 1938, Bertrand Russell has taught at the University of Chicago, Smith College, the University of California at Los Angeles (1939-40) and is giving the William James Lectures at Harvard 1940 to 1941. Officials at Harvard University on March 31, 1940 declared that the New York Supreme Court decision would have no effect there. They reiterated their policy of allowing instructors "academic freedom." The appointment, made two years ago, brought protest from Massachusetts State Representative Thomas Dorgan, who cited arguments similar to those that brought the action in New York.

Bertrand Russell, the second son of Viscount Amberley, was born at Trelleck, England, on May 18, 1872. An earldom was created for his grandfather, Lord John Russell, Liberal Prime Minister and a follower of John Stuart Mill, in 1861. Bertrand Russell, who prefers to be known as plain Mr. Russell, succeeded to the title upon the death of his brother (March 1931), the second Earl Russell.

Orphaned at the age of three, Bertrand Russell was brought up at Pembroke Lodge in Richmond Park, Surrey, by his grandmother. Educated by governesses and tutors, he acquired a knowledge of German and French and laid the foundation for a lucid prose style. At Trinity College, Cambridge, he obtained a "First" in mathematics and moral sciences.

When he left Cambridge in 1894 Russell was attached to the British Embassy in Paris and there married Alyz Pearsall Smith in December of that year. They went to Berlin, where he studied social democracy, and later settled in a small cottage near Haslemere, Surrey, where Russell devoted himself to philosophy and wrote *German Social Democracy* (1896).

Russell became interested in the Italian mathematician Peano, whom he met at a mathematical congress in Paris, and after a study of his works Russell wrote *The Principles of Mathematics* (1903), his first important book. With Dr. A. N. Whitehead he developed the mathematical logic of Peano and Frere, and jointly they wrote *Principia Mathematica* (1910), which *Life* lists as one of the 100 Great Books of All Time.

Russell was appointed lecturer at Trinity College in 1910, where he had been made a fellow after graduation. "He made frequent trips to the Continent, and occasionally abandoned philosophy for politics. When the World War broke out he took an active part in the No Conscription Fellowship and was fined 100 pounds for issuing a pamphlet on conscientious objection. His library was seized in payment of the fine, and although it was sold to a friend, several valuable volumes were lost." His lectureship was canceled. Then he was offered an opportunity to lecture at Harvard, but the military authorities prevented his departure from England, sentencing him to six months' imprisonment for his pacifist views expressed in an article in the *Tribunal*. The *Introduction to Mathematical Philosophy* (1919) was written in prison.

After his release a group of Russell's friends arranged for him to give a series of lectures in London which resulted in his writing *Analysis of the Mind* (1921). Then he made a brief visit to Russia to study conditions, and wrote *Bolshevism: Practice and Theory* (1920). In 1920 and 1921 he lectured on philosophy at Peking University, China. Returning to England, after his wife had secured a divorce in 1921, he married Dora Winifred Black, author of *The Right to Be Happy* (1927). The following six years were divided between Chelsea and Land's End. He supported himself by lecturing, journalism and writing books.

In 1922 and 1923 Russell stood as a Labor candidate for Parliament in Chelsea, London and his wife was a candidate in 1924. In 1927 the Russells started a famous nursery school in Hampshire, which was a success in every way except financially. The heavy drain on his income forced him to write voluminously and make several lecture trips in America to cover the deficit. Russell's conception of freedom in the nursery school has shocked the English. According to one story, "a local rector, visiting the school, knocked on the door, which was opened by a nine-year-old girl, stark naked. Cried he: 'Good God!' Retorted she, slamming the door: 'There is no God!'"

Russell, on becoming a peer in 1931, announced he would take his seat in the House of Lords, where he would speak out not on partisan measures but on social questions such as divorce. He continued to lecture and to write, and was awarded the Sylvester Medal in Mathematics by the Royal Society, of which he had been a fellow since 1908.

Divorced a second time, Russell married his former red-haired, youthful secretary, Patricia Helen Spence, in 1935. Three years later Russell received an appointment to teach mathematics and logic at the University of California at Los Angeles, and they came to the United States. With them are their three-year-old son, Conrad, and the two children of a former marriage, John Conrad and Katherine Jane, both students at the University.

Mr. and Mrs. Russell plan to live on a farm in Chester County while he is lecturing at Barnes. His subject will be the historical development of ideas and cultural values from the Greeks to the present.

Burton Rascoe describes Russell as: "A thin, wiry man, a little below medium height, with a hatchet face, furrowed cheeks, a Scot's complexion, and a shock of white hair. He looks a little like Henry Ford. He has a quizzical smile and an alert

Hansel Mieth

BERTRAND RUSSELL

look of intense curiosity. He has a fund of anecdotes and tells them well. Amiable and human, he can enjoy a gay party and have a playful time. He is fond of adding malicious footnotes to his manuscripts."

Of his work, J. W. Cunliffe says: "His remarkable gift of clear expression has enabled him to bring to the knowledge of a wide public the implications of recent theories of mathematical physics, about which he speaks with disinterested authority; his radical views of public and international questions naturally meet with less general acceptance, but even those who disagree with him on political issues respect him for his independence of mind and his undoubted devotion to what he believes to be the truth."

Among Russell's many books not mentioned previously perhaps the best-known are: *Why Men Fight* (1917); *Proposed Roads to Freedom* (1918); *A B C of Atoms* (1923); *A B C of Relativity* (1925); *What I Believe* (1925); *Education and the Good Life* (1931); *Education and the Modern World* (1932); *Conquest of Happiness* (1933); *Religion and Science* (1935); *Which Way to Peace?* (1936); *The Amberley Papers* (with Patricia Russell) (1937); *Marriage and Morals* (1938); and *Power* (1938).

References

Liberty 17:57-9 My 18 '40 por; 17:51-2 My 25 '40
Life 8:23-6 Ap 1 '40 pors
Nation 150:732-3 Je 15 '40
New Repub 102:596 My 6 '40
N Y Times p1, 41 Mr 31 '40 por; p27 Ap 2 '40
Pub W 137:1214 Mr 23 '40; 138:1590 O 19 '40

Sat R Lit 21:8 Mr 30 '40; 21:9 Ap 13 '40
Time 35:61 Mr 25 '40
Cunliffe, J. W. Essays, Journalism and Travel *In* English Literature in the Twentieth Century p59-80 1933
Kunitz, S. J. ed. Living Authors 1937
Swinnerton, F. Bloomsbury *In* The Georgian Scene p337-77 1934
Who's Who
Wickham, H. Visual Black Dot Occurs: Bertrand Russell *In* The Unrealists p165-95 1930

RUSSELL, HERBRAND ARTHUR, 11TH DUKE OF BEDFORD *See* Bedford, H. A. R.

RUTHERFORD, JOSEPH FRANKLIN

1869- Leader of Jehovah's Witnesses
Address: 101 Henry St, Brooklyn, New York

According to Stanley High, Joseph Franklin Rutherford's "only rival to the title of the nation's most potent religious leader is Father Coughlin" (see sketch this issue). Rutherford, known as "Judge" to his followers, is the leader of Jehovah's Witnesses, who believe that Biblical prophecies govern every earthly event but who don't think of themselves as a religious group at all: "Religion . . . turns men away from God." More than six feet tall, hazel-eyed, portly, severe and senatorial in appearance, Judge Rutherford doesn't look like the standard version of a prophet. He wears old-fashioned stand-up collars with a little black string bow tie, has a long black ribbon for his glasses and often carries a cane. Still, to many thousands of people this seems not at all unsuitable for a man who must interpret "Jehovah's word" in the difficult year 1940.

Joseph Franklin Rutherford was born in Missouri in 1869, the son of James Calvin and Lenore (Strickland) Rutherford and grew up much like any other farmer's son. He studied law and practiced it in several small Missouri towns, and it is said that he was at one time a Missouri circuit judge. The "Judge" may be completely unofficial, however; he never uses the title himself. In 1896 he was campaigning for William Jennings Bryan; it is difficult to say exactly when he fell under the influence of "Pastor" Charles Taze Russell, whose Biblical interpretations formed the faith of the group known as the "Russellites" in the early 1900's and before. Russell attacked "hell," preached a doctrine of the "second chance," kept prophesying an Armageddon and a "second coming"— "a time of retribution upon all, who by fraud or force, sometimes in the name of the law and under its sanctions, have unrighteously grasped the rights and property of others. The retribution, as we have seen, will come from the Lord through the uprising of the masses." It is said that a Russellite called on the Judge and, as was customary, left him some literature and some Scriptural quotations; he read them, was interested, became a *Bible* student and eventually a Russellite.

Lawyers weren't too common in the movement, and a good lawyer was a valuable acquisition, for the Pastor and many of his followers were continually arousing the prejudices of the law. Sometime around 1907 the Judge became legal adviser for the movement and made frequent appearances in court in Russell's defense. When the latter died in 1916 he hadn't appointed any successor, but it seemed a natural thing for Rutherford to take over. He did—just about the time when the United States was entering World War I. No Russellite believed in worldly wars and much less in fighting them, and wherever Rutherford went conscientious objectors sprang up. The military authorities asked him to be quieter. He wouldn't. After a great many unpleasant experiences at the hands of "bloodthirsty clergymen" and others, he finally wound up in the Federal Penitentiary in Atlanta in 1917 with seven of his followers. He was there for nine months and managed to enroll more than a hundred prisoners in his *Bible* class during that time. That may or may not be why the United States Court of Appeals decided to reverse its decision and let him out—a petition signed with some 700,000 names demanding his release may also have had something to do with it, and maybe the Department of Justice grew tired of getting letters of protest. In any case it was March 26, 1919 when he walked out of Atlanta, and he immediately marshaled forces for a national convention at Cedar Point, Ohio.

Shortly afterward, the dogma of the Russellites was revised, a mythology of "invisible powers" substituted for the late Pastor's interpretations. There was nothing inconsistent about this, for his followers believed that the meaning of prophecy is only gradually revealed as the time becomes ripe for it. Armageddons had never taken place on their promised dates. But now all was understood—somewhere in the invisible world Satan's rule had already ended, in 1914; Jesus, son of the "Great Theocrat Jehovah God," had been enthroned as King that same year and would henceforth direct the work of his witnesses on earth. Though Satan was still operating, all governments being "devil's kingdoms," in 1918 Jesus came "to His Temple," and "Armageddon will come as soon as the Witness work is completed." It was 1925 when this Witness work officially began, for in that year the Russellites and the International Bible

G. Maillard Kesslère

JOSEPH RUTHERFORD

Students changed their name to Jehovah's Witnesses. And although the Pastor had said: "Let every soul be subject to the powers that be," it was now necessary actively to resist the now-dethroned Satan, who was grooming himself for a rapidly-approaching final conflict with Jehovah. Since when Jesus came back to earth he would set up his kingdom here and judge between the good and the bad, it was also necessary to warn as many people as possible so that they too might be saved. The slogan of Jehovah's Witnesses was: "Millions now living will never die!"

For these reasons the Witnesses hate war, Fascism, Big Business, the American Legion, the DAR, the Catholic Church (and, as a matter of fact, all organized religions), financiers, politicians, the League of Nations, and all governments including the "Anglo-American seventh empire" foretold by Daniel, which falsely "sees itself as the world's peacemaker." They acknowledge allegiance only to "Jehovah's theocratic organization," and refuse to salute even the American flag just as—one writer says—the early Christians refused to put a pinch of salt on the altars of the Roman emperor and the Quakers refused to doff their hats in the presence of royalty. Though they would not refuse to fight for Jehovah's government, they would not serve if drafted for the worldly war which they believe inevitable. "We, as Christian people, respect the flag of the nation where we reside and we willingly obey every law for which that flag stands. We deem it more important to obey the laws of the land, without violating our covenant with Almighty

God by saluting an earthly thing, than to salute and then immediately violate the law for which the flag stands."

Rutherford is said to have well over 2,000,000 followers in 36 nations. Until World War II he traveled widely, addressing gatherings of Witnesses in nearly all these countries. More than 200,000,000 copies of his writings—he has written 17 books and more than 70 pamphlets—are said to have been circulated in over 80 languages. In August 1939 active field workers were estimated at 41,902 in the United States, some 11,000 in Great Britain and Canada, 28 in Chile, 114 in Brazil and a bare handful in Africa. Jehovah's Witnesses operate not only by door-to-door visits, distributing and selling literature, but also own or rent several hundred sound trucks which go around spreading the word noisily and use phonographs to play Judge Rutherford's messages to prospective converts. More than 15,000 recordings have been sold at $10 each.

President of the Watch Tower Bible and Tract Societies of Pennsylvania and New York and also of the International Bible Students' Association of Great Britain, Judge Rutherford edits the semimonthly *Watch Tower* and the weekly *Golden Age*. The latter was described by the *Christian Century* as a "vigorously written and well-edited weekly with sections devoted to Labor, Big Business Bits, Educational Flashes, Political, Domestic and Foreign News. . . It plants vigorous and well-directed blows at commercial and military exploiters, is militantly anti-Fascist, and is spoiled mainly by its intemperate Catholic baiting."

The Witnesses have an imposing eight-story tabernacle near the Brooklyn end of Brooklyn Bridge, the ruby electric lights above it proclaiming "Riches," and there the "Bethel Family" of nearly 200 workers is employed printing and mailing literature, manufacturing phonograph and transcription machines, making ink, keeping books—and maintaining their own Staten Island radio station WBBR. On the West coast there are other quarters, Beth-Sarim, (the House of Princes), in San Diego. That was built to house the prophets—Daniel, Ezekiel and the rest—when they return to earth, and to avoid legal trouble the deed is drawn in the prophets' names. The Witnesses also have a printing plant at Berne, Switzerland, and there used to be another in pre-Hitler Germany.

All this takes money, but there must be a substantial profit from the sale of books and pamphlets alone. During the year ending September 30, 1939 there were 15,169,244 pieces of literature sold or distributed solely in the United States, and more than a million miles covered in doing it. Witnesses are not lazy.

The Witnesses often hold conventions, and these may be lively affairs. In Sep-

tember 1938 a hookup between the Royal Albert Hall in London and auditoriums in twenty-three states in America, ten Canadian, four New Zealand cities sent Judge Rutherford's "heavy, rounded" voice to something like 100,000 spellbound listeners. "A hideous monstrosity," he announced, "is rapidly moving to rule the world by dictators and to regiment the people. God, by his holy prophets, thousands of years ago, as recorded in the *Bible*, foretold this great menace, its cause, and what will be the result." In June 1939 the Judge again spoke at a convention in Madison Square Garden, New York City, and four people were hurt. A five-day convention of Witnesses at Detroit in July 1940 meant to Detroit citizens sandwich signs, handbills, pamphlets and sound cars roving the streets. It meant to the Witnesses "hundreds of converts" claimed and a mass baptism for 2,500 at the end. Fifty Witnesses were left behind in the clutches of the law, but they were, unfortunately, used to that.

John Haynes Holmes has likened the Witnesses to the early Christians—as they appeared to the "highly respectable and patriotic Romans of their day." They have been jailed from Maine to Texas without charges or on charges of being spies, radicals, Nazis, Fifth Columnists; their cars have been wrecked; their headquarters have been sacked and burned; private houses have been stoned, raided, Witnesses dragged out and beaten up or tarred and feathered; their literature has been seized and burned; they have been stricken from relief rolls. As early as 1935 teachers and children who were Witnesses had been expelled from schools for refusing to salute the flag, and the United States Supreme Court in June 1940 upheld the right of school officials to force children to salute.

It has also on more than one occasion upheld the right of Witnesses to distribute literature and to play their records, but although the Department of Justice has sent special circulars to United States district attorneys instructing them to prevent interference to the right of freedom of assembly, in many cases there has been a "complete unwillingness of local law-enforcement officers" to do so. The American Legion and the Ku Klux Klan have been especially active against the Witnesses. In August 1940 the American Civil Liberties Union was defending 1,300 of them in 200 legal cases. In Germany there are thousands of them in concentration camps; in Canada it is a prison offense to be a Witness; in Australia the demand for their suppression is said to be growing. In England, however, they are merely exempt from military service.

Judge Rutherford himself is something of a mystery. In Detroit he was seen by his flock only at the opening and closing sessions of the convention, stayed incommunicado at an unnamed hotel. There is a Mrs. Mary M. 'Rutherford and a son, Malcolm C. Rutherford. Still, this secrecy doesn't seem to reflect on his character. There has never been the slightest suspicion that he misuses the funds which he handles; he has never entered any supernatural claims for himself; and he signs his correspondence modestly "J. F." One unusual honor came to him when in 1933 and 1934 French versions of his books won first prizes for religious literature at expositions sponsored by the French Ministry of the Interior.

References

Christian Cent 53:396-7 Mr 11 '36; 53: 567-70 Ap 15 '36; 54:1548 D 15 '37; 57:896-8 Jl 17 '40
Life 9:20-1 Ag 12 '40 il
Lit Digest 121:18 My 2 '36 por
Nation 151:110-12 Ag 10 '40
New Repub 102:843+ Je 24 '40
N Y Times p5 Ja 11 '38
Newsweek 13:29 Je 26 '39; 14:29 Jl 3 '39; 16:42 Ag 5 '40 il
Sat Eve Post 213:18-19+ S 14 '40 il por
Time 26:59 N 18 '35; 30:34 D 27 '37; 32:52 S 19 '38 por; 35:54 Je 24 '40 il; 36:40-1 Jl 29 '40; 36:39 Ag 5 '40 il

Who's Who in New York

RUTLEDGE, BRETT, pseud. *See* Paul, E.

SABRY, HASSAN, PASHA 1879—Nov 14, 1940 Premier of Egypt; Foreign Minister; held many Ministerial posts before asked to form coalition Cabinet in June 1940, composed of representatives from all parties except those opposing Egyptian participation in war; appointed Military Governor of Egypt on July 2; under him diplomatic relations with Italy and Germany broken off, defensive alliance with Britain continued

References

Gt Brit & East 51:681 D 22 '38 por
N Y Times p12 Je 28 '40; p4 Ag 27 '40; p4 Ag 28 '40; p8 S 3 '40; p48 N 10 '40
International Who's Who

Obituaries

Gt Brit & East 55:395 N 21 '40
N Y Herald Tribune p16 N 15 '40 por
N Y Times p5 N 15 '40 por
Time 36:29-30+ N 25 '40 por

SAERCHINGER, CESAR (serch'inj-er sā'zar) Oct 23, 1889- Radio commentator; author
Address: h. 299 Riverside Drive, New York City

For many years a foreign correspondent and, since 1930, organizer of the first complete transatlantic broadcasting service for American radio listeners, César Saerchinger is an authority on underlying forces in the contemporary world situation. He utilizes his varied background experience in a weekly broadcast over the National Broadcasting System: *Stories Behind the Headlines,* a program arranged with the cooperation of the American Historical Association. His most recent book, *The Way Out of War* (January 1940), is a brief but penetrating and concisely written study of the forces that make for war, and what can be done to prevent war.

Mr. Saerchinger says that it is not nations but their leaders who make war; and that in the War in Europe today the social structure of civilized man is at stake. He traces the background events that led to the First World War, showing the development of nationalism and capitalistic enterprise that threatened the "balance of power." After the War, nationalism became the minorities' problem. An economic war continued between imperialism's theory of collective security and the growth of totalitarian economy with its ideas of self-sufficiency. It was the failure of the World Economic Conference (1933) that brought on an epidemic of dictatorships. The present struggle is to maintain the "free" cooperative economic system developed by the Western democracies against the alternative of totalitarian economy, as exemplified by Germany and Soviet Russia.

It is the business of statesmen of the "have" countries, Mr. Saerchinger believes, to provide the means to live for the "have-not" countries. There is also needed a revision of the League Covenant and the spirit in which its provisions are carried out. The underlying causes of war will not be removed until nationalism, industrialism and imperialism are curbed. Further, no peace can be permanent that does not take into account the law of perpetual change. Nothing short of a federation of European states can bring real security against war. America, says Mr. Saerchinger, must stay out of the European War. We must preserve our moral leadership, and be ready to render economic support when a peace is made.

Because of the authority represented in *The Way Out of War*, Mr. Saerchinger was asked to participate in the *Town Meeting of the Air* radio program March 28, 1940, on the subject, Are We on the Road to War? The speeches of Mr. Saerchinger, Frederick L. Schuman, Norman Thomas and James G. McDonald on this subject have been published in a pamphlet by *Town Meeting of the Air* (1940).

César Saerchinger was born in Aix-la-Chapelle, Germany, October 23, 1889, son

Roy Lee Jackson

CESAR SAERCHINGER

of Victor and Anna (Lange) Saerchinger. He came to the United States in 1898, becoming an American citizen in 1910. He was educated in the Realgymnasium Halle, Germany, and in the New York City public schools; he also studied music with private teachers. He sang as a boy soprano soloist at Christ Church, New York, played piano in a New Thought Church, and did hack writing to help swell the family income. He began his editorial work as assistant in a publishing firm in 1905, and in 1908 became editorial assistant on the *National Cyclopedia of American Biography*. He spent one year of study abroad; then at the outbreak of the War returned to the United States with a headful of information and ideas, and an installment-plan contract for a Steinway Grand. One day he heard of a project to put out a 14-volume musical encyclopedia. He spent six weeks working out a meticulous plan for one, submitted it to the publishers, and landed the contract to edit it. This, *The Art of Music*, he edited from 1913 to 1917. He served on the editorial staff of *Current Opinion* in 1917.

In 1915 he married Marion Wilson Ballin of New York. They have two children: Dagmar and Eugene Henry Benjamin.

At the end of the War Saerchinger became foreign correspondent for the New York *Evening Post* in Berlin, 1919 to 1921. He was one of the first foreign "peace" correspondents to turn up at Berlin, and a mere cub among the seasoned newshawks. But he had beginner's luck. He was the first foreign newspaperman to interview General Von Ludendorff—and all but got chewed up when he tried to sound out the General on Wilson's "humanity" pleas. He then landed an interview with Friedrich Ebert, and traced the famous War Manifesto of the German Intellectuals to its source, establishing to his satisfaction that the author was Herman Sudermann. He talked with Töller in Munich a few days after the Communists proclaimed a Soviet; and in Copenhagen in 1920, obtained the first exclusive interview, with Litvinov, the future Soviet Commissar for Foreign Affairs.

For some years he roamed over Europe recording its musical life. He obtained interviews with Richard Strauss, Felix Weingartner, and Artur Nikisch, went to Bayreuth in a Red Cross ambulance, and found aged Cosima Wagner still alive. He reviewed the works of the younger generation of musicians, took a decisive part in the founding of the International Society for Contemporary Music at Salzburg, discovered and brought considerable talent to the United States.

In the late '20s he settled in London with his family, dividing his time between his two interests, journalism and music, until he discovered the job that was to combine and absorb both: radio. It happened that in 1930 he was covering the London Naval Conference for the Philadelphia *Public Ledger* when he met radio commentator Frederic Wile of Washington. When Wile left London, he placed Saerchinger in charge of Columbia interests. After new scoops—in radio this time—Saerchinger landed Secretary of State Stimson (see sketch this issue) on the day the Tripartite Naval Agreement was perfected. He also brought the voice of the Prince of Wales for the first time to American listeners.

This was the beginning of Saerchinger's activity as first European director for a national broadcasting chain; during the next seven years he organized the first complete transatlantic broadcasting service for American listeners. He brought the voice of George Bernard Shaw (after some nine months' persuasion), H. G. Wells, Sir Oliver Lodge, Stanley Baldwin, and many more, as well as the important messages of King George, King Albert, Queen Wilhelmina (see sketch this issue), Hindenburg, Masaryk, De Valera (see sketch this issue), and dictators Mussolini and Hitler. Chancellor Dollfuss not only broadcast twice for Saerchinger, but took him into his confidences: one of the little Chancellor's last acts was to confer on him the Austrian Cross of Honor.

To keep his broadcasts from becoming commonplace, Saerchinger evolved new types of programs epitomizing the culture and the art of many lands. A brilliant array of such programs from the homes of Shakespeare, Milton, Wordsworth and Keats, from the ruins of Pompeii and the streets of Cairo and many other places, made radio history. The climax of Saerchinger's activities came with the abdication crisis in England, which he describes in his book, *Hello, America!* (1938), as "ten nights that shook the ether." His final assignment was the Coronation of George VI.

Saerchinger's radio series, *Stories Behind the Headlines,* has won nationwide popularity for its entertaining and penetrating analysis of cause and effect. All of his references are authenticated by a member of the American Historical Association. It was this program which the Ninth Institute for Education by Radio, conducted in Columbus, Ohio, chose to receive its First Award for an historical program broadcast over a coast-to-coast network during 1938.

He is the author of *A Narrative History of Music* (with Leland Hall, 1915); *The Opera* (1916); and *Hello, America!* (1938). In the last-named he describes his varied experiences as the arranger of broadcasts from all the chancelleries of Europe, including the Vatican. He tells of the significant personalities of contemporary life whose voices have been heard in America via radio, and closes with a chapter on the future possibilities of radio.

Searchinger is much interested in the subject of radio as a political instrument; and in a recent article on radio censorship he said: "The American radio must be concerned to safeguard the spirit of democracy if the industry is to remain free and untrammeled. This, indeed, is the difference between the American system and the systems of most European countries. The very fact that the present controversy has arisen shows how deeply ingrained is our feeling for independence and freedom of thought. We mean to preserve this freedom all along the line, and to make new media of expression subservient to it. We do not want radio, now that it has become such a powerful medium of publicity, to be controlled or bureaucratically censored from 'above.' On the other hand, we do not wish to see it exploited by unseen forces beyond our control."

References

Atlan 161:509-18 Ap '38
Foreign Affairs 16:244-59 Ja '38; 18: 337-49 Ja '40
Nation 150:340 Mr 9 '40
N Y Times Book R p18 F 18 '40
Scholastic 34:29E Mr 11 '39
Who's Who in America

SAINT EXUPERY, ANTOINE DE (sänt' ex-ü'pā-rē" ăn-twaN) 1900- Author
Address: c/o Appleton Century, 35 W 32nd St, New York City

Of that generation which came into its own in the years immediately following the War, few have the robust equilibrium of the French airman, poet and philosopher, Antoine de Saint Exupéry, who received the French Academy's Grand Prix in the summer of 1939. His *Wind, Sand and Stars* (1939) has, however, more than a sanity of integration. It represents the creation of a kind of new literary cosmos, sprung from

ANTOINE DE SAINT EXUPERY

such things as the symmetry of an engine and the timelessness of flight into the night.

Antoine de Saint Exupéry—known to his friends as "Saint-Ex"—was born in Lyon in 1900. His father's ancestors were natives of a small village, in the old province of Limousin, which bore their name. His mother belonged to the famous old Boyer de Fonscolombe family to whom Fragonard and other painters of the eighteenth century dedicated their finest pictures.

In the eyes of the orderly Jesuit Fathers at Montgré and Mans, young Antoine was a noisy fractious youngster, difficult to teach. But at the college of Fribourg in Switzerland he made an admirable record in philosophy and the classics. The World War brought an end to all this; but the intellectual tastes which he acquired at this time established his life's fundamental accent.

Near the town of Bugey where Antoine, at the castle of Saint Maurice de Remens, passed his holidays, was one of France's oldest airports. He watched the trial flights of the apprentice pilots, was initiated into the mysteries of motors, and listened to many a fabulous boast that enlivened the adolescence of aviation.

This love of vast horizons led naturally to a brief naval-school training. It was in the cards, for a while, that he was to be a marine officer; but he failed his subsequent examinations.

He took lessons from a civil pilot, was granted his license and entered the service at Strasbourg. He was sent off to Morocco as a cadet and came back an officer. Very shortly, however, he returned to civil life, entering a business concern. But after a few months he felt himself completely thwarted and again (1926) plunged into civil aviation.

SAINT EXUPERY, ANTOINE DE—*Cont.*

Before receiving his long-awaited first commission with the Latécoère Company (Toulouse-Dakar line) he underwent a novitiate that included some short miscellaneous courses at Perpignan. At the end of a year's heavy flying schedule on the Toulouse-Casablanca run, he was put in command of the airport of Cap-Juby, at Rio del Rio, a Spanish possession on the West coast of Africa. Except for occasional skirmishes with the Moors it was a tedious charge.

Saint Exupéry went to South America when the airmails were pushing their way down from Brazil, and he himself fixed a route to Punta Arenas, the Southernmost air base in the Argentine. Those were the days, says he, when "our planes frequently fell apart in mid-air."

He admits that he "succumbed" to the desert as soon as he saw it, despite the sense of the irreparable which sometimes came over him—"the thought that far away the whole world is ageing . . . trees have brought forth their fruit . . . grain has ripened in the fields. . ." But for three years he flew the African mails, with quarters at Port Etienne, on the edge of one of the most unsubdued regions in the Sahara.

The art of flying over both South America and Africa is told in two of his books. *Night Flight* (1932) is a story of the European mail and how it is flown by night. It won the Femina Prize and was a Book-of-the-Month Club choice. In it "both the glamor and terror of night-flying at high altitudes are invested by the author with a kind of metaphysical poetry." It established his reputation in the United States. In *Southern Mail* (1933) he tells both a love story and the story of a plane's flight in Morocco. A critic said he "writes of love like a Frenchman and of flying like a pilot."

In December 1935 he decided to try a long-distance flight from Paris to Saïgon. His wife, Countess Manuelo, put a razor and a change of shirt in his bag, and with Prévot, his mechanic, he took off on the 29th. He avoided Paris "with a jerk," headed for the valley of the Loire, skimmed Sardinia, and entered Africa at Bizerta. They were about 250 miles into the desert when they crashed. For three days they went without water. They survived on the will to live and the feeble comfort of a pint of coffee, a half-pint of white wine, some grapes and two oranges. A passing Arab came to their rescue.

Just before the outbreak of the Second World War, Saint Exupéry flew the North Atlantic as a member of the crew of the flying-boat, *Lieutenant de Vaisseau Paris*, which was making an experimental flight for Air France. He returned to America and was working on a new novel when the beginning of hostilities called him home. Assigned to an air training school at Toulouse, Saint Exupéry asked to be transferred to active duty at the front, as captain in an observation squadron. As he said to Dorothy Thompson (see sketch this issue) in an interview: "Nobody has the right to write a word today who does not participate to the fullest in the agony of his fellow human beings. If I did not resist with my life I should be unable to write. . . One must write with one's body."

During the War Saint Exupéry's observation plane was shot to pieces in action on the Western Front, but he escaped injury to the end of French hostilities. In the chaotic conditions following the fall of France he disappeared and efforts to make contact with him failed. In December 1940, however, he was able to inform his publishers that he was in Lisbon, awaiting transportation to America.

Saint Exupéry is a tall and somewhat massively built man, with a round, smooth face, large chestnut eyes and a friendly, inquiring, upturned nose. He is neither an obliging optimist nor a naïve sentimentalist, but life to him has much bigness.

References

Atlan 162:1-12, 166-77 Jl-Ag '38 (Same abr. Read Digest 33:6-9 S '38)
Liv Age 355:225-8 N '38
Time 33:81 Je 26 '39 por

Saint Exupéry, A. Wind, Sand and Stars 1939

SANDBURG, CARL Jan 6, 1878- Author

Address: Harbert, Michigan

Outstanding American poet and biographer, Carl Sandburg has been awarded the 1939 Pulitzer Prize (awarded May 1940) in history for his *Abraham Lincoln: The War Years*. These four large volumes, the result of thirteen years of intensive research, together with *The Prairie Years* (two volumes) which was published in 1926, make up a major monumental work in historical biography that has been called the greatest study of an American ever written by another American. And in November 1940 its author was elected to the American Academy of Arts and Letters, succeeding the late John H. Finley (see sketch this issue).

In their story of Lincoln's growing up and early career *The Prairie Years* are like a lyric prologue to the greatly written human tragedy of *The War Years*. The vividly recreated scenes and cumulative force of detail of the latter work make it a biography not only of Lincoln but of the whole Civil War, concerned less with events than with the men and women who made them. There are extended portraits of the main figures of the time, and there is also a great background of humanity, woven in with anecdote and incident, against which the massive, solitary, but warmly realized, wholly human figure of Abraham Lincoln rises. Sandburg's aim was to "restore Lincoln to the common people to whom he belongs." As readers of his poems, *The People,*

Yes, might expect, there is throughout a tender understanding and appreciation of these ordinary folks. Lincoln is built up from their belief in him, their stories about him, his words to them: a homely, neighborly man who could be austere as well as kind, whose salient characteristics were his sadness and his humor, who combined the spirit of a dreamer and poet with the mind of a far-seeing, calculating politician. Above all Sandburg stresses the indescribable loneliness and personal isolation of this man who had to carry on alone, tortured and almost broken under his superhuman task.

The biography extends from the time Lincoln boarded the train at Springfield to go to his inauguration, down to the black day his coffin was placed in the earth of the Springfield he had left. In between lies the drama of violence, intrigue, bloodshed; of dealings with generals, Congress, the press; draft riots, emancipation, Copperheads; the early failures and the later triumphs; the rising faith of the people in Lincoln; the dream that forecast his death; the assassination, the grief of a nation. Significant to our time is the book's store of material on what happens to a democracy when it goes to war. The whole is written with a simple, richly cadenced prose; Sandburg the poet emerges in many pages that have the impact of lyrical free verse, such as the concluding passage describing the return of Lincoln's body home. Allan Nevins' estimate reflects in general the unanimous critical opinion of *The War Years*: "It is not merely a biography; it is a magnificent piece of history, an epic story of the most stirring period of national life and a narrative which for decades will hearten all believers in the stability of democracy and the potentialities of democratic leadership."

Of all American writers Carl Sandburg is most particularly fitted to be Lincoln's biographer. He, too, was a poor boy who grew up on the prairies, worked at a number of jobs and got little schooling, but liked the common people and got on with them. He has the same earthy, genuine sense of humor; he loves folklore and is a teller of anecdotes and of parables. A poet, he understands the poet in Lincoln; a practical man also (he could never have handled voluminous biographical material, he says, if he hadn't known how to be scientifically efficient), he could understand Lincoln's shrewdness. And like Lincoln, he believes in the destiny of democratic America.

Thirteen years after Lincoln's death, while the Civil War was still being fought at the corner store, Sandburg was born on January 6, 1878 at Galesburg, Illinois, son of August and Clara (Anderson) Sandburg. His parents were Swedish immigrants, his father a worker in the railroad blacksmith shops at Galesburg. At 13 Carl became a milk-wagon driver; later he was a barbershop porter, a scene shifter in a theatre, a truck operator at a brick kiln. He didn't go to school much, but he read books: folk tales

CARL SANDBURG

and biography. He listened to the local lore about Lincoln, to the Fourth of July orators who made speeches about him and he read all that he could about Lincoln. When he was 17 he struck out for the West, riding freights; worked in Kansas wheat fields and washed dishes in city hotels. These hard jobs gave him an early sympathy for workers. Back again in Galesburg, he decided to be a house-painter. Then the Spanish-American War came and Sandburg served in the Sixth Illinois Volunteers for several months; he is proud of his army service and still wears a veteran's insignia.

Influenced by a friend he met in the army, he decided to get an education, and worked his way through Lombard College at Galesburg (1898-1902). At college he was captain of the basketball team, editor of the college monthly and annual; he won several declamation prizes and was a member of the Poor Writers' Club. After graduation he traveled around the country holding various jobs, such as selling stereoptican photographs, then settled in Milwaukee, working for a year as district organizer for the Wisconsin Socialist-Democratic Party He was secretary to the Mayor of Milwaukee from 1910 to 1912, and as associate editor of *System Magazine* in 1913 came in contact with employers of labor. Inevitably he got into newspaper work, first as Stockholm correspondent for Newspaper Enterprise Associates, then as editorial writer for the Chicago *Daily News.* He covered the Chicago race riots for that paper and several years later became its motion picture editor.

Sandburg married on June 15, 1908 Lillian Steichen, whose brother is Edward Steichen, the famous photographer. Sandburg wrote a biography of him, *Steichen, the Photographer,* in 1929. The Sandburgs have three children: Margaret, Janet and Helga.

SANDBURG, CARL—*Continued*

While still in college Sandburg had begun writing poetry; he won *Poetry* Magazine's Levinson Prize in 1914 for his poem, *Chicago*. When his *Chicago Poems* appeared in 1915, elegant poetry readers were shocked by his calling Chicago "hog-butcher of the world." Other sensibilities were outraged by his use of slang and the earthy, racy speech of workers. Still others objected to his loose free-verse lines. But further volumes of poetry followed: *Corn Huskers* (1918); *Smoke and Steel* (1920); *Slabs of the Sunburnt West* (1922). These were poems of tough, vivid realism about men who worked in the fields and in the factories, built from Sandburg's own experiences, on work shared with them, on the things he knew about their lives and difficulties; sensitive, also, to the beauty of earth, of the prairies, of harvest; and of the raw, lean potentialities of the Midwestern cities. The poems were psalms of life with human understanding and social meaning. The fullest realization of his themes and the culmination of his poetic powers appear in *The People, Yes* (1936). Sandburg himself has called this volume "my footnote to the last words of the Gettysburg Address."

He writes not only about, but for the people, in popular language that has no esthetic claims, no technical skill, no rhetorical embellishments. But it is writing rich from authentic experience, full of folklore and idiomatic speech—of talk from farms, mines, hobo campfires, section gangs, soap boxes. It tells what the common man thinks, it affirms his strength and value. Newton Arvin says that *The People, Yes* is "an eloquent and sometimes a passionate reassertion of the dignity, the fortitude, the unweariable creativeness, the historic and unrelinquished hopes of the laboring many." Sandburg's weaknesses lie in inconclusive statement, uncorrelated facts; he is content to pose the question: "Who knows the answer?" Earl H. Robinson, coauthor of *Ballad for Americans,* is to make a musical dramatization of *The People, Yes.*

Some excellent books for children have been written by Sandburg, among them *Rootabaga Stories* (1922); *Potato Face* (1930); and *Early Moon* (1930).

Many people had been reading Sandburg's poems, but many more actually got to know him when he started traveling around the country lecturing, reading his poems and singing folk songs. Sandburg is a natural entertainer, he likes to talk to people and they like his deep slow voice, his humor, his homely informality. He stands tall and erect, a shock of white hair falling forward over his forehead, his lined but strong face and deep-set blue eyes. He is not a fastidious dresser, but likes to wear old flannels and old shoes, his black bow tie his one concession to formality.

His friend Harry Hansen writes of him: "Although Carl uses no gestures and rarely alters his attitude, his face is a sensitized mirror of his moods. When he aims a thrust at some inhuman practice that has aroused his indignation, his lower jaw sticks out, his lip seems to curl and he drawls out his words as if taking careful aim. When he reads the *Rootabaga Stories* he is as a big boy among children." Sandburg had been collecting folk songs since boyhood, but it was not until 1920 that he began singing them for the public; since then they have become the most popular part of his programs. He accompanies his songs with a guitar, singing in a deep, natural baritone. His audiences have given him ballads and songs from their sections of the country; he added these to his collections and in 1927 published his *American Songbag,* containing many ballads put in print for the first time.

The Sandburgs live in Harbert, Michigan, among the sand dunes 60 miles east of Chicago across the lake, where Sandburg has done all his writing on *The War Years* He took over the attic, with a stove, a cot, a lot of book shelves, a typewriter on a crackerbox. "If Grant and Sherman could run campaigns from crackerboxes, so could I," he said. The shelves soon filled up with hundreds of source-books on Lincoln, gathered from libraries and from people all over the country during his lecture tours. "I sort of planned my singing tour so it would take me where I knew material was." He marked these books for copyists, who worked two at a time on the downstairs porch. Sandburg worked long and hard, but he had to learn from the examples set by Gene Tunney (see sketch this issue) and Ty Cobb to get more sleep. *The War Years* was originally conceived as an essay; he thinks now that he could still spend a good 10 years more writing about Lincoln's life.

But with several volumes of verse and six volumes of Lincoln biography behind him, Sandburg does not think he will again write anything so enormous as the latter. He has been urged to write his autobiography because of his interesting work and experiences, but he has an idea that his life story would make "melancholy reading." Of his work he says: "Among the biographers I am a first-rate poet, and among poets a good biographer; among singers I'm a good collector of songs and among song-collectors a nice judge of pipes. I don't care how I am rated. I'm thankful to keep out of jail. Friendships are welcome, but flowers of approval are not a requisite." This is Sandburg, awarded the Pulitzer Prize for the year's best history, who can also write, with quiet irony:

"I tell you the past is a bucket of ashes.
I tell you yesterday is a wind gone
    down, a sun dropped in the West.
I tell you there is nothing in the world,
    only an ocean of tomorrows, a sky
    of tomorrows."

References

Christian Sci Mon Mag p6 O 7 '39
N Y Herald Tribune p17 My 7 '40
    por; p18 O 24 '40
N Y Times p20 My 7 '40 por
Newsweek 14:29 D 4 '39
Rotarian 56:44-6 My '40 pors
Scholastic 36:20+ F 5 '40; 36:28 My 6
    '40 por
Time 34:84+ D 4 '39 por
Arvin, N. Carl Sandburg *In* Cowley,
    M. ed. After the Genteel Tradition
    p79-87 1937
Compton, C. H. Who Reads Carl
    Sandburg? *In* Who Reads What?
    p53-69 1934
Hansen, H. Carl Sandburg: Poet of
    the Streets and of the Prairie *In*
    Midwest Portraits p15-91 1923
Kunitz, S. J. ed. Living Authors 1937
Loggins, V. Revolution *In* I Hear
    America p249-81 1938
Who's Who in America
Zabel, M. D. ed. Sandburg's Testa-
    ment *In* Literary Opinion in Ameri-
    ca p406-15 1937

SANDEFER, JEFFERSON DAVIS Mar 13, 1868—Mar 22, 1940 President of Hardin-Simmons University since 1909; nationally known educator; took prominent part in the Baptist Church in Texas; noted as an ardent prohibitionist.

JEFFERSON DAVIS SANDEFER

References

Sandefer, I. W. Jefferson Davis San-
    defer, Christian Educator 1940
Who's Who in America
Who's Who in American Education

Obituaries

N Y Herald Tribune p8 Mr 23 '40
N Y Times p13 Mr 23 '40 por
Sch & Soc 51:409 Mr 30 '40

SAPOSS, DAVID Feb 22, 1886- Labor economist

Address: h. 2716 Woodley Pl, N W, Washington, D. C.

David Joseph Saposs, the "bushy, rumpled little expert" who was chief economist for the National Labor Relations Board, head of its research division, no longer has a department to head. On October 11, 1940 President Roosevelt signed the Civil Deficiency Appropriation Bill which abolishes his research division, by then known as the "technical" division. Although columnist Ludwell Denny pointed out back in March that "to abolish the division at a time when both employers and unions are criticizing the board for knowing too little about the economic facts" is the height of absurdity, the House Appropriations Committee recently swept it completely away on the grounds that "no need exists."

Senator Wagner later managed to get an amendment permitting the retention of its functions, however. These are many and varied: the formulation of monthly and annual reports; analyses of employment records; library and reference work; economic service to the legal division; work on economic material that may go into briefs; preparation of economic data in relation to jurisdictional problems. But since none of this work will be carried on by an independent body, *finis* is written "to a project which played a nightly significant rôle in virtually revolutionizing industrial relations in the United States."

Saposs, the economist who has been in charge of this work, has also been kept busy for a long time denying that he is a Communist or ever has been one. Senator Burke and Martin Dies (see sketches this issue) were the first to make the charge. In March 1940 Mapes Davidson resigned as trial examiner for the board, charging that a majority of its members "continue brazenly and openly to foster Communists and kindred radicals as they have done in the past." His fire was centered for the most part on Mr. Saposs, who was said to have lectured the examiners on "what should be gotten into the record of a Labor Board meeting, aside from direct evidence, to show by inference that employers are fostering company-dominated unions." He also spoke of Mr. Saposs' "smelly Fansteel decision in which you sought to bestow a paternal benediction on sit-down strikes." In April David Saposs was once more attacked as a possible Communist in a report by two minority members of the House Committee investigating the Labor Board: "If the excerpts from his writings which were read into the record are a fair example of his views we disapprove as strongly as our colleagues

Associated Press

DAVID SAPOSS

of a person entertaining such views holding an important position in the government." Mr. Saposs replied that the excerpts were not representative and submitted "a positive statement of his political and economic philosophy together with letters and writings of persons acquainted with his work and record."

He was supported by educators, labor leaders and writers and in the end exonerated by "some of the staunchest opposition Congressmen," but continued to be attacked in testimony before the Smith Committee. Said *Time*, when appropriations for the research division were abolished: "What the NLRB foes really sought was abolition of Economist Saposs," who, "though often denounced as a Communist, is neither Red nor useless, but a zealous watchdog of labor rights." According to the *New Republic*, "doing away with this arm of the Board was a considerable victory for those who oppose collective bargaining and for the Congressmen who respond to their pressure."

David Saposs was born on February 22, 1886 at Kiev, Russia, the son of Isaac and Shima (Erevesky) Saposs. His family came to the United States when he was nine, and he was educated at the University of Wisconsin, where from 1911 to 1919 he was labor economics research associate, making himself an expert on the labor movement. Later—from 1924 to 1926—he was also to study at Columbia University. As a labor economist, before coming to the National Labor Relations Board in 1935 he held such diverse positions as director of the Company Union Study of the United States Bureau of Statistics (1914), New York Department of Labor expert (1917-18), investigator for the Carnegie Corporation Americanization Study (1918-19), investigator for the Interchurch

World Movement Steel Strike Inquiry (1919-20).

Perhaps his most valuable experience, however, was as founder and co-director (1920-22) of the Labor Bureau, Incorporated, which served as consulting economist to labor organizations, for in that position he had a unique opportunity to find out how labor organizations worked from the inside. As head of the Labor Division of Columbia University (1926-30), which was making a study of post-War social and economic conditions of France, he also made two trips abroad, spending a year and a half learning about the European labor movement; from 1922 to 1933 he was a member of the faculty of Brookwood, the first resident labor college in the United States; and he has lectured at New York City's New School for Social Research and at the Rand School. Few men have been so well equipped by training and experience to tackle the multitudinous problems faced by the chief economist of the understaffed NLRB.

Mr. Saposs is the coauthor of *A History of the Labor Movement of the United States* (1918), known as the outstanding work on the subject; is the author of *Readings in Trade Unionism* (1926); *Left Wing Unionism* (1926); *The Labor Movement of Post-War France* (1930); coauthored *Labor and the Government* (1935); and has published numerous articles on labor in magazines, many in the *New Republic*. In 1935 he was writing that "a strong trade union movement is only possible when aided by the government," although advising labor to build a third party in preparation for the time when the Administration might grow hostile. He is a member of the American Economic Association.

Since 1934 Mr. Saposs has lived in Washington, D. C., with his wife, the former Bertha Tigay (also from Russia), whom he married in 1917, and his two daughters, Corinne, born in 1924, and Barbara, born in 1929. His hobbies, he says, are walking and farm work.

References

New Repub 103:621-2 N 4 '40
N Y Herald Tribune p25 O 13 '40
N Y Times p1, 33 Mr 20 '40 por; p23 O 11 '40
Time 35:14 Ap 1 '40 por
Who's Who in American Jewry
Who's Who in the Nation's Capital

SARNOFF, DAVID (sar'noff) Feb 27, 1891- President of the Radio Corporation of America

Address: b. 30 Rockefeller Plaza, New York City; h. 44 E 71st St, New York City

David Sarnoff is not only president of the Radio Corporation of America but chairman of the board of its subsidiaries, the National Broadcasting Company, the RCA Communications, Incorporated, RCA Manufacturing Company, and a director of the

Electric and Musical Industries, Limited. He is the "industry's No. 1 wonder boy in the United States."

The son of Abraham and Lena (Privin) Sarnoff, he was born in Minsk, Russia, February 27, 1891. As a Russian immigrant boy he came to the United States at the age of nine, and soon afterward was helping out the family finances by selling newspapers. His father died when he was fifteen, and David, the eldest of five children, was the man of the family. He got a $5-a-week job as a messenger boy with the Commercial Cable Company. Fascinated by the telegraph instruments, he taught himself the Morse code and applied for a job at the Marconi Wireless Telegraph Company.

He got a job as an office boy, and two years later received his first assignment as a wireless operator in a Marconi station on Nantucket Island off the coast of Massachusetts. An ambitious youth, Sarnoff studied technical books on engineering at night and decided he wanted to take some electrical engineering courses at Pratt Institute in Brooklyn. In order to attend the school he got a transfer to Sea Gate, New York, though it meant a $10 salary cut. The cut was soon made up, however, when he was made office manager of the Sea Gate station. He served next as wireless operator aboard the *S. S. Beothic* on an Arctic sealing expedition, and in 1910 came to the New York Marconi station at Wanamaker's department store.

The young telegraph operator distinguished himself and came to the attention of the world in 1912 when he picked up word that the *S. S. Titanic* was sinking. He stayed at his station unrelieved for 72 hours, helping to direct ships to the sinking vessel, and got first news of the survivors. All other stations were ordered closed so as not to interfere with his work.

Sarnoff's rise in the Marconi Company was rapid. He was in turn radio inspector; instructor at the Marconi Institute; chief inspector; assistant chief engineer; assistant traffic manager; and finally, in 1917, commercial manager. When the Radio Corporation of America was formed in 1919 and acquired the Marconi Company Sarnoff was taken over as commercial manager.

His rise with the Radio Corporation of America was equally rapid. By 1922 he was general manager and vice-president; in 1929 he was made executive vice-president; and on January 3, 1930, just before his thirty-ninth birthday, he became president of the Radio Corporation of America.

In the years of his connection with the Radio Corporation of America, Sarnoff has gained a reputation as a keen executive and a formulator of sure-footed, sound policies. He was active in organizing NBC, which first inaugurated network broadcasting; he assisted in the negotiations which resulted in combining radio and phonograph machines; and he took

Kaiden-Keystone

DAVID SARNOFF

an important part in giving voice to the silent pictures.

Long before radio was thought of in terms of entertainment, Sarnoff dreamed of its broadcasting possibilities. As far back as 1915, when he was traffic manager of the Marconi Company, he made a recommendation to the company's general manager urging that the already proven facilities of wireless communication be carried further than mere message-sending, through the development of a music box to be used in the home for the reception of music. Nothing was done with the idea, which seemed fantastic at the time. Later, when the General Electric Company was organizing RCA, Sarnoff, in a report to the chairman of the board, again referred to his "plan of development which would make radio a 'household utility' in the same sense as a piano or phonograph." He suggested a portable household reception unit, predicting it could sell for about $75; and he also figured out the possible earnings in the first three years of production. Sarnoff's figures tallied close to the actual selling prices of radio sets from 1922 to 1924. But while he calculated sales returns at $75,000,000, sales for the first three years after RCA adopted Sarnoff's "music box" idea amounted to $83,500,000.

When RCA was first organized it was little more than a selling agency for the General Electric and Westinghouse companies. Under Sarnoff's unification plan it became a completely integrated research, manufacturing and selling organization, independent of its original parent companies.

Music has been one of Sarnoff's most important hobbies, and many of NBC's musical programs were his ideas. He established the weekly music appreciation hour under Dr. Walter Damrosch, which

SARNOFF, DAVID—*Continued*

became part of the curriculum of thousands of schools; he arranged for grand opera to be broadcast from the stage of the New York Metropolitan Opera House, when such things were startling innovations; and in 1937 he engaged Arturo Toscanini to conduct a series of 10 symphonic programs over the NBC networks with a newly created NBC symphony orchestra. He is a director of the Metropolitan Opera Company and director and chairman of the board of the Chatham Square Music School.

As he foresaw the possibilities of radio broadcasting long before it was thought of as a practical commercial household vehicle, so Sarnoff has been predicting that television can be commercially successful. RCA has been a pioneer in the television field under Sarnoff's direction. In 1935 he obtained from his directors a million-dollar appropriation to take television out of the laboratory and give it the benefit of exhaustive engineering field tests under actual service conditions.

In May 1940, at an RCA stockholders' meeting, fruits of that research were shown when stockholders were treated to the first public demonstration of a television program on a new, large, six-by-four-foot screen. The program included an hour of music and dramatic features and a news broadcast. David Sarnoff's television dream was about to come true, as his radio broadcasting dream had come true.

The Federal Communications Commission, however, ruled in that month that television broadcasting must remain longer on an experimental basis. Testifying before the United States Senate Interstate Commerce Committee that television had received a tremendous setback by this ruling, Sarnoff said RCA had no intention of "freezing" television and called it a potential billion-dollar-a year business capable of rising to greater heights than the $600,000,000 radio industry. As a result of his testimony and that of others, the FCC decided not to fix standards immediately.

Sarnoff's career is one of the most romantic in American industry. He has been decorated by three foreign countries, Luxembourg, France and Poland, and has been honored with degrees by five universities. Square-set, of medium height, blue-eyed, Sarnoff speaks slowly and quietly, with none of the Hollywood mannerisms of the big executive. In addition to heading the vast RCA, Sarnoff maintains an active interest in various civic and social organizations. He was married in 1917 to Miss Lizette Hermant of Paris, France. The couple have three sons.

References

Am Mag 121:16-17+ My '36 por
Etude 54:541+ S '36
Fortune 17:62-8+ Ja '38 por
N Y Herald Tribune p22 Ap 11 '40

Pop Mech 58:370-3+ S '32 por
Pop Sci 137:76-7 S '40 il
Sci ns 91:129-31 F 9 '40
Sci Am 155:251 N '36 por
Smith, A. D. H. David Sarnoff *In* Men Who Run America p191-200 1935
Who's Who in America
Who's Who in American Jewry
Who's Who in Broadcasting
Who's Who in Commerce and Industry

SAROYAN, WILLIAM (sor-rō'yän) Aug 31, 1908- Author; playwright; winner of Pulitzer Prize for best American play of 1939 to 1940 season

Address: 1821 15th Ave, San Francisco, California

William Saroyan began writing when he was 16 years old, and decided to give himself until he was 30 to prove that he could write, or as he calls it, "to win recognition." Saroyan was working in his uncle's vineyard at Fresno, California at the time, but in hours away from pruning the vines he studied the pulp magazines avidly. "I aimed at getting $50 a story—that seemed riches then," he says.

After a careful study of the pulp magazine stories, Saroyan dashed off 10 stories which he thought followed the pulp pattern and sent them to the editors. Every one came back with rejection slips.

This, Saroyan says, convinced him that he had to write in his own way, and not according to any set pattern. It has resulted in his highly subjective style that follows no formal narrative, and that has been both berated by critics and enthusiastically praised as "imaginative, fresh, and original." But while the editors paid scant attention to Saroyan's determination to be himself in his writing, Saroyan kept right on writing, confident that he had something important to say.

He finally made his literary debut as "Sirak Goryan" with a short story, *The Broken Wheel,* which appeared in 1933 in *Hairenik,* an Armenian daily published in Boston, and which was reprinted by Edward J. O'Brien in his *Best Short Stories of 1934.*

When in the same year *Story* Magazine accepted his short story, *The Daring Young Man on the Flying Trapeze,* Saroyan was evidently beside himself. He wrote critics throughout the country, sent them messages, bursting with the news of the great Saroyan. He deluged *Story* with his work. Sometimes the postman deposited two stories a day from Saroyan at the door of the magazine. *Story* published several of these, others were turned over to the *American Mercury* and other magazines. In the fall of 1934 twenty-six of the tales were gathered into Saroyan's first book, *The Daring Young Man on the Flying Trapeze and Other Stories.*

But when the book was published the critics to whom Saroyan had written so enthusiastically of his powers as a writer were laying for him with brickbats. They decided that he didn't write short stories at all; he didn't even write English; he was a "flash in the pan, a fraud, an egomaniac, a fool."

The book, however, became a best-seller, and Saroyan remarked: "Maybe American criticism is too far ahead of American writing or American writing is too far ahead of American criticism. I take heads." When critics contend that his short stories cannot properly be called short stories at all, or label them merely as "poetic shouts" written in prose, Saroyan replies: "What the hell difference does it make what you call it just so it breathes?"

Saroyan shouts loudly that he cares nothing for art or art forms, but that he is concerned with life. In a story called *Myself on Earth* he wrote: "I am a story-teller and I have but a single story—man. I want to tell this simple story in my own way, forgetting the rules of rhetoric, the tricks of composition. I am not a writer at all. I write because there is nothing more civilized or decent for me to do."

The profits from *The Daring Young Man on the Flying Trapeze* (the first edition of which became a collector's item) enabled the young author to go to Armenia and Russia for a visit in the summer of 1935. Some of his travel notes found their way into his second book, *Inhale and Exhale,* a collection of more than 70 new stories, published in 1936.

Saroyan is a prolific writer. He is frank in describing himself as a "natural." His writing flows without impediment. And he always has stories to tell. "What else is a natural?" he asks. But he maintains he is not a hard worker. After turning out three stories a day for a week, he is likely to spend a month loafing. He likes to travel and can work wherever he happens to be: London, Moscow, New York, Fresno. During a furious bout of typing he often takes time out to play his portable phonograph, preferably noisy jazz and cowboy songs.

Even Saroyan's severest critics had to admit that he was no "flash in the pan." His name appeared on the covers of a long list of American magazines and his short stories were collected in half a dozen volumes. They included *Peace It's Wonderful; Little Children; Love, Here Is My Hat; Three Times Three;* and *The Trouble with Tigers.* Saroyan was finding champions among the best known critics, many of whom were now applauding him as a genius.

Saroyan's debut as a playwright was made in 1938 with *My Heart's in the Highlands,* produced by the Group Theatre first and later taken over by the Theatre Guild. No two critics seemed to agree on what the play really meant. A fable of an ineffectual poet, his young son and a bearded trumpeter, it was called "modern, arty, experimental." Critics found it strangely touching and said it won for Saroyan an important niche in the hall of playwrights. Average playgoers,

however, didn't seem to know what it was all about.

While *My Heart's in the Highlands* was being produced on Broadway, Saroyan wrote his second play, *The Time of Your Life,* which won him the Pulitzer Prize and the New York Critics' Circle Prize. He is said to have written it in six days in a New York hotel. At the same time he was busying himself sending telegrams to friendly admirers and others telling them that *My Heart's in the Highlands* was the best play in town. Then, having polished off *The Time of Your Life* and sold it to Eddie Dowling, who later produced it with the Theatre Guild, Saroyan suddenly ceased his deluge of telegrams and left town.

When *The Time of Your Life* opened on Broadway in the fall of 1939, it received, on the whole, excellent reviews. Even those who damned it with faint praise admitted that it was a moving piece of work. Described as a "robust fantasia of love, lust, life, liberty and the pursuit of happiness" by a group of characters who parade in and out of a San Francisco waterfront barroom, it had as its chief character one Joe, who spent his time drinking, dreaming, and trying to help the other lost souls in the barroom.

Critics talked of its "originality, force, freshness and humor." George Jean Nathan inquired of those who would ask what it was all about, if they would ask "what some of the greatest music ever composed is about." Another critic wrote: "The content of the play is much the same as is everything that Saroyan writes, a hymn to the human heart expressed in terms of a poet's imagination." Such reviews made up for those few who found it merely "inconsequential, ingratiating, witty" or "drifting, sentimental, garrulous."

The Time of Your Life played twenty-two and one-half weeks on Broadway, and closed April 6, 1940 without earning back the cost of its production, estimated at about $25,000.

It was chosen the best new play of the 1939 to 1940 season by the New York Critics' Circle in May 1940, a few weeks after Saroyan's third play, *Love's Old Sweet Song,* opened. In choosing *The Time of Your Life* as the best play of the season the critics declared in their citation that the honor went to Saroyan because his play was "an exhilarating demonstration of the fresh, original and imaginative talent he has brought to our American Theatre."

Three days after the Critics' Circle announced its award, the Pulitzer Prize Committee also chose *The Time of Your Life* as the best American play of the season. It was the first time that the Critics' Circle and the Pulitzer Prize committee had agreed on a choice. The Critics' Circle had been making independent choices for several years because it had disapproved in the past of the Pulitzer Prize conception of a best play.

WILLIAM SAROYAN

Saroyan should have been a happy young man in May 1940 with two of the major theatre awards to his credit, but there was a fly in the ointment of success. He was disappointed over the reviews his new play *Love's Old Sweet Song* was receiving. It had received "mixed reviews"—some good, some bad. This time Saroyan had written a play with more plot than his usually formless dramas. *Love's Old Sweet Song* was a humorous, sometimes sentimental story revolving about an old maid who is led to believe by a messenger boy that an itinerant patent-medicine hawker is the man who filled her dreams of love back in her girlhood. Although the hawker is a fraud, the woman's faith and trust transforms him into something satisfyingly true. Some critics raved about the play but others didn't, and Saroyan was disappointed.

Saroyan created a seven-day sensation when he refused the $1,000 award that went with the Pulitzer Prize. In a long-winded statement explaining his refusal, Saroyan declared with his customary candor, "I believe that *The Time of Your Life* is a good, and perhaps great theatrical work. However, I also believe in the essential and possible greatness of all my work, in the theatre as well as in the short story form.

"While I am deeply grateful that formal, and one might say official, recognition has come to a piece of my work, I have always been opposed to awards in general in the realm of art, and particularly material awards, which seem to be dangerous both to the recipient and to the art form which has been awarded." Wealth patronizing art, he added, seemed to him to be in bad taste. Saroyan was taking the same stand Sinclair Lewis had taken in 1926 when he rejected the $1,000 prize for his novel, *Arrowsmith*.

Some found Saroyan's action inconsistent, since he had apparently been pleased with the Critics' Circle Prize. One magazine editorial suggested that the resultant publicity Saroyan got from his rejection of the Pulitzer Award "he couldn't have bought for less than $1,500."

In January 1940 the Ballet Theatre staged the world première of *The Great American Goof*, described by Saroyan as a "ballet-play" and "a new American form." It used music, dialogue, dancing and stereopticon effects. Some critics were merely baffled and some thought the experiment good.

In the summer of 1940 three new Saroyan plays, *Sweeney in the Trees, Hero of the World* and *Something About a Soldier*, the last of which took him a year to write, were produced at various summer theatres in the East. Although critics didn't seem to think them up to standard, Saroyan wanted to act as producer and director for *Sweeney* on Broadway. The autumn of 1940 found *Time of Your Life* opening for its second short but successful run, all three of Saroyan's Broadway successes published in book-form, and the playwright himself visiting New York and announcing his intentions of finishing four new plays in a couple of weeks or so, according to Leonard Lyons. "But my work will probably be interrupted," he feared, "by my being conscripted into the army." (Saroyan's opinion of army life and the War in general wouldn't influence any young man to run for the nearest recruiting station.) "Then why don't you get married and raise a family?" asked Lillian Hellman. "It's too late," he replied. "There isn't enough time." "There is," said Miss Hellman, "for Saroyan."

Saroyan's latest book, *My Name Is Aram*, was the January 1940 choice of the Book-of-the-Month Club and describes the "imaginative life of an Armenian boy in California." Christopher Morley says it shows him at last as the "grown and many-colored artist; the genuine poet in prose, and spokesman for the youth of the world."

Saroyan wrote another pretty comprehensive autobiography of his early life for the *New Yorker*:

"Born August 31, 1908,
In Fresno, California;
Student at Emerson Public School
On L Street, between San Benito and
    Santa Clara;
Holder of the First Prize for Street
    Sales,
    The Fresno *Evening Herald*, 1917;
Twice Winner of the Around-the-
    Block Race, 1918;
Founder, Manager, and Boss of
    Henry-and-
Willie's Empty Lot for Sons of Ar-
    menians,
Assyrians, and Other Immigrants;
Winner of Highest Third-Grade Binet-
    Simon Intelligence Rating,
"Far Above Average, Although Poor
    at Arithmetic;"

Official Letter-Writer to Mayor Toomey
For the Fifth Grade;
Speaker at the First Meeting
Of the Parent-Teachers' Association;
Singer of "The River Shannon;"
Author of "How I Earned My First Dollar;"
First to Dive from the Oak Tree
Into Thompson Ditch at Malaga;
First to Climb Guggenheim's Water Tank
And Drop a Cat;
Most Frequent Visitor of the Public Library;
Borrower of the Most and Best Books;
First Reader of the *Autobiography of Benjamin Franklin*;
First to Subscribe to Lionel Strongfort's
Body-Building Course;
Holder of the Certificate for Freehand Penmanship;
Fastest Postal Telegraph Messenger
In the San Joaquin Valley, 1921,
And Other Things Too Recent
Or Too Numerous to Mention. . ."

He doesn't mind mentioning most of them, though.

References

Am Mag 129:16-17+ Je '40
Bk-of-the-Month Club News p7 D '40
Life 9:96-100+ N 18 '40 il por
Liv Age 358:348-51 Je '40 por
New Yorker 16:16 Je 22 '40; 16:14 Ag 31 '40
Scholastic 35:12 N 6 '39; 36:26 Ap 22 '40 por
Theatre Arts 23:716-17 O '39; 23:870-5 D '39
Wilson Lib Bul 10:568 My '36
McCole, C. J. That Daring Young Man, Mr. Saroyan *In* Lucifer at Large p257-73 1937
Nathan, G. J. Encyclopedia of the Theatre 1940
Sobel, B. ed. Theatre Handbook 1940
Who's Who in America

SAUNDERS, JOHN MONK Nov 22, 1897—Mar 10, 1940 Scenario writer; wrote scenario for *Wings; Legion of the Condemned; Dawn Patrol*

References

Who's Who in America 1938-39

Obituaries

N Y Post p1 Mr 11 '40 por
N Y Sun p1 Mr 11 '40
Newsweek 15:8 Mr 18 '40
Springf'd Republican p1-2 Mr 12 '40
Variety 138:47 Mr 13 '40

SAVAGE, MICHAEL JOSEPH Mar 7, 1872—Mar 26, 1940 Prime Minister of New Zealand since 1935; social security champion; introduced 40-hour week; labor lead-

er; member of Parliament from 1919 until his death

References

International Who's Who
Who's Who

Obituaries

N Y Herald Tribune p22 Mr 27 '40 por
N Y Times p21 Mr 27 '40
N Y World-Telegram p30 Mr 26 '40
Newsweek 15:8 Ap 8 '40
Time 35:58 Ap 8 '40

SAYRE, FRANCIS BOWES Apr 30, 1885- Lawyer; United States High Commissioner to the Philippines
Address: Manila, Philippine Islands

Francis Bowes Sayre is a lawyer and a diplomat who because of his special diplomatic service in the Far East and Europe holds enough foreign decorations to cover the most expanded chest. In July 1939 President Roosevelt appointed him High Commissioner to the Philippines, and at that time President Manuel Quezon of the Philippine Commonwealth said: "No better appointment could have been made."

Before he took office Francis Sayre was familiar with the commonwealth's problems. Since 1934 he has been a member of the body planning new economic ties between the United States and the Philippines when the Philippines get their independence in 1946. He was also chairman of the Joint Preparatory Committee on Philippine Affairs which in November 1938 turned in the most complete report ever made on the Islands. Unlike Paul V. McNutt (see sketch this issue), his predecessor, Sayre had an open-minded attitude toward Philippine independence. McNutt frankly said that the Islands should be retained, at least as a dominion, but when Sayre arrived in Manila he declared that the Philippines would be cut loose in 1946. Since he has been in Manila he has occasionally clashed with Quezon, however. With 10 years for the Filipinos to learn how a democracy should be run, he finds some indications that they are being steered toward a dictatorship. Nevertheless there has been cooperation, and frequent conferences have been held between the two governments on military and civil problems which would arise in the event of an emergency affecting the Philippines.

Francis Bowes Sayre was born in South Bethlehem, Pennsylvania, the son of Robert Heysham and Martha Finley (Nevin) Sayre, on April 30, 1885. In 1909 he received his B. A. from Williams College and in 1912 was graduated from Harvard Law School. He became deputy district attorney for New York County and stayed in that position until 1914, when he returned to Williams as assistant to its president and instructor in government.

FRANCIS BOWES SAYRE

On November 25, 1913, before his return, he had married Jessie Woodrow, the daughter of President Woodrow Wilson, at the White House. It has been said that Sayre not only resembles Wilson in looks but is the "residuary legatee of Wilson's enthusiasms." Mrs. Sayre died in 1933, leaving three children. In 1937 Mr. Sayre was married again, to Elizabeth Evans Graves.

From 1919 until he left in 1933 to become assistant Secretary of State, Sayre was connected in one way or another with Harvard University. From 1919 to 1924 he was assistant professor of law, and professor of law from 1924 to 1933. In 1923 he took a leave of absence to become adviser in foreign affairs to the Siamese government, and on behalf of Siam negotiated new political and commercial treaties with France, Great Britain, the Netherlands, Spain, Portugal, Denmark, Norway, Sweden and Italy. For his services he received many honors from King Rama VI of Siam.

Mr. Sayre became the director of the Harvard Institute of Criminal Law in 1929 and in January 1933 was appointed Massachusetts State Commissioner of Correction. In November 1933 President Roosevelt appointed him Assistant Secretary of State.

Because of his academic background and in view of the recent housecleaning of "brain-trusters," Sayre's appearance in Washington was at first greeted with suspicion by the old-timers, but "his magnetic and attractive personality, his rapidly moving mind, his extreme energy" broke down all opposition and he was soon felt to be one of the real finds of the Roosevelt Administration.

In Washington, Sayre worked directly under Secretary of State Cordell Hull (see sketch this issue) and was Hull's "right-hand man in the making of our recent reciprocal trade treaties." Sayre, it has been said, be-lieved in the reciprocal trade treaties as Saint Augustine believed in God. In 1939 his book, *The American Trade Agreements Program*, appeared.

Francis Sayre is also the author of numerous books on law and international affairs, among them *Experiments in International Administration* (1919); *Cases on Labor Law* (1922); *Cases on Criminal Law* (1927); *Siam Treaties with Foreign Powers* (1920-27, 1928); *Cases on the Law of Admiralty* (1929); *America Must Act* (1935); and *The Way Forward* (1939).

"With a prominent nose, long face, thin hair retreating from a high forehead, and wearing spectacles," there does seem some ground for the belief that he resembles his father-in-law, Woodrow Wilson.

References

Cur Hist 50:10, 33 S '39 por
Fortune 17:144 Ja '38
Harper 174:229 F '37
Lit Digest 116:13 D 30 '33 por
New Outlook 163:35 My '34
N Y Times p33 N 10 '39; p49 D 3 '39; p46 D 10 '39; IV p5 Mr 3 '40; p9 My 7 '40; p7 Jl 27 '40; p38 O 13 '40
Sat R Lit 21:3 N 11 '39
Time 34:11 Ag 7 '39; 34:30 N 27 '39; 36:16-17 S 2 '40 por
Who's Who in America
Who's Who in the Nation's Capital

SCHELLING, ERNEST HENRY (shĕl'-ing) July 26, 1876—Dec 8, 1939 Pianist; composer; conductor

"What this boy needs is more oatmeal, more fresh air!" said the great composer Brahms upon hearing the 10-year-old Ernest Schelling play, after which "he took me toward him, leaned over and kissed me, his huge beard smothering me as he did so," recalled Schelling.

Ernest Schelling, one of the most brilliant figures in the musical life of New York, died suddenly of a cerebral embolism at the age of 63. Born in Belvedere, New Jersey, son of a Swiss philosopher and theosophist, Felix, and Rose (White) Schelling, he was a piano prodigy. He made his first public appearance at the age of four, spending much of his youth abroad, where his father's social position gave him entree into the great salons of Paris. Before he was eight he was studying at the Paris Conservatoire with Mathias, a pupil of Chopin; and at ten he was a pupil of the great Leschetizky. Then started concentrated hard work as he gave concerts before many of the crowned heads of Europe. Such tremendous demands took their toll and the full-fledged virtuoso of 16 could play no more—crippled with neuritis of the hands.

At 20 he had regained his health and played for Paderewski, who said: "You have little technique, not much flexibility, but I see a spark still in you. Come to Switzer-

Musical America

ERNEST H. SCHELLING

land and I will take you under my wing as my only disciple." After four years of unrelenting study for eight hours a day, Schelling became discouraged at his first concert and sought forgetfulness at a monastery, but the musical fire still burned and he returned to take up a brilliant career.

During the First World War he went to France with the rank of captain, received the decoration of the Legion of Honor, the Distinguished Service Medal, and was mustered out as a major. He was married to Lucy How Draper in 1905. She died in 1938. Four months before his death he married the 21-year-old Peggy Marshall, niece of Mrs. Vincent Astor, musical patroness.

Perhaps Schelling is best known for his conducting of special children's concerts. From 1924 onward these concerts, where children learned to love and understand fine music and musical history, grew in popularity until he had enthusiastic audiences in all the large cities of America, England and Holland. To the children he was always "Uncle Ernest." Radio broadcasts of these concerts with the Philharmonic Symphony had increased his prestige tremendously all over the country.

Most critics believed that Schelling was greater as a concert pianist than as conductor and that his work as a composer was lacking fundamental originality, but when he was stirred by strong emotions he was capable of effects of great power. His *Victory Ball,* based on a satirical verse of savage impact by Alfred Noyes was a direct result of the bitter disillusion, he suffered in the World War. It always made a dramatic sensation when a leading symphony performed it. Other of his works are *Impressions of an Artist's Life*; *Morocco*;

Concerto for Violin and Orchestra; and *Légende Symphonique.*

References

N Y Times p41 N 5 '39 pors

Ewen, D. ed. Composers of Today 1934

Howard, J. T. Our Contemporary Composers *In* Our American Music p462-579 1939

Thompson, O. ed. International Cyclopedia of Music and Musicians 1939

Who's Who in America 1938-39

Wier, A. E. ed. Macmillan Encyclopedia of Music and Musicians 1938

Obituaries

Etude 58:144 F '40

N Y Herald Tribune p29 Ja 21 '40

N Y Times p14 D 9 '39; p15 D 9 '39; p27 D 12 '39

Newsweek 14:47 D 18 '39 por

Time 34:59 D 18 '39

SCHERESCHEWSKY, JOSEPH WILLIAMS (shĕr-ĭ-chĕf'skĭ) Mar 6, 1873—July 9, 1940 Cancer specialist; founder of the Cancer Research Center at Harvard University and of the United States Public Health Service Research Station in Georgia; urged United States to spend $10,000,000 yearly to save 35,000 victims of cancer; noted for his contributions in field of industrial hygiene and occupational diseases

References

American Men of Science

Who's Who in America

Obituaries

N Y Herald Tribune p16 Jl 11 '40

N Y Times p19 Jl 11 '40

SCHIAPARELLI, ELSA (skyä'pä-rĕl'lē äl'sä) Parisian couturière

Address: 610 Fifth Ave, New York City

A "style refugee" to this country after the fall of France, during the early autumn of 1940 Elsa Schiaparelli lectured in 30 United States cities before women's clubs and department stores on *Clothes and the Woman,* wearing costumes which she had designed. Part of the royalties for their reproduction went to a fund for unemployed Parisian midinettes. Mme. Schiaparelli planned to return to Paris in November, where her house had been turned over to the Quakers for the benefit of the homeless, only one room reserved for herself. During her tour she insisted that as a style center no other city could take the place of Paris. "I am not pessimistic about our future," she said. . . There may be ashes on the fire, but the flames are still there."

Elsa Schiaparelli is of remote Egyptian descent on her mother's side; her Italian father was dean of the University of Rome, professor of Oriental lore, and in his lighter moods dabbler in numismatics; and her uncle, Giovanni Schiaparelli, was the discoverer of the canals on Mars. At six she ran

ELSA SCHIAPARELLI

away from home, and was found three days later leading a parade. She was sent to an English dame's school, and lyric summers spent in Capri or on Lake Como soon found her writing verse. *Arethusa*—for the Homeric guardian of the fount of forgetfulness—was her first bold try in her sixteenth year. It was published, but her father refused to read it and sent her off to a convent in Switzerland, where not only the mountains but the school itself gave her two years of complete joy.

At 17 she was enrolled in a school in England, and shortly after the outbreak of the First World War she was married to a Polish gentleman. They came to New York, and here their only child, Marisa, was born. Madame Schiaparelli was living in Greenwich Village, working for the movies in New Jersey, doing translations and taking part-time jobs from importers. At the end of five years she returned to France, did a little gold sculpture, and read a lot of French, English, Italian and German.

It was the chance designing of a black sweater for herself that decided her career in 1927. This piece of "chic melancholy." was hailed by her friends as something rather hard to forget. She began furiously to design clothes, and in two years she moved into her own attic shop in the Rue de la Paix. Her salon grew steadily in size and inimitability, and in 1935 she moved into a pretentious establishment in the old house of Chéruit, 21 Place Vendome.

Madame Schiaparelli has wisely conserved her "sense of inexperience" (she was certainly slated for an intellectual rather than professional life), and she has been described as "Tanagra-like" in build, with an "exotic hierarchy of feature."

References

N Y Times p31 D 7 '39; IV p2 D 10 '39; VII p7 D 24 '39; p24 S 24 '40; p35 S 25 '40

N Y World-Telegram p18 Jl 24 '40 por; p13 S 24 '40

New Yorker 8:19-23 Je 18 '32; 16:12 Ag 24 '40

PM p29 Ag 23 '40 il

Time 36:80-1 O 21 '40 por

Flanner, J. An American in Paris 1940

Flanner, J. Comet *In* New Yorker (periodical). Profiles from the New Yorker p239-46 1938

SCHOONMAKER, EDWIN DAVIES Feb 1, 1873—May 4, 1940 Author; lecturer; member United States mission to Russia 1918; author of books on world affairs; advocate of neutrality

References

Who's Who Among North American Authors

Who's Who in America

Obituaries

N Y Times p17 My 6 '40

SCHRATT, KATHARINA 1856—Apr 17, 1940 For 30 years mistress and confidante of Emperor Francis Joseph; called "uncrowned queen of Austria"; former actress; offered large sums for her memoirs by publishers but refused out of loyalty to the Emperor

Camera Features

KATHARINA SCHRATT

References

Lit Digest 116:13 O 28 '33 por

Obituaries

    N Y Herald Tribune p16 Ap 19 '40 pors
    N Y World-Telegram p1, 2 Ap 18 '40 por
    Newsweek 50:27 Ap 29 '40 por
    Time 35:29-30 Ap 29 '40 por

SCOTT, ARTHUR CARROLL July 12, 1865—Oct 27, 1940 Physician; specialist in diagnosis and treatment of cancer, especially known for his use of the hot (cautery) knife in the removal of cancer and his development of the "shadow" test in the diagnosis of cancer of the breast; pioneer in use of gas anesthesia; since 1904 president and senior surgeon of Scott and White Hospital in Temple, Texas; for many years a member of the board of governors of the American College of Surgeons and president, in 1929, of the Southern Surgical Association

References

    American Medical Directory
    Who's Who in America

Obituaries

    N Y Herald Tribune p10 O 28 '40
    N Y Times p17 O 28 '40

SCUDDER, JANET Oct 27, 1873—June 9, 1940 American sculptor; lived in Paris for 45 years; one of the world's foremost women sculptors; noted for fountain groups containing children; works shown in 14 museums; also noted as a painter and author

William Grimm

JANET SCUDDER

References

    American Women
    Kirkland, W. M. and Kirkland, F. Janet Scudder, a Girl Who Made

Her Own Name *In* Girls Who Became Artists p86-97 1934
McSpadden, J. W. Women Sculptors of Note *In* Famous Sculptors of America p329-68 1924
Scudder, J. Janet Scudder [from her Modeling My Life] *In* Ferris, H. J. comp. When I Was a Girl p74-133 1930
Scudder, J. Modeling My Life 1925
Who's Who Among North American Authors
Who's Who in America
Who's Who in American Art

Obituaries

    N Y Herald Tribune p22 Je 11 '40 por
    N Y Times p25 Je 11 '40 por

SEABROOK, WILLIAM Feb 22, 1886- Author

Address: b. c/o Harcourt, Brace & Co, 383 Madison Ave, New York City; h. Rhinebeck, New York

Like the man who didn't believe in ghosts but was afraid of them just the same, William Buehler Seabrook, whose tales of adventure in strange lands have been filled with investigations of the supernatural, goes on to discover (and debunk, maybe) vampires, werewolves, doll-image making and other diabolical doings right on our own civilized doorsteps. Of *Witchcraft: Its Power in the World Today* (September 1940) Seabrook solemnly says in his foreword that he is addressing the book to "rational people" only. "While witchcraft is not demoniac, it is a specific, real and dangerous force, evil when used for evil, mysterious in some of its manifestations, but always analyzable, always understandable within the bounds of reason, and combatable in consequence like crime, snake bite, insanity and yellow fever." He emphasizes the fact that witchcraft is successful only (like the induced auto-suggestion known to psychiatric science) provided the victim himself knows that he is being worked upon.

In the Ozarks, in Southern France, in Pennsylvania hexings, even in modern social and intellectual circles, doll-images of people have been made, pierced with pins in vital spots, and sure enough the victim—informed by supposed friends of what is being done to his image—gets terrible pains and wastes away. Unless, of course, the doll is found and destroyed. In Brooklyn there was a girl who had read all about vampires and knew, because of her uncontrollable craving for blood, that she was one. (It turns out that she suffered from pernicious anemia.) In Washington Square at a party, another girl (a Russian refugee "addicted to occult escape mechanisms") stared at a Chinese magic hexagram and went through the "slit in time" to imagine herself a wolf. A girl named Justine could hang by her wrists till her mind slipped into the future:

WILLIAM SEABROOK

once she saw a misbehaving lion in a circus in Avignon. Six months later she and Seabrook happened to be in Avignon: there was the circus, and there was the same anti-social lion behaving just as Justine had foreseen. The trouble with Justine (as with many other clairvoyants) was that she never foresaw anything she might turn a profitable penny on. "One person possessed of telepathic or clairvoyant power and capable of using it could make world history for good or evil, wreck all the stock markets in less than a week, smash governments"—and, presumably, do something about Hitler.

William Seabrook was born at Westminster, Maryland on Washington's birthday, 1886, son of William Levin and Myra Phelps (Buehler) Seabrook. Environment scarcely explains why a boy whose father was a Lutheran minister and who grew up in ordinary small American South and Midwest towns should become a traveler in strange lands and in the realms of the occult. Seabrook thinks heredity had something to do with it. "There was bad blood in me," he says in the book on witchcraft, "from the angle of magic, and it came, mandragora-like, from the best roots of my family. My only distinguished ancestor was a great-great-grandfather on the maternal side, Peter Boehler, a bishop of the Moravian Church." He was a missionary who worked among the Indians, the Negroes, etc. Family tradition had it that "he was up to his ears in black magic." Once church leaders nearly had him deposed; his defense was that he dabbled in magic in order "to fight the Devil with his own fire." From his nursery days Seabrook remembers hair-raising tales of this ancestor. He was also brought up on ghost-stories told him by a South Carolina nurse.

He was educated at academies in Pennsylvania and Virginia and in 1906 received his M. A. degree from Newberry College, South Carolina. He then got a job on the Augusta, Georgia *Chronicle* as a cub reporter. In 1908 he went to Switzerland and studied philosophy and metaphysics at the University of Geneva. After traveling in Europe for two years he returned to Atlanta, Georgia to operate an advertising agency. In 1912 he married Katherine Pauline Edmondson. Then the War broke out; he enrolled as a private in the French Army, was gassed at Verdun. He began his writing career as a reporter for the New York *Times*; encouraged by H. L. Mencken, for seven years thereafter he was a special feature writer for newspaper syndication.

In 1924 Seabrook and his wife went to Arabia. His first book, *Adventures in Arabia* (1927), was about their experiences among the Bedouins, Whirling Dervishes, etc. A visit to the Haitian voodoo country produced *The Magic Island* (1929). In 1931 came *Jungle Ways,* best remembered for Seabrook's description of a cannibal barbecue (recipes furnished). "The meat," he said, "tasted like good, fully developed veal." *Air Adventure* (1933) concerned a trip by plane from Paris to Timbuctoo. There he found Père Yakouba, whose life story was recounted in *The White Monk of Timbuctoo* (1934).

About this time Seabrook became a heavy drinker, needing one or two quarts of liquor a day. He got into such a bad physical and mental state that he entered an institution in Westchester County, New York, where he took a six months' cure. The frank account of what he underwent there, published in *Asylum* (1935) brought him more publicity than any other of his books. After its publication Seabrook received hundreds of letters from drunkards or their families asking about the institution. A further book followed his return to sobriety, *These Foreigners* (1938), sound studies of five immigrant groups in the United States and their contributions to American culture.

Seabrook and his first wife were divorced in 1934; in 1935 he married Marjorie Muir Worthington. (His first wife in turn married Mrs. Worthington's former husband, Lyman Worthington.) Marjorie Worthington is a successful popular novelist; a tall, strikingly handsome brunette who likes best to live in the country, where she can wear slacks and work among her flowers. Her husband ("Willie" to his many friends and Westchester County neighbors) is big and hearty, with a thick thatch of brown hair and warm blue eyes, fond of good talk and good food. They have an eight-acre farm near Rhinebeck, New York. Marjorie Seabrook has taken over the furnishing of the attractive farmhouse, and Seabrook himself has successfully converted the barn on the place into a handsome studio. There is a big, combined living and dining room; an upstairs study decorated with trophies from his many travels: rare rugs, Arabian guns and swords; and all kinds of African handicraft, including a remarkable assortment of devil masks.

References

Am Mag 122:54-5+ Jl '36 pors
N Y World-Telegram p23 S 5 '40
Newsweek 16:56 S 9 '40
Wilson Lib Bul 10:440 Mr '36 por
Bridges, T. C. and Tiltman, H. H. In the Heart of the Desert *In* More Heroes of Modern Adventure p173-87 1930
Seabrook, W. B. Asylum 1935
Who's Who Among North American Authors
Who's Who in America

SEGER, GEORGE N. Jan 4, 1866—Aug 26, 1940 Republican member of the House of Representatives since 1923; dean of the New Jersey delegation; Mayor of Passaic, New Jersey in 1911, serving two terms; known in Congress as an opponent of President Roosevelt's Supreme Court and government reorganization bills

References

Who's Who in America
Who's Who in the Nation's Capital

Obituaries

N Y Herald Tribune p14 Ag 27 '40 por
N Y Times p21 Ag 27 '40 por

SEMON, WALDO LONSBURY (sē-mŭn) Sept 10, 1898- Chemist
Address: c/o Goodrich Rubber Company, Akron, Ohio

On July 31, 1940 the B. F. Goodrich Company and the Phillips Petroleum Company announced the formation of the Hydrocarbon Chemical and Rubber Company for the production of synthetic rubber, the Phillips Company to provide the petroleum and the Goodrich Company the skill and experience in manufacturing.

Actually most of the credit for this skill and experience must go to Dr. Waldo Lonsbury Semon, inventor of *Ameripol* and head of chemical research for B. F. Goodrich. His synthetic rubber is the outgrowth of years of experimentation and the culmination of continual application and tireless effort.

The manufacture of American synthetic rubber is well timed. With war in progress and international trade stagnant, we need our own rubber to manufacture our own tires, insulate our own wires, chew our own gum. Yet the manufacture of synthetic rubber is not an American idea. It was begun by Germany during the last War. Isolated, it was impossible for her to buy any rubber products, and her ingenious chemists and research scientists set to work to devise a synthetic rubber (*Buna*) strong

WALDO SEMON

enough to make serviceable tires for automobiles and airplanes. Other attempts at synthetic rubber were made by the Du Ponts and by the Russians, who call theirs *Sovprene*. *Ameripol*, however, is the newest and most refined of the synthetic rubbers.

When Dr. Semon, whose discoveries eventually led to *Ameripol*, started out in 1928 his only aim was to preserve rubber. By 1932 he had learned to use those materials that made his later work more simple, and from July to December of 1933 he focused his attention on one single method of preserving rubber, part of which he discarded, part of which he extended into further research.

In August 1934 he found, finally, that he was able to retard the aging process of rubber and increase the resistance to the formation of cracks upon flexing. A month later he produced his first synthetic rubber-like composition. A group of organic substances were combined at a high temperature, treated to form a stiff resistant gel and then cooled. The result was an excellent insulator, capable of resisting high voltage and corrosion. Not only had Dr. Semon found the nucleus of his future work but with each experiment the process had grown simpler and the idea more clarified.

On December 11, 1935 Dr. Semon discovered *Koroseal*, made from salt, coke and limestone. It is usually classed as a plastic, even though it is a rubbery synthetic, and though it cannot be vulcanized, it can be made in any consistency from jelly-soft to bone-hard. Resistant to nitric and hydrofluoric acids, it makes good linings for pickling tanks. It also goes into beer pipes, gaskets, waterproof fabrics, fabrics for holding parts to be coated in chromium plating baths.

SEMON, WALDO—*Continued*

After four years of experimentation, after four years of searching and after making more than 5,000 synthetic rubbers, Dr. Semon compounded *Ameripol*. Its basic raw material is petroleum and other materials in it are gas, air and soap. Scientifically, the complex petroleum unit is broken into a mixture of simple molecules from which is extracted a gas which, under pressure, produces the basis of *Ameripol*. This is again mixed with other ingredients prepared from natural gas and air, and then this resultant combination is made into a milky emulsion, using soap. Again an agitation process and the ingredients react to form an emulsion of synthetic rubber.

The Goodrich Company announced *Ameripol* in June 1940 and in July 1940 *Ameripol* tires were put on the market, priced at $5 higher than rubber tires. It was claimed that they would wear as long as natural tires while being more resistant to heat, aging and sunlight. According to Dr. Semon, *Ameripol*, not only in tires but in other products, "in many of its important properties is equal or superior to natural rubber." A factory with a production capacity of several tons of *Ameripol* daily is under construction in late 1940.

Waldo Semon was born at Demopolis, Alabama. His father, Frank Emerson Semon, was a civil engineer who built the town's light and power plant and whose profession kept his family on the move. It wasn't until Waldo was seven that the Semons settled down for a while. Then Mr. Semon took a position in the city engineering office in Seattle, Washington and Waldo was able to get through the sixth grade before the next jump—to Medford, Oregon, where he finished grade school and started high school. Then on to Ashland, Oregon and Eugene, Oregon, and finally back to Seattle, where Waldo finished high school.

All this time Waldo had been working summers, picking strawberries, prunes and hops in the Northwest; working as a water boy on a construction project; digging ditches; even working with a surveying crew. When he got out of high school he continued to work, mostly for the state highway commission. But he quit this to enter the University of Washington in 1916. Here he majored in chemistry, spent one summer working for the United States Geological Survey, another helping build a spur of the Milwaukee railroad and analyzing inks for code messages for the United States Intelligence Service. He was graduated with honors in 1920.

Immediately he married Marjorie Gunn, whom he had known since freshman chemistry. The two of them settled down at the University of Washington. Semon studied for his doctorate while teaching and Mrs. Semon tutored would-be chemists. Dr. Semon also acted as consulting chemist to private industry and published several technical papers. It was in 1926, three years after he received his doctorate, that the Goodrich Company asked him to join its department of chemical research. Without any fanfare Dr. Semon piled his family into a wheezing second-hand car, climbed behind the wheel and headed Eastward. He reached Akron in 16 days and has stayed there ever since.

Six-foot-two, Dr. Semon has the physique of a lumberjack and uses it to good advantage swimming and boating. This doesn't happen often, however. Mostly he spends hours in the laboratory over his test tubes and beakers—long hours without a break, away from his wife and three daughters. And Sundays he conducts a class at the First Congregational Church in Cuyahoga Falls, Ohio.

References

> Harper 181:362-9 S '40
> N Y Times p24, p27 Je 6 '40; X p24 Je 16 '40
> Newsweek 15:64-5 Je 17 '40 por
> Time 35:50-1 Je 17 '40; 36:34 Jl 29 '40
>
> American Men of Science

SENARENS, LUIS PHILIP Apr 24, 1863 —Dec 26, 1939 Author; creator of the famous character, Frank Reade; called the Jules Verne of the dime novel; used "Noname" as pseudonym

Obituaries

> N Y Herald Tribune D 28 '39
> Newsweek 15:5 Ja 8 '40
> Pub W 137:789 F 17 '40

SEREDY, KATE (shĕr'ĕ-dē) Author; artist

Address: c/o Viking Press, 18 E 48th St, New York City

One of the most popular author-illustrators of children's books is Kate Seredy, who won the Newbery Medal in 1938 with *The White Stag*. Her latest book is *The Singing Tree* (1939), and she has since done the illustrations for other children's books, and one translation from the Hungarian, *Who Is Johnny?*, by Leopold Gedö (1939).

Kate Seredy was born in Hungary, and grew up in Budapest and the surrounding country. She was well-known for her illustrations before she began writing books. She says: "I started to draw for children as soon as I was old enough to go to school. These first drawings were highly successful as far as my classmates were concerned, but my teachers didn't think much of them. Perhaps because they were not very flattering portraits!" After high school she went to the Academy of Arts in Budapest and studied during summer vacations in Italy, France and Germany. When the War broke out she became a nurse and her experiences made her a confirmed pacifist.

KATE SEREDY

On coming to America in 1922, she already had a number of children's books to her credit. But she couldn't speak English—and that handicapped her for some time. Nevertheless she learned, in 12 years, to speak and write English so well that she wrote *The Good Master* (1935), a lasting favorite with boys and girls. This was followed by *Listening*, the story of her house in the Ramapo Mountains of New Jersey. In 1937 came *The White Stag*, the Newbery Prize winner. In connection with this book Miss Seredy feels that she owes much to her father, and pays him warm tribute. He was a man beloved by the neighborhood children: he collected the carvings and paintings of the countryside, and he told stories that taught young people how to think, how to live. His favorite story was that of the White Stag, one of the great legends of mankind. It is a tale of the legendary founding of Hungary, particularly of the hero Attila who, guided by the White Stag and the Red Eagle, led his people to their promised land.

The Singing Tree is a sequel to *The Good Master*. It covers the era 1914 to 1918, when Hungary, like the rest of Europe, was surrounded by the horror of warfare. The mischievous children of the previous book have grown older. Jancsi, now the Young Master, and Kate, no longer a tomboy, share the solace of their farm with Russian prisoners and German war orphans. The whole doctrine of the story is the world's need for tolerance and peace.

Miss Seredy has a farm of her own. She loves animals, gardens and making things for herself, such as clothes, furniture and pottery. She likes playing the piano and chasing hunters away when they intrude on her land. She hates caterpillars with the exception of a caterpillar tractor. Her tractor is named Attila because it has a one-track mind and mows down everything in its path. Attila does every job on the farm, aided by Ferdinand, a docile and very powerful disc-harrow.

References

El Engl R 15:217-20 O '38
Horn Book Jl '35
Library J 63:488-9 Je 15 '38 il por
Pub W 133:2355-6 Je 18 '38

SERKIN, RUDOLF Mar 28, 1903- Pianist and composer
Address: National Broadcasting System Artists' Service, RCA Building, New York City

Rudolf Serkin took American music-lovers by storm when he made his first United States appearance in 1935. Since that first concert Serkin has been rated one of the finest pianists of today. On June 20 he inaugurated the 1940 Lewisohn Stadium Concerts under the baton of Arturo Rodzinski (see sketch this issue), and was slated to play several concerts during the summer and autumn.

Rudolf Serkin was born in Eger, Bohemia, of Russian-Jewish parents. At four he could play the piano creditably and was able to read music with facility. On the advice of the celebrated Viennese pianist, Alfred Gruenfeld, his parents placed him under the tutelage of Professor Richard Robert in Vienna. At that time his parents were so poor that they had only one room for themselves and eight children. There, in the din and clatter, Rudolf learned to play, and at 12 made his debut as guest artist with the Vienna Symphony Orchestra.

Though he achieved great success and was offered a long tour by enthusiastic managers, his teacher and parents decided that he was still too young to undertake anything so strenuous. For several years he continued his studies, rounding out his technical knowledge of music by studying composition under Arnold Schönberg. When he finally inaugurated his career he established himself quickly as an important artist, giving concerts in France, Switzerland, Italy, Spain and Austria.

Herbert F. Peyser, writing in Berlin for the New York *Times* in 1931 made the comment that "Mr. Serkin is not a sensational pianist, though he can storm the clouds and summon the mellowest of thunders and dazzle like the best of them in the sheer resplendence of mechanics." He added: "a tall, gangling, bespectacled young man of 25 to 30, suggesting in his general appearance a somewhat overgrown high-school student, his demeanor at the keyboard is, on the whole, tranquil and unmannered." His playing, in its limpid and subtle loveliness, called to mind the famous Gieseking.

In 1935 Serkin appeared in the United States for the first time with Adolf Busch, the violinist, at the Coolidge Festival in Wash-

RUDOLF SERKIN

ington. When he made his American debut the following winter as soloist under the baton of Arturo Toscanini, conductor of the New York Philharmonic Symphony Orchestra, Leonard Liebling called "an artist of unusual and impressive talents in possession of a crystalline technique, plenty of power, delicacy, and tone pure and full." Not to be outdone, Olin Downes claimed that he was "a masterly musician . . . a scholar and a profound one, without pedantry, with the loftiest conception of beauty, whose every thought and emotion is for the glory of his art."

In 1937 he gave his first New York recital in Carnegie Hall, and Downes described him as: "a curious figure on the platform, because of his slightness and the fact that he is not tall, and the nervous intensity of his walk to the piano, and his fantastical intentness on the work in hand. . . He played significantly, always with a magnificent control and with a sovereign sense of form. Richness and complexity of detail never distracted him from issues, but only added to the richness of the effect, and in lyrical passages his tone was lovely in color, in nuance, in capacity to carry, even when the key was barely pressed down by the finger."

In 1937 Serkin, appearing with the National Orchestral Association under the direction of Leon Barzin, received the following comment from the well-known critic, Jerome D. Bohm: "His treatment of the music was perfectly proportioned, teeming with sensitively applied nuances, and invested with unceasing tonal loveliness and astonishing technical finish."

Since his first appearance in this country with Adolf Busch, Serkin has played several series in concert with the German violinist. As a matter of fact, so closely

attached did they become musically, that Serkin stepped forward to tighten the bond by marrying Busch's daughter in 1936.

References

Musician 41:57 Mr '36 por
Springf'd Repub E p6 Mr 3 '40
Time 28:22 D 28 '36 por

Thompson, O. ed. International Cyclopedia of Music and Musicians 1939
Wier, A. E. ed. Macmillan Encyclopedia of Music and Musicians 1938

SERRANO SUNER, RAMON (sĕr-rä'nō sōōn'yâr) 1901- Spanish Foreign Minister; head of Falange Española Tradicionalista

Address: b. Madrid, Spain; h. Saragossa, San Clemente 25, Spain

That Spain had definitely hitched its wagon to the Axis star became apparent on October 18, 1940 when Ramón Serrano Suñer, brother-in-law of Generalissimo Franco, succeeded Colonel Juan Beigbeder as Foreign Minister. Franco himself took over the Ministry of the Interior which Serrano Suñer had held since 1939, but it was significant that the staff of the Ministry remained unchanged under the same Under-Secretary that Serrano Suñer had. Possibly Serrano Suñer is in late 1940 running foreign affairs in person and the Interior through his former assistant. Upon assuming office he declared that his appointment meant Spain's acceptance of the "New Order" in Europe and that Spain "must not lose a single moment" in coming to grips with world affairs. Since then he has admittedly discussed with Hitler Spain's possible territorial gains if it should join the Axis.

Serrano Suñer's appointment is the culmination of great activity on his part. In September he went to Germany to confer with Von Ribbentrop and then on to Rome, where he made headlines by snubbing the Vatican and exchanged greetings with his good friend Ciano (see sketch this issue) after the latest Brenner conference.

The New York *Times* has called Serrano Suñer "Spain's second most prominent figure," but there is reason to believe that, although content to stay in the background, he is Spain's most powerful figure, without any qualifications. It has been often and openly stated that Ramón Serrano Suñer is Spain's real ruler, the power behind the throne occupied by his more publicized brother-in-law, Generalissimo Francesco Franco.

Before Señor Serrano Suñer became Foreign Minister he held the post of Minister of the Interior. This post also included the Ministry of Communications and gave him full control of the post office, telephone, telegraph and cable systems. As Minister of Press and Propaganda, he had the absolute say over what the Spanish people read or hear. He still is the president of the *Junta Politica* of the Falange Española Tradicionalista and has in his hands the control of Spain's

sole political party with its membership of
2,000,000, not counting the auxiliary organizations. No wonder then that there has
grown up around him a legend of omnis-
cience and omnipotence that has a sinister
flavor.

El Cuñadissimo—the "brother-in-law-issimo,"
as the Spaniards call him—has always had
much to say about Spain's foreign policy. He
has always favored close ties with Italy and
Germany, hated France and scoffed at England's "countinghouse diplomacy." He is an
ardent admirer of Hitler and Mussolini and he
is a good friend of Count Ciano (see sketch
this issue). In 1939, on the occasion of
celebrating the third anniversary of the
Rightist Rebellion, he claimed that Gibraltar would soon be returned to Spain—a
statement that found echo in Franco's public demand in 1940 that England give up The
Rock.

Like so many present-day key-men in the
destinies of Europe, Ramón Serrano Suñer,
whom *Time* has called "the fastest climbing
of Europe's modern politicos," comes from
rather humble origin and was generally unknown before swiftly moving events brought
him to the top. Before the Civil War broke
out he was an obscure lawyer. Probably
the most significant thing he did at that
time, from the point of view of his career,
was to marry the handsome Señorita Zita
Polo, sister of Franco's wife, and so obtain
a vital stake in Franco's fortunes. Another
important relationship was his close friendship with José Antonio Primo de Rivera,
son of the erstwhile Spanish dictator and
founder of the Falangist movement.

Serrano Suñer was born in 1901 in Saragossa. He studied law in the Italian universities—in Rome and in the famous University of Bologna. There he obtained his
admiration for Fascism as a philosophy and
a practical method of wielding power. Upon
coming back to Spain he practiced law in
Saragossa, obtained a certain amount of
recognition as a good lawyer and held a few
minor judicial posts.

In 1933 he went to the Cortes as the
deputy of the Catholic Party from Saragossa. He was still in Madrid when the
death of General Sanjurjo placed his
brother-in-law at the head of the rebellion.
He was taken into custody in 1936 and held
in one of Madrid's "model prisons," from
which he managed to escape in 1937 in a
rather picturesque way: he disguised himself as an Argentine sailor and was able to
board an Argentine ship unrecognized.
Then he made his way to Burgos, where
Franco was entrenched.

Once in Burgos he began his climb to
power. He was given the portfolio of the
Ministry for Press and Propaganda and
instituted strict censorship in Franco-owned
territory. He was sent on a good-will trip
to Germany, where he got an enthusiastic
reception, attended the 1937 Nuremberg
Nazi Congress and met Hitler. He came

European

RAMON SERRANO SUNER

back to Spain full of admiration for the
Nazi efficiency and was soon given a chance
to try out Nazi methods as Minister of the
Interior. At the same time Franco made
him Governor of Valladolid.

Señor Serrano Suñer's work was done
mainly behind the lines. While Franco
fought his way to the domination of Spain,
he, as an expert on national administrative
matters, was charged with the task of keeping order in the rebel-owned territory.
Much of his attention was given to organizing and strengthening the Falange, in
which all of Spain's heterogeneous Rightist
elements, from Fascists to Carlists, were
gradually fused. This party was later to
serve him as a bulwark in his struggle with
the military diehards who were campaigning with Franco and who held for him a
soldier's characteristic mistrust for the administrator.

As Franco's forces cut deeper into the
Republican territory, forcing the desper-
ately-fighting Loyalists to give up one city
after another, Señor Serrano Suñer's functions began to assume a grimly paradoxical
character: his was the task of eradicating
the Leftist elements of the population—
which he did with grisly efficiency, the
number of executions mounting into thousands—and feeding the rest. In September
1938, after the Civil War was over, he embarked on the gigantic task of reconstruction which today, after a year and a half,
has made hardly a dent on the general situation. He organized the Auxilio Social
(originally called the Winter Aid after the
similar German organization—another sign
of German influence), a nationwide social
service supported by a sales tax; enforced
government-fixed prices; established a distribution of free milk and set up govern-

SERRANO SUNER, RAMON—*Cont.*

ment-financed orphanages to take care of children left alone and destitute by the War.

The height of his personal triumph came in June 1939, when he, together with a retinue of Spanish generals, accompanied the Italian "volunteers" back to Rome. He was a huge social success, completely overshadowing the rest of his compatriots; also he cemented his friendship with Count Galeazzo Ciano, another "in-law" significant in European politics. His return to Spain marked an important crisis in his political life. Reports had been current that Franco was seriously contemplating making his brother-in-law Premier. But in August this step was forestalled by a near insurrection among the ranks of the blunt old-guard army leaders who detested Serrano Suñer.

Here the soft-spoken Minister showed his claws: one after another his opponents—Juan Yagüe, the bibulous Queipo de Llano, the popular Miguel Aranda—were relieved of their commands. Then followed a series of decrees that sapped the power of the opposition and strengthened Serrano Suñer's position to that of a virtual dictator, as well as marked the Falange's victory over the older aristocratic military clique. Serrano Suñer suspended all public meetings, forbade all gatherings except with his written permission, speeded up the reorganization of the army by recalling the demobilized officers.

Serrano Suñer's name for the system under which Spain is ruled is syndical nationalism. The syndicates which he has set up are reminiscent of the Labor Front in Germany in their complete subjection to the state. His totalitarian attitude includes business: he is as hard on the intransigent businessmen clinging to the idea of individual enterprise as Hitler. Reminiscent of Germany and Italy, too, is the all-pervasive character of the Falange, the sole political party: every village has some sort of an organization connected with the Falange, such as *Prensa y Propaganda, Informationes y Investigationes.* And the supreme authority is vested in the 20 members of the *Junta Politica* headed by Serrano Suñer himself.

One of the reasons why the all-powerful Serrano Suñer was content to stay in the background is his lack of popularity. Franco is much more appealing, a bluff and hearty soldier. Serrano Suñer is distant and forbidding in his manner, although he can be very charming when it is necessary. He has been described spitefully as "that pulpy olive fashioned in the likeness of man." That is unfair: his appearance in his austere black Falange uniform is impressive although somewhat Mephistophelian. His face, beneath its cap of graying hair, is narrow, ascetic and worried, his eyes are rather hard. He is hard-working, tenacious and ambitious. Little is known of his personal life, except that he has six children.

That his rôle in their country's destiny is well realized by his countrymen is evidenced by the amount of the brother-in-law jokes going the rounds in Spain. Here is one told toward the end of the Civil War:

Franco goes to heaven and is stopped at the gate by St. Peter who asks him his name.

Franco: "I am Franco."
St. Peter: "Never heard of you."
Franco: "El Caudillo."
St. Peter: " Never heard of him."
Franco (in despair): "The brother-in-law of Serrano Suñer."

St. Peter: "Oh, come right in! Why didn't you say in the first place that you were a friend of his?"

References

> Liv Age 357:49 S '39
> Newsweek 14:21 Ag 7 '39 por
> R Deux Mondes s8 57:442-7 Je 1 '40
> Scholastic 34:8 Mr 18 '39 por
> Time 33:15 F 6 '39; 34:19 Jl 31 '39 por; 36:24+ Ag 19 '40 por
> International Who's Who

SEVIER, HENRY HULME (sĕ-vēr') Mar 16, 1878—Mar 10, 1940 United States Ambassador to Chile 1933 to 1936; member of Texas House of Representatives 1902 to 1906; first president, Austin, Texas Public Library Association

References

> Who's Who in America 1936-37

Obituaries

> N Y Herald Tribune p12 Mr 11 '40
> N Y Sun p19 Mr 11 '40

SHAMBAUGH, BENJAMIN FRANKLIN Jan 29, 1871—Apr 7, 1940 Head of the political science department of the

BENJAMIN F. SHAMBAUGH

University of Iowa; eminent historian; president of the Political Science Association

References

Who's Who in America
Who's Who in American Education

Obituaries

N Y Herald Tribune p12 Ap 8 '40
Time 35:38 Ap 22 '40 por

SHARP, HARRY CLAY 1871—Oct 31, 1940 Chief medical officer of the United States Veterans' Administration Hospital at Lyons, New Jersey; nationally known expert on institutional medicine and one of the first doctors to advocate sterilization of defectives and degenerates; during First World War was head of surgical operating unit of the Army Medical Corps in France and after brief period of private practice became a surgeon of the United States Public Health Service

HARRY CLAY SHARP

References

American Medical Directory

Obituaries

N Y Herald Tribune p18 N 1 '40
N Y Times p25 N 1 '40

SHAW, LOUIS AGASSIZ Sept 25, 1886— Aug 27, 1940 Assistant professor at the Harvard University School of Public Health; co-inventor of the Drinker respirator used in the treatment of infantile paralysis and respiratory failure; considered one of the nation's leading authorities on compressed-air illness, or "the bends"; in 1931 awarded the John Scott Medal (with co-inventor Dr. Philip Drinker of Harvard)

for the Drinker respirator, which was the discovery "most conducive to the comfort, welfare and happiness of mankind"

References

American Men of Science

Obituaries

N Y Herald Tribune p22 Ag 28 '40
N Y Times p19 Ag 28 '40

SHERMAN, FREDERIC FAIRCHILD 1874—Oct 23, 1940 Writer on art and artists; publisher of the quarterly, *Art in America,* and of many books and pamphlets on art; wrote, among other works, *Early American Painting* and *Landscape and Figure Painters of America;* as collector specialized in paintings of Ryder; was dealer on a small scale

Obituaries

N Y Times p21 O 25 '40

SHERWOOD, ROBERT Apr 4, 1896- Dramatist; author

Address: 630 Fifth Ave, New York City

There Shall Be No Night, Robert Sherwood's latest play, opened in New York on April 29, 1940. "Writing with tremendous sincerity, burning indignation and occasional high eloquence, Mr. Sherwood says in it that unless the rest of the world unites in arms against Fascism, we are all headed back to the Dark Ages." Immediately a stir was created. The *Daily Worker* assailed him as the stooge of the imperialist war mongers; a group of "Christian Frontists" accused him of following the Communist line; Raymond Clapper (see sketch this issue), writing in the New York *World-Telegram,* stated: "This play, depicting the tragedy of Finland, seemed to me a rank inflammatory job, pleading for intervention, sneering at our reluctance to go in"; the Boston *Transcript* said that Sherwood's conclusion that this War were better fought to a conclusion by men with no illusions of patriotic glory, in whose minds "there shall be no night," is more than a brave statement. "It seems the only one in which there is any hope at all. . ."

Sherwood himself, in answer to those who claim that he has dealt the case for American neutrality a "nasty uppercut," says: "There's a frightful conspiracy of silence that's turning Washington into an orgy of unreality. . . It's a 'peace hysteria' clouding all attempts at intelligent thought about the War. Congress is one mass of Chamberlains. The United States is in exactly the same ostrich-escapism as England up to the insanity of Munich."

On Christmas Day 1939 Robert Sherwood listened to a broadcast from Finland by William L. White, American newspaper correspondent, called *Christmas in the Mannerheim Line.* Out of that broadcast came the idea for his play. For 20 days he turned the idea over in his mind and on January 15

S. J. Woolf

ROBERT SHERWOOD

he started writing. In 26 days the play was completed. He sent it to the Lunts. They read it on the train on their way to Wisconsin. Lynn Fontanne tells it thus: "We had planned, Alfred and I, to rest for the summer. . . At Harrisburg I wired Mr. Sherwood: 'This half of the combination returns in two weeks for rehearsals.' At Chicago Mr. Lunt sent a telegram: 'So does this half.'"

The chief character of *There Shall Be No Night,* played by Alfred Lunt, is an eminent Finnish neurologist who has just received the Nobel Prize for research into the causes of mental diseases. Being a free man intellectually, he does not believe in war. It is stupid, reactionary, weak minded. Thoroughly absorbed in research, Dr. Kaarlo Valkonen postpones thinking about the possibilities of Russia's invading his native land. But the Russian invasion does come, and Finnish freedom is shattered. The doctor's son goes to battle and is lost. The doctor himself is forced to lay down the ideals of the physician and take up the gun in defense of Viipuri.

Of the impact of *There Shall Be No Night* all critics are agreed. Richard Watts Jr., says: "It is not a tidy or consistent play. Yet it is a play of stature, dignity and high emotion, thoughtful, eloquent and heartfelt." Brooks Atkinson says: "As a play, *There Shall Be No Night* is not a masterpiece; it has a shiftless second act and less continuity of story than one likes to see" . . . but although it is uneven drama, "it honors the theatre and the best parts of it speak for the truth with enkindling faith and passionate conviction." He says, too, that in it is "some of the best prose writing in the modern theatre," although Wolcott Gibbs, writing in the *New Yorker,* feels that "too often the message, in the form of nearly interminable monologues by Mr. Lunt, brings the

action to a standstill, and much too often Mr. Sherwood's deep feeling betrays him into the kind of prose that sets a Hearst editorial apart from any other writing in the world."

Robert Sherwood, who was gassed and wounded in the First World War and spent many months in a hospital, has written of war before. *Waterloo Bridge* (1930) (in May 1940 released as a motion picture) was a play about the last War, showing what it was like through the characters of two Americans, a stranded chorus girl and a young soldier from Syracuse who enlisted with the Canadians. *Idiot's Delight* (1936), which won him his first Pulitzer Prize, told of the war that looms ahead, an international devastating war that is to bring the structure of the world tumbling down around our heads. Indeed, it has been said that "Sherwood seems never to have been able consciously or subconsciously to forget the War. . . The terror and the stupidity, the brutality and waste of those days and the disillusion that followed them remain constantly with him, in one way or another showing through everything of importance that he has written."

Robert Emmet Sherwood (he does not use his middle name) was born in New Rochelle, New York, on April 4, 1896, the son of Arthur Murray and Rosina (Emmet) Sherwood. He left New Rochelle at the age of two "because my parents, who had the upper hand of me at the time, decided that I should be moved." Before he was out of short pants, Robert was writing. At seven he edited for a year a magazine called *Children's Life;* at eight he had planned a revision of *A Tale of Two Cities;* and by the time he was ten his first play, *Tom Ruggles' Surprise,* had been written.

He attended Milton Academy in Massachusetts and then went to Harvard in 1914, where he did such a good job editing the "Vanity Fair" number of the *Harvard Lampoon* that he was offered the position of movie critic on the real *Vanity Fair* magazine when he returned from service in France. He went there in 1917 with the 42nd Battalion, Black Watch, of the Canadian Expeditionary Force after he had been rejected by virtually every branch of the American service because of his unusual height.

He started working on *Vanity Fair* when he returned from the War in 1919 and stayed there until he became associate editor of the old *Life* in 1920. In 1924 he became editor of *Life* as well as its motion picture editor, and stayed there until 1928. It has been said that because of his movie reviews for *Life* he "may justly be called the founder of American film criticism. Until he began paying the movies the compliment of treating them as an art form . . . film reviews had been merely publicity blurbs of reporters' paragraphs recounting the plot." It was while he was at *Life* that Sherwood was first married, on October 29, 1922, to Mary Brandon of Indianapolis. His daughter, Mary, was born of this marriage. He was married a second time, in 1935, to Madeline Hurlock.

While he was at *Life,* Sherwood was also literary editor of *Scribner's Magazine* and motion picture editor of the New York *Herald.* His first play hit, *The Road to Rome,* was produced in 1927 by the Theatre Guild. Its story is that of Hannibal, who saw the gates of Rome but didn't shatter them, who met tribulations with elephants and women. This was considered a most actable comedy, as proved by its long and successful run. Next came *Love Nest,* an unsuccessful dramatization of a Ring Lardner story.

The Queen's Husband (1928) was a burlesque on a member of European royalty, given point by the visit of Queen Marie. *This Is New York* (1930) has been called "a banal and negligible melodrama with vigorous dialogue and a gangster-Park Avenue plot." *Waterloo Bridge,* about the First World War, followed in 1930, and in 1931 came *Reunion in Vienna,* which was a great success both as a play and as a movie, a "mad slapstick comedy with undertones of philosophy concerning the final contest between the old and the new order." In 1931, too, Sherwood wrote *The Virtuous Knight,* his only novel.

In 1934 appeared *The Petrified Forest,* "with one of the best first acts Sherwood has ever written," a play dealing with problems raised by the depression. In 1936 *Idiot's Delight* was produced—"successful melodrama with a strong after-taste of ideas that are worth expressing." *Idiot's Delight,* unlike *There Shall Be No Night,* takes a purely personal interest in its people and only glances sidelong at war itself as one of mankind's fantastic and sinister follies whose action may begin "in any imminent year." "But the sidelong glances are penetrating, the impression is vivid, the effect is sensational."

The Playwrights' Producing Company was founded in 1938 by Maxwell Anderson, Elmer Rice, S. N. Behrman, the late Sidney Howard and Robert Sherwood, to produce their own and others' plays. Sherwood is its youngest member, and it was his *Abe Lincoln in Illinois* which set it off to "a brilliant start." It was this play, too, which won for Sherwood his second Pulitzer Prize. It is built about the familiar crises of Lincoln's life—his tragic love affair with Ann Rutledge, his marriage to Mary Todd, the debates against Douglas and his assumption of the Presidency—but the emphasis is original. For 20 years Sherwood had pondered this play and it says what all Sherwood's other serious plays and serious prefaces had tried to say. For Sherwood, Lincoln "had saved the Union and the right of its citizens to the liberty which today in a world disrupted with hatred, oppression and bestial brutality we still enjoy."

In 1937 Sherwood was elected president of the Dramatists' Guild of the Authors' League, a post which he held until he was succeeded in late 1940 by Elmer Rice. He is president of the American National Theatre and Academy, an organization chartered by Congress, whose purpose is to bring the American theatre to the whole American people.

In November 1940 he was elected to the National Institute of Arts and Letters and in January 1941 will be presented with the Institute's gold medal for distinguished service in the field of drama.

As the man who made the European War an issue in the Broadway theatre, today Mr. Sherwood would be expected to speak with intensity when questioned about the meaning of his latest play and his intentions in it. He is six-foot-seven and not immune from the habit of the tall of bowing their heads when they speak. His eyes remain glued to the object of his remarks. He talks directly to the point. "Ever since this War started the isolationists have had the floor. Practically every one agreed we must say nothing out loud, we must whisper nothing, we must think nothing which might involve the United States in this War. When I started to write this play I had come to the conclusion that the isolationists were leading us into a position of really awful peril for this country." Now, he believes, we should join an economic blockade with the Allies and let this country be proclaimed as "an arsenal" for them; supports Clarence Streit's (see sketch this issue) plan for an English Speaking Union to stop Hitler; was the author of the *Stop Hitler Now* advertisements inserted in newspapers throughout the country in the summer of 1940 by the Committee to Defend America by Aiding the Allies. In speeches he has assailed Lindbergh, Ford, Hugh Johnson (see sketch this issue) as members of an anti-democratic "appeasement" clique. He was a "fanatical" supporter of President Roosevelt in the 1940 Presidential campaign.

Noel Coward once asked Sherwood's sister: "What is that nine foot of gloom you call your brother?" Actually Robert Sherwood is far from gloomy. But he believes the final optimism that is expressed in *There Shall Be No Night* is entirely dependent on this country.

References

Christian Sci Mon Mag p5 D 7 '38
Nation 147:487-8 N 5 '38
N Y Times X p1 My 5 '40; IX p1 My 12 '40; VII p8+ Jl 7 '40 por; IX p1+ O 13 '40
New Yorker 16:33-40 Je 1 '40 il; 16:23-36 Je 8 '40 il
Sat R Lit 20:6-8 My 6 '39
Scholastic 36:18 F 12 '40 por
Theatre Arts 22:410-11 Je '38; 23:31-40 Ja '39
Time 35:22 My 13 '40 por (p52)

Flexner, E. Comedy *In* American Playwrights: 1918-1938 p198-282 1938
Krutch, J. W. Comedy *In* American Drama Since 1918 p134-225 1939
Kunitz, S. J. ed. Authors Today and Yesterday 1933
Mantle, B. Contemporary American Playwrights p20-27 1938
Who's Who in America
Who's Who in the Theatre

SHINN, FLORENCE SCOVEL Died Oct 17, 1940 Illustrator; writer and lecturer on metaphysics; connected for many years with Unity Truth Center but recently conducted lectures of her own; author of *The Game of Life and How to Play It* and *The Secret Door to Success*; career before First World War devoted to illustrating many popular works of fiction, including *Mrs. Wiggs of the Cabbage Patch* and *Coniston*, but gave up art work to devote herself to teaching, writing and lecturing in the field of metaphysics

References

Who's Who in America 1914-15

Obituaries

N Y Times p21 O 18 '40

SHINN, MILICENT WASHBURN Apr 15, 1858—Aug 14, 1940 Authority on child psychology; author of *The Biography of a Baby*, which is widely used as a college textbook; her books on the psychology of children, the first in the field, brought her international fame; edited *The Californian* in 1882 and from 1883 to 1894 edited *The Overland Monthly*, both landmarks in the literary history of the West; was one of the early discoverers of Jack London

References

American Women
Leaders In Education 1932
Who's Who in America 1930-31

Obituaries

N Y Herald Tribune p10 Ag 16 '40
N Y Times p19 Ag 15 '40
Sch & Soc 52:125 Ag 24 '40

SHOUP, OLIVER HENRY Dec 13, 1869 —Sept 30, 1940 Governor of Colorado from 1919 to 1923; prominent in mining and oil affairs in Colorado before he was elected Governor on the Republican ticket; was president of the Midwest Oil Company and the Midwest Refining Company

References

Who's Who in America

Obituaries

N Y Herald Tribune p22 O 1 '40

SIGERIST, HENRY ERNEST (sĭ'gĕ-rĭst) Apr 7, 1891- Professor of the history of medicine

Address: b. Institute of the History of Medicine, Johns Hopkins University, Baltimore, Maryland; h. 3946 Cloverhill Rd, Baltimore

Dr. Henry Ernest Sigerist, who is considered by many to be the world's greatest medical historian and who is director of the Institute of the History of Medicine at Johns Hopkins University, is one of this country's foremost proponents of socialized medicine. To him medicine "is not only a science whose triumphs are technical improvements, but a service whose success is measured by the ability of a small group of men to make mankind's life more livable."

In the early 1930's Dr. Sigerist became known to American doctors as a strong and articulate advocate of socialized medicine, and today "no man's arguments are read by either side of the socialized medicine controversy with greater respect." Dr. Sigerist has pointed out time and again that "one-third of the population has no medical care or not enough." He has urged "socialized medicine, under which medical care is not sold to the population or given as a matter of charity. Medical care under such a system has become a function of the state, a public service to which every citizen is entitled."

In the many years that he has fought the American Medical Association and those physicians who believe in an individualistic system of dispensing medicine, Dr. Sigerist has brought forth answers to all the objections to socialized medicine that are inevitably raised, both by those who oppose it and by those who are curious as to how it can work out, if it can.

To those who raise the cry of "regimentation," he points out that socialized medicine doesn't mean regimentation at all, but "organization." "Why should anybody feel regimented," he asks, "by having the possibility to budget the cost of illness and by having the privilege to receive all the medical care he needs?" When people say that doctors may neglect patients when they haven't the money-making incentive Dr. Sigerist calls such an assumption "an insult to the medical profession." To fears of politics interfering if medicine were government controlled, he states firmly: "Political interference can be opposed by public opinion." He points out, too, that "our present system allows only very few people to choose their own doctor"; that with socialized medicine physicians would have opportunities for postgraduate training and incompetent elements could be eliminated; and that state control of medicine, actually, isn't a radical departure: "more than 60 per cent of all hospital beds are owned and operated by the government" and nine-tenths of the work of the Public Health Service "consists of new tasks which private medicine was unable to fulfill."

Since 1932 Professor Sigerist has been at Johns Hopkins University. Before then, he admits, he had "an adventurous career." He was born in Paris, the son of Ernest Henry and Emma (Wiskemann) Sigerist, on April 7, 1891. When he was still young he and his family moved to Zurich, in Switzerland, and he studied at the Gymnasium there from 1904 to 1910. It was while he was at the Gymnasium that Dr. Sigerist decided to become an Orientalist. He ordered an Arabic grammar and got up at dawn every morning to study. From Arabic he plunged into Hebrew, Syriac, Persian and Chinese. (Today he knows 14 languages well.)

When his teachers insisted that he specialize young Henry Sigerist rebelled. He went into science and then medicine. In 1911 he attended University College in London and a few years later the University of Munich in Germany. In 1917 he got his M. D. from the University of Zurich.

After the World War Dr. Sigerist intended to become a country doctor in a Swiss valley: "I would love my valley and keep it in order." It wasn't long, however, before he realized that his ambitions were broader than that and in 1921 he returned to the academic field to become a lecturer in the history of medicine at the University of Zurich. From 1925 to 1932 he was a professor in the history of medicine at the University of Leipzig.

During these years of teaching Dr. Sigerist became famous as the author of books on medical history: among his most famous is *Man and Medicine* (1932), which was translated into six languages. During these years he traveled in almost all of Europe's countries, studying their medical systems, their histories, their social systems.

In 1931 Dr. Sigerist was invited to become head of the History of Medicine Institute at Johns Hopkins University, but before he accepted he explored all the great medical centers of the United States and visited the institutions of small towns. Up and down the country he roamed, investigating history, economics and folkways as well as medical practice. He found the United States "a great world, a gigantic historical process, strange and alluring," and felt that the center of gravity of medicine was shifting from Germany to this country. So he accepted the Johns Hopkins position.

With his wife, Emmy M. Escher of Zurich, whom he had married in 1916, and his two daughters he settled in Baltimore, where for more than eight years hundreds of enthusiastic students have been flocking to his lectures. In 1939 he gave the first course in practical socialized medicine ever held in the United States. This course and his others are always lively, for Dr. Sigerist "doesn't mind expounding his dynamic conception of medical history in hand-to-hand argument." Once a student argued a point he raised and when asked the authority for his contention, replied: "You." "When?" asked Dr. Sigerist. "Three years ago," replied the student. "Ah," said Sigerist, "three years is a long time. I've learned a great deal since then."

When not giving classes, stockily built Dr. Sigerist spends most of his time at the Institute, surrounded by books and filing a three-volume series on the history of Latin medical literature in the early Middle Ages; in another are notes for a definitive four-volume history of medicine and a two-volume sociology of medicine— notes that he has been compiling for seventeen years. His most recent books published in the United States are *American*

Althausen

HENRY ERNEST SIGERIST

Medicine (1934) and *Socialized Medicine in the Soviet Union* (1937). And month after month, year after year, innumerable reports, bulletins and articles come forth under his authorship or editorship. In late 1940 he is writing a series of articles on Group Health Plans in the United States, their difficulties and successes.

References

Atlan 163:794-804 Je '39
Time 33:51-3 Ja 30 '39 pors
Yale R ns 27 no3:463-81 [Mr] '38
American Men of Science
America's Young Men 1936-37
Who's Who in America

SIKORSKI, WLADYSLAW (sǐ-kôr'skē vwä-dĭs'swäf) May 20, 1881- Commander eral Wladyslaw Sikorski has been in England. Premier of the Polish government

Since the downfall of France in 1940, General Wladyslaw Sikorski has been in England. A representative of the Polish government is at Vichy, France. A little less than 200 miles from Paris, at Angers, the sedate and historic capital of the old duchy of Anjou, the expatriate "Capital of Poland" was established in late 1939. Resourceful, confident and handsome General Sikorski, a past master in military strategy, was its Premier.

Wladyslaw Sikorski was born in Tuszów, near Sandomierz, Central Poland on May 20, 1881. He was graduated from the Lwów High School in 1902 and was conscripted into the Austrian Army in 1905. In the year following he was placed on the reserve list with the rank of lieutenant and afterward returned to the Polytechnic Institute of Lwów. At the University he was president of a benevolent organization which was, actually, the very center of

SIKORSKI, WLADYSLAW—*Continued*

Polish patriotic activities, and he became a ranking organizer of military units. Six years after his graduation (1908) he was called to the Austrian legions, but Polish political influence had him transferred to the Polish legions, with the rank of lieutenant colonel. He was arrested by the Austrians following the Brest-Litovsk Treaty. His rise in military power was all the while fast and sure, and he was shortly advanced to a generalship. Moreover his prestige was greatly strengthened in the Battle of Warsaw when he strategically forced the Bolsheviks into retreat.

After the assassination of President Narutowicz late in 1922 Sikorski, now Chief of the General Staff, was called upon to form a government. He accepted, took over the Ministry of the Interior for himself and proclaimed a state of siege (martial law) in Warsaw. He and his cabinet resigned not long afterward but were asked to withdraw their resignations. Despite an apparent vote of confidence the government's position was basically unstable. In March 1923 nicely veiled but nevertheless bitter resolutions were passed, and within two months the Sikorski government was overthrown. It resigned immediately. In the new (Grabski) régime Sikorski in 1924 was made Minister of War.

It has been intimated that some of the tempting offers which Sikorski made to Pilsudski, then in retirement, were not the military plums they appeared to be. This would depend, it would seem, on how deep the rift between these two figures had become at this time. In any event it was in the face of considerable opposition that Sikorski clung to his long-held conviction that although it would be a great mistake to base Europe's peace on bayonets alone Poland must not allow herself to become defenseless. His successor in the War Office seemed to undo much of what he himself had done.

Sikorski retired from active duty in 1926 and devoted a good deal of time to writing, one piece of which was an account of the Polish-Russian campaign of 1920. His *Future War* was translated into French, enjoyed a wide circulation and won him election to the French Academy. Marshal Foch, who wrote the preface to the French edition, which was called *La Guerre Moderne,* considered Sikorski one of the most capable of military strategists.

After the establishment of the Polish Government at Angers, Poland's attitude toward Czechoslovakia was clarified. The Czechs had bitterly remarked that Poland, in its seizure of the Teschen area in 1939, had done to them what the Soviet Union later did to Poland—took advantage of a Nazi smash to fill their own pockets. But Sikorski conferred with Edvard Beneš, former President of Czechoslovakia, and reported: "Past errors between our two countries have been repaired and in the future we shall cooperate."

References

Contemp 158:177-80 Ag '40
Nat R 115:160-4 Ag '40
N Y Herald Tribune p5 Ja 21 '40
N Y Times p3 N 11 '39; N 15 '39; pl N 17 '39; p9 D 25 '39
Time 34:29 D 4 '39 por
International Who's Who

SIKORSKY, IGOR IVAN (sĭ-kôr′skē).

May 25, 1889- Airplane designer
Address: b. Vought-Sikorsky Aircraft, Stratford, Connecticut; h. Newtown, Connecticut

Igor Sikorsky, famous aeronautical engineer, treated newspaper and newsreel men to a strange spectacle in a field adjoining the Vought-Sikorsky airplane plant near Bridgeport, Connecticut on May 20, 1940. He took over the controls of his latest flying machine—a new type of helicopter—and rose vertically into the air like some object in a vaudeville magician's act. First he rose five feet and descended, then thirty feet, and finally he rose sixty feet in his strange machine, flew forward fifty yards or more and came down on the spot from which he had taken off.

The idea of helicopters is not new and Sikorsky himself tried his hand at constructing them back in 1909 when he was only 20. The real importance of this demonstration was that if Sikorsky was putting his creative genius into studying helicopters now, the chances of their becoming commercially practical before long are good. By September 1940, as a matter of fact, he was making the personnel of his airplane manufacturing division nervous by landing the eccentric little craft among the cars in the plant's parking lot and doing other humming-bird tricks with it. They were immensely relieved when he shipped it off to an exposition.

Sikorsky's demonstration of his helicopter was reminiscent of his early days in aviation. He is one of the few active airplane designers who began their careers during aviation's infancy. The story of his career is the story of aviation. Sikorsky was the first man to build a successful multi-motored plane; he designed the first of the Pan-American Airways' transoceanic clippers; he designed the United States' large patrol bomber, the *Flying Dreadnought,* as the *XPBS-A* was nicknamed.

Igor Sikorsky was born in Kiev, Russia, youngest of a family of five children. His father, Dr. Ivan S. Sikorsky, professor of psychology in the St. Vladimir University at Kiev, imbued him with an early interest in science. One of his mother's heroes was Leonardo da Vinci and her stories of his flying machine filled young Igor with dreams of huge flying transports. At 12 he made a rubber-powered helicopter. It did not fly, but the young mechanic was not discouraged. He continued to tinker, disturbing the neighborhood with homemade bombs and other less explosive gadgets.

In 1903 he entered the Naval College in St. Petersburg but after being graduated in 1906 he lost interest. Later he decided that his real career lay in the field of engineering, and entered the Polytechnic Institute in Kiev in the fall of 1907. He continued tinkering in his workshop at home and, in fact, gave his work there more attention than his theoretical studies at the Institute. It was at this time that the flight of Count Zeppelin in one of the early dirigibles and the first successful flight of the Wright brothers in America set Sikorsky dreaming about flying machines again.

He started to study all available literature on flying and went to Paris, cradle of the aviation industry in Europe, to observe the early efforts of plane builders there. He came back home determined to build his own flying machine. Contrary to the advice he received in Paris, he decided to build a helicopter rather than an airplane and started constructing the machine, in 1909, with money borrowed from his sister. He spent several months assembling it, but it never budged from the ground. He built another helicopter, then an airplane, but neither left the ground under its own power. Neighbors of the Sikorskys shook their heads sadly at these goings-on of Igor. That Sikorsky boy was just a crackpot, they decided.

Sikorsky spent two fruitless years designing planes that did not fly. He used up all his family's money and fell behind in his studies at the Polytechnic Institute with nothing to show for his pains but a few brief hops in the *S-2*. This made thirteen embryonic flights totaling seven minutes before it crashed and nearly ruined its designer, who, like all fliers of the period, had no practical flying experience and had to feel his way at the controls. Nevertheless, this small success impressed the elder Sikorsky, who decided to see his son through. Igor quit school, devoted himself to building two new planes and by the summer of 1911 was able to stay aloft half an hour at a thousand-foot altitude in his latest plane, the *S-5*. He got a pilot's license and took part in the army maneuvers in his plane.

The *S-5* set a world's record, flying 70 miles an hour and carrying three men. It made a cross-country flight of 30 miles, which was phenomenal then. One time during a demonstration flight its motor stopped and Sikorsky had to make a forced landing. He found that a mosquito had flown into the gasoline and had been drawn into the carburetor. The accident gave him the idea for a multi-motored plane which would continue to fly even after one motor failed.

Before he built his first multi-motored plane, Sikorsky won the highest award in the Moscow Aircraft Exhibition in 1912 with another plane, the *S-6A*. As a result he was given a contract by the Russo-Baltic Railroad Car Works as chief designer and engineer of its new airplane division. He also was given the privilege of building one

IGOR SIKORSKY

experimental plane a year at the company's expense.

Sikorsky's *Grand,* his first four-motored, dual control, 9,000-pound, four-passenger plane, made aviation history—it established a world's record for staying aloft with eight persons for an hour and fifty-four minutes. Czar Nicholas II inspected it and sent Sikorsky a watch with the Imperial eagle, which the designer still wears on important occasions. During the First World War he became rich and his bomber versions of his four-motored plane made a sensational record. This ended with the Russian Revolution. Sikorsky fled the country, leaving $500,000 in government bonds and real estate. After a brief period in London and Paris he arrived in the United States in March 1919 with only $600 in his pocket and unable to speak a word of English.

For a time the famous designer had to go on a diet of bread and beans as his capital dwindled and he could find no place in aviation after the First World War slump in that industry. He lectured to Russian immigrant groups on aviation, mathematics and astronomy, earning from $3 to $10 a lecture. It was 1923 before he finally got a start in aviation in the United States with the aid of a few hundred dollars raised by Russian friends who gave their savings to the Sikorsky Aero Engineering Corporation.

Sikorsky and his workers used second-hand parts, made their own tools, worked for weeks without money to build the first American-made Sikorsky plane. Despite all the sacrifice, the plane was damaged in its first test flight. Sikorsky refused to give up and demanded $2,500 more from his stockholders. He got it and the *S-29*, one of the first twin-engined planes made in America, a 14-passenger cabin job with a speed of 115 miles an hour, was the result. With its

SIKORSKY, IGOR—*Continued*

success, Sikorsky found it easy to get new backing and the Sikorsky Manufacturing Corporation was organized in 1925.

The designer next turned his attention to amphibians, and the popularity of the *S-38*, an amphibian 10-seater, brought the company Wall Street backing. In 1928 the company was reorganized as the Sikorsky Aviation Corporation. In 1929, a month before the stock market crash, the company was sold to the United Aircraft and Transport and at present is known as the United Aircraft Corporation's Vought-Sikorsky Aircraft Division. Sikorsky is not an officer of the company; he is its engineering manager at a salary of about $20,000 a year. Bonuses and dividends bring his income to about $25,000 a year. It is at the Vought-Sikorsky plant near Bridgeport that Sikorsky's big flying boats have been built.

A short, bald, mild-mannered man with a broad Slavic nose and gray-green eyes, Sikorsky has an old-world courtesy and politeness which he carries into the factory with him. He addresses a workman with "If I may make a suggestion," instead of giving orders. His best work he does at night with a pot full of coffee by his side.

Sikorsky has been married twice. His first wife, whom he married in his early 20's in Russia, died. He met his present wife, the former Elizabeth Semion, a Russian like himself, when he gave a lecture at the Russian People's Home, a mutual-aid society where she was a teacher. He married her on January 27, 1924. By his first marriage he has a daughter whose husband works for the Vought-Sikorsky Company, and he has four sons by his second marriage. Sikorsky was naturalized in 1928 and sharply resents being taken for a Soviet sympathizer.

Sikorsky lives in a white colonial house near Newtown, Connecticut, where he has a large study with an ample library of scientific, philosophical and religious books and a large selection of fine phonograph records. He has a garden there, too, which he likes to plough with a tractor. Recently he built a second, smaller house near Litchfield, Connecticut which he uses as a hideaway when he wants to read and work in complete solitude.

References

Christian Sci Mon Mag p14 Ag 10 '40 por
Liv Age 358:348-51 Je '40 por
N Y Herald Tribune p14 My 21 '40 p3 S 15 '40
New Yorker 16:23-8+ Ag 10 '40; 16: 22-6+ Ag 17 '40 pors
Newsweek 3:23 Mr 24 '34 por
Scrib Mag 105:9-13+ Ap '39 il por
Blue Book of American Aviation
Sikorsky, I. I. The Story of the Winged-S; an Autobiography 1938
Who's Who in America

SILLANPAA, FRANS EEMIL (sil″on-pä′ fränts ĕ′mil) Sept 16, 1888- Author
Address: c/o Alfred A. Knopf, 510 Madison Ave, New York City

After the outbreak of the Russo-Finnish conflict late in 1939 many Americans turned with increasing interest to an understanding of Finnish history and culture. Little of the work of modern Finnish writers has become known in this country. But Frans Eemil Sillanpää, Finnish novelist, was awarded the 1939 Nobel Prize for Literature by the Swedish Academy. Those novels by him which have been translated into English should serve to acquaint American readers with his work.

He was born in southwestern Finland, in the rural parish of Hämeenkyrö. His parents were small farmers and had pioneered the land themselves; they had moved into the forest country, built their own dwelling and cleared off enough trees to give them a small farmstead. The youngest of their three children, and the only one to survive, was Frans Eemil, the author. Despite the hardships of his boyhood, he managed to get a good education—not only in elementary and secondary school, but also at the University of Helsinki, through which he worked his way. He matriculated there in 1908 and studied the natural sciences, but it soon became apparent that his real interest lay in writing.

His first productions were short stories and articles which began to appear in magazines and newspapers about 1913. These established for him both a popular audience and a critical reputation; and he was soon approached by a book publisher who asked him if he would consider writing a novel. An agreement was accordingly made and the young author set to work. According to his own story, he spent the next two years alternately writing the book and explaining to his publisher why it wasn't completed. Finally the publisher, growing desperate, bodily kidnapped the author and settled him in a hotel room in Helsinki, where he finished the book under forced draft. Called *Elämä Ja Aurinko* (*Life and the Sun*), it was published in 1916. It had a considerable success and definitely established its author as an important writer.

Since that time his output has been steady and his reputation has spread all over Europe, especially in the Scandinavian countries. He has been regarded for years as a likely Nobel Prize winner. His published works now include at least fifteen volumes; nine of these are collections of stories and other short pieces, while six are full-length novels. Two of the novels have been translated into English—*Nuorena Nukkunut* (*The Maid Silja*), published in 1933, and *Hurskas Kurjuus* (*Meek Heritage*), 1938. This latter, brought out in Finland in 1919, first brought him an audience outside his own country. It is the story of a typical uneducated Finnish peasant of the older generation, from his birth in the "hungry sixties" to his death

FRANS EEMIL SILLANPAA

before a White firing squad in the War of
1918. The War was still in progress when
Sillanpää commenced this work; and while
he took no sides in the struggle he had
enough actual contact with the rival forces
to let him know what they represented, and
to write with truth and force of the gap,
still unbridged today, between Russian and
Finnish viewpoints.

Meek Heritage was published in Finland less
than a year after the fighting was over, and
its impact was tremendous—so much so that
the author was granted a life-time government pension in 1920 to enable him to
devote his time entirely to creative writing.
Other honors than this have come his way;
he has had government prizes for most of
his novels and in 1936 he received an honorary Doctorate in Philosophy from the three-
century-old State University of Finland.

The simple peasant origins of the new
Nobel Prize winner continue to set the pattern for his living. He was married in 1916,
the year of his first book, to a crofter's
daughter from a nearby farm, and with his
bride went to live in a little cottage in their
home district. They stayed there for several
years, and there the first of their seven children was born. Later they moved into
Helsinki where they lived for a while in a
large apartment. But they maintained the
old family farm as a country home and
there the author now lives most of the time.

Sillanpää, a great bearish person weighing
at least 250 pounds, is a devoted parent,
raising his children in accordance with his
own ideas. These include teaching them
to handle spiders, beetles and other insects
without fear.

His work even in its most grimly realistic
sections is marked by a fine feeling for landscape and the forces of nature, by a certain
nationalistic feeling and by a remarkable
quality of mystery and poetry.

Sillanpää is now completing a new novel
on which he has been at work for several
years.

References

Am Scand R 28:49-53 Mr '40 pors
Christian Sci Mon Mag p11 Ja 27 '40
  por
Deutsch Rundsch 258:113-14 F '39
Mercure Fr 296:728-32 Mr '40
International Who's Who

SILZER, GEORGE SEBASTIAN Apr 14,
1870—Oct 16, 1940 Former Governor of
New Jersey; member of New Jersey Senate
from 1907 to 1912; circuit judge from 1914
to 1922, when he resigned to run for Governor on the Democratic ticket; after
retiring from the Governorship in 1926 became active in law and banking; was chairman of the Port of New York Authority
planning the construction of the George
Washington Bridge

References

Who's Who in America

Obituaries

N Y Herald Tribune p28 O 17 '40 por
N Y Times p25 O 17 '40 por

SIMMONS, FURNIFOLD MCLENDELL
Jan 20, 1854—Apr 30, 1940 North Carolina
Senator for 30 years; chairman of the Senate
Finance Committee during the Wilson Administration; attracted national attention in
1928 as foe of Alfred E. Smith's Presidential
campaign

FURNIFOLD M. SIMMONS
(Continued next page)

SIMMONS, FURNIFOLD—*Continued*

References

Outlook 155:55-6 My 14 '30
Who's Who in America

Obituaries

N Y Herald Tribune p22 My 1 '40
N Y Times p23 My 1 '40 por

SIMON, JOHN ALLSEBROOK, 1ST VISCOUNT (si'mon) Feb 28, 1873- Lord Chancellor of England; former Chancellor of the Exchequer
Address: 11 Downing St, S. W. 1, London England

In May 1940 Sir John Simon was created Lord Chancellor of England, the highest judicial authority in the British State. Twenty-five years ago he refused this office, for his ambitions then were political rather than judicial. Now, when his efforts as Chancellor of the Exchequer have won little sympathy, when any aspirations to the Premiership seem doomed, he has quit the hurly-burly of competitive politics for the Speakership of the House of Lords.

His proposed tax schedule and budget, offered in April 1940, were the heaviest in British history. Taxes were put on cigarettes, whiskey, matches; income taxes were increased; a "purchase tax," the first sales tax in England, was proposed—to bring in an annual revenue of 1,234,000,000 pounds. And yet the main criticism was that the budget was too small—"a cowardly budget," Mr. Keynes called it. The thin, gray-haired Chancellor of the Exchequer said sadly in answer to the stormy debate: "I have proposed unprecedented taxes and yet the main complaint has been that they should be greater."

Unpopular, too, in his schedule was the absence of luxury taxes on cosmetics, for instance, or on an obvious source of revenue like advertising. But Sir John has never been popular in Great Britain, except during the period in the last War when he vigorously opposed conscription. His splendid legal brain has won him respect, but his temperament is remote, frosty and legalistic. By the orthodox Liberals he is regarded as a renegade to Toryism—he strongly supported Chamberlain, even after the defeat in Norway. By the Labor Party he is esteemed a deadly enemy because of his speeches after the General Strike of 1926. In the minds of the general public he is associated with a whole series of crushing taxes which recent economic difficulties and the War have forced him to impose.

John Allsebrook Simon, on May 13, 1940 raised to the peerage as Viscount Simon of Stackpole Elidor, is not a Jew, though he has often been thought one because of his name and, some think, because of his facial characteristics. He was born of a Welsh father and an English mother. His father, the Reverend Edwin Simon, the son of a stone-mason, was a Congregational minister who married Fanny Allsebrook. John Simon went to kindergarten in Manchester and at 10 to the Bristol Grammar School. At 14 he won a scholarship to Fettes, the Edinburgh public school. From there he won another scholarship to Wadham College, Oxford. He played Rugby for his college, became known and feared for his cynical and pungent speeches at the Union (debating society), won high academic honors and in 1898 was called to the Bar.

Simon made rapid progress as a junior counsel—so rapid that in 1899 he was able to marry Ethel Mary Venables, whom he had met at Oxford. She died in 1902 in childbirth, leaving him with two daughters and a son just born. In the following year his management of an intricate railroad case put him in a fair way to fortune. Later he was one of the counsel engaged in the arbitration between the United States and Russia over the Alaska question. He became known as a masterly exponent of difficult Chancery cases, but practiced also at the King's Bench, the Court of Appeal, the House of Lords, the Privy Council and even occasionally the Divorce Court. He was never a spectacular criminal lawyer and it was not until he attained political eminence that his name became known to the public at large, though in a few years he built up a huge practice and began to earn colossal fees. In 1908 he "took silk" as a King's Counsel, at the very early age of 35.

Meanwhile Simon had begun his political career by going into Parliament for the North-London constituency of Walthamstow as a Liberal in 1906. He was returned again in 1910, though with a reduced majority, and continued to sit for this division until 1918. In 1910 Mr. Asquith (later Lord Oxford) chose him, in spite of his comparative youth, for the office of Solicitor General. In 1913 he was promoted to Attorney General, with a seat in the Cabinet, and from 1915 to 1916 served as Home Secretary. Unlike many of his colleagues he supported Great Britain's entry into the War in 1914; but in the following year conducted a vigorous campaign against universal military service. Simon went out to the Air Staff in France, where he served as a major and was mentioned in dispatches.

In the 1918 election Simon lost his parliamentary seat, but came back in 1922 as member for Spen Valley, which he has represented ever since. He was associated with Asquith's so-called "Wee Free" Liberals, not the Lloyd George group, so there was no office for him for many years. Nevertheless he presided over sundry judicial inquiries and commissions, the most famous of which was the India Reform Commission, appointed to consider the practical application of the Montagu-Chelmsford reforms.

In 1931 the second Labor administration was dislodged and its place taken by the so-called "National" Government, consisting mainly of a solid block of Tories, with a sprinkling of Labor and Liberal members. Simon and his group supported this coalition, and have since been known to the Independent Liberals (led by Sir Archibald Sinclair [see sketch this issue]) as the "Simonites." The propaganda value of the name is obvious.

Simon served as Secretary for Foreign Affairs from 1931 to 1935. By this time he seems to have lost all traces of Liberalism and is hardly to be distinguished from the highest Tory. His record as Foreign Secretary is very far from edifying. In some quarters it was considered that he took the wrong line over Manchukuo and Spain, helped to weaken the authority of the League of Nations and annoyed the United States. He was one of the most outspoken members of the "appeasement" clique, and is remembered for his happy statement that German rearmament would make for peace. Later, at the time of Munich, "it was his steadfast intention to out-Chamberlain Chamberlain." From 1935 until 1937 he was Home Secretary, and since then, until early 1940, Chancellor of the Exchequer.

The tale of his social and academic distinctions is a long one. Knighted in 1910, sworn to the Privy Council in 1912, he has since advanced two more grades of knighthood in the Victorian order and has been invested with the Grand Cross of the Order of the Star of India. He holds the honorary degree of D. C. L. from Oxford (for which University he was for some years standing counsel); he is an honorary Fellow of All Souls, and has been made LL. D. by Edinburgh, Cambridge, St. Andrews, Manchester, Leeds, McGill, Toronto and Columbia.

Simon has excited the admiration that brilliant gifts call forth but has won little affection. John Gunther calls him "the greatest lawyer in modern England and the least successful foreign minister" and reports an acid saying of Mr. Lloyd George: "John Simon has sat on the fence so long that the iron has entered into his soul." He is calm, imperturbable, but lacking in warm human feelings.

In 1917 Simon was married a second time, to an Irish lady from Wexford, Kathleen Manning Harvey, who was created a Dame of the British Empire in 1933. She personally concocts a throat mixture of lemon juice, brown sugar and honey with which Simon refreshes himself when he has a long speech to make. They live at Walton Heath close to a famous golf course where he frequently plays. Anything he wins—and he wins often—is sent to the League for the Abolition of Slavery.

References
Great Brit & East 48:718 My 20 '37 por
Liv Age 334:873-4 Je '28; 335:257-9 D '28 pors; 339:60-2 S '30

S. J. Woolf

VISCOUNT SIMON

N Y Times p4 Ap 24 '40 por; p7 Ap 26 '40; IV p1 Ap 28 '40
R of Rs 71:278-81 Mr '25 pors
R Deux Mondes s8 26:947-52 Ap 15 '35
Sat R (England) 158:325-6 N 3 '34
Strand Mag F '39
Time 35:30+ My 6 '40 por

Audax, pseud. Sir John Simon *In* Men in Our Times p101-20 1940
Author's and Writer's Who's Who
Cato [pseud.] Guilty Men 1940
Gunther, J. Men of Whitehall *In* Inside Europe p237-55 1936
Hodgson, S. Sir John Simon *In* Portraits and Reflections p146-51 1929
Nicholson, A. P. The Real Men in Public Life 1928
Roberts, C. E. B. Sir John Simon 1938
Who's Who

SIMPSON, HELEN DE GUERRY Dec 1, 1897—Oct 15, 1940 English novelist; among her books are *Boomerang*, which won the James Tait Black Memorial Prize in 1932; *Saraband for Dead Lovers* (1935); *Under Capricorn* (1937); and *Maid No More*, her latest, published in July 1940; collaborated on three books with Clemence Dane

References
Sat R Lit 17:19 Ja 15 '38
Author's and Writer's Who's Who
Who's Who

Obituaries
N Y Herald Tribune p26 O 16 '40

SINCLAIR, SIR ARCHIBALD, 4TH BART Oct 22, 1890- British Secretary of State for Air

Address: b. Thorney Court, Kensington, London W. 8, England; h. Thurso Court, Caithness, England

For 20 years Liberalism (with a capital) has been under a cloud in Great Britain, though there are many liberal minds in all three parties—Conservative, Liberal and Labor. In the great heyday of official Liberalism, in 1910, young Archibald Sinclair was just passing from his military college into the Life Guards; in 1922, the year in which what remained of the party was split in two, he began his political career; and in 1935, the year which confirmed the National Government in its huge majority, he became head of that section of the party which remained independent, outside the coalition.

Sir Archibald Sinclair was born 20 years too late to have any real hopes of ever being Prime Minister of England and despite his prestige and distinction had been, until Winston Churchill's (see sketch this issue) government came into power, only the leader of a small band of opposition Liberals in the House of Commons. Today, as Secretary of State for Air, his ability in economic and military affairs is finally matched by opportunity, for while the task of producing airplanes falls to Lord Beaverbrook (see sketch this issue), it is Sinclair who must see that they are put to the best possible use. Since air and naval power will probably decide the issue of the War, Sinclair, with Sir Cyril Newall, Chief of the Air Staff (see sketch this issue), controls a department vital to the very survival of his country.

Acme

SIR ARCHIBALD SINCLAIR

Archibald Henry Macdonald Sinclair, fourth baronet, is one of the greatest chieftains of the Scottish Northern Kingdom, but he is also half American. His father, Clarence Granville Sinclair, the third baronet, married Miss Mabel Sands, "a famous New York beauty." Born heir to a tremendously rich inheritance—he is supposed to have inherited more than $1,000,000 on his twenty-first birthday from his American relations, who include the Vanderbilts and the Rutherfords—he was educated at Eton and at the Royal Military College, Sandhurst. From Sandhurst, in 1910, he passed as a subaltern into the Second Life Guards.

For 12 years Sinclair pursued the career of an army officer, serving right through the European War. In 1916 he was second in command to Winston Churchill in the Sixth Royal Scots Fusiliers, and by 1918 he had risen to the rank of major. In that year he married Marigold Forbes, and the year after became Lord Lieutenant (head of the county magistracy) of Caithness.

Three years later, in 1922, Sinclair was elected to Parliament for the division of Caithness and Sutherland, one of the few safe Liberal seats. That same year he was made Companion of the Order of St. Michael and St. George. He devoted himself to economic studies, took his Parliamentary work very seriously and took up flying as a hobby.

Although he showed himself a radical during his early years in Parliament, Sir Archibald was no friend of the Labor Party and especially resented Labor's attitude when it took office in 1924—to him the Labor Party seemed unappreciative and unaccommodating in light of the Liberals' support of them. He stayed in Parliament, always returned to the same seat, and in 1930 and 1931 was chief Liberal Whip (the Whips look after party discipline and summon members to divisions). When, in 1931, the National Government was formed, he adhered to it and was given the post of Secretary of State for Scotland. When the Ottawa Trade Agreements were signed in 1932 he resigned, however, for he had always been a free trader.

During the troubled period of the Abyssinian War Sinclair tried to make the government take a stronger line toward the totalitarian countries. He greatly condemned England's policy of paying lip service to the League of Nations while allowing its authority to be undermined. On the Abyssinian question, on the League of Nations and on the dangers of the rising Nazi power he made rousing and masterly speeches.

In 1935 Sinclair became head of the Independent Liberals in succession to Sir Herbert Samuel. At that time the Liberal Party was split into two parts, the "Simonites," followers of Sir John Simon (see sketch this issue) and coadjutors of the Conservatives, and the "Samuelites," a small independent fragment. For many years before then and since Sinclair concentrated his forces against Sir John Simon, whom he called "the evil genius of British politics." Since he became head of the "Samuelites" Sir Archibald's attitude toward Labor has become somewhat more sympathetic, though there has always been a broad gulf between his Liberal views and those of a party dedicated to socialism in one form or another.

It was Sinclair who was one of the first to raise his voice in protest against England's conduct during Hitler's invasion of Norway. "Furiously and attractively eloquent," he demanded "a grand inquest" on the whole matter. "I hope," said he thunderously to an Edinburgh audience, "that it is not too late for craven and irresolute counsels to be suppressed. . . I am amazed at the false prophets telling us that Hitler missed the bus, that we have turned the corner and that we are now ten times more confident than six months ago. That reminds me of the prophesy that Munich meant 'peace in our time.' "

At 50 Sir Archibald Sinclair shares with Mr. Anthony Eden (see sketch this issue) the distinction of being the best-looking man in Parliament and one of its most appealing. According to A. J. Cummings, a Liberal journalist: "He abounds in mental and physical energy. His judgment has matured. He knows his own mind. He has made a close study of the political and military problems of the moment. His almost joyous gaiety conceals a keen and resolute spirit and yet hints at that touch of boldness which seems at present to so many people the one thing needed in British statesmanship."

Sinclair has a big mock-Gothic castle at Thurso, "one of the most famed and imposing in the realm." During vacations he shoots, fishes or saws wood with his boys there. He has two sons, Robin and Angus, both at Eton, and two daughters, Elizabeth and Catherine. He was made LL. D. of Edinburgh in 1932 and is a Chevalier of the Légion d'Honneur.

References

N Y Sun p28 My 3 '40
Picture Post 7:21-4 Je 1 '40
Time 35:32+ My 13 '40 por
Watchman, pseud. Right Honorable Gentlemen 1939
Who's Who

SINCLAIR-COWAN, BERTHA MUZZY
See Bower, B. M., pseud.

SINGER, RICHARD   May 9, 1879—Feb 28, 1940   Hungarian concert pianist

References

Wier, A. E. ed. Macmillan Encyclopedia of Music & Musicians 1938

Obituaries

N Y Herald Tribune p16 Mr 1 '40
    por
N Y World-Telegram p7 F 29 '40
Variety 137:54 Mr 6 '40

SLOAN, ALFRED PRITCHARD JR.
May 23, 1875- Chairman of the board of General Motors Corporation

Address: b. 1775 Broadway, New York City; h. Great Neck, New York

The man responsible for the operation of the United States' second biggest manufacturing enterprise (Big Steel is the first) is Alfred P. Sloan Jr., chairman of the board of General Motors Corporation.

Born in New Haven, Connecticut on May 23, 1875, son of the late Alfred Pritchard and Katherine (Mead) Sloan, Alfred grew up in Brooklyn, New York, where his family moved when he was five. Among other things, his father was a partner in a tea and coffee importing business, and a contributor to Wesleyan charities; one grandfather was a schoolteacher, another a Methodist minister. But his own bent was mechanical and scientific. After attending Brooklyn public schools he entered the Polytechnic Institute, acquired a reputation as a sort of minor prodigy, passed examinations for the Massachusetts Institute of Technology with great ease but wasn't allowed to enter because of his youth. In order to make up for the delay young Alfred finished its four-year course in three years when he did get inside, and took his B. S. in electrical engineering in 1895, at the age of twenty. He was the youngest in his class.

After graduation he found a job as draftsman in the Hyatt Roller Bearing Company of Harrison, New Jersey, in which his father had a considerable investment. At Cambridge he had met Irene Jackson of Boston, Massachusetts and he married her three years later.

He was only 26 when he became Hyatt's president and general manager, and he held that position for 15 years. At first billiard balls were the company's chief manufactured product, but it wasn't long before young Sloan saw the possibilities in manufacturing steel roller bearings for the rapidly expanding auto industry. With this product perfected, he devoted his energy to selling it, and often went out on the road himself. He learned to know personally all the great names of the automobile industry, learned the business of building cars at firsthand, sold Ford his first order of Hyatt bearings, and retained him as a friend and as his best customer. During Sloan's first month at Hyatt the gross business had been under $2,000; in time the net profits reached as much as $4,000,000 a year. Still Sloan was worried. His two gigantic customers were Ford and General Motors—suppose one or the other or both decided to make their own bearings? "I had put my whole life's energy into Hyatt," he said later. "Every-

ALFRED P. SLOAN JR

thing I had earned was there in bricks, machinery and materials." With his father, Sloan owned about 75 per cent of Hyatt by this time, and, when in 1916 Durant of General Motors started linking accessory companies into United Motors, Sloan brought Hyatt into the accessory combine for $13,500,000 and became its president. By the time he was 41 he was worth nearly $5,000,000.

In 1918 Durant joined United Motors with General Motors, and Sloan became a vice-president and member of its executive committee. In November 1920, in the midst of the post-War depression, 2,500,000 shares of General Motors passed from the ownership of President Durant to the Du Ponts. Pierre du Pont (see sketch this issue) therefore took over as president of the company, but with the understanding that most of the operating burden would be on the man who was by this time the corporation's "heavy-duty trouble shooter," the man who had shown "he could straighten out almost any kind of a snarl." It was in December 1930 that Alfred Sloan was put in charge of operations as "operating vice-president, also sitting on the finance committee." And when on May 10, 1923 Du Pont resigned from the presidency of General Motors to become chairman of the board, Sloan succeeded him as president, and a few days later found himself a director of the E. I. Du Pont de Nemours Company and on the board of the Chase National Bank. He later became a member of the board of directors of the Pullman Company as well.

During Sloan's first year as president of General Motors he doubled the company's manufacturing capacity and sold more cars than ever before in its history. Under his administration a decentralized plan of management was set up in which the initiative

of each of General Motors' executives was exploited to the utmost, the immense corporation being tied together by a committee system and by Sloan's famous "standard procedures," which provided a "free and orderly circulation of information." Sloan said that in his opinion "the organization of which I am now president would be impossible without the principle of individual initiative."

The system proved itself so sound from the point of view of the stockholder that even during the depression General Motors took no losses, omitted no dividends, even after a drop in sales of more than 70 per cent. In 1936 there was a return of 24 per cent on the book value of the capital stock and surplus, as compared with an average return of 18 per cent, and in the same year Sloan was listed as the highest-paid executive in the United States.

It was also in December of that year that the sit-down strikes in General Motors plants began, after Sloan had refused to confer with representatives of the United Automobile Workers about employee grievances. Not until months later did the President consent to negotiations with Lewis and the auto unions, Governor Murphy (see sketch this issue) acting as go-between.

In May 1937 Sloan became chairman of the board of directors. He owned 750,000 shares of GM—at least in 1938.

The first half of war-year 1940 found General Motors handling a quarter more business than during the first half of 1939, but in September 1940 Sloan warned that, although business in general was facing an expanding market due to munitions orders, the years following the War are sure to be lean years.

Mr. Sloan is a staunch Republican and has contributed consistently and substantially to Republican Presidential campaign funds. He believes that "attempts to improve the economic status of our people, especially those who have so little, through wage-hour laws, shorter hours and all the other panaceas that have been imposed on the economy in recent years, are nothing but wishful thinking." Increased production is his own recipe for a higher standard of living for the American people, and he sees increased production as made possible only by "cooperation with mutual respect and confidence" between capital and labor. And "we just can't keep up with the politicians' ability to spend our money," he complains. It was Sloan who in November 1940 suggested that in the interests of national defense the six-day week should supplant the five-day week in American industry, and the overtime premium be eliminated "as soon as the slack in employment is taken up." He also expressed the fear that "unjustified" increases in wage rates would result in inflation.

General Motors' executives are notoriously well paid, for Mr. Sloan believes in recognizing "outstanding ability." His corporation he sees as "a pyramid of opportunity from the bottom toward the top, with thousands of chances for advancement. Only capacity limited any worker's chances to grow." He also sees it as performing a tremendous public service. *Fortune* agrees with him in so far as General Motors has contributed to technological advance, to making prices of cars lower for the consumer, to rewarding its executives and stockholders, but thinks the labor-minded might think some of the money should go toward stabilizing employment. Although the average wages paid by General Motors are comparatively high, there is little or no security for labor.

On the board of the Massachusetts Institute of Technology, Mr. Sloan has made substantial contributions to education. In June 1940 he made a gift to M. I. T. for the expansion of its airplane engine laboratory. He is also the founder of the Sloan Foundation, of which his brother Harold is director, for "Studies Bearing Directly Upon Human Relations and Devoted to the Increase and Diffusion of Economic Knowledge." The income from one of the funds goes to the University of Chicago to help underwrite a weekly national radio round-table on current affairs, income from another toward underwriting consumer education at Stephens College, Columbia, Missouri.

Sloan is almost six feet tall, "gaunt, lanky, with long, bony hands," and wears collars "of an arresting height and as stiff as a Buick mudguard." His long forehead is topped by a "tuft of gray-white forelock that valiantly defies baldness." He has "intense blue eyes." He is an impeccable dresser, though his valet buys most of his clothes for him, but likes to keep warm. Sometimes known as "silent Sloan" because of the deafness that makes him quiet in a large gathering, he is actually far from that. "His physical activity is varied but continual: when in action he squirms, he taps his fingers, he gestures, he puts his head in his hands, he draws one of his feet into his chair and sits on it; sometimes he speaks softly, sometimes he shouts, in a voice that has more than a trace of a Brooklyn accent."

Few men have been so devoted to business. Sloan has never found time to learn golf; he rarely drives his own car; when on a vacation abroad he has usually found GM's foreign branches more interesting than anything else; he doesn't go in for "culture" in the usual sense; he has no children to take up his time; he retires early; he seldom even gets aboard his yacht, the 235-foot $1,250,000 *Rene* (which, by the way, was incorporated under the name of the Rene Corporation, and from 1931 to 1936 showed operating "losses" of $278,474). The list of clubs of which he is a member—from the Detroit Club to Palm Beach's Bath and Tennis Club—doesn't make him a real clubman. His fraternity is Delta Upsilon.

In his work Mr. Sloan is said to have "an almost inhuman detachment from personalities." "We never give an order in GM," he says. "We 'sell' the idea to those who must carry it out." One typical story tells of a young executive making a suggestion with the comment: "I suppose you will bawl me out for this." "Why," was Mr. Sloan's answer, "did you ever hear of me bawling anybody out?"

References

Christian Sci Mon p12 N 21 '40
Fortune 17:72-7+ Ap 38 il pors
Good H 102:26-7+ F '36 il por
N Y Herald Tribune p17 N 14 '40 por
N Y Times p1+ N 14 '40
R of Rs 74:258-63 S '26 il por
Sat Eve Post 213:9-11+ Ag 17 '40 pors; 213:26-7+ Ag 24 '40 il; 213: 24-5+ Ag 31 '40 il pors; 213:26-7+ S 14 '40 pors; 213:22-3+ S 21 '40 il; 213:27+ S 28 '40
Time 26:68+ D 16 '35

Forbes, B. C. Alfred P. Sloan Jr. *In* Automotive Giants of America p237-51 1926
Who's Who in America
Who's Who in Commerce and Industry

SLYE, MAUD Feb 8, 1879- Pathologist
Address: h. 5822 Drexel Ave, Chicago, Illinois

Sometimes called the "American Curie," Maud Slye is a University of Chicago pathologist who since 1908 has been tending, breeding and writing the biographies of thousands of mice, in an effort to learn more about cancer and its causes. Cancer kills one out of ten men who reach the age of thirty-five, one out of five women; yet Dr. Slye has good reason for asserting that by selective-breeding care cancer could be stamped out in a generation. If more progress in cancer research has been made in the past 30 years than in the preceding 30 centuries, it is in large part due to her refusal to accept the old theory that it is not in any way inheritable, and to her persistence in attempting to find out just how it can be bred out.

Maud Slye was born in Minneapolis, Minnesota, on February 8, 1879, the daughter of James Alvin and Florence Alden (Wheeler) Slye. Her parents were poor, and she came to the University of Chicago as an undergraduate with only $40. For three years she put herself through school without help as one of the under-secretaries to President William Harper, carrying full academic work at the same time. A nervous breakdown resulted and she went to Woods Hole, Massachusetts to recuperate. She then finished her course at Brown University and acquired her B. A. there in 1899. Next she worked as a professor of psychology and pedagogy at Rhode Island State Normal School until 1905, but already

Helen B. Morrison

MAUD SLYE

her chief scientific interest was in the laws of heredity, and when in 1908 she was given a small grant to do postgraduate work at the University of Chicago she took it.

One of the first things Maud Slye did at Chicago was to spend $6 for six Japanese dancing mice, whose peculiar waltzing motion is due to a nervous disarrangement. In a corner of the basement of the zoological laboratory she began breeding them with albino mice with the idea of learning something about the factors in the inheritance of nervous abnormalities. Working 18 hours a day and longer, without an assistant, often going hungry herself because her mice required so much food, Maud Slye soon got on the trail of something—though that something had very little to do with nervous abnormalities. She learned that several cattle at the Chicago stock yards were afflicted with cancer of the eye—and that all of these cattle came from the same ranch. She began acquiring other data about cancer that seemed to point to the conclusion that there was an inheritable factor among its causes. Then she went to her superior and asked if she couldn't use her mice to prove that there was. He said: "That was settled long ago—it is not inherited."

Just the same, Maud Slye went ahead. Every time a mouse died it was autopsied. It was 1910 before her first mouse developed breast cancer. After that cancerous mice were bred with other cancerous mice; healthy mice were given healthy mates.

In 1911 Otho S. A. Sprague died and left millions of dollars for medical research; the Sprague Memorial Institute was set up at the University. Maud Slye became a member of its staff as well as instructor in pathology, and for the first time was provided with a steady, adequate income.

More than that, she was given a two-story building for her laboratory, and the director of the Institute, the pathologist, H. Gideon Wells, began to collaborate with her in microscopic analyses. Her first paper on cancer was read before the American Society for Cancer Research on May 1913, and at that time the theory that cancer might be contagious, caused by a filterable virus, was given a deathblow when she proved that healthy mice could mingle with doomed ones without any ill effects—at least that was what had been going on in her laboratory.

In 1919 Miss Slye left the staff of the Institute, becoming director of the Cancer Laboratory at the University of Chicago. In 1922 she was promoted to an assistant professorship in pathology, and in 1926 to an associate professorship. That same year she announced her belief in the possibility of controlling and preventing human cancer, for mice come closest to man in the percentage that have cancer and in types and locations of such growths. If it was being controlled and prevented in her laboratory, as she claimed it was, why not?

But other people had been doing research in cancer, too, and her theory wasn't accepted so easily. Some of their experiments seemed to point to radically different conclusions from hers. For instance, Japanese scientists found that tar painted on a rabbit's ears produces cancer, and concluded that it could therefore be caused merely by an irritation. Still Maud Slye wasn't defeated. She countered with the theory that the *disposition* toward cancer must have already been present in those rabbits, that it was the *disposition* that was inherited—and demonstrated by producing one strain of mice which uniformly developed lip cancer when their teeth were not filed down, another strain that did not.

Cancer is generally held to be an abnormal method of cell growth, in which cells keep multiplying because some normal factor in the cell itself is missing. From working with her mice over a period of years Maud Slye finally concluded that cancer susceptibility was a recessive characteristic, determined by only one gene and following Mendelian laws in a very regular sort of way; that the stimuli which will actually produce cancer, however, are extremely diverse. In 1936 she amended her theory, saying that there seemed to be three types of genes—one determining the location of the cancer, one its type, and the third its degree of malignancy. According to her final theory a man susceptible to one type of cancer could marry a woman susceptible to another type and the children would probably escape both types, but if the man and his wife were susceptible to the same type of cancer it might very easily be disastrous for their offspring.

This does not mean that everyone accepts her conclusions. In 1936 Dr. Clarence Cook Little of Jackson Memorial Laboratory at

Bar Harbor, Maine, who has also been working with mice over a period of years, called her contentions "pure poppy-cock." He wanted Miss Slye to furnish a herd of male, non-susceptible mice which a "neutral, properly qualified laboratory" could work with in order to test the validity of her hypothesis. Miss Slye replied that she had offered to do this five years ago, and he had not responded to her offer; that the non-tumor strains with which she had done her preliminary work were no longer in existence.

More than 140,000 mice have been on Miss Slye's autopsy table. The Cancer Laboratory is a three-story building in whose basement will be found steam-sterilizing equipment; on the first floor, cages where the offspring of cancerous mice begin and end their lives; on the second floor, examination and autopsy rooms; on the third floor, quarters for healthy mice. On each cage door is the history of its occupant, date of birth, matings, etc., and a pedigree going back 100 generations (which is something like 3,000 years in man's life span). In this laboratory, says Miss Slye, "the mice are kings, and we workers of secondary importance." It is a mouse Utopia, for all diseases but cancer must be prevented, and the mice kept alive and well to the oldest possible age. The life span of the average mouse has been just about doubled here.

If something should happen to her laboratory and its occupants—an epidemic, an accident—it might wipe out the work of a lifetime. Miss Slye therefore moved across the street after one blizzardy night when she feared for its safety and had to rush through the storm to reach it. When her mother was ill in California she rented a boxcar and took her mice with her to the coast. In fact, the first time she was brave enough to leave her laboratory in the care of an assistant was in 1936, when she took her first vacation in 26 years and went to Europe. There she addressed the International Congress for the Control of Cancer in Brussels and also visited Amsterdam, Berlin, Paris, London and other cities.

Miss Slye said in 1937: "I can go through this laboratory and predict for each of these 9,000 mice here whether any individual mouse will have a cancer and if so what type it will be, where it will appear and at what age. . . If we had records for human beings comparable to those of my mice we could stamp out cancer in a generation." She believes "only romance stops us" from taking advantage of the facts which her experiments have put at our disposal. Permitting more human autopsies and keeping adequate medical records for every individual would be only a first step, but "so long as there's life in my body, I shall continue to fight for that first step in the long battle that lies ahead."

Forty-two brochures on the nature and inheritability of cancer have been published by Miss Slye. In 1914 she received the gold medal of the American Medical Asso-ciation for outstanding research; in 1915 the Ricketts Prize; in 1922 the gold medal of the American Radiological Society. She holds an honorary D. Sc. degree from Brown University and honorary memberships in the Seattle Academy of Surgery and the Southern California Medical Society, and is a member of the Association for Cancer Research, the Chicago Institute of Medicine, the American Medical Association and other scientific societies.

Maud Slye is strong-featured, dark-browed, and wears her white hair cropped short. Away from her mice, she has a multitude of interests: music, nature, gardening, painting, poetry. She has, in fact, published books of poetry, *Songs and Solaces* (1934) and *I in the Wind* (1936).

References

Cur Hist 49:35-6 S '38
N Y Sun p8 Ja 11 '40
Newsweek 9:38 Ja 9 '37; 9:26-8 Ap 10 '37 il pors
Read Digest 28:77-80 Mr '36
Scholastic 30:11 My 15 '37 por; 36:17 Mr 11 '40 por
Time 28:24 Ag 31 '36 il por; 28:77 N 16 '36 por
American Men of Science
American Women
Jaffe, B. Cancer *In* Outposts of Science p129-60 1935
Jaffe, B. Woman Scientist *In* Compton, R. and Nettels, C. H. eds. Conquests of Science p255-68 1939
Who's Who in America

SMITH, CLYDE HAROLD June 9, 1876 —Apr 8, 1940 Republican representative of Maine; member of labor committee in the House; helped formulate Wages and Hours Act; backed Old-Age Pension Bill in Maine

References

Who's Who in America
Who's Who in the Nation's Capital

Obituaries

N Y Herald Tribune p21-2 Ap 9 '40 por (p23)
N Y Times p23 Ap 9 '40

SMITH, KATE May 1, 1909- Radio singer; actress

Address: 1819 Broadway, New York City

"Undisputed first lady of radio" is Kathryn Elizabeth Smith (she uses only Kate), 235-pound singer, who, at the age of 30, has achieved a position never before occupied by any broadcasting entertainer.

During the past years she was selected for the annual listing of the Ten Outstanding Women of the Year; the Red Cross awarded her its Legion of Valor Medal for her $4,000,000 campaign in their behalf; and, in addition, she was asked to sign at the White House in a "command perform-

KATE SMITH

ance" for King George VI and Queen Elizabeth of England.

Financially, Kate Smith is "sitting pretty" as the possessor of a unique three-year-non-cancelable radio contract guaranteeing her not less than $7,000 a week. In her nine successful years as a radio entertainer she has "used her booming, unschooled voice, plus occasional bursts of hearty Americanism, to sell millions of dollars worth of cigars, automobiles, coffee, and, since 1937, General Foods' cake flour, baking powder and salt."

the singer's career according to her, really began when she was only four years old. At that early age she delighted in accompanying her parents to church in Washington, D. C., where she would stand, the hymnbook upside down before her, and sing religious songs with great enthusiasm. Her birthplace is Greenville, Virginia, where she was born May 1, 1909, the daughter of William and Charlotte Smith.

The biggest day of her life, Kate claims, was the one in 1917 on which she was allowed to sing for the Blue Devils, a band of a hundred veteran French soldiers who were sent to the United States by the Allies to participate in Liberty Loan rallies. Kathryn Elizabeth's popularity was a thrilling experience and the singer still remembers the moment when the captain stepped up on the platform, planted a Blue Devil cap on the side of her head and kissed her on both cheeks.

After this, Kate continued to sing at school and church concerts and at local amateur nights and benefits. She added the Charleston to her acts and won numerous contests. But her father, who was a wholesale distributor of magazines, did not want a vaudeville performer in his family and insisted that she go in training to become a

nurse. "The family arguments won out for a time," Kate says, "but after several months of probation work, standing on my feet some 10 or 12 hours a day, I decided that as a nurse I was a pretty good entertainer."

In 1926, the girl, still in her teens, was invited to go to New York for a musical comedy rôle in Eddie Dowling's *Honeymoon Lane.* The show opened in Atlantic City August 29 with Kate cast as Tiny Little. Newspapers were kind to "the youngster with no stage experience whatever, who literally stopped the show." On September 20 *Honeymoon Lane* opened at the Knickerbocker Theatre in New York City, where it ran two years.

Kate's second stage appearance in the road company of *Hit the Deck* was more pleasant than her first because it gave her a chance to "shake the rafters" with the syncopated spiritual, *Hallelujah,* which she thoroughly enjoyed. But, upon her return to New York, she found that she was remembered not as a singer but as a fat girl. "Being fat didn't worry me in the least," she says. "It was the problem of making people realize its unimportance which floored me temporarily."

An opportunity to solve this problem was not immediately forthcoming, for Kate was costarred with Bert Lahr in *Flying High,* the story of a fat girl! The humiliation of Lahr's "double-entendre" jests was almost unbearable, and Kate was on the verge of leaving the show business forever and becoming a nurse when Ted Collins stepped into the picture. "Whatever success I have had or may have," she says, "is due entirely to Ted Collins, the man who took me and my work seriously and made it his chief concern."

As "patient stooge" for all the comedians in *Flying High* Kate had been very unhappy. Previously when she had appeared in *Honeymoon Lane* and *Hit the Deck,* it was always the same story. No one was willing to judge her for her "infinitely sentimental contralto" alone. Critics claimed that "Kate Smith is immense in more ways than one", "she is sitting on top of the world—nothing else would bear that weight," she is "a theatrical find of huge proportion," etc.

Ted Collins' first move as Kate's self-appointed manager was to persuade the management of *Flying High* to ease up on the wisecracks about her weight. Secondly, he had records made of her voice at the Columbia Phonograph Company, where he was an executive. Before long he had arranged with William S. Paley (see sketch this issue), president of the Columbia Broadcasting System, to audition the blues singer, and she was given a 15-minute "spot" on the air. This was in February 1931; within seven months she had her first radio commercial contract, and by autumn of that same year her weekly salary had climbed to four figures.

Kate wanted to put on a friendly, neighborly program, so Ted originated the greeting, "Hello, everybody! This is Kate Smith." As a theme song, the entertainer chose *When the Moon Comes Over the Mountain,* and to express her appreciation to the radio audience, she asked to be allowed to end each program by saying, "Thanks for listenin'." These three parts of her show are now world-famous.

Kate Smith's career is handled by the Kated Corporation, one of the most remarkable organizations in show business. The corporation is capitalized at $400,000 and was, in June 1940, producing the *Kate Smith* weekly hour program, six *Kate Smith* daily talks and several other radio acts, such as the *Aldrich Family* and *My Son and I.* It manages a professional basketball team, the *Kate Smith Celtics,* and handles the singer's philanthropies, of which there are many. In spite of all these activities, Kate Smith and Ted Collins have never had a written agreement. "You do the singing," said Ted, "and I'll fight the battles."

In 1932 Kate Smith was on the West Coast making *Hello, Everybody,* a scenario written especially for her by Fanny Hurst. "Hollywood frightened me," she recalls. "It lingers in my mind as a huge stage, enhanced by impossibly brilliant colors in sky and vegetation, filled with extraordinarily dressed actors and actresses mouthing lines and going through their paces for the benefit of an ever-present audience."

"Road fever" hit Kate Smith and her gang in October 1933, and they left radio to make a vaudeville tour of the United States. On this trip the singer appeared before audiences aggregating a million. She was made a Texas Ranger by "Ma" Ferguson, Governor of that state, and an honorary member of the Winnebago Tribe of Sioux Indians with the name of Hom-O-Goo-Winga (Glory of the Morn).

After the tour sponsors clamored for Kate Smith's services, but the "discriminating diva," as she was called, "turned down a high-salaried medicine contract, snubbed her nose at a chance to sing on a tempting skin-cleansing program." Instead, Kate accepted an offer from CBS to appear on a sustaining "matinee hour," a show designed for the entire family.

In January 1935 "Kate Smith, a star in her own right, set out to become a constellation." Sponsored by the Hudson Motor Corporation with a weekly outlay of $30,500, the singer toured the country trying to find new talent. Because of the size of the task she was obliged to abandon the idea, however.

Since 1937 Kate has been working for General Foods Corporation. In addition to her own songs, on her Friday night show she usually presents a brief drama with an outstanding radio, stage or screen star, a comedy act, *Snow Village Sketches,* and a chorus. During the week, she presents a 15-minute noonday chat from her rose and apple-green apartment on lower Park Avenue. Here she lives quietly with her maid Maria, her cat Mittsy, and two parrots who invariably greet her with "hello, baby."

The singer has often been accused of having a "hospital complex." To this taunt her only reply is: "It is true that I've been hurt many times in the past by some smart newspaper writer who sent up a shout of "publicity" whenever I appeared at one of the veterans' hospitals, sent flowers to shut-ins, or collected dolls at Christmas for youngsters who had never had a brand-new doll in all their lives." But these critics do not bother Kate and she bears them no malice because they do not understand the girl who still clings to her "childhood illusions." Today she is the only star in radio who is permitted, in violation of the Communication Commission's rules, to address directly on the air the people for whom she sings her special songs.

For her Armistice Eve program in 1938 the chanteuse, "sensitive to the rising tide of Broadway patrioteering," got Irving Berlin, composer of *God Bless America,* to give her the exclusive right to sing it on the air. This "badgered ballad" she sang week after week on her program until it was finally released for use by other patrioteers.

Kate's hobbies are numerous. At Lake Placid, where she has a cottage next door to Mr. and Mrs. Ted Collins and their eighteen-year old daughter, Kate lives the life of an athlete. Golf, tennis and swimming amuse her in summer, and winter finds her skating, tobogganing or skiing. She loves to dance at any time but dislikes night clubs because they are "stuffy and overcrowded."

Amateur photography is another hobby; her collections include odd perfume bottles and first editions. She is reputed to be the only private citizen in the United States allowed to use the President's entrance at Union Station, Washington, D. C.

In 1938 Kate Smith wrote the story of her career, *Living in a Great Big Way.* The book is not only a record of her achievements but is also a sincere declaration of her philosophy of life. It paints a picture of the singer as a genuine, unaffected person who has managed to "be herself" in a business where "phonies" flourish. She has been described as "a gay and gallant spirit, one of the most winning figures before' the public's eyes and ears." She has "regular features, lovely eyes and a peachy-creamy skin."

References

   Liberty 17:45-8 Je 8 '40 por
   Newsweek 4:36 S 8 '34; 5:37 Mr 2 '35
      por (cover)
   Time 33:41 My 15 '39 por; 36:60-1 S
      30 '40 por
   American Women
   Smith, K. Living in a Great Big
      Way 1938
   Who's Who in America

SMITH, WILBUR FISK May 21, 1856—Aug 9, 1940 President emeritus of the University of Baltimore; former principal of Baltimore City College; taught English and mathematics; professor since 1873

References
Who's Who in America

Obituaries
N Y Times p31 Ag 11 '40

SOGLOW, OTTO (sŏg'lō) Dec 23, 1900- Cartoonist
Address: h. 330 W 72nd St, New York City

Otto Soglow's cartoons enliven books, articles, advertisements, stories, but it is probably the Little King, that portly, bearded monarch, who has made him best known. The first drawing of the Little King appeared in the *New Yorker*. The editor called for another and then another, turning down six of every eight early ones submitted. Finally he made the Little King a weekly feature until Hearst's King Features Syndicate signed a contract with Soglow calling for a weekly Sunday page of his creation.

When the Little King first caught on and when he came out in a book (1933), psychoanalysts analyzed his personality, manufacturing companies put him on glasses and ties, made dolls of him; and Russia's then-important Litvinov begged Ambassador Bullitt (see sketch this issue) not to return to the Soviet Union without a copy of the book. More recently the Little King made his appearance in a New York ballet produced by the Monte Carlo Company, choreography by Massine (see sketch this issue).

OTTO SOGLOW

The main charm of the Little King has always been his complete simplicity, so incongruous in the royal setting about him. In one typical sequence, for instance, he arises from a magnificent royal bed, walks through sumptuous halls across a drawbridge and then takes in his morning quart of milk just like any tenement dweller. In another, escorted by a cortege of exquisite flunkies, he makes a stately ascent of a stately stairway and then slides down the bannister.

Otto Soglow was born far from scenes of such splendor, on New York's lower East Side. He attended public school in New York and then got himself jobs as a packer, dishwasher, errand boy, machinist's helper and baby-rattle painter in a sweatshop. From his hard work he was able to save enough money to study at the Art Students League. For a short while, in the days of silent films, he thought of being a movie actor, but nothing came of it.

What Soglow learned at the Art Students League enabled him to get jobs as an illustrator. He started with the cheap pulp magazines, doing conventional hackwork on cowboy pictures or gangster thrillers. Eventually he worked himself up until he was able to sell his drawings to the old *Life, Collier's, Judge, American Magazine* and the *New Yorker*. Commissions to illustrate books came in—today he has illustrated over 20, the latest of which is Frank Case's *Do Not Disturb*; advertisers began to use his work; his own books came out—*Pretty Pictures* (1931); *Everything's Rosy* (1932); *The Little King* (1933); *Wasn't the Depression Terrible?*, written with David G. Plotkin, (1934), and *Soglow's Confidential History of Modern England* (1939).

Most people consider Otto Soglow "quiet, retiring, almost shy." His hobby, he says, is "drawing very detailed pen and ink allegorical and grotesque drawings." In 1928 he was married to Anna Rosen of New York, a painter who also does wood carving. They have one daughter, Tona.

References
Am Mag 117:44 My '34 por
Collier's 106:44-5 D 28 '40 il self por
New Outlook 165:64 My '35
America's Young Men
Birchman, W. Otto Soglow *In* Faces & Facts 1937
Who's Who in America
Who's Who in American Art

SOUKUP, FRANTISEK 1871—Nov 1940 Minister of Justice of Czechoslovakia in 1918; member of executive committee of Labor and Socialist International; last President of Czechoslovakian Senate; oldest member of Czech Social Democratic Party; in black books of Germans; said to have died in nursing home where confined by Gestapo

References
  International Who's Who
  Who's Who in Central and East-
    Europe
Obituaries
  N Y Herald Tribune p16 N 15 '40 por

SPELLMAN, FRANCIS JOSEPH, ARCHBISHOP May 4, 1889- Archbishop
Address: 452 Madison Ave, New York City

When Pope Pius XII appointed Bishop Spellman on May 23, 1939 to be Archbishop of the million-odd Catholics of the See of New York, Archbishop Spellman promised to dedicate himself in every possible way to the welfare of children, whom he called the "hope of the future." He said: "I shall welcome the participation of all in the doing of good things for God, for country, for the poor, the sick, the suffering, and the underprivileged. For my part I shall give my all and do my best."

On March 12, 1940, in St. Patrick's Cathedral, Archbishop Spellman received the sacred pallium, the symbol of unity and loyalty to the Pope, and commemorating also the Archbishop's authority over souls in the Archdiocese of New York. This Archdiocese, probably the richest in the United States, includes Manhattan, the Bronx, Staten Island and the up-state counties of Westchester, Dutchess, Orange, Putnam, Rockland, Sullivan and Ulster. Archbishop Spellman also has authority as "metropolitan over the suffragan sees of Brooklyn, Albany, Buffalo, Rochester, Syracuse and Ogdensburg."

At the ceremony Archbishop Spellman publicly professed his Catholic faith. He also said: "I profess and glory in my American citizenship, and I pledge myself to maintain and defend our fundamental liberties. I am opposed to tyranny, even though it calls itself freedom. I am opposed to anarchy, even though it calls itself liberty. I am opposed to traitors to the United States, even though they wave American flags and call themselves patriots."

Archbishop Spellman was born on May 4, 1889 in Whitman, Massachusetts, the son of a grocer. In 1911 he received his Bachelor of Arts degree from Fordham University, and on the recommendation of William Henry Cardinal O'Connell of Boston was sent to the North American College in Rome, where he was ordained in 1916.

Father Spellman returned with his Doctorate in Sacred Theology to Boston, where in 1922 he became vice-chancellor and, shortly after, Director of Catholic Literature for the archdiocese. He served on the staff of *The Pilot,* the diocesan paper.

In 1925 the Vatican summoned Father Spellman to Rome, where he remained in the service of the Papal Secretariat of State for seven years, the first American so to serve. While at the Vatican he gave

ARCHBISHOP SPELLMAN

the English translations of the international broadcasts and encyclicals of Pope Pius XI. In 1931, when feeling between the Vatican and Fascist Italy ran high, the Pope entrusted to Monsignor Spellman an encyclical on Catholic Action which he feared might be suppressed in Italy. The American priest flew with it to Paris and there released it to the world. He did not pilot the plane on that trip, although Monsignor Spellman held an Italian pilot's license and later obtained an American license in Massachusetts.

On September 8, 1932, Francis Spellman was consecrated a bishop in the Vatican Basilica, where, 16 years before, he had said his first Mass—the first United States bishop ever consecrated there. He returned to this country as the Auxiliary Bishop of Boston, and was appointed pastor of the Sacred Heart Church, Newton Center, Massachusetts, where, until his appointment as Archbishop, he devoted himself earnestly to running a large parish. Modestly, he has often said (with a touch of brogue): "I have always been a parish priest."

When Archbishop Spellman received the sacred pallium, he announced a plan for a new $2,500,000 Catholic high school for boys to be built in The Bronx. Later he explained that he had "just happened to say that it would be a wonderful thing to have a high school in The Bronx"; 24 hours later a priest came in to tell him the land had been obtained; soon afterward he saw a picture of the architect's drawing.

References
  Cath World 149:363 Je '39
  Life 8:41 Je 24 '40 por
  N Y Herald Tribune p10 Ap 1 '40
  N Y Times p1, 19 Mr 13 '40; p10 Ag
    29 '40; p1, 8 S 23 '40

SPELLMAN, ARCHBISHOP—*Continued*

Time 33:54 My 1 '39; 33:30+ Je 5 '39 por

American Catholic Who's Who

Who's Who in America

SPENDER, STEPHEN Feb 28, 1909-
Author

Address: c/o Longmans, Green & Company, 55 Fifth Ave, New York City

With a revolutionary vigor that has caused some of his critics to compare him to Shelley, Stephen Spender has lent a rational fearlessness and a resonant lyricism to the harvests of that group of young English Left-wing poets who "care for freedom more than for the privileges which have given freedom of intellect to individuals in one particular class."

Stephen Spender was born on May 28, 1909, of German-Jewish-English lineage. His father was the late Edward Harold Spender, author, journalist and lecturer, who afterwards became a War-savings propagandist. As a small child he delighted in painting, but at 17 he had set up his own press and supported himself by the printing of chemists' labels; and during the year following he issued his *Nine Experiments,* a paper-back pamphlet of verse. After attending University College School in Hampstead, London, he went up to University College, Oxford, at the age of 19, but found campus life very hostile to his temperament; after some travel abroad he returned to Oxford, and then went down from the University in 1931.

As an undergraduate Spender published *Twenty Poems,* in which there were a palpable independence of language and a gusty imagination; and for the *Spectator's* pres-

STEPHEN SPENDER

entation of "the younger point of view" Spender wrote an article asserting the new poets' need of good constructive criticism. "Too many," he said, "have been ridiculed, excessively admired, and . . . now tolerated, without ever having been criticized." He was largely concerned at this time with the importance of style, the "'schema' of all great poetry."

In 1933 Spender's first substantial book of *Poems* (published in the United States in 1934) appeared in London, and even those critics who demurred at his Communist ideology could not deny his lyrical vehemence. A year later came *Vienna* (American publication date 1935), with imagery of disturbing literalism and some grim mockery that has now become even more grimly significant.

The Destructive Element (1935) was Spender's attempt at a critical analysis of the (probable and actual) expedients of Henry James, Yeats, Eliot, D. H. Lawrence, etc., when they were confronted by "that experience of an all-pervading Present, which is a world without belief." *Burning Cactus* (1936) was his first volume of stories. In *Forward From Liberalism* (1937) he drafted his politico-poetic credo. His *Trial of a Judge* (1938), a verse tragedy on European misrule which was produced by the Group Theatre on the day after its publication, was heralded by the *Spectator* as the "finest English poetic drama written since Otway's *Venice Preserv'd.*" And his work as a cotranslator of Federico García Lorca, Ernst Toller and Rainer Maria Rilke introduced some of their most significant work to the American public in 1939.

In 1936 Spender married Agnes Marie (Inez) Pearn, eldest daughter of the late William Henry Pearn.

Unlike most of the English delegates to the International Writers' Congress, Spender refused to be thwarted by the Foreign Office's ban on visas, and with the aid of French colleagues who had made complicated arrangements for getting the Britishers across the frontier, he proceeded in the summer of 1937 to Valencia, Barcelona for the Congress in which 28 nations participated, as no purely literary affair but rather as an "emphatic assertion that the creation of literature today is inseparable from the struggle in which the standards of culture" must be kept from destruction by Fascism. The "mob," he observed, generally "destroys things not because they are given three stars in *Baedeker* but because they symbolize tyranny, injustice and superstition."

Spender became a firm friend of André Malraux and of José Bergamin, the Spanish Catholic writer who has so effectively aided the Loyalists; and among the Spanish poems which he has translated are several by Manuel Altolaguirre.

Spender is tall and slim, with a high forehead and wavy hair. During the summer he wears a shirt open at the collar, and assumes an extraordinary resemblance (which obviously strengthens the parallel of literary temperaments) to the familiar portrait of Shelley. Malcolm Cowley, who was in Spain with Spender in 1939, credits him with a personality that is "serious, subtle, generous and full of charm." He has remained in England during the War.

References

Nation 144:354-6 Mr 27 '37
Poetry 50:280-4 Ag '37; 52:292-7 Ag '38
Va Q R 14 no4:502-18 [O] '38
Greene, G. The Old School 1934
Who's Who

SPERTI, GEORGE SPERI Jan 17, 1900- Research scientist

Address: b. 6616 Beechmont Ave, Cincinnati, Ohio; h. Fort Mitchell, Kentucky

Since he received his degree in electrical engineering from the University of Cincinnati in 1923, Professor Sperti has interested himself in research. In the practical realm this has resulted in his invention of the K-va Meter, Sperti sunlamps, and light-treatment processes for production of vitamin D. He is the cofounder of the Basic Science Laboratory of the University of Cincinnati and of the Institutum Divi Thomae, Cincinnati, Ohio, where he is in 1940 research professor and director of research. The Institutum was founded to provide research in the various fields of science and to give postgraduate courses in science.

Professor Sperti started his career in the laboratories of large industrial companies. He was assistant chief of the Meter Laboratories of the Union Electric Company, Cincinnati, Ohio; assistant research director of the Duncan Electric and Manufacturing Company, Lafayette, Indiana and research assistant at the University of Cincinnati.

Pope Pius XI honored him by appointing him to the Pontifical Academy of Sciences, November 1936. Professor Sperti is the co-author of *Quantum Theory in Biology* and *Correlated Investigations in the Basic Sciences*. He is editor of the Bulletin of Basic Science Research and Studies of the Institutum Divi Thomae.

Born in Covington, Kentucky, and still living in Kentucky at Fort Mitchell, he is single. Farming, fishing, horses are his hobbies.

References

American Catholic Who's Who
American Men of Science
America's Young Men
Who's Who in America

SPILLER, WILLIAM GIBSON Sept 13, 1863—Mar 18, 1940 Professor emeritus of neurology at the University of Pennsylvania Medical School; writer on medical subjects; ex-president of the American Neurological Association

WILLIAM GIBSON SPILLER

References

American Men of Science
Who's Who in America

Obituaries

N Y Herald Tribune p30 Mr 19 '40
N Y Times p25 Mr 19 '40

SPITALNY, PHIL (spĭ-tăl'nē) Nov 7, 1900- Orchestra leader

Address: c/o National Broadcasting Company, 30 Rockefeller Plaza, New York City

For six years Phil Spitalny and his all-girl orchestra have been appearing in the-

GEORGE SPERI SPERTI

SPITALNY, PHIL—*Continued*

atres and movie houses and broadcasting the *Hour of Charm* program over NBC. This female orchestra has come a long way from the days when to get his first audition Phil Spitalny had to list his band simply as "Phil Spitalny and His Orchestra" and "pipe" the program from a studio blocks away from his prospective sponsors.

The kind of music which the orchestra plays is light dance music, but music in which, according to Mr. Spitalny, "there has been no compromise with cheapness— only good melodic airs have been arranged." After considering for a long time "what sort of music we can offer the masses who love music without having studied it" he decided that the answer was "light music, melodic, rhythmic, well-played tunes which will satisfy the ear and the emotions without overtaxing an intellect which has not been trained so that it may grasp the beauties of the greater classics." The results, says Mr. Spitalny, have proved that "my belief is far from wrong."

To him the relation between this kind of music and an all-girl orchestra is clear. Long ago, when he first set out, Phil Spitalny discovered that light music, to be entirely pleasing, "must give the listener an impression of sweetness, of charm. And where in the world can you find a better exponent of charm than a charming young woman?" He decided on this kind of orchestra, too, because he felt that women should be able to have a future in music. In fact, even before he had his all-girl group he was one of the first band leaders to use a feminine violinist and vocalist with his band.

When he engages women, Spitalny's main requirement is real musicianship. No performer is hired who can't give a finished rendition of two sonatas and two concerti, who hasn't "individual gifts of rhythm and melodic perception," who can't read music fluently and who hasn't had a good deal of experience. In his orchestra eight of the first violins are graduates of the Juilliard School of Music; the concertmaster is a well-known virtuoso; Frances Blaisdell, the flautist, is considered one of the finest in the world.

Surprisingly enough, Phil Spitalny finds women musicians easier to work with than men. "Give me women to work with every time," he says. "They're more cooperative and they don't waste their emotions on much except their music." His girls follow a strict and rigid routine, rehearsing five days a week for five or six hours each day. Their ages range from seventeen to thirty, and as part of their contract they pledge not to

Roy Lee Jackson

PHIL SPITALNY

marry while members of the unit without giving six months' notice. And they manage to get along together without evidences of feminine temperament. They themselves choose a governing board which has the last say about all problems of costumes, hotel rooms, the assignment of upper and lower berths, dressing rooms and general behavior.

Like the members of his orchestra Phil Spitalny is a popular musician whose training has been along strictly classical lines. He was born in Odessa, Russia, the son of Jacob Spitalny, into a family which had been musicians for many generations. His musical education started early and at the age of nine he is supposed to have played the clarinet all night long to earn a few cents. At the Conservatory of Music in Odessa he studied piano, violin and clarinet, but the clarinet became his favorite instrument, and it was as a clarinetist that he toured Russia as a musical prodigy.

When Phil was 15 he came to America with his mother and his brother Leopold, who is now a member of the NBC Symphony Orchestra. After staying in New York for a short time, the Spitalnys moved to Cleveland, Ohio, where Phil served a further musical apprenticeship under his brother Leo, playing in local bands until he began to develop his own ideas of orchestral work.

In the original Cleveland Symphony Orchestra Phil Spitalny used to play the clarinet, and later he founded and conducted his own symphony orchestra in Cleveland which gave Sunday morning concerts of classical and symphonic programs. Then he came East to Boston, where he directed a 50-piece symphony orchestra in one of the larger motion picture houses. After two years there he was well-known as a leader of theatre, hotel, radio and recording bands, so well-known that he was able to make a successful world tour.

Back from the tour, in 1932, he decided to break up his orchestra and organize a group of talented girl musicians. His brother and all his friends told him he was crazy, but he persisted. He spent six months and twenty thousand dollars searching for talent, traveling all over the country, giving auditions, visiting amateur groups, persuading parents to allow their daughters to come to New York. Then he had trouble getting sponsors, until he adopted the ruse of not letting them know they were listening to women until it was too late.

Today Spitalny's orchestra has grown from 22 to 34 girls and today has smooth sailing: there are broadcasts, successful tours, movie shorts. But still Spitalny warns his girls to be careful. It's all right if a male trumpet player breaks a note, he tells them, but if one of them did it people would say, "Well, what can you expect from a woman?"

This five-foot-three conductor with dark complexion and dark, slightly thinning hair, is one of the hardest workers in his field. Often he spends as much as 15 hours a day rehearsing, making arrangements, doing research for special programs and even designing some of the dresses the girls wear. But he keeps up with the latest news, books, pictures and concerts; manages, too, to spend time with his equally musical wife and daughter, and to find a few moments once in a while for a card game or the amusements on the Atlantic City boardwalk.

References
Etude 56:639-40 O '38 por
N Y Herald Tribune VI p3 Ag 1 '40
Variety Radio Directory

SPOTTSWOOD, JAMES 1882—Oct 11, 1940 Character actor; began stage career in 1906 and made recent appearance as Dr Gibbs in *Our Town*; was in a number of motion pictures; took up radio work in 1937 and had rôles in Helen Menken's weekly dramatic program and in *Young Widder Brown*

Obituaries
N Y Herald Tribune p12 O 12 '40 por
N Y Times p17 O 12 '40 por
Variety 140:62 O 16 '40

SPRAGUE, EMBERT HIRAM Dec 20, 1875—Mar 9, 1940 Professor of civil engineering and head of the engineering department at the University of Maine

EMBERT HIRAM SPRAGUE

References
Who's Who in Engineering
Obituaries
N Y Times p48 Mr 10 '40

SPRY, CONSTANCE Dec 5, 1886- Horticulturist
Address: 64 S Audley St, London, England

Mrs. Spry, long noted in English gardening circles as an outstanding master of the art of flower arrangement, achieved international fame when she was asked to design the garden and interior flower decorations for the wedding of the Duke of Windsor and Mrs. Simpson. Her latest book, *Garden Notebook* (1940), is a charmingly informal book which does not mind mixing the recipe for a particularly good potato salad to serve with cold meat with discussions of little-known annuals for the garden. Critics believe that she has "something of the magic" of Beverley Nichols and Richardson Wright as a gardener-writer. She uses the time-tried procedure of dividing her material into twelve chapters, one for each month. Although Mrs. Spry is an English gardener, much of her material relates to American gardens.

She was born in Derby, England, December 5, 1886, and spent her childhood and early married life in Ireland. To an American used to making a garden from virgin woodland, her stories of the century-old gardens she owned at various times are enchanting. During the First World War she was a social worker in a dreary part of northern England. In order to relax herself in this depressing environment, she turned to flower arrangement. Her vases

SPRY, CONSTANCE—*Continued*

and bowls of flowers, so different from the formal Japanese influence (she feels that Americans have overdone the Japanese type), caused enthusiastic comments. She was consequently asked to design window arrangements for Atkinson's, a well-known perfume shop in Bond Street, London.

"I think," she says, "that I had unconsciously struck a moment when people were getting tired of the conventional set pieces made by professional florists and were not entirely satisfied with purely amateur arrangements." Soon she opened her own shop, having, as she says, "no preconceived ideas about what were really florists' flowers." She therefore "used quite naturally whatever I thought was decorative, going each morning to Covent Garden and buying there, but adding all sorts of odds and ends from my own garden. It was the use of these odds and ends, quite natural to me, which seemed to interest people."

In England she has done a great deal toward popularizing various unusual flowers and the use of twigs, seed heads, weeds, grasses, green leaves and vegetables in flower arrangements. This material she uses as enthusiastically as she would use the choicest orchids. She recalls that she would visit the Royal Horticultural Society's flower shows, pick out a few unknown flowers with good decorative qualities, buy a few plants or bulbs and grow them in her own garden. She has always found that anything unusual sells well. Growers would soon become interested and the flowers would appear in quantity on the market. Illustrations of Mrs. Spry's unconventional but charming flower arrangements began to appear in periodicals. Unusual, to Mrs. Spry, does not mean bizarre arrangements which are not in harmony with the surroundings of the vase. Mrs. Spry says: "When I first came to America I was laughed at quite a lot for introducing vegetable leaves and fruits into my flower arrangement. Provided the plant is beautiful, I cannot see why I should not use it for decoration just because it has the added advantage that it can also be eaten."

In the beginning of 1938 she was asked to come to New York at the invitation of the Women's Auxiliary of the Brooklyn Botanical Garden to give two lectures on modern flower arrangement. Her decorations, which show not the slightest trace of Japanese influence but stem instead from the Dutch flower painters, were enthusiastically received. She toured the States in connection with the Garden Clubs of America; spoke over the radio; and found such an interest in flower arrangements that she was enabled to obtain American backing for a shop in New York City's exclusive 50's. She returned to England to collect necessary materials and opened the shop in late November 1938.

The next year she delivered lectures in many cities of the United States and returned to New York for the opening of the World's Fair, where, at the request of the British Government, she arranged two large groups of flowers for the Hall of Honor in the British Pavilion. Every week these were changed by her staff, for Mrs. Spry was off to London again. She lives in an old Kentish farmhouse an hour from London. Every morning she motors down with flowers grown in her nursery for her London shop.

Aside from contributions on flower arrangement to English periodicals, she has written for *Harper's Bazaar, Vogue, House and Garden* and *Ladies' Home Journal*. In addition to her latest book she has written two others. The first, *Flower Decoration* (1935), is a book on the use of flowers as decoration, in which the author explains and illustrates her thesis that floral decoration should bear a distinct relationship to the architecture and general decorative scheme of the room—"that our object should be to reveal and emphasize the particular qualities or beauties in our houses by using our flowers as an artist might use colors." Her second book is *Flowers in House and Garden* (1938). It presents a more detailed treatment than her earlier book. Ten chapters are devoted to flower growing and house decoration, arranged by the months of the year. Of it one reviewer wrote: "Mrs. Spry can arrange almost anything to look beautiful, whether it be kale leaves, orchids or common flowers."

References

House & Gard 73:61-3+ Ap '38 pors

SQUIRES, RICHARD ANDERSON Jan 18, 1880—Mar 26, 1940 Master of the Supreme Court of Newfoundland; twice Prime Minister (1919-23) and (1928-32); knighted in 1921

References

Who's Who

Obituaries

Manchester Guardian p8 Mr 27 '40
N Y Times p21 Mr 26 '40
Newsweek 15:8 Ap 8 '40

STANLEY, FREELAN O. June 1, 1849—Oct 2, 1940 Motorcar inventor, who, with his twin brother, Francis E. Stanley, gained international fame when he invented the Stanley Steamer, forerunner of the modern automobile; steam-driven car was invented in 1896 and appeared in competition with the early gasoline-driven motorcar; more than 10,000 cars were sold before the business was sold in 1918

References

Who's Who in America

Obituaries
N Y Herald Tribune p18 O 3 '40
N Y Times p25 O 3 '40

STARK, HAROLD RAYNSFORD Nov 12, 1880-   Chief of United States naval operations

Address: Navy Department, Washington, D. C.

With national defense a topic of primary interest in the face of developments in Europe in 1940, Admiral Harold R. Stark, chief of naval operations for the United States, occupies a more spotlighted position than any Navy man has since 1914. Appointed chief of naval operations by President Roosevelt in 1939, Admiral Stark carried the burden of appearing before the United States House and Senate Naval Affairs Committees to plug the cause of "building a Navy second to none," and urging appropriations for the Navy's greatest peace time expansion.

Stark was commander of the cruiser division of the United States Battle Force, with the rank of rear admiral, when he was jumped over the heads of 10 ranking admirals, of vice-admirals and rear admirals to the position of chief of naval operations with full rank of admiral, to relieve Admiral William D. Leahy, due for retirement in May 1939 and slated as Ambassador to France in 1941. Stark was then 58 years old, and, as admirals go, a youngster. His appointment assured the Navy of comparatively long-term leadership, for he was six years from the compulsory retirement age.

President Roosevelt first met Admiral Stark in 1914, when the President, then assistant secretary of the United States Navy, was on board the destroyer *Patterson* off the coast of Maine. He said to young Lieutenant Stark at the helm: "May I relieve you for a while? I am an experienced navigator, and I know this coast." The young lieutenant replied: "I am in command here and responsible for the ship. I doubt your authority to supersede me. If you can offer any helpful suggestions I should be glad to hear them." Mr. Roosevelt evidently liked that kind of sea talk. At any rate he picked Stark over 59 others who outranked him for the No. 1 post in the United States Navy.

Admiral Stark, white-haired, capable, professorial and mild in manner, is considered by those acquainted with naval affairs a good choice for the position of chief of naval operations. He is said to be a fortunate combination of activist tradition and studious, informed knowledge on the overlapping zones of naval and foreign policies. He believes that the navy should operate its own air fleet and should always be ready for quick, hard-hitting action. Primarily he is a "big gun" expert, and thinks that decisions go to the biggest and best guns despite all modern improvements in the big battle wagons.

HAROLD R. STARK

An inlander, born at Wilkes-Barre, Pennsylvania, November 12, 1880, Admiral Stark was graduated from the United States Naval Academy in 1903, and was promoted through the ranks until he reached the rank of rear admiral in November 1934. From 1903 to 1917 he served on various ships and at various stations. From 1917 to 1919 he was aide on the staff of Admiral Sims, who was commanding the United States naval forces in European waters.

During the First World War Admiral Stark distinguished himself by taking a flotilla of reconditioned, broken-down destroyers from Philippine waters to harry German and Austrian submarines in the Mediterranean. For this he won the Distinguished Service Medal and the Order of the Crown of Italy.

After the War he occupied a number of posts, including that of aide to both Secretary of Navy Claude A. Swanson and former Secretary of Navy Charles Francis Adams, before he became commander of cruisers of the United States battle force in 1937. Stark was successively: inspector in charge of ordnance at the Naval Proving Ground, Dahlgren, Virginia and at the Naval Powder Factory, Indian Head, Maryland; chief of staff, Destroyer Squadrons, Battle Fleet; commander of the *U. S. S. Virginia*; and, from 1934 to 1937, chief of the Bureau of Ordnance of the Navy Department, Washington, D. C.

The Admiral (sometimes known as "Betty" in the ranks) was married in 1907 to Katherine Rhoades of Wilkes-Barre, Pennsylvania. They have two daughters, both married.

Appearing before the United States House and Senate Naval Affairs Committees in the spring of 1940, Admiral Stark recommended a 25 per cent increase in the size of the

STARK, HAROLD R.—*Continued*

United States Navy in order to maintain the 5-3 ratio with Japan, set by treaty. According to Admiral Stark, with a 25 per cent increase the Navy would be able to defend the Continental United States, the Panama Canal and Hawaii against any aggression, but in case of the worst possible danger—a coalition attack by Japan, Germany, Italy and Russia—it could not guarantee to defend the whole Western hemisphere. "We might," said the Admiral, "have to sacrifice southern Brazil."

Asked by a member of the Senate Naval Committee if a state of emergency existed in the international situation as it bears on United States defense, Admiral Stark answered: "My position is that we should have a Navy second to none, and I feel that I would be derelict in my duty if I found out that we were deteriorating and did not take steps to recover our position." The international situation, he stated, "was an emergency and should be dealt with by America as such."

Tables submitted by Admiral Stark showed that in ships built or being built, measured in terms of modern craft, the United States was in third place, with Britain first and Japan second in first-class navies. The ratio between the United States and Japanese Navies he declared was nearing parity, because of the building the Japanese Navy was doing. "We are uncomfortably close to a 5-5 ratio. We are asking Congress to reaffirm the 5-3 ratio."

By June 1940 the Admiral was asking for a 70 per cent increase in the strength of the United States fleet. And in a nationwide broadcast on Navy Day, October 27, he warned that the United States must envisage "the possibility of simultaneous attacks in either or both oceans." He expressed himself as satisfied with the shipbuilding yards' ahead-of-schedule pace, however.

References

Life 8:18 Ja 22 '40 por
N Y Herald Tribune p10 Ap 17 '40
N Y Post p14 Ap 20 '40 por
N Y Sun p9 Ap 16 '40; p26 Ap 17 '40
N Y Times p12 Ap 16 '40 por; p12 Ap 17 '40
N Y World-Telegram p3 Ap 18 '40; p1 Ap 17 '40; p1 Je 18 '40
Newsweek 13:14 Mr 27 '39 por
Time 33:11 Mr 27 '39 por
Who's Who in America
Who's Who in Government

STASSEN, HAROLD EDWARD (stăs'ĕn) Apr 13, 1907- Governor of Minnesota; Keynoter Republican National Convention, 1940
Address: State Capitol, St Paul, Minnesota

Governor Harold Edward Stassen is the wonder boy of Minnesota. At 31 he was elected Governor; he made sweeping reforms in the state government; and in one year as Governor he had made such a record for himself that, had he been old enough, he would have been considered tall Presidential timber in 1940. Since that was impossible, he was chosen to deliver the keynote address at the Republican National Convention in Philadelphia. He is the youngest Governor ever elected in the United States—young enough to have registered for the draft in October 1940.

Governor Stassen's career reads like an American success story of the old-fashioned kind. Born on a Dakota County, Minnesota farm about six miles from the Twin Cities, on April 13, 1907, the son of William Andrew and Elsie Emma (Mueller) Stassen, who were of German, Czech and Norwegian descent, Harold Edward Stassen attended a little red schoolhouse two miles from his home. He finished the six grades in four years, and entered the Humboldt High School in St. Paul, where, in order to earn money, he got himself a newspaper route (which he tripled in two months).

The spring young Stassen was graduated from high school his father was ill, and the 15-year-old Harold took over for a year, planting, harvesting and selling the crops. The next year, 1922, he matriculated at the University of Minnesota. To earn money, he worked as a grocery clerk, Pullman car conductor for three years, and grease boy in a bakery between semesters.

Stassen really started his political career in college. He was a topflight campus politician. By the time he was a sophomore he knew everybody, and everybody knew him. He was intercollegiate debater, champion intercollegiate orator, captain of a national championship rifle team, holder of almost every campus office including that of all-university class president, and was an honor student to boot. He was so involved in campus politics that he had to hire a fraternity brother as personal secretary.

In college, too, he gathered around him a group of young Republicans, and laid the groundwork for the Young Republican League, of which he became the first chairman.

He received his B. A. degree from the University of Minnesota in 1927, and his law degree two years later. The ink was hardly dry on his diploma when he and a fellow graduate, Elmer J. Ryan, now in Democratic politics, opened a law office in South St. Paul, a stockyard town of 10,000. Within several years their business had grown so that they had four other attorneys in the office. Stassen says he made more money than he makes now as Governor ($7,000 a year).

In 1930 Stassen was elected to his first political office, County Attorney of Dakota County. He won the election without any extensive personal campaigning. During the heat of the campaign he was taken ill, and his partner, Ryan, went out and did the talking for him. Stassen was re-elected County Attorney in 1934, and held the office until he was elected Governor.

Meanwhile, Stassen and his Young Republicans had been busy. Gradually they were wresting power from the old guard Republicans in party politics, and in 1937 Stassen announced himself as a candidate for Governor. He overcame the conservatives in his party easily, and in 1938 faced the formidable opposition of the incumbent Governor Elmer A. Benson and his Farmer-Labor machine, entrenched for eight years.

But Stassen was a. far more energetic campaigner than Benson. He went on a tour of the state that touched every village, town and city. He spoke morning, noon and night, sometimes making as many as four speeches in one evening. He had a way with audiences. Strapping, six-foot-three, ruddy, blue-eyed, with a wide, contagious smile and a friendly manner, Stassen made it a rule never to speak longer than 20 minutes. He wound up his speeches by telling the audience he wanted to shake hands with all before he left. With that he made a "bee line" for the door, and actually shook the hand of every departing listener. It "wowed" the audiences.

Stassen promised the voters clean politics, and preached a liberal brand of fundamental democratic principles. He promised a cleanup of scandals in government, a reduction of operating costs without reduction in relief, and an end to the "labor front" reign of terror. When the votes were counted Stassen had 678,839; Benson, 387,263.

Stassen kept his campaign promises. In one short legislative session he cleaned up scandals, put through his promised Civil Service Law and his labor and antiloan-shark bills, reduced state operating costs $5,000,000 without cutting relief, launched a program to find work for unemployed youth and to boom the state's tourist business. His Labor Law provides that neither strike nor lockout can be instituted in Minnesota until both disputants have waited a 10-day "cooling-off" period (30 days additional if the public welfare is involved). He keeps in touch with his constituents by weekly radio talks, and solicits letters and criticism. The voters like it. A poll in the summer of 1940 showed the state 68 per cent behind Stassen, although he was re-elected in November by a considerably smaller plurality than in 1938. His handling of patronage and his close connections with Willkie (see sketch this issue), who failed to carry the state, possibly accounted for the lower Republican vote.

Governor Stassen is married to the former Esther Glewwe, daughter of a South St. Paul storekeeper, whom he has known since his school days. They have one child, four-year-old Glen Stassen.

References

Am Mag 127:46-7+ Je '39
Christian Sci Mon Mag p1-2 D 14 '38 por; p1-2+ Mr 23 '40 por

HAROLD STASSEN

Cur Hist & Forum 51:37+ Je '40 por
N Y Herald Tribune X p4+ Mr 31 '40 por; pl, 3 Ap 17 '40 por
Newsweek 13:50 My 1 '39 por
Scholastic 34:20 F 4 '39 por
Survey G 29:400-1 Jl '40 por (Same abr. Read Digest 37:75-9 Jl '40)
Time 32:13 O 31 '38 por; 35:16-17 Ap 29 '40 por; 36:21-2 O 21 '40
Streyckmans, F. B. Today's Young Men p125-6 1940
Who's Who in America
Who Who in Government

STEINBECK, JOHN Feb 27, 1902- Author
Address: c/o McIntosh & Otis, 18 E 41st St, New York City

Considered by many critics the best novel of the last 10 years and awarded the Pulitzer Prize in May 1940, *The Grapes of Wrath*, by John Steinbeck, published in 1939, certainly became the most widely read and best-known book of the year. There were 450,000 copies printed by May 1940. Since it has been made into an excellent motion picture playing to capacity audiences, the story of *The Grapes of Wrath* has deservedly become known to a great many more.

A social novel with a powerful theme, excitingly and intensely written, it tells of a great modern trek—a broken-down jallopy and truck caravan—of poverty-stricken people from the Dust Bowl region to the promise of work and plenty in California. Typical of these migrating families, the folks called "Okies," are the Joads from Oklahoma: great-hearted, toughly-courageous Ma, who must hold the family together; Tom, the oldest boy, out of prison on parole; skirt-stricken Al; the two youngster Joads; Grampa, lively, mean and ribald;

JOHN STEINBECK

the diction of the original are tempered, but the story loses none of its emotional impact. Throughout taste, economy, balance and artistry make it one of the best productions to come out of Hollywood.

John Ernst Steinbeck (he does not use his middle name) was born in Salinas, California, February 27, 1902, of mixed German and Irish ancestry. His father, John Ernst Steinbeck, was born in Florida but lived most of his life in Salinas, where he was county treasurer for many years. Sixty years ago his mother, Olive (Hamilton) Steinbeck, taught in the tiny red schoolhouse of the Big Sur, that rugged country of ranges and cliffs which provides the locale for some of Steinbeck's work. Steinbeck was a member of the first surveying party that ever went down into the Big Sur country, when there was no motor road but only steep, precipitous bridle paths and mule tracks. He remembers the time when many families lived down there. "It was not always as deserted as it is now," he says, "and I think one has that feeling, very definitely that people lived there long, long ago, and have left their presence."

He was a graduate of the Salinas High School, 1918. At intervals from 1919 to 1925 he attended Stanford University but was not entirely happy there until it was understood that he wasn't anxious for a degree but wanted to study only what interested him. In between times he traveled about the country getting jobs wherever he could, on cattle ranches and in a sugar refinery. Then he went to New York and worked as a reporter on a New York newspaper but got fired because he couldn't or wouldn't report facts as he found them—only the poetry or philosophy he saw in them. He helped carry bricks for the building of Madison Square Garden and tried free-lancing.

Back again in California, Steinbeck had his first novel, Cup of Gold (the fourth he had written) published while he was living up in the High Sierras near Lake Tahoe's Emerald Bay, where he had a job as winter caretaker for an estate. When the owners found that a pine tree had crashed through their roof, he lost his job —but got one the next day in a trout hatchery.

His first book, Cup of Gold, was published in 1929; Pastures of Heaven, the second, was issued in 1932; and his third, To a God Unknown, came out in 1933. They were not successful financially, for the three together did not sell more than 3000 copies. Steinbeck had almost given up hope of making a living at writing by the time his fourth novel, Tortilla Flat, was published in 1935. It attracted considerable attention, no fewer than eight editions were published, and with the sale of the motion picture rights (though the picture was never made). Steinbeck, for the first time in his life, was able to look forward to at least a year or so of economic comfort. With its success he gained some recognition, and his fifth book, In Dubious Battle (1936), achieved a moderate sale.

Rosasharn, who is expecting a baby—all of them, with their friend the ex-preacher Casey, starving their way West in an old truck. Grampa and Gramma are left in unmarked graves along the road; the family stops in the disreputable camps dotting Highway 66. Finally they reach California, where they do have a pleasant interlude in a Government-run camp. But later, hungry and trying to get the work glowingly promised by handbills, they are hounded from place to place by sheriffs and labor contractors. Tom Joad is forced to go into hiding for killing a vigilante who had clubbed to death his friend Casey; Rosasharn's baby is born dead. But Ma says: "We ain't gonna die out. People is goin' on—changin' a little maybe, but goin' right on."

The Grapes of Wrath is about people, real Americans today: migrant farmers whose lives become tragedy through no fault of their own. Steinbeck understands these lives; through the Joads he has presented a whole culture that is not only uniquely American, but which has the lasting quality of a folk-myth. The narrative is vigorous, colorful, dramatic—though at times, particularly in its concluding episode, falsely dramatic; the speech of the people—honest, colloquial, coarse—is faithfully rendered; many of the minor incidents and situations are faultlessly and unforgettably told. It is not a novel of propaganda, but an inspired human tract, angry at a great injustice, but full of the affirmation of human dignity.

The movie version of The Grapes of Wrath sets a high standard of excellence in adaptation, direction, acting and photography. The last few scenes of the book are left out— but these were the least significant and convincing—and the picture closes with Tom Joad fleeing from the camp. The tone,

While some people called it the best strike novel ever written, *In Dubious Battle* was criticized by Leftists who disliked its portrayal of radical leadership and by reactionaries who thought there was too "Red" a sympathy in his description of strike-breaking. But the Commonwealth Club of California awarded it the gold medal for the best novel by a Californian during the year.

His next book, *Of Mice and Men* (1937) became, however, a best seller, and made Steinbeck widely known. It is a tender, human story of the strong attachment of two "bindle stiffs," or tramps, on a California grain ranch. One is George, shrewd, sophisticated job-getter and protector-in-general of big, dim-witted Lennie, who loves small, soft animals to their peril and death. The two have a wonderful dream of getting a little farm all their own on which to settle down. But the soft hair of Mae, a "floozie" ranch wife, attracts Lennie; and the end is tragedy for Lennie, and for George. A dramatization of the book in 1938 had a successful run on Broadway. Early in 1940 a moving picture version was released, with Burgess Meredith (see sketch this issue) and Lon Chaney Jr., in the title roles. Focusing on action and the building of tension rather than on a sentimental relationship between the two men, the picture presents a tough, raw and at times bleakly tender tale moving toward a powerful climax.

Steinbeck has been described as "of giant height, with fair hair and fair moustache, and eyes the blue of the Pacific on a sunny day, and a deep, quiet, slow voice. He belongs to the coast, the Monterey bay, the ranges and cliffs of the Big Sur country." He reads books on physics, philosophy and biology, but very little fiction, although he likes the writers who had leisure to think deeply about what they wrote—Thackeray, for instance. He was married in 1930 to Carol Henning of San Jose, California, and after their marriage he and his wife lived a while in Monterey, the scene of his novel *Tortilla Flat*. There they owned a launch and spent much of their time sailing and fishing. The fish were a valuable addition to their meager budget, for they lived on $25 a month. At present they live near the small town of Los Gatos, California.

Actually very little is known about Steinbeck, a shy, publicity-abhorring man who prefers the quiet, simple life on his ranch. It is said that when he came to New York in the summer of 1937 he was beset with such a fanfare of literary teas and lionizing that he cleared out as soon as possible on a Norway-bound freighter. He dislikes Hollywood almost as much as New York. Public dinners are anathema to him, and he avoids speech-making—his own or others'. He hates being photographed. Once he was poor, living the life of a working "stiff" on fruit ranches. Now, though royalties pile up, he has neither time nor taste for luxuries. In Mexico he is hard at work in 1940 gathering material for a movie with Herbert Kline, producer of the documentary films, *Crisis* and *Lights Out in Europe*. Steinbeck will write the screen story, which will concern itself with Mexican conditions, and Kline will direct and produce it. Steinbeck had another contract, paying a bare fraction of what he could command from any Hollywood studio, to write *Behold the Man* for the United States Film Service. Since no provision was made for the latter in the latest Federal budget, however, this contract has been abandoned.

References

Canad Forum 20:185-6 S '40
Forum 102:232-8 N '39 il (Same abr. Read Digest 35:89-95 N '39)
Nation 143:302-4 S 12 '36; 149:576-9 N 25 '39
No Am R 243:406-13 Je '37
Sat R Lit 16:11-12+ S 25 '37 (Same abr. Scholastic 32:5+ F 19 '38); 19:3-4 Ap 15 '39 il por (p1); 22:10 Ap 27 '40
Survey G 28:401-2 Je '39; 28:521 S '39 por
Time 30:79 O 11 '37 por; 33:87 Ap 17 '39 por
Va Q R no4:630-2 [O] '39
Gannett, L. John Steinbeck pam 1939
Miron, G. T. Truth About John Steinbeck and the Migrants pam 1939
Steinbeck, J. Grapes of Wrath [biographical preface by Joseph Henry Jackson] 1940
Van Doren, C. C. Revisions *In* American Novel, 1789-1939 p349-66 1940
Who's Who in America

STEINBERG, HANS WILHELM 1899-
Conductor

Address: c/o National Broadcasting Co, 30 Rockefeller Plaza, New York City

Hans Steinberg has been in America only two years but in those two years he has conducted the NBC Symphony Orchestra, he has appeared with the Philadelphia Orchestra in Robin Hood Dell, he has led the New York Philharmonic Orchestra at the Lewisohn Stadium concerts and he has been engaged by NBC as one of the four regular conductors for its orchestras in the 1940 to 1941 season.

Steinberg came to this country well recommended, however. His work as guest conductor in most of Europe's capitals had brought him fame, and Toscanini had singled him out as one of the most competent and inspiring of the younger modern conductors.

Steinberg's life has been one devoted to music with a singleness of purpose. Born in Cologne, Germany in 1899, he began to study the violin almost as soon as he was big enough to hold one. While at grammar school he attended the School of Higher Musical Studies in Cologne. When he was about 15 he started taken piano lessons with Professor Uzielli, who was perfectly certain that the boy would become a virtuoso with this instrument. But he not only studied the piano and violin, he stud-

Roy Lee Jackson

HANS WILHELM STEINBERG

ied the theory of music and composition, and at the end of his studies won the Wullner Prize for conducting, presented by the city of Cologne.

In 1929 Steinberg's musical career began when he was made "Correpititor" and personal assistant to Otto Klemperer at the Cologne Opera House. In 1924 he was made first conductor. Because of his success in Cologne, Zemlinski engaged him as conductor for the German Theatre in Prague, where after a very short time he became opera director.

From 1926 on Steinberg became a regular guest conductor at the Berlin State Opera House and in 1929 accepted the post of General Musical Director of the Frankfurt Opera House and conductor of the Museum Concerts in that city. Frequently he appeared as guest conductor with the great orchestras of Europe—in Paris, London, Prague, where after a very short time he was engaged by Huberman to conduct the Palestine Orchestra after he had been made an exile from Germany.

Toscanini was scheduled to appear with the Palestine Orchestra, and when he came there was delighted with the preliminary groundwork that Steinberg had done for his concerts. Immediately he chose him as his assistant in preparing for the NBC concert broadcasts in 1939. He assisted Toscanini, and after Toscanini left conducted the NBC Orchestra himself in a number of broadcasts.

Like Toscanini, Steinberg conducts without a score, but unlike Toscanini "he waggles his head both for cues and for umph." And "when the pinches come he winds up like Dizzy Dean and lets them have it."

References

Stadium Concerts R 23:5 Jl 25 '40
Time 33:72 Mr 13 '39 por

STEINBERG, MILTON, RABBI Nov 25, 1903- Rabbi of the Park Avenue Synagogue in New York City; author

Address: b. 50 E 87th St, New York City

Rabbi Milton Steinberg's first work in fiction form is an excellent novel whose central figure is Elisha Ben Abuyah, a second-century apostate from the Jewish faith. A student of classical literature and history, particularly the Greco-Roman period, Rabbi Steinberg has imbued the background of *As a Driven Leaf* (1940) with carefully authentic detail. This, together with a vivid, sensitive and dramatic handling, makes the book not only a convincing document but a highly moving piece of creative writing.

The wealthy and gifted Elisha, admitted to the highest Jewish council, the *Sanhedrin,* and married to a conventional woman who has no sympathy with his intellectual interests, turns in his search for "absolute truth" from the Talmud to the logic of Euclid. His wife is outraged, and a separation follows. His pupils leave him. He goes to Antioch, center of Greek learning, where he rises high in the favor of Manto, the brilliant mistress of Rufus, governor of Palestine. But finding no faith in either the Greek or the Roman world, Elisha, having forsaken his own, is indeed lost. Rufus forces him to help stamp out Judaism, and he comes to be despised by both Jews and Romans. In a final scene of dramatic intensity he is compelled to witness the deliberately cruel executions of his friends in the rabbinate whom he has betrayed.

Thus, unlike that other famed apostate, Spinoza, Elisha does not transcend his apostasy, but falls victim to it. His tragedy, as Rabbi Steinberg shows us, lies in an over-intellectuality, a rigid super-fidelity in the search for a logical theology. But the character of the man is glowing and real;

RABBI STEINBERG

and the book's theme is freshly pertinent to contemporary conflicts.

Rabbi Steinberg was born in Rochester, New York, November 25, 1903, and received his early schooling there. He was not, however, reared for the rabbinate, the profession first chosen for him being medicine. But at the College of the City of New York he became interested in classical languages. He took his M. A. at Columbia University. Then, under the influence of Rabbi Jacob Kohn of Los Angeles, he studied for the rabbinate and was ordained at the Jewish Theological Seminary.

He taught Jewish history and religion at the Teachers Institute of the Seminary, but his first congregation after ordination was in Indianapolis, Indiana (1928-33). Since then he has been Rabbi of the Park Avenue Synagogue in New York City. He was a member of the editorial board of *Reconstructionist,* 1936 to 1937; he has been a member of the administrative council of the Zionist Organization of America since 1934 and of the Rabbinical Assembly since 1936.

In 1929 he married Edith Alpert of New York City, and on his honeymoon visited Palestine, thus adding to his firsthand knowledge of the background for *As a Driven Leaf.* The Steinbergs have two children, Jonathan and David Joel.

Following numerous articles and reviews, Rabbi Steinberg published in 1934 *The Making of the Modern Jew,* an account of the history of the Jews beginning with medieval times, and an analysis of their situation today. The book was praised for its authoritative merits and for the vigor of its style. As one critic said—and this may be said also of *As a Driven Leaf*—"Steinberg writes as with a scalpel, in sharp, incisive, penetrating sentences. A vivid, communicative ardor illumines his pages."

References

Who's Who in American Jewry

STEKEL, WILHELM [WILLY BOJAN, DR. SERENUS, pseuds.] 1866—June 27, 1940 Viennese psychoanalyst; formerly assistant to the late Dr. Sigmund Freud; later separated from Freud because of disagreement with his theories; author of works on mental maladies; a violent anti-Fascist, he was forced to leave Vienna in 1938 and moved to London; listed by John Gunther as among the "ten most interesting people whom I have come to know"

References

Murchison, C. ed. Psychological Register 1932
Wer ist's?

Obituaries

N Y Herald Tribune p18 Je 28 '40
N Y Times p19 Je 28 '40 por

STEPHENS, WARD Sept 9, 1879— Sept 11, 1940 Pianist; composer; at one time assistant conductor at the late Oscar Hammerstein's Manhattan Opera House; was a musical prodigy at the age of five; had been a pupil of Johannes Brahms and other famous musicians; played in almost all European countries; served as accompanist for Fritz Kreisler; was composer of two symphonies, three light operas and a great number of secular and sacred songs; founded Mozart Festival at Harrisburg, Pennsylvania

References

Weir, A. E. ed. Macmillan Encyclopedia of Music and Musicians 1938
Who's Who in America 1938-39

Obituaries

N Y Times p23 S 13 '40

STETTINIUS, EDWARD REILLY JR. (stĕ-tĭn'nĭ-ŭs) Oct 22, 1900- Member of the National Defense Commission

Address: b. War Department, Washington, D. C.; h. 21 E 79th St, New York City

During the First World War a man named Edward Reilly Stettinius was called from the Diamond Match Company by J. P. Morgan to direct the munitions' purchases of the French and British governments in this country. His work earned him a Morgan partnership, and after the United States entered the War he was requisitioned for similiar work with our War Department. With World War II raging in Europe, another Stettinius, youthful, silver-haired Edward Reilly Jr., announced his resignation as chairman of the Board of Directors of the United States Steel Corporation and as director and member of its finance committee to accept full-time duties on President Roosevelt's new National Defense Commission. "As coordinator of industrial materials, his duty will be to see that the factories get all the material they need and get it quickly." His task is to render the United States independent of foreign sources for adequate supply of strategic materials. The Raw Materials Division under him has attempted to solve some of the more pressing problems by setting up emergency reserve supply of grease wool and achieving expansion of synthetic rubber production and tin-smelting plants.

Mr. Stettinius' qualifications for an important position in any such commission have been universally acknowledged by the press, one commentator calling him "all that the most critical Republican could ask." He was born in Chicago, Illinois on October 22, 1900, the son of the Morgan partner and of Virginia (Carrington) Stettinius, and from his days at prep school at Pomfret, Connecticut, he had to overcome "the handicaps of wealth, position and the reputation of a brilliant father." Matriculating at the University of Virginia in 1919, where "Big Stet" had been a student before him, young Stettinius acquired the title "Little Stet" and, in spite of the fact that he was already gray-haired and sober,

EDWARD R. STETTINIUS JR.

got himself elected to the Imps, "an honor usually conferred upon the Unversity's most rousing hell raiser." Somehow he never piled up enough credits to graduate, but his brilliant work as founder and manager of a student-employment bureau attracted the attention of a vice-president of General Motors, who offered him a job before he left school in 1924.

Before accepting it "Stet" took an educational trip abroad, and then went to Detroit to the Hyatt Bearings Division of General Motors as a 40-cent-an-hour laborer—"in overalls, though not without expectations." Whatever his expectations, they weren't disappointed. By 1931 Stettinius had become vice-president in charge of industrial and public relations, one year after having been appointed assistant to President Sloan (see sketch this issue). Then, during "the heyday of NRA," Stettinius went to Washington—first as liaison officer for General Motors with the New Deal authorities; in 1932 as director of the National Share-the-Work Movement for the Second Residential District; then, in 1933, as liaison officer between the Industrial Advisory Board and the National Industrial Recovery Administration. In Washington he won dozens of friends in the inner councils of the New Deal, astonished everyone by his "talents for soothing unreconstructed tycoons," and although "his friends were baffled by this open consorting with the enemy," acquired a reputation as a liberal, enlightened young businessman that was to be very helpful to United States Steel after Myron Taylor (see sketch this issue) called him in April 1934 to become vice-chairman of Big Steel's Finance Committee.

At that time Stettinius knew nothing about steel, and many people thought of him as merely a Morgan "stooge." He wasn't exactly that. For two years he read everything about steel he could lay his hands on, spent months knocking about the plants. In 1936 he became chairman of the Finance Committee and a director of the corporation, and on April 5, 1938 the steel world was dumbfounded by the promotion of a "37-year-old stripling" to the chairmanship of the Board, after the resignation of Myron Taylor, twice his age.

Taylor hadn't made a mistake, though. Evidently what "Steel" needed was young blood, and a man who could function acceptably as "Washington representative of the Corporation." Under the guidance of Stettinius United States Steel ceased being a "political scapegoat," and the revolution in the company's sales, management, labor and public relations policies was typified by the modernization of New York headquarters, once "a dark wilderness of unused gas jets, rolltop desks, internal politics."

In the fall of 1939 Stettinius once more came to Washington, this time as head of a War Resources Board appointed to study industrial mobilization of the United States in case of war. After a few weeks the board was disbanded and its unfinished report was never made public, but it seems reasonable to suppose that at that time Stettinius formed a rather good idea of industrial defense needs.

During the first three months of 1940 the 26 steel companies showed profits of $25,134,000, compared with $6,865,000 for a similar period last year, but Stettinius announced that in 1939 United States Steel stockholders had earned a "wage" of only 3 per cent, and gave it as his opinion that "a starvation wage for owners is as destructive as a starvation wage for workers." In May 1940 Stettinius gave up a position with a salary of $100,000 to become a government dollar-a-year man.

Shortly afterward President Roosevelt announced the sale of $200,000,000 worth of "antiquated" armaments to United States Steel for $50,000,000, for resale to the Allies.

"Genial, excessively energetic," Stettinius "has the happy faculty of charming even those whom he defeats." His heavy, black brows and ruddy complexion contrast with his white hair and teeth to make him extremely striking in appearance, and when restless Ed Stettinius "goes bounding through the board room hung with somber portraits of past great steelmen, he suggests a somewhat impudent tourist taking a gallery of old masters in his stride." Episcopalian, member of the Union Club and other clubs, he enjoys society with a Virginia wife (he married Virginia Gordon Wallace of that state in 1926), three young sons (only one of whom isn't a twin), an apartment in New York and a Virginia farm, where he tries to escape from business by raising "white-faced Hereford cattle, prize Belgian draft horses, and turkeys." His Washington home is in a large, outlying hotel, but as soon as he finishes work on Saturday afternoon he drives his own car to his farm.

References

Am Mag 130:71 O '40 por
Business Week p15 Ag 19 '39 por (cover); p22-3+ Ag 24 '40 por; p30 O 19 '40
Fortune 21:64-7+ Mr '40 il por
New Repub 102:791 Je 10 '40
N Y Herald Tribune p1, 10 My 29 '40; p13 Ap 12 '40
N Y Times p1, 15 My 29 '40 por; p1, 45 Je 5 '40 por
N Y World-Telegram p11 My 29 '40
Time 30:59-60+ N 8 '37

America's Young Men
Who's Who in America
Who's Who in Commerce and Industry

STEUER, MAX DAVID (stoi'ĕr) Sept 6, 1871—Aug 21, 1940 One of the nation's most prominent criminal lawyers; started as an immigrant boy from Austria; worked as a newsboy and tailor's helper while earning way through school; was a power behind Tammany Hall; at height of career was reputed to have made $1,000,000 a year; defended ex-Governor Gifford Pinchot of Pennsylvania, Tex Rickard, fight promotor, ex-Attorney General Harry M. Daugherty, and Charles E. Mitchell, ex-president of the National City Bank of New York, in addition to many of the nation's publicized gangsters

MAX STEUER

References

Boyer, R. O. Max Steuer 1932
Who's Who in America
Who's Who in American Jewry
Who's Who in Law

Obituaries

N Y Herald Tribune p16 Ag 22 '40 por
N Y Times p1, 19 Ag 22 '40 por
Time 36:47 S 2 '40

STEVENSON, E. ROBERT Aug 29, 1882- Editor in chief of the Waterbury (Connecticut) *Republican and American*

Address: b. Republican and American, Waterbury, Connecticut; h. Eastfield Rd, Waterbury, Connecticut

E. Robert Stevenson (he apparently doesn't like "Elias") has been an English teacher, a novelist, an historian and almost everything in the newspaper business—reporter, feature writer, city and managing editor, editor in chief. Since 1917 he has been editor of the Waterbury (Connecticut) *Re-*

E. ROBERT STEVENSON

publican (in 1922 consolidated with the *American*), which won the Pulitzer Gold Medal this year for its exposure of graft in the city administration.

Stevenson was born in New Haven, Connecticut, August 29, 1882, the son of Elias Gilbert and Mary Ann (Tighe) Stevenson. After graduating from the Hillhouse High School in 1903 he went to Yale in his hometown, at the same time working as reporter on the New Haven *Register* and *Journal Courier*. He was graduated in 1907 and spent two years away from the newspaper game: one as instructor in English at the Georgia School of Technology in Atlanta, another as English teacher in the Hartford, Connecticut High School. But 1909 found him working as a reporter on the Springfield (Massachusetts) *Republican,* and he hasn't gone back to teaching since. In 1911 he published the *Damnation of Sandy Mac-*

STEVENSON, E. ROBERT—*Continued*

Gregor. From 1912 to 1914 he was feature writer for the Springfield *Republican,* from 1914 to 1917 its city editor, and then in 1917 he joined the staff of the Waterbury *Republican* as editor, becoming managing editor of both the *Republican* and *American* when they merged in 1922 and, in 1927, editor in chief. In 1929 he made his debut as historian with a three-volume history entitled *Connecticut History Makers.*

Mr. Stevenson, an Episcopalian and a Mason, is a member of the American Society of Newspaper Editors, the Waterbury Chamber of Commerce, and the Mattatuck Historical Society. He belongs to the Waterbury, Rotary, University, Green Mountain and Waterbury Country Clubs.

References

St Louis Post-Dispatch p1C My 7 '40 por

Who's Who in America

STEWART, GEORGE CRAIG, BISHOP Aug 18, 1879—May 2, 1940 Bishop of the Protestant Episcopal Diocese of Chicago; entered the ministry in 1898

References

Time 28:50 O 26 '36 por

Who's Who in America

Obituaries

N Y Herald Tribune p20 My 3 '40 por

N Y Times p21 My 3 '40 por

STIEGLITZ, ALFRED (stĕg'lĭts) Jan 1, 1864- Photographer; editor

Address: b. 509 Madison Ave, New York City; h. Lake George, New York

"Philosopher, guide, teacher, discoverer of genius, inspirer of the machine age, prophet and Messiah"—that, according to John Gould Fletcher, is Alfred Stieglitz to the 25 famous people who contributed to *America and Alfred Stieglitz* (1934). To them and to many other Americans this photographer is "the man who has done the most for art in America."

Alfred Stieglitz was born January 1, 1864, in Hoboken, New Jersey, the son of a prosperous Jewish wool merchant. In 1871 Alfred's father with his family of six children moved to New York City, where Alfred was educated in private and public schools. He went to the City College of New York for a while and studied engineering because a professor there told his father it was a good field for a young man. In 1881 he was sent to Germany, to the Berlin Polytechnic, to study engineering further, but one day he saw a camera in a shop window. He bought it.

Stieglitz no longer was interested in engineering. He took courses in chemistry, with photography in view, and he used the Polytechnic laboratory for photographic experiments. He took pictures of the view from his window, of himself, and he came "to feel for the first time that he had a right to life and a right to be living in Berlin."

When Stieglitz started photographing it was in the days when it was necessary to have daylight, and when pictures needed a long exposure. From 1887, when he won first prize in an English competition of amateur photographers with pictures of Italy, Stieglitz has deepened and enriched the resources of his medium. He was the first to introduce figures in night photography. His was pioneering work in reproducing snow and rainstorms. He it was who insisted that photography had to be used to emphasize its ability to render substance, shape, texture and motion.

"One of the most active and experimental photographers in the world," Stieglitz turned his camera on the thing itself, not sprinkled with the eau de cologne of romance. "He gave the people back to themselves. He restored their world to them. The sea that cut a pattern in the sand; the shaggy, snow-capped Alps; a girl drawing water from a well; broad steps of stone endlessly rising." When Picasso saw Stieglitz's *Steerage* he was reported to have said: "This is exactly what I have been trying to say in paint."

Stieglitz always has seen photography as an art in itself, not a weak imitation of other forms of art. "His lucid sense of the fitting and authentic," says Frank Jewett Mather, "has kept him clear of the solecism of forcing the sensitive plate to compete with the painting of lithographic stone." Because photography is an art, Stieglitz is a perfectionist. A friend once asked him for a duplicate print from a certain negative he had made. "There will be but one print," said Stieglitz. "There will be no duplicates." "A waste print?" asked the friend. "You do not understand," said Stieglitz patiently. "There will be but one print that will express me. The others will not express me. They will be nothing."

In 1890 Stieglitz returned to America. His father bought for him and his brothers the Heliochrome Engraving Company in which he spent three years experimenting with three-color work. In 1893 he married Emeline Obermeyer of New York by whom he has one daughter, Katherine Stearns. In America, while with the Heliochrome Company and after, Stieglitz kept photographing. In his pictures are recorded the growth and change in New York. In *The Terminal,* for instance, "the whole mood and character of a period are caught for all eternity in the web of a photographic second."

In the 1890's Stieglitz edited the *American Amateur Photographer* and from 1897 to 1903 published and edited *Camera Notes.* But Stieglitz was not content just to be a photographer. He threw over the accepted commercial standards of the photo societies and journals from which he had accepted many medals and honors and effected a secession from the established ranks.

In 1905, at 291 Fifth Avenue, he opened a gallery for displaying the photographs of those whose work he thought stood above commercial standards. People came and asked questions, and Stieglitz found himself acting as official interpreter for photography, fighting for its right to life as a form of creative expression. *Camera Work,* the organ of the Photo-Secession, which he edited until its demise in 1917, has been called "perhaps the most distinguished work on art that America has ever seen."

Soon "291" widened its scope to include works of artists and sculptors. The early masters of the new art movement in France— Cézanne, Picasso, Matisse, Rodin, Toulouse-Lautrec, Picabia, Brancusi, Bráque, Rousseau—had their first American representation under the Stieglitz aegis, and this was a considerable time before the modern movement had got under way in America. He set the ball rolling in 1907 with his exhibition of Rodin drawings and gave the town another shock a few months later with a series of Matisse drawings. John Gould Fletcher gives a less flattering connotation to these activities of Stieglitz. He says that in Paris a new primitivism and abstractionism were preparing to sweep over the world and Stieglitz had merely to show examples of this new art—"in the case of selection he relied, I suspect, on the sensation-hunting energies of his friend, Miss Gertrude Stein—in order to give Americans the impression that he knew a good deal."

From 1907 until 1917, when "291" ceased to exist, an important group of American artists became associated with Stieglitz. Georgia O'Keeffe (whom he married on December 11, 1924), John Marin, Charles Demuth, Arthur Dove, Max Weber, Abraham Walkowitz are but a few of those whom he inspired, showed, helped. According to most critics, Stieglitz "has been a primary factor in forwarding the work of some of the most important of modern artists." But John Gould Fletcher feels that in surrounding himself with American painters and advising them he "probably wrecked and thwarted talents which, without his misdirection, would have found themselves engaged in more significant ways."

From 1917 to 1925 Stieglitz devoted himself completely to photography. In 1925 he opened the "Intimate Gallery" with an exhibition of John Marin, and in 1930 "An American Place" at 509 Madison Avenue, New York City, where he still is. In "An American Place" Stieglitz has continued to demonstrate the essential purpose of "291" through regular exhibitions, publications and manifestoes from time to time.

Here, as in his other galleries, he has continued to maintain the same indifference to commerce. One day, when there were pictures on the wall, a woman who had been walking about, suddenly addressed Stieglitz. "This is a very exciting show. What else ought I to see in New York?" Stieglitz replied: "I have no idea what else you ought to see in New York." The woman asked him:

Dorothy Norman

ALFRED STIEGLITZ

"Could you tell me by any chance where Mr. Stieglitz' gallery is? I hear he has the finest things in New York, but I can't find his gallery listed anywhere." The reply: "Mr. Stieglitz has no gallery." The woman insisted he was mistaken, but Stieglitz raised his voice: "Well, I ought to know. I am Mr. Stieglitz, and I tell you he has no gallery."

When she had left, someone standing there suggested that she might have bought something. But Stieglitz said: "Something more was at stake than her knowing where she was for the moment. I am not in business. I am not interested in exhibitions and pictures. I am not a salesman, nor are the pictures here for sale, although under certain circumstances certain pictures may be acquired. But if people seek something, really need a thing, and there is something here that they actually seek and need; then they will find it in time. The rest does not interest me."

References

Am Mag Art 26:542-5 D '33; 28:36-42 Ja '35

Am Phot 30:199-206 Ap '36

Am R 4:588-602 Mr '35

Christian Sci Mon Mag p5 N 17 '37 por

Newsweek 4:19 D 8 '34

Sat R Lit 11:337 D 8 '34

Frank, W. and others, eds. America and Alfred Stieglitz 1934

Rosenfeld, P. Alfred Stieglitz *In* Port of New York p237-79 1933

Who's Who in America

Who's Who in American Jewry

STIMSON, HENRY LEWIS Sept 21, 1867- Secretary of War

Address: b. United States War Department, Washington, D. C.; h. Huntington, Long Island, New York

On July 2, 1940 the Senate Military Affairs Committee voted to recommend confirmation of Henry L. Stimson's appointment as Secretary of War. On July 9 the Senate took its advice. Senate approval of the appointment had been expected, in spite of the flurry caused in isolationist and certain Republican circles by Roosevelt's nomination of a former Secretary of State in Hoover's Cabinet to the strategic post of War Secretary the day after he had made a speech calling for governmental aid to Britain "in our own ships and under convoy if necessary."

The veteran lawyer and diplomat was born in New York City on September 21, 1867, the son of Lewis Atterbury and Candace (Wheeler) Stimson. From Phillips Andover Academy he went to Yale, spending his vacations hunting big game. He was graduated in 1888, a Skull and Bonester, and proceeded to take an M. A. degree at Harvard in 1889 and an LL. B. at the Harvard University Law School in 1890. The next year he was admitted to the Bar, and then became understudy to the late Elihu Root by joining the law firm of Root and Clarke. By 1897 he had become a partner in the firm, which was then known as Root, Howard, Winthrop and Stimson, and which in 1901 took the name of Winthrop and Stimson. From 1898 to 1907 he was also a member of the New York National Guard.

It was in 1906 that Mr. Stimson received his first appointment to a governmental post —from Roosevelt I. He became United States District Attorney for the Southern District of New York, won Roosevelt's support by his prosecution of a famous embezzler, and in 1909 resigned to become the Republican nominee for the Governorship of New York (1910). The opposition called him the "human icicle." Defeated, he was made Secretary of War the following year by President Taft upon the recommendation of Elihu Root, and it was in this office that he acquired the nickname "Light-Horse Harry." Wilson's Administration interrupted his government service, but in 1915 he was attending the New York Constitutional Convention as a delegate at large and helping Al Smith in reforming the State Constitution; during the First World War serving in the A.E.F. as lieutenant colonel of the 305th Field Artillery and colonel of the 31st Field Artillery. For the most part, however, he was occupied with his private law practice, with fox-hunting, with building up a fortune, and with acquiring Highgold, his Long Island estate. In 1927 Coolidge appointed him special representative to arbitrate a dispute regarding the Presidency of Nicaragua; from 1927 to 1929 he was Governor General of the Philippines, where he performed "one of the best jobs he had ever done"; and in 1929 he became Secretary of State in the Cabinet of President Hoover.

As Secretary of State Stimson became known both for his strong interventionist stand and as "the original anti-appeaser." He was disliked in Latin America for his book, *American Policy in Nicaragua* (1927), which was considered propaganda for the State Department's policy there. Chairman of the American delegation to the London Naval Conference in 1930, he and Ramsay MacDonald were talking naval limitation. With Japan's repudiation of the Nine-Power Treaty through the Manchukuo invasion in 1931 he tried to persuade Great Britain to help the United States crack down on Japan, finally formulated the Hoover-Stimson doctrine of non-recognition of territories and agreements achieved by aggression. The Kellogg Pact, signed the following year, he declared, was not merely a negative policy putting the United States on record against war, but a positive policy obligating our country to consult with other nations in the endeavor to make the pact a "living reality." That same year (1932) he headed the American delegation to the Disarmament Conference at Geneva, where he could still "take tactful boat rides with Mussolini."

Stimson was also something of an enigma. He spent frequent week ends—from early Friday until Tuesday—away from the State Department, and his $800,000 estate at Woodley "was the scene of an interminable series of garden parties, dinners and luncheons"; yet he believed in the redistributing of wealth and increased income taxes for the wealthy. He advocated universal military conscription, "yet was the most hard-hitting enemy the militarists had where they opposed a naval reduction treaty." On some counts he was called "revolutionary and radical," on others "bull-headed, militaristic and inept." He had four personal secretaries, each with one or more assistants; he had a military aide—the first in history to a Secretary of State.

After 1932 Stimson resumed his long-interrupted law practice with the firm of Winthrop, Stimson, Putnam and Roberts, but continued to concern himself with the international scene. "A croquet-playing crony of Secretary Hull" (see sketch this issue), he had few complaints to make regarding his Democratic successor—indeed, it is said that he believed Hull one of the greatest of all Secretaries and would dash off letters to the New York *Times* whenever his policies were criticized. Strongly conservative, he was still sympathetic to some of the New Deal policies, made frequent trips to Washington and more than once publicly supported President Roosevelt's foreign policies and called for nonpartisanship in the field of foreign relations. His radio speech in May 1934 backing a bill to give wide tariff-bargaining powers to Roosevelt was found "most untimely" by Republican Senators.

In 1937 he was elected president of the Association of the Bar of the City of New York.

In his writings Stimson grew increasingly critical of Japanese policy, called for the cessation of United States' aid to Japan. He advocated a firm attitude toward Hitler and Mussolini, bewailed the "amoral" drift of neutrality legislation, was one of the strongest opponents of the Ludlow Amendment. Shortly before the fall of the Spanish Republic he was fighting for the lifting of the Spanish embargo. Hull's proposed neutrality bill allowing the Allies to purchase munitions under the cash-and-carry plan was given Stimson's support before the outbreak of World War II. And although early in 1939 it was still his opinion that the United States "enjoyed a unique and powerful advantage in its geographical situation and freedom from bomb attack," it was also his opinion that we must drop our isolationism.

With the beginning of hostilities Stimson's quarrel with United States isolationists naturally became more serious. He became a leading member of the Committee to Defend America by Aiding the Allies, organized by William Allen White (see sketch this issue) and one of the leading "Air Plattsburgers." He was often accused of being an "interventionist," having "suggested by his tone if not his words that even war would not be too high a price to pay for Hitler's scalp."

On June 18 a speech given by Mr. Stimson at New Haven, Connecticut laid down a line for United States' foreign policy and defense. He called for immediate compulsory military training, urged the repeal of "our ill-starred, so-called neutrality venture," accelerated shipment of planes and munitions to Great Britain with the use of the United States Navy to convoy shipments, if necessary, and the opening of American ports to British naval and merchant marine vessels. On June 20, 1940 the resignation of Secretary of War Woodring from President Roosevelt's Cabinet was followed by the announcement of Stimson's appointment, at the same time that Colonel Franklin Knox (see sketch this issue) was called to the post of Secretary of the Navy.

Although the two men were promptly read out of the Republican Party, many leading Republicans expressed their approval of the appointments, while some Democrats crossed party lines to condemn the coup as a prelude to war, an effort to disrupt opposition on the political front, or a retreat from the former liberal policies of the Administration. In Great Britain and in China the press was unanimous in its approval, however.

At the session of the Senate Military Affairs Committee which recommended confirmation of Mr. Stimson's appointment, the former Secretary of State defended his views during two hours of questioning. He explained his New Haven

HENRY L. STIMSON

speech as "having been made as a private citizen and at a time when the British situation seemed more desperate than it does at present." Queried as to his accord with all the Administration's policies, he replied: "I have abandoned everything except a consideration of the defense of the country since my acceptance."

Since his appointment he has been an ardent advocate of conscription and was one of the most gratified men in Washington when he drew the first number in the Draft Lottery on October 29, 1940. Under him United States defenses in Hawaii will be strengthened, and he has already ordered 65 per cent speed-up in army munitions production by the six Federal arsenals.

Mr. Stimson married the former Mabel Wellington White. He has no children, but many pets; he is fond of exercise, and is an excellent rider and tennis player. He holds the rank of brigadier general in the Inactive Section of the Officers' Reserve Corps. He has been described as "a strange mixture of conservatism and liberalism, of pacifism and militarism, of gentility and democracy."

References

Cong Digest 17:59-62 F '38
Fortune 16:154 Jl '37 por
Int Concil 334:721-32 N '37 (Same abr. Read Digest 31:63-7 D '37); 348:117-24 Mr '39; 350:255-62 My '39
New Repub 103:4-5 Jl 1 '40
New Yorker 6:30-3 O 4 '30 por
Newsweek 3:8 My 5 '34; 10:9 O 18 '37 por
Time 34:19 Jl 17 '39 por; 35:16 Ja 8 '40 por; 36:11 Jl 1 '40
U S News 9:22-3 Jl 12 '40

STIMSON, HENRY L.—*Continued*

Allen, R. S. and Pearson, D. Wrong-horse Harry (H. L. Stimson) *In* Washington Merry-Go-Round p103-36 1931
Who's Who in America
Who's Who in Law
Who's Who in the Nation's Capital

STIMSON, JULIA CATHERINE May 26, 1881- Chairman of the Nursing Council on National Defense

Address: b. American Nurses' Association, 50 W 50th St, New York City; h. Horse Chestnut Rd, Briarcliff Manor, New York

Major Julia C. Stimson, chairman of the Nursing Council on National Defense and veteran of the First World War, is urging young women to enter the nursing profession during the present emergency. "Even in ordinary times no highly qualified nurse need ever be unemployed," she says. "The expansion of the Public Health Service and the greater administrative positions now opening for women in the nursing field assure brilliant careers in the future."

Major Stimson herself has had a distinguished career in the nursing profession. She was born in Worcester, Massachusetts, the daughter of Dr. Henry A. and Alice Wheaton (Bartlett) Stimson, and the cousin of Henry L. Stimson, Secretary of War (see sketch this issue). She is the sister of Dr. Phillip Moen Stimson, specialist in communicable diseases, and of Dr. Barbara E. Stimson, specialist in orthopedic surgery. Julia Stimson was sent to the Brearley School in New York City and later to Vassar College, from which she received her B. A. in 1901. When she left college Miss Stimson was undecided about a career, but knew she was

JULIA CATHERINE STIMSON

interested in biology and sociology. She enrolled as a graduate student at Columbia University and spent the years until she entered the New York Hospital Training School in 1904 studying.

Miss Stimson's first job was that of superintendent of nurses at Harlem Hospital and in 1908 she became head of the nursing department of the Hospital. In this position she became interested in the possibilities of a hospital social service department and helped develop one. It was because of this interest that she received her next position in 1911—that of administrator of hospital social service at Washington University, St. Louis, Missouri.

Besides acting as social service administrator, Miss Stimson became, in 1913, superintendent of nurses of the hospitals and dispensaries associated with the Washington University Medical School. These jobs ended when the United States entered the War. Immediately Miss Stimson became a reserve nurse of the Army Nurse Corps and sailed for Europe on May 19, 1917 as chief nurse of Base Hospital No. 21, the St. Louis Red Cross Unit. This hospital served with the British Expeditionary Force at Rouen, France and much of its important and successful work has been attributed to Miss Stimson's guidance and ability.

In April 1918 Miss Stimson was ordered away from the St. Louis unit and was assigned to duty with the American Red Cross in Paris. There she was made chief nurse of the Red Cross Nursing Service in France and became coordinator of Red Cross and Army Nursing. In letters to her family she told of the trials and turmoils which had to be met, the uncertainties and anguishes. It was her success in meeting them, undoubtedly, that brought her the appointment of director of Nursing Service for the American Expeditionary Force—a job that meant the supervision of more than 10,000 members of the Army Nurse Corps.

In the United States, meanwhile, the need for nurses had greatly increased and to meet this need the Army School of Nursing had been organized. When Miss Stimson returned home from Europe in July 1919 she was made acting superintendent of the Army Nurse Corps and dean of the Army School of Nursing. Later in that same year she was appointed superintendent of the Army Nurse Corps, a post that gave her the rank of major and the coveted gold leaf on her epaulet, a post that raised her to the highest rank in the nursing field.

For 20 years Miss Stimson, the first nurse to hold the rank of major, served in this position, studying the status and opportunities of 'the Army Nurse Corps, the possible promotion of its place in the military service and its relationship to other nursing organizations. Due to her activities the requirements for appointments to the Corps were raised, relative rank for nurses, improved housing condi-

tions, retirement privileges, post graduate
courses, and statistical studies were instituted. In May 1937 Major Stimson retired. Today she continues as president
of the American Nurses' Association, a
position she has held since 1938.

"A tall vigorous woman with short graying hair, deep blue eyes and the firm handclasp of a man," Major Stimson is now
busily engaged in carrying on the work
of the Nursing Council on National Defense. She continues to contribute to
nursing literature in articles and continues
to lecture. In her spare time she plays
the violin or goes swimming.

Major Stimson is the author of *Drugs and
Solutions for Nurses* (1910) and *Finding
Themselves* (1919). For her work in the
nursing field she has been awarded the American Distinguished Service Medal, the
British Royal Red Cross, 1st Class, the
Medaille de la Reconnaissance Française,
the Medaille d'Honneur de l'Hygiène Pub-
lique and the International Florence Night-
ingale Medal.

References

N Y Sun p14 Ag 29 '40 por

STINE, CHARLES MILTON ALTLAND
Oct 18, 1882- Chemist

Address: b. E. I. du Pont de Nemours &
Co, Wilmington, Delaware; h. 1100 Green-
hill Ave, Wilmington, Delaware

Dr. Stine, the chemist who initiated the
research for making big molecules out of
little ones that led to the discovery of nylon,
the remarkable organic material out of which
chemistry can make anything from sheer
silk-like hosiery to toothbrush bristles and
fish line leaders, was presented with the Perkin Medal on January 12, 1940. The Perkin
Medal was established in 1906 in com-
memoration of the fiftieth anniversary of the
coal-tar products industry and may be
awarded annually by the American section of
the Society of Chemical Industry for the
most valuable work in applied chemistry.

Directly or indirectly, from the results of
intensive research in organic chemistry, Dr.
Stine has been responsible for advances in
the following fields: modern plastics, motion
picture films using synthetic camphor, me-
dicinal chemicals like sulfanilamide and sul-
fapyridine, superior dyes, improved cheap
and safe refrigerant fluids like Freon, the
development of synthetic rubber, safety
glass, superior lubricants for motor cars,
superior gasolines and fuels, better and safer
explosives, synthetic urea for fertilizer, new
plant hormones and vitamins.

Charles Milton Altland Stine, the son of
the Reverend Milton Henry and Mary Jane
(Altland) Stine, was born in Norwich, Connecticut in 1882. After some years spent in
trying to prove false the saying about ministers' sons he was graduated, Phi Beta Kappa, with a B. A. degree from Gettysburg
College, Pennsylvania in 1901; received his

C. M. A. STINE

B. S. there in 1903; M. A. the next year;
M. S. in 1905; and Sc. D. in 1926. While
studying for his M. A. he taught chemistry
at the Maryland College for Women. He
became a fellow at Johns Hopkins University in 1906 and received his Ph. D. in 1907.
He was awarded an LL. D. by Cumberland
University in 1932.

After graduation Dr. Stine started a long
period of employment with E. I. du Pont de
Nemours and Company, Incorporated. He
was first assigned to the Eastern Laboratory
at Gibbstown, New Jersey for research on
explosives. From 1909 to 1916 he was in
charge of chemical research and worked
on many compounds used in explosives. For
years all the aromatic nitro compounds used
by the Du Pont Company were prepared according to processes developed under his
direction. He also played a part in improving safety explosives for use in coal mines,
and low freezing dynamites. The first commercial trinitrotoluol was made as a result
of work done under his direction. With C. C.
Ahlum he demonstrated the value of sodium
sulphite as a purifying agent for extracting
crude TNT and with his own hands made
the first 25,000 pounds of trinitrotoluol which
the company produced on a navy contract.
He made the crude material, recrystallized it,
dried it, sieved and packed it into boxes.

Dr. Stine devised ways to improve the
manufacture of ammonium nitrate at the time
when this salt was made from crude ammonia liquor. He studied leakage of nitro-
glycerine and other liquid ingredients of dynamite, and his work on permissible explosives resulted in a new series much safer
for use in gassy mines. As a result of his
study of dynamite caps he developed a
method for nitrating ivory nut waste. Dr.
Stine also developed methods for making
tetryl from dimethylaniline; for picric acid

STINE, CHARLES—*Continued*

starting from chlorobenzene; and for chlorinating benzene.

In 1916 Dr. Stine was in charge of a group of chemists sent to England to study the manufacture of dye intermediates. Then followed a preliminary investigation at the Eastern Laboratory while the Jackson Laboratory was being built. He was in charge of all the chemical research in the early stages of this work, leading to the manufacture of dye intermediates. From 1919 to 1921 he had a large part in building up the reorganized chemical department of the Experimental Station for research aimed at the development of new industries and improvements in products beyond the scope of plant or departmental laboratories. Among the products and processes developed during the years 1921 to 1930 were finishes made with nitrocellulose and later with synthetic resins, synthetic methanol and higher alcohols; an improved process for nitric acid by the oxidation of ammonia; and improved catalysts for the contact process for manufacturing sulphuric acid.

After six years, in 1930, Dr. Stine succeeded in his efforts to have the company set aside a substantial sum for basic research. He initially directed this work along with the activities of the chemical department. He felt that great promise was offered by a fundamental study of the polymerization of organic chemicals. Programs of research were also initiated in physical and colloid chemistry and chemical engineering. Out of this fundamental research there have come neoprene and chloroprene rubber and the protein-like polyamide compound known as "fiber 66" or nylon. It is made from air, water and coal, and is said to be more elastic and durable than silk, more versatile than rayon. It is already used for toothbrush bristles and may yet make United States hosiery manufacturing independent of Japanese raw silk.

In 1919 Dr. Stine was appointed assistant director of the Du Pont chemical department and became director in 1924. In 1930 he was elected a vice-president and was made a member of the executive committee and of the board of directors. At present he is serving the company in all three of these capacities.

Speaking in opposition to the popular belief that the development of science encourages warfare, Dr. Stine says that "though science is able to confer the richest blessings upon mankind, it is not able to change the heart of man and insure that the great increases in scientific knowledge will be beneficently applied." Nevertheless he believes that "the great contribution which the development of the organic chemical industry has made to the self-sufficiency of this country is a definite contribution toward the maintenance of peace."

Dr. Stine has maintained an active interest in scientific societies: he is a past councilor-at-large and past chairman of the Delaware section of the American Chemical Society, a director of the American Institute of Chemical Engineers, a life member of the Franklin Institute, a member of the American Association for the Advancement of Science, a member of the Advisory Committee of the Philadelphia Academy of Natural Sciences and a committee member of the National Research Council. He is active also as a lecturer and as a contributor to scientific and popular journals.

Fortune selected Dr. Stine as one of the "outstanding faces of 1938"; he is ranked as among the 175 most important chemists in the United States by *American Men of Science* and has received medals from the Society of Chemical Industry.

Dr. H. E. Howe, in an address on the presentation of the Perkin Medal, said: "It would be difficult to find a better example to justify the saying 'if you want something done, get a busy man to do it' than is found in the interests and activities of Charles Stine."

In 1912 Dr. Stine married Martha E. Molly of Lewistown, Pennsylvania. They have two daughters.

References

Can Chem & Process Ind 24:36 Ja '40
Chem & Ind 59:180-1 Mr 16 '40
Fortune 19:122 Ja '39 por
Ind & Eng Chem 32:137 F '40
Oil Paint & Drug Rep 137:3 Ja 15 '40
Sci ns 91:sup8 Ja 19 '40
American Men of Science
Chemical Who's Who
Who's Who in America
Who's Who in Commerce and Industry

STODDARD, FREDERICK LINCOLN
Mar 7, 1861—Feb 24, 1940 Artist

Frederick Lincoln Stoddard, painter and muralist, who left the imprint of his work in public buildings in various parts of the United States, died at his home in Gloucester, Massachusetts, two weeks before his seventy-ninth birthday. Born in Coaticook, Quebec, Canada, he spent his youth in the West, and studied art at the St. Louis School of Fine Arts and in France under famous artists.

He returned to the United States in the '90s, and was instructor of design at the St. Louis School of Fine Arts from 1894 to 1905. His paintings were exhibited in the Paris Salon in the early '90s, and in 1904 he won a silver medal at the St. Louis Exposition, where he was chairman of art education.

He designed murals for the St. Louis City Hall, the Memorial Church in Baltimore and several high schools.

Mr. Stoddard moved to New York in 1906 and worked there until 1922, when he moved to Gloucester. In New York he painted murals for various schools, including the Hebrew Technical School for Girls and the Eastern District High School.

In Gloucester he was active in the artists' colony, serving as second president of the Gloucester Society of Artists and secretary of the North Shore Artists' Association. He was also a member of the Salmagundi Club, New York.

FREDERICK L. STODDARD

During the 17 years of his residence in Gloucester he painted murals for several public buildings there, and designed the wall decorations for the Sawyer Free Library.

Surviving him is his widow, the former Henrietta Ravet.

References
  Who's Who in American Art

Obituaries
  N Y Herald Tribune p12 F 26 '40
  N Y Times p38 F 25 '40

STONE, JOHN CHARLES Jan 11, 1867 —May 21, 1940 Professor emeritus of New Jersey State Teachers College; mathematician; author; estimated a few years ago that one of every five school children in the United States used his textbooks

References
  Who's Who Among North American Authors
  Who's Who in America

JOHN C. STONE

Obituaries
  N Y Herald Tribune p24 My 22 '40
  Pub W 137:2224 Je 8 '40

STOOKEY, CHARLEY May 4, 1900- Farm radio reporter for CBS and Station KMOX

Address: b. Mart Bldg, St. Louis, Missouri

Charley Stookey was born on a farm near Belleville, Illinois, and attended elementary and high schools in Belleville. Shortly after graduation he joined the navy and served until the end of the First World War. After returning home in 1919 he entered the University of Illinois and received a degree from the College of Agriculture. He is married and the father of four children.

Upon leaving the University he covered the entire Midwest as a reporter for the *Prairie Farmer,* and later was made farm director of a radio station in Chicago. He is a real veteran in radio, having started in 1929. Since 1932 he has been with station KMOX in St. Louis.

A man of tremendous vitality, he has driven the seventeen miles from his farm to the radio studio in St. Louis every morning for years to give his daily 5:30 a. m. broadcast. In these early morning programs he has supplied thousands of rural listeners in Missouri and Illinois with latest market reports and farm service features. He was the first announcer in the country to take portable broadcasting equipment into the fields and announce a national cornhusking contest direct from the scene.

Since July 1939 farmers throughout the country have become familiar with Stookey, for then CBS appointed him farm reporter. His duties take him over the entire country for his Saturday broadcasts on a nation-

CHARLEY STOOKEY

wide hook-up. These programs present a cross section of agriculture in the United States, as well as opinions of representative farmers. Whenever possible, Stookey continues with his regular KMOX early morning broadcasts.

Recently he decided to give up active farming, but he still finds time to make personal tours in Missouri and Illinois each week. Thus he is able to present firsthand knowledge of farming conditions to his 5:30 a. m. listeners.

STORR, VERNON FAITHFULL, REV.
Dec 4, 1869—Oct 26, 1940 Canon of Westminster Abbey since 1921 and rector of St. Margaret's Church, Westminster, England since 1936; lectured at Cambridge University; among published writings are *The Development of English Theology in the Nineteenth Century* (1913) and *The Living God* (1925)

References

Author's and Writer's Who's Who
Who's Who

Obituaries

N Y Times p44 O 27 '40

STOWE, LELAND Nov 10, 1899- Newspaper correspondent
Address: b. c/o Chicago Daily News, Chicago, Illinois; h. 121 Delwood Rd, Bronxville, New York

The foreign correspondent who has to date cabled the ablest, sensationally far-reaching reports on the War in Europe, and who is expected to win a 1940 Pulitzer Award for his work, is Leland Stowe. He has already been given an award for "faithful reporting" by the Overseas Press Club.

The two most important scoops to his credit are his exposé of the "Trojan-horse" treason and treachery by which Germany invaded Norway with incredible dispatch; and his equally authentic reports of the British blundering and inefficiency that lost the Norway campaign. His story of the Nazi invasion was said to have put other European nations on guard against Fifth Column activities in their own territory. His revelations on the unprepared and tragically mismanaged British expedition—though the story was censored by the British press—led to a shake-up in the British cabinet and the ultimate ousting of Chamberlain as Prime Minister.

Leland Stowe's achievements become more interesting in view of the fact that in the fall of 1939 the New York *Herald Tribune* told him he was "too old" to be a war correspondent. Stowe was 40, youthful and physically energetic despite his shock of white hair, and had served his paper well for 18 years. But three hours after the *Tribune* had refused him a post abroad, Colonel Frank Knox (see sketch this issue), editor of the Chicago *Daily News*, sent him a telegram asking if he cared to cover the War for the *Daily News* and other papers. "There is a God!" Stowe telephoned his wife; and a few days later, September 10, he was flying to Europe.

The ace correspondent for the Chicago *Daily News,* the New York *Post* and 14 other American newspapers was born in Southbury, Connecticut November 10, 1899, the son of Frank Philip and Eva Sarah (Noe) Stowe. A Methodist, he took his B. A. at Wesleyan University, Middletown, Connecticut in 1921. He held his first newspaper job at the age of 18 as campus correspondent for the Springfield (Massachusetts) *Republican*. While at college he earned his letter as a cross-country runner—training that later made him literally a master leg-man in covering war maneuvers. Paul Mowrer, of the Chicago *Daily News*, says that when Stowe "can't get a plane, a car or a horse, he starts out to walk." He hiked 10 miles through mud and snow over a mountain range near Trondheim, Norway to reach the Swedish border and file his exclusive story of the Nazi invasion.

The year following his graduation from college Stowe was a reporter on the Worcester *Telegram*, and in 1922 began his newspaper career in New York City. From 1922 to 1926 he worked for the New York *Herald* and for *Pathé News*. He was married to Dr. Ruth F. Bernot in 1924. Mrs. Stowe, like her husband, is a New Englander. She studied dentistry at Tufts College and was a dentist at the time of their marriage. They have two sons, both born in Paris while Stowe was Paris correspondent for the New York *Herald Tribune* from 1926 to 1935.

Young, ambitious and conscientious, as head of the *Tribune's* Paris Bureau Leland Stowe became well-grounded in French politics and finance. Although censured occasionally for over-stressing detail in his cables to the home office, it was precisely his careful attention to details that won for him in 1930 a Pulitzer Prize for his work on the Young Conference. He was decorated with the French Légion d'Honneur in 1931. In 1933 his book, *Nazi Means War*, was published.

As foreign correspondent since 1932 Stowe has covered important world events from positions ranging from London to Istanbul. He reported Pan-American conferences at Buenos Aires and Lima and covered Franco's rebellion in Spain, where his sympathies were distinctly with the Loyalist forces.

He was back at work in his office at the *Herald Tribune* in September 1939 when Germany invaded Poland and England declared war. When the *Tribune* refused him a foreign post and he got one through Colonel Knox of the Chicago *Daily News*, he flew to London and was first assigned to Finland. He sent back eloquent dispatches on the Russo-Finnish situation—stories that have been called "reportorial masterpieces—though seldom allowed to come very near the scene of the events he described so graphically. It was in Finland that he learned to use skis."

In the spring of 1940 the alert-minded correspondent was in Stockholm, considering a trip to Riga. But something in his bones said, "Get to Oslo first." So with his friend Edmund Stevens of the *Christian Science Monitor* he reached Oslo April 4, where the only other United States correspondent was about to leave. On hand, however, was another friend, Warren Irvin, of NBC. Everything was peaceful, but Stowe stayed on. His hunch was right—on April 8 Nazi bombers roared over the Norwegian housetops. By two in the afternoon the conquerors—not more than 1,500 of them—marched through Oslo's streets. Stowe got busy investigating this fantastically easy conquest. He found his story—that of a country infested with spies and traitors in key positions. Escaping to Stockholm, the 40-year-old veteran "too old to cover a war" cabled on April 15 his scoop on the Trojan-horse invasion.

During the Norway campaign he followed the British troops, interviewed officers and men near Namsos. They were being mercilessly bombed, with no anti-aircraft guns for defense, no field guns, few supplies. "They've let us down in London," said a young territorial whose battalion had been decimated. The Norwegians were bitter about the B. E. F.'s lack of equipment. "It looks as if the British were going to fight to the last Norwegian," an officer remarked to Stowe. When extracts from this news reached London (via New York) the Labor Party came out in open opposition to the government; it was said that if the full report had then been published in London the Chamberlain government would have fallen in less than a week.

LELAND STOWE

Leland Stowe was in June 1940 in Romania, cabling news of the situation in that section to his papers. He was also at work on a book, begun some time ago, on the Second World War, which his publishers reported would be ready for publication in 1940. Quincy Howe says of him that he has "tended more and more to editorialize. He hit an all-time high when he wired a long dispatch from the Balkans in late June stating that if the United States would at once send 2,000 planes to Britain, Hitler would be stopped."

References

Am Observer 9:6 My 13 '40
Liberty 17:27-9 Je 22 '40
Life 8:90+ My 6 '40 por
New Outlook 162:30 D '33
N Y Post p1, 9 Ap 26 '40 por
N Y Times p1 Ap 14 '40; p4 Ap 18 '40
Scholastic 36:16 My 6 '40 por
Time 35:63 Ap 22 '40 por; 35:36 Je 10 '40

Howe, Q. The News and How to Understand It p115-16 1940
Who's Who in America (Addenda)

STRASSER, OTTO (shträs'ĕr) Sept 10, 1897- Exiled German leader
Address: c/o Houghton Mifflin Co, 432 Fourth Ave, New York City

For six years now Adolf Hitler has been trying to "get" Otto Strasser. According to a July 1940 Associated Press dispatch he had finally succeeded, but late in August Strasser turned up safe in Portugal, after a two months' flight across France and Spain.

This man whom Hitler hates and fears has been fighting him since 1930 as head of the German Black Front, organized to fight

Keystone—Underwood

OTTO STRASSER

the Nazis from within. Today he swears
that the Black Front is a real danger to
Hitler and that he, Otto Strasser, will be
the leader of the "second revolution." Even
when the Black Front was threatened with
being stamped out after Strasser was accused
of the Munich bombing plot, Strasser insisted: "We have nothing to fear. . . The
Black Front has men in it whom they will
never discover. They are working not only
in the Nazi Party organization, but in the
Gestapo itself."

The hairbreadth story of the Black Front
and of Otto Strasser, the story of Hitler
and his rise to power was told by Douglas
Reid in *Nemesis?* (1940) and is now told
by Strasser himself in his *Hitler and I,*
published in August 1940. In with Hitler
from the beginning, this man whom Goebbels
now calls "Hitler's Public Enemy No. 1"
has finally told his whole history and the
history of those with whom he was once
so closely associated and whom he now so
violently hates. His *Germany Tomorrow* was
published in England at the same time.

Otto Strasser was born on September 10,
1897 at Windsheim in Franconia, Bavaria.
His father was a "quiet, diligent, middle-
rank civil servant in the judicial service,"
a Socialist at heart and a devout Catholic.
He studied at the Realschule of Diggendorf
in Lower Bavaria, and later at the Ober-
realschule of Munich. There was no money
for Otto to go to the university, so in
1913 he left school to spend "a terrible
year" as an apprentice in a textile factory.
Then came the War. When it ended Otto
was captain of an artillery battery, twice
wounded and decorated with the Iron Cross
and the Bavarian Distinguished Service
Order. He immediately entered Von Epp's
Free Corps and fought with him to end
Munich's Communist government.

The fighting over, he entered the University of Munich, struggling to support
himself by stenographic jobs, by teaching
workmen in the evenings. During these
years he had been an active member of the
Socialist Party, but when he left with his
law degree in 1921 he had resigned from
the party, disgusted with its aims and
tactics.

After leaving the University Strasser
entered the Ministry of Agriculture and
Food Supply in a very minor position.
Through his brother Gregory he had already met Hitler, in 1920, and in 1925 he
joined the National Socialist Party. At that
time Gregory, the party's head in the important region of North Germany, was
more important than Hitler. Otto became
active in the party; he edited the *National-
sozialistische Briefe,* the *Berliner Arbeiter-
zeitung* and the *Sächsischer Beobachter,* Nazi
organ.

During these years, however, Otto Strasser distrusted Hitler, and relations between
him and his brother, who still believed in
Hitler, became strained. Otto disliked
Hitler personally—he even called him a
fraud and a lying cheat to his face. And
his own theories of Socialism differed from
those Hitler was developing. He emphasized the Socialist part of National Socialism; he would abolish private ownership
of land or mineral resources and the products of the earth, as well as of the means
of production. The expropriated land,
etc., would be leased according to modified
feudal arrangements and all *Volksgenos-
sen* would have a share in the ownership,
direction and profit of the total economy
according to capability and worthiness.
Hitler told him: "What you call socialism
is pure Marxism and your whole system is
a writing-desk job and has nothing to do
with real life." Actually it isn't Marxism
at all. Strasser has stated firmly that:
"We must be equally implacable and hostile
in our attitude toward capitalism and
toward international Marxism."

Strasser quarreled with Hitler, too, over
"racial" theories, and although he agreed
with him in considering Jews as foreigners
in Germany, unlike Hitler he was "unag-
gressive about it." Lately, it might be
added, he has favored giving German Jews
a minority status and has even ventured
that a very few Jews might "pass" into
the German people.

As Hitler became more powerful in the
Nazi Party an open breach with Otto
Strasser was inevitable, and in 1930 Strasser
was expelled. His brother Gregory stayed
in until 1933; in 1934 he was murdered by
Hitler. Otto immediately announced that
he was setting up a "fighting union of
revolutionary National Socialists." Hitler's
reply was to close down the Kampfverlag
which published the papers which Strasser
edited and to announce that anyone who
joined with Strasser would be expelled
from the party. "So," says Strasser, "I

found myself without resources on the threshold of a new life and confronted with a colossal task."

The Black Front ("black" here means "secret") was organized from dissident groups; newspapers were set up to publish its message; and by the end of 1932 it was becoming "quite a power in the land." Shortly after the Reichstag fire, when Hitler began to rule, it was suppressed. Strasser's life was in danger.

What happened to Strasser from then on is "an astounding story of adventure and hairbreadth escape." He fled into Austria and started sending pamphlets over the border. Leaflets were smuggled into Germany by ingenious methods. Once he made 50,000 facsimiles of the envelopes of the German Medical Association, filled them with literature and mailed them within Germany itself at cheap postal rates. Always his life was in danger. One day he returned to Vienna, after a trip to Prague, to find that 19 of his assistants and friends had been arrested. He escaped to Prague.

From Prague, Strasser kept up his activities. He set up his *Schwarze Sender*, a secret broadcasting station that pestered the Nazis for a year until it was discovered by the Gestapo. He continued to organize his forces within Germany itself. He continued to escape death. Once in Prague he was invited to address some Black Front members. His hosts insisted he must want a bath after his long journey. Suspicious, as ever, Strasser examined the bathtub and found it wired for electrocution. He escaped through the bathroom window.

When Germany took over Czechoslovakia, Strasser escaped into Switzerland. When, in November 1939, the Reich was pressing Switzerland to extradite him in connection with the Munich bombing (Strasser insists it was done by Himmler and his Gestapo themselves), he skipped across the Swiss border into France. And it was there, according to all reports, that he was when the Nazis took over.

A "mild-mannered, soft-spoken Bavarian with a big, egg-shaped head, square and stocky in person, earnestly persuasive and a bit pedantic," Strasser is personally the complete antithesis of Hitler. He who talks of his "second revolution" talks of it quietly, simply and, according to some observers, makes it seem "an eminently reasonable enterprise. You just couldn't see this nice Bavarian who could talk like a Heidelberg professor making heads roll."

References

N Y Herald Tribune p2 Jl 25 '40 por
N Y Times VII p9+ Mr 3 '40 il por; p3 Ag 23 '40
Newsweek 14:24 D 4 '39 por; 15:46 Je 24 '40
Read Digest 36:123-35 Je '40
Time 35:94-6 Je 24 '40; 36:63 Ag 26 '40 pors
International Who's Who
Reed, D. Nemesis? the Story of Otto Strasser and the Black Front 1940
Strasser, O. Hitler and I 1940

STRAVINSKY, IGOR (strä-vĕn'ske ē'gor) June 17, 1882- Composer and conductor
Address: c/o Harvard University, Boston, Massachusetts

Igor Stravinsky, world famous composer and conductor, holds the Elliot Norton chair at Harvard University for 1940. He plans to stay in the United States and has accepted a number of engagements as guest conductor with American symphony orchestras. He conducted the Boston Symphony Orchestra at Carnegie Hall, New York, January 4 to 7, 1940; and was guest conductor of the New York Philharmonic-Symphony Orchestra April 3 to 7, 1940, concluding with an all Stravinsky program on Sunday, April 7.

Igor Fedorovich Stravinsky was born at Oranienbaum, near St. Petersburg, Russia, June 17, 1882. His father was a singer at the Imperial Opera, but he was sent to the University to study law. However, at the age of 20 he began to study music with Nikolai Rimsky-Korsakoff; his first important work, an orchestral fantasy, *Fireworks* (1908), was produced just after his famous master's death. His name became known in musical circles with the performances in 1908 of his *First Symphony* and of *Le Faune et la Bergère*. These compositions brought him to the attention of Sergei Diaghilev, who was then organizing his *Ballet Russe* in Paris. Diaghilev commissioned Stravinsky to write an original work on the subject of the Russian fairy-tale, *The Fire Bird,* and the ballet, staged by the dancer Nijinsky (see sketch this issue), was produced in 1910. The audience, puzzled and outraged, staged a riot; but *The Fire Bird* remains Stravinsky's first masterpiece. His second ballet was *Petrushka*, on the pathetic hero of the Russian marionette show. Produced in 1911, it used two keys together for polytonal effect. More far-reaching was the production of *Le Sacre du Printemps* (1913). Creating entirely new musical values, it established him as a world figure in music. Perhaps its most unusual presentation was Walt Disney's (see sketch this issue) interpretation in *Fantasia*. Although it was radically cut and used as the background for the story of prehistoric life, with nightmarish monsters stalking the screen, the composer announced that it was what he had in mind all along.

A period of works typically Russian in character followed. Stravinsky's *Histoire du Soldat* (1918) was based on a Russian tale about a deserting soldier. In search of new musical resources, he wrote *Ragtime* (1918) in the spirit of American jazz, and, in 1920, a Pergolesi ballet. *Mavra* (1922) a one-act opera, was his last work based on Russian themes; but his *Les Noces*, introduced by

Musical America

IGOR STRAVINSKY

the *Ballet Russe* in 1923, belongs also to this period of his career.

Stravinsky's post-War period was marked by a new austerity and economy in composition; his music was no longer vitriolic, but cool. This was illustrated in his *Concerto* (1924) for piano and orchestra; and the negation of the esthetic code was further pronounced in the oratorio, *Oedipus Rex* (1927).

He went on his first American tour early in 1925, as conductor of his own works with the New York Philharmonic Orchestra, and as pianist with the Boston Symphony Orchestra. The world première of his *Apollon Musagètes* was performed in Washington in 1928. A new ballet, *Le Baiser de la Fée*, was produced in Paris in 1928. His *Symphony of Psalms*, written for the fiftieth anniversary of the Boston Symphony Orchestra, was completed in 1930. He wrote the music for Madame Rubenstein's ballet, *Persephone*, which had its première in Paris in 1934. For his 1937 American tour, he wrote a ballet on a poker game, *Card Party*, called "a ballet in three deals," and it was produced at the Metropolitan Opera House under his direction.

There are two opposing camps with regard to the second and third periods of Stravinsky's compositions. One feels that the new classical simplicity and restraint represents him at his best—and Stravinsky himself is of this opinion. The other group yearns for his return to the bold color and vitality of the earlier work.

Whatever the opinions regarding Stravinsky's individual periods of composition, critics and musicians in general are agreed on his importance. Of him Marc Blitzstein (see sketch this issue) writes: "A composer with genius only partially realized, with only one or two works fixed for immortality, has nevertheless become *the* figure, *the* influence in the music of his day; and, although lacking in ultimate greatness, he occupies a position in musical time the exact opposite of, and not less important than, the position occupied by Beethoven."

Stravinsky's *Autobiography*, which appeared in this country in 1936, is the terse, candid chronicle of his first 38 years. In this volume he tells us a great deal about his childhood and youth; and his ready wit is evident in several of the anecdotes he relates about Rimsky-Korsakoff, with whom he studied.

His appearance has been described as follows: "Igor Stravinsky is small and thin; his chest appears hollow. His face, long and lean, has an expression of indefinable sadness. His eyes have a particularly piercing intensity which not even heavy lenses can obscure. An aquiline nose descends sharply from a majestic brow, and overlooks lips of uncompromising firmness." He gives an impression of enormous vitality, is very fond of good living and good conversation, but maintains usually a frigid silence with regard to his own music. Wagner he detests; his favorite composers are Mozart and Tschaikowsky. He has a keen appreciation of art and literature, and religion plays an important rôle in his life. He likes to play bridge and poker, and takes his camera with him wherever he goes."

As an orchestra conductor Stravinsky has become well known to the music-loving public. Though lean, his figure is erect and commanding, and he makes an impressive presence. He conducts his own works from a score, quietly and precisely, and with a notable grace. He has his idiosyncracies, one being his dislike of the cold. Once at a Philharmonic rehearsal the orchestra was amazed to see him peel down to his shirt-sleeves, since he dreads a draft and usually wears a couple of sweaters, snuggling into a fur-lined overcoat during rest periods. When playing the works of other composers, Stravinsky meticulously follows the score. He says he detests "star" conductors who pride themselves on their interpretations: what the composer originally wrote is good enough for him.

On April 1, 1940 *Time* reported a second marriage (his first wife died in 1939) to Vera de Bossett Sudeikine, onetime dancer with Sergei Diaghilev's *Ballet Russe*. After Disney had completed *Fantasia,* Stravinsky signed a contract to do more music with the Hollywood artist. His newest Symphony, dedicated to the Chicago Symphony Orchestra in honor of its Golden Jubilee, is described as "a gesture in the direction of Joseph Haydn."

References

Arts & Dec 46:14-15+ My '37 il
Etude 55:155-6 Mr '37 por

Musical Q 21:330-47 Jl '35; 21:487-9
  O '35; 26:283-96 Jl '40
New Repub 91:18 My 12 '37
N Y Herald Tribune p20 Mr 15 '40
New Yorker 10:23-8 Ja 5 '35
Newsweek 9:24 Ja 23 '37 por
Time 28:38+ N 2 '36 por; 29:40+
  Ja 25 '37 por; 35:65 Mr 11 '40 por;
  35:67 Ap 1 '40
Armitage, M. ed. Igor Stravinsky
  1936
Brockway, W. and Weinstock, H.
  Igor Stravinsky In Men of Music
  p557-69 1939
Evans, E. The Fire Bird and Pe-
  trushka 1933
Ewen, D. ed. From Bach to Stra-
  vinsky p323-57 1933
Ewen, D. ed. Igor Stravinsky In
  Twentieth Century Composers p3-29
  1937
Flanner, J. An American in Paris
  1940
Leichtentritt, H. Twentieth Century
  In Music, History, and Ideas p243-
  68 1938
Pannain, G. Igor Stravinsky In Mod-
  ern Composers p35-56 1933
Rosenfeld, P. Evolution of Strawin-
  sky In Discoveries of a Music
  Critic p170-96 1936
Sabaneev, L. L. Igor Stravinski In
  Modern Russian Composers p64-86
  1927
Stravinsky, I. An Autobiography
  1936
Taylor, D. Of Men and Music p159-
  66 1937
Thompson, O. ed. International Cy-
  clopedia of Music and Musicians
  1939
Who's Who

STREIT, CLARENCE (strīt)   Jan 21,
1896-   Newspaper correspondent

Address: b. 10 E 40th St, New York City; h.
4701 Connecticut Ave, Washington, D. C.

Authors of first novels sometimes experience the thrill of leaping at once into the
best-seller class. The writers of books
setting forth far-reaching proposals in the
field of government, however, usually must
wait a long time for their ideas to be
recognized as practical by statesmen, political scientists and the general public.
Union Now was in its tenth printing six
months after publication.

Completely American, Clarence Kirshman
Streit was born in California, Missouri, the son
of Louis Leland and Emma (Kirshman)
Streit, and brought up in Montana. While a
student at Montana State University, Streit
enlisted for the First World War. He
served overseas in the American Expeditionary Force, with the Railway Engineers
because he had worked summers in the
Public Land Surveys of the Rockies and
Alaska. Later he was a sergeant in the

Intelligence Service and attached to the
Archives Division of the American Peace
Mission at Versailles. He was one of those
who guarded President Wilson on his return
from Paris to Washington, his job being
"mainly to smell bouquets sent him to see
they hid no bombs."

After he returned to Montana, while completing the work for his Bachelor of Arts
(1919), he was awarded a Rhodes Scholarship. He also studied at the Paris Sorbonne.

He was foreign correspondent for the
Philadelphia *Ledger* from 1920 to 1924, working in Rome, Constantinople, Paris and
other European capitals. He was expelled
from Romania when his frank dispatches
met the disfavor of that government.

In Paris he met Jeanne Defrance. They
were married on September 26, 1921 and
have three children, Traven Pierre, Jeanne
Emma, Colette Helen. His wife assists him
in his writing.

He has been with the New York *Times* since
1925, covering the Carthage excavation and
the Riff War; became first Vienna correspondent, and then in 1929 League of Nations correspondent, holding this position
until 1939. While there he was elected
president of the Association of Newspaper
Correspondents in Geneva.

As editor of the Montana college paper,
Streit had already started to develop a skeptical, questioning attitude toward war, an attitude further evolved by his experiences in
the A. E. F. and as foreign correspondent at
Geneva.

His ideas crystalized in the form of a
book, a book that had the reputation of
being one of the most unanimously rejected
books in publishing history. He had spent
five years, since 1933, in writing and rewriting *Union Now*, advocating a political and
economic organization of all the democracies of the world into a union similar to
the United States of America. Finally at
Ambilly, France, in 1938, he had 300 copies,
(not for sale), printed in English at his own
expense.

The following year Harper & Brothers
imported a modest edition and the Carnegie
Foundation distributed copies to educational
institutions. Simultaneously it was published in London. A *Town Hall of the Air*
radio discussion in New York City aroused
public interest and stimulated sales. Further
championship came from Russell Davenport, then editor of *Fortune*, with an editorial
in the April 1939 issue: "Mr. Streit's name
was coupled with that of Mr. Cordell Hull
(see sketch this issue) as co-worker in the
cause of a 'free libertarian' economy. Under
the somewhat unexpected caption of 'Business
and Government' an outline of Streit's scheme
was given as that of a gargantuan democracy
of 280,000,000 people; a vast economic opportunity—the greatest political and economic
opportunity in history."

Sales began to rise to 200 copies a week.
In June 1939 the *Reader's Digest* carried a
condensation of the *Fortune* article. In Octo-

CLARENCE STREIT

ber *Life* led off with an article on Streit and the United States of the World. Sales by December increased to 700 a week and approximately 10,000 copies had been sold by the end of 1939, with an abridged edition published in March 1940. It was awarded honors as "the outstanding book of 1939" by *Current History*. The book has been translated into French and Swedish. A German edition, published in Zurich, is to appear very soon and there are rumors of a Portugese translation for distribution in South America.

Besides *Union Now* (1939), Mr. Streit has written *Where Iron Is; There is the Fatherland* (1920) and *Hafiz—The Tongue of the Hidden* (1928), a translation from the *Rubaiyat*. On January 3, 1941 his new book *Union Now Begins* will be published. In it he restates his plan, in view of world conditions.

On extended leave of absence from the New York *Times*, Mr. Streit is chairman of the National Organizing Committee of the Inter-Democracy Federal Unionists (I. F. U.), an association that was formed last July to promote in this country the plan for a federal union of free peoples throughout the world—an association that was the natural outgrowth of his book.

Mr. Streit in 1940 made a nationwide lecture tour on behalf of I. F. U. Both from its national headquarters in New York City and through affiliated local Unionist committees in many parts of the United States, I. F. U. is conducting an intensive educational campaign. Part of the purpose of the educational campaign to show that Federal union is an American idea invented by the Fathers of the American Constitution when they were faced 150 years ago with the problem of creating a workable Federal government for the United States

without depriving the various states of local autonomy for matters of purely local concern. I. F. U. maintains that the leading democracies of the world today—Australia, Canada, Ireland, New Zealand, Sweden, Switzerland, Union of South Africa, England, United States—are faced with problems, which although different in many respects, are still nevertheless fundamentally similar to the problems solved by our founding fathers at the Constitutional Convention held in Philadelphia in 1778.

The proposal is that the leading democracies of the world should form a Union which would be the nucleus around which a world union could be formed, and other nations could, by setting up a government based on freedom and equality, become a part of the Union.

The Union government would be patterned on that of the United States, with executive, legislative and judicial branches. But Switzerland would be the model for the executive branch—a board of five members, with a Premier at the top, one elected each year, three by the people at large and one each by the House and Senate; representatives, elected on a basis of population; two Senators from each country; the Premier to be selected by the Board and to hold office while he had the confidence of the majority party in Congress.

Such problems as involve trade, money, tariff (the organization believes in free trade), communication and a union defense force would come under the jurisdiction of the Union government. They predict that under this system: "Good times would come back. Taxes would be reduced. Armaments could be cut tremendously, and the Union would still be stronger than any possible combination of enemies. The Union's stable, reliable money would start new enterprises rolling, ending depression and unemployment. Goods would move as freely and profitably among the member nations as they now do among our states."

Perhaps the essential contribution this theory makes to the science of government is best summed up by the *Christian Science Monitor*: "Mr. Streit's specific proposal—interesting and well thought out as it is—is not the important part of his book. His essential achievement has been that, after years of controversy and experiment, Mr. Streit has brought the discussion of the peace problem back to a basis where it might be solved."

The Union has had a phenomenal growth. Simultaneously with the book's publication Mr. Streit spoke over the radio. Roy Frazier Potts, former diplomat and banker, on the verge of turning off the radio, listened in to the talk. After meeting Streit, a plan for organization was worked out. Mr. Potts and his brother volunteered a desk in their office for first headquarters. In a single month activity had grown so that it overflowed desk and office both. An apartment with a staff of three was the next office, and now the local office occupies an entire floor in a New York business building. Mr. Potts has given up his business entirely, devoting all his time, without remuneration, to directing the work of the Union.

Numerous chapters have been organized in 141 communities in the United States, the largest ones in California, New Jersey and Massachusetts. England has even more chapters. A Gallup (see sketch this issue) poll released on January 28 shows that two million voters would answer "union of democracies" if asked today for their solution of the problem of maintaining world peace after the Second World War.

Mr. Streit is tall and thin, with bright blue eyes and a quiet, unpretentious manner. He is an admirer of Lincoln, Beethoven and Michelangelo and often quotes from the poetry of Walt Whitman and Byron. His lectures frequently end on a note of now— or never—for the *Union*, with the following words from Julius Caesar:

> "There is a tide in the affairs of men
> Which, taken at the flood, leads on to fortune.
> Omitted, all the voyage of their life Is bound in shallows and in miseries."

References

Friday 1:1-5 N 15 '40 il por
Scholastic 35:29-30+ N 6 '39 por
Time 35:89 F 19 '40 por
Streit, C. K. Union Now 1939
Who's Who in America

STUART, JESSE Aug 8, 1907- Author
Address: c/o E. P. Dutton and Co, 300 Fourth Ave, New York City; h. Riverton, Kentucky

Greenup County, Kentucky is Jesse Stuart's home territory, and anyone who has been exposed to his "mountain prose" isn't likely to forget it. There's a lot that happens in Greenup County, Kentucky: sorghum making and hog killing, lard rendering and square dancing, feuds and loving and whiskey-guzzling and the birth of a lamb on a cold winter night. And always there are the hills and the cows and shacks and trees, and the way things feel and taste and sound if you live in Greenup County, Kentucky. Jesse Stuart, "whose stories smell of fresh-turned sod and smell like mountain brooks," has written his first novel, *Trees of Heaven* (1940).

No man who has not lived in the hills nearly all his life could have written this book. Jesse Stuart's ancestors lived and died in these same hills. "My father's people, the Stuarts," he says, "were feudists, killers, drinkers, country preachers, Republicans and fine soldiers. My mother's people, the Hiltons, were country schoolteachers, moonshiners, rebels, and Democrats." (Stuart himself is a Methodist and a Republican). His grandfather, Mitch Stuart, who died in ambush at the age of 80, was the biggest and

Dee Allen

JESSE STUART

lustiest of the lot—an old sinner who had had two wives and 19 kids, a man who used to shock the devout at spiritualist meetings by calling: "Come out, all you dead babies, and have a drink on old Mitch Stuart!"

The son of Mitchell and Martha (Hilton) Stuart, Jesse Hilton Stuart was born on August 8, 1907 near Riverton, Kentucky. As a child he never finished more than two-thirds of a school term in any one year. Living at the head of W-Hollow, he fished in the little Sandy, "went coon hunting with a lantern and a volume of Burns, read poetry by lantern light until a dog's barking signaled a treed coon," at 9 hired out to a farmer for 25 cents a day. From the time he was 11 until he was 15 he stopped school to cut corn and timber and to work on a paving gang, then went to high school until at 18 he succumbed to the glamor of a carnival and ran away to join it. This adventure was followed by 11 months in a Birmingham steel mill which made Jesse write, of one of his most admired poets: "Carl Sandburg, [see sketch this issue], you don't know anything about steel. You got your ideas from walking around the mills at night or talking to the Mayor of Gary, Indiana."

Ever since he was any age at all Jesse had been writing poetry himself, scribbling his earliest poems, he says, on "redhorse tobacco sacks, shoe boxes, pieces of wallpaper, sugar sacks—some on wood—and many were written on poplar leaves when I was out in the wood and one came to me." Whether they were good poems or not no one knows, because Jesse didn't bother to save them. Once he had considered becoming the American Robert Burns, but soon he knew he didn't want to imitate anybody. And he knew he wanted an education: nobody in his family

STUART, JESSE—*Continued*

had ever finished college, but he would have to manage it somehow.

He finally did. Saying farewell to steel forever, young Jesse shipped his trunk to Berea College, Berea, Kentucky, and followed on the highway with only $30 in his pocket. They couldn't take him there, but there was a mountain college in Tennessee, Lincoln Memorial, which could. In his three years at Lincoln Memorial he wrote "about 500 poems," made a reputation as a fighter and as editor of the school paper, worked in a hay field, digging a waterline and cleaning out manholes, and finished school in 1929 owing the college "one hundred dollars and fifty cents."

After a while back home teaching school his uncle helped him rope his trunk and strap his suitcases for shipment to Nashville, Tennessee, where he intended to get his M. A. from Vanderbilt University, working seven hours and eating one meal a day. He never achieved that M. A. When he received his first grades his "legs weakened," nearly all his term papers were rejected, his final thesis was lost in a fire; but of his last term paper, an autobiography which turned out to be 322 pages long, his professor said: "I have been teaching school for 40 years and I have never read anything so crudely written and yet beautiful, tremendous and powerful as that term paper you have written." It was some comfort to Jesse to know that he had at last done "a fairly decent piece of prose," for he had always been told that he couldn't.

Next he was back home again, putting the fear of God into the town toughs as principal of the Greenup County High School. Then in 1932 he spent a year as County School Superintendent at a salary of $100 a month, battling unhappily with the various political factions that ran the school, but still finding it as impossible to stop writing poems as to stop breathing. "The extra steam I gather from living escapes in poetry," he said. In 11 months he wrote 703 sonnets, sort of "a diary in loose-jointed verse," and was encouraged by selling some of them to magazines like *American Mercury, Virginia Quarterly Review* and *Poetry.* He started sending stories to magazines, too, though at first they all came back. Finally he sold his first to *Story* magazine, a story about nothing at all, just about a man who died and wanted to be buried in his shirttails, and the next thing he knew there was a book contract for his entire collection of sonnets. Jesse Stuart was "the happiest man in the world," particularly since his stories and poems kept on selling. Together with this income and the money which he saved from teaching he was able to finish paying for a farm of his own.

When Stuart's collection of sonnets appeared in 1934 under the title of *Man with a Bull-Tongue Plow* the critics began paying attention to him. The attention wasn't entirely favorable, of course. John Gould Fletcher couldn't understand why he cast all feelings and all experiences into one single form, and spoke of an effect of "monotony and blind confusion"; William Rose Benét found the collection valuable chiefly as a "human document." But nearly all the critics were amazed at the freshness and naturalness of these technically imperfect poems, for it was true that Jesse Stuart wrote the sonnet "as if no one had ever written sonnets before."

In 1936 a collection of his short stories about Greenup County was published, *Head o' W-Hollow,* and in 1937 Jesse Stuart found himself with a Guggenheim Fellowship to travel abroad. Jerome Beatty tells a story about this year abroad in his *Americans All Over.* "In Athens Beatty strolled out from his hotel to buy a Paris *Herald.* When he asked for it a strange young man in plusfours came up and said eagerly, 'You're an American?' It was Jesse Stuart, of whom Beatty, strangely, had never heard; and he proceeded to pour forth his loneliness to Beatty's amazed ears. He had written a book and made a little money, and gone out from his native hills to see the world. Seeing the world had made him lonely, which is as it should be."

In 1938 Jesse Stuart returned to his own country to teach school and to become principal of the McKell High School in Fullerton, Kentucky, and the following year married Naomi Deane Norris. He kept on selling stories, and that same year his autobiography, *Beyond Dark Hills,* which he had rewritten in Scotland, was published. He also wrote editorials for the Greenup County paper, managed to get into a hospital through his attack on a certain Democratic political boss who was up for re-election as Congressman, and began threatening "10,000 words for every drop of blood." Ten thousand words wasn't much of a threat for Jesse Stuart, though; it is merely his daily output when he is teaching school, and he dislikes teaching because it cuts him down from 30,000. Although he still has to write poems in longhand, he has learned to use the typewriter for prose, and now that *Trees of Heaven* has been published he probably won't be able to stop at a first novel. He has a younger brother, James, and a still younger sister who also ought to amount to something in a literary way some day.

A muscular six-footer, weighing 207 pounds, Jesse Stuart never does anything by halves. He not only loves writing, but he "loves his hills there in Kentucky; he loves his hogs and his mules; he loves to work with his hands."

References
Lit Digest 118:11 S 29 '34 por
Newsweek 15:50-1 My 13 '40
Poetry 45:217-20 Ja '35
Pub W 137:2223 Je 8 '40
Sat R Lit 11:129 S 22 '34

Scholastic 25:9 N 17 '34; 34:24E+
Mr 18 '39 por; 35:12 O 23 '39 por
Time 31:77 Ap 18 '38 por; 32:62-3 N
7 '38 por; 35:94+ My 13 '40
Wilson Lib Bul 10:98 O '35
America's Young Men
Stuart, J. Beyond Dark Hills 1938
Who's Who in America

SUESSE, DANA (swēz) Dec 3, 1911-
Musician

Address: c/o Harms, Inc, 62 W 45th St, New
York City

Dana Nadine Suesse, a young composer of
twenty-eight, was known as the "Girl Gershwin" when she was eighteen and composed her
first song when she was eight.

She was born in Shreveport, Louisiana,
the daughter of J. C. and Nina Chilton
(Quarrier) Suesse. A child prodigy, she
began to "fool around with the piano"
when she was about two. She didn't take
lessons for seven years after that, but recalls that she could play the *Sextette* from
Lucia rather creditably at five—she learned
it from a phonograph record. Her first
piece, redundantly called *Evening Sunset,*
was composed when she was eight.

After six months of study, she gave her
first concert in Kansas City, where her
family had moved, when she was nine. Included on the program were the Rachmaninoff *C-Sharp Minor Prelude* and three of
her own compositions. A few weeks later
she won a prize given by the American
Federation of Music and toured the South
and Midwest, sometimes playing entire
programs of her own works. She would
also improvise on any theme suggested by
anyone in the audience.

When Miss Suesse was 16 she refused a
scholarship at the Chicago Conservatory.
Instead she came to New York to study
piano with Alexander Siloti and composition with Rubin Goldmark. She experimented with jazz and wrote several
successes. Her first melody, *Syncopated
Love Song*, written when she was 18, was a
hit. *Ho Hum,* her second, was written in
15 minutes, sold half a million copies and
made $10,000, "thanks, in part, to Rudy
Vallee's plugging." *Whistling in the Dark,
You're So Beautiful, You Ought To Be in
Pictures, The Night is Young, Another Mile*
and *My Silent Love* are other popular song
titles.

Paul Whiteman first presented her in the
dual rôle of composer and pianist at a
Carnegie Hall concert in 1933. Her composition *Valses for Piano and Orchestra*
"sounded much like Ravel, with misty
strings and florid piano decorations. . .
There was nothing tuneful about the *Valses,*
but they were ambitious enough to build
up for Dana Suesse the nickname of the
'Girl Gershwin.' "

She composes rapidly. When Whiteman
asked for a piece for his concert in February 1932, she did *Concerto in Three Rhythms*

Edward Nell Jr.

DANA SUESSE

in three weeks. In 1934 she was working
on a symphonic tone-poem, *Two Irish Fairy
Tales,* which the New Chamber Orchestra
played in Town Hall that same year, when,
on November 15, Whiteman asked her for
something for his annual concert. She
agreed, thinking that it was to be in February again. When she learned it was just a
month off "she just sat down and wrote
her *Eight Valses* in two weeks," including
notes for the orchestral coloring which
Adolph Deutsch used for his orchestrations.
She didn't know the piano part which she
was to play at the concert, but she wasn't
worried.

"Four days before her appearance, she'd
hire a room in Steinway Hall, practice for
a couple of hours and have it." That's all
she ever practices for her public appearances.

"I trust to the angels," she says, and
thinks she's pretty lucky to be, as far as she
knows, the only girl symphonic composer
in the world. "I haven't any competition,"
she says. "It's a cinch." Her latest work,
Young Man with a Harp, performed by the
Philadelphia Symphony in July 1939 and by
the Rochester Civic Orchestra later in the
summer, has recently been recorded. Other
instrumental compositions are *Afternoon of
a Black Faun, Evening in Harlem, Danza á
Media Nioche* and *Jazz Nocturne.*

She wrote all the original music for Billy
Rose's (see sketch this issue) production for
the Texas Centennial at Fort Worth and the
musical score for the motion picture, *Sweet
Surrender.* She was WJZ's symphonic program pianist in 1935. Formerly a staff writer
for Famous Music Corporation, she now is one
for Harms, Incorporated.

Miss Suesse is a member of the American
Society of Composers, Authors and Pub-
lishers, Authors' League of America and
Song Writers' Protective Association.

SUESSE, DANA—*Continued*

She is tall, very slender, has gray eyes and reddish hair. She has an astonishing memory. She learned all of *Hamlet* and *Macbeth* merely by hearing the plays read in class, and still remembers most of them. She also has "absolute pitch," and can compose sitting in bed, not needing a piano. Shoes are her hobby, but she is equally interested in second-hand book stores, interior decoration, junkshops, tennis and sailing.

References

Am Mag 113:73 My '32 por
N Y Times p8 D 10 '33 por; IX p13 Ap 14 '35
Time 22:28 D 25 '33 por
American Women

SUNER, RAMON SERRANO *See* Serrano Suñer, R.

SWING, RAYMOND GRAM Mar 25, 1887- News commentator

Address: b. 1440 Broadway, New York City; h. 36 E 40th St, New York City

The solidly friendly, though somewhat pedagogical voice of Mutual's news commentator, Raymond Gram Swing, has become, with the thickening of political intrigue in Europe, a kind of *pièce de résistance*—whether comforting or not—to America's radio audience.

Raymond Gram Swing (Gram is the maiden name of his second wife, who, feministically, refused to abandon it) was born in Cortland, New York, March 25, 1887, the son of Albert Temple and Alice Edwards (Mead) Swing. He was educated at Oberlin—both at the College and at the Conservatory of Music (non-graduate)—and in 1906 began newspaper work in Cleveland. From there he went to Orville, Ohio and then joined, successively, two Hoosier papers. After some further experience in Cincinnati, an appendectomy, and a variety of nervous breakdown, he escaped to Europe with Chicago *Daily News* credentials. The Berlin Association of Foreign Correspondents was puzzled at the substitution of young Swing for Albert C. Wilkie and, suspecting Swing of some kind of unethical conduct in his capture of the Berlin assignment, refused him membership in the Association. The *News* informed the A. F. C. that Wilkie's dismissal had nothing to do with Swing's application, but the newcomer was blackballed, nevertheless. Swing was unhurt professionally, however, and the incident was soon forgotten. When he returned to Berlin in 1920 the A. F. C. received him with open arms.

One of Swing's biggest World War scoops was his story of the mysterious large-bore gun that was shelling Liège. He eluded German censorship by paying a trustworthy American student, who was on his way to London, $25, teaching him the "copy" word for word and then instructing him to dictate it to a stenographer in the London office of the *News*. He also had a personal interview with the U-boat captain who pierced the British blockade into Constantinople, and wrote a description of the sinking of a Turkish transport on which Swing was a passenger. An incident took place at that time that landed him in the annals of naval history. To the sub officer's query: "Who are you?" Swing, the only English-speaking passenger replied: "I am Raymond Swing, of the Chicago *Daily News*."

After his return to the United States in 1917 Swing became an examiner (1918) with the War Labor Board. He was Berlin correspondent for the New York *Herald* from 1919 to 1922; director of foreign service for the *Wall Street Journal* during the two years following; served on the London bureau of the Philadelphia *Public Ledger* and the New York *Evening Post*; and then for eight years was foreign correspondent for these two papers. From 1934 to 1936 he was a member of the board of editors of *The Nation* and in 1935 he became news commentator on American affairs for the British Broadcasting Corporation. A little later he began serving Mutual and the Canadian networks in this same capacity.

In the 20's he was writing sonnets for *Outlook* and the *Literary Digest*. In 1935 he published his political interpretations, *Forerunners of American Fascism*. And in the light of recent events there is considerable timeliness in his warning that "our size is not a reason against our submission to tyranny; we submitted to one which was strangely like a Fascist terror during the War. We accepted it then because we preferred unity in the crisis to freedom; and we would accept it again if we found we preferred unity in another crisis. . .."

He was the first radio commentator to join William Allen White's (see sketch this issue) Committee to Defend America by Aiding the Allies and in October 1940 became chairman of the newly organized Council for Democracy.

His book, *How War Came* (1939), is a collection of running commentaries—from the background events of Prague and Danzig up through the "war of nerves" era and the awful 14 days directly preceding Britain's formal declaration of a state of war.

On July 9, 1912 Swing was married to Suzanne Morin, of Paris, and by her had two children, Albert George and Elizabeth Françoise. The marriage was terminated by divorce. When he was in Berlin eight years later he married Betty Gram, of Portland, Oregon, who was studying voice from German masters. By his second wife he has three children, Peter Gram, Sally Gram, and John Temple. Now his family is augmented by Gabriel, an English lad whom the Swings have adopted.

During the whole of the politically tense period of 1938 Swing was on vacation abroad, and on his return he enjoyed the distinction of being the first eye-witness to report over a local station on the betrayal of Prague—and for this he was given an award by the National Educational Conference on Radio.

Swing has a fortunate invulnerability against news-shriek jitters. Unlike his confrère Kaltenborn (see sketch this issue), however, he manages during crises to sleep—briefly mayhap—in his own apartment. And also unlike his fellow newscaster, he refuses to go on the air without something solidly prepared in advance. Swing—and broadcasting in general—leapt into a terrific tempo on the night of Von Ribbentrop's visit to Moscow. At 7:30 p. m. he got wind of the coming Nazi-Soviet pact, chucked his comfortably written script, and in an hour and a half pounded out an entirely new broadcast of some 2,000 words.

Swing has been before a microphone since 1935. In addition to his American broadcasts, he shortwaves a weekly quarter hour on American affairs to the British Dominions—thus giving him the biggest international audience of any news expert. Swing fans include such assorted personalties as Lord Lothian (see sketch this issue), British Ambassador; Tallulah Bankhead; Supreme Court Justice Felix Frankfurter; and Nicholas Murray Butler (see sketch this issue). In 1940 Swing asked to reduce his number of radio broadcasts, giving the poor state of his health as the reason. He devotes over ten hours a day to preparation for his fifteen-minute broadcast, reading eight papers from cover to cover every day, besides press association reports, magazines and books, and making personal contacts for additional information. He has been offered a syndicated column, but he hasn't decided yet whether to accept it or not. His relaxations are ping-pong, bridge, piano playing, listening to concerts and playing poker. Never have his newscasts gone overtime and only twice have they been too short. This is a result of a peculiar system which he has worked out for timing his scripts on the typewriter.

When his program is over he leisurely travels a few blocks to New York's East Side to get to his apartment. He spends his week ends with his family in an old Connecticut farmhouse. This is the only time he is able to get away from and forget about work. During these brief respites no one is allowed to mention war or the European situation. The only other rule is absolute silence at Sunday morning breakfast. Swing takes this time to read the Sunday papers and to listen to Sunday concerts on the radio.

In New York his apartment is roomy and decorated in modern style. He col-

Reves-Biro

RAYMOND GRAM SWING

lects maps of Europe, each one showing changes in geographical boundaries. Before retiring, Swing always drinks a glass of milk and eats an apple. It helps him forget the war news of the day. He has written several classical compositions for the piano but is very modest about them—never intends to have them published.

References

Look 4:56 O 22 '40 pors
N Y Times p9 N 16 '39
Time 35:34 Ja 8 '40 por

Howe, Q. The News and How to Understand It 1940
Swing, R. G. How War Came 1939
Variety Radio Directory
Who's Who in America

SWITZER, GEORGE Mar 6, 1900—Oct 8, 1940 Industrial designer; former art director of Wasey and Company, advertising agents, and later of Young and Rubicam; opened his own office as designer and consultant in 1929, designing everything from letterheads, sausage labels and messengers' uniforms to the Rolls-Royce automobile body; leader in development of artistic packaging and in 1937 won two of the three awards in the "All America Package Competition" against 12,000 entries

References

Art & Ind 24:174-8 My '38 il
Comm Art 14:13-15 Ja '33 il
Who's Who in American Art

Obituaries

N Y Times p25 O 9 '40 por
N Y World-Telegram p48 O 9 '40

SZIGETI, JOSEPH (sē-gĕt'ĭ) Sept 5
1892- Violinist
Address: c/o Columbia Concerts Corp, 113
W 57th St, New York City

Recently Joseph Szigeti made a remark
which violin students hailed with joy. "Two
hours of practice a day are enough," he
said. But then he qualified the heretical
statement. Those two hours should be
preceded with what football coaches call
"skull practice." It is because of his firm
belief in "skull practice" that Szigeti has
been called the "peerless thinker of the
violin."

Szigeti believes that musicians should
seek behind the notes to bring their meaning to the surface—just as one must look
behind a writer's words for the thoughts
they hide. The first step, says Szigeti, "has
nothing whatever to do with music. It has
to do solely with habits of thought. Would
you play Bach and Schumann in exactly
the same manner? Of course not! Because
they represent entirely different ways of
looking at the world... Certain tonal intervals, certain sweeps of melody all tell
the musician something about the composer, the age in which he lived, the ideals
which that age cherished; and by combining
those elements, he arrives at the plan of his
interpretation. . ." The next step is to
"play and read a composition until I have
actually absorbed it. I analyze it with
regard to its construction, its form and
design. . . I imagine the whole composition
from beginning to end . . . and detect its
form, design and structure together with
the full relationship of one section to every
other section."

Born in Budapest on September 5, 1892,
Szigeti comes from a country that has produced such great violinists as Leopold

JOSEPH SZIGETI

Auer, Joachim and Jeno Hubay. His first
violin instruction came from his father and
then from his uncle. When he outgrew his
relatives, he was placed under the guidance
of the great Hungarian violinist and teacher, Jeno Hubay.

When Szigeti was 14 years old, his
teacher brought him to Joachim, who accompanied him on the piano as he performed the Beethoven violin concerto.
Joachim said that the boy was ready for
concert appearances, and predicted a great
future for him. He played in Berlin and
Dresden, and finally went to England,
where he remained five years. In England
he gave concerts widely, in London and the
provinces, and appeared in joint recitals
with the singer, Melba, the pianist, Bachaus,
and the composer, Busoni and under the
batons of Sir Henry Wood, Sir Hamilton
Harty, and Sir Thomas Beecham.

From 1912 to 1917 Szigeti appeared in
recitals on the Continent. In 1917 he succeeded the celebrated Henri Marteau as
professor of the class of violin virtuosity at
the Geneva Conservatory and held this
position until 1924, when the pressure of
concert engagements caused him to leave.

Leopold Stokowski, conductor of the
Philadelphia Orchestra, heard Szigeti play
in Europe and invited him to America. In
the autumn of 1925 he made his American
debut as soloist with the Philadelphia Orchestra, playing the Beethoven concerto at
the Academy of Music. A week later he
repeated this performance in New York at
Carnegie Hall. Szigeti's latest American
tour opened in January 1940 with the
Boston and New York premières of the
Bloch *concerto*, played with the Boston Symphony under Koussevitzky (see sketch this
issue). It was this work which the *Manchester Guardian* has hailed in England as
"the crown of Szigeti's career." During the
1940 to 1941 season he plans 15 appearances
with major American orchestras. In March
1941 he will begin a tour of Australia under
the auspices of the Australian Broadcasting
Commission.

From May 1931 to May 1933 Szigeti
circled the globe twice, giving more than
200 performances. He played five consecutive nights in Tokyo and seven in
Buenos Aires. He was invited 12 times to
the Soviet Union. On this tour and on
his others he was accorded many honors.
In France he was made an officer of the
Légion d'Honneur; in Belgium, Commander
of the Order of Leopold; in Hungary he
was awarded the Officer's Cross of Ordre
pour le Mérite; in Japan, the Ji Ji Shimpo
Gold Medal.

The critics of two continents agree on
the art of Joseph Szigeti. "He is the one
virtuoso able to make an 18th century
masterpiece understandable to a Gershwin
admirer," writes one. According to the
Chicago *Tribune*: "He is superior to nearly
every other practitioner in his field, both
in sheer technical skill and in musical in-

sight." His concentration on the meaning of the music he is playing and his superior technique have combined to earn him the titles of "an interpreter of genius" and "greatest musician-violinist now living."

From composers he has received innumerable dedications of compositions. Three modern concerti—those of Busoni, Sir Hamilton Harty and Casellai—were written for him, as well as a composition of Ernest Bloch, a rhapsody for violin and orchestra on Hungarian folk tunes by Béla Bartók (see sketch this issue), Bartók's *Rhapsody for Clarinet, Violin and Piano*, and a sonata for solo violin by Ysaye.

His transcriptions for the violin are included in the repertoire of his fellow artists, and his recordings of Bach, Beethoven, Brahms, Mozart and Mendelssohn are considered standards of interpretation and permanent acquisitions to recorded musical literature. The list of his recordings includes perhaps the largest number of concerti and major works of any violinist: 17 album sets. He himself says that he believes the great works of the masters must be the foundation of a violinist's equipment.

Though he ranks as one of the three or four greatest violinists in the world, Szigeti is no high-brow. There are few things he likes better than a night club where good swing is to be heard. He appreciated the ovation he got from "jitterbugs" as well as serious musicians when he and Benny Goodman appeared together in Carnegie Hall in January 1939 to play Bartók's *Rhapsody for Clarinet, Violin and Piano*.

Tall and sparely built, Szigeti looks much younger than his years. During rehearsals he is informal and displays his keen sense of humor, but at concerts he attends strictly to business. He enjoys himself when on tour because a concert-tour isn't just a series of hotel rooms and auditoriums to him. "Traveling," he says, "is something like mental hygiene after the too-rich accumulations of a big city." He doesn't use airplanes because they get him where he has to go too rapidly. "I do all my reading and writing on trains . . . and I am unique in one way, at least. I write my wife (who lives in Paris) even while I'm riding in taxicabs. I'm like a war correspondent, sending back bulletins from the front."

References

Etude 56:9-10 Ja '38 por
N Y Herald Tribune p33 Ap 14 '40
Scrib Mag 103:88 My '38 por
Ewen, D. Szigeti *In* Men and Women Who Make Music p213-25 1939
Kaufmann, Mrs. H. L. and Hansl, Mrs. E. E. vom B. Joseph Szigeti *In* Artists in Music of Today p101 1933
Saleski, G. Famous Musicians of a Wandering Race 1927

Thompson, O. ed. International Cyclopedia of Music and Musicians 1939
Who's Who
Wier, A. E. ed. Macmillan Encyclopedia of Music and Musicians 1938

SZOLD, HENRIETTA (zōlt) Dec 21, 1860- Organizer of *Hadassah,* women's Zionist movement

Address: b. 1860 Broadway, New York City; h. Jerusalem, Palestine

Born in Baltimore, the daughter of a Hungarian Rabbi, Miss Szold began her career of service to the Jewish people by helping refugees from Russian pogroms. She organized the first "Americanization" classes. She also won distinction as a translator of Hebrew writings, discovering Shalom Asch and Israel Zangwill, and by her thorough knowledge of theology. But it was not until 1909 that she became interested in Zionism. On a visit to Palestine that year, she found it plagued with malaria, and with the eye disease, trachoma; she found 13 per cent of the babies in Palestine dying in infancy. Horrified, she came back to the United States and began the work of getting medical aid to Palestine.

By 1912, she and 13 other women had organized *Hadassah,* and had raised $700 to send the first two nurses to the Holy Land. Under Miss Szold's drive *Hadassah* (the name is a variant of the Biblical heroine Esther) grew as an important factor in the Zionists' aim to recreate a Jewish homeland in Palestine. By 1919 when Miss Szold went to Palestine to direct the organization's work, its medical staff totaled more than 50. Its hospital, its medical school, its clinics and playgrounds are open to Jew and Arab alike.

Gray-haired, slight, Miss Szold has never married, has devoted herself to *Hadassah's* work in Palestine, often working 17 hours a day on the many projects by which the organization seeks to help the young colonists settle in Zion. In 1935, at the age of 74, she was considering retiring, and had her trunks packed to return to America, when she was asked to help organize *Aliyah* (Hebrew for immigration) to remove German refugee children to Palestine.

She threw herself into the work of making less tragic the plight of the children uprooted from their homes and separated from their families. She personally met boats, escorted children to the cooperative agricultural settlement which was their new home. In five years 6,200 refugee children had made their home in Palestine under her supervision. Although she has not lived in the country for 20 years, Miss Szold is known to 4,000,000 Jews in the United States as the foremost American Jewess of her time. *Hadassah* celebrated her 79th birthday December 21, 1939 by a series of luncheons and meetings throughout the country.

She was the editor of the American-Jewish Yearbook (1904-10) and president of

HENRIETTA SZOLD

Hadassah (1912-26). She translated *Ethics of Judaism* by Lazarus; *Legends of the Jews* by Ginsberg; and *Hebrew Renaissance* by N. Slouschz.

On November 29, 1940 Miss Szold was cited as one of the hundred outstanding women of the past century by the Women's Centennial Congress. The citation was given to her "as a pioneer in bringing American standards of health and hospitalization to Palestine."

References

Ind Woman 19:4 Ja '40 por
N Y Times p24 D 21 '38 por; p42 N 24 '39; VII p11+ D 15 '40 il por p46 D 17 '39
Newsweek 15:28 Ja 1 '40 por
Survey G 25:68 F '36 por; 29:158-62 Mr '40 il
Who's Who in America
Who's Who in American Jewry

TABOUIS, GENEVIEVE (tăb-ōō-ē zhĕn'vyĕv') 1892- French journalist

December 1940 Bulletin: In the summer of 1940 Madame Tabouis fled from her homeland and arrived in the United States. She could not stay to cover the story of France's betrayal and the German entry into Paris. On her arrival here she said: "Today, a refugee from my country, I am being tried for treason before a court at Riom. I am deprived of all rights, including the elementary right of defending myself. In my absence I have been stripped of my citizenship and my fortune. My family are today hostages to my prosecutors. But this is not my greatest misfortune. Today, after 16 **years** of incessant work in behalf of an ideal, I am compelled to acknowledge that all my efforts as writer, teacher and public speaker have utterly failed." Madame Tabouis plans a lecture tour of the United States and is conducting a radio series over station WMCA in New York.

From June issue:

Called "perhaps the best-known woman journalist in Europe," in 1892 Madame Tabouis was born Geneviève Le Quesne, daughter of a well-known painter and niece of both General Cambon and Jules Cambon, French Ambassador to Germany prior to the First World War. She was educated until 15 at the Convent of the Assumption: "I regret to say I didn't learn very much—I remember I used to keep silk worms and a frog in my desk and I left it with a liking for history and poetry, and quite resolved to follow the advice of our charming poet, Alfred de Musset—'In this good world you must get to like a lot of things so that you know finally which you like the best.'"

In order to find out "which she liked the best," young Geneviève studied for three years at the Faculté des Lettres de Paris, and then enrolled at the School of Archeology at the Louvre, "convinced that there was nothing so exciting as writing books in which you revive the past." An odd off-shoot of all this learning was "one of the happiest days of my life, when I could write a love letter to my favorite dancing partner in hieroglyphs."

In 1916 she married Robert Tabouis, who later became administrator of radio for France. They have a son and a daughter. Madame Tabouis became interested in politics and through her uncle made the acquaintance of most of the political figures of the period. She began to write up interviews with some of them in Geneva during the early days of the League of Nations.

From 1924 to 1932 she became favorably known for her political and diplomatic interpretations of events in many newspapers. She became Foreign News Editor of *L'Oeuvre*, a French journal, in 1932 and since then has become a power in European journalism. She is considered a master in dissecting current events and in revealing the background in the developments of the danger zones of Europe. In this connection, the *New Yorker* of February 10, 1940 ran an amusing article under the title *What paper d'ya read?*:

"If a wise citizen of Paris wants to know what Hitler and Stalin are thinking, what will be the next fantastic episode in an improbable war, he reads what Geneviève Tabouis has to say in *L'Oeuvre,* then waits for the exact opposite to happen.—*Time*.

"Geneviève Tabouis is the Cassandra columnist of France. As the pessimistic political prophetess of the Paris press, in her daily rubric in *L'Oeuvre* she forecast with accurate melancholy this year's war, last year's Munich appeasement, the German

GENEVIEVE TABOUIS

army maneuvers that led to the Austrian Anschluss, the failure of the Franco-Anglo-Russo alliance, and on February 12, 1939, predicted that Prague would be taken on March 11—four days before even Herr Hitler got around to it.—*Harper's Bazaar."*

Madame Tabouis is described as "a delicate woman with a fine spiritual face." Her name is known in the English, German, Italian and Soviet press, and her opinions are frequently quoted. Throughout Europe her articles on foreign policy have given her newspaper, *L'Oeuvre,* a special significance.

"One of the worst snags of being a woman diplomatic writer," she maintains, "is that you can't answer the insults that your adversaries pour down on your neck" as men can by fighting a duel. "Moreover in France men don't much like being under the orders of a woman." She has neatly solved that difficulty by never appearing at the editorial offices of her paper. Before starting an article she has telephone conversations with several European capitals. Then she telephones in all her instructions to her paper as she writes day by day a record "of the European crisis in all its ramifications and involutions." By "remaining in the wings" she feels that the prestige of her men colleagues is safe.

She works constantly to accomplish all the research and writing for her French paper, special dispatches to *La Critica* of Buenos Aires and the *Sunday Dispatch* of London. To write in these critical times an interpretation of history in the making exhausts her until she says: "Mon Dieu, what petty worries, what expenditure of energy, what a terrific amount of work. I can scarcely remember an evening when I haven't worked—even over the weekends and at Christmas." Asked what her favorite

relaxation is, she replied: "Playing with my cats."

Madame Tabouis has received numerous foreign decorations for her journalistic achievements; for her three books on historical subjects—*Nebuchadnezzar, Private Life of Tutankhamen* and *Solomon*—she has received honors from the French Academy. In addition she has written *Blackmail or War; Perfidious Albion—Entente Cordiale* and a *Life of Jules Cambon.*

References

Christian Sci. Mon Mag p12 Jl 1 '39 por
Cur Hist & Forum 52:19-20 S '40
Ind Woman 19:319+ O '40 por
Liv Age 351:230-2 N '36; 356:563-6 Ag '39
Newsweek 16:53 Ag 12 '40
Time 34:58-9 D 11 '39 por
International Who's Who
Who's Who

TAFT, ROBERT ALPHONSO Sept 8, 1889- Senator from Ohio

Address: b. United States Senate, Washington, D. C.; h. Station M, R R I, Cincinnati, Ohio

Even when there was a possibility of getting Robert Taft the Republican nomination for the Presidency in 1940, he was the despair of those who believe that a Presidential candidate should have color. His speeches are "prosy, clumsy, flowerless," and he has absolutely no sense of publicity. His campaign photographs show him "irreproachably garbed in a blue serge business suit holding at arm's length a wild turkey somebody else killed," or poking the head of a cow with a neatly gloved hand. He himself told a reporter: "I'm afraid you won't find much color in me. I'm too darn normal."

People found other assets for his campaign. In the first place, he had a perfect background. His father was President, and "a really great justice of the Supreme Court." What's more, he came from Ohio, which is always a good state for the Republican Party. He was about the right age—50—and he "looked like a composite picture of 16,000,000 Republicans." His failure to get the Presidential nomination was the first defeat after a series of uninspired but decisive victories.

Robert Alphonso Taft was born in Cincinnati, the elder son of William Howard Taft. When he was still a small boy his father was made Governor General of the Philippines, whither Robert accompanied him to find "his vast chuckling sire regarded by the natives as a cross between Santa Claus and Buddha." He was sent to America to his Uncle Horace's famous Taft School in Connecticut. He was "a solemn, diffident boy who never had to be told twice to go to bed, who always stood at the head of his

TAFT, ROBERT A.—*Continued*

class and who never seemed to be aware that he was not popular with the kids."

He led his class at Yale, where he "seemed to have a dread of cashing in on the fame of his father," then President of the United States. He led his class again at Harvard Law School, from which he received his LL. B. in 1913. And he passed his Bar exams with the highest mark in Ohio.

Though he had the pick of the big New York law offices, Bob Taft told his father: "I have a prejudice against New York as a place to work." He went back to Cincinnati to practice law with the firm of Maxwell and Ramsey, and married Martha Bowers, daughter of Lloyd Bowers, solicitor general under William Howard Taft.

When the United States went to War Taft volunteered twice, but his nearsightedness kept him out of the army. He thereupon became assistant counsel for Herbert Hoover's United States Food Administration, where he acquired a permanent horror of price fixing. "Whatever price we fixed," he says ruefully, "everybody howled." When the War ended he was counsel for the American Relief Administration in Europe, and for his work was decorated by the governments of Poland, Finland and Belgium.

After the War Bob Taft and his brother Charles set up a one-room law office and rapidly expanded it into the biggest and most prosperous in the city, with the leading corporations as their clients. He started politics as a precinct worker, and went around ringing doorbells and urging citizens to vote.

In 1921 Taft really entered politics as a candidate for the State Legislature, was elected, and stayed in the House until 1926. He went to Columbus "with a reputation of a silk stocking politician and astonished his fellow lawmakers by choosing as his specialty, of all disagreeable and laborious tasks, the revision of the antiquated Ohio tax system" In 1925 he became Republican House Leader, and Speaker in 1926. In 1931 he spent a term in the State Senate. Except for the work in tax revision, Taft's stay in the State Legislature has been called "three fireless terms."

In 1936 Taft was Ohio's favorite son at the Republican Convention. By then he and his wife were pleasantly well off: they had four sons, many friends, an agreeable, bustling sort of life. He decided to run for the Senate in 1938, even though Roosevelt had just piled up a huge Democratic majority in Ohio.

He got the Senatorship through plugging and, according to one commentator, through the "injudicious expenditure throughout Ohio of a couple of hundred thousand dollars, plus the wit, will and wisdom of his politically acute wife, Martha Bowers Taft." His wife was a tremendous aid to him then. If Senator Taft hadn't

come into her life, Mrs. Taft might have spent her years as a language teacher. After passing her examinations for Bryn Mawr, she decided instead to go to Paris where she studied for two years at the Sorbonne and obtained her certificate as a teacher. But instead of a language teacher, she became Robert Taft's wife and political campaigner.

Like Mrs. Roosevelt (see sketch this issue), Mrs. Taft received her early training in public affairs from the National League of Women Voters. She was the first president of the Cincinnati, Ohio League. She began to campaign for her husband in the 1938 Senatorial race because state chairman Ed Schorr told her she shouldn't, causing her to march straight from his office to the platform of an opposition meeting in a Negro church.

Between them Bob and Martha Taft visited every county in the state, traveling 30,000 miles and sometimes making as many as a dozen speeches in a day. Her speeches, unlike his, were brilliant and witty. There was the time she told a group of coal miners who felt Taft wasn't a man of the people: "My husband is not a simple man. He did not start from humble beginnings. My husband is a very brilliant man. He had a fine education at Yale. He has been trained well for his job. Isn't that what you prefer when you pick leaders to work for you?" And the day after Taft was elected one Ohio newspaper announced: "Bob and Martha Taft were elected to the Senate yesterday."

Probably one of the most important factors in Taft's vote-getting was his success in the debates between him and Senator Bulkley, his opponent. Bulkley was a good speaker, Taft a dull one, and Bulkley was way in the lead when the debates started. At the first debate in Marietta, Bulkley was booed when he talked. He waited for the audience to subside, meanwhile letting the radio audience hear the boos. When Taft, in turn, was booed, he hugged the microphone close and talked into it, so the much larger radio audience could hear only him. "He all but obliterated Mr. Bulkley in that contest."

In his first year in the United States Senate, despite the tradition that new members should lie low their first year, he has "talked out on the floor, hit headlines, and rushed into some of the bitterest debates." And he has been appointed to important committees—Appropriations, Banking and Currency, Education and Labor. But neither in the Senate nor in Ohio, according to Oswald Garrison Villard (see sketch this issue), has he fathered one proposal of a progressive and constructive character.

In the spring of 1939 Taft debated by radio with the New Deal Texan, T. V. Smith, professor of philosophy at the University of Chicago. Mr. Smith has "a golden tongue, a silver wit," but when the series were over a Gallup (see sketch this issue) poll between "Professor Smith's

Peter A. Nyholm

ROBERT A. TAFT

soufflé and Senator Taft's economic pork and
beans" showed that 66 per cent of the people
felt that in his plodding way Taft had the
best of the arguments. In 1939 as joint
author with Thomas V. Smith, he published
his debates under the title, *Foundations of
Democracy.*

Everybody seems to agree that Taft is
shy and that he is a "plain" man, but on
the other sides of his personality there's a
lot of disagreement.   One commentator
says: "Nature did not give him the singularly great charm of his parent," while
another insists that "Taft is his father's
son under a smiling and, for the most part,
charming exterior."   Partly because he is
near-sighted, he is not quick to greet people
on the street—and even when he does
there's no professional smile on his face,
nor is his handshake a hearty one. He is
tall, large-framed, slightly paunchy, with
sandy eyebrows and wispy hair, and self-
contained to the last drop. He doesn't
smoke, has no favorite foods, authors,
singers, artists or movie stars. He's never
"without a large brief case out of which
he can pull any paper the moment calls for
without looking. About the only things he
ever forgets or loses are his hat, umbrella,
galoshes and the names of the people he
met at Mrs. Quimp's reception last night."

Probably the most effective facet of his
personality is his rather quiet sense of
humor. "He has a nice grin which dis-
closes rows of large protruding teeth," and
he sometimes makes funny comments. One
of the most appreciated stories is about the
time he and Martha, who live modestly,
emerged from a stately Washington reception.   The   splendid   doorman   shouted:
"Senator Taft's car."   "Thank you," said

Taft. "It's a good car, but it doesn't come
when it's called."

References

Am Mag 128:40-1+ S '39
Christian Sci Mon Mag p5+ Ja 13 '40
Collier's 105:11+ Ap 6 '40 por
Liberty 17:55-8 Ap 6 '40 por; 17:39-40
 Ap 13 '40 por
Life 8:90-2+ Mr 18 '40 pors
Newsweek 15:33 Ap 29 '40
Sat Eve Post 212:29+ My 4 '40 por
Time 34:13-14 D 18 '39; 35:20-3 Ja 29
 '40; 35:20 Ap 15 '40

Who's Who in America
Who's Who in Government
Who's Who in Law

TAINTER, CHARLES SUMNER Apr 25,
1854—Apr 20, 1940 Physicist; inventor;
once associated with Alexander Graham
Bell; first made phonograph commercially
possible; inventor of the dictograph; first
to transmit sound through the agency of
light; called "father of the talkies"

References

American Men of Science
Who's Who in America 1938-39

Obituaries

N Y Herald Tribune p12 Ap 22 '40
N Y Times p18 Ap 22 '40

TANNER, JOHN HENRY Mar 1, 1861—
Mar 12, 1940 Professor of mathematics at
Cornell University; author of college texts
on algebra and geometry

JOHN HENRY TANNER

References

American Men of Science
Who's Who in America 1938-39

TANNER, JOHN HENRY—*Continued*

Obituaries

    N Y Herald Tribune p22 Mr 12 '40
    N Y Times p23 Mr 12 '40

TATE, ALLEN (tāt) Nov 19, 1899- Poet; author

Address: c/o Princeton University, Princeton, New Jersey

Allen Tate is one of the three "regulars" on CBS's *Invitation to Learning* broadcasts, a program designed to stimulate listeners to read or re-read the classics. Each Sunday from 4:30 to 5:00, "books which the world has not been willing or able to let die" are discussed, not technically or pedantically, yet without talking down. Mr. Tate, author, poet, critic and teacher, along with Huntington Cairns and Mark Van Doren (see sketches this issue) is now bringing to the public the thoughts of the world's great men, a job for which he is eminently equipped.

Allen Tate, who was born in Clarke County, Kentucky, the son of John Orley and Nellie (Varnell) Tate, has given all but three months of his life to literature since his graduation from Vanderbilt University in 1922. These three months he worked for an elder brother in the coal business. Because he had his mind on poetry instead of coal, young Tate shipped some anthracite that should have gone a hundred miles North to the remote West. The company lost $700 and he was fired.

It was while he was in college that Tate became one of the founders of the *Fugitive*, a journal of poetry published at Nashville, Tennessee. This magazine grew out of the literary and philosophic discussions of seven friends who issued their first cooperative number in April 1922 and continued to publish it until December 1925. Considered by many critics one of the most brilliant groups in American letters since the New England group in the nineteenth century, they tended to foster original expression and mature and intricate verse form.

During the period he was active on the *Fugitive* and for some years after Tate was a free-lance reviewer. In 1928 he was awarded a Guggenheim Fellowship and with his wife, Caroline Gordon, the novelist, whom he had married in 1924, went abroad. It was while he was in Europe that his first books were published: *Stonewall Jackson—The Good Soldier* (1928) and *Jefferson Davis—His Rise and Fall* (1929), biographies springing from his great interest in American history of the nineteenth century; and *Mr. Pope and Other Poems* (1928), a collection of his poetry.

In 1930 Mr. and Mrs. Tate, with their small daughter Nancy Meriwether, returned to America and bought a farm in Tennessee, near Clarksville. Here Tate did some of his best writing and his wife produced some of her distinguished novels. Tate continued

ALLEN TATE

to increase his reputation as a poet and at the same time was developing those critical powers which later led Louis Untermeyer to call him "the best critic in America." His essays in criticism have appeared in the *Yale Review*, *The Nation*, the *New Republic*, the *American Scholar* and other distinguished publications, and when his *Reactionary Essays on Poetry and Ideas* was published in 1936 London's *Time and Tide* called it "the best book that has come out of America in many years." Mark Van Doren didn't hesitate to say that it represented "contemporary criticism at its best," and other critics pointed out the thoughtfulness and freshness that illuminate the book.

Tate's poetry continued to appear, too— in 1930, 1932 and in 1936 when *The Mediterranean and other Poems* was published. It was with the publication of this volume that adverse criticism began to be loudly heard. Tate, who at one time was "the most highly praised poet of his generation with the exception of Hart Crane," was criticized for his lack of emotional impact, for being "heavy and sententious." And these same criticisms were leveled against *Selected Poems* (1937). His poems here "are difficult, partly because of the great amount of specialized knowledge they contain, partly because of the language in which they are cast." Despite the evidences they give of "an acute critical intelligence, hard at work on the most stubborn and invigorating problems of our time," their obscurity hindered their impact on some, an obscurity frequently attributed "to a lack of poetic ability, a lack of any deep passion or intuitive grasp of life," as Eda Lou Walton put it in the New York *Times*.

Few poets make a living with verse, and a poet who is also a critic with a knowledge of literature naturally drifts into teaching.

Tate's first teaching job was at Southwestern College in Tennessee in 1934. His next, during the academic year of 1938 to 1939, was as professor of English at the Women's College of the University of North Carolina. From 1939 on he has been a resident fellow at Princeton University, in charge of creative writing under the Creative Arts Program. He has, of course, lectured frequently on modern poetry and criticism—at Yale, Harvard, Columbia, Cornell and other colleges.

The Fathers, Tate's first and so far only novel, was published in 1938, its theme "the conflict between a strong man who is not rooted in the peculiar Virginia culture of the period and the ancient traditions of the culture itself." Only one critic pointed out the book's "indirection and inconclusiveness"; the others called it "beautifully written and profoundly searching", "a fine novel by a fine poet." In it Tate's knowledge of the South, previously shown in his biographies of Jackson and Jefferson, is clearly apparent; the physical scene is minutely reconstructed, though the story's elements are imaginatively combined. Here Tate gave proof of his belief that literature, poetry as well as fiction, comes of observing things that nobody but the literary artist takes the trouble to see.

Tate is blond and has a youthful mildness which those who know him say is deceptive. Actually he has strong and definite convictions on matters literary and political, and has no hesitation in expressing them "with incisive and sometimes demolishing wit."

References

> Poetry 50:96-100 My '37; 51:262-6 F '38
> Southern R 5:419-38 winter '40
> Time 30:81 N 1 '37 por
> Kunitz, S. J. ed. Living Authors 1937
> Who's Who in America

TAUSSIG, FRANK WILLIAM Dec 28, 1859—Nov 11, 1940 Political economist; professor emeritus of Harvard University (retired in 1935); a founder of Harvard Graduate School of Business Administration; author of many books on economics and international trade; has been called "parent of modern American economic thought"; his *Principles of Economics* widely used as a textbook; for 40 years editor of *Quarterly Journal of Economics*

References

> Leaders in Education 1932
> Parsons, T. On Certain Sociological Elements in Professor Taussig's Thought *In* Explorations in Economics; notes and essays contributed in honor of F. W. Taussig by various authors p359-79 1936
> Viner, J. Professor Taussig's Contribution to the Theory of International Trade *In* Explorations in Economics; notes and essays con-

tributed in honor of F. W. Taussig by various authors p3-12 1936
> Who's Who Among North American Authors
> Who's Who in America
> Who's Who in American Education

Obituaries

> N Y Herald Tribune p20 N 12 '40 por
> N Y Times p23 N 12 '40 por

TAYLOR, DEEMS Dec 22, 1885- Music commentator; composer; author
Address: h. 2 E 60th St, New York City

A man of many musical activities, including commenting on and writing about music, Deems Taylor conducted a new half-hour radio program from January to August 1940 called *Musical Americana.* It was an all-American program, with a large symphony orchestra and a mixed choir, and a policy that all compositions played were to be exclusively by Americans—the only criterion that it be good of its kind, with no discrimination between the popular and the serious. Taylor served as master of ceremonies on the program. His performance as commentator for Walt Disney's (see sketch this issue) *Fantasia* received much favorable critical comment.

His new book of interpretations of music, *The Well-Tempered Listener,* appeared early in February 1940. Much of its material has been addressed to radio audiences in the intervals of symphony concerts. The book starts with the thesis that however beautiful music may be, the listener should be credited with a certain amount of courage and endurance. He says that the listener should give ear to and try to like and understand modern music. Besides listeners, Mr. Taylor's book also considers the composer and the performer.

Joseph Deems Taylor (he has discarded his first name) is a native New Yorker. He was born in New York December 22, 1885. He attended Ethical Culture School and New York University, where he wrote musical shows that were performed at student gatherings and was also on the track team. He wanted to be an architect, but found that it took too much mathematics. He can subtract, he says, but he can't add. He got a job as an assistant for the *Nelson Encyclopedia.* Meanwhile, however, he had collaborated with an undergraduate on a musical comedy good enough to reach Broadway, so decided to teach himself composition and orchestration. He studied counterpoint and harmony with Oscar Coon, an Oswego, New York bandsman. After winning a symphonic contest he decided on a joint career of journalism and music.

In 1916 to 1917 he was a war correspondent for the Sunday *Tribune,* and for some time after 1917, associate editor of *Collier's Weekly.* His first public success as a composer was with his prize tone poem, *The Siren Song* (1913). Other early successes were two choral works, *The Chambered Nautilus* and

DEEMS TAYLOR

The Highwayman. His orchestral suite, *Through the Looking Glass,* attracted attention, and he was commissioned by Walter Damrosch to compose the symphonic poem, *Jurgen.* He served as music critic on the New York *World* from 1921 to 1926, when he resigned to compose his first serious opera, *The King's Henchman,* with libretto by Edna St. Vincent Millay. It was given for three seasons' performances at the Metropolitan Opera House. Taylor's second opera, *Peter Ibbetson,* was given for four seasons.

In the field of musical literature, Taylor has acted as editor of the magazine, *Musical America,* and as music editor for the *Encyclopedia Britannica* and the *Nelson Encyclopedia.* He has written incidental music for the theatre, and has been by turns writer, critic, linguist and artist. As a radio commentator, he was for some time narrator for the opera broadcasts from the Metropolitan Opera House and is the well-known commentator for the New York Philharmonic Sunday afternoon broadcasts. The predecessor to his present book of comment on music, *The Well-Tempered Listener,* was *Of Men and Music,* which appeared in 1938. It is a book of observations written with the amateur music audience in mind, and discusses diverse personalities in music, with an insistence on the entertainment value of good music.

Deems Taylor is a versatile man in many fields. He has now given up his newspaper jobs; but in his spare time he does translating from three languages, paints for his own "amazement," is a candid camera fiend and a good cabinet maker. He practically built his own home in Stamford, Connecticut. Though a smallish, witty, mild-appearing man, he is forced to be firm when pestered by advice seekers, and won't help any aspir-

ing young musician who is not well recommended. He has one daughter, Joan, by his second wife, Mary Kennedy, the actress, from whom he is now divorced.

His occasional visits to the *Information, Please* program have been most successful. As a commentator Taylor is humorous, chatty, informal—with a casualness actually hard to achieve. Preparing the comment, he first looks up the subject. Then, in the modern study-bedroom of his old-fashioned Fifth Avenue apartment, he starts talking to himself, repeating a sentence over and over until he is sure it sounds completely natural. He pecks out—"I type by ear," he says—the final version. Once in a while, broadcasting, he makes a tongue slip, as when he turned "Kern fans" into "fern cans" and the Holy Family into the "Homely Family." Of his future he says: "I'll stay in radio until I'm thrown out, and I'll keep on writing music because I can't help it."

References

Christian Sci Mon p9 Ap 5 '40 pors
N Y Herald Tribune p9 F 3 '40
N Y Herald Tribune Books p5 F 4 '40
N Y Times F 11 '40
New Yorker 1:9-10 Je 6 '25
Newsweek 15:44 Ja 29 '40 por
Sat R Lit 17:24 N 27 '37 por
Scholastic 32:6 Ap 30 '38; 36:24 Mr 4 '40 por
Variety 137:40 Ja 31 '40
Ewen, D. ed. Composers of Today 1936
Gillis, A. and Ketchum, R. Deems Taylor: A New World Melodist *In* Our America p265-79 1936
Howard, J. T. Our Contemporary Composers *In* Our American Music p462-579 1939
Pierre Key's Musical Who's Who 1931
Taylor, D. The Well-Tempered Listener 1940
Thompson, O. ed. International Cyclopedia of Music and Musicians 1939
Variety Radio Directory
Who's Who in America

TAYLOR, FRANCIS HENRY Apr 23, 1903- Director of New York Metropolitan Museum of Art

Address: b. Metropolitan Museum of Art, New York City

The Metropolitan Museum of Art is a dusty, gray edifice stretching over four city blocks and crammed full of art masterpieces of the ages. Herbert Eustis Winlock, former director and famed as an Egyptologist, resigned in April 1939 because of ill health. In May 1940 the new director, Francis Henry Taylor, took over one of the most important museum posts in the country.

He has many problems to solve in his new undertaking—shrinking income; heavy operating expenses; fallen attendance;

FRANCIS HENRY TAYLOR

mounting public interest in the new shiny Museum of Modern Art. However, Mr. Taylor, who since 1931 has been director of the rather small but very distinguished Museum of Art in Worcester, Massachusetts, seems to be the man for the job. He made art history by sponsoring a Flemish painting exhibit at Worcester, which was acclaimed as the most comprehensive ever shown in America. Also, it is said, that the average American enters a museum once in five years. In one year Taylor disproved this statement considerably by raising the attendance at the Worcester Museum from 37,000 to 145,000.

In September 1940 he accepted the President's invitation to head the council formed to carry out National Art Week, which took place from November 25 to December 1. During this time about 1,000 exhibits of the work of American artists and craftsmen were held. The object, according to Mr. Taylor himself, was to "bring to the attention of the public the fact that works of art may come within the reach of the most modest pocket."

Mr. Taylor was born in Philadelphia on April 23, 1903, son of the late Dr. William Johnson Taylor, former president of the College of Physicians, and president of the Library Company in Philadelphia. His mother was the late Emily Buckley (Newbold) Taylor. He prepared at the Kent School for the University of Pennsylvania, from which he was graduated in 1924. He taught English for the French government in the Lycée de Chartres in 1924 to 1925, and from 1924 to 1926 did graduate work in the Universities of Paris and Florence, the Institut d'Estudis Catalans, Barcelona, and the American Academy in Rome. He traveled extensively in central Europe and in 1926 to 1927 was a Carnegie Fellow in the

Graduate College of Princeton. From 1928 to 1931 he was curator of medieval art and editor of publications at the Philadelphia Museum of Art.

While director of the Worcester Museum he served as regional director and advisor of the Federal Arts Project for the New England states. He is the author of numerous monographs and critical articles on art history and archeology. In 1928 he married Pamela Coyne of Watertown, New York. They have three children, two girls and a boy.

Mr. Taylor, an "amiable, rotund" man with prominent nose and thinning hair, thinks that a museum's function is not merely to acquire art objects. In addition, it must lure people in to see the objects and must endeavor to teach them to make art a part of their daily lives.

References

Mag Art 31:157+ Mr '38 por; 33: 114-15+ F '40
N Y Sun p20 Ja 12 '40
N Y Times p1, 15 Ja 12 '40; VII p8, 23 My 5 '40
Time 35:70 Ja 22 '40 por
Who's Who in America

TAYLOR, MYRON CHARLES Jan 18, 1874- Retired steel executive; appointed envoy (1939) to the Vatican

Address: b. United States Senate, Washington, D. C.; h. Gooding, Idaho

Myron C. Taylor, retired chairman of the United States Steel Corporation, was appointed during Christmas week 1939, by President Roosevelt as his personal envoy to Pope Pius XII to work for world peace. He sailed on February 17, 1940.

Taylor was born in Lyons, New York, the son of William and Mary Morgan (Underhill) Taylor. Although he was educated as a lawyer, it is as a businessman that Taylor is best known. He has been prominent in banking, finance, insurance and industry. For a time he practiced law and then ran a group of New England textile mills. As a banker he aided in forming a two billion dollar merger. In 1932 he entered the United States Steel Corporation, replacing J. P. Morgan. He is credited with making notable changes in that company and achieved first-page attention in 1936 when he sat down with John L. Lewis, CIO leader, and effected a peaceable agreement between the labor leader and a great corporation, long non-union, and thus averted a serious strike.

In 1939 he resigned from the corporation and told his friends that he planned to spend "a sabbatical year of philosophic meditation on the problems of modern civilization." This pleasant project was soon given up when President Roosevelt asked him to head the United States delegation to the Evian Refugee Conference, and to undertake refugee work, which has occupied a good deal of Mr. Taylor's time. He

MYRON C. TAYLOR

became the American member of the Inter-governmental Committee for Refugees in 1939.

In the new appointment to the Vatican, Mr. Taylor, an Episcopalian of early Quaker stock, received the rank of Ambassador, but without portfolio. He was the first United States envoy to visit the Vatican officially since Rufus King left Rome in 1868. The restoration of relations with the Holy See had been proposed, since the Vatican is now a temporal State.

"The new ambassador of peace," said one writer, "is more than a businessman of action. Although he looks like a caricaturist's tycoon type with a buffalo build, an aggressive chin and heavy jowls, his manner is just the opposite, gentle, modest and self-controlled. He is the kind of person who enjoys having only one overworked photograph of himself, who takes a great interest in all art institutions (especially the American Academy in Rome, the Metropolitan Opera Company and the Metropolitan Museum of Art), and who feels lost unless he is playing a leading rôle in world affairs."

His appointment was viewed with favor by most newspapers and church leaders, although some Baptists and certain other Protestant groups vigorously opposed Mr. Taylor's appointment. The *Christian Century* said: "To strip away all camouflage, the President has, in reality, established diplomatic relations with the Vatican without legal authority. He has done so, we believe, not as a peace move but as a political move." The Methodist Conference meeting in April 1940 asked President Roosevelt to revoke the appointment. The New York *Herald Tribune,* however, said: "The President has found a way of symbolizing the fact that peace and good will are practical prin-

ciples, as much deserving the services of a special envoy as are other principles that operate in the affairs of men." *Time* called Taylor "the first industrialist to match minds with the thoroughly schooled and skillful Catholic diplomats. But the wise pouches under Mr. Taylor's sad, deep-set, clear-green eyes are there by no accident; his stubborn, pugnacious nose, his mailbox-slit mouth, his underslung jaw are all testimonials of the strength and judicial balance of his mind."

Mr. Taylor returned from Italy after seven months' stay which was marred by a serious illness. He brought with him the Pope's assurances that the Vatican was "doing everything it possibly can to bring about world peace"—with little hope of success.

References

Cath World 150:620 F '40; 151:107-8 Ap '40; 151:573-81 Ag '40
Fortune 15:91-4+ My '37 il por (Same cond. Time 29:74+ My 3 '37)
Nation 143:240 Ag 29 '36
N Y World-Telegram p18 My 2 '40
Newsweek 6:23 D 28 '35 por; 15:13 Ja 1 '40 por
Scholastic 35:7 Ja 8 '40 por
Time 35:7 Ja 1 '40 por
U S News 8:45 Ja 5 '40 por
Who's Who in America
Who's Who in Commerce and Industry

TEMPLETON, ALEC July 4, 1910-
Pianist; composer

Address: 200 E Chestnut St, Chicago, Illinois

Alec Andrew Templeton, (he does not use his middle name), has been called "one of the musical marvels of modern times." He was born in Cardiff, Wales, July 4, 1910, blind from birth. Although his father and mother were amateur musicians and there were musicians on both sides of the family, none were concert artists.

"When I first got over the shock that I had a little boy who would never see," said his mother, "I decided I would never let him realize he was handicapped. We treated him exactly as we treated his sisters." The little boy had to put his toys away himself and was often sent to get things from upstairs bedrooms. This early training made him self-reliant. No mention of his blindness was made at home, and he was eight before he heard the word "blind" from an outsider. At the age of two he imitated perfectly on the piano the sound of the bell in a nearby church. At four he composed a lullaby which he still remembers as his "first known composition." His mother used it to put him to sleep. His family early noted that his ear became phenomenally sharp as a natural compensation for his loss of sight. At five he directed a choir of his playmates and showed promise as a piano student. "When he was six," his mother says, "he was so far advanced musically that the rest of the family practically gave up playing. He made us all feel silly."

The family moved to London so that the amazing child could start his musical education. Enrolled as a student in the Royal Academy of Music when he was 12, Alec studied under excellent masters; became acquainted. with musical literature by playing hundreds of records which he borrowed; and learned to read the Braille texts of music. He auditioned for the British Broadcasting Corporation in 1922. He was promptly engaged, and his novelty musical acts were presented almost daily for more than 12 years. At 16 he won a piano contest in which 20,000 pianists competed. Upon graduation from Worcester College, Oxford, where he made brilliant progress in the almost forgotten art of musical improvisation, he studied for four years at the Royal College of Music.

Templeton joined Jack Hylton's band as a specialty performer in England and came to the United States in 1935. His success on the air, in recordings and concerts, both as a serious pianist and as a musical satirist, has been remarkable. Critics have mentioned "his unorthodox way of holding his hands flat, his arms stiff," but they admire "his sure, supple tone." In appearances at New York's top-flight night clubs, Carnegie Hall and such radio programs as Rudy Vallee's *Variety Hour*, the *Chase and Sanborn Hour*, *Kraft Music Hall* and *Magic Key*, Templeton became known not so much for his classical piano playing as for his tricks.

Humor in music is a very difficult art and rarely practiced. Templeton, through satire, imitation and caricature, has convulsed audiences with his take-off on Wagnerian opera, in which he portrays "the guttural "ich's" and "ach's" of a strangling German tenor, the shrill high notes of the famous soprano, the grunting shouts of the basso; and the Wagnerian orchestra is there, too, introduced with marvelous insight into some of the harmonic and instrumental mannerisms peculiar to the master." Another favorite is his satire on an actual performance of *Pinafore* which he once heard in Connecticut. The chorus came in off key and one whole beat behind the orchestra. He asks his audience to name five notes, and then swiftly builds them into a theme "with variations in the manner of Bach, Mozart and Chopin." Critics have been amazed at his uncanny versatility as he plays a Mozart concerto and then goes into a swing version of one of Bach's major works. He can improvise in any classical composer's style and sound so much like the composer that most listeners are fooled. A favorite trick of his is to take a popular tune and play it in the individual styles of Mozart, Puccini, Debussy and Johann Strauss.

Once at a party Templeton was asked to accompany Nathan Milstein, the violinist, in Lalo's *Symphonie Espagnole*. The blind

Musical America

ALEC TEMPLETON

pianist said he did not know the work but would play it if someone ran over it first. While the 32-minute-long work was played, Templeton listened carefully, then accompanied Milstein easily, making only one error. Milstein, considerably awed by such an amazing memory, declared the error was an improvement over the original.

Templeton thoroughly understands the jazz idiom and thinks "it will set its stamp more and more upon the musical production on this side of the Atlantic." "The music of such American composers as Ferde Grofé, Cole Porter (see sketches this issue), George Gershwin and Jerome Kern," he declares, "is certainly very fine; and it will have a definite influence on music of a more serious character." Templeton has written many improvisations on classical works. In the realm of swing music his *Mr. Bach Goes to Town* is a classic, part of a pentateuch that includes *Mendelssohn Mows 'Em Down*; *Mozart Matriculates*; *Haydn Takes to Ridin'*; and *Debussy in Dubuque*. In August 1940 he made his Lewisohn Stadium debut delighting the audience with his *Grieg's in the Groove*, and the critics with his brilliant performance of the Rachmaninoff *Concerto*.

Critics describe Templeton as "an exceedingly affable, brown-eyed young man." Everything is associated with music in Templeton's mind. He thinks of people in terms of music—cataloguing the key of their voices and remembering them by name as soon as they speak to him. He says: "I adore people, and jokes, and music, and the fresh feeling of the wind. What I can't have, I don't think about."

He married Juliett Vaiani, a singer, on August 25, 1940

A French critic has summed him up in the following words: "Alec Templeton has never

TEMPLETON, ALEC—*Continued*

in his life seen the sun, nor the moon, nor the stars. He does not know what light is. The names of the colors have no meaning for him. Still, he hears, he feels, he receives countless impressions; he evaluates, he comes to conclusions, with an accuracy that is a subject for wonder. Throughout his successes he has remained unaffected, simple and gentle. He is an authentic genius; a genius in the full and exceptional French meaning of the word *génie*."

References

Am Mag 128:53-4+ Ag '39 por
Etude 57:433-4+ Jl '39 por
Lit Digest 125:22 Ja 8 '38
N Y World-Telegram p9 F 3 '40
Opera News 4:8-10 Ja 29 '40 pors
Scrib Mag 105:48 Mr '39
Time 27:80-1+ Ap 13 '36 por; 33:47-8 F 13 '39 por; 34:50-1 D 4 '39 il por
America's Young Men
Streyckmans, F. B. Today's Young Men p78 1940
Who's Who in America

TETRAZZINI, LUISA (tĕt'rät-sē'nē) June 29, 1874—Apr 28, 1940 Noted Italian soprano; made New York debut in 1908; acclaimed on three continents; sang at Manhattan Opera and Chicago Opera

LUISA TETRAZZINI

References

Henderson, W. J. Mme. Tetrazzini's Violetta *In* Art of Singing p233-40 1938
Thompson, O. ed. Cyclopedia of Music and Musicians 1938
Who's Who in America 1920-21

Wier, A. E. ed. Macmillan Encyclopedia of Music and Musicians 1938

Obituaries

Musical Am 60:5+ My 10 '40 pors
N Y Herald Tribune p10 Ap 29 '40 pors
N Y Times p15 Ap 29 '40 por
Variety 138:54 My 1 '40

THAYER, ERNEST LAWRENCE Aug 14, 1863—Aug 21, 1940 Newspaperman who worked for the Hearst newspapers, the San Francisco *Examiner* and the New York *Journal* during the '80s and '90s; achieved fame as the author of *Casey at the Bat*, the baseball ballad which created a legend and became an American classic; wrote it in a few hours for the San Francisco *Examiner* in 1888; the late De Wolfe Hopper, the actor, included it in his repertoire and said that he recited it more than 15,000 times

References

Who's Who in America

Obituaries

N Y Herald Tribune p18 Ag 22 '40
Newsweek 16:55 S 2 '40
Time 36:47 S 2 '40

THOMAS, LOWELL Apr 6, 1892- Radio commentator; author; lecturer

Address: b. RCA Bldg, Rockefeller Center, New York City; h. "Clover Brook," Pawling, New York

Possibly no one person in America has been longer, oftener, or more successfully in the public eye than Lowell Thomas. He has been a radio news commentator for the National Broadcasting Company since 1930 (on September 30, 1940 he observed his tenth anniversary as a news broadcaster), and a commentator for Twentieth Century-Fox Movietone since 1935. Renowned as a globe-trotter, he has lectured on subjects gleaned from his travels to millions of people in nearly every English-speaking city in the world. He is the author of some 20 books; and was an editor of the *Commentator*. He was recently awarded the bicentennial medal of the University of Pennsylvania.

Lowell Jackson Thomas (he does not use his middle name) was born in Woodington, Ohio, April 6, 1892, but grew up in the world-famous Rocky Mountain mining camp of Cripple Creek, Colorado. His training for his 'ecture and radio career actually began here, since his father, a scholarly physician, had a horror of slovenly speech, and taught the boy to speak clearly and correctly. In his home was one of the finest libraries west of the Mississippi. Contrasting with this richly cultivated atmosphere were the shafts, shacks and dance halls of a mining town.

When he was 11 years old, Lowell Thomas worked for a while in the gold mines; before that he had sold newspapers in the gambling halls and saloons. Associating with all types of adventurers, his imagination was fired by their many stories of far corners of the world, and his boyhood ambition was to see more of the earth and its people than anyone who ever lived. He began by attending as many as four universities: Valparaiso in Indiana; the University of Denver, where he took a degree; the Kent College of Law, where he later became a professor; and Princeton, where he took postgraduate work in English literature. He worked his way through these colleges by holding various jobs, such as cow-punching, tending furnace, acting as a cook and waiter, mining, assisting a geologist, reporting on daily newspapers.

In his early twenties he outfitted and headed two private expeditions into the sub-Arctic, taking along camera and notebook. He soon became known as an authority on these regions, started lecturing first before small groups, later before such organizations as the Smithsonian Institution. During the First World War he became known as a brilliant reporter and speaker; and Franklin K. Lane, then Secretary of the Interior, asked the President to assign him to record the history of the War. Financed by a group of wealthy men, Lowell Thomas with a staff of cameramen and assistants set out to do so. He was attached in turn to the Belgian, French, Italian, Serbian, American, British and Arabian Armies.

It was while with the Italian Army in the Alps that Thomas first heard of the appointment of General Allenby as commander of the Allied Forces in the Near East. On joining Allenby in the Holy Land, he kept hearing stories, half myth, of a man who had united the Arab tribes against the Turks. Then, in Jerusalem, he saw a man garbed as an Arab, but beardless and blue-eyed. Thus he met Colonel T. E. Lawrence, and soon after joined him in the Arabian Desert. On his return to New York Thomas had the exclusive story and pictures of the famous Revolt in the Desert. Later he showed the films in the British Isles, where over a million heard him. His best-known book, *With Lawrence in Arabia*, appeared in 1924; he wrote also *A Boy's Life of Colonel Lawrence*.

At the end of the World War, after 16 attempts, Lowell Thomas was the first person to enter Germany and bring back an eyewitness account of the German Revolution. President Wilson called upon him to make a special report to the Peace Delegates. From 1919 to 1922 he made an extensive tour of the world, during part of which time he accompanied the Prince of Wales on his famous trip through India. Thomas has traveled among the pygmy tribes of the East, penetrated the bush country of Australia and the Himalayan fastness of Upper Burma.

On the lecture platform Thomas has spoken in almost every town of over 5,000 population in the United States and Canada.

LOWELL THOMAS

On the radio he has talked to countless millions more. He likes broadcasting, and prepares his broadcast up to the last second before he steps before the microphone. It is said that his sponsors never see the script, which is a rare proceeding in radio. He is one of the most factual and objective of commentators, and tries not to take sides in any issue. His voice is friendly, virile, typically American, but without a trace of accent. Radio broadcasting is a form of reporting; and, as Thomas says, "I've always liked reporting. And I've always tried to write the kind of story that would enable me to come back and get another if that should be necessary... It is getting the story, watching it unfold, that fascinates me."

Thomas is a Fellow of the Royal Geographical Society, a Fellow of the American Geographical Society, an honorary life member of the English Speaking Union and of the Chicago Press Club, and a member of the Explorers' Club, the Princeton Club and the New York Advertising Club.

Among his books are: *Beyond the Khyber Pass* (1925); *The First World Flight* (1925); *Count Luckner, the Sea Devil* (1927); *Raiders of the Deep* (1928); *The Hero of Vincennes* (1929); *India, Land of the Black Pagoda* (1930); *Rolling Stone* (1931); *Kabluk of the Eskimo* (1932); *Adventures Among Immortals* (1937); and a number of travel books such as *Seeing Japan with Lowell Thomas* (1937). His latest books are *How to Keep Mentally Fit* (1940), about the benefits of public speaking; and *Pageant of Adventure* (1940).

Thomas married Frances Ryan of Denver in 1917; they have one son, Lowell Jackson Jr. Thomas takes a great deal of interest in his home in the Berkshires at Pawling, New York. There he has a library of 3,000 volumes, runs a local softball team, likes to

THOMAS, LOWELL—*Continued*

ride and, when he can, breakfasts in his riding boots. He tamed an unmanageable outlaw horse, so that now it is one of the best performers in his stable. He likes opera, the theatre and the one cigar he allows himself each day. And, among the treasures gathered from his travels, he particularly likes a magnificent teak chest covered with 30 thin layers of gold, given him by the abbot of a Buddhist monastery.

References

Lit Digest 121:24 Mr 21 '36 por
N Y Times IX p12 F 25 '40
N Y World-Telegram p8 F 22 '40
Pict R 37:66 Ag '36
Read Digest 28:61-3 Mr '36
America's Young Men
International Motion Picture Almanac
Kunitz, S. J. and Haycraft, H. eds.
  Junior Book of Authors 1935
Variety Radio Directory
Who's Who Among North American
  Authors
Who's Who in America

THOMPSON, DOROTHY July 9, 1894-
Columnist
Address: b. New York Herald Tribune, 230 W 41st St, New York City

In October 1940 Dorothy Thompson amazed quite a lot of people and dismayed the New York's Republican *Herald Tribune* for which she works by coming out for President Roosevelt. As a poet in *The Sun Dial* (New York *Sun*) commented:

"Willkie's good
And plenty hotty
To all the Reids. . .
But not to Dotty."

"The mistakes of the New Deal," she wrote, "have been mistakes in the right direction. . . The President *knows* the world . . . better than any other living democratic head of a state. . . No new President could acquire this knowledge in weeks or in months or in four years." She claimed that the President can be a great man in an emergency, looming "above that of any statesman except perhaps Churchill" (see sketch this issue). After endorsing the President, Miss Thompson rolled up her sleeves and waded into the battle with characteristic ardor. She crusaded on the air and in political rallies, enlivened the campaign by trading verbal punches with playwright Clare Boothe, and suggested that Wendell Willkie be put in the Cabinet now that the elections are over. Because her prognostications and advice mold the opinion of a vast number of readers, the influence of such a Thompsonian endorsement was by no means slight.

Dynamic Dorothy Thompson has, next to Eleanor Roosevelt (see sketch this issue), the "most power and prestige of any woman in America today." Since 1936 her widely-syndicated thrice-a-week *On the Record* columns have convinced not only women, for whom they were originally intended, but men readers of her vigor, brilliance, enthusiasm, uncanny knowledge and judgment of the world situation and uncompromising sincerity. A selection of these articles, *Let the Record Speak,* appeared in 1939: they include, with an I-told-you-so air, mostly those of her pronouncements that came true. Of the book Raymond Gram Swing (see sketch this issue), a staunch admirer, wrote: "Reading her comments in the light of what did happen becomes a fascination so that it is hard to lay down this collection. They move with the drama of history. . . The book contains some first-class writing. It has body and texture, clarity and feeling. It is good writing because it conveys its meaning smoothly and directly." Besides her column, Miss Thompson writes each month for the *Ladies' Home Journal* and occasionally for other periodicals. In 1938 and 1939 she had a radio program, but her sponsors worried about her violent attacks upon Hitler, Stalin *et al,* and her contract was not renewed. Up to the last year or two she has done much lecturing; she is an excellent speaker and receives yearly some 7,000 invitations to speak, with proffered high fees. Her combined earnings are considerable.

She returned late in May 1940 from a trip abroad to observe war developments in France, England, Italy, Holland, Finland and the Balkans. She could not go to Germany: Hitler expelled her from the Reich in 1934 because of her writings; and for her viewpoints on Communism she is *persona non grata* in Russia. Belligerently non-isolationist before her trip, back came her cabled columns whose increased "war mongering" (her direct ancestry is British, the fixed object of her hatred is Hitler) alarmed many besides isolationists. A prophesying Cassandra is less dangerous than a crusading one. "Her emotional zeal runs away with her intellectual analysis," John Chamberlain (see sketch this issue) has said, since she wants to preserve the British balance of power by destroying Hitler, when it was this same statecraft that created Hitler and may create another like him in the future.

There is a perpetual dualism in Dorothy Thompson's personality and mental make-up that colors her political observances. She is the torch-bearing Great Mother out to protect the Status Quo; she is also the rebel kicking with childish vehemence at restraint and opposition. She deplores some of the New Deal, but approves wide-scale planning on a strict non-political basis; she approves sound, private ownership. Old-style capitalism, she says, is doomed, but her capitalist friends do not mind her saying so; they know that at heart she is a conservative, or, as she prefers to call it, "preservative." Nor are they alarmed when she says that the present War is just one manifestation of a world revolution going on for some time. What opposition and attack Miss Thompson gets come consistently from the Left. Many women are highly flattered by the fact that most of her column readers are men. But to the latter sex her rapid leaps from subject to subject are disconcerting, as are her equally rapid shifts in judgment. She remains thoroughly feminine in reserving the right to change her mind. She changed it on Hitler, on Lindbergh, on Roosevelt. Of Roosevelt she has said: "When he is right I am for him. When he is wrong, I'm against him." Her humor is usually pretty heavy-footed; as a satirist she often misses the boat. Occasionally she gets back neatly. Father Coughlin (see sketch this issue) once referred to her as "Dottie," so when she wrote of him thereafter she always called him "Chuck."

It is proof of her influence and vitality that rival columnists (masculine) make numerous quips about her. *Time*, via Hugh Johnson (see sketch this issue), has called her the "No. 1 United States Breast-beater." Sir Wilmot Lewis says that she "has discovered the secret of perpetual emotion." The late Heywood Broun wrote: "Dorothy Thompson is greater than Eliza because not only does she cross the ice but breaks it as she goes. Moreover, she is her own bloodhound." Miss Thompson, an aggressive extrovert who has never had the time to look at herself with any sort of objectivity, takes all this in her stride. Men also admire her and know that she is a good fellow.

A study of Dorothy Thompson's childhood might give a psychologist the cue to her career and viewpoints. She was born in Lancaster, New York, July 9, 1894, eldest child of Peter and Margaret (Grierson) Thompson. Her father, from England, was a Methodist minister who transferred from one parsonage to another in upper New York State. Dorothy became the mentor and protector of younger brother and sister: Peggy, small and gentle; Willard, fat and adoring, fall-guy for Dorothy's "Little Lulu" escapades and rebellions. She was gawky and a tomboy: everything a parson's daughter shouldn't be. When her mother died, the 10-year-old Cassandra prophesied darkly that the church organist, Eliza Abbott, was setting her cap for the minister. It was true: father married Eliza, who turned out to be a typical terror of a stepmother whom Dorothy hated and rebelled against. She adored her father, whose idea of punishment was the memorizing and reciting of Bible passages. His coaching of her recitations doubtless helped make her the effective speaker she became.

Young Dorothy's feuds with her stepmother were over when she was sent to her aunt in Chicago. There she went to high school and to Lewis Institute: not a brilliant scholar, but popular as captain of the basketball team and a social leader.

G. Maillard Kesslère

DOROTHY THOMPSON

Entering Syracuse University in 1910, she got a reputation as a joiner and a cause-embracer. She worked her way through the college, became a more thoughtful student, and showed marked ability as an orator. The boy students remember that she wasn't a girl who had many dates, however: romance, to her, was discussing politics and economics while strolling in the moonlight. She had prepared to be a teacher but failed in grammar and, interested in the suffrage movement, went all over the state making stump speeches. When the War broke out she wanted overseas service but was turned down. She supported herself doing social work, which she didn't like, but she managed to save up $150 to sail for Europe. On the boat she met a group of Zionists, and got International News Service to let her cover their conference. This was the start of her adventurous career, reading much like the *Perils of Pauline,* in free-lance journalism.

Traveling over Europe, Miss Thompson managed to sell pieces at space rates to various papers. Luck was usually with her: she had some knack or instinct to be on the spot when news broke. Important events so nearly coincided with her arrival that other correspondents, when they heard she got into town at noon, would ask what happened at one o'clock. Through Wythe Williams, then editor of the Philadelphia *Public Ledger*, she got the post of Vienna correspondent. There, a year after the Karlist *putsch,* she succeeded, by flattering a guard, in getting into the castle and interviewing Empress Zita and getting her story past the censor. She followed rumors and revolutions, blazing through Europe, as John Gunther said, like "a blue-eyed tornado." Her get-there-or-else maneuvers

THOMPSON, DOROTHY—*Continued*

won the respect of the newspaper boys. If she had to hit below the ethical belt to get a story through, she hit; but if she was able to do a fellow correspondent a good turn, she always did.

Blonde and buxom, Dorothy Thompson fitted ideally into Vienna, where she was the center of a lively cosmopolitan literary group. She gave superb parties which women didn't usually like: these soirees had an unscented, intellectual aura. They were dominated by a hostess who, as Phyllis Bottome remarked, "had no foliage: she was like a tree rooted in the earth and reaching in a straight line to the sky." In 1923 she married Josef Bard, a romantic Hungarian writer. Their matrimonial difficulties came to a head during the World Economic Conference. The Thompson idea of marriage was Methodist, the Bard's Bohemian; at any rate, the wife's output and personality soon eclipsed the husband's, and they were divorced in 1927.

In 1925 she was appointed head of the New York *Evening Post's* Berlin office, and met Sinclair Lewis at a tea given for Stresemann. Lovesick and airsick, Lewis pursued her by plane all over Europe, proposing to her every chance he got. When Moscow reporters asked the distinguished author of *Main Street* what he found most important in the European situation, he replied, "Dorothy." They were married in London in 1928. In 1930 their son Michael was born. Mrs. Lewis is a devoted mother, and goes often to visit him at his school in Arizona.

On their return to America Dorothy Thompson led a domestic life for a few years—in the summer on their farm near Woodstock, Vermont; in a New York apartment for the winter, where she arranged books, easy chairs and cheery logs around a fireplace that turned out to be phony. She read a great deal and wrote her book, *I Saw Hitler* (1932). This was based on a Berlin interview with the future Führer, when he made so slight an impression on her that she called him an insignificant "little man" who could never be dictator. Since that gross error in judgment Miss Thompson has spent about three-fifths of her column attacking his régime. From her long residence in Germany and Austria, she grew to love the German scene and its people; her feeling about Hitler's desecrations is deep; she meant it when she said she would have given her life to save Austria from the Nazis. She speaks and writes excellent German and delights in German cooking. She makes Viennese dishes in her Vermont kitchen, where the shelves hold containers marked *Salz, Pfeffer, Brot,* etc. Most of her servants are blond Germans—and Nazis: she says she hired them for their service, not for their politics. But since the Vermont house often harbors a good many refugees from Nazi Germany, the harmony between these and the Nazi servants must be a trifle strained.

Begun in 1936, Dorothy Thompson's column for the *Herald Tribune* was popular from the start. Miss Thompson had a talk with the *Tribune's* Mrs. Ogden Reid when she heard that Walter Lippmann (see sketch this issue) was being paid more than she was; she emerged with a new contract. The columns are done with the help of three secretaries, all named Madeline. Miss Thompson often dictates in bed just after breakfast, leaving blanks for statistics which the secretaries look up and fill in. She has a large "brain trust" which she consults by telephone and cable, among them David Sarnoff, Morris Ernst, Wendell Willkie (see sketches this issue) and Alexander Sacks. German intellectual refugees bring her grapevine information. Her interest in these refugees and their plight was embodied in her book: *Refugees: Anarchy or Organization?* (1938), which influenced Roosevelt to call the refugee conference at Evian, France. She also wrote, in collaboration with Fritz Kortner, *Another Sun* (1940), a play for refugee benefit, about a Teutonic actor who came to New York. "So what?" several critics rudely said. Another wrote: "So many things happened at once to so many people that when one of the characters died in the middle of the stage the audience didn't notice it for 10 minutes." The play ran a little more than a week. Miss Thompson gave the actors large bonuses, but has not yet forgiven the critics.

In person Miss Thompson is imposing, femininely handsome with soft gray hair, dresses expensively, but with a visible disregard for clothes. "She is a master of the dramatic entrance and immediately makes herself the center of attention whenever she enters a roomful of people. This seems to be as unconscious and automatic with her as it would be with a Barrymore. . . Women who go to the same social affairs begin by being annoyed and wind up by sitting things out in cold fury. The men surround Miss Thompson and hang on her words." She is a noted spotlight stealer. At a huge 1939 Madison Square Garden Bund meeting she heckled the speaker with strident roars of laughter and was highly pleased when police escorted her out of the meeting. Her favorite pastime is discussing the international situation. This, as expounded by his wife, Mr. Lewis calls "it." When she has guests and he drops in (they are living amicably apart) he first asks someone in the hall, "Is she talking about *it*?" If the answer is yes, Lewis quietly steals away. When the American Women's Association suggested forming a "Dorothy Thompson for President" club, Lewis made the remark that has since become classic: "I wish they would elect Dorothy; then I could write *My Day*." It is probable that Dorothy Thompson, without running for President, will find enough interests. Besides Hitler, she has only one aversion: New York intellectuals. She likes hard work and she likes life, socially and in a larger sense. She says she would like best as her epitaph: "Died of extreme old age."

References

Christian Sci Mon p9 F 14 '40 pors
Mlle 11:123 My '40
N Y Herald Tribune p11 Ja 30 '40; p21 My 24 '40
N Y Times p21 F 25 '40
New Yorker 16:24 Ap 20 '40 por; 16:23-9 Ap 27 '40 por
Sat Eve Post 212:126 My 18 '40 por; 212:20+ My 25 '40 il pors
Time 35:34 Ja 15 '40; 35:21 My 27 '40
Variety 138:2 Mr 13 '40
American Women
Who's Who in America

THOMPSON, HOLLAND July 30, 1873—Oct 21, 1940 Author, editor and former professor of history at the College of the City of New York, where he taught from 1901 until his retirement in 1940; editor in chief of first edition of *The Book of Knowledge* and editor of later editions; contributor to encyclopedias and author of many books, among them *The New South* (1919) and *The Age of Invention* (1921)

HOLLAND THOMPSON

References

Who's Who in America

Obituaries

N Y Herald Tribune p24 O 22 '40 por
N Y Times p23 O 22 '40 por

THOMPSON, JOHN TALIAFERRO 1861—June 21, 1940 Retired brigadier general of the United States Army; coinventor of the Thompson submachine gun; director

JOHN T. THOMPSON

of arsenals in charge of all small arms production during the First World War

References

Who's Who in America 1934-35

Obituaries

N Y Times p15 Je 22 '40 por

THOMSON, SIR JOSEPH JOHN Dec 18, 1856—Aug 30, 1940 English Nobel Prize winner for physics in 1906; Cavendish professor of experimental physics at Cambridge University for more than 30 years; considered one of the great scientists of history; epoch-making discoveries on the conduction of electricity through gases led him to discover the electron in 1897; had been with Cambridge University continuously since 1876; was given 21 honorary degrees from universities all over the world, an unmatched record; was author of a great number of technical books and articles; his son Paget Thomson received the Nobel award in physics in 1937

References

Jaffe, B. Thomson *In* Crucibles p265-88 1940
Thomson, Sir J. J. Recollections and Reflections 1937
Who's Who

Obituaries

N Y Herald Tribune p10 Ag 31 '40 por
N Y Times p13 Ag 31 '40 por
Newsweek 16:6 S 9 '40 por
Time 36:38 S 9 '40

THOMSON, VIRGIL　Nov 25, 1896-
Composer

Address: c/o New York Herald Tribune, 230 W 41st St, New York City

Virgil Thomson, one of America's most important modern composers, has known three phases of society, and each has left its mark on his work. He was born in Kansas City, Missouri and spent his youth in the Midwest. From there he went to Harvard, received his degree in 1922 and in the austerely intellectual atmosphere of Boston alternately taught at Harvard and performed as organist and choirmaster of King's Chapel. From Boston he migrated to Paris in 1925 and stayed there until 1932, studying under Nadia Boulanger and coming under the influence of Eric Satie and the "French Six."

Most of the ideas, attitudes and opinions he developed in those many years are presented in *The State of Music* (1939), "a witty and at times brilliant book." The most striking section and the one which aroused the most controversy is called "How Composers Eat," in which Mr. Thomson analyzes the categories of musical jobs and considers the possibilities of enlisting financial security or of marrying it. "I have never known an artist of any kind who didn't do better work when he got properly paid for it," he writes, and in this chapter and a later one he discusses as sources of economic maintenance, a composer's own income, his wife's, other people's and finally the different categories of patronage—Mr. Thomson himself was supported for a number of years by the Naumburg and Payne Fellowships from Harvard, and fellowships from the Ecole Normal de Paris and the Juilliard School. He also gives advice to subsidized composers—the work done, he says "should be difficult to listen to and very difficult to comprehend, yet withal skillful enough in instrumentation that nobody could call the work incompetent."

In *The State of Music* there are, too interesting data on music for motion pictures, and a lamentation for the fact that Wagner came so many generations too soon for them. His own work with films includes the incidental music for *The Plow That Broke the Plains* (1936) and *The River* (1937), and critics agree that much of the effectiveness of these pieces was derived from his score.

The same brilliance that lightens Virgil Thomson's book is apparent in his other writings (he has been a music critic for the Boston *Transcript, Vanity Fair* and *Modern Music* and is now music critic for the New York *Herald Tribune*) and in the various comments on music and its phases which he occasionally makes. About conducting, for instance, he has some very definite ideas. Although he himself is on occasion a conductor, still he deplores the modern qualifications for this "national sport." "The first requirement," says he, "is a figure. The second is interpretive ability. The successful

Toppo

VIRGIL THOMSON

leader must depict in his own person at least the spirit of the pieces played. Josef Stransky, an admittedly incompetent leader, delighted the ladies of the Philharmonic for seven years by putting symphonies to gesture, quite regardless of sound or rhythm. Mr. Stokowski, on the other hand, panting in a frock-coat over the love music from *Tristan*, is giving his own show, just as if the director of the Louvre were to exhibit himself to visitors, posed and breathing through his nostrils, before a Rubens' *Venus*."

Mr. Thomson's greatest interest, however, is in opera. "No art form is so little understood or so stupidly practiced as the opera in this age of decline," he comments. His own idea is that a successful composer should see that the musical and dramatic elements in his opera completely balance each other. He should not create a vehicle for a virtuoso to bellow from one *arpeggio* to another; nor should he devise a sequence of incidents set to music. What he should achieve is a normal blending of both musical and dramatic elements.

Virgil Thomson's own opera, *Four Saints in Three Acts*, was presented in 1934, its libretto the work of Gertude Stein, whose *Capital Capital* he had already set to music. Beyond the fact that it seemed odd for a man whose music is as well formulated as Mr. Thomson's to choose for his libretto poetry as obtuse and apparently senseless as Miss Stein's, there wasn't much comment on this. There was, however, a good deal of comment on the music. Mr. Lawrence Gilman described the opera as "deceptively simple, a little self-consciously candid and naïve, actually very wily and deft and slick, often subtly and wittily illusive. . . This is a suave and charming score."

Other critics agree with Mr. Gilman— one says the score was written "in a mood of cerebral sadism," in which Miss Stein presents her composer with a stream of words and he matched her, sound for sound and utterance for utterance. He almost dared her to continue the contest. She did so, again and again, from act to act and Mr. Thomson's score soared around and about her words. There were critics, too, who said that Mr. Thomson's music was a direct outgrowth of the liturgical music of the past 100 years. It was cited that since the atmosphere of *Four Saints* was religious and since Mr. Thomson had once been a church organist, he was writing simple and modern music to an ecclesiastical theme.

It is true, of course, that Mr. Thomson knows church music. His chorals would not be so sonorous, nor his harmonies so clear if he did not. But it was felt, too, that no composer whose purpose was seriously religious would accept as companion piece to his music a continuity which includes stage settings like that of Act II: "Might it be Mountains if it were not Barcelona," or that of Act III: "Barcelona —St. Ignatius and one of two literally," and texts like the often quoted: "Let Lucy Lily Lily Lucy lct Lucy Lily Lily Lily Lily Lily let Lily Lucy. . ." etc.

Mr. Thomson has produced but this one opera, but there are a great many of his other compositions which are performed extensively in the United States and France, especially the scores for incidental music for stage productions. Some of this music expresses "sparkle, wit and malice"; some of it is sober and meditative. Among his compositions are two sonatas, a set of *Synthetic Waltzes*, *Five Inventions*, a set of *Seven Portraits*; *Two Sentimental Tangos* for piano; a *Sonata da Chiesa* for trombone, horn, viola, trumpet and clarinet; *Symphony of an American Hymn Tune* and four variations and fugues for organ on songs like *Shall We Gather at the River*. He has also written *Symphony Number Two*, *Missa Brevis*, *Filling Station* and *Three Antiphonal Psalms*.

Virgil Thomson is blond, slightly bald, square-faced and young-looking. He is "a gifted cook, a specialist in the preparation of salad dressings and in the treatment of rice." He is said to possess great social charm and his flow of conversation, often amusingly ironic, is facile. Little of it is about music, however; much of it is about food; and gossip is perhaps his favorite subject.

References

Am Mercury 32:104-8 My '34; 34:491 Ap '35
Cath World 139:87-8 Ap '34
Commonweal 19:525 Mr 9 '34
Nation 138:396+ Ap 4 '34
Theatre Arts 18:246-8 Ap '34
Thompson, O. ed. International Cyclopedia of Music and Musicians 1939
Thomson, V. The State of Music 1939
Wier, A. ed. Macmillan Encyclopedia of Music and Musicians 1938

THORBORG, KERSTIN (tor'borg kûrs'-tĭn) Operatic contralto

Address: c/o Metropolitan Opera Assn, Broadway and 39th St, New York City

On January 20, 1940, Gluck's opera *Orfeo ed Eurydice* was broadcast from the Metropolitan stage. The cast was headed by the brilliant Swedish contralto, Kerstin Thorborg, acclaimed by critics as one of the great Orfeos in operatic history.

This young contralto, who takes more pleasure in her singing than in anything else, has known from earliest childhood that she wanted to be a singer. She was born in the little town of Hedemora, in the north of Sweden. Both her parents had been musicians; her father, a newspaperman, had been ambitious to become an opera singer, a career denied him by the social prejudices of his parents; her mother was an accomplished amateur pianist. The story is told that, while Kerstin was little more than a baby in her carriage, she was singing one day when Madame Karolin Oestberg, reigning Swedish operatic idol, happened to pass by. She listened to the little girl's voice and predicted that she would some day become a great singer.

Kerstin Thorborg's childhood recollections are of late afternoon choir practices, when she sang the solo stanzas of the hymns. All through childhood and adolescence she practiced singing. At home, her mother played while her father, two brothers and she sang four-part vocal harmonies. The quartet, still intact, functions again when the great prima donna goes home for vacations. Her first professional singing teacher was a violinist, the Baronin Karin von Rosen.

Her stage career began at the Royal Opera in Stockholm. At that time she sang one performance of Amneris with a relatively obscure Norwegian soprano as Aïda. The two did not meet again till an evening in 1936, when at the Metropolitan Opera House in New York, Flagstad and Thorborg sang the first of their many memorable *Walküres* together. A great many people are confused, in reading billings of their names, to see the odd juxtaposition of the Norwegian "Kirsten" and the Swedish "Kerstin."

Madame Thorborg made her London debut in May 1936 at Covent Garden in Wagner's *Ring* cycle. She appeared subsequently in Vienna, Salzburg, Berlin, Prague, Munich and Buenos Aires. She has given recitals on the Continent and has been soloist with major symphony orchestras.

Her American debut was at the Metropolitan Opera House in New York as Fricka in *Die Walküre*, December 21, 1936. Present was her Stockholm colleague, Gustav Bergman, who, as stage manager at the Royal Opera, had bet the young artist five kroner

Musical America
KERSTIN THORBORG

the first time he heard her sing that she would be called to the Metropolitan before very long. When the wager was won he had a hard time collecting, for in the meantime the lady had become his wife. They recently celebrated the twelfth anniversary of their marriage. Herr Bergman has given up his own career to become Madame Thorborg's coach, accompanist and business manager, and (she says) most feared of her critics.

Her rôles have included Fricka, Magdalena, Brangäne, Waltraute. She sang Klytemnestra in the Metropolitan revival of *Elektra* (1938); and Octavian in the *Rosenkavalier* revival. During the 1939 to 1940 season she appeared in several Wagnerian rôles, and in the rôle of Orfeo. In the latter, her favorite rôle, she wears a vivid blue tunic —for blue is the color of fidelity—with a bronze cloak. The rôle of Orfeo was added to Madame Thorborg's repertory early in her career, when she first sang in Prague. It was an immediate success: whenever *Orfeo* was billed, Madame Thorborg's name became a box-office enthusiast. Later Bruno Walter revived *Orfeo* for her when she became a member of the Vienna Opera Company.

Until World War II Madame Thorborg and her husband traveled around the world filling concert and opera engagements during eight months of each year. They work together at the piano four or five hours a day. They have other mutual enthusiasms also: bridge, the stage shows at the Radio City Music Hall, tomato juice and strong coffee. The rest of the year they used to spend at home—a medieval style Swedish peasant farmhouse set among the birch forests along the River Dal.

References

Etude 57:295-6+ My '39 pors
Metropolitan Opera Program p6 Ja 4 '40 por
Musician 42:213 D '37 por
Opera News p17 Ja 15 '40
Thompson, O. ed. International Cyclopedia of Music and Musicians 1939

THURBER, JAMES Dec 8, 1894- Author
Address: c/o The New Yorker, 25 W 43rd St, New York City

Before he became popularly associated with drawings of melancholy hounds and contentedly frustrated humans, James Thurber, as old-timers know, began his career as a writing humorist. *Is Sex Necessary?* has gone into the history of the libido; many who found the owl in the attic and the seal in the bedroom now let their minds alone. But they still turn to the pages of the *New Yorker* for those fascinating Thurber line sketches, with captions, drawn from the prankish edge of the subconscious. Now they can also be found in *PM*—every Tuesday and Thursday, illustrating the ramblings of the Thurber mind on any subject from football to the Martians.

Perhaps it is quite in the order of predestined things that some of the Thurberiana should take the form of a play. *The Male Animal*, coauthored by James Thurber and Elliott Nugent, opened on Broadway, January 9, 1940. It is a happily mad, semi-scandalous comedy hit with a sweet-water college setting. Nonplotted, nonconforming, fraily motivated, untidy, with some satire and much good-natured comment, *The Male Animal* depends for effect on its astral aura. For characters: a meek professor and his wife, with other stock campus figures. For action: a party, a football re-enactment, a fight, a drunk scene. When the mildly liberal professor wants to read one of Vanzetti's letters to his class, he is branded as a Red. But worse looms on the horizon when his wife's ex-sweetheart, an old football hero, comes to town. Fortifying himself with the emboldening cup, the professor decides he is man, not mouse, and fights for his mate. The play is directed shrewdly and brilliantly by Herman Shumlin; and coauthor Nugent, as the professor, is in perfect Thurberian fettle from his first entrance cue. Remarkably enough, the characters manage to sound the way Thurber's drawings look, preserving that same quality of grave lunacy combined with moronic, God-like yearning.

James Grover Thurber (he does not use his middle name) was born in Columbus, Ohio in 1894, and grew up with a fondness, legend has it, for peppering passing legislators with electric light bulbs dropped from the State House dome. Apparently he came by his talents honestly, since it is rumored that the doings of the Thurber household, from Grandfather on down, are still remembered with real awe around Columbus. He began to write at the age of 10, producing *Horse Sandusky, the Intrepid Boy Scout,* and to draw when he was 14.

Thurber attended Ohio State University (there is a chapter on his college career in *My Life and Hard Times,* leaving in his senior year to become a code clerk, first in Washington, then in the American Embassy in Paris (1918-20).

This was in the nature of war service, since in a childhood accident the loss of the sight of one eye made him unfit for front-line duty. He worked thereafter as a newspaperman on the Columbus *Dispatch,* the Paris Edition of the Chicago *Tribune,* and the New York *Evening Post.*

Having contributed a couple of pieces to the *New Yorker,* he found his real home on that magazine when Editor Harold Ross hired him (according to a trial-and-error method) as managing editor. Thurber, knowing nothing of the problems involved in running a magazine, had to work his way down to a position on the paper where he felt safe. He took care of the *Talk of the Town* department, which left him time for his own writing as well. There he developed a fruitful friendship with E. B. White, who was writing the *Notes and Comment* department. As his first book, Thurber in combine with White wrote a parody on the books-on-sex fad, the Schmalhausen-Wittels-Calverton popularizations. *Is Sex Necessary?* (1929) became a success, selling 40,000 copies—a success due not only to its hilarious satire, but to its embellishment with those odd drawings which marked Thurber's first appearance as a humorist-artist. It seems that the editor, on seeing these limp, neolithic, gap-mouthed figures, was doubtful. Thurber has become more widely known since for his drawings than for his essays, though he prefers to think of himself as a writer. The story is told that at a recent showing of his sketches in London, where the sales were high, a remark by a lady spoiled it all for Thurber. When someone to whom they were both talking mentioned one of his books, she exclaimed in surprise, "Oh, you write, too, then?"

After *Is Sex Necessary?* came *The Owl in the Attic* (1931) and *The Seal in the Bedroom* (1932), both collections of nonsense essays with appropriate illustrations. In 1934 appeared Thurber's "autobiography"— *My Life and Hard Times.* Here he affirms that humorists, far from being carefree and gay of heart, lead an existence of twitchy apprehension. "In the House of Life, they have the feeling that they have never taken off their overcoats." He recalls the night the bed fell on his father, and his mother's strange fear that the Victrola might blow up; he tells of Grandfather's brother Zenas, who died of the same disease that was killing off the chestnut trees; and of the night a ghost got in the Thurber house. Though he sometimes fails to make these episodes in his life convincing, Ernest Hemingway called this book "superior to the autobiogra-

JAMES THURBER

phy of Henry Adams." *The Middle-aged Man on the Flying Trapeze* (1935) was another collection of short pieces containing some major triumphs. In *Let Your Mind Alone* (1937) Thurber satirizes the best-seller inspirational books on the how-to-wake-up-and-win-friends order.

In 1939 he wrote *The Last Flower,* an antiwar fable in pictures, with the drawings telling most of the story. It shows the cyclic progress of humankind from civilization to war, from war to barbarity and destruction (the happy dogs leave, rabbits grow huge and swaggering), back again to civilization through the rediscovery of love when a girl finds the last flower on earth, etc. The drawings, first-rate Thurber, make a profoundly eloquent argument. His latest book is *Fables for Our Time, and Famous Poems Illustrated* (1940), with typically daft morals and dough-like illustrations.

Thurber's first marriage in 1922, to Althea Adams of Columbus, was dissolved in 1934. The following year he married his present wife, the former Helen Wismer. The Thurbers have traveled a great deal, and live in New York only a small part of the time. They contemplate owning some day a place in the country, but at present just rent places for winter sojourns. It is said they go winters instead of summers because Thurber always works in reverse, such as sleeping during the day and getting up at night. Mrs. Thurber, however, has succeeded in getting him onto a more normal schedule.

His self-portraits reveal him as a harrassed, wild-haired, hand-on-chin brooder-type. But he has been thus described by his friend, Robert M. Coates: "Tall, shy, loose-jointed and absent-minded, he has the physical equipment for getting into involuntary mischief and the artist's detach-

THURBER, JAMES—*Continued*

ment for making the most of it after it has happened." His fellow playwright, Elliott Nugent, who has known Thurber since they were at Ohio State together, says that there are several Thurbers, probably six. In college days he wandered around on cold winter days in an old pair of pants, no vest, no overcoat, no hat. Now in New York he does likewise. Thurber, in fact, suffered more from the California sun on a recent Hollywood trip, when he took umbrage with a green umbrella, than he does from New York's cold. As for his character: "Unstimulated, he is the mildest of men," writes Nugent. "When a cloud is over him he reacts to nothing. Even with friends he is shy and reluctant to disagree when in this mood of low vitality. . . The whirlwind comes later. Suddenly the mild, patient Thurber is gone like a forgotten zephyr, and a new piercing hurricane is upon you, piling up waves of argument and invective. . . Next day, while you are patching your sails and cutting away the wreckage, Thurber appears in a canoe bearing fruit and flowers."

Fond of rifle shooting but unable to concentrate, he usually fires the gun off into the air when handing it to the next marksman. He was recently blackballed when brought up for membership in the Fairfield County, Connecticut, Skeet Shooting Club. He has never been defeated at singles in crokinole. He can hold a grand slam hand in contract and be set six, but he has never been taken at fan-tan.

Thurber never listens when anybody else is talking, preferring to keep his mind a blank until the other finishes so he can talk. His favorite book is *The Great Gatsby*. His favorite author is Henry James.

Caught in their off-moments, humorists may sometimes be philosophers. Thurber really has a philosophy of humor—and of life. He defines humor as "a kind of emotional chaos told about calmly and quietly in retrospect." He feels that the answer to where we are going if anywhere, and why, has eluded everyone from Francis Bacon to John Kieran (see sketch this issue). Asked to state his beliefs in a series of *Intimate Credos* edited by Clifton Fadiman, he did so in a nutshell: "I have never been able to maintain a consistent attitude toward life or reality, or toward anything else."

References

Life 8:108-9 Ap 22 '40 il pors
N Y Post p4 Ja 27 '40
N Y Times X p3 F 25 '40
N Y World-Telegram p25 Ja 12 '40; p6 Ja 27 '40; p6 F 3 '40
New Yorker Ap 18 '36
Newsweek 15:33 Ja 22 '40
Sat R Lit 20:3-4+ Ap 29 '39 por; 21: 10-11+ D 2 '39
Time 35:49 Ja 22 '40 por
Birchman, W. James Thurber *In* Faces & Facts 1937
Fadiman, C. ed. I Believe 1939
Millett, F. B. Contemporary American Authors 1940
Thurber, J. My Life and Hard Times 1934

THYSSEN, FRITZ (tĭs'sĕn) Nov 9, 1873- Former German industrialist

In December 1939 there was an official announcement in Berlin: "On the basis of the law of July 14, 1933, regarding confiscation of property inimical to the state and nation, the entire movable possessions of Dr. Fritz Thyssen, formerly of Mühlheim in the Ruhr and now abroad, as well as his real estate, are confiscated by the state of Prussia. No legal appeal can be made against this action."

This was the final break between Fritz Thyssen and the Third Reich. Thyssen, once one of the wealthiest men in Europe and an industrialist whose support did much to raise Adolf Hitler to power, was made a man without a country. But his Rhine Valley industries continue working for the Reich, and his factories and mines have been incorporated into Goering's four-year plan.

For many months there was speculation as to what were the exact reasons for Thyssen's leaving Germany in September 1939. Then Thyssen himself told them in the correspondence between himself and Nazi leaders published in *Life* (April 29, 1940). He told them because he said he felt that "everything should be done that might contribute to ending the War, that might prevent the useless sacrifice of countless young lives, that might spare Europe so much sorrow, so many tears."

Fritz Thyssen was born in 1873, the son of August Thyssen, a "hard-headed, ruthless and brilliant businessman who forged spectacular industrial empires during the years of German economic expansion before the [First World] War." August Thyssen was both a tycoon and a "character." He was miserly, always shabbily dressed and used to drink beer and eat wurst with his workmen. Always he kept away from politicians and society, and when it was suggested that he appear at the German Imperial Court, said he had no suitable clothes. When August Thyssen died in 1926, he left as a monument 160,000,000 marks, coal mines, rolling mills, private railroads and ports, power stations and iron foundries.

He left them all to his son Fritz, for his other two sons had been a disappointment to him. Heinrich, the eldest, who had married a Hungarian noblewoman, was made a baron of the old Austro-Hungarian empire and spent his time collecting art. August, the youngest, wanted an empire of his own and was sent into bankruptcy by his father. In retaliation he spent much money in aiding the workers when they went on strike at his father's plants. But Fritz was a son after his father's heart.

When he received his father's empire, he was a "tall, impressive figure" who had served through the War in the German Army and had been jailed for shutting down his mines to resist the French occupation of the Ruhr. Within a year he had merged his own with other companies into the Vereinigte Stahlwerke, the largest mining trust in the world, reaching out into France, India, Russia and Brazil. This was supposed to be an imposing stroke of business, but the important industrialist Krupp von Bohlen refused to join because he felt that it "suffered from top-heavy bureaucratic organization to an unparalleled degree." There were so many people at the directors' meetings that people used to say they had to be introduced to one another.

As early as 1923 Fritz Thyssen joined the National Socialist Party, and in 1929 he admitted it, which was a daring thing to do. Thyssen believed in Hitler and liked Goering. These, he felt, were the men to make the strong, united Germany for which he longed. As the depression came on, he felt even more strongly that the Nazi way was the only way out. "None of us can get the country out of this mess," he would say defiantly. Thyssen knew that the continuation of liberal, capitalistic, economic measures would have meant, in 1931, "announcing his company's bankruptcy" and reducing its common stock by about 50 per cent. He also felt very strongly that the "Socialists are our great enemies," and feared the spread of socialistic ideas in the Reich.

He urged his fellow industrialists to support Hitler, and his persuasiveness smoothed Hitler's way in quarters which were naturally averse to revolution. Within a short time he had swung the backing of the most powerful industrial combines behind him. By the time the Presidential elections of 1932 were under way the big industrialists contributed to Hitler's and not Hindenburg's election funds. When, in November 1932, the National Socialist Party lost 2,000,000 votes and was broke, the big industrialists footed the bill for a last-minute effort. Fritz Thyssen alone is "reported to have spent 3,000,000 marks on the Nazis in 1932." There is no doubt but that he was "the most potent single factor behind Hitler's struggle for power."

Soon after Hitler reached power in 1933, all was rosy for Thyssen. The reorganization of the Vereinigte Stahlwerke was carried out, in the course of which the Reich's holdings of stock were reduced from 80 per cent to 22 per cent and Thyssen's grew correspondingly greater. There were no labor troubles and German rearmament meant money. When Thyssen was made economic dictator of the Ruhr, he felt that his position as capitalist was firmly secured. His first statement was: "Wild competition has no place in the new professional order."

FRITZ THYSSEN

Under Hitler, Thyssen received other honors and other important positions. He became Prussian state councilor, leader of the Amalgamated Union of West German Industry and supreme state authority for West German Industry.

As early as 1936, however, there were rumors of trouble between him and Hitler, as the "Socialism" of the Nazis ran counter to Thyssen's ironclad capitalism. There were complaints that his mail had been opened and telephone wire tapped. When, in this year, Thyssen spent some time in South America, some thought he had left Germany for good. "His departure, it was said, followed an interview at which he and other big industrialists had handed a memorandum to Hitler. The Führer was reported to have trampled the memorandum under foot and shouted angrily, in effect: 'Did you saps really believe that I would go to all this trouble just to make Germany safe for the steel barons?'"

Thyssen, too, strongly resented Hitler's persecution of the Jews and the Catholics. Fritz Thyssen had Jews among his friends and close business associates, and his father had been a devout Catholic. He himself said, in a letter to Goering: "I was a good Catholic and I shall always keep allegiance to my faith, and now even more so than ever before." "To Hitler's industrialist friend, religious and racial persecution seemed a stupid and unnecessary degradation which was losing Germany the good-will of the world."

More and more Hitler went counter to Thyssen's political creed, which was that Germany must be capitalistic, anti-Bolshevist and friendly with Great Britain. When the German-Soviet pact was signed, Thyssen was vocal against it. Before the War began he was against it and after it started

THYSSEN, FRITZ—*Continued*

he said: "Germany ought to try to put an end to it as soon as possible, for the longer it lasts, the worse will be the peace terms for Germany." Its outcome, he told the Führer, could only be Bolshevist chaos all over Europe. A few days after the War broke out Thyssen and his family crossed the frontier into Switzerland. According to anti-Nazi sources he bought his way out by turning over much of his fortune to the Nazis.

In a letter dated December 11, 1939 Thyssen told Hitler that he has "been pressed for an explanation of the reasons that prompted me to leave," and that he had not spoken as yet. "I do not intend to at a time when my Fatherland is struggling so hard to furnish the enemy with moral weapons. . . I shall keep silent." But if this letter to the German people does not reach them, "I shall call upon the conscience of the world and shall let the world pass judgment."

In Switzerland he established a residence at Locarno and told the world that he was "still a German" though "no longer a Nazi." In December 1939 the official confiscation announcement was made and the German government got from him an estimated 300,000,000 marks of property.

When Thyssen left Switzerland for France in March 1940 it was reported that it was because the strict rule of silence imposed on all political refugees was too much for him. In that country, unlike humbler German refugees in wartime, he was wined and dined and fêted. From Paris he published his correspondence with Nazi leaders in which he protested that the confiscation of his property was "an undisguised and brutal violation of law, a measure contrary to the Constitution, to law and to rights," and declared that "the time will come when my righs will be unrestrictedly respected."

"My conscience," said Thyssen, "is clear. I feel free of any guilt. My sole error was that I believed in you, Adolf Hitler, the Führer, and the movement you led. I believed with all the ardor of one passionately German." And then he begged Hitler to "listen to me and you will hear the voice of the tormented German nation that is crying out to you: 'Turn back, let freedom, right and humaneness rise again in the German Reich.'"

A few days before the fall of France Thyssen stated by radio to the *American Magazine* that Hitler would lose the War eventually, that the German people would get rid of him when they understood how they had been betrayed. Since that time no news of his fate has been received.

References

Am Mag 130:16-17+ Jl '40
Life 8:11-14+ Ap 29 '40 por
Liv Age 345:117-23 O '33; 347:121-8 O '34

N Y Times VII p9+ Mr 3 '40 por, Je 9 '40
Time 34:19 D 25 '39 por
International Who's Who
Who's Who in Commerce and Industry

TOKUGAWA, IYESATO, PRINCE (tō'-kōō-gä'wä) July 11, 1863—June 4, 1940 Former president of the House of Peers in Japan; leader in most of the country's progressive movements; called "aristocrat democrat"; rated next to Hirohito in influence; as prince, was heir to the famous Shogun family, military rulers who controlled Japan for 300 years

References

Lit Digest 117:15 Mr 10 '34 por
International Who's Who
Who's Who in Japan

Obituaries

N Y Herald Tribune p26 Je 5 '40 por
N Y Times p25 Je 5 '40

TOLEDANO, VICENTE LOMBARDO *See* Lombardo Toledano, V.

TOLISCHUS, OTTO DAVID (tō-lĭsh'ŭs) Nov 20, 1890- Journalist
Address: c/o New York Times, 229 W 43rd St, New York City

If the authorities of the German government had anything equivalent to the Pulitzer Prize it is fairly certain that it would not be awarded to Otto D. Tolischus, longtime member of the New York *Times* in Berlin, for Mr. Tolischus is now forced to do reporting far from Berlin, at their request. But on May 6, 1940 it was Mr. Tolischus, then in Stockholm, who was announced as the winner of the American 1939 Pulitzer Award for best foreign correspondence.

In July 1940 he published his book, *They Wanted War*, in which he looks back over the years he spent as *Times'* correspondent in Berlin. Called "a vivid, truthful, most objective account of Herr Hitler's preparations for a successful war," in it Mr. Tolischus gives firsthand accounts of life in Germany during the Second World War, "brilliant chapters" on the economics of war and rearmament, close-up studies of Hitler, analyses of the operation of Fifth Columns outside Germany, and of the workings of domestic propaganda.

Mr. Tolischus is Lithuanian by birth. He was born November 20, 1890, in Russ, the Memel territory which belonged to Germany before the First World War and which was recently taken back from Lithuania. When he was 17 he renounced his German citizenship through his father and came to America. Five years later he was attending the Columbia School of Journalism, paying his way by working in factories in Syracuse, New

Globe Press

OTTO D. TOLISCHUS

York and Trenton, New Jersey, and when he was graduated in 1916 he promptly entered the newspaper business as a cub reporter on the Cleveland *Press*. During the First World War he was a member of the Training Corps of Camp Gorden, near Atlanta, Georgia, but the Armistice came before he saw service in France. He returned to the *Press,* and in 1923, when he joined the Berlin staff of Hearst's Universal Service after a trip to Europe, he was managing editor of the Cleveland paper.

Tolischus was with Universal for eight years, then joined International News Service as Berlin correspondent. In 1931 he spent a year as head of International in London; returned to the United States in 1932 to work as a free-lance magazine writer for another year; and in 1933 joined the Berlin staff of the New York *Times,* where he has been until recently.

He watched the rise and expansion of the National Socialist régime, and covered it in its economic, political and cultural aspects. Before the War he made extensive studies of Poland and Czechoslovakia. He predicted the Nazi-Soviet pact three months before it happened. In July 1939 a casual appendage to one of his "learned, heavily statisticized" summaries of an official survey of Nazi economics, giving unofficial estimates of the German secret debt, caused the SEC to embarrass the German government by asking it to tell all about its "hush-hush bookkeeping." He covered the German angles of the outbreak of the present War and remained in Poland during the German campaign there.

Finally, in March 1940, the Nazi government told him that his permit to remain in Germany would not be renewed, but that if he would leave the country for six weeks he would be readmitted. When Mr. Tolischus,

traveling in Scandinavia, applied for re-admission he was told he would be permitted only eight days—just long enough for him to obtain any personal belongings he might have left behind and to settle any business affairs. In the meanwhile he had gone from Copenhagen to Oslo and thence to Stockholm. He was in Stockholm—still in the center of events—when the German Army invaded Norway, and there he remained as keen, analytical New York *Times'* correspondent until his arrival in the United States in August 1940. Back in America his plans included a badly needed vacation and what he calls "taking a look at the American scene." Before the winter is over, however, Tolischus expects to be back in a foreign post. Whatever the post, readers of his dispatches and his book know that his reports will be solid, able, readable and often brilliant.

References
N Y Herald Tribune p17 My 7 '40 por
N Y Times p20 My 7 '40 por
Time 34:53 Ag 14 '39 por; 36:60 Jl 29 '40 por

TONE, FRANCHOT (frăn-shō) Feb 27, 1905- Actor

Franchot Tone is back in Hollywood in November 1940 after having bought back his contract for Ernest Hemingway's *The Fifth Column* because he felt his throat could not stand the strain of regular performances.

This play, most critics agreed when it opened in New York in March 1940, owed a good deal of its force and conviction to the acting of Franchot Tone. Mr. Tone, who has acted rôles of boyish charm as well as tough gangsters, in *The Fifth Column* "turns in the best performance of his stage career." He gave the part all the bitterness, frustration and passion that it needs, and according to the *New Yorker* played the ex-journalist and counter-espionage agent of Hemingway's play "with maturity and a disregard for romantic attitudes that would never have got him anywhere in Hollywood."

Tone, who went to Hollywood in 1932, returned to the stage in 1939 and went back to Hollywood again in 1940, is "crazy about the stage. You get a chance to go deep into a character, work on it, and find out what sort of person a character is when you play it over and over." But he still feels that the movies are a better medium for telling a story. "On the screen you can do something with the flick of an eyelash," he says. "You can get close to an idea and you can direct the camera at a bit of action or an idea and the audience just has to look where you make them. They have no alternative. . . The realm of possibility expands so greatly when you tell a story with the films."

Franchot Tone's statement of loyalty to the screen is important because of his success in both fields of acting and because of "the shabby way Hollywood has treated

FRANCHOT TONE

him in recent years." When he first went there he was given a variety of rôles, most of them in good or nearly-good pictures— *Gabriel Over the White House, Dancing Lady, Lives of a Bengal Lancer* and *Mutiny on the Bounty,* among others. After *Mutiny,* in 1935, he began to have difficulty in getting the sort of parts he wanted, and when he found himself appearing in "B" pictures, he quit.

While in Hollywood, Tone made a reputation for himself as an actor—he was nominated by the Academy of Motion Picture Arts and Sciences as one of the ten best performers in 1935—as a liberal and as the husband of Joan Crawford. He was director of the Screen Actors' Guild, its vice-president in 1937, and because of his frequent outspokenness got himself called a Red by the producers. He was called one, too, when he sent money to Spain and got other actors to do the same.

It was in his first Hollywood picture, *Today We Live,* that he met Joan Crawford, the former wife of Douglas Fairbanks Jr. He married her two years afterward, in October 1935. On April 11, 1939 they were divorced "after one of the most denied, affirmed and re-denied romances Hollywood ever had witnessed."

Franchot Tone was born in Niagara Falls, New York on February 27, 1905, the son of Frank Jerome and Gertrude (Franchot) Tone. His father has been awarded medals for valuable work in applied chemistry, and is president of the Carborundum Company of America. When he was five his father took him with him on a business trip to Paris, where Franchot saw his first movie, a flickering, green sort of an affair. Then his father became ill and he and his brother Jerry were taken to Tucson, Arizona, where they were given a

burro. "The poor beast had a horrible existence," says Franchot. "We were never off his back for a moment."

In 1919 he was sent to the Hill School in Pottstown, Pennsylvania, where he was manager of the football team and only a "subtle influence for disorder" until he ran afoul of the Rules Committee in 1923. Then he went to Cornell, where he was graduated with Phi Beta Kappa honors in 1927. At Cornell his only interest was in the dramatic classes taught by Professor Drummond, the head of the public speaking department, and before he left he had played 40 different rôles.

From Cornell, Franchot Tone went to Buffalo, where a cousin, Pascal Franchot, headed the Garry McGarry Players. There he was assistant stage manager until the juvenile lead became ill. Then he became an actor. His first real chance came when Eleanor O'Reilly saw him in *Holy Night* and suggested him as a possibility to Guthrie McClintic, who was then (1928) casting Katharine Cornell in the *Age of Innocence.* The play was a success. Franchot saved $2,000 but lost it in the 1929 stock market.

From 1929 to 1931 he acted in Theatre Guild plays—*Red Rust, Meteor, Hotel Universe*—and played his first starring rôle as Curly McLain in *Green Grow the Lilacs.* When the Group Theatre split off from the Theatre Guild in 1931, Tone went along with the Group and for them played Will Connelly in *The House of Connelly,* Frederico in *Night Over Taos* and Raymond Merritt in *A Thousand Summers.* He said then and still says that the Group Theatre and Lee Strassberg taught him more about acting than he had ever known.

When, after 15 screen tests in New York City, Franchot Tone was finally signed by MGM and left for Hollywood, Stark Young wrote: "Mr. Tone is one of the best of the young actors in the New York Theatre and the most promising in his chances of development. He does not have to go to Hollywood to get a good rôle, many rôles in the theatre are open to him. And for the same reason he doesn't have to stay in Hollywood when he gets there."

When he came back, after seven years, it was to act in a Group Theatre play, *The Gentle People.* In it he took the part of Goff, a menacing citizen who "protects" his neighbors for so much a week. Tone was told by George Jean Nathan that he had reached his "top achievement." His rôle in *The Gentle People,* however, didn't receive the unanimous acclaim which his work in *The Fifth Column* has evoked.

Franchot Tone, who is six feet tall and weighs 160 pounds, finds his pleasure and exercise in golf and swimming. His interests are in music, in little theatre groups. He's far from a back-slapper or hail-fellow-well-met, though he is the kind of man who can "strain the seams of staid Baltimore hospitality in the early hours of the morning." And he is the kind of person who enjoys Hemingway's play, not only for its acting opportunities, but because "my own sympathies were on the same side as Hemingway's so far as the civil war was concerned."

References

Collier's 93:15+ Je 30 '34 pors
New Repub 73:16-17 N 16 '32; 102: 408 Mr 25 '40
N Y Herald Tribune p9 Mr 2 '40
N Y World-Telegram p9 Mr 2 '40; p20 Mr 20 '40
New Yorker 16:44 Mr 16 '40
Photoplay 48:52, 78 S '35; 51:34-5, 82, 84-5 My '37 por (p72); 51:56-7, 84-8 Je '37
America's Young Men
Who's Who in America
Who's Who in the Theatre

TOTTY, CHARLES H. 1874—Dec 6, 1939
Horticulturist

Charles H. Totty was born in England, and came to the United States in 1893. After 10 years with commercial firms and private estates, he established his own business and

CHARLES H. TOTTY

eventually was conceded by horticulturists to be the leader in the field. His widely-known work with English, Australian and French hybridizers resulted in his origination of new roses, chrysanthemums, delphinium and a wide range of perennial plants. These plants were in time distributed to foreign lands.

Totty's nurseries at Madison, New Jersey became a mecca for garden lovers from the whole country. Thousands of prizes were awarded for plants grown under his supervision. For 30 years he was associated with garden shows and believed that the advancement of American gardening could be directly traceable to such shows. Some years ago 500 gardeners from the whole United States gathered in New York for a dinner to honor Mr. Totty.

References

Am Mag 125:92 Je '38 por

Obituaries

N Y Times p23 D 11 '40

TOVEY, SIR DONALD FRANCIS (tö-vē) July 17, 1875—July 10, 1940 Reid professor of music at Edinburgh University since 1914; noted as musical theorist, writer and executant; compositions have been performed in European and American cities; contributor to the *Encyclopedia Britannica;* author of the opera *The Bride of Dionysius;* knighted in 1935

References

Who's Who

Obituaries

N Y Herald Tribune p12 Jl 12 '40
N Y Times p15 Jl 12 '40

TRAMMELL, NILES (tră'měl) July 6, 1894- President of National Broadcasting Company

Address: b. 30 Rockefeller Plaza, New York City; h. 730 Park Ave, New York City

In July 1940 Niles Trammell was elected president of the National Broadcasting Company after 12 years with the company and 17 in the radio industry. David Sarnoff (see sketch this issue), chairman of the board of NBC, said when the election was announced: "The directors of the National Broadcasting Company have promoted to the presidency a man who has risen from the ranks of the company. . . His intimate knowledge of broadcasting, his popularity and wide acquaintanceship in all segments of the industry and his contributions to the development of nationwide broadcasting are important assets of the company he now heads."

Niles Trammell's career in radio covers the rise of the industry from an infant entertainment art to the position it now holds. Born in Marietta, Georgia, the son of Bessie (Niles) and William J. Trammell, he received his education at Sewanee Military Academy and the University of the South. When the United States entered the First World War he was commissioned a second lieutenant in the regular army at Fort Leavenworth, Kansas. Later he served at Fort Snelling, Minnesota, Camp Devins in Massachusetts and at the infantry school at Fort Benning, Georgia. When the War ended he was a first lieutenant in the 36th infantry of the 12th Division.

Mr. Trammell remained in the army until 1923. In that year he married Elizabeth Huff of Greensburg, Pennsylvania and re-

NILES TRAMMELL

signed from the army to become commercial representative in the traffic department of the Radio Corporation of America. This early job in San Francisco wasn't an easy one. Trammell tells how he used to be "out prowling through smelly importers' places trying to persuade some Japanese to use our facilities instead of the cables." After a year of it, however, he was made district manager of the Pacific Northwest for RCA and by 1925 had risen to assistant sales manager.

In 1928 Trammell joined the staff of NBC as a salesman and sailed right up to the top. His first main job was that of manager of NBC in Chicago and in a few months he was made vice-president in charge of the central division. When he came to Chicago NBC headquarters consisted of one studio and two offices. "Combining talents of resourceful program producer and forceful salesman," Trammell quickly accomplished revolutionary changes in radio programs. It had been hoped he could raise the income of his office to $1,000,000 annually; within a year he had raised it to $1,000,000 a month, with more than 1,800 programs originating in his studios.

In his years in Chicago Niles Trammell "left a lasting imprint on the program structure. . . He comes as close as anyone to being the father of the soap operas, the serials that fill most of the networks' mornings and afternoons." It is these serials that are now a cornerstone of the radio business, much more successful than recipes and household aids ever were in selling products. Trammell started on their way *Clara, Lu and Em, Fibber McGee and Molly, Betty and Bob, Ma Perkins, Today's Children* and many other programs. But he is pretty modest about it: "Pushing those serials," he says, "was no sudden inspiration

of mine. A number of things made them inevitable. First of all out in Chicago we couldn't compete with the Broadway names the networks put on from New York. Chicago did have a lot of actors available. . . And we had the great success of *Amos and Andy* to point the way." Incidentally, it was Trammell who was responsible for the commercial success of *Amos and Andy*.

Among the firsts for which he gets the credit are the commercial network series of Eddie Cantor, Al Jolson (see sketch this issue), Phil Baker, Ben Bernie, Jane Froman and Wayne King. He was responsible, too, for securing sponsorship for orchestral music, though his first venture in this line wasn't too successful. The Chicago Symphony Orchestra was to play and the top floor of the old Masonic Temple had been rented, hung with drapes and filled with baffle boards to kill echoes. "The night the orchestra was to present its first broadcast," Trammel still remembers, "the makeshift studio was so hot that the musicians played in their undershirts. But things went along well enough until, right in the middle of a Wagnerian opus, a hail storm struck. And then we realized that we had overlooked one thing—the Masonic Temple had a tin roof!"

Other important programs which originated under Trammell's direction are the University of Chicago *Round Table*, the *Farm and Home Hour*, the Chicago Opera Company programs and the famous Grant Park concerts.

In January 1939 Trammell was transferred to New York by NBC and elected executive vice-president. Until his election as president he was in charge of the whole network operation, "obviously the man chosen for the day when Lennox R. Lohr should decide to retire from the arduous seat at the head of NBC." Soon after he became executive vice-president Trammell set up separate sales staffs for the Red and Blue network groups, each with its own vice-president, and during his year and a half in this position increased sales and reduced operating expenses.

Trammell is the kind of man who "inspires a quick confidence and affection in business associates. A great deal of work passes across his desk every day without destroying his even-tempered air of casual leisure." Even newspaper interviewers have been known to come away from him and write stories "with the warmth of praise usually reserved to house organs."

Trammell works hard, but he plays hard, too. In school he played football and in the years since then has always relaxed with golf and fishing. He won't tell his golf score, but it is rumored to be in the low 80's; he won't tell about his fishing, either, but there is a 30-pound muskellunge on the wall of his office in Radio City which seems information enough.

References

N Y Herald Tribune p6 Jl 13 '40 por
N Y Times p17 Jl 13 '40 por

N Y World-Telegram p20 Jl 12 '40
    por; p10 Jl 13 '40 por
Opera News 5:7-8 N 11 '40 por
Variety Radio Directory

TRAUBEL, HELEN (trou'bel) Soprano

Address: c/o Metropolitan Opera Assn,
Broadway and 39th St, New York City

One of the largest Metropolitan Opera
House welcomes of the 1939 to 1940 season
went to Miss Helen Traubel when she sang
her first Sieglinde in New York in *Die
Walküre*, and her Town Hall concert in October 1940 was called "the first major recital
event of the season."

Miss Traubel is an American and went to
public school in St. Louis, Missouri. In her
childhood home, her parents, though good
Americans for two generations or more, spoke
German among themselves and spent their
evenings in typical German music making. Her
mother, Clara (Stuhr) Traubel, gave up a professional concert career at her marriage, but her
critical instincts as a lieder singer were not forgotten. Grandfather Stuhr had brought the
classical dramatic repertory of his native land
to St. Louis in founding the Apollo Theatre,
the first serious German stage in the Midwest.
"The home atmosphere tingled with artistic
appreciation."

After Helen Traubel left school she studied
for seven years with Madame Vetter-Karst,
an old friend of her mother's. Miss Traubel
made her debut with the St. Louis Symphony
Orchestra under the direction of Rudolph
Ganz in 1925 and in the summer of the same
year in a Wagnerian concert with the New
York Oratorio Society and Philharmonic
under Stock at the Lewisohn Stadium. She
was successively soloist at a Worcester
Festival, with the Philadelphia Symphony
under Stokowski, and with the Minneapolis
and St. Louis Symphony Orchestras.

Besides her first teacher two other personalities made a profound impression upon her
future. One was Walter Damrosch, who was
officiating as conductor at an orchestral concert of the National Saengerfest in St. Louis
in 1935. After a few measures of her
Liebestod he turned to the rehearsing soloist
and smiled. "You are not made for concert
work alone," he said. "You will be an opera
singer, and your first part must be the heroine
of my own opera, *The Man Without a
Country*."

Thus Miss Traubel was introduced to the
Metropolitan in the spring of 1937 as leading
soprano in the rôle of Mary Rutledge. She
sang in both New York and Chicago. But it
was an "ungrateful rôle," and she did not sing
at the Metropolitan again until 1939. In the
meantime she studied with Giuseppe Boghetti,
who also trained Marion Anderson (see sketch
this issue) and who is famous for making
"Philadelphia debutantes easier to listen to."

Kirsten Flagstad is the other influence which
Miss Traubel recalls with much gratitude. Her
introduction to the great Norwegian took place
at the outset of her opera career at her first

Abresch

HELEN TRAUBEL

performance of *Die Walküre* in Chicago. The
young soprano, at once terrified and thrilled
by the thought of singing with such famous
stars as Flagstad, Melchior and List, approached her task with trepidation. She will
never forget the "kindness of the great Brünnhilde, her whispered stage directions, and the
support she gave the young Sieglinde as she
half carried her from the stage at her faint-
ing exit in the third act."

In the fall of 1939 Miss Traubel "bowled
over concertgoers at her Town Hall (New
York) recital and at her appearance as soloist
with the Philharmonic Symphony." She had
much the same effect on the Metropolitan's
audience. Her Sieglinde "put her high in the
scale of Wagnerian singers," and the first-
nighters who trooped in droves to hear her
stayed to cheer, for they heard what one
critic called one of the "finest heavyweight
Wagnerian soprano voices to turn up at the
Metropolitan since Kirsten Flagstad's debut
in 1935."

As Elizabeth in *Tannhäuser* she "won the
manifest approval of the audience. She is not
only fortunate in the qualities of her voice,
but also in her musicianship and in her evident
capacity for thorough study. Every detail of
her interpretation has been thoughtfully prepared and brought its well-considered results." But the *New Yorker* reported: "Miss
Traubel demonstrated her remarkable voice,
her clean unaffected German diction, and the
sincerity of her singing. It wasn't a complete
impersonation, but that wasn't to be expected
from a singer whose stage career began so
recently."

Helen Traubel has reddish hair and hazel
eyes. In a city of women trying to look small,
fragile and sensitive, her handsome figure
stands up straight to its full five-feet-eight
and one-quarter inches and her expression

TRAUBEL, HELEN—*Continued*

is one of slightly amused serenity. She laughs a great deal, but on the days when she is going to sing she tries to achieve solemnity because a big laugh opens the mouth and stretches the throat muscles.

She works hard at the slow business of learning opera parts and practices two hours a day, six days a week "to keep her voice going." The exigencies of caring for her voice regulate her life in a way that might be thought dull in the extreme. She does not smoke; her drink is a modest glass of sherry; she cannot afford ever to go short on sleep. Her recreations are walks, the movies and good food. "Nature has done a marvelous job on her," says *Cue*. "Here is a fine, big voice, amply housed and managed by a good brain."

She was formerly the wife of Louis F. Carpenter, a St. Louis automobile dealer whom she divorced in 1938. Later she married William Bass, a New York real estate and investment broker.

References

    Collier's 102:18 Ag 27 '38
    Cue 8:13 D 30 '40 por
    Musical Am 60:15 Ja 10 '40
    Musician 43:12 Ja '38; 45:12 Ja '40
    Opera News 4:34 D '39 por
    Time 35:36 Ja 8 '40
    Thompson, O. ed. International Cyclopedia of Music and Musicians 1938
    Wier, A. E. ed. Macmillan Encyclopedia of Music and Musicians 1938

TROTSKY, LEON (trôt-skĭ) Nov 1879— Aug 21, 1940 One of the world's foremost revolutionists; victim of an assassin alleged to be under orders of the Soviet secret police; born in Russia (real name Lev Davydovich Bronstein), early embraced Socialism and Marxism; suffered exile in Siberia; escaped to London in 1902 to work on revolutionary theories; returned to Russia to become head of the first secret Petrograd Soviet; for 12 years before the 1917 Revolution worked out famous theory of Permanent Revolution; with Lenin was cofather of the Russian Revolution of 1917; was made first Commissar of Foreign Affairs by Lenin; organized a Red Army which fought on fourteen fronts for more than four years; clashed with Stalin; was driven from the country permanently in 1929; in 1937 found a haven in Mexico after no other country would have him; wrote many articles agitating for the Fourth International; wrote *History of the Russian Revolution* and autobiography, *My Life*

References

    Lit Digest 119:9 Je 29 '35; 123:12 Ja 9 '37
    Nation 143:409 O 10 '36
    New Repub 86:254 Ap 8 '36
    Sat R Lit 14:10 Jl 11 '36
    Time 28:17 D 28 '36
    Bernstein, H. Leo Trotsky *In* Celebrities of Our Time p205-12 1924
    Campbell, J. R. Soviet Policy and Its Critics 1939
    Catlin, G. E. G. Kautsky, Lenin, Trotsky, Stalin *In* Story of the Political Philosophers p602-48 1939
    Churchill, W. L. S. Leon Trotsky, Alias Bronstein *In* Great Contemporaries p167-74 1937
    Eastman, M. F. Leon Trotsky 1925
    Jackson, J. H. Leon Trotsky *In* Bolitho, H. ed. Twelve Jews p249-69 1934
    Laski, H. J. Trotsky *In* Men of Turmoil p123-9 1935
    Marcosson, I. F. Trotsky *In* Turbulent Years p396-428 1938
    Namier, L. B. Trotsky *In* Skyscrapers p81-94 1934
    Trotsky, L. My Life 1930
    Who's Who
    Who's Who in American Jewry

Obituaries

    Christian Cent 57:1067-8 S 4 '40
    Christian Sci Mon Mag p6+ S 7 '40 pors
    Life 9:17-21 S 2 '40 il pors
    Nation 151:165 Ag 31 '40; 151:191-2 S 7 '40
    N Y Herald Tribune p1, 9 Ag 22 '40 pors
    N Y Times p1, 14 Ag 22 '40 por
    Newsweek 16:23-4 S 2 '40 pors
    Time 36:21-2 S 2 '40 il por

S. J. Woolf

LEON TROTSKY

TROTTER, FRANK BUTLER Feb 27, 1863—Mar 7, 1940 Former president of West Virginia University; entered the University faculty as professor of Latin in 1907; served as dean of the College of Arts and Sciences (1911-16); president of the University (1916-28)

FRANK BUTLER TROTTER

References
Who's Who in America 1938-39
Obituaries
N Y Herald Tribune p22 Mr 8 '40
N Y Times p22 Mr 8 '40

Blackstone

RODNEY H. TRUE

TRUE, RODNEY HOWARD Oct 14, 1866—Apr 8, 1940 Botanist; physiologist; emeritus professor of botany at the University of Pennsylvania; frequently has been called a "Sherlock Holmes" of the plant world; ex-director of the Morris Arboretum

References
Am Mag 107:24-5 Ap '29
American Men of Science
Who's Who in America
Who's Who in American Education
Obituaries
N Y Herald Tribune p22 Ap 9 '40 por
N Y Times p24 Ap 9 '40 por

TSAI YUAN-PEI 1867—Mar 5, 1940 Chinese statesman; educator; historian; held post of Educational Minister under both Sun Yat-sen and General Chiang Kai-shek (see sketch this issue)

References
International Who's Who
Who's Who in China
Obituaries
Boston Transcript p7 Mr 5 '40
N Y Herald Tribune p22 Mr 6 '40 por
N Y World-Telegram p32 Mr 5 '40
Sch & Soc 51:341 Mr 16 '40

TUNNEY, GENE (tŭn'ê) May 25, 1898- Ex-heavyweight world champion
Address: b. 135 E 42nd St, New York City; h. Stamford, Connecticut

Winner of the world's heavyweight boxing championship in 1926 and only champion to retire undefeated from the ring, James Joseph "Gene" Tunney has recently put on the gloves to challenge the "Americanism" of the American Youth Congress. One of the attacks was the announcement that he would serve as temporary national chairman of a National Foundation for American Youth, a new organization which would "serve as a clearing house and coordinating center for the pro-American youth groups" opposed to the AYC.

That was on August 13, 1940. The month before he had lost his first bout in political fisticuffs when he challenged the AYC meetings at Lake Geneva, Wisconsin held from July 3 to July 7. Mr. Tunney is a director of the Boy Scouts and of the Catholic Youth Club, organizations which have refused to affiliate with the Youth Congress under its present set-up. Taking up the cause of Murray Plavner, a founder of the Congress who has now been appointed national director of the rival organization, the one-time prize fighter headed a drive to purge the AYC of its "pro-Communist" forces. Tunney deplored the fact that the AYC had been under "the protective arms of certain well-meaning but misinformed people of prominence" without naming Mrs. Roosevelt (see sketch this issue), who was one of its staunch defenders. Tunney also

GENE TUNNEY

claimed that the AYC was led by "professional youths" over 30. The organization's leaders replied that Tunney himself, at 42, was scarcely a youth, and had not been interested in youth activities until very recently.

When Tunney's "pro-American" group arrived at the Congress meeting place the executive secretary of the AYC announced that his delegates had not complied with the registration rule that registration blanks be sent to the AYC office not later than June 24. Hence the Congress refused to honor the credentials of Tunney's anti-Red bloc. Tunney called his delegates to a separate meeting at Lake Geneva at which he condemned all enactments passed by the Congress. Instead of taking a peace stand he said he thought that young men should pledge themselves at once to universal selective service. Plans were announced for a rival group to the "Trojan horse AYC"—a group to be organized on a strictly "American" basis. While at Lake Geneva, Tunney was invited by officers of the AYC to address the Congress, which he refused to do.

Tunney continued his youth work in September 1940, when he set up a Young Voters' Exchange to bring 9,000,000 first voters to the polls in November.

Gene Tunney's life is a true Horatio Alger story of a poor lad's rise to fame, a million dollars (which he made in 40 minutes by the clock) and marriage to a wealthy society girl. As extra trimmings to Arrow-collar looks and two-fisted glory were his cultural and literary qualifications. A seeker of sweetness and light, a prize fighter who also read Shakespeare, Tunney violated the popular concept of a pugilist and had to overcome real antagonism in his ring career.

He was born May 25, 1898 in Greenwich Village, New York City, of Irish Catholic parents, John Joseph and Mary (Lydon) Tunney. He was a graduate of St. Veronica's Parochial School in 1911 and of La Salle Academy in 1915. The handsome but obscure young man held a job as clerk with the Ocean Steamship Company of New York until the outbreak of war in 1917. He enlisted with the Marine Corps and went to France with the American Expeditionary Force. He soon demonstrated his fistic ability behind the lines, and in Paris in 1919 won the A. E. F. light heavyweight championship.

Back in America in 1924 he knocked out France's idol, Georges Carpentier, and after that entered the heavyweight class. When he stepped into the arena at Philadelphia in 1926 to meet Champion Jack Dempsey, Gene Tunney had behind him a record of having lost only one of some sixty bouts. Although the bets were all on Dempsey the latter was in a nervous, run-down condition after having gone through a legal battle instigated by his former manager, Jack Kearns. The ex-marine bravely arrived by plane for the fight, which was held in a downpour of rain. It was in the tenth round that the "Manassa Mauler" went out on his feet. Gene Tunney was the new champion.

Just a year later (September 1927) Dempsey fought Tunney in a return battle. Things went well for Tunney till the seventh round, when he went down under seven smashing blows. But because Dempsey failed to go to a neutral corner the referee gave Tunney extra time on the "long count" and he was on his feet again, to out-guess and out-general his opponent and win the bout. Tunney fought once more, scoring a technical knockout over Tom Heeney in 1928; then he retired from the ring. Boxing experts agree that, while Tunney was not a "natural" fighter, he won because he made of boxing an exact science. His style was correct by the book; he left nothing to chance. Tunney himself has written: "The way to know about championship quality is to learn from the champions, and that I did, studying them with professional purpose during my time in the ring and from habitual interest afterward. . . My slant always put emphasis on the mental side of prize-fighting."

In Rome, Italy on October 3, 1928 Gene Tunney married Mary Josephine (Polly) Lauder, a debutante heiress, of Greenwich, Connecticut. They have four children. In July 1940 Tunney purchased a 375-acre Rapajo farm on the Choptank River near the Chrysler and Du Pont (see sketch this issue) properties in Maryland.

Since 1938 Tunney has been board chairman of the American Distilling Company. He has written numerous magazine articles on boxing, on championships and on the psychology of fighting and in 1932 published a book, *A Man Must Fight*. In much that he has written he has embodied his philosophy of life. "Religion is my highest and most encompassing ideal," he has said. Next to that he lists patriotism, human friendship and the rules of health.

References

Atlan 163:839-41 Je '39
N Y Herald Tribune p22 Je 20 '40; p7 Jl 5 '40
N Y Times p21 Jl 23 '40; p20 Jl 28 '40; Ag 14 '40
N Y World-Telegram p4 Jl 3 '40; p3 Jl 6 '40; p6 Jl 9 '40
Newsweek 16:35-6 Jl 15 '40; 16:4 Ag 12 '40; 16:15 Ag 26 '40
PM p50 Je 30 '40 por; p25 Jl 3 '40
Sat Eve Post 212:18-19+ F 10 '40 pors; 212:22-3+ Je 1 '40 pors
Gallico, P. W. "By Horatio Alger Jr." *In* Farewell to Sport p81-91 1938
Inglis, W. O. Gene Tunney, Captain of Fistic Industry *In* Champions off Guard p284-311 1932
Johnson, C. H. L. James Joseph ("Gene") Tunney: Champion Heavyweight Boxer of the World *In* Famous American Athletes of To-day 1st ser. p67-95 1928
Who's Who in America
Who's Who in Commerce and Industry

TURPIN, BEN (tŭr'pĭn) Sept 17, 1874— July 1, 1940 Motion picture comedian whose crossed eyes brought him fame in silent films; one of the first slapstick comedians on the screen and mainstay of Mack Sennett comedies; insured his eyes against normalcy for $100,000

BEN TURPIN

References

International Motion Picture Almanac 1937-38

Obituaries

N Y Herald Tribune p20 Jl 2 '40 por
N Y Times p21 Jl 2 '40
Variety 139:46 Jl 3 '40

TWEED, THOMAS FREDERIC 1890— Apr 30, 1940 Political adviser to Lloyd George since 1926; leader in Liberal Party councils in England; author of *Gabriel Over the White House*, published anonymously in 1933 and made into one of the most widely discussed motion pictures of that year

References

Who's Who

Obituaries

N Y Herald Tribune p22 My 1 '40
N Y Times p23 My 1 '40

TWEEDIE, MRS. ALEC Died Apr 16, 1940 Artist; author of numerous books; pioneer British woman journalist; active in welfare work; for last 50 years known as world traveler

References

Who's Who

Obituaries

N Y Herald Tribune p22 Ap 16 '40
N Y Times p23 Ap 16 '40 por

TWEEDSMUIR, JOHN BUCHAN, 1ST BARON *See* Buchan, J.

UNDSET, SIGRID May 20, 1882- Author *Address:* c/o Alfred A. Knopf, Inc, 501 Madison Ave, New York City

The famous Norwegian novelist and Nobel Prize winner, Sigrid Undset, and her son Hans arrived in the United States in September 1940 to fill lecture engagements and probably to take up permanent residence. She came from Sweden where she had been an exile since the Nazi invasion of Norway in April 1940 and the destruction of her home at Lillehammer. Prior to her flight into Sweden she had finished her new novel, *Madame Dorthea,* now published (August 1940) in this country.

With the valiance of one of her own fictional heroines, Sigrid Undset in her late fifties met the fury of sudden war and resisted the aggressors until forced at peril of her life—she had taken an anti-Nazi stand in her writings—to leave her home. When the first German bombers flew over Oslo she returned to her Lillehammer retreat, an old Norse dwelling dating from the year 1000. She offered her services to the government and worked as a censor. Her youngest boy joined an ambulance unit; her eldest son entered army service and was killed in action three weeks later. When the Norwegians were forced back and the fighting lines drew near to Lillehammer

SIGRID UNDSET

she left with a neighbor family, going by auto to the coast at Andalsnes. They lay in the snow for hours near Dombas to escape machine-gunning planes, then pushed on over bomb-cratered roads to the sea at Molde. From that destroyed port they took a boat to Mo at the edge of the Arctic Circle. The last stage of the journey, through snow and ice across the frontier, with a sick companion on a stretcher, was the worst. Finally they reached Sweden.

Sigrid Undset was born May 20, 1882 in Kallundborg, Denmark. Her mother was a Dane; her father, Dr. Ingvald Martin Undset, a distinguished Norwegian archeologist. Eldest of three daughters, she assisted her father in his research work, developing her interest in Scandinavian life of earlier times. She was educated in the Oslo public schools, and at her father's death attended a commercial school there. From 1899 to 1909 she supported herself doing clerical work in business offices. Her evenings and holidays she devoted to a study of fiction writing.

Her earliest writing showed those two special interests which she was to develop richly in later work: the Middle Ages and modern living. Her first novel, *Frau Marta Oulie,* published in 1907, received only mild praise. It was a story of marriage, parenthood, and human relationships—a theme that was to underlie many of her subsequent novels. With the publication of her second book she decided to devote herself wholly to writing; and in 1911, when her novel, *Jenny,* appeared it won a popular ovation. In 1912 she married A. C. Svarstad, a painter. Three children were born to them; but the marriage was dissolved in 1925. After this unsuccessful marriage, and despite her Lutheran upbringing, Madame

Undset entered the Catholic Church. This faith, to which she has paid tribute in several essays, including the collection *Men, Women and Places* (1939) has given her work its moral focus.

Several of her novels have had a modern setting, among them *The Wild Orchid* (1931) and *The Faithful Wife* (1937). It has been remarked by critics that the events of her own life do not wholly explain the richness of emotional understanding found in her work. She is an instinctive artist. "Her realism is so delicate and serene, and the direct, unflinching candor of her vision is so sweetly softened by native tenderness, by infinite pity . . . that the final effect of her novels is as unforgettable as the spectacle of a human heart laid bare."

But her great historical novels have overshadowed her work in the modern field. Her talents found their finest expression with the publication, in 1920, of *The Bridal Wreath,* the first volume of the great Kristin Lavransdatter trilogy, the succeeding two being *The Mistress of Husaby,* 1925 and *The Cross,* 1927. The study of Kristin Lavransdatter, a splendid woman who loves an essentially unworthy man, set against a background of the Middle Ages, was immediately recognized as an outstanding work not only in Norway but throughout the world. It has been translated into almost all European languages, and the American edition ran over 300,000 copies. Equally important was the Olav Audunsson historical tetralogy, called in English *The Master of Hestviken,* the first volume of which appeared in 1925. It has been said that in her studies of the "contemporaneousness of the past" Madame Undset has made the thirteenth and fourteenth centuries as timely as the latest war bulletin. The Nobel Prize for literature was awarded Sigrid Undset in 1928, the citation mentioning especially her remarkable delineation of medieval life.

Since 1937 Madame Undset has written many essays and articles. Her ideas have been given a great deal of publicity in Europe; up to the coming of Hitler her works were widely read in Germany. But the Nazi papers have angrily denounced her defense of racial and religious tolerance. Today her novels are banned throughout Norway on the grounds that she is in sympathy with the exiled Norwegian government in London.

In her speeches in this country Mme. Undset has warned America to preserve its democracy, has warned Americans "against feeling too safe." "The United States," she said, "has something to learn from what happened to the small countries of Scandinavia. It must act before it is too late."

Those qualities of human nature that are universal and timeless, remarked in her previous work, pervade Sigrid Undset's *Madame Dorthea,* a story of Norwegian life at the end of the eighteenth century. At forty, vigorous and capable, Madame

Dorthea has a second husband, Jorgen Thestrup, seven children, and lives a conventional middle-class life. The story opens one late winter night when her two oldest boys have been away all day with their tutor and fail to return. The boys later turn up safely at their grandmother's, but their father who has gone in search of them never comes back. Dorthea is left to cope with the loss of her husband, the subsequent loss of their farm and income and the necessity of finding work for the older boys. Most of the story concerns her relations with her children, her lusty mother and various neighbors in the little community. Because the novel ends inconclusively, with Dorthea's character just approaching development, several critics feel that it may be the first in a new historical series.

References

Christian Sci Mon Mag p12 N 6 '35 por
Life 8:90+ Je 10 '40 por
N Y Herald Tribune Books p15 Je 30 '40; p3 Ag 4 '40 por
N Y Times p19 Ap 26 '40; p11 Ag 5 '40
N Y Times Book R p2 S 8 '40
Sat R Lit 16:40 O 9 '37
Wilson Lib Bul 3:370 D '28

Beach, J. W.   Variations: Sigrid Undset   *In*   Twentieth Century Novel: Studies in Technique p263-72 1932
Drake, W. A.   Sigrid Undset   *In* Contemporary European Writers p72-9 1928
Gustafson, A.   Christian Ethics in a Pagan World: Sigrid Undset   *In* Six Scandinavian Novelists p286-365 1940
Kunitz, S. J. ed.   Living Authors 1937
Marble, Mrs. A. R.   Sigrid Undset: Novelist of Medieval Norway and Ageless Humanity   *In* Nobel Prize Winners in Literature, 1901-1931 p327-45 1932
Vinde, V.   Sigrid Undset 1930
Who's Who

UNTERMYER, SAMUEL   (ŭn'ter-mī'er) June 6, 1858—Mar 16, 1940   Lawyer

Samuel Untermyer died in his Palm Springs, California home on March 16, 1940 at the age of 81. He was a man "whose career was unique and made a lasting impression on his times."

Mr. Untermyer was born in Lynchburg, Virginia on June 6, 1858, the son of Isadore and Therese Untermyer. His father was a Bavarian-born tobacco planter who fell dead at the news of Lee's surrender. Both his father and mother had planned for Samuel to become a rabbi, but instead when he moved to New York after his father's death, he attended the College of the City of New York. In 1873 he entered a law office as

SAMUEL UNTERMYER

clerk and office boy and continued his studies at Columbia Law School, from which he received his LL. B. in 1878.

While young Untermyer was in college, when he was only 17, he appeared in court wearing a beard he had grown to conceal his boyishness. When he was 21 years old he was admitted to the Bar, and he proceeded in his twenty-first year to earn $75,000.

Before he was 24 Mr. Untermyer was representing many important business interests and had acted as trial counsel in some of the most important cases of that time. He defended Asa Bird Gardiner when an attempt was made to remove Mr. Gardiner as District Attorney of New York County. He was counsel for the Wertheimers, English art dealers, in their controversy with the Count de Castellane. As counsel for James Hazen Hyde in the struggle to oust Mr. Hyde from the control of the Equitable Life Assurance Society, Mr. Untermyer helped to bring on the great insurance investigation of 1905, conducted by Charles Evans Hughes. Another case which Mr. Untermyer handled and which was said to have resulted in the largest fee ever paid to a lawyer in this country up to that time, $775,000, was the merger of the Utah Copper Company with the Boston Consolidated and the Nevada Consolidated Companies.

In private practice Untermyer brought about the settlement which resulted in the formation of the Bethlehem Steel Corporation, and argued before the Supreme Court the case of William Randolph Hearst in a suit brought by Hearst's International News Service against the contention of the Associated Press of a property right in news.

UNTERMYER, SAMUEL—*Continued*

In December 1911 Mr. Untermyer delivered before the Finance Forum in New York an address entitled "Is There a Money Trust?" In it he expressed his opinion of financial conditions in this country and suggested legislative enactments to remedy what he considered abuses. This address was followed by a Congressional investigation for the purpose of formulating remedial legislation, which was known as the "Pujo Money Trust Investigation" from the name of the committee's chairman.

Mr. Untermyer was counsel of the House Committee on Banking and Currency which conducted the inquiry. He called the banking giants of the day, including J. P. Morgan, to the stand and fearlessly pursued his questioning. As an outgrowth of his exposures the Federal Reserve Bank law came into being, and Untermyer had a prominent part in the preparation of the bill and in advocating its passage before Congress.

Mr. Untermyer worked for the public good, too, as counsel of the Lockwood legislative housing investigating committee. Serving without pay, he uncovered abuses in the building trades which resulted in the conviction and imprisonment of Robert P. Brindell, "czar" of the Building Trades Council. The investigation was followed by remedial housing legislation and extended from time to time under constant hammering by Mr. Untermyer. During the investigation "there were many who whispered that he was not far from being the committee itself."

One of Mr. Untermyer's most conspicuous efforts in public service was as special counsel of the Transit Commission. The commission undertook to prepare a plan for unification of the New York Rapid Transit Railways and Mr. Untermyer conducted an exhaustive investigation while at the same time fighting strongly for the maintenance of the five-cent fare. In a resolution on his death the Transit Commission said: "It was through his invaluable services that the five-cent fare was saved."

Mr. Untermyer's career was a strange combination of paradoxes and contradictions. One of the highest paid corporation counselors in the country, serving men like J. D. Rockefeller, William Randolph Hearst and the Lewisohn banking interests, he earned for himself a reputation in the Pujo investigations as a foe of the trusts. He who denounced Wall Street made six million dollars profit from the purchase of 15,000 shares of Bethlehem Steel before the War. He who advocated the public ownership of utilities also devoted some of his shrewdest and most expensive advice to entrenching Tammany in office. In the pay of the largest capitalists in the country, he devoted time and money to defending labor unions.

Toward the close of his life Samuel Untermyer devoted more and more time to the championing of humanitarian causes. The coming of Hitler to power and the German drive against the Jews found a strong antagonist in him. He was one of the earliest and most outspoken critics of the Hitler régime and in July 1934 was elected the first president of the World Non-Sectarian Anti-Nazi Council. He was one of the first Americans to urge a boycott against Germany and once carried on a one-man demonstration on board a Bermuda bound liner when he found that the table decorations at the captain's dinner had been made in Germany. He was active against the use of German steel in the construction of the Triborough Bridge and was successful in getting the order for its use rescinded by Mayor La Guardia (see sketch this issue).

In politics Untermyer was a progressive Democrat, but refused to play any very active part, with the exception of making speaking trips for Woodrow Wilson in 1912 and 1916. He was a delegate to the national conventions of 1904, 1908, 1912 and 1916 but is reported to have refused the offer of Ambassador to France under Wilson.

When Untermyer grew older he used to go to Palm Springs for the winters "to sit in the sun and not worry." Even in his old age he looked as dapper as in his youth. Five-feet-five in height with martial moustaches, he had the neat and erect appearance of a much younger man. He was seldom seen without an orchid in his lapel. His fellow lawyers used to say that he carried a damp bag of orchids into court so as to have a fresh one whenever the one he was wearing wilted.

He "lived with a flair for the sumptuous and the picturesque." His gardens at Greystone, his estate near Yonkers, were filled with rare flowers. The walls of his home there and in New York City were hung with choice Old Masters. He was a connoisseur of the arts and a patron of them.

In 1880 Mr. Untermyer married Miss Minnie Carl of New York, who died in 1924. She was a Gentile who became converted to Judaism. There are three children: Alvin Untermyer, a lawyer; Irwin Untermyer, justice of the appellate division of the Supreme Court; and Mrs. Irene Richter.

References

New Yorker 6:29-32 My 17 '30; 6: 24-27 My 24 '30

Who's Who in America 1938-39
Who's Who in American Jewry
Who's Who in Law

Obituaries

    Christian Cent 57:425 Mr 27 '40
    N Y Herald Tribune p1, 38 Mr 17
    '40 por
    N Y Times p1, 48 Mr 17 '40 por
    Newsweek 15:8 Mr 25 '40 por
    Time 35:71 Mr 25 '40

VALERA, EAMON DE *See* De Valera, E.

VANCE, WILLIAM REYNOLDS May 9, 1870—Oct 23, 1940 Professor emeritus of Yale University Law School and nationally known authority on insurance law; professor of law and dean of law department at Washington and Lee University; left to become professor of law and dean of the law department of George Washington

WILLIAM REYNOLDS VANCE

University; dean of University of Minnesota Law School from 1912 to 1920; from 1920 to 1938 Foster professor of law at Yale; former president and secretary of Association of American Law Schools and active in American Bar Association; champion of legal aid bureaus and small claims courts; author of many books, his most widely used *Case Book on Insurance Law* (1914); general counsel for Bureau of War Risk Insurance in Washington in 1918

References

    Leaders In Education 1932
    Who's Who in America
    Who's Who in American Education
    Who's Who in Law

Obituaries

    N Y Times p25 O 24 '40

VANDENBERG, ARTHUR HENDRICK Mar 22, 1884- United States Senator from Michigan

Address: h. 316 Morris Ave, Grand Rapids, Michigan

It has been said that a Hollywood director would cast Arthur Vandenberg, re-elected in November 1940, for a United States Senator on sight. He not only looks the part, he acts it. On every political issue of the past 12 years his voice has been heard and listened to, for the Republican Senator from Michigan plays an influential part in the determination of this country's political activities. This was proved in the spring of 1940 when his name was frequently mentioned for the Presidential nomination and was brought before the Republican Convention.

Recently Senator Vandenberg raised his voice against the Burke-Wadsworth (see Burke sketch this issue) selective service bill. "Say what you please," he said, "something precious goes out of the American way of life and something sinister takes its place under conscription." To many people this stand is consistent with the reputation for being an isolationist which Senator Vandenberg has achieved since the last War. His natural Midwest isolationism fortified by his service as a member of Senator Nye's committee which investigated munitions in 1934 and 1935, Vandenberg came out in 1939 as the leader of the battle against modifying the Neutrality Act. In his campaign for the Presidential nomination he accused the New Deal of jeopardizing the nation's peace "by meddling internationally where it is none of our concern." Yet this isolationist Senator was in favor of the World Court and was the author of a Senate resolution to terminate the 1911 treaty of amity and commerce with Japan—according to Walter Lippmann (see sketch this issue) "the longest step on the road to war that the United States has taken since . . . 1915." He, too, demanded that we withdraw our recognition of the Soviet Union when Russia invaded Finland. And in June 1940, calling himself an "insulationist," he urged all help to the Allies short of war.

Other governmental issues seem to have been approached in the same way. As one editorial writer puts it, "Vandenberg has stood squarely on both sides of every issue of the past 10 years." Some call him an "opportunist" and a "trimmer"; others say he is a "liberal conservative." In the New Deal, according to one observer, he "discards what seems to him to be the bad and accepts what strikes him as the good, always proposing a substitute for what he discards." But in a different interpretation, based on his article, *The New Deal Must Be Salvaged*, his idea is "that the New Deal must be scrapped, melted over, recast into a new engine, going slowly and rather on the bias in slightly different directions."

Actually the record supports both points of view. For instance, Senator Vandenberg

ARTHUR H. VANDENBERG

voted for the creation of the Securities and Exchange Commission, a measure hated by "Big Business," and as a member of the Senate committee investigating munitions he won the hatred of the Du Pont (see sketch this issue) and other big interests. But on the other side of the scale are his consistent opposition to the excess-profits tax, his defense of holding companies, his fight against the TVA.

Vandenberg voted against the Wagner Act, yet he has repeatedly stated that collective bargaining is labor's bill of rights and is here to stay. He voted against the NRA, the AAA and the Wage and Hour Act, yet was the sponsor of a liberal anti-child-labor amendment and helped get the revision that made Social Security benefit payments more liberal and more quickly available. The way he himself explains it is that frequently he is in favor of New Deal objectives, but irked by the methods used to achieve them—by government in business, by the theory of spending into prosperity, by punitive taxation, by government handling of relief. After Roosevelt's re-election he announced that he didn't want unity "at the expense of constructive criticism."

It has been said that when Vandenberg argues about matters like the Florida ship canal and the Passamaquoddy development, both of which he strongly opposed, he is a good and convincing speaker. However, "in matters where public opinion is uncertain, he becomes uncertain, too. He starts out boldly, then wavers, qualifies, draws back until it is hard to follow him." Once he delivered a long and laboriously prepared speech on the work relief bill. When he had finished Hugo Black said he had listened fully and carefully and had

only one question to ask—"Was Vandenberg for or against the bill?"

Vandenberg still talks and writes in the "sometimes florid, sometimes pedantic style of the small town editor," and has been called "one of alliteration's most conspicuous and pitiable victims." Still he is an effective speaker and his desire to polish off a period or present the *mot juste* is often successful. He is good at phrases like "Dr. Jekyll and Mr. Hyde Park," for instance. And his speeches are always conspicuous for the amount of study and research he puts in them. For the Supreme Court fight of 1937 he wrote an address of 80,000 words as "a prelude to a real speech"—and never got a chance to deliver it.

It has been reported that on his deathbed Senator Vandenberg's father said to him: "Son, always be a good Republican." Aaron Vandenberg was a harness manufacturer, the descendant of Dutch settlers of New York, who was ruined in the panic of 1893 and attributed the disaster to the Democrats. Vandenberg's mother, Alpha (Hendrick) Vandenberg, was also of Dutch pioneer descent and her father was a delegate from New York to the convention which nominated Lincoln for President in 1860.

Arthur Vandenberg was born in Grand Rapids, Michigan and went to school there. He was only nine when his father lost his factory and his mother opened a boarding house, but he went to work. He bought himself a pushcart and started in the delivery business. Soon he was successful enough to buy another cart and hire helpers. In 1900 he was graduated from high school. There he had made his first speech, on Alexander Hamilton's greatness, his firm belief in which inspired three "fiercely partisan" books written later—*Alexander Hamilton, the Greatest American* (1921); *If Hamilton Were Here Today* (1923) and *The Trail of a Tradition* (1925).

After high school he got a job as clerk in a cracker factory. When he was fired for going to see Theodore Roosevelt in a parade he went to work for the Grand Rapids *Herald* as office boy and copy boy. Later he was promoted to the job of state editor and general reporter, at $8 a week. After 12 months of this he went to the University of Michigan in 1901, but after a year of studying days and working nights had a breakdown and returned to Grand Rapids, to the *Herald*. In his spare time he wrote stories that were accepted by *Lippincott's* and *Pearson's* magazines and on the basis of this success got himself a job on *Collier's Weekly* in New York. A year of this was enough for him and he went back to the *Herald* as City Hall reporter. He got to know the political bigwigs and, when in 1906 one of them, Representative (later Senator) William Alden Smith, bought the *Herald*, 22-year-old Arthur Vandenberg was made managing editor.

As the *Herald's* editor Vandenberg wrote editorials, solicited advertising, pepped up the circulation. At the same time he joined the Masons, the Shriners, the Elks and the Woodmen. He broadened his interests in politics and at 26 was a member of the Grand Rapids Charter Commission and at 28 a member of the Michigan Republican Central Committee. Before he was 30 Vandenberg was "the editor, oracle, orator and big shot of Grand Rapids."

Vandenberg's first wife, Elizabeth Watson, died in 1916 and Vandenberg, the father of three small children (the two girls are now married and the boy is now his father's secretary and "spittin' image"), didn't enlist when the War came. Instead he made hundreds of speeches in Liberty Loan drives. He also courted and married a second wife, Hazel H. Whittaker, a newspaper woman. When the War was over he was an important Republican. He consulted with Warren G. Harding on the 1920 Republican plank on the League and helped write parts of his campaign speeches. His paper helped build up the Michigan Republican machine and was strong enough to put Fred Green in the Governor's post. When Senator Woodbridge Ferris died Vandenberg was appointed to succeed him and in 1928 was elected for a full term "with the largest plurality ever given any Michigan candidate."

When Vandenberg first came to the Senate it was said he "could strut sitting down." He took himself very seriously and the boys in the press gallery gleefully nicknamed him "the pouter pigeon with the kewpie smile" and quoted the fancy verbiage in his *Alexander Hamilton*. But Vandenberg settled down soon enough and in 1930 was largely responsible for the decennial reapportionment law which requires Congress to remake the Congressional districts after each national census.

In 1934 Vandenberg was one of the very few Republican Senators to be elected, "a feat that is still the basis of his prestige among politicians," and according to some from 1934 to 1938 *was* the Republican Party, rising to the top "by the simple expedient of being the only man in it." After the Republican defeat of 1936, when he had been mentioned for the Presidency, he began to talk coalition—coalition of the conservative Democrats with the loyal Republicans—and "as much as anyone" he was responsible for the success of the coalition in the Senate. James Farley was among the many who realized his effectiveness and went so far as to say in 1938, "Senator Vandenberg is the Republican to defeat in 1940."

Vandenberg has always "worked slavishly" as a Senator. He attends Senate sessions and committee meetings conscientiously and stays up long nights reading, studying and pecking at his typewriter. According to the night porters, "he's the workin'est man" in Washington. Yet he and Mrs.

Vandenberg manage to get in a good deal of social life. And the Senator occasionally gets off to bowl duckpins or read Sax Rohmer and E. Phillips Oppenheim.

A big man, more than six feet tall and weighing more than 200 pounds, Senator Vandenberg is "good looking without the conspicuous handsomeness of a McNutt" (see sketch June issue). He has "dark brown eyes under heavy black brows" and graying hair parted far to one side to conceal his baldness. He smokes denicotinized cigars, drinks highballs (he hates cocktails and cigarettes) and chews gum vigorously. And yet, "during Senate inquiries, his rimless spectacles, his quizzical glance, his trick of shrouding the lower half of his face with his hand and his extreme patience in questioning witnesses often create the feeling of an extraordinarily wise, kindly professor."

References

Christian Sci Mon Mag p3+ Ja 27 '40 pors
Ed Research Reports 1:277-9 Ap 8 '40
Nation 150:587-90 My 11 '40 por
New Repub 86:274-5 Ap 15 '36; 102: 461-3 Ap 8 '40
N Y Herald Tribune II p2 F 18 '40 pors
N Y Times p15 My 17 '40; p7 Je 10 '40; pl Ag 13 '40
Newsweek 7:29-30 F 22 '36 por
Time 34:13+ O 2 '39 il por
Cuncannon, P. M. Arthur H. Vandenberg *In* Salter, J. T. ed. American Politician p47-61 1938
Who's Who in America
Who's Who in Government
Who's Who in the Nation's Capital

VAN DOREN, HAROLD LIVINGSTON
Mar 2, 1895- Industrial designer
Address: b. 1217 Madison Ave, Toledo, Ohio; h. 604 Winthrop St, Toledo, Ohio

According to Harold Van Doren, the goal of industrial designing "stripped of hocus-pocus . . . is sales—at a profit." For more than 10 years he has been considering our modern machine-made appliances and equipment and remaking them. He has increased the adaptability of their form to their function and the esthetic appeal of their shape, color and texture. Sleds, meat grinders, a dough divider for bakeries— these are only a few of the items he has changed for us.

Like most industrial designers, Van Doren trained for another branch of the arts. He started as a painter. He was born in Chicago, Illinois on March 2, 1895 the son of Charles Luther and Harriet (Clark) Van Doren; moved to East Orange, New Jersey in time to go to high school there; and was graduated from Williams College in 1917. He spent a year as art editor of the *Survey Graphic* but left

HAROLD VAN DOREN

to become a member of the Art Students League.

Then, in 1922, came the conventional years abroad, with Van Doren financing himself by lecturing at the Louvre, serving as artist on the Chicago *Tribune's* Paris edition, acting in one of the films produced by Jean Renoir, translating biographies of Cézanne and Renoir.

Back in New York after two years, he began to ghost-write articles for the *Saturday Evening Post* and for the *Encyclopedia Britannica* and to contribute to a good many magazines. From 1927 to 1930 he was at the same time assistant director of the Minneapolis Art Museum and art editor of two Minneapolis newspapers.

In 1930 Van Doren set up as an industrial designer in Toledo, Ohio, with the Toledo Scale Company his one and only client. His first fame was achieved in the field of plastics, and it wasn't long before Harold Van Doren and Associates were being called in to meet the designing problems of many companies.

In 1933 he married Mary Huggins of Emporia, Kansas. They have one daughter, Patricia.

In the 10 years he has been in business he has become one of the nation's leading and most articulate stylists. *Industrial Design, a Practical Guide* (February 1940) is the summary of his years of work and discovery. In it there is little of the press-agentry that so often distinguishes discussions of industrial design. *Industrial Design* shows that the daily job of designing merchandise for appearance is a serious profession requiring persistence, industry, technical skills and knowledge. Its first part surveys the field, its second is an elementary presentation of designing in

three dimensions, its third deals with the technique of design production, and the fourth offers various problems for the beginner, concluding with case histories of several products now on the market. There are chapters on streamlining, fees, materials and processes, design patents, color technique and the operation of a free-lance studio. There also are descriptions of how to make art renderings and presentation models.

Van Doren himself is a "shirt-sleeve" designer—the kind who gets out in overalls and learns how a product is built before he touches pencil to drawing paper. With him industrial design is no penthouse product. Today, his agency in Toledo is one of the three or four largest in the country. Last year he stole a march on fellow designers (nearly all of whom were trying to outdo each other in display architecture at the New York World's Fair) by walking off with commissions to do the 1940 models of some of the largest electrical appliance products—a Westinghouse range, a Maytag washing machine and Philco refrigerators.

References

Van Doren, H. Industrial Design, a
  Practical Guide 1940
Who's Who in America

VAN DOREN, MARK June 13, 1894-
Author

Address: h. 393 Bleecker St, New York City

Last year it was Carl Van Doren who was honored with a Pulitzer Award of $1,000 for his biography of Benjamin Franklin. This year his younger brother Mark has achieved the same recognition for his *Collected Poems.* Even this does not exhaust the list of literary Van Dorens, however, for there remains Irita, former wife of Carl, editor of *Herald Tribune Books* as well as Mark's wife, Dorothy, who does the brief book reviews for the *New Yorker* and who is herself the author of several books.

"More the artist, less the literary figure" than his brother, Mark Van Doren is a "spare, shrewd, genial gentleman with a wide mouth, bright, dark eyes and close-cropped head" who is associate professor of English at Columbia and one of the three "regulars" on CBS's *Invitation to Learning* Sunday broadcasts. He seems to belong to the English tradition, and a large part of his poetry was surely bred in New England, but facts state that he was born in Hope, Illinois on June 13, 1894, the son of Charles Lucius and Dora Anne (Butz) Van Doren. Mark grew up in the university town of Urbana, where the family moved when he was six. Like Carl, he attended the University of Illinois there, was graduated Phi Beta Kappa in 1914 and received his M. A. in English literature the following year, and then, still like Carl, proceeded to desert the Midwest permanently for New York City. While still working for his

Doctor's degree at Columbia University he published his first book, entitled *Henry David Thoreau—a Critical Study,* in 1916. The War interrupted scholarly pursuits, however. He spent two years in the Infantry, in 1918 spent a year abroad with Joseph Wood Krutch on a traveling fellowship from Columbia, and it was not until 1920 that he received his Ph. D. and joined the English department at Columbia. He had already published that same year his second book, another critical study entitled *The Poetry of John Dryden.*

In 1922 Mark Van Doren married Dorothy Graffe, and two years later he published his first book of poems, *Spring Thunder and Other Poems,* and became literary editor of *The Nation,* a position which he held until 1928. A poet himself, Mark Van Doren's scholarly preoccupation continued to be largely with poets. He published critical analyses of American and British literature, a biography of Edwin Arlington Robinson, several anthologies, and was editor of a number of works, for the most part early Americana. The three volumes of his poetry published up to 1928 have probably won more praise from critics than anything he has published since, unless it is *Winter Diary* (1935). In 1928 Allen Tate (see sketch this issue) named him "if not the most brilliant stylist of our time, one of the most accomplished craftsmen." In 1931 there appeared a long narrative poem, *Jonathan Gentry,* which received mixed reviews, and in 1935 he published his first novel, a puzzling and poetic psychological fantasy entitled *The Transients.* From 1935 to 1938 he was motion picture critic for *The Nation.*

Last year most critics found Mark Van Doren's *Shakespeare,* a collection of 36 essays on what is usually considered a scholarly subject, not only thoughtful and stimulating, but a positive delight to read—probably for the same reasons that fill his classes in English 35 and 36 at Columbia, where all the plays of Shakespeare are read through one after the other, and make his occasional lectures at the New School for Social Research so well attended. The appearance of his *Collected Poems* last year was also well received, and a second psychological novel, *Windless Cabins,* published in 1940, served to focus more critical attention on him. The awarding of the 1939 Pulitzer Prize for poetry to Mark Van Doren on May 6, 1940 was merely a form of tangible recognition for a long and distinguished literary career.

Mark Van Doren once said: "My only conception of the poet is that he is a person who writes poetry," and certainly aside from writing poetry he himself has little in common with the common conception of the poet. He has never had the opportunity to starve in a garret and has never sought the opportunity. He believes, in fact, that the best physical conditions for writing poetry include neither too

MARK VAN DOREN

many material comforts nor too few—just about as many as he has always had. With his "husky wife, Dorothy," and his two sons, Charles Lincoln and John, he lives in a pleasant Bleecker Street duplex apartment in New York City's Greenwich Village during the winters and spends his summers on the 150 wooded acres of their farm in the mountains of Connecticut. There is much of the past and the present of this New England in his poetry, and some critics have found an elegiac note in his voice. John Peale Bishop once said: "He seems while young to have become accustomed to the fact that his own particular world was already lost. And these things make him not altogether of our time. He is not solitary, but remote." Another critic attempted to describe him as a poet by saying: "He has no furies; rather a few fireside ghosts." As for Van Doren himself:

> "Wit is the only wall
> Between us and the dark.
> Wit is perpetual daybreak
> And skylark
> Springing off the unshaken stone
> Of man's blood and the mind's bone."

References

Nation 149 :714-16 D 23 '39
N Y Times p20 My 7 '40 por
Poetry 51 :164-7 D '37; 54 :157-60 Je '39
Sat R Lit 20:7 O 7 '39; 22:5+ My 11 '40
Scholastic 33:21-2E+ O 8 '38 por
Time 34 :69 O 2 '39
America's Young Men 1936-37
Kunitz, S. J. ed. Living Authors 1937
Van Doren, C. Three Worlds 1936
Who's Who in America

VANN, ROBERT LEE Aug 29, 1887—
Oct 24, 1940 Negro editor and publisher of
The Pittsburgh *Courier*, a newspaper with a
wide circulation among Negroes; practiced
law in Pittsburgh; from 1917 to 1921 Assistant City Solicitor of Pittsburgh and
from 1933 to 1936 Special Assistant Attorney General of the United States in Pittsburgh; gave up law in 1936 to devote entire
time to newspaper, which he had edited
since 1912; active Republican until 1932, national director of Negro publicity in campaigns
of Harding and Coolidge and first campaign
of Hoover; supported Franklin D. Roosevelt in 1932 and 1936 and was delegate-at-
large to Democratic National Convention in
1936; recently had been conducting campaign for equal participation by Negroes
in defense program

References

Who's Who in Colored America

Obituaries

N Y Herald Tribune p20 O 25 '40

VARGAS, GETULIO DORNELLAS (vär'-
gȧsh zhĕ-tōō'yōō) Apr 19, 1882- President
of Brazil

Address: Rio de Janeiro, Brazil, South America

On June 11, 1940 President Getulio Vargas
of Brazil made a speech, the reverberations
of which rolled around the world. He said
in it: "Virile people must follow the line
of their aspirations instead of standing still
and gazing at a structure that is crumbling
down. . . . There is no longer a place
for régimes founded on privilege and
distinction; only those subsist which incorporate all the nation in the same duties
and offer social justice and opportunities in
the fight for equality."

Immediately, United States' reaction was
that Vargas had aligned himself "morally"
with Mussolini; that Brazil was, more than
ever, a totalitarian state with pro-Nazi, pro-
Fascist sympathies. Germany was quick
to remark about the speech: "It is not acci-
dental that those valiant words were announced by the chief of one of the greatest
and most advanced American nations." But
the Brazilian government issued a formal
statement insisting that the speech referred
only to Brazil's internal life ("it was addressed to Brazilians and those who feel
that Brazil is their own country") and that
Brazil's foreign policy was based on "full
Pan-American solidarity and common defense of the Western Hemisphere against
any attacks from the outside."

Secretary of State Cordell Hull (see sketch
this issue) backed this up, for his reaction
to the speech was that relations between
the United States and Brazil "have never
been more intimate, whole-hearted, understanding, friendly and cooperative than now."
This is a state of affairs the United States
has been working hard to achieve, for our

interest in Brazil has been to counteract
the economic and political influence of Nazi
Germany there. With the recent successes
of Hitler in Europe, "the Nazi cause in
South America has been tremendously
strengthened" and our task has become a
more complicated and difficult one.

The consensus of opinion here is that
although Nazi ideology and Nazi forms
play a part in Brazilian government, nevertheless this government is "following a
distinctly nationalistic policy." Vargas, according to many commentators, wants merely
to build up a strong Brazil "and will play
ball with the side most likely to realize that
ambition for him." Symbolical of his attitude is the fact that he sent one son to Germany and Italy for his education and another to the United States; that his Foreign
Minister, Oswaldo Aranha, is pro-Democratic
and pro-Ally, while his War and Marine
Ministers are pro-Nazi. "Vargas, the dictator of Brazil for 10 years, is playing the
rôle of a man walking a tight rope with
democracy on one end and dictatorship of
vague promise on the other."

For 10 years Getulio Vargas, a "mild
appearing, soft-spoken, gentle little man,"
has been supreme dictator over 44 millions
of South America's 88 million population,
over a territory larger than the United
States. Of Spanish ancestry, he was born
in the prairie town of São Borja in the
state of Rio Grande do Sul, the son of
Candida Dornellas Vargas and of General
Manoel do Nascimento Vargas, who played
a distinguished part in the overthrow of
the monarchy and the establishment of
the Republic in 1889. Young Vargas
attended the Brazilian school of Porto Alegre
and the Military School of Rio Pardo in
his home state and was graduated from it
with distinction in 1900.

From 1903 to 1907 he was a law student
in Porto Alegre and in 1907 received the
degree of Bachelor of Juridical and Social
Sciences. He began to practice law in São
Borja and in 1909 was made a Deputy for
the state of Rio Grande do Sul. Immediately he became a leader of the Republican
Party but refused re-election in 1911 because
he wanted to devote himself to his law
practice. It wasn't until 1919 that he ran
for State Deputy again. Once in the State
Legislature, he became a member of its
budget committee and in 1922 president of
its committee on ways and means.

Vargas organized the Seventh Provisional
Corps which defended the legal government
in the revolutionary movement of 1923 and
shortly after was elected Federal Deputy
from the state of Rio Grande do Sul. In
the Federal House of Deputies he distinguished himself by his legal writings and
opinions and was one of a committee of 21
appointed to revise the Constitution in 1926.
In that same year he was made Minister of
Finance.

In 1927 Vargas was "unanimously" elected
President of his state of Rio Grande do Sul

and his political shrewdness was immediately apparent. His native state had been for years a battleground for opposing political factions. To these he came as a peacemaker —already one of the smartest politicians in South America.

In 1930 Vargas ran for President of Brazil, as the candidate of the Liberal opposition, against Julio Prestes, the administration candidate. He ran as a friend of the people, building his campaign on a fight against "the plutocratic coffee barons" of the São Paulo. He was badly defeated, but instead of accepting the defeat or charging that the ballot boxes had been stuffed or that the election had been dishonest, he got together a few of his friends and quietly took over the country. In October 1930 he was named provisional President by a junta of army and naval officers. His revolution had personified a popular reaction to the misdeeds of a political caste which had come to dominate the country like feudal magnates, but when Vargas took power the result was not quite what the nation had expected.

The time-honored Republican constitution of 1891 was abrogated and, for the alleged purpose of maintaining law and order, dictatorship was declared, Congress was dissolved, civil rights suspended and Vargas' own appointees put into state offices. In 1932 the state of São Paulo led a revolt with the objective of restoring the constitution, but the revolt was crushed. Still, Vargas saw it would be necessary to have a constitution of some sort and so summoned a Constituent Assembly in 1933, securing a majority by "carefully selected processes."

A constitution was finally adopted on July 16, 1934 and under it Vargas was elected President for four years. One Brazilian said that this constitution "witn its Bolshevist, Fascist, Syndicalist and Clerical ideas" was "an absolutely indigestible fruit salad." Shortly after it was adopted Vargas discovered a "Communist plot" against the government, declared martial law—and continued martial law.

Under it Vargas did something to improve conditions in Brazil. He established minimum wages, restricted immigration, set up an eight-hour, six-day-week, encouraged the extension of manufacturing, abolished internal tariff duties, tried to improve the prices of sugar, coffee and other basic products, reformed the schools to some extent and improved the utilities. In fact, it has been said that President Vargas "has shown unusual diligence in working to improve the condition of his country." In 1940 he has been very active working out plans to develop the rich resources of the Amazon Valley and to expand Brazil's rubber industry. On the other hand, however, 80 per cent of his country is illiterate and according to most commentators exploited—Carleton Beals calls it "a brutal slave system."

Under the constitution a Presidential election for Brazil was set for January 1938.

Wide World

GETULIO VARGAS

On November 10, 1937, using the economic situation and political unrest as an excuse, Vargas canceled the election, set aside the constitution and proclaimed a "corporative" one to be approved by plebiscite. The plebiscite was never held.

This *coup d'état* merely ended the fiction that Brazil was a free republic. Actually, since he first seized power in October 1930 Vargas "had been paramount in Brazil." Now he became "a dictator with more absolute power in Brazil than Mussolini in Italy or Stalin in Russia." The 1937 constitution began with the words: "Political power emanates from the people," but ended with "a state of emergency is declared throughout the country." It abolished the parliament, replaced it with "two impotent handpicked, consultative bodies" which Vargas could dismiss or jail. It established Vargas' complete control over "written communications and the spoken word," his power to make treaties valid without recognition and his power to nominate his successor after his six-year term is up.

Shortly after it was declared that "movements of political thought directed or oriented by private persons cannot be tolerated," and all political parties, domestic and foreign, were abolished, as well as all brown shirt and black shirt uniforms, swastika flags, insignias and Nazi and Fascist salutes. The only exception was the green shirt Integralist Party which had helped Vargas to power. At the same time Vargas decreed nationalization of a large number of German, Italian and Japanese private schools and forbade them to receive subsidies from their governments, to engage in political propaganda, to fly or to salute foreign flags. Vargas also established military posts of non-German troops in southern Brazil and

VARGAS, GETULIO—*Continued*

ruled, recently, that the pilots of domestic airlines must be native Brazilians. Nevertheless, he continued to allow and encourage economic ties with Germany, he bought many arms from her and continued to allow Germans to own dye works, paint plants, machine factories and to run retail establishments in Brazil.

When the Integralists, irked by the government's failure to respond fully to Nazi and Fascist influence tried a *Putsch* on May 11, 1938 they were defeated, the Green Shirts were put in jail by the hundreds and they were ordered disbanded except for cultural purposes. In the *Putsch* the Presidential palace was attacked and Vargas, armed with a pistol, moved from window to window sniping at the rebels until rescuers came.

Vargas was now free of threats from the Right. In April 1940 he freed himself from threats from the Left. The chiefs of the Brazilian Communist Party—about 200 of them—were captured, their newspaper was shut down, documents were seized and the Party dissolved.

Vargas is complete master, though his power, some think, is not endorsed by the masses and so rests on a shaky foundation. The states nominally have Governors, but the ruling is actually done by "Federal interventors" who work "always with both ears glued to the Palace in Rio." A national propaganda bureau tells the newspapers what to print; there is no free speech; there is an efficient secret police which taps telephone wires and snoops about. And all this is supported by the army, which, paid well and well-treated, is strongly behind Vargas.

There is a saying in Brazil that this "swarthy, stocky, little" dictator is so clever he can take off his socks without removing his shoes. He has been clever in always seeming more able and plausible than most dictators. "He isn't given to casual shooting or hanging and he says very little and this in a low voice, never in a sports palast or on a balcony." Conciliatory of manner, quick to forgive and forget, Vargas "goes about running Brazil with old Portuguese courtesy."

Vargas is happily married to Darcy Sarmanho and has a large family of children. His tastes are simple—his hobbies are walking and going to the movies. Sometimes he has private film showings or with a friend or two goes to the nearest movie house, scorning a bodyguard, to enjoy the excitement of a wild West picture.

References

Bul Pan Am Union 68:693-4 O '34 por
Christian Sci Mon Mag p3+ D 1 '37 il por
Collier's 103:24+ Ja 28 '39 por
Lit Digest 121:39 Ap 4 '36; 122:15-16 S 26 '36; 124:10-11 N 27 '37

Nation 145:528-9 N 13 '37
N Y Times p1, 8 Je 12 '40 por; p6 Je 13 '40; p20 Je 14 '40; p29 Je 16 '40; p18 Je 30 '40; p10 Jl 1 '40
Newsweek 2:14 N 25 '33; 10:19-21 N 22 '37 il; 11:13 My 23 '38 il por; 15:28 Je 24 '40
Time 35:45 Ja 15 '40 por; 35:32+ Je 24 '40 por; 36:18-20 Ag 12 '40 por (cover); 36:34-8 N 4 '40

International Who's Who
Who's Who in Latin America

VASSALLO, ERNESTO 1875—May 6, 1940 Under-secretary of Foreign Affairs in Mussolini's Cabinet; Senator; former Catholic deputy who was expelled from the Catholic Party and became an adherent of the Fascist Party in 1923

References

Chi è? 1936
International Who's Who

Obituaries

N Y Times p23 My 8 '40

VERDIER, JEAN, CARDINAL Feb 19, 1864—Apr 9, 1940 Archbishop of Paris since 1929; taught at Sulpician Seminary for 40 years; advocate of democracy and a foe of dictators; championed the cause of the oppressed

CARDINAL VERDIER

References

Cath World 130:363-4 D '29
Commonweal 11:185 D 18 '29
N Y Times p43 S 17 '39; p6 F 7 '40
International Who's Who

Obituaries

Illustration 205:389-91 Ap 20 '40 il
  pors
Manchester Guardian p12 Ap 10 '40
N Y Herald Tribune p28 Ap 10 '40
  por
N Y Times p23 Ap 9 '40

VIERECK, GEORGE SYLVESTER Dec 31, 1884- Journalist; poet
Address: 305 Riverside Drive, New York City

During the First World War George Sylvester Viereck was a staunch partisan of Germany, vilified, expelled from professional associations. He is just as staunch a partisan of Germany today, and the same hue and cry against him has been raised. Accused of spreading pro-Nazi propaganda, of furthering Germany's interests, Mr. Viereck issued a strong denial. "I am a poet, a journalist, I have even mixed in politics in a small way," he said, "but I am not a propagandist."

Actually, there doesn't seem much doubt that he is. In 1934, before a group investigating Nazi propaganda he admitted that an American publicity firm was paying him $1,750 a month for swinging a contract with German interests to that firm and that he had received $2,000 from the German Consul in New York for services "concerning the general aspects of public relations." Today he is registered in Washington as the American correspondent of the *Münchner Neuste Nachrichten*, a German newspaper.

According to *PM*, Viereck is employed by the German Library of Information, his job to prepare news for *Facts in Review*, "official Hitler upper level propaganda organ, to hold himself at all times for consultation on Nazi propaganda problems in the United States and to interpret the news to favor Germany." What he says about Nazi Germany is made to seem, according to *PM*, "superficially harmless, legal, even praiseworthy, to millions of Americans." For instance, in an article in *Nation's Business*, Viereck points out that although he doesn't suggest that we imitate the systems of government of the totalitarian countries, still they have many things we might well adopt—things such as the strength through joy movement, athletic facilities, parks, etc. And he himself has admitted: "Behind the scenes I do all I can to better relations between Germany and the United States."

George Sylvester Viereck, poet, author, journalist, propagandist and naturalized American, was born in Munich, Germany. His maternal grandfather, William Viereck, emigrated from Germany to the United States in 1848 and went to San Francisco, where he was a journalist and where he founded the German Theatre. His daughter Laura returned to Germany and married her first cousin, Louis, a son of Edwina Viereck, the famous German actress. Louis Viereck, George Sylvester's father, was a

GEORGE SYLVESTER VIERECK

Socialist member of the Reichstag whose political activities got him into difficulties, and after a term in prison he came to New York. His wife and son followed a year later.

George was 11 when he arrived in New York and had already attended school in Munich and a Gymnasium in Berlin. In New York he went to public school and later to the College of the City of New York, from which he was graduated in 1906. In college he was the class poet and on the staff of the college papers, but steadily flunked or squeezed through physics, mathematics, geometry and the sciences. There was one examination he passed by writing a scornful sonnet against the subject in question.

Viereck's first job on *Current Opinion* was obtained for him by the late John H. Finley (see sketch this issue), then president of City College, and he stayed with this magazine until 1915. In 1912, however, he began to edit *International* and in 1914 *Fatherland*, the name of which was later changed to the *American Monthly* and which was published until 1927. *Fatherland* was undoubtedly a pro-German magazine and when Viereck printed in it (1917) one of his own poems, *William II, Prince of Peace*, with the line, "For if thou fail a world shall fall," the fireworks began. Immediately the Authors' League and the Poetry Society of America expelled him. When to this expulsion was added the charge that he was receiving money from the German government, a mob threatened to lynch him and stormed his house in Mount Vernon, New York. Viereck left his wife, Margaret Edith Hein (whom he had married in 1915), and escaped to New York City, there to hide out in a hotel. Persecution of himself and his family continued—they used to call

VIERECK, GEORGE SYLVESTER—
Continued

him things like "venom-bloated toad of treason."

The uproar was the greater because Viereck was well-known as a poet and author. His first book of poems, *Nineveh*, had appeared in 1907 and was followed by others, and in 1911 Viereck was the first exchange lecturer on American poetry at the University of Berlin. The poems he wrote in those years and continued to write— the latest, *My Flesh and Blood*, "a lyric autobiography with indiscreet annotations" (1931) —called forth an extraordinary amount of favorable criticism. Richard Le Gallienne once called him "a poet of original mind and an exceptionally forcible and magnetic literary gift," and Frank Harris went so far as to term him "the most distinguished poet in America." Viereck himself points out that "few poets have met with more instant recognition than I . . . I have given a new lyric impetus to my country." Also he informs us, "I am perhaps the only American poet whose book of lyric verse has made money for himself and his publishers."

In the years since the First World War Viereck has continued as a journalist and author, sometimes using George Four Corners as a pseudonym. One of his many books and the one that has in recent years roused much comment was *My First 2000 Years* (1929), written in collaboration with Paul Eldridge. This book, its hero the Wandering Jew, was confiscated and burned in Nazi Germany in 1934. But Viereck, who states "I have always liked the Jews," said that was "entirely logical." "What," he asked, "is the fate of a book compared to the fate of a nation? Although I have warmly defended National Socialist Germany, I do not accept its anti-Semitic doctrine. Why should National Socialist Germany accept my Wandering Jew?"

Another of Viereck's books that caused a stir was *Spreading Germs of Hate* (1931), published with a foreword by Colonel Edward House. This study of propaganda was discovered to be "straightforward and objective," and called "the most effective history of war propaganda yet written and one of the most valuable antidotes for war hysteria." His two latest books are *The Kaiser on Trial* (1937) and *The Temptation of Jonathan* (1938).

George Sylvester Viereck is a "slim, blond man who looks 10 years younger than his age. . . His gray eyes seem small behind horn-rimmed glasses and he is given to restless gestures. He is almost oppressively neat in his dress." On the walls of his study in his 10-room, $3,500-a-year apartment hangs a surprising collection of photographs—Kaiser Wilhelm, Hitler, Goebbels, Freud and Albert Einstein. He explains it by saying: "All these people I have known and admired."

References

Nation 138:460 Ap 25 '34
Nation's Business 26:18-21+ Ap '38
New Yorker 16:15-6 Je 15 '40
Newsweek 12:11 Ag 15 '38 por
PM p8 Ag 13 '40
Viereck, G. S. My Flesh and Blood 1931
Who's Who in America

VILLARD, OSWALD GARRISON
(vĭl-lard') Mar 13, 1872- Journalist
Address: h. Thomaston, Connecticut

On June 29, 1940 Oswald Garrison Villard's valedictory to *The Nation* was published nearly 47 years after his first contribution appeared in that magazine. His retirement was precipitated he says, "by the editors' abandonment of *The Nation's* steadfast opposition to all preparations for war, to universal military service, to a great navy, and to *all* war, for this in my judgment has been the chief glory of its great and honorable past."

In the 47 years that Oswald Garrison Villard has been associated with *The Nation* he has fought for peace, he has fought for civil liberties, he has fought for the rights of the underprivileged. His platform has been "to be opposed to war, to hold no hate for any people; to be determined to champion a better world; to believe in the equality of all men and women; and to be opposed to all tyrants and all suppression of liberty of conscience and beliefs."

A list of the causes for which Villard battled covers most of the major controversies of the late nineteenth and of the twentieth centuries. He worked to improve the status of the Negro and was one of the founders of the National Association for the Advancement of Colored People; he lifted his voice for the emancipation of women; he struggled to keep America out of the Spanish-American War; he fought long and hard to keep America out of the First World War and later sought to secure just treatment of Germany; he battled for the conscientious objectors in that War and for the victims of the Espionage Act and Palmer's Red Raids; always he attacked tariffs, trusts, Wall Street, corrupt politics. Today he is again fighting to keep America at peace.

More often than not Villard was fighting a lost cause—one commentator said that "Villard had a genius for choosing the unpopular side of every issue." More often than not it cost him dearly to fight it. To some there has always been a touch of the dilettante reformer about him—he is "the aristocrat of liberalism." To others he has been a surviving voice of an "old-fashioned democratic liberalism, a genuine liberalism which they feel can alone preserve democracy through the ominous and regimented years ahead." But this liberalism to which Villard has been devoted has also been called "an inadequate weapon, for pacificism and passivism are not enough," and Max Lerner says that hard as he fought, Villard had "no clear outlines of a conception of social causation, a theory of history, a program of action."

Most of Villard's outspoken liberalism appeared in *The Nation,* which he received from his father, Henry Villard. Henry Villard came to America as a refugee from Germany unable to speak a word of English. Within five years he was reporting the Lincoln-Douglas debates. He became one of Horace Greeley's bright young men on the New York *Tribune,* explored the West and married the daughter of the famous abolitionist, William Lloyd Garrison.

Within thirteen years Henry Villard had become president of the Oregon Railway and Navigation Company and two years later of the Northern Pacific Railroad which he completed in 1883. He and his wife gave their son Oswald, born in Wiesbaden, Germany, a legacy "compounded of New England abolitionism, the German Revolution of '48 and Northern Pacific Railroad shares."

Oswald Garrison Villard's was a "boyhood of wonder and hope," made up of New York in the '80s, country life at Dobbs Ferry, trips across the wild West on the Northern Pacific, journeys to Europe and Harvard from which he received his B. A. in 1893 and his M. A. in 1896, and at which he was an assistant in the history department from 1894 to 1896. From Harvard young Villard went to Philadelphia where he spent half a year as reporter for the Philadelphia *Press.* From there he went, in 1897, to the New York *Evening Post* which his father had bought, together with *The Nation* which thereafter served as its weekly literary supplement, in 1881.

As editorial writer and president of the *Post,* Villard had "a sharp nose for news and an extraordinary talent, amounting almost to genius, for presenting it in a manner that would attract attention in places of power." He and his paper came out strongly against the Spanish-American War and played a large part in uncovering the insurance scandals and corruption in the New York legislature. "Single handed he drove Senator Allds, acting Lieutenant Governor of the state, out of public office." He and his paper came out strongly for Wilson. Villard who was an early admirer of Wilson, also supported him for the Governorship of New Jersey and in 1912 and in 1916 for the Presidency. When Wilson was nominated Villard said "my joy was greater than that I have ever felt over any political happening."

In Wilson, Villard saw the best promise of the liberal spirit and in Wilson, Villard found his greatest disillusionment. "I have long since come to believe," he said once, "that it would have been better for the country had Champ Clark been nominated." Always a strong pacifist, Villard fought

OSWALD GARRISON VILLARD

against our entrance into the War and as late as 1921 had to be smuggled out of Cincinnati by the police after a speaking engagement before the American Legion of the town could get him. His wife, Julia Breckinridge Sandford, whom he married in 1903, and his children suffered all the discomforts of ostracism.

A staunch independent like Villard, running a staunchly independent paper like the New York *Evening Post,* making no concessions to the popular mood of the moment, had a hard row to hoe. By July 1918 Villard had sold the *Post,* while retaining *The Nation* which he edited and owned until 1932.

The Nation under Villard in the 1920's was avowedly and outspokenly a fighting, muckraking magazine. Villard wrote then: "I had the complete satisfaction of molding a historic journal according to my exact wishes and beliefs." After the War *The Nation* worked at getting the Allies out of Russia; it called for a just peace of reconciliation and for tolerance and fair play. Villard dashed into Germany in 1919 and furnished his magazine with evidence of starvation under the blockade; it denounced the Versailles Treaty; it urged the freedom of Eire. This was called "treason" and "Bolshevism" by many and there were batches of cancellations from "grieved and scandalized oldest subscribers."

Villard's financial and intellectual independence made him a thorn in the side of other journals. The *Times* and the *Tribune* "pursued him with inveterate hate," and the *Times* went so far as to describe *The Nation* as "if not actually Bolshevik, so near it that the distinction is not visible to the naked eye." Villard was unperturbed. He continued his "infectious moral

VILLARD, OSWALD G.—*Continued*

indignation," and his paper had then, and continued to have, a power far beyond its circulation.

In 1932 he and others contributed to *The Nation's* support and in 1935 it was sold. But from 1933 until June 1940 each week, "in sickness or health, whether I was here or in Europe," Villard's *Issues and Men,* was a weekly feature of the journal.

During these years of editorship Villard wrote a number of books, three of them about Germany. *Germany Embattled* appeared in 1915; *The German Phoenix* in 1933 and in 1940 he wrote *Within Germany,* a firsthand account of conditions under Hitler in which he pulled no punches. He has written *John Brown, 1800-1859: a Biography Fifty Years After* (1910); *Some Newspapers and Newspaper-men* (1923); *Prophets True and False* (1928). In 1939 two books by him appeared: *Our Military Chaos,* a sharp criticism of our defense policy, and *Fighting Years,* a personal narrative and a record of contemporary history, a "brave, fine story," which has been compared by some with Lincoln Steffens' *Autobiography.* In it is a record of his life as a fighting liberal; in it is his philosophy. And part of his philosophy is this: "I have never been able to work happily with men or women who are incapable of hot indignation at something or other—whether small or big, whether it stirred me personally or not, if only it was *something.*"

References

    Am Mercury 47:240-1 Je '39
    Christian Cent 56:546 Ap 26 '39
    Nation 148:437-8 Ap 15 '39; 150:155-8 F 10 '40; 150:782 Je 29 '40; 151:58+ Jl 20 '40; 151:80 Jl 27 '40
    New Repub 98:342-4 Ap 26 '39
    N Y Times Book R p1 Ap 30 '39
    Newsweek 5:32 My 4 '35
    Survey G 29:24 Ja '40 por
    Time 35:28 Ja 29 '40

    Lerner, M. Liberalism of O. G. Villard *In* Ideas Are Weapons p178-85 1939
    Villard, O. G. Fighting Years 1939
    Who's Who Among North American Authors
    Who's Who in America

VOLTERRA, VITO (vôl-tĕr'rä) 1860—Oct 11, 1940 Italian professor and Senator; in 1883, at age of 23, became professor of physics and mechanics at Pisa University and later went to Turin University and in 1900 to the University of Rome; though a Senator, had not entered the Senate chamber since 1931, when he refused to take oath of allegiance to the Fascist régime imposed on scholars by the government; dismissed from University of Rome but invited later by Pope Pius XI to join the Papal Academy, where he was one of the few Jews serving as a member; taught in the United States at Princeton, Clarke University and the Universities of Illinois, California and Chicago; during First World War directed Italian Bureau of Inventions; former president of the International Committee of Weights and Measures and former head of Accademia dei Lincei and the National Research Council

References

    Chi è?
    International Who's Who

Obituaries

    N Y Herald Tribune p12 O 12 '40

VON ARCO, GEORG WILHELM ALEXANDER HANS, GRAF *See* Arco, G. W. A. H., Graf von

VON BRAUCHITSCH, HEINRICH ALFRED HERMANN WALTHER *See* Brauchitsch, H. A. H. W. von

VON HEIDENSTAM, KARL GUSTAF VERNER *See* Heidenstam, V. von

VON KEITEL, WILHELM *See* Keitel, W. von

VON MANNERHEIM, CARL GUSTAF EMIL, BARON *See* Mannerheim, C. G. E., Baron von

VON WAGNER-JAUREGG, JULIUS *See* Wagner-Jauregg, J. von

WADIYAR, SRI KRISHNARAJA, BAHADUR MAHARAJA of MYSORE (väd'yär srē krĭsh-nä-rä'yä) June 4, 1884—Aug

SRI KRISHNARAJA WADIYAR

3, 1940 Indian ruler of a native state whose title was Maharaja of Mysore; one of the wealthiest men in the world, with a personal fortune estimated at $400,000,000; ruler of more than 6,500,000 persons; was renowned for his lavish entertaining of European and American friends; considered a man of culture who introduced far-reaching reforms in government; in 1927 celebrated his silver jubilee

References

Gt Brit & East 47:45 Jl 9 '36 por
International Who's Who (under Mysore)
Who's Who (under Mysore)

Obituaries

N Y Herald Tribune p28 Ag 4 '40 il por
N Y Times p33 Ag 4 '40 por
Time 36:62 Ag 12 '40

WAGNER-JAUREGG, JULIUS VON (väg'nûr-you'rĕg yo͞ol'yo͞os) Mar 7, 1857— Oct 1, 1940 Viennese physician and professor who gained international fame and won a Nobel Prize in 1927 for his work in the use of malaria and other artificially induced fevers in treating syphilitic paralysis: honored in 1937 with an award of $1,000 and a medal in the United States for syphilis research; was noted for his method of treating cretinism with thyroid gland preparations and for treating goiter with iodine; made notable researches in the field of sleeping sickness

References

Forum 88:225-30 O '32 por
Good H 100:46-7+ F '35 por
Sci Mo 26:190-2 F '28 por; 44:483-6 My '37 por
De Kruif, P. H. Wagner-Jauregg: the Friendly Fever *In* Men Against Death p249-79 1932
International Who's Who

Obituaries

N Y Herald Tribune p22 O 1 '40 por
N Y Times p23 O 1 '40 por

WALD, LILLIAN D. Mar 10, 1867—Sept 2, 1940 Founder of the Henry Street Settlement House in New York City's lower East Side; organizer of the first non-sectarian public health nursing system in the world; won international fame as social worker and nurse among the poor; wrote several books on the Henry Street Settlement which became classics in their field; raised fabulous sums to improve the organization; noted as militant liberal; supported woman suffrage and pacifism during the First World War; received gold medals from the National Institute of Social Sciences, the Rotary Club and the Better Times organization

LILLIAN D. WALD

References

Forum 96:70-3 Ag '36
Lit Digest 121:34 F 1 '36 por
New Repub 97:152-3 D 7 '38
Scholastic 28:23 F 22 '36 por
Survey G 26:22-3 Ap '37 por
American Women
Duffus, R. L. Lillian Wald, Neighbor and Crusader 1939
Gillis, A. and Ketchum, R. Lillian D. Wald: Healer in the Slums *In* Our America p219-33 1936
Who's Who in America
Who's Who in American Jewry

Obituaries

N Y Herald Tribune p1, 14 S 2 '40; p20 S 3 '40 por
N Y Times p15 S 2 '40 por
Newsweek 16:6 S 9 '40
Time 36:38 S 9 '40

WALES, GEORGE CANNING Dec 23, 1868—Mar 21, 1940 Etcher and lithographer; specialist in old square-rigged ships since 1917; contributor of prints to museums in the United States and abroad

References

Who's Who in America 1938-39
Who's Who in American Art 1938-39

Obituaries

N Y Herald Tribune p18 Mr 22 '40

WALKER, FRANK COMERFORD May 30, 1886- Newly appointed United States Postmaster General

Address: b. Post Office Building, Washington, D. C.; h. 1035 Fifth Ave, New York City

"Quiet, diffident" Frank Walker, who in December 1935 resigned his position as

FRANK C. WALKER

works-relief chief to return to private life, is the man appointed by President Roosevelt to succeed Postmaster General James A. Farley. The announcement came as a "surprise" at the annual meeting of the Franklin D. Roosevelt Club at Hyde Park on August 31, 1940, although actually Mr. Walker has been mentioned for years as Mr. Farley's probable successor. Said President Roosevelt of his old friend: "He came from Montana and lived in New York and then, because of his interests, became a citizen of Pennsylvania, which is a pretty good record. In other words, he knows the country and is going to know a lot about the mails and communications of the country from now on."

Frank Walker, together with James Farley and Edward Flynn (see sketch this issue), has for a long time been a member of a triumvirate both personally and politically intimate with the President. Up to this time, however, his Washington service has been intermittent: he has been virtually drafted to the important posts which he has held under the New Deal, and has left them "as expeditiously as possible." One of the wealthiest men in the New Deal, a Roman Catholic who for years has been active in Roman Catholic charities, Mr. Walker is vice-president and general counsel of the Comerford Theatres, Incorporated, the Meco Realty Company and the Comerford-Publix Corporation. The conservative New York *Times* greeted his appointment with approval, finding him a "cool-headed pioneer" in the New Deal who nevertheless "has no share in the fads and fanaticisms of some of its acolytes."

He was born in Plymouth, Pennsylvania on May 30, 1886, the son of David and Ellen (Comerford) Walker. He was only three when his family moved to Montana,

however, and it was in Butte that he grew up. At one time during his boyhood he was hired as a grocer's delivery boy, and the story goes that his only fault was that he could never make the horse back up! After attending Gonzaga University at Spokane, Washington from 1903 to 1906, young Walker went to Notre Dame's Law School, starred in its debating society, acquired his LL. B. in 1909 and was admitted to the Montana Bar the same year.

Six months after Walker had hung out his shingle in Butte he ran for assistant district attorney of Silver Bay County, was elected and held the office from 1909 to 1912. In 1913 he was elected to the Montana legislature and the following year married Hallie Boucher of Butte and became a member of the firm of Walker and Walker. (His older brother, State Senator Thomas J. Walker, was also an attorney.) Soon he acquired an imposing list of clients, among them the late John D. Ryan, head of the Anaconda Copper Company, whose chief aide he became. His law practice was interrupted only by service as first lieutenant in the army during the First World War.

In 1920 Mr. Walker had first encountered Franklin Delano Roosevelt, when as the head of a local committee he received the Democratic Vice-Presidential candidate. In 1925 he came to New York City with his wife and two children, Thomas and Laura, to be general counsel and manager of Comerford Theatres, Incorporated, a chain of movie houses in New York and Pennsylvania owned by his uncle. There he met Roosevelt once more, became a Roosevelt booster and in 1928 contributed $10,000 to his re-election as Governor of New York. One of the inner circle of friends and advisers even before the 1932 Democratic nominating convention, Walker was one of three raisers of a pre-convention fund to promote the Roosevelt boom, once more contributing $10,000 himself. He helped to organize the Northwest for Roosevelt, and in 1932 served as treasurer of the Democratic National Committee. He was so retiring, however, that no one seemed to know quite who he was, and at Chicago the local press had him spotted as a hired field agent.

With Roosevelt's election it was well-known that Frank Walker could have had any government position he wanted except a Cabinet post. And although he showed no desire for office high or low, in July 1933 Roosevelt made him executive secretary of the Executive Council set up on his arrival in the White House—sometimes known as the "Super Cabinet." As such Walker was known as the coordinator, "the central point of contact with the Cabinet and the new recovery agencies." It was his duty to decide questions of "function, jurisdiction, duplication and administration." Liberals thought of him as an "enlightened conservative," conservatives thought of him as a sort of brakeman who would keep one eye on excesses and almost everybody thought of him as "Assistant President."

Then in December 1933 Walker was given an even more important coordinating position: head of the National Emergency Council. Said the London *Evening Standard*: "He will be more powerful than any Cabinet Minister. His real function will be that of Lord High Coordinator." Codes needed to be coordinated; information furnished; Consumers' Councils set up all over the country; the Central Statistical Board created. But the authority that had actually been delegated to Mr. Walker was very vague, and he resigned some time later, perhaps "somewhat discouraged by his inability to coordinate the various governmental agencies" and also anxious to return to private life. He had been commuting from New York to Washington for a stay of three or four days each week, devoting the rest of his time to the theatre business.

It seemed that his services were indispensable, however. He and his wife were in Atlantic City in April 1935 when he was called to Washington unexpectedly again— this time to serve as head of the Division of Application and Information of the $4,000,000,000 works relief program, a position no less important than those of Harold Ickes and Harry Hopkins. Colloquially he was sometimes known as Roosevelt's "fall guy," for it was his job to say "no" to all kinds of projects for spending the government's billions, picking out only the good ones. But in December 1935 personal affairs forced him to resign this post, too, though he promised to return when it was possible.

Mr. Walker has since been chairman of a committee that raised funds to establish the memorial library at President Roosevelt's Hyde Park estate which houses his personal papers, was one of a group of third-term strategists at the Chicago convention in July 1940 and has worked with the new Democratic National Chairman in helping to get him started in his new office.

"A chunky, round-headed, large-jowled man, Walker is as tight-lipped as an earthworm. . . He knows Big Business and Wall Street finance, and he knows how the average man feels about them, being more than inclined to share that opinion. . . Walker is a man of the Tom Walsh ('Teapot Dome' Walsh) type: tenacious, patient, and scrupulously honest." He can be seen cheering at prize fights and football games, but is as "phlegmatic as a Joffre in the face of trouble," never makes speeches, gives interviews nor holds press conferences, and probably goes by the slogan that no publicity is good publicity. Everyone agrees that he is an extremely able man for his new job.

References

Christian Sci Mon p2 S 3 '40 por
Collier's 96:26 Jl 6 '35 por
Lit Digest 120:6 D 28 '35 por
New Repub 82:365 My 8 '35
N Y Times p1+ S 1 '40
Newsweek 1:20 Jl 22 '33 por; 5:8-9 My 4 '35 por; 16:19 S 9 '40 por
R of Rs 92:13 Jl '35 por
Scholastic 26:21 My 25 '35 por
American Catholic Who's Who
Who's Who in America

WALL, EVANDER BERRY 1860—May 5, 1940 Leader in American colony of Paris called "fin de siècle dandy"; famous for his clothes; former New Yorker; one of the most colorful figures in France since the World War

Acme

BERRY WALL

References

Wall, E. B. Neither Pest Nor Puritan; Memoirs 1940

Obituaries

N Y Herald Tribune p14 My 6 '40 por
N Y Times p17 My 6 '40 por
Newsweek 15:8 My 13 '40 por
Time 36:90-2 S 16 '40 por

WALLACE, HENRY AGARD Oct 7, 1888- Vice-President-elect of the United States

Address: h. 3821 John Lynde Rd, Des Moines, Iowa

On November 5, 1940 former Secretary of Agriculture Henry Wallace was elected Vice-President of the United States. With President Roosevelt's backing he had won the Democratic nomination in July against a strong and vocal field. The lack of cheering demonstrations and the occasional boos when his name was presented to the Convention were not, most commentators agreed, directed against Wallace personally: some of the reaction was sectional; some of it strictly political. It was felt that he wouldn't add as much pulling power to the ticket as some of the

Acme

HENRY A. WALLACE

other Vice-Presidential possibilities, despite his farmer support.

The choice, however, was far from unexpected. Ever since 1933 Henry Wallace's name has cropped up from time to time as a Presidential possibility, and in 1937 Stanley High wrote: "A good many people believe that Henry Wallace is Mr. Roosevelt's heir apparent." They believed that because "no other department of the New Deal is so deeply indoctrinated with New Deal ideas or has so faithfully sought to make those ideas work" as Wallace's. They believed it because of Wallace's ardent support of the New Deal program beyond agriculture (his *America Must Choose*, 1934, is "a remarkably clear exposition of New Deal philosophy"). Today he is not Roosevelt's heir, but his partner, working with him in even closer harmony than he has for the past seven years. This was shown by the life of Mexico at the inauguration of Comacho (see sketch this issue), at which he represented the United States Government in an effort to establish the utmost friendliness between our country and its neighbor.

Henry Agard Wallace holds a position in the government today which his father, Henry Cantwell Wallace held before him, under Harding. His grandfather was a member of President Theodore Roosevelt's Country Life Commission. Henry Wallace I, was a United Presbyterian preacher who at the age of 60 launched the magazine, *Wallace's Farmer* with the masthead "Good Farming. Clear Thinking. Right Living." In his 80's he was "Uncle Henry" to half of Iowa, "the idol of prairie men throughout the West."

Henry Wallace II took over *Wallace's Farmer* when his father died and stayed with it until 1921 when he went as Secretary of Agriculture to Washington and "wore himself out in jurisdictional disputes with Hoover's Department of Commerce." He died in 1924. Henry III, like his father, was born in Iowa, on a farm in Adair County, the eldest of six children. He went to Iowa grade schools and to high school and then to Iowa State College where he majored in agriculture and from which he was graduated in 1910. While there he already demonstrated his "painfully acquiring mind." When a corn judge picked out certain corn as producing the highest yields, Henry set to work and proved that this corn was not as high yielding as corn which was less attractive in appearance.

As soon as he left college Henry went to work on the staff of *Wallace's Farmer*. In 1914 he was married to Miss Ilo Browne of Indianola, Iowa whom he had met in college. While on his father's journal, Henry began to study prices and price trends and produced the first corn-hog ratio charts which indicated the probable course of the markets. Because of his studies, in 1919 he was able to predict the agricultural collapse of 1920 and to write *Agricultural Prices* (1920). In 1921, when his father went to Washington and the editorship of *Wallace's Farmer* was his responsibility, Henry began to hammer home to his thousands of farmer-readers the same policies of farm relief which his father was enunciating in the Capital, and after his father died he continued to hammer them home until he gave up *Wallace's Farmer* (in 1929 incorporated with the Iowa *Homestead*) when he came to Washington in 1933.

All this time he was leading the life of a practical agriculturist. He devised a system for forecasting corn yields on the basis of rainfall and temperature records and, most important, conducted experiments which succeeded in producing high yielding strains of corn. His experiments are now ranked among the four or five important contributions to genetics in the last twenty years, and for many years farmers throughout the Corn Belt have been using his strains of hybrid corn, distributed through the Hi-Bred Seed Company which he organized and of which he was president.

Like his father and grandfather, Henry Wallace was a Republican while editing *Wallace's Farmer,* but in 1928 he bolted to Al Smith because he thought he had "social vision." It was for the same reason that he supported Roosevelt in 1932 and "is credited with having been a major factor in swinging Iowa into the Roosevelt column on election day." He wasn't actually registered as a Democrat until 1936, however.

Henry Wallace, whose ambition as a child was "to make the world safe for corn breeders," was, because of his clear-cut farm policies and practical farming contributions, a "natural" for the position of Secretary of Agriculture. "A tall young man with a lantern jaw and a logical, scientific turn of mind," Henry came to Washington, "first and last a friend of the farmer." One of his earliest statements was: "This department will make good for the farmer or I will go back home and grow corn."

"With his hat tilted well back on a head of unruly reddish-brown hair, a folksy manner of speech and a general appearance of being constantly attired in his Sunday best, Henry Wallace looked for all the world like the dressed-up country jake of the Eastern school boy's imagination." People didn't think too much of him at first—to them he was "a corn-hog farmer from Iowa virtually without political experience and with little more influence."

But Wallace proceeded to evolve the Agricultural Adjustment Act—and both farmers and Washington politicians took sharp notice. He called together farm leaders and created a program to raise farm prices. When the Act went into effect it was praised as "the most farsighted and heaven-sent piece of remedial legislation ever conceived by the mind of man" and "damned as the most vicious class-ridden measure which ever saddled some people's burden on other people's backs."

Under Wallace's direction corn and cotton were ploughed under, pigs killed, crops controlled; farm prices rose and millions of checks poured into the farmers' pockets out of the Federal Treasury. He who had worked years to produce high-yielding corn now told the farmers why they must grow less. He traveled all over the country, explaining the AAA in terms of simple horse sense; he wrote articles and books. He broadcasted on *The Farm and Home Hour*; he held frequent conferences with farm leaders to get agreement on farm legislation; and he held referenda on governmental policy among the farmers themselves.

When the first AAA was declared unconstitutional Wallace rewrote the act as it now stands on the books. Its major objective is to stabilize farm income at satisfactory levels and to bring about a better division of this income among all farmers, this to be achieved mainly through soil conservation, the storage of reserves, the control of price and production. Wallace and his department of 67,490 people pioneered, too, in the problem of farm tenancy, "the first venture of the American government into the field of economic and social uplift for agriculture's downtrodden."

During the years since Wallace took office until he resigned in August 1940 to campaign for the Vice-Presidency the policies of his department have remained largely unchanged. In his latest report he stated firmly. "There is no question of going back to *laissez-faire*. For agriculture the program is simply to get the nearest approach to a permanent equitable farm adjustment with the least drawback in national disadvantage." Today when the world and world trade are in a difficult situation he believes that the government should be in a position to adopt rigid price controls, if necessary, to prevent collapse in markets.

With this program, most of the farmers and much of the country agree. But there is and always has been a strong opposition which believes, as stated in the New York *Times*, that this policy of pegging prices "has kept American crops off the world markets; it has stuffed warehouses... The Treasury has tied up or lost hundreds of millions of dollars through the policy, but it has still not prevented farm prices from falling."

Undeterred by criticism, Wallace has always gone ahead with "intense sincerity and burning idealism." One of his friends in commenting on his devotion to his ideals said: "What gripes me most of all about Henry is that you know he would cut off his hand for an abstract ideal, and cut off yours, too, just as readily." Somehow he seems to believe himself *called* to his mission in a way that the ordinary politician does not.

"One of the best writers in the New Deal" (his latest book is *The American Choice*, 1940), according to Arthur Krock, Henry Wallace relies heavily on a Biblical simplicity of style for his articles and many books. He is a deeply religious man, the Bible his most frequent source of quotation. He tells critics that "the Biblical record is heavily loaded on the side of the Progressive Independents," and he is supposed to have evolved his fundamental theory of the "ever normal granary" from the *Bible's* story of the lean years and the fat.

Wallace is one of the most widely read men in public life. Within one page of his writing, for instance, he can applaud observations by Pope Pius XI and Karl Marx. He "has an insatiable curiosity and one of the keenest minds in Washington, well-disciplined and subtle, with a range of interests and accomplishments from agrarian genetics to astronomy." He also likes to climb Pike's Peak.

According to Peggy Bacon (see sketch this issue) he "looks as if he were going somewhere on a bus, possibly to the fair, self-conscious, all dressed up and scrubbed, determined to behave, taking it all in and simply thrilled." He is a non-smoker and non-drinker and sometimes is seen at Washington parties gingerly holding the highball his host has given him, unwilling to hurt his feelings by refusing it.

In Washington Wallace lives a quiet life in a hotel with Mrs. Wallace and one of his two sons and daughter. The other son, now married, lives in Iowa. But he still keeps a farm in Iowa and still carries on experimental work there.

References
　Am Mag 118:36-7+ Jl '34 por
　Am Mercury 34:319-27 Mr '35
　Collier's 91:8-9+ Ap 1 '33 por; 92:18+
　　S 9 '33 por
　Cur Hist & Forum 52:10 D 24 '40
　Life 9:80-7 S 2 '40 il pors; 9:17-23
　　D 16 '40 il
　Lit Digest 117:8 Mr 3 '34; 117:29 My
　　26 '34 por
　Nation 140:535-8 My 8 '35

WALLACE, HENRY A.—*Continued*

No Am R 244 no2:284-302 [D] '37;
247 no 1:100-8 [Mr] '39
Sat Eve Post 210:5-7+ Jl 3 '37 por;
213:18-9+ N 24 '40 il pors
Sat R Lit 21:3-4+ Mr 30 '40 por
Time 32:12-14 D 19 '38 pors; 36:13-14
Jl 29 '40; 36:2 Ag 5 '40 por; 36:12-14
S 23 '40 por; 36:17 O 7 '40 por; 36:
14 N 25 '40 por
American Men of Science
Babson, R. W. "Young Henry" *In*
Washington and the Revolutionists
p156-68 1934
De Kruif, P. H. Maize Finders: An-
cient and Anonymous *In* Hunger
Fighters p169-93 1928
Unofficial Observer [pseud.] Fren-
zied Farming *In* New Dealers
p74-103 1934
Who's Who in America
Who's Who in the Nation's Capital

WALLENSTEIN, ALFRED (wäl-n-stīn')
Oct 7, 1898- Radio musical director; conductor; cellist

Address: 333 E 57th St, New York City

It is his "nose for music" that has enabled
Alfred Wallenstein, WOR's musical director and guest conductor during the season
of .1940 and 1941 of the NBC symphony orchestra to present new and original programs and to discover new talent. He has
won the approval of the radio audience by
playing the works not only of unknown composers, but those of the great masters which
have been allowed to fade into limbo.
During 1940 Wallenstein performed two
radio series that exemplify his love of
unknown, classical music. One was his
Sunday night concerts of the entire Bach
Cantata series which is relatively unknown
outside of Leipzig, and nowhere to be found
in this country in orchestrated form. The
other was the Mozart piano concerto series,
which Wallenstein performed in its entirety for the first time. Each Tuesday
night WOR brings to the air as part of its
weekly musical agenda concerts featuring
guest soloists accompanied by full symphony
orchestra.

Alfred Franz Wallenstein, the son of Franz
Albrecht and Anna (Klinger) von Wallenstein, was born in Chicago October 7, 1898.
Shortly after his birth, his family moved to
California. When he was eight years old his
father gave him a choice between a bicycle and
a cello; son Alfred (with a little persuasion on
the part of his father) chose the cello. Studying music with the mother of the composer
Ferde Grofé (see sketch this issue), he made
such remarkable progress that he became
known as a child prodigy and won a contract
to tour the country. He made his debut as a
cellist in Los Angeles in 1912.

In 1916 Wallenstein was invited to join
the San Francisco Symphony Orchestra—
on condition that he don long pants. The
following season the young cellist was en-

gaged by dancer Pavlova as her accompanist on her tour of Central and South
America. Then he studied with Klengel at
Leipzig; later he played with the Los Angeles Philharmonic. For seven years (1922-
29) he played in the Chicago Symphony
Orchestra as first cellist. In 1929 he came
to New York with his wife Virginia Wilson,
whom he had married in 1924, to play with
the Philharmonic as solo cellist under Arturo
Toscanini, and remained till 1936. He has
appeared as guest conductor with the Philadelphia Orchestra, Cleveland Symphony and
Los Angeles Philharmonic, and also has been
one of the principal conductors at the Hollywood Bowl. He has been active in radio work
since 1931, but it was not until 1935 that he
assumed the musical directorship of WOR.

Neither hackneyed programming nor
music that has already an assured acceptance
by the listening public are to be found on
Wallenstein's WOR programs. Tuning in
on any one of his programs, the listener is
almost certain to hear at least one piece of
music he has not heard before. But the
audience likes it—enjoys particularly the
seldom-heard symphonies of the great composers. Communications pour into the
studio, Wallenstein says, asking for the performances of whole symphonies and for the
music of Bach, Wagner, Debussy.

According to him, radio enables an enter-
prising conductor to go far in his field.
"Through radio you get a much more
symptomatic cross section of opinion than
you do by using the concert hall as a
medium." He quotes the responses to an
appeal for suggestions made in the hinterlands of Canada. There were requests for
the second symphony of Tschaikowsky, the
second of Mahler, Sacchini's *Oedipus Colon-
neus* overture and Scarlatti's *Ballad of Good-
humored Ladies.* A good many of these
selections had never previously been given
over the air.

Wallenstein likes nothing so much as to
present the work of a contemporary composer, especially if the musician happens to
be an American. Of American talent he has
this to say: "We have a large percentage
of excellent raw talent here waiting to be
utilized. And yet it is much harder for an
American artist to get a start in his own
country than it is for any foreigner. I
don't mean to be chauvinistic, mind you.
But we have been loath to make the most
of our native musical resources. One encouraging factor is that leading talented
composers are now looking to radio even
more than to orchestral associations for the
playing of their new works. During the
past year I examined more than 300 scores,
many showing great signs of promise. I do
not believe that orchestra societies receive
more than our average of 20 new compositions each week."

As a sample of what a typical day brings,
Wallenstein lists a viola concerto by George
Steiner, a composition by Rudolf Forst, a
Political Suite by Arcady Dunesky, and
Harlequin and Columbine by Robert Braine.

ALFRED WALLENSTEIN

An example of Wallenstein's interest in young talent is the case of 27-year-old Morton Gould. Wallenstein encouraged Gould to compose "American" symphonies, using musical idioms native to this country. Negro, Western and jazz expressions are to be found in his music; his works have been performed by Fritz Reiner, Leopold Stokowski and Eugene Ormandy; during the season of 1939 to 1940 the Pittsburgh Symphony offered the première performance of his composition written for that organization's celebration of the Stephen Foster centennial. Among the groups Wallenstein has encouraged are the *Song Spinners,* a troupe of four vocalists specializing in folk songs from the deep South, the plains and the hills.

Wallenstein hopes to do much to make radio a tool of unparalleled influence in shaping the cultural destinies of America. Under his direction, the Mutual Broadcasting System outlet now has a concert program every night in the week and since there are some 20 million radio homes in America, the potential audience for a young composer's new work is tremendous.

References

    Time 35:74 My 13 '40 por
    Woman's Home Companion 67:28+ N '40 il pors
    America's Young Men
    Thompson, O. ed. International Cyclopedia of Music and Musicians 1939
    Who's Who in America

WALN, NORA June 4, 1895- Author
Address: c/o Provident Trust Co, Philadelphia, Pennsylvania

In April 1938 Herr Hitler flatteringly ordered 35 copies of a book about China written by Nora Waln. And before Nora Waln left Germany she had finished her *Reaching for the Stars* (1939), a layman's observations on Nazi society. She mailed—each from different postal stations—her only three copies of the manuscript. None of these was ever delivered. Every word of the book had to be rewritten from notes.

In *Reaching for the Stars* she tried to portray impartially and from all sides Germany today and the German people. Troubled by what she saw of totalitarianism in action, she still believed in the real Germany, convinced that the philosophy of Hitler and the heart of the German people are two distinct things.

Nora Waln was born on June 4, 1895, at Grampian, Pennsylvania, the daughter of Thomas Lincoln Waln, descended from Nicholas Waln whose house appears in the first plan of the city of Philadelphia, and Lillia (Quest) Waln, one of whose forefathers was a signer of the Declaration of Independence.

When she was nine she discovered some 1805 issues of the *United States Gazette* in her grandmother's attic. The marine notices listed a number of brigs, sloops and schooners serving one J. S. Waln; Canton, China, became her "favorite port of purchase." She began to read Chinese philosophy, memorized analects from Confucius, collected maps, log-books and old letters and wrote a "sad ballad" about the Emperor.

She entered Swarthmore College with the class of 1919; and left on our entry into the War to conduct a newspaper page in Washington called *Woman's Work in the War.* For two years she was publicity director of the Near East Relief Committee, New York.

In 1920 she sailed for China, proceeding from Peking by sledge-boat to the *House of Exile,* the homestead of the Lins, an old family in Hopei Province, with whom the early Walns had been traders. On a brief return journey to America she met an Englishman, George Edward Osland-Hill, who was in the foreign service at Peking. With this "alarmingly self-assured" gentleman she soon found herself "most confusedly in love." Because she, a Quaker, had never been baptized, the Dean of the Cathedral of the Church of England (in Shanghai) at first threatened to refuse her the Christian sacrament of marriage. But he was directly won over. They were married in 1922.

With the rise of the Nationalists, anti-Westernism became unbearably tense at Canton. Nora Waln went to England in the fall of 1926, and when the Nationalists began to aim at control of Tientsin her husband cabled her not to return to China until there was some glimmer of safety. She stuck it out as long as she could in Italy, but on March 2 of the year following she boarded a German vessel bound for the Orient. At Manila word came to her that the Nationalist army had marched to the Yangtze almost without battle. She went eventually to

C. LeRoy Baldridge

NORA WALN

Tientsin, and here passed two years of "waiting for what might happen."

By May 1931 it was rumored that Nanking officials were demanding the surrender of all foreign concessions—those few square acres which had become oases during perpetual civil war—in China. Early in 1932 Nora Waln and her daughter Marie left Tientsin and by way of Nanking and Shanghai went on to Japan. She was on the high seas bound for America, however, when fighting began at Shanghai. And she has returned once since for a stay in the *House of Exile*. It was on this occasion that the Family Council of the Lins passed judgment on her illuminating day-book covering those years in China. Ninety-six-year-old Kuei-tzu said curtly: "Scholarship is useless to a woman. All she needs to know is how to manage men, which any woman can do if she is a good cook." Others damned it with faint praise but did not forbid her to submit it for publication: *House of Exile*, issued in 1933, lost no time in finding its audience.

In June 1934 she went to Germany with her husband, who had meanwhile retired from the British civil service and wanted to study music. She has always had a solid admiration for the German people themselves, and four years of Hitlerism in no wise weakened her faith in a fundamental Quaker belief that "peoples can be a society of friends living peacefully and profitably together in a frontierless and unfortified world."

In the fall of 1940 Miss Waln is doing war work in London. Her college sorority has established the Nora Waln Fund for Refugee Children and cables money to London regularly.

References

Sat R Lit 20:12 My 20 '39 por
Who's Who in America

WALTON, WILLIAM TURNER Mar 29, 1902- Composer
Address: 56A South Eaton Pl, S. W. 1, London, England

Long regarded as the most important of the younger English composers, William Walton first received international notice when his fiery oratorio, *Belshazzar's Feast,* was produced at the Leeds Festival in 1931. An even stronger impression was made by the performance of his *First Symphony* in 1934 (its finale was completed a year later) by the London Philharmonic Orchestra. That it showed the influence of Sibelius was regarded by critics as evidence of the young composer's growth.

Among those impressed by his work was violinist Jascha Heifetz, who asked Walton in 1936 to write him a violin concerto. In three years' time the manuscript was completed, and in December 1939 Heifetz, with Artur Rodzinski's (see sketch this issue) Cleveland Orchestra, gave the first performance of the new concerto. Intricate, but solid and warm in feeling, the opus won enthusiastic reception. And of it Rodzinski said: "This is one of the most important violin works of the century." Walton, unfortunately, did not hear the performance, since he was busy driving an ambulance somewhere in England. The concerto was not broadcast; but at Walton's request Heifetz planned to make a private recording for him.

Born in Oldham, Lancashire, March 29, 1902, William Walton, son of a music teacher, revealed considerable talent early in childhood. He studied at Christ Church Cathedral Choir School at Oxford. He was influenced by Edward J. Dent, who brought him to the notice of the International Society for Contemporary Music, at whose Salzburg Festival in 1923 his *String Quartet* was performed. This, though described by some critics as "horrible," nonetheless showed technical assurance.

For a series of satirical poems by the English poetess, Edith Sitwell, Walton wrote his brilliant musical parodies, *Façade,* produced in London in 1926. Adding new numbers, he turned the work into two orchestral suites (1936 and 1938). In this form it has been used as a comic ballet.

Outstanding among Walton's earlier works are: *The Passionate Shepherd* for tenor and small orchestra (1920); *Dr. Syntax,* pedagogic overture (1921); *Bucolic Comedies* for voice and piano (1924); *Siesta* for chamber orchestra (1926); *Portsmouth Point,* concert overture (1926); and two songs, *The Winds* and *The Tritons.*

At Liège in 1929 his viola concerto was produced and accredited as a fully matured work. Walton was now seen as "an artist capable of lyrical and sometimes poignant expression as well as of high spirits tempered by fine taste." He was no longer imitating and experimenting, but had achieved originality by being himself.

Belshazzar's Feast and the *First Symphony,* mentioned above, assured Walton's position as one of the noteworthy composers of his time. Among his compositions since the *First Symphony* are *Crown Imperial,* written for the coronation of George VI in 1937; and *In Honor of the City of London,* for chorus and orchestra, produced at the Leeds Festival of 1937. These consolidated his position; but the 1939 performance of his violin concerto seems to have made an indelible impression of real genius.

R. M. G., Inc.

EUGENE WAMBAUGH

Obituaries

N Y Herald Tribune p15 Ag 7 '40
N Y Times p19 Ag 7 '40

WANG CHING-WEI (wäng' jing-wä)
1883- Puppet ruler of Japanese-sponsored Chinese National Government

Wang Ching-wei was considered a great Chinese revolutionist and patriot until he declared himself at peace with Japan, and was chosen the puppet ruler of Japanese-occupied China in 1940. Then he was berated as a traitor to his country. Chinese patriots in Chungking, provisional capital of the fighting part of China, circulated chain letters asking for money to be used for Wang's assassination.

The chain letters asked receivers to contribute a dollar to a "kill Wang Ching-wei Fund," and to send 11 copies of the letter to friends. Funds would be collected by the Kuomintang, or Nationalist Party, according to the letters, and would go to a successful assassin. Men who attempted to kill Mr. Wang but failed and fell into Japanese hands would have the satisfaction of knowing that one percent of the fund would go to members of their families.

What gauge of popular opinion the letters were, it would be hard to make out in the complex situations arising from China's long war with Japan. But certainly they reflected the general opinion, shared strongly in America and Britain, that Wang Ching-wei had sold his country down the river when he made secret terms with Japan and became head of Japanese-occupied China. In November 1940 he was formally recognized by Japan as China's ruler, and made a "last" plea for peace in China.

As a young law student, Wang had joined the forces of China's George Washington,

Musical America

WILLIAM T. WALTON

References

Musical Q 26:456-66 O '40 por
Time 34:55 D 18 '39

Thompson, O. ed. International Cyclopedia of Music and Musicians 1939

Tovey, D. F. William Walton. *In* Essays in Musical Analysis p220-26 1935-36

Who's Who

WAMBAUGH, EUGENE (wäm'bä) Feb 29, 1856—Aug 6, 1940 Professor emeritus of the Harvard Law School; on staff for 33 years; widely known authority on international and constitutional law; served as special counsel to the United States State Department on war problems, 1914; writer of numerous books

References

Who's Who in America

WANG CHING-WEI—*Continued*

Sun Yat-sen, founder of the Chinese Republic. Wang and Chiang Kai-shek (see sketch this issue) were Dr. Sun's foremost disciples. Wang was a favorite student of Dr. Sun, wrote many of his manifestoes, and even took down the famous will the great revolutionist delivered on his deathbed.

On Dr. Sun's death in 1925 his party split, and Wang and Chiang Kai-shek fought for the mantle of their leader. Wang joined the Cantonese and led several revolts. Chiang Kai-shek, with the aid of Communist advisers, won in the vicious, bloody civil war. Politics eventually brought the two men together again. After Canton made peace with Nanking, Wang became Premier of China.

Wang resigned as Premier in 1932, and ironically enough it was with loud charges that Chinese generals should fight Japan more aggressively. The following year he again took the post of Premier, and again resigned in 1935, giving ill health as his reason.

When the war with Japan started Generalissimo Chiang Kai-shek and Wang continued together. As deputy leader of the Nationalist (Kuomintang) Party, Wang followed the Chinese government from Nanking to Hankow and to Chungking, as the Japanese made inroads into China. But in 1938, in the mountain fastness of Western China's provisional capital, Wang addressed peace pleas to Chiang Kai-shek and members of the embattled Kuomintang. Chiang refused to consider cessation of hostilities as Wang advised. Wang then took his two sons out of school, sent them out of the country, packed his own belongings and one night left Chungking secretly for Hanoi, French Indo-China. Chiang Kai-shek read him out of the party, branded him as a traitor and arrested his followers. Wang was found in Indo-China and several attempts on his life were made.

But the erstwhile Chinese patriot had declared himself at peace with the Japanese. From Indo-China he went to Hong Kong, then Shanghai, and later to the Japanese-conquered Kankow. The Japanese recognized him as a good catch for their puppet régimes in China. And since he was the only Chinese leader they could win over, they entered into negotiations with him to set up a central Chinese government in those parts of China which they had occupied.

The "all China" Japanese-sponsored régime headed by the former Chinese Premier Wang Ching-wei was proclaimed March 30, 1940 in brief ceremonies at Nanking. The purpose of the new régime was to establish peace between China and Japan and to put an end to the 33 months of war. It was a strange installation of what Wang and the Japanese declared was a new Chinese government. With the exception of Japan, no foreign nation sent diplomatic representatives to the ceremony. The American, French, British and Soviet Ambassadors were in Chungking, where Generalissimo Chiang Kai-shek's government was recognized by their countries as the sole legal government of China, although the British Ambassador had made a speech conciliatory to Japan two days before.

The installation was not without its incidents. Wang's home in Shanghai for months had been ringed with pill boxes in which Japanese soldiers stood guard. Five Japanese boats escorted the steamer bringing Wang from Shanghai to Nanking. And a Japanese-operated train bringing Japanese officials and foreign correspondents to the Japanese-guarded walls of Nanking was derailed by unidentified persons, believed to have been Chinese guerrillas. Chungking held a huge outdoor demonstration, burning wooden effigies of Wang and his wife.

In a broadcast from Chungking, President Lin Sen of China bitterly denounced Wang as a traitor, and declared that he (Lin) and Chiang Kai-shek would lead China to fight "to the end for her liberty, sovereignty and territorial integrity." He appealed to the world to continue to support China, which he declared would live despite the Japanese and their puppets.

President Lin Sen pointed out that Wang was already under death sentence as a traitor, and ordered all responsible government organizations to arrest him. Wang was carrying on a large scale rebellion under cover of a peace campaign, he declared.

A peculiar phase of the Wang situation was that Lin had been elected as President in the Japanese conference with Wang in Nanking, and Wang merely named as acting President until such time as Lin might decide to "play ball" with the Japanese. Lin's speech was his first personal answer to the Nanking election. Wang, despite all this, at his inauguration as the puppet premier blandly acted as if he represented all China. While Japanese armed soldiers guarded the city, he spoke of cooperation with "our Japanese neighbors so that our sovereign independence and territorial integrity may be safeguarded." He suavely proclaimed the new Chinese government at Nanking the only legal government of the country. Hereafter, he announced, any decree issued to the nation and any treaty or agreement entered into by the Chungking régime with foreign powers will be automatically invalid. "Chungking," he said, "has now been reduced to the status of a regional refugee régime." He formally ordered the cessation of the 33 months' hostilities with Japan.

The domestic political strategy Wang sought to use to win over the Chinese was revealed when he called on all civil servants still serving Chungking and various local governments to report for duty at the capital within the shortest possible time. He added that on proper identification they would be appointed to the same rank they now held and at the same salary.

But although Wang set himself up as the successor to the Chiang Kai-shek government, his authority actually extended only to the areas occupied by the Japanese Army, the seaports and principal cities of North and Central China. In those areas he contemplates a system of stringent passport control in order to raise revenue and to refuse to return to China persons considered anti-Japanese.

In his 50's, the new puppet ruler looks about 20 years younger. He is handsome, a dapper dresser, witty, and an eloquent speaker. Japanese-educated, a graduate of the law college at Tokyo, he has traveled often in Europe. He learned to speak French fluently and several times took diabetes cures in Germany.

He has gone a long way since his early days as a young revolutionist seeking to overthrow the Manchu dynasty. As a young man he was imprisoned in 1910 for plotting the assassination of the Prince regent of Imperial China. Meanwhile the revolution of 1911 led by Dr. Sun Yat-sen broke out, and he was released. The chains which he wore in prison were displayed in a Peking museum.

By 1940 the "Chinese patriot" was proclaiming peace with Japan. He did not make public his terms with Japan, however. His inauguration had been put off for months. The terms which Wang's followers gave out sought to prove that Wang stubbornly refused to head a Central Chinese government unless the Japanese lived up to certain pledges to respect China's territorial integrity and independence.

He was said to have held out against Japanese political and military advisers for his government, accepting only economic advisers. His agreement also is said to have called for the eventual withdrawal of Japanese troops in China. And he was said to have insisted on the use of the Chinese flag, with pennants attached to distinguish it from the old Chinese Nationalist flag. Rumors were current in November 1940 that fighting had broken out between Wang's troops and Japanese troops and that rather than accede to harsh Japanese demands Wang has twice tried to give up his régime and leave for Hong Kong.

But in Chungking they are still sure of what Japan meant when she spoke of "the new order in East Asia." No one can change Japan's traditional policy of conquest any more than the leopard can change his spots, Chiang Kai-shek declares.

References

Amerasia 3:542-8 F '40
Asia 40:151-3 Mr '40
Christian Sci Mon p4 Mr 30 '40 por
Cur Hist 50:11 Ag '39
Life 8:16 Ja 29 '40 por; 9:58+ S 30 '40 por
Liv Age 358:260-6 My '40
Newsweek 6:14 Ag 17 '35 por; 15:27 Ja 15 '40; 15:26 Ap 8 '40
Time 34:23 Jl 10 '39 por; 35:39 Mr 25 '40; 35:28-9 Ap 1 '40
International Who's Who
Who's Who in China

WARING, FRED June 9, 1900- Orchestra leader
Address: b. 1697 Broadway, New York City

Five times a week at 7 o'clock Fred Waring and his Pennsylvanians appear over the NBC network for Chesterfield cigarettes. The program features no outside talent or visiting stars; it is made up only of the orchestra and chorus, spiced with impromptu gags and general madcapping. Fred Waring, who has been a successful band leader for 21 years, "directs production, helps write continuity, coaches the gang in rehearsal: 'come lively, lively', 'stay with me', 'give it rapture!'"

Frederic Malcolm Waring (he uses only Fred) has been a success for 21 years because his orchestra has "never gone too hot or too sweet for catholic tastes"; because he has always managed to produce "admirable precision and nuance in his numbers seldom duplicated on radio shows and certainly not eclipsed." He gets this precision through plenty of rehearsals. There have been times when he has spent hours on a single passage until it reached that state of perfection he wanted. All his shows, whether for radio, stage or screen, are built with infinite care.

Fred Waring's orchestra started when he failed to make his college glee club. He was born in the little town of Tyrone, Pennsylvania, the son of Frank M. and Jessie (Calderwood) Waring, and spent much of his life before college on a farm there. Even before he went to Pennsylvania State College, which his great-grandfather William G. Waring founded, he and his brother Tom, together with two neighbors, had formed a band to play for local parties. It was a small affair, but Fred kept it up while he was studying engineering and architecture. When the Pennsylvania Glee Club refused to have him he began to work seriously at an orchestra.

He began signing up promising collegiate musicians and he began getting engagements for them. In 1921 Fred landed a date for his band at the University of Michigan. A "name" band had been hired to play for the dance, and his band was supposed merely to handle the overflow crowd. But it stole the show and a Detroit theatre offered him a two weeks' engagement that lasted four weeks. By 1924 his band was really going. Fred figured out a novelty number called "Collegiate." Dressed in knickers, loud striped sweaters and big flowing ties, he and his men "put themselves definitely on the entertainment map as collegiate hot stuff." After they appeared in Harold Lloyd's picture, *The Freshman,* and started the fad for bell-bottomed trousers, they were definitely made.

FRED WARING

In 1929 the Pennsylvanians appeared in *Syncopation,* one of the first big movie musicals. They continued playing all over the country and in 1932 were a six months' hit at the Roxy Theatre in New York. Their first big radio engagement came in 1933 when they appeared for the Old Gold program. The next year they started a three-year radio engagement for the Ford Motor Company and the year after that were hired by Bromo-Quinine. Ford paid them $13,500 a week and Chesterfield is now giving them $12,000 a week. Between radio contracts and movie engagements (they starred in *Varsity Show*) Fred Waring and his Pennsylvanians are kept busy making personal appearances on hotel roofs and in theatres.

Waring, who is a "small dark man with wavy hair and blue eyes," spends his winters with his wife, Evalyn Nair Fall, (whom he married in September 1933) and three children in a Park Avenue duplex penthouse. His summers he spends in a lodge at Shawnee-on-Delaware, where his whole orchestra romps during vacations. But most of his time winters and summers is spent in his Broadway offices in New York, which take up a whole floor in the theatrical district.

Twelve hours a day five days a week he works—with his orchestra and with his other enterprises. His main side lines are a music publishing business called "Words and Music," which specializes in glee club arrangements that the Pennsylvanians have popularized, and a mixer, called the "Blendor", "that will turn you out an icy frappé while you look at it." Right now he is busy with a new steam electric iron which he expects to put on the market in the fall of 1940. When he relaxes from his business and his music, it is to play golf in the 70's. His musical friends say he probably "spends more time hanging around with big-name golfers than he does with members of his own profession."

References

> Am Mag 117:44 Je '34 por
> Etude 58:374+ Je '40 il por
> N Y World-Telegram p17 Jl 1 '40
> 　pors
> Newsweek 13:40 Je 19 '39
> PM p21 Jl 17 '40
> Time 33:52-3 Je 26 '39 il por
> America's Young Men

WASTE, WILLIAM HARRISON Oct 31, 1868—June 6, 1940 Chief justice of California for last 14 years; as head of Supreme Court of State heard appeals in Tom Mooney, Billings, Lamson cases

References

> Who's Who in America
> Who's Who in Government
> Who's Who in Law

Obituaries

> N Y Herald Tribune p18 Je 7 '40

WATROUS, GEORGE DUTTON Sept 18, 1858—Nov 14, 1940 Professor of Law at Yale Law School for many years; officer, director or attorney of numerous industrial, public utility and financial institutions; former president of Connecticut State Bar Association, New Haven County Bar Association; son of first president of New York, New Haven & Hartford Railroad

References

> Who's Who in Law

Obituaries

> N Y Herald Tribune p16 N 15 '40
> N Y Times p21 N 15 '40

WATROUS, HARRY WILLSON (wŏt'rŭs) Sept 17, 1857—May 10, 1940 Artist; former president of the National Academy of Design; won many prizes; known as genre painter; gave first one-man show in 1937

References

> Newsweek 9:18 F 6 '37 il por
> Who's Who in American Art
> Who's Who in New York

Obituaries

> N Y Herald Tribune p16 My 11 '40
> 　por
> N Y World-Telegram p39 My 10 '40

WATSON, CLARENCE WAYLAND May 8, 1864—May 25, 1940 Democratic United States Senator from West Virginia from 1911 to 1913; retired coal company executive who started as a miner

References

> Who's Who in America
> Who's Who in Commerce and Industry

Obituaries

N Y Herald Tribune p30 My 26 '40
por
N Y Times p17 My 25 '40

WATSON, THOMAS JOHN   Feb 17, 1874-   President of International Business Machines Corporation

Address: b. 590 Madison Ave, New York City; h. 4 E 75th St, New York City

For many years Thomas J. Watson, president of the International Business Machines Corporation, honorary president of the International Chamber of Commerce and trustee of the Carnegie Endowment for International Peace, has believed that "the only solution to the problem of peace must come through sound economics between countries." He has worked hard most of his life for international trade and in 1940 was twice honored for his efforts: he received the Captain Robert Dollar Memorial Award for his contribution to the Advancement of American foreign trade and he was honored at the Court of Peace exercises at the New York World's Fair in May 1940 "for his important contributions to the laying of a solid foundation on which a permanent world peace of the future may rest."

Year after year Mr. Watson has been traveling all over the world to build up trade. In 1937, for instance, he made a five months' tour of Europe in which he visited and talked with Hitler, Mussolini, King Leopold of Belgium; in which he was decorated by Sweden, France, Yugoslavia and Italy; in which he talked to financial leaders from all parts of the world. He came back from that trip believing that "it is important to think in terms of moving goods, not armies, across borders." Less than three years later he sent back to Hitler the Merit Cross of the German Eagle "because the present policies of your government are contrary to the causes for which I have been working and for which I received the decoration."

Even today, when armies and not goods are moving across borders all over the world, Thomas J. Watson stoutly maintains, "I believe the world is going to improve." And he is sure that "when this War is over there will be enough intelligent people in the world to get together and see to it that the settlements which are made are just to the small as well as to the large countries."

Mr. Watson, who heads one of the most profitable corporations in the United States with factories and branches in many parts of the world, was born in Campbell, New York, the son of Thomas and Jane (White) Watson. Young Tom went to Addison Academy until he was 17. His father, a lumber dealer and a very strict Methodist, wanted him to go to Cornell to study law, but Tom wasn't interested in education. He wanted to get a job and make money right

THOMAS J. WATSON

away. Father and son compromised on a year at the Elmira School of Commerce.

After Elmira, Watson spent two rather humdrum years as a clerk in a piano-sewing-machine-organ store in Painted Post, New York. He left this to go to Buffalo, where he eventually landed a job as a salesman with the local office of the National Cash Register Company. When he started he was "a lanky, earnest youth given to rationalizing his actions and ruminating upon his experiences. His general appearance and behavior were those of a somewhat puzzled divinity student."

In his first 10 days of selling for the Cash Register Company, Tom Watson earned nothing but refusals. Disappointed, he "took earnest counsel with his sales manager" and started all over again. Within 15 years he had become sales manager. Most of his experience came under John Henry Patterson, head of the company, who has been "conservatively described as an amalgam of St. Paul, Poor Richard and Adolf Hitler." He was Patterson's right-hand man and both he and Patterson benefited from the association.

In 1913, after a disagreement with Patterson, Watson left the National Cash Register Company. In 1914 he was offered the job of running the Computing-Tabulating-Recording Company, "an ineffective struggling outfit" then employing 235 people. Watson took over this company and the various enterprises under its control and it prospered. Renamed the International Business Machines Corporation in 1924, in 1940 it employs 11,250 persons and in 1938 earned a profit of $8,700,000.

As president of this corporation, Thomas Watson earns a fixed salary of $100,000 a year plus five per cent of the net profits after a $6 dividend has been paid on the

WATSON, THOMAS JOHN—*Continued*

stock. The income tax report of 1937 salaries showed that his ($419,938) was the highest for any ordinary businessman. His company has always prospered, for it has a virtual monopoly on many intricate business machines. Watson says: "The IBM is a world institution and is going on forever."

It has been said that Watson's "personality and force have saturated the IBM until now the personality of the man and the personality of the corporation are so closely identified as to be practically one and the same." Watson has always believed in the value of stimulating phrases for selling and his salesmen and employees live by them, too. On the walls of the classrooms where new workers are trained are signs reading: "Aim High and Think in Big Figures"; "Serve and Sell"; "Ever Onward"; "Be Better than Average." But the most successful and all-pervading motto is the single word: "THINK."

This word is on the most conspicuous wall of every room in every IBM building. Each employee carries a THINK notebook in which to record inspirations. The company stationery, matches, scratch pads all bear the inscription, THINK. A monthly magazine called *Think* is distributed to the employees.

There is a photograph of Mr. Watson in every room of IBM buildings and all employees are expected to have a copy of *Men, Minutes and Money*, a collection of Mr. Watson's speeches and essays. Mr. Watson dresses with "relentless conservatism—a dark suit of expensive worsted relieved by a timid stripe, a decorous tie of moiré knotted perfectly in a dazzling collar"—and IBM employees, whether in the New York main office or in the factory at Endicott, New York, "shave their faces and shine their shoes daily, are never without a haircut and whenever possible wear white shirts."

Mr. Watson, the super-salesman of them all, doesn't look like a salesman. When he begins to talk he is "the kind of slightly bashful, dignified gentleman who would be the last person on earth to try to sell you anything." What happens is that those who talk to him forget their sales resistance and only when they leave discover the size of the order they have given.

Mr. Watson never takes a vacation, works about 16 hours a day and spends many evenings at the functions of his many employees' clubs. His wife attends most of the company affairs with him; his son Thomas, who joined the sales force of IBM a few years ago, is now a crack salesman, member of the select Hundred Per Cent Club. Mr. Watson has another son, still in Yale, and two daughters.

His main interest apart from his business is art. Mr. Watson was only 24 when he bought his first painting, a pleasant scene on a Maine farm, and since then has acquired quite a number. He believes that "directly or indirectly artists must depend on business for support. It is our opinion that mutual benefit would result if the interest of business in art and of artists in business should be increased." Toward that end he presented, first at the San Francisco World's Fair and then at the New York World's Fair, an "exhibition of contemporary American art," selected by local art juries throughout the country as representative of the art and character of their respective localities. One critic called it "a random assemblage with no common characteristic save a distinct lack of offensiveness." After the Fair was over the pictures were exhibited in the IBM clubroom.

References

Christian Sci Mon p15 My 24 '40 por
Fortune 21:36-43+ Ja '40 il pors
N Y Sun p34 My 11 '40; p6 My 13 '40; p15 Je 7 '40; p28 Je 13 '40
Newsweek 10:5 N 22 '37 por; 15:41 Je 17 '40
R of Rs 91:29-34+ Je '35 il por
Time 27:73 Ap 20 '36 por; 35:57 Je 17 '40
Who's Who in America
Who's Who in Commerce and Industry

WAUGH, FREDERICK JUDD (wô) Sept 13, 1861—Sept 10, 1940 American painter principally of marine scenes; internationally known for paintings; represented in major galleries in the United States and Europe; sold every painting made and averaged about $30,000 per year; from 1934 through 1938 won the $200 popularity prize of the Carnegie Institute in Pittsburgh and many other awards; wrote and illustrated treatises on

FREDERICK J. WAUGH

painting; was a highly skilled woodcarver; designed church of St. Mary's of the Harbor at Provincetown, Massachusetts

References

> Time 26:49-50 D 16 '35 il; 30:67 D 6 '37 por
>
> Who's Who in America
>
> Who's Who in American Art

Obituaries

> N Y Herald Tribune p26 S 11 '40 por
>
> N Y Times p25 S 11 '40

WEBER, LOUIS LAWRENCE Jan 10, 1872—Feb 22, 1940 Theatrical producer who brought Miriam Hopkins, Ruby Keeler, John Boles, Judith Anderson and Claire Luce to the stage

References

> Who's Who in American Jewry

Obituaries

> N Y Herald Tribune p18 F 23 '40 por
>
> N Y Sun p23 F 23 '40
>
> N Y World-Telegram p36 F 23 '40
>
> Variety 137:44 F 28 '40

WEBSTER, MARGARET Mar 15, 1905- Theatrical director; actress

Address: b. c/o Theatre Guild, 245 W 52nd St, New York City

Recently listed as one of America's 10 outstanding women, Margaret Webster, for her 'distinguished work as a theatrical producer, has been called the feminine Belasco. She began staging and directing plays in London, but resounding success came to her in New York when, in 1937, she directed three notable Shakespearean productions starring Maurice Evans (see sketch this issue). Actress as well as director, Miss Webster played a memorable rôle during the 1939 season in *Family Portrait*, a story of the life of Jesus, which she also staged and directed.

Margaret Webster comes of a distinguished line of theatrical folk. Her great-grandfather, Benjamin N. Webster, was a leading English actor-manager. Her mother, Dame May Whitty, and her father, Ben Webster, are famous Shakespearean actors today. Margaret (known to all her friends as "Peggy") was born in New York City March 15, 1905; her parents had come to this country on one of their American tours. When Peggy was three they returned to England. She was sent to Queen Anne's School, Caversham, and studied for the stage at Eltinger's Dramatic School. Her first speaking part on the stage was at the age of seven or eight, in a play starring the great Ellen Terry; in 1917 she appeared as Youth in *Women's Tribute*. She contemplated going to Oxford to take a degree, but changed her mind, decided on a career in the theatre and went to Paris to study plays.

Her stage debut in London was as the Gentlewoman in John Barrymore's *Hamlet*. Since Barrymore was incessantly playing tricks in the wings, young Margaret was in constant terror that she might giggle just as she walked on the stage in her sedate rôle. In 1924 she acted with Sybil Thorndike in *The Trojan Woman*. Thereafter she played a number of parts in stock, met Maurice Evans and in 1931 played with him in *After All*. It was the following year that she decided to become a director, and her first assignment was with a stock company. Then she directed several West End plays. Since her own opportunity to direct plays came through London Sunday night performances, she feels that for this one reason the London stage is superior to the American. It has "more amateur productions where young people have a chance to work, to rehearse and to get experience."

In 1937 Evans heard glowing reports of her directing talents, and called Margaret Webster to New York to help with his *Richard II*. During two years (1937-39) she directed three Shakespearean plays for him: *Richard II*, immediately a success, averaged $17,500 weekly for 23 weeks; an uncut production of *Hamlet* did almost as well; and *Henry IV* soon earned $17,000 a week. Miss Webster had discovered how to make Shakespeare live, to be breathlessly absorbing to the modern audience. The Webster productions were fresh and exciting, swiftly paced and lacked the confusion often encountered in Shakespearean staging At the New York World's Fair, during the summer of 1939, Miss Webster staged several tabloid Shakespearean dramas for popular entertainment. The versions of his better-known comedies were condensed to 45 acting minutes, and seven performances a day were given.

Despite her directing successes, Miss Webster is, at heart, an actress. She played successfully several rôles in London; and besides her work in New York in *Family Portrait*, will be remembered as Masha in the Lunt-Fontanne production of *The Sea Gull*. "I never get the kick out of directing," she has said, "that comes from being out in front, playing a part." Her solution at present is to be both director and actress.

Margaret Webster is "a slender, pretty girl with hair that is perhaps more brown than red, and with a booming laugh. At work, she is undeniably grubby. She gets smudges on her face, and her hair is soon a tangled mess due to her habit of running her hands through it." As a director she is sane, calm, cheerful. But there is that bit of red in her hair, and on occasion she can lose her temper. She comes nearest to doing so when an actor is late for rehearsal. Once Mr. Evans, the star performer, was late. "A star has finally risen," said Miss Webster as he walked in, just loud enough for everyone to hear. Evans hasn't been tardy since.

Miss Webster has a definitely established credo as a director. She believes that the

Vandamm

MARGARET WEBSTER

director can only be judged according to whether or not the show he directs emerges as a satisfying whole. She emphasizes the differences in directing Shakespearean and modern plays, and says that the direction of the latter is actually handling an author. It means seeing that what the author says is said more cogently and dramatically in terms of the theatre. There must be close collaboration between director, author and scene designer. With regard to the actors, the director should remain flexible, since actors, even the most inexperienced, have personalities of their own which are a vital contribution to the play. The greatest thing the Anglo-Saxon director has to overcome, she believes, is self-consciousness. The director must make his actors trust him, and feel both easy and safe in his hands. "Stamina, the courage of a lion and the hide of a rhinoceros" are the qualities she lists as being most essential for a good director.

During the summer of 1939 Miss Webster directed summer theatricals in Maine. It is her ambition, with Maurice Evans, to establish a permanent repertory theatre of both classic and modern plays at the St. James Theatre in New York. After putting the finishing touches to his 1940 production of *Richard II*, Miss Webster left New York for Hollywood in April to begin a six months' period "without assignment," during which she "may write, act or work with any producer or director" in filmdom. She said that she was not deserting the theatre, however, but has a "definite yearly period, September to January, kept sacrosanct for Broadway." After five months with Paramount Miss Webster canceled her contract in October 1940 because of disagreement on contractual arrangements. She devoted her-

self to staging *Twelfth Night* for Maurice Evans and Helen Hayes. Critics praised the direction, saying: "The highest praise of all must go to Margaret Webster, who once again has proved herself a brilliant Shakespearean director."

She will start work on *Battle of Angels* for 1941 production. Having directed both of her parents in London productions in the past, she will also direct her mother's play, *Viceroy Sarah*, when it comes to Broadway. She is now working on a book of reminiscences about her parents.

"No, I'm not married—or anything," is the only information she will give about her private life. Her public life keeps her happy and busy; and her office is a hive of activity. Her dream, she says, is to live peacefully in the English countryside, sometime, and grow cabbages.

References

Arts & Dec 51:22-3+ N '39 il por
Collier's 104:11+ Jl 8 '39 por
Ind Woman 18:65 Mr '39 por
N Y Post p13 Mr 21 '40
N Y Times p13 Mr 18 '40; p28 O 4 '40
N Y World-Telegram p15 Ap 16 '40
St Louis Post-Dispatch F 20 '40 por
Theatre Arts 22:343-8 My '38; 24:334-6+ My/'40
American Women
Who's Who in the Theatre

WEISSE, FANEUIL SUYDAM Apr 20, 1875—Feb 25, 1940 Medical director of the Mutual Life Insurance Company of New York from 1911 until his retirement in 1938

FANEUIL SUYDAM WEISSE

Obituaries

N Y Herald Tribune p10 F 26 '40

WELD, JOHN 1905- Author

Address: c/o Charles Scribner's Sons, 597 Fifth Ave, New York City

There have been a good many American novels written about American pioneer life and the trek of covered wagons across the plains. One of the latest of these, *Don't You Cry for Me* (March 1940), has been called by some reviewers "the best of all the native migratory literature," and a "tremendous achievement" even by those who find it far from a great or faultless novel.

Don't You Cry for Me is the story of the memorable and tragic Donner party which set out from Independence, Missouri in 1846 for California. They were a group of gay and hardy people, more than 100 wagons and almost 500 persons strong when they started, loaded down with cooking implements, trunks of pretty clothes and china, food supplies, cosmetics and drugs. Beyond Fort Laramie the party split. A scatterbrained writer named Hastings persuaded the more adventurous members of the group to try a new trail south of Great Salt Lake, claiming that it would cut off 200 miles and contact with dangerous Indians. He did not tell them that it would lead past his own trading post.

The little band became caught in an endless sea of salt, its members dropping out as they dragged their way across. Then fearful mountain passes had to be traversed, the way often hacked out of virgin wilderness. After the mountains came the desert, and after the desert the foot of the Sierras. The terrible winter descended on them, already stripped of their possessions, of half the flesh on their bones, of the will to live. And out of this degradation came forth one of "the most desperately heroic ventures in the annals of American pioneering."

Some reviewers agree with John Breen that "the first 300 pages are crowded with infinite detail," but all are unanimous on the "powerful effect," the "tragedy and high drama" of the last push over the mountains, of the epic of human fortitude that it reveals.

This is not only the story of the band itself, but of the individual people who were part of it. There is the indomitable Captain Dan Johnson with his family and magnificent slave Amos. There is the frail, kindly George Lansing, a 42-year-old schoolmaster with a disturbingly beautiful wife. There is Asa Harper, who joined the party as it wound its way out of Independence, and who fell in love with Lansing's wife. There is the octoroon, Ida, who wore a veil and masqueraded as a white woman. And there are many others. The details of their daily lives are told, gaited to the speed of the slowly rolling ox-drawn wagons. All the individual hates and loves of these people combine with hopes and hardships to mold the novel into "an extraordinary and moving piece of historical realism."

John Weld, the author of *Don't You Cry for Me,* was born in 1905 in Birmingham, Alabama, and went to school there until, at the age of 12, he was sent to a ranch in

Joseph McElliott

JOHN WELD

Colorado, where he worked as a "half cattle-hand and chore boy." After attending two military schools and spending a year at Alabama Polytechnic Institute he set out at the age of 16 to see the world. Lots of times he just scraped along. For instance, in the days when "Dishwasher Wanted" signs still showed on Third Avenue in New York City he answered one after he hadn't eaten for 48 hours. "He started on a few dishes, and hunger barely let him stand up. He asked for a chance to eat. He ate all he could. Then he got so filled he couldn't work. He just departed via the alley, leaving his hat and coat."

Except for a voyage to Europe, as bell-boy on the United States liner *President Monroe,* he didn't see the world until much later. What he did see was America, a large, varied, exciting part. "I worked at a number of jobs," Mr. Weld recalls, "including pitching steel in Kansas City, selling candy through New England and soap through New York State. I landed in New York in January 1922 with 15 cents in my pocket, determined to go on the stage. I wrote a vaudeville act and made my only appearance on the stage of the famous Palace Theatre.

"In February 1923 I came to California in one of the early jallopies. I dove 137 feet from a cliff on Santa Cruz Island (for $60) and for three years thereafter continued working in moving pictures as a stunt man." Three years of doubling for Tom Mix, Buck Jones, Gloria Swanson, Leatrice Joy, Anna Q. Nilsson and others left Mr. Weld with a fortune of $100 with which he proceeded to New York to start his writing.

In New York Weld got a job on the New York *American,* then on the *World,* the Paris *Times* and the Paris *Herald.* He covered the Rothstein and the Snyder murders, the

WELD, JOHN—*Continued*

Communist riots, and got one of his jobs, on the *World,* after a stunt of his identified the body of a murder victim of 1929.

The idea of *Don't You Cry for Me,* which is Mr. Weld's first major work, "although he has had two others luridly and unsuccessfully published," grew out of a movie experience. He'd been on location on Donner Lake, along the trail of the famed Donner Party. "The picture was planned as an ice-skating picture but the lake turned out to be unfrozen. There was some snow on the hills, so everybody set to work and re-wrote the script on the back of some envelopes to make it a skiing picture. Mr. Weld had to learn hastily to ski. While he did, he saw a monument to the Donner caravan and got absorbed in its history." After his years of newspaper work he returned to California, spent a year on research, made 100,000 words of notes and then spent four years writing *Don't You Cry for Me.*

References

Boston Transcript p19 Mr 30 '40
N Y Herald Tribune Books p11 Mr 24 '40
N Y Times Book R p1 Mr 24 '40
N Y World-Telegram p8 Mr 25 '40 por
Sat R Lit 21:7 Mr 30 '40

WELLES, SUMNER Oct 14, 1892- United States Under-Secretary of State

Address: b. Department of State, Washington, D. C.; h. Oxon Hill Manor, Oxon Hill, Maryland

On February 17, 1940, Sumner Welles, Under-Secretary of State, sailed for Europe as diplomatic emissary from the United States to discuss political and economic problems with European leaders. The President did not authorize Mr. Welles to make any proposals or commitments for the United States; the journey, and the conversations, were to be "strictly on business." Mr. Welles' main object was to try to formulate an approach to a method of settling international disputes; if possible, to ascertain some method of guaranteeing freedom from threats of force. Long diplomatic experience, an acute mind and firm character are qualities Mr. Welles brought to his important mission. An accomplished linguist, and also able to keep a secret, it has been said of him that he "can hold his tongue" in English, Spanish, French, Italian and German.

On March 28, 1940 Sumner Welles returned from his month-long European trip "radiating elegance and uninformative urbanity." He had talked with Halifax, Daladier (see sketches this issue), Mussolini, Hitler, with all the leaders of Europe's great nations, but he had nothing to say to reporters when he returned. He gave them a polite, "No comment," and hustled to the State Department, and thence to the White House. The next day President Roosevelt told his press conference that there was "scant prospect for the establishment of any just and lasting peace." But he added that when the time comes for such a peace, the information collected by Mr. Welles "will undoubtedly be of the greatest value in helping solve problems that must be solved if the world is to be saved from conflict. . . "

One of the conspicuously able men of the State Department, Sumner Welles has the background and equipment of the perfect diplomat. He was born in New York City, October 14, 1892, the son of Benjamin and Frances (Swan) Welles. He was educated at Groton and Harvard and was graduated from the latter in 1914. He married Mathilde Townsend of Washington, D. C., and has two sons, Benjamin and Arnold.

Welles' diplomatic career began with his appointment as Secretary of the Tokyo Embassy (1915-17). It soon became evident that he was studious, brilliant and a natural diplomat. With these qualifications he might have gone on to Paris or London, but instead he asked for a post in the Argentine capital. Welles had come to the conclusion, soon after entering the Foreign Service, that the destiny of the United States lies largely in the Western Hemisphere. In Buenos Aires, 1917 to 1919, he mastered Spanish so that he could speak directly with the people. He also learned the essentials of the inter-American problem, for in Argentina Pan-American solidarity faces its most difficult economic obstacles.

Welles became assistant chief, then chief of the Latin American Affairs Division, (1920-22); was sent on a commission to the Dominican Republic in 1922; subsequently went there on the Dawes mission in 1929. He was also commissioned to offer mediation in the Honduras Revolution in 1924. His skilled negotiations in the Dominican Republic and in Central America laid the groundwork for the American "Good Neighbor Policy."

His most difficult assignment came in 1933 when he was appointed Ambassador to Cuba. He arrived at a moment when Leftist elements were in the saddle. The story of Welles' activities there is still a controversial one: he has been accused of exerting pressure in favor of conservative elements, contrary to the dominant Cuban radicalism, temporarily hindering the cause of Cuban-American good will. And he had the doubtful pleasure of seeing himself hanged in effigy. After the Machado régime, Welles made De Cespedes President and picked a Cabinet for him; but the Cubans turned him out, putting in Grau San Martin. Welles would not yield, despite the unpopularity of his act, and worked until the Leftists were forced out of power. His supporters say he refused to recognize the régime of Grau because of the instability of Grau's government, not because of ulterior sympathies or motives.

Harris & Ewing

SUMNER WELLES

Welles is known to be sincerely devoted to the promotion of human and political liberty as he interprets them. His basic viewpoint is conservative, as might be expected from his background and training. But in his handling of the recent Mexican oil dispute, he sought to maintain fair balance. Sympathetic to the oil companies, he recognized at the same time the value of the Leftist Cárdenas government and preferred to take a middle-of-the-road policy.

Because of his work in the Latin-American countries, Welles played an important part as a delegate to the Pan-American Congress at Buenos Aires in 1936. At these consultations he displayed an understanding of Latin-American ways that impressed all who worked with him. In May 1937 he was guest of honor at a luncheon given by the Pan American Union on the occasion of his promotion to Under-Secretary of State and in 1940 he was awarded the gold medal of the Pan American Union on the occasion of his contribution to good will among the American republics.

Sumner Welles is playing a more and more important part, too, in the other activities and negotiations of the United States Department of State. It was he who announced our firm stand in the Far East and our willingness, at the same time, to resume negotiations on American extraterritorial rights in China. It was he who discussed problems of American defense, of colonial possessions of conquered nations in this hemisphere, of Spain's position in the present War. And it has been he who has been holding conferences with Soviet Ambassador Oumansky to try to establish more harmonious relations.

Welles has a personality formal and austere, forbidding to all but his closest friends. He is reserved, his will inflexible.

His figure is tall, correct, disciplined. "Aquiline of feature, clear-blue of eye, clean-shaven except for a crisp white moustache matching the white at his temples, he has the vigor of youth tempered with a maturity that seems always to have been his." He has had an exceptionally full and distinguished career. He is a hard worker and takes his only relaxation on his estate at Oxon Hill Manor, Maryland. There he reads, rides horseback and is an enthusiastic amateur gardener.

References

Cath World 151:108 Ap '40
Christian Cent 57:267 F 28 '40
Christian Sci Mon p6+ N 25 '39 il por; p1 Mr 12 '40 por; p6 Ap 20 '40
Foreign Affairs 15:443-54 Ap '37
Harper 174:228 F '37
Life 8:22 F 19 '40 por; 8:30 Ap 1 '40 pors; 8:35+ Ap 8 '40 pors
Newsweek 11:12 Je 6 '38; 15:15-16 F 19 '40 por
Time 39:16 My 31 '37; 35:15 F 19 '40 por
America's Young Men 1936-37
Who's Who in America

WENCKEBACH, KAREL FRIEDRICH Mar 24, 1864—Nov 14, 1940 Famous heart expert; wrote two classical books on heart disease, often considered best on their subjects; head of Vienna's first medical clinic for many years; hundreds of United States physicians among his former students

References

International Who's Who
Wer Ist Wer
Who's Who in Central and East-Europe

Obituaries

N Y Times p21 N 15 '40

WENDT, GERALD LOUIS Mar 3, 1891-
Chemist; educator
Address: 320 E 42nd St, New York City

Famed as a humanitarian, scientist, author of articles and books on the social consequences of new scientific knowledge, Dr. Gerald Wendt became in 1939 director of science and education at the New York World's Fair, which position he held during the 1940 Fair season. His most recent book, *Science for the World of Tomorrow* (1939), highly praised by critics, and written in terms that the layman can understand, deals with the main aspects of modern living. It explains how science affects our present life, with clear accounts of important technical processes, and of the workings of transportation, communication, agriculture, medicine, etc. Dr. Wendt maintains that some of the main evils of modern life—war, poverty, unemployment, mental disease—exist because we do not

GERALD WENDT

recognize economic interdependence and follow from the fact that use of new scientific devices has not affected our thinking. He has drawn upon the World's Fair for the book's title, has paralleled the chapters of the book with the main divisions of the Fair and utilized the exhibits as illustrations of his thesis.

Since Dr. Wendt's task at the Fair was presumably made difficult by the fact that the managers of the Fair assumed that the industrial exhibits were in themselves so scientific no special Hall of Science was necessary, and since only the external aspects of social science were represented, the present volume effects the integration that a Hall of Science would have effected at the Fair. *Science for the World of Tomorrow* is a book that should be read with profit by those who visited the Fair.

Gerald Wendt was born in Davenport, Iowa, March 3, 1891. After being graduated from the Davenport High School he went to Harvard University, where he took the advanced degrees of M. A. and Ph. D. He was research student in radioactivity at Gif, France, in 1916. In that year he married Elsie Paula Lerch of Davenport. They have one son, Robert Louis. During the War Wendt was captain of the Research Division, Chemical Warfare Service.

He has been associate professor of chemistry at the University of Chicago and dean of the School of Chemistry and Physics as well as assistant to the president in charge of research at Pennsylvania State College. In the industrial world he has been director of research for the Standard Oil Company, Indiana; director of research for the General Printing Corporation; and president of the Coffee Products Corporation. He was associate editor of the *Journal of Radiology*

(1920-21), and served as editor of *Chemical Reviews* (1927-38). He has reviewed books on science for the New York *Herald Tribune Books* since 1925. Prior to his appointment at the New York World's Fair, he was director of the Battelle Memorial Institute for Industrial Research at Columbus, Ohio and director of the American Institute of the City of New York.

Dr. Wendt does considerable lecturing before clubs and organizations. Among the subjects on which he will speak for the 1940 to 1941 season are: The World at War and After; The Challenge of Science; The Science Revue for 1940; and Looking Into Science. The last named is illustrated with three-dimensional pictures in color.

Besides *Science for the World of Tomorrow*, Dr. Wendt is also the author of *Matter and Energy* (1930) and of the article on science in *America Now* edited by H. E. Stearns (1938). In this article Dr. Wendt states that the age of science still lies in the future. He believes that if science is to give us anything in terms of human happiness, 'research must be conceived not as the technical study of electrons and atoms, i.e., of nature, but as the best use of human intelligence to improve the conditions under which we live. It is in science that research has proved its value. If civilization can learn that lesson from science it stands at the threshold of a great new epoch. Thus will science at last be justified when it has revealed its true spirit and humanity."

In between lecture engagements, Dr. Wendt is at present working on a six-volume survey of science for colleges, entitled *The Sciences*, which is to be published soon. He is general editor of the series and the writer in particular of the volume on chemistry.

References

Sci Mo 48:577-80 Je '37
American Men of Science
America's Young Men 1936-37
Chemical Who's Who
Stearns, H. E. ed. America Now 1938
Who's Who in America

WERFEL, FRANZ (věr'fl fränts) Sept 10, 1890-　Author; playwright; poet

Address: c/o Viking Press, 18 E 48th St, New York City

Among the distinguished exiles from war-torn Europe—poets, writers, diplomats now without a country—is Franz Werfel, whose plays have been produced in the United States, and whose *The Forty Days of Musa Dagh* caused a sensation here when it was published in 1934. His latest novel, *Embezzled Heaven*, which was chosen as the Book-of-the-Month-Club selection for December 1940, is a revealing one. It chronicles the wanderings of an exiled writer uprooted from his country—the Nazified Austria—and desperately seeking a refuge where he can rebuild his philosophy of life on a newer, stronger foundation. Representative of a new type of literature—exile literature—the hero of this book seeks to find a homeland in something that transcends nationalism: in humanity at large.

Probably many of Werfel's own plans and ambitions could be found in this book. "Would the day ever come," one passage reads, "when we of the modern age were no longer condemned to hypercritical materialism but could at last take our place without supercilious mental reservations in an ordered universe, in a radiant cosmic system reaching from the skies above to the earth beneath." The hero of *Embezzled Heaven* finds his solution in Catholicism. Franz Werfel's visa for Mexico describes his own new faith as Roman Catholicism.

One of the proscribed writers whose lives were endangered by Hitler's occupation of France, Werfel had to make his way to Spain by secret pathways. In the course of his wanderings he had to destroy about 20 of his manuscripts because it was too dangerous to have them in his possession. He hoped, however, to be able to get some of his writings back and in the meantime to go about getting American citizenship "and a little peace." His wife, Alma Marie Schindler, widow of the great composer Gustav Mahler, came with him to the United States.

Franz Werfel used a Czechoslovakian passport to get to the United States. Although famous for his German-language works, he is a Czech. He was born in Prague, in 1890, a son of a wealthy and cultured Jewish manufacturer, Rudolf Werfel. From his youth he showed signs of great intellectual attainment, for which his proud parents provided every opportunity. Young Franz traveled extensively. After he was graduated from the Gymnasium at Prague he attended the Prague University and later the University of Leipzig. His *Fakultät* was philosophy and that proved a solid grounding for his later literary works. At the same time he became well-known in the famous literary circles of Prague, rubbing elbows with Max Brod, Gustave Meyrink and Otakar Brezina, the great national poet whose works Werfel later translated. It was when he was studying in Hamburg, in 1911, that he made his first bow as a poet with a volume of poems called *Der Weltfreund*. His other volumes of poetry, entitled *Wir Sind* (1913) and *Einander* (1915), added to his reputation as a poet. Mystic, tragic in tenor, his poetry brought him fame as a "new spirit of spiritual renascence." In 1915 he translated Euripides' *Troades*. His work of that period showed signs of what later became his most striking characteristic —love for the symbolic, a tragic fear of evil and the strange feeling of "personal responsibility for all of mankind's shortcomings."

The First World War found Franz Werfel teaching at the University of Leipzig, after having served his term in the army in

Foyer

FRANZ WERFEL

1912 and entered the civil service. He fought on the Russian front from 1915 to 1917. The experience had a shattering effect on him. It was as if he had seen in actual crystallized form all the evil of which the premonition had always haunted him. After the War was over he settled in Vienna, where he lived in studious retirement, writing copiously. His first novels of that period dealt mostly with the then-popular theme of revolt of youth—among them *Nicht der Mörder, der Ermordete ist Schuldig* (1915); *The Man Who Conquered Death* (1927); and *Class Reunion* (1929). He broke into the American market with his historical novel, *Verdi* (1925).

It was natural for Werfel to turn to the theatre as a medium for his ideas, "not as a dramatist hoping to amuse or excite but as a prophet whose word must be carried to larger audiences." His first attempt was a "magic trilogy in verse" called *Spiegelmensch* (1920). It expressed his doctrine of abnegation of self as a means of attaining perfection, of the conflict of the individual against the evil inherent in himself. Other plays with profound psychological implications followed: *Schweiger* (1922), a study of split personality; *Paulus unter den Juden* (1925); *The Goat Song* (1926), which was produced by the Theatre Guild in New York. His *Juarez and Maximilian* (1926) was a series of dramatic tableaus.

Werfel as a dramatist is perhaps best known for his *Goat Song,* a symbolic drama. An extraordinarily effective stage production, its hidden thesis was that natural impulses held down by traditional shackles of shame grow evil and eventually destroy their jailers. Pan, shackled, becomes an evil monster, in whose train follow "arson, revolution and rape."

WERFEL, FRANZ—*Continued*

Werfel is an unusually prolific author, counting something like 35 books to his credit. Best known in the United States are: *The Hidden Child* (1933); *The Forty Days of Musa Dagh* (1934); *Pascarella Family* (1935); *Twilight of a World* (1937). All of these works are remarkable for the lucidity of their style and the profundity of thought and emotion. The *Forty Days of Musa Dagh* was hailed in the United States as "a contemporary novel full of the breath, the flesh and blood, and bone and spirit of life." Another critic said: "It raises the name of Franz Werfel to new dignity in letters. . . It could make a great poem. Werfel has made of it a noble novel." It also set the style for mammoth novels like *Anthony Adverse* and *Gone with the Wind*. The book was placed on the Nazi "undesirable" list shortly after its publication.

Not so successful as his novels was his play, *The Eternal Road*, which was produced in New York by Max Reinhardt in 1937. George Jean Nathan described it spitefully as "a super Sears-Roebuck catalogue of Old Testament gods with an elaborate index of Reinhardt mobs, Bel Geddes (see sketch this issue) scenic devices and Westinghouse Electrical Company 'dinguses.'" Werfel's preoccupation with Biblical subjects continued, however, and in 1938 his *Hearken unto the Voice*, dealing with the life of Jeremiah, was published in America.

Werfel is a diffident, dark-haired, moon-faced man with dark brown eyes behind round horn-rimmed glasses. He has a rather withdrawn air, and has been very retiring ever since he fought in the War in his youth. He hates to talk about himself. When Georges Schreiber asked Werfel to write a brief autobiography to accompany a sketch of himself in the former's book, *Portraits and Self-Portraits*, Werfel wrote the briefest and most reluctant one in the book. He said: "I have an insuperable aversion to writing my autobiography. . . My lifework is to be objective and to formulate ideas but not to chat idly about myself. Aside from that I have nothing more to say except that I was born on September 10, 1890, that I have written many books and that I took part in the War."

References

N Y Times p16 O 14 '40 por
Sat R Lit 15:17+ F 27 '37; 26:4 O 19 '40
Block, Mrs. A. C. Contemporary Drama: the Conflict Within the Individual *In* Changing World in Plays and Theatre p133-93 1939
Chandler, F. W. Expressionism at Its Best: Kaiser, Toller, Werfel *In* Modern Continental Playwrights p407-37 1931
Drake, W. A. Franz Werfel *In* Contemporary European Writers p28-42 1928

Kunitz, S. J. ed. Living Authors 1937
Schreiber, G. ed. Franz Werfel *In* Portraits and Self-Portraits p159-61 1936
Who's Who
Who's Who in American Jewry

WERNE, ISAAC, RABBI Dec 2, 1876— Mar 10, 1940 Chief rabbi of the Los Angeles Orthodox Rabbinate; contributor to Jewish and other periodicals

References

Who's Who in American Jewry

Obituaries

N Y Herald Tribune p22 Mr 12 '40

WEYGAND, MAXIME (vā'-gäN) Jan 21, 1867- Former commander in chief of the Allied Armies

On May 19, 1940 General Weygand replaced General Gamelin (see sketch this issue) as commander in chief of the Allied Armies. Just as in 1918, the Germans were threatening Amiens; as in 1918, its possession would separate the British and French forces, with tragic consequences to the Allied cause. It seemed entirely appropriate for the French to turn to General Weygand when nothing less than a miracle was expected, for as Foch's chief of staff he had once assisted at this same miracle. And about this "bandy-legged, undersized, tight-lipped, hard-boiled" little general had been woven the kind of personal legend that inspires belief in his wonder-working qualities. Less than one month later General Weygand and his army had capitulated to Germany.

There is a dash of mystery in Weygand's parentage. He was born in Brussels, Belgium on January 21, 1867 above Waterloo Tavern, but brought up on the Belgian estate of the childless Empress Charlotte. Germans say he is "supposed to be the illegitimate issue of a Hapsburg, namely of that Emperor of Mexico, Maximilian, who met such an adventurous end"—and although this is hardly possible, it is true that his mother was a German from the Saar district. After attending preparatory school at the Lycée Louis-le-Grand, he was sent in 1886 to St. Cyr, French training school for officers, by old Leopold II of Belgium. Here he showed a remarkable talent for mathematics that might have made him a great tactician, but Maxime Weygand was not primarily interested in the academic side of military life: he wanted to be a cavalryman, and eventually to command. When he was graduated in 1888 with high honors he was posted as sub-lieutenant to the 4th Dragoons at Chambéry, and since as a foreigner his opportunity for advancement in the army would be limited, he elected to become a French citizen.

Next Weygand was found at the Cavalry School at Saumur, where he emerged a captain; he was second in command of a squadron, a squadron commander, aide-de-camp to General de Broissia; in 1902, back at Saumur as an instructor; in 1907, a major in the 7th Hussars; in 1909, chief instructor in tactics at Saumur. He was now eligible for the Ecole de Guerre, but his ambition had not changed: he still wanted to lead troops. In 1913 he finally attracted the attention of General Joffre, chief of the general staff, during a course at the Centre des Hautes Etudes Militaires, was taken by Joffre on a mission to Russia, found himself commander of a Hussar Regiment—yet when the World War actually came, it was no command that he was given, but the position of chief of staff to Marshal Foch. On September 21, 1914 a 47-year-old cavalryman, "slightly bow-legged, black-haired, with soft brown eyes and a clipped mustache," began to serve as Foch's official shadow, and was to remain in Foch's shade until 1923.

Weygand adjusted himself to his position so well that the combination of Foch and Weygand has since become one of the most famous in French history, and Foch has given credit to Weygand as chief organizer of victory. The great marshal often said: "Weygand, il est moi." But, as Liddell Hart (see sketch this issue) suggested: "That he fitted his rôle so perfectly, not only in work but in self-effacement, was a jest of fate at the expense of a man who, imbued with the cavalry spirit, longed to command troops." With unfailing tact he protected his chief from annoyance and from the irritation of detail, carried out orders, was available when Foch told others, as he often did: "See Weygand about this." The two men were so close that "toward the end of their association it was said that Foch could mutter a few unintelligible syllables, wave his hands a few times and Weygand would produce a fully detailed order for the movement into battle of half a million men." Foch's military theory of "attaque, attaque, attaque" left an indelible impression on Weygand which was invaluable when added to his own strategical caution and insistence upon detail.

In 1916 Weygand was made brigadier general; in December 1917 he succeeded Foch on the Supreme Inter-Allied War Council at Versailles; and when, in the spring of 1918, there was appointed one supreme commander for the Allies and America, and that commander Foch, Weygand's title was chief of the general staff of the Allied Armies. At the end of the War he was a lieutenant general, and in 1918 he was made commander of the Légion d'Honneur, cited for "activity, vigilance, decision."

For a short time after the War Maxime Weygand remained in obscurity; then in July 1920, at a time when the Allied Armies of Intervention were determined to crush the Bolsheviki, Foch received word from Marshal Pilsudski of Poland: "Send us Foch or we perish." Pilsudski had marched on Kiev with his forces, but in the Ukraine his armies had been routed by the Russians,

International

MAXIME WEYGAND

the tide had been turned, and the Red cavalry was now storming the gates of Warsaw. Foch announced: "Send them Weygand. He will do just as well as I would." Rushing across Germany in a special train, taking with him 600 French Army officers, Weygand arrived in Poland to act as adviser (and, in fact, commander) for the Polish Army. That his tactics were remarkably sound is shown by his terse report: "August 16: Start of the offensive. August 21-24: Surrender of routed Bolshevist troops." When he returned to France, hailed as the "Savior of Poland," he gave credit to "the heroic Polish Army" for the victory.

Weygand was at one time particularly hated by the Germans as a leading figure in the "tragi-comedy of disarming and humiliating Germany," and is said to have represented the spirit of the military clauses of the Peace Treaty. In 1923, in the chaos following the French occupation of the Ruhr, he was acting as sort of a "high coordinator" in that region, but was called from Germany to Syria in April of the same year, appointed high commissioner in Syria. He was not in Syria long either, for his clerical and royalist background made him suspect to the French government that came to power in 1924 (he had been accused by Clemenceau of being "knee deep in Priests," went to Mass nearly every day, and there had always been those in France who feared that "Weygand the militarist may be Weygand the monarchist"). He was immediately made director of the Centre of High Military Studies, however, and, since French governments change, he was to be chief of the general staff in 1930. Before his death in 1929 Foch had advised a certain French Senator to call on Weygand

WEYGAND, MAXIME—*Continued*

if military peril ever threatened France—
"You will be tranquil," he said.

In 1931 Gamelin took Weygand's place
as chief of the general staff and Weygand
became vice-president of the Higher Council
of War and general inspector of the Army.
Aggressively nationalistic, in May 1933 he
was advocating the plan of a preventive war
against Germany. But this did not mean
that the political (as opposed to the military) implications of Hitler's rise to power
upset him, for after 1934, when the Stavisky
scandal brought a near-revolution in France,
Weygand himself was continually expected
to emerge as the "man on horseback" to
overthrow the republic and to proclaim a
dictatorship. He was a patron of the *Jeu-
nesses Patriotes,* a semi-fascist youth organization; he was one of the guiding spirits of
the *Cagoulards,* or "hooded men," who plotted
to overthrow the French Republic, and who
were supposed to be subsidized by French industrial magnates and a foreign country. The
expected *putsch* never took place, however,
and the following year, having reached the
retirement age of 68, Weygand was relieved
of all active duties, though continued by
special statute on the active list of the
Army.

Retirement was not easy for Weygand; although nearly 70, he still demanded activity.
But everyone believed his military life over.
Sir George Aston's dedication to his biography of Marshal Foch strikes a conclusive
note: "Dedicated to General Weygand in
token of admiration of the example of
loyalty and devotion to a great chief which
he set to the staff officers of all armies for
all time." Weygand announced: "I can still
serve the Army by writing its history.
An old soldier can make a historian of military affairs"—and began working industriously on his *Histoire de l'Armée Française.* In 1936, when Hitler marched into
the Rhineland, he proclaimed from out of
his semi-retirement: "I am not pessimistic
—if only France will learn the lessons of her
experience." He wrote dozens of articles
and delivered countless speeches on military
affairs, analyzing France's situation, and before the War made the assertion that her
military strength was geared primarily for a
defensive war.

In August 1939, with war imminent, 72-
year-old Maxime Weygand "at last realized
his lifelong ambition to command a great
French Army: he was returned to Syria as
commander in chief of the French Forces in
the Levant." When war came a month
later he was commander in chief of the
Theatre of Operations of the Near East.
In this office it was necessary for him to
get along not only with his British allies
and his near-allies, the Turks, but to preserve friendly relations among his strangely
mixed French colonial troops and to retain
the loyalty of the colonials. "The touch of
mystery about the man himself" helped, and
"the whispers that he is of royal, perhaps even

of Napoleonic descent" were magnified into
"splendid and alluring mysteries in the mys-
tery-loving East." When he went to horse
races, the Arabs whom he passed en route to
the bookmaker were likely to salute him by
falling on their knees. A man of great personal magnetism, Weygand was said to be
idolized by his own soldiers as well, and there
was little but confidence in the generalship of
France's Eastern commander.

In December 1939 it is reported that Weygand came uninvited to a session of the Allied
Supreme War Council and wanted an immediate declaration of war against Italy and
Russia. The Russians also believed that
their old enemy for nine months plotted the
seizure of the Baku oil fields while stationed
in the East.

By May 1940 there had been no action
in the East. Holland had been conquered
by the Germans, Belgium occupied; the
Germans were rapidly moving toward the
Channel, threatening to separate the British and
French forces. French Premier Paul Reynaud
(see sketch this issue) announced that in such
a crisis changes in leadership might have to be
made; on May 19 he followed his announcement with the appointment of General
Maxime Weygand as commander in chief of
the Allied Armies, replacing the less aggressive General Maurice Gamelin. It was
expected that if any commander could save
the situation Weygand could. He did not save
the situation, for after complaining privately
that he had been called in two weeks too late
to correct "Gamelin's blunders" and that there
was little chance of holding out, after emphasizing the menace of a Communist revolution
in France, he joined with Pétain (see sketch
this issue) and other members of Reynaud's
Cabinet in voting for an armistice with the
Germans. In the succeeding Pétain government he was made Minister of Defense.

Apologists say that Weygand was misled
by others, that he underestimated the strength
of France's ally, Britain, and that he was persuaded that Hitler would really grant honorable peace terms to France. There are rumors that he afterward realized his mistake
and that he is not thoroughly trusted by the
Vichy government. In October 1940, having
recovered from minor injuries sustained in an
airplane accident in September, he left France
to take up his duties in French Colonial Africa
as general delegate of the Vichy government
for civil and military affairs—supposedly to
bolster the allegiance of the French colonies
to Vichy and weaken the influence of De
Gaulle's (see sketch this issue) "Free French"
movement there. Some say that this is not
precisely what he is doing, however.

This "small, spare, bullet-headed general
with the quizzical smile" once defined his job,
to a correspondent (who found the rest of the
interview productive of "all the professional
satisfaction of a quiet chat with King Tutankhamen," and who stated in despair that
Weygand has "the most unreadable face
east of Damon Runyon"): "I am a fireman.
If a fire breaks out anywhere within my
reach, I shall try to put it out."

He has preserved the energy of a man much younger. Until recently he rode every day of his life; as a retired officer his chief exercise was a five-mile morning walk. During his first term in Syria he was celebrated for his ability to vault into the saddle of his Arabian horse without touching the stirrups, and he is known as a tennis player. Although he doesn't smoke, he drinks wine with every meal except breakfast and is something of a gourmet. His favorite food is corn on the cob, however, and in Paris, on Sunday nights when the servants had gone out, he and his wife used to have a private banquet. He has always been intensely interested in the press and reads every word written about him and his army, perhaps because he himself has published many books: *Turenne* (1929); *Le 11 Novembre* (1932); *Histoire Militaire de Mohammed Aly et de Ses Fils* (1926) and *Histoire de l'Armée Francaise* (1938). For several years he has been a member of the French Academy, taking the seat of Joffre, who died in 1931.

In 1900 Maxime Weygand married Renée de Forsanz, and they have two sons, the younger of whom was an officer in the regular army, now in the War Office, the other a civil engineer.

References

Collier's 105:17+ Ap 27 '40 il por
Illustration 204:91 S 23 '39
Life 8:94-6+ My 20 '40 pors
Liv Age 348:104-7 Ap '35; 352:399-403 Jl '37; 357:108-14 O '39
N Y Times p5 My 20 '40; p1+ My 20 '40 por; p3 O 23 '40
R Deux Mondes s8 4:140-55 Jl 1 '31
Scholastic 36:10 F 26 '40 por
Spec 164:712 My 24 '40
Dictionnaire National des Contemporains 1936
Gunther, J. More about Frenchmen *In* Inside Europe p182-99 1940
Simone, A. J'Accuse 1940
Who's Who

WHEELER, BURTON KENDALL Feb 27, 1882- United States Senator from Montana, 1923-

Address: b. United States Senate, Washington, D. C.; h. Butte, Montana

The man whom the La Follette brothers called "a fearless fighter for the common people" was born in Hudson, Massachusetts on February 27, 1882. He was the tenth son of a poor shoemaker, Asa Leonard, and his wife, Mary Elizabeth (Tyler) Wheeler, and the descendant of Quakers who had settled in Massachusetts in the seventeenth century. Burton took a commercial course at Hudson High School, was graduated in 1900 and then worked as a bookkeeper in Boston until by the second September after graduation he had $750 in the bank. With the money he had earned he intended to study law at the University of

BURTON K. WHEELER

Michigan (he had relatives in Ann Arbor), and although before he left for the university he lost $500 of his fortune in a bank crash he managed to work his way through by waiting on tables, hiring himself out as a stenographer to the dean, and peddling *Old Doctor Chase's Receipt Book* around the countryside during summer vacations. He was president of his class, leader of the anti-fraternity group, but when he received his LL. B. in 1905, "an overworked, emaciated lad of 23," there was no job waiting for him.

During one vacation he had met Lulu M. White, the daughter of an Albany, Illinois farmer, while trying to sell her father a book. *Old Doctor Chase* had unwittingly brought about a romance. Lulu's uncle was in Colorado, and for a while Burton worked in a law office in Telluride, but then was off again— to Salt Lake City; to Portland, Oregon; to San Francisco; Los Angeles; Tucson, Arizona. On October 15, 1905, he reached Butte, Montana, with just $50 in his pocket. The only job offered him there was one collecting bills for $50 a month. He refused it and was planning to catch a train for other parts when he was fleeced of his $50 in a poker game. There was nothing to do but to accept the job, stay in Butte. Burt Wheeler stayed there for a long, long time.

His office was in the same building with that of the prosecutor, and from time to time Wheeler was appointed to defend someone without counsel, taking labor cases for the most part. In 1906 he was actually admitted to the Montana Bar, and by September 1907 he was able to marry Lulu. Butte was the general headquarters for the copper kings, notably the Anaconda Copper Company. In the panic of 1907 the mines were shut down, and the young attorney found himself with a jobless clientele. Offered a partnership, he accepted it, and in turn found himself shoved

WHEELER, BURTON K.—*Continued*

into politics by his partner as delegate to a
local convention from the Seventh Ward.
The smell of Butte politics he found "almost
as noxious as the sulphur dioxide burned
from the ore before it was sent to the
smelter." As a philosophic rancher once observed, "no one in Montana really sets easy
'till he decides whether he's for or agin' the
Company." But Burton Wheeler was to be
in politics, too, for a long, long time. In
1910 the copper barons staged one of their
periodic fake "reform" campaigns, and innocent of what was expected of him, in 1911
Wheeler was elected on their ticket to the
State House of Representatives.

During the first session (he was in the
Legislature until 1913) he voted generally
with the conservatives, but then he began to
rebel, to fight for laws to better working
conditions in the mines. When ordered not
to support for Senator "mustachioed, fearless
Thomas J. Walsh," who was opposed to the
copper interests, Wheeler turned around and
campaigned for him. Walsh was defeated
in that election, and so was Wheeler when
he ran for Attorney General, but in 1913
Walsh, grateful for Wheeler's support, induced President Wilson to appoint him United States District Attorney for Montana. In
the next election Walsh himself was elected
Senator.

Wheeler was a "born prosecutor": while he
was in office it was one indictment after
another. But in Butte they didn't consider
his victims well chosen. Before and during
the First World War he refused to take action
against the pacifists and the I. W. W., and
upon investigation of a violent labor conflict
in the mines reported that the strikes were
being provoked by the mine owners as part
of a scheme to force the government to raise
the fixed price for copper. During the War
he was considered a dangerous radical, was
once driven out of a Montana town when
he tried to speak. In 1918 Walsh was
threatened with defeat in the next election
unless he sacked Wheeler; Wheeler resigned,
was offered a Federal judgeship, refused, saying he wanted "to fight it out with the people
of Montana."

He did. In 1920 Wheeler ran for Governor on a Non-Partisan League ticket which
included also a Negro and a Blackfoot Indian. It was a Republican year, and in
addition "every weapon was used against him
except the Anaconda smokestack." Posters
charged him with fealty to both the Kaiser
and Lenin; it was said that if he were elected
the mines would close. He was not elected,
but even so the depression that followed
closed the mines, the Red scare began to
abate, and people began to wonder. In 1922
the charge brought by Wheeler's enemies
that he wanted to introduce free love into
Montana didn't alarm anyone very much, and
when he ran for the Senate the farmers and
miners and railroad men elected him. They
have stuck by him, and he has been Senator
from Montana ever since.

Within his first three months in the Senate
in 1923 Wheeler became spokesman for a
group of "New Democrats," corresponding
roughly to the La Follette group among the
Republicans. In 1924 he got a whiff of the
Teapot Dome scandal, introduced a resolution asking Attorney General Daugherty to
resign, demanded an investigation of the
Department of Justice. Daugherty was
eventually forced out, but he didn't forgive
Wheeler. His Department of Justice agents
were sent to Montana, and after several
months and an expenditure of $250,000 in-
dicted Wheeler on a charge of unlawfully
receiving money as a retainer fee to influence
the issuance of oil and gas prospecting permits. The indictment came just in time to
embarrass him in the coming election. A
Senate Committee headed by Senator Borah
(see sketch this issue) reported "no foundation" for the charge, however, and Wheeler
was acquitted in ten minutes—just as a telegram arrived telling of the birth of one of
his three daughters, Marion Montana. Several
times since, Wheeler has requested that his
dossier in the files be either returned or
destroyed, but his requests have been refused.

"During the subsequent doldrums of the
Republican heyday, Wheeler was one of the
most militant dissidents in Congress." In
1924, "sickened by a party that found John
W. Davis the best it could do" (at that time
Franklin Roosevelt was the Vice-Presidential
nominee on the same ticket), he strayed from
the Democratic fold, became La Follette's
running mate on a Progressive ticket that
advocated public control of natural resources,
labor legislation, federal aid for farmers and
subordination of the Supreme Court to Congress. Oswald Garrison Villard (see sketch
this issue) was with him in the 1924 campaign
and found him "sound by my tests and beliefs, courageous, quite willing to be on the
unpopular side and an extremely effective
campaigner . . . a remarkable actor, with a
great sense of the dramatic."

In 1928 Wheeler was back with the Democrats, supporting Alfred E. Smith, and he
was for Roosevelt for President even before
his re-election to the New York Governorship
in 1930—the first member of the Senate to
propose him for the office. In the spring of
1932 he toured the West, convincing many
liberals Roosevelt was the man to support,
lining up votes from Northwest and mountain delegations. He even won Huey Long
over to the Roosevelt camp. There was little
patronage for Wheeler after Roosevelt
reached the White House, however, and it
is said that as Wheeler had hopes of being
rewarded with the Vice-Presidential nomination and was disappointed when it went to
Garner, likewise he was disappointed when
Tom Walsh died and his post as Attorney
General was given to Homer Cummings, an
intimate of Wheeler's bitterest enemy in
Montana. The support of the Railroad
Brotherhood had kept Wheeler on his feet
when the Democratic Party was collapsing
all around him; in turn, Wheeler was faithful

to his supporters; he didn't understand any other brand of political loyalty.

Nevertheless he supported the greater part of the New Deal legislation. His first move of public opposition to Roosevelt was over the creation of the NRA, in which he saw the negation of the Sherman Antitrust Law and its supporting legislative and judicial interpretations. In 1935 he, more than any other man, got the Public Utilities Holding Company Act, for which President Roosevelt was fighting, passed intact with the death sentence clause. But in 1937 came Roosevelt's proposal to "pack" the Supreme Court. Almost immediately after it was proposed, before much opposition had become evident, Wheeler declared himself against it, denouncing it as a reactionary scheme to acquire "dictatorial power." He argued that although he thought the present Court wrong more often than right, if the Democrats destroyed the respect for the Court by adding enough justices to attain a majority, there would be nothing to prevent a more reactionary administration from enlarging it to their advantage when an opportunity came. He found particular danger in the section permitting any administration to send special hand-picked judges anywhere in the country to try cases in which the government was interested. "Where would anybody's civil liberties be?" he asked.

There were powerful conservative forces aligned against the measure, and the leadership of Wheeler, a Democrat, a Westerner, and a progressive, was immensely helpful. The bill was garroted; the conservatives were grateful. But the mildest name labor spokesmen called him was "traitor." It became a political fashion to point out that Wheeler's "past career had been done with mirrors and that he really was a 'reactionary' at heart." His support of Jacob Thorkelson, who as a Congressman had turned out to be a bitter anti-Semite, was remembered. Although Wheeler's voting record couldn't have given the vested interests much comfort, although he was even then conducting a major investigation into railroad financing in which he attacked the House of Morgan and the Guaranty Trust Company, it was almost universally claimed that he had "sold out to Anaconda." For years Wheeler had been saying: "When you see my name on the front pages of the corporation papers you will know that I have sold out." Now his picture and name were "a fixture in the corporation press of Montana." Students in Montana State University formed a "Wheeler for Ex-Senator Club," miners and railroad men in his own state vowed they would never vote for him again.

Said Wheeler: "I will be fighting for democracy with a small 'd' when many of the office-holding liberals of today will desert the New Deal ship for fat jobs with economic royalists in the caves of Wall Street." And when the wife of one influential citizen congratulated him on his "change," he told her: "Madam, I haven't changed. Perhaps

you have changed, perhaps the times have changed, but the Wheeler you now want to put in the White House is the same one you wanted put in jail a few years ago."

When the storm blew over Wheeler was found still sitting in the Senate and supporting liberal measures, although he was one of those who voted against the New Deal "spend-lend" bill in the summer of 1939. Roosevelt regained his support. In 1939 he said: "Franklin Delano Roosevelt is the one President since Lincoln who has done more for the workers and average people than any other." It was only with the coming of World War II that another break came. Before the War Wheeler had been concerned mainly with domestic problems—as chairman of the Senate Committee on Interstate Commerce, as a student of the railroad problem, as an opponent of the extension of Hull's (see sketch this issue) reciprocal trade agreements, as an advocate of the remonetization of silver. He had never labeled himself an isolationist. But he voted against the repeal of the arms embargo, he mildly denounced Roosevelt for paying more attention to matters abroad than to United States affairs, and later he came out publicly against permitting the United States to rearm the Allies. Finally, after giving his approval to Roosevelt's *fait accompli* of sending planes to the Allies, he almost immediately reversed himself by saying: "I do not want to have to break with the Democratic Party, I shall break with it if it is going to be a war party."

On June 30 Wheeler declared that a "new and great antiwar party" would be formed unless the Democrats pledged not to send American soldiers "to a foreign shore." He opposed Roosevelt's Cabinet appointments of Knox and Stimson (see sketches this issue), suggesting a coalition of "peacemakers"— not "war-makers." And on the same day Senator Johnson, Democrat from Colorado, made the statement that Wheeler was the only Democrat who could defeat Willkie (see sketch this issue), and that if a non-interventionist Democratic candidate was not selected, a third party, a "peace party," would be created. Shortly afterward John L. Lewis threw in his full support, and Wheeler announced himself as a candidate for the nomination whether or not Roosevelt was a candidate for a third term. Actually, by the time of the convention, he was no longer in the running.

After the convention, Wheeler began a campaign against conscription. "Conscription" he said, was "the farthest step yet in the direction of war" and might lead to a "military tyranny," might "ruin our entire industrial establishment by building a false economy." He lost his campaign, but was, nevertheless, re-elected to the Senate in November 1940.

It is said that on many issues Wheeler finds himself more at home with Senators Norris and La Follette than with most members of his own party. "A politician with principles," he is a firm believer in what he

WHEELER, BURTON K.—*Continued*

calls "Economic Democracy." "The principles of democracy," he has said, "can become effective only if they prevail in the industrial as well as the political life of a nation." He is against great corporations dominating the business of the United States and would bring about decentralization by heavy taxes. He believes that the people should own all natural resources, that public utilities should be operated by federal, state or municipal government. (But he has repudiated the public ownership of railroads, one plank in his 1924 La Follette platform.) While supporting Roosevelt's enormous defense budget, to Wheeler "the solution of our domestic problems is the first line of our defense. Give to a people who already enjoy the blessings of liberty and freedom the opportunity to live in modest comfort and we will need to fear neither foreign aggression nor the penetration of economic and social ideologies."

Methodist, Mason, Elk, Wheeler is something of a "joiner." He is "a lanky, rumpled man who walks with a rapid shamble, smiling quizzically, his glance a friendly, direct glare through octagonal spectacles, smoking a cigar with the superb nonchalance of Groucho Marx." His hat is a dented Stetson. Talkative, jovial, with only a hint of Massachusetts in either enunciation or manner, he has "no more stuffing to his shirt than husky arms and chest provide," is democratic in behavior without being a backslapper." He has been around the world twice; on Lake MacDonald in Glacier National Park he has a log cabin whose woodshed and sleeping porch he built with the help of his three sons; says he consults his wife on every important political move. Occasionally he threatens to retire from politics, but such threats are "like a sea captain growling against the sea." In spite of occasional stress and strain he manages to remain philosophical, saying "nearly everything, except perhaps dinner, seems less important after a nap."

References

Cong Digest 18:213-15 Ag '39
Cur Hist 46:29-31 Ag '37 por; 51:25-7 Mr '40 por (cover)
Harper 180:609-18 My '40
Nation 145:217-19 Ag 28 '37; 145:304 S 18 '37; 145:415 O 16 '37; 150:532-6 Ap 27 '40
New Repub 90:261 Ap 7 '37; 102:527-30 Ap 22 '40
Sat Eve Post 210:8-9+ N 13 '37 il pors
Time 34:11 O 9 '39 por; 35:21-2 Ap 15 '40 pors; 35:15 Je 24 '40
Va Q R 16 no2:279-84 [Ap] '40
Manly, B. M. Leading Facts in the Wheeler Case 1925
Tucker, R. T. and Barkley, F. R. "Burt" Wheeler: Montana Maverick *In* Sons of the Wild Jackass p269-91 1932

Unofficial Observer [pseud.] One-to-Sixteen! (B. K. Wheeler) *In* American Messiahs p118-33 1935
Who's Who in America
Who's Who in Law
Who's Who in the Nation's Capital

WHEELOCK, WARREN　Jan 15, 1880-
Artist

Address: 1931 Broadway, New York City

Warren Wheelock, known for his paintings and sculptures of men who have made American history, was represented at the Whitney, Museum's Contemporary American Art Show, January 10 to February 10, 1940, with a painting, *Washington at Valley Forge.* The painting shows Washington, as general, standing in the bitter cold, leaning against the blowing wind, his cape flying out behind him; and stern upon his face the weight of the problems before him. It has aroused much noteworthy critical comment.

An exhibition of his sculpture was held at the Robinson Galleries, March 18 to April 7, 1940. Of the 37 pieces on display, several were casts in bronze and plaster; others were carvings in walnut, applewood, oak, teakwood, satinwood, ebony, butternut and mahogany. Among these were his *Black Dancer, Dictator, Roosevelt Head, Sailor and Girl, Eve, Walt Whitman* and several *Lincoln* subjects.

He has exhibited his works in numerous one-man shows, such as at the Western Museum Association, Ehrich Galleries, Dudensing Gallery, American Group Galleries, Dartmouth College, and also at many group shows in New York and other cities.

Wheelock was born in Sutton, Massachusetts, January 15, 1880, of an old New England family. His first American ancestor was the Rev. Ralph Wheelock, born in 1600 in England and educated at Cambridge, who came from Shropshire to the Massachusetts Bay Colony with his wife Rebecca in 1637. Later he founded and taught the first public school in America. Dr. Eleazar Wheelock, founder and first president of Dartmouth College was also a direct descendant of the Rev. Ralph Wheelock but is not in the same direct line of descent as Warren Wheelock. Other ancestors were Simeon Wheelock, who led a company of Minute Men at Lexington and Concord at the beginning of the Revolutionary War; an uncle Simeon who distinguished himself during the Civil War. Warren Wheelock himself enlisted in the Spanish American War. This background no doubt accounts for his absorbing interests in the American historical scene. From boyhood on, American leaders have been his heroes, especially Paul Revere, who became the subject of his famous carved sculpture *Paul Revere's Ride.*

Growing up at Webster, Massachusetts, young Wheelock was accustomed to constructing things out of wood: his father was a carpenter and house painter, and he had access to his tools. During his high school days he built a rowboat and even made the oars for it; with the help of other boys he designed and constructed an indoor running track. He considers carpentry an excellent foundation training for sculpture.

He enlisted in the Spanish-American War two months before he was graduated from high school. On his return he worked at several jobs: in a woodworking shop, as a plumber's helper and as a draftsman for a civil engineer.

In 1902 Wheelock went to Pratt Institute, Brooklyn, where he studied painting for three years; and from 1905 to 1910 he taught drawing there. In 1910 he entered the field of commercial art, in which he was intermittently engaged for 12 years. During this period he spent several years in North Carolina where he remodeled houses and designed and built a house for himself. Most of the work he did himself, splitting shingles by hand, and even making tools for special windows and doors. His first carving was the wood pattern or model for andirons for his fireplace.

During these years in the South he painted a few landscapes, and several portraits of Blue Ridge Mountain folks. Wheelock is noted for his many sculptures of Lincoln; among these Carolina mountaineers he observed Lincoln prototypes: men long, lean, lanky and round-shouldered; men with large feet and powerful hands; men who had little schooling, whose faces were molded by hard work, who made their fences out of split rails just as Lincoln did.

In 1917 he returned to New York and worked three years in the art department of a magazine, painting in his spare time. He began free-lancing in 1920, his work including covers for *Current Opinion*, drawings for the New York *Times* and other publications and advertising illustrations. He first showed paintings in the Society of Independent Artists in 1921 and again in 1922. In that year he began to carve in wood and stone. He is self-taught in sculpture.

Having decided to devote himself entirely to painting and sculpture, Wheelock in 1923 went to Woodstock, New York, where he has lived and worked several years. In 1925 his painting *Old Man and Child* received honorable mention at the Pan-American exhibition in Los Angeles and was acquired by the Los Angeles Museum. Since then his work has been extensively exhibited; his paintings and sculptures have been acquired by numerous private collectors such as Juliana Force, Edsel Ford, M. R. Goldsmith, Mrs. Eugene Meyer, C. B. Warren, David

WARREN WHEELOCK

Jacobson, Walter D. Teague and by museums and public institutions. Wheelock is also an inventor and has created several industrial designs for American manufacturers.

He married Marinobel Smith in 1925. They have no children.

In strong contrast to his interest in American leaders who have devoted their lives to liberty and democracy are Wheelock's paintings of other subjects and personalities. Of his carving of Hitler, *Voice of Destruction*, a dictator who has no consideration for human rights, Wheelock has said: "Here is the rudimentary upraised arm, and the large hole for torrents to pour through; no eyes—only holes, for this robot doesn't see; but jutting brows are there—a small front for skull and brain that does not exist."

References

> Am Artist 4:18 F '40
> Art Instruction S '37
> Life 8:114-17 My 20 '40 il
> N Y Herald Tribune p15 Ja 10 '40
> N Y Times p16 Ja 11 '40; p20 F 1 '40
> Time 35:53 Ap 1 '40 il
> Who's Who in American Art

WHEELWRIGHT, JOHN B. 1897—Sept 15, 1940 American poet; wrote four books of poetry, *Northwest Passage* (1917); *Rock and Shell* (1933); *Mirrors of Venus* (1938) and *Political Self-Portrait* (1940); at time of death (in an automobile accident in Boston) was at work on a book of American architecture

JOHN B. WHEELWRIGHT

References

Christian Sci Mon Mag p14 Jl 13 '40

Obituaries

N Y Times p21 S 16 '40

WHITE, FRANK Dec 12, 1856—Mar 23, 1940 Treasurer of the United States from 1921 to 1928; Governor of North Dakota from 1901 to 1905

References

Who's Who in America 1938-39
Who's Who in the Nation's Capital

Obituaries

N Y Herald Tribune p30 Mr 24 '40
N Y Times p1 Mr 24 '40 por
Newsweek 15:7 Ap 1 '40

WHITE, MARGARET BOURKE (bûrk) June 14, 1906- Industrial photographer

Address: c/o Life Magazine, Time Life Bldg, New York City; h. Darien, Connecticut

Because Margaret Bourke-White (she does not use the library form of her name above), a woman, made better pictures of factories, smoke stacks, bridges, water tanks and other industrial and more or less masculine subjects than most men, the world literally beat a path to her door. Her pictures have the artistic and realistic quality of bringing out the feeling and atmosphere of an industry or country.

Although she had taken art courses and photography courses, photography as a livelihood was more or less of an accident for Margaret Bourke-White. She was born in New York City, the daughter of Joseph and Minnie Elizabeth (Bourke) White. Her father was a naturalist, and she had started her college career with the idea of becoming

a biologist. In her junior year her father died, and she was faced with the responsibility of earning her own way. She began taking pictures of campus buildings and campus scenes. Everyone exclaimed, "how extraordinary", "how wonderful," and she sold many pictures. Next she did some work for an architect. In 1927 she tucked her diploma from Cornell University under her arm, and came to New York.

She succeeded in getting a prominent architect to look at her photographs. It was the beginning of her career as a successful industrial photographer. Since then Miss Bourke-White has been commissioned to take pictures of the 1934 drought in the Dakotas, of America's Cup yacht races in Narragansett Bay, and of the smoke stacks, turbines and flywheels of the country's largest industries. She has made three trips to Russia to record photographically the progress of the Five Year Plan. Her two travelogues, *Eyes on Russia* (1931), and *Red Republic* (1934) were the first moving pictures to be made in Soviet Russia with full permission of Soviet authorities. She has written and illustrated *U. S. S. R., A Portfolio of Photographs* (1934). She "has taken photographs in 21 countries, including the Arctic region."

The first large permanent photo-mural for the NBC studios in Rockefeller Center was done by her in 1933. She is unable to fill all the assignments sent her by leading magazines, advertising agencies, and private business moguls. She is a contributor to national magazines using photographs. In 1936 she was selected by American women as one of the ten outstanding women in the country. She was married first to Everett Chapman in 1925 and after a divorce married on February 27, 1939 to Erskine Caldwell, the writer (see sketch this issue).

Prerequisites for an industrial photographer, Miss Bourke-White says, are good health and strength, ability to do hard work, and readiness to work under unusual and sometimes dangerous conditions, such as standing on cranes, atop freight cars or rafters, lying in the snow to get just the right shot.

Early in October 1939, shortly after the start of the War in Europe, *Life* sent Miss Bourke-White on an assignment abroad. Her first stop was London, where she remained until early December. While in London she took pictures of the blackouts, of Winston Churchill (see sketch this issue) on his birthday (a full-sized one appeared on the cover of the April 29, 1940 issue of *Life* and of Emperor Haile Selassie. From London she traveled to Romania, taking pictures of the oil fields there, and through Bessarabia, where, she says, "I nearly froze my legs off while I was working in a blizzard." From Romania she sailed to Constanta on the Black Sea, then on to Istanbul, Turkey, where she took pictures of the President of Turkey, and was arrested for taking pictures in a Moslem

MARGARET BOURKE-WHITE

Temple during a prayer meeting. In Beirut, Syria, she took pictures of General Weygand (see sketch this issue), then commander of the Allied Forces in the Near East, and learned to ride a military camel. From Syria she went to Egypt, where she photographed the King of Egypt and the numerous French and British colonial troops stationed at the foot of the pyramids near the Nile.

"Kit," as Miss Bourke-White is called by her close friends, is an intense person. She loves her work, leaves no stone unturned in the accomplishment of an assignment. Besides being a distinguished artist in her field, she is an extremely able and devoted wife. When at home in Connecticut, she gets much pleasure from working about in her garden, and takes great pride in managing her home, Horseplay Hill.

In April 1940 her appointment as chief photographer for the new publication *PM* was announced. Previously she had been associate editor of *Fortune* (1929-33) and of *Life* (1933-40). In the fall of 1940 she left *PM* and returned to *Life* Magazine.

Her name, Bourke-White, is a combination of her mother's maiden name, Bourke, and her paternal name. She attended Columbia University (1922-23), the University of Michigan (1923-25), and received her B. A. from Cornell in 1927. In 1934 she illustrated Terhune's *Book of Sunnybank*. She also has illustrated *Freighter of Fortune; Story of Steel* and *One Thing Leads to Another*. In 1937 she collaborated with her husband in writing and illustrating *You Have Seen Their Faces*, a record of a trip through the cotton states from South Carolina, west to Arkansas and Louisiana. It has been called "a stirring and painful document, magnificently produced." The 64 photographs which Miss White took to illustrate her hus-

band's *North of the Danube* (1939) are called by critics the best work she has ever done. "Without them this memorial fresco could never have attained its breadth of expression nor its fullness of power. Words cannot capture the breathless beauty of some of these pictures or convey their peculiar moving quality."

References
    Christian Sci Mon Mag p5+ S 25 '35 pors
    Pict R 38:24+ D '36 por
    Sat R Lit 21:1 F 24 '40
    Scholastic 30:18-19+ My 15 '37 pors
    Kirkland, W. M. and Kirkland, F. Margaret Bourke-White Photographer of Steel *In* Girls Who Became Artists p34-45 1934
    Who's Who in America (under Bourke-White)

WHITE, PAUL W. June 9, 1902- Radio director of public affairs for Columbia Broadcasting System

Address: b. 485 Madison Ave, New York City; h. 400 E 52d St, New York City

Director of public affairs for the Columbia Broadcasting System, Paul Welrose White has a highly responsible position in these days of national tension and international crises. Since the Czechoslovakian crisis of 1938, which commanded all of radio's resources, White has made elaborate reconstruction and reorganization plans; he is now all set for the next crisis to come up. A trained newspaperman, White hates to go home, even to leave his desk, when something seems to be brewing, for fear the *big* story will break the minute he takes his eyes from teletype machine, cables, reports of foreign broadcasts and other details connected with his job.

He was born in Pittsburg, Kansas, June 9, 1902, the son of Anna (Pickard) and Paul Wichard White. He was already a reporter when he entered high school—on the Pittsburg *Headlight* and the Salina *Sun*. By the time his college career was under way at the University of Kansas, he was telegraph editor for a while on the Kansas City *Journal*. He married Sue Taylor of New York City in 1937 and they have two children, Joan and Susanne. He attended the Columbia University School of Journalism from 1921 to 1924.

After graduation White joined the city staff of the New York *Evening Bulletin* and in August 1924, the staff of the United Press. He remained with the UP in various capacities for more than six years. Then he was editor for a year of the United Features Syndicate and also head of the UP mail service. During these years White's name became one of the best known by-lines in the country. He covered the Hall-Mills trial, the anthracite coal strike, the Snyder-Gray trial, and the transatlantic flights of

PAUL W. WHITE

Lindbergh, Byrd, Ruth Elder, Chamberlin-Levine and others.

In December 1930 he was named news editor of the Columbia Broadcasting System, and became successively publicity director, vice-president and general manager of news service and director of public relations for the Columbia Broadcasting System. Studio 9 is his stronghold as public affairs director. From its efficient confines come strictly factual, unsensational reports of every last moment's news, by a staff which maintains a seven-day, 24-hour schedule.

White directs CBS's European commentators. Before these go on the air each evening, there is a brief period of five to ten minutes during which White chats informally and privately with his men in London and Paris. This is made possible, as are the subsequent broadcasts, by means of what radio technicians call a "cue channel": a two-way short-wave hookup which White arranged while in Europe during the summer of 1939. It is all part of his preparation for the string of 1940 history-making European war crises. A remarkable thing about the "cue channel" is that it enables White to converse with England and France simultaneously. To him, trans-Atlantic conversations are by this time a routine matter. He is ready for any big news which breaks and which electrifies the studio into action. The job of the director of public affairs for CBS is, in 1940, more than a full-time proposition.

References

Collier's 103:78 Ap 29 '39 por
New Yorker p16 Ja 20 '40
Variety Radio Directory

WHITE, WILLIAM ALLEN Feb 10, 1868- Editor of Emporia *Gazette*
Address: Emporia, Kansas

William Allen White, called "Bill" by everyone who knows him, has since 1895 been editor of a paper in a small Kansas town of less than 15,000 population. But his Emporia *Gazette* has become one of the most famous papers in the world, and Bill White's influence on national affairs cannot be gauged even by the number of his readers. There are very few twentieth-century issues that he hasn't taken a strong position on—his wife once confided that "he can't be an hour on an ocean liner without telling the captain how to run the ship"—and when he takes up the cudgels in any cause there are always people to listen. As an ardent Republican since pre-voting age he threw his editorial weight behind Wendell Willkie (see sketch this issue) in the 1940 Presidential election.

Editor White is short, fleshy, white-haired, with "a small, pinkish bald spot," and in his 70's looks like "an apple dumpling with a smile carved into its outer crust"—or, as he himself expressed it, "like a rear view of Cupid." He has lived in Kansas all his life and around newspaper offices nearly as long. Born in Emporia on February 10, 1868, the son of Dr. Allen White, a Jeffersonian Democrat, and Mary Ann (Hatton) White, a Republican Abolitionist, as a boy he earned his first dollar playing for dances in Butler County (his family moved to El Dorado when he was a year old). After graduation from the El Dorado High School in 1884 he went back to Emporia for a while, attending college; in 1885 he was back in El Dorado, working as a printer's devil on the *Democrat* and learning to compose copy while setting type by hand; then he was in Emporia again, setting type on the *News* and the *Democrat*, working as reporter on the *News*; and from 1886 to 1890 he attended the State University of Kansas, taking tramp trips over the country when not in school.

He didn't graduate because he quit college to take a job on the weekly El Dorado *Republican* at $18 a month. At the *Republican* he was successively printer, circulation manager, reporter, advertising hustler, finally manager, and with no more heights to aspire to he left to become editorial writer and Topeka correspondent for the Kansas City *Journal*; later (1892) editorial writer for the *Star*. At that time his aspirations were apparently more purely literary than later, for in 1893 he published a volume of poetry with Albert Bigelow Paine —*Rhymes by Two Friends* (which he afterward regretted and tried to buy up). The same year he married a school teacher, Sallie Moss Lindsay (which he has never shown any signs of regretting at all). Their honeymoon being contemporary with the crash of '93, all the young couple's savings vanished in a bank at Manitou, and Bill came back to Kansas to find himself jobless.

In 1895 he showed up in Emporia with $1.25 in his pocket, promptly borrowed $3,000 and bought the Emporia *Gazette*— "and so they lived happily ever after." Their son, William Lindsay White, a "taller, more stalwart" edition of his father and also a newspaperman, was born in 1900. Mary Katherine White was born in 1904 and is still remembered by readers of her father's moving, much-anthologized tribute to her which was published at the time of her death in 1921.

The young editor's statement of his editorial purpose that first year wasn't unusual: "The main thing is to have this paper represent the average thought of the best people of Emporia and Lyon County in all their varied interests." Only a year afterward his paper became famous. William Jennings Bryan's free silver-Populist following was growing everywhere: Kansas had already elected a Populist Governor, a Populist legislature. But the growing spirit of economic revolt made Bill White angry. On August 15, 1896, his paper came out with an editorial, written in haste and heat after an argument. "What's the Matter with Kansas?" was the title, and in hard-hitting, effectively turned phrases he described the struggle for social change as "raising hell," suggested "raising corn" instead. Mark Hanna got hold of the editorial, put over a million copies in circulation in pamphlet form, and it was reprinted all over the country. McKinley was elected, and Bill White began to find himself besieged with requests to back political campaigns and candidacies, to write articles and editorials on what's the matter with life, death and women's hats, to leave Emporia and edit everybody else's newspaper, to take any office he wanted under McKinley. The last requests didn't interest him, but he did become interested in politics "and took a hand in state matters," becoming known as "the Sage of Emporia."

During the Spanish-American War Editor White was writing: "'Some great sentient power—destiny, evolution or the Lord of Hosts—is guiding the course of this war." When his editorials were collected into a book in 1937 his footnote to that was: "Probably the devil." He was persistent in calling Bryan "a shallow fellow" and Eugene V. Debs "a charlatan," phrases he was also to apologize for later. He started his career as a reactionary. But from supporting such mild reforms as the short ballot, anti-pass laws for railroads and the direct election of United States Senators, he later came to acquire the "bug" of Rooseveltian progressivism. In 1912, elected Republican national committeeman, he broke away temporarily from the party to join the Bull Moose movement. And although he came back to his party, he was never quite the same.

White's attitude toward the First World War was at first isolationist, gradually grew more belligerent, until on the day war was declared he, too, was declaring it a war "to

WILLIAM ALLEN WHITE

save the soul of humanity." In 1917 he was sent to France by the American Red Cross as an observer; he was at the Paris Peace Conference in 1918, sending back articles; in 1919 he was a delegate to the Russian Conference at Prinkip. He came back persuaded that another war could be prevented not through isolation but through participation in European affairs, and became an advocate of the League of Nations. He was also one of the first to declare for recognition of Russia by the United States.

White's career from that time on has been summed up in the phrase: "the patient liberal." Some found him too patient. William Clugston is bitter: "No living journalist has done more to uphold the existing order of society by preying upon the emotions of the people and patting the Main Street Overlords upon the back." Admittedly he has been inconsistent. And party loyalty brought him back into the Republican fold at the time of every election, regardless of the admiration he has expressed for certain things he believed Wilson, La Follette or Roosevelt II stood for. Although he voted against Harding at the Republican Nominating Convention, he grew to think of him as "honest and courageous" until the Teapot Dome scandal broke; he supported Coolidge; Hoover was and is his great friend; he told Kansans to vote for their native son, Landon, in 1936. It is true that in 1924 he ran independently for Governor of Kansas—"in order to have my say against the Ku Klux Klan," he said—though Clugston claims it was in order to split the liberal vote so that the Republicans could get power back from the dirt-farmer dynasty then in control.

To some he has seemed contradictory. He wrote an editorial upholding the guilt of Sacco and Vanzetti (though changing his

WHITE, WILLIAM ALLEN—*Continued*

mind after their death), and yet, during the period when the "Red scare" was at its height, joined a delegation asking for Eugene Debs' pardon, proclaimed the innocence of Tom Mooney. In 1922 he won a Pulitzer Award for an editorial on freedom of speech—written after he himself had been arrested as a test case for displaying a placard expressing sympathy with striking railroad workers. He favored the graduated income tax, old-age pensions, abolition of child labor, "social security" and similar measures of social legislation before they became commonplace; yet opposed many others. On the whole he seems to be equally shocked by the present-day behavior of large-letter Capital and large-letter Labor: to him it is the "ordinary everyday man" who keeps the world going. In 1938 he made the statement that "our American experiment has succeeded in bringing comfort, some luxuries, to probably 85, certainly 80 per cent of the American people," figures which Upton Sinclair claimed were incredibly optimistic.

Editor White is not always preoccupied with politics. A great deal of his energy has gone into defending Emporia and towns like it against all challengers, including H. L. Mencken. He has written also in defense of unmarried mothers, the younger generation and swing (which he, personally, detests); he has eulogized babies, the latest scientific discovery, movie stars and corn-syrup. A collection of his editorials, *Forty Years on Main Street* (1937), is described as "an interesting bit of Americana combining a Main Street diary, a graph of the devious political path of a Progressive of Roosevelt's 'Bull Moose' Class of 1912, and an all-but-extinct type of personal journalism."

Considering his other activities, Bill White has published an amazing number of books—one every two or three years since *The Real Issue*, a collection of short stories which came out in 1896. Other short story collections and even novels have followed, but he has become most noted for Sullivanesque commentaries on American statesmen and politics. Taft, Wilson, Harding, Coolidge and Al Smith have been "ground under the keys of his typewriter again and again" in such books as *Politics: The Citizen's Business* (1924); *Calvin Coolidge: The Man Who Is President* (1925); *Masks in a Pageant* (1928); *Woodrow Wilson the Man* (1929). In 1938 appeared a second biography of Coolidge, *A Puritan in Babylon*, and in 1939 came *The Changing West: An Economic Theory About Our Golden Age*. All are distinguished by his "vigorous and pungent style," but one critic claims that the book which has most chance of living in "the literature of the future" is still *The Court of Boyville*, an imaginative juvenile published when he was only 31.

Editor White knows other countries than the United States and other states than Kansas, even though he is thoroughly sold on both. In 1930 he was a member of Hoover's Commission for Conciliation which went to Haiti. He has been abroad several times, in 1933 visited Russia ("I think the Russians are mad" was his verdict) and in the fall of 1935 sailed to the Orient. A Congregationalist and a Rotarian, he is an untiring "joiner." The list of educational and philanthropic associations of which he is a director is almost endless. In 1931 he was a member of President Hoover's Organization for Unemployment Relief and in April 1938 was elected president of the American Society of Newspaper Editors. He is in 1940 head of the Committee to Defend America by Aiding the Allies.

Never "high hat," never inhospitable, never afraid to change his mind, known for his "kindly, generous tolerance in his personal contacts", "Ol' Bill White" and his family are undoubtedly Emporia's best-loved and most-consulted citizens. In 1933 he wrote: "I have never had a major quarrel with anyone." The Whites live in a rambling house built of sandstone from the Garden of the Gods. Money doesn't mean much to them—"it has come easy and gone easy"—but the editor of the *Gazette* keeps his bills paid on the tenth of the month, "shaves every Sunday, Tuesday, Thursday and Saturday," and still writes even three-line "locals" himself.

References

Christian Sci Mon Mag p6 Ap 15 '39
Lit Digest 119:5 Ap 6 '35; 123:29-32 Ap 24 '37
Nation 146:693-5 Je 18 '38
New Repub 96:177-80 S 21 '38; 97:132 D 7 '38; 102:809 Je 17 '40
New Yorker 1:9-10 My 30 '25
Sat R Lit 16:6 My 8 '37 il
Scholastic 31:9 O 23 '37; 32:16S Mr 26 '38
Time 29:84+ Ap 26 '37 por; 31:42-3 My 16 '38; 35:41 My 20 '40 por; 36:12+ Ag 19 '40

Clugston, W. G. Rascals in Democracy 1940
Kunitz, S. J. ed. Authors Today and Yesterday 1933
Who's Who in America
Who's Who in Commerce and Industry
Who's Who in Journalism

WHITEMAN, WILBERFORCE JAMES
Sept 1, 1857—Dec 17, 1939 Music teacher; father of Paul Whiteman, band leader

Obituaries

Musical Am 60:32 Ja 10 '40
Time 35:41 Ja 1 '40

WIART, ADRIAN CARTON DE *See* Carton de Wiart, A.

WICKARD, CLAUDE RAYMOND Feb 28, 1893- United States Secretary of Agriculture

Address: b. Department of Agriculture, Washington, D. C.; h. 2101 New Hampshire Ave, N W, Washington, D. C.

In his first speech after he was made Secretary of Agriculture in August 1939 Claude R. Wickard stated: "I intend to carry out the policies of Henry A. Wallace." For more than six years Mr. Wickard has been a member of the Department of Agriculture under Wallace (see sketch this issue) and his promotion was made, according to Stephen Early, secretary to the President, because of Roosevelt's desire to have the department directed by someone from within its own organization. Whether Mr. Wickard will play the part in broad administration policy-making that Mr. Wallace has played has been doubted in some quarters; but there is no doubt that this "thorough-going New Dealer" will "continue and strengthen" the programs initiated by his predecessor.

According to Secretary Wickard the Federal farm program has enabled American agriculture to right itself, regain its strength and "look to the future with renewed hope." In these days of war and possible famine he feels that more than ever we must have a strong American agriculture, based on the "tried and sound two-horse team of soil conservation and production control." Right now agriculture is better prepared than any other industry to help bulwark democracy, he says, and it must remain so.

The Department of Agriculture in the past years has had its share of theorists; it also had members "with honestly calloused hands." Claude Wickard, whose 380-acre farm in Carroll County, Indiana grows wheat, corn, and alfalfa and raises Hampshire hogs and Aberdeen Angus cattle, came to the Department of Agriculture as a farmer and during the years he has risen from a minor administrative job to the department's head he has stayed a farmer. As director of the North Central Division, Secretary Wickard stressed farmer-administration of the AAA and was chiefly responsible for developing the effective farmer-committeeman set-up which now exists in the corn belt.

Claude Wickard was born on an Indiana farm near Camden, Indiana which his family has owned since 1840. His father, Andrew Jackson Wickard, still helps run the farm. His mother was Iva L. Kirkpatrick. Claude went to high school in Delphi, Indiana and later to Purdue University, from which he received his Bachelor of Science degree in agriculture in 1915. After Purdue, Wickard went back to his family's farm to put to practical test the scientific theories he had learned at college. He found they were practical and he was able to do important pioneering work in the growing of soil-

Peter Killian

CLAUDE R. WICKARD

building crops. He also gave time to farm-bureau work.

After three years on the farm, Wickard married Louise E. Eckert of Logansport, Indiana, and the Wickards, with their two daughters, continued to live on the farm until Mr. Wickard went to Washington in 1933. The farm was a success and Wickard himself had the honor of being listed by the *Prairie Farmer,* a Midwestern magazine, as "Master Farmer of Indiana." In all these years Wickard's only political experience was as a member of the Indiana State Senate, to which he was elected in 1932.

In 1933 Wickard, who still looks and acts like a dirt farmer, came to Washington as assistant chief of the corn and hog section of the AAA and in 1935 he became chief of this division. In 1936, after the Supreme Court had invalidated the old AAA, he was named assistant director and then later in the same year appointed director of the North Central Division of the new AAA, which includes most of the corn-belt states. This post was an important but not a very prominent one, and eight months ago Wickard was comparatively unknown. Yet, though credit wasn't always given him, he is supposed to have been responsible for several of the New Deal's agricultural programs. His ability and effectiveness were recognized in February 1940 when he was made Under-Secretary of Agriculture and in August 1940 when he was promoted to the head of his department. In all these years Wickard has demonstrated that he understands the "mystic mathematics of agriculture." A few weeks ago he impressed his associates by forecasting the 1940 corn yield, hitting very close to the later official estimate.

Wickard is a thick-set man of medium height with blue eyes and dark brown hair

WICKARD, CLAUDE R.—*Continued*

that is starting to thin. He looks as though he "might well be named O'Leary." He has been devoted to his old jobs and will be to his new one, but nothing is going to make him happier than to steal away for a few days to his farm and help the hired hands with the haying, the hog feeding or the planting.

References

N Y Herald Tribune p9 Ag 28 '40
PM p8 Ag 16 '40 por
Time 9:13 Ag 26 '40 por
U S News p33 Ag 30 '40 por
Who's Who in the Nation's Capital

WICKWARE, FRANCIS GRAHAM Jan 31, 1883—Oct 12, 1940 Editor of D. Appleton-Century Company; former associate editor of the *Engineering Magazine;* from 1911 to 1920 editor of *American Yearbook*, joined D. Appleton Company as editor in 1920 and remained with company after merger to the Century Company in 1933; spent much time studying archeological remnants in southern France and Spain

References

Who's Who in America

Obituaries

N Y Herald Tribune O 13 '40
Pub W 138:1602 O 19 '40

WIEDOEFT, RUDY 1894—Feb 18, 1940 Musician; saxophone expert who is said to have put that instrument into modern jazz

Obituaries

N Y Herald Tribune p14 F 19 '40 por
N Y World-Telegram p19 F 19 '40

WILGUS, SIDNEY DEAN Feb 16, 1872 —Feb 23, 1940 Psychiatrist in New York and Illinois

References

Who's Who in America 1938-39

Obituaries

N Y Herald Tribune p10 F 24 '40
N Y Times p13 F 24 '40

WILHELMINA, QUEEN OF THE NETHERLANDS (wil"u-mē'nu) Aug 31, 1880-

On May 10, 1940 the Germans invaded The Netherlands. Immediately Queen Wilhelmina addressed a proclamation to her people: "I herewith direct a flaming protest against this unprecedented violation of good faith and violation of all that is decent in relations between cultured states. I and my government will now do our duty." On May 14 The Netherlands surrendered.

For 100 years The Netherlands had been at peace. For 42 years, through troubled times, Queen Wilhelmina had kept it at peace. This was not too difficult in the first years of her reign. It is true there was some friction with Venezuela over the Dutch-owned islands of Curacao; there was the problem of protecting trade interests in Turkey and China; there was concern over Mexico's program, even then taking shape, of annexing foreign oil properties. But it wasn't until the World War in 1914 that Queen Wilhelmina found herself faced with real problems. Then came a food shortage because of the British blockade. Then, trade was disrupted, Dutch ships were sunk, the country was full of refugees. Yet Wilhelmina kept The Netherlands at peace.

She intended and hoped to keep it at peace during the Second World War. Before Holland's invasion the Queen "has opened her mouth in many a peace appeal, but kept it closed in many a case of violated neutrality during the past few months in a desperate effort to keep her political hot corner out of the war play." Because of forces beyond her control, she has failed.

Her little country, which has a population of 8,639,000 and is no larger in area than Connecticut or Massachusetts, had most to lose from the War. With "its little policeman's army" it hadn't the barest fighting chance of defending itself. With defeat its valuable colonial empire is now endangered, its high standard of living will go. Yet Wilhemina's subjects trust her now, as they have always trusted her, to guide them and to save whatever can be saved from the debacle of defeat.

Queen Wilhelmina, in Holland and now in England, has a cabinet of able advisers and a corps of efficient officials, but they themselves are the first to admit "that for statecraft, diplomacy, energy and experience the Queen is their superior." The final responsibility is hers. "The only King in Europe," a French diplomat once remarked, "is the Queen of The Netherlands." Her ministers consult her on every move, for she knows as much or more than they about most national problems. When she receives her ministers, "woe be to him who does not know his subject well." If he can't answer her difficult questions he is asked: "Don't you think you had better study that a bit more?" and sent home.

Until the Germans took over The Netherlands they were a constitutional monarchy with a Parliament and a government responsible to it. Wilhelmina, who had more rights than most of her fellow sovereigns, had the power of absolute veto, which she never used, of dissolving Parliament and of appointing the 14 members of the Council of State. Only once was her reign in danger. In 1918, just after the War, the Socialist movement had an upswing in Europe and her country, impoverished by the British blockade, called upon the government to resign. Thousands gathered outside the palace in The Hague to overthrow the monarchy. But Wilhelmina rode out to the crowds in an open carriage. Demonstrations started for her on the street and troops drew her landau through the parade grounds in triumph. There was no revolution.

That evening, however, she issued a proclamation: "Social reforms shall be carried through with a speed fitting to the pulsations of our times." And she kept her promise. "Nowhere in Europe has so thorough a social program been completed—slum clearance, community housing and hospitalization, unemployment and old age insurance, wage and hour control—all with a maximum of efficiency and a minimum of noise."

Under Wilhelmina, too, The Netherlands as a whole progressed materially. Its population increased from 5,000,000 to over 8,500,000. The country changed from an agricultural to a predominately industrial economy. It still produces cheese and tulip bulbs, there are still dikes and wooden shoes, but it is mainly a country of busy manufacturers and an international banking center. It is richer abroad, with "a colonial atmosphere hailed as far healthier than the British." And Wilhelmina herself "has a moneyed finger in the pie of nearly every enterprise of magnitude in Holland."

Wilhelmina is the eleventh of her line to govern The Netherlands. The House of Nassau can trace its origin to 800, and its members settled in the Lowlands in 1400. The Orange-Nassau line barely missed dying out with Wilhelmina's father, William III. William's first wife and two sons died one after the other. At 62 he married the 20-year-old Princess Emma of Waldeck-Pyrmont, a small German state. Of that marriage the sole issue was Wilhelmina Helena Pauline Maria, born August 31, 1880. A repeal of the Salic law forbidding female rulers allowed her to succeed to the throne.

She became queen when she was 10, with her mother acting as Regent. On her first appearance on the balcony of the royal palace in Amsterdam she is said to have asked: "Mamma, do all these people belong to me?" Queen Emma answered: "No, my child, it is you who belong to all these people." Wilhelmina was brought up to be a queen. Her childhood wasn't a happy one, for Queen Emma allowed her no playmates and laid out a course of studies that would have staggered the average grown-up. At 16 she spoke German, French and English and was learning military and naval strategy from generals and admirals. Her economics lessons were so practical that she manages her own estate, which is reported to bring her about $5,000,000 a year.

When Wilhelmina was 18, in 1898, she was crowned in the New Church at Amsterdam, swearing to support the constitution and uphold the liberties of the people. Characteristically, she refused to allow her Prime Minister to write her first public speech. One year later she began her peace and neutrality offensive by offering her palace at The Hague for the first International Peace Conference at which many of the present conventions governing war, the rights of neutrals and the principles of arbitration were laid down.

QUEEN WILHELMINA

Two years after her coronation Queen Wilhelmina married a young lieutenant of the Prussian Guards, Henry Wladimir Albert Ernst, Duke of Mecklenburg-Schwerin—"a young man as round and pink as herself." "Prince Henry was fond of meeting up with sea captains and artists and led a hard life playing second fiddle for 33 years in a severely formal and moral court." Parliament steadily refused to make him a Prince of The Netherlands or to grant him funds, and his duties were limited to being the president of the Dutch Red Cross. In 1934 he died.

Juliana, the only child of this marriage, was born in 1909. She didn't lead the lonely life her mother suffered. She had friends, went to camp like any other girl, attended the University at Leyden for two years and took a degree in constitutional law. In 1937 Princess Juliana was married to Prince Bernhard zu Lippe-Biesterfeld, who met the specifications of royal blood, Protestantism and perfect health. It was at their marriage that Queen Wilhelmina had a run-in with Adolf Hitler. When the Nazis confiscated the passports of the German bridesmaids and guests at the wedding she told him firmly: "This is the marriage of my daughter to the man she loves, whom I have found worthy of her love; this is not the marriage of The Netherlands to Germany." The passports were returned.

At first there was a bit of scandal about the marriage. Prince Bernhard had a few mildly modern ideas. He liked an occasional cocktail, for instance, and liked to speed in his car. There was almost a government crisis when an indignant Dutchman once discovered Juliana and Bernhard on the French Riviera sipping cocktails on a Sunday afternoon and communicated with his newspaper, which broadcast the horrible

WILHELMINA, QUEEN OF THE NETHERLANDS—*Continued*

news throughout The Netherlands. After Bernhard got over the shock of suddenly finding himself minus debts and with a yearly allowance of $106,000 and after his and Juliana's two daughters, Beatrix and Irene, were born, both Wilhelmina and her people softened. Juliana and the children have been in Canada since the summer of 1940, while Bernhard has remained in London in a military capacity.

The exemplary private life that Queen Wilhelmina herself has lived blended well with her shrewd qualities as a ruler. Not a breath of scandal has ever touched her. "Few if any bits of gossip ever got through the cold, exclusive circle of Dutch nobility that surrounded the court. She was the good mother, the conscientious leader, the faithful church-goer." Because of her strong Calvinism, her words came to carry "almost a scriptural weight among the nobility of The Hague and Utrecht, the patrician families of Amsterdam, and all the older townspeople and villagers in the strongly Protestant North." Even Jews and Catholics "came to idolize her."

Because of her exemplary private life, the court at The Hague was called the dullest in Europe. At official receptions so much as a light laugh caused eyebrows to rise. "A lady-in-waiting turned up one day in a gorgeous Paris creation. Wilhelmina took one look. 'Where did you get that hat, young woman?' she asked in the Victorian manner. 'In Paris, Your Majesty,' the unfortunate answered. 'We wear Dutch clothes here,' said the Queen with an unforgettable look."

Dressed in a worn raincoat and a shapeless hat she used to pedal gravely on her bicycle through the streets of The Hague. Her Majesty's grocer used the same entrance to her Palace that she did. She was often seen by the people of The Hague sewing by the palace window. One of her greatest charms for her people is the fact that she is such a good housewife. She was that particularly in her white rambling Palace of Het Loo near Apeldoorn, where she skated in winter and worked in her gardens in a droopy old felt hat and cotton gloves. Her relaxation there was always painting, and when Wilhelmina painted a tree you knew it was a tree.

When the War between Germany and the Allies began, Wilhelmina continued to be both housewife and leader. Her only excursions were to the frontier posts where The Netherlands Army was mobilized. She poked into the troops' living quarters and if the blankets were too light or the kitchen not clean enough, there was trouble. When the War reached her country the lights in the palace could be seen burning all night as she went over dispatches and issued her quick, clear and final orders.

On May 13, 1940 Wilhelmina, Princess Juliana, Prince Bernhard and the two children arrived in London, advised to go there by her Cabinet, for "the German military authorities, with every intention of completing their nefarious practices, had started bombing her Majesty's destination." It was then Wilhelmina's intention "to return as soon as possible to her people in their great distress and their heroic fight against overwhelming odds."

On May 14 the Dutch surrendered to the invading German forces, but Wilhelmina, who is now guiding the destinies of her people from abroad, declared that the spirit of The Netherlands is unbroken because its conscience is clear. Netherlanders will never give up their faith in the cause of freedom and justice. And she prayed "that the dawn of the day when freedom will be restored to The Netherlands and to other victims of German aggression is near."

References

Atlan 162:474-82 O '38
Good H 110:24-5+ Ja '40 il
Illustration 201:65 S 17 '38 pors
Liv Age 357:344-7 D '39
N Y Times p1, 4 My 14 '40; p4 My 16 '40
Read Digest 36:62-7 Ap '40
R Deux Mondes s8 47:479-80 S 15 '38
Time 34:22-4+ N 27 '39 por
Barnouw, A. J. Holland under Queen Wilhelmina 1923
Forbes, R. Queen Wilhelmina *In* These Men I Know p209-15 1940
International Who's Who
Power, L. J. B. Royal Ladies of The Netherlands: Queen Wilhelmina and Princess Juliana 1939

WILLIAMS, ALFORD JOSEPH JR. July 26, 1896- Aviator

Address: b. Gulf Oil Corporation, Gulf Building, Pittsburgh, Pennsylvania

"I get a great kick out of being in trouble," Al Williams once confided. He has been amazingly successful at getting into it. The commander of the 400,000 Scripps-Howard Junior Aviators, writing a daily aviation column for the Scripps-Howard newspapers, has been recently stepping on the United States Navy's toes.

Since April 1935 Williams had been a major in the United States Marine Corps Reserve, after a long career of navy service. In February 1939 his column tore into the navy's selection board for having arranged to dismiss eight flying officers who were not Annapolis trained. A few months later he received a memorandum: "Further destructive criticism . . . will be considered sufficient cause . . . that your commission . . . be revoked." After an angry inquiry he was notified that he wasn't actually subject to control but was under the navy's orders by "custom and usage." Unable to restrain himself from campaigning with increasing vituperation in his columns for a strong and independent air force that would be free from army or navy interference, in July 1940

Williams finally resigned his commission, writing: "My services will always be at the command of the United States Marine Corps." In the summer of 1940 *Airpower* was published—developing this same unpopular plea for an independent air force into a book length thesis.

Lewis Gannett calls *Airpower* "a book filled with eloquently intimate descriptions of Europe's air forces, fantastically ignorant dogmatisms about politics and economics, and with that right-to-the-chin pattern of rhetoric which passes for argument among the fraternity of Scripps-Howard columnists," but says, too, that no reader "is likely to doubt the Major's knowledge of aircraft or his passionate faith in the air as the battleground of the present and of the future."

Al Williams in his book lights into the admirals and generals who cling to their prejudices "with the tenacity of a glue distilled from the roots of ignorance." Although he doesn't believe Germany can attack the United States, he finds the present defense program based on an outworn theory—that sea power is more important than air power. He knows the Nazi air power well: in 1938 he was flying their Messerschmitts and Storches before they flew across Poland and Flanders. He has inspected German air plants, noted their methods of production and believes we could profit by imitation.

Italians, too, Williams admires, but he has little but contempt for the British, who shrugged off the specific information and warnings he brought them about the development of German aircraft. He was disgusted with French delay and thinks the Soviets incapable of producing first-class planes for 10 or 15 years. His political views are rather strange: he believes that during the Ethiopian War England was scared off by the Italian air fleet, states that the British favored the "Red" cause in Spain (which he very definitely did not). But in aviation he knows his way around. Eddie Rickenbacker (see sketch this issue) called him "an airman's pilot, with true contempt for armchair goggles."

He was born in New York City on July 26, 1896, the son of Alford Joseph Williams, a civil engineer influential in New York politics, and of Emma Elizabeth (Madden) Williams, a gifted singer and musician. After attending public schools he entered Fordham Preparatory School at the age of 14, soon became its best baseball pitcher, but in his last year decided he was through with studying. His father gave him permission to quit school in order to work, but said he would do the job-finding for him. He did. After a summer at a steel foundry in Long Island City, Al found himself quite willing to start studying again and entered Fordham College. He was graduated in 1915 and by that time a career was cut out for him. As Fordham's star pitcher he had been spotted by Sam Crane, a sports writer, who called up Manager McGraw of the New York Giants to announce his "find."

ALFORD WILLIAMS JR.

McGraw offered young Williams a job and until the United States entered the First World War he pitched for the Giants.

Then he left to learn to fly for the navy, took a ground course at the Massachusetts Institute of Technology before going to the aviation camp at Bay Shore, Long Island, took to flying as if he had been made for it, but never got abroad. He was too useful in training pilots at the advanced flying school at Pensacola, Florida to be spared and by the time the Armistice came that was what he was still doing.

Williams remained with the navy as research aviator. There has been much talk of his "stunts," but Williams himself is rather contemptuous of stunts and calls what he did "aerobatics . . . the scientific investigations which take the mystery out of any and every situation in the air." It was Williams who wrote the first report on how to right a ship after getting into an upside-down position (in the past there had been crashes when this happened); he put his ships into innumerable tailspins without crashing, after the number of previous accidents had made officials fear the fault was the plane's; he became noted for inverted flights; and he showed how the human body could adjust itself to the unusual positions and stresses it was subjected to in out-of-the-ordinary flying situations.

In 1922 Williams was a navy entry in the Pulitzer Races at Detroit. His plane burst into flames in the air but he landed safely, beat out the flames—and then proceeded to discover something about faulty ignition. He tested out new ideas at the Naval Air Station at Hampton Roads, Virginia and then in 1923 helped design a new racing plane which won the Pulitzer Race at St. Louis, Missouri and established a new world's speed record which remained official until 1931.

WILLIAMS, ALFORD JR.—Continued

He was next called to Washington to help design a new combat plane and risked his life to test out the new designs. His first real crash found him miraculously unhurt.

In 1926 Williams won the Pulitzer Trophy; that same year he received his LL. B. from Georgetown University (he had been studying evenings), was admitted to the New York State Bar and married Florence Hawes Selby. Both in 1927 and 1929 he was working on a navy speed plane which was to enter the International Schneider Cup Races, and though something went wrong both times and the plane never was fit for the races, the Distinguished Flying Cross presented to him on May 17, 1929 was some consolation. Williams' articles both in the Scripps-Howard papers and in magazines had already made his name a familiar one. The naval citation said: "In his articles written for the public he has shown himself to be a scholar as well as a master pilot, and the beneficial effect on the public mind of his example, his clear exposition and his loyalty to the service has been great and it has reflected untold credit to the service." That same year he received the trophy of the American Society of Mechanical Engineers.

It was 1930 when Williams resigned his lieutenancy in the navy to become a consultant engineer. Manufacturers came to him for the correction of faults in newly designed ships; engineers brought him their problems. In July 1932 he became a captain in the Marine Corps Aviation Reserve, on their inactive list, but continued to fly for the Gulf Oil Corporation, becoming the manager of their aviation department in 1933. In April 1935 he was promoted to the rank of major in the Marine Corps Reserve.

Williams is more than six feet tall, young-looking, with reddish-brown, closely cropped hair and straight, firm features that might make him look as grim as Dick Tracy if it weren't for his Irish blue eyes. When he is around planes he doesn't like to be interrupted and some people mistake his concentration for unfriendliness. Flying is almost everything to him; it is his religion. He is inclined to be as poetic about the construction of a dive-bomber as about a sunset experienced from the air. In the year 1940 he can write a passage such as this: "What lucky people we are, born at the right time, breathing and living in this particular period of the world's history and, without effort or merit, entitled to live the dreams of only the greatest poets of the ages." He continues: "The flying man all but forgets his wings and motors. Spiritually he is enraptured with Nature's might and beauty in the great church of the universe, where all men think alike. And in this great church, where all men think alike, he is on wings."

References

Am Mag 115:24-6+ Ja '33 por
Collier's 81:22 Mr 31 '28 por; 90:24+ S 10 '32
Lit Digest 120:28 D 21 '35; 124:23 D 25 '37
Sat Eve Post 203:6-7+ My 23 '31 por; 203:14-15+ Je 13 '31; 204:10-11+ O 10 '31
Time 29:30 Ja 11 '37; 36:17 Jl 22 '40 por
Vital Speeches 6:565-8 Jl 1 '40
Who's Who in America

WILLIAMS, AUBREY　Aug 23, 1890-

Social worker; head of the National Youth Administration

Address: b. Washington Bldg, New York Ave and 15th St, Washington, D. C.; h. 5107 Wilson Blvd, Arlington, Virginia

"The most dangerous man in the government," according to Hamilton Fish, is Aubrey Willis Williams, head of the National Youth Administration. Mr. Fish made this statement before the House of Representatives on March 25, 1940 and, together with other representatives, urged that Mr. Williams be ousted from his position. Referring to the proposed good will tour to South America to be led by Leopold Stokowski, Representative Taber of New York said that Mr. Williams was "planning to take 109 American youths and turn them over to a man whose record is Communistic." But Representative Tarver of Georgia assured the House that Mr. Williams himself was no Communist, merely "a dreamer and an idealist who needs to be guided and restrained."

Aubrey Williams, "the gaunt, zealous, wavy-haired, hollow-eyed social worker" who is head of the NYA, has had a faculty for getting himself into hot water. In June 1938, addressing 800 delegates of the Workers' Alliance in Washington, he made what has been called "one of the most injudicious and foolish extemporaneous speeches that any New Dealer—including even Messrs. Harold L. Ickes and Robert Jackson (see sketch this issue)—has made." To these delegates he said: "You know who your friends are. Keep your friends in power!" There was a good deal of disturbed comment throughout the country when the man who was at that time temporarily in charge of the relief administration urged people on relief to vote for the New Deal on the ground that the New Deal would continue to give them money.

Williams' next important *gaffe* came in November 1938, when he was addressing the Southern Conference for Human Welfare. To them he said: "I am not sure that class warfare is not all right." He did explain that by class warfare he meant such accomplished facts as collective bargaining, "the clash of employee and employer, the clash of one industrial group against another," but concluded, "there are other forms than class warfare of solving these problems, but realistically it may not be possible to avoid it."

In June 1935, President Roosevelt created the National Youth Administration to meet the needs of the three and one-half million boys and girls between the ages of 16 and 24 who are unemployed, who can get neither jobs nor schooling. Aubrey Williams was put in charge as part of his duties as WPA deputy administrator, and took this over as his only job in December 1938.

It is probably because of his inability to "coddle Congressmen" and his rather tactless single-mindedness that Aubrey Williams is now head of the Youth Administration. Before Harry Hopkins became Secretary of Commerce, Williams had been his Deputy Administrator and "right-hand man" in the WPA. He seemed in line for the job of Administrator when Hopkins left in December 1938. But because Colonel Harrington was a "first-rate politician" he got Hopkins' job and Williams became NYA head.

Aubrey Williams was born in Springfield, Alabama on August 23, 1890, the son of Charles Evans and Eva (Taylor) Williams. According to his mother, he is a "self-made man." His grandfather had freed a thousand slaves and lost all his possessions in the Civil War, and Williams had to start work early. "When he was a little fellow, he went to work on a laundry wagon at $1 a week." But that was only a part-time job, and when he was 10 years old Williams had to leave school to take a full-time one. He worked in a Birmingham, Alabama department store as a stock boy at $3 a week, and he worked in a coal mine while going to night school.

With church aid, and by taking a number of jobs ranging from sign painting to social work Williams was able to attend Maryville College in 1911 to study for the ministry. When the War began he eagerly took the opportunity to go to Paris with the Y. M. C. A. With America's entrance into the War he enlisted in the artillery and remained in France until the Armistice. Then he got leave to attend the University of Bordeaux, from which he received a degree in 1919 while still officially in the army.

When Williams returned to the United States he became pastor of an Evangelical Lutheran Church near Cincinnati, and from there he moved on to Cincinnati to enter recreational work and get his B. A. from the University of Cincinnati in 1920. In this year he married Anita Schreck of Cincinnati. They have four sons. From 1922 to 1932 he was executive director of the Wisconsin Conference of Social Work, where he introduced many civic advances, including the first complete State Children's Code. In 1932 he became the field representative of the American Public Welfare Association.

Williams' first job under the New Deal was as field representative for the Federal Emergency Relief Administration in 1933;

AUBREY WILLIAMS

his second was as assistant administrator of the FERA and Civil Works Administration (1933-35); his third, as assistant administrator of the Works Progress Administration and executive director of NYA; his fourth, as deputy administrator of the Works Progress Administration, appointed December 31, 1936; and, finally, his single job as head of the National Youth Administration.

For hundreds of thousands of destitute boys and girls the NYA under Aubrey Williams has "meant work, self-respect, and the opportunity to continue their education on at least a part-time basis." It has taught them to build parks, to make surveys, to run farms, to manage libraries, to cook, sew and carpenter. It "has done more to create a feeling of self-reliance in young America than anything since the Alger books."

Aubrey Williams points out that in the services of the NYA "we have the means for supplying the young people, on an honorable basis, with some of that indispensable cash which all civilized persons, even young ones, have to have to get along. We have helped young people escape from the dilemma of no experience, no job; no job, no experience, and most important, we have made a new and valuable addition to our means of education for citizenship."

References
N Y Herald Tribune p20 Mr 26 '40
N Y Sun p1 Mt 25 '40
Scholastic 27:14 S 21 '35 por
Time 32:10 Jl 4 '38; 32:15 D 5 '38; 33:
8 Ja 2 '39
Vital Speeches 5:659-62 Ag 15 '39
Lindley, E. K. and Lindley, B. A
New Deal for Youth 1938
Who's Who in America
Who's Who in the Nation's Capital

WILLIAMS, JOSEPH JOHN, FATHER
Dec 1, 1875—Oct 28, 1940 Clergyman, author
and anthropologist; ordained a Roman Catholic priest in 1907 and served as missionary in
Jamaica for five years; spent many years
studying the Negro in the West Indies and
Africa and wrote books on his research;
professor of anthropology in the graduate
school of Boston College since 1934; former
managing editor of *America*, weekly Catholic
review

FATHER WILLIAMS

References

American Catholic Who's Who
American Men of Science
Who's Who in America
Williams, J. J. Whisperings of the
Caribbean 1925

Obituaries

N Y Times p23 O 30 '40 por

WILLIAMS, RALPH E. Sept 14, 1870—
May 16, 1940 Vice-president of the Republican National Committee; planner of Republican conventions since 1908; former
bank president

References

Who's Who in America
Who's Who in Finance, Banking and
Insurance

Obituaries

N Y Sun p23 My 17 '40
N Y Times p19 My 17 '40 por

WILLIAMS, THOMAS SUTLER Feb
14, 1872—Apr 5, 1940 Member of the United
States Court of Claims for more than 10
years; former Republican member of Congress for 14 years

References

Who's Who in America
Who's Who in the Nation's Capital

Obituaries

N Y Herald Tribune p8 Ap 6 '40
N Y Times p17 Ap 6 '40 por

WILLKIE, WENDELL LEWIS Feb 18,
1892- Nominated by Republican Party for
President June 29, 1940; lawyer; public
utility executive
Address: h. 1010 Fifth Ave, New York City

On November 5, 1940 Wendell L. Willkie
was defeated for the Presidency of the
United States by Franklin Delano Roosevelt. More than four strenuous months of
campaigning had resulted in over 22,000,000
votes for him. On November 12, one week
after his defeat, he announced to the American people in a radio address that their
"function during the next four years is that
of the loyal opposition." "Ours," said Mr.
Willkie, "is a two party system. Should
we ever permit one party to dominate our
lives entirely democracy would collapse."
An opposition party is necessary, but, he
emphasized, its opposition must be constructive, working honestly for the betterment of the nation.

In his message Wendell Willkie hoped
that the many Willkie clubs formed all over
the country would be continued. "It is not,
however," he said, "appropriate to continue
these organizations in my name. I do not
want this great cause to be weakened by
even a semblance of any personal advantage
to any individual. I feel too deeply about
it for that."

As early as 1939 General Hugh S. Johnson
(see sketch this issue) called Mr. Willkie a
"very strong candidate" for the Presidency of
the United States. To this Willkie, who has
tangled frequently with New Deal agencies—
especially the Tennessee Valley Authority—
replied: "If the government continues to take
over my business, I may be looking shortly for
some kind of a new job. General Johnson's·is the best offer I have had so far."
On January 30, 1940 he said further: "If
the nomination were given to me without
any strings I would have to accept it. No
man in middle life and in good health could
do otherwise."

By May 1940 Wendell Willkie had become the chief Republican dark horse for
the nomination. Oren Root Jr. (see sketch
this issue), impressed by Willkie's idea of
a platform for America called *We the
People* which appeared in *Fortune*, organized
a Willkie-for-President group in New York
and issued petitions which were signed
widely all over the country. Russell Davenport, managing editor of *Fortune*, resigned
his position to devote his full time to
furthering his nomination. By June, men
like Raymond Clapper (see sketch this
issue) were saying that Wendell Willkie
was the only man the Republicans "can put

up who would have a ghost- of a chance in the campaign." And on June 27 he received the nomination on the sixth ballot.

Almost immediately Willkie started his campaigning. Almost immediately the Democrats began presenting their opposition arguments. They, and others, criticized the combination of Willkie and McNary; they pointed out that he was a Big Business man, a utilities leader ("a simple barefoot Wall Street lawyer," Ickes called him); that he had never held public office; that his foreign policies actually differed little from Roosevelt's; that his labor policies were "paradoxical." As the campaign progressed Willkie was charged with making a number of "blunders," such as that in which he accused Roosevelt of selling "Czechoslovakia down the river." But with the aid of Joseph Martin Jr., (see sketch this issue), his campaign manager, it wasn't long before the trend began to swing more and more in his direction.

During the campaign ("there had never been anything like it," said *Time*. . . "It was an extraordinary phenomenon almost certain to make a notable exhibit in the museum of political history") Wendell Willkie stumped up and down the country, smilingly meeting hecklers ("Boos don't hurt me. . . All I ask is a square shake"), his voice growing hoarser and hoarser, his platform becoming more and more clear. Perhaps its main idea was that while wanting to preserve New Deal reforms, he felt they should be enforced along lines that would help business and encourage investment.

The New Deal's tax structure, he declared, was unscientific, repressive, loaded with punitive measures. The answer was "to stimulate production immediately and revise the tax system so that it will not act as a brake upon industry." In foreign policy he favored aid to Great Britain and China but condemned the Administration's reckless statements in foreign affairs and executive secrecy. He also condemned its "negligence in the face of great national need" in the matter of defense, favored conscription and suggested that the Defense Commission be given more authority."

Willkie advocated the public development of power. He said, too, "I stand for the National Labor Relations Act and the right of free collective bargaining. I stand for minimum wages and maximum hours, and for legislation to enforce them. I stand for social security benefits and believe that they should be extended." But over and over again, his main thesis was that the only real remedy for labor problems, for farm problems was an Administration that would encourage business to launch the enterprises that would make more jobs. Unemployment is the greatest American problem, he stated again and again. It was probably because of belief in his labor statements that John L. Lewis endorsed Willkie shortly before the elections.

WENDELL L. WILLKIE

As a boy, Willkie called himself Lewis Wendell Willkie. When he entered the army in 1917, his first and middle names became transposed on the records. He remonstrated and was advised: "By the time we get them corrected through all the red tape of Washington, the War will be over." Although later Willkie was to challenge the government on many scores, that time he meekly changed his name to conform to the records.

His family is a very unusual one. His ancestors in Europe were in frequent conflict with their several governments, for as he says: "Those who did not observe the restrictions under which they were forced to live got into trouble; one had to flee his native land because he adopted the religion of his choice; another was ostracized because he believed in the principles of the French Revolution; and still another was jailed for expressing his own opinions. In 1848 my father and grandparents [who spelled their name Willcke] came to America to escape this repression of individual liberties." This ancestry may explain the character of Willkie, a very articulate man who likes to "talk back" to the government, and who has become the leading critic of the business and power utility decisions of the New Deal.

Willkie was born in Elwood, Indiana, third in a family of six children. His father, Herman, was a prosperous lawyer and landowner in the then booming manufacturing town. Natural gas was used for its industries—indeed so plentiful was it that it was cheaper to allow street lights to burn all day than to pay a man to turn them off. At the exhaustion of the natural gas wells, the town fell into desolation and with it the fortunes of the Willkie family. His mother, besides taking care of her children,

WILLKIE, WENDELL—*Continued*

taught school and practiced law. She was the first woman ever admitted to the Indiana Bar. His grandmother was a Presbyterian minister. Again Willkie showed his nonconformity by becoming an Episcopalian. One brother (6-feet-5) was all-American tackle while at Annapolis and also an Olympic wrestler, and is in 1940 in charge of salmon-canning for the Libby Company. Willkie explains that he always buys Libby salmon, and also orders Seagram whisky because two of his other brothers are with Seagram, one as vice-president. One sister is a wine merchant; another is married to a naval attaché at the Berlin Embassy.

As a boy and college student Willkie helped support himself by harvesting grain, acting as "barker" for a tent hotel during a land boom in South Dakota, and moving houses out of the fast-disappearing town of Elwood to nearby farms. In their home the Willkie children led a stimulating life: "They kept more than 6,000 books around the house and old Herman Willkie . . . woke his children in the mornings by shouting quotations from the classics. Their home was a sort of perpetual debating society."

Willkie attended Culver Military Academy, then went to the University of Indiana in 1909. There he "became known as a red-sweatered campus radical spreading socialistic ideas, including the abolition of all inheritance as unfair to persons who inherit nothing. He raged against fraternities . . . and fumed against the law faculty." Paul Vories McNutt (see sketch this issue), prominent 1940 possibility as United States Presidential candidate was a fellow student, a conservative, snobbish fraternity man and no friend of the radical Willkie.

In 1913 Willkie received a B. A. degree and in 1916 his LL. B. degree. Then he joined his father in the practice of law but quit to enlist in the army. He likes to tell that when he met Edith Wilk, librarian in Rushville, Indiana, he told her: "Edith, I'd like to change that Wilk to Willkie." Their wedding on January 14, 1918 was delayed for two days by a blizzard, but he finally arrived, clutching a frozen, disheveled bouquet which she carried to the church. They have a son, Philip, at 20 a senior at Princeton, voted the "most likely to succeed" of his class.

After making a brilliant record as a lawyer in the legal department of the Firestone Company and the law firm of Mather and Newbitt, the president of the Commonwealth and Southern, a giant utility holding company, wrote of Willkie: "Do not let this young man get away from us. . . He is a comer and we should keep our eye on him." Willkie in 1929 was summoned to New York to become the attorney for Commonwealth and Southern. When the president retired in 1933, Willkie took his place. He made an enviable record as a utility executive until his Tennessee utility system became embroiled with the New Deal—a spectacular feud which ended when the TVA paid his company $78,600,000 for its Tennessee properties. For an attitude typified by warnings against concentration of power in either industry or government the National Institute of Social Science honored him with a gold medal award "for distinguished services to humanity" on May 7, 1940.

Although a lifelong Democrat who gave $150 to the Democratic Campaign fund in 1932 ("I wish I had my money back," he said in 1935) he voted against Roosevelt in 1936. "I won't be dropped into a mold. I want to be a free spirit. If I wasn't one, I would be still sitting on a cracker box in Indiana," he says.

In 1940 "the biggest political figure in United States business," until his resignation to campaign he received from the Commonwealth and Southern Company $75,000 a year, not considered a high salary for a billion-dollar corporation president. He has never owned an automobile, goes downtown from his Fifth Avenue, New York apartment by subway or taxi. "It is an asset in my business," he explains, "to look like an Indiana farmer." So he accounts for his "unpressed, shiny-seated suit, his disheveled mop of graying hair."

He is widely read and has done research on the economics of the South before the Civil War; the early settlement of Indiana; the rise of trade-unionism, communism and socialism. Fishing, a little poker and "fussing around" on his five Indiana farms give him his relaxation. He hasn't played golf for years, he says: "That's no fun, just chasing a pill around."

References

Collier's 106:15+ S 21 '40 por; 106:11+ O 26 '40
Cur Hist 51:21+ F '40 por
Fortune 15:89 My '37; 21:46-7 Ap '40
Harper 181:477-85 O '40 (Same abr. Read Digest 37:46-50 O '40)
Life 8:97-107 My 13 '40 il pors; 8:25-7 Je 24 '40 pors
Lit Digest 124:13 D 25 '37 pors
Nation 150:469+ Ap 13 '40
New Repub 103:48-9 Jl 8 '40; 103:315-32 S 2 '40 por tab (special section "This Man Willkie"); 103:855 D 23 '40
New Yorker 16:19 Jl 13 '40; 16:27-32+ O 12 '40
No Am 248 no2:259-64 [D] '39 (Same abr. Read Digest 35:1-4 D '39)
Sat Eve Post 211:10-11+ F 25 '39 il pors; 213:12-3+ Ag 24 '40 por
Time 32:15 D 5 '38 por; 34:42-5 Jl 31 '39 por (cover); 35:19 My 6 '40; 36:16-19 Je 24 '40 pors; 36:9-15 Jl 8 '40 por; 36:16 Jl 15 '40 por; 36:15-7 S 9 '40 por; 36:16-17 S 16 '40 il por; 36:14-5 S 23 '40 pors; 36:26-30 O 14 '40

Chapple, J. M. Willkie and American Unity 1940

Who's Who in America
Willkie, W. L. Meet Mr. Willkie
pam 1940
Willkie, W. This is Wendell Willkie
1940

WINTER, GEORGE B. Apr 19, 1878—
Mar 28, 1940 President of the American
Dental Association in 1935 and 1936; professor of exodontia—extraction of teeth—at
Washington University School of Dentistry
in St. Louis; after studying 10,000 cases of
impacted molars, he perfected a technique
for removing them which has since come
to be widely used by dentists throughout
the world

Taylor

GEORGE B. WINTER

References

Who's Who in America

Obituaries

N Y Herald Tribune p10 Mr 30 '40
por

WINTHROP, BEEKMAN 1874—Nov 10,
1940 Retired banker; governed Puerto
Rico, 1904 to 1907; close personal friend of
President Taft's; served as executive secre-
tary of Philippine Islands and as judge of
Court of First Instance during his Admin-
istration; Assistant Secretary of United
States Treasury, 1907 to 1909; Assistant
Secretary of Navy, 1909 to 1913; senior
partner of banking firm of Robert Winthrop
& Company, 1914 to 1939

References

Who's Who in America

Obituaries

N Y Herald Tribune p12 N 11 '40 por
N Y Times p19 N 11 '40

WOLFE, HUMBERT July 5, 1885—Jan
5, 1940 British poet; playwright; Deputy
Secretary of the Ministry of Labor

References

International Who's Who
Who's Who

Obituaries

Poetry 55:345 Mr '40
Pub W 137:719 F 10 '40

**WOOD, EDWARD FREDERICK LIND-
LEY, 3RD VISCOUNT** *See* Halifax, E.
F. L. W.

WOOD, GRANT Feb 13, 1892- Artist
Address: h. 1142 Court St, Iowa City, Iowa

Grant Wood, the "most celebrated white
hope of 100 per cent Americanism in art,"
created quite a stir 'with *Parson Weems'
Fable*, one of his latest paintings. This portrait
of George Washington, complete with powdered
wig and all the attributes of father of his
country, chopping down the cherry tree while
Parson Weems looks on slightly cynically
from behind the curtain he is lifting, raised
the dander of serious patriots all over the
country. But Grant Wood denied any charge
of debunking: "I have taken a tip from the
good parson," he says, "and have used my
imagination freely." The next American
legend he is tackling is the story of Captain
John Smith's rescue by Pocahontas. Wood
and a group of eight American artists went
to Hollywood to paint scenes from Walter
Wanger's film, *The Long Voyage Home*, in
1940. Wood's picture, *Sentimental Ballad*,
was very well received by critics.

It was as a painter of the Midwestern
scene of Iowa, however, that Grant Wood
won national recognition. He has painted
the Iowa fields at the time of spring plowing
and harvest; he has shown threshers at dinner, children planting a tree in a country
school yard, the strong faces of Iowa men
and women. Grant Wood paints "out of the
land and the people he knows best." He
believes in regional art and especially in "the
encouragement given to it by the United
States government." But he cautions us—
"the same artists who did fake impressionist
pictures in Paris a few years ago are now
busy with the American scene. God save
it from them!"

Of course Wood himself is one of those
artists who 10 years ago were painting misty
impressionist pictures of southern France.
He is that no longer. His painting now
steers clear of impressionism and gives the
literal, sharpened image. The color is clear,
the outlines unblurred and the surfaces un-
polished. His is a "brittle objective style
that is at once adapted to his own matter-
of-fact personality and to the homely subjects with which he has chosen to deal."
It is a style of which "the mechanical perfection would enchant the neatest of interior
decorators." In some of his landscapes the

Arthur O'Neill

GRANT WOOD

criticism is: "the design half consumes the subjects, and the trees and natural forms arbitrarily forced into a fixed pattern lose their specific character and become implements in a scheme of self-conscious stylization." But always the intent is easily understood—Wood's work is popular among simple people.

"Precisely meticulous in detail," Wood paints on the average two pictures a year. He works slowly. First he picks his subject and then he mulls it over in his mind. He may think a picture out in detail for a year before lifting a pencil. Then comes a series of sketches and one or more detailed working drawings; then the canvas itself on which he applies eight coats of paint. Wood has a fetish for authenticity. He uses mail order catalogues for details of hay rakes and milk separators; he checks even the rightness of the kinds of hay in wagons; and once he advertised in Chicago newspapers for a pair of genuine red flannel drawers.

Grant Wood's father, too, was a factual man. It is told that in his youth he returned a copy of Grimm's fairy tales to the giver saying, "We Quakers can read only true things." He died when Grant was only 10. The farm at Anamosa, Iowa where Grant was born was taken away, and Grant, with his mother and sister, moved to Cedar Rapids.

Here he mowed lawns, milked cows, was a truck gardener, house painter and carpenter for nine years, teaching himself to draw at night after the day's work was over. He finally decided to depend on crafts for a living until he could support himself with his art and in 1910 enrolled in the Handicraft Guild of Minneapolis, taking advanced courses in wood and metal work. Part of the year he worked by day as a paid assistant

in the forge and studied design in night classes. The rest of the term he studied by day and worked nights as a watchman in a morgue.

After 18 months of this Wood returned to Cedar Rapids and started a handicraft shop of his own. It prospered and Wood was able to paint more. One day he turned up at a life class at the University of Iowa, taught by an absent-minded instructor. When asked for his admission ticket he said he had forgotten it. The teacher didn't ask for it again, and Wood stayed there for a whole academic year without being enrolled or paying tuition. His conscience never hurt him: "When you don't get anything," he said, "you shouldn't pay. That's the way to run a college."

This session made him realize more than ever that he wanted training and in 1912 he went to Chicago where he worked days in a jewelry shop and attended night classes at the Chicago Art Institute. While there, he and a friend started a shop to design and execute beautiful metal objects. The War interfered and Wood, who had invested all he had, again found himself back in Cedar Rapids with no job and no money—at 23 merely a handy man around town.

Then came America's entrance into the War. Wood remained in this country, with the camouflage division. At training camp he made sketches of the soldiers and sold them —25 cents for a doughboy and $1 for an officer. After the Armistice Wood got a job teaching art in Cedar Rapids and stayed at it for six years.

During these years and after he traveled to Europe and even spent some months studying at the Academy Julian in Paris. He became bohemian and grew pink whiskers. As he put it: "I lived in Paris a couple of years and grew a very spectacular beard that didn't match my face or hair and read Mencken and was convinced that the Midwest was inhibited and barren." His work was full of "the sleazy artifices of impressionism." He painted fragments of nature, old French doorways and "picturesque landscapes slumbering in veils of atmospheric tone." But he soon saw that his canvases were indistinguishable from thousands of others. He went to Germany where he saw the works of the early German masters— patient, detailed characterizations of simple folk. "I started out to analyze what it was I really knew . . . it was Iowa. Suddenly I realized that all the really good ideas I'd ever had came to me when I was milking a cow. So I went back to Iowa."

Back in Cedar Rapids he began to sell some of his work,—at prices from $10 to $40 —and the people there paid him $2 an hour for advice on the improvement of their homes. It was there that he painted his first important picture, *John B. Turner, Pioneer*. Turner was a undertaker who had befriended him and who, the year before, had lured him to Chicago to address the National Selected Morticians on "The Interior Decoration of Mortuaries." "I had a jolly time," Wood said, "and the selected morticians bought a picture."

After his portrait of Turner, Wood was determined to paint his own Iowa people with all the integrity that had gone into the old European masterpieces. *Woman with Plants* came next, a portrait about which Thomas Craven says, "In draughtsmanship and sheer control of medium this picture of Wood's mother is superior to Whistler's *Mother*; and in vitality and endurance, substance of sacrificial devotion it reduces the Whistler tribute to a fragile silhouette."

With *American Gothic* Grant Wood became famous. This picture, exhibited in Chicago in 1930, was the most popular painting at the Century of Progress Exposition a few years later. With its typical and gaunt Iowa farmer and his tight-lipped daughter standing in front of their typical Gothic farmhouse, this picture "at once became the chief icon of the past decade's resurgent move to 'paint America.'"

Since *American Gothic* Grant Wood has produced not a large number of pictures, but "a substantial body of work in portraiture and figure painting." *Dinner for Threshers,* a design for a mural, is one of his more famous, "original in conception and superbly planned." *The Midnight Ride of Paul Revere* and the *Birthplace of President Hoover* are landscapes in which a "decorative realism prevails, mixed with a delightfully humorous fantasy." *Young Corn* is pure Iowa and *Spring Turning* is again Iowa, though in it the country has been "simplified into an abstraction." A portrait of Vice-President-elect Henry Wallace is his latest work.

Frequently in Wood's paintings there is a touch of satire, but the only thoroughly satirical painting he ever did was *Daughters of the American Revolution,* which shows three elderly, hard-bitten ladies, one holding a tea cup before a portrait of Washington crossing the Delaware. This caused a furor, and Wood believes that only the fact that he is a member of the American Legion and that his ancestors on both sides came to America in colonial times saved him from patriots who threatened him with arrest.

In 1933 Grant Wood founded "one of the nation's most significant art colony experiments at Stone City, Iowa," and under the New Deal's Public Works Art Project he supervised 24 of the 34 Iowa projects. It was he who was one of the first men appointed to do a decoration for the Post Office Department Building in Washington.

In 1935 he was married to Sara Sherman Maton, from whom he was divorced in 1940.

For a good many years, until the fall of 1940 when he resigned in order to take a year off just to paint, Grant Wood has been teaching art at Iowa State University, trying not to teach any special style or technique of painting but only to help young artists paint the things they know about in whatever way they see them. There is no formality in his teaching. All work on brown wrapping paper—"I use nothing else," Wood says. "It has a fine tone and it is free from impurities and for the classroom you can't beat it."

Wood used to teach three afternoons a week and twice a month conduct classes in criticism which about two hundred aspiring artists attended. Now he paints almost all day long and every Sunday drives around the country in an old Ford to visit and observe types and faces. In Iowa City he lives in a red brick house (it is the house in *Parson Weems' Fable*) which he remodeled himself, "able with equal facility to fix the plumbing, repair a broken clock, dress stone for his garden wall or paint a picture."

A "calm, self-contained person who looks at life with a clear serenity," he intends to stay in Iowa—the only American artist to get national recognition without a New York show, he "has no need of New York." He intends to continue painting and spreading his belief that "the hope of a native art in America," as he says in his pamphlet, *Revolt Against the City,* "lies in the development of regional art centers and the free competition between them. That is the only way in which we can win our independence."

References

Am Mag 120:44 S '35 por
Am Mag Art 28:285+ My '35
Life 8:32-3 F 19 '40 il
Lit Digest 114:13-14 Ag 13 '32 il; 121: 30 Ap 18 '36 il
Lond Studio 15 (Studio 115):88-93 F '38 il
No Am R 240:271-7 S '35
Scrib Mag 101:16-22 Je '37 il
Survey G 23:322-3 Jl '34 il
Time 35:41 Ja 8 '40 il; 36:53 S 23 '40
Bolton, T. American Book Illustrators 1938
Craven, T. Our Art Becomes American *In* Bower, W. ed. New Directions p303-20 1937
Who's Who in America
Who's Who in American Art

WOOD, SIR KINGSLEY 1881- Chancellor of the English Exchequer
Address: b. Broomhill Bank, Tunbridge Wells, England

For years a certain witty British columnist has been speaking of "colorful" Kingsley Wood. The irony may perhaps be lost on American readers, but actually "colorful" is the last adjective that could accurately apply to Wood, a "small, precise and puritanical" lawyer who belongs to the Wesleyan Church and is primarily interested in insurance, pensions, housing and public health. Wood is also almost the last man one would expect to find high in the councils of the Conservative Party, for he did not attend one of the "public schools" or either of the universities of Oxford or Cambridge, nor is he a member of the Anglican

Underwood & Underwood

SIR KINGSLEY WOOD

Church. Yet he is chairman of the executive committee of the Conservative Party and Grand Master of the Primrose League, a body devoted to "the maintenance of religion [the Anglican], of the estates of the realm and of the imperial ascendancy of Great Britain," and in Churchill's (see sketch this issue) National Government occupies a post from which men have often advanced to the Premiership. In October 1940 it was expected that he would be among those to go in the mild shakeup of Churchill's Cabinet, but after it was all over he was still clinging tenaciously to the chancellorship of the Exchequer and had moved up to join the War Cabinet.

Sir Kingsley Wood has been in Parliament for 22 years without interruption, and has moved steadily on to greater and greater responsibility "because he is heart and soul Tory and because he is not only a clever organizer but an astute and subtle politician." Not that he has not been responsible for some very beneficent legislation and administration. He has worked hard for social insurance legislation in Britain; the creation of a Ministry of Health was due to him more than to any other man; and it was also he who introduced measures providing for the earlier closing of shops and the introduction of daylight saving. Not known for picturesque speech or any kind of dramatic pose, he has applied business methods to government. As Chancellor of the Exchequer he has the job of finding a tremendous amount of money for the conduct of the War, and the budget he announced on July 23, 1940 was the most drastic ever presented to the British people. He called on the "little man" to carry most of the War burden, since, he said, there were not enough "big men" left to carry it.

Born in London in 1881, Sir Kingsley Wood is the son of the late Reverend Arthur Wood, a Wesleyan minister. From the fact that his school is nowhere recorded it may be assumed that he went to one of the lesser-known secondary schools. He studied to be a lawyer, passed his final law examination with honors and was admitted to practice in 1903. After a time he became head of Kingsley Wood, Williams and Murphy, a London law firm. Then in 1911, at the age of 30, Wood entered the outer fringes of politics as a Conservative member of the London County Council, the body which controls the municipal life of Greater London. He was elected by the working-class district of Woolwich and he continued to represent it until 1918.

Wood soon showed himself a very able committee member, and he took special interest in questions of building, insurance, the Old Age Pension and the fixing of adequate allowances for women legally separated from their husbands. He was chairman of the London Insurance Committee from 1916 to 1919 (acting as its president in 1920, 1922 and 1923); in 1917 he presented a petition to the Food Controller that all bread should be sold by weight; and in 1918 he put forward a much more important petition to the Prime Minister advocating the establishment of a Ministry of Health. Lloyd George, then Premier, adopted the suggestion, abolishing the old Local Government Board and merging its functions into the new and wider Ministry. In this same year a knighthood was conferred on Wood, and he was elected to Parliament as a Conservative for West Woolwich.

Lloyd George appointed the new knight and member to be Parliamentary Private Secretary to the Ministry he had virtually founded. In 1922 the Carlton Club meeting of the Conservatives decided to break up the coalition government of which Lloyd George was Premier, and installed Bonar Law in his place; Wood remained loyal to Lloyd George, and accepted no office under Bonar Law. But when the first short-lived Labor administration was replaced by a Conservative one under Stanley Baldwin in November 1924, Sir Kingsley was again made Parliamentary Secretary to the Ministry of Health. In 1928 he was nominated to the Privy Council (the King's advisory council). He remained in the Ministry of Health until Labor came in again in June 1929, and in that year's elections he held his seat by only a narrow margin.

Until the constitution of the National Government in 1931 Wood remained in opposition. Then he was appointed Parliamentary Secretary to the Board of Education, and, soon after the 1931 general election, Postmaster General. At the Post Office Wood gave the first real indication of his abilities, not only modernizing its administration but making it a paying service. He also introduced cheap night telephone service for long-distance telephone calls (familiarly known as the "Kingsley bobsworth"), a much-appreciated service not withdrawn until the War made it necessary; and as the Minister ultimately responsible to Parliament for broadcasting, he managed to work in harmony with the director general of the British Broadcasting Corporation of that day, the grim and dictatorial Sir John Reith (see sketch this issue).

In addition to this Ministerial post Sir Kingsley was also appointed, in 1931, chairman of the National Government Propaganda Committee. He had already, in the previous few years, assisted Neville Chamberlain in the Labor government's downfall; and he now proved an excellent propagandist and publicist. He continued at the Post Office until after the general election of 1935, when Stanley Baldwin made him Minister of Health. He was the first post office chief ever to be made a Cabinet Minister. Then early in 1938 he was transferred to the Air Ministry, and there he worked on the pressing job of aerial rearmament, replacing the brusque and inaccessible Lord Swinton. His own success at the job later seemed dubious to many critics of Chamberlain's government, however.

After the Munich pact in September 1938 it was Wood who is supposed to have given Chamberlain the idea of "going to the country" and asking for its votes while the mood of the day was still relief that war had been avoided. It was therefore a surprise when, soon after the outbreak of World War II, Wood was replaced at the Air Ministry by Sir Samuel Hoare (see sketch this issue). In Churchill's National Government of May 1940, however, he was placed in charge of the nation's finances as Chancellor of the Exchequer.

Sir Kingsley Wood lives at Tunbridge Wells, a pleasant spa one hour south of London. He is married to Agnes Fawcett. Plump, five-feet-five inches tall, with sparse gray hair and a "spiky little mustache," almost cherubically smiling through his horn-rimmed spectacles, Wood is popular as a departmental chief and knows how to get the best out of his subordinates. He is no orator, but can deliver a very capable speech, reading it from a manuscript. He has written many legal works on insurance and housing.

References

    Collier's 105:18-19 Ja 13 '40 il por
    N Y Times p1+, p11 Jl 24 '40
    Newsweek 16:27-8 Ag 5 '40
    Picture Post 7:30-1 Je 1 '40
    Strand Mag O '38
    Audax, pseud. Sir Kingsley Wood
      In Men in Our Time p181-98 1940

    Watchman, pseud. Right Honourable
      Gentlemen 1939
    Who's Who

WOOD, PHILIP 1895—Mar 3, 1940 Actor; author; playwright

Obituaries

    N Y Herald Tribune p20 Mr 5 '40
    Variety 137:54 Mr 6 '40

WOODBRIDGE, FREDERICK JAMES EUGENE Mar 26, 1867—June 1, 1940 Ex-dean of the graduate faculties of Columbia University; served institution for 38 years; was called "chief guide and counsellor in the development of all the university's policies"

FREDERICK J. E. WOODBRIDGE

References

    Leaders in Education
    Who's Who in America

Obituaries

    N Y Herald Tribune p34 Je 2 '40 por
    N Y Times p45 Je 2 '40 por
    Sch & Soc 51:731 Je 8 '40
    Time 35:88 Je 10 '40

WOODBURY, CHARLES HERBERT July 14, 1864—Jan 21, 1940 Marine painter; founder of the artists' colony at Ogunquit, Maine

References

    Who's Who in America 1938-39

Obituaries

    Boston Transcript p8 Ja 25 '40
    Mag Art 33:121 F '40
    N Y Herald Tribune p10 Ja 22 '40

WOODCOCK, CHARLES EDWARD, BISHOP June 12, 1854—Mar 12, 1940 Retired Protestant Episcopal Bishop of Kentucky; preached at the Cathedral of St.

WOODCOCK, CHARLES EDWARD—
Continued

John the Divine, New York City, in the summers of 1930 and 1931

References
Who's Who in America 1938-39

Obituaries
N Y Herald Tribune p22 Mr 13 '40
N Y Times p23 Mr 13 '40

WOOLLEY, EDGAR MONTILLION
See Woolley, M.

WOOLLEY, MONTY 1888- Actor; director

Address: Astor Hotel, Broadway and 44th St, New York City

Monty Woolley, who currently plays the part of Sheridan Whiteside in Kaufman and Hart's (see sketch this issue) *The Man Who Came to Dinner*, is famous not only as an actor and director but as the owner of the finest beard on Broadway and one of its loudest voices. "For years," says Lucius Beebe (see sketch this issue), "there have been divided schools of thought over which of these attributes constitutes his greatest claim to the attention of posterity. Adherents of the roaring school point out that Woolley was famous long before he became the Barbarossa of Broadway, while whisker enthusiasts say that anybody can make loud lion noises, but that the beard is of a unique magnificence, a museum piece in its own right."

Woolley values his beard at about $8,000. A few years ago Paramount Pictures asked if he would shave it off to play a part they had in mind for him. Woolley said he would part with his white plume for a bonus of $2,000 down plus $500 a week while it was growing back, a process which certainly would take three months. Paramount hired another actor. But Woolley wore it to great advantage as the ballet impresario in *On Your Toes* and as the visiting lecturer counterpart of Alexander Woolcott in *The Man Who Came to Dinner*.

The Man Who Came to Dinner is only Woolley's third appearance as an actor on the professional stage, but he has been in, of and about the drama ever since he went to Yale in 1907. He was born Edgar Montillion Woolley in the summer of 1888 in the old Hotel Bristol in New York City which his father owned, together with a number of other prosperous hotels. Except when he was away at school or traveling abroad with his parents, Monty spent all of his formative years in or near one of his father's hotels. In them or near them he met Lillian Russell, Victor Herbert and even Sarah Bernhardt.

Woolley attended the Mackenzie School, in Dobbs Ferry, New York until he went to Yale, where "he became the ringleader of a clique which dabbled in dramatics and profligacy." Every year he appeared in the Yale Dramatic Association's productions and was its president in his last year. At Yale he roomed with the late Thomas Beer and was friends with Cole Porter (see sketch this issue) and Gerald Murphy and others whom he was to know the rest of his life.

Woolley stayed at Yale to get his master's degree and then went to Harvard, intending to take a Ph. D. At Harvard he studied under George Lyman Kittredge, famous for his teaching of Shakespeare and his crisp, snowy-white beard. He left, however, before he earned his Ph. D., for Professor Kittredge had advised him to follow his bent for practical stage work.

He returned to Yale and for the next three years was an instructor of English there, as well as coach for the undergraduate dramatic productions. During the War he received a lieutenant's commission and spent eight uneventful months in France in 1918. When the Armistice came, he got his old job back at Yale and stayed there, "except for occasional ventures in New York," until 1927. These ventures included a couple of temporary jobs as stage manager for New York productions and one as assistant director and cutter in the old Famous Players-Lasky studio in Astoria.

At Yale Woolley was getting a small salary from the English department; he was getting an allowance from his father; and the drama in New Haven "had a little renaissance." Three boys who studied under him are still in the theatre: Dwight Deere Wiman, the producer; Jock Whitney, the perennial "angel"; and Jack Wilson, Noel Coward's manager. Woolley was happy there and intended to stay. But the late Edward Harkness presented Yale with a million dollars to be used for an experimental theatre, and Professor George Pierce Baker, who was conducting his "47 Workshop" at Harvard, was asked to direct the enterprise, despite the demonstrations on the campus against this choice. Woolley resigned and came to New York.

After he left Yale, "three important things happened": his father died, leaving him a small but comfortable income; he raised his famous beard at Saratoga Springs; and he "made a solid success of his first professional job of directing"—*Fifty Million Frenchmen*. Ray Goetz, the producer, engaged him overnight on the recommendation of Cole Porter. He directed, just as successfully, the *Second Little Show* and *Jubilee*. He now tells pupils of the drama: "Scorn not the lowly musical comedy as a training ground for your talents."

Then he went to Hollywood where nothing much, except a few small parts, happened until Wiman phoned him one day and asked him to return to New York to act. Woolley says: "Everybody said for me not to think of it, but a job on Broadway is worth millions in promises in Sunset Boulevard. That's one of the troubles with Hollywood anyhow. You may get an assignment at a simply staggering figure or you may get nothing. There's no simple

G. Maillard Kesslère

MONTY WOOLLEY

substantial middle ground of $200-a-week parts."

Woolley took the part of ballet impresario in *On Your Toes* and enjoyed doing it. He says he became a prima donna "ham all over" and used to shout to Mr. Wiman: "If you cut out that line of mine I'm going to cry. That's what I'll do." Then he appeared as the Prince of Wales in the short-lived musical romance about Gilbert and Sullivan, *Knights of Song*, and finally landed as Sheridan Whiteside in *The Man Who Came to Dinner*, where as the famous lecturer who goes to a dinner party in an Ohio town, gets hurt and has to stay on in the house for weeks, he commandeers the house, is crochety, mischief-making, selfish—and "excellent in the fattest of parts."

Woolley became well-known through his playing of Sheridan Whiteside, but in no way did this part raise him from obscurity. For many years he has been "a member in good standing of the international set: among the sparkplugs of café society the name of dear Monty is as well respected as those of dear Noel, dear Elsa and dear Cole." He basks at Antibes and the Lido; he's gone on a world cruise, reading Booth Tarkington "Little Orvie" stories to Moss Hart and Cole Porter; he holds levees in his hotel room at five in the afternoon to which the important come.

His life is made simple, however, by the fact that he has no possessive instinct at all. All he owns is an old Cadillac touring car and the usual amount of clothing—nothing else. He's never had an apartment and has always lived in hotels. His present room at the Astor "is usually a horrid welter of letters, linen and empty bottles. All he wants is a bed, a bathroom and a tele-

phone." Once when his friends complained about his hotel room's lack of individuality, he stopped at an art store and bought three identical prints to decorate it.

References
N Y Herald Tribune (drama section)
   p1 Ap 12 '36
N Y Times IX p1 Ag 16 '36
New Yorker 15:25-9 Ja 20 '40 por
Time 34:42-3 O 30 '39

WOOLTON, FREDERICK JAMES MARQUIS, 1ST BARON (wŏŏl'tŭn) Aug 24, 1883- British Minister of Food
Address: Hillfoot House, Woolton, Liverpool, England

For 20 years Frederick Marquis was known (especially in the North of England) as the incarnation of ruthless efficiency—director and more recently chairman of the big chain of provincial general stores called Lewis's, Limited. He would appoint men and women to executive positions at excellent salaries, but if they didn't come up to expectations their commercial lives in his concern were short. Now in 1940 this same Mr. Marquis, later Lord Woolton, is controller of a nation's food, manager of the "biggest shop the world has ever seen." Thousands of people carry out the work of the Ministry, but Woolton's job is to see to it that the people of Britain have enough food kept in reserve in different parts of the country so "that in the worst days we can imagine we shall have enough."

Frederick James Marquis was born in Manchester, England, the only child of Thomas Robert and Margaret (Ormerod) Marquis. He attended the Manchester Grammar School and continued his education at the University of Manchester, where he took B. S. and M. A. degrees and was awarded a research fellowship in economics. It was 1908 when he migrated to the rival city of Liverpool, 40 miles away, as warden of the University Settlement and of the David Lewis Club. His work there was to guide and supervise the practical side of the curriculum of students of the University School of Social Science, and it involved living in a slum. It was pure social work, at a moderate salary.

In 1912 Marquis married Maud Mathews of Manchester. (The couple now have a son and a daughter, the heir's name being Roger David Marquis.)

Then came the First World War. Marquis was judged unfit to fight, but got a job at the War Office and later became secretary to the Leather Control Board and controller of the Civilian Boots Department. He mastered the administrative side of this trade so well that he spent the next two years, from 1918 to 1920, reorganizing the Boot Manufacturers' Federation at its own invitation.

Marquis's plunge into big business hadn't really come yet, though. The firm of Lewis's, Limited, which has a large store in Liverpool and others in Manchester and

LORD WOOLTON

Birmingham, is controlled by a family named Cohen. The late Alderman L. Cohen, chairman of Lewis's at the end of the War, had his eye on the Settlement warden, and, recognizing ability even if it wasn't founded on commercial experience, asked Marquis to join his board of directors. "It is the first time," he said, "I have asked anyone who is not of my faith and family to join the board." And Marquis did—at first as staff controller.

Lewis's stores (not to be confused with the well-known London house of John Lewis) are not exactly for the carriage trade, but aim at producing good, cheap merchandise for customers of very moderate incomes. Nevertheless Marquis, having gone into business himself from academic circles, decided to recruit an administrative staff from the university. A number of young men and women who weren't attracted to teaching, journalism or law therefore began trying their luck in retail trade. Some only considered Lewis's as a stopgap; others fell by the wayside; but others did well, and even reached the directorial board.

Marquis himself became director of merchandising and in 1928 joint managing director. By this time he was the complete businessman, and soon he added directorships of other large Liverpool concerns such as the Bon Marché store, Martin's Bank, the Royal Insurance Company, the Liverpool, London and Globe Insurance Company, the Westpool Investment Trust, and S. Reece and Sons, the largest restaurateurs in the city.

He didn't lose his early interests, however. Marquis remained honorary secretary of the University Settlement and chairman of the David Lewis Club, became a governor of his old school, and served on a Board

of Education committee for the reconstitution of the Royal College of Art as a national training school for art masters. He acted as chairman of the Liverpool Medical Research Council, became a member of the University Council and served the University as deputy treasurer from 1931 to 1936, after which he became treasurer.

Meanwhile the powers in London, 200 miles away, became aware of his administrative ability. From 1930 to 1933 he was a member of the Overseas Trade Development Council; from 1930 to 1934 a member of the advisory council of the Board of Trade; and from 1933 a member of the advisory council to the Post Office. He was president of the Incorporated Association of Retail Distributors from 1930 to 1933, and became its chairman in 1934. In 1935 he was knighted and a year later advanced to the chairmanship of Lewis's, Limited, and all its associated companies.

Marquis was put in charge of army clothing at the outbreak of World War II, and shortly afterwards was raised to the peerage and asked by Prime Minister Chamberlain to take over food control. He chose his title from the pleasant outer suburb of Liverpool, where he has his home. Churchill (see sketch this issue) is felt to have done well in retaining him as Food Minister, for he combines a faculty for large-scale planning with an appreciation of the ordinary consumer's needs. Much of his success at Lewis's has been due to the talent for seeing into the housewife's mind which now enables him to buy and market on favorable terms for the housewives of all England; he knows something of the domestic problems that poor people have to face because of his experience in working-class neighborhoods in the cotton towns of Lancashire and the slums of Liverpool; and he has given evidence of the broadest views on commercial policy in general. Not even in Labor's ranks has there been adverse criticism of the appointment of Lord Woolton, sociologist and shopkeeper, philosopher and financier.

References

Collier's 106:15+ N 9 '40 por
Manchester Guardian p13 Ap 6 '40;
p12 Ap 9 '40
Who's Who

WORDEN, EDWARD CHAUNCEY Apr 17, 1875—Sept 22, 1940 Chemist; authority on cellulose chemistry; was consulted by private industries, governmental agencies and chemists the world over on matters pertaining to cellulose; his library contained 20,000 books on cellulose, probably the greatest collection on the subject in the world; was owner of a notable collection of stamps valued at $500,000

References

American Men of Science
Chemical Who's Who
Who's Who in America

Obituaries

N Y Herald Tribune p12 S 23 '40
N Y Times p17 S 23 '40

WRAY, JOHN GRIFFITH 1888—Apr 5, 1940 Actor and writer; acted on stage for years; went to Hollywood in 1929 for rôle in *All Quiet on the Western Front;* co-author of the play *Alibi*

References

International Motion Picture Almanac
Who's Who in the Theatre

Obituaries

N Y Times p44 Ap 7 '40
Variety 138:46 Ap 10 '40

WRIGHT, RICHARD Sept 4, 1908- Author

Address: b. c/o Harper and Bros, 49 E 33rd St, New York City

Richard Wright is a brilliant young Negro writer whose collection of short stories, *Uncle Tom's Children,* won a $500-prize competition in 1938. *Native Son,* the March 1940 selection of the Book-of-the-Month Club, is his first full-length novel. It is a powerful, intensely gripping story of a Negro boy driven to crime by reason of a Chicago tenement environment and the pressure of racial injustice. *Native Son* has been called the most striking novel to appear since *The Grapes of Wrath.* It has been acclaimed by critics as the most honest and important work yet written about the American Negro; daring because its author, himself a Negro, has presented in frank terms the savage brutality of a black boy "gone bad." Mr. Wright has a good reportorial style: simple, direct, at times staccato, on occasion rising to heights of poetic intensity.

Though compared to Dostoievsky because it is a study of crime and punishment, the story more closely parallels, in pattern and theme, Dreiser's *An American Tragedy.* Dreiser's white boy and Wright's black boy are both social misfits; both are victims of the adolescent lure of sex and money; both commit crime not deliberately but accidentally; both are condemned to the electric chair. And the conclusion is the same: that environment was responsible for their crimes—though in the case of Wright's character there is also the frustrating, neurosis-producing effect of racial suppression.

Bigger Thomas, who is 20 years old, lives with his mother, sister and younger brother in one rat-infested room, for which they pay $8, in Chicago's South Side Black Belt. He has been in a reform school; he and his gang commit petty neighborhood thieving; he is surly, fearful and a bully. He and his friend Gus like to imagine what they'd do if they were white. "'If you

RICHARD WRIGHT

wasn't black and if you had some money and if they'd let you go to that aviation school, you could fly a plane,' Gus said. For a moment Bigger contemplated all the if's Gus had mentioned; then both boys broke into hard laughter."

But Bigger gets a job as chauffeur to a millionaire philanthropist, Dalton, who makes his money in Negro tenement real estate. His daughter, Mary, is a radical; she asks Bigger to drive her that evening to a meeting with her Communist friend, Jan. When they try to treat him as an equal—shake hands with him, make him eat with them—Bigger is puzzled, scared, resentful. They all have drinks; Mary, very intoxicated, is brought, half-carried, to her room at two in the morning by Bigger. Her mother, who is blind, comes into the bedroom and calls to the daughter. Crazed by the fear that Mary will answer and betray his presence, Bigger puts a pillow over the girl's face, and without meaning to, smothers her. Frantic then, he burns her body in the furnace, hoping to leave no trace of the crime, and tries to implicate Jan, the Communist: dimly he knows that the Reds are also an object of mob hatred. When his Negro mistress, Bessie, learns of his crime, he kills her to protect himself, and throws her body down the air shaft of an old building. It is not long, however, before the death of Mary Dalton is traced to him (to the authorities, the Negro girl's death was negligible, as he knew it would be) and Bigger is caught while trying to escape over the tenement housetops.

The bloodshed, the horror, the tension—the swiftly paced melodramatic sequence of events—are at this point over. The latter part of the book is about Bigger's trial and defense: an exposition of an individual tragedy that symbolizes the tragedy of a

WRIGHT, RICHARD—*Continued*

race. It is Jan, the Communist, who calls on Bigger in his cell (and this time Bigger knows him for a friend) and arranges to have Max, a radical lawyer, defend him. Max's plea for Bigger, which the author bases to some extent on the arguments used by Clarence Darrow in the Loeb-Leopold case, follows the social premise that the hate of the whites toward Bigger is a subconscious feeling of guilt: by keeping him within rigid and sordid limits, they themselves actually were responsible for the murder of Mary Dalton. Bigger killed in order to keep from being killed, i. e., to preserve his integrity as a person, an individual. Max's plea becomes a defense of the twelve million Negroes in America—a nation without social, economic or property rights.

Naturally, no plea can save Bigger. He is sentenced to die. As he says: "Now I come to think of it, it seems like something that just had to be." And Bigger, searching for some meaning in his act, some self-justification, tells Max: "When a man kills, it's for something. . . I didn't know I was really alive in this world until I felt things hard enough to kill for 'em." And, for the first time in his life, because he had done something the white world really noticed, he felt a sense of freedom and power. He had always wanted, in his confused, groping way, to belong, to feel an equality with other men. In prison he at last comes to know that Max, and Jan, accept him on man-to-man terms. And he can accept them. Bigger's last words, implicit with his self-realization and self-redemption, are: "Tell Mister. . . Tell Jan hello."

Richard Wright was born September 4, 1908, on a plantation 25 miles from Natchez, Mississippi; his father, Nathan Wright, was a mill-worker and his mother, Ellen Wright, a country school teacher. His family was continually on the move, so his education was pretty much neglected. When his mother was stricken with paralysis during the First World War, he was sent to an uncle's house to live. He says he did so much fighting, lying and school-cutting that he was sent back to his grandmother, who predicted that he would end on the gallows. He was put in a Seventh Day Adventist school taught by his aunt; when he was beaten he got a razor and said he'd cut the next person who beat him.

At 15 he left home, went to Memphis and got a job as porter and messenger. He read a newspaper one day which criticized H. L. Mencken, and got interested in Mencken, thinking anybody the South didn't like must be all right. Since the Negro libraries in Memphis had few books, he had a white friend borrow books for him at the public library. He read all the books mentioned in Mencken's *Book of Prefaces*, and himself got the urge to write. For a

few years he bummed his way all over the country, working at any kind of job from ditch-digging to clerking in a post office. He drifted to Chicago, where he had heard Negroes stood a better chance of getting jobs. He was a clerk for awhile; and in 1933 had a taste of politics. "I became an assistant precinct captain in the Republican primary election," he said. "I was promised a job. I didn't get it. Next time I became an assistant precinct captain for the Democrats and was promised a job, which I didn't get. So then I became a Red. Now I'm what the papers refer to as a card-carrying Communist."

In 1935 Wright got on the Federal Writers' Project in Chicago. By this time he had sold poetry, articles and some stories to little magazines, and was working on his first book, *Uncle Tom's Children*. He came to New York in 1937, lived from hand to mouth for some months, then got on the Writers' Project. He wrote the essay on Harlem in *New York Panorama*. He also did some work on the *Daily Worker* (he says he never got orders from Stalin to cover anything) and became a contributing editor of the *New Masses*. His book of four long short stories, *Uncle Tom's Children*, part of which had originally appeared in the *New Caravan*, was a success. The stories won high critical praise; what one critic had to say of them is characteristic: "*Uncle Tom's Children* has its full share of violence and brutality; violent deaths occur in three stories and the mob goes to work in all four. Violence has long been an important element in fiction about Negroes, just as it is in their life. But where Julia Peterkin in her pastorals and Roark Bradford in his levee farces show violence to be the reaction of primitives unadjusted to modern civilization, Richard Wright shows it as the way in which civilization keeps the Negro in his place. And he knows what he is writing about."

In 1939 Wright got a Guggenheim Fellowship, which enabled him to quit the Project and complete his novel, *Native Son*. The material for this, he says, was based partly on boys he met in a Chicago rehabilitation school for Negro "Dead End" kids, and partly on the Robert Nixon case. Nixon was a young Negro who died in the electric chair in Chicago in August 1938 for killing a white woman with a brick.

Wright likes to read a lot and also likes the movies, which are a form of relaxation for him from a great deal of writing. But he doesn't exactly approve of Hollywood. He realizes that there are a lot of taboos in writing for pictures, so far as presenting Negroes in them is concerned. He wouldn't go to Hollywood if he had to write around those taboos, he says. Recently he made a trip back to Chicago, where, with the first money from his *Native Son*, he bought a home for his mother. After living for many months in Mexico, in November 1940 he was back in the United States completing a new

novel dealing with the plight of Negro female
servants in Manhattan and Brooklyn.

References

Atlan 165:659-61 My '40
Boston Transcript p1 Mr 2 '40
Commonweal 31:438 Mr 8 '40
N Y Herald Tribune Books p5 Mr 3
'40
N Y Sun p3 Mr 4 '40
N Y World-Telegram p15 Ap 29 '40
Sat R Lit 21:1 Mr 2 '40; 22:3+ Je 1
'40 por
Time 35:72 Mr 4 '40
Who's Who in America (Addenda)

WRIGHT, RUSSEL Apr 3, 1905- Industrial designer

Address: 4 E 39th St, New York City

Russel Wright stands high among industrial designers who have put the stamp of
their creativeness on the modern American
home, introducing into it accessories and
furniture of functional design: that is, objects
designed specifically for the purpose they
are to serve. He is one of the youngest of
industrial designers of note.

Mr. Wright is known for taking prosaic,
commonplace materials and transforming
them into highly decorative and brilliant
designs. He was a pioneer in bringing
aluminum out of the kitchen; spun aluminum
accessories and aluminum "from stove to
table" pieces are spectacular successes. He
has lifted wood from the kitchen to give
it a place in the dining room in a variety
of decorative forms such as cheese boards,
salad bowls and trays. He has done wonders
with copper, transforming it into original
modern decorative pieces, and in lamps he
has used natural fibre, such as bamboo,
rattan and cane, with talent and freshness.

"Blond" maple, now a familiar term in
furniture vernacular, owes much of its popularity, as do other light-colored woods, to
Russel Wright, for he was one of the first
designers to use a bleached maple finish
for commercial modern furniture. The imprint of his designing genius has been felt
in many fields—lamps, furniture, wall paper,
fabrics, radio, metalware and even machines
for manufacturers have all been within the
range of his work.

Russel Wright was born April 3, 1905 in
Lebanon, Ohio, where his father was county
judge. He traces his ancestry back to two
signers of the Declaration of Independence,
Whipple and Morris. As a boy, Wright
showed a feeling for art, and his Saturday
afternoons were spent at the Cincinnati
Art Academy. During the First World
War he worked after school hours in an
ammunition factory to earn money for
courses at the Academy, and studied painting there with Frank Duveneck.

When he was 16 years old he came to New
York for a year at the Art Students League,
studying under Kenneth Hayes Miller and
Leo Lentelli. As a climax to his year at
the school he won both the first and second

RUSSEL WRIGHT

Tiffany Prizes in a student competition for
the best war memorial.

Because Princeton and a legal career
were family traditions, the young artist found
himself enrolled at Princeton when he was
17. He distinguished himself at the college
as director of the campus playhouse and
for his Triangle Show sets. His outstanding
work on the show sets led to an offer to go
to Paris with Norman Bel Geddes (see
sketch this issue), and Wright cut short
his college career for theatrical work.

There followed a short span as a theatrical
designer during which Mr. Wright worked
with Lee Simonson, Robert Edmond Jones and
Rouben Mamoulian. He designed sets for the
Theatre Guild, the Neighborhood Playhouse,
the Group Theatre and for various New York
and out-of-town productions.

At this period the ambitious young designer started a workshop in which theatrical
properties were produced. Later on he
added custom-made furniture and decorative
accessories to his work. As local decorators
spread the word and the originality of
Wright's designs became known, many of
New York's department stores became
customers. Next the informal serving accessories of spun aluminum and wood for
which Wright became so popular were
added, and as the business grew, stock
articles were produced to fill reorders. It
was inevitable that a small factory would
be set up when Mr. Wright began getting
orders from all over the country and achieving a national distribution for his products.

Because of the success and reputation of
his own products Mr. Wright received commissions from manufacturers to design their
merchandise. Thus within a comparatively
short time he was designing rugs, wallpapers, radios, pianos, furniture, pottery,
displays, showrooms and exhibits. When

WRIGHT, RUSSEL—*Continued*

he was little over 30 he was already one of America's leading industrial designers.

Russel Wright's work all has a stream-lined, modern look. He is frankly a modernist, and functional design is his forte. He has lectured and written many articles on modern design. Economy, he says, can become an esthetic principle. In an article pointing out the incongruity of furniture and accessories designed for use in another age in the modern home, he wrote that absolute beauty in home furnishings depends on its adaptability to the demands of modern life. He advocates rooms "with muscles and bones that do things rather than imitate things they are not." Thus, he explained, while a canopied bed may have been a fine thing during the period it was designed to keep out drafts in early American homes, it has little excuse now in a modern, centrally heated home. It does not represent functional design.

Mr. Wright has exhibited in important museums of large cities in the United States, including the Metropolitan Museum of Art. His workshop is known as the Russel Wright Associates, and he is helped in his business by his wife, who works with him.

His newest venture is the formation of an "American-Way" merchandising project, a group effort among industrial designers, artists, and manufacturers and craftsmen to stimulate modern design of inherently American character. "American-Way" gave its first presentation of its merchandise at the Merchandise Mart in Chicago from August 1 to August 14, 1940.

References

Am Home 11:60-2 Ja '34 il por
Arch Forum 67:283-5 O '37 por
Arts & Dec 42:26-9 F '35
Home & F 44(House B 75):30-3 Ap '34 il
Pict R 37:55 O '35
Who's Who in American Art

WYLIE, MAX May 12, 1904- Radio director; writer

Address: 485 Madison Ave, New York City

Buyer of antique furniture for Macy's and professor at a university in Lahore, India have been only two of the occupations that Max Wylie has managed to cram into a busy life. He was born at Beverly, Massachusetts, the second son of the Rev. Edmund M. and Edna (Edwards) Wylie. As Edna Edwards, his mother was an author of best sellers during the early 1900's. Two of her best-known books were *The Blue Valley Feud* and *The Ward of the Sewing Circle,* the latter still in print and highly relished by lovers of early tear-jerkers. Wylie's younger brother is Philip Wylie, popular and prolific novelist, short story writer and motion picture scenarist. Another brother, Ted, was killed in Warsaw, Poland in 1936. He had been junior editor at Farrar and Rinehart's and

MAX WYLIE

had published one novel at the age of 20—*Altogether Now*. All three brothers have one curious thing in common—all were born on May 12 and every year therefore cheated of two additional ice-cream-and-cake celebrations. On their maternal side, the Wylies are direct descendants of the fierce New England preacher, Jonathan Edwards (their tenth great-grandfather, to be exact). On their father's side they are descendants of Aaron Burr.

Max Wylie attended grammar and high schools in Ohio and New Jersey. He received his B. A. from Hamilton College in 1928, then did graduate work at the University of Pennsylvania. The next few years were spent in a succession of occupations. For one year he was a buyer of antique furniture for Macy's Department Store in New York and for the next two, (1929-31) was professor of philosophy and history of the English novel at Punjab University, Lahore, British India. That stay furnished the background for his first novel *Hindu Heaven* (1933), a book about Englishmen and missionaries in India. It has been called an "engrossing narrative of fanaticism, racial discord and kindred ailments," in style derivative of Hemingway's he-man sentimentality and "marred by a terrible straining after effect."

Wylie became an instructor of English at the University of Pennsylvania after he returned from India in 1931. Evidently one year of academic life was enough for the restless young man for the next year he joined *Time* as a staff writer. After a year he flitted to the firm of Cape and Ballou, publishers. In 1933 he seems to have found his real occupation, for he joined the Columbia Broadcasting System, and has been there ever since. The same year he married Isobel Winans Lamb; they have one daughter, Pamela. For one year he was a producer of radio programs, then became director of script and continuity. He has brought more new writers to the radio field than any other editor and has himself produced and written many hundreds of shows of every type "except gag comedy" for which he admits he "has no talent." For three years he has lectured at New York University in the Adult Education Department on radio script writing.

With all these duties he still has found time to write *Radio Writing* (1939), a "comprehensive textbook of the entire field of writing for the radio industry." Mr. Wylie, a realist with deep respect for the radio medium, does not think that radio writing is a special art and he is suspicious of theories about "radio technique." He insists that to write a "good script or continuity demands imagination, dramatic sense, a gift for dialogue, a sense of timing, and a knowledge of the radio's particular techniques, especially sound effects."

After 16 months of "lost week ends and lonely nights" spent in the examination of some 6,000 radio scripts, he has selected 32 for *Best Broadcasts of 1938-39,* an anthology of representative programs. "The experience," he admits, "was a considerable chore because it was necessary to eat so much stale popcorn before finding a prize." The volume is probably the first of a series of yearly books on the order of the Burns Mantle theatre books. It is valuable as a record of the most impermanent of the arts—the work that "dies with the program sign-off."

Lewis Gannett, the critic, feels that this collection may "some day be as valuable, and as revealing, as a collection of early Sears Roebuck catalogues is today."

References

N Y Herald Tribune Books p21 Mr 17 '40
N Y Times IX p12 D 31 '39
Time 35:34 Ja 8 '40
Variety Radio Directory

YANCEY, LEWIS Q. ALONZO 1896— Mar 2, 1940 Navigator and co-pilot with Roger Q. Williams on a flight from Old Orchard, Maine to Rome in 1929

Obituaries

N Y Herald Tribune p12 Mr 4 '40
N Y World-Telegram p24 Mr 4 '40
Newsweek 15:9 Mr 11 '40
Time 35:64 Mr 11 '40

YBARRA, THOMAS RUSSELL (ē-bä'-rä) Oct 8, 1880- Ex-foreign correspondent; journalist; traveler
Address: c/o Dodd Mead & Co, 449 Fourth Ave, New York City

When Nazi penetration into South America at last awakened the United States to the fact that she would do well to revamp her attitude toward the republics to the South, *America Faces South* (1939), by T. R. Ybarra, veteran foreign correspondent and authority on the Latin-American question, made a very timely appearance.

Thomas Russell Ybarra was born October 8, 1880, in Boston, Massachusetts. His father was General Alejandro Ybarra, of Caracas, Venezuela, several times Governor of six of the states comprising the Republic of Venezuela, and Minister of War and Foreign Affairs; and his mother, Ellen Taylor Russell, daughter of Judge Thomas Russell of Boston. His great-grandfather on his mother's side was "Father" Taylor, long-famous New England preacher to the sailors in the flush days of windjammers.

Young Ybarra's father was, for a number of years, in business in the States, and Thomas was sent first to primary and grammar schools in Boston and then to Roxbury and Cambridge Latin schools. He spent three years at Harvard, was graduated with the Class of 1905, and studied in Venezuela and on the Continent.

After college he came to New York and began to bombard various magazines and dailies with samples of his prose and verse. Late in 1905 he joined the staff of the New York *Times,* where he began as a reporter and eventually became Sunday editor. In 1908 he published a book of jolly ballads called *Davy Jones's Yarns and Other Salted Songs.*

The *Times,* in 1924, made him correspondent in Berlin—just when the mark was taking its astronomical plunge. He was transferred 18 months later to London, where he remained about a year and a half; and in 1926 was appointed traveling European correspondent. Between 1929 and 1931 his three biographies—of Bolivar, Cervantes and Von Hindenberg—had made their way to the reading public. In 1930 he married Penelope O'Leary of New York City.

He left the *Times* in order to give more attention to writing for magazines, and for six years (1931-37) he was European editor of *Collier's,* doing, at the same time, considerable free-lance work for the American press. Within his circuit came almost every Continental country. He traveled also in North Africa, Egypt and Asiatic Turkey; toured South America for *Collier's* in 1933 and 1934; and made a return visit to Montevideo at the time of the Pan-American Conference. The log of his 1938 to 1939 tour of South and Central America appeared, for the most part, in the New York *Times* and became the basis of his *America Faces South.*

It is Mr. Ybarra's North American experience as a trained journalist, plus his South American heritage, that makes *America Faces South* of outstanding value. If his book seems something of a "hodgepodge" (his own term) it is justifiably so, for the one thing he stresses is that these South American countries are utterly dissimilar. They have no common center of culture, no unified formula, social or political.

THOMAS R. YBARRA

He gives us the history of these countries, and a glance at Central America and Mexico as well. He apprises Nazi, Fascist and Japanese penetration in various localities. The whole book is framed by a workman-like presentation of the Monroe Doctrine and the Good Neighbor Policy.

References
Cath World 150:627 F '40
Christian Sci Mon Mag p4+ D 7 '38
Collier's 96:26+ O 26 '35; 97:30+ Ja 4 '36; 97:25+ My 9 '36; 99:22+ F 13 '37; 100:21-2 S 4 '37
N Y Herald Tribune Books p7 N 20 '39
N Y Sun p15 Ap 16 '40
N Y Times Book R p9 N 5 '39
Sat R Lit 21:19 Ja 20 '40

YELLIN, SAMUEL   Mar 2, 1885—Oct 3, 1940 Artist; master craftsman in hand-wrought metal work; has been called "the master iron craftsman of all time"; his decorations on buildings throughout the country are examples of skill in ironwork such as marked buildings in medieval times; was recipient of many awards, among them the Bok Civic Award as "outstanding citizen of Philadelphia" in 1925

References
Am Mercury 21:199-207 O '30
Outlook 138:714-17 D 31 '24 il
Who's Who in America
Who's Who in American Art
Who's Who in American Jewry

Obituaries
N Y Herald Tribune p18 O 4 '40 por
N Y Times p23 O 4 '40 por

YODER, ALBERT HENRY   Feb 15, 1866—Sept 22, 1940 Child psychologist; educator; president of Vincennes University from 1896 to 1901; lecturer at the New York School of Philanthropy from 1910 to 1912; president of the Wisconsin State Normal School for next seven years; director of the University of Wisconsin extension service from 1920 to 1934

References
Leaders in Education 1932
Who's Who in America 1934-35

Obituaries
N Y Herald Tribune p18 S 24 '40
N Y Times p23 S 24 '40

YONAI, MITSUMASA   Mar 1880- (yô-nī mĭ-tsōō-mä-sä)   Former Premier of Japan
Address: Tokyo, Japan

The Japanese Emperor's appointment of Admiral Mitsumasa Yonai on January 14, 1940 as Premier to form a new Cabinet came as a surprise to Japanese and international circles, for the Admiral was little known in international politics and was not among the strong men considered as candidates. Premier Yonai succeeded Nobuyuki Abe, whose Cabinet was the third to fall in 12 months.

Premier Yonai's first speech before the Diet was a huge success. "He said nothing, and said it briefly, elegantly, forcefully." But soon he found himself faced with the problem of a food shortage in Japan, with a scarcity of labor, with a housing shortage, with the problem of American armament expansion, which was a matter of "grave concern" to him. He wasn't upset. "He was born to debts, weaned on trouble, schooled in adversity."

He was born in Iwateken in 1880, the son of a Samurai—"one of those ferocious retainer-warriors who wore two swords sharp enough to shave with, who scorned money because their liege lords supplied them with houses, clothes, food, concubines, whatever else they needed." But a few years before Mitsumasa was born Japan suddenly was turned from a feudal to a capitalist state. The elder Yonai, who had been given an inadequate political job, cracked up and deserted his family when Mitsumasa was six. His mother then worked as a seamstress and sewing teacher.

While Mitsumasa was in school, he got a job copying documents and gave his pay envelope to his mother each week, unopened. He went on to the Naval Academy where he was a "popular mediocrity": he finished at the center of his class in 1901—sixtieth among 125 cadets. At 21 he wrote a self portrait: "My strongest characteristic: gluttony—I never get enough to eat. My credo: self respect—I believe in myself. My weak points: none."

Yonai went up through the Navy "pushing himself ahead with alternate fits of rebellion and unctuousness, in alternate shifts of deck and desk duty. He lost the hearing of his

Times—Wide World

MITSUMASA YONAI

left ear in target practice, and quickly learned the political uses of deafness." He was commander of the Sasebo Naval Station from 1933 to 1934; commander in chief of the Second Squadron in 1934 and 1935; and commander in chief of the Imperial Japanese Fleet in 1936. Entering the government as Minister of the Navy in the Cabinet of Hayaski in February 1937, he served as Minister in the Navy in the two succeeding Cabinets, Konoye's and Hiranuma's.

Yonai is said to be one of the most popular and best informed men in the Japanese Navy. Nearly six feet tall, weighing 188 pounds, "with airplane shoulders and a trimotor voice," big of hands and feet and manner, with a fair complexion, he has been nicknamed "The White Elephant," with none of the Occidental connotations of the phrase. He is amiable and friendly and gives an appearance of strength and wisdom.

Yonai is a liberal, an opponent of military dictatorship and an advocate of closer relations with the United States and Britain. As Minister of the Navy in the summer of 1939 he stood firmly against the proposed military alliance with Germany. "The Japanese Navy," he said, "belongs to the Emperor. It is not for hire by Hitler, or anyone else."

It was probably because of his liberal policies that Yonai and his entire Cabinet were forced out of the Premiership in July 1940. Army circles by then had come to the conclusion that it was the urgent task of Japan to establish a new national political structure to carry out rearmament effectively, tighten State control of economy and renovate foreign policy with the construction of a new order in east Asia as the ultimate object. Yonai was not the man to do these, obviously, and so he either stepped or was pushed down, to be suc-

ceeded by Prince Konoye (see sketch this issue).

References

Cur Hist 51:12 F '40
Life 8:16 Ja 29 '40 por
Liv Age 353:233-4 N '37
Manchester Guardian p3 Ja 15 '40
N Y Herald Tribune p2 Ja 15 '40 por; p8 Ja 21 '40; p26 Mr 24 '40 por
N Y Sun p15 Ja 16 '40
N Y Times Ja 15 '40
Newsweek 15:25-6 Ja 22 '40 por; 15: 30 Ja 29 '40
Scholastic 36:10 F 5 '40 por
Time 35:35 Ja 22 '40 por; 35:24+ Mr 4 '40 por (cover)
Who's Who in Japan 1936

YOUNG, ART Jan 14, 1866- Cartoonist; author

Address: Bethel, Connecticut

The drawings of Arthur Henry Young (to give his full name, although he never uses it) have been for some 40 years "among both the least well advertised and the most distinguished features of American satiric art." He was born in 1866 on a farm near Orangeville, Stephenson County, Illinois, as his father was also, in 1838, six years after the Black Hawk War. The town was only 10 miles from Monroe, Wisconsin, and it was there the prosperous family repaired to run the general store. Art went to the little red schoolhouse for a while and then clerked in his father's store. As a boy he had made caricatures of all the town's leading characters and knew from the start that his life was to be devoted to art.

At 18, in 1884, he went to Chicago and studied at the Academy of Design. He found it easy to support himself by selling cartoons to newspapers and periodicals. The next year he went to New York and enrolled at the Art Students League, then he went to Paris, where for six months he studied painting at the Académie Julian and received honorable mention in a prize contest. This was the extent of his foreign study, for he became gravely ill and was taken home by his father. He married Elizabeth North of Monroe in 1885 and they had two sons. For some eight years they lived amicably, then separated: "I am an artist," he said, "and the duties and courtesies of married life are too much for me."

He was the first man in the world to draw a daily political cartoon. This he did for the Chicago *Inter-Ocean*. He was optimistic and conventional—cheerfully drawing to order cartoons on any subject. In his middle 30's he went to New York and began to read and study, and listen to debates at Cooper Union. Slowly he found himself a passionate hater of cruelty and falsehood in government and business. His art took on new power, became striking in its simplicity. To eliminate non-essentials became his constant striving. Among his

Harry Godfrey

ART YOUNG

most famous cartoons from *The Masses* (of which for a while he was coeditor) is the picture of a wife and husband captioned: "There you go," she says, "you're tired. Here I be a-standin' over a hot stove all day and you workin' in a nice cool sewer." Another was a picture of two slum children looking up at the sky: "Chee, Annie, look at the stars, thick as bedbugs!" In each he introduced humor, a sharp social protest and infinite love for his characters.

One reason he feels that he never made much money is that his humor always accompanied "savage assaults on every kind of organized meanness, cruelty, hypocrisy." During the years he has been active in campaigns for woman suffrage, labor organization, abolition of child labor and race discrimination. Always a crusader, he was arrested as a pacifist during the World War. The Associated Press once accused him of libel. His political leanings were socialistic and he ran for office twice. Now in his '70s he lives quietly in an old farmhouse in Bethel where he maintains a little Art Young gallery to which he welcomes visitors. In 1939 he published a genial autobiography, *Art Young: His Life and Times.*

He is described thus by his good friend Max Eastman: "He looks a little like a cigar-end-chewing Schopenhauer or Henrik Ibsen, notwithstanding his kind mouth and mild blue eyes, and his ability to look awfully funny when he gives an imitation of a Southern Congressman making a speech on the tariff. He looks that way when he greets you, but he will thaw out after a while and begin to look more like P. T. Barnum, his predecessor as the most illustrious citizen of Bethel."

Art Young has written *Trees at Night* (1927); *On My Way* (1928) (autobiographical); *Art Young's Inferno* (1933); and *The*

Best of Art Young (1936). Two other books which are parodies of Gustave Doré and Dante are out of print.

References

Art Digest 8:13 Ja 15 '34; 9:15 D 1 '34
Art N 37:13 Ap 1 '39
Milwaukee J p8 Ja 3 '40 self por
New Repub 57:217-18 Ja 9 '29; 102: 60 Ja 8 '40 il
New Yorker 11:21-5 Mr 2 '35
Time 34:46 D 11 '39 il
Birchman, W. Art Young *In* Faces & Facts 1937
Who's Who in America
Who's Who in American Art
Young, A. Art Young: His Life and Times 1939
Young, A. On My Way 1928

YOUNG, CHARLES JAC Dec 21, 1880— Mar 4, 1940 Artist

A native of Bavaria, Charles Jac Young was brought to this country by his parents when he was two years old. He studied art in New York at the National Academy of Design and under Robert Henri. Although both a painter and an etcher, Mr. Young preferred etching and was known for his landscapes, especially for his realistic snow scenes. His works are included in permanent collections in museums in many parts of the country. Mr. Young died March 4, 1940, leaving a wife and a son.

References

Who's Who in America 1938-39
Who's Who in American Art 1938-39

Obituaries

N Y Herald Tribune p22 Mr 5 '40
N Y World-Telegram p32 Mr 5 '40

YU-T'ANG, LIN *See* Lin Yu-t'ang

ZEIDLER, CARL FREDERICK Jan 4, 1908- Mayor of Milwaukee

Address: b. City Hall, Milwaukee, Wisconsin; h. 504 N 33rd St, Milwaukee, Wisconsin

A Mayoralty campaign which attracted national attention in 1940 was that of Carl F. Zeidler, who ousted the Socialist incumbent of Milwaukee, Daniel Webster Hoan, who had held the office for 24 consecutive years. Waging a rip-roaring campaign of song and music and handshaking, Zeidler became the youngest Mayor of a major American city.

It was a campaign of youth and good looks against age and experience. Hoan, fifty-nine, tall, lanky and unkempt, had successfully defeated candidates in six Mayoralty campaigns. Affectionately known as "Uncle Dan," he had the gratitude of Milwaukee's voters for cleaning up a corrupt city government. His tenure of 24 years as Mayor was unequaled in any metropolitan community in the United States.

Zeidler was 32, tall, broad-shouldered, handsome, had reddish blond wavy hair and a brilliant smile. He was single and the best looking Mayoralty candidate that Milwaukee had seen in years.

Hoan reminded the voters that he had served them faithfully and well for thirty years, for six years as city attorney, for twenty-four as Mayor. Under his régime, Milwaukee, once one of the most corrupt cities in the country, had become one of the best-governed cities. Mayor Hoan asked the voters to remember that he had given them a city free of political scandal, free of crime, a city with model police and fire departments and with a city debt that was the smallest in the country on a per capita basis. Milwaukee voters had made no mistake when they quit old-time party lines to elect Socialist Hoan their Mayor in 1916.

Zeidler had no such impressive record to offer. He had been appointed assistant city attorney in 1936 when he was 28, a job from which he resigned to run for Mayor. It was his first campaign for an elective office. The son of a Milwaukee barber, he had worked his way through Marquette University, finishing the law course in six years instead of the usual seven. In high school he had excelled in football and track. At Marquette University he won acclaim as an orator and was graduated with honors in 1929. His classmates voted him as one of ten most likely to succeed. In the year preceding his Mayoralty campaign he received five civic awards for service to his community.

Friends said he set his eye on a political career, and went about getting it systematically. He decided to use his fine baritone voice as a success vehicle. He joined dozens of fraternal and civic organizations, including the Young Men's Christian Association, where he kept in trim swimming in the pool. At meetings he could always be counted on to make a speech or to sing. He said, "I gravitate toward my fellow man." He claimed he knew 50,000 Milwaukeeans by their first names.

The politically impeccable Hoan talked to the voters of the excellent government he had given them. Carl F. Zeidler flashed his brilliant smile, sang and shook hands with the voters. Typical of the rah-rah campaign he waged was an incident at an Elks Club one afternoon when 600 astonished women saw handsome Candidate Zeidler step out beside a lovely brunette mannequin in a bridal gown, walk down the aisle with her singing *I Love You Truly* in a rich baritone. Lumps filled 600 throats, and Zeidler probably won 600 votes.

The energetic young Zeidler sang at dozens of funerals, wedding and church services, addressed 293 meetings, shook hands and sang *When Irish Eyes Are Smiling* appealingly. He admitted that Milwaukee was one of the best-governed cities in the country, but declared that there was room

CARL F. ZEIDLER

for improvement, and anyway Milwaukee needed a change. It was time to drive out the Socialists, he exhorted.

While Hoan was a Socialist, Socialism had played little part as an economic doctrine in his practical reforms. In 1935, when the Socialists merged with the Progressives, he ran for re-election as a member of the Farmer-Labor Progressive Federation. He was branded as a Red by complaining bankers, utility men and real estate owners in Milwaukee, however. Zeidler ran on a non-partisan ticket, but with the Red issue raised, conservative Democrats and Republicans lined up for him.

Hoan was a little worried when Zeidler ran up 50,515 votes to his 75,313 in a field of eight candidates in the primary. But observers who knew Hoan's fine record declared he could not be beaten. When the votes were counted in the election, however, there were 111,957 for Zeidler, only 99,798 for Hoan, and the city had turned out for a record vote. Going down to defeat with Hoan was Carl Zeidler's brother Frank, the Wisconsin secretary of the Socialist Party, who ran for county supervisor.

Zeidler, Mayor of the United States' twelfth largest city, is the second youngest Mayor in his city's history, the youngest having been Sherburn M. Becker, now of New York, who was elected in 1906 at the age of 29, and who served one term. Zeidler's comment on his election was, "I used nothing else than modern merchandising methods: See 'em, tell 'em, sell 'em." Hoan said, "I leave my public duties without rancor. Said papa Zeidler: The wave in Carl's hair is absolutely natural."

References

Look 4:38-43 Je 4 '40 il pors
Nation 150:523 Ap 20 '40

ZEIDLER, CARL F.—*Continued*

N Y Sun p4 Mr 29 '40 por
N Y Times p14 Ap 4 '40 por
Newsweek 15:19 Ap 15 '40 il por
Time 35:22-3 Ap 15 '40 por
Who's Who in America (Addenda)

ZHABOTINSKII, VLADIMIR EVGEN'-EVICH [ATALENA, pseud.] *See* Jabotinsky, V. E.

ZIMMERMAN, ALFRED F. M. May 8, 1859—June 6, 1940 Ex-World War Foreign Minister in Germany; author of the "Zimmerman note" which influenced the United States' entry into the First World War

Obituaries

N Y Herald Tribune p12 Je 8 '40 por
N Y Times p15 Je 8 '40 por
Newsweek 15:8 Je 17 '40 por
Time 35:64 Je 17 '40

ZINSSER, HANS Nov 17, 1878—Sept 4, 1940 Professor of bacteriology and immunology at the Harvard Medical School; author of two best-selling books, *Rats, Lice and History* (1937), and an autobiography, *As I Remember Him; The Biography of R. S.* (initials stood for Romantic Self) (1940), in which he forecast his own death; considered the world's leading authority on typhus; in 1936 isolated the typhus germ; in 1939 announced perfection of a method of producing enough anti-typhus to protect an entire nation; was sent to Serbia and Russia as Sanitary Commissioner; recipient of many high honors —United States awarded him the D. S. O., France made him a member of the Legion of Honor and Serbia decorated him

HANS ZINSSER

References

Atlan 165:117-50 Ja '40; 165:267-96 F '40; 165:417-44 Mr '40; 165:562-92 Ap '40; 165:638-46 My '40
Scholastic 27:5 O 5 '35
Sci ns 89:599 Je 30 '39
Wilson Lib Bul 15:10 S '40

American Medical Directory
American Men of Science
Leaders in Education 1932
Who's Who in America
Zinsser, H. As I Remember Him 1940

Obituaries

N Y Herald Tribune p18 S 5 '40 **por**
N Y Times p23 S 5 '40 por
Newsweek 16:8 S 16 '40 por

BIOGRAPHICAL DICTIONARIES CONSULTED

The publication dates listed are those of volumes in CURRENT BIOGRAPHY's reference collection. When no date appears for biographical dictionaries in the list of references at end of sketches, latest edition has been used.

American Catholic Who's Who 1940-41
American Medical Directory 1938
American Men of Science 1938
American Women 1939-40
America's Young Men 1938-39
Australian Biographical Dictionary 1934
Author's and Writer's Who's Who 1934

Blue Book of American Aviation 1940
Bolton, T. American Book Illustrators 1938

Catholic Who's Who 1936
Chambers's Biographical Dictionary 1938
Chemical Who's Who 1937
Chi è? 1936
China Year Book 1935

Dictionary of the American Hierarchy 1940
Directory of Medical Specialists 1939

Europa v2
Ewen, D. ed. Composers of Today 1936

Film Daily Year Book 1939

International Motion Picture Almanac 1939-40
International Press Who's Who; New Zealand 1938
International Who's Who 1940

Japan-Manchoukuo Year Book 1937

Keesing's Contemporary Archives 1937-40; 1940-43
Kunitz, S. J. ed. Authors Today and Yesterday 1933
Kunitz, S. J. ed. Living Authors 1937
Kunitz, S. J., and Haycraft, H. eds. American Authors 1600-1900 1938

Kunitz, S. J., and Haycraft, H. eds. Junior Book of Authors 1935
Leaders in Education 1932

Mantle, B. Contemporary American Playwrights 1938
Millett, F. B. Contemporary American Authors 1940
Murchison, C. ed. Psychological Register 1932

New Standard Encyclopedia of Art 1939
New York City. Museum of Modern Art Twenty Centuries of Mexican Art 1940

Pierre Key's Musical Who's Who 1931

Qui Etes-Vous? 1924

Ringel, F. J. ed. America as Americans See It 1932
Rus 1930

Saleski, G. Famous Musicians of a Wandering Race 1927
Sobel, B. ed. Theatre Handbook 1940

Thompson, O. ed. International Cyclopedia of Music and Musicians 1939

Variety Radio Directory 1940-41
Vodarsky-Shiraeff, A. comp. Russian Composers and Musicians 1940

Wer ist Wer 1937
Wer ist's? 1935
Who's Who 1940
Who's Who Among North American Authors 1936-39
Who's Who in America 1940-41
Who's Who in American Art 1940-41
Who's Who in American Education 1933-34

Who's Who in American Jewry 1938-39
Who's Who in Art 1934
Who's Who in Australia 1938
Who's Who in Broadcasting 1933
Who's Who in Canada 1936-37
Who's Who in Central and East-Europe 1935-36
Who's Who in China 1936
Who's Who in Colored America 1938-40
Who's Who in Commerce and Industry 1940-41
Who's Who in Engineering 1937
Who's Who in Finance, Banking and Insurance 1925-26
Who's Who in Government 1932
Who's Who in Japan 1937
Who's Who in Journalism 1928
Who's Who in Jurisprudence 1925
Who's Who in Latin America 1935
Who's Who in Law 1937
Who's Who in Library Service 1933
Who's Who in Major League Baseball 1933
Who's Who in Music Education 1925
Who's Who in New York 1938
Who's Who in New Zealand and the Western Pacific 1932
Who's Who in Railroading 1940
Who's Who in the East 1930
Who's Who in the Major Leagues 1937
Who's Who in the Nation's Capital 1938-39
Who's Who in the Regular Army 1925
Who's Who in the Theatre 1939

Wier, A. E. ed. Macmillan Encyclopedia of Music and Musicians 1938

PERIODICALS AND NEWSPAPERS CONSULTED

Adv & Selling—Advertising and Selling $2. Robbins Pub Co, Inc, 9 E 38th St, New York

A. L. A. Bul—American Library Association Bulletin 25c single copy. American Library Assn, 520 N Michigan Ave, Chicago

Am Artist—American Artist $3. Watson-Guptill Publications, Inc, 330 W 42nd St, New York Formerly Art Instruction

Am Assn Univ Women J—American Association of University Women Journal $1. American Assn of University Women, 1634 I St, N. W., Washington, D. C.

Am Hist R—American Historical Review $5; free to members of the American Historical Assn. Macmillan Co, 60 Fifth Ave, New York

Am Home—American Home $1. American Home Magazine Corp, 251 Fourth Ave, New York

Am Mag— merican Magazine $2.50. Crowell-Collier Pub Co, 386 Fourth Ave, New York

Am Mag Art See Mag Art

Am Mercury—American Mercury $3. American Mercury, Inc, 570 Lexington Ave, New York

Am Phot American Photography $2.50. American Photographic Pub Co, 353 Newbury St, Boston

Am Scand R—American Scandinavian Review $2; free to members. American Scandinavian Foundation, 116 E 64th St, New York

Am Scholar—American Scholar $2. United Chapters of the Phi Beta Kappa, 12 E 44th St, New York

Amerasia—Amerasia $2.50. Amerasia, Inc, 125 E 52nd St, New York

Amour Art—L'Amour de l'Art 170fr; foreign postage 40fr and 60fr. Editions Hypérion, 21 rue de Berri, Paris (8e)
    Name changed to Prométhée, L'Amour de l'Art January 1939

Ann Am Acad—Annals of the American Academy of Political and Social Science $5; free to members. 3457 Walnut St, Philadelphia

Apollo—Apollo 35s. Field Press, Ltd, Field House, Bream's Bldgs, Chancery Lane, London, EC 4 ($7.50, 18 E 48th St, New York)
    Temporary Address: 16 Whittington Court, London, N 2

Art Digest—Art Digest $3. Art Digest, Inc, 116 E 59th St, New York

Art N—Art News $7. Art News, Inc, 136 E 57th St, New York

Arts & Dec—Arts and Decoration $3. McBride, Andrews & Co, Inc, 116 E 16th St, New York

Asia—Asia $4. Editorial Publications, Inc, 40 E 49th St, New York

Asiatic R—Asiatic Review £1. East and West, Ltd, 3 Victoria St, London, SW 1

Assn Am Col Bul—Association of American Colleges Bulletin $3. Assn of American Colleges, 19 W 44th St, New York

Atlan—Atlantic Monthly $5. Atlantic Monthly Co, 8 Arlington St, Boston

Baltimore Sun—Baltimore Sun $15.60. A. S. Abell Co, Baltimore and Charles Sts, Baltimore

Beaux Arts—Beaux-Arts. Chronique des Arts et de la Curiosité 70fr; foreign postage 30fr and 50fr. La Gazette des Beaux Arts, 140 faubourg Saint Honoré, Paris (VIIIe)

Bet Homes & Gard—Better Homes & Gardens $1. Meredith Pub Co, 1714 Locust St, Des Moines, Iowa

Bookm—Bookman (discontinued)

Books (N Y Herald Tribune)—See N Y Herald Tribune Books

Books (N Y Times)—See N Y Times Book R

Boston Transcript—Boston Transcript $11. Boston Transcript Co, Inc, Pub, 324 Washington St, Boston

Bücherei—Bücherei; Zeitschrift der Reichsstelle für Volksbüchereiweisen Rm 12.50. Einkaufshaus für Büchereien G. m. b. H., Rossstrasse 11, Leipzig, C 1

Bul Museum Modern Art See New York City. Museum of Modern Art Bul

Bul Pan Am Union See Pan Am Union Bul

Business Week—Business Week $5. McGraw-Hill Pub Co, Inc, 330 W 42nd St, New York

Cahiers Art—Cahiers d'Art 170fr; foreign postage 50fr and 100fr. Editions Cahiers d'Art, 14 rue du Dragon, Paris (VIe)

Canad Forum—Canadian Forum $2. Canadian Forum, Ltd, 28 Wellington St, W, Toronto 5, Canada

Canad Hist R—Canadian Historical Review $2. University of Toronto Press, Toronto

Cath School J—Catholic School Journal $2. Bruce Pub Co, 524 N Milwaukee St, Milwaukee

Cath World—Catholic World $4. Catholic World, 401 W 59th St, New York

Chicago Daily News—Chicago Daily News $10.80. Col. Frank Knox, 400 W Madison St, Chicago

China W R—China Weekly Review $8. Millard Pub Co, 160 Ave Edward VII, Shanghai

Christian Cent—Christian Century $4. Christian Century Press, 440 S Dearborn St, Chicago

Christian Sci Mon—Christian Science Monitor (Atlantic ed) $9. Christian Science Pub Society, 1 Norway St, Boston

Christian Sci Mon Mag—Christian Science Monitor Weekly Magazine Section $2.60. Christian Science Pub Society, 1 Norway St, Boston

Churchman—The Churchman $4. Churchman Co, 425 Fourth Ave, New York

Cleveland Press—Cleveland Press $9.36. Scripps Pub Co, E 9th St and Rockwell Ave, Cleveland

Col Engl—College English $3. University of Chicago Press, 5750 Ellis Ave, Chicago Formerly English Journal (College Edition)

Collier's—Collier's $2. Crowell-Collier Pub Co, 386 Fourth Ave, New York

Commonweal—Commonweal $5. Commonweal Pub Co, Inc, 386 Fourth Ave, New York

Cong Digest—Congressional Digest $5. Congressional Digest, 2131 LeRoy Place, Washington, D. C.

Connoisseur—Connoisseur 30s. Connoisseur, Ltd, 28 & 30 Grosvenor Gardens, London SW 1 ($7.50, Connoisseur and International Studio, 572 Madison Ave, New York)

Contemp—Contemporary Review $9.50. Contemporary Review Co, Ltd, 19, 19a Cursitor St, London, EC 4

Coronet—Coronet $4. Esquire-Coronet, Inc, 919 N Michigan Ave, Chicago

Country Life—Country Life $5. Polo Magazine, Inc, 1270 Sixth Ave, New York

Cue—Cue (Manhattan ed) $3. Cue Publishing Co, Inc, 6 E 39th St, New York

Cur Hist—Current History See Cur Hist & Forum

Cur Hist & Forum—Current History and Forum $3. C-H Pub Corp, 420 Madison Ave, New York
    Forum combined with Current History July 1940

Dance—Dance $2.50. Tempo Magazines, Inc, 49 W 45th St, New York

Darien R—The Darien Review $2.25. The Review Corp, Darien, Conn.

Design—Design $3. Design Pub Co, Box 267, Columbus, Ohio

Die Bücherei See Bücherei

Dublin R—Dublin Review 15s. Burns Oates & Washbourne, Ltd, 43 Newgate St, London, EC 1

Eccl R—Ecclesiastical Review $4. American Ecclesiastical Review, 1722 Archer St, Philadelphia

Editor & Publisher—Editor and Publisher—The Fourth Estate $4. Editor and Publisher Co, Inc, 1475 Broadway, New York

Educa—Education $4. Palmer Co, 370 Atlantic Ave, Boston

El Engl R—Elementary English Review $2.50. Elementary English Review, Box 67, North End Station, Detroit

Engl J—English Journal $3. University of Chicago Press, 5750 Ellis Ave, Chicago
Formerly English Journal (High School edition)

Engl R—English Review See Nat R

Esquire—Esquire $5. Esquire, Inc, 919 N Michigan Ave, Chicago

Etude—Etude $2. Theodore Presser Co, 1712 Chestnut St, Philadelphia

Eur Nouv—L'Europe Nouvelle 150fr. 73bis quai d'Orsay, Paris (VIIe)

Far East R—Far Eastern Review $5. 24 The Bund, Shanghai

Foreign Affairs—Foreign Affairs $5. Council on Foreign Relations, Inc, 45 E 65th St, New York

Foreign Policy Rep—Foreign Policy Reports $5. (to libraries subscription includes Foreign Policy Bulletins and 6 headline books); $3 to F. P. A. members. Foreign Policy Assn, Inc, 8 W 40th St, New York

Fortnightly—Fortnightly $8.50. Fortnightly Review, Ltd, 13 Buckingham St, London, WC 2

Fortune—Fortune $10. Time, Inc, 330 E 22d St, Chicago

Forum—Forum See Cur Hist & Forum

Friday—Friday $4. Friday, Inc, 114 E 32nd St, New York

Good H—Good Housekeeping $2.50. Hearst Magazines, Inc, 57th St & Eighth Ave, New York

Harper—Harper's Magazine $4. Harper & Bros, 49 E 33rd St, New York

Harper's Bazaar—Harper's Bazaar $5. Hearst Magazines, Inc, 572 Madison Ave, New York

Home & F—Home and Field See House B

Horn Book—Horn Book $2.50. Horn Book, Inc, 264 Boylston St, Boston

House & Gard—House and Garden $3. Condé Nast Publications, Inc, Graybar Bldg, 420 Lexington Ave, New York

House B—House Beautiful $3. Hearst Magazines, Inc, 572 Madison Ave, New York Combined with Home and Field

Illustration—L'Illustration 490fr. 13 rue Saint-Georges, Paris (IXe) ($13. French and European Publications, Inc, 610 Fifth Ave, New York)

Ind Woman—Independent Woman $1.50. National Federation of Business and Professional Women's Clubs' Inc, 1819 Broadway, New York

Int Concil—International Conciliation 25c a year. Carnegie Endowment for International Peace, 405 W 117th St, New York

J Adult Ed—Journal of Adult Education 75c single copy. American Assn for Adult Education, 60 E 42nd St, New York

Kansas City Star—Kansas City Star $7.80. Kansas City Star Co, 1729 Grand Ave, Kansas City, Missouri

Ladies' H J—Ladies' Home Journal $1. Curtis Pub Co, Independence Sq, Philadelphia

Liberty—Liberty $2. Macfadden Publications, Inc, 122 E 42nd St, New York

Library J—Library Journal $5. R. R. Bowker Co, 62 W 45th St, New York

Life—Life $4.50. Time, Inc, 330 E 22nd St, Chicago

Lit Digest—Literary Digest (discontinued)

Liv Age—Living Age $6. Living Age Co, Inc, 420 Madison Ave, New York

London Mercury—London Mercury and Bookman 27s. Statesman and Nation Publishing Co, Ltd, 10 Great Turnstile, High Holborn, London, WC 1 (International News Co, 131 Varick St, New York)

London Studio (Studio)—London Studio, American edition of the Studio $6. Studio Publications, Inc, 381 Fourth Ave, New York (28s; foreign postage 2s; The Studio, Ltd, 44 Leicester Sq, London, WC 2)

Look—Look $2. Look, Inc, 715 Locust St, Des Moines, Iowa

Mag Art—Magazine of Art $5; free to members. American Federation of Arts, Barr Bldg, Farragut Sq, Washington, D. C.
Formerly American Magazine of Art

Manchester Guardian—Manchester Guardian 78s. Manchester Guardian, 3 Cross St, Manchester 2. Guardian Newspapers, Inc, 220 W 42nd St, New York

Mercure Fr—Mercure de France 140fr. 26 rue de Condé, Paris (VIe)

Mis R—Missionary Review of the World (discontinued)

Mo Labor R—Monthly Labor Review $3.50. Superintendent of Documents, Washington, D. C.

Musical Am—Musical America $3. Musical American Corp, 113 W 57th St, New York

Musical Courier—Musical Courier $3. Music Periodicals Corp, 119 W 57th St, New York

Musical Q—Musical Quarterly $3. G. Schirmer, Inc, 3 E 43rd St, New York

Musician—Musician $3. Eugene Belier, 113 W 57th St, New York

Nat Bd of R Mag—National Board of Review Magazine $1; free to members. National Board of Review of Motion Pictures, 70 Fifth Ave, New York

Nat Educ Assn J—National Education Association Journal $2; free to members. National Education Assn, 1201 16th St, N W, Washington, D. C.

Nation—The Nation $5. The Nation, Inc, 55 Fifth Ave, New York

Nation's Bus—Nation's Business $3. Chamber of Commerce of the United States, 1615 H St, N W, Washington, D. C.

Nat R—National Review 30s. 35 Wellington St, London, WC 2
Absorbed English Review August 1937

Nature—Nature Magazine $3. American Nature Assn, 1214 16th St, N W, Washington, D. C.

New Orleans Times-Picayune—New Orleans Times-Picayune $13.85, including Sunday Times-Picayune-States edition. Times-Picayune Pub Co, 615 North St, New Orleans

New Outlook—New Outlook (discontinued)

New Repub—New Republic $5. Editorial Publications, Inc, 40 E 49th St, New York

New Statesman & Nation—New Statesman & Nation—Week-end Review 30s. 10 Great Turnstile, London, WC 1

New York City. Museum of Modern Art Bul—Bulletin of the Museum of Modern Art. Membership. Museum of Modern Art, 11 W 53rd St, New York

New Yorker—New Yorker $5. F-R. Pub Corp, 25 W 43rd St, New York

Newsdom—Newsdom $2. Newsdom, Inc, Pub, 63 Park Row, New York

Newsweek—Newsweek $4. Weekly Publications, Inc, Rockefeller Center, 1270 Sixth Ave, New York

19th Cent—Nineteenth Century and After $8.75. Constable & Co, Ltd, 10 & 12 Orange St, London, WC 2

No Am R—North American Review $4. North American Review Corp, 123 William St, New York

Nuova Antol—Nuova Antologia 180 l. Via del Collegio Romano 10, Rome

N Y Herald Tribune—New York Herald Tribune $17, including Sunday edition. New York Tribune, Inc, 230 W 41st St, New York

N Y Herald Tribune Books—New York Herald Tribune Books $1. New York Tribune, Inc, 230 W 41st St, New York

N Y Post—New York Post $10. New York Post, Inc, 75 West St, New York

N Y Sun—New York Sun $12. New York Sun, Inc, 280 Broadway, New York

N Y Times—New York Times $17, including Sunday edition. The New York Times Co, Pub, 229 W 43rd St, New York

N Y Times Book R—New York Times Book Review $2. The New York Times Co, Pub, 229 W 43rd St, New York

N Y World-Telegram—New York World-Telegram $12. New York World-Telegram Corp, 125 Barclay St, New York

Opera News—Opera News $2; free to members. Metropolitan Opera Guild, Inc, 654 Madison Ave, New York

Outlook—Outlook (discontinued)

Pan Am Union Bul—Bulletin of the Pan American Union $1.50. Pan American Union, 17th St and Constitution Ave, N W, Washington, D. C.

Parnassus—Parnassus $2.50; free to members. College Art Association, 137 E 57th St, New York

Photoplay—Photoplay $1. Macfadden Publications, Inc, 122 E 42nd St, New York
  Combined with Movie Mirror

Pictures on Exhibit—Pictures on Exhibit $1. Pictures Pub Co, 724 Fifth Ave, New York

PM—PM $14, including Sunday edition. The Newspaper PM, Inc, 27 Sixth Ave, Brooklyn, New York

Poetry—Poetry $3. 232 E Erie St, Chicago

Pol Sci Q—Political Science Quarterly $5; free to members. Academy of Political Science, Columbia University, New York

Pop Mech—Popular Mechanics Magazine $2.50. Popular Mechanics Co, 200 E Ontario St, Chicago

Progressive Educ—Progressive Education $3. Progressive Education Assn, 221 W 57th St, New York

Pub W—Publishers' Weekly $5. R. R. Bowker Co, 62 W 45th St, New York

Queen's Q—Queen's Quarterly $2. Queen's University, Kingston, Canada

R Deux Mondes—Revue des Deux Mondes 230fr. 15 rue de l'Université, Paris (VIIe)

Read Digest—Reader's Digest $3. Reader's Digest Assn, Inc, Pleasantville, New York

Recreation—Recreation $2. National Recreation Assn, 315 Fourth Ave, New York

Ref Shelf—Reference Shelf $6 per volume of ten bound numbers, published irregularly. The H. W. Wilson Co, 950-972 University Ave, New York

R of Rs—Review of Reviews (discontinued)

Rotarian—Rotarian $1.50. Rotary International, 35 E Wacker Drive, Chicago

Royal Inst Brit Arch J—Royal Institute of British Architects Journal £1 16s postpaid. The Institute, 66 Portland Pl, London, W 1

San Francisco Chronicle—San Francisco Chronicle $15.60. Chronicle Publishing Co, 901 Mission St, San Francisco

Sat Eve Post—Saturday Evening Post $2. The Curtis Pub Co, Independence Sq, Philadelphia

Sat R Lit—Saturday Review of Literature $4. Saturday Review Co, Inc, 420 Madison Ave, New York

Sch & Soc—School and Society $5; free to members of the Society for the Advancement of Education. Science Press, Grand Central Terminal, New York

Sch Arts—School Arts $3. School Arts, Printers Bldg, Worcester, Mass.

Scholastic—Scholastic (High School Teacher edition) $2. (combined, or teacher ed. only); school group rate (two or more subscriptions to one address) $1 for special eds. $1.30 for combined ed. Scholastic Corp, 430 Kinnard Ave, Dayton, Ohio

Sci Am—Scientific American $4. Munn & Co, Inc, 24 W 40th St, New York

Sci Bk Club R—Scientific Book Club Review. Subscription. Scientific Book Club, Inc, 80 Lafayette St, New York

Sci Mo—Scientific Monthly $5. Science Press, Grand Central Terminal, New York

Sci N L—Science News Letter $5. Science Service, Inc, 2101 Constitution Ave, Washington, D. C.

Sci ns—Science $6. Science Press, Grand Central Terminal, New York

Scrib Com—Scribner's Commentator $3. P. & S. Publishing, Inc, 654 Madison Ave, New York
  Scribner's Magazine combined with Commentator November 1939

Scrib Mag—Scribner's Magazine See Scrib Commentator

So Atlan Q—South Atlantic Quarterly $3. Duke University Press, Durham, N. C.

Spec—Spectator 30s. 99 Gower St, London, WC 1

Stage—Stage $2.50. Ince Pub Co, Inc, 7 E 44th St, New York

Studio (Am edition) See London Studio

Survey—Survey $3. Survey Associates, Inc, 112 E 19th St, New York

Survey G—Survey Graphic $3. Survey Associates, Inc, 112 E 19th St, New York

Theatre Arts—Theatre Arts $3.50. Theatre Arts, Inc, 40 E 49th St, New York
  Formerly Theatre Arts Monthly

Time—Time $5. Time, Inc, 330 E 22nd St, Chicago

Times [London] Lit Sup—Times Literary Supplement 17s 4d; $4.15. The Times (London), North American Office, 280 Broadway, New York

Travel—Travel $4. Robert M. McBride & Co, Inc, 116 E 16th St, New York

U S Bur Labor—Monthly Labor R See Mo Labor R

U S Bur Labor Bul—United States Bureau of Labor Statistics. Bulletins. Free to libraries. Bureau of Labor Statistics, Washington, D. C. Purchase orders, Superintendent of Documents, Washington, D. C.

U S News—United States News $2. United States News Bldg, 22nd and M Sts, N W, Washington, D. C.

U S Office Educ Bul—United States Office of Education. Bulletins. Free to libraries. Office of Education, Washington, D. C. Purchase orders, Superintendent of Documents, Washington, D. C.

Va Q R—Virginia Quarterly Review $3. University of Virginia, Charlottesville, Virginia

Variety—Variety $10. Variety, Inc, 154 W 46th St, New York

Vital Speeches—Vital Speeches of the Day $3. City News Pub Co, 33 W 42nd St, New York

Wilson Lib Bul—Wilson Library Bulletin $1. The H. W. Wilson Co, 950-972 University Ave, New York
  Formerly Wilson Bulletin

Woman's H C—Woman's Home Companion $1. Crowell-Collier Pub Co, 386 Fourth Ave, New York

Writer—The Writer $3. The Writer, Inc, 8 Arlington St, Boston

Yale R ns—Yale Review $3. Yale University Press, 143 Elm St, New Haven

NECROLOGY

Abbott, Robert Sengstacke
Adams, Thomas
Addington, Sarah
Adler, Cyrus
Adler, Harry Clay
Allen, Joel Nott
Allyn, Lewis B.
Alsberg, Carl Lucas
Altenburg, Alexander
Alter, George Elias
Anderson, Abraham Archibald
Anderson, George Everett
Anderson, John Crawford
Anderson, Mary See Navarro, M. de
Arco, Georg Wilhelm Alexander Hans, Graf von
Aronson, Louis V.
Ashmun, Margaret Eliza
Atalena, pseud. See Jabotinsky, V. E.
Azaña, Manuel

Bachrach, Elise Wald
Bailey, Sir Abe, 1st Bart
Bailey, Guy Winfred
Baker, Asa George
Balbo, Italo
Bankhead, William Brockman
Barney, Samuel E.
Barrère, Camille Eugène Pierre
Barrett, Wilton Agnew
Barry, Patrick Frank, Bishop
Bartol, William Cyrus
Barton, George
Bates, Ernest Sutherland
Bates, Granville
Baur, Bertha
Bedford, Herbrand Arthur Russell, 11th Duke of
Beer, Thomas
Begg, Alexander Swanson
Benjamin, William Evarts
Bennett, James O'Donnell
Benson, Allan Louis
Benson, Edward Frederic
Bentley, Irene
Besteiro Y Fernandez, Julian
Binet-Valmer, Jean
Binkley, Robert Cedric
Black, Alexander
Blaker, Richard
Blatchley, Willis Stanley
Blau, Bela
Bloch, Charles Edward
Block, Rudolph See Lessing, B., pseud.
Blumer, George Alder
Bodanzky, Artur
Boggs, Charles Reid
Bonci, Alessandro
Booth, Ballington
Borah, William Edgar

Bosch, Carl
Bourne, Jonathan Jr.
Bower, Bertha Muzzy, pseud. of Bertha Muzzy Sinclair-Cowan
Bradbury, James H.
Brandenburg, William A.
Branly, Edouard
Breckenridge, Lester Paige
Bronshtein, Lev Davidovich See Trotsky, L.
Broun, Heywood
Brown, A. Ten Eyck
Brown, Francis Shunk
Brown, John Franklin
Bryce, Elizabeth Marion, Viscountess
Buchan, John, 1st Baron Tweedsmuir
Buchanan, Thomas Drysdale
Bulgakov, Michael Afanasievich
Bunau-Varilla, Philippe
Burdick, Charles Kellogg
Burleigh, George William
Burns, James Aloysius, Father
Burton, Charles Emerson, Rev.
Burton, Lewis William, Bishop
Burton, Richard
Butler, Smedley Darlington

Cahill, Michael Harrison
Callow, John Michael
Camac, Charles Nicoll Bancker
Campbell, Mrs. Patrick
Canavan, Joseph J.
Canby, Al H.
Canton, Allen A.
Cantu, Giuseppe
Carewe, Edwin
Carpenter, Sir Henry Cort Harold
Carpenter, Lewis Van
Carson, John Renshaw
Casey, Edward Pearce
Caturáni, Michele Gaëtano
Cavero, Salvador
Chaddock, Robert Emmet
Chadwick, Helene
Chamberlain, Neville
Chamberlain, Paul Mellen
Chang Shan-tze
Chappedelaine, Louis de
Chase, Charley
Chase, William Sheafe, Rev.
Chesser, Elizabeth Sloan
Chrysler, Walter Percy
Churchill, Berton
Clark, Marguerite
Clive, Edward E.
Cole, Jessie Duncan Savage
Coleman, Georgia
Collins, Eddie

Collins, Edward Day
Collins, George Lewis
Collins, Lorin Cone
Colquitt, Oscar Branch
Companys, Luis
Conley, William Gustavus
Connolly, Walter
Converse, Frederick Shepherd
Cook, Frederick Albert
Coolidge, Dane
Cooper, Courtney Ryley
Cordier, Constant
Cortelyou, George Bruce
Cotton, Joseph Bell
Coulter, Calvin Brewster
Cramer, Stuart Warren
Cravath, Paul Drennan
Crawford, Morris Barker
Crawshaw, William Henry
Crompton, Rookes Evelyn Bell
Crowley, John J., Father
Cullen, Glenn Ernest

Damon, Lindsay Todd
Daniels, Arthur Hill
Davidovitch, Ljuba
Davies, William Henry
Dawes, Rufus Cutler
Deasy, Luere B.
De Chappedelaine, Louis See Chappedelaine, L. de
De Guise, Jean Pierre Clément Marie, Duc See Guise, J. P. C. M., Duc de
Dell, Robert Edward
De Navarro, Mary See Navarro, M. de
Dermot, Jessie See Elliott, M.
Des Graz, Sir Charles Louis
Dieterich, William H.
Dillard, James Hardy
Dodd, William Edward
Doherty, Henry Latham
Dolmetsch, Arnold
Dornay, Louis
Dörpfeld, Wilhelm
Dover, Elmer
Drossaerts, Arthur Jerome, Archbishop
Drouet, Bessie Clarke
Du Fournet, Louis René Marie Charles Dartige
Dugan, Raymond Smith
Dusser de Barenne, Joannes Gregorius

Edey, Birdsall Otis
Eisen, Gustav
Ellerman, Ferdinand
Elliot, Kathleen Morrow
Elliott, Maxine
Elliott, William Thompson, Rev.
Elson, Arthur

Morton, Henry Holdich
Morton, James Madison Jr.
Moscovitch, Maurice
Moton, Robert Russa
Motta, Giuseppe
Muck, Karl
Mumford, Ethel Watts
Mundy, Talbot Chetwynd
Murphy, Frederick E.
Murray, Augustus Taber
Myers, Jerome
Mysore, Maharaja of   See
    Wadiyar, S. K.

Navarro, Mary de
Neal, Herbert Vincent
Neumann, Heinrich
Newton, Alfred Edward
Nipkow, Paul Gottlieb
Nixon, Lewis
Nordmann, Charles
Norris, Henry Hutchinson
Norris, James Flack
Northrup, Edwin Fitch

Oberteuffer, George
O'Gorman, Patrick F., Father
O'Neil, George
Osborne, Oliver Thomas
Owens, Robert Bowie

Paddon, Harry Locke
Page, Marie Danforth
Palmer, Albert deForest
Pasternack, Josef Alexander
Patrick, Mary Mills
Perla, David
Peynado, Jacinto B.
Phillips, Albert
Pick, Behrendt
Pierce, Palmer Eddy
Pirie, John Taylor
Pittman, Key
Pollain, René
Poore, Henry Rankin
Post, William Stone
Potter, Alfred Claghorn
Powys, Llewelyn
Prall, David Wight
Prellwitz, Henry
Prentiss, Henrietta
Pritchard, Stuart
Pusey, William Allen
Putnam, James William

Quinn, Daniel Joseph, Father

Ragon, Heartsill
Rautenberg, Robert
Reavis, Smith Freeman
Reed, Edward Bliss
Reed, Herbert Calhoun
Reed, John Howard
Reisner, Christian Fichthorne,
    Rev.
Revueltas, Silvestro
Reynolds, James A.
Richard, Louis
Richardson, Norval
Richmond, Charles Alexander,
    Rev.
Ricketts, Louis Davidson
Riesman, David

Riggs, Austen Fox
Ripley, Joseph
Robb, Hunter
Roberts, Florence
Rodriguez, Nicolas
Rogers, Norman McLeod
Rosett, Joshua
Ross, Sir Edward Denison
Rumpler, Edmund
Rushmore, David Barker
Russell, Herbrand Arthur, 11th
    Duke of Bedford   See Bed-
    ford, H. A. R., 11th Duke of

Sabry, Hassan, Pasha
Sandefer, Jefferson Davis
Saunders, John Monk
Savage, Michael Joseph
Schelling, Ernest Henry
Schereschewsky, Joseph Wil-
    liams
Schoonmaker, Edwin Davies
Schratt, Katharina
Scott, Arthur Carroll
Scudder, Janet
Seger, George N.
Senarens, Luis Philip
Sevier, Henry Hulme
Shambaugh, Benjamin Franklin
Sharp, Harry Clay
Shaw, Louis Agassiz
Sherman, Frederic Fairchild
Shinn, Florence Scovel
Shinn, Milicent Washburn
Shoup, Oliver Henry
Silzer, George Sebastian
Simmons, Furnifold McLendell
Simpson, Helen de Guerry
Sinclair-Cowan, Bertha Muzzy
    See Bower, B. M., pseud.
Singer, Richard
Smith, Clyde Harold
Smith, Wilbur Fisk
Soukup, Frantisek
Spiller, William Gibson
Spottswood, James
Sprague, Embert Hiram
Squires, Richard Anderson
Stanley, Freelan O.
Stekel, Wilhelm [Willy Bojan,
    Dr. Serenus, pseuds.]
Stephens, Ward
Steuer, Max David
Stewart, George Craig, Bishop
Stoddard, Frederick Lincoln
Stone, John Charles
Storr, Vernon Faithfull, Rev.
Switzer, George

Tainter, Charles Sumner
Tanner, John Henry
Taussig, Frank William
Tetrazzini, Luisa
Thayer, Ernest Lawrence
Thompson, Holland
Thompson, John Taliaferro
Thomson, Sir Joseph John
Tokugawa, Iyesato, Prince
Totty, Charles H.
Tovey, Sir Donald Francis
Trotsky, Leon

Trotter, Frank Butler
True, Rodney Howard
Tsai Yuan-pei
Turpin, Ben
Tweed, Thomas Frederic
Tweedie, Mrs. Alec
Tweedsmuir, John Buchan, 1st
    Baron   See Buchan, J.

Untermyer, Samuel

Vance, William Reynolds
Vann, Robert Lee
Vassallo, Ernesto
Verdier, Jean, Cardinal
Volterra, Vito
Von Arco, Georg Wilhelm
    Alexander Hans, Graf   See
    Arco, G. W. A. H., Graf von
Von Heidenstam, Karl Gustaf
    Verner   See Heidenstam, V.
    von
Von Wagner-Jauregg, Julius
    See Wagner-Jauregg J. von

Wadiyar, Sri Krishnaraja, Ba-
    hadur Maharaja of Mysore
Wagner-Jauregg, Julius von
Wald, Lillian D.
Wales, George Canning
Wall, Evander Berry
Wambaugh, Eugene
Waste, William Harrison
Watrous, George Dutton
Watrous, Harry Willson
Watson, Clarence Wayland
Waugh, Frederick Judd
Weber, Louis Lawrence
Weisse, Faneuil Suydam
Wenckebach, Karel Friedrich
Werne, Isaac, Rabbi
Wheelwright, John B.
White, Frank
Whiteman, Wilberforce James
Wickware, Francis Graham
Wiedoeft, Rudy
Wilgus, Sidney Dean
Williams, Joseph John, Father
Williams, Ralph E.
Williams, Thomas Sutler
Winter, George B.
Winthrop, Beekman
Wolfe, Humbert
Wood, Philip
Woodbridge, Frederick James
    Eugene
Woodbury, Charles Herbert
Woodcock, Charles Edward,
    Bishop
Worden, Edward Chauncey
Wray, John Griffith

Yancey, Lewis Q. Alonzo
Yellin, Samuel
Yoder, Albert Henry
Young, Charles Jac

Zhabotinskii, Vladimir Evgen'-
    evich [Atalena, pseud.] See
    Jabotinsky, V. E.
Zimmerman, Alfred F. M.
Zinsser, Hans

WHO'S NEWS AND WHY—1940

This is a cumulation of all names which have appeared in the monthly issues of CURRENT BIOGRAPHY during 1940.

All names marked [Dec] have not appeared in any previous issues.

All names marked [obit] are obituary notices.

Abbott, George
Abbott, Robert Sengstacke [obit]
Adamic, Louis [Dec]
Adams, Thomas [obit]
Addington, Sarah [obit] [Dec]
Addis Ababa, Pietro Badoglio, Duca d'
Additon, Henrietta Silvis
Adler, Cyrus [obit]
Adler, Harry Clay [obit]
Adler, Mortimer Jerome
Aitken, William Maxwell, 1st Baron Beaverbrook See Beaverbrook, W. M. A., 1st Baron
Aldrich, Winthrop Williams
Alexander, Albert Victor [Dec]
Allen, Gracie
Allen, Joel Nott [obit]
Allyn, Lewis B. [obit]
Almazán, Juan Andreu
Alsberg, Carl Lucas [obit] [Dec]
Altenburg, Alexander [obit]
Alter, George Elias [obit]
Amsterdam, Birdie
Anderson, Abraham Archibald [obit]
Anderson, George Everett [obit]
Anderson, John Crawford [obit]
Anderson, Marian
Anderson, Mary
Anderson, Mary See Navarro, M. de [obit]
Angell, James Rowland [Dec]
Antonescu, Ion
Arco, Georg Wilhelm Alexander Hans, Graf von [obit]
Armstrong, Edwin Howard
Arnold, Thurman Wesley
Aronson, Louis V. [obit] [Dec]
Ashmun, Margaret Eliza [obit]
Astor, Nancy Witcher, Viscountess
Atalena, pseud. See Jabotinsky, V. E. [obit]
Atherton, Gertrude
Attlee, Clement Richard
Aulaire, Ingri d' and Aulaire, Edgar Parin d'

Austin, William Lane
Avenol, Joseph Louis Anne
Ayres, Leonard Porter
Azaña, Manuel [obit] [Dec]

Bachrach, Elise Wald [obit]
Bacon, Peggy
Badoglio, Pietro See Addis Ababa, P. B., Duca d'
Bailey, Sir Abe, 1st Bart [obit]
Bailey, Guy Winfred [obit] [Dec]
Baker, Asa George [obit]
Baker, Ray Stannard [David Grayson, pseud.]
Balbo, Italo [obit]
Baldwin, Roger Nash
Bampton, Rose
Bankhead, William Brockman [obit]
Banning, Margaret Culkin
Barbirolli, John [Dec]
Barclay, McClelland
Barlow, Howard
Barney, Samuel E. [obit]
Barnouw, Erik
Barr, Frank Stringfellow
Barrère, Camille Eugène Pierre [obit] [Dec]
Barrett, Wilton Agnew [obit]
Barringer, Emily Dunning
Barrow, Joseph Louis See Louis, J.
Barry, Patrick Frank, Bishop [obit]
Barthé, Richmond
Bartók, Béla
Bartol, William Cyrus [obit] [Dec]
Barton, George [obit]
Bates, Ernest Sutherland [obit]
Bates, Granville [obit]
Batista Y Zaldivar, Fulgencio
Baur, Bertha [obit]
Beaverbrook, William Maxwell Aitken, 1st Baron
Bedford, Herbrand Arthur Russell, 11th Duke of [obit]
Beebe, Lucius
Beer, Thomas [obit]
Begg, Alexander Swanson [obit]
Bel Geddes, Norman See Geddes, N. B.
Benchley, Belle Jennings

Benjamin, William Evarts [obit]
Bennett, James O'Donnell [obit]
Benson, Allan Louis [obit]
Benson, Edward Frederic [obit]
Benson, John
Bentley, Irene [obit]
Benton, Thomas Hart
Berg, Patricia Jane
Bergman, Ingrid
Berle, Adolf Augustus Jr.
Berry, Martha McChesney
Besteiro Y Fernandez, Julian [obit]
Bethe, Hans Albrecht
Bevin, Ernest
Bevis, Howard Landis
Binet-Valmer, Jean [obit]
Binkley, Robert Cedric [obit]
Birge, Raymond Thayer
Black, Alexander [obit]
Blake, Nicholas, pseud. See Day-Lewis, C.
Blaker, Richard [obit]
Blanch, Arnold
Blatchley, Willis Stanley [obit]
Blau, Bela [obit] [Dec]
Blitzstein, Marc
Bloch, Charles Edward [obit]
Block, Rudolph See Lessing, B., pseud. [obit]
Blodgett, Katharine Burr
Blum, Léon
Blumer, George Alder [obit]
Boas, Franz
Bodanzky, Artur [obit]
Boggs, Charles Reid [obit]
Bolton, Frances Payne
Bonci, Alessandro [obit]
Booker, Edna Lee
Booth, Ballington [obit]
Borah, William Edgar [obit]
Bosch, Carl [obit]
Bourke-White, Margaret See White, M. B.
Bourne, Jonathan Jr. [obit]
Bower, Bertha Muzzy, pseud. of Bertha Muzzy Sinclair-Cowan [obit]
Bradbury, James H. [obit] [Dec]
Brandenburg, William A. [obit] [Dec]
Branly, Edouard [obit]

Brauchitsch, Heinrich Alfred
  Hermann Walther von
Breckenridge, Lester Paige
  [obit]
Bridges, Alfred Bryant Renton
  See Bridges, H.
Bridges, Harry
Bristow, Gwen [Dec]
Bronshtein, Lev Davidovich
  See Trotsky, L. [obit]
Brookes, George S., Rev.
Broun, Heywood [obit]
Brown, A. Ten Eyck [obit]
Brown, Francis Shunk [obit]
Brown, John Franklin [obit]
Brownson, Josephine
Bryan, Julien Hequembourg
Bryce, Elizabeth Marion, Vis-
  countess [obit]
Bryson, Lyman
Buchan, John, 1st Baron
  Tweedsmuir [obit]
Buchanan, Thomas Drysdale
  [obit]
Buchman, Frank Nathan
  Daniel, Rev.
Budd, Ralph
Bulgakov, Michael Afanasie-
  vich [obit]
Bullitt, William Christian
Bunau-Varilla, Philippe [obit]
Burdick, Charles Kellogg
  [obit]
Burke, Edward Raymond
Burleigh, George William
  [obit]
Burliuk, David
Burns, George See Allen, G.
Burns, James Aloysius, Father
  [obit]
Burton, Charles Emerson, Rev.
  [obit]
Burton, Lewis William, Bishop
  [obit] [Dec]
Burton, Richard [obit]
Bush, Vannevar
Butler, Nicholas Murray
Butler, Smedley Darlington
  [obit]

Cahill, Michael Harrison
  [obit]
Cairns, Huntington
Caldwell, Erskine
Caldwell, Mrs. Erskine   See
  White, M. B.
Caldwell, Taylor
Callow, John Michael [obit]
Camac, Charles Nicoll Bancker
  [obit]
Camacho, Manuel Avila
Campbell, Mrs. Patrick [obit]
Canavan, Joseph J. [obit]
  [Dec]
Canby, Al H. [obit] [Dec]
Canton, Allen A. [obit]
Cantu, Giuseppe [obit]
  [Dec]
Carewe, Edwin [obit]
Carmody, John Michael
Carol II

Carpenter, Sir Henry Cort
  Harold [obit]
Carpenter, Lewis Van [obit]
Carrel, Alexis
Carson, John Renshaw [obit]
  [Dec]
Carton de Wiart, Adrian
Carver, George Washington
Casey, Edward Pearce [obit]
Casey, Richard Gardiner
Catt, Carrie Chapman
Caturáni, Michele Gaëtano
  [obit]
Cavero, Salvador [obit]
Chaddock, Robert Emmet
  [obit] [Dec]
Chadwick, Helene [obit]
Chamberlain, John Rensselaer
Chamberlain, Neville [obit]
  [Dec]
Chamberlain, Paul Mellen
  [obit]
Chang Shan-tze [obit] [Dec]
Chapin, James
Chaplin, Charlie [Dec]
Chappedelaine, Louis de
  [obit]
Chase, Charley [obit]
Chase, Edna Woolman
Chase, Mary Ellen
Chase, Stuart
Chase, William Sheafe, Rev.
  [obit]
Cherne, Leo M. [Dec]
Chesser, Elizabeth Sloan
  [obit]
Chiang Kai-shek
Chiang Kai-shek, Mme.   See
  Chiang M.
Chiang Mei-ling [Mme.
  Chiang Kai-shek]
Chotzinoff, Samuel
Christie, Agatha
Chrysler, Walter Percy [obit]
Churchill, Berton [obit]
  [Dec]
Churchill, Winston Leonard
  Spencer
Ciano, Galeazzo, Conte
Clapper, Raymond
Clark, Marguerite [obit]
Clive, Edward E. [obit]
Cochran, Charles Blake
Cochran, Jacqueline
Cole, Jessie Duncan Savage
  [obit] [Dec]
Coleman, Georgia [obit]
Collins, Eddie [obit]
Collins, Edward Day [obit]
Collins, George Lewis [obit]
Collins, Lorin Cone [obit]
  [Dec]
Colquitt, Oscar Branch [obit]
Companys, Luis [obit] [Dec]
Compton, Arthur Holly
Conley, William Gustavus
  [obit] [Dec]
Connolly, Walter [obit]
Converse, Frederick Shepherd
  [obit]

Cook, Frederick Albert [obit]
Coolidge, Dane [obit]
Cooper, Alfred Duff
Cooper, Courtney Ryley
  [obit]
Copland, Aaron
Corcoran, Thomas Gardiner
Cordier, Constant [obit]
Corey, Paul [Dec]
Cortelyou, George Bruce
  [obit] [Dec]
Corwin, Norman [Dec]
Cotton, Joseph Bell [obit]
Coughlin, Charles Edward,
  Father
Coulter, Calvin Brewster
  [obit]
Covarrubias, Miguel
Cramer, Stuart Warren [obit]
Cravath, Paul Drennan [obit]
Crawford, Morris Barker
  [obit] [Dec]
Crawford, Phyllis
Crawshaw, William Henry
  [obit]
Cripps, Sir Stafford
Crompton, Rookes Evelyn Bell
  [obit]
Cromwell, James H. R.
Cross, Milton John
Crowley, John J., Father
  [obit]
Culbertson, Ely
Cullen, Glenn Ernest [obit]
Culver, Essae Martha
Curie, Eve
Curie, Irène   See Joliot-Curie,
  I.

Daladier, Edouard
Dali, Salvador
Damon, Lindsay Todd [obit]
Daniels, Arthur Hill [obit]
Dannay, Frederic   See Queen,
  E., pseud.
Daugherty, James Henry
D'Aulaire, Ingri and D'Aulaire,
  Edgar Parin   See Aulaire,
  I. d' and Aulaire, E. P. d'
Davidovitch, Ljuba [obit]
Davies, William Henry [obit]
Davis, Chester Charles
Davis, Elmer
Davis, Herbert John
Davis, Norman H.
Davis, Stuart
Davis, William Ellsworth
Dawes, Rufus Cutler [obit]
Day-Lewis, Cecil [Nicholas
  Blake, pseud.]
Deasy, Luere B. [obit]
De Chappedelaine, Louis See
  Chappedelaine, L. de [obit]
Defauw, Désiré
De Gaulle, Charles
De Guise, Jean Pierre Clé-
  ment Marie, Duc See Guise,
  J. P. C. M., Duc de [obit]
Dell, Robert Edward [obit]
De Navarro, Mary See Na-
  varro, M. de [obit]

Denny, George Vernon Jr.
Dermot, Jessie See Elliott, M. [obit]
Des Graz, Sir Charles Louis [obit] [Dec]
De Valera, Eamon
Dewey, Thomas Edmund
De Wiart, Adrian Carton See Carton de Wiart, A.
Dies, Martin
Dieterich, William H. [obit] [Dec]
Dietz, David
Dillard, James Hardy [obit]
Disney, Walt
Ditmars, Raymond Lee
Dix, Dorothy, pseud. of Elizabeth Meriwether Gilmer
Dodd, William Edward [obit]
Doherty, Henry Latham [obit]
Dolmetsch, Arnold [obit]
Doriot, Jacques
Dornay, Louis [obit]
Dörpfeld, Wilhelm [obit]
Dos Passos, John
Dover, Elmer [obit]
Dowding, Sir Hugh Caswell Tremenheere
Drossaerts, Arthur Jerome, Archbishop [obit]
Drouet, Bessie Clarke [obit]
Du Bois, William Edward Burghardt
Duff Cooper, Alfred See Cooper, A. D.
Duffy, Edmund
Du Fournet, Louis René Marie Charles Dartige [obit]
Dugan, Raymond Smith [obit]
Du Maurier, Daphne
Du Pont, Pierre Samuel
Durocher, Leo
Dusser de Barenne, Joannes Gregorius [obit]

Eden, Anthony [Dec]
Edey, Birdsall Otis [obit]
Edison, Charles
Egloff, Gustav
Eilshemius, Louis Michel
Eisen, Gustav [obit] [Dec]
Eliot, George Fielding
Ellerman, Ferdinand [obit]
Elliot, Kathleen Morrow [obit]
Elliott, Harriet Wiseman
Elliott, Maxine [obit]
Elliott, William Thompson, Rev. [obit]
Elson, Arthur [obit]
Enters, Angna
Erlanger, Mitchell Louis [obit]
Ernst, Morris Leopold
Estigarribia, José Félix [obit]
Evans, Maurice
Eves, Reginald Grenville
Eyde, Samuel [obit]

Fairbanks, Douglas [obit]
Faversham, William [obit]
Fedorova, Nina

Fenimore-Cooper, Susan de Lancey [obit]
Ferris, Harry Burr [obit] [Dec]
Few, William Preston [obit] [Dec]
Finch, Flora [obit]
Finkelstein, Louis, Rabbi
Finley, John Huston [obit]
Finn, William Joseph, Father
Fischer, Israel Frederick [obit]
Fischer, Louis
Fishbein, Morris
Fisher, John Stuchell [obit]
Fisher, Sterling [Dec]
Fitzmaurice, George [obit]
Flagg, James Montgomery
Fleming, Arthur Henry [obit]
Fleming, John Adam
Fleming, Philip Bracken
Fly, James Lawrence
Flynn, Edward J.
Folks, Homer [Dec]
Forbes, Guillaume, Archbishop [obit]
Fosdick, Harry Emerson, Rev.
Fournet, Louis René Marie Charles Dartige du See Du Fournet, L. R. M. C. D. [obit]
Fowler, Alfred [obit]
Fowler-Billings, Katharine
Fox, John McDill [obit]
Frank, Glenn [obit]
Frank, Waldo David
Fratellini, Paul [obit] [Dec]
Frazer, Spaulding [obit]
Frazier, Edward Franklin
Freedlander, Arthur R. [obit]
Freyberg, Bernard Cyril
Fuller, Clara Cornelia [obit] [Dec]
Fuller, George Washington [obit] [Dec]
Funk, Walther
Fyfe, H. Hamilton [Dec]

Galli, Rosina [obit]
Gallup, George Horace
Gamelin, Marie Gustave See Gamelin, M. G.
Gamelin, Maurice Gustave
Ganfield, William Arthur [obit] [Dec]
Garland, Hamlin [obit]
Garvey, Marcus [obit]
Gates, William [obit]
Gatti-Casazza, Giulio [obit]
Gaulle, Charles de See De Gaulle, C.
Gauthier, Joseph Alexandre George, Archbishop [obit]
Gayda, Virginio
Geddes, Norman Bel
Gehrig, Lou
George, Albert Bailey [obit]
Géraud, André [Pertinax, pseud.]
Gesell, Arnold
Gibbs, George [obit]

Gibson, Ernest Willard [obit]
Gideonse, Harry David
Gilbreth, Lillian Evelyn
Gilder, Robert Fletcher [obit]
Gildersleeve, Virginia Crocheron
Gilmer, Elizabeth Meriwether See Dix, D., pseud.
Gilmore, Melvin Randolph [obit]
Gilmour, Sir John [obit]
Glenn, Mary Wilcox [obit] [Dec]
Goldenweiser, Alexander A. [obit]
Goldman, Emma [obit]
Goldmark, Peter Carl
Goldsmith, Lester Morris
Goler, George Washington [obit]
Gomá Y Tomás, Isidoro, Cardinal [obit]
Goodrich, James Putnam [obit]
Gordon, John Sloan [obit] [Dec]
Gorman, Herbert Sherman
Gort, John Standish Surtees Prendergast Vereker, 6th Viscount
Goudge, Elizabeth
Grafton, Samuel
Grant, Ethel Watts Mumford See Mumford, E. W. [obit]
Grant, Robert [obit]
Graves, Frederick Rogers, Bishop [obit]
Graves, William Sidney [obit]
Grayson, David, pseud. See Baker, R. S.
Green, Julian
Greene, Frank Russell [obit]
Greenwood, Arthur
Grenfell, Sir Wilfred Thomason [obit] [Dec]
Griswold, Augustus H. [obit]
Grofé, Ferde
Gropper, William
Gruenberg, Sidonie Matsner
Gruppe, Charles Paul [obit]
Guillaumat, Marie Louis Adolphe [obit]
Guise, Jean Pierre Clément Marie, Duc de [obit]
Gunter, Julius Caldeen [obit] [Dec]
Guthrie, Charles Ellsworth, Rev. [obit]
Guthrie, William Buck [obit] [Dec]

Haakon VII, King of Norway
Haddon, Alfred Cort [obit]
Hadfield, Sir Robert Abbott, 1st Bart [obit]
Haggard, William David [obit]
Hainisch, Michael [obit]
Haldane, John Burdon Sanderson
Hale, Arthur, Rev. [obit]

Halifax, Edward Frederick Lindley Wood, 3rd Viscount
Hall, James [obit]
Hambro, Carl Joachim
Hamilton, George Livingston [obit]
Hamlin, Clarence Clark [obit] [Dec]
Hammond, Aubrey Lindsay [obit]
Hanson, Ole [obit]
Harada, Tasuku, Rev. [obit]
Harden, Sir Arthur [obit]
Hardy, Ashley Kingsley [obit]
Harington, Sir Charles [obit] [Dec]
Harkness, Edward Stephen [obit]
Harlan, Otis [obit]
Harper, Alexander James [obit]
Harriman, Florence Jaffray Hurst
Harrington, Francis Clark [obit]
Harris, Roy
Hart, Basil Henry Liddell- See Liddell Hart, B. H.
Hart, Lorenz   See Rodgers, R. and Hart, L.
Hart, Moss
Hawes, Elizabeth
Haynes, Roy Asa [obit] [Dec]
Head, Sir Henry [obit] [Dec]
Heath, S. Burton
Hedin, Sven Anders
Heidenstam, Verner von [obit]
Heming, Arthur Henry Howard [obit] [Dec]
Henderson, Leon
Henderson, Sir Nevile Meyrick
Henie, Sonja
Henry-Haye, Gaston
Hering, Hermann S. [obit]
Herrick, Francis Hobart [obit]
Hertz, Emanuel [obit]
Heyward, Du Bose [obit]
Hill, Edwin C.
Hill, Howard Copeland [obit]
Hillman, Sidney
Hillyer, Robert Silliman
Hitz, Ralph [obit]
Hoare, Sir Samuel John Gurney, 2nd Bart
Hobson, John Atkinson [obit]
Hoellering, Franz
Hoffman, Malvina [Dec]
Hohenlohe-Waldenburg, Stefanie Richter, Princess
Hollander, Jacob Harry [obit]
Honeywell, Harry E. [obit]
Hooper, Franklin Henry [obit]
Hooton, Earnest Albert [Dec]
Hoover, J. Edgar
Hopkins, Louis Bertram [obit]
Horlick, William Jr. [obit]

Horner, Henry [obit]
Horthy de Nagybánya, Nicholas
Hoshino, Naoki
Houston, David Franklin [obit]
Howard, Bart B.
Howard, Roy Wilson
Howe, Frederic Clemson [obit]
Howe, Quincy
Huckel, Oliver, Rev. [obit]
Hughes, Edward Everett [obit]
Hughes, Langston
Hull, Cordell
Hull, Helen R.
Hutchins, Robert Maynard [Dec]
Hutchinson, Ray Coryton
Hutton, Maurice [obit]

Iglesias, Santiago [obit]
Ingersoll, Ralph McAllister
Ingersoll, Raymond Vail [obit]
Ironside, Sir Edmund

Jabotinsky, Vladimir Evgenevich [Atalena, pseud.] [obit]
Jackson, Chevalier
Jackson, Robert Houghwout
Jacobs, Joe [obit]
Jacobs, Philip Peter [obit]
James, Arthur Horace
Jenkins, MacGregor [obit]
Jenks, Leon E. [obit]
Johnson, Arthur Newhall [obit]
Johnson, Clifton [obit]
Johnson, Harold Ogden   See Olsen, J. S. and Johnson, H. O.
Johnson, Hugh Samuel
Johnson, Nelson Trusler
Johnson, Osa
Joliot-Curie, Irène
Jolson, Al
Jones, E. Stanley, Rev.
Jones, Grover [obit]
Jones, Jack   See Jones, J. J.
Jones, Jesse Holman
Jones, Joe
Jones, John Joseph
Jones, Sam Houston
Josephson, Walter S. [obit]

Kai-shek, Chiang   See Chiang Kai-shek
Kaltenborn, Hans von
Kander, Lizzie Black [obit]
Kaup, Felix F., Father [obit]
Keenan, Walter Francis Jr. [obit]
Keitel, Wilhelm
Kelberine, Alexander [obit]
Kelly, Florence Finch [obit]
Kennedy, Joseph Patrick
Kettering, Charles Franklin
Key, Ben Witt [obit]
Kieran, John
Kimball, Wilbur R. [obit]

King, William Lyon Mackenzie
Kipling, Caroline Starr Balestier [obit]
Klee, Paul [obit]
Knickerbocker, Hubert Renfro
Knopf, Sigard Adolphus [obit]
Knox, Frank
Knudsen, William S.
Kohler, Walter Jodok [obit]
Konoye, Fumimaro, Prince
Koussevitzky, Serge
Krueger, Maynard C.

Lagerlöf, Selma [obit]
La Guardia, Fiorello Henry
Laidlaw, Sir Patrick Playfair [obit]
Lamond, Felix [obit]
Lamont, Thomas William
Langmuir, Irving
Lansbury, George [obit]
Latouche, John Treville
Laval, Pierre
Lawrence, Charles Edward [obit]
Lawrence, Ernest Orlando
Lawrence, Gertrude
Lawrence, Marjorie
Laycock, Craven [obit]
Lee, John Clarence, Rev. [obit]
Lee, Manfred B.   See Queen, E., pseud.
Lehrbas, Lloyd
Leigh, Douglas
Leinsdorf, Erich
Lenroot, Katharine Fredrica
Lessing, Bruno, pseud. of Rudolph Block [obit]
Levant, Oscar
Levene, Phoebus Aaron Theodore [obit]
Levin, Meyer
Lewis, Albert Buell [obit] [Dec]
Lewis, Cecil Day-   See Day-Lewis, C.
Lewis, Francis Park [obit]
Lewis, Mary
Ley, Robert
Lichtenberger, André [obit]
Liddell Hart, Basil Henry
Lie, Jonas [obit]
Lillard, George W. [obit] [Dec]
Lin Yu-t'ang
Lindbergh, Anne
Lindley, Ernest Hiram [obit]
Lippincott, Joshua Bertram [obit]
Lippmann, Walter
Little, William Lawson Jr.
Llewellyn, Richard, pseud. of Richard David Vivian Llewellyn Lloyd
Llewellyn Lloyd, Richard David Vivien   See Llewellyn, R., pseud.
Locke, Charles Edward, Bishop [obit]
Lockridg , Richard

Lodge, Sir Oliver Joseph [obit]
Loeb, Fritz [obit]
Loftus, Cissie
Logan, Walter [obit]
Lombardo Toledano, Vicente
Longman, Sir Hubert Harry [obit]
Loram, Charles Templeman [obit]
Lorentz, Pare
Lothian, Philip Henry Kerr, 11th Marquis of [obit] [Dec]
Louis, Joe
Louise Caroline Alberta, Duchess of Argyll, Princess [obit]
Low, David
Luhan, Mabel Dodge
Lundeen, Ernest [obit]
Lunn, Katharine Fowler See Fowler-Billings, K.
Lupescu, Magda
Luquiens, Frederick Bliss [obit]
Lyndon, Edward [obit] [Dec]

Macartney, William Napier [obit]
McCarl, John Raymond [obit]
McCormick, Anne O'Hare
MacCormick, Austin H.
McCormick, William Patrick Glyn, Rev. [obit] [Dec]
MacCracken, Henry Noble
McCullers, Carson
McCune, Charles Andrew [obit] [Dec]
McDaniel, Hattie
MacDonald, Sir George [obit]
McGuire, William Anthony [obit]
Mackenzie, Clinton [obit]
McKenzie, Roderick Duncan [obit]
MacLean, Malcolm Shaw
MacLeish, Archibald
McNary, Charles Linza
MacNeil, Neil
McNutt, Paul Vories
MacRossie, Allan, Rev. [obit]
Maltz, Albert
Mamlok, Hans J. [obit] [Dec]
Mandel, Georges [Dec]
Manly, John Matthews [obit]
Mann, Erika [Dec]
Mann, Klaus [Dec]
Mannerheim, Carl Gustaf Emil, Baron von
Manning, William Thomas, Bishop
Manship, Paul
Marble, Alice
Margoliouth, David Samuel [obit]
Marius, Emilie Alexander [obit]
Markham, Edwin [obit]

Marquis, Frederick James, 1st Baron Woolton See Woolton, F. J. M., 1st Baron
Marshall, George Catlett
Martin, Edgar Stanley [obit]
Martin, Joseph William Jr.
Martland, Harrison Stanford
Marvin, Dwight Edwards, Rev. [obit]
Marvin, Harry [obit]
Mary Joseph Butler, Mother [obit]
Massine, Léonide
Maurier, Daphne du See Du Maurier, D.
Max, Adolphe [obit]
May, Henry John [obit]
Maynor, Dorothy
Mayo, Katherine [obit] [Dec]
Mead, Margaret
Mearns, Hughes
Mellor, Walter [obit]
Mendenhall, Harlan George, Rev. [obit]
Meredith, Burgess
Merrill, John Douglas [obit]
Messerschmitt, Willy
Meštrović, Ivan
Metaxas, John
Meyers, George Julian [obit]
Michelin, Edouard [obit]
Michelson, Charles
Millar, Alexander Copeland, Rev. [obit] [Dec]
Miller, Max
Miller, Webb [obit]
Miller, William Lash [obit]
Milles, Carl [Dec]
Millikan, Robert Andrews
Millis, Harry Alvin
Minard, George Cann [obit]
Miró, Joán
Mix, Tom [obit] [Dec]
Modjeski, Ralph [obit]
Molotov, Viacheslav Mikhailovich
Montessori, Maria
Moore, Raymond [obit]
Moore, T. Albert, Rev. [obit]
Moorland, Jesse Edward, Rev. [obit]
Mora, Francis Luis [obit]
Morehouse, Ward
Morgenthau, Henry Jr.
Morrison, Herbert Stanley
Morrow, Honoré Willsie [obit]
Morse, John Lovett [obit]
Morton, Henry Holdich [obit]
Morton, James Madison Jr. [obit]
Moscovitch, Maurice [obit]
Moses, Robert
Mosley, Sir Oswald Ernald
Moton, Robert Russa [obit]
Motta, Giuseppe [obit]
Mowrer, Lilian Thomson
Muck, Karl [obit]
Mumford, Ethel Watts [obit]
Mumford, Lewis
Munch, Edvard [Dec]

Mundy, Talbot Chetwynd [obit]
Murphy, Frank
Murphy, Frederick E. [obit]
Murray, Augustus Taber [obit]
Myers, Jerome [obit]
Mysore, Maharaja of See Wadiyar, S. K. [obit]

Navarro, Mary de [obit]
Neal, Herbert Vincent [obit]
Neumann, Heinrich [obit]
Newall, Sir Cyril Louis Norton
Newton, Alfred Edward [obit]
Nicolson, Marjorie Hope
Nijinsky, Waslaw
Nipkow, Paul Gottlieb [obit]
Nixon, Lewis [obit]
Nordmann, Charles [obit] [Dec]
Norman, Montagu [Dec]
Norris, Henry Hutchinson [obit]
Norris, James Flack [obit]
Northrup, Edwin Fitch [obit]
Novotna, Jarmila

Oberteuffer, George [obit]
Oboler, Arch
O'Gorman, Patrick F., Father [obit]
Olsen, John Sigvard and Johnson, Harold Ogden
O'Neil, George [obit]
Orozco, José Clemente
Osborne, Oliver Thomas [obit] [Dec]
Owens, Robert Bowie [obit] [Dec]

Paddon, Harry Locke [obit]
Page, Marie Danforth [obit]
Paley, William Samuel
Palmer, Albert deForest [obit]
Pape, William Jamieson
Parran, Thomas
Parsons, Louella
Passos, John Dos See Dos Passos, J.
Pasternack, Josef Alexander [obit]
Patri, Angelo
Patrick, Mary Mills [obit]
Patterson, Eleanor Medill
Paul, Elliot
Peabody, Endicott, Rev.
Peattie, Donald Culross
Pegler, Westbrook
Peñaranda, Enrique
Perkins, Frances [Dec]
Perla, David [obit]
Pertinax, pseud. See Géraud, A.
Pétain, Henri Philippe
Petrillo, James Caesar [Dec]
Peynado, Jacinto B. [obit]
Phillips, Albert [obit]
Phillips, William
Pick, Behrendt [obit]
Pierce, Palmer Eddy [obit]

BY PROFESSION

Architecture

Adams, Thomas [obit]
Brown, A. Ten Eyck [obit]
Casey, Edward Pearce [obit]
Harper, Alexander James [obit]
Mackenzie, Clinton [obit]
Mellor, Walter [obit]
Post, William Stone [obit]

Art

Allen, Joel Nott [obit]
Altenburg, Alexander [obit]
Anderson, Abraham Archibald [obit]
Aulaire, Ingri d' and Aulaire, Edgar Parin d'
Bachrach, Elise Wald [obit]
Bacon, Peggy
Barclay, McClelland
Barthé, Richmond
Benton, Thomas Hart
Black, Alexander [obit]
Blanch, Arnold
Bourke-White, Margaret See White, M. B.
Bryan, Julien Hequembourg
Burliuk, David
Chang Shan-tze [obit]
Chapin, James
Cole, Jessie Duncan Savage [obit]
Covarrubias, Miguel
Dali, Salvador
Daugherty, James Henry
Davis, Stuart
Duffy, Edmund
Eilshemius, Louis Michel
Eves, Reginald Grenville
Flagg, James Montgomery
Freedlander, Arthur R. [obit]
Gordon, John Sloan [obit]
Greene, Frank Russell [obit]
Gropper, William
Gruppe, Charles Paul [obit]
Hammond, Aubrey Lindsay [obit]
Heming, Arthur Henry Howard [obit]
Hoffman, Malvina
Jones, Joe
Klee, Paul [obit]
Lie, Jonas [obit]
Louise Caroline Alberta, Duchess of Argyll, Princess [obit]
Low, David
Manship, Paul

Meštrović, Ivan
Milles, Carl
Miró, Joán
Mora, Francis Luis [obit]
Munch, Edvard
Myers, Jerome [obit]
Oberteuffer, George [obit]
Orozco, José Clemente
Page, Marie Danforth [obit]
Poore, Henry Rankin [obit]
Portinari, Cândido
Prellwitz, Henry [obit]
Quintanilla, Luis
Rautenberg, Robert [obit]
Richard, Louis [obit]
Romano, Emanuel
Scudder, Janet [obit]
Seredy, Kate
Shinn, Florence Scovel [obit]
Soglow, Otto
Stieglitz, Alfred
Stoddard, Frederick Lincoln [obit]
Taylor, Francis Henry
Wales, George Canning [obit]
Watrous, Harry Willson [obit]
Waugh, Frederick Judd [obit]
Wheelock, Warren
White, Margaret Bourke
Wood, Grant
Woodbury, Charles Herbert [obit]
Yellin, Samuel [obit]
Young, Art
Young, Charles Jac [obit]

Aviation

Cochran, Jacqueline
Rickenbacker, Edward
Sikorsky, Igor Ivan
Williams, Alford Joseph Jr.
Yancey, Lewis Q. Alonzo [obit]

Diplomacy

Anderson, George Everett [obit]
Avenol, Joseph Louis Anne
Barrère, Camille Eugène Pierre [obit]
Bullitt, William Christian
Casey, Richard Gardiner
Cripps, Sir Stafford
Des Graz, Sir Charles Louis [obit]

Dodd, William Edward [obit]
Harriman, Florence Jaffray Hurst
Henderson, Sir Nevile Meyrick
Henry-Haye, Gaston
Hoare, Sir Samuel John Gurney, 2nd Bart
Johnson, Nelson Trusler
Kennedy, Joseph Patrick
Lothian, Philip Henry Kerr, 11th Marquis of [obit]
Phillips, William
Procopé, Hjalmar Johan
Richardson, Norval [obit]
Sevier, Henry Hulme [obit]
Taylor, Myron Charles

Education

Adler, Cyrus [obit]
Adler, Mortimer Jerome
Angell, James Rowland
Bailey, Guy Winfred [obit]
Barr, Frank Stringfellow
Bartol, William Cyrus [obit]
Bevis, Howard Landis
Binkley, Robert Cedric [obit]
Brandenburg, William A. [obit]
Brown, John Franklin [obit]
Bryson, Lyman
Burdick, Charles Kellogg [obit]
Butler, Nicholas Murray
Chaddock, Robert Emmet [obit]
Collins, Edward Day [obit]
Crawford, Morris Barker [obit]
Crawshaw, William Henry [obit]
Culver, Essae Martha
Damon, Lindsay Todd [obit]
Daniels, Arthur Hill [obit]
Davis, Herbert John
Dillard, James Hardy [obit]
Elliott, Harriet Wiseman
Fenimore-Cooper, Susan de Lancey [obit]
Ferris, Harry Burr [obit]
Few, William Preston [obit]
Frank, Glenn [obit]
Frazier, Edward Franklin
Fuller, Clara Cornelia [obit]
Fuller, George Washington [obit]
Ganfield, William Arthur [obit]
Gates, William [obit]

Gesell, Arnold
Gideonse, Harry David
Gildersleeve, Virginia
Crocheron
Goldenweiser, Alexander A.
[obit]
Guthrie, William Buck
[obit]
Hamilton, George Livingston
[obit]
Harada, Tasuku, Rev. [obit]
Hardy, Ashley Kingsley
[obit]
Hill, Howard Copeland
[obit]
Hobson, John Atkinson
[obit]
Hollander, Jacob Harry
[obit]
Hopkins, Louis Bertram
[obit]
Hutchins, Robert Maynard
Hutton, Maurice [obit]
Krueger, Maynard C.
Laycock, Craven [obit]
Lindley, Ernest Hiram [obit]
Loram, Charles Templeman
[obit]
Luquiens, Frederick Bliss
[obit]
MacCracken, Henry Noble
MacDonald, Sir George
[obit]
McKenzie, Roderick Duncan
[obit]
MacLean, Malcolm Shaw
Manly, John Matthews
[obit]
Margoliouth, David Samuel
[obit]
Mearns, Hughes
Millar, Alexander Copeland,
Rev. [obit]
Minard, George Cann [obit]
Montessori, Maria
Moton, Robert Russa [obit]
Murray, Augustus Taber
[obit]
Nicolson, Marjorie Hope
O'Gorman, Patrick F.,
Father [obit]
Palmer, Albert deForest
[obit]
Patri, Angelo
Patrick, Mary Mills [obit]
Peabody, Endicott, Rev.
Pick, Behrendt [obit]
Potter, Alfred Claghorn
[obit]
Prall, David Wight [obit]
Prentiss, Henrietta [obit]
Putnam, James William
[obit]
Reed, Edward Bliss [obit]
Ross, Sir Edward Denison
[obit]
Russell, Bertrand Arthur
William, 3rd Earl
Sandefer, Jefferson Davis
[obit]

Shambaugh, Benjamin Franklin [obit]
Smith, Wilbur Fisk [obit]
Sprague, Embert Hiram
[obit]
Stone, John Charles [obit]
Tanner, John Henry [obit]
Taussig, Frank William [obit]
Thompson, Holland [obit]
Trotter, Frank Butler [obit]
Vance, William Reynolds
[obit]
Volterra, Vito [obit]
Wambaugh, Eugene [obit]
Woodbridge, Frederick
James Eugene [obit]
Yoder, Albert Henry [obit]

Engineering

Arco, Georg Wilhelm Alexander Hans, Graf von
[obit]
Armstrong, Edwin Howard
Barney, Samuel E. [obit]
Breckenridge, Lester Paige
[obit]
Bunau-Varilla, Philippe
[obit]
Callow, John Michael [obit]
Canton, Allen A. [obit]
Carpenter, Lewis Van [obit]
Carson, John Renshaw [obit]
Chamberlain, Paul Mellen
[obit]
Crompton, Rookes Evelyn
Bell [obit]
Gibbs, George [obit]
Gilbreth, Lillian Evelyn
Goldsmith, Lester Morris
Johnson, Arthur Newhall
[obit]
Keenan, Walter Francis Jr.
[obit]
Kimball, Wilbur R. [obit]
McCune, Charles Andrew
[obit]
Modjeski, Ralph [obit]
Nixon, Lewis [obit]
Norris, Henry Hutchinson
[obit]
Northrup, Edwin Fitch [obit]
Owens, Robert Bowie [obit]
Reynolds, James A. [obit]
Ricketts, Louis Davidson
[obit]
Ripley, Joseph [obit]
Rumpler, Edmund [obit]
Rushmore, David Barker
[obit]
Stanley, Freelan O. [obit]

Finance

Aldrich, Winthrop Williams
Ayres, Leonard Porter
Benjamin, William Evarts
[obit]
Dawes, Rufus Cutler [obit]

Harkness, Edward Stephen
[obit]
Lamont, Thomas William
Norman, Montagu
Pirie, John Taylor [obit]
Williams, Ralph E. [obit]

Government—International

(See also heading
Diplomacy)

Antonescu, Ion
Astor, Nancy Witcher, Viscountess
Attlee, Clement Richard
Azaña, Manuel [obit]
Bailey, Sir Abe, 1st Bart
[obit]
Batista Y Zaldivar, Fulgencio
Beaverbrook, William Maxwell Aitken, 1st Baron
Besteiro Y Fernandez, Julian
[obit]
Bevin, Ernest
Blum, Léon
Camacho, Manuel Avila
Carol II
Cavero, Salvador [obit]
Chamberlain, Neville [obit]
Chappedelaine, Louis de
[obit]
Chiang Kai-shek
Chiang Mei-ling [Mme.
Chiang Kai-shek]
Churchill, Winston Leonard
Spencer
Ciano, Galeazzo, Conte
Companys, Luis [obit]
Cooper, Alfred Duff
Daladier, Edouard
Davidovitch, Ljuba [obit]
De Valera, Eamon
Doriot, Jacques
Eden, Anthony
Estigarribia, José Félix
[obit]
Funk, Walther
Gilmour, Sir John [obit]
Greenwood, Arthur
Guise, Jean Pierre Clément
Marie, Duc de [obit]
Haakon VII, King of Norway
Hainisch, Michael [obit]
Halifax, Edward Frederick
Lindley Wood, 3rd Viscount
Hambro, Carl Joachim
Horthy de Nagybánya,
Nicholas
Hoshino, Naoki
King, William Lyon Mackenzie
Konoye, Fumimaro, Prince
Lansbury, George [obit]
Laval, Pierre
Ley, Robert
Mandel, Georges
Max, Adolphe [obit]

Metaxas, John
Molotov, Viacheslav Mikhailovich
Morrison, Herbert Stanley
Motta, Giuseppe [obit]
Peñaranda, Enrique
Pétain, Henri Philippe
Peynado, Jacinto B. [obit]
Quisling, Vidkun
Reith, John Charles Walsham, 1st Baron
Reynaud, Paul
Rogers, Norman McLeod [obit]
Sabry, Hassan, Pasha [obit]
Savage, Michael Joseph [obit]
Serrano Suñer, Ramón
Sikorski, Wladyslaw
Simon, John Allsebrook, 1st Viscount
Sinclair, Sir Archibald, 4th Bart
Soukup, Frantisek [obit]
Squires, Richard Anderson [obit]
Tokugawa, Iyesato, Prince [obit]
Tsai Yuan-pei [obit]
Tweed, Thomas Frederic [obit]
Vargas, Getulio Dornellas
Vassallo, Ernesto [obit]
Wadiyar, Sri Krishnaraja, Bahadur Maharaja of Mysore [obit]
Wang Ching-wei
Wilhelmina, Queen of The Netherlands
Wood, Sir Kingsley
Woolton, Frederick James Marquis, 1st Baron
Yonai, Mitsumasa
Zimmerman, Alfred F. M. [obit]

Government— United States

(See also heading Diplomacy)

Anderson, John Crawford [obit]
Anderson, Mary
Arnold, Thurman Wesley
Austin, William Lane
Bankhead, William Brockman [obit]
Berle, Adolf Augustus Jr.
Bolton, Frances Payne
Borah, William Edgar [obit]
Bourne, Jonathan Jr. [obit]
Burke, Edward Raymond
Carmody, John Michael
Colquitt, Oscar Branch [obit]
Conley, William Gustavus [obit]
Corcoran, Thomas Gardiner

Cortelyou, George Bruce [obit]
Davis, Chester Charles
Davis, Norman H.
Deasy, Luere B. [obit]
Dewey, Thomas Edmund
Dies, Martin
Dieterich, William H. [obit]
Dover, Elmer [obit]
Edison, Charles
Erlanger, Mitchell Louis [obit]
Fischer, Israel Frederick [obit]
Fisher, John Stuchell [obit]
Fleming, Philip Bracken
Fly, James Lawrence
George, Albert Bailey [obit]
Gibson, Ernest Willard [obit]
Goodrich, James Putnam [obit]
Harrington, Francis Clark [obit]
Henderson, Leon
Hoover, J. Edgar
Horner, Henry [obit]
Houston, David Franklin [obit]
Howe, Frederic Clemson [obit]
Hull, Cordell
Iglesias, Santiago [obit]
Ingersoll, Raymond Vail [obit]
Jackson, Robert Houghwout
James, Arthur Horace
Jones, Jesse Holman
Jones, Sam Houston
Knox, Frank
La Guardia, Fiorello Henry
Lenroot, Katharine Fredrica
Lundeen, Ernest [obit]
McCarl, John Raymond [obit]
McNary, Charles Linza
McNutt, Paul Vories
Martin, Joseph William Jr.
Morgenthau, Henry Jr.
Moses, Robert
Murphy, Frank
Perkins, Frances
Pittman, Key [obit]
Ragon, Heartsill [obit]
Rayburn, Sam
Reynolds, Robert Rice
Ross, Nellie Tayloe
Sayre, Francis Bowes
Seger, George N. [obit]
Shoup, Oliver Henry [obit]
Silzer, George Sebastian [obit]
Simmons, Furnifold McLendell [obit]
Smith, Clyde Harold [obit]
Stassen, Harold Edward
Stimson, Henry Lewis
Taft, Robert Alphonso
Vandenberg, Arthur Hendrick
Walker, Frank Comerford

Wallace, Henry Agard
Waste, William Harrison [obit]
Watson, Clarence Wayland [obit]
Welles, Sumner
Wheeler, Burton Kendall
White, Frank [obit]
Wickard, Claude Raymond
Williams, Aubrey
Williams, Thomas Sutler [obit]
Winthrop, Beekman [obit]
Zeidler, Carl Frederick

Industry

Aronson, Louis V. [obit]
Baker, Asa George [obit]
Benson, John
Bloch, Charles Edward [obit]
Budd, Ralph
Cahill, Michael Harrison [obit]
Chrysler, Walter Percy [obit]
Cramer, Stuart Warren [obit]
Cromwell, James H. R.
Doherty, Henry Latham [obit]
Du Pont, Pierre Samuel
Fleming, Arthur Henry [obit]
Gallup, George Horace
Griswold, Augustus H. [obit]
Hanson, Ole [obit]
Hitz, Ralph [obit]
Horlick, William Jr. [obit]
Hughes, Edward Everett [obit]
Josephson, Walter S. [obit]
Kettering, Charles Franklin
Knudsen, William S.
Kohler, Walter Jodok [obit]
Leigh, Douglas
Lewis, Mary
Lippincott, Joshua Bertram [obit]
Longman, Sir Hubert Harry [obit]
Marvin, Harry [obit]
Messerschmitt, Willy
Michelin, Edouard [obit]
Prentis, Henning Webb Jr.
Schiaparelli, Elsa
Sloan, Alfred Pritchard Jr.
Spry, Constance
Stettinius, Edward Reilly Jr.
Switzer, George [obit]
Totty, Charles H. [obit]
Tunney, Gene
Van Doren, Harold Livingston
Watson, Thomas John
Willkie, Wendell Lewis
Wright, Russel

Journalism

Abbott, Robert Sengstacke [obit]
Adler, Harry Clay [obit]
Barton, George [obit]
Beebe, Lucius
Bennett, James O'Donnell [obit]
Booker, Edna Lee
Broun, Heywood [obit]
Chamberlain, John Rensselaer
Chase, Edna Woolman
Clapper, Raymond
Cooper, Courtney Ryley [obit]
Dix, Dorothy, pseud. of Elizabeth Meriwether Gilmer
Finley, John Huston [obit]
Fischer, Louis
Fyfe, H. Hamilton
Gayda, Virginio
Géraud, André [Pertinax, pseud.]
Gilder, Robert Fletcher [obit]
Grafton, Samuel
Hawes, Elizabeth
Haynes, Roy Asa [obit]
Heath, S. Burton
Hohenlohe-Waldenburg, Stefanie Richter, Princess
Hooper, Franklin Henry [obit]
Howard, Bart B.
Howard, Roy Wilson
Ingersoll, Ralph McAllister
Johnson, Hugh Samuel
Kelly, Florence Finch [obit]
Knickerbocker, Hubert Renfro
Lehrbas, Lloyd
Lessing, Bruno, pseud. of Rudolph Block [obit]
Lippmann, Walter
McCormick, Anne O'Hare
MacNeil, Neil
Merrill, John Douglas [obit]
Michelson, Charles
Miller, Webb [obit]
Morehouse, Ward
Mowrer, Lilian Thomson
Murphy, Frederick E. [obit]
Pape, William Jamieson
Patterson, Eleanor Medill
Pegler, Westbrook
Reavis, Smith Freeman [obit]
Roosevelt, Eleanor
Rowell, Chester H.
Sherman, Frederic Fairchild [obit]
Stevenson, E. Robert
Stowe, Leland
Streit, Clarence
Tabouis, Geneviève
Thayer, Ernest Lawrence [obit]
Thompson, Dorothy
Tolischus, Otto David

Vann, Robert Lee [obit]
Viereck, George Sylvester
Villard, Oswald Garrison
White, William Allen
Wickware, Francis Graham [obit]
Ybarra, Thomas Russell

Labor

Bridges, Harry
Hillman, Sidney
Jones, John Joseph
Lombardo Toledano, Vicente
Millis, Harry Alvin
Petrillo, James Caesar
Saposs, David

Law

Alter, George Elias [obit]
Amsterdam, Birdie
Brown, Francis Shunk [obit]
Burleigh, George William [obit]
Cairns, Huntington
Collins, Lorin Cone [obit]
Cotton, Joseph Bell [obit]
Cravath, Paul Drennan [obit]
Ernst, Morris Leopold
Flynn, Edward J.
Fox, John McDill [obit]
Frazer, Spaulding [obit]
Gunter, Julius Caldeen [obit]
Hamlin, Clarence Clark [obit]
Hertz, Emanuel [obit]
Lillard, George W. [obit]
Morton, James Madison Jr. [obit]
Root, Oren Jr.
Steuer, Max David [obit]
Untermyer, Samuel [obit]
Watrous, George Dutton [obit]

Literature

Adamic, Louis
Addington, Sarah [obit]
Ashmun, Margaret Eliza [obit]
Atherton, Gertrude
Baker, Ray Stannard [David Grayson, pseud.]
Banning, Margaret Culkin
Bates, Ernest Sutherland [obit]
Beer, Thomas [obit]
Benson, Allan Louis [obit]
Benson, Edward Frederic [obit]
Binet-Valmer, Jean [obit]
Blaker, Richard [obit]
Bower, Bertha Muzzy, pseud. of Bertha Muzzy Sinclair-Cowan [obit]

Bristow, Gwen
Buchan, John, 1st Baron Tweedsmuir [obit]
Bulgakov, Michael Afanasievich [obit]
Burton, Richard Eugene [obit]
Caldwell, Erskine
Caldwell, Taylor
Chase, Mary Ellen
Chase, Stuart
Cherne, Leo M.
Christie, Agatha
Coolidge, Dane [obit]
Corey, Paul
Crawford, Phyllis
Curie, Eve
Davies, William Henry [obit]
Day-Lewis, Cecil [Nicholas Blake, pseud.]
Dell, Robert Edward [obit]
Dos Passos, John
Drouet, Bessie Clarke [obit]
Du Bois, William Edward Burghardt
Du Maurier, Daphne
Eliot, George Fielding
Elliot, Kathleen Morrow [obit]
Fedorova, Nina
Frank, Waldo David
Garland, Hamlin [obit]
Gorman, Herbert Sherman
Goudge, Elizabeth
Grant, Robert [obit]
Green, Julian
Hedin, Sven Anders
Heidenstam, Verner von [obit]
Heyward, Du Bose [obit]
Hillyer, Robert Silliman
Hoellering, Franz
Hughes, Langston
Hull, Helen R.
Hutchinson, Ray Coryton
Jabotinsky, Vladimir Evgenevich [Atalena, pseud.] [obit]
Jenkins, MacGregor [obit]
Johnson, Clifton [obit]
Johnson, Osa
Lagerlöf, Selma [obit]
Lawrence, Charles Edward [obit]
Levin, Meyer
Lichtenberger, André [obit]
Liddell Hart, Basil Henry
Lin Yu-t'ang
Lindbergh, Anne
Llewellyn, Richard, pseud. of Richard David Vivian Llewellyn Lloyd
Luhan, Mabel Dodge
McCullers, Carson
McGuire, William Anthony [obit]
MacLeish, Archibald
Maltz, Albert
Mann, Erika
Mann, Klaus

Markham, Edwin [obit]
Mayo, Katherine [obit]
Miller, Max
Morrow, Honoré Willsie [obit]
Mumford, Ethel Watts [obit]
Mumford, Lewis
Mundy, Talbot Chetwynd [obit]
Newton, Alfred Edward [obit]
Paul, Elliot
Pinkerton, Kathrene Sutherland
Porter, Katherine Anne
Powys, Llewelyn [obit]
Queen, Ellery, pseud. of Frederic Dannay and Manfred B. Lee
Saint Exupéry, Antoine de
Sandburg, Carl
Saroyan, William
Schoonmaker, Edwin Davies [obit]
Seabrook, William
Senarens, Luis Philip [obit]
Shinn, Milicent Washburn [obit]
Sillanpää, Frans Eemil
Simpson, Helen de Guerry [obit]
Spender, Stephen
Steinbeck, John
Stuart, Jesse
Tate, Allen
Thurber, James
Tweedie, Mrs. Alec [obit]
Undset, Sigrid
Van Doren, Mark
Waln, Nora
Weld, John
Werfel, Franz
Wheelwright, John B. [obit]
Wolfe, Humbert [obit]
Wright, Richard

Medicine

Barringer, Emily Dunning
Begg, Alexander Swanson [obit]
Blumer, George Alder [obit]
Buchanan, Thomas Drysdale [obit]
Camac, Charles Nicoll Bancker [obit]
Carrel, Alexis
Caturáni, Michele Gaëtano [obit]
Chesser, Elizabeth Sloan [obit]
Collins, George Lewis [obit]
Cook, Frederick Albert [obit]
Coulter, Calvin Brewster [obit]
Cullen, Glenn Ernest [obit]
Davis, William Ellsworth

Dusser de Barenne, Joannes Gregorius [obit]
Fishbein, Morris
Goler, George Washington [obit]
Grenfell, Sir Wilfred Thomason [obit]
Haggard, William David [obit]
Head, Sir Henry [obit]
Jackson, Chevalier
Key, Ben Witt [obit]
Knopf, Sigard Adolphus [obit]
Laidlaw, Sir Patrick Playfair [obit]
Lewis, Francis Park [obit]
Macartney, William Napier [obit]
Mamlok, Hans J. [obit]
Martland, Harrison Stanford
Morse, John Lovett [obit]
Morton, Henry Holdich [obit]
Neumann, Heinrich [obit]
Osborne, Oliver Thomas [obit]
Paddon, Harry Locke [obit]
Parran, Thomas
Perla, David [obit]
Pritchard, Stuart [obit]
Pusey, William Allen [obit]
Reed, John Howard [obit]
Riesman, David [obit]
Riggs, Austen Fox [obit]
Robb, Hunter [obit]
Rosett, Joshua [obit]
Schereschewsky, Joseph Williams [obit]
Scott, Arthur Carroll [obit]
Sharp, Harry Clay [obit]
Shaw, Louis Agassiz [obit]
Sigerist, Henry Ernest
Slye, Maud
Spiller, William Gibson [obit]
Stimson, Julia Catherine
Wagner-Jauregg, Julius von [obit]
Weisse, Faneuil Suydam [obit]
Wenckebach, Karel Friedrich [obit]
Wilgus, Sidney Dean [obit]
Winter, George B. [obit]
Zinsser, Hans [obit]

Military

Addis, Ababa, Pietro Badoglio, Duca d'
Alexander, Albert Victor
Almazán, Juan Andreu
Balbo, Italo [obit]
Brauchitsch, Heinrich Alfred Hermann Walther von
Butler, Smedley Darlington [obit]
Cantu, Giuseppe [obit]
Carton de Wiart, Adrian

Cordier, Constant [obit]
De Gaulle, Charles
Dowding, Sir Hugh Caswell Tremenheere
Du Fournet, Louis René Marie Charles Dartige [obit]
Freyberg, Bernard Cyril
Gamelin, Maurice Gustave
Gort, John Standish Surtees Prendergast Vereker, 6th Viscount
Graves, William Sidney [obit]
Guillaumat, Marie Louis Adolphe [obit]
Harington, Sir Charles [obit]
Ironside, Sir Edmund
Keitel, Wilhelm
Loeb, Fritz [obit]
Mannerheim, Carl Gustaf Emil, Baron von
Marshall, George Catlett
Meyers, George Julian [obit]
Newall, Sir Cyril Louis Norton
Pierce, Palmer Eddy [obit]
Stark, Harold Raynsford
Thompson, John Taliaferro [obit]
Weygand, Maxime

Motion Pictures

Barrett, Wilton Agnew [obit]
Bates, Granville [obit]
Bergman, Ingrid
Carewe, Edwin [obit]
Chadwick, Helene [obit]
Chaplin, Charlie
Chase, Charley [obit]
Clark, Marguerite [obit]
Clive, Edward E. [obit]
Collins, Eddie [obit]
Connolly, Walter [obit]
Disney, Walt
Fairbanks, Douglas [obit]
Finch, Flora [obit]
Fitzmaurice, George [obit]
Hall, James [obit]
Jones, Grover [obit]
Lorentz, Pare
McDaniel, Hattie
Mix, Tom [obit]
Moscovitch, Maurice [obit]
O'Neil, George [obit]
Parsons, Louella
Roberts, Florence [obit]
Saunders, John Monk [obit]
Turpin, Ben [obit]
Wray, John Griffith [obit]

Music

Anderson, Marian
Bampton, Rose

Barbirolli, John
Barlow, Howard
Bartók, Béla
Baur, Bertha [obit]
Blitzstein, Marc
Bodanzky, Artur [obit]
Bonci, Alessandro [obit]
Chotzinoff, Samuel
Converse, Frederick Shepherd [obit]
Copland, Aaron
Defauw, Désiré
Dolmetsch, Arnold [obit]
Dornay, Louis [obit]
Elson, Arthur [obit]
Gatti-Casazza, Giulio [obit]
Grofé, Ferde
Harris, Roy
Kelberine, Alexander [obit]
Koussevitzky, Serge
Lamond, Felix [obit]
Lawrence, Marjorie
Leinsdorf, Erich
Logan, Walter [obit]
Marius, Emilie Alexander [obit]
Maynor, Dorothy
Muck, Karl [obit]
Novotna, Jarmila
Pasternack, Josef Alexander [obit]
Pollain, René
Revueltas, Silvestro [obit]
Rodzinski, Artur
Schelling, Ernest Henry [obit]
Serkin, Rudolf
Singer, Richard [obit]
Spitalny, Phil
Steinberg, Hans Wilhelm
Stephens, Ward [obit]
Stravinsky, Igor
Suesse, Dana
Szigeti, Joseph
Taylor, Deems
Templeton, Alec
Tetrazzini, Luisa [obit]
Thomson, Virgil
Thorborg, Kerstin
Tovey, Sir Donald Francis [obit]
Traubel, Helen
Wallenstein, Alfred
Walton, William Turner
Waring, Fred
Whiteman, Wilberforce James [obit]
Wiedoeft, Rudy [obit]

Radio

Allen, Gracie
Barnouw, Erik
Corwin, Norman
Cross, Milton John
Davis, Elmer
Denny, George Vernon Jr.
Fisher, Sterling
Hill, Edwin C.

Howe, Quincy
Kaltenborn, Hans von
Kieran, John
Levant, Oscar
Oboler, Arch
Paley, William Samuel
Saerchinger, César
Sarnoff, David
Smith, Kate
Stookey, Charley
Swing, Raymond Gram
Thomas, Lowell
Trammell, Niles
White, Paul W.
Wylie, Max

Religion

Barry, Patrick Frank, Bishop [obit]
Booth, Ballington [obit]
Brookes, George S., Rev.
Brownson, Josephine
Buchman, Frank Nathan Daniel, Rev.
Burns, James Aloysius, Father [obit]
Burton, Charles Emerson, Rev. [obit]
Burton, Lewis William, Bishop [obit]
Chase, William Sheafe, Rev. [obit]
Coughlin, Charles Edward, Father
Crowley, John J., Father [obit]
Dossaerts, Arthur Jerome, Archbishop [obit]
Elliott, William Thompson, Rev. [obit]
Finkelstein, Louis, Rabbi
Finn, William Joseph, Father
Forbes, Guillaume, Archbishop [obit]
Fosdick, Harry Emerson, Rev.
Gauthier, Joseph Alexandre George, Archbishop [obit]
Gomá Y Tomás, Isidoro, Cardinal [obit]
Graves, Frederick Rogers, Bishop [obit]
Guthrie, Charles Ellsworth, Rev. [obit]
Hale, Arthur, Rev. [obit]
Hering, Hermann S. [obit]
Huckel, Oliver, Rev. [obit]
Jones, E. Stanley, Rev.
Kaup, Felix F., Father [obit]
Lee, John Clarence, Rev. [obit]
Locke, Charles Edward, Bishop [obit]
McCormick, William Patrick Glyn, Rev. [obit]
MacRossie, Allan, Rev. [obit]

Manning, William Thomas, Bishop
Marvin, Dwight Edwards, Rev. [obit]
Mary Joseph Butler, Mother [obit]
Mendenhall, Harlan George, Rev. [obit]
Moore, T. Albert, Rev. [obit]
Moorland, Jesse Edward, Rev. [obit]
Quinn, Daniel Joseph, Father [obit]
Reisner, Christian Fichthorne, Rev. [obit]
Richmond, Charles Alexander, Rev. [obit]
Rutherford, Joseph Franklin
Spellman, Francis Joseph, Archbishop
Steinberg, Milton, Rabbi
Stewart, George Craig, Bishop [obit]
Storr, Vernon Faithfull, Rev. [obit]
Verdier, Jean, Cardinal [obit]
Werne, Isaac, Rabbi [obit]
Williams, Joseph John, Father [obit]
Woodcock, Charles Edward, Bishop [obit]

Science

Allyn, Lewis B. [obit]
Alsberg, Carl Lucas [obit]
Bethe, Hans Albrecht
Birge, Raymond Thayer
Blatchley, Willis Stanley [obit]
Blodgett, Katharine Burr
Boas, Franz
Boggs, Charles Reid [obit]
Bosch, Carl [obit]
Branly, Edouard [obit]
Bush, Vannevar
Carpenter, Sir Henry Cort Harold [obit]
Carver, George Washington
Compton, Arthur Holly
Curie, Irène See Joliot-Curie, I.
Dietz, David
Ditmars, Raymond Lee
Dörpfeld, Wilhelm [obit]
Dugan, Raymond Smith [obit]
Egloff, Gustav
Eisen, Gustav [obit]
Ellerman, Ferdinand [obit]
Eyde, Samuel [obit]
Fleming, John Adam
Fowler, Alfred [obit]
Fowler-Billings, Katharine
Gilmore, Melvin Randolph [obit]
Goldmark, Peter Carl
Haddon, Alfred Cort [obit]

Hadfield, Sir Robert Abbott, 1st Bart [obit]
Haldane, John Burdon Sanderson
Harden, Sir Arthur [obit]
Herrick, Francis Hobart [obit]
Hooton, Earnest Albert
Jenks, Leon E. [obit]
Joliot-Curie, Irène
Langmuir, Irving
Lawrence, Ernest Orlando
Levene, Phoebus Aaron Theodore [obit]
Lewis, Albert Buell [obit]
Lodge, Sir Oliver Joseph [obit]
Lyndon, Edward [obit]
Mead, Margaret
Miller, William Lash [obit]
Millikan, Robert Andrews
Neal, Herbert Vincent [obit]
Nipkow, Paul Gottlieb [obit]
Nordmann, Charles [obit]
Norris, James Flack [obit]
Peattie, Donald Culross
Reed, Herbert Calhoun [obit]
Semon, Waldo Lonsbury
Sperti, George Speri
Stekel, Wilhelm [Willy Bojan, Dr. Serenus, pseuds.] [obit]
Stine, Charles Milton Altland
Tainter, Charles Sumner [obit]
Thomson, Sir Joseph John [obit]
True, Rodney Howard [obit]
Wendt, Gerald Louis
Worden, Edward Chauncey [obit]

Social Service

Additon, Henrietta Silvis
Baldwin, Roger Nash
Berry, Martha McChesney

Bryce, Elizabeth Marion, Viscountess [obit]
Canavan, Joseph J. [obit]
Catt, Carrie Chapman
Edey, Birdsall Otis [obit]
Folks, Homer
Gehrig, Lou
Glenn, Mary Wilcox [obit]
Gruenberg, Sidonie Matsner
Jacobs, Philip Peter [obit]
Kander, Lizzie Black [obit]
MacCormick, Austin H.
Martin, Edgar Stanley [obit]
May, Henry John [obit]
Szold, Henrietta
Wald, Lillian D. [obit]

Sports

Berg, Patricia Jane
Coleman, Georgia [obit]
Durocher, Leo
Henie, Sonja
Jacobs, Joe [obit]
Little, William Lawson Jr.
Louis, Joe
Marble, Alice

Theatre

Abbott, George
Bentley, Irene [obit]
Blau, Bela [obit]
Bradbury, James H. [obit]
Campbell, Mrs. Patrick [obit]
Canby, Al H. [obit]
Churchill, Berton [obit]
Cochran, Charles Blake
Elliott, Maxine [obit]
Enters, Angna
Evans, Maurice
Faversham, William [obit]
Fratellini, Paul [obit]
Galli, Rosina [obit]
Geddes, Norman Bel
Harlan, Otis [obit]
Hart, Lorenz See Rodgers, R. and Hart, L.
Hart, Moss

Johnson, Harold Ogden See Olsen, J. S. and Johnson, H. O.
Jolson, Al
Latouche, John Treville
Lawrence, Gertrude
Lockridge, Richard
Loftus, Cissie
Massine, Léonide
Meredith, Burgess
Moore, Raymond [obit]
Navarro, Mary de [obit]
Nijinsky, Waslaw
Olsen, John Sigvard and Johnson, Harold Ogden
Phillips, Albert [obit]
Porter, Cole
Rodgers, Richard and Hart, Lorenz
Rose, Billy
Schratt, Katharina [obit]
Sherwood, Robert
Spottswood, James [obit]
Tone, Franchot
Weber, Louis Lawrence [obit]
Webster, Margaret
Wood, Philip [obit]
Woolley, Monty

Other Professions

Bedford, Herbrand Arthur Russell, 11th Duke of [obit]
Benchley, Belle Jennings
Culbertson, Ely
Garvey, Marcus [obit]
Goldman, Emma [obit]
Honeywell, Harry E. [obit]
Kipling, Caroline Starr Balestier [obit]
Lupescu, Magda
Mosley, Sir Oswald Ernald
Randolph, Asa Philip
Rodriguez, Nicolas [obit]
Strasser, Otto
Thyssen, Fritz
Trotsky, Leon [obit]
Wall, Evander Berry [obit]